BeComing-One Bible

Old and New Testament – 2021

Third Edition

An English Translation
of the
Holy Scriptures

Translated

by

Walter R. Dolen

President of the Becoming-One Church

Becoming-One Publications

Copyright © 1993-2021 by Walter R. Dolen

BeComing-One Bible
Old and New Testament – 2021

Third Edition

Trade Softback
ISBN: 978-161918-105-0
Two Column Edition

Third Printing June 2022
with corrections

[The BCB (BeComingOne Bible) text may be quoted and/or reprinted up to and inclusive of one thousand (1,000) verses without express written permission of the publisher, providing the verses quoted do not amount to a complete book of the Bible nor do the verses quoted account for 50% of the total work in which they are quoted.]

Text herein taken from and improved from earlier versions of the
BeComing-One Bible

Earlier Versions of Text:
1993 Version:
ISBN: 1877981249
1998 Version:
ISBN: 1877981338
2010 Version:
ISBN: 9781619181050

BeComing-One Publication / Press
www.becomingone.org/books.htm

"**All silencing of discussion is an assumption of infallibility** ... But the peculiar evil of silencing the expression of opinion is, that it is robbing the human race ... If the opinion is right, they are deprived of the opportunity of exchanging error for truth; if wrong, they lose, what is almost as great a benefit, the clearer perception and livelier impression of truth, produced by its collision with error."

(John Stuart Mill, On Liberty,
Chapter 2; see the quote here:
[https://www.beone.ws/resources/OnLiberty-40.pdf])

Preface

This translation is a new and more literal translation of the English Bible. Using my fifty plus years experience with the Bible, improvements were made over other English translations by unitizing the best Hebrew and Greek texts, as well as the best language tools such as:

> *The Interlinear Bible: Hebrew, Greek, English* (1976-83) Ed. by Jay P. Green; *The NIV Interlinear Hebrew-English Old Testament* (1979-85) Ed. by John R. Kohlenberger III; *Gesenius Hebrew Grammar* (1910, 1980); *The New Englishman's Hebrew and Chaldee Concordance*; *A Grammar of the Greek New Testament* (1934) by A. T. Robertson; *Analytical Greek New Testament* (1981) Ed. by Barbara Friberg & Timothy Friberg; *The Analytical Greek Lexicon* (1969); *The New Thayer's Greek-English Lexicon* (1974); *The New Analytical Greek Lexicon* (1990); *Bible Works* (v.5-9) software; *Analytical Key to the Old Testament* (1989-92) by John Joseph Owens; *The New Brown Driver Briggs Gesenius' Hebrew and English Lexicon* (1979); *Old Testament Parsing Guide* (1986) by Todd S. Beall & William A. Banks; WordPerfect; Nota Bene; etc.

God's Name in the Old Testament was **YHWH** [יהוה] and has been wrongly translated into "Lord" in most modern English translations. We have correctly translated the very meaning of the Name into "**Becoming-One**." The Hebrew NAME of God meant, "He (who) Will-Be." It did *not* mean, "I am," or "the Being" as wrongly translated in the Greek (LXX) version of the Old Testament. Instead of translating God's Name into, "He (who) Will-Be," we have used, "Becoming-One," as suggested by Joseph Bryant Rotherham in the "Introduction" of his, *The Emphasized Bible*, published by Kregel Publications in 1974. See the *God Papers* to see who or what is the true God. The apparent paradoxes pertaining to God is explained and they actually help to prove the reliability of the Bible's rendition on God.

Also the correct translation for the Hebrew *olam*, the Greek *aion* and *aionious* was used. These words have been mistranslated into such words as, "forever," "eternal," "everlasting," and so forth which has given a perverse meaning to hundreds of verses. The best translation would be "age" or "aeonian" or "aeon," which is an age of unknown length. The length of time can only be ascertained by the context in which it is used. The *New International Version* translates the Hebrew *olam* in over 60 different ways (words or phrases) including: lasting, ancient, ever, regular, never, of old, eternal, forever, long ago, always, age-old, long, more, permanent, again, ages, all time, any time, continued, early times, endless, for life, etc. See *New Mind* book, part seven [NM 7], for more information on this. In the *Becoming-One Bible* words that deal with time were carefully translated so those studying prophecy could better understand how time is dealt with in the Bible.

The word "**soul**" has been more consistently translated to reflect its real meaning. (See Genesis 2:7; see NM6; etc.)

For your information: The word translated "***thousand***" in the Old Testament of the Bible is in most cases the Hebrew word ***eleph***. The earliest basic meaning was *not* the number "one thousand," but apparently referred to a group (*herd* of cattle or *company* of men) of various quantities. In some cases the word referred to as little as 5 to 14 men, not one thousand. At some later time the word began to refer to the number one-thousand.
See, www.becomingone.org/exodusnumbers.html.

And/or see:

https://biblearchaeology.org/research/chronological-categories/exodus-era/3943-the-number-of-israelites-in-the-exodus or https://beone.ws/exodusnumbers.pdf

(links were good as of Feb 6, 2022)

This brings up the possibility that in some of the history recorded in the Bible, some places where *eleph* is translated as "1000" or "thousand," may actually be a smaller number. Yes, Exodus 38:25-26, when you understand that a half a shekel equals one person, seems to confirm the large number of Israelites 20 years and older (at 603,550 men), and seems to confirm that Moses translated the Hebrew *eleph* as "1000" **IF** our understanding of the value the talent shekel is correct. Otherwise 603 thousand means only 603 *eleph*s (leaders or commanders) of companies of men.

Words in this translation were carefully and systematically translated so that this Bible can be used for studying doctrine. Although not always possible for some, you should always check doctrinal verses with the original languages.

One problem with translating from *Biblical* Hebrew into English, as well as *Biblical* Greek to English, is the impossibility of translating the **differences in verbal tense usage between languages**. For example, in Hebrew there are only two tenses: perfect and imperfect. Both tenses speak of complete and incomplete action, not about time. Books such as S. R. Driver's *Hebrew Tenses* attempt to explain this to the English reader. Readers of any English translation should bear this in mind – it is impossible to translate Biblical Hebrew verbs literally into English verbs.

The archaic use of thy, ye, thou, makest, lovest, and other such words was not employed in this translation.

In the BeComing-One Bible's New Testament, some **Greek aorist** verbs are marked with an * in the NT for some difficult verses. An aorist verb is a verb without any time element attached to. The following quote was taken from the *Prophecy Papers*:

Aorist Verbs & Other Timeless Verbs

One must also know that the book of Revelation is full of the aorist vverbs. The aorist verb is a verb of action, not time. An aorist verb by itself tells us nothing about the time of the action. It speaks of action without denoting the duration of the action or time of the action:

> "The aorist stem presents action in its simplest form (a-oristos 'undefined'). This action is simply presented as a point by the tense. This action is timeless ... The aorist is a sort of flashlight picture, the imperfect a time exposure." (pp. 824, 1380 in, *A Grammar Of The Greek New Testament*, by A.T. Robertson; see also such books as, *Do It Yourself Hebrew and Greek*, by E.W. Goodrick, pp. 4.4-4.5)

In fact, in Greek, the aorist, present, and perfect is timeless:

1. "These ideas (punctiliar, durative, perfected state) lie behind the three tenses (aorist, present, perfect) that run through all the moods ... The present is also timeless in itself as in the perfect ... These three tenses (aorist, present, perfect) were first developed irrespective of time. Dionysius Thrax erred in explaining the Greek tenses from the notion of time, and he has been followed by a host of imitators. The study of Homer ought to have prevented this error" (p. 824, A.T. Robertson).

2. "The terms aorist, imperfect, and perfect (past, present, future) are properly named from the point of view of the state of the action, but present and future are named from the standpoint of the time element. There is no time element in the present subjunctive, for instance. But the names cannot now be changed, though very unsatisfactory" (pp. 825-826, A.T. Robertson).

Because of errors some Greek verbs were misnamed; many today read the idea of *time* into Greek verbs, when they should read the state of the *action*.

We used classical versions of the Bible as a model or template which gives this translation a vintage feel.

Chronological dates: numbers in this Bible within square brackets [xxxx YM] with "YM" following number indicate the "year of man" as explained in the Walter R. Dolen's *New Chronology Papers*.

For the true **location of the first Temple** see information at 1 Chr 26:18 and 2 Kings 23:11.

May Grace abound to you and to all,

Walter R. Dolen,

February 2021

Note: Dolen's books or papers referenced to in this Bible (*i.e.* NM7) can be found on the Internet (www.becomingone.org) and on Amazon or Barnes and Noble's websites.

Table of Contents

Genesis	9
Exodus	46
Leviticus	78
Numbers	101
Deuteronomy	134
Joshua	161
Judges	179
Ruth	197
1 Samuel	200
2 Samuel	224
1 Kings	244
2 Kings	268
1 Chronicles	290
2 Chronicles	312
Ezra	338
Nehemiah	346
Esther	357
Job	363
Psalms	382
Proverbs	429
Ecclesiastes	445
Song of Solomon	451
Isaiah	454
Jeremiah	490
Lamentations	531
Ezekiel	535
Daniel	573
Hosea	585
Joel	591
Amos	593
Obadiah	597
Jonah	598
Micah	600
Nahum	603

Habakkuk	605
Zephaniah	607
Haggai	609
Zechariah	611
Malachi	618
Matthew	621
Mark	646
Luke	662
John	689
Acts	710
Romans	736
1 Corinthians	747
2 Corinthians	757
Galatians	764
Ephesians	768
Philippians	772
Colossians	775
1 Thessalonians	778
2 Thessalonians	781
1 Timothy	783
2 Timothy	786
Titus	788
Philemon	790
Hebrews	791
James	799
1 Peter	802
2 Peter	805
1 John	807
2 John	810
3 John	811
Jude	812
Revelation	813
About the Author	825

Genesis

Gen 1:1 In the beginning God[1] created[2] the heavens and the earth.

2 And the earth was[3] without form, and void; and darkness was upon the face of the deep. And the Spirit of God moved upon the face of the waters.

3 And God said, Let there be[4] light: and there was[5] light.

4 And God saw the light, that it was good[6]: and God divided the light from the darkness.

5 And God called the light Day, and the darkness he called Night. And thus was evening and morning: **one day**.

6 And God said, Let there be an expanse in the midst of the waters, and let it divide the waters from the waters.

7 And God made the expanse, and divided the waters which were under the expanse from the waters which were above the expanse: and it was so.

8 And God called the expanse, the heavens. And thus was evening and morning: **second day**.

9 And God said, Let the waters under the heavens be gathered together unto one place, and let the dry land appear: and it was so.

10 And God called the dry land Earth; and the gathering together of the waters called he Seas: and God saw that it was good.

11 And God said, Let the earth bring forth grass, the herb yielding seed, and the fruit tree yielding fruit after his kind, whose seed is in itself, upon the earth: and it was so.

12 And the earth brought forth grass, and herb yielding seed after his kind, and the tree yielding fruit, whose seed was in itself, after his kind: and God saw that it was good.

13 And thus was evening and morning: **third day**.

14 And God said, Let there be luminaries in the expanse of the heavens to divide the day from the night; and let them be for signs, and for set times,[7] and for days and years:

15 And let them be for luminaries in the expanse of the heavens to give light upon the earth: and it was so.

16 And God made two great luminaries; the greater luminary to rule the day, and the lesser luminary to rule the night: he made the stars also.

17 And God set them in the expanse of the heavens to give light upon the earth,

18 And to rule over the day and over the night, and to divide the light from the darkness: and God saw that it was good.

19 And thus was evening and morning: **fourth day**.

20 And God said, Let the waters swarm with the swarming soul that has life, and fowl that may fly above the earth across the expanse of the heavens.

21 And God created great sea-animals, and every living soul that moves, with which the waters swarm, after their kind, and every winged fowl after his kind: and God saw that it was good.

22 And God blessed them, saying, Be fruitful, and multiply, and fill the waters in the seas, and let fowl multiply in the earth.

23 And thus was evening and morning: **fifth day**.

24 And God said, Let the earth bring forth the living soul after her kind, animal, and creeping thing, and living things of the earth after her kind: and it was so.

25 And God made the living things of the earth after her kind, and animal after her kind, and every thing that creeps upon the earth after his kind: and God saw that it was good.

26 And **God said, Let us make man in our image**, after our likeness: and let them have dominion over the fish of the sea, and over the fowl of the air, and over the animal, and over all the earth, and over every creeping thing that creeps , upon the earth.

27 So **God created the man in his own image, in the image of God he created him; male and female**[8] **he created them. [1 YM – first Year of Man]**

28 And God blessed them, and God said unto them, Be fruitful, and multiply, and fill the earth, and subdue her: and have dominion over the fish of the sea, and over the fowl of the air, and over every living thing that moves upon the earth.

29 And God said, Behold, I have given you every herb bearing seed, which is upon the face of all the earth, and every tree, in the which is the fruit of a tree yielding seed; to you it shall be for food.

30 And to every beast of the earth, and to every fowl of the air, and to every thing that creeps upon the earth, wherein there is soul of life, I have given every green herb for food: and it was so.

---

[1] When you see "God" in this translation of the OT it is translated from its plural/dual form (*elohim*), which means powers in the plural or dual depending on context. See Gesenius § 87(a) & 88(a)(e). See GP8, re: Holy of holies & 2 Cor 4:4 note.

[2] Heb. *Bara* verb, perfect, 3rd person, singular; used with *elohim*, a dual/plural noun that means "power" translated as God or gods; *bara* with *elohim* is used only 5 times in the OT (Gen 1:1, Gen 1:27 [twice]; Gen 2:3' Gen 4:32).

[3] In the Hebrew the verb translated "was" is in the perfect or complete tense. The earth did not become, it was already "in the beginning" in a state of incompleteness.

[4] Imperfect verb

[5] Imperfect verb. Imperfect verbs appear in Gen 1:6; 1:9; 1:11, etc.

[6] The Hebrew means agreeable, functional, good

[7] Or appointed times or festivals

[8] Male and female are both corresponding and complementary to one another as well as opposite to one another [Gen 2:18, 20], yet - the two are one [Gen 2:24], both together are called Adam or mankind [Gen 5:1-2] *and* they both were made in the image of Elohim [Gen 1:27]. See GP8, Ex 25:20

Note: "Becoming-One" = YHWH; "God" = *Elohim*; "gods" = *elohim*; "GOD" = *El* or *Eloah*

31 And God saw every thing that he had made, and, behold, it was very good. And thus was evening and morning: **sixth day**.

Gen 2:1 Thus the heavens and the earth were being finished [imp[9]] and all the host of them.

2 And **on the seventh day** God will end [imp] his work which he had made; and he will rest [imp] on the seventh day from all his work which he had made.

3 And God blessed [imp] the seventh day, and sanctified [imp] it: because on it he rested from all his work which God created and made.

4 These the generations of the heavens and of the earth when they were created, in the day that the Becoming-One[10] God made the earth and the heavens,

5 And every plant of the field before it was in the earth, and every herb of the field before it grew: for the Becoming-One God had not caused it to rain upon the earth, and there was not a man to till the ground.

6 But there went up a mist from the earth, and watered the whole face of the ground.

7 And the Becoming-One God formed man of the dust of the ground, and breathed into his nostrils the breath of life; and man became a living soul.

8 And the Becoming-One God planted a garden eastward in Eden; and there he put the man whom he had formed.

9 And out of the ground made the Becoming-One God to grow every tree that is pleasant to the sight, and good for food; the **tree of life** also in the midst of the garden, and the **tree of knowledge of good and evil**[11].

10 And a river went out of Eden to water the garden; and from there it was parted, and became into four heads.

11 The name of the first is Pison: that is it which compasses the whole land of Havilah, where there is gold;

12 And the gold of that land is good: there is bdellium and the onyx stone.

13 And the name of the second river is Gihon: the same is it that compasses the whole land of Ethiopia.

14 And the name of the third river is Hiddekel: that is it which goes toward the east of Assyria. And the fourth river is Euphrates.

15 And the Becoming-One God took the man, and put him into the garden of Eden to dress it and to keep it.

16 And the Becoming-One God commanded the man, saying, Of every tree of the garden you may freely eat:

17 But of the tree of the knowledge of good and evil, you shall not eat of It: for in the day that you eat from it, in dying, you will die.[12]

18 And the Becoming-One God said, **It is not good that the man should be alone**; I will make him a helpmate corresponding[13] to him.

19 And out of the ground the Becoming-One God formed every beast of the field, and every fowl of the air; and brought them unto Adam to see what he would call them: and whatsoever Adam called every living soul, that was the name thereof.

20 And Adam gave names to every animal, and to the fowl of the air, and to every beast of the field; but for Adam there was not found a helpmate corresponding[14] to him.

21 And the Becoming-One God caused a deep sleep to fall upon Adam, and he slept: and one [fem gender] he took from his side, and closed up her place with flesh;

22 And the side [fem] which the Becoming-One God had taken from man, made he a woman, and brought her unto the man.

23 And Adam said, This is now bone from my bones, and flesh from my flesh: she shall be called Woman, because she was taken out of Man.

24 Therefore shall a man leave his father and his mother, and shall cleave unto his wife: and **they shall be one flesh**.

25 And they were both naked, the man and his wife, and were not ashamed.

Gen 3:1 Now the serpent[15] was more subtle than any beast of the field which the Becoming-One God had made. And he said unto the woman, Yes, has God said, you shall not eat of every tree of the garden?

2 And the woman said unto the serpent, We may eat of the fruit of the trees of the garden:

3 But of the fruit of the tree which is in the midst of the garden, God has said, you shall not eat of it, neither shall you touch it, lest you die.

4 And **the serpent said unto the woman, not in dying shall you be dead**. [First lie lead to man's death]

5 For God does know that in the day you eat thereof, then your eyes shall be opened, and you shall be as God, knowing good and evil.

6 And when the woman saw that the tree was good for food, and that it was pleasant to the eyes, and a tree to be desired to make one wise, she took of the fruit thereof, and did eat, and gave also unto her husband with her; and he did eat.

7 And the eyes of them both were opened, and they knew that they were naked; and they sewed fig leaves together, and made themselves aprons.

8 And they heard the voice of the Becoming-One God walking in the garden in the wind of the day: and Adam and his wife hid themselves from the presence

---

[9] Imp = imperfect verb

[10] Becoming-One = "He (who) will-be" ; יהוה ; YHWH. "God" = elohim, which is the plural/dual of God. Thus literally, "Becoming-One God" = "He (who) will-be Gods." The people who witnesses answered prayer put it this way: "Yehowah, He **the** Gods" (1 Kings 18:39, repeated twice in the verse, see Hebrew text). The Hebrew equivalent for the English "the" is in the Hebrew text. And see Heb. in 2 Kings 19:15.

[11] The Hebrew means disagreeable, dysfunctional, bad

[12] מוֹת תָּמוּת – "in dying, you will die": the repetition here of the word die or death emphasized the death Adam would die; or when he died, he would be dead – when he died he would be part of the group called the "dead"; Adam also died in the first 1000 year "day," therefore he died in the first anti-typical day in which he ate from the tree.

[13] Or *opposite* to him, see Hebrew

[14] Or *opposite* to him, see Hebrew

[15] Satan, See Rev 20:2

of the Becoming-One God among the trees of the garden.

9 And the Becoming-One God called unto Adam, and said unto him, Where are you?

10 And he said, I heard your voice in the garden, and I was afraid, because I was naked; and I hid myself.

11 And he said, Who told you that you were naked? have you eaten of the tree, whereof I commanded you that you should not eat?

12 And the man said, The woman whom you gave to be with me, she gave me of the tree, and I did eat.

13 And the Becoming-One God said unto the woman, What is this that you have done? And the woman said, The serpent beguiled me, and I did eat.

14 **And the Becoming-One God said unto the serpent,** Because you have done this, you are cursed above every animal, and above every beast of the field; upon your belly shall you go, and dust shall you eat all the days of your life:

15 And I will put enmity between you and the woman, and between your seed and her seed; he shall bruise your head, and you shall bruise his heel.

16 **Unto the woman he said**, I will greatly multiply your pain and your conception; in pain you shall bring forth children; and your desire shall be to your husband, and he shall rule over you.

17 **And unto Adam he said**, Because you have listened unto the voice of your wife, and have eaten of the tree, of which I commanded you, saying, you shall not eat of it: cursed is the ground for your sake; in toil shall you eat of it all the days of your life;

18 Thorns also and thistles shall it bring forth to you; and you shall eat the herb of the field;

19 In the sweat of your face shall you eat bread, till you return unto the ground; for out of it were you taken: for dust you are, and unto dust shall you return.

20 And Adam called his wife's name Eve; because she was the mother of all living.

21 Unto Adam also and to his wife did the Becoming-One God make coats of skins, and clothed them.

22 And the Becoming-One God said, Behold, the man is become as one from us, to know good and evil: and now, lest he put forth his hand, and take also of the tree of life, and eat, and live for olam . . .

23 Therefore the Becoming-One God sent him forth from the garden of Eden, to till the ground from where he was taken.

24 **So he drove out the man; and he placed at the east of the garden of Eden Cherubs,[16] and a flaming sword which turned every way, to guard the way of the tree of life.**

Gen 4:1 And Adam knew Eve his wife; and she conceived, and bare Cain, and said, I have gotten a man by means of the Becoming-One.

2 And she again bare his brother Abel. And Abel was a keeper of sheep, but Cain was a tiller of the ground.

3 And being the end of days, Cain brought of the fruit of the ground an offering unto the Becoming-One.

4 And Abel, he also brought of the firstlings of his flock and of the fat thereof. And the Becoming-One had regard unto Abel and to his offering:

5 But unto Cain and to his offering he had no regard. And Cain was very angry, and his face fell.

6 And the Becoming-One said unto Cain, Why are you angry? and why is your face fallen?

7 If you do well, shall you not be accepted? and if you do not well, sin lies at the door. And unto you shall be his [sin's] desire, but you must begin to master him.

8 And Cain talked with Abel his brother: and it came to pass, when they were in the field, that Cain rose up against Abel his brother, and killed him.

9 And the Becoming-One said unto Cain, Where is Abel your brother? And he said, I know not: Am I my brother's keeper?

10 And he said, What have you done? the voice of your brother's blood cries unto me from the ground.

11 And now are you cursed from the earth, which has opened her mouth to receive your brother's blood from your hand;

12 When you till the ground, it shall not henceforth yield unto you her strength; a fugitive and a vagabond shall you be in the earth.

13 And Cain said unto the Becoming-One, My punishment is greater than I can bear.

14 Behold, you have driven me out this day from the face of the earth; and from your face shall I be hid; and I shall be a fugitive and a vagabond in the earth; and it shall come to pass, that every one that finds me shall slay me.

15 And the Becoming-One said unto him, Therefore whosoever slays Cain, vengeance shall be taken on him sevenfold. And the Becoming-One set a mark upon Cain, lest any finding him should kill him.

16 And Cain went out from the presence of the Becoming-One, and dwelt in the land of Nod, east of Eden.

17 And Cain knew his wife; and she conceived, and bare **Enoch: and he built a city**, and called the name of the city, after the name of his son, Enoch.

18 And unto Enoch was born Irad: and Irad begat Mehujael: and Mehujael begat Methusael: and Methusael begat Lamech.

19 And Lamech took unto him two wives: the name of the one was Adah, and the name of the other Zillah.

20 And Adah bare Jabal: **he was the father of such as dwell in tents**, and of such as have cattle.

21 And his brother's name was Jubal: **he was the father of all such as handle the harp and organ**.

22 And Zillah, she also bare Tubalcain, **an instructor of every artificer in brass and iron**: and the sister of Tubalcain was Naamah.

23 And Lamech said unto his wives, Adah and Zillah, Hear my voice; you wives of Lamech, listen unto my speech: for I have slain a man to my wounding, and a young man to my hurt.

24 If Cain shall be avenged sevenfold, truly Lamech seventy and sevenfold.

25 And Adam knew his wife again; and she bare a son, and called his name Seth: For God, said she, has appointed me another seed instead of Abel, whom Cain killed.

---

[16] *Cherubim*, See Holy of holies & GP8

26 And to Seth, to him also there was born a son; and he called his name Enos: **then began men to call in [with or by] the name of the Becoming-One**.

Gen 5:1 This is **the book of the generations of Adam**. In the day that God created man, in the likeness of God he made him;

2 Male and female created he them; and blessed them, and called their name Adam, in the day when they were created. **[1 - 930 YM]**

3 And Adam lived a hundred and thirty years, and begat a son in his own likeness, after his image; and called his name Seth:

4 And the days of Adam after he had begotten Seth were eight hundred years: and he begat sons and daughters:

5 And all the days that Adam lived were nine hundred and thirty years: and he died.

6 And Seth lived a hundred and five years, and begat Enos:

7 And Seth lived after he begat Enos eight hundred and seven years, and begat sons and daughters:

8 And all the days of Seth were nine hundred and twelve years: and he died.

9 And Enos lived ninety years, and begat Cainan:

10 And Enos lived after he begat Cainan eight hundred and fifteen years, and begat sons and daughters:

11 And all the days of Enos were nine hundred and five years: and he died.

12 And Cainan lived seventy years, and begat Mahalaleel:

13 And Cainan lived after he begat Mahalaleel eight hundred and forty years, and begat sons and daughters:

14 And all the days of Cainan were nine hundred and ten years: and he died.

15 And Mahalaleel lived sixty and five years, and begat Jared:

16 And Mahalaleel lived after he begat Jared eight hundred and thirty years, and begat sons and daughters:

17 And all the days of Mahalaleel were eight hundred ninety and five years: and he died.

18 And Jared lived a hundred sixty and two years, and he begat Enoch:

19 And Jared lived after he begat Enoch eight hundred years, and begat sons and daughters:

20 And all the days of Jared were nine hundred sixty and two years: and he died.

21 And Enoch lived sixty and five years, and begat Methuselah:

22 And Enoch walked with God after he begat Methuselah three hundred years, and begat sons and daughters:

23 And all the days of Enoch were three hundred sixty and five years:

24 And Enoch walked with God: and he was not; for God took him.

25 And Methuselah lived a hundred eighty and seven years, and begat Lamech:

26 And Methuselah lived after he begat Lamech seven hundred eighty and two years, and begat sons and daughters:

27 And all the days of Methuselah were nine hundred sixty and nine years: and he died.

28 And Lamech lived a hundred eighty and two years, and begat a son:

29 And he called his name **Noah**, saying, This same shall comfort us concerning our work and toil of our hands, because of the ground which the Becoming-One has cursed. **[1056 - 2006 YM]**

30 And Lamech lived after he begat Noah five hundred ninety and five years, and begat sons and daughters:

31 And all the days of Lamech were seven hundred seventy and seven years: and he died.

32 And Noah was a son of five hundred years: and **Noah** begat Shem, Ham, and Japheth.

Gen 6:1 And it was that when men began to multiply on the face of the earth, and daughters were born unto them,

2 That the sons of God saw the daughters of men that they were fair; and they took them wives of all which they chose.

3 And the Becoming-One said, My spirit shall not for olam plead with man, for he is flesh: **so his days shall be a hundred and twenty years**.

4 There were giants in the earth in those days; and also after that, when the sons of God came in unto the daughters of men, and they bare children to them, the same became mighty men which were from olam men of renown.

5 **And God saw that the wickedness of man was great in the earth, and that every imagination of the thoughts of his heart was only evil daily**.

6 And the Becoming-One was sorry that he had made man on the earth, and it grieved him to his heart.

7 And the Becoming-One said, I will destroy man whom I have created from the face of the earth; both man, and beast, and the creeping thing, and the fowls of the air; for I am lament [grieved repented] that I have made them.

8 But Noah found grace in the eyes of the Becoming-One.

9 **These are the generations of Noah**: Noah was a just man and he was cut off with his generation, for Noah walked with God.

10 And Noah begat three sons, Shem, Ham, and Japheth.

11 The earth also was corrupt before God, and the earth was filled with violence.

12 And God looked upon the earth, and, behold, it was corrupt; for all flesh had corrupted his way upon the earth.

13 And God said unto Noah, The end of all flesh is come before me; for the earth is filled with violence through them; and, behold, I will destroy them with the earth.

14 Make you an ark of gopher wood; rooms shall you make in the ark, and shall pitch [atone] it within and without with pitch [atonement or covering]

15 And this is the fashion which you shall make it of: The length of the ark shall be three hundred cubits, the breadth of it fifty cubits, and the height of it thirty cubits.

16 A window shall you make to the ark, and in a cubit shall you finish it above; and the door of the ark

shall you set in the side thereof; with lower, second, and third stories shall you make it.

17 And, behold, I, even I, do bring a flood of waters upon the earth, to destroy all flesh, wherein is the breath of life, from under the heavens; and every thing that is in the earth shall die.

18 But with you will I establish my covenant; and you shall come into the ark, you, and your sons, and your wife, and your sons' wives with you.

19 And of every living thing of all flesh, two of every sort shall you bring into the ark, to keep them alive with you; they shall be male and female.

20 Of fowls after their kind, and of animal after their kind, of every creeping thing of the earth after his kind, two of every sort shall come unto you, to keep them alive.

21 And take you unto you of all food that is eaten, and you shall gather it to you; and it shall be for food for you, and for them.

22 Thus did Noah; according to all that God commanded him, so did he.

Gen 7:1 And the Becoming-One said unto Noah, Come you and all your household into the ark; for I have seen that you are righteous before me in this generation.

2 Of every clean beast you shall take to you by sevens, the male and his female: and of beasts that are not clean by two, the male and his female.

3 Of fowls also of the air by sevens, the male and the female; to keep seed alive upon the face of all the earth.

4 For yet seven days, and I will cause it to rain upon the earth forty days and forty nights; and every living substance that I have made will I destroy from off the face of the earth.

5 And Noah did according unto all that the Becoming-One commanded him.

6 And Noah was a son of six hundred years when the flood of waters was upon the earth. **[1656 YM]**

7 And Noah went in, and his sons, and his wife, and his sons' wives with him, into the ark, because of the waters of the flood.

8 Of clean beasts, and of beasts that are not clean, and of fowls, and of every thing that creeps upon the earth,

9 There went in two and two unto Noah into the ark, the male and the female, as God had commanded Noah.

10 And it came to pass after seven days, that the waters of the flood were upon the earth.

11 In the six hundredth year of Noah's life, in the second month, the seventeenth day of the month, the same day were all the fountains of the great deep burst forth, and the windows of the heavens were opened.

12 And the rain was upon the earth forty days and forty nights.

13 In the selfsame day entered Noah, and Shem, and Ham, and Japheth, the sons of Noah, and Noah's wife, and the three wives of his sons with them, into the ark;

14 They, and every beast after his kind, and every animal after their kind, and every creeping thing that creeps upon the earth after his kind, and every fowl after his kind, every bird of every sort.

15 And they went in unto Noah into the ark, two and two of all flesh, wherein is the breath of life.

16 And they that went in, went in male and female of all flesh, as God had commanded him: and the Becoming-One shut him in.

17 And the flood was forty days upon the earth; and the waters increased, and bare up the ark, and it was lift up above the earth.

18 And the waters prevailed, and were increased greatly upon the earth; and the ark went upon the face of the waters.

19 And the waters prevailed exceedingly upon the earth; and all the high hills, that were under the whole heavens, were covered.

20 Fifteen cubits upwards the waters prevail; and were covering the mountains.

21 And all flesh died that moved upon the earth, both of fowl, and of animal, and of beast, and of every creeping thing that creeps upon the earth, and every man:

22 All in whose nostrils was the breath of the spirit of lives, of all that was in the dry land, died.

23 And every living substance was destroyed which was upon the face of the ground, both man, and animal, and the creeping things, and the fowl of the heavens; and they were destroyed from the earth: and Noah only remained alive, and they that were with him in the ark.

24 And the waters prevailed upon the earth a hundred and fifty days.

Gen 8:1 And God remembered Noah, and every living thing, and every animal that was with him in the ark: and God made a wind to pass over the earth, and the waters subsided;

2 The fountains also of the deep and the windows of the heavens were stopped, and the rain from the heavens was restrained;

3 And the waters returned from off the earth continually: and after the end of the hundred and fifty days the waters were abated.

4 And the ark rested in the seventh month, on the seventeenth day of the month, upon the mountains of Ararat.

5 And the waters decreased continually until the tenth month: in the tenth month, on the first day of the month, were the tops of the mountains seen.

6 And it came to pass at the end of forty days, that Noah opened the window of the ark which he had made:

7 And he sent forth a raven, which went forth back and forth, until the waters were dried up from off the earth.

8 Also he sent forth a dove from him, to see if the waters were abated from off the face of the ground;

9 But the dove found no rest for the sole of her foot, and she returned unto him into the ark, for the waters were on the face of the whole earth: then he put forth his hand, and took her, and pulled her in unto him into the ark.

10 And he stayed yet other seven days; and again he sent forth the dove out of the ark;

11 And the dove came in to him in the time of the evening; and, lo, in her mouth was an olive leaf plucked off: so Noah knew that the waters were abated from off the earth.

12 And he stayed yet other seven days; and sent forth the dove; which returned not again unto him any more.

13 And it came to pass in the six hundredth and first year, in the first month, the first day of the month, the waters were dried up from off the earth: and Noah removed the covering of the ark, and looked, and, behold, the face of the ground was dry.

14 And in the second month, on the seven and twentieth day of the month, was the earth dried.

15 And God spoke unto Noah, saying,

16 Go forth of the ark, you, and your wife, and your sons, and your sons' wives with you.

17 Bring forth with you every living thing that is with you, of all flesh, both of fowl, and of animal, and of every creeping thing that creeps upon the earth; that they may breed abundantly in the earth, and be fruitful, and multiply upon the earth.

18 And Noah went forth, and his sons, and his wife, and his sons' wives with him:

19 Every beast, every creeping thing, and every fowl, and all that creeps upon the earth, after their kinds, went forth out of the ark.

20 And Noah built an altar unto the Becoming-One; and took of every clean beast, and of every clean fowl, and offered burnt offerings on the altar.

21 And the Becoming-One smelled a sweet aroma; and the Becoming-One said in his heart, I will not again curse the ground any more for man's sake; for the imagination of man's heart is evil from his youth; neither will I again smite any more every thing living, as I have done.

22 For all the days of the earth, seedtime and harvest, and cold and heat, and summer and winter, and day and night shall not cease.

Gen 9:1 And God blessed Noah and his sons, and said unto them, Be fruitful, and multiply, and fill the earth.

2 And the fear of you and the dread of you shall be upon every beast of the earth, and upon every fowl of the air, upon all that moves upon the earth, and upon all the fishes of the sea; into your hand are they delivered.

3 Every moving thing that lives shall be food for you; even as the green herb I have given you all things.

4 But flesh with the soul thereof, which is the blood thereof, shall you not eat.

5 And surely your blood of your soul will I require; at the hand of every beast will I require it, and at the hand of man; at the hand of every man's brother will I require the soul of man.

6 Whoso sheds man's blood, by man shall his blood be shed: for in the image of God made he man.

7 And you, be you fruitful, and multiply; bring forth abundantly in the earth, and multiply therein.

8 And God spoke unto Noah, and to his sons with him, saying,

9 And I, behold, I establish my covenant with you, and with your seed after you;

10 And with every living soul that is with you, of the fowl, of the animal, and of every beast of the earth with you; from all that go out of the ark, to every beast of the earth.

11 And I will establish my covenant with you; neither shall all flesh be cut off any more by the waters of a flood; neither shall there any more be a flood to destroy the earth.

12 And God said, This is the token of the covenant which I make between me and you and every living soul that is with you, for generations of olam.

13 I do set my bow in the cloud, and it shall be for a token of a covenant between me and the earth.

14 And it shall come to pass, when I bring a cloud over the earth, that the bow shall be seen in the cloud:

15 And I will remember my covenant, which is between me and you and every living soul of all flesh; and the waters shall no more become a flood to destroy all flesh.

16 And the bow shall be in the cloud; and I will look upon it, that I may remember the covenant of olam between God and every living soul of all flesh that is upon the earth.

17 And God said unto Noah, This is the token of the covenant, which I have established between me and all flesh that is upon the earth.

18 And the sons of Noah, that went forth of the ark, were Shem, and Ham, and Japheth: and Ham is the father of Canaan.

19 These are the three sons of Noah: and from them was the whole earth overspread.

20 And Noah began to be a husbandman, and he planted a vineyard:

21 And he drank of the wine, and was drunken; and he was uncovered within his tent.

22 And Ham, the father of Canaan, saw the nakedness of his father, and told his two brethren outside.

23 And Shem and Japheth took a garment, and laid it upon both their shoulders, and went backward, and covered the nakedness of their father; and their faces were backward, and they saw not their father's nakedness.

24 And Noah awoke from his wine, and knew what his younger son had done unto him.

25 And he said, Cursed be Canaan; a servant of servants shall he be unto his brethren.

26 And he said, Blessed be the Becoming-One, God of Shem; and Canaan shall be his servant.

27 God shall enlarge Japheth, and he shall dwell in the tents of Shem; and Canaan shall be his servant.

28 And Noah lived after the flood three hundred and fifty years.

29 And all the days of Noah were nine hundred and fifty years: and he died.

Gen 10:1 Now these are the **generations of the sons of Noah**, Shem, Ham, and Japheth: and unto them were sons born after the flood.

2 The sons of Japheth; Gomer, and Magog, and Madai, and Javan, and Tubal, and Meshech, and Tiras.

3 And the sons of Gomer; Ashkenaz, and Riphath, and Togarmah.

4 And the sons of Javan; Elishah, and Tarshish, Kittim, and Dodanim.

5 By these were the isles of the nations divided in their lands; every one after his tongue, after their families, in their nations.

6 And the sons of Ham; Cush, and Mizraim, and Phut, and Canaan.

7 And the sons of Cush; Seba, and Havilah, and Sabtah, and Raamah, and Sabtechah: and the sons of Raamah; Sheba, and Dedan.

8 And Cush begat Nimrod: he began to be a mighty one in the earth.

9 He was a mighty hunter before the Becoming-One; therefore it is said, Even as Nimrod the mighty hunter before the Becoming-One.

10 And the beginning of his kingdom was Babel, and Erech, and Accad, and Calneh, in the land of Shinar.

11 Out of that land went forth Asshur, and built Nineveh, and the city Rehoboth, and Calah,

12 And Resen between Nineveh and Calah: the same is a great city.

13 And Mizraim begat Ludim, and Anamim, and Lehabim, and Naphtuhim,

14 And Pathrusim, and Casluhim, out of whom came Philistim, and Caphtorim.

15 And Canaan begat Sidon his firstborn, and Heth,

16 And the Jebusite, and the Amorite, and the Girgasite,

17 And the Hivite, and the Arkite, and the Sinite,

18 And the Arvadite, and the Zemarite, and the Hamathite: and afterward were the families of the Canaanites spread abroad.

19 And the border of the Canaanites was from Sidon, as you come to Gerar, unto Gaza; as you go, unto Sodom, and Gomorrah, and Admah, and Zeboim, even unto Lasha.

20 These are the sons of Ham, after their families, after their tongues, in their countries, and in their nations.

21 Unto Shem also, the father of all the children of Eber, the brother of Japheth the elder, even to him were children born.

22 The children of Shem; Elam, and Asshur, and Arphaxad, and Lud, and Aram.

23 And the children of Aram; Uz, and Hul, and Gether, and Mash.

24 And Arphaxad begat Salah; and Salah begat Eber.

25 And unto Eber were born two sons: the name of one was Peleg; for in his days was the earth divided [see two] and his brother's name was Joktan.

26 And Joktan begat Almodad, and Sheleph, and Hazarmaveth, and Jerah,

27 And Hadoram, and Uzal, and Diklah,

28 And Obal, and Abimael, and Sheba,

29 And Ophir, and Havilah, and Jobab: all these were the sons of Joktan.

30 And their dwelling was from Mesha, as you go unto Sephar a mount of the east.

31 These are the sons of Shem, after their families, after their tongues, in their lands, after their nations.

32 These are the families of the sons of Noah, after their generations, in their nations: and by these were the nations divided in the earth after the flood.

Gen 11:1 And the whole earth was of one language, and of few words [or same words]

2 And it came to pass, as they journeyed from the east, that they found a plain in the land of Shinar; and they dwelt there.

3 And they said one to another, Go to, let us make brick, and burn them thoroughly. And they had brick for stone, and bitumen had they for mortar.

4 And they said, Go to, let us build us a city and a tower, whose top may reach unto the heavens; and let us make us a name, lest we be scattered abroad upon the face of the whole earth.

5 And the Becoming-One came down to see the city and the tower, which the children of men built.

6 And the Becoming-One said, Behold, the people is one, and they have all one language; and this they begin to do: and now nothing will be restrained from them, which they have imagined to do.

7 Go to, let us go down, and there confound their language, that they may not understand one another's speech.

8 So the Becoming-One scattered them abroad from there upon the face of all the earth: and they left off building the city.

9 Therefore is the name of it called Babel; because the Becoming-One did there confound the language of all the earth: and from there did the Becoming-One scatter them abroad upon the face of all the earth.

10 These are the generations of Shem: Shem was a son of a hundred years, and begat Arphaxad two years after the flood:

11 And Shem lived after he begat Arphaxad five hundred years, and begat sons and daughters.

12 And Arphaxad lived five and thirty years, and begat Salah:

13 And Arphaxad lived after he begat Salah four hundred and three years, and begat sons and daughters.

14 And Salah lived thirty years, and begat Eber:

15 And Salah lived after he begat Eber four hundred and three years, and begat sons and daughters.

16 And Eber lived four and thirty years, and begat Peleg:

17 And Eber lived after he begat Peleg four hundred and thirty years, and begat sons and daughters.

18 And Peleg lived thirty years, and begat Reu:

19 And Peleg lived after he begat Reu two hundred and nine years, and begat sons and daughters.

20 And Reu lived two and thirty years, and begat Serug:

21 And Reu lived after he begat Serug two hundred and seven years, and begat sons and daughters.

22 And Serug lived thirty years, and begat Nahor:

23 And Serug lived after he begat Nahor two hundred years, and begat sons and daughters.

24 And Nahor lived nine and twenty years, and begat Terah:

25 And Nahor lived after he begat Terah a hundred and nineteen years, and begat sons and daughters.

26 And Terah lived seventy years, and begat **Abram**, Nahor, and Haran.

27 Now these are the generations of Terah: Terah begat Abram, Nahor, and Haran; and Haran begat Lot.

28 And Haran died before his father Terah in the land of his nativity, in Ur of the Chaldees.

29 And Abram and Nahor took them wives: the name of Abram's wife was Sarai; and the name of Nahor's wife, Milcah, the daughter of Haran, the father of Milcah, and the father of Iscah.

30 But Sarai was barren; she had no child.

31 And Terah took Abram his son, and Lot the son of Haran his son's son, and Sarai his daughter-in-law, his son Abram's wife; and they went forth with them from Ur of the Chaldees, to go into the land of Canaan; and they came unto Haran, and dwelt there.

32 And the days of Terah were two hundred and five years: and Terah died in Haran.

Gen 12:1 Now the Becoming-One said unto **Abram**, Get you out of your country, and from your kindred, and from your father's house, unto a land that I will show you:

2 And I will make of you a great nation, and I will bless you, and make your name great; and you shall be a blessing:

3 And I will bless them that bless you, and curse him that curses you: and in you shall all families of the earth be blessed.

4 So Abram departed, as the Becoming-One had spoken unto him; and Lot went with him: and **Abram was a son of seventy and five years when he departed out of Haran. [2083 YM]**

5 And Abram took Sarai his wife, and Lot his brother's son, and all their substance that they had gathered, and the souls that they had gotten in Haran; and **they went forth to go into the land of Canaan**; and into the land of Canaan they came.

6 And Abram passed through the land unto the place of Sichem, unto the oak of Moreh. And the Canaanite was then in the land.

7 **And the Becoming-One appeared unto Abram, and said, Unto your seed will I give this land: and there built he an altar unto the Becoming-One, who appeared unto him.**

8 **And he removed from there unto a mountain on the east of Bethel, and pitched his tent, having Bethel on the west, and Hai [Ai] on the east: and there he built an altar unto the Becoming-One, and called upon the name of the Becoming-One.**

9 And Abram journeyed, going on still toward the south.

10 **And there was a famine in the land: and Abram went down into Egypt to sojourn there; for the famine was grievous in the land.**

11 **And it came to pass, when he was come near to enter into Egypt**, that he said unto Sarai his wife, Behold now, I know that you are a fair woman to look upon:

12 Therefore it shall come to pass, when the Egyptians shall see you, that they shall say, This is his wife: and they will kill me, but they will save you alive.

13 Say, I pray you, you are my sister: that it may be well with me for your sake; and my soul shall live because of you.

14 And it came to pass, that, when Abram was come into Egypt, the Egyptians beheld the woman that she was very fair.

15 The princes also of Pharaoh saw her, and commended her before Pharaoh: and the woman was taken into Pharaoh's house.

16 And he entreated Abram well for her sake: and he had sheep, and oxen, and he donkeys, and menservants, and maidservants, and she donkeys, and camels.

17 And the Becoming-One plagued Pharaoh and his house with great plagues for the word of Sarai, Abram's wife.

18 And Pharaoh called Abram, and said, What is this that you have done unto me? why did you not tell me that she was your wife?

19 Why say you, She is my sister? so I might have taken her to me to wife: now therefore behold your wife, take her, and go your way.

20 And Pharaoh commanded his men concerning him: and they sent him away, and his wife, and all that he had.

Gen 13:1 And Abram went up out of Egypt, he, and his wife, and all that he had, and Lot with him, into the south.

2 **And Abram was very rich in cattle, in silver, and in gold.**

3 **And he went on his journeys from the south even to Bethel, unto the place where his tent had been at the beginning, between Bethel and Hai;**

4 **Unto the place of the altar, which he had made there at the first: and there Abram called in [by or with] the name of the Becoming-One.**

5 And Lot also, which went with Abram, had flocks, and herds, and tents.

6 And the land was not able to bear them, that they might dwell together: for their substance was great, so that they could not dwell together.

7 And there was a strife between the herdmen of Abram's cattle and the herdmen of Lot's cattle: and the Canaanite and the Perizzite dwelled then in the land.

8 And Abram said unto Lot, Let there be no strife, I pray you, between me and you, and between my herdmen and your herdmen; for we be brethren.

9 Is not the whole land before you? separate thyself, I pray you, from me: if you will take the left hand, then I will go to the right; or if you depart to the right hand, then I will go to the left.

10 **And Lot lifted up his eyes, and beheld all the plain of Jordan, that it was well watered every where, before the Becoming-One destroyed Sodom and Gomorrah, even as the garden of the Becoming-One, like the land of Egypt, as you come unto Zoar.**

11 Then Lot chose him all the plain of Jordan; and Lot journeyed east: and they separated themselves the one from the other.

12 **Abram dwelled in the land of Canaan, and Lot dwelled in the cities of the plain, and pitched his tent toward Sodom.**

13 But the men of Sodom were evil and sinners before the Becoming-One exceedingly.

14 And the Becoming-One said unto Abram, after that Lot was separated from him, Lift up now your eyes, and look from the place where you are northward, and southward, and eastward, and westward:

15 For all the land which you see, to you will I give it, and to your seed for olam.

16 And I will make your seed as the dust of the earth: so that if a man can number the dust of the earth, then shall your seed also be numbered.

17 Arise, walk through the land in the length of it and in the breadth of it; for I will give it unto you.

18 Then Abram removed his tent, and came and dwelt in the plain of Mamre, which is in Hebron, and built there an altar unto the Becoming-One.

Gen 14:1 And it came to pass in the days of Amraphel king of Shinar, Arioch king of Ellasar, Chedorlaomer king of Elam, and Tidal king of nations;

2 That these made war with Bera king of Sodom, and with Birsha king of Gomorrah, Shinab king of Admah, and Shemeber king of Zeboiim, and the king of Bela, which is Zoar.

3 All these were joined together in the vale of Siddim, which is the salt sea.

4 Twelve years they served Chedorlaomer, and in the thirteenth year they rebelled.

5 And in the fourteenth year came Chedorlaomer, and the kings that were with him, and smote the Rephaims [giants] in Ashteroth Karnaim, and the Zuzims in Ham, and the Emims in Shaveh Kiriathaim,

6 And the Horites in their mount Seir, unto Elparan, which is by the wilderness.

7 And they returned, and came to Enmishpat, which is Kadesh, and smote all the country of the Amalekites, and also the Amorites, that dwelt in Hazezontamar.

8 And there went out the king of Sodom, and the king of Gomorrah, and the king of Admah, and the king of Zeboiim, and the king of Bela the same is Zoar; and they joined battle with them in the vale of Siddim;

9 With Chedorlaomer the king of Elam, and with Tidal king of nations, and Amraphel king of Shinar, and Arioch king of Ellasar; four kings with five.

10 **And the vale of Siddim was full of pits of bitumen;** and the kings of Sodom and Gomorrah fled, and fell there; and they that remained fled to the mountain.

11 And they took all the goods of Sodom and Gomorrah, and all their victuals, and went their way.

12 And they took Lot, Abram's brother's son, who dwelt in Sodom, and his goods, and departed.

13 And there came one that had escaped, and told Abram the Hebrew; for he dwelt in the plain of Mamre the Amorite, brother of Eshcol, and brother of Aner: and these were confederate with Abram.

14 And when Abram heard that his brother was taken captive, he armed his trained servants, born in his own house, three hundred and eighteen, and pursued them unto Dan.

15 And he divided himself against them, he and his servants, by night, and smote them, and pursued them unto Hobah, which is north of Damascus.

16 And he brought back all the goods, and also brought again his brother Lot, and his goods, and the women also, and the people.

17 And the king of Sodom went out to meet him after his return from the slaughter of Chedorlaomer, and of the kings that were with him, at the valley of Shaveh, which is the king's road.

18 And **Melchizedek** king of Salem brought forth bread and wine: and he was the priest of the most high GOD.

19 And he blessed him, and said, Blessed be Abram of the most high GOD, maker of the heavens and earth:

20 And blessed be the most high GOD, which has delivered your enemies into your hand. And he [Abram] gave him tithes of all.

21 And the king of Sodom said unto Abram, Give me the souls, and take the goods to thyself.

22 And Abram said to the king of Sodom, I have lift up mine hand unto the Becoming-One, the most high GOD, the maker of the heavens and earth,

23 That I will not take from a thread even to a shoelatchet, and that I will not take any thing that is yours, lest you should say, I have made Abram rich:

24 Save only that which the young men have eaten, and the portion of the men which went with me, Aner, Eshcol, and Mamre; let them take their portion.

Gen 15:1 After these things the word of the Becoming-One came unto Abram in a vision, saying, Fear not, Abram: I am your shield, and your exceeding great reward.

2 And Abram said, My Lord(s) the Becoming-One, what will you give me, seeing I go childless, and the acquisition heir of my house is this Eliezer of Damascus?

3 And Abram said, Behold, to me you have given no seed: and, lo, a son [adopted son or servant] of my house is taking possession of my house.

4 And, behold, the word of the Becoming-One came unto him, saying, This shall not be your heir; but he that shall come forth out of your own bowels shall be your heir.

5 And he brought him forth abroad, and said, Look now toward the heavens, and tell the stars, if you be able to number them: and he said unto him, So shall your seed be.

6 And he believed in the Becoming-One; and He counted it to him for righteousness.

7 And He said unto him, I am the Becoming-One that brought you out of Ur of the Chaldees, to give you this land to inherit it.

8 And he said, My Lord(s) the Becoming-One, whereby shall I know that I shall inherit it?

9 And He said unto him, Take me a heifer of three years, and a she goat of three years, and a ram of three years, and a turtledove, and a young pigeon.

10 And he took unto him all these, and divided them in the midst, and laid each piece one against another: but the birds divided he not.

11 And when the fowls came down upon the carcases, Abram drove them away.

12 And when the sun was going down, a deep sleep fell upon Abram; and, lo, a horror of great darkness fell upon him.

13 And He said unto Abram, Know of a surety that your seed shall be a stranger in a land that is not theirs, and shall serve them; and they shall afflict them four hundred years; [2113 - 2513 YM]

14 And also that nation, whom they shall serve, will I judge: and afterward shall they come out with great substance.

15 And you shall go to your fathers in peace; you shall be buried in a good old age.

16 But in the **fourth generation** they shall come here again: for the iniquity of the Amorites is not yet full.

17 And it came to pass, that, when the sun went down, and it was dark, behold a smoking furnace, and a burning lamp that passed between those pieces.

18 **In the same day the Becoming-One made a covenant with Abram, saying, Unto your seed I have given this land, from the river of Egypt unto the great river, the river Euphrates:**

19 The Kenites, and the Kenizzites, and the Kadmonites,

20 And the Hittites, and the Perizzites, and the Rephaims [giants]

21 And the Amorites, and the Canaanites, and the Girgashites, and the Jebusites.

Gen 16:1 Now Sarai Abram's wife bare him no children: and she had a handmaid, an Egyptian, whose name was Hagar.

2 And Sarai said unto Abram, Behold now, the Becoming-One has restrained me from bearing: I pray you, go in unto my maid; it may be that I may obtain children by her. And Abram listened to the voice of Sarai.

3 And Sarai Abram's wife took Hagar her maid the Egyptian, at the end of ten years Abram had dwelt in the land of Canaan, and gave her to her husband Abram to be his wife.

4 And he went in unto Hagar, and she conceived: and when she saw that she had conceived, her mistress was despised in her eyes.

5 And Sarai said unto Abram, The wrong done to me is on you [of your doing] I have given my maid into your bosom; and when she saw that she had conceived, I was despised in her eyes: the Becoming-One judge between me and you.

6 But Abram said unto Sarai, Behold, your maid is in your hand; do to her as it pleases you. And when Sarai dealt contemptuous with her, she fled from her face.

7 And the angel of the Becoming-One found her by a fountain of water in the wilderness, by the fountain in the way to Shur.

8 And he said, Hagar, Sarai's maid, where are you from? and where are you going? And she said, I flee from the face of my mistress Sarai.

9 And the angel of the Becoming-One said unto her, Return to your mistress, and submit yourself under her hands.

10 And the angel of the Becoming-One said unto her, I will multiply your seed exceedingly, that it shall not be numbered for multitude.

11 And the angel of the Becoming-One said unto her, Behold, you are with child, and shall bear a son, and shall call his name **Ishmael**; because the Becoming-One has heard your affliction.

12 **And he will be a wild man;** his hand will be against every man, and every man's hand against him; and he shall dwell in the presence of all his brethren.

13 And she called the name of the Becoming-One that spoke unto her, you GOD see me: for she said, Have I also here looked after him that sees me?

14 Therefore the well was called Beerlahairoi; behold, it is between Kadesh and Bered.

15 And Hagar bare Abram a son: and Abram called his son's name, which Hagar bare, Ishmael.

16 And Abram was a son of fourscore and six years, **when Hagar bare Ishmael to Abram**.

Gen 17:1 And when Abram was a son of ninety years and nine, the Becoming-One appeared to Abram, and said unto him, I am GOD Almighty walk before me, and be you complete [sound, whole]

2 And I will make my covenant between me and you, and will multiply you exceedingly.

3 And Abram fell on his face: and God talked with him, saying,

4 As for me, behold, my covenant is with you, and you shall be a father of many nations.

5 Neither shall your name any more be called Abram, but your name shall be **Abraham**; for a father of many nations I have made you.

6 And I will make you exceeding fruitful, and I will make nations of you, and kings shall come out of you.

7 And I will establish my covenant between me and you and your seed after you in their generations for a covenant of olam to be God unto you, and to your seed after you.

8 And I will give unto you, and to your seed after you, the land wherein you are a stranger, all the land of Canaan, for a possession of olam, and I will be their God.

9 And God said unto Abraham, you shall keep my covenant therefore, you, and your seed after you in their generations.

10 This is my covenant, which you shall keep, between me and you and your seed after you; **Every man child among you shall be circumcised.**

11 And you shall circumcise the flesh of your foreskin; and it shall be a token of the covenant between me and you.

12 And he that is a son of **eight days** shall be circumcised among you, every man child in your generations, he that is born in the house, or bought with money of any stranger, which is not of your seed.

13 He that is born in your house, and he that is bought with your money, must be circumcised: and my covenant shall be in your flesh for a covenant of olam.

14 And the uncircumcised male whose flesh of his foreskin is not circumcised, that soul shall be cut off from his people; he has broken my covenant.

15 And God said unto Abraham, As for Sarai your wife, you shall not call her name Sarai, but Sarah shall her name be.

16 And I will bless her, and give you a son also of her: yes, I will bless her, and she shall be a mother of nations; kings of people shall be from her.

17 Then Abraham fell upon his face, and laughed, and said in his heart, Shall a child be born unto him that is the son of a hundred years? and shall Sarah, the daughter of ninety years, bear?

18 And Abraham said unto God, O that Ishmael might live before you!

19 And God said, Sarah your wife shall bear you a son indeed; and you shall call his name **Isaac**: and I will establish my covenant with him for a covenant of olam, and with his seed after him.

20 And as for Ishmael, I have heard you: Behold, I have blessed him, and will make him fruitful, and will

multiply him exceedingly; twelve princes shall he beget, and I will make him a great nation.

21 But my covenant will I establish with Isaac, which Sarah shall bear unto you at this set time[17] in the next year.

22 And he finished talking with him, and God went up from Abraham.

23 And Abraham took Ishmael his son, and all that were born in his house, and all that were bought with his money, every male among the men of Abraham's house; and circumcised the flesh of their foreskin in the selfsame day, as God had said unto him.

24 And Abraham was a son of ninety years and nine, when he was circumcised in the flesh of his foreskin.

25 And Ishmael his son was a son of thirteen years, when he was circumcised in the flesh of his foreskin.

26 In the selfsame day was Abraham circumcised, and Ishmael his son.

27 And all the men of his house, born in the house, and bought with money of the stranger, were circumcised with him.

Gen 18:1 And the Becoming-One appeared unto him in the plains of Mamre: and he sat in the tent door in the heat of the day;

2 And he lift up his eyes and looked, and, lo, **three men stood by him**: and when he saw them, he ran to meet them from the tent door, and bowed himself toward the ground,

3 And said, My Lord(s), if now I have found favor in your sight, pass not away, I pray you, from your servant:

4 Let a little water, I pray you, be fetched, and wash your feet, and rest yourselves under the tree:

5 And I will fetch a morsel of bread, and comfort you your hearts; after that you shall pass on: since you have come to your servant. And they said, So do, as you have said.

6 And Abraham hurried into the tent unto Sarah, and said, Make ready quickly three measures of fine meal, knead it, and make cakes upon the hearth.

7 And Abraham ran unto the herd, and fetched a calf tender and good, and gave it unto a young man; and he hasted to dress it.

8 And he took butter, and milk, and the calf which he had dressed, and set it before them; and he stood by them under the tree, and they did eat.

9 And they said unto him, Where is Sarah your wife? And he said, Behold, in the tent.

10 And he said, I will certainly return unto you according to the time of life; and, lo, Sarah your wife shall have a son. And Sarah heard it in the tent door, which was behind him.

11 Now Abraham and Sarah were old and well stricken in age; and it ceased to be with Sarah after the manner of women.

12 Therefore Sarah laughed within herself, saying, After I am worn out, shall I have pleasure, my lord being old also?

13 And the Becoming-One said unto Abraham, Why did Sarah laugh, saying, Shall I of a surety bear a child, which am old?

14 Is any word too hard for the Becoming-One? At the set time[18] I will return unto you, according to the time of life, and Sarah shall have a son.

15 Then Sarah denied, saying, I laughed not; for she was afraid. And he said, Nay; but you did laugh.

16 And the men rose up from there, and looked toward Sodom: and Abraham went with them to bring them on the way.

17 And the Becoming-One said, Shall I hide from Abraham that thing which I do;

18 Seeing that Abraham shall surely become a great and mighty nation, and all the nations of the earth shall be blessed in him?

19 For I know him, that he will command his children and his household after him, and they shall keep the way of the Becoming-One, to do justice and judgment; that the Becoming-One may bring upon Abraham that which he has spoken of him.

20 **And the Becoming-One said, Because the cry of Sodom and Gomorrah is great, and because their sin is very grievous;**

21 I will go down now, and see whether they have done altogether according to the cry of it, which is come unto me; and if not, I will know.

22 And the men turned their faces from there, and went toward Sodom: but Abraham stood yet before the Becoming-One.

23 And Abraham drew near, and said, will you also destroy the righteous with the wicked?

24 Perhaps there be fifty righteous within the city: will you also destroy and not spare the place for the fifty righteous that are therein?

25 That be far from you to do after this manner, to slay the righteous with the wicked: and that the righteous should be as the wicked, that be far from you: Shall not the Judge of all the earth do right?

26 And the Becoming-One said, If I find in Sodom fifty righteous within the city, then I will spare all the place for their sakes.

27 And Abraham answered and said, Behold now, I have taken upon me to speak unto my Lord(s), which am but dust and ashes:

28 Perhaps there shall lack five of the fifty righteous: will you destroy all the city for lack of five? And he said, If I find there forty and five, I will not destroy it.

29 And he spoke unto him yet again, and said, Perhaps there shall be forty found there. And he said, I will not do it for forty's sake.

30 And he said unto him, Oh let not my Lord(s) be angry, and I will speak: Perhaps there shall thirty be found there. And he said, I will not do it, if I find thirty there.

31 And he said, Behold now, I have taken upon me to speak unto my Lord(s): Perhaps there shall be twenty found there. And he said, I will not destroy it for twenty's sake.

32 And he said, Oh let not my Lord(s) be angry, and I will speak yet but this once: Perhaps ten shall be

---

[17] Appointed time or appointed festival

[18] Appointed time or festival

found there. And he said, **I will not destroy it for ten's sake.**

33 And the Becoming-One went his way, as soon as he had left communing with Abraham: and Abraham returned unto his place.

Gen 19:1 And there came two angels to Sodom at evening; and Lot sat in the gate of Sodom: and Lot seeing them rose up to meet them; and he bowed himself with his face toward the ground;

2 And he said, Behold now, my Lord(s), turn in, I pray you, into your servant's house, and tarry all night, and wash your feet, and you shall rise up early, and go on your ways. And they said, Nay; but we will abide in the street all night.

3 And he pressed upon them greatly; and they turned in unto him, and entered into his house; and he made them a feast, and did bake unleavened bread, and they did eat.

4 But before they lay down, the men of the city, even the men of Sodom, compassed the house round, both old and young, all the people from every quarter:

5 And they called unto Lot, and said unto him, Where are the men which came in to you this night? bring them out unto us, that we may know them.

6 And Lot went out at the door unto them, and shut the door after him,

7 And said, I pray you, brethren, do not so wickedly.

8 Behold now, I have two daughters [2] which have not known man; let me, I pray you, bring them out unto you, and do you to them as is good in your eyes: only unto these men do nothing; for therefore came they under the shadow of my roof.

9 And they said, Stand back. And they said again, This one came in to sojourn, and now he wants to be a judge: now we will deal worse with you, than with them. And they pressed greatly upon the man, even Lot, and came near to break the door.

10 But the men put forth their hand, and pulled Lot into the house to them, and shut to the door.

11 And they smote the men that were at the door of the house with blindness, both small and great: so that they wearied themselves to find the door.

12 And the men said unto Lot [1], have you here any besides? son-in-law, and your sons [2], and your daughters [2], and whatsoever you have in the city, bring them out of this place:

13 For we will destroy this place, because the cry of them is waxen great before the face of the Becoming-One; and the Becoming-One has sent us to destroy it.

14 And Lot went out, and spoke unto his sons-in-law [2], which married his daughters [v. 12], and said, Up, get you out of this place; for the Becoming-One will destroy this city. But he seemed as one that mocked unto his sons-in-law.

15 And when the dawn arose, then the angels hurried Lot, saying, Arise, take your wife, and your two daughters, which are here; lest you be consumed in the iniquity of the city.

16 And while he lingered, the men laid hold upon his hand, and upon the hand of his wife, and upon the hand of his two daughters; the Becoming-One being merciful unto him: and they brought him forth, and set him outside the city.

17 And it came to pass, when they had brought them forth abroad, that he said, Escape for your soul; look not behind you, neither stay you in all the plain; escape to the mountain, lest you be consumed.

18 And Lot said unto them, Oh, not so, my Lord(s):

19 Behold now, your servant has found grace in your sight, and you have magnified your mercy, which you have showed unto me in saving my soul; and I cannot escape to the mountain, lest some evil take me, and I die:

20 Behold now, this city is near to flee unto, and it is a little one: Oh, let me escape there, is it not a little one? and my soul shall live.

21 And he said unto him, See, I have accepted you concerning this thing also, that I will not overthrow this city, for the which you have spoken.

22 Haste you, escape there; for I cannot do any thing till you get there. Therefore the name of the city was called **Zoar**.

23 The sun was risen upon the earth when Lot entered into Zoar.

24 Then the Becoming-One rained upon Sodom and upon Gomorrah brimstone and fire from the Becoming-One out of the heavens;

25 And he overthrew those cities, and all the plain, and all the inhabitants of the cities, and that which grew upon the ground.

26 **But his wife looked back from behind him, and she became a pillar of salt.** [only 9 of 10]

27 And Abraham got up early in the morning to the place where he stood before the Becoming-One: 28 And he looked toward Sodom and Gomorrah, and toward all the land of the plain, and beheld, and, lo, the smoke of the country went up as the smoke of a furnace.

29 And it came to pass, when God destroyed the cities of the plain, that God remembered Abraham, and sent Lot out of the midst of the overthrow, when He overthrew the cities in the which Lot dwelt.

30 And Lot went up out of Zoar, and dwelt in the mountain, and his two daughters with him; for he feared to dwell in Zoar: and he dwelt in a cave, he and his two daughters.

31 And the firstborn said unto the younger, Our father is old, and there is not a man in the earth to come in unto us after the manner of all the earth:

32 Come, let us make our father drink wine, and we will lie with him, that we may preserve seed of our father.

33 And they made their father drink wine that night: and the firstborn went in, and lay with her father; and he perceived not when she lay down, nor when she arose.

34 And it came to pass on the next day, that the firstborn said unto the younger, Behold, I lay yesternight with my father: let us make him drink wine this night also; and go you in, and lie with him, that we may preserve seed of our father.

35 And they made their father drink wine that night also: and the younger arose, and lay with him; and he perceived not when she lay down, nor when she arose.

36 Thus were both the daughters of Lot with child by their father.

37 And the firstborn bare a son, and called his name Moab: the same is the father of the Moabites unto this day.

38 And the younger, she also bare a son, and called his name Ben-Ammi: the same is the father of the children of Ammon unto this day.

Gen 20:1 And Abraham journeyed from there toward the south country, and dwelled between Kadesh and Shur, and sojourned in Gerar.

2 And Abraham said of Sarah his wife, She is my sister: and Abimelech king of Gerar sent, and took Sarah.

3 But God came to Abimelech in a dream by night, and said to him, Behold, you are but a dead man, for the woman which you have taken; for she is a man's wife.

4 But Abimelech had not come near her: and he said, My Lord(s), will you slay also a righteous nation?

5 Said he not unto me, She is my sister? and she, even she herself said, He is my brother: in the integrity of my heart and innocency of my hands I have done this.

6 And God said unto him in a dream, Yes, I know that you did this in the integrity of your heart; for I also withheld you from sinning against me: therefore I permitted you not to touch her.

7 Now therefore restore the man his wife; for he is a prophet, and he shall pray for you, and you shall live: and if you restore her not, know you that, in dying, you will die,[19] you, and all that are yours.

8 Therefore Abimelech rose early in the morning, and called all his servants, and told all these things in their ears: and the men were greatly afraid.

9 Then Abimelech called Abraham, and said unto him, What have you done unto us? and what have I offended you, that you have brought on me and on my kingdom a great sin? you have done deeds unto me that ought not to be done.

10 And Abimelech said unto Abraham, What did you see, that you have done this thing?

11 And Abraham said, Because I thought, Surely the fear of God is not in this place; and they will slay me for my wife's word.

12 And yet indeed she is my sister; she is the daughter of my father, but not the daughter of my mother; and she became my wife.

13 And it came to pass, when God caused me to wander from my father's house, that I said unto her, This is your kindness which you shall show unto me; at every place to which we shall come, say of me, He is my brother.

14 And Abimelech took sheep, and oxen, and menservants, and women servants, and gave them unto Abraham, and restored him Sarah his wife.

15 And Abimelech said, Behold, my land is before you: dwell where it pleases you.

16 And unto Sarah he said, Behold, I have given your brother an *eleph*[20] pieces of silver: behold, he is to you a covering of the eyes, unto all that are with you, and with all other: thus she was righted.

17 So Abraham prayed unto God: and God healed Abimelech, and his wife, and his maidservants; and they bare children.

18 For the Becoming-One had fast closed up all the wombs of the house of Abimelech, for the word of Sarah, Abraham's wife.

Gen 21:1 And the Becoming-One visited Sarah as he had said, and the Becoming-One did unto Sarah as he had spoken.

2 For Sarah conceived, and bare Abraham a son in his old age, at the set time[21] of which God had spoken to him.

3 And Abraham called the name of his son that was born unto him, whom Sarah bare to him, **Isaac**. **[2108 YM]**

4 And Abraham circumcised his son Isaac being a son of eight days, as God had commanded him.

5 And Abraham was a son of hundred years, when his son Isaac was born unto him.

6 And Sarah said, God has made me to laugh, so that all that hear will laugh with me.

7 And she said, Who would have said unto Abraham, that Sarah should have given children suck? for I have born him a son in his old age.

8 And the child grew, and was weaned: and Abraham made a great feast the same day that Isaac was weaned.

9 And Sarah saw the son of Hagar the Egyptian, which she had born unto Abraham, mocking.

10 Therefore she said unto Abraham, Cast out this bondwoman and her son: for the son of this bondwoman shall not be heir with my son, even with Isaac.

11 And the word was very grievous in Abraham's sight because of his son.

12 And God said unto Abraham, Let it not be grievous in your sight because of the lad, and because of your bondwoman; in all that Sarah has said unto you, listen unto her voice; for in Isaac shall your seed be called.

13 And also of the son of the bondwoman will I make a nation, because he is your seed.

14 And Abraham rose up early in the morning, and took bread, and a bottle of water, and gave it unto Hagar, putting it on her shoulder, and the child, and sent her away: and she departed, and wandered in the wilderness of Beersheba.

15 And the water was spent in the bottle, and she cast the child under one of the shrubs.

16 And she went, and sat her down over against him a good way off, as it were a bowshot: for she said, Let me not see the death of the child. And she sat over against him, and lift up her voice, and wept.

17 And God heard the voice of the lad; and the angel of God called to Hagar out of the heavens, and said unto her, What ails you, Hagar? fear not; for God has heard the voice of the lad where he is.

18 Arise, lift up the lad, and hold him in your hand; for I will make him a great nation.

---

[19] מוֹת תָּמוּת - "in dying, you will die" or when you die, you will be dead – a part of the group called the "dead"

[20] Or thousand, see Preface

[21] Appointed time or festival

19 And God opened her eyes, and she saw a well of water; and she went, and filled the bottle with water, and gave the lad drink.

20 And God was with the lad; and he grew, and dwelt in the wilderness, and became an archer.

21 And he dwelt in the wilderness of Paran: and his mother took him a wife out of the land of Egypt.

22 And it came to pass at that time, that Abimelech and Phichol the chief captain of his host spoke unto Abraham, saying, God is with you in all that you do:

23 Now therefore swear unto me here by God that you will not deal falsely with me, nor with my son, nor with my son's son: but according to the kindness that I have done unto you, you shall do unto me, and to the land wherein you have sojourned.

24 And Abraham said, I will swear.

25 And Abraham reproved Abimelech because of a well of water, which Abimelech's servants had violently taken away.

26 And Abimelech said, I know not who has done this thing: neither did you tell me, neither yet heard I of it, but today.

27 And Abraham took sheep and oxen, and gave them unto Abimelech; and both of them made a covenant.

28 And Abraham set seven ewe lambs of the flock by themselves.

29 And Abimelech said unto Abraham, What do you mean by these seven ewe lambs which you have set by themselves?

30 And he said, For these seven ewe lambs shall you take of my hand, that they may be a witness unto me, that I have digged this well.

31 Therefore he called that place Beersheba; because there they swore both of them.

32 Thus they made a covenant at Beersheba: then Abimelech rose up, and Phichol the chief captain of his host, and they returned into the land of the Philistines.

33 And Abraham planted a grove in Beersheba, and called there on the name of the Becoming-One, GOD of olam.

34 And Abraham sojourned in the Philistines' land many days.

Gen 22:1 And it came to pass after these things, that God did tempt Abraham, and said unto him, Abraham: and he said, Behold, here I am.

2 And he said, Take now your son, your only son Isaac, whom you love, and get you into the land of Moriah; and offer him there for a burnt offering upon one of the mountains which I will tell you of.

3 And Abraham rose up early in the morning, and saddled his donkey, and took two of his young men with him, and Isaac his son, and clave the wood for the burnt offering, and rose up, and went unto the place of which God had told him.

4 Then on the third day Abraham lifted up his eyes, and saw the place afar off.

5 And Abraham said unto his young men, Abide you here with the donkey; and I and the lad will go yonder and worship, and come again to you.

6 And Abraham took the wood of the burnt offering, and laid it upon Isaac his son; and he took the fire in his hand, and a knife; and they went both of them together.

7 And Isaac spoke unto Abraham his father, and said, My father: and he said, Here I am, my son. And he said, Behold the fire and the wood: but where is the lamb for a burnt offering?

8 And Abraham said, My son, God will provide himself a lamb for a burnt offering: so they went both of them together.

9 And they came to the place which God had told him of; and Abraham built an altar there, and laid the wood in order, and bound Isaac his son, and laid him on the altar upon the wood.

10 And Abraham stretched forth his hand, and took the knife to slay his son.

11 And the angel of the Becoming-One called unto him out of the heavens, and said, Abraham, Abraham: and he said, Here I am.

12 And he said, Lay not your hand upon the lad, neither do you any thing unto him: for now I know that you fear God, seeing you have not withheld your son, your only son from me.

13 And Abraham lifted up his eyes, and looked, and behold behind him a ram caught in a thicket by his horns: and Abraham went and took the ram, and offered him up for a burnt offering in the stead of his son.

14 And Abraham called the name of that place Yehowah-yireh: as it is said to this day, In the mount of the Becoming-One it shall be seen.

15 And the angel of the Becoming-One called unto Abraham out of the heavens the second time,

16 And said, By myself I have sworn, says the Becoming-One, for because you have done this thing, and have not withheld your son, your only son:

17 That in blessing I will bless you, and in multiplying I will multiply your seed as the stars of the heavens, and as the sand which is upon the sea shore; and your seed shall possess the gate of his enemies;

18 And in your seed shall all the nations of the earth be blessed; because you have obeyed my voice.

19 So Abraham returned unto his young men, and they rose up and went together to Beersheba; and Abraham dwelt at Beersheba.

20 And it came to pass after these things, that it was told Abraham, saying, Behold, Milcah, she has also born children unto your brother Nahor;

21 Huz his firstborn, and Buz his brother, and Kemuel the father of Aram,

22 And Chesed, and Hazo, and Pildash, and Jidlaph, and Bethuel.

23 And Bethuel begat Rebekah: these eight Milcah did bear to Nahor, Abraham's brother.

24 And his concubine, whose name was Reumah, she bare also Tebah, and Gaham, and Thahash, and Maachah.

Gen 23:1 And Sarah lived a hundred and seven and twenty years: these were the years of the life of Sarah.

2 And Sarah died in Kirjatharba; the same is Hebron in the land of Canaan: and Abraham came to mourn for Sarah, and to weep for her.

3 And Abraham stood up from before his dead, and spoke unto the sons of Heth, saying,

4 I am a stranger and a sojourner with you: give me a possession of a burying place with you, that I may bury my dead out of my sight.

5 And the children of Heth answered Abraham, saying unto him,

6 Hear us, my lord: you are a mighty prince among us: in the choice of our tombs bury your dead; none of us shall withhold from you his tomb, but that you may bury your dead.

7 And Abraham stood up, and bowed himself to the people of the land, even to the children of Heth.

8 And he communed with them, saying, If it be your soul that I should bury my dead out of my sight; hear me, and entreat for me to Ephron the son of Zohar,

9 That he may give me the cave of Machpelah, which he has, which is in the end of his field; for as much money as it is worth he shall give it me for a possession of a burying place among you.

10 And Ephron dwelt among the children of Heth: and Ephron the Hittite answered Abraham in the audience of the children of Heth, even of all that went in at the gate of his city, saying,

11 Nay, my lord, hear me: the field give I you, and the cave that is therein, I give it you; in the presence of the sons of my people give I it you: bury your dead.

12 And Abraham bowed down himself before the people of the land.

13 And he spoke unto Ephron in the audience of the people of the land, saying, But if you will give it, I pray you, hear me: I will give you money for the field; take it of me, and I will bury my dead there.

14 And Ephron answered Abraham, saying unto him,

15 My lord, listen unto me: the land is worth four hundred shekels of silver; what is that between me and you? bury therefore your dead.

16 And Abraham listened unto Ephron; and Abraham weighed to Ephron the silver, which he had named in the audience of the sons of Heth, four hundred shekels of silver, current money with the merchant.

17 And the field of Ephron, which was in Machpelah, which was before Mamre, the field, and the cave which was therein, and all the trees that were in the field, that were in all the borders round about, were made sure

18 Unto Abraham for a possession in the presence of the children of Heth, before all that went in at the gate of his city.

19 And after this, Abraham buried Sarah his wife in the cave of the field of Machpelah before Mamre: the same is Hebron in the land of Canaan.

20 And the field, and the cave that is therein, were made sure unto Abraham for a possession of a burying place by the sons of Heth.

Gen 24:1 And Abraham was old, and well stricken in age: and the Becoming-One had blessed Abraham in all things.

2 And Abraham said unto his eldest servant of his house, that ruled over all that he had, Put, I pray you, your hand under my thigh:

3 And I will make you swear by the Becoming-One, God of the heavens, and God of the earth, that you shall not take a wife unto my son of the daughters of the Canaanites, among whom I dwell:

4 But you shall go unto my country, and to my kindred, and take a wife unto my son Isaac.

5 And the servant said unto him, Perhaps the woman will not be willing to follow me unto this land: must I needs bring your son again unto the land from where you came?

6 And Abraham said unto him, Beware you that you bring not my son there again.

7 The Becoming-One, God of the heavens, which took me from my father's house, and from the land of my kindred, and which spoke unto me, and that swore unto me, saying, Unto your seed will I give this land; he shall send his angel before you, and you shall take a wife unto my son from there.

8 And if the woman will not be willing to follow you, then you shall be clear from this my oath: only bring not my son there again.

9 And the servant put his hand under the thigh of Abraham his master, and swore to him concerning that matter.

10 And the servant took ten camels of the camels of his master, and departed; for all the goods of his master were in his hand: and he arose, and went to Mesopotamia [Aram Syria of two rivers] unto the city of Nahor.

11 And he made his camels to kneel down outside the city by a well of water at the time of the evening, even the time that women go out to draw water.

12 And he said, O Becoming-One, God of my master Abraham, I pray you, send me good speed this day, and show kindness unto my master Abraham.

13 Behold, I stand here by the well of water; and the daughters of the men of the city come out to draw water:

14 And let it come to pass, that the damsel to whom I shall say, Let down your pitcher, I pray you, that I may drink; and she shall say, Drink, and I will give your camels drink also: let the same be she that you have appointed for your servant Isaac; and thereby shall I know that you have showed kindness unto my master.

15 And it came to pass, before he had done speaking, that, behold, Rebekah came out, who was born to Bethuel, son of Milcah, the wife of Nahor, Abraham's brother, with her pitcher upon her shoulder.

16 And the damsel was very fair to look upon, a virgin, neither had any man known her: and she went down to the well, and filled her pitcher, and came up.

17 And the servant ran to meet her, and said, Let me, I pray you, drink a little water of your pitcher.

18 And she said, Drink, my lord: and she hasted, and let down her pitcher upon her hand, and gave him drink.

19 And when she had done giving him drink, she said, I will draw water for your camels also, until they have finished drinking.

20 And she hasted, and emptied her pitcher into the trough, and ran again unto the well to draw water, and drew for all his camels.

21 And the man wondering at her held his peace, to know whether the Becoming-One had made his journey prosperous or not.

22 And it came to pass, as the camels had finished drinking, that the man took a golden earring of half a shekel weight, and two bracelets for her hands of ten shekels weight of gold;

23 And said, Whose daughter are you? tell me, I pray you: is there room in your father's house for us to lodge in?

24 And she said unto him, I am the daughter of Bethuel the son of Milcah, which she bare unto Nahor.

25 She said moreover unto him, We have both straw and feed enough, and room to lodge in.

26 And the man bowed down his head, and worshiped the Becoming-One.

27 And he said, Blessed be the Becoming-One, God of my master Abraham, who has not left destitute my master of his mercy and his truth: I being in the way, the Becoming-One led me to the house of my master's brethren.

28 And the damsel ran, and told them of her mother's house these things.

29 And Rebekah had a brother, and his name was Laban: and Laban ran out unto the man, unto the well.

30 And it came to pass, when he saw the earring and bracelets upon his sister's hands, and when he heard the words of Rebekah his sister, saying, Thus spoke the man unto me; that he came unto the man; and, behold, he stood by the camels at the well.

31 And he said, Come in, you blessed of the Becoming-One; why stand you outside? for I have prepared the house, and room for the camels.

32 And the man came into the house: and he ungirded his camels, and gave straw and feed for the camels, and water to wash his feet, and the men's feet that were with him.

33 And there was set food before him to eat: but he said, I will not eat, until I have told mine errand. And he said, Speak on.

34 And he said, I am Abraham's servant.

35 And the Becoming-One has blessed my master greatly; and he is become great: and he has given him flocks, and herds, and silver, and gold, and menservants, and maidservants, and camels, and donkeys.

36 And Sarah my master's wife bare a son to my master when she was old: and unto him has he given all that he has.

37 And my master made me swear, saying, you shall not take a wife to my son of the daughters of the Canaanites, in whose land I dwell:

38 But you shall go unto my father's house, and to my kindred, and take a wife unto my son.

39 And I said unto my master, Perhaps the woman will not follow me.

40 And he said unto me, The Becoming-One, before whom I walk, will send his angel with you, and prosper your way; and you shall take a wife for my son of my kindred, and of my father's house:

41 Then shall you be clear from this my oath, when you come to my kindred; and if they give not you one, you shall be clear from my oath.

42 And I came this day unto the well, and said, O Becoming-One, God of my master Abraham, if now you do prosper my way which I go:

43 Behold, I stand by the well of water; and it shall come to pass, that when the virgin comes forth to draw water, and I say to her, Give me, I pray you, a little water of your pitcher to drink;

44 And she say to me, Both drink you, and I will also draw for your camels: let the same be the woman whom the Becoming-One has appointed out for my master's son.

45 And before I had done speaking in mine heart, behold, Rebekah came forth with her pitcher on her shoulder; and she went down unto the well, and drew water: and I said unto her, Let me drink, I pray you.

46 And she made haste, and let down her pitcher from her shoulder, and said, Drink, and I will give your camels drink also: so I drank, and she made the camels drink also.

47 And I asked her, and said, Whose daughter are you? And she said, The daughter of Bethuel, Nahor's son, whom Milcah bare unto him: and I put the earring upon her face, and the bracelets upon her hands.

48 And I bowed down my head, and worshiped the Becoming-One, and blessed the Becoming-One, God of my master Abraham, which had led me in the right way to take my master's brother's daughter unto his son.

49 And now if you will deal kindly and truly with my master, tell me: and if not, tell me; that I may turn to the right hand, or to the left.

50 Then Laban and Bethuel answered and said, The word proceeds from the Becoming-One:we cannot speak unto you evil or good.

51 Behold, Rebekah is before you, take her, and go, and let her be your master's son's wife, as the Becoming-One has spoken.

52 And it came to pass, that, when Abraham's servant heard their words, he worshiped the Becoming-One, bowing himself to the earth.

53 And the servant brought forth jewels of silver, and jewels of gold, and raiment, and gave them to Rebekah: he gave also to her brother and to her mother precious things.

54 And they did eat and drink, he and the men that were with him, and tarried all night; and they rose up in the morning, and he said, Send me away unto my master.

55 And her brother and her mother said, Let the damsel abide with us a few days, at the least ten; after that she shall go.

56 And he said unto them, Hinder me not, seeing the Becoming-One has prospered my way; send me away that I may go to my master.

57 And they said, We will call the damsel, and inquire at her mouth.

58 And they called Rebekah, and said unto her, will you go with this man? And she said, I will go.

59 And they sent away Rebekah their sister, and her nurse, and Abraham's servant, and his men.

60 And they blessed Rebekah, and said unto her, you are our sister, be you the mother of *elephs*,[22] multiplied, and let your seed possess the gate of those which hate them.

61 And Rebekah arose, and her damsels, and they rode upon the camels, and followed the man: and the servant took Rebekah, and went his way.

62 And Isaac came from the way of the well Lahairoi; for he dwelt in the south country.

---

[22] Or thousands, see Preface

63 And Isaac went out to meditate in the field at the eventide: and he lifted up his eyes, and saw, and, behold, the camels were coming.

64 And Rebekah lifted up her eyes, and when she saw Isaac, she lighted off the camel.

65 For she had said unto the servant, What man is this that walks in the field to meet us? And the servant had said, It is my master: therefore she took a veil, and covered herself.

66 And the servant told Isaac all things that he had done.

67 And Isaac brought her into his mother Sarah's tent, and took Rebekah, and she became his wife; and he loved her: and Isaac was comforted after his mother's death.

Gen 25:1 Then again Abraham took a wife, and her name was Keturah.

2 And she bare him Zimran, and Jokshan, and Medan, and Midian, and Ishbak, and Shuah.

3 And Jokshan begat Sheba, and Dedan. And the sons of Dedan were Asshurim, and Letushim, and Leummim.

4 And the sons of Midian; Ephah, and Epher, and Hanoch, and Abidah, and Eldaah. All these were the children of Keturah.

5 And Abraham gave all that he had unto Isaac.

6 But unto the sons of the concubines, which Abraham had, Abraham gave gifts, and sent them away from Isaac his son, while he yet lived, eastward, unto the east country.

7 And these are the days of the years of Abraham's life which he lived, a hundred threescore and fifteen years.

8 Then Abraham gave up the ghost, and died in a good old age, an old man, and full of years; and was gathered to his people.

9 And his sons Isaac and Ishmael buried him in the cave of Machpelah, in the field of Ephron the son of Zohar the Hittite, which is before Mamre;

10 The field which Abraham purchased of the sons of Heth: there was Abraham buried, and Sarah his wife.

11 And it came to pass after the death of Abraham, that God blessed his son Isaac; and Isaac dwelt by the well Lahairoi.

12 Now these are the generations of Ishmael, Abraham's son, whom Hagar the Egyptian, Sarah's handmaid, bare unto Abraham:

13 And these are the names of the sons of Ishmael, by their names, according to their generations: the firstborn of Ishmael, Nebajoth; and Kedar, and Adbeel, and Mibsam,

14 And Mishma, and Dumah, and Massa,

15 Hadar, and Tema, Jetur, Naphish, and Kedemah:

16 These are the sons of Ishmael, and these are their names, by their towns, and by their castles; twelve princes according to their nations.

17 And these are the years of the life of Ishmael, a hundred and thirty and seven years: and he gave up the ghost and died; and was gathered unto his people.

18 And they dwelt from Havilah unto Shur, that is before Egypt, as you go toward Assyria: and he died in the presence of all his brethren.

19 And these are the generations of Isaac, Abraham's son: Abraham begat Isaac:

20 And Isaac was a son of forty years when he took Rebekah to wife, the daughter of Bethuel the Syrian of Padan-Aram, the sister to Laban the Syrian.

21 And Isaac entreated the Becoming-One for his wife, because she was barren: and the Becoming-One was entreated of him, and Rebekah his wife conceived.

22 And the children struggled together within her; and she said, If it be so, why am I thus? And she went to inquire of the Becoming-One.

23 And the Becoming-One said unto her, Two nations are in your womb, and two manner of people shall be separated from your bowels; and the one people shall be stronger than the other people; and the elder shall serve the younger.

24 And when her days to be delivered were fulfilled, behold, there were twins in her womb.

25 And the first came out red, all over like a hairy garment; and they called his name Esau.

26 And after that came his brother out, and his hand took hold on Esau's heel; and his name was called **Jacob**: and Isaac was a son of threescore years when she bare them. **[2168 YM]**

27 And the boys grew: and Esau was a cunning hunter, a man of the field; and Jacob was a plain man, dwelling in tents.

28 And Isaac loved Esau, because he did eat of his venison: but Rebekah loved Jacob.

29 And Jacob boiled pottage: and Esau came from the field, and he was faint:

30 And Esau said to Jacob, Feed me, I pray you, with that same red pottage; for I am faint: therefore was his name called Edom.

31 And Jacob said, Sell me this day your birthright.

32 And Esau said, Behold, I am at the point to die: and what profit shall this birthright do to me?

33 And Jacob said, Swear to me this day; and he swore unto him: and he sold his birthright unto Jacob.

34 Then Jacob gave Esau bread and pottage of lentiles; and he did eat and drink, and rose up, and went his way: thus Esau despised his birthright.

Gen 26:1 And there was a famine in the land, beside the first famine that was in the days of Abraham. And Isaac went unto Abimelech king of the Philistines unto Gerar.

2 And the Becoming-One appeared unto him, and said, Go not down into Egypt; dwell in the land which I shall tell you of:

3 Sojourn in this land, and I will be with you, and will bless you; for unto you, and unto your seed, I will give all these countries, and I will perform the oath which I swore unto Abraham your father;

4 And I will make your seed to multiply as the stars of the heavens, and will give unto your seed all these countries; and in your seed shall all the nations of the earth be blessed;

5 Because that Abraham obeyed my voice, and kept my charge, my commandments, my statutes, and my laws.

6 And Isaac dwelt in Gerar:

7 And the men of the place asked him of his wife; and he said, She is my sister: for he feared to say, She is my wife; lest, said he, the men of the place should kill me for Rebekah; because she was fair to look upon.

8 And it came to pass, when he had been there a long time, that Abimelech king of the Philistines looked out at a window, and saw, and, behold, Isaac was sporting with Rebekah his wife.

9 And Abimelech called Isaac, and said, Behold, of a surety she is your wife: and how say you, She is my sister? And Isaac said unto him, Because I said, Lest I die for her.

10 And Abimelech said, What is this you have done unto us? one of the people might lightly have lain with your wife, and you should have brought guiltiness upon us.

11 And Abimelech charged all his people, saying, He that touches this man or his wife in dying he shall be put to death.

12 Then Isaac sowed in that land, and received in the same year a hundredfold: and the Becoming-One blessed him.

13 And the man grew great, and went forward, and grew until he became very great:

14 For he had possession of flocks, and possession of herds, and great store of servants: and the Philistines envied him.

15 For all the wells which his father's servants had dug in the days of Abraham his father, the Philistines had stopped them, and filled them with earth.

16 And Abimelech said unto Isaac, Go from us; for you are much mightier than we.

17 And Isaac departed there, and pitched his tent in the valley of Gerar, and dwelt there.

18 And Isaac dug again the wells of water, which they had dug in the days of Abraham his father; for the Philistines had stopped them after the death of Abraham: and he called their names after the names by which his father had called them.

19 And Isaac's servants dug in the valley, and found there a well of springing water.

20 And the herdmen of Gerar did strive with Isaac's herdmen, saying, The water is ours: and he called the name of the well Esek; because they strove with him.

21 And they dug another well, and strove for that also: and he called the name of it Sitnah.

22 And he removed from there, and dug another well; and for that they strove not: and he called the name of it Rehoboth; and he said, For now the Becoming-One has made room for us, and we shall be fruitful in the land.

23 And he went up from there to Beersheba.

24 And the Becoming-One appeared unto him the same night, and said, I am God of Abraham your father: fear not, for I am with you, and will bless you, and multiply your seed for my servant Abraham's sake.

25 And he built an altar there, and called upon the name of the Becoming-One, and pitched his tent there: and there Isaac's servants dug a well.

26 Then Abimelech went to him from Gerar, and Ahuzzath one of his friends, and Phichol the chief captain of his army.

27 And Isaac said unto them, Why have you come to me, seeing you hate me, and have sent me away from you?

28 And they said, We saw certainly that the Becoming-One was with you: and we said, Let there be now an oath between us, even between us and you, and let us make a covenant with you;

29 That you will do us no evil, as we have not touched you, and as we have done unto you nothing but good, and have sent you away in peace: you are now the blessed of the Becoming-One.

30 And he made them a feast, and they did eat and drink.

31 And they rose up early in the morning, and swore one to another: and Isaac sent them away, and they departed from him in peace.

32 And it came to pass the same day, that Isaac's servants came, and told him concerning the well which they had dug, and said unto him, We have found water.

33 And he called it Shebah: therefore the name of the city is Beersheba unto this day.

34 And Esau was a son of forty years when he took to wife Judith the daughter of Beeri the Hittite, and Bashemath the daughter of Elon the Hittite:

35 Which were a grief of spirit unto Isaac and to Rebekah.

Gen 27:1 And it came to pass, that when Isaac was old, and his eyes were dim, so that he could not see, he called Esau his eldest son, and said unto him, My son: and he said unto him, Behold, here I am.

2 And he said, Behold now, I am old, I know not the day of my death:

3 Now therefore take, I pray you, your weapons, your quiver and your bow, and go out to the field, and take me some venison;

4 And make me savoury food, such as I love, and bring it to me, that I may eat; that my soul may bless you before I die.

5 And Rebekah heard when Isaac spoke to Esau his son. And Esau went to the field to hunt for venison, and to bring it.

6 And Rebekah spoke unto Jacob her son, saying, Behold, I heard your father speak unto Esau your brother, saying,

7 Bring me venison, and make me savoury food, that I may eat, and bless you before the Becoming-One before my death.

8 Now therefore, my son, obey my voice according to that which I command you.

9 Go now to the flock, and fetch me from there two good kids of the goats; and I will make them savoury food for your father, such as he loves:

10 And you shall bring it to your father, that he may eat, and that he may bless you before his death.

11 And Jacob said to Rebekah his mother, Behold, Esau my brother is a hairy man, and I am a smooth man:

12 My father perhaps will feel me, and I shall seem to him as a deceiver; and I shall bring a curse upon me, and not a blessing.

13 And his mother said unto him, Upon me be your curse, my son: only obey my voice, and go fetch me them.

14 And he went, and fetched, and brought them to his mother: and his mother made savoury food, such as his father loved.

15 And Rebekah took goodly raiment of her eldest son Esau, which were with her in the house, and put them upon Jacob her younger son:

16 And she put the skins of the kids of the goats upon his hands, and upon the smooth of his neck:

17 And she gave the savoury food and the bread, which she had prepared, into the hand of her son Jacob.

18 And he came unto his father, and said, My father: and he said, Here I am; who are you, my son?

19 And Jacob said unto his father, I am Esau your firstborn; I have done according as you told me: arise, I pray you, sit and eat of my venison, that your soul may bless me.

20 And Isaac said unto his son, How is it that you have found it so quickly, my son? And he said, Because the Becoming-One your God brought it to me.

21 And Isaac said unto Jacob, Come near, I pray you, that I may feel you, my son, whether you be my very son Esau or not.

22 And Jacob went near unto Isaac his father; and he felt him, and said, The voice is Jacob's voice, but the hands are the hands of Esau.

23 And he discerned him not, because his hands were hairy, as his brother Esau's hands: so he blessed him.

24 And he said, are you my very son Esau? And he said, I am.

25 And he said, Bring it near to me, and I will eat of my son's venison, that my soul may bless you. And he brought it near to him, and he did eat: and he brought him wine, and he drank.

26 And his father Isaac said unto him, Come near now, and kiss me, my son.

27 And he came near, and kissed him: and he smelled the smell of his raiment, and blessed him, and said, See, the smell of my son is as the smell of a field which the Becoming-One has blessed:

28 Therefore God give you of the dew of the heavens, and the fatness of the earth, and plenty of grain and wine:

29 Let people serve you, and nations bow down to you: be lord over your brethren, and let your mother's sons bow down to you: cursed be every one that curses you, and blessed be he that blesses you.

30 And it came to pass, as soon as Isaac had made an end of blessing Jacob, and Jacob was yet scarce gone out from the presence of Isaac his father, that Esau his brother came in from his hunting.

31 And he also had made savoury food, and brought it unto his father, and said unto his father, Let my father arise, and eat of his son's venison, that your soul may bless me.

32 And Isaac his father said unto him, Who are you? And he said, I am your son, your firstborn Esau.

33 And Isaac trembled very exceedingly, and said, Who? where is he that has taken venison, and brought it me, and I have eaten of all before you came, and have blessed him? yes, and he shall be blessed.

34 And when Esau heard the words of his father, he cried with a great and exceeding bitter cry, and said unto his father, Bless me, even me also, O my father.

35 And he said, your brother came with subtlety, and has taken away your blessing.

36 And he said, Is not he rightly named Jacob? for he has supplanted me these two times: he took away my birthright; and, behold, now he has taken away my blessing. And he said, have you not reserved a blessing for me?

37 And Isaac answered and said unto Esau, Behold, I have made him your lord, and all his brethren I have given to him for servants; and with grain and wine I have sustained him: and what shall I do now unto you, my son?

38 And Esau said unto his father, have you but one blessing, my father? bless me, even me also, O my father. And Esau lifted up his voice, and wept.

39 And Isaac his father answered and said unto him, Behold, your dwelling shall be the fatness of the earth, and of the dew of the heavens from above;

40 And by your sword shall you live, and shall serve your brother; and it shall come to pass when you shall have the dominion, that you shall break his yoke from off your neck.

41 And Esau hated Jacob because of the blessing wherewith his father blessed him: and Esau said in his heart, The days of mourning for my father are at hand; then will I slay my brother Jacob.

42 And these words of Esau her elder son were told to Rebekah: and she sent and called Jacob her younger son, and said unto him, Behold, your brother Esau, as touching you, does comfort himself, purposing to kill you.

43 Now therefore, my son, obey my voice; and arise, flee you to Laban my brother to Haran;

44 And tarry with him a few days, until your brother's fury turn away;

45 Until your brother's anger turn away from you, and he forget that which you have done to him: then I will send, and fetch you from there: why should I be deprived also of you both in one day?

46 And Rebekah said to Isaac, I am weary of my life because of the daughters of Heth: if Jacob take a wife of the daughters of Heth, such as these which are of the daughters of the land, what good shall my life do me?

Gen 28:1 And Isaac called Jacob, and blessed him, and charged him, and said unto him, you shall not take a wife of the daughters of Canaan.

2 Arise, go to Padan-aram, to the house of Bethuel your mother's father; and take you a wife from there of the daughters of Laban your mother's brother.

3 And GOD Almighty bless you, and make you fruitful, and multiply you, that you may be a multitude of people;

4 And give you the blessing of Abraham, to you, and to your seed with you; that you may inherit the land wherein you are a stranger, which God gave unto Abraham.

5 And Isaac sent away Jacob: and he went to Padan-Aram unto Laban, son of Bethuel the Syrian, the brother of Rebekah, Jacob's and Esau's mother.

6 When Esau saw that Isaac had blessed Jacob, and sent him away to Padan-Aram, to take him a wife from there; and that as he blessed him he gave him a charge, saying, you shall not take a wife of the daughters of Canaan;

7 And that Jacob obeyed his father and his mother, and was gone to Padan-Aram;

8 And Esau seeing that the daughters of Canaan pleased not Isaac his father;

9 Then went Esau unto Ishmael, and took unto the wives which he had Mahalath the daughter of

Ishmael Abraham's son, the sister of Nebajoth, to be his wife.

10 And Jacob went out from Beersheba, and went toward Haran.

11 And he lighted upon a certain place, and tarried there all night, because the sun was set; and he took of the stones of that place, and put them for his pillows, and lay down in that place to sleep.

12 And he dreamed, and behold a ladder set up on the earth, and the top of it reached to the heavens: and behold the angels of God ascending and descending on it.

13 And, behold, the Becoming-One stood above it, and said, I am the Becoming-One, God of Abraham your father, and God of Isaac: the land whereon you lie, to you will I give it, and to your seed;

14 And your seed shall be as the dust of the earth, and you shall spread abroad to the west, and to the east, and to the north, and to the south: and in you and in your seed shall all the families of the earth be blessed.

15 And, behold, I am with you, and will keep you in all places to which you go, and will bring you again into this land; for I will not leave you, until I have done that which I have spoken to you of.

16 And Jacob awaked out of his sleep, and he said, Surely the Becoming-One is in this place; and I knew it not.

17 And he was afraid, and said, How dreadful is this place! this is none other but the house of God [Bethel], and this is the gate of the heavens.

18 And Jacob rose up early in the morning, and took the stone that he had put for his pillows, and set it up for a pillar, and poured oil upon the top of it.

19 And he called the name of that place Bethel: but the name of that city was called Luz at the first.

20 And Jacob vowed a vow, saying, If God will be with me, and will keep me in this way that I go, and will give me bread to eat, and raiment to put on,

21 So that I come again to my father's house in peace; then shall the Becoming-One be my God:

22 And this stone, which I have set for a pillar, shall be God' house: and of all that you shall give me I will surely give the tenth unto you. [tithing I tithe to you, see Deut two]

Gen 29:1 Then Jacob went on his journey, and came into the land of the people of the east.

2 And he looked, and behold a well in the field, and, lo, there were three flocks of sheep lying by it; for out of that well they watered the flocks: and a great stone was upon the well's mouth.

3 And there were all the flocks gathered: and they rolled the stone from the well's mouth, and watered the sheep, and put the stone again upon the well's mouth in his place.

4 And Jacob said unto them, My brethren, where are you from? And they said, From Haran are we.

5 And he said unto them, Know you Laban the son of Nahor? And they said, We know him.

6 And he said unto them, Is he well? And they said, He is well: and, behold, Rachel his daughter comes with the sheep.

7 And he said, Lo, it is yet high day, neither is it time that the cattle should be gathered together: water you the sheep, and go and feed them.

8 And they said, We cannot, until all the flocks be gathered together, and till they roll the stone from the well's mouth; then we water the sheep.

9 And while he yet spoke with them, Rachel came with her father's sheep: for she kept them.

10 And it came to pass, when Jacob saw Rachel the daughter of Laban his mother's brother, and the sheep of Laban his mother's brother, that Jacob went near, and rolled the stone from the well's mouth, and watered the flock of Laban his mother's brother.

11 And Jacob kissed Rachel, and lifted up his voice, and wept.

12 And Jacob told Rachel that he was her father's brother, and that he was Rebekah's son: and she ran and told her father.

13 And it came to pass, when Laban heard the tidings of Jacob his sister's son, that he ran to meet him, and embraced him, and kissed him, and brought him to his house. And he told Laban all these things.

14 And Laban said to him, Surely you are my bone and my flesh. And he abode with him a month of days.

15 And Laban said unto Jacob, Because you are my brother, should you therefore serve me for nothing? tell me, what shall your wages be?

16 And Laban had two daughters: the name of the elder was Leah, and the name of the younger was Rachel.

17 Leah was tender eyed; but Rachel was beautiful and well favored.

18 And Jacob loved Rachel; and said, I will serve you seven years for Rachel your younger daughter.

19 And Laban said, It is better that I give her to you, than that I should give her to another man: abide with me.

20 And Jacob served seven years for Rachel; and they seemed unto him but a few days, for the love he had to her.

21 And Jacob said unto Laban, Give me my wife, for my days are fulfilled, that I may go in unto her.

22 And Laban gathered together all the men of the place, and made a feast.

23 And it came to pass in the evening, that he took Leah his daughter, and brought her to him; and he went in unto her.

24 And Laban gave unto his daughter Leah Zilpah his maid for a handmaid.

25 And it came to pass, that in the morning, behold, it was Leah: and he said to Laban, What is this you have done unto me? did not I serve with you for Rachel? why then have you beguiled me?

26 And Laban said, It must not be so done in our country, to give the younger before the firstborn.

27 Fulfil her week, and we will give you this also for the service which you shall serve with me yet seven other years.

28 And Jacob did so, and fulfilled her week: and he gave him Rachel his daughter to wife also.

29 And Laban gave to Rachel his daughter Bilhah his handmaid to be her maid.

30 And he went in also unto Rachel, and he loved also Rachel more than Leah, and served with him yet seven other years.

31 And when the Becoming-One saw that Leah was hated, he opened her womb: but Rachel was barren.

32 And Leah conceived, and bare a son, and she called his name Reuben: for she said, Surely the Becoming-One has looked upon my affliction; now therefore my husband will love me.

33 And she conceived again, and bare a son; and said, Because the Becoming-One has heard that I was hated, he has therefore given me this son also: and she called his name Simeon.

34 And she conceived again, and bare a son; and said, Now this time will my husband be joined unto me, because I have born him three sons: therefore was his name called Levi.

35 And she conceived again, and bare a son: and she said, Now will I praise the Becoming-One:therefore she called his name Judah; and left bearing.

Gen 30:1 And when Rachel saw that she bare Jacob no children, Rachel envied her sister; and said unto Jacob, Give me children, or else I die.

2 And Jacob's anger was kindled against Rachel: and he said, Am I in God' stead, who has withheld from you the fruit of the womb?

3 And she said, Behold my maid Bilhah, go in unto her; and she shall bear upon my knees, that I may also have children by her.

4 And she gave him Bilhah her handmaid to wife: and Jacob went in unto her.

5 And Bilhah conceived, and bare Jacob a son.

6 And Rachel said, God has judged me, and has also heard my voice, and has given me a son: therefore called she his name Dan.

7 And Bilhah Rachel's maid conceived again, and bare Jacob a second son.

8 And Rachel said, With great wrestlings have I wrestled with my sister, and I have prevailed: and she called his name Naphtali.

9 When Leah saw that she had left bearing, she took Zilpah her maid, and gave her Jacob to wife.

10 And Zilpah Leah's maid bare Jacob a son.

11 And Leah said, A troop comes: and she called his name Gad.

12 And Zilpah Leah's maid bare Jacob a second son.

13 And Leah said, Happy am I, for the daughters will call me blessed: and she called his name Asher.

14 And Reuben went in the days of wheat harvest, and found mandrakes in the field, and brought them unto his mother Leah. Then Rachel said to Leah, Give me, I pray you, of your son's mandrakes.

15 And she said unto her, Is it a small matter that you have taken my husband? and would you take away my son's mandrakes also? And Rachel said, Therefore he shall lie with you to night for your son's mandrakes.

16 And Jacob came out of the field in the evening, and Leah went out to meet him, and said, you must come in unto me; for surely I have hired you with my son's mandrakes. And he lay with her that night.

17 And God listened unto Leah, and she conceived, and bare Jacob the fifth son.

18 And Leah said, God has given me my hire, because I have given my maiden to my husband: and she called his name Issachar.

19 And Leah conceived again, and bare Jacob the sixth son.

20 And Leah said, God has endued me with a good dowry; now will my husband dwell with me, because I have born him six sons: and she called his name Zebulun.

21 And afterwards she bare a daughter, and called her name Dinah.

22 And God remembered Rachel, and God listened to her, and opened her womb.

23 And she conceived, and bare a son; and said, God has taken away my reproach:

24 And she called his name **Joseph**; and said, The Becoming-One shall add to me another son.

25 And it came to pass, when Rachel had born Joseph, that Jacob said unto Laban, Send me away, that I may go unto mine own place, and to my country.
[2259 YM]

26 Give me my wives and my children, for whom I have served you, and let me go: for you know my service which I have done you.

27 And Laban said unto him, I pray you, if I have found favor in your eyes, tarry: for I have seen omens that the Becoming-One has blessed me for your sake.

28 And he said, Appoint me your wages, and I will give it.

29 And he said unto him, you know how I have served you, and how your cattle was with me.

30 For it was little which you had before I came, and it is now increased unto a multitude; and the Becoming-One has blessed you since my coming: and now when shall I provide for mine own house also?

31 And he said, What shall I give you? And Jacob said, you shall not give me any thing: if you will do this thing for me, I will again feed and keep your flock.

32 I will pass through all your flock today, removing from there all the speckled and spotted cattle, and all the brown cattle among the sheep, and the spotted and speckled among the goats: and of such shall be my hire.

33 So shall my righteousness answer for me in a day to come, when you shall come about my wages: every one that is not speckled and spotted among the goats, and brown among the sheep, will be considered stolen by me.

34 And Laban said, Behold, Let it be according to your word.

35 And he removed that day the he goats that were ring-streaked and spotted, and all the she goats that were speckled and spotted, and every one that had some white in it, and all the brown among the sheep, and gave them into the hand of his sons.

36 And he set three days' journey between himself and Jacob: and Jacob fed the rest of Laban's flocks.

37 And Jacob took him rods of green poplar, and of the hazel and chestnut tree; and pilled white streaks in them, and made the white appear which was in the rods.

38 And he set the rods which he had pilled before the flocks in the gutters in the watering troughs when the flocks came to drink, that they should conceive when they came to drink.

39 And the flocks conceived before the rods, and brought forth cattle ring-streaked, speckled, and spotted.

40 And Jacob did separate the lambs, and set the faces of the flocks toward the ring-streaked, and all

the brown in the flock of Laban; and he put his own flocks by themselves, and put them not unto Laban's cattle.

41 And it came to pass, whensoever the stronger cattle did conceive, that Jacob laid the rods before the eyes of the cattle in the gutters, that they might conceive among the rods.

42 But when the cattle were feeble, he put them not in: so the feebler were Laban's, and the stronger Jacob's.

43 And the man increased exceedingly, and had much cattle, and maidservants, and menservants, and camels, and donkeys.

Gen 31:1 And he heard the words of Laban's sons, saying, Jacob has taken away all that was our father's; and of that which was our father's has he gotten all this glory.

2 And Jacob beheld the countenance of Laban, and, behold, it was not toward him as before.

3 And the Becoming-One said unto Jacob, Return unto the land of your fathers, and to your kindred; and I will be with you.

4 And Jacob sent and called Rachel and Leah to the field unto his flock,

5 And said unto them, I see your father's countenance, that it is not toward me as before; but God of my father has been with me.

6 And you know that with all my power I have served your father.

7 And your father has deceived me, and changed my wages ten times; but God permitted him not to hurt me.

8 If he said thus, The speckled shall be your wages; then all the cattle bare speckled: and if he said thus, The ring-streaked shall be your hire; then bare all the cattle ring-streaked.

9 Thus God has taken away the cattle of your father, and given them to me.

10 And it came to pass at the time that the cattle conceived, that I lifted up mine eyes, and saw in a dream, and, behold, the rams which leaped upon the cattle were ring-streaked, speckled, and grisled.

11 And the angel of God spoke unto me in a dream, saying, Jacob: And I said, Here I am.

12 And he said, Lift up now your eyes, and see, all the rams which leap upon the cattle are ring-streaked, speckled, and grisled: for I have seen all that Laban does to you.

13 I am GOD of Bethel, where you anointed the pillar, and where you vowed a vow unto me: now arise, get you out from this land, and return unto the land of your birth.

14 And Rachel and Leah answered and said unto him, Is there yet any portion or inheritance for us in our father's house?

15 Are we not counted of him strangers? for he has sold us, and has quite devoured also our money.

16 For all the riches which God has taken from our father, that is ours, and our children's: now then, whatsoever God has said unto you, do.

17 Then Jacob rose up, and set his sons and his wives upon camels;

18 And he carried away all his cattle, and all his goods which he had gotten, the cattle of his getting, which he had gotten in Padan-Aram, for to go to Isaac his father in the land of Canaan.

19 And Laban went to shear his sheep: and Rachel had stolen the images [teraphim] that were her father's.

20 And Jacob stole away unawares to Laban the Syrian, in that he told him not that he fled.

21 So he fled with all that he had; and he rose up, and passed over the river, and set his face toward the mount Gilead.

22 And it was told Laban on the third day that Jacob was fled.

23 And he took his brethren with him, and pursued after him seven days' journey; and they overtook him in the mount Gilead.

24 And God came to Laban the Syrian in a dream by night, and said unto him, Take heed that you speak not to Jacob either good or evil.

25 Then Laban overtook Jacob. Now Jacob had pitched his tent in the mount: and Laban with his brethren pitched in the mount of Gilead.

26 And Laban said to Jacob, What have you done, that you have stolen away unawares to me, and carried away my daughters, as captives taken with the sword?

27 Why did you flee away secretly, and steal away from me; and did not tell me, that I might have sent you away with mirth, and with songs, with tabret, and with harp?

28 And have not permitted me to kiss my sons and my daughters? you have now done foolishly in so doing.

29 It is in the power of GOD to do you evil: but GOD of your father spoke unto me yesternight, saying, Take you heed that you speak not to Jacob either good or evil.

30 And now, though you have gone away, because you greatly longed for your father's house, yet why have you stolen my gods?

31 And Jacob answered and said to Laban, Because I was afraid: for I said, Perhaps you would take by force your daughters from me.

32 With whomsoever you find your gods, let him not live: before our brethren discern you what is yours with me, and take it to you. For Jacob knew not that Rachel had stolen them.

33 And Laban went into Jacob's tent, and into Leah's tent, and into the two maidservants' tents; but he found them not. Then went he out of Leah's tent, and entered into Rachel's tent.

34 Now Rachel had taken the images [teraphim] and put them in the camel's furniture, and sat upon them. And Laban searched all the tent, but found them not.

35 And she said to her father, Let it not displease my lord that I cannot rise up before you; for the custom of women is upon me. And he searched, but found not the images [teraphim].

36 And Jacob was angry, and chided with Laban: and Jacob answered and said to Laban, What is my trespass? what is my sin, that you have so hotly pursued after me?

37 Whereas you have searched all my stuff, what have you found of all your household stuff? set it here before my brethren and your brethren, that they may judge between us both.

38 This twenty years I have been with you; your ewes and your she goats have not cast their young, and the rams of your flock I have not eaten.

39 That which was torn of beasts I brought not unto you; I bare the loss of it; of my hand didst you require it, whether stolen by day, or stolen by night.

40 Thus I was; in the day the drought consumed me, and the frost by night; and my sleep departed from mine eyes.

41 Thus I have been twenty years in your house; I served you fourteen years for your two daughters, and six years for your cattle: and you have changed my wages ten times.

42 Except God of my father, God of Abraham, and the fear of Isaac, had been with me, surely you have sent me away now empty. God has seen mine affliction and the labor of my hands, and rebuked you yesternight.

43 And Laban answered and said unto Jacob, These daughters are my daughters, and these children are my children, and these cattle are my cattle, and all that you see is mine: and what can I do this day unto these my daughters, or unto their children which they have born?

44 Now therefore you come, let us make a covenant, I and you; and let it be for a witness between me and you.

45 And Jacob took a stone, and set it up for a pillar.

46 And Jacob said unto his brethren, Gather stones; and they took stones, and made a heap: and they did eat there upon the heap.

47 And Laban called it Jegarsahadutha: but Jacob called it Galeed.

48 And Laban said, This heap is a witness between me and you this day. Therefore was the name of it called Galeed;

49 And Mizpah; for he said, The Becoming-One watch between me and you, when we are absent one from another.

50 If you shall afflict my daughters, or if you shall take other wives beside my daughters, no man is with us; see, God is witness between me and you.

51 And Laban said to Jacob, Behold this heap, and behold this pillar, which I have cast between me and you;

52 This heap be witness, and this pillar be witness, that I will not pass over this heap to you, and that you shall not pass over this heap and this pillar unto me, for evil.

53 God of Abraham, and God of Nahor, God of their father, judge between us. And Jacob swore by the fear of his father Isaac.

54 Then Jacob offered sacrifice upon the mount, and called his brethren to eat bread: and they did eat bread, and tarried all night in the mount.

55 And early in the morning Laban rose up, and kissed his sons and his daughters, and blessed them: and Laban departed, and returned unto his place.

Gen 32:1 And Jacob went on his way, and the angels of God met him.

2 And when Jacob saw them, he said, This is the host [army] of God: and he called the name of that place Mahanaim [two armies]

3 And Jacob sent messengers before him to Esau his brother unto the land of Seir, the country of Edom.

4 And he commanded them, saying, Thus shall you speak unto my lord Esau; your servant Jacob says thus, I have sojourned with Laban, and stayed there until now:

5 And I have oxen, and donkeys, flocks, and menservants, and women servants: and I have sent to tell my lord, that I may find grace in your sight.

6 And the messengers returned to Jacob, saying, We came to your brother Esau, and also he comes to meet you, and four hundred men with him.

7 Then Jacob was greatly afraid and distressed: and he divided the people that was with him, and the flocks, and herds, and the camels, into two bands;

8 And said, If Esau come to the one company, and smite it, then the other company which is left shall escape.

9 And Jacob said, O God of my father Abraham, and God of my father Isaac, the Becoming-One which say unto me, Return unto your country, and to your kindred, and I will deal well with you:

10 I am not worthy of the least of all the mercies, and of all the truth, which you have showed unto your servant; for with my staff I passed over this Jordan; and now I am become two bands.

11 Deliver me, I pray you, from the hand of my brother, from the hand of Esau: for I fear him, lest he will come and smite me, and the mother with the children.

12 And you said, I will surely do you good, and make your seed as the sand of the sea, which cannot be numbered for multitude.

13 And he lodged there that same night; and took of that which came to his hand a present for Esau his brother;

14 Two hundred she goats, and twenty he goats, two hundred ewes, and twenty rams,

15 Thirty milch camels with their colts, forty cows, and ten bulls, twenty she donkeys, and ten foals.

16 And he delivered them into the hand of his servants, every herd by themselves; and said unto his servants, Pass over before me, and put a space between herd and herd.

17 And he commanded the foremost, saying, When Esau my brother meets you, and asks you, saying, Whose are you? and where do you go? and whose are these before you?

18 Then you shall say, They be your servant Jacob's; it is a present sent unto my lord Esau: and, behold, also he is behind us.

19 And so commanded he the second, and the third, and all that followed the herds, saying, On this manner shall you speak unto Esau, when you find him.

20 And say you moreover, Behold, your servant Jacob is behind us. For he said, I will appease him with the present that goes before me, and afterward I will see his face; perhaps he will accept of me.

21 So went the present over before him: and himself lodged that night in the company.

22 And he rose up that night, and took his two wives, and his two women servants, and his eleven sons, and passed over the ford Jabbok.

23 And he took them, and sent them over the brook, and sent over that he had.

24 And Jacob was left alone; and there wrestled a man with him until the breaking of the dawn.

25 And when he saw that he prevailed not against him, he touched the hollow of his thigh; and the hollow of Jacob's thigh was out of joint, as he wrestled with him.

26 And he said, Let me go, for the dawn breaks. And he said, I will not let you go, except you bless me.

27 And he said unto him, What is your name? And he said, Jacob.

28 And he said, your name shall be called no more Jacob, but Israel: for as a prince have you power with God and with men, and have prevailed.

29 And Jacob asked him, and said, Tell me, I pray you, your name. And he said, Why is it that you do ask after my name? And he blessed him there.

30 And Jacob called the name of the place Peniel: for I have seen God face to face, and my soul is preserved.

31 And as he passed over Penuel the sun rose upon him, and he halted upon his thigh.

32 Therefore the children of Israel eat not of the tendon, which is upon the hollow [socket] of the thigh, unto this day: because he touched the hollow of Jacob's thigh in the tendon.

Gen 33:1 And Jacob lifted up his eyes, and looked, and, behold, Esau came, and with him four hundred men. And he divided the children unto Leah, and unto Rachel, and unto the two handmaids.

2 And he put the handmaids and their children foremost, and Leah and her children after, and Rachel and Joseph hindermost.

3 And he passed over before them, and bowed himself to the ground seven times, until he came near to his brother.

4 And Esau ran to meet him, and embraced him, and fell on his neck, and kissed him: and they wept.

5 And he lifted up his eyes, and saw the women and the children; and said, Who are those with you? And he said, The children which God has graciously given your servant.

6 Then the handmaidens came near, they and their children, and they bowed themselves.

7 And Leah also with her children came near, and bowed themselves: and after came Joseph near and Rachel, and they bowed themselves.

8 And he said, What do you mean by all this camp which I met? And he said, These are to find grace in the sight of my lord.

9 And Esau said, I have enough, my brother; keep that you have unto thyself.

10 And Jacob said, Nay, I pray you, if now I have found grace in your sight, then receive my present at my hand: for therefore I have seen your face, as though I had seen the face of God, and you were pleased with me.

11 Take, I pray you, my blessing that is brought to you; because God has dealt graciously with me, and because I have all. And he urged him, and he took it.

12 And he said, Let us take our journey, and let us go, and I will go before you.

13 And he said unto him, My lord knows that the children are tender, and the flocks and herds with young are with me: and if men should overdrive them one day, all the flock will die.

14 Let my lord, I pray you, pass over before his servant: and I will lead on softly, according as the cattle that goes before me and the children be able to endure, until I come unto my lord unto Seir.

15 And Esau said, Let me now leave with you some of the folk that are with me. And he said, What need is there? let me find grace in the sight of my lord.

16 So Esau returned that day on his way unto Seir.

17 And Jacob journeyed to Succoth, and built himself a house, and made booths for his cattle: therefore the name of the place is called Succoth [booths]

18 And Jacob came to Shalem, a city of Shechem, which is in the land of Canaan, when he came from Padan-Aram; and pitched his tent before the city.

19 And he bought a parcel of a field, where he had spread his tent, at the hand of the children of Hamor, Shechem's father, for a hundred pieces of money.

20 And he erected there an altar, and called it El elohe-Israel [god GOD of israel]

Gen 34:1 And Dinah the daughter of Leah, which she bare unto Jacob, went out to see the daughters of the land.

2 And when Shechem the son of Hamor the Hivite, prince of the country, saw her, he took her, and lay with her, and defiled her.

3 And his soul clave unto Dinah the daughter of Jacob, and he loved the damsel, and spoke kindly unto the damsel.

4 And Shechem spoke unto his father Hamor, saying, Get me this damsel to wife.

5 And Jacob heard that he had defiled Dinah his daughter: now his sons were with his cattle in the field: and Jacob held his peace until they were come.

6 And Hamor the father of Shechem went out unto Jacob to commune with him.

7 And the sons of Jacob came out of the field when they heard it: and the men were grieved, and they were very angry, because he had worked folly in Israel in lying with Jacob's daughter; which thing ought not to be done.

8 And Hamor communed with them, saying, The soul of my son Shechem longs for your daughter: I pray you give her him to wife.

9 And make you marriages with us, and give your daughters unto us, and take our daughters unto you.

10 And you shall dwell with us: and the land shall be before you; dwell and trade you therein, and get you possessions therein.

11 And Shechem said unto her father and unto her brethren, Let me find grace in your eyes, and what you shall say unto me I will give.

12 Ask me ever so much dowry and gift, and I will give according as you shall say unto me: but give me the damsel to wife.

13 And the sons of Jacob answered Shechem and Hamor his father deceitfully, and said, because he had defiled Dinah their sister:

14 And they said unto them, We cannot do this thing, to give our sister to one that is uncircumcised; for that were a reproach unto us:

15 But in this will we consent unto you: If you will be as we be, that every male of you be circumcised;

16 Then will we give our daughters unto you, and we will take your daughters to us, and we will dwell with you, and we will become one people.

17 But if you will not listen unto us, to be circumcised; then will we take our daughter, and we will be gone.

18 And their words pleased Hamor, and Shechem Hamor's son.

19 And the young man did not hesitate to do the thing, because he had delight in Jacob's daughter: and he was more honorable than all the house of his father.

20 And Hamor and Shechem his son came unto the gate of their city, and communed with the men of their city, saying,

21 These men are peaceable with us; therefore let them dwell in the land, and trade therein; for the land, behold, it is large enough for them; let us take their daughters to us for wives, and let us give them our daughters.

22 Only herein will the men consent unto us for to dwell with us, to be one people, if every male among us be circumcised, as they are circumcised.

23 Shall not their cattle and their substance and every animal of theirs be ours? only let us consent unto them, and they will dwell with us.

24 And unto Hamor and unto Shechem his son listened all that went out of the gate of his city; and every male was circumcised, all that went out of the gate of his city.

25 And it came to pass on the third day, when they were sore, that two of the sons of Jacob, Simeon and Levi, Dinah's brethren, took each man his sword, and came upon the city boldly, and killed all the males.

26 And they killed Hamor and Shechem his son with the mouth of the sword, and took Dinah out of Shechem's house, and went out.

27 The sons of Jacob came upon the slain, and spoiled the city, because they had defiled their sister.

28 They took their sheep, and their oxen, and their donkeys, and that which was in the city, and that which was in the field,

29 And all their wealth, and all their little ones, and their wives took they captive, and spoiled even all that was in the house.

30 And Jacob said to Simeon and Levi, you have troubled me to make me to stink among the inhabitants of the land, among the Canaanites and the Perizzites: and I being few in number, they shall gather themselves together against me, and slay me; and I shall be destroyed, I and my house.

31 And they said, Should he deal with our sister as with a harlot?

Gen 35:1 And God said unto Jacob, Arise, go up to Bethel, and dwell there: and make there an altar unto GOD, that appeared unto you when you fled from the face of Esau your brother.

2 Then Jacob said unto his household, and to all that were with him, Put away the strange gods that are among you, and be clean, and change your garments:

3 And let us arise, and go up to Bethel; and I will make there an altar unto GOD, who answered me in the day of my distress, and was with me in the way which I went.

4 And they gave unto Jacob all the strange gods which were in their hand, and all their earrings which were in their ears; and Jacob hid them under the oak which was by Shechem.

5 And they journeyed: and the terror of God was upon the cities that were round about them, and they did not pursue after the sons of Jacob.

6 So Jacob came to Luz, which is in the land of Canaan, that is, Bethel, he and all the people that were with him.

7 And he built there an altar, and called the place El-bethel: because there God appeared unto him, when he fled from the face of his brother.

8 But Deborah Rebekah's nurse died, and she was buried beneath Bethel under an oak: and the name of it was called Allonbachuth.

9 And God appeared unto Jacob again, when he came out of Padan-Aram, and blessed him.

10 And God said unto him, your name is Jacob: your name shall not be called any more Jacob, but Israel shall be your name: and he called his name Israel.

11 And God said unto him, I am GOD Almighty: be fruitful and multiply; a nation and a company of nations shall be of you, and kings shall come out of your loins;

12 And the land which I gave Abraham and Isaac, to you I will give it, and to your seed after you will I give the land.

13 And God went up from him in the place where he talked with him.

14 And Jacob set up a pillar in the place where he talked with him, even a pillar of stone: and he poured a drink offering thereon, and he poured oil thereon.

15 And Jacob called the name of the place where God spoke with him, Bethel.

16 And they journeyed from Bethel; and there was but a little way to come to Ephrath: and Rachel travailed, and she had hard labor.

17 And it came to pass, when she was in hard labor, that the midwife said unto her, Fear not; you shall have this son also.

18 And it came to pass, as her soul was in departing, for she died that she called his name Benoni: but his father called him Benjamin.

19 And Rachel died, and was buried in the way to Ephrath, which is Bethlehem.

20 And Jacob set a pillar upon her grave: that is the pillar of Rachel's grave unto this day.

21 And Israel journeyed, and spread his tent beyond the tower of Edar.

22 And it came to pass, when Israel dwelt in that land, that Reuben went and lay with Bilhah his father's concubine: and Israel heard it. Now the sons of Jacob were twelve:

23 The sons of Leah; Reuben, Jacob's firstborn, and Simeon, and Levi, and Judah, and Issachar, and Zebulun:

24 The sons of Rachel; Joseph, and Benjamin:

25 And the sons of Bilhah, Rachel's handmaid; Dan, and Naphtali:

26 And the sons of Zilpah, Leah's handmaid; Gad, and Asher: these are the sons of Jacob, which were born to him in Padan-Aram.

27 And Jacob came unto Isaac his father unto Mamre, unto the city of Arbah, which is Hebron, where Abraham and Isaac sojourned.

28 And the days of Isaac were a hundred and fourscore years.

29 And Isaac gave up the ghost, and died, and was gathered unto his people, being old and full of days: and his sons Esau and Jacob buried him.

Gen 36:1 Now these are the generations of Esau, who is Edom.

2 Esau took his wives of the daughters of Canaan; Adah the daughter of Elon the Hittite, and Aholibamah the daughter of Anah the daughter of Zibeon the Hivite;

3 And Bashemath Ishmael's daughter, sister of Nebajoth.

4 And Adah bare to Esau Eliphaz; and Bashemath bare Reuel;

5 And Aholibamah bare Jeush, and Jaalam, and Korah: these are the sons of Esau, which were born unto him in the land of Canaan.

6 And Esau took his wives, and his sons, and his daughters, and all the souls of his house, and his cattle, and all his beasts, and all his substance, which he had got in the land of Canaan; and went into the country from the face of his brother Jacob.

7 For their riches were more than that they might dwell together; and the land wherein they were strangers could not bear them because of their cattle.

8 Thus dwelt Esau in mount Seir: Esau is Edom.

9 And these are the generations of Esau the father of the Edomites in mount Seir:

10 These are the names of Esau's sons; Eliphaz the son of Adah the wife of Esau, Reuel the son of Bashemath the wife of Esau.

11 And the sons of Eliphaz were Teman, Omar, Zepho, and Gatam, and Kenaz.

12 And Timna was concubine to Eliphaz Esau's son; and she bare to Eliphaz Amalek: these were the sons of Adah Esau's wife.

13 And these are the sons of Reuel; Nahath, and Zerah, Shammah, and Mizzah: these were the sons of Bashemath Esau's wife.

14 And these were the sons of Aholibamah, the daughter of Anah the daughter of Zibeon, Esau's wife: and she bare to Esau Jeush, and Jaalam, and Korah.

15 These were chiefs of the sons of Esau: the sons of Eliphaz the firstborn son of Esau; chief Teman, chief Omar, chief Zepho, chief Kenaz,

16 Chief Korah, chief Gatam, and chief Amalek: these are the chiefs that came of Eliphaz in the land of Edom; these were the sons of Adah.

17 And these are the sons of Reuel Esau's son; chief Nahath, chief Zerah, chief Shammah, chief Mizzah: these are the chiefs that came of Reuel in the land of Edom; these are the sons of Bashemath Esau's wife.

18 And these are the sons of Aholibamah Esau's wife; chief Jeush, chief Jaalam, chief Korah: these were the chiefs that came of Aholibamah the daughter of Anah, Esau's wife.

19 These are the sons of Esau, who is Edom, and these are their chiefs.

20 These are the sons of Seir the Horite, who inhabited the land; Lotan, and Shobal, and Zibeon, and Anah,

21 And Dishon, and Ezer, and Dishan: these are the chiefs of the Horites, the children of Seir in the land of Edom.

22 And the children of Lotan were Hori and Hemam; and Lotan's sister was Timna.

23 And the children of Shobal were these; Alvan, and Manahath, and Ebal, Shepho, and Onam.

24 And these are the children of Zibeon; both Ajah, and Anah: this was that Anah that found the mules in the wilderness, as he fed the donkeys of Zibeon his father.

25 And the children of Anah were these; Dishon, and Aholibamah the daughter of Anah.

26 And these are the children of Dishon; Hemdan, and Eshban, and Ithran, and Cheran.

27 The children of Ezer are these; Bilhan, and Zaavan, and Akan.

28 The children of Dishan are these; Uz, and Aran.

29 These are the chiefs that came of the Horites; chief Lotan, chief Shobal, chief Zibeon, chief Anah,

30 Chief Dishon, chief Ezer, chief Dishan: these are the chiefs that came of Hori, among their chiefs in the land of Seir.

31 And these are the kings that reigned in the land of Edom, before there reigned any king over the children of Israel.

32 And Bela the son of Beor reigned in Edom: and the name of his city was Dinhabah.

33 And Bela died, and Jobab the son of Zerah of Bozrah reigned in his stead.

34 And Jobab died, and Husham of the land of Temani reigned in his stead.

35 And Husham died, and Hadad the son of Bedad, who smote Midian in the field of Moab, reigned in his stead: and the name of his city was Avith.

36 And Hadad died, and Samlah of Masrekah reigned in his stead.

37 And Samlah died, and Saul of Rehoboth by the river reigned in his stead.

38 And Saul died, and Baal-Hanan the son of Achbor reigned in his stead.

39 And Baal-Hanan the son of Achbor died, and Hadar reigned in his stead: and the name of his city was Pau; and his wife's name was Mehetabel, the daughter of Matred, the daughter of Mezahab.

40 And these are the names of the chiefs that came of Esau, according to their families, after their places, by their names; chief Timnah, chief Alvah, chief Jetheth,

41 Chief Aholibamah, chief Elah, chief Pinon,

42 Chief Kenaz, chief Teman, chief Mibzar,

43 Chief Magdiel, chief Iram: these be the chiefs of Edom, according to their habitations in the land of their possession: he is Esau the father of the Edomites.

Gen 37:1 And Jacob dwelt in the land wherein his father was a stranger, in the land of Canaan.

2 These are the generations of Jacob. Joseph, being a son of seventeen years, was feeding the flock with his brethren; and the lad was with the sons of Bilhah, and with the sons of Zilpah, his father's wives: and Joseph brought unto his father their evil report.

3 Now Israel loved Joseph more than all his children, because he was the son of his old age: and he made him a coat of many colors.

4 And when his brethren saw that their father loved him more than all his brethren, they hated him, and could not speak peaceably unto him.

5 And Joseph dreamed a dream, and he told it his brethren: and they hated him yet the more.

6 And he said unto them, Hear, I pray you, this dream which I have dreamed:

7 For, behold, we were binding sheaves in the field, and, lo, my sheaf arose, and also stood upright; and, behold, your sheaves stood round about, and made obeisance to my sheaf.

8 And his brethren said to him, shall you indeed reign over us? or shall you indeed have dominion over us? And they hated him yet the more for his dreams, and for his words.

9 And he dreamed yet another dream, and told it his brethren, and said, Behold, I have dreamed a dream more; and, behold, the sun and the moon and the eleven stars made obeisance to me.

10 And he told it to his father, and to his brethren: and his father rebuked him, and said unto him, What is this dream that you have dreamed? Shall I and your mother and your brethren indeed come to bow down ourselves to you to the earth?

11 And his brethren envied him; but his father observed the saying.

12 And his brethren went to feed their father's flock in Shechem.

13 And Israel said unto Joseph, Do not your brethren feed the flock in Shechem? come, and I will send you unto them. And he said to him, Here I am.

14 And he said to him, Go, I pray you, see whether it be well with your brethren, and well with the flocks; and bring me word again. So he sent him out of the vale of Hebron, and he came to Shechem.

15 And a certain man found him, and, behold, he was wandering in the field: and the man asked him, saying, What seek you?

16 And he said, I seek my brethren: tell me, I pray you, where they feed their flocks.

17 And the man said, They are departed hence; for I heard them say, Let us go to Dothan. And Joseph went after his brethren, and found them in Dothan.

18 And when they saw him afar off, even before he came near unto them, they conspired against him to slay him.

19 And they said one to another, Behold, this dreamer comes.

20 Come now therefore, and let us slay him, and cast him into some pit, and we will say, Some evil beast has devoured him: and we shall see what will become of his dreams.

21 And Reuben heard it, and he delivered him out of their hands; and said, Let us not kill him, the soul.

22 And Reuben said unto them, Shed no blood, but cast him into this pit that is in the wilderness, and lay no hand upon him; that he might rid him out of their hands, to deliver him to his father again.

23 And it came to pass, when Joseph was come unto his brethren, that they stripped Joseph out of his coat, his coat of many colors that was on him;

24 And they took him, and cast him into a pit: and the pit was empty, there was no water in it.

25 And they sat down to eat bread: and they lifted up their eyes and looked, and, behold, a company of Ishmeelites came from Gilead with their camels bearing spicery and balm and myrrh, going to carry it down to Egypt.

26 And Judah said unto his brethren, What profit is it if we slay our brother, and conceal his blood?

27 Come, and let us sell him to the Ishmeelites, and let not our hand be upon him; for he is our brother and our flesh. And his brethren were content.

28 Then there passed by Midianites merchantmen; and they drew and lifted up Joseph out of the pit, and sold Joseph to the Ishmeelites for twenty pieces of silver: and they brought Joseph into Egypt.

29 And Reuben returned unto the pit; and, behold, Joseph was not in the pit; and he rent his clothes.

30 And he returned unto his brethren, and said, The child is not; and I, to where shall I go?

31 And they took Joseph's coat, and killed a kid of the goats, and dipped the coat in the blood;

32 And they sent away the coat of many colors, and they brought it to their father; and said, We found this: and we know not if it is your son's coat or not.

33 And he knew it, and said, It is my son's coat; an evil beast has devoured him; Joseph is outside no doubt ripped in pieces.

34 And Jacob rent his clothes, and put sackcloth upon his loins, and mourned for his son many days.

35 And all his sons and all his daughters rose up to comfort him; but he refused to be comforted; and he said, For I will go down into Sheol to my son mourning. Thus his father wept for him.

36 And the Midianites sold him into Egypt unto Potiphar, an eunuch of Pharaoh's, and captain of the guard.

Gen 38:1 And it came to pass at that time, that Judah went down from his brethren, and turned in to a certain Adullamite, whose name was Hirah.

2 And Judah saw there a daughter of a certain Canaanite, whose name was Shuah; and he took her, and went in unto her.

3 And she conceived, and bare a son; and he called his name Er.

4 And she conceived again, and bare a son; and she called his name Onan.

5 And she yet again conceived, and bare a son; and called his name Shelah: and he was at Chezib, when she bare him.

6 And Judah took a wife for Er his firstborn, whose name was Tamar.

7 And Er, Judah's firstborn, was wicked in the sight of the Becoming-One; and the Becoming-One killed him.

8 And Judah said unto Onan, Go in unto your brother's wife, and marry her, and raise up seed to your brother.

9 And Onan knew that the seed should not be his; and it came to pass, when he went in unto his brother's wife, that he spilled it on the ground, lest that he should give seed to his brother.

10 And the thing which he did displeased the Becoming-One:therefore he killed him also.

11 Then said Judah to Tamar his daughter-in-law, Remain a widow at your father's house, till Shelah my son be grown: for he said, Lest perhaps he die also, as his brethren did. And Tamar went and dwelt in her father's house.

12 And in process of time the daughter of Shuah Judah's wife died; and Judah was comforted, and went up unto his sheepshearers to Timnath, he and his friend Hirah the Adullamite.

13 And it was told Tamar, saying, Behold your father-in-law goes up to Timnath to shear his sheep.

14 And she put her widow's garments off from her, and covered her with a veil, and wrapped herself, and sat in an open place, which is by the way to Timnath; for she saw that Shelah was grown, and she was not given unto him to wife.

15 When Judah saw her, he thought her to be a harlot; because she had covered her face.

16 And he turned unto her by the way, and said, Go to, I pray you, let me come in unto you; for he knew not that she was his daughter-in-law. And she said, What will you give me, that you may come in unto me?

17 And he said, I will send you a kid from the flock. And she said, will you give me a pledge, till you send it?

18 And he said, What pledge shall I give you? And she said, your signet, and your bracelets, and your staff that is in your hand. And he gave it her, and came in unto her, and she conceived by him.

19 And she arose, and went away, and took off her veil, and put on the garments of her widowhood.

20 And Judah sent the kid by the hand of his friend the Adullamite, to receive his pledge from the woman's hand: but he found her not.

21 Then he asked the men of that place, saying, Where is the harlot, that was openly by the way side? And they said, There was no harlot in this place.

22 And he returned to Judah, and said, I cannot find her; and also the men of the place said, that there was no harlot in this place.

23 And Judah said, Let her keep the things as her own, lest we be shamed: behold, I sent this kid, and you have not found her.

24 And it came to pass about three months after, that it was told Judah, saying, Tamar your daughter-in-law has played the harlot; and also, behold, she is with child by whoredom. And Judah said, Bring her forth, and let her be burnt.

25 When she was brought forth, she sent to her father-in-law, saying, By the man, whose these are, I am with child: and she said, Discern, I pray you, whose are these, the signet, and bracelets, and staff.

26 And Judah acknowledged them, and said, She has been more righteous than I; because that I gave her not to Shelah my son. And he knew her again no more.

27 And it came to pass in the time of her travail, that, behold, twins were in her womb.

28 And it came to pass, when she travailed, that the one put out his hand: and the midwife took and bound upon his hand a scarlet thread, saying, This came out first.

29 And it came to pass, as he drew back his hand, that, behold, his brother came out: and she said, How have you broken forth? this breach be upon you: therefore his name was called Pharez.

30 And afterward came out his brother, that had the scarlet thread upon his hand: and his name was called Zarah.

Gen 39:1 And Joseph was brought down to Egypt; and Potiphar, an eunuch of Pharaoh, captain of the guard, an Egyptian, bought him of the hands of the Ishmeelites, which had brought him down there.

2 And the Becoming-One was with Joseph, and he was a prosperous man; and he was in the house of his master the Egyptian.

3 And his master saw that the Becoming-One was with him, and that the Becoming-One made all that he did to prosper in his hand.

4 And Joseph found grace in his sight, and he served him: and he made him overseer over his house, and all that he had he put into his hand.

5 And it came to pass from the time that he had made him overseer in his house, and over all that he had, that the Becoming-One blessed the Egyptian's house for Joseph's sake; and the blessing of the Becoming-One was upon all that he had in the house, and in the field.

6 And he left all that he had in Joseph's hand; and he knew not what he had, except the bread which he did eat. And Joseph was well formed, and good looking.

7 And it came to pass after these things, that his master's wife cast her eyes upon Joseph; and she said, Lie with me.

8 But he refused, and said unto his master's wife, Behold, my master knows not what is with me in the house, and he has committed all that he has to my hand;

9 There is none greater in this house than I; neither has he kept back any thing from me but you, because you are his wife: how then can I do this great evil, and sin against God?

10 And it came to pass, as she spoke to Joseph day by day, that he listened not unto her, to lie by her, or to be with her.

11 And it came to pass about this time, that Joseph went into the house to do his business; and there was none of the men of the house there within.

12 And she caught him by his garment, saying, Lie with me: and he left his garment in her hand, and fled, and got him out.

13 And it came to pass, when she saw that he had left his garment in her hand, and was fled forth,

14 That she called unto the men of her house, and spoke unto them, saying, See, he has brought in a Hebrew unto us to mock us; he came in unto me to lie with me, and I cried with a loud voice:

15 And it came to pass, when he heard that I lifted up my voice and cried, that he left his garment with me, and fled, and got him out.

16 And she laid up his garment by her, until his lord came home.

17 And she spoke unto him according to these words, saying, The Hebrew servant, which you have brought unto us, came in unto me to mock me:

18 And it came to pass, as I lifted up my voice and cried, that he left his garment with me, and fled out.

19 And it came to pass, when his master heard the words of his wife, which she spoke unto him, saying, After this manner did your servant to me; that his wrath was kindled.

20 And Joseph's master took him, and put him into the prison, a place where the king's prisoners were bound: and he was there in the prison.

21 But the Becoming-One was with Joseph, and showed him mercy, and gave him favor in the sight of the keeper of the prison.

22 And the keeper of the prison committed to Joseph's hand all the prisoners that were in the prison; and whatsoever they did there, he was the doer of it.

23 The keeper of the prison looked not to any thing that was under his hand; because the Becoming-One was with him, and that which he did, the Becoming-One made it to prosper.

Gen 40:1 And it came to pass after these things, that the cupbearer of the king of Egypt and his baker had offended their lords the king of Egypt.

2 And Pharaoh was angry against two of his eunuchs, against the chief of the butlers, and against the chief of the bakers.

3 And he put them in prison in the house of the captain of the guard, into the prison, the place where Joseph was bound.

4 And the captain of the guard charged Joseph with them, and he served them: and they continued a season in ward.

5 And they dreamed a dream both of them, each man his dream in one night, each man according to the interpretation of his dream, the cupbearer and the baker of the king of Egypt, which were bound in the prison.

6 And Joseph came in unto them in the morning, and looked upon them, and, behold, they were sad.

7 And he asked Pharaoh's eunuchs that were with him in the prison of his lords' house, saying, Why look you so bad today?

8 And they said unto him, We have dreamed a dream, and there is no interpreter of it. And Joseph said unto them, Do not interpretations belong to God? tell me them, I pray you.

9 And the chief cupbearer told his dream to Joseph, and said to him, In my dream, behold, a vine was before me;

10 And in the vine were three branches: and it was as though it budded, and her blossoms shot forth; and the clusters thereof brought forth ripe grapes:

11 And Pharaoh's cup was in my hand: and I took the grapes, and pressed them into Pharaoh's cup, and I gave the cup into Pharaoh's hand.

12 And Joseph said unto him, This is the interpretation of it: The three branches are three days:

13 Yet within three days shall Pharaoh lift up your head, and restore you unto your place: and you shall deliver Pharaoh's cup into his hand, after the former manner when you were his cupbearer.

14 But think on me when it shall be well with you, and show kindness, I pray you, unto me, and make mention of me unto Pharaoh, and bring me out of this house:

15 For indeed I was stolen away out of the land of the Hebrews: and here also have I done nothing that they should put me into the dungeon.

16 When the chief baker saw that the interpretation was good, he said unto Joseph, I also was in my dream, and, behold, I had three white baskets on my head:

17 And in the uppermost basket there was of all manner of baked goods for Pharaoh; and the birds did eat them out of the basket upon my head.

18 And Joseph answered and said, This is the interpretation thereof: The three baskets are three days:

19 Yet within three days shall Pharaoh lift up your head from off you, and shall hang you on a tree; and the birds shall eat your flesh from off you.

20 And it came to pass the third day, which was Pharaoh's birthday, that he made a feast unto all his servants: and he lifted up the head of the chief cupbearer and of the chief baker among his servants.

21 And he restored the chief cupbearer unto his cupbearer's office again; and he gave the cup into Pharaoh's hand:

22 But he hanged the chief baker: as Joseph had interpreted to them.

23 Yet did not the chief cupbearer remember Joseph, but forgot him.

Gen 41:1 And it came to pass at the end of two full years, that Pharaoh dreamed: and, behold, he stood by the river.

2 And, behold, there came up out of the river seven well favored cows and fatfleshed; and they fed in a meadow.

3 And, behold, seven other cows came up after them out of the river, ill favored and leanfleshed; and stood by the other cows upon the brink of the river.

4 And the ill favored and lean fleshed cows did eat up the seven well favored and fat cows. So Pharaoh awoke.

5 And he slept and dreamed the second time: and, behold, seven ears of grain came up upon one stalk, rank and good.

6 And, behold, seven thin ears and blasted with the east wind sprung up after them.

7 And the seven thin ears devoured the seven rank and full ears. And Pharaoh awoke, and, behold, it was a dream.

8 And it came to pass in the morning that his spirit was troubled; and he sent and called for all the magicians of Egypt, and all the wise men thereof: and Pharaoh told them his dream; but there was none that could interpret them unto Pharaoh.

9 Then spoke the chief cupbearer unto Pharaoh, saying, I do remember my faults this day:

10 Pharaoh was angry with his servants, and put me in prison in the captain of the guard's house, both me and the chief baker:

11 And we dreamed a dream in one night, I and he; we dreamed each man according to the interpretation of his dream.

12 And there was there with us a young man, a Hebrew, servant to the captain of the guard; and we told him, and he interpreted to us our dreams; to each man according to his dream he did interpret.

13 And it came to pass, as he interpreted to us, so it was; me he restored unto mine office, and him he hanged.

14 Then Pharaoh sent and called Joseph, and they brought him hastily out of the dungeon: and he shaved himself, and changed his raiment, and came in unto Pharaoh.

15 And Pharaoh said unto Joseph, I have dreamed a dream, and there is none that can interpret it: and I have heard say of you, that you can understand a dream to interpret it.

16 And Joseph answered Pharaoh, saying, It is not in me: God shall give Pharaoh an answer of peace.

17 And Pharaoh said unto Joseph, In my dream, behold, I stood upon the bank of the river:

18 And, behold, there came up out of the river seven cows, fatfleshed and well favored; and they fed in a meadow:

19 And, behold, seven other cows came up after them, poor and very ill favored and leanfleshed, such as I never saw in all the land of Egypt for badness:

20 And the lean and the ill favored cows did eat up the first seven fat cows:

21 And when they had eaten them up, it could not be known that they had eaten them; but they were still ill favored, as at the beginning. So I awoke.

22 And I saw in my dream, and, behold, seven ears came up in one stalk, full and good:

23 And, behold, seven ears, withered, thin, and blasted with the east wind, sprung up after them:

24 And the thin ears devoured the seven good ears: and I told this unto the magicians; but there was none that could declare it to me.

25 And Joseph said unto Pharaoh, The dream of Pharaoh is one: God has showed Pharaoh what he is about to do.

26 The seven good cows are seven years; and the seven good ears are seven years: the dream is one.

27 And the seven thin and ill favored cows that came up after them are seven years; and the seven empty ears blasted with the east wind shall be seven years of famine.

28 This is the thing which I have spoken unto Pharaoh: What God is about to do he shows unto Pharaoh.

29 Behold, there come seven years of great plenty throughout all the land of Egypt:

30 And there shall arise after them seven years of famine; and all the plenty shall be forgotten in the land of Egypt; and the famine shall consume the land;

31 And the plenty shall not be known in the land by reason of that famine following; for it shall be very grievous.

32 And for that the dream was doubled unto Pharaoh twice; it is because the thing is established by God, and God will shortly bring it to pass.

33 Now therefore let Pharaoh seek out a man discreet and wise, and set him over the land of Egypt.

34 Let Pharaoh do this, and let him appoint officers over the land, and take up the fifth part of the land of Egypt in the seven plenteous years.

35 And let them gather all the food of those good years that come, and lay up grain under the hand of Pharaoh, and let them keep food in the cities.

36 And that food shall be for store to the land against the seven years of famine, which shall be in the land of Egypt; that the land perish not through the famine.

37 And the thing was good in the eyes of Pharaoh, and in the eyes of all his servants.

38 And Pharaoh said unto his servants, Can we find such a one as this is, a man in whom the Spirit of God is?

39 And Pharaoh said unto Joseph, Forasmuch as God has showed you all this, there is none so discreet and wise as you are:

40 you shall be over my house, and according unto your word shall all my people be ruled: only in the throne will I be greater than you.

41 And Pharaoh said unto Joseph, See, I have set you over all the land of Egypt.

42 And Pharaoh took off his ring from his hand, and put it upon Joseph's hand, and arrayed him in vestures of fine linen, and put a gold chain about his neck;

43 And he made him to ride in the second chariot which he had; and they cried before him, Bow the knee: and he made him ruler over all the land of Egypt.

44 And Pharaoh said unto Joseph, I am Pharaoh, and outside you shall no man lift up his hand or foot in all the land of Egypt.

45 And Pharaoh called Joseph's name Zaphnathpaaneah; and he gave him to wife Asenath the daughter of Potipherah priest of On. And Joseph went out over all the land of Egypt.

46 And Joseph was a son of thirty years when he stood before Pharaoh king of Egypt. And Joseph went out from the presence of Pharaoh, and went throughout all the land of Egypt. [2289 YM / 1685 BC]

47 And in the seven plenteous years the earth brought forth by handfuls.

48 And he gathered up all the food of the seven years, which were in the land of Egypt, and laid up the food in the cities: the food of the field, which was round about every city, laid he up in the same.

49 And Joseph gathered grain as the sand of the sea, very much, until he left numbering; for it was without number.

50 And unto Joseph were born two sons before the years of famine came, which Asenath the daughter of Potipherah priest of On bare unto him.

51 And Joseph called the name of the firstborn Manasseh: For God, said he, has made me forget all my toil, and all my father's house.

52 And the name of the second called he Ephraim: For God has caused me to be fruitful in the land of my affliction.

53 And the seven years of plenteousness, that was in the land of Egypt, were ended.

54 And the seven years of dearth began to come, according as Joseph had said: and the dearth was in all lands; but in all the land of Egypt there was bread.

55 And when all the land of Egypt was famished, the people cried to Pharaoh for bread: and Pharaoh said unto all the Egyptians, Go unto Joseph; what he says to you, do.

56 And the famine was over all the face of the earth: And Joseph opened all the storehouses, and sold unto the Egyptians; and the famine grew great in the land of Egypt.

57 And all countries came into Egypt to Joseph for to buy grain; because that the famine was so great in all lands.

Gen 42:1 Now when Jacob saw that there was grain in Egypt, Jacob said unto his sons, Why do you look one upon another?

2 And he said, Behold, I have heard that there is grain in Egypt: get you down there, and buy for us from there; that we may live, and not die.

3 And Joseph's ten brethren went down to buy grain in Egypt.

4 But Benjamin, Joseph's brother, Jacob sent not with his brethren; for he said, Lest perhaps mischief befall him.

5 And the sons of Israel came to buy grain among those that came: for the famine was in the land of Canaan.

6 And Joseph was the governor over the land, and he it was that sold to all the people of the land: and Joseph's brethren came, and bowed down themselves before him with their faces to the earth.

7 And Joseph saw his brethren, and he knew them, but made himself strange unto them, and spoke roughly unto them; and he said unto them, From where have you come? And they said, From the land of Canaan to buy food.

8 And Joseph knew his brethren, but they knew not him.

9 And Joseph remembered the dreams which he dreamed of them, and said unto them, you are spies; to see the nakedness of the land you are come.

10 And they said unto him, Nay, my lord, but to buy food are your servants come.

11 We are all one man's sons; we are true men, your servants are no spies.

12 And he said unto them, Nay, but to see the nakedness of the land you are come.

13 And they said, your servants are twelve brethren, the sons of one man in the land of Canaan; and, behold, the youngest is this day with our father, and one is not.

14 And Joseph said unto them, That is it that I spoke unto you, saying, you are spies:

15 Hereby you shall be proved: By the life of Pharaoh you shall not go forth hence, except your youngest brother come here.

16 Send one of you, and let him fetch your brother, and you shall be kept in prison, that your words may be proved, whether there be any truth in you: or else by the life of Pharaoh surely you are spies.

17 And he put them all together into prison three days.

18 And Joseph said unto them the third day, This do, and live; for I fear God:

19 If you be true men, let one of your brethren be bound in the house of your prison: go ye, carry grain for the famine of your houses:

20 But bring your youngest brother unto me; so shall your words be verified, and you shall not die. And they did so.

21 And they said one to another, We are truly guilty concerning our brother, in that we saw the anguish of his soul, when he besought us, and we would not hear; therefore is this distress come upon us.

22 And Reuben answered them, saying, Spoke I not unto you, saying, Do not sin against the child; and you would not hear? therefore, behold, also his blood is required.

23 And they knew not that Joseph understood them; for he spoke unto them by an interpreter.

24 And he turned himself about from them, and wept; and returned to them again, and communed with them, and took from them Simeon, and bound him before their eyes.

25 Then Joseph commanded to fill their sacks with grain, and to restore every man's money into his sack, and to give them provision for the way: and thus did he unto them.

26 And they laded their donkeys with the grain, and departed there.

27 And as one of them opened his sack to give his donkey feed in the inn, he saw his money; for, behold, it was in his sack's mouth.

28 And he said unto his brethren, My money is restored; and, lo, it is even in my sack: and their heart failed them, and they were afraid, saying one to another, What is this that God has done unto us?

29 And they came unto Jacob their father unto the land of Canaan, and told him all that befell unto them; saying,

30 The man, lords of the land, spoke roughly to us, and took us for spies of the country.

31 And we said unto him, We are true men; we are no spies:

32 We be twelve brethren, sons of our father; one is not, and the youngest is this day with our father in the land of Canaan.

33 And the man, lords of the country, said unto us, Hereby shall I know that you are true men; leave one of your brethren here with me, and take food for the famine of your households, and be gone:

34 And bring your youngest brother unto me: then shall I know that you are no spies, but that you are true men: so will I deliver you your brother, and you shall traffic in the land.

35 And it came to pass as they emptied their sacks, that, behold, every man's bundle of money was in his sack: and when both they and their father saw the bundles of money, they were afraid.

36 And Jacob their father said unto them, You have made me sad for my children: Joseph is not, and Simeon is not, and you will take Benjamin away: all these things are against me.

37 And Reuben spoke unto his father, saying, Slay my two sons, if I bring him not to you: deliver him into my hand, and I will bring him to you again.

38 And he said, My son shall not go down with you; for his brother is dead, and he is left alone: if mischief befall him by the way in the which you go, then shall you bring down my gray hairs with sorrow to Sheol.

Gen 43:1 And the famine was great in the land.

2 And it came to pass, when they had eaten up the grain which they had brought out of Egypt, their father said unto them, Go again, buy us a little food.

3 And Judah spoke unto him, saying, The man did solemnly protest unto us, saying, you shall not see my face, except your brother be with you.

4 If you will send our brother with us, we will go down and buy you food:

5 But if you will not send him, we will not go down: for the man said unto us, you shall not see my face, except your brother be with you.

6 And Israel said, Why dealt you so ill with me, as to tell the man whether you had yet a brother?

7 And they said, The man asked us straitly of our state, and of our kindred, saying, Is your father yet alive? have you another brother? and we told him according to the tenor of these words: could we certainly know that he would say, Bring your brother down?

8 And Judah said unto Israel his father, Send the lad with me, and we will arise and go; that we may live, and not die, both we, and you, and also our little ones.

9 I will be surety for him; of my hand shall you require him: if I bring him not unto you, and set him before you, then let me bear the blame for all the days:

10 For except we had lingered, surely now we had returned this second time.

11 And their father Israel said unto them, If it must be so now, do this; take of the best fruits in the land in your vessels, and carry down the man a present, a little balm, and a little honey, spices, and myrrh, nuts, and almonds:

12 And take double money in your hand; and the money that was brought again in the mouth of your sacks, carry it again in your hand; perhaps it was an oversight:

13 Take also your brother, and arise, go again unto the man:

14 And GOD Almighty give you mercy before the man, that he may send away your other brother, and Benjamin. If I be bereaved of my children, I am bereaved.

15 And the men took that present, and they took double money in their hand, and Benjamin; and rose up, and went down to Egypt, and stood before Joseph.

16 And when Joseph saw Benjamin with them, he said to the ruler of his house, Bring these men home, and slay, and make ready; for these men shall dine with me at noon.

17 And the man did as Joseph bade; and the man brought the men into Joseph's house.

18 And the men were afraid, because they were brought into Joseph's house; and they said, Because of the money that was returned in our sacks at the first time are we brought in; that he may seek occasion against us, and fall upon us, and take us for bondmen, and our donkeys.

19 And they came near to the steward of Joseph's house, and they communed with him at the door of the house,

20 And said, O sir, we came indeed down at the first time to buy food:

21 And it came to pass, when we came to the inn, that we opened our sacks, and, behold, every man's money was in the mouth of his sack, our money in full weight: and we have brought it again in our hand.

22 And other money have we brought down in our hands to buy food: we cannot tell who put our money in our sacks.

23 And he said, Peace be to you, fear not: your God, and God of your father, has given you treasure in your sacks: I had your money. And he brought Simeon out unto them.

24 And the man brought the men into Joseph's house, and gave them water, and they washed their feet; and he gave their donkeys feed.

25 And they made ready the present for Joseph was to come at noon: for they heard that they should eat bread there.

26 And when Joseph came home, they brought him the present which was in their hand into the house, and bowed themselves to him to the earth.

27 And he asked them of their welfare, and said, Is your father well, the old man of whom you spoke? Is he yet alive?

28 And they answered, your servant our father is in good health, he is yet alive. And they bowed down their heads, and made obeisance.

29 And he lifted up his eyes, and saw his brother Benjamin, his mother's son, and said, Is this your younger brother, of whom you spoke unto me? And he said, God be gracious unto you, my son.

30 And Joseph made haste; for his bowels did yearn upon his brother: and he sought where to weep; and he entered into his chamber, and wept there.

31 And he washed his face, and went out, and refrained himself, and said, Set on bread.

32 And they set on for him by himself, and for them by themselves, and for the Egyptians, which did eat with him, by themselves: because the Egyptians might not eat bread with the Hebrews; for that is an abomination unto the Egyptians.

33 And they sat before him, the firstborn according to his birthright, and the youngest according to his youth: and the men marvelled one at another.

34 And he took and sent portions unto them from before him: but Benjamin's portion was five times so much as any of theirs. And they drank, and were merry with him.

Gen 44:1 And he commanded the steward of his house, saying, Fill the men's sacks with food, as much as they can carry, and put every man's money in his sack's mouth.

2 And put my cup, the silver cup, in the sack's mouth of the youngest, and his grain money. And he did according to the word that Joseph had spoken.

3 As soon as the morning was light, the men were sent away, they and their donkeys.

4 And when they were gone out of the city, and not yet far off, Joseph said unto his steward, Up, follow after the men; and when you do overtake them, say unto them, Why have you rewarded evil for good?

5 Is not this it in which my lord drinks, and whereby indeed he divines? you have done evil in so doing.

6 And he overtook them, and he spoke unto them these same words.

7 And they said unto him, Why says my lord these words? Forbid that your servants should do according to this thing:

8 Behold, the money, which we found in our sacks' mouths, we brought again unto you out of the land of Canaan: how then should we steal out of your lords' house silver or gold?

9 With whomsoever of your servants it be found, both let him die, and we also will be my lord's bondmen.

10 And he said, Now also let it be according unto your words: he with whom it is found shall be my servant; and you shall be blameless.

11 Then they speedily took down every man his sack to the ground, and opened every man his sack.

12 And he searched, and began at the eldest, and left at the youngest: and the cup was found in Benjamin's sack.

13 Then they rent their clothes, and laded every man his donkey, and returned to the city.

14 And Judah and his brethren came to Joseph's house; for he was yet there: and they fell before him on the ground.

15 And Joseph said unto them, What deed is this that you have done? Don't you know that such a man as I can certainly divine?

16 And Judah said, What shall we say unto my lord? what shall we speak? or how shall we clear ourselves? God has found out the iniquity of your servants: behold, we are my lord's servants, both we, and he also with whom the cup is found.

17 And he said, forbid that I should do so: but the man in whose hand the cup is found, he shall be my servant; and as for you, get you up in peace unto your father.

18 Then Judah came near unto him, and said, Oh my lord, let your servant, I pray you, speak a word in my lord's ears, and let not your anger burn against your servant: for you are even as Pharaoh.

19 My lord asked his servants, saying, Have you a father, or a brother?

20 And we said unto my lord, We have a father, an old man, and a child of his old age, a little one; and his brother is dead, and he alone is left of his mother, and his father loves him.

21 And you say unto your servants, Bring him down unto me, that I may set mine eyes upon him.

22 And we said unto my lord, The lad cannot leave his father: for if he should leave his father, his father would die.

23 And you say unto your servants, Except your youngest brother come down with you, you shall see my face no more.

24 And it came to pass when we came up unto your servant my father, we told him the words of my lord.

25 And our father said, Go again, and buy us a little food.

26 And we said, We cannot go down: if our youngest brother be with us, then will we go down: for we may not see the man's face, except our youngest brother be with us.

27 And your servant my father said unto us, you know that my wife bare me two sons:

28 And the one went out from me, and I said, Surely he is torn in pieces; and I saw him not since:

29 And if you take this also from me, and mischief befall him, you shall bring down my gray hairs with sorrow to Sheol.

30 Now therefore when I come to your servant my father, and the lad be not with us; seeing that his soul is bound up in the lad's soul;

31 It shall come to pass, when he sees that the lad is not with us, that he will die: and your servants shall bring down the gray hairs of your servant our father with sorrow to Sheol.

32 For your servant became surety for the lad unto my father, saying, If I bring him not unto you, then I shall bear the blame to my father for all the days.

33 Now therefore, I pray you, let your servant abide instead of the lad a bondman to my lord; and let the lad go up with his brethren.

34 For how shall I go up to my father, and the lad be not with me? lest perhaps I see the evil that shall come on my father.

Gen 45:1 Then Joseph could not refrain himself before all them that stood by him; and he cried, Cause every man to go out from me. And there stood no man with him, while Joseph made himself known unto his brethren.

2 And he wept aloud: and the Egyptians and the house of Pharaoh heard.

3 And Joseph said unto his brethren, I am Joseph; does my father yet live? And his brethren could not answer him; for they were troubled at his presence.

4 And Joseph said unto his brethren, Come near to me, I pray you. And they came near. And he said, I am Joseph your brother, whom you sold into Egypt.

5 Now therefore be not grieved, nor angry with yourselves, that you sold me here: for God did send me before you to preserve life.

6 For these two years has the famine been in the land: and yet there are five years, in the which there shall neither be earing nor harvest.

7 And God sent me before you to preserve you a posterity in the earth, and to save your lives by a great deliverance.

8 So now it was not you that sent me here, but God: and he has made me a father to Pharaoh, and lord of all his house, and a ruler throughout all the land of Egypt.

9 Make haste, and go up to my father, and say unto him, Thus says your son Joseph, God has made me lord of all Egypt: come down unto me, tarry not:

10 And you shall dwell in the land of Goshen, and you shall be near unto me, you, and your children, and your children's children, and your flocks, and your herds, and all that you have:

11 And there will I nourish you; for yet there are five years of famine; lest you, and your household, and all that you hast, come to poverty.

12 And, behold, your eyes see, and the eyes of my brother Benjamin, that it is my mouth that speaks unto you.

13 And you shall tell my father of all my glory in Egypt, and of all that you have seen; and you shall haste and bring down my father here.

14 And he fell upon his brother Benjamin's neck, and wept; and Benjamin wept upon his neck.

15 Moreover he kissed all his brethren, and wept upon them: and after that his brethren talked with him.

16 And the report thereof was heard in Pharaoh's house, saying, Joseph's brethren are come: and it pleased Pharaoh well, and his servants.

17 And Pharaoh said unto Joseph, Say unto your brethren, This you do; lade your beasts, and go, get you unto the land of Canaan;

18 And take your father and your households, and come unto me: and I will give you the good of the land of Egypt, and you shall eat the fat of the land.

19 Now you are commanded, this you do; take you wagons out of the land of Egypt for your little ones, and for your wives, and bring your father, and come.

20 Also regard not your stuff; for the good of all the land of Egypt is yours.

21 And the children of Israel did so: and Joseph gave them wagons, according to the commandment of Pharaoh, and gave them provision for the way.

22 To all of them he gave each man changes of raiment; but to Benjamin he gave three hundred pieces of silver, and five changes of raiment.

23 And to his father he sent after this manner; ten donkeys loaded with the good things of Egypt, and ten she donkeys loaded with grain and bread and food for his father by the way.

24 So he sent his brethren away, and they departed: and he said unto them, See that you fall not out by the way.

25 And they went up out of Egypt, and came into the land of Canaan unto Jacob their father,

26 And told him, saying, Joseph is yet alive, and he is governor over all the land of Egypt. And Jacob's heart fainted, for he believed them not.

27 And they told him all the words of Joseph, which he had said unto them: and when he saw the wagons which Joseph had sent to carry him, the spirit of Jacob their father revived:

28 And Israel said, It is enough; Joseph my son is yet alive: I will go and see him before I die.

Gen 46:1 And Israel took his journey with all that he had, and came to Beersheba, and offered sacrifices unto God of his father Isaac.

2 And God spoke unto Israel in the visions of the night, and said, Jacob, Jacob. And he said, Here I am.

3 And he said, I am GOD, God of your father: fear not to go down into Egypt; for I will there make of you a great nation:

4 I will go down with you into Egypt; and I will also surely bring you up again: and Joseph shall put his hand upon your eyes.

5 And Jacob rose up from Beersheba: and the sons of Israel carried Jacob their father, and their little ones, and their wives, in the wagons which Pharaoh had sent to carry him.

6 And they took their cattle, and their goods, which they had gotten in the land of Canaan, and came into Egypt, Jacob, and all his seed with him:

7 His sons, and his sons' sons with him, his daughters, and his sons' daughters, and all his seed brought he with him into Egypt.

8 And these are the names of the children of Israel, which came into Egypt, Jacob and his sons: Reuben, Jacob's firstborn.

9 And the sons of Reuben; Hanoch, and Phallu, and Hezron, and Carmi.

10 And the sons of Simeon; Jemuel, and Jamin, and Ohad, and Jachin, and Zohar, and Shaul the son of a Canaanitish woman.

11 And the sons of Levi; Gershon, Kohath, and Merari.

12 And the sons of Judah; Er, and Onan, and Shelah, and Pharez, and Zarah: but Er and Onan died in the land of Canaan. And the sons of Pharez were Hezron and Hamul.

13 And the sons of Issachar; Tola, and Phuvah, and Job, and Shimron.

14 And the sons of Zebulun; Sered, and Elon, and Jahleel.

15 These be the sons of Leah, which she bare unto Jacob in Padan-Aram, with his daughter Dinah: all the souls of his sons and his daughters were thirty and three.

16 And the sons of Gad; Ziphion, and Haggi, Shuni, and Ezbon, Eri, and Arodi, and Areli.

17 And the sons of Asher; Jimnah, and Ishuah, and Isui, and Beriah, and Serah their sister: and the sons of Beriah; Heber, and Malchiel.

18 These are the sons of Zilpah, whom Laban gave to Leah his daughter, and these she bare unto Jacob, even sixteen souls.

19 The sons of Rachel Jacob's wife; Joseph, and Benjamin.

20 And unto Joseph in the land of Egypt were born Manasseh and Ephraim, which Asenath the daughter of Potipherah priest of On bare unto him.

21 And the sons of Benjamin were Belah, and Becher, and Ashbel, Gera, and Naaman, Ehi, and Rosh, Muppim, and Huppim, and Ard.

22 These are the sons of Rachel, which were born to Jacob: all the souls were fourteen.

23 And the sons of Dan; Hushim.

24 And the sons of Naphtali; Jahzeel, and Guni, and Jezer, and Shillem.

25 These are the sons of Bilhah, which Laban gave unto Rachel his daughter, and she bare these unto Jacob: all the souls were seven.

26 All the souls that came with Jacob into Egypt, which came out of his loins, besides Jacob's sons' wives, all the souls were threescore and six;

27 And the sons of Joseph, which were born him in Egypt, were two souls: all the souls of the house of Jacob, which came into Egypt, were threescore and ten.

28 And he sent Judah before him unto Joseph, to direct his face unto Goshen; and they came into the land of Goshen.

29 And Joseph made ready his chariot, and went up to meet Israel his father, to Goshen, and presented himself unto him; and he fell on his neck, and wept on his neck a good while.

30 And Israel said unto Joseph, Now let me die, since I have seen your face, because you are yet alive.

31 And Joseph said unto his brethren, and unto his father's house, I will go up, and show Pharaoh, and say unto him, My brethren, and my father's house, which were in the land of Canaan, are come unto me;

32 And the men are shepherds, for their trade has been to feed cattle; and they have brought their flocks, and their herds, and all that they have.

33 And it shall come to pass, when Pharaoh shall call you, and shall say, What is your occupation?

34 That you shall say, your servants' trade has been about cattle from our youth even until now, both we, and also our fathers: that you may dwell in the land of Goshen; for every shepherd is an abomination unto the Egyptians.

Gen 47:1 Then Joseph came and told Pharaoh, and said, My father and my brethren, and their flocks, and their herds, and all that they have, are come out of the land of Canaan; and, behold, they are in the land of Goshen.

2 And he took some of his brethren, even five men, and presented them unto Pharaoh.

3 And Pharaoh said unto his brethren, What is your occupation? And they said unto Pharaoh, your servants are shepherds, both we, and also our fathers.

4 They said moreover unto Pharaoh, For to sojourn in the land are we come; for your servants have no pasture for their flocks; for the famine is great in the land of Canaan: now therefore, we pray you, let your servants dwell in the land of Goshen.

5 And Pharaoh spoke unto Joseph, saying, your father and your brethren are come unto you:

6 The land of Egypt is before you; in the best of the land make your father and brethren to dwell; in the land of Goshen let them dwell: and if you know any men of activity among them, then make them rulers over my cattle.

7 And Joseph brought in Jacob his father, and set him before Pharaoh: and Jacob blessed Pharaoh.

8 And Pharaoh said unto Jacob, How many days of the years of your life?

9 And Jacob said unto Pharaoh, The days of the years of my pilgrimage are a hundred and thirty years: few and evil have the days of the years of my life been, and have not attained unto the days of the years of the life of my fathers in the days of their pilgrimage.

[2298 YM]

10 And Jacob blessed Pharaoh, and went out from before Pharaoh.

11 And Joseph placed his father and his brethren, and gave them a possession in the land of Egypt, in the best of the land, in the land of Rameses, as Pharaoh had commanded.

12 And Joseph nourished his father, and his brethren, and all his father's household, with bread, according to their families.

13 And there was no bread in all the land; for the famine was very great, so that the land of Egypt and all the land of Canaan fainted by reason of the famine.

14 And Joseph gathered up all the money that was found in the land of Egypt, and in the land of Canaan, for the grain which they bought: and Joseph brought the money into Pharaoh's house.

15 And when money failed in the land of Egypt, and in the land of Canaan, all the Egyptians came unto Joseph, and said, Give us bread: for why should we die in your presence? for the money fails.

16 And Joseph said, Give your cattle; and I will give you for your cattle, if money fail.

17 And they brought their cattle unto Joseph: and Joseph gave them bread in exchange for horses, and for the flocks, and for the cattle of the herds, and for the donkeys: and he fed them with bread for all their cattle for that year.

18 When that year was ended, they came unto him the second year, and said unto him, We will not hide it from my lord, how that our money is spent; my lord also has our herds of animals; there is not ought left in the sight of my lord, but our bodies, and our lands:

19 Why shall we die before your eyes, both we and our land? buy us and our land for bread, and we and our land will be servants unto Pharaoh: and give us seed, that we may live, and not die, that the land be not desolate.

20 And Joseph bought all the land of Egypt for Pharaoh; for the Egyptians sold every man his field, because the famine prevailed over them: so the land became Pharaoh's.

21 And as for the people, he removed them to cities from one end of the borders of Egypt even to the other end thereof.

22 Only the land of the priests bought he not; for the priests had a portion assigned them of Pharaoh, and did eat their portion which Pharaoh gave them: therefore they sold not their lands.

23 Then Joseph said unto the people, Behold, I have bought you this day and your land for Pharaoh: lo, here is seed for you, and you shall sow the land.

24 And it shall come to pass in the increase, that you shall give the fifth part unto Pharaoh, and four parts shall be your own, for seed of the field, and for your food, and for them of your households, and for food for your little ones.

25 And they said, you have saved our lives: let us find grace in the sight of my lord, and we will be Pharaoh's servants.

26 And Joseph made it a law over the land of Egypt unto this day, that Pharaoh should have the fifth part; except the land of the priests only, which became not Pharaoh's.

27 And Israel dwelt in the land of Egypt, in the country of Goshen; and they had possessions therein, and grew, and multiplied exceedingly.

28 And Jacob lived in the land of Egypt seventeen years: so the days of the years of his life was a hundred forty and seven years.

29 And the time drew near that Israel must die: and he called his son Joseph, and said unto him, If now I have found grace in your sight, put, I pray you, your hand under my thigh, and deal kindly and truly with me; bury me not, I pray you, in Egypt:

30 But I will lie with my fathers, and you shall carry me out of Egypt, and bury me in their burying place. And he said, I will do as you have said.

31 And he said, Swear unto me. And he swore unto him. And Israel bowed himself upon the bed's head.

Gen 48:1 And it came to pass after these things, that one told Joseph, Behold, your father is sick: and he took with him his two sons, Manasseh and Ephraim.

2 And one told Jacob, and said, Behold, your son Joseph comes unto you: and Israel strengthened himself, and sat upon the bed.

3 And Jacob said unto Joseph, GOD Almighty appeared unto me at Luz in the land of Canaan, and blessed me,

4 And said unto me, Behold, I will make you fruitful, and multiply you, and I will make of you a multitude of people; and will give this land to your seed after you for a possession of olam.

5 And now your two sons, Ephraim and Manasseh, which were born unto you in the land of Egypt before I came unto you into Egypt, are mine; as Reuben and Simeon, they shall be mine.

6 And your issue, which you beget after them, shall be yours, and shall be called after the name of their brethren in their inheritance.

7 And as for me, when I came from Padan, Rachel died by me in the land of Canaan in the way, when yet there was but a little way to come unto Ephrath: and I buried her there in the way of Ephrath; the same is Bethlehem.

8 And Israel beheld Joseph's sons, and said, Who are these?

9 And Joseph said unto his father, They are my sons, whom God has given me in this place. And he said, Bring them, I pray you, unto me, and I will bless them.

10 Now the eyes of Israel were dim for age, so that he could not see. And he brought them near unto him; and he kissed them, and embraced them.

11 And Israel said unto Joseph, I had not thought to see your face: and, lo, God has showed me also your seed.

12 And Joseph brought them out from between his knees, and he bowed himself with his face to the earth.

13 And Joseph took them both, Ephraim in his right hand toward Israel's left hand, and Manasseh in his left hand toward Israel's right hand, and brought them near unto him.

14 And Israel stretched out his right hand, and laid it upon Ephraim's head, who was the younger, and his left hand upon Manasseh's head, guiding his hands knowingly; for Manasseh was the firstborn.

15 And he blessed Joseph, and said, God, before whom my fathers Abraham and Isaac did walk, God which fed me all my life long unto this day,

16 The Angel which redeemed me from all evil, bless the lads; and let my name be named on them, and the name of my fathers Abraham and Isaac; and let them grow into a multitude in the midst of the earth.

17 And when Joseph saw that his father laid his right hand upon the head of Ephraim, it displeased him: and he held up his father's hand, to remove it from Ephraim's head unto Manasseh's head.

18 And Joseph said unto his father, Not so, my father: for this is the firstborn; put your right hand upon his head.

19 And his father refused, and said, I know it, my son, I know it: he also shall become a people, and he also shall be great: but truly his younger brother shall be greater than he, and his seed shall become a multitude of nations.

20 And he blessed them that day, saying, In you shall Israel bless, saying, God make you as Ephraim and as Manasseh: and he set Ephraim before Manasseh.

21 And Israel said unto Joseph, Behold, I die: but God shall be with you, and bring you again unto the land of your fathers.

22 Moreover I have given to you one portion above your brethren, which I took out of the hand of the Amorite with my sword and with my bow.

Gen 49:1 And Jacob called unto his sons, and said, Gather yourselves together, that I may tell you that which shall befall you in the end of days.

2 Gather yourselves together, and hear, you sons of Jacob; and listen unto Israel your father.

3 Reuben, you are my firstborn, my might, and the beginning of my strength, the excellency of dignity, and the excellency of power:

4 Unstable as water, you shall not excel; because you went up to your father's bed; then defiled you it: he went up to my couch.

5 Simeon and Levi are brethren; instruments of cruelty are in their habitations.

6 O my soul, come not you into their secret; unto their assembly, mine honor, be not you united: for in their anger they killed a man, and in their selfwill they dug down a wall.

7 Cursed be their anger, for it was fierce; and their wrath, for it was cruel: I will divide them in Jacob, and scatter them in Israel.

8 Judah, you are he whom your brethren shall praise: your hand shall be in the neck of your enemies; your father's children shall bow down before you.

9 Judah is a lion's whelp: from the prey, my son, you are gone up: he stooped down, he couched as a lion, and as an old lion; who shall rouse him up?

10 The scepter shall not depart from Judah, nor a lawgiver from between his feet, until Shiloh come; and unto him shall the gathering of the people be.

11 Binding his foal unto the vine, and his ass's colt unto the choice vine; he washed his garments in wine, and his clothes in the blood of grapes:

12 His eyes shall be red with wine, and his teeth white with milk.

13 Zebulun shall dwell at the haven of the sea; and he shall be for a haven of ships; and his border shall be unto Zidon.

14 Issachar is a strong donkey couching down between two burdens:

15 And he saw that rest was good, and the land that it was pleasant; and bowed his shoulder to bear, and became a servant unto tribute.

16 Dan shall judge his people, as one of the tribes of Israel.

17 Dan shall be a serpent by the way, an adder in the path, that bits the horse heels, so that his rider shall fall backward.

18 I have waited for your salvation, O Becoming-One.

19 Gad, a troop shall overcome him: but he shall overcome at the last.

20 Out of Asher his bread shall be fat, and he shall yield royal dainties.

21 Naphtali is a hind let loose: he gives goodly words.

22 Joseph is a fruitful bough, even a fruitful bough by a well; whose branches run over the wall:

23 The archers have sorely grieved him, and shot at him, and hated him:

24 But his bow abode in strength, and the arms of his hands were made strong by the hands of the mighty God of Jacob; from there is the shepherd, the stone of Israel:

25 Even by GOD of your father, who shall help you; and by the Almighty, who shall bless you with blessings of the heavens above, blessings of the deep that lies under, blessings of the breasts, and of the womb:

26 The blessings of your father have prevailed above the blessings of my progenitors unto the utmost bound of the hills of olam; they shall be on the head of Joseph, and on the crown of the head of him that was separate from his brethren.

27 Benjamin shall ravin as a wolf: in the morning he shall devour the prey, and at night he shall divide the spoil.

28 All these are the twelve tribes of Israel: and this is it that their father spoke unto them, and blessed them; every one according to his blessing he blessed them.

29 And he charged them, and said unto them, I am to be gathered unto my people: bury me with my fathers in the cave that is in the field of Ephron the Hittite,

30 In the cave that is in the field of Machpelah, which is before Mamre, in the land of Canaan, which Abraham bought with the field of Ephron the Hittite for a possession of a burying place.

31 There they buried Abraham and Sarah his wife; there they buried Isaac and Rebekah his wife; and there I buried Leah.

32 The purchase of the field and of the cave that is therein was from the children of Heth.

33 And when Jacob had made an end of commanding his sons, he gathered up his feet into the bed, and yielded up the ghost, and was gathered unto his people.

Gen 50:1 And Joseph fell upon his father's face, and wept upon him, and kissed him.

2 And Joseph commanded his servants the physicians to embalm his father: and the physicians embalmed Israel.

3 And forty days were fulfilled for him; for so are fulfilled the days of those which are embalmed: and the Egyptians mourned for him threescore and ten days.

4 And when the days of his mourning were past, Joseph spoke unto the house of Pharaoh, saying, If now I have found grace in your eyes, speak, I pray you, in the ears of Pharaoh, saying,

5 My father made me swear, saying, Lo, I die: in my grave which I have dug for me in the land of Canaan, there shall you bury me. Now therefore let me go up, I pray you, and bury my father, and I will come again.

6 And Pharaoh said, Go up, and bury your father, according as he made you swear.

7 And Joseph went up to bury his father: and with him went up all the servants of Pharaoh, the elders of his house, and all the elders of the land of Egypt,

8 And all the house of Joseph, and his brethren, and his father's house: only their little ones, and their flocks, and their herds, they left in the land of Goshen.

9 And there went up with him both chariots and horsemen: and it was a very great company.

10 And they came to the threshing floor of Atad, which is over [beyond] the Jordan, and there they mourned with a great and very great lamentation: and he made a mourning for his father seven days.

11 And when the inhabitants of the land, the Canaanites, saw the mourning in the floor of Atad, they said, This is a grievous mourning to the Egyptians: therefore the name of it was called Able-mizraim, which is over Jordan.

12 And his sons did unto him according as he commanded them:

13 For his sons carried him into the land of Canaan, and buried him in the cave of the field of Machpelah, which Abraham bought with the field for a possession of a burying place of Ephron the Hittite, before Mamre.

14 And Joseph returned into Egypt, he, and his brethren, and all that went up with him to bury his father, after he had buried his father.

15 And when Joseph's brethren saw that their father was dead, they said, Joseph will perhaps hate us, and will certainly requite us all the evil which we did unto him.

16 And they sent a messenger unto Joseph, saying, your father did command before he died, saying,

17 So shall you say unto Joseph, Forgive, I pray you now, the trespass of your brethren, and their sin; for they did unto you evil: and now, we pray you, forgive the trespass of the servants of God of your father. And Joseph wept when they spoke unto him.

18 And his brethren also went and fell down before his face; and they said, Behold, we be your servants.

19 And Joseph said unto them, Fear not: for I am in the place of God?

20 But as for you, you thought evil against me; but God meant it unto good, to bring to pass, as it is this day, to save much people alive.

21 Now therefore fear you not: I will nourish you, and your little ones. And he comforted them, and spoke kindly unto them.

22 And Joseph dwelt in Egypt, he, and his father's house: and Joseph lived a hundred and ten years. **[2369 YM/ 1605 BC]**

23 And Joseph saw Ephraim's children of the third generation: the children also of Machir the son of Manasseh were brought up upon Joseph's knees.

24 And Joseph said unto his brethren, I die: and God will surely visit you, and bring you out of this land unto the land which he swore to Abraham, to Isaac, and to Jacob.

25 And Joseph took an oath of the children of Israel, saying, God will surely visit you, and you shall carry up my bones from hence.

26 So Joseph died, being a son of hundred and ten years: and they embalmed him, and he was put in a coffin in Egypt.

Exodus

Ex 1:1 Now these are the names of the children of Israel, which came into Egypt; every man and his household came with Jacob.

2 Reuben, Simeon, Levi, and Judah,

3 Issachar, Zebulun, and Benjamin,

4 Dan, and Naphtali, Gad, and Asher.

5 And all the souls that came out of the loins of Jacob were seventy souls: for Joseph was in Egypt already.

6 And Joseph died, and all his brethren, and all that generation.

7 And the children of Israel were fruitful, and increased abundantly, and multiplied, and grew exceeding mighty; and the land was filled with them.

8 Now there arose up a new king over Egypt, which knew not Joseph.

9 And he said unto his people, Behold, the people of the children of Israel are more and mightier than we:

10 Come on, let us deal wisely with them; lest they multiply, and it come to pass, that, when there falls out any war, they join also unto our enemies, and fight against us, and so get them up out of the land.

11 Therefore they did set over them taskmasters to afflict them with their burdens. And they built for Pharaoh treasure cities, Pithom and Raamses.

12 But the more they afflicted them, the more they multiplied and grew. And they were grieved because of the children of Israel.

13 And the Egyptians made the children of Israel to serve with rigor:

14 And they made their lives bitter with hard bondage, in mortar, and in brick, and in all manner of service in the field: all their service, wherein they made them serve, was with rigor.

15 And the king of Egypt spoke to the Hebrew midwives, of which the name of the one was Shiphrah, and the name of the other Puah:

16 And he said, When you do the office of a midwife to the Hebrew women, and see them upon the stools; if it be a son, then you shall kill him: but if it be a daughter, then she shall live.

17 But the midwives feared God, and did not as the king of Egypt commanded them, but saved the men children alive.

18 And the king of Egypt called for the midwives, and said unto them, Why have you done this thing, and have saved the men children alive?

19 And the midwives said unto Pharaoh, Because the Hebrew women are not as the Egyptian women; for they are lively, and are delivered before the midwives come in unto them.

20 Therefore God dealt well with the midwives: and the people multiplied, and grew very mighty.

21 And it came to pass, because the midwives feared God, that he made them houses [familes]

22 And Pharaoh charged all his people, saying, Every son that is born you shall cast into the river, and every daughter you shall save alive.

Ex 2:1 And there went a man of the house of Levi, and took to wife a daughter of Levi.

2 And the woman conceived, and bare a son: and when she saw him that he was a goodly child, she hid him three months.

3 And when she could not longer hide him, she took for him an ark of bulrushes, and daubed it with bitumen and with pitch, and put the child therein; and she laid it in the reeds by the river's brink.

4 And his sister stood afar off, to know what would be done to him.

5 And the daughter of Pharaoh came down to wash herself at the river; and her maidens walked along by the river's side; and when she saw the ark among the reeds, she sent her maid to fetch it.

6 And when she had opened it, she saw the child: and, behold, the babe wept. And she had compassion on him, and said, This is one of the Hebrews' children.

7 Then said his sister to Pharaoh's daughter, Shall I go and call to you a nurse of the Hebrew women, that she may nurse the child for you?

8 And Pharaoh's daughter said to her, Go. And the maid went and called the child's mother.

9 And Pharaoh's daughter said unto her, Take this child away, and nurse it for me, and I will give you your wages. And the woman took the child, and nursed it.

10 And the child grew, and she brought him unto Pharaoh's daughter, and he became her son. And she called his name **Moses**: and she said, Because I drew him out of the water.

11 And it came to pass in those days, when Moses was grown, that he went out unto his brethren, and looked on their burdens: and he saw an Egyptian smiting a Hebrew, one of his brethren.

12 And he looked this way and that way, and when he saw that there was no man, he killed the Egyptian, and hid him in the sand.

13 And when he went out the second day, behold, two men of the Hebrews strove together: and he said to him that did the wrong, Why smite you your fellow?

14 And he said, Who made you a prince and a judge over us? intend you to kill me, as you killed the Egyptian? And Moses feared, and said, Surely this thing is known.

15 Now when Pharaoh heard this thing, he sought to slay Moses. But Moses fled from the face of Pharaoh, and dwelt in the land of Midian: and he sat down by a well.

16 Now the priest of Midian had seven daughters: and they came and drew water, and filled the troughs to water their father's flock.

17 And the shepherds came and drove them away: but Moses stood up and helped them, and watered their flock.

18 And when they came to Reuel their father, he said, How is it that you are come so soon today?

19 And they said, An Egyptian delivered us out of the hand of the shepherds, and also drew water enough for us, and watered the flock.

20 And he said unto his daughters, And where is he? why is it that you have left the man? call him, that he may eat bread.

21 And Moses was content to dwell with the man: and he gave Moses Zipporah his daughter.

22 And she bare him a son, and he called his name Gershom: for he said, I have been a stranger in a strange land.

23 And in the course of many days, that the king of Egypt died: and the children of Israel sighed by reason of the bondage, and they cried, and their cry came up unto God by reason of the bondage.

24 And God heard their groaning, and God remembered his covenant with Abraham, with Isaac, and with Jacob.

25 And God looked upon the children of Israel, and God had respect unto them.

Ex 3:1 Now Moses kept the flock of Jethro his father-in-law, the priest of Midian: and he led the flock to the backside of the desert, and came to the mountain of God, even to Horeb.

2 And the angel of the Becoming-One appeared unto him in a flame of fire out of the midst of a bush: and he looked, and, behold, the bush burned with fire, and the bush was not consumed.

3 And Moses said, I will now turn aside, and see this great sight, why the bush is not burnt.

4 And when the Becoming-One saw that he turned aside to see, God called unto him out of the midst of the bush, and said, Moses, Moses. And he said, Here I am.

5 And He said, Draw not near here: put off your shoes from off your feet, for the place whereon you stand is holy ground.

6 Moreover He said, I am God of your father, God of Abraham, God of Isaac, and God of Jacob. And Moses hid his face; for he was afraid to look upon God.

7 And the Becoming-One said, I have surely seen the affliction of my people which are in Egypt, and have heard their cry by reason of their taskmasters; for I know their sorrows;

8 And I am come down to deliver them out of the hand of the Egyptians, and to bring them up out of that land unto a good land and a large, unto a land flowing with milk and honey; unto the place of the Canaanites, and the Hittites, and the Amorites, and the Perizzites, and the Hivites, and the Jebusites.

9 Now therefore, behold, the cry of the children of Israel is come unto me: and I have also seen the oppression wherewith the Egyptians oppress them.

10 Come now therefore, and I will send you unto Pharaoh, that you may bring forth my people the children of Israel out of Egypt.

11 And Moses said unto God, Who am I, that I should go unto Pharaoh, and that I should bring forth the children of Israel out of Egypt?

12 And he said, Certainly I-will-be[23] with you; and this shall be a sign unto you, that I have sent you: When you have brought forth the people out of Egypt, you shall serve God upon this mountain.

13 And Moses said unto God, Behold, when I come unto the children of Israel, and shall say unto them, God of your fathers has sent me unto you; and they shall say to me, What is his name? what shall I say unto them?

14 And God said unto Moses, I-Will-Be that I-Will-Be:[24] and he said, Thus shall you say unto the children of Israel, **I-Will-Be**[1] has sent me unto you.

15 And God said moreover unto Moses, Thus shall you say unto the children of Israel,**Becoming-One**, God of your fathers, God of Abraham, God of Isaac, and God of Jacob, has sent me unto you: this is my name for olam, and this is my memorial unto all generations.

16 Go, and gather the elders of Israel together, and say unto them, The Becoming-One,[3] God of your fathers, God of Abraham, of Isaac, and of Jacob, appeared unto me, saying, I have surely visited you, and seen that which is done to you in Egypt:

17 And I have said, I will bring you up out of the affliction of Egypt unto the land of the Canaanites, and the Hittites, and the Amorites, and the Perizzites, and the Hivites, and the Jebusites, unto a land flowing with milk and honey.

18 And they shall listen to your voice: and you shall come, you and the elders of Israel, unto the king of Egypt, and you shall say unto him, The Becoming-One, God of the Hebrews has met with us: and now let us go, we beg you, three days' journey into the wilderness, that we may sacrifice to the Becoming-One our God.

19 And I am sure that the king of Egypt will not let you go, no, not by a mighty hand.

20 And I will stretch out my hand, and smite Egypt with all my wonders which I will do in the midst thereof: and after that he will let you go.

21 And I will give this people favor in the sight of the Egyptians: and it shall come to pass, that, when you go, you shall not go empty:

22 But every woman shall borrow of her neighbor, and of her that sojourns in her house, jewels of silver, and jewels of gold, and raiment: and you shall put them upon your sons, and upon your daughters; and you shall spoil the Egyptians.

Ex 4:1 And Moses answered and said, But, behold, they will not believe me, nor listen unto my voice: for they will say, Becoming-One has not appeared unto you.

2 And the Becoming-One said unto him, What is that in your hand? And he said, A rod.

3 And he said, Cast it on the ground. And he cast it on the ground, and it became a serpent; and Moses fled from before it.

4 And the Becoming-One said unto Moses, Put forth your hand, and take it by the tail. And he put forth his hand, and caught it, and it became a rod in his hand:

5 That they may believe that the Becoming-One, God of their fathers, God of Abraham, God of Isaac, and God of Jacob, has appeared unto you.

6 And the Becoming-One said furthermore unto him, Put now your hand into your bosom. And he put his hand into his bosom: and when he took it out, behold, his hand was leprous as snow.

7 And he said, Put your hand into your bosom again. And he put his hand into his bosom again; and

---

[23] אֶהְיֶה or "I will be"

[24] אֶהְיֶה אֲשֶׁר אֶהְיֶה or "I will be that I will be" ; see Exodus 3:12

plucked it out of his bosom, and, behold, it was turned again as his other flesh.

8 And it shall come to pass, if they will not believe you, neither listen to the voice of the first sign, that they will believe the voice of the latter sign.

9 And it shall come to pass, if they will not believe also these two signs, neither listen unto your voice, that you shall take of the water of the river, and pour it upon the dry land: and the water which you take out of the river shall become blood upon the dry land.

10 And Moses said unto the Becoming-One, O my Lord(s), I am not eloquent, neither yesterday or the third day, nor since you have spoken unto your servant: but I am slow of mouth, and of a slow tongue.

11 And the Becoming-One said unto him, Who has made man's mouth? or who makes the mute, or deaf, or the seeing, or the blind? have not I the Becoming-One?

12 Now therefore go, and I will be with your mouth, and teach you what you shall say.

13 And he said, O my Lord(s), send, I pray you, by the hand of him whom you will send.

14 And the anger of the Becoming-One was kindled against Moses, and he said, Is not Aaron the Levite your brother? I know that he can speak well. And also, behold, he comes forth to meet you: and when he sees you, he will be glad in his heart.

15 And you shall speak unto him, and put words in his mouth: and I will be with your mouth, and with his mouth, and will teach you what you shall do.

16 And he shall be your spokesman unto the people: and he shall be, even he shall be to you instead of a mouth, and you shall be to him instead of God.

17 And you shall take this rod in your hand, wherewith you shall do signs.

18 And Moses went and returned to Jethro his father-in-law, and said unto him, Let me go, I pray you, and return unto my brethren which are in Egypt, and see whether they be yet alive. And Jethro said to Moses, Go in peace.

19 And the Becoming-One said unto Moses in Midian, Go, return into Egypt: for all the men are dead which sought your soul.

20 And Moses took his wife and his sons, and set them upon an donkey, and he returned to the land of Egypt: and Moses took the rod of God in his hand.

21 And the Becoming-One said unto Moses, When you go to return into Egypt, see that you do all those wonders before Pharaoh, which I have put in your hand: but I will harden his heart, that he shall not let the people go.

22 And you shall say unto Pharaoh, Thus says the Becoming-One, Israel is my son, even my firstborn:

23 And I say unto you, Let my son go, that he may serve me: and if you refuse to let him go, behold, I will slay your son, even your firstborn.

24 And it came to pass by the way in the inn, that the Becoming-One met him, and sought to kill him.

25 Then Zipporah took a sharp stone, and cut off the foreskin of her son, and cast it at his feet, and said, Surely a bloody husband are you to me.

26 So he let him go: then she said, A bloody husband you are, because of the circumcision.

27 And the Becoming-One said to Aaron, Go into the wilderness to meet Moses. And he went, and met him in the mount of God, and kissed him.

28 And Moses told Aaron all the words of the Becoming-One who had sent him, and all the signs which he had commanded him.

29 And Moses and Aaron went and gathered together all the elders of the children of Israel:

30 And Aaron spoke all the words which the Becoming-One had spoken unto Moses, and did the signs in the sight of the people.

31 And the people believed: and when they heard that the Becoming-One had visited the children of Israel, and that he had looked upon their affliction, then they bowed their heads and worshiped.

Ex 5:1 And afterward Moses and Aaron went in, and told Pharaoh, Thus says the Becoming-One, God of Israel, Let my people go, that they may hold a feast unto me in the wilderness.

2 And Pharaoh said, Who is the Becoming-One, that I should obey his voice to let Israel go? I know not the Becoming-One, neither will I let Israel go.

3 And they said, God of the Hebrews has met with us: let us go, we pray you, three days' journey into the desert, and sacrifice unto the Becoming-One our God; lest he fall upon us with pestilence, or with the sword.

4 And the king of Egypt said unto them, Why do you, Moses and Aaron, let the people from their works? get you unto your burdens.

5 And Pharaoh said, Behold, the people of the land now are many, and you make them rest from their burdens.

6 And Pharaoh commanded the same day the taskmasters of the people, and their officers, saying,

7 you shall no more give the people straw to make brick, as yesterday or the third day: let them go and gather straw for themselves.

8 And the tale of the bricks, which they did make yesterday or the third day, you shall lay upon them; you shall not lessen thereof: for they be idle; therefore they cry, saying, Let us go and sacrifice to our God.

9 Let there more work be laid upon the men, that they may labor therein; and let them not regard vain words.

10 And the taskmasters of the people went out, and their officers, and they spoke to the people, saying, Thus says Pharaoh, I will not give you straw.

11 Go, get you straw where you can find it: yet not any of your work shall be diminished.

12 So the people were scattered abroad throughout all the land of Egypt to gather stubble instead of straw.

13 And the taskmasters hasted them, saying, Fulfil your works, your daily tasks, as when there was straw.

14 And the officers of the children of Israel, which Pharaoh's taskmasters had set over them, were beaten, and demanded, Why have you not fulfilled your task in making brick both yesterday and today, as yesterday and the third day?

15 Then the officers of the children of Israel came and cried unto Pharaoh, saying, Why deal you thus with your servants?

16 There is no straw given unto your servants, and they say to us, Make brick: and, behold, your servants are beaten; but the fault is in your own people.

17 But he said, you are idle, you are idle: therefore you say, Let us go and do sacrifice to the Becoming-One.

18 Go therefore now, and work; for there shall no straw be given you, yet shall you deliver the number of bricks.

19 And the officers of the children of Israel did see that they were in evil case, after it was said, you shall not diminish from any of your bricks of your daily task.

20 And they met Moses and Aaron, who stood in the way, as they came forth from Pharaoh:

21 And they said unto them, The Becoming-One look upon you, and judge; because you have made our aroma to be abhorred in the eyes of Pharaoh, and in the eyes of his servants, to put a sword in their hand to slay us.

22 And Moses returned unto the Becoming-One, and said, my Lord(s), why have you so evil entreated this people? why is it that you have sent me?

23 For since I came to Pharaoh to speak in your name, he has done evil to this people; neither have you delivered your people at all.

Ex 6:1 Then the Becoming-One said unto Moses, Now shall you see what I will do to Pharaoh: for with a strong hand shall he let them go, and with a strong hand shall he drive them out of his land.

2 And God spoke unto Moses, and said unto him, I am the Becoming-One: 3 And I appeared unto Abraham, unto Isaac, and unto Jacob, by the name of GOD Almighty, but by my name Yehowah [becoming one] was I not known to them.

4 And I have also established my covenant with them, to give them the land of Canaan, the land of their pilgrimage, wherein they were strangers.

5 And I have also heard the groaning of the children of Israel, whom the Egyptians keep in bondage; and I have remembered my covenant.

6 Therefore say unto the children of Israel, I am the Becoming-One, and I will bring you out from under the burdens of the Egyptians, and I will rid you out of their bondage, and I will redeem you with a stretched out arm, and with great judgments:

7 And I will take you to me for a people, and I will be to you God: and you shall know that I am the Becoming-One your God, which brings you out from under the burdens of the Egyptians.

8 And I will bring you in unto the land, concerning the which I did swear to give it to Abraham, to Isaac, and to Jacob; and I will give it you for a heritage: I am the Becoming-One.

9 And Moses spoke so unto the children of Israel: but they listened not unto Moses for anguish of spirit, and for cruel bondage.

10 And the Becoming-One spoke unto Moses, saying,

11 Go in, speak unto Pharaoh king of Egypt, that he let the children of Israel go out of his land.

12 And Moses spoke before the Becoming-One, saying, Behold, the children of Israel have not listened unto me; how then shall Pharaoh hear me, who am of uncircumcised lips?

13 And the Becoming-One spoke unto Moses and unto Aaron, and gave them a charge unto the children of Israel, and unto Pharaoh king of Egypt, to bring the children of Israel out of the land of Egypt.

14 These be the heads of their fathers' houses: The sons of Reuben the firstborn of Israel; Hanoch, and Pallu, Hezron, and Carmi: these be the families of Reuben.

15 And the sons of Simeon; Jemuel, and Jamin, and Ohad, and Jachin, and Zohar, and Shaul the son of a Canaanitish woman: these are the families of Simeon.

16 And these are the names of the sons of Levi according to their generations; Gershon, and Kohath, and Merari: and the years of the life of Levi were a hundred thirty and seven years.

17 The sons of Gershon; Libni, and Shimi, according to their families.

18 And the sons of Kohath; Amram, and Izhar, and Hebron, and Uzziel: and the years of the life of Kohath were a hundred thirty and three years.

19 And the sons of Merari; Mahali and Mushi: these are the families of Levi according to their generations.

20 And Amram took him Jochebed his father's sister to wife; and she bare him Aaron and Moses: and the years of the life of Amram were a hundred and thirty and seven years.

21 And the sons of Izhar; Korah, and Nepheg, and Zichri.

22 And the sons of Uzziel; Mishael, and Elzaphan, and Zithri.

23 And Aaron took him Elisheba, daughter of Amminadab, sister of Naashon, to wife; and she bare him Nadab, and Abihu, Eleazar, and Ithamar.

24 And the sons of Korah; Assir, and Elkanah, and Abiasaph: these are the families of the Korhites.

25 And Eleazar Aaron's son took him one of the daughters of Putiel to wife; and she bare him Phinehas: these are the heads of the fathers of the Levites according to their families.

26 These are that Aaron and Moses, to whom the Becoming-One said, Bring out the children of Israel from the land of Egypt according to their armies.

27 These are they which spoke to Pharaoh king of Egypt, to bring out the children of Israel from Egypt: these are that Moses and Aaron.

28 And it came to pass on the day when the Becoming-One spoke unto Moses in the land of Egypt,

29 That the Becoming-One spoke unto Moses, saying, I am the Becoming-One:speak you unto Pharaoh king of Egypt all that I say unto you.

30 And Moses said before the Becoming-One, Behold, I am of uncircumcised lips, and how shall Pharaoh listen unto me?

Ex 7:1 And the Becoming-One said unto Moses, See, I have made you a god to Pharaoh: and Aaron your brother shall be your prophet.

2 you shall speak all that I command you: and Aaron your brother shall speak unto Pharaoh, that he send the children of Israel out of his land.

3 And I will harden Pharaoh's heart, and multiply my signs and my wonders in the land of Egypt.

4 But Pharaoh shall not listen unto you, that I may lay my hand upon Egypt, and bring forth mine armies, and my people the children of Israel, out of the land of Egypt by great judgments.

5 And the Egyptians shall know that I am the Becoming-One, when I stretch forth mine hand upon Egypt, and bring out the children of Israel from among them.

6 And Moses and Aaron did as the Becoming-One commanded them, so did they.

7 And Moses was a son of fourscore years, and Aaron a son of fourscore and three years, when they spoke unto Pharaoh. **[2512 YM / 1462 BC]**

8 And the Becoming-One spoke unto Moses and unto Aaron, saying,

9 When Pharaoh shall speak unto you, saying, Show a miracle for you: then you shall say unto Aaron, Take your rod, and cast it before Pharaoh, and it shall become a serpent.

10 And Moses and Aaron went in unto Pharaoh, and they did so as the Becoming-One had commanded: and Aaron cast down his rod before Pharaoh, and before his servants, and it became a serpent.

11 Then Pharaoh also called the wise men and the sorcerers: now the magicians of Egypt, they also did in like manner with their enchantments.

12 For they cast down every man his rod, and they became serpents: but Aaron's rod swallowed up their rods.

13 And he hardened Pharaoh's heart, that he listened not unto them; as the Becoming-One had said.

14 And the Becoming-One said unto Moses, Pharaoh's heart is hardened, he refuses to let the people go.

15 Get you unto Pharaoh in the morning; lo, he goes out unto the water; and you shall stand by the river's brink and wait for him; and the rod which was turned to a serpent shall you take in your hand.

16 And you shall say unto him, The Becoming-One, God of the Hebrews has sent me unto you, saying, Let my people go, that they may serve me in the wilderness: and, behold, hitherto you would not hear.

17 Thus says the Becoming-One, In this you shall know that I am the Becoming-One:behold, I will smite with the rod that is in mine hand upon the waters which are in the river, and they shall be turned to blood.

18 And the fish that is in the river shall die, and the river shall stink; and the Egyptians shall loathe to drink of the water of the river.

19 And the Becoming-One spoke unto Moses, Say unto Aaron, Take your rod, and stretch out your hand upon the waters of Egypt, upon their streams, upon their rivers, and upon their ponds, and upon all their pools of water, that they may become blood; and that there may be blood throughout all the land of Egypt, both in vessels of wood, and in vessels of stone.

20 And Moses and Aaron did so, as the Becoming-One commanded; and he lifted up the rod, and smote the waters that were in the river, in the sight of Pharaoh, and in the sight of his servants; and all the waters that were in the river were turned to blood.

21 And the fish that was in the river died; and the river stank, and the Egyptians could not drink of the water of the river; and there was blood throughout all the land of Egypt.

22 And the magicians of Egypt did so with their enchantments: and Pharaoh's heart was hardened, neither did he listen unto them; as the Becoming-One had said.

23 And Pharaoh turned and went into his house, neither did he set his heart to this also.

24 And all the Egyptians dug round about the river for water to drink; for they could not drink of the water of the river.

25 And seven days were fulfilled, after that the Becoming-One had struck the river.

Ex 8:1 And the Becoming-One spoke unto Moses, Go unto Pharaoh, and say unto him, Thus says the Becoming-One, Let my people go, that they may serve me.

2 And if you refuse to let them go, behold, I will smite all your borders with frogs:

3 And the river shall bring forth frogs abundantly, which shall go up and come into your house, and into your bedchamber, and upon your bed, and into the house of your servants, and upon your people, and into your ovens, and into your kneading bowls:

4 And the frogs shall come up both on you, and upon your people, and upon all your servants.

5 And the Becoming-One spoke unto Moses, Say unto Aaron, Stretch forth your hand with your rod over the streams, over the rivers, and over the ponds, and cause frogs to come up upon the land of Egypt.

6 And Aaron stretched out his hand over the waters of Egypt; and the frogs came up, and covered the land of Egypt.

7 And the magicians did so with their enchantments, and brought up frogs upon the land of Egypt.

8 Then Pharaoh called for Moses and Aaron, and said, Entreat the Becoming-One, that he may take away the frogs from me, and from my people; and I will let the people go, that they may do sacrifice unto the Becoming-One.

9 And Moses said unto Pharaoh, Glory for me: when shall I entreat for you, and for your servants, and for your people, to destroy the frogs from you and your houses, that they may remain in the river only?

10 And he said, tomorrow. And he said, Be it according to your word: that you may know that there is none like unto the Becoming-One our God.

11 And the frogs shall depart from you, and from your houses, and from your servants, and from your people; they shall remain in the river only.

12 And Moses and Aaron went out from Pharaoh: and Moses cried unto the Becoming-One because of the frogs which he had brought against Pharaoh.

13 And the Becoming-One did according to the word of Moses; and the frogs died out of the houses, out of the villages, and out of the fields.

14 And they gathered them together upon heaps: and the land stank.

15 But when Pharaoh saw that there was respite, he hardened his heart, and listened not unto them; as the Becoming-One had said.

16 And the Becoming-One said unto Moses, Say unto Aaron, Stretch out your rod, and smite the dust of the land, that it may become gnats throughout all the land of Egypt.

17 And they did so; for Aaron stretched out his hand with his rod, and smote the dust of the earth, and it became gnats in man, and in beast; all the dust of the land became gnats throughout all the land of Egypt.

18 And the magicians did so with their enchantments to bring forth gnats, but they could not: so there were gnats upon man, and upon beast.

19 Then the magicians said unto Pharaoh, This is the finger of God: and Pharaoh's heart was hardened, and he listened not unto them; as the Becoming-One had said.

20 And the Becoming-One said unto Moses, Rise up early in the morning, and stand before Pharaoh; lo, he comes forth to the water; and say unto him, Thus says the Becoming-One, Let my people go, that they may serve me.

21 Else, if you will not let my people go, behold, I will send swarms of flies upon you, and upon your servants, and upon your people, and into your houses: and the houses of the Egyptians shall be full of swarms of flies, and also the ground whereon they are.

22 And I will sever in that day the land of Goshen, in which my people dwell, that no swarms of flies shall be there; to the end you may know that I am the Becoming-One in the midst of the earth.

23 And I will put a division between my people and your people: tomorrow shall this sign be.

24 And the Becoming-One did so; and there came a grievous swarm of flies into the house of Pharaoh, and into his servants' houses, and into all the land of Egypt: the land was corrupted by reason of the swarm of flies.

25 And Pharaoh called for Moses and for Aaron, and said, Go, sacrifice to your God in the land.

26 And Moses said, It is not meet so to do; for we shall sacrifice the abomination of the Egyptians to the Becoming-One our God: lo, shall we sacrifice the abomination of the Egyptians before their eyes, and will they not stone us?

27 We will go three days' journey into the wilderness, and sacrifice to the Becoming-One our God, as he shall command us.

28 And Pharaoh said, I will let you go, that you may sacrifice to the Becoming-One your God in the wilderness; only you shall not go very far away: entreat for me.

29 And Moses said, Behold, I go out from you, and I will entreat the Becoming-One that the swarms of flies may depart from Pharaoh, from his servants, and from his people, tomorrow: but let not Pharaoh deal deceitfully any more in not letting the people go to sacrifice to the Becoming-One.

30 And Moses went out from Pharaoh, and entreated the Becoming-One.

31 And the Becoming-One did according to the word of Moses; and he removed the swarms of flies from Pharaoh, from his servants, and from his people; there remained not one.

32 And Pharaoh hardened his heart at this time also, neither would he let the people go.

Ex 9:1 Then the Becoming-One said unto Moses, Go in unto Pharaoh, and tell him, Thus says the Becoming-One, God of the Hebrews, Let my people go, that they may serve me.

2 For if you refuse to let them go, and will hold them still,

3 Behold, the hand of the Becoming-One is upon your cattle which is in the field, upon the horses, upon the donkeys, upon the camels, upon the oxen, and upon the sheep: there shall be a very grievous plague.

4 And the Becoming-One shall divide between the cattle of Israel and the cattle of Egypt: and there shall nothing die of all that is the children's of Israel.

5 And the Becoming-One appointed a set time,[25] saying, tomorrow the Becoming-One shall do this thing in the land.

6 And the Becoming-One did that thing on the next day, and all the cattle of Egypt died: but of the cattle of the children of Israel died not one.

7 And Pharaoh sent, and, behold, there was not one of the cattle of the Israelites dead. And the heart of Pharaoh was hardened, and he did not let the people go.

8 And the Becoming-One said unto Moses and unto Aaron, Take to you handfuls of ashes of the furnace, and let Moses sprinkle it toward the heavens in the sight of Pharaoh.

9 And it shall become small dust in all the land of Egypt, and shall be a boil breaking forth with inflammation upon man, and upon beast, throughout all the land of Egypt.

10 And they took ashes of the furnace, and stood before Pharaoh; and Moses sprinkled it up toward the heavens; and it became a boil breaking forth with inflammations upon man, and upon beast.

11 And the magicians could not stand before Moses because of the boils; for the boil was upon the magicians, and upon all the Egyptians.

12 And the Becoming-One hardened the heart of Pharaoh, and he listened not unto them; as the Becoming-One had spoken unto Moses.

13 And the Becoming-One said unto Moses, Rise up early in the morning, and stand before Pharaoh, and say unto him, Thus says the Becoming-One, God of the Hebrews, Let my people go, that they may serve me.

14 For I will at this time send all my plagues upon your heart, and upon your servants, and upon your people; that you may know that there is none like me in all the earth.

15 For now I will stretch out my hand, that I may smite you and your people with pestilence; and you shall be cut off from the earth.

16 And in very deed for this cause I have raised you up, for to show in you my power; and that my name may be declared throughout all the earth.

17 As yet exalt you yourself against my people, that you will not let them go?

18 Behold, tomorrow about this time I will cause it to rain a very grievous hail, such as has not been in Egypt since the foundation thereof even until now.

19 Send therefore now, and gather your cattle, and all that you have in the field; for upon every man and beast which shall be found in the field, and shall not be brought home, the hail shall come down upon them, and they shall die.

20 He that feared the word of the Becoming-One among the servants of Pharaoh made his servants and his cattle flee into the houses:

---

[25] Appointed time or festival

21 And he that regarded not the word of the Becoming-One left his servants and his cattle in the field.

22 And the Becoming-One said unto Moses, Stretch forth your hand toward the heavens, that there may be hail in all the land of Egypt, upon man, and upon beast, and upon every herb of the field, throughout the land of Egypt.

23 And Moses stretched forth his rod toward the heavens: and the Becoming-One sent thunder and hail, and the fire ran along upon the ground; and the Becoming-One rained hail upon the land of Egypt.

24 So there was hail, and fire mingled with the hail, very grievous, such as there was none like it in all the land of Egypt since it became a nation.

25 And the hail smote throughout all the land of Egypt all that was in the field, both man and beast; and the hail smote every herb of the field, and brake every tree of the field.

26 Only in the land of Goshen, where the children of Israel were, was there no hail.

27 And Pharaoh sent, and called for Moses and Aaron, and said unto them, I have sinned this time: the Becoming-One is righteous, and I and my people are wicked.

28 Entreat the Becoming-One for it is enough that there be no more mighty thunderings and hail; and I will let you go, and you shall stay no longer.

29 And Moses said unto him, As soon as I am gone out of the city, I will spread abroad my hands unto the Becoming-One; and the thunder shall cease, neither shall there be any more hail; that you may know how that the earth is the Becoming-One's.

30 But as for you and your servants, I know that you will not yet fear the Becoming-One God.

31 And the flax and the barley was ruined: for the barley was young (in the ear), and the flax was in bud.

32 But the wheat and the rye were not ruined: for they were not ripe yet.

33 And Moses went out of the city from Pharaoh, and spread abroad his hands unto the Becoming-One:and the thunders and hail ceased, and the rain was not poured upon the earth.

34 And when Pharaoh saw that the rain and the hail and the thunders were ceased, he sinned yet more, and hardened his heart, he and his servants.

35 And the heart of Pharaoh was hardened, neither would he let the children of Israel go; as the Becoming-One had spoken by Moses.

Ex 10:1 And the Becoming-One said unto Moses, Go in unto Pharaoh: for I have hardened his heart, and the heart of his servants, that I might show these my signs before him:

2 And that you may tell in the ears of your son, and of your son's son, what things I have worked in Egypt, and my signs which I have done among them; that you may know how that I am the Becoming-One.

3 And Moses and Aaron came in unto Pharaoh, and said unto him, Thus says the Becoming-One, God of the Hebrews, How long will you refuse to humble yourself before me? let my people go, that they may serve me.

4 Else, if you refuse to let my people go, behold, tomorrow will I bring the locusts into your coast:

5 And they shall cover the face of the earth, that one cannot be able to see the earth: and they shall eat the residue of that which is escaped, which remains unto you from the hail, and shall eat every tree which grows for you out of the field:

6 And they shall fill your houses, and the houses of all your servants, and the houses of all the Egyptians; which neither your fathers, nor your fathers' fathers have seen, since the day that they were upon the earth unto this day. And he turned himself, and went out from Pharaoh.

7 And Pharaoh's servants said unto him, How long shall this man be a snare unto us? let the men go, that they may serve the Becoming-One their God: don't you know yet that Egypt is destroyed?

8 And Moses and Aaron were brought again unto Pharaoh: and he said unto them, Go, serve the Becoming-One your God: but who will be going?

9 And Moses said, We will go with our young and with our old, with our sons and with our daughters, with our flocks and with our herds will we go; for we must hold a feast unto the Becoming-One.

10 And he said unto them, Let the Becoming-One be so with you, if I let you go, and your little ones: look! But only for a evil purpose you ask.

11 No! Go only you men, and serve the Becoming-One; for that you did desire. And they were driven out from Pharaoh's presence.

12 And the Becoming-One said unto Moses, Stretch out your hand over the land of Egypt for the locusts, that they may come up upon the land of Egypt, and eat every herb of the land, even all that the hail has left.

13 And Moses stretched forth his rod over the land of Egypt, and the Becoming-One brought an east wind upon the land all that day, and all that night; and when it was morning, the east wind brought the locusts.

14 And the locusts went up over all the land of Egypt, and rested in all the coasts of Egypt: very grievous were they; before them there were no such locusts as they, neither after them shall be such.

15 For they covered the face of the whole earth, so that the land was darkened; and they did eat every herb of the land, and all the fruit of the trees which the hail had left: and there remained not any green thing in the trees, or in the herbs of the field, through all the land of Egypt.

16 Then Pharaoh called for Moses and Aaron in haste; and he said, I have sinned against the Becoming-One your God, and against you.

17 Now therefore forgive, I pray you, my sin only this once, and entreat the Becoming-One your God, that he may take away from me this death only.

18 And he went out from Pharaoh, and entreated the Becoming-One.

19 And the Becoming-One turned a mighty strong west wind, which took away the locusts, and cast them into the boundary sea[26]; there remained not one locust in all the coasts of Egypt.

20 But the Becoming-One hardened Pharaoh's heart, so that he would not let the children of Israel go.

---

[26]*Aka* "red sea." Southern boundary of Israel

21 And the Becoming-One said unto Moses, Stretch out your hand toward the heavens, that there may be darkness over the land of Egypt, even darkness which may be felt.

22 And Moses stretched forth his hand toward the heavens; and there was a thick darkness in all the land of Egypt three days:

23 They saw not one another, neither rose any from his place for three days: but all the children of Israel had light in their dwellings.

24 And Pharaoh called unto Moses, and said, Go ye, serve the Becoming-One; only let your flocks and your herds be stayed: let your little ones also go with you.

25 And Moses said, you must give us also sacrifices and burnt offerings, that we may sacrifice unto the Becoming-One our God.

26 Our cattle also shall go with us; there shall not a hoof be left behind; for thereof must we take to serve the Becoming-One our God; and we know not with what we must serve the Becoming-One, until we come there.

27 But the Becoming-One hardened Pharaoh's heart, and he would not let them go.

28 And Pharaoh said unto him, Get you from me, take heed to thyself, see my face no more; for in that day you see my face you shall die.

29 And Moses said, you have spoken well, I will see your face again no more.

Ex 11:1 And the Becoming-One said unto Moses, Yet will I bring one plague more upon Pharaoh, and upon Egypt; afterwards he will let you go hence: when he shall let you go, he shall surely thrust you out hence altogether.

2 Speak now in the ears of the people, and let every man borrow of his neighbor, and every woman of her neighbor, jewels of silver, and jewels of gold.

3 And the Becoming-One gave the people favor in the sight of the Egyptians. Moreover the man Moses was very great in the land of Egypt, in the sight of Pharaoh's servants, and in the sight of the people.

4 And Moses said, Thus says the Becoming-One, About midnight will I go out into the midst of Egypt:

5 And all the firstborn in the land of Egypt shall die, from the firstborn of Pharaoh that sits upon his throne, even unto the firstborn of the maidservant that is behind the mill; and all the firstborn of beasts.

6 And there shall be a great cry throughout all the land of Egypt, such as there was none like it, nor shall be like it any more.

7 But against any of the children of Israel shall not a dog move his tongue, against man or beast: that you may know how that the Becoming-One does put a difference between the Egyptians and Israel.

8 And all these your servants shall come down unto me, and bow down themselves unto me, saying, Get you out, and all the people that follow you: and after that I will go out. And he went out from Pharaoh in a great anger.

9 And the Becoming-One said unto Moses, Pharaoh shall not listen unto you; that my wonders may be multiplied in the land of Egypt.

10 And Moses and Aaron did all these wonders before Pharaoh: and the Becoming-One hardened Pharaoh's heart, so that he would not let the children of Israel go out of his land.

Ex 12:1 And the Becoming-One spoke unto Moses and Aaron in the land of Egypt, saying,

2 This new moon [month] shall be unto you the beginning of months: it shall be the first month of the year to you. **[2512 YM]**

3 Speak you unto all the congregation of Israel, saying, In the tenth day of this month they shall take to them every man a lamb, according to the house of their fathers, a lamb for a house:

4 And if the household be too little for the lamb, let him and his neighbor next unto his house take it according to the number of the souls; every man according to his eating shall make your count for the lamb.

5 Your lamb shall be without blemish, a male of the first year: you shall take it out from the sheep, or from the goats:

6 And you shall watch it until the fourteenth day of the same month: and the whole assembly of the congregation of Israel shall kill it between the evenings.

7 And they shall take of the blood, and strike it on the two side posts and on the upper door post of the houses, wherein they shall eat it.

8 And they shall eat the flesh in that night, roast with fire, and unleavened bread; and with bitter herbs they shall eat it.

9 Eat not of it raw, nor sodden at all with water, but roast with fire; his head with his legs, and with the inner parts thereof.

10 And you shall let nothing of it remain until the morning; and that which remains of it until the morning you shall burn with fire.

11 And thus shall you eat it; with your loins girded, your shoes on your feet, and your staff in your hand; and you shall eat it in haste: it is the Becoming-One's Passover.

12 For I will pass through the land of Egypt this night, and will smite all the firstborn in the land of Egypt, both man and beast; and against all the gods of Egypt I will execute judgment: I am the Becoming-One.

13 And the blood shall be to you for a token upon the houses where you are: and when I see the blood, I will pass over you, and the plague shall not be upon you to destroy you, when I smite the land of Egypt.

14 And this day shall be unto you for a memorial; and you shall keep it a feast to the Becoming-One throughout your generations; you shall keep it a feast by an ordinance for olam.

15 Seven days shall you eat unleavened bread; even the first day you shall put away leaven out of your houses: for whosoever eats leavened bread from the first day until the seventh day, that soul shall be cut off from Israel.

16 And in the first day there shall be a holy convocation, and in the seventh day there shall be a holy convocation to you; no manner of work shall be done in them, save that which every soul must eat, that only may be done of you.

17 And you shall observe the feast of unleavened bread; for in this selfsame day I have brought your armies out of the land of Egypt: therefore shall you

observe this day in your generations by an ordinance for olam.

18 In the first month, on the fourteenth day of the month at evening, you shall eat unleavened bread, until the one and twentieth day of the month at evening.

19 Seven days shall there be no leaven found in your houses: for whosoever eats that which is leavened, even that soul shall be cut off from the congregation of Israel, whether he be a stranger, or born in the land.

20 you shall eat nothing leavened; in all your habitations shall you eat unleavened bread.

21 Then Moses called for all the elders of Israel, and said unto them, Draw out and take you a lamb according to your families, and kill the Passover.

22 And you shall take a bunch of hyssop, and dip it in the blood that is in the basin, and strike the lintel and the two side posts with the blood that is in the basin; and none of you shall go out at the door of his house until the morning.

23 For the Becoming-One will pass through to smite the Egyptians; and when he sees the blood upon the lintel, and on the two side posts, the Becoming-One will pass over the door, and will not permit the destroyer to come in unto your houses to smite you.

24 And you shall observe this thing for an ordinance to you and to your sons for olam.

25 And it shall come to pass, when you be come to the land which the Becoming-One will give you, according as he has promised, that you shall keep this service.

26 And it shall come to pass, when your children shall say unto you, What do you mean by this service?

27 That you shall say, It is the sacrifice of the Becoming-One's Passover, who passed over the houses of the children of Israel in Egypt, when he smote the Egyptians, and delivered our houses. And the people bowed the head and worshiped.

28 And the children of Israel went away, and did as the Becoming-One had commanded Moses and Aaron, so did they.

29 And it came to pass, that at midnight the Becoming-One smote all the firstborn in the land of Egypt, from the firstborn of Pharaoh that sat on his throne unto the firstborn of the captive that was in the dungeon; and all the firstborn of animal.

30 And Pharaoh rose up in the night, he, and all his servants, and all the Egyptians; and there was a great cry in Egypt; for there was not a house where there was not one dead.

31 And he called for Moses and Aaron by night, and said, Rise up, and get you forth from among my people, both you and the children of Israel; and go, serve the Becoming-One, as you have said.

32 Also take your flocks and your herds, as you have said, and be gone; and bless me also.

33 And the Egyptians were urgent upon the people, that they might send them out of the land in haste; for they said, We be all dead men.

34 And the people took their dough before it was leavened, their kneading bowls being bound up in their clothes upon their shoulders.

35 And the children of Israel did according to the word of Moses; and they borrowed of the Egyptians jewels of silver, and jewels of gold, and raiment:

36 And the Becoming-One gave the people favor in the sight of the Egyptians, so that they gave unto them such things as they asked for. And they spoiled the Egyptians.

37 And the children of Israel journeyed from Rameses to Succoth, **about six hundred thousand [*eleph*[27]] on foot that were men, beside children.**

38 And a mixed multitude went up also with them; and flocks, and herds, even very much cattle.

39 And they baked unleavened cakes of the dough which they brought forth out of Egypt, for it was not leavened; because they were thrust out of Egypt, and could not tarry, neither had they prepared for themselves any victual.

40 Now the sojourning of the children of Israel, who dwelt in Egypt, **was four hundred and thirty years. [2083 - 2512 YM]**

41 And it came to pass at the end of the four hundred and thirty years, even the selfsame day it came to pass, that all the hosts of the Becoming-One went out from the land of Egypt.

42 It is a night to be much observed unto the Becoming-One for bringing them out from the land of Egypt: this is that night of the Becoming-One to be observed of all the children of Israel in their generations.

43 And the Becoming-One said unto Moses and Aaron, This is the ordinance of the Passover: There shall no stranger eat thereof:

44 But every man's servant that is bought for money, when you have circumcised him, then shall he eat thereof.

45 A foreigner and a hired servant shall not eat thereof.

46 In one house shall it be eaten; you shall not carry forth of the flesh abroad out of the house; neither shall you break a bone thereof.

47 All the congregation of Israel shall keep it.

48 And when a stranger shall sojourn with you, and will keep the Passover to the Becoming-One, let all his males be circumcised, and then let him come near and keep it; and he shall be as one that is born in the land: for no uncircumcised person shall eat thereof.

49 One law shall be to him that is homeborn, and unto the stranger that sojourns among you.

50 Thus did all the children of Israel; as the Becoming-One commanded Moses and Aaron, so did they.

51 And it came to pass the selfsame day, that the Becoming-One did bring the children of Israel out of the land of Egypt by their hosts.

Ex 13:1 And the Becoming-One spoke unto Moses, saying,

2 Sanctify unto me all the firstborn, whatsoever opens the womb among the children of Israel, both of man and of beast: it is mine.

3 And Moses said unto the people, Remember this day, in which you came out from Egypt, out of the house of bondage; for by strength of hand the Becoming-One brought you out from this place: there shall no leavened bread be eaten.

---

[27] Could be an early Hebrew troop name such as *battalion* instead of the number 1000, see Preface

4 This day came you out in the month Abib.

5 And it shall be when the Becoming-One shall bring you into the land of the Canaanites, and the Hittites, and the Amorites, and the Hivites, and the Jebusites, which he swore unto your fathers to give you, a land flowing with milk and honey, that you shall keep this service in this month.

6 Seven days you shall eat unleavened bread, and in the seventh day shall be a feast to the Becoming-One.

7 Unleavened bread shall be eaten seven days; and there shall no leavened bread be seen with you, neither shall there be leaven seen with you in all your quarters.

8 And you shall show your son in that day, saying, This is done because of that which the Becoming-One did unto me when I came forth out of Egypt.

9 And it shall be for a sign unto you upon your hand, and for a memorial between your eyes, that of the law of the Becoming-One may be in your mouth: for with a strong hand has the Becoming-One brought you out of Egypt.

10 you shall therefore keep this ordinance at her set time[28] from day to day.

11 And it shall be when the Becoming-One shall bring you into the land of the Canaanites, as he swore unto you and to your fathers, and shall give it you,

12 That you shall set apart unto the Becoming-One all that opens the matrix, and every firstling that comes of a beast which you have; the males shall be the Becoming-One's.

13 And every firstling of an donkey you shall redeem with a lamb; and if you will not redeem it, then you shall break his neck: and all the firstborn of man among your children shall you redeem.

14 And it shall be when your son asks you in time to come, saying, What is this? that you shall say unto him, By strength of hand the Becoming-One brought us out from Egypt, from the house of bondage:

15 And it came to pass, when Pharaoh would hardly let us go, that the Becoming-One killed all the firstborn in the land of Egypt, both the firstborn of man, and the firstborn of beast: therefore I sacrifice to the Becoming-One all that opens the matrix, being males; but all the firstborn of my children I redeem.

16 And it shall be for a token upon your hand, and for frontlets between your eyes: for by strength of hand the Becoming-One brought us forth out of Egypt.

17 And it came to pass, when Pharaoh had let the people go, that God led them not through the way of the land of the Philistines, although that was near; for God said, Lest perhaps the people repent when they see war, and they return to Egypt:

18 But God led the people about, through the way of the wilderness, boundary sea [red sea] and the children of Israel went up in battle array out of the land of Egypt.

19 And **Moses took the bones of Joseph with him: for he had straitly sworn the children of Israel, saying, God will surely visit you; and you shall carry up my bones away hence with you.**

20 And they took their journey from Succoth, and encamped in Etham, in the edge of the wilderness.

21 And the Becoming-One went before them by day in a pillar of a cloud, to lead them the way; and by night in a pillar of fire, to give them light; to go by day and night:

22 He took not away the pillar of the cloud by day, nor the pillar of fire by night, from before the people.

Ex 14:1 And the Becoming-One spoke unto Moses, saying,

2 Speak unto the children of Israel, that they turn and encamp before Pihahiroth, between Migdol and the sea, over against Baal-Zephon: before it shall you encamp by the sea.

3 For Pharaoh will say of the children of Israel, They are entangled in the land, the wilderness has shut them in.

4 And I will harden Pharaoh's heart, that he shall follow after them; and I will be honored upon Pharaoh, and upon all his host; that the Egyptians may know that I am the Becoming-One. And they did so.

5 And it was told the king of Egypt that the people fled: and the heart of Pharaoh and of his servants was turned against the people, and they said, Why have we done this, that we have let Israel go from serving us?

6 And he made ready his chariot, and took his people with him:

7 And he took six hundred chosen chariots, and all the chariots of Egypt, and captains over every one of them.

8 And the Becoming-One hardened the heart of Pharaoh king of Egypt, and he pursued after the children of Israel: and the children of Israel went out with a high hand.

9 But the Egyptians pursued after them, all the horses and chariots of Pharaoh, and his horsemen, and his army, and overtook them encamping by the sea, beside Pihahiroth, before Baal-Zephon.

10 And when Pharaoh drew near, the children of Israel lifted up their eyes, and, behold, the Egyptians marched after them; and they were greatly afraid: and the children of Israel cried out unto the Becoming-One.

11 And they said unto Moses, Because there were no graves in Egypt, have you taken us away to die in the wilderness? why have you dealt thus with us, to carry us forth out of Egypt?

12 Is not this the word that we did tell you in Egypt, saying, Let us alone, that we may serve the Egyptians? For it had been better for us to serve the Egyptians, than that we should die in the wilderness.

13 And Moses said unto the people, Fear you not, stand still, and see the salvation of the Becoming-One, which he will show to you today: for the Egyptians whom you have seen today, you shall see them again no more for olam.

14 The Becoming-One shall fight for you, and you shall hold your peace.

15 And the Becoming-One said unto Moses, Why cry you unto me? speak unto the children of Israel, that they go forward:

16 But lift you up your rod, and stretch out your hand over the sea, and divide it: and the children of Israel shall go on dry ground through the midst of the sea.

---

[28] Appointed time or festival

17 And I, behold, I will harden the hearts of the Egyptians, and they shall follow them: and I will get me honor upon Pharaoh, and upon all his host, upon his chariots, and upon his horsemen.

18 And the Egyptians shall know that I am the Becoming-One, when I have gotten me honor upon Pharaoh, upon his chariots, and upon his horsemen.

19 And the angel of God, which went before the camp of Israel, removed and went behind them; and the pillar of the cloud went from before their face, and stood behind them:

20 And it came between the camp of the Egyptians and the camp of Israel; and it was a cloud and darkness to them, but it gave light by night to these: so that the one came not near the other all the night.

21 And Moses stretched out his hand over the sea; and the Becoming-One caused the sea to go back by a strong east wind all that night, and made the sea dry land, and the waters were divided.

22 And the children of Israel went into the midst of the sea upon the dry ground: and the waters were a wall unto them on their right hand, and on their left.

23 And the Egyptians pursued, and went in after them to the midst of the sea, even all Pharaoh's horses, his chariots, and his horsemen.

24 And it came to pass, that in the morning watch the Becoming-One looked unto the host of the Egyptians through the pillar of fire and of the cloud, and troubled the host of the Egyptians,

25 And took off their chariot wheels, that they drove them heavily: so that the Egyptians said, Let us flee from the face of Israel; for the Becoming-One fights for them against the Egyptians.

26 And the Becoming-One said unto Moses, Stretch out your hand over the sea, that the waters may come again upon the Egyptians, upon their chariots, and upon their horsemen.

27 And Moses stretched forth his hand over the sea, and the sea returned to his strength when the morning appeared; and the Egyptians fled against it; and the Becoming-One overthrew the Egyptians in the midst of the sea.

28 And the waters returned, and covered the chariots, and the horsemen, and all the host of Pharaoh that came into the sea after them; there remained not so much as one of them.

29 But the children of Israel walked upon dry land in the midst of the sea; and the waters were a wall unto them on their right hand, and on their left.

30 Thus the Becoming-One saved Israel that day out of the hand of the Egyptians; and Israel saw the Egyptians dead upon the sea shore.

31 And Israel saw that great work which the Becoming-One did upon the Egyptians: and the people feared the Becoming-One, and believed the Becoming-One, and his servant Moses.

Ex 15:1 Then sang Moses and the children of Israel this song unto the Becoming-One, and spoke, saying, I will sing unto the Becoming-One, for he has triumphed gloriously: the horse and his rider has he thrown into the sea.

2 The Becoming-One is my strength and song, and he is become my salvation: he is my GOD, and I will prepare him a habitation; my father's God, and I will exalt him.

3 The Becoming-One is a man of war: the Becoming-One is his name.

4 Pharaoh's chariots and his host has he cast into the sea: his chosen captains also are drowned in the boundary sea.

5 The depths have covered them: they sank into the bottom as a stone.

6 your right hand, O Becoming-One, is become glorious in power: your right hand, O Becoming-One, has dashed in pieces the enemy.

7 And in the greatness of your excellency you have overthrown them that rose up against you: you sent forth your wrath, which consumed them as stubble.

8 And with the blast of your nostrils the waters were gathered together, the floods stood upright as a heap, and the depths were congealed in the heart of the sea.

9 The enemy said, I will pursue, I will overtake, I will divide the spoil; my soul shall be satisfied upon them; I will draw my sword, my hand shall destroy them.

10 you didst blow with your wind, the sea covered them: they sank as lead in the mighty waters.

11 Who is like unto you, O Becoming-One, among the gods? who is like you, glorious in holiness, fearful in praises, doing wonders?

12 you stretched out your right hand, the earth swallowed them.

13 you in your mercy have led forth the people which you have redeemed: you have guided them in your strength unto your holy habitation.

14 The people shall hear, and be afraid: sorrow shall take hold on the inhabitants of Palestina.

15 Then the chiefs of Edom shall be amazed; the mighty men of Moab, trembling shall take hold upon them; all the inhabitants of Canaan shall melt away.

16 Fear and dread shall fall upon them; by the greatness of your arm they shall be as still as a stone; till your people pass over, O Becoming-One, till the people pass over, which you have purchased.

17 you shall bring them in, and plant them in the mountain of your inheritance, in the place, O Becoming-One, which you have made for you to dwell in, in the Sanctuary, O my Lord(s), which your hands have established.

18 The Becoming-One shall reign for olam and beyond.

19 For the horse of Pharaoh went in with his chariots and with his horsemen into the sea, and the Becoming-One brought again the waters of the sea upon them; but the children of Israel went on dry land in the midst of the sea.

20 And Miriam the prophetess, the sister of Aaron, took a timbrel in her hand; and all the women went out after her with timbrels and with dances.

21 And Miriam answered them, Sing you to the Becoming-One, for he has triumphed gloriously; the horse and his rider has he thrown into the sea.

22 **So Moses brought Israel from the boundary sea, and they went out into the wilderness of Shur; and they went three days in the wilderness, and found no water.**

23 And when they came to Marah, they could not drink of the waters of Marah, for they were bitter: therefore the name of it was called Marah.

24 And the people murmured against Moses, saying, What shall we drink?

25 And he cried unto the Becoming-One; and the Becoming-One showed him a tree, which when he had cast into the waters, the waters were made sweet: there he made for them a statute and an ordinance, and there he proved them,

26 And said, If you will diligently listen to the voice of the Becoming-One your God, and will do that which is right in his sight, and will give ear to his commandments, and keep all his statutes, I will put none of these diseases upon you, which I have brought upon the Egyptians: for I am the Becoming-One that heals you.

27 And they came to **Elim**, where were **twelve wells of water**, and threescore and ten palm trees: and they encamped there by the waters.

Ex 16:1 And **they took their journey from Elim**, and all the congregation of the children of Israel came unto the wilderness of Sin, which is between Elim and Sinai, **on the fifteenth day of the second month** relating to their departing out of the land of Egypt.

2 And the whole congregation of the children of Israel murmured against Moses and Aaron in the wilderness:

3 And the children of Israel said unto them, Would that we had died by the hand of the Becoming-One in the land of Egypt, when we sat by the flesh pots, and when we did eat bread to the full; for you have brought us forth into this wilderness, to kill this whole assembly with hunger.

4 Then said the Becoming-One unto Moses, Behold, **I will rain bread from the heavens for you**; and the people shall go out and gather a certain rate every day, that I may prove them, whether they will walk in my law, or not.

5 **And it shall come to pass, that on the sixth day they shall prepare that which they bring in; and it shall be twice as much as they gather daily.**

6 And Moses and Aaron said unto all the children of Israel, At evening, then you shall know that the Becoming-One has brought you out from the land of Egypt:

7 And in the morning, then you shall see the glory of the Becoming-One; for that he hears your murmurings against the Becoming-One: and what are we, that you murmur against us?

8 And Moses said, This shall be, when the Becoming-One shall give you in the evening flesh to eat, and in the morning bread to the full; for that the Becoming-One hears your murmurings which you murmur against him: and what are we? your murmurings are not against us, but against the Becoming-One.

9 And Moses spoke unto Aaron, Say unto all the congregation of the children of Israel, Come near before the Becoming-One: for he has heard your murmurings.

10 And it came to pass, as Aaron spoke unto the whole congregation of the children of Israel, that they looked toward the wilderness, and, behold, the glory of the Becoming-One appeared in the cloud.

11 And the Becoming-One spoke unto Moses, saying,

12 I have heard the murmurings of the children of Israel: speak unto them, saying, Between the evenings you shall eat flesh, and in the morning you shall be filled with bread; and you shall know that I am the Becoming-One your God.

13 And it came to pass, that at evening the quails came up, and covered the camp: and in the morning the dew lay round about the host.

14 And when the dew that lay was gone up, behold, upon the face of the wilderness there lay a small round thing, as small as the hoar frost on the ground.

15 And when the children of Israel saw it, they said one to another, It is manna: for they knew not what it was. And Moses said unto them, This is the bread which the Becoming-One has given you to eat.

16 This is the thing which the Becoming-One has commanded, Gather of it every man according to his eating, an omer for every man, according to the number of your souls; take you every man for them which are in his tents.

17 And the children of Israel did so, and gathered, some more, some less.

18 And when they did measured it with an omer, he that gathered much had nothing over, and he that gathered little had no lack; they gathered every man according to his eating.

19 And Moses said, Let no man leave of it till the morning.

20 Notwithstanding they listened not unto Moses; but some of them left of it until the morning, and it bred worms, and stank: and Moses was angry with them.

21 And they gathered it every morning, every man according to his eating: and when the sun grew hot, it melted.

22 And it came to pass, that on the sixth day they gathered twice as much bread, two omers for one man: and all the rulers of the congregation came and told Moses.

23 And he said unto them, This is that which the Becoming-One has said, tomorrow is the rest of the holy Sabbath unto the Becoming-One:bake that which you will bake today, and seethe that you will seethe; and all that which remains over lay up for you to be kept until the morning.

24 And they laid it up till the morning, as Moses bade: and it did not stink, neither was there any worm therein.

25 And Moses said, Eat that today; for today is a Sabbath unto the Becoming-One: today you shall not find it in the field.

26 **Six days you shall gather it; but on the seventh day, which is the Sabbath, in it there shall be none**.

27 And it came to pass, that there went out some of the people on the seventh day for to gather, and they found none.

28 And the Becoming-One said unto Moses, How long refuse you to keep my commandments and my laws?

29 See, for that the Becoming-One has given you the Sabbath, therefore he gives you on the sixth day the bread of two days; abide you every man in his place, let no man go out of his place on the seventh day.

30 So the people rested on the seventh day.

31 And the house of Israel called the name thereof Manna: and it was like coriander seed, white; and the taste of it was like wafers made with honey.

32 And Moses said, This is the thing which the Becoming-One commands, Fill an omer of it to be kept for your generations; that they may see the bread wherewith I have fed you in the wilderness, when I brought you forth from the land of Egypt.

33 And Moses said unto Aaron, Take a pot, and put an omer full of manna therein, and lay it up before the Becoming-One, to be kept for your generations.

34 As the Becoming-One commanded Moses, so Aaron laid it up before the Testimony, to be kept.

35 And the children of Israel did eat manna forty years, until they came to a land inhabited; they did eat manna, until they came unto the borders of the land of Canaan.

36 Now an omer is the tenth part of an ephah.

Ex 17:1 And all the congregation of the children of Israel journeyed from the wilderness of Sin, after their journeys, according to the commandment of the Becoming-One, and pitched in Rephidim: and there was no water for the people to drink.

2 Therefore the people did chide with Moses, and said, Give us water that we may drink. And Moses said unto them, Why chide you with me? why do you tempt the Becoming-One?

3 And the people thirsted there for water; and the people murmured against Moses, and said, Is this why you have brought us up out of Egypt, to kill us and our children and our cattle with thirst?

4 And Moses cried unto the Becoming-One, saying, What shall I do unto this people? they be almost ready to stone me.

5 And the Becoming-One said unto Moses, Go on before the people, and take with you of the elders of Israel; and your rod, wherewith you smote the river, take in your hand, and go.

6 Behold, I will stand before you there upon the rock in Horeb; and you shall smite the rock, and there shall come water out of it, that the people may drink. And Moses did so in the sight of the elders of Israel.

7 And he called the name of the place Massah, and Meribah, because of the chiding of the children of Israel, and because they tempted the Becoming-One, saying, Is the Becoming-One among us, or not?

8 Then came Amalek, and fought with Israel in Rephidim.

9 And Moses said unto Joshua, Choose us out men, and go out, fight with Amalek: tomorrow I will stand on the top of the hill with the rod of God in mine hand.

10 So Joshua did as Moses had said to him, and fought with Amalek: and Moses, Aaron, and Hur went up to the top of the hill.

11 And it came to pass, when Moses held up his hand, that Israel prevailed: and when he let down his hand, Amalek prevailed.

12 But Moses' hands were heavy; and they took a stone, and put it under him, and he sat thereon; and Aaron and Hur stayed up his hands, the one on the one side, and the other on the other side; and his hands were steady until the going down of the sun.

13 And Joshua discomfited Amalek and his people with the edge of the sword.

14 And the Becoming-One said unto Moses, Write this for a memorial in a book, and rehearse it in the ears of Joshua: for I will utterly put out the remembrance of Amalek from under the heavens.

15 And Moses built an altar, and called the name of it Yehowah-nissi:

16 For he said, Because the Becoming-One has sworn that the Becoming-One will have war with Amalek from generation to generation.

Ex 18:1 When Jethro, the priest of Midian, Moses' father-in-law, heard of all that God had done for Moses, and for Israel his people, and that the Becoming-One had brought Israel out of Egypt;

2 Then Jethro, Moses' father-in-law, took Zipporah, Moses' wife, after he had sent her back,

3 And her two sons; of which the name of the one was Gershom; for he said, I have been an alien in a strange land:

4 And the name of the other was Eliezer; for God of my father, said he, was mine help, and delivered me from the sword of Pharaoh:

5 And Jethro, Moses' father-in-law, came with his sons and his wife unto Moses into the wilderness, where he encamped at the mount of God:

6 And he said unto Moses, I your father-in-law Jethro am come unto you, and your wife, and her two sons with her.

7 And Moses went out to meet his father-in-law, and did obeisance, and kissed him; and they asked each other of their welfare; and they came into the tent.

8 And Moses told his father-in-law all that the Becoming-One had done unto Pharaoh and to the Egyptians for Israel's sake, and all the travail that had come upon them by the way, and how the Becoming-One delivered them.

9 And Jethro rejoiced for all the goodness which the Becoming-One had done to Israel, whom he had delivered out of the hand of the Egyptians.

10 And Jethro said, Blessed be the Becoming-One, who has delivered you out of the hand of the Egyptians, and out of the hand of Pharaoh, who has delivered the people from under the hand of the Egyptians.

11 Now I know that the Becoming-One is greater than all gods: for in the thing wherein they dealt proudly he was above them.

12 And Jethro, Moses' father-in-law, took a burnt offering and sacrifices for God: and Aaron came, and all the elders of Israel, to eat bread with Moses' father-in-law before God.

13 And it came to pass on the next day, that Moses sat to judge the people: and the people stood by Moses from the morning unto the evening.

14 And when Moses' father-in-law saw all that he did to the people, he said, What is this thing that you do to the people? why sit you yourself alone, and all the people stand by you from morning unto even?

15 And Moses said unto his father-in-law, Because the people come unto me to inquire of God:

16 When they have a matter, they come unto me; and I judge between one and another, and I do make them know the statutes of God, and his laws.

17 And Moses' father-in-law said unto him, The thing that you do is not good.

18 you will surely wear away, both you, and this people that is with you: for this thing is too heavy for you; you are not able to perform it yourself alone.

19 listen now unto my voice, I will give you counsel, and God shall be with you: Be you the people before God, that you may bring their cases unto God:

20 And you shall teach them ordinances and laws, and shall show them the way wherein they must walk, and the work that they must do.

21 Moreover you shall provide out of all the people able men, such as fear God, men of truth, hating covetousness; and place such over them, to be rulers of *eleph*,[29] and rulers of hundreds, rulers of fifties, and rulers of tens:

22 And let them judge the people at all seasons: and it shall be, that every great matter they shall bring unto you, but every small matter they shall judge: so shall it be easier for thyself, and they shall bear the burden with you.

23 If you shall do this thing, and God command you so, then you shall be able to endure, and all this people shall also go to their place in peace.

24 So Moses listened to the voice of his father-in-law, and did all that he had said.

25 And Moses chose able men out of all Israel, and made them heads over the people, rulers of *eleph*,[30] rulers of hundreds, rulers of fifties, and rulers of tens.

26 And they judged the people at all seasons: the hard causes they brought unto Moses, but every small matter they judged themselves.

27 And Moses let his father-in-law depart; and he went his way into his own land.

Ex 19:1 In the third month, after the children of Israel were gone forth out of the land of Egypt, the same day came they into the wilderness of Sinai.

2 For they were departed from Rephidim, and were come to the desert of Sinai, and had pitched in the wilderness; and there Israel camped before the mount.

3 And Moses went up unto God, and the Becoming-One called unto him out of the mountain, saying, Thus shall you say to the house of Jacob, and tell the children of Israel;

4 you have seen what I did unto the Egyptians, and how I bare you on eagles' wings, and brought you unto myself.

5 Now therefore, if you will obey my voice indeed, and keep my covenant, then you shall be a treasure unto me above all the nations: for all the earth is mine:

6 And you shall be unto me a kingdom of priests, and a holy nation. These are the words which you shall speak unto the children of Israel.

7 And Moses came and called for the elders of the people, and laid before their faces all these words which the Becoming-One commanded him.

8 And all the nation answered together, and said, All that the Becoming-One has spoken we will do. And Moses returned the words of the people unto the Becoming-One.

9 And the Becoming-One said unto Moses, Lo, I come unto you in a thick cloud, that the people may hear when I speak with you, and believe you for olam. And Moses told the words of the people unto the Becoming-One.

10 And the Becoming-One said unto Moses, Go unto the people, and sanctify them today and tomorrow, and let them wash their clothes,

11 And be ready against the third day: for the third day the Becoming-One will come down in the sight of all the people upon mount Sinai.

12 And you shall set bounds unto the people round about, saying, Take heed to yourselves, that you go not up into the mount, or touch the border of it: whosoever touches the mount shall be surely put to death:

13 There shall not a hand touch it, but he shall surely be stoned, or shot through; whether it be beast or man, it shall not live: when the trumpet sounds long, they shall come up to the mount.

14 And Moses went down from the mount unto the people, and sanctified the people; and they washed their clothes.

15 And he said unto the people, Be ready against the third day: come not at your wives.

16 And it came to pass on the third day in the morning, that there were thunders and lightning, and a thick cloud upon the mount, and the voice of the trumpet exceeding loud; so that all the people that was in the camp trembled.

17 And Moses brought forth the people out of the camp to meet with God; and they stood at the foot of the mount.

18 And mount Sinai was wrapped in smoke, because the Becoming-One descended upon it in fire: and the smoke thereof ascended as the smoke of a furnace, and the whole mount quaked greatly.

19 And when the voice of the trumpet sounded long, and grew louder and louder, Moses spoke, and God answered him by a voice.

20 And the Becoming-One came down upon mount Sinai, on the top of the mount: and the Becoming-One called Moses up to the top of the mount; and Moses went up.

21 And the Becoming-One said unto Moses, Go down, charge the people, lest they break through unto the Becoming-One to gaze, and many of them perish.

22 And let the priests also, which come near to the Becoming-One, sanctify themselves, lest the Becoming-One break forth upon them.

23 And Moses said unto the Becoming-One, The people cannot come up to mount Sinai: for you charged us, saying, Set bounds about the mount, and sanctify it.

24 And the Becoming-One said unto him, Away, get you down, and you shall come up, you, and Aaron with you: but let not the priests and the people break through to come up unto the Becoming-One, lest he break forth upon them.

25 So Moses went down unto the people, and spoke unto them.

Ex 20:1 And God spoke all these words, saying,

2 I am the Becoming-One your God, which have brought you out of the land of Egypt, out of the house of bondage.

---

[29] Or thousands, see Preface
[30] Or thousands, see Preface

3 you shall have no other gods before/over/above me.

4 you shall not make unto you any graven image, or any likeness of any thing that is in the heavens above, or that is in the earth beneath, or that is in the water under the earth:

5 you shall not bow down yourself to them, nor serve them: for I the Becoming-One your God, a jealous GOD, visiting the iniquity of the fathers upon the children unto the third and fourth generation of them that hate me;

6 And showing mercy unto thousands of them that love me, and keep my commandments.

7 you shall not take the name of the Becoming-One your God for falsehood; for the Becoming-One will not hold him guiltless that takes his name for falsehood [in vain]

8 Remember the Sabbath day, to keep it holy.

9 Six days shall you labor, and do all your work:

10 But the seventh day is the Sabbath of the Becoming-One your God: in it you shall not do any work, you, nor your son, nor your daughter, your manservant, nor your maidservant, nor your animals, nor your stranger that is within your gates:

11 For in six days the Becoming-One made the heavens and earth, the sea, and all that in them is, and shall rest the seventh day: therefore the Becoming-One blessed the Sabbath day, and hallowed it.

12 Honor your father and your mother: that your days may be long upon the land which the Becoming-One your God gives you.

13 you shall not kill [murder].

14 you shall not commit adultery.

15 you shall not steal.

16 you shall not bear false witness against your neighbor.

17 you shall not covet your neighbor's house, you shall not covet your neighbor's wife, nor his manservant, nor his maidservant, nor his ox, nor his donkey, nor any thing that is your neighbor's.

18 And all the people saw the thunderings, and the lightning, and the noise of the trumpet, and the mountain smoking: and when the people saw it, they removed, and stood afar off.

19 And they said unto Moses, Speak you with us, and we will hear: but let not God speak with us, lest we die.

20 And Moses said unto the people, Fear not: for God is come to prove you, and that his fear may be before your faces, that you sin not.

21 And the people stood afar off, and Moses drew near unto the thick darkness where God was.

22 And the Becoming-One said unto Moses, Thus you shall say unto the children of Israel, you have seen that I have talked with you from the heavens.

23 you shall not make with me gods of silver, neither shall you make unto you gods of gold.

24 An altar of earth you shall make unto me, and shall sacrifice thereon your burnt offerings, and your peace offerings, your sheep, and your oxen: in all places where I record my name I will come unto you, and I will bless you.

25 And if you will make me an altar of stone, you shall not build it of hewn stone: for if you lift up your tool upon it, you have polluted it.

26 Neither shall you go up by steps unto mine altar, that your nakedness be not discovered thereon.

Ex 21:1 Now **these are the judgments** which you shall set before them.

2 If you buy a Hebrew servant, six years he shall serve: and in the seventh he shall go out free for nothing.

3 If he came in by himself, he shall go out by himself: if he were married, then his wife shall go out with him.

4 If his master have given him a wife, and she have born him sons or daughters; the wife and her children shall be her master's, and he shall go out by himself.

5 And if the servant shall plainly say, I love my master, my wife, and my children; I will not go out free:

6 Then his master shall bring him unto God; he shall also bring him to the door, or unto the door post; and his master shall bore his ear through with an awl; and he shall serve him for olam.

7 And if a man sell his daughter to be a maidservant, she shall not go out as the menservants do.

8 If she please not her master, who has betrothed her to himself, then shall he let her be redeemed: to sell her unto a strange nation he shall have no power, seeing he has dealt deceitfully with her.

9 And if he have betrothed her unto his son, he shall deal with her after the manner of daughters.

10 If he take him another wife; her food, her raiment, and her duty of marriage, shall he not diminish.

11 And if he do not these three unto her, then shall she go out free without money.

12 He that smites a man, so that he die, in dying he shall be put to death.

13 And if a man lie not in wait, but God deliver him into his hand; then I will appoint you a place to which he shall flee.

14 But if a man come presumptuously upon his neighbor, to slay him with guile; you shall take him from mine altar, that he may die.

15 And he that smites his father, or his mother, in dying he shall be put to death.

16 And he that steals a man, and sells him, or if he be found in his hand, in dying he shall be put to death.

17 And he that curses his father, or his mother, shall surely be put to death.

18 And if men strive together, and one smite another with a stone, or with his fist, and he die not, but keeps his bed:

19 If he rise again, and walk abroad upon his staff, then shall clear he that smote him: only he shall pay for the loss of his time, and shall cause him to be thoroughly healed.

20 And if a man smite his servant, or his maid, with a rod, and he die under his hand; he shall be surely punished.

21 Notwithstanding, if he continue two days, he shall not be punished: for he is his money.

22 If men strive, and hurt a woman with child, so that her fruit depart from her, and yet no mischief follow: he shall be surely punished, according as the

woman's husband will lay upon him; and he shall pay as the judges determine.

23 And if any mischief follow, then you shall give soul for soul,

24 Eye for eye, tooth for tooth, hand for hand, foot for foot,

25 Burning for burning, wound for wound, stripe for stripe.

26 And if a man smite the eye of his servant, or the eye of his maid, that it perish; he shall let him go free for his eye's sake.

27 And if he smite out his manservant's tooth, or his maidservant's tooth; he shall let him go free for his tooth's sake.

28 If an ox gore a man or a woman, that they die: then the ox shall be surely stoned, and his flesh shall not be eaten; but the owner of the ox shall be clear.

29 But if the ox were wont to push with his horn yesterday and the third day, and it has been testified to his owner, and he has not kept him in, but that he has killed a man or a woman; the ox shall be stoned, and his owner also shall be put to death.

30 If there be laid on him a sum of money, then he shall give for the ransom of his soul whatsoever is laid upon him.

31 Whether he have gored a son, or have gored a daughter, according to this judgment shall it be done unto him.

32 If the ox shall push a manservant or a maidservant; he shall give unto their master thirty shekels of silver, and the ox shall be stoned.

33 And if a man shall open a pit, or if a man shall dig a pit, and not cover it, and an ox or an donkey fall therein;

34 The owner of the pit shall make it good, and give money unto the owner of them; and the dead beast shall be his.

35 And if one man's ox hurt another's, that he die; then they shall sell the live ox, and divide the money of it; and the dead ox also they shall divide.

36 Or if it be known that the ox has used to push yesterday and the third day, and his owner has not kept him in; he shall surely pay ox for ox; and the dead shall be his own.

Ex 22:1 If a man shall steal an ox, or a sheep, and kill it, or sell it; he shall restore five oxen for an ox, and four sheep for a sheep.

2 If a thief be found breaking up, and be struck that he die, there shall no blood be shed for him.

3 If the sun be risen upon him, there shall be blood shed for him; he thief should make full restitution; if he have nothing, then he shall be sold for his theft.

4 If the theft be certainly found in his hand alive, whether it be ox, or donkey, or sheep; he shall restore double.

5 If a man shall cause a field or vineyard to be eaten, and shall put in his beast, and shall feed in another man's field; of the best of his own field, and of the best of his own vineyard, shall he make restitution.

6 If fire break out, and catch in thorns, so that the stacks of grain, or the standing grain, or the field, be consumed therewith; he that kindled the fire shall surely make restitution.

7 If a man shall deliver unto his neighbor money or stuff to keep, and it be stolen out of the man's house; if the thief be found, let him pay double.

8 If the thief be not found, then the master of the house shall be brought unto God, to see whether he have put his hand unto his neighbor's goods.

9 For all manner of trespass, whether it be for ox, for donkey, for sheep, for raiment, or for any manner of lost thing, which another challenges to be his, the cause of both parties shall come before God; and whom the judges shall condemn, he shall pay double unto his neighbor.

10 If a man deliver unto his neighbor an donkey, or an ox, or a sheep, or any beast, to keep; and it die, or be hurt, or driven away, no man seeing it:

11 Then shall an oath of the Becoming-One be between them both, that he has not put his hand unto his neighbor's goods; and the owner of it shall accept thereof, and he shall not make it good.

12 And if it be stolen from him, he shall make restitution unto the owner thereof.

13 If it be torn in pieces, then let him bring it for witness, and he shall not make good that which was torn.

14 And if a man borrow of his neighbor, and it be hurt, or die, the owner thereof being not with it, he shall surely make it good.

15 But if the owner thereof be with it, he shall not make it good: if it be a hired thing, it came for his hire.

16 And if a man entice a maid that is not betrothed, and lie with her, he shall surely endow her to be his wife.

17 If her father utterly refuse to give her unto him, he shall pay money according to the dowry of virgins.

18 you shall not permit a witch to live.

19 Whosoever lies with a beast shall surely be put to death.

20 He that sacrifices unto any god, save unto the Becoming-One only, he shall be utterly destroyed.

21 you shall neither vex a stranger, nor oppress him: for you were strangers in the land of Egypt.

22 you shall not afflict any widow, or fatherless child.

23 If you afflict them in any way, and they cry at all unto me, I will surely hear their cry;

24 And my wrath shall wax hot, and I will kill you with the sword; and your wives shall be widows, and your children fatherless.

25 If you lend money to any of my people with you that is poor, you shall not be to him as an usurer, neither shall you lay upon him usury.

26 If you at all take your neighbor's raiment to pledge, you shall deliver it unto him by that the sun goes down:

27 For that is his covering only, it is his raiment for his skin: wherein shall he sleep? and it shall come to pass, when he cries unto me, that I will hear; for I am gracious.

28 you shall not revile the gods, nor curse the ruler of your people.

29 you shall not delay to offer the first of your ripe fruits, and of your liquors: the firstborn of your sons shall you give unto me.

30 Likewise shall you do with your oxen, and with your sheep: seven days it shall be with his dam; on the eighth day you shall give it me.

31 And you shall be holy men unto me: neither shall you eat any flesh that is torn of beasts in the field; you shall cast it to the dogs.

Ex 23:1 you shall not raise a false report: put not your hand with the wicked to be an unrighteous witness.

2 you shall not follow a multitude to do evil; neither shall you speak in a law case to follow a crowd to pervert judgment:

3 Neither shall you partial to a poor man in his law case.

4 If you meet your enemy's ox or his donkey going astray, you shall surely bring it back to him again.

5 If you see the donkey of him that hates you lying under his burden, and would forbear to help him, you shall surely help with him.

6 you shall not pervert the judgment of your poor in his cause.

7 Keep you far from a false matter; and the innocent and righteous slay you not: for I will not justify the wicked.

8 And you shall take no gift: for the gift blinds the wise, and perverts the words of the righteous.

9 Also you shall not oppress a stranger: for you know the soul of a stranger, seeing you were strangers in the land of Egypt.

10 And six years you shall sow your land, and shall gather in the fruits thereof:

11 But the seventh year you shall let it rest and lie still; that the poor of your people may eat: and what they leave the beasts of the field shall eat. In like manner you shall deal with your vineyard, and with your oliveyard.

12 Six days you shall do your work, and on the seventh day you shall rest: that your ox and your donkey may rest, and the son of your handmaid, and the stranger, may be refreshed.

13 And in all things that I have said unto you be circumspect: and make no mention of the name of other gods, neither let it be heard out of your mouth.

14 Three times you shall keep a feast unto me in the year.

15 you shall keep the feast of unleavened bread: you shall eat unleavened bread seven days, as I commanded you, in the set time[31] of the month Abib; for in it you came out from Egypt: and none shall appear before me empty:

16 And the feast of harvest, the firstfruits of your labors, which you have sown in the field: and the feast of ingathering, in the produce of the year, when you have gathered in your labors out of the field.

17 Three times in the year all your males shall appear before the Lord Becoming-One.

18 you shall not offer the blood of my sacrifice with leavened bread; neither shall the fat of my feast remain until the morning.

19 The first of the firstfruits of your land you shall bring into the house of the Becoming-One your God. you shall not seethe a kid in his mother's milk.

20 Behold, I send an Angel before you, to keep you in the way, and to bring you into the place which I have prepared.

21 Beware of him, and obey his voice, provoke him not; for he will not pardon your transgressions: for my name is in him.

22 But if you shall indeed obey his voice, and do all that I speak; then I will be an enemy unto your enemies, and an adversary unto your adversaries.

23 For mine Angel shall go before you, and bring you in unto the Amorites, and the Hittites, and the Perizzites, and the Canaanites, the Hivites, and the Jebusites: and I will cut them off.

24 you shall not bow down to their gods, nor serve them, nor do after their works: but you shall utterly overthrow them, and completely break down their images.

25 And you shall serve the Becoming-One your God, and He shall bless your bread, and your water; and I will take sickness away from the midst of you.

26 There shall nothing cast their young, nor be barren, in your land: the number of your days I will fulfil.

27 I will send my fear before you, and will destroy all the people to whom you shall come, and I will make all your enemies turn their backs unto you.

28 And I will send hornets before you, which shall drive out the Hivite, the Canaanite, and the Hittite, from before you.

29 I will not drive them out from before you in one year; lest the land become desolate, and the beast of the field multiply against you.

30 By little and little I will drive them out from before you, until you be increased, and inherit the land.

31 And I will set your bounds from the boundary sea even unto the sea of the Philistines, and from the desert unto the river: for I will deliver the inhabitants of the land into your hand; and you shall drive them out before you.

32 you shall make no covenant with them, nor with their gods.

33 They shall not dwell in your land, lest they make you sin against me: for if you serve their gods, it will surely be a snare unto you.

Ex 24:1 And he said unto Moses, Come up unto the Becoming-One, you, and Aaron, Nadab, and Abihu, and seventy of the elders of Israel; and worship you afar off.

2 And Moses alone shall come near the Becoming-One: but they shall not come near; neither shall the people go up with him.

3 And Moses came and told the people all the words of the Becoming-One, and all the judgments: and all the people answered with one voice, and said, All the words which the Becoming-One has said will we do.

4 And Moses wrote all the words of the Becoming-One, and rose up early in the morning, and built an altar under the hill, and twelve pillars, according to the twelve tribes of Israel.

5 And he sent young men of the children of Israel, which offered burnt offerings, and sacrificed peace offerings of oxen unto the Becoming-One.

---

[31] Appointed time or festival

6 And Moses took half of the blood, and put it in basins; and half of the blood he sprinkled on the altar.

7 And he took the book of the covenant, and read in the audience of the people: and they said, All that the Becoming-One has said will we do, and be obedient.

8 And Moses took the blood, and sprinkled it on the people, and said, Behold the blood of the covenant, which the Becoming-One has made with you concerning all these words.

9 Then went up Moses, and Aaron, Nadab, and Abihu, and seventy of the elders of Israel:

10 And they saw God of Israel: and there was under his feet as it were a paved work of a sapphire stone, and as it were the body of the heavens in his clearness.

11 And upon the nobles of the children of Israel he laid not his hand: also they saw God, and did eat and drink.

12 And the Becoming-One said unto Moses, Come up to me into the mount, and be there: and I will give you tables of stone, and a law, and commandments which I have written; that you may teach them.

13 And Moses rose up, and his minister Joshua: and Moses went up into the mount of God.

14 And he said unto the elders, Tarry you here for us, until we come again unto you: and, behold, Aaron and Hur are with you: if any man have any matters to do, let him come unto them.

15 And Moses went up into the mount, and a cloud covered the mount.

16 And the glory of the Becoming-One abode upon mount Sinai, and the cloud covered it six days: and the seventh day he called unto Moses out of the midst of the cloud.

17 And the sight of the glory of the Becoming-One was like devouring fire on the top of the mount in the eyes of the children of Israel.

18 And Moses went into the midst of the cloud, and got him up into the mount: and Moses was in the mount forty days and forty nights.

Ex 25:1 And the Becoming-One spoke unto Moses, saying,

2 Speak unto the children of Israel, that they bring me an offering: of every man that gives it willingly with his heart you shall take my offering.

3 And this is the offering which you shall take of them; gold, and silver, and brass,

4 And blue, and purple, and scarlet, and fine linen, and goats' hair,

5 And rams' skins dyed red, and badgers' skins, and shittim wood,

6 Oil for the light, spices for anointing oil, and for sweet incense,

7 Onyx stones, and stones to be set in the ephod, and in the breastplate.

8 **And let them make me a sanctuary; that I may dwell among them.**

9 **According to all that I show you, after the pattern of the tabernacle, and the pattern of all the instruments thereof, even so shall you make it.**

10 And they shall make an **ark of shittim wood**: two cubits and a half shall be the length thereof, and a cubit and a half the breadth thereof, and a cubit and a half the height thereof.

11 And you shall **overlay it with pure gold**, within and without shall you overlay it, and shall make upon it a crown of gold round about.

12 And you shall cast four rings of gold for it, and put them in the four corners thereof; and two rings shall be in the one side of it, and two rings in the other side of it.

13 And you shall make staves of shittim wood, and overlay them with gold.

14 And you shall put the staves into the rings by the sides of the ark, that the ark may be borne with them.

15 The staves shall be in the rings of the ark: they shall not be taken from it.

16 And you shall put into the ark the testimony which I shall give you.

17 **And you shall make a mercy seat of pure gold**: two cubits and a half shall be the length thereof, and a cubit and a half the breadth thereof.

18 And **you shall make two cherubs of gold**, of beaten work shall you make them, in the two ends of the mercy seat.

19 And make one cherub on the one end, and the other cherub on the other end: even of the mercy seat shall you make the cherubs on the two ends thereof.

20 And the cherubs shall stretch forth their wings on high, covering the mercy seat with their wings, and **their faces shall look one to another**; toward the mercy seat shall the faces of the cherubs be.[32]

21 **And you shall put the mercy seat above upon the ark; and in the ark you shall put the testimony that I shall give you.**

22 **And there I will meet with you, and I will commune with you from above the mercy seat, from between the two cherubs** which are upon the ark of the testimony, of all things which I will give you in commandment unto the children of Israel.

23 you shall also make a table of shittim wood: two cubits shall be the length thereof, and a cubit the breadth thereof, and a cubit and a half the height thereof.

24 And you shall overlay it with pure gold, and make thereto a crown of gold round about.

25 And you shall make unto it a border of a hand breadth round about, and you shall make a golden crown to the border thereof round about.

26 And you shall make for it four rings of gold, and put the rings in the four corners that are on the four feet thereof.

27 Over against the border shall the rings be for places of the staves to bear the table.

28 And you shall make the staves of shittim wood, and overlay them with gold, that the table may be borne with them.

29 And you shall make the dishes thereof, and spoons thereof, and covers thereof, and bowls thereof, to cover withal: of pure gold shall you make them.

30 And you shall set upon the table showbread of the presence before me always.

31 And you shall make a candlestick of pure gold: of beaten work shall the candlestick be made: his

---

[32] See GP8

shaft, and his branches, his bowls, his gourds, and his flowers, shall be of the same.

32 And six branches shall come out of the sides of it; three branches of the candlestick out of the one side, and three branches of the candlestick out of the other side:

33 Three bowls made like unto almonds, with a knop and a flower in one branch; and three bowls made like almonds in the other branch, with a knop and a flower: so in the six branches that come out of the candlestick.

34 And in the candlestick shall be four bowls made like unto almonds, with their gourds and their flowers.

35 And there shall be a knop under two branches of the same, and a knop under two branches of the same, and a knop under two branches of the same, according to the six branches that proceed out of the candlestick.

36 Their gourds and their branches shall be of the same: all it shall be one beaten work of pure gold.

37 And you shall make the seven lamps thereof: and they shall light the lamps thereof, that they may give light over against it.

38 And the tongs thereof, and the snuffdishes thereof, shall be of pure gold.

39 Of a talent of pure gold shall he make it, with all these vessels.

40 And look that you make them after their pattern, which was showed you in the mount.

Ex 26:1 Moreover you shall make the tabernacle with ten curtains of fine twined linen, and blue, and purple, and scarlet: with cherubs of cunning work shall you make them.

2 The length of one curtain shall be eight and twenty cubits, and the breadth of one curtain four cubits: and every one of the curtains shall have one measure.

3 The five curtains shall be coupled together one to another; and other five curtains shall be coupled one to another.

4 And you shall make loops of blue upon the edge of the one curtain at the end in the coupling; and likewise shall you make in the uttermost edge of another curtain, in the coupling of the second.

5 Fifty loops shall you make in the one curtain, and fifty loops shall you make in the edge of the curtain that is in the coupling of the second; that the loops may take hold one of another.

6 And you shall make fifty taches of gold, and couple the curtains together with the taches: and it shall be one tabernacle.

7 And you shall make curtains of goats' hair to be a covering upon the tabernacle: eleven curtains shall you make.

8 The length of one curtain shall be thirty cubits, and the breadth of one curtain four cubits: and the eleven curtains shall be all of one measure.

9 And you shall couple five curtains by themselves, and six curtains by themselves, and shall double the sixth curtain in the forefront of the tabernacle.

10 And you shall make fifty loops on the edge of the one curtain that is outmost in the coupling, and fifty loops in the edge of the curtain which couples the second.

11 And you shall make fifty taches of brass, and put the taches into the loops, and couple the tent together, that it may be one.

12 And the remnant that remains of the curtains of the tent, the half curtain that remains, shall hang over the backside of the tabernacle.

13 And a cubit on the one side, and a cubit on the other side of that which remains in the length of the curtains of the tent, it shall hang over the sides of the tabernacle on this side and on that side, to cover it.

14 And you shall make a covering for the tent of rams' skins dyed red, and a covering above of badgers' skins.

15 And you shall make boards for the tabernacle of shittim wood standing up.

16 Ten cubits shall be the length of a board, and a cubit and a half shall be the breadth of one board.

17 Two tenons shall there be in one board, set in order one against another: thus shall you make for all the boards of the tabernacle.

18 And you shall make the boards for the tabernacle, twenty boards on the south side southward.

19 And you shall make forty sockets of silver under the twenty boards; two sockets under one board for his two tenons, and two sockets under another board for his two tenons.

20 And for the second side of the tabernacle on the north side there shall be twenty boards:

21 And their forty sockets of silver; two sockets under one board, and two sockets under another board.

22 And for the sides of the tabernacle westward you shall make six boards.

23 And two boards shall you make for the corners of the tabernacle in the two sides.

24 And they shall be coupled together beneath, and they shall be coupled together above the head of it unto one ring: thus shall it be for them both; they shall be for the two corners.

25 And they shall be eight boards, and their sockets of silver, sixteen sockets; two sockets under one board, and two sockets under another board.

26 And you shall make bars of shittim wood; five for the boards of the one side of the tabernacle,

27 And five bars for the boards of the other side of the tabernacle, and five bars for the boards of the side of the tabernacle, for the two sides westward.

28 And the middle bar in the midst of the boards shall reach from end to end.

29 And you shall overlay the boards with gold, and make their rings of gold for places for the bars: and you shall overlay the bars with gold.

30 And you shall rear up the tabernacle according to the fashion thereof which was showed you in the mount.

31 And you shall make a veil of blue, and purple, and scarlet, and fine twined linen of skilled work: with cherubs shall it be made:

32 And you shall hang it upon four pillars of shittim wood overlaid with gold: their hooks shall be of gold, upon the four sockets of silver.

33 And you shall hang up the veil under the taches, that you may bring in there within the veil the

ark of the testimony: and the veil shall divide unto you between the holy place and the most holy.

34 And you shall put the mercy seat upon the ark of the testimony in the most holy place.

35 And you shall set the table outside the veil, and the candlestick over against the table on the side of the tabernacle toward the south: and you shall put the table on the north side.

36 And you shall make a hanging for the door of the tent, of blue, and purple, and scarlet, and fine twined linen, worked with needlework.

37 And you shall make for the hanging five pillars of shittim wood, and overlay them with gold, and their hooks shall be of gold: and you shall cast five sockets of brass for them.

Ex 27:1 And you shall make an altar of shittim wood, five cubits long, and five cubits broad; the altar shall be foursquare: and the height thereof shall be three cubits.

2 And you shall make the horns of it upon the four corners thereof: his horns shall be of the same: and you shall overlay it with brass.

3 And you shall make his pans to receive his ashes, and his shovels, and his basins, and his fleshhooks, and his firepans: all the vessels thereof you shall make of brass.

4 And you shall make for it a grate of network of brass; and upon the net shall you make four brazen rings in the four corners thereof.

5 And you shall put it under the rim of the altar beneath, that the net may be even to the midst of the altar.

6 And you shall make staves for the altar, staves of shittim wood, and overlay them with brass.

7 And the staves shall be put into the rings, and the staves shall be upon the two sides of the altar, to bear it.

8 Hollow with boards shall you make it: as it was showed you in the mount, so shall they make it.

9 And you shall make the court of the tabernacle: for the south side southward there shall be hangings for the court of fine twined linen of a hundred cubits long for one side:

10 And the twenty pillars thereof and their twenty sockets shall be of brass; the hooks of the pillars and their bands shall be of silver.

11 And likewise for the north side in length there shall be hangings of a hundred cubits long, and his twenty pillars and their twenty sockets of brass; the hooks of the pillars and their bands of silver.

12 And for the breadth of the court on the west side shall be hangings of fifty cubits: their pillars ten, and their sockets ten.

13 And the breadth of the court on the east side eastward shall be fifty cubits.

14 The hangings of one side of the gate shall be fifteen cubits: their pillars three, and their sockets three.

15 And on the other side shall be hangings fifteen cubits: their pillars three, and their sockets three.

16 And for the gate of the court shall be a hanging of twenty cubits, of blue, and purple, and scarlet, and fine twined linen, worked with needlework: and their pillars shall be four, and their sockets four.

17 All the pillars round about the court shall be banded with silver; their hooks shall be of silver, and their sockets of brass.

18 The length of the court shall be a hundred cubits, and the breadth fifty every where, and the height five cubits of fine twined linen, and their sockets of brass.

19 All the vessels of the tabernacle in all the service thereof, and all the pins thereof, and all the pins of the court, shall be of brass.

20 And you shall command the children of Israel, that they bring you pure oil olive beaten for the light, to cause the lamp to burn always.

21 In the tabernacle of the set time[33] outside the veil, which is before the testimony, Aaron and his sons shall order it from evening to morning before the Becoming-One: it shall be a statute for olam unto their generations on the behalf of the children of Israel.

Ex 28:1 And take you unto you Aaron your brother, and his sons with him, from among the children of Israel, that he may minister unto me in the priest's office, even Aaron, Nadab and Abihu, Eleazar and Ithamar, Aaron's sons.

2 And you shall make holy garments for Aaron your brother for glory and for beauty.

3 And you shall speak unto all that are wise hearted, whom I have filled with the spirit of wisdom, that they may make Aaron's garments to consecrate him, that he may minister unto me in the priest's office.

4 And these are the garments which they shall make; a breastplate, and an ephod, and a robe, and a broidered coat, a turban, and a girdle: and they shall make holy garments for Aaron your brother, and his sons, that he may minister unto me in the priest's office.

5 And they shall take gold, and blue, and purple, and scarlet, and fine linen.

6 And they shall make the ephod of gold, of blue, and of purple, of scarlet, and fine twined linen, with skilled work.

7 It shall have the two shoulder pieces thereof joined at the two edges thereof; and so it shall be joined together.

8 And the curious girdle of the ephod, which is upon it, shall be of the same, according to the work thereof; even of gold, of blue, and purple, and scarlet, and fine twined linen.

9 And you shall take two onyx stones, and grave on them the names of the children of Israel:

10 Six of their names on one stone, and the other six names of the rest on the other stone, according to their birth.

11 With the work of an engraver in stone, like the engravings of a signet, shall you engrave the two stones with the names of the children of Israel: you shall make them to be set in ouches of gold.

12 And you shall put the two stones upon the shoulders of the ephod for stones of memorial unto the children of Israel: and Aaron shall bear their

---

[33] Appointed time or festival

names before the Becoming-One upon his two shoulders for a memorial.

13 And you shall make settings of gold;

14 And two chains of pure gold at the ends; of braided work shall you make them, and fasten the braided chains to the settings.

15 And you shall make the breastplate of judgment with skilled work; after the work of the ephod you shall make it; of gold, of blue, and of purple, and of scarlet, and of fine twined linen, shall you make it.

16 Foursquare it shall be being doubled; a span shall be the length thereof, and a span shall be the breadth thereof.

17 And you shall set in it settings of stones, even four rows of stones: the first row shall be a sardius, a topaz, and a carbuncle: this shall be the first row.

18 And the second row shall be an emerald, a sapphire, and a diamond.

19 And the third row a ligure, an agate, and an amethyst.

20 And the fourth row a beryl, and an onyx, and a jasper: they shall be set in gold in their enclosings.

21 And the stones shall be with the names of the children of Israel, twelve, according to their names, like the engravings of a signet; every one with his name shall they be according to the twelve tribes.

22 And you shall make upon the breastplate chains at the ends of braided work of pure gold.

23 And you shall make upon the breastplate two rings of gold, and shall put the two rings on the two ends of the breastplate.

24 And you shall put the two braided chains of gold in the two rings which are on the ends of the breastplate.

25 And the other two ends of the two braided chains you shall fasten in the two settings, and put them on the shoulder pieces of the ephod before it.

26 And you shall make two rings of gold, and you shall put them upon the two ends of the breastplate in the border thereof, which is in the side of the ephod inward.

27 And two other rings of gold you shall make, and shall put them on the two sides of the ephod underneath, toward the forepart thereof, over against the other coupling thereof, above the curious girdle of the ephod.

28 And they shall bind the breastplate by the rings thereof unto the rings of the ephod with a lace of blue, that it may be above the curious girdle of the ephod, and that the breastplate be not loosened from the ephod.

29 And Aaron shall bear the names of the children of Israel in the breastplate of judgment upon his heart, when he goes in unto the holy place, for a memorial before the Becoming-One continually.

30 And you shall put in the breastplate of judgment the Urim and the Thummim; and they shall be upon Aaron's heart, when he goes in before the Becoming-One: and Aaron shall bear the judgment of the children of Israel upon his heart before the Becoming-One continually.

31 And you shall make the robe of the ephod all of blue.

32 And there shall be a hole in the top of it, in the midst thereof: it shall have a binding of woven work round about the opening of it, as it were the opening of a collar that it not tear.

33 And beneath upon the hem of it you shall make pomegranates of blue, and of purple, and of scarlet, round about the hem thereof; and bells of gold between them round about:

34 A golden bell and a pomegranate, a golden bell and a pomegranate, upon the hem of the robe round about.

35 And it shall be upon Aaron to minister: and his sound shall be heard when he goes in unto the holy place before the Becoming-One, and when he comes out, that he die not.

36 And you shall make a plate of pure gold, and grave upon it, like the engravings of a signet, Holiness to the Becoming-One.

37 And you shall put it on a blue lace, that it may be upon the turban; upon the forefront of the turban it shall be.

38 And it shall be upon Aaron's forehead, that Aaron may bear the iniquity of the holy things, which the children of Israel shall hallow in all their holy gifts; and it shall be always upon his forehead, that they may be accepted before the Becoming-One.

39 And you shall embroider the coat of fine linen, and you shall make the turban of fine linen, and you shall make the girdle of needlework.

40 And for Aaron's sons you shall make coats, and you shall make for them girdles, and caps shall you make for them, for glory and for beauty.

41 And you shall put them upon Aaron your brother, and his sons with him; and shall anoint them, and consecrate them, and sanctify them, that they may minister unto me in the priest's office.

42 And you shall make them linen breeches to cover their nakedness; from the loins even unto the thighs they shall reach:

43 And they shall be upon Aaron, and upon his sons, when they come in unto the tabernacle of the set time,[34] or when they come near unto the altar to minister in the holy place; that they bear not iniquity, and die: it shall be a statute for olam unto him and his seed after him.

Ex 29:1 And this is the thing that you shall do unto them to hallow them, to minister unto me in the priest's office: Take one young bullock, and two rams without blemish,

2 And unleavened bread, and cakes unleavened tempered with oil, and wafers unleavened anointed with oil: of wheaten flour shall you make them.

3 And you shall put them into one basket, and bring them in the basket, with the bullock and the two rams.

4 And Aaron and his sons you shall bring unto the door of the tabernacle of the set time,[35] and shall wash them with water.

5 And you shall take the garments, and put upon Aaron the coat, and the robe of the ephod, and the ephod, and the breastplate, and gird him with the curious girdle of the ephod:

---

[34] Appointed time or festival
[35] Appointed time or festival

6 And you shall put the turban upon his head, and put the holy crown upon the turban.

7 Then shall you take the anointing oil, and pour it upon his head, and anoint him.

8 And you shall bring his sons, and put coats upon them.

9 And you shall gird them with girdles, Aaron and his sons, and put the caps on them: and the priest's office shall be theirs for a statute of olam, and you shall consecrate Aaron and his sons.

10 And you shall cause a bullock to be brought before the tabernacle of the set time:[36] and Aaron and his sons shall put their hands upon the head of the bullock.

11 And you shall kill the bullock before the Becoming-One, by the door of the tabernacle of the set time.[37]

12 And you shall take of the blood of the bullock, and put it upon the horns of the altar with your finger, and pour all the blood beside the bottom of the altar.

13 And you shall take all the fat that covers the inwards, and the covering of the liver, and the two kidneys, and the fat that is upon them, and burn them upon the altar.

14 But the flesh of the bullock, and his skin, and his dung, shall you burn with fire outside the camp: it is a sin offering.

15 you shall also take one ram; and Aaron and his sons shall put their hands upon the head of the ram.

16 And you shall slay the ram, and you shall take his blood, and sprinkle it round about upon the altar.

17 And you shall cut the ram in pieces, and wash the inwards of him, and his legs, and put them unto his pieces, and unto his head.

18 And you shall burn the whole ram upon the altar: it is a burnt offering unto the Becoming-One: it is a sweet aroma, an offering made by fire unto the Becoming-One.

19 And you shall take the other ram; and Aaron and his sons shall put their hands upon the head of the ram.

20 Then shall you kill the ram, and take of his blood, and put it upon the tip of the right ear of Aaron, and upon the tip of the right ear of his sons, and upon the thumb of their right hand, and upon the great toe of their right foot, and sprinkle the blood upon the altar round about.

21 And you shall take of the blood that is upon the altar, and of the anointing oil, and sprinkle it upon Aaron, and upon his garments, and upon his sons, and upon the garments of his sons with him: and he shall be hallowed, and his garments, and his sons, and his sons' garments with him.

22 Also you shall take of the ram the fat and the rump, and the fat that covers the inwards, and the caul above the liver, and the two kidneys, and the fat that is upon them, and the right shoulder; for it is a ram of consecration:

23 And one loaf of bread, and one cake of oiled bread, and one wafer out of the basket of the unleavened bread that is before the Becoming-One: 24 And you shall put all in the hands of Aaron, and in the hands of his sons; and shall wave them for a wave offering before the Becoming-One.

25 And you shall receive them of their hands, and burn them upon the altar for a burnt offering, for a sweet aroma before the Becoming-One: it is an offering made by fire unto the Becoming-One.

26 And you shall take the breast of the ram of Aaron's consecration, and wave it for a wave offering before the Becoming-One: and it shall be your part.

27 And you shall sanctify the breast of the wave offering, and the shoulder of the heave offering, which is waved, and which is heaved up, of the ram of the consecration, even of that which is for Aaron, and of that which is for his sons:

28 And it shall be Aaron's and his sons' by a statute for olam from the children of Israel: for it is a heave offering: and it shall be a heave offering from the children of Israel of the sacrifice of their peace offerings, even their heave offering unto the Becoming-One.

29 And the holy garments of Aaron shall be his sons' after him, to be anointed therein, and to be consecrated in them.

30 And that son that is priest in his stead shall put them on seven days, when he comes into the tabernacle of the set time[38] to minister in the holy place.

31 And you shall take the ram of the consecration, and seethe his flesh in the holy place.

32 And Aaron and his sons shall eat the flesh of the ram, and the bread that is in the basket, by the door of the tabernacle of the set time.[39]

33 And they shall eat those things wherewith the atonement was made, to consecrate and to sanctify them: but a stranger shall not eat thereof, because they are holy.

34 And if of the flesh of the consecrations, or of the bread, remain unto the morning, then you shall burn the remainder with fire: it shall not be eaten, because it is holy.

35 And thus shall you do unto Aaron, and to his sons, according to all things which I have commanded you: seven days shall you consecrate them.

36 And you shall offer every day a bullock for a sin offering for atonement: and you shall cleanse the altar, when you have made an atonement for it, and you shall anoint it, to sanctify it.

37 Seven days you shall make an atonement for the altar, and sanctify it; and it shall be an altar most holy: whatsoever touches the altar shall be holy.

38 Now this is that which you shall offer upon the altar; two lambs of the first year day by day continually.

39 The one lamb you shall offer in the morning; and the other lamb you shall offer between the evenings:

40 And with the one lamb a tenth deal of flour mingled with the fourth part of a hin of beaten oil; and the fourth part of a hin of wine for a drink offering.

41 And the other lamb you shall offer between the evenings, and shall do thereto according to the food offering of the morning, and according to the drink

---

[36] Appointed time or festival
[37] Appointed time or festival
[38] Appointed time or festival
[39] Appointed time or festival

offering thereof, for a sweet aroma, an offering made by fire unto the Becoming-One.

42 This shall be a continual burnt offering throughout your generations at the door of the tabernacle of the set time[40] before the Becoming-One: where I will meet you, to speak there unto you.

43 And there I will meet with the children of Israel, and the tabernacle shall be sanctified by my glory.

44 And I will sanctify the tabernacle of the set time,[41] and the altar: I will sanctify also both Aaron and his sons, to minister to me in the priest's office.

45 And I will dwell among the children of Israel, and will be their God.

46 And they shall know that I am the Becoming-One their God, that brought them forth out of the land of Egypt, that I may dwell among them: I am the Becoming-One their God.

Ex 30:1 And you shall make an altar to burn incense upon: of shittim wood shall you make it.

2 A cubit shall be the length thereof, and a cubit the breadth thereof; foursquare shall it be: and two cubits shall be the height thereof: the horns thereof shall be of the same.

3 And you shall overlay it with pure gold, the top thereof, and the sides thereof round about, and the horns thereof; and you shall make unto it a crown of gold round about.

4 And two golden rings shall you make to it under the crown of it, by the two corners thereof, upon the two sides of it shall you make it; and they shall be for places for the staves to bear it withal.

5 And you shall make the staves of shittim wood, and overlay them with gold.

6 And you shall put it before the veil that is by the ark of the testimony, before the mercy seat that is over the testimony, where I will meet with you.

7 And Aaron shall burn thereon sweet incense every morning: when he dresses the lamps, he shall burn incense upon it.

8 And when Aaron lights the lamps between the evenings, he shall burn incense upon it, a perpetual incense before the Becoming-One throughout your generations.

9 you shall offer no strange incense thereon, nor burnt sacrifice, nor food offering; neither shall you pour drink offering thereon.

10 And Aaron shall make an atonement upon the horns of it once in a year with the blood of the sin offering of atonements: once in the year shall he make atonement upon it throughout your generations: it is most holy unto the Becoming-One.

11 And the Becoming-One spoke unto Moses, saying,

12 When you take the sum of the children of Israel after their number, then shall they give every man a ransom for his soul unto the Becoming-One, when you number them; that there be no plague among them, when you number them.

13 This they shall give, every one that passes among them that are numbered, half a shekel after the shekel of the sanctuary: a shekel is twenty gerahs: a half shekel shall be the offering of the Becoming-One.

14 Every one that passes among them that are numbered, from a son of twenty years and above, shall give an offering unto the Becoming-One.

15 The rich shall not give more, and the poor shall not give less than half a shekel, when they give an offering unto the Becoming-One, to make an atonement for your souls.

16 And you shall take the atonement money of the children of Israel, and shall appoint it for the service of the tabernacle of the set time;[42] that it may be a memorial unto the children of Israel before the Becoming-One, to make an atonement for your souls.

17 And the Becoming-One spoke unto Moses, saying,

18 you shall also make a laver of brass, and his foot also of brass, to wash withal: and you shall put it between the tabernacle of the set time[43] and the altar, and you shall put water therein.

19 For Aaron and his sons shall wash their hands and their feet thereat:

20 When they go into the tabernacle of the set time,[44] they shall wash with water, that they die not; or when they come near to the altar to minister, to burn offering made by fire unto the Becoming-One: 21 So they shall wash their hands and their feet, that they die not: and it shall be a statute for olam to them, even to him and to his seed throughout their generations.

22 Moreover the Becoming-One spoke unto Moses, saying,

23 Take you also unto you principal spices, of pure myrrh five hundred shekels, and of sweet cinnamon half so much, even two hundred and fifty shekels, and of sweet calamus two hundred and fifty shekels,

24 And of cassia five hundred shekels, after the shekel of the sanctuary, and of oil olive a hin:

25 And you shall make it an oil of holy ointment, an ointment compound after the art of the apothecary ointment maker: it shall be a holy anointing oil.

26 And you shall anoint the tabernacle of the set time[45] therewith, and the ark of the testimony,

27 And the table and all his vessels, and the candlestick and his vessels, and the altar of incense,

28 And the altar of burnt offering with all his vessels, and the laver and his foot.

29 And you shall sanctify them, that they may be most holy: whatsoever touches them shall be holy.

30 And you shall anoint Aaron and his sons, and consecrate them, that they may minister unto me in the priest's office.

31 And you shall speak unto the children of Israel, saying, This shall be a holy anointing oil unto me throughout your generations.

32 Upon man's flesh shall it not be poured, neither shall you make any other like it, after the composition of it: it is holy, and it shall be holy unto you.

---

[40] Appointed time or festival
[41] Appointed time or festival
[42] Appointed time or festival
[43] Appointed time or festival
[44] Appointed time or festival
[45] Appointed time or festival

33 Whosoever compounds any like it, or whosoever puts any of it upon a stranger, shall even be cut off from his people.

34 And the Becoming-One said unto Moses, Take unto you sweet spices, stacte, and onycha, and galbanum; these sweet spices with pure frankincense: of each shall there be a like weight:

35 And you shall make it a perfume, a confection after the art of the apothecary, tempered together, pure and holy:

36 And you shall beat some of it very small, and put of it before the testimony in the tabernacle of the set time,[46] where I will meet with you: it shall be unto you most holy.

37 And as for the perfume which you shall make, you shall not make to yourselves according to the composition thereof: it shall be unto you holy for the Becoming-One.

38 Whosoever shall make like unto that, to smell thereto, shall even be cut off from his people.

Ex 31:1 And the Becoming-One spoke unto Moses, saying,

2 See, I have called by name Bezaleel the son of Uri, the son of Hur, of the tribe of Judah:

3 And I have filled him with the spirit of God, in wisdom, and in understanding, and in knowledge, and in all manner of workmanship,

4 To devise skilled works, to work in gold, and in silver, and in brass,

5 And in cutting of stones, to set them, and in carving of timber, to work in all manner of workmanship.

6 And I, behold, I have given with him Aholiab, the son of Ahisamach, of the tribe of Dan: and in the hearts of all that are wise hearted I have put wisdom, that they may make all that I have commanded you;

7 The tabernacle of the set time,[47] and the ark of the testimony, and the mercy seat that is thereupon, and all the furniture of the tabernacle,

8 And the table and his furniture, and the pure candlestick with all his furniture, and the altar of incense,

9 And the altar of burnt offering with all his furniture, and the laver and his foot,

10 And the cloths of service, and the holy garments for Aaron the priest, and the garments of his sons, to minister in the priest's office,

11 And the anointing oil, and sweet incense for the holy place: according to all that I have commanded you shall they do.

12 And the Becoming-One spoke unto Moses, saying,

13 Speak you also unto the children of Israel, saying, Truly my sabbaths you shall keep: for it is a sign between me and you throughout your generations; that you may know that I am the Becoming-One that does sanctify you.

14 you shall keep the Sabbath therefore; for it is holy unto you: every one that defiles it in dying he shall be put to death: for whosoever did any work therein, that soul shall be cut off from among his people.

15 Six days may work be done; but in the seventh day is the Sabbath of rest, holy to the Becoming-One: whosoever did any work in the Sabbath day, in dying he shall be put to death.

16 Therefore the children of Israel shall keep the Sabbath, to observe the Sabbath throughout their generations, for a covenant of olam.

17 It is a sign between me and the children of Israel for olam, for in six days the Becoming-One made the heavens and earth, and on the seventh day he rested, and and will be refreshed.

18 And he gave unto Moses, when he had made an end of communing with him upon mount Sinai, two tables of testimony, tables of stone, written with the finger of God.

Ex 32:1 And when the people saw that Moses delayed to come down out of the mount, the people gathered themselves together unto Aaron, and said unto him, Up, make us gods, which shall go before us; for as for this Moses, the man that brought us up out of the land of Egypt, we know not what is become of him.

2 And Aaron said unto them, Break off the golden earrings, which are in the ears of your wives, of your sons, and of your daughters, and bring them unto me.

3 And all the people brake off the golden earrings which were in their ears, and brought them unto Aaron.

4 And he received them at their hand, and fashioned it with a graving tool, after he had made it a molten calf: and they said, These be your gods, O Israel, which brought you up out of the land of Egypt.

5 And when Aaron saw it, he built an altar before it; and Aaron made proclamation, and said, tomorrow is a feast to the Becoming-One.

6 And they rose up early on the next day, and offered burnt offerings, and brought peace offerings; and the people sat down to eat and to drink, and rose up to play.

7 And the Becoming-One said unto Moses, Go, get you down; for your people, which you brought out of the land of Egypt, have corrupted themselves:

8 They have turned aside quickly out of the way which I commanded them: they have made them a molten calf, and have worshiped it, and have sacrificed thereunto, and said, These be your gods, O Israel, which have brought you up out of the land of Egypt.

9 And the Becoming-One said unto Moses, I have seen this people, and, behold, it is a stiffnecked people:

10 Now therefore let me alone, that my wrath may wax hot against them, and that I may consume them: and I will make of you a great nation.

11 And Moses besought the Becoming-One his God, and said, Becoming-One, why does your wrath wax hot against your people, which you have brought forth out of the land of Egypt with great power, and with a mighty hand?

12 Why should the Egyptians speak, and say, For mischief did he bring them out, to slay them in the mountains, and to consume them from the face of the earth? Turn from your fierce wrath, and repent of this evil against your people.

13 Remember Abraham, Isaac, and Israel, your servants, to whom you swore by your own self, and

---

[46] Appointed time or festival
[47] Appointed time or festival

say unto them, I will multiply your seed as the stars of the heavens, and all this land that I have spoken of will I give unto your seed, and they shall inherit it for olam.

14 And the Becoming-One repented of the evil which he thought to do unto his people.

15 And Moses turned, and went down from the mount, and the two tables of the testimony were in his hand: the tables were written on both their sides; on the one side and on the other were they written.

16 And the tables were the work of God, and the writing was the writing of God, graven upon the tables.

17 And when Joshua heard the noise of the people as they shouted, he said unto Moses, There is a noise of war in the camp.

18 And he said, It is not the voice of them that shout for mastery, neither is it the voice of them that cry for being overcome: but the noise of them that sing do I hear.

19 And it came to pass, as soon as he came near unto the camp, that he saw the calf, and the dancing: and Moses' anger grew hot, and he cast the tables out of his hands, and brake them beneath the mount.

20 And he took the calf which they had made, and burnt it in the fire, and ground it to powder, and strowed it upon the water, and made the children of Israel drink of it.

21 And Moses said unto Aaron, What did this people unto you, that you have brought so great a sin upon them?

22 And Aaron said, Let not the anger of my lord wax hot: you know the people, that they are set on mischief.

23 For they said unto me, Make us gods, which shall go before us: for as for this Moses, the man that brought us up out of the land of Egypt, we know not what is become of him.

24 And I said unto them, Whosoever has any gold, let them break it off. So they gave it me: then I cast it into the fire, and there came out this calf.

25 And when Moses saw that the people were naked; for Aaron had made them naked unto their shame among their enemies:

26 Then Moses stood in the gate of the camp, and said, Who is on the Becoming-One's side? let him come unto me. And all the sons of Levi gathered themselves together unto him.

27 And he said unto them, Thus says the Becoming-One, God of Israel, Put every man his sword by his side, and go in and out from gate to gate throughout the camp, and slay every man his brother, and every man his companion, and every man his neighbor.

28 And the children of Levi did according to the word of Moses: and there fell of the people that day about three thousand men.

29 For Moses had said, Consecrate yourselves today to the Becoming-One, even every man upon his son, and upon his brother; that he may bestow upon you a blessing this day.

30 And it came to pass on the next day, that Moses said unto the people, you have sinned a great sin: and now I will go up unto the Becoming-One; perhaps I can make an atonement for your sin.

31 And Moses returned unto the Becoming-One, and said, Oh, this people have sinned a great sin, and have made them gods of gold.

32 Yet now, if you will forgive their sin; and if not, blot me, I pray you, out of your book which you have written.

33 And the Becoming-One said unto Moses, Whosoever has sinned against me, him will I blot out of my book.

34 Therefore now go, lead the people unto the place of which I have spoken unto you: behold, mine Angel shall go before you: nevertheless in the day when I visit I will visit their sin upon them.

35 And the Becoming-One plagued the people, because they made the calf, which Aaron made.

Ex 33:1 And the Becoming-One said unto Moses, Depart, and go up hence, you and the people which you have brought up out of the land of Egypt, unto the land which I swore unto Abraham, to Isaac, and to Jacob, saying, Unto your seed will I give it:

2 And I will send an angel before you; and I will drive out the Canaanite, the Amorite, and the Hittite, and the Perizzite, the Hivite, and the Jebusite:

3 Unto a land flowing with milk and honey: for I will not go up in the midst of you; for you are a stiffnecked people: lest I consume you in the way.

4 And when the people heard these evil tidings, they mourned: and no man did put on him his ornaments.

5 For the Becoming-One had said unto Moses, Say unto the children of Israel, you are a stiffnecked people: I will come up into the midst of you in a moment, and consume you: therefore now put off your ornaments from you, that I may know what to do unto you.

6 And the children of Israel stripped themselves of their ornaments by the mount Horeb.

7 And Moses took the tabernacle, and pitched it outside the camp, afar off from the camp, and called it the Tabernacle of the set time.[48] And it came to pass, that every one which sought the Becoming-One went out unto the tabernacle of the set time,[49] which was outside the camp.

8 And it came to pass, when Moses went out unto the tabernacle, that all the people rose up, and stood every man at his tent door, and looked after Moses, until he was gone into the tabernacle.

9 And it came to pass, as Moses entered into the tabernacle, the cloudy pillar descended, and stood at the door of the tabernacle, and the Becoming-One talked with Moses.

10 And all the people saw the cloudy pillar stand at the tabernacle door: and all the people rose up and worshiped, every man in his tent door.

11 And the Becoming-One spoke unto Moses face to face, as a man speaks unto his friend. And he turned again into the camp: but his servant Joshua, the son of Nun, a young man, departed not out of the tabernacle.

12 And Moses said unto the Becoming-One, See, you say unto me, Bring up this people: and you have not let me know whom you will send with me. Yet you have said, I know you by name, and you have also found grace in my sight.

---

[48] Appointed time or festival
[49] Appointed time or festival

13 Now therefore, I pray you, if I have found grace in your sight, show me now your way, that I may know you, that I may find grace in your sight: and consider that this nation is your people.

14 And he said, My presence shall go with you, and I will give you rest.

15 And he said unto him, If your presence go not with me, do not carry us up from here.

16 For wherein shall it be known here that I and your people have found grace in your sight? is it not in that you go with us? so shall we be separated, I and your people, from all the people that are upon the face of the earth.

17 And the Becoming-One said unto Moses, I will do this thing also that you have spoken: for you have found grace in my sight, and I know you by name.

18 And he said, I beg you, show me your glory.

19 And He said, I will make all my goodness pass before you, and I will proclaim the name of the Becoming-One before you; and will be gracious to whom I will be gracious, and will show mercy on whom I will show mercy.

20 And he said, you can not see my face: for there shall no man see me, and live.

21 And the Becoming-One said, Behold, there is a place by me, and you shall stand upon a rock:

22 And it shall come to pass, while my glory passes by, that I will put you in a clift of the rock, and will cover you with my hand while I pass by:

23 And I will take away mine hand, and you shall see my back parts: but my face shall not be seen.

Ex 34:1 And the Becoming-One said unto Moses, Hew you two tables of stone like unto the first: and I will write upon these tables the words that were in the first tables, which you broke.

2 And be ready in the morning, and come up in the morning unto mount Sinai, and present yourself there to me in the top of the mount.

3 And no man shall come up with you, neither let any man be seen throughout all the mount; neither let the flocks nor herds feed before that mount.

4 And he hewed two tables of stone like unto the first; and Moses rose up early in the morning, and went up unto mount Sinai, as the Becoming-One had commanded him, and took in his hand the two tables of stone.

5 And the Becoming-One descended in the cloud, and stood with him there, and proclaimed the name of the Becoming-One.

6 And the Becoming-One passed by before him, and proclaimed, The Becoming-One, The Becoming-One, GOD merciful and gracious, patient, and abundant in goodness and truth,

7 Keeping mercy for thousands, forgiving iniquity and transgression and sin, and that will by no means clear the guilty; visiting the iniquity of the fathers upon the children, and upon the children's children, unto the third and to the fourth generation.

8 And Moses made haste, and bowed his head toward the earth, and worshiped.

9 And he said, If now I have found grace in your sight, O my Lord(s), let my Lord(s), I pray you, go among us; for it is a stiffnecked people; and pardon our iniquity and our sin, and take us for your inheritance.

10 And he said, Behold, I make a covenant: before all your people I will do marvels, such as have not been done in all the earth, nor in any nation: and all the people among which you are shall see the work of the Becoming-One: for it is a terrible thing that I will do with you.

11 Observe you that which I command you this day: behold, I drive out before you the Amorite, and the Canaanite, and the Hittite, and the Perizzite, and the Hivite, and the Jebusite.

12 Take heed to thyself, lest you make a covenant with the inhabitants of the land to which you go, lest it be for a snare in the midst of you:

13 But you shall destroy their altars, break their images, and cut down Asherahs [astarte]

14 For you shall worship no other god: for the Becoming-One, whose name is Zealous[50], is a zealous GOD:

15 Lest you make a covenant with the inhabitants of the land, and they go a whoring after their gods, and do sacrifice unto their gods, and one call you, and you eat of his sacrifice;

16 And you take of their daughters unto your sons, and their daughters go a whoring after their gods, and make your sons go a whoring after their gods.

17 you shall make you no molten gods.

18 The feast of unleavened bread shall you keep. Seven days you shall eat unleavened bread, as I commanded you, in the time of the month Abib: for in the month Abib you came out from Egypt.

19 All that opens the matrix is mine; and every firstling among your cattle, whether ox or sheep, that is male.

20 But the firstling of an donkey you shall redeem with a lamb: and if you redeem him not, then shall you break his neck. All the firstborn of your sons you shall redeem. And none shall appear before me empty.

21 Six days you shall work, but on the seventh day you shall rest: in earing time and in harvest you shall rest.

22 And you shall observe the feast of weeks, of the firstfruits of wheat harvest, and the feast of ingathering at the revolution of the year.

23 Three times in the year shall all your menchildren appear before the Lord Becoming-One, God of Israel.

24 For I will cast out the nations before you, and enlarge your borders: neither shall any man desire your land, when you shall go up to appear before the Becoming-One your God three times in the year.

25 you shall not offer the blood of my sacrifice with leaven; neither shall the sacrifice of the feast of the Passover be left unto the morning.

26 The first of the firstfruits of your land you shall bring unto the house of the Becoming-One your God. you shall not seethe a kid in his mother's milk.

27 And the Becoming-One said unto Moses, Write you these words: for according to these words I have made a covenant with you and with Israel.

28 And he was there with the Becoming-One forty days and forty nights; he did neither eat bread, nor

---

[50] Because YHWH is a cohortative verb

drink water. And he wrote upon the tables the words of the covenant, the ten commandments.

29 And it came to pass, when Moses came down from mount Sinai with the two tables of testimony in Moses' hand, when he came down from the mount, that Moses knew not that the skin of his face shone while he talked with him.

30 And when Aaron and all the children of Israel saw Moses, behold, the skin of his face shone; and they were afraid to come near him.

31 And Moses called unto them; and Aaron and all the rulers of the congregation returned unto him: and Moses talked with them.

32 And afterward all the children of Israel came near: and he gave them in commandment all that the Becoming-One had spoken with him in mount Sinai.

33 And till Moses had done speaking with them, he put a veil on his face.

34 But when Moses went in before the Becoming-One to speak with him, he took the veil off, until he came out. And he came out, and spoke unto the children of Israel that which he was commanded.

35 And the children of Israel saw the face of Moses, that the skin of Moses' face shone: and Moses put the veil upon his face again, until he went in to speak with him.

Ex 35:1 And Moses gathered all the congregation of the children of Israel together, and said unto them, These are the words which the Becoming-One has commanded, that you should do them.

2 Six days shall work be done, but on the seventh day there shall be to you a holy day, a Sabbath of rest to the Becoming-One: whosoever did work therein shall be put to death.

3 you shall kindle no fire throughout your habitations upon the Sabbath day.

4 And Moses spoke unto all the congregation of the children of Israel, saying, This is the thing which the Becoming-One commanded, saying,

5 Take you from among you an offering unto the Becoming-One: all that is of a willing heart, let him bring it, an offering of the Becoming-One; gold, and silver, and brass,

6 And blue, and purple, and scarlet, and fine linen, and goats' hair,

7 And rams' skins dyed red, and badgers' skins, and shittim wood,

8 And oil for the light, and spices for anointing oil, and for the sweet incense,

9 And onyx stones, and stones to be set for the ephod, and for the breastplate.

10 And every wise hearted among you shall come, and make all that the Becoming-One has commanded;

11 The tabernacle, his tent, and his covering, his taches, and his boards, his bars, his pillars, and his sockets,

12 The ark, and the staves thereof, with the mercy seat, and the veil of the covering,

13 The table, and his staves, and all his vessels, and the showbread,

14 The candlestick also for the light, and his furniture, and his lamps, with the oil for the light,

15 And the incense altar, and his staves, and the anointing oil, and the sweet incense, and the hanging for the door at the entering in of the tabernacle,

16 The altar of burnt offering, with his brazen grate, his staves, and all his vessels, the laver and his foot,

17 The hangings of the court, his pillars, and their sockets, and the hanging for the door of the court,

18 The pins of the tabernacle, and the pins of the court, and their cords,

19 The cloths of service, to do service in the holy place, the holy garments for Aaron the priest, and the garments of his sons, to minister in the priest's office.

20 And all the congregation of the children of Israel departed from the presence of Moses.

21 And they came, every one whose heart stirred him up, and every one whom his spirit made willing, and they brought the Becoming-One's offering to the work of the tabernacle of the congregation, and for all his service, and for the holy garments.

22 And they came, both men and women, all as were willing hearted, and brought bracelets, and earrings, and rings, and tablets, all jewels of gold: and every man that offered offered an offering of gold unto the Becoming-One.

23 And every man, with whom was found blue, and purple, and scarlet, and fine linen, and goats' hair, and red skins of rams, and badgers' skins, brought them.

24 Every one that did offer an offering of silver and brass brought the Becoming-One's offering: and every man, with whom was found shittim wood for any work of the service, brought it.

25 And all the women that were wise hearted did spin with their hands, and brought that which they had spun, both of blue, and of purple, and of scarlet, and of fine linen.

26 And all the women whose heart stirred them up in wisdom spun goats' hair.

27 And the rulers brought onyx stones, and stones to be set, for the ephod, and for the breastplate;

28 And spice, and oil for the light, and for the anointing oil, and for the sweet incense.

29 The children of Israel brought a willing offering unto the Becoming-One, every man and woman, whose heart made them willing to bring for all manner of work, which the Becoming-One had commanded to be made by the hand of Moses.

30 And Moses said unto the children of Israel, See, the Becoming-One has called by name Bezaleel the son of Uri, the son of Hur, of the tribe of Judah;

31 And he has filled him with the spirit of God, in wisdom, in understanding, and in knowledge, and in all manner of workmanship;

32 And to devise skilled works, to work in gold, and in silver, and in brass,

33 And in the cutting of stones, to set them, and in carving of wood, to make any manner of skilled work.

34 And he has put in his heart that he may teach, both he, and Aholiab, the son of Ahisamach, of the tribe of Dan.

35 Them has he filled with wisdom of heart, to work all manner of work, of the engraver, and of the skilled workman, and of the embroiderer, in blue, and in purple, in scarlet, and in fine linen, and of the weaver, even of them that do any work, and of those that devise skilled work.

Ex 36:1 Then worked Bezaleel and Aholiab, and every wise hearted man, in whom the Becoming-One put wisdom and understanding to know how to work all manner of work for the service of the sanctuary, according to all that the Becoming-One had commanded.

2 And Moses called Bezaleel and Aholiab, and every wise hearted man, in whose heart the Becoming-One had put wisdom, even every one whose heart stirred him up to come unto the work to do it:

3 And they received of Moses all the offering, which the children of Israel had brought for the work of the service of the sanctuary, to make it withal. And they brought yet unto him free offerings every morning.

4 And all the wise men, that worked all the work of the sanctuary, came every man from his work which they made;

5 And they spoke unto Moses, saying, The people bring much more than enough for the service of the work, which the Becoming-One commanded to make.

6 And Moses gave commandment, and they caused it to be proclaimed throughout the camp, saying, Let neither man nor woman make any more work for the offering of the sanctuary. So the people were restrained from bringing.

7 For the stuff they had was sufficient for all the work to make it, and too much.

8 And every wise hearted man among them that worked the work of the tabernacle made ten curtains of fine twined linen, and blue, and purple, and scarlet: with cherubs of skilled work made he them.

9 The length of one curtain was twenty and eight cubits, and the breadth of one curtain four cubits: the curtains were all of one size.

10 And he coupled the five curtains one unto another: and the other five curtains he coupled one unto another.

11 And he made loops of blue on the edge of one curtain from the selvedge in the coupling: likewise he made in the uttermost side of another curtain, in the coupling of the second.

12 Fifty loops made he in one curtain, and fifty loops made he in the edge of the curtain which was in the coupling of the second: the loops held one curtain to another.

13 And he made fifty taches of gold, and coupled the curtains one unto another with the taches: so it became one tabernacle.

14 And he made curtains of goats' hair for the tent over the tabernacle: eleven curtains he made them.

15 The length of one curtain was thirty cubits, and four cubits was the breadth of one curtain: the eleven curtains were of one size.

16 And he coupled five curtains by themselves, and six curtains by themselves.

17 And he made fifty loops upon the uttermost edge of the curtain in the coupling, and fifty loops made he upon the edge of the curtain which couple the second.

18 And he made fifty taches of brass to couple the tent together, that it might be one.

19 And he made a covering for the tent of rams' skins dyed red, and a covering of badgers' skins above that.

20 And he made boards for the tabernacle of shittim wood, standing up.

21 The length of a board was ten cubits, and the breadth of a board one cubit and a half.

22 One board had two tenons, equally distant one from another: thus did he make for all the boards of the tabernacle.

23 And he made boards for the tabernacle; twenty boards for the south side southward:

24 And forty sockets of silver he made under the twenty boards; two sockets under one board for his two tenons, and two sockets under another board for his two tenons.

25 And for the other side of the tabernacle, which is toward the north corner, he made twenty boards,

26 And their forty sockets of silver; two sockets under one board, and two sockets under another board.

27 And for the sides of the tabernacle westward he made six boards.

28 And two boards made he for the corners of the tabernacle in the two sides.

29 And they were coupled beneath, and coupled together at the head thereof, to one ring: thus he did to both of them in both the corners.

30 And there were eight boards; and their sockets were sixteen sockets of silver, under every board two sockets.

31 And he made bars of shittim wood; five for the boards of the one side of the tabernacle,

32 And five bars for the boards of the other side of the tabernacle, and five bars for the boards of the tabernacle for the sides westward.

33 And he made the middle bar to shoot through the boards from the one end to the other.

34 And he overlaid the boards with gold, and made their rings of gold to be places for the bars, and overlaid the bars with gold.

35 And he made a veil of blue, and purple, and scarlet, and fine twined linen: with cherubs made he it of skilled work.

36 And he made thereunto four pillars of shittim wood, and overlaid them with gold: their hooks were of gold; and he cast for them four sockets of silver.

37 And he made a hanging for the tabernacle door of blue, and purple, and scarlet, and fine twined linen, of needlework;

38 And the five pillars of it with their hooks: and he overlaid their capitals and their bands with gold: but their five sockets were of brass.

Ex 37:1 And Bezaleel made the ark of shittim wood: two cubits and a half was the length of it, and a cubit and a half the breadth of it, and a cubit and a half the height of it:

2 And he overlaid it with pure gold within and without, and made a crown of gold to it round about.

3 And he cast for it four rings of gold, to be set by the four corners of it; even two rings upon the one side of it, and two rings upon the other side of it.

4 And he made staves of shittim wood, and overlaid them with gold.

5 And he put the staves into the rings by the sides of the ark, to bear the ark.

6 And he made the mercy seat of pure gold: two cubits and a half was the length thereof, and one cubit and a half the breadth thereof.

7 And he made two cherubs of gold, beaten out of one piece made he them, on the two ends of the mercy seat;

8 One cherub on the end on this side, and another cherub on the other end on that side: out of the mercy seat made he the cherubs on the two ends thereof.

9 And the cherubs spread out their wings on high, and covered with their wings over the mercy seat, with their faces one to another; even to the mercy seatward were the faces of the cherubs.

10 And he made the table of shittim wood: two cubits was the length thereof, and a cubit the breadth thereof, and a cubit and a half the height thereof:

11 And he overlaid it with pure gold, and made thereunto a crown of gold round about.

12 Also he made thereunto a border of a handbreadth round about; and made a crown of gold for the border thereof round about.

13 And he cast for it four rings of gold, and put the rings upon the four corners that were in the four feet thereof.

14 Over against the border were the rings, the places for the staves to bear the table.

15 And he made the staves of shittim wood, and overlaid them with gold, to bear the table.

16 And he made the vessels which were upon the table, his dishes, and his spoons, and his bowls, and his covers to cover withal, of pure gold.

17 And he made the candlestick of pure gold: of beaten work made he the candlestick; his shaft, and his branch, his bowls, his knops, and his flowers, were of the same:

18 And six branches going out of the sides thereof; three branches of the candlestick out of the one side thereof, and three branches of the candlestick out of the other side thereof:

19 Three bowls made after the fashion of almonds in one branch, a knop and a flower; and three bowls made like almonds in another branch, a knop and a flower: so throughout the six branches going out of the candlestick.

20 And in the candlestick were four bowls made like almonds, his gourds, and his flowers:

21 And a knop under two branches of the same, and a knop under two branches of the same, and a knop under two branches of the same, according to the six branches going out of it.

22 Their gourds and their branches were of the same: all of it was one beaten work of pure gold.

23 And he made his seven lamps, and his snuffers, and his snuffdishes, of pure gold.

24 Of a talent of pure gold made he it, and all the vessels thereof.

25 And he made the incense altar of shittim wood: the length of it was a cubit, and the breadth of it a cubit; it was foursquare; and two cubits was the height of it; the horns thereof were of the same.

26 And he overlaid it with pure gold, both the top of it, and the sides thereof round about, and the horns of it: also he made unto it a crown of gold round about.

27 And he made two rings of gold for it under the crown thereof, by the two corners of it, upon the two sides thereof, to be places for the staves to bear it withal.

28 And he made the staves of shittim wood, and overlaid them with gold.

29 And he made the holy anointing oil, and the pure incense of sweet spices, according to the work of the apothecary.

Ex 38:1 And he made the altar of burnt offering of shittim wood: five cubits was the length thereof, and five cubits the breadth thereof; it was foursquare; and three cubits the height thereof.

2 And he made the horns thereof on the four corners of it; the horns thereof were of the same: and he overlaid it with brass.

3 And he made all the vessels of the altar, the pots, and the shovels, and the basins, and the fleshhooks, and the firepans: all the vessels thereof made he of brass.

4 And he made for the altar a brazen grate of network under the compass thereof beneath unto the midst of it.

5 And he cast four rings for the four ends of the grate of brass, to be places for the staves.

6 And he made the staves of shittim wood, and overlaid them with brass.

7 And he put the staves into the rings on the sides of the altar, to bear it withal; he made the altar hollow with boards.

8 And he made the laver of brass, and the foot of it of brass, of the mirrors of the women assembling, which assembled at the door of the tabernacle of the set time.

9 And he made the court: on the south side southward the hangings of the court were of fine twined linen, a hundred cubits:

10 Their pillars were twenty, and their brazen sockets twenty; the hooks of the pillars and their bands were of silver.

11 And for the north side the hangings were a hundred cubits, their pillars were twenty, and their sockets of brass twenty; the hooks of the pillars and their bands of silver.

12 And for the west side were hangings of fifty cubits, their pillars ten, and their sockets ten; the hooks of the pillars and their bands of silver.

13 And for the east side eastward fifty cubits.

14 The hangings of the one side of the gate were fifteen cubits; their pillars three, and their sockets three.

15 And for the other side of the court gate, on this hand and that hand, were hangings of fifteen cubits; their pillars three, and their sockets three.

16 All the hangings of the court round about were of fine twined linen.

17 And the sockets for the pillars were of brass; the hooks of the pillars and their bands of silver; and the overlaying of their capitals of silver; and all the pillars of the court were banded with silver.

18 And the hanging for the gate of the court was needlework, of blue, and purple, and scarlet, and fine twined linen: and twenty cubits was the length, and the height in the breadth was five cubits, answerable to the hangings of the court.

19 And their pillars were four, and their sockets of brass four; their hooks of silver, and the overlaying of their capitals and their bands of silver.

20 And all the pins of the tabernacle, and of the court round about, were of brass.

21 This is the sum of the tabernacle, even of the tabernacle of testimony, as it was counted, according to the mouth of Moses, for the service of the Levites, by the hand of Ithamar, son to Aaron the priest.

22 And Bezaleel the son of Uri, the son of Hur, of the tribe of Judah, made all that the Becoming-One commanded Moses.

23 And with him was Aholiab, son of Ahisamach, of the tribe of Dan, an engraver, and a skilled workman, and an embroiderer in blue, and in purple, and in scarlet, and fine linen.

24 All the gold that was occupied for the work in all the work of the holy place, even the gold of the offering, was twenty and nine talents, and seven hundred and thirty shekels, after the shekel of the sanctuary.

25 And the silver of them that were numbered of the congregation was a hundred talents, and a thousand seven hundred and threescore and fifteen shekels, after the shekel of the sanctuary:

26 A bekah for every man, that is, half a shekel, after the shekel of the sanctuary, for every one that went to be numbered, from a son of twenty years and upward, for six hundred thousand and three thousand and five hundred and fifty men. [603,550]

27 And of the hundred talents of silver were cast the sockets of the sanctuary, and the sockets of the veil; a hundred sockets of the hundred talents, a talent for a socket.

28 And of the thousand seven hundred seventy and five shekels he made hooks for the pillars, and overlaid their capitals, and banded them.

29 And the brass of the offering was seventy talents, and two thousand and four hundred shekels.

30 And therewith he made the sockets to the door of the tabernacle of the set time, and the brazen altar, and the brazen grate for it, and all the vessels of the altar,

31 And the sockets of the court round about, and the sockets of the court gate, and all the pins of the tabernacle, and all the pins of the court round about.

Ex 39:1 And of the blue, and purple, and scarlet, they made cloths of service, to do service in the holy place, and made the holy garments for Aaron; as the Becoming-One commanded Moses.

2 And he made the ephod of gold, blue, and purple, and scarlet, and fine twined linen.

3 And they did beat the gold into thin plates, and cut it into wires, to work it in the blue, and in the purple, and in the scarlet, and in the fine linen, with skilled work.

4 They made shoulderpieces for it, to couple it together: by the two edges was it coupled together.

5 And the skilled girdle of his ephod, that was upon it, was of the same, according to the work thereof; of gold, blue, and purple, and scarlet, and fine twined linen; as the Becoming-One commanded Moses.

6 And they worked onyx stones enclosed in ouches of gold, graven, as signets are graven, with the names of the children of Israel.

7 And he put them on the shoulders of the ephod, that they should be stones for a memorial to the children of Israel; as the Becoming-One commanded Moses.

8 And he made the breastplate of skilled work, like the work of the ephod; of gold, blue, and purple, and scarlet, and fine twined linen.

9 It was foursquare; they made the breastplate double: a span was the length thereof, and a span the breadth thereof, being doubled.

10 And they set in it four rows of stones: the first row was a sardius, a topaz, and a carbuncle: this was the first row.

11 And the second row, an emerald, a sapphire, and a diamond.

12 And the third row, a ligure, an agate, and an amethyst.

13 And the fourth row, a beryl, an onyx, and a jasper: they were enclosed in ouches of gold in their enclosings.

14 And the stones were according to the names of the children of Israel, twelve, according to their names, like the engravings of a signet, every one with his name, according to the twelve tribes.

15 And they made upon the breastplate chains at the ends, of braided work of pure gold.

16 And they made two ouches of gold, and two gold rings; and put the two rings in the two ends of the breastplate.

17 And they put the two braided chains of gold in the two rings on the ends of the breastplate.

18 And the two ends of the two braided chains they fastened in the two settings, and put them on the shoulderpieces of the ephod, before it.

19 And they made two rings of gold, and put them on the two ends of the breastplate, upon the border of it, which was on the side of the ephod inward.

20 And they made two other golden rings, and put them on the two sides of the ephod underneath, toward the forepart of it, over against the other coupling thereof, above the skilled girdle of the ephod.

21 And they did bind the breastplate by his rings unto the rings of the ephod with a lace of blue, that it might be above the skilled girdle of the ephod, and that the breastplate might not be loosened from the ephod; as the Becoming-One commanded Moses.

22 And he made the robe of the ephod of woven work, all of blue.

23 And there was a hole in the midst of the robe, as the hole of a habergeon, with a band round about the hole, that it should not rend.

24 And they made upon the hems of the robe pomegranates of blue, and purple, and scarlet, and twined linen.

25 And they made bells of pure gold, and put the bells between the pomegranates upon the hem of the robe, round about between the pomegranates;

26 A bell and a pomegranate, a bell and a pomegranate, round about the hem of the robe to minister in; as the Becoming-One commanded Moses.

27 And they made coats of fine linen of woven work for Aaron, and for his sons,

28 And a turban of fine linen, and goodly caps of fine linen, and linen breeches of fine twined linen,

29 And a girdle of fine twined linen, and blue, and purple, and scarlet, of needlework; as the Becoming-One commanded Moses.

30 And they made the plate of the holy crown of pure gold, and wrote upon it a writing, like to the engravings of a signet, Holiness to the Becoming-One.

31 And they tied unto it a lace of blue, to fasten it on high upon the turban; as the Becoming-One commanded Moses.

32 Thus was all the work of the tabernacle of the tent of the set time finished: and the children of Israel did according to all that the Becoming-One commanded Moses, so did they.

33 And they brought the tabernacle unto Moses, the tent, and all his furniture, his taches, his boards, his bars, and his pillars, and his sockets,

34 And the covering of rams' skins dyed red, and the covering of badgers' skins, and the veil of the covering,

35 The ark of the testimony, and the staves thereof, and the mercy seat,

36 The table, and all the vessels thereof, and the showbread,

37 The pure candlestick, with the lamps thereof, even with the lamps to be set in order, and all the vessels thereof, and the oil for light,

38 And the golden altar, and the anointing oil, and the sweet incense, and the hanging for the tabernacle door,

39 The brazen altar, and his grate of brass, his staves, and all his vessels, the laver and his foot,

40 The hangings of the court, his pillars, and his sockets, and the hanging for the court gate, his cords, and his pins, and all the vessels of the service of the tabernacle, for the tent of the set time,

41 The cloths of service to do service in the holy place, and the holy garments for Aaron the priest, and his sons' garments, to minister in the priest's office.

42 According to all that the Becoming-One commanded Moses, so the children of Israel made all the work.

43 And Moses did look upon all the work, and, behold, they had done it as the Becoming-One had commanded, even so had they done it: and Moses blessed them.

Ex 40:1 And the Becoming-One spoke unto Moses, saying,

2 On the first day of the first month shall you set up the tabernacle of the tent of the set time.

3 And you shall put therein the ark of the testimony, and cover the ark with the veil.

4 And you shall bring in the table, and set in order the things that are to be set in order upon it; and you shall bring in the candlestick, and light the lamps thereof.

5 And you shall set the altar of gold for the incense before the ark of the testimony, and put the hanging of the door to the tabernacle.

6 And you shall set the altar of the burnt offering before the door of the tabernacle of the tent of the set time.

7 And you shall set the laver between the tent of the set time and the altar, and shall put water therein.

8 And you shall set up the court round about, and hang up the hanging at the court gate.

9 And you shall take the anointing oil, and anoint the tabernacle, and all that is therein, and shall hallow it, and all the vessels thereof: and it shall be holy.

10 And you shall anoint the altar of the burnt offering, and all his vessels, and sanctify the altar: and it shall be an altar most holy.

11 And you shall anoint the laver and his foot, and sanctify it.

12 And you shall bring Aaron and his sons unto the door of the tabernacle of the set time, and wash them with water.

13 And you shall put upon Aaron the holy garments, and anoint him, and sanctify him; that he may minister unto me in the priest's office.

14 And you shall bring his sons, and clothe them with coats:

15 And you shall anoint them, as you didst anoint their father, that they may minister unto me in the priest's office: for their anointing shall surely be a priesthood of olam throughout their generations.

16 Thus did Moses: according to all that the Becoming-One commanded him, so did he.

17 And it came to pass in the first month in the second year, on the first day of the month, that the tabernacle was reared up.

18 And Moses reared up the tabernacle, and fastened his sockets, and set up the boards thereof, and put in the bars thereof, and reared up his pillars.

19 And he spread abroad the tent over the tabernacle, and put the covering of the tent above upon it; as the Becoming-One commanded Moses.

20 And he took and put the testimony into the ark, and set the staves on the ark, and put the mercy seat above upon the ark:

21 And he brought the ark into the tabernacle, and set up the veil of the covering, and covered the ark of the testimony; as the Becoming-One commanded Moses.

22 And he put the table in the tabernacle of the set time,[51] upon the side of the tabernacle northward, outside the veil.

23 And he set the bread in order upon it before the Becoming-One; as the Becoming-One had commanded Moses.

24 And he put the candlestick in the tabernacle of the set time,[52] over against the table, on the side of the tabernacle southward.

25 And he lighted the lamps before the Becoming-One; as the Becoming-One commanded Moses.

26 And he put the golden altar in the tabernacle of the set time[53] before the veil:

27 And he burnt sweet incense thereon; as the Becoming-One commanded Moses.

28 And he set up the hanging at the door of the tabernacle.

29 And he put the altar of burnt offering by the door of the tabernacle of the tent of the set time, and offered upon it the burnt offering and the food offering; as the Becoming-One commanded Moses.

---

[51] Appointed time or festival
[52] Appointed time or festival
[53] Appointed time or festival

30 And he set the laver between the tent of the set time and the altar, and put water there, to wash withal.

31 And Moses and Aaron and his sons washed their hands and their feet thereat:

32 When they went into the tent of the set time, and when they came near unto the altar, they washed; as the Becoming-One commanded Moses.

33 And he reared up the court round about the tabernacle and the altar, and set up the hanging of the court gate. So Moses finished the work.

34 Then a cloud covered the tent of the set time, and the glory of the Becoming-One filled the tabernacle.

35 And Moses was not able to enter into the tent of the set time, because the cloud abode thereon, and the glory of the Becoming-One filled the tabernacle.

36 And when the cloud was taken up from over the tabernacle, the children of Israel went onward in all their journeys:

37 But if the cloud were not taken up, then they journeyed not till the day that it was taken up.

38 For the cloud of the Becoming-One was upon the tabernacle by day, and fire was on it by night, in the sight of all the house of Israel, throughout all their journeys.

Leviticus

Lev 1:1 And the Becoming-One called unto Moses, and spoke unto him out of the tabernacle of the set time, saying,

2 Speak unto the children of Israel, and say unto them, If any man of you bring an offering unto the Becoming-One, you shall bring your offering of the cattle, even of the herd, and of the flock.

3 If his offering be a burnt sacrifice of the herd, let him offer a male without blemish: he shall offer it of his own voluntary will at the door of the tabernacle of the set time before the Becoming-One.

4 And he shall put his hand upon the head of the burnt offering; and it shall be accepted for him to make atonement for him.

5 And he shall kill the bullock before the Becoming-One: and the priests, Aaron's sons, shall bring the blood, and sprinkle the blood round about upon the altar that is by the door of the tabernacle of the set time.

6 And he shall flay the burnt offering, and cut it into his pieces.

7 And the sons of Aaron the priest shall put fire upon the altar, and lay the wood in order upon the fire:

8 And the priests, Aaron's sons, shall lay the parts, the head, and the fat, in order upon the wood that is on the fire which is upon the altar:

9 But his inwards and his legs shall he wash in water: and the priest shall burn all on the altar, to be a burnt sacrifice, an offering made by fire, of a sweet aroma unto the Becoming-One.

10 And if his offering be of the flocks, namely, of the sheep, or of the goats, for a burnt sacrifice; he shall bring it a male without blemish.

11 And he shall kill it on the side of the altar northward before the Becoming-One: and the priests, Aaron's sons, shall sprinkle his blood round about upon the altar.

12 And he shall cut it into his pieces, with his head and his fat: and the priest shall lay them in order on the wood that is on the fire which is upon the altar:

13 But he shall wash the inwards and the legs with water: and the priest shall bring it all, and burn it upon the altar: it is a burnt sacrifice, an offering made by fire, of a sweet aroma unto the Becoming-One.

14 And if the burnt sacrifice for his offering to the Becoming-One be of fowls, then he shall bring his offering of turtledoves, or of young pigeons.

15 And the priest shall bring it unto the altar, and wring off his head, and burn it on the altar; and the blood thereof shall be wrung out at the side of the altar:

16 And he shall pluck away his crop with his feathers, and cast it beside the altar on the east part, by the place of the ashes:

17 And he shall cleave it with the wings thereof, but shall not divide it asunder: and the priest shall burn it upon the altar, upon the wood that is upon the fire: it is a burnt sacrifice, an offering made by fire, of a sweet aroma unto the Becoming-One.

Lev 2:1 And a soul when he will offer a food offering unto the Becoming-One, his offering shall be of fine flour; and he shall pour oil upon it, and put frankincense thereon:

2 And he shall bring it to Aaron's sons the priests: and he shall take thereout his handful of the flour thereof, and of the oil thereof, with all the frankincense thereof; and the priest shall burn the memorial of it upon the altar, to be an offering made by fire, of a sweet aroma unto the Becoming-One: 3 And the remnant of the food offering shall be Aaron's and his sons': it is a thing most holy of the offerings of the Becoming-One made by fire.

4 And if you bring an offering of a food offering baken in the oven, it shall be unleavened cakes of fine flour mingled with oil, or unleavened wafers anointed with oil.

5 And if your offering be a food offering baken in a pan, it shall be of fine flour unleavened, mingled with oil.

6 you shall part it in pieces, and pour oil thereon: it is a food offering.

7 And if your offering be a food offering baken in the frying pan, it shall be made of fine flour with oil.

8 And you shall bring the food offering that is made of these things unto the Becoming-One: and when it is presented unto the priest, he shall bring it unto the altar.

9 And the priest shall take from the food offering a memorial thereof, and shall burn it upon the altar: it is an offering made by fire, of a sweet aroma unto the Becoming-One.

10 And that which is left of the food offering shall be Aaron's and his sons': it is a thing most holy of the offerings of the Becoming-One made by fire.

11 No food offering, which you shall bring unto the Becoming-One, shall be made with leaven: for you shall burn no leaven, nor any honey, in any offering of the Becoming-One made by fire.

12 As for the offering of the beginning firstfruits, you shall offer them unto the Becoming-One: but they shall not be burnt on the altar for a sweet aroma.

13 And every offering of your food offering shall you season with salt; neither shall you permit the salt of the covenant of your God to be lacking from your food offering: with all your offerings you shall offer salt.

14 And if you offer a food offering of your firstfruits unto the Becoming-One, you shall offer for the food offering of your firstfruits green ears of corn dried by the fire, even grain beaten out of full ears.

15 And you shall put oil upon it, and lay frankincense thereon: it is a food offering.

16 And the priest shall burn the memorial of it, part of the beaten grain thereof, and part of the oil thereof, with all the frankincense thereof: it is an offering made by fire unto the Becoming-One.

Lev 3:1 And if his offering be a sacrifice of peace offering, if he offer it of the herd; whether it be a male or female, he shall offer it without blemish before the Becoming-One.

2 And he shall lay his hand upon the head of his offering, and kill it at the door of the tabernacle of the set time: and Aaron's sons the priests shall sprinkle the blood upon the altar round about.

3 And he shall offer of the sacrifice of the peace offering an offering made by fire unto the Becoming-

One; the fat that coveres the inwards, and all the fat that is upon the inwards,

4 And the two kidneys, and the fat that is on them, which is by the flanks, and the diaphragm around the liver, with the kidneys, it shall he take away.

5 And Aaron's sons shall burn it on the altar upon the burnt sacrifice, which is upon the wood that is on the fire: it is an offering made by fire, of a sweet aroma unto the Becoming-One.

6 And if his offering for a sacrifice of peace offering unto the Becoming-One be of the flock; male or female, he shall offer it without blemish.

7 If he offer a lamb for his offering, then shall he offer it before the Becoming-One.

8 And he shall lay his hand upon the head of his offering, and kill it before the tabernacle of the set time: and Aaron's sons shall sprinkle the blood thereof round about upon the altar.

9 And he shall offer of the sacrifice of the peace offering an offering made by fire unto the Becoming-One; the fat thereof, and the whole rump, he shall take it off close by the backbone; and the fat that coveres the inwards, and all the fat that is upon the inwards,

10 And the two kidneys, and the fat that is upon them, which is by the flanks, and the diaphragm around the liver, with the kidneys, it shall he take away.

11 And the priest shall burn it upon the altar: it is the food of the offering made by fire unto the Becoming-One.

12 And if his offering be a goat, then he shall offer it before the Becoming-One.

13 And he shall lay his hand upon the head of it, and kill it before the tabernacle of the set time: and the sons of Aaron shall sprinkle the blood thereof upon the altar round about.

14 And he shall offer thereof his offering, even an offering made by fire unto the Becoming-One; the fat that coveres the inwards, and all the fat that is upon the inwards,

15 And the two kidneys, and the fat that is upon them, which is by the flanks, and the diaphragm around the liver, with the kidneys, it shall he take away.

16 And the priest shall burn them upon the altar: it is the food of the offering made by fire for a sweet aroma: all the fat is the Becoming-One's.

17 It shall be a statute of olam for your generations throughout all your dwellings, that you eat neither fat nor blood.

Lev 4:1 And the Becoming-One spoke unto Moses, saying,

2 Speak unto the children of Israel, saying, If a soul shall sin through ignorance against any of the commandments of the Becoming-One concerning things which ought not to be done, and shall do against any of them:

3 If the priest that is anointed do sin according to the sin of the people; then let him bring for his sin, which he has sinned, a young bullock without blemish unto the Becoming-One for a sin offering.

4 And he shall bring the bullock unto the door of the tabernacle of the set time before the Becoming-One; and shall lay his hand upon the bullock's head, and kill the bullock before the Becoming-One.

5 And the priest that is anointed shall take of the bullock's blood, and bring it to the tabernacle of the set time:

6 And the priest shall dip his finger in the blood, and sprinkle of the blood seven times before the Becoming-One, before the veil of the sanctuary.

7 And the priest shall put some of the blood upon the horns of the altar of sweet incense before the Becoming-One, which is in the tabernacle of the set time;[54] and shall pour all the blood of the bullock at the bottom of the altar of the burnt offering, which is at the door of the tabernacle of the set time.[55]

8 And he shall take off from it all the fat of the bullock for the sin offering; the fat that coveres the inwards, and all the fat that is upon the inwards,

9 And the two kidneys, and the fat that is upon them, which is by the flanks, and the diaphragm around the liver, with the kidneys, it shall he take away,

10 As it was taken off from the bullock of the sacrifice of peace offerings: and the priest shall burn them upon the altar of the burnt offering.

11 And the skin of the bullock, and all his flesh, with his head, and with his legs, and his inwards, and his dung,

12 Even the whole bullock shall he carry forth outside the camp unto a clean place, where the ashes are poured out, and burn him on the wood with fire: where the ashes are poured out shall he be burnt.

13 And if the whole congregation of Israel sin through ignorance, and the thing be hid from the eyes of the assembly, and they have done somewhat against any of the commandments of the Becoming-One concerning things which should not be done, and are guilty;

14 When the sin, which they have sinned against it, is known, then the congregation shall offer a young bullock for the sin, and bring him before the tabernacle of the set time.

15 And the elders of the congregation shall lay their hands upon the head of the bullock before the Becoming-One: and the bullock shall be killed before the Becoming-One.

16 And the priest that is anointed shall bring of the bullock's blood to the tabernacle of the set time:

17 And the priest shall dip his finger in some of the blood, and sprinkle it seven times before the Becoming-One, even before the veil.

18 And he shall put some of the blood upon the horns of the altar which is before the Becoming-One, that is in the tabernacle of the set time,[56] and shall pour out all the blood at the bottom of the altar of the burnt offering, which is at the door of the tabernacle of the set time.[57]

19 And he shall take all his fat from him, and burn it upon the altar.

20 And he shall do with the bullock as he did with the bullock for a sin offering, so shall he do with this: and the priest shall make an atonement for them, and it shall be forgiven them.

---

[54] Appointed time or festival
[55] Appointed time or festival
[56] Appointed time or festival
[57] Appointed time or festival

21 And he shall carry forth the bullock outside the camp, and burn him as he burned the first bullock: it is a sin offering for the congregation.

22 When a ruler has sinned, and done somewhat through ignorance against any of the commandments of the Becoming-One his God concerning things which should not be done, and is guilty;

23 Or if his sin, wherein he has sinned, come to his knowledge; he shall bring his offering, a kid of the goats, a male without blemish:

24 And he shall lay his hand upon the head of the goat, and kill it in the place where they kill the burnt offering before the Becoming-One: it is a sin offering.

25 And the priest shall take of the blood of the sin offering with his finger, and put it upon the horns of the altar of burnt offering, and shall pour out his blood at the bottom of the altar of burnt offering.

26 And he shall burn all his fat upon the altar, as the fat of the sacrifice of peace offerings: and the priest shall make an atonement for him as concerning his sin, and it shall be forgiven him.

27 And if any soul of the common people sin through ignorance, while he did somewhat against any of the commandments of the Becoming-One concerning things which ought not to be done, and be guilty;

28 Or if his sin, which he has sinned, come to his knowledge: then he shall bring his offering, a kid of the goats, a female without blemish, for his sin which he has sinned.

29 And he shall lay his hand upon the head of the sin offering, and slay the sin offering in the place of the burnt offering.

30 And the priest shall take of the blood thereof with his finger, and put it upon the horns of the altar of burnt offering, and shall pour out all the blood thereof at the bottom of the altar.

31 And he shall take away all the fat thereof, as the fat is taken away from off the sacrifice of peace offerings; and the priest shall burn it upon the altar for a sweet aroma unto the Becoming-One; and the priest shall make an atonement for him, and it shall be forgiven him.

32 And if he bring a lamb for a sin offering, he shall bring it a female without blemish.

33 And he shall lay his hand upon the head of the sin offering, and slay it for a sin offering in the place where they kill the burnt offering.

34 And the priest shall take of the blood of the sin offering with his finger, and put it upon the horns of the altar of burnt offering, and shall pour out all the blood thereof at the bottom of the altar:

35 And he shall take away all the fat thereof, as the fat of the lamb is taken away from the sacrifice of the peace offerings; and the priest shall burn them upon the altar, according to the offerings made by fire unto the Becoming-One: and the priest shall make an atonement for his sin that he has committed, and it shall be forgiven him.

Lev 5:1 And if a soul sin, and hear the voice of swearing, and is a witness, whether he has seen or known of it; if he do not utter it, then he shall bear his iniquity.

2 Or if a soul touch any unclean thing, whether it be a carcase of an unclean beast, or a carcase of unclean cattle, or the carcase of unclean creeping things, and if it be hidden from him; he also shall be unclean, and guilty.

3 Or if he touch the uncleanness of man, whatsoever uncleanness it be that a man shall be defiled withal, and it be hid from him; when he knows of it, then he shall be guilty.

4 Or if a soul swear, pronouncing with his lips to do evil, or to do good, whatsoever it be that a man shall pronounce with an oath, and it be hid from him; when he knows of it, then he shall be guilty in one of these.

5 And it shall be, when he shall be guilty in one of these things, that he shall confess that he has sinned in that thing:

6 And he shall bring his trespass offering unto the Becoming-One for his sin which he has sinned, a female from the flock, a lamb or a kid of the goats, for a sin offering; and the priest shall make an atonement for him concerning his sin.

7 And if he be not able to bring a lamb, then he shall bring for his trespass, which he has committed, two turtledoves, or two young pigeons, unto the Becoming-One; one for a sin offering, and the other for a burnt offering.

8 And he shall bring them unto the priest, who shall offer that which is for the sin offering first, and wring off his head from his neck, but shall not divide it asunder:

9 And he shall sprinkle of the blood of the sin offering upon the side of the altar; and the rest of the blood shall be wrung out at the bottom of the altar: it is a sin offering.

10 And he shall offer the second for a burnt offering, according to the manner: and the priest shall make an atonement for him for his sin which he has sinned, and it shall be forgiven him.

11 But if he be not able to bring two turtledoves, or two young pigeons, then he that sinned shall bring for his offering the tenth part of an ephah of fine flour for a sin offering; he shall put no oil upon it, neither shall he put any frankincense thereon: for it is a sin offering.

12 Then shall he bring it to the priest, and the priest shall take his handful of it, even a memorial thereof, and burn it on the altar, according to the offerings made by fire unto the Becoming-One: it is a sin offering.

13 And the priest shall make an atonement for him as touching his sin that he has sinned in one of these, and it shall be forgiven him: and the remnant shall be the priest's, as a food offering.

14 And the Becoming-One spoke unto Moses, saying,

15 If a soul commit a trespass, and sin through ignorance, in the holy things of the Becoming-One; then he shall bring for his trespass unto the Becoming-One a ram without blemish out of the flocks, with your estimation by shekels of silver, after the shekel of the sanctuary, for a trespass offering:

16 And he shall make amends for the harm that he has done in the holy thing, and shall add the fifth part thereto, and give it unto the priest: and the priest shall make an atonement for him with the ram of the trespass offering, and it shall be forgiven him.

17 And if a soul sin, and commit any of these things which are forbidden to be done by the commandments of the Becoming-One; though he knew it not, yet is he guilty, and shall bear his iniquity.

18 And he shall bring a ram without blemish out of the flock, with your estimation, for a trespass offering, unto the priest: and the priest shall make an atonement for him concerning his ignorance wherein he erred and knew it not, and it shall be forgiven him.

19 It is a trespass offering: he has certainly trespassed against the Becoming-One.

Lev 6:1 And the Becoming-One spoke unto Moses, saying,

2 If a soul sin, and commit a trespass against the Becoming-One, and lie unto his neighbor in that which was delivered him to keep, or in fellowship, or in a thing taken away by violence, or has deceived his neighbor;

3 Or have found that which was lost, and lies concerning it, and swears falsely; in any of all these that a man does, sinning therein:

4 Then it shall be, because he has sinned, and is guilty, that he shall restore that which he took violently away, or the thing which he has deceitfully gotten, or that which was delivered him to keep, or the lost thing which he found,

5 Or all that about which he has sworn falsely; he shall even restore it in the principal, and shall add the fifth part more thereto, and give it unto him to whom it appertains, in the day of his trespass offering.

6 And he shall bring his trespass offering unto the Becoming-One, a ram without blemish out of the flock, with your estimation, for a trespass offering, unto the priest:

7 And the priest shall make an atonement for him before the Becoming-One: and it shall be forgiven him for any thing of all that he has done in trespassing therein.

8 And the Becoming-One spoke unto Moses, saying,

9 Command Aaron and his sons, saying, This is the law of the burnt offering: It is the burnt offering, because of the burning upon the altar all night unto the morning, and the fire of the altar shall be burning in it.

10 And the priest shall put on his linen garment, and his linen breeches shall he put upon his flesh, and take up the ashes which the fire has consumed with the burnt offering on the altar, and he shall put them beside the altar.

11 And he shall put off his garments, and put on other garments, and carry forth the ashes outside the camp unto a clean place.

12 And the fire upon the altar shall be burning in it; it shall not be put out: and the priest shall burn wood on it every morning, and lay the burnt offering in order upon it; and he shall burn thereon the fat of the peace offerings.

13 The fire continually shall be burning on the altar; it shall not go out.

14 And this is the law of the food offering: the sons of Aaron shall offer it before the Becoming-One, before the altar.

15 And he shall take of it his handful, of the flour of the food offering, and of the oil thereof, and all the frankincense which is upon the food offering, and shall burn it upon the altar for a sweet aroma, even the memorial of it, unto the Becoming-One.

16 And the remainder thereof shall Aaron and his sons eat: with unleavened bread shall it be eaten in the holy place; in the court of the tabernacle of the set time they shall eat it.

17 It shall not be baken with leaven. I have given it unto them for their portion of my offerings made by fire; it is most holy, as is the sin offering, and as the trespass offering.

18 All the males among the children of Aaron shall eat of it. It shall be a statute for olam in your generations concerning the offerings of the Becoming-One made by fire: every one that touches them shall be holy.

19 And the Becoming-One spoke unto Moses, saying,

20 This is the offering of Aaron and of his sons, which they shall offer unto the Becoming-One in the day when he is anointed; the tenth part of an ephah of fine flour for a food offering perpetual, half of it in the morning, and half thereof at night.

21 In a pan it shall be made with oil; and when it is baken, you shall bring it in: and the baken pieces of the food offering shall you offer for a sweet aroma unto the Becoming-One.

22 And the priest of his sons that is anointed in his stead shall offer it: it is a statute for olam unto the Becoming-One; it shall be wholly burnt.

23 For every food offering for the priest shall be wholly burnt: it shall not be eaten.

24 And the Becoming-One spoke unto Moses, saying,

25 Speak unto Aaron and to his sons, saying, This is the law of the sin offering: In the place where the burnt offering is killed shall the sin offering be killed before the Becoming-One: it is most holy.

26 The priest that offers it for sin shall eat it: in the holy place shall it be eaten, in the court of the tabernacle of the set time.

27 Whatsoever shall touch the flesh thereof shall be holy: and when there is sprinkled of the blood thereof upon any garment, you shall wash that whereon it was sprinkled in the holy place.

28 But the earthen vessel wherein it is sodden shall be broken: and if it be sodden in a brazen pot, it shall be both scoured, and rinsed in water.

29 All the males among the priests shall eat thereof: it is most holy.

30 And no sin offering, whereof any of the blood is brought into the tabernacle of the set time to reconcile withal in the holy place, shall be eaten: it shall be burnt in the fire.

Lev 7:1 Likewise this is the law of the trespass offering: it is most holy.

2 In the place where they kill the burnt offering shall they kill the trespass offering: and the blood thereof shall he sprinkle round about upon the altar.

3 And he shall offer of it all the fat thereof; the rump, and the fat that covers the inwards,

4 And the two kidneys, and the fat that is on them, which is by the flanks, and the caul that is above the liver, with the kidneys, it shall he take away:

5 And the priest shall burn them upon the altar for an offering made by fire unto the Becoming-One: it is a trespass offering.

6 Every male among the priests shall eat thereof: it shall be eaten in the holy place: it is most holy.

7 As the sin offering is, so is the trespass offering: there is one law for them: the priest that makes atonement therewith shall have it.

8 And the priest that offers any man's burnt offering, even the priest shall have to himself the skin of the burnt offering which he has offered.

9 And all the food offering that is baken in the oven, and all that is dressed in the frying pan, and in the pan, shall be the priest's that offers it.

10 And every food offering, mingled with oil, and dry, shall all the sons of Aaron have, one as much as another.

11 And this is the law of the sacrifice of peace offerings, which he shall offer unto the Becoming-One.

12 If he offer it for a thanksgiving, then he shall offer with the sacrifice of thanksgiving unleavened cakes mingled with oil, and unleavened wafers anointed with oil, and cakes mingled with oil, of fine flour, fried.

13 Besides the cakes, he shall offer for his offering leavened bread with the sacrifice of thanksgiving of his peace offerings.

14 And of it he shall offer one out of the whole offering for a heave offering unto the Becoming-One, and it shall be the priest's that sprinkles the blood of the peace offerings.

15 And the flesh of the sacrifice of his peace offerings for thanksgiving shall be eaten the same day that it is offered; he shall not leave any of it until the morning.

16 But if the sacrifice of his offering be a vow, or a voluntary offering, it shall be eaten the same day that he offers his sacrifice: and on the next day also the remainder of it shall be eaten:

17 But the remainder of the flesh of the sacrifice on the third day shall be burnt with fire.

18 And if any of the flesh of the sacrifice of his peace offerings be eaten at all on the third day, it shall not be accepted, neither shall it be imputed unto him that offers it: it shall be an abomination, and the soul that eats of it shall bear his iniquity.

19 And the flesh that touches any unclean thing shall not be eaten; it shall be burnt with fire: and as for the flesh, all that be clean shall eat thereof.

20 But the soul that eats of the flesh of the sacrifice of peace offerings, that pertain unto the Becoming-One, having his uncleanness upon him, even that soul shall be cut off from his people.

21 Moreover the soul that shall touch any unclean thing, as the uncleanness of man, or any unclean beast, or any abominable unclean thing, and eat of the flesh of the sacrifice of peace offerings, which pertain unto the Becoming-One, even that soul shall be cut off from his people.

22 And the Becoming-One spoke unto Moses, saying,

23 Speak unto the children of Israel, saying, you shall eat no manner of fat, of ox, or of sheep, or of goat.

24 And the fat of the beast that dies of itself, and the fat of that which is torn with beasts, may be used in any other use: but you shall in no wise eat of it.

25 For whosoever eats the fat of the beast, of which men offer an offering made by fire unto the Becoming-One, even the soul that eats it shall be cut off from his people.

26 Moreover you shall eat no manner of blood, whether it be of fowl or of beast, in any of your dwellings.

27 Whatsoever soul it be that eats any manner of blood, even that soul shall be cut off from his people.

28 And the Becoming-One spoke unto Moses, saying,

29 Speak unto the children of Israel, saying, He that offers the sacrifice of his peace offerings unto the Becoming-One shall bring his offering unto the Becoming-One of the sacrifice of his peace offerings.

30 His own hands shall bring the offerings of the Becoming-One made by fire, the fat with the breast, it shall he bring, that the breast may be waved for a wave offering before the Becoming-One.

31 And the priest shall burn the fat upon the altar: but the breast shall be Aaron's and his sons.'

32 And the right shoulder shall you give unto the priest for a heave offering of the sacrifices of your peace offerings.

33 He among the sons of Aaron, that offers the blood of the peace offerings, and the fat, shall have the right shoulder for his part.

34 For the wave breast and the heave shoulder have I taken of the children of Israel from off the sacrifices of their peace offerings, and have given them unto Aaron the priest and unto his sons by a statute for olam from among the children of Israel.

35 This is the portion of the anointing of Aaron, and of the anointing of his sons, out of the offerings of the Becoming-One made by fire, in the day when he presented them to minister unto the Becoming-One in the priest's office;

36 Which the Becoming-One commanded to be given them of the children of Israel, in the day that he anointed them, by a statute for olam throughout their generations.

37 This is the law of the burnt offering, of the food offering, and of the sin offering, and of the trespass offering, and of the consecrations, and of the sacrifice of the peace offerings;

38 Which the Becoming-One commanded Moses in mount Sinai, in the day that he commanded the children of Israel to offer their offerings unto the Becoming-One, in the wilderness of Sinai.

Lev 8:1 And the Becoming-One spoke unto Moses, saying,

2 Take Aaron and his sons with him, and the garments, and the anointing oil, and a bullock for the sin offering, and two rams, and a basket of unleavened bread;

3 And gather you all the congregation together unto the door of the tabernacle of the set time.

4 And Moses did as the Becoming-One commanded him; and the assembly was gathered together unto the door of the tabernacle of the set time.

5 And Moses said unto the congregation, This is the thing which the Becoming-One commanded to be done.

6 And Moses brought Aaron and his sons, and washed them with water.

7 And he put upon him the coat, and girded him with the girdle, and clothed him with the robe, and put the ephod upon him, and he girded him with the skilled girdle of the ephod, and bound it unto him therewith.

8 And he put the breastplate upon him: also he put in the breastplate the Urim and the Thummim.

9 And he put the turban upon his head; also upon the turban, even upon his forefront, did he put the golden plate, the holy crown; as the Becoming-One commanded Moses.

10 And Moses took the anointing oil, and anointed the tabernacle and all that was therein, and sanctified them.

11 And he sprinkled thereof upon the altar seven times, and anointed the altar and all his vessels, both the laver and his foot, to sanctify them.

12 And he poured of the anointing oil upon Aaron's head, and anointed him, to sanctify him.

13 And Moses brought Aaron's sons, and put coats upon them, and girded them with girdles, and put caps upon them; as the Becoming-One commanded Moses.

14 And he brought the bullock for the sin offering: and Aaron and his sons laid their hands upon the head of the bullock for the sin offering.

15 And he killed it; and Moses took the blood, and put it upon the horns of the altar round about with his finger, and purified the altar, and poured the blood at the bottom of the altar, and sanctified it, to make reconciliation upon it.

16 And he took all the fat that was upon the inwards, and the diaphragm around the liver, and the two kidneys, and their fat, and Moses burned it upon the altar.

17 But the bullock, and his hide, his flesh, and his dung, he burnt with fire outside the camp; as the Becoming-One commanded Moses.

18 And he brought the ram for the burnt offering: and Aaron and his sons laid their hands upon the head of the ram.

19 And he killed it; and Moses sprinkled the blood upon the altar round about.

20 And he cut the ram into pieces; and Moses burnt the head, and the pieces, and the fat.

21 And he washed the inwards and the legs in water; and Moses burnt the whole ram upon the altar: it was a burnt sacrifice for a sweet aroma, and an offering made by fire unto the Becoming-One; as the Becoming-One commanded Moses.

22 And he brought the other ram, the ram of consecration: and Aaron and his sons laid their hands upon the head of the ram.

23 And he killed it; and Moses took of the blood of it, and put it upon the tip of Aaron's right ear, and upon the thumb of his right hand, and upon the great toe of his right foot.

24 And he brought Aaron's sons, and Moses put of the blood upon the tip of their right ear, and upon the thumbs of their right hands, and upon the great toes of their right feet: and Moses sprinkled the blood upon the altar round about.

25 And he took the fat, and the rump, and all the fat that was upon the inwards, and the diaphragm around the liver, and the two kidneys, and their fat, and the right shoulder:

26 And out of the basket of unleavened bread, that was before the Becoming-One, he took one unleavened cake, and a cake of oiled bread, and one wafer, and put them on the fat, and upon the right shoulder:

27 And he put all upon Aaron's hands, and upon his sons' hands, and waved them for a wave offering before the Becoming-One.

28 And Moses took them from off their hands, and burnt them on the altar upon the burnt offering: they were consecrations for a sweet aroma: it is an offering made by fire unto the Becoming-One.

29 And Moses took the breast, and waved it for a wave offering before the Becoming-One: for of the ram of consecration it was Moses' part; as the Becoming-One commanded Moses.

30 And Moses took of the anointing oil, and of the blood which was upon the altar, and sprinkled it upon Aaron, and upon his garments, and upon his sons, and upon his sons' garments with him; and sanctified Aaron, and his garments, and his sons, and his sons' garments with him.

31 And Moses said unto Aaron and to his sons, Boil the flesh at the door of the tabernacle of the set time: and there eat it with the bread that is in the basket of consecrations, as I commanded, saying, Aaron and his sons shall eat it.

32 And that which remains of the flesh and of the bread shall you burn with fire.

33 And you shall not go out of the door of the tabernacle of the set time in seven days, until the days of your consecration be at an end: for seven days shall he consecrate you.

34 As he has done this day, so the Becoming-One has commanded to do, to make an atonement for you.

35 Therefore shall you abide at the door of the tabernacle of the set time day and night seven days, and keep the charge of the Becoming-One, that you die not: for so I am commanded.

36 So Aaron and his sons did all things which the Becoming-One commanded by the hand of Moses.

Lev 9:1 And it came to pass on the eighth day, that Moses called Aaron and his sons, and the elders of Israel;

2 And he said unto Aaron, Take you a young calf for a sin offering, and a ram for a burnt offering, without blemish, and offer them before the Becoming-One.

3 And unto the children of Israel you shall speak, saying, Take you a kid of the goats for a sin offering; and a calf and a lamb, both of the first year, without blemish, for a burnt offering;

4 Also a bullock and a ram for peace offerings, to sacrifice before the Becoming-One; and a food offering mingled with oil: for today the Becoming-One will appear unto you.

5 And they brought that which Moses commanded before the tabernacle of the set time: and all the congregation drew near and stood before the Becoming-One.

6 And Moses said, This is the thing which the Becoming-One commanded that you should do: and the glory of the Becoming-One shall appear unto you.

7 And Moses said unto Aaron, Go unto the altar, and offer your sin offering, and your burnt offering, and make an atonement for thyself, and for the people: and offer the offering of the people, and make an atonement for them; as the Becoming-One commanded.

8 Aaron therefore went unto the altar, and killed the calf of the sin offering, which was for himself.

9 And the sons of Aaron brought the blood unto him: and he dipped his finger in the blood, and put it upon the horns of the altar, and poured out the blood at the bottom of the altar:

10 But the fat, and the kidneys, and the diaphragm around the liver of the sin offering, he burnt upon the altar; as the Becoming-One commanded Moses.

11 And the flesh and the hide he burnt with fire outside the camp.

12 And he killed the burnt offering; and Aaron's sons presented unto him the blood, which he sprinkled round about upon the altar.

13 And they presented the burnt offering unto him, with the pieces thereof, and the head: and he burnt them upon the altar.

14 And he did wash the inwards and the legs, and burnt them upon the burnt offering on the altar.

15 And he brought the people's offering, and took the goat, which was the sin offering for the people, and killed it, and offered it for sin, as the first.

16 And he brought the burnt offering, and offered it according to the manner.

17 And he brought the food offering, and took a handful thereof, and burnt it upon the altar, beside the burnt sacrifice of the morning.

18 He killed also the bullock and the ram for a sacrifice of peace offerings, which was for the people: and Aaron's sons presented unto him the blood, which he sprinkled upon the altar round about,

19 And the fat of the bullock and of the ram, the rump, and that which covers the inwards, and the kidneys, and the diaphragm around the liver:

20 And they put the fat upon the breasts, and he burnt the fat upon the altar:

21 And the breasts and the right shoulder Aaron waved for a wave offering before the Becoming-One; as Moses commanded.

22 And Aaron lifted up his hand toward the people, and blessed them, and came down from offering of the sin offering, and the burnt offering, and peace offerings.

23 And Moses and Aaron went into the tabernacle of the set time, and came out, and blessed the people: and the glory of the Becoming-One appeared unto all the people.

24 And there came a fire out from before the Becoming-One, and consumed upon the altar the burnt offering and the fat: which when all the people saw, they shouted, and fell on their faces.

Lev 10:1 And Nadab and Abihu, the sons of Aaron, took either of them his censer, and put fire therein, and put incense thereon, and offered strange fire before the Becoming-One, which he commanded them not.

2 And there went out fire from the Becoming-One, and devoured them, and they died before the Becoming-One.

3 Then Moses said unto Aaron, This is it that the Becoming-One spoke, saying, I will be sanctified in them that come near me, and before all the people I will be glorified. And Aaron held his peace.

4 And Moses called Mishael and Elzaphan, the sons of Uzziel the uncle of Aaron, and said unto them, Come near, carry your brethren from before the sanctuary out of the camp.

5 So they went near, and carried them in their coats out of the camp; as Moses had said.

6 And Moses said unto Aaron, and unto Eleazar and unto Ithamar, his sons, Uncover not your heads, neither rend your clothes; lest you die, and lest wrath come upon all the people: but let your brethren, the whole house of Israel, bewail the burning which the Becoming-One has kindled.

7 And you shall not go out from the door of the tabernacle of the set time, lest you die: for the anointing oil of the Becoming-One is upon you. And they did according to the word of Moses.

8 And the Becoming-One spoke unto Aaron, saying,

9 Do not drink wine nor strong drink, you, nor your sons with you, when you go into the tabernacle of the set time, lest you die: it shall be a statute for olam throughout your generations:

10 And that you may put difference between holy and unholy, and between unclean and clean;

11 And that you may teach the children of Israel all the statutes which the Becoming-One has spoken unto them by the hand of Moses.

12 And Moses spoke unto Aaron, and unto Eleazar and unto Ithamar, his sons that were left, Take the food offering that remains of the offerings of the Becoming-One made by fire, and eat it without leaven beside the altar: for it is most holy:

13 And you shall eat it in the holy place, because it is your due, and your sons' due, of the sacrifices of the Becoming-One made by fire: for so I am commanded.

14 And the wave breast and heave shoulder shall you eat in a clean place; you, and your sons, and your daughters with you: for they be your due, and your sons' due, which are given out of the sacrifices of peace offerings of the children of Israel.

15 The heave shoulder and the wave breast shall they bring with the offerings made by fire of the fat, to wave it for a wave offering before the Becoming-One; and it shall be yours, and your sons' with you, by a statute for olam as the Becoming-One has commanded.

16 And Moses diligently sought the goat of the sin offering, and, behold, it was burnt: and he was angry with Eleazar and Ithamar, the sons of Aaron which were left alive, saying,

17 Why have you not eaten the sin offering in the holy place, seeing it is most holy, and God has given it you to bear the iniquity of the congregation, to make atonement for them before the Becoming-One?

18 Behold, the blood of it was not brought in within the holy place: you should indeed have eaten it in the holy place, as I commanded.

19 And Aaron said unto Moses, Behold, this day have they offered their sin offering and their burnt offering before the Becoming-One; and such things have befallen me: and if I had eaten the sin offering

today, should it have been accepted in the sight of the Becoming-One?

20 And when Moses heard that, he was content.

Lev 11:1 And the Becoming-One spoke unto Moses and to Aaron, saying unto them,

2 Speak unto the children of Israel, saying, These are the beasts which you shall eat among all the beasts that are on the earth.

3 Whatsoever parts the hoof, and is clovenfooted, and chews the cud, among the beasts, that shall you eat.

4 Nevertheless these shall you not eat of them that chew the cud, or of them that divide the hoof: as the camel, because he chews the cud, but divides not the hoof; he is unclean unto you.

5 And the coney, because he chews the cud, but divides not the hoof; he is unclean unto you.

6 And the rabbit, because he chews the cud, but divides not the hoof; he is unclean unto you.

7 And the swine, though he divide the hoof, and be clovenfooted, yet he chews not the cud; he is unclean to you.

8 Of their flesh shall you not eat, and their carcase shall you not touch; they are unclean to you.

9 These shall you eat of all that are in the waters: whatsoever has fins and scales in the waters, in the seas, and in the rivers, them shall you eat.

10 And all that have not fins and scales in the seas, and in the rivers, of all that move in the waters, and of any living soul which is in the waters, they shall be an abomination unto you:

11 They shall be even an abomination unto you; you shall not eat of their flesh, but you shall have their carcases in abomination.

12 Whatsoever has no fins nor scales in the waters, that shall be an abomination unto you.

13 And these are they which you shall have in abomination among the fowls; they shall not be eaten, they are an abomination: the eagle, and the ossifrage, and the osprey,

14 And the vulture, and the kite after his kind;

15 Every raven after his kind;

16 And the owl, and the night hawk, and the sea gull, and the hawk after his kind,

17 And the little owl, and the cormorant, and the great owl,

18 And the swan, and the pelican, and the gier eagle,

19 And the stork, the heron after her kind, and the lapwing, and the bat.

20 All fowls that creep, going upon all four, shall be an abomination unto you.

21 Yet these may you eat of every flying creeping thing that goes upon all four, which have legs above their feet, to leap withal upon the earth;

22 Even these of them you may eat; the locust after his kind, and the bald locust after his kind, and the beetle after his kind, and the grasshopper after his kind.

23 But all other flying creeping things, which have four feet, shall be an abomination unto you.

24 And for these you shall be unclean: whosoever touches the carcase of them shall be unclean until the evening.

25 And whosoever bears of the carcase of them shall wash his clothes, and be unclean until the evening.

26 The carcases of every beast which divides the hoof, and is not clovenfooted, nor chews the cud, are unclean unto you: every one that touches them shall be unclean.

27 And whatsoever goes upon his paws, among all manner of beasts that go on all four, those are unclean unto you: whoso touches their carcase shall be unclean until the evening.

28 And he that bears the carcase of them shall wash his clothes, and be unclean until the evening: they are unclean unto you.

29 These also shall be unclean unto you among the creeping things that creep upon the earth; the weasel, and the mouse, and the tortoise after his kind,

30 And the ferret, and the chameleon, and the lizard, and the snail, and the mole.

31 These are unclean to you among all that creep: whosoever does touch them, when they be dead, shall be unclean until the evening.

32 And upon whatsoever any of them, when they are dead, does fall, it shall be unclean; whether it be any vessel of wood, or raiment, or skin, or sack, whatsoever vessel it be, wherein any work is done, it must be put into water, and it shall be unclean until the evening; so it shall be cleansed.

33 And every earthen vessel, whereinto any of them falls, whatsoever is in it shall be unclean; and you shall break it.

34 Of all food which may be eaten, that on which such water comes shall be unclean: and all drink that may be drunk in every such vessel shall be unclean.

35 And every thing whereupon any part of their carcase falls shall be unclean; whether it be oven, or ranges for pots, they shall be broken down: for they are unclean, and shall be unclean unto you.

36 Nevertheless a fountain or pit, wherein there is plenty of water, shall be clean: but that which touches their carcase shall be unclean.

37 And if any part of their carcase fall upon any sowing seed which is to be sown, it shall be clean.

38 But if any water be put upon the seed, and any part of their carcase fall thereon, it shall be unclean unto you.

39 And if any beast, of which you may eat, die; he that touches the carcase thereof shall be unclean until the evening.

40 And he that eats of the carcase of it shall wash his clothes, and be unclean until the evening: he also that bears the carcase of it shall wash his clothes, and be unclean until the evening.

41 And every creeping thing that creeps upon the earth shall be an abomination; it shall not be eaten.

42 Whatsoever goes upon the belly, and whatsoever goes upon all four, or whatsoever has more feet among all creeping things that creep upon the earth, them you shall not eat; for they are an abomination.

43 you shall not make your souls abominable with any creeping thing that creeps, neither shall you make yourselves unclean with them, that you should be defiled thereby.

44 For I am the Becoming-One your God: you shall therefore sanctify yourselves, and you shall be holy;

for I am holy: neither shall you defile your souls with any manner of creeping thing that creeps upon the earth.

45 For I am the Becoming-One that brings you up out of the land of Egypt, to be your God: you shall therefore be holy, for I am holy.

46 This is the law of the beasts, and of the fowl, and of every living soul that moves in the waters, and of every soul that creeps upon the earth:

47 To make a difference between the unclean and the clean, and between the beast that may be eaten and the beast that may not be eaten.

Lev 12:1 And the Becoming-One spoke unto Moses, saying,

2 Speak unto the children of Israel, saying, If a woman have conceived seed, and born a male child: then she shall be unclean seven days; according to the days of the separation for her menstruous period shall she be unclean.

3 And in the eighth day the flesh of his foreskin shall be circumcised.

4 And she shall then continue in the blood of her purifying three and thirty days; she shall touch no hallowed thing, nor come into the sanctuary, until the days of her purifying be fulfilled.

5 But if she bear a female, then she shall be unclean two weeks, as in her separation: and she shall continue in the blood of her purifying threescore and six days.

6 And when the days of her purifying are fulfilled, for a son, or for a daughter, she shall bring a lamb of the first year for a burnt offering, and a young pigeon, or a turtledove, for a sin offering, unto the door of the tabernacle of the set time, unto the priest:

7 Who shall offer it before the Becoming-One, and make an atonement for her; and she shall be cleansed from the issue of her blood. This is the law for her that has born a male or a female.

8 And if she be not able to bring a lamb, then she shall bring two turtles, or two young pigeons; the one for the burnt offering, and the other for a sin offering: and the priest shall make an atonement for her, and she shall be clean.

Lev 13:1 And the Becoming-One spoke unto Moses and Aaron, saying,

2 When a man shall have in the skin of his flesh a rising, a scab, or bright spot, and it be in the skin of his flesh like the plague of leprosy; then he shall be brought unto Aaron the priest, or unto one of his sons the priests:

3 And the priest shall look on the plague in the skin of the flesh: and when the hair in the plague is turned white, and the plague in sight be deeper than the skin of his flesh, it is a plague of leprosy: and the priest shall look on him, and pronounce him unclean.

4 If the bright spot be white in the skin of his flesh, and in sight be not deeper than the skin, and the hair thereof be not turned white; then the priest shall shut up him that has the plague seven days:

5 And the priest shall look on him the seventh day: and, behold, if the plague in his sight be at a stay, and the plague spread not in the skin; then the priest shall shut him up seven days more:

6 And the priest shall look on him again the seventh day: and, behold, if the plague be somewhat dark, and the plague spread not in the skin, the priest shall pronounce him clean: it is but a scab: and he shall wash his clothes, and be clean.

7 But if the scab spread much abroad in the skin, after that he has been seen of the priest for his cleansing, he shall be seen of the priest again:

8 And if the priest see that, behold, the scab spreads in the skin, then the priest shall pronounce him unclean: it is a leprosy.

9 When the plague of leprosy is in a man, then he shall be brought unto the priest;

10 And the priest shall see him: and, behold, if the rising be white in the skin, and it have turned the hair white, and there be quick raw flesh in the rising;

11 It is an old leprosy in the skin of his flesh, and the priest shall pronounce him unclean, and shall not shut him up: for he is unclean.

12 And if a leprosy break out abroad in the skin, and the leprosy cover all the skin of him that has the plague from his head even to his foot, wheresoever the priest looks;

13 Then the priest shall consider: and, behold, if the leprosy have covered all his flesh, he shall pronounce him clean that has the plague: it is all turned white: he is clean.

14 But when raw flesh appears in him, he shall be unclean.

15 And the priest shall see the raw flesh, and pronounce him to be unclean: for the raw flesh is unclean: it is a leprosy.

16 Or if the raw flesh turn again, and be changed unto white, he shall come unto the priest;

17 And the priest shall see him: and, behold, if the plague be turned into white; then the priest shall pronounce him clean that has the plague: he is clean.

18 The flesh also, in which, even in the skin thereof, was a boil, and is healed,

19 And in the place of the boil there be a white rising, or a bright spot, white, and somewhat reddish, and it be showed to the priest;

20 And if, when the priest sees it, behold, it be in sight lower than the skin, and the hair thereof be turned white; the priest shall pronounce him unclean: it is a plague of leprosy broken out of the boil.

21 But if the priest look on it, and, behold, there be no white hairs therein, and if it be not lower than the skin, but be somewhat dark; then the priest shall shut him up seven days:

22 And if it spread much abroad in the skin, then the priest shall pronounce him unclean: it is a plague.

23 But if the bright spot stay in his place, and spread not, it is a burning boil; and the priest shall pronounce him clean.

24 Or if there be any flesh, in the skin whereof there is a hot burning, and the quick flesh that burns have a white bright spot, somewhat reddish, or white;

25 Then the priest shall look upon it: and, behold, if the hair in the bright spot be turned white, and it be in sight deeper than the skin; it is a leprosy broken out of the burning: therefore the priest shall pronounce him unclean: it is the plague of leprosy.

26 But if the priest look on it, and, behold, there be no white hair in the bright spot, and it be no lower

than the other skin, but be somewhat dark; then the priest shall shut him up seven days:

27 And the priest shall look upon him the seventh day: and if it be spread much abroad in the skin, then the priest shall pronounce him unclean: it is the plague of leprosy.

28 And if the bright spot stay in his place, and spread not in the skin, but it be somewhat dark; it is a rising of the burning, and the priest shall pronounce him clean: for it is an inflammation of the burning.

29 If a man or woman have a plague upon the head or the beard;

30 Then the priest shall see the plague: and, behold, if it be in sight deeper than the skin; and there be in it a yellow thin hair; then the priest shall pronounce him unclean: it is a dry scab, even a leprosy upon the head or beard.

31 And if the priest look on the plague of the scab, and, behold, it be not in sight deeper than the skin, and that there is no black hair in it; then the priest shall shut up him that has the plague of the scab seven days:

32 And in the seventh day the priest shall look on the plague: and, behold, if the scab spread not, and there be in it no yellow hair, and the scab be not in sight deeper than the skin;

33 He shall be shaven, but the scab shall he not shave; and the priest shall shut up him that has the scab seven days more:

34 And in the seventh day the priest shall look on the scab: and, behold, if the scab be not spread in the skin, nor be in sight deeper than the skin; then the priest shall pronounce him clean: and he shall wash his clothes, and be clean.

35 But if the scab spread much in the skin after his cleansing;

36 Then the priest shall look on him: and, behold, if the scab be spread in the skin, the priest shall not seek for yellow hair; he is unclean.

37 But if the scab be in his sight is checked, and that there is black hair grown up therein; the scab is healed, he is clean: and the priest shall pronounce him clean.

38 If a man also or a woman have in the skin of their flesh bright spots, even white bright spots;

39 Then the priest shall look: and, behold, if the bright spots in the skin of their flesh be darkish white; it is a freckled spot that grows in the skin; he is clean.

40 And the man whose hair is fallen off his head, he is bald; yet is he clean.

41 And he that has his hair fallen off from the part of his head toward his face, he is forehead bald: yet is he clean.

42 And if there be in the bald head, or bald forehead, a white reddish sore; it is a leprosy sprung up in his bald head, or his bald forehead.

43 Then the priest shall look upon it: and, behold, if the rising of the sore be white reddish in his bald head, or in his bald forehead, as the leprosy appears in the skin of the flesh;

44 He is a leprous man, he is unclean: the priest shall pronounce him utterly unclean; his plague is in his head.

45 And the leper in whom the plague is, his clothes shall be rent, and his head bare, and he shall put a covering upon his upper lip, and shall cry, Unclean, unclean.

46 All the days wherein the plague shall be in him he shall be defiled; he is unclean: he shall dwell alone; outside the camp shall his habitation be.

47 The garment also that the plague of leprosy is in, whether it be a woollen garment, or a linen garment;

48 Whether it be in the warp, or woof; of linen, or of woollen; whether in a skin, or in any thing made of skin;

49 And if the plague be greenish or reddish in the garment, or in the skin, either in the warp, or in the woof, or in any thing of skin; it is a plague of leprosy, and shall be showed unto the priest:

50 And the priest shall look upon the plague, and shut up it that has the plague seven days:

51 And he shall look on the plague on the seventh day: if the plague be spread in the garment, either in the warp, or in the woof, or in a skin, or in any work that is made of skin; the plague is a fretting leprosy; it is unclean.

52 He shall therefore burn that garment, whether warp or woof, in woollen or in linen, or any thing of skin, wherein the plague is: for it is a fretting leprosy; it shall be burnt in the fire.

53 And if the priest shall look, and, behold, the plague be not spread in the garment, either in the warp, or in the woof, or in any thing of skin;

54 Then the priest shall command that they wash the thing wherein the plague is, and he shall shut it up seven days more:

55 And the priest shall look on the plague, after that it is washed: and, behold, if the plague have not changed his color, and the plague be not spread; it is unclean; you shall burn it in the fire; it is fret inward, whether it be bare within or without.

56 And if the priest look, and, behold, the plague be somewhat dark after the washing of it; then he shall rend it out of the garment, or out of the skin, or out of the warp, or out of the woof:

57 And if it appear still in the garment, either in the warp, or in the woof, or in any thing of skin; it is a spreading plague: you shall burn that wherein the plague is with fire.

58 And the garment, either warp, or woof, or whatsoever thing of skin it be, which you shall wash, if the plague be departed from them, then it shall be washed the second time, and shall be clean.

59 This is the law of the plague of leprosy in a garment of woollen or linen, either in the warp, or woof, or any thing of skins, to pronounce it clean, or to pronounce it unclean.

Lev 14:1 And the Becoming-One spoke unto Moses, saying,

2 This shall be the law of the leper in the day of his cleansing: He shall be brought unto the priest:

3 And the priest shall go forth out of the camp; and the priest shall look, and, behold, if the plague of leprosy be healed in the leper;

4 Then shall the priest command to take for him that is to be cleansed two birds alive and clean, and cedar wood, and scarlet, and hyssop:

5 And the priest shall command that one of the birds be killed in an earthen vessel over running water:

6 As for the living bird, he shall take it, and the cedar wood, and the scarlet, and the hyssop, and shall dip them and the living bird in the blood of the bird that was killed over the running water:

7 And he shall sprinkle upon him that is to be cleansed from the leprosy seven times, and shall pronounce him clean, and shall let the living bird loose into the open field.

8 And he that is to be cleansed shall wash his clothes, and shave off all his hair, and wash himself in water, that he may be clean: and after that he shall come into the camp, and shall tarry abroad out of his tent seven days.

9 But it shall be on the seventh day, that he shall shave all his hair off his head and his beard and his eyebrows, even all his hair he shall shave off: and he shall wash his clothes, also he shall wash his flesh in water, and he shall be clean.

10 And on the eighth day he shall take two he lambs without blemish, and one ewe lamb of the first year without blemish, and three tenth deals of fine flour for a food offering, mingled with oil, and one log of oil.

11 And the priest that makes him clean shall present the man that is to be made clean, and those things, before the Becoming-One, at the door of the tabernacle of the set time:

12 And the priest shall take one he lamb, and offer him for a trespass offering, and the log of oil, and wave them for a wave offering before the Becoming-One: 13 And he shall slay the lamb in the place where he shall kill the sin offering and the burnt offering, in the holy place: for as the sin offering is the priest's, so is the trespass offering: it is most holy:

14 And the priest shall take some of the blood of the trespass offering, and the priest shall put it upon the tip of the right ear of him that is to be cleansed, and upon the thumb of his right hand, and upon the great toe of his right foot:

15 And the priest shall take some of the log of oil, and pour it into the palm of his own left hand:

16 And the priest shall dip his right finger in the oil that is in his left hand, and shall sprinkle of the oil with his finger seven times before the Becoming-One: 17 And of the rest of the oil that is in his hand shall the priest put upon the tip of the right ear of him that is to be cleansed, and upon the thumb of his right hand, and upon the great toe of his right foot, upon the blood of the trespass offering:

18 And the remnant of the oil that is in the priest's hand he shall pour upon the head of him that is to be cleansed: and the priest shall make an atonement for him before the Becoming-One.

19 And the priest shall offer the sin offering, and make an atonement for him that is to be cleansed from his uncleanness; and afterward he shall kill the burnt offering:

20 And the priest shall offer the burnt offering and the food offering upon the altar: and the priest shall make an atonement for him, and he shall be clean.

21 And if he be poor, and cannot get so much; then he shall take one lamb for a trespass offering to be waved, to make an atonement for him, and one tenth deal of fine flour mingled with oil for a food offering, and a log of oil;

22 And two turtledoves, or two young pigeons, such as he is able to get; and the one shall be a sin offering, and the other a burnt offering.

23 And he shall bring them on the eighth day for his cleansing unto the priest, unto the door of the tabernacle of the set time, before the Becoming-One.

24 And the priest shall take the lamb of the trespass offering, and the log of oil, and the priest shall wave them for a wave offering before the Becoming-One: 25 And he shall kill the lamb of the trespass offering, and the priest shall take some of the blood of the trespass offering, and put it upon the tip of the right ear of him that is to be cleansed, and upon the thumb of his right hand, and upon the great toe of his right foot:

26 And the priest shall pour of the oil into the palm of his own left hand:

27 And the priest shall sprinkle with his right finger some of the oil that is in his left hand seven times before the Becoming-One: 28 And the priest shall put of the oil that is in his hand upon the tip of the right ear of him that is to be cleansed, and upon the thumb of his right hand, and upon the great toe of his right foot, upon the place of the blood of the trespass offering:

29 And the rest of the oil that is in the priest's hand he shall put upon the head of him that is to be cleansed, to make an atonement for him before the Becoming-One.

30 And he shall offer the one of the turtledoves, or of the young pigeons, such as he can get;

31 Even such as he is able to get, the one for a sin offering, and the other for a burnt offering, with the food offering: and the priest shall make an atonement for him that is to be cleansed before the Becoming-One.

32 This is the law of him in whom is the plague of leprosy, whose hand is not able to get that which pertains to his cleansing.

33 And the Becoming-One spoke unto Moses and unto Aaron, saying,

34 When you be come into the land of Canaan, which I give to you for a possession, and I put the plague of leprosy in a house of the land of your possession;

35 And he that owns the house shall come and tell the priest, saying, It seems to me there is as it were a plague in the house:

36 Then the priest shall command that they empty the house, before the priest go into it to see the plague, that all that is in the house be not made unclean: and afterward the priest shall go in to see the house:

37 And he shall look on the plague, and, behold, if the plague be in the walls of the house with hollow streaks, greenish or reddish, which in sight are lower than the wall;

38 Then the priest shall go out of the house to the door of the house, and shut up the house seven days:

39 And the priest shall come again the seventh day, and shall look: and, behold, if the plague be spread in the walls of the house;

40 Then the priest shall command that they take away the stones in which the plague is, and they shall cast them into an unclean place outside the city:

41 And he shall cause the house to be scraped within round about, and they shall pour out the dust that they scrape off outside the city into an unclean place:

42 And they shall take other stones, and put them in the place of those stones; and he shall take other mortar, and shall plaster the house.

43 And if the plague come again, and break out in the house, after that he has taken away the stones, and after he has scraped the house, and after it is plastered;

44 Then the priest shall come and look, and, behold, if the plague be spread in the house, it is a fretting leprosy in the house: it is unclean.

45 And he shall break down the house, the stones of it, and the timber thereof, and all the mortar of the house; and he shall carry them forth out of the city into an unclean place.

46 Moreover he that goes into the house all the while that it is shut up shall be unclean until the evening.

47 And he that lies in the house shall wash his clothes; and he that eats in the house shall wash his clothes.

48 And if the priest shall come in, and look upon it, and, behold, the plague has not spread in the house, after the house was plastered: then the priest shall pronounce the house clean, because the plague is healed.

49 And he shall take to cleanse the house two birds, and cedar wood, and scarlet, and hyssop:

50 And he shall kill the one of the birds in an earthen vessel over running water:

51 And he shall take the cedar wood, and the hyssop, and the scarlet, and the living bird, and dip them in the blood of the slain bird, and in the running water, and sprinkle the house seven times:

52 And he shall cleanse the house with the blood of the bird, and with the running water, and with the living bird, and with the cedar wood, and with the hyssop, and with the scarlet:

53 But he shall let go the living bird out of the city into the open fields, and make an atonement for the house: and it shall be clean.

54 This is the law for all manner of plague of leprosy, and scab,

55 And for the leprosy of a garment, and of a house,

56 And for a rising, and for a scab, and for a bright spot:

57 To teach when it is unclean, and when it is clean: this is the law of leprosy.

Lev 15:1 And the Becoming-One spoke unto Moses and to Aaron, saying,

2 Speak unto the children of Israel, and say unto them, When any man has a running issue out of his flesh, because of his issue he is unclean.

3 And this shall be his uncleanness in his issue: whether his flesh run with his issue, or his flesh be stopped from his issue, it is his uncleanness.

4 Every bed, whereon he lies that has the issue, is unclean: and every thing, whereon he sits, shall be unclean.

5 And whosoever touches his bed shall wash his clothes, and bathe himself in water, and be unclean until the evening.

6 And he that sits on any thing whereon he sat that has the issue shall wash his clothes, and bathe himself in water, and be unclean until the evening.

7 And he that touches the flesh of him that has the issue shall wash his clothes, and bathe himself in water, and be unclean until the evening.

8 And if he that has the issue spit upon him that is clean; then he shall wash his clothes, and bathe himself in water, and be unclean until the evening.

9 And what saddle soever he rides upon that has the issue shall be unclean.

10 And whosoever touches any thing that was under him shall be unclean until the evening: and he that bears any of those things shall wash his clothes, and bathe himself in water, and be unclean until the evening.

11 And whomsoever he touches that has the issue, and has not rinsed his hands in water, he shall wash his clothes, and bathe himself in water, and be unclean until the evening.

12 And the vessel of earth, that he touches which has the issue, shall be broken: and every vessel of wood shall be rinsed in water.

13 And when he that has an issue is cleansed of his issue; then he shall number to himself seven days for his cleansing, and wash his clothes, and bathe his flesh in running water, and shall be clean.

14 And on the eighth day he shall take to him two turtledoves, or two young pigeons, and come before the Becoming-One unto the door of the tabernacle of the set time, and give them unto the priest:

15 And the priest shall offer them, the one for a sin offering, and the other for a burnt offering; and the priest shall make an atonement for him before the Becoming-One for his issue.

16 And if any man's seed of copulation go out from him, then he shall wash all his flesh in water, and be unclean until the evening.

17 And every garment, and every skin, whereon is the seed of copulation, shall be washed with water, and be unclean until the evening.

18 The woman also with whom man shall lie with seed of copulation, they shall both bathe themselves in water, and be unclean until the evening.

19 And if a woman have an issue, and her issue in her flesh be blood, she shall be put apart seven days: and whosoever touches her shall be unclean until the evening.

20 And every thing that she lies upon in her separation shall be unclean: every thing also that she sits upon shall be unclean.

21 And whosoever touches her bed shall wash his clothes, and bathe himself in water, and be unclean until the evening.

22 And whosoever touches any thing that she sat upon shall wash his clothes, and bathe himself in water, and be unclean until the evening.

23 And if it be on her bed, or on any thing whereon she sits, when he touches it, he shall be unclean until the evening.

24 And if any man lie with her at all, and her separation be upon him, he shall be unclean seven days; and all the bed whereon he lies shall be unclean.

25 And if a woman have an issue of her blood many days out of the time of her separation, or if it run beyond the time of her separation; all the days of the issue of her uncleanness shall be as the days of her separation: she shall be unclean.

26 Every bed whereon she lies all the days of her issue shall be unto her as the bed of her separation: and whatsoever she sits upon shall be unclean, as the uncleanness of her separation.

27 And whosoever touches those things shall be unclean, and shall wash his clothes, and bathe himself in water, and be unclean until the evening.

28 But if she be cleansed of her issue, then she shall number to herself seven days, and after that she shall be clean.

29 And on the eighth day she shall take unto her two turtles, or two young pigeons, and bring them unto the priest, to the door of the tabernacle of the set time.

30 And the priest shall offer the one for a sin offering, and the other for a burnt offering; and the priest shall make an atonement for her before the Becoming-One for the issue of her uncleanness.

31 Thus shall you separate the children of Israel from their uncleanness; that they die not in their uncleanness, when they defile my tabernacle that is among them.

32 This is the law of him that has an issue, and of him whose seed goes from him, and is defiled therewith;

33 And of her that is in her menstruous period, and of him that has an issue, male or female, and for the man that lies with a woman who is unclean.

Lev 16:1 And the Becoming-One spoke unto Moses after the death of the two sons of Aaron, when they offered before the Becoming-One, and died;

2 And the Becoming-One said unto Moses, Speak unto Aaron your brother, that he come not at any time [at all times] into the holy place within the veil before the mercy seat, which is upon the ark; that he die not: for I will appear in the cloud upon the mercy seat.

3 Thus shall Aaron come into the holy place: with a young bullock for a sin offering, and a ram for a burnt offering.

4 He shall put on the holy linen coat, and he shall have the linen breeches upon his flesh, and shall be girded with a linen girdle, and with the linen turban shall he be attired: these are holy garments; therefore shall he wash his flesh in water, and so put them on.

5 And he shall take of the congregation of the children of Israel two kids of the goats for a sin offering, and one ram for a burnt offering.

6 And Aaron shall offer his bullock of the sin offering, which is for himself, and make an atonement for himself, and for his house.

7 And he shall take the two goats, and present them before the Becoming-One at the door of the tabernacle of the set time.

8 And Aaron shall cast lots upon the two goats; one lot for the Becoming-One, and the other lot for Azazel [entire removal, scapegoat]

9 And Aaron shall bring the goat upon which the Becoming-One's lot fell, and offer him for a sin offering.

10 But the goat, on which the lot fell to be the scapegoat [azazel] shall be presented alive before the Becoming-One, to make an atonement with him, and to let him go for a scapegoat [azazel] into the wilderness.

11 And Aaron shall bring the bullock of the sin offering, which is for himself, and shall make an atonement for himself, and for his house, and shall kill the bullock of the sin offering which is for himself:

12 And he shall take a censer full of burning coals of fire from off the altar before the Becoming-One, and his hands full of sweet incense beaten small, and bring it within the veil:

13 And he shall put the incense upon the fire before the Becoming-One, that the cloud of the incense may cover the mercy seat that is upon the testimony, that he die not:

14 And he shall take of the blood of the bullock, and sprinkle it with his finger upon the mercy seat eastward; and before the mercy seat shall he sprinkle of the blood with his finger seven times.

15 Then shall he kill the goat of the sin offering, that is for the people, and bring his blood within the veil, and do with that blood as he did with the blood of the bullock, and sprinkle it upon the mercy seat, and before the mercy seat:

16 And he shall make an atonement for the holy place, because of the uncleanness of the children of Israel, and because of their transgressions in all their sins: and so shall he do for the tabernacle of the set time, that remains among them in the midst of their uncleanness.

17 And there shall be no man [all of Adam, there shall not be] in the tabernacle of the set time[58] when he goes in to make an atonement in the holy place, until he come out, and have made an atonement for himself, and for his household, and for all the congregation of Israel.

18 And he shall go out unto the altar that is before the Becoming-One, and make an atonement for it; and shall take of the blood of the bullock, and of the blood of the goat, and put it upon the horns of the altar round about.

19 And he shall sprinkle of the blood upon it with his finger seven times, and cleanse it, and hallow it from the uncleanness of the children of Israel.

20 And when he has made an end of reconciling the holy place, and the tabernacle of the set time, and the altar, he shall bring the live goat:

21 And Aaron shall lay both his hands upon the head of the live goat, and confess over him all the iniquities of the children of Israel, and all their transgressions in all their sins, putting them upon the head of the goat, and shall send him away by the hand of a fit man into the wilderness:

22 And the goat shall bear upon him all their iniquities unto a land not inhabited: and he shall let go the goat in the wilderness.

23 And Aaron shall come into the tabernacle of the set time, and shall put off the linen garments, which he put on when he went into the holy place, and shall leave them there:

---

[58] Appointed time or festival

24 And he shall wash his flesh with water in the holy place, and put on his garments, and come forth, and offer his burnt offering, and the burnt offering of the people, and make an atonement for himself, and for the people.

25 And the fat of the sin offering shall he burn upon the altar.

26 And he that let go the goat for the scapegoat [azazel] shall wash his clothes, and bathe his flesh in water, and afterward come into the camp.

27 And the bullock for the sin offering, and the goat for the sin offering, whose blood was brought in to make atonement in the holy place, shall one carry forth outside the camp; and they shall burn in the fire their skins, and their flesh, and their dung.

28 And he that burns them shall wash his clothes, and bathe his flesh in water, and afterward he shall come into the camp.

29 And this shall be a statute for olam unto you: that in the seventh month, on the tenth day of the month, you shall afflict your souls, and do no work at all, whether it be one of your own country, or a stranger that sojourns among you:

30 For on that day shall the priest make an atonement for you, to cleanse you, that you may be clean from all your sins before the Becoming-One.

31 It shall be a Sabbath of rest unto you, and you shall afflict your souls, by a statute for olam.

32 And the priest, whom he shall anoint, and whom he shall consecrate to minister in the priest's office in his father's stead, shall make the atonement, and shall put on the linen clothes, even the holy garments:

33 And he shall make an atonement for the holy sanctuary, and he shall make an atonement for the tabernacle of the set time, and for the altar, and he shall make an atonement for the priests, and for all the people of the congregation.

34 And this shall be a statute of olam unto you, to make an atonement for the children of Israel for all their sins once a year. And he did as the Becoming-One commanded Moses.

Lev 17:1 And the Becoming-One spoke unto Moses, saying,

2 Speak unto Aaron, and unto his sons, and unto all the children of Israel, and say unto them; This is the thing which the Becoming-One has commanded, saying,

3 What man soever there be of the house of Israel, that kills an ox, or lamb, or goat, in the camp, or that kills it out of the camp,

4 And brings it not unto the door of the tabernacle of the set time, to offer an offering unto the Becoming-One before the tabernacle of the Becoming-One; blood shall be imputed unto that man; he has shed blood; and that man shall be cut off from among his people:

5 To the end that the children of Israel may bring their sacrifices, which they offer in the open field, even that they may bring them unto the Becoming-One, unto the door of the tabernacle of the set time, unto the priest, and offer them for peace offerings unto the Becoming-One.

6 And the priest shall sprinkle the blood upon the altar of the Becoming-One at the door of the tabernacle of the set time, and burn the fat for a sweet aroma unto the Becoming-One.

7 And they shall no more offer their sacrifices unto devils, after whom they have gone a whoring. This shall be a statute for olam unto them throughout their generations.

8 And you shall say unto them, Whatsoever man there be of the house of Israel, or of the strangers which sojourn among you, that offers a burnt offering or sacrifice,

9 And brings it not unto the door of the tabernacle of the set time, to offer it unto the Becoming-One; even that man shall be cut off from among his people.

10 And whatsoever man there be of the house of Israel, or of the strangers that sojourn among you, that eats any manner of blood; I will even set my face against that soul that eats blood, and will cut him off from among his people.

11 For the life of the flesh is in the blood: and I have given it to you upon the altar to make an atonement for your souls: for it is the blood that makes an atonement for the soul.

12 Therefore I said unto the children of Israel, No soul of you shall eat blood, neither shall any stranger that sojourns among you eat blood.

13 And whatsoever man there be of the children of Israel, or of the strangers that sojourn among you, which hunts and catches any beast or fowl that may be eaten; he shall even pour out the blood thereof, and cover it with dust.

14 For it is the soul of all flesh; the blood of it is for the soul thereof: therefore I said unto the children of Israel, you shall eat the blood of no manner of flesh: for the soul of all flesh is the blood thereof: whosoever eats it shall be cut off.

15 And every soul that eats that which died of itself, or that which was torn with beasts, whether it be one of your own country, or a stranger, he shall both wash his clothes, and bathe himself in water, and be unclean until the evening: then shall he be clean.

16 But if he wash them not, nor bathe his flesh; then he shall bear his iniquity.

Lev 18:1 And the Becoming-One spoke unto Moses, saying,

2 Speak unto the children of Israel, and say unto them, I am the Becoming-One your God.

3 After the doings of the land of Egypt, wherein you dwelt, shall you not do: and after the doings of the land of Canaan, to where I bring you, shall you not do: neither shall you walk in their ordinances.

4 you shall do my judgments, and keep mine ordinances, to walk therein: I am the Becoming-One your God.

5 you shall therefore keep my statutes, and my judgments: which if a man [adam male and female] do them, he shall live: I am the Becoming-One.

6 None of you shall approach to any that is near of kin to him, to uncover their nakedness: I am the Becoming-One.

7 The nakedness of your father, or the nakedness of your mother, shall you not uncover: she is your mother; you shall not uncover her nakedness.

8 The nakedness of your father's wife shall you not uncover: it is your father's nakedness.

9 The nakedness of your sister, the daughter of your father, or daughter of your mother, whether she be born at home, or born abroad, even their nakedness you shall not uncover.

10 The nakedness of your son's daughter, or of your daughter's daughter, even their nakedness you shall not uncover: for theirs is your own nakedness.

11 The nakedness of your father's wife's daughter, begotten of your father, she is your sister, you shall not uncover her nakedness.

12 you shall not uncover the nakedness of your father's sister: she is your father's near kinswoman.

13 you shall not uncover the nakedness of your mother's sister; for she is your mother's near kinswoman.

14 you shall not uncover the nakedness of your father's brother, you shall not approach to his wife: she is your aunt.

15 you shall not uncover the nakedness of your daughter-in-law: she is your son's wife; you shall not uncover her nakedness.

16 you shall not uncover the nakedness of your brother's wife: it is your brother's nakedness.

17 you shall not uncover the nakedness of a woman and her daughter, neither shall you take her son's daughter, or her daughter's daughter, to uncover her nakedness; for they are her near kinswomen: it is wickedness.

18 Neither shall you take a wife to her sister, to vex her, to uncover her nakedness, beside the other in her life time.

19 Also you shall not approach unto a woman to uncover her nakedness, as long as she is put apart for her uncleanness.

20 Moreover you shall not lie carnally with your neighbor's wife, to defile yourself with her.

21 And you shall not let any of your seed pass through the fire to Molech, neither shall you profane the name of your God: I am the Becoming-One.

22 you shall not lie with male, as with a woman: it is abomination.

23 Neither shall you lie with any beast to defile yourself therewith: neither shall any woman stand before a beast to lie down thereto: it is confusion.

24 Defile not you yourselves in any of these things: for in all these the nations are defiled which I cast out before you:

25 And the land is defiled: therefore I do visit the iniquity thereof upon it, and the land itself vomits out her inhabitants.

26 you shall therefore keep my statutes and my judgments, and shall not commit any of these abominations; neither any of your own nation, nor any stranger that sojourns among you:

27 For all these abominations have the men of the land done, which were before you, and the land is defiled;

28 That the land spue not you out also, when you defile it, as it spued out the nations that were before you.

29 For whosoever shall commit any of these abominations, even the souls that commit them shall be cut off from among their people.

30 Therefore shall you keep mine ordinance, that you commit not any one of these abominable customs, which were committed before you, and that you defile not yourselves therein: I am the Becoming-One your God.

Lev 19:1 And the Becoming-One spoke unto Moses, saying,

2 Speak unto all the congregation of the children of Israel, and say unto them, you shall be holy: for I the Becoming-One your God am holy.

3 you shall fear every man his mother, and his father, and keep my sabbaths: I am the Becoming-One your God.

4 Turn you not unto idols, nor make to yourselves molten gods: I am the Becoming-One your God.

5 And if you offer a sacrifice of peace offerings unto the Becoming-One, you shall offer it at your own will.

6 It shall be eaten the same day you offer it, and on the next day: and if anything remain until the third day, it shall be burnt in the fire.

7 And if it be eaten at all on the third day, it is abominable; it shall not be accepted.

8 Therefore every one that eats it shall bear his iniquity, because he has profaned the hallowed thing of the Becoming-One: and that soul shall be cut off from among his people.

9 And when you reap the harvest of your land, you shall not wholly reap the corners of your field, neither shall you gather the gleanings of your harvest.

10 And you shall not glean your vineyard, neither shall you gather every grape of your vineyard; you shall leave them for the poor and stranger: I am the Becoming-One your God.

11 you shall not steal, neither deal falsely, neither lie one to his neighbor.

12 And you shall not swear by my name falsely, neither shall you profane the name of your God: I am the Becoming-One.

13 you shall not defraud your neighbor, neither rob him: the wages of him that is hired shall not abide with you all night until the morning.

14 you shall not curse the deaf, nor put a stumbling block before the blind, but shall fear your God: I am the Becoming-One.

15 you shall do no unrighteousness in judgment: you shall not respect the person of the poor, nor honor the person of the mighty: but in righteousness shall you judge your neighbor.

16 you shall not go up and down as a talebearer among your people: neither shall you stand against the blood of your neighbor: I am the Becoming-One.

17 you shall not hate your brother in your heart: you shall in any way rebuke your neighbor, and not permit sin upon him.

18 you shall not avenge, nor bear any grudge against the children of your people, but you shall love your neighbor as thyself: I am the Becoming-One.

19 you shall keep my statutes. you shall not let your cattle gender with a diverse kind: you shall not sow your field with mingled seed: neither shall a garment mingled of linen and woollen come upon you.

20 And whosoever lying with seed with a woman, that is a bondmaid, betrothed to a husband, and not at all redeemed, nor freedom given her; she shall be scourged; they shall not be put to death, because she was not free.

21 And he shall bring his trespass offering unto the Becoming-One, unto the door of the tabernacle of the set time, even a ram for a trespass offering.

22 And the priest shall make an atonement for him with the ram of the trespass offering before the Becoming-One for his sin which he has done: and the sin which he has done shall be forgiven him.

23 And when you shall come into the land, and shall have planted all manner of trees for food, then you shall count the fruit thereof as uncircumcised: three years shall it be as uncircumcised unto you: it shall not be eaten of.

24 But in the fourth year all the fruit thereof shall be holy to praise the Becoming-One withal.

25 And in the fifth year shall you eat of the fruit thereof, that it may yield unto you the increase thereof: I am the Becoming-One your God.

26 you shall not eat any thing with the blood: neither shall you use enchantment, nor observe times.

27 you shall not round the corners of your heads, neither shall you mar the corners of your beard.

28 you shall not make any cuttings in your flesh for the soul, nor print any marks upon you: I am the Becoming-One.

29 Do not prostitute your daughter, to cause her to be a whore; lest the land fall to whoredom, and the land become full of wickedness.

30 you shall keep my sabbaths, and reverence my sanctuary: I am the Becoming-One.

31 Regard not mediums; neither seek after fortune-tellers, to be defiled by them: I am the Becoming-One your God.

32 you shall rise up before the aged head, and honor the face of the old man, and fear your God: I am the Becoming-One.

33 And if a stranger sojourn with you in your land, you shall not vex him.

34 But the stranger that dwells with you shall be unto you as one born among you, and you shall love him as thyself; for you were strangers in the land of Egypt: I am the Becoming-One your God.

35 you shall do no unrighteousness in judgment, in measures, in weight, or in quantity.

36 Just balances, just weights, a just ephah, and a just hin, shall you have: I am the Becoming-One your God, which brought you out of the land of Egypt.

37 Therefore shall you observe all my statutes, and all my judgments, and do them: I am the Becoming-One.

Lev 20:1 And the Becoming-One spoke unto Moses, saying,

2 Again, you shall say to the children of Israel, Whosoever he be of the children of Israel, or of the strangers that sojourn in Israel, that gives any of his seed unto Molech; in dying he shall be put to death: the people of the land shall stone him with stones.

3 And I will set my face against that man, and will cut him off from among his people; because he has given of his seed unto Molech, to defile my sanctuary, and to profane my holy name.

4 And if the people of the land do in any way hide their eyes from the man, when he gives of his seed unto Molech, and kill him not:

5 Then I will set My face against that man, and against his family, and will cut him off, and all that go a whoring after him, to commit whoredom with Molech, from among their people.

6 And the soul that turns after the mediums, and after fortune-tellers, to go a whoring after them, I will even set my face against that soul, and will cut him off from among his people.

7 Sanctify yourselves therefore, and be you holy: for I am the Becoming-One your God.

8 And you shall keep my statutes, and do them: I am the Becoming-One which sanctify you.

9 For every one that curses his father or his mother in dying he shall be put to death: he has cursed his father or his mother; his blood shall be upon him.

10 And the man that commits adultery with another man's wife, even he that commits adultery with his neighbor's wife, the adulterer and the adulteress in dying he shall be put to death.

11 And the man that lies with his father's wife has uncovered his father's nakedness: both of them in dying they shall be put to death; their blood shall be upon them.

12 And if a man lie with his daughter-in-law, both of them in dying they shall be put to death: they have worked confusion; their blood shall be upon them.

13 If a man also lie with mankind, as he lies with a woman, both of them have committed an abomination: in dying they shall be put to death; their blood shall be upon them.

14 And if a man take a wife and her mother, it is wickedness: they shall be burnt with fire, both he and they; that there be no wickedness among you.

15 And if a man lie with a beast, in dying he shall be put to death: and you shall slay the beast.

16 And if a woman approach unto any beast, and lie down thereto, you shall kill the woman, and the beast: in dying they shall be put to death; their blood shall be upon them.

17 And if a man shall take his sister, his father's daughter, or his mother's daughter, and see her nakedness, and she see his nakedness; it is a wicked thing; and they shall be cut off in the sight of their people: he has uncovered his sister's nakedness; he shall bear his iniquity.

18 And if a man shall lie with a woman having her menstruous period, and shall uncover her nakedness; he has discovered her fountain, and she has uncovered the fountain of her blood: and both of them shall be cut off from among their people.

19 And you shall not uncover the nakedness of your mother's sister, nor of your father's sister: for he uncovers his near kin: they shall bear their iniquity.

20 And if a man shall lie with his uncle's wife, he has uncovered his uncle's nakedness: they shall bear their sin; they shall die childless.

21 And if a man shall take his brother's wife, it is an unclean thing: he has uncovered his brother's nakedness; they shall be childless.

22 you shall therefore keep all my statutes, and all my judgments, and do them: that the land, to which I bring you to dwell therein, spue you not out.

23 And you shall not walk in the manners of the nation, which I cast out before you: for they committed all these things, and therefore I abhorred them.

24 But I have said unto you, you shall inherit their land, and I will give it unto you to possess it, a land that flows with milk and honey: I am the Becoming-

One your God, which have separated you from other people.

25 you shall therefore put difference between clean beasts and unclean, and between unclean fowls and clean: and you shall not make your souls abominable by beast, or by fowl, or by any manner of living thing that creeps on the ground, which I have separated from you as unclean.

26 And you shall be holy unto me: for I the Becoming-One am holy, and have severed you from other people, that you should be mine.

27 A man also or woman that has a medium, or that is a fortune-teller, in dying they shall be put to death: they shall stone them with stones: their blood shall be upon them.

Lev 21:1 And the Becoming-One said unto Moses, Speak unto the priests the sons of Aaron, and say unto them, There shall none be defiled for the soul among his people:

2 But for his kin, that is near unto him, that is, for his mother, and for his father, and for his son, and for his daughter, and for his brother,

3 And for his sister a virgin, that is near unto him, which has had no husband; for her may he be defiled.

4 But he shall not defile himself, being a chief man among his people, to profane himself.

5 They shall not make baldness upon their head, neither shall they shave off the corner of their beard, nor make any cuttings in their flesh.

6 They shall be holy unto their God, and not profane the name of their God: for the offerings of the Becoming-One made by fire, and the bread of their God, they do offer: therefore they shall be holy.

7 They shall not take a wife that is a whore, or profane; neither shall they take a woman put away from her husband: for he is holy unto his God.

8 you shall sanctify him therefore; for he offers the bread of your God: he shall be holy unto you: for I the Becoming-One, which sanctify you, am holy.

9 And the daughter of any priest, if she profane herself by playing the whore, she profanes her father: she shall be burnt with fire.

10 And he that is the high priest among his brethren, upon whose head the anointing oil was poured, and that is consecrated to put on the garments, shall not uncover his head, nor rend his clothes;

11 Neither shall he go in to any dead soul, nor defile himself for his father, or for his mother;

12 Neither shall he go out of the sanctuary, nor profane the sanctuary of his God; for the crown of the anointing oil of his God is upon him: I am the Becoming-One.

13 And he shall take a wife in her virginity.

14 A widow, or a divorced woman, or profane, or a harlot, these shall he not take: but he shall take a virgin of his own people to wife.

15 Neither shall he profane his seed among his people: for I the Becoming-One do sanctify him.

16 And the Becoming-One spoke unto Moses, saying,

17 Speak unto Aaron, saying, Whosoever he be of your seed in their generations that has any blemish, let him not approach to offer the bread of his God.

18 For whatsoever man he be that has a blemish, he shall not approach: a blind man, or a lame, or he that has a flat nose, or any thing superfluous,

19 Or a man that is broken-footed, or broken-handed,

20 Or crook-backed, or a dwarf, or that has a blemish in his eye, or be scurvy, or scabbed, or has his stones broken;

21 No man that has a blemish of the seed of Aaron the priest shall come near to offer the offerings of the Becoming-One made by fire: he has a blemish; he shall not come near to offer the bread of his God.

22 He shall eat the bread of his God, both of the most holy, and of the holy.

23 Only he shall not go in unto the veil, nor come near unto the altar, because he has a blemish; that he profane not my sanctuaries: for I the Becoming-One do sanctify them.

24 And Moses told it unto Aaron, and to his sons, and unto all the children of Israel.

Lev 22:1 And the Becoming-One spoke unto Moses, saying,

2 Speak unto Aaron and to his sons, that they separate themselves from the holy things of the children of Israel, and that they profane not my holy name in those things which they hallow unto me: I am the Becoming-One.

3 Say unto them, Whosoever he be of all your seed among your generations, that goes unto the holy things, which the children of Israel hallow unto the Becoming-One, having his uncleanness upon him, that soul shall be cut off from my presence: I am the Becoming-One.

4 What man soever of the seed of Aaron is a leper, or has a running issue; he shall not eat of the holy things, until he be clean. And whoso touches any thing that is unclean by the [dead] soul, or a man whose seed goes from him;

5 Or whosoever touches any creeping thing, whereby he may be made unclean, or a man of whom he may take uncleanness, whatsoever uncleanness he has;

6 The soul which has touched any such shall be unclean until even, and shall not eat of the holy things, unless he wash his flesh with water.

7 And when the sun is down, he shall be clean, and shall afterward eat of the holy things; because it is his food.

8 That which dies of itself, or is torn with beasts, he shall not eat to defile himself therewith: I am the Becoming-One.

9 They shall therefore keep mine ordinance, lest they bear sin for it, and die therefore, if they profane it: I the Becoming-One do sanctify them.

10 There shall no stranger eat of the holy thing: a sojourner of the priest, or a hired servant, shall not eat of the holy thing.

11 But if the priest buy any soul with his money, he shall eat of it, and he that is born in his house: they shall eat of his food.

12 If the priest's daughter also be married unto a stranger, she may not eat of an offering of the holy things.

13 But if the priest's daughter be a widow, or divorced, and have no seed, and is returned unto her

father's house, as in her youth, she shall eat of her father's food: but there shall no stranger eat thereof.

14 And if a man eat of the holy thing unknowingly, then he shall put the fifth part thereof unto it, and shall give it unto the priest with the holy thing.

15 And they shall not profane the holy things of the children of Israel, which they offer unto the Becoming-One;

16 Or permit them to bear the iniquity of trespass, when they eat their holy things: for I the Becoming-One do sanctify them.

17 And the Becoming-One spoke unto Moses, saying,

18 Speak unto Aaron, and to his sons, and unto all the children of Israel, and say unto them, Whatsoever he be of the house of Israel, or of the strangers in Israel, that will offer his offering for all his vows, and for all his freewill offerings, which they will offer unto the Becoming-One for a burnt offering;

19 you shall offer at your own will a male without blemish, of the cattle, of the sheep, or of the goats.

20 But whatsoever has a blemish, that shall you not offer: for it shall not be acceptable for you.

21 And whosoever offers a sacrifice of peace offerings unto the Becoming-One to accomplish his vow, or a freewill offering in cattle or sheep, it shall be perfect to be accepted; there shall be no blemish therein.

22 Blind, or broken, or maimed, or having a wen, or scurvy, or scabbed, you shall not offer these unto the Becoming-One, nor make an offering by fire of them upon the altar unto the Becoming-One.

23 Either a bullock or a lamb that has anything superfluous or lacking in his parts, that may you offer for a freewill offering; but for a vow it shall not be accepted.

24 you shall not offer unto the Becoming-One that which is bruised, or crushed, or broken, or cut; neither shall you make any offering thereof in your land.

25 Neither from a stranger's hand shall you offer the bread of your God of any of these; because their corruption is in them, and blemishes be in them: they shall not be accepted for you.

26 And the Becoming-One spoke unto Moses, saying,

27 When a bullock, or a sheep, or a goat, is brought forth, then it shall be seven days under the dam; and from the eighth day and thereforth it shall be accepted for an offering made by fire unto the Becoming-One.

28 And whether it be cow or ewe, you shall not kill it and her young both in one day.

29 And when you will offer a sacrifice of thanksgiving unto the Becoming-One, offer it at your own will.

30 On the same day it shall be eaten up; you shall leave none of it until the morrow: I am the Becoming-One.

31 Therefore shall you keep my commandments, and do them: I am the Becoming-One.

32 Neither shall you profane my holy name; but I will be hallowed among the children of Israel: I am the Becoming-One which hallow you,

33 That brought you out of the land of Egypt, to be your God: I am the Becoming-One.

Lev 23:1 And the Becoming-One spoke unto Moses, saying,

2 Speak unto the children of Israel, and say unto them, Concerning the set times[59] of the Becoming-One, which you shall proclaim to be holy convocations, even these are my set times.[60]

3 Six days shall work be done: but the seventh day is the Sabbath of rest, a holy convocation; you shall do no work therein: it is the Sabbath of the Becoming-One in all your dwellings.

4 These are the set times[61] of the Becoming-One, even holy convocations, which you shall proclaim in their seasons.

5 In the fourteenth day of the first month between the evenings is the Becoming-One's Passover.

6 And on the fifteenth day of the same month is the feast of unleavened bread unto the Becoming-One: seven days you must eat unleavened bread.

7 In the first day you shall have a holy convocation: you shall do no servile work therein.

8 But you shall offer an offering made by fire unto the Becoming-One seven days: in the seventh day is a holy convocation: you shall do no servile work therein.

9 And the Becoming-One spoke unto Moses, saying,

10 Speak unto the children of Israel, and say unto them, When you be come into the land which I give unto you, and shall reap the harvest thereof, then you shall bring a sheaf of the beginning firstfruit of your harvest unto the priest:

11 And he shall wave the sheaf before the Becoming-One, to be accepted for you: on the next day after the Sabbath the priest shall wave it.

12 And you shall offer that day when you wave the sheaf a he lamb without blemish of the first year for a burnt offering unto the Becoming-One.

13 And the food offering thereof shall be two tenth deals of fine flour mingled with oil, an offering made by fire unto the Becoming-One for a sweet aroma: and the drink offering thereof shall be of wine, the fourth part of a hin.

14 And you shall eat neither bread, nor parched grain, nor green ears, until the selfsame day that you have brought an offering unto your God: it shall be a statute for olam throughout your generations in all your dwellings.

15 And you shall count unto you from the morrow after the Sabbath, from the day that you brought the sheaf of the wave offering; seven sabbaths shall be complete:

16 Even unto the morrow after the seventh Sabbath shall you number fifty days; and you shall offer a new food offering unto the Becoming-One.

17 you shall bring out of your habitations two wave loaves of two tenth deals: they shall be of fine flour; they shall be baken with leaven; they are the firstfruits unto the Becoming-One.

18 And you shall offer with the bread seven lambs without blemish of the first year, and one young bullock, and two rams: they shall be for a burnt offering unto the Becoming-One, with their food

---

[59] Appointed times or festivals
[60] Appointed times or festivals
[61] Appointed times or festivals

offering, and their drink offerings, even an offering made by fire, of sweet aroma unto the Becoming-One.

19 Then you shall sacrifice one kid of the goats for a sin offering, and two lambs of the first year for a sacrifice of peace offerings.

20 And the priest shall wave them with the bread of the firstfruits for a wave offering before the Becoming-One with the two lambs: they shall be holy to the Becoming-One for the priest.

21 And you shall proclaim on the selfsame day, that it may be a holy convocation unto you: you shall do no servile work therein: it shall be a statute for olam in all your dwellings throughout your generations.

22 And when you reap the harvest of your land, you shall not make clean riddance of the corners of your field when you reap, neither shall you gather any gleaning of your harvest: you shall leave them unto the poor, and to the stranger: I am the Becoming-One your God.

23 And the Becoming-One spoke unto Moses, saying,

24 Speak unto the children of Israel, saying, In the seventh month, in the first day of the month, shall you have a Sabbath, a memorial of blowing of trumpets, a holy convocation.

25 you shall do no servile work therein: but you shall offer an offering made by fire unto the Becoming-One.

26 And the Becoming-One spoke unto Moses, saying,

27 Also on the tenth day of this seventh month there shall be a day of atonement: it shall be a holy convocation unto you; and you shall afflict your souls, and offer an offering made by fire unto the Becoming-One.

28 And you shall do no work in that same day: for it is a day of atonement, to make an atonement for you before the Becoming-One your God.

29 For whatsoever soul it be that shall not be afflicted in that same day, he shall be cut off from among his people.

30 And whatsoever soul it be that did any work in that same day, the same soul will I destroy from among his people.

31 you shall do no manner of work: it shall be a statute for olam throughout your generations in all your dwellings.

32 It shall be unto you a Sabbath of rest, and you shall weaken [by the fast] your souls: in the ninth day of the month at evening, from evening unto evening, shall you celebrate your Sabbath.

33 And the Becoming-One spoke unto Moses, saying,

34 Speak unto the children of Israel, saying, The fifteenth day of this seventh month shall be the feast of tabernacles [booths] for seven days unto the Becoming-One.

35 On the first day shall be a holy convocation: you shall do no servile work therein.

36 Seven days you shall offer an offering made by fire unto the Becoming-One: on the eighth day shall be a holy convocation unto you; and you shall offer an offering made by fire unto the Becoming-One: it is a solemn assembly; and you shall do no servile work therein.

37 These are the set times[62] of the Becoming-One, which you shall proclaim to be holy set time,[63] to offer an offering made by fire unto the Becoming-One, a burnt offering, and a food offering, a sacrifice, and drink offerings, every thing upon his day:

38 Beside the sabbaths of the Becoming-One, and beside your gifts, and beside all your vows, and beside all your freewill offerings, which you give unto the Becoming-One.

39 Also in the fifteenth day of the seventh month, when you have gathered in the fruit of the land, you shall keep a feast unto the Becoming-One seven days: on the first day shall be a Sabbath, and on the eighth day shall be a Sabbath.

40 And you shall take you on the first day the boughs of goodly trees, branches of palm trees, and the boughs of thick trees, and willows of the brook; and you shall rejoice before the Becoming-One your God seven days.

41 And you shall keep it a feast unto the Becoming-One seven days in the year. It shall be a statute for olam in your generations: you shall celebrate it in the seventh month.

42 you shall dwell in booths seven days; all that are Israelites born shall dwell in booths:

43 That your generations may know that I made the children of Israel to dwell in booths, when I brought them out of the land of Egypt: I am the Becoming-One your God.

44 And Moses declared unto the children of Israel the set times[64] of the Becoming-One.

Lev 24:1 And the Becoming-One spoke unto Moses, saying,

2 Command the children of Israel, that they bring unto you pure oil olive beaten for the light, to cause the lamps to burn continually.

3 Outside the veil of the testimony, in the tabernacle of the set time,[65] shall Aaron order it from the evening unto the morning before the Becoming-One continually: it shall be a statute for olam in your generations.

4 He shall order the lamps upon the pure candlestick before the Becoming-One continually.

5 And you shall take fine flour, and bake twelve cakes thereof: two tenth deals shall be in one cake.

6 And you shall set them in two rows, six on a row, upon the pure table before the Becoming-One.

7 And you shall put pure frankincense upon each row, that it may be on the bread for a memorial, even an offering made by fire unto the Becoming-One.

8 Every Sabbath he shall set it in order before the Becoming-One continually, being taken from the children of Israel by a covenant of olam.

9 And it shall be Aaron's and his sons'; and they shall eat it in the holy place: for it is most holy unto him of the offerings of the Becoming-One made by fire by a statute of olam.

10 And the son of an Israelitish woman, whose father was an Egyptian, went out among the children

---

[62] Appointed times or festivals
[63] Appointed times or festivals
[64] Appointed times or festivals
[65] Appointed time or festival

of Israel: and this son of the Israelitish woman and a man of Israel strove together in the camp;

11 And the Israelitish woman's son blasphemed the name of the Becoming-One, and cursed. And they brought him unto Moses: and his mother's name was Shelomith, the daughter of Dibri, of the tribe of Dan:

12 And they put him in prison, that the mind of the Becoming-One might be showed them.

13 And the Becoming-One spoke unto Moses, saying,

14 Bring forth him that has cursed outside the camp; and let all that heard him lay their hands upon his head, and let all the congregation stone him.

15 And you shall speak unto the children of Israel, saying, Whosoever curses his God shall bear his sin.

16 And he that blasphemies the name of the Becoming-One, in dying he shall be put to death, and all the congregation shall certainly stone him: as well the stranger, as he that is born in the land, when he blasphemies the name of the Becoming-One, shall be put to death.

17 And he that kills any soul of a man in dying he shall be put to death.

18 And he that kills the soul of a beast shall make it good; soul for soul.

19 And if a man cause a blemish in his neighbor; as he has done, so shall it be done to him;

20 Breach for breach, eye for eye, tooth for tooth: as he has caused a blemish in a man, so shall it be done to him again.

21 And he that kills a beast, he shall restore it: and he that kills a man, he shall be put to death.

22 you shall have one manner of law, as well for the stranger, as for one of your own country: for I am the Becoming-One your God.

23 And Moses spoke to the children of Israel, that they should bring forth him that had cursed out of the camp, and stone him with stones. And the children of Israel did as the Becoming-One commanded Moses.

Lev 25:1 And the Becoming-One spoke unto Moses in mount Sinai, saying,

2 Speak unto the children of Israel, and say unto them, When you come into the land which I give you, then shall the land keep a Sabbath unto the Becoming-One.

3 Six years you shall sow your field, and six years you shall prune your vineyard, and gather in the fruit thereof;

4 But in the seventh year shall be a Sabbath of rest unto the land, a Sabbath for the Becoming-One: you shall neither sow your field, nor prune your vineyard.

5 That which grows of its own accord of your harvest you shall not reap, neither gather the grapes of your vine undressed: for it is a year of rest unto the land.

6 And the Sabbath of the land shall be food for you; for you, and for your servant, and for your maid, and for your hired servant, and for your stranger that sojourns with you,

7 And for your cattle, and for the beast that are in your land, shall all the increase thereof be food.

8 And you shall number seven sabbaths of years unto you, seven times seven years; and the space of the seven sabbaths of years shall be unto you forty and nine years.

9 Then shall you cause the trumpet of the jubilee to sound on the tenth day of the seventh month, in the day of atonement shall you make the trumpet sound throughout all your land.

10 And you shall hallow the fiftieth year, and proclaim liberty throughout all the land unto all the inhabitants thereof: it shall be a jubilee unto you; and you shall return every man unto his possession, and you shall return every man unto his family.

11 A jubilee shall that fiftieth year be unto you: you shall not sow, neither reap that which grows of itself in it, nor gather the grapes in it of your vine undressed.

12 For it is the jubilee; it shall be holy unto you: you shall eat the increase thereof out of the field.

13 In the year of this jubilee you shall return every man unto his possession.

14 And if you sell anything unto your neighbor, or buy anything of your neighbor's hand, you shall not oppress one another:

15 According to the number of years after the jubilee you shall buy of your neighbor, and according unto the number of years of the fruits he shall sell unto you:

16 According to the multitude of years you shall increase the price thereof, and according to the fewness of years you shall diminish the price of it: for according to the number of the years of the fruits does he sell unto you.

17 you shall not therefore oppress one another; but you shall fear your God: for I am the Becoming-One your God.

18 Therefore you shall do my statutes, and keep my judgments, and do them; and you shall dwell in the land in safety.

19 And the land shall yield her fruit, and you shall eat your fill, and dwell therein in safety.

20 And if you shall say, What shall we eat the seventh year? behold, we shall not sow, nor gather in our increase:

21 Then I will command my blessing upon you in the sixth year, and it shall bring forth fruit for three years.

22 And when you shall sow the eighth year, you will be eating the old fruit until the ninth year; until her fruits [of the eight year] come in you shall eat of the old store.

23 The land shall not be sold for olam, for the land is mine; for you are strangers and sojourners with me.

24 And in all the land of your possession you shall grant a redemption for the land.

25 If your brother be waxen poor, and has sold away some of his possession, and if any of his kin come to redeem it, then shall he redeem that which his brother sold.

26 And if the man have none to redeem it, and himself be able to redeem it;

27 Then let him count the years of the sale thereof, and restore the overpayment unto the man to whom he sold it; that he may return unto his possession.

28 But if he be not able to restore it to him, then that which is sold shall remain in the hand of him that has bought it until the year of jubilee: and in the

jubilee it shall go out, and he shall return unto his possession.

29 And if a man sell a dwelling house in a walled city, then he may redeem it till the end of the year of its sell; for days [until the end of the year] may he redeem it.

30 And if it be not redeemed within the space of a full year, then the house that is in the walled city shall be established for olam to him that bought it throughout his generations: it shall not go out in the jubilee.

31 But the houses of the villages which have no wall round about them shall be counted as the fields of the country: they may be redeemed, and they shall go out in the jubilee.

32 Notwithstanding the cities of the Levites, and the houses of the cities of their possession, may the Levites redeem for olam.

33 And if a man purchase of the Levites, then the house that was sold, and the city of his possession, shall go out in the year of jubilee: for the houses of the cities of the Levites are their possession among the children of Israel.

34 But the field of the suburbs of their cities may not be sold; for it is their olam possession.

35 And if your brother be waxen poor, and fallen in decay with you; then you shall relieve him: yes, though he be a stranger, or a sojourner; that he may live with you.

36 Take you no usury of him, or increase: but fear your God; that your brother may live with you.

37 you shall not give him your money upon usury, nor lend him your victuals for increase.

38 I am the Becoming-One your God, which brought you forth out of the land of Egypt, to give you the land of Canaan, and to be your God.

39 And if your brother that dwells by you be waxen poor, and be sold unto you; you shall not compel him to serve as a bondservant:

40 But as a hired servant, and as a sojourner, he shall be with you, and shall serve you unto the year of jubilee:

41 And then shall he depart from you, both he and his children with him, and shall return unto his own family, and unto the possession of his fathers shall he return.

42 For they are my servants, which I brought forth out of the land of Egypt: they shall not be sold as bondmen.

43 you shall not rule over him with rigor; but shall fear your God.

44 Both your bondmen, and your bondmaids, which you shall have, shall be of the nations that are round about you; of them shall you buy bondmen and bondmaids.

45 Moreover of the children of the strangers that do sojourn among you, of them shall you buy, and of their families that are with you, which they begat in your land: and they shall be your possession.

46 And you shall take them as an inheritance for your children after you, to inherit them for a possession; they shall be your bondmen for olam, but over your brethren the children of Israel, you shall not rule one over another with rigor.

47 And if a sojourner or stranger wax rich by you, and your brother that dwells by him wax poor, and sell himself unto the stranger or sojourner by you, or to the stock of the stranger's family:

48 After that he is sold he may be redeemed again; one of his brethren may redeem him:

49 Either his uncle, or his uncle's son, may redeem him, or any that is near of kin unto him of his family may redeem him; or if he be able, he may redeem himself.

50 And he shall reckon with him that bought him from the year that he was sold to him unto the year of jubilee: and the price of his sale shall be according unto the number of years, according to the time of a hired servant shall it be with him.

51 If there be yet many years behind, according unto them he shall give again the price of his redemption out of the money that he was bought for.

52 And if there remain but few years unto the year of jubilee, then he shall count with him, and according unto his years shall he give him again the price of his redemption.

53 And as a yearly hired servant shall he be with him: and the other shall not rule with rigor over him in your sight.

54 And if he be not redeemed in these years, then he shall go out in the year of jubilee, both he, and his children with him.

55 For unto me the children of Israel are servants; they are my servants whom I brought forth out of the land of Egypt: I am the Becoming-One your God.

Lev 26:1 you shall make you no idols nor graven image, neither rear you up a standing image, neither shall you set up any image of stone in your land, to bow down unto it: for I am the Becoming-One your God.

2 you shall keep my sabbaths, and reverence my sanctuary: I am the Becoming-One.

3 If you walk in my statutes, and keep my commandments, and do them;

4 Then I will give you rain in due season, and the land shall yield her increase, and the trees of the field shall yield their fruit.

5 And your threshing shall reach unto the vintage, and the vintage shall reach unto the sowing time: and you shall eat your bread to the full, and dwell in your land safely.

6 And I will give peace in the land, and you shall lie down, and none shall make you afraid: and I will rid evil beasts out of the land, neither shall the sword go through your land.

7 And you shall chase your enemies, and they shall fall before you by the sword.

8 And five of you shall chase a hundred, and a hundred of you shall put multitude to flight: and your enemies shall fall before you by the sword.

9 For I will have respect unto you, and make you fruitful, and multiply you, and establish my covenant with you.

10 And you shall eat old store, and bring forth the old because of the new.

11 And I will set my tabernacle among you: and my soul shall not abhor you.

12 And I will walk among you, and will be your God, and you shall be my people.

13 I am the Becoming-One your God, which brought you forth out of the land of Egypt, that you

should not be their bondmen; and I have broken the bands of your yoke, and made you go upright.

14 But if you will not listen unto me, and will not do all these commandments;

15 And if you shall despise my statutes, or if your soul abhor my judgments, so that you will not do all my commandments, but that you break my covenant:

16 I also will do this unto you; I will even appoint over you terror, consumption, and the burning fever, that shall consume the eyes, and cause sorrow of soul: and you shall sow your seed in vain, for your enemies shall eat it.

17 And I will set my face against you, and you shall be slain before your enemies: they that hate you shall reign over you; and you shall flee when none pursues you.

18 And if you will not yet for all this listen unto me, then I will punish you seven times more for your sins.

19 And I will break the pride of your power; and I will make your heavens as iron, and your earth as brass:

20 And your strength shall be spent in vain: for your land shall not yield her increase, neither shall the trees of the land yield their fruits.

21 And if you walk contrary unto me, and will not listen unto me; I will bring seven times more plagues upon you according to your sins.

22 I will also send wild beasts among you, which shall rob you of your children, and destroy your cattle, and make you few in number; and your high ways shall be desolate.

23 And if you will not be reformed by me by these things, but will walk contrary unto me;

24 Then will I also walk contrary unto you, and will punish you yet seven times for your sins.

25 And I will bring a sword upon you, that shall avenge the quarrel of my covenant: and when you are gathered together within your cities, I will send the pestilence among you; and you shall be delivered into the hand of the enemy.

26 And when I have broken the staff of your bread, ten women shall bake your bread in one oven, and they shall deliver you your bread again by weight: and you shall eat, and not be satisfied.

27 And if you will not for all this listen unto me, but walk contrary unto me;

28 Then I will walk contrary unto you also in fury; and I, even I, will chastise you seven times for your sins.

29 And you shall eat the flesh of your sons, and the flesh of your daughters shall you eat.

30 And I will destroy your high places, and cut down your images, and cast your carcases upon the carcases of your idols, and my soul shall abhor you.

31 And I will make your cities waste, and bring your sanctuaries unto desolation, and I will not smell the aroma of your sweet odors.

32 And I will bring the land into desolation: and your enemies which dwell therein shall be astonished at it.

33 And I will scatter you among the nations, and will draw out a sword after you: and your land shall be desolate, and your cities waste.

34 Then shall the land enjoy her sabbaths, as long as it lies desolate, and you be in your enemies' land; even then shall the land rest, and enjoy her sabbaths.

35 As long as it lies desolate it shall rest; because it did not rest in your sabbaths, when you dwelt upon it.

36 And upon them that are left alive of you I will send a faintness into their hearts in the lands of their enemies; and the sound of a shaken leaf shall chase them; and they shall flee, as fleeing from a sword; and they shall fall when none pursued.

37 And they shall fall one upon another, as it were before a sword, when none pursue: and you shall have no power to stand before your enemies.

38 And you shall perish among the nations, and the land of your enemies shall eat you up.

39 And they that are left of you shall pine away in their iniquity in your enemies' lands; and also in the iniquities of their fathers shall they pine away with them.

40 If they shall confess their iniquity, and the iniquity of their fathers, with their trespass which they trespassed against me, and that also they have walked contrary unto me;

41 And that I also have walked contrary unto them, and have brought them into the land of their enemies; if then their uncircumcised hearts be humbled, and they then accept of the punishment of their iniquity:

42 Then will I remember my covenant with Jacob, and also my covenant with Isaac, and also my covenant with Abraham will I remember; and I will remember the land.

43 The land also shall be left of them, and shall enjoy her sabbaths, while she lies desolate without them: and they shall accept of the punishment of their iniquity: because, even because they despised my judgments, and because their soul abhorred my statutes.

44 And yet for all that, when they be in the land of their enemies, I will not cast them away, neither will I abhor them, to destroy them utterly, and to break my covenant with them: for I am the Becoming-One their God.

45 But I will for their sakes remember the covenant of their ancestors, whom I brought forth out of the land of Egypt in the sight of the nations, that I might be their God: I am the Becoming-One.

46 These are the statutes and judgments and laws, which the Becoming-One made between him and the children of Israel in mount Sinai by the hand of Moses.

Lev 27:1 And the Becoming-One spoke unto Moses, saying,

2 Speak unto the children of Israel, and say unto them, When a man shall make a singular vow, the souls shall be for the Becoming-One by your valuation.

3 And your estimation shall be of the male from a son of twenty years even unto a son of sixty years, even your estimation shall be fifty shekels of silver, after the shekel of the sanctuary.

4 And if it be a female, then your estimation shall be thirty shekels.

5 And if it be from a son five years even unto a son of twenty years, then your estimation shall be of

the male twenty shekels, and for the female ten shekels.

6 And if it be from a son of one month old even unto a son of five years, then your estimation shall be of the male five shekels of silver, and for the female your estimation shall be three shekels of silver.

7 And if it be from a son of sixty years and above; if it be a male, then your estimation shall be fifteen shekels, and for the female ten shekels.

8 But if he be poorer than your estimation, then he shall present himself before the priest, and the priest shall value him; according to his ability that vowed shall the priest value him.

9 And if it be a beast, whereof men bring an offering unto the Becoming-One, all that any man gives of such unto the Becoming-One shall be holy.

10 He shall not alter it, nor change it, a good for a bad, or a bad for a good: and if he shall at all change beast for beast, then it and the exchange thereof shall be holy.

11 And if it be any unclean beast, of which they do not offer a sacrifice unto the Becoming-One, then he shall present the beast before the priest:

12 And the priest shall value it, whether it be good or bad: as you value it, who are the priest, so shall it be.

13 But if he will at all redeem it, then he shall add a fifth part thereof unto your estimation.

14 And when a man shall sanctify his house to be holy unto the Becoming-One, then the priest shall estimate it, whether it be good or bad: as the priest shall estimate it, so shall it stand.

15 And if he that sanctified it will redeem his house, then he shall add the fifth part of the money of your estimation unto it, and it shall be his.

16 And if a man shall sanctify unto the Becoming-One some part of a field of his possession, then your estimation shall be according to the seed thereof: a homer of barley seed shall be valued at fifty shekels of silver.

17 If he sanctify his field from the year of jubilee, according to your estimation it shall stand.

18 But if he sanctify his field after the jubilee, then the priest shall reckon unto him the money according to the years that remain, even unto the year of the jubilee, and it shall be deducted from your valuation.

19 And if he that sanctified the field will in any way redeem it, then he shall add the fifth part of the money of your estimation unto it, and it shall be assured to him.

20 And if he will not redeem the field, or if he have sold the field to another man, it shall not be redeemed any more.

21 But the field, when it goes out in the jubilee, shall be holy unto the Becoming-One, as a field devoted; the possession thereof shall be the priest's.

22 And if a man sanctify unto the Becoming-One a field which he has bought, which is not of the fields of his possession;

23 Then the priest shall reckon unto him the worth of your estimation, even unto the year of the jubilee: and he shall give your estimation in that day, as a holy thing unto the Becoming-One.

24 In the year of the jubilee the field shall return unto him of whom it was bought, even to him to whom the possession of the land did belong.

25 And all your estimations shall be according to the shekel of the sanctuary: twenty gerahs shall be the shekel.

26 But the firstling of the beasts, which should be the Becoming-One's firstling, no man shall sanctify it; whether it be ox, or sheep: it is the Becoming-One's.

27 And if it be of an unclean beast, then he shall redeem it according to your estimation, and shall add a fifth part of it thereto: or if it be not redeemed, then it shall be sold according to your estimation.

28 Notwithstanding no devoted thing, that a man shall devote unto the Becoming-One of all that he hath, both of man and beast, and of the field of his possession, shall be sold or redeemed: every devoted thing is most holy unto the Becoming-One.

29 None devoted, which shall be devoted of men, shall be redeemed; but in dying he shall be put to death.

30 And all the tithe of the land, whether of the seed of the land, or of the fruit of the tree, is the Becoming-One's: it is holy unto the Becoming-One.

31 And if a man will at all redeem any of his tithes, he shall add thereto the fifth part thereof.

32 And concerning the tithe of the herd, or of the flock, even of whatsoever passes under the rod, the tenth shall be holy unto the Becoming-One.

33 He shall not search whether it be good or bad, neither shall he change it: and if he change it at all, then both it and the change thereof shall be holy; it shall not be redeemed.

34 These are the commandments, which the Becoming-One commanded Moses for the children of Israel in mount Sinai.

Numbers

Num 1:1 And the Becoming-One spoke unto Moses in the wilderness of Sinai, in the tabernacle of the set time,[66] on the first day of the second month, in the second year after they were come out of the land of Egypt, saying,

2 Take you the sum of all the congregation of the children of Israel, after their families, by the house of their fathers, with the number of their names, every male by their polls;

3 From a son of twenty years and upward, all that are able to go forth to war in Israel: you and Aaron shall number them by their armies.

4 And with you there shall be a man of every tribe; every one head of the house of his fathers.

5 And these are the names of the men that shall stand with you: of the tribe of Reuben; Elizur the son of Shedeur.

6 Of Simeon; Shelumiel the son of Zurishaddai.

7 Of Judah; Nahshon the son of Amminadab.

8 Of Issachar; Nethaneel the son of Zuar.

9 Of Zebulun; Eliab the son of Helon.

10 Of the children of Joseph: of Ephraim; Elishama the son of Ammihud: of Manasseh; Gamaliel the son of Pedahzur.

11 Of Benjamin; Abidan the son of Gideoni.

12 Of Dan; Ahiezer the son of Ammishaddai.

13 Of Asher; Pagiel the son of Ocran.

14 Of Gad; Eliasaph the son of Deuel.

15 Of Naphtali; Ahira the son of Enan.

16 These were the renowned of the congregation, princes of the tribes of their fathers, heads of thousands in Israel.

17 And Moses and Aaron took these men which are expressed by their names:

18 And they assembled all the congregation together on the first day of the second month, and they declared their pedigrees after their families, by the house of their fathers, according to the number of the names, from a son of twenty years and upward, by their polls.

19 As the Becoming-One commanded Moses, so he numbered them in the wilderness of Sinai.

20 And the children of Reuben, Israel's eldest son, by their generations, after their families, by the house of their fathers, according to the number of the names, by their polls, every male from a son of twenty years and upward, all that were able to go forth to war;

21 Those that were numbered of them, even of the tribe of Reuben, were forty and six thousand and five hundred.

22 Of the children of Simeon, by their generations, after their families, by the house of their fathers, those that were numbered of them, according to the number of the names, by their polls, every male from a son of twenty years and upward, all that were able to go forth to war;

23 Those that were numbered of them, even of the tribe of Simeon, were fifty and nine thousand and three hundred.

24 Of the children of Gad, by their generations, after their families, by the house of their fathers, according to the number of the names, from a son of twenty years and upward, all that were able to go forth to war;

25 Those that were numbered of them, even of the tribe of Gad, were forty and five thousand six hundred and fifty.

26 Of the children of Judah, by their generations, after their families, by the house of their fathers, according to the number of the names, from a son of twenty years and upward, all that were able to go forth to war;

27 Those that were numbered of them, even of the tribe of Judah, were threescore and fourteen thousand and six hundred.

28 Of the children of Issachar, by their generations, after their families, by the house of their fathers, according to the number of the names, from a son of twenty years and upward, all that were able to go forth to war;

29 Those that were numbered of them, even of the tribe of Issachar, were fifty and four thousand and four hundred.

30 Of the children of Zebulun, by their generations, after their families, by the house of their fathers, according to the number of the names, from a son of twenty years and upward, all that were able to go forth to war;

31 Those that were numbered of them, even of the tribe of Zebulun, were fifty and seven thousand and four hundred.

32 Of the children of Joseph, namely, of the children of Ephraim, by their generations, after their families, by the house of their fathers, according to the number of the names, from a son of twenty years and upward, all that were able to go forth to war;

33 Those that were numbered of them, even of the tribe of Ephraim, were forty thousand and five hundred.

34 Of the children of Manasseh, by their generations, after their families, by the house of their fathers, according to the number of the names, from a son of twenty years and upward, all that were able to go forth to war;

35 Those that were numbered of them, even of the tribe of Manasseh, were thirty and two thousand and two hundred.

36 Of the children of Benjamin, by their generations, after their families, by the house of their fathers, according to the number of the names, from a son of twenty years and upward, all that were able to go forth to war;

37 Those that were numbered of them, even of the tribe of Benjamin, were thirty and five thousand and four hundred.

38 Of the children of Dan, by their generations, after their families, by the house of their fathers, according to the number of the names, from a son of twenty years and upward, all that were able to go forth to war;

39 Those that were numbered of them, even of the tribe of Dan, were threescore and two thousand and seven hundred.

40 Of the children of Asher, by their generations, after their families, by the house of their fathers,

---

[66] Appointed time or festival

according to the number of the names, from a son of twenty years and upward, all that were able to go forth to war;

41 Those that were numbered of them, even of the tribe of Asher, were forty and one thousand and five hundred.

42 Of the children of Naphtali, throughout their generations, after their families, by the house of their fathers, according to the number of the names, from a son of twenty years and upward, all that were able to go forth to war;

43 Those that were numbered of them, even of the tribe of Naphtali, were fifty and three thousand and four hundred.

44 These are those that were numbered, which Moses and Aaron numbered, and the princes of Israel, being twelve men: each one was for the house of his fathers.

45 So were all those that were numbered of the children of Israel, by the house of their fathers, from a son of twenty years and upward, all that were able to go forth to war in Israel;

46 Even all they that were numbered were six hundred thousand and three thousand and five hundred and fifty.

47 But the Levites after the tribe of their fathers were not numbered among them.

48 For the Becoming-One had spoken unto Moses, saying,

49 Only you shall not number the tribe of Levi, neither take the sum of them among the children of Israel:

50 But you shall appoint the Levites over the tabernacle of testimony, and over all the vessels thereof, and over all things that belong to it: they shall bear the tabernacle, and all the vessels thereof; and they shall minister unto it, and shall encamp round about the tabernacle.

51 And when the tabernacle sets forward, the Levites shall take it down: and when the tabernacle is to be pitched, the Levites shall set it up: and the stranger that comes near shall be put to death.

52 And the children of Israel shall pitch their tents, every man by his own camp, and every man by his own standard, throughout their hosts.

53 But the Levites shall pitch round about the tabernacle of testimony, that there be no wrath upon the congregation of the children of Israel: and the Levites shall keep the charge of the tabernacle of testimony.

54 And the children of Israel did according to all that the Becoming-One commanded Moses, so did they.

Num 2:1 And the Becoming-One spoke unto Moses and unto Aaron, saying,

2 Every man of the children of Israel shall pitch by his own standard, with the ensign of their father's house: far off about the tabernacle of the set time shall they pitch.

3 And on the east side toward the rising of the sun shall they of the standard of the camp of Judah pitch throughout their armies: and Nahshon the son of Amminadab shall be captain of the children of Judah.

4 And his host, and those that were numbered of them, were threescore and fourteen thousand and six hundred.

5 And those that do pitch next unto him shall be the tribe of Issachar: and Nethaneel the son of Zuar shall be captain of the children of Issachar.

6 And his host, and those that were numbered thereof, were fifty and four thousand and four hundred.

7 Then the tribe of Zebulun: and Eliab the son of Helon shall be captain of the children of Zebulun.

8 And his host, and those that were numbered thereof, were fifty and seven thousand and four hundred.

9 All that were numbered in the camp of Judah were a hundred thousand and fourscore thousand and six thousand and four hundred, throughout their armies. These shall first set forth.

10 On the south side shall be the standard of the camp of Reuben according to their armies: and the captain of the children of Reuben shall be Elizur the son of Shedeur.

11 And his host, and those that were numbered thereof, were forty and six thousand and five hundred.

12 And those which pitch by him shall be the tribe of Simeon: and the captain of the children of Simeon shall be Shelumiel the son of Zurishaddai.

13 And his host, and those that were numbered of them, were fifty and nine thousand and three hundred.

14 Then the tribe of Gad: and the captain of the sons of Gad shall be Eliasaph the son of Reuel.

15 And his host, and those that were numbered of them, were forty and five thousand and six hundred and fifty.

16 All that were numbered in the camp of Reuben were a hundred thousand and fifty and one thousand and four hundred and fifty, throughout their armies. And they shall set forth in the second rank.

17 Then the tabernacle of the set time shall set forward with the camp of the Levites in the midst of the camp: as they encamp, so shall they set forward, every man in his place by their standards.

18 On the west side shall be the standard of the camp of Ephraim according to their armies: and the captain of the sons of Ephraim shall be Elishama the son of Ammihud.

19 And his host, and those that were numbered of them, were forty thousand and five hundred.

20 And by him shall be the tribe of Manasseh: and the captain of the children of Manasseh shall be Gamaliel the son of Pedahzur.

21 And his host, and those that were numbered of them, were thirty and two thousand and two hundred.

22 Then the tribe of Benjamin: and the captain of the sons of Benjamin shall be Abidan the son of Gideoni.

23 And his host, and those that were numbered of them, were thirty and five thousand and four hundred.

24 All that were numbered of the camp of Ephraim were a hundred thousand and eight thousand and a hundred, throughout their armies. And they shall go forward in the third rank.

25 The standard of the camp of Dan shall be on the north side by their armies: and the captain of the children of Dan shall be Ahiezer the son of Ammishaddai.

26 And his host, and those that were numbered of them, were threescore and two thousand and seven hundred.

27 And those that encamp by him shall be the tribe of Asher: and the captain of the children of Asher shall be Pagiel the son of Ocran.

28 And his host, and those that were numbered of them, were forty and one thousand and five hundred.

29 Then the tribe of Naphtali: and the captain of the children of Naphtali shall be Ahira the son of Enan.

30 And his host, and those that were numbered of them, were fifty and three thousand and four hundred.

31 All they that were numbered in the camp of Dan were a hundred thousand and fifty and seven thousand and six hundred. They shall go hindmost with their standards.

32 These are those which were numbered of the children of Israel by the house of their fathers: all those that were numbered of the camps throughout their hosts were six hundred thousand and three thousand and five hundred and fifty.

33 But the Levites were not numbered among the children of Israel; as the Becoming-One commanded Moses.

34 And the children of Israel did according to all that the Becoming-One commanded Moses: so they pitched by their standards, and so they set forward, every one after their families, according to the house of their fathers.

Num 3:1 These also are the generations of Aaron and Moses in the day that the Becoming-One spoke with Moses in mount Sinai.

2 And these are the names of the sons of Aaron; Nadab the firstborn, and Abihu, Eleazar, and Ithamar.

3 These are the names of the sons of Aaron, the priests which were anointed, whom he consecrated to minister in the priest's office.

4 And Nadab and Abihu died before the Becoming-One, when they offered strange fire before the Becoming-One, in the wilderness of Sinai, and they had no children: and Eleazar and Ithamar ministered in the priest's office in the sight of Aaron their father.

5 And the Becoming-One spoke unto Moses, saying,

6 Bring the tribe of Levi near, and present them before Aaron the priest, that they may minister unto him.

7 And they shall keep his charge, and the charge of the whole congregation before the tabernacle of the set time, to do the service of the tabernacle.

8 And they shall keep all the instruments of the tabernacle of the set time, and the charge of the children of Israel, to do the service of the tabernacle.

9 And you shall give the Levites unto Aaron and to his sons: they are wholly given unto him out of the children of Israel.

10 And you shall appoint Aaron and his sons, and they shall wait on their priest's office: and the stranger that comes near shall be put to death.

11 And the Becoming-One spoke unto Moses, saying,

12 And I, behold, I have taken the Levites from among the children of Israel instead of all the firstborn that opens the matrix among the children of Israel: therefore the Levites shall be mine;

13 Because all the firstborn are mine; for on the day that I smote all the firstborn in the land of Egypt I hallowed unto me all the firstborn in Israel, both man and beast: mine shall they be: I am the Becoming-One.

14 And the Becoming-One spoke unto Moses in the wilderness of Sinai, saying,

15 Number the children of Levi after the house of their fathers, by their families: every male from a month old and upward shall you number them.

16 And Moses numbered them according to the mouth of the Becoming-One, as he was commanded.

17 And these were the sons of Levi by their names; Gershon, and Kohath, and Merari.

18 And these are the names of the sons of Gershon by their families; Libni, and Shimei.

19 And the sons of Kohath by their families; Amram, and Izehar, Hebron, and Uzziel.

20 And the sons of Merari by their families; Mahli, and Mushi. These are the families of the Levites according to the house of their fathers.

21 Of Gershon was the family of the Libnites, and the family of the Shimites: these are the families of the Gershonites.

22 Those that were numbered of them, according to the number of all the males, from a month old and upward, even those that were numbered of them were seven thousand and five hundred.

23 The families of the Gershonites shall pitch behind the tabernacle westward.

24 And the chief of the house of the father of the Gershonites shall be Eliasaph the son of Lael.

25 And the charge of the sons of Gershon in the tabernacle of the set time[67] shall be the tabernacle, and the tent, the covering thereof, and the hanging for the door of the tabernacle of the set time.[68]

26 And the hangings of the court, and the curtain for the door of the court, which is by the tabernacle, and by the altar round about, and the cords of it for all the service thereof.

27 And of Kohath was the family of the Amramites, and the family of the Izeharites, and the family of the Hebronites, and the family of the Uzzielites: these are the families of the Kohathites.

28 In the number of all the males, from a month old and upward, were eight thousand and six hundred, keeping the charge of the sanctuary.

29 The families of the sons of Kohath shall pitch on the side of the tabernacle southward.

30 And the chief of the house of the father of the families of the Kohathites shall be Elizaphan the son of Uzziel.

31 And their charge shall be the ark, and the table, and the candlestick, and the altars, and the vessels of the sanctuary wherewith they minister, and the hanging, and all the service thereof.

32 And Eleazar the son of Aaron the priest shall be chief over the chief of the Levites, and have the oversight of them that keep the charge of the sanctuary.

33 Of Merari was the family of the Mahlites, and the family of the Mushites: these are the families of Merari.

---

[67] Appointed time or festival
[68] Appointed time or festival

34 And those that were numbered of them, according to the number of all the males, from a month old and upward, were six thousand and two hundred.

35 And the chief of the house of the father of the families of Merari was Zuriel the son of Abihail: these shall pitch on the side of the tabernacle northward.

36 And under the custody and charge of the sons of Merari shall be the boards of the tabernacle, and the bars thereof, and the pillars thereof, and the sockets thereof, and all the vessels thereof, and all that serves thereto,

37 And the pillars of the court round about, and their sockets, and their pins, and their cords.

38 But those that encamp before the tabernacle toward the east, even before the tabernacle of the set time eastward, shall be Moses, and Aaron and his sons, keeping the charge of the sanctuary for the charge of the children of Israel; and the stranger that comes near shall be put to death.

39 All that were numbered of the Levites, which Moses and Aaron numbered at the mouth of the Becoming-One, throughout their families, all the males from a month old and upward, were twenty and two thousand.

40 And the Becoming-One said unto Moses, Number all the firstborn of the males of the children of Israel from a month old and upward, and take the number of their names.

41 And you shall take the Levites for me I am the Becoming-One instead of all the firstborn among the children of Israel; and the cattle of the Levites instead of all the firstlings among the cattle of the children of Israel.

42 And Moses numbered, as the Becoming-One commanded him, all the firstborn among the children of Israel.

43 And all the firstborn males by the number of names, from a month old and upward, of those that were numbered of them, were twenty and two thousand two hundred and threescore and thirteen.

44 And the Becoming-One spoke unto Moses, saying,

45 Take the Levites instead of all the firstborn among the children of Israel, and the cattle of the Levites instead of their cattle; and the Levites shall be mine: I am the Becoming-One.

46 And for those that are to be redeemed of the two hundred and threescore and thirteen of the firstborn of the children of Israel, which are more than the Levites;

47 you shall even take five shekels apiece by the poll, after the shekel of the sanctuary shall you take them: the shekel is twenty gerahs;

48 And you shall give the money, wherewith the odd number of them is to be redeemed, unto Aaron and to his sons.

49 And Moses took the redemption money of them that were over and above them that were redeemed by the Levites:

50 Of the firstborn of the children of Israel took he the money; an thousand three hundred and threescore and five shekels, after the shekel of the sanctuary:

51 And Moses gave the money of them that were redeemed unto Aaron and to his sons, according to the word of the Becoming-One, as the Becoming-One commanded Moses.

Num 4:1 And the Becoming-One spoke unto Moses and unto Aaron, saying,

2 Take the sum of the sons of Kohath from among the sons of Levi, after their families, by the house of their fathers,

3 From a son of thirty years and upward even until a son of fifty years, all that enter into the host, to do the work in the tabernacle of the set time.[69]

4 This shall be the service of the sons of Kohath in the tabernacle of the set time,[70] about the most holy things:

5 And when the camp sets forward, Aaron shall come, and his sons, and they shall take down the covering veil, and cover the ark of testimony with it:

6 And shall put thereon the covering of badgers' skins, and shall spread over it a cloth wholly of blue, and shall put in the staves thereof.

7 And upon the table of showbread they shall spread a cloth of blue, and put thereon the dishes, and the spoons, and the bowls, and covers to cover withal: and the continual bread shall be thereon:

8 And they shall spread upon them a cloth of scarlet, and cover the same with a covering of badgers' skins, and shall put in the staves thereof.

9 And they shall take a cloth of blue, and cover the candlestick of the light, and his lamps, and his tongs, and his snuffdishes, and all the oil vessels thereof, wherewith they minister unto it:

10 And they shall put it and all the vessels thereof within a covering of badgers' skins, and shall put it upon a bar.

11 And upon the golden altar they shall spread a cloth of blue, and cover it with a covering of badgers' skins, and shall put to the staves thereof:

12 And they shall take all the instruments of ministry, wherewith they minister in the sanctuary, and put them in a cloth of blue, and cover them with a covering of badgers' skins, and shall put them on a bar:

13 And they shall take away the ashes from the altar, and spread a purple cloth thereon:

14 And they shall put upon it all the vessels thereof, wherewith they minister about it, even the censers, the fleshhooks, and the shovels, and the basins, all the vessels of the altar; and they shall spread upon it a covering of badgers' skins, and put to the staves of it.

15 And when Aaron and his sons have made an end of covering the sanctuary, and all the vessels of the sanctuary, as the camp is to set forward; after that, the sons of Kohath shall come to bear it: but they shall not touch any holy thing, lest they die. These things are the burden of the sons of Kohath in the tabernacle of the set time.[71]

16 And to the office of Eleazar the son of Aaron the priest pertains the oil for the light, and the sweet incense, and the daily food offering, and the anointing oil, and the oversight of all the tabernacle, and of all that therein is, in the sanctuary, and in the vessels thereof.

17 And the Becoming-One spoke unto Moses and unto Aaron, saying,

---

[69] Appointed time or festival
[70] Appointed time or festival
[71] Appointed time or festival

18 Cut you not off the tribe of the families of the Kohathites from among the Levites:

19 But thus do unto them, that they may live, and not die, when they approach unto the most holy things: Aaron and his sons shall go in, and appoint them every one to his service and to his burden:

20 But they shall not go in to see when the holy things are covered, lest they die.

21 And the Becoming-One spoke unto Moses, saying,

22 Take also the sum of the sons of Gershon, throughout the houses of their fathers, by their families;

23 From a son of thirty years and upward until a son of fifty years shall you number them; all that enter in to perform the service, to do the work in the tabernacle of the set time.[72]

24 This is the service of the families of the Gershonites, to serve, and for burdens:

25 And they shall bear the curtains of the tabernacle, and the tabernacle of the set time, his covering, and the covering of the badgers' skins that is above upon it, and the hanging for the door of the tabernacle of the set time,

26 And the hangings of the court, and the hanging for the door of the gate of the court, which is by the tabernacle and by the altar round about, and their cords, and all the instruments of their service, and all that is made for them: so shall they serve.

27 At the appointment of Aaron and his sons shall be all the service of the sons of the Gershonites, in all their burdens, and in all their service: and you shall appoint unto them in charge all their burdens.

28 This is the service of the families of the sons of Gershon in the tabernacle of the set time:[73] and their charge shall be under the hand of Ithamar the son of Aaron the priest.

29 As for the sons of Merari, you shall number them after their families, by the house of their fathers;

30 From a son of thirty years and upward even unto a son of fifty years shall you number them, every one that enters into the service, to do the work of the tabernacle of the set time.

31 And this is the charge of their burden, according to all their service in the tabernacle of the set time;[74] the boards of the tabernacle, and the bars thereof, and the pillars thereof, and sockets thereof,

32 And the pillars of the court round about, and their sockets, and their pins, and their cords, with all their instruments, and with all their service: and by name you shall reckon the instruments of the charge of their burden.

33 This is the service of the families of the sons of Merari, according to all their service, in the tabernacle of the set time,[75] under the hand of Ithamar the son of Aaron the priest.

34 And Moses and Aaron and the chief of the congregation numbered the sons of the Kohathites after their families, and after the house of their fathers,

35 From a son of thirty years and upward even unto a son of fifty years, every one that enters into the service, for the work in the tabernacle of the set time:[76]

36 And those that were numbered of them by their families were two thousand[77] seven hundred and fifty.

37 These were they that were numbered of the families of the Kohathites, all that might do service in the tabernacle of the set time,[78] which Moses and Aaron did number according to the commandment of the Becoming-One by the hand of Moses.

38 And those that were numbered of the sons of Gershon, throughout their families, and by the house of their fathers,

39 From a son of thirty years and upward even unto a son of fifty years, every one that enters into the service, for the work in the tabernacle of the set time,[79]

40 Even those that were numbered of them, throughout their families, by the house of their fathers, were two thousand and six hundred and thirty.

41 These are they that were numbered of the families of the sons of Gershon, of all that might do service in the tabernacle of the set time,[80] whom Moses and Aaron did number according to the commandment of the Becoming-One.

42 And those that were numbered of the families of the sons of Merari, throughout their families, by the house of their fathers,

43 From a son of thirty years and upward even unto a son of fifty years, every one that enters into the service, for the work in the tabernacle of the set time,[81]

44 Even those that were numbered of them after their families, were three thousand and two hundred.

45 These be those that were numbered of the families of the sons of Merari, whom Moses and Aaron numbered according to the word of the Becoming-One by the hand of Moses.

46 All those that were numbered of the Levites, whom Moses and Aaron and the chief of Israel numbered, after their families, and after the house of their fathers,

47 From a son of thirty years and upward even unto a son of fifty years, every one that came to do the service of the ministry, and the service of the burden in the tabernacle of the set time,[82]

48 Even those that were numbered of them, were eight thousand and five hundred and fourscore.

49 According to the commandment of the Becoming-One they were numbered by the hand of Moses, every one according to his service, and according to his burden: thus were they numbered of him, as the Becoming-One commanded Moses.

Num 5:1 And the Becoming-One spoke unto Moses, saying,

---

[72] Appointed time or festival
[73] Appointed time or festival
[74] Appointed time or festival
[75] Appointed time or festival
[76] Appointed time or festival
[77] See Preface
[78] Appointed time or festival
[79] Appointed time or festival
[80] Appointed time or festival
[81] Appointed time or festival
[82] Appointed time or festival

2 Command the children of Israel, that they put out of the camp every leper, and every one that has an issue, and whosoever is defiled by the [dead] soul:

3 Both male and female shall you put out, outside the camp shall you put them; that they defile not their camps, in the midst whereof I dwell.

4 And the children of Israel did so, and put them out outside the camp: as the Becoming-One spoke unto Moses, so did the children of Israel.

5 And the Becoming-One spoke unto Moses, saying,

6 Speak unto the children of Israel, When a man or woman shall commit any sin that men commit, to do a trespass against the Becoming-One, and that soul be guilty;

7 Then they shall confess their sin which they have done: and he shall recompense his trespass with the principal thereof, and add unto it the fifth part thereof, and give it unto him against whom he has trespassed.

8 But if the man have no kinsman to recompense the trespass unto, let the trespass be recompensed unto the Becoming-One, even to the priest; beside the ram of the atonement, whereby an atonement shall be made for him.

9 And every offering of all the holy things of the children of Israel, which they bring unto the priest, shall be his.

10 And every man's hallowed things shall be his: whatsoever any man gives the priest, it shall be his.

11 And the Becoming-One spoke unto Moses, saying,

12 Speak unto the children of Israel, and say unto them, If any man's wife go aside, and commit a trespass against him,

13 And a man lie with her with seed, and it be hid from the eyes of her husband, and be kept close, and she be defiled, and there be no witness against her, neither she be taken with the manner;

14 And the spirit of jealousy come upon him, and he be jealous of his wife, and she be defiled: or if the spirit of jealousy come upon him, and he be jealous of his wife, and she be not defiled:

15 Then shall the man bring his wife unto the priest, and he shall bring her offering for her, the tenth part of an ephah of barley meal; he shall pour no oil upon it, nor put frankincense thereon; for it is an offering of jealousy, an offering of memorial, bringing iniquity to remembrance.

16 And the priest shall bring her near, and set her before the Becoming-One: 17 And the priest shall take holy water in an earthen vessel; and of the dust that is in the floor of the tabernacle the priest shall take, and put it into the water:

18 And the priest shall set the woman before the Becoming-One, and uncover the woman's head, and put the offering of memorial in her hands, which is the jealousy offering: and the priest shall have in his hand the bitter water that causes the curse:

19 And the priest shall charge her by an oath, and say unto the woman, If no man have lain with you, and if you have not gone aside to uncleanness with another instead of your husband, be you free from this bitter water that causes the curse:

20 But if you have gone aside to another instead of your husband, and if you be defiled, and some man have lain with you beside your husband:

21 Then the priest shall charge the woman with an oath of cursing, and the priest shall say unto the woman, The Becoming-One make you a curse and an oath among your people, when the Becoming-One does make your thigh to rot, and your belly to swell;

22 And this water that causes the curse shall go into your bowels, to make your belly to swell, and your thigh to rot: And the woman shall say, Amen, amen.

23 And the priest shall write these curses in a book, and he shall blot them out with the bitter water:

24 And he shall cause the woman to drink the bitter water that causes the curse: and the water that causes the curse shall enter into her, and become bitter.

25 Then the priest shall take the jealousy offering out of the woman's hand, and shall wave the offering before the Becoming-One, and offer it upon the altar:

26 And the priest shall take a handful of the offering, even the memorial thereof, and burn it upon the altar, and afterward shall cause the woman to drink the water.

27 And when he has made her to drink the water, then it shall come to pass, that, if she be defiled, and have done trespass against her husband, that the water that causes the curse shall enter into her, and become bitter, and her belly shall swell, and her thigh shall rot: and the woman shall be a curse among her people.

28 And if the woman be not defiled, but be clean; then she shall be free, and shall conceive seed.

29 This is the law of jealousies, when a wife goes aside to another instead of her husband, and is defiled;

30 Or when the spirit of jealousy comes upon him, and he be jealous over his wife, and shall set the woman before the Becoming-One, and the priest shall execute upon her all this law.

31 Then shall the man be guiltless from iniquity, and this woman shall bear her iniquity.

Num 6:1 And the Becoming-One spoke unto Moses, saying,

2 Speak unto the children of Israel, and say unto them, When either man or woman shall separate themselves to vow a vow of a Nazarite, to separate themselves unto the Becoming-One: 3 He shall separate himself from wine and strong drink, and shall drink no vinegar of wine, or vinegar of strong drink, neither shall he drink any liquor of grapes, nor eat moist grapes, or dried.

4 All the days of his separation shall he eat nothing that is made of the vine tree, from the kernels even to the husk.

5 All the days of the vow of his separation there shall no razor come upon his head: until the days be fulfilled, for which he separates himself unto the Becoming-One, he shall be holy, and shall let the locks of the hair of his head grow.

6 All the days that he separates himself unto the Becoming-One he shall come at no dead soul.

7 He shall not make himself unclean for his father, or for his mother, for his brother, or for his sister, when they die: because the consecration of his God is upon his head.

8 All the days of his separation he is holy unto the Becoming-One.

9 And if any man die very suddenly by him, and he has defiled the head of his consecration; then he shall shave his head in the day of his cleansing, on the seventh day shall he shave it.

10 And on the eighth day he shall bring two turtles, or two young pigeons, to the priest, to the door of the tabernacle of the set time:

11 And the priest shall offer the one for a sin offering, and the other for a burnt offering, and make an atonement for him, for that he sinned by the [dead] soul, and shall hallow his head that same day.

12 And he shall consecrate unto the Becoming-One the days of his separation, and shall bring a lamb of the first year for a trespass offering: but the days that were before shall be lost, because his separation was defiled.

13 And this is the law of the Nazarite, when the days of his separation are fulfilled: he shall be brought unto the door of the tabernacle of the set time:

14 And he shall offer his offering unto the Becoming-One, one he lamb of the first year without blemish for a burnt offering, and one ewe lamb of the first year without blemish for a sin offering, and one ram without blemish for peace offerings,

15 And a basket of unleavened bread, cakes of fine flour mingled with oil, and wafers of unleavened bread anointed with oil, and their food offering, and their drink offerings.

16 And the priest shall bring them before the Becoming-One, and shall offer his sin offering, and his burnt offering:

17 And he shall offer the ram for a sacrifice of peace offerings unto the Becoming-One, with the basket of unleavened bread: the priest shall offer also his food offering, and his drink offering.

18 And the Nazarite shall shave the head of his separation at the door of the tabernacle of the set time, and shall take the hair of the head of his separation, and put it in the fire which is under the sacrifice of the peace offerings.

19 And the priest shall take the sodden shoulder of the ram, and one unleavened cake out of the basket, and one unleavened wafer, and shall put them upon the hands of the Nazarite, after the hair of his separation is shaven:

20 And the priest shall wave them for a wave offering before the Becoming-One: this is holy for the priest, with the wave breast and heave shoulder: and after that the Nazarite may drink wine.

21 This is the law of the Nazarite who has vowed, and of his offering unto the Becoming-One for his separation, beside that that his hand shall get: according to the vow which he vowed, so he must do after the law of his separation.

22 And the Becoming-One spoke unto Moses, saying,

23 Speak unto Aaron and unto his sons, saying, In this way you shall bless the children of Israel, saying unto them,

24 The Becoming-One bless you, and keep you:

25 The Becoming-One make his face shine upon you, and be gracious unto you:

26 The Becoming-One lift up his countenance upon you, and give you peace.

27 And they shall put my name upon the children of Israel; and I will bless them.

Num 7:1 And it came to pass on the day that Moses had fully set up the tabernacle, and had anointed it, and sanctified it, and all the instruments thereof, both the altar and all the vessels thereof, and had anointed them, and sanctified them;

2 That the princes of Israel, heads of the house of their fathers, who were the princes of the tribes, and were over them that were numbered, offered:

3 And they brought their offering before the Becoming-One, six covered wagons, and twelve oxen; a wagon for two of the princes, and for each one an ox: and they brought them before the tabernacle.

4 And the Becoming-One spoke unto Moses, saying,

5 Take it of them, that they may be to do the service of the tabernacle of the set time; and you shall give them unto the Levites, to every man according to his service.

6 And Moses took the wagons and the oxen, and gave them unto the Levites.

7 Two wagons and four oxen he gave unto the sons of Gershon, according to their service:

8 And four wagons and eight oxen he gave unto the sons of Merari, according unto their service, under the hand of Ithamar the son of Aaron the priest.

9 But unto the sons of Kohath he gave none: because the service of the sanctuary belonging unto them was that they should bear upon their shoulders.

10 And the princes offered for dedicating of the altar in the day that it was anointed, even the princes offered their offering before the altar.

11 And the Becoming-One said unto Moses, They shall offer their offering, each prince on his day, for the dedicating of the altar.

12 And he that offered his offering the first day was Nahshon the son of Amminadab, of the tribe of Judah:

13 And his offering was one silver charger, the weight thereof was a hundred and thirty shekels, one silver bowl of seventy shekels, after the shekel of the sanctuary; both of them were full of fine flour mingled with oil for a food offering:

14 One spoon of ten shekels of gold, full of incense:

15 One young bullock, one ram, one lamb of the first year, for a burnt offering:

16 One kid of the goats for a sin offering:

17 And for a sacrifice of peace offerings, two oxen, five rams, five he goats, five lambs of the first year: this was the offering of Nahshon the son of Amminadab.

18 On the second day Nethaneel the son of Zuar, prince of Issachar, did offer:

19 He offered for his offering one silver charger, the weight whereof was a hundred and thirty shekels, one silver bowl of seventy shekels, after the shekel of the sanctuary; both of them full of fine flour mingled with oil for a food offering:

20 One spoon of gold of ten shekels, full of incense:

21 One young bullock, one ram, one lamb of the first year, for a burnt offering:

22 One kid of the goats for a sin offering:

23 And for a sacrifice of peace offerings, two oxen, five rams, five he goats, five lambs of the first year: this was the offering of Nethaneel the son of Zuar.

24 On the third day Eliab the son of Helon, prince of the children of Zebulun, did offer:

25 His offering was one silver charger, the weight whereof was a hundred and thirty shekels, one silver bowl of seventy shekels, after the shekel of the sanctuary; both of them full of fine flour mingled with oil for a food offering:

26 One golden spoon of ten shekels, full of incense:

27 One young bullock, one ram, one lamb of the first year, for a burnt offering:

28 One kid of the goats for a sin offering:

29 And for a sacrifice of peace offerings, two oxen, five rams, five he goats, five lambs of the first year: this was the offering of Eliab the son of Helon.

30 On the fourth day Elizur the son of Shedeur, prince of the children of Reuben, did offer:

31 His offering was one silver charger of the weight of a hundred and thirty shekels, one silver bowl of seventy shekels, after the shekel of the sanctuary; both of them full of fine flour mingled with oil for a food offering:

32 One golden spoon of ten shekels, full of incense:

33 One young bullock, one ram, one lamb of the first year, for a burnt offering:

34 One kid of the goats for a sin offering:

35 And for a sacrifice of peace offerings, two oxen, five rams, five he goats, five lambs of the first year: this was the offering of Elizur the son of Shedeur.

36 On the fifth day Shelumiel the son of Zurishaddai, prince of the children of Simeon, did offer:

37 His offering was one silver charger, the weight whereof was a hundred and thirty shekels, one silver bowl of seventy shekels, after the shekel of the sanctuary; both of them full of fine flour mingled with oil for a food offering:

38 One golden spoon of ten shekels, full of incense:

39 One young bullock, one ram, one lamb of the first year, for a burnt offering:

40 One kid of the goats for a sin offering:

41 And for a sacrifice of peace offerings, two oxen, five rams, five he goats, five lambs of the first year: this was the offering of Shelumiel the son of Zurishaddai.

42 On the sixth day Eliasaph the son of Deuel, prince of the children of Gad, offered:

43 His offering was one silver charger of the weight of a hundred and thirty shekels, a silver bowl of seventy shekels, after the shekel of the sanctuary; both of them full of fine flour mingled with oil for a food offering:

44 One golden spoon of ten shekels, full of incense:

45 One young bullock, one ram, one lamb of the first year, for a burnt offering:

46 One kid of the goats for a sin offering:

47 And for a sacrifice of peace offerings, two oxen, five rams, five he goats, five lambs of the first year: this was the offering of Eliasaph the son of Deuel.

48 On the seventh day Elishama the son of Ammihud, prince of the children of Ephraim, offered:

49 His offering was one silver charger, the weight whereof was a hundred and thirty shekels, one silver bowl of seventy shekels, after the shekel of the sanctuary; both of them full of fine flour mingled with oil for a food offering:

50 One golden spoon of ten shekels, full of incense:

51 One young bullock, one ram, one lamb of the first year, for a burnt offering:

52 One kid of the goats for a sin offering:

53 And for a sacrifice of peace offerings, two oxen, five rams, five he goats, five lambs of the first year: this was the offering of Elishama the son of Ammihud.

54 On the eighth day offered Gamaliel the son of Pedahzur, prince of the children of Manasseh:

55 His offering was one silver charger of the weight of a hundred and thirty shekels, one silver bowl of seventy shekels, after the shekel of the sanctuary; both of them full of fine flour mingled with oil for a food offering:

56 One golden spoon of ten shekels, full of incense:

57 One young bullock, one ram, one lamb of the first year, for a burnt offering:

58 One kid of the goats for a sin offering:

59 And for a sacrifice of peace offerings, two oxen, five rams, five he goats, five lambs of the first year: this was the offering of Gamaliel the son of Pedahzur.

60 On the ninth day Abidan the son of Gideoni, prince of the children of Benjamin, offered:

61 His offering was one silver charger, the weight whereof was a hundred and thirty shekels, one silver bowl of seventy shekels, after the shekel of the sanctuary; both of them full of fine flour mingled with oil for a food offering:

62 One golden spoon of ten shekels, full of incense:

63 One young bullock, one ram, one lamb of the first year, for a burnt offering:

64 One kid of the goats for a sin offering:

65 And for a sacrifice of peace offerings, two oxen, five rams, five he goats, five lambs of the first year: this was the offering of Abidan the son of Gideoni.

66 On the tenth day Ahiezer the son of Ammishaddai, prince of the children of Dan, offered:

67 His offering was one silver charger, the weight whereof was a hundred and thirty shekels, one silver bowl of seventy shekels, after the shekel of the sanctuary; both of them full of fine flour mingled with oil for a food offering:

68 One golden spoon of ten shekels, full of incense:

69 One young bullock, one ram, one lamb of the first year, for a burnt offering:

70 One kid of the goats for a sin offering:

71 And for a sacrifice of peace offerings, two oxen, five rams, five he goats, five lambs of the first year: this was the offering of Ahiezer the son of Ammishaddai.

72 On the eleventh day Pagiel the son of Ocran, prince of the children of Asher, offered:

73 His offering was one silver charger, the weight whereof was a hundred and thirty shekels, one silver bowl of seventy shekels, after the shekel of the sanctuary; both of them full of fine flour mingled with oil for a food offering:

74 One golden spoon of ten shekels, full of incense:

75 One young bullock, one ram, one lamb of the first year, for a burnt offering:

76 One kid of the goats for a sin offering:

77 And for a sacrifice of peace offerings, two oxen, five rams, five he goats, five lambs of the first year: this was the offering of Pagiel the son of Ocran.

78 On the twelfth day Ahira the son of Enan, prince of the children of Naphtali, offered:

79 His offering was one silver charger, the weight whereof was a hundred and thirty shekels, one silver bowl of seventy shekels, after the shekel of the sanctuary; both of them full of fine flour mingled with oil for a food offering:

80 One golden spoon of ten shekels, full of incense:

81 One young bullock, one ram, one lamb of the first year, for a burnt offering:

82 One kid of the goats for a sin offering:

83 And for a sacrifice of peace offerings, two oxen, five rams, five he goats, five lambs of the first year: this was the offering of Ahira the son of Enan.

84 This was the dedication of the altar, in the day when it was anointed, by the princes of Israel: twelve chargers of silver, twelve silver bowls, twelve spoons of gold:

85 Each charger of silver weighing a hundred and thirty shekels, each bowl seventy: all the silver vessels weighed two thousand and four hundred shekels, after the shekel of the sanctuary:

86 The golden spoons were twelve, full of incense, weighing ten shekels apiece, after the shekel of the sanctuary: all the gold of the spoons was a hundred and twenty shekels.

87 All the oxen for the burnt offering were twelve bullocks, the rams twelve, the lambs of the first year twelve, with their food offering: and the kids of the goats for sin offering twelve.

88 And all the oxen for the sacrifice of the peace offerings were twenty and four bullocks, the rams sixty, the he goats sixty, the lambs of the first year sixty. This was the dedication of the altar, after that it was anointed.

89 And when Moses was gone into the tabernacle of the set time to speak with him, then he heard the voice of one speaking unto him from off the mercy seat that was upon the ark of testimony, from between the two cherubs: and he spoke unto him.

Num 8:1 And the Becoming-One spoke unto Moses, saying,

2 Speak unto Aaron, and say unto him, When you light the lamps, the seven lamps shall give light over against the candlestick.

3 And Aaron did so; he lighted the lamps thereof over against the candlestick, as the Becoming-One commanded Moses.

4 And this work of the candlestick was of beaten gold, unto the shaft thereof, unto the flowers thereof, was beaten work: according unto the pattern which the Becoming-One had showed Moses, so he made the candlestick.

5 And the Becoming-One spoke unto Moses, saying,

6 Take the Levites from among the children of Israel, and cleanse them.

7 And thus shall you do unto them, to cleanse them: Sprinkle water of purifying upon them, and let them shave all their flesh, and let them wash their clothes, and so make themselves clean.

8 Then let them take a young bullock with his food offering, even fine flour mingled with oil, and another young bullock shall you take for a sin offering.

9 And you shall bring the Levites before the tabernacle of the set time: and you shall gather the whole assembly of the children of Israel together:

10 And you shall bring the Levites before the Becoming-One: and the children of Israel shall put their hands upon the Levites:

11 And Aaron shall offer the Levites before the Becoming-One for an offering of the children of Israel, that they may execute the service of the Becoming-One.

12 And the Levites shall lay their hands upon the heads of the bullocks: and you shall offer the one for a sin offering, and the other for a burnt offering, unto the Becoming-One, to make an atonement for the Levites.

13 And you shall set the Levites before Aaron, and before his sons, and offer them for an offering unto the Becoming-One.

14 Thus shall you separate the Levites from among the children of Israel: and the Levites shall be mine.

15 And after that shall the Levites go in to do the service of the tabernacle of the set time: and you shall cleanse them, and offer them for an offering.

16 For they are wholly given unto me from among the children of Israel; instead of such as open every womb, even instead of the firstborn of all the children of Israel, I have taken them unto me.

17 For all the firstborn of the children of Israel are mine, both man and beast: on the day that I smote every firstborn in the land of Egypt I sanctified them for myself.

18 And I have taken the Levites for all the firstborn of the children of Israel.

19 And I have given the Levites as a gift to Aaron and to his sons from among the children of Israel, to do the service of the children of Israel in the tabernacle of the set time,[83] and to make an atonement for the children of Israel: that there be no plague among the children of Israel, when the children of Israel come near unto the sanctuary.

20 And Moses, and Aaron, and all the congregation of the children of Israel, did to the Levites according unto all that the Becoming-One commanded Moses concerning the Levites, so did the children of Israel unto them.

21 And the Levites were purified, and they washed their clothes; and Aaron offered them as an offering before the Becoming-One; and Aaron made an atonement for them to cleanse them.

22 And after that went the Levites in to do their service in the tabernacle of the set time[84] before Aaron, and before his sons: as the Becoming-One had

---

[83] Appointed time or festival
[84] Appointed time or festival

commanded Moses concerning the Levites, so did they unto them.

23 And the Becoming-One spoke unto Moses, saying,

24 This is it that belongs unto the Levites: from a son of twenty and five years and upward they shall go in to wait upon the service of the tabernacle of the set time:

25 And from the age of fifty years they shall cease waiting upon the service thereof, and shall serve no more:

26 But shall minister with their brethren in the tabernacle of the set time,[85] to keep the charge, and shall do no service. Thus shall you do unto the Levites touching their charge.

Num 9:1 And the Becoming-One spoke unto Moses in the wilderness of Sinai, in the first month of the second year after they were come out of the land of Egypt, saying,

2 Let the children of Israel also keep the Passover at his set time.[86]

3 In the fourteenth day of this month, between the evenings, you shall keep it in his set time:[87] according to all the rites of it, and according to all the judgments thereof, shall you keep it.

4 And Moses spoke unto the children of Israel, that they should keep the Passover.

5 And they kept the Passover on the fourteenth day of the first month between the evenings in the wilderness of Sinai: according to all that the Becoming-One commanded Moses, so did the children of Israel.

6 And there were certain men, who were defiled by the dead soul of a man, that they could not keep the Passover on that day: and they came before Moses and before Aaron on that day:

7 And those men said unto him, We are defiled by the dead soul of a man: why are we kept back, that we may not offer an offering of the Becoming-One in his set time[88] among the children of Israel?

8 And Moses said unto them, Stand still, and I will hear what the Becoming-One will command concerning you.

9 And the Becoming-One spoke unto Moses, saying,

10 Speak unto the children of Israel, saying, If any man of you or of your posterity shall be unclean by reason of a dead soul, or be in a journey afar off, yet he shall keep the Passover unto the Becoming-One.

11 The fourteenth day of the second month between the evenings they shall keep it, and eat it with unleavened bread and bitter herbs.

12 They shall leave none of it unto the morning, nor break any bone of it: according to all the ordinances of the Passover they shall keep it.

13 But the man that is clean, and is not in a journey, and forbears to keep the Passover, even the same soul shall be cut off from among his people: because he brought not the offering of the Becoming-One in his set time,[89] that man shall bear his sin.

14 And if a stranger shall sojourn among you, and will keep the Passover unto the Becoming-One; according to the ordinance of the Passover, and according to the judgement thereof, so shall he do: you shall have one ordinance, both for the stranger, and for him that was born in the land.

15 And on the day that the tabernacle was reared up the cloud covered the tabernacle, namely, the tent of the testimony: and at evening there was upon the tabernacle as it were the appearance of fire, until the morning.

16 So it was always: the cloud covered it by day, and the appearance of fire by night.

17 And when the cloud was taken up from the tabernacle, then after that the children of Israel journeyed: and in the place where the cloud abode, there the children of Israel pitched their tents.

18 At the mouth of the Becoming-One the children of Israel journeyed, and at the mouth of the Becoming-One they pitched: all the days of the cloud upon the tabernacle they rested in their tents.

19 And when the cloud tarried long upon the tabernacle many days, then the children of Israel kept the charge of the Becoming-One, and journeyed not.

20 And so it was, when the cloud was a few days upon the tabernacle; according to the mouth of the Becoming-One they abode in their tents, and according to the mouth of the Becoming-One they journeyed.

21 And so it was, when the cloud abode from even unto the morning, and that the cloud was taken up in the morning, then they journeyed: whether it was by day or by night that the cloud was taken up, they journeyed.

22 Or whether it were two days, or a month, or a year, that the cloud tarried upon the tabernacle, remaining thereon, the children of Israel abode in their tents, and journeyed not: but when it was taken up, they journeyed.

23 At the mouth of the Becoming-One they rested in the tents, and at the mouth of the Becoming-One they journeyed: they kept the charge of the Becoming-One, at the mouth of the Becoming-One by the hand of Moses.

Num 10:1 And the Becoming-One spoke unto Moses, saying,

2 Make you two trumpets of silver; of a whole piece shall you make them: that you may use them for the calling of the assembly, and for the journeying of the camps.

3 And when they shall blow with them, all the assembly shall assemble themselves to you at the door of the tabernacle of the set time.

4 And if they blow but with one trumpet, then the princes, which are heads of the thousands of Israel, shall gather themselves unto you.

5 When you blow an alarm, then the camps that lie on the east parts shall go forward.

---

[85] Appointed time or festival
[86] Appointed time or festival
[87] Appointed time or festival
[88] Appointed time or festival

[89] Appointed time or festival

6 When you blow an alarm the second time, then the camps that lie on the south side shall take their journey: they shall blow an alarm for their journeys.

7 But when the congregation is to be gathered together, you shall blow, but you shall not sound an alarm.

8 And the sons of Aaron, the priests, shall blow with the trumpets; and they shall be to you for an ordinance for olam throughout your generations.

9 And if you go to war in your land against the enemy that oppresses you, then you shall blow an alarm with the trumpets; and you shall be remembered before the Becoming-One your God, and you shall be saved from your enemies.

10 Also in the day of your gladness, and in your set times,[90] and in the beginnings of your months, you shall blow with the trumpets over your burnt offerings, and over the sacrifices of your peace offerings; that they may be to you for a memorial before your God: I am the Becoming-One your God.

11 And it came to pass on the twentieth day of the second month, in the second year, that the cloud was taken up from off the tabernacle of the testimony.

12 And the children of Israel took their journeys out of the wilderness of Sinai; and the cloud rested in the wilderness of Paran.

13 And they first took their journey according to the mouth of the Becoming-One by the hand of Moses.

14 In the first place went the standard of the camp of the children of Judah according to their armies: and over his host was Nahshon the son of Amminadab.

15 And over the host of the tribe of the children of Issachar was Nethaneel the son of Zuar.

16 And over the host of the tribe of the children of Zebulun was Eliab the son of Helon.

17 And the tabernacle was taken down; and the sons of Gershon and the sons of Merari set forward, bearing the tabernacle.

18 And the standard of the camp of Reuben set forward according to their armies: and over his host was Elizur the son of Shedeur.

19 And over the host of the tribe of the children of Simeon was Shelumiel the son of Zurishaddai.

20 And over the host of the tribe of the children of Gad was Eliasaph the son of Deuel.

21 And the Kohathites set forward, bearing the sanctuary: and the other did set up the tabernacle against they came.

22 And the standard of the camp of the children of Ephraim set forward according to their armies: and over his host was Elishama the son of Ammihud.

23 And over the host of the tribe of the children of Manasseh was Gamaliel the son of Pedahzur.

24 And over the host of the tribe of the children of Benjamin was Abidan the son of Gideoni.

25 And the standard of the camp of the children of Dan set forward, which was the rear-guard of all the camps throughout their hosts: and over his host was Ahiezer the son of Ammishaddai.

26 And over the host of the tribe of the children of Asher was Pagiel the son of Ocran.

27 And over the host of the tribe of the children of Naphtali was Ahira the son of Enan.

28 Thus were the journeyings of the children of Israel according to their armies, when they set forward.

29 And Moses said unto Hobab, the son of Raguel the Midianite, Moses' father-in-law, We are journeying unto the place of which the Becoming-One said, I will give it you: you come with us, and we will do you good: for the Becoming-One has spoken good concerning Israel.

30 And he said unto him, I will not go; but I will depart to mine own land, and to my kindred.

31 And he said, Leave us not, I pray you; forasmuch as you know how we are to encamp in the wilderness, and you may be to us instead of eyes.

32 And it shall be, if you go with us, yes, it shall be, that what goodness the Becoming-One shall do unto us, the same will we do unto you.

33 And they departed from the mount of the Becoming-One three days' journey: and the ark of the covenant of the Becoming-One went before them in the three days' journey, to search out a resting place for them.

34 And the cloud of the Becoming-One was upon them by day, when they went out of the camp.

35 And it came to pass, when the ark set forward, that Moses said, Rise up, Becoming-One, and let your enemies be scattered; and let them that hate you flee before you.

36 And when it rested, he said, Return, O Becoming-One, unto the multitude of thousands of Israel.

Num 11:1 And when the people complained, it displeased the Becoming-One: and the Becoming-One heard it; and his anger was kindled; and the fire of the Becoming-One burnt among them, and consumed them that were in the uttermost parts of the camp.

2 And the people cried unto Moses; and when Moses prayed unto the Becoming-One, the fire was quenched.

3 And he called the name of the place Taberah: because the fire of the Becoming-One burnt among them.

4 And the mixed multitude that was among them fell a lusting: and the children of Israel also wept again, and said, Who shall give us flesh to eat?

5 We remember the fish, which we did eat in Egypt freely; the cucumbers, and the melons, and the leeks, and the onions, and the garlic:

6 But now our soul is dried away: there is nothing at all, beside this manna, before our eyes.

7 And the manna was as coriander seed, and the color thereof as the color of bdellium.

8 And the people went about, and gathered it, and ground it in mills, or beat it in a mortar, and baked it in pans, and made cakes of it: and the taste of it was as the taste of fresh oil.

9 And when the dew fell upon the camp in the night, the manna fell upon it.

10 Then Moses heard the people weep throughout their families, every man in the door of his tent: and the anger of the Becoming-One was kindled greatly; Moses also was displeased.

---

[90] Appointed times or festivals

11 And Moses said unto the Becoming-One, Why have you afflicted your servant? and why have I not found favor in your sight, that you lay the burden of all this people upon me?

12 Have I conceived all this people? have I begotten them, that you should say unto me, Carry them in your bosom, as the nurse carries the sucking child, unto the land which you swore unto their fathers?

13 From where do I have food to give unto all this people? for they weep unto me, saying, Give us flesh, that we may eat.

14 I am not able to bear all this people alone, because it is too heavy for me.

15 And if you deal thus with me, kill me, I pray you, out of hand, if I have found favor in your sight; and let me not see my wretchedness.

16 And the Becoming-One said unto Moses, Gather unto me seventy men of the elders of Israel, whom you know to be the elders of the people, and officers over them; and bring them unto the tabernacle of the set time, that they may stand there with you.

17 And I will come down and talk with you there: and I will take of the spirit which is upon you, and will put it upon them; and they shall bear the burden of the people with you, that you bear it not yourself alone.

18 And say you unto the people, Sanctify yourselves against tomorrow, and you shall eat flesh: for you have wept in the ears of the Becoming-One, saying, Who shall give us flesh to eat? for it was well with us in Egypt: therefore the Becoming-One will give you flesh, and you shall eat.

19 you shall not eat one day, nor two days, nor five days, neither ten days, nor twenty days;

20 But even a whole month, until it come out at your nostrils, and it be loathsome unto you: because that you have despised the Becoming-One which is among you, and have wept before him, saying, Why came we forth out of Egypt?

21 And Moses said, The people, among whom I am, are six hundred thousand of footmen; and you have said, I will give them flesh, that they may eat a whole month.

22 Shall the flocks and the herds be slain for them, to suffice them? or shall all the fish of the sea be gathered together for them, to suffice them?

23 And the Becoming-One said unto Moses, Is the Becoming-One's hand grown short? you shall see now whether my word shall come to pass unto you or not.

24 And Moses went out, and told the people the words of the Becoming-One, and gathered the seventy men of the elders of the people, and set them round about the tabernacle.

25 And the Becoming-One came down in a cloud, and spoke unto him, and took of the spirit that was upon him, and gave it unto the seventy elders: and it came to pass, that, when the spirit rested upon them, they prophesied, and did not cease.

26 But there remained two of the men in the camp, the name of the one was Eldad, and the name of the other Medad: and the spirit rested upon them; and they were of them that were written, but went not out unto the tabernacle: and they prophesied in the camp.

27 And there ran a young man, and told Moses, and said, Eldad and Medad do prophesy in the camp.

28 And Joshua the son of Nun, the servant of Moses, one of his young men, answered and said, My lord Moses, forbid them.

29 And Moses said unto him, Envy you for my sake? would God that all the Becoming-One's people were prophets, and that the Becoming-One would put his spirit upon them!

30 And Moses got him into the camp, he and the elders of Israel.

31 And there went forth a wind from the Becoming-One, and brought quails from the sea, and let them fall by the camp, as it were a day's journey on this side, and as it were a day's journey on the other side, round about the camp, and as it were two cubits high upon the face of the earth.

32 And the people stood up all that day, and all that night, and all the next day, and they gathered the quails: he that gathered least gathered ten homers: and they spread them all abroad for themselves round about the camp.

33 And while the flesh was yet between their teeth, ere it was chewed, the wrath of the Becoming-One was kindled against the people, and the Becoming-One smote the people with a very great plague.

34 And he called the name of that place Kibrothhattaavah: because there they buried the people that lusted.

35 And the people journeyed from Kibrothhattaavah unto Hazeroth; and abode at Hazeroth.

Num 12:1 And Miriam and Aaron spoke against Moses because of the Ethiopian woman whom he had married: for he had married an Ethiopian woman.

2 And they said, has the Becoming-One indeed spoken only by Moses? has he not spoken also by us? And the Becoming-One heard it.

3 Now the man Moses was very meek, above all the men which were upon the face of the earth.

4 And the Becoming-One spoke suddenly unto Moses, and unto Aaron, and unto Miriam, Come out you three unto the tabernacle of the set time. And they three came out.

5 And the Becoming-One came down in the pillar of the cloud, and stood in the door of the tabernacle, and called Aaron and Miriam: and they both came forth.

6 And he said, Hear now my words: If there be a prophet among you, I the Becoming-One will make myself known unto him in a vision, and will speak unto him in a dream.

7 My servant Moses is not so, who is faithful in all mine house.

8 With him will I speak mouth to mouth, even apparently, and not in dark speeches; and the similitude of the Becoming-One shall he behold: why then were you not afraid to speak against my servant Moses?

9 And the anger of the Becoming-One was kindled against them; and he departed.

10 And the cloud departed from off the tabernacle; and, behold, Miriam became leprous, white as snow: and Aaron looked upon Miriam, and, behold, she was leprous.

11 And Aaron said unto Moses, Alas, my lord, I beg you, lay not the sin upon us, wherein we have done foolishly, and wherein we have sinned.

12 Let her not be as one dead, of whom the flesh is half consumed when he comes out of his mother's womb.

13 And Moses cried unto the Becoming-One, saying, Heal her now, O GOD, I beg you.

14 And the Becoming-One said unto Moses, If her father had but spit in her face, should she not be ashamed seven days? let her be shut out from the camp seven days, and after that let her be received in again.

15 And Miriam was shut out from the camp seven days: and the people journeyed not till Miriam was brought in again.

16 And afterward the people removed from Hazeroth, and pitched in the wilderness of Paran.

Num 13:1 And the Becoming-One spoke unto Moses, saying,

2 Send you men, that they may search the land of Canaan, which I give unto the children of Israel: of every tribe of their fathers shall you send a man, every one a ruler among them.

3 And Moses by the mouth of the Becoming-One sent them from the wilderness of Paran: all those men were heads of the children of Israel.

4 And these were their names: of the tribe of Reuben, Shammua the son of Zaccur.

5 Of the tribe of Simeon, Shaphat the son of Hori.

6 Of the tribe of Judah, Caleb the son of Jephunneh.

7 Of the tribe of Issachar, Igal the son of Joseph.

8 Of the tribe of Ephraim, Oshea the son of Nun.

9 Of the tribe of Benjamin, Palti the son of Raphu.

10 Of the tribe of Zebulun, Gaddiel the son of Sodi.

11 Of the tribe of Joseph, namely, of the tribe of Manasseh, Gaddi the son of Susi.

12 Of the tribe of Dan, Ammiel the son of Gemalli.

13 Of the tribe of Asher, Sethur the son of Michael.

14 Of the tribe of Naphtali, Nahbi the son of Vophsi.

15 Of the tribe of Gad, Geuel the son of Machi.

16 These are the names of the men which Moses sent to spy out the land. And Moses called Oshea the son of Nun Jehoshua.

17 And Moses sent them to spy out the land of Canaan, and said unto them, Get you up this way southward, and go up into the mountain:

18 And see the land, what it is; and the people that dwells therein, whether they be strong or weak, few or many;

19 And what the land is that they dwell in, whether it be good or bad; and what cities they be that they dwell in, whether in tents, or in strong holds;

20 And what the land is, whether it be fat or lean, whether there be wood therein, or not. And be you of good courage, and bring of the fruit of the land. Now the time was the time of the firstripe grapes.

21 So they went up, and searched the land from the wilderness of Zin unto Rehob, as men come to Hamath.

22 And they ascended by the south, and came unto Hebron; where Ahiman, Sheshai, and Talmai, the children of Anak, were. Now Hebron was built seven years before Zoan in Egypt.

23 And they came unto the brook of Eshcol, and cut down from there a branch with one cluster of grapes, and they bare it between two upon a staff; and they brought of the pomegranates, and of the figs.

24 The place was called the brook Eshcol, because of the cluster of grapes which the children of Israel cut down from there.

25 And they returned from searching of the land after forty days.

26 And they went and came to Moses, and to Aaron, and to all the congregation of the children of Israel, unto the wilderness of Paran, to Kadesh; and brought back word unto them, and unto all the congregation, and showed them the fruit of the land.

27 And they told him, and said, We came unto the land where you sent us, and surely it flows with milk and honey; and this is the fruit of it.

28 Nevertheless the people be strong that dwell in the land, and the cities are walled, and very great: and moreover we saw the children of Anak there.

29 The Amalekites dwell in the land of the south: and the Hittites, and the Jebusites, and the Amorites, dwell in the mountains: and the Canaanites dwell by the sea, and by the coast of Jordan.

30 And Caleb stilled the people before Moses, and said, Let us go up at once, and possess it; for we are well able to overcome it.

31 But the men that went up with him said, We be not able to go up against the people; for they are stronger than we.

32 And they brought up an evil report of the land which they had searched unto the children of Israel, saying, The land, through which we have gone to search it, is a land that eats up the inhabitants thereof; and all the people that we saw in it are men of a great stature.

33 And there we saw the giants, the sons of Anak, which come of the giants: and we were in our own sight as grasshoppers, and so we were in their sight.

Num 14:1 And all the congregation lifted up their voice, and cried; and the people wept that night.

2 And all the children of Israel murmured against Moses and against Aaron: and the whole congregation said unto them, If only we had died in the land of Egypt! or we had died in this wilderness!

3 And why has the Becoming-One brought us unto this land, to fall by the sword, that our wives and our children should be a prey? were it not better for us to return into Egypt?

4 And they said one to another, Let us make a captain, and let us return into Egypt.

5 Then Moses and Aaron fell on their faces before all the assembly of the congregation of the children of Israel.

6 And Joshua the son of Nun, and Caleb the son of Jephunneh, which were of them that searched the land, ripped their clothes:

7 And they spoke unto all the company of the children of Israel, saying, The land, which we passed through to search it, is an exceeding good land.

8 If the Becoming-One delight in us, then he will bring us into this land, and give it us; a land which flows with milk and honey.

9 Only rebel not you against the Becoming-One, neither fear you the people of the land; for they are bread for us: their defense is departed from them, and the Becoming-One is with us: fear them not.

10 But all the congregation bade stone them with stones. And the glory of the Becoming-One appeared in the tabernacle of the set time[91] before all the children of Israel.

11 And the Becoming-One said unto Moses, How long will this people provoke me? and how long will it be before they believe me, for all the signs which I have showed among them?

12 I will smite them with the pestilence, and disinherit them, and will make of you a greater nation and mightier than they.

13 And Moses said unto the Becoming-One, Then the Egyptians shall hear it, for you brought up this people in your might from among them;

14 And they will tell it to the inhabitants of this land: for they have heard that you Becoming-One are among this people, that you Becoming-One are seen face to face, and that your cloud stands over them, and that you go before them, by day time in a pillar of a cloud, and in a pillar of fire by night.

15 Now if you shall kill all this people as one man, then the nations which have heard the fame of you will speak, saying,

16 Because the Becoming-One was not able to bring this people into the land which he swore unto them, therefore he has slain them in the wilderness.

17 And now, I beg you, let the power of my Becoming-One be great, according as you have spoken, saying,

18 The Becoming-One is patient, and of great mercy, forgiving iniquity and transgression, and by no means clearing the guilty, visiting the iniquity of the fathers upon the children unto the third and fourth generation.

19 Pardon, I beg you, the iniquity of this people according unto the greatness of your mercy, and as you have forgiven this people, from Egypt even until now.

20 And the Becoming-One said, I have pardoned according to your word:

21 But as truly as I live, all the earth shall be filled with the glory of the Becoming-One.

22 Because all those men which have seen my glory, and my miracles, which I did in Egypt and in the wilderness, and have tempted me now these ten times, and have not listened to my voice;

23 Surely they shall not see the land which I swore unto their fathers, neither shall any of them that provoked me see it:

24 But my servant Caleb, because he had another spirit with him, and has followed me fully, him will I bring into the land whereinto he went; and his seed shall possess it.

25 Now the Amalekites and the Canaanites dwelt in the valley. tomorrow turn you, and get you into the wilderness by the way of the boundary sea.

26 And the Becoming-One spoke unto Moses and unto Aaron, saying,

27 How long shall I bear with this evil congregation, which murmur against me? I have heard the murmurings of the children of Israel, which they murmur against me.

28 Say unto them, As truly as I live, says the Becoming-One, as you have spoken in mine ears, so will I do to you:

29 Your carcases shall fall in this wilderness; and all that were numbered of you, according to your whole number, from a son of twenty years and upward, which have murmured against me,

30 Doubtless you shall not come into the land, concerning which I swore to make you dwell therein, save Caleb the son of Jephunneh, and Joshua the son of Nun.

31 But your little ones, which you said should be a prey, them will I bring in, and they shall know the land which you have despised.

32 But as for you, your carcases shall fall in this wilderness.

33 And your children shall wander in the wilderness forty years, and bear your whoredoms, until your carcases be wasted in the wilderness.

34 After the number of the days in which you searched the land, even forty days, each day for a year, shall you bear your iniquities, even forty years, and you shall know my breach of promise.

35 I the Becoming-One have said, I will surely do it unto all this evil congregation, that are gathered together against me: in this wilderness they shall be consumed, and there they shall die.

36 And the men, which Moses sent to search the land, who returned, and made all the congregation to murmur against him, by bringing up a slander upon the land,

37 Even those men that did bring up the evil report upon the land, died by the plague before the Becoming-One.

38 But Joshua the son of Nun, and Caleb the son of Jephunneh, which were of the men that went to search the land, lived still.

39 And Moses told these sayings unto all the children of Israel: and the people mourned greatly.

40 And they rose up early in the morning, and got them up into the top of the mountain, saying, Lo, we be here, and will go up unto the place which the Becoming-One has promised: for we have sinned.

41 And Moses said, Why now do you transgress the mouth of the Becoming-One? but it shall not prosper.

42 Go not up, for the Becoming-One is not among you; that you be not struck before your enemies.

43 For the Amalekites and the Canaanites are there before you, and you shall fall by the sword: because you are turned away from the Becoming-One, therefore the Becoming-One will not be with you.

44 But they presumed to go up unto the hill top: nevertheless the ark of the covenant of the Becoming-One, and Moses, departed not out of the camp.

45 Then the Amalekites came down, and the Canaanites which dwelt in that hill, and smote them, and discomfited them, even unto Hormah.

Num 15:1 And the Becoming-One spoke unto Moses, saying,

---

[91] Appointed time or festival

2 Speak unto the children of Israel, and say unto them, When you be come into the land of your habitations, which I give unto you,

3 And will make an offering by fire unto the Becoming-One, a burnt offering, or a sacrifice in performing a vow, or in a freewill offering, or in your set times,[92] to make a sweet aroma unto the Becoming-One, of the herd, or of the flock:

4 Then shall he that offers his offering unto the Becoming-One bring a food offering of a tenth deal of flour mingled with the fourth part of a hin of oil.

5 And the fourth part of a hin of wine for a drink offering shall you prepare with the burnt offering or sacrifice, for one lamb.

6 Or for a ram, you shall prepare for a food offering two tenth deals of flour mingled with the third part of a hin of oil.

7 And for a drink offering you shall offer the third part of a hin of wine, for a sweet aroma unto the Becoming-One.

8 And when you prepare a bullock for a burnt offering, or for a sacrifice in performing a vow, or peace offerings unto the Becoming-One: 9 Then shall he bring with a bullock a food offering of three tenth deals of flour mingled with half a hin of oil.

10 And you shall bring for a drink offering half a hin of wine, for an offering made by fire, of a sweet aroma unto the Becoming-One.

11 Thus shall it be done for one bullock, or for one ram, or for a lamb, or a kid.

12 According to the number that you shall prepare, so shall you do to every one according to their number.

13 All that are born of the country shall do these things after this manner, in offering an offering made by fire, of a sweet aroma unto the Becoming-One.

14 And if a stranger sojourn with you, or whosoever be among you in your generations, and will offer an offering made by fire, of a sweet aroma unto the Becoming-One; as you do, so he shall do.

15 One ordinance shall be both for you of the congregation, and also for the stranger that sojourns with you, an ordinance for olam in your generations: as you are, so shall the stranger be before the Becoming-One.

16 One law and one manner shall be for you, and for the stranger that sojourns with you.

17 And the Becoming-One spoke unto Moses, saying,

18 Speak unto the children of Israel, and say unto them, When you come into the land to which I bring you,

19 Then it shall be, that, when you eat of the bread of the land, you shall offer up a heave offering unto the Becoming-One.

20 you shall offer up a cake of the first of your dough for a heave offering: as you do the heave offering of the threshing floor, so shall you heave it.

21 Of the first of your dough you shall give unto the Becoming-One a heave offering in your generations.

22 And if you have erred, and not observed all these commandments, which the Becoming-One has spoken unto Moses,

23 Even all that the Becoming-One has commanded you by the hand of Moses, from the day that the Becoming-One commanded Moses, and henceforward among your generations;

24 Then it shall be, if any be committed by ignorance without the knowledge of the congregation, that all the congregation shall offer one young bullock for a burnt offering, for a sweet aroma unto the Becoming-One, with his food offering, and his drink offering, according to the manner, and one kid of the goats for a sin offering.

25 And the priest shall make an atonement for all the congregation of the children of Israel, and it shall be forgiven them; for it is ignorance: and they shall bring their offering, a sacrifice made by fire unto the Becoming-One, and their sin offering before the Becoming-One, for their ignorance:

26 And it shall be forgiven all the congregation of the children of Israel, and the stranger that sojourns among them; seeing all the people were in ignorance.

27 And if any soul sin through ignorance, then he shall bring a she goat of the first year for a sin offering.

28 And the priest shall make an atonement for the soul that sins ignorantly, when he sins by ignorance before the Becoming-One, to make an atonement for him; and it shall be forgiven him.

29 you shall have one law for him that sins through ignorance, both for him that is born among the children of Israel, and for the stranger that sojourns among them.

30 But the soul that did anything presumptuously, whether he be born in the land, or a stranger, the same reproaches the Becoming-One; and that soul shall be cut off from among his people.

31 Because he has despised the word of the Becoming-One, and has broken his commandment, that soul shall utterly be cut off; his iniquity shall be upon him.

32 And while the children of Israel were in the wilderness, they found a man that gathered sticks upon the Sabbath day.

33 And they that found him gathering sticks brought him unto Moses and Aaron, and unto all the congregation.

34 And they put him in ward, because it was not declared what should be done to him.

35 And the Becoming-One said unto Moses, The man shall be surely put to death: all the congregation shall stone him with stones outside the camp.

36 And all the congregation brought him outside the camp, and stoned him with stones, and he died; as the Becoming-One commanded Moses.

37 And the Becoming-One spoke unto Moses, saying,

38 Speak unto the children of Israel, and bid them that they make them fringes in the borders of their garments throughout their generations, and that they put upon the fringe of the borders a ribband of blue:

39 And it shall be unto you for a fringe, that you may look upon it, and remember all the commandments of the Becoming-One, and do them; and that you seek not after your own heart and your own eyes, after which you use to go a whoring:

---

[92] Appointed times or festivals

40 That you may remember, and do all my commandments, and be holy unto your God.

41 I am the Becoming-One your God, which brought you out of the land of Egypt, to be your God: I am the Becoming-One your God.

Num 16:1 Now Korah, the son of Izhar, the son of Kohath, the son of Levi, and Dathan and Abiram, the sons of Eliab, and On, the son of Peleth, sons of Reuben, took men:

2 And they rose up before Moses, with certain of the children of Israel, two hundred and fifty princes of the assembly, famous in the congregation, men of renown:

3 And they gathered themselves together against Moses and against Aaron, and said unto them, you take too much upon you, seeing all the congregation are holy, every one of them, and the Becoming-One is among them: why then lift you up yourselves above the congregation of the Becoming-One?

4 And when Moses heard it, he fell upon his face:

5 And he spoke unto Korah and unto all his company, saying, Even tomorrow the Becoming-One will show who are his, and who is holy; and will cause him to come near unto him: even him whom he has chosen will he cause to come near unto him.

6 This do; Take you censers, Korah, and all his company;

7 And put fire therein, and put incense in them before the Becoming-One tomorrow: and it shall be that the man whom the Becoming-One does choose, he shall be holy: you take too much upon you, you sons of Levi.

8 And Moses said unto Korah, Hear, I pray you, you sons of Levi:

9 Seems it but a small thing unto you, that God of Israel has separated you from the congregation of Israel, to bring you near to himself to do the service of the tabernacle of the Becoming-One, and to stand before the congregation to minister unto them?

10 And he has brought you near to him, and all your brethren the sons of Levi with you: and seek you the priesthood also?

11 For which cause both you and all your company are gathered together against the Becoming-One: and what is Aaron, that you murmur against him?

12 And Moses sent to call Dathan and Abiram, the sons of Eliab: which said, We will not come up:

13 Is it a small thing that you have brought us up out of a land that flows with milk and honey, to kill us in the wilderness, except you make yourself altogether a prince over us?

14 Moreover you have not brought us into a land that flows with milk and honey, or given us inheritance of fields and vineyards: will you put out the eyes of these men? we will not come up.

15 And Moses was very angry, and said unto the Becoming-One, Respect not you their offering: I have not taken one donkey from them, neither have I hurt one of them.

16 And Moses said unto Korah, Be you and all your company before the Becoming-One, you, and they, and Aaron, tomorrow:

17 And take every man his censer, and put incense in them, and bring you before the Becoming-One every man his censer, two hundred and fifty censers; you also, and Aaron, each of you his censer.

18 And they took every man his censer, and put fire in them, and laid incense thereon, and stood in the door of the tabernacle of the congregation with Moses and Aaron.

19 And Korah gathered all the congregation against them unto the door of the tabernacle of the congregation: and the glory of the Becoming-One appeared unto all the congregation.

20 And the Becoming-One spoke unto Moses and unto Aaron, saying,

21 Separate yourselves from among this congregation, that I may consume them in a moment.

22 And they fell upon their faces, and said, O GOD, God of the spirits of all flesh, shall one man sin, and will you be angry with all the congregation?

23 And the Becoming-One spoke unto Moses, saying,

24 Speak unto the congregation, saying, Get you up from about the tabernacle of Korah, Dathan, and Abiram.

25 And Moses rose up and went unto Dathan and Abiram; and the elders of Israel followed him.

26 And he spoke unto the congregation, saying, Depart, I pray you, from the tents of these wicked men, and touch nothing of theirs, lest you be consumed in all their sins.

27 So they got up from the tabernacle of Korah, Dathan, and Abiram, on every side: and Dathan and Abiram came out, and stood in the door of their tents, and their wives, and their sons, and their little children.

28 And Moses said, Hereby you shall know that the Becoming-One has sent me to do all these works; for I have not done them of mine own mind.

29 If these men die the common death of all men, or if they be visited after the visitation of all men; then the Becoming-One has not sent me.

30 But if the Becoming-One make a new thing, and the earth open her mouth, and swallow them up, with all that belongs unto them, and they go down quick into Sheol; then you shall understand that these men have provoked the Becoming-One.

31 And it came to pass, as he had made an end of speaking all these words, that the ground clave asunder that was under them:

32 And the earth opened her mouth, and swallowed them up, and their houses, and all the men that belonged unto Korah, and all their goods.

33 They, and all that belonged to them, went down alive into Sheol, and the earth closed upon them: and they perished from among the congregation.

34 And all Israel that were round about them fled at the cry of them: for they said, Lest the earth swallow us up also.

35 And there came out a fire from the Becoming-One, and consumed the two hundred and fifty men that offered incense.

36 And the Becoming-One spoke unto Moses, saying,

37 Speak unto Eleazar the son of Aaron the priest, that he take up the censers out of the burning, and scatter you the fire yonder; for they are hallowed.

38 The censers of these sinners against their own souls, let them make them broad plates for a covering

of the altar: for they offered them before the Becoming-One, therefore they are hallowed: and they shall be a sign unto the children of Israel.

39 And Eleazar the priest took the brazen censers, wherewith they that were burnt had offered; and they were made broad plates for a covering of the altar:

40 To be a memorial unto the children of Israel, that no stranger, which is not of the seed of Aaron, come near to offer incense before the Becoming-One; that he be not as Korah, and as his company: as the Becoming-One said to him by the hand of Moses.

41 But on the next day all the congregation of the children of Israel murmured against Moses and against Aaron, saying, you have killed the people of the Becoming-One.

42 And it came to pass, when the congregation was gathered against Moses and against Aaron, that they looked toward the tabernacle of the congregation: and, behold, the cloud covered it, and the glory of the Becoming-One appeared.

43 And Moses and Aaron came before the tabernacle of the congregation.

44 And the Becoming-One spoke unto Moses, saying,

45 Get you up from among this congregation, that I may consume them as in a moment. And they fell upon their faces.

46 And Moses said unto Aaron, Take a censer, and put fire therein from off the altar, and put on incense, and go quickly unto the congregation, and make an atonement for them: for there is wrath gone out from the Becoming-One; the plague is begun.

47 And Aaron took as Moses commanded, and ran into the midst of the congregation; and, behold, the plague was begun among the people: and he put on incense, and made an atonement for the people.

48 And he stood between the dead and the living; and the plague was stayed.

49 Now they that died in the plague were fourteen thousand and seven hundred, beside them that died about the matter of Korah.

50 And Aaron returned unto Moses unto the door of the tabernacle of the set time: and the plague was stayed.

Num 17:1 And the Becoming-One spoke unto Moses, saying,

2 Speak unto the children of Israel, and take of every one of them a rod according to the house of their fathers, of all their princes according to the house of their fathers twelve rods: write you every man's name upon his rod.

3 And you shall write Aaron's name upon the rod of Levi: for one rod shall be for the head of the house of their fathers.

4 And you shall lay them up in the tabernacle of the set time[93] before the testimony, where I will meet with you.

5 And it shall come to pass, that the man's rod, whom I shall choose, shall blossom: and I will make to cease from me the murmurings of the children of Israel, whereby they murmur against you.

6 And Moses spoke unto the children of Israel, and every one of their princes gave him a rod apiece, for each prince one, according to their fathers' houses, even twelve rods: and the rod of Aaron was among their rods.

7 And Moses laid up the rods before the Becoming-One in the tabernacle of witness.

8 And it came to pass, that on the next day Moses went into the tabernacle of witness; and, behold, the rod of Aaron for the house of Levi was budded, and brought forth buds, and bloomed blossoms, and yielded almonds.

9 And Moses brought out all the rods from before the Becoming-One unto all the children of Israel: and they looked, and took every man his rod.

10 And the Becoming-One said unto Moses, Bring Aaron's rod again before the testimony, to be kept for a token against the rebels; and you shall quite take away their murmurings from me, that they die not.

11 And Moses did so: as the Becoming-One commanded him, so did he.

12 And the children of Israel spoke unto Moses, saying, Behold, we die, we perish, we all perish.

13 Whosoever comes any thing near unto the tabernacle of the Becoming-One shall die: shall we be consumed with dying?

Num 18:1 And the Becoming-One said unto Aaron, you and your sons and your father's house with you shall bear the iniquity of the sanctuary: and you and your sons with you shall bear the iniquity of your priesthood.

2 And your brethren also of the tribe of Levi, the tribe of your father, bring you with you, that they may be joined unto you, and minister unto you: but you and your sons with you shall minister before the tabernacle of witness.

3 And they shall keep your charge, and the charge of all the tabernacle: only they shall not come near the vessels of the sanctuary and the altar, that neither they, nor you also, die.

4 And they shall be joined unto you, and keep the charge of the tabernacle of the set time, for all the service of the tabernacle: and a stranger shall not come near unto you.

5 And you shall keep the charge of the sanctuary, and the charge of the altar: that there be no wrath any more upon the children of Israel.

6 And I, behold, I have taken your brethren the Levites from among the children of Israel: to you they are given as a gift for the Becoming-One, to do the service of the tabernacle of the congregation.

7 Therefore you and your sons with you shall keep your priest's office for every thing of the altar, and within the veil; and you shall serve: I have given your priest's office unto you as a service of gift: and the stranger that comes near shall be put to death.

8 And the Becoming-One spoke unto Aaron, Behold, I also have given you the charge of mine heave offerings of all the hallowed things of the children of Israel; unto you have I given them by reason of the anointing, and to your sons, by an ordinance for olam.

9 This shall be your of the most holy things, reserved from the fire: every offering of theirs, every food offering of theirs and every sin offering of theirs, and every trespass offering of theirs, which they shall

---

[93] Appointed time or festival

render unto me, shall be most holy for you and for your sons.

10 In the most holy place shall you eat it; every male shall eat it: it shall be holy unto you.

11 And this is yours; the heave offering of their gift, with all the wave offerings of the children of Israel: I have given them unto you, and to your sons and to your daughters with you, by a statute for olam, every one that is clean in your house shall eat of it.

12 All the best of the oil, and all the best of the wine, and of the wheat, the beginning of them which they shall offer unto the Becoming-One, them have I given you.

13 And whatsoever is first ripe in the land, which they shall bring unto the Becoming-One, shall be yours; every one that is clean in your house shall eat of it.

14 Everything devoted in Israel shall be yours.

15 Every thing that opens the matrix in all flesh, which they bring unto the Becoming-One, whether it be of men or beasts, shall be yours: nevertheless the firstborn of man shall you surely redeem, and the firstling of unclean beasts shall you redeem.

16 And those that are to be redeemed from a month old shall you redeem, according to your estimation, for the money of five shekels, after the shekel of the sanctuary, which is twenty gerahs.

17 But the firstling of a cow, or the firstling of a sheep, or the firstling of a goat, you shall not redeem; they are holy: you shall sprinkle their blood upon the altar, and shall burn their fat for an offering made by fire, for a sweet aroma unto the Becoming-One.

18 And the flesh of them shall be yours, as the wave breast and as the right shoulder are yours.

19 All the heave offerings of the holy things, which the children of Israel offer unto the Becoming-One, have I given you, and your sons and your daughters with you, by a statute for olam, it is a covenant of salt for olam before the Becoming-One unto you and to your seed with you.

20 And the Becoming-One spoke unto Aaron, you shall have no inheritance in their land, neither shall you have any part among them: I am your part and your inheritance among the children of Israel.

21 And, behold, I have given the children of Levi all the tenth in Israel for an inheritance, for their service which they serve, even the service of the tabernacle of the set time.

22 Neither must the children of Israel henceforth come near the tabernacle of the set time, lest they bear sin, and die.

23 But the Levites shall do the service of the tabernacle of the set time, and they shall bear their iniquity: it shall be a statute for olam throughout your generations, that among the children of Israel they have no inheritance.

24 But the tithes of the children of Israel, which they offer as a heave offering unto the Becoming-One, I have given to the Levites to inherit: therefore I have said unto them, Among the children of Israel they shall have no inheritance.

25 And the Becoming-One spoke unto Moses, saying,

26 Thus speak unto the Levites, and say unto them, When you take of the children of Israel the tithes which I have given you from them for your inheritance, then you shall offer up a heave offering of it for the Becoming-One, even a tenth part from the tithe.

27 And this your heave offering shall be reckoned unto you, as though it were the grain of the threshing floor, and as the fullness of the winepress.

28 Thus you also shall offer a heave offering unto the Becoming-One of all your tithes, which you receive of the children of Israel; and you shall give thereof the Becoming-One's heave offering to Aaron the priest.

29 Out of all your gifts you shall offer every heave offering of the Becoming-One, of all the best thereof, even the hallowed part thereof out of it.

30 Therefore you shall say unto them, When you have heaved the best thereof from it, then it shall be counted unto the Levites as the increase of the threshing floor, and as the increase of the winepress.

31 And you shall eat it in every place, you and your households: for it is your reward for your service in the tabernacle of the set time.[94]

32 And you shall bear no sin by reason of it, when you have heaved from it the best of it: neither shall you pollute the holy things of the children of Israel, lest you die.

Num 19:1 And the Becoming-One spoke unto Moses and unto Aaron, saying,

2 This is the ordinance of the law which the Becoming-One has commanded, saying, Speak unto the children of Israel, that they bring you a red heifer without spot, wherein is no blemish, and upon which never came yoke:

3 And you shall give her unto Eleazar the priest, that he may bring her forth outside the camp, and one shall slay her before his face:

4 And Eleazar the priest shall take of her blood with his finger, and sprinkle of her blood directly before the tabernacle of the set time seven times:

5 And one shall burn the heifer in his sight; her skin, and her flesh, and her blood, with her dung, shall he burn:

6 And the priest shall take cedar wood, and hyssop, and scarlet, and cast it into the midst of the burning of the heifer.

7 Then the priest shall wash his clothes, and he shall bathe his flesh in water, and afterward he shall come into the camp, and the priest shall be unclean until the evening.

8 And he that burns her shall wash his clothes in water, and bathe his flesh in water, and shall be unclean until the evening.

9 And a man that is clean shall gather up the ashes of the heifer, and lay them up outside the camp in a clean place, and it shall be kept for the congregation of the children of Israel for a water of separation: it is a purification for sin.

10 And he that gathers the ashes of the heifer shall wash his clothes, and be unclean until the evening: and it shall be unto the children of Israel, and unto the stranger that sojourns among them, for a statute for olam.

---

[94] Appointed time or festival

11 He that touches the dead soul of any man shall be unclean seven days.

12 He shall purify himself on the third day, and on the seventh day he shall be clean: but if he purify not himself the third day, then the seventh day he shall not be clean.

13 Whosoever touches the dead soul of any man that is dead, and purifies not himself, defiles the tabernacle of the Becoming-One; and that soul shall be cut off from Israel: because the water of separation was not sprinkled upon him, he shall be unclean; his uncleanness is yet upon him.

14 This is the law, when a man dies in a tent: all that come into the tent, and all that is in the tent, shall be unclean seven days.

15 And every open vessel, which has no covering bound upon it, is unclean.

16 And whosoever touches one that is slain with a sword in the open fields, or a dead body, or a bone of a man, or a grave, shall be unclean seven days.

17 And for an unclean person they shall take of the ashes of the burnt heifer of purification for sin, and running water shall be put thereto in a vessel:

18 And a clean person shall take hyssop, and dip it in the water, and sprinkle it upon the tent, and upon all the vessels, and upon the souls that were there, and upon him that touched a bone, or one slain, or one dead, or a grave:

19 And the clean person shall sprinkle upon the unclean on the third day, and on the seventh day: and on the seventh day he shall purify himself, and wash his clothes, and bathe himself in water, and shall be clean at evening.

20 But the man that shall be unclean, and shall not purify himself, that soul shall be cut off from among the congregation, because he has defiled the sanctuary of the Becoming-One: the water of separation has not been sprinkled upon him; he is unclean.

21 And it shall be a statute of olam unto them, that he that sprinkles the water of separation shall wash his clothes; and he that touches the water of separation shall be unclean until even.

22 And whatsoever the unclean person touches shall be unclean; and the soul that touches it shall be unclean until even.

Num 20:1 Then came the children of Israel, even the whole congregation, into the desert of Zin in the first month: and the people abode in Kadesh; and Miriam died there, and was buried there.

2 And there was no water for the congregation: and they gathered themselves together against Moses and against Aaron.

3 And the people chided with Moses, and spoke, saying, Would God that we had died when our brethren died before the Becoming-One!

4 And why have you brought up the congregation of the Becoming-One into this wilderness, that we and our cattle should die there?

5 And why have you made us to come up out of Egypt, to bring us in unto this evil place? it is no place of seed, or of figs, or of vines, or of pomegranates; neither is there any water to drink.

6 And Moses and Aaron went from the presence of the assembly unto the door of the tabernacle of the set time, and they fell upon their faces: and the glory of the Becoming-One appeared unto them.

7 And the Becoming-One spoke unto Moses, saying,

8 Take the rod, and gather you the assembly together, you, and Aaron your brother, and speak you unto the rock before their eyes; and it shall give forth his water, and you shall bring forth to them water out of the rock: so you shall give the congregation and their beasts drink.

9 And Moses took the rod from before the Becoming-One, as he commanded him.

10 And Moses and Aaron gathered the congregation together before the rock, and he said unto them, Hear now, you rebels; must we fetch you water out of this rock?

11 And Moses lifted up his hand, and with his rod he smote the rock twice: and the water came out abundantly, and the congregation drank, and their beasts also.

12 And the Becoming-One spoke unto Moses and Aaron, Because you believed me not, to sanctify me in the eyes of the children of Israel, therefore you shall not bring this congregation into the land which I have given them.

13 This is the water of Meribah, because the children of Israel strove with the Becoming-One, and he was sanctified in them.

14 And Moses sent messengers from Kadesh unto the king of Edom, Thus says your brother Israel, you know all the travail that has befallen us:

15 How our fathers went down into Egypt, and we have dwelt in Egypt a long time; and the Egyptians vexed us, and our fathers:

16 And when we cried unto the Becoming-One, he heard our voice, and sent an angel, and has brought us forth out of Egypt: and, behold, we are in Kadesh, a city in the uttermost of your border:

17 Let us pass, I pray you, through your country: we will not pass through the fields, or through the vineyards, neither will we drink of the water of the wells: we will go by the king's high way, we will not turn to the right hand nor to the left, until we have passed your borders.

18 And Edom said unto him, you shall not pass by me, lest I come out against you with the sword.

19 And the children of Israel said unto him, We will go by the high way: and if I and my cattle drink of your water, then I will pay for it: I will only, without doing any thing else, go through on my feet.

20 And he said, you shall not go through. And Edom came out against him with much people, and with a strong hand.

21 Thus Edom refused to give Israel passage through his border: therefore Israel turned away from him.

22 And the children of Israel, even the whole congregation, journeyed from Kadesh, and came unto mount Hor.

23 And the Becoming-One spoke unto Moses and Aaron in mount Hor, by the coast of the land of Edom, saying,

24 Aaron shall be gathered unto his people: for he shall not enter into the land which I have given unto the children of Israel, because you rebelled against my word at the water of Meribah.

25 Take Aaron and Eleazar his son, and bring them up unto mount Hor:

26 And strip Aaron of his garments, and put them upon Eleazar his son: and Aaron shall be gathered unto his people, and shall die there.

27 And Moses did as the Becoming-One commanded: and they went up into mount Hor in the sight of all the congregation.

28 And Moses stripped Aaron of his garments, and put them upon Eleazar his son; and Aaron died there in the top of the mount: and Moses and Eleazar came down from the mount.

29 And when all the congregation saw that Aaron was dead, they mourned for Aaron thirty days, even all the house of Israel.

Num 21:1 And when king Arad the Canaanite, which dwelt in the south, heard tell that Israel came by the way of the spies; then he fought against Israel, and took some of them prisoners.

2 And Israel vowed a vow unto the Becoming-One, and said, If you will indeed deliver this people into my hand, then I will utterly destroy their cities.

3 And the Becoming-One listened to the voice of Israel, and delivered up the Canaanites; and they utterly destroyed them and their cities: and he called the name of the place Hormah.

4 And they journeyed from mount Hor by the way of the boundary sea, to compass the land of Edom: and the soul of the people was much discouraged because of the way.

5 And the people spoke against God, and against Moses, Why have you brought us up out of Egypt to die in the wilderness? for there is no bread, neither is there any water; and our soul loathes this light bread.

6 And the Becoming-One sent fiery serpents among the people, and they bit the people; and much people of Israel died.

7 Therefore the people came to Moses, and said, We have sinned, for we have spoken against the Becoming-One, and against you; pray unto the Becoming-One, that he take away the serpents from us. And Moses prayed for the people.

8 And the Becoming-One said unto Moses, Make you a fiery serpent, and set it upon a pole: and it shall come to pass, that every one that is bitten, when he looks upon it, shall live.

9 And Moses made a serpent of brass, and put it upon a pole, and it came to pass, that if a serpent had bitten any man, when he beheld the serpent of brass, he lived.

10 And the children of Israel set forward, and pitched in Oboth.

11 And they journeyed from Oboth, and pitched at Ijeabarim, in the wilderness which is before Moab, toward the sunrising.

12 From there they removed, and pitched in the valley of Zared.

13 From there they removed, and pitched on the other side of Arnon, which is in the wilderness that comes out of the coasts of the Amorites: for Arnon is the border of Moab, between Moab and the Amorites.

14 Therefore it is said in the book of the wars of the Becoming-One, Waheb in Suphah [meaning uncertain] and in the brooks of Arnon,

15 And at the stream of the brooks that goes down to the dwelling of Ar, and lies upon the border of Moab.

16 And from there they went to Beer: that is the well whereof the Becoming-One spoke unto Moses, Gather the people together, and I will give them water.

17 Then Israel sang this song, Spring up, O well; sing you unto it:

18 The princes dug the well, the nobles of the people dug it, by the direction of the lawgiver, with their staves. And from the wilderness they went to Mattanah:

19 And from Mattanah to Nahaliel: and from Nahaliel to Bamoth:

20 And from Bamoth in the valley that is in the country of Moab, to the top of Pisgah, which looks toward Jeshimon.

21 And Israel sent messengers unto Sihon king of the Amorites, saying,

22 Let me pass through your land: we will not turn into the fields, or into the vineyards; we will not drink of the waters of the well: but we will go along by the king's high way, until we be past your borders.

23 And Sihon would not permit Israel to pass through his border: but Sihon gathered all his people together, and went out against Israel into the wilderness: and he came to Jahaz, and fought against Israel.

24 And Israel smote him with the mouth of the sword, and possessed his land from Arnon unto Jabbok, even unto the children of Ammon: for the border of the children of Ammon was strong.

25 And Israel took all these cities: and Israel dwelt in all the cities of the Amorites, in Heshbon, and in all the villages thereof.

26 For Heshbon was the city of Sihon the king of the Amorites, who had fought against the former king of Moab, and taken all his land out of his hand, even unto Arnon.

27 Therefore they that speak in proverbs say, Come into Heshbon, let the city of Sihon be built and prepared:

28 For there is a fire gone out of Heshbon, a flame from the city of Sihon: it has consumed Ar of Moab, lords of the high places of Arnon.

29 Woe to you, Moab! you are undone, O people of Chemosh: he has given his sons that escaped, and his daughters, into captivity unto Sihon king of the Amorites.

30 We have shot at them; Heshbon is perished even unto Dibon, and we have laid them waste even unto Nophah, which reaches unto Medeba.

31 Thus Israel dwelt in the land of the Amorites.

32 And Moses sent to spy out Jaazer, and they took the villages thereof, and drove out the Amorites that were there.

33 And they turned and went up by the way of Bashan: and Og the king of Bashan went out against them, he, and all his people, to the battle at Edrei.

34 And the Becoming-One said unto Moses, Fear him not: for I have delivered him into your hand, and all his people, and his land; and you shall do to him as you did unto Sihon king of the Amorites, which dwelt at Heshbon.

35 So they smote him, and his sons, and all his people, until there was none left him alive: and they possessed his land.

Num 22:1 And the children of Israel set forward, and pitched in the plains of Moab beyond Jordan by Jericho.

2 And Balak the son of Zippor saw all that Israel had done to the Amorites.

3 And Moab was greatly afraid of the people, because they were many: and Moab was distressed because of the children of Israel.

4 And Moab said unto the elders of Midian, Now shall this company lick up all that are round about us, as the ox licks up the grass of the field. And Balak the son of Zippor was king of the Moabites at that time.

5 He sent messengers therefore unto Balaam the son of Beor to Pethor, which is by the river of the land of the children of his people, to call him, saying, Behold, there is a people come out from Egypt: behold, they cover the face of the earth, and they abide over against me:

6 Come now therefore, I pray you, curse me this people; for they are too mighty for me: perhaps I can prevail, that we may smite them, and that I may drive them out of the land: for I know that he whom you bless is blessed, and he whom you curse is cursed.

7 And the elders of Moab and the elders of Midian departed with the rewards of divination in their hand; and they came unto Balaam, and spoke unto him the words of Balak.

8 And he said unto them, Lodge here this night, and I will bring you word again, as the Becoming-One shall speak unto me: and the princes of Moab abode with Balaam.

9 And God came unto Balaam, and said, What men are these with you?

10 And Balaam said unto God, Balak the son of Zippor, king of Moab, has sent unto me, saying,

11 Behold, there is a people come out of Egypt, which coveres the face of the earth: come now, curse me them; perhaps I shall be able to overcome them, and drive them out.

12 And God said unto Balaam, you shall not go with them; you shall not curse the people: for they are blessed.

13 And Balaam rose up in the morning, and said unto the princes of Balak, Get you into your land: for the Becoming-One refuses to give me leave to go with you.

14 And the princes of Moab rose up, and they went unto Balak, and said, Balaam refuses to come with us.

15 And Balak sent yet again princes, more, and more honorable than they.

16 And they came to Balaam, and said to him, Thus says Balak the son of Zippor, Let nothing, I pray you, hinder you from coming unto me:

17 For I will promote you unto very great honor, and I will do whatsoever you say unto me: come therefore, I pray you, curse me this people.

18 And Balaam answered and said unto the servants of Balak, If Balak would give me his house full of silver and gold, I cannot go beyond the word of the Becoming-One my God, to do less or more.

19 Now therefore, I pray you, tarry you also here this night, that I may know what the Becoming-One will say unto me more.

20 And God came unto Balaam at night, and said unto him, If the men come to call you, rise up, and go with them; but yet the word which I shall say unto you, that shall you do.

21 And Balaam rose up in the morning, and saddled his donkey, and went with the princes of Moab.

22 And God' anger was kindled because he went: and the angel of the Becoming-One stood in the way for an adversary against him. Now he was riding upon his donkey, and his two servants were with him.

23 And the donkey saw the angel of the Becoming-One standing in the way, and his sword drawn in his hand: and the donkey turned aside out of the way, and went into the field: and Balaam smote the donkey, to turn her into the way.

24 But the angel of the Becoming-One stood in a path of the vineyards, a wall being on this side, and a wall on that side.

25 And when the donkey saw the angel of the Becoming-One, she thrust herself unto the wall, and crushed Balaam's foot against the wall: and he smote her again.

26 And the angel of the Becoming-One went further, and stood in a narrow place, where was no way to turn either to the right hand or to the left.

27 And when the donkey saw the angel of the Becoming-One, she fell down under Balaam: and Balaam's anger was kindled, and he smote the donkey with a staff.

28 And the Becoming-One opened the mouth of the donkey, and she said unto Balaam, What have I done unto you, that you have struck me these three times?

29 And Balaam said unto the donkey, Because you have mocked me: I wish I had a sword in my hand, for then I would kill you.

30 And the donkey said unto Balaam, Am not I your donkey, upon which you have ridden all your life long unto this day? was I ever accustoned to do so unto you? And he said, Nay.

31 Then the Becoming-One opened the eyes of Balaam, and he saw the angel of the Becoming-One standing in the way, and his sword drawn in his hand: and he bowed down his head, and fell flat on his face.

32 And the angel of the Becoming-One said unto him, Why have you struck your donkey these three times? behold, I went out to withstand you, because your way is perverse before me:

33 And the donkey saw me, and turned from me these three times: unless she had turned from me, surely now also I had slain you, and saved her alive.

34 And Balaam said unto the angel of the Becoming-One, I have sinned; for I knew not that you stood in the way against me: now therefore, if it displease you, I will get me back again.

35 And the angel of the Becoming-One said unto Balaam, Go with the men: but only the word that I shall speak unto you, that you shall speak. So Balaam went with the princes of Balak.

36 And when Balak heard that Balaam was come, he went out to meet him unto a city of Moab, which is in the border of Arnon, which is in the utmost coast.

37 And Balak said unto Balaam, Did I not earnestly send unto you to call you? why came you not unto me? am I not able indeed to promote you to honor?

38 And Balaam said unto Balak, Lo, I am come unto you: have I now any power at all to say any thing? the word that God puts in my mouth, that shall I speak.

39 And Balaam went with Balak, and they came unto Kirjathhuzoth.

40 And Balak offered oxen and sheep, and sent to Balaam, and to the princes that were with him.

41 And it came to pass on the next day, that Balak took Balaam, and brought him up into the high places of the Lord [baal] that there he might see the utmost part of the people.

Num 23:1 And Balaam said unto Balak, Build me here seven altars, and prepare me here seven oxen and seven rams.

2 And Balak did as Balaam had spoken; and Balak and Balaam offered on every altar a bullock and a ram.

3 And Balaam said unto Balak, Stand by your burnt offering, and I will go: perhaps the Becoming-One will come to meet me: and whatsoever he shows me I will tell you. And he went to a high place.

4 And God met Balaam: and he said unto him, I have prepared seven altars, and I have offered upon every altar a bullock and a ram.

5 And the Becoming-One put a word in Balaam's mouth, and said, Return unto Balak, and thus you shall speak.

6 And he returned unto him, and, lo, he stood by his burnt sacrifice, he, and all the princes of Moab.

7 And he took up his parable, and said, Balak the king of Moab has brought me from Aram, out of the mountains of the east, saying, Come, curse me Jacob, and come, defy Israel.

8 How shall I curse, whom GOD has not cursed? or how shall I defy, whom the Becoming-One has not defied?

9 For from the top of the rocks I see him, and from the hills I behold him: lo, the people shall dwell alone, and shall not be reckoned among the nations.

10 Who can count the dust of Jacob, and the number of the fourth part of Israel? Let my soul die the death of the righteous, and let my last end be like his!

11 And Balak said unto Balaam, What have you done unto me? I took you to curse mine enemies, and, behold, you have blessed them altogether.

12 And he answered and said, Must I not take heed to speak that which the Becoming-One has put in my mouth?

13 And Balak said unto him, Come, I pray you, with me unto another place, from where you may see them: you shall see but the utmost part of them, and shall not see them all: and curse me them from there.

14 And he brought him into the field of Zophim, to the top of Pisgah, and built seven altars, and offered a bullock and a ram on every altar.

15 And he said unto Balak, Stand here by your burnt offering, while I meet the Becoming-One yonder.

16 And the Becoming-One met Balaam, and put a word in his mouth, and said, Go again unto Balak, and say thus.

17 And when he came to him, behold, he stood by his burnt offering, and the princes of Moab with him. And Balak said unto him, What has the Becoming-One spoken?

18 And he took up his parable, and said, Rise up, Balak, and hear; listen unto me, you son of Zippor:

19 GOD is not a man, that he should lie; neither the son of man, that he should repent: has he said, and shall he not do it? or has he spoken, and shall he not make it good?

20 Behold, I have received commandment to bless: and he has blessed; and I cannot reverse it.

21 He has not beheld iniquity in Jacob, neither has he seen perverseness in Israel: the Becoming-One his God is with him, and the shout of a king is among them.

22 GOD brought them out of Egypt; he has as it were the strength of a reem [wild ox or beast]

23 Surely there is no enchantment against Jacob, neither is there any divination against Israel: according to this time it shall be said of Jacob and of Israel, What has GOD worked!

24 Behold, the people shall rise up as a great lion, and lift up himself as a young lion: he shall not lie down until he eat of the prey, and drink the blood of the slain.

25 And Balak said unto Balaam, Neither curse them at all, nor bless them at all.

26 But Balaam answered and said unto Balak, Told not I you, saying, All that the Becoming-One speaks, that I must do?

27 And Balak said unto Balaam, Come, I pray you, I will bring you unto another place; perhaps it will please God that you may curse me them from there.

28 And Balak brought Balaam unto the top of Peor, that looks toward Jeshimon.

29 And Balaam said unto Balak, Build me here seven altars, and prepare me here seven bullocks and seven rams.

30 And Balak did as Balaam had said, and offered a bullock and a ram on every altar.

Num 24:1 And when Balaam saw that it pleased the Becoming-One to bless Israel, he went not, as at other times, to seek for enchantments, but he set his face toward the wilderness.

2 And Balaam lifted up his eyes, and he saw Israel abiding in his tents according to their tribes; and the spirit of God came upon him.

3 And he took up his parable, and said, Balaam the son of Beor has said, and the man whose eyes are open has said:

4 He has said, which heard the words of GOD, which saw the vision of the Almighty, falling into a trance, but having his eyes open:

5 How goodly are your tents, O Jacob, and your tabernacles, O Israel!

6 As the valleys are they spread forth, as gardens by the river's side, as the trees of aloes which the Becoming-One has planted, and as cedar trees beside the waters.

7 He shall pour the water out of his buckets, and his seed shall be in many waters, and his king shall be higher than Agag, and his kingdom shall be exalted.

8 GOD brought him forth out of Egypt; he has as it were the strength of a reem: he shall eat up the nations his enemies, and shall break their bones, and pierce them through with his arrows.

9 He couched, he lay down as a lion, and as a great lion: who shall stir him up? Blessed is he that blesses you, and cursed is he that curses you.

10 And Balak's anger was kindled against Balaam, and he smote his hands together: and Balak said unto Balaam, I called you to curse mine enemies, and, behold, you have altogether blessed them these three times.

11 Therefore now flee you to your place: I thought to promote you unto great honor; but, lo, the Becoming-One has kept you back from honor.

12 And Balaam said unto Balak, spoke I not also to your messengers which you sent unto me, saying,

13 If Balak would give me his house full of silver and gold, I cannot go beyond the mouth of the Becoming-One, to do either good or bad of mine own mind; but what the Becoming-One says, that will I speak?

14 And now, behold, I go unto my people: come therefore, and I will advertise you what this people shall do to your people in the end of days.

15 And he took up his parable, and said, Balaam the son of Beor has said, and the man whose eyes are open has said:

16 He has said, which heard the words of God, and knew the knowledge of the most High, which saw the vision of the Almighty, falling into a trance, but having his eyes open:

17 I shall see him, but not now: I shall behold him, but not near: there shall come a Star out of Jacob, and a Sceptre shall rise out of Israel, and shall smite the corners of Moab, and destroy all the children of Sheth.

18 And Edom shall be a possession, Seir also shall be a possession for his enemies; and Israel shall do valiantly.

19 Out of Jacob shall come he that shall have dominion, and shall destroy him that remains of the city.

20 And when he looked on Amalek, he took up his parable, and said, Amalek was the first of the nations; but his latter end shall be for destruction.

21 And he looked on the Kenites, and took up his parable, and said, Strong is your dwellingplace, and you put your nest in a rock.

22 Nevertheless the Kenite shall be wasted, until Asshur shall carry you away captive.

23 And he took up his parable, and said, Alas, who shall live when GOD did this!

24 And ships shall come from the coast of Chittim, and shall afflict Asshur, and shall afflict Eber, and he also shall come to destruction.

25 And Balaam rose up, and went and returned to his place: and Balak also went his way.

Num 25:1 And Israel abode in Shittim, and the people began to commit whoredom with the daughters of Moab.

2 And they called the people unto the sacrifices of their gods: and the people did eat, and bowed down to their gods.

3 And Israel joined himself unto Baal-Peor: and the anger of the Becoming-One was kindled against Israel.

4 And the Becoming-One said unto Moses, Take all the heads of the people, and hang them up before the Becoming-One against the sun, that the fierce anger of the Becoming-One may be turned away from Israel.

5 And Moses said unto the judges of Israel, Slay you every one his men that were joined unto Baal-Peor.

6 And, behold, one of the children of Israel came and brought unto his brethren a Midianitish woman in the sight of Moses, and in the sight of all the congregation of the children of Israel, who were weeping before the door of the tabernacle of the set time.

7 And when Phinehas, the son of Eleazar, the son of Aaron the priest, saw it, he rose up from among the congregation, and took a javelin in his hand;

8 And he went after the man of Israel into the tent, and thrust both of them through, the man of Israel, and the woman through her belly. So the plague was stayed from the children of Israel.

9 And those that died in the plague were twenty and four thousand.

10 And the Becoming-One spoke unto Moses, saying,

11 Phinehas, the son of Eleazar, the son of Aaron the priest, has turned my wrath away from the children of Israel, while he was zealous for my sake among them, that I consumed not the children of Israel in my jealousy.

12 Therefore say, Behold, I give unto him my covenant of peace:

13 And he shall have it, and his seed after him, even the covenant of a priesthood of olam, because he was zealous for his God, and made an atonement for the children of Israel.

14 Now the name of the Israelite that was slain, even that was slain with the Midianitish woman, was Zimri, the son of Salu, a prince of a chief house among the Simeonites.

15 And the name of the Midianitish woman that was slain was Cozbi, the daughter of Zur; he was head over a people, and of a chief house in Midian.

16 And the Becoming-One spoke unto Moses, saying,

17 Vex the Midianites, and smite them:

18 For they vex you with their wiles, wherewith they have beguiled you in the matter of Peor, and in the matter of Cozbi, the daughter of a prince of Midian, their sister, which was slain in the day of the plague for Peor's sake.

Num 26:1 And it came to pass after the plague, that the Becoming-One spoke unto Moses and unto Eleazar the son of Aaron the priest, saying,

2 Take the sum of all the congregation of the children of Israel, from a son of twenty years and upward, throughout their fathers' house, all that are able to go to war in Israel.

3 And Moses and Eleazar the priest spoke with them in the plains of Moab by Jordan near Jericho, saying,

4 Take the sum of the people, from a son of twenty years and upward; as the Becoming-One commanded Moses and the children of Israel, which went forth out of the land of Egypt.

5 Reuben, the eldest son of Israel: the children of Reuben; Hanoch, of whom comes the family of the Hanochites: of Pallu, the family of the Palluites:

6 Of Hezron, the family of the Hezronites: of Carmi, the family of the Carmites.

7 These are the families of the Reubenites: and they that were numbered of them were forty and three thousand and seven hundred and thirty.

8 And the sons of Pallu; Eliab.

9 And the sons of Eliab; Nemuel, and Dathan, and Abiram. This is that Dathan and Abiram, which were famous in the congregation, who strove against Moses and against Aaron in the company of Korah, when they strove against the Becoming-One: 10 And the earth opened her mouth, and swallowed them up together with Korah, when that company died, what time the fire devoured two hundred and fifty men: and they became a sign.

11 Notwithstanding the children of Korah died not.

12 The sons of Simeon after their families: of Nemuel, the family of the Nemuelites: of Jamin, the family of the Jaminites: of Jachin, the family of the Jachinites:

13 Of Zerah, the family of the Zarhites: of Shaul, the family of the Shaulites.

14 These are the families of the Simeonites, twenty and two thousand and two hundred.

15 The children of Gad after their families: of Zephon, the family of the Zephonites: of Haggi, the family of the Haggites: of Shuni, the family of the Shunites:

16 Of Ozni, the family of the Oznites: of Eri, the family of the Erites:

17 Of Arod, the family of the Arodites: of Areli, the family of the Arelites.

18 These are the families of the children of Gad according to those that were numbered of them, forty thousand and five hundred.

19 The sons of Judah were Er and Onan: and Er and Onan died in the land of Canaan.

20 And the sons of Judah after their families were; of Shelah, the family of the Shelanites: of Pharez, the family of the Pharzites: of Zerah, the family of the Zarhites.

21 And the sons of Pharez were; of Hezron, the family of the Hezronites: of Hamul, the family of the Hamulites.

22 These are the families of Judah according to those that were numbered of them, threescore and sixteen thousand and five hundred.

23 Of the sons of Issachar after their families: of Tola, the family of the Tolaites: of Pua, the family of the Punites:

24 Of Jashub, the family of the Jashubites: of Shimron, the family of the Shimronites.

25 These are the families of Issachar according to those that were numbered of them, threescore and four thousand and three hundred.

26 Of the sons of Zebulun after their families: of Sered, the family of the Sardites: of Elon, the family of the Elonites: of Jahleel, the family of the Jahleelites.

27 These are the families of the Zebulunites according to those that were numbered of them, threescore thousand and five hundred.

28 The sons of Joseph after their families were Manasseh and Ephraim.

29 Of the sons of Manasseh: of Machir, the family of the Machirites: and Machir begat Gilead: of Gilead come the family of the Gileadites.

30 These are the sons of Gilead: of Jeezer, the family of the Jeezerites: of Helek, the family of the Helekites:

31 And of Asriel, the family of the Asrielites: and of Shechem, the family of the Shechemites:

32 And of Shemida, the family of the Shemidaites: and of Hepher, the family of the Hepherites.

33 And Zelophehad the son of Hepher had no sons, but daughters: and the names of the daughters of Zelophehad were Mahlah, and Noah, Hoglah, Milcah, and Tirzah.

34 These are the families of Manasseh, and those that were numbered of them, fifty and two thousand and seven hundred.

35 These are the sons of Ephraim after their families: of Shuthelah, the family of the Shuthalhites: of Becher, the family of the Bachrites: of Tahan, the family of the Tahanites.

36 And these are the sons of Shuthelah: of Eran, the family of the Eranites.

37 These are the families of the sons of Ephraim according to those that were numbered of them, thirty and two thousand and five hundred. These are the sons of Joseph after their families.

38 The sons of Benjamin after their families: of Bela, the family of the Belaites: of Ashbel, the family of the Ashbelites: of Ahiram, the family of the Ahiramites:

39 Of Shupham, the family of the Shuphamites: of Hupham, the family of the Huphamites.

40 And the sons of Bela were Ard and Naaman: of Ard, the family of the Ardites: and of Naaman, the family of the Naamites.

41 These are the sons of Benjamin after their families: and they that were numbered of them were forty and five thousand and six hundred.

42 These are the sons of Dan after their families: of Shuham, the family of the Shuhamites. These are the families of Dan after their families.

43 All the families of the Shuhamites, according to those that were numbered of them, were threescore and four thousand and four hundred.

44 Of the children of Asher after their families: of Jimna, the family of the Jimnites: of Jesui, the family of the Jesuites: of Beriah, the family of the Beriites.

45 Of the sons of Beriah: of Heber, the family of the Heberites: of Malchiel, the family of the Malchielites.

46 And the name of the daughter of Asher was Sarah.

47 These are the families of the sons of Asher according to those that were numbered of them; who were fifty and three thousand and four hundred.

48 Of the sons of Naphtali after their families: of Jahzeel, the family of the Jahzeelites: of Guni, the family of the Gunites:

49 Of Jezer, the family of the Jezerites: of Shillem, the family of the Shillemites.

50 These are the families of Naphtali according to their families: and they that were numbered of them were forty and five thousand and four hundred.

51 These were the numbered of the children of Israel, six hundred thousand and a thousand seven hundred and thirty.

52 And the Becoming-One spoke unto Moses, saying,

53 Unto these the land shall be divided for an inheritance according to the number of names.

54 To many you shall give the more inheritance, and to few you shall give the less inheritance: to every one shall his inheritance be given according to those that were numbered of him.

55 Notwithstanding the land shall be divided by lot: according to the names of the tribes of their fathers they shall inherit.

56 According to the lot shall the possession thereof be divided between many and few.

57 And these are they that were numbered of the Levites after their families: of Gershon, the family of the Gershonites: of Kohath, the family of the Kohathites: of Merari, the family of the Merarites.

58 These are the families of the Levites: the family of the Libnites, the family of the Hebronites, the family of the Mahlites, the family of the Mushites, the family of the Korathites. And Kohath begat Amram.

59 And the name of Amram's wife was Jochebed, the daughter of Levi, whom her mother bare to Levi in Egypt: and she bare unto Amram Aaron and Moses, and Miriam their sister.

60 And unto Aaron was born Nadab, and Abihu, Eleazar, and Ithamar.

61 And Nadab and Abihu died, when they offered strange fire before the Becoming-One.

62 And those that were numbered of them were twenty and three thousand all males from a month old and upward: for they were not numbered among the children of Israel, because there was no inheritance given them among the children of Israel.

63 These are they that were numbered by Moses and Eleazar the priest, who numbered the children of Israel in the plains of Moab by Jordan near Jericho.

64 But among these there was not a man of them whom Moses and Aaron the priest numbered, when they numbered the children of Israel in the wilderness of Sinai.

65 For the Becoming-One had said of them, They shall surely die in the wilderness. And there was not left a man of them, save Caleb the son of Jephunneh, and Joshua the son of Nun.

Num 27:1 Then came the daughters of Zelophehad, the son of Hepher, the son of Gilead, the son of Machir, the son of Manasseh, of the families of Manasseh the son of Joseph: and these are the names of his daughters; Mahlah, Noah, and Hoglah, and Milcah, and Tirzah.

2 And they stood before Moses, and before Eleazar the priest, and before the princes and all the congregation, by the door of the tabernacle of the set time, saying,

3 Our father died in the wilderness, and he was not in the company of them that gathered themselves together against the Becoming-One in the company of Korah; but died in his own sin, and had no sons.

4 Why should the name of our father be done away from among his family, because he has no son? Give unto us therefore a possession among the brethren of our father.

5 And Moses brought their cause before the Becoming-One.

6 And the Becoming-One spoke unto Moses, saying,

7 The daughters of Zelophehad speak right: you shall surely give them a possession of an inheritance among their father's brethren; and you shall cause the inheritance of their father to pass unto them.

8 And you shall speak unto the children of Israel, saying, If a man die, and have no son, then you shall cause his inheritance to pass unto his daughter.

9 And if he have no daughter, then you shall give his inheritance unto his brethren.

10 And if he have no brethren, then you shall give his inheritance unto his father's brethren.

11 And if his father have no brethren, then you shall give his inheritance unto his kinsman that is next to him of his family, and he shall possess it: and it shall be unto the children of Israel a statute of judgment, as the Becoming-One commanded Moses.

12 And the Becoming-One said unto Moses, Get you up into this mount Abarim, and see the land which I have given unto the children of Israel.

13 And when you have seen it, you also shall be gathered unto your people, as Aaron your brother was gathered.

14 For you rebelled against my mouth in the desert of Zin, in the strife of the congregation, to sanctify me at the water before their eyes: that is the water of Meribah in Kadesh in the wilderness of Zin.

15 And Moses spoke unto the Becoming-One, saying,

16 Let the Becoming-One, God of the spirits of all flesh, set a man over the congregation,

17 Which may go out before them, and which may go in before them, and which may lead them out, and which may bring them in; that the congregation of the Becoming-One be not as sheep which have no shepherd.

18 And the Becoming-One said unto Moses, Take you Joshua the son of Nun, a man in whom is the spirit, and lay your hand upon him;

19 And set him before Eleazar the priest, and before all the congregation; and give him a charge in their sight.

20 And you shall put some of your honor upon him, that all the congregation of the children of Israel may be obedient.

21 And he shall stand before Eleazar the priest, who shall ask counsel for him after the judgment of Urim before the Becoming-One: at his mouth shall they go out, and at his mouth they shall come in, both he, and all the children of Israel with him, even all the congregation.

22 And Moses did as the Becoming-One commanded him: and he took Joshua, and set him before Eleazar the priest, and before all the congregation:

23 And he laid his hands upon him, and gave him a charge, as the Becoming-One commanded by the hand of Moses.

Num 28:1 And the Becoming-One spoke unto Moses, saying,

2 Command the children of Israel, and say unto them, My offering, and my bread for my sacrifices

made by fire, for a sweet aroma unto me, shall you observe to offer unto me in their set time.[95]

3 And you shall say unto them, This is the offering made by fire which you shall offer unto the Becoming-One; lambs, sons of a year, without blemish, two per day, for a continual burnt offering.

4 The one lamb shall you offer in the morning, and the other lamb shall you offer between the evenings;

5 And a tenth part of an ephah of flour for a food offering, mingled with the fourth part of a hin of beaten oil.

6 It is a continual burnt offering, which was ordained in mount Sinai for a sweet aroma, a sacrifice made by fire unto the Becoming-One.

7 And the drink offering thereof shall be the fourth part of a hin for the one lamb: in the holy place shall you cause the strong wine to be poured unto the Becoming-One for a drink offering.

8 And the other lamb shall you offer between the evenings: as the food offering of the morning, and as the drink offering thereof, you shall offer it, a sacrifice made by fire, of a sweet aroma unto the Becoming-One.

9 And on the Sabbath day two lambs of the first year without spot, and two tenth deals of flour for a food offering, mingled with oil, and the drink offering thereof:

10 This is the burnt offering of every Sabbath, beside the continual burnt offering, and his drink offering.

11 And in the beginnings of your months you shall offer a burnt offering unto the Becoming-One; two young bullocks, and one ram, seven lambs of the first year without spot;

12 And three tenth deals of flour for a food offering, mingled with oil, for one bullock; and two tenth deals of flour for a food offering, mingled with oil, for one ram;

13 And a several tenth deal of flour mingled with oil for a food offering unto one lamb; for a burnt offering of a sweet aroma, a sacrifice made by fire unto the Becoming-One.

14 And their drink offerings shall be half a hin of wine unto a bullock, and the third part of a hin unto a ram, and a fourth part of a hin unto a lamb: this is the burnt offering of every month throughout the months of the year.

15 And one kid of the goats for a sin offering unto the Becoming-One shall be offered, beside the continual burnt offering, and his drink offering.

16 And in the fourteenth day of the first month is the Passover of the Becoming-One.

17 And in the fifteenth day of this month is the feast: seven days shall unleavened bread be eaten.

18 In the first day shall be a holy convocation; you shall do no manner of servile work therein:

19 But you shall offer a sacrifice made by fire for a burnt offering unto the Becoming-One; two young bullocks, and one ram, and seven lambs of the first year: they shall be unto you without blemish:

20 And their food offering shall be of flour mingled with oil: three tenth deals shall you offer for a bullock, and two tenth deals for a ram;

21 A several tenth deal shall you offer for every lamb, throughout the seven lambs:

22 And one goat for a sin offering, to make an atonement for you.

23 you shall offer these beside the burnt offering in the morning, which is for a continual burnt offering.

24 After this manner you shall offer daily, throughout the seven days, the food of the sacrifice made by fire, of a sweet aroma unto the Becoming-One: it shall be offered beside the continual burnt offering, and his drink offering.

25 And on the seventh day you shall have a holy convocation; you shall do no servile work.

26 Also in the day of the firstfruits, when you bring a new food offering unto the Becoming-One, after your weeks be out, you shall have a holy convocation; you shall do no servile work:

27 But you shall offer the burnt offering for a sweet aroma unto the Becoming-One; two young bullocks, one ram, seven lambs of the first year;

28 And their food offering of flour mingled with oil, three tenth deals unto one bullock, two tenth deals unto one ram,

29 A several tenth deal unto one lamb, throughout the seven lambs;

30 And one kid of the goats, to make an atonement for you.

31 you shall offer them beside the continual burnt offering, and his food offering, they shall be unto you without blemish and their drink offerings.

Num 29:1 And in the seventh month, on the first day of the month, you shall have a holy convocation; you shall do no servile work: it is a day of blowing the trumpets unto you.

2 And you shall offer a burnt offering for a sweet aroma unto the Becoming-One; one young bullock, one ram, and seven lambs of the first year without blemish:

3 And their food offering shall be of flour mingled with oil, three tenth deals for a bullock, and two tenth deals for a ram,

4 And one tenth deal for one lamb, throughout the seven lambs:

5 And one kid of the goats for a sin offering, to make an atonement for you:

6 Beside the burnt offering of the month, and his food offering, and the daily burnt offering, and his food offering, and their drink offerings, according unto their manner, for a sweet aroma, a sacrifice made by fire unto the Becoming-One.

7 And you shall have on the tenth day of this seventh month a holy convocation; and you shall weaken [by fasting] your souls: you shall not do any work therein:

8 But you shall offer a burnt offering unto the Becoming-One for a sweet aroma; one young bullock, one ram, and seven lambs of the first year; they shall be unto you without blemish:

9 And their food offering shall be of flour mingled with oil, three tenth deals to a bullock, and two tenth deals to one ram,

---

[95] Appointed time or festival

10 A several tenth deal for one lamb, throughout the seven lambs:

11 One kid of the goats for a sin offering; beside the sin offering of atonement, and the continual burnt offering, and the food offering of it, and their drink offerings.

12 And on the fifteenth day of the seventh month you shall have a holy convocation; you shall do no servile work, and you shall keep a feast unto the Becoming-One seven days:

13 And you shall offer a burnt offering, a sacrifice made by fire, of a sweet aroma unto the Becoming-One; thirteen young bullocks, two rams, and fourteen lambs of the first year; they shall be without blemish:

14 And their food offering shall be of flour mingled with oil, three tenth deals unto every bullock of the thirteen bullocks, two tenth deals to each ram of the two rams,

15 And a several tenth deal to each lamb of the fourteen lambs:

16 And one kid of the goats for a sin offering; beside the continual burnt offering, his food offering, and his drink offering.

17 And on the second day you shall offer twelve young bullocks, two rams, fourteen lambs of the first year without spot:

18 And their food offering and their drink offerings for the bullocks, for the rams, and for the lambs, shall be according to their number, after the manner:

19 And one kid of the goats for a sin offering; beside the continual burnt offering, and the food offering thereof, and their drink offerings.

20 And on the third day eleven bullocks, two rams, fourteen lambs of the first year without blemish;

21 And their food offering and their drink offerings for the bullocks, for the rams, and for the lambs, shall be according to their number, after the manner:

22 And one goat for a sin offering; beside the continual burnt offering, and his food offering, and his drink offering.

23 And on the fourth day ten bullocks, two rams, and fourteen lambs of the first year without blemish:

24 Their food offering and their drink offerings for the bullocks, for the rams, and for the lambs, shall be according to their number, after the manner:

25 And one kid of the goats for a sin offering; beside the continual burnt offering, his food offering, and his drink offering.

26 And on the fifth day nine bullocks, two rams, and fourteen lambs of the first year without spot:

27 And their food offering and their drink offerings for the bullocks, for the rams, and for the lambs, shall be according to their number, after the manner:

28 And one goat for a sin offering; beside the continual burnt offering, and his food offering, and his drink offering.

29 And on the sixth day eight bullocks, two rams, and fourteen lambs of the first year without blemish:

30 And their food offering and their drink offerings for the bullocks, for the rams, and for the lambs, shall be according to their number, after the manner:

31 And one goat for a sin offering; beside the continual burnt offering, his food offering, and his drink offering.

32 And on the seventh day seven bullocks, two rams, and fourteen lambs of the first year without blemish:

33 And their food offering and their drink offerings for the bullocks, for the rams, and for the lambs, shall be according to their number, after the manner:

34 And one goat for a sin offering; beside the continual burnt offering, his food offering, and his drink offering.

35 On the eighth day you shall have a solemn assembly: you shall do no servile work therein:

36 But you shall offer a burnt offering, a sacrifice made by fire, of a sweet aroma unto the Becoming-One: one bullock, one ram, seven lambs of the first year without blemish:

37 Their food offering and their drink offerings for the bullock, for the ram, and for the lambs, shall be according to their number, after the manner:

38 And one goat for a sin offering; beside the continual burnt offering, and his food offering, and his drink offering.

39 These things you shall do unto the Becoming-One in your set times,[96] beside your vows, and your freewill offerings, for your burnt offerings, and for your food offerings, and for your drink offerings, and for your peace offerings.

40 And Moses told the children of Israel according to all that the Becoming-One commanded Moses.

Num 30:1 And Moses spoke unto the heads of the tribes concerning the children of Israel, saying, This is the thing which the Becoming-One has commanded.

2 If a man vow a vow unto the Becoming-One, or swear an oath to bind his soul with a bond; he shall not break his word, he shall do according to all that proceeds out of his mouth.

3 If a woman also vow a vow unto the Becoming-One, and bind herself by a bond, being in her father's house in her youth;

4 And her father hear her vow, and her bond wherewith she has bound her soul, and her father shall hold his peace at her: then all her vows shall stand, and every bond wherewith she has bound her soul shall stand.

5 But if her father disallow her in the day that he hears; not any of her vows, or of her bonds wherewith she has bound her soul, shall stand: and the Becoming-One shall forgive her, because her father disallowed her.

6 And if she had at all a husband, when she vowed, or uttered anything out of her lips, wherewith she bound her soul;

7 And her husband heard it, and held his peace at her in the day that he heard it: then her vows shall stand, and her bonds wherewith she bound her soul shall stand.

8 But if her husband disallowed her on the day that he heard it; then he shall make her vow which she

---

[96] Appointed times or festivals

vowed, and that which she uttered with her lips, wherewith she bound her soul, of none effect: and the Becoming-One shall forgive her.

9 But every vow of a widow, and of her that is divorced, wherewith they have bound their souls, shall stand against her.

10 And if she vowed in her husband's house, or bound her soul by a bond with an oath;

11 And her husband heard it, and held his peace at her, and disallowed her not: then all her vows shall stand, and every bond wherewith she bound her soul shall stand.

12 But if her husband has utterly made them void on the day he heard them; then whatsoever proceeded out of her lips concerning her vows, or concerning the bond of her soul, shall not stand: her husband has made them void; and the Becoming-One shall forgive her.

13 Every vow, and every binding oath to afflict the soul, her husband may establish it, or her husband may make it void.

14 But if her husband altogether hold his peace at her from day to day; then he establishes all her vows, or all her bonds, which are upon her: he confirms them, because he held his peace at her in the day that he heard them.

15 But if he shall in any way make them void after that he has heard them; then he shall bear her iniquity.

16 These are the statutes, which the Becoming-One commanded Moses, between a man and his wife, between the father and his daughter, being yet in her youth in her father's house.

Num 31:1 And the Becoming-One spoke unto Moses, saying,

2 Avenge the children of Israel of the Midianites: afterward shall you be gathered unto your people.

3 And Moses spoke unto the people, saying, Arm some of yourselves unto the war, and let them go against the Midianites, and avenge the Becoming-One of Midian.

4 Of every tribe a thousand, throughout all the tribes of Israel, shall you send to the war.

5 So there were delivered out of the thousands of Israel, a thousand of every tribe, twelve thousand armed for war.

6 And Moses sent them to the war, a thousand of every tribe, them and Phinehas the son of Eleazar the priest, to the war, with the holy instruments, and the trumpets to blow in his hand.

7 And they warred against the Midianites, as the Becoming-One commanded Moses; and they killed all the males.

8 And they killed the kings of Midian, beside the rest of them that were slain; namely, Evi, and Rekem, and Zur, and Hur, and Reba, five kings of Midian: Balaam also the son of Beor they killed with the sword.

9 And the children of Israel took all the women of Midian captives, and their little ones, and took the spoil of all their cattle, and all their flocks, and all their goods.

10 And they burnt all their cities wherein they dwelt, and all their goodly castles, with fire.

11 And they took all the spoil, and all the prey, both of men and of beasts.

12 And they brought the captives, and the prey, and the spoil, unto Moses, and Eleazar the priest, and unto the congregation of the children of Israel, unto the camp at the plains of Moab, which are by Jordan near Jericho.

13 And Moses, and Eleazar the priest, and all the princes of the congregation, went forth to meet them outside the camp.

14 And Moses was angry with the officers of the host, with the captains over thousands, and captains over hundreds, which came from the battle.

15 And Moses said unto them, Have you saved all the female alive?

16 Behold, these caused the children of Israel, through the counsel of Balaam, to commit trespass against the Becoming-One in the matter of Peor, and there was a plague among the congregation of the Becoming-One.

17 Now therefore kill every male among the little ones, and kill every woman that has known man by lying with him.

18 But all the women children, that have not known a man by lying with him, keep alive for yourselves.

19 And do you abide outside the camp seven days: whosoever has killed any soul, and whosoever has touched any slain, purify both yourselves and your captives on the third day, and on the seventh day.

20 And purify all your raiment, and all that is made of skins, and all work of goats' hair, and all things made of wood.

21 And Eleazar the priest said unto the men of war which went to the battle, This is the ordinance of the law which the Becoming-One commanded Moses;

22 Only the gold, and the silver, the brass, the iron, the tin, and the lead,

23 Every thing that may abide the fire, you shall make it go through the fire, and it shall be clean: nevertheless it shall be purified with the water of separation: and all that abides not the fire you shall make go through the water.

24 And you shall wash your clothes on the seventh day, and you shall be clean, and afterward you shall come into the camp.

25 And the Becoming-One spoke unto Moses, saying,

26 Take the sum of the prey that was taken, both of man and of beast, you, and Eleazar the priest, and the chief fathers of the congregation:

27 And divide the prey into two parts; between them that took the war upon them, who went out to battle, and between all the congregation:

28 And levy a tribute unto the Becoming-One of the men of war which went out to battle: one soul of five hundred, from the man, from the herd, from the donkeys. and from the flock:

29 Take it of their half, and give it unto Eleazar the priest, for a heave offering of the Becoming-One.

30 And of the children of Israel's half, you shall take one portion of fifty, from the man, from the herd, from the donkeys, and from the flocks, and from all manner of beasts, and give them unto the Levites, which keep the charge of the tabernacle of the Becoming-One.

31 And Moses and Eleazar the priest did as the Becoming-One commanded Moses.

32 And the booty, being the rest of the prey which the men of war had caught, was six hundred thousand and seventy thousand and five thousand of sheep.

33 And threescore and twelve thousand of cattle,

34 And threescore and one thousand of donkeys,

35 And thirty and two thousand souls of man in all, of women that had not known man by lying with him.

36 And the half, which was the portion of them that went out to war, was in number three hundred thousand and seven and thirty thousand and five hundred sheep:

37 And the Becoming-One's tribute of the sheep was six hundred and threescore and fifteen.

38 And the cattle were thirty and six thousand; of which the Becoming-One's tribute was threescore and twelve.

39 And the donkeys were thirty thousand and five hundred; of which the Becoming-One's tribute was threescore and one.

40 And the souls of man were sixteen thousand; of which the Becoming-One's tribute was thirty and two souls.

41 And Moses gave the tribute, which was the Becoming-One's heave offering, unto Eleazar the priest, as the Becoming-One commanded Moses.

42 And of the children of Israel's half, which Moses divided from the men that warred,

43 Now the half that pertained unto the congregation was three hundred thousand and thirty thousand and seven thousand and five hundred sheep,

44 And thirty and six thousand of cattle,

45 And thirty thousand of donkeys and five hundred,

46 And sixteen thousand souls of man;

47 Even of the children of Israel's half, Moses took one portion of fifty, both of man and of beast, and gave them unto the Levites, which kept the charge of the tabernacle of the Becoming-One; as the Becoming-One commanded Moses.

48 And the officers which were over thousand of the host, the captains of thousand, and captains of hundreds, came near unto Moses:

49 And they said unto Moses, your servants have taken the sum of the men of war which are under our charge, and there lacks not one man of us.

50 We have therefore brought an offering for the Becoming-One, what every man has gotten, of jewels of gold, chains, and bracelets, rings, earrings, and tablets, to make an atonement for our souls before the Becoming-One.

51 And Moses and Eleazar the priest took the gold of them, even all worked jewels.

52 And all the gold of the offering that they offered up to the Becoming-One, of the captains of thousands, and of the captains of hundreds, was sixteen thousand seven hundred and fifty shekels.

53 For the men of war had taken spoil, every man for himself.

54 And Moses and Eleazar the priest took the gold of the captains of thousands and of hundreds, and brought it into the tabernacle of the set time, for a memorial for the children of Israel before the Becoming-One.

Num 32:1 Now the children of Reuben and the children of Gad had a very great multitude of cattle: and when they saw the land of Jazer, and the land of Gilead, that, behold, the place was a place for cattle;

2 The children of Gad and the children of Reuben came and spoke unto Moses, and to Eleazar the priest, and unto the princes of the congregation, saying,

3 Ataroth, and Dibon, and Jazer, and Nimrah, and Heshbon, and Elealeh, and Shebam, and Nebo, and Beon,

4 Even the country which the Becoming-One smote before the congregation of Israel, is a land for cattle, and your servants have cattle:

5 Therefore, said they, if we have found grace in your sight, let this land be given unto your servants for a possession, and bring us not over Jordan.

6 And Moses said unto the children of Gad and to the children of Reuben, Shall your brethren go to war, and shall you sit here?

7 And why discourage you the heart of the children of Israel from going over into the land which the Becoming-One has given them?

8 Thus did your fathers, when I sent them from Kadeshbarnea to see the land.

9 For when they went up unto the valley of Eshcol, and saw the land, they discouraged the heart of the children of Israel, that they should not go into the land which the Becoming-One had given them.

10 And the Becoming-One's anger was kindled the same time, and he swore, saying,

11 Surely none of the men that came up out of Egypt, from a son of twenty years and upward, shall see the land which I swore unto Abraham, unto Isaac, and unto Jacob; because they have not wholly followed me:

12 Save Caleb the son of Jephunneh the Kenezite, and Joshua the son of Nun: for they have wholly followed the Becoming-One.

13 And the Becoming-One's anger was kindled against Israel, and he made them wander in the wilderness forty years, until all the generation, that had done evil in the sight of the Becoming-One, was consumed.

14 And, behold, you are risen up in your fathers' stead, an increase of sinful men, to augment yet the fierce anger of the Becoming-One toward Israel.

15 For if you turn away from after him, he will yet again leave them in the wilderness; and you shall destroy all this people.

16 And they came near unto him, and said, We will build sheepfolds here for our cattle, and cities for our little ones:

17 But we ourselves will go ready armed before the children of Israel, until we have brought them unto their place: and our little ones shall dwell in the fenced cities because of the inhabitants of the land.

18 We will not return unto our houses, until the children of Israel have inherited every man his inheritance.

19 For we will not inherit with them beyond Jordan, or further beyond; because our inheritance is fallen to us beyond Jordan eastward.

20 And Moses said unto them, If you will do this thing, if you will go armed before the Becoming-One to war,

21 And will go all of you armed over Jordan before the Becoming-One, until he has driven out his enemies from before him,

22 And the land be subdued before the Becoming-One: then afterward you shall return, and be guiltless before the Becoming-One, and before Israel; and this land shall be your possession before the Becoming-One.

23 But if you will not do so, behold, you have sinned against the Becoming-One: and be sure your sin will find you out.

24 Build you cities for your little ones, and folds for your sheep; and do that which has proceeded out of your mouth.

25 And the children of Gad and the children of Reuben spoke unto Moses, saying, your servants will do as my lord commands.

26 Our little ones, our wives, our flocks, and all our cattle, shall be there in the cities of Gilead:

27 But your servants will pass over, every man armed for war, before the Becoming-One to battle, as my lord says.

28 So concerning them Moses commanded Eleazar the priest, and Joshua the son of Nun, and the chief fathers of the tribes of the children of Israel:

29 And Moses said unto them, If the children of Gad and the children of Reuben will pass with you over Jordan, every man armed to battle, before the Becoming-One, and the land shall be subdued before you; then you shall give them the land of Gilead for a possession:

30 But if they will not pass over with you armed, they shall have possessions among you in the land of Canaan.

31 And the children of Gad and the children of Reuben answered, saying, As the Becoming-One has said unto your servants, so will we do.

32 We will pass over armed before the Becoming-One into the land of Canaan, that the possession of our inheritance beyond Jordan may be ours.

33 And Moses gave unto them, even to the children of Gad, and to the children of Reuben, and unto half the tribe of Manasseh the son of Joseph, the kingdom of Sihon king of the Amorites, and the kingdom of Og king of Bashan, the land, with the cities thereof in the coasts, even the cities of the country round about.

34 And the children of Gad built Dibon, and Ataroth, and Aroer,

35 And Atroth, Shophan, and Jaazer, and Jogbehah,

36 And Beth-nimrah, and Beth-haran, fenced cities: and folds for sheep.

37 And the children of Reuben built Heshbon, and Elealeh, and Kirjathaim,

38 And Nebo, and Baal-Meon, their names being changed and Shibmah: and gave other names unto the cities which they built.

39 And the children of Machir the son of Manasseh went to Gilead, and took it, and dispossessed the Amorite which was in it.

40 And Moses gave Gilead unto Machir the son of Manasseh; and he dwelt therein.

41 And Jair the son of Manasseh went and took the small towns thereof, and called them Havothjair.

42 And Nobah went and took Kenath, and the villages thereof, and called it Nobah, after his own name.

Num 33:1 These are the journeys of the children of Israel, which went forth out of the land of Egypt with their armies under the hand of Moses and Aaron.

2 And Moses wrote their goings out according to their journeys by the mouth of the Becoming-One: and these are their journeys according to their goings out.

3 And they departed from Rameses in the first month, on the fifteenth day of the first month; on the next day after the Passover the children of Israel went out with a high hand in the sight of all the Egyptians.

4 For the Egyptians buried all their firstborn, which the Becoming-One had struck among them: upon their gods also the Becoming-One executed judgments.

5 And the children of Israel removed from Rameses, and pitched in Succoth.

6 And they departed from Succoth, and pitched in Etham, which is in the edge of the wilderness.

7 And they removed from Etham, and turned again unto Pihahiroth, which is before Baal-Zephon: and they pitched before Migdol.

8 And they departed from before Pihahiroth, and passed through the midst of the sea into the wilderness, and went three days' journey in the wilderness of Etham, and pitched in Marah.

9 And they removed from Marah, and came unto Elim: and in Elim were twelve fountains of water, and threescore and ten palm trees; and they pitched there.

10 And they removed from Elim, and encamped by the boundary sea.

11 And they removed from the boundary sea, and encamped in the wilderness of Sin.

12 And they took their journey out of the wilderness of Sin, and encamped in Dophkah.

13 And they departed from Dophkah, and encamped in Alush.

14 And they removed from Alush, and encamped at Rephidim, where was no water for the people to drink.

15 And they departed from Rephidim, and pitched in the wilderness of Sinai.

16 And they removed from the desert of Sinai, and pitched at Kibrothhattaavah.

17 And they departed from Kibrothhattaavah, and encamped at Hazeroth.

18 And they departed from Hazeroth, and pitched in Rithmah.

19 And they departed from Rithmah, and pitched at Rimmonparez.

20 And they departed from Rimmonparez, and pitched in Libnah.

21 And they removed from Libnah, and pitched at Rissah.

22 And they journeyed from Rissah, and pitched in Kehelathah.

23 And they went from Kehelathah, and pitched in mount Shapher.

24 And they removed from mount Shapher, and encamped in Haradah.

25 And they removed from Haradah, and pitched in Makheloth.

26 And they removed from Makheloth, and encamped at Tahath.

27 And they departed from Tahath, and pitched at Tarah.

28 And they removed from Tarah, and pitched in Mithcah.

29 And they went from Mithcah, and pitched in Hashmonah.

30 And they departed from Hashmonah, and encamped at Moseroth.

31 And they departed from Moseroth, and pitched in Benejaakan.

32 And they removed from Benejaakan, and encamped at Horhagidgad.

33 And they went from Horhagidgad, and pitched in Jotbathah.

34 And they removed from Jotbathah, and encamped at Ebronah.

35 And they departed from Ebronah, and encamped at Eziongaber.

36 And they removed from Eziongaber, and pitched in the wilderness of Zin, which is Kadesh.

37 And they removed from Kadesh, and pitched in mount Hor, in the edge of the land of Edom.

38 And Aaron the priest went up into mount Hor at the mouth of the Becoming-One, and died there, in the fortieth year after the children of Israel were come out of the land of Egypt, in the first day of the fifth month.

39 And Aaron was a son of a hundred and twenty and three years when he died in mount Hor.

40 And king Arad the Canaanite, which dwelt in the south in the land of Canaan, heard of the coming of the children of Israel.

41 And they departed from mount Hor, and pitched in Zalmonah.

42 And they departed from Zalmonah, and pitched in Punon.

43 And they departed from Punon, and pitched in Oboth.

44 And they departed from Oboth, and pitched in Ijeabarim, in the border of Moab.

45 And they departed from Iim, and pitched in Dibongad.

46 And they removed from Dibongad, and encamped in Almondiblathaim.

47 And they removed from Almondiblathaim, and pitched in the mountains of Abarim, before Nebo.

48 And they departed from the mountains of Abarim, and pitched in the plains of Moab by Jordan near Jericho.

49 And they pitched by Jordan, from Beth-jesimoth even unto Able-shittim in the plains of Moab.

50 And the Becoming-One spoke unto Moses in the plains of Moab by Jordan near Jericho, saying,

51 Speak unto the children of Israel, and say unto them, When you are passed over Jordan into the land of Canaan;

52 Then you shall drive out all the inhabitants of the land from before you, and destroy all their pictures, and destroy all their molten images, and quite pluck down all their high places:

53 And you shall dispossess the inhabitants of the land, and dwell therein: for I have given you the land to possess it.

54 And you shall divide the land by lot for an inheritance among your families: and to the more you shall give the more inheritance, and to the fewer you shall give the less inheritance: every man's inheritance shall be in the place where his lot falls; according to the tribes of your fathers you shall inherit.

55 But if you will not drive out the inhabitants of the land from before you; then it shall come to pass, that those which you let remain of them shall be pricks in your eyes, and thorns in your sides, and shall vex you in the land wherein you dwell.

56 Moreover it shall come to pass, that I shall do unto you, as I thought to do unto them.

Num 34:1 And the Becoming-One spoke unto Moses, saying,

2 Command the children of Israel, and say unto them, When you come into the land of Canaan; this is the land that shall fall unto you for an inheritance, even the land of Canaan with the coasts thereof:

3 Then your south quarter shall be from the wilderness of Zin along by the coast of Edom, and your south border shall be the outmost coast of the salt sea eastward:

4 And your border shall turn from the south to the ascent of Akrabbim, and pass on to Zin: and the going forth thereof shall be from the south to Kadeshbarnea, and shall go on to Hazaraddar, and pass on to Azmon:

5 And the border shall fetch a compass from Azmon unto the river of Egypt, and the goings out of it shall be at the sea.

6 And as for the western border, you shall even have the great sea for a border: this shall be your west border.

7 And this shall be your north border: from the great sea you shall point out for you mount Hor:

8 From mount Hor you shall point out your border unto the entrance of Hamath; and the goings forth of the border shall be to Zedad:

9 And the border shall go on to Ziphron, and the goings out of it shall be at Hazarenan: this shall be your north border.

10 And you shall point out your east border from Hazarenan to Shepham:

11 And the coast shall go down from Shepham to Riblah, on the east side of Ain; and the border shall descend, and shall reach unto the side of the sea of Chinnereth eastward:

12 And the border shall go down to Jordan, and the goings out of it shall be at the salt sea: this shall be your land with the coasts thereof round about.

13 And Moses commanded the children of Israel, saying, This is the land which you shall inherit by lot, which the Becoming-One commanded to give unto the nine tribes, and to the half tribe:

14 For the tribe of the children of Reuben according to the house of their fathers, and the tribe of the children of Gad according to the house of their fathers, have received their inheritance; and half the tribe of Manasseh have received their inheritance:

15 The two tribes and the half tribe have received their inheritance on beyond Jordan near Jericho eastward, toward the sunrising.

16 And the Becoming-One spoke unto Moses, saying,

17 These are the names of the men which shall divide the land unto you: Eleazar the priest, and Joshua the son of Nun.

18 And you shall take one prince of every tribe, to divide the land by inheritance.

19 And the names of the men are these: Of the tribe of Judah, Caleb the son of Jephunneh.

20 And of the tribe of the children of Simeon, Shemuel the son of Ammihud.

21 Of the tribe of Benjamin, Elidad the son of Chislon.

22 And the prince of the tribe of the children of Dan, Bukki the son of Jogli.

23 The prince of the children of Joseph, for the tribe of the children of Manasseh, Hanniel the son of Ephod.

24 And the prince of the tribe of the children of Ephraim, Kemuel the son of Shiphtan.

25 And the prince of the tribe of the children of Zebulun, Elizaphan the son of Parnach.

26 And the prince of the tribe of the children of Issachar, Paltiel the son of Azzan.

27 And the prince of the tribe of the children of Asher, Ahihud the son of Shelomi.

28 And the prince of the tribe of the children of Naphtali, Pedahel the son of Ammihud.

29 These are they whom the Becoming-One commanded to divide the inheritance unto the children of Israel in the land of Canaan.

Num 35:1 And the Becoming-One spoke unto Moses in the plains of Moab by Jordan near Jericho, saying,

2 Command the children of Israel, that they give unto the Levites of the inheritance of their possession cities to dwell in; and you shall give also unto the Levites suburbs for the cities round about them.

3 And the cities shall they have to dwell in; and the suburbs of them shall be for their cattle, and for their goods, and for all their beasts.

4 And the suburbs of the cities, which you shall give unto the Levites, shall reach from the wall of the city and outward a thousand cubits round about.

5 And you shall measure from outside the city on the east side two thousand cubits, and on the south side two thousand cubits, and on the west side two thousand cubits, and on the north side two thousand cubits; and the city shall be in the midst: this shall be to them the suburbs of the cities.

6 And among the cities which you shall give unto the Levites there shall be six cities for refuge, which you shall appoint for the manslayer, that he may flee there: and to them you shall add forty and two cities.

7 So all the cities which you shall give to the Levites shall be forty and eight cities: them shall you give with their suburbs.

8 And the cities which you shall give shall be of the possession of the children of Israel: from them that have many you shall give many; but from them that have few you shall give few: every one shall give of his cities unto the Levites according to his inheritance which he inherited.

9 And the Becoming-One spoke unto Moses, saying,

10 Speak unto the children of Israel, and say unto them, When you be come over Jordan into the land of Canaan;

11 Then you shall appoint you cities to be cities of refuge for you; that the slayer may flee there, which kills any soul at unawares.

12 And they shall be unto you cities for refuge from the avenger; that the manslayer die not, until he stand before the congregation in judgment.

13 And of these cities which you shall give six cities shall you have for refuge.

14 you shall give three cities on this side Jordan, and three cities shall you give in the land of Canaan, which shall be cities of refuge.

15 These six cities shall be a refuge, both for the children of Israel, and for the stranger, and for the sojourner among them: that every one that kills any soul unawares may flee there.

16 And if he smite him with an instrument of iron, so that he die, he is a murderer: the murderer in dying he shall be put to death.

17 And if he smite him with throwing a stone, wherewith he may die, and he die, he is a murderer: the murderer in dying he shall be put to death.

18 Or if he smite him with a hand weapon of wood, wherewith he may die, and he die, he is a murderer: the murderer in dying he shall be put to death.

19 The revenger of blood himself shall slay the murderer: when he meets him, he shall slay him.

20 But if he thrust him of hatred, or hurl at him by laying of wait, that he die;

21 Or in enmity smite him with his hand, that he die: he that smote him in dying he shall be put to death; for he is a murderer: the revenger of blood shall slay the murderer, when he meets him.

22 But if he thrust him suddenly without enmity, or have cast upon him any thing without laying of wait,

23 Or with any stone, wherewith a man may die, seeing him not, and cast it upon him, that he die, and was not his enemy, neither sought his harm:

24 Then the congregation shall judge between the slayer and the revenger of blood according to these judgments:

25 And the congregation shall deliver the slayer out of the hand of the revenger of blood, and the congregation shall restore him to the city of his refuge, to which he fled: and he shall abide in it unto the death of the high priest, which was anointed with the holy oil.

26 But if the slayer shall at any time come outside the border of the city of his refuge, to which he fled;

27 And the revenger of blood find him outside the borders of the city of his refuge, and the revenger of blood kill the slayer; he shall not be guilty of blood:

28 Because he should have remained in the city of his refuge until the death of the high priest: but after the death of the high priest the slayer shall return into the land of his possession.

29 So these things shall be for a statute of judgment unto you throughout your generations in all your dwellings.

30 Whoso kills any soul, the murderer shall be put to death by the mouth of witnesses: but one witness shall not testify against any soul to cause him to die.

31 Moreover you shall take no satisfaction for the soul of a murderer, which is guilty of death: but in dying he shall be put to death.

32 And you shall take no satisfaction for him that is fled to the city of his refuge, that he should come again to dwell in the land, until the death of the priest.

33 So you shall not pollute the land wherein you are: for blood it defiles the land: and the land cannot be cleansed of the blood that is shed therein, but by the blood of him that shed it.

34 Defile not therefore the land which you shall inhabit, wherein I dwell: for I the Becoming-One dwell among the children of Israel.

Num 36:1 And the chief fathers of the families of the children of Gilead, the son of Machir, the son of Manasseh, of the families of the sons of Joseph, came near, and spoke before Moses, and before the princes, the chief fathers of the children of Israel:

2 And they said, The Becoming-One commanded my lord to give the land for an inheritance by lot to the children of Israel: and my lord was commanded by the Becoming-One to give the inheritance of Zelophehad our brother unto his daughters.

3 And if they be married to any of the sons of the other tribes of the children of Israel, then shall their inheritance be taken from the inheritance of our fathers, and shall be put to the inheritance of the tribe whereunto they are received: so shall it be taken from the lot of our inheritance.

4 And when the jubile of the children of Israel shall be, then shall their inheritance be put unto the inheritance of the tribe whereunto they are received: so shall their inheritance be taken away from the inheritance of the tribe of our fathers.

5 And Moses commanded the children of Israel according to the word of the Becoming-One, saying, The tribe of the sons of Joseph has said well.

6 This is the thing which the Becoming-One does command concerning the daughters of Zelophehad, saying, Let them marry to whom they think best; only to the family of the tribe of their father shall they marry.

7 So shall not the inheritance of the children of Israel remove from tribe to tribe: for every one of the children of Israel shall keep himself to the inheritance of the tribe of his fathers.

8 And every daughter, that possesses an inheritance in any tribe of the children of Israel, shall be wife unto one of the family of the tribe of her father, that the children of Israel may enjoy every man the inheritance of his fathers.

9 Neither shall the inheritance remove from one tribe to another tribe; but every one of the tribes of the children of Israel shall keep himself to his own inheritance.

10 Even as the Becoming-One commanded Moses, so did the daughters of Zelophehad:

11 For Mahlah, Tirzah, and Hoglah, and Milcah, and Noah, the daughters of Zelophehad, were married unto their father's brothers' sons:

12 And they were married into the families of the sons of Manasseh the son of Joseph, and their inheritance remained in the tribe of the family of their father.

13 These are the commandments and the judgments, which the Becoming-One commanded by the hand of Moses unto the children of Israel in the plains of Moab by Jordan near Jericho.

Deuteronomy

Deu 1:1 These be the words which Moses spoke unto all Israel on beyond Jordan in the wilderness, in the plain over against the boundary sea, between Paran, and Tophel, and Laban, and Hazeroth, and Dizahab.

2 There are eleven days' journey from Horeb by the way of mount Seir unto Kadeshbarnea.

3 And it came to pass in the fortieth year, in the eleventh month, on the first day of the month, that Moses spoke unto the children of Israel, according unto all that the Becoming-One had given him in commandment unto them;

4 After he had slain Sihon the king of the Amorites, which dwelt in Heshbon, and Og the king of Bashan, which dwelt at Astaroth in Edrei:

5 Beyond Jordan, in the land of Moab, began Moses to declare this law, saying,

6 The Becoming-One our God spoke unto us in Horeb, saying, you have dwelt long enough in this mount:

7 Turn you, and take your journey, and go to the mount of the Amorites, and unto all the places near thereunto, in the plain, in the hills, and in the vale, and in the south, and by the sea side, to the land of the Canaanites, and unto Lebanon, unto the great river, the river Euphrates.

8 Behold, I have set the land before you: go in and possess the land which the Becoming-One swore unto your fathers, Abraham, Isaac, and Jacob, to give unto them and to their seed after them.

9 And I spoke unto you at that time, saying, I am not able to bear you myself alone:

10 The Becoming-One your God has multiplied you, and, behold, you are this day as the stars of the heavens for multitude.

11 The Becoming-One, God of your fathers make you a thousand times more than you are, and bless you, as he has promised you!

12 How can I myself alone bear your cumbrance, and your burden, and your strife?

13 Take you wise men, and understanding, and known among your tribes, and I will make them rulers over you.

14 And you answered me, and said, The thing which you have spoken is good for us to do.

15 So I took the chief of your tribes, wise men, and known, and made them heads over you, captains over thousands, and captains over hundreds, and captains over fifties, and captains over tens, and officers among your tribes.

16 And I charged your judges at that time, saying, Hear the causes between your brethren, and judge righteously between every man and his brother, and the stranger that is with him.

17 you shall not respect persons in judgment; but you shall hear the small as well as the great; you shall not be afraid of the face of man; for the judgment is God': and the cause that is too hard for you, bring it unto me, and I will hear it.

18 And I commanded you at that time all the things which you should do.

19 And when we departed from Horeb, we went through all that great and terrible wilderness, which you saw by the way of the mountain of the Amorites, as the Becoming-One our God commanded us; and we came to Kadeshbarnea.

20 And I said unto you, you are come unto the mountain of the Amorites, which the Becoming-One our God does give unto us.

21 Behold, the Becoming-One your God has set the land before you: go up and possess it, as the Becoming-One, God of your fathers has said unto you; fear not, neither be discouraged.

22 And you came near unto me every one of you, and said, We will send men before us, and they shall search us out the land, and bring us word again by what way we must go up, and into what cities we shall come.

23 And the saying pleased me well: and I took twelve men of you, one of a tribe:

24 And they turned and went up into the mountain, and came unto the valley of Eshcol, and searched it out.

25 And they took of the fruit of the land in their hands, and brought it down unto us, and brought us word again, and said, It is a good land which the Becoming-One our God does give us.

26 Notwithstanding you would not go up, but rebelled against the mouth of the Becoming-One your God:

27 And you murmured in your tents, and said, Because the Becoming-One hated us, he has brought us forth out of the land of Egypt, to deliver us into the hand of the Amorites, to destroy us.

28 Where shall we go up? our brethren have discouraged our heart, saying, The people is greater and taller than we; the cities are great and walled up to the heavens; and moreover we have seen the sons of the Anakims there.

29 Then I said unto you, Dread not, neither be afraid of them.

30 The Becoming-One your God which goes before you, he shall fight for you, according to all that he did for you in Egypt before your eyes;

31 And in the wilderness, where you have seen how that the Becoming-One your God bare you, as a man does bear his son, in all the way that you went, until you came into this place.

32 Yet in this thing you did not believe the Becoming-One your God,

33 Who went in the way before you, to search you out a place to pitch your tents in, in fire by night, to show you by what way you should go, and in a cloud by day.

34 And the Becoming-One heard the voice of your words, and was angry, and swore, saying,

35 Surely there shall not one of these men of this evil generation see that good land, which I swore to give unto your fathers,

36 Save Caleb the son of Jephunneh; he shall see it, and to him will I give the land that he has trodden upon, and to his children, because he has wholly followed the Becoming-One.

37 Also the Becoming-One was angry with me for your sakes, saying, you also shall not go in there.

38 But Joshua the son of Nun, which stands before you, he shall go in there: encourage him: for he shall cause Israel to inherit it.

39 Moreover your little ones, which you said should be a prey, and your children, which in that day had no knowledge between good and evil, they shall go in there, and unto them will I give it, and they shall possess it.

40 But as for you, turn you, and take your journey into the wilderness by the way of the boundary sea.

41 Then you answered and said unto me, We have sinned against the Becoming-One, we will go up and fight, according to all that the Becoming-One our God commanded us. And when you had girded on every man his weapons of war, you were ready to go up into the hill.

42 And the Becoming-One said unto me, Say unto them, Go not up, neither fight; for I am not among you; lest you be struck before your enemies.

43 So I spoke unto you; and you would not hear, but rebelled against the commandment of the Becoming-One, and went presumptuously up into the hill.

44 And the Amorites, which dwelt in that mountain, came out against you, and chased you, as bees do, and destroyed you in Seir, even unto Hormah.

45 And you returned and wept before the Becoming-One; but the Becoming-One would not listen to your voice, nor give ear unto you.

46 So you abode in Kadesh many days, according unto the days that you abode there.

Deu 2:1 Then we turned, and took our journey into the wilderness by the way of the boundary sea, as the Becoming-One spoke unto me: and we compassed mount Seir many days.

2 And the Becoming-One spoke unto me, saying,

3 you have compassed this mountain long enough: turn you northward.

4 And command you the people, saying, you are to pass through the coast of your brethren the children of Esau, which dwell in Seir; and they shall be afraid of you: take you good heed unto yourselves therefore:

5 Meddle not with them; for I will not give you of their land, no, not so much as a foot breadth; because I have given mount Seir unto Esau for a possession.

6 you shall buy food of them for money, that you may eat; and you shall also buy water of them for money, that you may drink.

7 For the Becoming-One your God has blessed you in all the works of your hand: he knows your walking through this great wilderness: these forty years the Becoming-One your God has been with you; you have lacked nothing.

8 And when we passed by from our brethren the children of Esau, which dwelt in Seir, through the way of the plain from Elath, and from Eziongaber, we turned and passed by the way of the wilderness of Moab.

9 And the Becoming-One said unto me, Distress not the Moabites, neither contend with them in battle: for I will not give you of their land for a possession; because I have given Ar unto the children of Lot for a possession.

10 The Emims dwelt therein in times past, a people great, and many, and tall, as the Anakims;

11 Which also were accounted giants [rephaims] as the Anakims; but the Moabites call them Emims.

12 The Horims also dwelt in Seir beforetime; but the children of Esau succeeded them, when they had destroyed them from before them, and dwelt in their stead; as Israel did unto the land of his possession, which the Becoming-One gave unto them.

13 Now rise up, said I, and get you over the brook Zered. And we went over the brook Zered.

14 And the days in which we came from Kadeshbarnea, until we were come over the brook Zered, was thirty and eight years; until all the generation of the men of war were wasted out from among the host, as the Becoming-One swore unto them.

15 For indeed the hand of the Becoming-One was against them, to destroy them from among the host, until they were consumed.

16 So it came to pass, when all the men of war were consumed and dead from among the people,

17 That the Becoming-One spoke unto me, saying,

18 you are to pass over through Ar, the coast of Moab, this day:

19 And when you come near over against the children of Ammon, distress them not, nor meddle with them: for I will not give you of the land of the children of Ammon any possession; because I have given it unto the children of Lot for a possession.

20 That also was accounted a land of giants: giants dwelt therein in old time; and the Ammonites call them Zamzummims;

21 A people great, and many, and tall, as the Anakims; but the Becoming-One destroyed them before them; and they succeeded them, and dwelt in their stead:

22 As he did to the children of Esau, which dwelt in Seir, when he destroyed the Horims from before them; and they succeeded them, and dwelt in their stead even unto this day:

23 And the Avims which dwelt in Hazerim, even unto Azzah, the Caphtorims, which came forth out of Caphtor, destroyed them, and dwelt in their stead.

24 Rise you up, take your journey, and pass over the river Arnon: behold, I have given into your hand Sihon the Amorite, king of Heshbon, and his land: begin to possess it, and contend with him in battle.

25 This day will I begin to put the dread of you and the fear of you upon the nations that are under the whole of the heavens, who shall hear report of you, and shall tremble, and be in anguish because of you.

26 And I sent messengers out of the wilderness of Kedemoth unto Sihon king of Heshbon with words of peace, saying,

27 Let me pass through your land: I will go along by the high way, I will neither turn unto the right hand nor to the left.

28 you shall sell me food for money, that I may eat; and give me water for money, that I may drink: only I will pass through on my feet;

29 As the children of Esau which dwell in Seir, and the Moabites which dwell in Ar, did unto me; until I shall pass over Jordan into the land which the Becoming-One our God gives us.

30 But Sihon king of Heshbon would not let us pass by him: for the Becoming-One your God hardened his spirit, and made his heart obstinate, that he might deliver him into your hand, as appears this day.

31 And the Becoming-One said unto me, Behold, I have begun to give Sihon and his land before you: begin to possess, that you may inherit his land.

32 Then Sihon came out against us, he and all his people, to fight at Jahaz.

33 And the Becoming-One our God delivered him before us; and we smote him, and his sons, and all his people.

34 And we took all his cities at that time, and utterly destroyed the men, and the women, and the little ones, of every city, we left none to remain:

35 Only the cattle we took for a prey unto ourselves, and the spoil of the cities which we took.

36 From Aroer, which is by the brink of the river of Arnon, and from the city that is by the river, even unto Gilead, there was not one city too strong for us: the Becoming-One our God delivered all unto us:

37 Only unto the land of the children of Ammon you came not, nor unto any place of the river Jabbok, nor unto the cities in the mountains, nor unto whatsoever the Becoming-One our God forbad us.

Deu 3:1 Then we turned, and went up the way to Bashan: and Og the king of Bashan came out against us, he and all his people, to battle at Edrei.

2 And the Becoming-One said unto me, Fear him not: for I will deliver him, and all his people, and his land, into your hand; and you shall do unto him as you didst unto Sihon king of the Amorites, which dwelt at Heshbon.

3 So the Becoming-One our God delivered into our hands Og also, the king of Bashan, and all his people: and we smote him until none was left to him remaining.

4 And we took all his cities at that time, there was not a city which we took not from them, threescore cities, all the region of Argob, the kingdom of Og in Bashan.

5 All these cities were fenced with high walls, gates, and bars; beside unwalled towns a great many.

6 And we utterly destroyed them, as we did unto Sihon king of Heshbon, utterly destroying the men, women, and children, of every city.

7 But all the cattle, and the spoil of the cities, we took for a prey to ourselves.

8 And we took at that time out of the hand of the two kings of the Amorites the land that was beyond Jordan, from the river of Arnon unto mount Hermon;

9 Which Hermon the Sidonians call Sirion; and the Amorites call it Shenir;

10 All the cities of the plain, and all Gilead, and all Bashan, unto Salchah and Edrei, cities of the kingdom of Og in Bashan.

11 For only Og king of Bashan remained of the remnant of giants; behold, his bedstead was a bedstead of iron; is it not in Rabbath of the children of Ammon? nine cubits was the length thereof, and four cubits the breadth of it, after the cubit of a man.

12 And this land, which we possessed at that time, from Aroer, which is by the river Arnon, and half mount Gilead, and the cities thereof, gave I unto the Reubenites and to the Gadites.

13 And the rest of Gilead, and all Bashan, being the kingdom of Og, gave I unto the half tribe of Manasseh; all the region of Argob, with all Bashan, which was called the land of giants.

14 Jair the son of Manasseh took all the country of Argob unto the coasts of Geshuri and Maachathi; and called them after his own name, Bashanhavothjair, unto this day.

15 And I gave Gilead unto Machir.

16 And unto the Reubenites and unto the Gadites I gave from Gilead even unto the river Arnon half the valley, and the border even unto the river Jabbok, which is the border of the children of Ammon;

17 The plain also, and Jordan, and the coast thereof, from Chinnereth even unto the sea of the plain, even the salt sea, under Ashdothpisgah eastward.

18 And I commanded you at that time, saying, The Becoming-One your God has given you this land to possess it: you shall pass over armed before your brethren the children of Israel, all the sons of might.

19 But your wives, and your little ones, and your cattle, for I know that you have much cattle, shall abide in your cities which I have given you;

20 Until the Becoming-One have given rest unto your brethren, as well as unto you, and until they also possess the land which the Becoming-One your God has given them beyond Jordan: and then shall you return every man unto his possession, which I have given you.

21 And I commanded Joshua at that time, saying, your eyes have seen all that the Becoming-One your God has done unto these two kings: so shall the Becoming-One do unto all the kingdoms to which you pass.

22 you shall not fear them: for the Becoming-One your God he shall fight for you.

23 And I besought the Becoming-One at that time, saying,

24 O my Lord(s) the Becoming-One, you have begun to show your servant your greatness, and your mighty hand: for what god is there in the heavens or in the earth, that can do according to your works, and according to your might?

25 I pray you, let me go over, and see the good land that is beyond Jordan, that goodly mountain, and Lebanon.

26 But the Becoming-One was angry with me for your sakes, and would not hear me: and the Becoming-One said unto me, Let it suffice you; speak no more unto me of this matter.

27 Get you up into the top of Pisgah, and lift up your eyes westward, and northward, and southward, and eastward, and behold it with your eyes: for you shall not go over this Jordan.

28 But charge Joshua, and encourage him, and strengthen him: for he shall go over before this people, and he shall cause them to inherit the land which you shall see.

29 So we abode in the valley over against Beth-peor.

Deu 4:1 Now therefore listen, O Israel, unto the statutes and unto the judgments, which I teach you, for to do them, that you may live, and go in and possess the land which the Becoming-One, God of your fathers gives you.

2 you shall not add unto the word which I command you, neither shall you diminish anything

from it, that you may keep the commandments of the Becoming-One your God which I command you.

3 Your eyes have seen what the Becoming-One did because of Baal-Peor: for all the men that followed Baal-Peor, the Becoming-One your God has destroyed them from among you.

4 But you that did cleave unto the Becoming-One your God are alive every one of you this day.

5 Behold, I have taught you statutes and judgments, even as the Becoming-One my God commanded me, that you should do so in the land to which you go to possess it.

6 Keep therefore and do them; for this is your wisdom and your understanding in the sight of the nations, which shall hear all these statutes, and say, Surely this great nation is a wise and understanding people.

7 For what nation is there so great, who has God so near unto them, as the Becoming-One our God is in all things that we call upon him for?

8 And what nation is there so great, that has statutes and judgments so righteous as all this law, which I set before you this day?

9 Only take heed to thyself, and keep your soul diligently, lest you forget the things which your eyes have seen, and lest they depart from your heart all the days of your life: but teach them your sons, and your sons' sons;

10 Specially the day that you stood before the Becoming-One your God in Horeb, when the Becoming-One said unto me, Gather me the people together, and I will make them hear my words, that they may learn to fear me all the days that they shall live upon the earth, and that they may teach their children.

11 And you came near and stood under the mountain; and the mountain burned with fire unto the midst of the heavens, with darkness, clouds, and thick darkness.

12 And the Becoming-One spoke unto you out of the midst of the fire: you heard the voice of the words, but saw no similitude; only you heard a voice.

13 And he declared unto you his covenant, which he commanded you to perform, even ten commandments; and he wrote them upon two tables of stone.

14 And the Becoming-One commanded me at that time to teach you statutes and judgments, that you might do them in the land to which you go over to possess it.

15 Take you therefore good heed unto your souls; for you saw no manner of similitude on the day that the Becoming-One spoke unto you in Horeb out of the midst of the fire:

16 Lest you corrupt yourselves, and make you a graven image, the similitude of any figure, the likeness of male or female,

17 The likeness of any beast that is on the earth, the likeness of any winged fowl that flies in the air,

18 The likeness of any thing that creeps on the ground, the likeness of any fish that is in the waters beneath the earth:

19 And lest you lift up your eyes unto the heavens, and when you see the sun, and the moon, and the stars, even all the host of the heavens, should be driven to worship them, and serve them, which the Becoming-One your God has allotted unto all nations under the whole heavens.

20 But the Becoming-One has taken you, and brought you forth out of the iron furnace, even out of Egypt, to be unto him a people of inheritance, as you are this day.

21 Furthermore the Becoming-One was angry with me for your sakes, and swore that I should not go over Jordan, and that I should not go in unto that good land, which the Becoming-One your God gives you for an inheritance:

22 But I must die in this land, I must not go over Jordan: but you shall go over, and possess that good land.

23 Take heed unto yourselves, lest you forget the covenant of the Becoming-One your God, which he made with you, and make you a graven image, or the likeness of any thing, which the Becoming-One your God has forbidden you.

24 For the Becoming-One your God is a consuming fire, even a jealous GOD.

25 When you shall beget children, and children's children, and you shall have remained long in the land, and shall corrupt yourselves, and make a graven image, or the likeness of any thing, and shall do evil in the sight of the Becoming-One your God, to provoke him to anger:

26 I call the heavens and earth to witness against you this day, that you shall soon utterly perish from off the land whereunto you go over Jordan to possess it; you shall not prolong your days upon it, but shall utterly be destroyed.

27 And the Becoming-One shall scatter you among the nations, and you shall be left few in number among the nations, to which the Becoming-One shall lead you.

28 And there you shall serve gods, the work of men's hands, wood and stone, which neither see, nor hear, nor eat, nor smell.

29 But if from there you shall seek the Becoming-One your God, you shall find him, if you seek him with all your heart and with all your soul.

30 When you are in tribulation, and all these things are come upon you, even in the end of days, if you turn to the Becoming-One your God, and shall be obedient unto his voice;

31 For the Becoming-One your God is a merciful GOD; he will not forsake you, neither destroy you, nor forget the covenant of your fathers which he swore unto them.

32 For ask now of the days that are past, which were before you, since the day that God created man upon the earth, and ask from the one side of the heavens unto the other, whether there has been any such thing as this great thing is, or has been heard like it?

33 Did ever people hear the voice of God speaking out of the midst of the fire, as you have heard, and live?

34 Or has God assayed to go and take him a nation from the midst of another nation, by temptations, by signs, and by wonders, and by war, and by a mighty hand, and by a stretched out arm, and by great terrors, according to all that the Becoming-One your God did for you in Egypt before your eyes?

35 Unto you it was showed, that you might know that the Becoming-One he is God; there is none else beside him.

36 Out of the heavens he made you to hear his voice, that he might instruct you: and upon earth he showed you his great fire; and you heard his words out of the midst of the fire.

37 And because he loved your fathers, therefore he chose their seed after them, and brought you out in his sight with his mighty power out of Egypt;

38 To drive out nations from before you greater and mightier than you are, to bring you in, to give you their land for an inheritance, as it is this day.

39 Know therefore this day, and consider it in your heart, that the Becoming-One he is God in the heavens above, and upon the earth beneath: there is none else.

40 you shall keep therefore his statutes, and his commandments, which I command you this day, that it may go well with you, and with your children after you, and that you may prolong your days upon the earth, for the Becoming-One your God gives you all the days.

41 Then Moses severed three cities beyond Jordan toward the sun rising;

42 That the slayer might flee there, which should kill his neighbor unawares, and hated him not yesterday and the third day; and that fleeing unto one of these cities he might live:

43 Namely, Bezer in the wilderness, in the plain country, of the Reubenites; and Ramoth in Gilead, of the Gadites; and Golan in Bashan, of the Manassites.

44 And this is the law which Moses set before the children of Israel:

45 These are the testimonies, and the statutes, and the judgments, which Moses spoke unto the children of Israel, after they came forth out of Egypt,

46 Beyond Jordan, in the valley over against Beth-peor, in the land of Sihon king of the Amorites, who dwelt at Heshbon, whom Moses and the children of Israel smote, after they were come forth out of Egypt:

47 And they possessed his land, and the land of Og king of Bashan, two kings of the Amorites, which were beyond Jordan toward the sun rising;

48 From Aroer, which is by the bank of the river Arnon, even unto mount Sion, which is Hermon,

49 And all the plain beyond Jordan eastward, even unto the sea of the plain, under the springs of Pisgah.

Deu 5:1 And Moses called all Israel, and said unto them, Hear, O Israel, the statutes and judgments which I speak in your ears this day, that you may learn them, and keep, and do them.

2 The Becoming-One our God made a covenant with us in Horeb.

3 The Becoming-One made not this covenant with our fathers, but with us, even us, who are all of us here alive this day.

4 The Becoming-One talked with you face to face in the mount out of the midst of the fire,

5 I stood between the Becoming-One and you at that time, to show you the word of the Becoming-One: for you were afraid by reason of the fire, and went not up into the mount; saying,

6 I am the Becoming-One your God, which brought you out of the land of Egypt, from the house of bondage.

7 you shall have none other gods before me.

8 you shall not make you any graven image, or any likeness of any thing that is in the heavens above, or that is in the earth beneath, or that is in the waters beneath the earth:

9 you shall not bow down yourself unto them, nor serve them: for I the Becoming-One your God am a jealous GOD, visiting the iniquity of the fathers upon the children unto the third and fourth generation of them that hate me,

10 And showing mercy unto thousands of them that love me and keep my commandments.

11 you shall not take the name of the Becoming-One your God for falsehood for the Becoming-One will not hold him guiltless that takes his name for falsehood.

12 Keep the Sabbath day to sanctify it, as the Becoming-One your God has commanded you.

13 Six days you shall labor, and do all your work:

14 But the seventh day is the Sabbath of the Becoming-One your God: in it you shall not do any work, you, nor your son, nor your daughter, nor your manservant, nor your maidservant, nor your ox, nor your donkey, nor any of your cattle, nor your stranger that is within your gates; that your manservant and your maidservant may rest as well as you.

15 And remember that you were a servant in the land of Egypt, and that the Becoming-One your God brought you out there through a mighty hand and by a stretched out arm: therefore the Becoming-One your God commanded you to keep the Sabbath day.

16 Honor your father and your mother, as the Becoming-One your God has commanded you; that your days may be prolonged, and that it may go well with you, in the land which the Becoming-One your God gives you.

17 you shall not kill.

18 Neither shall you commit adultery.

19 Neither shall you steal.

20 Neither shall you bear false witness against your neighbor.

21 Neither shall you desire your neighbor's wife, neither shall you covet your neighbor's house, his field, or his manservant, or his maidservant, his ox, or his donkey, or any thing that is your neighbor's.

22 These words the Becoming-One spoke unto all your assembly in the mount out of the midst of the fire, of the cloud, and of the thick darkness, with a great voice: and he added no more. And he wrote them in two tables of stone, and delivered them unto me.

23 And it came to pass, when you heard the voice out of the midst of the darkness, for the mountain did burn with fire, that you came near unto me, even all the heads of your tribes, and your elders;

24 And you said, Behold, the Becoming-One our God has showed us his glory and his greatness, and we have heard his voice out of the midst of the fire: we have seen this day that God does talk with man, and he lives.

25 Now therefore why should we die? for this great fire will consume us: if we hear the voice of the Becoming-One our God any more, then we shall die.

26 For who is there of all flesh, that has heard the voice of the living God speaking out of the midst of the fire, as we have, and lived?

27 Go you near, and hear all that the Becoming-One our God shall say: and speak you unto us all that the Becoming-One our God shall speak unto you; and we will hear it, and do it.

28 And the Becoming-One heard the voice of your words, when you spoke unto me; and the Becoming-One said unto me, I have heard the voice of the words of this people, which they have spoken unto you: they have well said all that they have spoken.

29 O that there were such a heart in them, that they would fear me, and keep all my commandments all days, that it might be well with them, and with their children for olam.

30 Go say to them, Get you into your tents again.

31 But as for you, stand you here by me, and I will speak unto you all the commandments, and the statutes, and the judgments, which you shall teach them, that they may do them in the land which I give them to possess it.

32 you shall observe to do therefore as the Becoming-One your God has commanded you: you shall not turn aside to the right hand or to the left.

33 you shall walk in all the ways which the Becoming-One your God has commanded you, that you may live, and that it may be well with you, and that you may prolong your days in the land which you shall possess.

Deu 6:1 Now these are the commandments, the statutes, and the judgments, which the Becoming-One your God commanded to teach you, that you might do them in the land to which you go to possess it:

2 That you might fear the Becoming-One your God, to keep all his statutes and his commandments, which I command you, you, and your son, and your son's son, all the days of your life; and that your days may be prolonged.

3 Hear therefore, O Israel, and observe to do it; that it may be well with you, and that you may increase mightily, as the Becoming-One, God of your fathers has promised you, in the land that flows with milk and honey.

4 Hear, O Israel: The Becoming-One our God, the Becoming-One [is] one:

5 And you shall love the Becoming-One your God with all your heart, and with all your soul, and with all your might.

6 And these words, which I command you this day, shall be in your heart:

7 And you shall teach them diligently unto your children, and shall talk of them when you sit in your house, and when you walk by the way, and when you lie down, and when you rise up.

8 And you shall bind them for a sign upon your hand, and they shall be as frontlets between your eyes.

9 And you shall write them upon the posts of your house, and on your gates.

10 And it shall be, when the Becoming-One your God shall have brought you into the land which he swore unto your fathers, to Abraham, to Isaac, and to Jacob, to give you great and goodly cities, which you built not,

11 And houses full of all good things, which you filled not, and wells dug, which you dug not, vineyards and olive trees, which you planted not; when you shall have eaten and be full;

12 Then beware lest you forget the Becoming-One, which brought you forth out of the land of Egypt, from the house of bondage.

13 you shall fear the Becoming-One your God, and serve him, and shall swear by his name.

14 you shall not go after other gods, of the gods of the people which are round about you;

15 For the Becoming-One your God is a jealous GOD among you lest the anger of the Becoming-One your God be kindled against you, and destroy you from off the face of the earth.

16 you shall not tempt the Becoming-One your God, as you tempted him in Massah.

17 you shall diligently keep the commandments of the Becoming-One your God, and his testimonies, and his statutes, which he has commanded you.

18 And you shall do that which is right and good in the sight of the Becoming-One: that it may be well with you, and that you may go in and possess the good land which the Becoming-One swore unto your fathers,

19 To cast out all your enemies from before you, as the Becoming-One has spoken.

20 And when your son asks you in time to come, saying, What is the meaning of the testimonies, and the statutes, and the judgments, which the Becoming-One our God has commanded you?

21 Then you shall say unto your son, We were Pharaoh's bondmen in Egypt; and the Becoming-One brought us out of Egypt with a mighty hand:

22 And the Becoming-One showed signs and wonders, great and sore, upon Egypt, upon Pharaoh, and upon all his household, before our eyes:

23 And he brought us out from there, that he might bring us in, to give us the land which he swore unto our fathers.

24 And the Becoming-One commanded us to do all these statutes, to fear the Becoming-One our God, for our good all days, that he might preserve us alive, as it is at this day.

25 And it shall be our righteousness, if we observe to do all these commandments before the Becoming-One our God, as he has commanded us.

Deu 7:1 When the Becoming-One your God shall bring you into the land to which you go to possess it, and has cast out many nations before you, the Hittites, and the Girgashites, and the Amorites, and the Canaanites, and the Perizzites, and the Hivites, and the Jebusites, seven nations greater and mightier than you;

2 And when the Becoming-One your God shall deliver them before you; you shall smite them, and utterly destroy them; you shall make no covenant with them, nor show mercy unto them:

3 Neither shall you make marriages with them; your daughter you shall not give unto his son, nor his daughter shall you take unto your son.

4 For they will turn away your son from following me, that they may serve other gods: so will the anger of the Becoming-One be kindled against you, and destroy you suddenly.

5 But thus shall you deal with them; you shall destroy their altars, and break down their images, and cut down Asherahs, and burn their graven images with fire.

6 For you are a holy people unto the Becoming-One your God: the Becoming-One your God has chosen you to be a nation of treasure unto himself, above all people that are upon the face of the earth.

7 The Becoming-One did not set his love upon you, nor choose you, because you were more in number than any people; for you were the fewest of all people:

8 But because the Becoming-One loved you, and because he would keep the oath which he had sworn unto your fathers, has the Becoming-One brought you out with a mighty hand, and redeemed you out of the house of bondmen, from the hand of Pharaoh king of Egypt.

9 Know therefore that the Becoming-One your God, he is God, the faithful GOD, which keeps covenant and mercy with them that love him and keep his commandments to a thousand generations;

10 And repays them that hate him to their face, to destroy them: he will not be slack to him that hates him, he will repay him to his face.

11 you shall therefore keep the commandments, and the statutes, and the judgments, which I command you this day, to do them.

12 Therefore it shall come to pass, if you listen to these judgments, and keep, and do them, that the Becoming-One your God shall keep unto you the covenant and the mercy which he swore unto your fathers:

13 And he will love you, and bless you, and multiply you: he will also bless the fruit of your womb, and the fruit of your land, your grain, and your wine, and your oil, the increase of your herd, and the flocks of your sheep, in the land which he swore unto your fathers to give you.

14 you shall be blessed above all people: there shall not be male or female barren among you, or among your cattle.

15 And the Becoming-One will take away from you all sickness, and will put none of the evil diseases of Egypt, which you know, upon you; but will lay them upon all them that hate you.

16 And you shall consume all the people which the Becoming-One your God shall deliver you; your eye shall have no pity upon them: neither shall you serve their gods; for that will be a snare unto you.

17 If you shall say in your heart, These nations are more than I; how can I dispossess them?

18 you shall not be afraid of them: but shall well remember what the Becoming-One your God did unto Pharaoh, and unto all Egypt;

19 The great temptations which your eyes saw, and the signs, and the wonders, and the mighty hand, and the stretched out arm, whereby the Becoming-One your God brought you out: so shall the Becoming-One your God do unto all the people of whom you are afraid.

20 Moreover the Becoming-One your God will send the hornet among them, until they that are left, and hide themselves from you, be destroyed.

21 you shall not be affrighted at them: for the Becoming-One your God is among you, a mighty GOD and terrible.

22 And the Becoming-One your God will put out those nations before you by little and little: you may not consume them at once, lest the beasts of the field increase upon you.

23 But the Becoming-One your God shall deliver them unto you, and shall destroy them with a mighty destruction, until they be destroyed.

24 And he shall deliver their kings into your hand, and you shall destroy their name from under the heavens: there shall no man be able to stand before you, until you have destroyed them.

25 The graven images of their gods shall you burn with fire: you shall not desire the silver or gold that is on them, nor take it unto you, lest you be snared therein: for it is an abomination to the Becoming-One your God.

26 Neither shall you bring an abomination into your house, lest you be a cursed thing like it: but you shall utterly detest it, and you shall utterly abhor it; for it is a cursed thing.

Deu 8:1 All the commandments which I command you this day shall you observe to do, that you may live, and multiply, and go in and possess the land which the Becoming-One swore unto your fathers.

2 And you shall remember all the way which the Becoming-One your God led you these forty years in the wilderness, to humble you, and to prove you, to know what was in your heart, whether you would keep his commandments, or not.

3 And he humbled you, and permitted you to hunger, and fed you with manna, which you knew not, neither did your fathers know; that he might make you know that man does not live by bread only, but by every word that proceeds out of the mouth of the Becoming-One does man live.

4 your raiment grew not old upon you, neither did your foot swell, these forty years.

5 you shall also consider in your heart, that, as a man chastens his son, so the Becoming-One your God chastens you.

6 Therefore you shall keep the commandments of the Becoming-One your God, to walk in his ways, and to fear him.

7 For the Becoming-One your God brings you into a good land, a land of brooks of water, of fountains and depths that spring out of valleys and hills;

8 A land of wheat, and barley, and vines, and fig trees, and pomegranates; a land of oil olive, and honey;

9 A land wherein you shall eat bread without scarceness, you shall not lack any thing in it; a land whose stones are iron, and out of whose hills you may dig brass.

10 When you have eaten and are full, then you shall bless the Becoming-One your God for the good land which he has given you.

11 Beware that you forget not the Becoming-One your God, in not keeping his commandments, and his judgments, and his statutes, which I command you this day:

12 Lest when you have eaten and are full, and have built goodly houses, and dwelt therein;

13 And when your herds and your flocks multiply, and your silver and your gold is multiplied, and all that you have is multiplied;

14 Then your heart be lifted up, and you forget the Becoming-One your God, which brought you forth out of the land of Egypt, from the house of bondage;

15 Who led you through that great and terrible wilderness, wherein were fiery serpents, and scorpions, and drought, where there was no water; who brought you forth water out of the rock of flint;

16 Who fed you in the wilderness with manna, which your fathers knew not, that he might humble you, and that he might prove you, to do you good at your latter end;

17 And you say in your heart, My power and the might of mine hand has gotten me this wealth.

18 But you shall remember the Becoming-One your God: for it is he that gives you power to get wealth, that he may establish his covenant which he swore unto your fathers, as it is this day.

19 And it shall be, if you do at all forget the Becoming-One your God, and walk after other gods, and serve them, and worship them, I testify against you this day that you shall surely perish.

20 As the nations which the Becoming-One destroys before your face, so shall you perish; because you would not be obedient unto the voice of the Becoming-One your God.

Deu 9:1 Hear, O Israel: you are to pass over Jordan this day, to go in to possess nations greater and mightier than thyself, cities great and fenced up to the heavens,

2 A people great and tall, the children of the Anakims, whom you know, and of whom you have heard say, Who can stand before the children of Anak!

3 Understand therefore this day, that the Becoming-One your God is he which goes over before you; as a consuming fire he shall destroy them, and he shall bring them down before your face: so shall you drive them out, and destroy them quickly, as the Becoming-One has said unto you.

4 Speak not you in your heart, after that the Becoming-One your God has cast them out from before you, saying, For my righteousness the Becoming-One has brought me in to possess this land: but for the wickedness of these nations the Becoming-One does drive them out from before you.

5 Not for your righteousness, or for the uprightness of your heart, do you go to possess their land: but for the wickedness of these nations the Becoming-One your God does drive them out from before you, and that he may perform the word which the Becoming-One swore unto your fathers, Abraham, Isaac, and Jacob.

6 Understand therefore, that the Becoming-One your God gives you not this good land to possess it for your righteousness; for you are a stiffnecked people.

7 Remember, and forget not, how you provoked the Becoming-One your God to wrath in the wilderness: from the day that you did depart out of the land of Egypt, until you came unto this place, you have been rebellious against the Becoming-One.

8 Also in Horeb you provoked the Becoming-One to wrath, so that the Becoming-One was angry with you to have destroyed you.

9 When I was gone up into the mount to receive the tables of stone, even the tables of the covenant which the Becoming-One made with you, then I abode in the mount forty days and forty nights, I neither did eat bread nor drink water:

10 And the Becoming-One delivered unto me two tables of stone written with the finger of God; and on them was written according to all the words, which the Becoming-One spoke with you in the mount out of the midst of the fire in the day of the assembly.

11 And it came to pass at the end of forty days and forty nights, that the Becoming-One gave me the two tables of stone, even the tables of the covenant.

12 And the Becoming-One said unto me, Arise, get you down quickly from hence; for your people which you have brought forth out of Egypt have corrupted themselves; they are quickly turned aside out of the way which I commanded them; they have made them a molten image.

13 Furthermore the Becoming-One spoke unto me, saying, I have seen this people, and, behold, it is a stiffnecked people:

14 Let me alone, that I may destroy them, and blot out their name from under the heavens: and I will make of you a nation mightier and greater than they.

15 So I turned and came down from the mount, and the mount burned with fire: and the two tables of the covenant were in my two hands.

16 And I looked, and, behold, you had sinned against the Becoming-One your God, and had made you a molten calf: you had turned aside quickly out of the way which the Becoming-One had commanded you.

17 And I took the two tables, and cast them out of my two hands, and brake them before your eyes.

18 And I fell down before the Becoming-One, as at the first, forty days and forty nights: I did neither eat bread, nor drink water, because of all your sins which you sinned, in doing wickedly in the sight of the Becoming-One, to provoke him to anger.

19 For I was afraid of the anger and hot displeasure, wherewith the Becoming-One was angry against you to destroy you. But the Becoming-One listened unto me at that time also.

20 And the Becoming-One was very angry with Aaron to have destroyed him: and I prayed for Aaron also the same time.

21 And I took your sin, the calf which you had made, and burnt it with fire, and stamped it, and ground it very small, even until it was as small as dust: and I cast the dust thereof into the brook that descended out of the mount.

22 And at Taberah, and at Massah, and at Kibroth-hattaavah, you provoked the Becoming-One to wrath.

23 Likewise when the Becoming-One sent you from Kadesh-barnea, saying, Go up and possess the land which I have given you; then you rebelled against the mouth of the Becoming-One your God, and you believed him not, nor listened to his voice.

24 you have been rebellious against the Becoming-One from the day that I knew you.

25 Thus I fell down before the Becoming-One forty days and forty nights, as I fell down at the first; because the Becoming-One had said he would destroy you.

26 I prayed therefore unto the Becoming-One, and said, O my Lord(s) the Becoming-One, destroy not your people and your inheritance, which you have redeemed through your greatness, which you have brought forth out of Egypt with a mighty hand.

27 Remember your servants, Abraham, Isaac, and Jacob; look not unto the stubbornness of this people, nor to their wickedness, nor to their sin:

28 Lest the land from where you brought us out say, Because the Becoming-One was not able to bring them into the land which he promised them, and because he hated them, he has brought them out to slay them in the wilderness.

29 Yet they are your people and your inheritance, which you brought out by your mighty power and by your stretched out arm.

Deu 10:1 At that time the Becoming-One said unto me, Hew you two tables of stone like unto the first, and come up unto me into the mount, and make you an ark of wood.

2 And I will write on the tables the words that were in the first tables which you broke, and you shall put them in the ark.

3 And I made an ark of shittim wood, and hewed two tables of stone like unto the first, and went up into the mount, having the two tables in mine hand.

4 And he wrote on the tables, according to the first writing, the ten commandments, which the Becoming-One spoke unto you in the mount out of the midst of the fire in the day of the assembly: and the Becoming-One gave them unto me.

5 And I turned myself and came down from the mount, and put the tables in the ark which I had made; and there they be, as the Becoming-One commanded me.

6 And the children of Israel took their journey from Beeroth of the children of Jaakan to Mosera: there Aaron died, and there he was buried; and Eleazar his son ministered in the priest's office in his stead.

7 From there they journeyed unto Gudgodah; and from Gudgodah to Jotbath, a land of rivers of waters.

8 At that time the Becoming-One separated the tribe of Levi, to bear the ark of the covenant of the Becoming-One, to stand before the Becoming-One to minister unto him, and to bless in his name, unto this day.

9 Therefore Levi has no part nor inheritance with his brethren; the Becoming-One is his inheritance, according as the Becoming-One your God promised him.

10 And I stayed in the mount, according to the first time, forty days and forty nights; and the Becoming-One listened unto me at that time also, and the Becoming-One would not destroy you.

11 And the Becoming-One said unto me, Arise, take your journey before the people, that they may go in and possess the land, which I swore unto their fathers to give unto them.

12 And now, Israel, what does the Becoming-One your God require of you, but to fear the Becoming-One your God, to walk in all his ways, and to love him, and to serve the Becoming-One your God with all your heart and with all your soul,

13 To keep the commandments of the Becoming-One, and his statutes, which I command you this day for your good?

14 Behold, the heavens and the heavens of the heavens is for the Becoming-One's your God, the earth also, with all that therein is.

15 Only the Becoming-One had a delight in your fathers to love them, and he chose their seed after them, even you above all people, as it is this day.

16 Circumcise therefore the foreskin of your heart, and be no more stiffnecked.

17 For the Becoming-One your God is God of gods, and lords of lords, the great GOD, the mighty, and the terrible, which regards not persons, nor takes reward:

18 He does execute the judgment of the fatherless and widow, and loves the stranger, in giving him food and raiment.

19 Love you therefore the stranger: for you were strangers in the land of Egypt.

20 you shall fear the Becoming-One your God; him shall you serve, and to him shall you cleave, and swear by his name.

21 He is your praise, and he is your God, that has done for you these great and terrible things, which your eyes have seen.

22 your fathers went down into Egypt with threescore and ten souls; and now the Becoming-One your God has made you as the stars of the heavens for multitude.

Deu 11:1 Therefore you shall love the Becoming-One your God, and keep his charge, and his statutes, and his judgments, and his commandments, all days.

2 And know you this day: for I speak not with your children which have not known, and which have not seen the chastisement of the Becoming-One your God, his greatness, his mighty hand, and his stretched out arm,

3 And his miracles, and his acts, which he did in the midst of Egypt unto Pharaoh the king of Egypt, and unto all his land;

4 And what he did unto the army of Egypt, unto their horses, and to their chariots; how he made the water of the boundary sea to overflow them as they pursued after you, and how the Becoming-One has destroyed them unto this day;

5 And what he did unto you in the wilderness, until you came into this place;

6 And what he did unto Dathan and Abiram, the sons of Eliab, the son of Reuben: how the earth opened her mouth, and swallowed them up, and their households, and their tents, and all the substance that was in their possession, in the midst of all Israel:

7 But your eyes have seen all the great acts of the Becoming-One which he did.

8 Therefore shall you keep all the commandments which I command you this day, that you may be strong, and go in and possess the land, to which you go to possess it;

9 And that you may prolong your days in the land, which the Becoming-One swore unto your fathers to give unto them and to their seed, a land that flows with milk and honey.

10 For the land, to which you go in to possess it, is not as the land of Egypt, from where you came out,

where you sowed your seed, and wateredst it with your foot, as a garden of herbs:

11 But the land, to which you go to possess it, is a land of hills and valleys, and drinks water of the rain of the heavens:

12 A land which the Becoming-One your God cares for: the eyes of the Becoming-One your God are always upon it, from the beginning of the year even unto the end of the year.

13 And it shall come to pass, if you shall listen diligently unto my commandments which I command you this day, to love the Becoming-One your God, and to serve him with all your heart and with all your soul,

14 That I will give you the rain of your land in his due season, the first rain and the latter rain, that you may gather in your grain, and your wine, and your oil.

15 And I will send grass in your fields for your cattle, that you may eat and be full.

16 Take heed to yourselves, that your heart be not deceived, and you turn aside, and serve other gods, and worship them;

17 And then the Becoming-One's wrath be kindled against you, and he shut up the heavens, that there be no rain, and that the land yield not her fruit; and lest you perish quickly from off the good land which the Becoming-One gives you.

18 Therefore shall you lay up these my words in your heart and in your soul, and bind them for a sign upon your hand, that they may be as frontlets between your eyes.

19 And you shall teach them your children, speaking of them when you sit in your house, and when you walk by the way, when you lie down, and when you rise up.

20 And you shall write them upon the door posts of your house, and upon your gates:

21 That your days may be multiplied, and the days of your children, in the land which the Becoming-One swore unto your fathers to give them, as the days of the heavens upon the earth.

22 For if you shall diligently keep all these commandments which I command you, to do them, to love the Becoming-One your God, to walk in all his ways, and to cleave unto him;

23 Then will the Becoming-One drive out all these nations from before you, and you shall possess greater nations and mightier than yourselves.

24 Every place whereon the soles of your feet shall tread shall be yours: from the wilderness and Lebanon, from the river, the river Euphrates, even unto the uttermost sea shall your coast be.

25 There shall no man be able to stand before you: for the Becoming-One your God shall lay the fear of you and the dread of you upon all the land that you shall tread upon, as he has said unto you.

26 Behold, I set before you this day a blessing and a curse;

27 A blessing, if you obey the commandments of the Becoming-One your God, which I command you this day:

28 And a curse, if you will not obey the commandments of the Becoming-One your God, but turn aside out of the way which I command you this day, to go after other gods, which you have not known.

29 And it shall come to pass, when the Becoming-One your God has brought you in unto the land to which you go to possess it, that you shall put the blessing upon mount Gerizim, and the curse upon mount Ebal.

30 Are they not beyond Jordan, by the way where the sun goes down, in the land of the Canaanites, which dwell in the champaign over against Gilgal, beside the plains of Moreh?

31 For you shall pass over Jordan to go in to possess the land which the Becoming-One your God gives you, and you shall possess it, and dwell therein.

32 And you shall observe to do all the statutes and judgments which I set before you this day.

Deu 12:1 These are the statutes and judgments, which you shall observe to do in the land, which the Becoming-One, God of your fathers gives you to possess it, all the days that you live upon the earth.

2 you shall utterly destroy all the places, wherein the nations which you shall possess served their gods, upon the high mountains, and upon the hills, and under every green tree:

3 And you shall overthrow their altars, and break their pillars, and burn Asherahs with fire; and you shall hew down the graven images of their gods, and destroy the names of them out of that place.

4 you shall not do so unto the Becoming-One your God.

5 But unto the place which the Becoming-One your God shall choose out of all your tribes to put his name there, even unto his habitation shall you seek, and there you shall come:

6 And there you shall bring your burnt offerings, and your sacrifices, and your tithes, and heave offerings of your hand, and your vows, and your freewill offerings, and the firstlings of your herds and of your flocks:

7 And there you shall eat before the Becoming-One your God, and you shall rejoice in all that you put your hand unto, you and your households, wherein the Becoming-One your God has blessed you.

8 you shall not do after all the things that we do here this day, every man whatsoever is right in his own eyes.

9 For you are not as yet come to the rest and to the inheritance, which the Becoming-One your God gives you.

10 But when you go over Jordan, and dwell in the land which the Becoming-One your God gives you to inherit, and when he gives you rest from all your enemies round about, so that you dwell in safety;

11 Then there shall be a place which the Becoming-One your God shall choose to cause his name to dwell there; there shall you bring all that I command you; your burnt offerings, and your sacrifices, your tithes, and the heave offering of your hand, and all your choice vows which you vow unto the Becoming-One: 12 And you shall rejoice before the Becoming-One your God, ye, and your sons, and your daughters, and your menservants, and your maidservants, and the Levite that is within your gates; forasmuch as he has no part nor inheritance with you.

13 Take heed to yourself that you offer not your burnt offerings in every place that you see:

14 But in the place which the Becoming-One shall choose in one of your tribes, there you shall offer your

burnt offerings, and there you shall do all that I command you.

15 Notwithstanding you may kill and eat flesh in all your gates, whatsoever your soul lusts after, according to the blessing of the Becoming-One your God which he has given you: the unclean and the clean may eat thereof, as of the roebuck, and as of the hart.

16 Only you shall not eat the blood; you shall pour it upon the earth as water.

17 you may not eat within your gates the tithe of your grain, or of your wine, or of your oil, or the firstlings of your herds or of your flock, nor any of your vows which you vowed, nor your freewill offerings, or heave offering of your hand:

18 But you must eat them before the Becoming-One your God in the place which the Becoming-One your God shall choose, you, and your son, and your daughter, and your manservant, and your maidservant, and the Levite that is within your gates: and you shall rejoice before the Becoming-One your God in all that you put your hands unto.

19 Take heed to yourself that you forsake not the Levite as long as you live upon the earth.

20 When the Becoming-One your God shall enlarge your border, as he has promised you, and you shall say, I will eat flesh, because your soul longs to eat flesh; you may eat flesh, whatsoever your soul lusts after.

21 If the place which the Becoming-One your God has chosen to put his name there be too far from you, then you shall kill of your herd and of your flock, which the Becoming-One has given you, as I have commanded you, and you shall eat in your gates whatsoever your soul lusts after.

22 Even as the roebuck and the hart is eaten, so you shall eat them: the unclean and the clean shall eat of them alike.

23 Only be sure that you eat not the blood: for the blood is the soul; and you may not eat the soul with the flesh.

24 you shall not eat it; you shall pour it upon the earth as water.

25 you shall not eat it; that it may go well with you, and with your children after you, when you shall do that which is right in the sight of the Becoming-One.

26 Only your holy things which you hast, and your vows, you shall take, and go unto the place which the Becoming-One shall choose.

27 And you shall offer your burnt offerings, the flesh and the blood, upon the altar of the Becoming-One your God: and the blood of your sacrifices shall be poured out upon the altar of the Becoming-One your God, and you shall eat the flesh.

28 Observe and hear all these words which I command you, that it may go well with you, and with your children after you for olam, when you do that which is good and right in the sight of the Becoming-One your God.

29 When the Becoming-One your God shall cut off the nations from before you, to which you go to possess them, and you succeed them, and dwell in their land;

30 Take heed to yourself that you be not snared by following them, after that they be destroyed from before you; and that you inquire not after their gods, saying, How did these nations serve their gods? even so will I do likewise.

31 you shall not do so unto the Becoming-One your God: for every abomination to the Becoming-One, which he hates, have they done unto their gods; for even their sons and their daughters they have burnt in the fire to their gods.

32 What thing soever I command you, observe to do it: you shall not add thereto, nor diminish from it.

Deu 13:1 If there arise among you a prophet, or a dreamer of dreams, and gives you a sign or a wonder,

2 And the sign or the wonder come to pass, whereof he spoke unto you, saying, Let us go after other gods, which you have not known, and let us serve them;

3 you shall not listen unto the words of that prophet, or that dreamer of dreams: for the Becoming-One your God proves you, to know whether you love the Becoming-One your God with all your heart and with all your soul.

4 you shall walk after the Becoming-One your God, and fear him, and keep his commandments, and obey his voice, and you shall serve him, and cleave unto him.

5 And that prophet, or that dreamer of dreams, shall be put to death; because he has spoken to turn you away from the Becoming-One your God, which brought you out of the land of Egypt, and redeemed you out of the house of bondage, to thrust you out of the way which the Becoming-One your God commanded you to walk in. So shall you put the evil away from the midst of you.

6 If your brother, the son of your mother, or your son, or your daughter, or the wife of your bosom, or your friend, which is as your own soul, entice you secretly, saying, Let us go and serve other gods, which you have not known, you, nor your fathers;

7 Namely, of the gods of the people which are round about you, near unto you, or far off from you, from the one end of the earth even unto the other end of the earth;

8 you shall not consent unto him, nor listen unto him; neither shall your eye pity him, neither shall you spare, neither shall you conceal him:

9 But you shall surely kill him; your hand shall be first upon him to put him to death, and afterwards the hand of all the people.

10 And you shall stone him with stones, that he die; because he has sought to thrust you away from the Becoming-One your God, which brought you out of the land of Egypt, from the house of bondage.

11 And all Israel shall hear, and fear, and shall do no more any such wickedness as this is among you.

12 If you shall hear say in one of your cities, which the Becoming-One your God has given you to dwell there, saying,

13 Certain men, the children of Belial, are gone out from among you, and have withdrawn the inhabitants of their city, saying, Let us go and serve other gods, which you have not known;

14 Then shall you inquire, and make search, and ask diligently; and, behold, if it be truth, and the thing certain, that such abomination is worked among you;

15 you shall surely smite the inhabitants of that city with the edge of the sword, destroying it utterly,

and all that is therein, and the cattle thereof, with the edge of the sword.

16 And you shall gather all the spoil of it into the midst of the street thereof, and shall burn with fire the city, and all the spoil thereof every bit, for the Becoming-One your God: and it shall be a heap for olam, it shall not be built again.

17 And there shall cleave nothing of the cursed thing to your hand: that the Becoming-One may turn from the fierceness of his anger, and show you mercy, and have compassion upon you, and multiply you, as he has sworn unto your fathers;

18 When you shall listen to the voice of the Becoming-One your God, to keep all his commandments which I command you this day, to do that which is right in the eyes of the Becoming-One your God.

Deu 14:1 you are the children of the Becoming-One your God: you shall not cut yourselves, nor make any baldness between your eyes for the dead.

2 For you are a holy nation unto the Becoming-One your God, and the Becoming-One has chosen you to be a nation of treasure unto himself, above all the nations that are upon the earth.

3 you shall not eat any abominable thing.

4 These are the beasts which you shall eat: the ox, the sheep, and the goat,

5 The hart, and the roebuck, and the fallow deer, and the wild goat, and the pygarg, and the wild ox, and the chamois.

6 And every beast that parts the hoof, and cleaves the cleft into two claws, and chews the cud among the beasts, that you shall eat.

7 Nevertheless these you shall not eat of them that chew the cud, or of them that divide the cloven hoof; as the camel, and the rabbit, and the coney: for they chew the cud, but divide not the hoof; therefore they are unclean unto you.

8 And the swine, because it divides the hoof, yet chews not the cud, it is unclean unto you: you shall not eat of their flesh, nor touch their dead carcase.

9 These you shall eat of all that are in the waters: all that have fins and scales shall you eat:

10 And whatsoever has not fins and scales you may not eat; it is unclean unto you.

11 Of all clean birds you shall eat.

12 But these are they of which you shall not eat: the eagle, and the ossifrage, and the osprey,

13 And the glede, and the kite, and the vulture after his kind,

14 And every raven after his kind,

15 And the owl, and the night hawk, and the sea gull, and the hawk after his kind,

16 The little owl, and the great owl, and the swan,

17 And the pelican, and the gier eagle, and the cormorant,

18 And the stork, and the heron after her kind, and the lapwing, and the bat.

19 And every creeping thing that flies is unclean unto you: they shall not be eaten.

20 But of all clean fowls you may eat.

21 you shall not eat of anything that dies of itself: you shall give it unto the stranger that is in your gates, that he may eat it; or you may sell it unto an alien: for you are a holy people unto the Becoming-One your God. you shall not seethe a kid in his mother's milk.

22 you shall truly tithe all the increase of your seed, that the field brings forth year by year.

23 And you shall eat before the Becoming-One your God, in the place which he shall choose to place his name there, the tithe of your grain, of your wine, and of your oil, and the firstlings of your herds and of your flocks; that you may learn to fear the Becoming-One your God all days.

24 And if the way be too long for you, so that you are not able to carry it; or if the place be too far from you, which the Becoming-One your God shall choose to set his name there, when the Becoming-One your God has blessed you:

25 Then shall you turn it into money, and bind up the money in your hand, and shall go unto the place which the Becoming-One your God shall choose:

26 And you shall bestow that money for whatsoever your soul lusts after, for oxen, or for sheep, or for wine, or for strong drink, or for whatsoever your soul desires: and you shall eat there before the Becoming-One your God, and you shall rejoice, you, and your household,

27 And the Levite that is within your gates; you shall not forsake him; for he has no part nor inheritance with you.

28 At the end of three years you shall bring forth all the tithe of your increase the same year, and shall lay it up within your gates:

29 And the Levite, because he has no part nor inheritance with you, and the stranger, and the fatherless, and the widow, which are within your gates, shall come, and shall eat and be satisfied; that the Becoming-One your God may bless you in all the work of your hand which you do.

Deu 15:1 At the end of every seven years you shall make a release.

Deu 15:1 At the end of every seven years you shall make a release.

2 And this is the manner of the release: Every creditor that lends anything unto his neighbor shall release it; he shall not exact it of his neighbor, or of his brother; because it is called the Becoming-One's release.

3 Of a foreigner you may exact it again: but that which is your with your brother your hand shall release;

4 Save when there shall be no poor among you; for the Becoming-One shall greatly bless you in the land which the Becoming-One your God gives you for an inheritance to possess it:

5 Only if you carefully listen unto the voice of the Becoming-One your God, to observe to do all these commandments which I command you this day.

6 For the Becoming-One your God blesses you, as he promised you: and you shall lend unto many nations, but you shall not borrow; and you shall reign over many nations, but they shall not reign over you.

7 If there be among you a poor man of one of your brethren within any of your gates in your land which the Becoming-One your God gives you, you shall not harden your heart, nor shut your hand from your poor brother:

8 But you shall open your hand wide unto him, and shall surely lend him sufficient for his need, in that which he lacks.

9 Beware that there be not a thought in your wicked heart, saying, The seventh year, the year of release, is at hand; and your eye be evil against your poor brother, and you give him nothing; and he cry unto the Becoming-One against you, and it be sin unto you.

10 you shall surely give him, and your heart shall not be grieved when you give unto him: because that for this thing the Becoming-One your God shall bless you in all your works, and in all that you put your hand unto.

11 For the poor shall never cease out of the land: therefore I command you, saying, you shall open your hand wide unto your brother, to your poor, and to your needy, in your land.

12 And if your brother, a Hebrew man, or a Hebrew woman, be sold unto you, and serve you six years; then in the seventh year you shall let him go free from you.

13 And when you send him out free from you, you shall not let him go away empty:

14 you shall furnish him liberally out of your flock, and out of your floor, and out of your winepress: of that wherewith the Becoming-One your God has blessed you you shall give unto him.

15 And you shall remember that you were a servant in the land of Egypt, and the Becoming-One your God redeemed you: therefore I command you this thing today.

16 And it shall be, if he say unto you, I will not go away from you; because he loves you and your house, because he is well with you;

17 Then you shall take an awl, and thrust it through his ear unto the door, and he shall be your servant for olam. And also unto your maidservant you shall do likewise.

18 It shall not seem hard unto you, when you send him away free from you; for he has been worth a double hired servant to you, in serving you six years: and the Becoming-One your God shall bless you in all that you do.

19 All the firstling males that come of your herd and of your flock you shall sanctify unto the Becoming-One your God: you shall do no work with the firstling of your bullock, nor shear the firstling of your sheep.

20 you shall eat it before the Becoming-One your God year by year in the place which the Becoming-One shall choose, you and your household.

21 And if there be any blemish therein, as if it be lame, or blind, or have any ill blemish, you shall not sacrifice it unto the Becoming-One your God.

22 you shall eat it within your gates: the unclean and the clean person shall eat it alike, as the roebuck, and as the hart.

23 Only you shall not eat the blood thereof; you shall pour it upon the ground as water.

Deu 16:1 Observe the new moon[97] of young [barley] ears [Abib], and keep the Passover unto the Becoming-One your God: for in the moon of young [barley] ears [Abib] the Becoming-One your God brought you forth out of Egypt by night.

2 you shall therefore sacrifice the Passover unto the Becoming-One your God, of the flock and the herd, in the place which the Becoming-One shall choose to place his name there.

3 you shall eat no leavened bread with it; seven days shall you eat unleavened bread therewith, even the bread of affliction: for you came forth out of the land of Egypt in haste: that you may remember the day when you came forth out of the land of Egypt all the days of your life.

4 And there shall be no leavened bread seen with you in all your coast seven days; neither shall there remain any thing of the flesh, which you sacrificed the first day at evening, into the morning.

5 you may not sacrifice the Passover within any of your gates, which the Becoming-One your God gives you:

6 But at the place which the Becoming-One your God shall choose to place his name in, there you shall sacrifice the Passover at evening, at the going down of the sun, at the set time[98] that you came forth out of Egypt.

7 And you shall roast and eat it in the place which the Becoming-One your God shall choose: and you shall turn in the morning, and go unto your tents.

8 Six days you shall eat unleavened bread: and on the seventh day shall be a solemn assembly to the Becoming-One your God: you shall do no work therein.

9 Seven weeks shall you number unto you: begin to number the seven weeks from such time as you begin to put the sickle to the standing grain.

10 And you shall keep the feast of weeks unto the Becoming-One your God with a tribute of a freewill offering of your hand, which you shall give unto the Becoming-One your God, according as the Becoming-One your God has blessed you:

11 And you shall rejoice before the Becoming-One your God, you, and your son, and your daughter, and your manservant, and your maidservant, and the Levite that is within your gates, and the stranger, and the fatherless, and the widow, that are among you, in the place which the Becoming-One your God has chosen to place his name there.

12 And you shall remember that you were a servant in Egypt: and you shall observe and do these statutes.

13 you shall observe the feast of tabernacles seven days, after that you have gathered in your grain and your wine:

14 And you shall rejoice in your feast, you, and your son, and your daughter, and your manservant, and your maidservant, and the Levite, the stranger, and the fatherless, and the widow, that are within your gates.

15 Seven days shall you keep a solemn feast unto the Becoming-One your God in the place which the Becoming-One shall choose: because the Becoming-One your God shall bless you in all your increase, and

---

[97] Moon or month

[98] Appointed time or festival

in all the works of your hands, therefore you shall surely rejoice.

16 Three times in a year shall all your males appear before the Becoming-One your God in the place which he shall choose; in the feast of unleavened bread, and in the feast of weeks, and in the feast of tabernacles: and they shall not appear before the Becoming-One empty:

17 Every man shall give as he is able, according to the blessing of the Becoming-One your God which he has given you.

18 Judges and officers shall you make you in all your gates, which the Becoming-One your God gives you, throughout your tribes: and they shall judge the people with just judgment.

19 you shall not wrest judgment; you shall not respect persons, neither take a gift: for a gift does blind the eyes of the wise, and pervert the words of the righteous.

20 That which is altogether just shall you follow, that you may live, and inherit the land which the Becoming-One your God gives you.

21 you shall not plant you a Asherah, or any wooden image near unto the altar of the Becoming-One your God, which you shall make you.

22 Neither shall you set you up any image; which the Becoming-One your God hates.

Deu 17:1 you shall not sacrifice unto the Becoming-One your God any bullock, or sheep, wherein is blemish, or any evil flaw: for that is an abomination unto the Becoming-One your God.

2 If there be found among you, within any of your gates which the Becoming-One your God gives you, man or woman, that has worked wickedness in the sight of the Becoming-One your God, in transgressing his covenant,

3 And has gone and served other gods, and worshiped them, either the sun, or moon, or any of the host of the heavens, which I have not commanded;

4 And it be told you, and you have heard of it, and inquired diligently, and, behold, it be true, and the thing certain, that such abomination is worked in Israel:

5 Then shall you bring forth that man or that woman, which have committed that wicked thing, unto your gates, even that man or that woman, and shall stone them with stones, till they die.

6 At the mouth of two witnesses, or three witnesses, shall he that is worthy of death be put to death; but at the mouth of one witness he shall not be put to death.

7 The hands of the witnesses shall be first upon him to put him to death, and afterward the hands of all the people. So you shall put the evil away from among you.

8 If there arise a matter too hard for you in judgment, between blood and blood, between plea and plea, and between stroke and stroke, being matters of controversy within your gates: then shall you arise, and get you up into the place which the Becoming-One your God shall choose;

9 And you shall come unto the priests the Levites, and unto the judge that shall be in those days, and inquire; and they shall show you the sentence of judgment:

10 And you shall do according to the sentence, which they of that place which the Becoming-One shall choose shall show you; and you shall observe to do according to all that they inform you:

11 According to the sentence of the law which they shall teach you, and according to the judgment which they shall tell you, you shall do: you shall not decline from the sentence which they shall show you, to the right hand, nor to the left.

12 And the man that will do presumptuously, and will not listen unto the priest that stands to minister there before the Becoming-One your God, or unto the judge, even that man shall die: and you shall put away the evil from Israel.

13 And all the people shall hear, and fear, and do no more presumptuously.

14 When you are come unto the land which the Becoming-One your God gives you, and shall possess it, and shall dwell therein, and shall say, I will set a king over me, like as all the nations that are about me;

15 you shall in any way set him king over you, whom the Becoming-One your God shall choose: one from among your brethren shall you set king over you: you may not set a stranger over you, which is not your brother.

16 But he shall not multiply horses to himself, nor cause the people to return to Egypt, to the end that he should multiply horses: forasmuch as the Becoming-One has said unto you, you shall henceforth return no more that way.

17 Neither shall he multiply wives to himself, that his heart turn not away: neither shall he greatly multiply to himself silver and gold.

18 And it shall be, when he sits upon the throne of his kingdom, that he shall write him a copy of this law in a book out of that which is before the priests the Levites:

19 And it shall be with him, and he shall read therein all the days of his life: that he may learn to fear the Becoming-One his God, to keep all the words of this law and these statutes, to do them:

20 That his heart be not lifted up above his brethren, and that he turn not aside from the commandment, to the right hand, or to the left: to the end that he may prolong his days in his kingdom, he, and his children, in the midst of Israel.

Deu 18:1 The priests the Levites, and all the tribe of Levi, shall have no part nor inheritance with Israel: they shall eat the offerings of the Becoming-One made by fire, and his inheritance.

2 Therefore shall they have no inheritance among their brethren: the Becoming-One is their inheritance, as he has said unto them.

3 And this shall be the priest's due from the people, from them that offer a sacrifice, whether it be ox or sheep; and they shall give unto the priest the shoulder, and the two cheeks, and the maw.

4 The beginning also of your grain, of your wine, and of your oil, and the first of the fleece of your sheep, shall you give him.

5 For the Becoming-One your God has chosen him out of all your tribes, to stand to minister in the name of the Becoming-One, him and his sons all days.

6 And if a Levite come from any of your gates out of all Israel, where he sojourned, and come with all the

desire of his soul unto the place which the Becoming-One shall choose;

7 Then he shall minister in the name of the Becoming-One his God, as all his brethren the Levites do, which stand there before the Becoming-One.

8 They shall have like portions to eat, beside that which comes of the sale of his patrimony.

9 When you are come into the land which the Becoming-One your God gives you, you shall not learn to do after the abominations of those nations.

10 There shall not be found among you any one that makes his son or his daughter to pass through the fire, or that uses divination, or a soothsayer, or an enchanter, or a witch,

11 Or a charmer, or a consulter with mediums, or a fortune-teller, or a necromancer [inquiring of the dead]

12 For all that do these things are an abomination unto the Becoming-One: and because of these abominations the Becoming-One your God does drive them out from before you.

13 you shall be perfect with the Becoming-One your God.

14 For these nations, which you shall possess, listened unto observers of times, and unto diviners: but as for you, the Becoming-One your God has not permitted you so to do.

15 The Becoming-One your God will raise up unto you a Prophet from the midst of you, of your brethren, like unto me; unto him you shall listen;

16 According to all that you desired of the Becoming-One your God in Horeb in the day of the assembly, saying, Let me not hear again the voice of the Becoming-One my God, neither let me see this great fire any more, that I die not.

17 And the Becoming-One said unto me, They have well spoken that which they have spoken.

18 I will raise them up a Prophet from among their brethren, like unto you, and will put my words in his mouth; and he shall speak unto them all that I shall command him.

19 And it shall come to pass, that whosoever will not listen unto my words which he shall speak in my name, I will require it of him.

20 But the prophet, which shall presume to speak a word in my name, which I have not commanded him to speak, or that shall speak in the name of other gods, even that prophet shall die.

21 And if you say in your heart, How shall we know the word which the Becoming-One has not spoken?

22 When a prophet speaks in the name of the Becoming-One, if the thing follow not, nor come to pass, that is the thing which the Becoming-One has not spoken, but the prophet has spoken it presumptuously: you shall not be afraid of him.

Deu 19:1 When the Becoming-One your God has cut off the nations, whose land the Becoming-One your God gives you, and you succeed them, and dwell in their cities, and in their houses;

2 you shall separate three cities for you in the midst of your land, which the Becoming-One your God gives you to possess it.

3 you shall prepare you a way, and divide the coasts of your land, which the Becoming-One your God gives you to inherit, into three parts, that every slayer may flee there.

4 And this is the case of the slayer, which shall flee there, that he may live: Whoso kills his neighbor ignorantly, whom he hated not yesterday and the third day;

5 As when a man goes into the wood with his neighbor to hew wood, and his hand fetches a stroke with the ax to cut down the tree, and the head slips from the helve, and lands upon his neighbor, that he die; he shall flee unto one of those cities, and live:

6 Lest the avenger of the blood pursue the slayer, while his heart is hot, and overtake him, because the way is long, and slay his soul; whereas he was not worthy of death, inasmuch as he hated him not yesterday and the third day.

7 Therefore I command you, saying, you shall separate three cities for you.

8 And if the Becoming-One your God enlarge your coast, as he has sworn unto your fathers, and give you all the land which he promised to give unto your fathers;

9 If you shall keep all these commandments to do them, which I command you this day, to love the Becoming-One your God, and to walk all days in his ways; then shall you add three cities more for you, beside these three:

10 That innocent blood be not shed in your land, which the Becoming-One your God gives you for an inheritance, and so blood be upon you.

11 But if any man hate his neighbor, and lie in wait for him, and rise up against him, and smite his soul that he die, and flees into one of these cities:

12 Then the elders of his city shall send and fetch him there, and deliver him into the hand of the avenger of blood, that he may die.

13 your eye shall not pity him, but you shall put away the guilt of innocent blood from Israel, that it may go well with you.

14 you shall not remove your neighbor's landmark, which they of old time have set in your inheritance, which you shall inherit in the land that the Becoming-One your God gives you to possess it.

15 One witness shall not rise up against a man for any iniquity, or for any sin, in any sin that he sins: at the mouth of two witnesses, or at the mouth of three witnesses, shall the matter be established.

16 If a false witness rise up against any man to testify against him that which is wrong;

17 Then both the men, between whom the controversy is, shall stand before the Becoming-One, before the priests and the judges, which shall be in those days;

18 And the judges shall make diligent inquisition: and, behold, if the witness be a false witness, and has testified falsely against his brother;

19 Then shall you do unto him, as he had thought to have done unto his brother: so shall you put the evil away from among you.

20 And those which remain shall hear, and fear, and shall henceforth commit no more any such evil among you.

21 And your eye shall not pity; but soul shall go for soul, eye for eye, tooth for tooth, hand for hand, foot for foot.

Deu 20:1 When you go out to battle against your enemies, and see horses, and chariots, and a people more than you, be not afraid of them: for the Becoming-One your God is with you, which brought you up out of the land of Egypt.

2 And it shall be, when you are come near unto the battle, that the priest shall approach and speak unto the people,

3 And shall say unto them, Hear, O Israel, you approach this day unto battle against your enemies: let not your hearts faint, fear not, and do not tremble, neither be you terrified because of them;

4 For the Becoming-One your God is he that goes with you, to fight for you against your enemies, to save you.

5 And the officers shall speak unto the people, saying, What man is there that has built a new house, and has not dedicated it? let him go and return to his house, lest he die in the battle, and another man dedicate it.

6 And what man is he that has planted a vineyard, and has not yet eaten of it? let him also go and return unto his house, lest he die in the battle, and another man eat of it.

7 And what man is there that has betrothed a wife, and has not taken her? let him go and return unto his house, lest he die in the battle, and another man take her.

8 And the officers shall speak further unto the people, and they shall say, What man is there that is fearful and fainthearted? let him go and return unto his house, lest his brethren's heart faint as well as his heart.

9 And it shall be, when the officers have made an end of speaking unto the people, that they shall make captains of the armies to lead the people.

10 When you come near unto a city to fight against it, then proclaim peace unto it.

11 And it shall be, if it make you answer of peace, and open unto you, then it shall be, that all the people that is found therein shall be tributaries unto you, and they shall serve you.

12 And if it will make no peace with you, but will make war against you, then you shall besiege it:

13 And when the Becoming-One your God has delivered it into your hands, you shall smite every male thereof with the edge of the sword:

14 But the women, and the little ones, and the cattle, and all that is in the city, even all the spoil thereof, shall you take unto thyself; and you shall eat the spoil of your enemies, which the Becoming-One your God has given you.

15 Thus shall you do unto all the cities which are very far off from you, which are not of the cities of these nations.

16 But of the cities of these people, which the Becoming-One your God does give you for an inheritance, you shall save alive nothing that breaths:

17 But you shall utterly destroy them; namely, the Hittites, and the Amorites, the Canaanites, and the Perizzites, the Hivites, and the Jebusites; as the Becoming-One your God has commanded you:

18 That they teach you not to do after all their abominations, which they have done unto their gods; so should you sin against the Becoming-One your God.

19 When you shall besiege a city a long time, in making war against it to take it, you shall not destroy the trees thereof by forcing an ax against them: for you may eat of them, and you shall not cut them down for the tree of the field is man's life to employ them in the siege:

20 Only the trees which you know that they be not trees for food, you shall destroy and cut them down; and you shall build bulwarks against the city that makes war with you, until it be subdued.

Deu 21:1 If one be found slain in the land which the Becoming-One your God gives you to possess it, lying in the field, and it be not known who has slain him:

2 Then your elders and your judges shall come forth, and they shall measure unto the cities which are round about him that is slain:

3 And it shall be, that the city which is next unto the slain man, even the elders of that city shall take a heifer, which has not been worked with, and which has not drawn in the yoke;

4 And the elders of that city shall bring down the heifer unto a rough valley, which is neither eared nor sown, and shall strike off the heifer's neck there in the valley:

5 And the priests the sons of Levi shall come near; for them the Becoming-One your God has chosen to minister unto him, and to bless in the name of the Becoming-One; and by their word shall every controversy and every stroke be tried:

6 And all the elders of that city, that are next unto the slain man, shall wash their hands over the heifer that is beheaded in the valley:

7 And they shall answer and say, Our hands have not shed this blood, neither have our eyes seen it.

8 Be merciful, O Becoming-One, unto your people Israel, whom you have redeemed, and lay not innocent blood unto your people of Israel's charge. And the blood shall be forgiven them.

9 So shall you put away the guilt of innocent blood from among you, when you shall do that which is right in the sight of the Becoming-One.

10 When you go forth to war against your enemies, and the Becoming-One your God has delivered them into your hands, and you have taken them captive,

11 And see among the captives a beautiful woman, and have a desire unto her, that you would have her to your wife;

12 Then you shall bring her home to your house; and she shall shave her head, and pare her nails;

13 And she shall put the raiment of her captivity from off her, and shall remain in your house, and bewail her father and her mother a full month: and after that you shall go in unto her, and be her husband, and she shall be your wife.

14 And it shall be, if you have no delight in her, then you shall let her go to her soul; but you shall not sell her at all for money, you shall not make merchandise of her, because you have humbled her.

15 If a man have two wives, one beloved, and another hated, and they have born him children, both the beloved and the hated; and if the firstborn son be hers that was hated:

16 Then it shall be, in the day he makes his sons to inherit that which he has, that he may not make the son of the beloved firstborn before the son of the hated, which is indeed the firstborn:

17 But he shall acknowledge the son of the hated for the firstborn, by giving him a double portion of all that he hath: for he is the beginning of his strength; the right of the firstborn is his.

18 If a man have a stubborn and rebellious son, which will not obey the voice of his father, or the voice of his mother, and that, when they have chastened him, will not listen unto them:

19 Then shall his father and his mother lay hold on him, and bring him out unto the elders of his city, and unto the gate of his place;

20 And they shall say unto the elders of his city, This our son is stubborn and rebellious, he will not obey our voice; he is a glutton, and a drunkard.

21 And all the men of his city shall stone him with stones, that he die: so shall you put evil away from among you; and all Israel shall hear, and fear.

22 And if a man have committed a sin worthy of death, and he be to be put to death, and you hang him on a tree:

23 His body shall not remain [or pass the might] upon the tree, but you shall bury him that same day; for he that is hanged is accursed of God; that your land be not defiled, which the Becoming-One your God gives you for an inheritance.

Deu 22:1 you shall not see your brother's ox or his sheep go astray, and hide yourself from them: you shall in any case bring them again unto your brother.

2 And if your brother be not near unto you, or if you know him not, then you shall bring it unto your own house, and it shall be with you until your brother seek after it, and you shall restore it to him again.

3 In like manner shall you do with his donkey; and so shall you do with his raiment; and with all lost thing of your brother's, which he has lost, and you have found, shall you do likewise: you may not hide thyself.

4 you shall not see your brother's donkey or his ox fall down by the way, and hide yourself from them: you shall surely help him to lift them up again.

5 The woman shall not wear that which pertains unto a man, neither shall a man put on a woman's garment: for all that do so are abomination unto the Becoming-One your God.

6 If a bird's nest chance to be before you in the way in any tree, or on the ground, whether they be young ones, or eggs, and the dam sitting upon the young, or upon the eggs, you shall not take the dam with the young:

7 But you shall in any way let the dam go, and take the young to you; that it may be well with you, and that you may prolong your days.

8 When you build a new house, then you shall make a battlement for your roof, that you bring not blood upon your house, if any man fall from there.

9 you shall not sow your vineyard with diverse seeds: lest the fruit of your seed which you have sown, and the fruit of your vineyard, be defiled.

10 you shall not plow with an ox and an donkey together.

11 you shall not wear a garment of diverse sorts, as of woollen and linen together.

12 you shall make you fringes upon the four quarters of your vesture, wherewith you cover yourself.

13 If any man take a wife, and go in unto her, and hate her,

14 And give occasions of speech against her, and bring up an evil name upon her, and say, I took this woman, and when I came to her, I found her not a maid:

15 Then shall the father of the damsel, and her mother, take and bring forth the tokens of the damsel's virginity unto the elders of the city in the gate:

16 And the damsel's father shall say unto the elders, I gave my daughter unto this man to wife, and he hates her;

17 And, lo, he has given occasions of speech against her, saying, I found not your daughter a maid; and yet these are the tokens of my daughter's virginity. And they shall spread the cloth before the elders of the city.

18 And the elders of that city shall take that man and chastise him;

19 And they shall amerce him in a hundred shekels of silver, and give them unto the father of the damsel, because he has brought up an evil name upon a virgin of Israel: and she shall be his wife; he may not put her away all his days.

20 But if this thing be true, and the tokens of virginity be not found for the damsel:

21 Then they shall bring out the damsel to the door of her father's house, and the men of her city shall stone her with stones that she die: because she has worked folly in Israel, to play the whore in her father's house: so shall you put evil away from among you.

22 If a man be found lying with a woman married to a husband, then they shall both of them die, both the man that lay with the woman, and the woman: so shall you put away evil from Israel.

23 If a damsel that is a virgin be betrothed unto a husband, and a man find her in the city, and lie with her;

24 Then you shall bring them both out unto the gate of that city, and you shall stone them with stones that they die; the damsel, because she cried not, being in the city; and the man, because he has humbled his neighbor's wife: so you shall put away evil from among you.

25 But if a man find a betrothed damsel in the field, and the man force her, and lie with her: then the man only that lay with her shall die:

26 But unto the damsel you shall do nothing; there is in the damsel no sin worthy of death: for as when a man rises against his neighbor, and slays his soul, even so is this matter:

27 For he found her in the field, and the betrothed damsel cried, and there was none to save her.

28 If a man find a damsel that is a virgin, which is not betrothed, and lay hold on her, and lie with her, and they be found;

29 Then the man that lay with her shall give unto the damsel's father fifty shekels of silver, and she shall

be his wife; because he has humbled her, he may not put her away all his days.

30 A man shall not take his father's wife, nor discover his father's skirt.

Deu 23:1 He that is wounded in the stones, or has his privy member cut off, shall not enter into the congregation of the Becoming-One.

2 A bastard shall not enter into the congregation of the Becoming-One; even to his tenth generation shall he not enter into the congregation of the Becoming-One.

3 An Ammonite or Moabite shall not enter into the congregation of the Becoming-One; even to their tenth generation shall they not enter into the congregation of the Becoming-One for olam.

4 Because they met you not with bread and with water in the way, when you came forth out of Egypt; and because they hired against you Balaam the son of Beor of Pethor of Mesopotamia, to curse you.

5 Nevertheless the Becoming-One your God would not listen unto Balaam; but the Becoming-One your God turned the curse into a blessing unto you, because the Becoming-One your God loved you.

6 you shall not seek their peace nor their prosperity all your days for olam.

7 you shall not abhor an Edomite; for he is your brother: you shall not abhor an Egyptian; because you were a stranger in his land.

8 The children that are begotten of them shall enter into the congregation of the Becoming-One in their third generation.

9 When the host goes forth against your enemies, then keep you from every wicked thing.

10 If there be among you any man, that is not clean by reason of uncleanness that chances him by night, then shall he go abroad out of the camp, he shall not come within the camp:

11 But it shall be, when evening comes on, he shall wash himself with water: and when the sun is down, he shall come into the camp again.

12 you shall have a place also outside the camp, to which you shall go forth abroad:

13 And you shall have a paddle upon your weapon; and it shall be, when you will ease yourself abroad, you shall dig therewith, and shall turn back and cover that which comes from you:

14 For the Becoming-One your God walks in the midst of your camp, to deliver you, and to give up your enemies before you; therefore shall your camp be holy: that he see no unclean thing in you, and turn away from you.

15 you shall not deliver unto his master the servant which is escaped from his master unto you:

16 He shall dwell with you, even among you, in that place which he shall choose in one of your gates, where it likes him best: you shall not oppress him.

17 There shall be no whore of the daughters of Israel, nor a sodomite of the sons of Israel.

18 you shall not bring the hire of a whore, or the price of a dog, into the house of the Becoming-One your God for any vow: for even both these are abomination unto the Becoming-One your God.

19 you shall not lend upon usury to your brother; usury of money, usury of victuals, usury of any thing that is lent upon usury:

20 Unto a stranger you may lend upon usury; but unto your brother you shall not lend upon usury: that the Becoming-One your God may bless you in all that you set your hand to in the land to which you go to possess it.

21 When you shall vow a vow unto the Becoming-One your God, you shall not be slack to pay it: for the Becoming-One your God will surely require it of you; and it would be sin in you.

22 But if you shall forbear to vow, it shall be no sin in you.

23 That which is gone out of your lips you shall keep and perform; even a freewill offering, according as you have vowed unto the Becoming-One your God, which you have promised with your mouth.

24 When you come into your neighbor's vineyard, then you may eat grapes your fill to your soul; but you shall not put any in your vessel.

25 When you come into the standing grain of your neighbor, then you may pluck the ears with your hand; but you shall not move a sickle unto your neighbor's standing grain.

Deu 24:1 When a man has taken a wife, and married her, and it come to pass that she find no favor in his eyes, because he has found some uncleanness in her: then let him write her a bill of divorcement, and give it in her hand, and send her out of his house.

2 And when she is departed out of his house, she may go and be another man's wife.

3 And if the latter husband hate her, and write her a bill of divorcement, and gives it in her hand, and sends her out of his house; or if the latter husband die, which took her to be his wife;

4 Her former husband, which sent her away, may not take her again to be his wife, after that she is defiled; for that is abomination before the Becoming-One: and you shall not cause the land to sin, which the Becoming-One your God gives you for an inheritance.

5 When a man has taken a new wife, he shall not go out to war, neither shall he be charged with any business: but he shall be free at home one year, and shall cheer up his wife which he has taken.

6 No man shall take the nether or the upper millstone to pledge: for he takes a man's soul to pledge.

7 If a man be found stealing a soul of his brethren of the children of Israel, and makes merchandise of him, or sells him; then that thief shall die; and you shall put evil away from among you.

8 Take heed in the plague of leprosy, that you observe diligently, and do according to all that the priests the Levites shall teach you: as I commanded them, so you shall observe to do.

9 Remember what the Becoming-One your God did unto Miriam by the way, after that you were come forth out of Egypt.

10 When you do lend your brother anything, you shall not go into his house to fetch his pledge.

11 you shall stand abroad, and the man to whom you do lend shall bring out the pledge abroad unto you.

12 And if the man be poor, you shall not sleep with his pledge:

13 In any case you shall deliver him the pledge again when the sun goes down, that he may sleep in

his own raiment, and bless you: and it shall be righteousness unto you before the Becoming-One your God.

14 you shall not oppress a hired servant that is poor and needy, whether he be of your brethren, or of your strangers that are in your land within your gates:

15 At his day you shall give him his hire, neither shall the sun go down upon it; for he is poor, and sets his soul upon it: lest he cry against you unto the Becoming-One, and it be sin unto you.

16 The fathers shall not be put to death for the children, neither shall the children be put to death for the fathers: every man shall be put to death for his own sin.

17 you shall not pervert the judgment of the stranger, nor of the fatherless; nor take a widow's raiment to pledge:

18 But you shall remember that you were a servant in Egypt, and the Becoming-One your God redeemed you there: therefore I command you to do this thing.

19 When you cut down your harvest in your field, and have forgot a sheaf in the field, you shall not go again to fetch it: it shall be for the stranger, for the fatherless, and for the widow: that the Becoming-One your God may bless you in all the work of your hands.

20 When you beat your olive tree, you shall not go over the boughs again: it shall be for the stranger, for the fatherless, and for the widow.

21 When you gather the grapes of your vineyard, you shall not glean it afterward: it shall be for the stranger, for the fatherless, and for the widow.

22 And you shall remember that you were a servant in the land of Egypt: therefore I command you to do this thing.

Deu 25:1 If there be a controversy between men, and they come unto judgment, that the judges may judge them; then they shall justify the righteous, and condemn the wicked.

2 And it shall be, if the wicked man be worthy to be beaten, that the judge shall cause him to lie down, and to be beaten before his face, according to his fault, by a certain number.

3 Forty stripes he may give him, and not exceed: lest, if he should exceed, and beat him above these with many stripes, then your brother should seem vile unto you.

4 you shall not muzzle the ox when he treads out the grain.

5 If brethren dwell together, and one of them die, and have no child, the wife of the dead shall not marry outside unto a stranger: her husband's brother shall go in unto her, and take her to him to wife, and perform the duty of a husband's brother unto her.

6 And it shall be, that the firstborn which she bears shall succeed in the name of his brother which is dead, that his name be not put out of Israel.

7 And if the man like not to take his brother's wife, then let his brother's wife go up to the gate unto the elders, and say, My husband's brother refuses to raise up unto his brother a name in Israel, he will not perform the duty of my husband's brother.

8 Then the elders of his city shall call him, and speak unto him: and if he stand to it, and say, I like not to take her;

9 Then shall his brother's wife come unto him in the presence of the elders, and loose his shoe from off his foot, and spit in his face, and shall answer and say, So shall it be done unto that man that will not build up his brother's house.

10 And his name shall be called in Israel, The house of him that has his shoe loosened.

11 When men strive together one with another, and the wife of the one draws near for to deliver her husband out of the hand of him that smites him, and puts forth her hand, and takes him by the secrets:

12 Then you shall cut off her hand, your eye shall not pity her.

13 you shall not have in your bag diverse weights, a great and a small.

14 you shall not have in your house diverse measures, a great and a small.

15 But you shall have a perfect and just weight, a perfect and just measure shall you have: that your days may be lengthened in the land which the Becoming-One your God gives you.

16 For all that do such things, and all that do unrighteously, are an abomination unto the Becoming-One your God.

17 Remember what Amalek did unto you by the way, when you were come forth out of Egypt;

18 How he met you by the way, and smote the hindmost of you, even all that were feeble behind you, when you were faint and weary; and he feared not God.

19 Therefore it shall be, when the Becoming-One your God has given you rest from all your enemies round about, in the land which the Becoming-One your God gives you for an inheritance to possess it, that you shall blot out the remembrance of Amalek from under the heavens; you shall not forget it.

Deu 26:1 And it shall be, when you are come in unto the land which the Becoming-One your God gives you for an inheritance, and possess it, and dwell therein;

2 That you shall take of the beginning of all the fruit of the earth, which you shall bring of your land that the Becoming-One your God gives you, and shall put it in a basket, and shall go unto the place which the Becoming-One your God shall choose to place his name there.

3 And you shall go unto the priest that shall be in those days, and say unto him, I profess this day unto the Becoming-One your God, that I am come unto the country which the Becoming-One swore unto our fathers for to give us.

4 And the priest shall take the basket out of your hand, and set it down before the altar of the Becoming-One your God.

5 And you shall speak and say before the Becoming-One your God, A Syrian ready to perish was my father, and he went down into Egypt, and sojourned there with a few, and became there a nation, great, mighty, and populous:

6 And the Egyptians evil entreated us, and afflicted us, and laid upon us hard bondage:

7 And when we cried unto the Becoming-One, God of our fathers, the Becoming-One heard our voice, and looked on our affliction, and our labor, and our oppression:

8 And the Becoming-One brought us forth out of Egypt with a mighty hand, and with an outstretched arm, and with great terribleness, and with signs, and with wonders:

9 And he has brought us into this place, and has given us this land, even a land that flows with milk and honey.

10 And now, behold, I have brought the beginning of the land, which you, O Becoming-One, have given me. And you shall set it before the Becoming-One your God, and worship before the Becoming-One your God:

11 And you shall rejoice in every good thing which the Becoming-One your God has given unto you, and unto your house, you, and the Levite, and the stranger that is among you.

12 When you have made an end of tithing all the tithes of your increase the third year, which is the year of tithing, and have given it unto the Levite, the stranger, the fatherless, and the widow, that they may eat within your gates, and be filled;

13 Then you shall say before the Becoming-One your God, I have brought away the hallowed things out of mine house, and also have given them unto the Levite, and unto the stranger, to the fatherless, and to the widow, according to all your commandments which you have commanded me: I have not transgressed your commandments, neither have I forgotten them:

14 I have not eaten thereof in my mourning, neither have I taken away anything thereof for any unclean use, nor given anything thereof for the dead: but I have listened to the voice of the Becoming-One my God, and have done according to all that you have commanded me.

15 Look down from your holy habitation, from the heavens, and bless your people Israel, and the land which you have given us, as you swore unto our fathers, a land that flows with milk and honey.

16 This day the Becoming-One your God has commanded you to do these statutes and judgments: you shall therefore keep and do them with all your heart, and with all your soul.

17 you have declared the Becoming-One this day to be your God, and to walk in his ways, and to keep his statutes, and his commandments, and his judgments, and to listen unto his voice:

18 And the Becoming-One has declared you this day to be his nation of treasure, as he has promised you, and that you should keep all his commandments;

19 And to make you high above all nations which he has made, in praise, and in name, and in honor; and that you may be a holy people unto the Becoming-One your God, as he has spoken.

Deu 27:1 And Moses with the elders of Israel commanded the people, saying, Keep all the commandments which I command you this day.

2 And it shall be on the day when you shall pass over Jordan unto the land which the Becoming-One your God gives you, that you shall set you up great stones, and plaster them with plaster:

3 And you shall write upon them all the words of this law, when you are passed over, that you may go in unto the land which the Becoming-One your God gives you, a land that flows with milk and honey; as the Becoming-One, God of your fathers has promised you.

4 Therefore it shall be when you be gone over Jordan, that you shall set up these stones, which I command you this day, in mount Ebal, and you shall plaster them with plaster.

5 And there shall you build an altar unto the Becoming-One your God, an altar of stones: you shall not lift up any iron tool upon them.

6 you shall build the altar of the Becoming-One your God of whole stones: and you shall offer burnt offerings thereon unto the Becoming-One your God:

7 And you shall offer peace offerings, and shall eat there, and rejoice before the Becoming-One your God.

8 And you shall write upon the stones all the words of this law very plainly.

9 And Moses and the priests the Levites spoke unto all Israel, saying, Take heed, and listen, O Israel; this day you are become the people of the Becoming-One your God.

10 you shall therefore obey the voice of the Becoming-One your God, and do his commandments and his statutes, which I command you this day.

11 And Moses charged the people the same day, saying,

12 These shall stand upon mount Gerizim to bless the people, when you are come over Jordan; Simeon, and Levi, and Judah, and Issachar, and Joseph, and Benjamin:

13 And these shall stand upon mount Ebal to curse; Reuben, Gad, and Asher, and Zebulun, Dan, and Naphtali.

14 And the Levites shall speak, and say unto all the men of Israel with a loud voice,

15 Cursed be the man that makes any graven or molten image, an abomination unto the Becoming-One, the work of the hands of the craftsman, and puts it in a secret place. And all the people shall answer and say, Amen.

16 Cursed be he that dishonors by his father or his mother. And all the people shall say, Amen.

17 Cursed be he that removes his neighbor's landmark. And all the people shall say, Amen.

18 Cursed be he that makes the blind to wander out of the way. And all the people shall say, Amen.

19 Cursed be he that perverts the judgment of the stranger, fatherless, and widow. And all the people shall say, Amen.

20 Cursed be he that lies with his father's wife; because he uncoveres his father's skirt. And all the people shall say, Amen.

21 Cursed be he that lies with any manner of beast. And all the people shall say, Amen.

22 Cursed be he that lies with his sister, the daughter of his father, or the daughter of his mother. And all the people shall say, Amen.

23 Cursed be he that lies with his mother-in-law. And all the people shall say, Amen.

24 Cursed be he that smites his neighbor secretly. And all the people shall say, Amen.

25 Cursed be he that takes reward to slay an innocent soul. And all the people shall say, Amen.

26 Cursed be he that confirms not all the words of this law to do them. And all the people shall say, Amen.

Deu 28:1 And it shall come to pass, if you shall listen diligently unto the voice of the Becoming-One your God, to observe and to do all his commandments which I command you this day, that the Becoming-One your God will set you on high above all nations of the earth:

2 And all these blessings shall come on you, and overtake you, if you shall listen unto the voice of the Becoming-One your God.

3 Blessed shall you be in the city, and blessed shall you be in the field.

4 Blessed shall be the fruit of your body, and the fruit of your ground, and the fruit of your cattle, the increase of your kine, and the flocks of your sheep.

5 Blessed shall be your basket and your store.

6 Blessed shall you be when you come in, and blessed shall you be when you go out.

7 The Becoming-One shall cause your enemies that rise up against you to be struck before your face: they shall come out against you one way, and flee before you seven ways.

8 The Becoming-One shall command the blessing upon you in your storehouses, and in all that you set your hand unto; and he shall bless you in the land which the Becoming-One your God gives you.

9 The Becoming-One shall establish you a holy people unto himself, as he has sworn unto you, if you shall keep the commandments of the Becoming-One your God, and walk in his ways.

10 And all nations of the earth shall see that you are called by the name of the Becoming-One; and they shall be afraid of you.

11 And the Becoming-One shall make you plenteous in goods, in the fruit of your body, and in the fruit of your cattle, and in the fruit of your ground, in the land which the Becoming-One swore unto your fathers to give you.

12 The Becoming-One shall open unto you his good treasure, the heavens to give the rain unto your land in his season, and to bless all the work of your hand: and you shall lend unto many nations, and you shall not borrow.

13 And the Becoming-One shall make you the head, and not the tail; and you shall be above only, and you shall not be beneath; if that you listen unto the commandments of the Becoming-One your God, which I command you this day, to observe and to do them:

14 And you shall not go aside from any of the words which I command you this day, to the right hand, or to the left, to go after other gods to serve them.

15 But it shall come to pass, if you will not listen unto the voice of the Becoming-One your God, to observe to do all his commandments and his statutes which I command you this day; that all these curses shall come upon you, and overtake you:

16 Cursed shall you be in the city, and cursed shall you be in the field.

17 Cursed shall be your basket and your store.

18 Cursed shall be the fruit of your body, and the fruit of your land, the increase of your kine, and the flocks of your sheep.

19 Cursed shall you be when you come in, and cursed shall you be when you go out.

20 The Becoming-One shall send upon you cursing, vexation, and rebuke, in all that you set your hand unto for to do, until you be destroyed, and until you perish quickly; because of the wickedness of your doings, whereby you have forsaken me.

21 The Becoming-One shall make the pestilence cleave unto you, until he have consumed you from off the land, whither you go to possess it.

22 The Becoming-One shall smite you with a consumption, and with a fever, and with an inflammation, and with an extreme burning, and with the sword, and with blasting, and with mildew; and they shall pursue you until you perish.

23 And your heavens that is over your head shall be brass, and the earth that is under you shall be iron.

24 The Becoming-One shall make the rain of your land powder and dust: from the heavens shall it come down upon you, until you be destroyed.

25 The Becoming-One shall cause you to be struck before your enemies: you shall go out one way against them, and flee seven ways before them: and shall be removed into all the kingdoms of the earth.

26 And your carcase shall be food unto all fowls of the air, and unto the beasts of the earth, and no man shall fray them away.

27 The Becoming-One will smite you with the botch of Egypt, and with the hemorrhoids, and with the scab, and with the itch, whereof you canst not be healed.

28 The Becoming-One shall smite you with madness, and blindness, and astonishment of heart:

29 And you shall grope at noonday, as the blind gropes in darkness, and you shall not prosper in your ways: and you shall be only oppressed and spoiled all the days, and no man shall save you.

30 you shall betroth a wife, and another man shall lie with her: you shall build a house, and you shall not dwell therein: you shall plant a vineyard, and shall not gather the grapes thereof.

31 your ox shall be slain before your eyes, and you shall not eat thereof: your donkey shall be violently taken away from before your face, and shall not be restored to you: your sheep shall be given unto your enemies, and you shall have none to rescue them.

32 your sons and your daughters shall be given unto another people, and your eyes shall look, and fail with longing for them all the day long: and there shall be no god in your hand.

33 The fruit of your land, and all your labors, shall a nation which you know not eat up; and you shall be only oppressed and crushed all days:

34 So that you shall be mad for the sight of your eyes which you shall see.

35 The Becoming-One shall smite you in the knees, and in the legs, with a great botch that cannot be healed, from the sole of your foot unto the top of your head.

36 The Becoming-One shall bring you, and your king which you shall set over you, unto a nation which neither you nor your fathers have known; and there shall you serve other gods, wood and stone.

37 And you shall become an astonishment, a proverb, and a byword, among all nations to which the Becoming-One shall lead you.

38 you shall carry much seed out into the field, and shall gather but little in; for the locust shall consume it.

39 you shall plant vineyards, and dress them, but shall neither drink of the wine, nor gather the grapes; for the worms shall eat them.

40 you shall have olive trees throughout all your coasts, but you shall not anoint yourself with the oil; for your olive shall cast his fruit.

41 you shall beget sons and daughters, but you shall not enjoy them; for they shall go into captivity.

42 All your trees and fruit of your land shall the locust consume.

43 The stranger that is within you shall get up above you very high; and you shall come down very low.

44 He shall lend to you, and you shall not lend to him: he shall be the head, and you shall be the tail.

45 Moreover all these curses shall come upon you, and shall pursue you, and overtake you, till you be destroyed; because you listenedst not unto the voice of the Becoming-One your God, to keep his commandments and his statutes which he commanded you:

46 And they shall be upon you for a sign and for a wonder, and upon your seed for olam.

47 Because you served not the Becoming-One your God with joyfullness, and with gladness of heart, for the abundance of all things;

48 Therefore shall you serve your enemies which the Becoming-One shall send against you, in hunger, and in thirst, and in nakedness, and in want of all things: and he shall put a yoke of iron upon your neck, until he have destroyed you.

49 The Becoming-One shall bring a nation against you from far, from the end of the earth, as swift as the eagle flies; a nation whose tongue you shall not understand;

50 A nation of fierce countenance, which shall not regard the person of the old, nor show favor to the young:

51 And he shall eat the fruit of your cattle, and the fruit of your land, until you be destroyed: which also shall not leave you either grain, wine, or oil, or the increase of your kine, or flocks of your sheep, until he have destroyed you.

52 And he shall besiege you in all your gates, until your high and fenced walls come down, wherein you trusted, throughout all your land: and he shall besiege you in all your gates throughout all your land, which the Becoming-One your God has given you.

53 And you shall eat the fruit of your own body, the flesh of your sons and of your daughters, which the Becoming-One your God has given you, in the siege, and in the straitness, wherewith your enemies shall distress you:

54 So that the man that is tender among you, and very delicate, his eye shall be evil toward his brother, and toward the wife of his bosom, and toward the remnant of his children which he shall leave:

55 So that he will not give to any of them of the flesh of his children whom he shall eat: because he has nothing left him in the siege, and in the straitness, wherewith your enemies shall distress you in all your gates.

56 The tender and delicate woman among you, which would not adventure to set the sole of her foot upon the ground for delicateness and tenderness, her eye shall be evil toward the husband of her bosom, and toward her son, and toward her daughter,

57 And toward her young one that comes out from between her feet, and toward her children which she shall bear: for she shall eat them for lack of all things secretly in the siege and straitness, wherewith your enemy shall distress you in your gates.

58 If you will not observe to do all the words of this law that are written in this book, that you may fear this glorious and fearful name, The Becoming-One your Becoming-One;

59 Then the Becoming-One will make your plagues wonderful, and the plagues of your seed, even great plagues, and of long continuance, and great sicknesses, and of long continuance.

60 Moreover he will bring upon you all the diseases of Egypt, which you were afraid of; and they shall cleave unto you.

61 Also every sickness, and every plague, which is not written in the book of this law, them will the Becoming-One bring upon you, until you be destroyed.

62 And you shall be left few in number, whereas you were as the stars of the heavens for multitude; because you would not obey the voice of the Becoming-One your God.

63 And it shall come to pass, that as the Becoming-One rejoiced over you to do you good, and to multiply you; so the Becoming-One will rejoice over you to destroy you, and to bring you to nothing; and you shall be plucked from off the land to which you go to possess it.

64 And the Becoming-One shall scatter you among all people, from the one end of the earth even unto the other; and there you shall serve other gods, which neither you nor your fathers have known, even wood and stone.

65 And among these nations shall you find no ease, neither shall the sole of your foot have rest: but the Becoming-One shall give you there a trembling heart, and failing of eyes, and sorrow of soul:

66 And your life shall hang in doubt before you; and you shall fear day and night, and shall have none assurance of your life:

67 In the morning you shall say, Wish it were evening! and at evening you shall say, Wish it were morning! for the fear of your heart wherewith you shall fear, and for the sight of your eyes which you shall see.

68 And the Becoming-One shall bring you into Egypt again with ships, by the way whereof I spoke unto you, you shall see it no more again: and there you shall be sold unto your enemies for bondmen and bondwomen, and no man shall buy you.

Deu 29:1 These are the words of the covenant, which the Becoming-One commanded Moses to make with the children of Israel in the land of Moab, beside the covenant which he made with them in Horeb.

2 And Moses called unto all Israel, and said unto them, you have seen all that the Becoming-One did before your eyes in the land of Egypt unto Pharaoh, and unto all his servants, and unto all his land;

3 The great temptations which your eyes have seen, the signs, and those great miracles:

4 Yet the Becoming-One has not given you a heart to perceive, and eyes to see, and ears to hear, unto this day.

5 And I have led you forty years in the wilderness: your clothes are not waxen old upon you, and your shoe is not waxen old upon your foot.

6 you have not eaten bread, neither have you drunk wine or strong drink: that you might know that I am the Becoming-One your God.

7 And when you came unto this place, Sihon the king of Heshbon, and Og the king of Bashan, came out against us unto battle, and we smote them:

8 And we took their land, and gave it for an inheritance unto the Reubenites, and to the Gadites, and to the half tribe of Manasseh.

9 Keep therefore the words of this covenant, and do them, that you may prosper in all that you do.

10 you stand this day all of you before the Becoming-One your God; your captains of your tribes, your elders, and your officers, with all the men of Israel,

11 Your little ones, your wives, and your stranger that is in your camp, from the hewer of your wood unto the drawer of your water:

12 That you should enter into covenant with the Becoming-One your God, and into his oath, which the Becoming-One your God makes with you this day:

13 That he may establish you today for a people unto himself, and that he may be unto you God, as he has said unto you, and as he has sworn unto your fathers, to Abraham, to Isaac, and to Jacob.

14 Neither with you only do I make this covenant and this oath;

15 But with him that stands here with us this day before the Becoming-One our God, and also with him that is not here with us this day:

16 For you know how we have dwelt in the land of Egypt; and how we came through the nations which you passed by;

17 And you have seen their abominations, and their idols, wood and stone, silver and gold, which were among them:

18 Lest there should be among you man, or woman, or family, or tribe, whose heart turns away this day from the Becoming-One our God, to go and serve the gods of these nations; lest there should be among you a root that bears gall and wormwood;

19 And it come to pass, when he hears the words of this curse, that he bless himself in his heart, saying, I shall have peace, though I walk in the imagination of mine heart, to add drunkenness to thirst:

20 The Becoming-One will not spare him, but then the anger of the Becoming-One and his jealousy shall smoke against that man, and all the curses that are written in this book shall lie upon him, and the Becoming-One shall blot out his name from under the heavens.

21 And the Becoming-One shall separate him unto evil out of all the tribes of Israel, according to all the curses of the covenant that are written in this book of the law:

22 So that the generation to come of your children that shall rise up after you, and the stranger that shall come from a far land, shall say, when they see the plagues of that land, and the sicknesses which the Becoming-One has laid upon it;

23 And that the whole land thereof is brimstone, and salt, and burning, that it is not sown, nor bears, nor any grass grows therein, like the overthrow of Sodom, and Gomorrah, Admah, and Zeboim, which the Becoming-One overthrew in his anger, and in his wrath:

24 Even all nations shall say, Why has the Becoming-One done thus unto this land? what does the heat of this great anger mean?

25 Then men shall say, Because they have forsaken the covenant of the Becoming-One, God of their fathers, which he made with them when he brought them forth out of the land of Egypt:

26 For they went and served other gods, and worshiped them, gods whom they knew not, and whom he had not given unto them:

27 And the anger of the Becoming-One was kindled against this land, to bring upon it all the curses that are written in this book:

28 And the Becoming-One rooted them out of their land in anger, and in wrath, and in great indignation, and cast them into another land, as it is this day.

29 The secret things belong unto the Becoming-One our God: but those things which are revealed belong unto us and to our children for olam that we may do all the words of this law.

Deu 30:1 And it shall come to pass, when all these things are come upon you, the blessing and the curse, which I have set before you, and you shall call them to mind among all the nations, to which the Becoming-One your God has driven you,

2 And shall return unto the Becoming-One your God, and shall obey his voice according to all that I command you this day, you and your children, with all your heart, and with all your soul;

3 That then the Becoming-One your God will turn your captivity, and have compassion upon you, and will return and gather you from all the nations, to which the Becoming-One your God has scattered you.

4 If any of your be driven out unto the outmost parts of the heavens, from there will the Becoming-One your God gather you, and from there will he fetch you:

5 And the Becoming-One your God will bring you into the land which your fathers possessed, and you shall possess it; and he will do you good, and multiply you above your fathers.

6 And the Becoming-One your God will circumcise your heart, and the heart of your seed, to love the Becoming-One your God with all your heart, and with all your soul, that you may live.

7 And the Becoming-One your God will put all these curses upon your enemies, and on them that hate you, which persecuted you.

8 And you shall return and obey the voice of the Becoming-One, and do all his commandments which I command you this day.

9 And the Becoming-One your God will make you plenteous in every work of your hand, in the fruit of your body, and in the fruit of your cattle, and in the fruit of your land, for good: for the Becoming-One will again rejoice over you for good, as he rejoiced over your fathers:

10 If you shall listen unto the voice of the Becoming-One your God, to keep his commandments and his statutes which are written in this book of the law, and if you turn unto the Becoming-One your God with all your heart, and with all your soul.

11 For this commandment which I command you this day, it is not hidden from you, neither is it far off.

12 It is not in the heavens, that you should say, Who shall go up for us to the heavens, and bring it unto us, that we may hear it, and do it?

13 Neither is it beyond the sea, that you should say, Who shall go beyond the sea for us, and bring it unto us, that we may hear it, and do it?

14 But the word is very near unto you, in your mouth, and in your heart, that you may do it.

15 See, I have set before you this day life and good, and death and evil;

16 In that I command you this day to love the Becoming-One your God, to walk in his ways, and to keep his commandments and his statutes and his judgments, that you may live and multiply: and the Becoming-One your God shall bless you in the land to which you go to possess it.

17 But if your heart turn away, so that you will not hear, but shall be drawn away, and worship other gods, and serve them;

18 I denounce unto you this day, that you shall surely perish, and that you shall not prolong your days upon the land, to which you pass over Jordan to go to possess it.

19 I call the heavens and earth to record this day against you, that I have set before you life and death, blessing and cursing: therefore choose life, that both you and your seed may live:

20 That you may love the Becoming-One your God, and that you may obey his voice, and that you may cleave unto him: for he is your life, and the length of your days: that you may dwell in the land which the Becoming-One swore unto your fathers, to Abraham, to Isaac, and to Jacob, to give them.

Deu 31:1 And Moses went and spoke these words unto all Israel.

2 And he said unto them, I am a son of a hundred and twenty years this day; I can no more go out and come in: also the Becoming-One has said unto me, you shall not go over this Jordan.

3 The Becoming-One your God, he will go over before you, and he will destroy these nations from before you, and you shall possess them: and Joshua, he shall go over before you, as the Becoming-One has said.

4 And the Becoming-One shall do unto them as he did to Sihon and to Og, kings of the Amorites, and unto the land of them, whom he destroyed.

5 And the Becoming-One shall give them up before your face, that you may do unto them according unto all the commandments which I have commanded you.

6 Be strong and of a good courage, fear not, nor be afraid of them: for the Becoming-One your God, he it is that does go with you; he will not fail you, nor forsake you.

7 And Moses called unto Joshua, and said unto him in the sight of all Israel, Be strong and of a good courage: for you must go with this people unto the land which the Becoming-One has sworn unto their fathers to give them; and you shall cause them to inherit it.

8 And the Becoming-One, he it is that does go before you; he will be with you, he will not fail you, neither forsake you: fear not, neither be dismayed.

9 And Moses wrote this law, and delivered it unto the priests the sons of Levi, which bare the ark of the covenant of the Becoming-One, and unto all the elders of Israel.

10 And Moses commanded them, saying, At the end of every seven years, in the set time[99] of the year of release, in the feast of tabernacles,

11 When all Israel is come to appear before the Becoming-One your God in the place which he shall choose, you shall read this law before all Israel in their hearing.

12 Gather the people together, men, and women, and children, and your stranger that is within your gates, that they may hear, and that they may learn, and fear the Becoming-One your God, and observe to do all the words of this law:

13 And that their children, which have not known any thing, may hear, and learn to fear the Becoming-One your God, all the days you live in the land to which you go over Jordan to possess it.

14 And the Becoming-One said unto Moses, Behold, your days approach that you must die: call Joshua, and present yourselves in the tabernacle of the set time,[100] that I may give him a charge. And Moses and Joshua went, and presented themselves in the tabernacle of the set time.[101]

15 And the Becoming-One appeared in the tabernacle in a pillar of a cloud: and the pillar of the cloud stood over the door of the tabernacle.

16 And the Becoming-One said unto Moses, Behold, you shall sleep with your fathers; and this people will rise up, and go a whoring after the gods of the strangers of the land, to which they go to be among them, and will forsake me, and break my covenant which I have made with them.

17 Then my anger shall be kindled against them in that day, and I will forsake them, and I will hide my face from them, and they shall be devoured, and many evils and troubles shall befall them; so that they will say in that day, Are not these evils come upon us, because our God is not among us?

18 And I will surely hide my face in that day for all the evils which they shall have worked, in that they are turned unto other gods.

19 Now therefore write you this song for you, and teach it the children of Israel: put it in their mouths, that this song may be a witness for me against the children of Israel.

20 For when I shall have brought them into the land which I swore unto their fathers, that flows with milk and honey; and they shall have eaten and filled themselves, and waxen fat; then will they turn unto other gods, and serve them, and provoke me, and break my covenant.

21 And it shall come to pass, when many evils and troubles are befallen them, that this song shall testify against them as a witness; for it shall not be forgotten out of the mouths of their seed: for I know their imagination which they go about, even now, before I have brought them into the land which I swore.

---

[99] Appointed time or festival
[100] Appointed time or festival
[101] Appointed time or festival

22 Moses therefore wrote this song the same day, and taught it the children of Israel.

23 And he gave Joshua the son of Nun a charge, and said, Be strong and of a good courage: for you shall bring the children of Israel into the land which I swore unto them: and I will be with you.

24 And it came to pass, when Moses had made an end of writing the words of this law in a book, until they were finished,

25 That Moses commanded the Levites, which bare the ark of the covenant of the Becoming-One, saying,

26 Take this book of the law, and put it in the side of the ark of the covenant of the Becoming-One your God, that it may be there for a witness against you.

27 For I know your rebellion, and your stiff neck: behold, while I am yet alive with you this day, you have been rebellious against the Becoming-One; and how much more after my death?

28 Gather unto me all the elders of your tribes, and your officers, that I may speak these words in their ears, and call the heavens and earth to record against them.

29 For I know that after my death you will utterly corrupt yourselves, and turn aside from the way which I have commanded you; and evil will befall you in the end of days; because you will do evil in the sight of the Becoming-One, to provoke him to anger through the work of your hands.

30 And Moses spoke in the ears of all the congregation of Israel the words of this song, until they were ended.

Deu 32:1 Give ear, O you heavens, and I will speak; and hear, O earth, the words of my mouth.

2 My doctrine shall drop as the rain, my speech shall distil as the dew, as the small rain upon the tender herb, and as the showers upon the grass:

3 Because I will publish the name of the Becoming-One: ascribe you greatness unto our God.

4 He is the Rock, his work is perfect: for all his ways are judgment: a GOD of truth and without iniquity, just and right is he.

5 They have corrupted themselves, their spot is not the spot of his children: they are a perverse and crooked generation.

6 Do you thus requite the Becoming-One, O foolish people and unwise? is not he your father that has bought you? has he not made you, and established you?

7 Remember the days of olam, consider the years of many generations: ask your father, and he will show you; your elders, and they will tell you.

8 When the Most High divided to the nations their inheritance, when he separated the sons of Adam, he set the bounds of the people according to the number of the children of Israel.

9 For the Becoming-One's portion is his people; Jacob is the lot of his inheritance.

10 He found him in a desert land, and in the waste howling wilderness; he led him about, he instructed him, he kept him as the apple of his eye.

11 As an eagle stirs up her nest, flutters over her young, spreads abroad her wings, takes them, bears them on her wings:

12 So the Becoming-One alone did lead him, and there was no strange god with him.

13 He made him ride on the high places of the earth, that he might eat the increase of the fields; and he made him to suck honey out of the rock, and oil out of the flinty rock;

14 Butter of cattle, and milk of sheep, with fat of lambs, and rams of the breed of Bashan, and goats, with the fat of kidneys of wheat; and you didst drink the pure blood of the grape.

15 But Jeshurun grew fat, and kicked: you are waxen fat, you are grown thick, you are covered with fatness; then he forsook God which made him, and lightly esteemed the Rock of his salvation.

16 They provoked him to jealousy with strange gods, with abominations provoked they him to anger.

17 They sacrificed unto devils, not to God; to gods whom they knew not, to new gods that came newly up, whom your fathers feared not.

18 Of the Rock that begat you you are unmindful, and have forgotten GOD that formed you.

19 And when the Becoming-One saw it, he abhorred them, because of the provoking of his sons, and of his daughters.

20 And he said, I will hide my face from them, I will see what their end shall be: for they are a very perverse generation, children in whom is no faith.

21 They have moved me to jealousy with that which is not god; they have provoked me to anger with their vanities: and I will move them to jealousy with those which are not a people; I will provoke them to anger with a foolish nation.

22 For a fire is kindled in mine anger, and shall burn unto the lowest Sheol, and shall consume the earth with her increase, and set on fire the foundations of the mountains.

23 I will heap mischiefs upon them; I will spend mine arrows upon them.

24 They shall be burnt with hunger, and devoured with burning heat, and with bitter destruction: I will also send the teeth of beasts upon them, with the poison of serpents of the dust.

25 The sword outside, and terror within, shall destroy both the young man and the virgin, the suckling also with the man of gray hairs.

26 I said, I would scatter them into corners, I would make the remembrance of them to cease from among men:

27 Were it not that I feared the wrath of the enemy, lest their adversaries should behave themselves strangely, and lest they should say, Our hand is high, and the Becoming-One has not done all this.

28 For they are a nation void of counsel, neither is there any understanding in them.

29 O that they were wise, that they understood this, that they would consider their latter end!

30 How should one chase a thousand, and two put multitude to flight, except their Rock had sold them, and the Becoming-One had shut them up?

31 For their rock is not as our Rock, even our enemies themselves being judges.

32 For their vine is of the vine of Sodom, and of the fields of Gomorrah: their grapes are grapes of gall, their clusters are bitter:

33 Their wine is the poison of monsters, and the cruel venom of asps.

34 Is not this laid up in store with me, and sealed up among my treasures?

35 To me belongs vengeance, and recompense; their foot shall slide in due time: for the day of their calamity is at hand, and the things that shall come upon them make haste.

36 For the Becoming-One shall judge his people, and he will repent for his servants, when he sees that their power is gone, and there is none shut up, or left.

37 And he shall say, Where are their gods, their rock in whom they trusted,

38 Which did eat the fat of their sacrifices, and drank the wine of their drink offerings? let them rise up and help you, and be your protection.

39 See now that I, even I, am he, and there is no god with me: I kill, and I make alive; I wound, and I heal: neither is there any that can deliver out of my hand.

40 For I lift up my hand to the heavens, and say, I live for olam.

41 If I sharpen my glittering sword, and mine hand take hold on judgment; I will render vengeance to mine enemies, and will reward them that hate me.

42 I will make mine arrows drunk with blood, and my sword shall devour flesh; and that with the blood of the slain and of the captives, from the beginning of revenges upon the enemy.

43 Rejoice, O you nations, with his people: for he will avenge the blood of his servants, and will render vengeance to his adversaries, and will be merciful unto his land, and to his people.

44 And Moses came and spoke all the words of this song in the ears of the people, he, and Hoshea the son of Nun.

45 And Moses made an end of speaking all these words to all Israel:

46 And he said unto them, Set your hearts unto all the words which I testify among you this day, which you shall command your children to observe to do, all the words of this law.

47 For it is not a vain thing for you; because it is your life: and through this thing you shall prolong your days in the land, to which you go over Jordan to possess it.

48 And the Becoming-One spoke unto Moses that selfsame day, saying,

49 Get you up into this mountain Abarim, unto mount Nebo, which is in the land of Moab, that is over against Jericho; and behold the land of Canaan, which I give unto the children of Israel for a possession:

50 And die in the mount to which you go up, and be gathered unto your people; as Aaron your brother died in mount Hor, and was gathered unto his people:

51 Because you trespassed against me among the children of Israel at the waters of Meribah-Kadesh, in the wilderness of Zin; because you sanctified me not in the midst of the children of Israel.

52 Yet you shall see the land before you; but you shall not go there unto the land which I give the children of Israel.

Deu 33:1 And this is the blessing, wherewith Moses the man of God blessed the children of Israel before his death.

2 And he said, The Becoming-One came from Sinai, and rose up from Seir unto them; he shined forth from mount Paran, and he came with multitude of saints: from his right hand went a fiery law for them.

3 Yes, he loved the people; all his saints are in your hand: and they sat down at your feet; every one shall receive of your words.

4 Moses commanded us a law, even the inheritance of the congregation of Jacob.

5 And he was king in Jeshurun, when the heads of the people and the tribes of Israel were gathered together.

6 Let Reuben live, and not die; and let not his men be few.

7 And this is the blessing of Judah: and he said, Hear, Becoming-One, the voice of Judah, and bring him unto his people: let his hands be sufficient for him; and be you a help to him from his enemies.

8 And of Levi he said, Let your Thummim and your Urim be with your holy one, whom you didst prove at Massah, and with whom you didst strive at the waters of Meribah;

9 Who said unto his father and to his mother, I have not seen him; neither did he acknowledge his brethren, nor knew his own children: for they have observed your word, and kept your covenant.

10 They shall teach Jacob your judgments, and Israel your law: they shall put incense before you, and whole burnt sacrifice upon your altar.

11 Bless, Becoming-One, his substance, and accept the work of his hands: smite through the loins of them that rise against him, and of them that hate him, that they rise not again.

12 And of Benjamin he said, The beloved of the Becoming-One shall dwell in safety by him; and the Becoming-One shall cover him all the day long, and he shall dwell between his shoulders.

13 And of Joseph he said, Blessed of the Becoming-One be his land, for the precious things of the heavens, for the dew, and for the deep that couches beneath,

14 And for the precious fruits brought forth by the sun, and for the precious things put forth by the moon,

15 And for the chief things of the ancient mountains, and for the precious things of the hills of olam.

16 And for the precious things of the earth and fullness thereof, and for the good will of him that dwelt in the bush: let the blessing come upon the head of Joseph, and upon the top of the head of him that was separated from his brethren.

17 His glory is like the firstling of his bullock, and his horns are like the horns of a reem: with them he shall push the people together to the ends of the earth: and they are the multitude of Ephraim, and they are the thousands of Manasseh.

18 And of Zebulun he said, Rejoice, Zebulun, in your going out; and, Issachar, in your tents.

19 They shall call the people unto the mountain; there they shall offer sacrifices of righteousness: for they shall suck of the abundance of the seas, and of treasures hid in the sand.

20 And of Gad he said, Blessed be he that enlarges Gad; he dwells as a lion, and tears the arm with the crown of the head.

21 And he provided the first part for himself, because there, in a portion of the lawgiver, was he seated; and he came with the heads of the people, he executed the justice of the Becoming-One, and his judgments with Israel.

22 And of Dan he said, Dan is a lion's whelp: he shall leap from Bashan.

23 And of Naphtali he said, O Naphtali, satisfied with favor, and full with the blessing of the Becoming-One: possess you the west and the south.

24 And of Asher he said, Let Asher be blessed with children; let him be acceptable to his brethren, and let him dip his foot in oil.

25 your shoes shall be iron and brass; and as your days, so shall your strength be.

26 There is none like unto GOD of Jeshurun, who rids upon the heavens in your help, and in his excellency on the sky.

27 God of old is your refuge, and underneath are the arms of olam, and he shall thrust out the enemy from before you; and shall say, Destroy them.

28 Israel then shall dwell in safety alone: the fountain of Jacob shall be upon a land of grain and wine; also his heavens shall drop down dew.

29 Happy are you, O Israel: who is like unto you, O people saved by the Becoming-One, the shield of your help, and who is the sword of your excellency! and your enemies shall be found liars unto you; and you shall tread upon their high places.

Deu 34:1 And Moses went up from the plains of Moab unto the mountain of Nebo, to the top of Pisgah, that is over against Jericho. And the Becoming-One showed him all the land of Gilead, unto Dan,

2 And all Naphtali, and the land of Ephraim, and Manasseh, and all the land of Judah, unto the utmost sea,

3 And the south, and the plain of the valley of Jericho, the city of palm trees, unto Zoar.

4 And the Becoming-One said unto him, This is the land which I swore unto Abraham, unto Isaac, and unto Jacob, saying, I will give it unto your seed: I have caused you to see it with your eyes, but you shall not go over there.

5 So Moses the servant of the Becoming-One died there in the land of Moab, according to the word of the Becoming-One.

6 And He buried him in a valley in the land of Moab, over against Beth-peor: but no man knows of his tomb unto this day.

7 And Moses was a son of a hundred and twenty years when he died: his eye was not dim, nor his natural force abated.

8 And the children of Israel wept for Moses in the plains of Moab thirty days: so the days of weeping and mourning for Moses were ended.

9 And Joshua the son of Nun was full of the spirit of wisdom; for Moses had laid his hands upon him: and the children of Israel listened unto him, and did as the Becoming-One commanded Moses.

10 And there arose not a prophet since in Israel like unto Moses, whom the Becoming-One knew face to face,

11 In all the signs and the wonders, which the Becoming-One sent him to do in the land of Egypt to Pharaoh, and to all his servants, and to all his land,

12 And in all that mighty hand, and in all the great terror which Moses showed in the sight of all Israel.

Joshua

Josh 1:1 Now after the death of Moses, the servant of the Becoming-One, it came to pass that the Becoming-One spoke unto Joshua the son of Nun, Moses' minister, saying,

2 Moses my servant is dead; now therefore arise, go over this Jordan, you, and all this people, unto the land which I do give to them, even to the children of Israel.

3 Every place that the sole of your foot shall tread upon, that have I given unto you, as I said unto Moses.

4 From the wilderness and this Lebanon even unto the great river, the river Euphrates, all the land of the Hittites, and unto the great sea toward the going down of the sun, shall be your coast.

5 There shall not any man be able to stand before you all the days of your life: as I was with Moses, so I will be with you: I will not fail you, nor forsake you.

6 Be strong and of a good courage: for unto this people shall you divide for an inheritance the land, which I swore unto their fathers to give them.

7 Only be you strong and very courageous, that you may observe to do according to all the law, which Moses my servant commanded you: turn not from it to the right hand or to the left, that you may prosper wheresoever you go.

8 This book of the law shall not depart out of your mouth; but you shall meditate therein day and night, that you may observe to do according to all that is written therein: for then you shall make your way prosperous, and then you shall have good success.

9 Have not I commanded you? Be strong and of a good courage; be not afraid, neither be you dismayed: for the Becoming-One your God is with you wheresoever you go.

10 Then Joshua commanded the officers of the people, saying,

11 Pass through the host, and command the people, saying, Prepare you victuals; for within three days you shall pass over this Jordan, to go in to possess the land, which the Becoming-One your God gives you to possess it.

12 And to the Reubenites, and to the Gadites, and to half the tribe of Manasseh, spoke Joshua, saying,

13 Remember the word which Moses the servant of the Becoming-One commanded you, saying, The Becoming-One your God has given you rest, and has given you this land.

14 Your wives, your little ones, and your cattle, shall remain in the land which Moses gave you beyond Jordan; but you shall pass before your brethren armed, all the mighty men of valor, and help them;

15 Until the Becoming-One have given your brethren rest, as he has given you, and they also have possessed the land which the Becoming-One your God gives them: then you shall return unto the land of your possession, and enjoy it, which Moses the Becoming-One's servant gave you beyond Jordan toward the sunrising.

16 And they answered Joshua, saying, All that you command us we will do, and wheresoever you send us, we will go.

17 According as we listened unto Moses in all things, so will we listen unto you: only the Becoming-One your God be with you, as he was with Moses.

18 Whosoever he be that does rebel against your mouth, and will not hear your words in all that you command him, he shall be put to death: only be strong and of a good courage.

Josh 2:1 And Joshua the son of Nun sent out of Shittim two men to spy secretly, saying, Go view the land, even Jericho. And they went, and came into a harlot's house, named Rahab, and lodged there.

2 And it was told the king of Jericho, saying, Behold, there came men in here to night of the children of Israel to search out the country.

3 And the king of Jericho sent unto Rahab, saying, Bring forth the men that are come to you, which are entered into your house: for they be come to search out all the country.

4 And the woman took the two men, and hid them, and said thus, There came men unto me, but I knew not from where they came:

5 And it came to pass about the time of shutting of the gate, when it was dark, that the men went out: where the men went I know not: pursue after them quickly; for you shall overtake them.

6 But she had brought them up to the roof of the house, and hid them with the stalks of flax, which she had laid in order upon the roof.

7 And the men pursued after them the way to Jordan unto the fords: and as soon as they which pursued after them were gone out, they shut the gate.

8 And before they were laid down, she came up unto them upon the roof;

9 And she said unto the men, I know that the Becoming-One has given you the land, and that your terror is fallen upon us, and that all the inhabitants of the land faint because of you.

10 For we have heard how the Becoming-One dried up the water of the boundary sea for you, when you came out of Egypt; and what you did unto the two kings of the Amorites, that were beyond Jordan, Sihon and Og, whom you utterly destroyed.

11 And as soon as we had heard these things, our hearts did melt, neither did there remain any more wind in any man, because of you: for the Becoming-One your God, he is God in the heavens above, and in earth beneath.

12 Now therefore, I pray you, swear unto me by the Becoming-One, since I have showed you kindness, that you will also show kindness unto my father's house, and give me a true token:

13 And that you will save alive my father, and my mother, and my brethren, and my sisters, and all that they have, and deliver our soul from death.

14 And the men answered her, Our soul for yours, if you utter not this our business. And it shall be, when the Becoming-One has given us the land, that we will deal kindly and truly with you.

15 Then she let them down by a cord through the window: for her house was upon the town wall, and she dwelt upon the wall.

16 And she said unto them, Get you to the mountain, lest the pursuers meet you; and hide yourselves there three days, until the pursuers be returned: and afterward may you go your way.

17 And the men said unto her, We will be blameless of this your oath which you have made us swear.

18 Behold, when we come into the land, you shall bind this line of scarlet thread in the window which you did let us down by: and you shall bring your father, and your mother, and your brethren, and all your father's household, home unto you.

19 And it shall be, that whosoever shall go out of the doors of your house into the street, his blood shall be upon his head, and we will be guiltless: and whosoever shall be with you in the house, his blood shall be on our head, if any hand be upon him.

20 And if you utter this our business, then we will be free from your oath which you have made us to swear.

21 And she said, According unto your words, so be it. And she sent them away, and they departed: and she bound the scarlet line in the window.

22 And they went, and came unto the mountain, and abode there three days, until the pursuers were returned: and the pursuers sought them throughout all the way, but found them not.

23 So the two men returned, and descended from the mountain, and passed over, and came to Joshua the son of Nun, and told him all things that befell them:

24 And they said unto Joshua, Truly the Becoming-One has delivered into our hands all the land; for even all the inhabitants of the country do faint because of us.

Josh 3:1 And Joshua rose early in the morning; and they removed from Shittim, and came to Jordan, he and all the children of Israel, and lodged there before they passed over.

2 And it came to pass after three days, that the officers went through the host;

3 And they commanded the people, saying, When you see the ark of the covenant of the Becoming-One your God, and the priests the Levites bearing it, then you shall remove from your place, and go after it.

4 Yet there shall be a space between you and it, about two thousand cubits by measure: come not near unto it, that you may know the way by which you must go: for you have not passed this way yesterday and the third day.

5 And Joshua said unto the people, Sanctify yourselves: for tomorrow the Becoming-One will do wonders among you.

6 And Joshua spoke unto the priests, saying, Take up the ark of the covenant, and pass over before the people. And they took up the ark of the covenant, and went before the people.

7 And the Becoming-One said unto Joshua, This day will I begin to magnify you in the sight of all Israel, that they may know that, as I was with Moses, so I will be with you.

8 And you shall command the priests that bear the ark of the covenant, saying, When you are come to the brink of the water of Jordan, you shall stand still in Jordan.

9 And Joshua said unto the children of Israel, Come here, and hear the words of the Becoming-One your God.

10 And Joshua said, Hereby you shall know that the living GOD is among you, and that he will without fail drive out from before you the Canaanites, and the Hittites, and the Hivites, and the Perizzites, and the Girgashites, and the Amorites, and the Jebusites.

11 Behold, the ark of the covenant of the Becoming-One of all the earth passes over before you into Jordan.

12 Now therefore take you twelve men out of the tribes of Israel, out of every tribe a man.

13 And it shall come to pass, as soon as the soles of the feet of the priests that bear the ark of the Becoming-One, Lord of all the earth, shall rest in the waters of Jordan, that the waters of Jordan shall be cut off from the waters that come down from above; and they shall stand upon a heap.

14 And it came to pass, when the people removed from their tents, to pass over Jordan, and the priests bearing the ark of the covenant before the people;

15 And as they that bare the ark were come unto Jordan, and the feet of the priests that bare the ark were dipped in the brim of the water, for Jordan overflows all his banks all the time of harvest,

16 That the waters which came down from above stood and rose up upon a heap very far from the city Adam, that is beside Zaretan: and those that came down toward the sea of the plain, even the salt sea, failed, and were cut off: and the people passed over right against Jericho.

17 And the priests that bare the ark of the covenant of the Becoming-One stood firm on dry ground in the midst of Jordan, and all the Israelites passed over on dry ground, until all the people were passed clean over Jordan.

Josh 4:1 And it came to pass, when all the people were clean passed over Jordan, that the Becoming-One spoke unto Joshua, saying,

2 Take you twelve men out of the people, out of every tribe a man,

3 And command you them, saying, Take you hence out of the midst of Jordan, out of the place where the priests' feet stood firm, twelve stones, and you shall carry them over with you, and leave them in the lodging place, where you shall lodge this night.

4 Then Joshua called the twelve men, whom he had prepared of the children of Israel, out of every tribe a man:

5 And Joshua said unto them, Pass over before the ark of the Becoming-One your God into the midst of Jordan, and take you up every man of you a stone upon his shoulder, according unto the number of the tribes of the children of Israel:

6 That this may be a sign among you, that when your children ask their fathers in time to come, saying, What do you mean by these stones?

7 Then you shall answer them, That the waters of Jordan were cut off before the ark of the covenant of the Becoming-One; when it passed over Jordan, the waters of Jordan were cut off: and these stones shall be for a memorial unto the children of Israel for olam.

8 And the children of Israel did so as Joshua commanded, and took up twelve stones out of the midst of Jordan, as the Becoming-One spoke unto Joshua, according to the number of the tribes of the children of Israel, and carried them over with them unto the place where they lodged, and laid them down there.

9 And Joshua set up twelve stones in the midst of Jordan, in the place where the feet of the priests which bare the ark of the covenant stood: and they are there unto this day.

10 For the priests which bare the ark stood in the midst of Jordan, until every thing was finished that the Becoming-One commanded Joshua to speak unto the people, according to all that Moses commanded Joshua: and the people hasted and passed over.

11 And it came to pass, when all the people were clean passed over, that the ark of the Becoming-One passed over, and the priests, in the presence of the people.

12 And the children of Reuben, and the children of Gad, and half the tribe of Manasseh, passed over armed before the children of Israel, as Moses spoke unto them:

13 About forty thousand prepared for war passed over before the Becoming-One unto battle, to the plains of Jericho.

14 On that day the Becoming-One magnified Joshua in the sight of all Israel; and they feared him, as they feared Moses, all the days of his life.

15 And the Becoming-One spoke unto Joshua, saying,

16 Command the priests that bear the ark of the testimony, that they come up out of Jordan.

17 Joshua therefore commanded the priests, saying, Come you up out of Jordan.

18 And it came to pass, when the priests that bare the ark of the covenant of the Becoming-One were come up out of the midst of Jordan, and the soles of the priests' feet were lifted up unto the dry land, that the waters of Jordan returned unto their place, and flowed over all his banks, as they did yesterday and the third day.

19 And the people came up out of Jordan on the tenth day of the first month, and encamped in Gilgal, in the east border of Jericho.

20 And those twelve stones, which they took out of Jordan, did Joshua pitch in Gilgal.

21 And he spoke unto the children of Israel, saying, When your children shall ask their fathers in time to come, saying, What do you mean by these stones?

22 Then you shall let your children know, saying, Israel came over this Jordan on dry land.

23 For the Becoming-One your God dried up the waters of Jordan from before you, until you were passed over, as the Becoming-One your God did to the boundary sea, which he dried up from before us, until we were gone over:

24 That all the people of the earth might know the hand of the Becoming-One, that it is mighty: that you might fear the Becoming-One your God all days.

Josh 5:1 And it came to pass, when all the kings of the Amorites, which were beyond Jordan westward, and all the kings of the Canaanites, which were by the sea, heard that the Becoming-One had dried up the waters of Jordan from before the children of Israel, until we were passed over, that their heart melted, neither was there spirit in them any more, because of the children of Israel.

2 At that time the Becoming-One said unto Joshua, Make you sharp knives, and circumcise again the children of Israel the second time.

3 And Joshua made him sharp knives, and circumcised the children of Israel at the hill of the foreskins.

4 And this is the cause why Joshua did circumcise: All the people that came out of Egypt, that were males, even all the men of war, died in the wilderness by the way, after they came out of Egypt.

5 Now all the people that came out were circumcised: but all the people that were born in the wilderness by the way as they came forth out of Egypt, them they had not circumcised.

6 For the children of Israel walked forty years in the wilderness, till all the people that were men of war, which came out of Egypt, were consumed, because they obeyed not the voice of the Becoming-One: unto whom the Becoming-One swore that he would not show them the land, which the Becoming-One swore unto their fathers that he would give us, a land that flows with milk and honey.

7 And their children, whom he raised up in their stead, them Joshua circumcised: for they were uncircumcised, because they had not circumcised them by the way.

8 And it came to pass, when they had done circumcising all the people, that they abode in their places in the camp, till they were whole.

9 And the Becoming-One said unto Joshua, This day have I rolled away the reproach of Egypt from off you. Therefore the name of the place is called Gilgal unto this day.

10 And the children of Israel encamped in Gilgal, and kept the Passover on the fourteenth day of the month at evening in the plains of Jericho.

11 And they did eat of the old grain of the land on the next day after the Passover, unleavened cakes, and parched grain in the selfsame day.

12 And the manna ceased on the next day after they had eaten of the old grain of the land; neither had the children of Israel manna any more; but they did eat of the fruit of the land of Canaan that year.

13 And it came to pass, when Joshua was by Jericho, that he lifted up his eyes and looked, and, behold, there stood a man over against him with his sword drawn in his hand: and Joshua went unto him, and said unto him, are you for us, or for our adversaries?

14 And he said, Nay; but as captain of the host of the Becoming-One I am now come. And Joshua fell on his face to the earth, and did worship, and said unto him, What says my lord unto his servant?

15 And the captain of the Becoming-One's host said unto Joshua, Loose your shoe from off your foot; for the place whereon you stand is holy. And Joshua did so.

Josh 6:1 Now Jericho was straitly shut up because of the children of Israel: none went out, and none came in.

2 And the Becoming-One said unto Joshua, See, I have given into your hand Jericho, and the king thereof, and the mighty men of valor.

3 And you shall compass the city, all you men of war, and go round about the city once. Thus shall you do six days.

4 And seven priests shall bear before the ark seven trumpets of rams' horns: and the seventh day you shall compass the city seven times, and the priests shall blow with the trumpets.

5 And it shall come to pass, that when they make a long blast with the ram's horn, and when you hear the sound of the trumpet, all the people shall shout with a great shout; and the wall of the city shall fall down flat, and the people shall ascend up every man straight before him.

6 And Joshua the son of Nun called the priests, and said unto them, Take up the ark of the covenant, and let seven priests bear seven trumpets of rams' horns before the ark of the Becoming-One.

7 And he said unto the people, Pass on, and compass the city, and let him that is armed pass on before the ark of the Becoming-One.

8 And it came to pass, when Joshua had spoken unto the people, that the seven priests bearing the seven trumpets of rams' horns passed on before the Becoming-One, and blew with the trumpets: and the ark of the covenant of the Becoming-One followed them.

9 And the armed men went before the priests that blew with the trumpets, and the rear guard came after the ark, the priests going on, and blowing with the trumpets.

10 And Joshua had commanded the people, saying, you shall not shout, nor make any noise with your voice, neither shall any word proceed out of your mouth, until the day I bid you shout; then shall you shout.

11 So the ark of the Becoming-One compassed the city, going about it once: and they came into the camp, and lodged in the camp.

12 And Joshua rose early in the morning, and the priests took up the ark of the Becoming-One.

13 And seven priests bearing seven trumpets of rams' horns before the ark of the Becoming-One went on continually, and blew with the trumpets: and the armed men went before them; but the rear-guard came after the ark of the Becoming-One, the priests going on, and blowing with the trumpets.

14 And the second day they compassed the city once, and returned into the camp: so they did six days.

15 And it came to pass on the seventh day, that they rose early about the rising of the dawn, and compassed the city after the same manner seven times: only on that day they compassed the city seven times.

16 And it came to pass at the seventh time, when the priests blew with the trumpets, Joshua said unto the people, Shout; for the Becoming-One has given you the city.

17 And the city shall be accursed, even it, and all that are therein, to the Becoming-One: only Rahab the harlot shall live, she and all that are with her in the house, because she hid the messengers that we sent.

18 And you, in any way keep yourselves from the accursed thing, lest you make yourselves accursed, when you take of the accursed thing, and make the camp of Israel a curse, and trouble it.

19 But all the silver, and gold, and vessels of brass and iron, are consecrated unto the Becoming-One: they shall come into the treasury of the Becoming-One.

20 So the people shouted when the priests blew with the trumpets: and it came to pass, when the people heard the sound of the trumpet, and the people shouted with a great shout, that the wall fell down flat, so that the people went up into the city, every man straight before him, and they took the city.

21 And they utterly destroyed all that was in the city, both man and woman, young and old, and ox, and sheep, and donkey, with the edge of the sword.

22 But Joshua had said unto the two men that had spied out the country, Go into the harlot's house, and bring out there the woman, and all that she has, as you swore unto her.

23 And the young men that were spies went in, and brought out Rahab, and her father, and her mother, and her brethren, and all that she had; and they brought out all her kindred, and left them outside the camp of Israel.

24 And they burnt the city with fire, and all that was therein: only the silver, and the gold, and the vessels of brass and of iron, they put into the treasury of the house of the Becoming-One.

25 And Joshua saved Rahab the harlot alive, and her father's household, and all that she had; and she dwells in Israel even unto this day; because she hid the messengers, which Joshua sent to spy out Jericho.

26 And Joshua adjured them at that time, saying, Cursed be the man before the Becoming-One, that rises up and builds this city Jericho: he shall lay the foundation thereof in his firstborn, and in his youngest son shall he set up the gates of it.

27 So the Becoming-One was with Joshua; and his fame was noised throughout all the country.

Josh 7:1 But the children of Israel committed a trespass in the accursed thing: for Achan, the son of Carmi, the son of Zabdi, the son of Zerah, of the tribe of Judah, took of the accursed thing: and the anger of the Becoming-One was kindled against the children of Israel.

2 And Joshua sent men from Jericho to Ai, which is beside Bethaven, on the east side of Bethel, and spoke unto them, saying, Go up and view the country. And the men went up and viewed Ai.

3 And they returned to Joshua, and said unto him, Let not all the people go up; but let about two or three thousand of men go up and smite Ai; and make not all the people to labor there; for they are but few.

4 So there went up there of the people about three thousand of men: and they fled before the men of Ai.

5 And the men of Ai smote of them about thirty and six men: for they chased them from before the gate even unto Shebarim, and smote them in the going down: therefore the hearts of the people melted, and became as water.

6 And Joshua ripped his clothes, and fell to the earth upon his face before the ark of the Becoming-One until the eveningtide, he and the elders of Israel, and put dust upon their heads.

7 And Joshua said, Alas, O my Lord(s) the Becoming-One, why have you at all brought this people over Jordan, to deliver us into the hand of the

Amorites, to destroy us? would that we had been content, and dwelt on the other side Jordan!

8 O my Lord(s), what shall I say, when Israel turns their backs before their enemies!

9 For the Canaanites and all the inhabitants of the land shall hear of it, and shall surround us, and cut off our name from the earth: and what will you do unto your great name?

10 And the Becoming-One said unto Joshua, Get you up; why lie you thus upon your face?

11 Israel has sinned, and they have also transgressed my covenant which I commanded them: for they have even taken of the accursed thing, and have also stolen, and dissembled also, and they have put it even among their own stuff.

12 Therefore the children of Israel could not stand before their enemies, but turned their backs before their enemies, because they were accursed: neither will I be with you any more, except you destroy the accursed from among you.

13 Up, sanctify the people, and say, Sanctify yourselves against tomorrow: for thus says the Becoming-One, God of Israel, There is an accursed thing in the midst of you, O Israel: you can not stand before your enemies, until you take away the accursed thing from among you.

14 In the morning therefore you shall be brought according to your tribes: and it shall be, that the tribe which the Becoming-One takes shall come according to the families thereof; and the family which the Becoming-One shall take shall come by households; and the household which the Becoming-One shall take shall come man by man.

15 And it shall be, that he that is taken with the accursed thing shall be burnt with fire, he and all that he has: because he has transgressed the covenant of the Becoming-One, and because he has worked folly in Israel.

16 So Joshua rose up early in the morning, and brought Israel by their tribes; and the tribe of Judah was taken:

17 And he brought the family of Judah; and he took the family of the Zarhites: and he brought the family of the Zarhites man by man; and Zabdi was taken:

18 And he brought his household man by man; and Achan, the son of Carmi, the son of Zabdi, the son of Zerah, of the tribe of Judah, was taken.

19 And Joshua said unto Achan, My son, give, I pray you, glory to the Becoming-One, God of Israel, and make confession unto him; and tell me now what you have done; hide it not from me.

20 And Achan answered Joshua, and said, Indeed I have sinned against the Becoming-One, God of Israel, and thus and thus I have done:

21 When I saw among the spoils a goodly Babylonish garment, and two hundred shekels of silver, and a wedge of gold of fifty shekels weight, then I coveted them, and took them; and, behold, they are hid in the earth in the midst of my tent, and the silver under it.

22 So Joshua sent messengers, and they ran unto the tent; and, behold, it was hid in his tent, and the silver under it.

23 And they took them out of the midst of the tent, and brought them unto Joshua, and unto all the children of Israel, and laid them out before the Becoming-One.

24 And Joshua, and all Israel with him, took Achan the son of Zerah, and the silver, and the garment, and the wedge of gold, and his sons, and his daughters, and his oxen, and his donkeys, and his sheep, and his tent, and all that he had: and they brought them unto the valley of Achor.

25 And Joshua said, Why have you troubled us? the Becoming-One shall trouble you this day. And all Israel stoned him with stones, and burned them with fire, after they had stoned them with stones.

26 And they raised over him a great heap of stones unto this day. So the Becoming-One turned from the fierceness of his anger. Therefore the name of that place was called, The valley of Achor, unto this day.

Josh 8:1 And the Becoming-One said unto Joshua, Fear not, neither be you dismayed: take all the people of war with you, and arise, go up to Ai: see, I have given into your hand the king of Ai, and his people, and his city, and his land:

2 And you shall do to Ai and her king as you did unto Jericho and her king: only the spoil thereof, and the cattle thereof, shall you take for a prey unto yourselves: lay you an ambush for the city behind it.

3 So Joshua arose, and all the people of war, to go up against Ai: and Joshua chose out thirty thousand mighty men of valor, and sent them away by night.

4 And he commanded them, saying, Behold, you shall lie in wait against the city, even behind the city: go not very far from the city, but be you all ready:

5 And I, and all the people that are with me, will approach unto the city: and it shall come to pass, when they come out against us, as at the first, that we will flee before them,

6 For they will come out after us till we have drawn them from the city; for they will say, They flee before us, as at the first: therefore we will flee before them.

7 Then you shall rise up from the ambush, and seize upon the city: for the Becoming-One your God will deliver it into your hand.

8 And it shall be, when you have taken the city, that you shall set the city on fire: according to the commandment of the Becoming-One shall you do. See, I have commanded you.

9 Joshua therefore sent them forth: and they went to lie in ambush, and abode between Bethel and Ai, on the west side of Ai: but Joshua lodged that night among the people.

10 And Joshua rose up early in the morning, and numbered the people, and went up, he and the elders of Israel, before the people to Ai.

11 And all the people, even the people of war that were with him, went up, and drew near, and came before the city, and pitched on the north side of Ai: now there was a valley between them and Ai.

12 And he took about five thousand of men, and set them to lie in ambush between Bethel and Ai, on the west side of the city.

13 And when they had set the people, even all the host that was on the north of the city, and their ambushers on the west of the city, Joshua went that night into the midst of the valley.

14 And it came to pass, when the king of Ai saw it, that they hasted and rose up early, and the men of the city went out against Israel to battle, he and all his people, at a set time,[102] before the plain; but he knew not that there were liers in ambush against him behind the city.

15 And Joshua and all Israel made as if they were beaten before them, and fled by the way of the wilderness.

16 And all the people that were in Ai were called together to pursue after them: and they pursued after Joshua, and were drawn away from the city.

17 And there was not a man left in Ai or Bethel, that went not out after Israel: and they left the city open, and pursued after Israel.

18 And the Becoming-One said unto Joshua, Stretch out the spear that is in your hand toward Ai; for I will give it into your hand. And Joshua stretched out the spear that he had in his hand toward the city.

19 And the ambush arose quickly out of their place, and they ran as soon as he had stretched out his hand: and they entered into the city, and took it, and hasted and set the city on fire.

20 And when the men of Ai looked behind them, they saw, and, behold, the smoke of the city ascended up to heaven, and they had no power to flee this way or that way: and the people that fled to the wilderness turned back upon the pursuers.

21 And when Joshua and all Israel saw that the ambush had taken the city, and that the smoke of the city ascended, then they turned again, and killed the men of Ai.

22 And the other issued out of the city against them; so they were in the midst of Israel, some on this side, and some on that side: and they smote them, so that they let none of them remain or escape.

23 And the king of Ai they took alive, and brought him to Joshua.

24 And it came to pass, when Israel had made an end of slaying all the inhabitants of Ai in the field, in the wilderness wherein they chased them, and when they were all fallen on the edge of the sword, until they were consumed, that all the Israelites returned unto Ai, and smote it with the edge of the sword.

25 And so it was, that all that fell that day, both of men and women, were twelve thousand, even all the men of Ai.

26 For Joshua drew not his hand back, wherewith he stretched out the spear, until he had utterly destroyed all the inhabitants of Ai.

27 Only the cattle and the spoil of that city Israel took for a prey unto themselves, according unto the word of the Becoming-One which he commanded Joshua.

28 And Joshua burnt Ai, and made it a heap for olam, even a desolation unto this day.

29 And the king of Ai he hanged on a tree until eventide: and as soon as the sun was down, Joshua commanded that they should take his carcase down from the tree, and cast it at the entering of the gate of the city, and raise thereon a great heap of stones, that remains unto this day.

30 Then Joshua built an altar unto the Becoming-One, God of Israel in mount Ebal,

31 As Moses the servant of the Becoming-One commanded the children of Israel, as it is written in the book of the law of Moses, an altar of whole stones, over which no man has lift up any iron: and they offered thereon burnt offerings unto the Becoming-One, and sacrificed peace offerings.

32 And he wrote there upon the stones a copy of the law of Moses, which he wrote in the presence of the children of Israel.

33 And all Israel, and their elders, and their officers and judges, stood on this side and on that side of the ark of the covenant of the Becoming-One, as well the stranger as the home-born [Israelite]; half of them toward mount Gerizim, and the other half of them toward mount Ebal; as Moses the servant of the Becoming-One had commanded, that they should bless the people of Israel, in the beginning.

34 And afterward he read all the words of the law, the blessings and cursings, according to all that is written in the book of the law.

35 There was not a word of all that Moses commanded, which Joshua read not before all the congregation of Israel, with the women, and the little ones, and the strangers that were conversant among them.

Josh 9:1 And it came to pass, when all the kings which were over the Jordan, in the hills, and in the valleys, and in all the coasts of the great sea over against Lebanon, the Hittite, and the Amorite, the Canaanite, the Perizzite, the Hivite, and the Jebusite, heard thereof;

2 That they gathered themselves together, to fight with Joshua and with Israel, with one accord.

3 And when the inhabitants of Gibeon heard what Joshua had done unto Jericho and to Ai,

4 They did work prudently, and went and made as if they had been ambassadors, and took old sacks upon their donkeys, and wine bottles, old, and rent, and bound up;

5 And old shoes and clouted upon their feet, and old garments upon them; and all the bread of their provision was dry and mouldy.

6 And they went to Joshua unto the camp at Gilgal, and said unto him, and to the men of Israel, We be come from a far country: now therefore make you a league with us.

7 And the men of Israel said unto the Hivites, Perhaps you dwell among us; and how shall we make a league with you?

8 And they said unto Joshua, We are your servants. And Joshua said unto them, Who are ye? and from where do you come?

9 And they said unto him, From a very far country your servants are come because of the name of the Becoming-One your God: for we have heard the fame of him, and all that he did in Egypt,

10 And all that he did to the two kings of the Amorites, that were beyond Jordan, to Sihon king of Heshbon, and to Og king of Bashan, which was at Ashtaroth.

11 Therefore our elders and all the inhabitants of our country spoke to us, saying, Take victuals with you for the journey, and go to meet them, and say unto

---

[102] Appointed time or festival

them, We are your servants: therefore now make you a league with us.

12 This our bread we took hot for our provision out of our houses on the day we came forth to go unto you; but now, behold, it is dry, and it is mouldy:

13 And these bottles of wine, which we filled, were new; and, behold, they be rent: and these our garments and our shoes are become old by reason of the very long journey.

14 And the men took of their victuals, and asked not counsel at the mouth of the Becoming-One.

15 And Joshua made peace with them, and made a league with them, to let them live: and the princes of the congregation swore unto them.

16 And it came to pass at the end of three days after they had made a league with them, that they heard that they were their neighbors, and that they dwelt among them.

17 And the children of Israel journeyed, and came unto their cities on the third day. Now their cities were Gibeon, and Chephirah, and Beeroth, and Kirjathjearim.

18 And the children of Israel smote them not, because the princes of the congregation had sworn unto them by the Becoming-One, God of Israel. And all the congregation murmured against the princes.

19 But all the princes said unto all the congregation, We have sworn unto them by the Becoming-One, God of Israel: now therefore we may not touch them.

20 This we will do to them; we will even let them live, lest wrath be upon us, because of the oath which we swore unto them.

21 And the princes said unto them, Let them live; but let them be hewers of wood and drawers of water unto all the congregation; as the princes had promised them.

22 And Joshua called for them, and he spoke unto them, saying, Why have you beguiled us, saying, We are very far from you; when you dwell among us?

23 Now therefore you are cursed, and there shall none of you be freed from being bondmen, and hewers of wood and drawers of water for the house of my God.

24 And they answered Joshua, and said, Because it was certainly told your servants, how that the Becoming-One your God commanded his servant Moses to give you all the land, and to destroy all the inhabitants of the land from before you, therefore we were greatly afraid of our souls because of you, and have done this thing.

25 And now, behold, we are in your hand: as it seems good and right unto you to do unto us, do.

26 And so did he unto them, and delivered them out of the hand of the children of Israel, that they killed them not.

27 And Joshua made them that day hewers of wood and drawers of water for the congregation, and for the altar of the Becoming-One, even unto this day, in the place which he should choose.

Josh 10:1 Now it came to pass, when Adonizedek king of Jerusalem had heard how Joshua had taken Ai, and had utterly destroyed it; as he had done to Jericho and her king, so he had done to Ai and her king; and how the inhabitants of Gibeon had made peace with Israel, and were among them;

2 That they feared greatly, because Gibeon was a great city, as one of the royal cities, and because it was greater than Ai, and all the men thereof were mighty.

3 Therefore Adonizedek king of Jerusalem sent unto Hoham king of Hebron, and unto Piram king of Jarmuth, and unto Japhia king of Lachish, and unto Debir king of Eglon, saying,

4 Come up unto me, and help me, that we may smite Gibeon: for it has made peace with Joshua and with the children of Israel.

5 Therefore the five kings of the Amorites, the king of Jerusalem, the king of Hebron, the king of Jarmuth, the king of Lachish, the king of Eglon, gathered themselves together, and went up, they and all their hosts, and encamped before Gibeon, and made war against it.

6 And the men of Gibeon sent unto Joshua to the camp to Gilgal, saying, Slack not your hand from your servants; come up to us quickly, and save us, and help us: for all the kings of the Amorites that dwell in the mountains are gathered together against us.

7 So Joshua ascended from Gilgal, he, and all the people of war with him, and all the mighty men of valor.

8 And the Becoming-One said unto Joshua, Fear them not: for I have delivered them into your hand; there shall not a man of them stand before you.

9 Joshua therefore came unto them suddenly, and went up from Gilgal all night.

10 And the Becoming-One discomfited them before Israel, and killed them with a great slaughter at Gibeon, and chased them along the way that goes up to Beth-horon, and smote them to Azekah, and unto Makkedah.

11 And it came to pass, as they fled from before Israel, and were in the going down to Beth-horon, that the Becoming-One cast down great stones from the heavens upon them unto Azekah, and they died: they were more which died with hailstones than they whom the children of Israel killed with the sword.

12 Then spoke Joshua to the Becoming-One in the day when the Becoming-One delivered up the Amorites before the children of Israel, and he said in the sight of Israel, Sun, stand you still upon Gibeon; and you, Moon, in the valley of Ajalon.

13 And the sun stood still, and the moon stayed, until the people had avenged themselves upon their enemies. Is not this written in the book of Jasher? So the sun stood still in the midst of heaven, and hasted not to go down about a whole day.

14 And there was no day like that before it or after it, that the Becoming-One listened unto the voice of a man: for the Becoming-One fought for Israel.

15 And Joshua returned, and all Israel with him, unto the camp to Gilgal.

16 But these five kings fled, and hid themselves in a cave at Makkedah.

17 And it was told Joshua, saying, The five kings are found hid in a cave at Makkedah.

18 And Joshua said, Roll great stones upon the mouth of the cave, and set men by it for to keep them:

19 And stay you not, but pursue after your enemies, and smite the hindmost of them; permit them

not to enter into their cities: for the Becoming-One your God has delivered them into your hand.

20 And it came to pass, when Joshua and the children of Israel had made an end of slaying them with a very great slaughter, till they were consumed, that the rest which remained of them entered into fenced cities.

21 And all the people returned to the camp to Joshua at Makkedah in peace: none moved his tongue against any of the children of Israel.

22 Then said Joshua, Open the mouth of the cave, and bring out those five kings unto me out of the cave.

23 And they did so, and brought forth those five kings unto him out of the cave, the king of Jerusalem, the king of Hebron, the king of Jarmuth, the king of Lachish, and the king of Eglon.

24 And it came to pass, when they brought out those kings unto Joshua, that Joshua called for all the men of Israel, and said unto the captains of the men of war which went with him, Come near, put your feet upon the necks of these kings. And they came near, and put their feet upon the necks of them.

25 And Joshua said unto them, Fear not, nor be dismayed, be strong and of good courage: for thus shall the Becoming-One do to all your enemies against whom you fight.

26 And afterward Joshua smote them, and killed them, and hanged them on five trees: and they were hanging upon the trees until the evening.

27 And it came to pass at the time of the going down of the sun, that Joshua commanded, and they took them down off the trees, and cast them into the cave wherein they had been hid, and laid great stones in the cave's mouth, which remain until this very day.

28 And that day Joshua took Makkedah, and smote it with the edge of the sword, and the king thereof he utterly destroyed, them, and all the souls that were therein; he let none remain: and he did to the king of Makkedah as he did unto the king of Jericho.

29 Then Joshua passed from Makkedah, and all Israel with him, unto Libnah, and fought against Libnah:

30 And the Becoming-One delivered it also, and the king thereof, into the hand of Israel; and he smote it with the edge of the sword, and all the souls that were therein; he let none remain in it; but did unto the king thereof as he did unto the king of Jericho.

31 And Joshua passed from Libnah, and all Israel with him, unto Lachish, and encamped against it, and fought against it:

32 And the Becoming-One delivered Lachish into the hand of Israel, which took it on the second day, and smote it with the edge of the sword, and all the souls that were therein, according to all that he had done to Libnah.

33 Then Horam king of Gezer came up to help Lachish; and Joshua smote him and his people, until he had left him none remaining.

34 And from Lachish Joshua passed unto Eglon, and all Israel with him; and they encamped against it, and fought against it:

35 And they took it on that day, and smote it with the edge of the sword, and all the souls that were therein he utterly destroyed that day, according to all that he had done to Lachish.

36 And Joshua went up from Eglon, and all Israel with him, unto Hebron; and they fought against it:

37 And they took it, and smote it with the edge of the sword, and the king thereof, and all the cities thereof, and all the souls that were therein; he left none remaining, according to all that he had done to Eglon; but destroyed it utterly, and all the souls that were therein.

38 And Joshua returned, and all Israel with him, to Debir; and fought against it:

39 And he took it, and the king thereof, and all the cities thereof; and they smote them with the edge of the sword, and utterly destroyed all the souls that were therein; he left none remaining: as he had done to Hebron, so he did to Debir, and to the king thereof; as he had done also to Libnah, and to her king.

40 So Joshua smote all the country of the hills, and of the south, and of the vale, and of the springs, and all their kings: he left none remaining, but utterly destroyed all that breathed, as the Becoming-One, God of Israel commanded.

41 And Joshua smote them from Kadeshbarnea even unto Gaza, and all the country of Goshen, even unto Gibeon.

42 And all these kings and their land did Joshua take at one time, because the Becoming-One, God of Israel fought for Israel.

43 And Joshua returned, and all Israel with him, unto the camp to Gilgal.

Josh 11:1 And it came to pass, when Jabin king of Hazor had heard those things, that he sent to Jobab king of Madon, and to the king of Shimron, and to the king of Achshaph,

2 And to the kings that were on the north of the mountains, and of the plains south of Chinneroth, and in the valley, and in the borders of Dor on the west,

3 And to the Canaanite on the east and on the west, and to the Amorite, and the Hittite, and the Perizzite, and the Jebusite in the mountains, and to the Hivite under Hermon in the land of Mizpeh.

4 And they went out, they and all their hosts with them, much people, even as the sand that is upon the sea shore in multitude, with horses and chariots very many.

5 And when all these kings were met together, they came and pitched together at the waters of Merom, to fight against Israel.

6 And the Becoming-One said unto Joshua, Be not afraid because of them: for tomorrow about this time will I deliver them up all slain before Israel: you shall hock their horses, and burn their chariots with fire.

7 So Joshua came, and all the people of war with him, against them by the waters of Merom suddenly; and they fell upon them.

8 And the Becoming-One delivered them into the hand of Israel, who smote them, and chased them unto great Zidon, and unto Misrephothmaim, and unto the valley of Mizpeh eastward; and they smote them, until they left them none remaining.

9 And Joshua did unto them as the Becoming-One bade him: he hocked their horses, and burnt their chariots with fire.

10 And Joshua at that time turned back, and took Hazor, and smote the king thereof with the sword: for Hazor beforetime was the head of all those kingdoms.

11 And they smote all the souls that were therein with the edge of the sword, utterly destroying them: there was not any left to breathe: and he burnt Hazor with fire.

12 And all the cities of those kings, and all the kings of them, did Joshua take, and smote them with the edge of the sword, and he utterly destroyed them, as Moses the servant of the Becoming-One commanded.

13 But as for the cities that stood still in their strength, Israel burned none of them, save Hazor only; that did Joshua burn.

14 And all the spoil of these cities, and the cattle, the children of Israel took for a prey unto themselves; but every man they smote with the edge of the sword, until they had destroyed them, neither left they any to breathe.

15 As the Becoming-One commanded Moses his servant, so did Moses command Joshua, and so did Joshua; he left nothing undone of all that the Becoming-One commanded Moses.

16 So Joshua took all that land, the hills, and all the south country, and all the land of Goshen, and the valley, and the plain, and the mountain of Israel, and the valley of the same;

17 Even from the mount Halak, that goes up to Seir, even unto Baal-Gad in the valley of Lebanon under mount Hermon: and all their kings he took, and smote them, and killed them.

18 Joshua made war a long time with all those kings.

19 There was not a city that made peace with the children of Israel, save the Hivites the inhabitants of Gibeon: all other they took in battle.

20 For it was of the Becoming-One to harden their hearts, that they should come against Israel in battle, that he might destroy them utterly, and that they might have no favor, but that he might destroy them, as the Becoming-One commanded Moses.

21 And at that time came Joshua, and cut off the Anakims from the mountains, from Hebron, from Debir, from Anab, and from all the mountains of Judah, and from all the mountains of Israel: Joshua destroyed them utterly with their cities.

22 There was none of the Anakims left in the land of the children of Israel: only in Gaza, in Gath, and in Ashdod, there remained.

23 So Joshua took the whole land, according to all that the Becoming-One said unto Moses; and Joshua gave it for an inheritance unto Israel according to their divisions by their tribes. And the land rested from war.

Josh 12:1 Now these are the kings of the land, which the children of Israel smote, and possessed their land beyond Jordan toward the rising of the sun, from the river Arnon unto mount Hermon, and all the plain on the east:

2 Sihon king of the Amorites, who dwelt in Heshbon, and ruled from Aroer, which is upon the bank of the river Arnon, and from the middle of the river, and from half Gilead, even unto the river Jabbok, which is the border of the children of Ammon;

3 And from the plain to the sea of Chinneroth on the east, and unto the sea of the plain, even the salt sea on the east, the way to Beth-jeshimoth; and from the south, under Ashdothpisgah:

4 And the coast of Og king of Bashan, which was of the remnant of the giants, that dwelt at Ashtaroth and at Edrei,

5 And reigned in mount Hermon, and in Salcah, and in all Bashan, unto the border of the Geshurites and the Maachathites, and half Gilead, the border of Sihon king of Heshbon.

6 Them did Moses the servant of the Becoming-One and the children of Israel smite: and Moses the servant of the Becoming-One gave it for a possession unto the Reubenites, and the Gadites, and the half tribe of Manasseh.

7 And these are the kings of the country which Joshua and the children of Israel smote over Jordan on the west, from Baal-Gad in the valley of Lebanon even unto the mount Halak, that goes up to Seir; which Joshua gave unto the tribes of Israel for a possession according to their divisions;

8 In the mountains, and in the valleys, and in the plains, and in the springs, and in the wilderness, and in the south country; the Hittites, the Amorites, and the Canaanites, the Perizzites, the Hivites, and the Jebusites:

9 The king of Jericho, one; the king of Ai, which is beside Bethel, one;

10 The king of Jerusalem, one; the king of Hebron, one;

11 The king of Jarmuth, one; the king of Lachish, one;

12 The king of Eglon, one; the king of Gezer, one;

13 The king of Debir, one; the king of Geder, one;

14 The king of Hormah, one; the king of Arad, one;

15 The king of Libnah, one; the king of Adullam, one;

16 The king of Makkedah, one; the king of Bethel, one;

17 The king of Tappuah, one; the king of Hepher, one;

18 The king of Aphek, one; the king of Lasharon, one;

19 The king of Madon, one; the king of Hazor, one;

20 The king of Shimronmeron, one; the king of Achshaph, one;

21 The king of Taanach, one; the king of Megiddo, one;

22 The king of Kedesh, one; the king of Jokneam of Carmel, one;

23 The king of Dor in the coast of Dor, one; the king of the nations of Gilgal, one;

24 The king of Tirzah, one: all the kings thirty and one.

Josh 13:1 Now Joshua was old and advanced in years; and the Becoming-One said unto him, you are old and advanced in years, and there remains yet very much land to be possessed.

2 This is the land that yet remains: all the borders of the Philistines, and all Geshuri,

3 From Sihor, which is before Egypt, even unto the borders of Ekron northward, which is counted to the Canaanite: five lords of the Philistines; the Gazathites, and the Ashdothites, the Eshkalonites, the Gittites, and the Ekronites; also the Avites:

4 From the south, all the land of the Canaanites, and Mearah that is beside the Sidonians unto Aphek, to the borders of the Amorites:

5 And the land of the Giblites, and all Lebanon, toward the sunrising, from Baal-Gad under mount Hermon unto the entering into Hamath.

6 All the inhabitants of the hill country from Lebanon unto Misrephothmaim, and all the Sidonians, them will I drive out from before the children of Israel: only divide you it by lot unto the Israelites for an inheritance, as I have commanded you.

7 Now therefore divide this land for an inheritance unto the nine tribes, and the half tribe of Manasseh,

8 With whom the Reubenites and the Gadites have received their inheritance, which Moses gave them, beyond Jordan eastward, even as Moses the servant of the Becoming-One gave them;

9 From Aroer, that is upon the bank of the river Arnon, and the city that is in the midst of the river, and all the plain of Medeba unto Dibon;

10 And all the cities of Sihon king of the Amorites, which reigned in Heshbon, unto the border of the children of Ammon;

11 And Gilead, and the border of the Geshurites and Maachathites, and all mount Hermon, and all Bashan unto Salcah;

12 All the kingdom of Og in Bashan, which reigned in Ashtaroth and in Edrei, who remained of the remnant of the giants: for these did Moses smite, and cast them out.

13 Nevertheless the children of Israel expelled not the Geshurites, nor the Maachathites: but the Geshurites and the Maachathites dwell among the Israelites until this day.

14 Only unto the tribe of Levi he gave none inheritance; the sacrifices of the Becoming-One, God of Israel made by fire are their inheritance, as he said unto them.

15 And Moses gave unto the tribe of the children of Reuben inheritance according to their families.

16 And their coast was from Aroer, that is on the bank of the river Arnon, and the city that is in the midst of the river, and all the plain by Medeba;

17 Heshbon, and all her cities that are in the plain; Dibon, and Bamoth-Baal, and Beth-Baal-Meon,

18 And Jahaza, and Kedemoth, and Mephaath,

19 And Kirjathaim, and Sibmah, and Zareth-Shahar in the mount of the valley,

20 And Beth-Peor, and Ashdothpisgah, and Beth-Jeshi-Moth,

21 And all the cities of the plain, and all the kingdom of Sihon king of the Amorites, which reigned in Heshbon, whom Moses smote with the princes of Midian, Evi, and Rekem, and Zur, and Hur, and Reba, which were chiefs of Sihon, dwelling in the country.

22 Balaam also the son of Beor, the soothsayer, did the children of Israel slay with the sword among them that were slain by them.

23 And the border of the children of Reuben was Jordan, and the border thereof. This was the inheritance of the children of Reuben after their families, the cities and the villages thereof.

24 And Moses gave inheritance unto the tribe of Gad, even unto the children of Gad according to their families.

25 And their coast was Jazer, and all the cities of Gilead, and half the land of the children of Ammon, unto Aroer that is before Rabbah;

26 And from Heshbon unto Ramathmizpeh, and Betonim; and from Mahanaim unto the border of Debir;

27 And in the valley, Beth-aram, and Beth-nimrah, and Succoth, and Zaphon, the rest of the kingdom of Sihon king of Heshbon, Jordan and his border, even unto the edge of the sea of Chinnereth over the Jordan eastward.

28 This is the inheritance of the children of Gad after their families, the cities, and their villages.

29 And Moses gave inheritance unto the half tribe of Manasseh: and this was the possession of the half tribe of the children of Manasseh by their families.

30 And their coast was from Mahanaim, all Bashan, all the kingdom of Og king of Bashan, and all the towns of Jair, which are in Bashan, threescore cities:

31 And half Gilead, and Ashtaroth, and Edrei, cities of the kingdom of Og in Bashan, were pertaining unto the children of Machir the son of Manasseh, even to the one half of the children of Machir by their families.

32 These are the countries which Moses did distribute for inheritance in the plains of Moab, over the Jordan, by Jericho, eastward.

33 But unto the tribe of Levi Moses gave not any inheritance: the Becoming-One, God of Israel was their inheritance, as he said unto them.

Josh 14:1 And these are the countries which the children of Israel inherited in the land of Canaan, which Eleazar the priest, and Joshua the son of Nun, and the heads of the fathers of the tribes of the children of Israel, distributed for inheritance to them.

2 By lot was their inheritance, as the Becoming-One commanded by the hand of Moses, for the nine tribes, and for the half tribe.

3 For Moses had given the inheritance of two tribes and a half tribe beyond Jordan: but unto the Levites he gave none inheritance among them.

4 For the children of Joseph were two tribes, Manasseh and Ephraim: therefore they gave no part unto the Levites in the land, save cities to dwell in, with their suburbs for their cattle and for their substance.

5 As the Becoming-One commanded Moses, so the children of Israel did, and they divided the land.

6 Then the children of Judah came unto Joshua in Gilgal: and Caleb the son of Jephunneh the Kenezite said unto him, you know the thing that the Becoming-One said unto Moses the man of God concerning me and you in Kadeshbarnea.

7 A son of forty years was I when Moses the servant of the Becoming-One sent me from Kadeshbarnea to spy out the land; and I brought him word again as it was in mine heart.

8 Nevertheless my brethren that went up with me made the heart of the people melt: but I wholly followed the Becoming-One my God.

9 And Moses swore on that day, saying, Surely the land whereon your feet have trodden shall be your inheritance, and your children's for olam, because you have wholly followed the Becoming-One my God.

10 And now, behold, the Becoming-One has kept me alive, as he said, these forty and five years, even since the Becoming-One spoke this word unto Moses,

while the children of Israel wandered in the wilderness: and now, lo, I am this day a son of fourscore and five years.

11 As yet I am as strong this day as I was in the day that Moses sent me: as my strength was then, even so is my strength now, for war, both to go out, and to come in.

12 Now therefore give me this mountain, whereof the Becoming-One spoke in that day; for you heard in that day how the Anakims were there, and that the cities were great and fenced: if so be the Becoming-One will be with me, then I shall be able to drive them out, as the Becoming-One said.

13 And Joshua blessed him, and gave unto Caleb the son of Jephunneh Hebron for an inheritance.

14 Hebron therefore became the inheritance of Caleb the son of Jephunneh the Kenezite unto this day, because that he wholly followed the Becoming-One, God of Israel.

15 And the name of Hebron before was Kirjatharba; which Arba was a great man among the Anakims. And the land had rest from war.

Josh 15:1 This then was the lot of the tribe of the children of Judah by their families; even to the border of Edom the wilderness of Zin southward was the uttermost part of the south coast.

2 And their south border was from the shore of the salt sea, from the bay that looks southward:

3 And it went out to the south side to Maalehacrabbim, and passed along to Zin, and ascended up on the south side unto Kadeshbarnea, and passed along to Hezron, and went up to Adar, and fetched a compass to Karkaa:

4 From there it passed toward Azmon, and went out unto the river of Egypt; and the goings out of that coast were at the sea: this shall be your south coast.

5 And the east border was the salt sea, even unto the end of Jordan. And their border in the north quarter was from the bay of the sea at the uttermost part of Jordan:

6 And the border went up to Beth-hogla, and passed along by the north of Beth-arabah; and the border went up to the stone of Bohan the son of Reuben:

7 And the border went up toward Debir from the valley of Achor, and so northward, looking toward Gilgal, that is before the going up to Adummim, which is on the south side of the river: and the border passed toward the waters of Enshemesh, and the goings out thereof were at Enrogel:

8 And the border went up by the valley of the son of Hinnom unto the south side of the Jebusite; the same is Jerusalem: and the border went up to the top of the mountain that lies before the valley of Hinnom westward, which is at the end of the valley of the giants northward;

9 And the border was drawn from the top of the hill unto the fountain of the water of Nephtoah, and went out to the cities of mount Ephron; and the border was drawn to Baalah, which is Kirjathjearim:

10 And the border compassed from Baalah westward unto mount Seir, and passed along unto the side of mount Jearim, which is Chesalon, on the north side, and went down to Beth-shemesh, and passed on to Timnah:

11 And the border went out unto the side of Ekron northward: and the border was drawn to Shicron, and passed along to mount Baalah, and went out unto Jabneel; and the goings out of the border were at the sea.

12 And the west border was to the great sea, and the coast thereof. This is the coast of the children of Judah round about according to their families.

13 And unto Caleb the son of Jephunneh he gave a part among the children of Judah, according to the commandment of the Becoming-One to Joshua, even the city of Arba the father of Anak, which city is Hebron.

14 And Caleb drove there the three sons of Anak, Sheshai, and Ahiman, and Talmai, the children of Anak.

15 And he went up there to the inhabitants of Debir: and the name of Debir before was Kirjathsepher.

16 And Caleb said, He that smites Kirjathsepher, and takes it, to him will I give Achsah my daughter to wife.

17 And Othniel the son of Kenaz, the brother of Caleb, took it: and he gave him Achsah his daughter to wife.

18 And it came to pass, as she came unto him, that she moved him to ask of her father a field: and she lighted off her donkey; and Caleb said unto her, What would you?

19 Who answered, Give me a blessing; for you have given me a south land; give me also springs of water. And he gave her the upper springs, and the nether springs.

20 This is the inheritance of the tribe of the children of Judah according to their families.

21 And the uttermost cities of the tribe of the children of Judah toward the coast of Edom southward were Kabzeel, and Eder, and Jagur,

22 And Kinah, and Dimonah, and Adadah,

23 And Kedesh, and Hazor, and Ithnan,

24 Ziph, and Telem, and Bealoth,

25 And Hazor, Hadattah, and Kerioth, and Hezron, which is Hazor,

26 Amam, and Shema, and Moladah,

27 And Hazargaddah, and Heshmon, and Beth-palet,

28 And Hazarshual, and Beersheba, and Bizjothjah,

29 Baalah, and Iim, and Azem,

30 And Eltolad, and Chesil, and Hormah,

31 And Ziklag, and Madmannah, and Sansannah,

32 And Lebaoth, and Shilhim, and Ain, and Rimmon: all the cities are twenty and nine, with their villages:

33 And in the valley, Eshtaol, and Zoreah, and Ashnah,

34 And Zanoah, and Engannim, Tappuah, and Enam,

35 Jarmuth, and Adullam, Socoh, and Azekah,

36 And Sharaim, and Adithaim, and Gederah, and Gederothaim; fourteen cities with their villages:

37 Zenan, and Hadashah, and Migdalgad,

38 And Dilean, and Mizpeh, and Jokyoul,

39 Lachish, and Bozkath, and Eglon,

40 And Cabbon, and Lahmam, and Kithlish,

41 And Gederoth, Beth-dagon, and Naamah, and Makkedah; sixteen cities with their villages:

42 Libnah, and Ether, and Ashan,

43 And Jiphtah, and Ashnah, and Nezib,

44 And Keilah, and Achzib, and Mareshah; nine cities with their villages:

45 Ekron, with her towns and her villages:

46 From Ekron even unto the sea, all that lay near Ashdod, with their villages:

47 Ashdod with her towns and her villages, Gaza with her towns and her villages, unto the river of Egypt, and the great sea, and the border thereof:

48 And in the mountains, Shamir, and Jattir, and Socoh,

49 And Dannah, and Kirjathsannah, which is Debir,

50 And Anab, and Eshtemoh, and Anim,

51 And Goshen, and Holon, and Giloh; eleven cities with their villages:

52 Arab, and Dumah, and Eshean,

53 And Janum, and Beth-tappuah, and Aphekah,

54 And Humtah, and Kirjatharba, which is Hebron, and Zior; nine cities with their villages:

55 Maon, Carmel, and Ziph, and Juttah,

56 And Jezreel, and Jokdeam, and Zanoah,

57 Cain, Gibeah, and Timnah; ten cities with their villages:

58 Halhul, Beth-zur, and Gedor,

59 And Maarath, and Beth-anoth, and Eltekon; six cities with their villages:

60 Kirjath-Baal, which is Kirjathjearim, and Rabbah; two cities with their villages:

61 In the wilderness, Beth-arabah, Middin, and Secacah,

62 And Nibshan, and the city of Salt, and Engedi; six cities with their villages.

63 As for the Jebusites the inhabitants of Jerusalem, the children of Judah could not drive them out: but the Jebusites dwell with the children of Judah at Jerusalem unto this day.

Josh 16:1 And the lot of the children of Joseph fell from Jordan by Jericho, unto the water of Jericho on the east, to the wilderness that goes up from Jericho throughout mount Bethel.

2 And goes out from Bethel to Luz, and passes along unto the borders of Archi to Ataroth,

3 And goes down westward to the coast of Japhleti, unto the coast of Beth-horon the nether, and to Gezer: and the goings out thereof are at the sea.

4 So the children of Joseph, Manasseh and Ephraim, took their inheritance.

5 And the border of the children of Ephraim according to their families was thus: even the border of their inheritance on the east side was Atarothaddar, unto Beth-horon the upper;

6 And the border went out toward the sea to Michmethah on the north side; and the border went about eastward unto Taanathshiloh, and passed by it on the east to Janohah;

7 And it went down from Janohah to Ataroth, and to Naarath, and came to Jericho, and went out at Jordan.

8 The border went out from Tappuah westward unto the river Kanah; and the goings out thereof were at the sea. This is the inheritance of the tribe of the children of Ephraim by their families.

9 And the separate cities for the children of Ephraim were among the inheritance of the children of Manasseh, all the cities with their villages.

10 And they drove not out the Canaanites that dwelt in Gezer: but the Canaanites dwell among the Ephraimites unto this day, and serve under tribute.

Josh 17:1 There was also a lot for the tribe of Manasseh; for he was the firstborn of Joseph; to wit, for Machir the firstborn of Manasseh, the father of Gilead: because he was a man of war, therefore he had Gilead and Bashan.

2 There was also a lot for the rest of the children of Manasseh by their families; for the children of Abiezer, and for the children of Helek, and for the children of Asriel, and for the children of Shechem, and for the children of Hepher, and for the children of Shemida: these were the male children of Manasseh the son of Joseph by their families.

3 But Zelophehad, the son of Hepher, the son of Gilead, the son of Machir, the son of Manasseh, had no sons, but daughters: and these are the names of his daughters, Mahlah, and Noah, Hoglah, Milcah, and Tirzah.

4 And they came near before Eleazar the priest, and before Joshua the son of Nun, and before the princes, saying, The Becoming-One commanded Moses to give us an inheritance among our brethren. Therefore according to the commandment of the Becoming-One he gave them an inheritance among the brethren of their father.

5 And there fell ten portions to Manasseh, beside the land of Gilead and Bashan, which were beyond Jordan;

6 Because the daughters of Manasseh had an inheritance among his sons: and the rest of Manasseh's sons had the land of Gilead.

7 And the coast of Manasseh was from Asher to Michmethah, that lies before Shechem; and the border went along on the right hand unto the inhabitants of Entappuah.

8 Now Manasseh had the land of Tappuah: but Tappuah on the border of Manasseh belonged to the children of Ephraim;

9 And the coast descended unto the river Kanah, southward of the river: these cities of Ephraim are among the cities of Manasseh: the coast of Manasseh also was on the north side of the river, and the outgoings of it were at the sea:

10 Southward it was Ephraim's, and northward it was Manasseh's, and the sea is his border; and they met together in Asher on the north, and in Issachar on the east.

11 And Manasseh had in Issachar and in Asher Beth-shean and her towns, and Ibleam and her towns, and the inhabitants of Dor and her towns, and the inhabitants of Endor and her towns, and the inhabitants of Taanach and her towns, and the inhabitants of Megiddo and her towns, even three countries.

12 Yet the children of Manasseh could not drive out the inhabitants of those cities; but the Canaanites would dwell in that land.

13 Yet it came to pass, when the children of Israel were waxen strong, that they put the Canaanites to tribute; but did not utterly drive them out.

14 And the children of Joseph spoke unto Joshua, saying, Why have you given me but one lot and one portion to inherit, seeing I am a great people, forasmuch as the Becoming-One has blessed me hitherto?

15 And Joshua answered them, If you be a great people, then get you up to the wood country, and cut down for yourself there in the land of the Perizzites and of the giants, if mount Ephraim be too narrow for you.

16 And the children of Joseph said, The hill is not enough for us: and all the Canaanites that dwell in the land of the valley have chariots of iron, both they who are of Beth-shean and her towns, and they who are of the valley of Jezreel.

17 And Joshua spoke unto the house of Joseph, even to Ephraim and to Manasseh, saying, you are a great people, and have great power: you shall not have one lot only:

18 But the mountain shall be yours; for it is a wood, and you shall cut it down: and the outgoings of it shall be yours: for you shall drive out the Canaanites, though they have iron chariots, and though they be strong.

Josh 18:1 And the whole congregation of the children of Israel assembled together at Shiloh, and set up the tabernacle of the set time there. And the land was subdued before them.

2 And there remained among the children of Israel seven tribes, which had not yet received their inheritance.

3 And Joshua said unto the children of Israel, How long will you show yourselves slack to go to possess the land, which the Becoming-One, God of your fathers has given you?

4 Give out from among you three men for each tribe: and I will send them, and they shall rise, and go through the land, and describe it according to the inheritance of them; and they shall come again to me.

5 And they shall divide it into seven parts: Judah shall abide in their coast on the south, and the house of Joseph shall abide in their coasts on the north.

6 you shall therefore describe the land into seven parts, and bring the description here to me, that I may cast lots for you here before the Becoming-One our God.

7 But the Levites have no part among you; for the priesthood of the Becoming-One is their inheritance: and Gad, and Reuben, and half the tribe of Manasseh, have received their inheritance beyond Jordan on the east, which Moses the servant of the Becoming-One gave them.

8 And the men arose, and went away: and Joshua charged them that went to describe the land, saying, Go and walk through the land, and describe it, and come again to me, that I may here cast lots for you before the Becoming-One in Shiloh.

9 And the men went and passed through the land, and described it by cities into seven parts in a book, and came again to Joshua to the host at Shiloh.

10 And Joshua cast lots for them in Shiloh before the Becoming-One: and there Joshua divided the land unto the children of Israel according to their divisions.

11 And the lot of the tribe of the children of Benjamin came up according to their families: and the coast of their lot came forth between the children of Judah and the children of Joseph.

12 And their border on the north side was from Jordan; and the border went up to the side of Jericho on the north side, and went up through the mountains westward; and the goings out thereof were at the wilderness of Beth-aven.

13 And the border went over from there toward Luz, to the side of Luz, which is Bethel, southward; and the border descended to Atarothadar, near the hill that lies on the south side of the nether Beth-horon.

14 And the border was drawn there, and compassed the corner of the sea southward, from the hill that lies before Beth-horon southward; and the goings out thereof were at Kirjath-Baal, which is Kirjathjearim, a city of the children of Judah: this was the west quarter.

15 And the south quarter was from the end of Kirjathjearim, and the border went out on the west, and went out to the well of waters of Nephtoah:

16 And the border came down to the end of the mountain that lies before the valley of the son of Hinnom, and which is in the valley of the giants on the north, and descended to the valley of Hinnom, to the side of Jebusi on the south, and descended to Enrogel,

17 And was drawn from the north, and went forth to Enshemesh, and went forth toward Geliloth, which is over against the going up of Adummim, and descended to the stone of Bohan the son of Reuben,

18 And passed along toward the side over against Arabah northward, and went down unto Arabah:

19 And the border passed along to the side of Beth-hoglah northward: and the outgoings of the border were at the north bay of the salt sea at the south end of Jordan: this was the south coast.

20 And Jordan was the border of it on the east side. This was the inheritance of the children of Benjamin, by the coasts thereof round about, according to their families.

21 Now the cities of the tribe of the children of Benjamin according to their families were Jericho, and Beth-hoglah, and the valley of Keziz.

22 And Beth-arabah, and Zemaraim, and Bethel,

23 And Avim, and Parah, and Ophrah,

24 And Chepharhaammonai, and Ophni, and Gaba; twelve cities with their villages:

25 Gibeon, and Ramah, and Beeroth,

26 And Mizpeh, and Chephirah, and Mozah,

27 And Rekem, and Irpeel, and Taralah,

28 And Zelah, Eleph, and Jebusi, which is Jerusalem, Gibeath, and Kirjath; fourteen cities with their villages. This is the inheritance of the children of Benjamin according to their families.

Josh 19:1 And the second lot came forth to Simeon, even for the tribe of the children of Simeon according to their families: and their inheritance was within the inheritance of the children of Judah.

2 And they had in their inheritance Beersheba, and Sheba, and Moladah,

3 And Hazarshual, and Balah, and Azem,

4 And Eltolad, and Bethul, and Hormah,

5 And Ziklag, and Beth-marcaboth, and Hazarsusah,

6 And Beth-lebaoth, and Sharuhen; thirteen cities and their villages:

7 Ain, Remmon, and Ether, and Ashan; four cities and their villages:

8 And all the villages that were round about these cities to Baal-Athbeer, Ramath of the south. This is the inheritance of the tribe of the children of Simeon according to their families.

9 Out of the portion of the children of Judah was the inheritance of the children of Simeon: for the part of the children of Judah was too much for them: therefore the children of Simeon had their inheritance within the inheritance of them.

10 And the third lot came up for the children of Zebulun according to their families: and the border of their inheritance was unto Sarid:

11 And their border went up toward the sea, and Maralah, and reached to Dabbasheth, and reached to the river that is before Jokneam;

12 And turned from Sarid eastward toward the sunrising unto the border of Chislothtabor, and then goes out to Daberath, and goes up to Japhia.

13 And from there passes on along on the east to Gittahhepher, to Ittahkazin, and goes out to Remmonmethoar to Neah;

14 And the border compasses it on the north side to Hannathon: and the outgoings thereof are in the valley of Jiphthahel:

15 And Kattath, and Nahallal, and Shimron, and Idalah, and Bethlehem: twelve cities with their villages.

16 This is the inheritance of the children of Zebulun according to their families, these cities with their villages.

17 And the fourth lot came out to Issachar, for the children of Issachar according to their families.

18 And their border was toward Jezreel, and Chesulloth, and Shunem,

19 And Haphraim, and Shihon, and Anaharath,

20 And Rabbith, and Kishion, and Abez,

21 And Remeth, and Engannim, and Enhaddah, and Beth-pazzez;

22 And the coast reaches to Tabor, and Shahazimah, and Beth-shemesh; and the outgoings of their border were at Jordan: sixteen cities with their villages.

23 This is the inheritance of the tribe of the children of Issachar according to their families, the cities and their villages.

24 And the fifth lot came out for the tribe of the children of Asher according to their families.

25 And their border was Helkath, and Hali, and Beten, and Achshaph,

26 And Alammelech, and Amad, and Misheal; and reaches to Carmel westward, and to Shihorlibnath;

27 And turns toward the sunrising to Beth-dagon, and reaches to Zebulun, and to the valley of Jiphthahel toward the north side of Beth-emek, and Neiel, and goes out to Cabul on the left hand,

28 And Hebron, and Rehob, and Hammon, and Kanah, even unto great Zidon;

29 And then the coast turns to Ramah, and to the strong city Tyre; and the coast turns to Hosah; and the outgoings thereof are at the sea from the coast to Achzib:

30 Ummah also, and Aphek, and Rehob: twenty and two cities with their villages.

31 This is the inheritance of the tribe of the children of Asher according to their families, these cities with their villages.

32 The sixth lot came out to the children of Naphtali, even for the children of Naphtali according to their families.

33 And their coast was from Heleph, from Allon to Zaanannim, and Adami, Nekeb, and Jabneel, unto Lakum; and the outgoings thereof were at Jordan:

34 And then the coast turns westward to Aznothtabor, and goes out from there to Hukkok, and reaches to Zebulun on the south side, and reaches to Asher on the west side, and to Judah upon Jordan toward the sunrising.

35 And the fenced cities are Ziddim, Zer, and Hammath, Rakkath, and Chinnereth,

36 And Adamah, and Ramah, and Hazor,

37 And Kedesh, and Edrei, and Enhazor,

38 And Iron, and Migdalel, Horem, and Beth-anath, and Beth-shemesh; nineteen cities with their villages.

39 This is the inheritance of the tribe of the children of Naphtali according to their families, the cities and their villages.

40 And the seventh lot came out for the tribe of the children of Dan according to their families.

41 And the coast of their inheritance was Zorah, and Eshtaol, and Irshemesh,

42 And Shaalabbin, and Ajalon, and Jethlah,

43 And Elon, and Thimnathah, and Ekron,

44 And Eltekeh, and Gibbethon, and Baalath,

45 And Jehud, and Bene-Berak, and Gath-Rimmon,

46 And Mejarkon, and Rakkon, with the border before Japho.

47 And the coast of the children of Dan went out too little for them: therefore the children of Dan went up to fight against Leshem, and took it, and smote it with the edge of the sword, and possessed it, and dwelt therein, and called Leshem, Dan, after the name of Dan their father.

48 This is the inheritance of the tribe of the children of Dan according to their families, these cities with their villages.

49 When they had made an end of dividing the land for inheritance by their coasts, the children of Israel gave an inheritance to Joshua the son of Nun among them:

50 According to the word of the Becoming-One they gave him the city which he asked, even Timnathserah in mount Ephraim: and he built the city, and dwelt therein.

51 These are the inheritances, which Eleazar the priest, and Joshua the son of Nun, and the heads of the fathers of the tribes of the children of Israel, divided for an inheritance by lot in Shiloh before the Becoming-One, at the door of the tabernacle of the set time. So they made an end of dividing the country.

Josh 20:1 The Becoming-One also spoke unto Joshua, saying,

2 Speak to the children of Israel, saying, Appoint out for you cities of refuge, whereof I spoke unto you by the hand of Moses:

3 That the slayer that kills any soul unawares and unwittingly may flee there: and they shall be your refuge from the avenger of blood.

4 And when he that does flee unto one of those cities shall stand at the entering of the gate of the city, and shall declare his cause in the ears of the elders of that city, they shall take him into the city unto them, and give him a place, that he may dwell among them.

5 And if the avenger of blood pursue after him, then they shall not deliver the slayer up into his hand; because he smote his neighbor unwittingly, and hated him not yesterday and the third day.

6 And he shall dwell in that city, until he stand before the congregation for judgment, and until the death of the high priest that shall be in those days: then shall the slayer return, and come unto his own city, and unto his own house, unto the city from where he fled.

7 And they appointed Kedesh in Galilee in mount Naphtali, and Shechem in mount Ephraim, and Kirjatharba, which is Hebron, in the mountain of Judah.

8 And over Jordan by Jericho eastward, they assigned Bezer in the wilderness upon the plain out of the tribe of Reuben, and Ramoth in Gilead out of the tribe of Gad, and Golan in Bashan out of the tribe of Manasseh.

9 These were the cities appointed for all the children of Israel, and for the stranger that sojourns among them, that whosoever kills any soul unawares might flee there, and not die by the hand of the avenger of blood, until he stood before the congregation.

Josh 21:1 Then came near the heads of the fathers of the Levites unto Eleazar the priest, and unto Joshua the son of Nun, and unto the heads of the fathers of the tribes of the children of Israel;

2 And they spoke unto them at Shiloh in the land of Canaan, saying, The Becoming-One commanded by the hand of Moses to give us cities to dwell in, with the suburbs thereof for our cattle.

3 And the children of Israel gave unto the Levites out of their inheritance, at the commandment of the Becoming-One, these cities and their suburbs.

4 And the lot came out for the families of the Kohathites: and the children of Aaron the priest, which were of the Levites, had by lot out of the tribe of Judah, and out of the tribe of Simeon, and out of the tribe of Benjamin, thirteen cities.

5 And the rest of the children of Kohath had by lot out of the families of the tribe of Ephraim, and out of the tribe of Dan, and out of the half tribe of Manasseh, ten cities.

6 And the children of Gershon had by lot out of the families of the tribe of Issachar, and out of the tribe of Asher, and out of the tribe of Naphtali, and out of the half tribe of Manasseh in Bashan, thirteen cities.

7 The children of Merari by their families had out of the tribe of Reuben, and out of the tribe of Gad, and out of the tribe of Zebulun, twelve cities.

8 And the children of Israel gave by lot unto the Levites these cities with their suburbs, as the Becoming-One commanded by the hand of Moses.

9 And they gave out of the tribe of the children of Judah, and out of the tribe of the children of Simeon, these cities which are here mentioned by name,

10 Which the children of Aaron, being of the families of the Kohathites, who were of the children of Levi, had: for theirs was the first lot.

11 And they gave them the city of Arba the father of Anak, which city is Hebron, in the hill country of Judah, with the suburbs thereof round about it.

12 But the fields of the city, and the villages thereof, gave they to Caleb the son of Jephunneh for his possession.

13 Thus they gave to the children of Aaron the priest Hebron with her suburbs, to be a city of refuge for the slayer; and Libnah with her suburbs,

14 And Jattir with her suburbs, and Eshtemoa with her suburbs,

15 And Holon with her suburbs, and Debir with her suburbs,

16 And Ain with her suburbs, and Juttah with her suburbs, and Beth-shemesh with her suburbs; nine cities out of those two tribes.

17 And out of the tribe of Benjamin, Gibeon with her suburbs, Geba with her suburbs,

18 Anathoth with her suburbs, and Almon with her suburbs; four cities.

19 All the cities of the children of Aaron, the priests, were thirteen cities with their suburbs.

20 And the families of the children of Kohath, the Levites which remained of the children of Kohath, even they had the cities of their lot out of the tribe of Ephraim.

21 For they gave them Shechem with her suburbs in mount Ephraim, to be a city of refuge for the slayer; and Gezer with her suburbs,

22 And Kibzaim with her suburbs, and Beth-horon with her suburbs; four cities.

23 And out of the tribe of Dan, Eltekeh with her suburbs, Gibbethon with her suburbs,

24 Aijalon with her suburbs, Gathrimmon with her suburbs; four cities.

25 And out of the half tribe of Manasseh, Tanach with her suburbs, and Gathrimmon with her suburbs; two cities.

26 All the cities were ten with their suburbs for the families of the children of Kohath that remained.

27 And unto the children of Gershon, of the families of the Levites, out of the other half tribe of Manasseh they gave Golan in Bashan with her suburbs, to be a city of refuge for the slayer; and Beeshterah with her suburbs; two cities.

28 And out of the tribe of Issachar, Kishon with her suburbs, Dabareh with her suburbs,

29 Jarmuth with her suburbs, Engannim with her suburbs; four cities.

30 And out of the tribe of Asher, Mishal with her suburbs, Abdon with her suburbs,

31 Helkath with her suburbs, and Rehob with her suburbs; four cities.

32 And out of the tribe of Naphtali, Kedesh in Galilee with her suburbs, to be a city of refuge for the slayer; and Hammothdor with her suburbs, and Kartan with her suburbs; three cities.

33 All the cities of the Gershonites according to their families were thirteen cities with their suburbs.

34 And unto the families of the children of Merari, the rest of the Levites, out of the tribe of Zebulun, Jokneam with her suburbs, and Kartah with her suburbs,

35 Dimnah with her suburbs, Nahalal with her suburbs; four cities.

36 And out of the tribe of Reuben, Bezer with her suburbs, and Jahazah with her suburbs,

37 Kedemoth with her suburbs, and Mephaath with her suburbs; four cities.

38 And out of the tribe of Gad, Ramoth in Gilead with her suburbs, to be a city of refuge for the slayer; and Mahanaim with her suburbs,

39 Heshbon with her suburbs, Jazer with her suburbs; four cities in all.

40 So all the cities for the children of Merari by their families, which were remaining of the families of the Levites, were by their lot twelve cities.

41 All the cities of the Levites within the possession of the children of Israel were forty and eight cities with their suburbs.

42 These cities were every one with their suburbs round about them: thus were all these cities.

43 And the Becoming-One gave unto Israel all the land which he swore to give unto their fathers; and they possessed it, and dwelt therein.

44 And the Becoming-One gave them rest round about, according to all that he swore unto their fathers: and there stood not a man of all their enemies before them; the Becoming-One delivered all their enemies into their hand.

45 There failed not of any good thing which the Becoming-One had spoken unto the house of Israel; all came to pass.

Josh 22:1 Then Joshua called the Reubenites, and the Gadites, and the half tribe of Manasseh,

2 And said unto them, you have kept all that Moses the servant of the Becoming-One commanded you, and have obeyed my voice in all that I commanded you:

3 you have not left your brethren these many days unto this day, but have kept the charge of the commandment of the Becoming-One your God.

4 And now the Becoming-One your God has given rest unto your brethren, as he promised them: therefore now return ye, and get you unto your tents, and unto the land of your possession, which Moses the servant of the Becoming-One gave you beyond Jordan.

5 But take diligent heed to do the commandment and the law, which Moses the servant of the Becoming-One charged you, to love the Becoming-One your God, and to walk in all his ways, and to keep his commandments, and to cleave unto him, and to serve him with all your heart and with all your soul.

6 So Joshua blessed them, and sent them away: and they went unto their tents.

7 Now to the one half of the tribe of Manasseh Moses had given possession in Bashan: but unto the other half thereof gave Joshua among their brethren over Jordan westward. And when Joshua sent them away also unto their tents, then he blessed them,

8 And he spoke unto them, saying, Return with much riches unto your tents, and with very much cattle, with silver, and with gold, and with brass, and with iron, and with very much raiment: divide the spoil of your enemies with your brethren.

9 And the children of Reuben and the children of Gad and the half tribe of Manasseh returned, and departed from the children of Israel out of Shiloh, which is in the land of Canaan, to go unto the country of Gilead, to the land of their possession, whereof they were possessed, according to the word of the Becoming-One by the hand of Moses.

10 And when they came unto the borders of Jordan, that are in the land of Canaan, the children of Reuben and the children of Gad and the half tribe of Manasseh built there an altar by Jordan, a great altar to see to.

11 And the children of Israel heard say, Behold, the children of Reuben and the children of Gad and the half tribe of Manasseh have built an altar over against the land of Canaan, in the borders of Jordan, at the passage of the children of Israel.

12 And when the children of Israel heard of it, the whole congregation of the children of Israel gathered themselves together at Shiloh, to go up to war against them.

13 And the children of Israel sent unto the children of Reuben, and to the children of Gad, and to the half tribe of Manasseh, into the land of Gilead, Phinehas the son of Eleazar the priest,

14 And with him ten princes, of each chief house a prince throughout all the tribes of Israel; and each one was a head of the house of their fathers among the thousands of Israel.

15 And they came unto the children of Reuben, and to the children of Gad, and to the half tribe of Manasseh, unto the land of Gilead, and they spoke with them, saying,

16 Thus says the whole congregation of the Becoming-One, What trespass is this that you have committed against God of Israel, to turn away this day from following the Becoming-One, in that you have built you an altar, that you might rebel this day against the Becoming-One?

17 Is the iniquity of Peor too little for us, from which we are not cleansed until this day, although there was a plague in the congregation of the Becoming-One,

18 But that you must turn away this day from following the Becoming-One? and it will be, seeing you rebel today against the Becoming-One, that tomorrow he will be angry with the whole congregation of Israel.

19 Notwithstanding, if the land of your possession be unclean, then pass you over unto the land of the possession of the Becoming-One, wherein the Becoming-One's tabernacle dwells, and take possession among us: but rebel not against the Becoming-One, nor rebel against us, in building you an altar beside the altar of the Becoming-One our God.

20 Did not Achan the son of Zerah commit a trespass in the accursed thing, and wrath fell on all the congregation of Israel? and that man perished not alone in his iniquity.

21 Then the children of Reuben and the children of Gad and the half tribe of Manasseh answered, and said unto the heads of the thousands of Israel,

22 The Becoming-One is GOD of gods, the Becoming-One is GOD of gods, he knows, and Israel he shall know; if it be in rebellion, or if in transgression against the Becoming-One, save us not this day,

23 That we have built us an altar to turn from following the Becoming-One, or if to offer thereon burnt offering or food offering, or if to offer peace

offerings thereon, let the Becoming-One himself require it;

24 And if we have not rather done it for fear of this thing, saying, In time to come your children might speak unto our children, saying, What have you to do with the Becoming-One, God of Israel?

25 For the Becoming-One has made Jordan a border between us and you, you children of Reuben and children of Gad; you have no part in the Becoming-One: so shall your children make our children cease from fearing the Becoming-One.

26 Therefore we said, Let us now prepare to build us an altar, not for burnt offering, nor for sacrifice:

27 But that it may be a witness between us, and you, and our generations after us, that we might do the service of the Becoming-One before him with our burnt offerings, and with our sacrifices, and with our peace offerings; that your children may not say to our children in time to come, you have no part in the Becoming-One.

28 Therefore said we, that it shall be, when they should so say to us or to our generations in time to come, that we may say again, Behold the pattern of the altar of the Becoming-One, which our fathers made, not for burnt offerings, nor for sacrifices; but it is a witness between us and you.

29 Forbid it that we should rebel against the Becoming-One, and turn this day from following the Becoming-One, to build an altar for burnt offerings, for food offerings, or for sacrifices, beside the altar of the Becoming-One our God that is before his tabernacle.

30 And when Phinehas the priest, and the princes of the congregation and heads of the thousands of Israel which were with him, heard the words that the children of Reuben and the children of Gad and the children of Manasseh spoke, it pleased them.

31 And Phinehas the son of Eleazar the priest said unto the children of Reuben, and to the children of Gad, and to the children of Manasseh, This day we perceive that the Becoming-One is among us, because you have not committed this trespass against the Becoming-One: now you have delivered the children of Israel out of the hand of the Becoming-One.

32 And Phinehas the son of Eleazar the priest, and the princes, returned from the children of Reuben, and from the children of Gad, out of the land of Gilead, unto the land of Canaan, to the children of Israel, and brought them word again.

33 And the thing pleased the children of Israel; and the children of Israel blessed God, and did not intend to go up against them in battle, to destroy the land wherein the children of Reuben and Gad dwelt.

34 And the children of Reuben and the children of Gad called the altar Ed: for it shall be a witness between us that the Becoming-One is God.

Josh 23:1 And it came to pass a long time after that the Becoming-One had given rest unto Israel from all their enemies round about, that Joshua grew old and stricken in age.

2 And Joshua called for all Israel, and for their elders, and for their heads, and for their judges, and for their officers, and said unto them, I am old and stricken in age:

3 And you have seen all that the Becoming-One your God has done unto all these nations because of you; for the Becoming-One your God is he that has fought for you.

4 Behold, I have divided unto you by lot these nations that remain, to be an inheritance for your tribes, from Jordan, with all the nations that I have cut off, even unto the great sea westward.

5 And the Becoming-One your God, he shall expel them from before you, and drive them from out of your sight; and you shall possess their land, as the Becoming-One your God has promised unto you.

6 Be you therefore very courageous to keep and to do all that is written in the book of the law of Moses, that you turn not aside therefrom to the right hand or to the left;

7 That you come not among these nations, these that remain among you; neither make mention of the name of their gods, nor cause to swear by them, neither serve them, nor bow yourselves unto them:

8 But cleave unto the Becoming-One your God, as you have done unto this day.

9 For the Becoming-One has driven out from before you great nations and strong: but as for you, no man has been able to stand before you unto this day.

10 One man of you shall chase a thousand: for the Becoming-One your God, he it is that fights for you, as he has promised you.

11 Take good heed therefore unto your souls, that you love the Becoming-One your God.

12 Else if you do in any way go back, and cleave unto the remnant of these nations, even these that remain among you, and shall make marriages with them, and go in unto them, and they to you:

13 Know for a certainty that the Becoming-One your God will no more drive out any of these nations from before you; but they shall be snares and traps unto you, and scourges in your sides, and thorns in your eyes, until you perish from off this good land which the Becoming-One your God has given you.

14 And, behold, this day I am going the way of all the earth: and you know in all your hearts and in all your souls, that not one thing has failed of all the good things which the Becoming-One your God spoke concerning you; all are come to pass unto you, and not one thing has failed thereof.

15 Therefore it shall come to pass, that as all good things are come upon you, which the Becoming-One your God promised you; so shall the Becoming-One bring upon you all evil things, until he have destroyed you from off this good land which the Becoming-One your God has given you.

16 When you have transgressed the covenant of the Becoming-One your God, which he commanded you, and have gone and served other gods, and bowed yourselves to them; then shall the anger of the Becoming-One be kindled against you, and you shall perish quickly from off the good land which he has given unto you.

Josh 24:1 And Joshua gathered all the tribes of Israel to Shechem, and called for the elders of Israel, and for their heads, and for their judges, and for their officers; and they presented themselves before God.

2 And Joshua said unto all the people, Thus says the Becoming-One, God of Israel, Your fathers dwelt over the river in past olam time, even Terah, the father

of Abraham, and the father of Nachor: and they served other gods.

3 And I took your father Abraham over the river, and led him throughout all the land of Canaan, and multiplied his seed, and gave him Isaac.

4 And I gave unto Isaac Jacob and Esau: and I gave unto Esau mount Seir, to possess it; but Jacob and his children went down into Egypt.

5 I sent Moses also and Aaron, and I plagued Egypt, according to that which I did among them: and afterward I brought you out.

6 And I brought your fathers out of Egypt: and you came unto the sea; and the Egyptians pursued after your fathers with chariots and horsemen unto the boundary sea.

7 And when they cried unto the Becoming-One, he put darkness between you and the Egyptians, and brought the sea upon them, and covered them; and your eyes have seen what I have done in Egypt: and you dwelt in the wilderness a long season.

8 And I brought you into the land of the Amorites, which dwelt over Jordan; and they fought with you: and I gave them into your hand, that you might possess their land; and I destroyed them from before you.

9 Then Balak the son of Zippor, king of Moab, arose and warred against Israel, and sent and called Balaam the son of Beor to curse you:

10 But I would not hear Balaam; nevertheless he blessed you still: so I delivered you out of his hand.

11 And you went over Jordan, and came unto Jericho: and the men of Jericho fought against you, the Amorites, and the Perizzites, and the Canaanites, and the Hittites, and the Girgashites, the Hivites, and the Jebusites; and I delivered them into your hand.

12 And I sent the hornet before you, which drove them out from before you, even the two kings of the Amorites; but not with your sword, nor with your bow.

13 And I have given you a land for which you did not labor, and cities which you built not, and you dwell in them; of the vineyards and oliveyards which you planted not do you eat.

14 Now therefore fear the Becoming-One, and serve him in sincerity and in truth: and put away the gods which your fathers served over the river, and in Egypt; and serve you the Becoming-One.

15 And if it seem evil unto you to serve the Becoming-One, choose you this day whom you will serve; whether the gods which your fathers served that were over the river, or the gods of the Amorites, in whose land you dwell: but as for me and my house, we will serve the Becoming-One.

16 And the people answered and said, forbid it that we should forsake the Becoming-One, to serve other gods;

17 For the Becoming-One our God, he it is that brought us up and our fathers out of the land of Egypt, from the house of bondage, and which did those great signs in our sight, and preserved us in all the way wherein we went, and among all the people through whom we passed:

18 And the Becoming-One drove out from before us all the people, even the Amorites which dwelt in the land: therefore will we also serve the Becoming-One; for he is our God.

19 And Joshua said unto the people, you cannot serve the Becoming-One: for God, Holies, is He; he is a jealous GOD; he will not forgive your transgressions nor your sins.

20 If you forsake the Becoming-One, and serve strange gods, then he will turn and do you hurt, and consume you, after that he has done you good.

21 And the people said unto Joshua, Nay; but we will serve the Becoming-One.

22 And Joshua said unto the people, you are witnesses against yourselves that you have chosen you the Becoming-One, to serve him. And they said, We are witnesses.

23 Now therefore put away, said he, the strange gods which are among you, and incline your heart unto the Becoming-One, God of Israel.

24 And the people said unto Joshua, The Becoming-One our God will we serve, and his voice will we obey.

25 So Joshua made a covenant with the people that day, and set them a statute and an ordinance in Shechem.

26 And Joshua wrote these words in the book of the law of God, and took a great stone, and set it up there under an oak, that was by the sanctuary of the Becoming-One.

27 And Joshua said unto all the people, Behold, this stone shall be a witness unto us; for it has heard all the words of the Becoming-One which he spoke unto us: it shall be therefore a witness unto you, lest you deny your God.

28 So Joshua let the people depart, every man unto his inheritance.

29 And it came to pass after these things, that Joshua the son of Nun, the servant of the Becoming-One, died, being a son of a hundred and ten years.

30 And they buried him in the border of his inheritance in Timnathserah, which is in mount Ephraim, on the north side of the hill of Gaash.

31 And Israel served the Becoming-One all the days of Joshua, and all the days of the elders that overlived Joshua, and which had known all the works of the Becoming-One, that he had done for Israel.

32 And the bones of Joseph, which the children of Israel brought up out of Egypt, buried they in Shechem, in a parcel of ground which Jacob bought of the sons of Hamor the father of Shechem for a hundred pieces of silver: and it became the inheritance of the children of Joseph.

33 And Eleazar the son of Aaron died; and they buried him in a hill that pertained to Phinehas his son, which was given him in mount Ephraim.

Judges

Judges 1:1 Now after the death of Joshua it came to pass, that the children of Israel asked the Becoming-One, saying, Who shall go up for us against the Canaanites first, to fight against them?

2 And the Becoming-One said, Judah shall go up: behold, I have delivered the land into his hand.

3 And Judah said unto Simeon his brother, Come up with me into my lot, that we may fight against the Canaanites; and I likewise will go with you into your lot. So Simeon went with him.

4 And Judah went up; and the Becoming-One delivered the Canaanites and the Perizzites into their hand: and they killed of them in Bezek ten thousand men.

5 And they found Adonibezek in Bezek: and they fought against him, and they killed the Canaanites and the Perizzites.

6 But Adonibezek fled; and they pursued after him, and caught him, and cut off his thumbs and his great toes.

7 And Adonibezek said, Threescore and ten kings, having their thumbs and their great toes cut off, gathered their food under my table: as I have done, so God has repaid me. And they brought him to Jerusalem, and there he died.

8 Now the children of Judah had fought against Jerusalem, and had taken it, and struck it with the edge of the sword, and set the city on fire.

9 And afterward the children of Judah went down to fight against the Canaanites, that dwelt in the mountain, and in the south, and in the valley.

10 And Judah went against the Canaanites that dwelt in Hebron: now the name of Hebron before was Kirjatharba: and they killed Sheshai, and Ahiman, and Talmai.

11 And from there he went against the inhabitants of Debir: and the name of Debir before was Kirjathsepher:

12 And Caleb said, He that smites Kirjathsepher, and takes it, to him will I give Achsah my daughter to wife.

13 And Othniel the son of Kenaz, Caleb's younger brother, took it: and he gave him Achsah his daughter to wife.

14 And it came to pass, when she came to him, that she moved him to ask of her father a field: and she lighted from off her donkey; and Caleb said unto her, What will you?

15 And she said unto him, Give me a blessing: for you have given me a south land; give me also springs of water. And Caleb gave her the upper springs and the lower springs.

16 And the children of the Kenite, Moses' father-in-law, went up out of the city of palm trees with the children of Judah into the wilderness of Judah, which lies in the south of Arad; and they went and dwelt among the people.

17 And Judah went with Simeon his brother, and they killed the Canaanites that inhabited Zephath, and utterly destroyed it. And the name of the city was called Hormah.

18 Also Judah took Gaza with the coast thereof, and Askelon with the coast thereof, and Ekron with the coast thereof.

19 And the Becoming-One was with Judah; and he drave out the inhabitants of the mountain; but could not drive out the inhabitants of the valley, because they had chariots of iron.

20 And they gave Hebron unto Caleb, as Moses said: and he expelled there the three sons of Anak.

21 And the children of Benjamin did not drive out the Jebusites that inhabited Jerusalem; but the Jebusites dwell with the children of Benjamin in Jerusalem unto this day.

22 And the house of Joseph, they also went up against Bethel: and the Becoming-One was with them.

23 And the house of Joseph sent to descry Bethel. Now the name of the city before was Luz.

24 And the spies saw a man come forth out of the city, and they said unto him, Show us, we pray you, the entrance into the city, and we will show you mercy.

25 And when he showed them the entrance into the city, they smote the city with the edge of the sword; but they let go the man and all his family.

26 And the man went into the land of the Hittites, and built a city, and called the name thereof Luz: which is the name thereof unto this day.

27 Neither did Manasseh drive out the inhabitants of Beth-shean and her towns, nor Taanach and her towns, nor the inhabitants of Dor and her towns, nor the inhabitants of Ibleam and her towns, nor the inhabitants of Megiddo and her towns: but the Canaanites would dwell in that land.

28 And it came to pass, when Israel was strong, that they put the Canaanites to tribute, and did not utterly drive them out.

29 Neither did Ephraim drive out the Canaanites that dwelt in Gezer; but the Canaanites dwelt in Gezer among them.

30 Neither did Zebulun drive out the inhabitants of Kitron, nor the inhabitants of Nahalol; but the Canaanites dwelt among them, and became tributaries.

31 Neither did Asher drive out the inhabitants of Accho, nor the inhabitants of Zidon, nor of Ahlab, nor of Achzib, nor of Helbah, nor of Aphik, nor of Rehob:

32 But the Asherites dwelt among the Canaanites, the inhabitants of the land: for they did not drive them out.

33 Neither did Naphtali drive out the inhabitants of Beth-shemesh, nor the inhabitants of Beth-anath; but he dwelt among the Canaanites, the inhabitants of the land: nevertheless the inhabitants of Beth-shemesh and of Beth-anath became tributaries unto them.

34 And the Amorites forced the children of Dan into the mountain: for they would not permit them to come down to the valley:

35 But the Amorites would dwell in mount Heres in Aijalon, and in Shaalbim: yet the hand of the house of Joseph prevailed, so that they became tributaries.

36 And the coast of the Amorites was from the going up to Akrabbim, from the rock, and upward.

Judges 2:1 And an angel of the Becoming-One came up from Gilgal to Bochim, and said, I made you to go up out of Egypt, and have brought you unto the land which I swore unto your fathers; and I said, I will not for olam break my covenant with you.

2 And you shall make no league with the inhabitants of this land; you shall throw down their altars: but you have not obeyed my voice: why have you done this?

3 Therefore I also said, I will not drive them out from before you; but they shall be as thorns in your sides, and their gods shall be a snare unto you.

4 And it came to pass, when the angel of the Becoming-One spoke these words unto all the children of Israel, that the people lifted up their voice, and wept.

5 And they called the name of that place Bochim: and they sacrificed there unto the Becoming-One.

6 And when Joshua had let the people go, the children of Israel went every man unto his inheritance to possess the land.

7 And the people served the Becoming-One all the days of Joshua, and all the days of the elders that outlived Joshua, who had seen all the great works of the Becoming-One, that he did for Israel.

8 And Joshua, the son of Nun, the servant of the Becoming-One, died, being a son of a hundred and ten years.

9 And they buried him in the border of his inheritance in Timnathheres, in the mount of Ephraim, on the north side of the hill Gaash.

10 And also all that generation were gathered unto their fathers: and there arose another generation after them, which knew not the Becoming-One, nor yet the works which he had done for Israel.

11 And the children of Israel did evil in the sight of the Becoming-One, and served the lords [baalim]

12 And they forsook the Becoming-One, God of their fathers, which brought them out of the land of Egypt, and followed other gods, of the gods of the people that were round about them, and bowed themselves unto them, and provoked the Becoming-One to anger.

13 And they forsook the Becoming-One, and served the lord [baal] and Ashtaroth.

14 And the anger of the Becoming-One was hot against Israel, and he delivered them into the hands of spoilers that spoiled them, and he sold them into the hands of their enemies round about, so that they could not any longer stand before their enemies.

15 Wheresoever they went out, the hand of the Becoming-One was against them for evil, as the Becoming-One had said, and as the Becoming-One had sworn unto them: and they were greatly distressed.

16 Nevertheless the Becoming-One raised up judges, which delivered them out of the hand of those that spoiled them.

17 And yet they would not listen unto their judges, but they went a whoring after other gods, and bowed themselves unto them: they turned quickly out of the way which their fathers walked in, obeying the commandments of the Becoming-One; but they did not so.

18 And when the Becoming-One raised them up judges, then the Becoming-One was with the judge, and delivered them out of the hand of their enemies all the days of the judge: for it repented the Becoming-One because of their groanings by reason of them that oppressed them and vexed them.

19 And it came to pass, when the judge was dead, that they returned, and corrupted themselves more than their fathers, in following other gods to serve them, and to bow down unto them; they ceased not from their own doings, nor from their stubborn way.

20 And the anger of the Becoming-One was hot against Israel; and he said, Because that this people has transgressed my covenant which I commanded their fathers, and have not listened unto my voice;

21 I also will not henceforth drive out any from before them of the nations which Joshua left when he died:

22 That through them I may prove Israel, whether they will keep the way of the Becoming-One to walk therein, as their fathers did keep it, or not.

23 Therefore the Becoming-One left those nations, without driving them out hastily; neither delivered he them into the hand of Joshua.

Judges 3:1 Now these are the nations which the Becoming-One left, to prove Israel by them, even as many of Israel as had not known all the wars of Canaan;

2 Only that the generations of the children of Israel might know, to teach them war, at the least such as before knew nothing thereof;

3 Namely, five lords of the Philistines, and all the Canaanites, and the Sidonians, and the Hivites that dwelt in mount Lebanon, from mount Baal-Hermon unto the entering in of Hamath.

4 And they were to prove Israel by them, to know whether they would listen unto the commandments of the Becoming-One, which he commanded their fathers by the hand of Moses.

5 And the children of Israel dwelt among the Canaanites, Hittites, and Amorites, and Perizzites, and Hivites, and Jebusites:

6 And they took their daughters to be their wives, and gave their daughters to their sons, and served their gods.

7 And the children of Israel did evil in the sight of the Becoming-One, and forgat the Becoming-One their God, and served the lords [baalim] and the Asherahs.

8 Therefore the anger of the Becoming-One was hot against Israel, and he sold them into the hand of Chushanrishathai king of Mesopotamia: and the children of Israel served Chushanrishathai eight years.

9 And when the children of Israel cried unto the Becoming-One, the Becoming-One raised up a deliverer to the children of Israel, who delivered them, even Othniel the son of Kenaz, Caleb's younger brother.

10 And the spirit of the Becoming-One came upon him, and he judged Israel, and went out to war: and the Becoming-One delivered Chushanrishathai king of Mesopotamia into his hand; and his hand prevailed against Chushanrishathai.

11 And the land had rest forty years. And Othniel the son of Kenaz died.

12 And the children of Israel did evil again in the sight of the Becoming-One: and the Becoming-One strengthened Eglon the king of Moab against Israel, because they had done evil in the sight of the Becoming-One.

13 And he gathered unto him the children of Ammon and Amalek, and went and smote Israel, and possessed the city of palm trees.

14 So the children of Israel served Eglon the king of Moab eighteen years.

15 But when the children of Israel cried unto the Becoming-One, the Becoming-One raised them up a deliverer, Ehud the son of Gera, a Benjamite, a man lefthanded: and by him the children of Israel sent a present unto Eglon the king of Moab.

16 But Ehud made him a dagger which had two edges, of a cubit length; and he did gird it under his raiment upon his right thigh.

17 And he brought the present unto Eglon king of Moab: and Eglon was a very fat man.

18 And when he had made an end to offer the present, he sent away the people that bare the present.

19 But he himself turned again from the quarries that were by Gilgal, and said, I have a secret errand unto you, O king: who said, Keep silence. And all that stood by him went out from him.

20 And Ehud came unto him; and he was sitting in a summer parlour, which he had for himself alone. And Ehud said, I have a message from God unto you. And he arose out of his seat.

21 And Ehud put forth his left hand, and took the dagger from his right thigh, and thrust it into his belly:

22 And the haft also went in after the blade; and the fat closed upon the blade, so that he could not draw the dagger out of his belly; and it came out the rectum.

23 Then Ehud went forth through the porch, and shut the doors of the parlour upon him, and locked them.

24 When he was gone out, his servants came; and when they saw that, behold, the doors of the parlour were locked, they said, Surely he coveres his feet in his summer chamber.

25 And they tarried till they were ashamed: and, behold, he opened not the doors of the parlour; therefore they took a key, and opened them: and, behold, their lords was fallen down dead on the earth.

26 And Ehud escaped while they tarried, and passed beyond the quarries, and escaped unto Seirath.

27 And it came to pass, when he was come, that he blew a trumpet in the mountain of Ephraim, and the children of Israel went down with him from the mount, and he before them.

28 And he said unto them, Follow after me: for the Becoming-One has delivered your enemies the Moabites into your hand. And they went down after him, and took the fords of Jordan toward Moab, and permitted not a man to pass over.

29 And they killed of Moab at that time about ten thousand men, all lusty, and all men of valor; and there escaped not a man.

30 So Moab was subdued that day under the hand of Israel. And the land had rest fourscore years.

31 And after him was Shamgar the son of Anath, which killed of the Philistines six hundred men with an ox goad: and he also delivered Israel.

Judges 4:1 And the children of Israel again did evil in the sight of the Becoming-One, when Ehud was dead.

2 And the Becoming-One sold them into the hand of Jabin king of Canaan, that reigned in Hazor; the captain of whose host was Sisera, which dwelt in Harosheth of the nations.

3 And the children of Israel cried unto the Becoming-One: for he had nine hundred chariots of iron; and twenty years he mightily oppressed the children of Israel.

4 And Deborah, a prophetess, the wife of Lapidoth, she judged Israel at that time.

5 And she dwelt under the palm tree of Deborah between Ramah and Bethel in mount Ephraim: and the children of Israel came up to her for judgment.

6 And she sent and called Barak the son of Abinoam out of Kedeshnaphtali, and said unto him, has not the Becoming-One, God of Israel commanded, saying, Go and draw toward mount Tabor, and take with you ten thousand men of the children of Naphtali and of the children of Zebulun?

7 And I will draw unto you to the river Kishon Sisera, the captain of Jabin's army, with his chariots and his multitude; and I will deliver him into your hand.

8 And Barak said unto her, If you will go with me, then I will go: but if you will not go with me, then I will not go.

9 And she said, I will surely go with you: notwithstanding the journey that you take shall not be for your honor; for the Becoming-One shall sell Sisera into the hand of a woman. And Deborah arose, and went with Barak to Kedesh.

10 And Barak called Zebulun and Naphtali to Kedesh; and he went up with ten thousand men at his feet: and Deborah went up with him.

11 Now Heber the Kenite, which was of the children of Hobab the father-in-law of Moses, had severed himself from the Kenites, and pitched his tent unto the plain of Zaanaim, which is by Kedesh.

12 And they showed Sisera that Barak the son of Abinoam was gone up to mount Tabor.

13 And Sisera gathered together all his chariots, even nine hundred chariots of iron, and all the people that were with him, from Harosheth of the nations unto the river of Kishon.

14 And Deborah said unto Barak, Up; for this is the day in which the Becoming-One has delivered Sisera into your hand: is not the Becoming-One gone out before you? So Barak went down from mount Tabor, and ten thousand men after him.

15 And the Becoming-One discomfited Sisera, and all his chariots, and all his host, with the edge of the sword before Barak; so that Sisera lighted down off his chariot, and fled away on his feet.

16 But Barak pursued after the chariots, and after the host, unto Harosheth of the nations: and all the host of Sisera fell upon the edge of the sword; and there was not a man left.

17 Howbeit Sisera fled away on his feet to the tent of Jael the wife of Heber the Kenite: for there was peace between Jabin the king of Hazor and the house of Heber the Kenite.

18 And Jael went out to meet Sisera, and said unto him, Turn in, my lord, turn in to me; fear not. And when he had turned in unto her into the tent, she covered him with a mantle.

19 And he said unto her, Give me, I pray you, a little water to drink; for I am thirsty. And she opened a bottle of milk, and gave him drink, and covered him.

20 Again he said unto her, Stand in the door of the tent, and it shall be, when any man does come and inquire of you, and say, Is there any man here? that you shall say, No.

21 Then Jael Heber's wife took a nail of the tent, and took a hammer in her hand, and went softly unto him, and smote the nail into his temples, and fastened it into the ground: for he was fast asleep and weary. So he died.

22 And, behold, as Barak pursued Sisera, Jael came out to meet him, and said unto him, Come, and I will show you the man whom you seek. And when he came into her tent, behold, Sisera lay dead, and the nail was in his temples.

23 So God subdued on that day Jabin the king of Canaan before the children of Israel.

24 And the hand of the children of Israel prospered, and prevailed against Jabin the king of Canaan, until they had destroyed Jabin king of Canaan.

Judges 5:1 Then sang Deborah and Barak the son of Abinoam on that day, saying,

2 Praise you the Becoming-One for the avenging of Israel, when the people willingly offered themselves.

3 Hear, O you kings; give ear, O you princes; I, even I, will sing unto the Becoming-One; I will sing praise to the Becoming-One, God of Israel.

4 Becoming-One, when you went out of Seir, when you marched out of the field of Edom, the earth trembled, and the heavens dropped, the clouds also dropped water.

5 The mountains melted from before the Becoming-One, even that Sinai from before the Becoming-One, God of Israel.

6 In the days of Shamgar the son of Anath, in the days of Jael, the highways were unoccupied, and the travellers walked through byways.

7 The inhabitants of the villages ceased, they ceased in Israel, until that I Deborah arose, that I arose a mother in Israel.

8 They chose new gods; then was war in the gates: was there a shield or spear seen among forty thousand in Israel?

9 My heart is toward the governors of Israel, that offered themselves willingly among the people. Bless you the Becoming-One.

10 Speak, you that ride on white donkeys, you that sit in judgment, and walk by the way.

11 They that are delivered from the noise of archers in the places of drawing water, there shall they rehearse the righteous acts of the Becoming-One, even the righteous acts toward the inhabitants of his villages in Israel: then shall the people of the Becoming-One go down to the gates.

12 Awake, awake, Deborah: awake, awake, utter a song: arise, Barak, and lead your captivity captive, you son of Abinoam.

13 Then he made him that remains have dominion over the nobles among the people: the Becoming-One made me have dominion over the mighty.

14 Out of Ephraim was there a root of them against Amalek; after you, Benjamin, among your people; out of Machir came down governors, and out of Zebulun they that handle the pen of the writer.

15 And the princes of Issachar were with Deborah; even Issachar, and also Barak: he was sent on foot into the valley. For the divisions of Reuben there were great thoughts of heart.

16 Why abode you among the sheepfolds, to hear the bleatings of the flocks? For the divisions of Reuben there were great searchings of heart.

17 Gilead abode over Jordan: and why did Dan remain in ships? Asher continued on the sea shore, and abode in his creeks.

18 Zebulun and Naphtali were a people that jeoparded their souls unto the death in the high places of the field.

19 The kings came and fought, then fought the kings of Canaan in Taanach by the waters of Megiddo; they took no gain of money.

20 They fought from heaven; the stars in their courses fought against Sisera.

21 The river of Kishon swept them away, that ancient river, the river Kishon. O my soul, you have trodden down strength.

22 Then were the horsehoofs broken by the means of the prancings, the prancings of their mighty ones.

23 Curse you Meroz, said the angel of the Becoming-One, curse you bitterly the inhabitants thereof; because they came not to the help of the Becoming-One, to the help of the Becoming-One against the mighty.

24 Blessed above women shall Jael the wife of Heber the Kenite be, blessed shall she be above women in the tent.

25 He asked water, and she gave him milk; she brought forth butter in a lordly dish.

26 She put her hand to the nail, and her right hand to the workmen's hammer; and with the hammer she smote Sisera, she smote off his head, when she had pierced and stricken through his temples.

27 At her feet he bowed, he fell, he lay down: at her feet he bowed, he fell: where he bowed, there he fell down dead.

28 The mother of Sisera looked out at a window, and cried through the lattice, Why is his chariot so long in coming? why tarry the wheels of his chariots?

29 Her wise ladies answered her, yes, she returned answer to herself,

30 Have they not sped? have they not divided the prey; to every man a damsel or two; to Sisera a prey of diverse colors, a prey of diverse colors of needlework, of diverse colors of needlework on both sides, meet for the necks of them that take the spoil?

31 So let all your enemies perish, O Becoming-One: but let them that love him be as the sun when he goes forth in his might. And the land had rest forty years.

Judges 6:1 And the children of Israel did evil in the sight of the Becoming-One: and the Becoming-One delivered them into the hand of Midian seven years.

2 And the hand of Midian prevailed against Israel: and because of the Midianites the children of Israel made them the dens which are in the mountains, and caves, and strong holds.

3 And so it was, when Israel had sown, that the Midianites came up, and the Amalekites, and the children of the east, even they came up against them;

4 And they encamped against them, and destroyed the increase of the earth, till you come unto Gaza, and left no sustenance for Israel, neither sheep, nor ox, nor donkey.

5 For they came up with their cattle and their tents, and they came as grasshoppers for multitude; for both they and their camels were without number: and they entered into the land to destroy it.

6 And Israel was greatly impoverished because of the Midianites; and the children of Israel cried unto the Becoming-One.

7 And it came to pass, when the children of Israel cried unto the Becoming-One because of the Midianites,

8 That the Becoming-One sent a prophet unto the children of Israel, which said unto them, Thus says the Becoming-One, God of Israel, I brought you up from Egypt, and brought you forth out of the house of bondage;

9 And I delivered you out of the hand of the Egyptians, and out of the hand of all that oppressed you, and drave them out from before you, and gave you their land;

10 And I said unto you, I am the Becoming-One your God; fear not the gods of the Amorites, in whose land you dwell: but you have not obeyed my voice.

11 And there came an angel of the Becoming-One, and sat under an oak which was in Ophrah, that pertained unto Joash the Abiezrite: and his son Gideon threshed wheat by the winepress, to hide it from the Midianites.

12 And the angel of the Becoming-One appeared unto him, and said unto him, The Becoming-One is with you, you mighty man of valor.

13 And Gideon said unto him, Oh my lord, if the Becoming-One be with us, why then is all this befallen us? and where be all his miracles which our fathers told us of, saying, Did not the Becoming-One bring us up from Egypt? but now the Becoming-One has forsaken us, and delivered us into the hands of the Midianites.

14 And the Becoming-One looked upon him, and said, Go in this your might, and you shall save Israel from the hand of the Midianites: have not I sent you?

15 And he said unto him, Oh my Lord(s), wherewith shall I save Israel? behold, my family is poor in Manasseh, and I am the least in my father's house.

16 And the Becoming-One said unto him, Surely I will be with you, and you shall smite the Midianites as one man.

17 And he said unto him, If now I have found grace in your sight, then show me a sign that you talk with me.

18 Depart not hence, I pray you, until I come unto you, and bring forth my present, and set it before you. And he said, I will tarry until you come again.

19 And Gideon went in, and made ready a kid, and unleavened cakes of an ephah of flour: the flesh he put in a basket, and he put the broth in a pot, and brought it out unto him under the oak, and presented it.

20 And the angel of God said unto him, Take the flesh and the unleavened cakes, and lay them upon this rock, and pour out the broth. And he did so.

21 Then the angel of the Becoming-One put forth the end of the staff that was in his hand, and touched the flesh and the unleavened cakes; and there rose up fire out of the rock, and consumed the flesh and the unleavened cakes. Then the angel of the Becoming-One departed out of his sight.

22 And when Gideon perceived that he was an angel of the Becoming-One, Gideon said, Alas, O my Lord(s) the Becoming-One! for because I have seen an angel of the Becoming-One face to face.

23 And the Becoming-One said unto him, Peace be unto you; fear not: you shall not die.

24 Then Gideon built an altar there unto the Becoming-One, and called it Yehowah-shalom: unto this day it is yet in Ophrah of the Abiezrites.

25 And it came to pass the same night, that the Becoming-One said unto him, Take your father's young bullock, even the second bullock of seven years, and throw down the altar of the lord [baal] that your father hath, and cut down the Asherah that is by it:

26 And build an altar unto the Becoming-One your God upon the top of this rock, in the ordered place, and take the second bullock, and offer a burnt sacrifice with the wood of the Asherah which you shall cut down.

27 Then Gideon took ten men of his servants, and did as the Becoming-One had said unto him: and so it was, because he feared his father's household, and the men of the city, that he could not do it by day, that he did it by night.

28 And when the men of the city arose early in the morning, behold, the altar of the lord [baal] was cast down, and the Asherah was cut down that was by it, and the second bullock was offered upon the altar that was built.

29 And they said one to another, Who has done this thing? And when they inquired and asked, they said, Gideon the son of Joash has done this thing.

30 Then the men of the city said unto Joash, Bring out your son, that he may die: because he has cast down the altar of the lord [baal] and because he has cut down the Asherah that was by it.

31 And Joash said unto all that stood against him, Will you plead for the lord [baal] will you save him? he that will plead for him, let him be put to death while it is yet morning: if he be a god, let him plead for himself, because one has cast down his altar.

32 Therefore on that day he called him Jerub-Baal, saying, Let the lord [baal] plead against him, because he has thrown down his altar.

33 Then all the Midianites and the Amalekites and the children of the east were gathered together, and went over, and pitched in the valley of Jezreel.

34 But the spirit of the Becoming-One came upon Gideon, and he blew a trumpet; and Abiezer was gathered after him.

35 And he sent messengers throughout all Manasseh; who also was gathered after him: and he sent messengers unto Asher, and unto Zebulun, and unto Naphtali; and they came up to meet them.

36 And Gideon said unto God, If you will save Israel by mine hand, as you have said,

37 Behold, I will put a fleece of wool in the floor; and if the dew be on the fleece only, and it be dry upon all the earth beside, then shall I know that you will save Israel by mine hand, as you have said.

38 And it was so: for he rose up early on the next day, and thrust the fleece together, and wringed the dew out of the fleece, a bowl full of water.

39 And Gideon said unto God, Let not your anger be hot against me, and I will speak but this once: let me prove, I pray you, but this once with the fleece; let it now be dry only upon the fleece, and upon all the ground let there be dew.

40 And God did so that night: for it was dry upon the fleece only, and there was dew on all the ground.

Judges 7:1 Then Jerub-Baal, who is Gideon, and all the people that were with him, rose up early, and pitched beside the well of Harod: so that the host of the Midianites were on the north side of them, by the hill of Moreh, in the valley.

2 And the Becoming-One said unto Gideon, The people that are with you are too many for me to give the Midianites into their hands, lest Israel vaunt themselves against me, saying, Mine own hand has saved me.

3 Now therefore go to, proclaim in the ears of the people, saying, Whosoever is fearful and afraid, let him return and depart early from mount Gilead. And there returned of the people twenty and two thousand; and there remained ten thousand.

4 And the Becoming-One said unto Gideon, The people are yet too many; bring them down unto the water, and I will try them for you there: and it shall be, that of whom I say unto you, This shall go with you, the same shall go with you; and of whomsoever I say unto you, This shall not go with you, the same shall not go.

5 So he brought down the people unto the water: and the Becoming-One said unto Gideon, Every one that laps of the water with his tongue, as a dog laps, him shall you set by himself; likewise every one that bows down upon his knees to drink.

6 And the number of them that lapped, putting their hand to their mouth, were three hundred men: but all the rest of the people bowed down upon their knees to drink water.

7 And the Becoming-One said unto Gideon, By the three hundred men that lapped will I save you, and deliver the Midianites into your hand: and let all the other people go every man unto his place.

8 So the people took victuals in their hand, and their trumpets: and he sent all the rest of Israel every man unto his tent, and retained those three hundred men: and the host of Midian was beneath him in the valley.

9 And it came to pass the same night, that the Becoming-One said unto him, Arise, get you downåvnto the host; for I have delivered it into your hand.

10 But if you fear to go down, go you with Phurah your servant down to the host:

11 And you shall hear what they say; and afterward shall your hands be strengthened to go down unto the host. Then went he down with Phurah his servant unto the outside of the armed men that were in the host.

12 And the Midianites and the Amalekites and all the children of the east lay along in the valley like grasshoppers for multitude; and their camels were without number, as the sand by the sea side for multitude.

13 And when Gideon was come, behold, there was a man that told a dream unto his fellow, and said, Behold, I dreamed a dream, and, lo, a cake of barley bread tumbled into the host of Midian, and came unto a tent, and smote it that it fell, and overturned it, that the tent lay along.

14 And his fellow answered and said, This is nothing else save the sword of Gideon the son of Joash, a man of Israel: for into his hand has God delivered Midian, and all the host.

15 And it was so, when Gideon heard the telling of the dream, and the interpretation thereof, that he worshiped, and returned into the host of Israel, and said, Arise; for the Becoming-One has delivered into your hand the host of Midian.

16 And he divided the three hundred men into three companies, and he put a trumpet in every man's hand, with empty pitchers, and lamps within the pitchers.

17 And he said unto them, Look on me, and do likewise: and, behold, when I come to the outside of the camp, it shall be that, as I do, so shall you do.

18 When I blow with a trumpet, I and all that are with me, then blow you the trumpets also on every side of all the camp, and say, The sword of the Becoming-One, and of Gideon.

19 So Gideon, and the hundred men that were with him, came unto the outside of the camp in the beginning of the middle watch; and they had but newly set the watch: and they blew the trumpets, and brake the pitchers that were in their hands.

20 And the three companies blew the trumpets, and brake the pitchers, and held the lamps in their left hands, and the trumpets in their right hands to blow withal: and they cried, The sword of the Becoming-One, and of Gideon.

21 And they stood every man in his place round about the camp: and all the host ran, and cried, and fled.

22 And the three hundred blew the trumpets, and the Becoming-One set every man's sword against his fellow, even throughout all the host: and the host fled to Beth-shittah in Zererath, and to the border of Able-meholah, unto Tabbath.

23 And the men of Israel gathered themselves together out of Naphtali, and out of Asher, and out of all Manasseh, and pursued after the Midianites.

24 And Gideon sent messengers throughout all mount Ephraim, saying, Come down against the Midianites, and take before them the waters unto Beth-barah and Jordan. Then all the men of Ephraim gathered themselves together, and took the waters unto Beth-barah and Jordan.

25 And they took two princes of the Midianites, Oreb and Zeeb; and they killed Oreb upon the rock Oreb, and Zeeb they killed at the winepress of Zeeb, and pursued Midian, and brought the heads of Oreb and Zeeb to Gideon over the Jordan.

Judges 8:1 And the men of Ephraim said unto him, Why have you served us thus, that you called us not, when you went to fight with the Midianites? And they did chide with him sharply.

2 And he said unto them, What have I done now in comparison of you? Is not the gleaning of the grapes of Ephraim better than the vintage of Abiezer?

3 God has delivered into your hands the princes of Midian, Oreb and Zeeb: and what was I able to do in comparison of you? Then their spirit was abated toward him, when he had said that.

4 And Gideon came to Jordan, and passed over, he, and the three hundred men that were with him, faint, yet pursuing them.

5 And he said unto the men of Succoth, Give, I pray you, loaves of bread unto the people that follow me; for they be faint, and I am pursuing after Zebah and Zalmunna, kings of Midian.

6 And the princes of Succoth said, Are the hands of Zebah and Zalmunna now in your hand, that we should give bread unto your army?

7 And Gideon said, Therefore when the Becoming-One has delivered Zebah and Zalmunna into mine hand, then I will tear your flesh with the thorns of the wilderness and with briers.

8 And he went up there to Penuel, and spoke unto them likewise: and the men of Penuel answered him as the men of Succoth had answered him.

9 And he spoke also unto the men of Penuel, saying, When I come again in peace, I will break down this tower.

10 Now Zebah and Zalmunna were in Karkor, and their hosts with them, about fifteen thousand men, all that were left of all the hosts of the children of the east: for there fell a hundred and twenty thousand men that drew sword.

11 And Gideon went up by the way of them that dwelt in tents on the east of Nobah and Jogbehah, and smote the host: for the host was secure.

12 And when Zebah and Zalmunna fled, he pursued after them, and took the two kings of Midian, Zebah and Zalmunna, and discomfited all the host.

13 And Gideon the son of Joash returned from battle before the sun was up,

14 And caught a young man of the men of Succoth, and inquired of him: and he described unto him the princes of Succoth, and the elders thereof, even threescore and seventeen men.

15 And he came unto the men of Succoth, and said, Behold Zebah and Zalmunna with whom you did upbraid me, saying, Are the hands of Zebah and Zalmunna now in your hand, that we should give bread unto your men that are weary?

16 And he took the elders of the city, and thorns of the wilderness and briers, and with them he taught the men of Succoth.

17 And he beat down the tower of Penuel, and killed the men of the city.

18 Then said he unto Zebah and Zalmunna, What manner of men were they whom you killed at Tabor? And they answered, As you are, so were they; each one resembled the children of a king.

19 And he said, They were my brethren, even the sons of my mother: as the Becoming-One lives, if you had saved them alive, I would not slay you.

20 And he said unto Jether his firstborn, Up, and slay them. But the youth drew not his sword: for he feared, because he was yet a youth.

21 Then Zebah and Zalmunna said, Rise you, and fall upon us: for as the man is, so is his strength. And Gideon arose, and killed Zebah and Zalmunna, and took away the ornaments that were on their camels' necks.

22 Then the men of Israel said unto Gideon, Rule you over us, both you, and your son, and your son's son also: for you have delivered us from the hand of Midian.

23 And Gideon said unto them, I will not rule over you, neither shall my son rule over you: the Becoming-One shall rule over you.

24 And Gideon said unto them, I would desire a request of you, that you would give me every man the earrings of his prey. For they had golden earrings, because they were Ishmaelites.

25 And they answered, We will willingly give them. And they spread a garment, and did cast therein every man the earrings of his prey.

26 And the weight of the golden earrings that he requested was a thousand and seven hundred shekels of gold; beside ornaments, and collars, and purple raiment that was on the kings of Midian, and beside the chains that were about their camels' necks.

27 And Gideon made an ephod thereof, and put it in his city, even in Ophrah: and all Israel went there a whoring after it: which thing became a snare unto Gideon, and to his house.

28 Thus was Midian subdued before the children of Israel, so that they lifted up their heads no more. And the country was in quietness forty years in the days of Gideon.

29 And Jerub-Baal the son of Joash went and dwelt in his own house.

30 And Gideon had threescore and ten sons of his body begotten: for he had many wives.

31 And his concubine that was in Shechem, she also bare him a son, whose name he called Abimelech.

32 And Gideon the son of Joash died in a good old age, and was buried in the tomb of Joash his father, in Ophrah of the Abiezrites.

33 And it came to pass, as soon as Gideon was dead, that the children of Israel turned again, and went a whoring after the lords [baalim] and made Baal-Berith their god.

34 And the children of Israel remembered not the Becoming-One their God, who had delivered them out of the hands of all their enemies on every side:

35 Neither showed they kindness to the house of Jerub-Baal, namely, Gideon, according to all the goodness which he had showed unto Israel.

Judges 9:1 And Abimelech the son of Jerub-Baal went to Shechem unto his mother's brethren, and communed with them, and with all the family of the house of his mother's father, saying,

2 Speak, I pray you, in the ears of all the men of Shechem, Whether is better for you, either that all the sons of Jerub-Baal, which are threescore and ten persons, reign over you, or that one reign over you? remember also that I am your bone and your flesh.

3 And his mother's brethren spoke of him in the ears of all the men of Shechem all these words: and their hearts inclined to follow Abimelech; for they said, He is our brother.

4 And they gave him threescore and ten pieces of silver out of the house of Baal-Berith, wherewith Abimelech hired vain and light persons, which followed him.

5 And he went unto his father's house at Ophrah, and killed his brethren the sons of Jerub-Baal, being threescore and ten persons, upon one stone: notwithstanding yet Jotham the youngest son of Jerub-Baal was left; for he hid himself.

6 And all the men of Shechem gathered together, and all the house of Millo, and went, and made Abimelech king, by the plain of the pillar that was in Shechem.

7 And when they told it to Jotham, he went and stood in the top of mount Gerizim, and lifted up his voice, and cried, and said unto them, listen unto me, you men of Shechem, that God may listen unto you.

8 The trees went forth on a time to anoint a king over them; and they said unto the olive tree, Reign you over us.

9 But the olive tree said unto them, Should I leave my fatness, wherewith by me they honor God and man, and go to be promoted over the trees?

10 And the trees said to the fig tree, You come, and reign over us.

11 But the fig tree said unto them, Should I forsake my sweetness, and my good fruit, and go to be promoted over the trees?

12 Then said the trees unto the vine, You come, and reign over us.

13 And the vine said unto them, Should I leave my wine, which cheers God and man, and go to be promoted over the trees?

14 Then said all the trees unto the bramble, You come, and reign over us.

15 And the bramble said unto the trees, If in truth you anoint me king over you, then come and put your trust in my shadow: and if not, let fire come out of the bramble, and devour the cedars of Lebanon.

16 Now therefore, if you have done truly and sincerely, in that you have made Abimelech king, and if you have dealt well with Jerub-Baal and his house, and have done unto him according to the deserving of his hands;

17 For my father fought for you, and cast his soul aside, and delivered you out of the hand of Midian:

18 And you are risen up against my father's house this day, and have slain his sons, threescore and ten persons, upon one stone, and have made Abimelech, the son of his maidservant, king over the men of Shechem, because he is your brother;

19 If you then have dealt truly and sincerely with Jerub-Baal and with his house this day, then rejoice you in Abimelech, and let him also rejoice in you:

20 But if not, let fire come out from Abimelech, and devour the men of Shechem, and the house of Millo; and let fire come out from the men of Shechem, and from the house of Millo, and devour Abimelech.

21 And Jotham ran away, and fled, and went to Beer, and dwelt there, for fear of Abimelech his brother.

22 When Abimelech had reigned three years over Israel,

23 Then God sent an evil spirit between Abimelech and the men of Shechem; and the men of Shechem dealt treacherously with Abimelech:

24 That the cruelty done to the threescore and ten sons of Jerub-Baal might come, and their blood be laid upon Abimelech their brother, which killed them; and upon the men of Shechem, which aided him in the killing of his brethren.

25 And the men of Shechem set ambushers for him in the top of the mountains, and they robbed all that came along that way by them: and it was told Abimelech.

26 And Gaal the son of Ebed came with his brethren, and went over to Shechem: and the men of Shechem put their confidence in him.

27 And they went out into the fields, and gathered their vineyards, and trode the grapes, and made merry, and went into the house of their god, and did eat and drink, and cursed Abimelech.

28 And Gaal the son of Ebed said, Who is Abimelech, and who is Shechem, that we should serve him? is not he the son of Jerub-Baal? and Zebul his officer? serve the men of Hamor the father of Shechem: for why should we serve him?

29 And would to God this people were under my hand! then would I remove Abimelech. And he said to Abimelech, Increase your army, and come out.

30 And when Zebul the ruler of the city heard the words of Gaal the son of Ebed, his anger was kindled.

31 And he sent messengers unto Abimelech privily, saying, Behold, Gaal the son of Ebed and his brethren be come to Shechem; and, behold, they fortify the city against you.

32 Now therefore up by night, you and the people that is with you, and lie in wait in the field:

33 And it shall be, that in the morning, as soon as the sun is up, you shall rise early, and set upon the city: and, behold, when he and the people that is with him come out against you, then may you do to them as you shall find occasion.

34 And Abimelech rose up, and all the people that were with him, by night, and they laid wait against Shechem in four companies.

35 And Gaal the son of Ebed went out, and stood in the entering of the gate of the city: and Abimelech rose up, and the people that were with him, from lying in wait.

36 And when Gaal saw the people, he said to Zebul, Behold, there come people down from the top of the mountains. And Zebul said unto him, you see the shadow of the mountains as if they were men.

37 And Gaal spoke again and said, See there come people down by the middle of the land, and another company come along by the plain of Meonenim.

38 Then said Zebul unto him, Where is now your mouth, wherewith you said, Who is Abimelech, that we should serve him? is not this the people that you have despised? go out, I pray now, and fight with them.

39 And Gaal went out before the men of Shechem, and fought with Abimelech.

40 And Abimelech chased him, and he fled before him, and many were overthrown and wounded, even unto the entering of the gate.

41 And Abimelech dwelt at Arumah: and Zebul thrust out Gaal and his brethren, that they should not dwell in Shechem.

42 And it came to pass on the next day, that the people went out into the field; and they told Abimelech.

43 And he took the people, and divided them into three companies, and laid wait in the field, and looked, and, behold, the people were come forth out of the city; and he rose up against them, and smote them.

44 And Abimelech, and the company that was with him, rushed forward, and stood in the entering of the gate of the city: and the two other companies ran upon all the people that were in the fields, and killed them.

45 And Abimelech fought against the city all that day; and he took the city, and killed the people that was therein, and beat down the city, and sowed it with salt.

46 And when all the men of the tower of Shechem heard that, they entered into a hold of the house of God Berith.

47 And it was told Abimelech, that all the men of the tower of Shechem were gathered together.

48 And Abimelech got him up to mount Zalmon, he and all the people that were with him; and Abimelech took an ax in his hand, and cut down a bough from the trees, and took it, and laid it on his shoulder, and said unto the people that were with him, What you have seen me do, make haste, and do as I have done.

49 And all the people likewise cut down every man his bough, and followed Abimelech, and put them to the hold, and set the hold on fire upon them; so that all the men of the tower of Shechem died also, about a thousand men and women.

50 Then went Abimelech to Thebez, and encamped against Thebez, and took it.

51 But there was a strong tower within the city, and there fled all the men and women, and all they of the city, and shut it to them, and got them up to the top of the tower.

52 And Abimelech came unto the tower, and fought against it, and went hard unto the door of the tower to burn it with fire.

53 And a certain woman cast a piece of a millstone upon Abimelech's head, and all to brake his skull.

54 Then he called hastily unto the young man his armor bearer, and said unto him, Draw your sword, and slay me, that men say not of me, A woman killed him. And his young man thrust him through, and he died.

55 And when the men of Israel saw that Abimelech was dead, they departed every man unto his place.

56 Thus God rendered the wickedness of Abimelech, which he did unto his father, in slaying his seventy brethren:

57 And all the evil of the men of Shechem did God render upon their heads: and upon them came the curse of Jotham the son of Jerub-Baal.

Judges 10:1 And after Abimelech there arose to defend Israel Tola the son of Puah the son of Dodo, a man of Issachar, and he dwelt in Shamir in mount Ephraim.

2 And he judged Israel twenty and three years, and died, and was buried in Shamir.

3 And after him arose Jair, a Gileadite, and judged Israel twenty and two years.

4 And he had thirty sons that rode on thirty donkey colts, and they had thirty cities, which are called Havothjair unto this day, which are in the land of Gilead.

5 And Jair died, and was buried in Camon.

6 And the children of Israel did evil again in the sight of the Becoming-One, and served the lords [baalim] and Ashtaroth, and the gods of Syria, and the gods of Zidon, and the gods of Moab, and the gods of the children of Ammon, and the gods of the Philistines, and forsook the Becoming-One, and served not him.

7 And the anger of the Becoming-One was hot against Israel, and he sold them into the hands of the Philistines, and into the hands of the children of Ammon.

8 And that year they vexed and oppressed the children of Israel: eighteen years, all the children of Israel that were over the Jordan in the land of the Amorites, which is in Gilead.

9 Moreover the children of Ammon passed over Jordan to fight also against Judah, and against Benjamin, and against the house of Ephraim; so that Israel was greatly distressed.

10 And the children of Israel cried unto the Becoming-One, saying, We have sinned against you, both because we have forsaken our God, and also served the lords [baalim]

11 And the Becoming-One said unto the children of Israel, Did not I deliver you from the Egyptians, and from the Amorites, from the children of Ammon, and from the Philistines?

12 The Zidonians also, and the Amalekites, and the Maonites, did oppress you; and you cried to me, and I delivered you out of their hand.

13 Yet you have forsaken me, and served other gods: therefore I will deliver you no more.

14 Go and cry unto the gods which you have chosen; let them deliver you in the time of your tribulation.

15 And the children of Israel said unto the Becoming-One, We have sinned: do you unto us whatsoever seems good unto you; deliver us only, we pray you, this day.

16 And they put away the strange gods from among them, and served the Becoming-One: and his soul was grieved for the misery of Israel.

17 Then the children of Ammon were gathered together, and encamped in Gilead. And the children of Israel assembled themselves together, and encamped in Mizpeh.

18 And the people and princes of Gilead said one to another, What man is he that will begin to fight against the children of Ammon? he shall be head over all the inhabitants of Gilead.

Judges 11:1 Now Jephthah the Gileadite was a mighty man of valor, and he was the son of a harlot: and Gilead begat Jephthah.

2 And Gilead's wife bare him sons; and his wife's sons grew up, and they thrust out Jephthah, and said unto him, you shall not inherit in our father's house; for you are the son of a strange woman.

3 Then Jephthah fled from his brethren, and dwelt in the land of Tob: and there were gathered vain men to Jephthah, and went out with him.

4 And it came to pass after days, that the children of Ammon made war against Israel.

5 And it was so, that when the children of Ammon made war against Israel, the elders of Gilead went to fetch Jephthah out of the land of Tob:

6 And they said unto Jephthah, Come, and be our captain, that we may fight with the children of Ammon.

7 And Jephthah said unto the elders of Gilead, Did not you hate me, and expel me out of my father's house? and why are you come unto me now when you are in distress?

8 And the elders of Gilead said unto Jephthah, Therefore we turn again to you now, that you may go with us, and fight against the children of Ammon, and be our head over all the inhabitants of Gilead.

9 And Jephthah said unto the elders of Gilead, If you bring me home again to fight against the children of Ammon, and the Becoming-One deliver them before me, shall I be your head?

10 And the elders of Gilead said unto Jephthah, The Becoming-One be witness between us, if we do not so according to your words.

11 Then Jephthah went with the elders of Gilead, and the people made him head and captain over them: and Jephthah uttered all his words before the Becoming-One in Mizpeh.

12 And Jephthah sent messengers unto the king of the children of Ammon, saying, What have you to do with me, that you are come against me to fight in my land?

13 And the king of the children of Ammon answered unto the messengers of Jephthah, Because Israel took away my land, when they came up out of Egypt, from Arnon even unto Jabbok, and unto Jordan: now therefore restore those lands again peaceably.

14 And Jephthah sent messengers again unto the king of the children of Ammon:

15 And said unto him, Thus says Jephthah, Israel took not away the land of Moab, nor the land of the children of Ammon:

16 But when Israel came up from Egypt, and walked through the wilderness unto the boundary sea, and came to Kadesh;

17 Then Israel sent messengers unto the king of Edom, saying, Let me, I pray you, pass through your land: but the king of Edom would not listen thereto. And in like manner they sent unto the king of Moab: but he would not consent: and Israel abode in Kadesh.

18 Then they went along through the wilderness, and compassed the land of Edom, and the land of Moab, and came by the east side of the land of Moab, and camped over Arnon, but came not within the border of Moab: for Arnon was the border of Moab.

19 And Israel sent messengers unto Sihon king of the Amorites, the king of Heshbon; and Israel said unto him, Let us pass, we pray you, through your land into my place.

20 But Sihon trusted not Israel to pass through his coast: but Sihon gathered all his people together, and pitched in Jahaz, and fought against Israel.

21 And the Becoming-One, God of Israel delivered Sihon and all his people into the hand of Israel, and they smote them: so Israel possessed all the land of the Amorites, the inhabitants of that country.

22 And they possessed all the coasts of the Amorites, from Arnon even unto Jabbok, and from the wilderness even unto Jordan.

23 So now the Becoming-One, God of Israel has dispossessed the Amorites from before his people Israel, and should you possess it?

24 will not you possess that which Chemosh your god gives you to possess? So whomsoever the Becoming-One our God shall drive out from before us, them will we possess.

25 And now are you any thing better than Balak the son of Zippor, king of Moab? did he ever strive against Israel, or did he ever fight against them,

26 While Israel dwelt in Heshbon and her towns, and in Aroer and her towns, and in all the cities that be along by the coasts of Arnon, three hundred years? why therefore did you not recover them within that time?

27 Therefore I have not sinned against you, but you do me wrong to war against me: the Becoming-One the Judge be judge this day between the children of Israel and the children of Ammon.

28 Howbeit the king of the children of Ammon listened not unto the words of Jephthah which he sent him.

29 Then the spirit of the Becoming-One came upon Jephthah, and he passed over Gilead, and Manasseh, and passed over Mizpeh of Gilead, and from Mizpeh of Gilead he passed over unto the children of Ammon.

30 And Jephthah vowed a vow unto the Becoming-One, and said, If you shall without fail deliver the children of Ammon into mine hands,

31 Then it shall be, that whatsoever comes forth of the doors of my house to meet me, when I return in peace from the children of Ammon, shall surely be the Becoming-One's, and I will offer it up for a burnt offering.

32 So Jephthah passed over unto the children of Ammon to fight against them; and the Becoming-One delivered them into his hands.

33 And he smote them from Aroer, even till you come to Minnith, even twenty cities, and unto the plain of the vineyards, with a very great slaughter. Thus the children of Ammon were subdued before the children of Israel.

34 And Jephthah came to Mizpeh unto his house, and, behold, his daughter came out to meet him with timbrels and with dances: and she was his only child; beside her he had neither son nor daughter.

35 And it came to pass, when he saw her, that he ripped his clothes, and said, Alas, my daughter! you have brought me very low, and you are one of them that trouble me: for I have opened my mouth unto the Becoming-One, and I cannot go back.

36 And she said unto him, My father, if you have opened your mouth unto the Becoming-One, do to me according to that which has proceeded out of your mouth; forasmuch as the Becoming-One has taken vengeance for you of your enemies, even of the children of Ammon.

37 And she said unto her father, Let this thing be done for me: let me alone two months, that I may go up and down upon the mountains, and bewail my virginity, I and my fellows.

38 And he said, Go. And he sent her away for two months: and she went with her companions, and bewailed her virginity upon the mountains.

39 And it came to pass at the end of two months, that she returned unto her father, who did with her according to his vow which he had vowed: and she knew no man. And it was a custom in Israel,

40 That the daughters of Israel went from days to days to lament the daughter of Jephthah the Gileadite four days in a year.

Judges 12:1 And the men of Ephraim gathered themselves together, and went northward, and said unto Jephthah, Why did you pass over to fight against the children of Ammon, and did not call us to go with you? we will burn your house upon you with fire.

2 And Jephthah said unto them, I and my people were at great strife with the children of Ammon; and when I called you, you delivered me not out of their hands.

3 And when I saw that you delivered me not, I put my soul in my hands, and passed over against the children of Ammon, and the Becoming-One delivered them into my hand: why then are you come up unto me this day, to fight against me?

4 Then Jephthah gathered together all the men of Gilead, and fought with Ephraim: and the men of Gilead smote Ephraim, because they said, you Gileadites are fugitives of Ephraim among the Ephraimites, and among the Manassites.

5 And the Gileadites took the passages of Jordan before the Ephraimites: and it was so that when those Ephraimites which were escaped said, Let me go over; that the men of Gilead said unto him, are you an Ephraimite? If he said, Nay;

6 Then said they unto him, Say now Shibboleth: and he said Sibboleth: for he could not frame to pronounce it right. Then they took him, and killed him at the passages of Jordan: and there fell at that time of the Ephraimites forty and two thousand.

7 And Jephthah judged Israel six years. Then died Jephthah the Gileadite, and was buried in one of the cities of Gilead.

8 And after him Ibzan of Bethlehem judged Israel.

9 And he had thirty sons, and thirty daughters, whom he sent abroad, and took in thirty daughters from abroad for his sons. And he judged Israel seven years.

10 Then died Ibzan, and was buried at Bethlehem.

11 And after him Elon, a Zebulonite, judged Israel; and he judged Israel ten years.

12 And Elon the Zebulonite died, and was buried in Aijalon in the country of Zebulun.

13 And after him Abdon the son of Hillel, a Pirathonite, judged Israel.

14 And he had forty sons and thirty nephews, that rode on threescore and ten donkey colts: and he judged Israel eight years.

15 And Abdon the son of Hillel the Pirathonite died, and was buried in Pirathon in the land of Ephraim, in the mount of the Amalekites.

Judges 13:1 And the children of Israel did evil again in the sight of the Becoming-One; and the Becoming-One delivered them into the hand of the Philistines forty years.

2 And there was a certain man of Zorah, of the family of the Danites, whose name was Manoah; and his wife was barren, and bare not.

3 And the angel of the Becoming-One appeared unto the woman, and said unto her, Behold now, you are barren, and bear not: but you shall conceive, and bear a son.

4 Now therefore beware, I pray you, and drink not wine nor strong drink, and eat not any unclean thing:

5 For, lo, you shall conceive, and bear a son; and no razor shall come on his head: for the child shall be a Nazarite unto God from the womb: and he shall begin to deliver Israel out of the hand of the Philistines.

6 Then the woman came and told her husband, saying, A man of God came unto me, and his countenance was like the countenance of an angel of God, very terrible: but I asked him not where he was from, neither did he tell me his name:

7 But he said unto me, Behold, you shall conceive, and bear a son; and now drink no wine nor strong drink, neither eat any unclean thing: for the child shall be a Nazarite to God from the womb to the day of his death.

8 Then Manoah entreated the Becoming-One, and said, O my Lord(s), let the man of God which you did send come again unto us, and teach us what we shall do unto the child that shall be born.

9 And God listened to the voice of Manoah; and the angel of God came again unto the woman as she sat in the field: but Manoah her husband was not with her.

10 And the woman made haste, and ran, and showed her husband, and said unto him, Behold, the man has appeared unto me, that came unto me the other day.

11 And Manoah arose, and went after his wife, and came to the man, and said unto him, are you the man that spoke unto the woman? And he said, I am.

12 And Manoah said, Now let your words come to pass. How shall we order the child, and how shall we do unto him?

13 And the angel of the Becoming-One said unto Manoah, Of all that I said unto the woman let her beware.

14 She may not eat of any thing that comes of the vine, neither let her drink wine or strong drink, nor eat any unclean thing: all that I commanded her let her observe.

15 And Manoah said unto the angel of the Becoming-One, I pray you, let us detain you, until we shall have made ready a kid for you.

16 And the angel of the Becoming-One said unto Manoah, Though you detain me, I will not eat of your bread: and if you will offer a burnt offering, you must offer it unto the Becoming-One. For Manoah knew not that he was an angel of the Becoming-One.

17 And Manoah said unto the angel of the Becoming-One, What is your name, that when your sayings come to pass we may do you honor?

18 And the angel of the Becoming-One said unto him, Why ask you thus after my name, seeing it is secret?

19 So Manoah took a kid with a food offering, and offered it upon a rock unto the Becoming-One: and the angel did wonderously; and Manoah and his wife looked on.

20 For it came to pass, when the flame went up toward the heavens from off the altar, that the angel of the Becoming-One ascended in the flame of the altar.

And Manoah and his wife looked on it, and fell on their faces to the ground.

21 But the angel of the Becoming-One did no more appear to Manoah and to his wife. Then Manoah knew that he was an angel of the Becoming-One.

22 And Manoah said unto his wife, We shall surely die, because we have seen God.

23 But his wife said unto him, If the Becoming-One was pleased to kill us, he would not have received a burnt offering and a food offering at our hands, neither would he have showed us all these things, nor would as at this time have told us such things as these.

24 And the woman bare a son, and called his name Samson: and the child grew, and the Becoming-One blessed him.

25 And the spirit of the Becoming-One began to move him at times in the camp of Dan between Zorah and Eshtaol.

Judges 14:1 And Samson went down to Timnath, and saw a woman in Timnath of the daughters of the Philistines.

2 And he came up, and told his father and his mother, and said, I have seen a woman in Timnath of the daughters of the Philistines: now therefore get her for me to wife.

3 Then his father and his mother said unto him, Is there never a woman among the daughters of your brethren, or among all my people, that you go to take a wife of the uncircumcised Philistines? And Samson said unto his father, Get her for me; for she pleases me well.

4 But his father and his mother knew not that it was of the Becoming-One, that he sought an occasion against the Philistines: for at that time the Philistines had dominion over Israel.

5 Then went Samson down, and his father and his mother, to Timnath, and came to the vineyards of Timnath: and, behold, a young lion roared against him.

6 And the spirit of the Becoming-One came mightily upon him, and he ripped him as he would have ripped a kid, and he had nothing in his hand: but he told not his father or his mother what he had done.

7 And he went down, and talked with the woman; and she pleased Samson well.

8 And after a time he returned to take her, and he turned aside to see the carcase of the lion: and, behold, there was a swarm of bees and honey in the carcase of the lion.

9 And he took thereof in his hands, and went on eating, and came to his father and mother, and he gave them, and they did eat: but he told not them that he had taken the honey out of the carcase of the lion.

10 So his father went down unto the woman: and Samson made there a feast; for so used the young men to do.

11 And it came to pass, when they saw him, that they brought thirty companions to be with him.

12 And Samson said unto them, I will now put forth a riddle unto you: if you can certainly declare it me within the seven days of the feast, and find it out, then I will give you thirty sheets and thirty change of garments:

13 But if you cannot declare it me, then shall you give me thirty sheets and thirty change of garments. And they said unto him, Put forth your riddle, that we may hear it.

14 And he said unto them, Out of the eater came forth food, and out of the strong came forth sweetness. And they could not in three days expound the riddle.

15 And it came to pass on the seventh day, that they said unto Samson's wife, Entice your husband, that he may declare unto us the riddle, lest we burn you and your father's house with fire: have you called us to take that we have? is it not so?

16 And Samson's wife wept before him, and said, you do but hate me, and love me not: you have put forth a riddle unto the children of my people, and have not told it me. And he said unto her, Behold, I have not told it my father nor my mother, and shall I tell it you?

17 And she wept before him the seven days, while their feast lasted: and it came to pass on the seventh day, that he told her, because she lay great upon him: and she told the riddle to the children of her people.

18 And the men of the city said unto him on the seventh day before the sun went down, What is sweeter than honey? and what is stronger than a lion? And he said unto them, If you had not plowed with my heifer, you had not found out my riddle.

19 And the spirit of the Becoming-One came upon him, and he went down to Ashkelon, and killed thirty men of them, and took their spoil, and gave change of garments unto them which expounded the riddle. And his anger was kindled, and he went up to his father's house.

20 But Samson's wife was given to his companion, whom he had used as his friend.

Judges 15:1 But it came to pass within a while after, in the time of wheat harvest, that Samson visited his wife with a kid; and he said, I will go in to my wife into the chamber. But her father would not permit him to go in.

2 And her father said, I truly thought that you had utterly hated her; therefore I gave her to your companion: is not her younger sister fairer than she? take her, I pray you, instead of her.

3 And Samson said concerning them, Now shall I be more blameless than the Philistines, though I do them a displeasure.

4 And Samson went and caught three hundred foxes, and took firebrands, and turned tail to tail, and put a firebrand in the midst between two tails.

5 And when he had set the brands on fire, he let them go into the standing grain of the Philistines, and burnt up both the shocks, and also the standing grain, with the vineyards and olives.

6 Then the Philistines said, Who has done this? And they answered, Samson, the son-in-law of the Timnite, because he had taken his wife, and given her to his companion. And the Philistines came up, and burnt her and her father with fire.

7 And Samson said unto them, Though you have done this, yet will I be avenged of you, and after that I will cease.

8 And he smote them hip and thigh with a great slaughter: and he went down and dwelt in the top of the rock Etam.

9 Then the Philistines went up, and pitched in Judah, and spread themselves in Lehi.

10 And the men of Judah said, Why are you come up against us? And they answered, To bind Samson are we come up, to do to him as he has done to us.

11 Then three thousand men of Judah went to the top of the rock Etam, and said to Samson, don't you know that the Philistines are rulers over us? what is this that you have done unto us? And he said unto them, As they did unto me, so I have done unto them.

12 And they said unto him, We are come down to bind you, that we may deliver you into the hand of the Philistines. And Samson said unto them, Swear unto me, that you will not fall upon me yourselves.

13 And they spoke unto him, saying, No; but we will bind you fast, and deliver you into their hand: but surely we will not kill you. And they bound him with two new cords, and brought him up from the rock.

14 And when he came unto Lehi, the Philistines shouted against him: and the spirit of the Becoming-One came mightily upon him, and the cords that were upon his arms became as flax that was burnt with fire, and his bands loosened from off his hands.

15 And he found a new jawbone of an donkey, and put forth his hand, and took it, and killed a thousand men therewith.

16 And Samson said, With the jawbone of an donkey, heaps upon heaps, with the jaw of an donkey I have slain a thousand men.

17 And it came to pass, when he had made an end of speaking, that he cast away the jawbone out of his hand, and called that place Ramathlehi.

18 And he was greatly athirst, and called on the Becoming-One, and said, you have given this great deliverance into the hand of your servant: and now shall I die for thirst, and fall into the hand of the uncircumcised?

19 But God clave a hollow place that was in the jaw, and there came water thereout; and when he had drunk, his spirit came again, and he revived: therefore he called the name thereof Enhakkore, which is in Lehi unto this day.

20 And he judged Israel in the days of the Philistines twenty years.

Judges 16:1 Then went Samson to Gaza, and saw there a harlot, and went in unto her.

2 And it was told the Gazites, saying, Samson is come here. And they compassed him in, and laid wait for him all night in the gate of the city, and were quiet all the night, saying, In the morning, when it is day, we shall kill him.

3 And Samson lay till midnight, and arose at midnight, and took the doors of the gate of the city, and the two posts, and went away with them, bar and all, and put them upon his shoulders, and carried them up to the top of a hill that is before Hebron.

4 And it came to pass afterward, that he loved a woman in the valley of Sorek, whose name was Delilah.

5 And the lords of the Philistines came up unto her, and said unto her, Entice him, and see wherein his great strength lies, and by what means we may prevail against him, that we may bind him to afflict him: and we will give you every one of us eleven hundred pieces of silver.

6 And Delilah said to Samson, Tell me, I pray you, wherein does your great strength lie, and wherewith you might be bound to afflict you.

7 And Samson said unto her, If they bind me with seven green cords that were never dried, then shall I be weak, and be as another man.

8 Then the lords of the Philistines brought up to her seven green cords which had not been dried, and she bound him with them.

9 Now there were men lying in wait, abiding with her in the chamber. And she said unto him, The Philistines be upon you, Samson. And he brake the cords, as a thread of tow is broken when it touches the fire. So his strength was not known.

10 And Delilah said unto Samson, Behold, you have mocked me, and told me lies: now tell me, I pray you, wherewith you might be bound.

11 And he said unto her, If they bind me fast with new ropes that never were occupied, then shall I be weak, and be as another man.

12 Delilah therefore took new ropes, and bound him therewith, and said unto him, The Philistines be upon you, Samson. And there were ambushers abiding in the chamber. And he brake them from off his arms like a thread.

13 And Delilah said unto Samson, Hitherto you have mocked me, and told me lies: tell me wherewith you might be bound. And he said unto her, If you weave the seven locks of my head with the web.

14 And she fastened it with the pin, and said unto him, The Philistines be upon you, Samson. And he awaked out of his sleep, and went away with the pin of the beam, and with the web.

15 And she said unto him, How can you say, I love you, when your heart is not with me? you have mocked me these three times, and have not told me wherein your great strength lies.

16 And it came to pass, when she pressed him daily with her words, and urged him, so that his soul was vexed unto death;

17 That he told her all his heart, and said unto her, There has not come a razor upon mine head; for I have been a Nazarite unto God from my mother's womb: if I be shaven, then my strength will go from me, and I shall become weak, and be like any other man.

18 And when Delilah saw that he had told her all his heart, she sent and called for the lords of the Philistines, saying, Come up this once, for he has showed me all his heart. Then the lords of the Philistines came up unto her, and brought money in their hand.

19 And she made him sleep upon her knees; and she called for a man, and she caused him to shave off the seven locks of his head; and she began to afflict him, and his strength went from him.

20 And she said, The Philistines be upon you, Samson. And he awoke out of his sleep, and said, I will go out as at other times before, and shake myself. And he knew not that the Becoming-One was departed from him.

21 But the Philistines took him, and put out his eyes, and brought him down to Gaza, and bound him with fetters of brass; and he did grind in the prison house.

22 Howbeit the hair of his head began to grow again after he was shaven.

23 Then the lords of the Philistines gathered them together for to offer a great sacrifice unto Dagon their god, and to rejoice: for they said, Our god has delivered Samson our enemy into our hand.

24 And when the people saw him, they praised their god: for they said, Our god has delivered into our hands our enemy, and the destroyer of our country, which killed many of us.

25 And it came to pass, when their hearts were merry, that they said, Call for Samson, that he may make us sport. And they called for Samson out of the prison house; and he made them sport: and they set him between the pillars.

26 And Samson said unto the lad that held him by the hand, Permit me that I may feel the pillars, whereupon the house stands that I may lean upon them.

27 Now the house was full of men and women; and all the lords of the Philistines were there; and there were upon the roof about three thousand men and women, that beheld while Samson made sport.

28 And Samson called unto the Becoming-One, and said, O my Lord(s) the Becoming-One, remember me, I pray you, and strengthen me, I pray you, only this once, O God, that I may be at once avenged of the Philistines for my two eyes.

29 And Samson took hold of the two middle pillars upon which the house stood, and on which it was borne up, of the one with his right hand, and of the other with his left.

30 And Samson said, Let my soul die with the Philistines. And he bowed himself with all his might; and the house fell upon the lords, and upon all the people that were therein. So the dead which he killed at his death were more than they which he killed in his life.

31 Then his brethren and all the house of his father came down, and took him, and brought him up, and buried him between Zorah and Eshtaol in the buryingplace of Manoah his father. And he judged Israel twenty years.

Judges 17:1 And there was a man of mount Ephraim, whose name was Micah.

2 And he said unto his mother, The eleven hundred shekels of silver that were taken from you, about which you cursed, and spoke of also in mine ears, behold, the silver is with me; I took it. And his mother said, Blessed be you of the Becoming-One, my son.

3 And when he had restored the eleven hundred shekels of silver to his mother, his mother said, I had wholly dedicated the silver unto the Becoming-One from my hand for my son, to make a graven image and a molten image: now therefore I will restore it unto you.

4 Yet he restored the money unto his mother; and his mother took two hundred shekels of silver, and gave them to the founder, who made thereof a graven image and a molten image: and they were in the house of Micah.

5 And the man Micah had a house of gods, and made an ephod, and teraphim [images] and consecrated one of his sons, who became his priest.

6 In those days there was no king in Israel, but every man did that which was right in his own eyes.

7 And there was a young man out of Bethlehem-judah of the family of Judah, who was a Levite, and he sojourned there.

8 And the man departed out of the city from Bethlehem-judah to sojourn where he could find a place: and he came to mount Ephraim to the house of Micah, as he journeyed.

9 And Micah said unto him, From where are you from? And he said unto him, I am a Levite of Bethlehem-judah, and I go to sojourn where I may find a place.

10 And Micah said unto him, Dwell with me, and be unto me a father and a priest, and I will give you ten shekels of silver by the day, and a suit of apparel, and your victuals. So the Levite went in.

11 And the Levite was content to dwell with the man; and the young man was unto him as one of his sons.

12 And Micah consecrated the Levite; and the young man became his priest, and was in the house of Micah.

13 Then said Micah, Now know I that the Becoming-One will do me good, seeing I have a Levite to my priest.

Judges 18:1 In those days there was no king in Israel: and in those days the tribe of the Danites sought them an inheritance to dwell in; for unto that day all their inheritance had not fallen unto them among the tribes of Israel.

2 And the children of Dan sent of their family five men from their coasts, men of valor, from Zorah, and from Eshtaol, to spy out the land, and to search it; and they said unto them, Go, search the land: who when they came to mount Ephraim, to the house of Micah, they lodged there.

3 When they were by the house of Micah, they knew the voice of the young man the Levite: and they turned in there, and said unto him, Who brought you here? and what make you in this place? and what have you here?

4 And he said unto them, Thus and thus deals Micah with me, and has hired me, and I am his priest.

5 And they said unto him, Ask counsel, we pray you, of God, that we may know whether our way which we go shall be prosperous.

6 And the priest said unto them, Go in peace: before the Becoming-One is your way wherein you go.

7 Then the five men departed, and came to Laish, and saw the people that were therein, how they dwelt careless, after the manner of the Zidonians, quiet and secure; and there was no magistrate in the land, that might put them to shame in any thing; and they were far from the Zidonians, and had no business with any man.

8 And they came unto their brethren to Zorah and Eshtaol: and their brethren said unto them, What do you say?

9 And they said, Arise, that we may go up against them: for we have seen the land, and, behold, it is very good: and are you still? be not slothful to go, and to enter to possess the land.

10 When you go, you shall come unto a people secure, and to a large land: for God has given it into your hands; a place where there is no lack of anything that is in the earth.

11 And there went from there of the family of the Danites, out of Zorah and out of Eshtaol, six hundred men appointed with weapons of war.

12 And they went up, and pitched in Kirjathjearim, in Judah: therefore they called that place Mahanehdan unto this day: behold, it is behind Kirjathjearim.

13 And they passed there unto mount Ephraim, and came unto the house of Micah.

14 Then answered the five men that went to spy out the country of Laish, and said unto their brethren, Do you know that there is in these houses an ephod, and teraphim, and a graven image, and a molten image? now therefore consider what you have to do.

15 And they turned in there, and came to the house of the young man the Levite, even unto the house of Micah, and saluted him.

16 And the six hundred men appointed with their weapons of war, which were of the children of Dan, stood by the entering of the gate.

17 And the five men that went to spy out the land went up, and came in there, and took the graven image, and the ephod, and the teraphim, and the molten image: and the priest stood in the entering of the gate with the six hundred men that were appointed with weapons of war.

18 And these went into Micah's house, and fetched the carved image, the ephod, and the teraphim, and the molten image. Then said the priest unto them, What are you doing?

19 And they said unto him, Hold your peace, lay your hand upon your mouth, and go with us, and be to us a father and a priest: is it better for you to be a priest unto the house of one man, or that you be a priest unto a tribe and a family in Israel?

20 And the priest's heart was glad, and he took the ephod, and the teraphim, and the graven image, and went in the midst of the people.

21 So they turned and departed, and put the little ones and the cattle and the carriage before them.

22 And when they were a good way from the house of Micah, the men that were in the houses near to Micah's house were gathered together, and overtook the children of Dan.

23 And they cried unto the children of Dan. And they turned their faces, and said unto Micah, What ails you, that you come with such a company?

24 And he said, you have taken away my gods which I made, and the priest, and you are gone away: and what have I more? and what is this that you say unto me, What ails you?

25 And the children of Dan said unto him, Let not your voice be heard among us, lest angry of soul fellows run upon you, and you lose your soul, with the souls of your household.

26 And the children of Dan went their way: and when Micah saw that they were too strong for him, he turned and went back unto his house.

27 And they took the things which Micah had made, and the priest which he had, and came unto Laish, unto a people that were at quiet and secure: and they smote them with the edge of the sword, and burnt the city with fire.

28 And there was no deliverer, because it was far from Zidon, and they had no business with any man; and it was in the valley that lies by Beth-rehob. And they built a city, and dwelt therein.

29 And they called the name of the city Dan, after the name of Dan their father, who was born unto Israel: howbeit the name of the city was Laish at the first.

30 And the children of Dan set up the graven image: and Jonathan, the son of Gershom, the son of Manasseh, he and his sons were priests to the tribe of Dan until the day of the captivity of the land.

31 And they set them up Micah's graven image, which he made, all the time that the house of God was in Shiloh.

Judges 19:1 And it came to pass in those days, when there was no king in Israel, that there was a certain Levite sojourning on the side of mount Ephraim, who took to him a concubine out of Bethlehem-judah.

2 And his concubine played the whore against him, and went away from him unto her father's house to Behlehem-judah, and was there four whole months.

3 And her husband arose, and went after her, to speak friendly unto her, and to bring her again, having his servant with him, and a couple of donkeys: and she brought him into her father's house: and when the father of the damsel saw him, he rejoiced to meet him.

4 And his father-in-law, the damsel's father, retained him; and he abode with him three days: so they did eat and drink, and lodged there.

5 And it came to pass on the fourth day, when they arose early in the morning, that he rose up to depart: and the damsel's father said unto his son-in-law, Comfort your heart with a morsel of bread, and afterward go your way.

6 And they sat down, and did eat and drink both of them together: for the damsel's father had said unto the man, Be content, I pray you, and tarry all night, and let your heart be merry.

7 And when the man rose up to depart, his father-in-law urged him: therefore he lodged there again.

8 And he arose early in the morning on the fifth day to depart: and the damsel's father said, Comfort your heart, I pray you. And they tarried until afternoon, and they did eat both of them.

9 And when the man rose up to depart, he, and his concubine, and his servant, his father-in-law, the damsel's father, said unto him, Behold, now the day draws toward evening, I pray you tarry all night: behold, the day grows to an end, lodge here, that your heart may be merry; and tomorrow get you early on your way, that you may go home.

10 But the man would not tarry that night, but he rose up and departed, and came over against Jebus, which is Jerusalem; and there were with him two donkeys saddled, his concubine also was with him.

11 And when they were by Jebus, the day was far spent; and the servant said unto his master, Come, I pray you, and let us turn in into this city of the Jebusites, and lodge in it.

12 And his master said unto him, We will not turn aside here into the city of a stranger, that is not of the children of Israel; we will pass over to Gibeah.

13 And he said unto his servant, Come, and let us draw near to one of these places to lodge all night, in Gibeah, or in Ramah.

14 And they passed on and went their way; and the sun went down upon them when they were by Gibeah, which belongs to Benjamin.

15 And they turned aside there, to go in and to lodge in Gibeah: and when he went in, he sat him down in a street of the city: for there was no man that took them into his house to lodging.

16 And, behold, there came an old man from his work out of the field at evening, which was also of mount Ephraim; and he sojourned in Gibeah: but the men of the place were Benjamites.

17 And when he had lifted up his eyes, he saw a wayfaring man in the street of the city: and the old man said, Where to are you going? and from where are you from?

18 And he said unto him, We are passing from Bethlehem-judah toward the side of mount Ephraim; from there I am: and I went to Bethlehem-judah, but I am now going to the house of the Becoming-One; and there is no man that receives me to house.

19 Yet there is both straw and feed for our donkeys; and there is bread and wine also for me, and for your handmaid, and for the young man which is with your servants: there is no want of any thing.

20 And the old man said, Peace be with you; howsoever let all your wants lie upon me; only lodge not in the street.

21 So he brought him into his house, and gave feed unto the donkeys: and they washed their feet, and did eat and drink.

22 Now as they were making their hearts merry, behold, the men of the city, certain sons of Belial, beset the house round about, and beat at the door, and spoke to the master of the house, the old man, saying, Bring forth the man that came into your house, that we may know him.

23 And the man, the master of the house, went out unto them, and said unto them, Nay, my brethren, nay, I pray you, do not so wickedly; seeing that this man is come into mine house, do not this folly.

24 Behold, here is my daughter a maiden, and his concubine; them I will bring out now, and humble you them, and do with them what seems good unto you: but unto this man do not so vile a thing.

25 But the men would not listen to him: so the man took his concubine, and brought her forth unto them; and they knew her, and abused her all the night until the morning: and when the dawn arose, they let her go.

26 Then came the woman in the dawning of the day, and fell down at the door of the man's house where her lord(s) [was], till it was light.

27 And her lord(s) rose up in the morning, and opened the doors of the house, and went out to go his way: and, behold, the woman his concubine was fallen down at the door of the house, and her hands were upon the threshold.

28 And he said unto her, Up, and let us be going. But none answered. Then the man took her up upon an donkey, and the man rose up, and got him unto his place.

29 And when he was come into his house, he took a knife, and laid hold on his concubine, and divided her, together with her bones, into twelve pieces, and sent her into all the coasts of Israel.

30 And it was so, that all that saw it said, There was no such deed done nor seen from the day that the children of Israel came up out of the land of Egypt unto this day: consider of it, take advice, and speak your minds.

Judges 20:1 Then all the children of Israel went out, and the congregation was gathered together as one man, from Dan even to Beersheba, with the land of Gilead, unto the Becoming-One in Mizpeh.

2 And the chief of all the people, even of all the tribes of Israel, presented themselves in the assembly of the people of God, four hundred thousand footmen that drew sword.

3 Now the children of Benjamin heard that the children of Israel were gone up to Mizpeh. Then said the children of Israel, Tell us, how was this wickedness?

4 And the Levite, the husband of the woman that was slain, answered and said, I came into Gibeah that belongs to Benjamin, I and my concubine, to lodge.

5 And the men of Gibeah rose against me, and beset the house round about upon me by night, and thought to have slain me: and my concubine have they forced, that she is dead.

6 And I took my concubine, and cut her in pieces, and sent her throughout all the country of the inheritance of Israel: for they have committed lewdness and folly in Israel.

7 Behold, you are all children of Israel; give here your advice and counsel.

8 And all the people arose as one man, saying, We will not any of us go to his tent, neither will we any of us turn into his house.

9 But now this shall be the thing which we will do to Gibeah; we will go up by lot against it;

10 And we will take ten men of a hundred throughout all the tribes of Israel, and a hundred of a thousand, and an thousand out of multitude, to fetch

victual for the people, that they may do, when they come to Gibeah of Benjamin, according to all the folly that they have worked in Israel.

11 So all the men of Israel were gathered against the city, knit together as one man.

12 And the tribes of Israel sent men through all the tribe of Benjamin, saying, What wickedness is this that is done among you?

13 Now therefore deliver us the men, the children of Belial, which are in Gibeah, that we may put them to death, and put away evil from Israel. But the children of Benjamin would not listen to the voice of their brethren the children of Israel:

14 But the children of Benjamin gathered themselves together out of the cities unto Gibeah, to go out to battle against the children of Israel.

15 And the children of Benjamin were numbered at that time out of the cities twenty and six thousand of men that drew sword, beside the inhabitants of Gibeah, which were numbered seven hundred chosen men.

16 Among all this people there were seven hundred chosen men lefthanded; every one could sling stones at a hair breadth, and not miss.

17 And the men of Israel, beside Benjamin, were numbered four hundred thousand men that drew sword: all these were men of war.

18 And the children of Israel arose, and went up to the house of God, and asked counsel of God, and said, Which of us shall go up first to the battle against the children of Benjamin? And the Becoming-One said, Judah shall go up first.

19 And the children of Israel rose up in the morning, and encamped against Gibeah.

20 And the men of Israel went out to battle against Benjamin; and the men of Israel put themselves in array to fight against them at Gibeah.

21 And the children of Benjamin came forth out of Gibeah, and destroyed down to the ground of the Israelites that day twenty and two thousand men.

22 And the people the men of Israel encouraged themselves, and set their battle again in array in the place where they put themselves in array the first day.

23 And the children of Israel went up and wept before the Becoming-One until even, and asked counsel of the Becoming-One, saying, Shall I go up again to battle against the children of Benjamin my brother? And the Becoming-One said, Go up against him.

24 And the children of Israel came near against the children of Benjamin the second day.

25 And Benjamin went forth against them out of Gibeah the second day, and destroyed down to the ground of the children of Israel again eighteen thousand men; all these drew the sword.

26 Then all the children of Israel, and all the people, went up, and came unto the house of God, and wept, and sat there before the Becoming-One, and fasted that day until even, and offered burnt offerings and peace offerings before the Becoming-One.

27 And the children of Israel inquired of the Becoming-One, for the ark of the covenant of God was there in those days,

28 And Phinehas, the son of Eleazar, the son of Aaron, stood before it in those days, saying, Shall I yet again go out to battle against the children of Benjamin my brother, or shall I cease? And the Becoming-One said, Go up; for tomorrow I will deliver them into your hand.

29 And Israel set ambushers round about Gibeah.

30 And the children of Israel went up against the children of Benjamin on the third day, and put themselves in array against Gibeah, as at other times.

31 And the children of Benjamin went out against the people, and were drawn away from the city; and they began to smite of the people, and kill, as at other times, in the highways, of which one goes up to the house of God, and the other to Gibeah in the field, about thirty men of Israel.

32 And the children of Benjamin said, They are struck down before us, as at the first. But the children of Israel said, Let us flee, and draw them from the city unto the highways.

33 And all the men of Israel rose up out of their place, and put themselves in array at Baal-Tamar: and the ambushers of Israel came forth out of their places, even out of the meadows of Gibeah.

34 And there came against Gibeah ten thousand chosen men out of all Israel, and the battle was great: but they knew not that evil was near them.

35 And the Becoming-One smote Benjamin before Israel: and the children of Israel destroyed of the Benjamites that day twenty and five thousand and a hundred men: all these drew the sword.

36 So the children of Benjamin saw that they were struck: for the men of Israel gave place to the Benjamites, because they trusted unto the ambushers which they had set beside Gibeah.

37 And the ambushers hasted, and rushed upon Gibeah; and the ambushers drew themselves along, and smote all the city with the edge of the sword.

38 Now there was a set time between the men of Israel and the ambushers, that they should make a great flame with smoke rise up out of the city.

39 And when the men of Israel retired in the battle, Benjamin began to smite and kill of the men of Israel about thirty persons: for they said, Surely they are struck down before us, as in the first battle.

40 But when the flame began to arise up out of the city with a pillar of smoke, the Benjamites looked behind them, and, behold, the flame of the city ascended up to heaven.

41 And when the men of Israel turned again, the men of Benjamin were amazed: for they saw that evil was come upon them.

42 Therefore they turned their backs before the men of Israel unto the way of the wilderness; but the battle overtook them; and them which came out of the cities they destroyed in the midst of them.

43 Thus they enclosed the Benjamites round about, and chased them, and trode them down with ease over against Gibeah toward the sunrising.

44 And there fell of Benjamin eighteen thousand men; all these were men of valor.

45 And they turned and fled toward the wilderness unto the rock of Rimmon: and they gleaned of them in the highways five thousand men; and pursued hard after them unto Gidom, and killed two thousand men of them.

46 So that all which fell that day of Benjamin were twenty and five thousand men that drew the sword; all these were men of valor.

47 But six hundred men turned and fled to the wilderness unto the rock Rimmon, and abode in the rock Rimmon four months.

48 And the men of Israel turned again upon the children of Benjamin, and smote them with the edge of the sword, as well the men of every city, as the beast, and all that came to hand: also they set on fire all the cities that they came to.

Judges 21:1 Now the men of Israel had sworn in Mizpeh, saying, There shall not any of us give his daughter unto Benjamin to wife.

2 And the people came to the house of God, and abode there till even before God, and lifted up their voices, and wept greatly;

3 And said, O Becoming-One, God of Israel, why is this come to pass in Israel, that there should be today one tribe lacking in Israel?

4 And it came to pass on the next day, that the people rose early, and built there an altar, and offered burnt offerings and peace offerings.

5 And the children of Israel said, Who is there among all the tribes of Israel that came not up with the congregation unto the Becoming-One? For they had made a great oath concerning him that came not up to the Becoming-One to Mizpeh, saying, He shall surely be put to death.

6 And the children of Israel repented them for Benjamin their brother, and said, There is one tribe cut off from Israel this day.

7 How shall we do for wives for them that remain, seeing we have sworn by the Becoming-One that we will not give them of our daughters to wives?

8 And they said, What one is there of the tribes of Israel that came not up to Mizpeh to the Becoming-One? And, behold, there came none to the camp from Jabeshgilead to the assembly.

9 For the people were numbered, and, behold, there were none of the inhabitants of Jabeshgilead there.

10 And the congregation sent there twelve thousand men of the bravest, and commanded them, saying, Go and smite the inhabitants of Jabeshgilead with the edge of the sword, with the women and the children.

11 And this is the thing that you shall do, you shall utterly destroy every male, and every woman that has lain by man.

12 And they found among the inhabitants of Jabeshgilead four hundred young virgins, that had known no man by lying with any male: and they brought them unto the camp to Shiloh, which is in the land of Canaan.

13 And the whole congregation sent some to speak to the children of Benjamin that were in the rock Rimmon, and to call peaceably unto them.

14 And Benjamin came again at that time; and they gave them wives which they had saved alive of the women of Jabeshgilead: and yet so they sufficed them not.

15 And the people repented them for Benjamin, because that the Becoming-One had made a breach in the tribes of Israel.

16 Then the elders of the congregation said, How shall we do for wives for them that remain, seeing the women are destroyed out of Benjamin?

17 And they said, There must be an inheritance for them that be escaped of Benjamin, that a tribe be not destroyed out of Israel.

18 Howbeit we may not give them wives of our daughters: for the children of Israel have sworn, saying, Cursed be he that gives a wife to Benjamin.

19 Then they said, Behold, there is a feast of the Becoming-One in Shiloh from days to days in a place which is on the north side of Bethel, on the east side of the highway that goes up from Bethel to Shechem, and on the south of Lebonah.

20 Therefore they commanded the children of Benjamin, saying, Go and lie in wait in the vineyards;

21 And see, and, behold, if the daughters of Shiloh come out to dance in dances, then you come out of the vineyards, and catch you every man his wife of the daughters of Shiloh, and go to the land of Benjamin.

22 And it shall be, when their fathers or their brethren come unto us to complain, that we will say unto them, Be favorable unto them for our sakes: because we reserved not to each man his wife in the war: for you did not give unto them at this time, that you should be guilty.

23 And the children of Benjamin did so, and took them wives, according to their number, of them that danced, whom they caught: and they went and returned unto their inheritance, and repaired the cities, and dwelt in them.

24 And the children of Israel departed there at that time, every man to his tribe and to his family, and they went out from there every man to his inheritance.

25 In those days there was no king in Israel: every man did that which was right in his own eyes.

Ruth

Ruth 1:1 Now it came to pass in the days when the judges ruled, that there was a famine in the land. And a certain man of Bethlehem-judah went to sojourn in the country of Moab, he, and his wife, and his two sons.

2 And the name of the man was Elimelech, and the name of his wife Naomi, and the name of his two sons Mahlon and Chilion, Ephrathites of Bethlehem-judah. And they came into the country of Moab, and continued there.

3 And Elimelech Naomi's husband died; and she was left, and her two sons.

4 And they took them wives of the women of Moab; the name of the one was Orpah, and the name of the other Ruth: and they dwelled there about ten years.

5 And Mahlon and Chilion died also both of them; and the woman was left of her two sons and her husband.

6 Then she arose with her daughters-in-law, that she might return from the country of Moab: for she had heard in the country of Moab how that the Becoming-One had visited his people in giving them bread.

7 Therefore she went forth out of the place where she was, and her two daughters-in-law with her; and they went on the way to return unto the land of Judah.

8 And Naomi said unto her two daughters-in-law, Go, return each to her mother's house: the Becoming-One deal kindly with you, as you have dealt with the dead, and with me.

9 The Becoming-One grant you that you may find rest, each of you in the house of her husband. Then she kissed them; and they lifted up their voice, and wept.

10 And they said unto her, Surely we will return with you unto your people.

11 And Naomi said, Turn again, my daughters: why will you go with me? are there yet any more sons in my womb, that they may be your husbands?

12 Turn again, my daughters, go your way; for I am too old to have a husband. If I should say, I have hope, if I should have a husband also to night, and should also bear sons;

13 Would you tarry for them till they were grown? would you stay for them from having husbands? nay, my daughters; for it grieves me much for your sakes that the hand of the Becoming-One is gone out against me.

14 And they lifted up their voice, and wept again: and Orpah kissed her mother-in-law; but Ruth clave unto her.

15 And she said, Behold, your sister-in-law is gone back unto her people, and unto her gods: return you after your sister-in-law.

16 And Ruth said, Entreat me not to leave you, or to return from following after you: for wheresoever you go, I will go; and where you lodged, I will lodge: your people shall be my people, and your God my God:

17 Where you die, will I die, and there will I be buried: the Becoming-One do so to me, and more also, if anything but death part you and me.

18 When she saw that she was stedfastly minded to go with her, then she left speaking unto her.

19 So they two went until they came to Bethlehem. And it came to pass, when they were come to Bethlehem, that all the city was moved about them, and they said, Is this Naomi?

20 And she said unto them, Call me not Naomi, call me Mara: for the Almighty has dealt very bitterly with me.

21 I went out full, and the Becoming-One has brought me home again empty: why then call you me Naomi, seeing the Becoming-One has testified against me, and the Almighty has afflicted me?

22 So Naomi returned, and Ruth the Moabitess, her daughter-in-law, with her, which returned out of the country of Moab: and they came to Bethlehem in the beginning of barley harvest.

Ruth 2:1 And Naomi had a kinsman of her husband's, a mighty man of wealth, of the family of Elimelech; and his name was Boaz.

2 And Ruth the Moabitess said unto Naomi, Let me now go to the field, and glean ears of grain after him in whose sight I shall find grace. And she said unto her, Go, my daughter.

3 And she went, and came, and gleaned in the field after the reapers: and her hap was to light on a part of the field belonging unto Boaz, who was of the kindred of Elimelech.

4 And, behold, Boaz came from Bethlehem, and said unto the reapers, The Becoming-One be with you. And they answered him, The Becoming-One bless you.

5 Then said Boaz unto his servant that was set over the reapers, Whose damsel is this?

6 And the servant that was set over the reapers answered and said, It is the Moabitish damsel that came back with Naomi out of the country of Moab:

7 And she said, I pray you, let me glean and gather after the reapers among the sheaves: so she came, and has continued even from the morning until now, that she tarried a little in the house.

8 Then said Boaz unto Ruth, Hear you not, my daughter? Go not to glean in another field, neither go from hence, but abide here fast by my maidens:

9 Let your eyes be on the field that they do reap, and go you after them: have I not charged the young men that they shall not touch you? and when you are athirst, go unto the vessels, and drink of that which the young men have drawn.

10 Then she fell on her face, and bowed herself to the ground, and said unto him, Why have I found grace in your eyes, that you should take knowledge of me, seeing I am a stranger?

11 And Boaz answered and said unto her, It has fully been showed me, all that you have done unto your mother-in-law since the death of your husband: and how you have left your father and your mother, and the land of your nativity, and are come unto a people which you knew not yesterday and the third day.

12 The Becoming-One recompense your work, and a full reward be given you of the Becoming-One,

God of Israel, under whose wings you are come to trust.

13 Then she said, Let me find favor in your sight, my lord; for that you have comforted me, and for that you have spoken friendly unto your handmaid, though I be not like unto one of your handmaidens.

14 And Boaz said unto her, At mealtime you come here, and eat of the bread, and dip your morsel in the vinegar. And she sat beside the reapers: and he reached her parched grain, and she did eat, and was sufficed, and left.

15 And when she was risen up to glean, Boaz commanded his young men, saying, Let her glean even among the sheaves, and reproach her not:

16 And let fall also some of the handfuls of purpose for her, and leave them, that she may glean them, and rebuke her not.

17 So she gleaned in the field until evening, and beat out that she had gleaned: and it was about an ephah of barley.

18 And she took it up, and went into the city: and her mother-in-law saw what she had gleaned: and she brought forth, and gave to her that she had reserved after she was sufficed.

19 And her mother-in-law said unto her, Where have you gleaned today? and where worked you? blessed be he that did take knowledge of you. And she showed her mother-in-law with whom she had worked, and said, The man's name with whom I worked today is Boaz.

20 And Naomi said unto her daughter-in-law, Blessed be he of the Becoming-One, who has not left off his kindness to the living and to the dead. And Naomi said unto her, The man is near of kin unto us, one of our next kinsmen.

21 And Ruth the Moabitess said, He said unto me also, you shall keep fast by my young men, until they have ended all my harvest.

22 And Naomi said unto Ruth her daughter-in-law, It is good, my daughter, that you go out with his maidens, that they meet you not in any other field.

23 So she kept fast by the maidens of Boaz to glean unto the end of barley harvest and of wheat harvest; and dwelt with her mother-in-law.

Ruth 3:1 Then Naomi her mother-in-law said unto her, My daughter, shall I not seek rest for you, that it may be well with you?

2 And now is not Boaz of our kindred, with whose maidens you were? Behold, he winnows barley tonight in the threshing floor.

3 Wash your self therefore, and anoint you, and put your raiment upon you, and get you down to the floor: but make not yourself known unto the man, until he shall have done eating and drinking.

4 And it shall be, when he lies down, that you shall mark the place where he shall lie, and you shall go in, and uncover his feet, and lay you down; and he will tell you what you shall do.

5 And she said unto her, All that you say unto me I will do.

6 And she went down unto the floor, and did according to all that her mother-in-law bade her.

7 And when Boaz had eaten and drunk, and his heart was merry, he went to lie down at the end of the heap of grain: and she came softly, and uncovered his feet, and laid her down.

8 And it came to pass at midnight, that the man was afraid, and turned himself: and, behold, a woman lay at his feet.

9 And he said, Who are you? And she answered, I am Ruth your handmaid: spread therefore your skirt over your handmaid; for you are a near kinsman.

10 And he said, Blessed be you of the Becoming-One, my daughter: for you have showed more kindness in the latter end than at the beginning, inasmuch as you followed not young men, whether poor or rich.

11 And now, my daughter, fear not; I will do to you all that you require: for all the city of my people does know that you are a virtuous woman.

12 And now it is true that I am your near kinsman: howbeit there is a kinsman nearer than I.

13 Tarry this night, and it shall be in the morning, that if he will perform unto you the part of a kinsman, well; let him do the kinsman's part: but if he will not do the part of a kinsman to you, then will I do the part of a kinsman to you, as the Becoming-One lives: lie down until the morning.

14 And she lay at his feet until the morning: and she rose up before one could know another. And he said, Let it not be known that a woman came into the floor.

15 Also he said, Bring the veil that you have upon you, and hold it. And when she held it, he measured six measures of barley, and laid it on her: and she went into the city.

16 And when she came to her mother-in-law, she said, Who are you, my daughter? And she told her all that the man had done to her.

17 And she said, These six measures of barley gave he me; for he said to me, Go not empty unto your mother-in-law.

18 Then said she, Sit still, my daughter, until you know how the matter will fall: for the man will not be in rest, until he have finished the thing this day.

Ruth 4:1 Then went Boaz up to the gate, and sat him down there: and, behold, the kinsman of whom Boaz spoke came by; unto whom he said, Ho, such a one! turn aside, sit down here. And he turned aside, and sat down.

2 And he took ten men of the elders of the city, and said, Sit you down here. And they sat down.

3 And he said unto the kinsman, Naomi, that is come again out of the country of Moab, sells a parcel of land, which was our brother Elimelech's:

4 And I thought to advertise you, saying, Buy it before the inhabitants, and before the elders of my people. If you will redeem it, redeem it: but if you will not redeem it, then tell me, that I may know: for there is none to redeem it beside you; and I am after you. And he said, I will redeem it.

5 Then said Boaz, What day you buy the field of the hand of Naomi, you must buy it also of Ruth the Moabitess, the wife of the dead, to raise up the name of the dead upon his inheritance.

6 And the kinsman said, I cannot redeem it for myself, lest I mar mine own inheritance: redeem you my right to thyself; for I cannot redeem it.

7 Now this was the manner in former time in Israel concerning redeeming and concerning changing, for to confirm all things; a man plucked off his shoe, and gave it to his neighbor: and this was a testimony in Israel.

8 Therefore the kinsman said unto Boaz, Buy it for you. So he drew off his shoe.

9 And Boaz said unto the elders, and unto all the people, you are witnesses this day, that I have bought all that was Elimelech's, and all that was Chilion's and Mahlon's, of the hand of Naomi.

10 Moreover Ruth the Moabitess, the wife of Mahlon, have I purchased to be my wife, to raise up the name of the dead upon his inheritance, that the name of the dead be not cut off from among his brethren, and from the gate of his place: you are witnesses this day.

11 And all the people that were in the gate, and the elders, said, We are witnesses. The Becoming-One make the woman that is come into your house like Rachel and like Leah, which two did build the house of Israel: and do you worthily in Ephratah, and be famous in Bethlehem:

12 And let your house be like the house of Pharez, whom Tamar bare unto Judah, of the seed which the Becoming-One shall give you of this young woman.

13 So Boaz took Ruth, and she was his wife: and when he went in unto her, the Becoming-One gave her conception, and she bare a son.

14 And the women said unto Naomi, Blessed be the Becoming-One, which has not left you this day without a kinsman, that his name may be famous in Israel.

15 And he shall be unto you a restorer of your soul, and a nourisher of your old age: for your daughter-in-law, which loves you, which is better to you than seven sons, has borne him.

16 And Naomi took the child, and laid it in her bosom, and became nurse unto it.

17 And the women her neighbors gave it a name, saying, There is a son born to Naomi; and they called his name Obed: he is the father of Jesse, the father of **David**.

18 Now these are the generations of Pharez: Pharez begat Hezron,

19 And Hezron begat Ram, and Ram begat Amminadab,

20 And Amminadab begat Nahshon, and Nahshon begat Salmon,

21 And Salmon begat Boaz, and Boaz begat Obed,

22 And Obed begat Jesse, and Jesse begat David.

1 Samuel

1 Sam 1:1 Now there was a certain man of Ramathaim-zophim, of mount Ephraim, and his name was Elkanah, the son of Jeroham, the son of Elihu, the son of Tohu, the son of Zuph, an Ephrathite:

2 And he had two wives; the name of the one was Hannah, and the name of the other Peninnah: and Peninnah had children, but Hannah had no children.

3 And this man went up out of his city yearly to worship and to sacrifice unto the Becoming-One of hosts in Shiloh. And the two sons of Eli, Hophni and Phinehas, the priests of the Becoming-One, were there.

4 And when the time was that Elkanah offered, he gave to Peninnah his wife, and to all her sons and her daughters, portions:

5 But unto Hannah he gave a worthy portion; for he loved Hannah: but the Becoming-One had shut up her womb.

6 And her adversary also provoked her greatly, for to make her fret, because the Becoming-One had shut up her womb.

7 And as he did so year by year, when she went up to the house of the Becoming-One, so she provoked her; therefore she wept, and did not eat.

8 Then said Elkanah her husband to her, Hannah, why weep you? and why eat you not? and why is your heart grieved? am not I better to you than ten sons?

9 So Hannah rose up after they had eaten in Shiloh, and after they had drunk. Now Eli the priest sat upon a seat by a post of the temple of the Becoming-One.

10 And she was in bitterness of soul, and prayed unto the Becoming-One, and wept greatly.

11 And she vowed a vow, and said, O Becoming-One of hosts, if you will indeed look on the affliction of your handmaid, and remember me, and not forget your handmaid, but will give unto your handmaid a seed of men, then I will give him unto the Becoming-One all the days of his life, and there shall no razor come upon his head.

12 And it came to pass, as she continued praying before the Becoming-One, that Eli marked her mouth.

13 Now Hannah, she spoke in her heart; only her lips moved, but her voice was not heard: therefore Eli thought she had been drunken.

14 And Eli said unto her, How long will you be drunken? put away your wine from you.

15 And Hannah answered and said, No, my lord, I am a woman of a sorrowful spirit: I have drunk neither wine nor strong drink, but have poured out my soul before the Becoming-One.

16 Count not your handmaid for a daughter of Belial: for out of the abundance of my complaint and grief have I spoken hitherto.

17 Then Eli answered and said, Go in peace: and God of Israel grant you your petition that you have asked of him.

18 And she said, Let your handmaid find grace in your sight. So the woman went her way, and did eat, and her countenance was no more sad.

19 And they rose up in the morning early, and worshiped before the Becoming-One, and returned, and came to their house to Ramah: and Elkanah knew Hannah his wife; and the Becoming-One remembered her.

20 Therefore it came to pass, when in the revolution of days Hannah had conceived, that she bare a son, and called his name Samuel, saying, Because I have asked him of the Becoming-One.

21 And the man Elkanah, and all his house, went up to offer unto the Becoming-One the sacrifice of days, and his vow.

22 But Hannah went not up; for she said unto her husband, I will not go up until the child be weaned, and then I will bring him, that he may appear before the Becoming-One, and there abide for olam.

23 And Elkanah her husband said unto her, Do what seems you good; tarry until you have weaned him; only the Becoming-One establish his word. So the woman abode, and gave her son suck until she weaned him.

24 And when she had weaned him, she took him up with her, with three bullocks, and one ephah of flour, and a bottle of wine, and brought him unto the house of the Becoming-One in Shiloh: and the child was young.

25 And they killed a bullock, and brought the child to Eli.

26 And she said, Oh my lord, as your soul lives, my lord, I am the woman that stood by you here, praying unto the Becoming-One.

27 For this child I prayed; and the Becoming-One has given me my petition which I asked of him:

28 Therefore also I have lent him to the Becoming-One; as long as he lives he shall be lent to the Becoming-One. And he worshiped the Becoming-One there.

1 Sam 2:1 And Hannah prayed, and said, My heart rejoices in the Becoming-One, mine horn is exalted in the Becoming-One: my mouth is enlarged over mine enemies; because I rejoice in your salvation.

2 There is none holy as the Becoming-One: for there is none beside you: neither is there any rock like our God.

3 Talk no more so exceeding proudly; let not arrogance come out of your mouth: for the Becoming-One is a GOD of knowledge, and by him actions are weighed.

4 The bows of the mighty men are broken, and they that stumbled are girded with strength.

5 They that were full have hired out themselves for bread; and they that were hungry ceased: so that the barren has born seven; and she that has many children is grown feeble.

6 The Becoming-One kills, and makes alive: he brings down to Sheol, and brings up.

7 The Becoming-One makes poor, and makes rich: he brings low, and lifts up.

8 He raises up the poor out of the dust, and lifts up the beggar from the dunghill, to set them among princes, and to make them inherit the throne of glory: for the pillars of the earth are the Becoming-One's, and he has set the world upon them.

9 He will keep the feet of his saints, and the wicked shall be silent in darkness; for by strength shall no man prevail.

10 The adversaries of the Becoming-One shall be broken to pieces; out of the heavens shall he thunder upon them: the Becoming-One shall judge the ends of the earth; and he shall give strength unto his king, and exalt the horn of his anointed.

11 And Elkanah went to Ramah to his house. And the child did minister unto the Becoming-One before Eli the priest.

12 Now the sons of Eli were sons of Belial; they knew not the Becoming-One.

13 And the priests' custom with the people was, that, when any man offered sacrifice, the priest's servant came, while the flesh was in seething, with a fleshhook of three teeth in his hand;

14 And he struck it into the pan, or kettle, or caldron, or pot; all that the fleshhook brought up the priest took for himself. So they did in Shiloh, unto all the Israelites that came there.

15 Also before they burnt the fat, the priest's servant came, and said to the man that sacrificed, Give flesh to roast for the priest; for he will not have sodden flesh of you, but raw.

16 And if any man said unto him, Let them not fail to burn the fat on the day, and then take as much as your soul desires; then he would answer him, Nay; but you shall give it me now: and if not, I will take it by force.

17 Therefore the sin of the young men was very great before the Becoming-One: for men abhorred the offering of the Becoming-One.

18 But Samuel ministered before the Becoming-One, being a child, girded with a linen ephod.

19 Moreover his mother made him a little coat, and brought it to him from day to day, when she came up with her husband to offer the sacrifice of days.

20 And Eli blessed Elkanah and his wife, and said, The Becoming-One give you seed of this woman for the loan which is lent to the Becoming-One. And they went unto their own home.

21 And the Becoming-One visited Hannah, so that she conceived, and bare three sons and two daughters. And the child Samuel grew before the Becoming-One.

22 Now Eli was very old, and heard all that his sons did unto all Israel; and how they lay with the women that assembled at the door of the tabernacle of the set time.

23 And he said unto them, Why do you such things? for I hear of your evil dealings by all this people.

24 Nay, my sons; for it is no good report that I hear: you make the Becoming-One's nation to transgress.

25 If one man sin against another, the judge shall judge him: but if a man sin against the Becoming-One, who shall entreat for him? But they listened not unto the voice of their father, because the Becoming-One wished to slay them.

26 And the child Samuel grew on, and was in favor both with the Becoming-One, and also with men.

27 And there came a man of God unto Eli, and said unto him, Thus says the Becoming-One, Did I plainly appear unto the house of your father, when they were in Egypt in Pharaoh's house?

28 And did I choose him out of all the tribes of Israel to be my priest, to offer upon mine altar, to burn incense, to wear an ephod before me? and did I give unto the house of your father all the offerings made by fire of the children of Israel?

29 Why kick you at my sacrifice and at my offering, which I have commanded in my habitation; and honor your sons above me, to make yourselves fat with the beginning firstfruits of all the offerings of Israel my people?

30 Therefore the Becoming-One, God of Israel says, I said indeed that your house, and the house of your father, should walk before me for olam, but now the Becoming-One says, Be it far from me; for them that honor me I will honor, and they that despise me shall be lightly esteemed.

31 Behold, the days come, that I will cut off your arm, and the arm of your father's house, that there shall not be an old man in your house.

32 And you shall see an enemy in my habitation, in all the wealth which God shall give Israel: and there shall not be an old man in your house all the days.

33 And the man of yours, whom I shall not cut off from mine altar, shall be to consume your eyes, and to grieve your soul: and all the increase of your house shall die in the flower of their age.

34 And this shall be a sign unto you, that shall come upon your two sons, on Hophni and Phinehas; in one day they shall die both of them.

35 And I will raise me up a faithful priest, that shall do according to that which is in mine heart and in my soul: and I will build him a sure house; and he shall walk before mine anointed all the days.

36 And it shall come to pass, that every one that is left in your house shall come and crouch to him for a piece of silver and a morsel of bread, and shall say, Put me, I pray you, into one of the priests' offices, that I may eat a piece of bread.

1 Sam 3:1 And the child Samuel ministered unto the Becoming-One before Eli. And the word of the Becoming-One was precious in those days; there was no open vision.

2 And it came to pass at that time, when Eli was laid down in his place, and his eyes began to wax dim, that he could not see;

3 And where the lamp of God went out in the temple of the Becoming-One, where the ark of God was, and Samuel was laid down to sleep;

4 That the Becoming-One called Samuel: and he answered, Here I am.

5 And he ran unto Eli, and said, Here I am; for you calledst me. And he said, I called not; lie down again. And he went and lay down.

6 And the Becoming-One called yet again, Samuel. And Samuel arose and went to Eli, and said, Here I am; for you did call me. And he answered, I called not, my son; lie down again.

7 Now Samuel did not yet know the Becoming-One, neither was the word of the Becoming-One yet revealed unto him.

8 And the Becoming-One called Samuel again the third time. And he arose and went to Eli, and said, Here I am; for you did call me. And Eli perceived that the Becoming-One had called the child.

9 Therefore Eli said unto Samuel, Go, lie down: and it shall be, if He call you, that you shall say, Speak, Becoming-One; for your servant hears. So Samuel went and lay down in his place.

10 And the Becoming-One came, and stood, and called as at other times, Samuel, Samuel. Then Samuel answered, Speak; for your servant hears.

11 And the Becoming-One said to Samuel, Behold, I will do a thing in Israel, at which both the ears of every one that hears it shall tingle.

12 In that day I will perform against Eli all things which I have spoken concerning his house: when I begin, I will also make an end.

13 For I have told him that I will judge his house for olam, for the iniquity which he knows; because his sons made themselves vile, and he restrained them not.

14 And therefore I have sworn unto the house of Eli, that the iniquity of Eli's house shall not be purged with sacrifice nor offering for olam.

15 And Samuel lay until the morning, and opened the doors of the house of the Becoming-One. And Samuel feared to show Eli the vision.

16 Then Eli called Samuel, and said, Samuel, my son. And he answered, Here I am.

17 And he said, What is the thing that the Becoming-One has said unto you? I pray you hide it not from me: God do so to you, and more also, if you hide any thing from me of all the things that he said unto you.

18 And Samuel told him every thing, and hid nothing from him. And he said, It is the Becoming-One: let him do what seems him good.

19 And Samuel grew, and the Becoming-One was with him, and did let none of his words fall to the ground.

20 And all Israel from Dan even to Beersheba knew that Samuel was established to be a prophet of the Becoming-One.

21 And the Becoming-One appeared again in Shiloh: for the Becoming-One revealed himself to Samuel in Shiloh by the word of the Becoming-One.

1 Sam 4:1 And the word of Samuel came to all Israel. Now Israel went out against the Philistines to battle, and pitched beside Ebenezer: and the Philistines pitched in Aphek.

2 And the Philistines put themselves in array against Israel: and when they joined battle, Israel was struck before the Philistines: and they killed of the army in the field about four thousand men.

3 And when the people were come into the camp, the elders of Israel said, Why has the Becoming-One struck us today before the Philistines? Let us fetch the ark of the covenant of the Becoming-One out of Shiloh unto us, that, when it comes among us, it may save us out of the hand of our enemies.

4 So the people sent to Shiloh, that they might bring from there the ark of the covenant of the Becoming-One of hosts, which dwells between the cherubs: and the two sons of Eli, Hophni and Phinehas, were there with the ark of the covenant of God.

5 And when the ark of the covenant of the Becoming-One came into the camp, all Israel shouted with a great shout, so that the earth rang again.

6 And when the Philistines heard the noise of the shout, they said, What does it mean the noise of this great shout in the camp of the Hebrews? And they understood that the ark of the Becoming-One was come into the camp.

7 And the Philistines were afraid, for they said, God is come into the camp. And they said, Woe unto us! for there has not been such a thing yesterday and the third day.

8 Woe unto us! who shall deliver us out of the hand of these mighty God? these are God that smote the Egyptians with all the plagues in the wilderness.

9 Be strong, and make yourselves like men, O you Philistines, that you be not servants unto the Hebrews, as they have been to you: make yourselves like men, and fight.

10 And the Philistines fought, and Israel was struck, and they fled every man into his tent: and there was a very great slaughter; for there fell of Israel thirty thousand footmen.

11 And the ark of God was taken; and the two sons of Eli, Hophni and Phinehas, were slain.

12 And there ran a man of Benjamin out of the army, and came to Shiloh the same day with his clothes rent, and with earth upon his head.

13 And when he came, lo, Eli sat upon a seat by the wayside watching: for his heart trembled for the ark of God. And when the man came into the city, and told it, all the city cried out.

14 And when Eli heard the noise of the crying, he said, What does it mean the noise of this tumult? And the man came in hastily, and told Eli.

15 Now Eli was a son of ninety and eight years; and his eyes were dim, that he could not see.

16 And the man said unto Eli, I am he that came out of the army, and I fled today out of the army. And he said, What is there done, my son?

17 And the messenger answered and said, Israel is fled before the Philistines, and there has been also a great slaughter among the people, and your two sons also, Hophni and Phinehas, are dead, and the ark of God is taken.

18 And it came to pass, when he made mention of the ark of God, that he fell from off the seat backward by the side of the gate, and his neck brake, and he died: for he was an old man, and heavy. And he had judged Israel forty years.

19 And his daughter-in-law, Phinehas' wife, was with child, near to be delivered: and when she heard the tidings that the ark of God was taken, and that her father-in-law and her husband were dead, she bowed herself and travailed; for her pains came upon her.

20 And about the time of her death the women that stood by her said unto her, Fear not; for you have borne a son. But she answered not, neither did she regard it.

21 And she named the child Ichabod, saying, The glory is departed from Israel: because the ark of God was taken, and because of her father-in-law and her husband.

22 And she said, The glory is departed from Israel: for the ark of God is taken.

1 Sam 5:1 And the Philistines took the ark of God, and brought it from Ebenezer unto Ashdod.

2 When the Philistines took the ark of God, they brought it into the house of Dagon, and set it by Dagon.

3 And when they of Ashdod arose early on the next day, behold, Dagon was fallen upon his face to the earth before the ark of the Becoming-One. And they took Dagon, and set him in his place again.

4 And when they arose early on the next day morning, behold, Dagon was fallen upon his face to the ground before the ark of the Becoming-One; and the head of Dagon and both the palms of his hands were cut off upon the threshold; only the stump of Dagon was left to him.

5 Therefore neither the priests of Dagon, nor any that come into Dagon's house, tread on the threshold of Dagon in Ashdod unto this day.

6 But the hand of the Becoming-One was heavy upon them of Ashdod, and he destroyed them, and smote them with hemorrhoids, even Ashdod and the coasts thereof.

7 And when the men of Ashdod saw that it was so, they said, The ark of God of Israel shall not abide with us: for his hand is great upon us, and upon Dagon our god.

8 They sent therefore and gathered all the lords of the Philistines unto them, and said, What shall we do with the ark of God of Israel? And they answered, Let the ark of God of Israel be carried about unto Gath. And they carried the ark of God of Israel about there.

9 And it was so, that, after they had carried it about, the hand of the Becoming-One was against the city with a very great destruction: and he smote the men of the city, both small and great, and they had hemorrhoids in their secret parts.

10 Therefore they sent the ark of God to Ekron. And it came to pass, as the ark of God came to Ekron, that the Ekronites cried out, saying, They have brought about the ark of God of Israel to us, to slay us and our people.

11 So they sent and gathered together all the lords of the Philistines, and said, Send away the ark of God of Israel, and let it go again to his own place, that it slay us not, and our people: for there was a deadly destruction throughout all the city; the hand of God was very heavy there.

12 And the men that died not were struck with the hemorrhoids: and the cry of the city went up to heaven.

1 Sam 6:1 And the ark of the Becoming-One was in the country of the Philistines seven months.

2 And the Philistines called for the priests and the diviners, saying, What shall we do to the ark of the Becoming-One? tell us wherewith we shall send it to his place.

3 And they said, If you send away the ark of God of Israel, send it not empty; but in any way return him a trespass offering: then you shall be healed, and it shall be known to you why his hand is not removed from you.

4 Then said they, What shall be the trespass offering which we shall return to him? They answered, Five golden hemorrhoids, and five golden mice, according to the number of the lords of the Philistines: for one plague was on you all, and on your lords.

5 Therefore you shall make images of your hemorrhoids, and images of your mice that mar the land; and you shall give glory unto God of Israel: perhaps he will lighten his hand from off you, and from off your gods, and from off your land.

6 Why then do you harden your hearts, as the Egyptians and Pharaoh hardened their hearts? when he had worked wonderfully among them, did they not let the people go, and they departed?

7 Now therefore make a new cart, and take two suckling cows, on which there has come no yoke, and tie the cows to the cart, and bring their calves home from them:

8 And take the ark of the Becoming-One, and lay it upon the cart; and put the jewels of gold, which you return him for a trespass offering, in a coffer by the side thereof; and send it away, that it may go.

9 And see, if it goes up by the way of his own coast to Beth-shemesh, then he has done us this great evil: but if not, then we shall know that it is not his hand that smote us: it was a chance that happened to us.

10 And the men did so; and took two suckling cows, and tied them to the cart, and shut up their calves at home:

11 And they laid the ark of the Becoming-One upon the cart, and the coffer with the mice of gold and the images of their hemorrhoids.

12 And the cows took the straight way to the way of Beth-shemesh, and went along the highway, lowing as they went, and turned not aside to the right hand or to the left; and the lords of the Philistines went after them unto the border of Beth-shemesh.

13 And they of Beth-shemesh were reaping their wheat harvest in the valley: and they lifted up their eyes, and saw the ark, and rejoiced to see it.

14 And the cart came into the field of Joshua, a Beth-shemite, and stood there, where there was a great stone: and they clave the wood of the cart, and offered the cow a burnt offering unto the Becoming-One.

15 And the Levites took down the ark of the Becoming-One, and the coffer that was with it, wherein the jewels of gold were, and put them on the great stone: and the men of Beth-shemesh offered burnt offerings and sacrificed sacrifices the same day unto the Becoming-One.

16 And when the five lords of the Philistines had seen it, they returned to Ekron the same day.

17 And these are the golden hemorrhoids which the Philistines returned for a trespass offering unto the Becoming-One; for Ashdod one, for Gaza one, for Askelon one, for Gath one, for Ekron one;

18 And the golden mice, according to the number of all the cities of the Philistines belonging to the five lords, both of fenced cities, and of country villages, even unto the great stone of Abel, whereon they set down the ark of the Becoming-One: which stone remains unto this day in the field of Joshua, the Beth-shemite.

19 And he smote the men of Beth-shemesh, because they had looked into the ark of the Becoming-One, even he smote of the people fifty thousand and threescore and ten men: and the people lamented, because the Becoming-One had struck many of the people with a great slaughter.

20 And the men of Beth-shemesh said, Who is able to stand before the Becoming-One, the holy God? and to whom shall he go up from us?

21 And they sent messengers to the inhabitants of Kirjathjearim, saying, The Philistines have brought again the ark of the Becoming-One; you come down, and fetch it up to you.

1 Sam 7:1 And the men of Kirjathjearim came, and fetched up the ark of the Becoming-One, and brought it into the house of Abinadab in the hill, and sanctified Eleazar his son to keep the ark of the Becoming-One.

2 And it came to pass, while the ark abode in Kirjathjearim, that the days were multiplied; for it was twenty years: and all the house of Israel lamented after the Becoming-One.

3 And Samuel spoke unto all the house of Israel, saying, If you do return unto the Becoming-One with all your hearts, then put away the strange gods and Ashtaroth from among you, and prepare your hearts unto the Becoming-One, and serve him only: and he will deliver you out of the hand of the Philistines.

4 Then the children of Israel did put away the lords [baalim] and Ashtaroth, and served the Becoming-One only.

5 And Samuel said, Gather all Israel to Mizpeh, and I will pray for you unto the Becoming-One.

6 And they gathered together to Mizpeh, and drew water, and poured it out before the Becoming-One, and fasted on that day, and said there, We have sinned against the Becoming-One. And Samuel judged the children of Israel in Mizpeh.

7 And when the Philistines heard that the children of Israel were gathered together to Mizpeh, the lords of the Philistines went up against Israel. And when the children of Israel heard it, they were afraid of the Philistines.

8 And the children of Israel said to Samuel, Cease not to cry unto the Becoming-One our God for us, that he will save us out of the hand of the Philistines.

9 And Samuel took a sucking lamb, and offered it for a burnt offering wholly unto the Becoming-One: and Samuel cried unto the Becoming-One for Israel; and the Becoming-One heard him.

10 And as Samuel was offering up the burnt offering, the Philistines drew near to battle against Israel: but the Becoming-One thundered with a great thunder on that day upon the Philistines, and discomfited them; and they were struck before Israel.

11 And the men of Israel went out of Mizpeh, and pursued the Philistines, and smote them, until they came under Beth-car.

12 Then Samuel took a stone, and set it between Mizpeh and Shen, and called the name of it Ebenezer, saying, Hitherto has the Becoming-One helped us.

13 So the Philistines were subdued, and they came no more into the coast of Israel: and the hand of the Becoming-One was against the Philistines all the days of Samuel.

14 And the cities which the Philistines had taken from Israel were restored to Israel, from Ekron even unto Gath; and the coasts thereof did Israel deliver out of the hands of the Philistines. And there was peace between Israel and the Amorites.

15 And Samuel judged Israel all the days of his life.

16 And he went from year to year in circuit to Bethel, and Gilgal, and Mizpeh, and judged Israel in all those places.

17 And his return was to Ramah; for there was his house; and there he judged Israel; and there he built an altar unto the Becoming-One.

1 Sam 8:1 And it came to pass, when Samuel was old, that he made his sons judges over Israel.

2 Now the name of his firstborn was Joel; and the name of his second, Abiah: they were judges in Beersheba.

3 And his sons walked not in his ways, but turned aside after gain, and took bribes, and perverted judgment.

4 Then all the elders of Israel gathered themselves together, and came to Samuel unto Ramah,

5 And said unto him, Behold, you are old, and your sons walk not in your ways: now make us a king to judge us like all the nations.

6 But the thing displeased Samuel, when they said, Give us a king to judge us. And Samuel prayed unto the Becoming-One.

7 And the Becoming-One said unto Samuel, listen unto the voice of the people in all that they say unto you: for they have not rejected you, but they have rejected me, that I should not reign over them.

8 According to all the works which they have done since the day that I brought them up out of Egypt even unto this day, wherewith they have forsaken me, and served other gods, so do they also unto you.

9 Now therefore listen unto their voice: howbeit yet protest solemnly unto them, and show them the manner of the king that shall reign over them.

10 And Samuel told all the words of the Becoming-One unto the people that asked of him a king.

11 And he said, This will be the manner of the king that shall reign over you: He will take your sons, and appoint them for himself, for his chariots, and to be his horsemen; and some shall run before his chariots.

12 And he will appoint him captains over thousands and captains over fifties; and will set them to ear his ground, and to reap his harvest, and to make his instruments of war, and instruments of his chariots.

13 And he will take your daughters to be perfumers, and to be cooks, and to be bakers.

14 And he will take your fields, and your vineyards, and your oliveyards, even the best of them, and give them to his servants.

15 And he will take the tenth of your seed, and of your vineyards, and give to his eunuchs, and to his servants.

16 And he will take your menservants, and your maidservants, and your best young men, and your donkeys, and put them to his work.

17 He will take the tenth of your sheep: and you shall be his servants.

18 And you shall cry out in that day because of your king which you shall have chosen you; and the Becoming-One will not hear you in that day.

19 Nevertheless the people refused to obey the voice of Samuel; and they said, Nay; but we will have a king over us;

20 That we also may be like all the nations; and that our king may judge us, and go out before us, and fight our battles.

21 And Samuel heard all the words of the people, and he rehearsed them in the ears of the Becoming-One.

22 And the Becoming-One said to Samuel, listen unto their voice, and make them a king. And Samuel said unto the men of Israel, Go you every man unto his city.

1 Sam 9:1 Now there was a man of Benjamin, whose name was Kish, the son of Abiel, the son of Zeror, the son of Bechorath, the son of Aphiah, a Benjamite, a mighty man of power.

2 And he had a son, whose name was Saul, a choice young man, and a goodly: and there was not among the children of Israel a goodlier person than he: from his shoulders and upward he was higher than any of the people.

3 And the donkeys of Kish Saul's father were lost. And Kish said to Saul his son, Take now one of the servants with you, and arise, go seek the donkeys.

4 And he passed through mount Ephraim, and passed through the land of Shalisha, but they found them not: then they passed through the land of Shalim, and there they were not: and he passed through the land of the Benjamites, but they found them not.

5 And when they were come to the land of Zuph, Saul said to his servant that was with him, Come, and let us return; lest my father leave caring for the donkeys, and take thought for us.

6 And he said unto him, Behold now, there is in this city a man of God, and he is a honorable man; all that he says comes surely to pass: now let us go there; perhaps he can show us our way that we should go.

7 Then said Saul to his servant, But, behold, if we go, what shall we bring the man? for the bread is spent in our vessels, and there is not a present to bring to the man of God: what have we?

8 And the servant answered Saul again, and said, Behold, I have here at hand the fourth part of a shekel of silver: that will I give to the man of God, to tell us our way.

9 Beforetime in Israel, when a man went to inquire of God, thus he spoke, Come, and let us go to the seer: for he that is now called a Prophet was beforetime called a Seer.

10 Then said Saul to his servant, Well said; come, let us go. So they went unto the city where the man of God was.

11 And as they went up the hill to the city, they found young maidens going out to draw water, and said unto them, Is the seer here?

12 And they answered them, and said, He is; behold, he is before you: make haste now, for he came today to the city; for there is a sacrifice of the people today in the high place:

13 As soon as you be come into the city, you shall straightway find him, before he go up to the high place to eat: for the people will not eat until he come, because he does bless the sacrifice; and afterwards they eat that be bidden. Now therefore get you up; for about this time you shall find him.

14 And they went up into the city: and when they were come into the city, behold, Samuel came out against them, for to go up to the high place.

15 Now the Becoming-One had told Samuel in his ear a day before Saul came, saying,

16 tomorrow about this time I will send you a man out of the land of Benjamin, and you shall anoint him to be captain over my people Israel, that he may save my people out of the hand of the Philistines: for I have looked upon my people, because their cry is come unto me.

17 And when Samuel saw Saul, the Becoming-One said unto him, Behold the man whom I spoke to you of! this same shall reign over my people.

18 Then Saul drew near to Samuel in the gate, and said, Tell me, I pray you, where the seer's house is.

19 And Samuel answered Saul, and said, I am the seer: go up before me unto the high place; for you shall eat with me today, and tomorrow I will let you go, and will tell you all that is in your heart.

20 And as for your donkeys that were lost today three days, set not your mind on them; for they are found. And on whom is all the desire of Israel? Is it not on you, and on all your father's house?

21 And Saul answered and said, Am not I a Benjamite, of the smallest of the tribes of Israel? and my family the least of all the families of the tribe of Benjamin? why then speak you so to me?

22 And Samuel took Saul and his servant, and brought them into the parlour, and made them sit in the chief place among them that were bidden, which were about thirty persons.

23 And Samuel said unto the cook, Bring the portion which I gave you, of which I said unto you, Set it by you.

24 And the cook took up the shoulder, and that which was upon it, and set it before Saul. And Samuel said, Behold that which is left! set it before you, and eat: for unto this set time[103] has it been kept for you since I said, I have invited the people. So Saul did eat with Samuel that day.

25 And when they were come down from the high place into the city, Samuel communed with Saul upon the top of the house.

26 And they arose early: and it came to pass about the spring of the dawn, that Samuel called Saul to the top of the house, saying, Up, that I may send

---

[103] Appointed time or festival

you away. And Saul arose, and they went out both of them, he and Samuel, abroad.

27 And as they were going down to the end of the city, Samuel said to Saul, Bid the servant pass on before us, and he passed on, but stand you still today, that I may show you the word of God.

1 Sam 10:1 Then Samuel took a vial of oil, and poured it upon his head, and kissed him, and said, Is it not because the Becoming-One has anointed you to be captain over his inheritance?

2 When you are departed from me today, then you shall find two men by Rachel's tomb in the border of Benjamin at Zelzah; and they will say unto you, The donkeys which you went to seek are found: and, lo, your father has left the care of the donkeys, and sorrows for you, saying, What shall I do for my son?

3 Then shall you go on forward from there, and you shall come to the plain of Tabor, and there shall meet you three men going up to God to Bethel, one carrying three kids, and another carrying three loaves of bread, and another carrying a bottle of wine:

4 And they will salute you, and give you two loaves of bread; which you shall receive of their hands.

5 After that you shall come to the hill of God, where is the garrison of the Philistines: and it shall come to pass, when you are come there to the city, that you shall meet a company of prophets coming down from the high place with a psaltery, and a tabret, and a pipe, and a harp, before them; and they shall prophesy:

6 And the spirit of the Becoming-One will come upon you, and you shall prophesy with them, and shall be turned into another man.

7 And let it be, when these signs are come unto you, that you do as occasion serve you; for God is with you.

8 And you shall go down before me to Gilgal; and, behold, I will come down unto you, to offer burnt offerings, and to sacrifice sacrifices of peace offerings: seven days shall you tarry, till I come to you, and show you what you shall do.

9 And it was so, that when he had turned his back to go from Samuel, God gave him another heart: and all those signs came to pass that day.

10 And when they came there to the hill, behold, a company of prophets met him; and the spirit of God came upon him, and he prophesied among them.

11 And it came to pass, when all that knew him yesterday and the third day saw that, behold, he prophesied among the prophets, then the people said one to another, What is this that is come unto the son of Kish? Is Saul also among the prophets?

12 And one of the same place answered and said, But who is their father? Therefore it became a proverb, Is Saul also among the prophets?

13 And when he had made an end of prophesying, he came to the high place.

14 And Saul's uncle said unto him and to his servant, Where did you go? And he said, To seek the donkeys: and when we saw that they were no where, we came to Samuel.

15 And Saul's uncle said, Tell me, I pray you, what Samuel said unto you.

16 And Saul said unto his uncle, He told us plainly that the donkeys were found. But of the matter of the kingdom, whereof Samuel spoke, he told him not.

17 And Samuel called the people together unto the Becoming-One to Mizpeh;

18 And said unto the children of Israel, Thus says the Becoming-One, God of Israel, I brought up Israel out of Egypt, and delivered you out of the hand of the Egyptians, and out of the hand of all kingdoms, and of them that oppressed you:

19 And you have this day rejected your God, who himself saved you out of all your adversities and your tribulations; and you have said unto him, Nay, but set a king over us. Now therefore present yourselves before the Becoming-One by your tribes, and by your thousands.

20 And when Samuel had caused all the tribes of Israel to come near, the tribe of Benjamin was taken.

21 When he had caused the tribe of Benjamin to come near by their families, the family of Matri was taken, and Saul the son of Kish was taken: and when they sought him, he could not be found.

22 Therefore they inquired of the Becoming-One further, if the man should yet come there. And the Becoming-One answered, Behold, he has hid himself among the stuff.

23 And they ran and fetched him there: and when he stood among the people, he was higher than any of the people from his shoulders and upward.

24 And Samuel said to all the people, See you him whom the Becoming-One has chosen, that there is none like him among all the people? And all the people shouted, and said, may the king live.

25 Then Samuel told the people the manner of the kingdom, and wrote it in a book, and laid it up before the Becoming-One. And Samuel sent all the people away, every man to his house.

26 And Saul also went home to Gibeah; and there went with him a band of men, whose hearts God had touched.

27 But the children of Belial said, How shall this man save us? And they despised him, and brought him no presents. But he held his peace.

1 Sam 11:1 Then Nahash the Ammonite came up, and encamped against Jabeshgilead: and all the men of Jabesh said unto Nahash, Make a covenant with us, and we will serve you.

2 And Nahash the Ammonite answered them, On this condition will I make a covenant with you, that I may thrust out all your right eyes, and lay it for a reproach upon all Israel.

3 And the elders of Jabesh said unto him, Give us seven days' respite, that we may send messengers unto all the coasts of Israel: and then, if there be no man to save us, we will come out to you.

4 Then came the messengers to Gibeah of Saul, and told the tidings in the ears of the people: and all the people lifted up their voices, and wept.

5 And, behold, Saul came after the herd out of the field; and Saul said, What ails the people that they weep? And they told him the tidings of the men of Jabesh.

6 And the spirit of God came upon Saul when he heard those tidings, and his anger was kindled greatly.

7 And he took a yoke of oxen, and hewed them in pieces, and sent them throughout all the coasts of Israel by the hands of messengers, saying, Whosoever comes not forth after Saul and after Samuel, so shall it be done unto his oxen. And the fear of the Becoming-One fell on the people, and they came out with one consent.

8 And when he numbered them in Bezek, the children of Israel were three hundred thousand, and the men of Judah thirty thousand.

9 And they said unto the messengers that came, Thus shall you say unto the men of Jabeshgilead, tomorrow, by that time the sun be hot, you shall have help. And the messengers came and showed it to the men of Jabesh; and they were glad.

10 Therefore the men of Jabesh said, tomorrow we will come out unto you, and you shall do with us all that seems good unto you.

11 And it was so on the next day, that Saul put the people in three companies; and they came into the midst of the host in the morning watch, and killed the Ammonites until the heat of the day: and it came to pass, that they which remained were scattered, so that two of them were not left together.

12 And the people said unto Samuel, Who is he that said, Shall Saul reign over us? bring the men, that we may put them to death.

13 And Saul said, There shall not a man be put to death this day: for today the Becoming-One has worked salvation in Israel.

14 Then said Samuel to the people, Come, and let us go to Gilgal, and renew the kingdom there.

15 And all the people went to Gilgal; and there they made Saul king before the Becoming-One in Gilgal; and there they sacrificed sacrifices of peace offerings before the Becoming-One; and there Saul and all the men of Israel rejoiced greatly.

1 Sam 12:1 And Samuel said unto all Israel, Behold, I have listened unto your voice in all that you said unto me, and have made a king over you.

2 And now, behold, the king walks before you: and I am old and grayheaded; and, behold, my sons are with you: and I have walked before you from my childhood unto this day.

3 Behold, here I am: witness against me before the Becoming-One, and before his anointed: whose ox have I taken? or whose donkey have I taken? or whom have I defrauded? whom have I oppressed? or of whose hand have I received any bribe to blind mine eyes therewith? and I will restore it you.

4 And they said, you have not defrauded us, nor oppressed us, neither have you taken a bribe from any man's hand.

5 And he said unto them, The Becoming-One is witness against you, and his anointed is witness this day, that you have not found anything in my hand. And they answered, He is witness.

6 And Samuel said unto the people, It is the Becoming-One that advanced Moses and Aaron, and that brought your fathers up out of the land of Egypt.

7 Now therefore stand still, that I may reason with you before the Becoming-One of all the righteous acts of the Becoming-One, which he did to you and to your fathers.

8 When Jacob was come into Egypt, and your fathers cried unto the Becoming-One, then the Becoming-One sent Moses and Aaron, which brought forth your fathers out of Egypt, and made them dwell in this place.

9 And when they forgat the Becoming-One their God, he sold them into the hand of Sisera, captain of the host of Hazor, and into the hand of the Philistines, and into the hand of the king of Moab, and they fought against them.

10 And they cried unto the Becoming-One, and said, We have sinned, because we have forsaken the Becoming-One, and have served the lords [baalim] and Ashtaroth: but now deliver us out of the hand of our enemies, and we will serve you.

11 And the Becoming-One sent Jerub-Baal, and Bedan, and Jephthah, and Samuel, and delivered you out of the hand of your enemies on every side, and you dwelled safe.

12 And when you saw that Nahash the king of the children of Ammon came against you, you said unto me, Nay; but a king shall reign over us: when the Becoming-One your God was your king.

13 Now therefore behold the king whom you have chosen, and whom you have desired! and, behold, the Becoming-One has set a king over you.

14 If you will fear the Becoming-One, and serve him, and obey his voice, and not rebel against the commandment of the Becoming-One, then shall both you and also the king that reigns over you continue following the Becoming-One your God:

15 But if you will not obey the voice of the Becoming-One, but rebel against the commandment of the Becoming-One, then shall the hand of the Becoming-One be against you, as it was against your fathers.

16 Now therefore stand and see this great thing, which the Becoming-One will do before your eyes.

17 Is it not wheat harvest today? I will call unto the Becoming-One, and he shall send thunder and rain; that you may perceive and see that your wickedness is great, which you have done in the sight of the Becoming-One, in asking you a king.

18 So Samuel called unto the Becoming-One; and the Becoming-One sent thunder and rain that day: and all the people greatly feared the Becoming-One and Samuel.

19 And all the people said unto Samuel, Pray for your servants unto the Becoming-One your God, that we die not: for we have added unto all our sins this evil, to ask us a king.

20 And Samuel said unto the people, Fear not: you have done all this wickedness: yet turn not aside from following the Becoming-One, but serve the Becoming-One with all your heart;

21 And turn you not aside: for then should you go after vain things, which cannot profit nor deliver; for they are vain.

22 For the Becoming-One will not forsake his people for his great name's sake: because it has pleased the Becoming-One to make you his people.

23 Moreover as for me, forbid it that I should sin against the Becoming-One in ceasing to pray for you: but I will teach you the good and the right way:

24 Only fear the Becoming-One, and serve him in truth with all your heart; for consider how great things he has done for you.

25 But if you shall still do wickedly, you shall be consumed, both you and your king.

1 Sam 13:1 Saul reigned one year; and when he had reigned two years over Israel,

2 Saul chose him three thousand men of Israel; whereof two thousand were with Saul in Michmash and in mount Bethel, and a thousand were with Jonathan in Gibeah of Benjamin: and the rest of the people he sent every man to his tent.

3 And Jonathan smote the garrison of the Philistines that was in Geba, and the Philistines heard of it. And Saul blew the trumpet throughout all the land, saying, Let the Hebrews hear.

4 And all Israel heard say that Saul had struck a garrison of the Philistines, and that Israel also was had in abomination with the Philistines. And the people were called together after Saul to Gilgal.

5 And the Philistines gathered themselves together to fight with Israel, thirty thousand of chariots, and six thousand of horsemen, and people as the sand which is on the sea shore in multitude: and they came up, and pitched in Michmash, eastward from Beth-aven.

6 When the men of Israel saw that they were in a strait, for the people were distressed, then the people did hide themselves in caves, and in thickets, and in rocks, and in high places, and in pits.

7 And some of the Hebrews went over Jordan to the land of Gad and Gilead. As for Saul, he was yet in Gilgal, and all the people followed him trembling.

8 And he tarried seven days, according to the set time that Samuel had appointed: but Samuel came not to Gilgal; and the people were scattered from him.

9 And Saul said, Bring here a burnt offering to me, and peace offerings. And he offered the burnt offering.

10 And it came to pass, that as soon as he had made an end of offering the burnt offering, behold, Samuel came; and Saul went out to meet him, that he might salute him.

11 And Samuel said, What have you done? And Saul said, Because I saw that the people were scattered from me, and that you came not within the set time,[104] and that the Philistines gathered themselves together at Michmash;

12 Therefore said I, The Philistines will come down now upon me to Gilgal, and I have not made supplication unto the Becoming-One: I forced myself therefore, and offered a burnt offering.

13 And Samuel said to Saul, you have done foolishly: you have not kept the commandment of the Becoming-One your God, which he commanded you: for now would the Becoming-One have established your kingdom upon Israel for olam.

14 But now your kingdom shall not continue: the Becoming-One has sought him a man after his own heart, and the Becoming-One has commanded him to be captain over his people, because you have not kept that which the Becoming-One commanded you.

15 And Samuel arose, and got him up from Gilgal unto Gibeah of Benjamin. And Saul numbered the people that were present with him, about six hundred men.

16 And Saul, and Jonathan his son, and the people that were present with them, abode in Gibeah of Benjamin: but the Philistines encamped in Michmash.

17 And the spoilers came out of the camp of the Philistines in three companies: one company turned unto the way that leads to Ophrah, unto the land of Shual:

18 And another company turned the way to Beth-horon: and another company turned to the way of the border that looks to the valley of Zeboim toward the wilderness.

19 Now there was no smith found throughout all the land of Israel: for the Philistines said, Lest the Hebrews make them swords or spears:

20 But all the Israelites went down to the Philistines, to sharpen every man his share, and his coulter, and his ax, and his mattock.

21 Yet they had a file for the mattocks, and for the coulters, and for the forks, and for the axes, and to sharpen the goads.

22 So it came to pass in the day of battle, that there was neither sword nor spear found in the hand of any of the people that were with Saul and Jonathan: but with Saul and with Jonathan his son was there found.

23 And the garrison of the Philistines went out to the passage of Michmash.

1 Sam 14:1 Now it came to pass upon a day, that Jonathan the son of Saul said unto the young man that bare his armor, Come, and let us go over to the Philistines' garrison, that is on the other side. But he told not his father.

2 And Saul tarried in the uttermost part of Gibeah under a pomegranate tree which is in Migron: and the people that were with him were about six hundred men;

3 And Ahiah, the son of Ahitub, Ichabod's brother, the son of Phinehas, the son of Eli, the Becoming-One's priest in Shiloh, wearing an ephod. And the people knew not that Jonathan was gone.

4 And between the passages, by which Jonathan sought to go over unto the Philistines' garrison, there was a sharp rock on the one side, and a sharp rock on the other side: and the name of the one was Bozez, and the name of the other Seneh.

5 The forefront of the one was situate northward over against Michmash, and the other southward over against Gibeah.

6 And Jonathan said to the young man that bare his armor, Come, and let us go over unto the garrison of these uncircumcised: it may be that the Becoming-One will work for us: for there is no restraint to the Becoming-One to save by many or by few.

7 And his armor bearer said unto him, Do all that is in your heart: turn you; behold, I am with you according to your heart.

---

[104] Appointed time or festival

8 Then said Jonathan, Behold, we will pass over unto these men, and we will discover ourselves unto them.

9 If they say thus unto us, Tarry until we come to you; then we will stand still in our place, and will not go up unto them.

10 But if they say thus, Come up unto us; then we will go up: for the Becoming-One has delivered them into our hand: and this shall be a sign unto us.

11 And both of them presented themselves unto the garrison of the Philistines: and the Philistines said, Behold, the Hebrews come forth out of the holes where they had hid themselves.

12 And the men of the garrison answered Jonathan and his armor bearer, and said, Come up to us, and we will show you a thing. And Jonathan said unto his armor bearer, Come up after me: for the Becoming-One has delivered them into the hand of Israel.

13 And Jonathan climbed up upon his hands and upon his feet, and his armor bearer after him: and they fell before Jonathan; and his armor bearer killed after him.

14 And that first slaughter, which Jonathan and his armor bearer made, was about twenty men, within as it were a half acre of land, which a yoke of oxen might plow.

15 And there was trembling in the host, in the field, and among all the people: the garrison, and the spoilers, they also trembled, and the earth quaked: so it was a very great trembling.

16 And the watchmen of Saul in Gibeah of Benjamin looked; and, behold, the multitude melted away, and they went on beating down one another.

17 Then said Saul unto the people that were with him, Number now, and see who is gone from us. And when they had numbered, behold, Jonathan and his armor bearer were not there.

18 And Saul said unto Ahiah, Bring here the ark of God. For the ark of God was at that time with the children of Israel.

19 And it came to pass, while Saul talked unto the priest, that the noise that was in the host of the Philistines went on and increased: and Saul said unto the priest, Withdraw your hand.

20 And Saul and all the people that were with him assembled themselves, and they came to the battle: and, behold, every man's sword was against his fellow, and there was a very great discomfiture.

21 Moreover the Hebrews that were with the Philistines before that time, which went up with them into the camp from the country round about, even they also turned to be with the Israelites that were with Saul and Jonathan.

22 Likewise all the men of Israel which had hid themselves in mount Ephraim, when they heard that the Philistines fled, even they also followed hard after them in the battle.

23 So the Becoming-One saved Israel that day: and the battle passed over unto Beth-aven.

24 And the men of Israel were distressed that day: for Saul had adjured the people, saying, Cursed be the man that eats any food until evening, that I may be avenged on mine enemies. So none of the people tasted any food.

25 And all they of the land came to a wood; and there was honey upon the ground.

26 And when the people were come into the wood, behold, the honey dropped; but no man put his hand to his mouth: for the people feared the oath.

27 But Jonathan heard not when his father charged the people with the oath: therefore he put forth the end of the rod that was in his hand, and dipped it in a honeycomb, and put his hand to his mouth; and his eyes were enlightened.

28 Then answered one of the people, and said, your father straitly charged the people with an oath, saying, Cursed be the man that eats any food this day. And the people were faint.

29 Then said Jonathan, My father has troubled the land: see, I pray you, how mine eyes have been enlightened, because I tasted a little of this honey.

30 How much more, if haply the people had eaten freely today of the spoil of their enemies which they found? for had there not been now a much greater slaughter among the Philistines?

31 And they smote the Philistines that day from Michmash to Aijalon: and the people were very faint.

32 And the people flew upon the spoil, and took sheep, and oxen, and calves, and killed them on the ground: and the people did eat them with the blood.

33 Then they told Saul, saying, Behold, the people sin against the Becoming-One, in that they eat with the blood. And he said, you have transgressed: roll a great stone unto me this day.

34 And Saul said, Disperse yourselves among the people, and say unto them, Bring me here every man his ox, and every man his sheep, and slay them here, and eat; and sin not against the Becoming-One in eating with the blood. And all the people brought every man his ox with him that night, and killed them there.

35 And Saul built an altar unto the Becoming-One: the same was the first altar that he built unto the Becoming-One.

36 And Saul said, Let us go down after the Philistines by night, and spoil them until the morning light, and let us not leave a man of them. And they said, Do whatsoever seems good unto you. Then said the priest, Let us draw near here unto God.

37 And Saul asked counsel of God, Shall I go down after the Philistines? will you deliver them into the hand of Israel? But he answered him not that day.

38 And Saul said, Draw you near here, all the chief of the people: and know and see wherein this sin has been this day.

39 For, as the Becoming-One lives, which saves Israel, though it be in Jonathan my son, he shall surely die. But there was not a man among all the people that answered him.

40 Then said he unto all Israel, Be you on one side, and I and Jonathan my son will be on the other side. And the people said unto Saul, Do what seems good unto you.

41 Therefore Saul said unto the Becoming-One, God of Israel, Give a perfect lot. And Saul and Jonathan were taken: but the people escaped.

42 And Saul said, Cast lots between me and Jonathan my son. And Jonathan was taken.

43 Then Saul said to Jonathan, Tell me what you have done. And Jonathan told him, and said, I did but

taste a little honey with the end of the rod that was in mine hand, and, lo, I must die.

44 And Saul answered, God do so and more also: for, in death, you shall die, Jonathan.

45 And the people said unto Saul, Shall Jonathan die, who has worked this great salvation in Israel? Forbid it: as the Becoming-One lives, there shall not one hair of his head fall to the ground; for he has worked with God this day. So the people rescued Jonathan, that he died not.

46 Then Saul went up from following the Philistines: and the Philistines went to their own place.

47 So Saul took the kingdom over Israel, and fought against all his enemies on every side, against Moab, and against the children of Ammon, and against Edom, and against the kings of Zobah, and against the Philistines: and wheresoever he turned himself, he vexed them.

48 And he gathered a host, and smote the Amalekites, and delivered Israel out of the hands of them that spoiled them.

49 Now the sons of Saul were Jonathan, and Ishui, and Melchishua: and the names of his two daughters were these; the name of the firstborn Merab, and the name of the younger Michal:

50 And the name of Saul's wife was Ahinoam, the daughter of Ahimaaz: and the name of the captain of his host was Abner, the son of Ner, Saul's uncle.

51 And Kish was the father of Saul; and Ner the father of Abner was the son of Abiel.

52 And there was great war against the Philistines all the days of Saul: and when Saul saw any strong man, or any valiant man, he took him unto him.

1 Sam 15:1 Samuel also said unto Saul, The Becoming-One sent me to anoint you to be king over his people, over Israel: now therefore listen you unto the voice of the words of the Becoming-One.

2 Thus says the Becoming-One of hosts, I remember that which Amalek did to Israel, how he laid wait for him in the way, when he came up from Egypt.

3 Now go and smite Amalek, and utterly destroy all that they have, and spare them not; but slay both man and woman, infant and suckling, ox and sheep, camel and donkey.

4 And Saul gathered the people together, and numbered them in Telaim, two hundred thousand of footmen, and ten thousand men of Judah.

5 And Saul came to a city of Amalek, and laid wait in the valley.

6 And Saul said unto the Kenites, Go, depart, get you down from among the Amalekites, lest I destroy you with them: for you showed kindness to all the children of Israel, when they came up out of Egypt. So the Kenites departed from among the Amalekites.

7 And Saul smote the Amalekites from Havilah until you come to Shur, that is over against Egypt.

8 And he took Agag the king of the Amalekites alive, and utterly destroyed all the people with the edge of the sword.

9 But Saul and the people spared Agag, and the best of the sheep, and of the oxen, and of the fatlings, and the lambs, and all that was good, and would not utterly destroy them: but every thing that was vile and refuse, that they destroyed utterly.

10 Then came the word of the Becoming-One unto Samuel, saying,

11 It repents me that I have set up Saul to be king: for he is turned back from following me, and has not performed my commandments. And it grieved Samuel; and he cried unto the Becoming-One all night.

12 And when Samuel rose early to meet Saul in the morning, it was told Samuel, saying, Saul came to Carmel, and, behold, he set him up a place, and is gone about, and passed on, and gone down to Gilgal.

13 And Samuel came to Saul: and Saul said unto him, Blessed be you of the Becoming-One: I have performed the commandment of the Becoming-One.

14 And Samuel said, What does it mean then this bleating of the sheep in mine ears, and the lowing of the oxen which I hear?

15 And Saul said, They have brought them from the Amalekites: for the people spared the best of the sheep and of the oxen, to sacrifice unto the Becoming-One your God; and the rest we have utterly destroyed.

16 Then Samuel said unto Saul, Stay, and I will tell you what the Becoming-One has said to me this night. And he said unto him, Say on.

17 And Samuel said, When you were little in your own sight, were you not made the head of the tribes of Israel, and the Becoming-One anointed you king over Israel?

18 And the Becoming-One sent you on a journey, and said, Go and utterly destroy the sinners the Amalekites, and fight against them until they be consumed.

19 Why then did you not obey the voice of the Becoming-One, but did fly upon the spoil, and did evil in the sight of the Becoming-One?

20 And Saul said unto Samuel, Yes, I have obeyed the voice of the Becoming-One, and have gone the way which the Becoming-One sent me, and have brought Agag the king of Amalek, and have utterly destroyed the Amalekites.

21 But the people took of the spoil, sheep and oxen, the first of the things which should have been utterly destroyed, to sacrifice unto the Becoming-One your God in Gilgal.

22 And Samuel said, has the Becoming-One as great delight in burnt offerings and sacrifices, as in obeying the voice of the Becoming-One? Behold, to obey is better than sacrifice, and to listen than the fat of rams.

23 For rebellion is as the sin of witchcraft, and stubbornness is as iniquity and images [teraphim] Because you have rejected the word of the Becoming-One, he has also rejected you from being king.

24 And Saul said unto Samuel, I have sinned: for I have transgressed the commandment of the Becoming-One, and your words: because I feared the people, and obeyed their voice.

25 Now therefore, I pray you, pardon my sin, and turn again with me, that I may worship the Becoming-One.

26 And Samuel said unto Saul, I will not return with you: for you have rejected the word of the

Becoming-One, and the Becoming-One has rejected you from being king over Israel.

27 And as Samuel turned about to go away, he laid hold upon the skirt of his mantle, and it rent.

28 And Samuel said unto him, The Becoming-One has ripped the kingdom of Israel from you this day, and has given it to a neighbor of yours, that is better than you.

29 And also the glory of Israel will not lie nor repent: for he is not a man, that he should repent.

30 Then he said, I have sinned: yet honor me now, I pray you, before the elders of my people, and before Israel, and turn again with me, that I may worship the Becoming-One your God.

31 So Samuel turned again after Saul; and Saul worshiped the Becoming-One.

32 Then said Samuel, Bring you here to me Agag the king of the Amalekites. And Agag came unto him delicately. And Agag said, Surely the bitterness of death is past.

33 And Samuel said, As your sword has made women childless, so shall your mother be childless among women. And Samuel hewed Agag in pieces before the Becoming-One in Gilgal.

34 Then Samuel went to Ramah; and Saul went up to his house to Gibeah of Saul.

35 And Samuel came no more to see Saul until the day of his death: nevertheless Samuel mourned for Saul: and the Becoming-One repented that he had made Saul king over Israel.

1 Sam 16:1 And the Becoming-One said unto Samuel, How long will you mourn for Saul, seeing I have rejected him from reigning over Israel? fill your horn with oil, and go, I will send you to Jesse the Bethlehemite: for I have provided me a king among his sons.

2 And Samuel said, How can I go? if Saul hear it, he will kill me. And the Becoming-One said, Take a heifer with you, and say, I am come to sacrifice to the Becoming-One.

3 And call Jesse to the sacrifice, and I will show you what you shall do: and you shall anoint unto me him whom I name unto you.

4 And Samuel did that which the Becoming-One spoke, and came to Bethlehem. And the elders of the town trembled at his coming, and said, you come peaceably?

5 And he said, Peaceably: I am come to sacrifice unto the Becoming-One: sanctify yourselves, and come with me to the sacrifice. And he sanctified Jesse and his sons, and called them to the sacrifice.

6 And it came to pass, when they were come, that he looked on Eliab, and said, Surely the Becoming-One's anointed is before him.

7 But the Becoming-One said unto Samuel, Look not on his countenance, or on the height of his stature; because I have refused him: for the Becoming-One sees not as man sees; for man looks on the outward appearance, but the Becoming-One looks on the heart.

8 Then Jesse called Abinadab, and made him pass before Samuel. And he said, Neither has the Becoming-One chosen this.

9 Then Jesse made Shammah to pass by. And he said, Neither has the Becoming-One chosen this.

10 Again, Jesse made seven of his sons to pass before Samuel. And Samuel said unto Jesse, The Becoming-One has not chosen these.

11 And Samuel said unto Jesse, Are here all your children? And he said, There remains yet the youngest, and, behold, he keeps the sheep. And Samuel said unto Jesse, Send and fetch him: for we will not sit down till he come here.

12 And he sent, and brought him in. Now he was ruddy, and withal of a beautiful countenance, and goodly to look to. And the Becoming-One said, Arise, anoint him: for this is he.

13 Then Samuel took the horn of oil, and anointed him in the midst of his brethren: and the spirit of the Becoming-One came upon **David** from that day forward. So Samuel rose up, and went to Ramah.

14 But the spirit of the Becoming-One departed from Saul, and an evil spirit from the Becoming-One troubled him.

15 And Saul's servants said unto him, Behold now, an evil spirit from God troubles you.

16 Let our lord now command your servants, which are before you, to seek out a man, who is a cunning player on a harp: and it shall come to pass, when the evil spirit from God is upon you, that he shall play with his hand, and you shall be well.

17 And Saul said unto his servants, Provide me now a man that can play well, and bring him to me.

18 Then answered one of the servants, and said, Behold, I have seen a son of Jesse the Bethlehemite, that is cunning in playing, and a mighty valiant man, and a man of war, and prudent in matters, and a comely person, and the Becoming-One is with him.

19 Therefore Saul sent messengers unto Jesse, and said, Send me David your son, which is with the sheep.

20 And Jesse took a donkey loaded with bread, and a bottle of wine, and a kid, and sent them by David his son unto Saul.

21 And David came to Saul, and stood before him: and he loved him greatly; and he became his armor bearer.

22 And Saul sent to Jesse, saying, Let David, I pray you, stand before me; for he has found favor in my sight.

23 And it came to pass, when the evil spirit from God was upon Saul, that David took a harp, and played with his hand: so Saul was refreshed, and was well, and the evil spirit departed from him.

1 Sam 17:1 Now the Philistines gathered together their armies to battle, and were gathered together at Shochoh, which belongs to Judah, and pitched between Shochoh and Azekah, in Ephesdammim.

2 And Saul and the men of Israel were gathered together, and pitched by the valley of Elah, and set the battle in array against the Philistines.

3 And the Philistines stood on a mountain on the one side, and Israel stood on a mountain on the other side: and there was a valley between them.

4 And there went out a champion out of the camp of the Philistines, named Goliath, of Gath, whose height was six cubits and a span.

5 And he had a helmet of brass upon his head, and he was armed with a coat of mail; and the weight of the coat was five thousand shekels of brass.

6 And he had greaves of brass upon his legs, and a target of brass between his shoulders.

7 And the staff of his spear was like a weaver's beam; and his spear's head weighed six hundred shekels of iron: and one bearing a shield went before him.

8 And he stood and cried unto the armies of Israel, and said unto them, Why are you come out to set your battle in array? am not I a Philistine, and you servants to Saul? choose you a man for you, and let him come down to me.

9 If he be able to fight with me, and to kill me, then will we be your servants: but if I prevail against him, and kill him, then shall you be our servants, and serve us.

10 And the Philistine said, I defy the armies of Israel this day; give me a man, that we may fight together.

11 When Saul and all Israel heard those words of the Philistine, they were dismayed, and greatly afraid.

12 Now David was the son of that Ephrathite of Bethlehem-judah, whose name was Jesse; and he had eight sons: and the man went among men for an old man in the days of Saul.

13 And the three eldest sons of Jesse went and followed Saul to the battle: and the names of his three sons that went to the battle were Eliab the firstborn, and next unto him Abinadab, and the third Shammah.

14 And David was the youngest: and the three eldest followed Saul.

15 But David went and returned from Saul to feed his father's sheep at Bethlehem.

16 And the Philistine drew near morning [at rising early time] and evening, and presented himself forty days.

17 And Jesse said unto David his son, Take now for your brethren an ephah of this parched grain, and these ten loaves, and run to the camp to your brethren;

18 And carry these ten cheeses unto the captain of their thousand and look how your brethren fare, and take their pledge.

19 Now Saul, and they, and all the men of Israel, were in the valley of Elah, fighting with the Philistines.

20 And David rose up early in the morning, and left the sheep with a keeper, and took, and went, as Jesse had commanded him; and he came to the trench, as the host was going forth to the fight, and shouted for the battle.

21 For Israel and the Philistines had put the battle in array, army against army.

22 And David left his carriage in the hand of the keeper of the carriage, and ran into the army, and came and saluted his brethren.

23 And as he talked with them, behold, there came up the champion, the Philistine of Gath, Goliath by name, out of the armies of the Philistines, and spoke according to the same words: and David heard them.

24 And all the men of Israel, when they saw the man, fled from him, and were greatly afraid.

25 And the men of Israel said, Have you seen this man that is come up? surely to defy Israel is he come up: and it shall be, that the man who kills him, the king will enrich him with great riches, and will give him his daughter, and make his father's house free in Israel.

26 And David spoke to the men that stood by him, saying, What shall be done to the man that kills this Philistine, and takes away the reproach from Israel? for who is this uncircumcised Philistine, that he should defy the armies of the living God?

27 And the people answered him after this manner, saying, So shall it be done to the man that kills him.

28 And Eliab his eldest brother heard when he spoke unto the men; and Eliab's anger was kindled against David, and he said, Why came you down here? and with whom have you left those few sheep in the wilderness? I know your pride, and the naughtiness of your heart; for you are come down that you might see the battle.

29 And David said, What have I now done? Is there not a cause?

30 And he turned from him toward another, and spoke after the same manner: and the people answered him again after the former manner.

31 And when the words were heard which David spoke, they rehearsed them before Saul: and he sent for him.

32 And David said to Saul, Let no man's heart fail because of him; your servant will go and fight with this Philistine.

33 And Saul said to David, you are not able to go against this Philistine to fight with him: for you are but a youth, and he a man of war from his youth.

34 And David said unto Saul, your servant kept his father's sheep, and there came a lion, and a bear, and took a lamb out of the flock:

35 And I went out after him, and smote him, and delivered it out of his mouth: and when he arose against me, I caught him by his beard, and smote him, and killed him.

36 your servant killed both the lion and the bear: and this uncircumcised Philistine shall be as one of them, seeing he has defied the armies of the living God.

37 David said moreover, The Becoming-One that delivered me out of the paw of the lion, and out of the paw of the bear, he will deliver me out of the hand of this Philistine. And Saul said unto David, Go, and the Becoming-One be with you.

38 And Saul armed David with his armor, and he put a helmet of brass upon his head; also he armed him with a coat of mail.

39 And David girded his sword upon his armor, and he assayed to go; for he had not proved it. And David said unto Saul, I cannot go with these; for I have not proved them. And David put them off him.

40 And he took his staff in his hand, and chose him five smooth stones out of the brook, and put them in a shepherd's bag which he had, even in a scrip; and his sling was in his hand: and he drew near to the Philistine.

41 And the Philistine came on and drew near unto David; and the man that bare the shield went before him.

42 And when the Philistine looked about, and saw David, he disdained him: for he was but a youth, and ruddy, and of a fair countenance.

43 And the Philistine said unto David, Am I a dog, that you come to me with staves? And the Philistine cursed David by his gods.

44 And the Philistine said to David, Come to me, and I will give your flesh unto the fowls of the air, and to the beasts of the field.

45 Then said David to the Philistine, you come to me with a sword, and with a spear, and with a shield: but I come to you in the name of the Becoming-One of hosts, God of the armies of Israel, whom you have defied.

46 This day will the Becoming-One deliver you into mine hand; and I will smite you, and take your head from you; and I will give the carcases of the host of the Philistines this day unto the fowls of the air, and to the wild beasts of the earth; that all the earth may know that there is God in Israel.

47 And all this assembly shall know that the Becoming-One saves not with sword and spear: for the battle is the Becoming-One's and he will give you into our hands.

48 And it came to pass, when the Philistine arose, and came and drew near to meet David, that David hasted, and ran toward the army to meet the Philistine.

49 And David put his hand in his bag, and took there a stone, and slang it, and smote the Philistine in his forehead, that the stone sunk into his forehead; and he fell upon his face to the earth.

50 So David prevailed over the Philistine with a sling and with a stone, and smote the Philistine, and killed him; but there was no sword in the hand of David.

51 Therefore David ran, and stood upon the Philistine, and took his sword, and drew it out of the sheath thereof, and killed him, and cut off his head therewith. And when the Philistines saw their champion was dead, they fled.

52 And the men of Israel and of Judah arose, and shouted, and pursued the Philistines, until you come to the valley, and to the gates of Ekron. And the wounded of the Philistines fell down by the way to Shaaraim, even unto Gath, and unto Ekron.

53 And the children of Israel returned from chasing after the Philistines, and they spoiled their tents.

54 And David took the head of the Philistine, and brought it to Jerusalem; but he put his armor in his tent.

55 And when Saul saw David go forth against the Philistine, he said unto Abner, the captain of the host, Abner, whose son is this youth? And Abner said, As your soul lives, O king, I cannot tell.

56 And the king said, Inquire you whose son the stripling is.

57 And as David returned from the slaughter of the Philistine, Abner took him, and brought him before Saul with the head of the Philistine in his hand.

58 And Saul said to him, Whose son are you, you young man? And David answered, I am the son of your servant Jesse the Bethlehemite.

1 Sam 18:1 And it came to pass, when he had made an end of speaking unto Saul, that the soul of Jonathan was knit with the soul of David, and Jonathan loved him as his own soul.

2 And Saul took him that day, and would let him go no more home to his father's house.

3 Then Jonathan and David made a covenant, because he loved him as his own soul.

4 And Jonathan stripped himself of the robe that was upon him, and gave it to David, and his garments, even to his sword, and to his bow, and to his girdle.

5 And David went out wheresoever Saul sent him, and behaved himself wisely: and Saul set him over the men of war, and he was accepted in the sight of all the people, and also in the sight of Saul's servants.

6 And it came to pass as they came, when David was returned from the slaughter of the Philistine, that the women came out of all cities of Israel, singing and dancing, to meet king Saul, with tabrets, with joy, and with instruments of music.

7 And the women answered one another as they played, and said, Saul has slain his thousands, and David his multitude.

8 And Saul was very angry, and the saying displeased him; and he said, They have ascribed unto David ten myriads, and to me they have ascribed but thousands: and what can he have more but the kingdom?

9 And Saul eyed David from that day and forward.

10 And it came to pass on the next day, that the evil spirit from God came upon Saul, and he prophesied in the midst of the house: and David played with his hand the harp, as at other times: and there was a javelin in Saul's hand.

11 And Saul cast the javelin; for he said, I will smite David even to the wall with it. And David avoided out of his presence twice.

12 And Saul was afraid of David, because the Becoming-One was with him, and was departed from Saul.

13 Therefore Saul removed him from him, and made him his captain over a thousand; and he went out and came in before the people.

14 And David behaved himself wisely in all his ways; and the Becoming-One was with him.

15 Therefore when Saul saw that he behaved himself very wisely, he was afraid of him.

16 But all Israel and Judah loved David, because he went out and came in before them.

17 And Saul said to David, Behold my elder daughter Merab, her will I give you to wife: only be you valiant for me, and fight the Becoming-One's battles. For Saul said, Let not mine hand be upon him, but let the hand of the Philistines be upon him.

18 And David said unto Saul, Who am I? and what is my life, or my father's family in Israel, that I should be son-in-law to the king?

19 But it came to pass at the time when Merab Saul's daughter should have been given to David, that she was given unto Adriel the Meholathite to wife.

20 And Michal Saul's daughter loved David: and they told Saul, and the thing pleased him.

21 And Saul said, I will give him her, that she may be a snare to him, and that the hand of the Philistines may be against him. Therefore Saul said to David, you shall this day be my son-in-law in the one of the twain.

22 And Saul commanded his servants, saying, Commune with David secretly, and say, Behold, the king has delight in you, and all his servants love you: now therefore be the king's son-in-law.

23 And Saul's servants spoke those words in the ears of David. And David said, seems it to you a light thing to be a king's son-in-law, seeing that I am a poor man, and lightly esteemed?

24 And the servants of Saul told him, saying, On this manner spoke David.

25 And Saul said, Thus shall you say to David, The king desires not any dowry, but a hundred foreskins of the Philistines, to be avenged of the king's enemies. But Saul thought to make David fall by the hand of the Philistines.

26 And when his servants told David these words, it pleased David well to be the king's son-in-law: and the days were not expired.

27 Therefore David arose and went, he and his men, and killed of the Philistines two hundred men; and David brought their foreskins, and they gave them in full tale to the king, that he might be the king's son-in-law. And Saul gave him Michal his daughter to wife.

28 And Saul saw and knew that the Becoming-One was with David, and that Michal Saul's daughter loved him.

29 And Saul was yet the more afraid of David; and Saul became David's enemy all the days.

30 Then the princes of the Philistines went forth: and it came to pass, after they went forth, that David behaved himself more wisely than all the servants of Saul; so that his name was much set by.

1 Sam 19:1 And Saul spoke to Jonathan his son, and to all his servants, that they should kill David.

2 But Jonathan Saul's son delighted much in David: and Jonathan told David, saying, Saul my father seeks to kill you: now therefore, I pray you, take heed to yourself until the morning, and abide in a secret place, and hide thyself:

3 And I will go out and stand beside my father in the field where you are, and I will commune with my father of you; and what I see, that I will tell you.

4 And Jonathan spoke good of David unto Saul his father, and said unto him, Let not the king sin against his servant, against David; because he has not sinned against you, and because his works have been to you very good:

5 For he did put his soul in his hand, and killed the Philistine, and the Becoming-One worked a great salvation for all Israel: you saw it, and didst rejoice: why then will you sin against innocent blood, to slay David without a cause?

6 And Saul listened unto the voice of Jonathan: and Saul swore, As the Becoming-One lives, he shall not be slain.

7 And Jonathan called David, and Jonathan showed him all those things. And Jonathan brought David to Saul, and he was in his presence, as yesterday and the third day.

8 And there was war again: and David went out, and fought with the Philistines, and killed them with a great slaughter; and they fled from him.

9 And the evil spirit from the Becoming-One was upon Saul, as he sat in his house with his javelin in his hand: and David played with his hand the harp.

10 And Saul sought to smite David even to the wall with the javelin; but he slipped away out of Saul's presence, and he smote the javelin into the wall: and David fled, and escaped that night.

11 Saul also sent messengers unto David's house, to watch him, and to slay him in the morning: and Michal David's wife told him, saying, If you save not your soul to night, tomorrow you shall be slain.

12 So Michal let David down through a window: and he went, and fled, and escaped.

13 And Michal took an image [teraphim] and laid it in the bed, and put a pillow of goats' hair for his bolster, and covered it with a cloth.

14 And when Saul sent messengers to take David, she said, He is sick.

15 And Saul sent the messengers again to see David, saying, Bring him up to me in the bed, that I may slay him.

16 And when the messengers were come in, behold, there was an image [teraphim] in the bed, with a pillow of goats' hair for his bolster.

17 And Saul said unto Michal, Why have you deceived me so, and sent away mine enemy, that he is escaped? And Michal answered Saul, He said unto me, Let me go; why should I kill you?

18 So David fled, and escaped, and came to Samuel to Ramah, and told him all that Saul had done to him. And he and Samuel went and dwelt in Naioth.

19 And it was told Saul, saying, Behold, David is at Naioth in Ramah.

20 And Saul sent messengers to take David: and when they saw the company of the prophets prophesying, and Samuel standing as appointed over them, the spirit of God was upon the messengers of Saul, and they also prophesied.

21 And when it was told Saul, he sent other messengers, and they prophesied likewise. And Saul sent messengers again the third time, and they prophesied also.

22 Then went he also to Ramah, and came to a great well that is in Sechu: and he asked and said, Where are Samuel and David? And one said, Behold, they be at Naioth in Ramah.

23 And he went there to Naioth in Ramah: and the spirit of God was upon him also, and he went on, and prophesied, until he came to Naioth in Ramah.

24 And he stripped off his clothes also, and prophesied before Samuel in like manner, and lay down naked all that day and all that night. Why they say, Is Saul also among the prophets?

1 Sam 20:1 And David fled from Naioth in Ramah, and came and said before Jonathan, What have I done? what is mine iniquity? and what is my sin before your father, that he seeks my soul?

2 And he said unto him, Far be it; you shall not die: behold, my father will do nothing either great or

small, but that he will show it me: and why should my father hide this thing from me? it is not so.

3 And David swore moreover, and said, your father certainly knows that I have found grace in your eyes; and he said, Let not Jonathan know this, lest he be grieved: but truly as the Becoming-One lives, and as your soul lives, there is but a step between me and death.

4 Then said Jonathan unto David, Whatsoever your soul desires, I will even do it for you.

5 And David said unto Jonathan, Behold, tomorrow is the new moon, and I should not fail to sit with the king at food: but let me go, that I may hide myself in the field unto the third day at evening.

6 If your father at all miss me, then say, David earnestly asked leave of me that he might run to Bethlehem his city: for there is a yearly sacrifice there for all the family.

7 If he say thus, It is well; your servant shall have peace: but if he be very angry, then be sure that evil is determined by him.

8 Therefore you shall deal kindly with your servant; for you have brought your servant into a covenant of the Becoming-One with you: notwithstanding, if there be in me iniquity, slay me thyself; for why should you bring me to your father?

9 And Jonathan said, Far be it from you: for if I knew certainly that evil were determined by my father to come upon you, then would not I tell it you?

10 Then said David to Jonathan, Who shall tell me? or what if your father answer you roughly?

11 And Jonathan said unto David, Come, and let us go out into the field. And they went out both of them into the field.

12 And Jonathan said unto David, O Becoming-One, God of Israel, when I have sounded my father about tomorrow any time, or the third day, and, behold, if there be good toward David, and I then send not unto you, and show it you;

13 The Becoming-One do so and much more to Jonathan: but if it please my father to do you evil, then I will show it you, and send you away, that you may go in peace: and the Becoming-One be with you, as he has been with my father.

14 And you shall not only while yet I live show me the kindness of the Becoming-One, that I die not:

15 But also you shall not cut off your kindness from my house for olam, no, not when the Becoming-One has cut off the enemies of David every one from the face of the earth.

16 So Jonathan made a covenant with the house of David, saying, Let the Becoming-One even require it at the hand of David's enemies.

17 And Jonathan caused David to swear again, because he loved him: for he loved him as he loved his own soul.

18 Then Jonathan said to David, tomorrow is the new moon: and you shall be missed, because your seat will be empty.

19 And when you have stayed three days, then you shall go down quickly, and come to the place where you did hide yourself when the business was in hand, and shall remain by the stone Ezel.

20 And I will shoot three arrows on the side thereof, as though I shot at a mark.

21 And, behold, I will send a lad, saying, Go, find out the arrows. If I expressly say unto the lad, Behold, the arrows are on this side of you, take them; then you come: for there is peace to you, and no hurt; as the Becoming-One lives.

22 But if I say thus unto the young man, Behold, the arrows are beyond you; go your way: for the Becoming-One has sent you away.

23 And as touching the matter which you and I have spoken of, behold, the Becoming-One be between you and me for olam.

24 So David hid himself in the field: and when the new moon was come, the king sat him down to eat food.

25 And the king sat upon his seat, as at other times, even upon a seat by the wall: and Jonathan arose, and Abner sat by Saul's side, and David's place was empty.

26 Nevertheless Saul spoke not any thing that day: for he thought, Something has befallen him, he is not clean; surely he is not clean.

27 And it came to pass on the next day, which was the second day of the month, that David's place was empty: and Saul said unto Jonathan his son, Why comes not the son of Jesse to food, neither yesterday, nor today?

28 And Jonathan answered Saul, David earnestly asked leave of me to go to Bethlehem:

29 And he said, Let me go, I pray you; for our family has a sacrifice in the city; and my brother, he has commanded me to be there: and now, if I have found favor in your eyes, let me get away, I pray you, and see my brethren. Therefore he comes not unto the king's table.

30 Then Saul's anger was kindled against Jonathan, and he said unto him, you son of the perverse rebellious woman, do not I know that you have chosen the son of Jesse to your own confusion, and unto the confusion of your mother's nakedness?

31 For as long as the son of Jesse lives upon the ground, you shall not be established, nor your kingdom. Therefore now send and fetch him unto me, for he is a son of death.

32 And Jonathan answered Saul his father, and said unto him, Why shall he be slain? what has he done?

33 And Saul cast a javelin at him to smite him: whereby Jonathan knew that it was determined of his father to slay David.

34 So Jonathan arose from the table in fierce anger, and did eat no food the second day of the month: for he was grieved for David, because his father had done him shame.

35 And it came to pass in the morning, that Jonathan went out into the field at the set time[105] with David, and a little lad with him.

36 And he said unto his lad, Run, find out now the arrows which I shoot. And as the lad ran, he shot an arrow beyond him.

37 And when the lad was come to the place of the arrow which Jonathan had shot, Jonathan cried after the lad, and said, Is not the arrow beyond you?

---

[105] Appointed time or festival

38 And Jonathan cried after the lad, Make speed, haste, stay not. And Jonathan's lad gathered up the arrows, and came to his master.

39 But the lad knew not any thing: only Jonathan and David knew the matter.

40 And Jonathan gave his artillery unto his lad, and said unto him, Go, carry them to the city.

41 And as soon as the lad was gone, David arose out of a place toward the south, and fell on his face to the ground, and bowed himself three times: and they kissed one another, and wept one with another, until David exceeded.

42 And Jonathan said to David, Go in peace, forasmuch as we have sworn both of us in the name of the Becoming-One, saying, The Becoming-One be between me and you, and between my seed and your seed for olam. And he arose and departed: and Jonathan went into the city.

1 Sam 21:1 Then came David to Nob to Ahimelech the priest: and Ahimelech was afraid at the meeting of David, and said unto him, Why are you alone, and no man with you?

2 And David said unto Ahimelech the priest, The king has commanded me a business, and has said unto me, Let no man know any thing of the business whereabout I send you, and what I have commanded you: and I have appointed my servants to such and such a place.

3 Now therefore what is under your hand? give me five loaves of bread in mine hand, or what there is present.

4 And the priest answered David, and said, There is no common bread under mine hand, but there is hallowed bread; if the young men have kept themselves at least from women.

5 And David answered the priest, and said unto him, Of a truth women have been kept from us about as yesterday the third day, since I came out, and the vessels of the young men are holy, and the bread is in a manner common, yes, though it were sanctified this day in the vessel.

6 So the priest gave him hallowed bread: for there was no bread there but the showbread, that was taken from before the Becoming-One, to put hot bread in the day when it was taken away.

7 Now a certain man of the servants of Saul was there that day, detained before the Becoming-One; and his name was Doeg, an Edomite, the chief of the herdmen that belonged to Saul.

8 And David said unto Ahimelech, And is there not here under your hand spear or sword? for I have neither brought my sword nor my weapons with me, because the king's business required haste.

9 And the priest said, The sword of Goliath the Philistine, whom you killed in the valley of Elah, behold, it is here wrapped in a cloth behind the ephod: if you will take that, take it: for there is no other save that here. And David said, There is none like that; give it me.

10 And David arose, and fled that day for fear of Saul, and went to Achish the king of Gath.

11 And the servants of Achish said unto him, Is not this David the king of the land? did they not sing one to another of him in dances, saying, Saul has slain his thousands, and David his myriads?

12 And David laid up these words in his heart, and was greatly afraid of Achish the king of Gath.

13 And he changed his behavior before them, and pretended himself mad in their hands, and scrabbled on the doors of the gate, and let his spittle fall down upon his beard.

14 Then said Achish unto his servants, Lo, you see the man is mad: why then have you brought him to me?

15 Have I need of mad men, that you have brought this fellow to play the mad man in my presence? shall this fellow come into my house?

1 Sam 22:1 David therefore departed there, and escaped to the cave Adullam: and when his brethren and all his father's house heard it, they went down there to him.

2 And every one that was in distress, and every one that was in debt, and every one that was in bitterness of soul, gathered themselves unto him; and he became a captain over them: and there were with him about four hundred men.

3 And David went there to Mizpeh of Moab: and he said unto the king of Moab, Let my father and my mother, I pray you, come forth, and be with you, till I know what God will do for me.

4 And he brought them before the king of Moab: and they dwelt with him all the while that David was in the hold.

5 And the prophet Gad said unto David, Abide not in the hold; depart, and get you into the land of Judah. Then David departed, and came into the forest of Hareth.

6 When Saul heard that David was discovered, and the men that were with him, now Saul abode in Gibeah under a tree in Ramah, having his spear in his hand, and all his servants were standing about him;

7 Then Saul said unto his servants that stood about him, Hear now, you Benjamites; will the son of Jesse give every one of you fields and vineyards, and make you all captains of thousands, and captains of hundreds;

8 That all of you have conspired against me, and there is none that shows me that my son has made a league with the son of Jesse, and there is none of you that is sorry for me, or shows unto me that my son has stirred up my servant against me, to lie in wait, as at this day?

9 Then answered Doeg the Edomite, which was set over the servants of Saul, and said, I saw the son of Jesse coming to Nob, to Ahimelech the son of Ahitub.

10 And he inquired of the Becoming-One for him, and gave him victuals, and gave him the sword of Goliath the Philistine.

11 Then the king sent to call Ahimelech the priest, the son of Ahitub, and all his father's house, the priests that were in Nob: and they came all of them to the king.

12 And Saul said, Hear now, you son of Ahitub. And he answered, Here I am, my lord.

13 And Saul said unto him, Why have you conspired against me, you and the son of Jesse, in that you have given him bread, and a sword, and have inquired of God for him, that he should rise against me, to lie in wait, as at this day?

14 Then Ahimelech answered the king, and said, And who is so faithful among all your servants as David, which is the king's son-in-law, and goes at your bidding, and is honorable in your house?

15 Did I then begin to inquire of God for him? be it far from me: let not the king impute any thing unto his servant, nor to all the house of my father: for your servant knew nothing of all this, less or more.

16 And the king said, in dying you shall surely die, Ahimelech, you, and all your father's house.

17 And the king said unto the footmen that stood about him, Turn, and slay the priests of the Becoming-One; because their hand also is with David, and because they knew when he fled, and did not show it to me. But the servants of the king would not put forth their hand to fall upon the priests of the Becoming-One.

18 And the king said to Doeg, Turn you, and fall upon the priests. And Doeg the Edomite turned, and he fell upon the priests, and killed on that day fourscore and five persons that did wear a linen ephod.

19 And Nob, the city of the priests, smote he with the edge of the sword, both men and women, children and sucklings, and oxen, and donkeys, and sheep, with the edge of the sword.

20 And one of the sons of Ahimelech the son of Ahitub, named Abiathar, escaped, and fled after David.

21 And Abiathar showed David that Saul had slain the Becoming-One's priests.

22 And David said unto Abiathar, I knew it that day, when Doeg the Edomite was there, that he would surely tell Saul: I have occasioned the death of all the souls of your father's house.

23 Abide you with me, fear not: for he that seeks my soul seeks your soul: but with me you shall be in safeguard.

1 Sam 23:1 Then they told David, saying, Behold, the Philistines fight against Keilah, and they rob the threshing floors.

2 Therefore David inquired of the Becoming-One, saying, Shall I go and smite these Philistines? And the Becoming-One said unto David, Go, and smite the Philistines, and save Keilah.

3 And David's men said unto him, Behold, we be afraid here in Judah: how much more then if we come to Keilah against the armies of the Philistines?

4 Then David inquired of the Becoming-One yet again. And the Becoming-One answered him and said, Arise, go down to Keilah: for I will deliver the Philistines into your hand.

5 So David and his men went to Keilah, and fought with the Philistines, and brought away their cattle, and smote them with a great slaughter. So David saved the inhabitants of Keilah.

6 And it came to pass, when Abiathar the son of Ahimelech fled to David to Keilah, that he came down with an ephod in his hand.

7 And it was told Saul that David was come to Keilah. And Saul said, God has delivered him into mine hand; for he is shut in, by entering into a town that has gates and bars.

8 And Saul called all the people together to war, to go down to Keilah, to besiege David and his men.

9 And David knew that Saul secretly practiced mischief against him; and he said to Abiathar the priest, Bring here the ephod.

10 Then said David, O Becoming-One, God of Israel, your servant has certainly heard that Saul seeks to come to Keilah, to destroy the city for my sake.

11 Will the men of Keilah deliver me up into his hand? will Saul come down, as your servant has heard? O Becoming-One, God of Israel, I beg you, tell your servant. And the Becoming-One said, He will come down.

12 Then said David, Will the men of Keilah deliver me and my men into the hand of Saul? And the Becoming-One said, They will deliver you up.

13 Then David and his men, which were about six hundred, arose and departed out of Keilah, and went wheresoever they could go. And it was told Saul that David was escaped from Keilah; and he forbare to go forth.

14 And David abode in the wilderness in strong holds, and remained in a mountain in the wilderness of Ziph. And Saul sought him every day, but God delivered him not into his hand.

15 And David saw that Saul was come out to seek his soul: and David was in the wilderness of Ziph in a wood.

16 And Jonathan Saul's son arose, and went to David into the wood, and strengthened his hand in God.

17 And he said unto him, Fear not: for the hand of Saul my father shall not find you; and you shall be king over Israel, and I shall be next unto you; and that also Saul my father knows.

18 And they two made a covenant before the Becoming-One: and David abode in the wood, and Jonathan went to his house.

19 Then came up the Ziphites to Saul to Gibeah, saying, does not David hide himself with us in strong holds in the wood, in the hill of Hachilah, which is on the south of Jeshimon?

20 Now therefore, O king, come down according to all the desire of your soul to come down; and our part shall be to deliver him into the king's hand.

21 And Saul said, Blessed be you of the Becoming-One; for you have compassion on me.

22 Go, I pray you, prepare yet, and know and see his place where his haunt is, and who has seen him there: for it is told me that he deals very subtly.

23 See therefore, and take knowledge of all the lurking places where he hides himself, and you come again to me with the certainty, and I will go with you: and it shall come to pass, if he be in the land, that I will search him out throughout all the thousands of Judah.

24 And they arose, and went to Ziph before Saul: but David and his men were in the wilderness of Maon, in the plain on the south of Jeshimon.

25 Saul also and his men went to seek him. And they told David: therefore he came down into a rock, and abode in the wilderness of Maon. And when Saul heard that, he pursued after David in the wilderness of Maon.

26 And Saul went on this side of the mountain, and David and his men on that side of the mountain: and David made haste to get away for fear of Saul; for

Saul and his men compassed David and his men round about to take them.

27 But there came a messenger unto Saul, saying, Haste you, and come; for the Philistines have invaded the land.

28 Therefore Saul returned from pursuing after David, and went against the Philistines: therefore they called that place Selahammahlekoth.

29 And David went up from there, and dwelt in strong holds at Engedi.

1 Sam 24:1 And it came to pass, when Saul was returned from following the Philistines, that it was told him, saying, Behold, David is in the wilderness of Engedi.

2 Then Saul took three thousand of chosen men out of all Israel, and went to seek David and his men upon the rocks of the wild goats.

3 And he came to the sheepcotes by the way, where was a cave; and Saul went in to cover his feet: and David and his men remained in the sides of the cave.

4 And the men of David said unto him, Behold the day of which the Becoming-One said unto you, Behold, I will deliver your enemy into your hand, that you may do to him as it shall seem good unto you. Then David arose, and cut off the skirt of Saul's robe privily.

5 And it came to pass afterward, that David's heart smote him, because he had cut off Saul's skirt.

6 And he said unto his men, The Becoming-One forbid that I should do this thing unto my lord, the Becoming-One's anointed, to stretch forth mine hand against him, seeing he is the anointed of the Becoming-One.

7 So David stayed his servants with these words, and permitted them not to rise against Saul. But Saul rose up out of the cave, and went on his way.

8 David also arose afterward, and went out of the cave, and cried after Saul, saying, My lord the king. And when Saul looked behind him, David stooped with his face to the earth, and bowed himself.

9 And David said to Saul, Why hear you men's words, saying, Behold, David seeks your hurt?

10 Behold, this day your eyes have seen how that the Becoming-One had delivered you today into mine hand in the cave: and some bade me kill you: but mine eye spared you; and I said, I will not put forth mine hand against my lord; for he is the Becoming-One's anointed.

11 Moreover, my father, see, yes, see the skirt of your robe in my hand: for in that I cut off the skirt of your robe, and killed you not, know you and see that there is neither evil nor transgression in mine hand, and I have not sinned against you; yet you hunt my soul to take it.

12 The Becoming-One judge between me and you, and the Becoming-One avenge me of you: but mine hand shall not be upon you.

13 As says the proverb of the ancients, Wickedness proceeds from the wicked: but mine hand shall not be upon you.

14 After whom is the king of Israel come out? after whom do you pursue? after a dead dog, after a flea.

15 The Becoming-One therefore be judge, and judge between me and you, and see, and plead my cause, and deliver me out of your hand.

16 And it came to pass, when David had made an end of speaking these words unto Saul, that Saul said, Is this your voice, my son David? And Saul lifted up his voice, and wept.

17 And he said to David, you are more righteous than I: for you have rewarded me good, whereas I have rewarded you evil.

18 And you have showed this day how that you have dealt well with me: forasmuch as when the Becoming-One had delivered me into your hand, you killed me not.

19 For if a man find his enemy, will he let him go well away? therefore the Becoming-One reward you good for that you have done unto me this day.

20 And now, behold, I know well that you shall surely be king, and that the kingdom of Israel shall be established in your hand.

21 Swear now therefore unto me by the Becoming-One, that you will not cut off my seed after me, and that you will not destroy my name out of my father's house.

22 And David swore unto Saul. And Saul went home; but David and his men got them up unto the hold.

1 Sam 25:1 And Samuel died; and all the Israelites were gathered together, and lamented him, and buried him in his house at Ramah. And David arose, and went down to the wilderness of Paran.

2 And there was a man in Maon, whose possessions were in Carmel; and the man was very great, and he had three thousand of sheep, and an thousand of goats: and he was shearing his sheep in Carmel.

3 Now the name of the man was Nabal; and the name of his wife Abigail: and she was a woman of good understanding, and of a beautiful countenance: but the man was churlish and evil in his doings; and he was of the house of Caleb.

4 And David heard in the wilderness that Nabal did shear his sheep.

5 And David sent out ten young men, and David said unto the young men, Get you up to Carmel, and go to Nabal, and greet him in my name:

6 And thus shall you say to him that lives in prosperity, Peace be both to you, and peace be to your house, and peace be unto all that you hast.

7 And now I have heard that you have shearers: now your shepherds which were with us, we hurt them not, neither was there anything missing unto them, all the while they were in Carmel.

8 Ask your young men, and they will show you. Therefore let the young men find favor in your eyes: for we come in a good day: give, I pray you, whatsoever comes to your hand unto your servants, and to your son David.

9 And when David's young men came, they spoke to Nabal according to all those words in the name of David, and ceased.

10 And Nabal answered David's servants, and said, Who is David? and who is the son of Jesse? there be many servants now a days that break away every man from his master.

11 Shall I then take my bread, and my water, and my flesh that I have killed for my shearers, and give it unto men, whom I know not where they be?

12 So David's young men turned their way, and went again, and came and told him all those sayings.

13 And David said unto his men, Gird you on every man his sword. And they girded on every man his sword; and David also girded on his sword: and there went up after David about four hundred men; and two hundred abode by the stuff.

14 But one of the young men told Abigail, Nabal's wife, saying, Behold, David sent messengers out of the wilderness to salute our master; and he railed on them.

15 But the men were very good unto us, and we were not hurt, neither missed we any thing, as long as we were conversant with them, when we were in the fields:

16 They were a wall unto us both by night and day, all the while we were with them keeping the sheep.

17 Now therefore know and consider what you will do; for evil is determined against our master, and against all his household: for he is such a son of Belial, that a man cannot speak to him.

18 Then Abigail made haste, and took two hundred loaves, and two bottles of wine, and five sheep ready dressed, and five measures of parched grain, and a hundred clusters of raisins, and two hundred cakes of figs, and laid them on donkeys.

19 And she said unto her servants, Go on before me; behold, I come after you. But she told not her husband Nabal.

20 And it was so, as she rode on the donkey, that she came down by the covert on the hill, and, behold, David and his men came down against her; and she met them.

21 Now David had said, Surely in vain have I kept all that this fellow has in the wilderness, so that nothing was missed of all that pertained unto him: and he has requited me evil for good.

22 So and more also do God unto the enemies of David, if I leave of all that pertain to him by the morning light any that pisses against the wall.

23 And when Abigail saw David, she hasted, and lighted off the donkey, and fell before David on her face, and bowed herself to the ground,

24 And fell at his feet, and said, Upon me, my lord, upon me let this iniquity be: and let your handmaid, I pray you, speak in your audience, and hear the words of your handmaid.

25 Let not my lord, I pray you, regard this man of Belial, even Nabal: for as his name is, so is he; Nabal is his name, and folly is with him: but I your handmaid saw not the young men of my lord, whom you did send.

26 Now therefore, my lord, as the Becoming-One lives, and as your soul lives, seeing the Becoming-One has withheld you from coming to shed blood, and from avenging yourself with your own hand, now let your enemies, and they that seek evil to my lord, be as Nabal.

27 And now this blessing which your handmaid has brought unto my lord, let it even be given unto the young men that follow my lord.

28 I pray you, forgive the trespass of your handmaid: for the Becoming-One will certainly make my lord a sure house; because my lord fights the battles of the Becoming-One, and evil has not been found in you all your days.

29 Yet a man is risen to pursue you, and to seek your soul: but the soul of my lord shall be bound in the bundle of life with the Becoming-One your God; and the souls of your enemies, them shall he sling out, as out of the middle of a sling.

30 And it shall come to pass, when the Becoming-One shall have done to my lord according to all the good that he has spoken concerning you, and shall have appointed you ruler over Israel;

31 That this shall be no grief unto you, nor offence of heart unto my lord, either that you have shed blood causeless, or that my lord has avenged himself: but when the Becoming-One shall have dealt well with my lord, then remember your handmaid.

32 And David said to Abigail, Blessed be the Becoming-One, God of Israel, which sent you this day to meet me:

33 And blessed be your advice, and blessed be you, which have kept me this day from coming to shed blood, and from avenging myself with mine own hand.

34 For in very deed, as the Becoming-One, God of Israel lives, which has kept me back from hurting you, except you hadst hasted and come to meet me, surely there had not been left unto Nabal by the morning light any that pisses against the wall.

35 So David received of her hand that which she had brought him, and said unto her, Go up in peace to your house; see, I have listened to your voice, and have accepted your person.

36 And Abigail came to Nabal; and, behold, he held a feast in his house, like the feast of a king; and Nabal's heart was merry within him, for he was very drunken: therefore she told him nothing, less or more, until the morning light.

37 But it came to pass in the morning, when the wine was gone out of Nabal, and his wife had told him these things, that his heart died within him, and he became as a stone.

38 And it came to pass about ten days after, that the Becoming-One smote Nabal, that he died.

39 And when David heard that Nabal was dead, he said, Blessed be the Becoming-One, that has pleaded the cause of my reproach from the hand of Nabal, and has kept his servant from evil: for the Becoming-One has returned the wickedness of Nabal upon his own head. And David sent and communed with Abigail, to take her to him to wife.

40 And when the servants of David were come to Abigail to Carmel, they spoke unto her, saying, David sent us unto you, to take you to him to wife.

41 And she arose, and bowed herself on her face to the earth, and said, Behold, let your handmaid be a servant to wash the feet of the servants of my lord.

42 And Abigail hasted, and arose, and rode upon an donkey, with five damsels of hers that went after her; and she went after the messengers of David, and became his wife.

43 David also took Ahinoam of Jezreel; and they were also both of them his wives.

44 But Saul had given Michal his daughter, David's wife, to Phalti the son of Laish, which was of Gallim.

1 Sam 26:1 And the Ziphites came unto Saul to Gibeah, saying, does not David hide himself in the hill of Hachilah, which is before Jeshimon?

2 Then Saul arose, and went down to the wilderness of Ziph, having three thousand of chosen men of Israel with him, to seek David in the wilderness of Ziph.

3 And Saul pitched in the hill of Hachilah, which is before Jeshimon, by the way. But David abode in the wilderness, and he saw that Saul came after him into the wilderness.

4 David therefore sent out spies, and understood that Saul was come in very deed.

5 And David arose, and came to the place where Saul had pitched: and David beheld the place where Saul lay, and Abner the son of Ner, the captain of his host: and Saul lay in the trench, and the people pitched round about him.

6 Then answered David and said to Ahimelech the Hittite, and to Abishai the son of Zeruiah, brother to Joab, saying, Who will go down with me to Saul to the camp? And Abishai said, I will go down with you.

7 So David and Abishai came to the people by night: and, behold, Saul lay sleeping within the trench, and his spear stuck in the ground at his bolster: but Abner and the people lay round about him.

8 Then said Abishai to David, God has delivered your enemy into your hand this day: now therefore let me smite him, I pray you, with the spear even to the earth at once, and I will not smite him the second time.

9 And David said to Abishai, Destroy him not: for who can stretch forth his hand against the Becoming-One's anointed, and be guiltless?

10 David said furthermore, As the Becoming-One lives, the Becoming-One shall smite him; or his day shall come to die; or he shall descend into battle, and perish.

11 The Becoming-One forbid that I should stretch forth mine hand against the Becoming-One's anointed: but, I pray you, take you now the spear that is at his bolster, and the cruse of water, and let us go.

12 So David took the spear and the cruse of water from Saul's bolster; and they got them away, and no man saw it, nor knew it, neither awaked: for they were all asleep; because a deep sleep from the Becoming-One was fallen upon them.

13 Then David went over to the other side, and stood on the top of a hill afar off; a great space being between them:

14 And David cried to the people, and to Abner the son of Ner, saying, Answer you not, Abner? Then Abner answered and said, Who are you that cry to the king?

15 And David said to Abner, are not you a valiant man? and who is like to you in Israel? why then have you not kept thy lords the king? for there came one of the people in to destroy the king thy lords.

16 This thing is not good that you have done. As the Becoming-One lives, you are worthy to die, because you have not kept your master, the Becoming-One's anointed. And now see where the king's spear is, and the cruse of water that was at his bolster.

17 And Saul knew David's voice, and said, Is this your voice, my son David? And David said, It is my voice, my lord, O king.

18 And he said, Why does my lord thus pursue after his servant? for what have I done? or what evil is in mine hand?

19 Now therefore, I pray you, let my lord the king hear the words of his servant. If the Becoming-One have stirred you up against me, let him accept an offering: but if they be the children of men, cursed be they before the Becoming-One; for they have driven me out this day from abiding in the inheritance of the Becoming-One, saying, Go, serve other gods.

20 Now therefore, let not my blood fall to the earth before the face of the Becoming-One: for the king of Israel is come out to seek a flea, as when one does hunt a partridge in the mountains.

21 Then said Saul, I have sinned: return, my son David: for I will no more do you harm, because my soul was precious in your eyes this day: behold, I have played the fool, and have erred exceedingly.

22 And David answered and said, Behold the king's spear! and let one of the young men come over and fetch it.

23 The Becoming-One render to every man his righteousness and his faithfullness: for the Becoming-One delivered you into my hand today, but I would not stretch forth mine hand against the Becoming-One's anointed.

24 And, behold, as your soul was much set by this day in mine eyes, so let my soul be much set by in the eyes of the Becoming-One, and let him deliver me out of all tribulation.

25 Then Saul said to David, Blessed be you, my son David: you shall both do great things, and also shall still prevail. So David went on his way, and Saul returned to his place.

1 Sam 27:1 And David said in his heart, I shall now perish one day by the hand of Saul: there is nothing better for me than that I should speedily escape into the land of the Philistines; and Saul shall despair of me, to seek me any more in any coast of Israel: so shall I escape out of his hand.

2 And David arose, and he passed over with the six hundred men that were with him unto Achish, the son of Maoch, king of Gath.

3 And David dwelt with Achish at Gath, he and his men, every man with his household, even David with his two wives, Ahinoam the Jezreelitess, and Abigail the Carmelitess, Nabal's wife.

4 And it was told Saul that David was fled to Gath: and he sought no more again for him.

5 And David said unto Achish, If I have now found grace in your eyes, let them give me a place in some town in the country, that I may dwell there: for why should your servant dwell in the royal city with you?

6 Then Achish gave him Ziklag that day: therefore Ziklag pertains unto the kings of Judah unto this day.

7 And the time that David dwelt in the country of the Philistines was a full year and four months.

8 And David and his men went up, and invaded the Geshurites, and the Gezrites, and the Amalekites: for those nations were from olam past the inhabitants of the land, as you go to Shur, even unto the land of Egypt.

9 And David smote the land, and left neither man nor woman alive, and took away the sheep, and the oxen, and the donkeys, and the camels, and the apparel, and returned, and came to Achish.

10 And Achish said, To where have you made a road today? And David said, Against the south of Judah, and against the south of the Jerahmeelites, and against the south of the Kenites.

11 And David saved neither man nor woman alive, to bring tidings to Gath, saying, Lest they should tell on us, saying, So did David, and so will be his manner all the while he dwells in the country of the Philistines.

12 And Achish believed David, saying, He has made his people Israel utterly to abhor him; therefore he shall be my servant for olam.

1 Sam 28:1 And it came to pass in those days, that the Philistines gathered their armies together for warfare, to fight with Israel. And Achish said unto David, Know you assuredly, that you shall go out with me to battle, you and your men.

2 And David said to Achish, Surely you shall know what your servant can do. And Achish said to David, Therefore will I make you keeper of mine head all the days.

3 Now Samuel was dead, and all Israel had lamented him, and buried him in Ramah, even in his own city. And Saul had put away the mediums, and the fortune-tellers, out of the land.

4 And the Philistines gathered themselves together, and came and pitched in Shunem: and Saul gathered all Israel together, and they pitched in Gilboa.

5 And when Saul saw the host of the Philistines, he was afraid, and his heart greatly trembled.

6 And when Saul inquired of the Becoming-One, the Becoming-One answered him not, neither by dreams, nor by Urim, nor by prophets.

7 Then said Saul unto his servants, Seek me a woman that has a medium, that I may go to her, and inquire of her. And his servants said to him, Behold, there is a woman that has a familiar spirit at Endor.

8 And Saul disguised himself, and put on other raiment, and he went, and two men with him, and they came to the woman by night: and he said, I pray you, divine unto me by the medium, and bring me him up, whom I shall name unto you.

9 And the woman said unto him, Behold, you know what Saul has done, how he has cut off the mediums, and the fortune-tellers, out of the land: why then lay you a snare for my soul, to cause me to die?

10 And Saul swore to her by the Becoming-One, saying, As the Becoming-One lives, there shall no punishment happen to you for this thing.

11 Then said the woman, Whom shall I bring up unto you? And he said, Bring me up Samuel.

12 And when the woman saw Samuel, she cried with a loud voice: and the woman spoke to Saul, saying, Why have you deceived me? for you are Saul.

13 And the king said unto her, Be not afraid: for what saw you? And the woman said unto Saul, I saw gods ascending out of the earth.

14 And he said unto her, What form is he of? And she said, An old man comes up; and he is covered with a mantle. And Saul perceived that it was Samuel, and he stooped with his face to the ground, and bowed himself.

15 And Samuel said to Saul, Why have you disquieted me, to bring me up? And Saul answered, I am greatly distressed; for the Philistines make war against me, and God is departed from me, and answers me no more, neither by prophets, nor by dreams: therefore I have called you, that you may make known unto me what I shall do.

16 Then said Samuel, Why then do you ask of me, seeing the Becoming-One is departed from you, and is become your enemy?

17 And the Becoming-One has done to him, as he spoke by me: for the Becoming-One has ripped the kingdom out of your hand, and given it to your neighbor, even to David:

18 Because you obeyed not the voice of the Becoming-One, nor executedst his fierce wrath upon Amalek, therefore has the Becoming-One done this thing unto you this day.

19 Moreover the Becoming-One will also deliver Israel with you into the hand of the Philistines: and tomorrow shall you and your sons be with me: the Becoming-One also shall deliver the host of Israel into the hand of the Philistines.

20 Then Saul fell straightway all along on the earth, and was greatly afraid, because of the words of Samuel: and there was no strength in him; for he had eaten no bread all the day, nor all the night.

21 And the woman came unto Saul, and saw that he was greatly troubled, and said unto him, Behold, your handmaid has obeyed your voice, and I have put my soul in my hand, and have listened unto your words which you spoke unto me.

22 Now therefore, I pray you, listen you also unto the voice of your handmaid, and let me set a morsel of bread before you; and eat, that you may have strength, when you go on your way.

23 But he refused, and said, I will not eat. But his servants, together with the woman, compelled him; and he listened unto their voice. So he arose from the earth, and sat upon the bed.

24 And the woman had a fat calf in the house; and she hasted, and killed it, and took flour, and kneaded it, and did bake unleavened bread thereof:

25 And she brought it before Saul, and before his servants; and they did eat. Then they rose up, and went away that night.

1 Sam 29:1 Now the Philistines gathered together all their armies to Aphek: and the Israelites pitched by a fountain which is in Jezreel.

2 And the lords of the Philistines passed on by hundreds, and by thousands: but David and his men passed on in the rear with Achish.

3 Then said the princes of the Philistines, What do these Hebrews here? And Achish said unto the princes of the Philistines, Is not this David, the servant of Saul the king of Israel, which has been with

me these days, or these years, and I have found no fault in him since he fell unto me unto this day?

4 And the princes of the Philistines were angry with him; and the princes of the Philistines said unto him, Make this fellow return, that he may go again to his place which you have appointed him, and let him not go down with us to battle, lest in the battle he be an adversary to us: for wherewith should he reconcile himself unto his master? should it not be with the heads of these men?

5 Is not this David, of whom they sang one to another in dances, saying, Saul killed his thousands, and David his myriads?

6 Then Achish called David, and said unto him, Surely, as the Becoming-One lives, you have been upright, and your going out and your coming in with me in the host is good in my sight: for I have not found evil in you since the day of your coming unto me unto this day: nevertheless the lords favor you not.

7 Therefore now return, and go in peace, that you displease not the lords of the Philistines.

8 And David said unto Achish, But what have I done? and what have you found in your servant so long as I have been with you unto this day, that I may not go fight against the enemies of my lord the king?

9 And Achish answered and said to David, I know that you are good in my sight, as an angel of God: notwithstanding the princes of the Philistines have said, He shall not go up with us to the battle.

10 Therefore now rise up early in the morning with your lords' servants that are come with you: and as soon as you be up early in the morning, and have light, depart.

11 So David and his men rose up early to depart in the morning, to return into the land of the Philistines. And the Philistines went up to Jezreel.

1 Sam 30:1 And it came to pass, when David and his men were come to Ziklag on the third day, that the Amalekites had invaded the south, and Ziklag, and struck Ziklag, and burned it with fire;

2 And had taken the women captives, that were therein: they killed not any, either great or small, but carried them away, and went on their way.

3 So David and his men came to the city, and, behold, it was burned with fire; and their wives, and their sons, and their daughters, were taken captives.

4 Then David and the people that were with him lifted up their voice and wept, until they had no more power to weep.

5 And David's two wives were taken captives, Ahinoam the Jezreelitess, and Abigail the wife of Nabal the Carmelite.

6 And David was greatly distressed; for the people spoke of stoning him, because the soul of all the people was grieved, every man for his sons and for his daughters: but David encouraged himself in the Becoming-One, his God.

7 And David said to Abiathar the priest, Ahimelech's son, I pray you, bring me here the ephod. And Abiathar brought there the ephod to David.

8 And David inquired at the Becoming-One, saying, Shall I pursue after this troop? shall I overtake them? And he answered him, Pursue: for you shall surely overtake them, and without fail recover all.

9 So David went, he and the six hundred men that were with him, and came to the brook Besor, where those that were left behind stayed.

10 But David pursued, he and four hundred men: for two hundred abode behind, which were so faint that they could not go over the brook Besor.

11 And they found an Egyptian in the field, and brought him to David, and gave him bread, and he did eat; and they made him drink water;

12 And they gave him a piece of a cake of figs, and two clusters of raisins: and when he had eaten, his spirit came again to him: for he had eaten no bread, nor drunk any water, three days and three nights.

13 And David said unto him, To whom do you belong? and where are you from? And he said, I am a young man of Egypt, servant to an Amalekite; and my master left me, because three days ago I fell sick.

14 We made an invasion upon the south of the Cherethites, and upon the coast which belongs to Judah, and upon the south of Caleb; and we burned Ziklag with fire.

15 And David said to him, Canst you bring me down to this company? And he said, Swear unto me by God, that you will neither kill me, nor deliver me into the hands of my master, and I will bring you down to this company.

16 And when he had brought him down, behold, they were spread abroad upon all the earth, eating and drinking, and dancing, because of all the great spoil that they had taken out of the land of the Philistines, and out of the land of Judah.

17 And David smote them from the breeze time even near sunset unto the evening of the next day: and there escaped not a man of them, save four hundred young men, which rode upon camels, and fled.

18 And David recovered all that the Amalekites had carried away: and David rescued his two wives.

19 And there was nothing lacking to them, neither small nor great, neither sons nor daughters, neither spoil, nor anything that they had taken to them: David recovered all.

20 And David took all the flocks and the herds, which they drave before those other cattle, and said, This is David's spoil.

21 And David came to the two hundred men, which were so faint that they could not follow David, whom they had made also to abide at the brook Besor: and they went forth to meet David, and to meet the people that were with him: and when David came near to the people, he saluted them.

22 Then answered all the wicked men and men of Belial, of those that went with David, and said, Because they went not with us, we will not give them of the spoil that we have recovered, save to every man his wife and his children, that they may lead them away, and depart.

23 Then said David, you shall not do so, my brethren, with that which the Becoming-One has given us, who has preserved us, and delivered the company that came against us into our hand.

24 For who will listen unto you in this matter? but as his part is that goes down to the battle, so shall

his part be that tarries by the stuff: they shall part alike.

25 And it was so from that day forward, that he made it a statute and an ordinance for Israel unto this day.

26 And when David came to Ziklag, he sent of the spoil unto the elders of Judah, even to his friends, saying, Behold a present for you of the spoil of the enemies of the Becoming-One;

27 To them which were in Bethel, and to them which were in south Ramoth, and to them which were in Jattir,

28 And to them which were in Aroer, and to them which were in Siphmoth, and to them which were in Eshtemoa,

29 And to them which were in Rachal, and to them which were in the cities of the Jerahmeelites, and to them which were in the cities of the Kenites,

30 And to them which were in Hormah, and to them which were in Chorashan, and to them which were in Athach,

31 And to them which were in Hebron, and to all the places where David himself and his men were wont to haunt.

1 Sam 31:1 Now the Philistines fought against Israel: and the men of Israel fled from before the Philistines, and fell down slain in mount Gilboa.

2 And the Philistines followed hard upon Saul and upon his sons; and the Philistines killed Jonathan, and Abinadab, and Melchishua, Saul's sons.

3 And the battle went great against Saul, and the archers hit him; and he was greatly wounded of the archers.

4 Then said Saul unto his armor bearer, Draw your sword, and thrust me through therewith; lest these uncircumcised come and thrust me through, and abuse me. But his armor bearer would not; for he was greatly afraid. Therefore Saul took a sword, and fell upon it.

5 And when his armor bearer saw that Saul was dead, he fell likewise upon his sword, and died with him.

6 So Saul died, and his three sons, and his armor bearer, and all his men, that same day together.

7 And when the men of Israel that were on the other side of the valley, and they that were on the other side Jordan, saw that the men of Israel fled, and that Saul and his sons were dead, they forsook the cities, and fled; and the Philistines came and dwelt in them.

8 And it came to pass on the next day, when the Philistines came to strip the slain, that they found Saul and his three sons fallen in mount Gilboa.

9 And they cut off his head, and stripped off his armor, and sent into the land of the Philistines round about, to publish it in the house of their idols, and among the people.

10 And they put his armor in the house of Ashtaroth: and they fastened his body to the wall of Beth-shan.

11 And when the inhabitants of Jabeshgilead heard of that which the Philistines had done to Saul;

12 All the valiant men arose, and went all night, and took the body of Saul and the bodies of his sons from the wall of Beth-shan, and came to Jabesh, and burnt them there.

13 And they took their bones, and buried them under a tree at Jabesh, and fasted seven days.

2 Samuel

2 Sam 1:1 Now it came to pass after the death of Saul, when David was returned from the slaughter of the Amalekites, and David had abode two days in Ziklag;

2 It came even to pass on the third day, that, behold, a man came out of the camp from Saul with his clothes rent, and earth upon his head: and so it was, when he came to David, that he fell to the earth, and did obeisance.

3 And David said unto him, From where do you come? And he said unto him, Out of the camp of Israel am I escaped.

4 And David said unto him, How did the matter go? I pray you, tell me. And he answered, That the people are fled from the battle, and many of the people also are fallen and dead; and Saul and Jonathan his son are dead also.

5 And David said unto the young man that told him, How know you that Saul and Jonathan his son be dead?

6 And the young man that told him said, As I happened by chance upon mount Gilboa, behold, Saul leaned upon his spear; and, lo, the chariots and horsemen followed hard after him.

7 And when he looked behind him, he saw me, and called unto me. And I answered, Here I am.

8 And he said unto me, Who are you? And I answered him, I am an Amalekite.

9 He said unto me again, Stand, I pray you, upon me, and slay me: for anguish is come upon me, because my soul is yet whole in me.

10 So I stood upon him, and killed him, because I was sure that he could not live after that he was fallen: and I took the crown that was upon his head, and the bracelet that was on his arm, and have brought them here unto my lord.

11 Then David took hold on his clothes, and ripped them; and likewise all the men that were with him:

12 And they mourned, and wept, and fasted until even, for Saul, and for Jonathan his son, and for the people of the Becoming-One, and for the house of Israel; because they were fallen by the sword.

13 And David said unto the young man that told him, Where are you from? And he answered, I am the son of a stranger, an Amalekite.

14 And David said unto him, How were you not afraid to stretch forth your hand to destroy the Becoming-One's anointed?

15 And David called one of the young men, and said, Go near, and fall upon him. And he smote him that he died.

16 And David said unto him, your blood be upon your head; for your mouth has testified against you, saying, I have slain the Becoming-One's anointed.

17 And David lamented with this lamentation over Saul and over Jonathan his son:

18 Also he bade them teach the children of Judah the use of the bow: behold, it is written in the book of Jasher.

19 The beauty of Israel is slain upon your high places: how are the mighty fallen!

20 Tell it not in Gath, publish it not in the streets of Askelon; lest the daughters of the Philistines rejoice, lest the daughters of the uncircumcised triumph.

21 you mountains of Gilboa, let there be no dew, neither let there be rain, upon you, nor fields of offerings: for there the shield of the mighty is vilely cast away, the shield of Saul, as though he had not been anointed with oil.

22 From the blood of the slain, from the fat of the mighty, the bow of Jonathan turned not back, and the sword of Saul returned not empty.

23 Saul and Jonathan were lovely and pleasant in their lives, and in their death they were not divided: they were swifter than eagles, they were stronger than lions.

24 you daughters of Israel, weep over Saul, who clothed you in scarlet, with other delights, who put on ornaments of gold upon your apparel.

25 How are the mighty fallen in the midst of the battle! O Jonathan, you were slain in your high places.

26 I am distressed for you, my brother Jonathan: very pleasant have you been unto me: your love to me was wonderful, passing the love of women.

27 How are the mighty fallen, and the weapons of war perished!

2 Sam 2:1 And it came to pass after this, that David inquired of the Becoming-One, saying, Shall I go up into any of the cities of Judah? And the Becoming-One said unto him, Go up. And David said, To where shall I go up? And he said, Unto Hebron.

2 So David went up there, and his two wives also, Ahinoam the Jezreelitess, and Abigail Nabal's wife the Carmelite.

3 And his men that were with him did David bring up, every man with his household: and they dwelt in the cities of Hebron.

4 And the men of Judah came, and there they anointed David king over the house of Judah. And they told David, saying, That the men of Jabeshgilead were they that buried Saul.

5 And David sent messengers unto the men of Jabeshgilead, and said unto them, Blessed be you of the Becoming-One, that you have showed this kindness unto your lords, even unto Saul, and have buried him.

6 And now the Becoming-One show kindness and truth unto you: and I also will requite you this kindness, because you have done this thing.

7 Therefore now let your hands be strengthened, and be you valiant: for your master Saul is dead, and also the house of Judah have anointed me king over them.

8 But Abner the son of Ner, captain of Saul's host, took Ishbosheth the son of Saul, and brought him over to Mahanaim;

9 And made him king over Gilead, and over the Ashurites, and over Jezreel, and over Ephraim, and over Benjamin, and over all Israel.

10 Ishbosheth Saul's son was a son of forty years when he began to reign over Israel, and reigned two years. But the house of Judah followed David.

11 And the number of days that David was king in Hebron over the house of Judah was seven years and six months.

12 And Abner the son of Ner, and the servants of Ishbosheth the son of Saul, went out from Mahanaim to Gibeon.

13 And Joab the son of Zeruiah, and the servants of David, went out, and met together by the pool of Gibeon: and they sat down, the one on the one side of the pool, and the other on the other side of the pool.

14 And Abner said to Joab, Let the young men now arise, and play before us. And Joab said, Let them arise.

15 Then there arose and went over by number twelve of Benjamin, which pertained to Ishbosheth the son of Saul, and twelve of the servants of David.

16 And they caught every one his fellow by the head, and thrust his sword in his fellow's side; so they fell down together: therefore that place was called Helkathhazzurim, which is in Gibeon.

17 And there was a very great battle that day; and Abner was beaten, and the men of Israel, before the servants of David.

18 And there were three sons of Zeruiah there, Joab, and Abishai, and Asahel: and Asahel was as light of foot as a wild roe.

19 And Asahel pursued after Abner; and in going he turned not to the right hand nor to the left from following Abner.

20 Then Abner looked behind him, and said, are you Asahel? And he answered, I am.

21 And Abner said to him, Turn you aside to your right hand or to your left, and lay you hold on one of the young men, and take you his armor. But Asahel would not turn aside from following of him.

22 And Abner said again to Asahel, Turn you aside from following me: therefore should I smite you to the ground? how then should I hold up my face to Joab your brother?

23 Howbeit he refused to turn aside: therefore Abner with the hinder end of the spear smote him under the fifth rib, that the spear came out behind him; and he fell down there, and died in the same place: and it came to pass, that as many as came to the place where Asahel fell down and died stood still.

24 Joab also and Abishai pursued after Abner: and the sun went down when they were come to the hill of Ammah, that lies before Giah by the way of the wilderness of Gibeon.

25 And the children of Benjamin gathered themselves together after Abner, and became one troop, and stood on the top of a hill.

26 Then Abner called to Joab, and said, Shall the sword devour for glory? don't you know that it will be bitterness in the latter end? how long shall it be then, ere you bid the people return from following their brethren?

27 And Joab said, As God lives, unless you had spoken, surely then in the morning the people had gone up every one from following his brother.

28 So Joab blew a trumpet, and all the people stood still, and pursued after Israel no more, neither fought they any more.

29 And Abner and his men walked all that night through the plain, and passed over Jordan, and went through all Bithron, and they came to Mahanaim.

30 And Joab returned from following Abner: and when he had gathered all the people together, there lacked of David's servants nineteen men and Asahel.

31 But the servants of David had struck of Benjamin, and of Abner's men, so that three hundred and threescore men died.

32 And they took up Asahel, and buried him in the tomb of his father, which was in Bethlehem. And Joab and his men went all night, and they came to Hebron at break of day.

2 Sam 3:1 Now there was long war between the house of Saul and the house of David: but David grew stronger and stronger, and the house of Saul grew weaker and weaker.

2 And unto David were sons born in Hebron: and his firstborn was Amnon, of Ahinoam the Jezreelitess;

3 And his second, Chileab, of Abigail the wife of Nabal the Carmelite; and the third, Absalom the son of Maacah the daughter of Talmai king of Geshur;

4 And the fourth, Adonijah the son of Haggith; and the fifth, Shephatiah the son of Abital;

5 And the sixth, Ithream, by Eglah David's wife. These were born to David in Hebron.

6 And it came to pass, while there was war between the house of Saul and the house of David, that Abner made himself strong for the house of Saul.

7 And Saul had a concubine, whose name was Rizpah, the daughter of Aiah: and Ishbosheth said to Abner, Why have you gone in unto my father's concubine?

8 Then was Abner very angry for the words of Ishbosheth, and said, I am a dog's head, which against Judah do show kindness this day unto the house of Saul your father, to his brethren, and to his friends, and have not delivered you into the hand of David, that you charge me today with a fault concerning this woman?

9 So do God to Abner, and more also, except, as the Becoming-One has sworn to David, even so I do to him;

10 To translate the kingdom from the house of Saul, and to set up the throne of David over Israel and over Judah, from Dan even to Beersheba.

11 And he could not answer Abner a word again, because he feared him.

12 And Abner sent messengers to David on his behalf, saying, Whose is the land? saying also, Make your league with me, and, behold, my hand shall be with you, to bring about all Israel unto you.

13 And he said, Well; I will make a league with you: but one thing I require of you, that is, you shall not see my face, except you first bring Michal Saul's daughter, when you come to see my face.

14 And David sent messengers to Ishbosheth Saul's son, saying, Deliver me my wife Michal, which I espoused to me for a hundred foreskins of the Philistines.

15 And Ishbosheth sent, and took her from her husband, even from Phaltiel the son of Laish.

16 And her husband went with her along weeping behind her to Bahurim. Then said Abner unto him, Go, return. And he returned.

17 And Abner had communication with the elders of Israel, saying, you sought for David yesterday and the third day to be king over you:

18 Now then do it: for the Becoming-One has spoken of David, saying, By the hand of my servant David I will save my people Israel out of the hand of

the Philistines, and out of the hand of all their enemies.

19 And Abner also spoke in the ears of Benjamin: and Abner went also to speak in the ears of David in Hebron all that seemed good to Israel, and that seemed good to the whole house of Benjamin.

20 So Abner came to David to Hebron, and twenty men with him. And David made Abner and the men that were with him a feast.

21 And Abner said unto David, I will arise and go, and will gather all Israel unto my lord the king, that they may make a league with you, and that you may reign over all that your soul desires. And David sent Abner away; and he went in peace.

22 And, behold, the servants of David and Joab came from pursuing a troop, and brought in a great spoil with them: but Abner was not with David in Hebron; for he had sent him away, and he was gone in peace.

23 When Joab and all the host that was with him were come, they told Joab, saying, Abner the son of Ner came to the king, and he has sent him away, and he is gone in peace.

24 Then Joab came to the king, and said, What have you done? behold, Abner came unto you; why is it that you have sent him away, and he is quite gone?

25 you know Abner the son of Ner, that he came to deceive you, and to know your going out and your coming in, and to know all that you do.

26 And when Joab was come out from David, he sent messengers after Abner, which brought him again from the well of Sirah: but David knew it not.

27 And when Abner was returned to Hebron, Joab took him aside in the gate to speak with him quietly, and smote him there under the fifth rib, that he died, for the blood of Asahel his brother.

28 And afterward when David heard it, he said, I and my kingdom are guiltless before the Becoming-One for olam, from the blood of Abner the son of Ner:

29 Let it rest on the head of Joab, and on all his father's house; and let there not fail from the house of Joab one that has an issue, or that is a leper, or that leans on a staff, or that falls on the sword, or that lacks bread.

30 So Joab and Abishai his brother killed Abner, because he had slain their brother Asahel at Gibeon in the battle.

31 And David said to Joab, and to all the people that were with him, Rend your clothes, and gird you with sackcloth, and mourn before Abner. And king David himself followed the bier.

32 And they buried Abner in Hebron: and the king lifted up his voice, and wept at the grave of Abner; and all the people wept.

33 And the king lamented over Abner, and said, Died Abner as a fool dieth?

34 your hands were not bound, nor your feet put into fetters: as a man falls before wicked men, so fell you. And all the people wept again over him.

35 And when all the people came to cause David to eat food while it was yet day, David swore, saying, So do God to me, and more also, if I taste bread, or anything else, till the sun be down.

36 And all the people took notice of it, and it pleased them: as whatsoever the king did pleased all the people.

37 For all the people and all Israel understood that day that it was not of the king to slay Abner the son of Ner.

38 And the king said unto his servants, Don't you know that there is a prince and a great man fallen this day in Israel?

39 And I am this day weak, though anointed king; and these men the sons of Zeruiah be too hard for me: the Becoming-One shall reward the doer of evil according to his wickedness.

2 Sam 4:1 And when Saul's son heard that Abner was dead in Hebron, his hands were feeble, and all the Israelites were troubled.

2 And Saul's son had two men that were captains of bands: the name of the one was Baanah, and the name of the other Rechab, the sons of Rimmon a Beerothite, of the children of Benjamin: for Beeroth also was reckoned to Benjamin.

3 And the Beerothites fled to Gittaim, and were sojourners there until this day.

4 And Jonathan, Saul's son, had a son that was lame of his feet. He was a son of five years when the tidings came of Saul and Jonathan out of Jezreel, and his nurse took him up, and fled: and it came to pass, as she made haste to flee, that he fell, and became lame. And his name was Mephibosheth.

5 And the sons of Rimmon the Beerothite, Rechab and Baanah, went, and came about the heat of the day to the house of Ishbosheth, who lay on a bed at noon.

6 And they came there into the midst of the house, as though they would have fetched wheat; and they smote him under the fifth rib: and Rechab and Baanah his brother escaped.

7 For when they came into the house, he lay on his bed in his bedchamber, and they smote him, and killed him, and beheaded him, and took his head, and got them away through the plain all night.

8 And they brought the head of Ishbosheth unto David to Hebron, and said to the king, Behold the head of Ishbosheth the son of Saul your enemy, which sought your soul; and the Becoming-One has avenged my lord the king this day of Saul, and of his seed.

9 And David answered Rechab and Baanah his brother, the sons of Rimmon the Beerothite, and said unto them, As the Becoming-One lives, who has redeemed my soul out of all adversity,

10 When one told me, saying, Behold, Saul is dead, thinking to have brought good tidings, I took hold of him, and killed him in Ziklag, who thought that I would have given him a reward for his tidings:

11 How much more, when wicked men have slain a righteous person in his own house upon his bed? shall I not therefore now require his blood of your hand, and take you away from the earth?

12 And David commanded his young men, and they killed them, and cut off their hands and their feet, and hanged them up over the pool in Hebron. But they took the head of Ishbosheth, and buried it in the tomb of Abner in Hebron.

2 Sam 5:1 Then came all the tribes of Israel to David unto Hebron, and spoke, saying, Behold, we are your bone and your flesh.

2 Also yesterday and the third day, when Saul was king over us, you were he that led out and brought in Israel: and the Becoming-One said to you, you shall feed my people Israel, and you shall be a captain over Israel.

3 So all the elders of Israel came to the king to Hebron; and king David made a league with them in Hebron before the Becoming-One: and they anointed David king over Israel.

4 David was a son of thirty years when he began to reign, and he reigned forty years.

5 In Hebron he reigned over Judah seven years and six months: and in Jerusalem he reigned thirty and three years over all Israel and Judah.

6 And the king and his men went to Jerusalem unto the Jebusites, the inhabitants of the land: which spoke unto David, saying, Except you take away the blind and the lame, you shall not come in here: thinking, David cannot come in here.

7 Nevertheless David took the strong hold of Zion: the same is the city of David.

8 And David said on that day, Whosoever gets up to the gutter, and smites the Jebusites, and the lame and the blind, that are hated of David's soul, he shall be chief and captain. Therefore they said, The blind and the lame shall not come into the house.

9 So David dwelt in the fort, and called it the city of David. And David built round about from Millo and inward.

10 And David went on, and grew great, and the Becoming-One, God of hosts was with him.

11 And Hiram king of Tyre sent messengers to David, and cedar trees, and carpenters, and masons: and they built David a house.

12 And David perceived that the Becoming-One had established him king over Israel, and that he had exalted his kingdom for his people Israel's sake.

13 And David took him more concubines and wives out of Jerusalem, after he was come from Hebron: and there were yet sons and daughters born to David.

14 And these be the names of those that were born unto him in Jerusalem; Shammuah, and Shobab, and Nathan, and **Solomon**,

15 Ibhar also, and Elishua, and Nepheg, and Japhia,

16 And Elishama, and Eliada, and Eliphalet.

17 But when the Philistines heard that they had anointed David king over Israel, all the Philistines came up to seek David; and David heard of it, and went down to the hold.

18 The Philistines also came and spread themselves in the valley of Rephaim.

19 And David inquired of the Becoming-One, saying, Shall I go up to the Philistines? will you deliver them into mine hand? And the Becoming-One said unto David, Go up: for I will doubtless deliver the Philistines into your hand.

20 And David came to Baal-Perazim, and David smote them there, and said, The Becoming-One has broken forth upon mine enemies before me, as the breach of waters. Therefore he called the name of that place Baal-Perazim.

21 And there they left their images, and David and his men burned them.

22 And the Philistines came up yet again, and spread themselves in the valley of Rephaim.

23 And when David inquired of the Becoming-One, he said, you shall not go up; but fetch a compass behind them, and come upon them over against the mulberry trees.

24 And let it be, when you hear the sound of a going in the tops of the mulberry trees, that then you shall bestir thyself: for then shall the Becoming-One go out before you, to smite the host of the Philistines.

25 And David did so, as the Becoming-One had commanded him; and smote the Philistines from Geba until you come to Gazer.

2 Sam 6:1 Again, David gathered together all the chosen men of Israel, thirty thousand.

2 And David arose, and went with all the people that were with him from Baale of Judah, to bring up from there the ark of God, whose name is called by the name of the Becoming-One, the hosts that dwells between the cherubs.

3 And they set the ark of God upon a new cart, and brought it out of the house of Abinadab that was in Gibeah: and Uzzah and Ahio, the sons of Abinadab, drave the new cart.

4 And they brought it out of the house of Abinadab which was at Gibeah, accompanying the ark of God: and Ahio went before the ark.

5 And David and all the house of Israel played before the Becoming-One on all manner of instruments made of fir wood, even on harps, and on psalteries, and on timbrels, and on cornets, and on cymbals.

6 And when they came to Nachon's threshing floor, Uzzah put forth his hand to the ark of God, and took hold of it; for the oxen shook it.

7 And the anger of the Becoming-One was kindled against Uzzah; and God smote him there for his error; and there he died by the ark of God.

8 And David was displeased, because the Becoming-One had made a breach upon Uzzah: and he called the name of the place Perezuzzah to this day.

9 And David was afraid of the Becoming-One that day, and said, How shall the ark of the Becoming-One come to me?

10 So David would not remove the ark of the Becoming-One unto him into the city of David: but David carried it aside into the house of Obededom the Gittite.

11 And the ark of the Becoming-One continued in the house of Obededom the Gittite three months: and the Becoming-One blessed Obededom, and all his household.

12 And it was told king David, saying, The Becoming-One has blessed the house of Obededom, and all that pertains unto him, because of the ark of God. So David went and brought up the ark of God from the house of Obededom into the city of David with gladness.

13 And it was so, that when they that bare the ark of the Becoming-One had gone six paces, he sacrificed oxen and fatlings.

14 And David danced before the Becoming-One with all his might; and David was girded with a linen ephod.

15 So David and all the house of Israel brought up the ark of the Becoming-One with shouting, and with the sound of the trumpet.

16 And as the ark of the Becoming-One came into the city of David, Michal Saul's daughter looked through a window, and saw king David leaping and dancing before the Becoming-One; and she despised him in her heart.

17 And they brought in the ark of the Becoming-One, and set it in his place, in the midst of the tabernacle that David had pitched for it: and David offered burnt offerings and peace offerings before the Becoming-One.

18 And as soon as David had made an end of offering burnt offerings and peace offerings, he blessed the people in the name of the Becoming-One of hosts.

19 And he dealt among all the people, even among the whole multitude of Israel, as well to the women as men, to every one a cake of bread, and a good piece of flesh, and a flagon of wine. So all the people departed every one to his house.

20 Then David returned to bless his household. And Michal the daughter of Saul came out to meet David, and said, How glorious was the king of Israel today, who uncovered himself today in the eyes of the handmaids of his servants, as one of the vain fellows shamelessly uncovers himself!

21 And David said unto Michal, It was before the Becoming-One, which chose me before your father, and before all his house, to appoint me ruler over the people of the Becoming-One, over Israel: therefore will I play before the Becoming-One.

22 And I will yet be more vile than thus, and will be base in mine own sight: and of the maidservants which you have spoken of, of them shall I be had in honor.

23 Therefore Michal the daughter of Saul had no child unto the day of her death.

2 Sam 7:1 And it came to pass, when the king sat in his house, and the Becoming-One had given him rest round about from all his enemies;

2 That the king said unto Nathan the prophet, See now, I dwell in a house of cedar, but the ark of God dwells within curtains.

3 And Nathan said to the king, Go, do all that is in your heart; for the Becoming-One is with you.

4 And it came to pass that night, that the word of the Becoming-One came unto Nathan, saying,

5 Go and tell my servant David, Thus says the Becoming-One, shall you build me a house for me to dwell in?

6 Whereas I have not dwelt in any house since the time that I brought up the children of Israel out of Egypt, even to this day, but have walked in a tent and in a tabernacle.

7 In all the places wherein I have walked with all the children of Israel spoke I a word with any of the tribes of Israel, whom I commanded to feed my people Israel, saying, Why build you not me a house of cedar?

8 Now therefore so shall you say unto my servant David, Thus says the Becoming-One of hosts, I took you from the sheepcote, from following the sheep, to be ruler over my people, over Israel:

9 And I was with you wheresoever you went, and have cut off all your enemies out of your sight, and have made you a great name, like unto the name of the great men that are in the earth.

10 Moreover I will appoint a place for my people Israel, and will plant them, that they may dwell in a place of their own, and move no more; neither shall the children of wickedness afflict them any more, as beforetime,

11 And as since the time that I commanded judges to be over my people Israel, and have caused you to rest from all your enemies. Also the Becoming-One tells you that he will make you a house.

12 And when your days be fulfilled, and you shall sleep with your fathers, I will set up your seed after you, which shall proceed out of your bowels, and I will establish his kingdom.

13 He shall build a house for my name, and I will establish the throne of his kingdom for olam.

14 I will be his father, and he shall be my son. If he commit iniquity, I will chasten him with the rod of men, and with the stripes of the children of men:

15 But my mercy shall not depart away from him, as I took it from Saul, whom I put away before you.

16 And your house and your kingdom shall be established for olam before you: your throne shall be established for olam.

17 According to all these words, and according to all this vision, so did Nathan speak unto David.

18 Then went king David in, and sat before the Becoming-One, and he said, Who am I, O my Lord(s) the Becoming-One? and what is my house, that you have brought me hitherto?

19 And this was yet a small thing in your sight, O my Lord(s) the Becoming-One; but you have spoken also of your servant's house for a great while to come. And is this the manner of man, O my Lord(s) the Becoming-One?

20 And what can David say more unto you? for you, my Lord(s) the Becoming-One, know your servant.

21 For your word's sake, and according to your own heart, have you done all these great things, to make your servant know them.

22 Therefore you are great, O Becoming-One, God: for there is none like you, neither is there any gods beside you, according to all that we have heard with our ears.

23 And what one nation in the earth is like your people, even like Israel, whom God went to redeem for a people to himself, and to make him a name, and to do for you great things and terrible, for your land, before your people, which you redeemed to you from Egypt, from the nations and their gods?

24 For you have confirmed to yourself your people Israel to be a nation unto you for olam, and you, Becoming-One, are become their God.

25 And now, O Becoming-One God, the word that you have spoken concerning your servant, and concerning his house, establish it for olam, and do as you have said.

26 And let your name be magnified for olam, saying, The Becoming-One of hosts is God over Israel: and let the house of your servant David be established before you.

27 For you, O Becoming-One of hosts, God of Israel, have revealed to your servant, saying, I will build you a house: therefore has your servant found in his heart to pray this prayer unto you.

28 And now, O my Lord(s) the Becoming-One, you are God, and your words be true, and you have promised this goodness unto your servant:

29 Therefore now let it please you to bless the house of your servant, that it may continue for olam before you: for you, O my Lord(s) the Becoming-One, have spoken it: and with your blessing let the house of your servant be blessed for olam.

2 Sam 8:1 And after this it came to pass, that David smote the Philistines, and subdued them: and David took Methegammah out of the hand of the Philistines.

2 And he smote Moab, and measured them with a line, casting them down to the ground; even with two lines measured he to put to death, and with one full line to keep alive. And so the Moabites became David's servants, and brought gifts.

3 David smote also Hadadezer, the son of Rehob, king of Zobah, as he went to recover his border at the river Euphrates.

4 And David took from him a thousand chariots, and seven hundred horsemen, and twenty thousand of footmen: and David hocked all the chariot horses, but reserved of them for a hundred chariots.

5 And when the Syrians of Damascus came to succour Hadadezer king of Zobah, David killed of the Syrians two and twenty thousand of men.

6 Then David put garrisons in Syria of Damascus: and the Syrians became servants to David, and brought gifts. And the Becoming-One preserved David wheresoever he went.

7 And David took the shields of gold that were on the servants of Hadadezer, and brought them to Jerusalem.

8 And from Betah, and from Berothai, cities of Hadadezer, king David took exceeding much brass.

9 When Toi king of Hamath heard that David had struck all the host of Hadadezer,

10 Then Toi sent Joram his son unto king David, to salute him, and to bless him, because he had fought against Hadadezer, and struck him: for Hadadezer had wars with Toi. And Joram brought with him vessels of silver, and vessels of gold, and vessels of brass:

11 Which also king David did dedicate unto the Becoming-One, with the silver and gold that he had dedicated of all nations which he subdued;

12 Of Syria, and of Moab, and of the children of Ammon, and of the Philistines, and of Amalek, and of the spoil of Hadadezer, son of Rehob, king of Zobah.

13 And David got him a name when he returned from smiting of the Syrians in the valley of salt, being eighteen thousand of men.

14 And he put garrisons in Edom; throughout all Edom put he garrisons, and all they of Edom became David's servants. And the Becoming-One preserved David wheresoever he went.

15 And David reigned over all Israel; and David executed judgment and justice unto all his people.

16 And Joab the son of Zeruiah was over the host; and Jehoshaphat the son of Ahilud was recorder;

17 And Zadok the son of Ahitub, and Ahimelech the son of Abiathar, were the priests; and Seraiah was the scribe;

18 And Benaiah the son of Jehoiada was over both the Cherethites and the Pelethites; and David's sons were chief rulers.

2 Sam 9:1 And David said, Is there yet any that is left of the house of Saul, that I may show him kindness for Jonathan's sake?

2 And there was of the house of Saul a servant whose name was Ziba. And when they had called him unto David, the king said unto him, are you Ziba? And he said, your servant is he.

3 And the king said, Is there not yet any of the house of Saul, that I may show the kindness of God unto him? And Ziba said unto the king, Jonathan has yet a son, which is lame on his feet.

4 And the king said unto him, Where is he? And Ziba said unto the king, Behold, he is in the house of Machir, the son of Ammiel, in Lodebar.

5 Then king David sent, and fetched him out of the house of Machir, the son of Ammiel, from Lodebar.

6 Now when Mephibosheth, the son of Jonathan, the son of Saul, was come unto David, he fell on his face, and did reverence. And David said, Mephibosheth. And he answered, Behold your servant!

7 And David said unto him, Fear not: for I will surely show you kindness for Jonathan your father's sake, and will restore you all the land of Saul your father; and you shall eat bread at my table continually.

8 And he bowed himself, and said, What is your servant, that you should look upon such a dead dog as I am?

9 Then the king called to Ziba, Saul's servant, and said unto him, I have given unto your master's son all that pertained to Saul and to all his house.

10 You therefore, and your sons, and your servants, shall till the land for him, and you shall bring in the fruits, that your master's son may have food to eat: but Mephibosheth your master's son shall eat bread continually at my table. Now Ziba had fifteen sons and twenty servants.

11 Then said Ziba unto the king, According to all that my lord the king has commanded his servant, so shall your servant do. As for Mephibosheth, said the king, he shall eat at my table, as one of the king's sons.

12 And Mephibosheth had a young son, whose name was Micha. And all that dwelt in the house of Ziba were servants unto Mephibosheth.

13 So Mephibosheth dwelt in Jerusalem: for he did eat continually at the king's table; and was lame on both his feet.

2 Sam 10:1 And it came to pass after this, that the king of the children of Ammon died, and Hanun his son reigned in his stead.

2 Then said David, I will show kindness unto Hanun the son of Nahash, as his father showed

kindness unto me. And David sent to comfort him by the hand of his servants for his father. And David's servants came into the land of the children of Ammon.

3 And the princes of the children of Ammon said unto Hanun their lords, Think you that David does honor your father, that he has sent comforters unto you? has not David rather sent his servants unto you, to search the city, and to spy it out, and to overthrow it?

4 Therefore Hanun took David's servants, and shaved off the one half of their beards, and cut off their garments in the middle, even to their buttocks, and sent them away.

5 When they told it unto David, he sent to meet them, because the men were greatly ashamed: and the king said, Tarry at Jericho until your beards be grown, and then return.

6 And when the children of Ammon saw that they stank before David, the children of Ammon sent and hired the Syrians of Beth-rehob, and the Syrians of Zoba, twenty thousand of footmen, and of king Maacah a thousand men, and of Ishtob twelve thousand men.

7 And when David heard of it, he sent Joab, and all the host of the mighty men.

8 And the children of Ammon came out, and put the battle in array at the entering in of the gate: and the Syrians of Zoba, and of Rehob, and Ishtob, and Maacah, were by themselves in the field.

9 When Joab saw that the front of the battle was against him before and behind, he chose of all the choice men of Israel, and put them in array against the Syrians:

10 And the rest of the people he delivered into the hand of Abishai his brother, that he might put them in array against the children of Ammon.

11 And he said, If the Syrians be too strong for me, then you shall help me: but if the children of Ammon be too strong for you, then I will come and help you.

12 Be of good courage, and let us play the men for our people, and for the cities of our God: and the Becoming-One do that which seems him good.

13 And Joab drew near, and the people that were with him, unto the battle against the Syrians: and they fled before him.

14 And when the children of Ammon saw that the Syrians were fled, then fled they also before Abishai, and entered into the city. So Joab returned from the children of Ammon, and came to Jerusalem.

15 And when the Syrians saw that they were struck before Israel, they gathered themselves together.

16 And Hadarezer sent, and brought out the Syrians that were beyond the river: and they came to Helam; and Shobach the captain of the host of Hadarezer went before them.

17 And when it was told David, he gathered all Israel together, and passed over Jordan, and came to Helam. And the Syrians set themselves in array against David, and fought with him.

18 And the Syrians fled before Israel; and David killed the men of seven hundred chariots of the Syrians, and forty thousand of horsemen, and smote Shobach the captain of their host, who died there.

19 And when all the kings that were servants to Hadarezer saw that they were struck before Israel, they made peace with Israel, and served them. So the Syrians feared to help the children of Ammon any more.

2 Sam 11:1 And it came to pass, at the return of the year, at the time when kings go forth to battle, that David sent Joab, and his servants with him, and all Israel; and they destroyed the children of Ammon, and besieged Rabbah. But David tarried still at Jerusalem.

2 And it came to pass in an eveningtide, that David arose from off his bed, and walked upon the roof of the king's house: and from the roof he saw a woman washing herself; and the woman was very beautiful to look upon.

3 And David sent and inquired after the woman. And one said, Is not this Bathsheba, the daughter of Eliam, the wife of Uriah the Hittite?

4 And David sent messengers, and took her; and she came in unto him, and he lay with her; for she was purified from her uncleanness: and she returned unto her house.

5 And the woman conceived, and sent and told David, and said, I am with child.

6 And David sent to Joab, saying, Send me Uriah the Hittite. And Joab sent Uriah to David.

7 And when Uriah was come unto him, David demanded of him how Joab did, and how the people did, and how the war prospered.

8 And David said to Uriah, Go down to your house, and wash your feet. And Uriah departed out of the king's house, and there followed him a mess of food from the king.

9 But Uriah slept at the door of the king's house with all the servants of his lords, and went not down to his house.

10 And when they had told David, saying, Uriah went not down unto his house, David said unto Uriah, came you not from your journey? why then did you not go down unto your house?

11 And Uriah said unto David, The ark, and Israel, and Judah, abide in tents; and my lord Joab, and the servants of my lord, are encamped in the open fields; shall I then go into mine house, to eat and to drink, and to lie with my wife? as you live, and as your soul lives, I will not do this thing.

12 And David said to Uriah, Tarry here today also, and tomorrow I will let you depart. So Uriah abode in Jerusalem that day, and the morrow.

13 And when David had called him, he did eat and drink before him; and he made him drunk: and at evening he went out to lie on his bed with the servants of his lords, but went not down to his house.

14 And it came to pass in the morning, that David wrote a letter to Joab, and sent it by the hand of Uriah.

15 And he wrote in the letter, saying, Set you Uriah in the forefront of the hot battle, and retire you from him, that he may be struck, and die.

16 And it came to pass, when Joab observed the city, that he assigned Uriah unto a place where he knew that valiant men were.

17 And the men of the city went out, and fought with Joab: and there fell some of the people of the servants of David; and Uriah the Hittite died also.

18 Then Joab sent and told David all the things concerning the war;

19 And charged the messenger, saying, When you have made an end of telling the matters of the war unto the king,

20 And if so be that the king's wrath arise, and he say unto you, Why approached you so near unto the city when you did fight? knew you not that they would shoot from the wall?

21 Who smote Abimelech the son of Jerubbesheth? did not a woman cast a piece of a millstone upon him from the wall, that he died in Thebez? why went you near the wall? then say you, your servant Uriah the Hittite is dead also.

22 So the messenger went, and came and showed David all that Joab had sent him for.

23 And the messenger said unto David, Surely the men prevailed against us, and came out unto us into the field, and we were upon them even unto the entering of the gate.

24 And the shooters shot from off the wall upon your servants; and some of the king's servants be dead, and your servant Uriah the Hittite is dead also.

25 Then David said unto the messenger, Thus shall you say unto Joab, Let not this thing displease you, for the sword devours one as well as another: make your battle more strong against the city, and overthrow it: and encourage you him.

26 And when the wife of Uriah heard that Uriah her husband was dead, she mourned for her husband.

27 And when the mourning was past, David sent and fetched her to his house, and she became his wife, and bare him a son. But the thing that David had done displeased the Becoming-One.

2 Sam 12:1 And the Becoming-One sent Nathan unto David. And he came unto him, and said unto him, There were two men in one city; the one rich, and the other poor.

2 The rich man had exceeding many flocks and herds:

3 But the poor man had nothing, save one little ewe lamb, which he had bought and nourished up: and it grew up together with him, and with his children; it did eat of his own food, and drank of his own cup, and lay in his bosom, and was unto him as a daughter.

4 And there came a traveller unto the rich man, and he spared to take of his own flock and of his own herd, to dress for the wayfaring man that was come unto him; but took the poor man's lamb, and dressed it for the man that was come to him.

5 And David's anger was greatly kindled against the man; and he said to Nathan, As the Becoming-One lives, the man that has done this thing shall be a son of death:

6 And he shall restore the lamb fourfold, because he did this thing, and because he had no pity.

7 And Nathan said to David, you are the man. Thus says the Becoming-One, God of Israel, I anointed you king over Israel, and I delivered you out of the hand of Saul;

8 And I gave you your master's house, and your master's wives into your bosom, and gave you the house of Israel and of Judah; and if that had been too little, I would moreover have given unto you such and such things.

9 Therefore have you despised the commandment of the Becoming-One, to do evil in his sight? you have killed Uriah the Hittite with the sword, and have taken his wife to be your wife, and have slain him with the sword of the children of Ammon.

10 Now therefore the sword shall not for olam depart from your house; because you have despised me, and have taken the wife of Uriah the Hittite to be your wife.

11 Thus says the Becoming-One, Behold, I will raise up evil against you out of your own house, and I will take your wives before your eyes, and give them unto your neighbor, and he shall lie with your wives in the sight of this sun.

12 For you did it secretly: but I will do this thing before all Israel, and before the sun.

13 And David said unto Nathan, I have sinned against the Becoming-One. And Nathan said unto David, The Becoming-One also has put away your sin; you shall not die.

14 Howbeit, because by this deed you have given great occasion to the enemies of the Becoming-One to blaspheme, the child also that is born unto you, in dying, he will die.

15 And Nathan departed unto his house. And the Becoming-One struck the child that Uriah's wife bare unto David, and it was very sick.

16 David therefore besought God for the child; and David fasted, and went in, and lay all night upon the earth.

17 And the elders of his house arose, and went to him, to raise him up from the earth: but he would not, neither did he eat bread with them.

18 And it came to pass on the seventh day, that the child died. And the servants of David feared to tell him that the child was dead: for they said, Behold, while the child was yet alive, we spoke unto him, and he would not listen unto our voice: how will he then vex himself, if we tell him that the child is dead?

19 But when David saw that his servants whispered, David perceived that the child was dead: therefore David said unto his servants, Is the child dead? And they said, He is dead.

20 Then David arose from the earth, and washed, and anointed himself, and changed his apparel, and came into the house of the Becoming-One, and worshiped: then he came to his own house; and when he required, they set bread before him, and he did eat.

21 Then said his servants unto him, What thing is this that you have done? you did fast and weep for the child, while it was alive; but when the child was dead, you did rise and eat bread.

22 And he said, While the child was yet alive, I fasted and wept: for I said, Who can tell whether Becoming-One will be gracious to me, that the child may live?

23 But now he is dead, why should I fast? can I bring him back again? I shall go to him, but he shall not return to me.

24 And David comforted Bathsheba his wife, and went in unto her, and lay with her: and she bare a son, and he called his name Solomon: and the Becoming-One loved him.

25 And he sent by the hand of Nathan the prophet; and he called his name Jedidiah [loved by Yehowah Becoming-One] because of the Becoming-One.

26 And Joab fought against Rabbah of the children of Ammon, and took the royal city.

27 And Joab sent messengers to David, and said, I have fought against Rabbah, and have taken the city of waters.

28 Now therefore gather the rest of the people together, and encamp against the city, and take it: lest I take the city, and it be called after my name.

29 And David gathered all the people together, and went to Rabbah, and fought against it, and took it.

30 And he took their king's crown from off his head, the weight whereof was a talent of gold with the precious stones: and it was set on David's head. And he brought forth the spoil of the city in great abundance.

31 And he brought forth the people that were therein, and put them under saws, and under harrows of iron, and under axes of iron, and made them pass through the brickkiln: and thus did he unto all the cities of the children of Ammon. So David and all the people returned unto Jerusalem.

2 Sam 13:1 And it came to pass after this, that Absalom the son of David had a fair sister, whose name was Tamar; and Amnon the son of David loved her.

2 And Amnon was so vexed, that he fell sick for his sister Tamar; for she was a virgin; and Amnon thought it hard for him to do anything to her.

3 But Amnon had a friend, whose name was Jonadab, the son of Shimeah David's brother: and Jonadab was a very subtle man.

4 And he said unto him, Why are you, being the king's son, lean from day to day? will you not tell me? And Amnon said unto him, I love Tamar, my brother Absalom's sister.

5 And Jonadab said unto him, Lay you down on your bed, and make yourself sick: and when your father comes to see you, say unto him, I pray you, let my sister Tamar come, and give me food, and dress the food in my sight, that I may see it, and eat it at her hand.

6 So Amnon lay down, and made himself sick: and when the king was come to see him, Amnon said unto the king, I pray you, let Tamar my sister come, and make me a couple of cakes in my sight, that I may eat at her hand.

7 Then David sent home to Tamar, saying, Go now to your brother Amnon's house, and dress him food.

8 So Tamar went to her brother Amnon's house; and he was laid down. And she took flour, and kneaded it, and made cakes in his sight, and did bake the cakes.

9 And she took a pan, and poured them out before him; but he refused to eat. And Amnon said, Have out all men from me. And they went out every man from him.

10 And Amnon said unto Tamar, Bring the food into the chamber, that I may eat of your hand. And Tamar took the cakes which she had made, and brought them into the chamber to Amnon her brother.

11 And when she had brought them unto him to eat, he took hold of her, and said unto her, Come lie with me, my sister.

12 And she answered him, Nay, my brother, do not force me; for no such thing ought to be done in Israel: do not you this folly.

13 And I, where shall I cause my shame to go? and as for you, you shall be as one of the fools in Israel. Now therefore, I pray you, speak unto the king; for he will not withhold me from you.

14 Howbeit he would not listen unto her voice: but, being stronger than she, forced her, and lay with her.

15 Then Amnon hated her exceedingly; so that the hatred wherewith he hated her was greater than the love wherewith he had loved her. And Amnon said unto her, Arise, be gone.

16 And she said unto him, There is no cause: this evil in sending me away is greater than the other that you did unto me. But he would not listen unto her.

17 Then he called his servant that ministered unto him, and said, Put now this woman out from me, and bolt the door after her.

18 And she had a garment of diverse colors upon her: for with such robes were the king's daughters that were virgins appareled. Then his servant brought her out, and bolted the door after her.

19 And Tamar put ashes on her head, and ripped her garment of diverse colors that was on her, and laid her hand on her head, and went on crying.

20 And Absalom her brother said unto her, has Amnon your brother been with you? but hold now your peace, my sister: he is your brother; regard not this thing. So Tamar remained desolate in her brother Absalom's house.

21 But when king David heard of all these things, he was very angry.

22 And Absalom spoke unto his brother Amnon neither good nor bad: for Absalom hated Amnon, because he had forced his sister Tamar.

23 And it came to pass after two full years, that Absalom had sheepshearers in Baal-Hazor, which is beside Ephraim: and Absalom invited all the king's sons.

24 And Absalom came to the king, and said, Behold now, your servant has sheepshearers; let the king, I beg you, and his servants go with your servant.

25 And the king said to Absalom, Nay, my son, let us not all now go, lest we be chargeable unto you. And he pressed him: howbeit he would not go, but blessed him.

26 Then said Absalom, If not, I pray you, let my brother Amnon go with us. And the king said unto him, Why should he go with you?

27 But Absalom pressed him, that he let Amnon and all the king's sons go with him.

28 Now Absalom had commanded his servants, saying, Mark you now when Amnon's heart is merry with wine, and when I say unto you, Smite Amnon;

then kill him, fear not: have not I commanded you? be courageous, and be valiant.

29 And the servants of Absalom did unto Amnon as Absalom had commanded. Then all the king's sons arose, and every man got him up upon his mule, and fled.

30 And it came to pass, while they were in the way, that tidings came to David, saying, Absalom has slain all the king's sons, and there is not one of them left.

31 Then the king arose, and tare his garments, and lay on the earth; and all his servants stood by with their clothes rent.

32 And Jonadab, the son of Shimeah David's brother, answered and said, Let not my lord suppose that they have slain all the young men the king's sons; for Amnon only is dead: for by the appointment of Absalom this has been determined from the day that he forced his sister Tamar.

33 Now therefore let not my lord the king take the thing to his heart, to think that all the king's sons are dead: for Amnon only is dead.

34 But Absalom fled. And the young man that kept the watch lifted up his eyes, and looked, and, behold, there came much people by the way of the hill side behind him.

35 And Jonadab said unto the king, Behold, the king's sons come: as your servant said, so it is.

36 And it came to pass, as soon as he had made an end of speaking, that, behold, the king's sons came, and lifted up their voice and wept: and the king also and all his servants wept very greatly.

37 But Absalom fled, and went to Talmai, the son of Ammihud, king of Geshur. And David mourned for his son every day.

38 So Absalom fled, and went to Geshur, and was there three years.

39 And the soul of king David longed to go forth unto Absalom: for he was comforted concerning Amnon, seeing he was dead.

2 Sam 14:1 Now Joab the son of Zeruiah perceived that the king's heart was toward Absalom.

2 And Joab sent to Tekoah, and fetched there a wise woman, and said unto her, I pray you, pretend yourself to be a mourner, and put on now mourning apparel, and anoint not yourself with oil, but be as a woman that had a long time mourned for the dead:

3 And come to the king, and speak on this manner unto him. So Joab put the words in her mouth.

4 And when the woman of Tekoah spoke to the king, she fell on her face to the ground, and did obeisance, and said, Help, O king.

5 And the king said unto her, What ails you? And she answered, I am indeed a widow woman, and mine husband is dead.

6 And your handmaid had two sons, and they two strove together in the field, and there was none to part them, but the one smote the other, and killed him.

7 And, behold, the whole family is risen against your handmaid, and they said, Deliver him that smote his brother, that we may kill him, for the soul of his brother whom he killed; and we will destroy the heir also: and so they shall quench my coal which is left, and shall not leave to my husband neither name nor remainder upon the earth.

8 And the king said unto the woman, Go to your house, and I will give charge concerning you.

9 And the woman of Tekoah said unto the king, My lord, O king, the iniquity be on me, and on my father's house: and the king and his throne be guiltless.

10 And the king said, Whosoever says anything unto you, bring him to me, and he shall not touch you any more.

11 Then said she, I pray you, let the king remember the Becoming-One your God, that you would not permit the revengers of blood to destroy any more, lest they destroy my son. And he said, As the Becoming-One lives, there shall not one hair of your son fall to the earth.

12 Then the woman said, Let your handmaid, I pray you, speak one word unto my lord the king. And he said, Say on.

13 And the woman said, Why then have you thought such a thing against the people of God? for the king does speak this thing as one which is faulty, in that the king does not fetch home again his banished.

14 For we must needs die, and are as water spilled on the ground, which cannot be gathered up again; neither does God respect any soul: yet does he devise means, that his banished be not expelled from him.

15 Now therefore that I am come to speak of this thing unto my lord the king, it is because the people have made me afraid: and your handmaid said, I will now speak unto the king; it may be that the king will perform the request of his handmaid.

16 For the king will hear, to deliver his handmaid out of the hand of the man that would destroy me and my son together out of the inheritance of God.

17 Then your handmaid said, The word of my lord the king shall now be comfortable: for as an angel of God, so is my lord the king to discern good and bad: therefore the Becoming-One your God will be with you.

18 Then the king answered and said unto the woman, Hide not from me, I pray you, the thing that I shall ask you. And the woman said, Let my lord the king now speak.

19 And the king said, Is not the hand of Joab with you in all this? And the woman answered and said, As your soul lives, my lord the king, none can turn to the right hand or to the left from anything that my lord the king has spoken: for your servant Joab, he bade me, and he put all these words in the mouth of your handmaid:

20 To fetch about this form of speech has your servant Joab done this thing: and my lord is wise, according to the wisdom of an angel of God, to know all things that are in the earth.

21 And the king said unto Joab, Behold now, I have done this thing: go therefore, bring the young man Absalom again.

22 And Joab fell to the ground on his face, and bowed himself, and thanked the king: and Joab said, Today your servant knows that I have found grace in your sight, my lord, O king, in that the king has fulfilled the request of his servant.

23 So Joab arose and went to Geshur, and brought Absalom to Jerusalem.

24 And the king said, Let him turn to his own house, and let him not see my face. So Absalom returned to his own house, and saw not the king's face.

25 But in all Israel there was none to be so much praised as Absalom for his beauty: from the sole of his foot even to the crown of his head there was no blemish in him.

26 And when he polled his head, for it was at end of days of days that he polled it: because the hair was heavy on him, therefore he polled it: he weighed the hair of his head at two hundred shekels after the king's weight.

27 And unto Absalom there were born three sons, and one daughter, whose name was Tamar: she was a woman of a fair countenance.

28 So Absalom dwelt two full years in Jerusalem, and saw not the king's face.

29 Therefore Absalom sent for Joab, to have sent him to the king; but he would not come to him: and when he sent again the second time, he would not come.

30 Therefore he said unto his servants, See, Joab's field is near mine, and he has barley there; go and set it on fire. And Absalom's servants set the field on fire.

31 Then Joab arose, and came to Absalom unto his house, and said unto him, Why have your servants set my field on fire?

32 And Absalom answered Joab, Behold, I sent unto you, saying, Come here, that I may send you to the king, to say, Why am I come from Geshur? it had been good for me to have been there still: now therefore let me see the king's face; and if there be any iniquity in me, let him kill me.

33 So Joab came to the king, and told him: and when he had called for Absalom, he came to the king, and bowed himself on his face to the ground before the king: and the king kissed Absalom.

2 Sam 15:1 And it came to pass after this, that Absalom prepared him chariots and horses, and fifty men to run before him.

2 And Absalom rose up early, and stood beside the way of the gate: and it was so, that when any man that had a controversy came to the king for judgment, then Absalom called unto him, and said, Of what city are you? And he said, your servant is of one of the tribes of Israel.

3 And Absalom said unto him, See, your matters are good and right; but there is no man deputed of the king to hear you.

4 Absalom said moreover, Oh that I were made judge in the land, that every man which has any suit or cause might come unto me, and I would do him justice!

5 And it was so, that when any man came near to him to do him obeisance, he put forth his hand, and took him, and kissed him.

6 And on this manner did Absalom to all Israel that came to the king for judgment: so Absalom stole the hearts of the men of Israel.

7 And it came to pass after forty years, that Absalom said unto the king, I pray you, let me go and pay my vow, which I have vowed unto the Becoming-One, in Hebron.

8 For your servant vowed a vow while I abode at Geshur in Syria, saying, If the Becoming-One shall bring me again indeed to Jerusalem, then I will serve the Becoming-One.

9 And the king said unto him, Go in peace. So he arose, and went to Hebron.

10 But Absalom sent spies throughout all the tribes of Israel, saying, As soon as you hear the sound of the trumpet, then you shall say, Absalom reigns in Hebron.

11 And with Absalom went two hundred men out of Jerusalem, that were called; and they went in their simplicity, and they knew not anything.

12 And Absalom sent for Ahithophel the Gilonite, David's counselor, from his city, even from Giloh, while he offered sacrifices. And the conspiracy was strong; for the people increased continually with Absalom.

13 And there came a messenger to David, saying, The hearts of the men of Israel are after Absalom.

14 And David said unto all his servants that were with him at Jerusalem, Arise, and let us flee; for we shall not else escape from Absalom: make speed to depart, lest he overtake us suddenly, and bring evil upon us, and smite the city with the edge of the sword.

15 And the king's servants said unto the king, Behold, your servants are ready to do whatsoever my lord the king shall appoint.

16 And the king went forth, and all his household after him. And the king left ten women, which were concubines, to keep the house.

17 And the king went forth, and all the people after him, and tarried in a place that was far off.

18 And all his servants passed on beside him; and all the Cherethites, and all the Pelethites, and all the Gittites, six hundred men which came after him from Gath, passed on before the king.

19 Then said the king to Ittai the Gittite, Therefore go you also with us? return to your place, and abide with the king: for you are a stranger, and also an exile.

20 Whereas you came but yesterday, should I this day make you go up and down with us? seeing I go to where I may, return you, and take back your brethren: mercy and truth be with you.

21 And Ittai answered the king, and said, As the Becoming-One lives, and as my lord the king lives, surely in what place my lord the king shall be, whether in death or life, even there also will your servant be.

22 And David said to Ittai, Go and pass over. And Ittai the Gittite passed over, and all his men, and all the little ones that were with him.

23 And all the country wept with a loud voice, and all the people passed over: the king also himself passed over the brook Kidron, and all the people passed over, toward the way of the wilderness.

24 And lo Zadok also, and all the Levites were with him, bearing the ark of the covenant of God: and they set down the ark of God; and Abiathar went up, until all the people had done passing out of the city.

25 And the king said unto Zadok, Carry back the ark of God into the city: if I shall find favor in the eyes

of the Becoming-One, he will bring me again, and show me both it, and his habitation:

26 But if he thus say, I have no delight in you; behold, here I am, let him do to me as seems good unto him.

27 The king said also unto Zadok the priest, are not you a seer? return into the city in peace, and your two sons with you, Ahimaaz your son, and Jonathan the son of Abiathar.

28 See, I will tarry in the plain of the wilderness, until there come word from you to certify me.

29 Zadok therefore and Abiathar carried the ark of God again to Jerusalem: and they tarried there.

30 And David went up by the ascent of mount Olivet, and wept as he went up, and had his head covered, and he went barefoot: and all the people that was with him covered every man his head, and they went up, weeping as they went up.

31 And one told David, saying, Ahithophel is among the conspirators with Absalom. And David said, O Becoming-One, I pray you, turn the counsel of Ahithophel into foolishness.

32 And it came to pass, that when David was come to the top of the mount, where he worshiped God, behold, Hushai the Archite came to meet him with his coat rent, and earth upon his head:

33 Unto whom David said, If you pass on with me, then you shall be a burden unto me:

34 But if you return to the city, and say unto Absalom, I will be your servant, O king; as I have been your father's servant hitherto, so will I now also be your servant: then may you for me defeat the counsel of Ahithophel.

35 And have you not there with you Zadok and Abiathar the priests? therefore it shall be, that what thing soever you shall hear out of the king's house, you shall tell it to Zadok and Abiathar the priests.

36 Behold, they have there with them their two sons, Ahimaaz Zadok's son, and Jonathan Abiathar's son; and by them you shall send unto me every thing that you can hear.

37 So Hushai David's friend came into the city, and Absalom came into Jerusalem.

2 Sam 16:1 And when David was a little past the top of the hill, behold, Ziba the servant of Mephibosheth met him, with a couple of donkeys saddled, and upon them two hundred loaves of bread, and a hundred bunches of raisins, and a hundred of summer fruits, and a bottle of wine.

2 And the king said unto Ziba, What do you mean by these? And Ziba said, The donkeys be for the king's household to ride on; and the bread and summer fruit for the young men to eat; and the wine, that such as be faint in the wilderness may drink.

3 And the king said, And where is your master's son? And Ziba said unto the king, Behold, he abides at Jerusalem: for he said, Today shall the house of Israel restore me the kingdom of my father.

4 Then said the king to Ziba, Behold, you are all that pertained unto Mephibosheth. And Ziba said, I humbly beg you that I may find grace in your sight, my lord, O king.

5 And when king David came to Bahurim, behold, there came out a man of the family of the house of Saul, whose name was Shimei, the son of Gera: he came forth, and cursed still as he came.

6 And he cast stones at David, and at all the servants of king David: and all the people and all the mighty men were on his right hand and on his left.

7 And thus said Shimei when he cursed, Come out, come out, you bloody man, and you man of Belial:

8 The Becoming-One has returned upon you all the blood of the house of Saul, in whose stead you have reigned; and the Becoming-One has delivered the kingdom into the hand of Absalom your son: and, behold, you are taken in your mischief, because you are a bloody man.

9 Then said Abishai the son of Zeruiah unto the king, Why should this dead dog curse my lord the king? let me go over, I pray you, and take off his head.

10 And the king said, What have I to do with you, you sons of Zeruiah? so let him curse, because the Becoming-One has said unto him, Curse David. Who shall then say, Why have you done so?

11 And David said to Abishai, and to all his servants, Behold, my son, which came forth of my bowels, seeks my soul: how much more now may this Benjamite do it? let him alone, and let him curse; for the Becoming-One has bidden him.

12 It may be that the Becoming-One will look on mine affliction, and that the Becoming-One will return me good for his cursing this day.

13 And as David and his men went by the way, Shimei went along on the hill's side over against him, and cursed as he went, and threw stones at him, and cast dust.

14 And the king, and all the people that were with him, came weary, and refreshed themselves there.

15 And Absalom, and all the people the men of Israel, came to Jerusalem, and Ahithophel with him.

16 And it came to pass, when Hushai the Archite, David's friend, was come unto Absalom, that Hushai said unto Absalom, Let the king live, Let the king live.

17 And Absalom said to Hushai, Is this your kindness to your friend? why went you not with your friend?

18 And Hushai said unto Absalom, Nay; but whom the Becoming-One, and this people, and all the men of Israel, choose, his will I be, and with him will I abide.

19 And again, whom should I serve? should I not serve in the presence of his son? as I have served in your father's presence, so will I be in your presence.

20 Then said Absalom to Ahithophel, Give counsel among you what we shall do.

21 And Ahithophel said unto Absalom, Go in unto your father's concubines, which he has left to keep the house; and all Israel shall hear that you are abhorred of your father: then shall the hands of all that are with you be strong.

22 So they spread Absalom a tent upon the top of the house; and Absalom went in unto his father's concubines in the sight of all Israel.

23 And the counsel of Ahithophel, which he counselled in those days, was as if a man had inquired at the oracle of God: so was all the counsel of Ahithophel both with David and with Absalom.

2 Sam 17:1 Moreover Ahithophel said unto Absalom, Let me now choose out twelve thousand of men, and I will arise and pursue after David this night:

2 And I will come upon him while he is weary and weak handed, and will make him afraid: and all the people that are with him shall flee; and I will smite the king only:

3 And I will bring back all the people unto you: the man whom you seek is as if all returned: so all the people shall be in peace.

4 And the saying pleased Absalom well, and all the elders of Israel.

5 Then said Absalom, Call now Hushai the Archite also, and let us hear likewise what he said.

6 And when Hushai was come to Absalom, Absalom spoke unto him, saying, Ahithophel has spoken after this manner: shall we do after his saying? if not; speak you.

7 And Hushai said unto Absalom, The counsel that Ahithophel has given is not good at this time.

8 For, said Hushai, you know your father and his men, that they be mighty men, and they be chafed in their bitterness of soul, as a bear robbed of her whelps in the field: and your father is a man of war, and will not lodge with the people.

9 Behold, he is hid now in some pit, or in some other place: and it will come to pass, when some of them be overthrown at the first, that whosoever hears it will say, There is a slaughter among the people that follow Absalom.

10 And he also that is valiant, whose heart is as the heart of a lion, shall utterly melt: for all Israel knows that your father is a mighty man, and they which be with him are valiant men.

11 Therefore I counsel that all Israel be generally gathered unto you, from Dan even to Beersheba, as the sand that is by the sea for multitude; and that you go to battle in your own person.

12 So shall we come upon him in some place where he shall be found, and we will light upon him as the dew falls on the ground: and of him and of all the men that are with him there shall not be left so much as one.

13 Moreover, if he be gotten into a city, then shall all Israel bring ropes to that city, and we will draw it into the river, until there be not one small stone found there.

14 And Absalom and all the men of Israel said, The counsel of Hushai the Archite is better than the counsel of Ahithophel. For the Becoming-One had appointed to defeat the good counsel of Ahithophel, to the intent that the Becoming-One might bring evil upon Absalom.

15 Then said Hushai unto Zadok and to Abiathar the priests, Thus and thus did Ahithophel counsel Absalom and the elders of Israel; and thus and thus have I counselled.

16 Now therefore send quickly, and tell David, saying, Lodge not this night in the plains of the wilderness, but speedily pass over; lest the king be swallowed up, and all the people that are with him.

17 Now Jonathan and Ahimaaz stayed by Enrogel; for they might not be seen to come into the city: and a wench went and told them; and they went and told king David.

18 Nevertheless a lad saw them, and told Absalom: but they went both of them away quickly, and came to a man's house in Bahurim, which had a well in his court; to which they went down.

19 And the woman took and spread a covering over the well's mouth, and spread ground grain thereon; and the thing was not known.

20 And when Absalom's servants came to the woman to the house, they said, Where is Ahimaaz and Jonathan? And the woman said unto them, They be gone over the brook of water. And when they had sought and could not find them, they returned to Jerusalem.

21 And it came to pass, after they were departed, that they came up out of the well, and went and told king David, and said unto David, Arise, and pass quickly over the water: for thus has Ahithophel counselled against you.

22 Then David arose, and all the people that were with him, and they passed over Jordan: by the morning light there lacked not one of them that was not gone over Jordan.

23 And when Ahithophel saw that his counsel was not followed, he saddled his donkey, and arose, and got him home to his house, to his city, and put his household in order, and hanged himself, and died, and was buried in the tomb of his father.

24 Then David came to Mahanaim. And Absalom passed over Jordan, he and all the men of Israel with him.

25 And Absalom made Amasa captain of the host instead of Joab: which Amasa was a man's son, whose name was Ithra an Israelite, that went in to Abigail the daughter of Nahash, sister to Zeruiah Joab's mother.

26 So Israel and Absalom pitched in the land of Gilead.

27 And it came to pass, when David was come to Mahanaim, that Shobi the son of Nahash of Rabbah of the children of Ammon, and Machir the son of Ammiel of Lodebar, and Barzillai the Gileadite of Rogelim,

28 Brought beds, and basins, and earthen vessels, and wheat, and barley, and flour, and parched grain, and beans, and lentiles, and parched pulse,

29 And honey, and butter, and sheep, and cheese of cows, for David, and for the people that were with him, to eat: for they said, The people is hungry, and weary, and thirsty, in the wilderness.

2 Sam 18:1 And David numbered the people that were with him, and set captains of thousands and captains of hundreds over them.

2 And David sent forth a third part of the people under the hand of Joab, and a third part under the hand of Abishai the son of Zeruiah, Joab's brother, and a third part under the hand of Ittai the Gittite. And the king said unto the people, I will surely go forth with you myself also.

3 But the people answered, you shall not go forth: for if we flee away, they will not care for us; neither if half of us die, will they care for us: but now you are worth ten thousand of us: therefore now it is better that you succour us out of the city.

4 And the king said unto them, What seems you best I will do. And the king stood by the gate side, and

all the people came out by hundreds and by thousands.

5 And the king commanded Joab and Abishai and Ittai, saying, Deal gently for my sake with the young man, even with Absalom. And all the people heard when the king gave all the captains charge concerning Absalom.

6 So the people went out into the field against Israel: and the battle was in the wood of Ephraim;

7 Where the people of Israel were slain before the servants of David, and there was there a great slaughter that day of twenty thousand men.

8 For the battle was there scattered over the face of all the country: and the wood devoured more people that day than the sword devoured.

9 And Absalom met the servants of David. And Absalom rode upon a mule, and the mule went under the thick boughs of a great oak, and his head caught hold of the oak, and he was taken up between the heavens and the earth; and the mule that was under him went away.

10 And a certain man saw it, and told Joab, and said, Behold, I saw Absalom hanged in an oak.

11 And Joab said unto the man that told him, And, behold, you saw him, and why did you not smite him there to the ground? And I would have given you ten shekels of silver, and a girdle.

12 And the man said unto Joab, Though I should receive a thousand shekels of silver in mine hand, yet would I not put forth mine hand against the king's son: for in our hearing the king charged you and Abishai and Ittai, saying, Beware that none touch the young man Absalom.

13 Otherwise I should have worked falsehood against mine own soul: for there is no matter hid from the king, and you yourself would have set yourself against me.

14 Then said Joab, I may not tarry thus with you. And he took three darts in his hand, and thrust them through the heart of Absalom, while he was yet alive in the midst of the oak.

15 And ten young men that bare Joab's armor compassed about and smote Absalom, and killed him.

16 And Joab blew the trumpet, and the people returned from pursuing after Israel: for Joab held back the people.

17 And they took Absalom, and cast him into a great pit in the wood, and laid a very great heap of stones upon him: and all Israel fled every one to his tent.

18 Now Absalom in his lifetime had taken and reared up for himself a pillar, which is in the king's dale: for he said, I have no son to keep my name in remembrance: and he called the pillar after his own name: and it is called unto this day, Absalom's place.

19 Then said Ahimaaz the son of Zadok, Let me now run, and bear the king tidings, how that the Becoming-One has avenged him of his enemies.

20 And Joab said unto him, you shall not bear tidings this day, but you shall bear tidings another day: but this day you shall bear no tidings, because the king's son is dead.

21 Then said Joab to Cushi, Go tell the king what you have seen. And Cushi bowed himself unto Joab, and ran.

22 Then said Ahimaaz the son of Zadok yet again to Joab, But howsoever, let me, I pray you, also run after Cushi. And Joab said, Why will you run, my son, seeing that you have no tidings ready?

23 But howsoever, said he, let me run. And he said unto him, Run. Then Ahimaaz ran by the way of the plain, and overran Cushi.

24 And David sat between the two gates: and the watchman went up to the roof over the gate unto the wall, and lifted up his eyes, and looked, and behold a man running alone.

25 And the watchman cried, and told the king. And the king said, If he be alone, there is tidings in his mouth. And he came apace, and drew near.

26 And the watchman saw another man running: and the watchman called unto the gatekeeper, and said, Behold another man running alone. And the king said, He also brings tidings.

27 And the watchman said, Me thinks the running of the foremost is like the running of Ahimaaz the son of Zadok. And the king said, He is a good man, and comes with good tidings.

28 And Ahimaaz called, and said unto the king, All is well. And he fell down to the earth upon his face before the king, and said, Blessed be the Becoming-One your God, which has delivered up the men that lifted up their hand against my lord the king.

29 And the king said, Is the young man Absalom safe? And Ahimaaz answered, When Joab sent the king's servant, and me your servant, I saw a great tumult, but I knew not what it was.

30 And the king said unto him, Turn aside, and stand here. And he turned aside, and stood still.

31 And, behold, Cushi came; and Cushi said, Tidings, my lord the king: for the Becoming-One has avenged you this day of all them that rose up against you.

32 And the king said unto Cushi, Is the young man Absalom safe? And Cushi answered, The enemies of my lord the king, and all that rise against you to do you hurt, be as that young man is.

33 And the king was much moved, and went up to the chamber over the gate, and wept: and as he went, thus he said, O my son Absalom, my son, my son Absalom! would God I had died for you, O Absalom, my son, my son!

2 Sam 19:1 And it was told Joab, Behold, the king weeps and mourns for Absalom.

2 And the victory that day was turned into mourning unto all the people: for the people heard say that day how the king was grieved for his son.

3 And the people got them by sneaking that day into the city, as people being ashamed steal away when they flee in battle.

4 But the king covered his face, and the king cried with a loud voice, O my son Absalom, O Absalom, my son, my son!

5 And Joab came into the house to the king, and said, you have shamed this day the faces of all your servants, which this day have saved your soul, and the souls of your sons and of your daughters, and the souls of your wives, and the souls of your concubines;

6 In that you love your enemies, and hate your friends. For you have declared this day, that you regard neither princes nor servants: for this day I

perceive, that if Absalom had lived, and all we had died this day, then it had pleased you well.

7 Now therefore arise, go forth, and speak comfortably unto your servants: for I swear by the Becoming-One, if you go not forth, there will not tarry one with you this night: and that will be worse unto you than all the evil that befell you from your youth until now.

8 Then the king arose, and sat in the gate. And they told unto all the people, saying, Behold, the king does sit in the gate. And all the people came before the king: for Israel had fled every man to his tent.

9 And all the people were at strife throughout all the tribes of Israel, saying, The king saved us out of the hand of our enemies, and he delivered us out of the hand of the Philistines; and now he is fled out of the land for Absalom.

10 And Absalom, whom we anointed over us, is dead in battle. Now therefore why speak you not a word of bringing the king back?

11 And king David sent to Zadok and to Abiathar the priests, saying, Speak unto the elders of Judah, saying, Why are you the last to bring the king back to his house? seeing the speech of all Israel is come to the king, even to his house.

12 you are my brethren, you are my bones and my flesh: why then are you the last to bring back the king?

13 And say you to Amasa, are you not of my bone, and of my flesh? God do so to me, and more also, if you be not captain of the host before me continually in the room of Joab.

14 And he bowed the heart of all the men of Judah, even as the heart of one man; so that they sent this word unto the king, Return you, and all your servants.

15 So the king returned, and came to Jordan. And Judah came to Gilgal, to go to meet the king, to conduct the king over Jordan.

16 And Shimei the son of Gera, a Benjamite, which was of Bahurim, hasted and came down with the men of Judah to meet king David.

17 And there were a thousand men of Benjamin with him, and Ziba the servant of the house of Saul, and his fifteen sons and his twenty servants with him; and they went over Jordan before the king.

18 And there went over a ferry boat to carry over the king's household, and to do what he thought good. And Shimei the son of Gera fell down before the king, as he was come over Jordan;

19 And said unto the king, Let not my lord impute iniquity unto me, neither do you remember that which your servant did perversely the day that my lord the king went out of Jerusalem, that the king should take it to his heart.

20 For your servant does know that I have sinned: therefore, behold, I am come the first this day of all the house of Joseph to go down to meet my lord the king.

21 But Abishai the son of Zeruiah answered and said, Shall not Shimei be put to death for this, because he cursed the Becoming-One's anointed?

22 And David said, What have I to do with you, you sons of Zeruiah, that you should this day be adversaries unto me? shall there any man be put to death this day in Israel? for do not I know that I am this day king over Israel?

23 Therefore the king said unto Shimei, you shall not die. And the king swore unto him.

24 And Mephibosheth the son of Saul came down to meet the king, and had neither dressed his feet, nor trimmed his beard, nor washed his clothes, from the day the king departed until the day he came again in peace.

25 And it came to pass, when he was come to Jerusalem to meet the king, that the king said unto him, Why went not you with me, Mephibosheth?

26 And he answered, My lord, O king, my servant deceived me: for your servant said, I will saddle me an donkey, that I may ride thereon, and go to the king; because your servant is lame.

27 And he has slandered your servant unto my lord the king; but my lord the king is as an angel of God: do therefore what is good in your eyes.

28 For all of my father's house were but dead men before my lord the king: yet did you set your servant among them that did eat at your own table. What right therefore have I yet to cry any more unto the king?

29 And the king said unto him, Why speak you any more of your matters? I have said, you and Ziba divide the land.

30 And Mephibosheth said unto the king, Yes, let him take all, forasmuch as my lord the king is come again in peace unto his own house.

31 And Barzillai the Gileadite came down from Rogelim, and went over Jordan with the king, to conduct him over Jordan.

32 Now Barzillai was a very aged man, even a son of fourscore years: and he had provided the king of sustenance while he lay at Mahanaim; for he was a very great man.

33 And the king said unto Barzillai, You come over with me, and I will feed you with me in Jerusalem.

34 And Barzillai said unto the king, How long have I to live, that I should go up with the king unto Jerusalem?

35 I am this day a son of fourscore years: and can I discern between good and evil? can your servant taste what I eat or what I drink? can I hear any more the voice of singing men and singing women? why then should your servant be yet a burden unto my lord the king?

36 your servant will go a little way over Jordan with the king: and why should the king recompense it me with such a reward?

37 Let your servant, I pray you, turn back again, that I may die in mine own city, and be buried by the grave of my father and of my mother. But behold your servant Chimham; let him go over with my lord the king; and do to him what shall seem good unto you.

38 And the king answered, Chimham shall go over with me, and I will do to him that which shall seem good unto you: and whatsoever you shall require of me, that will I do for you.

39 And all the people went over Jordan. And when the king was come over, the king kissed Barzillai, and blessed him; and he returned unto his own place.

40 Then the king went on to Gilgal, and Chimham went on with him: and all the people of Judah conducted the king, and also half the people of Israel.

41 And, behold, all the men of Israel came to the king, and said unto the king, Why have our brethren the men of Judah stolen you away, and have brought the king, and his household, and all David's men with him, over Jordan?

42 And all the men of Judah answered the men of Israel, Because the king is near of kin to us: why then be you angry for this matter? have we eaten at all of the king's cost? or has he given us any gift?

43 And the men of Israel answered the men of Judah, and said, We have ten parts in the king, and we have also more right in David than you: why then did you despise us, that our advice should not be first had in bringing back our king? And the words of the men of Judah were fiercer than the words of the men of Israel.

2 Sam 20:1 And there happened to be there a man of Belial, whose name was Sheba, the son of Bichri, a Benjamite: and he blew a trumpet, and said, We have no part in David, neither have we inheritance in the son of Jesse: every man to his tents, O Israel.

2 So every man of Israel went up from after David, and followed Sheba the son of Bichri: but the men of Judah clave unto their king, from Jordan even to Jerusalem.

3 And David came to his house at Jerusalem; and the king took the ten women his concubines, whom he had left to keep the house, and put them in ward, and fed them, but went not in unto them. So they were shut up unto the day of their death, living in widowhood.

4 Then said the king to Amasa, Assemble me the men of Judah within three days, and be you here present.

5 So Amasa went to assemble the men of Judah: but he tarried longer than the set time which he had appointed him.

6 And David said to Abishai, Now shall Sheba the son of Bichri do us more harm than did Absalom: take you thy lords' servants, and pursue after him, lest he get him fenced cities, and escape us.

7 And there went out after him Joab's men, and the Cherethites, and the Pelethites, and all the mighty men: and they went out of Jerusalem, to pursue after Sheba the son of Bichri.

8 When they were at the great stone which is in Gibeon, Amasa went before them. And Joab's garment that he had put on was girded unto him, and upon it a girdle with a sword fastened upon his loins in the sheath thereof; and as he went forth it fell out.

9 And Joab said to Amasa, are you in health, my brother? And Joab took Amasa by the beard with the right hand to kiss him.

10 But Amasa took no heed to the sword that was in Joab's hand: so he smote him therewith in the fifth rib, and shed out his bowels to the ground, and struck him not again; and he died. So Joab and Abishai his brother pursued after Sheba the son of Bichri.

11 And one of Joab's men stood by him, and said, He that favors Joab, and he that is for David, let him go after Joab.

12 And Amasa wallowed in blood in the midst of the highway. And when the man saw that all the people stood still, he removed Amasa out of the highway into the field, and cast a cloth upon him, when he saw that every one that came by him stood still.

13 When he was removed out of the highway, all the people went on after Joab, to pursue after Sheba the son of Bichri.

14 And he went through all the tribes of Israel unto Abel, and to Beth-maachah, and all the Berites: and they were gathered together, and went also after him.

15 And they came and besieged him in Abel of Beth-maachah, and they cast up a bank against the city, and it stood in the trench: and all the people that were with Joab battered the wall, to throw it down.

16 Then cried a wise woman out of the city, Hear, hear; say, I pray you, unto Joab, Come near here, that I may speak with you.

17 And when he was come near unto her, the woman said, are you Joab? And he answered, I am he. Then she said unto him, Hear the words of your handmaid. And he answered, I do hear.

18 Then she spoke, saying, They were wont to speak in old time, saying, They shall surely ask counsel at Abel: and so they ended the matter.

19 I am one of them that are peaceable and faithful in Israel: you seek to destroy a city and a mother in Israel: why will you swallow up the inheritance of the Becoming-One?

20 And Joab answered and said, Far be it, far be it from me, that I should swallow up or destroy.

21 The matter is not so: but a man of mount Ephraim, Sheba the son of Bichri by name, has lifted up his hand against the king, even against David: deliver him only, and I will depart from the city. And the woman said unto Joab, Behold, his head shall be thrown to you over the wall.

22 Then the woman went unto all the people in her wisdom. And they cut off the head of Sheba the son of Bichri, and cast it out to Joab. And he blew a trumpet, and they retired from the city, every man to his tent. And Joab returned to Jerusalem unto the king.

23 Now Joab was over all the host of Israel: and Benaiah the son of Jehoiada was over the Cherethites and over the Pelethites:

24 And Adoram was over the tribute: and Jehoshaphat the son of Ahilud was recorder:

25 And Sheva was scribe: and Zadok and Abiathar were the priests:

26 And Ira also the Jairite was a chief ruler about David.

2 Sam 21:1 Then there was a famine in the days of David three years, year after year; and David inquired of the Becoming-One. And the Becoming-One answered, It is for Saul, and for his bloody house, because he killed the Gibeonites.

2 And the king called the Gibeonites, and said unto them; now the Gibeonites were not of the children of Israel, but of the remnant of the Amorites;

and the children of Israel had sworn unto them: and Saul sought to slay them in his zeal to the children of Israel and Judah.

3 Therefore David said unto the Gibeonites, What shall I do for you? and wherewith shall I make the atonement, that you may bless the inheritance of the Becoming-One?

4 And the Gibeonites said unto him, We will have no silver nor gold of Saul, nor of his house; neither for us shall you kill any man in Israel. And he said, What you shall say, that will I do for you.

5 And they answered the king, The man that consumed us, and that devised against us that we should be destroyed from remaining in any of the coasts of Israel,

6 Let seven men of his sons be delivered unto us, and we will hang them up unto the Becoming-One in Gibeah of Saul, whom the Becoming-One did choose. And the king said, I will give them.

7 But the king spared Mephibosheth, the son of Jonathan the son of Saul, because of the Becoming-One's oath that was between them, between David and Jonathan the son of Saul.

8 But the king took the two sons of Rizpah the daughter of Aiah, whom she bare unto Saul, Armoni and Mephibosheth; and the five sons of Michal the daughter of Saul, whom she brought up for Adriel the son of Barzillai the Meholathite:

9 And he delivered them into the hands of the Gibeonites, and they hanged them in the hill before the Becoming-One: and they fell all seven together, and were put to death in the days of harvest, in the first days, in the beginning of barley harvest.

10 And Rizpah the daughter of Aiah took sackcloth, and spread it for her upon the rock, from the beginning of harvest until water dropped upon them out of heaven, and permitted neither the birds of the air to rest on them by day, nor the beasts of the field by night.

11 And it was told David what Rizpah the daughter of Aiah, the concubine of Saul, had done.

12 And David went and took the bones of Saul and the bones of Jonathan his son from the men of Jabeshgilead, which had stolen them from the street of Beth-shan, where the Philistines had hanged them, when the Philistines had slain Saul in Gilboa:

13 And he brought up from there the bones of Saul and the bones of Jonathan his son; and they gathered the bones of them that were hanged.

14 And the bones of Saul and Jonathan his son buried they in the country of Benjamin in Zelah, in the tomb of Kish his father: and they performed all that the king commanded. And after that God was entreated for the land.

15 Moreover the Philistines had yet war again with Israel; and David went down, and his servants with him, and fought against the Philistines: and David grew faint.

16 And Ishbibenob, which was of the sons of the giant, the weight of whose spear weighed three hundred shekels of brass in weight, he being girded with a new sword, thought to have slain David.

17 But Abishai the son of Zeruiah succoured him, and smote the Philistine, and killed him. Then the men of David swore unto him, saying, you shall go no more out with us to battle, that you quench not the light of Israel.

18 And it came to pass after this, that there was again a battle with the Philistines at Gob: then Sibbechai the Hushathite killed Saph, which was of the sons of the giant.

19 And there was again a battle in Gob with the Philistines, where Elhanan the son of Jaareoregim, a Bethlehemite, killed the brother of Goliath the Gittite, the staff of whose spear was like a weaver's beam.

20 And there was yet a battle in Gath, where was a man of great stature, that had on every hand six fingers, and on every foot six toes, four and twenty in number; and he also was born to the giant.

21 And when he defied Israel, Jonathan the son of Shimeah the brother of David killed him.

22 These four were born to the giant in Gath, and fell by the hand of David, and by the hand of his servants.

2 Sam 22:1 And David spoke unto the Becoming-One the words of this song in the day that the Becoming-One had delivered him out of the hand of all his enemies, and out of the hand of Saul:

2 And he said, The Becoming-One is my rock, and my fortress, and my deliverer;

3 God of my rock; in him will I trust: he is my shield, and the horn of my salvation, my high tower, and my refuge, my Savior; you save me from violence.

4 I will call on the Becoming-One, who is worthy to be praised: so shall I be saved from mine enemies.

5 When the waves of death compassed me, the floods of ungodly men made me afraid;

6 The sorrows of Sheol compassed me about; the snares of death prevented me;

7 In my distress I called upon the Becoming-One, and cried to my God: and he did hear my voice out of his temple, and my cry did enter into his ears.

8 Then the earth shook and trembled; the foundations of the heavens moved and shook, because he was angry.

9 There went up a smoke out of his nostrils, and fire out of his mouth devoured: coals were kindled by it.

10 He bowed the heavens also, and came down; and darkness was under his feet.

11 And he rode upon a cherub, and did fly: and he was seen upon the wings of the wind.

12 And he made darkness pavilions round about him, dark waters, and thick clouds of the skies.

13 Through the brightness before him were coals of fire kindled.

14 The Becoming-One thundered from heaven, and the most High uttered his voice.

15 And he sent out arrows, and scattered them; lightning, and discomfited them.

16 And the channels of the sea appeared, the foundations of the world were discovered, at the rebuking of the Becoming-One, at the blast of the breath of his nostrils.

17 He sent from above, he took me; he drew me out of many waters;

18 He delivered me from my strong enemy, and from them that hated me: for they were too strong for me.

19 They prevented me in the day of my calamity: but the Becoming-One was my stay.

20 He brought me forth also into a large place: he delivered me, because he delighted in me.

21 The Becoming-One rewarded me according to my righteousness: according to the cleanness of my hands has he recompensed me.

22 For I have kept the ways of the Becoming-One, and have not wickedly departed from my God.

23 For all his judgments were before me: and as for his statutes, I did not depart from them.

24 I was also upright before him, and have kept myself from mine iniquity.

25 Therefore the Becoming-One has recompensed me according to my righteousness; according to my cleanness in his eye sight.

26 With the merciful you will show yourself merciful, and with the upright man you will show yourself upright.

27 With the pure you will show yourself pure; and with the perverse you will show yourself perverse.

28 And the afflicted people you will save: but your eyes are upon the haughty, that you may bring them down.

29 For you are my lamp, O Becoming-One: and the Becoming-One will lighten my darkness.

30 For by you I have run through a troop: by my God have I leaped over a wall.

31 As for GOD, his way is perfect; the word of the Becoming-One is tried: he is a buckler to all them that trust in him.

32 For who is GOD, save the Becoming-One? and who is a rock, save our God?

33 GOD is my strength and power: And he makes my way perfect.

34 He makes my feet like hinds' feet: and sets me upon my high places.

35 He teaches my hands to war; so that a bow of steel is broken by mine arms.

36 you have also given me the shield of your salvation: and your gentleness has made me great.

37 you have enlarged my steps under me; so that my feet did not slip.

38 I have pursued mine enemies, and destroyed them; and turned not again until I had consumed them.

39 And I have consumed them, and wounded them, that they could not arise: yes, they are fallen under my feet.

40 For you have girded me with strength to battle: them that rose up against me have you subdued under me.

41 you have also given me the necks of mine enemies, that I might destroy them that hate me.

42 They looked, but there was none to save; even unto the Becoming-One, but he answered them not.

43 Then did I beat them as small as the dust of the earth, I did stamp them as the mire of the street, and did spread them abroad.

44 you also have delivered me from the strivings of my people, you have kept me to be head of the nations: a people which I knew not shall serve me.

45 Strangers shall submit themselves unto me: as soon as they hear, they shall be obedient unto me.

46 Strangers shall fade away, and they shall be afraid out of their close places.

47 The Becoming-One lives; and blessed be my rock; and exalted be God of the rock of my salvation.

48 It is GOD that avenges me, and that brings down the people under me,

49 And that brings me forth from mine enemies: you also have lifted me up on high above them that rose up against me: you have delivered me from the violent man.

50 Therefore I will give thanks unto you, O Becoming-One, among the nations, and I will sing praises unto your name.

51 He is the tower of salvation for his king: and shows mercy to his anointed, unto David, and to his seed for olam.

2 Sam 23:1 Now these be the last words of David. David the son of Jesse said, and the man who was raised up on high, the anointed of God of Jacob, and the sweet psalmist of Israel, said,

2 The spirit of the Becoming-One spoke by me, and his word was in my tongue.

3 God of Israel said, the Rock of Israel spoke to me, He that rules over men must be just, ruling in the fear of God.

4 And he shall be as the light of the morning, when the sun rises, even a morning without clouds; as the tender grass springing out of the earth by clear shining after rain.

5 Although my house be not so with GOD; yet he has made with me a covenant of olam, ordered in all things, and sure: for this is all my salvation, and all my desire, although he make it not to grow.

6 But the sons of Belial shall be all of them as thorns thrust away, because they cannot be taken with hands:

7 But the man that shall touch them must be fenced with iron and the staff of a spear; and they shall be utterly burned with fire in the same place.

8 These be the names of the mighty men whom David had: The Tachmonite that sat in the seat, chief among the captains; the same was Adino the Eznite: he lift up his spear against eight hundred, whom he killed at one time.

9 And after him was Eleazar the son of Dodo the Ahohite, one of the three mighty men with David, when they defied the Philistines that were there gathered together to battle, and the men of Israel were gone away:

10 He arose, and smote the Philistines until his hand was weary, and his hand clave unto the sword: and the Becoming-One worked a great victory that day; and the people returned after him only to spoil.

11 And after him was Shammah the son of Agee the Hararite. And the Philistines were gathered together into a troop, where was a piece of ground full of lentiles: and the people fled from the Philistines.

12 But he stood in the midst of the ground, and defended it, and killed the Philistines: and the Becoming-One worked a great victory.

13 And three of the thirty chief went down, and came to David in the harvest time unto the cave of Adullam: and the troop of the Philistines pitched in the valley of Rephaim.

14 And David was then in a hold, and the garrison of the Philistines was then in Bethlehem.

15 And David longed, and said, Oh that one would give me drink of the water of the well of Bethlehem, which is by the gate!

16 And the three mighty men brake through the host of the Philistines, and drew water out of the well of Bethlehem, that was by the gate, and took it, and brought it to David: nevertheless he would not drink thereof, but poured it out unto the Becoming-One.

17 And he said, Be it far from me, O Becoming-One, that I should do this: is not this the blood of the men that went in jeopardy of their souls? therefore he would not drink it. These things did these three mighty men.

18 And Abishai, the brother of Joab, the son of Zeruiah, was chief among three. And he lifted up his spear against three hundred, and killed them, and had the name among three.

19 Was he not most honorable of three? therefore he was their captain: howbeit he attained not unto the first three.

20 And Benaiah the son of Jehoiada, the son of a valiant man, of Kabzeel, who had done many acts, he killed two lionlike men of Moab: he went down also and killed a lion in the midst of a pit in time of snow:

21 And he killed an Egyptian, a goodly man: and the Egyptian had a spear in his hand; but he went down to him with a staff, and plucked the spear out of the Egyptian's hand, and killed him with his own spear.

22 These things did Benaiah the son of Jehoiada, and had the name among three mighty men.

23 He was more honorable than the thirty, but he attained not to the first three. And David set him over his guard.

24 Asahel the brother of Joab was one of the thirty; Elhanan the son of Dodo of Bethlehem,

25 Shammah the Harodite, Elika the Harodite,

26 Helez the Paltite, Ira the son of Ikkesh the Tekoite,

27 Abiezer the Anethothite, Mebunnai the Hushathite,

28 Zalmon the Ahohite, Maharai the Netophathite,

29 Heleb the son of Baanah, a Netophathite, Ittai the son of Ribai out of Gibeah of the children of Benjamin,

30 Benaiah the Pirathonite, Hiddai of the brooks of Gaash,

31 Abialbon the Arbathite, Azmaveth the Barhumite,

32 Eliahba the Shaalbonite, of the sons of Jashen, Jonathan,

33 Shammah the Hararite, Ahiam the son of Sharar the Hararite,

34 Eliphelet the son of Ahasbai, the son of the Maachathite, Eliam the son of Ahithophel the Gilonite,

35 Hezrai the Carmelite, Paarai the Arbite,

36 Igal the son of Nathan of Zobah, Bani the Gadite,

37 Zelek the Ammonite, Nahari the Beerothite, armor bearer to Joab the son of Zeruiah,

38 Ira an Ithrite, Gareb an Ithrite,

39 Uriah the Hittite: thirty and seven in all.

2 Sam 24:1 And again the anger of the Becoming-One was kindled against Israel, and he moved David against them to say, Go, number Israel and Judah.

2 For the king said to Joab the captain of the host, which was with him, Go now through all the tribes of Israel, from Dan even to Beersheba, and number you the people, that I may know the number of the people.

3 And Joab said unto the king, Now the Becoming-One your God add unto the people, how many soever they be, a hundredfold, and that the eyes of my lord the king may see it: but why does my lord the king delight in this thing?

4 Notwithstanding the king's word prevailed against Joab, and against the captains of the host. And Joab and the captains of the host went out from the presence of the king, to number the people of Israel.

5 And they passed over Jordan, and pitched in Aroer, on the right side of the city that lies in the midst of the river of Gad, and toward Jazer:

6 Then they came to Gilead, and to the land of Tahtimhodshi; and they came to Danjaan, and about to Zidon,

7 And came to the strong hold of Tyre, and to all the cities of the Hivites, and of the Canaanites: and they went out to the south of Judah, even to Beersheba.

8 So when they had gone through all the land, they came to Jerusalem at the end of nine months and twenty days.

9 And Joab gave up the sum of the number of the people unto the king: and there were in Israel eight hundred thousand of valiant men that drew the sword; and the men of Judah were five hundred thousand men.

10 And David's heart smote him after that he had numbered the people. And David said unto the Becoming-One, I have sinned greatly in that I have done: and now, I beg you, O Becoming-One, take away the iniquity of your servant; for I have done very foolishly.

11 For when David was up in the morning, the word of the Becoming-One came unto the prophet Gad, David's seer, saying,

12 Go and say unto David, Thus says the Becoming-One, I offer you three things; choose you one of them, that I may do it unto you.

13 So Gad came to David, and told him, and said unto him, Shall seven years of famine come unto you in your land? or will you flee three months before your enemies, while they pursue you? or that there be three days' pestilence in your land? now advise, and see what answer I shall return to him that sent me.

14 And David said unto Gad, I am in a great strait: let us fall now into the hand of the Becoming-One; for his mercies are great: and let me not fall into the hand of man.

15 So the Becoming-One sent a pestilence upon Israel from the morning even to the set time:[106] and

---

[106] Appointed time or festival

there died of the people from Dan even to Beersheba seventy thousand men.

16 And when the angel stretched out his hand upon Jerusalem to destroy it, the Becoming-One repented him of the evil, and said to the angel that destroyed the people, It is enough: stay now your hand. And the angel of the Becoming-One was by the threshing place of Araunah the Jebusite.

17 And David spoke unto the Becoming-One when he saw the angel that smote the people, and said, Lo, I have sinned, and I have done wickedly: but these sheep, what have they done? let your hand, I pray you, be against me, and against my father's house.

18 And Gad came that day to David, and said unto him, Go up, rear an altar unto the Becoming-One in the threshing floor of Araunah the Jebusite.

19 And David, according to the saying of Gad, went up as the Becoming-One commanded.

20 And Araunah looked, and saw the king and his servants coming on toward him: and Araunah went out, and bowed himself before the king on his face upon the ground.

21 And Araunah said, Why is my lord the king come to his servant? And David said, To buy the threshing floor of you, to build an altar unto the Becoming-One, that the plague may be stayed from the people.

22 And Araunah said unto David, Let my lord the king take and offer up what seems good unto him: behold, here be oxen for burnt sacrifice, and threshing instruments and other instruments of the oxen for wood.

23 All these things did Araunah, as a king, give unto the king. And Araunah said unto the king, The Becoming-One your God accept you.

24 And the king said unto Araunah, Nay; but I will surely buy it of you at a price: neither will I offer burnt offerings unto the Becoming-One my God of that which does cost me nothing. So David bought the threshing floor and the oxen for fifty shekels of silver.

25 And David built there an altar unto the Becoming-One, and offered burnt offerings and peace offerings. So the Becoming-One was entreated for the land, and the plague was stayed from Israel.

1 Kings

1 Ki 1:1 Now king David was old and advanced in years; and they covered him with clothes, but he got no heat.

2 Therefore his servants said unto him, Let there be sought for my lord the king a young virgin: and let her stand before the king, and let her cherish him, and let her lie in your bosom, that my lord the king may get heat.

3 So they sought for a fair damsel throughout all the coasts of Israel, and found Abishag a Shunammite, and brought her to the king.

4 And the damsel was very fair, and cherished the king, and ministered to him: but the king knew her not.

5 Then Adonijah the son of Haggith exalted himself, saying, I will be king: and he prepared him chariots and horsemen, and fifty men to run before him.

6 And his father had not displeased him at any time in saying, Why have you done so? and he also was a very goodly man; and his mother bare him after Absalom.

7 And he conferred with Joab the son of Zeruiah, and with Abiathar the priest: and they following Adonijah helped him.

8 But Zadok the priest, and Benaiah the son of Jehoiada, and Nathan the prophet, and Shimei, and Rei, and the mighty men which belonged to David, were not with Adonijah.

9 And Adonijah killed sheep and oxen and fat cattle by the stone of Zoheleth, which is by Enrogel, and called all his brethren the king's sons, and all the men of Judah the king's servants:

10 But Nathan the prophet, and Benaiah, and the mighty men, and Solomon his brother, he called not.

11 Therefore Nathan spoke unto Bathsheba the mother of Solomon, saying, have you not heard that Adonijah the son of Haggith does reign, and David our lord knows it not?

12 Now therefore come, let me, I pray you, give you counsel, that you may save your own soul, and the soul of your son Solomon.

13 Go and get you in unto king David, and say unto him, Did not you, my lord, O king, swear unto your handmaid, saying, Assuredly Solomon your son shall reign after me, and he shall sit upon my throne? why then does Adonijah reign?

14 Behold, while you yet talk there with the king, I also will come in after you, and confirm your words.

15 And Bathsheba went in unto the king into the chamber: and the king was very old; and Abishag the Shunammite ministered unto the king.

16 And Bathsheba bowed, and did obeisance unto the king. And the king said, What shall I do for you?

17 And she said unto him, My lord, you swore by the Becoming-One your God unto your handmaid, saying, Assuredly Solomon your son shall reign after me, and he shall sit upon my throne.

18 And now, behold, Adonijah reigns; and now, my lord the king, you know it not:

19 And he has slain oxen and fat cattle and sheep in abundance, and has called all the sons of the king, and Abiathar the priest, and Joab the captain of the host: but Solomon your servant has he not called.

20 And you, my lord, O king, the eyes of all Israel are upon you, that you should tell them who shall sit on the throne of my lord the king after him.

21 Otherwise it shall come to pass, when my lord the king shall sleep with his fathers, that I and my son Solomon shall be counted offenders.

22 And, lo, while she yet talked with the king, Nathan the prophet also came in.

23 And they told the king, saying, Behold Nathan the prophet. And when he was come in before the king, he bowed himself before the king with his face to the ground.

24 And Nathan said, My lord, O king, have you said, Adonijah shall reign after me, and he shall sit upon my throne?

25 For he is gone down this day, and has slain oxen and fat cattle and sheep in abundance, and has called all the king's sons, and the captains of the host, and Abiathar the priest; and, behold, they eat and drink before him, and say, Let live the king Adonijah.

26 But me, even me your servant, and Zadok the priest, and Benaiah the son of Jehoiada, and your servant Solomon, has he not called.

27 Is this thing done by my lord the king, and you have not showed it unto your servant, who should sit on the throne of my lord the king after him?

28 Then king David answered and said, Call me Bathsheba. And she came into the king's presence, and stood before the king.

29 And the king swore, and said, As the Becoming-One lives, that has redeemed my soul out of all distress,

30 Even as I swore unto you by the Becoming-One, God of Israel, saying, Assuredly Solomon your son shall reign after me, and he shall sit upon my throne in my stead; even so will I certainly do this day.

31 Then Bathsheba bowed with her face to the earth, and did reverence to the king, and said, Let my lord king David live for olam.

32 And king David said, Call me Zadok the priest, and Nathan the prophet, and Benaiah the son of Jehoiada. And they came before the king.

33 The king also said unto them, Take with you the servants of your lord, and cause Solomon my son to ride upon mine own mule, and bring him down to Gihon:

34 And let Zadok the priest and Nathan the prophet anoint him there king over Israel: and blow you with the trumpet, and say, Let king Solomon live.

35 Then you shall come up after him, that he may come and sit upon my throne; for he shall be king in my stead: and I have appointed him to be ruler over Israel and over Judah.

36 And Benaiah the son of Jehoiada answered the king, and said, Amen: the Becoming-One, God of my lord the king say so too.

37 As the Becoming-One has been with my lord the king, even so be he with Solomon, and make his throne greater than the throne of my lord king David.

38 So Zadok the priest, and Nathan the prophet, and Benaiah the son of Jehoiada, and the Cherethites, and the Pelethites, went down, and caused Solomon

to ride upon king David's mule, and brought him to Gihon.

39 And Zadok the priest took a horn of oil out of the tabernacle, and anointed Solomon. And they blew the trumpet; and all the people said, Let king Solomon live.

40 And all the people came up after him, and the people piped with pipes, and rejoiced with great joy, so that the earth ripped with the sound of them.

41 And Adonijah and all the guests that were with him heard it as they had made an end of eating. And when Joab heard the sound of the trumpet, he said, Why is this noise of the city being in an uproar?

42 And while he yet spoke, behold, Jonathan the son of Abiathar the priest came: and Adonijah said unto him, Come in; for you are a valiant man, and bring good tidings.

43 And Jonathan answered and said to Adonijah, Truly our lord king David has made Solomon king.

44 And the king has sent with him Zadok the priest, and Nathan the prophet, and Benaiah the son of Jehoiada, and the Cherethites, and the Pelethites, and they have caused him to ride upon the king's mule:

45 And Zadok the priest and Nathan the prophet have anointed him king in Gihon: and they are come up from there rejoicing, so that the city rang again. This is the noise that you have heard.

46 And also Solomon sits on the throne of the kingdom.

47 And moreover the king's servants came to bless our lord king David, saying, God make the name of Solomon better than your name, and make his throne greater than your throne. And the king bowed himself upon the bed.

48 And also thus said the king, Blessed be the Becoming-One, God of Israel, which has given one to sit on my throne this day, mine eyes even seeing it.

49 And all the guests that were with Adonijah were afraid, and rose up, and went every man his way.

50 And Adonijah feared because of Solomon, and arose, and went, and caught hold on the horns of the altar.

51 And it was told Solomon, saying, Behold, Adonijah fears king Solomon: for, lo, he has caught hold on the horns of the altar, saying, Let king Solomon swear unto me today that he will not slay his servant with the sword.

52 And Solomon said, If he will show himself a worthy man, there shall not a hair of him fall to the earth: but if wickedness shall be found in him, he shall die.

53 So king Solomon sent, and they brought him down from the altar. And he came and bowed himself to king Solomon: and Solomon said unto him, Go to your house.

1 Ki 2:1 Now the days of David drew near that he should die; and he charged Solomon his son, saying,

2 I go the way of all the earth: be you strong therefore, and show yourself a man;

3 And keep the charge of the Becoming-One your God, to walk in his ways, to keep his statutes, and his commandments, and his judgments, and his testimonies, as it is written in the law of Moses, that you may prosper in all that you do, and wheresoever you turn thyself:

4 That the Becoming-One may continue his word which he spoke concerning me, saying, If your children take heed to their way, to walk before me in truth with all their heart and with all their soul, there shall not fail you said he a man on the throne of Israel.

5 Moreover you know also what Joab the son of Zeruiah did to me, and what he did to the two captains of the hosts of Israel, unto Abner the son of Ner, and unto Amasa the son of Jether, whom he killed, and shed the blood of war in peace, and put the blood of war upon his girdle that was about his loins, and in his shoes that were on his feet.

6 Do therefore according to your wisdom, and let not his aged head go down to Sheol in peace.

7 But show kindness unto the sons of Barzillai the Gileadite, and let them be of those that eat at your table: for so they came to me when I fled because of Absalom your brother.

8 And, behold, you have with you Shimei the son of Gera, a Benjamite of Bahurim, which cursed me with a grievous curse in the day when I went to Mahanaim: but he came down to meet me at Jordan, and I swore to him by the Becoming-One, saying, I will not put you to death with the sword.

9 Now therefore hold him not guiltless: for you are a wise man, and know what you ought to do unto him; but his aged head bring you down to Sheol with blood.

10 So David slept with his fathers, and was buried in the city of David.

11 And the days that David reigned over Israel were forty years: seven years reigned he in Hebron, and thirty and three years reigned he in Jerusalem.

12 Then sat Solomon upon the throne of David his father; and his kingdom was established greatly.

13 And Adonijah the son of Haggith came to Bathsheba the mother of Solomon. And she said, you come peaceably? And he said, Peaceably.

14 He said moreover, I have somewhat to say unto you. And she said, Say on.

15 And he said, you know that the kingdom was mine, and that all Israel set their faces on me, that I should reign: howbeit the kingdom is turned about, and is become my brother's: for it was his from the Becoming-One.

16 And now I ask one petition of you, deny me not. And she said unto him, Say on.

17 And he said, Speak, I pray you, unto Solomon the king, for he will not say you nay, that he give me Abishag the Shunammite to wife.

18 And Bathsheba said, Well; I will speak for you unto the king.

19 Bathsheba therefore went unto king Solomon, to speak unto him for Adonijah. And the king rose up to meet her, and bowed himself unto her, and sat down on his throne, and caused a seat to be set for the king's mother; and she sat on his right hand.

20 Then she said, I desire one small petition of you; I pray you, say me not nay. And the king said unto her, Ask on, my mother: for I will not say you nay.

21 And she said, Let Abishag the Shunammite be given to Adonijah your brother to wife.

22 And king Solomon answered and said unto his mother, And why do you ask Abishag the Shunammite for Adonijah? ask for him the kingdom also; for he is mine elder brother; even for him, and for Abiathar the priest, and for Joab the son of Zeruiah.

23 Then king Solomon swore by the Becoming-One, saying, God do so to me, and more also, if Adonijah have not spoken this word against his own soul.

24 Now therefore, as the Becoming-One lives, which has established me, and set me on the throne of David my father, and who has made me a house, as he promised, Adonijah shall be put to death this day.

25 And king Solomon sent by the hand of Benaiah the son of Jehoiada; and he fell upon him that he died.

26 And unto Abiathar the priest said the king, Get you to Anathoth, unto your own fields; for you are worthy of death: but I will not at this time put you to death, because you bare the ark of my Lord(s) the, the Becoming-One, before David my father, and because you have been afflicted in all wherein my father was afflicted.

27 So Solomon thrust out Abiathar from being priest unto the Becoming-One; that he might fulfil the word of the Becoming-One, which he spoke concerning the house of Eli in Shiloh.

28 Then tidings came to Joab: for Joab had turned after Adonijah, though he turned not after Absalom. And Joab fled unto the tabernacle of the Becoming-One, and caught hold on the horns of the altar.

29 And it was told king Solomon that Joab was fled unto the tabernacle of the Becoming-One; and, behold, he is by the altar. Then Solomon sent Benaiah the son of Jehoiada, saying, Go, fall upon him.

30 And Benaiah came to the tabernacle of the Becoming-One, and said unto him, Thus says the king, Come forth. And he said, Nay; but I will die here. And Benaiah brought the king word again, saying, Thus said Joab, and thus he answered me.

31 And the king said unto him, Do as he has said, and fall upon him, and bury him; that you may take away the innocent blood, which Joab shed, from me, and from the house of my father.

32 And the Becoming-One shall return his blood upon his own head, who fell upon two men more righteous and better than he, and killed them with the sword, my father David not knowing it, Abner the son of Ner, captain of the host of Israel, and Amasa the son of Jether, captain of the host of Judah.

33 Their blood shall therefore return upon the head of Joab, and upon the head of his seed for olam; but upon David, and upon his seed, and upon his house, and upon his throne, shall there be peace for olam from the Becoming-One.

34 So Benaiah the son of Jehoiada went up, and fell upon him, and killed him: and he was buried in his own house in the wilderness.

35 And the king put Benaiah the son of Jehoiada in his room over the host: and Zadok the priest did the king put in the room of Abiathar.

36 And the king sent and called for Shimei, and said unto him, Build you a house in Jerusalem, and dwell there, and go not forth there any where.

37 For it shall be, that on the day you go out, and pass over the brook Kidron, you shall know for certain that, in dying, you will die:[107] your blood shall be upon your own head.

38 And Shimei said unto the king, The saying is good: as my lord the king has said, so will your servant do. And Shimei dwelt in Jerusalem many days.

39 And it came to pass at the end of three years, that two of the servants of Shimei ran away unto Achish son of Maachah king of Gath. And they told Shimei, saying, Behold, your servants be in Gath.

40 And Shimei arose, and saddled his donkey, and went to Gath to Achish to seek his servants: and Shimei went, and brought his servants from Gath.

41 And it was told Solomon that Shimei had gone from Jerusalem to Gath, and was come again.

42 And the king sent and called for Shimei, and said unto him, Did I not make you to swear by the Becoming-One, and protested unto you, saying, Know for a certain, on the day you go out, and walk abroad anywhere, that, in dying, you will die?[108] and you say unto me, The word that I have heard is good.

43 Why then have you not kept the oath of the Becoming-One, and the commandment that I have charged you with?

44 The king said moreover to Shimei, you know all the wickedness which your heart is privy to, that you did to David my father: therefore the Becoming-One shall return your wickedness upon your own head;

45 And king Solomon shall be blessed, and the throne of David shall be established before the Becoming-One for olam.

46 So the king commanded Benaiah the son of Jehoiada; which went out, and fell upon him, that he died. And the kingdom was established in the hand of Solomon.

1 Ki 3:1 And Solomon made affinity with Pharaoh king of Egypt, and took Pharaoh's daughter, and brought her into the city of David, until he had made an end of building his own house, and the house of the Becoming-One, and the wall of Jerusalem round about.

2 Only the people sacrificed in high places, because there was no house built unto the name of the Becoming-One, until those days.

3 And Solomon loved the Becoming-One, walking in the statutes of David his father: only he sacrificed and burnt incense in high places.

4 And the king went to Gibeon to sacrifice there; for that was the great high place: a thousand of burnt offerings did Solomon offer upon that altar.

5 In Gibeon the Becoming-One appeared to Solomon in a dream by night: and God said, Ask what I shall give you.

---

[107] מוֹת תָּמוּת – "in dying, you will die" or when you die, you will be dead – a part of the group called the "dead"

[108] מוֹת תָּמוּת – "in dying, you will die" or when you die, you will be dead – a part of the group called the "dead"

6 And Solomon said, you have showed unto your servant David my father great mercy, according as he walked before you in truth, and in righteousness, and in uprightness of heart with you; and you have kept for him this great kindness, that you have given him a son to sit on his throne, as it is this day.

7 And now, O Becoming-One my God, you have made your servant king instead of David my father: and I am but a little child: I know not how to go out or come in.

8 And your servant is in the midst of your people which you have chosen, a great people, that cannot be numbered nor counted for multitude.

9 Give therefore your servant an understanding heart to judge your people, that I may discern between good and bad: for who is able to judge this your so great a people?

10 And the speech pleased my Lord(s), that Solomon had asked this thing.

11 And God said unto him, Because you have asked this thing, and have not asked for yourself long life; neither have asked riches for thyself, nor have asked the life of your enemies; but have asked for yourself understanding to discern judgment;

12 Behold, I have done according to your words: lo, I have given you a wise and an understanding heart; so that there was none like you before you, neither after you shall any arise like unto you.

13 And I have also given you that which you have not asked, both riches, and honor: so that there shall not be any among the kings like unto you all your days.

14 And if you will walk in my ways, to keep my statutes and my commandments, as your father David did walk, then I will lengthen your days.

15 And Solomon awoke; and, behold, it was a dream. And he came to Jerusalem, and stood before the ark of the covenant of the Becoming-One, and offered up burnt offerings, and offered peace offerings, and made a feast to all his servants.

16 Then came there two women, that were harlots, unto the king, and stood before him.

17 And the one woman said, O my lord, I and this woman dwell in one house; and I was delivered of a child with her in the house.

18 And it came to pass the third day after that I was delivered, that this woman was delivered also: and we were together; there was no stranger with us in the house, save we two in the house.

19 And this woman's child died in the night; because she overlaid it.

20 And she arose at midnight, and took my son from beside me, while your handmaid slept, and laid it in her bosom, and laid her dead child in my bosom.

21 And when I rose in the morning to give my child suck, behold, it was dead: but when I had considered it in the morning, behold, it was not my son, which I did bear.

22 And the other woman said, Nay; but the living is my son, and the dead is your son. And this said, No; but the dead is your son, and the living is my son. Thus they spoke before the king.

23 Then said the king, The one says, This is my son that lives, and your son is the dead: and the other says, Nay; but your son is the dead, and my son is the living.

24 And the king said, Bring me a sword. And they brought a sword before the king.

25 And the king said, Divide the living child in two, and give half to the one, and half to the other.

26 Then spoke the woman whose the living child was unto the king, for her bowels yearned upon her son, and she said, O my lord, give her the living child, and in no way slay it. But the other said, Let it be neither mine nor yours, but divide it.

27 Then the king answered and said, Give her the living child, and in no way slay it: she is the mother thereof.

28 And all Israel heard of the judgment which the king had judged; and they feared the king: for they saw that the wisdom of God was in him, to do judgment.

1 Ki 4:1 So king Solomon was king over all Israel.

2 And these were the princes which he had; Azariah the son of Zadok the priest,

3 Elihoreph and Ahiah, the sons of Shisha, scribes; Jehoshaphat the son of Ahilud, the recorder.

4 And Benaiah the son of Jehoiada was over the host: and Zadok and Abiathar were the priests:

5 And Azariah the son of Nathan was over the officers; and Zabud the son of Nathan was principal officer, and the king's friend:

6 And Ahishar was over the household: and Adoniram the son of Abda was over the tribute.

7 And Solomon had twelve officers over all Israel, which provided victuals for the king and his household: each man his month in a year made provision.

8 And these are their names: The son of Hur, in mount Ephraim:

9 The son of Dekar, in Makaz, and in Shaalbim, and Beth-shemesh, and Elon-beth-hanan:

10 The son of Hesed, in Aruboth; to him pertained Sochoh, and all the land of Hepher:

11 The son of Abinadab, in all the region of Dor; which had Taphath the daughter of Solomon to wife:

12 Baana the son of Ahilud; to him pertained Taanach and Megiddo, and all Beth-shean, which is by Zartanah beneath Jezreel, from Beth-shean to Able-meholah, even unto the place that is beyond Jokneam:

13 The son of Geber, in Ramothgilead; to him pertained the towns of Jair the son of Manasseh, which are in Gilead; to him also pertained the region of Argob, which is in Bashan, threescore great cities with walls and brazen bars:

14 Ahinadab the son of Iddo had Mahanaim:

15 Ahimaaz was in Naphtali; he also took Basmath the daughter of Solomon to wife:

16 Baanah the son of Hushai was in Asher and in Aloth:

17 Jehoshaphat the son of Paruah, in Issachar:

18 Shimei the son of Elah, in Benjamin:

19 Geber the son of Uri was in the country of Gilead, in the country of Sihon king of the Amorites, and of Og king of Bashan; and he was the only officer which was in the land.

20 Judah and Israel were many, as the sand which is by the sea in multitude, eating and drinking, and making merry.

21 And Solomon reigned over all kingdoms from the river unto the land of the Philistines, and unto the border of Egypt: they brought presents, and served Solomon all the days of his life.

22 And Solomon's provision for one day was thirty measures of fine flour, and threescore measures of meal,

23 Ten fat oxen, and twenty oxen out of the pastures, and a hundred sheep, beside harts, and roebucks, and fallowdeer, and fatted fowl.

24 For he had dominion over all the region over the river, from Tiphsah even to Azzah, over all the kings over the river: and he had peace on all sides round about him.

25 And Judah and Israel dwelt safely, every man under his vine and under his fig tree, from Dan even to Beersheba, all the days of Solomon.

26 And Solomon had forty thousand stalls of horses for his chariots, and twelve thousand of horsemen.

27 And those officers provided victual for king Solomon, and for all that came unto king Solomon's table, every man in his month: they lacked nothing.

28 Barley also and straw for the horses and mules brought they unto the place where the officers were, every man according to his charge.

29 And God gave Solomon wisdom and understanding exceeding much, and largeness of heart, even as the sand that is on the sea shore.

30 And Solomon's wisdom excelled the wisdom of all the children of the east country, and all the wisdom of Egypt.

31 For he was wiser than all men; than Ethan the Ezrahite, and Heman, and Chalcol, and Darda, the sons of Mahol: and his fame was in all nations round about.

32 And he spoke three thousand of proverbs: and his songs were a thousand and five.

33 And he spoke of trees, from the cedar tree that is in Lebanon even unto the hyssop that springs out of the wall: he spoke also of beasts, and of fowl, and of creeping things, and of fishes.

34 And there came of all people to hear the wisdom of Solomon, from all kings of the earth, which had heard of his wisdom.

1 Ki 5:1 And Hiram king of Tyre sent his servants unto Solomon; for he had heard that they had anointed him king in the room of his father: for Hiram was all the days a lover of David.

2 And Solomon sent to Hiram, saying,

3 you know how that David my father could not build a house unto the name of the Becoming-One his God for the wars which were about him on every side, until the Becoming-One put them under the soles of his feet.

4 But now the Becoming-One my God has given me rest on every side, so that there is neither adversary nor evil occurrent.

5 And, behold, I purpose to build a house unto the name of the Becoming-One my God, as the Becoming-One spoke unto David my father, saying, your son, whom I will set upon your throne in your room, he shall build a house unto my name.

6 Now therefore command you that they hew me cedar trees out of Lebanon; and my servants shall be with your servants: and unto you will I give hire for your servants according to all that you shall appoint: for you know that there is not among us any that can skill to hew timber like unto the Sidonians.

7 And it came to pass, when Hiram heard the words of Solomon, that he rejoiced greatly, and said, Blessed be the Becoming-One this day, which has given unto David a wise son over this great people.

8 And Hiram sent to Solomon, saying, I have considered the things which you sent to me for: and I will do all your desire concerning timber of cedar, and concerning timber of fir.

9 My servants shall bring them down from Lebanon unto the sea: and I will convey them by sea in floats unto the place that you shall appoint me, and will cause them to be discharged there, and you shall receive them: and you shall accomplish my desire, in giving food for my household.

10 So Hiram gave Solomon cedar trees and fir trees according to all his desire.

11 And Solomon gave Hiram twenty thousand measures of wheat for food to his household, and twenty measures of pure oil: thus gave Solomon to Hiram year by year.

12 And the Becoming-One gave Solomon wisdom, as he promised him: and there was peace between Hiram and Solomon; and they two made a league together.

13 And king Solomon raised a levy out of all Israel; and the levy was thirty thousand men.

14 And he sent them to Lebanon, ten thousand a month by courses: a month they were in Lebanon, and two months at home: and Adoniram was over the levy.

15 And Solomon had threescore and ten thousand that bare burdens, and fourscore thousand of hewers in the mountains;

16 Beside the chief of Solomon's officers which were over the work, three thousand and three hundred, which ruled over the people that worked in the work.

17 And the king commanded, and they brought great stones, costly stones, and hewed stones, to lay the foundation of the house.

18 And Solomon's builders and Hiram's builders did hew them, and the stonesquarers: so they prepared timber and stones to build the house.

1 Ki 6:1 And it came to pass in the four hundred and eightieth year [after] the children of Israel were come out of the land of Egypt, in the fourth year of Solomon's reign over Israel, in the month Zif, which is the second month, that he began to build the house of the Becoming-One. [2992 YM / 982 BC]

2 And the house which king Solomon built for the Becoming-One, the length thereof was threescore cubits, and the breadth thereof twenty cubits, and the height thereof thirty cubits.

3 And the porch before the temple of the house, twenty cubits was the length thereof, according to the breadth of the house; and ten cubits was the breadth thereof before the house.

4 And for the house he made windows of narrow lights.

5 And against the wall of the house he built chambers round about, against the walls of the house

round about, both of the temple and of the oracle: and he made chambers round about:

6 The nethermost chamber was five cubits broad, and the middle was six cubits broad, and the third was seven cubits broad: for outside in the wall of the house he made narrowed rests round about, that the beams should not be fastened in the walls of the house.

7 And the house, when it was in building, was built of stone made ready before it was brought there: so that there was neither hammer nor ax nor any tool of iron heard in the house, while it was in building.

8 The door for the middle chamber was in the right side of the house: and they went up with winding stairs into the middle chamber, and out of the middle into the third.

9 So he built the house, and finished it; and covered the house with beams and boards of cedar.

10 And then he built chambers against all the house, five cubits high: and they rested on the house with timber of cedar.

11 And the word of the Becoming-One came to Solomon, saying,

12 Concerning this house which you are in building, if you will walk in my statutes, and execute my judgments, and keep all my commandments to walk in them; then will I perform my word with you, which I spoke unto David your father:

13 And I will dwell among the children of Israel, and will not forsake my people Israel.

14 So Solomon built the house, and finished it.

15 And he built the walls of the house within with boards of cedar, both the floor of the house, and the walls of the ceiling: and he covered them on the inside with wood, and covered the floor of the house with planks of fir.

16 And he built twenty cubits on the sides of the house, both the floor and the walls with boards of cedar: he even built them for it within, even for the oracle, even for the most holy place.

17 And the house, that is, the temple before it, was forty cubits long.

18 And the cedar of the house within was carved with gourds and open flowers: all was cedar; there was no stone seen.

19 And the oracle he prepared in the house within, to set there the ark of the covenant of the Becoming-One.

20 And the oracle in the forepart was twenty cubits in length, and twenty cubits in breadth, and twenty cubits in the height thereof: and he overlaid it with pure gold; and so covered the altar which was of cedar.

21 So Solomon overlaid the house within with pure gold: and he made a partition by the chains of gold before the oracle; and he overlaid it with gold.

22 And the whole house he overlaid with gold, until he had finished all the house: also the whole altar that was by the oracle he overlaid with gold.

23 And within the oracle he made two cherubs of olive tree, each ten cubits high.

24 And five cubits was the one wing of the cherub, and five cubits the other wing of the cherub: from the uttermost part of the one wing unto the uttermost part of the other were ten cubits.

25 And the other cherub was ten cubits: both the cherubs were of one measure and one size.

26 The height of the one cherub was ten cubits, and so was it of the other cherub.

27 And he set the cherubs within the inner house: and they stretched forth the wings of the cherubs, so that the wing of the one touched the one wall, and the wing of the other cherub touched the other wall; and their wings touched one another in the midst of the house.

28 And he overlaid the cherubs with gold.

29 And he carved all the walls of the house round about with carved figures of cherubs and palm trees and open flowers, within and without.

30 And the floor of the house he overlaid with gold, within and without.

31 And for the entering of the oracle he made doors of olive tree: the lintel and side posts were a fifth part of the wall.

32 The two doors also were of olive tree; and he carved upon them carvings of cherubs and palm trees and open flowers, and overlaid them with gold, and spread gold upon the cherubs, and upon the palm trees.

33 So also made he for the door of the temple posts of olive tree, a fourth part of the wall.

34 And the two doors were of fir tree: the two leaves of the one door were folding, and the two leaves of the other door were folding.

35 And he carved thereon cherubs and palm trees and open flowers: and covered them with gold fitted upon the carved work.

36 And he built the inner court with three rows of hewed stone, and a row of cedar beams.

37 In the fourth year was the foundation of the house of the Becoming-One laid, in the month Zif:

38 And in the eleventh year, in the month Bul, which is the eighth month, was the house finished throughout all the parts thereof, and according to all the fashion of it. So was he seven years in building it.

1 Ki 7:1 But Solomon was building his own house thirteen years, and he finished all his house.

2 He built also the house of the forest of Lebanon; the length thereof was a hundred cubits, and the breadth thereof fifty cubits, and the height thereof thirty cubits, upon four rows of cedar pillars, with cedar beams upon the pillars.

3 And it was covered with cedar above upon the beams, that lay on forty five pillars, fifteen in a row.

4 And there were windows in three rows, and light was against light in three ranks.

5 And all the doors and posts were square, with the windows: and light was against light in three ranks.

6 And he made a porch of pillars; the length thereof was fifty cubits, and the breadth thereof thirty cubits: and the porch was before them: and the other pillars and the thick beam were before them.

7 Then he made a porch for the throne where he might judge, even the porch of judgment: and it was covered with cedar from one side of the floor to the other.

8 And his house where he dwelt had another court within the porch, which was of the like work.

Solomon made also a house for Pharaoh's daughter, whom he had taken to wife, like unto this porch.

9 All these were of costly stones, according to the measures of hewed stones, sawed with saws, within and without, even from the foundation unto the coping, and so on the outside toward the great court.

10 And the foundation was of costly stones, even great stones, stones of ten cubits, and stones of eight cubits.

11 And above were costly stones, after the measures of hewed stones, and cedars.

12 And the great court round about was with three rows of hewed stones, and a row of cedar beams, both for the inner court of the house of the Becoming-One, and for the porch of the house.

13 And king Solomon sent and fetched Hiram out of Tyre.

14 He was a widow's son of the tribe of Naphtali, and his father was a man of Tyre, a worker in brass: and he was filled with wisdom, and understanding, and cunning to work all works in brass. And he came to king Solomon, and worked all his work.

15 For he cast two pillars of brass, of eighteen cubits high apiece: and a line of twelve cubits did compass either of them about.

16 And he made two capitals of molten brass, to set upon the tops of the pillars: the height of the one capital was five cubits, and the height of the other capital was five cubits:

17 And nets of checker work, and wreaths of chain work, for the capitals which were upon the top of the pillars; seven for the one capital, and seven for the other capital.

18 And he made the pillars, and two rows round about upon the one network, to cover the capitals that were upon the top, with pomegranates: and so did he for the other capital.

19 And the capitals that were upon the top of the pillars were of lily work in the porch, four cubits.

20 And the capitals upon the two pillars had pomegranates also above, over against the belly which was by the network: and the pomegranates were two hundred in rows round about upon the other capital.

21 And he set up the pillars in the porch of the temple: and he set up the right pillar, and called the name thereof Jachin: and he set up the left pillar, and called the name thereof Boaz.

22 And upon the top of the pillars was lily work: so was the work of the pillars finished.

23 And he made a molten sea, ten cubits from the one brim to the other: it was round all about, and his height was five cubits: and a line of thirty cubits did compass it round about.

24 And under the brim of it round about there were gourds compassing it, ten in a cubit, compassing the sea round about: the gourds were cast in two rows, when it was cast.

25 It stood upon twelve oxen, three looking toward the north, and three looking toward the west, and three looking toward the south, and three looking toward the east: and the sea was set above upon them, and all their hinder parts were inward.

26 And it was a hand breadth thick, and the brim thereof was worked like the brim of a cup, with flowers of lilies: it contained two thousand of baths.

27 And he made ten bases of brass; four cubits was the length of one base, and four cubits the breadth thereof, and three cubits the height of it.

28 And the work of the bases was on this manner: they had borders, and the borders were between the ledges:

29 And on the borders that were between the ledges were lions, oxen, and cherubs: and upon the ledges there was a base above: and beneath the lions and oxen were certain additions made of thin work.

30 And every base had four brazen wheels, and the lords of brass: and the four corners thereof had undersetters: under the laver were undersetters molten, at the side of every addition.

31 And the mouth of it within the capital and above was a cubit: but the mouth thereof was round after the work of the base, a cubit and a half: and also upon the mouth of it were gravings with their borders, foursquare, not round.

32 And under the borders were four wheels; and the axletrees of the wheels were joined to the base: and the height of a wheel was a cubit and half a cubit.

33 And the work of the wheels was like the work of a chariot wheel: their axletrees, and their naves, and their felloes, and their spokes, were all molten.

34 And there were four undersetters to the four corners of one base: and the undersetters were of the very base itself.

35 And in the top of the base was there a round compass of half a cubit high: and on the top of the base the ledges thereof and the borders thereof were of the same.

36 For on the plates of the ledges thereof, and on the borders thereof, he graved cherubs, lions, and palm trees, according to the nakedness of every one, and additions round about.

37 After this manner he made the ten bases: all of them had one casting, one measure, and one size.

38 Then made he ten lavers of brass: one laver contained forty baths: and every laver was four cubits: and upon every one of the ten bases one laver.

39 And he put five bases on the right side of the house, and five on the left side of the house: and he set the sea on the right side of the house eastward over against the south.

40 And Hiram made the lavers, and the shovels, and the basins. So Hiram made an end of doing all the work that he made king Solomon for the house of the Becoming-One: 41 The two pillars, and the two bowls of the capitals that were on the top of the two pillars; and the two networks, to cover the two bowls of the capitals which were upon the top of the pillars;

42 And four hundred pomegranates for the two networks, even two rows of pomegranates for one network, to cover the two bowls of the capitals that were upon the pillars;

43 And the ten bases, and ten lavers on the bases;

44 And one sea, and twelve oxen under the sea;

45 And the pots, and the shovels, and the basins: and all these vessels, which Hiram made to king Solomon for the house of the Becoming-One, were of bright brass.

46 In the plain of Jordan did the king cast them, in the clay ground between Succoth and Zarthan.

47 And Solomon left all the vessels unweighed, because they were exceeding many: neither was the weight of the brass found out.

48 And Solomon made all the vessels that pertained unto the house of the Becoming-One: the altar of gold, and the table of gold, whereupon the showbread was,

49 And the candlesticks of pure gold, five on the right side, and five on the left, before the oracle, with the flowers, and the lamps, and the tongs of gold,

50 And the bowls, and the snuffers, and the basins, and the spoons, and the censers of pure gold; and the hinges of gold, both for the doors of the inner house, the most holy place, and for the doors of the house of the temple.

51 So was ended all the work that king Solomon made for the house of the Becoming-One. And Solomon brought in the things which David his father had dedicated; even the silver, and the gold, and the vessels, did he put among the treasures of the house of the Becoming-One.

1 Ki 8:1 Then Solomon assembled the elders of Israel, and all the heads of the tribes, the chief of the fathers of the children of Israel, unto king Solomon in Jerusalem, that they might bring up the ark of the covenant of the Becoming-One out of the city of David, which is Zion.

2 And all the men of Israel assembled themselves unto king Solomon at the feast in the month Ethanim, which is the seventh month.

3 And all the elders of Israel came, and the priests took up the ark.

4 And they brought up the ark of the Becoming-One, and the tabernacle of the set time,[109] and all the holy vessels that were in the tabernacle, even those did the priests and the Levites bring up.

5 And king Solomon, and all the congregation of Israel, that were assembled unto him, were with him before the ark, sacrificing sheep and oxen, that could not be told nor numbered for multitude.

6 And the priests brought in the ark of the covenant of the Becoming-One unto his place, into the oracle of the house, to the most holy place, even under the wings of the cherubs.

7 For the cherubs spread forth their two wings over the place of the ark, and the cherubs covered the ark and the staves thereof above.

8 And they drew out the staves, that the ends of the staves were seen out in the holy place before the oracle, and they were not seen outside: and there they are unto this day.

9 There was nothing in the ark save the two tables of stone, which Moses put there at Horeb, when the Becoming-One made a covenant with the children of Israel, when they came out of the land of Egypt.

10 And it came to pass, when the priests were come out of the holy place, that the cloud filled the house of the Becoming-One,

11 So that the priests could not stand to minister because of the cloud: for the glory of the Becoming-One had filled the house of the Becoming-One.

12 Then spoke Solomon, The Becoming-One said that he would dwell in the thick darkness.

13 I have surely built you a house to dwell in, a settled place for you to abide in for olams.

14 And the king turned his face about, and blessed all the congregation of Israel: and all the congregation of Israel stood;

15 And he said, Blessed be the Becoming-One, God of Israel, which spoke with his mouth unto David my father, and has with his hand fulfilled it, saying,

16 Since the day that I brought forth my people Israel out of Egypt, I chose no city out of all the tribes of Israel to build a house, that my name might be therein; but I chose David to be over my people Israel.

17 And it was in the heart of David my father to build a house for the name of the Becoming-One, God of Israel.

18 And the Becoming-One said unto David my father, Whereas it was in your heart to build a house unto my name, you did well that it was in your heart.

19 Nevertheless you shall not build the house; but your son that shall come forth out of your loins, he shall build the house unto my name.

20 And the Becoming-One has performed his word that he spoke, and I am risen up in the room of David my father, and sit on the throne of Israel, as the Becoming-One promised, and have built a house for the name of the Becoming-One, God of Israel.

21 And I have set there a place for the ark, wherein is the covenant of the Becoming-One, which he made with our fathers, when he brought them out of the land of Egypt.

22 And Solomon stood before the altar of the Becoming-One in the presence of all the congregation of Israel, and spread forth his hands toward heaven:

23 And he said, Becoming-One, God of Israel, there is no God like you, in the heavens above, or on earth beneath, who keep covenant and mercy with your servants that walk before you with all their heart:

24 Who have kept with your servant David my father that you promised him: you spoke also with your mouth, and have fulfilled it with your hand, as it is this day.

25 Therefore now, Becoming-One, God of Israel, keep with your servant David my father that you promised him, saying, There shall not fail you a man in my sight to sit on the throne of Israel; so that your children take heed to their way, that they walk before me as you have walked before me.

26 And now, O God of Israel, let your word, I pray you, be verified, which you spoke unto your servant David my father.

27 But will God indeed dwell on the earth? behold, the heavens and heavens of the heavens cannot contain you; how much less this house that I have built?

28 Yet have you respect unto the prayer of your servant, and to his supplication, O Becoming-One my God, to listen unto the cry and to the prayer, which your servant prays before you today:

29 That your eyes may be open toward this house night and day, even toward the place of which

---

[109] Appointed time or festival

you have said, My name shall be there: that you may listen unto the prayer which your servant shall make toward this place.

30 And listen you to the supplication of your servant, and of your people Israel, when they shall pray toward this place: and hear you in the heavens your dwelling place: and when you hear, forgive.

31 If any man trespass against his neighbor, and an oath be laid upon him to cause him to swear, and the oath come before your altar in this house:

32 Then hear you in heaven, and do, and judge your servants, condemning the wicked, to bring his way upon his head; and justifying the righteous, to give him according to his righteousness.

33 When your people Israel be struck down before the enemy, because they have sinned against you, and shall turn again to you, and confess your name, and pray, and make supplication unto you in this house:

34 Then hear you in heaven, and forgive the sin of your people Israel, and bring them again unto the land which you gave unto their fathers.

35 When the heavens is shut up, and there is no rain, because they have sinned against you; if they pray toward this place, and confess your name, and turn from their sin, when you afflict them:

36 Then hear you in heaven, and forgive the sin of your servants, and of your people Israel, that you teach them the good way wherein they should walk, and give rain upon your land, which you have given to your people for an inheritance.

37 If there be in the land famine, if there be pestilence, blasting, mildew, locust, or if there be caterpillar; if their enemy besiege them in the land of their cities; whatsoever plague, whatsoever sickness there be;

38 What prayer and supplication soever be made by any man, or by all your people Israel, which shall know every man the plague of his own heart, and spread forth his hands toward this house:

39 Then hear you in the heavens your dwelling place, and forgive, and do, and give to every man according to his ways, whose heart you know; for you, even you only, know the hearts of all the children of men;

40 That they may fear you all the days that they live in the land which you gave unto our fathers.

41 Moreover concerning a stranger, that is not of your people Israel, but comes out of a far country for your name's sake;

42 For they shall hear of your great name, and of your strong hand, and of your stretched out arm; when he shall come and pray toward this house;

43 Hear you in the heavens your dwelling place, and do according to all that the stranger calls to you for: that all people of the earth may know your name, to fear you, as do your people Israel; and that they may know that this house, which I have built, is called by your name.

44 If your people go out to battle against their enemy, wheresoever you shall send them, and shall pray unto the Becoming-One toward the city which you have chosen, and toward the house that I have built for your name:

45 Then hear you in the heavens their prayer and their supplication, and maintain their cause.

46 If they sin against you, for there is no man that sins not, and you be angry with them, and deliver them to the enemy, so that they carry them away captives unto the land of the enemy, far or near;

47 Yet if they shall bethink themselves in the land to which they were carried captives, and repent, and make supplication unto you in the land of them that carried them captives, saying, We have sinned, and have done perversely, we have committed wickedness;

48 And so return unto you with all their heart, and with all their soul, in the land of their enemies, which led them away captive, and pray unto you toward their land, which you gave unto their fathers, the city which you have chosen, and the house which I have built for your name:

49 Then hear you their prayer and their supplication in the heavens your dwelling place, and maintain their cause,

50 And forgive your people that have sinned against you, and all their transgressions wherein they have transgressed against you, and give them compassion before them who carried them captive, that they may have compassion on them:

51 For they be your people, and your inheritance, which you brought forth out of Egypt, from the midst of the furnace of iron:

52 That your eyes may be open unto the supplication of your servant, and unto the supplication of your people Israel, to listen unto them in all that they call for unto you.

53 For you did separate them from among all the people of the earth, to be your inheritance, as you spoke by the hand of Moses your servant, when you brought our fathers out of Egypt, O my Lord(s) the Becoming-One.

54 And it was so, that when Solomon had made an end of praying all this prayer and supplication unto the Becoming-One, he arose from before the altar of the Becoming-One, from kneeling on his knees with his hands spread up to heaven.

55 And he stood, and blessed all the congregation of Israel with a loud voice, saying,

56 Blessed be the Becoming-One, that has given rest unto his people Israel, according to all that he promised: there has not failed one word of all his good promise, which he promised by the hand of Moses his servant.

57 The Becoming-One our God be with us, as he was with our fathers: let him not leave us, nor forsake us:

58 That he may incline our hearts unto him, to walk in all his ways, and to keep his commandments, and his statutes, and his judgments, which he commanded our fathers.

59 And let these my words, wherewith I have made supplication before the Becoming-One, be near unto the Becoming-One our God day and night, that he maintain the cause of his servant, and the cause of his people Israel at all times, as the matter shall require:

60 That all the people of the earth may know that the Becoming-One, He is God, and that there is none else.

61 Let your heart therefore be perfect with the Becoming-One our God, to walk in his statutes, and to keep his commandments, as at this day.

62 And the king, and all Israel with him, offered sacrifice before the Becoming-One.

63 And Solomon offered a sacrifice of peace offerings, which he offered unto the Becoming-One, two and twenty thousand of oxen, and a hundred and twenty thousand of sheep. So the king and all the children of Israel dedicated the house of the Becoming-One.

64 The same day did the king hallow the middle of the court that was before the house of the Becoming-One for there he offered burnt offerings, and food offerings, and the fat of the peace offerings: because the brazen altar that was before the Becoming-One was too little to receive the burnt offerings, and food offerings, and the fat of the peace offerings.

65 And at that time Solomon held a feast, and all Israel with him, a great congregation, from the entering in of Hamath unto the river of Egypt, before the Becoming-One our God, seven days and seven days, even fourteen days.

66 On the eighth day he sent the people away: and they blessed the king, and went unto their tents joyful and glad of heart for all the goodness that the Becoming-One had done for David his servant, and for Israel his people.

1 Ki 9:1 And it came to pass, when Solomon had finished the building of the house of the Becoming-One, and the king's house, and all Solomon's desire which he was pleased to do,

2 That the Becoming-One appeared to Solomon the second time, as he had appeared [in a dream] unto him at Gibeon.

3 And the Becoming-One said unto him, I have heard your prayer and your supplication, that you have made before me: I have hallowed this house, which you have built, to put my name there for olam, and mine eyes and mine heart shall be there perpetually.

4 And if you will walk before me, as David your father walked, in integrity of heart, and in uprightness, to do according to all that I have commanded you, and will keep my statutes and my judgments:

5 Then I will establish the throne of your kingdom upon Israel for olam, as I promised to David your father, saying, There shall not fail you a man upon the throne of Israel.

6 But if you shall at all turn from following me, you or your children, and will not keep my commandments and my statutes which I have set before you, but go and serve other gods, and worship them:

7 Then will I cut off Israel out of the land which I have given them; and this house, which I have hallowed for my name, will I cast out of my sight; and Israel shall be a proverb and a byword among all people:

8 And at this house, which is high, every one that passes by it shall be astonished, and shall hiss; and they shall say, Why has the Becoming-One done thus unto this land, and to this house?

9 And they shall answer, Because they forsook the Becoming-One their God, who brought forth their fathers out of the land of Egypt, and have taken hold upon other gods, and have worshiped them, and served them: therefore has the Becoming-One brought upon them all this evil.

10 And it came to pass at the end of twenty years, when Solomon had built the two houses, the house of the Becoming-One, and the king's house,

11 Now Hiram the king of Tyre had furnished Solomon with cedar trees and fir trees, and with gold, according to all his desire, that then king Solomon gave Hiram twenty cities in the land of Galilee.

12 And Hiram came out from Tyre to see the cities which Solomon had given him; and they pleased him not.

13 And he said, What cities are these which you have given me, my brother? And he called them the land of Cabul unto this day.

14 And Hiram sent to the king sixscore talents of gold.

15 And this is the reason of the levy which king Solomon raised; for to build the house of the Becoming-One, and his own house, and Millo, and the wall of Jerusalem, and Hazor, and Megiddo, and Gezer.

16 For Pharaoh king of Egypt had gone up, and taken Gezer, and burnt it with fire, and slain the Canaanites that dwelt in the city, and given it for a present unto his daughter, Solomon's wife.

17 And Solomon built Gezer, and Beth-horon the lower,

18 And Baalath, and Tadmor in the wilderness, in the land,

19 And all the cities of store that Solomon had, and cities for his chariots, and cities for his horsemen, and that which Solomon desired to build in Jerusalem, and in Lebanon, and in all the land of his dominion.

20 And all the people that were left of the Amorites, Hittites, Perizzites, Hivites, and Jebusites, which were not of the children of Israel,

21 Their children that were left after them in the land, whom the children of Israel also were not able utterly to destroy, upon those did Solomon levy a tribute of bondservice unto this day.

22 But of the children of Israel did Solomon make no bondmen: but they were men of war, and his servants, and his princes, and his captains, and rulers of his chariots, and his horsemen.

23 These were the chief of the officers that were over Solomon's work, five hundred and fifty, which bare rule over the people that worked in the work.

24 But Pharaoh's daughter came up out of the city of David unto her house which Solomon had built for her: then did he build Millo.

25 And three times in a year did Solomon offer burnt offerings and peace offerings upon the altar which he built unto the Becoming-One, and he burnt incense upon the altar that was before the Becoming-One. So he finished the house.

26 And king Solomon made a navy of ships in Eziongeber, which is beside Eloth, on the shore of the boundary sea, in the land of Edom.

27 And Hiram sent in the navy his servants, shipmen that had knowledge of the sea, with the servants of Solomon.

28 And they came to Ophir, and fetched from there gold, four hundred and twenty talents, and brought it to king Solomon.

1 Ki 10:1 And when the queen of Sheba heard of the fame of Solomon concerning the name of the Becoming-One, she came to prove him with hard questions.

2 And she came to Jerusalem with a very great train, with camels that bare spices, and very much gold, and precious stones: and when she was come to Solomon, she communed with him of all that was in her heart.

3 And Solomon answered her all her questions: there was not anything hid from the king, which he told her not.

4 And when the queen of Sheba had seen all Solomon's wisdom, and the house that he had built,

5 And the food of his table, and the sitting of his servants, and the attendance of his ministers, and their apparel, and his cupbearers, and his ascent by which he went up unto the house of the Becoming-One; there was no more spirit in her.

6 And she said to the king, It was a true report that I heard in mine own land of your acts and of your wisdom.

7 Howbeit I believed not the words, until I came, and mine eyes had seen it: and, behold, the half was not told me: your wisdom and prosperity exceeds the fame which I heard.

8 Happy are your men, happy are these your servants, which stand continually before you, and that hear your wisdom.

9 Blessed be the Becoming-One your God, which delighted in you, to set you on the throne of Israel: because the Becoming-One loved Israel for olam; therefore he made you king, to do judgment and justice.

10 And she gave the king a hundred and twenty talents of gold, and of spices very great store, and precious stones: there came no more such abundance of spices as these which the queen of Sheba gave to king Solomon.

11 And the navy also of Hiram, that brought gold from Ophir, brought in from Ophir great plenty of almug trees, and precious stones.

12 And the king made of the almug trees pillars for the house of the Becoming-One, and for the king's house, harps also and psalteries for singers: there came no such almug trees, nor were seen unto this day.

13 And king Solomon gave unto the queen of Sheba all her desire, whatsoever she asked, beside that which Solomon gave her of his royal bounty. So she turned and went to her own country, she and her servants.

14 Now the weight of gold that came to Solomon in one year was six hundred threescore and six talents of gold,

15 Beside that he had of the merchantmen, and of the traffic of the spice merchants, and of all the kings of Arabia, and of the governors of the country.

16 And king Solomon made two hundred targets of beaten gold: six hundred shekels of gold went to one target.

17 And he made three hundred shields of beaten gold; three pound of gold went to one shield: and the king put them in the house of the forest of Lebanon.

18 Moreover the king made a great throne of ivory, and overlaid it with the best gold.

19 The throne had six steps, and the top of the throne was round behind: and there were stays on either side on the place of the seat, and two lions stood beside the stays.

20 And twelve lions stood there on the one side and on the other upon the six steps: there was not the like made in any kingdom.

21 And all king Solomon's drinking vessels were of gold, and all the vessels of the house of the forest of Lebanon were of pure gold; none were of silver: it was nothing accounted of in the days of Solomon.

22 For the king had at sea a navy of Tharshish with the navy of Hiram: once in three years came the navy of Tharshish, bringing gold, and silver, ivory, and apes, and peacocks.

23 So king Solomon exceeded all the kings of the earth for riches and for wisdom.

24 And all the earth sought to Solomon, to hear his wisdom, which God had put in his heart.

25 And they brought every man his present, vessels of silver, and vessels of gold, and garments, and armor, and spices, horses, and mules, a rate year by year.

26 And Solomon gathered together chariots and horsemen: and he had a thousand and four hundred chariots, and twelve thousand of horsemen, whom he bestowed in the cities for chariots, and with the king at Jerusalem.

27 And the king made silver to be in Jerusalem as stones, and cedars made he to be as the sycamore trees that are in the vale, for abundance.

28 And Solomon had horses brought out of Egypt, and linen yarn: the king's merchants received the linen yarn at a price.

29 And a chariot came up and went out of Egypt for six hundred shekels of silver, and a horse for a hundred and fifty: and so for all the kings of the Hittites, and for the kings of Syria, did they bring them out by their means.

1 Ki 11:1 But king Solomon loved many strange women, together with the daughter of Pharaoh, women of the Moabites, Ammonites, Edomites, Zidonians, and Hittites;

2 Of the nations concerning which the Becoming-One said unto the children of Israel, you shall not go in to them, neither shall they come in unto you: for surely they will turn away your heart after their gods: Solomon clave unto these in love.

3 And he had seven hundred wives, princesses, and three hundred concubines: and his wives turned away his heart.

4 For it came to pass, when Solomon was old, that his wives turned away his heart after other gods: and his heart was not perfect with the Becoming-One his God, as was the heart of David his father.

5 For Solomon went after Ashtoreth the goddess of the Zidonians, and after Milcom the abomination of the Ammonites.

6 And Solomon did evil in the sight of the Becoming-One, and went not fully after the Becoming-One, as did David his father.

7 Then did Solomon build a high place for Chemosh, the abomination of Moab, in the hill that is before Jerusalem, and for Molech, the abomination of the children of Ammon.

8 And likewise did he for all his strange wives, which burnt incense and sacrificed unto their gods.

9 And the Becoming-One was angry with Solomon, because his heart was turned from the Becoming-One, God of Israel, which had appeared unto him twice,

10 And had commanded him concerning this thing, that he should not go after other gods: but he kept not that which the Becoming-One commanded.

11 Therefore the Becoming-One said unto Solomon, Forasmuch as this is done of you, and you have not kept my covenant and my statutes, which I have commanded you, I will surely rend the kingdom from you, and will give it to your servant.

12 Notwithstanding in your days I will not do it for David your father's sake: but I will rend it out of the hand of your son.

13 Howbeit I will not rend away all the kingdom; but will give one tribe to your son for David my servant's sake, and for Jerusalem's sake which I have chosen.

14 And the Becoming-One stirred up an adversary unto Solomon, Hadad the Edomite: he was of the king's seed in Edom.

15 For it came to pass, when David was in Edom, and Joab the captain of the host was gone up to bury the slain, after he had struck every male in Edom;

16 For six months did Joab remain there with all Israel, until he had cut off every male in Edom:

17 That Hadad fled, he and certain Edomites of his father's servants with him, to go into Egypt; Hadad being yet a little child.

18 And they arose out of Midian, and came to Paran: and they took men with them out of Paran, and they came to Egypt, unto Pharaoh king of Egypt; which gave him a house, and appointed him victuals, and gave him land.

19 And Hadad found great favor in the sight of Pharaoh, so that he gave him to wife the sister of his own wife, the sister of Tahpenes the queen.

20 And the sister of Tahpenes bare him Genubath his son, whom Tahpenes weaned in Pharaoh's house: and Genubath was in Pharaoh's household among the sons of Pharaoh.

21 And when Hadad heard in Egypt that David slept with his fathers, and that Joab the captain of the host was dead, Hadad said to Pharaoh, Let me depart, that I may go to mine own country.

22 Then Pharaoh said unto him, But what have you lacked with me, that, behold, you seek to go to your own country? And he answered, Nothing: howbeit let me go any way.

23 And God stirred him up another adversary, Rezon the son of Eliadah, which fled from his lords Hadadezer king of Zobah:

24 And he gathered men unto him, and became captain over a band, when David killed them of Zobah: and they went to Damascus, and dwelt therein, and reigned in Damascus.

25 And he was an adversary to Israel all the days of Solomon, beside the mischief that Hadad did: and he abhorred Israel, and reigned over Syria.

26 And Jeroboam the son of Nebat, an Ephrathite of Zereda, Solomon's servant, whose mother's name was Zeruah, a widow woman, even he lifted up his hand against the king.

27 And this was the cause that he lifted up his hand against the king: Solomon built Millo, and repaired the breaches of the city of David his father.

28 And the man Jeroboam was a mighty man of valor: and Solomon seeing the young man that he was industrious, he made him ruler over all the charge of the house of Joseph.

29 And it came to pass at that time when Jeroboam went out of Jerusalem, that the prophet Ahijah the Shilonite found him in the way; and he had clad himself with a new garment; and they two were alone in the field:

30 And Ahijah caught the new garment that was on him, and ripped it in twelve pieces:

31 And he said to Jeroboam, Take you ten pieces: for thus says the Becoming-One, God of Israel, Behold, I will rend the kingdom out of the hand of Solomon, and will give ten tribes to you:

32 But he shall have one tribe for my servant David's sake, and for Jerusalem's sake, the city which I have chosen out of all the tribes of Israel:

33 Because that they have forsaken me, and have worshiped Ashtoreth the goddess of the Zidonians, Chemosh God of the Moabites, and Milcom God of the children of Ammon, and have not walked in my ways, to do that which is right in mine eyes, and to keep my statutes and my judgments, as did David his father.

34 Howbeit I will not take the whole kingdom out of his hand: but I will make him prince all the days of his life for David my servant's sake, whom I chose, because he kept my commandments and my statutes:

35 But I will take the kingdom out of his son's hand, and will give it unto you, even ten tribes.

36 And unto his son will I give one tribe, that David my servant may have a light always before me in Jerusalem, the city which I have chosen me to put my name there.

37 And I will take you, and you shall reign according to all that your soul desires, and shall be king over Israel.

38 And it shall be, if you will listen unto all that I command you, and will walk in my ways, and do that is right in my sight, to keep my statutes and my commandments, as David my servant did; that I will be with you, and build you a sure house, as I built for David, and will give Israel unto you.

39 And I will for this afflict the seed of David, but not all the days.

40 Solomon sought therefore to kill Jeroboam. And Jeroboam arose, and fled into Egypt, unto Shishak king of Egypt, and was in Egypt until the death of Solomon.

41 And the rest of the acts of Solomon, and all that he did, and his wisdom, are they not written in the book of the acts of Solomon?

42 And the time that Solomon reigned in Jerusalem over all Israel was forty years.

43 And Solomon slept with his fathers, and was buried in the city of David his father: and Rehoboam his son reigned in his stead.

1 Ki 12:1 And Rehoboam went to Shechem: for all Israel were come to Shechem to make him king.

2 And it came to pass, when Jeroboam the son of Nebat, who was yet in Egypt, heard of it, for he was fled from the presence of king Solomon, and Jeroboam dwelt in Egypt;

3 That they sent and called him. And Jeroboam and all the congregation of Israel came, and spoke unto Rehoboam, saying,

4 your father made our yoke grievous: now therefore make you the grievous service of your father, and his heavy yoke which he put upon us, lighter, and we will serve you.

5 And he said unto them, Depart yet for three days, then come again to me. And the people departed.

6 And king Rehoboam consulted with the old men, that stood before Solomon his father while he yet lived, and said, How do you advise that I may answer this people?

7 And they spoke unto him, saying, If you will be a servant unto this people this day, and will serve them, and answer them, and speak good words to them, then they will be your servants all the days.

8 But he forsook the counsel of the old men, which they had given him, and consulted with the young men that were grown up with him, and which stood before him:

9 And he said unto them, What counsel give you that we may answer this people, who have spoken to me, saying, Make the yoke which your father did put upon us lighter?

10 And the young men that were grown up with him spoke unto him, saying, Thus shall you speak unto this people that spoke unto you, saying, your father made our yoke heavy, but make you it lighter unto us; thus shall you say unto them, My little finger shall be thicker than my father's loins.

11 And now whereas my father did lade you with a heavy yoke, I will add to your yoke: my father has chastised you with whips, but I will chastise you with scorpions.

12 So Jeroboam and all the people came to Rehoboam the third day, as the king had appointed, saying, Come to me again the third day.

13 And the king answered the people roughly, and forsook the old men's counsel that they gave him;

14 And spoke to them after the counsel of the young men, saying, My father made your yoke heavy, and I will add to your yoke: my father also chastised you with whips, but I will chastise you with scorpions.

15 Therefore the king listened not unto the people; for the cause was from the Becoming-One, that he might perform his saying, which the Becoming-One spoke by Ahijah the Shilonite unto Jeroboam the son of Nebat.

16 So when all Israel saw that the king listened not unto them, the people answered the king, saying, What portion have we in David? neither have we inheritance in the son of Jesse: to your tents, O Israel: now see to your own house, David. So Israel departed unto their tents.

17 But as for the children of Israel which dwelt in the cities of Judah, Rehoboam reigned over them.

18 Then king Rehoboam sent Adoram, who was over the tribute; and all Israel stoned him with stones, that he died. Therefore king Rehoboam made speed to get him up to his chariot, to flee to Jerusalem.

19 So Israel rebelled against the house of David unto this day.

20 And it came to pass, when all Israel heard that Jeroboam was come again, that they sent and called him unto the congregation, and made him king over all Israel: there was none that followed the house of David, but the tribe of Judah only.

21 And when Rehoboam was come to Jerusalem, he assembled all the house of Judah, with the tribe of Benjamin, a hundred and fourscore thousand of chosen men, which were warriors, to fight against the house of Israel, to bring the kingdom again to Rehoboam the son of Solomon.

22 But the word of God came unto Shemaiah the man of God, saying,

23 Speak unto Rehoboam, the son of Solomon, king of Judah, and unto all the house of Judah and Benjamin, and to the remnant of the people, saying,

24 Thus says the Becoming-One, you shall not go up, nor fight against your brethren the children of Israel: return every man to his house; for this thing is from me. They listened therefore to the word of the Becoming-One, and returned to depart, according to the word of the Becoming-One.

25 Then Jeroboam built Shechem in mount Ephraim, and dwelt therein; and went out from there, and built Penuel.

26 And Jeroboam said in his heart, Now shall the kingdom return to the house of David:

27 If this people go up to do sacrifice in the house of the Becoming-One at Jerusalem, then shall the heart of this people turn again unto their lords, even unto Rehoboam king of Judah, and they shall kill me, and go again to Rehoboam king of Judah.

28 Whereupon the king took counsel, and made two calves of gold, and said unto them, It is too much for you to go up to Jerusalem: behold your gods, O Israel, which brought you up out of the land of Egypt.

29 And he set the one calf in Bethel, and the other calf put he in Dan.

30 And this thing became a sin: for the people went to worship before the one calf, even unto Dan.

31 And he made a house of high places, and made priests of the lowest of the people, which were not of the sons of Levi.

32 And Jeroboam ordained a feast in the eighth month, on the fifteenth day of the month, like unto the feast that is in Judah, and he offered upon the altar. So did he in Bethel, sacrificing unto the calves that he had made: and he placed in Bethel the priests of the high places which he had made.

33 So he offered upon the altar which he had made in Bethel the fifteenth day of the eighth month, even in the month which he had devised of his own heart; and ordained a feast unto the children of Israel: and he offered upon the altar, and burnt incense.

1 Ki 13:1 And, behold, there came a man of God out of Judah by the word of the Becoming-One unto Bethel: and Jeroboam stood by the altar to burn incense.

2 And he cried against the altar in the word of the Becoming-One, and said, O altar, altar, thus says the Becoming-One; Behold, a child shall be born unto the house of David, Josiah by name; and upon you shall he offer the priests of the high places that burn incense upon you, and men's bones shall be burnt upon you.

3 And he gave a sign the same day, saying, This is the sign which the Becoming-One has spoken; Behold, the altar shall be rent, and the ashes that are upon it shall be poured out.

4 And it came to pass, when king Jeroboam heard the saying of the man of God, which had cried against the altar in Bethel, that he put forth his hand from the altar, saying, Lay hold on him. And his hand, which he put forth against him, dried up, so that he could not pull it in again to him.

5 The altar also was rent, and the ashes poured out from the altar, according to the sign which the man of God had given by the word of the Becoming-One.

6 And the king answered and said unto the man of God, Entreat now the face of the Becoming-One your God, and pray for me, that my hand may be restored me again. And the man of God besought the Becoming-One, and the king's hand was restored him again, and became as it was before.

7 And the king said unto the man of God, Come home with me, and refresh thyself, and I will give you a reward.

8 And the man of God said unto the king, If you will give me half your house, I will not go in with you, neither will I eat bread nor drink water in this place:

9 For so was it charged me by the word of the Becoming-One, saying, Eat no bread, nor drink water, nor turn again by the same way that you came.

10 So he went another way, and returned not by the way that he came to Bethel.

11 Now there dwelt an old prophet in Bethel; and his sons came and told him all the works that the man of God had done that day in Bethel: the words which he had spoken unto the king, them they told also to their father.

12 And their father said unto them, What way went he? For his sons had seen what way the man of God went, which came from Judah.

13 And he said unto his sons, Saddle me the donkey. So they saddled him the donkey: and he rode thereon,

14 And went after the man of God, and found him sitting under an oak: and he said unto him, are you the man of God that came from Judah? And he said, I am.

15 Then he said unto him, Come home with me, and eat bread.

16 And he said, I may not return with you, nor go in with you: neither will I eat bread nor drink water with you in this place:

17 For it was said to me by the word of the Becoming-One, you shall eat no bread nor drink water there, nor turn again to go by the way that you came.

18 He said unto him, I am a prophet also as you are; and an angel spoke unto me by the word of the Becoming-One, saying, Bring him back with you into your house, that he may eat bread and drink water. But he lied unto him.

19 So he went back with him, and did eat bread in his house, and drank water.

20 And it came to pass, as they sat at the table, that the word of the Becoming-One came unto the prophet that brought him back:

21 And he cried unto the man of God that came from Judah, saying, Thus says the Becoming-One, Forasmuch as you have disobeyed the mouth of the Becoming-One, and have not kept the commandment which the Becoming-One your God commanded you,

22 But came back, and have eaten bread and drunk water in the place, of the which the Becoming-One did say to you, Eat no bread, and drink no water; your carcase shall not come unto the tomb of your fathers.

23 And it came to pass, after he had eaten bread, and after he had drunk, that he saddled for him the donkey, for the prophet whom he had brought back.

24 And when he was gone, a lion met him by the way, and killed him: and his carcase was cast in the way, and the donkey stood by it, the lion also stood by the carcase.

25 And, behold, men passed by, and saw the carcase cast in the way, and the lion standing by the carcase: and they came and told it in the city where the old prophet dwelt.

26 And when the prophet that brought him back from the way heard thereof, he said, It is the man of God, who was disobedient unto the word of the Becoming-One: therefore the Becoming-One has delivered him unto the lion, which has torn him, and slain him, according to the word of the Becoming-One, which he spoke unto him.

27 And he spoke to his sons, saying, Saddle me the donkey. And they saddled him.

28 And he went and found his carcase cast in the way, and the donkey and the lion standing by the carcase: the lion had not eaten the carcase, nor torn the donkey.

29 And the prophet took up the carcase of the man of God, and laid it upon the donkey, and brought it back: and the old prophet came to the city, to mourn and to bury him.

30 And he laid his carcase in his own grave; and they mourned over him, saying, Alas, my brother!

31 And it came to pass, after he had buried him, that he spoke to his sons, saying, When I am dead, then bury me in the tomb wherein the man of God is buried; lay my bones beside his bones:

32 For the saying which he cried by the word of the Becoming-One against the altar in Bethel, and against all the houses of the high places which are in the cities of Samaria, shall surely come to pass.

33 After this thing Jeroboam returned not from his evil way, but made again of the lowest of the people priests of the high places: whosoever would, he consecrated him, and he became one of the priests of the high places.

34 And this thing became sin unto the house of Jeroboam, even to cut it off, and to destroy it from off the face of the earth.

1 Ki 14:1 At that time Abijah the son of Jeroboam fell sick.

2 And Jeroboam said to his wife, Arise, I pray you, and disguise thyself, that you be not known to be the wife of Jeroboam; and get you to Shiloh: behold, there is Ahijah the prophet, which told me that I should be king over this people.

3 And take with you ten loaves, and cracknels, and a cruse of honey, and go to him: he shall tell you what shall become of the child.

4 And Jeroboam's wife did so, and arose, and went to Shiloh, and came to the house of Ahijah. But Ahijah could not see; for his eyes were set by reason of his age.

5 And the Becoming-One said unto Ahijah, Behold, the wife of Jeroboam comes to ask a thing of you for her son; for he is sick: thus and thus shall you say unto her: for it shall be, when she comes in, that she shall pretend herself to be another woman.

6 And it was so, when Ahijah heard the sound of her feet, as she came in at the door, that he said, Come in, you wife of Jeroboam; why pretend you yourself to be another? for I am sent to you with heavy tidings.

7 Go, tell Jeroboam, Thus says the Becoming-One, God of Israel, Forasmuch as I exalted you from among the people, and made you prince over my people Israel,

8 And ripped the kingdom away from the house of David, and gave it you: and yet you have not been as my servant David, who kept my commandments, and who followed me with all his heart, to do that only which was right in mine eyes;

9 But have done evil above all that were before you: for you have gone and made you other gods, and molten images, to provoke me to anger, and have cast me behind your back:

10 Therefore, behold, I will bring evil upon the house of Jeroboam, and will cut off from Jeroboam him that pisses against the wall, and him that is shut up and left in Israel, and will take away the remnant of the house of Jeroboam, as a man takes away dung, till it be all gone.

11 Him that dies of Jeroboam in the city shall the dogs eat; and him that dies in the field shall the fowls of the air eat: for the Becoming-One has spoken it.

12 Arise you therefore, get you to your own house: and when your feet enter into the city, the child shall die.

13 And all Israel shall mourn for him, and bury him: for he only of Jeroboam shall come to the grave, because in him there is found some good thing toward the Becoming-One, God of Israel in the house of Jeroboam.

14 Moreover the Becoming-One shall raise him up a king over Israel, who shall cut off the house of Jeroboam that day: but what? even now.

15 For the Becoming-One shall smite Israel, as a reed is shaken in the water, and he shall root up Israel out of this good land, which he gave to their fathers, and shall scatter them beyond the river, because they have made their Asherahs, provoking the Becoming-One to anger.

16 And he shall give Israel up because of the sins of Jeroboam, who did sin, and who made Israel to sin.

17 And Jeroboam's wife arose, and departed, and came to Tirzah: and when she came to the threshold of the door, the child died;

18 And they buried him; and all Israel mourned for him, according to the word of the Becoming-One, which he spoke by the hand of his servant Ahijah the prophet.

19 And the rest of the acts of Jeroboam, how he warred, and how he reigned, behold, they are written in the book of the chronicles of the kings of Israel.

20 And the days which Jeroboam reigned were two and twenty years: and he slept with his fathers, and Nadab his son reigned in his stead.

21 And Rehoboam the son of Solomon reigned in Judah. Rehoboam was a son of forty and one years when he began to reign, and he reigned seventeen years in Jerusalem, the city which the Becoming-One did choose out of all the tribes of Israel, to put his name there. And his mother's name was Naamah an Ammonitess.

22 And Judah did evil in the sight of the Becoming-One, and they provoked him to jealousy with their sins which they had committed, above all that their fathers had done.

23 For they also built them high places, and images, and Asherahs, on every high hill, and under every green tree.

24 And there were also sodomites in the land: and they did according to all the abominations of the nations which the Becoming-One cast out before the children of Israel.

25 And it came to pass in the fifth year of king Rehoboam, that Shishak king of Egypt came up against Jerusalem:

26 And he took away the treasures of the house of the Becoming-One, and the treasures of the king's house; he even took away all: and he took away all the shields of gold which Solomon had made.

27 And king Rehoboam made in their stead brazen shields, and committed them unto the hands of the chief of the guard, which kept the door of the king's house.

28 And it was so, when the king went into the house of the Becoming-One, that the guard bare them, and brought them back into the guard chamber.

29 Now the rest of the acts of Rehoboam, and all that he did, are they not written in the book of the words of the days [chronicles] of the kings of Judah?

30 And there was war between Rehoboam and Jeroboam all their days.

31 And Rehoboam slept with his fathers, and was buried with his fathers in the city of David. And his mother's name was Naamah an Ammonitess. And Abijam his son reigned in his stead.

1 Ki 15:1 Now in the eighteenth year of king Jeroboam the son of Nebat reigned Abijam over Judah.

2 Three years reigned he in Jerusalem. And his mother's name was Maachah, the daughter of Abishalom.

3 And he walked in all the sins of his father, which he had done before him: and his heart was not perfect with the Becoming-One his God, as the heart of David his father.

4 Nevertheless for David's sake did the Becoming-One his God give him a lamp in Jerusalem, to set up his son after him, and to establish Jerusalem:

5 Because David did that which was right in the eyes of the Becoming-One, and turned not aside from anything that he commanded him all the days of his life, save only in the matter of Uriah the Hittite.

6 And there was war between Rehoboam and Jeroboam all the days of his life.

7 Now the rest of the acts of Abijam, and all that he did, are they not written in the book of the word of the days [chronicles] of the kings of Judah? And there was war between Abijam and Jeroboam.

8 And Abijam slept with his fathers; and they buried him in the city of David: and Asa his son reigned in his stead.

9 And in the twentieth year of Jeroboam king of Israel reigned Asa over Judah.

10 And forty and one years reigned he in Jerusalem. And his mother's name was Maachah, the daughter of Abishalom.

11 And Asa did that which was right in the eyes of the Becoming-One, as did David his father.

12 And he took away the sodomites out of the land, and removed all the idols that his fathers had made.

13 And also Maachah his mother, even her he removed from being queen, because she had made an idol in a Asherah; and Asa destroyed her idol, and burnt it by the brook Kidron.

14 But the high places were not removed: nevertheless Asa's heart was perfect with the Becoming-One all his days.

15 And he brought in the things which his father had dedicated, and the things which himself had dedicated, into the house of the Becoming-One, silver, and gold, and vessels.

16 And there was war between Asa and Baasha king of Israel all their days.

17 And Baasha king of Israel went up against Judah, and built Ramah, that he might not permit any to go out or come in to Asa king of Judah.

18 Then Asa took all the silver and the gold that were left in the treasures of the house of the Becoming-One, and the treasures of the king's house, and delivered them into the hand of his servants: and king Asa sent them to Benhadad, the son of Tabrimon, the son of Hezion, king of Syria, that dwelt at Damascus, saying,

19 There is a league between me and you, and between my father and your father: behold, I have sent unto you a present of silver and gold; come and break your league with Baasha king of Israel, that he may depart from me.

20 So Benhadad listened unto king Asa, and sent the captains of the hosts which he had against the cities of Israel, and smote Ijon, and Dan, and Abel-beth-maachah, and all Cinneroth, with all the land of Naphtali.

21 And it came to pass, when Baasha heard thereof, that he left off building of Ramah, and dwelt in Tirzah.

22 Then king Asa made a proclamation throughout all Judah; none was exempted: and they took away the stones of Ramah, and the timber thereof, wherewith Baasha had built; and king Asa built with them Geba of Benjamin, and Mizpah.

23 The rest of all the acts of Asa, and all his might, and all that he did, and the cities which he built, are they not written in the book of the words of the days [chronicles] of the kings of Judah? Nevertheless in the time of his old age he was diseased in his feet.

24 And Asa slept with his fathers, and was buried with his fathers in the city of David his father: and Jehoshaphat his son reigned in his stead.

25 And Nadab the son of Jeroboam began to reign over Israel in the second year of Asa king of Judah, and reigned over Israel two years.

26 And he did evil in the sight of the Becoming-One, and walked in the way of his father, and in his sin wherewith he made Israel to sin.

27 And Baasha the son of Ahijah, of the house of Issachar, conspired against him; and Baasha smote him at Gibbethon, which belonged to the Philistines; for Nadab and all Israel laid siege to Gibbethon.

28 Even in the third year of Asa king of Judah did Baasha slay him, and reigned in his stead.

29 And it came to pass, when he reigned, that he smote all the house of Jeroboam; he left not to Jeroboam any that breathed, until he had destroyed him, according unto the saying of the Becoming-One, which he spoke by his servant Ahijah the Shilonite:

30 Because of the sins of Jeroboam which he sinned, and which he made Israel sin, by his provocation wherewith he provoked the Becoming-One, God of Israel to anger.

31 Now the rest of the acts of Nadab, and all that he did, are they not written in the book of the words of the days [chronicles] of the kings of Israel?

32 And there was war between Asa and Baasha king of Israel all their days.

33 In the third year of Asa king of Judah began Baasha the son of Ahijah to reign over all Israel in Tirzah, twenty and four years.

34 And he did evil in the sight of the Becoming-One, and walked in the way of Jeroboam, and in his sin wherewith he made Israel to sin.

1 Ki 16:1 Then the word of the Becoming-One came to Jehu the son of Hanani against Baasha, saying,

2 Forasmuch as I exalted you out of the dust, and made you prince over my people Israel; and you have walked in the way of Jeroboam, and have made my people Israel to sin, to provoke me to anger with their sins;

3 Behold, I will take away the posterity of Baasha, and the posterity of his house; and will make your house like the house of Jeroboam the son of Nebat.

4 Him that dies of Baasha in the city shall the dogs eat; and him that dies of his in the fields shall the fowls of the air eat.

5 Now the rest of the acts of Baasha, and what he did, and his might, are they not written in the book of the words of the days [chronicles] of the kings of Israel?

6 So Baasha slept with his fathers, and was buried in Tirzah: and Elah his son reigned in his stead.

7 And also by the hand of the prophet Jehu the son of Hanani came the word of the Becoming-One against Baasha, and against his house, even for all the evil that he did in the sight of the Becoming-One, in provoking him to anger with the work of his hands, in being like the house of Jeroboam; and because he killed him.

8 In the twenty and sixth year of Asa king of Judah began Elah the son of Baasha to reign over Israel in Tirzah, two years.

9 And his servant Zimri, captain of half his chariots, conspired against him, as he was in Tirzah, drinking himself drunk in the house of Arza steward of his house in Tirzah.

10 And Zimri went in and smote him, and killed him, in the twenty and seventh year of Asa king of Judah, and reigned in his stead.

11 And it came to pass, when he began to reign, as soon as he sat on his throne, that he killed all the house of Baasha: he left him not one that pisses against a wall, neither of his kinsfolks, nor of his friends.

12 Thus did Zimri destroy all the house of Baasha, according to the word of the Becoming-One, which he spoke against Baasha by Jehu the prophet,

13 For all the sins of Baasha, and the sins of Elah his son, by which they sinned, and by which they made Israel to sin, in provoking the Becoming-One, God of Israel to anger with their vanities.

14 Now the rest of the acts of Elah, and all that he did, are they not written in the book of the words of the days [chronicles] of the kings of Israel?

15 In the twenty and seventh year of Asa king of Judah did Zimri reign seven days in Tirzah. And the people were encamped against Gibbethon, which belonged to the Philistines.

16 And the people that were encamped heard say, Zimri has conspired, and has also slain the king: therefore all Israel made Omri, the captain of the host, king over Israel that day in the camp.

17 And Omri went up from Gibbethon, and all Israel with him, and they besieged Tirzah.

18 And it came to pass, when Zimri saw that the city was taken, that he went into the palace of the king's house, and burnt the king's house over him with fire, and died,

19 For his sins which he sinned in doing evil in the sight of the Becoming-One, in walking in the way of Jeroboam, and in his sin which he did, to make Israel to sin.

20 Now the rest of the acts of Zimri, and his treason that he worked, are they not written in the book of the words of the days [chronicles] of the kings of Israel?

21 Then were the people of Israel divided into two parts: half of the people followed Tibni the son of Ginath, to make him king; and half followed Omri.

22 But the people that followed Omri prevailed against the people that followed Tibni the son of Ginath: so Tibni died, and Omri reigned.

23 In the thirty and first year of Asa king of Judah began Omri to reign over Israel, twelve years: six years reigned he in Tirzah.

24 And he bought the hill Samaria of Shemer for two talents of silver, and built on the hill, and called the name of the city which he built, after the name of Shemer, owner of the hill, Samaria.

25 But Omri worked evil in the eyes of the Becoming-One, and did worse than all that were before him.

26 For he walked in all the way of Jeroboam the son of Nebat, and in his sin wherewith he made Israel to sin, to provoke the Becoming-One, God of Israel to anger with their vanities.

27 Now the rest of the acts of Omri which he did, and his might that he showed, are they not written in the book of the words of the days [chronicles] of the kings of Israel?

28 So Omri slept with his fathers, and was buried in Samaria: and Ahab his son reigned in his stead.

29 And in the thirty and eighth year of Asa king of Judah began Ahab the son of Omri to reign over Israel: and Ahab the son of Omri reigned over Israel in Samaria twenty and two years.

30 And Ahab the son of Omri did evil in the sight of the Becoming-One above all that were before him.

31 And it came to pass, as if it had been a light thing for him to walk in the sins of Jeroboam the son of Nebat, that he took to wife Jezebel the daughter of Ethbaal king of the Zidonians, and went and served the lord [baal] and worshiped him.

32 And he reared up an altar for the lord [baal] in the house of the lord [baal] which he had built in Samaria.

33 And Ahab made a Asherah; and Ahab did more to provoke the Becoming-One, God of Israel to anger than all the kings of Israel that were before him.

34 In his days did Hiel the Bethelite build Jericho: he laid the foundation thereof in Abiram his firstborn, and set up the gates thereof in his youngest son Segub, according to the word of the Becoming-One, which he spoke by Joshua the son of Nun.

1 Ki 17:1 And **Elijah** the Tishbite, who was of the inhabitants of Gilead, said unto Ahab, As the Becoming-One, God of Israel lives, before whom I stand, there shall not be dew nor rain these years, but according to my word.

2 And the word of the Becoming-One came unto him, saying,

3 Get you hence, and turn you eastward, and hide yourself by the brook Cherith, that is before Jordan.

4 And it shall be, that you shall drink of the brook; and I have commanded the ravens to feed you there.

5 So he went and did according unto the word of the Becoming-One: for he went and dwelt by the brook Cherith, that is before Jordan.

6 And the ravens brought him bread and flesh in the morning, and bread and flesh in the evening; and he drank of the brook.

7 And it came to pass at the end of days, that the brook dried up, because there had been no rain in the land.

8 And the word of the Becoming-One came unto him, saying,

9 Arise, get you to Zarephath, which belongs to Zidon, and dwell there: behold, I have commanded a widow woman there to sustain you.

10 So he arose and went to Zarephath. And when he came to the gate of the city, behold, the widow woman was there gathering of sticks: and he called to her, and said, Fetch me, I pray you, a little water in a vessel, that I may drink.

11 And as she was going to fetch it, he called to her, and said, Bring me, I pray you, a morsel of bread in your hand.

12 And she said, As the Becoming-One your God lives, I have not a cake, but a handful of meal in a barrel, and a little oil in a cruse: and, behold, I am gathering two sticks, that I may go in and dress it for me and my son, that we may eat it, and die.

13 And Elijah said unto her, Fear not; go and do as you have said: but make me thereof a little cake first, and bring it unto me, and after make for you and for your son.

14 For thus says the Becoming-One, God of Israel, The barrel of meal shall not waste, neither shall the cruse of oil fail, until the day that the Becoming-One sends rain upon the earth.

15 And she went and did according to the saying of Elijah: and she, and he, and her house, did eat many days.

16 And the barrel of meal wasted not, neither did the cruse of oil fail, according to the word of the Becoming-One, which he spoke by Elijah.

17 And it came to pass after these things, that the son of the woman, the mistress of the house, fell sick; and his sickness was so great, that there was no breath left in him.

18 And she said unto Elijah, What have I to do with you, O you man of God? are you come unto me to call my sin to remembrance, and to slay my son?

19 And he said unto her, Give me your son. And he took him out of her bosom, and carried him up into a loft, where he abode, and laid him upon his own bed.

20 And he cried unto the Becoming-One, and said, O Becoming-One my God, have you also brought evil upon the widow with whom I sojourn, by slaying her son?

21 And he stretched himself upon the child three times, and cried unto the Becoming-One, and said, O Becoming-One my God, I pray you, let this child's soul come into him again.

22 And the Becoming-One heard the voice of Elijah; and the soul of the child came into him again, and he revived.

23 And Elijah took the child, and brought him down out of the chamber into the house, and delivered him unto his mother: and Elijah said, See, your son lives.

24 And the woman said to Elijah, Now by this I know that you are a man of God, and that the word of the Becoming-One in your mouth is truth.

1 Ki 18:1 And it came to pass after many days, that the word of the Becoming-One came to Elijah in the third year, saying, Go, show yourself unto Ahab; and I will send rain upon the earth.

2 And Elijah went to show himself unto Ahab. And there was a great famine in Samaria.

3 And Ahab called Obadiah, which was the governor of his house. Now Obadiah feared the Becoming-One greatly:

4 For it was so, when Jezebel cut off the prophets of the Becoming-One, that Obadiah took a hundred prophets, and hid them by fifty in a cave, and fed them with bread and water.

5 And Ahab said unto Obadiah, Go into the land, unto all fountains of water, and unto all brooks: perhaps we may find grass to save the horses and mules alive, that we lose not all the beasts.

6 So they divided the land between them to pass throughout it: Ahab went one way by himself, and Obadiah went another way by himself.

7 And as Obadiah was in the way, behold, Elijah met him: and he knew him, and fell on his face, and said, are you that my lord Elijah?

8 And he answered him, I am: go, tell thy lords, Behold, Elijah is here.

9 And he said, What have I sinned, that you would deliver your servant into the hand of Ahab, to slay me?

10 As the Becoming-One your God lives, there is no nation or kingdom, to which my lord has not sent to seek you: and when they said, He is not there; he took an oath of the kingdom and nation, that they found you not.

11 And now you say, Go, tell thy lords, Behold, Elijah is here.

12 And it shall come to pass, as soon as I am gone from you, that the spirit of the Becoming-One shall carry you to where I know not; and so when I come and tell Ahab, and he cannot find you, he shall slay me: but I your servant fear the Becoming-One from my youth.

13 Was it not told my lord what I did when Jezebel killed the prophets of the Becoming-One, how I hid a hundred men of the Becoming-One's prophets by fifty in a cave, and fed them with bread and water?

14 And now you say, Go, tell thy lords, Behold, Elijah is here: and he shall slay me.

15 And Elijah said, As the Becoming-One of hosts lives, before whom I stand, I will surely show myself unto him today.

16 So Obadiah went to meet Ahab, and told him: and Ahab went to meet Elijah.

17 And it came to pass, when Ahab saw Elijah, that Ahab said unto him, are you he that troubles Israel?

18 And he answered, I have not troubled Israel; but you, and your father's house, in that you have forsaken the commandments of the Becoming-One, and you have followed the lords [baalim]

19 Now therefore send, and gather to me all Israel unto mount Carmel, and the prophets of the lord [baal] four hundred and fifty, and the prophets of

the Asherahs four hundred, which eat at Jezebel's table.

20 So Ahab sent unto all the children of Israel, and gathered the prophets together unto mount Carmel.

21 And Elijah came unto all the people, and said, How long will you be between two opinions? if the Becoming-One be God, follow him: but if the lord [baal] then follow him. And the people answered him not a word.

22 Then said Elijah unto the people, I, even I only, remain a prophet of the Becoming-One; but the lord's [baal] prophets are four hundred and fifty men.

23 Let them therefore give us two bullocks; and let them choose one bullock for themselves, and cut it in pieces, and lay it on wood, and put no fire under: and I will dress the other bullock, and lay it on wood, and put no fire under:

24 And call you on the name of your gods, and I will call on the name of the Becoming-One: and God that answers by fire, He be God. And all the people answered and said, It is well spoken.

25 And Elijah said unto the prophets of the lord [baal] Choose you one bullock for yourselves, and dress it first; for you are many; and call on the name of your gods, but put no fire under.

26 And they took the bullock which was given them, and they dressed it, and called on the name of the lord [baal] from morning even until noon, saying, O lord [baal] hear us. But there was no voice, nor any that answered. And they leaped upon the altar which was made.

27 And it came to pass at noon, that Elijah mocked them, and said, Cry aloud: for he is a god; either he is talking, or he is pursuing, or he is in a journey, or perhaps he sleeps, and must be awaked.

28 And they cried aloud, and cut themselves after their manner with knives and lancets, till the blood gushed out upon them.

29 And it came to pass, when midday was past, and they prophesied until the time of the offering of the evening sacrifice, that there was neither voice, nor any to answer, nor any that regarded.

30 And Elijah said unto all the people, Come near unto me. And all the people came near unto him. And he repaired the altar of the Becoming-One that was broken down.

31 And Elijah took twelve stones, according to the number of the tribes of the sons of Jacob, unto whom the word of the Becoming-One came, saying, Israel shall be your name:

32 And with the stones he built an altar in the name of the Becoming-One: and he made a trench about the altar, as great as would contain two measures of seed.

33 And he put the wood in order, and cut the bullock in pieces, and laid him on the wood, and said, Fill four barrels with water, and pour it on the burnt sacrifice, and on the wood.

34 And he said, Do it the second time. And they did it the second time. And he said, Do it the third time. And they did it the third time.

35 And the water ran round about the altar; and he filled the trench also with water.

36 And it came to pass at the time of the offering of the evening sacrifice, that Elijah the prophet came near, and said, Becoming-One, God of Abraham, Isaac, and of Israel, let it be known this day that you are God in Israel, and that I am your servant, and that I have done all these things at your word.

37 Hear me, O Becoming-One, hear me, that this people may know that you Becoming-One be God, and that you have turned their heart back again.

38 Then the fire of the Becoming-One fell, and consumed the burnt sacrifice, and the wood, and the stones, and the dust, and licked up the water that was in the trench.

39 And when all the people saw it, they fell on their faces: and they said, The Becoming-One, he is **the** God; the Becoming-One, he is **the** God.

40 And Elijah said unto them, Take the prophets of the lord [baal] let not one of them escape. And they took them: and Elijah brought them down to the brook Kishon, and killed them there.

41 And Elijah said unto Ahab, Get you up, eat and drink; for there is a sound of abundance of rain.

42 So Ahab went up to eat and to drink. And Elijah went up to the top of Carmel; and he cast himself down upon the earth, and put his face between his knees,

43 And said to his servant, Go up now, look toward the sea. And he went up, and looked, and said, There is nothing. And he said, Go again seven times.

44 And it came to pass at the seventh time, that he said, Behold, there arises a little cloud out of the sea, like a man's hand. And he said, Go up, say unto Ahab, Prepare your chariot, and get you down, that the rain stop you not.

45 And it came to pass in the mean while, that the heavens was black with clouds and wind, and there was a great rain. And Ahab rode, and went to Jezreel.

46 And the hand of the Becoming-One was on Elijah; and he girded up his loins, and ran before Ahab to the entrance of Jezreel.

1 Ki 19:1 And Ahab told Jezebel all that Elijah had done, and withal how he had slain all the prophets with the sword.

2 Then Jezebel sent a messenger unto Elijah, saying, So let the gods do to me, and more also, if I make not your soul as the soul of one of them by tomorrow about this time.

3 And when he saw that, he arose, and went for his soul, and came to Beersheba, which belongs to Judah, and left his servant there.

4 But he himself went a day's journey into the wilderness, and came and sat down under a juniper tree: and he requested for his soul that he might die; and said, It is enough; now, O Becoming-One, take away my soul; for I am not better than my fathers.

5 And as he lay and slept under a juniper tree, behold, then an angel touched him, and said unto him, Arise and eat.

6 And he looked, and, behold, there was a cake baken on the coals, and a cruse of water at his head. And he did eat and drink, and laid him down again.

7 And the angel of the Becoming-One came again the second time, and touched him, and said, Arise and eat; because the journey is too great for you.

8 And he arose, and did eat and drink, and went in the strength of that food forty days and forty nights unto Horeb the mount of God.

9 And he came there unto a cave, and lodged there; and, behold, the word of the Becoming-One came to him, and he said unto him, Why are you here, Elijah?

10 And he said, I have been very jealous for the Becoming-One, God of hosts: for the children of Israel have forsaken your covenant, thrown down your altars, and slain your prophets with the sword; and I, even I only, am left; and they seek my life, to take it away.

11 And he said, Go forth, and stand upon the mount before the Becoming-One. And, behold, the Becoming-One passed by, and a great and strong wind ripped the mountains, and brake in pieces the rocks before the Becoming-One; but the Becoming-One was not in the wind: and after the wind an earthquake; but the Becoming-One was not in the earthquake:

12 And after the earthquake a fire; but the Becoming-One was not in the fire: and after the fire a still small voice.

13 And it was so, when Elijah heard it that he wrapped his face in his mantle, and went out, and stood in the entering in of the cave. And, behold, there came a voice unto him, and said, Why are you here, Elijah?

14 And he said, I have been very jealous for the Becoming-One, God of hosts: because the children of Israel have forsaken your covenant, thrown down your altars, and slain your prophets with the sword; and I, even I only, am left; and they seek my life, to take it away.

15 And the Becoming-One said unto him, Go, return on your way to the wilderness of Damascus: and when you come, anoint Hazael to be king over Syria:

16 And Jehu the son of Nimshi shall you anoint to be king over Israel: and Elisha the son of Shaphat of Able-meholah shall you anoint to be prophet in your room.

17 And it shall come to pass, that him that escapes the sword of Hazael shall Jehu slay: and him that escapes from the sword of Jehu shall Elisha slay.

18 Yet I have left me seven thousand in Israel, all the knees which have not bowed unto the lord [baal] and every mouth which has not kissed him.

19 So he departed there, and found Elisha the son of Shaphat, who was plowing with twelve yoke of oxen before him, and he with the twelfth: and Elijah passed by him, and cast his mantle upon him.

20 And he left the oxen, and ran after Elijah, and said, Let me, I pray you, kiss my father and my mother, and then I will follow you. And he said unto him, Go back again: for what have I done to you?

21 And he returned back from him, and took a yoke of oxen, and killed them, and boiled their flesh with the instruments of the oxen, and gave unto the people, and they did eat. Then he arose, and went after Elijah, and ministered unto him.

1 Ki 20:1 And Benhadad the king of Syria gathered all his host together: and there were thirty and two kings with him, and horses, and chariots: and he went up and besieged Samaria, and warred against it.

2 And he sent messengers to Ahab king of Israel into the city, and said unto him, Thus says Benhadad,

3 your silver and your gold is mine; your wives also and your children, even the best, are mine.

4 And the king of Israel answered and said, My lord, O king, according to your saying, I am yours, and all that I have.

5 And the messengers came again, and said, Thus speaks Benhadad, saying, Although I have sent unto you, saying, you shall deliver me your silver, and your gold, and your wives, and your children;

6 Yet I will send my servants unto you tomorrow about this time, and they shall search your house, and the houses of your servants; and it shall be, that whatsoever is pleasant in your eyes, they shall put it in their hand, and take it away.

7 Then the king of Israel called all the elders of the land, and said, Mark, I pray you, and see how this man seeks mischief: for he sent unto me for my wives, and for my children, and for my silver, and for my gold; and I denied him not.

8 And all the elders and all the people said unto him, listen not unto him, nor consent.

9 Therefore he said unto the messengers of Benhadad, Tell my lord the king, All that you did send for to your servant at the first I will do: but this thing I may not do. And the messengers departed, and brought him word again.

10 And Benhadad sent unto him, and said, The gods do so unto me, and more also, if the dust of Samaria shall suffice for handfuls for all the people that follow me.

11 And the king of Israel answered and said, Tell him, Let not him that girds on his harness boast himself as he that puts it off.

12 And it came to pass, when Benhadad heard this message, as he was drinking, he and the kings in the pavilions, that he said unto his servants, Set yourselves in array. And they set themselves in array against the city.

13 And, behold, there came a prophet unto Ahab king of Israel, saying, Thus says the Becoming-One, have you seen all this great multitude? behold, I will deliver it into your hand this day; and you shall know that I am the Becoming-One.

14 And Ahab said, By whom? And he said, Thus says the Becoming-One, Even by the young men of the princes of the provinces. Then he said, Who shall order the battle? And he answered, you.

15 Then he numbered the young men of the princes of the provinces, and they were two hundred and thirty two: and after them he numbered all the people, even all the children of Israel, being seven thousand.

16 And they went out at noon. But Benhadad was drinking himself drunk in the pavilions, he and the kings, the thirty and two kings that helped him.

17 And the young men of the princes of the provinces went out first; and Benhadad sent out, and they told him, saying, There are men come out of Samaria.

18 And he said, Whether they be come out for peace, take them alive; or whether they be come out for war, take them alive.

19 So these young men of the princes of the provinces came out of the city, and the army which followed them.

20 And they killed every one his man: and the Syrians fled; and Israel pursued them: and Benhadad the king of Syria escaped on a horse with the horsemen.

21 And the king of Israel went out, and smote the horses and chariots, and killed the Syrians with a great slaughter.

22 And the prophet came to the king of Israel, and said unto him, Go, strengthen thyself, and mark, and see what you do: for at the return of the year the king of Syria will come up against you.

23 And the servants of the king of Syria said unto him, Their God are gods of the hills; therefore they were stronger than we; but let us fight against them in the plain, and surely we shall be stronger than they.

24 And do this thing, Take the kings away, every man out of his place, and put captains in their rooms:

25 And number you an army, like the army that you have lost, horse for horse, and chariot for chariot: and we will fight against them in the plain, and surely we shall be stronger than they. And he listened unto their voice, and did so.

26 And it came to pass at the return of the year, that Benhadad numbered the Syrians, and went up to Aphek, to fight against Israel.

27 And the children of Israel were numbered, and were all present, and went against them: and the children of Israel pitched before them like two little flocks of kids; but the Syrians filled the country.

28 And there came a man of God, and spoke unto the king of Israel, and said, Thus says the Becoming-One, Because the Syrians have said, The Becoming-One is God of the hills, but he is not God of the valleys, therefore will I deliver all this great multitude into your hand, and you shall know that I am the Becoming-One.

29 And they pitched one over against the other seven days. And so it was, that in the seventh day the battle was joined: and the children of Israel killed of the Syrians a hundred thousand of footmen in one day.

30 But the rest fled to Aphek, into the city; and there a wall fell upon twenty and seven thousand of the men that were left. And Benhadad fled, and came into the city, into an inner chamber.

31 And his servants said unto him, Behold now, we have heard that the kings of the house of Israel are merciful kings: let us, I pray you, put sackcloth on our loins, and ropes upon our heads, and go out to the king of Israel: perhaps he will save your soul.

32 So they girded sackcloth on their loins, and put ropes on their heads, and came to the king of Israel, and said, your servant Benhadad says, I pray you, let me live. And he said, Is he yet alive? he is my brother.

33 Now the men did diligently observe whether anything would come from him, and did hastily catch it: and they said, your brother Benhadad. Then he said, Go, bring him. Then Benhadad came forth to him; and he caused him to come up into the chariot.

34 And Benhadad said unto him, The cities, which my father took from your father, I will restore; and you shall make streets for you in Damascus, as my father made in Samaria. Then said Ahab, I will send you away with this covenant. So he made a covenant with him, and sent him away.

35 And a certain man of the sons of the prophets said unto his neighbor in the word of the Becoming-One, Smite me, I pray you. And the man refused to smite him.

36 Then said he unto him, Because you have not obeyed the voice of the Becoming-One, behold, as soon as you are departed from me, a lion shall slay you. And as soon as he was departed from him, a lion found him, and killed him.

37 Then he found another man, and said, Smite me, I pray you. And the man smote him, so that in smiting he wounded him.

38 So the prophet departed, and waited for the king by the way, and disguised himself with ashes upon his face.

39 And as the king passed by, he cried unto the king: and he said, your servant went out into the midst of the battle; and, behold, a man turned aside, and brought a man unto me, and said, Keep this man: if by any means he be missing, then shall your soul be for his soul, or else you shall pay a talent of silver.

40 And as your servant was busy here and there, he was gone. And the king of Israel said unto him, So shall your judgment be; yourself have decided it.

41 And he hasted, and took the ashes away from his face; and the king of Israel discerned him that he was of the prophets.

42 And he said unto him, Thus says the Becoming-One, Because you have let go out of your hand a man whom I appointed to utter destruction, therefore your soul shall go for his soul, and your people for his people.

43 And the king of Israel went to his house heavy and displeased, and came to Samaria.

1 Ki 21:1 And it came to pass after these things, that Naboth the Jezreelite had a vineyard, which was in Jezreel, hard by the palace of Ahab king of Samaria.

2 And Ahab spoke unto Naboth, saying, Give me your vineyard, that I may have it for a garden of herbs, because it is near unto my house: and I will give you for it a better vineyard than it; or, if it seem good to you, I will give you the worth of it in money.

3 And Naboth said to Ahab, The Becoming-One forbid it me, that I should give the inheritance of my fathers unto you.

4 And Ahab came into his house heavy and displeased because of the word which Naboth the Jezreelite had spoken to him: for he had said, I will not give you the inheritance of my fathers. And he laid him down upon his bed, and turned away his face, and would eat no bread.

5 But Jezebel his wife came to him, and said unto him, Why is your spirit so sad, that you eat no bread?

6 And he said unto her, Because I spoke unto Naboth the Jezreelite, and said unto him, Give me your vineyard for money; or else, if it please you, I will give you another vineyard for it: and he answered, I will not give you my vineyard.

7 And Jezebel his wife said unto him, do you now govern the kingdom of Israel? arise, and eat bread,

and let your heart be merry: I will give you the vineyard of Naboth the Jezreelite.

8 So she wrote letters in Ahab's name, and sealed them with his seal, and sent the letters unto the elders and to the nobles that were in his city, dwelling with Naboth.

9 And she wrote in the letters, saying, Proclaim a fast, and set Naboth on high among the people:

10 And set two men, sons of Belial, before him, to bear witness against him, saying, you did blaspheme God and the king. And then carry him out, and stone him, that he may die.

11 And the men of his city, even the elders and the nobles who were the inhabitants in his city, did as Jezebel had sent unto them, and as it was written in the letters which she had sent unto them.

12 They proclaimed a fast, and set Naboth on high among the people.

13 And there came in two men, children of Belial, and sat before him: and the men of Belial witnessed against him, even against Naboth, in the presence of the people, saying, Naboth did blaspheme God and the king. Then they carried him forth out of the city, and stoned him with stones, that he died.

14 Then they sent to Jezebel, saying, Naboth is stoned, and is dead.

15 And it came to pass, when Jezebel heard that Naboth was stoned, and was dead, that Jezebel said to Ahab, Arise, take possession of the vineyard of Naboth the Jezreelite, which he refused to give you for money: for Naboth is not alive, but dead.

16 And it came to pass, when Ahab heard that Naboth was dead, that Ahab rose up to go down to the vineyard of Naboth the Jezreelite, to take possession of it.

17 And the word of the Becoming-One came to Elijah the Tishbite, saying,

18 Arise, go down to meet Ahab king of Israel, which is in Samaria: behold, he is in the vineyard of Naboth, to which he is gone down to possess it.

19 And you shall speak unto him, saying, Thus says the Becoming-One, have you killed, and also taken possession? And you shall speak unto him, saying, Thus says the Becoming-One, In the place where dogs licked the blood of Naboth shall dogs lick your blood, even yours.

20 And Ahab said to Elijah, have you found me, O mine enemy? And he answered, I have found you; because you have sold yourself to work evil in the sight of the Becoming-One.

21 Behold, I will bring evil upon you, and will take away your posterity, and will cut off from Ahab him that pisses against the wall, and him that is shut up and left in Israel,

22 And will make your house like the house of Jeroboam the son of Nebat, and like the house of Baasha the son of Ahijah, for the provocation wherewith you have provoked me to anger, and made Israel to sin.

23 And of Jezebel also spoke the Becoming-One, saying, The dogs shall eat Jezebel by the wall of Jezreel.

24 Him that dies of Ahab in the city the dogs shall eat; and him that dies in the field shall the fowls of the air eat.

25 But there was none like unto Ahab, which did sell himself to work wickedness in the sight of the Becoming-One, whom Jezebel his wife stirred up.

26 And he did very abominably in following idols, according to all things as did the Amorites, whom the Becoming-One cast out before the children of Israel.

27 And it came to pass, when Ahab heard those words, that he ripped his clothes, and put sackcloth upon his flesh, and fasted, and lay in sackcloth, and went softly.

28 And the word of the Becoming-One came to Elijah the Tishbite, saying,

29 see you how Ahab humbles himself before me? because he humbles himself before me, I will not bring the evil in his days: but in his son's days will I bring the evil upon his house.

1 Ki 22:1 And they continued three years without war between Syria and Israel.

2 And it came to pass in the third year, that Jehoshaphat the king of Judah came down to the king of Israel.

3 And the king of Israel said unto his servants, Know you that Ramoth in Gilead is ours, and we be still, and take it not out of the hand of the king of Syria?

4 And he said unto Jehoshaphat, will you go with me to battle to Ramothgilead? And Jehoshaphat said to the king of Israel, I am as you are, my people as your people, my horses as your horses.

5 And Jehoshaphat said unto the king of Israel, Inquire, I pray you, at the word of the Becoming-One today.

6 Then the king of Israel gathered the prophets together, about four hundred men, and said unto them, Shall I go against Ramothgilead to battle, or shall I forbear? And they said, Go up; for my Lord(s) shall deliver it into the hand of the king.

7 And Jehoshaphat said, Is there not here a prophet of the Becoming-One besides, that we might inquire of him?

8 And the king of Israel said unto Jehoshaphat, There is yet one man, Micaiah the son of Imlah, by whom we may inquire of the Becoming-One: but I hate him; for he does not prophesy good concerning me, but evil. And Jehoshaphat said, Let not the king say so.

9 Then the king of Israel called an eunuch, and said, Hasten here Micaiah the son of Imlah.

10 And the king of Israel and Jehoshaphat the king of Judah sat each on his throne, having put on their robes, in a void place in the entrance of the gate of Samaria; and all the prophets prophesied before them.

11 And Zedekiah the son of Chenaanah made him horns of iron: and he said, Thus says the Becoming-One, With these shall you push the Syrians, until you have consumed them.

12 And all the prophets prophesied so, saying, Go up to Ramothgilead, and prosper: for the Becoming-One shall deliver it into the king's hand.

13 And the messenger that was gone to call Micaiah spoke unto him, saying, Behold now, the words of the prophets declare good unto the king

with one mouth: let your word, I pray you, be like the word of one of them, and speak that which is good.

14 And Micaiah said, As the Becoming-One lives, what the Becoming-One says unto me, that will I speak.

15 So he came to the king. And the king said unto him, Micaiah, shall we go against Ramothgilead to battle, or shall we forbear? And he answered him, Go, and prosper: for the Becoming-One shall deliver it into the hand of the king.

16 And the king said unto him, How many times shall I adjure you that you tell me nothing but that which is true in the name of the Becoming-One?

17 And he said, I saw all Israel scattered upon the hills, as sheep that have not a shepherd: and the Becoming-One said, These have no master: let them return every man to his house in peace.

18 And the king of Israel said unto Jehoshaphat, Did I not tell you that he would prophesy no good concerning me, but evil?

19 And he said, Hear you therefore the word of the Becoming-One: I saw the Becoming-One sitting on his throne, and all the host of the heavens standing by him on his right hand and on his left.

20 And the Becoming-One said, Who shall persuade Ahab, that he may go up and fall at Ramothgilead? And one said on this manner, and another said on that manner.

21 And there came forth a spirit, and stood before the Becoming-One, and said, I will persuade him.

22 And the Becoming-One said unto him, Wherewith? And he said, I will go forth, and I will be a lying spirit in the mouth of all his prophets. And he said, you shall persuade him, and prevail also: go forth, and do so.

23 Now therefore, behold, the Becoming-One has put a lying spirit in the mouth of all these your prophets, and the Becoming-One has spoken evil concerning you.

24 But Zedekiah the son of Chenaanah went near, and smote Micaiah on the cheek, and said, Which way went the spirit of the Becoming-One from me to speak unto you?

25 And Micaiah said, Behold, you shall see in that day, when you shall go into an inner chamber to hide thyself.

26 And the king of Israel said, Take Micaiah, and carry him back unto Amon the governor of the city, and to Joash the king's son;

27 And say, Thus says the king, Put this fellow in the prison, and feed him with bread of affliction and with water of affliction, until I come in peace.

28 And Micaiah said, If you return at all in peace, the Becoming-One has not spoken by me. And he said, listen, O people, every one of you.

29 So the king of Israel and Jehoshaphat the king of Judah went up to Ramothgilead.

30 And the king of Israel said unto Jehoshaphat, I will disguise myself, and enter into the battle; but put you on your robes. And the king of Israel disguised himself, and went into the battle.

31 But the king of Syria commanded his thirty and two captains that had rule over his chariots, saying, Fight neither with small nor great, save only with the king of Israel.

32 And it came to pass, when the captains of the chariots saw Jehoshaphat, that they said, Surely it is the king of Israel. And they turned aside to fight against him: and Jehoshaphat cried out.

33 And it came to pass, when the captains of the chariots perceived that it was not the king of Israel, that they turned back from pursuing him.

34 And a certain man drew a bow at a venture, and smote the king of Israel between the joints of the harness: therefore he said unto the driver of his chariot, Turn your hand, and carry me out of the host; for I am wounded.

35 And the battle increased that day: and the king was stayed up in his chariot against the Syrians, and died at evening: and the blood ran out of the wound into the midst of the chariot.

36 And there went a proclamation throughout the host about the going down of the sun, saying, Every man to his city, and every man to his own country.

37 So the king died, and was brought to Samaria; and they buried the king in Samaria.

38 And one washed the chariot in the pool of Samaria; and the dogs licked up his blood; and they washed his armor; according unto the word of the Becoming-One which he spoke.

39 Now the rest of the acts of Ahab, and all that he did, and the ivory house which he made, and all the cities that he built, are they not written in the book of the words of the days [chronicles] of the kings of Israel?

40 So Ahab slept with his fathers; and Ahaziah his son reigned in his stead.

41 And Jehoshaphat the son of Asa began to reign over Judah in the fourth year of Ahab king of Israel.

42 Jehoshaphat was a son of thirty and five years when he began to reign; and he reigned twenty and five years in Jerusalem. And his mother's name was Azubah the daughter of Shilhi.

43 And he walked in all the ways of Asa his father; he turned not aside from it, doing that which was right in the eyes of the Becoming-One: nevertheless the high places were not taken away; for the people offered and burnt incense yet in the high places.

44 And Jehoshaphat made peace with the king of Israel.

45 Now the rest of the acts of Jehoshaphat, and his might that he showed, and how he warred, are they not written in the book of the words of the days [chronicles] of the kings of Judah?

46 And the remnant of the sodomites, which remained in the days of his father Asa, he took out of the land.

47 There was then no king in Edom: a deputy was king.

48 Jehoshaphat made ships of Tharshish to go to Ophir for gold: but they went not; for the ships were broken at Eziongeber.

49 Then said Ahaziah the son of Ahab unto Jehoshaphat, Let my servants go with your servants in the ships. But Jehoshaphat would not.

50 And Jehoshaphat slept with his fathers, and was buried with his fathers in the city of David his father: and Jehoram his son reigned in his stead.

51 Ahaziah the son of Ahab began to reign over Israel in Samaria the seventeenth year of Jehoshaphat king of Judah, and reigned two years over Israel.

52 And he did evil in the sight of the Becoming-One, and walked in the way of his father, and in the way of his mother, and in the way of Jeroboam the son of Nebat, who made Israel to sin:

53 For he served the lord [baal] and worshiped him, and provoked to anger the Becoming-One, God of Israel, according to all that his father had done.

2 Kings

2 Ki 1:1 Then Moab rebelled against Israel after the death of Ahab.

2 And Ahaziah fell down through a lattice in his upper chamber that was in Samaria, and was sick: and he sent messengers, and said unto them, Go, inquire of Baal-Zebub God of Ekron whether I shall recover of this disease.

3 But the angel of the Becoming-One said to Elijah the Tishbite, Arise, go up to meet the messengers of the king of Samaria, and say unto them, Is it not because there is not God in Israel, that you go to inquire of Baal-Zebub God of Ekron?

4 Now therefore thus says the Becoming-One, you shall not come down from that bed on which you are gone up, for in dying, you will die.[110] And Elijah departed.

5 And when the messengers turned back unto him, he said unto them, Why are you now turned back?

6 And they said unto him, There came a man up to meet us, and said unto us, Go, turn again unto the king that sent you, and say unto him, Thus says the Becoming-One, Is it not because there is not God in Israel, that you send to inquire of Baal-Zebub God of Ekron? therefore you shall not come down from that bed on which you are gone up, for in dying, you will die.[111]

7 And he said unto them, What manner of man was he which came up to meet you, and told you these words?

8 And they answered him, He was a hairy man, and girt with a girdle of leather about his loins. And he said, It is Elijah the Tishbite.

9 Then the king sent unto him a captain of fifty with his fifty. And he went up to him: and, behold, he sat on the top of a hill. And he spoke unto him, you man of God, the king has said, Come down.

10 And Elijah answered and said to the captain of fifty, If I be a man of God, then let fire come down from heaven, and consume you and your fifty. And there came down fire from heaven, and consumed him and his fifty.

11 Again also he sent unto him another captain of fifty with his fifty. And he answered and said unto him, O man of God, thus has the king said, Come down quickly.

12 And Elijah answered and said unto them, If I be a man of God, let fire come down from heaven, and consume you and your fifty. And the fire of God came down from heaven, and consumed him and his fifty.

13 And he sent again a captain of the third fifty with his fifty. And the third captain of fifty went up, and came and fell on his knees before Elijah, and besought him, and said unto him, O man of God, I pray you, let my soul, and the soul of these fifty your servants, be precious in your sight.

14 Behold, there came fire down from heaven, and burnt up the two captains of the former fifties with their fifties: therefore let my soul now be precious in your sight.

15 And the angel of the Becoming-One said unto Elijah, Go down with him: be not afraid of him. And he arose, and went down with him unto the king.

16 And he said unto him, Thus says the Becoming-One, Forasmuch as you have sent messengers to inquire of Baal-Zebub God of Ekron, is it not because there is no God in Israel to inquire of his word? therefore you shall not come down off that bed on which you are gone up, for in dying, you will die.[112] 2 Ki 1:17 So he died according to the word of the Becoming-One which Elijah had spoken. And Jehoram reigned in his stead in the second year of Jehoram the son of Jehoshaphat king of Judah; because he had no son.

18 Now the rest of the acts of Ahaziah which he did, are they not written in the book of the words of the days [chronicles] of the kings of Israel?

2 Ki 2:1 And it came to pass, when the Becoming-One was about to take up Elijah into the heavens by a whirlwind, that Elijah went with Elisha from Gilgal.

2 And Elijah said unto Elisha, Tarry here, I pray you; for the Becoming-One has sent me to Bethel. And Elisha said unto him, As the Becoming-One lives, and as your soul lives, I will not leave you. So they went down to Bethel.

3 And the sons of the prophets that were at Bethel came forth to Elisha, and said unto him, know you that the Becoming-One will take away your master from your head today? And he said, Yes, I know it; hold you your peace.

4 And Elijah said unto him, Elisha, tarry here, I pray you; for the Becoming-One has sent me to Jericho. And he said, As the Becoming-One lives, and as your soul lives, I will not leave you. So they came to Jericho.

5 And the sons of the prophets that were at Jericho came to Elisha, and said unto him, know you that the Becoming-One will take away your master from your head today? And he answered, Yes, I know it; hold you your peace.

6 And Elijah said unto him, Tarry, I pray you, here; for the Becoming-One has sent me to Jordan. And he said, As the Becoming-One lives, and as your soul lives, I will not leave you. And they two went on.

7 And fifty men of the sons of the prophets went, and stood to view afar off: and they two stood by Jordan.

8 And Elijah took his mantle, and wrapped it together, and smote the waters, and they were divided here and there, so that they two went over on dry ground.

9 And it came to pass, when they were gone over, that Elijah said unto Elisha, Ask what I shall do for you, before I be taken away from you. And Elisha said, I pray you, let a double portion of your spirit be upon me.

10 And he said, you have asked a hard thing: nevertheless, if you see me when I am taken from

---

[110] מוֹת תָּמוּת – "in dying, you will die" or when you die, you will be dead – a part of the group called the "dead"
[111] מוֹת תָּמוּת – "in dying, you will die" or when you die, you will be dead – a part of the group called the "dead"

[112] מוֹת תָּמוּת – "in dying, you will die" or when you die, you will be dead – a part of the group called the "dead"

you, it shall be so unto you; but if not, it shall not be so.

11 And it came to pass, as they still went on, and talked, that, behold, there appeared a chariot of fire, and horses of fire, and parted them both asunder; and Elijah went up by a whirlwind into heaven.

12 And Elisha saw it, and he cried, My father, my father, the chariot of Israel, and the horsemen thereof. And he saw him no more: and he took hold of his own clothes, and ripped them in two pieces.

13 He took up also the mantle of Elijah that fell from him, and went back, and stood by the bank of Jordan;

14 And he took the mantle of Elijah that fell from him, and smote the waters, and said, Where is the Becoming-One, God of Elijah? and when he also had struck the waters, they parted here and there: and Elisha went over.

15 And when the sons of the prophets which were to view at Jericho saw him, they said, The spirit of Elijah does rest on Elisha. And they came to meet him, and bowed themselves to the ground before him.

16 And they said unto him, Behold now, there be with your servants fifty strong men; let them go, we pray you, and seek your master: lest perhaps the spirit of the Becoming-One has taken him up, and cast him upon some mountain, or into some valley. And he said, you shall not send.

17 And when they urged him till he was ashamed, he said, Send. They sent therefore fifty men; and they sought three days, but found him not.

18 And when they came again to him, for he tarried at Jericho, he said unto them, Did I not say unto you, Go not?

19 And the men of the city said unto Elisha, Behold, I pray you, the situation of this city is pleasant, as my lord sees: but the water is nothing, and the ground barren.

20 And he said, Bring me a new cruse, and put salt therein. And they brought it to him.

21 And he went forth unto the spring of the waters, and cast the salt in there, and said, Thus says the Becoming-One, I have healed these waters; there shall not be from there any more death or barren land.

22 So the waters were healed unto this day, according to the saying of Elisha which he spoke.

23 And he went up from there unto Bethel: and as he was going up by the way, there came forth little children out of the city, and mocked him, and said unto him, Go up, you bald head; go up, you bald head.

24 And he turned back, and looked on them, and cursed them in the name of the Becoming-One. And there came forth two she bears out of the wood, and tare forty and two children of them.

25 And he went from there to mount Carmel, and from there he returned to Samaria.

2 Ki 3:1 Now Jehoram the son of Ahab began to reign over Israel in Samaria the eighteenth year of Jehoshaphat king of Judah, and reigned twelve years.

2 And he worked evil in the sight of the Becoming-One; but not like his father, and like his mother: for he put away the image of the lord [baal] that his father had made.

3 Nevertheless he cleaved unto the sins of Jeroboam the son of Nebat, which made Israel to sin; he departed not therefrom.

4 And Mesha king of Moab was a sheepmaster, and rendered unto the king of Israel a hundred thousand of lambs, and a hundred thousand of rams, with the wool.

5 But it came to pass, when Ahab was dead, that the king of Moab rebelled against the king of Israel.

6 And king Jehoram went out of Samaria the same time, and numbered all Israel.

7 And he went and sent to Jehoshaphat the king of Judah, saying, The king of Moab has rebelled against me: will you go with me against Moab to battle? And he said, I will go up: I am as you are, my people as your people, and my horses as your horses.

8 And he said, Which way shall we go up? And he answered, The way through the wilderness of Edom.

9 So the king of Israel went, and the king of Judah, and the king of Edom: and they fetched a compass of seven days' journey: and there was no water for the host, and for the cattle that followed them.

10 And the king of Israel said, Alas! that the Becoming-One has called these three kings together, to deliver them into the hand of Moab!

11 But Jehoshaphat said, Is there not here a prophet of the Becoming-One, that we may inquire of the Becoming-One by him? And one of the king of Israel's servants answered and said, Here is Elisha the son of Shaphat, which poured water on the hands of Elijah.

12 And Jehoshaphat said, The word of the Becoming-One is with him. So the king of Israel and Jehoshaphat and the king of Edom went down to him.

13 And Elisha said unto the king of Israel, What have I to do with you? get you to the prophets of your father, and to the prophets of your mother. And the king of Israel said unto him, Nay: for the Becoming-One has called these three kings together, to deliver them into the hand of Moab.

14 And Elisha said, As the Becoming-One of hosts lives, before whom I stand, surely, were it not that I regard the presence of Jehoshaphat the king of Judah, I would not look toward you, nor see you.

15 But now bring me a minstrel. And it came to pass, when the minstrel played, that the hand of the Becoming-One came upon him.

16 And he said, Thus says the Becoming-One, Make this valley full of ditches.

17 For thus says the Becoming-One, you shall not see wind, neither shall you see rain; yet that valley shall be filled with water, that you may drink, both you, and your cattle, and your beasts.

18 And this is but a light thing in the sight of the Becoming-One: he will deliver the Moabites also into your hand.

19 And you shall smite every fenced city, and every choice city, and shall fell every good tree, and stop all wells of water, and mar every good piece of land with stones.

20 And it came to pass in the morning, when the food offering was offered, that, behold, there came water by the way of Edom, and the country was filled with water.

21 And when all the Moabites heard that the kings were come up to fight against them, they gathered all that were able to put on armor, and upward, and stood in the border.

22 And they rose up early in the morning, and the sun shone upon the water, and the Moabites saw the water on the other side as red as blood:

23 And they said, This is blood: the kings are surely slain, and they have struck one another: now therefore, Moab, to the spoil.

24 And when they came to the camp of Israel, the Israelites rose up and smote the Moabites, so that they fled before them: but they went forward smiting the Moabites, even in their country.

25 And they beat down the cities, and on every good piece of land cast every man his stone, and filled it; and they stopped all the wells of water, and felled all the good trees: only in Kirharaseth left they the stones thereof; howbeit the slingers went about it, and smote it.

26 And when the king of Moab saw that the battle was too great for him, he took with him seven hundred men that drew swords, to break through even unto the king of Edom: but they could not.

27 Then he took his eldest son that should have reigned in his stead, and offered him for a burnt offering upon the wall. And there was great indignation against Israel: and they departed from him, and returned to their own land.

2 Ki 4:1 Now there cried a certain woman of the wives of the sons of the prophets unto Elisha, saying, your servant my husband is dead; and you know that your servant did fear the Becoming-One: and the creditor is come to take unto him my two sons to be bondmen.

2 And Elisha said unto her, What shall I do for you? tell me, what have you in the house? And she said, your handmaid has not anything in the house, save a pot of oil.

3 Then he said, Go, borrow you vessels abroad of all your neighbors, even empty vessels; borrow not a few.

4 And when you are come in, you shall shut the door upon you and upon your sons, and shall pour out into all those vessels, and you shall set aside that which is full.

5 So she went from him, and shut the door upon her and upon her sons, who brought the vessels to her; and she poured out.

6 And it came to pass, when the vessels were full, that she said unto her son, Bring me yet a vessel. And he said unto her, There is not a vessel more. And the oil stayed.

7 Then she came and told the man of God. And he said, Go, sell the oil, and pay your debt, and live you and your children of the rest of the money.

8 And it fell on a day, that Elisha passed to Shunem, where was a great woman; and she constrained him to eat bread. And so it was, that as oft as he passed by, he turned in there to eat bread.

9 And she said unto her husband, Behold now, I perceive that this is a holy man of God, which passes by us continually.

10 Let us make a little chamber, I pray you, on the wall; and let us set for him there a bed, and a table, and a stool, and a candlestick: and it shall be, when he comes to us, that he shall turn in there.

11 And it fell on a day, that he came there, and he turned into the chamber, and lay there.

12 And he said to Gehazi his servant, Call this Shunammite. And when he had called her, she stood before him.

13 And he said unto him, Say now unto her, Behold, you have been careful for us with all this care; what is to be done for you? would you be spoken for to the king, or to the captain of the host? And she answered, I dwell among mine own people.

14 And he said, What then is to be done for her? And Gehazi answered, Truly she has no child, and her husband is old.

15 And he said, Call her. And when he had called her, she stood in the door.

16 And he said, About this set time,[113] according to the time of life, you shall embrace a son. And she said, Nay, my lord, you man of God, do not lie unto your handmaid.

17 And the woman conceived, and bare a son at that set time[114] that Elisha had said unto her, according to the time of life.

18 And when the child was grown, it fell on a day, that he went out to his father to the reapers.

19 And he said unto his father, My head, my head. And he said to a lad, Carry him to his mother.

20 And when he had taken him, and brought him to his mother, he sat on her knees till noon, and then died.

21 And she went up, and laid him on the bed of the man of God, and shut the door upon him, and went out.

22 And she called unto her husband, and said, Send me, I pray you, one of the young men, and one of the donkeys, that I may run to the man of God, and come again.

23 And he said, Why will you go to him today? it is neither new moon, nor Sabbath. And she said, It shall be well.

24 Then she saddled an donkey, and said to her servant, Drive, and go forward; slack not your riding for me, except I bid you.

25 So she went and came unto the man of God to mount Carmel. And it came to pass, when the man of God saw her afar off, that he said to Gehazi his servant, Behold, yonder is that Shunammite:

26 Run now, I pray you, to meet her, and say unto her, Is it well with you? is it well with your husband? is it well with the child? And she answered, It is well.

27 And when she came to the man of God to the hill, she caught him by the feet: but Gehazi came near to thrust her away. And the man of God said, Let her alone; for her soul is vexed within her: and the Becoming-One has hid it from me, and has not told me.

28 Then she said, Did I desire a son of my lord? did I not say, Do not deceive me?

29 Then he said to Gehazi, Gird up your loins, and take my staff in your hand, and go your way: if you

---

[113] Appointed time or festival
[114] Appointed time or festival

meet any man, salute him not; and if any salute you, answer him not again: and lay my staff upon the face of the child.

30 And the mother of the child said, As the Becoming-One lives, and as your soul lives, I will not leave you. And he arose, and followed her.

31 And Gehazi passed on before them, and laid the staff upon the face of the child; but there was neither voice, nor hearing. Therefore he went again to meet him, and told him, saying, The child is not awaked.

32 And when Elisha was come into the house, behold, the child was dead, and laid upon his bed.

33 He went in therefore, and shut the door upon them both, and prayed unto the Becoming-One.

34 And he went up, and lay upon the child, and put his mouth upon his mouth, and his eyes upon his eyes, and his hands upon his hands: and he stretched himself upon the child; and the flesh of the child grew warm.

35 Then he returned, and walked in the house back and forth; and went up, and stretched himself upon him: and the child sneezed seven times, and the child opened his eyes.

36 And he called Gehazi, and said, Call this Shunammite. So he called her. And when she was come in unto him, he said, Take up your son.

37 Then she went in, and fell at his feet, and bowed herself to the ground, and took up her son, and went out.

38 And Elisha came again to Gilgal: and there was a dearth in the land; and the sons of the prophets were sitting before him; and he said unto his servant, Set on the great pot, and boil pottage for the sons of the prophets.

39 And one went out into the field to gather herbs, and found a wild vine, and gathered thereof wild gourds his lap full, and came and shred them into the pot of pottage: for they knew them not.

40 So they poured out for the men to eat. And it came to pass, as they were eating of the pottage, that they cried out, and said, O you man of God, there is death in the pot. And they could not eat thereof.

41 But he said, Then bring meal. And he cast it into the pot; and he said, Pour out for the people, that they may eat. And there was no harm in the pot.

42 And there came a man from Baal-Shalisha, and brought the man of God bread of the firstfruits, twenty loaves of barley, and full ears of grain in the husk thereof. And he said, Give unto the people, that they may eat.

43 And his servitor said, What, should I set this before a hundred men? He said again, Give the people, that they may eat: for thus says the Becoming-One, They shall eat, and shall leave thereof.

44 So he set it before them, and they did eat, and left thereof, according to the word of the Becoming-One.

2 Ki 5:1 Now Naaman, captain of the host of the king of Syria, was a great man with his master, and honorable, because by him the Becoming-One had given deliverance unto Syria: he was also a mighty man in valor, but he was a leper.

2 And the Syrians had gone out by companies, and had brought away captive out of the land of Israel a little maid; and she waited on Naaman's wife.

3 And she said unto her mistress, If only my lord were with the prophet that is in Samaria! for he would recover him of his leprosy.

4 And one went in, and told his lords, saying, Thus and thus said the maid that is of the land of Israel.

5 And the king of Syria said, Go to, go, and I will send a letter unto the king of Israel. And he departed, and took with him ten talents of silver, and six thousand pieces of gold, and ten changes of raiment.

6 And he brought the letter to the king of Israel, saying, Now when this letter is come unto you, behold, I have therewith sent Naaman my servant to you, that you may recover him of his leprosy.

7 And it came to pass, when the king of Israel had read the letter, that he ripped his clothes, and said, Am I God, to kill and to make alive, that this man does send unto me to recover a man of his leprosy? therefore consider, I pray you, and see how he seeks a quarrel against me.

8 And it was so, when Elisha the man of God had heard that the king of Israel had ripped his clothes, that he sent to the king, saying, Why have you ripped your clothes? let him come now to me, and he shall know that there is a prophet in Israel.

9 So Naaman came with his horses and with his chariot, and stood at the door of the house of Elisha.

10 And Elisha sent a messenger unto him, saying, Go and wash in Jordan seven times, and your flesh shall come again to you, and you shall be clean.

11 But Naaman was angry, and went away, and said, Behold, I thought, He will surely come out to me, and stand, and call on the name of the Becoming-One his God, and strike his hand over the place, and recover the leper.

12 Are not Abana and Pharpar, rivers of Damascus, better than all the waters of Israel? may I not wash in them, and be clean? So he turned and went away in a rage.

13 And his servants came near, and spoke unto him, and said, My father, if the prophet had bid you do some great thing, would you not have done it? how much rather then, when he says to you, Wash, and be clean?

14 Then went he down, and dipped himself seven times in Jordan, according to the saying of the man of God: and his flesh came again like unto the flesh of a little child, and he was clean.

15 And he returned to the man of God, he and all his company, and came, and stood before him: and he said, Behold, now I know that there is no God in all the earth, but in Israel: now therefore, I pray you, take a blessing of your servant.

16 But he said, As the Becoming-One lives, before whom I stand, I will receive none. And he urged him to take it; but he refused.

17 And Naaman said, Shall there not then, I pray you, be given to your servant two mules' burden of earth? for your servant will henceforth offer neither burnt offering nor sacrifice unto other gods, but unto the Becoming-One.

18 In this thing the Becoming-One pardon your servant, that when my master goes into the house of

Rimmon to worship there, and he leans on my hand, and I bow myself in the house of Rimmon: when I bow down myself in the house of Rimmon, the Becoming-One pardon your servant in this thing.

19 And he said unto him, Go in peace. So he departed from him a little way.

20 But Gehazi, the servant of Elisha the man of God, said, Behold, my master has spared Naaman this Syrian, in not receiving at his hands that which he brought: but, as the Becoming-One lives, I will run after him, and take somewhat of him.

21 So Gehazi followed after Naaman. And when Naaman saw him running after him, he lighted down from the chariot to meet him, and said, Is all well?

22 And he said, All is well. My master has sent me, saying, Behold, even now there be come to me from mount Ephraim two young men of the sons of the prophets: give them, I pray you, a talent of silver, and two changes of garments.

23 And Naaman said, Be content, take two talents. And he urged him, and bound two talents of silver in two bags, with two changes of garments, and laid them upon two of his servants; and they bare them before him.

24 And when he came to the tower, he took them from their hand, and bestowed them in the house: and he let the men go, and they departed.

25 But he went in, and stood before his master. And Elisha said unto him, Where are you from, Gehazi? And he said, your servant went nowhere.

26 And he said unto him, Went not mine heart with you, when the man turned again from his chariot to meet you? Is it a time to receive money, and to receive garments, and oliveyards, and vineyards, and sheep, and oxen, and menservants, and maidservants?

27 The leprosy therefore of Naaman shall cleave unto you, and unto your seed for olam. And he went out from his presence a leper as white as snow.

2 Ki 6:1 And the sons of the prophets said unto Elisha, Behold now, the place where we dwell with you is too strait for us.

2 Let us go, we pray you, unto Jordan, and take there every man a beam, and let us make us a place there, where we may dwell. And he answered, Go.

3 And one said, Be content, I pray you, and go with your servants. And he answered, I will go.

4 So he went with them. And when they came to Jordan, they cut down wood.

5 But as one was felling a beam, the ax head fell into the water: and he cried, and said, Alas, master! for it was borrowed.

6 And the man of God said, Where fell it? And he showed him the place. And he cut down a stick, and cast it in there; and the iron did swim.

7 Therefore said he, Take it up to you. And he put out his hand, and took it.

8 Then the king of Syria warred against Israel, and took counsel with his servants, saying, In such and such a place shall be my camp.

9 And the man of God sent unto the king of Israel, saying, Beware that you pass not such a place; for there the Syrians are come down.

10 And the king of Israel sent to the place which the man of God told him and warned him of, and saved himself there, not once nor twice.

11 Therefore the heart of the king of Syria was greatly troubled for this thing; and he called his servants, and said unto them, Will you not show me which of us is for the king of Israel?

12 And one of his servants said, None, my lord, O king: but Elisha, the prophet that is in Israel, tells the king of Israel the words that you speak in your bedchamber.

13 And he said, Go and spy where he is, that I may send and fetch him. And it was told him, saying, Behold, he is in Dothan.

14 Therefore sent he there horses, and chariots, and a great host: and they came by night, and compassed the city about.

15 And when the servant of the man of God was risen early, and gone forth, behold, a host compassed the city both with horses and chariots. And his servant said unto him, Alas, my master! what shall we do?

16 And he answered, Fear not: for they that be with us are more than they that be with them.

17 And Elisha prayed, and said, Becoming-One, I pray you, open his eyes, that he may see. And the Becoming-One opened the eyes of the young man; and he saw: and, behold, the mountain was full of horses and chariots of fire round about Elisha.

18 And when they came down to him, Elisha prayed unto the Becoming-One, and said, Smite this people, I pray you, with blindness. And he smote them with blindness according to the word of Elisha.

19 And Elisha said unto them, This is not the way, neither is this the city: follow me, and I will bring you to the man whom you seek. But he led them to Samaria.

20 And it came to pass, when they were come into Samaria, that Elisha said, Becoming-One, open the eyes of these men, that they may see. And the Becoming-One opened their eyes, and they saw; and, behold, they were in the midst of Samaria.

21 And the king of Israel said unto Elisha, when he saw them, My father, shall I smite them? shall I smite them?

22 And he answered, you shall not smite them: would you smite those whom you have taken captive with your sword and with your bow? set bread and water before them, that they may eat and drink, and go to their master.

23 And he prepared great provision for them: and when they had eaten and drunk, he sent them away, and they went to their master. So the bands of Syria came no more into the land of Israel.

24 And it came to pass after this, that Benhadad king of Syria gathered all his host, and went up, and besieged Samaria.

25 And there was a great famine in Samaria: and, behold, they besieged it, until an ass's head was sold for fourscore pieces of silver, and the fourth part of a cab of dove's dung for five pieces of silver.

26 And as the king of Israel was passing by upon the wall, there cried a woman unto him, saying, Help, my lord, O king.

27 And he said, If the Becoming-One do not help you, from where shall I help you? out of the barnfloor, or out of the winepress?

28 And the king said unto her, What ails you? And she answered, This woman said unto me, Give your son, that we may eat him today, and we will eat my son tomorrow.

29 So we boiled my son, and did eat him: and I said unto her on the next day, Give your son, that we may eat him: and she has hid her son.

30 And it came to pass, when the king heard the words of the woman, that he ripped his clothes; and he passed by upon the wall, and the people looked, and, behold, he had sackcloth within upon his flesh.

31 Then he said, God do so and more also to me, if the head of Elisha the son of Shaphat shall stand on him this day.

32 But Elisha sat in his house, and the elders sat with him; and the king sent a man from before him: but ere the messenger came to him, he said to the elders, See you how this son of a murderer has sent to take away mine head? look, when the messenger comes, shut the door, and hold him fast at the door: is not the sound of his master's feet behind him?

33 And while he yet talked with them, behold, the messenger came down unto him: and he said, Behold, this evil is of the Becoming-One; what should I wait for the Becoming-One any longer?

2 Ki 7:1 Then Elisha said, Hear you the word of the Becoming-One; Thus says the Becoming-One, Tomorrow about this time shall a measure of fine flour be sold for a shekel, and two measures of barley for a shekel, in the gate of Samaria.

2 Then a officer on whose hand the king leaned answered the man of God, and said, Behold, if the Becoming-One would make windows in heaven, might this thing be? And he said, Behold, you shall see it with your eyes, but shall not eat thereof.

3 And there were four leprous men at the entering in of the gate: and they said one to another, Why sit we here until we die?

4 If we say, We will enter into the city, then the famine is in the city, and we shall die there: and if we sit still here, we die also. Now therefore come, and let us fall unto the host of the Syrians: if they save us alive, we shall live; and if they kill us, we shall but die.

5 And they rose up in the breeze time of the evening, to go unto the camp of the Syrians: and when they were come to the uttermost part of the camp of Syria, behold, there was no man there.

6 For my Lord(s) had made the host of the Syrians to hear a noise of chariots, and a noise of horses, even the noise of a great host: and they said one to another, Lo, the king of Israel has hired against us the kings of the Hittites, and the kings of the Egyptians, to come upon us.

7 Therefore they arose and fled in the breeze time of the evening and left their tents, and their horses, and their donkeys, even the camp as it was, and fled for their soul.

8 And when these lepers came to the uttermost part of the camp, they went into one tent, and did eat and drink, and carried there silver, and gold, and raiment, and went and hid it; and came again, and entered into another tent, and carried there also, and went and hid it.

9 Then they said one to another, We do not well: this day is a day of good tidings, and we hold our peace: if we tarry till the morning light, some mischief will come upon us: now therefore come, that we may go and tell the king's household.

10 So they came and called unto the gatekeeper of the city: and they told them, saying, We came to the camp of the Syrians, and, behold, there was no man there, neither voice of man, but horses tied, and donkeys tied, and the tents as they were.

11 And he called the gatekeepers; and they told it to the king's house within.

12 And the king arose in the night, and said unto his servants, I will now show you what the Syrians have done to us. They know that we be hungry; therefore are they gone out of the camp to hide themselves in the field, saying, When they come out of the city, we shall catch them alive, and get into the city.

13 And one of his servants answered and said, Let some take, I pray you, five of the horses that remain, which are left in the city, behold, they are as all the multitude of Israel that are left in it: behold, I say, they are even as all the multitude of the Israelites that are consumed: and let us send and see.

14 They took therefore two chariot horses; and the king sent after the host of the Syrians, saying, Go and see.

15 And they went after them unto Jordan: and, lo, all the way was full of garments and vessels, which the Syrians had cast away in their haste. And the messengers returned, and told the king.

16 And the people went out, and spoiled the tents of the Syrians. So a measure of fine flour was sold for a shekel, and two measures of barley for a shekel, according to the word of the Becoming-One.

17 And the king appointed the officer on whose hand he leaned to have the charge of the gate: and the people trode upon him in the gate, and he died, as the man of God had said, who spoke when the king came down to him.

18 And it came to pass as the man of God had spoken to the king, saying, Two measures of barley for a shekel, and a measure of fine flour for a shekel, shall be tomorrow about this time in the gate of Samaria:

19 And that officer answered the man of God, and said, Now, behold, if the Becoming-One should make windows in heaven, might such a thing be? And he said, Behold, you shall see it with your eyes, but shall not eat thereof.

20 And so it fell out unto him: for the people trode upon him in the gate, and he died.

2 Ki 8:1 Then spoke Elisha unto the woman, whose son he had restored to life, saying, Arise, and go you and your household, and sojourn wheresoever you can sojourn: for the Becoming-One has called for a famine; and it shall also come upon the land seven years.

2 And the woman arose, and did after the saying of the man of God: and she went with her household, and sojourned in the land of the Philistines seven years.

3 And it came to pass at the seven years' end, that the woman returned out of the land of the Philistines: and she went forth to cry unto the king for her house and for her land.

4 And the king talked with Gehazi the servant of the man of God, saying, Tell me, I pray you, all the great things that Elisha has done.

5 And it came to pass, as he was telling the king how he had restored a dead body to life, that, behold, the woman, whose son he had restored to life, cried to the king for her house and for her land. And Gehazi said, My lord, O king, this is the woman, and this is her son, whom Elisha restored to life.

6 And when the king asked the woman, she told him. So the king appointed unto her a certain eunuch, saying, Restore all that was hers, and all the fruits of the field since the day that she left the land, even until now.

7 And Elisha came to Damascus; and Benhadad the king of Syria was sick; and it was told him, saying, The man of God is come here.

8 And the king said unto Hazael, Take a present in your hand, and go, meet the man of God, and inquire of the Becoming-One by him, saying, Shall I recover of this disease?

9 So Hazael went to meet him, and took a present with him, even of every good thing of Damascus, forty camels' burden, and came and stood before him, and said, your son Benhadad king of Syria has sent me to you, saying, Shall I recover of this disease?

10 And Elisha said unto him, Go, say unto him, you may certainly recover: howbeit the Becoming-One has showed me that he shall surely die.

11 And he settled his countenance stedfastly, until he was ashamed: and the man of God wept.

12 And Hazael said, Why weeps my lord? And he answered, Because I know the evil that you will do unto the children of Israel: their strong holds will you set on fire, and their young men will you slay with the sword, and will dash their children, and rip up their women with child.

13 And Hazael said, But what, is your servant a dog, that he should do this great thing? And Elisha answered, The Becoming-One has showed me that you shall be king over Syria.

14 So he departed from Elisha, and came to his master; who said to him, What said Elisha to you? And he answered, He told me that you should surely recover.

15 And it came to pass on the next day, that he took a thick cloth, and dipped it in water, and spread it on his face, so that he died: and Hazael reigned in his stead.

16 And in the fifth year of Joram the son of Ahab king of Israel, Jehoshaphat being then king of Judah, Jehoram the son of Jehoshaphat king of Judah began to reign.

17 A son of thirty and two years old he when he began to reign; and he reigned eight years in Jerusalem.

18 And he walked in the way of the kings of Israel, as did the house of Ahab: for the daughter of Ahab was his wife: and he did evil in the sight of the Becoming-One.

19 Yet the Becoming-One would not destroy Judah for David his servant's sake, as he promised him to give him always a light, and to his children.

20 In his days Edom revolted from under the hand of Judah, and made a king over themselves.

21 So Joram went over to Zair, and all the chariots with him: and he rose by night, and smote the Edomites which compassed him about, and the captains of the chariots: and the people fled into their tents.

22 Yet Edom revolted from under the hand of Judah unto this day. Then Libnah revolted at the same time.

23 And the rest of the acts of Joram, and all that he did, are they not written in the book of the words of the days [chronicles] of the kings of Judah?

24 And Joram slept with his fathers, and was buried with his fathers in the city of David: and Ahaziah his son reigned in his stead.

25 In the twelfth year of Joram the son of Ahab king of Israel did Ahaziah the son of Jehoram king of Judah begin to reign.

26 A son of two and twenty years was Ahaziah when he began to reign; and he reigned one year in Jerusalem. And his mother's name was Athaliah, the daughter of Omri king of Israel.

27 And he walked in the way of the house of Ahab, and did evil in the sight of the Becoming-One, as did the house of Ahab: for he was the son-in-law of the house of Ahab.

28 And he went with Joram the son of Ahab to the war against Hazael king of Syria in Ramothgilead; and the Syrians wounded Joram.

29 And king Joram went back to be healed in Jezreel of the wounds which the Syrians had given him at Ramah, when he fought against Hazael king of Syria. And Ahaziah the son of Jehoram king of Judah went down to see Joram the son of Ahab in Jezreel, because he was sick.

2 Ki 9:1 And Elisha the prophet called one of the children of the prophets, and said unto him, Gird up your loins, and take this box of oil in your hand, and go to Ramothgilead:

2 And when you come there, and you shall see there Jehu the son of Jehoshaphat the son of Nimshi, and go in, and make him arise up from among his brethren, and carry him to an inner chamber;

3 Then take the box of oil, and pour it on his head, and say, Thus says the Becoming-One, I have anointed you king over Israel. Then open the door, and flee, and tarry not.

4 So the young man, even the young man the prophet, went to Ramothgilead.

5 And when he came, behold, the captains of the host were sitting; and he said, I have an errand to you, O captain. And Jehu said, Unto which of all us? And he said, To you, O captain.

6 And he arose, and went into the house; and he poured the oil on his head, and said unto him, Thus says the Becoming-One, God of Israel, I have anointed you king over the people of the Becoming-One, even over Israel.

7 And you shall smite the house of Ahab your master, that I may avenge the blood of my servants

the prophets, and the blood of all the servants of the Becoming-One, at the hand of Jezebel.

8 For the whole house of Ahab shall perish: and I will cut off from Ahab him that pisses against the wall, and him that is shut up and left in Israel:

9 And I will make the house of Ahab like the house of Jeroboam the son of Nebat, and like the house of Baasha the son of Ahijah:

10 And the dogs shall eat Jezebel in the portion of Jezreel, and there shall be none to bury her. And he opened the door, and fled.

11 Then Jehu came forth to the servants of his lords: and one said unto him, Is all well? why came this mad fellow to you? And he said unto them, you know the man, and his communication.

12 And they said, It is false; tell us now. And he said, Thus and thus spoke he to me, saying, Thus says the Becoming-One, I have anointed you king over Israel.

13 Then they hasted, and took every man his garment, and put it under him on the top of the stairs, and blew with trumpets, saying, Jehu is king.

14 So Jehu the son of Jehoshaphat the son of Nimshi conspired against Joram. Now Joram had kept Ramothgilead, he and all Israel, because of Hazael king of Syria.

15 But king Joram was returned to be healed in Jezreel of the wounds which the Syrians had given him, when he fought with Hazael king of Syria. And Jehu said, If it be your souls, then let none go forth nor escape out of the city to go to tell it in Jezreel.

16 So Jehu rode in a chariot, and went to Jezreel; for Joram lay there. And Ahaziah king of Judah was come down to see Joram.

17 And there stood a watchman on the tower in Jezreel, and he spied the company of Jehu as he came, and said, I see a company. And Joram said, Take a horseman, and send to meet them, and let him say, Is it peace?

18 So there went one on horseback to meet him, and said, Thus says the king, Is it peace? And Jehu said, What have you to do with peace? turn you behind me. And the watchman told, saying, The messenger came to them, but he comes not again.

19 Then he sent out a second on horseback, which came to them, and said, Thus says the king, Is it peace? And Jehu answered, What have you to do with peace? turn you behind me.

20 And the watchman told, saying, He came even unto them, and comes not again: and the driving is like the driving of Jehu the son of Nimshi; for he drives furiously.

21 And Joram said, Make ready. And his chariot was made ready. And Joram king of Israel and Ahaziah king of Judah went out, each in his chariot, and they went out against Jehu, and met him in the portion of Naboth the Jezreelite.

22 And it came to pass, when Joram saw Jehu, that he said, Is it peace, Jehu? And he answered, What peace, so long as the whoredoms of your mother Jezebel and her witchcrafts are so many?

23 And Joram turned his hands, and fled, and said to Ahaziah, There is treachery, O Ahaziah.

24 And Jehu drew a bow with his full strength, and smote Jehoram between his arms, and the arrow went out at his heart, and he sunk down in his chariot.

25 Then said Jehu to Bidkar his captain, Take up, and cast him in the portion of the field of Naboth the Jezreelite: for remember how that, when I and you rode together after Ahab his father, the Becoming-One laid this burden upon him;

26 Surely I have seen yesterday the blood of Naboth, and the blood of his sons, says the Becoming-One; and I will pay you for this plot, says the Becoming-One. Now therefore take and cast him into the plot of ground, according to the word of the Becoming-One.

27 But when Ahaziah the king of Judah saw this, he fled by the way of the garden house. And Jehu followed after him, and said, Smite him also in the chariot. And they did so at the going up to Gur, which is by Ibleam. And he fled to Megiddo, and died there.

28 And his servants carried him in a chariot to Jerusalem, and buried him in his tomb with his fathers in the city of David.

29 And in the eleventh year of Joram the son of Ahab began Ahaziah to reign over Judah.

30 And when Jehu was come to Jezreel, Jezebel heard of it; and she painted her face, and made up her hair, and looked out at a window.

31 And as Jehu entered in at the gate, she said, Had Zimri peace, who killed his master?

32 And he lifted up his face to the window, and said, Who is on my side? who? And there looked out to him two or three eunuchs.

33 And he said, Throw her down. So they threw her down: and some of her blood was sprinkled on the wall, and on the horses: and he trode her under foot.

34 And when he was come in, he did eat and drink, and said, Go, see now this cursed woman, and bury her: for she is a king's daughter.

35 And they went to bury her: but they found no more of her than the skull, and the feet, and the palms of her hands.

36 Therefore they came again, and told him. And he said, This is the word of the Becoming-One, which he spoke by his servant Elijah the Tishbite, saying, In the portion of Jezreel shall dogs eat the flesh of Jezebel:

37 And the carcase of Jezebel shall be as dung upon the face of the field in the portion of Jezreel; so that they shall not say, This is Jezebel.

2 Ki 10:1 And Ahab had seventy sons in Samaria. And Jehu wrote letters, and sent to Samaria, unto the rulers of Jezreel, to the elders, and to them that brought up Ahab's children, saying,

2 Now as soon as this letter comes to you, seeing your master's sons are with you, and there are with you chariots and horses, a fenced city also, and armor;

3 Look even out the best and meet of your master's sons, and set him on his father's throne, and fight for your master's house.

4 But they were exceedingly afraid, and said, Behold, two kings stood not before him: how then shall we stand?

5 And he that was over the house, and he that was over the city, the elders also, and the bringers up

of the children, sent to Jehu, saying, We are your servants, and will do all that you shall bid us; we will not make any king: do you that which is good in your eyes.

6 Then he wrote a letter the second time to them, saying, If you be mine, and if you will listen unto my voice, take you the heads of the men your master's sons, and come to me to Jezreel by tomorrow this time. Now the king's sons, being seventy persons, were with the great men of the city, which brought them up.

7 And it came to pass, when the letter came to them, that they took the king's sons, and killed seventy persons, and put their heads in baskets, and sent him them to Jezreel.

8 And there came a messenger, and told him, saying, They have brought the heads of the king's sons. And he said, Lay you them in two heaps at the entering in of the gate until the morning.

9 And it came to pass in the morning, that he went out, and stood, and said to all the people, you be righteous: behold, I conspired against my master, and killed him: but who killed all these?

10 Know now that there shall fall unto the earth nothing of the word of the Becoming-One, which the Becoming-One spoke concerning the house of Ahab: for the Becoming-One has done that which he spoke by his servant Elijah.

11 So Jehu killed all that remained of the house of Ahab in Jezreel, and all his great men, and his kinsfolks, and his priests, until he left him none remaining.

12 And he arose and departed, and came to Samaria. And as he was at the shearing house in the way,

13 Jehu met with the brethren of Ahaziah king of Judah, and said, Who are you? And they answered, We are the brethren of Ahaziah; and we go down to salute the children of the king and the children of the queen.

14 And he said, Take them alive. And they took them alive, and killed them at the pit of the shearing house, even two and forty men; neither left he any of them.

15 And when he was departed there, he lighted on Jehonadab the son of Rechab coming to meet him: and he saluted him, and said to him, Is your heart right, as my heart is with your heart? And Jehonadab answered, It is. If it be, give me your hand. And he gave him his hand; and he took him up to him into the chariot.

16 And he said, Come with me, and see my zeal for the Becoming-One. So they made him ride in his chariot.

17 And when he came to Samaria, he killed all that remained unto Ahab in Samaria, till he had destroyed him, according to the saying of the Becoming-One, which he spoke to Elijah.

18 And Jehu gathered all the people together, and said unto them, Ahab served the lord [baal] a little; but Jehu shall serve him much.

19 Now therefore call unto me all the prophets of the lord [baal] all his servants, and all his priests; let no one be missing: for I have a great sacrifice to do to the lord [baal] whosoever shall be missing, he shall not live. But Jehu did it in subtlety, to the intent that he might destroy the worshippers of the lord [baal]

20 And Jehu said, Proclaim a solemn assembly for the lord [baal] And they proclaimed it.

21 And Jehu sent through all Israel: and all the worshippers of the lord [baal] came, so that there was not a man left that came not. And they came into the house of the lord [baal] and the house of the lord [baal] was full from one end to another.

22 And he said unto him that was over the vestry, Bring forth vestments for all the worshippers of the lord [baal] And he brought them forth vestments.

23 And Jehu went, and Jehonadab the son of Rechab, into the house of the lord [baal] and said unto the worshippers of the lord [baal] Search, and look that there be here with you none of the servants of the Becoming-One, but the worshippers of the lord [baal] only.

24 And when they went in to offer sacrifices and burnt offerings, Jehu appointed fourscore men outside, and said, If any of the men whom I have brought into your hands escape, he that lets him go, his soul shall be for the soul of him.

25 And it came to pass, as soon as he had made an end of offering the burnt offering, that Jehu said to the guard and to the captains, Go in, and slay them; let none come forth. And they smote them with the edge of the sword; and the guard and the captains cast them out, and went to the city of the house of the lord [baal]

26 And they brought forth the images out of the house of the lord [baal] and burned them.

27 And they broke down the image of the lord [baal] and brake down the house of the lord [baal] and made it a draught house unto this day.

28 Thus Jehu destroyed the lord [baal] out of Israel.

29 Howbeit from the sins of Jeroboam the son of Nebat, who made Israel to sin, Jehu departed not from after them: the golden calves that were in Bethel, and that were in Dan.

30 And the Becoming-One said unto Jehu, Because you have done well in executing that which is right in mine eyes, and have done unto the house of Ahab according to all that was in mine heart, your children of the fourth generation shall sit on the throne of Israel.

31 But Jehu took no heed to walk in the law of the Becoming-One, God of Israel, with all his heart: for he departed not from the sins of Jeroboam, which made Israel to sin.

32 In those days the Becoming-One began to cut Israel short: and Hazael smote them in all the coasts of Israel;

33 From Jordan eastward, all the land of Gilead, the Gadites, and the Reubenites, and the Manassites, from Aroer, which is by the river Arnon, even Gilead and Bashan.

34 Now the rest of the acts of Jehu, and all that he did, and all his might, are they not written in the book of the words of the days [chronicles] of the kings of Israel?

35 And Jehu slept with his fathers: and they buried him in Samaria. And Jehoahaz his son reigned in his stead.

36 And the time that Jehu reigned over Israel in Samaria was twenty and eight years.

2 Ki 11:1 And when Athaliah the mother of Ahaziah saw that her son was dead, she arose and destroyed all the seed royal.

2 But Jehosheba, the daughter of king Joram, sister of Ahaziah, took Joash the son of Ahaziah, and stole him from among the king's sons which were slain; and they hid him, even him and his nurse, in the bedchamber from Athaliah, so that he was not slain.

3 And he was with her hid in the house of the Becoming-One six years. And Athaliah did reign over the land.

4 And the seventh year Jehoiada sent and fetched the rulers over hundreds, with the captains and the guard, and brought them to him into the house of the Becoming-One, and made a covenant with them, and took an oath of them in the house of the Becoming-One, and showed them the king's son.

5 And he commanded them, saying, This is the thing that you shall do; A third part of you that enter in on the Sabbath shall even be keepers of the watch of the king's house;

6 And a third part shall be at the gate of Sur; and a third part at the gate behind the guard: so shall you keep the watch of the house, that it be not broken down.

7 And two parts of all you that go forth on the Sabbath, even they shall keep the watch of the house of the Becoming-One about the king.

8 And you shall compass the king round about, every man with his weapons in his hand: and he that comes within the ranges, let him be slain: and be you with the king as he goes out and as he comes in.

9 And the captains over the hundreds did according to all things that Jehoiada the priest commanded: and they took every man his men that were to come in on the Sabbath, with them that should go out on the Sabbath, and came to Jehoiada the priest.

10 And to the captains over hundreds did the priest give king David's spears and shields, that were in the temple of the Becoming-One.

11 And the guard stood, every man with his weapons in his hand, round about the king, from the right corner of the temple to the left corner of the temple, along by the altar and the temple.

12 And he brought forth the king's son, and put the crown upon him, and gave him the testimony; and they made him king, and anointed him; and they clapped their hands, and said, Let the king live.

13 And when Athaliah heard the noise of the guard and of the people, she came to the people into the temple of the Becoming-One.

14 And when she looked, behold, the king stood by a pillar, as the manner was, and the princes and the trumpeters by the king, and all the people of the land rejoiced, and blew with trumpets: and Athaliah ripped her clothes, and cried, Treason, Treason.

15 But Jehoiada the priest commanded the captains of the hundreds, the officers of the host, and said unto them, Have her forth outside the ranges: and him that follows her kill with the sword. For the priest had said, Let her not be slain in the house of the Becoming-One.

16 And they laid hands on her; and she went by the way by the which the horses came into the king's house: and there was she slain.

17 And Jehoiada made a covenant between the Becoming-One and the king and the people, that they should be people for the Becoming-One; between the king also and the people.

18 And all the people of the land went into the house of the lord [baal] and brake it down; his altars and his images brake they in pieces thoroughly, and killed Mattan the priest of the lord [baal] before the altars. And the priest appointed officers over the house of the Becoming-One.

19 And he took the rulers over hundreds, and the captains, and the guard, and all the people of the land; and they brought down the king from the house of the Becoming-One, and came by the way of the gate of the guard to the king's house. And he sat on the throne of the kings.

20 And all the people of the land rejoiced, and the city was in quiet: and they killed Athaliah with the sword beside the king's house.

21 A son of Seven years was Jehoash when he began to reign.

2 Ki 12:1 In the seventh year of Jehu Jehoash began to reign; and forty years reigned he in Jerusalem. And his mother's name was Zibiah of Beersheba.

2 And Jehoash did that which was right in the sight of the Becoming-One all his days wherein Jehoiada the priest instructed him.

3 But the high places were not taken away: the people still sacrificed and burnt incense in the high places.

4 And Jehoash said to the priests, All the money of the dedicated things that is brought into the house of the Becoming-One, even the money of every one that passes the account, the money that every soul is set at, and all the money that comes into any man's heart to bring into the house of the Becoming-One,

5 Let the priests take it to them, every man of his acquaintance: and let them repair the breaches of the house, wheresoever any breach shall be found.

6 But it was so, that in the three and twentieth year of king Jehoash the priests had not repaired the breaches of the house.

7 Then king Jehoash called for Jehoiada the priest, and the other priests, and said unto them, Why repair you not the breaches of the house? now therefore receive no more money of your acquaintance, but deliver it for the breaches of the house.

8 And the priests consented to receive no more money of the people, neither to repair the breaches of the house.

9 But Jehoiada the priest took a chest, and bored a hole in the lid of it, and set it beside the altar, on the right side as one comes into the house of the Becoming-One: and the priests that kept the door put therein all the money that was brought into the house of the Becoming-One.

10 And it was so, when they saw that there was much money in the chest, that the king's scribe and

the high priest came up, and they put up in bags, and told the money that was found in the house of the Becoming-One.

11 And they gave the money, being told, into the hands of them that did the work, that had the oversight of the house of the Becoming-One: and they laid it out to the carpenters and builders, that worked upon the house of the Becoming-One,

12 And to masons, and hewers of stone, and to buy timber and hewed stone to repair the breaches of the house of the Becoming-One, and for all that was laid out for the house to repair it.

13 Howbeit there were not made for the house of the Becoming-One bowls of silver, snuffers, basins, trumpets, any vessels of gold, or vessels of silver, of the money that was brought into the house of the Becoming-One: 14 But they gave that to the workmen, and repaired therewith the house of the Becoming-One.

15 Moreover they reckoned not with the men, into whose hand they delivered the money to be bestowed on workmen: for they dealt faithfully.

16 The trespass money and sin money was not brought into the house of the Becoming-One: it was the priests.'

17 Then Hazael king of Syria went up, and fought against Gath, and took it: and Hazael set his face to go up to Jerusalem.

18 And Jehoash king of Judah took all the hallowed things that Jehoshaphat, and Jehoram, and Ahaziah, his fathers, kings of Judah, had dedicated, and his own hallowed things, and all the gold that was found in the treasures of the house of the Becoming-One, and in the king's house, and sent it to Hazael king of Syria: and he went away from Jerusalem.

19 And the rest of the acts of Joash, and all that he did, are they not written in the book of the words of the days [chronicles] of the kings of Judah?

20 And his servants arose, and made a conspiracy, and killed Joash in the house of Millo, which goes down to Silla.

21 For Jozachar the son of Shimeath, and Jehozabad the son of Shomer, his servants, smote him, and he died; and they buried him with his fathers in the city of David: and Amaziah his son reigned in his stead.

2 Ki 13:1 In the three and twentieth year of Joash the son of Ahaziah king of Judah Jehoahaz the son of Jehu began to reign over Israel in Samaria, and reigned seventeen years.

2 And he did that which was evil in the sight of the Becoming-One, and followed the sins of Jeroboam the son of Nebat, which made Israel to sin; he departed not therefrom.

3 And the anger of the Becoming-One was kindled against Israel, and he delivered them into the hand of Hazael king of Syria, and into the hand of Benhadad the son of Hazael, all their days.

4 And Jehoahaz besought the Becoming-One, and the Becoming-One listened unto him: for he saw the oppression of Israel, because the king of Syria oppressed them.

5 And the Becoming-One gave Israel a Savior, so that they went out from under the hand of the Syrians: and the children of Israel dwelt in their tents, as yesterday and the third day.

6 Nevertheless they departed not from the sins of the house of Jeroboam, who made Israel sin, but walked therein: and there remained the Asherah also in Samaria.

7 Neither did he leave of the people to Jehoahaz but fifty horsemen, and ten chariots, and ten thousand of footmen; for the king of Syria had destroyed them, and had made them like the dust by threshing.

8 Now the rest of the acts of Jehoahaz, and all that he did, and his might, are they not written in the book of the words of the days [chronicles] of the kings of Israel?

9 And Jehoahaz slept with his fathers; and they buried him in Samaria: and Joash his son reigned in his stead.

10 In the thirty and seventh year of Joash king of Judah began Jehoash the son of Jehoahaz to reign over Israel in Samaria, and reigned sixteen years.

11 And he did that which was evil in the sight of the Becoming-One; he departed not from all the sins of Jeroboam the son of Nebat, who made Israel sin: but he walked therein.

12 And the rest of the acts of Joash, and all that he did, and his might wherewith he fought against Amaziah king of Judah, are they not written in the book of the words of the days [chronicles] of the kings of Israel?

13 And Joash slept with his fathers; and Jeroboam sat upon his throne: and Joash was buried in Samaria with the kings of Israel.

14 Now Elisha was fallen sick of his sickness whereof he died. And Joash the king of Israel came down unto him, and wept over his face, and said, O my father, my father, the chariot of Israel, and the horsemen thereof.

15 And Elisha said unto him, Take bow and arrows. And he took unto him bow and arrows.

16 And he said to the king of Israel, Put your hand upon the bow. And he put his hand upon it: and Elisha put his hands upon the king's hands.

17 And he said, Open the window eastward. And he opened it. Then Elisha said, Shoot. And he shot. And he said, The arrow of the Becoming-One's deliverance, and the arrow of deliverance from Syria: for you shall smite the Syrians in Aphek, till you have consumed them.

18 And he said, Take the arrows. And he took them. And he said unto the king of Israel, Smite upon the ground. And he smote three times, and stopped.

19 And the man of God was angry with him, and said, you should have struck five or six times; then had you struck Syria till you had consumed it: whereas now you shall smite Syria but three times.

20 And Elisha died, and they buried him. And the bands of the Moabites invaded the land at the coming in of the year.

21 And it came to pass, as they were burying a man, that, behold, they spied a band of men; and they cast the man into the tomb of Elisha: and when the man was let down, and touched the bones of Elisha, he revived, and stood up on his feet.

22 But Hazael king of Syria oppressed Israel all the days of Jehoahaz.

23 And the Becoming-One was gracious unto them, and had compassion on them, and had respect unto them, because of his covenant with Abraham, Isaac, and Jacob, and would not destroy them, neither cast he them from his presence as yet.

24 So Hazael king of Syria died; and Benhadad his son reigned in his stead.

25 And Jehoash the son of Jehoahaz took again out of the hand of Benhadad the son of Hazael the cities, which he had taken out of the hand of Jehoahaz his father by war. Three times did Joash beat him, and recovered the cities of Israel.

2 Ki 14:1 In the second year of Joash son of Jehoahaz king of Israel reigned Amaziah the son of Joash king of Judah.

2 He was a son of twenty and five years when he began to reign, and reigned twenty and nine years in Jerusalem. And his mother's name was Jehoaddan of Jerusalem.

3 And he did that which was right in the sight of the Becoming-One, yet not like David his father: he did according to all things as Joash his father did.

4 Howbeit the high places were not taken away: as yet the people did sacrifice and burnt incense on the high places.

5 And it came to pass, as soon as the kingdom was confirmed in his hand, that he killed his servants which had slain the king his father.

6 But the children of the murderers he killed not: according unto that which is written in the book of the law of Moses, wherein the Becoming-One commanded, saying, The fathers shall not be put to death for the children, nor the children be put to death for the fathers; but every man shall be put to death for his own sin.

7 He killed of Edom in the valley of salt ten thousand, and took Selah by war, and called the name of it Jokyoul unto this day.

8 Then Amaziah sent messengers to Jehoash, the son of Jehoahaz son of Jehu, king of Israel, saying, Come, let us look one another in the face.

9 And Jehoash the king of Israel sent to Amaziah king of Judah, saying, The thistle that was in Lebanon sent to the cedar that was in Lebanon, saying, Give your daughter to my son to wife: and there passed by a wild beast that was in Lebanon, and trode down the thistle.

10 you have indeed struck Edom, and your heart has lifted you up: glory of this, and tarry at home: for why should you meddle to your hurt, that you should fall, even you, and Judah with you?

11 But Amaziah would not hear. Therefore Jehoash king of Israel went up; and he and Amaziah king of Judah looked one another in the face at Beth-shemesh, which belongs to Judah.

12 And Judah was put to the worse before Israel; and they fled every man to their tents.

13 And Jehoash king of Israel took Amaziah king of Judah, the son of Jehoash the son of Ahaziah, at Beth-shemesh, and came to Jerusalem, and brake down the wall of Jerusalem from the gate of Ephraim unto the corner gate, four hundred cubits.

14 And he took all the gold and silver, and all the vessels that were found in the house of the Becoming-One, and in the treasures of the king's house, and hostages, and returned to Samaria.

15 Now the rest of the acts of Jehoash which he did, and his might, and how he fought with Amaziah king of Judah, are they not written in the book of the words of the days [chronicles] of the kings of Israel?

16 And Jehoash slept with his fathers, and was buried in Samaria with the kings of Israel; and Jeroboam his son reigned in his stead.

17 And Amaziah the son of Joash king of Judah lived after the death of Jehoash son of Jehoahaz king of Israel fifteen years.

18 And the rest of the acts of Amaziah, are they not written in the book of the words of the days [chronicles] of the kings of Judah?

19 Now they made a conspiracy against him in Jerusalem: and he fled to Lachish; but they sent after him to Lachish, and killed him there.

20 And they brought him on horses: and he was buried at Jerusalem with his fathers in the city of David.

21 And all the people of Judah took Azariah, which was a son of sixteen years, and made him king instead of his father Amaziah.

22 He built Elath, and restored it to Judah, after that the king slept with his fathers.

23 In the fifteenth year of Amaziah the son of Joash king of Judah Jeroboam the son of Joash king of Israel began to reign in Samaria, and reigned forty and one years.

24 And he did that which was evil in the sight of the Becoming-One: he departed not from all the sins of Jeroboam the son of Nebat, who made Israel to sin.

25 He restored the coast of Israel from the entering of Hamath unto the sea of the plain, according to the word of the Becoming-One, God of Israel, which he spoke by the hand of his servant Jonah, the son of Amittai, the prophet, which was of Gathhepher.

26 For the Becoming-One saw the affliction of Israel, that it was very bitter: for there was not any shut up, nor any left, nor any helper for Israel.

27 And the Becoming-One said not that he would blot out the name of Israel from under heaven: but he saved them by the hand of Jeroboam the son of Joash.

28 Now the rest of the acts of Jeroboam, and all that he did, and his might, how he warred, and how he recovered Damascus, and Hamath, which belonged to Judah, for Israel, are they not written in the book of the words of the days [chronicles] of the kings of Israel?

29 And Jeroboam slept with his fathers, even with the kings of Israel; and Zachariah his son reigned in his stead.

2 Ki 15:1 In the twenty and seventh year of Jeroboam king of Israel began Azariah son of Amaziah king of Judah to reign.

2 A son of sixteen years was he when he began to reign, and he reigned two and fifty years in Jerusalem. And his mother's name was Jecholiah of Jerusalem.

3 And he did that which was right in the sight of the Becoming-One, according to all that his father Amaziah had done;

4 Save that the high places were not removed: the people sacrificed and burnt incense still on the high places.

5 And the Becoming-One smote the king, so that he was a leper unto the day of his death, and dwelt in a set apart house. And Jotham the king's son was over the house, judging the people of the land.

6 And the rest of the acts of Azariah, and all that he did, are they not written in the book of the words of the days [chronicles] of the kings of Judah?

7 So Azariah slept with his fathers; and they buried him with his fathers in the city of David: and Jotham his son reigned in his stead.

8 In the thirty and eighth year of Azariah king of Judah did Zachariah the son of Jeroboam reign over Israel in Samaria six months.

9 And he did that which was evil in the sight of the Becoming-One, as his fathers had done: he departed not from the sins of Jeroboam the son of Nebat, who made Israel to sin.

10 And Shallum the son of Jabesh conspired against him, and smote him before the people, and killed him, and reigned in his stead.

11 And the rest of the acts of Zachariah, behold, they are written in the book of the words of the days [chronicles] of the kings of Israel.

12 This was the word of the Becoming-One which he spoke unto Jehu, saying, your sons shall sit on the throne of Israel unto the fourth generation. And so it came to pass.

13 Shallum the son of Jabesh began to reign in the nine and thirtieth year of Uzziah king of Judah; and he reigned a full month in Samaria. **[3231 YM]**

14 For Menahem the son of Gadi went up from Tirzah, and came to Samaria, and smote Shallum the son of Jabesh in Samaria, and killed him, and reigned in his stead.

15 And the rest of the acts of Shallum, and his conspiracy which he made, behold, they are written in the book of the words of the days [chronicles] of the kings of Israel.

16 Then Menahem smote Tiphsah, and all that were therein, and the coasts thereof from Tirzah: because they opened not to him, therefore he smote it; and all the women therein that were with child he ripped up.

17 In the nine and thirtieth year of Azariah king of Judah began Menahem the son of Gadi to reign over Israel, and reigned ten years in Samaria.

18 And he did that which was evil in the sight of the Becoming-One: he departed not all his days from the sins of Jeroboam the son of Nebat, who made Israel to sin.

19 And Pul the king of Assyria came against the land: and Menahem gave Pul a thousand talents of silver, that his hand might be with him to confirm the kingdom in his hand.

20 And Menahem exacted the money of Israel, even of all the mighty men of wealth, of each man fifty shekels of silver, to give to the king of Assyria. So the king of Assyria turned back, and stayed not there in the land.

21 And the rest of the acts of Menahem, and all that he did, are they not written in the book of the words of the days [chronicles] of the kings of Israel?

22 And Menahem slept with his fathers; and Pekahiah his son reigned in his stead.

23 In the fiftieth year of Azariah king of Judah Pekahiah the son of Menahem began to reign over Israel in Samaria, and reigned two years.

24 And he did that which was evil in the sight of the Becoming-One: he departed not from the sins of Jeroboam the son of Nebat, who made Israel to sin.

25 But Pekah the son of Remaliah, a captain of his, conspired against him, and smote him in Samaria, in the palace of the king's house, with Argob and Arieh, and with him fifty men of the Gileadites: and he killed him, and reigned in his room.

26 And the rest of the acts of Pekahiah, and all that he did, behold, they are written in the book of the words of the days [chronicles] of the kings of Israel.

27 In the two and fiftieth year of Azariah king of Judah Pekah the son of Remaliah began to reign over Israel in Samaria, and reigned twenty years **[3244 YM]**.

28 And he did that which was evil in the sight of the Becoming-One: he departed not from the sins of Jeroboam the son of Nebat, who made Israel to sin.

29 In the days of Pekah king of Israel came Tiglathpileser king of Assyria, and took Ijon, and Abel-beth-maachah, and Janoah, and Kedesh, and Hazor, and Gilead, and Galilee, all the land of Naphtali, and carried them captive to Assyria. [ab. 3262 YM]

30 And Hoshea the son of Elah made a conspiracy against Pekah the son of Remaliah, and smote him, and killed him, and reigned in his stead, in the twentieth year of Jotham the son of Uzziah.

31 And the rest of the acts of Pekah, and all that he did, behold, they are written in the book of the words of the days [chronicles] of the kings of Israel.

32 In the second year of Pekah the son of Remaliah king of Israel began Jotham the son of Uzziah king of Judah to reign.

33 A son of five and twenty years was he when he began to reign, and he reigned sixteen years in Jerusalem. And his mother's name was Jerusha, the daughter of Zadok.

34 And he did that which was right in the sight of the Becoming-One: he did according to all that his father Uzziah had done.

35 Howbeit the high places were not removed: the people sacrificed and burned incense still in the high places. He built the higher gate of the house of the Becoming-One.

36 Now the rest of the acts of Jotham, and all that he did, are they not written in the book of the words of the days [chronicles] of the kings of Judah?

37 In those days the Becoming-One began to send against Judah Rezin the king of Syria, and Pekah the son of Remaliah.

38 And Jotham slept with his fathers, and was buried with his fathers in the city of David his father: and Ahaz his son reigned in his stead.

2 Ki 16:1 In the seventeenth year of Pekah the son of Remaliah Ahaz the son of Jotham king of Judah began to reign. **[3260 YM]**

2 A son of twenty years was Ahaz when he began to reign, and reigned sixteen years in Jerusalem, and did not that which was right in the sight of the Becoming-One his God, like David his father.

3 But he walked in the way of the kings of Israel, yes, and made his son to pass through the fire, according to the abominations of the nations, whom the Becoming-One cast out from before the children of Israel.

4 And he sacrificed and burnt incense in the high places, and on the hills, and under every green tree.

5 Then Rezin king of Syria and Pekah son of Remaliah king of Israel came up to Jerusalem to war: and they besieged Ahaz, but could not overcome him.

6 At that time Rezin king of Syria recovered Elath to Syria, and drove the Jews from Elath: and the Syrians came to Elath, and dwelt there unto this day.

7 So Ahaz sent messengers to Tiglathpileser king of Assyria, saying, I am your servant and your son: come up, and save me out of the hand of the king of Syria, and out of the hand of the king of Israel, which rise up against me.

8 And Ahaz took the silver and gold that was found in the house of the Becoming-One, and in the treasures of the king's house, and sent it for a present to the king of Assyria.

9 And the king of Assyria listened unto him: for the king of Assyria went up against Damascus, and took it, and carried the people of it captive to Kir, and killed Rezin.

10 And king Ahaz went to Damascus to meet Tiglathpileser king of Assyria, and saw an altar that was at Damascus: and king Ahaz sent to Urijah the priest the fashion of the altar, and the pattern of it, according to all the workmanship thereof.

11 And Urijah the priest built an altar according to all that king Ahaz had sent from Damascus: so Urijah the priest made it before king Ahaz came from Damascus.

12 And when the king was come from Damascus, the king saw the altar: and the king approached to the altar, and offered thereon.

13 And he burnt his burnt offering and his food offering, and poured his drink offering, and sprinkled the blood of his peace offerings, upon the altar.

14 And he brought also the brazen altar, which was before the Becoming-One, from the forefront of the house, from between the altar and the house of the Becoming-One, and put it on the north side of the altar.

15 And king Ahaz commanded Urijah the priest, saying, Upon the great altar burn the morning burnt offering, and the evening food offering, and the king's burnt sacrifice, and his food offering, with the burnt offering of all the people of the land, and their food offering, and their drink offerings; and sprinkle upon it all the blood of the burnt offering, and all the blood of the sacrifice: and the brazen altar shall be for me to inquire by

16 Thus did Urijah the priest, according to all that king Ahaz commanded.

17 And king Ahaz cut off the borders of the bases, and removed the laver from off them; and took down the sea from off the brazen oxen that were under it, and put it upon a pavement of stones.

18 And the covert for the Sabbath that they had built in the house, and the king's entry outside, turned he from the house of the Becoming-One for the king of Assyria.

19 Now the rest of the acts of Ahaz which he did, are they not written in the book of the words of the days [chronicles] of the kings of Judah?

20 And Ahaz slept with his fathers, and was buried with his fathers in the city of David: and Hezekiah his son reigned in his stead.

2 Ki 17:1 In the twelfth year of Ahaz king of Judah began Hoshea the son of Elah to reign in Samaria over Israel nine years.

2 And he did that which was evil in the sight of the Becoming-One, but not as the kings of Israel that were before him.

3 Against him came up Shalmaneser king of Assyria; and Hoshea became his servant, and gave him presents.

4 And the king of Assyria found conspiracy in Hoshea: for he had sent messengers to So king of Egypt, and brought no present to the king of Assyria, as he had done year by year: therefore the king of Assyria shut him up, and bound him in prison.

5 Then the king of Assyria came up throughout all the land, and went up to Samaria, and besieged it three years.

6 In the ninth year of Hoshea the king of Assyria took Samaria, and carried Israel away into Assyria, and placed them in Halah and in Habor by the river of Gozan, and in the cities of the Medes.

7 For so it was, that the children of Israel had sinned against the Becoming-One their God, which had brought them up out of the land of Egypt, from under the hand of Pharaoh king of Egypt, and had feared other gods,

8 And walked in the statutes of the nations, whom the Becoming-One cast out from before the children of Israel, and of the kings of Israel, which they had made.

9 And the children of Israel did secretly those things that were not right against the Becoming-One their God, and they built them high places in all their cities, from the tower of the watchmen to the fenced city.

10 And they set them up images and Asherahs in every high hill, and under every green tree:

11 And there they burnt incense in all the high places, as did the nations whom the Becoming-One carried away before them; and worked wicked things to provoke the Becoming-One to anger:

12 For they served idols, whereof the Becoming-One had said unto them, you shall not do this thing.

13 Yet the Becoming-One testified against Israel, and against Judah, by all the prophets, and by all the seers, saying, Turn you from your evil ways, and keep my commandments and my statutes, according to all the law which I commanded your fathers, and which I sent to you by my servants the prophets.

14 Notwithstanding they would not hear, but hardened their necks, like to the neck of their fathers, that did not believe in the Becoming-One their God.

15 And they rejected his statutes, and his covenant that he made with their fathers, and his testimonies which he testified against them; and they followed vanity, and became vain, and went after the nations that were round about them, concerning whom the Becoming-One had charged them, that they should not do like them.

16 And they left all the commandments of the Becoming-One their God, and made them molten images, even two calves, and made a Asherah, and worshiped all the host of heaven, and served the lord [baal]

17 And they caused their sons and their daughters to pass through the fire, and used divination and enchantments, and sold themselves to do evil in the sight of the Becoming-One, to provoke him to anger.

18 Therefore the Becoming-One was very angry with Israel, and removed them out of his sight: there was none left but the tribe of Judah only.

19 Also Judah kept not the commandments of the Becoming-One their God, but walked in the statutes of Israel which they made.

20 And the Becoming-One rejected all the seed of Israel, and afflicted them, and delivered them into the hand of spoilers, until he had cast them out of his sight.

21 For he ripped Israel from the house of David; and they made Jeroboam the son of Nebat king: and Jeroboam drave Israel from following the Becoming-One, and made them sin a great sin.

22 For the children of Israel walked in all the sins of Jeroboam which he did; they departed not from them;

23 Until the Becoming-One removed Israel out of his sight, as he had said by all his servants the prophets. So was Israel carried away out of their own land to Assyria unto this day.

24 And the king of Assyria brought men from Babylon, and from Cuthah, and from Ava, and from Hamath, and from Sepharvaim, and placed them in the cities of Samaria instead of the children of Israel: and they possessed Samaria, and dwelt in the cities thereof.

25 And so it was at the beginning of their dwelling there, that they feared not the Becoming-One: therefore the Becoming-One sent lions among them, which killed some of them.

26 Therefore they spoke to the king of Assyria, saying, The nations which you have removed, and placed in the cities of Samaria, know not the manner of God of the land: therefore he has sent lions among them, and, behold, they slay them, because they know not the manner of God of the land.

27 Then the king of Assyria commanded, saying, Carry there one of the priests whom you brought from there; and let them go and dwell there, and let him teach them the manner of God of the land.

28 Then one of the priests whom they had carried away from Samaria came and dwelt in Bethel, and taught them how they should fear the Becoming-One.

29 Howbeit every nation made gods of their own, and put them in the houses of the high places which the Samaritans had made, every nation in their cities wherein they dwelt.

30 And the men of Babylon made Succothbenoth, and the men of Cuth made Nergal, and the men of Hamath made Ashima,

31 And the Avites made Nibhaz and Tartak, and the Sepharvites burnt their children in fire to Adrammelech and Anammelech, the gods of Sepharvaim.

32 So they feared the Becoming-One, and made unto themselves of the lowest of them priests of the high places, which sacrificed for them in the houses of the high places.

33 They feared the Becoming-One, and served their own gods, after the manner of the nations whom they carried away from there.

34 Unto this day they do after the former manners: they fear not the Becoming-One, neither do they after their statutes, or after their ordinances, or after the law and commandment which the Becoming-One commanded the children of Jacob, whom he named Israel;

35 With whom the Becoming-One had made a covenant, and charged them, saying, you shall not fear other gods, nor bow yourselves to them, nor serve them, nor sacrifice to them:

36 But the Becoming-One, who brought you up out of the land of Egypt with great power and a stretched out arm, him shall you fear, and him shall you worship, and to him shall you do sacrifice.

37 And the statutes, and the ordinances, and the law, and the commandment, which he wrote for you, you shall observe to do all the days; and you shall not fear other gods.

38 And the covenant that I have made with you you shall not forget; neither shall you fear other gods.

39 But the Becoming-One your God you shall fear; and he shall deliver you out of the hand of all your enemies.

40 Howbeit they did not listen, but they did after their former manner.

41 So these nations feared the Becoming-One, and served their graven images, both their children, and their children's children: as did their fathers, so do they unto this day.

2 Ki 18:1 Now it came to pass in the third year of Hoshea son of Elah king of Israel, that Hezekiah the son of Ahaz king of Judah began to reign.

2 A son of twenty and five years was he when he began to reign; and he reigned twenty and nine years in Jerusalem. His mother's name also was Abi, the daughter of Zachariah.

3 And he did that which was right in the sight of the Becoming-One, according to all that David his father did.

4 He removed the high places, and brake the images, and cut down the Asherahs, and brake in pieces the brazen serpent that Moses had made: for unto those days the children of Israel did burn incense to it: and he called it Nehushtan.

5 He trusted in the Becoming-One, God of Israel; so that after him was none like him among all the kings of Judah, nor any that were before him.

6 For he clave to the Becoming-One, and departed not from following him, but kept his commandments, which the Becoming-One commanded Moses.

7 And the Becoming-One was with him; and he prospered whereoever he went forth: and he rebelled against the king of Assyria, and served him not.

8 He smote the Philistines, even unto Gaza, and the borders thereof, from the tower of the watchmen to the fenced city.

9 And it came to pass in the fourth year of king Hezekiah, which was the seventh year of Hoshea son of Elah king of Israel, that **Shalmaneser king of Assyria** came up against Samaria, and besieged it.

10 And at the end of three years they took it: even in the sixth year of Hezekiah, that is the ninth year of Hoshea king of Israel, **Samaria was taken**. [3279 YM / 695 BC]

11 And the king of Assyria did carry away Israel unto Assyria, and put them in Halah and in Habor by the river of Gozan, and in the cities of the Medes:

12 Because they obeyed not the voice of the Becoming-One their God, but transgressed his covenant, and all that Moses the servant of the Becoming-One commanded, and would not hear them, nor do them.

13 Now in the fourteenth year of king Hezekiah did Sennacherib king of Assyria come up against all the fenced cities of Judah, and took them.

14 And Hezekiah king of Judah sent to the king of Assyria to Lachish, saying, I have offended; return from me: that which you put on me will I bear. And the king of Assyria appointed unto Hezekiah king of Judah three hundred talents of silver and thirty talents of gold.

15 And Hezekiah gave him all the silver that was found in the house of the Becoming-One, and in the treasures of the king's house.

16 At that time did Hezekiah cut off the gold from the doors of the temple of the Becoming-One, and from the pillars which Hezekiah king of Judah had overlaid, and gave it to the king of Assyria.

17 And the king of Assyria sent Tartan [general] and the chief of the eunuchs and chief of the cupbearers from Lachish to king Hezekiah with a great host against Jerusalem. And they went up and came to Jerusalem. And when they were come up, they came and stood by the conduit of the upper pool, which is in the highway of the fuller's [a washer of garments] field.

18 And when they had called to the king, there came out to them Eliakim the son of Hilkiah, which was over the household, and Shebna the scribe, and Joah the son of Asaph the recorder.

19 And Rabshakeh said unto them, Speak you now to Hezekiah, Thus says the great king, the king of Assyria, What confidence is this wherein you trust?

20 You say, but they are but vain words, I have counsel and strength for the war. Now on whom do you trust, that you rebell against me?

21 Now, behold, you trust upon the staff of this bruised reed, even upon Egypt, on which if a man lean, it will go into his hand, and pierce it: so is Pharaoh king of Egypt unto all that trust on him.

22 But if you say unto me, We trust in the Becoming-One our God: is not that he, whose high places and whose altars Hezekiah has taken away, and has said to Judah and Jerusalem, you shall worship before this altar in Jerusalem?

23 Now therefore, I pray you, give pledges to my lord the king of Assyria, and I will deliver you two thousand of horses, if you be able on your part to set riders upon them.

24 How then will you turn away the face of one captain of the least of my master's servants, and put your trust on Egypt for chariots and for horsemen?

25 Am I now come up without the Becoming-One against this place to destroy it? The Becoming-One said to me, Go up against this land, and destroy it.

26 Then said Eliakim the son of Hilkiah, and Shebna, and Joah, unto Rabshakeh, Speak, I pray you, to your servants in the Syrian language; for we understand it: and talk not with us in the Jews' language in the ears of the people that are on the wall.

27 But Rabshakeh said unto them, has my master sent me to your master, and to you, to speak these words? has he not sent me to the men which sit on the wall, that they may eat their own dung, and drink their own piss with you?

28 Then Rabshakeh stood and cried with a loud voice in the Jews' language, and spoke, saying, Hear the word of the great king, the king of Assyria:

29 Thus says the king, Let not Hezekiah deceive you: for he shall not be able to deliver you out of his hand:

30 Neither let Hezekiah make you trust in the Becoming-One, saying, The Becoming-One will surely deliver us, and this city shall not be delivered into the hand of the king of Assyria.

31 Listen not to Hezekiah: for thus says the king of Assyria, Make an agreement with me by a present, and come out to me, and then eat you every man of his own vine, and every one of his fig tree, and drink you every one the waters of his cistern:

32 Until I come and take you away to a land like your own land, a land of grain and wine, a land of bread and vineyards, a land of oil olive and of honey, that you may live, and not die: and listen not unto Hezekiah, when he persuades you, saying, The Becoming-One will deliver us.

33 Has any of the gods of the nations delivered at all his land out of the hand of the king of Assyria?

34 Where are the gods of Hamath, and of Arpad? where are the gods of Sepharvaim, Hena, and Ivah? have they delivered Samaria out of mine hand?

35 Who are they among all the gods of the countries, that have delivered their country out of mine hand, that the Becoming-One should deliver Jerusalem out of mine hand?

36 But the people held their peace, and answered him not a word: for the king's commandment was, saying, Answer him not.

37 Then came Eliakim the son of Hilkiah, which was over the household, and Shebna the scribe, and Joah the son of Asaph the recorder, to Hezekiah with their clothes rent, and told him the words of Rabshakeh.

2 Ki 19:1 And it came to pass, when king Hezekiah heard it, that he ripped his clothes, and covered himself with sackcloth, and went into the house of the Becoming-One.

2 And he sent Eliakim, which was over the household, and Shebna the scribe, and the elders of the priests, covered with sackcloth, to Isaiah the prophet the son of Amoz.

3 And they said unto him, Thus says Hezekiah, This day is a day of trouble, and of rebuke, and blasphemy: for the children are come to the birth, and there is not strength to bring forth.

4 It may be the Becoming-One your God will hear all the words of Rabshakeh, whom the king of Assyria his master has sent to reproach the living God; and will reprove the words which the Becoming-One your God has heard: therefore lift up your prayer for the remnant that are left.

5 So the servants of king Hezekiah came to Isaiah.

6 And Isaiah said unto them, Thus shall you say to your master, Thus says the Becoming-One, Be not afraid of the words which you have heard, with which the servants of the king of Assyria have blasphemed me.

7 Behold, I will send a spirit [wind] upon him, and he shall hear a rumor, and shall return to his own land; and I will cause him to fall by the sword in his own land.

8 So Rabshakeh returned, and found the king of Assyria warring against Libnah: for he had heard that he was departed from Lachish.

9 And when he heard say of Tirhakah king of Ethiopia, Behold, he is come out to fight against you: he sent messengers again unto Hezekiah, saying,

10 Thus shall you speak to Hezekiah king of Judah, saying, Let not your God in whom you trust deceive you, saying, Jerusalem shall not be delivered into the hand of the king of Assyria.

11 Behold, you have heard what the kings of Assyria have done to all lands, by destroying them utterly: and shall you be delivered?

12 Have the gods of the nations delivered them which my fathers have destroyed; as Gozan, and Haran, and Rezeph, and the children of Eden which were in Thelasar?

13 Where is the king of Hamath, and the king of Arpad, and the king of the city of Sepharvaim, of Hena, and Ivah?

14 And Hezekiah received the letter of the hand of the messengers, and read it: and Hezekiah went up into the house of the Becoming-One, and spread it before the Becoming-One.

15 And Hezekiah prayed before the Becoming-One, and said, O Becoming-One, God of Israel, which dwells **the** cherubs, you alone **the** God, even you alone, for all the kingdoms of the earth you have made the heavens and earth.

16 Becoming-One, bow down your ear, and hear: open, Becoming-One, your eyes, and see: and hear the words of Sennacherib, which has sent him to reproach the living God.

17 Of a truth, Becoming-One, the kings of Assyria have destroyed the nations and their lands,

18 And have cast their gods into the fire: for they were no gods, but the work of men's hands, wood and stone: therefore they have destroyed them.

19 Now therefore, O Becoming-One our God, I beg you, save you us out of his hand, that all the kingdoms of the earth may know that you are the Becoming-One, you alone God.

20 Then Isaiah the son of Amoz sent to Hezekiah, saying, Thus says the Becoming-One, God of Israel, That which you have prayed to me against Sennacherib king of Assyria I have heard.

21 This is the word that the Becoming-One has spoken concerning him; The virgin the daughter of Zion has despised you, and laughed you to scorn; the daughter of Jerusalem has shaken her head at you.

22 Whom have you reproached and blasphemed? and against whom have you exalted your voice, and lifted up your eyes on high? even against the Holy One of Israel.

23 By your messengers you have reproached my lord, and have said, With the multitude of my chariots I am come up to the height of the mountains, to the sides of Lebanon, and will cut down the tall cedar trees thereof, and the choice fir trees thereof: and I will enter into the lodgings of his borders, and into the forest of his Carmel.

24 I have dug and drunk strange waters, and with the sole of my feet have I dried up all the rivers of besieged places.

25 have you not heard long ago how I have done it, and of ancient times that I have formed it? now have I brought it to pass, that you should be to lay waste fenced cities into ruinous heaps.

26 Therefore their inhabitants were of small power, they were dismayed and confounded; they were as the grass of the field, and as the green herb, as the grass on the house tops, and as grain blasted before it be grown up.

27 But I know your abode, and your going out, and your coming in, and your rage against me.

28 Because your rage against me and your tumult is come up into mine ears, therefore I will put my hook in your nose, and my bridle in your lips, and I will turn you back by the way by which you came.

29 And this shall be a sign unto you, you shall eat this year such things as grow of themselves, and in the second year that which springs of the same; and in the third year sow ye, and reap, and plant vineyards, and eat the fruits thereof.

30 And the remnant that is escaped of the house of Judah shall yet again take root downward, and bear fruit upward.

31 For out of Jerusalem shall go forth a remnant, and they that escape out of mount Zion: the zeal of the Becoming-One of hosts shall do this.

32 Therefore thus says the Becoming-One concerning the king of Assyria, He shall not come into this city, nor shoot an arrow there, nor come before it with shield, nor cast a bank against it.

33 By the way that he came, by the same shall he return, and shall not come into this city, says the Becoming-One.

34 For I will defend this city, to save it, for mine own sake, and for my servant David's sake.

35 And it came to pass that night, that the angel of the Becoming-One went out, and smote in the camp of the Assyrians a hundred fourscore and five thousand: and when they arose early in the morning, behold, they were all dead corpses.

36 So Sennacherib king of Assyria departed, and went and returned, and dwelt at Nineveh.

37 And it came to pass, as he was worshipping in the house of Nisroch his god, that Adrammelech and Sharezer his sons smote him with the sword: and they escaped into the land of Armenia. And Esarhaddon his son reigned in his stead.

2 Ki 20:1 In those days was Hezekiah sick unto death. And the prophet Isaiah the son of Amoz came to him, and said unto him, Thus says the Becoming-One, Set your house in order; for you shall die, and not live.

2 Then he turned his face to the wall, and prayed unto the Becoming-One, saying,

3 I beg you, O Becoming-One, remember now how I have walked before you in truth and with a perfect heart, and have done that which is good in your sight. And Hezekiah wept greatly.

4 And it came to pass, afore Isaiah was gone out into the middle court, that the word of the Becoming-One came to him, saying,

5 Turn again, and tell Hezekiah the captain of my people, Thus says the Becoming-One, God of David your father, I have heard your prayer, I have seen your tears: behold, I will heal you: on the third day you shall go up unto the house of the Becoming-One.

6 And I will add unto your days fifteen years; and I will deliver you and this city out of the hand of the king of Assyria; and I will defend this city for mine own sake, and for my servant David's sake. [3287 YM 687 BC – a Jubilee year, see CP5]

7 And Isaiah said, Take a lump of figs. And they took and laid it on the boil, and he recovered.

8 And Hezekiah said unto Isaiah, What shall be the sign that the Becoming-One will heal me, and that I shall go up into the house of the Becoming-One the third day?

9 And Isaiah said, This sign shall you have of the Becoming-One, that the Becoming-One will do the thing that he has spoken: shall the shadow go forward ten degrees, or go back ten degrees?

10 And Hezekiah answered, It is a light thing for the shadow to go down ten degrees: nay, but let the shadow return backward ten degrees.

11 And Isaiah the prophet cried unto the Becoming-One: and he brought the shadow ten degrees backward, by which it had gone down in the dial of Ahaz.

12 At that time Berodachbaladan, the son of Baladan, king of Babylon, sent letters and a present unto Hezekiah: for he had heard that Hezekiah had been sick.

13 And Hezekiah listened unto them, and showed them all the house of his precious things, the silver, and the gold, and the spices, and the precious ointment, and all the house of his armor, and all that was found in his treasures: there was nothing in his house, nor in all his dominion, that Hezekiah showed them not.

14 Then came Isaiah the prophet unto king Hezekiah, and said unto him, What said these men? and from where came they unto you? And Hezekiah said, They are come from a far country, even from Babylon.

15 And he said, What have they seen in your house? And Hezekiah answered, All the things that are in mine house have they seen: there is nothing among my treasures that I have not showed them.

16 And Isaiah said unto Hezekiah, Hear the word of the Becoming-One.

17 Behold, the days come, that all that is in your house, and that which your fathers have laid up in store unto this day, shall be carried into Babylon: nothing shall be left, says the Becoming-One.

18 And of your sons that shall issue from you, which you shall beget, shall they take away; and they shall be eunuchs in the palace of the king of Babylon.

19 Then said Hezekiah unto Isaiah, Good is the word of the Becoming-One which you have spoken. And he said, Is it not good, if peace and truth be in my days?

20 And the rest of the acts of Hezekiah, and all his might, and how he made a pool, and a conduit, and brought water into the city, are they not written in the book of the words of the days [chronicles] of the kings of Judah?

21 And Hezekiah slept with his fathers: and Manasseh his son reigned in his stead.

2 Ki 21:1 Manasseh was a son of twelve years when he began to reign, and reigned fifty and five years in Jerusalem. And his mother's name was Hephzibah.

2 And he did that which was evil in the sight of the Becoming-One, after the abominations of the nations, whom the Becoming-One cast out before the children of Israel.

3 For he built up again the high places which Hezekiah his father had destroyed; and he reared up altars for the lord [baal] and made a Asherah, as did Ahab king of Israel; and worshiped all the host of heaven, and served them.

4 And he built altars in the house of the Becoming-One, of which the Becoming-One said, In Jerusalem will I put my name.

5 And he built altars for all the host of the heavens in the two courts of the house of the Becoming-One.

6 And he made his son pass through the fire, and observed times, and used enchantments, and dealt with mediums and fortune-tellers: he worked much wickedness in the sight of the Becoming-One, to provoke him to anger.

7 And he set a graven image of the Asherah that he had made in the house, of which the Becoming-One said to David, and to Solomon his son, In this house, and in Jerusalem, which I have chosen out of all tribes of Israel, will I put my name for olam.

8 Neither will I make the feet of Israel move any more out of the land which I gave their fathers; only if they will observe to do according to all that I have commanded them, and according to all the law that my servant Moses commanded them.

9 But they listened not: and Manasseh seduced them to do more evil than did the nations whom the Becoming-One destroyed before the children of Israel.

10 And the Becoming-One spoke by his servants the prophets, saying,

11 Because Manasseh king of Judah has done these abominations, and has done wickedly above all that the Amorites did, which were before him, and has made Judah also to sin with his idols:

12 Therefore thus says the Becoming-One, God of Israel, Behold, I am bringing such evil upon Jerusalem and Judah, that whosoever hears of it, both his ears shall tingle.

13 And I will stretch over Jerusalem the line of Samaria, and the plummet of the house of Ahab: and I

will wipe Jerusalem as a man wipes a dish, wiping it, and turning it upside down.

14 And I will forsake the remnant of mine inheritance, and deliver them into the hand of their enemies; and they shall become a prey and a spoil to all their enemies;

15 Because they have done that which was evil in my sight, and have provoked me to anger, since the day their fathers came forth out of Egypt, even unto this day.

16 Moreover Manasseh shed innocent blood very much, till he had filled Jerusalem from one end to another; beside his sin wherewith he made Judah to sin, in doing that which was evil in the sight of the Becoming-One.

17 Now the rest of the acts of Manasseh, and all that he did, and his sin that he sinned, are they not written in the book of the words of the days [chronicles] of the kings of Judah?

18 And Manasseh slept with his fathers, and was buried in the garden of his own house, in the garden of Uzza: and Amon his son reigned in his stead.

19 Amon was a son of twenty and two years when he began to reign, and he reigned two years in Jerusalem. And his mother's name was Meshullemeth, the daughter of Haruz of Jotbah.

20 And he did that which was evil in the sight of the Becoming-One, as his father Manasseh did.

21 And he walked in all the way that his father walked in, and served the idols that his father served, and worshiped them:

22 And he forsook the Becoming-One, God of his fathers, and walked not in the way of the Becoming-One.

23 And the servants of Amon conspired against him, and killed the king in his own house.

24 And the people of the land killed all them that had conspired against king Amon; and the people of the land made Josiah his son king in his stead.

25 Now the rest of the acts of Amon which he did, are they not written in the book of the words of the days [chronicles] of the kings of Judah?

26 And he was buried in his tomb in the garden of Uzza: and Josiah his son reigned in his stead.

2 Ki 22:1 Josiah was a son of eight years when he began to reign, and he reigned thirty and one years in Jerusalem. And his mother's name was Jedidah, the daughter of Adaiah of Boscath.

2 And he did that which was right in the sight of the Becoming-One, and walked in all the way of David his father, and turned not aside to the right hand or to the left.

3 And it came to pass in the eighteenth year of king Josiah, that the king sent Shaphan the son of Azaliah, the son of Meshullam, the scribe, to the house of the Becoming-One, saying,

4 Go up to Hilkiah the high priest, that he may sum the silver which is brought into the house of the Becoming-One, which the keepers of the door have gathered of the people:

5 And let them deliver it into the hand of the doers of the work, that have the oversight of the house of the Becoming-One: and let them give it to the doers of the work which is in the house of the Becoming-One, to repair the breaches of the house,

6 Unto carpenters, and builders, and masons, and to buy timber and hewn stone to repair the house.

7 Howbeit there was no reckoning made with them of the money that was delivered into their hand, because they dealt faithfully.

8 And Hilkiah the high priest said unto Shaphan the scribe, I have found the book of the law in the house of the Becoming-One. And Hilkiah gave the book to Shaphan, and he read it.

9 And Shaphan the scribe came to the king, and brought the king word again, and said, your servants have gathered the money that was found in the house, and have delivered it into the hand of them that do the work, that have the oversight of the house of the Becoming-One.

10 And Shaphan the scribe showed the king, saying, Hilkiah the priest has delivered me a book. And Shaphan read it before the king.

11 And it came to pass, when the king had heard the words of the book of the law, that he ripped his clothes.

12 And the king commanded Hilkiah the priest, and Ahikam the son of Shaphan, and Achbor the son of Michaiah, and Shaphan the scribe, and Asahiah a servant of the king's, saying,

13 Go, inquire of the Becoming-One for me, and for the people, and for all Judah, concerning the words of this book that is found: for great is the wrath of the Becoming-One that is kindled against us, because our fathers have not listened unto the words of this book, to do according unto all that which is written concerning us.

14 So Hilkiah the priest, and Ahikam, and Achbor, and Shaphan, and Asahiah, went unto Huldah the prophetess, the wife of Shallum the son of Tikvah, the son of Harhas, keeper of the wardrobe; now she dwelt in Jerusalem in the college; and they communed with her.

15 And she said unto them, Thus says the Becoming-One, God of Israel, Tell the man that sent you to me,

16 Thus says the Becoming-One, Behold, I will bring evil upon this place, and upon the inhabitants thereof, even all the words of the book which the king of Judah has read:

17 Because they have forsaken me, and have burned incense unto other gods, that they might provoke me to anger with all the works of their hands; therefore my wrath shall be kindled against this place, and shall not be quenched.

18 But to the king of Judah which sent you to inquire of the Becoming-One, thus shall you say to him, Thus says the Becoming-One, God of Israel, As touching the words which you have heard;

19 Because your heart was tender, and you have humbled yourself before the Becoming-One, when you heard what I spoke against this place, and against the inhabitants thereof, that they should become a desolation and a curse, and have ripped your clothes, and wept before me; I also have heard you, says the Becoming-One.

20 Behold therefore, I will gather you unto your fathers, and you shall be gathered into your grave in peace; and your eyes shall not see all the evil which I

will bring upon this place. And they brought the king word again.

2 Ki 23:1 And the king sent, and they gathered unto him all the elders of Judah and of Jerusalem.

2 And the king went up into the house of the Becoming-One, and all the men of Judah and all the inhabitants of Jerusalem with him, and the priests, and the prophets, and all the people, both small and great: and he read in their ears all the words of the book of the covenant which was found in the house of the Becoming-One.

3 And the king stood by a pillar, and made a covenant before the Becoming-One, to walk after the Becoming-One, and to keep his commandments and his testimonies and his statutes with all their heart and all their soul, to perform the words of this covenant that were written in this book. And all the people stood to the covenant.

4 And the king commanded Hilkiah the high priest, and the priests of the second order, and the keepers of the door, to bring forth out of the temple of the Becoming-One all the vessels that were made for the lord [baal] and for the Asherah, and for all the host of heaven: and he burned them outside Jerusalem in the fields of Kidron, and carried the ashes of them unto Bethel.

5 And he put down the idolatrous priests, whom the kings of Judah had ordained to burn incense in the high places in the cities of Judah, and in the places round about Jerusalem; them also that burned incense unto the lord [baal] to the sun, and to the moon, and to the planets, and to all the host of heaven.

6 And he brought out the Asherah from the house of the Becoming-One, outside Jerusalem, unto the brook Kidron, and burned it at the brook Kidron, and stamped it small to powder, and cast the powder thereof upon the graves of the children of the people.

7 And he brake down the houses of the sodomites, that were by the house of the Becoming-One, where the women wove hangings for the Asherah.

8 And he brought all the priests out of the cities of Judah, and defiled the high places where the priests had burned incense, from Geba to Beersheba, and brake down the high places of the gates that were in the entering in of the gate of Joshua the governor of the city, which were on a man's left hand at the gate of the city.

9 Nevertheless the priests of the high places came not up to the altar of the Becoming-One in Jerusalem, but they did eat of the unleavened bread among their brethren.

10 And he defiled Topheth, which is in the valley of the children of Hinnom, that no man might make his son or his daughter to pass through the fire to Molech.

11 And he took away the horses that the kings of Judah had given to the sun, at the entrance to the house of the Becoming-One, by the chamber of <u>Nathan-melech</u> the chamberlain [of the king], which was in the **Parbar**,[115] and burned the chariots of the sun with fire.

[**For location of the "Parbar" see:** *https://youtu.be/adtNyATL4Tw* **or read:** *https://www.timesofisrael.com/two-tiny-first-temple-inscriptions-vastly-enlarge-picture-of-ancient-jerusalem/amp/*]

12 And the altars that were on the top of the upper chamber of Ahaz, which the kings of Judah had made, and the altars which Manasseh had made in the two courts of the house of the Becoming-One, did the king beat down, and brake them down from there, and cast the dust of them into the brook Kidron.

13 And the high places that were before Jerusalem, which were on the right hand of the mount of corruption, which Solomon the king of Israel had built for Ashtoreth the abomination of the Zidonians, and for Chemosh the abomination of the Moabites, and for Milcom the abomination of the children of Ammon, did the king defile.

14 And he brake in pieces the images, and cut down the Asherahs, and filled their places with the bones of men.

15 Moreover the altar that was at Bethel, and the high place which Jeroboam the son of Nebat, who made Israel to sin, had made, both that altar and the high place he brake down, and burned the high place, and stamped it small to powder, and burned the Asherah.

16 And as Josiah turned himself, he spied the tombs that were there in the mount, and sent, and took the bones out of the tombs, and burned them upon the altar, and polluted it, according to the word of the Becoming-One which the man of God proclaimed, who proclaimed these words.

17 Then he said, What title is that that I see? And the men of the city told him, It is the tomb of the man of God, which came from Judah, and proclaimed these things that you have done against the altar of Bethel.

18 And he said, Let him alone; let no man move his bones. So they let his bones alone, with the bones of the prophet that came out of Samaria.

19 And all the houses also of the high places that were in the cities of Samaria, which the kings of Israel had made to provoke the Becoming-One to anger, Josiah took away, and did to them according to all the acts that he had done in Bethel.

20 And he killed all the priests of the high places that were there upon the altars, and burned men's bones upon them, and returned to Jerusalem.

21 And the king commanded all the people, saying, Keep the Passover unto the Becoming-One your God, as it is written in the book of this covenant.

22 Surely there was not held such a Passover from the days of the judges that judged Israel, nor in all the days of the kings of Israel, nor of the kings of Judah;

23 But in the eighteenth year of king Josiah, wherein this Passover was held to the Becoming-One in Jerusalem.

24 Moreover the workers with mediums, and the fortune-tellers, and the images [teraphim] and the

---

[115] 1Chr 26:18 in context indicates this location was on the west side of the first Temple

idols, and all the abominations that were spied in the land of Judah and in Jerusalem, did Josiah put away, that he might perform the words of the law which were written in the book that Hilkiah the priest found in the house of the Becoming-One.

25 And like unto him was there no king before him, that turned to the Becoming-One with all his heart, and with all his soul, and with all his might, according to all the law of Moses; neither after him arose there any like him.

26 Notwithstanding the Becoming-One turned not from the fierceness of his great wrath, wherewith his anger was kindled against Judah, because of all the provocations that Manasseh had provoked him withal.

27 And the Becoming-One said, I will remove Judah also out of my sight, as I have removed Israel, and will cast off this city Jerusalem which I have chosen, and the house of which I said, My name shall be there.

28 Now the rest of the acts of Josiah, and all that he did, are they not written in the book of the words of the days [chronicles] of the kings of Judah?

29 In his days Pharaoh-nechoh king of Egypt went up against the king of Assyria to the river Euphrates: and king Josiah went against him; and he killed him at Megiddo, when he had seen him.

30 And his servants carried him in a chariot dead from Megiddo, and brought him to Jerusalem, and buried him in his own tomb. And the people of the land took Jehoahaz the son of Josiah, and anointed him, and made him king in his father's stead.

31 Jehoahaz was a son of twenty and three years when he began to reign; and he reigned three months in Jerusalem. And his mother's name was Hamutal, the daughter of Jeremiah of Libnah.

32 And he did that which was evil in the sight of the Becoming-One, according to all that his fathers had done.

33 And Pharaoh-nechoh put him in bands at Riblah in the land of Hamath, that he might not reign in Jerusalem; and put the land to a tribute of a hundred talents of silver, and a talent of gold.

34 And Pharaoh-nechoh made Eliakim the son of Josiah king in the room of Josiah his father, and turned his name to Jehoiakim, and took Jehoahaz away: and he came to Egypt, and died there.

35 And Jehoiakim gave the silver and the gold to Pharaoh; but he taxed the land to give the money according to the commandment of Pharaoh: he exacted the silver and the gold of the people of the land, of every one according to his taxation, to give it unto Pharaoh-nechoh.

36 Jehoiakim was a son of twenty and five years when he began to reign; and he reigned eleven years in Jerusalem. And his mother's name was Zebudah, the daughter of Pedaiah of Rumah.

37 And he did that which was evil in the sight of the Becoming-One, according to all that his fathers had done.

2 Ki 24:1 In his days Nebuchadnezzar king of Babylon came up, and Jehoiakim became his servant three years: then he turned and rebelled against him.

2 And the Becoming-One sent against him bands of the Chaldees, and bands of the Syrians, and bands of the Moabites, and bands of the children of Ammon, and sent them against Judah to destroy it, according to the word of the Becoming-One, which he spoke by his servants the prophets.

3 Surely at the commandment of the Becoming-One came this upon Judah, to remove them out of his sight, for the sins of Manasseh, according to all that he did;

4 And also for the innocent blood that he shed: for he filled Jerusalem with innocent blood; which the Becoming-One would not pardon.

5 Now the rest of the acts of Jehoiakim, and all that he did, are they not written in the book of the words of the days [chronicles] of the kings of Judah?

6 So Jehoiakim slept with his fathers: and Jehoiachin his son reigned in his stead.

7 And the king of Egypt came not again any more out of his land: for the king of Babylon had taken from the river of Egypt unto the river Euphrates all that pertained to the king of Egypt.

8 Jehoiachin was a son of eighteen years when he began to reign, and he reigned in Jerusalem three months. And his mother's name was Nehushta, the daughter of Elnathan of Jerusalem.

9 And he did that which was evil in the sight of the Becoming-One, according to all that his father had done.

10 At that time the servants of Nebuchadnezzar king of Babylon came up against Jerusalem, and the city was besieged.

11 And Nebuchadnezzar king of Babylon came against the city, and his servants did besiege it.

12 And Jehoiachin the king of Judah went out to the king of Babylon, he, and his mother, and his servants, and his princes, and his eunuchs: and the king of Babylon took him in the eighth year of his reign.

13 And he carried out there all the treasures of the house of the Becoming-One, and the treasures of the king's house, and cut in pieces all the vessels of gold which Solomon king of Israel had made in the temple of the Becoming-One, as the Becoming-One had said.

14 And he carried away all Jerusalem, and all the princes, and all the mighty men of valor, even ten thousand of captives, and all the craftsmen and smiths: none remained, save the poorest sort of the people of the land.

15 And he carried away Jehoiachin to Babylon, and the king's mother, and the king's wives, and his eunuchs, and the mighty of the land, those carried he into captivity from Jerusalem to Babylon.

16 And all the men of might, even seven thousand, and craftsmen and smiths a thousand, all that were strong and apt for war, even them the king of Babylon brought captive to Babylon.

17 And the king of Babylon made Mattaniah his father's brother king in his stead, and changed his name to Zedekiah.

18 Zedekiah was a son of twenty and one years when he began to reign, and he reigned eleven years in Jerusalem. And his mother's name was Hamutal, the daughter of Jeremiah of Libnah.

19 And he did that which was evil in the sight of the Becoming-One, according to all that Jehoiakim had done.

20 For through the anger of the Becoming-One it came to pass in Jerusalem and Judah, until he had cast them out from his presence, that Zedekiah rebelled against the king of Babylon.

2 Ki 25:1 And it came to pass in the ninth year of his reign, in the tenth month, in the tenth day of the month, that Nebuchadnezzar king of Babylon came, he, and all his host, against Jerusalem, and pitched against it: and they built forts against it round about.

2 And the city was besieged unto the eleventh year of king Zedekiah.

3 And on the ninth day of the fourth month the famine prevailed in the city, and there was no bread for the people of the land.

4 And the city was broken up, and all the men of war fled by night by the way of the gate between two walls, which is by the king's garden: now the Chaldees were against the city round about: and the king went the way toward the plain.

5 And the army of the Chaldees pursued after the king, and overtook him in the plains of Jericho: and all his army were scattered from him.

6 So they took the king, and brought him up to the king of Babylon to Riblah; and they gave judgment upon him.

7 And they killed the sons of Zedekiah before his eyes, and put out the eyes of Zedekiah, and bound him with fetters of brass, and carried him to Babylon.

8 And in the fifth month, on the seventh day of the month, which is the nineteenth year of king Nebuchadnezzar king of Babylon, came Nebuzaradan, captain of the guard, a servant of the king of Babylon, unto Jerusalem: [3388 YM / 586 BC]

9 And he burnt the house of the Becoming-One, and the king's house, and all the houses of Jerusalem, and every great man's house burnt he with fire.

10 And all the army of the Chaldees, that were with the captain of the guard, brake down the walls of Jerusalem round about.

11 Now the rest of the people that were left in the city, and the fugitives that fell away to the king of Babylon, with the remnant of the multitude, did Nebuzaradan the captain of the guard carry away.

12 But the captain of the guard left of the poor of the land to be vinedressers and husbandmen.

13 And the pillars of brass that were in the house of the Becoming-One, and the bases, and the brazen sea that was in the house of the Becoming-One, did the Chaldees break in pieces, and carried the brass of them to Babylon.

14 And the pots, and the shovels, and the snuffers, and the spoons, and all the vessels of brass wherewith they ministered, took they away.

15 And the firepans, and the bowls, and such things as were of gold, in gold, and of silver, in silver, the captain of the guard took away.

16 The two pillars, one sea, and the bases which Solomon had made for the house of the Becoming-One; the brass of all these vessels was without weight.

17 The height of the one pillar was eighteen cubits, and the capital upon it was brass: and the height of the capital three cubits; and the braided work, and pomegranates upon the capital round about, all of brass: and like unto these had the second pillar with braided work.

18 And the captain of the guard took Seraiah the chief priest, and Zephaniah the second priest, and the three keepers of the door:

19 And out of the city he took an eunuch that was set over the men of war, and five men of them that were in the king's presence, which were found in the city, and the principal scribe of the host, which mustered the people of the land, and threescore men of the people of the land that were found in the city:

20 And Nebuzaradan captain of the guard took these, and brought them to the king of Babylon to Riblah:

21 And the king of Babylon smote them, and killed them at Riblah in the land of Hamath. So Judah was carried away out of their land.

22 And as for the people that remained in the land of Judah, whom Nebuchadnezzar king of Babylon had left, even over them he made Gedaliah the son of Ahikam, the son of Shaphan, ruler.

23 And when all the captains of the armies, they and their men, heard that the king of Babylon had made Gedaliah governor, there came to Gedaliah to Mizpah, even Ishmael the son of Nethaniah, and Johanan the son of Careah, and Seraiah the son of Tanhumeth the Netophathite, and Jaazaniah the son of a Maachathite, they and their men.

24 And Gedaliah swore to them, and to their men, and said unto them, Fear not to be the servants of the Chaldees: dwell in the land, and serve the king of Babylon; and it shall be well with you.

25 But it came to pass in the seventh month, that Ishmael the son of Nethaniah, the son of Elishama, of the seed royal, came, and ten men with him, and smote Gedaliah, that he died, and the Jews and the Chaldees that were with him at Mizpah.

26 And all the people, both small and great, and the captains of the armies, arose, and came to Egypt: for they were afraid of the Chaldees.

27 And it came to pass in the seven and thirtieth year of the captivity of Jehoiachin king of Judah, in the twelfth month, on the seven and twentieth day of the month, that Evil-merodach king of Babylon in the year that he began to reign did lift up the head of Jehoiachin king of Judah out of prison;

28 And he spoke kindly to him, and set his throne above the throne of the kings that were with him in Babylon;

29 And changed his prison garments: and he did eat bread continually before him all the days of his life.

30 And his allowance was a continual allowance given him of the king, a daily rate for every day, all the days of his life.

1 Chronicles

1 Chr 1:1 Adam, Sheth, Enosh,

2 Kenan, Mahalaleel, Jered,

3 Henoch, Methuselah, Lamech,

4 Noah, Shem, Ham, and Japheth.

5 The sons of Japheth; Gomer, and Magog, and Madai, and Javan, and Tubal, and Meshech, and Tiras.

6 And the sons of Gomer; Ashchenaz, and Riphath, and Togarmah.

7 And the sons of Javan; Elishah, and Tarshish, Kittim, and Dodanim.

8 The sons of Ham; Cush, and Mizraim, Put, and Canaan.

9 And the sons of Cush; Seba, and Havilah, and Sabta, and Raamah, and Sabtecha. And the sons of Raamah; Sheba, and Dedan.

10 And Cush begat Nimrod: he began to be mighty upon the earth.

11 And Mizraim begat Ludim, and Anamim, and Lehabim, and Naphtuhim,

12 And Pathrusim, and Casluhim, of whom came the Philistines, and Caphthorim.

13 And Canaan begat Zidon his firstborn, and Heth,

14 The Jebusite also, and the Amorite, and the Girgashite,

15 And the Hivite, and the Arkite, and the Sinite,

16 And the Arvadite, and the Zemarite, and the Hamathite.

17 The sons of Shem; Elam, and Asshur, and Arphaxad, and Lud, and Aram, and Uz, and Hul, and Gether, and Meshech.

18 And Arphaxad begat Shelah, and Shelah begat Eber.

19 And unto Eber were born two sons: the name of the one was Peleg; because in his days the earth was divided: and his brother's name was Joktan.

20 And Joktan begat Almodad, and Sheleph, and Hazarmaveth, and Jerah,

21 Hadoram also, and Uzal, and Diklah,

22 And Ebal, and Abimael, and Sheba,

23 And Ophir, and Havilah, and Jobab. All these were the sons of Joktan.

24 Shem, Arphaxad, Shelah,

25 Eber, Peleg, Reu,

26 Serug, Nahor, Terah,

27 Abram; the same is Abraham.

28 The sons of Abraham; Isaac, and Ishmael.

29 These are their generations: The firstborn of Ishmael, Nebaioth; then Kedar, and Adbeel, and Mibsam,

30 Mishma, and Dumah, Massa, Hadad, and Tema,

31 Jetur, Naphish, and Kedemah. These are the sons of Ishmael.

32 Now the sons of Keturah, Abraham's concubine: she bare Zimran, and Jokshan, and Medan, and Midian, and Ishbak, and Shuah. And the sons of Jokshan; Sheba, and Dedan.

33 And the sons of Midian; Ephah, and Epher, and Henoch, and Abida, and Eldaah. All these are the sons of Keturah.

34 And Abraham begat Isaac. The sons of Isaac; Esau and Israel.

35 The sons of Esau; Eliphaz, Reuel, and Jeush, and Jaalam, and Korah.

36 The sons of Eliphaz; Teman, and Omar, Zephi, and Gatam, Kenaz, and Timna, and Amalek.

37 The sons of Reuel; Nahath, Zerah, Shammah, and Mizzah.

38 And the sons of Seir; Lotan, and Shobal, and Zibeon, and Anah, and Dishon, and Ezar, and Dishan.

39 And the sons of Lotan; Hori, and Homam: and Timna was Lotan's sister.

40 The sons of Shobal; Alian, and Manahath, and Ebal, Shephi, and Onam. And the sons of Zibeon; Aiah, and Anah.

41 The sons of Anah; Dishon. And the sons of Dishon; Amram, and Eshban, and Ithran, and Cheran.

42 The sons of Ezer; Bilhan, and Zavan, and Jakan. The sons of Dishan; Uz, and Aran.

43 Now these are the kings that reigned in the land of Edom before any king reigned over the children of Israel; Bela the son of Beor: and the name of his city was Dinhabah.

44 And when Bela was dead, Jobab the son of Zerah of Bozrah reigned in his stead.

45 And when Jobab was dead, Husham of the land of the Temanites reigned in his stead.

46 And when Husham was dead, Hadad the son of Bedad, which smote Midian in the field of Moab, reigned in his stead: and the name of his city was Avith.

47 And when Hadad was dead, Samlah of Masrekah reigned in his stead.

48 And when Samlah was dead, Shaul of Rehoboth by the river reigned in his stead.

49 And when Shaul was dead, Baal-Hanan the son of Achbor reigned in his stead.

50 And when Baal-Hanan was dead, Hadad reigned in his stead: and the name of his city was Pai; and his wife's name was Mehetabel, the daughter of Matred, the daughter of Mezahab.

51 Hadad died also. And the chiefs of Edom were; chief Timnah, chief Aliah, chief Jetheth,

52 Chief Aholibamah, chief Elah, chief Pinon,

53 Chief Kenaz, chief Teman, chief Mibzar,

54 Chief Magdiel, chief Iram. These are the chiefs of Edom.

1 Chr 2:1 These are the sons of Israel; Reuben, Simeon, Levi, and Judah, Issachar, and Zebulun,

2 Dan, Joseph, and Benjamin, Naphtali, Gad, and Asher.

3 The sons of Judah; Er, and Onan, and Shelah: which three were born unto him of the daughter of Shua the Canaanitess. And Er, the firstborn of Judah, was evil in the sight of the Becoming-One; and he killed him.

4 And Tamar his daughter-in-law bare him Pharez and Zerah. All the sons of Judah were five.

5 The sons of Pharez; Hezron, and Hamul.

6 And the sons of Zerah; Zimri, and Ethan, and Heman, and Calcol, and Dara: five of them in all.

7 And the sons of Carmi; Achar, the troubler of Israel, who transgressed in the thing accursed.

8 And the sons of Ethan; Azariah.

9 The sons also of Hezron, that were born unto him; Jerahmeel, and Ram, and Chelubai.

10 And Ram begat Amminadab; and Amminadab begat Nahshon, prince of the children of Judah;

11 And Nahshon begat Salma, and Salma begat Boaz,

12 And Boaz begat Obed, and Obed begat Jesse.

13 And Jesse begat his firstborn Eliab, and Abinadab the second, and Shimma the third,

14 Nethaneel the fourth, Raddai the fifth,

15 Ozem the sixth, David the seventh:

16 Whose sisters were Zeruiah, and Abigail. And the sons of Zeruiah; Abishai, and Joab, and Asahel, three.

17 And Abigail bare Amasa: and the father of Amasa was Jether the Ishmeelite.

18 And Caleb the son of Hezron begat children of Azubah his wife, and of Jerioth: her sons are these; Jesher, and Shobab, and Ardon.

19 And when Azubah was dead, Caleb took unto him Ephrath, which bare him Hur.

20 And Hur begat Uri, and Uri begat Bezaleel.

21 And afterward Hezron went in to the daughter of Machir the father of Gilead, whom he married when he was a son of threescore years; and she bare him Segub.

22 And Segub begat Jair, who had three and twenty cities in the land of Gilead.

23 And he took Geshur, and Aram, with the towns of Jair, from them, with Kenath, and the towns thereof, even threescore cities. All these belonged to the sons of Machir, the father of Gilead.

24 And after that Hezron was dead in Calebephratah, then Abiah Hezron's wife bare him Ashur the father of Tekoa.

25 And the sons of Jerahmeel the firstborn of Hezron were, Ram the firstborn, and Bunah, and Oren, and Ozem, and Ahijah.

26 Jerahmeel had also another wife, whose name was Atarah; she was the mother of Onam.

27 And the sons of Ram the firstborn of Jerahmeel were, Maaz, and Jamin, and Eker.

28 And the sons of Onam were, Shammai, and Jada. And the sons of Shammai; Nadab, and Abishur.

29 And the name of the wife of Abishur was Abihail, and she bare him Ahban, and Molid.

30 And the sons of Nadab; Seled, and Appaim: but Seled died without children.

31 And the sons of Appaim; Ishi. And the sons of Ishi; Sheshan. And the children of Sheshan; Ahlai.

32 And the sons of Jada the brother of Shammai; Jether, and Jonathan: and Jether died without children.

33 And the sons of Jonathan; Peleth, and Zaza. These were the sons of Jerahmeel.

34 Now Sheshan had no sons, but daughters. And Sheshan had a servant, an Egyptian, whose name was Jarha.

35 And Sheshan gave his daughter to Jarha his servant to wife; and she bare him Attai.

36 And Attai begat Nathan, and Nathan begat Zabad,

37 And Zabad begat Ephlal, and Ephlal begat Obed,

38 And Obed begat Jehu, and Jehu begat Azariah,

39 And Azariah begat Helez, and Helez begat Eleasah,

40 And Eleasah begat Sisamai, and Sisamai begat Shallum,

41 And Shallum begat Jekamiah, and Jekamiah begat Elishama.

42 Now the sons of Caleb the brother of Jerahmeel were, Mesha his firstborn, which was the father of Ziph; and the sons of Mareshah the father of Hebron.

43 And the sons of Hebron; Korah, and Tappuah, and Rekem, and Shema.

44 And Shema begat Raham, the father of Jorkoam: and Rekem begat Shammai.

45 And the son of Shammai was Maon: and Maon was the father of Beth-zur.

46 And Ephah, Caleb's concubine, bare Haran, and Moza, and Gazez: and Haran begat Gazez.

47 And the sons of Jahdai; Regem, and Jotham, and Gesham, and Pelet, and Ephah, and Shaaph.

48 Maachah, Caleb's concubine, bare Sheber, and Tirhanah.

49 She bare also Shaaph the father of Madmannah, Sheva the father of Machbenah, and the father of Gibea: and the daughter of Caleb was Achsa.

50 These were the sons of Caleb the son of Hur, the firstborn of Ephratah; Shobal the father of Kirjathjearim,

51 Salma the father of Bethlehem, Hareph the father of Beth-gader.

52 And Shobal the father of Kirjathjearim had sons; Haroeh, and half of the Manahethites.

53 And the families of Kirjathjearim; the Ithrites, and the Puhites, and the Shumathites, and the Mishraites; of them came the Zareathites, and the Eshtaulites.

54 The sons of Salma; Bethlehem, and the Netophathites, Ataroth, the house of Joab, and half of the Manahethites, the Zorites.

55 And the families of the scribes which dwelt at Jabez; the Tirathites, the Shimeathites, and Suchathites. These are the Kenites that came of Hemath, the father of the house of Rechab.

1 Chr 3:1 Now these were the sons of David, which were born unto him in Hebron; the firstborn Amnon, of Ahinoam the Jezreelitess; the second Daniel, of Abigail the Carmelitess:

2 The third, Absalom the son of Maachah the daughter of Talmai king of Geshur: the fourth, Adonijah the son of Haggith:

3 The fifth, Shephatiah of Abital: the sixth, Ithream by Eglah his wife.

4 These six were born unto him in Hebron; and there he reigned seven years and six months: and in Jerusalem he reigned thirty and three years.

5 And these were born unto him in Jerusalem; Shimea, and Shobab, and Nathan, and Solomon, four, of Bathshua the daughter of Ammiel:

6 Ibhar also, and Elishama, and Eliphelet,

7 And Nogah, and Nepheg, and Japhia,

8 And Elishama, and Eliada, and Eliphelet, nine.

9 These were all the sons of David, beside the sons of the concubines, and Tamar their sister.

10 And Solomon's son was Rehoboam, Abia his son, Asa his son, Jehoshaphat his son,

11 Joram his son, Ahaziah his son, Joash his son,

12 Amaziah his son, Azariah his son, Jotham his son,

13 Ahaz his son, Hezekiah his son, Manasseh his son,

14 Amon his son, Josiah his son.

15 And the sons of Josiah were, the firstborn Johanan, the second Jehoiakim, the third Zedekiah, the fourth Shallum.

16 And the sons of Jehoiakim: Jeconiah his son, Zedekiah his son.

17 And the sons of Jeconiah; Assir, Salathiel his son,

18 Malchiram also, and Pedaiah, and Shenazar, Jecamiah, Hoshama, and Nedabiah.

19 And the sons of Pedaiah were, Zerubbabel, and Shimei: and the sons of Zerubbabel; Meshullam, and Hananiah, and Shelomith their sister:

20 And Hashubah, and Ohel, and Berechiah, and Hasadiah, Jushabhesed, five.

21 And the sons of Hananiah; Pelatiah, and Jesaiah: the sons of Rephaiah, the sons of Arnan, the sons of Obadiah, the sons of Shechaniah.

22 And the sons of Shechaniah; Shemaiah: and the sons of Shemaiah; Hattush, and Igeal, and Bariah, and Neariah, and Shaphat, six.

23 And the sons of Neariah; Elioenai, and Hezekiah, and Azrikam, three.

24 And the sons of Elioenai were, Hodaiah, and Eliashib, and Pelaiah, and Akkub, and Johanan, and Dalaiah, and Anani, seven.

1 Chr 4:1 The sons of Judah; Pharez, Hezron, and Carmi, and Hur, and Shobal.

2 And Reaiah the son of Shobal begat Jahath; and Jahath begat Ahumai, and Lahad. These are the families of the Zorathites.

3 And these were of the father of Etam; Jezreel, and Ishma, and Idbash: and the name of their sister was Hazelelponi:

4 And Penuel the father of Gedor, and Ezer the father of Hushah. These are the sons of Hur, the firstborn of Ephratah, the father of Bethlehem.

5 And Ashur the father of Tekoa had two wives, Helah and Naarah.

6 And Naarah bare him Ahuzam, and Hepher, and Temeni, and Haahashtari. These were the sons of Naarah.

7 And the sons of Helah were, Zereth, and Jezoar, and Ethnan.

8 And Coz begat Anub, and Zobebah, and the families of Aharhel the son of Harum.

9 And Jabez was more honorable than his brethren: and his mother called his name Jabez, saying, Because I bare him with sorrow.

10 And Jabez called on God of Israel, saying, Oh that you would bless me indeed, and enlarge my coast, and that your hand might be with me, and that you would keep me from evil, that it may not grieve me! And God granted him that which he requested.

11 And Chelub the brother of Shuah begat Mehir, which was the father of Eshton.

12 And Eshton begat Beth-rapha, and Paseah, and Tehinnah the father of Irnahash. These are the men of Rechah.

13 And the sons of Kenaz; Othniel, and Seraiah: and the sons of Othniel; Hathath.

14 And Meonothai begat Ophrah: and Seraiah begat Joab, the father of the valley of Charashim; for they were craftsmen.

15 And the sons of Caleb the son of Jephunneh; Iru, Elah, and Naam: and the sons of Elah, even Kenaz.

16 And the sons of Jehaleleel; Ziph, and Ziphah, Tiria, and Asareel.

17 And the sons of Ezra were, Jether, and Mered, and Epher, and Jalon: and she bare Miriam, and Shammai, and Ishbah the father of Eshtemoa.

18 And his wife Jehudijah bare Jered the father of Gedor, and Heber the father of Socho, and Jekuthiel the father of Zanoah. And these are the sons of Bithiah the daughter of Pharaoh, which Mered took.

19 And the sons of his wife Hodiah the sister of Naham, the father of Keilah the Garmite, and Eshtemoa the Maachathite.

20 And the sons of Shimon were, Amnon, and Rinnah, Benhanan, and Tilon. And the sons of Ishi were, Zoheth, and Benzoheth.

21 The sons of Shelah the son of Judah were, Er the father of Lecah, and Laadah the father of Mareshah, and the families of the house of them that worked fine linen, of the house of Ashbea,

22 And Jokim, and the men of Chozeba, and Joash, and Saraph, who had the dominion in Moab, and Jashubilehem. And these are ancient things.

23 These were the potters, and those that dwelt among plants and hedges: there they dwelt with the king for his work.

24 The sons of Simeon were, Nemuel, and Jamin, Jarib, Zerah, and Shaul:

25 Shallum his son, Mibsam his son, Mishma his son.

26 And the sons of Mishma; Hamuel his son, Zacchur his son, Shimei his son.

27 And Shimei had sixteen sons and six daughters; but his brethren had not many children, neither did all their family multiply, like to the children of Judah.

28 And they dwelt at Beersheba, and Moladah, and Hazarshual,

29 And at Bilhah, and at Ezem, and at Tolad,

30 And at Bethuel, and at Hormah, and at Ziklag,

31 And at Beth-marcaboth, and Hazarsusim, and at Beth-birei, and at Shaaraim. These were their cities unto the reign of David.

32 And their villages were, Etam, and Ain, Rimmon, and Tochen, and Ashan, five cities:

33 And all their villages that were round about the same cities, unto the lord [baal] These were their habitations, and their genealogy.

34 And Meshobab, and Jamlech, and Joshah, the son of Amaziah,

35 And Joel, and Jehu the son of Josibiah, the son of Seraiah, the son of Asiel,

36 And Elioenai, and Jaakobah, and Jeshohaiah, and Asaiah, and Adiel, and Jesimiel, and Benaiah,

37 And Ziza the son of Shiphi, the son of Allon, the son of Jedaiah, the son of Shimri, the son of Shemaiah;

38 These mentioned by their names were princes in their families: and the house of their fathers increased greatly.

39 And they went to the entrance of Gedor, even unto the east side of the valley, to seek pasture for their flocks.

40 And they found fat pasture and good, and the land was wide, and quiet, and peaceable; for they of Ham had dwelt there of old.

41 And these written by name came in the days of Hezekiah king of Judah, and smote their tents, and the habitations that were found there, and destroyed them utterly unto this day, and dwelt in their rooms: because there was pasture there for their flocks.

42 And some of them, even of the sons of Simeon, five hundred men, went to mount Seir, having for their captains Pelatiah, and Neariah, and Rephaiah, and Uzziel, the sons of Ishi.

43 And they smote the rest of the Amalekites that were escaped, and dwelt there unto this day.

1 Chr 5:1 Now the sons of Reuben the firstborn of Israel, for he was the firstborn; but, forasmuch as he defiled his father's bed, his birthright was given unto the sons of Joseph the son of Israel: and the genealogy is not to be reckoned after the birthright.

2 For Judah prevailed above his brethren, and of him comes the chief ruler; but the birthright was Joseph's:

3 The sons, I say, of Reuben the firstborn of Israel were, Hanoch, and Pallu, Hezron, and Carmi.

4 The sons of Joel; Shemaiah his son, Gog his son, Shimei his son,

5 Micah his son, Reaia his son, the lord [baal] his son,

6 Beerah his son, whom Tilgathpilneser king of Assyria carried away captive: he was prince of the Reubenites.

7 And his brethren by their families, when the genealogy of their generations was reckoned, were the chief, Jeiel, and Zechariah,

8 And Bela the son of Azaz, the son of Shema, the son of Joel, who dwelt in Aroer, even unto Nebo and Baal-Meon:

9 And eastward he inhabited unto the entering in of the wilderness from the river Euphrates: because their cattle were multiplied in the land of Gilead.

10 And in the days of Saul they made war with the Hagarites, who fell by their hand: and they dwelt in their tents throughout all the east land of Gilead.

11 And the children of Gad dwelt over against them, in the land of Bashan unto Salcah:

12 Joel the chief, and Shapham the next, and Jaanai, and Shaphat in Bashan.

13 And their brethren of the house of their fathers were, Michael, and Meshullam, and Sheba, and Jorai, and Jachan, and Zia, and Heber, seven.

14 These are the children of Abihail the son of Huri, the son of Jaroah, the son of Gilead, the son of Michael, the son of Jeshishai, the son of Jahdo, the son of Buz;

15 Ahi the son of Abdiel, the son of Guni, chief of the house of their fathers.

16 And they dwelt in Gilead in Bashan, and in her towns, and in all the suburbs of Sharon, upon their borders.

17 All these were reckoned by genealogies in the days of Jotham king of Judah, and in the days of Jeroboam king of Israel.

18 The sons of Reuben, and the Gadites, and half the tribe of Manasseh, of valiant men, men able to bear buckler and sword, and to shoot with bow, and skillful in war, were four and forty thousand seven hundred and threescore, that went out to the war.

19 And they made war with the Hagarites, with Jetur, and Nephish, and Nodab.

20 And they were helped against them, and the Hagarites were delivered into their hand, and all that were with them: for they cried to God in the battle, and he was entreated of them; because they put their trust in him.

21 And they took away their cattle; of their camels fifty thousand, and of sheep two hundred and fifty thousand, and of donkeys two thousand, and souls of men a hundred thousand.

22 For there fell down many slain, because the war was from God. And they dwelt in their steads until the captivity.

23 And the children of the half tribe of Manasseh dwelt in the land: they increased from Bashan unto Baal-Hermon and Senir, and unto mount Hermon.

24 And these were the heads of the house of their fathers, even Epher, and Ishi, and Eliel, and Azriel, and Jeremiah, and Hodaviah, and Jahdiel, mighty men of valor, famous men, and heads of the house of their fathers.

25 And they transgressed against God of their fathers, and went a whoring after the gods of the people of the land, whom God destroyed before them.

26 And God of Israel stirred up the spirit of Pul king of Assyria, and the spirit of Tilgathpilneser king of Assyria, and he carried them away, even the Reubenites, and the Gadites, and the half tribe of Manasseh, and brought them unto Halah, and Habor, and Hara, and to the river Gozan, unto this day.

1 Chr 6:1 The sons of Levi; Gershon, Kohath, and Merari.

2 And the sons of Kohath; Amram, Izhar, and Hebron, and Uzziel.

3 And the children of Amram; Aaron, and Moses, and Miriam. The sons also of Aaron; Nadab, and Abihu, Eleazar, and Ithamar.

4 Eleazar begat Phinehas, Phinehas begat Abishua,

5 And Abishua begat Bukki, and Bukki begat Uzzi,

6 And Uzzi begat Zerahiah, and Zerahiah begat Meraioth,

7 Meraioth begat Amariah, and Amariah begat Ahitub,

8 And Ahitub begat Zadok, and Zadok begat Ahimaaz,

9 And Ahimaaz begat Azariah, and Azariah begat Johanan,

10 And Johanan begat Azariah, he it is that executed the priest's office in the temple that Solomon built in Jerusalem:

11 And Azariah begat Amariah, and Amariah begat Ahitub,

12 And Ahitub begat Zadok, and Zadok begat Shallum,

13 And Shallum begat Hilkiah, and Hilkiah begat Azariah,

14 And Azariah begat Seraiah, and Seraiah begat Jehozadak,

15 And Jehozadak went into captivity, when the Becoming-One carried away Judah and Jerusalem by the hand of Nebuchadnezzar.

16 The sons of Levi; Gershom, Kohath, and Merari.

17 And these be the names of the sons of Gershom; Libni, and Shimei.

18 And the sons of Kohath were, Amram, and Izhar, and Hebron, and Uzziel.

19 The sons of Merari; Mahli, and Mushi. And these are the families of the Levites according to their fathers.

20 Of Gershom; Libni his son, Jahath his son, Zimmah his son,

21 Joah his son, Iddo his son, Zerah his son, Jeaterai his son.

22 The sons of Kohath; Amminadab his son, Korah his son, Assir his son,

23 Elkanah his son, and Ebiasaph his son, and Assir his son,

24 Tahath his son, Uriel his son, Uzziah his son, and Shaul his son.

25 And the sons of Elkanah; Amasai, and Ahimoth.

26 As for Elkanah: the sons of Elkanah; Zophai his son, and Nahath his son,

27 Eliab his son, Jeroham his son, Elkanah his son.

28 And the sons of Samuel; the firstborn Vashni, and Abiah.

29 The sons of Merari; Mahli, Libni his son, Shimei his son, Uzza his son,

30 Shimea his son, Haggiah his son, Asaiah his son.

31 And these are they whom David set over the service of song in the house of the Becoming-One, after that the ark had rest.

32 And they ministered before the dwelling place of the tabernacle of the set time with singing, until Solomon had built the house of the Becoming-One in Jerusalem: and then they waited on their office according to their order.

33 And these are they that waited with their children. Of the sons of the Kohathites: Heman a singer, the son of Joel, the son of Shemuel,

34 The son of Elkanah, the son of Jeroham, the son of Eliel, the son of Toah,

35 The son of Zuph, the son of Elkanah, the son of Mahath, the son of Amasai,

36 The son of Elkanah, the son of Joel, the son of Azariah, the son of Zephaniah,

37 The son of Tahath, the son of Assir, the son of Ebiasaph, the son of Korah,

38 The son of Izhar, the son of Kohath, the son of Levi, the son of Israel.

39 And his brother Asaph, who stood on his right hand, even Asaph the son of Berachiah, the son of Shimea,

40 The son of Michael, the son of Baaseiah, the son of Malchiah,

41 The son of Ethni, the son of Zerah, the son of Adaiah,

42 The son of Ethan, the son of Zimmah, the son of Shimei,

43 The son of Jahath, the son of Gershom, the son of Levi.

44 And their brethren the sons of Merari stood on the left hand: Ethan the son of Kishi, the son of Abdi, the son of Malluch,

45 The son of Hashabiah, the son of Amaziah, the son of Hilkiah,

46 The son of Amzi, the son of Bani, the son of Shamer,

47 The son of Mahli, the son of Mushi, the son of Merari, the son of Levi.

48 Their brethren also the Levites were appointed unto all manner of service of the tabernacle of the house of God.

49 But Aaron and his sons offered upon the altar of the burnt offering, and on the altar of incense, and were appointed for all the work of the place most holy, and to make an atonement for Israel, according to all that Moses the servant of God had commanded.

50 And these are the sons of Aaron; Eleazar his son, Phinehas his son, Abishua his son,

51 Bukki his son, Uzzi his son, Zerahiah his son,

52 Meraioth his son, Amariah his son, Ahitub his son,

53 Zadok his son, Ahimaaz his son.

54 Now these are their dwelling places throughout their castles in their coasts, of the sons of Aaron, of the families of the Kohathites: for theirs was the lot.

55 And they gave them Hebron in the land of Judah, and the suburbs thereof round about it.

56 But the fields of the city, and the villages thereof, they gave to Caleb the son of Jephunneh.

57 And to the sons of Aaron they gave the cities of Judah, namely, Hebron, the city of refuge, and Libnah with her suburbs, and Jattir, and Eshtemoa, with their suburbs,

58 And Hilen with her suburbs, Debir with her suburbs,

59 And Ashan with her suburbs, and Beth-shemesh with her suburbs:

60 And out of the tribe of Benjamin; Geba with her suburbs, and Alemeth with her suburbs, and Anathoth with her suburbs. All their cities throughout their families were thirteen cities.

61 And unto the sons of Kohath, which were left of the family of that tribe, were cities given out of the half tribe, namely, out of the half tribe of Manasseh, by lot, ten cities.

62 And to the sons of Gershom throughout their families out of the tribe of Issachar, and out of the tribe of Asher, and out of the tribe of Naphtali, and out of the tribe of Manasseh in Bashan, thirteen cities.

63 Unto the sons of Merari were given by lot, throughout their families, out of the tribe of Reuben, and out of the tribe of Gad, and out of the tribe of Zebulun, twelve cities.

64 And the children of Israel gave to the Levites these cities with their suburbs.

65 And they gave by lot out of the tribe of the children of Judah, and out of the tribe of the children of Simeon, and out of the tribe of the children of Benjamin, these cities, which are called by their names.

66 And the residue of the families of the sons of Kohath had cities of their coasts out of the tribe of Ephraim.

67 And they gave unto them, of the cities of refuge, Shechem in mount Ephraim with her suburbs; they gave also Gezer with her suburbs,

68 And Jokmeam with her suburbs, and Bethhoron with her suburbs,

69 And Aijalon with her suburbs, and Gathrimmon with her suburbs:

70 And out of the half tribe of Manasseh; Aner with her suburbs, and Bileam with her suburbs, for the family of the remnant of the sons of Kohath.

71 Unto the sons of Gershom were given out of the family of the half tribe of Manasseh, Golan in Bashan with her suburbs, and Ashtaroth with her suburbs:

72 And out of the tribe of Issachar; Kedesh with her suburbs, Daberath with her suburbs,

73 And Ramoth with her suburbs, and Anem with her suburbs:

74 And out of the tribe of Asher; Mashal with her suburbs, and Abdon with her suburbs,

75 And Hukok with her suburbs, and Rehob with her suburbs:

76 And out of the tribe of Naphtali; Kedesh in Galilee with her suburbs, and Hammon with her suburbs, and Kirjathaim with her suburbs.

77 Unto the rest of the children of Merari were given out of the tribe of Zebulun, Rimmon with her suburbs, Tabor with her suburbs:

78 And over the Jordan by Jericho, on the east side of Jordan, were given them out of the tribe of Reuben, Bezer in the wilderness with her suburbs, and Jahzah with her suburbs,

79 Kedemoth also with her suburbs, and Mephaath with her suburbs:

80 And out of the tribe of Gad; Ramoth in Gilead with her suburbs, and Mahanaim with her suburbs,

81 And Heshbon with her suburbs, and Jazer with her suburbs.

1 Chr 7:1 Now the sons of Issachar were, Tola, and Puah, Jashub, and Shimrom, four.

2 And the sons of Tola; Uzzi, and Rephaiah, and Jeriel, and Jahmai, and Jibsam, and Shemuel, heads of their father's house, to wit, of Tola: they were valiant men of might in their generations; whose number was in the days of David two and twenty thousand and six hundred.

3 And the sons of Uzzi; Izrahiah: and the sons of Izrahiah; Michael, and Obadiah, and Joel, Ishiah, five: all of them chief men.

4 And with them, by their generations, after the house of their fathers, were bands of soldiers for war, six and thirty thousand of men: for they had many wives and sons.

5 And their brethren among all the families of Issachar were valiant men of might, reckoned in all by their genealogies fourscore and seven thousand.

6 The sons of Benjamin; Bela, and Becher, and Jediael, three.

7 And the sons of Bela; Ezbon, and Uzzi, and Uzziel, and Jerimoth, and Iri, five; heads of the house of their fathers, mighty men of valor; and were reckoned by their genealogies twenty and two thousand and thirty and four.

8 And the sons of Becher; Zemira, and Joash, and Eliezer, and Elioenai, and Omri, and Jerimoth, and Abiah, and Anathoth, and Alameth. All these are the sons of Becher.

9 And the number of them, after their genealogy by their generations, heads of the house of their fathers, mighty men of valor, was twenty thousand and two hundred.

10 The sons also of Jediael; Bilhan: and the sons of Bilhan; Jeush, and Benjamin, and Ehud, and Chenaanah, and Zethan, and Tharshish, and Ahishahar.

11 All these the sons of Jediael, by the heads of their fathers, mighty men of valor, were seventeen thousand and two hundred soldiers, fit to go out for war and battle.

12 Shuppim also, and Huppim, the children of Ir, and Hushim, the sons of Aher.

13 The sons of Naphtali; Jahziel, and Guni, and Jezer, and Shallum, the sons of Bilhah.

14 The sons of Manasseh; Ashriel, whom she bare: but his concubine the Aramitess bare Machir the father of Gilead:

15 And Machir took to wife the sister of Huppim and Shuppim, whose sister's name was Maachah; and the name of the second was Zelophehad: and Zelophehad had daughters.

16 And Maachah the wife of Machir bare a son, and she called his name Peresh; and the name of his brother was Sheresh; and his sons were Ulam and Rakem.

17 And the sons of Ulam; Bedan. These were the sons of Gilead, the son of Machir, the son of Manasseh.

18 And his sister Hammoleketh bare Ishod, and Abiezer, and Mahalah.

19 And the sons of Shemidah were, Ahian, and Shechem, and Likhi, and Aniam.

20 And the sons of Ephraim; Shuthelah, and Bered his son, and Tahath his son, and Eladah his son, and Tahath his son,

21 And Zabad his son, and Shuthelah his son, and Ezer, and Elead, whom the men of Gath that were born in that land killed, because they came down to take away their cattle.

22 And Ephraim their father mourned many days, and his brethren came to comfort him.

23 And when he went in to his wife, she conceived, and bare a son, and he called his name Beriah, because it went evil with his house.

24 And his daughter was Sherah, who built Bethhoron the nether, and the upper, and Uzzensherah.

25 And Rephah was his son, also Resheph, and Telah his son, and Tahan his son,

26 Laadan his son, Ammihud his son, Elishama his son,

27 Non his son, Jehoshuah his son.

28 And their possessions and habitations were, Bethel and the towns thereof, and eastward Naaran, and westward Gezer, with the towns thereof; Shechem also and the towns thereof, unto Gaza and the towns thereof:

29 And by the borders of the children of Manasseh, Beth-shean and her towns, Taanach and

her towns, Megiddo and her towns, Dor and her towns. In these dwelt the children of Joseph the son of Israel.

30 The sons of Asher; Imnah, and Isuah, and Ishuai, and Beriah, and Serah their sister.

31 And the sons of Beriah; Heber, and Malchiel, who is the father of Birzavith.

32 And Heber begat Japhlet, and Shomer, and Hotham, and Shua their sister.

33 And the sons of Japhlet; Pasach, and Bimhal, and Ashvath. These are the children of Japhlet.

34 And the sons of Shamer; Ahi, and Rohgah, Jehubbah, and Aram.

35 And the sons of his brother Helem; Zophah, and Imna, and Shelesh, and Amal.

36 The sons of Zophah; Suah, and Harnepher, and Shual, and Beri, and Imrah,

37 Bezer, and Hod, and Shamma, and Shilshah, and Ithran, and Beera.

38 And the sons of Jether; Jephunneh, and Pispah, and Ara.

39 And the sons of Ulla; Arah, and Haniel, and Rezia.

40 All these were the children of Asher, heads of their father's house, choice and mighty men of valor, chief of the princes. And the number throughout the genealogy of them that were apt to the war and to battle was twenty and six thousand of men.

1 Chr 8:1 Now Benjamin begat Bela his firstborn, Ashbel the second, and Aharah the third,

2 Nohah the fourth, and Rapha the fifth.

3 And the sons of Bela were, Addar, and Gera, and Abihud,

4 And Abishua, and Naaman, and Ahoah,

5 And Gera, and Shephuphan, and Huram.

6 And these are the sons of Ehud: these are the heads of the fathers of the inhabitants of Geba, and they removed them to Manahath:

7 And Naaman, and Ahiah, and Gera, he removed them, and begat Uzza, and Ahihud.

8 And Shaharaim begat children in the country of Moab, after he had sent them away; Hushim and Baara were his wives.

9 And he begat of Hodesh his wife, Jobab, and Zibia, and Mesha, and Malcham,

10 And Jeuz, and Shachia, and Mirma. These were his sons, heads of the fathers.

11 And of Hushim he begat Abitub, and Elpaal.

12 The sons of Elpaal; Eber, and Misham, and Shamed, who built Ono, and Lod, with the towns thereof:

13 Beriah also, and Shema, who were heads of the fathers of the inhabitants of Aijalon, who drove away the inhabitants of Gath:

14 And Ahio, Shashak, and Jeremoth,

15 And Zebadiah, and Arad, and Ader,

16 And Michael, and Ispah, and Joha, the sons of Beriah;

17 And Zebadiah, and Meshullam, and Hezeki, and Heber,

18 Ishmerai also, and Jezliah, and Jobab, the sons of Elpaal;

19 And Jakim, and Zichri, and Zabdi,

20 And Elienai, and Zilthai, and Eliel,

21 And Adaiah, and Beraiah, and Shimrath, the sons of Shimhi;

22 And Ishpan, and Heber, and Eliel,

23 And Abdon, and Zichri, and Hanan,

24 And Hananiah, and Elam, and Antothijah,

25 And Iphedeiah, and Penuel, the sons of Shashak;

26 And Shamsherai, and Shehariah, and Athaliah,

27 And Jaresiah, and Eliah, and Zichri, the sons of Jeroham.

28 These were heads of the fathers, by their generations, chief men. These dwelt in Jerusalem.

29 And at Gibeon dwelt the father of Gibeon; whose wife's name was Maachah:

30 And his firstborn son Abdon, and Zur, and Kish, and the lord [baal] and Nadab,

31 And Gedor, and Ahio, and Zacher.

32 And Mikloth begat Shimeah. And these also dwelt with their brethren in Jerusalem, over against them.

33 And Ner begat Kish, and Kish begat Saul, and Saul begat Jonathan, and Malchishua, and Abinadab, and Eshbaal.

34 And the son of Jonathan was Meribbaal; and Meribbaal begat Micah.

35 And the sons of Micah were, Pithon, and Melech, and Tarea, and Ahaz.

36 And Ahaz begat Jehoadah; and Jehoadah begat Alemeth, and Azmaveth, and Zimri; and Zimri begat Moza,

37 And Moza begat Binea: Rapha was his son, Eleasah his son, Azel his son:

38 And Azel had six sons, whose names are these, Azrikam, Bocheru, and Ishmael, and Sheariah, and Obadiah, and Hanan. All these were the sons of Azel.

39 And the sons of Eshek his brother were, Ulam his firstborn, Jehush the second, and Eliphelet the third.

40 And the sons of Ulam were mighty men of valor, archers, and had many sons, and sons' sons, a hundred and fifty. All these are of the sons of Benjamin.

1 Chr 9:1 So all Israel were reckoned by genealogies; and, behold, they were written in the book of the kings of Israel and Judah, who were carried away to Babylon for their transgression.

2 Now the first inhabitants that dwelt in their possessions in their cities were, the Israelites, the priests, Levites, and the Nethinims.

3 And in Jerusalem dwelt of the children of Judah, and of the children of Benjamin, and of the children of Ephraim, and Manasseh;

4 Uthai the son of Ammihud, the son of Omri, the son of Imri, the son of Bani, of the children of Pharez the son of Judah.

5 And of the Shilonites; Asaiah the firstborn, and his sons.

6 And of the sons of Zerah; Jeuel, and their brethren, six hundred and ninety.

7 And of the sons of Benjamin; Sallu the son of Meshullam, the son of Hodaviah, the son of Hasenuah,

8 And Ibneiah the son of Jeroham, and Elah the son of Uzzi, the son of Michri, and Meshullam the son of Shephathiah, the son of Reuel, the son of Ibnijah;

9 And their brethren, according to their generations, nine hundred and fifty and six. All these men were chief of the fathers in the house of their fathers.

10 And of the priests; Jedaiah, and Jehoiarib, and Jachin,

11 And Azariah the son of Hilkiah, the son of Meshullam, the son of Zadok, the son of Meraioth, the son of Ahitub, the ruler of the house of God;

12 And Adaiah the son of Jeroham, the son of Pashur, the son of Malchijah, and Maasiai the son of Adiel, the son of Jahzerah, the son of Meshullam, the son of Meshillemith, the son of Immer;

13 And their brethren, heads of the house of their fathers, a thousand and seven hundred and threescore; very able men for the work of the service of the house of God.

14 And of the Levites; Shemaiah the son of Hasshub, the son of Azrikam, the son of Hashabiah, of the sons of Merari;

15 And Bakbakkar, Heresh, and Galal, and Mattaniah the son of Micah, the son of Zichri, the son of Asaph;

16 And Obadiah the son of Shemaiah, the son of Galal, the son of Jeduthun, and Berechiah the son of Asa, the son of Elkanah, that dwelt in the villages of the Netophathites.

17 And the gatekeepers were, Shallum, and Akkub, and Talmon, and Ahiman, and their brethren: Shallum was the chief;

18 Who hitherto waited in the king's gate eastward: they were gatekeepers in the companies of the children of Levi.

19 And Shallum the son of Kore, the son of Ebiasaph, the son of Korah, and his brethren, of the house of his father, the Korahites, were over the work of the service, keepers of the gates of the tabernacle: and their fathers, being over the host of the Becoming-One, were keepers of the entry.

20 And Phinehas the son of Eleazar was the ruler over them in time past, and the Becoming-One was with him.

21 And Zechariah the son of Meshelemiah was doorkeeper of the door of the tabernacle of the set time.

22 All these which were chosen to be gatekeepers in the gates were two hundred and twelve. These were reckoned by their genealogy in their villages, whom David and Samuel the seer did ordain in their set office.

23 So they and their children had the oversight of the gates of the house of the Becoming-One, namely, the house of the tabernacle, by wards.

24 In the four winds were the gatekeepers, toward the east, west, north, and south.

25 And their brethren, which were in their villages, were to come after seven days from time to time with them.

26 For these Levites, the four chief gatekeepers, were in their set office, and were over the chambers and treasuries of the house of God.

27 And they lodged round about the house of God, because the charge was upon them, and the opening thereof every morning pertained to them.

28 And certain of them had the charge of the ministering vessels, that they should bring them in and out by tale.

29 Some of them also were appointed to oversee the vessels and all the instruments of the sanctuary, and the fine flour, and the wine, and the oil, and the frankincense, and the spices.

30 And some of the sons of the priests made the ointment of the spices.

31 And Mattithiah, one of the Levites, who was the firstborn of Shallum the Korahite, had the set office over the things that were made in the pans.

32 And other of their brethren, of the sons of the Kohathites, were over the showbread, to prepare it every Sabbath.

33 And these are the singers, chief of the fathers of the Levites, who remaining in the chambers were free: for they were employed in that work day and night.

34 These chief fathers of the Levites were chief throughout their generations; these dwelt at Jerusalem.

35 And in Gibeon dwelt the father of Gibeon, Jehiel, whose wife's name was Maachah:

36 And his firstborn son Abdon, then Zur, and Kish, and Baal, and Ner, and Nadab,

37 And Gedor, and Ahio, and Zechariah, and Mikloth.

38 And Mikloth begat Shimeam. And they also dwelt with their brethren at Jerusalem, over against their brethren.

39 And Ner begat Kish; and Kish begat Saul; and Saul begat Jonathan, and Malchishua, and Abinadab, and Eshbaal.

40 And the son of Jonathan was Meribbaal: and Meribbaal begat Micah.

41 And the sons of Micah were, Pithon, and Melech, and Tahrea, and Ahaz.

42 And Ahaz begat Jarah; and Jarah begat Alemeth, and Azmaveth, and Zimri; and Zimri begat Moza;

43 And Moza begat Binea; and Rephaiah his son, Eleasah his son, Azel his son.

44 And Azel had six sons, whose names are these, Azrikam, Bocheru, and Ishmael, and Sheariah, and Obadiah, and Hanan: these were the sons of Azel.

1 Chr 10:1 Now the Philistines fought against Israel; and the men of Israel fled from before the Philistines, and fell down slain in mount Gilboa.

2 And the Philistines followed hard after Saul, and after his sons; and the Philistines killed Jonathan, and Abinadab, and Malchishua, the sons of Saul.

3 And the battle went great against Saul, and the archers hit him, and he was wounded of the archers.

4 Then said Saul to his armor bearer, Draw your sword, and thrust me through therewith; lest these uncircumcised come and abuse me. But his armor bearer would not; for he was greatly afraid. So Saul took a sword, and fell upon it.

5 And when his armor bearer saw that Saul was dead, he fell likewise on the sword, and died.

6 So Saul died, and his three sons, and all his house died together.

7 And when all the men of Israel that were in the valley saw that they fled, and that Saul and his sons

were dead, then they forsook their cities, and fled: and the Philistines came and dwelt in them.

8 And it came to pass on the next day, when the Philistines came to strip the slain, that they found Saul and his sons fallen in mount Gilboa.

9 And when they had stripped him, they took his head, and his armor, and sent into the land of the Philistines round about, to carry tidings unto their idols, and to the people.

10 And they put his armor in the house of their gods, and fastened his head in the temple of Dagon.

11 And when all Jabeshgilead heard all that the Philistines had done to Saul,

12 They arose, all the valiant men, and took away the body of Saul, and the bodies of his sons, and brought them to Jabesh, and buried their bones under the oak in Jabesh, and fasted seven days.

13 So Saul died for his transgression which he committed against the Becoming-One, even against the word of the Becoming-One, which he kept not, and also for asking counsel of one that had a medium, to inquire of it;

14 And inquired not of the Becoming-One: therefore he killed him, and turned the kingdom unto David the son of Jesse.

1 Chr 11:1 Then all Israel gathered themselves to David unto Hebron, saying, Behold, we are your bone and your flesh.

2 And moreover yesterday and the third day, even when Saul was king, you were he that led out and brought in Israel: and the Becoming-One your God said unto you, you shall feed my people Israel, and you shall be ruler over my people Israel.

3 Therefore came all the elders of Israel to the king to Hebron; and David made a covenant with them in Hebron before the Becoming-One; and they anointed David king over Israel, according to the word of the Becoming-One by Samuel.

4 And David and all Israel went to Jerusalem, which is Jebus; where the Jebusites were, the inhabitants of the land.

5 And the inhabitants of Jebus said to David, you shall not come here. Nevertheless David took the castle of Zion, which is the city of David.

6 And David said, Whosoever smites the Jebusites first shall be chief and captain. So Joab the son of Zeruiah went first up, and was chief.

7 And David dwelt in the castle; therefore they called it the city of David.

8 And he built the city round about, even from Millo round about: and Joab repaired the rest of the city.

9 So David grew greater and greater: for the Becoming-One of hosts was with him.

10 These also are the chief of the mighty men whom David had, who strengthened themselves with him in his kingdom, and with all Israel, to make him king, according to the word of the Becoming-One concerning Israel.

11 And this is the number of the mighty men whom David had; Jashobeam, a hachmonite, the chief of the captains: he lifted up his spear against three hundred slain by him at one time.

12 And after him was Eleazar the son of Dodo, the Ahohite, who was one of the three mighties.

13 He was with David at Pasdammim, and there the Philistines were gathered together to battle, where was a parcel of ground full of barley; and the people fled from before the Philistines.

14 And they set themselves in the midst of that parcel, and delivered it, and killed the Philistines; and the Becoming-One saved them by a great deliverance.

15 Now three of the thirty captains went down to the rock to David, into the cave of Adullam; and the host of the Philistines encamped in the valley of Rephaim.

16 And David was then in the hold, and the Philistines' garrison was then at Bethlehem.

17 And David longed, and said, Oh that one would give me drink of the water of the well of Bethlehem, that is at the gate!

18 And the three brake through the host of the Philistines, and drew water out of the well of Bethlehem, that was by the gate, and took it, and brought it to David: but David would not drink of it, but poured it out to the Becoming-One,

19 And said, Forbid it me, that I should do this thing: shall I drink the blood of these men that have put their souls in jeopardy? for with the jeopardy of their souls they brought it. Therefore he would not drink it. These things did these three mightiest.

20 And Abishai the brother of Joab, he was chief of the three: for lifting up his spear against three hundred, he killed them, and had a name among the three.

21 Of the three, he was more honorable than the two; for he was their captain: howbeit he attained not to the first three.

22 Benaiah the son of Jehoiada, the son of a valiant man of Kabzeel, who had done many acts; he killed two lionlike men of Moab: also he went down and killed a lion in a pit in a snowy day.

23 And he killed an Egyptian, a man of great stature, five cubits high; and in the Egyptian's hand was a spear like a weaver's beam; and he went down to him with a staff, and plucked the spear out of the Egyptian's hand, and killed him with his own spear.

24 These things did Benaiah the son of Jehoiada, and had the name among the three mighties.

25 Behold, he was honorable among the thirty, but attained not to the first three: and David set him over his guard.

26 Also the valiant men of the armies were, Asahel the brother of Joab, Elhanan the son of Dodo of Bethlehem,

27 Shammoth the Harorite, Helez the Pelonite,

28 Ira the son of Ikkesh the Tekoite, Abiezer the Antothite,

29 Sibbecai the Hushathite, Ilai the Ahohite,

30 Maharai the Netophathite, Heled the son of Baanah the Netophathite,

31 Ithai the son of Ribai of Gibeah, that pertained to the children of Benjamin, Benaiah the Pirathonite,

32 Hurai of the brooks of Gaash, Abiel the Arbathite,

33 Azmaveth the Baharumite, Eliahba the Shaalbonite,

34 The sons of Hashem the Gizonite, Jonathan the son of Shage the Hararite,

35 Ahiam the son of Sacar the Hararite, Eliphal the son of Ur,

36 Hepher the Mecherathite, Ahijah the Pelonite,

37 Hezro the Carmelite, Naarai the son of Ezbai,

38 Joel the brother of Nathan, Mibhar the son of Haggeri,

39 Zelek the Ammonite, Naharai the Berothite, the armor bearer of Joab the son of Zeruiah,

40 Ira the Ithrite, Gareb the Ithrite,

41 Uriah the Hittite, Zabad the son of Ahlai,

42 Adina the son of Shiza the Reubenite, a captain of the Reubenites, and thirty with him,

43 Hanan the son of Maachah, and Joshaphat the Mithnite,

44 Uzzia the Ashterathite, Shama and Jehiel the sons of Hothan the Aroerite,

45 Jediael the son of Shimri, and Joha his brother, the Tizite,

46 Eliel the Mahavite, and Jeribai, and Joshaviah, the sons of Elnaam, and Ithmah the Moabite,

47 Eliel, and Obed, and Jasiel the Mesobaite.

1 Chr 12:1 Now these are they that came to David to Ziklag, while he yet kept himself close because of Saul the son of Kish: and they were among the mighty men, helpers of the war.

2 They were armed with bows, and could use both the right hand and the left in hurling stones and shooting arrows out of a bow, even of Saul's brethren of Benjamin.

3 The chief was Ahiezer, then Joash, the sons of Shemaah the Gibeathite; and Jeziel, and Pelet, the sons of Azmaveth; and Berachah, and Jehu the Antothite,

4 And Ismaiah the Gibeonite, a mighty man among the thirty, and over the thirty; and Jeremiah, and Jahaziel, and Johanan, and Josabad the Gederathite,

5 Eluzai, and Jerimoth, and Bealiah, and Shemariah, and Shephatiah the Haruphite,

6 Elkanah, and Jesiah, and Azareel, and Joezer, and Jashobeam, the Korhites,

7 And Joelah, and Zebadiah, the sons of Jeroham of Gedor.

8 And of the Gadites there separated themselves unto David into the hold to the wilderness men of might, and men of war fit for the battle, that could handle shield and buckler, whose faces were like the faces of lions, and were as swift as the roes upon the mountains;

9 Ezer the first, Obadiah the second, Eliab the third,

10 Mishmannah the fourth, Jeremiah the fifth,

11 Attai the sixth, Eliel the seventh,

12 Johanan the eighth, Elzabad the ninth,

13 Jeremiah the tenth, Machbanai the eleventh.

14 These were of the sons of Gad, captains of the host: one of the least was over a hundred, and the greatest over a thousand.

15 These are they that went over Jordan in the first month, when it had overflown all his banks; and they put to flight all them of the valleys, both toward the east, and toward the west.

16 And there came of the children of Benjamin and Judah to the hold unto David.

17 And David went out to meet them, and answered and said unto them, If you be come peaceably unto me to help me, mine heart shall be knit unto you: but if you be come to betray me to mine enemies, seeing there is no wrong in mine hands, God of our fathers look thereon, and rebuke it.

18 Then the spirit came upon Amasai, who was chief of the captains, and he said, yours are we, David, and on your side, you son of Jesse: peace, peace be unto you, and peace be to your helpers; for your God, He will help you. Then David received them, and made them captains of the band.

19 And there fell some of Manasseh to David, when he came with the Philistines against Saul to battle: but they helped them not: for the lords of the Philistines upon advisement sent him away, saying, He will fall to his master Saul to the jeopardy of our heads.

20 As he went to Ziklag, there fell to him of Manasseh, Adnah, and Jozabad, and Jediael, and Michael, and Jozabad, and Elihu, and Zilthai, captains of the thousands that were of Manasseh.

21 And they helped David against the band of the rovers: for they were all mighty men of valor, and were captains in the host.

22 For at that time day by day there came to David to help him, until it was a great host, like the host of God.

23 And these are the numbers of the bands that were ready armed to the war, and came to David to Hebron, to turn the kingdom of Saul to him, according to the word of the Becoming-One.

24 The children of Judah that bare shield and spear were six thousand and eight hundred, ready armed to the war.

25 Of the children of Simeon, mighty men of valor for the war, seven thousand and one hundred.

26 Of the children of Levi four thousand and six hundred.

27 And Jehoiada was the leader of the Aaronites, and with him were three thousand and seven hundred;

28 And Zadok, a young man mighty of valor, and of his father's house twenty and two captains.

29 And of the children of Benjamin, the kindred of Saul, three thousand: for hitherto the greatest part of them had kept the prison of the house of Saul.

30 And of the children of Ephraim twenty thousand and eight hundred, mighty men of valor, famous throughout the house of their fathers.

31 And of the half tribe of Manasseh eighteen thousand, which were expressed by name, to come and make David king.

32 And of the children of Issachar, which were men that had understanding of the times, to know what Israel ought to do; the heads of them were two hundred; and all their brethren were at their commandment.

33 Of Zebulun, such as went forth to battle, expert in war, with all instruments of war, fifty thousand, which could keep rank: they were not of double heart.

34 And of Naphtali a thousand captains, and with them with shield and spear thirty and seven thousand.

35 And of the Danites expert in war twenty and eight thousand and six hundred.

36 And of Asher, such as went forth to battle, expert in war, forty thousand.

37 And over the Jordan, of the Reubenites, and the Gadites, and of the half tribe of Manasseh, with all manner of instruments of war for the battle, a hundred and twenty thousand.

38 All these men of war, that could keep rank, came with a perfect heart to Hebron, to make David king over all Israel: and all the rest also of Israel were of one heart to make David king.

39 And there they were with David three days, eating and drinking: for their brethren had prepared for them.

40 Moreover they that were near them, even unto Issachar and Zebulun and Naphtali, brought bread on donkeys, and on camels, and on mules, and on oxen, and food, meal, cakes of figs, and bunches of raisins, and wine, and oil, and oxen, and sheep abundantly: for there was joy in Israel.

1 Chr 13:1 And David consulted with the captains of thousands, and hundreds, and with every leader.

2 And David said unto all the congregation of Israel, If it seem good unto you, and that it be of the Becoming-One our God, let us send abroad unto our brethren every where, that are left in all the land of Israel, and with them also to the priests and Levites which are in their cities and suburbs, that they may gather themselves unto us:

3 And let us bring again the ark of our God to us: for we inquired not at it in the days of Saul.

4 And all the congregation said that they would do so: for the thing was right in the eyes of all the people.

5 So David gathered all Israel together, from Shihor of Egypt even unto the entering of Hemath, to bring the ark of God from Kirjathjearim.

6 And David went up, and all Israel, to Baalah, that is, to Kirjathjearim, which belonged to Judah, to bring up there the ark of God, the Becoming-One, that dwells between the cherubs, whose name is called on it.

7 And they carried the ark of God in a new cart out of the house of Abinadab: and Uzza and Ahio drave the cart.

8 And David and all Israel played before God with all their might, and with singing, and with harps, and with psalteries, and with timbrels, and with cymbals, and with trumpets.

9 And when they came unto the threshing floor of Chidon, Uzza put forth his hand to hold the ark; for the oxen stumbled.

10 And the anger of the Becoming-One was kindled against Uzza, and he smote him, because he put his hand to the ark: and there he died before God.

11 And David was displeased, because the Becoming-One had made a breach upon Uzza: therefore that place is called Perezuzza to this day.

12 And David was afraid of God that day, saying, How shall I bring the ark of God home to me?

13 So David brought not the ark home to himself to the city of David, but carried it aside into the house of Obededom the Gittite.

14 And the ark of God remained with the family of Obededom in his house three months. And the Becoming-One blessed the house of Obededom, and all that he had.

1 Chr 14:1 Now Hiram king of Tyre sent messengers to David, and timber of cedars, with masons and carpenters, to build him a house.

2 And David perceived that the Becoming-One had confirmed him king over Israel, for his kingdom was lifted up on high, because of his people Israel.

3 And David took more wives at Jerusalem: and David begat more sons and daughters.

4 Now these are the names of his children which he had in Jerusalem; Shammua, and Shobab, Nathan, and Solomon,

5 And Ibhar, and Elishua, and Elpalet,

6 And Nogah, and Nepheg, and Japhia,

7 And Elishama, and Beeliada, and Eliphalet.

8 And when the Philistines heard that David was anointed king over all Israel, all the Philistines went up to seek David. And David heard of it, and went out against them.

9 And the Philistines came and spread themselves in the valley of Rephaim.

10 And David inquired of God, saying, Shall I go up against the Philistines? and will you deliver them into mine hand? And the Becoming-One said unto him, Go up; for I will deliver them into your hand.

11 So they came up to Baal-Perazim; and David smote them there. Then David said, God has broken in upon mine enemies by mine hand like the breaking forth of waters: therefore they called the name of that place Baal-Perazim.

12 And when they had left their gods there, David gave a commandment, and they were burned with fire.

13 And the Philistines yet again spread themselves abroad in the valley.

14 Therefore David inquired again of God; and God said unto him, Go not up after them; turn away from them, and come upon them over against the mulberry trees.

15 And it shall be, when you shall hear a sound of going in the tops of the mulberry trees, that then you shall go out to battle: for God is gone forth before you to smite the host of the Philistines.

16 David therefore did as God commanded him: and they smote the host of the Philistines from Gibeon even to Gazer.

17 And the fame of David went out into all lands; and the Becoming-One brought the fear of him upon all nations.

1 Chr 15:1 And David made him houses in the city of David, and prepared a place for the ark of God, and pitched for it a tent.

2 Then David said, None ought to carry the ark of God but the Levites: for them has the Becoming-One chosen to carry the ark of God, and to minister unto him for olam.

3 And David gathered all Israel together to Jerusalem, to bring up the ark of the Becoming-One unto his place, which he had prepared for it.

4 And David assembled the children of Aaron, and the Levites:

5 Of the sons of Kohath; Uriel the chief, and his brethren a hundred and twenty:

6 Of the sons of Merari; Asaiah the chief, and his brethren two hundred and twenty:

7 Of the sons of Gershom; Joel the chief, and his brethren a hundred and thirty:

8 Of the sons of Elizaphan; Shemaiah the chief, and his brethren two hundred:

9 Of the sons of Hebron; Eliel the chief, and his brethren fourscore:

10 Of the sons of Uzziel; Amminadab the chief, and his brethren a hundred and twelve.

11 And David called for Zadok and Abiathar the priests, and for the Levites, for Uriel, Asaiah, and Joel, Shemaiah, and Eliel, and Amminadab,

12 And said unto them, you are the chief of the fathers of the Levites: sanctify yourselves, both you and your brethren, that you may bring up the ark of the Becoming-One, God of Israel unto the place that I have prepared for it.

13 For because you did it not at the first, the Becoming-One our God made a breach upon us, for that we sought him not after the due order.

14 So the priests and the Levites sanctified themselves to bring up the ark of the Becoming-One, God of Israel.

15 And the children of the Levites bare the ark of God upon their shoulders with the staves thereon, as Moses commanded according to the word of the Becoming-One.

16 And David spoke to the chief of the Levites to appoint their brethren to be the singers with instruments of music, psalteries and harps and cymbals, sounding, by lifting up the voice with joy.

17 So the Levites appointed Heman the son of Joel; and of his brethren, Asaph the son of Berechiah; and of the sons of Merari their brethren, Ethan the son of Kushaiah;

18 And with them their brethren of the second degree, Zechariah, Ben, and Jaaziel, and Shemiramoth, and Jehiel, and Unni, Eliab, and Benaiah, and Maaseiah, and Mattithiah, and Elipheleh, and Mikneiah, and Obededom, and Jeiel, the gatekeepers.

19 So the singers, Heman, Asaph, and Ethan, were appointed to sound with cymbals of brass;

20 And Zechariah, and Aziel, and Shemiramoth, and Jehiel, and Unni, and Eliab, and Maaseiah, and Benaiah, with psalteries on Alamoth;

21 And Mattithiah, and Elipheleh, and Mikneiah, and Obededom, and Jeiel, and Azaziah, with harps on the Sheminith to excel.

22 And Chenaniah, chief of the Levites, was for song: he instructed about the song, because he was skillful.

23 And Berechiah and Elkanah were doorkeepers for the ark.

24 And Shebaniah, and Jehoshaphat, and Nethaneel, and Amasai, and Zechariah, and Benaiah, and Eliezer, the priests, did blow with the trumpets before the ark of God: and Obededom and Jehiah were doorkeepers for the ark.

25 So David, and the elders of Israel, and the captains over thousands, went to bring up the ark of the covenant of the Becoming-One out of the house of Obededom with joy.

26 And it came to pass, when God helped the Levites that bare the ark of the covenant of the Becoming-One, that they offered seven bullocks and seven rams.

27 And David was clothed with a robe of fine linen, and all the Levites that bare the ark, and the singers, and Chenaniah the master of the song with the singers: David also had upon him an ephod of linen.

28 Thus all Israel brought up the ark of the covenant of the Becoming-One with shouting, and with sound of the cornet, and with trumpets, and with cymbals, making a noise with psalteries and harps.

29 And it came to pass, as the ark of the covenant of the Becoming-One came to the city of David, that Michal the daughter of Saul looking out at a window saw king David dancing and playing: and she despised him in her heart.

1 Chr 16:1 So they brought the ark of God, and set it in the midst of the tent that David had pitched for it: and they offered burnt sacrifices and peace offerings before God.

2 And when David had made an end of offering the burnt offerings and the peace offerings, he blessed the people in the name of the Becoming-One.

3 And he dealt to every one of Israel, both man and woman, to every one a loaf of bread, and a good piece of flesh, and a flagon of wine.

4 And he appointed certain of the Levites to minister before the ark of the Becoming-One, and to record, and to thank and praise the Becoming-One, God of Israel:

5 Asaph the chief, and next to him Zechariah, Jeiel, and Shemiramoth, and Jehiel, and Mattithiah, and Eliab, and Benaiah, and Obededom: and Jeiel with psalteries and with harps; but Asaph made a sound with cymbals;

6 Benaiah also and Jahaziel the priests with trumpets continually before the ark of the covenant of God.

7 Then on that day David delivered first this psalm to thank the Becoming-One into the hand of Asaph and his brethren.

8 Give thanks unto the Becoming-One, call upon his name, make known his deeds among the people.

9 Sing unto him, sing psalms unto him, talk you of all his wondrous works.

10 Glory you in his holy name: let the heart of them rejoice that seek the Becoming-One.

11 Seek the Becoming-One and his strength, seek his face continually.

12 Remember his marvelous works that he has done, his wonders, and the judgments of his mouth;

13 O you seed of Israel his servant, you children of Jacob, his chosen ones.

14 He is the Becoming-One our God; his judgments are in all the earth.

15 Be you mindful for olam of his covenant; the word which he commanded to a thousand of generations;

16 Even of the covenant which he made with Abraham, and of his oath unto Isaac;

17 And has confirmed the same to Jacob for a law, and to Israel for a covenant of olam.

18 Saying, Unto you will I give the land of Canaan, the lot of your inheritance;

19 When you were but few, even a few, and strangers in it.

20 And when they went from nation to nation, and from one kingdom to another people;

21 He permitted no man to do them wrong: yes, he reproved kings for their sakes,

22 Saying, Touch not mine anointed, and do my prophets no harm.

23 Sing unto the Becoming-One, all the earth; show forth from day to day his salvation.

24 Declare his glory among the nations; his marvelous works among all nations.

25 For great is the Becoming-One, and greatly to be praised: he also is to be feared above all gods.

26 For all the gods of the people are idols: but the Becoming-One made the heavens.

27 Glory and honor are in his presence; strength and gladness are in his place.

28 Give unto the Becoming-One, you kindreds of the people, give unto the Becoming-One glory and strength.

29 Give unto the Becoming-One the glory due unto his name: bring an offering, and come before him: worship the Becoming-One in the beauty of holiness.

30 Fear before him, all the earth: the world also shall be stable, that it be not moved.

31 Let the heavens be glad, and let the earth rejoice: and let men say among the nations, The Becoming-One reigns.

32 Let the sea roar, and the fullness thereof: let the fields rejoice, and all that is therein.

33 Then shall the trees of the wood sing out at the presence of the Becoming-One, because he comes to judge the earth.

34 O give thanks unto the Becoming-One; surely goodness, surely mercy for olam.

35 And say ye, Save us, O God of our salvation, and gather us together, and deliver us from the nations, that we may give thanks to your holy name, and glory in your praise.

36 Blessed be the Becoming-One, God of Israel for olam and beyond. And all the people said, Amen, and praised the Becoming-One.

37 So he left there before the ark of the covenant of the Becoming-One Asaph and his brethren, to minister before the ark continually, as every day's work required:

38 And Obededom with their brethren, threescore and eight; Obededom also the son of Jeduthun and Hosah to be gatekeepers:

39 And Zadok the priest, and his brethren the priests, before the tabernacle of the Becoming-One in the high place that was at Gibeon,

40 To offer burnt offerings unto the Becoming-One upon the altar of the burnt offering continually morning and evening, and to do according to all that is written in the law of the Becoming-One, which he commanded Israel;

41 And with them Heman and Jeduthun, and the rest that were chosen, who were expressed by name, to give thanks to the Becoming-One, because his mercy endures for olam.

42 And with them Heman and Jeduthun with trumpets and cymbals for those that should make a sound, and with musical instruments of God. And the sons of Jeduthun were gatekeepers.

43 And all the people departed every man to his house: and David returned to bless his house.

1 Chr 17:1 Now it came to pass, as David sat in his house, that David said to Nathan the prophet, Lo, I dwell in a house of cedars, but the ark of the covenant of the Becoming-One remains under curtains.

2 Then Nathan said unto David, Do all that is in your heart; for God is with you.

3 And it came to pass the same night, that the word of God came to Nathan, saying,

4 Go and tell David my servant, Thus says the Becoming-One, you shall not build me a house to dwell in:

5 For I have not dwelt in a house since the day that I brought up Israel unto this day; but have gone from tent to tent, and from one tabernacle to another.

6 Wheresoever I have walked with all Israel, spoke I a word to any of the judges of Israel, whom I commanded to feed my people, saying, Why have you not built me a house of cedars?

7 Now therefore thus shall you say unto my servant David, Thus says the Becoming-One of hosts, I took you from the sheepcote, even from following the sheep, that you should be ruler over my people Israel:

8 And I have been with you wheresoever you have walked, and have cut off all your enemies from before you, and have made you a name like the name of the great men that are in the earth.

9 Also I will ordain a place for my people Israel, and will plant them, and they shall dwell in their place, and shall be moved no more; neither shall the children of wickedness waste them any more, as at the beginning,

10 And since the time that I commanded judges to be over my people Israel. Moreover I will subdue all your enemies. Furthermore I tell you that the Becoming-One will build you a house.

11 And it shall come to pass, when your days be expired that you must go to be with your fathers, that I will raise up your seed after you, which shall be of your sons; and I will establish his kingdom.

12 He shall build me a house, and I will establish his throne for olam.

13 I will be his father, and he shall be my son: and I will not take my mercy away from him, as I took it from him that was before you:

14 But I will settle him in mine house and in my kingdom for olam, and his throne shall be established for olam.

15 According to all these words, and according to all this vision, so did Nathan speak unto David.

16 And David the king came and sat before the Becoming-One, and said, Who am I, O Becoming-One God, and what is mine house, that you have brought me hitherto?

17 And yet this was a small thing in your eyes, O God; for you have also spoken of your servant's house for a great while to come, and have regarded me according to the estate of a man of high degree, O Becoming-One, God.

18 What can David speak more to you for the honor of your servant? for you know your servant.

19 O Becoming-One, for your servant's sake, and according to your own heart, have you done all this greatness, in making known all these great things.

20 O Becoming-One, there is none like you, neither is there any God beside you, according to all that we have heard with our ears.

21 And what one nation in the earth is like your people Israel, whom God went to redeem to be his own people, to make you a name of greatness and terribleness, by driving out nations from before your people, whom you have redeemed out of Egypt?

22 For your people Israel did you make your own people for olam, and you, Becoming-One, became their God.

23 Therefore now, Becoming-One, let the thing that you have spoken concerning your servant and concerning his house be established for olam, and do as you have said.

24 Let it even be established, that your name may be magnified for olam, saying, The Becoming-One, hosts, is God of Israel, even God to Israel: and let the house of David your servant be established before you.

25 For you, O my God, have told your servant that you will build him a house: therefore your servant has found in his heart to pray before you.

26 And now, Becoming-One, you are God, and have promised this goodness unto your servant:

27 Now therefore let it please you to bless the house of your servant, that it may be before you for olam, for you bless, O Becoming-One, and it shall be blessed for olam.

1 Chr 18:1 Now after this it came to pass, that David smote the Philistines, and subdued them, and took Gath and her towns out of the hand of the Philistines.

2 And he smote Moab; and the Moabites became David's servants, and brought gifts.

3 And David smote Hadarezer king of Zobah unto Hamath, as he went to establish his dominion by the river Euphrates.

4 And David took from him an thousand of chariots, and seven thousand of horsemen, and twenty thousand of footmen: David also hocked all the chariot horses, but reserved of them a hundred chariots.

5 And when the Syrians of Damascus came to help Hadarezer king of Zobah, David killed of the Syrians two and twenty thousand of men.

6 Then David put garrisons in Syriadamascus; and the Syrians became David's servants, and brought gifts. Thus the Becoming-One preserved David wheresoever he went.

7 And David took the shields of gold that were on the servants of Hadarezer, and brought them to Jerusalem.

8 Likewise from Tibhath, and from Chun, cities of Hadarezer, brought David very much brass, wherewith Solomon made the brazen sea, and the pillars, and the vessels of brass.

9 Now when Tou king of Hamath heard how David had struck all the host of Hadarezer king of Zobah;

10 He sent Hadoram his son to king David, to inquire of his welfare, and to congratulate him, because he had fought against Hadarezer, and struck him; for Hadarezer had war with Tou; and with him all manner of vessels of gold and silver and brass.

11 Them also king David dedicated unto the Becoming-One, with the silver and the gold that he brought from all these nations; from Edom, and from Moab, and from the children of Ammon, and from the Philistines, and from Amalek.

12 Moreover Abishai the son of Zeruiah killed of the Edomites in the valley of salt eighteen thousand.

13 And he put garrisons in Edom; and all the Edomites became David's servants. Thus the Becoming-One preserved David wheresoever he went.

14 So David reigned over all Israel, and executed judgment and justice among all his people.

15 And Joab the son of Zeruiah was over the host; and Jehoshaphat the son of Ahilud, recorder.

16 And Zadok the son of Ahitub, and Abimelech the son of Abiathar, were the priests; and Shavsha was scribe;

17 And Benaiah the son of Jehoiada was over the Cherethites and the Pelethites; and the sons of David were chief about the king.

1 Chr 19:1 Now it came to pass after this, that Nahash the king of the children of Ammon died, and his son reigned in his stead.

2 And David said, I will show kindness unto Hanun the son of Nahash, because his father showed kindness to me. And David sent messengers to comfort him concerning his father. So the servants of David came into the land of the children of Ammon to Hanun, to comfort him.

3 But the princes of the children of Ammon said to Hanun, Think you that David does honor your father, that he has sent comforters unto you? are not his servants come unto you for to search, and to overthrow, and to spy out the land?

4 Therefore Hanun took David's servants, and shaved them, and cut off their garments in the midst by their buttocks, and sent them away.

5 Then there went [certain people], and told David how the men were served. And he sent to meet them: for the men were greatly ashamed. And the king said, Tarry at Jericho until your beards be grown, and then return.

6 And when the children of Ammon saw that they had made themselves odious to David, Hanun and the children of Ammon sent a thousand talents of silver to hire them chariots and horsemen out of Mesopotamia, and out of Syriamaachah, and out of Zobah.

7 So they hired thirty and two thousand of chariots, and the king of Maachah and his people; who came and pitched before Medeba. And the children of Ammon gathered themselves together from their cities, and came to battle.

8 And when David heard of it, he sent Joab, and all the host of the mighty men.

9 And the children of Ammon came out, and put the battle in array before the gate of the city: and the kings that were come were by themselves in the field.

10 Now when Joab saw that the battle was set against him before and behind, he chose out of all the choice of Israel, and put them in array against the Syrians.

11 And the rest of the people he delivered unto the hand of Abishai his brother, and they set themselves in array against the children of Ammon.

12 And he said, If the Syrians be too strong for me, then you shall help me: but if the children of Ammon be too strong for you, then I will help you.

13 Be of good courage, and let us behave ourselves valiantly for our people, and for the cities of our God: and let the Becoming-One do that which is good in his sight.

14 So Joab and the people that were with him drew near before the Syrians unto the battle; and they fled before him.

15 And when the children of Ammon saw that the Syrians were fled, they likewise fled before Abishai his brother, and entered into the city. Then Joab came to Jerusalem.

16 And when the Syrians saw that they were put to the worse before Israel, they sent messengers, and drew forth the Syrians that were over the river: and Shophach the captain of the host of Hadarezer went before them.

17 And it was told David; and he gathered all Israel, and passed over Jordan, and came upon them, and set the battle in array against them. So when David had put the battle in array against the Syrians, they fought with him.

18 But the Syrians fled before Israel; and David killed of the Syrians seven thousand of men which fought in chariots, and forty thousand of footmen, and killed Shophach the captain of the host.

19 And when the servants of Hadarezer saw that they were put to the worse before Israel, they made peace with David, and became his servants: neither would the Syrians help the children of Ammon any more.

1 Chr 20:1 And it came to pass, at the return of the year, at the time that kings go out to battle, Joab led forth the power of the army, and wasted the country of the children of Ammon, and came and besieged Rabbah. But David tarried at Jerusalem. And Joab smote Rabbah, and destroyed it.

2 And David took the crown of their king from off his head, and found it to weigh a talent of gold, and there were precious stones in it; and it was set upon David's head: and he brought also exceeding much spoil out of the city.

3 And he brought out the people that were in it, and cut them with saws, and with harrows of iron, and with axes. Even so dealt David with all the cities of the children of Ammon. And David and all the people returned to Jerusalem.

4 And it came to pass after this, that there arose war at Gezer with the Philistines; at which time Sibbechai the Hushathite killed Sippai, that was of the children of the giant: and they were subdued.

5 And there was war again with the Philistines; and Elhanan the son of Jair killed Lahmi the brother of Goliath the Gittite, whose spear staff was like a weaver's beam.

6 And yet again there was war at Gath, where was a man of great stature, whose fingers and toes were four and twenty, six on each hand, and six on each foot: and he also was the son of the giant.

7 But when he defied Israel, Jonathan the son of Shimea David's brother killed him.

8 These were born unto the giant in Gath; and they fell by the hand of David, and by the hand of his servants.

1 Chr 21:1 And Satan stood up against Israel, and provoked David to number Israel.

2 And David said to Joab and to the rulers of the people, Go, number Israel from Beersheba even to Dan; and bring the number of them to me, that I may know it.

3 And Joab answered, The Becoming-One make his people a hundred times so many more as they be: but, my lord the king, are they not all my lord's servants? why then does my lord require this thing? why will he be a cause of trespass to Israel?

4 Nevertheless the king's word prevailed against Joab. Therefore Joab departed, and went throughout all Israel, and came to Jerusalem.

5 And Joab gave the sum of the number of the people unto David. And all they of Israel were a thousand thousand and a hundred thousand of men that drew sword: and Judah was four hundred threescore and ten thousand of men that drew sword.

6 But Levi and Benjamin counted he not among them: for the king's word was abominable to Joab.

7 And God being displeased with this thing; therefore he smote Israel.

8 And David said unto God, I have sinned greatly, because I have done this thing: but now, I beg you, do away the iniquity of your servant; for I have done very foolishly.

9 And the Becoming-One spoke unto Gad, David's seer, saying,

10 Go and tell David, saying, Thus says the Becoming-One, I offer you three things: choose you one of them, that I may do it unto you.

11 So Gad came to David, and said unto him, Thus says the Becoming-One, Choose you

12 Either three years' famine; or three months to be destroyed before your foes, while that the sword of your enemies overtake you; or else three days the sword of the Becoming-One, even the pestilence, in the land, and the angel of the Becoming-One destroying throughout all the coasts of Israel. Now therefore advise yourself what word I shall bring again to him that sent me.

13 And David said unto Gad, I am in a great strait: let me fall now into the hand of the Becoming-One; for very great are his mercies: but let me not fall into the hand of man.

14 So the Becoming-One sent pestilence upon Israel: and there fell of Israel seventy thousand of men.

15 And God sent an angel unto Jerusalem to destroy it: and as he was destroying, the Becoming-One beheld, and he repented him of the evil, and said to the angel that destroyed, It is enough, stay now your hand. And the angel of the Becoming-One stood by the threshing floor of Ornan the Jebusite.

16 And David lifted up his eyes, and saw the angel of the Becoming-One standing between the earth and the heaven, having a drawn sword in his hand stretched out over Jerusalem. Then David and

the elders of Israel, who were clothed in sackcloth, fell upon their faces.

17 And David said unto God, Is it not I that commanded the people to be numbered? even I it is that have sinned and done evil indeed; but as for these sheep, what have they done? let your hand, I pray you, O Becoming-One my God, be on me, and on my father's house; but not on your people, that they should be plagued.

18 Then the angel of the Becoming-One commanded Gad to say to David, that David should go up, and set up an altar unto the Becoming-One in the threshing floor of Ornan the Jebusite.

19 And David went up at the saying of Gad, which he spoke in the name of the Becoming-One.

20 And Ornan turned back, and saw the angel; and his four sons with him hid themselves. Now Ornan was threshing wheat.

21 And as David came to Ornan, Ornan looked and saw David, and went out of the threshingfloor, and bowed himself to David with his face to the ground.

22 Then David said to Ornan, Grant me the place of this threshing floor, that I may build an altar therein unto the Becoming-One: you shall grant it me for the full price: that the plague may be stayed from the people.

23 And Ornan said unto David, Take it to you, and let my lord the king do that which is good in his eyes: lo, I give you the oxen also for burnt offerings, and the threshing instruments for wood, and the wheat for the food offering; I give it all.

24 And king David said to Ornan, Nay; but I will truly buy it for the full price: for I will not take that which is yours for the Becoming-One, nor offer burnt offerings without cost.

25 So David gave to Ornan for the place six hundred shekels of gold by weight.

26 And David built there an altar unto the Becoming-One, and offered burnt offerings and peace offerings, and called upon the Becoming-One; and he answered him from the heavens by fire upon the altar of burnt offering.

27 And the Becoming-One commanded the angel; and he put up his sword again into the sheath thereof.

28 At that time when David saw that the Becoming-One had answered him in the threshing floor of Ornan the Jebusite, then he sacrificed there.

29 For the tabernacle of the Becoming-One, which Moses made in the wilderness, and the altar of the burnt offering, were at that season in the high place at Gibeon.

30 But David could not go before it to inquire of God: for he was afraid because of the sword of the angel of the Becoming-One.

1 Chr 22:1 Then David said, This is the house of the Becoming-One God, and this is the altar of the burnt offering for Israel.

2 And David commanded to gather together the strangers that were in the land of Israel; and he set masons to hew worked stones to build the house of God.

3 And David prepared iron in abundance for the nails for the doors of the gates, and for the joinings; and brass in abundance without weight;

4 Also cedar trees in abundance: for the Zidonians and they of Tyre brought much cedar wood to David.

5 And David said, Solomon my son is young and tender, and the house that is to be built for the Becoming-One must be exceeding magnifical, of fame and of glory throughout all countries: I will therefore now make preparation for it. So David prepared abundantly before his death.

6 Then he called for Solomon his son, and charged him to build a house for the Becoming-One, God of Israel.

7 And David said to Solomon, My son, as for me, it was in my mind to build a house unto the name of the Becoming-One my God:

8 But the word of the Becoming-One came to me, saying, you have shed blood abundantly, and have made great wars: you shall not build a house unto my name, because you have shed much blood upon the earth in my sight.

9 Behold, a son shall be born to you, who shall be a man of rest; and I will give him rest from all his enemies round about: for his name shall be Solomon, and I will give peace and quietness unto Israel in his days.

10 He shall build a house for my name; and he shall be my son, and I will be his father; and I will establish the throne of his kingdom over Israel for olam.

11 Now, my son, the Becoming-One be with you; and prosper you, and build the house of the Becoming-One your God, as he has said of you.

12 Only the Becoming-One give you wisdom and understanding, and give you charge concerning Israel, that you may keep the law of the Becoming-One your God.

13 Then shall you prosper, if you take heed to fulfil the statutes and judgments which the Becoming-One charged Moses with concerning Israel: be strong, and of good courage; dread not, nor be dismayed.

14 Now, behold, in my trouble I have prepared for the house of the Becoming-One a hundred thousand talents of gold, and a thousand thousand talents of silver; and of brass and iron without weight; for it is in abundance: timber also and stone have I prepared; and you may add thereto.

15 Moreover there are workmen with you in abundance, hewers and workers of stone and timber, and all manner of cunning men for every manner of work.

16 Of the gold, the silver, and the brass, and the iron, there is no number. Arise therefore, and be doing, and the Becoming-One be with you.

17 David also commanded all the princes of Israel to help Solomon his son, saying,

18 Is not the Becoming-One your God with you? and has he not given you rest on every side? for he has given the inhabitants of the land into mine hand; and the land is subdued before the Becoming-One, and before his people.

19 Now set your heart and your soul to seek the Becoming-One your God; arise therefore, and build

you the sanctuary of the Becoming-One, God, to bring the ark of the covenant of the Becoming-One, and the holy vessels of God, into the house that is to be built to the name of the Becoming-One.

1 Chr 23:1 So when David was old and full of days, he made Solomon his son king over Israel.

2 And he gathered together all the princes of Israel, with the priests and the Levites.

3 Now the Levites were numbered from the age of thirty years and upward: and their number by their polls, man by man, was thirty and eight thousand.

4 Of which, twenty and four thousand were to set forward the work of the house of the Becoming-One; and six thousand were officers and judges:

5 Moreover four thousand were gatekeepers; and four thousand praised the Becoming-One with the instruments which I made, said David, to praise therewith.

6 And David divided them into courses among the sons of Levi, namely, Gershon, Kohath, and Merari.

7 Of the Gershonites were, Laadan, and Shimei.

8 The sons of Laadan; the chief was Jehiel, and Zetham, and Joel, three.

9 The sons of Shimei; Shelomith, and Haziel, and Haran, three. These were the chief of the fathers of Laadan.

10 And the sons of Shimei were, Jahath, Zina, and Jeush, and Beriah. These four were the sons of Shimei.

11 And Jahath was the chief, and Zizah the second: but Jeush and Beriah had not many sons; therefore they were in one reckoning, according to their father's house.

12 The sons of Kohath; Amram, Izhar, Hebron, and Uzziel, four.

13 The sons of Amram; Aaron and Moses: and Aaron was separated, that he should sanctify the most holy things, he and his sons for olam to burn incense before the Becoming-One, to minister unto him, and to bless in his name for olam.

14 Now concerning Moses the man of God, his sons were named of the tribe of Levi.

15 The sons of Moses were, Gershom, and Eliezer.

16 Of the sons of Gershom, Shebuel was the chief.

17 And the sons of Eliezer were, Rehabiah the chief. And Eliezer had none other sons; but the sons of Rehabiah were very many.

18 Of the sons of Izhar; Shelomith the chief.

19 Of the sons of Hebron; Jeriah the first, Amariah the second, Jahaziel the third, and Jekameam the fourth.

20 Of the sons of Uzziel; Micah the first, and Jesiah the second.

21 The sons of Merari; Mahli, and Mushi. The sons of Mahli; Eleazar, and Kish.

22 And Eleazar died, and had no sons, but daughters: and their brethren the sons of Kish took them.

23 The sons of Mushi; Mahli, and Eder, and Jeremoth, three.

24 These were the sons of Levi after the house of their fathers; even the chief of the fathers, as they were counted by number of names by their polls, that did the work for the service of the house of the Becoming-One, from the age of twenty years and upward.

25 For David said, The Becoming-One, God of Israel, has given rest unto his people, that they may dwell in Jerusalem for olam.

26 And also unto the Levites; they shall no more carry the tabernacle, nor any vessels of it for the service thereof.

27 For by the last words of David the Levites were numbered from a son of twenty years and above:

28 Because their office was to wait on the sons of Aaron for the service of the house of the Becoming-One, in the courts, and in the chambers, and in the purifying of all holy things, and the work of the service of the house of God;

29 Both for the showbread, and for the fine flour for food offering, and for the unleavened cakes, and for that which is baked in the pan, and for that which is fried, and for all manner of measure and size;

30 And to stand every morning to thank and praise the Becoming-One, and likewise at evening;

31 And to offer all burnt sacrifices unto the Becoming-One in the sabbaths, in the new moons, and on the set time,[116] by number, according to the order commanded unto them, continually before the Becoming-One: 32 And that they should keep the charge of the tabernacle of the set time, and the charge of the holy place, and the charge of the sons of Aaron their brethren, in the service of the house of the Becoming-One.

1 Chr 24:1 Now these are the divisions of the sons of Aaron. The sons of Aaron; Nadab, and Abihu, Eleazar, and Ithamar.

2 But Nadab and Abihu died before their father, and had no children: therefore Eleazar and Ithamar executed the priest's office.

3 And David distributed them, both Zadok of the sons of Eleazar, and Ahimelech of the sons of Ithamar, according to their offices in their service.

4 And there were more chief men found of the sons of Eleazar than of the sons of Ithamar; and thus were they divided. Among the sons of Eleazar there were sixteen chief men of the house of their fathers, and eight among the sons of Ithamar according to the house of their fathers.

5 Thus were they divided by lot, one sort with another; for the governors of the sanctuary, and governors of the house of God, were of the sons of Eleazar, and of the sons of Ithamar.

6 And Shemaiah the son of Nethaneel the scribe, one of the Levites, wrote them before the king, and the princes, and Zadok the priest, and Ahimelech the son of Abiathar, and before the chief of the fathers of the priests and Levites: one principal household being taken for Eleazar, and one taken for Ithamar.

---

[116] Appointed time or festival

7 Now the first lot came forth to Jehoiarib, the second to Jedaiah,

8 The third to Harim, the fourth to Seorim,

9 The fifth to Malchijah, the sixth to Mijamin,

10 The seventh to Hakkoz, the eighth to Abijah,

11 The ninth to Jeshuah, the tenth to Shecaniah,

12 The eleventh to Eliashib, the twelfth to Jakim,

13 The thirteenth to Huppah, the fourteenth to Jeshebeab,

14 The fifteenth to Bilgah, the sixteenth to Immer,

15 The seventeenth to Hezir, the eighteenth to Aphses,

16 The nineteenth to Pethahiah, the twentieth to Jehezekel,

17 The one and twentieth to Jachin, the two and twentieth to Gamul,

18 The three and twentieth to Delaiah, the four and twentieth to Maaziah.

19 These were the orderings of them in their service to come into the house of the Becoming-One, according to their manner, under Aaron their father, as the Becoming-One, God of Israel had commanded him.

20 And the rest of the sons of Levi were these: Of the sons of Amram; Shubael: of the sons of Shubael; Jehdeiah.

21 Concerning Rehabiah: of the sons of Rehabiah, the first was Isshiah.

22 Of the Izharites; Shelomoth: of the sons of Shelomoth; Jahath.

23 And the sons of Hebron; Jeriah the first, Amariah the second, Jahaziel the third, Jekameam the fourth.

24 Of the sons of Uzziel; Michah: of the sons of Michah; Shamir.

25 The brother of Michah was Isshiah: of the sons of Isshiah; Zechariah.

26 The sons of Merari were Mahli and Mushi: the sons of Jaaziah; Beno.

27 The sons of Merari by Jaaziah; Beno, and Shoham, and Zaccur, and Ibri.

28 Of Mahli came Eleazar, who had no sons.

29 Concerning Kish: the son of Kish was Jerahmeel.

30 The sons also of Mushi; Mahli, and Eder, and Jerimoth. These were the sons of the Levites after the house of their fathers.

31 These likewise cast lots over against their brethren the sons of Aaron in the presence of David the king, and Zadok, and Ahimelech, and the chief of the fathers of the priests and Levites, even the principal fathers over against their younger brethren.

1 Chr 25:1 Moreover David and the captains of the host separated to the service of the sons of Asaph, and of Heman, and of Jeduthun, who should prophesy with harps, with psalteries, and with cymbals: and the number of the workmen according to their service was:

2 Of the sons of Asaph; Zaccur, and Joseph, and Nethaniah, and Asarelah, the sons of Asaph under the hands of Asaph, which prophesied according to the order of the king.

3 Of Jeduthun: the sons of Jeduthun; Gedaliah, and Zeri, and Jeshaiah, Hashabiah, and Mattithiah, six, under the hands of their father Jeduthun, who prophesied with a harp, to give thanks and to praise the Becoming-One.

4 Of Heman: the sons of Heman; Bukkiah, Mattaniah, Uzziel, Shebuel, and Jerimoth, Hananiah, Hanani, Eliathah, Giddalti, and Romamtiezer, Joshbekashah, Mallothi, Hothir, and Mahazioth:

5 All these were the sons of Heman the king's seer in the words of God, to lift up the horn. And God gave to Heman fourteen sons and three daughters.

6 All these were under the hands of their father for song in the house of the Becoming-One, with cymbals, psalteries, and harps, for the service of the house of God, according to the king's order to Asaph, Jeduthun, and Heman.

7 So the number of them, with their brethren that were instructed in the songs of the Becoming-One, even all that were cunning, was two hundred fourscore and eight.

8 And they cast lots, ward against ward, as well the small as the great, the teacher as the scholar.

9 Now the first lot came forth for Asaph to Joseph: the second to Gedaliah, who with his brethren and sons were twelve:

10 The third to Zaccur, he, his sons, and his brethren, were twelve:

11 The fourth to Izri, he, his sons, and his brethren, were twelve:

12 The fifth to Nethaniah, he, his sons, and his brethren, were twelve:

13 The sixth to Bukkiah, he, his sons, and his brethren, were twelve:

14 The seventh to Jesharelah, he, his sons, and his brethren, were twelve:

15 The eighth to Jeshaiah, he, his sons, and his brethren, were twelve:

16 The ninth to Mattaniah, he, his sons, and his brethren, were twelve:

17 The tenth to Shimei, he, his sons, and his brethren, were twelve:

18 The eleventh to Azareel, he, his sons, and his brethren, were twelve:

19 The twelfth to Hashabiah, he, his sons, and his brethren, were twelve:

20 The thirteenth to Shubael, he, his sons, and his brethren, were twelve:

21 The fourteenth to Mattithiah, he, his sons, and his brethren, were twelve:

22 The fifteenth to Jeremoth, he, his sons, and his brethren, were twelve:

23 The sixteenth to Hananiah, he, his sons, and his brethren, were twelve:

24 The seventeenth to Joshbekashah, he, his sons, and his brethren, were twelve:

25 The eighteenth to Hanani, he, his sons, and his brethren, were twelve:

26 The nineteenth to Mallothi, he, his sons, and his brethren, were twelve:

27 The twentieth to Eliathah, he, his sons, and his brethren, were twelve:

28 The one and twentieth to Hothir, he, his sons, and his brethren, were twelve:

29 The two and twentieth to Giddalti, he, his sons, and his brethren, were twelve:

30 The three and twentieth to Mahazioth, he, his sons, and his brethren, were twelve:

31 The four and twentieth to Romamtiezer, he, his sons, and his brethren, were twelve.

1 Chr 26:1 Concerning the divisions of the gatekeepers: Of the Korhites was Meshelemiah the son of Kore, of the sons of Asaph.

2 And the sons of Meshelemiah were, Zechariah the firstborn, Jediael the second, Zebadiah the third, Jathniel the fourth,

3 Elam the fifth, Jehohanan the sixth, Elioenai the seventh.

4 Moreover the sons of Obededom were, Shemaiah the firstborn, Jehozabad the second, Joah the third, and Sacar the fourth, and Nethaneel the fifth,

5 Ammiel the sixth, Issachar the seventh, Peulthai the eighth: for God blessed him.

6 Also unto Shemaiah his son were sons born, that ruled throughout the house of their father: for they were mighty men of valor.

7 The sons of Shemaiah; Othni, and Rephael, and Obed, Elzabad, whose brethren were strong men, Elihu, and Semachiah.

8 All these of the sons of Obededom: they and their sons and their brethren, able men for strength for the service, were threescore and two of Obededom.

9 And Meshelemiah had sons and brethren, strong men, eighteen.

10 Also Hosah, of the children of Merari, had sons; Simri the chief, for though he was not the firstborn, yet his father made him the chief;

11 Hilkiah the second, Tebaliah the third, Zechariah the fourth: all the sons and brethren of Hosah were thirteen.

12 Among these were the divisions of the gatekeepers, even among the chief men, having wards one against another, to minister in the house of the Becoming-One.

13 And they cast lots, as well the small as the great, according to the house of their fathers, for every gate.

14 And the lot eastward fell to Shelemiah. Then for Zechariah his son, a wise counselor, they cast lots; and his lot came out northward.

15 To Obededom southward; and to his sons the house of Asuppim.

16 To Shuppim and Hosah the lot came forth westward, with the gate Shallecheth, by the causeway of the going up, ward against ward.

17 Eastward were six Levites, northward four a day, southward four a day, and toward Asuppim two and two.

18 At **Parbar** on the westside [of the Temple – cf. 23:4-5], four [gatekeepers – cf. 26:1, 12, 19] at the road, and two at the Parbar.

19 These are the divisions of the gatekeepers among the sons of Kore, and among the sons of Merari.

20 And of the Levites, Ahijah was over the treasures of the house of God, and over the treasures of the dedicated things.

21 As concerning the sons of Laadan; the sons of the Gershonite Laadan, chief fathers, even of Laadan the Gershonite, were Jehieli.

22 The sons of Jehieli; Zetham, and Joel his brother, which were over the treasures of the house of the Becoming-One.

23 Of the Amramites, and the Izharites, the Hebronites, and the Uzzielites:

24 And Shebuel the son of Gershom, the son of Moses, was ruler of the treasures.

25 And his brethren by Eliezer; Rehabiah his son, and Jeshaiah his son, and Joram his son, and Zichri his son, and Shelomith his son.

26 Which Shelomith and his brethren were over all the treasures of the dedicated things, which David the king, and the chief fathers, the captains over thousands and hundreds, and the captains of the host, had dedicated.

27 Out of the spoils won in battles did they dedicate to maintain the house of the Becoming-One.

28 And all that Samuel the seer, and Saul the son of Kish, and Abner the son of Ner, and Joab the son of Zeruiah, had dedicated; and whosoever had dedicated anything, it was under the hand of Shelomith, and of his brethren.

29 Of the Izharites, Chenaniah and his sons were for the outward business over Israel, for officers and judges.

30 And of the Hebronites, Hashabiah and his brethren, men of valor, a thousand and seven hundred, were officers among them of Israel over the Jordan westward in all the business of the Becoming-One, and in the service of the king.

31 Among the Hebronites was Jerijah the chief, even among the Hebronites, according to the generations of his fathers. In the fortieth year of the reign of David they were sought for, and there were found among them mighty men of valor at Jazer of Gilead.

32 And his brethren, men of valor, were two thousand and seven hundred chief fathers, whom king David made rulers over the Reubenites, the Gadites, and the half tribe of Manasseh, for every matter pertaining to God, and affairs of the king.

1 Chr 27:1 Now the children of Israel after their number: the chief fathers and captains of thousands, and hundreds, and their officers that served the king in any matter of the courses, which came in and went out month by month throughout all the months of the year, of every course were twenty and four thousand.

2 Over the first course for the first month was Jashobeam the son of Zabdiel: and in his course were twenty and four thousand.

3 Of the children of Perez was the chief of all the captains of the host for the first month.

4 And over the course of the second month was Dodai an Ahohite, and of his course was Mikloth also the ruler: in his course likewise were twenty and four thousand.

5 The third captain of the host for the third month was Benaiah the son of Jehoiada, a chief priest: and in his course were twenty and four thousand.

6 This is that Benaiah, who was mighty among the thirty, and above the thirty: and in his course was Ammizabad his son.

7 The fourth captain for the fourth month was Asahel the brother of Joab, and Zebadiah his son after

him: and in his course were twenty and four thousand.

8 The fifth captain for the fifth month was Shamhuth the Izrahite: and in his course were twenty and four thousand.

9 The sixth captain for the sixth month was Ira the son of Ikkesh the Tekoite: and in his course were twenty and four thousand.

10 The seventh captain for the seventh month was Helez the Pelonite, of the children of Ephraim: and in his course were twenty and four thousand.

11 The eighth captain for the eighth month was Sibbecai the Hushathite, of the Zarhites: and in his course were twenty and four thousand.

12 The ninth captain for the ninth month was Abiezer the Anetothite, of the Benjamites: and in his course were twenty and four thousand.

13 The tenth captain for the tenth month was Maharai the Netophathite, of the Zarhites: and in his course were twenty and four thousand.

14 The eleventh captain for the eleventh month was Benaiah the Pirathonite, of the children of Ephraim: and in his course were twenty and four thousand.

15 The twelfth captain for the twelfth month was Heldai the Netophathite, of Othniel: and in his course were twenty and four thousand.

16 Furthermore over the tribes of Israel: the ruler of the Reubenites was Eliezer the son of Zichri: of the Simeonites, Shephatiah the son of Maachah:

17 Of the Levites, Hashabiah the son of Kemuel: of the Aaronites, Zadok:

18 Of Judah, Elihu, one of the brethren of David: of Issachar, Omri the son of Michael:

19 Of Zebulun, Ishmaiah the son of Obadiah: of Naphtali, Jerimoth the son of Azriel:

20 Of the children of Ephraim, Hoshea the son of Azaziah: of the half tribe of Manasseh, Joel the son of Pedaiah:

21 Of the half tribe of Manasseh in Gilead, Iddo the son of Zechariah: of Benjamin, Jaasiel the son of Abner:

22 Of Dan, Azareel the son of Jeroham. These were the princes of the tribes of Israel.

23 But David took not the number of them from a son of twenty years and under: because the Becoming-One had said he would increase Israel like to the stars of the heavens.

24 Joab the son of Zeruiah began to number, but he finished not, because there fell wrath for it against Israel; neither was the number put in the account of the chronicles of king David.

25 And over the king's treasures was Azmaveth the son of Adiel: and over the storehouses in the fields, in the cities, and in the villages, and in the castles, was Jehonathan the son of Uzziah:

26 And over them that did the work of the field for tillage of the ground was Ezri the son of Chelub:

27 And over the vineyards was Shimei the Ramathite: over the increase of the vineyards for the wine cellars was Zabdi the Shiphmite:

28 And over the olive trees and the sycamore trees that were in the low plains was Baal-Hanan the Gederite: and over the cellars of oil was Joash:

29 And over the herds that fed in Sharon was Shitrai the Sharonite: and over the herds that were in the valleys was Shaphat the son of Adlai:

30 Over the camels also was Obil the Ishmaelite: and over the donkeys was Jehdeiah the Meronothite:

31 And over the flocks was Jaziz the Hagerite. All these were the rulers of the substance which was king David's.

32 Also Jonathan David's uncle was a counselor, a wise man, and a scribe: and Jehiel the son of Hachmoni was with the king's sons:

33 And Ahithophel was the king's counselor: and Hushai the Archite was the king's companion:

34 And after Ahithophel was Jehoiada the son of Benaiah, and Abiathar: and the general of the king's army was Joab.

1 Chr 28:1 And David assembled all the princes of Israel, the princes of the tribes, and the captains of the companies that ministered to the king by course, and the captains over the thousands, and captains over the hundreds, and the stewards over all the substance and possession of the king, and of his sons, with the eunuchs, and with the mighty men, and with all the valiant men, unto Jerusalem.

2 Then David the king stood up upon his feet, and said, Hear me, my brethren, and my people: As for me, I had in mine heart to build a house of rest for the ark of the covenant of the Becoming-One, and for the footstool of our God, and had made ready for the building:

3 But God said unto me, you shall not build a house for my name, because you have been a man of war, and have shed blood.

4 Howbeit the Becoming-One, God of Israel chose me before all the house of my father to be king over Israel for olam, for he has chosen Judah to be the ruler; and of the house of Judah, the house of my father; and among the sons of my father he liked me to make me king over all Israel:

5 And of all my sons, for the Becoming-One has given me many sons, he has chosen Solomon my son to sit upon the throne of the kingdom of the Becoming-One over Israel.

6 And he said unto me, Solomon your son, he shall build my house and my courts: for I have chosen him to be my son, and I will be his father.

7 Moreover I will establish his kingdom for olam, if he be constant to do my commandments and my judgments, as at this day.

8 Now therefore in the sight of all Israel the congregation of the Becoming-One, and in the audience of our God, keep and seek for all the commandments of the Becoming-One your God: that you may possess this good land, and leave it for an inheritance for your children after you for olam.

9 And you, Solomon my son, know you God of your father, and serve him with a perfect heart and with a willing soul: for the Becoming-One searches all hearts, and understands all the imaginations of the thoughts: if you seek him, he will be found of you; but if you forsake him, he will cast you off to the beyond.

10 Take heed now; for the Becoming-One has chosen you to build a house for the sanctuary: be strong, and do it.

11 Then David gave to Solomon his son the pattern of the porch, and of the houses thereof, and of the treasuries thereof, and of the upper chambers

thereof, and of the inner parlours thereof, and of the place of the mercy seat,

12 And the pattern of all that he had by the spirit, of the courts of the house of the Becoming-One, and of all the chambers round about, of the treasuries of the house of God, and of the treasuries of the dedicated things:

13 Also for the courses of the priests and the Levites, and for all the work of the service of the house of the Becoming-One, and for all the vessels of service in the house of the Becoming-One.

14 He gave of gold by weight for things of gold, for all instruments of all manner of service; silver also for all instruments of silver by weight, for all instruments of every kind of service:

15 Even the weight for the candlesticks of gold, and for their lamps of gold, by weight for every candlestick, and for the lamps thereof: and for the candlesticks of silver by weight, both for the candlestick, and also for the lamps thereof, according to the use of every candlestick.

16 And by weight he gave gold for the tables of showbread, for every table; and likewise silver for the tables of silver:

17 Also pure gold for the fleshhooks, and the bowls, and the cups: and for the golden basins he gave gold by weight for every basin; and likewise silver by weight for every basin of silver:

18 And for the altar of incense refined gold by weight; and gold for the pattern of the chariot of the cherubs, that spread out their wings, and covered the ark of the covenant of the Becoming-One.

19 All this, said David, the Becoming-One made me understand in writing by his hand upon me, even all the works of this pattern.

20 And David said to Solomon his son, Be strong and of good courage, and do it: fear not, nor be dismayed: for the Becoming-One, God, even my God, will be with you; he will not fail you, nor forsake you, until you have finished all the work for the service of the house of the Becoming-One.

21 And, behold, the courses of the priests and the Levites, even they shall be with you for all the service of the house of God: and there shall be with you for all manner of workmanship every willing skillful man, for any manner of service: also the princes and all the people will be wholly at your commandment.

1 Chr 29:1 Furthermore David the king said unto all the congregation, Solomon my son, whom alone God has chosen, is yet young and tender, and the work is great: for the palace is not for man, but for the Becoming-One, God.

2 Now I have prepared with all my might for the house of my God the gold for things to be made of gold, and the silver for things of silver, and the brass for things of brass, the iron for things of iron, and wood for things of wood; onyx stones, and stones to be set, glistering stones, and of diverse colors, and all manner of precious stones, and marble stones in abundance.

3 Moreover, because I have set my affection to the house of my God, I have of mine own treasure, of gold and silver, which I have given to the house of my God, over and above all that I have prepared for the holy house,

4 Even three thousand talents of gold, of the gold of Ophir, and seven thousand talents of refined silver, to overlay the walls of the houses withal:

5 The gold for things of gold, and the silver for things of silver, and for all manner of work to be made by the hands of artificers. And who then is willing to consecrate his service this day unto the Becoming-One?

6 Then the chief of the fathers and princes of the tribes of Israel, and the captains of thousands, and of hundreds, with the rulers of the king's work, offered willingly,

7 And gave for the service of the house of God of gold five thousand talents and ten myriads of drams, and of silver ten thousand talents, and of brass eighteen thousand talents, and one hundred thousand talents of iron.

8 And they with whom precious stones were found gave them to the treasure of the house of the Becoming-One, by the hand of Jehiel the Gershonite.

9 Then the people rejoiced, for that they offered willingly, because with perfect heart they offered willingly to the Becoming-One: and David the king also rejoiced with great joy.

10 Therefore David blessed the Becoming-One before all the congregation: and David said, Blessed be you, Becoming-One, God of Israel our father, from olam and into olam.

11 Yours, O Becoming-One, is the greatness, and the power, and the glory, and the victory, and the majesty: for all that is in the heavens and in the earth is yours; yours is the kingdom, O Becoming-One, and you are exalted as head above all.

12 Both riches and honor come from you, and you reign over all; and in your hand is power and might; and in your hand it is to make great, and to give strength unto all.

13 Now therefore, our God, we thank you, and praise your glorious name.

14 But who am I, and what is my people, that we should be able to offer so willingly after this sort? for all things come from you, and from your own have we given you.

15 For we are strangers before you, and sojourners, as were all our fathers: our days on the earth are as a shadow, and there is none abiding.

16 O Becoming-One our God, all this store that we have prepared to build you a house for your holy name comes of your hand, and is all your own.

17 I know also, my God, that you try the heart, and have pleasure in uprightness. As for me, in the uprightness of mine heart I have willingly offered all these things: and now have I seen with joy your people, which are present here, to offer willingly unto you.

18 O Becoming-One, God of Abraham, Isaac, and of Israel, our fathers, keep this for olam in the imagination of the thoughts of the heart of your people, and prepare their heart unto you:

19 And give unto Solomon my son a perfect heart, to keep your commandments, your testimonies, and your statutes, and to do all these things, and to build the palace, for the which I have made provision.

20 And David said to all the congregation, Now bless the Becoming-One your God. And all the congregation blessed the Becoming-One, God of their fathers, and bowed down their heads, and worshiped the Becoming-One, and the king.

21 And they sacrificed sacrifices unto the Becoming-One, and offered burnt offerings unto the Becoming-One, on the next day after that day, even a thousand of bullocks, a thousand of rams, and a thousand of lambs, with their drink offerings, and sacrifices in abundance for all Israel:

22 And did eat and drink before the Becoming-One on that day with great gladness. And they made Solomon the son of David king the second time, and anointed him unto the Becoming-One to be the ruler, and Zadok to be priest.

23 Then Solomon sat on the throne of the Becoming-One as king instead of David his father, and prospered; and all Israel obeyed him.

24 And all the princes, and the mighty men, and all the sons likewise of king David, submitted themselves unto Solomon the king.

25 And the Becoming-One magnified Solomon exceedingly in the sight of all Israel, and bestowed upon him such royal majesty as had not been on any king before him in Israel.

26 Thus David the son of Jesse reigned over all Israel.

27 And the time that he reigned over Israel was forty years; seven years reigned he in Hebron, and thirty and three years reigned he in Jerusalem.

28 And he died in a good old age, full of days, riches, and honor: and Solomon his son reigned in his stead.

29 Now the acts of David the king, first and last, behold, they are written in the book of Samuel the seer, and in the book of Nathan the prophet, and in the book of Gad the seer,

30 With all his reign and his might, and the times that went over him, and over Israel, and over all the kingdoms of the countries.

2 Chronicles

2 Chr 1:1 And Solomon the son of David was strengthened in his kingdom, and the Becoming-One his God was with him, and magnified him exceedingly.

2 Then Solomon spoke unto all Israel, to the captains of thousands, and of hundreds, and to the judges, and to every governor in all Israel, the chief of the fathers.

3 So Solomon, and all the congregation with him, went to the high place that was at Gibeon; for there was the tabernacle of the set time of God, which Moses the servant of the Becoming-One had made in the wilderness.

4 But the ark of God had David brought up from Kirjathjearim to the place which David had prepared for it: for he had pitched a tent for it at Jerusalem.

5 Moreover the brazen altar, that Bezaleel the son of Uri, the son of Hur, had made, he put before the tabernacle of the Becoming-One: and Solomon and the congregation sought unto it.

6 And Solomon went up there to the brazen altar before the Becoming-One, which was at the tabernacle of the set time, and offered a thousand of burnt offerings upon it.

7 In that night did He appear, God, unto Solomon, and said unto him, Ask what I shall give you.

8 And Solomon said unto God, you have showed great mercy unto David my father, and have made me to reign in his stead.

9 Now, O Becoming-One, God, let your promise unto David my father be established: for you have made me king over a people like the dust of the earth in multitude.

10 Give me now wisdom and knowledge, that I may go out and come in before this people: for who can judge this your people, that is so great?

11 And God said to Solomon, Because this was in your heart, and you have not asked riches, wealth, or honor, nor the soul of your enemies, neither yet have asked long life; but have asked wisdom and knowledge for thyself, that you may judge my people, over whom I have made you king:

12 Wisdom and knowledge is granted unto you; and I will give you riches, and wealth, and honor, such as none of the kings have had that have been before you, neither shall there any after you have the like.

13 Then Solomon came from his journey to the high place that was at Gibeon to Jerusalem, from before the tabernacle of the set time, and reigned over Israel.

14 And Solomon gathered chariots and horsemen: and he had a thousand and four hundred chariots, and twelve thousand of horsemen, which he placed in the chariot cities, and with the king at Jerusalem.

15 And the king made silver and gold at Jerusalem as plenteous as stones, and cedar trees made he as the sycamore trees that are in the vale for abundance.

16 And Solomon had horses brought out of Egypt, and linen yarn: the king's merchants received the linen yarn at a price.

17 And they fetched up, and brought forth out of Egypt a chariot for six hundred shekels of silver, and a horse for a hundred and fifty: and so brought they out horses for all the kings of the Hittites, and for the kings of Syria, by their means.

2 Chr 2:1 And Solomon determined to build a house for the name of the Becoming-One, and a house for his kingdom.

2 And Solomon told out threescore and ten thousand of men to bear burdens, and fourscore thousand to hew in the mountain, and three thousand and six hundred to oversee them.

3 And Solomon sent to Huram the king of Tyre, saying, As you did deal with David my father, and did send him cedars to build him a house to dwell therein, even so deal with me.

4 Behold, I build a house to the name of the Becoming-One my God, to dedicate it to him, and to burn before him sweet incense, and for the continual showbread, and for the burnt offerings morning and evening, on the sabbaths, and on the new moons, and on the set times[117] of the Becoming-One our God. This is an ordinance for olam to Israel.

5 And the house which I build is great: for great is our God above all gods.

6 But who is able to build him a house, seeing the heavens and heavens of the heavens cannot contain him? who am I then, that I should build him a house, save only to burn sacrifice before him?

7 Send me now therefore a man cunning to work in gold, and in silver, and in brass, and in iron, and in purple, and crimson, and blue, and that can skill to grave with the cunning men that are with me in Judah and in Jerusalem, whom David my father did provide.

8 Send me also cedar trees, fir trees, and algum trees, out of Lebanon: for I know that your servants can skill to cut timber in Lebanon; and, behold, my servants shall be with your servants,

9 Even to prepare me timber in abundance: for the house which I am about to build shall be wonderfully great.

10 And, behold, I will give to your servants, the hewers that cut timber, twenty thousand measures of beaten wheat, and twenty thousand measures of barley, and twenty thousand baths of wine, and twenty thousand baths of oil.

11 Then Huram the king of Tyre answered in writing, which he sent to Solomon, Because the Becoming-One has loved his people, he has made you king over them.

12 Huram said moreover, Blessed be the Becoming-One, God of Israel, that made the heavens and earth, who has given to David the king a wise son, endued with prudence and understanding, that might build a house for the Becoming-One, and a house for his kingdom.

13 And now I have sent a cunning man, endued with understanding, of Huram my father's,

14 the son of a woman of the daughters of Dan, and whose father was a man of Tyre, experienced in working in gold, and in silver, in bronze, in iron, in

---

[117] Appointed times or festivals

stone, and in timber, in purple, in blue, and in byssus, and in crimson, and for doing any manner of engraving, and for inventing every device which shall be put to him, besides your skillful men, and the skillful men of my lord David your father

15 Now therefore the wheat, and the barley, the oil, and the wine, which my lord has spoken of, let him send unto his servants:

16 And we will cut wood out of Lebanon, as much as you shall need: and we will bring it to you in floats by sea to Joppa; and you shall carry it up to Jerusalem.

17 And Solomon numbered all the strangers that were in the land of Israel, after the numbering wherewith David his father had numbered them; and they were found a hundred and fifty thousand and three thousand and six hundred.

18 And he set threescore and ten thousand of them to be bearers of burdens, and fourscore thousand to be hewers in the mountain, and three thousand and six hundred overseers to set the people to work.

2 Chr 3:1 Then Solomon began to build the house of the Becoming-One at Jerusalem in mount Moriah, where He appeared unto David his father, in the place that David had prepared in the threshing floor of Ornan the Jebusite.

2 And he began to build in the second day of the second month, in the fourth year of his reign.

3 Now these are the things wherein Solomon was instructed for the building of the house of God. The length by cubits after the first measure was threescore cubits, and the breadth twenty cubits.

4 And the porch that was in the front of the house, the length of it was according to the breadth of the house, twenty cubits, and the height was a hundred and twenty: and he overlaid it within with pure gold.

5 And the greater house he ceiled with fir tree, which he overlaid with fine gold, and set thereon palm trees and chains.

6 And he garnished the house with precious stones for beauty: and the gold was gold of Parvaim.

7 He overlaid also the house, the beams, the posts, and the walls thereof, and the doors thereof, with gold; and graved cherubs on the walls.

8 And he made the most holy house, the length whereof was according to the breadth of the house, twenty cubits, and the breadth thereof twenty cubits: and he overlaid it with fine gold, amounting to six hundred talents.

9 And the weight of the nails was fifty shekels of gold. And he overlaid the upper chambers with gold.

10 And in the most holy house he made two cherubs of image work, and overlaid them with gold.

11 And the wings of the cherubs were twenty cubits long: one wing of the one cherub was five cubits, reaching to the wall of the house: and the other wing was likewise five cubits, reaching to the wing of the other cherub.

12 And one wing of the other cherub was five cubits, reaching to the wall of the house: and the other wing was five cubits also, joining to the wing of the other cherub.

13 The wings of these cherubs spread themselves forth twenty cubits: and they stood on their feet, and their faces were inward.

14 And he made the veil of blue, and purple, and crimson, and fine linen, and worked cherubs thereon.

15 Also he made before the house two pillars of thirty and five cubits high, and the capital that was on the top of each of them was five cubits.

16 And he made chains, as in the oracle, and put them on the heads of the pillars; and made a hundred pomegranates, and put them on the chains.

17 And he reared up the pillars before the temple, one on the right hand, and the other on the left; and called the name of that on the right hand Jachin, and the name of that on the left Boaz.

2 Chr 4:1 Moreover he made an altar of brass, twenty cubits the length thereof, and twenty cubits the breadth thereof, and ten cubits the height thereof.

2 Also he made a molten sea of ten cubits from brim to brim, round in compass, and five cubits the height thereof; and a line of thirty cubits did compass it round about.

3 And under it was the similitude of oxen, which did compass it round about: ten in a cubit, compassing the sea round about. Two rows of oxen were cast, when it was cast.

4 It stood upon twelve oxen, three looking toward the north, and three looking toward the west, and three looking toward the south, and three looking toward the east: and the sea was set above upon them, and all their back sides were towards the center.

5 And the thickness of it was a handbreadth, and the brim of it like the work of the brim of a cup, with flowers of lilies; and it received and held three thousand baths.

6 He made also ten lavers, and put five on the right hand, and five on the left, to wash in them: such things as they offered for the burnt offering they washed in them; but the sea was for the priests to wash in.

7 And he made ten candlesticks of gold according to their form, and set them in the temple, five on the right hand, and five on the left.

8 He made also ten tables, and placed them in the temple, five on the right side, and five on the left. And he made a hundred basins of gold.

9 Furthermore he made the court of the priests, and the great court, and doors for the court, and overlaid the doors of them with brass.

10 And he set the sea on the right side of the east end, over against the south.

11 And Huram made the pots, and the shovels, and the basins. And Huram finished the work that he was to make for king Solomon for the house of God;

12 To wit, the two pillars, and the pommels, and the capitals which were on the top of the two pillars, and the two wreaths to cover the two pommels of the capitals which were on the top of the pillars;

13 And four hundred pomegranates on the two wreaths; two rows of pomegranates on each wreath, to cover the two pommels of the capitals which were upon the pillars.

14 He made also bases, and lavers made he upon the bases;

15 One sea, and twelve oxen under it.

16 The pots also, and the shovels, and the fleshhooks, and all their instruments, did Huram his father make to king Solomon for the house of the Becoming-One of bright brass.

17 In the plain of Jordan did the king cast them, in the clay ground between Succoth and Zeredathah.

18 Thus Solomon made all these vessels in great abundance: for the weight of the brass could not be found out.

19 And Solomon made all the vessels that were for the house of God, the golden altar also, and the tables whereon the showbread was set;

20 Moreover the candlesticks with their lamps, that they should burn after the manner before the oracle, of pure gold;

21 And the flowers, and the lamps, and the tongs, made he of gold, and that perfect gold;

22 And the snuffers, and the basins, and the spoons, and the censers, of pure gold: and the entry of the house, the inner doors thereof for the most holy place, and the doors of the house of the temple, were of gold.

2 Chr 5:1 Thus all the work that Solomon made for the house of the Becoming-One was finished: and Solomon brought in all the things that David his father had dedicated; and the silver, and the gold, and all the instruments, put he among the treasures of the house of God.

2 Then Solomon assembled the elders of Israel, and all the heads of the tribes, the chief of the fathers of the children of Israel, unto Jerusalem, to bring up the ark of the covenant of the Becoming-One out of the city of David, which is Zion.

3 Therefore all the men of Israel assembled themselves unto the king in the feast which was in the seventh month.

4 And all the elders of Israel came; and the Levites took up the ark.

5 And they brought up the ark, and the tabernacle of the set time,[118] and all the holy vessels that were in the tabernacle, these did the priests and the Levites bring up.

6 Also king Solomon, and all the congregation of Israel that were assembled unto him before the ark, sacrificed sheep and oxen, which could not be told nor numbered for multitude.

7 And the priests brought in the ark of the covenant of the Becoming-One unto his place, to the oracle of the house, into the most holy place, even under the wings of the cherubs:

8 For the cherubs spread forth their wings over the place of the ark, and the cherubs covered the ark and the staves thereof above.

9 And they drew out the staves of the ark, that the ends of the staves were seen from the ark before the oracle; but they were not seen outside. And there it is unto this day.

10 There was nothing in the ark save the two tables which Moses put therein at Horeb, when the Becoming-One made a covenant with the children of Israel, when they came out of Egypt.

11 And it came to pass, when the priests were come out of the holy place: for all the priests that were present were sanctified, and did not then wait by course:

12 Also the Levites which were the singers, all of them of Asaph, of Heman, of Jeduthun, with their sons and their brethren, being arrayed in white linen, having cymbals and psalteries and harps, stood at the east end of the altar, and with them a hundred and twenty priests sounding with trumpets:

13 It came even to pass, as the trumpeters and singers were as one, to make one sound to be heard in praising and thanking the Becoming-One; and when they lifted up their voice with the trumpets and cymbals and instruments of music, and praised the Becoming-One, saying, Surely goodness, surely mercy for olam, then the house was filled with a cloud, even the house of the Becoming-One;

14 So that the priests could not stand to minister by reason of the cloud: for the glory of the Becoming-One had filled the house of God.

2 Chr 6:1 Then said Solomon, The Becoming-One has said that he would dwell in the thick darkness.

2 But I have built a house of habitation for you, and a place for your dwelling for olams.

3 And the king turned his face, and blessed the whole congregation of Israel: and all the congregation of Israel stood.

4 And he said, Blessed be the Becoming-One, God of Israel, who has with his hands fulfilled that which he spoke with his mouth to my father David, saying,

5 Since the day that I brought forth my people out of the land of Egypt I chose no city among all the tribes of Israel to build a house in, that my name might be there; neither chose I any man to be a ruler over my people Israel:

6 But I have chosen Jerusalem, that my name might be there; and have chosen David to be over my people Israel.

7 Now it was in the heart of David my father to build a house for the name of the Becoming-One, God of Israel.

8 But the Becoming-One said to David my father, Forasmuch as it was in your heart to build a house for my name, you did well in that it was in your heart:

9 Notwithstanding you shall not build the house; but your son which shall come forth out of your loins, he shall build the house for my name.

10 The Becoming-One therefore has performed his word that he has spoken: for I am risen up in the room of David my father, and am set on the throne of Israel, as the Becoming-One promised, and have built the house for the name of the Becoming-One, God of Israel.

11 And in it have I put the ark, wherein is the covenant of the Becoming-One, that he made with the children of Israel.

12 And he stood before the altar of the Becoming-One in the presence of all the congregation of Israel, and spread forth his hands:

13 For Solomon had made a brazen scaffold, of five cubits long, and five cubits broad, and three cubits high, and had set it in the midst of the court:

---

[118] Appointed time or festival

and upon it he stood, and kneeled down upon his knees before all the congregation of Israel, and spread forth his hands toward heaven,

14 And said, O Becoming-One, God of Israel, there is no God like you in the heaven, nor in the earth; which keep covenant, and show mercy unto your servants, that walk before you with all their hearts:

15 you which have kept with your servant David my father that which you have promised him; and spoke with your mouth, and have fulfilled it with your hand, as it is this day.

16 Now therefore, O Becoming-One, God of Israel, keep with your servant David my father that which you have promised him, saying, There shall not fail you a man in my sight to sit upon the throne of Israel; yet so that your children take heed to their way to walk in my law, as you have walked before me.

17 Now then, O Becoming-One, God of Israel, let your word be verified, which you have spoken unto your servant David.

18 But will God truly dwell with men on the earth? behold, the heavens and the heavens of the heavens cannot contain you; how much less this house which I have built!

19 Have respect therefore to the prayer of your servant, and to his supplication, O Becoming-One my God, to listen unto the cry and the prayer which your servant prays before you:

20 That your eyes may be open upon this house day and night, upon the place whereof you have said that you would put your name there; to listen unto the prayer which your servant prays toward this place.

21 listen therefore unto the supplications of your servant, and of your people Israel, which they shall make toward this place: hear you from your dwelling place, even from heaven; and when you hear, forgive.

22 If a man sin against his neighbor, and an oath be laid upon him to make him swear, and the oath come before your altar in this house;

23 Then hear you from heaven, and do, and judge your servants, by repaying the wicked, by recompensing his way upon his own head; and by justifying the righteous, by giving him according to his righteousness.

24 And if your people Israel be put to the worse before the enemy, because they have sinned against you; and shall return and confess your name, and pray and make supplication before you in this house;

25 Then hear you from the heavens, and forgive the sin of your people Israel, and bring them again unto the land which you gave to them and to their fathers.

26 When the heavens is shut up, and there is no rain, because they have sinned against you; yet if they pray toward this place, and confess your name, and turn from their sin, when you do afflict them;

27 Then hear you from heaven, and forgive the sin of your servants, and of your people Israel, when you have taught them the good way, wherein they should walk; and send rain upon your land, which you have given unto your people for an inheritance.

28 If there be dearth in the land, if there be pestilence, if there be blasting, or mildew, locusts, or caterpillars; if their enemies besiege them in the cities of their land; whatsoever sore or whatsoever sickness there be:

29 Then what prayer or what supplication soever shall be made of any man, or of all your people Israel, when every one shall know his own sore and his own grief, and shall spread forth his hands in this house:

30 Then hear you from the heavens your dwelling place, and forgive, and render unto every man according unto all his ways, whose heart you know; for you only know the hearts of the children of men:

31 That they may fear you, to walk in your ways, so long as they live in the land which you gave unto our fathers.

32 Moreover concerning the stranger, which is not of your people Israel, but is come from a far country for your great name's sake, and your mighty hand, and your stretched out arm; if they come and pray in this house;

33 Then hear you from the heavens, even from your dwelling place, and do according to all that the stranger calls to you for; that all people of the earth may know your name, and fear you, as does your people Israel, and may know that this house which I have built is called by your name.

34 If your people go out to war against their enemies by the way that you shall send them, and they pray unto you toward this city which you have chosen, and the house which I have built for your name;

35 Then hear you from the heavens their prayer and their supplication, and maintain their cause.

36 If they sin against you, for there is no man which sins not, and you be angry with them, and deliver them over before their enemies, and they carry them away captives unto a land far off or near;

37 Yet if they bethink themselves in the land to which they are carried captive, and turn and pray unto you in the land of their captivity, saying, We have sinned, we have done amiss, and have dealt wickedly;

38 If they return to you with all their heart and with all their soul in the land of their captivity, to which they have carried them captives, and pray toward their land, which you gave unto their fathers, and toward the city which you have chosen, and toward the house which I have built for your name:

39 Then hear you from the heavens, even from your dwelling place, their prayer and their supplications, and maintain their cause, and forgive your people which have sinned against you.

40 Now, my God, let, I beg you, your eyes be open, and let your ears be attent unto the prayer that is made in this place.

41 Now therefore arise, O Becoming-One God, into your resting place, you, and the ark of your strength: let your priests, O Becoming-One, God, be clothed with salvation, and let your saints rejoice in goodness.

42 O Becoming-One, God, turn not away the face of your anointed: remember the mercies of David your servant.

2 Chr 7:1 Now when Solomon had made an end of praying, the fire came down from heaven, and consumed the burnt offering and the sacrifices; and the glory of the Becoming-One filled the house.

2 And the priests could not enter into the house of the Becoming-One, because the glory of the Becoming-One had filled the Becoming-One's house.

3 And when all the children of Israel saw how the fire came down, and the glory of the Becoming-One upon the house, they bowed themselves with their faces to the ground upon the pavement, and worshiped, and praised the Becoming-One, saying, Surely goodness, surely mercy for olam.

4 Then the king and all the people offered sacrifices before the Becoming-One.

5 And king Solomon offered a sacrifice of twenty and two thousand of oxen, and a hundred and twenty thousand of sheep: so the king and all the people dedicated the house of God.

6 And the priests waited on their offices: the Levites also with instruments of music of the Becoming-One, which David the king had made to praise the Becoming-One, because his mercy endures for olam, when David praised by their ministry; and the priests sounded trumpets before them, and all Israel stood.

7 Moreover Solomon hallowed the middle of the court that was before the house of the Becoming-One: for there he offered burnt offerings, and the fat of the peace offerings, because the brazen altar which Solomon had made was not able to receive the burnt offerings, and the food offerings, and the fat.

8 Also at the same time Solomon kept the feast seven days, and all Israel with him, a very great congregation, from the entering in of Hamath unto the river of Egypt.

9 And in the eighth day they made a solemn assembly: for they kept the dedication of the altar seven days, and the feast seven days.

10 And on the three and twentieth day of the seventh month he sent the people away into their tents, glad and merry in heart for the goodness that the Becoming-One had showed unto David, and to Solomon, and to Israel his people.

11 Thus Solomon finished the house of the Becoming-One, and the king's house: and all that came into Solomon's heart to make in the house of the Becoming-One, and in his own house, he prosperously effected.

12 And the Becoming-One appeared to Solomon by night, and said unto him, I have heard your prayer, and have chosen this place to myself for a house of sacrifice.

13 If I shut up the heavens that there be no rain, or if I command the locusts to devour the land, or if I send pestilence among my people;

14 If my people, which are called by my name, shall humble themselves, and pray, and seek my face, and turn from their wicked ways; then will I hear from heaven, and will forgive their sin, and will heal their land.

15 Now mine eyes shall be open, and mine ears attend unto the prayer that is made in this place.

16 For now have I chosen and sanctified this house, that my name may be there for olam, and mine eyes and mine heart shall be there all the days.

17 And as for you, if you will walk before me, as David your father walked, and do according to all that I have commanded you, and shall observe my statutes and my judgments;

18 Then will I establish the throne of your kingdom, according as I have covenanted with David your father, saying, There shall not fail you a man to be ruler in Israel.

19 But if you turn away, and forsake my statutes and my commandments, which I have set before you, and shall go and serve other gods, and worship them;

20 Then will I pluck them up by the roots out of my land which I have given them; and this house, which I have sanctified for my name, will I cast out of my sight, and will make it to be a proverb and a byword among all nations.

21 And this house, which is high, shall be an astonishment to every one that passes by it; so that he shall say, Why has the Becoming-One done thus unto this land, and unto this house?

22 And it shall be answered, Because they forsook the Becoming-One, God of their fathers, which brought them forth out of the land of Egypt, and laid hold on other gods, and worshiped them, and served them: therefore has he brought all this evil upon them.

2 Chr 8:1 And it came to pass at the end of twenty years, wherein Solomon had built the house of the Becoming-One, and his own house,

2 That the cities which Huram had restored to Solomon, Solomon built them, and caused the children of Israel to dwell there.

3 And Solomon went to Hamathzobah, and prevailed against it.

4 And he built Tadmor in the wilderness, and all the store cities, which he built in Hamath.

5 Also he built Beth-horon the upper, and Beth-horon the nether, fenced cities, with walls, gates, and bars;

6 And Baalath, and all the store cities that Solomon had, and all the chariot cities, and the cities of the horsemen, and all that Solomon desired to build in Jerusalem, and in Lebanon, and throughout all the land of his dominion.

7 As for all the people that were left of the Hittites, and the Amorites, and the Perizzites, and the Hivites, and the Jebusites, which were not of Israel,

8 But of their children, who were left after them in the land, whom the children of Israel consumed not, them did Solomon make to pay tribute until this day.

9 But of the children of Israel did Solomon make no servants for his work; but they were men of war, and chief of his captains, and captains of his chariots and horsemen.

10 And these were the chief of king Solomon's officers, even two hundred and fifty, that bare rule over the people.

11 And Solomon brought up the daughter of Pharaoh out of the city of David unto the house that he had built for her: for he said, My wife shall not dwell in the house of David king of Israel, because the places are holy, whereunto the ark of the Becoming-One has come.

12 Then Solomon offered burnt offerings unto the Becoming-One on the altar of the Becoming-One, which he had built before the porch,

13 Even after a certain rate every day, offering according to the commandment of Moses, on the sabbaths, and on the new moons, and on the set times,[119] three times in the year, even in the feast of unleavened bread, and in the feast of weeks, and in the feast of tabernacles.

14 And he appointed, according to the order of David his father, the courses of the priests to their service, and the Levites to their charges, to praise and minister before the priests, as the duty of every day required: the gatekeepers also by their courses at every gate: for so had David the man of God commanded.

15 And they departed not from the commandment of the king unto the priests and Levites concerning any matter, or concerning the treasures.

16 Now all the work of Solomon was prepared unto the day of the foundation of the house of the Becoming-One, and until it was finished. So the house of the Becoming-One was finished.

17 Then went Solomon to Eziongeber, and to Eloth, at the sea side in the land of Edom.

18 And Huram sent him by the hands of his servants ships, and servants that had knowledge of the sea; and they went with the servants of Solomon to Ophir, and took there four hundred and fifty talents of gold, and brought them to king Solomon.

2 Chr 9:1 And when the queen of Sheba heard of the fame of Solomon, she came to prove Solomon with hard questions at Jerusalem, with a very great company, and camels that bare spices, and gold in abundance, and precious stones: and when she was come to Solomon, she communed with him of all that was in her heart.

2 And Solomon answered her all her questions: and there was nothing too hard for Solomon to answer her.

3 And when the queen of Sheba had seen the wisdom of Solomon, and the house that he had built,

4 And the food of his table, and the sitting of his servants, and the attendance of his ministers, and their apparel; his cupbearers also, and their apparel; and his ascent by which he went up into the house of the Becoming-One; there was no more spirit in her.

5 And she said to the king, It was a true report which I heard in mine own land of your acts, and of your wisdom:

6 Howbeit I believed not their words, until I came, and mine eyes had seen it: and, behold, the one half of the greatness of your wisdom was not told me: for you exceed the fame that I heard.

7 Happy are your men, and happy are these your servants, which stand continually before you, and hear your wisdom.

8 Blessed be the Becoming-One your God, which delighted in you to set you on his throne, to be king for the Becoming-One your God: because your God loved Israel, to establish them for olam, therefore made he you king over them, to do judgment and justice.

9 And she gave the king a hundred and twenty talents of gold, and of spices great abundance, and precious stones: neither was there any such spice as the queen of Sheba gave king Solomon.

10 And the servants also of Huram, and the servants of Solomon, which brought gold from Ophir, brought algum trees and precious stones.

11 And the king made of the algum trees terraces to the house of the Becoming-One, and to the king's palace, and harps and psalteries for singers: and there were none such seen before in the land of Judah.

12 And king Solomon gave to the queen of Sheba all her desire, whatsoever she asked, beside that which she had brought unto the king. So she turned, and went away to her own land, she and her servants.

13 Now the weight of gold that came to Solomon in one year was six hundred and threescore and six talents of gold;

14 Beside that which chapmen and merchants brought. And all the kings of Arabia and governors of the country brought gold and silver to Solomon.

15 And king Solomon made two hundred targets of beaten gold: six hundred shekels of beaten gold went to one target.

16 And three hundred shields made he of beaten gold: three hundred shekels of gold went to one shield. And the king put them in the house of the forest of Lebanon.

17 Moreover the king made a great throne of ivory, and overlaid it with pure gold.

18 And there were six steps to the throne, with a footstool of gold, which were fastened to the throne, and stays on each side of the sitting place, and two lions standing by the stays:

19 And twelve lions stood there on the one side and on the other upon the six steps. There was not the like made in any kingdom.

20 And all the drinking vessels of king Solomon were of gold, and all the vessels of the house of the forest of Lebanon were of pure gold: none were of silver; it was not anything accounted of in the days of Solomon.

21 For the king's ships went to Tarshish with the servants of Huram: every three years once came the ships of Tarshish bringing gold, and silver, ivory, and apes, and peacocks.

22 And king Solomon passed all the kings of the earth in riches and wisdom.

23 And all the kings of the earth sought the presence of Solomon, to hear his wisdom, that God had put in his heart.

24 And they brought every man his present, vessels of silver, and vessels of gold, and raiment, harness, and spices, horses, and mules, a rate year by year.

25 And Solomon had four thousand stalls for horses and chariots, and twelve thousand of horsemen; whom he bestowed in the chariot cities, and with the king at Jerusalem.

26 And he reigned over all the kings from the river even unto the land of the Philistines, and to the border of Egypt.

27 And the king made silver in Jerusalem as stones, and cedar trees made he as the sycamore trees that are in the low plains in abundance.

---

[119] Appointed times or festivals

28 And they brought unto Solomon horses out of Egypt, and out of all lands.

29 Now the rest of the acts of Solomon, first and last, are they not written in the book of Nathan the prophet, and in the prophecy of Ahijah the Shilonite, and in the visions of Iddo the seer against Jeroboam the son of Nebat?

30 And Solomon reigned in Jerusalem over all Israel forty years.

31 And Solomon slept with his fathers, and he was buried in the city of David his father: and Rehoboam his son reigned in his stead.

2 Chr 10:1 And Rehoboam went to Shechem: for to Shechem were all Israel come to make him king.

2 And it came to pass, when Jeroboam the son of Nebat, who was in Egypt, to which he had fled from the presence of Solomon the king, heard it, that Jeroboam returned out of Egypt.

3 And they sent and called him. So Jeroboam and all Israel came and spoke to Rehoboam, saying,

4 your father made our yoke grievous: now therefore ease you somewhat the grievous servitude of your father, and his heavy yoke that he put upon us, and we will serve you.

5 And he said unto them, Come again unto me after three days. And the people departed.

6 And king Rehoboam took counsel with the old men that had stood before Solomon his father while he yet lived, saying, What counsel give you me to return answer to this people?

7 And they spoke unto him, saying, If you be kind to this people, and please them, and speak good words to them, they will be your servants all the days.

8 But he forsook the counsel which the old men gave him, and took counsel with the young men that were brought up with him, that stood before him.

9 And he said unto them, What advice give you that we may return answer to this people, which have spoken to me, saying, Ease somewhat the yoke that your father did put upon us?

10 And the young men that were brought up with him spoke unto him, saying, Thus shall you answer the people that spoke unto you, saying, your father made our yoke heavy, but make you it somewhat lighter for us; thus shall you say unto them, My little finger shall be thicker than my father's loins.

11 For whereas my father put a heavy yoke upon you, I will put more to your yoke: my father chastised you with whips, but I will chastise you with scorpions.

12 So Jeroboam and all the people came to Rehoboam on the third day, as the king bade, saying, Come again to me on the third day.

13 And the king answered them roughly; and king Rehoboam forsook the counsel of the old men,

14 And answered them after the advice of the young men, saying, My father made your yoke heavy, but I will add thereto: my father chastised you with whips, but I will chastise you with scorpions.

15 So the king listened not unto the people: for the cause was of God, that the Becoming-One might perform his word, which he spoke by the hand of Ahijah the Shilonite to Jeroboam the son of Nebat.

16 And when all Israel saw that the king would not listen unto them, the people answered the king, saying, What portion have we in David? and we have none inheritance in the son of Jesse: every man to your tents, O Israel: and now, David, see to your own house. So all Israel went to their tents.

17 But as for the children of Israel that dwelt in the cities of Judah, Rehoboam reigned over them.

18 Then king Rehoboam sent Hadoram that was over the tribute; and the children of Israel stoned him with stones, that he died. But king Rehoboam made speed to get him up to his chariot, to flee to Jerusalem.

19 And Israel rebelled against the house of David unto this day.

2 Chr 11:1 And when Rehoboam was come to Jerusalem, he gathered of the house of Judah and Benjamin a hundred and fourscore thousand of chosen men, which were warriors, to fight against Israel, that he might bring the kingdom again to Rehoboam.

2 But the word of the Becoming-One came to Shemaiah the man of God, saying,

3 Speak unto Rehoboam the son of Solomon, king of Judah, and to all Israel in Judah and Benjamin, saying,

4 Thus says the Becoming-One, you shall not go up, nor fight against your brethren: return every man to his house: for this thing is done from me. And they obeyed the words of the Becoming-One, and returned from going against Jeroboam.

5 And Rehoboam dwelt in Jerusalem, and built cities for defense in Judah.

6 He built even Bethlehem, and Etam, and Tekoa,

7 And Beth-zur, and Shoco, and Adullam,

8 And Gath, and Mareshah, and Ziph,

9 And Adoraim, and Lachish, and Azekah,

10 And Zorah, and Aijalon, and Hebron, which are in Judah and in Benjamin fenced cities.

11 And he fortified the strong holds, and put captains in them, and store of victual, and of oil and wine.

12 And in every several city he put shields and spears, and made them exceeding strong, having Judah and Benjamin on his side.

13 And the priests and the Levites that were in all Israel resorted to him out of all their coasts.

14 For the Levites left their suburbs and their possession, and came to Judah and Jerusalem: for Jeroboam and his sons had cast them off from executing the priest's office unto the Becoming-One:

15 And he ordained him priests for the high places, and for the devils, and for the calves which he had made.

16 And after them out of all the tribes of Israel such as set their hearts to seek the Becoming-One, God of Israel came to Jerusalem, to sacrifice unto the Becoming-One, God of their fathers.

17 So they strengthened the kingdom of Judah, and made Rehoboam the son of Solomon strong, three years: for three years they walked in the way of David and Solomon.

18 And Rehoboam took him Mahalath the daughter of Jerimoth the son of David to wife, and Abihail the daughter of Eliab the son of Jesse;

19 Which bare him children; Jeush, and Shamariah, and Zaham.

20 And after her he took Maachah the daughter of Absalom; which bare him Abijah, and Attai, and Ziza, and Shelomith.

21 And Rehoboam loved Maachah the daughter of Absalom above all his wives and his concubines: for he took eighteen wives, and threescore concubines; and begat twenty and eight sons, and threescore daughters.

22 And Rehoboam made Abijah the son of Maachah the chief, to be ruler among his brethren: for he thought to make him king.

23 And he dealt wisely, and dispersed of all his children throughout all the countries of Judah and Benjamin, unto every fenced city: and he gave them victual in abundance. And he desired many wives.

2 Chr 12:1 And it came to pass, when Rehoboam had established the kingdom, and had strengthened himself, he forsook the law of the Becoming-One, and all Israel with him.

2 And it came to pass, that in the fifth year of king Rehoboam Shishak king of Egypt came up against Jerusalem, because they had transgressed against the Becoming-One,

3 With twelve hundred chariots, and threescore thousand of horsemen: and the people were without number that came with him out of Egypt; the Lubims, the Sukkiims, and the Ethiopians.

4 And he took the fenced cities which pertained to Judah, and came to Jerusalem.

5 Then came Shemaiah the prophet to Rehoboam, and to the princes of Judah, that were gathered together to Jerusalem because of Shishak, and said unto them, Thus says the Becoming-One, you have forsaken me, and therefore have I also left you in the hand of Shishak.

6 Whereupon the princes of Israel and the king humbled themselves; and they said, The Becoming-One is righteous.

7 And when the Becoming-One saw that they humbled themselves, the word of the Becoming-One came to Shemaiah, saying, They have humbled themselves; therefore I will not destroy them, but I will grant them some deliverance; and my wrath shall not be poured out upon Jerusalem by the hand of Shishak.

8 Nevertheless they shall be his servants; that they may know my service, and the service of the kingdoms of the countries.

9 So Shishak king of Egypt came up against Jerusalem, and took away the treasures of the house of the Becoming-One, and the treasures of the king's house; he took all: he carried away also the shields of gold which Solomon had made.

10 Instead of which king Rehoboam made shields of brass, and committed them to the hands of the chief of the guard, that kept the entrance of the king's house.

11 And when the king entered into the house of the Becoming-One, the guard came and fetched them, and brought them again into the guard chamber.

12 And when he humbled himself, the wrath of the Becoming-One turned from him, that he would not destroy him altogether: and also in Judah things went well.

13 So king Rehoboam strengthened himself in Jerusalem, and reigned: for Rehoboam was a son of one and forty years when he began to reign, and he reigned seventeen years in Jerusalem, the city which the Becoming-One had chosen out of all the tribes of Israel, to put his name there. And his mother's name was Naamah an Ammonitess.

14 And he did evil, because he prepared not his heart to seek the Becoming-One.

15 Now the acts of Rehoboam, first and last, are they not written in the book of Shemaiah the prophet, and of Iddo the seer concerning genealogies? And there were wars between Rehoboam and Jeroboam all the days.

16 And Rehoboam slept with his fathers, and was buried in the city of David: and Abijah his son reigned in his stead.

2 Chr 13:1 Now in the eighteenth year of king Jeroboam began Abijah to reign over Judah.

2 He reigned three years in Jerusalem. His mother's name also was Michaiah the daughter of Uriel of Gibeah. And there was war between Abijah and Jeroboam.

3 And Abijah set the battle in array with an army of valiant men of war, even four hundred thousand of chosen men: Jeroboam also set the battle in array against him with eight hundred thousand of chosen men, being mighty men of valor.

4 And Abijah stood up upon mount Zemaraim, which is in mount Ephraim, and said, Hear me, you Jeroboam, and all Israel;

5 Ought you not to know that the Becoming-One, God of Israel gave the kingdom over Israel to David for olam, even to him and to his sons by a covenant of salt?

6 Yet Jeroboam the son of Nebat, the servant of Solomon the son of David, is risen up, and has rebelled against his lords.

7 And there are gathered unto him vain men, the children of Belial, and have strengthened themselves against Rehoboam the son of Solomon, when Rehoboam was young and tenderhearted, and could not withstand them.

8 And now you think to withstand the kingdom of the Becoming-One in the hand of the sons of David; and you be a great multitude, and there are with you golden calves, which Jeroboam made you for gods.

9 Have you not cast out the priests of the Becoming-One, the sons of Aaron, and the Levites, and have made you priests after the manner of the nations of other lands? so that whosoever comes to consecrate himself with a young bullock and seven rams, the same may be a priest of them that are no gods.

10 But as for us, the Becoming-One is our God, and we have not forsaken him; and the priests, which minister unto the Becoming-One, are the sons of Aaron, and the Levites wait upon their business:

11 And they burn unto the Becoming-One every morning and every evening burnt sacrifices and sweet incense: the showbread also set they in order upon the pure table; and the candlestick of gold with the lamps thereof, to burn every evening: for we keep

the charge of the Becoming-One our God; but you have forsaken him.

12 And, behold, God himself is with us for our captain, and his priests with sounding trumpets to cry alarm against you. O children of Israel, fight you not against the Becoming-One, God of your fathers; for you shall not prosper.

13 But Jeroboam caused an ambushment to come about behind them: so they were before Judah, and the ambushment was behind them.

14 And when Judah looked back, behold, the battle was before and behind: and they cried unto the Becoming-One, and the priests sounded with the trumpets.

15 Then the men of Judah gave a shout: and as the men of Judah shouted, it came to pass, that God smote Jeroboam and all Israel before Abijah and Judah.

16 And the children of Israel fled before Judah: and God delivered them into their hand.

17 And Abijah and his people killed them with a great slaughter: so there fell down slain of Israel five hundred thousand of chosen men.

18 Thus the children of Israel were brought under at that time, and the children of Judah prevailed, because they relied upon the Becoming-One, God of their fathers.

19 And Abijah pursued after Jeroboam, and took cities from him, Bethel with the towns thereof, and Jeshanah with the towns thereof, and Ephrain with the towns thereof.

20 Neither did Jeroboam recover strength again in the days of Abijah: and the Becoming-One struck him, and he died.

21 But Abijah grew mighty, and married fourteen wives, and begat twenty and two sons, and sixteen daughters.

22 And the rest of the acts of Abijah, and his ways, and his sayings, are written in the story of the prophet Iddo.

2 Chr 14:1 So Abijah slept with his fathers, and they buried him in the city of David: and Asa his son reigned in his stead. In his days the land was quiet ten years.

2 And Asa did that which was good and right in the eyes of the Becoming-One his God:

3 For he took away the altars of the strange gods, and the high places, and brake down the images, and cut down the Asherahs:

4 And commanded Judah to seek the Becoming-One, God of their fathers, and to do the law and the commandment.

5 Also he took away out of all the cities of Judah the high places and the images: and the kingdom was quiet before him.

6 And he built fenced cities in Judah: for the land had rest, and he had no war in those years; because the Becoming-One had given him rest.

7 Therefore he said unto Judah, Let us build these cities, and make about them walls, and towers, gates, and bars, while the land is yet before us; because we have sought the Becoming-One our God, we have sought him, and he has given us rest on every side. So they built and prospered.

8 And Asa had an army of men that bare targets and spears, out of Judah three hundred thousand; and out of Benjamin, that bare shields and drew bows, two hundred and fourscore thousand: all these were mighty men of valor.

9 And there came out against them Zerah the Ethiopian with a host of a thousand thousand, and three hundred chariots; and came unto Mareshah.

10 Then Asa went out against him, and they set the battle in array in the valley of Zephathah at Mareshah.

11 And Asa cried unto the Becoming-One his God, and said, Becoming-One, it is nothing with you to help, whether with many, or with them that have no power: help us, O Becoming-One our God; for we rest on you, and in your name we go against this multitude. O Becoming-One, you are our God; let not man prevail against you.

12 So the Becoming-One smote the Ethiopians before Asa, and before Judah; and the Ethiopians fled.

13 And Asa and the people that were with him pursued them unto Gerar: and the Ethiopians were overthrown, that they could not recover themselves; for they were destroyed before the Becoming-One, and before his host; and they carried away very much spoil.

14 And they smote all the cities round about Gerar; for the fear of the Becoming-One came upon them: and they spoiled all the cities; for there was exceeding much spoil in them.

15 They smote also the tents of cattle, and carried away sheep and camels in abundance, and returned to Jerusalem.

2 Chr 15:1 And the Spirit of God came upon Azariah the son of Oded:

2 And he went out to meet Asa, and said unto him, Hear you me, Asa, and all Judah and Benjamin; The Becoming-One is with you, while you be with him; and if you seek him, he will be found of you; but if you forsake him, he will forsake you.

3 Now for a long season Israel has been without the true God, and without a teaching priest, and without law.

4 But when they in their trouble did turn unto the Becoming-One, God of Israel, and sought him, he was found of them.

5 And in those times there was no peace to him that went out, nor to him that came in, but great vexations were upon all the inhabitants of the countries.

6 And nation was destroyed of nation, and city of city: for God did vex them with all adversity.

7 Be you strong therefore, and let not your hands be weak: for your work shall be rewarded.

8 And when Asa heard these words, and the prophecy of Oded the prophet, he took courage, and put away the abominable idols out of all the land of Judah and Benjamin, and out of the cities which he had taken from mount Ephraim, and renewed the altar of the Becoming-One, that was before the porch of the Becoming-One.

9 And he gathered all Judah and Benjamin, and the strangers with them out of Ephraim and Manasseh, and out of Simeon: for they fell to him out

of Israel in abundance, when they saw that the Becoming-One his God was with him.

10 So they gathered themselves together at Jerusalem in the third month, in the fifteenth year of the reign of Asa.

11 And they offered unto the Becoming-One the same time, of the spoil which they had brought, seven hundred oxen and seven thousand of sheep.

12 And they entered into a covenant to seek the Becoming-One, God of their fathers with all their heart and with all their soul;

13 That whosoever would not seek the Becoming-One, God of Israel should be put to death, whether small or great, whether man or woman.

14 And they swore unto the Becoming-One with a loud voice, and with shouting, and with trumpets, and with cornets.

15 And all Judah rejoiced at the oath: for they had sworn with all their heart, and sought him with their whole desire; and he was found of them: and the Becoming-One gave them rest round about.

16 And also concerning Maachah the mother of Asa the king, he removed her from being queen, because she had made for Asherah a horrible idol: and Asa cut down her idol, and stamped it, and burnt it at the brook Kidron.

17 But the high places were not taken away out of Israel: nevertheless the heart of Asa was perfect all his days.

18 And he brought into the house of God the things that his father had dedicated, and that he himself had dedicated, silver, and gold, and vessels.

19 And there was no more war unto the five and thirtieth year of the reign of Asa.

2 Chr 16:1 In the six and thirtieth year of the reign of Asa Baasha king of Israel came up against Judah, and built Ramah, to the intent that he might let none go out or come in to Asa king of Judah.

2 Then Asa brought out silver and gold out of the treasures of the house of the Becoming-One and of the king's house, and sent to Benhadad king of Syria, that dwelt at Damascus, saying,

3 There is a league between me and you, as there was between my father and your father: behold, I have sent you silver and gold; go, break your league with Baasha king of Israel, that he may depart from me.

4 And Benhadad listened unto king Asa, and sent the captains of his armies against the cities of Israel; and they smote Ijon, and Dan, and Able-maim, and all the store cities of Naphtali.

5 And it came to pass, when Baasha heard it, that he left off building of Ramah, and let his work cease.

6 Then Asa the king took all Judah; and they carried away the stones of Ramah, and the timber thereof, wherewith Baasha was building; and he built therewith Geba and Mizpah.

7 And at that time Hanani the seer came to Asa king of Judah, and said unto him, Because you have relied on the king of Syria, and not relied on the Becoming-One your God, therefore is the host of the king of Syria escaped out of your hand.

8 Were not the Ethiopians and the Lubims a huge host, with very many chariots and horsemen? yet, because you did rely on the Becoming-One, he delivered them into your hand.

9 For the eyes of the Becoming-One run back and forth throughout the whole earth, to show himself strong in the behalf of them whose heart is perfect toward him. Herein you have done foolishly: therefore from henceforth you shall have wars.

10 Then Asa was angry with the seer, and put him in a prison house; for he was in a rage with him because of this thing. And Asa oppressed some of the people the same time.

11 And, behold, the acts of Asa, first and last, lo, they are written in the book of the kings of Judah and Israel.

12 And Asa in the thirty and ninth year of his reign was diseased in his feet, until his disease was exceeding great: yet in his disease he sought not to the Becoming-One, but to the physicians.

13 And Asa slept with his fathers, and died in the one and fortieth year of his reign.

14 And they buried him in his own tombs, which he had made for himself in the city of David, and laid him in the bed which was filled with sweet odors and diverse kinds of spices prepared by the apothecaries' art: and they made a very great burning for him.

2 Chr 17:1 And Jehoshaphat his son reigned in his stead, and strengthened himself against Israel.

2 And he placed forces in all the fenced cities of Judah, and set garrisons in the land of Judah, and in the cities of Ephraim, which Asa his father had taken.

3 And the Becoming-One was with Jehoshaphat, because he walked in the first ways of his father David, and sought not unto the lords [baalim]

4 But sought to the Becoming-One, God of his father, and walked in his commandments, and not after the doings of Israel.

5 Therefore the Becoming-One established the kingdom in his hand; and all Judah brought to Jehoshaphat presents; and he had riches and honor in abundance.

6 And his heart was lifted up in the ways of the Becoming-One: moreover he took away the high places and Asherahs out of Judah.

7 Also in the third year of his reign he sent to his princes, even to Benhail, and to Obadiah, and to Zechariah, and to Nethaneel, and to Michaiah, to teach in the cities of Judah.

8 And with them he sent Levites, even Shemaiah, and Nethaniah, and Zebadiah, and Asahel, and Shemiramoth, and Jehonathan, and Adonijah, and Tobijah, and Tobadonijah, Levites; and with them Elishama and Jehoram, priests.

9 And they taught in Judah, and had the book of the law of the Becoming-One with them, and went about throughout all the cities of Judah, and taught the people.

10 And the fear of the Becoming-One fell upon all the kingdoms of the lands that were round about Judah, so that they made no war against Jehoshaphat.

11 Also some of the Philistines brought Jehoshaphat presents, and tribute silver; and the Arabians brought him flocks, seven thousand and seven hundred rams, and seven thousand and seven hundred he goats.

12 And Jehoshaphat grew great exceedingly; and he built in Judah castles, and cities of store.

13 And he had much business in the cities of Judah: and the men of war, mighty men of valor, were in Jerusalem.

14 And these are the numbers of them according to the house of their fathers: Of Judah, the captains of thousands; Adnah the chief, and with him mighty men of valor three hundred thousand.

15 And next to him was Jehohanan the captain, and with him two hundred and fourscore thousand.

16 And next him was Amasiah the son of Zichri, who willingly offered himself unto the Becoming-One; and with him two hundred thousand of mighty men of valor.

17 And of Benjamin; Eliada a mighty man of valor, and with him armed men with bow and shield two hundred thousand.

18 And next him was Jehozabad, and with him a hundred and fourscore thousand ready prepared for the war.

19 These waited on the king, beside those whom the king put in the fenced cities throughout all Judah.

2 Chr 18:1 Now Jehoshaphat had riches and honor in abundance, and joined affinity with Ahab.

2 And at the end of years he went down to Ahab to Samaria. And Ahab killed sheep and oxen for him in abundance, and for the people that he had with him, and persuaded him to go up with him to Ramothgilead.

3 And Ahab king of Israel said unto Jehoshaphat king of Judah, will you go with me to Ramothgilead? And he answered him, I am as you are, and my people as your people; and we will be with you in the war.

4 And Jehoshaphat said unto the king of Israel, Inquire, I pray you, at the word of the Becoming-One today.

5 Therefore the king of Israel gathered together of prophets four hundred men, and said unto them, Shall we go to Ramothgilead to battle, or shall I forbear? And they said, Go up; for God will deliver it into the king's hand.

6 But Jehoshaphat said, Is there not here a prophet of the Becoming-One besides, that we might inquire of him?

7 And the king of Israel said unto Jehoshaphat, There is yet one man, by whom we may inquire of the Becoming-One: but I hate him; for he never prophesied good unto me, but all his days evil: the same is Micaiah the son of Imla. And Jehoshaphat said, Let not the king say so.

8 And the king of Israel called for one of his eunuchs, and said, Fetch quickly Micaiah the son of Imla.

9 And the king of Israel and Jehoshaphat king of Judah sat either of them on his throne, clothed in their robes, and they sat in a void place at the entering in of the gate of Samaria; and all the prophets prophesied before them.

10 And Zedekiah the son of Chenaanah had made him horns of iron, and said, Thus says the Becoming-One, With these you shall push Syria until they be consumed.

11 And all the prophets prophesied so, saying, Go up to Ramothgilead, and prosper: for the Becoming-One shall deliver it into the hand of the king.

12 And the messenger that went to call Micaiah spoke to him, saying, Behold, the words of the prophets declare good to the king with one assent; let your word therefore, I pray you, be like one of theirs, and speak you good.

13 And Micaiah said, As the Becoming-One lives, even what my God says, that will I speak.

14 And when he was come to the king, the king said unto him, Micaiah, shall we go to Ramothgilead to battle, or shall I forbear? And he said, Go you up, and prosper, and they shall be delivered into your hand.

15 And the king said to him, How many times shall I adjure you that you say nothing but the truth to me in the name of the Becoming-One?

16 Then he said, I did see all Israel scattered upon the mountains, as sheep that have no shepherd: and the Becoming-One said, These have no master; let them return therefore every man to his house in peace.

17 And the king of Israel said to Jehoshaphat, Did I not tell you that he would not prophesy good unto me, but evil?

18 Again he said, Therefore hear the word of the Becoming-One; I saw the Becoming-One sitting upon his throne, and all the host of the heavens standing on his right hand and on his left.

19 And the Becoming-One said, Who shall entice Ahab king of Israel, that he may go up and fall at Ramothgilead? And one spoke saying after this manner, and another saying after that manner.

20 Then there came out a spirit, and stood before the Becoming-One, and said, I will entice him. And the Becoming-One said unto him, Wherewith?

21 And he said, I will go out, and be a lying spirit in the mouth of all his prophets. And the Becoming-One said, you shall entice him, and you shall also prevail: go out, and do even so.

22 Now therefore, behold, the Becoming-One has put a lying spirit in the mouth of these your prophets, and the Becoming-One has spoken evil against you.

23 Then Zedekiah the son of Chenaanah came near, and smote Micaiah upon the cheek, and said, Which way went the Spirit of the Becoming-One from me to speak unto you?

24 And Micaiah said, Behold, you shall see on that day when you shall go into an inner chamber to hide thyself.

25 Then the king of Israel said, Take you Micaiah, and carry him back to Amon the governor of the city, and to Joash the king's son;

26 And say, Thus says the king, Put this fellow in the prison, and feed him with bread of affliction and with water of affliction, until I return in peace.

27 And Micaiah said, If you certainly return in peace, then has not the Becoming-One spoken by me. And he said, listen, all you people.

28 So the king of Israel and Jehoshaphat the king of Judah went up to Ramothgilead.

29 And the king of Israel said unto Jehoshaphat, I will disguise myself, and will go to the battle; but put you on your robes. So the king of Israel disguised himself; and they went to the battle.

30 Now the king of Syria had commanded the captains of the chariots that were with him, saying, Fight you not with small or great, save only with the king of Israel.

31 And it came to pass, when the captains of the chariots saw Jehoshaphat, that they said, It is the king of Israel. Therefore they compassed about him to fight: but Jehoshaphat cried out, and the Becoming-One helped him; and God moved them to depart from him.

32 For it came to pass, that, when the captains of the chariots perceived that it was not the king of Israel, they turned back again from pursuing him.

33 And a certain man drew a bow at a venture, and smote the king of Israel between the joints of the harness: therefore he said to his chariot man, Turn your hand, that you may carry me out of the host; for I am wounded.

34 And the battle increased that day: howbeit the king of Israel stayed himself up in his chariot against the Syrians until the evening: and about the time of the sun going down he died.

2 Chr 19:1 And Jehoshaphat the king of Judah returned to his house in peace to Jerusalem.

2 And Jehu the son of Hanani the seer went out to meet him, and said to king Jehoshaphat, should you help the ungodly, and love them that hate the Becoming-One? therefore is wrath upon you from before the Becoming-One.

3 Nevertheless there are good things found in you, in that you have taken away the Asherahs out of the land, and have prepared your heart to seek God.

4 And Jehoshaphat dwelt at Jerusalem: and he went out again through the people from Beersheba to mount Ephraim, and brought them back unto the Becoming-One, God of their fathers.

5 And he set judges in the land throughout all the fenced cities of Judah, city by city,

6 And said to the judges, Take heed what you do: for you judge not for man, but for the Becoming-One, who is with you in the judgment.

7 Therefore now let the fear of the Becoming-One be upon you; take heed and do it: for there is no iniquity with the Becoming-One our God, nor respect of persons, nor taking of gifts.

8 Moreover in Jerusalem did Jehoshaphat set of the Levites, and of the priests, and of the chief of the fathers of Israel, for the judgment of the Becoming-One, and for controversies, when they returned to Jerusalem.

9 And he charged them, saying, Thus shall you do in the fear of the Becoming-One, faithfully, and with a perfect heart.

10 And what cause soever shall come to you of your brethren that dwell in their cities, between blood and blood, between law and commandment, statutes and judgments, you shall even warn them that they trespass not against the Becoming-One, and so wrath come upon you, and upon your brethren: this do, and you shall not trespass.

11 And, behold, Amariah the chief priest is over you in all matters of the Becoming-One; and Zebadiah the son of Ishmael, the ruler of the house of Judah, for all the king's matters: also the Levites shall be officers before you. Deal courageously, and the Becoming-One shall be with the good.

2 Chr 20:1 It came to pass after this also, that the children of Moab, and the children of Ammon, and with them other beside the Ammonites, came against Jehoshaphat to battle.

2 Then there came some that told Jehoshaphat, saying, There comes a great multitude against you from over the sea from Syria [Aram] and, behold, they be in Hazazontamar, which is Engedi.

3 And Jehoshaphat feared, and set himself to seek the Becoming-One, and proclaimed a fast throughout all Judah.

4 And Judah gathered themselves together, to ask help of the Becoming-One: even out of all the cities of Judah they came to seek the Becoming-One.

5 And Jehoshaphat stood in the congregation of Judah and Jerusalem, in the house of the Becoming-One, before the new court,

6 And said, O Becoming-One, God of our fathers, are not you God in heaven? and rule not you over all the kingdoms of the nations? and in your hand is there not power and might, so that none is able to withstand you?

7 Are not you our God, who did drive out the inhabitants of this land before your people Israel, and gave it to the seed of Abraham your friend for olam.

8 And they dwelt therein, and have built you a sanctuary therein for your name, saying,

9 If, when evil comes upon us, as the sword, judgment, or pestilence, or famine, we stand before this house, and in your presence, for your name is in this house, and cry unto you in our affliction, then you will hear and help.

10 And now, behold, the children of Ammon and Moab and mount Seir, whom you would not let Israel invade, when they came out of the land of Egypt, but they turned from them, and destroyed them not;

11 Behold, I say, how they reward us, to come to cast us out of your possession, which you have given us to inherit.

12 O our God, will you not judge them? for we have no might against this great company that comes against us; neither know we what to do: but our eyes are upon you.

13 And all Judah stood before the Becoming-One, with their little ones, their wives, and their children.

14 Then upon Jahaziel the son of Zechariah, the son of Benaiah, the son of Jeiel, the son of Mattaniah, a Levite of the sons of Asaph, came the Spirit of the Becoming-One in the midst of the congregation;

15 And he said, listen ye, all Judah, and you inhabitants of Jerusalem, and you king Jehoshaphat, Thus says the Becoming-One unto you, Be not afraid nor dismayed by reason of this great multitude; for the battle is not yours, but God.'

16 tomorrow go you down against them: behold, they come up by the cliff of Ziz; and you shall find them at the end of the brook, before the wilderness of Jeruel.

17 You shall not need to fight in this battle: set yourselves, stand you still, and see the salvation of the Becoming-One with you, O Judah and Jerusalem: fear not, nor be dismayed; tomorrow go out against them: for the Becoming-One will be with you.

18 And Jehoshaphat bowed his head with his face to the ground: and all Judah and the inhabitants of Jerusalem fell before the Becoming-One, worshipping the Becoming-One.

19 And the Levites, of the children of the Kohathites, and of the children of the Korhites, stood up to praise the Becoming-One, God of Israel with a loud voice on high.

20 And they rose early in the morning, and went forth into the wilderness of Tekoa: and as they went forth, Jehoshaphat stood and said, Hear me, O Judah, and you inhabitants of Jerusalem; Believe in the Becoming-One your God, so shall you be established; believe his prophets, so shall you prosper.

21 And when he had consulted with the people, he appointed singers unto the Becoming-One, and that should praise the beauty of holiness, as they went out before the army, and to say, Praise the Becoming-One; for his mercy endures for olam.

22 And when they began to sing and to praise, the Becoming-One set ambushments against the children of Ammon, Moab, and mount Seir, which were come against Judah; and they were struck.

23 For the children of Ammon and Moab stood up against the inhabitants of mount Seir, utterly to slay and destroy them: and when they had made an end of the inhabitants of Seir, every one helped to destroy another.

24 And when Judah came toward the watch tower in the wilderness, they looked unto the multitude, and, behold, they were dead bodies fallen to the earth, and none escaped.

25 And when Jehoshaphat and his people came to take away the spoil of them, they found among them in abundance both riches with the dead bodies, and precious jewels, which they stripped off for themselves, more than they could carry away: and they were three days in gathering of the spoil, it was so much.

26 And on the fourth day they assembled themselves in the valley of Berachah; for there they blessed the Becoming-One: therefore the name of the same place was called, The valley of Berachah, unto this day.

27 Then they returned, every man of Judah and Jerusalem, and Jehoshaphat in the forefront of them, to go again to Jerusalem with joy; for the Becoming-One had made them to rejoice over their enemies.

28 And they came to Jerusalem with psalteries and harps and trumpets unto the house of the Becoming-One.

29 And the fear of God was on all the kingdoms of those countries, when they had heard that the Becoming-One fought against the enemies of Israel.

30 So the realm of Jehoshaphat was quiet: for his God gave him rest round about.

31 And Jehoshaphat reigned over Judah: he was a son of thirty and five years when he began to reign, and he reigned twenty and five years in Jerusalem. And his mother's name was Azubah the daughter of Shilhi.

32 And he walked in the way of Asa his father, and departed not from it, doing that which was right in the sight of the Becoming-One.

33 Howbeit the high places were not taken away: for as yet the people had not prepared their hearts unto God of their fathers.

34 Now the rest of the acts of Jehoshaphat, first and last, behold, they are written in the book of Jehu the son of Hanani, who is mentioned in the book of the kings of Israel.

35 And after this did Jehoshaphat king of Judah join himself with Ahaziah king of Israel, who did very wickedly:

36 And he joined himself with him to make ships to go to Tarshish: and they made the ships in Eziongaber.

37 Then Eliezer the son of Dodavah of Mareshah prophesied against Jehoshaphat, saying, Because you have joined yourself with Ahaziah, the Becoming-One has broken your works. And the ships were broken, that they were not able to go to Tarshish.

2 Chr 21:1 Now Jehoshaphat slept with his fathers, and was buried with his fathers in the city of David. And Jehoram his son reigned in his stead.

2 And he had brethren the sons of Jehoshaphat, Azariah, and Jehiel, and Zechariah, and Azariah, and Michael, and Shephatiah: all these were the sons of Jehoshaphat king of Israel.

3 And their father gave them great gifts of silver, and of gold, and of precious things, with fenced cities in Judah: but the kingdom gave he to Jehoram; because he was the firstborn.

4 Now when Jehoram was risen up to the kingdom of his father, he strengthened himself, and killed all his brethren with the sword, and divers also of the princes of Israel.

5 Jehoram was a son of thirty and two years when he began to reign, and he reigned eight years in Jerusalem.

6 And he walked in the way of the kings of Israel, like as did the house of Ahab: for he had the daughter of Ahab to wife: and he worked that which was evil in the eyes of the Becoming-One.

7 Howbeit the Becoming-One would not destroy the house of David, because of the covenant that he had made with David, and as he promised to give a light to him and to his sons all the days.

8 In his days the Edomites revolted from under the dominion of Judah, and made themselves a king.

9 Then Jehoram went forth with his princes, and all his chariots with him: and he rose up by night, and smote the Edomites which compassed him in, and the captains of the chariots.

10 So the Edomites revolted from under the hand of Judah unto this day. The same time also did Libnah revolt from under his hand; because he had forsaken the Becoming-One, God of his fathers.

11 Moreover he made high places in the mountains of Judah, and caused the inhabitants of Jerusalem to commit fornication, and compelled Judah thereto.

12 And there came a writing to him from Elijah the prophet, saying, Thus says the Becoming-One, God of David your father, Because you have not walked in the ways of Jehoshaphat your father, nor in the ways of Asa king of Judah,

13 But have walked in the way of the kings of Israel, and have made Judah and the inhabitants of

Jerusalem to go a whoring, like to the whoredoms of the house of Ahab, and also have slain your brethren of your father's house, which were better than thyself:

14 Behold, with a great plague will the Becoming-One smite your people, and your children, and your wives, and all your goods:

15 And you shall have great sickness by disease of your bowels, until your bowels fall out by reason of the sickness day by day.

16 Moreover the Becoming-One stirred up against Jehoram the spirit of the Philistines, and of the Arabians, that were near the Ethiopians:

17 And they came up into Judah, and brake into it, and carried away all the substance that was found in the king's house, and his sons also, and his wives; so that there was never a son left him, save Jehoahaz, the youngest of his sons.

18 And after all this the Becoming-One smote him in his bowels with an incurable disease.

19 And it was days after days that in process of time, after the end of days, two [years] his bowels fell out by reason of his sickness: so he died of great diseases. And his people made no burning for him, like the burning of his fathers.

20 A son of thirty and two years was he when he began to reign, and he reigned in Jerusalem eight years, and departed without being desired. Howbeit they buried him in the city of David, but not in the tombs of the kings.

2 Chr 22:1 And the inhabitants of Jerusalem made Ahaziah his youngest son king in his stead: for the band of men that came with the Arabians to the camp had slain all the eldest. So Ahaziah the son of Jehoram king of Judah reigned.

2 A son of forty and two years was Ahaziah when he began to reign, and he reigned one year in Jerusalem. His mother's name also was Athaliah the daughter of Omri.

3 He also walked in the ways of the house of Ahab: for his mother was his counselor to do wickedly.

4 Therefore he did evil in the sight of the Becoming-One like the house of Ahab: for they were his councelors after the death of his father to his destruction.

5 He walked also after their counsel, and went with Jehoram the son of Ahab king of Israel to war against Hazael king of Syria at Ramothgilead: and the Syrians smote Joram.

6 And he returned to be healed in Jezreel because of the wounds which were given him at Ramah, when he fought with Hazael king of Syria. And Azariah the son of Jehoram king of Judah went down to see Jehoram the son of Ahab at Jezreel, because he was sick.

7 And the destruction of Ahaziah was from God by coming to Joram: for when he was come, he went out with Jehoram against Jehu the son of Nimshi, whom the Becoming-One had anointed to cut off the house of Ahab.

8 And it came to pass, that, when Jehu was executing judgment upon the house of Ahab, and found the princes of Judah, and the sons of the brethren of Ahaziah, that ministered to Ahaziah, he killed them.

9 And he sought Ahaziah: and they caught him, for he was hid in Samaria, and brought him to Jehu: and when they had slain him, they buried him: Because, said they, he is the son of Jehoshaphat, who sought the Becoming-One with all his heart. So the house of Ahaziah had no power to keep still the kingdom.

10 But when Athaliah the mother of Ahaziah saw that her son was dead, she arose and destroyed all the seed royal of the house of Judah.

11 But Jehoshabeath, the daughter of the king, took Joash the son of Ahaziah, and stole him from among the king's sons that were slain, and put him and his nurse in a bedchamber. So Jehoshabeath, the daughter of king Jehoram, the wife of Jehoiada the priest, for she was the sister of Ahaziah, hid him from Athaliah, so that she killed him not.

12 And he was with them hid in the house of God six years: and Athaliah reigned over the land.

2 Chr 23:1 And in the seventh year Jehoiada strengthened himself, and took the captains of hundreds, Azariah the son of Jeroham, and Ishmael the son of Jehohanan, and Azariah the son of Obed, and Maaseiah the son of Adaiah, and Elishaphat the son of Zichri, into covenant with him.

2 And they went about in Judah, and gathered the Levites out of all the cities of Judah, and the chief of the fathers of Israel, and they came to Jerusalem.

3 And all the congregation made a covenant with the king in the house of God. And he said unto them, Behold, the king's son shall reign, as the Becoming-One has said of the sons of David.

4 This is the thing that you shall do; A third part of you entering on the Sabbath, of the priests and of the Levites, shall be gatekeepers of the doors;

5 And a third part shall be at the king's house; and a third part at the gate of the foundation: and all the people shall be in the courts of the house of the Becoming-One.

6 But let none come into the house of the Becoming-One, save the priests, and they that minister of the Levites; they shall go in, for they are holy: but all the people shall keep the watch of the Becoming-One.

7 And the Levites shall compass the king round about, every man with his weapons in his hand; and whosoever else comes into the house, he shall be put to death: but be you with the king when he comes in, and when he goes out.

8 So the Levites and all Judah did according to all things that Jehoiada the priest had commanded, and took every man his men that were to come in on the Sabbath, with them that were to go out on the Sabbath: for Jehoiada the priest dismissed not the courses.

9 Moreover Jehoiada the priest delivered to the captains of hundreds spears, and bucklers, and shields, that had been king David's, which were in the house of God.

10 And he set all the people, every man having his weapon in his hand, from the right side of the temple to the left side of the temple, along by the altar and the temple, by the king round about.

11 Then they brought out the king's son, and put upon him the crown, and gave him the testimony, and made him king. And Jehoiada and his sons anointed him, and said, Let the king live.

12 Now when Athaliah heard the noise of the people running and praising the king, she came to the people into the house of the Becoming-One: 13 And she looked, and, behold, the king stood at his pillar at the entering in, and the princes and the trumpets by the king: and all the people of the land rejoiced, and sounded with trumpets, also the singers with instruments of music, and such as taught to sing praise. Then Athaliah ripped her clothes, and said, Treason, Treason.

14 Then Jehoiada the priest brought out the captains of hundreds that were set over the host, and said unto them, Have her forth of the ranges: and whoso follows her, let him be slain with the sword. For the priest said, Slay her not in the house of the Becoming-One.

15 So they laid hands on her; and when she was come to the entering of the horse gate by the king's house, they killed her there.

16 And Jehoiada made a covenant between him, and between all the people, and between the king, that they should be the Becoming-One's people.

17 Then all the people went to the house of the lord [baal] and brake it down, and brake his altars and his images in pieces, and killed Mattan the priest of the lord [baal] before the altars.

18 Also Jehoiada appointed the offices of the house of the Becoming-One by the hand of the priests the Levites, whom David had distributed in the house of the Becoming-One, to offer the burnt offerings of the Becoming-One, as it is written in the law of Moses, with rejoicing and with singing, as it was ordained by David.

19 And he set the gatekeepers at the gates of the house of the Becoming-One, that none which was unclean in anything should enter in.

20 And he took the captains of hundreds, and the nobles, and the governors of the people, and all the people of the land, and brought down the king from the house of the Becoming-One: and they came through the high gate into the king's house, and set the king upon the throne of the kingdom.

21 And all the people of the land rejoiced: and the city was quiet, after that they had slain Athaliah with the sword.

2 Chr 24:1 Joash was a son of seven years when he began to reign, and he reigned forty years in Jerusalem. His mother's name also was Zibiah of Beersheba.

2 And Joash did that which was right in the sight of the Becoming-One all the days of Jehoiada the priest.

3 And Jehoiada took for him two wives; and he begat sons and daughters.

4 And it came to pass after this, that Joash was minded to repair the house of the Becoming-One.

5 And he gathered together the priests and the Levites, and said to them, Go out unto the cities of Judah, and gather of all Israel money to repair the house of your God from year to year, and see that you hasten the matter. Howbeit the Levites hurried it not.

6 And the king called for Jehoiada the chief, and said unto him, Why have you not required of the Levites to bring in out of Judah and out of Jerusalem the collection, according to the commandment of Moses the servant of the Becoming-One, and of the congregation of Israel, for the tabernacle of witness?

7 For the sons of Athaliah, that wicked woman, had broken up the house of God; and also all the dedicated things of the house of the Becoming-One did they bestow upon the lords [baalim]

8 And at the king's commandment they made a chest, and set it outside at the gate of the house of the Becoming-One.

9 And they made a proclamation through Judah and Jerusalem, to bring in to the Becoming-One the collection that Moses the servant of God laid upon Israel in the wilderness.

10 And all the princes and all the people rejoiced, and brought in, and cast into the chest, until they had made an end.

11 Now it came to pass, that at what time the chest was brought unto the king's office by the hand of the Levites, and when they saw that there was much money, the king's scribe and the high priest's officer came and emptied the chest, and took it, and carried it to his place again. Thus they did day by day, and gathered money in abundance.

12 And the king and Jehoiada gave it to such as did the work of the service of the house of the Becoming-One, and hired masons and carpenters to repair the house of the Becoming-One, and also such as worked iron and brass to mend the house of the Becoming-One.

13 So the workmen worked, and the work was perfected by them, and they set the house of God in his state, and strengthened it.

14 And when they had finished it, they brought the rest of the money before the king and Jehoiada, whereof were made vessels for the house of the Becoming-One, even vessels to minister, and to offer withal, and spoons, and vessels of gold and silver. And they offered burnt offerings in the house of the Becoming-One continually all the days of Jehoiada.

15 But Jehoiada grew old, and was full of days when he died; a son of hundred and thirty years was he when he died.

16 And they buried him in the city of David among the kings, because he had done good in Israel, both toward God, and toward his house.

17 Now after the death of Jehoiada came the princes of Judah, and made obeisance to the king. Then the king listened unto them.

18 And they left the house of the Becoming-One, God of their fathers, and served Asherahs and idols: and wrath came upon Judah and Jerusalem for this their trespass.

19 Yet he sent prophets to them, to bring them again unto the Becoming-One; and they testified against them: but they would not give ear.

20 And the Spirit of God came upon Zechariah the son of Jehoiada the priest, which stood above the people, and said unto them, Thus says God, Why transgress you the commandments of the Becoming-One, that you cannot prosper? because you have forsaken the Becoming-One, he has also forsaken you.

21 And they conspired against him, and stoned him with stones at the commandment of the king in the court of the house of the Becoming-One.

22 Thus Joash the king remembered not the kindness which Jehoiada his father had done to him, but killed his son. And as he lay dying, he said, The Becoming-One look upon this, and call you to account.

23 And it came to pass in the revolution of the year, that the host of Syria came up against him: and they came to Judah and Jerusalem, and destroyed all the princes of the people from among the people, and sent all the spoil of them unto the king of Damascus.

24 For the army of the Syrians came with a small company of men, and the Becoming-One delivered a very great host into their hand, because they had forsaken the Becoming-One, God of their fathers. So they executed judgment against Joash.

25 And when they were departed from him, for they left him in great diseases, his own servants conspired against him for the blood of the sons of Jehoiada the priest, and killed him on his bed, and he died: and they buried him in the city of David, but they buried him not in the tombs of the kings.

26 And these are they that conspired against him; Zabad the son of Shimeath an Ammonitess, and Jehozabad the son of Shimrith a Moabitess.

27 Now concerning his sons, and the greatness of the burdens laid upon him, and the repairing of the house of God, behold, they are written in the story of the book of the kings. And Amaziah his son reigned in his stead.

2 Chr 25:1 Amaziah was a son of twenty and five years when he began to reign, and he reigned twenty and nine years in Jerusalem. And his mother's name was Jehoaddan of Jerusalem.

2 And he did that which was right in the sight of the Becoming-One, but not with a perfect heart.

3 Now it came to pass, when the kingdom was established to him, that he killed his servants that had killed the king his father.

4 But he killed not their children, but did as it is written in the law in the book of Moses, where the Becoming-One commanded, saying, The fathers shall not die for the children, neither shall the children die for the fathers, but every man shall die for his own sin.

5 Moreover Amaziah gathered Judah together, and made them captains over thousands, and captains over hundreds, according to the houses of their fathers, throughout all Judah and Benjamin: and he numbered them from a son of twenty years and above, and found them three hundred thousand of choice men, able to go forth to war, that could handle spear and shield.

6 He hired also a hundred thousand of mighty men of valor out of Israel for a hundred talents of silver.

7 But there came a man of God to him, saying, O king, let not the army of Israel go with you; for the Becoming-One is not with Israel, to wit, with all the children of Ephraim.

8 But if you will go, do it, be strong for the battle: God shall make you fall before the enemy: for God has power to help, and to cast down.

9 And Amaziah said to the man of God, But what shall we do for the hundred talents which I have given to the army of Israel? And the man of God answered, The Becoming-One is able to give you much more than this.

10 Then Amaziah separated them, to wit, the army that was come to him out of Ephraim, to go home again: therefore their anger was greatly kindled against Judah, and they returned home in great anger.

11 And Amaziah strengthened himself, and led forth his people, and went to the valley of salt, and smote of the children of Seir ten thousand.

12 And other ten thousand left alive did the children of Judah carry away captive, and brought them unto the top of the rock, and cast them down from the top of the rock, that they all were broken in pieces.

13 But the soldiers of the army which Amaziah sent back, that they should not go with him to battle, fell upon the cities of Judah, from Samaria even unto Beth-horon, and smote three thousand of them, and took much spoil.

14 Now it came to pass, after that Amaziah was come from the slaughter of the Edomites, that he brought the gods of the children of Seir, and set them up to be his gods, and bowed down himself before them, and burned incense unto them.

15 Therefore the anger of the Becoming-One was kindled against Amaziah, and he sent unto him a prophet, which said unto him, Why have you sought after the gods of the people, which could not deliver their own people out of your hand?

16 And it came to pass, as he talked with him, that the king said unto him, are you made of the king's counsel? forbear; why should you be struck? Then the prophet forbare, and said, I know that God has determined to destroy you, because you have done this, and have not listened unto my counsel.

17 Then Amaziah king of Judah took advice, and sent to Joash, the son of Jehoahaz, the son of Jehu, king of Israel, saying, Come, let us see one another in the face.

18 And Joash king of Israel sent to Amaziah king of Judah, saying, The thistle that was in Lebanon sent to the cedar that was in Lebanon, saying, Give your daughter to my son to wife: and there passed by a wild beast that was in Lebanon, and trode down the thistle.

19 You say, Lo, you have struck the Edomites; and your heart lifts you up to boast: abide now at home; why should you meddle to your hurt, that you should fall, even you, and Judah with you?

20 But Amaziah would not hear; for it came from God, that he might deliver them into the hand of their enemies, because they sought after the gods of Edom.

21 So Joash the king of Israel went up; and they saw one another in the face, both he and Amaziah king of Judah, at Beth-shemesh, which belongs to Judah.

22 And Judah was put to the worse before Israel, and they fled every man to his tent.

23 And Joash the king of Israel took Amaziah king of Judah, the son of Joash, the son of Jehoahaz, at Beth-shemesh, and brought him to Jerusalem, and brake down the wall of Jerusalem from the gate of Ephraim to the corner gate, four hundred cubits.

24 And he took all the gold and the silver, and all the vessels that were found in the house of God with Obededom, and the treasures of the king's house, the hostages also, and returned to Samaria.

25 And Amaziah the son of Joash king of Judah lived after the death of Joash son of Jehoahaz king of Israel fifteen years.

26 Now the rest of the acts of Amaziah, first and last, behold, are they not written in the book of the kings of Judah and Israel?

27 Now after the time that Amaziah did turn away from following the Becoming-One they made a conspiracy against him in Jerusalem; and he fled to Lachish: but they sent to Lachish after him, and killed him there.

28 And they brought him upon horses, and buried him with his fathers in the city of Judah.

2 Chr 26:1 Then all the people of Judah took Uzziah, who was a son of sixteen years, and made him king in the room of his father Amaziah.

2 He built Eloth, and restored it to Judah, after that the king slept with his fathers.

3 A son of sixteen years was Uzziah when he began to reign, and he reigned fifty and two years in Jerusalem. His mother's name also was Jecoliah of Jerusalem.

4 And he did that which was right in the sight of the Becoming-One, according to all that his father Amaziah did.

5 And he sought God in the days of Zechariah, who had understanding in the visions of God: and as long as he sought the Becoming-One, God made him to prosper.

6 And he went forth and warred against the Philistines, and brake down the wall of Gath, and the wall of Jabneh, and the wall of Ashdod, and built cities about Ashdod, and among the Philistines.

7 And God helped him against the Philistines, and against the Arabians that dwelt in Gurbaal, and the Mehunims.

8 And the Ammonites gave gifts to Uzziah: and his name spread abroad even to the entering in of Egypt; for he strengthened himself exceedingly.

9 Moreover Uzziah built towers in Jerusalem at the corner gate, and at the valley gate, and at the turning of the wall, and fortified them.

10 Also he built towers in the desert, and dug many wells: for he had much cattle, both in the low country, and in the plains: husbandmen also, and vine dressers in the mountains, and in Carmel: for he loved husbandry.

11 Moreover Uzziah had a host of fighting men, that went out to war by bands, according to the number of their account by the hand of Jeiel the scribe and Maaseiah the ruler, under the hand of Hananiah, one of the king's captains.

12 The whole number of the chief of the fathers of the mighty men of valor were two thousand and six hundred.

13 And under their hand was an army, three hundred thousand and seven thousand and five hundred, that made war with mighty power, to help the king against the enemy.

14 And Uzziah prepared for them throughout all the host shields, and spears, and helmets, and habergeons, and bows, and slings to cast stones.

15 And he made in Jerusalem engines, invented by cunning men, to be on the towers and upon the bulwarks, to shoot arrows and great stones withal. And his name spread far abroad; for he was marvellously helped, till he was strong.

16 But when he was strong, his heart was lifted up to his destruction: for he transgressed against the Becoming-One his God, and went into the temple of the Becoming-One to burn incense upon the altar of incense.

17 And Azariah the priest went in after him, and with him fourscore priests of the Becoming-One, that were valiant men:

18 And they withstood Uzziah the king, and said unto him, It's not unto you, Uzziah, to burn incense unto the Becoming-One, but to the priests the sons of Aaron, that are consecrated to burn incense: go out of the sanctuary; for you have trespassed; neither shall it be for your honor from the Becoming-One, God.

19 Then Uzziah was angry, and had a censer in his hand to burn incense: and while he was angry with the priests, the leprosy even rose up in his forehead before the priests in the house of the Becoming-One, from beside the incense altar.

20 And Azariah the chief priest, and all the priests, looked upon him, and, behold, he was leprous in his forehead, and they thrust him out from there; yes, himself hasted also to go out, because the Becoming-One had struck him.

21 And Uzziah the king was a leper unto the day of his death, and dwelt in a several house, being a leper; for he was cut off from the house of the Becoming-One: and Jotham his son was over the king's house, judging the people of the land.

22 Now the rest of the acts of Uzziah, first and last, did Isaiah the prophet, the son of Amoz, write.

23 So Uzziah slept with his fathers, and they buried him with his fathers in the field of the burial which belonged to the kings; for they said, He is a leper: and Jotham his son reigned in his stead.

2 Chr 27:1 Jotham was a son of twenty and five years when he began to reign, and he reigned sixteen years in Jerusalem. His mother's name also was Jerushah, the daughter of Zadok.

2 And he did that which was right in the sight of the Becoming-One, according to all that his father Uzziah did: howbeit he entered not into the temple of the Becoming-One. And the people did yet corruptly.

3 He built the high gate of the house of the Becoming-One, and on the wall of Ophel he built much.

4 Moreover he built cities in the mountains of Judah, and in the forests he built castles and towers.

5 He fought also with the king of the Ammonites, and prevailed against them. And the children of Ammon gave him the same year a hundred talents of silver, and ten thousand measures of wheat, and ten thousand of barley. So much did the children of Ammon pay unto him, both the second year, and the third.

6 So Jotham became mighty, because he prepared his ways before the Becoming-One his God.

7 Now the rest of the acts of Jotham, and all his wars, and his ways, lo, they are written in the book of the kings of Israel and Judah.

8 He was a son of five and twenty years when he began to reign, and reigned sixteen years in Jerusalem.

9 And Jotham slept with his fathers, and they buried him in the city of David: and Ahaz his son reigned in his stead.

2 Chr 28:1 Ahaz was a son of twenty years when he began to reign, and he reigned sixteen years in Jerusalem: but he did not that which was right in the sight of the Becoming-One, like David his father:

2 For he walked in the ways of the kings of Israel, and made also molten images for the lords [baalim]

3 Moreover he burnt incense in the valley of the son of Hinnom, and burnt his children in the fire, after the abominations of the nations whom the Becoming-One had cast out before the children of Israel.

4 He sacrificed also and burnt incense in the high places, and on the hills, and under every green tree.

5 Therefore the Becoming-One his God delivered him into the hand of the king of Syria; and they smote him, and carried away a great multitude of them captives, and brought them to Damascus. And he was also delivered into the hand of the king of Israel, who smote him with a great slaughter.

6 For Pekah the son of Remaliah killed in Judah a hundred and twenty thousand in one day, which were all valiant men; because they had forsaken the Becoming-One, God of their fathers.

7 And Zichri, a mighty man of Ephraim, killed Maaseiah the king's son, and Azrikam the governor of the house, and Elkanah that was next to the king.

8 And the children of Israel carried away captive of their brethren two hundred thousand, women, sons, and daughters, and took also away much spoil from them, and brought the spoil to Samaria.

9 But a prophet of the Becoming-One was there, whose name was Oded: and he went out before the host that came to Samaria, and said unto them, Behold, because the Becoming-One, God of your fathers was angry with Judah, he has delivered them into your hand, and you have slain them in a rage that reaches up unto heaven.

10 And now you purpose to keep under the children of Judah and Jerusalem for bondmen and bondwomen unto you: but are there not with you, even with you, sins against the Becoming-One your God?

11 Now hear me therefore, and deliver the captives again, which you have taken captive of your brethren: for the fierce wrath of the Becoming-One is upon you.

12 Then certain of the heads of the children of Ephraim, Azariah the son of Johanan, Berechiah the son of Meshillemoth, and Jehizkiah the son of Shallum, and Amasa the son of Hadlai, stood up against them that came from the war,

13 And said unto them, you shall not bring in the captives here: for whereas we have offended against the Becoming-One already, you intend to add more to our sins and to our trespass: for our trespass is great, and there is fierce wrath against Israel.

14 So the armed men left the captives and the spoil before the princes and all the congregation.

15 And the men which were expressed by name rose up, and took the captives, and with the spoil clothed all that were naked among them, and arrayed them, and shod them, and gave them to eat and to drink, and anointed them, and carried all the feeble of them upon donkeys, and brought them to Jericho, the city of palm trees, to their brethren: then they returned to Samaria.

16 At that time did king Ahaz send unto the kings of Assyria to help him.

17 For again the Edomites had come and struck Judah, and carried away captives.

18 The Philistines also had invaded the cities of the low country, and of the south of Judah, and had taken Beth-shemesh, and Ajalon, and Gederoth, and Shocho with the villages thereof, and Timnah with the villages thereof, Gimzo also and the villages thereof: and they dwelt there.

19 For the Becoming-One brought Judah low because of Ahaz king of Israel; for he made Judah naked, and transgressed greatly against the Becoming-One.

20 And Tilgathpilneser king of Assyria came unto him, and distressed him, but strengthened him not.

21 For Ahaz took away a portion out of the house of the Becoming-One, and out of the house of the king, and of the princes, and gave it unto the king of Assyria: but he helped him not.

22 And in the time of his distress did he trespass yet more against the Becoming-One: this is that king Ahaz.

23 For he sacrificed unto the gods of Damascus, which smote him: and he said, Because the gods of the kings of Syria help them, therefore will I sacrifice to them, that they may help me. But they were the ruin of him, and of all Israel.

24 And Ahaz gathered together the vessels of the house of God, and cut in pieces the vessels of the house of God, and shut up the doors of the house of the Becoming-One, and he made him altars in every corner of Jerusalem.

25 And in every several city of Judah he made high places to burn incense unto other gods, and provoked to anger the Becoming-One, God of his fathers.

26 Now the rest of his acts and of all his ways, first and last, behold, they are written in the book of the kings of Judah and Israel.

27 And Ahaz slept with his fathers, and they buried him in the city, even in Jerusalem: but they brought him not into the tombs of the kings of Israel: and Hezekiah his son reigned in his stead.

2 Chr 29:1 Hezekiah began to reign when he was a son of five and twenty years, and he reigned nine and twenty years in Jerusalem. And his mother's name was Abijah, the daughter of Zechariah.

2 And he did that which was right in the sight of the Becoming-One, according to all that David his father had done.

3 He in the first year of his reign, in the first month, opened the doors of the house of the Becoming-One, and repaired them.

4 And he brought in the priests and the Levites, and gathered them together into the east street,

5 And said unto them, Hear me, you Levites, sanctify now yourselves, and sanctify the house of the Becoming-One, God of your fathers, and carry forth the filthiness out of the holy place.

6 For our fathers have trespassed, and done that which was evil in the eyes of the Becoming-One our God, and have forsaken him, and have turned away their faces from the habitation of the Becoming-One, and turned their backs.

7 Also they have shut up the doors of the porch, and put out the lamps, and have not burned incense nor offered burnt offerings in the holy place unto God of Israel.

8 Therefore the wrath of the Becoming-One was upon Judah and Jerusalem, and he has delivered them to trouble, to astonishment, and to hissing, as you see with your eyes.

9 For, lo, our fathers have fallen by the sword, and our sons and our daughters and our wives are in captivity for this.

10 Now it is in mine heart to make a covenant with the Becoming-One, God of Israel, that his fierce wrath may turn away from us.

11 My sons, be not now negligent: for the Becoming-One has chosen you to stand before him, to serve him, and that you should minister unto him, and burn incense.

12 Then the Levites arose, Mahath the son of Amasai, and Joel the son of Azariah, of the sons of the Kohathites: and of the sons of Merari, Kish the son of Abdi, and Azariah the son of Jehalelel: and of the Gershonites; Joah the son of Zimmah, and Eden the son of Joah:

13 And of the sons of Elizaphan; Shimri, and Jeiel: and of the sons of Asaph; Zechariah, and Mattaniah:

14 And of the sons of Heman; Jehiel, and Shimei: and of the sons of Jeduthun; Shemaiah, and Uzziel.

15 And they gathered their brethren, and sanctified themselves, and came, according to the commandment of the king, by the words of the Becoming-One, to cleanse the house of the Becoming-One.

16 And the priests went into the inner part of the house of the Becoming-One, to cleanse it, and brought out all the uncleanness that they found in the temple of the Becoming-One into the court of the house of the Becoming-One. And the Levites took it, to carry it out abroad into the brook Kidron.

17 Now they began on the first day of the first month to sanctify, and on the eighth day of the month came they to the porch of the Becoming-One: so they sanctified the house of the Becoming-One in eight days; and in the sixteenth day of the first month they made an end.

18 Then they went in to Hezekiah the king, and said, We have cleansed all the house of the Becoming-One, and the altar of burnt offering, with all the vessels thereof, and the showbread table, with all the vessels thereof.

19 Moreover all the vessels, which king Ahaz in his reign did cast away in his transgression, have we prepared and sanctified, and, behold, they are before the altar of the Becoming-One.

20 Then Hezekiah the king rose early, and gathered the rulers of the city, and went up to the house of the Becoming-One.

21 And they brought seven bullocks, and seven rams, and seven lambs, and seven he goats, for a sin offering for the kingdom, and for the sanctuary, and for Judah. And he commanded the priests the sons of Aaron to offer them on the altar of the Becoming-One.

22 So they killed the bullocks, and the priests received the blood, and sprinkled it on the altar: likewise, when they had killed the rams, they sprinkled the blood upon the altar: they killed also the lambs, and they sprinkled the blood upon the altar.

23 And they brought forth the he goats for the sin offering before the king and the congregation; and they laid their hands upon them:

24 And the priests killed them, and they made reconciliation with their blood upon the altar, to make an atonement for all Israel: for the king commanded that the burnt offering and the sin offering should be made for all Israel.

25 And he set the Levites in the house of the Becoming-One with cymbals, with psalteries, and with harps, according to the commandment of David, and of Gad the king's seer, and Nathan the prophet: for so was the commandment of the Becoming-One by his prophets.

26 And the Levites stood with the instruments of David, and the priests with the trumpets.

27 And Hezekiah commanded to offer the burnt offering upon the altar. And when the burnt offering began, the song of the Becoming-One began also with the trumpets, and with the instruments ordained by David king of Israel.

28 And all the congregation worshiped, and the singers sang, and the trumpeters sounded: and all this continued until the burnt offering was finished.

29 And when they had made an end of offering, the king and all that were present with him bowed themselves, and worshiped.

30 Moreover Hezekiah the king and the princes commanded the Levites to sing praise unto the Becoming-One with the words of David, and of Asaph the seer. And they sang praises with gladness, and they bowed their heads and worshiped.

31 Then Hezekiah answered and said, Now you have consecrated yourselves unto the Becoming-One, come near and bring sacrifices and thank offerings into the house of the Becoming-One. And the congregation brought in sacrifices and thank offerings; and as many as were of a free heart burnt offerings.

32 And the number of the burnt offerings, which the congregation brought, was threescore and ten bullocks, a hundred rams, and two hundred lambs: all these were for a burnt offering to the Becoming-One.

33 And the consecrated things were six hundred oxen and three thousand of sheep.

34 But the priests were too few, so that they could not flay all the burnt offerings: therefore their brethren the Levites did help them, till the work was

ended, and until the other priests had sanctified themselves: for the Levites were more upright in heart to sanctify themselves than the priests.

35 And also the burnt offerings were in abundance, with the fat of the peace offerings, and the drink offerings for every burnt offering. So the service of the house of the Becoming-One was set in order.

36 And Hezekiah rejoiced, and all the people, that God had prepared the people: for the thing was done suddenly.

2 Chr 30:1 And Hezekiah sent to all Israel and Judah, and wrote letters also to Ephraim and Manasseh, that they should come to the house of the Becoming-One at Jerusalem, to keep the Passover unto the Becoming-One, God of Israel.

2 For the king had taken counsel, and his princes, and all the congregation in Jerusalem, to keep the Passover in the second month.

3 For they could not keep it at that time, because the priests had not sanctified themselves sufficiently, neither had the people gathered themselves together to Jerusalem.

4 And the thing pleased the king and all the congregation.

5 So they established a decree to make proclamation throughout all Israel, from Beersheba even to Dan, that they should come to keep the Passover unto the Becoming-One, God of Israel at Jerusalem: for they had not done it of a long time in such sort as it was written.

6 So the runners went with the letters from the king and his princes throughout all Israel and Judah, and according to the commandment of the king, saying, you children of Israel, turn again unto the Becoming-One, God of Abraham, Isaac, and Israel, and he will return to the remnant of you, that are escaped out of the hand of the kings of Assyria.

7 And be not you like your fathers, and like your brethren, which trespassed against the Becoming-One, God of their fathers, who therefore gave them up to desolation, as you see.

8 Now be you not stiffnecked, as your fathers were, but yield yourselves unto the Becoming-One, and enter into his sanctuary, which he has sanctified for olam, and serve the Becoming-One your God, that the fierceness of his wrath may turn away from you.

9 For if you turn again unto the Becoming-One, your brethren and your children shall find compassion before them that lead them captive, so that they shall come again into this land: for the Becoming-One your God is gracious and merciful, and will not turn away his face from you, if you return unto him.

10 So the runners passed from city to city through the country of Ephraim and Manasseh even unto Zebulun: but they laughed them to scorn, and mocked them.

11 Nevertheless diverse of Asher and Manasseh and of Zebulun humbled themselves, and came to Jerusalem.

12 Also in Judah the hand of God was to give them one heart to do the commandment of the king and of the princes, by the word of the Becoming-One.

13 And there assembled at Jerusalem much people to keep the feast of unleavened bread in the second month, a very great congregation.

14 And they arose and took away the altars that were in Jerusalem, and all the altars for incense took they away, and cast them into the brook Kidron.

15 Then they killed the Passover on the fourteenth day of the second month: and the priests and the Levites were ashamed, and sanctified themselves, and brought in the burnt offerings into the house of the Becoming-One.

16 And they stood in their place after their manner, according to the law of Moses the man of God: the priests sprinkled the blood, which they received of the hand of the Levites.

17 For there were many in the congregation that were not sanctified: therefore the Levites had the charge of the killing of the passovers for every one that was not clean, to sanctify them unto the Becoming-One.

18 For a multitude of the people, even many of Ephraim, and Manasseh, Issachar, and Zebulun, had not cleansed themselves, yet did they eat the Passover otherwise than it was written. But Hezekiah prayed for them, saying, the Becoming-One: the good atonement for them.

19 That prepares his heart to seek God, the Becoming-One, God of his fathers, though he be not cleansed according to the purification of the sanctuary.

20 And the Becoming-One listened to Hezekiah, and healed the people.

21 And the children of Israel that were present at Jerusalem kept the feast of unleavened bread seven days with great gladness: and the Levites and the priests praised the Becoming-One day by day, singing with loud instruments unto the Becoming-One.

22 And Hezekiah spoke comfortably unto all the Levites that taught the good knowledge of the Becoming-One: and they did eat throughout the set time[120] seven days, offering peace offerings, and making confession to the Becoming-One, God of their fathers.

23 And the whole assembly took counsel to keep other seven days: and they kept other seven days with gladness.

24 For Hezekiah king of Judah did give to the congregation a thousand bullocks and seven thousand of sheep; and the princes gave to the congregation a thousand of bullocks and ten thousand of sheep: and a great number of priests sanctified themselves.

25 And all the congregation of Judah, with the priests and the Levites, and all the congregation that came out of Israel, and the strangers that came out of the land of Israel, and that dwelt in Judah, rejoiced.

26 So there was great joy in Jerusalem: for since the time of Solomon the son of David king of Israel there was not the like in Jerusalem.

27 Then the priests the Levites arose and blessed the people: and their voice was heard, and their

---

[120] Appointed time or festival

prayer came up to his holy dwelling place, even unto heaven.

2 Chr 31:1 Now when all this was finished, all Israel that were present went out to the cities of Judah, and brake the images in pieces, and cut down the Asherahs, and threw down the high places and the altars out of all Judah and Benjamin, in Ephraim also and Manasseh, until they had utterly destroyed them all. Then all the children of Israel returned, every man to his possession, into their own cities.

2 And Hezekiah appointed the courses of the priests and the Levites after their courses, every man according to his service, the priests and Levites for burnt offerings and for peace offerings, to minister, and to give thanks, and to praise in the gates of the tents of the Becoming-One.

3 He appointed also the king's portion of his substance for the burnt offerings, to wit, for the morning and evening burnt offerings, and the burnt offerings for the sabbaths, and for the new moons, and for the set times,[121] as it is written in the law of the Becoming-One.

4 Moreover he commanded the people that dwelt in Jerusalem to give the portion due to the priests and the Levites, that they might devote themselves in the law of the Becoming-One.

5 And as soon as the commandment came abroad, the children of Israel brought in abundance the beginning of grain, wine, and oil, and honey, and of all the increase of the field; and the tithe of all things brought they in abundantly.

6 And concerning the children of Israel and Judah, that dwelt in the cities of Judah, they also brought in the tithe of oxen and sheep, and the tithe of holy things which were consecrated unto the Becoming-One their God, and laid them by heaps.

7 In the third month they began to lay the foundation of the heaps, and finished them in the seventh month.

8 And when Hezekiah and the princes came and saw the heaps, they blessed the Becoming-One, and his people Israel.

9 Then Hezekiah questioned with the priests and the Levites concerning the heaps.

10 And Azariah the chief priest of the house of Zadok answered him, and said, Since the people began to bring the offerings into the house of the Becoming-One, we have had enough to eat, and have left plenty: for the Becoming-One has blessed his people; and that which is left is this great store.

11 Then Hezekiah commanded to prepare chambers in the house of the Becoming-One; and they prepared them,

12 And brought in the offerings and the tithes and the dedicated things faithfully: over which Cononiah the Levite was ruler, and Shimei his brother was the next.

13 And Jehiel, and Azaziah, and Nahath, and Asahel, and Jerimoth, and Jozabad, and Eliel, and Ismachiah, and Mahath, and Benaiah, were overseers under the hand of Cononiah and Shimei his brother, at the commandment of Hezekiah the king, and Azariah the ruler of the house of God.

14 And Kore the son of Imnah the Levite, the gatekeeper toward the east, was over the freewill offerings of God, to distribute the offerings of the Becoming-One, and the most holy things.

15 And next him were Eden, and Miniamin, and Jeshua, and Shemaiah, Amariah, and Shecaniah, in the cities of the priests, in their set office, to give to their brethren by courses, as well to the great as to the small:

16 Beside their genealogy of males, from a son of three years and upward, even unto every one that enters into the house of the Becoming-One, his daily portion for their service in their charges according to their courses;

17 Both to the genealogy of the priests by the house of their fathers, and the Levites from a son of twenty years and upward, in their charges by their courses;

18 And to the genealogy of all their little ones, their wives, and their sons, and their daughters, through all the congregation: for in their set office they sanctified themselves in holiness:

19 Also of the sons of Aaron the priests, which were in the fields of the suburbs of their cities, in every several city, the men that were expressed by name, to give portions to all the males among the priests, and to all that were reckoned by genealogies among the Levites.

20 And thus did Hezekiah throughout all Judah, and worked that which was good and right and truth before the Becoming-One his God.

2 Chr 32:1 After these things, and the establishment thereof, Sennacherib king of Assyria came, and entered into Judah, and encamped against the fenced cities, and thought to win them for himself.

2 And when Hezekiah saw that Sennacherib was come, and that he was purposed to fight against Jerusalem,

3 He took counsel with his princes and his mighty men to stop the waters of the fountains which were outside the city: and they did help him.

4 So there was gathered much people together, who stopped all the fountains, and the brook that ran through the midst of the land, saying, Why should the kings of Assyria come, and find much water?

5 Also he strengthened himself, and built up all the wall that was broken, and raised it up to the towers, and another wall outside, and repaired Millo in the city of David, and made darts and shields in abundance.

6 And he set captains of war over the people, and gathered them together to him in the street of the gate of the city, and spoke comfortably to them, saying,

7 Be strong and courageous, be not afraid nor dismayed for the king of Assyria, nor for all the multitude that is with him: for there be more with us than with him:

8 With him is an arm of flesh; but with us is the Becoming-One our God to help us, and to fight our battles. And the people rested themselves upon the words of Hezekiah king of Judah.

---

[121] Appointed times or festivals

9 After this did Sennacherib king of Assyria send his servants to Jerusalem, but he himself laid siege against Lachish, and all his power with him, unto Hezekiah king of Judah, and unto all Judah that were at Jerusalem, saying,

10 Thus says Sennacherib king of Assyria, Whereon do you trust, that you abide in the siege in Jerusalem?

11 Does not Hezekiah persuade you to give over yourselves to die by famine and by thirst, saying, The Becoming-One our God shall deliver us out of the hand of the king of Assyria?

12 Has not the same Hezekiah taken away his high places and his altars, and commanded Judah and Jerusalem, saying, you shall worship before one altar, and burn incense upon it?

13 Don't you know what I and my fathers have done unto all the people of other lands? were the gods of the nations of those lands any ways able to deliver their lands out of mine hand?

14 Who was there among all the gods of those nations that my fathers utterly destroyed, that could deliver his people out of mine hand, that your God should be able to deliver you out of mine hand?

15 Now therefore let not Hezekiah deceive you, nor persuade you on this manner, neither yet believe him: for no god of any nation or kingdom was able to deliver his people out of mine hand, and out of the hand of my fathers: how much less shall your God deliver you out of mine hand?

16 And his servants spoke yet more against the Becoming-One, God, and against his servant Hezekiah.

17 He wrote also letters to rail on the Becoming-One, God of Israel, and to speak against him, saying, As the gods of the nations of other lands have not delivered their people out of mine hand, so shall not God of Hezekiah deliver his people out of mine hand.

18 Then they cried with a loud voice in the Jews' speech unto the people of Jerusalem that were on the wall, to affright them, and to trouble them; that they might take the city.

19 And they spoke against God of Jerusalem, as against the gods of the people of the earth, which were the work of the hands of man.

20 And for this cause Hezekiah the king, and the prophet Isaiah the son of Amoz, prayed and cried to heaven.

21 And the Becoming-One sent an angel, which cut off all the mighty men of valor, and the leaders and captains in the camp of the king of Assyria. So he returned with shame of face to his own land. And when he was come into the house of his god, they that came forth of his own bowels killed him there with the sword.

22 Thus the Becoming-One saved Hezekiah and the inhabitants of Jerusalem from the hand of Sennacherib the king of Assyria, and from the hand of all other, and guided them on every side.

23 And many brought gifts unto the Becoming-One to Jerusalem, and presents to Hezekiah king of Judah: so that he was magnified in the sight of all nations from thereforth.

24 In those days Hezekiah was sick to the death, and prayed unto the Becoming-One: and he spoke unto him, and he gave him a sign.

25 But Hezekiah rendered not again according to the benefit done unto him; for his heart was lifted up: therefore there was wrath upon him, and upon Judah and Jerusalem.

26 Notwithstanding Hezekiah humbled himself for the pride of his heart, both he and the inhabitants of Jerusalem, so that the wrath of the Becoming-One came not upon them in the days of Hezekiah.

27 And Hezekiah had exceeding much riches and honor: and he made himself treasuries for silver, and for gold, and for precious stones, and for spices, and for shields, and for all manner of pleasant jewels;

28 Storehouses also for the increase of grain, and wine, and oil; and stalls for all manner of beasts, and cotes for flocks.

29 Moreover he provided him cities, and possessions of flocks and herds in abundance: for God had given him substance very much.

30 This same Hezekiah also stopped the upper watercourse of Gihon, and brought it straight down to the west side of the city of David. And Hezekiah prospered in all his works.

31 Howbeit in the business of the ambassadors of the princes of Babylon, who sent unto him to inquire of the wonder that was done in the land, God left him, to try him, that he might know all that was in his heart.

32 Now the rest of the acts of Hezekiah, and his goodness, behold, they are written in the vision of Isaiah the prophet, the son of Amoz, and in the book of the kings of Judah and Israel.

33 And Hezekiah slept with his fathers, and they buried him in the chief of the tombs of the sons of David: and all Judah and the inhabitants of Jerusalem did him honor at his death. And Manasseh his son reigned in his stead.

2 Chr 33:1 Manasseh was a son of twelve years when he began to reign, and he reigned fifty and five years in Jerusalem:

2 But did that which was evil in the sight of the Becoming-One, like unto the abominations of the nations, whom the Becoming-One had cast out before the children of Israel.

3 For he built again the high places which Hezekiah his father had broken down, and he reared up altars for the lords [baalim] and made Asherahs, and worshiped all the host of heaven, and served them.

4 Also he built altars in the house of the Becoming-One, whereof the Becoming-One had said, In Jerusalem shall my name be for olam.

5 And he built altars for all the host of the heavens in the two courts of the house of the Becoming-One.

6 And he caused his children to pass through the fire in the valley of the son of Hinnom: also he observed times, and used enchantments, and used witchcraft, and dealt with a medium, and with fortune-tellers: he worked much evil in the sight of the Becoming-One, to provoke him to anger.

7 And he set a carved image, the idol which he had made, in the house of God, of which God had said to David and to Solomon his son, In this house, and in Jerusalem, which I have chosen before all the tribes of Israel, will I put my name for olam.

8 Neither will I any more remove the foot of Israel from out of the land which I have appointed for your fathers; so that they will take heed to do all that I have commanded them, according to the whole law and the statutes and the ordinances by the hand of Moses.

9 So Manasseh made Judah and the inhabitants of Jerusalem to err, and to do worse than the nations, whom the Becoming-One had destroyed before the children of Israel.

10 And the Becoming-One spoke to Manasseh, and to his people: but they would not listen.

11 Therefore the Becoming-One brought upon them the captains of the host of the king of Assyria, which took Manasseh among the thorns, and bound him with brass chains, and carried him to Babylon.

12 And when he was in affliction, he besought the Becoming-One his God, and humbled himself greatly before God of his fathers,

13 And prayed unto him: and he was entreated of him, and heard his supplication, and brought him again to Jerusalem into his kingdom. Then Manasseh knew that the Becoming-One he was God.

14 Now after this he built a wall outside the city of David, on the west side of Gihon, in the valley, even to the entering in at the fish gate, and compassed about Ophel, and raised it up a very great height, and put captains of war in all the fenced cities of Judah.

15 And he took away the strange gods, and the idol out of the house of the Becoming-One, and all the altars that he had built in the mount of the house of the Becoming-One, and in Jerusalem, and cast them out of the city.

16 And he repaired the altar of the Becoming-One, and sacrificed thereon peace offerings and thank offerings, and commanded Judah to serve the Becoming-One, God of Israel.

17 Nevertheless the people did sacrifice still in the high places, yet unto the Becoming-One their God only.

18 Now the rest of the acts of Manasseh, and his prayer unto his God, and the words of the seers that spoke to him in the name of the Becoming-One, God of Israel, behold, they are written in the book of the kings of Israel.

19 His prayer also, and how God was entreated of him, and all his sins, and his trespass, and the places wherein he built high places, and set up Asherahs and graven images, before he was humbled: behold, they are written among the sayings of the seers.

20 So Manasseh slept with his fathers, and they buried him in his own house: and Amon his son reigned in his stead.

21 Amon was a son of two and twenty years when he began to reign, and reigned two years in Jerusalem.

22 But he did that which was evil in the sight of the Becoming-One, as did Manasseh his father: for Amon sacrificed unto all the carved images which Manasseh his father had made, and served them;

23 And humbled not himself before the Becoming-One, as Manasseh his father had humbled himself; but Amon trespassed more and more.

24 And his servants conspired against him, and killed him in his own house.

25 But the people of the land killed all them that had conspired against king Amon; and the people of the land made Josiah his son king in his stead.

2 Chr 34:1 Josiah was a son of eight years when he began to reign, and he reigned in Jerusalem one and thirty years.

2 And he did that which was right in the sight of the Becoming-One, and walked in the ways of David his father, and declined neither to the right hand, nor to the left.

3 For in the eighth year of his reign, while he was yet young, he began to seek after God of David his father: and in the twelfth year he began to purge Judah and Jerusalem from the high places, and the Asherahs, and the carved images, and the molten images.

4 And they broke down the altars of the lords [baalim] in his presence; and the images, that were on high above them, he cut down; and the Asherahs, and the carved images, and the molten images, he brake in pieces, and made dust of them, and strowed it upon the graves of them that had sacrificed unto them.

5 And he burnt the bones of the priests upon their altars, and cleansed Judah and Jerusalem.

6 And so did he in the cities of Manasseh, and Ephraim, and Simeon, even unto Naphtali, with their mattocks round about.

7 And when he had broken down the altars and the Asherahs, and had beaten the graven images into powder, and cut down all the idols throughout all the land of Israel, he returned to Jerusalem.

8 Now in the eighteenth year of his reign, when he had purged the land, and the house, he sent Shaphan the son of Azaliah, and Maaseiah the governor of the city, and Joah the son of Joahaz the recorder, to repair the house of the Becoming-One his God.

9 And when they came to Hilkiah the high priest, they delivered the money that was brought into the house of God, which the Levites that kept the doors had gathered of the hand of Manasseh and Ephraim, and of all the remnant of Israel, and of all Judah and Benjamin; and they returned to Jerusalem.

10 And they put it in the hand of the workmen that had the oversight of the house of the Becoming-One, and they gave it to the workmen that worked in the house of the Becoming-One, to repair and amend the house:

11 Even to the artificers and builders gave they it, to buy hewn stone, and timber for couplings, and to floor the houses which the kings of Judah had destroyed.

12 And the men did the work faithfully: and the overseers of them were Jahath and Obadiah, the Levites, of the sons of Merari; and Zechariah and Meshullam, of the sons of the Kohathites, to set it forward; and other of the Levites, all that could skill of instruments of music.

13 Also they were over the bearers of burdens, and were overseers of all that worked the work in any manner of service: and of the Levites there were scribes, and officers, and gatekeepers.

14 And when they brought out the money that was brought into the house of the Becoming-One,

Hilkiah the priest found a book of the law of the Becoming-One given by Moses.

15 And Hilkiah answered and said to Shaphan the scribe, I have found the book of the law in the house of the Becoming-One. And Hilkiah delivered the book to Shaphan.

16 And Shaphan carried the book to the king, and brought the king word back again, saying, All that was committed to your servants, they do it.

17 And they have gathered together the money that was found in the house of the Becoming-One, and have delivered it into the hand of the overseers, and to the hand of the workmen.

18 Then Shaphan the scribe told the king, saying, Hilkiah the priest has given me a book. And Shaphan read it before the king.

19 And it came to pass, when the king had heard the words of the law, that he ripped his clothes.

20 And the king commanded Hilkiah, and Ahikam the son of Shaphan, and Abdon the son of Micah, and Shaphan the scribe, and Asaiah a servant of the king's, saying,

21 Go, inquire of the Becoming-One for me, and for them that are left in Israel and in Judah, concerning the words of the book that is found: for great is the wrath of the Becoming-One that is poured out upon us, because our fathers have not kept the word of the Becoming-One, to do after all that is written in this book.

22 And Hilkiah, and they that the king had appointed, went to Huldah the prophetess, the wife of Shallum the son of Tikvath, the son of Hasrah, keeper of the wardrobe; now she dwelt in Jerusalem in the college: and they spoke to her to that effect.

23 And she answered them, Thus says the Becoming-One, God of Israel, Tell you the man that sent you to me,

24 Thus says the Becoming-One, Behold, I will bring evil upon this place, and upon the inhabitants thereof, even all the curses that are written in the book which they have read before the king of Judah:

25 Because they have forsaken me, and have burned incense unto other gods, that they might provoke me to anger with all the works of their hands; therefore my wrath shall be poured out upon this place, and shall not be quenched.

26 And as for the king of Judah, who sent you to inquire of the Becoming-One, so shall you say unto him, Thus says the Becoming-One, God of Israel concerning the words which you have heard;

27 Because your heart was tender, and you did humble yourself before God, when you heard his words against this place, and against the inhabitants thereof, and humbled yourself before me, and did rip your clothes, and weep before me; I have even heard you also, says the Becoming-One.

28 Behold, I will gather you to your fathers, and you shall be gathered to your grave in peace, neither shall your eyes see all the evil that I will bring upon this place, and upon the inhabitants of the same. So they brought the king word again.

29 Then the king sent and gathered together all the elders of Judah and Jerusalem.

30 And the king went up into the house of the Becoming-One, and all the men of Judah, and the inhabitants of Jerusalem, and the priests, and the Levites, and all the people, great and small: and he read in their ears all the words of the book of the covenant that was found in the house of the Becoming-One.

31 And the king stood in his place, and made a covenant before the Becoming-One, to walk after the Becoming-One, and to keep his commandments, and his testimonies, and his statutes, with all his heart, and with all his soul, to perform the words of the covenant which are written in this book.

32 And he caused all that were present in Jerusalem and Benjamin to stand to it. And the inhabitants of Jerusalem did according to the covenant of God, God of their fathers.

33 And Josiah took away all the abominations out of all the countries that pertained to the children of Israel, and made all that were present in Israel to serve, even to serve the Becoming-One their God. And all his days they departed not from following the Becoming-One, God of their fathers.

2 Chr 35:1 Moreover Josiah kept a Passover unto the Becoming-One in Jerusalem: and they killed the Passover on the fourteenth day of the first month.

2 And he set the priests in their charges, and encouraged them to the service of the house of the Becoming-One,

3 And said unto the Levites that taught all Israel, which were holy unto the Becoming-One, Put the holy ark in the house which Solomon the son of David king of Israel did build; it shall not be a burden upon your shoulders: serve now the Becoming-One your God, and his people Israel,

4 And prepare yourselves by the houses of your fathers, after your courses, according to the writing of David king of Israel, and according to the writing of Solomon his son.

5 And stand in the holy place according to the divisions of the families of the fathers of your brethren the people, and after the division of the families of the Levites.

6 So kill the Passover, and sanctify yourselves, and prepare your brethren, that they may do according to the word of the Becoming-One by the hand of Moses.

7 And Josiah gave to the people, of the flock, lambs and kids, all for the Passover offerings, for all that were present, to the number of thirty thousand, and three thousand of bullocks: these were of the king's substance.

8 And his princes gave willingly unto the people, to the priests, and to the Levites: Hilkiah and Zechariah and Jehiel, rulers of the house of God, gave unto the priests for the Passover offerings two thousand and six hundred small cattle, and three hundred oxen.

9 Conaniah also, and Shemaiah and Nethaneel, his brethren, and Hashabiah and Jeiel and Jozabad, chief of the Levites, gave unto the Levites for Passover offerings five thousand of small cattle, and five hundred oxen.

10 So the service was prepared, and the priests stood in their place, and the Levites in their courses, according to the king's commandment.

11 And they killed the Passover, and the priests sprinkled the blood from their hands, and the Levites flayed them.

12 And they removed the burnt offerings, that they might give according to the divisions of the families of the people, to offer unto the Becoming-One, as it is written in the book of Moses. And so did they with the oxen.

13 And they roasted the Passover with fire according to the ordinance: but the other holy offerings boiled they in pots, and in caldrons, and in pans, and divided them speedily among all the people.

14 And afterward they made ready for themselves, and for the priests: because the priests the sons of Aaron were busied in offering of burnt offerings and the fat until night; therefore the Levites prepared for themselves, and for the priests the sons of Aaron.

15 And the singers the sons of Asaph were in their place, according to the commandment of David, and Asaph, and Heman, and Jeduthun the king's seer; and the gatekeepers waited at every gate; they might not depart from their service; for their brethren the Levites prepared for them.

16 So all the service of the Becoming-One was prepared the same day, to keep the Passover, and to offer burnt offerings upon the altar of the Becoming-One, according to the commandment of king Josiah.

17 And the children of Israel that were present kept the Passover at that time, and the feast of unleavened bread seven days.

18 And there was no Passover like to that kept in Israel from the days of Samuel the prophet; neither did all the kings of Israel keep such a Passover as Josiah kept, and the priests, and the Levites, and all Judah and Israel that were present, and the inhabitants of Jerusalem.

19 In the eighteenth year of the reign of Josiah was this Passover kept.

20 After all this, when Josiah had prepared the temple, Necho king of Egypt came up to fight against Charchemish by Euphrates: and Josiah went out against him.

21 But he sent ambassadors to him, saying, What have I to do with you, you king of Judah? I come not against you this day, but against the house wherewith I have war: for God commanded me to make haste: forbear you from meddling with God, who is with me, that he destroy you not.

22 Nevertheless Josiah would not turn his face from him, but disguised himself, that he might fight with him, and listened not unto the words of Necho from the mouth of God, and came to fight in the valley of Megiddo.

23 And the archers shot at king Josiah; and the king said to his servants, Take me away; for I am greatly wounded.

24 His servants therefore took him out of that chariot, and put him in the second chariot that he had; and they brought him to Jerusalem, and he died, and was buried in one of the tombs of his fathers. And all Judah and Jerusalem mourned for Josiah.

25 And Jeremiah lamented for Josiah: and all the singing men and the singing women spoke of Josiah in their lamentations to this day, and made them an ordinance in Israel: and, behold, they are written in the lamentations.

26 Now the rest of the acts of Josiah, and his goodness, according to that which was written in the law of the Becoming-One,

27 And his deeds, first and last, behold, they are written in the book of the kings of Israel and Judah.

2 Chr 36:1 Then the people of the land took Jehoahaz the son of Josiah, and made him king in his father's stead in Jerusalem.

2 Jehoahaz was a son of twenty and three years when he began to reign, and he reigned three months in Jerusalem.

3 And the king of Egypt put him down at Jerusalem, and condemned the land in a hundred talents of silver and a talent of gold.

4 And the king of Egypt made Eliakim his brother king over Judah and Jerusalem, and turned his name to Jehoiakim. And Necho took Jehoahaz his brother, and carried him to Egypt.

5 Jehoiakim was a son of twenty and five years when he began to reign, and he reigned eleven years in Jerusalem: and he did that which was evil in the sight of the Becoming-One his God.

6 Against him came up Nebuchadnezzar king of Babylon, and bound him in brass chains, to carry him to Babylon.

7 Nebuchadnezzar also carried of the vessels of the house of the Becoming-One to Babylon, and put them in his temple at Babylon.

8 Now the rest of the acts of Jehoiakim, and his abominations which he did, and that which was found in him, behold, they are written in the book of the kings of Israel and Judah: and Jehoiachin his son reigned in his stead.

9 Jehoiachin was a son of eight years when he began to reign, and he reigned three months and ten days in Jerusalem: and he did that which was evil in the sight of the Becoming-One.

10 And at the turn of the year, king Nebuchadnezzar sent, and brought him to Babylon, with the goodly vessels of the house of the Becoming-One, and made Zedekiah his brother king over Judah and Jerusalem.

11 Zedekiah was a son of one and twenty years when he began to reign, and reigned eleven years in Jerusalem.

12 And he did that which was evil in the sight of the Becoming-One his God, and humbled not himself before Jeremiah the prophet speaking from the mouth of the Becoming-One.

13 And he also rebelled against king Nebuchadnezzar, who had made him swear by God: but he stiffened his neck, and hardened his heart from turning unto the Becoming-One, God of Israel.

14 Moreover all the chief of the priests, and the people, transgressed very much after all the abominations of the nations; and polluted the house of the Becoming-One which he had hallowed in Jerusalem.

15 And the Becoming-One, God of their fathers sent to them by his messengers, rising up early, and sending; because he had compassion on his people, and on his dwelling place:

16 But they mocked the messengers of God, and despised his words, and misused his prophets, until the wrath of the Becoming-One arose against his people, till there was no remedy.

17 Therefore he brought upon them the king of the Chaldees, who killed their young men with the sword in the house of their sanctuary, and had no compassion upon young man or maiden, old man, or him that stooped for age: he gave them all into his hand.

18 And all the vessels of the house of God, great and small, and the treasures of the house of the Becoming-One, and the treasures of the king, and of his princes; all these he brought to Babylon.

19 And they burnt the house of God, and brake down the wall of Jerusalem, and burnt all the palaces thereof with fire, and destroyed all the goodly vessels thereof.

20 And them that had escaped from the sword carried he away to Babylon; where they were servants to him and his sons until the reign of the kingdom of Persia:

21 To fulfil the word of the Becoming-One by the mouth of Jeremiah, until the land had enjoyed her sabbaths: for as long as she lay desolate she kept Sabbath, to fulfil threescore and ten years.

22 Now in the first year of Cyrus king of Persia, that the word of the Becoming-One spoken by the mouth of Jeremiah might be accomplished, the Becoming-One stirred up the spirit of Cyrus king of Persia, that he made a proclamation throughout all his kingdom, and put it also in writing, saying,

23 Thus says Cyrus king of Persia, All the kingdoms of the earth has the Becoming-One, God of the heavens given me; and he has charged me to build him a house in Jerusalem, which is in Judah. Who is there among you of all his people? The Becoming-One his God be with him, and let him go up.

Ezra

Ezra 1:1 Now in the first year of **Cyrus** king of Persia, that the word of the Becoming-One by the mouth of Jeremiah might be fulfilled, the Becoming-One stirred up the spirit of Cyrus king of Persia, that he made a proclamation throughout all his kingdom, and put it also in writing, saying, [3435/6 YM; 539/8 BC]

2 Thus says Cyrus king of Persia, The Becoming-One, God of the heavens has given me all the kingdoms of the earth; and he has charged me to build him a house at Jerusalem, which is in Judah.

3 Who is there among you of all his people? his God be with him, and let him go up to Jerusalem, which is in Judah, and build the house of the Becoming-One, God of Israel, he is God, which is in Jerusalem.

4 And whosoever remains in any place where he sojourns, let the men of his place help him with silver, and with gold, and with goods, and with beasts, beside the freewill offering for the house of God that is in Jerusalem.

5 Then rose up the chief of the fathers of Judah and Benjamin, and the priests, and the Levites, with all them whose spirit God had raised, to go up to build the house of the Becoming-One which is in Jerusalem.

6 And all they that were about them strengthened their hands with vessels of silver, with gold, with goods, and with beasts, and with precious things, beside all that was willingly offered.

7 Also Cyrus the king brought forth the vessels of the house of the Becoming-One, which Nebuchadnezzar had brought forth out of Jerusalem, and had put them in the house of his gods;

8 Even those did Cyrus king of Persia bring forth by the hand of Mithredath the treasurer, and numbered them unto Sheshbazzar, the prince of Judah.

9 And this is the number of them: thirty chargers of gold, a thousand chargers of silver, nine and twenty knives,

10 Thirty basins of gold, silver basins of a second sort four hundred and ten, and other vessels a thousand.

11 All the vessels of gold and of silver were five thousand and four hundred. All these did Sheshbazzar bring up with them of the captivity that were brought up from Babylon unto Jerusalem.

Ezra 2:1 Now these are the children of the province that went up out of the captivity, of those which had been carried away, whom Nebuchadnezzar the king of Babylon had carried away unto Babylon, and came again unto Jerusalem and Judah, every one unto his city;

2 Which came with **Zerubbabel**: **Jeshua**, Nehemiah, Seraiah, Reelaiah, Mordecai, Bilshan, Mizpar, Bigvai, Rehum, Baanah. The number of the men of the people of Israel:

3 The children of Parosh, two thousand a hundred seventy and two.

4 The children of Shephatiah, three hundred seventy and two.

5 The children of Arah, seven hundred seventy and five.

6 The children of Pahathmoab, of the children of Jeshua and Joab, two thousand eight hundred and twelve.

7 The children of Elam, a thousand two hundred fifty and four.

8 The children of Zattu, nine hundred forty and five.

9 The children of Zaccai, seven hundred and threescore.

10 The children of Bani, six hundred forty and two.

11 The children of Bebai, six hundred twenty and three.

12 The children of Azgad, a thousand two hundred twenty and two.

13 The children of Adonikam, six hundred sixty and six.

14 The children of Bigvai, two thousand fifty and six.

15 The children of Adin, four hundred fifty and four.

16 The children of Ater of Hezekiah, ninety and eight.

17 The children of Bezai, three hundred twenty and three.

18 The children of Jorah, a hundred and twelve.

19 The children of Hashum, two hundred twenty and three.

20 The children of Gibbar, ninety and five.

21 The children of Bethlehem, a hundred twenty and three.

22 The men of Netophah, fifty and six.

23 The men of Anathoth, a hundred twenty and eight.

24 The children of Azmaveth, forty and two.

25 The children of Kirjatharim, Chephirah, and Beeroth, seven hundred and forty and three.

26 The children of Ramah and Gaba, six hundred twenty and one.

27 The men of Michmas, a hundred twenty and two.

28 The men of Bethel and Ai, two hundred twenty and three.

29 The children of Nebo, fifty and two.

30 The children of Magbish, a hundred fifty and six.

31 The children of the other Elam, a thousand two hundred fifty and four.

32 The children of Harim, three hundred and twenty.

33 The children of Lod, Hadid, and Ono, seven hundred twenty and five.

34 The children of Jericho, three hundred forty and five.

35 The children of Senaah, three thousand and six hundred and thirty.

36 The priests: the children of Jedaiah, of the house of Jeshua, nine hundred seventy and three.

37 The children of Immer, a thousand fifty and two.

38 The children of Pashur, a thousand two hundred forty and seven.

39 The children of Harim, a thousand and seventeen.

40 The Levites: the children of Jeshua and Kadmiel, of the children of Hodaviah, seventy and four.

41 The singers: the children of Asaph, a hundred twenty and eight.

42 The children of the gatekeepers: the children of Shallum, the children of Ater, the children of Talmon, the children of Akkub, the children of Hatita, the children of Shobai, in all a hundred thirty and nine.

43 The Nethinims: the children of Ziha, the children of Hasupha, the children of Tabbaoth,

44 The children of Keros, the children of Siaha, the children of Padon,

45 The children of Lebanah, the children of Hagabah, the children of Akkub,

46 The children of Hagab, the children of Shalmai, the children of Hanan,

47 The children of Giddel, the children of Gahar, the children of Reaiah,

48 The children of Rezin, the children of Nekoda, the children of Gazzam,

49 The children of Uzza, the children of Paseah, the children of Besai,

50 The children of Asnah, the children of Mehunim, the children of Nephusim,

51 The children of Bakbuk, the children of Hakupha, the children of Harhur,

52 The children of Bazluth, the children of Mehida, the children of Harsha,

53 The children of Barkos, the children of Sisera, the children of Thamah,

54 The children of Neziah, the children of Hatipha.

55 The children of Solomon's servants: the children of Sotai, the children of Sophereth, the children of Peruda,

56 The children of Jaalah, the children of Darkon, the children of Giddel,

57 The children of Shephatiah, the children of Hattil, the children of Pochereth of Zebaim, the children of Ami.

58 All the Nethinims, and the children of Solomon's servants, were three hundred ninety and two.

59 And these were they which went up from Telmelah, Telharsa, Cherub, Addan, and Immer: but they could not show their father's house, and their seed, whether they were of Israel:

60 The children of Delaiah, the children of Tobiah, the children of Nekoda, six hundred fifty and two.

61 And of the children of the priests: the children of Habaiah, the children of Koz, the children of Barzillai; which took a wife of the daughters of Barzillai the Gileadite, and was called after their name:

62 These sought their register among those that were reckoned by genealogy, but they were not found: therefore were they, as polluted, put from the priesthood.

63 And the Tirshatha said unto them, that they should not eat of the most holy things, till there stood up a priest with Urim and with Thummim.

64 The whole congregation together was forty and two thousand three hundred and threescore,

65 Beside their servants and their maids, of whom there were seven thousand three hundred thirty and seven: and there were among them two hundred singing men and singing women.

66 Their horses were seven hundred thirty and six; their mules, two hundred forty and five;

67 Their camels, four hundred thirty and five; their donkeys, six thousand seven hundred and twenty.

68 And some of the chief of the fathers, when they came to the house of the Becoming-One which is at Jerusalem, offered freely for the house of God to set it up in his place:

69 They gave after their ability unto the treasure of the work threescore and one thousand drams of gold, and five thousand pounds of silver, and one hundred priests' garments.

70 So the priests, and the Levites, and some of the people, and the singers, and the gatekeepers, and the Nethinims, dwelt in their cities, and all Israel in their cities.

Ezra 3:1 And when the seventh month was come, and the children of Israel were in the cities, the people gathered themselves together as one man to Jerusalem.

2 Then stood up Jeshua the son of Jozadak, and his brethren the priests, and Zerubbabel the son of Shealtiel, and his brethren, and built the altar of God of Israel, to offer burnt offerings thereon, as it is written in the law of Moses the man of God.

3 And they set the altar upon his bases; for fear was upon them because of the people of those countries: and they offered burnt offerings thereon unto the Becoming-One, even burnt offerings morning and evening.

4 They kept also the feast of tabernacles, as it is written, and offered the daily burnt offerings by number, according to the custom, as the duty of every day required;

5 And afterward offered the continual burnt offering, both of the new moons, and of all the set times[122] of the Becoming-One that were consecrated, and of every one that willingly offered a freewill offering unto the Becoming-One.

6 From the first day of the seventh month began they to offer burnt offerings unto the Becoming-One. But the foundation of the temple of the Becoming-One was not yet laid.

7 They gave money also unto the masons, and to the carpenters; and food, and drink, and oil, unto them of Zidon, and to them of Tyre, to bring cedar trees from Lebanon to the sea of Joppa, according to the grant that they had of Cyrus king of Persia.

8 Now in the second year of their coming unto the house of God at Jerusalem, in the second month, began Zerubbabel the son of Shealtiel, and Jeshua the son of Jozadak, and the remnant of their brethren the priests and the Levites, and all they that were come out of the captivity unto Jerusalem; and appointed the Levites, from a son of twenty years and upward, to

---

[122] Appointed times or festivals

set forward the work of the house of the Becoming-One.

9 Then stood Jeshua with his sons and his brethren, Kadmiel and his sons, the sons of Judah, together, to set forward the workmen in the house of God: the sons of Henadad, with their sons and their brethren the Levites.

10 And when the builders laid the foundation of the temple of the Becoming-One, they set the priests in their apparel with trumpets, and the Levites the sons of Asaph with cymbals, to praise the Becoming-One, after the ordinance of David king of Israel.

11 And they sang together by course in praising and giving thanks unto the Becoming-One; because he is good, for his mercy endures for olam toward Israel. And all the people shouted with a great shout, when they praised the Becoming-One, because the foundation of the house of the Becoming-One was laid.

12 But many of the priests and Levites and chief of the fathers, who were ancient men, that had seen the first house, when the foundation of this house was laid before their eyes, wept with a loud voice; and many shouted aloud for joy:

13 So that the people could not discern the noise of the shout of joy from the noise of the weeping of the people: for the people shouted with a loud shout, and the noise was heard afar off.

Ezra 4:1 Now when the adversaries of Judah and Benjamin heard that the children of the captivity built the temple unto the Becoming-One, God of Israel;

2 Then they came to Zerubbabel, and to the chief of the fathers, and said unto them, Let us build with you: for we seek your God, as you do; and we do sacrifice unto him since the days of Esarhaddon king of Assur, which brought us up here.

3 But Zerubbabel, and Jeshua, and the rest of the chief of the fathers of Israel, said unto them, you have nothing to do with us to build a house unto our God; but we ourselves together will build unto the Becoming-One, God of Israel, as king Cyrus the king of Persia has commanded us.

4 Then the people of the land weakened the hands of the people of Judah, and troubled them in building,

5 And hired councelors against them, to frustrate their purpose, all the days of Cyrus king of Persia, even until the reign of **Darius** king of **Persia**.

6 And in the reign of **Ahasuerus**, in the beginning of his reign, wrote they unto him an accusation against the inhabitants of Judah and Jerusalem.

7 And in the days of **Artaxerxes** wrote Bishlam, Mithredath, Tabeel, and the rest of their companions, unto Artaxerxes king of Persia; and the writing of the letter was written in the Syrian [Aramaic] tongue, and interpreted in the Syrian tongue.

8 Rehum the chancellor and Shimshai the scribe wrote a letter against Jerusalem to Artaxerxes the king in this sort:

9 Then wrote Rehum the chancellor, and Shimshai the scribe, and the rest of their companions; the Dinaites, the Apharsathchites, the Tarpelites, the Apharsites, the Archevites, the Babylonians, the Susanchites, the Dehavites, and the Elamites,

10 And the rest of the nations whom the great and noble Asnapper brought over, and set in the cities of Samaria, and the rest that are on this side the river, and at such a time.

11 This is the copy of the letter that they sent unto him, even unto Artaxerxes the king; your servants the men on this side the river, and at such a time.

12 Be it known unto the king, that the Jews which came up from you to us are come unto Jerusalem, building the rebellious and the bad city, and have set up the walls thereof, and joined the foundations.

13 Be it known now unto the king, that, **if** this city be built, and the walls set up again, then will they not pay toll, tribute, and custom, and so you shall endamage the revenue of the kings.

14 Now because we have maintenance from the king's palace, and it was not meet for us to see the king's dishonor, therefore have we sent and certified the king;

15 That search may be made in the book of the records of your fathers: so shall you find in the book of the records, and know that this city is a rebellious city, and hurtful unto kings and provinces, and that they have moved sedition within the same from the days of olam [alam], for which cause was this city destroyed.

16 We certify the king that, **if** this city be built again, and the walls thereof set up, by this means you shall have no portion on this side the river.

17 Then sent the king an answer unto Rehum the chancellor, and to Shimshai the scribe, and to the rest of their companions that dwell in Samaria, and unto the rest beyond the river, Peace, and at such a time.

18 The letter which you sent unto us has been plainly read before me.

19 And I commanded, and search has been made, and it is found that this city from the days of olam [alam] has made insurrection against kings, and that rebellion and sedition have been made therein.

20 There have been mighty kings also over Jerusalem, which have ruled over all countries beyond the river; and toll, tribute, and custom, was paid unto them.

21 Give you now commandment to cause these men to cease, and that this city be not built, until another commandment shall be given from me.

22 Take heed now that you fail not to do this: why should damage grow to the hurt of the kings?

23 Now when the copy of king Artaxerxes' letter was read before Rehum, and Shimshai the scribe, and their companions, they went up in haste to Jerusalem unto the Jews, and made them to cease by force and power.

24 Then ceased the work of the house of GOD which is at Jerusalem. So it ceased unto the second year of the reign of **Darius** king of **Persia**.

Ezra 5:1 Now the prophets, Haggai the prophet, and Zechariah the son of Iddo, prophesied unto the Jews that were in Judah and Jerusalem in the name of GOD of Israel, even unto them.

2 Then rose up Zerubbabel the son of Shealtiel, and Jeshua the son of Jozadak, and began to build the house of GOD which is at Jerusalem: and with them were the prophets of GOD helping them.

3 At the same time came to them Tatnai, governor on this side the river, and Shetharboznai, and their companions, and said thus unto them, Who has commanded you to build this house, and to make up this wall?

4 Then said we unto them after this manner, What are the names of the men that make this building?

5 But the eye of their GOD was upon the elders of the Jews, that they could not cause them to cease, till the matter came to Darius: and then they returned answer by letter concerning this matter.

6 The copy of the letter that Tatnai, governor on this side the river, and Shetharboznai, and his companions the Apharsachites, which were on this side the river, sent unto Darius the king:

7 They sent a letter unto him, wherein was written thus; Unto Darius the king, all peace.

8 Be it known unto the king, that we went into the province of Judea, to the house of the great GOD, which is built with great stones, and timber is laid in the walls, and this work goes fast on, and prospers in their hands.

9 Then asked we those elders, and said unto them thus, Who commanded you to build this house, and to make up these walls?

10 We asked their names also, to certify you, that we might write the names of the men that were the chief of them.

11 And thus they returned us answer, saying, We are the servants of GOD of the heavens and earth, and build the house that was built these many years ago, which a great king of Israel built and set up.

12 But after that our fathers had provoked GOD of the heavens unto wrath, he gave them into the hand of Nebuchadnezzar the king of Babylon, the Chaldean, who destroyed this house, and carried the people away into Babylon.

13 But in the first year of Cyrus the king of Babylon the same king Cyrus made a decree to build this house of GOD.

14 And the vessels also of gold and silver of the house of GOD, which Nebuchadnezzar took out of the temple that was in Jerusalem, and brought them into the temple of Babylon, those did Cyrus the king take out of the temple of Babylon, and they were delivered unto one, whose name was Sheshbazzar, whom he had made governor;

15 And said unto him, Take these vessels, go, carry them into the temple that is in Jerusalem, and let the house of GOD be built in his place.

16 Then came the same Sheshbazzar, and laid the foundation of the house of GOD which is in Jerusalem: and since that time even until now has it been in building, and yet it is not finished.

17 Now therefore, if it seem good to the king, let there be search made in the king's treasure house, which is there at Babylon, whether it be so, that a decree was made of Cyrus the king to build this house of GOD at Jerusalem, and let the king send his pleasure to us concerning this matter.

Ezra 6:1 Then Darius [of Persia] the king made a decree, and search was made in the house of the rolls, where the treasures were laid up in Babylon.

2 And there was found at Achmetha, in the palace that is in the province of the Medes, a roll, and therein was a record thus written:

3 In the first year of Cyrus the king the same Cyrus the king made a decree concerning the house of GOD at Jerusalem, Let the house be built, the place where they offered sacrifices, and let the foundations thereof be strongly laid; the height thereof threescore cubits, and the breadth thereof threescore cubits;

4 With three rows of great stones, and a row of new timber: and let the expenses be given out of the king's house:

5 And also let the golden and silver vessels of the house of GOD, which Nebuchadnezzar took forth out of the temple which is at Jerusalem, and brought unto Babylon, be restored, and brought again unto the temple which is at Jerusalem, every one to his place, and place them in the house of GOD.

6 Now therefore, Tatnai, governor beyond the river, Shetharboznai, and your companions the Apharsachites, which are beyond the river, be you far from there:

7 Let the work of this house of GOD alone; let the governor of the Jews and the elders of the Jews build this house of GOD in his place.

8 Moreover I make a decree what you shall do to the elders of these Jews for the building of this house of GOD: that of the king's goods, even of the tribute beyond the river, forthwith expenses be given unto these men, that they be not hindered.

9 And that which they have need of, both young bullocks, and rams, and lambs, for the burnt offerings of GOD of the heavens, wheat, salt, wine, and oil, according to the appointment of the priests which are at Jerusalem, let it be given them day by day without fail:

10 That they may offer sacrifices of sweet savours unto GOD of the heavens, and pray for the life of the king, and of his sons.

11 Also I have made a decree, that whosoever shall alter this word, let timber be pulled down from his house, and being set up, let him be hanged thereon; and let his house be made a dunghill for this.

12 And GOD that has caused his name to dwell there destroy all kings and people, that shall put to their hand to alter and to destroy this house of GOD which is at Jerusalem. I Darius have made a decree; let it be done with speed.

13 Then Tatnai, governor on this side the river, Shetharboznai, and their companions, according to that which Darius the king had sent, so they did speedily.

14 And the elders of the Jews built, and they prospered through the prophesying of Haggai the prophet and Zechariah the son of Iddo. And they built, and finished it, according to the commandment of GOD of Israel, and according to the commandment of Cyrus, and Darius, and Artaxerxes king of Persia.

15 And this house was finished on the third day of the month Adar, which was in the sixth year of the reign of Darius the king [of Persia].

16 And the children of Israel, the priests, and the Levites, and the rest of the children of the captivity, kept the dedication of this house of GOD with joy,

17 And offered at the dedication of this house of GOD a hundred bullocks, two hundred rams, four hundred lambs; and for a sin offering for all Israel, twelve he goats, according to the number of the tribes of Israel.

18 And they set the priests in their divisions, and the Levites in their courses, for the service of GOD, which is at Jerusalem; as it is written in the book of Moses.

19 And the children of the captivity kept the Passover upon the fourteenth day of the first month.

20 For the priests and the Levites were purified together, all of them were pure, and killed the Passover for all the children of the captivity, and for their brethren the priests, and for themselves.

21 And the children of Israel, which were come again out of captivity, and all such as had separated themselves unto them from the filthiness of the nations of the land, to seek the Becoming-One, God of Israel, did eat,

22 And kept the feast of unleavened bread seven days with joy: for the Becoming-One had made them joyful, and turned the heart of the king of Assyria unto them, to strengthen their hands in the work of the house of God, God of Israel.

Ezra 7:1 Now after these things, in the reign of Artaxerxes king of Persia, Ezra the son of Seraiah, the son of Azariah, the son of Hilkiah,

2 The son of Shallum, the son of Zadok, the son of Ahitub,

3 The son of Amariah, the son of Azariah, the son of Meraioth,

4 The son of Zerahiah, the son of Uzzi, the son of Bukki,

5 The son of Abishua, the son of Phinehas, the son of Eleazar, the son of Aaron the chief priest:

6 This **Ezra** went up from Babylon; and he was a ready scribe in the law of Moses, which the Becoming-One, God of Israel had given: and the king granted him all his request, according to the hand of the Becoming-One his God upon him.

7 And there went up some of the children of Israel, and of the priests, and the Levites, and the singers, and the gatekeepers, and the Nethinims, unto Jerusalem, **in the seventh year of Artaxerxes the king.**

8 And he came to Jerusalem in the fifth month, which was in the seventh year of the king.

9 For upon the first day of the first month began he to go up from Babylon, and on the first day of the fifth month came he to Jerusalem, according to the good hand of his God upon him.

10 For Ezra had prepared his heart to seek the law of the Becoming-One, and to do it, and to teach in Israel statutes and judgments.

11 Now this is the copy of the letter that the king Artaxerxes gave unto Ezra the priest, the scribe, even a scribe of the words of the commandments of the Becoming-One, and of his statutes to Israel.

12 Artaxerxes, king of kings, unto Ezra the priest, a scribe of the law of GOD of heaven, perfect peace, and at such a time.

13 I make a decree, that all they of the people of Israel, and of his priests and Levites, in my realm, which are minded of their own freewill to go up to Jerusalem, go with you.

14 Forasmuch as you are sent of the king, and of his seven counselors, to inquire concerning Judah and Jerusalem, according to the law of your GOD which is in your hand;

15 And to carry the silver and gold, which the king and his counselors have freely offered unto GOD of Israel, whose habitation is in Jerusalem,

16 And all the silver and gold that you can find in all the province of Babylon, with the freewill offering of the people, and of the priests, offering willingly for the house of their GOD which is in Jerusalem:

17 That you may buy speedily with this money bullocks, rams, lambs, with their food offerings and their drink offerings, and offer them upon the altar of the house of your GOD which is in Jerusalem.

18 And whatsoever shall seem good to you, and to your brethren, to do with the rest of the silver and the gold, that do after the will of your GOD.

19 The vessels also that are given you for the service of the house of your GOD, those deliver you before GOD of Jerusalem.

20 And whatsoever more shall be needful for the house of your GOD, which you shall have occasion to bestow, bestow it out of the king's treasure house.

21 And I, even I Artaxerxes the king, do make a decree to all the treasurers which are beyond the river, that whatsoever Ezra the priest, the scribe of the law of GOD of heaven, shall require of you, it be done speedily,

22 Unto a hundred talents of silver, and to a hundred measures of wheat, and to a hundred baths of wine, and to a hundred baths of oil, and salt without prescribing how much.

23 Whatsoever is commanded by GOD of heaven, let it be diligently done for the house of GOD of heaven: for why should there be wrath against the realm of the king and his sons?

24 Also we certify you, that touching any of the priests and Levites, singers, gatekeepers, Nethinims, or ministers of this house of GOD, it shall not be lawful to impose toll, tribute, or custom, upon them.

25 And you, Ezra, after the wisdom of your GOD, that is in your hand, set magistrates and judges, which may judge all the people that are beyond the river, all such as know the laws of your GOD; and teach you them that know them not.

26 And whosoever will not do the law of your GOD, and the law of the king, let judgment be executed speedily upon him, whether it be unto death, or to banishment, or to confiscation of goods, or to imprisonment.

27 Blessed be the Becoming-One, God of our fathers, which has put such a thing as this in the king's heart, to beautify the house of the Becoming-One which is in Jerusalem:

28 And has extended mercy unto me before the king, and his counselors, and before all the king's mighty princes. And I was strengthened as the hand of the Becoming-One my God was upon me, and I

gathered together out of Israel chief men to go up with me.

Ezra 8:1 These are now the chief of their fathers, and this is the genealogy of them that went up with me from Babylon, in the reign of Artaxerxes the king.

2 Of the sons of Phinehas; Gershom: of the sons of Ithamar; Daniel: of the sons of David; Hattush.

3 Of the sons of Shechaniah, of the sons of Pharosh; Zechariah: and with him were reckoned by genealogy of the males a hundred and fifty.

4 Of the sons of Pahathmoab; Elihoenai the son of Zerahiah, and with him two hundred males.

5 Of the sons of Shechaniah; the son of Jahaziel, and with him three hundred males.

6 Of the sons also of Adin; Ebed the son of Jonathan, and with him fifty males.

7 And of the sons of Elam; Jeshaiah the son of Athaliah, and with him seventy males.

8 And of the sons of Shephatiah; Zebadiah the son of Michael, and with him fourscore males.

9 Of the sons of Joab; Obadiah the son of Jehiel, and with him two hundred and eighteen males.

10 And of the sons of Shelomith; the son of Josiphiah, and with him a hundred and threescore males.

11 And of the sons of Bebai; Zechariah the son of Bebai, and with him twenty and eight males.

12 And of the sons of Azgad; Johanan the son of Hakkatan, and with him a hundred and ten males.

13 And of the last sons of Adonikam, whose names are these, Eliphelet, Jeiel, and Shemaiah, and with them threescore males.

14 Of the sons also of Bigvai; Uthai, and Zabbud, and with them seventy males.

15 And I gathered them together to the river that runs to Ahava; and there abode we in tents three days: and I viewed the people, and the priests, and found there none of the sons of Levi.

16 Then sent I for Eliezer, for Ariel, for Shemaiah, and for Elnathan, and for Jarib, and for Elnathan, and for Nathan, and for Zechariah, and for Meshullam, chief men; also for Joiarib, and for Elnathan, men of understanding.

17 And I sent them with commandment unto Iddo the chief at the place Casiphia, and I told them what they should say unto Iddo, and to his brethren the Nethinims, at the place Casiphia, that they should bring unto us ministers for the house of our God.

18 And by the good hand of our God upon us they brought us a man of understanding, of the sons of Mahli, the son of Levi, the son of Israel; and Sherebiah, with his sons and his brethren, eighteen;

19 And Hashabiah, and with him Jeshaiah of the sons of Merari, his brethren and their sons, twenty;

20 Also of the Nethinims, whom David and the princes had appointed for the service of the Levites, two hundred and twenty Nethinims: all of them were expressed by name.

21 Then I proclaimed a fast there, at the river of Ahava, that we might afflict ourselves before our God, to seek of him a right way for us, and for our little ones, and for all our substance.

22 For I was ashamed to require of the king a band of soldiers and horsemen to help us against the enemy in the way: because we had spoken unto the king, saying, The hand of our God is upon all them for good that seek him; but his power and his wrath is against all them that forsake him.

23 So we fasted and besought our God for this: and he was entreated of us.

24 Then I separated twelve of the chief of the priests, Sherebiah, Hashabiah, and ten of their brethren with them,

25 And weighed unto them the silver, and the gold, and the vessels, even the offering of the house of our God, which the king, and his councelors, and his officials, and all Israel there present, had offered:

26 I even weighed unto their hand six hundred and fifty talents of silver, and silver vessels a hundred talents, and of gold a hundred talents;

27 Also twenty basins of gold, of a thousand of drams; and two vessels of fine copper, precious as gold.

28 And I said unto them, you are holy unto the Becoming-One; the vessels are holy also; and the silver and the gold are a freewill offering unto the Becoming-One, God of your fathers.

29 Watch ye, and keep them, until you weigh them before the chief of the priests and the Levites, and chief of the fathers of Israel, at Jerusalem, in the chambers of the house of the Becoming-One.

30 So took the priests and the Levites the weight of the silver, and the gold, and the vessels, to bring them to Jerusalem unto the house of our God.

31 Then we departed from the river of Ahava on the twelfth day of the first month, to go unto Jerusalem: and the hand of our God was upon us, and he delivered us from the hand of the enemy, and of such as lay in wait by the way.

32 And we came to Jerusalem, and abode there three days.

33 Now on the fourth day was the silver and the gold and the vessels weighed in the house of our God by the hand of Meremoth the son of Uriah the priest; and with him was Eleazar the son of Phinehas; and with them was Jozabad the son of Jeshua, and Noadiah the son of Binnui, Levites;

34 By number and by weight of every one: and all the weight was written at that time.

35 Also the children of those that had been carried away, which were come out of the captivity, offered burnt offerings unto God of Israel, twelve bullocks for all Israel, ninety and six rams, seventy and seven lambs, twelve he goats for a sin offering: all this was a burnt offering unto the Becoming-One.

36 And they delivered the king's laws unto the king's lieutenants, and to the governors over the river: and they furthered the people, and the house of God.

Ezra 9:1 Now when these things were done, the princes came to me, saying, The people of Israel, and the priests, and the Levites, have not separated themselves from the people of the lands, doing according to their abominations, even of the Canaanites, the Hittites, the Perizzites, the Jebusites, the Ammonites, the Moabites, the Egyptians, and the Amorites.

2 For they have taken of their daughters for themselves, and for their sons: so that the holy seed

have mingled themselves with the people of those lands: yes, the hand of the princes and rulers has been chief in this trespass.

3 And when I heard this thing, I ripped my garment and my mantle, and plucked off the hair of my head and of my beard, and sat down astonished.

4 Then were assembled unto me every one that trembled at the words of God of Israel, because of the transgression of those that had been carried away; and I sat astonied until the evening sacrifice.

5 And at the evening sacrifice I arose up from my heaviness; and having ripped my garment and my mantle, I fell upon my knees, and spread out my hands unto the Becoming-One my God,

6 And said, O my God, I am ashamed and blush to lift up my face to you, my God: for our iniquities are increased over our head, and our trespass is grown up unto the heavens.

7 Since the days of our fathers have we been in a great trespass unto this day; and for our iniquities have we, our kings, and our priests, been delivered into the hand of the kings of the lands, to the sword, to captivity, and to a spoil, and to confusion of face, as it is this day.

8 And now for a little space grace has been showed from the Becoming-One our God, to leave us a remnant to escape, and to give us a nail in his holy place, that our God may lighten our eyes, and give us a little reviving in our bondage.

9 For we were bondmen; yet our God has not forsaken us in our bondage, but has extended mercy unto us in the sight of the kings of Persia, to give us a reviving, to set up the house of our God, and to repair the desolations thereof, and to give us a wall in Judah and in Jerusalem.

10 And now, O our God, what shall we say after this? for we have forsaken your commandments,

11 Which you have commanded by your servants the prophets, saying, The land, unto which you go to possess it, is an unclean land with the filthiness of the people of the lands, with their abominations, which have filled it from one end to another with their uncleanness.

12 Now therefore give not your daughters unto their sons, neither take their daughters unto your sons, nor seek their peace or their wealth for olam that you may be strong, and eat the good of the land, and leave it for an inheritance to your children for olam.

13 And after all that is come upon us for our evil deeds, and for our great trespass, seeing that you our God have punished us less than our iniquities deserve, and have given us such deliverance as this;

14 Should we again break your commandments, and join in affinity with the people of these abominations? would not you be angry with us till you had consumed us, so that there should be no remnant nor escaping?

15 O Becoming-One, God of Israel, you are righteous: for we remain yet escaped, as it is this day: behold, we are before you in our trespasses: for we cannot stand before you because of this.

Ezra 10:1 Now when Ezra had prayed, and when he had confessed, weeping and casting himself down before the house of God, there assembled unto him out of Israel a very great congregation of men and women and children: for the people wept very greatly.

2 And Shechaniah the son of Jehiel, one of the sons of Elam, answered and said unto Ezra, We have trespassed against our God, and have taken strange wives of the people of the land: yet now there is hope in Israel concerning this thing.

3 Now therefore let us make a covenant with our God to put away all the wives, and such as are born of them, according to the counsel of my Lord(s), and of those that tremble at the commandment of our God; and let it be done according to the law.

4 Arise; for this matter belongs unto you: we also will be with you: be of good courage, and do it.

5 Then arose Ezra, and made the chief priests, the Levites, and all Israel, to swear that they should do according to this word. And they swore.

6 Then Ezra rose up from before the house of God, and went into the chamber of Johanan the son of Eliashib: and when he came there, he did eat no bread, nor drink water: for he mourned because of the transgression of them that had been carried away.

7 And they made proclamation throughout Judah and Jerusalem unto all the children of the captivity, that they should gather themselves together unto Jerusalem;

8 And that whosoever would not come within three days, according to the counsel of the princes and the elders, all his substance should be forfeited, and himself separated from the congregation of those that had been carried away.

9 Then all the men of Judah and Benjamin gathered themselves together unto Jerusalem within three days. It was the ninth month, on the twentieth day of the month; and all the people sat in the street of the house of God, trembling because of this matter, and for the great rain.

10 And Ezra the priest stood up, and said unto them, you have transgressed, and have taken strange wives, to increase the trespass of Israel.

11 Now therefore make confession unto the Becoming-One, God of your fathers, and do his pleasure: and separate yourselves from the people of the land, and from the strange wives.

12 Then all the congregation answered and said with a loud voice, As you have said, so must we do.

13 But the people are many, and it is a time of much rain, and we are not able to stand outside, neither is this a work of one day or two: for we are many that have transgressed in this thing.

14 Let now our rulers of all the congregation stand, and let all them which have taken strange wives in our cities come at appointed times, and with them the elders of every city, and the judges thereof, until the fierce wrath of our God for this matter be turned from us.

15 Only Jonathan the son of Asahel and Jahaziah the son of Tikvah were employed about this matter: and Meshullam and Shabbethai the Levite helped them.

16 And the children of the captivity did so. And Ezra the priest, with certain chief of the fathers, after the house of their fathers, and all of them by their

names, were separated, and sat down in the first day of the tenth month to examine the matter.

17 And they made an end with all the men that had taken strange wives by the first day of the first month.

18 And among the sons of the priests there were found that had taken strange wives: namely, of the sons of Jeshua the son of Jozadak, and his brethren; Maaseiah, and Eliezer, and Jarib, and Gedaliah.

19 And they gave their hands that they would put away their wives; and being guilty, they offered a ram of the flock for their trespass.

20 And of the sons of Immer; Hanani, and Zebadiah.

21 And of the sons of Harim; Maaseiah, and Elijah, and Shemaiah, and Jehiel, and Uzziah.

22 And of the sons of Pashur; Elioenai, Maaseiah, Ishmael, Nethaneel, Jozabad, and Elasah.

23 Also of the Levites; Jozabad, and Shimei, and Kelaiah, the same is Kelita, Pethahiah, Judah, and Eliezer.

24 Of the singers also; Eliashib: and of the gatekeepers; Shallum, and Telem, and Uri.

25 Moreover of Israel: of the sons of Parosh; Ramiah, and Jeziah, and Malchiah, and Miamin, and Eleazar, and Malchijah, and Benaiah.

26 And of the sons of Elam; Mattaniah, Zechariah, and Jehiel, and Abdi, and Jeremoth, and Eliah.

27 And of the sons of Zattu; Elioenai, Eliashib, Mattaniah, and Jeremoth, and Zabad, and Aziza.

28 Of the sons also of Bebai; Jehohanan, Hananiah, Zabbai, and Athlai.

29 And of the sons of Bani; Meshullam, Malluch, and Adaiah, Jashub, and Sheal, and Ramoth.

30 And of the sons of Pahathmoab; Adna, and Chelal, Benaiah, Maaseiah, Mattaniah, Bezaleel, and Binnui, and Manasseh.

31 And of the sons of Harim; Eliezer, Ishijah, Malchiah, Shemaiah, Shimeon,

32 Benjamin, Malluch, and Shemariah.

33 Of the sons of Hashum; Mattenai, Mattathah, Zabad, Eliphelet, Jeremai, Manasseh, and Shimei.

34 Of the sons of Bani; Maadai, Amram, and Uel,

35 Benaiah, Bedeiah, Chelluh,

36 Vaniah, Meremoth, Eliashib,

37 Mattaniah, Mattenai, and Jaasau,

38 And Bani, and Binnui, Shimei,

39 And Shelemiah, and Nathan, and Adaiah,

40 Machnadebai, Shashai, Sharai,

41 Azareel, and Shelemiah, Shemariah,

42 Shallum, Amariah, and Joseph.

43 Of the sons of Nebo; Jeiel, Mattithiah, Zabad, Zebina, Jadau, and Joel, Benaiah.

44 All these had taken strange wives: and some of them had wives by whom they had children.

Nehemiah

Neh 1:1 The words of Nehemiah the son of Hachaliah. And it came to pass in the month Chisleu, in the twentieth year, as I was in Shushan the palace,

2 That Hanani, one of my brethren, came, he and certain men of Judah; and I asked them concerning the Jews that had escaped, which were left of the captivity, and concerning Jerusalem.

3 And they said unto me, The remnant that are left of the captivity there in the province are in great affliction and reproach: the wall of Jerusalem also is broken down, and the gates thereof are burned with fire.

4 And it came to pass, when I heard these words, that I sat down and wept, and mourned certain days, and fasted, and prayed before God of heaven,

5 And said, I beg you, O Becoming-One, God of heaven, the great and terrible GOD, that keeps covenant and mercy for them that love him and observe his commandments:

6 Let your ear now be attentive, and your eyes open, that you may hear the prayer of your servant, which I pray before you now, day and night, for the children of Israel your servants, and confess the sins of the children of Israel, which we have sinned against you: both I and my father's house have sinned.

7 We have dealt very corruptly against you, and have not kept the commandments, nor the statutes, nor the judgments, which you commanded your servant Moses.

8 Remember, I beg you, the word that you commanded your servant Moses, saying, If you transgress, I will scatter you abroad among the nations:

9 But if you turn unto me, and keep my commandments, and do them; though there were of you cast out unto the uttermost part of the heaven, yet will I gather them from there, and will bring them unto the place that I have chosen to set my name there.

10 Now these are your servants and your people, whom you have redeemed by your great power, and by your strong hand.

11 O my Lord(s), I beg you, let now your ear be attentive to the prayer of your servant, and to the prayer of your servants, who desire to fear your name: and prosper, I pray you, your servant this day, and grant him mercy in the sight of this man. For I was the king's cupbearer.

Neh 2:1 And it came to pass in the month Nisan, in the twentieth year of Artaxerxes the king, that wine was before him: and I took up the wine, and gave it unto the king. Now I had not been beforetime sad in his presence.

2 Therefore the king said unto me, Why is your countenance sad, seeing you are not sick? this is nothing else but sorrow of heart. Then I was very greatly afraid,

3 And said unto the king, Let the king live for olam, why should not my countenance be sad, when the city, the place of my fathers' tombs, lies waste, and the gates thereof are consumed with fire?

4 Then the king said unto me, For what do you make request? So I prayed to God of heaven.

5 And I said unto the king, If it please the king, and if your servant have found favor in your sight, that you would send me unto Judah, unto the city of my fathers' tombs, that I may build it.

6 And the king said unto me, the queen also sitting by him, For how long shall your journey be? and when will you return? So it pleased the king to send me; and I set him a time.

7 Moreover I said unto the king, If it please the king, let letters be given me to the governors over the river, that they may convey me over till I come into Judah;

8 And a letter unto Asaph the keeper of the king's forest, that he may give me timber to make beams for the gates of the palace which appertained to the house, and for the wall of the city, and for the house that I shall enter into. And the king granted me, according to the good hand of my God upon me.

9 Then I came to the governors over the river, and gave them the king's letters. Now the king had sent captains of the army and horsemen with me.

10 When Sanballat the Horonite, and Tobiah the servant, the Ammonite, heard of it, it grieved them exceedingly that there was come a man to seek the welfare of the children of Israel.

11 So I came to Jerusalem, and was there three days.

12 And I arose in the night, I and some few men with me; neither told I any man what my God had put in my heart to do at Jerusalem: neither was there any beast with me, save the beast that I rode upon.

13 And I went out by night by the gate of the valley, even before the monster well, and to the dung port, and viewed the walls of Jerusalem, which were broken down, and the gates thereof were consumed with fire.

14 Then I went on to the gate of the fountain, and to the king's pool: but there was no place for the beast that was under me to pass.

15 Then went I up in the night by the brook, and viewed the wall, and turned back, and entered by the gate of the valley, and so returned.

16 And the rulers knew not where I went, or what I did; neither had I as yet told it to the Jews, nor to the priests, nor to the nobles, nor to the rulers, nor to the rest that did the work.

17 Then said I unto them, you see the distress that we are in, how Jerusalem lies waste, and the gates thereof are burned with fire: come, and let us build up the wall of Jerusalem, that we be no more a reproach.

18 Then I told them of the hand of my God which was good upon me; as also the king's words that he had spoken unto me. And they said, Let us rise up and build. So they strengthened their hands for this good work.

19 But when Sanballat the Horonite, and Tobiah the servant, the Ammonite, and Geshem the Arabian, heard it, they laughed us to scorn, and despised us, and said, What is this thing that you do? will you rebel against the king?

20 Then answered I them, and said unto them, God of heaven, he will prosper us; therefore we his

servants will arise and build: but you have no portion, nor right, nor memorial, in Jerusalem.

Neh 3:1 Then Eliashib the high priest rose up with his brethren the priests, and they built the sheep gate; they sanctified it, and set up the doors of it; even unto the tower of Meah they sanctified it, unto the tower of Hananeel.

2 And next unto him built the men of Jericho. And next to them built Zaccur the son of Imri.

3 But the fish gate did the sons of Hassenaah build, who also laid the beams thereof, and set up the doors thereof, the locks thereof, and the bars thereof.

4 And next unto them repaired Meremoth the son of Urijah, the son of Koz. And next unto them repaired Meshullam the son of Berechiah, the son of Meshezabeel. And next unto them repaired Zadok the son of Baana.

5 And next unto them the Tekoites repaired; but their nobles put not their necks to the work of their lords.

6 Moreover the old gate repaired Jehoiada the son of Paseah, and Meshullam the son of Besodeiah; they laid the beams thereof, and set up the doors thereof, and the locks thereof, and the bars thereof.

7 And next unto them repaired Melatiah the Gibeonite, and Jadon the Meronothite, the men of Gibeon, and of Mizpah, unto the throne of the governor over the river.

8 Next unto him repaired Uzziel the son of Harhaiah, of the goldsmiths. Next unto him also repaired Hananiah the son of one of the apothecaries, and they fortified Jerusalem unto the broad wall.

9 And next unto them repaired Rephaiah the son of Hur, the ruler of the half part of Jerusalem.

10 And next unto them repaired Jedaiah the son of Harumaph, even over against his house. And next unto him repaired Hattush the son of Hashabniah.

11 Malchijah the son of Harim, and Hashub the son of Pahathmoab, repaired the other piece, and the tower of the furnaces.

12 And next unto him repaired Shallum the son of Halohesh, the ruler of the half part of Jerusalem, he and his daughters.

13 The valley gate repaired Hanun, and the inhabitants of Zanoah; they built it, and set up the doors thereof, the locks thereof, and the bars thereof, and a thousand cubits on the wall unto the dung gate.

14 But the dung gate repaired Malchiah the son of Rechab, the ruler of part of Beth-haccerem; he built it, and set up the doors thereof, the locks thereof, and the bars thereof.

15 But the gate of the fountain repaired Shallun the son of Colhozeh, the ruler of part of Mizpah; he built it, and covered it, and set up the doors thereof, the locks thereof, and the bars thereof, and the wall of the pool of Siloah by the king's garden, and unto the stairs that go down from the city of David.

16 After him repaired Nehemiah the son of Azbuk, the ruler of the half part of Beth-zur, unto the place over against the tombs of David, and to the pool that was made, and unto the house of the mighty.

17 After him repaired the Levites, Rehum the son of Bani. Next unto him repaired Hashabiah, the ruler of the half part of Keilah, in his part.

18 After him repaired their brethren, Bavai the son of Henadad, the ruler of the half part of Keilah.

19 And next to him repaired Ezer the son of Jeshua, the ruler of Mizpah, another piece over against the going up to the armory at the corner of the wall.

20 After him Baruch the son of Zabbai earnestly repaired the other piece, from the corner of the wall unto the door of the house of Eliashib the high priest.

21 After him repaired Meremoth the son of Urijah the son of Koz another piece, from the door of the house of Eliashib even to the end of the house of Eliashib.

22 And after him repaired the priests, the men of the plain.

23 After him repaired Benjamin and Hashub over against their house. After him repaired Azariah the son of Maaseiah the son of Ananiah by his house.

24 After him repaired Binnui the son of Henadad another piece, from the house of Azariah unto the corner of the wall, even unto the corner.

25 Palal the son of Uzai, over against the corner of the wall, and the tower which lies out from the king's high house, that was by the court of the prison. After him Pedaiah the son of Parosh.

26 Moreover the Nethinims dwelt in Ophel, unto the place over against the water gate toward the east, and the tower that lies out.

27 After them the Tekoites repaired another piece, over against the great tower that lies out, even unto the wall of Ophel.

28 From above the horse gate repaired the priests, every one over against his house.

29 After them repaired Zadok the son of Immer over against his house. After him repaired also Shemaiah the son of Shechaniah, the keeper of the east gate.

30 After him repaired Hananiah the son of Shelemiah, and Hanun the sixth son of Zalaph, another piece. After him repaired Meshullam the son of Berechiah over against his chamber.

31 After him repaired Malchiah the goldsmith's son unto the place of the Nethinims, and of the merchants, over against the gate Miphkad, and to the going up of the corner.

32 And between the going up of the corner unto the sheep gate repaired the goldsmiths and the merchants.

Neh 4:1 But it came to pass, that when Sanballat heard that we built the wall, he was angry, and took great indignation, and mocked the Jews.

2 And he spoke before his brethren and the army of Samaria, and said, What do these feeble Jews? will they fortify themselves? will they sacrifice? will they make an end in a day? will they revive the stones out of the heaps of the rubbish which are burned?

3 Now Tobiah the Ammonite was by him, and he said, Even that which they build, if a fox go up, he shall even break down their stone wall.

4 Hear, O our God; for we are despised: and turn their reproach upon their own head, and give them for a prey in the land of captivity:

5 And cover not their iniquity, and let not their sin be blotted out from before you: for they have provoked you to anger before the builders.

6 So built we the wall; and all the wall was joined together unto the half thereof: for the people had a mind to work.

7 But it came to pass, that when Sanballat, and Tobiah, and the Arabians, and the Ammonites, and the Ashdodites, heard that the walls of Jerusalem were made up, and that the breaches began to be stopped, then they were very angry,

8 And conspired all of them together to come and to fight against Jerusalem, and to hinder it.

9 Nevertheless we made our prayer unto our God, and set a watch against them day and night, because of them.

10 And Judah said, The strength of the bearers of burdens is decayed, and there is much rubbish; so that we are not able to build the wall.

11 And our adversaries said, They shall not know, neither see, till we come in the midst among them, and slay them, and cause the work to cease.

12 And it came to pass, that when the Jews which dwelt by them came, they said unto us ten times, From all places where you shall return unto us they will be upon you.

13 Therefore set I in the lower places behind the wall, and on the higher places, I even set the people after their families with their swords, their spears, and their bows.

14 And I looked, and rose up, and said unto the nobles, and to the rulers, and to the rest of the people, Be not you afraid of them: remember my Lord(s), the great and terrible one, and fight for your brethren, your sons, and your daughters, your wives, and your houses.

15 And it came to pass, when our enemies heard that it was known unto us, and God had brought their counsel to nothing, that we returned all of us to the wall, every one unto his work.

16 And it came to pass from that time forth, that the half of my servants worked in the work, and the other half of them held both the spears, the shields, and the bows, and the habergeons; and the rulers were behind all the house of Judah.

17 They which built on the wall, and they that bare burdens, with those that laded, every one with one of his hands worked in the work, and with the other hand held a weapon.

18 For the builders, every one had his sword girded by his side, and so built. And he that sounded the trumpet was by me.

19 And I said unto the nobles, and to the rulers, and to the rest of the people, The work is great and large, and we are separated upon the wall, one far from another.

20 In what place therefore you hear the sound of the trumpet, resort you there unto us: our God shall fight for us.

21 So we labored in the work: and half of them held the spears from the rising of the dawn till the stars appeared.

22 Likewise at the same time said I unto the people, Let every one with his servant lodge within Jerusalem, that in the night they may be a guard to us, and labor on the day.

23 So neither I, nor my brethren, nor my servants, nor the men of the guard which followed me, none of us put off our clothes, saving that every one put them off for washing.

Neh 5:1 And there was a great cry of the people and of their wives against their brethren the Jews.

2 For there were that said, We, our sons, and our daughters, are many: therefore we take up grain for them, that we may eat, and live.

3 Some also there were that said, We have mortgaged our lands, vineyards, and houses, that we might buy grain, because of the dearth.

4 There were also that said, We have borrowed money for the king's tribute, and that upon our lands and vineyards.

5 Yet now our flesh is as the flesh of our brethren, our children as their children: and, lo, we bring into bondage our sons and our daughters to be servants, and some of our daughters are brought unto bondage already: neither is it in god of our hand to redeem them; for other men have our lands and vineyards.

6 And I was very angry when I heard their cry and these words.

7 Then I consulted with myself, and I rebuked the nobles, and the rulers, and said unto them, you exact usury, every one of his brother. And I set a great assembly against them.

8 And I said unto them, We after our ability have redeemed our brethren the Jews, which were sold unto the nations; and will you even sell your brethren? or shall they be sold unto us? Then held they their peace, and found nothing to answer.

9 Also I said, It is not good that you do: ought you not to walk in the fear of our God because of the reproach of the nations our enemies?

10 I likewise, and my brethren, and my servants, might exact of them money and grain: I pray you, let us leave off this usury.

11 Restore, I pray you, to them, even this day, their lands, their vineyards, their oliveyards, and their houses, also the hundredth part of the money, and of the grain, the wine, and the oil, that you exact of them.

12 Then said they, We will restore them, and will require nothing of them; so will we do as you say. Then I called the priests, and took an oath of them, that they should do according to this promise.

13 Also I shook my lap, and said, So God shake out every man from his house, and from his labor, that performs not this promise, even thus be he shaken out, and emptied. And all the congregation said, Amen, and praised the Becoming-One. And the people did according to this promise.

14 Moreover from the time that I was appointed to be their governor in the land of Judah, from the twentieth year even unto the two and thirtieth year of Artaxerxes the king, that is, twelve years, I and my brethren have not eaten the bread of the governor.

15 But the former governors that had been before me were chargeable unto the people, and had taken of them bread and wine, beside forty shekels of silver; yes, even their servants bare rule over the people: but so did not I, because of the fear of God.

16 Yes, also I continued in the work of this wall, neither bought we any land: and all my servants were gathered there unto the work.

17 Moreover there were at my table a hundred and fifty of the Jews and rulers, beside those that came unto us from among the nations that are about us.

18 Now that which was prepared for me daily was one ox and six choice sheep; also fowls were prepared for me, and once in ten days store of all sorts of wine: yet for all this required not I the bread of the governor, because the bondage was heavy upon this people.

19 Think upon me, my God, for good, according to all that I have done for this people.

Neh 6:1 Now it came to pass, when Sanballat, and Tobiah, and Geshem the Arabian, and the rest of our enemies, heard that I had built the wall, and that there was no breach left therein; though at that time I had not set up the doors upon the gates;

2 That Sanballat and Geshem sent unto me, saying, Come, let us meet together in some one of the villages in the plain of Ono. But they thought to do me mischief.

3 And I sent messengers unto them, saying, I am doing a great work, so that I cannot come down: why should the work cease, why leave it, and come down to you?

4 Yet they sent unto me four times after this sort; and I answered them after the same manner.

5 Then sent Sanballat his servant unto me in like manner the fifth time with an open letter in his hand;

6 Wherein was written, It is reported among the nations, and Gashmu says it, that you and the Jews think to rebel: for which cause you build the wall, that you may be their king, according to these words.

7 And you have also appointed prophets to preach of you at Jerusalem, saying, There is a king in Judah: and now shall it be reported to the king according to these words. Come now therefore, and let us take counsel together.

8 Then I sent unto him, saying, There are no such things done as you say, but you fake them out of your own heart.

9 For they all made us afraid, saying, Their hands shall be weakened from the work, that it be not done. Now therefore, O God, strengthen my hands.

10 Afterward I came unto the house of Shemaiah the son of Delaiah the son of Mehetabeel, who was shut up; and he said, Let us meet together in the house of God, within the temple, and let us shut the doors of the temple: for they will come to slay you; yes, in the night will they come to slay you.

11 And I said, Should such a man as I flee? and who is there, that, being as I am, would go into the temple to save his life? I will not go in.

12 And, lo, I perceived that God had not sent him; but that he pronounced this prophecy against me: for Tobiah and Sanballat had hired him.

13 Therefore was he hired, that I should be afraid, and do so, and sin, and that they might have matter for an evil report, that they might reproach me.

14 My God, think you upon Tobiah and Sanballat according to these their works, and on the prophetess Noadiah, and the rest of the prophets, that would have put me in fear.

15 So the wall was finished in the twenty and fifth day of the month Elul, in fifty and two days.

16 And it came to pass, that when all our enemies heard thereof, and all the nations that were about us saw these things, they were much cast down in their own eyes: for they perceived that this work was worked of our God.

17 Moreover in those days the nobles of Judah sent many letters unto Tobiah, and the letters of Tobiah came unto them.

18 For there were many in Judah sworn unto him, because he was the son-in-law of Shechaniah the son of Arah; and his son Johanan had taken the daughter of Meshullam the son of Berechiah.

19 Also they reported his good deeds before me, and uttered my words to him. And Tobiah sent letters to put me in fear.

Neh 7:1 Now it came to pass, when the wall was built, and I had set up the gates, and the gatekeepers and the singers and the Levites were appointed,

2 That I gave my brother Hanani, and Hananiah the ruler of the palace, charge over Jerusalem: for he was a faithful man, and feared God above many.

3 And I said unto them, Let not the gates of Jerusalem be opened until the sun be hot; and while they stand by, let them shut the doors, and bar them: and appoint watches of the inhabitants of Jerusalem, every one in his watch, and every one to be over against his house.

4 Now the city was large and great: but the people were few therein, and the houses were not built.

5 And my God put into mine heart to gather together the nobles, and the rulers, and the people, that they might be reckoned by genealogy. **And I found a register of the genealogy of them which came up at the first, and found written therein**,

6 These are the children of the province, that went up out of the captivity, of those that had been carried away, whom Nebuchadnezzar the king of Babylon had carried away, and came again to Jerusalem and to Judah, every one unto his city;

7 Who came with Zerubbabel, Jeshua, Nehemiah, Azariah, Raamiah, Nahamani, Mordecai, Bilshan, Mispereth, Bigvai, Nehum, Baanah. The number, I say, of the men of the people of Israel was this;

8 The children of Parosh, two thousand a hundred seventy and two.

9 The children of Shephatiah, three hundred seventy and two.

10 The children of Arah, six hundred fifty and two.

11 The children of Pahathmoab, of the children of Jeshua and Joab, two thousand and eight hundred and eighteen.

12 The children of Elam, a thousand two hundred fifty and four.

13 The children of Zattu, eight hundred forty and five.

14 The children of Zaccai, seven hundred and threescore.

15 The children of Binnui, six hundred forty and eight.

16 The children of Bebai, six hundred twenty and eight.

17 The children of Azgad, two thousand three hundred twenty and two.

18 The children of Adonikam, six hundred threescore and seven.

19 The children of Bigvai, two thousand threescore and seven.

20 The children of Adin, six hundred fifty and five.

21 The children of Ater of Hezekiah, ninety and eight.

22 The children of Hashum, three hundred twenty and eight.

23 The children of Bezai, three hundred twenty and four.

24 The children of Hariph, a hundred and twelve.

25 The children of Gibeon, ninety and five.

26 The men of Bethlehem and Netophah, a hundred fourscore and eight.

27 The men of Anathoth, a hundred twenty and eight.

28 The men of Beth-azmaveth, forty and two.

29 The men of Kirjathjearim, Chephirah, and Beeroth, seven hundred forty and three.

30 The men of Ramah and Gaba, six hundred twenty and one.

31 The men of Michmas, a hundred and twenty and two.

32 The men of Bethel and Ai, a hundred twenty and three.

33 The men of the other Nebo, fifty and two.

34 The children of the other Elam, a thousand two hundred fifty and four.

35 The children of Harim, three hundred and twenty.

36 The children of Jericho, three hundred forty and five.

37 The children of Lod, Hadid, and Ono, seven hundred twenty and one.

38 The children of Senaah, three thousand nine hundred and thirty.

39 The priests: the children of Jedaiah, of the house of Jeshua, nine hundred seventy and three.

40 The children of Immer, a thousand fifty and two.

41 The children of Pashur, a thousand two hundred forty and seven.

42 The children of Harim, a thousand and seventeen.

43 The Levites: the children of Jeshua, of Kadmiel, and of the children of Hodevah, seventy and four.

44 The singers: the children of Asaph, a hundred forty and eight.

45 The gatekeepers: the children of Shallum, the children of Ater, the children of Talmon, the children of Akkub, the children of Hatita, the children of Shobai, a hundred thirty and eight.

46 The Nethinims: the children of Ziha, the children of Hashupha, the children of Tabbaoth,

47 The children of Keros, the children of Sia, the children of Padon,

48 The children of Lebana, the children of Hagaba, the children of Shalmai,

49 The children of Hanan, the children of Giddel, the children of Gahar,

50 The children of Reaiah, the children of Rezin, the children of Nekoda,

51 The children of Gazzam, the children of Uzza, the children of Phaseah,

52 The children of Besai, the children of Meunim, the children of Nephishesim,

53 The children of Bakbuk, the children of Hakupha, the children of Harhur,

54 The children of Bazlith, the children of Mehida, the children of Harsha,

55 The children of Barkos, the children of Sisera, the children of Tamah,

56 The children of Neziah, the children of Hatipha.

57 The children of Solomon's servants: the children of Sotai, the children of Sophereth, the children of Perida,

58 The children of Jaala, the children of Darkon, the children of Giddel,

59 The children of Shephatiah, the children of Hattil, the children of Pochereth of Zebaim, the children of Amon.

60 All the Nethinims, and the children of Solomon's servants, were three hundred ninety and two.

61 And these were they which went up also from Telmelah, Telharesha, Cherub, Addon, and Immer: but they could not show their father's house, nor their seed, whether they were of Israel.

62 The children of Delaiah, the children of Tobiah, the children of Nekoda, six hundred forty and two.

63 And of the priests: the children of Habaiah, the children of Koz, the children of Barzillai, which took one of the daughters of Barzillai the Gileadite to wife, and was called after their name.

64 These sought their register among those that were reckoned by genealogy, but it was not found: therefore were they, as polluted, put from the priesthood.

65 And the Tirshatha said unto them, that they should not eat of the most holy things, till there stood up a priest with Urim and Thummim.

66 The whole congregation together was forty and two thousand three hundred and threescore,

67 Beside their manservants and their maidservants, of whom there were seven thousand three hundred thirty and seven: and they had two hundred forty and five singing men and singing women.

68 Their horses, seven hundred thirty and six: their mules, two hundred forty and five:

69 Their camels, four hundred thirty and five: six thousand seven hundred and twenty donkeys.

70 And some of the chief of the fathers gave unto the work. The Tirshatha gave to the treasure a thousand drams of gold, fifty basins, five hundred and thirty priests' garments.

71 And some of the chief of the fathers gave to the treasure of the work twenty myriads drams of gold, and two thousand and two hundred pound of silver.

72 And that which the rest of the people gave was twenty thousand drams of gold, and two thousand pound of silver, and threescore and seven priests' garments.

73 So the priests, and the Levites, and the gatekeepers, and the singers, and some of the people, and the Nethinims, and all Israel, dwelt in their cities; and when the seventh month came, the children of Israel were in their cities.

Neh 8:1 And all the people gathered themselves together as one man into the street that was before the water gate; **and they spoke unto Ezra the scribe to bring the book of the law of Moses, which the Becoming-One had commanded to Israel.**

2 And Ezra the priest brought the law before the congregation both of men and women, and all that could hear with understanding, upon the first day of the seventh month.

3 And he read therein before the street that was before the water gate from the morning until midday, before the men and the women, and those that could understand; and the ears of all the people were attentive unto the book of the law.

4 And Ezra the scribe stood upon a pulpit of wood, which they had made for the purpose; and beside him stood Mattithiah, and Shema, and Anaiah, and Urijah, and Hilkiah, and Maaseiah, on his right hand; and on his left hand, Pedaiah, and Mishael, and Malchiah, and Hashum, and Hashbadana, Zechariah, and Meshullam.

5 And Ezra opened the book in the sight of all the people; for he was above all the people; and when he opened it, all the people stood up:

6 And Ezra blessed the Becoming-One, the great God. And all the people answered, Amen, Amen, with lifting up their hands: and they bowed their heads, and worshiped the Becoming-One with their faces to the ground.

7 Also Jeshua, and Bani, and Sherebiah, Jamin, Akkub, Shabbethai, Hodijah, Maaseiah, Kelita, Azariah, Jozabad, Hanan, Pelaiah, and the Levites, caused the people to understand the law: and the people stood in their place.

8 So they read in the book in the law of God distinctly, and gave the sense, and caused them to understand the reading.

9 And Nehemiah, which is the Tirshatha, and Ezra the priest the scribe, and the Levites that taught the people, said unto all the people, This day is holy unto the Becoming-One your God; mourn not, nor weep. For all the people wept, when they heard the words of the law.

10 Then he said unto them, Go your way, eat the fat, and drink the sweet, and send portions unto them for whom nothing is prepared: for this day is holy unto our Lords: neither be you sorry; for the joy of the Becoming-One is your strength.

11 So the Levites stilled all the people, saying, Hold your peace, for the day is holy; neither be you grieved.

12 And all the people went their way to eat, and to drink, and to send portions, and to make great mirth, because they had understood the words that were declared unto them.

13 And on the second day were gathered together the chief of the fathers of all the people, the priests, and the Levites, unto Ezra the scribe, even to understand the words of the law.

14 And they found written in the law which the Becoming-One had commanded by Moses, that the children of Israel should dwell in booths in the feast of the seventh month:

15 And that they should publish and proclaim in all their cities, and in Jerusalem, saying, Go forth unto the mount, and fetch olive branches, and pine branches, and myrtle branches, and palm branches, and branches of thick trees, to make booths, as it is written.

16 So the people went forth, and brought them, and made themselves booths, every one upon the roof of his house, and in their courts, and in the courts of the house of God, and in the street of the water gate, and in the street of the gate of Ephraim.

17 And all the congregation of them that were come again out of the captivity made booths, and sat under the booths: for since the days of Jeshua the son of Nun unto that day had not the children of Israel done so. And there was very great gladness.

18 Also day by day, from the first day unto the last day, he read in the book of the law of God. And they kept the feast seven days; and on the eighth day was a solemn assembly, according unto the manner.

Neh 9:1 Now in the twenty and fourth day of this month the children of Israel were assembled with fasting, and with sackclothes, and earth upon them.

2 And the seed of Israel separated themselves from all strangers, and stood and confessed their sins, and the iniquities of their fathers.

3 And they stood up in their place, and read in the book of the law of the Becoming-One their God one fourth part of the day; and another fourth part they confessed, and worshiped the Becoming-One their God.

4 Then stood up upon the stairs, of the Levites, Jeshua, and Bani, Kadmiel, Shebaniah, Bunni, Sherebiah, Bani, and Chenani, and cried with a loud voice unto the Becoming-One their God.

5 Then the Levites, Jeshua, and Kadmiel, Bani, Hashabniah, Sherebiah, Hodijah, Shebaniah, and Pethahiah, said, Stand up and bless the Becoming-One your God for olam and beyond: and blessed be your glorious name, which is exalted above all blessing and praise.

6 You, even you, are Becoming-One alone; you have made heaven, the heavens of the heavens, with all their host, the earth, and all things that are therein, the seas, and all that is therein, and you preserve them all; and the host of heaven worships you.

7 you are the Becoming-One God, who did choose Abram, and brought him forth out of Ur of the Chaldees, and gave him the name of Abraham;

8 And found his heart faithful before you, and made a covenant with him to give the land of the Canaanites, the Hittites, the Amorites, and the Perizzites, and the Jebusites, and the Girgashites, to give it, I say, to his seed, and have performed your words; for you are righteous:

9 And did see the affliction of our fathers in Egypt, and heard their cry by the boundary sea;

10 And showed signs and wonders upon Pharaoh, and on all his servants, and on all the people of his land: for you knew that they dealt proudly

against them. So did you get you a name, as it is this day.

11 And you did divide the sea before them, so that they went through the midst of the sea on the dry land; and their persecutors you threw into the deeps, as a stone into the mighty waters.

12 Moreover you led them in the day by a cloudy pillar; and in the night by a pillar of fire, to give them light in the way wherein they should go.

13 you came down also upon mount Sinai, and spoke with them from heaven, and gave them right judgments, and true laws, good statutes and commandments:

14 And made known unto them your holy Sabbath, and commanded them precepts, statutes, and laws, by the hand of Moses your servant:

15 And gave them bread from the heavens for their hunger, and brought forth water for them out of the rock for their thirst, and promised them that they should go in to possess the land which you had sworn to give them.

16 But they and our fathers dealt proudly, and hardened their necks, and listened not to your commandments,

17 And refused to obey, neither were mindful of your wonders that you did among them; but hardened their necks, and in their rebellion appointed a captain to return to their bondage: but you are God ready to pardon, gracious and merciful, slow to anger, and of great kindness, and forsook them not.

18 Yes, when they had made them a molten calf, and said, This is your God that brought you up out of Egypt, and had worked great provocations;

19 Yet you in your manifold mercies forsook them not in the wilderness: the pillar of the cloud departed not from them by day, to lead them in the way; neither the pillar of fire by night, to show them light, and the way wherein they should go.

20 you gave also your good spirit to instruct them, and withheld not your manna from their mouth, and gave them water for their thirst.

21 Yes, forty years did you sustain them in the wilderness, so that they lacked nothing; their clothes grew not old, and their feet swelled not.

22 Moreover you gave them kingdoms and nations, and did divide them into corners: so they possessed the land of Sihon, and the land of the king of Heshbon, and the land of Og king of Bashan.

23 Their children also multiplied you as the stars of heaven, and brought them into the land, concerning which you had promised to their fathers, that they should go in to possess it.

24 So the children went in and possessed the land, and you subdued before them the inhabitants of the land, the Canaanites, and gave them into their hands, with their kings, and the people of the land, that they might do with them as they would.

25 And they took strong cities, and a fat land, and possessed houses full of all goods, wells dug, vineyards, and oliveyards, and fruit trees in abundance: so they did eat, and were filled, and became fat, and delighted themselves in your great goodness.

26 Nevertheless they were disobedient, and rebelled against you, and cast your law behind their backs, and killed your prophets which testified against them to turn them to you, and they worked great provocations.

27 Therefore you delivered them into the hand of their enemies, who vexed them: and in the time of their trouble, when they cried unto you, you heard them from heaven; and according to your manifold mercies you gave them saviors, who saved them out of the hand of their enemies.

28 But after they had rest, they did evil again before you: therefore left you them in the hand of their enemies, so that they had the dominion over them: yet when they returned, and cried unto you, you heard them from heaven; and many times did you deliver them according to your mercies;

29 And testified against them, that you might bring them again unto your law: yet they dealt proudly, and listened not unto your commandments, but sinned against your judgments, which if a man do, he shall live in them; and withdrew the shoulder, and hardened their neck, and would not hear.

30 Yet many years did you forbear them, and testified against them by your spirit in your prophets: yet would they not give ear: therefore gave you them into the hand of the people of the lands.

31 Nevertheless for your great mercies' sake you did not utterly consume them, nor forsake them; for you are a gracious and merciful GOD.

32 Now therefore, our God, the great, the mighty, and the terrible GOD, who keep covenant and mercy, let not all the trouble seem little before you, that has come upon us, on our kings, on our princes, and on our priests, and on our prophets, and on our fathers, and on all your people, since the time of the kings of Assyria unto this day.

33 Howbeit you are just in all that is brought upon us; for you have done right, but we have done wickedly:

34 Neither have our kings, our princes, our priests, nor our fathers, kept your law, nor listened unto your commandments and your testimonies, wherewith you did testify against them.

35 For they have not served you in their kingdom, and in your great goodness that you gave them, and in the large and fat land which you gave before them, neither turned they from their wicked works.

36 Behold, we are servants this day, and for the land that you gave unto our fathers to eat the fruit thereof and the good thereof, behold, we are servants in it:

37 And it yields much increase unto the kings whom you have set over us because of our sins: also they have dominion over our bodies, and over our cattle, at their pleasure, and we are in great distress.

38 And because of all this we make a sure covenant, and write it; and our princes, Levites, and priests, seal unto it.

Neh 10:1 Now those that sealed were, Nehemiah, the Tirshatha, the son of Hachaliah, and Zidkijah,

2 Seraiah, Azariah, Jeremiah,

3 Pashur, Amariah, Malchijah,

4 Hattush, Shebaniah, Malluch,

5 Harim, Meremoth, Obadiah,

6 Daniel, Ginnethon, Baruch,

7 Meshullam, Abijah, Mijamin,

8 Maaziah, Bilgai, Shemaiah: these were the priests.

9 And the Levites: both Jeshua the son of Azaniah, Binnui of the sons of Henadad, Kadmiel;

10 And their brethren, Shebaniah, Hodijah, Kelita, Pelaiah, Hanan,

11 Micha, Rehob, Hashabiah,

12 Zaccur, Sherebiah, Shebaniah,

13 Hodijah, Bani, Beninu.

14 The chief of the people; Parosh, Pahathmoab, Elam, Zatthu, Bani,

15 Bunni, Azgad, Bebai,

16 Adonijah, Bigvai, Adin,

17 Ater, Hizkijah, Azzur,

18 Hodijah, Hashum, Bezai,

19 Hariph, Anathoth, Nebai,

20 Magpiash, Meshullam, Hezir,

21 Meshezabeel, Zadok, Jaddua,

22 Pelatiah, Hanan, Anaiah,

23 Hoshea, Hananiah, Hashub,

24 Hallohesh, Pileha, Shobek,

25 Rehum, Hashabnah, Maaseiah,

26 And Ahijah, Hanan, Anan,

27 Malluch, Harim, Baanah.

28 And the rest of the people, the priests, the Levites, the gatekeepers, the singers, the Nethinims, and all they that had separated themselves from the people of the lands unto the law of God, their wives, their sons, and their daughters, every one having knowledge, and having understanding;

29 They clave to their brethren, their nobles, and entered into a curse, and into an oath, to walk in God' law, which was given by Moses the servant of God, and to observe and do all the commandments of the Becoming-One our my Lord(s), and his judgments and his statutes;

30 And that we would not give our daughters unto the people of the land, nor take their daughters for our sons:

31 And if the people of the land bring ware or any victuals on the Sabbath day to sell, that we would not buy it of them on the Sabbath, or on the holy day: and that we would leave the seventh year, and the exaction of every debt.

32 Also we made ordinances for us, to charge ourselves yearly with the third part of a shekel for the service of the house of our God;

33 For the showbread, and for the continual food offering, and for the continual burnt offering, of the sabbaths, of the new moons, for the set times,[123] and for the holy things, and for the sin offerings to make an atonement for Israel, and for all the work of the house of our God.

34 And we cast the lots among the priests, the Levites, and the people, for the wood offering, to bring it into the house of our God, after the houses of our fathers, at times appointed year by year, to burn upon the altar of the Becoming-One our God, as it is written in the law:

35 And to bring the firstfruits of our ground, and the firstfruits of all fruit of all trees, year by year, unto the house of the Becoming-One: 36 Also the firstborn of our sons, and of our cattle, as it is written in the law, and the firstlings of our herds and of our flocks, to bring to the house of our God, unto the priests that minister in the house of our God:

37 And that we should bring the beginning of our dough, and our offerings, and the fruit of all manner of trees, of wine and of oil, unto the priests, to the chambers of the house of our God; and the tithes of our ground unto the Levites, that the same Levites might have the tithes in all the cities of our tillage.

38 And the priest the son of Aaron shall be with the Levites, when the Levites take tithes: and the Levites shall bring up the tithe of tithe unto the house of our God, to the chambers, into the treasure house.

39 For the children of Israel and the children of Levi shall bring the offering of the grain, of the new wine, and the oil, unto the chambers, where are the vessels of the sanctuary, and the priests that minister, and the gatekeepers, and the singers: and we will not forsake the house of our God.

Neh 11:1 And the rulers of the people dwelt at Jerusalem: the rest of the people also cast lots, to bring one of ten to dwell in Jerusalem the holy city, and nine parts to dwell in other cities.

2 And the people blessed all the men, that willingly offered themselves to dwell at Jerusalem.

3 Now these are the chief of the province that dwelt in Jerusalem: but in the cities of Judah dwelt every one in his possession in their cities, to wit, Israel, the priests, and the Levites, and the Nethinims, and the children of Solomon's servants.

4 And at Jerusalem dwelt certain of the children of Judah, and of the children of Benjamin. Of the children of Judah; Athaiah the son of Uzziah, the son of Zechariah, the son of Amariah, the son of Shephatiah, the son of Mahalaleel, of the children of Perez;

5 And Maaseiah the son of Baruch, the son of Colhozeh, the son of Hazaiah, the son of Adaiah, the son of Joiarib, the son of Zechariah, the son of Shiloni.

6 All the sons of Perez that dwelt at Jerusalem were four hundred threescore and eight valiant men.

7 And these are the sons of Benjamin; Sallu the son of Meshullam, the son of Joed, the son of Pedaiah, the son of Kolaiah, the son of Maaseiah, the son of Ithiel, the son of Jesaiah.

8 And after him Gabbai, Sallai, nine hundred twenty and eight.

9 And Joel the son of Zichri was their overseer: and Judah the son of Senuah was second over the city.

10 Of the priests: Jedaiah the son of Joiarib, Jachin.

11 Seraiah the son of Hilkiah, the son of Meshullam, the son of Zadok, the son of Meraioth, the son of Ahitub, was the ruler of the house of God.

12 And their brethren that did the work of the house were eight hundred twenty and two: and Adaiah the son of Jeroham, the son of Pelaliah, the son of Amzi, the son of Zechariah, the son of Pashur, the son of Malchiah,

13 And his brethren, chief of the fathers, two hundred forty and two: and Amashai the son of

---

[123] Appointed times or festivals

Azareel, the son of Ahasai, the son of Meshillemoth, the son of Immer,

14 And their brethren, mighty men of valor, a hundred twenty and eight: and their overseer was Zabdiel, the son of one of the great men.

15 Also of the Levites: Shemaiah the son of Hashub, the son of Azrikam, the son of Hashabiah, the son of Bunni;

16 And Shabbethai and Jozabad, of the chief of the Levites, had the oversight of the outward business of the house of God.

17 And Mattaniah the son of Micha, the son of Zabdi, the son of Asaph, was the principal to begin the thanksgiving in prayer: and Bakbukiah the second among his brethren, and Abda the son of Shammua, the son of Galal, the son of Jeduthun.

18 All the Levites in the holy city were two hundred fourscore and four.

19 Moreover the gatekeepers, Akkub, Talmon, and their brethren that kept the gates, were a hundred seventy and two.

20 And the residue of Israel, of the priests, and the Levites, were in all the cities of Judah, every one in his inheritance.

21 But the Nethinims dwelt in Ophel: and Ziha and Gispa were over the Nethinims.

22 The overseer also of the Levites at Jerusalem was Uzzi the son of Bani, the son of Hashabiah, the son of Mattaniah, the son of Micha. Of the sons of Asaph, the singers were over the business of the house of God.

23 For it was the king's commandment concerning them, that a certain portion should be for the singers, due for every day.

24 And Pethahiah the son of Meshezabeel, of the children of Zerah the son of Judah, was at the king's hand in all matters concerning the people.

25 And for the villages, with their fields, some of the children of Judah dwelt at Kirjatharba, and in the villages thereof, and at Dibon, and in the villages thereof, and at Jekabzeel, and in the villages thereof,

26 And at Jeshua, and at Moladah, and at Beth-phelet,

27 And at Hazarshual, and at Beersheba, and in the villages thereof,

28 And at Ziklag, and at Mekonah, and in the villages thereof,

29 And at Enrimmon, and at Zareah, and at Jarmuth,

30 Zanoah, Adullam, and in their villages, at Lachish, and the fields thereof, at Azekah, and in the villages thereof. And they dwelt from Beersheba unto the valley of Hinnom.

31 The children also of Benjamin from Geba dwelt at Michmash, and Aija, and Bethel, and in their villages,

32 And at Anathoth, Nob, Ananiah,

33 Hazor, Ramah, Gittaim,

34 Hadid, Zeboim, Neballat,

35 Lod, and Ono, the valley of craftsmen.

36 And of the Levites were divisions in Judah, and in Benjamin.

Neh 12:1 Now these are the priests and the Levites that went up with Zerubbabel the son of Shealtiel, and Jeshua: Seraiah, Jeremiah, Ezra,

2 Amariah, Malluch, Hattush,

3 Shechaniah, Rehum, Meremoth,

4 Iddo, Ginnetho, Abijah,

5 Miamin, Maadiah, Bilgah,

6 Shemaiah, and Joiarib, Jedaiah,

7 Sallu, Amok, Hilkiah, Jedaiah. These were the chief of the priests and of their brethren in the days of Jeshua.

8 Moreover the Levites: Jeshua, Binnui, Kadmiel, Sherebiah, Judah, and Mattaniah, which was over the thanksgiving, he and his brethren.

9 Also Bakbukiah and Unni, their brethren, were over against them in the watches.

10 And Jeshua begat Joiakim, Joiakim also begat Eliashib, and Eliashib begat Joiada,

11 And Joiada begat Jonathan, and Jonathan begat Jaddua.

12 And in the days of Joiakim were priests, the chief of the fathers: of Seraiah, Meraiah; of Jeremiah, Hananiah;

13 Of Ezra, Meshullam; of Amariah, Jehohanan;

14 Of Melicu, Jonathan; of Shebaniah, Joseph;

15 Of Harim, Adna; of Meraioth, Helkai;

16 Of Iddo, Zechariah; of Ginnethon, Meshullam;

17 Of Abijah, Zichri; of Miniamin, of Moadiah, Piltai;

18 Of Bilgah, Shammua; of Shemaiah, Jehonathan;

19 And of Joiarib, Mattenai; of Jedaiah, Uzzi;

20 Of Sallai, Kallai; of Amok, Eber;

21 Of Hilkiah, Hashabiah; of Jedaiah, Nethaneel.

22 The Levites in the days of Eliashib, Joiada, and Johanan, and Jaddua, were recorded chief of the fathers: also the priests, to the reign of Darius the Persian.

23 The sons of Levi, the chief of the fathers, were written in the book of the chronicles, even until the days of Johanan the son of Eliashib.

24 And the chief of the Levites: Hashabiah, Sherebiah, and Jeshua the son of Kadmiel, with their brethren over against them, to praise and to give thanks, according to the commandment of David the man of God, ward over against ward.

25 Mattaniah, and Bakbukiah, Obadiah, Meshullam, Talmon, Akkub, were gatekeepers keeping the ward at the thresholds of the gates.

26 These were in the days of Joiakim the son of Jeshua, the son of Jozadak, and in the days of Nehemiah the governor, and of Ezra the priest, the scribe.

27 And at the dedication of the wall of Jerusalem they sought the Levites out of all their places, to bring them to Jerusalem, to keep the dedication with gladness, both with thanksgivings, and with singing, with cymbals, psalteries, and with harps.

28 And the sons of the singers gathered themselves together, both out of the plain country round about Jerusalem, and from the villages of Netophathi;

29 Also from the house of Gilgal, and out of the fields of Geba and Azmaveth: for the singers had built them villages round about Jerusalem.

30 And the priests and the Levites purified themselves, and purified the people, and the gates, and the wall.

31 Then I brought up the princes of Judah upon the wall, and appointed two great companies of them that gave thanks, whereof one went on the right hand upon the wall toward the dung gate:

32 And after them went Hoshaiah, and half of the princes of Judah,

33 And Azariah, Ezra, and Meshullam,

34 Judah, and Benjamin, and Shemaiah, and Jeremiah,

35 And certain of the priests' sons with trumpets; namely, Zechariah the son of Jonathan, the son of Shemaiah, the son of Mattaniah, the son of Michaiah, the son of Zaccur, the son of Asaph:

36 And his brethren, Shemaiah, and Azarael, Milalai, Gilalai, Maai, Nethaneel, and Judah, Hanani, with the musical instruments of David the man of God, and Ezra the scribe before them.

37 And at the fountain gate, which was over against them, they went up by the stairs of the city of David, at the going up of the wall, above the house of David, even unto the water gate eastward.

38 And the other company of them that gave thanks went over against them, and I after them, and the half of the people upon the wall, from beyond the tower of the furnaces even unto the broad wall;

39 And from above the gate of Ephraim, and above the old gate, and above the fish gate, and the tower of Hananeel, and the tower of Meah, even unto the sheep gate: and they stood still in the prison gate.

40 So stood the two companies of them that gave thanks in the house of God, and I, and the half of the rulers with me:

41 And the priests; Eliakim, Maaseiah, Miniamin, Michaiah, Elioenai, Zechariah, and Hananiah, with trumpets;

42 And Maaseiah, and Shemaiah, and Eleazar, and Uzzi, and Jehohanan, and Malchijah, and Elam, and Ezer. And the singers sang loud, with Jezrahiah their overseer.

43 Also that day they offered great sacrifices, and rejoiced: for God had made them rejoice with great joy: the wives also and the children rejoiced: so that the joy of Jerusalem was heard even afar off.

44 And at that time were some appointed over the chambers for the treasures, for the offerings, for the firstfruits, and for the tithes, to gather into them out of the fields of the cities the portions of the law for the priests and Levites: for Judah rejoiced for the priests and for the Levites that waited.

45 And both the singers and the gatekeepers kept the ward of their God, and the ward of the purification, according to the commandment of David, and of Solomon his son.

46 For in the days of David and Asaph of old there were chief of the singers, and songs of praise and thanksgiving unto God.

47 And all Israel in the days of Zerubbabel, and in the days of Nehemiah, gave the portions of the singers and the gatekeepers, every day his portion: and they sanctified holy things unto the Levites; and the Levites sanctified them unto the children of Aaron.

Neh 13:1 On that day they read in the book of Moses in the audience of the people; and therein was found written, that the Ammonite and the Moabite should not come into the congregation of God for olam.

2 Because they met not the children of Israel with bread and with water, but hired Balaam against them, that he should curse them: howbeit our God turned the curse into a blessing.

3 Now it came to pass, when they had heard the law, that they separated from Israel all the mixed multitude.

4 And before this, Eliashib the priest, having the oversight of the chamber of the house of our God, was allied unto Tobiah:

5 And he had prepared for him a great chamber, where aforetime they laid the food offerings, the frankincense, and the vessels, and the tithes of the grain, the new wine, and the oil, which was commanded to be given to the Levites, and the singers, and the gatekeepers; and the offerings of the priests.

6 But in all this time was not I at Jerusalem: for in the two and thirtieth year of Artaxerxes king of Babylon came I unto the king, and at the end of days I obtained leave of the king:

7 And I came to Jerusalem, and understood of the evil that Eliashib did for Tobiah, in preparing him a chamber in the courts of the house of God.

8 And it grieved me greatly: therefore I cast forth all the household stuff of Tobiah out of the chamber.

9 Then I commanded, and they cleansed the chambers: and there brought I again the vessels of the house of God, with the food offering and the frankincense.

10 And I perceived that the portions of the Levites had not been given them: for the Levites and the singers, that did the work, were fled every one to his field.

11 Then contended I with the rulers, and said, Why is the house of God forsaken? And I gathered them together, and set them in their place.

12 Then brought all Judah the tithe of the grain and the new wine and the oil unto the treasuries.

13 And I made treasurers over the treasuries, Shelemiah the priest, and Zadok the scribe, and of the Levites, Pedaiah: and next to them was Hanan the son of Zaccur, the son of Mattaniah: for they were counted faithful, and their office was to distribute unto their brethren.

14 Remember me, O my God, concerning this, and wipe not out my good deeds that I have done for the house of my God, and for the offices thereof.

15 In those days saw I in Judah some treading wine presses on the Sabbath, and bringing in sheaves, and loading donkeys; as also wine, grapes, and figs, and all manner of burdens, which they brought into Jerusalem on the Sabbath day: and I testified against them in the day wherein they sold victuals.

16 There dwelt men of Tyre also therein, which brought fish, and all manner of ware, and sold on the Sabbath unto the children of Judah, and in Jerusalem.

17 Then I contended with the nobles of Judah, and said unto them, What evil thing is this that you do, and profane the Sabbath day?

18 Did not your fathers thus, and did not our God bring all this evil upon us, and upon this city? yet you bring more wrath upon Israel by profaning the Sabbath.

19 And it came to pass, that when the gates of Jerusalem began to be dark before the Sabbath, I commanded that the gates should be shut, and charged that they should not be opened till after the Sabbath: and some of my servants set I at the gates, that there should no burden be brought in on the Sabbath day.

20 So the merchants and sellers of all kind of ware lodged outside Jerusalem once or twice.

21 Then I testified against them, and said unto them, Why lodge you about the wall? if you do so again, I will lay hands on you. From that time forth came they no more on the Sabbath.

22 And I commanded the Levites that they should cleanse themselves, and that they should come and keep the gates, to sanctify the Sabbath day. Remember me, O my God, concerning this also, and spare me according to the greatness of your mercy.

23 In those days also saw I Jews that had married wives of Ashdod, of Ammon, and of Moab:

24 And their children spoke half in the speech of Ashdod, and could not speak in the Jews' language, but according to the language of each people.

25 And I contended with them, and cursed them, and smote certain of them, and plucked off their hair, and made them swear by God, saying, you shall not give your daughters unto their sons, nor take their daughters unto your sons, or for yourselves.

26 Did not Solomon king of Israel sin by these things? yet among many nations was there no king like him, who was beloved of his God, and God made him king over all Israel: nevertheless even him did outlandish women cause to sin.

27 Shall we then listen unto you to do all this great evil, to transgress against our God in marrying strange wives?

28 And one of the sons of Joiada, the son of Eliashib the high priest, was son-in-law to Sanballat the Horonite: therefore I chased him from me.

29 Remember them, O my God, because they have defiled the priesthood, and the covenant of the priesthood, and of the Levites.

30 Thus cleansed I them from all strangers, and appointed the wards of the priests and the Levites, every one in his business;

31 And for the wood offering, at times appointed, and for the firstfruits. Remember me, O my God, for good.

Esther

Est 1:1 Now it came to pass in the days of Ahasuerus, this is Ahasuerus which reigned, from India even unto Ethiopia, over a hundred and seven and twenty provinces:

2 That in those days, when the king Ahasuerus sat on the throne of his kingdom, which was in Shushan the palace,

3 In the third year of his reign, he made a feast unto all his princes and his servants; the power of Persia and Media, the nobles and princes of the provinces, being before him:

4 When he showed the riches of his glorious kingdom and the honor of his excellent majesty many days, even and hundred and fourscore days.

5 And when these days were expired, the king made a feast unto all the people that were present in Shushan the palace, both unto great and small, seven days, in the court of the garden of the king's palace;

6 Where were white, green, and blue, hangings, fastened with cords of fine linen and purple to silver rings and pillars of marble: the beds were of gold and silver, upon a pavement of red, and blue, and white, and black, marble.

7 And they gave them drink in vessels of gold, the vessels being diverse one from another, and royal wine in abundance, according to the state of the king.

8 And the drinking was according to the law; none did compel: for so the king had appointed to all the officers of his house, that they should do according to every man's pleasure.

9 Also Vashti the queen made a feast for the women in the royal house which belonged to king Ahasuerus.

10 On the seventh day, when the heart of the king was merry with wine, he commanded Mehuman, Biztha, Harbona, Bigtha, and Abagtha, Zethar, and Carcas, the seven eunuchs that served in the presence of Ahasuerus the king,

11 To bring Vashti the queen before the king with the crown royal, to show the people and the princes her beauty: for she was fair to look on.

12 But the queen Vashti refused to come at the king's commandment by his eunuchs: therefore was the king very angry, and his anger burned in him.

13 Then the king said to the wise men, which knew the times, for so was the king's manner toward all that knew law and judgment:

14 And the next unto him was Carshena, Shethar, Admatha, Tarshish, Meres, Marsena, and Memucan, the seven princes of Persia and Media, which saw the king's face, and which sat the first in the kingdom;

15 What shall we do unto the queen Vashti according to law, because she has not performed the commandment of the king Ahasuerus by the eunuchs?

16 And Memucan answered before the king and the princes, Vashti the queen has not done wrong to the king only, but also to all the princes, and to all the people that are in all the provinces of the king Ahasuerus.

17 For this deed of the queen shall come abroad unto all women, so that they shall despise their husbands in their eyes, when it shall be reported, The king Ahasuerus commanded Vashti the queen to be brought in before him, but she came not.

18 Likewise shall the ladies of Persia and Media say this day unto all the king's princes, which have heard of the deed of the queen. Thus shall there arise too much contempt and wrath.

19 If it please the king, let there go a royal commandment from him, and let it be written among the laws of the Persians and the Medes, that it be not altered, That Vashti come no more before king Ahasuerus; and let the king give her royal estate unto another that is better than she.

20 And when the king's decree which he shall make shall be published throughout all his empire, for it is great, all the wives shall give to their husbands honor, both to great and small.

21 And the saying pleased the king and the princes; and the king did according to the word of Memucan:

22 For he sent letters into all the king's provinces, into every province according to the writing thereof, and to every people after their language, that every man should bear rule in his own house, and that it should be published according to the language of every people.

Est 2:1 After these things, when the wrath of king Ahasuerus was appeased, he remembered Vashti, and what she had done, and what was decreed against her.

2 Then said the king's servants that ministered unto him, Let there be fair young virgins sought for the king:

3 And let the king appoint officers in all the provinces of his kingdom, that they may gather together all the fair young virgins unto Shushan the palace, to the house of the women, unto the custody of Hege the king's eunuch, keeper of the women; and let their things for purification be given them:

4 And let the maiden which pleases the king be queen instead of Vashti. And the thing pleased the king; and he did so.

5 Now in Shushan the palace there was a certain Jew, whose name was Mordecai, the son of Jair, the son of Shimei, the son of Kish, a Benjamite;

6 Who had been carried away from Jerusalem with the captivity which had been carried away with Jeconiah king of Judah, whom Nebuchadnezzar the king of Babylon had carried away.

7 And he brought up Hadassah, that is, Esther, his uncle's daughter: for she had neither father nor mother, and the maid was fair and beautiful; whom Mordecai, when her father and mother were dead, took for his own daughter.

8 So it came to pass, when the king's commandment and his law was heard, and when many maidens were gathered together unto Shushan the palace, to the custody of Hegai, that Esther was brought also unto the king's house, to the custody of Hegai, keeper of the women.

9 And the maiden pleased him, and she obtained kindness of him; and he speedily gave her her things for purification, with such things as belonged to her, and seven maidens, which were meet to be given her, out of the king's house: and he preferred her and her maids unto the best place of the house of the women.

10 Esther had not showed her people nor her kindred: for Mordecai had charged her that she should not show it.

11 And Mordecai walked every day before the court of the women's house, to know how Esther did, and what should become of her.

12 Now when every maid's turn was come to go in to king Ahasuerus, after that she had been twelve months, according to the law of the women, for so were the days of their purification accomplished, to wit, six months with oil of myrrh, and six months with sweet odors, and with other things for the purifying of the women;

13 Then thus came every maiden unto the king; whatsoever she desired was given her to go with her out of the house of the women unto the king's house.

14 In the evening she went, and on the next day she returned into the second house of the women, to the custody of Shaashgaz, the king's eunuch, which kept the concubines: she came in unto the king no more, except the king delighted in her, and that she were called by name.

15 Now when the turn of Esther, the daughter of Abihail the uncle of Mordecai, who had taken her for his daughter, was come to go in unto the king, she required nothing but what Hegai the king's eunuch, the keeper of the women, appointed. And Esther obtained favor in the sight of all them that looked upon her.

16 So Esther was taken unto king Ahasuerus into his house royal in the tenth month, which is the month Tebeth, in the seventh year of his reign.

17 And the king loved Esther above all the women, and she obtained grace and favor in his sight more than all the virgins; so that he set the royal crown upon her head, and made her queen instead of Vashti.

18 Then the king made a great feast unto all his princes and his servants, even Esther's feast; and he made a release to the provinces, and gave gifts, according to the state of the king.

19 And when the virgins were gathered together the second time, then Mordecai sat in the king's gate.

20 Esther had not yet showed her kindred nor her people; as Mordecai had charged her: for Esther did the commandment of Mordecai, like as when she was brought up with him.

21 In those days, while Mordecai sat in the king's gate, two of the king's eunuchs, Bigthan and Teresh, of those which kept the door, were wrath, and sought to lay hand on the king Ahasuerus.

22 And the thing was known to Mordecai, who told it unto Esther the queen; and Esther certified the king thereof in Mordecai's name.

23 And when inquisition was made of the matter, it was found out; therefore they were both hanged on a tree: and it was written in the book of the chronicles before the king.

Est 3:1 After these things did king Ahasuerus promote Haman the son of Hammedatha the Agagite, and advanced him, and set his seat above all the princes that were with him.

2 And all the king's servants, that were in the king's gate, bowed, and reverenced Haman: for the king had so commanded concerning him. But Mordecai bowed not, nor did him reverence.

3 Then the king's servants, which were in the king's gate, said unto Mordecai, Why transgress you the king's commandment?

4 Now it came to pass, when they spoke daily unto him, and he listened not unto them, that they told Haman, to see whether Mordecai's matters would stand: for he had told them that he was a Jew.

5 And when Haman saw that Mordecai bowed not, nor did him reverence, then was Haman full of wrath.

6 And he thought scorn to lay hands on Mordecai alone; for they had showed him the people of Mordecai: therefore Haman sought to destroy all the Jews that were throughout the whole kingdom of Ahasuerus, even the people of Mordecai.

7 In the first month, that is, the month Nisan, in the twelfth year of king Ahasuerus, they cast Pur, that is, the lot, before Haman from day to day, and from month to month, to the twelfth month, that is, the month Adar.

8 And Haman said unto king Ahasuerus, There is a certain people scattered abroad and dispersed among the people in all the provinces of your kingdom; and their laws are diverse from all people; neither keep they the king's laws: therefore it is not for the king's profit to permit them.

9 If it please the king, let it be written that they may be destroyed: and I will pay ten thousand talents of silver to the hands of those that have the charge of the business, to bring it into the king's treasuries.

10 And the king took his ring from his hand, and gave it unto Haman the son of Hammedatha the Agagite, the Jews' enemy.

11 And the king said unto Haman, The silver is given to you, the people also, to do with them as it seems good to you.

12 Then were the king's scribes called on the thirteenth day of the first month, and there was written according to all that Haman had commanded unto the king's lieutenants, and to the governors that were over every province, and to the rulers of every people of every province according to the writing thereof, and to every people after their language; in the name of king Ahasuerus was it written, and sealed with the king's ring

13 And the letters were sent by runners into all the king's provinces, to destroy, to kill, and to cause to perish, all Jews, both young and old, little children and women, in one day, even upon the thirteenth day of the twelfth month, which is the month Adar, and to take the spoil of them for a prey.

14 The copy of the writing for a law to be given in every province was published unto all people, that they should be ready against that day.

15 The runners went out, being hurried by the king's commandment, and the law was given in Shushan the palace. And the king and Haman sat down to drink; but the city Shushan was perplexed.

Est 4:1 When Mordecai perceived all that was done, Mordecai ripped his clothes, and put on sackcloth with ashes, and went out into the midst of the city, and cried with a loud and a bitter cry;

2 And came even before the king's gate: for none might enter into the king's gate clothed with sackcloth.

3 And in every province, wheresoever the king's commandment and his law came, there was great mourning among the Jews, and fasting, and weeping, and wailing; and many lay in sackcloth and ashes.

4 So Esther's maids and her eunuchs came and told it her. Then was the queen exceedingly grieved; and she sent raiment to clothe Mordecai, and to take away his sackcloth from him: but he received it not.

5 Then called Esther for Hatach, one of the king's eunuchs, whom he had appointed to attend upon her, and gave him a commandment to Mordecai, to know what it was, and why it was.

6 So Hatach went forth to Mordecai unto the street of the city, which was before the king's gate.

7 And Mordecai told him of all that had happened unto him, and of the sum of the money that Haman had promised to pay to the king's treasuries for the Jews, to destroy them.

8 Also he gave him the copy of the writing of the law that was given at Shushan to destroy them, to show it unto Esther, and to declare it unto her, and to charge her that she should go in unto the king, to make supplication unto him, and to make request before him for her people.

9 And Hatach came and told Esther the words of Mordecai.

10 Again Esther spoke unto Hatach, and gave him commandment unto Mordecai;

11 All the king's servants, and the people of the king's provinces, do know, that whosoever, whether man or woman, shall come unto the king into the inner court, who is not called, there is one law of his to put him to death, except such to whom the king shall hold out the golden scepter, that he may live: but I have not been called to come in unto the king these thirty days.

12 And they told to Mordecai Esther's words.

13 Then Mordecai commanded to answer Esther, Think not with your soul that you shall escape in the king's house, more than all the Jews.

14 For if you altogether hold your peace at this time, then shall there enlargement and deliverance arise to the Jews from another place; but you and your father's house shall be destroyed: and who knows whether you are come to the kingdom for such a time as this?

15 Then Esther bade them return Mordecai this answer,

16 Go, gather together all the Jews that are present in Shushan, and fast you for me, and neither eat nor drink three days, night or day: I also and my maidens will fast likewise; and so will I go in unto the king, which is not according to the law: and if I perish, I perish.

17 So Mordecai went his way, and did according to all that Esther had commanded him.

Est 5:1 Now it came to pass on the third day, that Esther put on her royal apparel, and stood in the inner court of the king's house, over against the king's house: and the king sat upon his royal throne in the royal house, over against the gate of the house.

2 And it was so, when the king saw Esther the queen standing in the court, that she obtained favor in his sight: and the king held out to Esther the golden scepter that was in his hand. So Esther drew near, and touched the top of the scepter.

3 Then said the king unto her, What will you, queen Esther? and what is your request? it shall be even given you to the half of the kingdom.

4 And Esther answered, If it seem good unto the king, let the king and Haman come this day unto the banquet that I have prepared for him.

5 Then the king said, Cause Haman to make haste, that he may do as Esther has said. So the king and Haman came to the banquet that Esther had prepared.

6 And the king said unto Esther at the banquet of wine, What is your petition? and it shall be granted you: and what is your request? even to the half of the kingdom it shall be performed.

7 Then answered Esther, and said, My petition and my request is;

8 If I have found favor in the sight of the king, and if it please the king to grant my petition, and to perform my request, let the king and Haman come to the banquet that I shall prepare for them, and I will do tomorrow as the king has said.

9 Then went Haman forth that day joyful and with a glad heart: but when Haman saw Mordecai in the king's gate, that he stood not up, nor moved for him, he was full of indignation against Mordecai.

10 Nevertheless Haman refrained himself: and when he came home, he sent and called for his friends, and Zeresh his wife.

11 And Haman told them of the glory of his riches, and the multitude of his children, and all the things wherein the king had promoted him, and how he had advanced him above the princes and servants of the king.

12 Haman said moreover, Yes, Esther the queen did let no man come in with the king unto the banquet that she had prepared but myself; and tomorrow I am invited unto her also with the king.

13 Yet all this avails me nothing, so long as I see Mordecai the Jew sitting at the king's gate.

14 Then said Zeresh his wife and all his friends unto him, Let a gallows be made of fifty cubits high, and tomorrow speak you unto the king that Mordecai may be hanged thereon: then go you in merrily with the king unto the banquet. And the thing pleased Haman; and he caused the gallows to be made.

Est 6:1 On that night could not the king sleep, and he commanded to bring the book of records of the chronicles; and they were read before the king.

2 And it was found written, that Mordecai had told of Bigthana and Teresh, two of the king's eunuchs, the keepers of the door, who sought to lay hand on the king Ahasuerus.

3 And the king said, What honor and dignity has been done to Mordecai for this? Then said the king's servants that ministered unto him, There is nothing done for him.

4 And the king said, Who is in the court? Now Haman was come into the outward court of the king's house, to speak unto the king to hang Mordecai on the gallows that he had prepared for him.

5 And the king's servants said unto him, Behold, Haman stands in the court. And the king said, Let him come in.

6 So Haman came in. And the king said unto him, What shall be done unto the man whom the king delights to honor? Now Haman thought in his heart, To whom would the king delight to do honor more than to myself?

7 And Haman answered the king, For the man whom the king delights to honor,

8 Let the royal apparel be brought which the king uses to wear, and the horse that the king rides upon, and the crown royal which is set upon his head:

9 And let this apparel and horse be delivered to the hand of one of the king's most noble princes, that they may array the man withal whom the king delights to honor, and bring him on horseback through the street of the city, and proclaim before him, Thus shall it be done to the man whom the king delights to honor.

10 Then the king said to Haman, Make haste, and take the apparel and the horse, as you have said, and do even so to Mordecai the Jew, that sits at the king's gate: let nothing fail of all that you have spoken.

11 Then took Haman the apparel and the horse, and arrayed Mordecai, and brought him on horseback through the street of the city, and proclaimed before him, Thus shall it be done unto the man whom the king delights to honor.

12 And Mordecai came again to the king's gate. But Haman hasted to his house mourning, and having his head covered.

13 And Haman told Zeresh his wife and all his friends every thing that had befallen him. Then said his wise men and Zeresh his wife unto him, If Mordecai be of the seed of the Jews, before whom you have begun to fall, you shall not prevail against him, but shall surely fall before him.

14 And while they were yet talking with him, came the king's eunuchs, and hasted to bring Haman unto the banquet that Esther had prepared.

Est 7:1 So the king and Haman came to banquet with Esther the queen.

2 And the king said again unto Esther on the second day at the banquet of wine, What is your petition, queen Esther? and it shall be granted you: and what is your request? and it shall be performed, even to the half of the kingdom.

3 Then Esther the queen answered and said, If I have found favor in your sight, O king, and if it please the king, let my soul be given me at my petition, and my people at my request:

4 For we are sold, I and my people, to be destroyed, to be slain, and to perish. But if we had been sold for bondmen and bondwomen, I had held my tongue, although the enemy could not countervail the king's damage.

5 Then the king Ahasuerus answered and said unto Esther the queen, Who is he, and where is he, that durst presume in his heart to do so?

6 And Esther said, The adversary and enemy is this wicked Haman. Then Haman was afraid before the king and the queen.

7 And the king arising from the banquet of wine in his wrath went into the palace garden: and Haman stood up to make request for his soul to Esther the queen; for he saw that there was evil determined against him by the king.

8 Then the king returned out of the palace garden into the place of the banquet of wine; and Haman was fallen upon the bed whereon Esther was. Then said the king, Will he force the queen also before me in the house? As the word went out of the king's mouth, they covered Haman's face.

9 And Harbonah, one of the eunuchs, said before the king, Behold also, the gallows fifty cubits high, which Haman had made for Mordecai, who had spoken good for the king, stands in the house of Haman. Then the king said, Hang him thereon.

10 So they hanged Haman on the gallows that he had prepared for Mordecai. Then was the king's wrath pacified.

Est 8:1 On that day did the king Ahasuerus give the house of Haman the Jews' enemy unto Esther the queen. And Mordecai came before the king; for Esther had told what he was unto her.

2 And the king took off his ring, which he had taken from Haman, and gave it unto Mordecai. And Esther set Mordecai over the house of Haman.

3 And Esther spoke yet again before the king, and fell down at his feet, and besought him with tears to put away the mischief of Haman the Agagite, and his device that he had devised against the Jews.

4 Then the king held out the golden scepter toward Esther. So Esther arose, and stood before the king,

5 And said, If it please the king, and if I have found favor in his sight, and the thing seem right before the king, and I be pleasing in his eyes, let it be written to reverse the letters devised by Haman the son of Hammedatha the Agagite, which he wrote to destroy the Jews which are in all the king's provinces:

6 For how can I endure to see the evil that shall come unto my people? or how can I endure to see the destruction of my kindred?

7 Then the king Ahasuerus said unto Esther the queen and to Mordecai the Jew, Behold, I have given Esther the house of Haman, and him they have hanged upon the gallows, because he laid his hand upon the Jews.

8 Write you also for the Jews, as it likes you, in the king's name, and seal it with the king's ring: for the writing which is written in the king's name, and sealed with the king's ring, may no man reverse.

9 Then were the king's scribes called at that time, in the third month, that is, the month Sivan, on the three and twentieth [day] thereof; and it was written according to all that Mordecai commanded, to the Jews, and to the satraps, and the governors, and the princes of the provinces which are from India even to Ethiopia, a hundred and twenty-seven provinces, to every province according to the writing thereof, and to every people according to their language, and to the Jews according to their writing and according to their language.

10 And he wrote in the king Ahasuerus' name, and sealed it with the king's ring, and sent letters by

runners on horseback, and riders on mules, camels, and young dromedaries:

11 Wherein the king granted the Jews which were in every city to gather themselves together, and to stand for their soul, to destroy, to slay, and to cause to perish, all the power of the people and province that would assault them, both little ones and women, and to take the spoil of them for a prey,

12 Upon one day in all the provinces of king Ahasuerus, namely, upon the thirteenth day of the twelfth month, which is the month Adar.

13 The copy of the writing for a law to be given in every province was published unto all people, and that the Jews should be ready against that day to avenge themselves on their enemies.

14 So the runners that rode upon mules and camels went out, being hurried and pressed on by the king's commandment. And the law was given at Shushan the palace.

15 And Mordecai went out from the presence of the king in royal apparel of blue and white, and with a great crown of gold, and with a garment of fine linen and purple: and the city of Shushan rejoiced and was glad.

16 The Jews had light, and gladness, and joy, and honor.

17 And in every province, and in every city, wheresoever the king's commandment and his law came, the Jews had joy and gladness, a feast and a good day. And many of the people of the land became Jews; for the fear of the Jews fell upon them.

Est 9:1 Now in the twelfth month, that is, the month Adar, on the thirteenth day of the same, when the king's commandment and his law drew near to be put in execution, in the day that the enemies of the Jews hoped to have power over them, though it was turned to the contrary, that the Jews had rule over them that hated them;

2 The Jews gathered themselves together in their cities throughout all the provinces of the king Ahasuerus, to lay hand on such as sought their hurt: and no man could withstand them; for the fear of them fell upon all people.

3 And all the rulers of the provinces, and the lieutenants, and the deputies, and officers of the king, helped the Jews; because the fear of Mordecai fell upon them.

4 For Mordecai was great in the king's house, and his fame went out throughout all the provinces: for this man Mordecai grew greater and greater.

5 Thus the Jews smote all their enemies with the stroke of the sword, and slaughter, and destruction, and did what they would unto those that hated them.

6 And in Shushan the palace the Jews killed and destroyed five hundred men.

7 And Parshandatha, and Dalphon, and Aspatha,

8 And Poratha, and Adalia, and Aridatha,

9 And Parmashta, and Arisai, and Aridai, and Vajezatha,

10 The ten sons of Haman the son of Hammedatha, the enemy of the Jews, killed they; but on the spoil laid they not their hand.

11 On that day the number of those that were slain in Shushan the palace was brought before the king.

12 And the king said unto Esther the queen, The Jews have slain and destroyed five hundred men in Shushan the palace, and the ten sons of Haman; what have they done in the rest of the king's provinces? now what is your petition? and it shall be granted you: or what is your request further? and it shall be done.

13 Then said Esther, If it please the king, let it be granted to the Jews which are in Shushan to do tomorrow also according unto this day's law, and let Haman's ten sons be hanged upon the gallows.

14 And the king commanded it so to be done: and the law was given at Shushan; and they hanged Haman's ten sons.

15 For the Jews that were in Shushan gathered themselves together on the fourteenth day also of the month Adar, and killed three hundred men at Shushan; but on the prey they laid not their hand.

16 But the other Jews that were in the king's provinces gathered themselves together, and stood for their souls, and had rest from their enemies, and killed of their foes seventy and five thousand, but they laid not their hands on the prey,

17 On the thirteenth day of the month Adar; and on the fourteenth day of the same rested they, and made it a day of feasting and gladness.

18 But the Jews that were at Shushan assembled together on the thirteenth day thereof, and on the fourteenth thereof; and on the fifteenth day of the same they rested, and made it a day of feasting and gladness.

19 Therefore the Jews of the villages, that dwelt in the unwalled towns, made the fourteenth day of the month Adar a day of gladness and feasting, and a good day, and of sending portions one to another.

20 And Mordecai wrote these things, and sent letters unto all the Jews that were in all the provinces of the king Ahasuerus, both near and far,

21 To establish this among them, that they should keep the fourteenth day of the month Adar, and the fifteenth day of the same, yearly,

22 As the days wherein the Jews rested from their enemies, and the month which was turned unto them from sorrow to joy, and from mourning into a good day: that they should make them days of feasting and joy, and of sending portions one to another, and gifts to the poor.

23 And the Jews undertook to do as they had begun, and as Mordecai had written unto them;

24 Because Haman the son of Hammedatha, the Agagite, the enemy of all the Jews, had devised against the Jews to destroy them, and had cast Pur, that is, the lot, to consume them, and to destroy them;

25 But when Esther came before the king, he commanded by letters that his wicked device, which he devised against the Jews, should return upon his own head, and that he and his sons should be hanged on the gallows.

26 Therefore they called these days Purim after the name of Pur. Therefore for all the words of this letter, and of that which they had seen concerning this matter, and which had come unto them,

27 The Jews ordained, and took upon them, and upon their seed, and upon all such as joined themselves unto them, so as it should not fail, that they would keep these two days according to their

writing, and according to their appointed time every year;

28 And that these days should be remembered and kept throughout every generation, every family, every province, and every city; and that these days of Purim should not fail from among the Jews, nor the memorial of them perish from their seed.

29 Then Esther the queen, the daughter of Abihail, and Mordecai the Jew, wrote with all authority, to confirm this second letter of Purim.

30 And he sent the letters unto all the Jews, to the hundred twenty and seven provinces of the kingdom of Ahasuerus, with words of peace and truth,

31 To confirm these days of Purim in their times appointed, according as Mordecai the Jew and Esther the queen had enjoined them, and as they had decreed for their souls and for their seed, the matters of the fasting and their cry.

32 And the decree of Esther confirmed these matters of Purim; and it was written in the book.

Est 10:1 And the king Ahasuerus laid a tribute upon the land, and upon the isles of the sea.

2 And all the acts of his power and of his might, and the declaration of the greatness of Mordecai, whereunto the king advanced him, are they not written in the book of the chronicles of the kings of Media and Persia?

3 For Mordecai the Jew was next unto king Ahasuerus, and great among the Jews, and accepted of the multitude of his brethren, seeking the wealth of his people, and speaking peace to all his seed.

Job

Job 1:1 There was a man in the land of Uz, whose name was Job; and that man was perfect and upright, and one that feared God, and eschewed evil.

2 And there were born unto him seven sons and three daughters.

3 His substance also was seven thousand of sheep, and three thousand of camels, and five hundred yoke of oxen, and five hundred she donkeys, and a very great household; so that this man was the greatest of all the men of the east.

4 And his sons went and feasted in their houses, every one his day; and sent and called for their three sisters to eat and to drink with them.

5 And it was so, when the days of their feasting were gone about, that Job sent and sanctified them, and rose up early in the morning, and offered burnt offerings according to the number of them all: for Job said, It may be that my sons have sinned, and cursed God in their hearts. Thus did Job all the days.

6 Now there was a day when the sons of God came to present themselves before the Becoming-One, and Satan came also among them.

7 And the Becoming-One said unto Satan, Where are you from? Then Satan answered the Becoming-One, and said, From going back and forth in the earth, and from walking up and down in it.

8 And the Becoming-One said unto Satan, have you considered my servant Job, that there is none like him in the earth, a perfect and an upright man, one that fears God, and eschews evil?

9 Then Satan answered the Becoming-One, and said, does Job fear God for nothing?

10 have not you made a hedge about him, and about his house, and about all that he has on every side? you have blessed the work of his hands, and his substance is increased in the land.

11 But put forth your hand now, and touch all that he hath, and he will curse you to your face.

12 And the Becoming-One said unto Satan, Behold, all that he has is in your power; only upon himself put not forth your hand. So Satan went forth from the presence of the Becoming-One.

13 And there was a day when his sons and his daughters were eating and drinking wine in their eldest brother's house:

14 And there came a messenger unto Job, and said, The oxen were plowing, and the donkeys feeding beside them:

15 And the Sabeans fell upon them, and took them away; yes, they have slain the servants with the edge of the sword; and I only am escaped alone to tell you.

16 While he was yet speaking, there came also another, and said, The fire of God is fallen from heaven, and has burned up the sheep, and the servants, and consumed them; and I only am escaped alone to tell you.

17 While he was yet speaking, there came also another, and said, The Chaldeans made out three bands, and fell upon the camels, and have carried them away, yes, and slain the servants with the edge of the sword; and I only am escaped alone to tell you.

18 While he was yet speaking, there came also another, and said, your sons and your daughters were eating and drinking wine in their eldest brother's house:

19 And, behold, there came a great wind from the wilderness, and smote the four corners of the house, and it fell upon the young men, and they are dead; and I only am escaped alone to tell you.

20 Then Job arose, and ripped his mantle, and shaved his head, and fell down upon the ground, and worshiped,

21 And said, Naked came I out of my mother's womb, and naked shall I return there: the Becoming-One gave, and the Becoming-One has taken away; blessed be the name of the Becoming-One.

22 In all this Job sinned not, nor charged God foolishly.

Job 2:1 Again there was a day when the sons of God came to present themselves before the Becoming-One, and Satan came also among them to present himself before the Becoming-One.

2 And the Becoming-One said unto Satan, From where do you come? And Satan answered the Becoming-One, and said, From going back and forth in the earth, and from walking up and down in it.

3 And the Becoming-One said unto Satan, have you considered my servant Job, that there is none like him in the earth, a perfect and an upright man, one that fears God, and eschews evil? and still he holds fast his integrity, although you moved me against him, to destroy him without cause.

4 And Satan answered the Becoming-One, and said, Skin for skin, yes, all that a man has will he give for his soul.

5 But put forth your hand now, and touch his bone and his flesh, and he will curse you to your face.

6 And the Becoming-One said unto Satan, Behold, he is in your hand; but save his soul.

7 So went Satan forth from the presence of the Becoming-One, and smote Job with great boils from the sole of his foot unto his crown.

8 And he took him a potsherd to scrape himself withal; and he sat down among the ashes.

9 Then said his wife unto him, do you still retain your integrity? curse God, and die.

10 But he said unto her, you speak as one of the foolish women speaks. What? shall we receive good at the hand of God, and shall we not receive evil? In all this did not Job sin with his lips.

11 Now when Job's three friends heard of all this evil that was come upon him, they came every one from his own place; Eliphaz the Temanite, and Bildad the Shuhite, and Zophar the Naamathite: for they had made an appointment together to come to mourn with him and to comfort him.

12 And when they lifted up their eyes afar off, and knew him not, they lifted up their voice, and wept; and they ripped every one his mantle, and sprinkled dust upon their heads toward heaven.

13 So they sat down with him upon the ground seven days and seven nights, and none spoke a word unto him: for they saw that his grief was very great.

Job 3:1 After this opened Job his mouth, and cursed his day.

2 And Job spoke, and said,

3 Let the day perish wherein I was born, and the night in which it was said, There is a man child conceived.

4 Let that day be darkness; let not God regard it from above, neither let the light shine upon it.

5 Let darkness and the shadow of death stain it; let a cloud dwell upon it; let the blackness of the day terrify it.

6 As for that night, let darkness seize upon it; let it not be joined unto the days of the year, let it not come into the number of the months.

7 Lo, let that night be solitary, let no joyful voice come therein.

8 Let them curse it that curse the day, who are ready to raise up their mourning [leviathan]

9 Let the stars of the breeze time of the evening thereof be dark; let it look for light, but have none; neither let it see the eyelids of dawn:

10 Because it shut not up the doors of my mother's womb, nor hid sorrow from mine eyes.

11 Why died I not from the womb? why did I not give up the ghost when I came out of the belly?

12 Why did the knees prevent me? or why the breasts that I should suck?

13 For now should I have lain still and been quiet, I should have slept: then had I been at rest,

14 With kings and councelors of the earth, which built desolate places for themselves;

15 Or with princes that had gold, who filled their houses with silver:

16 Or as a hidden untimely birth I had not been; as infants which never saw light.

17 There the wicked cease from troubling; and there the weary be at rest.

18 There the prisoners rest together; they hear not the voice of the oppressor.

19 The small and great are there; and the servant is free from his master.

20 Therefore is light given to him that is in misery, and life unto the bitter in soul;

21 Which long for death, but it comes not; and dig for it more than for hid treasures;

22 Which rejoice exceedingly, and are glad, when they can find the grave?

23 Why is light given to a man whose way is hid, and whom God has hedged in?

24 For my sighing comes before I eat, and my roarings are poured out like the waters.

25 For the thing which I greatly feared is come upon me, and that which I was afraid of is come unto me.

26 I was not in safety, neither had I rest, neither was I quiet; yet trouble came.

Job 4:1 Then Eliphaz the Temanite answered and said,

2 If we assay to commune with you, will you be grieved? but who can withhold himself from speaking?

3 Behold, you have instructed many, and you have strengthened the weak hands.

4 your words have upheld him that was falling, and you have strengthened the feeble knees.

5 But now it is come upon you, and you faint; it touches you, and you are troubled.

6 Is not this your fear, your confidence, your hope, and the uprightness of your ways?

7 Remember, I pray you, who ever perished, being innocent? or where were the righteous cut off?

8 Even as I have seen, they that plow iniquity, and sow wickedness, reap the same.

9 By the blast of God they perish, and by the breath of his nostrils are they consumed.

10 The roaring of the lion, and the voice of the fierce lion, and the teeth of the young lions, are broken.

11 The old lion perishes for lack of prey, and the stout lion's whelps are scattered abroad.

12 Now a thing was secretly brought to me, and mine ear received a little thereof.

13 In thoughts from the visions of the night, when deep sleep falls on men,

14 Fear came upon me, and trembling, which made all my bones to shake.

15 Then a spirit passed before my face; the hair of my flesh stood up:

16 It stood still, but I could not discern the form thereof: an image was before mine eyes, there was silence, and I heard a voice, saying,

17 Shall mortal man be more just than God? shall a man be more pure than his maker?

18 Behold, he put no trust in his servants; and his angels he charged with folly:

19 How much less in them that dwell in houses of clay, whose foundation is in the dust, which are crushed before the moth?

20 They are destroyed from morning to evening: they perish for glory without any regarding it.

21 does not their excellency which is in them go away? they die, even without wisdom.

Job 5:1 Call now, if there be any that will answer you; and to which of the saints will you turn?

2 For wrath kills the foolish man, and envy slays the silly one.

3 I have seen the foolish taking root: but suddenly I cursed his habitation.

4 His children are far from safety, and they are crushed in the gate, neither is there any to deliver them.

5 Whose harvest the hungry eats up, and takes it even out of the thorns, and the robber swallows up their substance.

6 Although affliction comes not forth of the dust, neither does trouble spring out of the ground;

7 Yet man is born unto trouble, as the sparks fly upward.

8 I would seek unto GOD, and unto God would I commit my cause:

9 Which did great things and unsearchable; marvelous things without number:

10 Who gives rain upon the earth, and sends waters upon the fields:

11 To set up on high those that be low; that those which mourn may be exalted to safety.

12 He disappoints the devices of the crafty, so that their hands cannot perform their enterprise.

13 He takes the wise in their own craftiness: and the counsel of the perverse is carried headlong.

14 They meet with darkness in the daytime, and grope in the noonday as in the night.

15 But he saves the poor from the sword, from their mouth, and from the hand of the mighty.

16 So the poor has hope, and iniquity stops her mouth.

17 Behold, happy is the man whom God corrects: therefore despise not you the chastening of the Almighty:

18 For he makes sore, and binds up: he wounds, and his hands make whole.

19 He shall deliver you in six troubles: yes, in seven there shall no evil touch you.

20 In famine he shall redeem you from death: and in war from the power of the sword.

21 you shall be hid from the scourge of the tongue: neither shall you be afraid of destruction when it comes.

22 At destruction and famine you shall laugh: neither shall you be afraid of the beasts of the earth.

23 For you shall be in league with the stones of the field: and the beasts of the field shall be at peace with you.

24 And you shall know that your tabernacle shall be in peace; and you shall visit your habitation, and shall not sin.

25 you shall know also that your seed shall be great, and your offspring as the grass of the earth.

26 you shall come to your grave in a full age, like as a shock of grain comes in in his season.

27 Lo this, we have searched it, so it is; hear it, and know you it for your good.

Job 6:1 But Job answered and said,

2 Oh that my grief were thoroughly weighed, and my calamity laid in the balances together!

3 For now it would be heavier than the sand of the sea: therefore my words are swallowed up.

4 For the arrows of the Almighty are within me, the poison whereof drinks up my spirit: the terrors of God do set themselves in array against me.

5 does the wild donkey bray when he has grass? or low the ox over his fodder?

6 Can that which is unsavoury be eaten without salt? or is there any taste in the white of an egg?

7 The things that my soul refused to touch are as my sorrowful food.

8 Oh that I might have my request; and that God would grant me the thing that I long for!

9 Even that it would please God to destroy me; that he would let loose his hand, and cut me off!

10 Then should I yet have comfort; yes, I would harden myself in sorrow: let him not spare; for I have not concealed the words of the Holy One.

11 What is my strength, that I should hope? and what is mine end, that I should prolong my soul?

12 Is my strength the strength of stones? or is my flesh of brass?

13 Is not my help in me? and is wisdom driven quite from me?

14 To him that is afflicted pity should be showed from his friend; but he forsakes the fear of the Almighty.

15 My brethren have dealt deceitfully as a brook, and as the stream of brooks they pass away;

16 Which are blackish by reason of the ice, and wherein the snow is hid:

17 What time they wax warm, they vanish: when it is hot, they are consumed out of their place.

18 The paths of their way are turned aside; they go to nothing, and perish.

19 The troops of Tema looked, the companies of Sheba waited for them.

20 They were confounded because they had hoped; they came there, and were ashamed.

21 For now you are nothing; you see my casting down, and are afraid.

22 Did I say, Bring unto me? or, Give a reward for me of your substance?

23 Or, Deliver me from the enemy's hand? or, Redeem me from the hand of the terrible?

24 Teach me, and I will hold my tongue: and cause me to understand wherein I have erred.

25 How forcible are right words! but what does your arguing reprove?

26 Do you imagine to reprove words, and the speeches of one that is desperate, which are as wind?

27 Yes, you overwhelm the fatherless, and you dig a pit for your friend.

28 Now therefore be content, look upon me; for it is evident unto you if I lie.

29 Return, I pray you, let it not be iniquity; yes, return again, my righteousness is in it.

30 Is there iniquity in my tongue? cannot my taste discern perverse things?

Job 7:1 Is there not an appointed time to man upon earth? are not his days also like the days of a hireling?

2 As a servant earnestly desires the shadow, and as a hireling looks for the reward of his work:

3 So I am made to possess months of vanity, and wearisome nights are appointed to me.

4 When I lie down, I say, When shall I arise, and the evening be gone? and I am full of tossing back and forth unto the breeze time.

5 My flesh is clothed with worms and clods of dust; my skin is broken, and become loathsome.

6 My days are swifter than a weaver's shuttle, and are spent without hope.

7 O remember that my life is wind: mine eye shall no more see good.

8 The eye of him that has seen me shall see me no more: your eyes are upon me, and I am not.

9 As the cloud is consumed and vanishes away: so he that goes down to Sheol shall come up no more.

10 He shall return no more to his house, neither shall his place know him any more.

11 Therefore I will not refrain my mouth; I will speak in the anguish of my spirit; I will complain in the bitterness of my soul.

12 Am I a sea, or a whale, that you set a watch over me?

13 When I say, My bed shall comfort me, my couch shall ease my complaint;

14 Then you scare me with dreams, and terrifies me through visions:

15 So that my soul chooses strangling, and death rather than my life.

16 I loathe it; I would not live for olam, let me alone; for my days are vanity.

17 What is man, that you should magnify him? and that you should set your heart upon him?

18 And that you should visit him every morning, and try him every moment?

19 How long will you not depart from me, nor let me alone till I swallow down my spittle?

20 I have sinned; what shall I do unto you, O you preserver of men? why have you set me as a mark against you, so that I am a burden to myself?

21 And why do you not pardon my transgression, and take away mine iniquity? for now shall I sleep in the dust; and you shall seek me in the morning, but I shall not be.

Job 8:1 Then answered Bildad the Shuhite, and said,

2 How long will you speak these things? and how long shall the words of your mouth be like a strong wind?

3 does GOD pervert judgment? or does the Almighty pervert justice?

4 If your children have sinned against him, and he have cast them away for their transgression;

5 If you would seek unto GOD, and make your supplication to the Almighty;

6 If you were pure and upright; surely now he would awake for you, and make the habitation of your righteousness prosperous.

7 Though your beginning was small, yet your latter end should greatly increase.

8 For inquire, I pray you, of the former age, and prepare yourself to the search of their fathers:

9 For we are but of yesterday, and know nothing, because our days upon earth are a shadow.

10 Shall not they teach you, and tell you, and utter words out of their heart?

11 Can the rush grow up without mire? can the flag grow without water?

12 While it is yet in his greenness, and not cut down, it withers before any other herb.

13 So are the paths of all that forget GOD; and the hypocrite's hope shall perish:

14 Whose hope shall be cut off, and whose trust shall be a spider's web.

15 He shall lean upon his house, but it shall not stand: he shall hold it fast, but it shall not endure.

16 He is green before the sun, and his branch shoots forth in his garden.

17 His roots are wrapped about the heap, and sees the place of stones.

18 If he destroy him from his place, then it shall deny him, saying, I have not seen you.

19 Behold, this is the joy of his way, and out of the earth shall others grow.

20 Behold, GOD will not cast away a perfect man, neither will he help the evil doers:

21 Till he fill your mouth with laughing, and your lips with rejoicing.

22 They that hate you shall be clothed with shame; and the dwelling place of the wicked shall come to nothing.

Job 9:1 Then Job answered and said,

2 I know it is so of a truth: but how should man be just with GOD?

3 If he will contend with him, he cannot answer him one of a thousand.

4 He is wise in heart, and mighty in strength: who has hardened himself against him, and has prospered?

5 Which removes the mountains, and they know not: which overturns them in his anger.

6 Which shakes the earth out of her place, and the pillars thereof tremble.

7 Which commands the sun, and it rises not; and seals up the stars.

8 Which alone spreads out the heavens, and treads upon the waves of the sea.

9 Which makes Arcturus, Orion, and Pleiades [cluster] and the chambers of the south.

10 Which did great things past finding out; yes, and wonders without number.

11 Lo, he goes by me, and I see him not: he passes on also, but I perceive him not.

12 Behold, he takes away, who can hinder him? who will say unto him, What do you?

13 If God will not withdraw his anger, the proud helpers do stoop under him.

14 How much less shall I answer him, and choose out my words to reason with him?

15 Whom, though I were righteous, yet would I not answer, but I would make supplication to my judge.

16 If I had called, and he had answered me; yet would I not believe that he had heard my voice.

17 For he breaks me with a tempest, and multiplies my wounds without cause.

18 He will not permit me to take my breath, but fills me with bitterness.

19 If I speak of strength, lo, he is strong: and if of judgment, who shall set me a time to plead?

20 If I justify myself, mine own mouth shall condemn me: if I say, I am perfect, it shall also prove me perverse.

21 Though I were perfect, yet would I not know my soul: I would despise my life.

22 This is one thing, therefore I said it, He destroys the perfect and the wicked.

23 If the scourge slay suddenly, he will laugh at the trial of the innocent.

24 The earth is given into the hand of the wicked: he covers the faces of the judges thereof; if not, where, and who is he?

25 Now my days are swifter than a post: they flee away, they see no good.

26 They are passed away as the swift ships: as the eagle that hastens to the prey.

27 If I say, I will forget my complaint, I will leave off my heaviness, and comfort myself:

28 I am afraid of all my sorrows, I know that you will not hold me innocent.

29 If I be wicked, why then labor I in vain?

30 If I wash myself with snow water, and make my hands never so clean;

31 Yet shall you plunge me in the ditch, and mine own clothes shall abhor me.

32 For he is not a man, as I am, that I should answer him, and we should come together in judgment.

33 Neither is there any daysman between us, that might lay his hand upon us both.

34 Let him take his rod away from me, and let not his fear terrify me:

35 Then would I speak, and not fear him; but it is not so with me.

Job 10:1 My soul is weary of my life; I will leave my complaint upon myself; I will speak in the bitterness of my soul.

2 I will say unto God, Do not condemn me; show me therefore you contend with me.

3 Is it good unto you that you should oppress, that you should despise the work of your hands, and shine upon the counsel of the wicked?

4 have you eyes of flesh? or see you as man sees?

5 Are your days as the days of man? are your years as man's days,

6 That you inquire after mine iniquity, and search after my sin?

7 you know that I am not wicked; and there is none that can deliver out of your hand.

8 your hands have made me and fashioned me together round about; yet you do destroy me.

9 Remember, I beg you, that you have made me as the clay; and will you bring me into dust again?

10 have you not poured me out as milk, and curdled me like cheese?

11 you have clothed me with skin and flesh, and have fenced me with bones and tendons.

12 you have granted me life and favor, and your visitation has preserved my spirit.

13 And these things have you hid in your heart: I know that this is with you.

14 If I sin, then you mark me, and you will not acquit me from mine iniquity.

15 If I be wicked, woe unto me; and if I be righteous, yet will I not lift up my head. I am full of confusion; therefore see you mine affliction;

16 For it increases. you hunt me as a fierce lion: and again you show yourself marvelous upon me.

17 you renew your witnesses against me, and increase your indignation upon me; changes and war are against me.

18 Why then have you brought me forth out of the womb? Oh that I had given up the ghost, and no eye had seen me!

19 I should have been as though I had not been; I should have been carried from the womb to the grave.

20 Are not my days few? cease then, and let me alone, that I may take comfort a little,

21 Before I go where I shall not return, even to the land of darkness and the shadow of death;

22 A land of darkness, as darkness itself; and of the shadow of death, without any order, and where the light is as darkness.

Job 11:1 Then answered Zophar the Naamathite, and said,

2 Should not the multitude of words be answered? and should a man full of talk be justified?

3 Should your lies make men hold their peace? and when you mock, shall no man make you ashamed?

4 For you have said, My doctrine is pure, and I am clean in your eyes.

5 But oh that God would speak, and open his lips against you;

6 And that he would show you the secrets of wisdom, that they are double to that which is! Know therefore that God exacts of you less than your iniquity deserves.

7 Can you by searching find out God? can you find out the Almighty unto perfection?

8 It is as high as heaven; what can you do? deeper than Sheol; what can you know?

9 The measure thereof is longer than the earth, and broader than the sea.

10 If he cut off, and shut up, or gather together, then who can hinder him?

11 For he knows vain men: he sees wickedness also; will he not then consider it?

12 For vain man would be wise, though man be born like a wild ass's colt.

13 If you prepare your heart, and stretch out your hands toward him;

14 If iniquity be in your hand, put it far away, and let not wickedness dwell in your tabernacles.

15 For then shall you lift up your face without spot; yes, you shall be stedfast, and shall not fear:

16 Because you shall forget your misery, and remember it as waters that pass away:

17 And your age shall be clearer than the noonday; you shall shine forth, you shall be as the morning.

18 And you shall be secure, because there is hope; yes, you shall dig about you, and you shall take your rest in safety.

19 Also you shall lie down, and none shall make you afraid; yes, many shall make suit unto you.

20 But the eyes of the wicked shall fail, and they shall not escape, and their hope shall be as the giving up of the breath of the soul.

Job 12:1 And Job answered and said,

2 No doubt but you are the people, and wisdom shall die with you.

3 But I have understanding as well as you; I am not inferior to you: yes, who knows not such things as these?

4 I am as one mocked of his neighbor, who calls upon God, and he answers him: the just upright man is laughed to scorn.

5 He that is ready to slip with his feet is as a lamp despised in the thought of him that is at ease.

6 The tabernacles of robbers prosper, and they that provoke GOD are secure; into whose hand God brings abundantly.

7 But ask now the beasts, and they shall teach you; and the fowls of the air, and they shall tell you:

8 Or speak to the earth, and it shall teach you: and the fishes of the sea shall declare unto you.

9 Who knows not in all these that the hand of the Becoming-One has worked this?

10 In whose hand is the soul of every living thing, and the spirit of all mankind.

11 does not the ear try words? and the mouth taste his food?

12 With the ancient is wisdom; and in length of days understanding.

13 With him is wisdom and strength, he has counsel and understanding.

14 Behold, he breaks down, and it cannot be built again: he shuts up a man, and there can be no opening.

15 Behold, he withholds the waters, and they dry up: also he sends them out, and they overturn the earth.

16 With him is strength and wisdom: the deceived and the deceiver are his.

17 He leads councelors away spoiled, and makes the judges fools.

18 He looses the bond of kings, and girds their loins with a girdle.

19 He leads princes away spoiled, and overthrows the mighty.

20 He removes away the speech of the trusty, and takes away the understanding of the aged.

21 He pours contempt upon princes, and weakens the strength of the mighty.

22 He discovers deep things out of darkness, and brings out to light the shadow of death.

23 He increases the nations, and destroys them: he enlarges the nations, and straitens them again.

24 He takes away the heart of the chief of the people of the earth, and causes them to wander in a wilderness where there is no way.

25 They grope in the dark without light, and he makes them to stagger like a drunken man.

Job 13:1 Lo, mine eye has seen all this, mine ear has heard and understood it.

2 What you know, the same do I know also: I am not inferior unto you.

3 Surely I would speak to the Almighty, and I desire to reason with GOD.

4 But you are forgers of lies, you are all physicians of no value.

5 O that you would altogether hold your peace! and it should be your wisdom.

6 Hear now my reasoning, and listen to the pleadings of my lips.

7 Will you speak wickedly for GOD? and talk deceitfully for him?

8 Will you accept his person? will you contend for GOD?

9 Is it good that he should search you out? or as one man mocks another, do you so mock him?

10 He will surely reprove you, if you do secretly accept persons.

11 Shall not his excellency make you afraid? and his dread fall upon you?

12 Your remembrances are like unto ashes, your bodies to bodies of clay.

13 Hold your peace, let me alone, that I may speak, and let come on me what will.

14 Therefore do I take my flesh in my teeth, and put my soul in mine hand?

15 Though he slay me, yet will I trust in him: but I will maintain mine own ways before him.

16 He also shall be my salvation: for a hypocrite shall not come before him.

17 Hear diligently my speech, and my declaration with your ears.

18 Behold now, I have ordered my cause; I know that I shall be justified.

19 Who is he that will plead with me? for now, if I hold my tongue, I shall give up the ghost.

20 Only do not two things unto me: then will I not hide myself from you.

21 Withdraw your hand far from me: and let not your dread make me afraid.

22 Then call you, and I will answer: or let me speak, and answer you me.

23 How many are mine iniquities and sins? make me to know my transgression and my sin.

24 Why hide you your face, and hold me for your enemy?

25 will you break a leaf driven back and forth? and will you pursue the dry stubble?

26 For you write bitter things against me, and make me to possess the iniquities of my youth.

27 you put my feet also in the stocks, and look narrowly unto all my paths; you set a print upon the heels of my feet.

28 And he, as a rotten thing, consumes as a garment that is moth eaten.

Job 14:1 Man that is born of a woman is of few days, and full of trouble.

2 He comes forth like a flower, and is cut down: he flees also as a shadow, and continues not.

3 And do you open your eyes upon such an one, and bring me into judgment with you?

4 Who can bring a clean thing out of an unclean? not one.

5 Seeing his days are determined, the number of his months are with you, you have appointed his bounds that he cannot pass;

6 Turn from him, that he may rest, till he shall accomplish, as a hireling, his day.

7 For there is hope of a tree, if it be cut down, that it will sprout again, and that the tender branch thereof will not cease.

8 Though the root thereof wax old in the earth, and the stock thereof die in the ground;

9 Yet through the scent of water it will bud, and bring forth boughs like a plant.

10 But man dies, and wastes away: yes, man gives up the ghost, and where is he?

11 As the waters fail from the sea, and the flood decays and dries up:

12 So man lies down, and rises not: till the heavens be no more, they shall not awake, nor be raised out of their sleep.

13 O that you would hide me in Sheol, that you would keep me secret, until your wrath be past, that you would appoint me a set time, and remember me!

14 If a man die, shall he live again? all the days of my appointed time will I wait, till my change come.

15 you shall call, and I will answer you: you will have a desire to the work of your hands.

16 For now you number my steps: do you not watch over my sin?

17 My transgression is sealed up in a bag, and you sew up mine iniquity.

18 And surely the mountain falling comes to nothing, and the rock is removed out of his place.

19 The waters wear the stones: you wash away the things which grow out of the dust of the earth; and you destroy the hope of man.

20 you prevail for glory against him, and he passes: you change his countenance, and send him away.

21 His sons come to honor, and he knows it not; and they are brought low, but he perceives it not of them.

22 But his flesh upon him shall have pain, and his soul within him shall mourn.

Job 15:1 Then answered Eliphaz the Temanite, and said,

2 Should a wise man utter knowledge of the wind, and fill his belly with the east wind?

3 Should he reason with unprofitable talk? or with speeches wherewith he can do no good?

4 Yes, you cast off fear, and restrain prayer before GOD.

5 For your mouth utters your iniquity, and you choose the tongue of the crafty.

6 your own mouth condemns you, and not I: yes, your own lips testify against you.

7 are you the first man that was born? or were you made before the hills?

8 have you heard the secret of God? and do you restrain wisdom to thyself?

9 What know you, that we know not? what understand you, which is not in us?

10 With us are both the grayheaded and very aged men, much elder than your father.

11 Are the consolations of GOD small with you? is there any secret thing with you?

12 Why does your heart carry you away? and what do your eyes wink at,

13 That you turn your spirit against GOD, and let such words go out of your mouth?

14 What is man, that he should be clean? and he which is born of a woman, that he should be righteous?

15 Behold, he puts no trust in his saints; yes, the heavens are not clean in his sight.

16 How much more abominable and filthy is man, which drinks iniquity like water?

17 I will show you, hear me; and that which I have seen I will declare;

18 Which wise men have told from their fathers, and have not hid it:

19 Unto whom alone the earth was given, and no stranger passed among them.

20 The wicked man travails, with pain all his days, and the number of years is hidden to the terrible.

21 A dreadful sound is in his ears: in prosperity the destroyer shall come upon him.

22 He believes not that he shall return out of darkness, and he is waited for of the sword.

23 He wanders abroad for bread, saying, Where is it? he knows that the day of darkness is ready at his hand.

24 Trouble and anguish shall make him afraid; they shall prevail against him, as a king ready to the battle.

25 For he stretches out his hand against GOD, and strengthens himself against the Almighty.

26 He runs upon him, even on his neck, upon the thick bosses of his bucklers:

27 Because he covers his face with his fatness, and makes collops of fat on his flanks.

28 And he dwells in desolate cities, and in houses which no man inhabits, which are ready to become heaps.

29 He shall not be rich, neither shall his substance continue, neither shall he prolong the perfection thereof upon the earth.

30 He shall not depart out of darkness; the flame shall dry up his branches, and by the breath of his mouth shall he go away.

31 Let not him that is deceived trust in vanity: for vanity shall be his recompense.

32 It shall be accomplished before his time, and his branch shall not be green.

33 He shall shake off his unripe grape as the vine, and shall cast off his flower as the olive.

34 For the congregation of hypocrites shall be desolate, and fire shall consume the tabernacles of bribery.

35 They conceive mischief, and bring forth vanity, and their belly prepares deceit.

Job 16:1 Then Job answered and said,

2 I have heard many such things: miserable comforters are you all.

2 I have heard many such things: miserable comforters are you all.

3 Shall words of the wind have an end? or what emboldens you that you answer?

4 I also could speak as you do: if your soul were in my soul's stead, I could heap up words against you, and shake mine head at you.

5 But I would strengthen you with my mouth, and the moving of my lips should assuage your grief.

6 Though I speak, my grief is not assuaged: and though I forbear, what am I eased?

7 But now he has made me weary: you have made desolate all my company.

8 And you have filled me with wrinkles, which is a witness against me: and my leanness rising up in me bears witness to my face.

9 He tears me in his wrath, who hates me: he gnashes upon me with his teeth; mine enemy sharpens his eyes upon me.

10 They have gaped upon me with their mouth; they have struck me upon the cheek reproachfully; they have gathered themselves together against me.

11 GOD has delivered me to the ungodly, and turned me over into the hands of the wicked.

12 I was at ease, but he has broken me asunder: he has also taken me by my neck, and shaken me to pieces, and set me up for his mark.

13 His archers compass me round about, he cleaves my reins asunder, and does not spare; he pours out my gall upon the ground.

14 He breaks me with breach upon breach, he runs upon me like a giant.

15 I have sewed sackcloth upon my skin, and defiled my horn in the dust.

16 My face is foul with weeping, and on my eyelids is the shadow of death;

17 Not for any injustice in mine hands: also my prayer is pure.

18 O earth, cover not you my blood, and let my cry have no place.

19 Also now, behold, my witness is in heaven, and my record is on high.

20 My friends scorn me: but mine eye pours out tears unto God.

21 O that one might plead for a man with God, as a man pleads for his neighbor!

22 When a few years are come, then I shall go the way where I shall not return.

Job 17:1 My breath is corrupt, my days are extinct, the graves are ready for me.

2 Are there not mockers with me? and does not mine eye continue in their provocation?

3 Lay down now, put me in a surety with you; who is he that will strike hands with me?

4 For you have hid their heart from understanding: therefore shall you not exalt them.

5 He that speaks flattery to his friends, even the eyes of his children shall fail.

6 He has made me also a byword of the people; and aforetime I was as a tabret.

7 Mine eye also is dim by reason of sorrow, and all my members are as a shadow.

8 Upright men shall be astonied at this, and the innocent shall stir up himself against the hypocrite.

9 The righteous also shall hold on his way, and he that has clean hands shall be stronger and stronger.

10 But as for you all, do you return, and come now: for I cannot find one wise man among you.

11 My days are past, my purposes are broken off, even the thoughts of my heart.

12 They change the night into day: the light is short because of darkness.

13 If I wait, Sheol is mine house: I have made my bed in the darkness.

14 I have said to corruption, you are my father: to the worm, you are my mother, and my sister.

15 And where is now my hope? as for my hope, who shall see it?

16 They shall go down to the bars of Sheol, when our rest together is in the dust.

Job 18:1 Then answered Bildad the Shuhite, and said,

2 How long will it be ere you make an end of words? mark, and afterwards we will speak.

3 Why are we counted as beasts, and reputed vile in your sight?

4 He tears his soul in his anger: shall the earth be forsaken for you? and shall the rock be removed out of his place?

5 Yes, the light of the wicked shall be put out, and the spark of his fire shall not shine.

6 The light shall be dark in his tabernacle, and his candle shall be put out with him.

7 The steps of his strength shall be hampered, and his own counsel shall cast him down.

8 For he is cast into a net by his own feet, and he walks upon a snare.

9 The gin shall take him by the heel, and the robber shall prevail against him.

10 The snare is laid for him in the ground, and a trap for him in the way.

11 Terrors shall make him afraid on every side, and shall drive him to his feet.

12 His strength shall be hungerbitten, and destruction shall be ready at his side.

13 It shall devour the strength of his skin: even the firstborn of death shall devour his strength.

14 His confidence shall be rooted out of his tabernacle, and it shall bring him to the king of terrors.

15 It shall dwell in his tabernacle, because it is none of his: brimstone shall be scattered upon his habitation.

16 His roots shall be dried up beneath, and above shall his branch be cut off.

17 His remembrance shall perish from the earth, and he shall have no name in the street.

18 He shall be driven from light into darkness, and chased out of the world.

19 He shall neither have son nor nephew among his people, nor any remaining in his dwellings.

20 They that come after him shall be astonied at his day, as they that went before were affrighted.

21 Surely such are the dwellings of the wicked, and this is the place of him that knows not GOD.

Job 19:1 Then Job answered and said,

2 How long will you vex my soul, and break me in pieces with words?

3 These ten times have you reproached me: you are not ashamed that you make yourselves strange to me.

4 And be it indeed that I have erred, mine error remains with myself.

5 If indeed you will magnify yourselves against me, and plead against me my reproach:

6 Know now that God has overthrown me, and has compassed me with his net.

7 Behold, I cry out of wrong, but I am not heard: I cry aloud, but there is no judgment.

8 He has fenced up my way that I cannot pass, and he has set darkness in my paths.

9 He has stripped me of my glory, and taken the crown from my head.

10 He has destroyed me on every side, and I am gone: and mine hope has he removed like a tree.

11 He has also kindled his wrath against me, and he counts me unto him as one of his enemies.

12 His troops come together, and raise up their way against me, and encamp round about my tabernacle.

13 He has put my brethren far from me, and mine acquaintance are truly estranged from me.

14 My kinsfolk have failed, and my familiar friends have forgotten me.

15 They that dwell in mine house, and my maids, count me for a stranger: I am an alien in their sight.

16 I called my servant, and he gave me no answer; I entreated him with my mouth.

17 My breath is strange to my wife, though I entreated for the children's sake of mine own body.

18 Yes, young children despised me; I arose, and they spoke against me.

19 All my inward friends abhorred me: and they whom I loved are turned against me.

20 My bone cleaves to my skin and to my flesh, and I am escaped with the skin of my teeth.

21 Have pity upon me, have pity upon me, O you my friends; for the hand of God has touched me.

22 Why do you persecute me as GOD, and are not satisfied with my flesh?

23 Oh that my words were now written! oh that they were printed in a book!
24 That they were graven with an iron pen and lead in the rock to the beyond.
25 For I know that my redeemer lives, and that he shall stand at the latter day upon the earth:
26 And though after my skin worms destroy this body, yet in my flesh shall I see God:
27 Whom I shall see for myself, and mine eyes shall behold, and not another; though my reins be consumed within me.
28 But you should say, Why persecute we him, seeing the root of the matter is found in me?
29 Be you afraid of the sword: for wrath brings the punishments of the sword, that you may know there is a judgment.

Job 20:1 Then answered Zophar the Naamathite, and said,
2 Therefore do my thoughts cause me to answer, and for this I make haste.
3 I have heard the check of my reproach, and the spirit of my understanding causes me to answer.
4 Don't you know this from beyond, since man was placed upon earth,
5 That the triumphing of the wicked is short, and the joy of the hypocrite but for a moment?
6 Though his excellency mount up to the heavens, and his head reach unto the clouds;
7 Yet he shall perish altogether like his own dung: they which have seen him shall say, Where is he?
8 He shall fly away as a dream, and shall not be found: yes, he shall be chased away as a vision of the night.
9 The eye also which saw him shall see him no more; neither shall his place any more behold him.
10 His children shall seek to please the poor, and his hands shall restore their goods.
11 His bones are full of the sin of his youth, which shall lie down with him in the dust.
12 Though wickedness be sweet in his mouth, though he hide it under his tongue;
13 Though he spare it, and forsake it not; but keep it still within his mouth:
14 Yet his food in his bowels is turned, it is the gall of asps within him.
15 He has swallowed down riches, and he shall vomit them up again: GOD shall cast them out of his belly.
16 He shall suck the poison of asps: the viper's tongue shall slay him.
17 He shall not see the rivers, the floods, the brooks of honey and butter.
18 That which he labored for shall he restore, and shall not swallow it down: according to his substance shall the restitution be, and he shall not rejoice therein.
19 Because he has oppressed and has forsaken the poor; because he has violently taken away a house which he built not;
20 Surely he shall not feel quietness in his belly, he shall not save of that which he desired.
21 There shall none of his food be left; therefore shall no man look for his goods.
22 In the fullness of his sufficiency he shall be in straits: every hand of the wicked shall come upon him.
23 When he is about to fill his belly, God shall cast the fury of his wrath upon him, and shall rain it upon him while he is eating.
24 He shall flee from the iron weapon, and the bow of steel shall strike him through.
25 It is drawn, and comes out of the body; yes, the glittering sword comes out of his gall: terrors are upon him.
26 All darkness shall be hid in his secret places: a fire not blown shall consume him; it shall go ill with him that is left in his tabernacle.
27 The heavens shall reveal his iniquity; and the earth shall rise up against him.
28 The increase of his house shall depart, and his goods shall flow away in the day of his wrath.
29 This is the portion of a wicked man from God, and the heritage appointed unto him by GOD.

Job 21:1 But Job answered and said,
2 Hear diligently my speech, and let this be your consolations.
3 Permit me that I may speak; and after that I have spoken, mock on.
4 As for me, is my complaint to man? and if it were so, why should not my spirit be troubled?
5 Mark me, and be astonished, and lay your hand upon your mouth.
6 Even when I remember I am afraid, and trembling takes hold on my flesh.
7 Why do the wicked live, become old, yes, are mighty in power?
8 Their seed is established in their sight with them, and their offspring before their eyes.
9 Their houses are safe from fear, neither is the rod of God upon them.
10 Their bull genders and fails not; their cow calves, and casts not her calf.
11 They send forth their little ones like a flock, and their children dance.
12 They take the timbrel and harp, and rejoice at the sound of the organ.
13 They spend their days in wealth, and in a moment go down to Sheol.
14 Therefore they say unto GOD, Depart from us; for we desire not the knowledge of your ways.
15 What is the Almighty, that we should serve him? and what profit should we have, if we pray unto him?
16 Lo, their good is not in their hand: the counsel of the wicked is far from me.
17 How oft is the candle of the wicked put out! and how oft comes their destruction upon them! God distributes sorrows in his anger.
18 They are as stubble before the wind, and as chaff that the storm carries away.
19 God lays up his iniquity for his children: he rewards him, and he shall know it.
20 His eyes shall see his destruction, and he shall drink of the wrath of the Almighty.
21 For what pleasure has he in his house after him, when the number of his months is cut off in the midst?

22 Shall any teach GOD knowledge? seeing he judges those that are high.

23 One dies in his full strength, being wholly at ease and quiet.

24 His breasts are full of milk, and his bones are moistened with marrow.

25 And another dies in the bitterness of his soul, and never eats with pleasure.

26 They shall lie down alike in the dust, and the worms shall cover them.

27 Behold, I know your thoughts, and the devices which you wrongfully imagine against me.

28 For you say, Where is the house of the prince? and where are the dwelling places of the wicked?

29 Have you not asked them that go by the way? and do you not know their tokens,

30 That the wicked is reserved to the day of destruction? they shall be brought forth to the day of wrath.

31 Who shall declare his way to his face? and who shall repay him what he has done?

32 Yet shall he be brought to the grave, and shall remain in the tomb.

33 The clods of the valley shall be sweet unto him, and every man shall draw after him, as there are innumerable before him.

34 How then comfort you me in vain, seeing in your answers there remains falsehood?

Job 22:1 Then Eliphaz the Temanite answered and said,

2 Can a man be profitable unto GOD, as he that is wise may be profitable unto himself?

3 Is it any pleasure to the Almighty, that you are righteous? or is it gain to him, that you make your ways perfect?

4 Will he reprove you for fear of you? will he enter with you into judgment?

5 Is not your wickedness great? and is there no end to your iniquities?

6 For you have taken a pledge from your brother for nothing, and stripped the naked of their clothing.

7 you have not given water to the weary to drink, and you have withheld bread from the hungry.

8 But as for the mighty man, he had the earth; and the honorable man dwelt in it.

9 you have sent widows away empty, and the arms of the fatherless have been broken.

10 Therefore snares are round about you, and sudden fear troubles you;

11 Or darkness, that you can not see; and abundance of waters cover you.

12 Is not God in the height of heaven? and behold the height of the stars, how high they are!

13 And you say, How does GOD know? can he judge through the dark cloud?

14 Thick clouds are a covering to him, that he sees not; and he walks in the circuit of heaven.

15 have you marked the way of olam past which wicked men have trodden?

16 Which were cut down out of time, whose foundation was overflown with a flood:

17 Which said unto GOD, Depart from us: and what can the Almighty do for them?

18 Yet he filled their houses with good things: but the counsel of the wicked is far from me.

19 The righteous see it, and are glad: and the innocent laugh them to scorn.

20 Whereas our substance is not cut down, but the remnant of them the fire consumeth.

21 Acquaint now yourself with him, and be at peace: thereby good shall come unto you.

22 Receive, I pray you, the law from his mouth, and lay up his words in your heart.

23 If you return to the Almighty, you shall be built up, you shall put away iniquity far from your tabernacles.

24 Then shall you lay up gold as dust, and the gold of Ophir as the stones of the brooks.

25 Yes, the Almighty shall be your defense, and you shall have plenty of silver.

26 For then shall you have your delight in the Almighty, and shall lift up your face unto God.

27 you shall make your prayer unto him, and he shall hear you, and you shall pay your vows.

28 you shall also decree a thing, and it shall be established unto you: and the light shall shine upon your ways.

29 When men are cast down, then you shall say, There is lifting up; and he shall save the humble person.

30 He shall deliver the island of the innocent: and it is delivered by the pureness of your hands.

Job 23:1 Then Job answered and said,

2 Even today is my complaint bitter: my stroke is heavier than my groaning.

3 Oh that I knew where I might find him! that I might come even to his seat!

4 I would order my cause before him, and fill my mouth with arguments.

5 I would know the words which he would answer me, and understand what he would say unto me.

6 Will he plead against me with his great power? No; but he would put strength in me.

7 There the righteous might dispute with him; so should I be delivered altother from my judge.

8 Behold, I go forward, but he is not there; and backward, but I cannot perceive him:

9 On the left hand, where he does work, but I cannot behold him: he hides himself on the right hand, that I cannot see him:

10 But he knows the way that I take: when he has tried me, I shall come forth as gold.

11 My foot has held his steps, his way have I kept, and not declined.

12 Neither have I gone back from the commandment of his lips; I have esteemed the words of his mouth more than my necessary food.

13 But he is in one mind, and who can turn him? and what his soul desires, even that he does.

14 For he performs the thing that is appointed for me: and many such things are with him.

15 Therefore I am troubled at his presence: when I consider, I am afraid of him.

16 For GOD makes my heart soft, and the Almighty troubles me:

17 Because I was not cut off before the darkness, neither has he covered the darkness from my face.

Job 24:1 Why, seeing times are not hidden from the Almighty, do they that know him not see his days?

2 Some remove the landmarks; they violently take away flocks, and feed thereof.

3 They drive away the donkey of the fatherless, they take the widow's ox for a pledge.

4 They turn the needy out of the way: the poor of the earth hide themselves together.

5 Behold, as wild donkeys in the desert, go they forth to their work; rising early for a prey: the wilderness yields food for them and for their children.

6 They reap every one his grain in the field: and they gather the vintage of the wicked.

7 They cause the naked to lodge without clothing, that they have no covering in the cold.

8 They are wet with the showers of the mountains, and embrace the rock for want of a shelter.

9 They pluck the fatherless from the breast, and take a pledge of the poor.

10 They cause him to go naked without clothing, and they take away the sheaf from the hungry;

11 Which make oil within their walls, and tread their winepresses, and suffer thirst.

12 Men groan from out of the city, and the soul of the wounded cries out: yet God lays not folly to them.

13 They are of those that rebel against the light; they know not the ways thereof, nor abide in the paths thereof.

14 The murderer rising with the light kills the poor and needy, and in the night is as a thief.

15 The eye also of the adulterer waits for the breeze time of the evening, saying, No eye shall see me: and disguises his face.

16 In the dark they dig through houses, which they had marked for themselves in the daytime: they know not the light.

17 For the morning is to them even as the shadow of death: if one know them, they are in the terrors of the shadow of death.

18 He is swift as the waters; their portion is cursed in the earth: he beholds not the way of the vineyards.

19 Drought and heat consume the snow waters: so does Sheol to those which have sinned.

20 The womb shall forget him; the worm shall feed sweetly on him; he shall be no more remembered; and wickedness shall be broken as a tree.

21 He evil entreats the barren that bears not: and did not good to the widow.

22 He draws also the mighty with his power: he rises up, and no man is sure of life.

23 Though it be given him to be in safety, whereon he rests; yet his eyes are upon their ways.

24 They are exalted for a little while, but are gone and brought low; they are taken out of the way as all other, and cut off as the tops of the ears of grain.

25 And if it be not so now, who will make me a liar, and make my speech nothing worth?

Job 25:1 Then answered Bildad the Shuhite, and said,

2 Dominion and fear are with him, he makes peace in his high places.

3 Is there any number of his armies? and upon whom does not his light arise?

4 How then can man be justified with GOD? or how can he be clean that is born of a woman?

5 Behold even to the moon, and it shines not; yes, the stars are not pure in his sight.

6 How much less man, that is a worm? and the son of man, which is a worm?

Job 26:1 But Job answered and said,

2 How have you helped him that is without power? how save you the arm that has no strength?

3 How have you counselled him that has no wisdom? and how have you plentifully declared the thing as it is?

4 To whom have you uttered words? and whose spirit came from you?

5 Dead things are formed from under the waters, and the inhabitants thereof.

6 Sheol is naked before him, and destruction has no covering.

7 He stretches out the north over the empty place, and hangs the earth upon nothing.

8 He binds up the waters in his thick clouds; and the cloud is not ripped under them.

9 He holds back the face of his throne, and spreads his cloud upon it.

10 He has compassed the waters with bounds, until the day and night come to an end.

11 The pillars of the heavens tremble and are astonished at his reproof.

12 He divides the sea with his power, and by his understanding he smites through the proud.

13 By his spirit he has garnished the heavens; his hand has formed the crooked serpent.

14 Lo, these are parts of his ways: but how little a portion is heard of him? but the thunder of his power who can understand?

Job 27:1 Moreover Job continued his parable, and said,

2 As GOD lives, who has taken away my judgment; and the Almighty, who has vexed my soul;

3 All the while my breath is in me, and the spirit of God is in my nostrils;

4 My lips shall not speak wickedness, nor my tongue utter deceit.

5 Forbid it that I should justify you: till I die I will not remove mine integrity from me.

6 My righteousness I hold fast, and will not let it go: my heart shall not reproach me so long as I live.

7 Let mine enemy be as the wicked, and he that rises up against me as the unrighteous.

8 For what is the hope of the hypocrite, though he has gained, when God takes away his soul?

9 Will GOD hear his cry when trouble comes upon him?

10 Will he delight himself in the Almighty? will he always call upon God?

11 I will teach you by the hand of GOD: that which is with the Almighty will I not conceal.

12 Behold, all you yourselves have seen it; why then are you thus altogether vain?

13 This is the portion of a wicked man with GOD, and the heritage of terrible ones, which they shall receive of the Almighty.

14 If his children be multiplied, it is for the sword: and his offspring shall not be satisfied with bread.

15 Those that remain of him shall be buried in death: and his widows shall not weep.

16 Though he heap up silver as the dust, and prepare raiment as the clay;

17 He may prepare it, but the just shall put it on, and the innocent shall divide the silver.

18 He builds his house as a moth, and as a booth that the keeper makes.

19 The rich man shall lie down, but he shall not be gathered: he opens his eyes, and he is not.

20 Terrors take hold on him as waters, a tempest steals him away in the night.

21 The east wind carries him away, and he departs: and as a storm hurls him out of his place.

22 For God shall cast upon him, and not spare: he would fain flee out of his hand.

23 Men shall clap their hands at him, and shall hiss him out of his place.

Job 28:1 Surely there is a vein for the silver, and a place for gold where they fine it.

2 Iron is taken out of the earth, and brass is molten out of the stone.

3 He sets an end to darkness, and searches out all perfection: the stones of darkness, and the shadow of death.

4 The flood breaks out from the inhabitant; even the waters forgotten of the foot: they are dried up, they are gone away from men.

5 As for the earth, out of it comes bread: and under it is turned up as it were fire.

6 The stones of it are the place of sapphires: and it has dust of gold.

7 There is a path which no fowl knows, and which the vulture's eye has not seen:

8 The lion's whelps have not trodden it, nor the fierce lion passed by it.

9 He puts forth his hand upon the rock; he overturns the mountains by the roots.

10 He cuts out rivers among the rocks; and his eye sees every precious thing.

11 He binds the floods from overflowing; and the thing that is hid brings he forth to light.

12 But where shall wisdom be found? and where is the place of understanding?

13 Man knows not the price thereof; neither is it found in the land of the living.

14 The depth says, It is not in me: and the sea says, It is not with me.

15 It cannot be gotten for gold, neither shall silver be weighed for the price thereof.

16 It cannot be valued with the gold of Ophir, with the precious onyx, or the sapphire.

17 The gold and the crystal cannot equal it: and the exchange of it shall not be for jewels of fine gold.

18 No mention shall be made of coral, or of pearls: for the price of wisdom is above rubies.

19 The topaz of Ethiopia shall not equal it, neither shall it be valued with pure gold.

20 From where then comes wisdom? and where is the place of understanding?

21 Seeing it is hid from the eyes of all living, and kept close from the fowls of the air.

22 Destruction and death say, We have heard the fame thereof with our ears.

23 God understands the way thereof, and he knows the place thereof.

24 For he looks to the ends of the earth, and sees under the whole heaven;

25 To make the weight for the winds; and he weighs the waters by measure.

26 When he made a decree for the rain, and a way for the lightning of the thunder:

27 Then did he see it, and declare it; he prepared it, yes, and searched it out.

28 And unto man he said, Behold, the fear of my Lord(s), that is wisdom; and to depart from evil is understanding.

Job 29:1 Moreover Job continued his parable, and said,

2 Oh that I were as in months past, as in the days when God preserved me;

3 When his candle shined upon my head, and when by his light I walked through darkness;

4 As I was in the days of my youth, when the secret of God was upon my tabernacle;

5 When the Almighty was yet with me, when my children were about me;

6 When I washed my steps with butter, and the rock poured me out rivers of oil;

7 When I went out to the gate through the city, when I prepared my seat in the street!

8 The young men saw me, and hid themselves: and the aged arose, and stood up.

9 The princes refrained talking, and laid their hand on their mouth.

10 The nobles held their peace, and their tongue cleaved to the roof of their mouth.

11 When the ear heard me, then it blessed me; and when the eye saw me, it gave witness to me:

12 Because I delivered the poor that cried, and the fatherless, and him that had none to help him.

13 The blessing of him that was ready to perish came upon me: and I caused the widow's heart to sing for joy.

14 I put on righteousness, and it clothed me: my judgment was as a robe and a diadem.

15 I was eyes to the blind, and feet was I to the lame.

16 I was a father to the poor: and the cause which I knew not I searched out.

17 And I brake the jaws of the wicked, and plucked the spoil out of his teeth.

18 Then I said, I shall die in my nest, and I shall multiply my days as the sand.

19 My root was spread out by the waters, and the dew lay all night upon my branch.

20 My glory was fresh in me, and my bow was renewed in my hand.

21 Unto me men gave ear, and waited, and kept silence at my counsel.

22 After my words they spoke not again; and my speech dropped upon them.

23 And they waited for me as for the rain; and they opened their mouth wide as for the latter rain.

24 If I laughed on them, they believed it not; and the light of my countenance they cast not down.

25 I chose out their way, and sat chief, and dwelt as a king in the army, as one that comforts the mourners.

Job 30:1 But now they that are younger than I have me in derision, whose fathers I would have disdained to have set with the dogs of my flock.

2 Yes, whereto might the strength of their hands profit me, in whom old age was perished?

3 For want and famine they were solitary; fleeing into the wilderness in former time desolate and waste.

4 Who cut up mallows by the bushes, and juniper roots for their food.

5 They were driven forth from among men, they cried after them as after a thief;

6 To dwell in the cliffs of the valleys, in caves of the earth, and in the rocks.

7 Among the bushes they brayed; under the nettles they were gathered together.

8 They were children of fools, yes, children of base men: they were viler than the earth.

9 And now I am their song, yes, I am their byword.

10 They abhor me, they flee far from me, and spare not to spit in my face.

11 Because he has loosened my cord, and afflicted me, they have also let loose the bridle before me.

12 Upon my right hand rise the youth; they push away my feet, and they raise up against me the ways of their destruction.

13 They mar my path, they set forward my calamity, they have no helper.

14 They came upon me as a wide breaking in of waters: in the desolation they rolled themselves upon me.

15 Terrors are turned upon me: they pursue my soul as the wind: and my welfare passes away as a cloud.

16 And now my soul is poured out upon me; the days of affliction have taken hold upon me.

17 My bones are pierced in me in the night season: and my sinews take no rest.

18 By the great force of my disease is my garment changed: it binds me about as the collar of my coat.

19 He has cast me into the mire, and I am become like dust and ashes.

20 I cry unto you, and you do not hear me: I stand up, and you regard me not.

21 you are become cruel to me: with your strong hand you oppose yourself against me.

22 you lift me up to the wind; you cause me to ride upon it, and dissolve my substance.

23 For I know that you will bring me to death, and to the house appointed for all living.

24 Howbeit he will not stretch out his hand to the grave, though they cry in his destruction.

25 Did not I weep for him that was in trouble? was not my soul grieved for the poor?

26 When I looked for good, then evil came unto me: and when I waited for light, there came darkness.

27 My bowels boiled, and rested not: the days of affliction prevented me.

28 I went mourning without the sun: I stood up, and I cried in the congregation.

29 I am a brother to monsters, and a companion to owls.

30 My skin is black upon me, and my bones are burned with heat.

31 My harp also is turned to mourning, and my organ into the voice of them that weep.

Job 31:1 I made a covenant with mine eyes; why then should I think upon a maid?

2 For what portion of God is there from above? and what inheritance of the Almighty from on high?

3 Is not destruction to the wicked? and a strange punishment to the workers of iniquity?

4 does not he see my ways, and count all my steps?

5 If I have walked with vanity, or if my foot has hasted to deceit;

6 Let me be weighed in an even balance that God may know mine integrity.

7 If my step has turned out of the way, and mine heart walked after mine eyes, and if any blot has cleaved to mine hands;

8 Then let me sow, and let another eat; yes, let my offspring be rooted out.

9 If mine heart have been deceived by a woman, or if I have laid wait at my neighbor's door;

10 Then let my wife grind unto another, and let others bow down upon her.

11 For this is a heinous crime; yes, it is an iniquity to be punished by the judges.

12 For it is a fire that consumes to destruction, and would root out all mine increase.

13 If I did despise the cause of my manservant or of my maidservant, when they contended with me;

14 What then shall I do when GOD rises up? and when he visits, what shall I answer him?

15 Did not he that made me in the womb make him? and did not one fashion us in the womb?

16 If I have withheld the poor from their desire, or have caused the eyes of the widow to fail;

17 Or have eaten my morsel myself alone, and the fatherless has not eaten thereof;

18 For from my youth he was brought up with me, as with a father, and I have guided her from my mother's womb;

19 If I have seen any perish for want of clothing, or any poor without covering;

20 If his loins have not blessed me, and if he were not warmed with the fleece of my sheep;

21 If I have lifted up my hand against the fatherless, when I saw my help in the gate:

22 Then let mine arm fall from my shoulder blade, and mine arm be broken from the bone.

23 For destruction from GOD was a terror to me, and by reason of his highness I could not endure.

24 If I have made gold my hope, or have said to the fine gold, you are my confidence;

25 If I rejoiced because my wealth was great, and because mine hand had gotten much;

26 If I beheld the sun when it shined, or the moon walking in brightness;

27 And my heart has been secretly enticed, or my mouth has kissed my hand:

28 This also were an iniquity to be punished by the judge: for I should have denied GOD that is above.

29 If I rejoiced at the destruction of him that hated me, or lifted up myself when evil found him:

30 Neither have I permitted my mouth to sin by wishing a curse to his soul.

31 If the men of my tabernacle said not, Oh that we had of his flesh! we cannot be satisfied.

32 The stranger did not lodge in the street: but I opened my doors to the traveller.

33 If I covered my transgressions as Adam, by hiding mine iniquity in my bosom:

34 Did I fear a great multitude, or did the contempt of families terrify me, that I kept silence, and went not out of the door?

35 Oh that one would hear me! behold, my desire is, that the Almighty would answer me, and that mine adversary had written a book.

36 Surely I would take it upon my shoulder, and bind it as a crown to me.

37 I would declare unto him the number of my steps; as a prince would I go near unto him.

38 If my land cry against me, or that the furrows likewise thereof complain;

39 If I have eaten the fruits thereof without money, or have caused the owners thereof to lose their soul:

40 Let thistles grow instead of wheat, and cockle instead of barley. The words of Job are ended.

Job 32:1 So these three men ceased to answer Job, because he was righteous in his own eyes.

2 Then was kindled the wrath of Elihu the son of Barachel the Buzite, of the kindred of Ram: against Job was his wrath kindled, because he justified his soul rather than God.

3 Also against his three friends was his wrath kindled, because they had found no answer, and yet had condemned Job.

4 Now Elihu had waited till Job had spoken, because they were elder than he.

5 When Elihu saw that there was no answer in the mouth of these three men, then his wrath was kindled.

6 And Elihu the son of Barachel the Buzite answered and said, I am young, and you are very old; therefore I was afraid, and durst not show you mine opinion.

7 I said, Days should speak, and multitude of years should teach wisdom.

8 But there is a spirit in man: but the spirit [breath] of the Almighty gives them understanding.

9 Great men are not always wise: neither do the aged understand judgment.

10 Therefore I said, listen to me; I also will show mine opinion.

11 Behold, I waited for your words; I gave ear to your reasons, while you searched out what to say.

12 Yes, I attended unto you, and, behold, there was none of you that convinced Job, or that answered his words:

13 Lest you should say, We have found out wisdom: GOD thrusts him down, not man.

14 Now he has not directed his words against me: neither will I answer him with your speeches.

15 They were amazed, they answered no more: they left off speaking.

16 When I had waited, for they spoke not, but stood still, and answered no more;

17 I said, I will answer also my part, I also will show mine opinion.

18 For I am full of matter, the spirit within me constrains me.

19 Behold, my belly is as wine which has no vent; it is ready to burst like new bottles.

20 I will speak, that I may be refreshed: I will open my lips and answer.

21 Let me not, I pray you, accept any man's person, neither let me give flattering titles unto man.

22 For I know not to give flattering titles; in so doing my maker would soon take me away.

Job 33:1 Therefore, Job, I pray you, hear my speeches, and listen to all my words.

2 Behold, now I have opened my mouth, my tongue has spoken in my mouth.

3 My words shall be of the uprightness of my heart: and my lips shall utter knowledge clearly.

4 The spirit of GOD has made me, and the spirit [breath] of the Almighty has given me life.

5 If you can't answer me, set your words in order before me, stand up.

6 Behold, I am your mouth towards GOD: I also am formed out of the clay.

7 Behold, my terror shall not make you afraid, neither shall my hand be heavy upon you.

8 Surely you have spoken in mine hearing, and I have heard the voice of your words, saying,

9 I am clean without transgression, I am innocent; neither is there iniquity in me.

10 Behold, he finds occasions against me, he counts me for his enemy,

11 He puts my feet in the stocks, he markes all my paths.

12 Behold, in this you are not just: I will answer you, that God is greater than man.

13 Why do you strive against him? for he gives not account of any of his matters.

14 For GOD speaks once, yes twice, yet man perceives it not.

15 In a dream, in a vision of the night, when deep sleep falls upon men, in slumber upon the bed;

16 Then he opens the ears of men, and seals their instruction,

17 That he may withdraw man from his purpose, and hide pride from man.

18 He keeps back his soul from the pit, and his life from perishing by the sword.

19 He is chastened also with pain upon his bed, and the multitude of his bones with strong pain:

20 So that his life abhors bread, and his soul dainty food.

21 His flesh is consumed away, that it cannot be seen; and his bones that were not seen stick out.

22 Yes, his soul draws near unto the grave, and his life to the destroyers.

23 If there be a messenger with him, an interpreter, one among a thousand, to show unto man his uprightness:

24 Then he is gracious unto him, and says, Deliver him from going down to the pit: I have found a ransom.

25 His flesh shall be fresher than a child's: he shall return to the days of his youth:

26 He shall pray unto God, and he will be favorable unto him: and he shall see his face with joy: for he will render unto man his righteousness.

27 He looks upon men, and if any say, I have sinned, and perverted that which was right, and it profited me not;

28 He will deliver his soul from going into the pit, and his life shall see the light.

29 Lo, all these things works GOD oftentimes with man,

30 To bring back his soul from the pit, to be enlightened with the light of the living.

31 Mark well, O Job, listen unto me: hold your peace, and I will speak.

32 If you have anything to say, answer me: speak, for I desire to justify you.

33 If not, listen unto me: hold your peace, and I shall teach you wisdom.

Job 34:1 Furthermore Elihu answered and said,

2 Hear my words, O you wise men; and give ear unto me, you that have knowledge.

3 For the ear tries words, as the mouth tastes food.

4 Let us choose to us judgment: let us know among ourselves what is good.

5 For Job has said, I am righteous: and GOD has taken away my judgment.

6 Should I lie against my right? my wound is incurable without transgression.

7 What man is like Job, who drinks up scorning like water?

8 Which goes in company with the workers of iniquity, and walks with wicked men.

9 For he has said, It profits a man nothing that he should delight himself with God.

10 Therefore listen unto me, you men of understanding: far be it from GOD, that he should do wickedness; and from the Almighty, that he should commit iniquity.

11 For the work of a man shall he render unto him, and cause every man to find according to his ways.

12 Yes, surely GOD will not do wickedly, neither will the Almighty pervert judgment.

13 Who has given him a charge over the earth? or who has disposed the whole world?

14 If he set his heart upon man, if he gather unto himself his spirit and his breath;

15 All flesh shall perish together, and man shall turn again unto dust.

16 If now you have understanding, hear this: listen to the voice of my words.

17 Shall even he that hates right govern? and will you condemn him that is most just?

18 Is it fit to say to a king, you are wicked? and to princes, you are ungodly?

19 How much less to him that accepts not the persons of princes, nor regards the rich more than the poor? for they all are the work of his hands.

20 In a moment shall they die, and the people shall be troubled at midnight, and pass away: and the mighty shall be taken away without hand.

21 For his eyes are upon the ways of man, and he sees all his goings.

22 There is no darkness, nor shadow of death, where the workers of iniquity may hide themselves.

23 For he will not lay upon man more than right; that he should enter into judgment with GOD.

24 He shall break in pieces mighty men without number, and set others in their stead.

25 Therefore he knows their works, and he overturns them in the night, so that they are destroyed.

26 He strikes them as wicked men in the open sight of others;

27 Because they turned back from him, and would not consider any of his ways:

28 So that they cause the cry of the poor to come unto him, and he hears the cry of the afflicted.

29 When he gives quietness, who then can make trouble? and when he hides his face, who then can behold him? whether it be done against a nation, or against a man only:

30 That the hypocrite reign not, lest the people be ensnared.

31 Surely it is meet to be said unto GOD, I have borne chastisement, I will not offend any more:

32 That which I see not teach you me: if I have done iniquity, I will do no more.

33 Should it be according to your mind? he will recompense it, whether you refuse, or whether you choose; and not I: therefore speak what you know.

34 Let men of understanding tell me, and let a wise man listen unto me.

35 Job has spoken without knowledge, and his words were without wisdom.

36 My desire is that Job may be tried altogether because of his answers for wicked men.

37 For he adds rebellion unto his sin, he claps his hands among us, and multiplies his words against GOD.

Job 35:1 Elihu spoke moreover, and said,

2 Think you this to be right, that you said, My righteousness is more than God's?

3 For you said, What advantage will it be unto you? and, What profit shall I have, if I be cleansed from my sin?

4 I will answer you, and your companions with you.

5 Look unto the heavens, and see; and behold the clouds which are higher than you.

6 If you sin, what do you against him? or if your transgressions be multiplied, what do you unto him?

7 If you be righteous, what give you him? or what receives he of your hand?

8 your wickedness may hurt a man as you are; and your righteousness may profit the son of man.

9 By reason of the multitude of oppressions they make the oppressed to cry: they cry out by reason of the arm of the mighty.

10 But none says, Where is God my maker, who gives songs in the night;

11 Who teaches us more than the beasts of the earth, and makes us wiser than the fowls of heaven?

12 There they cry, but none gives answer, because of the pride of evil men.

13 Surely GOD will not hear vanity, neither will the Almighty regard it.

14 Although you say you shall not see him, yet judgment is before him; therefore trust you in him.

15 But now, because it is not so, he has visited in his anger; yet he knows it not in great extremity:

16 Therefore does Job open his mouth in vain; he multiplies words without knowledge.

Job 36:1 Elihu also proceeded, and said,

2 Permit me a little, and I will show you that I have yet to speak on God' behalf.

3 I will fetch my knowledge from afar, and will ascribe righteousness to my Maker.

4 For truly my words shall not be false: he that is perfect in knowledge is with you.

5 Behold, GOD is mighty, and despises not any: he is mighty in strength and wisdom.

6 He preserves not the life of the wicked: but gives right to the poor.

7 He withdraws not his eyes from the righteous: but with kings are they on the throne; yes, he does establish them for glory, and they are exalted.

8 And if they be bound in fetters, and be held in cords of affliction;

9 Then he shows them their work, and their transgressions that they have exceeded.

10 He opens also their ear to discipline, and commands that they return from iniquity.

11 If they obey and serve him, they shall spend their days in prosperity, and their years in pleasures.

12 But if they obey not, they shall perish by the sword, and they shall die without knowledge.

13 But the hypocrites in heart heap up wrath: they cry not when he binds them.

14 Their souls die in youth, and their life is among the unclean.

15 He delivers the poor in his affliction, and opens their ears in oppression.

16 Even so would he have removed you out of the strait into a broad place, where there is no straitness; and that which should be set on your table should be full of fatness.

17 But you have fulfilled the judgment of the wicked: judgment and justice take hold on you.

18 Because there is wrath, beware lest he take you away with his stroke: then a great ransom cannot deliver you.

19 Will he esteem your riches? no, not gold, nor all the forces of strength.

20 Desire not the night, when people are cut off in their place.

21 Take heed, regard not iniquity: for this have you chosen rather than affliction.

22 Behold, GOD exalts by his power: who teaches like him?

23 Who has enjoined him his way? or who can say, you have worked iniquity?

24 Remember that you magnify his work, which men behold.

25 Every man may see it; man may behold it afar off.

26 Behold, GOD is great, and we know him not, neither can the number of his years be searched out.

27 For he makes small the drops of water: they pour down rain according to the vapour thereof:

28 Which the clouds do drop and distil upon man abundantly.

29 Also can any understand the spreadings of the clouds, or the noise of his tabernacle?

30 Behold, he spreads his light upon it, and covers the bottom of the sea.

31 For by them judges he the people; he gives food in abundance.

32 With clouds he covers the light; and commands it not to shine by the cloud that comes between.

33 The noise thereof shows concerning it, the cattle also concerning the vapour.

Job 37:1 At this also my heart trembles, and is moved out of his place.

2 Hear attentively the noise of his voice, and the sound that goes out of his mouth.

3 He directs it under the whole heaven, and his lightning unto the ends of the earth.

4 After it a voice roars: he thunders with the voice of his excellency; and he will not stay them when his voice is heard.

5 GOD thunders marvelously with his voice; great things did he, which we cannot comprehend.

6 For he says to the snow, Be you on the earth; likewise to the small rain, and to the great rain of his strength.

7 He seals up the hand of every man; that all men may know his work.

8 Then the beasts go into dens, and remain in their places.

9 Out of the south comes the whirlwind: and cold out of the north.

10 By the breath of GOD frost is given: and the breadth of the waters is hampered.

11 Also by watering he wearies the thick cloud: he scatters his bright cloud:

12 And it is turned round about by his counsels: that they may do whatsoever he commands them upon the face of the world in the earth.

13 He causes it to come, whether for correction, or for his land, or for mercy.

14 listen unto this, O Job: stand still, and consider the wondrous works of GOD.

15 do you know when God disposed them, and caused the light of his cloud to shine?

16 do you know the balancings of the clouds, the wondrous works of him which is perfect in knowledge?

17 How your garments are warm, when he quiets the earth by the south wind?

18 have you with him spread out the sky, which is strong, and as a molten looking glass?

19 Teach us what we shall say unto him; for we cannot order our speech by reason of darkness.

20 Shall it be told him that I speak? if a man speak, surely he shall be swallowed up.

21 And now men see not the bright light which is in the clouds: but the wind passes, and cleanses them.

22 Fair weather comes out of the north: with God is terrible majesty.

23 Touching the Almighty, we cannot find him out: he is excellent in power, and in judgment, and in plenty of justice: he will not afflict.

24 Men do therefore fear him: he respects not any that are wise of heart.

Job 38:1 Then the Becoming-One answered Job out of the whirlwind, and said,

2 Who is this that darkens counsel by words without knowledge?

3 Gird up now your loins like a man; for I will demand of you, and answer you me.

4 Where were you when I laid the foundations of the earth? declare, if you have understanding.

5 Who has laid the measures thereof, if you know? or who has stretched the line upon it?

6 Whereupon are the foundations thereof fastened? or who laid the corner stone thereof;

7 When the morning stars sang together, and all the sons of God shouted for joy?

8 Or who shut up the sea with doors, when it brake forth, as if it had issued out of the womb?

9 When I made the cloud the garment thereof, and thick darkness a swaddlingband for it,

10 And brake up for it my decreed place, and set bars and doors,

11 And said, Hitherto shall you come, but no further: and here shall your proud waves be stayed?

12 have you commanded the morning since your days; and caused the dawn to know his place;

13 That it might take hold of the ends of the earth, that the wicked might be shaken out of it?

14 It is turned as clay to the seal; and they stand as a garment.

15 And from the wicked their light is withheld, and the high arm shall be broken.

16 have you entered into the springs of the sea? or have you walked in the search of the depth?

17 Have the gates of death been opened unto you? or have you seen the doors of the shadow of death?

18 have you perceived the breadth of the earth? declare if you know it all.

19 Where is the way where light dwells? and as for darkness, where is the place thereof,

20 That you should take it to the bound thereof, and that you should know the paths to the house thereof?

21 know you it, because you were then born? or because the number of your days is great?

22 have you entered into the treasures of the snow? or have you seen the treasures of the hail,

23 Which I have reserved against the time of trouble, against the day of battle and war?

24 By what way is the light parted, which scatters the east wind upon the earth?

25 Who has divided a watercourse for the overflowing of waters, or a way for the lightning of thunder;

26 To cause it to rain on the earth, where no man is; on the wilderness, wherein there is no man;

27 To satisfy the desolate and waste ground; and to cause the bud of the tender herb to spring forth?

28 has the rain a father? or who has begotten the drops of dew?

29 Out of whose womb came the ice? and the hoary frost of heaven, who has gendered it?

30 The waters are hid as with a stone, and the face of the deep is frozen.

31 Can you bind the sweet influences of Pleiades, or loose the bands of Orion?

32 Can you bring forth Mazzaroth in his season? or can you guide Arcturus with his sons?

33 know you the ordinances of heaven? can you set the dominion thereof in the earth?

34 Can you lift up your voice to the clouds, that abundance of waters may cover you?

35 Can you send lightning, that they may go, and say unto you, Here we are?

36 Who has put wisdom in the inward parts? or who has given understanding to the heart?

37 Who can number the clouds in wisdom? or who can stay the bottles of heaven,

38 When the dust grows into hardness, and the clods cleave fast together?

39 will you hunt the prey for the lion? or fill the appetite of the young lions,

40 When they couch in their dens, and abide in the covert to lie in wait?

41 Who provides for the raven his food? when his young ones cry unto GOD, they wander for lack of food.

Job 39:1 know you the time when the wild goats of the rock bring forth? or can you mark when the hinds do calve?

2 Can you number the months that they fulfil? or know you the time when they bring forth?

3 They bow themselves, they bring forth their young ones, they cast out their sorrows.

4 Their young ones are in good liking, they grow up with grain; they go forth, and return not unto them.

5 Who has sent out the wild donkey free? or who has loosened the bands of the wild donkey?

6 Whose house I have made the wilderness, and the barren land his dwellings.

7 He scorns the multitude of the city, neither regards he the crying of the driver.

8 The range of the mountains is his pasture, and he searches after every green thing.

9 Will the reem [wild ox or beast] be willing to serve you, or abide by your crib?

10 Can you bind the reem with his band in the furrow? or will he harrow the valleys after you?

11 will you trust him, because his strength is great? or will you leave your labor to him?

12 will you believe him, that he will bring home your seed, and gather it into your barn?

13 gave you the goodly wings unto the peacocks? or wings and feathers unto the ostrich?

14 Which leaves her eggs in the earth, and warms them in dust,

15 And forgets that the foot may crush them, or that the wild beast may break them.

16 She is hardened against her young ones, as though they were not hers: her labor is in vain without fear;

17 Because God has deprived her of wisdom, neither has he imparted to her understanding.

18 What time she lifts up herself on high, she scorns the horse and his rider.

19 have you given the horse strength? have you clothed his neck with thunder?

20 Can you make him afraid as a grasshopper? the glory of his nostrils is terrible.

21 He paws in the valley, and rejoices in his strength: he goes on to meet the armed men.

22 He mocks at fear, and is not affrighted; neither turns he back from the sword.

23 The quiver rattles against him, the glittering spear and the shield.

24 He swallowes the ground with earthquakes and rage: neither believes he that it is the sound of the trumpet.

25 He says among the trumpets, Ha, ha; and he smells the battle afar off, the thunder of the captains, and the shouting.

26 does the hawk fly by your wisdom, and stretch her wings toward the south?

27 does the eagle mount up at your command, and make her nest on high?

28 She dwells and abides on the rock, upon the crag of the rock, and the strong place.

29 From there she seeks the prey, and her eyes behold afar off.

30 Her young ones also suck up blood: and where the slain are, there is she.

Job 40:1 Moreover the Becoming-One answered Job, and said,

2 Shall he that contends with the Almighty instruct him? he that reproves God, let him answer it.

3 Then Job answered the Becoming-One, and said,

4 Behold, I am vile; what shall I answer you? I will lay mine hand upon my mouth.

5 Once have I spoken; but I will not answer: yes, twice; but I will proceed no further.

6 Then answered the Becoming-One unto Job out of the whirlwind, and said,

7 Gird up your loins now like a man: I will demand of you, and declare you unto me.

8 will you also disannul my judgment? will you condemn me, that you may be righteous?

9 have you an arm like GOD? or can you thunder with a voice like him?

10 Deck yourself now with majesty and excellency; and array yourself with glory and beauty.

11 Cast abroad the rage of your wrath: and behold every one that is proud, and abase him.

12 Look on every one that is proud, and bring him low; and tread down the wicked in their place.

13 Hide them in the dust together; and bind their faces in secret.

14 Then will I also confess unto you that your own right hand can save you.

15 Behold now behemoth, which I made with you; he eats grass as an ox.

16 Lo now, his strength is in his loins, and his force is in the navel of his belly.

17 He moves his tail like a cedar: the tendons of his stones are wrapped together.

18 His bones are as strong pieces of brass; his bones are like bars of iron.

19 He is the chief of the ways of GOD: he that made him can make his sword to approach unto him.

20 Surely the mountains bring him forth food, where all the beasts of the field play.

21 He lies under the shady trees, in the covert of the reed, and fens.

22 The shady trees cover him with their shadow; the willows of the brook compass him about.

23 Behold, he drinks up a river, and hastens not: he trusts that he can draw up Jordan into his mouth.

24 He takes it with his eyes: his nose pierces through snares.

Job 41:1 Can you draw out leviathan with a hook? or his tongue with a cord which you let down?

2 Can you put a hook into his nose? or bore his jaw through with a thorn?

3 Will he make many supplications unto you? will he speak soft words unto you?

4 Will he make a covenant with you? will you take him for a servant for olam.

5 will you play with him as with a bird? or will you bind him for your maidens?

6 Shall the companions make a banquet of him? shall they part him among the merchants?

7 Can you fill his skin with barbed irons? or his head with fish spears?

8 Lay your hand upon him, remember the battle, do no more.

9 Behold, the hope of him is in vain; shall not one be cast down even at the sight of him?

10 None is so fierce that dare stir him up: who then is able to stand before me?

11 Who has prevented me, that I should repay him? whatsoever is under the whole heaven is mine.

12 I will not conceal his parts, nor his power, nor his comely proportion.

13 Who can discover the face of his garment? or who can come to him with his double bridle?

14 Who can open the doors of his face? his teeth are terrible round about.

15 His scales are his pride, shut up together as with a close seal.

16 One is so near to another, that no air can come between them.

17 They are joined one to another, they stick together, that they cannot be sundered.

18 By his neesings a light does shine, and his eyes are like the eyelids of the dawn.

19 Out of his mouth go burning lamps, and sparks of fire leap out.

20 Out of his nostrils goes smoke, as out of a seesing pot or caldron.

21 His soul kindles coals, and a flame goes out of his mouth.

22 In his neck remains strength, and sorrow is turned into joy before him.

23 The flakes of his flesh are joined together: they are firm in themselves; they cannot be moved.

24 His heart is as firm as a stone; yes, as hard as a piece of the nether millstone.

25 When he raises up himself, the mighty are afraid: by reason of breakings they purify themselves.

26 The sword of him that lays at him cannot hold: the spear, the dart, nor the habergeon.

27 He esteems iron as straw, and brass as rotten wood.

28 The arrow cannot make him flee: slingstones are turned with him into stubble.

29 Darts are counted as stubble: he laughs at the shaking of a spear.

30 Sharp stones are under him: he spreads sharp pointed things upon the mire.

31 He makes the deep to boil like a pot: he makes the sea like a pot of ointment.

32 He makes a path to shine after him; one would think the deep to be aged.

33 Upon earth there is not his like, who is made without fear.

34 He beholds all high things: he is a king over all the children of pride.

Job 42:1 Then Job answered the Becoming-One, and said,

2 I know that you can do every thing, and that no thought can be withheld from you.

3 Who is he that hides counsel without knowledge? therefore have I uttered that I understood not; things too wonderful for me, which I knew not.

4 Hear, I beg you, and I will speak: I will demand of you, and declare you unto me.

5 I have heard of you by the hearing of the ear: but now mine eye sees you.

6 Therefore I abhor myself, and repent in dust and ashes.

7 And it was so, that after the Becoming-One had spoken these words unto Job, the Becoming-One said to Eliphaz the Temanite, My wrath is kindled against you, and against your two friends: for you have not spoken of me the thing that is right, as my servant Job hath.

8 Therefore take unto you now seven bullocks and seven rams, and go to my servant Job, and offer up for yourselves a burnt offering; and my servant Job shall pray for you: for him will I accept: lest I deal with you after your folly, in that you have not spoken of me the thing which is right, like my servant Job.

9 So Eliphaz the Temanite and Bildad the Shuhite and Zophar the Naamathite went, and did according as the Becoming-One commanded them: the Becoming-One also accepted Job.

10 And the Becoming-One turned the captivity of Job, when he prayed for his friends: also the Becoming-One gave Job twice as much as he had before.

11 Then came there unto him all his brethren, and all his sisters, and all they that had been of his acquaintance before, and did eat bread with him in his house: and they bemoaned him, and comforted him over all the evil that the Becoming-One had brought upon him: every man also gave him a piece of money, and every one an earring of gold.

12 So the Becoming-One blessed the latter end of Job more than his beginning: for he had fourteen thousand of sheep, and six thousand of camels, and a thousand of yoke of oxen, and a thousand of she donkeys.

13 He had also seven sons and three daughters.

14 And he called the name of the first, Jemima; and the name of the second, Kezia; and the name of the third, Kerenhappuch.

15 And in all the land were no women found so fair as the daughters of Job: and their father gave them inheritance among their brethren.

16 After this lived Job a hundred and forty years, and saw his sons, and his sons' sons, even four generations.

17 So Job died, being old and full of days.

Psalms

Psa 1:1 Blessed is the man that walks not in the counsel of the ungodly, nor stands in the way of sinners, nor sits in the seat of the scornful.

2 But his delight is in the law of the Becoming-One; and in his law does he meditate day and night.

3 And he shall be like a tree planted by the rivers of water, that brings forth his fruit in his season; his leaf also shall not wither; and whatsoever he did shall prosper.

4 The ungodly are not so: but are like the chaff which the wind drives away.

5 Therefore the ungodly shall not stand in the judgment, nor sinners in the congregation of the righteous.

6 For the Becoming-One knows the way of the righteous: but the way of the ungodly shall perish.

Psa 2:1 Why do the nations rage, and the people imagine a vain thing?

2 The kings of the earth set themselves, and the rulers take counsel together, against the Becoming-One, and against his anointed [Messiah] , saying,

3 Let us break their bands asunder, and cast away their cords from us.

4 He that sits in the heavens shall laugh: my Lord(s) shall have them in derision.

5 Then shall he speak unto them in his wrath, and vex them in his great displeasure.

6 Yet have I set my king upon my holy hill of Zion.

7 I will declare the decree: the Becoming-One has said unto me, you are my Son; this day have I begotten you.

8 Ask of me, and I shall give you the nations for your inheritance, and the uttermost parts of the earth for your possession.

9 you shall break them with a rod of iron; you shall dash them in pieces like a potter's vessel.

10 Be wise now therefore, O you kings: be instructed, you judges of the earth.

11 Serve the Becoming-One with fear, and rejoice with trembling.

12 Kiss the Son, lest he be angry, and you perish from the way, when his wrath is kindled but a little. Blessed are all they that put their trust in him.

Psa 3:1 A Psalm of David, when he fled from Absalom his son. Becoming-One, how are they increased that trouble me! many are they that rise up against me.

2 Many there be which say of my soul, There is no help for him in God. Selah.

3 But you, O Becoming-One, are a shield for me; my glory, and the lifter up of mine head.

4 I cried unto the Becoming-One with my voice, and he heard me out of his holy hill. Selah.

5 I laid me down and slept; I awaked; for the Becoming-One sustained me.

6 I will not be afraid of multitude of people, that have set themselves against me round about.

7 Arise, O Becoming-One; save me, O my God: for you have struck all mine enemies upon the cheek bone; you have broken the teeth of the ungodly.

8 Salvation belongs unto the Becoming-One: your blessing is upon your people. Selah.

Psa 4:1 To the chief Musician on Neginoth, A Psalm of David. Hear me when I call, O God of my righteousness: you have enlarged me when I was in distress; have mercy upon me, and hear my prayer.

2 O you sons of men, how long will you turn my glory into shame? how long will you love vanity, and look up to lying? Selah.

3 But know that the Becoming-One has set apart him that is godly for himself: the Becoming-One will hear when I call unto him.

4 Stand in awe, and sin not: commune with your own heart upon your bed, and be still. Selah.

5 Offer the sacrifices of righteousness, and put your trust in the Becoming-One.

6 There be many that say, Who will show us any good? Becoming-One, lift you up the light of your countenance upon us.

7 you have put gladness in my heart, more than in the time that their grain and their wine increased.

8 I will both lay me down in peace, and sleep: for you, Becoming-One, only make me dwell in safety.

Psa 5:1 To the chief Musician upon Nehiloth, A Psalm of David. Give ear to my words, O Becoming-One, consider my meditation.

2 listen unto the voice of my cry, my King, and my God: for unto you will I pray.

3 My voice shall you hear in the morning, O Becoming-One; in the morning will I direct my prayer unto you, and will look up.

4 For you are not a GOD that has pleasure in wickedness: neither shall evil dwell with you.

5 The foolish shall not stand in your sight: you hate all workers of iniquity.

6 you shall destroy them that speak lies: the Becoming-One will abhor the bloody and deceitful man.

7 But as for me, I will come into your house in the multitude of your mercy: and in your fear will I worship toward your holy temple.

8 Lead me, O Becoming-One, in your righteousness because of mine enemies; make your way straight before my face.

9 For there is no faithfullness in their mouth; their inner thought is very wicked; their throat is an open tomb; they flatter with their tongue.

10 Destroy you them, O God; let them fall by their own counsels; cast them out in the multitude of their transgressions; for they have rebelled against you.

11 But let all those that put their trust in you rejoice: let them ever shout for joy, because you defend them: let them also that love your name be joyful in you.

12 For you, Becoming-One, will bless the righteous; with favor will you compass him as with a shield.

Psa 6:1 To the chief Musician on Neginoth upon Sheminith, A Psalm of David. O Becoming-One, rebuke me not in your anger, neither chasten me in your hot displeasure.

2 Have mercy upon me, O Becoming-One; for I am weak: O Becoming-One, heal me; for my bones are vexed.

3 My soul is also greatly vexed: but you, O Becoming-One, how long?

4 Return, O Becoming-One, deliver my soul: oh save me for your mercies' sake.

5 For in death there is no remembrance of you: in Sheol who shall give you thanks?

6 I am weary with my groaning; all the night make I my bed to swim; I water my couch with my tears.

7 Mine eye is consumed because of grief; it waxes old because of all mine enemies.

8 Depart from me, all you workers of iniquity; for the Becoming-One has heard the voice of my weeping.

9 The Becoming-One has heard my supplication; the Becoming-One will receive my prayer.

10 Let all mine enemies be ashamed and greatly vexed: let them return and be ashamed suddenly.

Psa 7:1 Shiggaion of David, which he sang unto the Becoming-One, concerning the words of Cush the Benjamite. O Becoming-One my God, in you do I put my trust: save me from all them that persecute me, and deliver me:

2 Lest he tear my soul like a lion, rending it in pieces, while there is none to deliver.

3 O Becoming-One my God, if I have done this; if there be iniquity in my hands;

4 If I have rewarded evil unto him that was at peace with me; yes, I have delivered him that without cause is mine enemy:

5 Let the enemy persecute my soul, and take it; yes, let him tread down my life upon the earth, and lay mine honor in the dust. Selah.

6 Arise, O Becoming-One, in your anger, lift up yourself because of the rage of mine enemies: and awake for me to the judgment that you have commanded.

7 So shall the congregation of the people compass you about: for their sakes therefore return you on high.

8 The Becoming-One shall judge the people: judge me, O Becoming-One, according to my righteousness, and according to mine integrity that is in me.

9 Oh let the wickedness of the wicked come to an end; but establish the just: for the righteous God tries the hearts and reins.

10 My defense is of God, which saves the upright in heart.

11 God judges the righteous, and GOD is angry with the wicked every day.

12 If he turn not, he will whet his sword; he has bent his bow, and made it ready.

13 He has also prepared for him the instruments of death; he ordains his arrows against the persecutors.

14 Behold, he travails with iniquity, and has conceived mischief, and brought forth falsehood.

15 He made a pit, and dug it, and is fallen into the ditch which he made.

16 His mischief shall return upon his own head, and his violent dealing shall come down upon his own pate.

17 I will praise the Becoming-One according to his righteousness: and will sing praise to the name of the Becoming-One most high.

Psa 8:1 To the chief Musician upon Gittith, A Psalm of David. O Becoming-One our Lords, how excellent is your name in all the earth! who have set your glory above the heavens.

2 Out of the mouth of babes and sucklings have you ordained strength because of your enemies, that you might still the enemy and the avenger.

3 When I consider your heavens, the work of your fingers, the moon and the stars, which you have ordained;

4 What is man, that you are mindful of him? and the son of man, that you visit him?

5 For you have made him a little lower than the angels, and have crowned him with glory and honor.

6 you made him to have dominion over the works of your hands; you have put all things under his feet:

7 All sheep and oxen, yes, and the beasts of the field;

8 The fowl of the air, and the fish of the sea, and whatsoever passes through the paths of the seas.

9 O Becoming-One our Lords, how excellent is your name in all the earth!

Psa 9:1 To the chief Musician upon Muthlabben, A Psalm of David. I will praise you, O Becoming-One, with my whole heart; I will show forth all your marvelous works.

2 I will be glad and rejoice in you: I will sing praise to your name, O you most High.

3 When mine enemies are turned back, they shall fall and perish at your presence.

4 For you have maintained my right and my cause; you sat in the throne judging right.

5 you have rebuked the nations, you have destroyed the wicked, you have put out their name for olam and beyond.

6 O you enemy, destructions are come to a complete end: and you have destroyed cities; their memorial is perished with them.

7 But the Becoming-One shall endure for olam, he has prepared his throne for judgment.

8 And he shall judge the world in righteousness, he shall minister judgment to the people in uprightness.

9 The Becoming-One also will be a refuge for the oppressed, a refuge in times of trouble.

10 And they that know your name will put their trust in you: for you, Becoming-One, have not forsaken them that seek you.

11 Sing praises to the Becoming-One, which dwells in Zion: declare among the people his doings.

12 When he makes inquisition for blood, he remembers them: he forgets not the cry of the humble.

13 Have mercy upon me, O Becoming-One; consider my trouble which I suffer of them that hate me, you that lift me up from the gates of death:

14 That I may show forth all your praise in the gates of the daughter of Zion: I will rejoice in your salvation.

15 The nations are sunk down in the pit that they made: in the net which they hid is their own foot taken.

16 The Becoming-One is known by the judgment which he executes: the wicked is snared in the work of his own hands. Higgaion. Selah.

17 The wicked shall be turned into Sheol, and all the nations that forget God.

18 For the needy shall not always be forgotten: the expectation of the poor shall not perish to the beyond.

19 Arise, O Becoming-One; let not man prevail: let the nations be judged in your sight.

20 Put them in fear, O Becoming-One: that the nations may know themselves to be but men. Selah.

Psa 10:1 Why stand you afar off, O Becoming-One? why hide you yourself in times of trouble?

2 The wicked in his pride does persecute the poor: let them be taken in the devices that they have imagined.

3 For the wicked boasts of his soul's desire, and blesses the covetous, whom the Becoming-One abhorreth.

4 The wicked, through the pride of his countenance, will not seek after God: God is not in all his thoughts.

5 His ways are always grievous; your judgments are far above out of his sight: as for all his enemies, he puffs at them.

6 He has said in his heart, I shall not be moved: for I shall never be in adversity.

7 His mouth is full of cursing and deceit and fraud: under his tongue is mischief and vanity.

8 He sits in the lurking places of the villages: in the secret places does he murder the innocent: his eyes are privily set against the poor.

9 He lies in wait secretly as a lion in his den: he lies in wait to catch the poor: he does catch the poor, when he draws him into his net.

10 He crouches, and humbles himself, that the poor may fall by his strong ones.

11 He has said in his heart, GOD has forgotten: he hides his face; he will never see it.

12 Arise, O Becoming-One; O God, lift up your hand: forget not the humble.

13 Why does the wicked contemn God? he has said in his heart, you will not require it.

14 you have seen it: for you behold mischief and spite, to requite it with your hand: the poor commits himself unto you; you are the helper of the fatherless.

15 Break you the arm of the wicked and the evil man: seek out his wickedness till you find none.

16 The Becoming-One is King for olam and beyond: the nations are perished out of his land.

17 Becoming-One, you have heard the desire of the humble: you will prepare their heart, you will cause your ear to hear:

18 To judge the fatherless and the oppressed, that the man of the earth may no more oppress.

Psa 11:1 To the chief Musician, A Psalm of David. In the Becoming-One put I my trust: how say you to my soul, Flee as a bird to your mountain?

2 For, lo, the wicked bend their bow, they make ready their arrow upon the string, that they may in darkness shoot at the upright in heart.

3 If the foundations be destroyed, what can the righteous do?

4 The Becoming-One is in his holy temple, the Becoming-One's throne is in heaven: his eyes behold, his eyelids try, the children of men.

5 The Becoming-One tries the righteous: but the wicked and him that loves violence his soul hates.

6 Upon the wicked he shall rain snares, fire and brimstone, and a horrible wind: this shall be the portion of their cup.

7 For the righteous Becoming-One loves righteousness; his countenance does behold the upright.

Psa 12:1 To the chief Musician upon Sheminith, A Psalm of David. Help, Becoming-One; for the godly man ceases; for the faithful fail from among the children of men.

2 They speak vanity every one with his neighbor: with flattering lips and with a double heart do they speak.

3 The Becoming-One shall cut off all flattering lips, and the tongue that speaks proud things:

4 Who have said, With our tongue will we prevail; our lips are our own: who is lord over us?

5 For the oppression of the poor, for the sighing of the needy, now will I arise, says the Becoming-One; I will set him in safety from him that puffs at him.

6 The words of the Becoming-One are pure words: as silver tried in a furnace of earth, purified seven times.

7 you shall keep them, O Becoming-One, you shall preserve them from this generation for olam.

8 The wicked walk on every side, when the vile men are exalted.

Psa 13:1 To the chief Musician, A Psalm of David. How long will you forget me, O Becoming-One? will you forget completely? how long will you hide your face from me?

2 How long shall I take counsel in my soul, having sorrow in my heart daily? how long shall mine enemy be exalted over me?

3 Consider and hear me, O Becoming-One my God: lighten mine eyes, lest I sleep the sleep of death;

4 Lest mine enemy say, I have prevailed against him; and those that trouble me rejoice when I am moved.

5 But I have trusted in your mercy; my heart shall rejoice in your salvation.

6 I will sing unto the Becoming-One, because he has dealt bountifully with me.

Psa 14:1 To the chief Musician, A Psalm of David. The fool has said in his heart, There is no God. They are corrupt, they have done abominable works, there is none that did good.

2 The Becoming-One looked down from the heavens upon the children of men, to see if there were any that did understand, and seek God.

3 They are all gone aside, they are all together become filthy: there is none that did good, no, not one.

4 Have all the workers of iniquity no knowledge? who eat up my people as they eat bread, and call not upon the Becoming-One.

5 There were they in great fear: for God is in the generation of the righteous.

6 you have shamed the counsel of the poor, because the Becoming-One is his refuge.

7 Oh that the salvation of Israel were come out of Zion! when the Becoming-One brings back the captivity of his people, Jacob shall rejoice, and Israel shall be glad.

Psa 15:1 A Psalm of David. Becoming-One, who shall abide in your tabernacle? who shall dwell in your holy hill?

2 He that walks uprightly, and works righteousness, and speaks the truth in his heart.

3 He that backbites not with his tongue, nor did evil to his neighbor, nor takes up a reproach against his neighbor.

4 In whose eyes a vile person is contemned; but he honors them that fear the Becoming-One. He that sweares to his own hurt, and changes not.

5 He that puts not out his money to usury, nor takes reward against the innocent. He that did these things shall not for olam be moved.

Psa 16:1 Michtam of David. Preserve me, O GOD: for in you do I put my trust.

2 O my soul, you have said unto the Becoming-One, you are my Lord(s): my goodness extends not to you;

3 But to the saints that are in the earth, and to the excellent, in whom is all my delight.

4 Their sorrows shall be multiplied that hasten after another god: their drink offerings of blood will I not offer, nor take up their names into my lips.

5 The Becoming-One is the portion of mine inheritance and of my cup: you maintain my lot.

6 The lines are fallen unto me in pleasant places; yes, I have a goodly heritage.

7 I will bless the Becoming-One, who has given me counsel: my reins also instruct me in the night seasons.

8 I have set the Becoming-One always before me: because he is at my right hand, I shall not be moved.

9 Therefore my heart is glad, and my glory rejoices: my flesh also shall rest in hope.

10 For you will not leave my soul in Sheol; neither will you permit your Holy One to see corruption.

11 you will show me the path of life: in your presence is fullness of joy; at your right hand there are pleasures altogether.

Psa 17:1 A prayer of David. Hear the right, O Becoming-One, attend unto my cry, give ear unto my prayer, that goes not out of deceitful lips.

2 Let my sentence come forth from your presence; let your eyes behold the things that are equal.

3 you have proved mine heart; you have visited me in the night; you have tried me, and shall find nothing; I am purposed that my mouth shall not transgress.

4 Concerning the works of men, by the word of your lips I have kept me from the paths of the destroyer.

5 Hold up my goings in your paths, that my footsteps slip not.

6 I have called upon you, for you will hear me, O GOD: incline your ear unto me, and hear my speech.

7 Show your marvelous loving-kindness, O you that save by your right hand them which put their trust in you from those that rise up against them.

8 Keep me as the apple of the eye, hide me under the shadow of your wings,

9 From the wicked that oppress me, from my enemies against my soul, who compass me about.

10 They are enclosed in their own fat: with their mouth they speak proudly.

11 They have now compassed us in our steps: they have set their eyes bowing down to the earth;

12 Like as a lion that is greedy of his prey, and as it were a young lion lurking in secret places.

13 Arise, O Becoming-One, disappoint him, cast him down: deliver my soul from the wicked, which is your sword:

14 From men which are your hand, O Becoming-One, from men of the world, which have their portion in this life, and whose belly you fill with your hid treasure: they are full of children, and leave the rest of their substance to their babes.

15 As for me, I will behold your face in righteousness: I shall be satisfied, when I awake, with your likeness.

Psa 18:1 To the chief Musician, A Psalm of David, the servant of the Becoming-One, who spoke unto the Becoming-One the words of this song in the day that the Becoming-One delivered him from the hand of all his enemies, and from the hand of Saul: And he said, I will love you, O Becoming-One, my strength.

2 The Becoming-One is my rock, and my fortress, and my deliverer; my GOD, my strength, in whom I will trust; my buckler, and the horn of my salvation, and my high tower.

3 I will call upon the Becoming-One, who is worthy to be praised: so shall I be saved from mine enemies.

4 The sorrows of death compassed me, and the floods of ungodly men made me afraid.

5 The sorrows of Sheol compassed me about: the snares of death prevented me.

6 In my distress I called upon the Becoming-One, and cried unto my God: he heard my voice out of his temple, and my cry came before him, even into his ears.

7 Then the earth shook and trembled; the foundations also of the hills moved and were shaken, because he was angry.

8 There went up a smoke out of his nostrils, and fire out of his mouth devoured: coals were kindled by it.

9 He bowed the heavens also, and came down: and darkness was under his feet.

10 And he rode upon a cherub, and did fly: yes, he did fly upon the wings of the wind.

11 He made darkness his secret place; his pavilion round about him were dark waters and thick clouds of the skies.

12 At the brightness that was before him his thick clouds passed, hail stones and coals of fire.

13 The Becoming-One also thundered in the heavens, and the High gave his voice; hail stones and coals of fire.

14 Yes, he sent out his arrows, and scattered them; and he shot out lightning, and discomfited them.

15 Then the channels of waters were seen, and the foundations of the world were discovered at your rebuke, O Becoming-One, at the blast of the breath of your nostrils.

16 He sent from above, he took me, he drew me out of many waters.

17 He delivered me from my strong enemy, and from them which hated me: for they were too strong for me.

18 They confronted me in the day of my calamity: but the Becoming-One was my stay.

19 He brought me forth also into a large place; he delivered me, because he delighted in me.

20 The Becoming-One rewarded me according to my righteousness; according to the cleanness of my hands has he recompensed me.

21 For I have kept the ways of the Becoming-One, and have not wickedly departed from my God.

22 For all his judgments were before me, and I did not put away his statutes from me.

23 I was also upright before him, and I kept myself from mine iniquity.

24 Therefore has the Becoming-One recompensed me according to my righteousness, according to the cleanness of my hands in his eyesight.

25 With the merciful you will show yourself merciful; with an upright man you will show yourself upright;

26 With the pure you will show yourself pure; and with the perverse you will show yourself perverse.

27 For you will save the afflicted people; but will bring down high looks.

28 For you will light my candle: the Becoming-One my God will enlighten my darkness.

29 For by you I have run through a troop; and by my God have I leaped over a wall.

30 As for GOD, his way is perfect: the word of the Becoming-One is tried: he is a buckler to all those that trust in him.

31 For who is God save the Becoming-One? or who is a rock save our God?

32 It is GOD that girds me with strength, and makes my way perfect.

33 He makes my feet like hinds' feet, and sets me upon my high places.

34 He teaches my hands to war, so that a bow of steel is broken by mine arms.

35 you have also given me the shield of your salvation: and your right hand has held me up, and your gentleness has made me great.

36 you have enlarged my steps under me, that my feet did not slip.

37 I have pursued mine enemies, and overtaken them: neither did I turn again till they were consumed.

38 I have wounded them that they were not able to rise: they are fallen under my feet.

39 For you have girded me with strength unto the battle: you have subdued under me those that rose up against me.

40 you have also given me the necks of mine enemies; that I might destroy them that hate me.

41 They cried, but there was none to save them: even unto the Becoming-One, but he answered them not.

42 Then did I beat them small as the dust before the wind: I did cast them out as the dirt in the streets.

43 you have delivered me from the strivings of the people; and you have made me the head of the nations: a people whom I have not known shall serve me.

44 As soon as they hear of me, they shall obey me: the strangers shall submit themselves unto me.

45 The strangers shall fade away, and be afraid out of their close places.

46 The Becoming-One lives; and blessed be my rock; and let God of my salvation be exalted.

47 It is GOD that avenges me, and subdues the people under me.

48 He deliveres me from mine enemies: yes, you lift me up above those that rise up against me: you have delivered me from the violent man

49 Therefore will I give thanks unto you, O Becoming-One, among the nations, and sing praises unto your name.

50 Great deliverance gives he to his king; and shows mercy to his anointed [Messiah], to David, and to his seed for olam.

Psa 19:1 To the chief Musician, A Psalm of David. The heavens declare the glory of GOD; and space shows his handiwork.

2 Day unto day utters speech, and night unto night shows knowledge.

3 There is no speech nor language, where their voice is not heard.

4 Their line is gone out through all the earth, and their words to the end of the world. In them has he set a tabernacle for the sun,

5 Which is as a bridegroom coming out of his chamber, and rejoices as a strong man to run a race.

6 His going forth is from the end of the heaven, and his circuit unto the ends of it: and there is nothing hid from the heat thereof.

7 The law of the Becoming-One is perfect, converting the soul: the testimony of the Becoming-One is sure, making wise the simple.

8 The statutes of the Becoming-One are right, rejoicing the heart: the commandment of the Becoming-One is pure, enlightening the eyes.

9 The fear of the Becoming-One is clean, enduring to the beyond: the judgments of the Becoming-One are true and righteous altogether.

10 More to be desired are they than gold, yes, than much fine gold: sweeter also than honey and the honeycomb.

11 Moreover by them is your servant warned: and in keeping of them there is great reward.

12 Who can understand his errors? cleanse you me from secret faults.

13 Keep back your servant also from presumptuous sins; let them not have dominion over me: then shall I be upright, and I shall be innocent from the great transgression.

14 Let the words of my mouth, and the meditation of my heart, be acceptable in your sight, O Becoming-One, my strength, and my redeemer.

Psa 20:1 To the chief Musician, A Psalm of David. The Becoming-One hear you in the day of trouble; the name of God of Jacob defend you;

2 Send you help from the sanctuary, and strengthen you out of Zion;

3 Remember all your offerings, and accept your burnt sacrifice; Selah.

4 Grant you according to your own heart, and fulfil all your counsel.

5 We will rejoice in your salvation, and in the name of our God we will set up our banners: the Becoming-One fulfil all your petitions.

6 Now know I that the Becoming-One saves his anointed [Messiah]; he will hear him from his holy heavens with the saving strength of his right hand.

7 Some trust in chariots, and some in horses: but we will remember the name of the Becoming-One our God.

8 They are brought down and fallen: but we are risen, and stand upright.

9 Save, Becoming-One: let the king hear us when we call.

Psa 21:1 To the chief Musician, A Psalm of David. The king shall joy in your strength, O Becoming-One; and in your salvation how greatly shall he rejoice!

2 you have given him his heart's desire, and have not withheld the request of his lips. Selah.

3 For you prevent him with the blessings of goodness: you set a crown of pure gold on his head.

4 He asked life of you, and you gave it him, even length of days for olam and beyond.

5 His glory is great in your salvation: honor and majesty have you laid upon him.

6 For you have made him most blessed to the beyond: you have made him exceeding glad with your countenance.

7 For the king trusts in the Becoming-One, and through the mercy of the most High he shall not be moved.

8 your hand shall find out all your enemies: your right hand shall find out those that hate you.

9 you shall make them as a fiery oven in the time of your anger: the Becoming-One shall swallow them up in his wrath, and the fire shall devour them.

10 Their fruit shall you destroy from the earth, and their seed from among the children of men.

11 For they intended evil against you: they imagined a mischievous device, which they are not able to perform.

12 Therefore shall you make them turn their back, when you shall make ready your arrows upon your strings against the face of them.

13 Be you exalted, Becoming-One, in your own strength: so will we sing and praise your power.

Psa 22:1 To the chief Musician upon Aijeleth Shahar, A Psalm of David. My GOD, my GOD, why have you forsaken me? why are you so far from helping me, and from the words of my roaring?

2 O my God, I cry in the daytime, but you hear not; and in the night season, and am not silent.

3 But you are holy, O you that inhabit the praises of Israel.

4 Our fathers trusted in you: they trusted, and you did deliver them.

5 They cried unto you, and were delivered: they trusted in you, and were not confounded.

6 But I am a worm, and no man; a reproach of men, and despised of the people.

7 All they that see me laugh me to scorn: they shoot out the lip, they shake the head, saying,

8 He trusted on the Becoming-One that he would deliver him: let him deliver him, seeing he delighted in him.

9 But you are he that took me out of the womb: you did make me hope when I was upon my mother's breasts.

10 I was cast upon you from the womb: you are my GOD from my mother's belly.

11 Be not far from me; for trouble is near; for there is none to help.

12 Many bulls have compassed me: strong bulls of Bashan have beset me round.

13 They gaped upon me with their mouths, as a ravening and a roaring lion.

14 I am poured out like water, and all my bones are out of joint: my heart is like wax; it is melted in the midst of my bowels.

15 My strength is dried up like a potsherd; and my tongue cleaves to my jaws; and you have brought me into the dust of death.

16 For dogs have compassed me: the assembly of the wicked have enclosed me: they pierced my hands and my feet.

17 I may tell all my bones: they look and stare upon me.

18 They part my garments among them, and cast lots upon my vesture.

19 But be not you far from me, O Becoming-One: O my strength, haste you to help me.

20 Deliver my soul from the sword; my darling from the power of the dog.

21 Save me from the lion's mouth: for you have heard me from the horns of the reem [wild ox or beast]

22 I will declare your name unto my brethren: in the midst of the congregation will I praise you.

23 you that fear the Becoming-One, praise him; all you the seed of Jacob, glorify him; and fear him, all you the seed of Israel.

24 For he has not despised nor abhorred the affliction of the afflicted; neither has he hid his face from him; but when he cried unto him, he heard.

25 My praise shall be of you in the great congregation: I will pay my vows before them that fear him.

26 The meek shall eat and be satisfied: they shall praise the Becoming-One that seek him: your heart shall live to the beyond.

27 All the ends of the world shall remember and turn unto the Becoming-One: and all the kindreds of the nations shall worship before you.

28 For the kingdom is the Becoming-One's: and he is the governor among the nations.

29 All they that be fat upon earth shall eat and worship: all they that go down to the dust shall bow before him: and none can keep alive his own soul.

30 A seed shall serve him; it shall be accounted to my Lord(s) for a generation.

31 They shall come, and shall declare his righteousness unto a people that shall be born, that he has done this.

Psa 23:1 A Psalm of David. The Becoming-One is my shepherd; I shall not want.

2 He makes me to lie down in green pastures: he leads me beside the still waters.

3 He restores my soul: he leads me in the paths of righteousness for his name's sake.

4 Yes, though I walk through the valley of the shadow of death, I will fear no evil: for you are with me; your rod and your staff they comfort me.

5 you prepare a table before me in the presence of mine enemies: you anoint my head with oil; my cup runs over.

6 Surely goodness and mercy shall follow me all the days of my life: and I will dwell in the house of the Becoming-One for length of days.

Psa 24:1 A Psalm of David. The earth is the Becoming-One's, and the fullness thereof; the world, and they that dwell therein.

2 For he has founded it upon the seas, and established it upon the floods.

3 Who shall ascend into the hill of the Becoming-One? or who shall stand in his holy place?

4 He that has clean hands, and a pure heart; who has not lifted up his soul unto vanity, nor sworn deceitfully.

5 He shall receive the blessing from the Becoming-One, and righteousness from God of his salvation.

6 This is the generation of them that seek him, that seek your face, O Jacob. Selah.

7 Lift up your heads, O you gates; and be you lift up, you doors of olam, and the King of glory shall come in.

8 Who is this King of glory? The Becoming-One strong and mighty, the Becoming-One mighty in battle.

9 Lift up your heads, O you gates; even lift them up, you doors of olam, and the King of glory shall come in.

10 Who is this King of glory? The Becoming-One of hosts, he is the King of glory. Selah.

Psa 25:1 A Psalm of David. Unto you, O Becoming-One, do I lift up my soul.

2 O my God, I trust in you: let me not be ashamed, let not mine enemies triumph over me.

3 Yes, let none that wait on you be ashamed: let them be ashamed which transgress without cause.

4 Show me your ways, O Becoming-One; teach me your paths.

5 Lead me in your truth, and teach me: for you are God of my salvation; on you do I wait all the day.

6 Remember, O Becoming-One, your tender mercies and your loving-kindnesses; for they have been from olam.

7 Remember not the sins of my youth, nor my transgressions: according to your mercy remember you me for your goodness' sake, O Becoming-One.

8 Good and upright is the Becoming-One: therefore will he teach sinners in the way.

9 The meek will he guide in judgment: and the meek will he teach his way.

10 All the paths of the Becoming-One are mercy and truth unto such as keep his covenant and his testimonies.

11 For your name's sake, O Becoming-One, pardon mine iniquity; for it is great.

12 What man is he that fears the Becoming-One? him shall he teach in the way that he shall choose.

13 His soul shall dwell at ease; and his seed shall inherit the earth.

14 The secret of the Becoming-One is with them that fear him; and he will show them his covenant.

15 Mine eyes are continually toward the Becoming-One; for he shall pluck my feet out of the net.

16 Turn you unto me, and have mercy upon me; for I am desolate and afflicted.

17 The troubles of my heart are enlarged: O bring you me out of my distresses.

18 Look upon mine affliction and my pain; and forgive all my sins.

19 Consider mine enemies; for they are many; and they hate me with cruel hatred.

20 O keep my soul, and deliver me: let me not be ashamed; for I put my trust in you.

21 Let integrity and uprightness preserve me; for I wait on you.

22 Redeem Israel, O God, out of all his troubles.

Psa 26:1 A Psalm of David. Judge me, O Becoming-One; for I have walked in mine integrity: I have trusted also in the Becoming-One; therefore I shall not slide.

2 Examine me, O Becoming-One, and prove me; try my reins and my heart.

3 For your loving-kindness is before mine eyes: and I have walked in your truth.

4 I have not sat with vain persons, neither will I go in with dissemblers.

5 I have hated the congregation of evildoers; and will not sit with the wicked.

6 I will wash mine hands in innocency: so will I compass your altar, O Becoming-One: 7 That I may publish with the voice of thanksgiving, and tell of all your wondrous works.

8 Becoming-One, I have loved the habitation of your house, and the place where your honor dwells.

9 Gather not my soul with sinners, nor my life with bloody men:

10 In whose hands is mischief, and their right hand is full of bribes.

11 But as for me, I will walk in mine integrity: redeem me, and be merciful unto me.

12 My foot stands in an even place: in the congregations will I bless the Becoming-One.

Psa 27:1 A Psalm of David. The Becoming-One is my light and my salvation; whom shall I fear? the Becoming-One is the strength of my life; of whom shall I be afraid?

2 When the wicked, even mine enemies and my foes, came upon me to eat up my flesh, they stumbled and fell.

3 Though a host should encamp against me, my heart shall not fear: though war should rise against me, in this will I be confident.

4 One thing have I desired of the Becoming-One, that will I seek after; that I may dwell in the house of the Becoming-One all the days of my life, to behold the beauty of the Becoming-One, and to inquire in his temple.

5 For in the time of trouble he shall hide me in his pavilion: in the secret of his tabernacle shall he hide me; he shall set me up upon a rock.

6 And now shall mine head be lifted up above mine enemies round about me: therefore will I offer in his tabernacle sacrifices of joy; I will sing, yes, I will sing praises unto the Becoming-One.

7 Hear, O Becoming-One, when I cry with my voice: have mercy also upon me, and answer me.

8 When you said, Seek you my face; my heart said unto you, your face, Becoming-One, will I seek.

9 Hide not your face far from me; put not your servant away in anger: you have been my help; leave me not, neither forsake me, O God of my salvation.

10 When my father and my mother forsake me, then the Becoming-One will take me up.

11 Teach me your way, O Becoming-One, and lead me in a plain path, because of mine enemies.

12 Deliver me not over unto the soul of mine enemies: for false witnesses are risen up against me, and such as breathe out cruelty.

13 I had fainted, unless I had believed to see the goodness of the Becoming-One in the land of the living.

14 Wait on the Becoming-One: be of good courage, and he shall strengthen your heart: wait, I say, on the Becoming-One.

Psa 28:1 A Psalm of David. Unto you will I cry, O Becoming-One my rock; be not silent to me: lest, if you be silent to me, I become like them that go down into the pit.

2 Hear the voice of my supplications, when I cry unto you, when I lift up my hands toward your holy oracle.

3 Draw me not away with the wicked, and with the workers of iniquity, which speak peace to their neighbors, but mischief is in their hearts.

4 Give them according to their deeds, and according to the wickedness of their endeavors: give them after the work of their hands; render to them their desert.

5 Because they regard not the works of the Becoming-One, nor the operation of his hands, he shall destroy them, and not build them up.

6 Blessed be the Becoming-One, because he has heard the voice of my supplications.

7 The Becoming-One is my strength and my shield; my heart trusted in him, and I am helped: therefore my heart greatly rejoices; and with my song will I praise him.

8 The Becoming-One is their strength, and he is the saving strength of his anointed [Messiah].

9 Save your people, and bless your inheritance: feed them also, and lift them up for olam.

Psa 29:1 A Psalm of David. Give unto the Becoming-One, O sons of gods, give unto the Becoming-One glory and strength.

2 Give unto the Becoming-One the glory due unto his name; worship the Becoming-One in the beauty of holiness.

3 The voice of the Becoming-One is upon the waters: GOD of glory thunders: the Becoming-One is upon many waters.

4 The voice of the Becoming-One is powerful; the voice of the Becoming-One is full of majesty.

5 The voice of the Becoming-One breaks the cedars; yes, the Becoming-One breaks the cedars of Lebanon.

6 He makes them also to skip like a calf; Lebanon and Sirion like a young reem [wild ox or beast]

7 The voice of the Becoming-One divides the flames of fire.

8 The voice of the Becoming-One shakes the wilderness; the Becoming-One shakes the wilderness of Kadesh.

9 The voice of the Becoming-One makes the hinds to calve, and discoveres the forests: and in his temple does every one speak of his glory.

10 The Becoming-One sits upon the flood; yes, the Becoming-One sits King for olam.

11 The Becoming-One will give strength unto his people; the Becoming-One will bless his people with peace.

Psa 30:1 A Psalm and Song at the dedication of the house of David. I will extol you, O Becoming-One; for you have lifted me up, and have not made my foes to rejoice over me.

2 O Becoming-One my God, I cried unto you, and you have healed me.

3 O Becoming-One, you have brought up my soul from Sheol: you have kept me alive, that I should not go down to the pit.

4 Sing unto the Becoming-One, O you saints of his, and give thanks at the remembrance of his holiness.

5 For his anger endures but a moment; in his favor is life: weeping may endure for a night, but joy comes in the morning.

6 And in my prosperity I said, I shall not for olam be moved.

7 Becoming-One, by your favor you have made my mountain to stand strong: you did hide your face, and I was troubled.

8 I cried to you, O Becoming-One; and unto the Becoming-One I made supplication.

9 What profit is there in my blood, when I go down to the pit? Shall the dust praise you? shall it declare your truth?

10 Hear, O Becoming-One, and have mercy upon me: Becoming-One, be you my helper.

11 you have turned for me my mourning into dancing: you have put off my sackcloth, and girded me with gladness;

12 To the end that my glory may sing praise to you, and not be silent. O Becoming-One my God, I will give thanks unto you for olam.

Psa 31:1 To the chief Musician, A Psalm of David. In you, O Becoming-One, do I put my trust; let me never be ashamed: deliver me in your righteousness.

2 Bow down your ear to me; deliver me speedily: be you my strong rock, for a house of defense to save me.

3 For you are my rock and my fortress; therefore for your name's sake lead me, and guide me.

4 Pull me out of the net that they have laid privily for me: for you are my strength.

5 Into your hand I commit my spirit: you have redeemed me, O Becoming-One GOD of truth.

6 I have hated them that regard lying vanities: but I trust in the Becoming-One.

7 I will be glad and rejoice in your mercy: for you have considered my trouble; you have known my soul in adversities;

8 And have not shut me up into the hand of the enemy: you have set my feet in a large room.

9 Have mercy upon me, O Becoming-One, for I am in trouble: mine eye is consumed with grief, yes, my soul and my belly.

10 For my life is spent with grief, and my years with sighing: my strength fails because of mine iniquity, and my bones are consumed.

11 I was a reproach among all mine enemies, but especially among my neighbors, and a fear to mine acquaintance: they that did see me outside fled from me.

12 I am forgotten as a dead man out of mind: I am like a broken vessel.

13 For I have heard the slander of many: fear was on every side: while they took counsel together against me, they devised to take away my soul.

14 But I trusted in you, O Becoming-One: I said, you are my God.

15 My times are in your hand: deliver me from the hand of mine enemies, and from them that persecute me.

16 Make your face to shine upon your servant: save me for your mercies' sake.

17 Let me not be ashamed, O Becoming-One; for I have called upon you: let the wicked be ashamed, and let them be silent in Sheol.

18 Let the lying lips be put to silence; which speak grievous things proudly and contemptuously against the righteous.

19 Oh how great is your goodness, which you have laid up for them that fear you; which you have worked for them that trust in you before the sons of men!

20 you shall hide them in the secret of your presence from the pride of man: you shall keep them secretly in a pavilion from the strife of tongues.

21 Blessed be the Becoming-One: for he has showed me his marvelous kindness in a strong city.

22 For I said in my haste, I am cut off from before your eyes: nevertheless you heard the voice of my supplications when I cried unto you.

23 O love the Becoming-One, all you his saints: for the Becoming-One preserves the faithful, and plentifully rewards the proud doer.

24 Be of good courage, and he shall strengthen your heart, all you that hope in the Becoming-One.

Psa 32:1 A Psalm of David, Maschil. Blessed is he whose transgression is forgiven, whose sin is covered.

2 Blessed is the man unto whom the Becoming-One imputes not iniquity, and in whose spirit there is no guile.

3 When I kept silence, my bones grew old through my roaring all the day long.

4 For day and night your hand was heavy upon me: my moisture is turned into the drought of summer. Selah.

5 I acknowledged my sin unto you, and mine iniquity have I not hid. I said, I will confess my transgressions unto the Becoming-One; and you forgave the iniquity of my sin. Selah.

6 For this shall every one that is godly pray unto you in a time when you may be found: surely in the floods of great waters they shall not come near unto him.

7 you are my hiding place; you shall preserve me from trouble; you shall compass me about with songs of deliverance. Selah.

8 I will instruct you and teach you in the way which you shall go: I will guide you with mine eye.

9 Be you not as the horse, or as the mule, which have no understanding: whose mouth must be held in with bit and bridle, lest they come near unto you.

10 Many sorrows shall be to the wicked: but he that trusts in the Becoming-One, mercy shall compass him about.

11 Be glad in the Becoming-One, and rejoice, you righteous: and shout for joy, all you that are upright in heart.

Psa 33:1 Rejoice in the Becoming-One, O you righteous: for praise is becoming for the upright.

2 Praise the Becoming-One with harp: sing unto him with the psaltery and an instrument of ten strings.

3 Sing unto him a new song; play skillfully with a loud noise.

4 For the word of the Becoming-One is right; and all his works are done in truth.

5 He loves righteousness and judgment: the earth is full of the goodness of the Becoming-One.

6 By the word of the Becoming-One were the heavens made; and all the host of them by the breath of his mouth.

7 He gathers the waters of the sea together as a heap: he lays up the depth in storehouses.

8 Let all the earth fear the Becoming-One: let all the inhabitants of the world stand in awe of him.

9 For he spoke, and it was done; he commanded, and it stood fast.

10 The Becoming-One brings the counsel of the nations to nothing: he makes the devices of the people of none effect.

11 The counsel of the Becoming-One stands for olam, the thoughts of his heart to all generations.

12 Blessed is the nation whose God is the Becoming-One; and the people whom he has chosen for his own inheritance.

13 The Becoming-One looks from heaven; he beholds all the sons of men.

14 From the place of his habitation he looks upon all the inhabitants of the earth.

15 He fashions their hearts alike; he considers all their works.

16 There is no king saved by the multitude of a host: a mighty man is not delivered by much strength.

17 a horse is a vain thing for safety: neither shall he deliver any by his great strength.

18 Behold, the eye of the Becoming-One is upon them that fear him, upon them that hope in his mercy;

19 To deliver their soul from death, and to keep them alive in famine.

20 Our soul waits for the Becoming-One: he is our help and our shield.

21 For our heart shall rejoice in him, because we have trusted in his holy name.

22 Let your mercy, O Becoming-One, be upon us, according as we hope in you.

Psa 34:1 A Psalm of David, when he changed his behavior before Abimelech; who drove him away, and he departed. I will bless the Becoming-One at all times: his praise shall continually be in my mouth.

2 My soul shall make her boast in the Becoming-One: the humble shall hear thereof, and be glad.

3 O magnify the Becoming-One with me, and let us exalt his name together.

4 I sought the Becoming-One, and he heard me, and delivered me from all my fears.

5 They looked unto him, and were lightened: and their faces were not ashamed.

6 This poor man cried, and the Becoming-One heard him, and saved him out of all his troubles.

7 The angel of the Becoming-One encamps round about them that fear him, and delivers them.

8 O taste and see that the Becoming-One is good: blessed is the man that trusts in him.

9 O fear the Becoming-One, you his saints: for there is no want to them that fear him.

10 The young lions do lack, and suffer hunger: but they that seek the Becoming-One shall not want any good thing.

11 Come, you children, listen unto me: I will teach you the fear of the Becoming-One.

12 What man is he that desires life, and loves many days, that he may see good?

13 Keep your tongue from evil, and your lips from speaking guile.

14 Depart from evil, and do good; seek peace, and pursue it.

15 The eyes of the Becoming-One are upon the righteous, and his ears are open unto their cry.

16 The face of the Becoming-One is against them that do evil, to cut off the remembrance of them from the earth.

17 The righteous cry, and the Becoming-One hears, and delivers them out of all their troubles.

18 The Becoming-One is near unto them that are of a broken heart; and saves such as be of a contrite spirit.

19 Many are the afflictions of the righteous: but the Becoming-One delivers him out of them all.

20 He keeps all his bones: not one of them is broken.

21 Evil shall slay the wicked: and they that hate the righteous shall be desolate.

22 The Becoming-One redeems the soul of his servants: and none of them that trust in him shall be desolate.

Psa 35:1 A Psalm of David. Plead my cause, O Becoming-One, with them that strive with me: fight against them that fight against me.

2 Take hold of shield and buckler, and stand up for mine help.

3 Draw out also the spear, and stop the way against them that persecute me: say unto my soul, I am your salvation.

4 Let them be confounded and put to shame that seek after my soul: let them be turned back and brought to confusion that devise my hurt.

5 Let them be as chaff before the wind: and let the angel of the Becoming-One chase them.

6 Let their way be dark and slippery: and let the angel of the Becoming-One persecute them.

7 For without cause have they hid for me their net in a pit, which without cause they have dug for my soul.

8 Let destruction come upon him at unawares; and let his net that he has hid catch himself: into that very destruction let him fall.

9 And my soul shall be joyful in the Becoming-One: it shall rejoice in his salvation.

10 All my bones shall say, Becoming-One, who is like unto you, which deliver the poor from him that is too strong for him, yes, the poor and the needy from him that spoils him?

11 False witnesses did rise up; they laid to my charge things that I knew not.

12 They rewarded me evil for good to the spoiling of my soul.

13 But as for me, when they were sick, my clothing was sackcloth: I humbled my soul with fasting; and my prayer returned into mine own bosom.

14 I behaved myself as though he had been my friend or brother: I bowed down heavily, as one that mourns for his mother.

15 But in mine adversity they rejoiced, and gathered themselves together: yes, the abjects gathered themselves together against me, and I knew it not; they did tear me, and ceased not:

16 With hypocritical mockers in feasts, they gnashed upon me with their teeth.

17 My Lord(s), how long will you look on? rescue my soul from their destructions, my darling from the lions.

18 I will give you thanks in the great congregation: I will praise you among much people.

19 Let not them that are mine enemies wrongfully rejoice over me: neither let them wink with the eye that hate me without a cause.

20 For they speak not peace: but they devise deceitful matters against them that are quiet in the land.

21 Yes, they opened their mouth wide against me, and said, Aha, aha, our eye has seen it.

22 This you have seen, O Becoming-One: keep not silence: O Becoming-One, be not far from me.

23 Stir up thyself, and awake to my judgment, even unto my cause, my God and my Lord(s).

24 Judge me, O Becoming-One my God, according to your righteousness; and let them not rejoice over me.

25 Let them not say in their hearts, Ah, so would we have it: let them not say, We have swallowed him up.

26 Let them be ashamed and brought to confusion together that rejoice at mine hurt: let them be clothed with shame and dishonor that magnify themselves against me.

27 Let them shout for joy, and be glad, that favor my righteous cause: yes, let them say continually, Let the Becoming-One be magnified, which has pleasure in the prosperity of his servant.

28 And my tongue shall speak of your righteousness and of your praise all the day long.

Psa 36:1 To the chief Musician, A Psalm of David the servant of the Becoming-One. The transgression of the wicked says within my heart, that there is no fear of God before his eyes.

2 For he flatters himself in his own eyes, until his iniquity be found to be hateful.

3 The words of his mouth are iniquity and deceit: he has left off to be wise, and to do good.

4 He devises mischief upon his bed; he sets himself in a way that is not good; he abhors not evil.

5 your mercy, O Becoming-One, is in the heavens; and your faithfullness reaches unto the clouds.

6 your righteousness is like the mountains of GOD; your judgments are a great deep: O Becoming-One, you preserve man and beast.

7 How excellent is your loving-kindness, O God! therefore the children of men put their trust under the shadow of your wings.

8 They shall be abundantly satisfied with the fatness of your house; and you shall make them drink of the river of your pleasures.

9 For with you is the fountain of life: in your light shall we see light.

10 O continue your loving-kindness unto them that know you; and your righteousness to the upright in heart.

11 Let not the foot of pride come against me, and let not the hand of the wicked remove me.

12 There are the workers of iniquity fallen: they are cast down, and shall not be able to rise.

Psa 37:1 A Psalm of David. Fret not yourself because of evildoers, neither be you envious against the workers of iniquity.

2 For they shall soon be cut down like the grass, and wither as the green herb.

3 Trust in the Becoming-One, and do good; so shall you dwell in the land, and truly you shall be fed.

4 Delight yourself also in the Becoming-One; and he shall give you the desires of your heart.

5 Commit your way unto the Becoming-One; trust also in him; and he shall bring it to pass.

6 And he shall bring forth your righteousness as the light, and your judgment as the noonday.

7 Rest in the Becoming-One, and wait patiently for him: fret not yourself because of him who prospers in his way, because of the man who brings wicked devices to pass.

8 Cease from anger, and forsake wrath: fret not yourself in any way to do evil.

9 For evildoers shall be cut off: but those that wait upon the Becoming-One, they shall inherit the earth.

10 For yet a little while, and the wicked shall not be: yes, you shall diligently consider his place, and it shall not be.

11 But the meek shall inherit the earth; and shall delight themselves in the abundance of peace.

12 The wicked plots against the just, and gnashes upon him with his teeth.

13 My Lord(s) shall laugh at him: for he sees that his day is coming.

14 The wicked have drawn out the sword, and have bent their bow, to cast down the poor and needy, and to slay such as be of upright behavior.

15 Their sword shall enter into their own heart, and their bows shall be broken.

16 A little that a righteous man has is better than the riches of many wicked.

17 For the arms of the wicked shall be broken: but the Becoming-One upholds the righteous.

18 The Becoming-One knows the days of the upright: and their inheritance shall be for olam.

19 They shall not be ashamed in the evil time: and in the days of famine they shall be satisfied.

20 But the wicked shall perish, and the enemies of the Becoming-One shall be as the fat of lambs: they shall consume; into smoke shall they consume away.

21 The wicked borrows, and pays not again: but the righteous shows mercy, and giveth.

22 For such as be blessed of him shall inherit the earth; and they that be cursed of him shall be cut off.

23 The steps of a good man are ordered by the Becoming-One: and he delights in his way.

24 Though he fall, he shall not be utterly cast down: for the Becoming-One upholds him with his hand.

25 I have been young, and now am old; yet have I not seen the righteous forsaken, nor his seed begging bread.

26 He is all the days merciful, and lends; and his seed is blessed.

27 Depart from evil, and do good; and dwell for olam.

28 For the Becoming-One loves judgment, and forsakes not his saints; they are preserved for olam, but the seed of the wicked shall be cut off.

29 The righteous shall inherit the land, and dwell therein to the beyond.

30 The mouth of the righteous speaks wisdom, and his tongue talks of judgment.

31 The law of his God is in his heart; none of his steps shall slide.

32 The wicked watches the righteous, and seeks to slay him.

33 The Becoming-One will not leave him in his hand, nor condemn him when he is judged.

34 Wait on the Becoming-One, and keep his way, and he shall exalt you to inherit the land: when the wicked are cut off, you shall see it.

35 I have seen the wicked, the terrible, and spreading himself like a green bay tree.

36 Yet he passed away, and, lo, he was not: yes, I sought him, but he could not be found.

37 Mark the perfect, and behold the upright: for the end to man is peace.

38 But the transgressors shall be destroyed together: in the end the wicked shall be cut off.

39 But the salvation of the righteous is from the Becoming-One: he is their strength in the time of trouble.

40 And the Becoming-One shall help them, and deliver them: he shall deliver them from the wicked, and save them, because they trust in him.

Psa 38:1 A Psalm of David, to bring to remembrance. O Becoming-One, rebuke me not in your wrath: neither chasten me in your hot displeasure.

2 For your arrows stick fast in me, and your hand presses me greatly.

3 There is no soundness in my flesh because of your anger; neither is there any rest in my bones because of my sin.

4 For mine iniquities are gone over mine head: as a heavy burden they are too heavy for me.

5 My wounds stink and are corrupt because of my foolishness.

6 I am troubled; I am bowed down greatly; I go mourning all the day long.

7 For my loins are filled with a loathsome disease: and there is no soundness in my flesh.

8 I am feeble and greatly broken: I have roared by reason of the disquietness of my heart.

9 My Lord(s), all my desire is before you; and my groaning is not hid from you.

10 My heart pants my strength fails me: as for the light of mine eyes, it also is gone from me.

11 My lovers and my friends stand aloof from my sore; and my kinsmen stand afar off.

12 They also that seek after my soul lay snares for me: and they that seek my hurt speak mischievous things, and imagine deceits all the day long.

13 But I, as a deaf man, heard not; and I was as a mute man that opens not his mouth.

14 Thus I was as a man that hears not, and in whose mouth are no reproofs.

15 For in you, O Becoming-One, do I hope: you will hear, O my Lord(s) my God.

16 For I said, Hear me, lest otherwise they should rejoice over me: when my foot slips, they magnify themselves against me.

17 For I am ready to halt, and my sorrow is continually before me.

18 For I will declare mine iniquity; I will be sorry for my sin.

19 But mine enemies are lively, and they are strong: and they that hate me wrongfully are multiplied.

20 They also that render evil for good are mine adversaries; because I follow the thing that good is.

21 Forsake me not, O Becoming-One: O my God, be not far from me.

22 Make haste to help me, O my Lord(s) my salvation.

Psa 39:1 To the chief Musician, even to Jeduthun, A Psalm of David. I said, I will take heed to my ways, that I sin not with my tongue: I will keep my mouth with a bridle, while the wicked is before me.

2 I was mute with silence, I held my peace, even from good; and my sorrow was stirred.

3 My heart was hot within me, while I was musing the fire burned: then spoke I with my tongue,

4 Becoming-One, make me to know mine end, and the measure of my days, what it is; that I may know how frail I am.

5 Behold, you have made my days as a handbreadth; and mine age is as nothing before you: truly every man at his best state is altogether vanity. Selah.

6 Surely every man walks in a vain show: surely they are disquieted in vain: he heaps up riches, and knows not who shall gather them.

7 And now, my Lord(s), what wait I for? my hope is in you.

8 Deliver me from all my transgressions: make me not the reproach of the foolish.

9 I was mute, I opened not my mouth; because you did it.

10 Remove your stroke away from me: I am consumed by the blow of your hand.

11 When you with rebukes do correct man for iniquity, you make his beauty to consume away like a moth: surely every man is vanity. Selah.

12 Hear my prayer, O Becoming-One, and give ear unto my cry; hold not your peace at my tears: for I am a stranger with you, and a sojourner, as all my fathers were.

13 O spare me, that I may recover strength, before I go hence, and be no more.

Psa 40:1 To the chief Musician, A Psalm of David. I waited patiently for the Becoming-One; and he inclined unto me, and heard my cry.

2 He brought me up also out of a horrible pit, out of the miry clay, and set my feet upon a rock, and established my goings.

3 And he has put a new song in my mouth, even praise unto our God: many shall see it, and fear, and shall trust in the Becoming-One.

4 Blessed is that man that makes the Becoming-One his trust, and respects not the proud, nor such as turn aside to lies.

5 Many, O Becoming-One my God, are your wonderful works which you have done, and your thoughts which are to us-ward: they cannot be reckoned up in order unto you: if I would declare and speak of them, they are more than can be numbered.

6 Sacrifice and offering you did not desire; mine ears have you opened: burnt offering and sin offering have you not required.

7 Then said I, Lo, I come: in the volume of the book it is written of me,

8 I delight to do your will, O my God: yes, your law is within my heart.

9 I have preached righteousness in the great congregation: lo, I have not refrained my lips, O Becoming-One, you know.

10 I have not hid your righteousness within my heart; I have declared your faithfullness and your salvation: I have not concealed your loving-kindness and your truth from the great congregation.

11 Withhold not you your tender mercies from me, O Becoming-One: let your loving-kindness and your truth continually preserve me.

12 For innumerable evils have compassed me about: mine iniquities have taken hold upon me, so that I am not able to look up; they are more than the hairs of mine head: therefore my heart fails me.

13 Be pleased, O Becoming-One, to deliver me: O Becoming-One, make haste to help me.

14 Let them be ashamed and confounded together that seek after my soul to destroy it; let them be driven backward and put to shame that wish me evil.

15 Let them be desolate for a reward of their shame that say unto me, Aha, aha.

16 Let all those that seek you rejoice and be glad in you: let such as love your salvation say continually, The Becoming-One be magnified.

17 But I am poor and needy; yet my Lord(s) thinks of me: you are my help and my deliverer; make no tarrying, O my God.

Psa 41:1 To the chief Musician, A Psalm of David. Blessed is he that considers the poor: the Becoming-One will deliver him in time of trouble.

2 The Becoming-One will preserve him, and keep him alive; and he shall be blessed upon the earth: and you will not deliver him unto the soul of his enemies.

3 The Becoming-One will strengthen him upon the bed of languishing: you will make all his bed in his sickness.

4 I said, Becoming-One, be merciful unto me: heal my soul; for I have sinned against you.

5 Mine enemies speak evil of me, When shall he die, and his name perish?

6 And if he come to see me, he speaks vanity: his heart gathers iniquity to itself; when he goes abroad, he tells it.

7 All that hate me whisper together against me: against me do they devise my hurt.

8 An evil disease, say they, cleaves fast unto him: and now that he lies he shall rise up no more.

9 Yes, mine own familiar friend, in whom I trusted, which did eat of my bread, has lifted up his heel against me.

10 But you, O Becoming-One, be merciful unto me, and raise me up, that I may requite them.

11 By this I know that you favor me, because mine enemy does not triumph over me.

12 And as for me, you uphold me in mine integrity, and set me before your face for olam.

13 Blessed be the Becoming-One, God of Israel from olam and till olam. Amen, and Amen.

Psa 42:1 To the chief Musician, Maschil, for the sons of Korah. As the hart pants after the water brooks, so pants my soul after you, O God.

2 My soul thirsts for God, for the living GOD: when shall I come and appear before God?

3 My tears have been my food day and night, while they all the day say unto me, Where is your God?

4 When I remember these things, I pour out my soul in me: for I had gone with the multitude, I went with them to the house of God, with the voice of joy and praise, with a multitude that kept holyday.

5 Why are you cast down, O my soul? and why are you disquieted in me? hope you in God: for I shall yet praise him for the help of his countenance.

6 O my God, my soul is cast down within me: therefore will I remember you from the land of Jordan, and of the Hermonites, from the hill Mizar.

7 Deep calls unto deep at the noise of your waterspouts: all your waves and your billows are gone over me.

8 Yet the Becoming-One will command his loving-kindness in the daytime, and in the night his song shall be with me, and my prayer unto GOD of my life.

9 I will say unto GOD my rock, Why have you forgotten me? why go I mourning because of the oppression of the enemy?

10 As with a sword in my bones, mine enemies reproach me; while they say all day unto me, Where is your God?

11 Why are you cast down, O my soul? and why are you disquieted within me? hope you in God: for I shall yet praise him, who is the health of my countenance, and my God.

Psa 43:1 Judge me, O God, and plead my cause against an ungodly nation: O deliver me from the deceitful and unjust man.

2 For you are God of my strength: why do you cast me off? why go I mourning because of the oppression of the enemy?

3 O send out your light and your truth: let them lead me; let them bring me unto your holy hill, and to your tabernacles.

4 Then will I go unto the altar of God, unto GOD my exceeding joy: yes, upon the harp will I praise you, O God my God.

5 Why are you cast down, O my soul? and why are you disquieted within me? hope in God: for I shall yet praise him, who is the health of my countenance, and my God.

Psa 44:1 To the chief Musician for the sons of Korah, Maschil. We have heard with our ears, O God, our fathers have told us, what work you did in their days, in the days of old.

2 How you did drive out the nations with your hand, and planted them; how you did afflict the people, and cast them out.

3 For they got not the land in possession by their own sword, neither did their own arm save them: but your right hand, and your arm, and the light of your countenance, because you had a favor unto them.

4 you are my King, O God: command deliverance for Jacob.

5 Through you will we push down our enemies: through your name will we tread them under that rise up against us.

6 For I will not trust in my bow, neither shall my sword save me.

7 But you have saved us from our enemies, and have put them to shame that hated us.

8 In God we boast all the day long, and praise your name for olam. Selah.

9 But you have cast off, and put us to shame; and go not forth with our armies.

10 you make us to turn back from the enemy: and they which hate us spoil for themselves.

11 you have given us like sheep appointed for food; and have scattered us among the nations.

12 you sell your people for nothing, and do not increase your wealth by their price.

13 you make us a reproach to our neighbors, a scorn and a derision to them that are round about us.

14 you make us a byword among the nations, a shaking of the head among the people.

15 My confusion is all the day before me, and the shame of my face has covered me,

16 For the voice of him that reproaches and blasphems; by reason of the enemy and avenger.

17 All this is come upon us; yet have we not forgotten you, neither have we dealt falsely in your covenant.

18 Our heart is not turned back, neither have our steps declined from your way;

19 Though you have greatly broken us in the place of monsters, and covered us with the shadow of death.

20 If we have forgotten the name of our God, or stretched out our hands to a strange god;

21 Shall not God search this out? for he knows the secrets of the heart.

22 Yes, for your sake are we killed all the day long; we are counted as sheep for the slaughter.

23 Awake, why sleep you, O my Lord(s)? arise, cast us not off completely.

24 Why hide you your face, and forget our affliction and our oppression?

25 For our soul is bowed down to the dust: our belly cleaves unto the earth.

26 Arise for our help, and redeem us for your mercies' sake.

Psa 45:1 To the chief Musician upon Shoshannim, for the sons of Korah, Maschil, A Song of loves. My heart is inditing a good matter: I speak of the things which I have made touching the king: my tongue is the pen of a ready writer.

2 you are fairer than the children of men: grace is poured into your lips: therefore God has blessed you for olam.

3 Gird your sword upon your thigh, O most mighty, with your glory and your majesty.

4 And in your majesty ride prosperously because of truth and meekness and righteousness; and your right hand shall teach you terrible things.

5 your arrows are sharp in the heart of the king's enemies; whereby the people fall under you.

6 your throne, O God, is for olam and beyond: the scepter of your kingdom is a right scepter.

7 you love righteousness, and hate wickedness: therefore God, your God, has anointed you with the oil of gladness above your fellows.

8 All your garments smell of myrrh, and aloes, and cassia, out of the ivory palaces, whereby they have made you glad.

9 Kings' daughters were among your honorable women: upon your right hand did stand the queen in gold of Ophir.

10 listen, O daughter, and consider, and incline your ear; forget also your own people, and your father's house;

11 So shall the king greatly desire your beauty: for he is your lords; and worship you him.

12 And the daughter of Tyre shall be there with a gift; even the rich among the people shall entreat your favor.

13 The king's daughter is all glorious within: her clothing is of worked gold.

14 She shall be brought unto the king in raiment of needlework: the virgins her companions that follow her shall be brought unto you.

15 With gladness and rejoicing shall they be brought: they shall enter into the king's palace.

16 Instead of your fathers shall be your children, whom you may make princes in all the earth.

17 I will make your name to be remembered in all generations: therefore shall the people praise you for olam and beyond.

Psa 46:1 To the chief Musician for the sons of Korah, A Song upon Alamoth. God is our refuge and strength, a very present help in trouble.

2 Therefore will not we fear, though the earth be removed, and though the mountains be carried into the midst of the sea;

3 Though the waters thereof roar and be troubled, though the mountains shake with the swelling thereof. Selah.

4 There is a river, the streams whereof shall make glad the city of God, the holy place of the tabernacles of the most High.

5 God is in the midst of her; she shall not be moved: God shall help her, and that right early.

6 The nations raged, the kingdoms were moved: he uttered his voice, the earth melted.

7 The Becoming-One of hosts is with us; God of Jacob is our refuge. Selah.

8 Come, behold the works of the Becoming-One, what desolations he has made in the earth.

9 He makes wars to cease unto the end of the earth; he breaks the bow, and cuts the spear in sunder; he burns the chariot in the fire.

10 Be still, and know that I am God: I will be exalted among the nations, I will be exalted in the earth.

11 The Becoming-One of hosts is with us; the the God of Jacob is our refuge. Selah.

Psa 47:1 To the chief Musician, A Psalm for the sons of Korah. O clap your hands, all you people; shout unto God with the voice of triumph.

2 For the Becoming-One most high is terrible; he is a great King over all the earth.

3 He shall subdue the people under us, and the nations under our feet.

4 He shall choose our inheritance for us, the excellency of Jacob whom he loved. Selah.

5 God is gone up with a shout, the Becoming-One with the sound of a trumpet.

6 Sing praises to God, sing praises: sing praises unto our King, sing praises.

7 For God is the King of all the earth: sing you praises with understanding.

8 God reigns over the nations: God sits upon the throne of his holiness.

9 The princes of the people are gathered together, even the people of God of Abraham: for the shields of the earth belong unto God: he is greatly exalted.

Psa 48:1 A Song and Psalm for the sons of Korah. Great is the Becoming-One, and greatly to be praised in the city of our God, in the mountain of his holiness.

2 Beautiful for situation, the joy of the whole earth, is mount Zion, on the sides of the north, the city of the great King.

3 God is known in her palaces for a refuge.

4 For, lo, the kings were assembled, they passed by together.

5 They saw it, and so they marveled; they were troubled, and hastened away.

6 Fear took hold upon them there, and pain, as of a woman in travail.

7 you break the ships of Tarshish with an east wind.

8 As we have heard, so have we seen in the city of the Becoming-One of hosts, in the city of our God: God will establish it for olam. Selah.

9 We have thought of your loving-kindness, O God, in the midst of your temple.

10 According to your name, O God, so is your praise unto the ends of the earth: your right hand is full of righteousness.

11 Let mount Zion rejoice, let the daughters of Judah be glad, because of your judgments.

12 Walk about Zion, and go round about her: tell the towers thereof.

13 Mark you well her bulwarks, consider her palaces; that you may tell it to the generation following.

14 For this God is our God for olam and beyond: he will be our guide even unto death.

Psa 49:1 To the chief Musician, A Psalm for the sons of Korah. Hear this, all you people; give ear, all you inhabitants of the world:

2 Both low and high, rich and poor, together.

3 My mouth shall speak of wisdom; and the meditation of my heart shall be of understanding.

4 I will incline mine ear to a parable: I will open my dark saying upon the harp.

5 Therefore should I fear in the days of evil, when the iniquity of my heels shall compass me about?

6 They that trust in their wealth, and boast themselves in the multitude of their riches;

7 None of them can by any means redeem his brother, nor give to God a ransom for him:

8 For the redemption of their soul is precious, and it ceases for olam.

9 Yet he will still live for glory, and not see corruption.

10 For he sees that wise men die, likewise the fool and the brutish person perish, and leave their wealth to others.

11 Their inward thought is, that their houses shall continue for olam, and their dwelling places to all generations; they call their lands after their own names.

12 Nevertheless man being in honor abides not: he is like the beasts that perish.

13 This their way is their folly: yet their posterity approve their sayings. Selah.

14 Like sheep they are laid in Sheol; death shall feed on them; and the upright shall have dominion over them in the morning; and their beauty shall consume in Sheol from their dwelling.

15 But God will redeem my soul from the power of Sheol: for he shall receive me. Selah.

16 Be not you afraid when one is made rich, when the glory of his house is increased;

17 For when he dies he shall carry nothing away: his glory shall not descend after him.

18 Though while he lived he blessed his soul: and men will praise you, when you do well to thyself.

19 He shall go to the generation of his fathers; they shall never see light.

20 Man that is in honor, and understands not, is like the beasts that perish.

Psa 50:1 A Psalm of Asaph. GOD of God, even the Becoming-One, has spoken, and called the earth from the rising of the sun unto the going down thereof.

2 Out of Zion, the perfection of beauty, God has shined.

3 Our God shall come, and shall not keep silence: a fire shall devour before him, and it shall be very tempestuous round about him.

4 He shall call to the heavens from above, and to the earth, that he may judge his people.

5 Gather my saints together unto me; those that have made a covenant with me by sacrifice.

6 And the heavens shall declare his righteousness: for God is judge himself. Selah.

7 Hear, O my people, and I will speak; O Israel, and I will testify against you: I am God, even your God.

8 I will not reprove you for your sacrifices or your burnt offerings, to have been continually before me.

9 I will take no bullock out of your house, nor he goats out of your folds.

10 For every beast of the forest is mine, and the cattle upon a thousand hills.

11 I know all the fowls of the mountains: and the wild beasts of the field are mine.

12 If I were hungry, I would not tell you: for the world is mine, and the fullness thereof.

13 Will I eat the flesh of bulls, or drink the blood of goats?

14 Offer unto God thanksgiving; and pay your vows unto the most High:

15 And call upon me in the day of trouble: I will deliver you, and you shall glorify me.

16 But unto the wicked, God says, What have you to do to declare my statutes, or that you should take my covenant in your mouth?

17 Seeing you hate instruction, and cast my words behind you.

18 When you saw a thief, then you consented with him, and have been partaker with adulterers.

19 you give your mouth to evil, and your tongue frames deceit.

20 you sit and speak against your brother; you slander your own mother's son.

21 These things have you done, and I kept silence; you thought that I was altogether such an one as thyself: but I will reprove you, and set them in order before your eyes.

22 Now consider this, you that forget God, lest I tear you in pieces, and there be none to deliver.

23 Whoso offers praise glorifies me: and to him that orders his behavior aright will I show the salvation of God.

Psa 51:1 To the chief Musician, A Psalm of David, when Nathan the prophet came unto him, after he had gone in to Bathsheba. Have mercy upon me, O God, according to your loving-kindness: according unto the multitude of your tender mercies blot out my transgressions.

2 Wash me thoroughly from mine iniquity, and cleanse me from my sin.

3 For I acknowledge my transgressions: and my sin is ever before me.

4 Against you, you only, have I sinned, and done this evil in your sight: that you might be justified when you speak, and be clear when you judge.

5 Behold, I was brought forth [in my mother's birth pains] in iniquity, and in sin did my mother conceive me.

6 Behold, you desire truth in the inward parts: and in the hidden part you shall make me to know wisdom.

7 Purge me with hyssop, and I shall be clean: wash me, and I shall be whiter than snow.

8 Make me to hear joy and gladness; that the bones which you have broken may rejoice.

9 Hide your face from my sins, and blot out all mine iniquities.

10 Create in me a clean heart, O God; and renew a right spirit within me.

11 Cast me not away from your presence; and take not your holy spirit from me.

12 Restore unto me the joy of your salvation; and uphold me with your free spirit.

13 Then will I teach transgressors your ways; and sinners shall be converted unto you.

14 Deliver me from blood guiltiness, O God, God of my salvation: and my tongue shall sing aloud of your righteousness.

15 O my Lord(s), open you my lips; and my mouth shall show forth your praise.

16 For you desire not sacrifice; else would I give it: you delight not in burnt offering.

17 The sacrifices of God are a broken spirit: a broken and a contrite heart, O God, you will not despise.

18 Do good in your good pleasure unto Zion: build you the walls of Jerusalem.

19 Then shall you be pleased with the sacrifices of righteousness, with burnt offering and whole burnt offering: then shall they offer bullocks upon your altar.

Psa 52:1 To the chief Musician, Maschil, A Psalm of David, when Doeg the Edomite came and told Saul, and said unto him, David is come to the house of Ahimelech. Why boast you yourself in mischief, O mighty man? the goodness of GOD endures every day.

2 your tongue devises mischiefs; like a sharp razor, working deceitfully.

3 you love evil more than good; and lying rather than to speak righteousness. Selah.

4 you love all devouring words, O you deceitful tongue.

5 GOD shall likewise destroy you completely, he shall take you away, and pluck you out of your dwelling place, and root you out of the land of the living. Selah.

6 The righteous also shall see, and fear, and shall laugh at him:

7 Lo, this is the man that made not God his strength; but trusted in the abundance of his riches, and strengthened himself in his wickedness.

8 But I am like a green olive tree in the house of God: I trust in the mercy of God for olam and beyond.

9 I will praise you for olam, because you have done it: and I will wait on your name; for it is good before your saints.

Psa 53:1 To the chief Musician upon Mahalath, Maschil, A Psalm of David. The fool has said in his heart, There is no God. Corrupt are they, and have done abominable iniquity: there is none that did good.

2 God looked down from the heavens upon the children of men, to see if there were any that did understand, that did seek God.

3 Every one of them is gone back: they are altogether become filthy; there is none that did good, no, not one.

4 Have the workers of iniquity no knowledge? who eat up my people as they eat bread: they have not called upon God.

5 There were they in great fear, where no fear was: for God has scattered the bones of him that encamps against you: you have put them to shame, because God has despised them.

6 Oh that the salvation of Israel were come out of Zion! When God brings back the captivity of his people, Jacob shall rejoice, and Israel shall be glad.

Psa 54:1 To the chief Musician on Neginoth, Maschil, A Psalm of David, when the Ziphims came and said to Saul, does not David hide himself with us? Save me, O God, by your name, and judge me by your strength.

2 Hear my prayer, O God; give ear to the words of my mouth.

3 For strangers are risen up against me, and the terrible ones seek after my soul: they have not set God before them. Selah.

4 Behold, God is mine helper: my Lord(s) is with them that uphold my soul.

5 He shall reward evil unto mine enemies: cut them off in your truth.

6 I will freely sacrifice unto you: I will praise your name, O Becoming-One; for it is good.

7 For he has delivered me out of all trouble: and mine eye has seen his desire upon mine enemies.

Psa 55:1 To the chief Musician on Neginoth, Maschil, A Psalm of David. Give ear to my prayer, O God; and hide not yourself from my supplication.

2 Attend unto me, and hear me: I mourn in my complaint, and make a noise;

3 Because of the voice of the enemy, because of the oppression of the wicked: for they cast iniquity upon me, and in wrath they hate me.

4 My heart is greatly pained within me: and the terrors of death are fallen upon me.

5 Fearfullness and trembling are come upon me, and horror has overwhelmed me.

6 And I said, Oh that I had wings like a dove! for then would I fly away, and be at rest.

7 Lo, then would I wander far off, and remain in the wilderness. Selah.

8 I would hasten my escape from the windy storm and tempest.

9 Destroy, O my Lord(s), and divide their tongues: for I have seen violence and strife in the city.

10 Day and night they go about it upon the walls thereof: mischief also and sorrow are in the midst of it.

11 Wickedness is in the midst thereof: deceit and guile depart not from her streets.

12 For it was not an enemy that reproached me; then I could have borne it: neither was it he that hated me that did magnify himself against me; then I would have hid myself from him:

13 But it was you, a man mine equal, my guide, and mine acquaintance.

14 We took sweet counsel together, and walked unto the house of God in company.

15 Let death seize upon them, and let them go down quick into Sheol: for wickedness is in their dwellings, and among them.

16 As for me, I will call upon God; and the Becoming-One shall save me.

17 Evening, and morning, and at noon, will I pray, and cry aloud: and he shall hear my voice.

18 He has delivered my soul in peace from the battle that was against me: for there were many with me.

19 GOD shall hear, and afflict them, even he that abides of old. Selah. Because they have no changes, therefore they fear not God.

20 He has put forth his hands against such as be at peace with him: he has broken his covenant.

21 The words of his mouth were smoother than butter, but war was in his heart: his words were softer than oil, yet were they drawn swords.

22 Cast your burden upon the Becoming-One, and he shall sustain you: he shall not for olam permit the righteous to be moved.

23 But you, O God, shall bring them down into the pit of destruction: bloody and deceitful men shall not live out half their days; but I will trust in you.

Psa 56:1 To the chief Musician upon Jonathelemrechok, Michtam of David, when the Philistines took him in Gath. Be merciful unto me, O God: for man would swallow me up; he fighting daily oppresses me.

2 Mine enemies would daily swallow me up: for they be many that fight against me, O you most High.

3 What time I am afraid, I will trust in you.

4 In God I will praise his word, in God I have put my trust; I will not fear what flesh can do unto me.

5 Every day they wrest my words: all their thoughts are against me for evil.

6 They gather themselves together, they hide themselves, they mark my steps, when they wait for my soul.

7 Shall they escape by iniquity? in your anger cast down the people, O God.

8 you tell my wanderings: put you my tears into your bottle: are they not in your book?

9 In the day I cry unto you, then shall mine enemies turn back: this I know; for God is for me.

10 In God will I praise his word: in the Becoming-One will I praise his word.

11 In God have I put my trust: I will not be afraid what man can do unto me.

12 your vows are upon me, O God: I will render praises unto you.

13 For you have delivered my soul from death: will not you deliver my feet from falling, that I may walk before God in the light of the living?

Psa 57:1 To the chief Musician, Altaschith, Michtam of David, when he fled from Saul in the cave. Be merciful unto me, O God, be merciful unto me: for my soul trusts in you: yes, in the shadow of your wings will I make my refuge, until these calamities be overpast.

2 I will cry unto God most high; unto GOD that performs all things for me.

3 He shall send from heaven, and save me from the reproach of him that would swallow me up. Selah. God shall send forth his mercy and his truth.

4 My soul is among lions: and I lie even among them that are set on fire, even the sons of men, whose teeth are spears and arrows, and their tongue a sharp sword.

5 Be you exalted, O God, above the heavens; let your glory be above all the earth.

6 They have prepared a net for my steps; my soul is bowed down: they have dug a pit before me, into the midst whereof they are fallen themselves. Selah.

7 My heart is fixed, O God, my heart is fixed: I will sing and give praise.

8 Awake up, my glory; awake, psaltery and harp: I myself will awake at dawn.

9 I will praise you, O my Lord(s), among the nations: I will sing unto you among the nations.

10 For your mercy is great unto the heavens, and your truth unto the clouds.

11 Be you exalted, O God, above the heavens: let your glory be above all the earth.

Psa 58:1 To the chief Musician, Altaschith, Michtam of David. Do you indeed speak righteousness, O congregation? do you judge uprightly, O you sons of men?

2 Yes, in heart you work wickedness; you weigh the violence of your hands in the earth.

3 The wicked are estranged from the womb: they go astray as soon as they be born, speaking lies.

4 Their poison is like the poison of a serpent: they are like the deaf adder that stops her ear;

5 Which will not listen to the voice of charmers, charming never so wisely.

6 Break their teeth, O God, in their mouth: break out the great teeth of the young lions, O Becoming-One.

7 Let them melt away as waters which run continually: when he bends his bow to shoot his arrows, let them be as cut in pieces.

8 As a snail which melts let every one of them pass away: like the untimely birth of a woman, that they may not see the sun.

9 Before your pots can feel the thorns, he shall take them away as with a whirlwind, both living, and in his wrath.

10 The righteous shall rejoice when he sees the vengeance: he shall wash his feet in the blood of the wicked.

11 So that a man shall say, Truly there is a reward for the righteous: truly he is God that judges in the earth.

Psa 59:1 To the chief Musician, Altaschith, Michtam of David; when Saul sent, and they watched the house to kill him. Deliver me from mine enemies, O my God: defend me from them that rise up against me.

2 Deliver me from the workers of iniquity, and save me from bloody men.

3 For, lo, they lie in wait for my soul: the mighty are gathered against me; not for my transgression, nor for my sin, O Becoming-One.

4 They run and prepare themselves without my fault: awake to help me, and behold.

5 you therefore, O Becoming-One, God of hosts, God of Israel, awake to visit all the nations: be not merciful to any wicked transgressors. Selah.

6 They return at evening: they make a noise like a dog, and go round about the city.

7 Behold, they belch out with their mouth: swords are in their lips: for who, say they, does hear?

8 But you, O Becoming-One, shall laugh at them; you shall have all the nations in derision.

9 Because of his strength will I wait upon you: for God is my defense.

10 God of my mercy shall prevent me: God shall let me see my desire upon mine enemies.

11 Slay them not, lest my people forget: scatter them by your power; and bring them down, O my Lord(s) our shield.

12 For the sin of their mouth and the words of their lips let them even be taken in their pride: and for cursing and lying which they speak.

13 Consume them in wrath, consume them, that they may not be: and let them know that God rules in Jacob unto the ends of the earth. Selah.

14 And at evening let them return; and let them make a noise like a dog, and go round about the city.

15 Let them wander up and down for food, and grudge if they be not satisfied.

16 But I will sing of your power; yes, I will sing aloud of your mercy in the morning: for you have been my defense and refuge in the day of my trouble.

17 Unto you, O my strength, will I sing: for God is my defense, and God of my mercy.

Psa 60:1 To the chief Musician upon Shushaneduth, Michtam of David, to teach; when he strove with Aram-naharaim and with Aramzobah, when Joab returned, and smote of Edom in the valley of salt twelve thousand. O God, you have cast us off, you have scattered us, you have been displeased; O turn yourself to us again.

2 you have made the earth to tremble; you have broken it: heal the breaches thereof; for it shaketh.

3 you have showed your people hard things: you have made us to drink the wine of astonishment.

4 you have given a banner to them that fear you, that it may be displayed because of the truth. Selah.

5 That your beloved may be delivered; save with your right hand, and hear me.

6 God has spoken in his holiness; I will rejoice, I will divide Shechem, and measured out the valley of Succoth.

7 Gilead is mine, and Manasseh is mine; Ephraim also is the strength of mine head; Judah is my lawgiver;

8 Moab is my washpot; over Edom will I cast out my shoe: Philistia, triumph you because of me.

9 Who will bring me into the strong city? who will lead me into Edom?

10 will not you, O God, which had cast us off? and you, O God, which did not go out with our armies?

11 Give us help from trouble: for vain is the help of man.

12 Through God we shall do valiantly: for he it is that shall tread down our enemies.

Psa 61:1 To the chief Musician upon Neginah, A Psalm of David. Hear my cry, O God; attend unto my prayer.

2 From the end of the earth will I cry unto you, when my heart is overwhelmed: lead me to the rock that is higher than I.

3 For you have been a shelter for me, and a strong tower from the enemy.

4 I will abide in your tabernacle for olams, I will trust in the covering of your wings. Selah.

5 For you, O God, have heard my vows: you have given me the heritage of those that fear your name.

6 you will prolong the king's life: and his years as many generations.

7 He shall abide before God for olam. O prepare mercy and truth, which may preserve him.

8 So will I sing praise unto your name to the beyond, that I may daily perform my vows.

Psa 62:1 To the chief Musician, to Jeduthun, A Psalm of David. Truly my soul waits upon God: from him comes my salvation.

2 He only is my rock and my salvation; he is my defense; I shall not be greatly moved.

3 How long will you imagine mischief against a man? you shall be slain all of you: as a bowing wall shall you be, and as a tottering fence.

4 They only consult to cast him down from his excellency: they delight in lies: they bless with their mouth, but they curse inwardly. Selah.

5 My soul, wait you only upon God; for my expectation is from him.

6 He only is my rock and my salvation: he is my defense; I shall not be moved.

7 In God is my salvation and my glory: the rock of my strength, and my refuge, is in God.

8 Trust in him at all times; you people, pour out your heart before him: God is a refuge for us. Selah.

9 Surely men of low degree are vanity, and men of high degree are a lie: to be laid in the balance, they are altogether lighter than vanity.

10 Trust not in oppression, and become not vain in robbery: if riches increase, set not your heart upon them.

11 God has spoken once; twice have I heard this; that power belongs unto God.

12 Also unto you, O my Lord(s), belongs love: for you render to every man according to his work.

Psa 63:1 A Psalm of David, when he was in the wilderness of Judah. O God, you are my GOD; early will I seek you: my soul thirsts for you, my flesh longs for you in a dry and thirsty land, where no water is;

2 To see your power and your glory, so as I have seen you in the sanctuary.

3 Because your loving-kindness is better than life, my lips shall praise you.

4 Thus will I bless you while I live: I will lift up my hands in your name.

5 My soul shall be satisfied as with marrow and fatness; and my mouth shall praise you with joyful lips:

6 When I remember you upon my bed, and meditate on you in the night watches.

7 Because you have been my help, therefore in the shadow of your wings will I rejoice.

8 My soul follows hard after you: your right hand upholds me.

9 But those that seek my soul, to destroy it, shall go into the lower parts of the earth.

10 They shall fall by the sword: they shall be a portion for foxes.

11 But the king shall rejoice in God; every one that sweares by him shall glory: but the mouth of them that speak lies shall be stopped.

Psa 64:1 To the chief Musician, A Psalm of David. Hear my voice, O God, in my prayer: preserve my life from fear of the enemy.

2 Hide me from the secret counsel of the wicked; from the insurrection of the workers of iniquity:

3 Who whet their tongue like a sword, and bend their bows to shoot their arrows, even bitter words:

4 That they may shoot in secret at the perfect: suddenly do they shoot at him, and fear not.

5 They encourage themselves in an evil matter: they commune of laying snares privily; they say, Who shall see them?

6 They search out iniquities; they accomplish a diligent search: both the inward thought of every one of them, and the heart, is deep.

7 But God shall shoot at them with an arrow; suddenly shall they be wounded.

8 So they shall make their own tongue to fall upon themselves: all that see them shall flee away.

9 And all men shall fear, and shall declare the work of God; for they shall wisely consider of his doing.

10 The righteous shall be glad in the Becoming-One, and shall trust in him; and all the upright in heart shall glory.

Psa 65:1 To the chief Musician, A Psalm and Song of David. Praise waits for you, O God, in Sion: and unto you shall the vow be performed.

2 O you that hear prayer, unto you shall all flesh come.

3 Iniquities prevail against me: as for our transgressions, you shall purge them away.

4 Blessed is the man whom you choose, and cause to approach unto you, that he may dwell in your courts: we shall be satisfied with the goodness of your house, even of your holy temple.

5 By terrible things in righteousness will you answer us, O God of our salvation; who are the confidence of all the ends of the earth, and of them that are afar off upon the sea:

6 Which by his strength sets fast the mountains; being girded with power:

7 Which stills the noise of the seas, the noise of their waves, and the tumult of the people.

8 They also that dwell in the uttermost parts are afraid at your tokens: you make the outgoings of the morning and evening to rejoice.

9 you visit the earth, and water it; you greatly enrich it with the river of God, which is full of water: you prepare them grain, when you have so provided for it.

10 you water the ridges thereof abundantly: you settle the furrows thereof: you make it soft with showers: you bless the springing thereof.

11 you crown the year with your goodness; and your paths drop fatness.

12 They drop upon the pastures of the wilderness: and the little hills rejoice on every side.

13 The pastures are clothed with flocks; the valleys also are covered over with grain; they shout for joy, they also sing.

Psa 66:1 To the chief Musician, A Song or Psalm. Make a joyful noise unto God, all you lands:

2 Sing forth the honor of his name: make his praise glorious.

3 Say unto God, How terrible are you in your works! through the greatness of your power shall your enemies submit themselves unto you.

4 All the earth shall worship you, and shall sing unto you; they shall sing to your name. Selah.

5 Come and see the works of God: he is terrible in his doing toward the children of men.

6 He turned the sea into dry land: they went through the flood on foot: there did we rejoice in him.

7 He rules by his power for olam, his eyes behold the nations: let not the rebellious exalt themselves. Selah.

8 O bless our God, you people, and make the voice of his praise to be heard:

9 Which holds our soul in life, and permit not our feet to be moved.

10 For you, O God, have proved us: you have tried us, as silver is tried.

11 you brought us into the net; you laidst affliction upon our loins.

12 you have caused men to ride over our heads; we went through fire and through water: but you brought us out into a wealthy place.

13 I will go into your house with burnt offerings: I will pay you my vows,

14 Which my lips have uttered, and my mouth has spoken, when I was in trouble.

15 I will offer unto you burnt sacrifices of fatlings, with the incense of rams; I will offer bullocks with goats. Selah.

16 Come and hear, all you that fear God, and I will declare what he has done for my soul.

17 I cried unto him with my mouth, and he was extolled with my tongue.

18 If I regard iniquity in my heart, my Lord(s) will not hear me:

19 But truly God has heard me; he has attended to the voice of my prayer.

20 Blessed be God, which has not turned away my prayer, nor his mercy from me.

Psa 67:1 To the chief Musician on Neginoth, A Psalm or Song. God be merciful unto us, and bless us; and cause his face to shine upon us; Selah.

2 That your way may be known upon earth, your saving health among all nations.

3 Let the people praise you, O God; let all the people praise you.

4 O let the nations be glad and sing for joy: for you shall judge the people righteously, and govern the nations upon earth. Selah.

5 Let the people praise you, O God; let all the people praise you.

6 Then shall the earth yield her increase; and God, even our own God, shall bless us.

7 God shall bless us; and all the ends of the earth shall fear him.

Psa 68:1 To the chief Musician, A Psalm or Song of David. Let God arise, let his enemies be scattered: let them also that hate him flee before him.

2 As smoke is driven away, so drive them away: as wax melts before the fire, so let the wicked perish at the presence of God.

3 But let the righteous be glad; let them rejoice before God: yes, let them exceedingly rejoice.

4 Sing unto God, sing praises to his name: extol him that rides upon the heavens by his name JAH, and rejoice before him.

5 A father of the fatherless, and a judge of the widows, is God in his holy habitation.

6 God sets the solitary in families: he brings out those which are bound with chains: but the rebellious dwell in a dry land.

7 O God, when you went forth before your people, when you did march through the wilderness; Selah:

8 The earth shook, the heavens also dropped at the presence of God: even Sinai itself was moved at the presence of God, God of Israel.

9 you, O God, did send a plentiful rain, whereby you did confirm your inheritance, when it was weary.

10 your congregation has dwelt therein: you, O God, have prepared of your goodness for the poor.

11 My Lord(s) gave the word: great was the company of those that proclaim it.

12 Kings of armies did flee apace: and she that tarried at home divided the spoil.

13 Though you have lien among the pots, yet shall you be as the wings of a dove covered with silver, and her feathers with yellow gold.

14 When the Almighty scattered kings in it, it was white as snow in Salmon.

15 The hill of God is as the hill of Bashan; a high hill as the hill of Bashan.

16 Why leap you, you high hills? this is the hill which God desires to dwell in; yes, the Becoming-One will dwell in it for glory.

17 The chariots of God are twenty myriads, even thousands of thousands: my Lord(s) is among them, as in Sinai, in the holy place.

18 you have ascended on high, you have led captivity captive: you have received gifts for men; yes, for the rebellious also, that the Becoming-One God might dwell among them.

19 Blessed be my Lord(s), who daily loads us with benefits, even GOD of our salvation. Selah.

20 He that is our GOD is GOD of salvation; and unto Becoming-One my Lord(s) belong the deliverance from death.

21 But God shall wound the head of his enemies, and the hairy scalp of such an one as goes on still in his trespasses.

22 My Lord(s) said, I will bring again from Bashan, I will bring my people again from the depths of the sea:

23 That your foot may be dipped in the blood of your enemies, and the tongue of your dogs in the same.

24 They have seen your goings, O God; even the goings of my GOD, my King, in the sanctuary.

25 The singers went before, the players on instruments followed after; among them were the damsels playing with timbrels.

26 Bless you God in the congregations, even the Becoming-One, from the assembly of Israel.

27 There is little Benjamin with their ruler, the princes of Judah and their council, the princes of Zebulun, and the princes of Naphtali.

28 your God has commanded your strength: strengthen, O God, that which you have worked for us.

29 Because of your temple at Jerusalem shall kings bring presents unto you.

30 Rebuke the company of spearmen, the multitude of the bulls, with the calves of the people, till every one submit himself with pieces of silver: scatter you the people that delight in war.

31 Princes shall come out of Egypt; Ethiopia shall soon stretch out her hands unto God.

32 Sing unto God, you kingdoms of the earth; O sing praises unto my Lord(s); Selah:

33 To him that rides upon the heavens of the heavens, which were of old; lo, he does send out his voice, and that a mighty voice.

34 Ascribe you strength unto God: his excellency is over Israel, and his strength is in the clouds.

35 O God, you are terrible out of your holy places: GOD of Israel is he that gives strength and power unto his people. Blessed be God.

Psa 69:1 To the chief Musician upon Shoshannim, A Psalm of David. Save me, O God; for the waters are come in unto my soul.

2 I sink in deep mire, where there is no standing: I am come into deep waters, where the floods overflow me.

3 I am weary of my crying: my throat is dried: mine eyes fail while I wait for my God.

4 They that hate me without a cause are more than the hairs of mine head: they that would destroy me, being mine enemies wrongfully, are mighty: then I restored that which I took not away.

5 O God, you know my foolishness; and my sins are not hid from you.

6 Let not them that wait on you, O my Lord(s) the Becoming-One of hosts, be ashamed for my sake: let not those that seek you be confounded for my sake, O God of Israel.

7 Because for your sake I have borne reproach; shame has covered my face.

8 I am become a stranger unto my brethren, and an alien unto my mother's children.

9 For the zeal of your house has eaten me up; and the reproaches of them that reproached you are fallen upon me.

10 When I wept, and chastened my soul with fasting, that was to my reproach.

11 I made sackcloth also my garment; and I became a proverb to them.

12 They that sit in the gate speak against me; and I was the song of the drunkards.

13 But as for me, my prayer is unto you, O Becoming-One, in an acceptable time: O God, in the multitude of your mercy hear me, in the truth of your salvation.

14 Deliver me out of the mire, and let me not sink: let me be delivered from them that hate me, and out of the deep waters.

15 Let not the waterflood overflow me, neither let the deep swallow me up, and let not the pit shut her mouth upon me.

16 Hear me, O Becoming-One; for your lovingkindness is good: turn unto me according to the multitude of your tender mercies.

17 And hide not your face from your servant; for I am in trouble: hear me speedily.

18 Draw near unto my soul, and redeem it: deliver me because of mine enemies.

19 you have known my reproach, and my shame, and my dishonor: mine adversaries are all before you.

20 Reproach has broken my heart; and I am full of heaviness: and I looked for some to take pity, but there was none; and for comforters, but I found none.

21 They gave me also gall for my food; and in my thirst they gave me vinegar to drink.

22 Let their table become a snare before them: and that which should have been for their welfare, let it become a trap.

23 Let their eyes be darkened, that they see not; and make their loins continually to shake.

24 Pour out your indignation upon them, and let your wrathful anger take hold of them.

25 Let their habitation be desolate; and let none dwell in their tents.

26 For they persecute him whom you have struck; and they talk to the grief of those whom you have wounded.

27 Add iniquity unto their iniquity: and let them not come into your righteousness.

28 Let them be blotted out of the book of the living, and not be written with the righteous.

29 But I am poor and sorrowful: let your salvation, O God, set me up on high.

30 I will praise the name of God with a song, and will magnify him with thanksgiving.

31 This also shall please the Becoming-One better than an ox or bullock that has horns and hoofs.

32 The humble shall see this, and be glad: and your heart shall live that seek God.

33 For the Becoming-One hears the poor, and despises not his prisoners.

34 Let the heavens and earth praise him, the seas, and every thing that moves therein.

35 For God will save Zion, and will build the cities of Judah: that they may dwell there, and have it in possession.

36 The seed also of his servants shall inherit it: and they that love his name shall dwell therein.

Psa 70:1 To the chief Musician, A Psalm of David, to bring to remembrance. Make haste, O God, to deliver me; make haste to help me, O Becoming-One.

2 Let them be ashamed and confounded that seek after my soul: let them be turned backward, and put to confusion, that desire my hurt.

3 Let them be turned back for a reward of their shame that say, Aha, aha.

4 Let all those that seek you rejoice and be glad in you: and let such as love your salvation say continually, Let God be magnified.

5 But I am poor and needy: make haste unto me, O God: you are my help and my deliverer; O Becoming-One, make no tarrying.

Psa 71:1 In you, O Becoming-One, do I put my trust: let me not for olam be put to confusion.

2 Deliver me in your righteousness, and cause me to escape: incline your ear unto me, and save me.

3 Be you my strong habitation, whereunto I may continually resort: you have given commandment to save me; for you are my rock and my fortress.

4 Deliver me, O my God, out of the hand of the wicked, out of the hand of the unrighteous and cruel man.

5 For you are my hope, O my Lord(s) the Becoming-One: you are my trust from my youth.

6 By you have I been held up from the womb: you are he that took me out of my mother's bowels: my praise shall be continually of you.

7 I am as a wonder unto many; but you are my strong refuge.

8 Let my mouth be filled with your praise and with your honor all the day.

9 Cast me not off in the time of old age; forsake me not when my strength fails.

10 For mine enemies speak against me; and they that lay wait for my soul take counsel together,

11 Saying, God has forsaken him: persecute and take him; for there is none to deliver him.

12 O God, be not far from me: O my God, make haste for my help.

13 Let them be confounded and consumed that are adversaries to my soul; let them be covered with reproach and dishonor that seek my hurt.

14 But I will hope continually, and will yet praise you more and more.

15 My mouth shall show forth your righteousness and your salvation all the day; for I know not the numbers thereof.

16 I will go in the strength of my Lord(s) the Becoming-One: I will make mention of your righteousness, even of your only.

17 O God, you have taught me from my youth: and hitherto have I declared your wondrous works.

18 Now also when I am old and greyheaded, O God, forsake me not; until I have showed your strength unto this generation, and your power to every one that is to come.

19 your righteousness also, O God, is very high, who have done great things: O God, who is like unto you!

20 you, which have showed me great and sore troubles, shall quicken me again, and shall bring me up again from the depths of the earth.

21 you shall increase my greatness, and comfort me on every side.

22 I will also praise you with the psaltery, even your truth, O my God: unto you will I sing with the harp, O you Holy One of Israel.

23 My lips shall greatly rejoice when I sing unto you; and my soul, which you have redeemed.

24 My tongue also shall talk of your righteousness all the day long: for they are confounded, for they are brought unto shame, that seek my hurt.

Psa 72:1 A Psalm for Solomon. Give the king your judgments, O God, and your righteousness unto the king's son.

2 He shall judge your people with righteousness, and your poor with judgment.

3 The mountains shall bring peace to the people, and the little hills, by righteousness.

4 He shall judge the poor of the people, he shall save the children of the needy, and shall break in pieces the oppressor.

5 They shall fear you as long as the sun and moon endure, throughout all generations.

6 He shall come down like rain upon the mown grass: as showers that water the earth.

7 In his days shall the righteous flourish; and abundance of peace so long as the moon endures.

8 He shall have dominion also from sea to sea, and from the river unto the ends of the earth.

9 They that dwell in the wilderness shall bow before him; and his enemies shall lick the dust.

10 The kings of Tarshish and of the isles shall bring presents: the kings of Sheba and Seba shall offer gifts.

11 Yes, all kings shall fall down before him: all nations shall serve him.

12 For he shall deliver the needy when he cries; the poor also, and him that has no helper.

13 He shall spare the poor and needy, and shall save the souls of the needy.

14 He shall redeem their soul from deceit and violence: and precious shall their blood be in his sight.

15 And he shall live, and to him shall be given of the gold of Sheba: prayer also shall be made for him continually; and all day shall he be praised.

16 There shall be a handful of corn in the earth upon the top of the mountains; the fruit thereof shall shake like Lebanon: and they of the city shall flourish like grass of the earth.

17 His name shall endure for olam, his name shall be continued as long as the sun: and men shall be blessed in him: all nations shall call him blessed.

18 Blessed be the Becoming-One God, God of Israel, who only did wondrous things.

19 And blessed be his glorious name for olam, and let the whole earth be filled with his glory; Amen, and Amen.

20 The prayers of David the son of Jesse are ended.

Psa 73:1 A Psalm of Asaph. Truly God is good to Israel, even to such as are of a clean heart.

2 But as for me, my feet were almost gone; my steps had well near slipped.

3 For I was envious at the foolish, when I saw the prosperity of the wicked.

4 For there are no bands in their death: but their strength is firm.

5 They are not in trouble as other men; neither are they plagued like other men.

6 Therefore pride compasses them about as a chain; violence covers them as a garment.

7 Their eyes stand out with fatness: they have more than heart could wish.

8 They are corrupt, and speak wickedly concerning oppression: they speak loftily.

9 They set their mouth against the heavens, and their tongue walks through the earth.

10 Therefore his people return here: and waters of a full cup are wrung out to them.

11 And they say, How does GOD know? and is there knowledge in the most High?

12 Behold, these are the ungodly, who prosper olam, they increase in riches.

13 Truly I have cleansed my heart in vain, and washed my hands in innocency.

14 For all the day long have I been plagued, and chastened every morning.

15 If I say, I will speak thus; behold, I should offend against the generation of your children.

16 When I thought to know this, it was too painful for me;

17 Until I went into the sanctuary of GOD; then understood I their end.

18 Surely you did set them in slippery places: you casked them down into destruction.

19 How are they brought into desolation, as in a moment! they are utterly consumed with terrors.

20 As a dream when one awakes; so, O my Lord(s), when you awake, you shall despise their image.

21 Thus my heart was grieved, and I was pricked in my reins.

22 So foolish was I, and ignorant: I was as a beast before you.

23 Nevertheless I am continually with you: you have held me by my right hand.

24 you shall guide me with your counsel, and afterward receive me to glory.

25 Whom have I in the heavens but you? and there is none upon earth that I desire beside you.

26 My flesh and my heart fails: but God is the strength of my heart, and my portion for olam.

27 For, lo, they that are far from you shall perish: you have destroyed all them that go a whoring from you.

28 But it is good for me to draw near to God: I have put my trust in my Lord(s) the Becoming-One, that I may declare all your works.

Psa 74:1 Maschil of Asaph. O God, why have you cast us off altogether? why does your anger smoke against the sheep of your pasture?

2 Remember your congregation, which you have purchased of old; the rod of your inheritance, which you have redeemed; this mount Zion, wherein you have dwelt.

3 Lift up your feet unto the complete desolations; even all that the enemy has done wickedly in the sanctuary.

4 your enemies roar in the midst of your congregations; they set up their ensigns for signs.

5 A man was famous according as he had lifted up axes upon the thick trees.

6 But now they break down the carved work thereof at once with axes and hammers.

7 They have cast fire into your sanctuary, they have defiled by casting down the dwelling place of your name to the ground.

8 They said in their hearts, Let us destroy them together: they have burned up all the synagogues of GOD in the land.

9 We see not our signs: there is no more any prophet: neither is there among us any that knows how long.

10 O God, how long shall the adversary reproach? shall the enemy blaspheme your name completely?

11 Why withdraw you your hand, even your right hand? pluck it out of your bosom.

12 For God is my King of old, working salvation in the midst of the earth.

13 you did divide the sea by your strength: you brake the heads of the monsters in the waters.

14 you brake the heads of leviathan in pieces, and gave him to be food to the people inhabiting the wilderness.

15 you did cleave the fountain and the flood: you dried up mighty rivers.

16 The day is yours, the night also is yours: you have prepared the light and the sun.

17 you have set all the borders of the earth: you have made summer and winter.

18 Remember this, that the enemy has reproached, O Becoming-One, and that the foolish people have blasphemed your name.

19 O deliver not the soul of your turtledove unto the multitude of the wicked: forget not the congregation of your poor completely.

20 Have respect unto the covenant: for the dark places of the earth are full of the habitations of cruelty.

21 O let not the oppressed return ashamed: let the poor and needy praise your name.

22 Arise, O God, plead your own cause: remember how the foolish man reproaches you daily.

23 Forget not the voice of your enemies: the tumult of those that rise up against you increases continually.

Psa 75:1 To the chief Musician, Altaschith, A Psalm or Song of Asaph. Unto you, O God, do we give thanks, unto you do we give thanks: for that your name is near your wondrous works declare.

2 When I shall receive the congregation I will judge uprightly.

3 The earth and all the inhabitants thereof are dissolved: I bear up the pillars of it. Selah.

4 I said unto the fools, Deal not foolishly: and to the wicked, Lift not up the horn:

5 Lift not up your horn on high: speak not with a stiff neck.

6 For promotion comes neither from the east, nor from the west, nor from the south.

7 But God is the judge: he puts down one, and sets up another.

8 For in the hand of the Becoming-One there is a cup, and the wine is red: it is full of mixture; and he pours out of the same: but the dregs thereof, all the wicked of the earth shall wring them out, and drink them.

9 But I will declare for olam, I will sing praises to God of Jacob.

10 All the horns of the wicked also will I cut off; but the horns of the righteous shall be exalted.

Psa 76:1 To the chief Musician on Neginoth, A Psalm or Song of Asaph. In Judah is God known: his name is great in Israel.

2 In Salem also is his tabernacle, and his dwelling place in Zion.

3 There brake he the arrows of the bow, the shield, and the sword, and the battle. Selah.

4 you are more glorious and excellent than the mountains of prey.

5 The stouthearted are spoiled, they have slept their sleep: and none of the men of might have found their hands.

6 At your rebuke, O God of Jacob, both the chariot and horse are cast into a dead sleep.

7 you, even you, are to be feared: and who may stand in your sight when once you are angry?

8 you did cause judgment to be heard from heaven; the earth feared, and was still,

9 When God arose to judgment, to save all the meek of the earth. Selah.

10 Surely the wrath of man shall praise you: the remainder of wrath shall you restrain.

11 Vow, and pay unto the Becoming-One your God: let all that be round about him bring presents unto him that ought to be feared.

12 He shall cut off the spirit of princes: he is terrible to the kings of the earth.

Psa 77:1 To the chief Musician, to Jeduthun, A Psalm of Asaph. I cried unto God with my voice, even unto God with my voice; and he gave ear unto me.

2 In the day of my trouble I sought my Lord(s): my sore ran in the night, and ceased not: my soul refused to be comforted.

3 I remembered God, and was troubled: I complained, and my spirit was overwhelmed. Selah.

4 you hold mine eyes waking: I am so troubled that I cannot speak.

5 I have considered the days of old, the years of olams [past].

6 I call to remembrance my song in the night: I commune with mine own heart: and my spirit made diligent search.

7 Will my Lord(s) cast off for olams and will he be favorable no more?

8 Is his mercy clean gone? does his word fail to all generations?

9 has GOD forgotten to be gracious? has he in anger shut up his tender mercies? Selah.

10 And I said, This is my infirmity: but I will remember the years of the right hand of the most High.

11 I will remember the works of the Becoming-One: surely I will remember your wonders of old.

12 I will meditate also of all your work, and talk of your doings.

13 your way, O God, is in the sanctuary: who is so great a GOD as our God?

14 you are GOD that do wonders: you have declared your strength among the people.

15 you have with your arm redeemed your people, the sons of Jacob and Joseph. Selah.

16 The waters saw you, O God, the waters saw you; they were afraid: the depths also were troubled.

17 The clouds poured out water: the skies sent out a sound: your arrows also went abroad.

18 The voice of your thunder was in the heaven: the lightning lightened the world: the earth trembled and shook.

19 your way is in the sea, and your path in the great waters, and your footsteps are not known.

20 you led your people like a flock by the hand of Moses and Aaron.

Psa 78:1 Maschil of Asaph. Give ear, O my people, to my law: incline your ears to the words of my mouth.

2 I will open my mouth in a parable: I will utter dark sayings of old:

3 Which we have heard and known, and our fathers have told us.

4 We will not hide them from their children, showing to the generation to come the praises of the Becoming-One, and his strength, and his wonderful works that he has done.

5 For he established a testimony in Jacob, and appointed a law in Israel, which he commanded our fathers, that they should make them known to their children:

6 That the generation to come might know them, even the children which should be born; who should arise and declare them to their children:

7 That they might set their hope in God, and not forget the works of GOD, but keep his commandments:

8 And might not be as their fathers, a stubborn and rebellious generation; a generation that set not their heart aright, and whose spirit was not steadfast with GOD.

9 The children of Ephraim, being armed, and carrying bows, turned back in the day of battle.

10 They kept not the covenant of God, and refused to walk in his law;

11 And forgot his works, and his wonders that he had showed them.

12 Marvelous things did he in the sight of their fathers, in the land of Egypt, in the field of Zoan.

13 He divided the sea, and caused them to pass through; and he made the waters to stand as a heap.

14 In the daytime also he led them with a cloud, and all the night with a light of fire.

15 He split the rocks in the wilderness, and gave them drink as out of the great depths.

16 He brought streams also out of the rock, and caused waters to run down like rivers.

17 And they sinned yet more against him by provoking the most High in the wilderness.

18 And they tempted GOD in their heart by asking food for their soul.

19 Yes, they spoke against God; they said, Can GOD furnish a table in the wilderness?

20 Behold, he smote the rock, that the waters gushed out, and the streams overflowed; can he give bread also? can he provide flesh for his people?

21 Therefore the Becoming-One heard this, and was angry: so a fire was kindled against Jacob, and anger also came up against Israel;

22 Because they believed not in God, and trusted not in his salvation:

23 Though he had commanded the clouds from above, and opened the doors of heaven,

24 And had rained down manna upon them to eat, and had given them of the corn of heaven.

25 Man did eat angels' food: he sent them food to the full.

26 He caused an east wind to blow in the heaven: and by his power he brought in the south wind.

27 He rained flesh also upon them as dust, and feathered fowls like as the sand of the sea:

28 And he let it fall in the midst of their camp, round about their habitations.

29 So they did eat, and were well filled: for he gave them their own desire;

30 They were not estranged from their lust. But while their food was yet in their mouths,

31 The wrath of God came upon them, and killed the fattest of them, and smote down the chosen men of Israel.

32 For all this they sinned still, and believed not for his wondrous works.

33 Therefore their days did he consume in vanity, and their years in trouble.

34 When he killed them, then they sought him: and they returned and inquired early after GOD.

35 And they remembered that God was their rock, and the high GOD their redeemer.

36 Nevertheless they did flatter him with their mouth, and they lied unto him with their tongues.

37 For their heart was not right with him, neither were they steadfast in his covenant.

38 But he, being full of compassion, forgave their iniquity, and destroyed them not: yes, many a time turned he his anger away, and did not stir up all his wrath.

39 For he remembered that they were but flesh; a wind that passes away, and comes not again.

40 How oft did they provoke him in the wilderness, and grieve him in the desert!

41 Yes, they turned back and tempted GOD, and limited the Holy One of Israel.

42 They remembered not his hand, nor the day when he delivered them from the enemy.

43 How he had worked his signs in Egypt, and his wonders in the field of Zoan:

44 And had turned their rivers into blood; and their floods, that they could not drink.

45 He sent diverse sorts of flies among them, which devoured them; and frogs, which destroyed them.

46 He gave also their increase unto the caterpillar, and their labor unto the locust.

47 He destroyed their vines with hail, and their sycamore trees with frost.

48 He gave up their cattle also to the hail, and their flocks to hot thunderbolts.

49 He cast upon them the fierceness of his anger, wrath, and indignation, and trouble, by sending evil angels among them.

50 He made a way to his anger; he spared not their soul from death, but gave their life over to the pestilence;

51 And smote all the firstborn in Egypt; the beginning of their strength in the tabernacles of Ham:

52 But made his own people to go forth like sheep, and guided them in the wilderness like a flock.

53 And he led them on safely, so that they feared not: but the sea overwhelmed their enemies.

54 And he brought them to the border of his sanctuary, even to this mountain, which his right hand had purchased.

55 He cast out the nations also before them, and divided them an inheritance by line, and made the tribes of Israel to dwell in their tents.

56 Yet they tempted and provoked the most high God, and kept not his testimonies:

57 But turned back, and dealt unfaithfully like their fathers: they were turned aside like a deceitful bow.

58 For they provoked him to anger with their high places, and moved him to jealousy with their graven images.

59 When God heard this, he was angry, and greatly abhorred Israel:

60 So that he forsook the tabernacle of Shiloh, the tent which he placed among men;

61 And delivered his strength into captivity, and his glory into the enemy's hand.

62 He gave his people over also unto the sword; and was angry with his inheritance.

63 The fire consumed their young men; and their maidens were not given to marriage.

64 Their priests fell by the sword; and their widows made no lamentation.

65 Then my Lord(s) awaked as one out of sleep, and like a mighty man that shouts by reason of wine.

66 And he smote his enemies in the hinder parts: he put them to a reproach of olam.

67 Moreover he refused the tabernacle of Joseph, and chose not the tribe of Ephraim:

68 But chose the tribe of Judah, the mount Zion which he loved.

69 And he built his sanctuary like high palaces, like the earth which he has established for olam.

70 He chose David also his servant, and took him from the sheep folds:

71 From following the ewes great with young he brought him to feed Jacob his people, and Israel his inheritance.

72 So he fed them according to the integrity of his heart; and guided them by the skillfullness of his hands.

Psa 79:1 A Psalm of Asaph. O God, the nations are come into your inheritance; your holy temple have they defiled; they have laid Jerusalem on heaps.

2 The dead bodies of your servants have they given to be food unto the fowls of the heaven, the flesh of your saints unto the beasts of the earth.

3 Their blood have they shed like water round about Jerusalem; and there was none to bury them.

4 We are become a reproach to our neighbors, a scorn and derision to them that are round about us.

5 How long, Becoming-One? will you be angry for glory? shall your jealousy burn like fire?

6 Pour out your wrath upon the nations that have not known you, and upon the kingdoms that have not called upon your name.

7 For they have devoured Jacob, and laid waste his dwelling place.

8 O remember not against us former iniquities: let your tender mercies speedily prevent us: for we are brought very low.

9 Help us, O God of our salvation, for the glory of your name: and deliver us, and purge away our sins, for your name's sake.

10 Therefore should the nations say, Where is their God? let him be known among the nations in our sight by the revenging of the blood of your servants which is shed.

11 Let the sighing of the prisoner come before you; according to the greatness of your power preserve you those that are appointed to die;

12 And render unto our neighbors sevenfold into their bosom their reproach, wherewith they have reproached you, O my Lord(s).

13 So we your people and sheep of your pasture will give you thanks for olam, we will show forth your praise to all generations.

Psa 80:1 To the chief Musician upon Shoshannimeduth, A Psalm of Asaph. Give ear, O Shepherd of Israel, you that lead Joseph like a flock; you that dwell between the cherubs, shine forth.

2 Before Ephraim and Benjamin and Manasseh stir up your strength, and come and save us.

3 Turn us again, O God, and cause your face to shine; and we shall be saved.

4 O Becoming-One, God of hosts, how long will you be angry against the prayer of your people?

5 you feed them with the bread of tears; and give them tears to drink in great measure.

6 you make us a strife unto our neighbors: and our enemies laugh among themselves.

7 Turn us again, O God of hosts, and cause your face to shine; and we shall be saved.

8 you have brought a vine out of Egypt: you have cast out the nations, and planted it.

9 you prepared room before it, and did cause it to take deep root, and it filled the land.

10 The hills were covered with the shadow of it, and the boughs thereof were like the cedars of GOD.

11 She sent out her boughs unto the sea, and her branches unto the river.

12 Why have you then broken down her hedges, so that all they which pass by the way do pluck her?

13 The boar out of the wood does waste it, and the wild beast of the field does devour it.

14 Return, we beg you, O God of hosts: look down from heaven, and behold, and visit this vine;

15 And the vineyard which your right hand has planted, and the branch that you made strong for thyself.

16 It is burned with fire, it is cut down: they perish at the rebuke of your countenance.

17 Let your hand be upon the man of your right hand, upon the son of man whom you made strong for thyself.

18 So will not we go back from you: quicken us, and we will call upon your name.

19 Turn us again, O Becoming-One, God of hosts, cause your face to shine; and we shall be saved.

Psa 81:1 To the chief Musician upon Gittith, A Psalm of Asaph. Sing aloud unto God our strength: make a joyful noise unto God of Jacob.

2 Take a psalm, and bring here the timbrel, the pleasant harp with the psaltery.

3 Blow up the trumpet in the new moon, in the time appointed, on our solemn feast day.

4 For this was a statute for Israel, and a law of God of Jacob.

5 This he ordained in Joseph for a testimony, when he went out through the land of Egypt: where I heard a language that I understood not.

6 I removed his shoulder from the burden: his hands were delivered from the pots.

7 you calledst in trouble, and I delivered you; I answered you in the secret place of thunder: I proved you at the waters of Meribah. Selah.

8 Hear, O my people, and I will testify unto you: O Israel, if you will listen unto me;

9 There shall no strange god be in you; neither shall you worship any strange god.

10 I am the Becoming-One your God, which brought you out of the land of Egypt: open your mouth wide, and I will fill it.

11 But my people would not listen to my voice; and Israel would none of me.

12 So I gave them up unto their own hearts' lust: and they walked in their own counsels.

13 Oh that my people had listened unto me, and Israel had walked in my ways!

14 I should soon have subdued their enemies, and turned my hand against their adversaries.

15 The haters of the Becoming-One should have submitted themselves unto him: but their time should have endured for olam.

16 He should have fed them also with the finest of the wheat: and with honey out of the rock should I have satisfied you.

Psa 82:1 A Psalm of Asaph. GOD stands in the congregation of GOD; he judges among the gods.

2 How long will you judge unjustly, and accept the persons of the wicked? Selah.

3 Defend the poor and fatherless: do justice to the afflicted and needy.

4 Deliver the poor and needy: rid them out of the hand of the wicked.

5 They know not, neither will they understand; they walk on in darkness: all the foundations of the earth are out of course.

6 I have said, you are God [elohim]; and all of you are children of the most High.

7 But you shall die like men, and fall like one of the princes.

8 Arise, O God, judge the earth: for you shall inherit all nations.

Psa 83:1 A Song or Psalm of Asaph. Keep not you silence, O GOD: hold not your peace, and be not still, O God.

2 For, lo, your enemies make a tumult: and they that hate you have lifted up the head.

3 They have taken crafty counsel against your people, and consulted against your hidden ones.

4 They have said, Come, and let us cut them off from being a nation; that the name of Israel may be no more in remembrance.

5 For they have consulted together with one consent: they are confederate against you:

6 The tabernacles of Edom, and the Ishmaelites; of Moab, and the Hagarenes;

7 Gebal, and Ammon, and Amalek; the Philistines with the inhabitants of Tyre;

8 Assur also is joined with them: they have holpen the children of Lot. Selah.

9 Do unto them as unto the Midianites; as to Sisera, as to Jabin, at the brook of Kison:

10 Which perished at Endor: they became as dung for the earth.

11 Make their nobles like Oreb, and like Zeeb: yes, all their princes as Zebah, and as Zalmunna:

12 Who said, Let us take to ourselves the houses of God in possession.

13 O my God, make them like a wheel; as the stubble before the wind.

14 As the fire burns a wood, and as the flame sets the mountains on fire;

15 So persecute them with your tempest, and make them afraid with your storm.

16 Fill their faces with shame; that they may seek your name, O Becoming-One.

17 Let them be confounded and troubled to the beyond; yes, let them be put to shame, and perish:

18 That men may know that you, whose name alone is, Becoming-One, are the most high over all the earth.

Psa 84:1 To the chief Musician upon Gittith, A Psalm for the sons of Korah. How amiable are your tabernacles, O Becoming-One of hosts!

2 My soul longs yes, even faints for the courts of the Becoming-One: my heart and my flesh cries out for the living GOD.

3 Yes, the sparrow has found a house, and the swallow a nest for herself, where she may lay her young, even your altars, O Becoming-One of hosts, my King, and my God.

4 Blessed are they that dwell in your house: they will be still praising you. Selah.

5 Blessed is the man whose strength is in you; in whose heart are the ways of them.

6 Who passing through the valley of Baca make it a well; the rain also fills the pools.

7 They go from strength to strength, every one of them in Zion appears before God.

8 O Becoming-One, God of hosts, hear my prayer: give ear, O God of Jacob. Selah.

9 Behold, O God our shield, and look upon the face of your anointed [Messiah].

10 For a day in your courts is better than a thousand. I had rather be a doorkeeper in the house of my God, than to dwell in the tents of wickedness.

11 For the Becoming-One God is a sun and shield: the Becoming-One will give grace and glory: no good thing will he withhold from them that walk uprightly.

12 O Becoming-One of hosts, blessed is the man that trusts in you.

Psa 85:1 To the chief Musician, A Psalm for the sons of Korah. Becoming-One, you have been favorable unto your land: you have brought back the captivity of Jacob.

2 you have forgiven the iniquity of your people, you have covered all their sin. Selah.

3 you have taken away all your wrath: you have turned yourself from the fierceness of your anger.

4 Turn us, O God of our salvation, and cause your anger toward us to cease.

5 will you be angry with us for olam, will you draw out your anger to all generations?

6 will you not revive us again: that your people may rejoice in you?

7 Show us your mercy, O Becoming-One, and grant us your salvation.

8 I will hear what GOD the Becoming-One will speak: for he will speak peace unto his people, and to his saints: but let them not turn again to folly.

9 Surely his salvation is near them that fear him; that glory may dwell in our land.

10 Mercy and truth are met together; righteousness and peace have kissed each other.

11 Truth shall spring out of the earth; and righteousness shall look down from heaven.

12 Yes, the Becoming-One shall give that which is good; and our land shall yield her increase.

13 Righteousness shall go before him; and shall set us in the way of his steps.

Psa 86:1 A Prayer of David. Bow down your ear, O Becoming-One, hear me: for I am poor and needy.

2 Preserve my soul; for I am holy: O you my God, save your servant that trusts in you.

3 Be merciful unto me, O my Lord(s): for I cry unto you daily.

4 Rejoice the soul of your servant: for unto you, O my Lord(s), do I lift up my soul.

5 For you, my Lord(s), are good, and ready to forgive; and plenteous in mercy unto all them that call upon you.

6 Give ear, O Becoming-One, unto my prayer; and attend to the voice of my supplications.

7 In the day of my trouble I will call upon you: for you will answer me.

8 Among the gods there is none like unto you, O my Lord(s); neither are there any works like unto your works.

9 All nations whom you have made shall come and worship before you, O my Lord(s); and shall glorify your name.

10 For you are great, and do wondrous things: you are God alone.

11 Teach me your way, O Becoming-One; I will walk in your truth: unite my heart to fear your name.

12 I will praise you, O my Lord(s) my God, with all my heart: and I will glorify your name for olam.

13 For great is your mercy toward me: and you have delivered my soul from the lowest Sheol.

14 O God, the proud are risen against me, and the assemblies of terrible men have sought after my soul; and have not set you before them.

15 But you, O my Lord(s), are a GOD full of compassion, and gracious, patient, and plenteous in mercy and truth.

16 O turn unto me, and have mercy upon me; give your strength unto your servant, and save the son of your handmaid.

17 Show me a token for good; that they which hate me may see it, and be ashamed: because you, Becoming-One, have holpen me, and comforted me.

Psa 87:1 A Psalm or Song for the sons of Korah. His foundation is in the holy mountains.

2 The Becoming-One loves the gates of Zion more than all the dwellings of Jacob.

3 Glorious things are spoken of you, O city of God. Selah.

4 I will make mention of Rahab pride and Babylon to them that know me: behold Philistia, and Tyre, with Ethiopia; this man was born there.

5 And of Zion it shall be said, This and that man was born in her: and the highest himself shall establish her.

6 The Becoming-One shall count, when he writes up the people, that this man was born there. Selah.

7 As well the singers as the players on instruments shall be there: all my springs are in you.

Psa 88:1 A Song or Psalm for the sons of Korah, to the chief Musician upon Mahalath Leannoth, Maschil of Heman the Ezrahite. O Becoming-One, God of my salvation, I have cried day and night before you:

2 Let my prayer come before you: incline your ear unto my cry;

3 For my soul is full of troubles: and my life draws near unto Sheol.

4 I am counted with them that go down into the pit: I am as a man that has no strength:

5 Free among the dead, like the slain that lie in the grave, whom you remember no more: and they are cut off from your hand.

6 you have laid me in the lowest pit, in darkness, in the deeps.

7 your wrath lies hard upon me, and you have afflicted me with all your waves. Selah.

8 you have put away mine acquaintance far from me; you have made me an abomination unto them: I am shut up, and I cannot come forth.

9 Mine eye mourns by reason of affliction: Becoming-One, I have called daily upon you, I have stretched out my hands unto you.

10 will you show wonders to the dead? shall the dead arise and praise you? Selah.

11 Shall your loving-kindness be declared in the grave? or your faithfullness in destruction?

12 Shall your wonders be known in the dark? and your righteousness in the land of forgetfullness?

13 But unto you have I cried, O Becoming-One; and in the morning shall my prayer prevent you.

14 Becoming-One, why cast you off my soul? why hide you your face from me?

15 I am afflicted and ready to die from my youth up: while I suffer your terrors I am distracted.

16 your fierce wrath goes over me; your terrors have cut me off.

17 They came round about me all day like water; they compassed me about together.

18 Lover and friend have you put far from me, and mine acquaintance into darkness.

Psa 89:1 Maschil of Ethan the Ezrahite. I will sing of the mercies of the Becoming-One for olam, with my mouth will I make known your faithfullness to all generations.

2 For I have said, Mercy shall be built up for olam, your faithfullness shall you establish in the very heavens.

3 I have made a covenant with my chosen, I have sworn unto David my servant,

4 your seed will I establish for olam, and build up your throne to all generations. Selah.

5 And the heavens shall praise your wonders, O Becoming-One: your faithfullness also in the congregation of the saints.

6 For who in the heavens can be compared unto the Becoming-One? who among the sons of GOD can be likened unto the Becoming-One?

7 GOD is greatly to be feared in the assembly of the saints, and to be had in reverence of all them that are about him.

8 O Becoming-One, God of hosts, who is a strong Becoming-One like unto you? or to your faithfullness round about you?

9 you rule the raging of the sea: when the waves thereof arise, you still them.

10 you have broken Rahab pride in pieces, as one that is slain; you have scattered your enemies with your strong arm.

11 The heavens are yours, the earth also is yours: as for the world and the fullness thereof, you have founded them.

12 The north and the south you have created them: Tabor and Hermon shall rejoice in your name.

13 you have a mighty arm: strong is your hand, and high is your right hand.

14 Justice and judgment are the habitation of your throne: mercy and truth shall go before your face.

15 Blessed is the people that know the joyful sound: they shall walk, O Becoming-One, in the light of your countenance.

16 In your name shall they rejoice all the day: and in your righteousness shall they be exalted.

17 For you are the glory of their strength: and in your favor our horn shall be exalted.

18 For the Becoming-One is our defense; and the Holy One of Israel is our king.

19 Then you spoke in vision to your holy one, and said, I have laid help upon one that is mighty; I have exalted one chosen out of the people.

20 I have found David my servant; with my holy oil have I anointed him:

21 With whom my hand shall be established: mine arm also shall strengthen him.

22 The enemy shall not exact upon him; nor the son of wickedness afflict him.

23 And I will beat down his foes before his face, and plague them that hate him.

24 But my faithfullness and my mercy shall be with him: and in my name shall his horn be exalted.

25 I will set his hand also in the sea, and his right hand in the rivers.

26 He shall cry unto me, you are my father, my GOD, and the rock of my salvation.

27 Also I will make him my firstborn, higher than the kings of the earth.

28 My mercy will I keep for him for olam, and my covenant shall stand firm with him.

29 His seed also will I make to endure to the beyond, and his throne as the days of heaven.

30 If his children forsake my law, and walk not in my judgments;

31 If they break my statutes, and keep not my commandments;

32 Then will I visit their transgression with the rod, and their iniquity with stripes.

33 Nevertheless my loving-kindness will I not utterly take from him, nor permit my faithfullness to fail.

34 My covenant will I not break, nor alter the thing that is gone out of my lips.

35 Once have I sworn by my holiness that I will not lie unto David.

36 His seed shall endure for olam, and his throne as the sun before me.

37 It shall be established for olam as the moon, and as a faithful witness in heaven. Selah.

38 But you have cast off and abhorred, you have been angry with your anointed [Messsiah].

39 you have made void the covenant of your servant: you have profaned his crown by casting it to the ground.

40 you have broken down all his hedges; you have brought his strong holds to ruin.

41 All that pass by the way spoil him: he is a reproach to his neighbors.

42 you have set up the right hand of his adversaries; you have made all his enemies to rejoice.

43 you have also turned the edge of his sword, and have not made him to stand in the battle.

44 you have made his glory to cease, and cast his throne down to the ground.

45 The days of his youth have you shortened: you have covered him with shame. Selah.

46 How long, Becoming-One? will you hide yourself completely? shall your wrath burn like fire?

47 Remember how short my time is: therefore have you made all men in vain?

48 What man is he that lives, and shall not see death? shall he deliver his soul from the hand of Sheol? Selah.

49 My Lord(s), where are your former lovingkindnesses, which you swore unto David in your truth?

50 Remember, my Lord(s), the reproach of your servants; how I do bear in my bosom the reproach of all the many nations;

51 Wherewith your enemies have reproached, O Becoming-One; wherewith they have reproached the footsteps of your anointed [Messiah].

52 Blessed be the Becoming-One for olam. Amen, and Amen.

Psa 90:1 A Prayer of Moses the man of God. Becoming-One, you have been our dwelling place in all generations.

2 Before the mountains were brought forth, or ever you had formed the earth and the world, even from olam to olam, you are GOD.

3 you turn man to destruction; and say, Return, you children of men.

4 For a **thousand years** in your sight are but as yesterday when it is past, and as a watch in the night.

5 you carried them away as with a flood; they are as a sleep: in the morning they are like grass which grows up.

6 In the morning it flourishes, and grows up; in the evening it is cut down, and withereth.

7 For we are consumed by your anger, and by your wrath are we troubled.

8 you have set our iniquities before you, our secret sins in the light of your countenance.

9 For all our days are passed away in your wrath: we spend our years as a tale that is told.

10 The days of our years are threescore years and ten; and if by reason of strength they be fourscore years, yet is their strength labor and sorrow; for it is soon cut off, and we fly away.

11 Who knows the power of your anger? even according to your fear, so is your wrath.

12 So teach us to number our days, that we may apply our hearts unto wisdom.

13 Return, O Becoming-One, how long? and let it repent you concerning your servants.

14 O satisfy us early with your mercy; that we may rejoice and be glad all our days.

15 Make us glad according to the days wherein you have afflicted us, and the years wherein we have seen evil.

16 Let your work appear unto your servants, and your glory unto their children.

17 And let the beauty of the Becoming-One our God be upon us: and establish you the work of our hands upon us; yes, the work of our hands establish you it.

Psa 91:1 He that dwells in the secret place of the most High shall abide under the shadow of the Almighty.

2 I will say of the Becoming-One, He is my refuge and my fortress: my God; in him will I trust.

3 Surely he shall deliver you from the snare of the fowler, and from the noisome pestilence.

4 He shall cover you with his feathers, and under his wings shall you trust: his truth shall be your shield and buckler.

5 you shall not be afraid for the terror by night; nor for the arrow that flies by day;

6 Nor for the pestilence that walks in darkness; nor for the destruction that wastes at noonday.

7 a thousand shall fall at your side, and a multitude at your right hand; but it shall not come near you.

8 Only with your eyes shall you behold and see the reward of the wicked.

9 Because you have made the Becoming-One, which is my refuge, even the most High, your habitation;

10 There shall no evil befall you, neither shall any plague come near your dwelling.

11 For he shall give his angels charge over you, to keep you in all your ways.

12 They shall bear you up in their hands, lest you dash your foot against a stone.

13 you shall tread upon the lion and adder: the young lion and the monster shall you trample under feet.

14 Because he has set his love upon me, therefore will I deliver him: I will set him on high, because he has known my name.

15 He shall call upon me, and I will answer him: I will be with him in trouble; I will deliver him, and honor him.

16 With long life will I satisfy him, and show him my salvation.

Psa 92:1 A Psalm or Song for the Sabbath day. It is a good thing to give thanks unto the Becoming-One, and to sing praises unto your name, O most High:

2 To show forth your loving-kindness in the morning, and your faithfullness every night,

3 Upon an instrument of ten strings, and upon the psaltery; upon the harp with a solemn sound.

4 For you, Becoming-One, have made me glad through your work: I will triumph in the works of your hands.

5 O Becoming-One, how great are your works! and your thoughts are very deep.

6 A brutish man knows not; neither does a fool understand this.

7 When the wicked spring as the grass, and when all the workers of iniquity do flourish; it is that they shall be destroyed to the beyond:

8 But you, Becoming-One, are most high for olam.

9 For, lo, your enemies, O Becoming-One, for, lo, your enemies shall perish; all the workers of iniquity shall be scattered.

10 But my horn shall you exalt like the horn of a reem [wild ox or beast] I shall be anointed with fresh oil.

11 Mine eye also shall see my desire on mine enemies, and mine ears shall hear my desire of the wicked that rise up against me.

12 The righteous shall flourish like the palm tree: he shall grow like a cedar in Lebanon.

13 Those that be planted in the house of the Becoming-One shall flourish in the courts of our God.

14 They shall still bring forth fruit in old age; they shall be fat and flourishing;

15 To show that the Becoming-One is upright: he is my rock, and there is no unrighteousness in him.

Psa 93:1 The Becoming-One reigns, he is clothed with majesty; the Becoming-One is clothed with strength, wherewith he has girded himself: the world also is established, that it cannot be moved.

2 your throne is established from that time: you are from olam.

3 The floods have lifted up, O Becoming-One, the floods have lifted up their voice; the floods lift up their waves.

4 The Becoming-One on high is mightier than the noise of many waters, yes, than the mighty waves of the sea.

5 your testimonies are very sure: holiness becomes your house, O Becoming-One, for length of days.

Psa 94:1 O Becoming-One, GOD to whom vengeance belongs; O GOD to whom vengeance belongs, show thyself.

2 Lift up thyself, you judge of the earth: render a reward to the proud.

3 Becoming-One, how long shall the wicked, how long shall the wicked triumph?

4 How long shall they utter and speak hard things? and all the workers of iniquity boast themselves?

5 They break in pieces your people, O Becoming-One, and afflict your heritage.

6 They slay the widow and the stranger, and murder the fatherless.

7 Yet they say, The Becoming-One shall not see, neither shall God of Jacob regard it.

8 Understand, you brutish among the people: and you fools, when will you be wise?

9 He that planted the ear, shall he not hear? he that formed the eye, shall he not see?

10 He that chastises the nations, shall not he correct? he that teaches man knowledge, shall not he know?

11 The Becoming-One knows the thoughts of man, that they are vanity.

12 Blessed is the man whom you chasten, O Becoming-One, and teach him out of your law;

13 That you may give him rest from the days of adversity, until the pit be dug for the wicked.

14 For the Becoming-One will not cast off his people, neither will he forsake his inheritance.

15 But judgment shall return unto righteousness: and all the upright in heart shall follow it.

16 Who will rise up for me against the evildoers? or who will stand up for me against the workers of iniquity?

17 Unless the Becoming-One had been my help, my soul had almost dwelt in silence.

18 When I said, My foot slips; your mercy, O Becoming-One, held me up.

19 In the multitude of my thoughts within me your comforts delight my soul.

20 Shall the throne of iniquity have fellowship with you, which frames mischief by a law?

21 They gather themselves together against the soul of the righteous, and condemn the innocent blood.

22 But the Becoming-One is my defense; and my God is the rock of my refuge.

23 And he shall bring upon them their own iniquity, and shall cut them off in their own wickedness; yes, the Becoming-One our God shall cut them off.

Psa 95:1 O come, let us sing unto the Becoming-One: let us make a joyful noise to the rock of our salvation.

2 Let us come before his presence with thanksgiving, and make a joyful noise unto him with psalms.

3 For the Becoming-One is a great GOD, and a great King above all gods.

4 In his hand are the deep places of the earth: the strength of the hills is his also.

5 The sea is his, and he made it: and his hands formed the dry land.

6 O come, let us worship and bow down: let us kneel before the Becoming-One our maker.

7 For he is our God; and we are the people of his pasture, and the sheep of his hand. Today if you will hear his voice,

8 Harden not your heart, as in the provocation, and as in the day of temptation in the wilderness:

9 When your fathers tempted me, proved me, and saw my work.

10 Forty years long was I grieved with this generation, and said, It is a people that do err in their heart, and they have not known my ways:

11 Unto whom I swore in my wrath that they should not enter into my rest.

Psa 96:1 O sing unto the Becoming-One a new song: sing unto the Becoming-One, all the earth.

2 Sing unto the Becoming-One, bless his name; show forth his salvation from day to day.

3 Declare his glory among the nations, his wonders among all people.

4 For the Becoming-One is great, and greatly to be praised: he is to be feared above all gods.

5 For all the gods of the nations are idols: but the Becoming-One made the heavens.

6 Honor and majesty are before him: strength and beauty are in his sanctuary.

7 Give unto the Becoming-One, O you kindreds of the people, give unto the Becoming-One glory and strength.

8 Give unto the Becoming-One the glory due unto his name: bring an offering, and come into his courts.

9 O worship the Becoming-One in the beauty of holiness: fear before him, all the earth.

10 Say among the nations that the Becoming-One reigns: the world also shall be established that it shall not be moved: he shall judge the people righteously.

11 Let the heavens rejoice, and let the earth be glad; let the sea roar, and the fullness thereof.

12 Let the field be joyful, and all that is therein: then shall all the trees of the wood rejoice

13 Before the Becoming-One: for he comes, for he comes to judge the earth: he shall judge the world with righteousness, and the people with his truth.

Psa 97:1 The Becoming-One reigns; let the earth rejoice; let the multitude of isles be glad thereof.

2 Clouds and darkness are round about him: righteousness and judgment are the habitation of his throne.

3 A fire goes before him, and burns up his enemies round about.

4 His lightning enlightened the world: the earth saw, and trembled.

5 The hills melted like wax at the presence of the Becoming-One, at the presence of the Lord of the whole earth.

6 The heavens declare his righteousness, and all the people see his glory.

7 Confounded be all they that serve graven images, that boast themselves of idols: worship him, all you gods.

8 Zion heard, and was glad; and the daughters of Judah rejoiced because of your judgments, O Becoming-One.

9 For you, Becoming-One, are high above all the earth: you are exalted far above all gods.

10 you that love the Becoming-One, hate evil: he preserves the souls of his saints; he delivers them out of the hand of the wicked.

11 Light is sown for the righteous, and gladness for the upright in heart.

12 Rejoice in the Becoming-One, you righteous; and give thanks at the remembrance of his holiness.

Psa 98:1 A Psalm. O sing unto the Becoming-One a new song; for he has done marvelous things: his right hand, and his holy arm, has gotten him the victory.

2 The Becoming-One has made known his salvation: his righteousness has he openly showed in the sight of the nations.

3 He has remembered his mercy and his truth toward the house of Israel: all the ends of the earth have seen the salvation of our God.

4 Make a joyful noise unto the Becoming-One, all the earth: make a loud noise, and rejoice, and sing praise.

5 Sing unto the Becoming-One with the harp; with the harp, and the voice of a psalm.

6 With trumpets and sound of cornet make a joyful noise before the Becoming-One, the King.

7 Let the sea roar, and the fullness thereof; the world, and they that dwell therein.

8 Let the floods clap their hands: let the hills be joyful together

9 Before the Becoming-One; for he comes to judge the earth: with righteousness shall he judge the world, and the people with equity.

Psa 99:1 The Becoming-One reigns; let the people tremble: he sits between the cherubs;[124] let the earth be moved.

2 The Becoming-One is great in Zion; and he is high above all the people.

3 Let them praise your great and terrible name; for it is holy.

4 The king's strength also loves judgment; you do establish equity, you execute judgment and righteousness in Jacob.

5 Exalt you the Becoming-One our God, and worship at his footstool; for he is holy.

6 Moses and Aaron among his priests, and Samuel among them that call upon his name; they called upon the Becoming-One, and he answered them.

7 He spoke unto them in the cloudy pillar: they kept his testimonies, and the ordinance that he gave them.

8 you answered them, O Becoming-One our God: you were a GOD that forgave them, though you took vengeance of their inventions.

9 Exalt the Becoming-One our God, and worship at his holy hill; for the Becoming-One our God is holy.

Psa 100:1 A Psalm of praise. Make a joyful noise unto the Becoming-One, all you lands.

2 Serve the Becoming-One with gladness: come before his presence with singing.

3 Know you that the Becoming-One he is God: it is he that has made us, and not we ourselves; we are his people, and the sheep of his pasture.

4 Enter into his gates with thanksgiving, and into his courts with praise: be thankful unto him, and bless his name.

5 For the Becoming-One surely good, surely mercy is for olam, and his truth endures to all generations.

Psa 101:1 A Psalm of David. I will sing of mercy and judgment: unto you, O Becoming-One, will I sing.

2 I will behave myself wisely in a perfect way. O when will you come unto me? I will walk within my house with a perfect heart.

3 I will set no wicked thing before mine eyes: I hate the work of them that turn aside; it shall not cleave to me.

4 A perverse heart shall depart from me: I will not know a wicked person.

5 Whoso privily slanders his neighbor, him will I cut off: him that has a high look and a proud heart will not I permit.

6 Mine eyes shall be upon the faithful of the land, that they may dwell with me: he that walks in a perfect way, he shall serve me.

---

[124] Or "He inhibits [the] cherubs"

7 He that works deceit shall not dwell within my house: he that tells lies shall not tarry in my sight.

8 I will early destroy all the wicked of the land; that I may cut off all wicked doers from the city of the Becoming-One.

Psa 102:1 A Prayer of the afflicted, when he is overwhelmed, and pours out his complaint before the Becoming-One. Hear my prayer, O Becoming-One, and let my cry come unto you.

2 Hide not your face from me in the day when I am in trouble; incline your ear unto me: in the day when I call answer me speedily.

3 For my days are consumed like smoke, and my bones are burned as a hearth.

4 My heart is struck, and withered like grass; so that I forget to eat my bread.

5 By reason of the voice of my groaning my bones cleave to my skin.

6 I am like a pelican of the wilderness: I am like an owl of the desert.

7 I watch, and am as a sparrow alone upon the house top.

8 Mine enemies reproach me all the day; and they that are mad against me are sworn against me.

9 For I have eaten ashes like bread, and mingled my drink with weeping,

10 Because of your indignation and your wrath: for you have lifted me up, and cast me down.

11 My days are like a shadow that declines; and I am withered like grass.

12 But you, O Becoming-One, shall endure for olam, and your remembrance unto all generations.

13 you shall arise, and have mercy upon Zion: for the time to favor her, yes, the set time,[125] is come.

14 For your servants take pleasure in her stones, and favor the dust thereof.

15 So the nations shall fear the name of the Becoming-One, and all the kings of the earth your glory.

16 When the Becoming-One shall build up Zion, he shall appear in his glory.

17 He will regard the prayer of the destitute, and not despise their prayer.

18 This shall be written for the generation to come: and the people which shall be created shall praise the Becoming-One.

19 For he has looked down from the height of his sanctuary; from the heavens did the Becoming-One behold the earth;

20 To hear the groaning of the prisoner; to loose those that are appointed to death;

21 To declare the name of the Becoming-One in Zion, and his praise in Jerusalem;

22 When the people are gathered together, and the kingdoms, to serve the Becoming-One.

23 He weakened my strength in the way; he shortened my days.

24 I said, O my GOD, take me not away in the midst of my days: your years are throughout all generations.

25 Of old have you laid the foundation of the earth: and the heavens are the work of your hands.

26 They shall perish, but you shall endure: yes, all of them shall wax old like a garment; as a vesture shall you change them, and they shall be changed:

27 But you are the same, and your years shall have no end.

28 The children of your servants shall continue, and their seed shall be established before you.

Psa 103:1 A Psalm of David. Bless the Becoming-One, O my soul: and all that is within me, bless his holy name.

2 Bless the Becoming-One, O my soul, and forget not all his benefits:

3 Who forgives all your iniquities; who heals all your diseases;

4 Who redeems your life from destruction; who crowns you with loving-kindness and tender mercies;

5 Who satisfies your mouth with good things; so that your youth is renewed like the eagle's.

6 The Becoming-One executes righteousness and judgment for all that are oppressed.

7 He made known his ways unto Moses, his acts unto the children of Israel.

8 The Becoming-One is merciful and gracious, slow to anger, and plenteous in mercy.

9 He will not always chide: neither will he keep his anger for olam.

10 He has not dealt with us after our sins; nor rewarded us according to our iniquities.

11 For as the heavens is high above the earth, so great is his mercy toward them that fear him.

12 As far as the east is from the west, so far has he removed our transgressions from us.

13 Like as a father pities his children, so the Becoming-One pities them that fear him.

14 For he knows our frame; he remembers that we are dust.

15 As for man, his days are as grass: as a flower of the field, so he flourishes.

16 For the wind passes over it, and it is gone; and the place thereof shall know it no more.

17 But the mercy of the Becoming-One is from olam to olam upon them that fear him, and his righteousness unto children's children;

18 To such as keep his covenant, and to those that remember his commandments to do them.

19 The Becoming-One has prepared his throne in the heavens; and his kingdom rules over all.

20 Bless the Becoming-One, you his angels, that excel in strength, that do his commandments, listening unto the voice of his word.

21 Bless you the Becoming-One, all you his hosts; you ministers of his, that do his pleasure.

22 Bless the Becoming-One, all his works in all places of his dominion: bless the Becoming-One, O my soul.

Psa 104:1 Bless the Becoming-One, O my soul. O Becoming-One my God, you are very great; you are clothed with honor and majesty.

2 Who cover yourself with light as with a garment: who stretch out the heavens like a curtain:

---

[125] Appointed time or festival

3 Who lays the beams of his chambers in the waters: who makes the clouds his chariot: who walks upon the wings of the wind:

4 Who makes his angels spirits; his ministers a flaming fire:

5 Who laid the foundations of the earth, that it should not be removed to the beyond.

6 you covered it with the deep as with a garment: the waters stood above the mountains.

7 At your rebuke they fled; at the voice of your thunder they hastened away.

8 They go up by the mountains; they go down by the valleys unto the place which you have founded for them.

9 you have set a bound that they may not pass over; that they turn not again to cover the earth.

10 He sends the springs into the valleys, which run among the hills.

11 They give drink to every beast of the field: the wild donkeys quench their thirst.

12 By them shall the fowls of the heavens have their habitation, which sing among the branches.

13 He waters the hills from his chambers: the earth is satisfied with the fruit of your works.

14 He causes the grass to grow for the cattle, and herb for the service of man: that he may bring forth food out of the earth;

15 And wine that makes glad the heart of man, and oil to make his face to shine, and bread which strengthens man's heart.

16 The trees of the Becoming-One are full of sap; the cedars of Lebanon, which he has planted;

17 Where the birds make their nests: as for the stork, the fir trees are her house.

18 The high hills are a refuge for the wild goats; and the rocks for the conies.

19 He appointed the moon for set time:[126] the sun knows his going down.

20 you make darkness, and it is night: wherein all the beasts of the forest do creep forth.

21 The young lions roar after their prey, and seek their food from GOD.

22 The sun arises, they gather themselves together, and lay them down in their dens.

23 Man goes forth unto his work and to his labor until the evening.

24 O Becoming-One, how manifold are your works! in wisdom have you made them all: the earth is full of your riches.

25 So is this great and wide sea, wherein are things creeping innumerable, both small and great beasts.

26 There go the ships: there is that leviathan, whom you have made to play therein.

27 These wait all upon you; that you may give them their food in due season.

28 That you give them they gather: you open your hand, they are filled with good.

29 you hide your face, they are troubled: you take away their breath, they die, and return to their dust.

30 you send forth your spirit, they are created: and you renew the face of the earth.

31 The glory of the Becoming-One shall endure for olam, the Becoming-One shall rejoice in his works.

32 He looks on the earth, and it trembles: he touches the hills, and they smoke.

33 I will sing unto the Becoming-One as long as I live: I will sing praise to my God while I have my being.

34 My meditation of him shall be sweet: I will be glad in the Becoming-One.

35 Let the sinners be consumed out of the earth, and let the wicked be no more. Bless you the Becoming-One, O my soul. Praise you the Becoming-One.

Psa 105:1 O give thanks unto the Becoming-One; call upon his name: make known his deeds among the people.

2 Sing unto him, sing psalms unto him: talk you of all his wondrous works.

3 Glory you in his holy name: let the heart of them rejoice that seek the Becoming-One.

4 Seek the Becoming-One, and his strength: seek his face continually.

5 Remember his marvelous works that he has done; his wonders, and the judgments of his mouth;

6 O you seed of Abraham his servant, you children of Jacob his chosen.

7 He is the Becoming-One our God: his judgments are in all the earth.

8 He has remembered his covenant for olam, the word which he commanded to a thousand generations.

9 Which covenant he made with Abraham, and his oath unto Isaac;

10 And confirmed the same unto Jacob for a law, and to Israel for a covenant of olam.

11 Saying, Unto you will I give the land of Canaan, the lot of your inheritance:

12 When they were but a few men in number; yes, very few, and strangers in it.

13 When they went from one nation to another, from one kingdom to another people;

14 He permitted no man to do them wrong: yes, he reproved kings for their sakes;

15 Saying, Touch not mine anointed [Messiah], and do my prophets no harm.

16 Moreover he called for a famine upon the land: he brake the whole staff of bread.

17 He sent a man before them, even Joseph, who was sold for a servant:

18 Whose feet they hurt with fetters: he was laid in iron:

19 Until the time that his word came: the word of the Becoming-One tried him.

20 The king sent and loosened him; even the ruler of the people, and let him go free.

21 He made him lord of his house, and ruler of all his substance:

22 To bind his princes of his soul; and teach his senators wisdom.

23 Israel also came into Egypt; and Jacob sojourned in the land of Ham.

24 And he increased his people greatly; and made them stronger than their enemies.

---

[126] Appointed time or festival

25 He turned their heart to hate his people, to deal subtly with his servants.

26 He sent Moses his servant; and Aaron whom he had chosen.

27 They showed his signs among them, and wonders in the land of Ham.

28 He sent darkness, and made it dark; and they rebelled not against his word.

29 He turned their waters into blood, and killed their fish.

30 Their land brought forth frogs in abundance, in the chambers of their kings.

31 He spoke, and there came diverse sorts of flies, and gnats in all their coasts.

32 He gave them hail for rain, and flaming fire in their land.

33 He smote their vines also and their fig trees; and brake the trees of their coasts.

34 He spoke, and the locusts came, and caterpillars, and that without number,

35 And did eat up all the herbs in their land, and devoured the fruit of their ground.

36 He smote also all the firstborn in their land, the beginning of all their strength.

37 He brought them forth also with silver and gold: and there was not one feeble person among their tribes.

38 Egypt was glad when they departed: for the fear of them fell upon them.

39 He spread a cloud for a covering; and fire to give light in the night.

40 The people asked, and he brought quails, and satisfied them with the bread of heaven.

41 He opened the rock, and the waters gushed out; they ran in the dry places like a river.

42 For he remembered his holy promise, and Abraham his servant.

43 And he brought forth his people with joy, and his chosen with gladness:

44 And gave them the lands of the nations: and they inherited the labor of the people;

45 That they might observe his statutes, and keep his laws. Praise you the Becoming-One.

Psa 106:1 Praise you the Becoming-One. O give thanks unto the Becoming-One; surely good, surely mercy is for olam.

2 Who can utter the mighty acts of the Becoming-One? who can show forth all his praise?

3 Blessed are they that keep judgment, and he that did righteousness at all times.

4 Remember me, O Becoming-One, with the favor that you bear unto your people: O visit me with your salvation;

5 That I may see the good of your chosen, that I may rejoice in the gladness of your nation, that I may glory with your inheritance.

6 We have sinned with our fathers, we have committed iniquity, we have done wickedly.

7 Our fathers understood not your wonders in Egypt; they remembered not the multitude of your mercies; but provoked him at the sea, even at the boundary sea.

8 Nevertheless he saved them for his name's sake, that he might make his mighty power to be known.

9 He rebuked the boundary sea also, and it was dried up: so he led them through the depths, as through the wilderness.

10 And he saved them from the hand of him that hated them, and redeemed them from the hand of the enemy.

11 And the waters covered their enemies: there was not one of them left.

12 Then believed they his words; they sang his praise.

13 They soon forgat his works; they waited not for his counsel:

14 But lusted exceedingly in the wilderness, and tempted GOD in the desert.

15 And he gave them their request; but sent leanness into their soul.

16 They envied Moses also in the camp, and Aaron the saint of the Becoming-One.

17 The earth opened and swallowed up Dathan, and covered the company of Abiram.

18 And a fire was kindled in their company; the flame burned up the wicked.

19 They made a calf in Horeb, and worshiped the molten image.

20 Thus they changed their glory into the similitude of an ox that eats grass.

21 They forgat GOD their Savior, which had done great things in Egypt;

22 Wondrous works in the land of Ham, and terrible things by the boundary sea.

23 Therefore he said that he would destroy them, had not Moses his chosen stood before him in the breach, to turn away his wrath, lest he should destroy them.

24 Yes, they despised the pleasant land, they believed not his word:

25 But murmured in their tents, and listened not unto the voice of the Becoming-One.

26 Therefore he lifted up his hand against them, to overthrow them in the wilderness:

27 To overthrow their seed also among the nations, and to scatter them in the lands.

28 They joined themselves also unto Baal-Peor, and ate the sacrifices of the dead.

29 Thus they provoked him to anger with their inventions: and the plague brake in upon them.

30 Then stood up Phinehas, and executed judgment: and so the plague was stayed.

31 And that was counted unto him for righteousness unto all generations for olam.

32 They angered him also at the waters of strife, so that it went ill with Moses for their sakes:

33 Because they provoked his spirit, so that he spoke unadvisedly with his lips.

34 They did not destroy the nations, concerning whom the Becoming-One commanded them:

35 But were mingled among the nations, and learned their works.

36 And they served their idols: which were a snare unto them.

37 Yes, they sacrificed their sons and their daughters unto devils,

38 And shed innocent blood, even the blood of their sons and of their daughters, whom they sacrificed unto the idols of Canaan: and the land was polluted with blood.

39 Thus were they defiled with their own works, and went a whoring with their own inventions.

40 Therefore was the wrath of the Becoming-One kindled against his people, insomuch that he abhorred his own inheritance.

41 And he gave them into the hand of the nations; and they that hated them ruled over them.

42 Their enemies also oppressed them, and they were brought into subjection under their hand.

43 Many times did he deliver them; but they provoked him with their counsel, and were brought low for their iniquity.

44 Nevertheless he regarded their affliction, when he heard their cry:

45 And he remembered for them his covenant, and repented according to the multitude of his mercies.

46 He made them also to be pitied of all those that carried them captives.

47 Save us, O Becoming-One our God, and gather us from among the nations, to give thanks unto your holy name, and to triumph in your praise.

48 Blessed be the Becoming-One, God of Israel from olam to olam, and let all the people say, Amen. Praise you the Becoming-One.

Psa 107:1 O give thanks unto the Becoming-One, for good: for his mercy endures for olam.

2 Let the redeemed of the Becoming-One say so, whom he has redeemed from the hand of the enemy;

3 And gathered them out of the lands, from the east, and from the west, from the north, and from the south.

4 They wandered in the wilderness in a solitary way; they found no city to dwell in.

5 Hungry and thirsty, their soul fainted in them.

6 Then they cried unto the Becoming-One in their trouble, and he delivered them out of their distresses.

7 And he led them forth by the right way, that they might go to a city of habitation.

8 Oh that men would praise the Becoming-One for his goodness, and for his wonderful works to the children of men!

9 For he satisfies the longing soul, and fills the hungry soul with goodness.

10 Such as sit in darkness and in the shadow of death, being bound in affliction and iron;

11 Because they rebelled against the words of GOD, and contemned the counsel of the most High:

12 Therefore he brought down their heart with labor; they fell down, and there was none to help.

13 Then they cried unto the Becoming-One in their trouble, and he saved them out of their distresses.

14 He brought them out of darkness and the shadow of death, and brake their bands in sunder.

15 Oh that men would praise the Becoming-One for his goodness, and for his wonderful works to the children of men!

16 For he has broken the gates of brass, and cut the bars of iron in sunder.

17 Fools because of their transgression, and because of their iniquities, are afflicted.

18 Their soul abhors all manner of food; and they draw near unto the gates of death.

19 Then they cry unto the Becoming-One in their trouble, and he saves them out of their distresses.

20 He sent his word, and healed them, and delivered them from their destructions.

21 Oh that men would praise the Becoming-One for his goodness, and for his wonderful works to the children of men!

22 And let them sacrifice the sacrifices of thanksgiving, and declare his works with rejoicing.

23 They that go down to the sea in ships, that do business in great waters;

24 These see the works of the Becoming-One, and his wonders in the deep.

25 For he commands, and raises the stormy wind, which lifts up the waves thereof.

26 They mount up to the heaven, they go down again to the depths: their soul is melted because of trouble.

27 They reel back and forth, and stagger like a drunken man, and are at their wit's end.

28 Then they cry unto the Becoming-One in their trouble, and he brings them out of their distresses.

29 He makes the storm a calm, so that the waves thereof are still.

30 Then are they glad because they be quiet; so he brings them unto their desired haven.

31 Oh that men would praise the Becoming-One for his goodness, and for his wonderful works to the children of men!

32 Let them exalt him also in the congregation of the people, and praise him in the assembly of the elders.

33 He turns rivers into a wilderness, and the water springs into dry ground;

34 A fruitful land into barrenness, for the wickedness of them that dwell therein.

35 He turns the wilderness into a standing water, and dry ground into water springs.

36 And there he makes the hungry to dwell, that they may prepare a city for habitation;

37 And sow the fields, and plant vineyards, which may yield fruits of increase.

38 He blesses them also, so that they are multiplied greatly; and permit not their cattle to decrease.

39 Again, they are diminished and brought low through oppression, affliction, and sorrow.

40 He pours contempt upon princes, and causes them to wander in the wilderness, where there is no way.

41 Yet sets he the poor on high from affliction, and makes him families like a flock.

42 The righteous shall see it, and rejoice: and all iniquity shall stop her mouth.

43 Whoso is wise, and will observe these things, even they shall understand the loving-kindness of the Becoming-One.

Psa 108:1 A Song or Psalm of David. O God, my heart is fixed; I will sing and give praise, even with my glory.

2 Awake, psaltery and harp: I myself will awake at dawn.

3 I will praise you, O Becoming-One, among the people: and I will sing praises unto you among the nations.

4 For your mercy is great above the heavens: and your truth reaches unto the clouds.

5 Be you exalted, O God, above the heavens: and your glory above all the earth;

6 That your beloved may be delivered: save with your right hand, and answer me.

7 God has spoken in his holiness; I will rejoice, I will divide Shechem, and measured out the valley of Succoth.

8 Gilead is mine; Manasseh is mine; Ephraim also is the strength of mine head; Judah is my lawgiver;

9 Moab is my washbasin; over Edom will I cast out my shoe; over Philistia will I triumph.

10 Who will bring me into the strong city? who will lead me into Edom?

11 will not you, O God, who have cast us off? and will not you, O God, go forth with our hosts?

12 Give us help from trouble: for vain is the help of man.

13 Through God we shall do valiantly: for he it is that shall tread down our enemies.

Psa 109:1 To the chief Musician, A Psalm of David. Hold not your peace, O God of my praise;

2 For the mouth of the wicked and the mouth of the deceitful are opened against me: they have spoken against me with a lying tongue.

3 They compassed me about also with words of hatred; and fought against me without a cause.

4 For my love they are my adversaries: but I give myself unto prayer.

5 And they have rewarded me evil for good, and hatred for my love.

6 Set you a wicked man over him: and let Satan stand at his right hand.

7 When he shall be judged, let him be condemned: and let his prayer become sin.

8 Let his days be few; and let another take his office.

9 Let his children be fatherless, and his wife a widow.

10 Let his children be continually vagabonds, and beg: let them seek their bread also out of their desolate places.

11 Let the extortionist catch all that he has; and let the strangers spoil his labor.

12 Let there be none to extend mercy unto him: neither let there be any to favor his fatherless children.

13 Let his end be cut off; and in the generation following let their name be blotted out.

14 Let the iniquity of his fathers be remembered with the Becoming-One; and let not the sin of his mother be blotted out.

15 Let them be before the Becoming-One continually, that he may cut off the memory of them from the earth.

16 Because that he remembered not to show mercy, but persecuted the poor and needy man, that he might even slay the broken in heart.

17 As he loved cursing, so let it come unto him: as he delighted not in blessing, so let it be far from him.

18 As he clothed himself with cursing like as with his garment, so let it come into his bowels like water, and like oil into his bones.

19 Let it be unto him as the garment which covers him, and for a girdle wherewith he is girded continually.

20 Let this be the reward of mine adversaries from the Becoming-One, and of them that speak evil against my soul.

21 But do you for me, O Becoming-One, my Lord(s), for your name's sake: because your mercy is good, deliver you me.

22 For I am poor and needy, and my heart is wounded within me.

23 I am gone like the shadow when it declines: I am tossed up and down as the locust.

24 My knees are weak through fasting; and my flesh fails of fatness.

25 I became also a reproach unto them: when they looked upon me they shaked their heads.

26 Help me, O Becoming-One my God: O save me according to your mercy:

27 That they may know that this is your hand; that you, Becoming-One, have done it.

28 Let them curse, but bless you: when they arise, let them be ashamed; but let your servant rejoice.

29 Let mine adversaries be clothed with shame, and let them cover themselves with their own confusion, as with a mantle.

30 I will greatly praise the Becoming-One with my mouth; yes, I will praise him among the multitude.

31 For he shall stand at the right hand of the poor, to save him from those that condemn his soul.

Psa 110:1 A Psalm of David. The Becoming-One said unto my Lord, Sit you at my right hand, until I make your enemies your footstool.

2 The Becoming-One shall send the rod of your strength out of Zion: rule you in the midst of your enemies.

3 your people shall be willing in the day of your power, in the beauties of holiness from the womb of the morning: you have the dew of your youth.

4 The Becoming-One has sworn, and will not repent, you are a priest for olam, after the order of Melchizedek.

5 My Lord(s),[127] at your right hand he shall strike through kings in the day of his wrath.

6 He shall judge among the nations, he shall fill the places with the dead bodies; he shall wound the heads over many countries.

7 He shall drink of the brook in the way: therefore shall he lift up the head.

Psa 111:1 Praise you the Becoming-One. I will praise the Becoming-One with my whole heart, in the assembly of the upright, and in the congregation.

2 The works of the Becoming-One are great, sought out of all them that have pleasure therein.

---

[127] "My Lords" = **Becoming-One** (see, Psa 140:7)

3 His work is honorable and glorious: and his righteousness endures to the beyond.

4 He has made his wonderful works to be remembered: the Becoming-One is gracious and full of compassion.

5 He has given food unto them that fear him: he will to olam be mindful of his covenant.

6 He has showed his people the power of his works, that he may give them the heritage of the nations.

7 The works of his hands are verity and judgment; all his commandments are sure.

8 They stand firm for olam and beyond, and are done in truth and uprightness.

9 He sent redemption unto his people: he has commanded his covenant for olam, holy and reverend is his name.

10 The fear of the Becoming-One is the beginning of wisdom: a good understanding have all they that do his commandments: his praise endures to the beyond.

Psa 112:1 Praise you the Becoming-One. Blessed is the man that fears the Becoming-One, that delights greatly in his commandments.

2 His seed shall be mighty upon earth: the generation of the upright shall be blessed.

3 Wealth and riches shall be in his house: and his righteousness endures to the beyond.

4 Unto the upright there arises light in the darkness: he is gracious, and full of compassion, and righteous.

5 A good man shows favor, and lends: he will guide his affairs with discretion.

6 Surely he shall not be moved for olam, the righteous shall be in remembrance of olam.

7 He shall not be afraid of evil tidings: his heart is fixed, trusting in the Becoming-One.

8 His heart is established, he shall not be afraid, until he see his desire upon his enemies.

9 He has dispersed, he has given to the poor; his righteousness endures to the beyond; his horn shall be exalted with honor.

10 The wicked shall see it, and be grieved; he shall gnash with his teeth, and melt away: the desire of the wicked shall perish.

Psa 113:1 Praise you the Becoming-One. Praise, O you servants of the Becoming-One, praise the name of the Becoming-One.

2 Blessed be the name of the Becoming-One from this time forth and for olam.

3 From the rising of the sun unto the going down of the same the Becoming-One's name is to be praised.

4 The Becoming-One is high above all nations, and his glory above the heavens.

5 Who is like unto the Becoming-One our God, who dwells on high,

6 Who humbles himself to behold the things that are in heaven, and in the earth!

7 He raises up the poor out of the dust, and lifts the needy out of the dunghill;

8 That he may set him with princes, even with the princes of his people.

9 He makes the barren woman to keep house, and to be a joyful mother of children. Praise you the Becoming-One.

Psa 114:1 When Israel went out of Egypt, the house of Jacob from a people of strange language;

2 Judah was his sanctuary, and Israel his dominion.

3 The sea saw it, and fled: Jordan was driven back.

4 The mountains skipped like rams, and the little hills like lambs.

5 What ailed you, O you sea, that you fled? you Jordan, that you were driven back?

6 you mountains, that you skipped like rams; and you little hills, like lambs?

7 Tremble, you earth, at the presence of the Lord, at the presence of GOD of Jacob;

8 Which turned the rock into a standing water, the flint into a fountain of waters.

Psa 115:1 Not unto us, O Becoming-One, not unto us, but unto your name give glory, for your mercy, and for your truth's sake.

2 Therefore should the nations say, Where is now their God?

3 But our God is in the heavens: he has done whatsoever he has pleased.

4 Their idols are silver and gold, the work of men's hands.

5 They have mouths, but they speak not: eyes have they, but they see not:

6 They have ears, but they hear not: noses have they, but they smell not:

7 They have hands, but they handle not: feet have they, but they walk not: neither speak they through their throat.

8 They that make them are like unto them; so is every one that trusts in them.

9 O Israel, trust you in the Becoming-One: he is their help and their shield.

10 O house of Aaron, trust in the Becoming-One: he is their help and their shield.

11 you that fear the Becoming-One, trust in the Becoming-One: he is their help and their shield.

12 The Becoming-One has been mindful of us: he will bless us; he will bless the house of Israel; he will bless the house of Aaron.

13 He will bless them that fear the Becoming-One, both small and great.

14 The Becoming-One shall increase you more and more, you and your children.

15 you are blessed of the Becoming-One which made the heavens and earth.

16 The heaven of the heavens, are for the Becoming-One: but the earth has he given to the children of men.

17 The dead praise not the Becoming-One, neither any that go down into silence.

18 But we will bless the Becoming-One from this time forth and for olam. Praise the Becoming-One.

Psa 116:1 I love the Becoming-One, because he has heard my voice and my supplications.

2 Because he has inclined his ear unto me, therefore will I call upon him as long as I live.

3 The sorrows of death compassed me, and the pains of Sheol got hold upon me: I found trouble and sorrow.

4 Then called I upon the name of the Becoming-One; O Becoming-One, I beg you, deliver my soul.

5 Gracious is the Becoming-One, and righteous; yes, our God is merciful.

6 The Becoming-One preserves the simple: I was brought low, and he helped me.

7 Return unto your rest, O my soul; for the Becoming-One has dealt bountifully with you.

8 For you have delivered my soul from death, mine eyes from tears, and my feet from falling.

9 I will walk before the Becoming-One in the land of the living.

10 I believed, therefore have I spoken: I was greatly afflicted:

11 I said in my haste, All men are liars.

12 What shall I render unto the Becoming-One for all his benefits toward me?

13 I will take the cup of salvation, and call upon the name of the Becoming-One.

14 I will pay my vows unto the Becoming-One now in the presence of all his people.

15 Precious in the sight of the Becoming-One is the death of his saints.

16 O Becoming-One, truly I am your servant; I am your servant, and the son of your handmaid: you have loosened my bonds.

17 I will offer to you the sacrifice of thanksgiving, and will call upon the name of the Becoming-One.

18 I will pay my vows unto the Becoming-One now in the presence of all his people,

19 In the courts of the Becoming-One's house, in the midst of you, O Jerusalem. Praise you the Becoming-One.

Psa 117:1 O Praise the Becoming-One, all you nations: praise him, all you people.

2 For his merciful kindness is great toward us: and the truth of the Becoming-One endures for olam. Praise you the Becoming-One.

Psa 118:1 O give thanks unto the Becoming-One; surely good, surely mercy is for olam.

2 Let Israel now say, that his mercy endures for olam.

3 Let the house of Aaron now say, that his mercy endures for olam.

4 Let them now that fear the Becoming-One say, that his mercy endures for olam.

5 I called upon the Becoming-One in distress: the Becoming-One answered me, and set me in a large place.

6 The Becoming-One is on my side; I will not fear: what can man do unto me?

7 The Becoming-One takes my part with them that help me: therefore shall I see my desire upon them that hate me.

8 It is better to trust in the Becoming-One than to put confidence in man.

9 It is better to trust in the Becoming-One than to put confidence in princes.

10 All nations compassed me about: but in the name of the Becoming-One will I destroy them.

11 They compassed me about; yes, they compassed me about: but in the name of the Becoming-One I will destroy them.

12 They compassed me about like bees; they are quenched as the fire of thorns: for in the name of the Becoming-One I will destroy them.

13 you have thrust greatly at me that I might fall: but the Becoming-One helped me.

14 The Becoming-One is my strength and song, and is become my salvation.

15 The voice of rejoicing and salvation is in the tabernacles of the righteous: the right hand of the Becoming-One did valiantly.

16 The right hand of the Becoming-One is exalted: the right hand of the Becoming-One did valiantly.

17 I shall not die, but live, and declare the works of the Becoming-One.

18 The Becoming-One has chastened me greatly: but he has not given me over unto death.

19 Open to me the gates of righteousness: I will go into them, and I will praise the Becoming-One: 20 This gate of the Becoming-One, into which the righteous shall enter.

21 I will praise you: for you have heard me, and are become my salvation.

22 The stone which the builders refused is become the head stone of the corner.

23 This is the Becoming-One's doing; it is marvelous in our eyes.

24 This is the day which the Becoming-One has made; we will rejoice and be glad in it.

25 Save now, I beg you, O Becoming-One: O Becoming-One, I beg you, send now prosperity.

26 Blessed be he that comes in the name of the Becoming-One: we have blessed you out of the house of the Becoming-One.

27 GOD is the Becoming-One, which has showed us light: bind the feast with cords, even unto the horns of the altar.

28 you are my GOD, and I will praise you: you are my God, I will exalt you.

29 O give thanks unto the Becoming-One; surely good, surely mercy is for olam.

Psa 119:1 ALEPH. Blessed are the undefiled in the way, who walk in the law of the Becoming-One.

2 Blessed are they that keep his testimonies, and that seek him with the whole heart.

3 They also do no iniquity: they walk in his ways.

4 you have commanded us to keep your precepts diligently.

5 O that my ways were directed to keep your statutes!

6 Then shall I not be ashamed, when I have respect unto all your commandments.

7 I will praise you with uprightness of heart, when I shall have learned your righteous judgments.

8 I will keep your statutes: O forsake me not utterly.

9 BETH. Wherewithal shall a young man cleanse his way? by taking heed thereto according to your word.

10 With my whole heart have I sought you: O let me not wander from your commandments.

11 your word have I hid in mine heart, that I might not sin against you.
12 Blessed are you, O Becoming-One: teach me your statutes.
13 With my lips have I declared all the judgments of your mouth.
14 I have rejoiced in the way of your testimonies, as much as in all riches.
15 I will meditate in your precepts, and have respect unto your ways.
16 I will delight myself in your statutes: I will not forget your word.
17 GIMEL. Deal bountifully with your servant, that I may live, and keep your word.
18 Open you mine eyes, that I may behold wondrous things out of your law.
19 I am a stranger in the earth: hide not your commandments from me.
20 My soul breaks for the longing that it has unto your judgments at all times.
21 you have rebuked the proud that are cursed, which do err from your commandments.
22 Remove from me reproach and contempt; for I have kept your testimonies.
23 Princes also did sit and speak against me: but your servant did meditate in your statutes.
24 your testimonies also are my delight and my counselors.
25 DALETH. My soul cleaves unto the dust: quicken you me according to your word.
26 I have declared my ways, and you heard me: teach me your statutes.
27 Make me to understand the way of your precepts: so shall I talk of your wondrous works.
28 My soul melts for heaviness: strengthen you me according unto your word.
29 Remove from me the way of lying: and grant me your law graciously.
30 I have chosen the way of truth: your judgments have I laid before me.
31 I have stuck unto your testimonies: O Becoming-One, put me not to shame.
32 I will run the way of your commandments, when you shall enlarge my heart.
33 HE. Teach me, O Becoming-One, the way of your statutes; and I shall keep it unto the end.
34 Give me understanding, and I shall keep your law; yes, I shall observe it with my whole heart.
35 Make me to go in the path of your commandments; for therein do I delight.
36 Incline my heart unto your testimonies, and not to covetousness.
37 Turn away mine eyes from beholding vanity; and quicken you me in your way.
38 Establish your word unto your servant, who is devoted to your fear.
39 Turn away my reproach which I fear: for your judgments are good.
40 Behold, I have longed after your precepts: quicken me in your righteousness.
41 VAU. Let your mercies come also unto me, O Becoming-One, even your salvation, according to your word.
42 So shall I have wherewith to answer him that reproaches me: for I trust in your word.
43 And take not the word of truth utterly out of my mouth; for I have hoped in your judgments.
44 So shall I keep your law continually for olam and beyond.
45 And I will walk at liberty: for I seek your precepts.
46 I will speak of your testimonies also before kings, and will not be ashamed.
47 And I will delight myself in your commandments, which I have loved.
48 My hands also will I lift up unto your commandments, which I have loved; and I will meditate in your statutes.
49 ZAIN. Remember the word unto your servant, upon which you have caused me to hope.
50 This is my comfort in my affliction: for your word has quickened me.
51 The proud have had me greatly in derision: yet have I not declined from your law.
52 I remembered your judgments of olam past, O Becoming-One; and have comforted myself.
53 Horror has taken hold upon me because of the wicked that forsake your law.
54 your statutes have been my songs in the house of my pilgrimage.
55 I have remembered your name, O Becoming-One, in the night, and have kept your law.
56 This I had, because I kept your precepts.
57 CHETH. you are my portion, O Becoming-One: I have said that I would keep your words.
58 I entreated your favor with my whole heart: be merciful unto me according to your word.
59 I thought on my ways, and turned my feet unto your testimonies.
60 I made haste, and delayed not to keep your commandments.
61 The bands of the wicked have robbed me: but I have not forgotten your law.
62 At midnight I will rise to give thanks unto you because of your righteous judgments.
63 I am a companion of all them that fear you, and of them that keep your precepts.
64 The earth, O Becoming-One, is full of your mercy: teach me your statutes.
65 TETH. you have dealt well with your servant, O Becoming-One, according unto your word.
66 Teach me good judgment and knowledge: for I have believed your commandments.
67 Before I was afflicted I went astray: but now have I kept your word.
68 you are good, and do good; teach me your statutes.
69 The proud have forged a lie against me: but I will keep your precepts with my whole heart.
70 Their heart is as fat as grease; but I delight in your law.
71 It is good for me that I have been afflicted; that I might learn your statutes.
72 The law of your mouth is better unto me than thousands of gold and silver.
73 JOD. your hands have made me and fashioned me: give me understanding, that I may learn your commandments.
74 They that fear you will be glad when they see me; because I have hoped in your word.

75 I know, O Becoming-One, that your judgments are right, and that you in faithfullness have afflicted me.

76 Let, I pray you, your merciful kindness be for my comfort, according to your word unto your servant.

77 Let your tender mercies come unto me, that I may live: for your law is my delight.

78 Let the proud be ashamed; for they dealt perversely with me without a cause: but I will meditate in your precepts.

79 Let those that fear you turn unto me, and those that have known your testimonies.

80 Let my heart be sound in your statutes; that I be not ashamed.

81 CAPH. My soul faints for your salvation: but I hope in your word.

82 Mine eyes fail for your word, saying, When will you comfort me?

83 For I am become like a bottle in the smoke; yet do I not forget your statutes.

84 How many are the days of your servant? when will you execute judgment on them that persecute me?

85 The proud have dug pits for me, which are not after your law.

86 All your commandments are faithful: they persecute me wrongfully; help you me.

87 They had almost consumed me upon earth; but I forsook not your precepts.

88 Quicken me after your loving-kindness; so shall I keep the testimony of your mouth.

89 LAMED. For olam, O Becoming-One, your word is settled in heaven.

90 your faithfullness is unto all generations: you have established the earth, and it abideth.

91 They continue this day according to your ordinances: for all are your servants.

92 Unless your law had been my delights, I should then have perished in mine affliction.

93 I will not for olam forget your precepts: for with them you have quickened me.

94 I am yours, save me; for I have sought your precepts.

95 The wicked have waited for me to destroy me: but I will consider your testimonies.

96 I have seen an end of all perfection: but your commandment is exceeding broad.

97 MEM. O how love I your law! it is my meditation all the day.

98 you through your commandments have made me wiser than mine enemies: for they are ever with me.

99 I have more understanding than all my teachers: for your testimonies are my meditation.

100 I understand more than the ancients, because I keep your precepts.

101 I have refrained my feet from every evil way, that I might keep your word.

102 I have not departed from your judgments: for you have taught me.

103 How sweet are your words unto my taste! yes, sweeter than honey to my mouth!

104 Through your precepts I get understanding: therefore I hate every false way.

105 NUN. your word is a lamp unto my feet, and a light unto my path.

106 I have sworn, and I will perform it, that I will keep your righteous judgments.

107 I am afflicted very much: quicken me, O Becoming-One, according unto your word.

108 Accept, I beg you, the freewill offerings of my mouth, O Becoming-One, and teach me your judgments.

109 My soul is continually in my hand: yet do I not forget your law.

110 The wicked have laid a snare for me: yet I erred not from your precepts.

111 your testimonies have I taken as a heritage for olam, for they are the rejoicing of my heart.

112 I have inclined mine heart to perform your statutes for olam unto the end.

113 SAMECH. I hate vain thoughts: but your law do I love.

114 you are my hiding place and my shield: I hope in your word.

115 Depart from me, you evildoers: for I will keep the commandments of my God.

116 Uphold me according unto your word, that I may live: and let me not be ashamed of my hope.

117 Hold you me up, and I shall be safe: and I will have respect unto your statutes continually.

118 you have trodden down all them that err from your statutes: for their deceit is falsehood.

119 you put away all the wicked of the earth like dross: therefore I love your testimonies.

120 My flesh trembles for fear of you; and I am afraid of your judgments.

121 AIN. I have done judgment and justice: leave me not to mine oppressors.

122 Be surety for your servant for good: let not the proud oppress me.

123 Mine eyes fail for your salvation, and for the word of your righteousness.

124 Deal with your servant according unto your mercy, and teach me your statutes.

125 I am your servant; give me understanding, that I may know your testimonies.

126 It is time for you, Becoming-One, to work: for they have made void your law.

127 Therefore I love your commandments above gold; yes, above fine gold.

128 Therefore I esteem all your precepts concerning all things to be right; and I hate every false way.

129 PE. your testimonies are wonderful: therefore does my soul keep them.

130 The entrance of your words gives light; it gives understanding unto the simple.

131 I opened my mouth, and panted: for I longed for your commandments.

132 Look you upon me, and be merciful unto me, as you use to do unto those that love your name.

133 Order my steps in your word: and let not any iniquity have dominion over me.

134 Deliver me from the oppression of man: so will I keep your precepts.

135 Make your face to shine upon your servant; and teach me your statutes.

136 Rivers of waters run down mine eyes, because they keep not your law.

137 TZADDI. Righteous are you, O Becoming-One, and upright are your judgments.

138 your testimonies that you have commanded are righteous and very faithful.

139 My zeal has consumed me, because mine enemies have forgotten your words.

140 your word is very pure: therefore your servant loves it.

141 I am small and despised: yet do not I forget your precepts.

142 your righteousness is a righteousness of olam, and your law is the truth.

143 Trouble and anguish have taken hold on me: yet your commandments are my delights.

144 The righteousness of your testimonies is for olam, give me understanding, and I shall live.

145 KOPH. I cried with my whole heart; hear me, O Becoming-One: I will keep your statutes.

146 I cried unto you; save me, and I shall keep your testimonies.

147 I go before the breeze time, and cry: I hoped in your word.

148 Mine eyes go to meet with eyes open the night watches, that I might meditate in your word.

149 Hear my voice according unto your lovingkindness: O Becoming-One, quicken me according to your judgment.

150 They draw near that follow after mischief: they are far from your law.

151 you are near, O Becoming-One; and all your commandments are truth.

152 Concerning your testimonies, I have known of old that you have founded them for olam.

153 RESH. Consider mine affliction, and deliver me: for I do not forget your law.

154 Plead my cause, and deliver me: quicken me according to your word.

155 Salvation is far from the wicked: for they seek not your statutes.

156 Great are your tender mercies, O Becoming-One: quicken me according to your judgments.

157 Many are my persecutors and mine enemies; yet do I not decline from your testimonies.

158 I beheld the transgressors, and was grieved; because they kept not your word.

159 Consider how I love your precepts: quicken me, O Becoming-One, according to your lovingkindness.

160 your word is true from the beginning: and every one of your righteous judgments endures for olam.

161 SCHIN. Princes have persecuted me without a cause: but my heart stands in awe of your word.

162 I rejoice at your word, as one that finds great spoil.

163 I hate and abhor lying: but your law do I love.

164 Seven times a day do I praise you because of your righteous judgments.

165 Great peace have they which love your law: and nothing shall offend them.

166 Becoming-One, I have hoped for your salvation, and done your commandments.

167 My soul has kept your testimonies; and I love them exceedingly.

168 I have kept your precepts and your testimonies: for all my ways are before you.

169 TAU. Let my cry come near before you, O Becoming-One: give me understanding according to your word.

170 Let my supplication come before you: deliver me according to your word.

171 My lips shall utter praise, when you have taught me your statutes.

172 My tongue shall speak of your word: for all your commandments are righteousness.

173 Let your hand help me; for I have chosen your precepts.

174 I have longed for your salvation, O Becoming-One; and your law is my delight.

175 Let my soul live, and it shall praise you; and let your judgments help me.

176 I have gone astray like a lost sheep; seek your servant; for I do not forget your commandments.

Psa 120:1 A Song of degrees. In my distress I cried unto the Becoming-One, and he heard me.

2 Deliver my soul, O Becoming-One, from lying lips, and from a deceitful tongue.

3 What shall be given unto you? or what shall be done unto you, you false tongue?

4 Sharp arrows of the mighty, with coals of juniper.

5 Woe is me, that I sojourn in Mesech, that I dwell in the tents of Kedar!

6 My soul has long dwelt with him that hates peace.

7 I am for peace: but when I speak, they are for war.

Psa 121:1 A Song of degrees. I will lift up mine eyes unto the hills, from where comes my help.

2 My help comes from the Becoming-One, which made the heavens and earth.

3 He will not permit your foot to be moved: he that keeps you will not slumber.

4 Behold, he that keeps Israel shall neither slumber nor sleep.

5 The Becoming-One is your keeper: the Becoming-One is your shade upon your right hand.

6 The sun shall not smite you by day, nor the moon by night.

7 The Becoming-One shall preserve you from all evil: he shall preserve your soul.

8 The Becoming-One shall preserve your going out and your coming in from this time forth, and even for olam.

Psa 122:1 A Song of degrees of David. I was glad when they said unto me, Let us go into the house of the Becoming-One.

2 Our feet shall stand within your gates, O Jerusalem.

3 Jerusalem is built as a city that is compact together:

4 To which the tribes go up, the tribes of the Becoming-One, unto the testimony of Israel, to give thanks unto the name of the Becoming-One.

5 For there are set thrones of judgment, the thrones of the house of David.

6 Pray for the peace of Jerusalem: they shall prosper that love you.

7 Peace be within your walls, and prosperity within your palaces.

8 For my brethren and companions' sakes, I will now say, Peace be within you.

9 Because of the house of the Becoming-One our God I will seek your good.

Psa 123:1 A Song of degrees. Unto you lift I up mine eyes, O you that dwell in the heavens.

2 Behold, as the eyes of servants look unto the hand of their masters, and as the eyes of a maiden unto the hand of her mistress; so our eyes wait upon the Becoming-One our God, until that he have mercy upon us.

3 Have mercy upon us, O Becoming-One, have mercy upon us: for we are exceedingly filled with contempt.

4 Our soul is exceedingly filled with the scorning of those that are at ease, and with the contempt of the proud.

Psa 124:1 A Song of degrees of David. If it had not been the Becoming-One who was on our side, now may Israel say;

2 If it had not been the Becoming-One who was on our side, when men rose up against us:

3 Then they had swallowed us up quick, when their wrath was kindled against us:

4 Then the waters had overwhelmed us, the stream had gone over our soul:

5 Then the proud waters had gone over our soul.

6 Blessed be the Becoming-One, who has not given us as a prey to their teeth.

7 Our soul is escaped as a bird out of the snare of the fowlers: the snare is broken, and we are escaped.

8 Our help is in the name of the Becoming-One, who made the heavens and earth.

Psa 125:1 A Song of degrees. They that trust in the Becoming-One shall be as mount Zion, which cannot be removed, but abides for olam.

2 As the mountains are round about Jerusalem, so the Becoming-One is round about his people from henceforth even for olam.

3 For the rod of the wicked shall not rest upon the lot of the righteous; lest the righteous put forth their hands unto iniquity.

4 Do good, O Becoming-One, unto those that be good, and to them that are upright in their hearts.

5 As for such as turn aside unto their crooked ways, the Becoming-One shall lead them forth with the workers of iniquity: but peace shall be upon Israel.

Psa 126:1 A Song of degrees. When the Becoming-One turned again the captivity of Zion, we were like them that dream.

2 Then was our mouth filled with laughter, and our tongue with singing: then said they among the nations, The Becoming-One has done great things for them.

3 The Becoming-One has done great things for us; whereof we are glad.

4 Turn again our captivity, O Becoming-One, as the streams in the south.

5 They that sow in tears shall reap in joy.

6 He that goes forth and weeps, bearing precious seed, shall doubtless come again with rejoicing, bringing his sheaves with him.

Psa 127:1 A Song of degrees for Solomon. Except the Becoming-One build the house, they labor in vain that build it: except the Becoming-One keep the city, the watchman stays awake but in vain.

2 It is vain for you to rise up early, to sit up late, to eat the bread of sorrows: for so he gives his beloved sleep.

3 Lo, children are a heritage of the Becoming-One: and the fruit of the womb is his reward.

4 As arrows are in the hand of a mighty man; so are children of the youth.

5 Happy is the man that has his quiver full of them: they shall not be ashamed, but they shall speak with the enemies in the gate.

Psa 128:1 A Song of degrees. Blessed is every one that fears the Becoming-One; that walks in his ways.

2 For you shall eat the labor of your hands: happy shall you be, and it shall be well with you.

3 your wife shall be as a fruitful vine by the sides of your house: your children like olive plants round about your table.

4 Behold, that thus shall the man be blessed that fears the Becoming-One.

5 The Becoming-One shall bless you out of Zion: and you shall see the good of Jerusalem all the days of your life.

6 Yes, you shall see your children's children, and peace upon Israel.

Psa 129:1 A Song of degrees. Many a time have they afflicted me from my youth, may Israel now say:

2 Many a time have they afflicted me from my youth: yet they have not prevailed against me.

3 The plowers plowed upon my back: they made long their furrows.

4 The Becoming-One is righteous: he has cut asunder the cords of the wicked.

5 Let them all be confounded and turned back that hate Zion.

6 Let them be as the grass upon the housetops, which withers afore it grows up:

7 Wherewith the mower fills not his hand; nor he that binds sheaves his bosom.

8 Neither do they which go by say, The blessing of the Becoming-One be upon you: we bless you in the name of the Becoming-One.

Psa 130:1 A Song of degrees. Out of the depths have I cried unto you, O Becoming-One.

2 My Lord(s), hear my voice: let your ears be attentive to the voice of my supplications.

3 If you, Becoming-One, should mark iniquities, O my Lord(s), who shall stand?

4 But there is forgiveness with you, that you may be feared.

5 I wait for the Becoming-One, my soul does wait, and in his word do I hope.

6 My soul waits for my Lord(s) more than they that watch for the morning: I say, more than they that watch for the morning.

7 Let Israel hope in the Becoming-One: for with the Becoming-One there is mercy, and with him is plenteous redemption.

8 And he shall redeem Israel from all his iniquities.

Psa 131:1 A Song of degrees of David. Becoming-One, my heart is not haughty, nor mine eyes lofty: neither do I exercise myself in great matters, or in things too high for me.

2 Surely I have behaved and quieted my soul, as a child that is weaned of his mother: my soul is even as a weaned child.

3 Let Israel hope in the Becoming-One from henceforth and for olam.

Psa 132:1 A Song of degrees. Becoming-One, remember David, and all his afflictions:

2 How he swore unto the Becoming-One, and vowed unto the mighty God of Jacob;

3 Surely I will not come into the tabernacle of my house, nor go up into my bed;

4 I will not give sleep to mine eyes, or slumber to mine eyelids,

5 Until I find out a place for the Becoming-One, a habitation for the mighty God of Jacob.

6 Lo, we heard of it at Ephratah: we found it in the fields of the wood.

7 We will go into his tabernacles: we will worship at his footstool.

8 Arise, O Becoming-One, into your rest; you, and the ark of your strength.

9 Let your priests be clothed with righteousness; and let your saints shout for joy.

10 For your servant David's sake turn not away the face of your anointed [Messiah].

11 The Becoming-One has sworn in truth unto David; he will not turn from it; Of the fruit of your body will I set upon your throne.

12 If your children will keep my covenant and my testimony that I shall teach them, their children shall also sit upon your throne to the beyond.

13 For the Becoming-One has chosen Zion; he has desired it for his habitation.

14 This is my rest to the beyond: here will I dwell; for I have desired it.

15 I will abundantly bless her provision: I will satisfy her poor with bread.

16 I will also clothe her priests with salvation: and her saints shall shout aloud for joy.

17 There will I make the horn of David to bud: I have ordained a lamp for mine anointed [Messiah].

18 His enemies will I clothe with shame: but upon himself shall his crown flourish.

Psa 133:1 A Song of degrees of David. Behold, how good and how pleasant it is for brethren to dwell together in unity!

2 It is like the precious ointment upon the head, that ran down upon the beard, even Aaron's beard: that went down to the skirts of his garments;

3 As the dew of Hermon, and as the dew that descended upon the mountains of Zion: for there the Becoming-One commanded the blessing, even life for olam.

Psa 134:1 A Song of degrees. Behold, bless you the Becoming-One, all you servants of the Becoming-One, which by night stand in the house of the Becoming-One.

2 Lift up your hands in the sanctuary, and bless the Becoming-One.

3 The Becoming-One that made the heavens and earth bless you out of Zion.

Psa 135:1 Praise you the Becoming-One. Praise you the name of the Becoming-One; praise him, O you servants of the Becoming-One.

2 you that stand in the house of the Becoming-One, in the courts of the house of our God,

3 Praise the Becoming-One; for the Becoming-One is good: sing praises unto his name; for it is pleasant.

4 For the Becoming-One has chosen Jacob unto himself, and Israel for his treasure.

5 For I know that the Becoming-One is great, and that our Lords is above all gods.

6 Whatsoever the Becoming-One pleased, that did he in heaven, and in earth, in the seas, and all deep places.

7 He causes the vapours to ascend from the ends of the earth; he makes lightning for the rain; he brings the wind out of his treasuries.

8 Who smote the firstborn of Egypt, both of man and beast.

9 Who sent tokens and wonders into the midst of you, O Egypt, upon Pharaoh, and upon all his servants.

10 Who smote great nations, and killed mighty kings;

11 Sihon king of the Amorites, and Og king of Bashan, and all the kingdoms of Canaan:

12 And gave their land for a heritage, a heritage unto Israel his people.

13 your name, O Becoming-One, endures for olam, and your memorial, O Becoming-One, throughout all generations.

14 For the Becoming-One will judge his people, and he will repent himself concerning his servants.

15 The idols of the nations are silver and gold, the work of men's hands.

16 They have mouths, but they speak not; eyes have they, but they see not;

17 They have ears, but they hear not; neither is there any breath in their mouths.

18 They that make them are like unto them: so is every one that trusts in them.

19 Bless the Becoming-One, O house of Israel: bless the Becoming-One, O house of Aaron:

20 Bless the Becoming-One, O house of Levi: you that fear the Becoming-One, bless the Becoming-One.

21 Blessed be the Becoming-One out of Zion, which dwells at Jerusalem. Praise you the Becoming-One.

Psa 136:1 O give thanks unto the Becoming-One; surely good, surely mercy is for olam.

2 O give thanks unto God of gods: for his mercy endures for olam.

3 O give thanks to my Lord(s) of the lords: for his mercy endures for olam.

4 To him who alone did great wonders: for his mercy endures for olam.

5 To him that by wisdom made the heavens: for his mercy endures for olam.

6 To him that stretched out the earth above the waters: for his mercy endures for olam.

7 To him that made great lights: for his mercy endures for olam.

8 The sun to rule by day: for his mercy endures for olam.

9 The moon and stars to rule by night: for his mercy endures for olam.

10 To him that smote Egypt in their firstborn: for his mercy endures for olam.

11 And brought out Israel from among them: for his mercy endures for olam.

12 With a strong hand, and with a stretched out arm: for his mercy endures for olam.

13 To him which divided the boundary sea into parts: for his mercy endures for olam.

14 And made Israel to pass through the midst of it: for his mercy endures for olam.

15 But overthrew Pharaoh and his host in the boundary sea: for his mercy endures for olam.

16 To him which led his people through the wilderness: for his mercy endures for olam.

17 To him which smote great kings: for his mercy endures for olam.

18 And killed famous kings: for his mercy endures for olam.

19 Sihon king of the Amorites: for his mercy endures for olam.

20 And Og the king of Bashan: for his mercy endures for olam.

21 And gave their land for a heritage: for his mercy endures for olam.

22 Even a heritage unto Israel his servant: for his mercy endures for olam.

23 Who remembered us in our low estate: for his mercy endures for olam.

24 And has redeemed us from our enemies: for his mercy endures for olam.

25 Who gives food to all flesh: for his mercy endures for olam.

26 O give thanks unto GOD of heaven: for his mercy endures for olam.

Psa 137:1 By the rivers of Babylon, there we sat down, yes, we wept, when we remembered Zion.

2 We hanged our harps upon the willows in the midst thereof.

3 For there they that carried us away captive required of us a song; and they that wasted us required of us mirth, saying, Sing us one of the songs of Zion.

4 How shall we sing the Becoming-One's song in a strange land?

5 If I forget you, O Jerusalem, let my right hand forget her cunning.

6 If I do not remember you, let my tongue cleave to the roof of my mouth; if I prefer not Jerusalem above my chief joy.

7 Remember, O Becoming-One, the children of Edom in the day of Jerusalem; who said, Raze it, raze it, even to the foundation thereof.

8 O daughter of Babylon, who are to be destroyed; happy shall he be, that rewards you as you have served us.

9 Happy shall he be, that takes and dashes your little ones against the stones.

Psa 138:1 A Psalm of David. I will praise you with my whole heart: before the gods will I sing praise unto you.

2 I will worship toward your holy temple, and praise your name for your loving-kindness and for your truth: for you have magnified your word above all your name.

3 In the day when I cried you answered me, and strengthened me with strength in my soul.

4 All the kings of the earth shall praise you, O Becoming-One, when they hear the words of your mouth.

5 Yes, they shall sing in the ways of the Becoming-One: for great is the glory of the Becoming-One.

6 Though the Becoming-One be high, yet has he respect unto the lowly: but the proud he knows afar off.

7 Though I walk in the midst of trouble, you will revive me: you shall stretch forth your hand against the wrath of mine enemies, and your right hand shall save me.

8 The Becoming-One will perfect that which concerns me: your mercy, O Becoming-One, endures for olam, forsake not the works of your own hands.

Psa 139:1 To the chief Musician, A Psalm of David. O Becoming-One, you have searched me, and known me.

2 you know when I sit and when I rise, you understand my thought afar off.

3 you compass my path and my lying down, and are acquainted with all my ways.

4 For there is not a word in my tongue, but, lo, O Becoming-One, you know it altogether.

5 you have beset me behind and before, and laid your hand upon me.

6 Such knowledge is too wonderful for me; it is high, I cannot attain unto it.

7 Where shall I go from your spirit? or where shall I flee from your presence?

8 If I ascend up into heaven, you are there: if I make my bed in Sheol, behold, you are there.

9 If I take the wings of the dawn, and dwell in the uttermost parts of the sea;

10 Even there shall your hand lead me, and your right hand shall hold me.

11 If I say, Surely the darkness shall cover me; even the night shall be light about me.

12 Yes, the darkness hides not from you; but the night shines as the day: the darkness and the light are both alike to you.

13 For you have possessed my reins: you have covered me in my mother's womb.

14 I will praise you; for I am fearfully and wonderfully made: marvelous are your works; and that my soul knows right well.

15 My substance was not hid from you, when I was made in secret, and curiously worked in the lowest parts of the earth.

16 your eyes did see my substance, yet being unperfect; and in your book all my members were written, which in continuance were fashioned, when as yet there was none of them.

17 How precious also are your thoughts unto me, O GOD! how great is the sum of them!

18 If I should count them, they are more in number than the sand: when I awake, I am still with you.

19 Surely you will slay the wicked, O God: depart from me therefore, you bloody men.

20 For they speak against you wickedly, and your enemies take your name in vain.

21 Do not I hate them, O Becoming-One, that hate you? and am not I grieved with those that rise up against you?

22 I hate them with perfect hatred: I count them mine enemies.

23 Search me, O GOD, and know my heart: try me, and know my thoughts:

24 And see if there be any wicked way in me, and lead me in the way of olam.

Psa 140:1 To the chief Musician, A Psalm of David. Deliver me, O Becoming-One, from the evil man: preserve me from the violent man;

2 Which imagine mischiefs in their heart; all day are they gathered together for war.

3 They have sharpened their tongues like a serpent; adders' poison is under their lips. Selah.

4 Keep me, O Becoming-One, from the hands of the wicked; preserve me from the violent man; who have purposed to overthrow my goings.

5 The proud have hid a snare for me, and cords; they have spread a net by the wayside; they have set gins for me. Selah.

6 I said unto the Becoming-One, you are my GOD: hear the voice of my supplications, O Becoming-One.

7 O Becoming-One, my Lord(s), the strength of my salvation, you have covered my head in the day of battle.

8 Grant not, O Becoming-One, the desires of the wicked: further not his wicked device; lest they exalt themselves. Selah.

9 As for the head of those that compass me about, let the mischief of their own lips cover them.

10 Let burning coals fall upon them: let them be cast into the fire; into deep pits, that they rise not up again.

11 Let not an evil speaker be established in the earth: evil shall hunt the violent man to overthrow him.

12 I know that the Becoming-One will maintain the cause of the afflicted, and the right of the poor.

13 Surely the righteous shall give thanks unto your name: the upright shall dwell in your presence.

Psa 141:1 A Psalm of David. Becoming-One, I cry unto you: make haste unto me; give ear unto my voice, when I cry unto you.

2 Let my prayer be set forth before you as incense; and the lifting up of my hands as the evening sacrifice.

3 Set a watch, O Becoming-One, before my mouth; keep the door of my lips.

4 Incline not my heart to any evil thing, to practice wicked works with men that work iniquity: and let me not eat of their dainties.

5 Let the righteous smite me; it shall be a kindness: and let him reprove me; it shall be an excellent oil, which shall not break my head: for yet my prayer also shall be in their calamities.

6 When their judges are overthrown in stony places, they shall hear my words; for they are sweet.

7 Our bones are scattered at hell's mouth, as when one cuts and cleaves wood upon the earth.

8 But mine eyes are unto you, O Becoming-One, my Lord(s): in you is my trust; leave not my soul destitute.

9 Keep me from the snares which they have laid for me, and the gins of the workers of iniquity.

10 Let the wicked fall into their own nets, while all of me will pass over.

Psa 142:1 Maschil of David; A Prayer when he was in the cave. I cried unto the Becoming-One with my voice; with my voice unto the Becoming-One did I make my supplication.

2 I poured out my complaint before him; I showed before him my trouble.

3 When my spirit was overwhelmed within me, then you knew my path. In the way wherein I walked have they privily laid a snare for me.

4 I looked on my right hand, and beheld, but there was no man that would know me: refuge failed me; no man cared for my soul.

5 I cried unto you, O Becoming-One: I said, you are my refuge and my portion in the land of the living.

6 Attend unto my cry; for I am brought very low: deliver me from my persecutors; for they are stronger than I.

7 Bring my soul out of prison, that I may praise your name: the righteous shall compass me about; for you shall deal bountifully with me.

Psa 143:1 A Psalm of David. Hear my prayer, O Becoming-One, give ear to my supplications: in your faithfullness answer me, and in your righteousness.

2 And enter not into judgment with your servant: for in your sight shall no man living be justified.

3 For the enemy has persecuted my soul; he has struck my life down to the ground; he has made me to dwell in darkness, as those that have been long dead.

4 Therefore is my spirit overwhelmed within me; my heart within me is desolate.

5 I remember the days of old; I meditate on all your works; I muse on the work of your hands.

6 I stretch forth my hands unto you: my soul thirsts after you, as a thirsty land. Selah.

7 Hear me speedily, O Becoming-One: my spirit fails: hide not your face from me, lest I be like unto them that go down into the pit.

8 Cause me to hear your loving-kindness in the morning; for in you do I trust: cause me to know the way wherein I should walk; for I lift up my soul unto you.

9 Deliver me, O Becoming-One, from mine enemies: I flee unto you to hide me.

10 Teach me to do your will; for you are my God: your spirit is good; lead me into the land of uprightness.

11 Quicken me, O Becoming-One, for your name's sake: for your righteousness' sake bring my soul out of trouble.

12 And of your mercy cut off mine enemies, and destroy all them that afflict my soul: for I am your servant.

Psa 144:1 A Psalm of David. Blessed be the Becoming-One my strength, which teaches my hands to war, and my fingers to fight:

2 My goodness, and my fortress; my high tower, and my deliverer; my shield, and he in whom I trust; who subdues my people under me.

3 Becoming-One, what is man, that you take knowledge of him! or the son of man, that you make account of him!

4 Man is like to vanity: his days are as a shadow that passes away.

5 Bow your heavens, O Becoming-One, and come down: touch the mountains, and they shall smoke.

6 Cast forth lightning, and scatter them: shoot out your arrows, and destroy them.

7 Send your hand from above; rid me, and deliver me out of great waters, from the hand of strange children;

8 Whose mouth speaks vanity, and their right hand is a right hand of falsehood.

9 I will sing a new song unto you, O God: upon a psaltery and an instrument of ten strings will I sing praises unto you.

10 It is he that gives salvation unto kings: who delivers David his servant from the hurtful sword.

11 Rid me, and deliver me from the hand of strange children, whose mouth speaks vanity, and their right hand is a right hand of falsehood:

12 That our sons may be as plants grown up in their youth; that our daughters may be as corner stones, polished after the similitude of a palace:

13 That our garners may be full, affording all manner of store: that our sheep may bring forth thousands and ten myriads in our fields:

14 That our oxen may be strong to labor; that there be no breaking in, nor going out; that there be no complaining in our streets.

15 Happy is that people, that is in such a case: yes, happy the people, whose God [elohim] (is the) Becoming-One.

Psa 145:1 David's Psalm of praise. I will extol you, my God, O king; and I will bless your name for olam and beyond.

2 Every day will I bless you; and I will praise your name for olam and beyond.

3 Great is the Becoming-One, and greatly to be praised; and his greatness is unsearchable.

4 One generation shall praise your works to another, and shall declare your mighty acts.

5 I will speak of the glorious honor of your majesty, and of your wondrous works.

6 And men shall speak of the might of your terrible acts: and I will declare your greatness.

7 They shall abundantly utter the memory of your great goodness, and shall sing of your righteousness.

8 The Becoming-One is gracious, and full of compassion; slow to anger, and of great mercy.

9 The Becoming-One is good to all: and his tender mercies are over all his works.

10 All your works shall praise you, O Becoming-One; and your saints shall bless you.

11 They shall speak of the glory of your kingdom, and talk of your power;

12 To make known to the sons of men his mighty acts, and the glorious majesty of his kingdom.

13 your kingdom is a kingdom of all olams, and your dominion endures throughout all generations.

14 The Becoming-One upholds all that fall, and raises up all those that be bowed down.

15 The eyes of all wait upon you; and you give them their food in due season.

16 you open your hand, and satisfy the desire of every living thing.

17 The Becoming-One is righteous in all his ways, and holy in all his works.

18 The Becoming-One is near unto all them that call upon him, to all that call upon him in truth.

19 He will fulfil the desire of them that fear him: he also will hear their cry, and will save them.

20 The Becoming-One preserves all them that love him: but all the wicked will he destroy.

21 My mouth shall speak the praise of the Becoming-One: and let all flesh bless his holy name for olam and beyond.

Psa 146:1 Praise you the Becoming-One. Praise the Becoming-One, O my soul.

2 While I live will I praise the Becoming-One: I will sing praises unto my God while I have any being.

3 Put not your trust in princes, nor in the son of man, in whom there is no help.

4 His breath goes forth, he returns to his earth; in that very day his thoughts perish.

5 Happy is he that has GOD of Jacob for his help, whose hope is in the Becoming-One his God:

6 Which made heaven, and earth, the sea, and all that therein is: which keeps truth for olam.

7 Which executes judgment for the oppressed: which gives food to the hungry. The Becoming-One releases the prisoners:

8 The Becoming-One opens the eyes of the blind: the Becoming-One raises them that are bowed down: the Becoming-One loves the righteous:

9 The Becoming-One preserves the strangers; he relieves the fatherless and widow: but the way of the wicked he turns upside down.

10 The Becoming-One shall reign for olam, even your God, O Zion, unto all generations. Praise you the Becoming-One.

Psa 147:1 Praise you the Becoming-One: for it is good to sing praises unto our God; for it is pleasant; and praise is becoming.

2 The Becoming-One does build up Jerusalem: he gathers together the outcasts of Israel.

3 He heals the broken in heart, and binds up their wounds.

4 He tells the number of the stars; he calls them all by their names.

5 Great is our Lords, and of great power: his understanding is not numbered.

6 The Becoming-One lifts up the meek: he casts the wicked down to the ground.

7 Sing unto the Becoming-One with thanksgiving; sing praise upon the harp unto our God:

8 Who covers the heavens with clouds, who prepares rain for the earth, who makes grass to grow upon the mountains.

9 He gives to the beast his food, and to the young ravens which cry.

10 He delights not in the strength of the horse: he takes not pleasure in the legs of a man.

11 The Becoming-One takes pleasure in them that fear him, in those that hope in his mercy.

12 Praise the Becoming-One, O Jerusalem; praise your God, O Zion.

13 For he has strengthened the bars of your gates; he has blessed your children within you.

14 He makes peace in your borders, and fills you with the finest of the wheat.

15 He sends forth his commandment upon earth: his word runs very swiftly.

16 He gives snow like wool: he scatters the hoar frost like ashes.

17 He castes forth his ice like morsels: who can stand before his cold?

18 He sends out his word, and melts them: he causes his wind to blow, and the waters flow.

19 He shows his word unto Jacob, his statutes and his judgments unto Israel.

20 He has not dealt so with any nation: and as for his judgments, they have not known them. Praise you the Becoming-One.

Psa 148:1 Praise you the Becoming-One. Praise you the Becoming-One from the heavens: praise him in the heights.

2 Praise you him, all his angels: praise you him, all his hosts.

3 Praise you him, sun and moon: praise him, all you stars of light.

4 Praise him, you heavens of heavens, and you waters that be above the heavens.

5 Let them praise the name of the Becoming-One: for he commanded, and they were created.

6 He has also established them for the beyond, for olam, he has made a decree which shall not pass.

7 Praise the Becoming-One from the earth, you monsters, and all deeps:

8 Fire, and hail; snow, and vapors; stormy wind fulfilling his word:

9 Mountains, and all hills; fruitful trees, and all cedars:

10 Beasts, and all cattle; creeping things, and flying fowl:

11 Kings of the earth, and all people; princes, and all judges of the earth:

12 Both young men, and maidens; old men, and children:

13 Let them praise the name of the Becoming-One: for his name alone is excellent; his glory is above the earth and heaven.

14 He also exalts the horn of his people, the praise of all his saints; even of the children of Israel, a people near unto him. Praise you the Becoming-One.

Psa 149:1 Praise you the Becoming-One. Sing unto the Becoming-One a new song, and his praise in the congregation of saints.

2 Let Israel rejoice in him that made him: let the children of Zion be joyful in their King.

3 Let them praise his name in the dance: let them sing praises unto him with the timbrel and harp.

4 For the Becoming-One takes pleasure in his people: he will beautify the meek with salvation.

5 Let the saints be joyful in glory: let them sing aloud upon their beds.

6 Let the high praises of GOD be in their mouth, and a two edged sword in their hand;

7 To execute vengeance upon the nations, and punishments upon the people;

8 To bind their kings with chains, and their nobles with fetters of iron;

9 To execute upon them the judgment written: this honor have all his saints. Praise you the Becoming-One.

Psa 150:1 Praise you the Becoming-One. Praise GOD in his sanctuary: praise him in his mighty space of the heavens.

2 Praise him for his mighty acts: praise him according to his excellent greatness.

3 Praise him with the sound of the trumpet: praise him with the psaltery and harp.

4 Praise him with the timbrel and dance: praise him with stringed instruments and organs.

5 Praise him upon the loud cymbals: praise him upon the high sounding cymbals.

6 Let every thing that has breath praise the Becoming-One. Praise you the Becoming-One.

Proverbs

Prov 1:1 The proverbs of Solomon the son of David, king of Israel;

2 To know wisdom and instruction; to perceive the words of understanding;

3 To receive the instruction of wisdom, justice, and judgment, and equity;

4 To give prudence to the simple, to the young man knowledge and discretion.

5 A wise man will hear, and will increase learning; and a man of understanding shall attain unto wise counsels:

6 To understand a proverb, and the interpretation; the words of the wise, and their dark sayings.

7 The fear of the Becoming-One is the beginning of knowledge: but fools despise wisdom and instruction.

8 My son, hear the instruction of your father, and forsake not the law of your mother:

9 For they shall be an ornament of grace unto your head, and chains about your neck.

10 My son, if sinners entice you, consent you not.

11 If they say, Come with us, let us lay wait for blood, let us ambush the innocent without cause:

12 Let us swallow them up alive as Sheol; and whole, as those that go down into the pit:

13 We shall find all precious substance, we shall fill our houses with spoil:

14 Cast in your lot among us; let us all have one purse:

15 My son, walk not you in the way with them; refrain your foot from their path:

16 For their feet run to evil, and make haste to shed blood.

17 Surely in vain the net is spread in the sight of any bird.

18 And they lay wait for their own blood; they ambush their own souls.

19 So are the ways of every one that is greedy of gain; which takes away the soul of the owners thereof.

20 Wisdom cries outside; she utters her voice in the streets:

21 She cries in the chief place of concourse, in the openings of the gates: in the city she utters her words, saying,

22 How long, you simple ones, will you love simplicity? and the scorners delight in their scorning, and fools hate knowledge?

23 Turn you at my reproof: behold, I will pour out my spirit unto you, I will make known my words unto you.

24 Because I have called, and you refused; I have stretched out my hand, and no man regarded;

25 But you have set at nothing all my counsel, and would none of my reproof:

26 I also will laugh at your calamity; I will mock when your fear comes;

27 When your fear comes as desolation, and your destruction comes as a whirlwind; when distress and anguish comes upon you.

28 Then shall they call upon me, but I will not answer; they shall seek me early, but they shall not find me:

29 For that they hated knowledge, and did not choose the fear of the Becoming-One: 30 They wanted none of my counsel: they despised all my reproof.

31 Therefore shall they eat of the fruit of their own way, and be filled with their own devices.

32 For the turning away of the simple shall slay them, and the prosperity of fools shall destroy them.

33 But whoso listens unto me shall dwell safely, and shall be quiet from fear of evil.

Prov 2:1 My son, if you will receive my words, and hide my commandments with you;

2 So that you incline your ear unto wisdom, and apply your heart to understanding;

3 Yes, if you cry after knowledge, and lift up your voice for understanding;

4 If you seek her as silver, and search for her as for hid treasures;

5 Then shall you understand the fear of the Becoming-One, and find the knowledge of God.

6 For the Becoming-One gives wisdom: out of his mouth comes knowledge and understanding.

7 He lays up sound wisdom for the righteous: he is a buckler to them that walk uprightly.

8 He keeps the paths of judgment, and preserves the way of his saints.

9 Then shall you understand righteousness, and judgment, and equity; yes, every good path.

10 When wisdom enters into your heart, and knowledge is pleasant unto your soul;

11 Discretion shall preserve you, understanding shall keep you:

12 To deliver you from the way of the evil man, from the man that speaks perverse things;

13 Who leave the paths of uprightness, to walk in the ways of darkness;

14 Who rejoice to do evil, and delight in the perverseness of the wicked;

15 Whose ways are crooked, and they are perverse in their paths:

16 To deliver you from the strange woman, even from the stranger which flatters with her words;

17 Which forsakes the guide of her youth, and forgets the covenant of her God.

18 For her house inclines unto death, and her paths unto the dead.

19 None that go unto her return again, neither take they hold of the paths of life.

20 That you may walk in the way of good men, and keep the paths of the righteous.

21 For the upright shall dwell in the land, and the perfect shall remain in it.

22 But the wicked shall be cut off from the earth, and the transgressors shall be rooted out of it.

Prov 3:1 My son, forget not my law; but let your heart keep my commandments:

2 For length of days, and long life, and peace, shall they add to you.

3 Let not mercy and truth forsake you: bind them about your neck; write them upon the table of your heart:

4 So shall you find favor and good understanding in the sight of God and man.

5 Trust in the Becoming-One with all your heart; and lean not unto your own understanding.

6 In all your ways acknowledge him, and he shall direct your paths.

7 Be not wise in your own eyes: fear the Becoming-One, and depart from evil.

8 It shall be health to your navel, and marrow to your bones.

9 Honor the Becoming-One with your substance, and with the beginning of all your increase:

10 So shall your barns be filled with plenty, and your presses shall burst out with new wine.

11 My son, despise not the chastening of the Becoming-One; neither be weary of his correction:

12 For whom the Becoming-One loves he corrects; even as a father the son in whom he delights.

13 Happy is the man that finds wisdom, and the man that gets understanding.

14 For the merchandise of it is better than the merchandise of silver, and the gain thereof than fine gold.

15 She is more precious than rubies: and all the things you can desire are not to be compared unto her.

16 Length of days is in her right hand; and in her left hand riches and honor.

17 Her ways are ways of pleasantness, and all her paths are peace.

18 She is a tree of life to them that lay hold upon her: and happy is every one that retains her.

19 The Becoming-One by wisdom has founded the earth; by understanding has he established the heavens.

20 By his knowledge the depths are broken up, and the clouds drop down the dew.

21 My son, let not them depart from your eyes: keep sound wisdom and discretion:

22 So shall they be life unto your soul, and grace to your neck.

23 Then shall you walk in your way safely, and your foot shall not stumble.

24 When you lie down, you shall not be afraid: yes, you shall lie down, and your sleep shall be sweet.

25 Be not afraid of sudden fear, neither of the desolation of the wicked, when it comes.

26 For the Becoming-One shall be your confidence, and shall keep your foot from being taken.

27 Withhold not good from them to whom it is due, when it is in the power [god] of your hand to do it.

28 Say not unto your neighbor, Go, and come again, and tomorrow I will give; when you have it by you.

29 Devise not evil against your neighbor, seeing he dwells securely by you.

30 Strive not with a man without cause, if he have done you no harm.

31 Envy you not the oppressor, and choose none of his ways.

32 For the perverse is abomination to the Becoming-One: but his secret is with the righteous.

33 The curse of the Becoming-One is in the house of the wicked: but he blesses the habitation of the just.

34 Surely he scorns the scorners: but he gives grace unto the lowly.

35 The wise shall inherit glory: but shame shall be the promotion of fools.

Prov 4:1 Hear, you children, the instruction of a father, and attend to know understanding.

2 For I give you good doctrine, forsake you not my law.

3 For I was my father's son, tender and only beloved in the sight of my mother.

4 He taught me also, and said unto me, Let your heart retain my words: keep my commandments, and live.

5 Get wisdom, get understanding: forget it not; neither decline from the words of my mouth.

6 Forsake her not, and she shall preserve you: love her, and she shall keep you.

7 Wisdom is the beginning thing; therefore get wisdom: and with all your getting get understanding.

8 Exalt her, and she shall promote you: she shall bring you to honor, when you do embrace her.

9 She shall give to your head an ornament of grace: a crown of glory shall she deliver to you.

10 Hear, O my son, and receive my sayings; and the years of your life shall be many.

11 I have taught you in the way of wisdom; I have led you in right paths.

12 When you go, your steps shall not be hampered; and when you run, you shall not stumble.

13 Take hold of instruction; let her not go: keep her; for she is your life.

14 Enter not into the path of the wicked, and go not in the way of evil men.

15 Avoid it, pass not by it, turn from it, and pass away.

16 For they sleep not, except they have done mischief; and their sleep is taken away, unless they cause some to fall.

17 For they eat the bread of wickedness, and drink the wine of violence.

18 But the path of the just is as the shining light, that shins more and more unto the perfect day.

19 The way of the wicked is as darkness: they know not at what they stumble.

20 My son, attend to my words; incline your ear unto my sayings.

21 Let them not depart from your eyes; keep them in the midst of your heart.

22 For they are life unto those that find them, and health to all their flesh.

23 Keep your heart with all diligence; for out of it are the issues of life.

24 Put away from you a perverse mouth, and perverse lips put far from you.

25 Let your eyes look right on, and let your eyelids look straight before you.

26 Ponder the path of your feet, and let all your ways be established.

27 Turn not to the right hand nor to the left: remove your foot from evil.

Prov 5:1 My son, attend unto my wisdom, and bow your ear to my understanding:

2 That you may regard discretion, and that your lips may keep knowledge.

3 For the lips of a strange woman drop as a honeycomb, and her mouth is smoother than oil:

4 But her end is bitter as wormwood, sharp as a two edged sword.

5 Her feet go down to death; her steps take hold on Sheol.

6 Lest you should ponder the path of life, her ways are moveable, that you can not know them.

7 Hear me now therefore, O you children, and depart not from the words of my mouth.

8 Remove your way far from her, and come not near the door of her house:

9 Lest you give your honor unto others, and your years unto the cruel:

10 Lest strangers be filled with your wealth; and your labors be in the house of a stranger;

11 And you mourn at the last, when your flesh and your body are consumed,

12 And say, How have I hated instruction, and my heart despised reproof;

13 And have not obeyed the voice of my teachers, nor inclined mine ear to them that instructed me!

14 I was almost in all evil in the midst of the congregation and assembly.

15 Drink waters out of your own cistern, and running waters out of your own well.

16 Let your fountains be dispersed abroad, and rivers of waters in the streets.

17 Let them be only your own, and not strangers' with you.

18 Let your fountain be blessed: and rejoice with the wife of your youth.

19 Let her be as the loving hind and pleasant roe; let her breasts satisfy you at all times; and be you ravished always with her love.

20 And why will you, my son, be ravished with a strange woman, and embrace the bosom of a stranger?

21 For the ways of man are before the eyes of the Becoming-One, and he ponders all his goings.

22 His own iniquities shall take the wicked himself, and he shall be held with the cords of his sins.

23 He shall die without instruction; and in the greatness of his folly he shall go astray.

Prov 6:1 My son, if you be surety for your friend, if you have pledged your hand with a stranger,

2 you are snared with the words of your mouth, you are taken with the words of your mouth.

3 Do this now, my son, and deliver thyself, when you are come into the hand of your friend; go, humble thyself, and make sure your friend.

4 Give not sleep to your eyes, nor slumber to your eyelids.

5 Deliver yourself as a roe from the hand of the hunter, and as a bird from the hand of the fowler.

6 Go to the ant, you sluggard; consider her ways, and be wise:

7 Which having no guide, overseer, or ruler,

8 Provides her food in the summer, and gathers her food in the harvest.

9 How long will you sleep, O sluggard? when will you arise out of your sleep?

10 Yet a little sleep, a little slumber, a little folding of the hands to sleep:

11 So shall your poverty come as one that travells and your want as an armed man.

12 A naughty person, a wicked man, walks with a perverse mouth.

13 He winks with his eyes, he speaks with his feet, he teaches with his fingers;

14 Forwardness is in his heart, he devises mischief continually; he sows discord.

15 Therefore shall his calamity come suddenly; suddenly shall he be broken without remedy.

16 These six things does the Becoming-One hate: yes, seven are an abomination unto him:

17 A proud look, a lying tongue, and hands that shed innocent blood,

18 a heart that devises wicked imaginations, feet that be swift in running to mischief,

19 A false witness that speaks lies, and he that sows discord among brethren.

20 My son, keep your father's commandment, and forsake not the law of your mother:

21 Bind them continually upon your heart, and tie them about your neck.

22 When you go it shall lead you; when you sleep, it shall keep you; and when you awake, it shall talk with you.

23 For the commandment is a lamp; and the law is light; and reproofs of instruction are the way of life:

24 To keep you from the evil woman, from the flattery of the tongue of a strange woman.

25 Lust not after her beauty in your heart; neither let her take you with her eyelids.

26 For by means of a whorish woman a man is brought to a piece of bread: and the adulteress will hunt for the precious soul.

27 Can a man take fire in his bosom, and his clothes not be burned?

28 Can one go upon hot coals, and his feet not be burned?

29 So he that goes in to his neighbor's wife; whosoever touches her shall not be innocent.

30 Men do not despise a thief, if he steal to satisfy his soul when he is hungry;

31 But if he be found, he shall restore sevenfold; he shall give all the substance of his house.

32 But whoso commits adultery with a woman lacks understanding: he that did it destroys his own soul.

33 A wound and dishonor shall he get; and his reproach shall not be wiped away.

34 For jealousy is the rage of a man: therefore he will not spare in the day of vengeance.

35 He will not regard any ransom; neither will he rest content, though you give many gifts.

Prov 7:1 My son, keep my words, and lay up my commandments with you.

2 Keep my commandments, and live; and my law as the apple of your eye.

3 Bind them upon your fingers, write them upon the table of your heart.

4 Say unto wisdom, you are my sister; and call understanding your kinswoman:

5 That they may keep you from the strange woman, from the stranger which flatters with her words.

6 For at the window of my house I looked through my casement,

7 And beheld among the simple ones, I discerned among the youths, a young man void of understanding,

8 Passing through the street near her corner; and he went the way to her house,

9 In the breeze time, in the evening of the day, in the black and dark night:

10 And, behold, there met him a woman with the attire of a harlot, and subtle of heart.

11 She is loud and stubborn; her feet abide not in her house:

12 Now is she outside, now in the streets, and lies in wait at every corner.

13 So she caught him, and kissed him, and with an impudent face said unto him,

14 I have peace offerings with me; this day have I payed my vows.

15 Therefore came I forth to meet you, diligently to seek your face, and I have found you.

16 I have decked my bed with coverings of tapestry, with carved works, with fine linen of Egypt.

17 I have perfumed my bed with myrrh, aloes, and cinnamon.

18 Come, let us take our fill of love until the morning: let us solace ourselves with loves.

19 For the goodman is not at home, he is gone a long journey:

20 He has taken a bag of money with him, and will come home at the day appointed.

21 With her much fair speech she caused him to yield, with the flattering of her lips she forced him.

22 He goes after her straightway, as an ox goes to the slaughter, or as a fool to the correction of the stocks;

23 Till a dart strike through his liver; as a bird hastens to the snare, and knows not that it is for his soul.

24 listen unto me now therefore, O you children, and attend to the words of my mouth.

25 Let not your heart decline to her ways, go not astray in her paths.

26 For she has cast down many wounded: yes, many strong men have been slain by her.

27 Her house is the way to Sheol, going down to the chambers of death.

Prov 8:1 does not wisdom cry? and understanding put forth her voice?

2 She stands in the top of high places, by the way in the places of the paths.

3 She cries at the gates, at the entry of the city, at the coming in at the doors.

4 Unto you, O men, I call; and my voice is to the sons of man.

5 O you simple, understand prudence: and, you fools, be you of an understanding heart.

6 Hear; for I will speak of excellent things; and the opening of my lips shall be right things.

7 For my mouth shall speak truth; and wickedness is an abomination to my lips.

8 All the words of my mouth are in righteousness; there is nothing twisted or perverse in them.

9 They are all plain to him that understands, and right to them that find knowledge.

10 Receive my instruction, and not silver; and knowledge rather than choice gold.

11 For wisdom is better than rubies; and all the things that may be desired are not to be compared to it.

12 I wisdom dwell with prudence, and find out knowledge of witty inventions.

13 The fear of the Becoming-One is to hate evil: pride, and arrogance, and the evil way, and the perverse mouth, do I hate.

14 Counsel is mine, and sound wisdom: I am understanding; I have strength.

15 By me kings reign, and princes decree justice.

16 By me princes rule, and nobles, even all the judges of the earth.

17 I love them that love me; and those that seek me early shall find me.

18 Riches and honor are with me; yes, durable riches and righteousness.

19 My fruit is better than gold, yes, than fine gold; and my revenue than choice silver.

20 I lead in the way of righteousness, in the midst of the paths of judgment:

21 That I may cause those that love me to inherit substance; and I will fill their treasures.

22 The Becoming-One possessed me in the beginning of his way, before his works of old.

23 I was set up from olam, from the beginning of the ancient earth.

24 When there were no depths, I was brought forth; when there were no fountains abounding with water.

25 Before the mountains were settled, before the hills was I brought forth:

26 While as yet he had not made the earth, nor the fields, nor the highest part of the dust of the world.

27 When he prepared the heavens, I was there: when he set a circle upon the face of the depth:

28 When he established the clouds above: when he strengthened the fountains of the deep:

29 When he gave to the sea his decree, that the waters should not pass his commandment: when he appointed the foundations of the earth:

30 Then I was by him, as one brought up with him: and I was daily his delight, rejoicing always before him;

31 Rejoicing in the habitable part of his earth; and my delights were with the sons of men.

32 Now therefore listen unto me, O you children: for blessed are they that keep my ways.

33 Hear instruction, and be wise, and refuse it not.

34 Blessed is the man that hears me, watching daily at my gates, waiting at the posts of my doors.

35 For whoso finds me finds life, and shall obtain favor of the Becoming-One.

36 But he that sins against me wrongs his own soul: all they that hate me love death.

Prov 9:1 Wisdom has built her house, she has hewn out her seven pillars:

2 She has killed her beasts; she has mingled her wine; she has also furnished her table.

3 She has sent forth her maidens: she cries upon the highest places of the city,

4 Whoso is simple, let him turn in here: as for him that wants understanding, she says to him,

5 Come, eat of my bread, and drink of the wine which I have mingled.

6 Forsake the foolish, and live; and go in the way of understanding.

7 He that reproves a scorner gets to himself shame: and he that rebukes a wicked man gets himself a blot.

8 Reprove not a scorner, lest he hate you: rebuke a wise man, and he will love you.

9 Give instruction to a wise man, and he will be yet wiser: teach a just man, and he will increase in learning.

10 The fear of the Becoming-One is the beginning of wisdom: and the knowledge of the holy is understanding.

11 For by me your days shall be multiplied, and the years of your life shall be increased.

12 If you be wise, you shall be wise for thyself: but if you scorn, you alone shall bear it.

13 A foolish woman is clamorous: she is simple, and knows nothing.

14 For she sits at the door of her house, on a seat in the high places of the city,

15 To call passengers who go right on their ways:

16 Whoso is simple, let him turn in here: and as for him that wants understanding, she says to him,

17 Stolen waters are sweet, and bread eaten in secret is pleasant.

18 But he knows not that the dead are there; and that her guests are in the depths of Sheol.

Prov 10:1 The proverbs of Solomon. A wise son makes a glad father: but a foolish son is the heaviness of his mother.

2 Treasures of wickedness profit nothing: but righteousness delivers from death.

3 The Becoming-One will not permit the soul of the righteous to famish: but he castes away the substance of the wicked.

4 He be comes poor that deals with a slack hand: but the hand of the diligent makes rich.

5 He that gathers in summer is a wise son: but he that sleeps in harvest is a son that causes shame.

6 Blessings are upon the head of the just: but violence covers the mouth of the wicked.

7 The memory of the just is blessed: but the name of the wicked shall rot.

8 The wise in heart will receive commandments: but a prating fool shall fall.

9 He that walks uprightly walks surely: but he that perverts his ways shall be known.

10 He that winks with the eye causes sorrow: but a prating fool shall fall.

11 The mouth of a righteous man is a well of life: but violence covers the mouth of the wicked.

12 Hatred stirs up strife: but love covers all sins.

13 In the lips of him that has understanding wisdom is found: but a rod is for the back of him that is void of understanding.

14 Wise men lay up knowledge: but the mouth of the foolish is near destruction.

15 The rich man's wealth is his strong city: the destruction of the poor is their poverty.

16 The labor of the righteous tends to life: the fruit of the wicked to sin.

17 He is in the way of life that keeps instruction: but he that refuses reproof errs.

18 He that hides hatred with lying lips, and he that utters a slander, is a fool.

19 In the multitude of words there lacks not sin: but he that refrains his lips is wise.

20 The tongue of the just is as choice silver: the heart of the wicked is little worth.

21 The lips of the righteous feed many: but fools die for want of wisdom.

22 The blessing of the Becoming-One, it makes rich, and he adds no sorrow with it.

23 It is as sport to a fool to do mischief: but a man of understanding has wisdom.

24 The fear of the wicked, it shall come upon him: but the desire of the righteous shall be granted.

25 As the whirlwind passes, so is the wicked no more: but the righteous is a foundation of olam.

26 As vinegar to the teeth, and as smoke to the eyes, so is the sluggard to them that send him.

27 The fear of the Becoming-One prolongs days: but the years of the wicked shall be shortened.

28 The hope of the righteous shall be gladness: but the expectation of the wicked shall perish.

29 The way of the Becoming-One is strength to the upright: but destruction shall be to the workers of iniquity.

30 The righteous shall never be removed: but the wicked shall not inhabit the earth.

31 The mouth of the just brings forth wisdom: but the perverse tongue shall be cut out.

32 The lips of the righteous know what is acceptable: but the mouth of the wicked speaks perverseness.

Prov 11:1 A false balance is abomination to the Becoming-One: but a just weight is his delight.

2 When pride comes, then comes shame: but with the lowly is wisdom.

3 The integrity of the upright shall guide them: but the perverseness of transgressors shall destroy them.

4 Riches profit not in the day of wrath: but righteousness delivers from death.

5 The righteousness of the perfect shall direct his way: but the wicked shall fall by his own wickedness.

6 The righteousness of the upright shall deliver them: but transgressors shall be taken in their own naughtiness.

7 When a wicked man dies, his expectation shall perish: and the hope of unjust men perishes.

8 The righteous is delivered out of trouble, and the wicked comes in his stead.

9 a hypocrite with his mouth destroys his neighbor: but through knowledge shall the just be delivered.

10 When it goes well with the righteous, the city rejoices: and when the wicked perish, there is shouting.

11 By the blessing of the upright the city is exalted: but it is overthrown by the mouth of the wicked.

12 He that is void of wisdom despises his neighbor: but a man of understanding holds his peace.

13 A talebearer reveals secrets: but he that is of a faithful spirit conceals the matter.

14 Where no counsel is, the people fall: but in the multitude of counselors there is safety.

15 He that is surety for a stranger shall suffer for it: and he that hates shaking hands is safe.

16 A gracious woman retains honor: and terrifying men retain riches.

17 The merciful man did good to his own soul: but he that is cruel troubles his own flesh.

18 The wicked works a deceitful work: but to him that sows righteousness shall be a sure reward.

19 As righteousness tends to life: so he that pursues evil pursues it to his own death.

20 They that are of a perverse heart are abomination to the Becoming-One: but such as are upright in their way are his delight.

21 Though hand join in hand, the wicked shall not be unpunished: but the seed of the righteous shall be delivered.

22 As a jewel of gold in a swine's snout, so is a fair woman which is without discretion.

23 The desire of the righteous is only good: but the expectation of the wicked is wrath.

24 There is that scatters and yet increases; and there is that withholds more than is meet, but it tends to poverty.

25 The liberal soul shall be made fat: and he that waters shall be watered also himself.

26 He that withholds corn, the people shall curse him: but blessing shall be upon the head of him that sells it.

27 He that diligently seeks good procures favor: but he that seeks mischief, it shall come unto him.

28 He that trusts in his riches shall fall: but the righteous shall flourish as a branch.

29 He that troubles his own house shall inherit the wind: and the fool shall be servant to the wise of heart.

30 The fruit of the righteous is a tree of life; and he that wins souls is wise.

31 Behold, the righteous shall be recompensed in the earth: much more the wicked and the sinner.

Prov 12:1 Whoso loves instruction loves knowledge: but he that hates reproof is brutish.

2 A good man obtains favor of the Becoming-One: but a man of wicked devices will he condemn.

3 A man shall not be established by wickedness: but the root of the righteous shall not be moved.

4 A virtuous woman is a crown to her husband: but she that makes ashamed is as rottenness in his bones.

5 The thoughts of the righteous are right: but the counsels of the wicked are deceit.

6 The words of the wicked are to lie in wait for blood: but the mouth of the upright shall deliver them.

7 The wicked are overthrown, and are not: but the house of the righteous shall stand.

8 A man shall be commended according to his wisdom: but he that is of a perverse heart shall be despised.

9 He that is despised, and has a servant, is better than he that honors himself, and lacks bread.

10 A righteous man regards the soul of his beast: but the tender mercies of the wicked are cruel.

11 He that tills his land shall be satisfied with bread: but he that follows vain persons is void of understanding.

12 The wicked desires the net of evil men: but the root of the righteous yields fruit.

13 The wicked is snared by the transgression of his lips: but the just shall come out of trouble.

14 A man shall be satisfied with good by the fruit of his mouth: and the recompense of a man's hands shall be rendered unto him.

15 The way of a fool is right in his own eyes: but he that listens unto counsel is wise.

16 A fool's wrath is presently known: but a prudent man covers shame.

17 He that speaks truth shows forth righteousness: but a false witness deceit.

18 There is that speaks like the piercings of a sword: but the tongue of the wise is health.

19 The lip of truth shall be established to the beyond: but a lying tongue is but for a moment.

20 Deceit is in the heart of them that imagine evil: but to the counselors of peace is joy.

21 There shall no evil happen to the just: but the wicked shall be filled with mischief.

22 Lying lips are abomination to the Becoming-One: but they that deal truly are his delight.

23 A prudent man conceals knowledge: but the heart of fools proclaims foolishness.

24 The hand of the diligent shall bear rule: but the slothful shall be under tribute.

25 Heaviness in the heart of man makes it stoop: but a good word makes it glad.

26 The righteous is more excellent than his neighbor: but the way of the wicked seduces them.

27 The slothful man roasts not that which he took in hunting: but the substance of a diligent man is precious.

28 In the way of righteousness is life; and in the pathway thereof there is no death.

Prov 13:1 A wise son hears his father's instruction: but a scorner hears not rebuke.

2 A man shall eat good by the fruit of his mouth: but the soul of the transgressors shall eat violence.

3 He that keeps his mouth keeps his life: but he that opens wide his lips shall have destruction.

4 The soul of the sluggard desires, and has nothing: but the soul of the diligent shall be made fat.

5 A righteous man hates lying: but a wicked man is loathsome, and comes to shame.

6 Righteousness keeps him that is upright in the way: but wickedness overthrows the sinner.

7 There is that makes himself rich, yet has nothing: there is that makes himself poor, yet has great riches.

8 The ransom of a man's life are his riches: but the poor hears not rebuke.

9 The light of the righteous rejoices: but the lamp of the wicked shall be put out.

10 Only by pride comes contention: but with the well advised is wisdom.

11 Wealth gotten by vanity shall be diminished: but he that gathers by labor shall increase.

12 Hope deferred makes the heart sick: but when the desire comes, it is a tree of life.

13 Whoso despises the word shall be destroyed: but he that fears the commandment shall be rewarded.

14 The law of the wise is a fountain of life, to depart from the snares of death.

15 Good understanding gives favor: but the way of transgressors is hard.

16 Every prudent man deals with knowledge: but a fool lays open his folly.

17 A wicked messenger falls into mischief: but a faithful ambassador is health.

18 Poverty and shame shall be to him that refuses instruction: but he that regards reproof shall be honored.

19 The desire accomplished is sweet to the soul: but it is abomination to fools to depart from evil.

20 He that walks with wise men shall be wise: but a companion of fools shall be destroyed.

21 Evil pursues sinners: but to the righteous good shall be repaid.

22 A good man leaves an inheritance to his children's children: and the wealth of the sinner is laid up for the just.

23 Much food is in the tillage of the poor: but there is that is destroyed for want of judgment.

24 He that spares his rod hates his son: but he that loves him chastens him early.

25 The righteous eats to the satisfying of his soul: but the belly of the wicked shall want.

Prov 14:1 Every wise woman builds her house: but the foolish plucks it down with her hands.

2 He that walks in his uprightness fears the Becoming-One: but he that is perverse in his ways despises him.

3 In the mouth of the foolish is a rod of pride: but the lips of the wise shall preserve them.

4 Where no oxen are, the crib is clean: but much increase is by the strength of the ox.

5 A faithful witness will not lie: but a false witness will utter lies.

6 A scorner seeks wisdom, and finds it not: but knowledge is easy unto him that understands.

7 Go from the presence of a foolish man, when you perceive not in him the lips of knowledge.

8 The wisdom of the prudent is to understand his way: but the folly of fools is deceit.

9 Fools make a mock at sin: but among the righteous there is favor.

10 The heart knows his own bitterness; and a stranger does not share with his joy.

11 The house of the wicked shall be overthrown: but the tabernacle of the upright shall flourish.

12 There is a way which seems right unto a man, but the end thereof are the ways of death.

13 Even in laughter the heart is sorrowful; and the end of that mirth is heaviness.

14 The backslider in heart shall be filled with his own ways: and a good man shall be satisfied from himself.

15 The simple believes every word: but the prudent man looks well to his going.

16 A wise man fears, and departs from evil: but the fool rages, and is confident.

17 He that is soon angry deals foolishly: and a man of wicked devices is hated.

18 The simple inherit folly: but the prudent are crowned with knowledge.

19 The evil bow before the good; and the wicked at the gates of the righteous.

20 The poor is hated even of his own neighbor: but the rich has many friends.

21 He that despises his neighbor sins: but he that has mercy on the poor, happy is he.

22 Do they not err that devise evil? but mercy and truth shall be to them that devise good.

23 In all labor there is profit: but the talk of the lips tends only to penury.

24 The crown of the wise is their riches: but the foolishness of fools is folly.

25 A true witness delivers souls: but a deceitful witness speaks lies.

26 In the fear of the Becoming-One is strong confidence: and his children shall have a place of refuge.

27 The fear of the Becoming-One is a fountain of life, to depart from the snares of death.

28 In the multitude of people is the king's honor: but in the lack of people is the destruction of the prince.

29 He that is slow to wrath is of great understanding: but he that is hasty of spirit exalts folly.

30 A sound heart is the life of the flesh: but envy the rottenness of the bones.

31 He that oppresses the poor reproaches his Maker: but he that honors him has mercy on the poor.

32 The wicked is driven away in his wickedness: but the righteous has hope in his death.

33 Wisdom rests in the heart of him that has understanding: but that which is in the midst of fools is made known.

34 Righteousness exalts a nation: but sin is a reproach to any people.

35 The king's favor is toward a wise servant: but his wrath is against him that causes shame.

Prov 15:1 A soft answer turns away wrath: but grievous words stir up anger.

2 The tongue of the wise uses knowledge aright: but the mouth of fools pours out foolishness.

3 The eyes of the Becoming-One are in every place, beholding the evil and the good.

4 A wholesome tongue is a tree of life: but perverseness therein is a breach in the spirit.

5 A fool despises his father's instruction: but he that regards reproof is prudent.

6 In the house of the righteous is much treasure: but in the revenues of the wicked is trouble.

7 The lips of the wise disperse knowledge: but the heart of the foolish did not so.

8 The sacrifice of the wicked is an abomination to the Becoming-One: but the prayer of the upright is his delight.

9 The way of the wicked is an abomination unto the Becoming-One: but he loves him that follows after righteousness.

10 Correction is grievous unto him that forsakes the way: and he that hates reproof shall die.

11 Sheol and destruction are before the Becoming-One: how much more then the hearts of the children of men?

12 A scorner loves not one that reproves him: neither will he go unto the wise.

13 A merry heart makes a cheerful countenance: but by sorrow of the heart the spirit is broken.

14 The heart of him that has understanding seeks knowledge: but the mouth of fools feeds on foolishness.

15 All the days of the afflicted are evil: but he that is of a merry heart has a continual feast.

16 Better is little with the fear of the Becoming-One than great treasure and trouble therewith.

17 Better is a dinner of herbs where love is, than a stalled ox and hatred therewith.

18 A wrathful man stirs up strife: but he that is slow to anger appeases strife.

19 The way of the slothful man is as a hedge of thorns: but the way of the righteous is made plain.

20 A wise son makes a glad father: but a foolish man despises his mother.

21 Folly is joy to him that is destitute of wisdom: but a man of understanding walks uprightly.

22 Without counsel purposes are disappointed: but in the multitude of counselors they are established.

23 A man has joy by the answer of his mouth: and a word spoken in due season, how good is it!

24 The way of life is above to the wise, that he may depart from Sheol beneath.

25 The Becoming-One will destroy the house of the proud: but he will establish the border of the widow.

26 The thoughts of the wicked are an abomination to the Becoming-One: but the words of the pure are pleasant words.

27 He that is greedy of gain troubles his own house; but he that hates gifts shall live.

28 The heart of the righteous studies to answer: but the mouth of the wicked pours out evil things.

29 The Becoming-One is far from the wicked: but he hears the prayer of the righteous.

30 The light of the eyes rejoices the heart: and a good report makes the bones fat.

31 The ear that hears the reproof of life abides among the wise.

32 He that refuses instruction despises his own soul: but he that hears reproof gets understanding.

33 The fear of the Becoming-One is the instruction of wisdom; and before honor is humility.

Prov 16:1 The preparations of the heart in man, and the answer of the tongue, is from the Becoming-One.

2 All the ways of a man are clean in his own eyes; but the Becoming-One weighs the spirits.

3 Commit your works unto the Becoming-One, and your thoughts shall be established.

4 The Becoming-One has made all things for himself: yes, even the wicked for the day of evil.

5 Every one that is proud in heart is an abomination to the Becoming-One: though hand join in hand, he shall not be unpunished.

6 By mercy and truth iniquity is purged: and by the fear of the Becoming-One men depart from evil.

7 When a man's ways please the Becoming-One, he makes even his enemies to be at peace with him.

8 Better is a little with righteousness than great revenues without right.

9 A man's heart devises his way: but the Becoming-One directs his steps.

10 A divine sentence is in the lips of the king: his mouth transgresses not in judgment.

11 A just weight and balance are the Becoming-One's: all the weights of the bag are his work.

12 It is an abomination to kings to commit wickedness: for the throne is established by righteousness.

13 Righteous lips are the delight of kings; and they love him that speaks right.

14 The wrath of a king is as messengers of death: but a wise man will pacify it.

15 In the light of the king's countenance is life; and his favor is as a cloud of the latter rain.

16 How much better is it to get wisdom than gold! and to get understanding to be chosen rather than silver!

17 The highway of the upright is to depart from evil: he that keeps his way preserves his soul.

18 Pride goes before destruction, and a haughty spirit before a fall.

19 Better it is to be of a humble spirit with the lowly, than to divide the spoil with the proud.

20 He that handles a matter wisely shall find good: and whoso trusts in the Becoming-One, happy is he.

21 The wise in heart shall be called prudent: and the sweetness of the lips increases learning.

22 Understanding is a wellspring of life unto him that has it: but the instruction of fools is folly.

23 The heart of the wise teaches his mouth, and adds learning to his lips.

24 Pleasant words are as a honeycomb, sweet to the soul, and health to the bones.

25 There is a way that seems right unto a man, but the end thereof are the ways of death.

26 The soul of him that labors labors for himself; for his mouth craves it of him.

27 An ungodly man digs up evil: and in his lips there is as a burning fire.

28 A perverse man sows strife: and a whisperer separates chief friends.

29 A violent man entices his neighbor, and leads him into the way that is not good.

30 He shuts his eyes to devise perverse things: moving his lips he brings evil to pass.

31 The hoary head is a crown of glory, if it be found in the way of righteousness.

32 He that is slow to anger is better than the mighty; and he that rules his spirit than he that takes a city.

33 The lot is cast into the lap; but the whole disposing thereof is of the Becoming-One.

Prov 17:1 Better is a dry morsel, and quietness therewith, than a house full of sacrifices with strife.

2 A wise servant shall have rule over a son that causes shame, and shall have part of the inheritance among the brethren.

3 The fining pot is for silver, and the furnace for gold: but the Becoming-One tries the hearts.

4 A wicked doer gives heed to false lips; and a liar gives ear to a naughty tongue.

5 Whoso mocks the poor reproaches his Maker: and he that is glad at calamities shall not be unpunished.

6 Children's children are the crown of old men; and the glory of children are their fathers.

7 Excellent speech becomes not a fool: much less do lying lips a prince.

8 A gift is as a precious stone in the eyes of him that has it: wheresoever it turns, it prospers.

9 He that covers a transgression seeks love; but he that repeats a matter separates very friends.

10 A reproof enters more into a wise man than a hundred stripes into a fool.

11 An evil man seeks only rebellion: therefore a cruel messenger shall be sent against him.

12 Let a bear robbed of her whelps meet a man, rather than a fool in his folly.

13 Whoso rewards evil for good, evil shall not depart from his house.

14 The beginning of strife is as when one lets out water: therefore leave off contention, before it be meddled with.

15 He that justifies the wicked, and he that condemns the just, even they both are abomination to the Becoming-One.

16 Therefore is there a price in the hand of a fool to get wisdom, seeing he has no heart to it?

17 A friend loves at all times, and a brother is born for adversity.

18 A man void of understanding strikes hands, and be comes surety in the presence of his friend.

19 He loves transgression that loves strife: and he that exalts his gate seeks destruction.

20 He that has a perverse heart finds no good: and he that has a perverse tongue falls into mischief.

21 He that begets a fool did it to his sorrow: and the father of a fool has no joy.

22 A merry heart did good like a medicine: but a broken spirit dries the bones.

23 A wicked man takes a gift out of the bosom to pervert the ways of judgment.

24 Wisdom is before him that has understanding; but the eyes of a fool are in the ends of the earth.

25 A foolish son is a grief to his father, and bitterness to her that bare him.

26 Also to punish the just is not good, nor to strike princes for equity.

27 He that has knowledge spares his words: and a man of understanding is of an excellent spirit.

28 Even a fool, when he holds his peace, is counted wise: and he that shuts his lips is esteemed a man of understanding.

Prov 18:1 Through desire, he, having separated himself, seeks to lay bare all wisdom.

2 A fool has no delight in understanding, but that his heart may discover itself.

3 When the wicked comes, then comes also contempt, and with ignominy reproach.

4 The words of a man's mouth are as deep waters, and the wellspring of wisdom as a flowing brook.

5 It is not good to accept the person of the wicked, to overthrow the righteous in judgment.

6 A fool's lips enter into contention, and his mouth calls for strokes.

7 A fool's mouth is his destruction, and his lips are the snare of his soul.

8 The words of a talebearer are as wounds, and they go down into the innermost parts of the belly.

9 He also that is slothful in his work is brother to him that is a great waster.

10 The name of the Becoming-One is a strong tower: the righteous runs into it, and is safe.

11 The rich man's wealth is his strong city, and as a high wall in his own conceit.

12 Before destruction the heart of man is haughty, and before honor is humility.

13 He that answers a matter before he hears it, it is folly and shame unto him.

14 The spirit of a man will sustain his infirmity; but a wounded spirit who can bear?

15 The heart of the prudent gets knowledge; and the ear of the wise seeks knowledge.

16 A man's gift makes room for him, and brings him before great men.

17 He that is first in his own cause seems just; but his neighbor comes and searches him.

18 The lot causes contentions to cease, and parts between the mighty.

19 A brother offended is harder to be won than a strong city: and their contentions are like the bars of a castle.

20 A man's belly shall be satisfied with the fruit of his mouth; and with the increase of his lips shall he be filled.

21 Death and life are in the power of the tongue: and they that love it shall eat the fruit thereof.

22 Whoso finds a wife finds a good thing, and obtains favor of the Becoming-One.

23 The poor uses entreaties; but the rich answers roughly.

24 A man that has friends must show himself friendly: and there is a friend that sticks closer than a brother.

Prov 19:1 Better is the poor that walks in his integrity, than he that is perverse in his lips, and is a fool.

2 Also, that the soul be without knowledge, it is not good; and he that hastens with his feet sins.

3 The foolishness of man perverts his way: and his heart frets against the Becoming-One.

4 Wealth makes many friends; but the poor is separated from his neighbor.

5 A false witness shall not be unpunished, and he that speaks lies shall not escape.

6 Many will entreat the favor of the prince: and every man is a friend to him that gives gifts.

7 All the brethren of the poor do hate him: how much more do his friends go far from him? he pursues them with words, yet they are wanting to him.

8 He that gets wisdom loves his own soul: he that keeps understanding shall find good.

9 A false witness shall not be unpunished, and he that speaks lies shall perish.

10 Delight is not seemly for a fool; much less for a servant to have rule over princes.

11 The discretion of a man defers his anger; and it is his glory to pass over a transgression.

12 The king's wrath is as the roaring of a lion; but his favor is as dew upon the grass.

13 A foolish son is the calamity of his father: and the contentions of a wife are a continual dropping.

14 House and riches are the inheritance of fathers: and a prudent wife is from the Becoming-One.

15 Slothfullness casts into a deep sleep; and an idle soul shall suffer hunger.

16 He that keeps the commandment keeps his own soul; but he that despises his ways shall die.

17 He that has pity upon the poor lends unto the Becoming-One; and that which he has given will he pay him again.

18 Chasten your son while there is hope, and let not your soul spare for his crying.

19 A man of great wrath shall suffer punishment: for if you deliver him, yet you must do it again.

20 Hear counsel, and receive instruction, that you may be wise in your latter end.

21 There are many devices in a man's heart; nevertheless the counsel of the Becoming-One, that shall stand.

22 The desire of a man is his kindness: and a poor man is better than a liar.

23 The fear of the Becoming-One tends to life: and he that has it shall abide satisfied; he shall not be visited with evil.

24 A slothful man hides his hand in his bosom, and will not so much as bring it to his mouth again.

25 Smite a scorner, and the simple will beware: and reprove one that has understanding, and he will understand knowledge.

26 He that wastes his father, and chases away his mother, is a son that causes shame, and brings reproach.

27 Cease, my son, to hear the instruction that causes to err from the words of knowledge.

28 An ungodly witness scorns judgment: and the mouth of the wicked devours iniquity.

29 Judgments are prepared for scorners, and stripes for the back of fools.

Prov 20:1 Wine is a mocker, strong drink is raging: and whosoever is deceived thereby is not wise.

2 The fear of a king is as the roaring of a lion: whoso provokes him to anger sins against his own soul.

3 It is a honor for a man to cease from strife: but every fool will be meddling.

4 The sluggard will not plow by reason of the cold; therefore shall he beg in harvest, and have nothing.

5 Counsel in the heart of man is like deep water; but a man of understanding will draw it out.

6 Most men will proclaim every one his own goodness: but a faithful man who can find?

7 The just man walks in his integrity: his children are blessed after him.

8 A king that sits in the throne of judgment scatters away all evil with his eyes.

9 Who can say, I have made my heart clean, I am pure from my sin?

10 Diverse weights, and diverse measures, both of them are alike abomination to the Becoming-One.

11 Even a child is known by his doings, whether his work be pure, and whether it be right.

12 The hearing ear, and the seeing eye, the Becoming-One has made even both of them.

13 Love not sleep, lest you come to poverty; open your eyes, and you shall be satisfied with bread.

14 It is naught, it is naught, says the buyer: but when he is gone his way, then he boasts.

15 There is gold, and a multitude of rubies: but the lips of knowledge are a precious jewel.

16 Take his garment that is surety for a stranger: and take a pledge of him for a strange woman.

17 Bread of deceit is sweet to a man; but afterwards his mouth shall be filled with gravel.

18 Every purpose is established by counsel: and with good advice make war.

19 He that goes about as a talebearer reveals secrets: therefore meddle not with him that flatters with his lips.

20 Whoso curses his father or his mother, his lamp shall be put out in obscure darkness.

21 An inheritance may be gotten hastily at the beginning; but the end thereof shall not be blessed.

22 Say not you, I will recompense evil; but wait on the Becoming-One, and he shall save you.

23 Diverse weights are an abomination unto the Becoming-One; and a false balance is not good.

24 Man's goings are of the Becoming-One; how can a man then understand his own way?

25 It is a snare to the man who devours that which is holy, and after vows to make inquiry.

26 A wise king scatters the wicked, and brings the wheel over them.

27 The spirit of man is the candle of the Becoming-One, searching all the inward parts of the belly.

28 Mercy and truth preserve the king: and his throne is held up by mercy.

29 The glory of young men is their strength: and the beauty of old men is the grey head.

30 The blueness of a wound cleanses away evil: so do stripes the inward parts of the belly.

Prov 21:1 The king's heart is in the hand of the Becoming-One, as the rivers of water: he turns it wheresoever he will.

2 Every way of a man is right in his own eyes: but the Becoming-One ponders the hearts.

3 To do justice and judgment is more acceptable to the Becoming-One than sacrifice.

4 a high look, and a proud heart, and the plowing of the wicked, is sin.

5 The thoughts of the diligent tend only to plenteousness; but of every one that is hasty only to want.

6 The getting of treasures by a lying tongue is a vanity tossed back and forth of them that seek death.

7 The robbery of the wicked shall destroy them; because they refuse to do judgment.

8 The way of man is perverse and strange: but as for the pure, his work is right.

9 It is better to dwell in a corner of the housetop, than with a contentious woman in a wide house.

10 The soul of the wicked desires evil: his neighbor finds no favor in his eyes.

11 When the scorner is punished, the simple is made wise: and when the wise is instructed, he receives knowledge.

12 The righteous man wisely considers the house of the wicked: but God overthrows the wicked for their wickedness.

13 Whoso stops his ears at the cry of the poor, he also shall cry himself, but shall not be heard.

14 A gift in secret pacifies anger: and a reward in the bosom strong wrath.

15 [It is] joy to the just to do judgment: but destruction [shall be] to the workers of iniquity

16 The man that wanders out of the way of understanding shall remain in the congregation of the dead

17 He that loves pleasure [shall be] a poor man: he that loves wine and oil shall not be rich.

18 The wicked [shall be] a ransom for the righteous, and the transgressor for the upright

19 [It is] better to dwell in the wilderness, than with a contentious and an angry woman.

20 [There is] treasure to be desired and oil in the dwelling of the wise; but a foolish man spends it up

21 He that follows after righteousness and mercy finds life, righteousness, and honor

22 A wise [man] scales the city of the mighty, and casts down the strength of the confidence thereof

23 Whoso keeps his mouth and his tongue keeps his soul from troubles

24 Proud [and] haughty scorner [is] his name, who deals in proud wrath.

25 The desire of the slothful kills him; for his hands refuse to labor

26 He covets greedily all the day long: but the righteous gives and spares not

27 The sacrifice of the wicked [is] abomination: how much more, [when] he brings it with a wicked mind?

28 A false witness shall perish: but the man that hears speaks constantly.

29 A wicked man hardens his face: but [as for] the upright, he directs his way.

30 [There is] no wisdom nor understanding nor counsel against the Becoming-One

31 The horse [is] prepared against the day of battle: but safety [is] of the Becoming-One.

Pro 22:1 A [good] name [is] rather to be chosen than great riches, [and] loving favor rather than silver and gold.

2 The rich and poor meet together: the Becoming-One [is] the maker of them all

3 A prudent [man] foresees the evil, and hides himself: but the simple pass on, and are punished

4 By humility [and] the fear of the Becoming-One [are] riches, and honor, and life.

5 Thorns [and] snares [are] in the way of the perverse: he that doth keep his soul shall be far from them

6 Train up a child in the way he should go: and when he is old, he will not depart from it.

7 The rich rules over the poor, and the borrower [is] servant to the lender.

8 He that sows iniquity shall reap vanity: and the rod of his anger shall fail.

9 He that hath a bountiful eye shall be blessed; for he giveth of his bread to the poor.

10 Cast out the scorner, and contention shall go out; yes, strife and reproach shall cease

11 He that loves pureness of heart, [for] the grace of his lips the king [shall be] his friend.

12 The eyes of the Becoming-One preserve knowledge, and he overthrows the words of the transgressor.

13 The slothful [man] says, [There is] a lion without, I shall be slain in the streets

14 The mouth of strange women [is] a deep pit: he that is abhorred of the Becoming-One shall fall therein

15 Foolishness [is] bound in the heart of a child; [but] the rod of correction shall drive it far from him

16 He that oppresses the poor to increase his [riches, and] he that giveth to the rich, [shall] surely [come] to want

17 Bow down thine ear, and hear the words of the wise, and apply thine heart unto my knowledge

18 For [it is] a pleasant thing if thou keep them within you; they shall withal be fitted in thy lips.

19 That thy trust may be in the Becoming-One, I have made known to you this day, even to you.

20 Have not I written to you excellent things in counsels and knowledge

21 That I might make you know the certainty of the words of truth; that you might answer the words of truth to them that send unto you?

22 Rob not the poor, because he [is] poor: neither oppress the afflicted in the gate

23 For the Becoming-One will plead their cause, and spoil the soul of those that spoiled them

24 Make no friendship with an angry man; and with a furious man thou shalt not go

25 Lest you learn his ways, and get a snare to thy soul

26 Be not you [one] of them that strike hands, [or] of them that are sureties for debts

27 If you hast nothing to pay, why should he take away thy bed from under you

28 Remove not the ancient landmark, which your fathers have set.

29 See you a man diligent in his business? he shall stand before kings; he shall not stand before mean [men].

Pro 23:1 When you sit to eat with a ruler, consider diligently what [is] before you

2 And put a knife to your throat, if you [be] a man given to appetite

3 Be not desirous of his dainties: for they [are] deceitful meat

4 labor not to be rich: cease from thine own wisdom

5 Wilt thou set thine eyes upon that which is not? for [riches] certainly make themselves wings; they fly away as an eagle toward heaven.

6 Eat thou not the bread of [him that hath] an evil eye, neither desire thou his dainty meats

7 For as he thinks in his heart, so [is] he: Eat and drink, says he to you; but his heart [is] not with you

8 The morsel [which] you have eaten shalt you vomit up, and lose your sweet words

9 Speak not in the ears of a fool: for he will despise the wisdom of your words

10 Remove not the old landmark; and enter not into the fields of the fatherless:

11 For their redeemer [is] mighty; he shall plead their cause with you

12 Apply your heart unto instruction, and your ears to the words of knowledge

13 Withhold not correction from the child: for [if] you hit him with the rod, he shall not die

14 You shall hit him with the rod, and shall deliver his soul from Sheol

15 My son, if your heart be wise, my heart shall rejoice, even mine.

16 Yes, my reins shall rejoice, when your lips speak right things

17 Let not your heart envy sinners: but [be thou] in the fear of the Becoming-One all the day long

18 For surely there is an end; and thine expectation shall not be cut off.

19 Hear you, my son, and be wise, and guide your heart in the way

20 Be not among wine bibbers; among riotous eaters of flesh:

21 For the drunkard and the glutton shall come to poverty: and drowsiness shall clothe [a man] with rags

22 Listen unto thy father that begat you, and despise not thy mother when she is old

23 Buy the truth, and sell it not; [also] wisdom, and instruction, and understanding

24 The father of the righteous shall greatly rejoice: and he that begets a wise [child] shall have joy of him

25 Thy father and thy mother shall be glad, and she that bare you shall rejoice

26 My son, give me thine heart, and let thine eyes observe my ways

27 For a whore [is] a deep ditch; and a strange woman [is] a narrow pit

28 She also lies in wait as [for] a prey, and increases the transgressors among men.

29 Who has woe? who has sorrow? who has contentions? who has babbling? who has wounds without cause? who has redness of eyes

30 They that tarry long at the wine; they that go to seek mixed wine

31 Look not upon the wine when it is red, when it giveth his color in the cup, [when] it moves itself aright

32 At the last it bites like a serpent, and stings like an adder.

33 your eyes shall behold strange women, and your heart shall utter perverse things.

34 Yes, you shall be as he that lies down in the midst of the sea, or as he that lies upon the top of a mast.

35 They have stricken me, shall you say, and I was not sick; they have beaten me, and I felt it not: when shall I awake? I will seek it yet again.

Prov 24:1 Be not you envious against evil men, neither desire to be with them.

2 For their heart studies destruction, and their lips talk of mischief.

3 Through wisdom is a house built; and by understanding it is established:

4 And by knowledge shall the chambers be filled with all precious and pleasant riches.

5 A wise man is strong; yes, a man of knowledge increases strength.

6 For by wise counsel you shall make your war: and in multitude of counselors there is safety.

7 Wisdom is too high for a fool: he opens not his mouth in the gate.

8 He that devises to do evil shall be called a mischievous person.

9 The thought of foolishness is sin: and the scorner is an abomination to men.

10 If you faint in the day of adversity, your strength is small.

11 If you forbear to deliver them that are drawn unto death, and those that are ready to be slain;

12 If you say, Behold, we knew it not; does not he that ponders the heart consider it? and he that keeps your soul, does not he know it? and shall not he render to every man according to his works?

13 My son, eat you honey, because it is good; and the honeycomb, which is sweet to your taste:

14 So shall the knowledge of wisdom be unto your soul: when you have found it, then there shall be a reward, and your expectation shall not be cut off.

15 Lay not wait, O wicked man, against the dwelling of the righteous; spoil not his resting place:

16 For a just man falls seven times, and rises up again: but the wicked shall fall into mischief.

17 Rejoice not when your enemy falls, and let not your heart be glad when he stumbles:

18 Lest the Becoming-One see it, and it displease him, and he turn away his wrath from him.

19 Fret not yourself because of evil men, neither be you envious at the wicked;

20 For there shall be no reward to the evil man; the candle of the wicked shall be put out.

21 My son, fear you the Becoming-One and the king: and meddle not with them that are given to change:

22 For their calamity shall rise suddenly; and who knows the ruin of them both?

23 These things also belong to the wise. It is not good to have respect of persons in judgment.

24 He that says unto the wicked, you are righteous; him shall the people curse, nations shall abhor him:

25 But to them that rebuke him shall be delight, and a good blessing shall come upon them.

26 Every man shall kiss his lips that gives a right answer.

27 Prepare your work outside, and make it fit for yourself in the field; and afterwards build your house.

28 Be not a witness against your neighbor without cause; and deceive not with your lips.

29 Say not, I will do so to him as he has done to me: I will render to the man according to his work.

30 I went by the field of the slothful, and by the vineyard of the man void of understanding;

31 And, lo, it was all grown over with thorns, and nettles had covered the face thereof, and the stone wall thereof was broken down.

32 Then I saw, and considered it well: I looked upon it, and received instruction.

33 Yet a little sleep, a little slumber, a little folding of the hands to sleep:

34 So shall your poverty come as one that travels; and your want as an armed man.

Prov 25:1 These are also proverbs of Solomon, which the men of Hezekiah king of Judah copied out.

2 It is the glory of God to conceal a thing: but the honor of kings is to search out a matter.

3 The heavens for height, and the earth for depth, and the heart of kings is unsearchable.

4 Take away the dross from the silver, and there shall come forth a vessel for the finer.

5 Take away the wicked from before the king, and his throne shall be established in righteousness.

6 Put not forth yourself in the presence of the king, and stand not in the place of great men:

7 For better it is that it be said unto you, Come up here; than that you should be put lower in the presence of the prince whom your eyes have seen.

8 Go not forth hastily to strive, lest you know not what to do in the end thereof, when your neighbor has put you to shame.

9 Debate your cause with your neighbor himself; and discover not a secret to another:

10 Lest he that hears it put you to shame, and your infamy turn not away.

11 A word fitly spoken is like apples of gold in pictures of silver.

12 As an earring of gold, and an ornament of fine gold, so is a wise reprover upon an obedient ear.

13 As the cold of snow in the time of harvest, so is a faithful messenger to them that send him: for he refreshs the soul of his masters.

14 Whoso boasts himself of a false gift is like clouds and wind without rain.

15 By long forbearing is a prince persuaded, and a soft tongue breaks the bone.

16 have you found honey? eat so much as is sufficient for you, lest you be filled therewith, and vomit it.

17 Withdraw your foot from your neighbor's house; lest he be weary of you, and so hate you.

18 A man that bears false witness against his neighbor is a maul, and a sword, and a sharp arrow.

19 Confidence in an unfaithful man in time of trouble is like a broken tooth, and a foot out of joint.

20 As he that takes away a garment in cold weather, and as vinegar upon nitre, so is he that sings songs to a heavy heart.

21 If your enemy be hungry, give him bread to eat; and if he be thirsty, give him water to drink:

22 For you shall heap coals of fire upon his head, and the Becoming-One shall reward you.

23 The north wind drives away rain: so does an angry countenance a backbiting tongue.

24 It is better to dwell in the corner of the housetop, than with a contentious woman and in a wide house.

25 As cold waters to a thirsty soul, so is good news from a far country.

26 A righteous man falling down before the wicked is as a troubled fountain, and a corrupt spring.

27 It is not good to eat much honey: so for men to search their own glory is not glory.

28 He that has no rule over his own spirit is like a city that is broken down, and without walls.

Prov 26:1 As snow in summer, and as rain in harvest, so honor is not seemly for a fool.

2 As the bird by wandering, as the swallow by flying, so the curse causeless shall not come.

3 A whip for the horse, a bridle for the donkey, and a rod for the fool's back.

4 Answer not a fool according to his folly, lest you also be like unto him.

5 Answer a fool according to his folly, lest he be wise in his own conceit.

6 He that sends a message by the hand of a fool cuts off the feet, and drinks damage.

7 The legs of the lame are not equal: so is a parable in the mouth of fools.

8 As he that binds a stone in a sling, so is he that gives honor to a fool.

9 As a thorn goes up into the hand of a drunkard, so is a parable in the mouth of fools.

10 The great God that formed all things both rewards the fool, and rewards transgressors.

11 As a dog returns to his vomit, so a fool returns to his folly.

12 see you a man wise in his own conceit? there is more hope of a fool than of him.

13 The slothful man says, There is a lion in the way; a lion is in the streets.

14 As the door turns upon his hinges, so does the slothful upon his bed.

15 The slothful hides his hand in his bosom; it grieves him to bring it again to his mouth.

16 The sluggard is wiser in his own conceit than seven men that can render a reason.

17 He that passes by, and meddles with strife belonging not to him, is like one that takes a dog by the ears.

18 As a mad man who casts firebrands, arrows, and death,

19 So is the man that deceives his neighbor, and says, Am not I in sport?

20 Where no wood is, there the fire goes out: so where there is no talebearer, the strife ceaseth.

21 As coals are to burning coals, and wood to fire; so is a contentious man to kindle strife.

22 The words of a talebearer are as wounds, and they go down into the innermost parts of the belly.

23 Burning lips and a wicked heart are like a potsherd covered with silver dross.

24 He that hates dissembles with his lips, and lays up deceit within him;

25 When he speaks fair, believe him not: for there are seven abominations in his heart.

26 Whose hatred is covered by deceit, his wickedness shall be showed before the whole congregation.

27 Whoso digs a pit shall fall therein: and he that rolls a stone, it will return upon him.

28 A lying tongue hates those that are afflicted by it; and a flattering mouth works ruin.

Prov 27:1 Boast not yourself of tomorrow; for you know not what a day may bring forth.

2 Let another man praise you, and not your own mouth; a stranger, and not your own lips.

3 A stone is heavy, and the sand weighty; but a fool's wrath is heavier than them both.

4 Wrath is cruel, and anger is outrageous; but who is able to stand before envy?

5 Open rebuke is better than secret love.

6 Faithful are the wounds of a friend; but the kisses of an enemy are deceitful.

7 The full soul loathes a honeycomb; but to the hungry soul every bitter thing is sweet.

8 As a bird that wanders from her nest, so is a man that wanders from his place.

9 Ointment and perfume rejoice the heart: so does the sweetness of a man's friend by soulful counsel.

10 your own friend, and your father's friend, forsake not; neither go into your brother's house in the day of your calamity: for better is a neighbor that is near than a brother far off.

11 My son, be wise, and make my heart glad, that I may answer him that reproaches me.

12 A prudent man foresees the evil, and hides himself; but the simple pass on, and are punished.

13 Take his garment that is surety for a stranger, and take a pledge of him for a strange woman.

14 He that blesses his friend with a loud voice, rising early in the morning, it shall be counted a curse to him.

15 A continual dropping in a very rainy day and a contentious woman are alike.

16 Whosoever hides her hides the wind, and as the oil his right hand touches.

17 Iron sharpens iron; so a man sharpens the countenance of his friend.

18 Whoso keeps the fig tree shall eat the fruit thereof: so he that waits on his master shall be honored.

19 As in water face answers to face, so the heart of man to man.

20 Sheol and destruction are never full; so the eyes of man are never satisfied.

21 As the fining pot for silver, and the furnace for gold; so is a man to his praise.

22 Though you should bray a fool in a mortar among wheat with a pestle, yet will not his foolishness depart from him.

23 Be you diligent to know the state of your flocks, and look well to your herds.

24 For riches are not for olam: and does the crown endure to every generation?

25 The hay appears, and the tender grass shows itself, and herbs of the mountains are gathered.

26 The lambs are for your clothing, and the goats are the price of the field.

27 And you shall have goats' milk enough for your food, for the food of your household, and for the maintenance for your maidens.

Prov 28:1 The wicked flee when no man pursues: but the righteous are bold as a lion.

2 For the transgression of a land many are the princes thereof: but by a man of understanding and knowledge the state thereof shall be prolonged.

3 A poor man that oppresses the poor is like a sweeping rain which leaves no food.

4 They that forsake the law praise the wicked: but such as keep the law contend with them.

5 Evil men understand not judgment: but they that seek the Becoming-One understand all things.

6 Better is the poor that walks in his uprightness, than he that is perverse in his ways, though he be rich.

7 Whoso keeps the law is a wise son: but he that is a companion of riotous men shames his father.

8 He that by usury and unjust gain increases his substance, he shall gather it for him that will pity the poor.

9 He that turns away his ear from hearing the law, even his prayer shall be abomination.

10 Whoso causes the righteous to go astray in an evil way, he shall fall himself into his own pit: but the upright shall have good things in possession.

11 The rich man is wise in his own conceit; but the poor that has understanding searches him out.

12 When righteous men do rejoice, there is great glory: but when the wicked rise, a man is hidden.

13 He that covers his sins shall not prosper: but whoso confesses and forsakes them shall have mercy.

14 Happy is the man that fears always: but he that hardens his heart shall fall into mischief.

15 As a roaring lion, and a ranging bear; so is a wicked ruler over the poor people.

16 The prince that lacks understanding is also a great oppressor: but he that hates covetousness shall prolong his days.

17 A man that did violence to the blood of any soul shall flee to the pit; let no man stay him.

18 Whoso walks uprightly shall be saved: but he that is perverse in his ways shall fall at once.

19 He that tills his land shall have plenty of bread: but he that follows after vain persons shall have poverty enough.

20 A faithful man shall abound with blessings: but he that makes haste to be rich shall not be innocent.

21 To have respect of persons is not good: for for a piece of bread that man will transgress.

22 He that hastens to be rich has an evil eye, and considers not that poverty shall come upon him.

23 He that rebukes a man afterwards shall find more favor than he that flatters with the tongue.

24 Whoso robs his father or his mother, and says, It is no transgression; the same is the companion of a destroyer.

25 He that is of a proud soul stirs up strife: but he that puts his trust in the Becoming-One shall be made fat.

26 He that trusts in his own heart is a fool: but whoso walks wisely, he shall be delivered.

27 He that gives unto the poor shall not lack: but he that hides his eyes shall have many a curse.

28 When the wicked rise, men hide themselves: but when they perish, the righteous increase.

Prov 29:1 He, that being often reproved hardens his neck, shall suddenly be destroyed, and that without remedy.

2 When the righteous are in authority, the people rejoice: but when the wicked bears rule, the people mourn.

3 Whoso loves wisdom rejoices his father: but he that keeps company with harlots spends his substance.

4 The king by judgment establishes the land: but he that receives gifts overthrows it.

5 A man that flatters his neighbor spreads a net for his feet.

6 In the transgression of an evil man there is a snare: but the righteous does sing and rejoice.

7 The righteous considers the cause of the poor: but the wicked regards not to know it.

8 Scornful men bring a city into a snare: but wise men turn away wrath.

9 If a wise man contends with a foolish man, whether he rage or laugh, there is no rest.

10 The bloodthirsty hate the upright: but the just seek his soul.

11 A fool utters all his spirit: but a wise man keeps it in till afterwards.

12 If a ruler listen to lies, all his servants are wicked.

13 The poor and the deceitful man meet together: the Becoming-One lightens both their eyes.

14 The king that faithfully judges the poor, his throne shall be established to the beyond.

15 The rod and reproof give wisdom: but a child left to himself brings his mother to shame.

16 When the wicked are multiplied, transgression increases: but the righteous shall see their fall.

17 Correct your son, and he shall give you rest; yes, he shall give delight unto your soul.

18 Where there is no vision, the people perish: but he that keeps the law, happy is he.

19 A servant will not be corrected by words: for though he understand he will not answer.

20 see you a man that is hasty in his words? there is more hope of a fool than of him.

21 He that delicately brings up his servant from a child shall have him become his son at the length.

22 An angry man stirs up strife, and a furious man abounds in transgression.

23 A man's pride shall bring him low: but honor shall uphold the humble in spirit.

24 Whoso is partner with a thief hates his own soul: he hears an oath, and reveals it not [to the judge].

25 The fear of man brings a snare: but whoso puts his trust in the Becoming-One shall be safe.

26 Many seek the ruler's favor; but every man's judgment comes from the Becoming-One.

27 An unjust man is an abomination to the just: and he that is upright in the way is abomination to the wicked.

Prov 30:1 The words of Agur the son of Jakeh, even the prophecy: the man spoke unto Ithiel, even unto Ithiel and Ucal,

2 Surely I am more brutish than any man, and have not the understanding of a man.

3 I neither learned wisdom, nor have the knowledge of the holy.

4 Who has ascended up into heaven, or descended? who has gathered the wind in his fists? who has bound the waters in a garment? who has established all the ends of the earth? what is his name, and what is his son's name, if you can tell?

5 Every word of God is pure: he is a shield unto them that put their trust in him.

6 Add you not unto his words, lest he reprove you, and you be found a liar.

7 Two things have I required of you; deny me them not before I die:

8 Remove far from me vanity and lies: give me neither poverty nor riches; feed me with food convenient for me:

9 Lest I be full, and deny you, and say, Who is the Becoming-One? or lest I be poor, and steal, and take the name of my God in vain.

10 Accuse not a servant unto his master, lest he curse you, and you be found guilty.

11 There is a generation that curses their father, and does not bless their mother.

12 There is a generation that are pure in their own eyes, and yet is not washed from their filthiness.

13 There is a generation, O how lofty are their eyes! and their eyelids are lifted up.

14 There is a generation, whose teeth are as swords, and their jaw teeth as knives, to devour the poor from off the earth, and the needy from among men.

15 The horse leach has two daughters, crying, Give, give. There are three things that are never satisfied, yes, four things say not, It is enough:

16 Sheol; and the barren womb; the earth that is not filled with water; and the fire that says not, It is enough.

17 The eye that mocks at his father, and despises to obey his mother, the ravens of the valley shall pick it out, and the young eagles shall eat it.

18 There be three things which are too wonderful for me, yes, four which I know not:

19 The way of an eagle in the air; the way of a serpent upon a rock; the way of a ship in the midst of the sea; and the way of a man with a maid.

20 Such is the way of an adulterous woman; she eats, and wipes her mouth, and says, I have done no wickedness.

21 For three things the earth is disquieted, and for four which it cannot bear:

22 For a servant when he reigns; and a fool when he is filled with food;

23 For an odious woman when she is married; and a handmaid that is heir to her mistress.

24 There be four things which are little upon the earth, but they are exceeding wise:

25 The ants are a people not strong, yet they prepare their food in the summer;

26 The conies are but a feeble folk, yet make they their houses in the rocks;

27 The locusts have no king, yet go they forth all of them by bands;

28 The spider takes hold with her hands, and is in kings' palaces.

29 There be three things which go well, yes, four are becoming in going:

30 A lion which is strongest among beasts, and turns not away for any;

31 A greyhound; a he goat also; and a king, against whom there is no rising up.

32 If you have done foolishly in lifting up thyself, or if you have thought evil, lay your hand upon your mouth.

33 Surely the churning of milk brings forth butter, and the wringing of the nose brings forth blood: so the forcing of wrath brings forth strife.

Prov 31:1 The words of king Lemuel, the prophecy that his mother taught him.

2 What, my son? and what, the son of my womb? and what, the son of my vows?

3 Give not your strength unto women, nor your ways to that which destroys kings.

4 It is not for kings, O Lemuel, it is not for kings to drink wine; nor for princes strong drink:

5 Lest they drink, and forget the law, and pervert the judgment of any of the afflicted.

6 Give strong drink unto him that is ready to perish, and wine unto those that be of heavy souls.

7 Let him drink, and forget his poverty, and remember his misery no more.

8 Open your mouth for the mute in the cause of all such as are appointed to destruction.

9 Open your mouth, judge righteously, and plead the cause of the poor and needy.

10 Who can find a virtuous woman? for her price is far above rubies.

11 The heart of her husband does safely trust in her, so that he shall have no need of spoil.

12 She will do him good and not evil all the days of her life.

13 She seeks wool, and flax, and works willingly with her hands.

14 She is like the merchants' ships; she brings her food from afar.

15 She rises also while it is yet night, and gives food to her household, and a portion to her maidens.

16 She considers a field, and buys it: with the fruit of her hands she plants a vineyard.

17 She girdes her loins with strength, and strengthens her arms.

18 She perceives that her merchandise is good: her candle goes not out by night.

19 She lays her hands to the spindle, and her hands hold the distaff.

20 She stretches out her hand to the poor; yes, she reaches forth her hands to the needy.

21 She is not afraid of the snow for her household: for all her household are clothed with scarlet.

22 She makes herself coverings of tapestry; her clothing is silk and purple.

23 Her husband is known in the gates, when he sits among the elders of the land.

24 She makes fine linen, and sells it; and delivers girdles unto the merchant.

25 Strength and honor are her clothing; and she shall rejoice in time to come.

26 She opens her mouth with wisdom; and in her tongue is the law of kindness.

27 She looks well to the ways of her household, and eats not the bread of idleness.

28 Her children arise up, and call her blessed; her husband also, and he praises her.

29 Many daughters have done virtuously, but you excel them all.

30 Favor is deceitful, and beauty is vain: but a woman that fears the Becoming-One, she shall be praised.

31 Give her of the fruit of her hands; and let her own works praise her in the gates.

Ecclesiastes

Eccl 1:1 The words of the Preacher, the son of David, king in Jerusalem.

2 Vanity of vanities, says the Preacher, vanity of vanities; all is vanity.

3 What profit has a man of all his labor which he takes under the sun?

4 One generation passes away, and another generation comes: but the earth abides for olam.

5 The sun also arises, and the sun goes down, and hastens to his place where he arose.

6 The wind goes toward the south, and turns about unto the north; it whirls about continually, and the wind returns again according to his circuits.

7 All the rivers run into the sea; yet the sea is not full; unto the place from where the rivers come, there they return again.

8 All things are full of labor; man cannot utter it: the eye is not satisfied with seeing, nor the ear filled with hearing.

9 The thing that has been, it is that which shall be; and that which is done is that which shall be done: and there is no new thing under the sun.

10 Is there anything whereof it may be said, See, this is new? it has been already for olams, which was before us.

11 There is no remembrance of former things; neither shall there be any remembrance of things that are to come with those that shall come after.

12 I the Preacher was king over Israel in Jerusalem.

13 And I gave my heart to seek and search out by wisdom concerning all things that are done under heaven: this great travail has God given to the sons of man to be exercised therewith.

14 I have seen all the works that are done under the sun; and, behold, all is vanity and vexation of spirit.

15 That which is crooked cannot be made straight: and that which is wanting cannot be numbered.

16 I communed with mine own heart, saying, Lo, I am come to great estate, and have gotten more wisdom than all they that have been before me in Jerusalem: yes, my heart had great experience of wisdom and knowledge.

17 And I gave my heart to know wisdom, and to know madness and folly: I perceived that this also is vexation of spirit.

18 For in much wisdom is much grief: and he that increases knowledge increases sorrow.

Eccl 2:1 I said in mine heart, Go to now, I will prove you with mirth, therefore enjoy pleasure: and, behold, this also is vanity.

2 I said of laughter, It is mad: and of mirth, What did it?

3 I sought in mine heart to give myself unto wine, yet acquainting mine heart with wisdom; and to lay hold on folly, till I might see what was that good for the sons of men, which they should do under the heavens all the days of their life.

4 I made me great works; I built me houses; I planted me vineyards:

5 I made me gardens and orchards, and I planted trees in them of all kind of fruits:

6 I made me pools of water, to water therewith the wood that brings forth trees:

7 I got me servants and maidens, and had servants born in my house; also I had great possessions of great and small cattle above all that were in Jerusalem before me:

8 I gathered me also silver and gold, and the treasure of kings and of the provinces: I got me men singers and women singers, and the delights of the sons of men, as musical instruments, and that of all sorts.

9 So I was great, and increased more than all that were before me in Jerusalem: also my wisdom remained with me.

10 And whatsoever mine eyes desired I kept not from them, I withheld not my heart from any joy; for my heart rejoiced in all my labor: and this was my portion of all my labor.

11 Then I looked on all the works that my hands had worked, and on the labor that I had labored to do: and, behold, all was vanity and vexation of spirit, and there was no profit under the sun.

12 And I turned myself to behold wisdom, and madness, and folly: for what can the man do that comes after the king? even that which has been already done.

13 Then I saw that wisdom excels folly, as far as light excels darkness.

14 The wise man's eyes are in his head; but the fool walks in darkness: and I myself perceived also that one event happens to them all.

15 Then said I in my heart, As it happens to the fool, so it happens even to me; and why was I then more wise? Then I said in my heart, that this also is vanity.

16 For there is no remembrance of the wise more than of the fool for olam; seeing that which now is in the days to come shall all be forgotten. And how dies the wise man? as the fool.

17 Therefore I hated life; because the work that is worked under the sun is grievous unto me: for all is vanity and vexation of spirit.

18 Yes, I hated all my labor which I had taken under the sun: because I should leave it unto the man that shall be after me.

19 And who knows whether he shall be a wise man or a fool? yet shall he have rule over all my labor wherein I have labored, and wherein I have showed myself wise under the sun. This is also vanity.

20 Therefore I went about to cause my heart to despair of all the labor which I took under the sun.

21 For there is a man whose labor is in wisdom, and in knowledge, and in equity; yet to a man that has not labored therein shall he leave it for his portion. This also is vanity and a great evil.

22 For what has man of all his labor, and of the vexation of his heart, wherein he has labored under the sun?

23 For all his days are sorrows, and his travail grief; yes, his heart takes not rest in the night. This is also vanity.

24 There is nothing better for a man, than that he should eat and drink, and that he should make his

soul enjoy good in his labor. This also I saw, that it was from the hand of God.

25 For who can eat, or who else can hasten hereunto, more than I?

26 For God gives to a man that is good in his sight wisdom, and knowledge, and joy: but to the sinner he gives travail, to gather and to heap up, that he may give to him that is good before God. This also is vanity and vexation of spirit.

Eccl 3:1 To every thing there is a season, and a time to every purpose under the heaven:

2 A time to be born, and a time to die; a time to plant, and a time to pluck up that which is planted;

3 A time to kill, and a time to heal; a time to break down, and a time to build up;

4 A time to weep, and a time to laugh; a time to mourn, and a time to dance;

5 A time to cast away stones, and a time to gather stones together; a time to embrace, and a time to refrain from embracing;

6 A time to get, and a time to lose; a time to keep, and a time to cast away;

7 A time to rend, and a time to sew; a time to keep silence, and a time to speak;

8 A time to love, and a time to hate; a time of war, and a time of peace.

9 What profit has the worker in his labor?

10 I have seen the occupation [work], which God has given to the sons of men to be occupied with.

11 He has made every thing beautiful in his time: also he has set the olam in their mind, without which no man can find out the work that God makes from the beginning to the end.

12 I know that there is no good in them, but for a man to rejoice, and to do good in his life.

13 And also that every man should eat and drink, and enjoy the good of all his labor, it is the gift of God.

14 I know that, whatsoever God do, it shall be for olam: nothing can be put to it, nor anything taken from it: and God did it, that men should fear before him.

15 That which has been is now; and that which is to be has already been; and God requires that which is past.

16 And moreover I saw under the sun the place of judgment, that wickedness was there; and the place of righteousness, that iniquity was there.

17 I said in mine heart, God shall judge the righteous and the wicked: for there is a time there for every purpose and for every work.

18 I said in mine heart concerning the estate of the sons of men, that God might manifest them, and that they might see that they themselves are beasts.

19 For that which befalls the sons of men befalls beasts; even one thing befalls them: as the one dies, so dies the other; yes, they have all one breath; so that a man has no preeminence above a beast: for all is vanity.

20 All go unto one place; all are of the dust, and all turn to dust again.

21 Who knows the spirit of man that goes upward, and the spirit of the beast that goes downward to the earth?

22 Therefore I perceive that there is nothing better, than that a man should rejoice in his own works; for that is his portion: for who shall bring him to see what shall be after him?

Eccl 4:1 So I returned, and considered all the oppressions that are done under the sun: and behold the tears of such as were oppressed, and they had no comforter; and on the side of their oppressors there was power; but they had no comforter.

2 Therefore I praised the dead which are already dead more than the living which are yet alive.

3 Yes, better is he than both they, which has not yet been, who has not seen the evil work that is done under the sun.

4 Again, I considered all travail, and every right work, that for this a man is envied of his neighbor. This is also vanity and vexation of spirit.

5 The fool folds his hands together, and eats his own flesh.

6 Better is a handful with quietness, than both the hands full with travail and vexation of spirit.

7 Then I returned, and I saw vanity under the sun.

8 There is one alone, and there is not a second; yes, he has neither child nor brother: yet is there no end of all his labor; neither is his eye satisfied with riches; neither says he, For whom do I labor, and bereave my soul of good? This is also vanity, yes, it is a great travail.

9 Two are better than one; because they have a good reward for their labor.

10 For if they fall, the one will lift up his fellow: but woe to him that is alone when he falls; for he has not another to help him up.

11 Again, if two lie together, then they have heat: but how can one be warm alone?

12 And if one prevail against him, two shall withstand him; and a threefold cord is not quickly broken.

13 Better is a poor and a wise child than an old and foolish king, who will no more be admonished.

14 For out of prison he comes to reign; whereas also he that is born in his kingdom be comes poor.

15 I considered all the living which walk under the sun, with the second child that shall stand up in his stead.

16 There is no end of all the people, even of all that have been before them: they also that come after shall not rejoice in him. Surely this also is vanity and vexation of spirit.

Eccl 5:1 Keep your foot when you go to the house of God, and be more ready to hear, than to give the sacrifice of fools: for they consider not that they do evil.

2 Be not rash with your mouth, and let not your heart be hasty to utter anything before God: for God is in heaven, and you upon earth: therefore let your words be few.

3 For a dream comes through the multitude of business; and a fool's voice is known by multitude of words.

4 When you vow a vow unto God, defer not to pay it; for he has no pleasure in fools: pay that which you have vowed.

5 Better is it that you should not vow, than that you should vow and not pay.

6 Permit not your mouth to cause your flesh to sin; neither say you before the angel, that it was an error: why should God be angry at your voice, and destroy the work of your hands?

7 For in the multitude of dreams and many words there are also diverse vanities: but fear you God.

8 If you see the oppression of the poor, and violent perverting of judgment and justice in a province, marvel not at the matter: for he that is higher than the highest regards; and there be higher than they.

9 Moreover the profit of the earth is for all: the king himself is served by the field.

10 He that loves silver shall not be satisfied with silver; nor he that loves abundance with increase: this is also vanity.

11 When goods increase, they are increased that eat them: and what good is there to the owners thereof, saving the beholding of them with their eyes?

12 The sleep of a laboring man is sweet, whether he eat little or much: but the abundance of the rich will not permit him to sleep.

13 There is a great evil which I have seen under the sun, namely, riches kept for the owners thereof to their hurt.

14 But those riches perish by evil travail: and he begets a son, and there is nothing in his hand.

15 As he came forth of his mother's womb, naked shall he return to go as he came, and shall take nothing of his labor, which he may carry away in his hand.

16 And this also is a great evil, that in all points as he came, so shall he go: and what profit has he that has labored for the wind?

17 All his days also he eats in darkness, and he has much sorrow and wrath with his sickness.

18 Behold that which I have seen: it is good and becoming for one to eat and to drink, and to enjoy the good of all his labor that he takes under the sun all the days of his life, which God gives him: for it is his portion.

19 Every man also to whom God has given riches and wealth, and has given him power to eat thereof, and to take his portion, and to rejoice in his labor; this is the gift of God.

20 For he shall not much remember the days of his life; because God answers him in the joy of his heart.

Eccl 6:1 There is an evil which I have seen under the sun, and it is common among men:

2 A man to whom God has given riches, wealth, and honor, so that he lacks nothing for his soul of all that he desires, yet God gives him not power to eat thereof, but a stranger eats it: this is vanity, and it is an evil disease.

3 If a man beget a hundred children, and live many years, so that the days of his years be many, and his soul be not filled with good, and also that he have no burial; I say, that an untimely birth is better than he.

4 For he comes in with vanity, and departs in darkness, and his name shall be covered with darkness.

5 Moreover he has not seen the sun, nor known anything: this has more rest than the other.

6 Yes, though he live a thousand years twice, yet does not see good: do not all go to one place?

7 All the labor of man is for his mouth, and yet the soul is not filled.

8 For what has the wise more than the fool? what has the poor, that knows to walk before the living?

9 Better is the sight of the eyes than the wandering of the soul: this is also vanity and vexation of spirit.

10 That which has been is named already, and it is known that it is man: neither may he contend with him that is mightier than he.

11 Seeing there be many things that increase vanity, what is man the better?

12 For who knows what is good for man in this life, all the days of his vain life which he spends as a shadow? for who can tell a man what shall be after him under the sun?

Eccl 7:1 A good name is better than precious ointment; and the day of death than the day of one's birth.

2 It is better to go to the house of mourning, than to go to the house of feasting: for that is the end of all men; and the living will lay it to his heart.

3 Sorrow is better than laughter: for by the sadness of the countenance the heart is made better.

4 The heart of the wise is in the house of mourning; but the heart of fools is in the house of mirth.

5 It is better to hear the rebuke of the wise, than for a man to hear the song of fools.

6 For as the crackling of thorns under a pot, so is the laughter of the fool: this also is vanity.

7 Surely oppression makes a wise man mad; and a gift destroys the heart.

8 Better is the end of a thing than the beginning thereof: and the patient in spirit is better than the proud in spirit.

9 Be not hasty in your spirit to be angry: for anger rests in the bosom of fools.

10 Say not you, What is the cause that the former days were better than these? for you do not inquire wisely concerning this.

11 Wisdom is good with an inheritance: and by it there is profit to them that see the sun.

12 For wisdom is a defense, and money is a defense: but the excellency of knowledge is, that wisdom gives life to them that have it.

13 Consider the work of God: for who can make that straight, which he has made crooked?

14 In the day of prosperity be joyful, but in the day of adversity consider: God also has set the one over against the other, to the end that man should find nothing after him.

15 All things have I seen in the days of my vanity: there is a just man that perishes in his righteousness, and there is a wicked man that prolongs his life in his wickedness.

16 Be not overly righteous; neither make yourself overly wise: why should you destroy thyself?

17 Be not over much wicked, neither be you foolish: why should you die before your time?

18 It is good that you should take hold of this; yes, also from this withdraw not your hand: for he that fears God shall come forth of them all.

19 Wisdom strengthens the wise more than ten mighty men which are in the city.

20 For there is not a just man upon earth, that did good, and sins not.

21 Also take no heed unto all words that are spoken; lest you hear your servant curse you:

22 For oftentimes also your own heart knows that you yourself likewise have cursed others.

23 All this have I proved by wisdom: I said, I will be wise; but it was far from me.

24 That which is far off, and exceeding deep, who can find it out?

25 I applied mine heart to know, and to search, and to seek out wisdom, and the reason of things, and to know the wickedness of folly, even of foolishness and madness:

26 And I find more bitter than death the woman, whose heart is snares and nets, and her hands as bands: whoso pleases God shall escape from her; but the sinner shall be taken by her.

27 Behold, this have I found, says the preacher, counting one by one, to find out the account:

28 Which yet my soul seeks, but I find not: one man among a thousand have I found; but a woman among all those have I not found.

29 Lo, this only have I found, that God has made man upright; but they have sought out many inventions.

Eccl 8:1 Who is as the wise man? and who knows the interpretation of a thing? a man's wisdom makes his face to shine, and the boldness of his face shall be changed.

2 I counsel you to keep the king's commandment, and that in regard of the oath of God.

3 Be not hasty to go out of his sight: stand not in an evil thing; for he did whatsoever pleases him.

4 Where the word of a king is, there is power: and who may say unto him, What do you?

5 Whoso keeps the commandment shall feel no evil thing: and a wise man's heart discerns both time and judgment.

6 Because to every purpose there is time and judgment, therefore the misery of man is great upon him.

7 For he knows not that which shall be: for who can tell him when it shall be?

8 There is no man that has power over the spirit to retain the spirit; neither has he power in the day of death: and there is no discharge in that war; neither shall wickedness deliver those that are given to it.

9 All this have I seen, and applied my heart unto every work that is done under the sun: there is a time wherein one man rules over another to his own hurt.

10 And so I saw the wicked buried, who had come and gone from the place of the holy, and they were forgotten in the city where they had so done: this is also vanity.

11 Because sentence against an evil work is not executed speedily, therefore the heart of the sons of men is fully set in them to do evil.

12 Though a sinner do evil a hundred times, and his days be prolonged, yet surely I know that it shall be well with them that fear God, which fear before him:

13 But it shall not be well with the wicked, neither shall he prolong his days, which are as a shadow; because he fears not before God.

14 There is a vanity which is done upon the earth; that there be just men, unto whom it happens according to the work of the wicked; again, there be wicked men, to whom it happens according to the work of the righteous: I said that this also is vanity.

15 Then I commended mirth, because a man has no better thing under the sun, than to eat, and to drink, and to be merry: for that shall abide with him of his labor the days of his life, which God gives him under the sun.

16 When I applied mine heart to know wisdom, and to see the business that is done upon the earth: for also there is that neither day nor night sees sleep with his eyes:

17 Then I beheld all the work of God, that a man cannot find out the work that is done under the sun: because though a man labor to seek it out, yet he shall not find it; yes farther; though a wise man think to know it, yet shall he not be able to find it.

Eccl 9:1 For all this I considered in my heart even to declare all this, that the righteous, and the wise, and their works, are in the hand of God: no man knows either love or hatred by all that is before them.

2 All things come alike to all: there is one event to the righteous, and to the wicked; to the good and to the clean, and to the unclean; to him that sacrifices, and to him that sacrifices not: as is the good, so is the sinner; and he that swears, as he that fears an oath.

3 This is an evil among all things that are done under the sun, that there is one event unto all: yes, also the heart of the sons of men is full of evil, and madness is in their heart while they live, and after that they go to the dead.

4 For to him that is joined to all the living there is hope: for a living dog is better than a dead lion.

5 For the living know that they shall die: but the dead know not anything, neither have they any more a reward; for the memory of them is forgotten.

6 Also their love, and their hatred, and their envy, is now perished; neither have they any more a portion for olam in anything that is done under the sun.

7 Go your way, eat your bread with joy, and drink your wine with a merry heart; for God now accepts your works.

8 Let your garments be always white; and let your head lack no ointment.

9 Live joyfully with the wife whom you love all the days of the life of your vanity, which he has given you under the sun, all the days of your vanity: for that is your portion in this life, and in your labor which you take under the sun.

10 Whatsoever your hand finds to do, do it with your might; for there is no work, nor device, nor knowledge, nor wisdom, in Sheol, to which you go.

11 I returned, and saw under the sun, that the race is not to the swift, nor the battle to the strong, neither yet bread to the wise, nor yet riches to men of understanding, nor yet favor to men of skill; but time and chance happens to them all.

12 For man also knows not his time: as the fishes that are taken in an evil net, and as the birds that are caught in the snare; so are the sons of men snared in an evil time, when it falls suddenly upon them.

13 This wisdom have I seen also under the sun, and it seemed great unto me:

14 There was a little city, and few men within it; and there came a great king against it, and besieged it, and built great bulwarks against it:

15 Now there was found in it a poor wise man, and he by his wisdom delivered the city; yet no man remembered that same poor man.

16 Then said I, Wisdom is better than strength: nevertheless the poor man's wisdom is despised, and his words are not heard.

17 The words of wise men are heard in quiet more than the cry of him that rules among fools.

18 Wisdom is better than weapons of war: but one sinner destroys much good.

Eccl 10:1 Dead flies cause the ointment of the apothecary to send forth a stinking aroma: so does a little folly him that is in reputation for wisdom and honor.

2 A wise man's heart is at his right hand; but a fool's heart at his left.

3 Yes also, when he that is a fool walks by the way, his wisdom fails him, and he says to every one that he is a fool.

4 If the spirit of the ruler rise up against you, leave not your place; for yielding pacifies great offences.

5 There is an evil which I have seen under the sun, as an error which proceeds from the ruler:

6 Folly is set in great dignity, and the rich sit in low place.

7 I have seen servants upon horses, and princes walking as servants upon the earth.

8 He that digs a pit shall fall into it; and whoso breaks a hedge, a serpent shall bite him.

9 Whoso removes stones shall be hurt therewith; and he that cleaves wood shall be endangered thereby.

10 If the iron be blunt, and he do not whet the edge, then must he put to more strength: but wisdom is profitable to direct.

11 Surely the serpent will bite without enchantment; and a babbler is no better.

12 The words of a wise man's mouth are gracious; but the lips of a fool will swallow up himself.

13 The beginning of the words of his mouth is foolishness: and the end of his talk is mischievous madness.

14 A fool also is full of words: a man cannot tell what shall be; and what shall be after him, who can tell him?

15 The labor of the foolish wearies everyone of them, because he knows not how to go to the city.

16 Woe to you, O land, when your king is a child, and your princes eat in the morning!

17 Blessed are you, O land, when your king is the son of nobles, and your princes eat in due season, for strength, and not for drunkenness!

18 By much slothfullness the building decays; and through idleness of the hands the house drops through.

19 A feast is made for laughter, and wine makes merry: but money answers all things.

20 Curse not the king, no not in your thought; and curse not the rich in your bedchamber: for a bird of the air shall carry the voice, and that which has wings shall tell the matter.

Eccl 11:1 Cast your bread upon the waters: for you shall find it after many days.

2 Give a portion to seven, and also to eight; for you know not what evil shall be upon the earth.

3 If the clouds be full of rain, they empty themselves upon the earth: and if the tree fall toward the south, or toward the north, in the place where the tree falls, there it shall be.

4 He that observes the wind shall not sow; and he that regards the clouds shall not reap.

5 As you know not what is the way of the spirit, nor how the bones do grow in the womb of her that is with child: even so you know not the works of God who makes all.

6 In the morning sow your seed, and in the evening withhold not your hand: for you know not whether shall prosper, either this or that, or whether they both shall be alike good.

7 Truly the light is sweet, and a pleasant thing it is for the eyes to behold the sun:

8 But if a man live many years, and rejoice in them all; yet let him remember the days of darkness; for they shall be many. All that comes is vanity.

9 Rejoice, O young man, in your youth; and let your heart cheer you in the days of your youth, and walk in the ways of your heart, and in the sight of your eyes: but know you, that for all these things God will bring you into judgment.

10 Therefore remove sorrow from your heart, and put away evil from your flesh: for childhood and youth are vanity.

Eccl 12:1 Remember now your Creator in the days of your youth, while the evil days come not, nor the years draw near, when you shall say, I have no pleasure in them;

2 While the sun, or the light, or the moon, or the stars, be not darkened, nor the clouds return after the rain:

3 In the day when the keepers of the house shall tremble, and the strong men shall bow themselves, and the grinders cease because they are few, and those that look out of the windows be darkened,

4 And the doors shall be shut in the streets, when the sound of the grinding is low, and he shall rise up at the voice of the bird, and all the daughters of music shall be brought low;

5 Also when they shall be afraid of that which is high, and fears shall be in the way, and the almond tree shall flourish, and the grasshopper shall be a burden, and desire shall fail: because man goes to his olam home, and the mourners go about the streets:

6 Or ever the silver cord be loosened, or the golden bowl be broken, or the pitcher be broken at the fountain, or the wheel broken at the cistern.

7 Then shall the dust return to the earth as it was: and the spirit shall return unto God who gave it.

8 Vanity of vanities, says the preacher; all is vanity.

9 And moreover, because the preacher was wise, he still taught the people knowledge; yes, he gave good heed, and sought out, and set in order many proverbs.

10 The preacher sought to find out acceptable words: and that which was written was upright, even words of truth.

11 The words of the wise are as goads, and as nails fastened by the masters of assemblies, which are given from one shepherd.

12 And further, by these, my son, be admonished: of making many books there is no end; and much study is a weariness of the flesh.

13 Let us hear the conclusion of the whole matter: Fear God, and keep his commandments: for this is the whole duty of man.

14 For God shall bring every work into judgment, with every secret thing, whether it be good, or whether it be evil.

Song of Solomon

Song 1:1 The song of songs, which is Solomon's.

2 Let him kiss me with the kisses of his mouth: for your love is better than wine.

3 Because of the aroma of your good ointments your name is as ointment poured forth, therefore do the virgins love you.

4 Draw me, we will run after you: the king has brought me into his chambers: we will be glad and rejoice in you, we will remember your love more than wine: the upright love you.

5 I am black, but becoming, O you daughters of Jerusalem, as the tents of Kedar, as the curtains of Solomon.

6 Look not upon me, because I am black, because the sun has looked upon me: my mother's children were angry with me; they made me the keeper of the vineyards; but mine own vineyard have I not kept.

7 Tell me, O you whom my soul loves, where you feed, where you make your flock to rest at noon: for why should I be as one that turns aside by the flocks of your companions?

8 If you know not, O you fair among women, go your way forth by the footsteps of the flock, and feed your kids beside the shepherds' tents.

9 I have compared you, O my love, to a company of horses in Pharaoh's chariots.

10 your cheeks are becoming with rows of jewels, your neck with chains of gold.

11 We will make you borders of gold with studs of silver.

12 While the king sits at his table, my spikenard sends forth the smell thereof.

13 A bundle of myrrh is my wellbeloved unto me; he shall lie all night between my breasts.

14 My beloved is unto me as a cluster of camphire in the vineyards of Engedi.

15 Behold, you are fair, my love; behold, you are fair; you have doves' eyes.

16 Behold, you are fair, my beloved, yes, pleasant: also our bed is green.

17 The beams of our house are cedar, and our rafters of fir.

Song 2:1 I am the rose of Sharon, and the lily of the valleys.

2 As the lily among thorns, so is my love among the daughters.

3 As the apple tree among the trees of the wood, so is my beloved among the sons. I sat down under his shadow with great delight, and his fruit was sweet to my taste.

4 He brought me to the banqueting house, and his banner over me was love.

5 Stay me with flagons, comfort me with apples: for I am sick of love.

6 His left hand is under my head, and his right hand does embrace me.

7 I charge you, O you daughters of Jerusalem, by the roes, and by the hinds of the field, that you stir not up, nor awake my love, till he please.

8 The voice of my beloved! behold, he comes leaping upon the mountains, skipping upon the hills.

9 My beloved is like a roe or a young hart: behold, he stands behind our wall, he looks forth at the windows, showing himself through the lattice.

10 My beloved spoke, and said unto me, Rise up, my love, my fair one, and come away.

11 For, lo, the winter is past, the rain is over and gone;

12 The flowers appear on the earth; the time of the singing of birds is come, and the voice of the turtle is heard in our land;

13 The fig tree puts forth her green figs, and the vines with the tender grape give a good smell. Arise, my love, my fair one, and come away.

14 O my dove, that are in the clefts of the rock, in the secret places of the stairs, let me see your countenance, let me hear your voice; for sweet is your voice, and your countenance is becoming.

15 Take us the foxes, the little foxes, that spoil the vines: for our vines have tender grapes.

16 My beloved is mine, and I am his: he feeds among the lilies.

17 Until the day break, and the shadows flee away, turn, my beloved, and be you like a roe or a young hart upon the mountains of Bether.

Song 3:1 By night on my bed I sought him whom my soul loves: I sought him, but I found him not.

2 I will rise now, and go about the city in the streets, and in the broad ways I will seek him whom my soul loves: I sought him, but I found him not.

3 The watchmen that go about the city found me: to whom I said, Did you see him whom my soul loves?

4 It was but a little that I passed from them, but I found him whom my soul loves: I held him, and would not let him go, until I had brought him into my mother's house, and into the chamber of her that conceived me.

5 I charge you, O you daughters of Jerusalem, by the roes, and by the hinds of the field, that you stir not up, nor awake my love, till he please.

6 Who is this that comes out of the wilderness like pillars of smoke, perfumed with myrrh and frankincense, with all powders of the merchant?

7 Behold his bed, which is Solomon's; threescore valiant men are about it, of the valiant of Israel.

8 They all hold swords, being expert in war: every man has his sword upon his thigh because of fear in the night.

9 King Solomon made himself a chariot of the wood of Lebanon.

10 He made the pillars thereof of silver, the bottom thereof of gold, the covering of it of purple, the midst thereof being paved with love, for the daughters of Jerusalem.

11 Go forth, O you daughters of Zion, and behold king Solomon with the crown wherewith his mother crowned him in the day of his espousals, and in the day of the gladness of his heart.

Song 4:1 Behold, you are fair, my love; behold, you are fair; you have doves' eyes within your locks: your hair is as a flock of goats, that appear from mount Gilead.

2 your teeth are like a flock of sheep that are even shorn, which came up from the washing;

whereof every one bear twins, and none is barren among them.

3 your lips are like a thread of scarlet, and your speech is becoming: your temples are like a piece of a pomegranate within your locks.

4 your neck is like the tower of David built for an armory, whereon there hang a thousand of bucklers, all shields of mighty men.

5 your two breasts are like two young roes that are twins, which feed among the lilies.

6 Until the day break, and the shadows flee away, I will get me to the mountain of myrrh, and to the hill of frankincense.

7 you are all fair, my love; there is no spot in you.

8 Come with me from Lebanon, my spouse, with me from Lebanon: look from the top of Amana, from the top of Shenir and Hermon, from the lions' dens, from the mountains of the leopards.

9 you have ravished my heart, my sister, my spouse; you have ravished my heart with one of your eyes, with one chain of your neck.

10 How fair is your love, my sister, my spouse! how much better is your love than wine! and the smell of your ointments than all spices!

11 your lips, O my spouse, drop as the honeycomb: honey and milk are under your tongue; and the smell of your garments is like the smell of Lebanon.

12 A garden enclosed is my sister, my spouse; a spring shut up, a fountain sealed.

13 your plants are an orchard of pomegranates, with pleasant fruits; Henna, with spikenard,

14 Spikenard and saffron; calamus and cinnamon, with all trees of frankincense; myrrh and aloes, with all the chief spices:

15 A fountain of gardens, a well of living waters, and streams from Lebanon.

16 Awake, O north wind; and come, you south; blow upon my garden, that the spices thereof may flow out. Let my beloved come into his garden, and eat his pleasant fruits.

Song 5:1 I am come into my garden, my sister, my spouse: I have gathered my myrrh with my spice; I have eaten my honeycomb with my honey; I have drunk my wine with my milk: eat, O friends; drink, yes, drink abundantly, O beloved.

2 I sleep, but my heart wakes: it is the voice of my beloved that knocks, saying, Open to me, my sister, my love, my dove, my undefiled: for my head is filled with dew, and my locks with the drops of the night.

3 I have put off my coat; how shall I put it on? I have washed my feet; how shall I defile them?

4 My beloved put in his hand by the hole of the door, and my bowels were moved for him.

5 I rose up to open to my beloved; and my hands dropped with myrrh, and my fingers with sweet smelling myrrh, upon the handles of the lock.

6 I opened to my beloved; but my beloved had withdrawn himself, and was gone: my soul failed when he spoke: I sought him, but I could not find him; I called him, but he gave me no answer.

7 The watchmen that went about the city found me, they smote me, they wounded me; the keepers of the walls took away my veil from me.

8 I charge you, O daughters of Jerusalem, if you find my beloved, that you tell him, that I am sick of love.

9 What is your beloved more than another beloved, O you fair among women? what is your beloved more than another beloved, that you do so charge us?

10 My beloved is white and ruddy, the chief among a multitude.

11 His head is as the most fine gold, his locks are wavy,[128] and black as a raven.

12 His eyes are as the eyes of doves by the rivers of waters, washed with milk, and fitly set.

13 His cheeks are as a bed of spices, as towers of perfumes: his lips like lilies, dropping sweet smelling myrrh.

14 His hands are as gold rings set with the beryl: his belly is as bright ivory overlaid with sapphires.

15 His legs are as pillars of marble, set upon sockets of fine gold: his countenance is as Lebanon, excellent as the cedars.

16 His mouth is most sweet: yes, he is altogether lovely. This is my beloved, and this is my friend, O daughters of Jerusalem.

Song 6:1 Where is your beloved gone, O you fairest among women? where is your beloved turned aside? that we may seek him with you.

2 My beloved is gone down into his garden, to the beds of spices, to feed in the gardens, and to gather lilies.

3 I am my beloved's, and my beloved is mine: he feeds among the lilies.

4 you are beautiful, O my love, as Tirzah, becoming as Jerusalem, terrible as an army with banners.

5 Turn away your eyes from me, for they have overcome me: your hair is as a flock of goats that appear from Gilead.

6 your teeth are as a flock of sheep which go up from the washing, whereof every one bears twins, and there is not one barren among them.

7 As a piece of a pomegranate are your temples within your locks.

8 There are threescore queens, and fourscore concubines, and virgins without number.

9 My dove, my undefiled is but one; she is the only one of her mother, she is the choice one of her that bare her. The daughters saw her, and blessed her; yes, the queens and the concubines, and they praised her.

10 Who is she that looks forth as the dawn, fair as the moon, clear as the sun, and terrible as an army with banners?

11 I went down into the garden of nuts to see the fruits of the valley, and to see whether the vine flourished, and the pomegranates budded.

12 Or ever I was aware, my soul made me like the chariots of Amminadib.

13 Return, return, O Shulamite; return, return, that we may look upon you. What will you see in the Shulamite? As it were the company of two armies.

---

[128] Wavy as in "waving palm-branches" [BDB, p. 1068]

Song 7:1 How beautiful are your feet with shoes, O prince's daughter! the joints of your thighs are like jewels, the work of the hands of a cunning workman.

2 your navel is like a round goblet, which lacks not liquor: your belly is like a heap of wheat set about with lilies.

3 your two breasts are like two young roes that are twins.

4 your neck is as a tower of ivory; your eyes like the fish pools in Heshbon, by the gate of Bathrabbim: your nose is as the tower of Lebanon which looks toward Damascus.

5 your head upon you is like Carmel, and the hair of your head like purple; the king is held in the galleries.

6 How fair and how pleasant are you, O love, for delights!

7 This your stature is like to a palm tree, and your breasts to clusters of grapes.

8 I said, I will go up to the palm tree, I will take hold of the boughs thereof: now also your breasts shall be as clusters of the vine, and the smell of your nose like apples;

9 And the roof of your mouth like the best wine for my beloved, that goes down sweetly, causing the lips of those that are asleep to speak.

10 I am my beloved's, and his desire is toward me.

11 Come, my beloved, let us go forth into the field; let us lodge in the villages.

12 Let us get up early to the vineyards; let us see if the vine flourish, whether the tender grape appear, and the pomegranates bud forth: there will I give you my loves.

13 The mandrakes give a smell, and at our gates are all manner of pleasant fruits, new and old, which I have laid up for you, O my beloved.

Song 8:1 O that you were as my brother, that sucked the breasts of my mother! when I should find you outside, I would kiss you; yes, I should not be despised.

2 I would lead you, and bring you into my mother's house, who would instruct me: I would cause you to drink of spiced wine of the juice of my pomegranate.

3 His left hand should be under my head, and his right hand should embrace me.

4 I charge you, O daughters of Jerusalem, that you stir not up, nor awake my love, until he please.

5 Who is this that comes up from the wilderness, leaning upon her beloved? I raised you up under the apple tree: there your mother brought you forth: there she brought you forth that bare you.

6 Set me as a seal upon your heart, as a seal upon your arm: for love is strong as death; jealousy is cruel as the Sheol: the coals thereof are coals of fire, which has a most vehement flame.

7 Many waters cannot quench love, neither can the floods drown it: if a man would give all the substance of his house for love, it would utterly be contemned.

8 We have a little sister, and she has no breasts: what shall we do for our sister in the day when she shall be spoken for?

9 If she be a wall, we will build upon her a palace of silver: and if she be a door, we will enclose her with boards of cedar.

10 I am a wall, and my breasts like towers: then was I in his eyes as one that found favor.

11 Solomon had a vineyard at Baal-Hamon; he let out the vineyard unto keepers; every one for the fruit thereof was to bring a thousand pieces of silver.

12 My vineyard, which is mine, is before me: you, O Solomon, must have a thousand, and those that keep the fruit thereof two hundred.

13 you that dwell in the gardens, the companions listen to your voice: cause me to hear it.

14 Make haste, my beloved, and be you like to a roe or to a young hart upon the mountains of spices.

Isaiah

Isa 1:1 The vision of Isaiah the son of Amoz, which he saw concerning Judah and Jerusalem in the days of Uzziah, Jotham, Ahaz, and Hezekiah, kings of Judah. **[ab. 747-687? BC]**

2 Hear, O heavens, and give ear, O earth: for the Becoming-One has spoken, I have nourished and brought up children, and they have rebelled against me.

3 The ox knows his owner, and the donkey his master's crib: but Israel does not know, my people does not consider.

4 Ah sinful nation, a people loaded with iniquity, a seed of evildoers, children that are corrupters: they have forsaken the Becoming-One, they have provoked the Holy One of Israel unto anger, they are gone away backward.

5 Why should you be stricken any more? you will revolt more and more: the whole head is sick, and the whole heart faint.

6 From the sole of the foot even unto the head there is no soundness in it; but wounds, and bruises, and putrifying sores: they have not been closed, neither bound up, neither mollified with ointment.

7 Your country is desolate, your cities are burned with fire: your land, strangers devour it in your presence, and it is desolate, as overthrown by strangers.

8 And the daughter of Zion is left as a cottage in a vineyard, as a lodge in a garden of cucumbers, as a besieged city.

9 Except the Becoming-One of hosts had left unto us a very small remnant, we should have been as Sodom, and we should have been like unto Gomorrah.

10 Hear the word of the Becoming-One, you rulers of Sodom; give ear unto the law of our God, you people of Gomorrah.

11 To what purpose is the multitude of your sacrifices unto me? says the Becoming-One: I am full of the burnt offerings of rams, and the fat of fed beasts; and I delight not in the blood of bullocks, or of lambs, or of he goats.

12 When you come to appear before me, who has required this at your hand, to tread my courts?

13 Bring no more vain offerings; incense is an abomination unto me; the new moons and sabbaths, the calling of assemblies, I cannot endure; it is iniquity, even the solemn meeting.

14 Your new moons and your set times[129] my soul hates: they are a trouble unto me; I am weary to bear them.

15 And when you spread forth your hands, I will hide mine eyes from you: yes, when you make many prayers, I will not hear: your hands are full of blood.

16 Wash you, make you clean; put away the evil of your doings from before mine eyes; cease to do evil;

17 Learn to do well; seek judgment, relieve the oppressed, judge the fatherless, plead for the widow.

18 Come now, and let us reason together, says the Becoming-One: though your sins be as scarlet, they shall be as white as snow; though they be red like crimson, they shall be as wool.

19 If you be willing and obedient, you shall eat the good of the land:

20 But if you refuse and rebel, you shall be devoured with the sword: for the mouth of the Becoming-One has spoken it.

21 How is the faithful city become a harlot! it was full of judgment; righteousness lodged in it; but now murderers.

22 your silver is become dross, your wine mixed with water:

23 your princes are rebellious, and companions of thieves: every one loves gifts, and follows after rewards: they judge not the fatherless, neither does the cause of the widow come unto them.

24 Therefore says the Lord, the Becoming-One of hosts, the mighty One of Israel, Ah, I will ease me of mine adversaries, and avenge me of mine enemies:

25 And I will turn my hand upon you, and purely purge away your dross, and take away all your tin:

26 And I will restore your judges as at the first, and your counselors as at the beginning: afterward you shall be called, The city of righteousness, the faithful city.

27 Zion shall be redeemed with judgment, and her converts with righteousness.

28 And the destruction of the transgressors and of the sinners shall be together, and they that forsake the Becoming-One shall be consumed.

29 For they shall be ashamed of the oaks which you have desired, and you shall be confounded for the gardens that you have chosen.

30 For you shall be as an oak whose leaf fades, and as a garden that has no water.

31 And the strong shall be as tow, and the maker of it as a spark, and they shall both burn together, and none shall quench them.

Isa 2:1 The word that Isaiah the son of Amoz saw concerning Judah and Jerusalem.

2 And it shall come to pass in the last days, that the mountain of the Becoming-One's house shall be established in the top of the mountains, and shall be exalted above the hills; and all nations shall flow unto it.

3 And many people shall go and say, Come ye, and let us go up to the mountain of the Becoming-One, to the house of God of Jacob; and he will teach us of his ways, and we will walk in his paths: for out of Zion shall go forth the law, and the word of the Becoming-One from Jerusalem.

4 And he shall judge among the nations, and shall rebuke many people: and they shall beat their swords into plowshares, and their spears into pruning hooks: nation shall not lift up sword against nation, neither shall they learn war any more.

5 O house of Jacob, come ye, and let us walk in the light of the Becoming-One.

6 Therefore you have forsaken your people the house of Jacob, because they be replenished from the east, and are soothsayers like the Philistines, and they please themselves in the children of strangers.

---

[129] Appointed times or festivals

7 Their land also is full of silver and gold, neither is there any end of their treasures; their land is also full of horses, neither is there any end of their chariots:

8 Their land also is full of idols; they worship the work of their own hands, that which their own fingers have made:

9 And the mean man bows down, and the great man humbles himself: therefore forgive them not.

10 Enter into the rock, and hide you in the dust, for fear of the Becoming-One, and for the glory of his majesty.

11 The lofty looks of man shall be humbled, and the haughtiness of men shall be bowed down, and the Becoming-One alone shall be exalted in that day.

12 For the day of the Becoming-One of hosts shall be upon every one that is proud and lofty, and upon every one that is lifted up; and he shall be brought low:

13 And upon all the cedars of Lebanon, that are high and lifted up, and upon all the oaks of Bashan,

14 And upon all the high mountains, and upon all the hills that are lifted up,

15 And upon every high tower, and upon every fenced wall,

16 And upon all the ships of Tarshish, and upon all pleasant pictures.

17 And the loftiness of man shall be bowed down, and the haughtiness of men shall be made low: and the Becoming-One alone shall be exalted in that day.

18 And the idols he shall utterly abolish.

19 And they shall go into the holes of the rocks, and into the caves of the earth, for fear of the Becoming-One, and for the glory of his majesty, when he arises to shake terribly the earth.

20 In that day a man shall cast his idols of silver, and his idols of gold, which they made each one for himself to worship, to the moles and to the bats;

21 To go into the clefts of the rocks, and into the tops of the ragged rocks, for fear of the Becoming-One, and for the glory of his majesty, when he arises to shake terribly the earth.

22 Cease you from man, whose breath is in his nostrils: for wherein is he to be accounted of?

Isa 3:1 For, behold, the Lord, the Becoming-One of hosts, does take away from Jerusalem and from Judah the stay and the staff, the whole stay of bread, and the whole stay of water.

2 The mighty man, and the man of war, the judge, and the prophet, and the prudent, and the ancient,

3 The captain of fifty, and the honorable man, and the counselor, and the cunning artificer, and the eloquent orator.

4 And I will give children to be their princes, and babes shall rule over them.

5 And the people shall be oppressed, every one by another, and every one by his neighbor: the child shall behave himself proudly against the ancient, and the base against the honorable.

6 When a man shall take hold of his brother of the house of his father, saying, you have clothing, be you our ruler, and let this ruin be under your hand:

7 In that day shall he swear, saying, I will not be a healer; for in my house is neither bread nor clothing: make me not a ruler of the people.

8 For Jerusalem is ruined, and Judah is fallen: because their tongue and their doings are against the Becoming-One, to provoke the eyes of his glory.

9 The show of their countenance does witness against them; and they declare their sin as Sodom, they hide it not. Woe unto their soul! for they have rewarded evil unto themselves.

10 Say you to the righteous, that it shall be well with him: for they shall eat the fruit of their doings.

11 Woe unto the wicked! it shall be ill with him: for the reward of his hands shall be given him.

12 As for my people, children are their oppressors, and women rule over them. O my people, they which lead you cause you to err, and destroy the way of your paths.

13 The Becoming-One stands up to plead, and stands to judge the people.

14 The Becoming-One will enter into judgment with the ancients of his people, and the princes thereof: for you have eaten up the vineyard; the spoil of the poor is in your houses.

15 What do you mean that you beat my people to pieces, and grind the faces of the poor? says my Lord(s), Becoming-One of hosts.

16 Moreover the Becoming-One says, Because the daughters of Zion are haughty, and walk with stretched forth necks and wanton eyes, walking and mincing as they go, and making a tinkling with their feet:

17 Therefore my Lord(s) will smite with a scab the crown of the head of the daughters of Zion, and the Becoming-One will discover their secret parts.

18 In that day my Lord(s) will take away the bravery of their tinkling ornaments about their feet, and their cauls, and their round tires like the moon,

19 The chains, and the bracelets, and the mufflers,

20 The bonnets, and the ornaments of the legs, and the headbands, and the houses of the soul, and the earrings,

21 The rings, and nose jewels,

22 The changeable suits of apparel, and the mantles, and the wimples, and the crisping pins,

23 The glasses, and the fine linen, and the hoods, and the veils.

24 And it shall come to pass, that instead of perfume there shall be rottenness; and instead of a girdle a rope; and instead of well set hair baldness; and instead of a rich robe a girding of sackcloth, instead of beauty.

25 your men shall fall by the sword, and your mighty in the war.

26 And her gates shall lament and mourn; and she being desolate shall sit upon the ground.

Isa 4:1 And in that day seven women shall take hold of one man, saying, We will eat our own bread, and wear our own apparel: only let us be called by your name, to take away our reproach.

2 In that day shall the branch of the Becoming-One be beautiful and glorious, and the fruit of the earth shall be excellent and becoming for them that are escaped of Israel.

3 And it shall come to pass, that he that is left in Zion, and he that remains in Jerusalem, shall be called holy, even every one that is written among the living in Jerusalem:

4 When my Lord(s) shall have washed away the filth of the daughters of Zion, and shall have purged the blood of Jerusalem from the midst thereof by the spirit of judgment, and by the spirit of burning.

5 And the Becoming-One will create upon every dwelling place of mount Zion, and upon her assemblies, a cloud and smoke by day, and the shining of a flaming fire by night: for upon all the glory shall be a defense.

6 And there shall be a tabernacle for a shadow in the daytime from the heat, and for a place of refuge, and for a covert from storm and from rain.

Isa 5:1 Now will I sing to my well beloved a song of my beloved touching his vineyard. My well beloved has a vineyard in a very fruitful hill:

2 And he fenced it, and gathered out the stones thereof, and planted it with the choicest vine, and built a tower in the midst of it, and also made a winepress therein: and he looked that it should bring forth grapes, and it brought forth wild grapes.

3 And now, O inhabitants of Jerusalem, and men of Judah, judge, I pray you, between me and my vineyard.

4 What could have been done more to my vineyard, that I have not done in it? why when I looked that it should bring forth grapes, brought it forth wild grapes?

5 And now go to; I will tell you what I will do to my vineyard: I will take away the hedge thereof, and it shall be eaten up; and break down the wall thereof, and it shall be trodden down:

6 And I will lay it waste: it shall not be pruned, nor dug; but there shall come up briers and thorns: I will also command the clouds that they rain no rain upon it.

7 For the vineyard of the Becoming-One of hosts is the house of Israel, and the men of Judah his pleasant plant: and he looked for judgment, but behold oppression; for righteousness, but behold a cry.

8 Woe unto them that join house to house, that lay field to field, till there be no place, that they may be placed alone in the midst of the earth!

9 In mine ears said the Becoming-One of hosts, Of a truth many houses shall be desolate, even great and fair, without inhabitant.

10 Yes, ten acres of vineyard shall yield one bath, and the seed of a homer shall yield an ephah.

11 Woe unto them that rise up early in the morning, that they may follow strong drink; that continue until the breeze time, till wine inflame them!

12 And the harp, and the viol, the tabret, and pipe, and wine, are in their feasts: but they regard not the work of the Becoming-One, neither consider the operation of his hands.

13 Therefore my people are gone into captivity, because they have no knowledge: and their honorable men are famished, and their multitude dried up with thirst.

14 Therefore Sheol has enlarged her soul, and opened her mouth without measure: and their glory, and their multitude, and their pomp, and he that rejoices, shall descend into it.

15 And the mean man shall be brought down, and the mighty man shall be humbled, and the eyes of the lofty shall be humbled:

16 But the Becoming-One of hosts shall be exalted in judgment, and GOD that is holy shall be sanctified in righteousness.

17 Then shall the lambs feed after their manner, and the waste places of the fat ones shall strangers eat.

18 Woe unto them that draw iniquity with cords of vanity, and sin as it were with a cart rope:

19 That say, Let him make speed, and hasten his work, that we may see it: and let the counsel of the Holy One of Israel draw near and come, that we may know it!

20 Woe unto them that call evil good, and good evil; that put darkness for light, and light for darkness; that put bitter for sweet, and sweet for bitter!

21 Woe unto them that are wise in their own eyes, and prudent in their own sight!

22 Woe unto them that are mighty to drink wine, and men of strength to mingle strong drink:

23 Which justify the wicked for reward, and take away the righteousness of the righteous from him!

24 Therefore as the fire devours the stubble, and the flame consumes the chaff, so their root shall be as rottenness, and their blossom shall go up as dust: because they have cast away the law of the Becoming-One of hosts, and despised the word of the Holy One of Israel.

25 Therefore is the anger of the Becoming-One kindled against his people, and he has stretched forth his hand against them, and has struck them: and the hills did tremble, and their carcases were torn in the midst of the streets. For all this his anger is not turned away, but his hand is stretched out still.

26 And he will lift up an ensign to the nations from far, and will hiss unto them from the end of the earth: and, behold, they shall come with speed swiftly:

27 None shall be weary nor stumble among them; none shall slumber nor sleep; neither shall the girdle of their loins be loosened, nor the latchet of their shoes be broken:

28 Whose arrows are sharp, and all their bows bent, their horses' hoofs shall be counted like flint, and their wheels like a whirlwind.

29 Their roaring shall be like a lion, they shall roar like young lions: yes, they shall roar, and lay hold of the prey, and shall carry it away safe, and none shall deliver it.

30 And in that day they shall roar against them like the roaring of the sea: and if one look unto the land, behold darkness and sorrow, and the light is darkened in the heavens thereof.

Isa 6:1 In the year that king Uzziah died I saw also my Lord(s) sitting upon a throne, high and lifted up, and his train filled the temple.[730 BC | 3260YM]

2 Above it stood the seraphims: each one had six wings; with twain he covered his face, and with twain he covered his feet, and with twain he did fly.

3 And one cried unto another, and said, Holy, holy, holy, is the Becoming-One of hosts: the whole earth is full of his glory.

4 And the posts of the door moved at the voice of him that cried, and the house was filled with smoke.

5 Then said I, Woe is me! for I am undone; because I am a man of unclean lips, and I dwell in the midst of a people of unclean lips: for mine eyes have seen the King, the Becoming-One of hosts.

6 Then flew one of the seraphims unto me, having a live coal in his hand, which he had taken with the tongs from off the altar:

7 And he laid it upon my mouth, and said, Lo, this has touched your lips; and your iniquity is taken away, and your sin purged.

8 Also I heard the voice of my Lord(s), saying, Whom shall I send, and who will go for us? Then said I, Here I am; send me.

9 And he said, Go, and tell this people, Hear you indeed, but understand not; and see you indeed, but perceive not.

10 Make the heart of this people fat, and make their ears heavy, and shut their eyes; lest they see with their eyes, and hear with their ears, and understand with their heart, and convert, and be healed.

11 Then said I, my Lord(s), how long? And he answered, Until the cities be wasted without inhabitant, and the houses without man, and the land be utterly desolate,

12 And the Becoming-One have removed men far away, and there be a great forsaking in the midst of the land.

13 But yet in it shall be a tenth, and it shall return, and shall be eaten: as a teil tree, and as an oak, whose substance is in them, when they cast their leaves: so the holy seed shall be the substance thereof.

Isa 7:1 And it came to pass in the days of Ahaz the son of Jotham, the son of Uzziah, king of Judah, that Rezin the king of Syria, and Pekah the son of Remaliah, king of Israel, went up toward Jerusalem to war against it, but could not prevail against it. [714-710? BC]

2 And it was told the house of David, saying, Syria is confederate with Ephraim. And his heart was moved, and the heart of his people, as the trees of the wood are moved with the wind.

3 Then said the Becoming-One unto Isaiah, Go forth now to meet Ahaz, you, and Shearjashub your son, at the end of the conduit of the upper pool in the highway of the fuller's field;

4 And say unto him, Take heed, and be quiet; fear not, neither be fainthearted for the two tails of these smoking firebrands, for the fierce anger of Rezin with Syria, and of the son of Remaliah.

5 Because Syria, Ephraim, and the son of Remaliah, have taken evil counsel against you, saying,

6 Let us go up against Judah, and vex it, and let us make a breach therein for us, and set a king in the midst of it, even the son of Tabeal:

7 Thus says my Lord(s) the Becoming-One, It shall not stand, neither shall it come to pass.

8 For the head of Syria is Damascus, and the head of Damascus is Rezin; and within threescore and five years shall Ephraim be broken, that it be not a people.

9 And the head of Ephraim is Samaria, and the head of Samaria is Remaliah's son. If you will not believe, surely you shall not be established.

10 Moreover the Becoming-One spoke again unto Ahaz, saying,

11 Ask you a sign of the Becoming-One your God; ask it either in the depth, or in the height above.

12 But Ahaz said, I will not ask, neither will I tempt the Becoming-One.

13 And he said, Hear you now, O house of David; Is it a small thing for you to weary men, but will you weary my God also?

14 Therefore my Lord(s) himself shall give you a sign; **Behold, a virgin shall conceive, and bear a son, and shall call his name, GOD with us [Immanuel]**

15 Butter and honey shall he eat, that he may know to refuse the evil, and choose the good.

16 For before the child shall know to refuse the evil, and choose the good, the land that you abhorr shall be forsaken of both her kings.

17 The Becoming-One shall bring upon you, and upon your people, and upon your father's house, days that have not come from the day that Ephraim departed from Judah; even the king of Assyria.

18 And it shall come to pass in that day, that the Becoming-One shall hiss for the fly that is in the uttermost part of the rivers of Egypt, and for the bee that is in the land of Assyria.

19 And they shall come, and shall rest all of them in the desolate valleys, and in the holes of the rocks, and upon all thorns, and upon all bushes.

20 In the same day shall my Lord(s) shave with a razor that is hired, namely, by them over the river, by the king of Assyria, the head, and the hair of the feet: and it shall also consume the beard.

21 And it shall come to pass in that day, that a man shall nourish a young cow, and two sheep;

22 And it shall come to pass, for the abundance of milk that they shall give he shall eat butter: for butter and honey shall every one eat that is left in the land.

23 And it shall come to pass in that day, that every place shall be, where there were a thousand vines at a thousand silverlings, it shall even be for briers and thorns.

24 With arrows and with bows shall men come there; because all the land shall become briers and thorns.

25 And on all hills that shall be dug with the mattock, there shall not come there the fear of briers and thorns: but it shall be for the sending forth of oxen, and for the treading of lesser cattle.

Isa 8:1 Moreover the Becoming-One said unto me, Take you a great roll, and write in it with a man's pen concerning Maher-shalal-hashb.

2 And I took unto me faithful witnesses to record, Uriah the priest, and Zechariah the son of Jeberechiah.

3 And I went unto the prophetess; and she conceived, and bare a son. Then said the Becoming-One to me, Call his name Maher-shalal-hashb.

4 For before the child shall have knowledge to cry, My father, and my mother, the riches of Damascus and the spoil of Samaria shall be taken away before the king of Assyria.

5 The Becoming-One spoke also unto me again, saying,

6 Forasmuch as this people refuses the waters of Shiloah that go softly, and rejoice in Rezin and Remaliah's son;

7 Now therefore, behold, my Lord(s) brings up upon them the waters of the river, strong and many, even the **king of Assyria**, and all his glory: and he shall come up over all his channels, and go over all his banks:

8 And he shall pass through Judah; he shall overflow and go over, he shall reach even to the neck; and the stretching out of his wings shall fill the breadth of your land, O GOD with us [Immanuel]

9 Associate yourselves, O you people, and you shall be broken in pieces; and give ear, all you of far countries: gird yourselves, and you shall be broken in pieces; gird yourselves, and you shall be broken in pieces.

10 Take counsel together, and it shall come to nothing; speak the word, and it shall not stand: for GOD with us [Immanuel]

11 For the Becoming-One spoke thus to me with a strong hand, and instructed me that I should not walk in the way of this people, saying,

12 Say you not, A confederacy, to all them to whom this people shall say, A confederacy; neither fear you their fear, nor be afraid.

13 Sanctify the Becoming-One of hosts himself; and let him be your fear, and let him be your dread.

14 And he shall be for a sanctuary; but for a stone of stumbling and for a rock of offence to both the houses of Israel, for a gin and for a snare to the inhabitants of Jerusalem.

15 And many among them shall stumble, and fall, and be broken, and be snared, and be taken.

16 Bind up the testimony, seal the law among my disciples.

17 And I will wait upon the Becoming-One, that hides his face from the house of Jacob, and I will look for him.

18 Behold, I and the children whom the Becoming-One has given me are for signs and for wonders in Israel from the Becoming-One of hosts, which dwells in mount Zion.

19 And when they shall say unto you, Seek unto them that have mediums, and unto fortune-tellers that chirp, and that mutter: should not a people seek unto their God? for the living to the dead?

20 To the law and to the testimony: if they speak not according to this word, it is because there is no dawn in them.

21 And they shall pass through it, hardly bestead and hungry: and it shall come to pass, that when they shall be hungry, they shall fret themselves, and curse their king and their God, and look upward.

22 And they shall look unto the earth; and behold trouble and darkness, dimness of anguish; and they shall be driven to darkness.

Isa 9:1 Nevertheless the dimness shall not be such as was in her vexation, when at the first he lightly afflicted the land of Zebulun and the land of Naphtali, and afterward did more grievously afflict her by the way of the sea, over the Jordan, in Galilee of the nations.

2 The people that walked in darkness have seen a great light: they that dwell in the land of the shadow of death, upon them has the light shined.

3 you have multiplied the nation, and not increased the joy: they joy before you according to the joy in harvest, and as men rejoice when they divide the spoil.

4 For you have broken the yoke of his burden, and the staff of his shoulder, the rod of his oppressor, as in the day of Midian.

5 For every battle of the warrior is with earthquakes, and garments rolled in blood; but this shall be with burning and fuel of fire.

6 For unto us a child is born, unto us a son is given: and the government shall be upon his shoulder: and his name shall be called Wonderful, Counselor, The mighty GOD, The enduring Father, The Prince of Peace.

7 Of the increase of his government and peace there shall be no end, upon the throne of David, and upon his kingdom, to order it, and to establish it with judgment and with justice from henceforth even for olam. The zeal of the Becoming-One of hosts will perform this.

8 My Lord(s) sent a word into Jacob, and it has lighted upon Israel.

9 And all the people shall know, even Ephraim and the inhabitant of Samaria, that say in the pride and stoutness of heart,

10 The bricks are fallen down, but we will build with hewn stones: the sycamores are cut down, but we will change them into cedars.

11 Therefore the Becoming-One shall set up the adversaries of Rezin against him, and join his enemies together;

12 The Syrians before, and the Philistines behind; and they shall devour Israel with open mouth. For all this his anger is not turned away, but his hand is stretched out still.

13 For the people turns not unto him that smites them, neither do they seek the Becoming-One of hosts.

14 Therefore the Becoming-One will cut off from Israel head and tail, branch and rush, in one day.

15 The ancient and honorable, he is the head; and the prophet that teaches lies, he is the tail.

16 For the leaders of this people cause them to err; and they that are led of them are destroyed.

17 Therefore my Lord(s) shall have no joy in their young men, neither shall have mercy on their fatherless and widows: for every one is a hypocrite and an evildoer, and every mouth speaks folly. For all this his anger is not turned away, but his hand is stretched out still.

18 For wickedness burns as the fire: it shall devour the briers and thorns, and shall kindle in the thickets of the forest, and they shall mount up like the lifting up of smoke.

19 Through the wrath of the Becoming-One of hosts is the land darkened, and the people shall be as the fuel of the fire: no man shall spare his brother.

20 And he shall snatch on the right hand, and be hungry; and he shall eat on the left hand, and they shall not be satisfied: they shall eat every man the flesh of his own arm:

21 Manasseh, Ephraim; and Ephraim, Manasseh: and they together shall be against Judah. For all this his anger is not turned away, but his hand is stretched out still.

Isa 10:1 Woe unto them that decree unrighteous decrees, and that write grievousness which they have prescribed;

2 To turn aside the needy from judgment, and to take away the right from the poor of my people, that widows may be their prey, and that they may rob the fatherless!

3 And what will you do in the day of visitation, and in the desolation which shall come from far? to whom will you flee for help? and where will you leave your glory?

4 Without me they shall bow down under the prisoners, and they shall fall under the slain. For all this his anger is not turned away, but his hand is stretched out still.

5 O Assyrian, the rod of mine anger, and the staff in their hand is mine indignation.

6 I will send him against a hypocritical nation, and against the people of my wrath will I give him a charge, to take the spoil, and to take the prey, and to tread them down like the mire of the streets.

7 Howbeit he doesn't mean it, neither does his heart think so; but it is in his heart to destroy and cut off nations not a few.

8 For he says, Are not my princes altogether kings?

9 Is not Calno as Carchemish? is not Hamath as Arpad? is not Samaria as Damascus?

10 As my hand has found the kingdoms of the idols, and whose graven images did excel them of Jerusalem and of Samaria:

11 Shall I not, as I have done unto Samaria and her idols, so do to Jerusalem and her idols?

12 Therefore it shall come to pass, that when my Lord(s) has performed his whole work upon mount Zion and on Jerusalem, I will punish the fruit of the stout heart of the king of Assyria, and the glory of his high looks.

13 For he says, By the strength of my hand I have done it, and by my wisdom; for I am prudent: and I have removed the bounds of the people, and have robbed their treasures, and I have put down the inhabitants like a valiant man:

14 And my hand has found as a nest the riches of the people: and as one gathers eggs that are left, have I gathered all the earth; and there was none that moved the wing, or opened the mouth, or peeped.

15 Shall the ax boast itself against him that hews therewith? or shall the saw magnify itself against him that shakes it? as if the rod should shake itself against them that lift it up, or as if the staff should lift up itself, as if it were no wood.

16 Therefore shall the Lord, Becoming-One of hosts, send among his fat ones leanness; and under his glory he shall kindle a burning like the burning of a fire.

17 And the light of Israel shall be for a fire, and his Holy One for a flame: and it shall burn and devour his thorns and his briers in one day;

18 And shall consume the glory of his forest, and of his fruitful field, both soul and body: and they shall be as when a standard bearer faints.

19 And the rest of the trees of his forest shall be few, that a child may write them.

20 And it shall come to pass in that day, that the remnant of Israel, and such as are escaped of the house of Jacob, shall no more again stay upon him that smote them; but shall stay upon the Becoming-One, the Holy One of Israel, in truth.

21 The remnant shall return, even the remnant of Jacob, unto the mighty GOD.

22 For though your people Israel be as the sand of the sea, yet a remnant of them shall return: the consumption decreed shall overflow with righteousness.

23 For my Lord(s), Becoming-One of hosts, shall make a consumption, even determined, in the midst of all the land.

24 Therefore thus says my Lord(s), Becoming-One of hosts, O my people that dwell in Zion, be not afraid of the Assyrian: he shall smite you with a rod, and shall lift up his staff against you, after the manner of Egypt.

25 For yet a very little while, and the indignation shall cease, and mine anger in their destruction.

26 And the Becoming-One of hosts shall stir up a scourge for him according to the slaughter of Midian at the rock of Oreb: and as his rod was upon the sea, so shall he lift it up after the manner of Egypt.

27 And it shall come to pass in that day, that his burden shall be taken away from off your shoulder, and his yoke from off your neck, and the yoke shall be destroyed because of the anointing.

28 He is come to Aiath, he is passed to Migron; at Michmash he has laid up his carriages:

29 They are gone over the passage: they have taken up their lodging at Geba; Ramah is afraid; Gibeah of Saul is fled.

30 Lift up your voice, O daughter of Gallim: cause it to be heard unto Laish, O poor Anathoth.

31 Madmenah is removed; the inhabitants of Gebim gather themselves to flee.

32 As yet shall he remain at Nob that day: he shall shake his hand against the mount of the daughter of Zion, the hill of Jerusalem.

33 Behold, the Lord, the Becoming-One of hosts, shall lop the bough with terror: and the high ones of stature shall be hewn down, and the haughty shall be humbled.

34 And he shall cut down the thickets of the forest with iron, and Lebanon shall fall by a mighty one.

Isa 11:1 And there shall come forth a rod out of the stem of Jesse, and a Branch shall grow out of his roots:

2 And the spirit of the Becoming-One shall rest upon him, the spirit of wisdom and understanding, the spirit of counsel and might,

the spirit of knowledge and of the fear of the Becoming-One;

3 And shall make him of quick understanding in the fear of the Becoming-One: and he shall not judge after the sight of his eyes, neither reprove after the hearing of his ears:

4 But with righteousness shall he judge the poor, and reprove with equity for the meek of the earth: and he shall smite the earth with the rod of his mouth, and with the breath of his lips shall he slay the wicked.

5 And righteousness shall be the girdle of his loins, and faithfullness the girdle of his reins.

6 **The wolf also shall dwell with the lamb**, and the leopard shall lie down with the kid; and the calf and the young lion and the fatling together; and a little child shall lead them.

7 And the cow and the bear shall feed; their young ones shall lie down together: and the lion shall eat straw like the ox.

8 And the sucking child shall play on the hole of the asp, and the weaned child shall put his hand on the cockatrice' den.

9 They shall not hurt nor destroy in all my holy mountain: for the earth shall be full of the knowledge of the Becoming-One, as the waters cover the sea.

10 And in that day there shall be a root of Jesse, which shall stand for an ensign of the people; to it shall the nations seek: and his rest shall be glorious.

11 And it shall come to pass in that day, that my Lord(s) shall set his hand again the second time to recover the remnant of his people, which shall be left, from Assyria, and from Egypt, and from Pathros, and from Cush, and from Elam, and from Shinar, and from Hamath, and from the coastlands of the sea.

12 And he shall set up an ensign for the nations, and shall assemble the outcasts of Israel, and gather together the dispersed of Judah from the four corners of the earth.

13 The envy also of Ephraim shall depart, and the adversaries of Judah shall be cut off: Ephraim shall not envy Judah, and Judah shall not vex Ephraim.

14 But they shall fly upon the shoulders of the Philistines toward the west; they shall spoil them of the east together: they shall lay their hand upon Edom and Moab; and the children of Ammon shall obey them.

15 And the Becoming-One shall utterly destroy the tongue of the Egyptian sea; and with his mighty wind shall he shake his hand over the river, and shall smite it in the seven streams, and make men go over dryshod.

16 And there shall be a highway for the remnant of his people, which shall be left, from Assyria; like as it was to Israel in the day that he came up out of the land of Egypt.

Isa 12:1 And in that day you shall say, O Becoming-One, I will praise you: though you were angry with me, your anger is turned away, and you comfortedst me.

2 Behold, GOD is my salvation; I will trust, and not be afraid: for the Yah Becoming-One is my strength and my song; he also is become my salvation.

3 Therefore with joy shall you draw water out of the wells of salvation.

4 And in that day shall you say, Praise the Becoming-One, call upon his name, declare his doings among the people, make mention that his name is exalted.

5 Sing unto the Becoming-One; for he has done excellent things: this is known in all the earth.

6 Cry out and shout, you inhabitant of Zion: for great is the Holy One of Israel in the midst of you.

Isa 13:1 The **burden of Babylon**, which Isaiah the son of Amoz did see.

2 Lift you up a banner upon the high mountain, exalt the voice unto them, shake the hand, that they may go into the gates of the nobles.

3 I have commanded my sanctified ones, I have also called my mighty ones for mine anger, even them that rejoice in my highness.

4 The noise of a multitude in the mountains, like as of a great people; a tumultuous noise of the kingdoms of nations gathered together: the Becoming-One of hosts musters the host of the battle.

5 They come from a far country, from the end of heaven, even the Becoming-One, and the weapons of his indignation, to destroy the whole land.

6 Howl ye; for the day of the Becoming-One is at hand; it shall come as a destruction from the Almighty.

7 Therefore shall all hands be faint, and every man's heart shall melt:

8 And they shall be afraid: pangs and sorrows shall take hold of them; they shall be in pain as a woman that travails: they shall be amazed one at another; their faces shall be as flames.

9 **Behold, the day of the Becoming-One comes, cruel both with wrath and fierce anger, to lay the land desolate: and he shall destroy the sinners thereof out of it.**

10 **For the stars of the heavens and the constellations thereof shall not give their light: the sun shall be darkened in his going forth, and the moon shall not cause her light to shine.**

11 And I will punish the world for their evil, and the wicked for their iniquity; and I will cause the arrogance of the proud to cease, and will lay low the haughtiness of the terrible.

12 I will make a man more precious than fine gold; even a man than the golden wedge of Ophir.

13 Therefore I will shake the heavens, and the earth shall remove out of her place, in the wrath of the Becoming-One of hosts, and in the day of his fierce anger.

14 And it shall be as the chased roe, and as a sheep that no man takes up: they shall every man turn to his own people, and flee every one into his own land.

15 Every one that is found shall be thrust through; and every one that is joined unto them shall fall by the sword.

16 Their children also shall be dashed to pieces before their eyes; their houses shall be spoiled, and their wives ravished.

17 Behold, **I will stir up the Medes against them**, which shall not regard silver; and as for gold, they shall not delight in it.

18 Their bows also shall dash the young men to pieces; and they shall have no pity on the fruit of the womb; their eye shall not spare children.

19 And Babylon, the glory of kingdoms, the beauty of the Chaldees' excellency, shall be as when God overthrew Sodom and Gomorrah.

20 It shall never be inhabited, neither shall it be dwelt in from generation to generation: neither shall the Arabian pitch tent there; neither shall the shepherds make their fold there.

21 But wild beasts of the desert shall lie there; and their houses shall be full of doleful creatures; and owls shall dwell there, and satyrs shall dance there.

22 And the wild beasts of the coastlands shall cry in their desolate houses, and monsters in their pleasant palaces: and her time is near to come, and her days shall not be prolonged.

Isa 14:1 For the Becoming-One will have mercy on Jacob, and will yet choose Israel, and set them in their own land: and the strangers shall be joined with them, and they shall cleave to the house of Jacob.

2 And the people shall take them, and bring them to their place: and the house of Israel shall possess them in the land of the Becoming-One for servants and handmaids: and they shall take them captives, whose captives they were; and they shall rule over their oppressors.

3 And it shall come to pass in the day that the Becoming-One shall give you rest from your sorrow, and from your fear, and from the hard bondage wherein you were made to serve.

4 That you **shall take up this proverb against the king of Babylon**, and say, How has the oppressor ceased! the golden city ceased!

5 The Becoming-One has broken the staff of the wicked, and the scepter of the rulers.

6 He who smote the people in wrath with a continual stroke, he that ruled the nations in anger, is persecuted, and none hinders.

7 The whole earth is at rest, and is quiet: they break forth into singing.

8 Yes, the fir trees rejoice at you, and the cedars of Lebanon, saying, Since you are laid down, no tree cutter is come up against us.

9 Sheol from beneath is moved for you to meet you at your coming: it stirs up the dead for you, even all the chief ones of the earth; it has raised up from their thrones all the kings of the nations.

10 All they shall speak and say unto you, are you also become weak as we? are you become like unto us?

11 your pomp is brought down to Sheol, and the noise of your viols: the worm is spread under you, and the worms cover you.

12 How are you fallen from heaven, O Lucifer, son of the dawn! how are you cut down to the ground, which did weaken the nations!

13 For you have said in your heart, I will ascend into heaven, I will exalt my throne above the stars of GOD: I will sit also upon the mount of the set time,[130] in the sides of the north:

14 I will ascend above the heights of the clouds; I will be like the most High.

15 Yet you shall be brought down to Sheol, to the sides of the pit.

16 They that see you shall narrowly look upon you, and consider you, saying, Is this the man that made the earth to tremble, that did shake kingdoms;

17 That made the world as a wilderness, and destroyed the cities thereof; that opened not the house of his prisoners?

18 All the kings of the nations, even all of them, lie in glory, every one in his own house.

19 But you are cast out of your grave like an abominable branch, and as the raiment of those that are slain, thrust through with a sword, that go down to the stones of the pit; as a carcase trodden under feet.

20 you shall not be joined with them in burial, because you have destroyed your land, and slain your people: the seed of evildoers shall not for olam be renowned.

21 Prepare slaughter for his children for the iniquity of their fathers; that they do not rise, nor possess the land, nor fill the face of the world with cities.

22 For I will rise up against them, says the Becoming-One of hosts, and cut off from Babylon the name, and remnant, and son, and nephew, says the Becoming-One.

23 I will also make it a possession for the bittern, and pools of water: and I will sweep it with the besom of destruction, says the Becoming-One of hosts.

24 The Becoming-One of hosts has sworn, saying, Surely as I have thought, so shall it come to pass; and as I have purposed, so shall it stand:

25 That **I will break the Assyrian in my land**, and upon my mountains tread him under foot: then shall his yoke depart from off them, and his burden depart from off their shoulders.

26 This is the purpose that is purposed upon the whole earth: and this is the hand that is stretched out upon all the nations.

27 For the Becoming-One of hosts has purposed, and who shall disannul it? and his hand is stretched out, and who shall turn it back?

28 In the year that king Ahaz died was this burden. **[699BC | 3275YM]**

29 Rejoice not you, whole Palestina, because the rod of him that smote you is broken: for out of the serpent's root shall come forth a cockatrice, and his fruit shall be a fiery flying serpent.

30 And the firstborn of the poor shall feed, and the needy shall lie down in safety: and I will kill your root with famine, and he shall slay your remnant.

31 Howl, O gate; cry, O city; you, whole Palestina, are dissolved: for there shall come from the north a smoke, and none shall be alone in his set times.[131]

32 What shall one then answer the messengers of the nation? That the Becoming-One has founded Zion, and the poor of his people shall trust in it.

---

[130] Appointed time or festival

[131] Appointed times or festivals

Isa 15:1 The **burden of Moab**. Because in the night Ar of Moab is laid waste, and brought to silence; because in the night Kir of Moab is laid waste, and brought to silence;

2 He is gone up to Bajith, and to Dibon, the high places, to weep: Moab shall howl over Nebo, and over Medeba: on all their heads shall be baldness, and every beard cut off.

3 In their streets they shall gird themselves with sackcloth: on the tops of their houses, and in their streets, every one shall howl, weeping abundantly.

4 And Heshbon shall cry, and Elealeh: their voice shall be heard even unto Jahaz: therefore the armed soldiers of Moab shall cry out; his soul shall be grievous unto him.

5 My heart shall cry out for Moab; his fugitives shall flee unto Zoar, a heifer of three years: for by the mounting up of Luhith with weeping shall they go it up; for in the way of Horonaim they shall raise up a cry of destruction.

6 For the waters of Nimrim shall be desolate: for the hay is withered away, the grass fails there is no green thing.

7 Therefore the abundance they have gotten, and that which they have laid up, shall they carry away to the brook of the willows.

8 For the cry is gone round about the borders of Moab; the howling thereof unto Eglaim, and the howling thereof unto Beerelim.

9 For the waters of Dimon shall be full of blood: for I will bring more upon Dimon, lions upon him that escapes of Moab, and upon the remnant of the land.

Isa 16:1 Send you the lamb to the ruler of the land from Sela to the wilderness, unto the mount of the daughter of Zion.

2 For it shall be, that, as a wandering bird cast out of the nest, so the daughters of Moab shall be at the fords of Arnon.

3 Take counsel, execute judgment; make your shadow as the night in the midst of the noonday; hide the outcasts; reveals not him that wanders.

4 Let mine outcasts dwell with you, Moab; be you a covert to them from the face of the spoiler: for the extortionist is at an end, the spoiler ceases, the oppressors are consumed out of the land.

5 And in mercy shall the throne be established: and he shall sit upon it in truth in the tabernacle of David, judging, and seeking judgment, and hasting righteousness.

6 We have heard of the pride of Moab; he is very proud: even of his haughtiness, and his pride, and his wrath: but his lies shall not be so.

7 Therefore shall Moab howl for Moab, every one shall howl: for the foundations of Kirhareseth shall you mourn; surely they are stricken.

8 For the fields of Heshbon languish, and the vine of Sibmah: the masters of the nations have broken down the principal plants thereof, they are come even unto Jazer, they wandered through the wilderness: her branches are stretched out, they are gone over the sea.

9 Therefore I will bewail with the weeping of Jazer the vine of Sibmah: I will water you with my tears, O Heshbon, and Elealeh: for the shouting for your summer fruits and for your harvest is fallen.

10 And gladness is taken away, and joy out of the plentiful field; and in the vineyards there shall be no singing, neither shall there be shouting: the treaders shall tread out no wine in their presses; I have made their vintage shouting to cease.

11 Therefore my bowels shall sound like a harp for Moab, and mine inward parts for Kirharesh.

12 And it shall come to pass, when it is seen that Moab is weary on the high place, that he shall come to his sanctuary to pray; but he shall not prevail.

13 This is the word that the Becoming-One has spoken concerning Moab since that time.

14 But now the Becoming-One has spoken, saying, Within three years, as the years of a hireling, and the glory of Moab shall be contemned, with all that great multitude; and the remnant shall be very small and feeble.

Isa 17:1 The **burden of Damascus**. Behold, Damascus is taken away from being a city, and it shall be a ruinous heap.

2 The cities of Aroer are forsaken: they shall be for flocks, which shall lie down, and none shall make them afraid.

3 The fortress also shall cease from Ephraim, and the kingdom from Damascus, and the remnant of Syria: they shall be as the glory of the children of Israel, says the Becoming-One of hosts.

4 And in that day it shall come to pass, that the glory of Jacob shall be made thin, and the fatness of his flesh shall wax lean.

5 And it shall be as when the harvestman gathers the corn, and reaps the ears with his arm; and it shall be as he that gathers ears in the valley of Rephaim giants,

6 Yet gleaning grapes shall be left in it, as the shaking of an olive tree, two or three berries in the top of the uppermost bough, four or five in the outmost fruitful branches thereof, says the Becoming-One, God of Israel.

7 At that day shall a man look to his Maker, and his eyes shall have respect to the Holy One of Israel.

8 And he shall not look to the altars, the work of his hands, neither shall respect that which his fingers have made, either the Asherahs or the images.

9 In that day shall his strong cities be as a forsaken bough, and an uppermost branch, which they left because of the children of Israel: and there shall be desolation.

10 Because you have forgotten God of your salvation, and have not been mindful of the rock of your strength, therefore shall you plant pleasant plants, and shall set it with strange slips:

11 In the day shall you make your plant to grow, and in the morning shall you make your seed to flourish: but the harvest shall be a heap in the day of grief and of desperate sorrow.

12 Woe to the multitude of many people, which make a noise like the noise of the seas; and to the rushing of nations, that make a rushing like the rushing of mighty waters!

13 The nations shall rush like the rushing of many waters: but God shall rebuke them, and they shall flee far off, and shall be chased as the chaff of the mountains before the wind, and like a rolling thing before the whirlwind.

14 And behold at eveningtide trouble; and before the morning he is not. This is the portion of them that spoil us, and the lot of them that rob us.

Isa 18:1 Woe to the land shadowing with wings, which is beyond the rivers of Ethiopia:

2 That sends ambassadors by the sea, even in vessels of bulrushes upon the waters, saying, Go, you swift messengers, to a nation scattered and peeled, to a people terrible from their beginning hitherto; a nation meted out and trodden down, whose land the rivers have spoiled!

3 All you inhabitants of the world, and dwellers on the earth, see, when he lifts up an ensign on the mountains; and when he blows a trumpet, hear.

4 For so the Becoming-One said unto me, I will take my rest, and I will consider in my dwelling place like a clear heat upon herbs, and like a cloud of dew in the heat of harvest.

5 For afore the harvest, when the bud is perfect, and the sour grape is ripening in the flower, he shall both cut off the sprigs with pruning hooks, and take away and cut down the branches.

6 They shall be left together unto the fowls of the mountains, and to the beasts of the earth: and the fowls shall summer upon them, and all the beasts of the earth shall winter upon them.

7 In that time shall the present be brought unto the Becoming-One of hosts of a people scattered and peeled, and from a people terrible from their beginning hitherto; a nation meted out and trodden under foot, whose land the rivers have spoiled, to the place of the name of the Becoming-One of hosts, the mount Zion.

Isa 19:1 The **burden of Egypt**. Behold, the Becoming-One rides upon a swift cloud, and shall come into Egypt: and the idols of Egypt shall be moved at his presence, and the heart of Egypt shall melt in the midst of it.

2 And I will set the Egyptians against the Egyptians: and they shall fight every one against his brother, and every one against his neighbor; city against city, and kingdom against kingdom.

3 And the spirit of Egypt shall fail in the midst thereof; and I will destroy the counsel thereof: and they shall seek to the idols, and to the charmers, and to them that have mediums, and to the fortune-tellers.

4 And the Egyptians will I give over into the hand of a cruel lords; and a fierce king shall rule over them, says the Lord, the Becoming-One of hosts.

5 And the waters shall fail from the sea, and the river shall be wasted and dried up.

6 And they shall turn the rivers far away; and the brooks of defense shall be emptied and dried up: the reeds and flags shall wither.

7 The paper reeds by the brooks, by the mouth of the brooks, and every thing sown by the brooks, shall wither, be driven away, and be no more.

8 The fishermen also shall mourn, and all they that cast angle into the brooks shall lament, and they that spread nets upon the waters shall languish.

9 Moreover they that work in fine flax, and they that weave networks, shall be confounded.

10 And the pillars of Egypt will be crushed; All the hired laborers will be grieved in soul.

11 Surely the princes of Zoan are fools, the counsel of the wise councelors of Pharaoh is become brutish: how say you unto Pharaoh, I am the son of the wise, the son of ancient kings?

12 Where are they? where are your wise men? and let them tell you now, and let them know what the Becoming-One of hosts has purposed upon Egypt.

13 The princes of Zoan are become fools, the princes of Noph are deceived; they have also seduced Egypt, even they that are the stay of the tribes thereof.

14 The Becoming-One has mingled a perverse spirit in the midst thereof: and they have caused Egypt to err in every work thereof, as a drunken man staggers in his vomit.

15 Neither shall there be any work for Egypt, which the head or tail, branch or rush, may do.

16 In that day shall Egypt be like unto women: and it shall be afraid and fear because of the shaking of the hand of the Becoming-One of hosts, which he shakes over it.

17 And the land of Judah shall be a terror unto Egypt, every one that makes mention thereof shall be afraid in himself, because of the counsel of the Becoming-One of hosts, which he has determined against it.

18 In that day shall five cities in the land of Egypt speak the language of Canaan, and swear to the Becoming-One of hosts; one shall be called, The city of destruction.

19 In that day shall there be an altar to the Becoming-One in the midst of the land of Egypt, and a pillar at the border thereof to the Becoming-One.

20 And it shall be for a sign and for a witness unto the Becoming-One of hosts in the land of Egypt: for they shall cry unto the Becoming-One because of the oppressors, and he shall send them a Savior, and a great one, and he shall deliver them.

21 And the Becoming-One shall be known to Egypt, and the Egyptians shall know the Becoming-One in that day, and shall do sacrifice and offering; yes, they shall vow a vow unto the Becoming-One, and perform it.

22 And the Becoming-One shall smite Egypt: he shall smite and heal it: and they shall return even to the Becoming-One, and he shall be entreated of them, and shall heal them.

23 In that day shall there be a highway out of Egypt to Assyria, and the Assyrian shall come into Egypt, and the Egyptian into Assyria, and the Egyptians shall serve with the Assyrians.

24 In that day shall Israel be the third with Egypt and with Assyria, even a blessing in the midst of the land:

25 Whom the Becoming-One of hosts shall bless, saying, Blessed be Egypt my people, and Assyria the work of my hands, and Israel mine inheritance.

Isa 20:1 In the year that Tartan came unto Ashdod **when Sargon the king of Assyria** sent him, and fought against Ashdod, and took it; **[695? BC]**

2 At the same time spoke the Becoming-One by Isaiah the son of Amoz, saying, Go and loose the sackcloth from off your loins, and put off your shoe

from your foot. And he did so, walking naked and barefoot.

3 And the Becoming-One said, Like as my servant Isaiah has walked naked and barefoot three years for a sign and wonder upon Egypt and upon Ethiopia;

4 So shall the king of Assyria lead away the Egyptians prisoners, and the Ethiopians captives, young and old, naked and barefoot, even with their buttocks uncovered, to the shame of Egypt.

5 And they shall be afraid and ashamed of Ethiopia their expectation, and of Egypt their glory.

6 And the inhabitant of this isle shall say in that day, Behold, such is our expectation, to which we flee for help to be delivered from the king of Assyria: and how shall we escape?

Isa 21:1 The burden of the desert of the sea. As whirlwinds in the south pass through; so it comes from the desert, from a terrible land.

2 A grievous vision is declared unto me; the treacherous dealer deals treacherously, and the spoiler spoils. Go up, O Elam: besiege, O Media; all the sighing thereof have I made to cease.

3 Therefore are my loins filled with pain: pangs have taken hold upon me, as the pangs of a woman that travails: I was bowed down at the hearing of it; I was dismayed at the seeing of it.

4 My heart panted, fearfullness frightened me: the night [breeze time] of my pleasure has he turned into fear unto me.

5 Prepare the table, watch in the watchtower, eat, drink: arise, you princes, and anoint the shield.

6 For thus has my Lord(s) said unto me, Go, set a watchman, let him declare what he sees.

7 And he saw a chariot with a couple of horsemen, a chariot of donkeys, and a chariot of camels; and he listened diligently with much heed:

8 And he cried, A lion: My Lord(s), I stand continually upon the watchtower in the daytime, and I am set in my ward whole nights:

9 And, behold, here comes a chariot of men, with a couple of horsemen. And he answered and said, Babylon is fallen, is fallen; and all the graven images of her gods he has broken unto the ground.

10 O my threshing, and the corn of my floor: that which I have heard of the Becoming-One of hosts, God of Israel, have I declared unto you.

11 The burden of Dumah. He calls to me out of Seir, Watchman, what of the night? Watchman, what of the night?

12 The watchman said, The morning comes, and also the night: if you will inquire, inquire ye: return, come.

13 The burden upon Arabia. In the forest in Arabia shall you lodge, O you travelling companies of Dedanim.

14 The inhabitants of the land of Tema brought water to him that was thirsty, they prevented with their bread him that fled.

15 For they fled from the swords, from the drawn sword, and from the bent bow, and from the grievousness of war.

16 For thus has my Lord(s) said unto me, Within a year, according to the years of a hireling, and all the glory of Kedar shall fail:

17 And the residue of the number of archers, the mighty men of the children of Kedar, shall be diminished: for the Becoming-One, God of Israel has spoken it.

Isa 22:1 The burden of the valley of vision. What ails you now, that you are wholly gone up to the housetops?

2 you that are full of stirs, a tumultuous city, a joyous city: your slain men are not slain with the sword, nor dead in battle.

3 All your rulers are fled together, they are bound by the archers: all that are found in you are bound together, which have fled from far.

4 Therefore said I, Look away from me: I will weep bitterly, labor not to comfort me, because of the spoiling of the daughter of my people.

5 For it is a day of trouble, and of treading down, and of perplexity by my Lord(s) the Becoming-One of hosts in the valley of vision, breaking down the walls, and of crying to the mountains.

6 And Elam bare the quiver with chariots of men and horsemen, and Kir uncovered the shield.

7 And it shall come to pass, that your choicest valleys shall be full of chariots, and the horsemen shall set themselves in array at the gate.

8 And he discovered the covering of Judah, and you did look in that day to the armor of the house of the forest.

9 you have seen also the breaches of the city of David, that they are many: and you gathered together the waters of the lower pool.

10 And you have numbered the houses of Jerusalem, and the houses have you broken down to fortify the wall.

11 you made also a ditch between the two walls for the water of the old pool: but you have not looked unto the maker thereof, neither had respect unto him that fashioned it long ago.

12 And in that day did my Lord(s) the Becoming-One of hosts call to weeping, and to mourning, and to baldness, and to girding with sackcloth:

13 And behold joy and gladness, slaying oxen, and killing sheep, eating flesh, and drinking wine: let us eat and drink; for tomorrow we shall die.

14 And it was revealed in mine ears by the Becoming-One of hosts, Surely this iniquity shall not be purged from you till you die, says my Lord(s) the Becoming-One of hosts.

15 Thus says my Lord(s) the Becoming-One of hosts, Go, get you unto this treasurer, even unto Shebna, which is over the house, and say,

16 What have you here? and whom have you here, that you have hewed you out a tomb here, as he that hews him out a tomb on high, and that graves a habitation for himself in a rock?

17 Behold, the Becoming-One will carry you away with a mighty captivity, and will surely cover you.

18 He will surely violently turn and toss you like a ball into a large country: there shall you die, and there the chariots of your glory shall be the shame of your lords' house.

19 And I will drive you from your station, and from your state shall he pull you down.

20 And it shall come to pass in that day, that I will call my servant Eliakim the son of Hilkiah:

21 And I will clothe him with your robe, and strengthen him with your girdle, and I will commit your government into his hand: and he shall be a father to the inhabitants of Jerusalem, and to the house of Judah.

22 And the key of the house of David will I lay upon his shoulder; so he shall open, and none shall shut; and he shall shut, and none shall open.

23 And I will fasten him as a nail in a sure place; and he shall be for a glorious throne to his father's house.

24 And they shall hang upon him all the glory of his father's house, the offspring and the issue, all vessels of small quantity, from the vessels of cups, even to all the vessels of flagons.

25 In that day, says the Becoming-One of hosts, shall the nail that is fastened in the sure place be removed, and be cut down, and fall; and the burden that was upon it shall be cut off: for the Becoming-One has spoken it.

Isa 23:1 The **burden of Tyre**. Howl, you ships of Tarshish; for it is laid waste, so that there is no house, no entering in: from the land of Chittim it is revealed to them.

2 Be still, you inhabitants of the isle; you whom the merchants of Zidon, that pass over the sea, have replenished.

3 And by great waters the seed of Sihor, the harvest of the river, is her revenue; and she is a mart of nations.

4 Be you ashamed, O Zidon: for the sea has spoken, even the strength of the sea, saying, I travail not, nor bring forth children, neither do I nourish up young men, nor bring up virgins.

5 As at the report concerning Egypt, so shall they be sorely pained at the report of Tyre.

6 Pass you over to Tarshish; howl, you inhabitants of the isle.

7 Is this your joyous city, whose antiquity is of ancient days? her own feet shall carry her afar off to sojourn.

8 Who has taken this counsel against Tyre, the crowning city, whose merchants are princes, whose traffickers are the honorable of the earth?

9 The Becoming-One of hosts has purposed it, to stain the pride of all glory, and to bring into contempt all the honorable of the earth.

10 Pass through your land as a river, O daughter of Tarshish: there is no more strength.

11 He stretched out his hand over the sea, he shook the kingdoms: the Becoming-One has given a commandment against the merchant city, to destroy the strong holds thereof.

12 And he said, you shall no more rejoice, O you oppressed virgin, daughter of Zidon: arise, pass over to Chittim; there also shall you have no rest.

13 Behold the land of the Chaldeans; this people was not, till the Assyrian founded it for them that dwell in the wilderness: they set up the towers thereof, they raised up the palaces thereof; and he brought it to ruin.

14 Howl, you ships of Tarshish: for your strength is laid waste.

15 And it shall come to pass in that day, that Tyre shall be forgotten seventy years, according to the days of one king: after the end of seventy years shall Tyre sing as a harlot.

16 Take a harp, go about the city, you harlot that have been forgotten; make sweet melody, sing many songs, that you may be remembered.

17 And it shall come to pass after the end of seventy years, that the Becoming-One will visit Tyre, and she shall turn to her hire, and shall commit fornication with all the kingdoms of the world upon the face of the earth.

18 And her merchandise and her hire shall be holiness to the Becoming-One: it shall not be treasured nor laid up; for her merchandise shall be for them that dwell before the Becoming-One, to eat sufficiently, and for durable clothing.

Isa 24:1 Behold, the Becoming-One makes the earth empty, and makes it waste, and turns it upside down, and scatters abroad the inhabitants thereof.

2 And it shall be, as with the people, so with the priest; as with the servant, so with his master; as with the maid, so with her mistress; as with the buyer, so with the seller; as with the lender, so with the borrower; as with the taker of usury, so with the giver of usury to him.

3 The land shall be utterly emptied, and utterly spoiled: for the Becoming-One has spoken this word.

4 The earth mourns and fades away, the world languishes and fades away, the haughty people of the earth do languish.

5 The earth also is defiled under the inhabitants thereof; because they have transgressed the laws, changed the ordinance, broken the covenant of olam.

6 Therefore has the curse devoured the earth, and they that dwell therein are desolate: therefore the inhabitants of the earth are burned, and few men left.

7 The new wine mourns, the vine languishes, all the merry hearted do sigh.

8 The mirth of tabrets ceases, the noise of them that rejoice ends, the joy of the harp ceases.

9 They shall not drink wine with a song; strong drink shall be bitter to them that drink it.

10 The city of confusion is broken down: every house is shut up, that no man may come in.

11 There is a crying for wine in the streets; all joy is darkened, the mirth of the land is gone.

12 In the city is left desolation, and the gate is struck with destruction.

13 When thus it shall be in the midst of the land among the people, there shall be as the shaking of an olive tree, and as the gleaning grapes when the vintage is done.

14 They shall lift up their voice, they shall sing for the majesty of the Becoming-One, they shall cry aloud from the sea.

15 Therefore glorify you the Becoming-One in the fires, even the name of the Becoming-One, God of Israel in the isles of the sea.

16 From the uttermost part of the earth have we heard songs, even glory to the righteous. But I said, My leanness, my leanness, woe unto me! the treacherous dealers have dealt treacherously; yes, the treacherous dealers have dealt very treacherously.

17 Fear, and the pit, and the snare, are upon you, O inhabitant of the earth.

18 And it shall come to pass, that he who flees from the noise of the fear shall fall into the pit; and he that comes up out of the midst of the pit shall be taken in the snare: for the windows from on high are open, and the foundations of the earth do shake.

19 The earth is utterly broken down, the earth is clean dissolved, the earth is moved exceedingly.

20 The earth shall reel back and forth like a drunkard, and shall be removed like a cottage; and the transgression thereof shall be heavy upon it; and it shall fall, and not rise again.

21 And it shall come to pass in that day, that the Becoming-One shall punish the host of the high ones that are on high, and the kings of the earth upon the earth.

22 And they shall be gathered together, as prisoners are gathered in the pit, and shall be shut up in the prison, and after many days shall they be visited.

23 Then the moon shall be confounded, and the sun ashamed, when the Becoming-One of hosts shall reign in mount Zion, and in Jerusalem, and before his ancients gloriously.

Isa 25:1 O Becoming-One, you are my God; I will exalt you, I will praise your name; for you have done wonderful things; your counsels of old are faithfullness and truth.

2 For you have made of a city a heap; of a fortified city a ruin: a palace of strangers to be no city; it shall not for olam be built.

3 Therefore shall the strong people glorify you, the city of the terrible nations shall fear you.

4 For you have been a strength to the poor, a strength to the needy in his distress, a refuge from the storm, a shadow from the heat, when the blast of the terrible ones is as a storm against the wall.

5 you shall bring down the noise of strangers, as the heat in a dry place; even the heat with the shadow of a cloud: the branch of the terrible ones shall be brought low.

6 And in this mountain shall the Becoming-One of hosts make unto all people a feast of fat things, a feast of wines on the lees, of fat things full of marrow, of wines on the lees well refined.

7 And he will destroy in this mountain the face of the covering cast over all people, and the veil that is spread over all nations.

8 He will swallow up death in victory; and my Lord(s) the Becoming-One will wipe away tears from off all faces; and the rebuke of his people shall he take away from off all the earth: for the Becoming-One has spoken it.

9 And it shall be said in that day, Lo, this is our God; we have waited for him, and he will save us: this is the Becoming-One; we have waited for him, we will be glad and rejoice in his salvation.

10 For in this mountain shall the hand of the Becoming-One rest, and Moab shall be trodden down under him, even as straw is trodden down for the dunghill.

11 And he shall spread forth his hands in the midst of them, as he that swims spreads forth his hands to swim: and he shall bring down their pride together with the spoils of their hands.

12 And the fortress of the high fort of your walls shall he bring down, lay low, and bring to the ground, even to the dust.

Isa 26:1 In that day shall this song be sung in the land of Judah; We have a strong city; salvation will God appoint for walls and bulwarks.

2 Open you the gates, that the righteous nation which keeps the truth may enter in.

3 you will keep him in perfect peace, whose mind is stayed on you: because he trusts in you.

4 Trust you in the Becoming-One to the beyond: for in Yah, the Becoming-One, is the Rock of olams:

5 For he brings down them that dwell on high; the lofty city, he lays it low; he lays it low, even to the ground; he brings it even to the dust.

6 The foot shall tread it down, even the feet of the poor, and the steps of the needy.

7 The way of the just is uprightness: you, most upright, do weigh the path of the just.

8 Yes, in the way of your judgments, O Becoming-One, have we waited for you; the desire of our soul is to your name, and to the remembrance of you.

9 With my soul have I desired you in the night; yes, with my spirit within me will I seek you early: for when your judgments are in the earth, the inhabitants of the world will learn righteousness.

10 Let favor be showed to the wicked, yet will he not learn righteousness: in the land of uprightness will he deal unjustly, and will not behold the majesty of the Becoming-One.

11 Becoming-One, when your hand is lifted up, they will not see: but they shall see, and be ashamed for their envy at the people; yes, the fire of your enemies shall devour them.

12 Becoming-One, you will ordain peace for us: for you also have worked all our works in us.

13 O Becoming-One our God, other lords beside you have had dominion over us: but by you only will we make mention of your name.

14 They are dead, they shall not live; they are dead, they shall not rise: therefore have you visited and destroyed them, and made all their memory to perish.

15 you have increased the nation, O Becoming-One, you have increased the nation: you are glorified: you had removed it far unto all the ends of the earth.

16 Becoming-One, in trouble have they visited you, they poured out a prayer when your chastening was upon them.

17 Like as a woman with child, that draws near the time of her delivery, is in pain, and cries out in her pangs; so have we been in your sight, O Becoming-One.

18 We have been with child, we have been in pain, we have as it were brought forth wind; we have not worked any deliverance in the earth; neither have the inhabitants of the world fallen.

19 your dead men shall live, together with my dead body shall they arise. Awake and sing, you that dwell in dust: for your dew is as the dew of herbs, and the earth shall cast out the dead.

20 Come, my people, enter you into your chambers, and shut your doors about you: hide yourself as it were for a little moment, until the indignation be overpast.

21 For, behold, the Becoming-One comes out of his place to punish the inhabitants of the earth for their iniquity: the earth also shall disclose her blood, and shall no more cover her slain.

Isa 27:1 In that day **the Becoming-One with his sore and great and strong sword shall punish leviathan the piercing serpent, even leviathan that crooked serpent; and he shall slay the monster that is in the sea.**

2 In that day sing you unto her, A vineyard of red wine.

3 I the Becoming-One do keep it; I will water it every moment: lest any hurt it, I will keep it night and day.

4 Fury is not in me: who would set the briers and thorns against me in battle? I would go through them, I would burn them together.

5 Or let him take hold of my strength, that he may make peace with me; and he shall make peace with me.

6 He shall cause them that come of Jacob to take root: Israel shall blossom and bud, and fill the face of the world with fruit.

7 has he struck him, as he smote those that smote him? or is he slain according to the slaughter of them that are slain by him?

8 In measure, when it shoots forth, you will debate with it: he stops his rough wind in the day of the east wind.

9 By this therefore shall the iniquity of Jacob be purged; and this is all the fruit to take away his sin; when he makes all the stones of the altar as chalk stones that are beaten in sunder, the Asherahs and images shall not stand up.

10 Yet the fortified city shall be desolate, and the habitation forsaken, and left like a wilderness: there shall the calf feed, and there shall he lie down, and consume the branches thereof.

11 When the boughs thereof are withered, they shall be broken off: the women come, and set them on fire: for it is a people of no understanding: therefore he that made them will not have mercy on them, and he that formed them will show them no favor.

12 And it shall come to pass in that day, that the Becoming-One shall beat off from the channel of the river unto the stream of Egypt, and you shall be gathered one by one, O you children of Israel.

13 And it shall come to pass in that day, that the great trumpet shall be blown, and they shall come which were ready to perish in the land of Assyria, and the outcasts in the land of Egypt, and shall worship the Becoming-One in the holy mount at Jerusalem.

Isa 28:1 Woe to the crown of pride, to the drunkards of Ephraim, whose glorious beauty is a fading flower, which are on the head of the fat valleys of them that are overcome with wine!

2 Behold, my Lord(s) has a mighty and strong one, which as a tempest of hail and a destroying storm, as a flood of mighty waters overflowing, shall cast down to the earth with the hand.

3 The crown of pride, the drunkards of Ephraim, shall be trodden under feet:

4 And the glorious beauty, which is on the head of the fat valley, shall be a fading flower, and as the hasty fruit before the summer; which when he that looks upon it sees, while it is yet in his hand he eats it up.

5 In that day shall the Becoming-One of hosts be for a crown of glory, and for a diadem of beauty, unto the residue of his people,

6 And for a spirit of judgment to him that sits in judgment, and for strength to them that turn the battle to the gate.

7 But they also have erred through wine, and through strong drink are out of the way; the priest and the prophet have erred through strong drink, they are swallowed up of wine, they are out of the way through strong drink; they err in vision, they stumble in judgment.

8 For all tables are full of vomit and filthiness, so that there is no place clean.

9 Whom shall he teach knowledge? and whom shall he make to understand doctrine? them that are weaned from the milk, and drawn from the breasts.

10 For precept must be upon precept, precept upon precept; line upon line, line upon line; here a little, and there a little:

11 For with stammering lips and another tongue will he speak to this people.

12 To whom he said, This is the rest wherewith you may cause the weary to rest; and this is the refreshing: yet they would not hear.

13 **But the word of the Becoming-One was unto them precept upon precept, precept upon precept; line upon line, line upon line; here a little, and there a little; that they might go, and fall backward, and be broken, and snared, and taken.**

14 Therefore hear the word of the Becoming-One, you scornful men, that rule this people which is in Jerusalem.

15 Because you have said, We have made a covenant with death, and with Sheol are we at agreement; when the overflowing scourge shall pass through, it shall not come unto us: for we have made lies our refuge, and under falsehood have we hid ourselves:

16 Therefore thus says my Lord(s) the Becoming-One, Behold, I lay in Zion for a foundation a stone, a tried stone, a precious corner stone, a sure foundation: he that believes shall not make haste.

17 Judgment also will I lay to the line, and righteousness to the plummet: and the hail shall sweep away the refuge of lies, and the waters shall overflow the hiding place.

18 And your covenant with death shall be disannulled, and your agreement with Sheol shall not stand; when the overflowing scourge shall pass through, then you shall be trodden down by it.

19 From the time that it goes forth it shall take you: for morning by morning shall it pass over, by day and by night: and it shall be a vexation only to understand the report.

20 For the bed is shorter than that a man can stretch himself on it: and the covering narrower than that he can wrap himself in it.

21 For the Becoming-One shall rise up as in mount Perazim, he shall be angry as in the valley of Gibeon, that he may do his work, his strange work; and bring to pass his act, his strange act.

22 Now therefore be you not mockers, lest your bands be made strong: for I have heard from my Lord(s) the Becoming-One of hosts a consumption, even determined upon the whole earth.

23 Give you ear, and hear my voice; listen, and hear my speech.

24 does the plowman plow all day to sow? does he open and break the clods of his ground?

25 When he has made plain the face thereof, does he not cast abroad the dill, and scatter the cummin, and cast in the principal wheat and the appointed barley and the rie in their place?

26 For his God does instruct him to discretion, and does teach him.

27 For the dill are not threshed with a threshing instrument, neither is a cart wheel turned about upon the cummin; but the dill are beaten out with a staff, and the cummin with a rod.

28 Bread corn is bruised; because he will not completely be threshing it, nor break it with the wheel of his cart, nor bruise it with his horsemen.

29 This also comes forth from the Becoming-One of hosts, which is wonderful in counsel, and excellent in working.

Isa 29:1 Woe to Ariel, to Ariel, the city where David dwelt! add you year to year; let feasts come around.

2 Yet I will distress Ariel, and there shall be heaviness and sorrow: and it shall be unto me as Ariel.

3 And I will camp against you round about, and will lay siege against you with a mount, and I will raise forts against you.

4 And you shall be brought down, and shall speak out of the ground, and your speech shall be low out of the dust, and your voice shall be, as of one that has a mediums, out of the ground, and your speech shall whisper out of the dust.

5 Moreover the multitude of your strangers shall be like small dust, and the multitude of the terrible ones shall be as chaff that passes away: yes, it shall be at an instant suddenly.

6 you shall be visited of the Becoming-One of hosts with thunder, and with earthquake, and great noise, with storm and tempest, and the flame of devouring fire.

7 And the multitude of all the nations that fight against Ariel, even all that fight against her and her munition, and that distress her, shall be as a dream of a night vision.

8 It shall even be as when a hungry man dreams, and, behold, he eats; but he awakes, and his soul is empty: or as when a thirsty man dreams, and, behold, he drinks; but he awakes, and, behold, he is faint, and his soul has appetite: so shall the multitude of all the nations be, that fight against mount Zion.

9 Stay yourselves, and wonder; cry you out, and cry: they are drunken, but not with wine; they stagger, but not with strong drink.

10 For the Becoming-One has poured out upon you the spirit of deep sleep, and has closed your eyes: the prophets and your rulers, the seers has he covered.

11 And the vision of all is become unto you as the words of a book that is sealed, which men deliver to one that is learned, saying, Read this, I pray you: and he said, I cannot; for it is sealed:

12 And the book is delivered to him that is not learned, saying, Read this, I pray you: and he said, I am not learned.

13 Therefore my Lord(s) said, Forasmuch as this people draw near me with their mouth, and with their lips do honor me, but have removed their heart far from me, and their fear toward me is taught by the precept of men:

14 Therefore, behold, I will proceed to do a marvelous work among this people, even a marvelous work and a wonder: for the wisdom of their wise men shall perish, and the understanding of their prudent men shall be hid.

15 Woe unto them that seek deep to hide their counsel from the Becoming-One, and their works are in the dark, and they say, Who sees us? and who knows us?

16 Surely your turning of things upside down shall be esteemed as the potter's clay: for shall the work say of him that made it, He made me not? or shall the thing framed say of him that framed it, He had no understanding?

17 Is it not yet a very little while, and Lebanon shall be turned into a fruitful field, and the fruitful field shall be esteemed as a forest?

18 And in that day shall the deaf hear the words of the book, and the eyes of the blind shall see out of obscurity, and out of darkness.

19 The meek also shall increase their joy in the Becoming-One, and the poor among men shall rejoice in the Holy One of Israel.

20 For the terrible one is brought to nothing, and the scorner is consumed, and all that watch for iniquity are cut off:

21 That make a man an offender for a word, and lay a snare for him that reproves in the gate, and turn aside the just for a thing of nothing.

22 Therefore thus says the Becoming-One, who redeemed Abraham, concerning the house of Jacob, Jacob shall not now be ashamed, neither shall his face now wax pale.

23 But when he sees his children, the work of mine hands, in the midst of him, they shall sanctify my name, and sanctify the Holy One of Jacob, and shall fear God of Israel.

24 They also that erred in spirit shall come to understanding, and they that murmured shall learn doctrine.

Isa 30:1 Woe to the rebellious children, says the Becoming-One, that take counsel, but not of me; and that cover with a covering, but not of my spirit, that they may add sin to sin:

2 That walk to go down into Egypt, and have not asked at my mouth; to strengthen themselves in the

strength of Pharaoh, and to trust in the shadow of Egypt!

3 Therefore shall the strength of Pharaoh be your shame, and the trust in the shadow of Egypt your confusion.

4 For his princes were at Zoan, and his ambassadors came to Hanes.

5 They were all ashamed of a people that could not profit them, nor be a help nor profit, but a shame, and also a reproach.

6 The burden of the beasts of the south: into the land of trouble and anguish, from where come the young and old lion, the viper and fiery flying serpent, they will carry their riches upon the shoulders of young donkeys, and their treasures upon the bunches of camels, to a people that shall not profit them.

7 For the Egyptians shall help in vain, and to no purpose: therefore have I cried concerning this, Their pride is to sit still.

8 Now go, write it before them in a table, and note it in a book, that it may be for the time to come to the beyond, til olam:

9 That this is a rebellious people, lying children, children that will not hear the law of the Becoming-One: 10 Which say to the seers, See not; and to the prophets, Prophesy not unto us right things, speak unto us smooth things, prophesy deceits:

11 Get you out of the way, turn aside out of the path, cause the Holy One of Israel to cease from before us.

12 Therefore thus says the Holy One of Israel, Because you despise this word, and trust in oppression and perverseness, and stay thereon:

13 Therefore this iniquity shall be to you as a breach ready to fall, swelling out in a high wall, whose breaking comes suddenly at an instant.

14 And he shall break it as the breaking of the potters' vessel that is broken in pieces; he shall not spare: so that there shall not be found in the bursting of it a sherd to take fire from the hearth, or to take water withal out of the pit.

15 For thus says my Lord(s) the Becoming-One, the Holy One of Israel; In returning and rest shall you be saved; in quietness and in confidence shall be your strength: and you would not.

16 But you said, No; for we will flee upon horses; therefore shall you flee: and, We will ride upon the swift; therefore shall they that pursue you be swift.

17 One thousand shall flee at the rebuke of one; at the rebuke of five shall you flee: till you be left as a beacon upon the top of a mountain, and as an ensign on a hill.

18 And therefore will the Becoming-One wait, that he may be gracious unto you, and therefore will he be exalted, that he may have mercy upon you: for the Becoming-One is God of judgment: blessed are all they that wait for him.

19 For the people shall dwell in Zion at Jerusalem: you shall weep no more: he will be very gracious unto you at the voice of your cry; when he shall hear it, he will answer you.

20 And though my Lord(s) give you the bread of adversity, and the water of affliction, yet shall not your teachers be removed into a corner any more, but your eyes shall see your teachers:

21 And your ears shall hear a word behind you, saying, This is the way, walk you in it, when you turn to the right hand, and when you turn to the left.

22 you shall defile also the covering of your graven images of silver, and the ornament of your molten images of gold: you shall cast them away as a menstruous cloth; you shall say unto it, Get you hence.

23 Then shall he give the rain of your seed, that you shall sow the ground withal; and bread of the increase of the earth, and it shall be fat and plenteous: in that day shall your cattle feed in large pastures.

24 The oxen likewise and the young donkeys that ear the ground shall eat clean feed, which has been winnowed with the shovel and with the fan.

25 And there shall be upon every high mountain, and upon every high hill, rivers and streams of waters in the day of the great slaughter, when the towers fall.

26 Moreover the light of the moon shall be as the light of the sun, and the light of the sun shall be sevenfold, as the light of seven days, in the day that the Becoming-One binds up the breach of his people, and heals the stroke of their wound.

27 Behold, the name of the Becoming-One comes from far, burning with his anger, and the burden thereof is heavy: his lips are full of indignation, and his tongue as a devouring fire:

28 And his breath, as an overflowing stream, shall reach to the midst of the neck, to sift the nations with the sieve of vanity: and there shall be a bridle in the jaws of the people, causing them to err.

29 you shall have a song, as in the night when a holy feast is kept; and gladness of heart, as when one goes with a pipe to come into the mountain of the Becoming-One, to the Rock of Israel.

30 And the Becoming-One shall cause his glorious voice to be heard, and shall show the lighting down of his arm, with the indignation of his anger, and with the flame of a devouring fire, with scattering, and tempest, and hailstones.

31 For through the voice of the Becoming-One shall the Assyrian be beaten down, which smote with a rod.

32 And in every place where the grounded staff shall pass, which the Becoming-One shall lay upon him, it shall be with tabrets and harps: and in battles of shaking will he fight with it.

33 For Tophet is ordained of old; yes, for the king it is prepared; he has made it deep and large: the pile thereof is fire and much wood; the breath of the Becoming-One, like a stream of brimstone, does kindle it.

Isa 31:1 Woe to them that go down to Egypt for help; and stay on horses, and trust in chariots, because they are many; and in horsemen, because they are very strong; but they look not unto the Holy One of Israel, neither seek the Becoming-One!

2 Yet he also is wise, and will bring evil, and will not call back his words: but will arise against the house of the evildoers, and against the help of them that work iniquity.

3 Now the Egyptians are men, and not GOD; and their horses flesh, and not spirit. When the Becoming-One shall stretch out his hand, both he that helps

shall fall, and he that is helped shall fall down, and they all shall fail together.

4 For thus has the Becoming-One spoken unto me, Like as the lion and the young lion roaring on his prey, when a multitude of shepherds is called forth against him, he will not be afraid of their voice, nor abase himself for the noise of them: so shall the Becoming-One of hosts come down to fight for mount Zion, and for the hill thereof.

5 As birds flying, so will the Becoming-One of hosts defend Jerusalem; defending also he will deliver it; and passing over he will preserve it.

6 Turn you unto him from whom the children of Israel have deeply revolted.

7 For in that day every man shall cast away his idols of silver, and his idols of gold, which your own hands have made unto you for a sin.

8 Then shall the Assyrian fall with the sword, not of a mighty man; and the sword, not of a mean man, shall devour him: but he shall flee from the sword, and his young men shall be discomfited.

9 And he shall pass over to his strong hold for fear, and his princes shall be afraid of the ensign, says the Becoming-One, whose fire is in Zion, and his furnace in Jerusalem.

Isa 32:1 Behold, a king shall reign in righteousness, and princes shall rule in judgment.

2 And a man shall be as a hiding place from the wind, and a covert from the tempest; as rivers of water in a dry place, as the shadow of a great rock in a weary land.

3 And the eyes of them that see shall not be dim, and the ears of them that hear shall listen.

4 The heart also of the rash shall understand knowledge, and the tongue of the stammerers shall be ready to speak plainly.

5 The vile person shall be no more called liberal, nor the churl said to be bountiful.

6 For the vile person will speak folly, and his heart will work iniquity, to practice hypocrisy, and to utter error against the Becoming-One, to make empty the soul of the hungry, and he will cause the drink of the thirsty to fail.

7 The instruments also of the churl are evil: he devises wicked devices to destroy the poor with lying words, even when the needy speaks right.

8 But the liberal devises liberal things; and by liberal things shall he stand.

9 Rise up, you women that are at ease; hear my voice, you careless daughters; give ear unto my speech.

10 Many days and years shall you be troubled, you careless women: for the vintage shall fail, the gathering shall not come.

11 Tremble, you women that are at ease; be troubled, you careless ones: strip you, and make you bare, and gird sackcloth upon your loins.

12 They shall lament for the teats, for the pleasant fields, for the fruitful vine.

13 Upon the land of my people shall come up thorns and briers; yes, upon all the houses of joy in the joyous city:

14 Because the palaces shall be forsaken; the multitude of the city shall be left; the forts and towers shall be for dens for olam, a joy of wild donkeys, a pasture of flocks;

15 Until the spirit be poured upon us from on high, and the wilderness be a fruitful field, and the fruitful field be counted for a forest.

16 Then judgment shall dwell in the wilderness, and righteousness remain in the fruitful field.

17 And the work of righteousness shall be peace; and the effect of righteousness quietness and assurance for olam.

18 And my people shall dwell in a peaceable habitation, and in sure dwellings, and in quiet resting places;

19 When it shall hail, coming down on the forest; and the city shall be low in a low place.

20 Blessed are you that sow beside all waters, that send forth there the feet of the ox and the donkey.

Isa 33:1 Woe to you that spoil, and you were not spoiled; and deal treacherously, and they dealt not treacherously with you! when you shall cease to spoil, you shall be spoiled; and when you shall make an end to deal treacherously, they shall deal treacherously with you.

2 O Becoming-One, be gracious unto us; we have waited for you: be you their arm every morning, our salvation also in the time of trouble.

3 At the noise of the tumult the people fled; at the lifting up of yourself the nations were scattered.

4 And your spoil shall be gathered like the gathering of the caterpillar: as the running back and forth of locusts shall he run upon them.

5 The Becoming-One is exalted; for he dwells on high: he has filled Zion with judgment and righteousness.

6 And wisdom and knowledge shall be the stability of your times, and strength of salvation: the fear of the Becoming-One is his treasure.

7 Behold, their valiant ones shall cry outside: the ambassadors of peace shall weep bitterly.

8 The highways lie waste, the wayfaring man ceases: he has broken the covenant, he has despised the cities, he regards no man.

9 The earth mourns and languishes: Lebanon is ashamed and hewn down: Sharon is like a wilderness; and Bashan and Carmel shake off their fruits.

10 Now will I rise, says the Becoming-One; now will I be exalted; now will I lift up myself.

11 you shall conceive chaff, you shall bring forth stubble: your breath, as fire, shall devour you.

12 And the people shall be as the burnings of lime: as thorns cut up shall they be burned in the fire.

13 Hear, you that are far off, what I have done; and, you that are near, acknowledge my might.

14 The sinners in Zion are afraid; fearfullness has surprised the hypocrites. Who among us shall dwell with the devouring fire? who among us shall dwell with burnings of olam?

15 He that walks righteously, and speaks uprightly; he that despises the gain of oppressions, that shakes his hands from holding of bribes, that stops his ears from hearing of blood, and shuts his eyes from seeing evil;

16 He shall dwell on high: his place of defense shall be the munitions of rocks: bread shall be given him; his waters shall be sure.

17 your eyes shall see the king in his beauty: they shall behold the land that is very far off.

18 your heart shall meditate terror. Where is the scribe? where is the receiver? where is he that counted the towers?

19 you shall not see a fierce people, a people of a deeper speech than you can perceive; of a stammering tongue, that you can not understand.

20 Look upon Zion, the city of our set times:[132] your eyes shall see Jerusalem a quiet habitation, a tabernacle that shall not be taken down; not one of the stakes thereof shall completely be removed, neither shall any of the cords thereof be broken.

21 But there the glorious Becoming-One will be unto us a place of broad rivers and streams; wherein shall go no galley with oars, neither shall gallant ship pass thereby.

22 For the Becoming-One is our judge, the Becoming-One is our lawgiver, the Becoming-One is our king; he will save us.

23 your tackling are loosened; they could not well strengthen their mast, they could not spread the sail: then is the prey of a great spoil divided; the lame take the prey.

24 And the inhabitant shall not say, I am sick: the people that dwell therein shall be forgiven their iniquity.

Isa 34:1 Come near, you nations, to hear; and listen, you people: let the earth hear, and all that is therein; the world, and all things that come forth of it.

2 **For the indignation of the Becoming-One is upon all nations, and his fury upon all their armies: he has utterly destroyed them, he has delivered them to the slaughter.**

3 Their slain also shall be cast out, and their stink shall come up out of their carcases, and the mountains shall be melted with their blood.

4 And all the host of the heavens shall be dissolved, and the heavens shall be rolled together as a scroll: and all their host shall fall down, as the leaf falls off from the vine, and as a falling fig from the fig tree.

5 For my sword shall be bathed in heaven: behold, it shall come down upon Idumea, and upon the people of my curse, to judgment.

6 The sword of the Becoming-One is filled with blood, it is made fat with fatness, and with the blood of lambs and goats, with the fat of the kidneys of rams: for the Becoming-One has a sacrifice in Bozrah, and a great slaughter in the land of Idumea.

7 And the reem [wild ox or beast] shall come down with them, and the bullocks with the bulls; and their land shall be soaked with blood, and their dust made fat with fatness.

8 For it is the day of for the Becoming-One's vengeance, and the year of recompenses for the controversy of Zion.

9 And the streams thereof shall be turned into pitch, and the dust thereof into brimstone, and the land thereof shall become burning pitch.

10 It shall not be quenched night nor day; the smoke thereof shall go up for olam of olams: from generation to generation it shall lie waste; none shall pass through it for sure, absolutely.

11 But the cormorant and the bittern shall possess it; the owl also and the raven shall dwell in it: and he shall stretch out upon it the line of confusion, and the stones of emptiness.

12 They shall call the nobles thereof to the kingdom, but none shall be there, and all her princes shall be nothing.

13 And thorns shall come up in her palaces, nettles and brambles in the fortresses thereof: and it shall be a habitation of monsters, and a court for owls.

14 The wild beasts of the desert shall also meet with the wild beasts of the island, and the satyr shall cry to his fellow; the screech owl also shall rest there, and find for herself a place of rest.

15 There shall the great owl make her nest, and lay, and hatch, and gather under her shadow: there shall the vultures also be gathered, every one with her mate.

16 Seek you out of the book of the Becoming-One, and read: no one of these shall fail, none shall want her mate: for my mouth it has commanded, and his spirit it has gathered them.

17 And he has cast the lot for them, and his hand has divided it unto them by line: they shall possess it for olam, from generation to generation shall they dwell therein.

Isa 35:1 The wilderness and the solitary place shall be glad for them; and the desert shall rejoice, and blossom as the rose.

2 It shall blossom abundantly, and rejoice even with joy and singing: the glory of Lebanon shall be given unto it, the excellency of Carmel and Sharon, they shall see the glory of the Becoming-One, and the excellency of our God.

3 Strengthen you the weak hands, and confirm the feeble knees.

4 Say to them that are of a fearful heart, Be strong, fear not: behold, your God will come with vengeance, even God with a recompense; he will come and save you.

5 Then the eyes of the blind shall be opened, and the ears of the deaf shall be unstopped.

6 Then shall the lame man leap as a hart, and the tongue of the mute sing: for in the wilderness shall waters break out, and streams in the desert.

7 And the parched ground shall become a pool, and the thirsty land springs of water: in the habitation of monsters, where each lay, shall be grass with reeds and rushes.

8 And a highway shall be there, and a way, and it shall be called The way of holiness; the unclean shall not pass over it; but it shall be for those: the wayfaring men, though fools, shall not err therein.

9 No lion shall be there, nor any ravenous beast shall go up thereon, it shall not be found there; but the redeemed shall walk there:

---

[132] Appointed times or festivals

10 And the ransomed of the Becoming-One shall return, and come to Zion with songs and joy of olam upon their heads: they shall obtain joy and gladness, and sorrow and sighing shall flee away.

Isa 36:1 Now it came to **pass in the fourteenth year of king Hezekiah**, that **Sennacherib** king of Assyria came up against all the fortified cities of Judah, and took them. **[687 BC | 3287YM]**

2 And the king of Assyria sent Rabshakeh from Lachish to Jerusalem unto king Hezekiah with a great army. And he stood by the conduit of the upper pool in the highway of the fuller's field.

3 Then came forth unto him Eliakim, Hilkiah's son, which was over the house, and Shebna the scribe, and Joah, Asaph's son, the recorder.

4 And Rabshakeh said unto them, Say you now to Hezekiah, Thus says the great king, the king of Assyria, What confidence is this wherein you trust?

5 I say, say you, but they are but vain words I have counsel and strength for war: now on whom do you trust, that you rebel against me?

6 Lo, you trust in the staff of this broken reed, on Egypt; whereon if a man lean, it will go into his hand, and pierce it: so is Pharaoh king of Egypt to all that trust in him.

7 But if you say to me, We trust in the Becoming-One our God: is it not he, whose high places and whose altars Hezekiah has taken away, and said to Judah and to Jerusalem, you shall worship before this altar?

8 Now therefore give pledges, I pray you, to my master the king of Assyria, and I will give you two thousand of horses, if you be able on your part to set riders upon them.

9 How then will you turn away the face of one captain of the least of my master's servants, and put your trust on Egypt for chariots and for horsemen?

10 And am I now come up without the Becoming-One against this land to destroy it? the Becoming-One said unto me, Go up against this land, and destroy it.

11 Then said Eliakim and Shebna and Joah unto Rabshakeh, Speak, I pray you, unto your servants in the Syrian language; for we understand it; and speak not to us in the Jews' language, in the ears of the people that are on the wall.

12 But Rabshakeh said, has my master sent me to your master and to you to speak these words? has he not sent me to the men that sit upon the wall, that they may eat their own dung, and drink their own piss with you?

13 Then Rabshakeh stood, and cried with a loud voice in the Jews' language, and said, Hear you the words of the great king, the king of Assyria.

14 Thus says the king, Let not Hezekiah deceive you: for he shall not be able to deliver you.

15 Neither let Hezekiah make you trust in the Becoming-One, saying, The Becoming-One will surely deliver us: this city shall not be delivered into the hand of the king of Assyria.

16 listen not to Hezekiah: for thus says the king of Assyria, Make an agreement with me by a present, and come out to me: and eat you every one of his vine, and every one of his fig tree, and drink you every one the waters of his own cistern;

17 Until I come and take you away to a land like your own land, a land of corn and wine, a land of bread and vineyards.

18 Beware lest Hezekiah persuade you, saying, The Becoming-One will deliver us. Has any of the gods of the nations delivered his land out of the hand of the king of Assyria?

19 Where are the gods of Hamath and Arphad? where are the gods of Sepharvaim? and have they delivered Samaria out of my hand?

20 Who are they among all the gods of these lands, that have delivered their land out of my hand, that the Becoming-One should deliver Jerusalem out of my hand?

21 But they held their peace, and answered him not a word: for the king's commandment was, saying, Answer him not.

22 Then came Eliakim, the son of Hilkiah, that was over the household, and Shebna the scribe, and Joah, the son of Asaph, the recorder, to Hezekiah with their clothes rent, and told him the words of Rabshakeh.

Isa 37:1 And it came to pass, when king Hezekiah heard it, that he ripped his clothes, and covered himself with sackcloth, and went into the house of the Becoming-One.

2 And he sent Eliakim, who was over the household, and Shebna the scribe, and the elders of the priests covered with sackcloth, unto Isaiah the prophet the son of Amoz.

3 And they said unto him, Thus says Hezekiah, This day is a day of trouble, and of rebuke, and of blasphemy: for the children are come to the birth, and there is not strength to bring forth.

4 It may be the Becoming-One your God will hear the words of Rabshakeh, whom the king of Assyria his master has sent to reproach the living God, and will reprove the words which the Becoming-One your God has heard: therefore lift up your prayer for the remnant that is left.

5 So the servants of king Hezekiah came to Isaiah.

6 And Isaiah said unto them, Thus shall you say unto your master, Thus says the Becoming-One, Be not afraid of the words that you have heard, wherewith the servants of the king of Assyria have blasphemed me.

7 Behold, I will send a blast upon him, and he shall hear a rumor, and return to his own land; and I will cause him to fall by the sword in his own land.

8 So Rabshakeh returned, and found the king of Assyria warring against Libnah: for he had heard that he was departed from Lachish.

9 And he heard say concerning Tirhakah king of Ethiopia, He is come forth to make war with you. And when he heard it, he sent messengers to Hezekiah, saying,

10 Thus shall you speak to Hezekiah king of Judah, saying, Let not your God, in whom you trust, deceive you, saying, Jerusalem shall not be given into the hand of the king of Assyria.

11 Behold, you have heard what the kings of Assyria have done to all lands by destroying them utterly; and shall you be delivered?

12 Have the gods of the nations delivered them which my fathers have destroyed, as Gozan, and Haran, and Rezeph, and the children of Eden which were in Telassar?

13 Where is the king of Hamath, and the king of Arphad, and the king of the city of Sepharvaim, Hena, and Ivah?

14 And Hezekiah received the letter from the hand of the messengers, and read it: and Hezekiah went up unto the house of the Becoming-One, and spread it before the Becoming-One.

15 And Hezekiah prayed unto the Becoming-One, saying,

16 O Becoming-One of hosts, God of Israel, that dwell between the cherubs, you are God, even you alone, of all the kingdoms of the earth: you have made the heavens and earth.

17 Incline your ear, O Becoming-One, and hear; open your eyes, O Becoming-One, and see: and hear all the words of **Sennacherib**, which has sent to reproach the living God.

18 Of a truth, Becoming-One, the **kings of Assyria** have laid waste all the nations, and their countries.

19 And have cast their gods into the fire: for they were no gods, but the work of men's hands, wood and stone: therefore they have destroyed them.

20 Now therefore, O Becoming-One our God, save us from his hand, that all the kingdoms of the earth may know that you are the Becoming-One, even you only.

21 Then Isaiah the son of Amoz sent unto Hezekiah, saying, Thus says the Becoming-One, God of Israel, Whereas you have prayed to me against **Sennacherib** king of Assyria:

22 This is the word which the Becoming-One has spoken concerning him; The virgin, the daughter of Zion, has despised you, and laughed you to scorn; the daughter of Jerusalem has shaken her head at you.

23 Whom have you reproached and blasphemed? and against whom have you exalted your voice, and lifted up your eyes on high? even against the Holy One of Israel.

24 By your servants have you reproached my Lord(s), and have said, By the multitude of my chariots I am come up to the height of the mountains, to the sides of Lebanon; and I will cut down the tall cedars thereof, and the choice fir trees thereof: and I will enter into the height of his border, and the forest of his Carmel.

25 I have dug, and drunk water; and with the sole of my feet have I dried up all the rivers of the besieged places.

26 have you not heard long ago, how I have done it; and of ancient times, that I have formed it? now have I brought it to pass, that you should be to lay waste fortified cities into ruinous heaps.

27 Therefore their inhabitants were of small power, they were dismayed and confounded: they were as the grass of the field, and as the green herb, as the grass on the housetops, and as corn blasted before it be grown up.

28 But I know your abode, and your going out, and your coming in, and your rage against me.

29 Because your rage against me, and your tumult, is come up into mine ears, therefore will I put my hook in your nose, and my bridle in your lips, and I will turn you back by the way by which you came.

30 And this shall be a sign unto you, you shall eat this year such as grows of itself; and the second year that which springs of the same: and in the third year sow ye, and reap, and plant vineyards, and eat the fruit thereof.

31 And the remnant that is escaped of the house of Judah shall again take root downward, and bear fruit upward:

32 For out of Jerusalem shall go forth a remnant, and they that escape out of mount Zion: the zeal of the Becoming-One of hosts shall do this.

33 Therefore thus says the Becoming-One concerning the king of Assyria, He shall not come into this city, nor shoot an arrow there, nor come before it with shields, nor cast a bank against it.

34 By the way that he came, by the same shall he return, and shall not come into this city, says the Becoming-One.

35 For I will defend this city to save it for mine own sake, and for my servant David's sake.

36 Then the angel of the Becoming-One went forth, and smote in the camp of the Assyrians a hundred and fourscore and five thousand: and when they arose early in the morning, behold, they were all dead corpses.

37 So **Sennacherib** king of Assyria departed, and went and returned, and dwelt at Nineveh.

38 And it came to pass, as he was worshipping in the house of Nisroch his god, that Adrammelech and Sharezer his sons smote him with the sword; and they escaped into the land of Armenia: and Esarhaddon his son reigned in his stead.

Isa 38:1 In those days was Hezekiah sick unto death. And Isaiah the prophet the son of Amoz came unto him, and said unto him, Thus says the Becoming-One, Set your house in order: for you shall die, and not live.

2 Then Hezekiah turned his face toward the wall, and prayed unto the Becoming-One,

3 And said, Remember now, O Becoming-One, I beg you, how I have walked before you in truth and with a perfect heart, and have done that which is good in your sight. And Hezekiah wept greatly.

4 Then came the word of the Becoming-One to Isaiah, saying,

5 Go, and say to Hezekiah, Thus says the Becoming-One, God of David your father, I have heard your prayer, I have seen your tears: behold, I will add unto your days fifteen years.

6 And I will deliver you and this city out of the hand of the king of Assyria: and I will defend this city.

7 And this shall be a sign unto you from the Becoming-One, that the Becoming-One will do this thing that he has spoken;

8 Behold, I will bring again the shadow of the degrees, which is gone down in the sun dial of Ahaz, ten degrees backward. So the sun returned ten degrees, by which degrees it was gone down.

9 The writing of Hezekiah king of Judah, when he had been sick, and was recovered of his sickness:

10 I said in the cutting off of my days, I shall go to the gates of Sheol: I am deprived of the residue of my years.

11 I said, I shall not see the Becoming-One, even the Becoming-One, in the land of the living: I shall behold man no more with the inhabitants of the world.

12 Mine age is departed, and is removed from me as a shepherd's tent: I have cut off like a weaver my life: he will cut me off with pining sickness: from day even to night will you make an end of me.

13 I reckoned till morning, that, as a lion, so will he break all my bones: from day even to night will you make an end of me.

14 Like a crane or a swallow, so did I chatter: I did mourn as a dove: mine eyes fail with looking upward: O Becoming-One, I am oppressed; undertake for me.

15 What shall I say? he has both spoken unto me, and himself has done it: I shall go softly all my years in the bitterness of my soul.

16 O my Lord(s), by these things men live, and in all these things is the life of my spirit: so will you recover me, and make me to live.

17 Behold, for peace I had great bitterness: but you have in love to my soul delivered it from the pit of corruption: for you have cast all my sins behind your back.

18 For Sheol cannot praise you, death can not celebrate you: they that go down into the pit cannot hope for your truth.

19 The living, the living, he shall praise you, as I do this day: the father to the children shall make known your truth.

20 The Becoming-One was ready to save me: therefore we will sing my songs to the stringed instruments all the days of our life in the house of the Becoming-One.

21 For Isaiah had said, Let them take a lump of figs, and lay it for a plaster upon the boil, and he shall recover.

22 Hezekiah also had said, What is the sign that I shall go up to the house of the Becoming-One?

Isa 39:1 At that time Merodach-baladan, the son of Baladan, king of Babylon, sent letters and a present to Hezekiah: for he had heard that he had been sick, and was recovered.

2 And Hezekiah was glad of them, and showed them the house of his precious things, the silver, and the gold, and the spices, and the precious ointment, and all the house of his armor, and all that was found in his treasures: there was nothing in his house, nor in all his dominion, that Hezekiah showed them not.

3 Then came Isaiah the prophet unto king Hezekiah, and said unto him, What said these men? and from where came they unto you? And Hezekiah said, They are come from a far country unto me, even from Babylon.

4 Then said he, What have they seen in your house? And Hezekiah answered, All that is in mine house have they seen: there is nothing among my treasures that I have not showed them.

5 Then said Isaiah to Hezekiah, Hear the word of the Becoming-One of hosts:

6 Behold, the days come, that all that is in your house, and that which your fathers have laid up in store until this day, shall be carried to Babylon: nothing shall be left, says the Becoming-One.

7 And of your sons that shall issue from you, which you shall beget, shall they take away; and they shall be eunuchs in the palace of the king of Babylon.

8 Then said Hezekiah to Isaiah, Good is the word of the Becoming-One which you have spoken. He said moreover, For there shall be peace and truth in my days.

Isa 40:1 Comfort ye, comfort you my people, says your God.

2 **Speak you comfortably to Jerusalem**, and cry unto her, that her warfare is accomplished, that her iniquity is pardoned: for she has received from the Becoming-One's hand double for all her sins.

3 The voice of him that cries in the wilderness, Prepare you the way of the Becoming-One, make straight in the desert a highway for our God.

4 Every valley shall be exalted, and every mountain and hill shall be made low: and the crooked shall be made straight, and the rough places plain:

5 And the glory of the Becoming-One shall be revealed, and all flesh shall see it together: for the mouth of the Becoming-One has spoken it.

6 The voice said, Cry. And he said, What shall I cry? All flesh is grass, and all the goodliness thereof is as the flower of the field:

7 The grass withers, the flower fades: because the spirit of the Becoming-One blows upon it: surely the people is grass.

8 The grass withers, the flower fades: but the word of our God shall stand for olam.

9 O Zion, that bring good tidings, get you up into the high mountain; O Jerusalem, that bring good tidings, lift up your voice with strength; lift it up, be not afraid; say unto the cities of Judah, Behold your God!

10 Behold, my Lord(s) the Becoming-One will come with strong hand, and his arm shall rule for him: behold, his reward is with him, and his work before him.

11 He shall feed his flock like a shepherd: he shall gather the lambs with his arm, and carry them in his bosom, and shall gently lead those that are with young.

12 Who has measured the waters in the hollow of his hand, and measured out the heavens with the span, and comprehended the dust of the earth in a measure, and weighed the mountains in scales, and the hills in a balance?

13 Who has directed the Spirit of the Becoming-One, or being his counselor has taught him?

14 With whom took he counsel, and who instructed him, and taught him in the path of judgment, and taught him knowledge, and showed to him the way of understanding?

15 Behold, the nations are as a drop of a bucket, and are counted as the small dust of the balance: behold, he takes up the isles as a very little thing.

16 And Lebanon is not sufficient to burn, nor the beasts thereof sufficient for a burnt offering.

17 All nations before him are as nothing; and they are counted to him less than nothing, and vanity.

18 To whom then will you liken GOD? or what likeness will you compare unto him?

19 The workman melts a graven image, and the goldsmith spreads it over with gold, and castes silver chains.

20 He that is so impoverished that he has no offering chooses a tree that will not rot; he seeks unto him a cunning workman to prepare a graven image, that shall not be moved.

21 Have you not known? have you not heard? has it not been told you from the beginning? have you not understood from the foundations of the earth?

22 It is he that sits upon the circle of the earth, and the inhabitants thereof are as grasshoppers; that stretches out the heavens as a curtain, and spreads them out as a tent to dwell in:

23 That brings the princes to nothing; he makes the judges of the earth as vanity.

24 Yes, they shall not be planted; yes, they shall not be sown: yes, their stock shall not take root in the earth: and he shall also blow upon them, and they shall wither, and the whirlwind shall take them away as stubble.

25 To whom then will you liken me, or shall I be equal? says the Holy One.

26 Lift up your eyes on high, and behold who has created these things, that brings out their host by number: he calls them all by names by the greatness of his might, for that he is strong in power; not one faileth.

27 Why say you, O Jacob, and speak, O Israel, My way is hid from the Becoming-One, and my judgment is passed over from my God?

28 have you not known? have you not heard, that God of olam, the Becoming-One, the Creator of the ends of the earth, faints not, neither is weary? there is no searching of his understanding.

29 He gives power to the faint; and to them that have no might he increases strength.

30 Even the youths shall faint and be weary, and the young men shall utterly fall:

31 But they that wait upon the Becoming-One shall renew their strength; they shall mount up with wings as eagles; they shall run, and not be weary; and they shall walk, and not faint.

Isa 41:1 Keep silence before me, O coastlands; and let the people renew their strength: let them come near; then let them speak: let us come near together to judgment.

2 Who raised up the righteous man from the east, called him to his foot, gave the nations before him, and made him rule over kings? he gave them as the dust to his sword, and as driven stubble to his bow.

3 He pursued them, and passed safely; even by the way that he had not gone with his feet.

4 Who has worked and done it, calling the generations from the beginning? I the Becoming-One, the first, and with the last ones; I am he.

5 The isles saw it, and feared; the ends of the earth were afraid, drew near, and came.

6 They helped every one his neighbor; and every one said to his brother, Be of good courage.

7 So the carpenter encouraged the goldsmith, and he that is smoothing with the hammer him that smote the anvil, saying, It is ready for the soldering: and he fastened it with nails, that it should not be moved.

8 But you, Israel, are my servant, Jacob whom I have chosen, the seed of Abraham my friend.

9 you whom I have taken from the ends of the earth, and called you from the chief men thereof, and said unto you, you are my servant; I have chosen you, and not cast you away.

10 Fear you not; for I am with you: be not dismayed; for I am your God: I will strengthen you; yes, I will help you; yes, I will uphold you with the right hand of my righteousness.

11 Behold, all they that were incensed against you shall be ashamed and confounded: they shall be as nothing; and they that strive with you shall perish.

12 you shall seek them, and shall not find them, even them that contended with you: they that war against you shall be as nothing, and as a thing of nothing.

13 For I the Becoming-One your God will hold your right hand, saying unto you, Fear not; I will help you.

14 Fear not, you worm Jacob, and you men of Israel; I will help you, says the Becoming-One, and your redeemer, the Holy One of Israel.

15 Behold, I will make you a new sharp threshing instrument having teeth: you shall thresh the mountains, and beat them small, and shall make the hills as chaff.

16 you shall fan them, and the wind shall carry them away, and the whirlwind shall scatter them: and you shall rejoice in the Becoming-One, and shall glory in the Holy One of Israel.

17 When the poor and needy seek water, and there is none, and their tongue fails for thirst, I the Becoming-One will hear them, I God of Israel will not forsake them.

18 I will open rivers in high places, and fountains in the midst of the valleys: I will make the wilderness a pool of water, and the dry land springs of water.

19 I will plant in the wilderness the cedar, the shittah tree, and the myrtle, and the oil tree; I will set in the desert the fir tree, and the pine, and the box tree together:

20 That they may see, and know, and consider, and understand together, that the hand of the Becoming-One has done this, and the Holy One of Israel has created it.

21 Produce your cause, says the Becoming-One; bring forth your strong reasons, says the King of Jacob.

22 Let them bring them forth, and show us what shall happen: let them show the former things, what they be, that we may consider them, and know the latter end of them; or declare us things for to come.

23 Show the things that are to come hereafter, that we may know that you are gods: yes, do good, or do evil, that we may be dismayed, and behold it together.

24 Behold, you are of nothing, and your work of nothing: an abomination is he that chooses you.

25 I have raised up one from the north, and he shall come: from the rising of the sun shall he call upon my name: and he shall come upon princes as upon mortar, and as the potter treads clay.

26 Who has declared from the beginning, that we may know? and beforetime, that we may say, He is righteous? yes, there is none that shows, yes, there is none that declares, yes, there is none that hears your words.

27 The first shall say to Zion, Behold, behold them: and I will give to Jerusalem one that brings good tidings.

28 For I beheld, and there was no man; even among them, and there was no counselor, that, when I asked of them, could answer a word.

29 Behold, they are all vanity; their works are nothing: their molten images are wind and confusion.

Isa 42:1 Behold my servant, whom I uphold; mine elect, in whom my soul delights; I have put my spirit upon him: he shall bring forth judgment to the nations.

2 He shall not cry, nor lift up, nor cause his voice to be heard in the street.

3 A bruised reed shall he not break, and the smoking flax shall he not quench: he shall bring forth judgment unto truth.

4 He shall not fail nor be discouraged, till he have set judgment in the earth: and the isles shall wait for his law.

5 Thus says GOD the Becoming-One, he that created the heavens, and stretched them out; he that spread forth the earth, and that which comes out of it; he that gives breath unto the people upon it, and spirit to them that walk therein:

6 I the Becoming-One have called you in righteousness, and will hold your hand, and will keep you, and give you for a covenant of the people, for a light of the nations;

7 To open the blind eyes, to bring out the prisoners from the prison, and them that sit in darkness out of the prison house.

8 I am the Becoming-One: that is my name: and my glory will I not give to another, neither my praise to graven images.

9 Behold, the former things are come to pass, and new things do I declare: before they spring forth I tell you of them.

10 Sing unto the Becoming-One a new song, and his praise from the end of the earth, you that go down to the sea, and all that is therein; the isles, and the inhabitants thereof.

11 Let the wilderness and the cities thereof lift up their voice, the villages that Kedar does inhabit: let the inhabitants of the rock sing, let them shout from the top of the mountains.

12 Let them give glory unto the Becoming-One, and declare his praise in the coastlands.

13 The Becoming-One shall go forth as a mighty man, he shall stir up jealousy like a man of war: he shall cry, yes, roar; he shall prevail against his enemies.

14 I have long time held my peace; I have been still, and refrained myself: now will I cry like a travailing woman; I will destroy and devour at once.

15 I will make waste mountains and hills, and dry up all their herbs; and I will make the rivers coastlands, and I will dry up the pools.

16 And I will bring the blind by a way that they knew not; I will lead them in paths that they have not known: I will make darkness light before them, and crooked things straight. These things will I do unto them, and not forsake them.

17 They shall be turned back, they shall be greatly ashamed, that trust in graven images, that say to the molten images, you are our gods.

18 Hear, you deaf; and look, you blind, that you may see.

19 Who is blind, but my servant? or deaf, as my messenger that I sent? who is blind as he that is perfect, and blind as the Becoming-One's servant?

20 Seeing many things, but you observe not; opening the ears, but he hears not.

21 The Becoming-One is well pleased for his righteousness' sake; he will magnify the law, and make it honorable.

22 But this is a people robbed and spoiled; they are all of them snared in holes, and they are hid in prison houses: they are for a prey, and none delivers; for a spoil, and none says, Restore.

23 Who among you will give ear to this? who will listen and hear for the time to come?

24 Who gave Jacob for a spoil, and Israel to the robbers? did not the Becoming-One, he against whom we have sinned? for they would not walk in his ways, neither were they obedient unto his law.

25 Therefore he has poured upon him the fury of his anger, and the strength of battle: and it has set him on fire round about, yet he knew not; and it burned him, yet he laid it not to heart.

Isa 43:1 But now thus says the Becoming-One that created you, O Jacob, and he that formed you, O Israel, Fear not: for I have redeemed you, I have called you by your name; you are mine.

2 When you pass through the waters, I will be with you; and through the rivers, they shall not overflow you: when you walk through the fire, you shall not be burned; neither shall the flame kindle upon you.

3 For I am the Becoming-One your God, the Holy One of Israel, your Savior: I gave Egypt for your ransom, Ethiopia and Seba for you.

4 Since you were precious in my sight, you have been honorable, and I have loved you: therefore will I give men for you, and people for your soul.

5 Fear not: for I am with you: I will bring your seed from the east, and gather you from the west;

6 I will say to the north, Give up; and to the south, Keep not back: bring my sons from far, and my daughters from the ends of the earth;

7 All are called by my name: for I have created him for my glory, I have formed him; yes, I have made him.

8 Bring forth the blind people that have eyes, and the deaf that have ears.

9 Let all the nations be gathered together, and let the people be assembled: who among them can declare this, and show us former things? let them bring forth their witnesses, that they may be justified: or let them hear, and say, It is truth.

10 you are my witnesses, says the Becoming-One, and my servant whom I have chosen: that you may know and believe me, and understand that I am he: before me there was no GOD formed, neither shall there be after me.

11 I, even I, am the Becoming-One; and beside me there is no Savior.

12 I have declared, and have saved, and I have showed, when there was no strange god among you: therefore you are my witnesses, says the Becoming-One, that I am GOD.

13 Yes, before the day was I am he; and there is none that can deliver out of my hand: I will work, and who shall let it?

14 Thus says the Becoming-One, your redeemer, the Holy One of Israel; For your sake I have sent to Babylon, and have brought down all their nobles, and the Chaldeans, whose cry is in the ships.

15 I am the Becoming-One, your Holy One, the creator of Israel, your King.

16 Thus says the Becoming-One, which makes a way in the sea, and a path in the mighty waters;

17 Which brings forth the chariot and horse, the army and the power; they shall lie down together, they shall not rise: they are extinct, they are quenched as tow.

18 Remember you not the former things, neither consider the things of old.

19 Behold, I will do a new thing; now it shall spring forth; shall you not know it? I will even make a way in the wilderness, and rivers in the desert.

20 The beast of the field shall honor me, the monsters and the owls: because I give waters in the wilderness, and rivers in the desert, to give drink to my people, my chosen.

21 This people have I formed for myself; they shall show forth my praise.

22 But you have not called upon me, O Jacob; but you have been weary of me, O Israel.

23 you have not brought me the small cattle of your burnt offerings; neither have you honored me with your sacrifices. I have not caused you to serve with an offering, nor wearied you with incense.

24 you have bought me no sweet cane with money, neither have you filled me with the fat of your sacrifices: but you have made me to serve with your sins, you have wearied me with your iniquities.

25 I, even I, am he that blots out your transgressions for mine own sake, and will not remember your sins.

26 Put me in remembrance: let us plead together: declare you, that you may be justified.

27 your first father has sinned, and your teachers have transgressed against me.

28 Therefore I have profaned the princes of the sanctuary, and have given Jacob to the curse, and Israel to reproaches.

Isa 44:1 Yet now hear, O Jacob my servant; and Israel, whom I have chosen:

2 Thus says the Becoming-One that made you, and formed you from the womb, which will help you; Fear not, O Jacob, my servant; and you, Jesurun, whom I have chosen.

3 For I will pour water upon him that is thirsty, and floods upon the dry ground: I will pour my spirit upon your seed, and my blessing upon your offspring:

4 And they shall spring up as among the grass, as willows by the water courses.

5 One shall say, I am for Becoming-One; and another shall call himself by the name of Jacob; and another shall subscribe with his hand unto the Becoming-One, and surname himself by the name of Israel.

6 Thus says the Becoming-One the King of Israel, and his redeemer the Becoming-One of hosts; I am the first, and I am the last; and beside me there is no God.

7 And who, as I, shall call, and shall declare it, and set it in order for me, since I appointed the nation of olam? and the things that are coming, and which shall absolutely come, let them show unto them.

8 Fear you not, neither be afraid: have not I told you from then, and have declared it? you are even my witnesses. Is there a GOD beside me? yes, there is no Rock; I know not any.

9 They that make a graven image are all of them vanity; and their delectable things shall not profit; and they are their own witnesses; they see not, nor know; that they may be ashamed.

10 Who has formed a god, or molten a graven image that is profitable for nothing?

11 Behold, all his fellows shall be ashamed: and the workmen, they are of men: let them all be gathered together, let them stand up; yet they shall fear, and they shall be ashamed together.

12 The smith with the tongs both works in the coals, and fashions it with hammers, and works it with the strength of his arms: yes, he is hungry, and his strength fails: he drinks no water, and is faint.

13 The carpenter stretches out his rule; he marks it out with a line; he fits it with planes, and he marks it out with the compass, and makes it after the figure of a man, according to the beauty of a man; that it may remain in the house.

14 He hews him down cedars, and takes the cypress and the oak, which he strengthens for himself among the trees of the forest: he plants an ash, and the rain does nourish it.

15 Then shall it be for a man to burn: for he will take thereof, and warm himself; yes, he kindles it, and bakes bread; yes, he makes a god, and worships it; he makes it a graven image, and falls down thereto.

16 He burns part thereof in the fire; with part thereof he eats flesh; he roasts the meat, and is satisfied: yes, he warms himself, and says, Aha, I am warm, I have seen the fire:

17 And the residue thereof he makes a god, even his graven image: he falls down unto it, and worships it, and prays unto it, and says, Deliver me; for you are my god.

18 They have not known nor understood: for he has shut their eyes, that they cannot see; and their hearts, that they cannot understand.

19 And none consider in his heart, neither is there knowledge nor understanding to say, I have burned part of it in the fire; yes, also I have baked bread upon the coals thereof; I have roasted flesh, and eaten it: and shall I make the residue thereof an abomination? shall I fall down to the stock of a tree?

20 He feeds on ashes: a deceived heart has turned him aside, that he cannot deliver his soul, nor say, Is there not a lie in my right hand?

21 Remember these, O Jacob and Israel; for you are my servant: I have formed you; you are my servant: O Israel, you shall not be forgotten of me.

22 I have blotted out, as a thick cloud, your transgressions, and, as a cloud, your sins: return unto me; for I have redeemed you.

23 Sing, O you heavens; for the Becoming-One has done it: shout, you lower parts of the earth: break forth into singing, you mountains, O forest, and every tree therein: for the Becoming-One has redeemed Jacob, and glorified himself in Israel.

24 Thus says the Becoming-One, your redeemer, and he that formed you from the womb, I am the Becoming-One that makes all things; that stretches forth the heavens alone; that spreads abroad the earth by myself;

25 That frustrates the tokens of the liars, and makes diviners mad; that turns wise men backward, and makes their knowledge foolish;

26 That confirms the word of his servant, and performs the counsel of his messengers; that says to Jerusalem, you shall be inhabited; and to the cities of Judah, you shall be built, and I will raise up the decayed places thereof:

27 That says to the deep, Be dry, and I will dry up your rivers:

28 That says of Cyrus, He is my shepherd, and shall perform all my pleasure: even saying to Jerusalem, you shall be built; and to the temple, your foundation shall be laid.

Isa 45:1 Thus says the Becoming-One to his anointed [Messiah], to Cyrus, whose right hand I have held, to subdue nations before him; and I will loose the loins of kings, to open before him the two leaved gates; and the gates shall not be shut;

2 I will go before you, and make the crooked places straight: I will break in pieces the gates of brass, and cut in sunder the bars of iron:

3 And I will give you the treasures of darkness, and hidden riches of secret places, that you may know that I, the Becoming-One, which call you by your name, am God of Israel.

4 For Jacob my servant's sake, and Israel mine elect, I have even called you by your name: I have surnamed you, though you have not known me.

5 **I am the Becoming-One, and there is none else, there is no God beside me**: I girded you, though you have not known me:

6 That they may know from the rising of the sun, and from the west, that there is none beside me. I am the Becoming-One, and there is none else.

7 **I form the light, and create darkness: I make peace, and create evil: I the Becoming-One do all these things.**

8 Drop down, you heavens, from above, and let the skies pour down righteousness: let the earth open, and let them bring forth salvation, and let righteousness spring up together; I the Becoming-One have created it.

9 Woe unto him that strives with his Maker! Let the potsherd strive with the potsherds of the earth. Shall the clay say to him that fashions it, What make you? or your work, He has no hands?

10 Woe unto him that says unto his father, What beget you? or to the woman, What have you brought forth?

11 Thus says the Becoming-One, the Holy One of Israel, and his Maker, Ask me of things to come concerning my sons, and concerning the work of my hands command you me.

12 I have made the earth, and created man upon it: I, even my hands, have stretched out the heavens, and all their host have I commanded.

13 I have raised him up in righteousness, and I will direct all his ways: he shall build my city, and he shall let go my captives, not for price nor reward, says the Becoming-One of hosts.

14 Thus says the Becoming-One, The labor of Egypt, and merchandise of Ethiopia and of the Sabeans, men of stature, shall come over unto you, and they shall be yours: they shall come after you; in chains they shall come over, and they shall fall down unto you, they shall make supplication unto you, saying, Surely GOD is in you; and none else, no [other] gods.

15 Truly you are a GOD that hides thyself, O God of Israel, the Savior.

16 They shall be ashamed, and also confounded, all of them: they shall go to confusion together that are makers of idols.

17 But Israel shall be saved in the Becoming-One with a salvation of olams: you shall not be ashamed nor confounded to olams and beyond.

18 For thus says the Becoming-One that created the heavens; God himself that formed the earth and made it; he has established it, he created it not in vain, he formed it to be inhabited: I am the Becoming-One; and there is none else.

19 I have not spoken in secret, in a dark place of the earth: I said not unto the seed of Jacob, Seek you me in vain: I the Becoming-One speak righteousness, I declare things that are right.

20 Assemble yourselves and come; draw near together, you that are escaped of the nations: they have no knowledge that set up the wood of their graven image, and pray unto a god that cannot save.

21 Tell ye, and bring them near; yes, let them take counsel together: who has declared this from ancient time? who has told it from that time? have not I the Becoming-One? and there is no God else beside me; a just GOD and a Savior; there is none beside me.

22 Look unto me, and be you saved, all the ends of the earth: for I am GOD, and there is none else.

23 I have sworn by myself, the word is gone out of my mouth in righteousness, and shall not return, That unto me every knee shall bow, every tongue shall swear.

24 Surely, shall one say, in the Becoming-One have I righteousness and strength: even to him shall men come; and all that are incensed against him shall be ashamed.

25 In the Becoming-One shall all the seed of Israel be justified, and shall glory.

Isa 46:1 Bel bows down, Nebo stoops, their idols were upon the beasts, and upon the cattle: your carriages were heavily loaded; they are a burden to the weary beast.

2 They stoop, they bow down together; they could not deliver the burden, but their souls are gone into captivity.

3 listen unto me, O house of Jacob, and all the remnant of the house of Israel, which are borne by me from the belly, which are carried from the womb:

4 And even to your old age I am he; and even to hoar hairs will I carry you: I have made, and I will bear; even I will carry, and will deliver you.

5 To whom will you liken me, and make me equal, and compare me, that we may be like?

6 They lavish gold out of the bag, and weigh silver in the balance, and hire a goldsmith; and he makes it a god: they fall down, yes, they worship.

7 They bear him upon the shoulder, they carry him, and set him in his place, and he stands; from his place shall he not remove: yes, one shall cry unto him, yet can he not answer, nor save him out of his trouble.

8 Remember this, and show yourselves men: bring it again to mind, O you transgressors.

9 Remember the former things of olam: for I am GOD, and there is none else; I am God, and there is none like me,

10 Declaring the end from the beginning, and from ancient times the things that are not yet done, saying, My counsel shall stand, and I will do all my pleasure:

11 Calling a ravenous bird from the east, the man that executes my counsel from a far country: yes, I have spoken it [perfect verb] I will also bring it to pass [imperf verb] yes, I have made it [perf] I will also do it [imperf]

12 listen unto me, you stouthearted, that are far from righteousness:

13 I bring near my righteousness: it shall not be far off, and my salvation shall not tarry: and I will place salvation in Zion for Israel my glory.

Isa 47:1 Come down, and sit in the dust, O virgin daughter of Babylon, sit on the ground: there is no throne, O daughter of the Chaldeans: for you shall no more be called tender and delicate.

2 Take the millstones, and grind meal: uncover your locks, make bare the leg, uncover the thigh, pass over the rivers.

3 your nakedness shall be uncovered, yes, your shame shall be seen: I will take vengeance, and I will not meet you as a man.

4 As for our redeemer, the Becoming-One of hosts is his name, the Holy One of Israel.

5 Sit you silent, and get you into darkness, O daughter of the Chaldeans: for you shall no more be called, The lady of kingdoms.

6 I was angry with my people, I have polluted mine inheritance, and given them into your hand: you did show them no mercy; upon the ancient have you very heavily laid your yoke.

7 And you said, I shall be a lady for olam: so that you did not lay these things to your heart, neither did remember the latter end of it.

8 Therefore hear now this, you that are given to pleasures, that dwell carelessly, that say in your heart, I am, and none else beside me; I shall not sit as a widow, neither shall I know the loss of children:

9 But these two things shall come to you in a moment in one day, the loss of children, and widowhood: they shall come upon you in their perfection for the multitude of your sorceries, and for the great abundance of your enchantments.

10 For you have trusted in your wickedness: you have said, None sees me. your wisdom and your knowledge, it has perverted you; and you have said in your heart, I am, and none else beside me.

11 Therefore shall evil come upon you; you shall not know the dawn of it: and mischief shall fall upon you; you shall not be able to atone it: and desolation shall come upon you suddenly, which you shall not know.

12 Stand now with your enchantments, and with the multitude of your sorceries, wherein you have labored from your youth; if so be you shall be able to profit, if so be you may prevail.

13 you are wearied in the multitude of your counsels. Let now the astrologers, the stargazers, the monthly prognosticators, stand up, and save you from these things that shall come upon you.

14 Behold, they shall be as stubble; the fire shall burn them; they shall not deliver their souls from the power of the flame: there shall not be a coal to warm at, nor fire to sit before it.

15 Thus shall they be unto you with whom you have labored, even your merchants, from your youth: they shall wander every one over; none shall save you.

Isa 48:1 Hear you this, O house of Jacob, which are called by the name of Israel, and are come forth out of the waters of Judah, which swear by the name of the Becoming-One, and make mention of God of Israel, but not in truth, nor in righteousness.

2 For they call themselves of the holy city, and stay themselves upon God of Israel; The Becoming-One of hosts is his name.

3 I have declared the former things from then; and they went forth out of my mouth, and I showed them; I did them suddenly, and they came to pass.

4 Because I knew that you are obstinate, and your neck is an iron tendon, and your brow brass;

5 I have even from then declared it to you; before it came to pass I showed it you: lest you should say, Mine idol has done them, and my graven image, and my molten image, has commanded them.

6 you have heard, see all this; and will not you declare it? I have showed you new things from this time, even hidden things, and you did not know them.

7 They are created now, and not from the beginning; even before the day when you heard them not; lest you should say, Behold, I knew them.

8 Yes, you heard not; yes, you knew not; yes, from that time that your ear was not opened: for I knew that you would deal very treacherously, and were called a transgressor from the womb.

9 For my name's sake will I defer mine anger, and for my praise will I refrain for you, that I cut you not off.

10 Behold, I have refined you, but not with silver; I have chosen you in the furnace of affliction.

11 For mine own sake, even for mine own sake, will I do it: for how should my name be polluted? and I will not give my glory unto another.

12 listen unto me, O Jacob and Israel, my called; I am he; I am the first, I also am the last.

13 Mine hand also has laid the foundation of the earth, and my right hand has spanned the heavens: when I call unto them, they stand up together.

14 All ye, assemble yourselves, and hear; which among them has declared these things? The Becoming-One has loved him: he will do his pleasure on Babylon, and his arm shall be on the Chaldeans.

15 I, even I, have spoken; yes, I have called him: I have brought him, and he shall make his way prosperous.

16 Come you near unto me, hear you this; I have not spoken in secret from the beginning; from the time that it was, there am I: and now my Lord(s) the Becoming-One, has sent me and his Spirit.

17 Thus says the Becoming-One, your Redeemer, the Holy One of Israel; I am the Becoming-One your God which teaches you to profit, which leads you by the way that you should go.

18 O that you had listened to my commandments! then had your peace been as a river, and your righteousness as the waves of the sea:

19 your seed also had been as the sand, and the offspring of your bowels like the gravel thereof; his name should not have been cut off nor destroyed from before me.

20 Go you forth of Babylon, flee you from the Chaldeans, with a voice of singing declare ye, tell this, utter it even to the end of the earth; say ye, The Becoming-One has redeemed his servant Jacob.

21 And they thirsted not when he led them through the deserts: he caused the waters to flow out of the rock for them: he split the rock also, and the waters gushed out.

22 There is no peace, says the Becoming-One, unto the wicked.

Isa 49:1 Listen, O isles, unto me; and listen, you people, from far; The Becoming-One has called me from the womb; from the bowels of my mother has he made mention of my name.

2 And he has made my mouth like a sharp sword; in the shadow of his hand has he hid me, and made me a polished shaft; in his quiver has he hid me;

3 And said unto me, you are my servant, O Israel, in whom I will be glorified.

4 Then I said, I have labored in vain, I have spent my strength for nothing, and in vain: yet surely my judgment is with the Becoming-One, and my work with my God.

4 Then I said, I have labored in vain, I have spent my strength for nothing, and in vain: yet surely my judgment is with the Becoming-One, and my work with my God.

5 And now, says the Becoming-One that formed me from the womb to be his servant, to bring Jacob again to him, Though Israel be not gathered, yet shall I be glorious in the eyes of the Becoming-One, and my God shall be my strength.

6 And he said, It is a light thing that you should be my servant to raise up the tribes of Jacob, and to restore the preserved of Israel: I will also give you for a light to the nations, that you may be my salvation unto the end of the earth.

7 Thus says the Becoming-One, the Redeemer of Israel, and his Holy One, to him whom man despises in soul, to him whom the nation abhors, to a servant of rulers, Kings shall see and arise, princes also shall worship, because of the Becoming-One that is faithful, and the Holy One of Israel, and he shall choose you.

8 Thus says the Becoming-One, In an acceptable time have I heard you, and in a day of salvation have I helped you: and I will preserve you, and give you for a covenant of the people, to establish the earth, to cause to inherit the desolate heritages;

9 That you may say to the prisoners, Go forth; to them that are in darkness, Show yourselves. They shall feed in the ways, and their pastures shall be in all high places.

10 They shall not hunger nor thirst; neither shall the heat nor sun smite them: for he that has mercy on them shall lead them, even by the springs of water shall he guide them.

11 And I will make all my mountains a way, and my highways shall be exalted.

12 Behold, these shall come from far: and, lo, these from the north and from the west; and these from the land of Sinim.

13 Sing, O heavens; and be joyful, O earth; and break forth into singing, O mountains: for the Becoming-One has comforted his people, and will have mercy upon his afflicted.

14 But Zion said, The Becoming-One has forsaken me, and my Lord(s) has forgotten me.

15 Can a woman forget her sucking child, that she should not have compassion on the son of her womb? yes, they may forget, yet will I not forget you.

16 Behold, I have graven you upon the palms of my hands; your walls are continually before me.

17 your children shall make haste; your destroyers and they that made you waste shall go forth of you.

18 Lift up your eyes round about, and behold: all these gather themselves together, and come to you. As I live, says the Becoming-One, you shall surely clothe you with them all, as with an ornament, and bind them on you, as a bride does.

19 For your waste and your desolate places, and the land of your destruction, shall even now be too narrow by reason of the inhabitants, and they that swallowed you up shall be far away.

20 The children which you shall have, after you have lost the other, shall say again in your ears, The place is too strait for me: give place to me that I may dwell.

21 Then shall you say in your heart, Who has begotten me these, seeing I have lost my children, and am desolate, a captive, and removing back and forth? and who has brought up these? Behold, I was left alone; these, where had they been?

22 Thus says my Lord(s) the Becoming-One, Behold, I will lift up mine hand to the nations, and set up my standard to the people: and they shall bring your sons in their arms, and your daughters shall be carried upon their shoulders.

23 And kings shall be your nursing fathers, and their queens your nursing mothers: they shall bow down to you with their face toward the earth, and lick up the dust of your feet; and you shall know that I am

the Becoming-One: for they shall not be ashamed that wait for me.

24 Shall the prey be taken from the mighty, or the lawful captive delivered?

25 But thus says the Becoming-One, Even the captives of the mighty shall be taken away, and the prey of the terrible shall be delivered: for I will contend with him that contends with you, and I will save your children.

26 And I will feed them that oppress you with their own flesh; and they shall be drunken with their own blood, as with sweet wine: and all flesh shall know that I the Becoming-One am your Savior and your Redeemer, the mighty One of Jacob.

Isa 50:1 Thus says the Becoming-One, Where is the bill of your mother's divorcement, whom I have put away? or which of my creditors is it to whom I have sold you? Behold, for your iniquities have you sold yourselves, and for your transgressions is your mother put away.

2 Therefore, when I came, was there no man? when I called, was there none to answer? Is my hand shortened at all, that it cannot redeem? or have I no power to deliver? behold, at my rebuke I dry up the sea, I make the rivers a wilderness: their fish stinks, because there is no water, and dies for thirst.

3 I clothe the heavens with blackness, and I make sackcloth their covering.

4 **My Lord(s) the Becoming-One has given me the tongue of the learned**, that I should know how to speak a word in season to him that is weary: he wakens morning by morning, he wakens mine ear to hear as the learned.

5 My Lord(s) the Becoming-One has opened mine ear, and I was not rebellious, neither turned away back.

6 **I gave my back to the smiters, and my cheeks to them that plucked off the hair: I hid not my face from shame and spitting**.

7 For my Lord(s) the Becoming-One will help me; therefore shall I not be confounded: therefore have I set my face like a flint, and I know that I shall not be ashamed.

8 He is near that justifies me; who will contend with me? let us stand together: who is mine adversary? let him come near to me.

9 Behold, my Lord(s) the Becoming-One will help me; who is he that shall condemn me? lo, they all shall wax old as a garment; the moth shall eat them up.

10 Who is among you that fears the Becoming-One, that obeys the voice of his servant, that walks in darkness, and has no light? let him trust in the name of the Becoming-One, and stay upon his God.

11 Behold, all you that kindle a fire, that compass yourselves about with sparks: walk in the light of your fire, and in the sparks that you have kindled. This shall you have of mine hand; you shall lie down in sorrow.

Isa 51:1 listen to me, you that follow after righteousness, you that seek the Becoming-One: look unto the rock from where you are hewn, and to the hole of the pit from where you are dug.

2 Look unto Abraham your father, and unto Sarah that bare you: for I called him alone, and blessed him, and increased him.

3 For the Becoming-One shall comfort Zion: he will comfort all her waste places; and he will make her wilderness like Eden, and her desert like the garden of the Becoming-One; joy and gladness shall be found therein, thanksgiving, and the voice of melody.

4 listen unto me, my people; and give ear unto me, O my nation: for a law shall proceed from me, and I will make my judgment to rest for a light of the people.

5 My righteousness is near; my salvation is gone forth, and mine arms shall judge the people; the isles shall wait upon me, and on mine arm shall they trust.

6 Lift up your eyes to the heavens, and look upon the earth beneath: for the heavens shall vanish away like smoke, and the earth shall wax old like a garment, and they that dwell therein shall die in like manner: but my salvation shall be for olam, and my righteousness shall not be abolished.

7 listen unto me, you that know righteousness, the people in whose heart is my law; fear you not the reproach of men, neither be you afraid of their revilings.

8 For the moth shall eat them up like a garment, and the worm shall eat them like wool: but my righteousness shall be for olam, and my salvation from generation to generation.

9 Awake, awake, put on strength, O arm of the Becoming-One; awake, as in the ancient days, in the generations of olams. are you not it that has cut pride Rahab, and wounded the monster?

10 are you not it which has dried the sea, the waters of the great deep; that has made the depths of the sea a way for the ransomed to pass over?

11 Therefore the redeemed of the Becoming-One shall return, and come with singing unto Zion; and joy of olam shall be upon their head: they shall obtain gladness and joy; and sorrow and mourning shall flee away.

12 I, even I, am he that comforts you: who are you, that you should be afraid of a man that shall die, and of the son of man which shall be made as grass;

13 And forget the Becoming-One your maker, that has stretched forth the heavens, and laid the foundations of the earth; and have feared continually every day because of the fury of the oppressor, as if he were ready to destroy? and where is the fury of the oppressor?

14 The captive exile hastens that he may be loosened, and that he should not die in the pit, nor that his bread should fail.

15 But I am the Becoming-One your God, that divided the sea, whose waves roared: The Becoming-One of hosts is his name.

16 And I have put my words in your mouth, and I have covered you in the shadow of mine hand, that I may plant the heavens, and lay the foundations of the earth, and say unto Zion, you are my people.

17 Awake, awake, stand up, O Jerusalem, which have drunk at the hand of the Becoming-One the cup of his fury; you have drunken the dregs of the cup of trembling, and wrung them out.

18 There is none to guide her among all the sons whom she has brought forth; neither is there any that takes her by the hand of all the sons that she has brought up.

19 These two things are come unto you; who shall be sorry for you? desolation, and destruction, and the famine, and the sword: by whom shall I comfort you?

20 your sons have fainted, they lie at the head of all the streets, as a wild bull in a net: they are full of the fury of the Becoming-One, the rebuke of your God.

21 Therefore hear now this, you afflicted, and drunken, but not with wine:

22 Thus says your Lords the Becoming-One, and your God that pleads the cause of his people, Behold, I have taken out of your hand the cup of trembling, even the dregs of the cup of my fury; you shall no more drink it again:

23 But I will put it into the hand of them that afflict you; which have said to your soul, Bow down, that we may go over: and you have laid your body as the ground, and as the street, to them that went over.

Isa 52:1 Awake, awake; put on your strength, O Zion; put on your beautiful garments, O Jerusalem, the holy city: for henceforth there shall no more come into you the uncircumcised and the unclean.

2 Shake yourself from the dust; arise, and sit down, O Jerusalem: loose yourself from the bands of your neck, O captive daughter of Zion.

3 For thus says the Becoming-One, you have sold yourselves for nothing; and you shall be redeemed without money.

4 For thus says my Lord(s) the Becoming-One, My people went down afore time into Egypt to sojourn there; and the Assyrian oppressed them without cause.

5 Now therefore, what have I here, says the Becoming-One, that my people is taken away for nothing? they that rule over them make them to howl, says the Becoming-One; and my name continually every day is blasphemed.

6 Therefore my people shall know my name: therefore they shall know in that day that I am he that does speak: behold, it is I.

7 How beautiful upon the mountains are the feet of him that brings good tidings, that declares peace; that brings good tidings of good, that declares salvation; that says unto Zion, your God reigns!

8 your watchmen shall lift up the voice; with the voice together shall they sing: for they shall see eye to eye, when the Becoming-One shall bring again Zion.

9 Break forth into joy, sing together, you waste places of Jerusalem: for the Becoming-One has comforted his people, he has redeemed Jerusalem.

10 The Becoming-One has made bare his holy arm in the eyes of all the nations; and all the ends of the earth shall see the salvation of our God.

11 Depart ye, depart ye, go you out from there, touch no unclean thing; go you out of the midst of her; be you clean, that bear the vessels of the Becoming-One.

12 For you shall not go out with haste, nor go by flight: for the Becoming-One will go before you; and God of Israel will be your rear-guard.

13 Behold, my servant shall deal prudently, he shall be exalted and extolled, and be very high.

14 As many were astonied at you; his visage was so marred more than any man, and his form more than the sons of men:

15 So shall he sprinkle many nations; the kings shall shut their mouths at him: for that which had not been told them shall they see; and that which they had not heard shall they consider.

Isa 53:1 Who has believed our report? and to whom is the arm of the Becoming-One revealed?

2 For he shall grow up before him as a tender plant, and as a root out of a dry ground: he has no form nor comeliness; and when we shall see him, there is no beauty that we should desire him.

3 He is despised and rejected of men; a man of sorrows, and acquainted with grief: and we hid as it were our faces from him; he was despised, and we esteemed him not.

4 Surely he has borne our griefs, and carried our sorrows: yet we did esteem him stricken, struck of God, and afflicted.

5 But he was wounded for our transgressions, he was bruised for our iniquities: the chastisement of our peace was upon him; and with his stripes we are healed.

6 All we like sheep have gone astray; we have turned every one to his own way; and the Becoming-One has laid on him the iniquity of us all.

7 He was oppressed, and he was afflicted, yet he opened not his mouth: he is brought as a lamb to the slaughter, and as a sheep before her shearers is mute, so he opens not his mouth.

8 He was taken from prison and from judgment: and who shall declare his generation? for he was cut off out of the land of the living: for the transgression of my people was he stricken.

9 And he made his grave with the wicked, and with the rich in his death; because he had done no violence, neither was any deceit in his mouth.

10 Yet it pleased the Becoming-One to bruise him; he has put him to grief: when you shall make his soul an offering for sin, he shall see his seed, he shall prolong his days, and the pleasure of the Becoming-One shall prosper in his hand.

11 He shall see of the travail of his soul, and shall be satisfied: by his knowledge shall my righteous servant justify many; for he shall bear their iniquities.

12 Therefore will I divide him a portion with the great, and he shall divide the spoil with the strong; because he has poured out his soul unto death: and he was numbered with the transgressors; and he bare the sin of many, and made intercession for the transgressors.

Isa 54:1 Sing, O barren, you that did not bear; break forth into singing, and cry aloud, you that did not travail with child: for more are the children of the desolate than the children of the married wife, says the Becoming-One.

2 Enlarge the place of your tent, and let them stretch forth the curtains of your habitations: spare not, lengthen your cords, and strengthen your stakes;

3 For you shall break forth on the right hand and on the left; and your seed shall inherit the nations, and make the desolate cities to be inhabited.

4 Fear not; for you shall not be ashamed: neither be you confounded; for you shall not be put to shame: for you shall forget the shame of your youth, and shall not remember the reproach of your widowhood any more.

5 For your Maker is your husband; the Becoming-One of hosts is his name; and your Redeemer the Holy One of Israel; God of the whole earth shall he be called.

6 For the Becoming-One has called you as a woman forsaken and grieved in spirit, and a wife of youth, when you were refused, says your God.

7 For a small moment have I forsaken you; but with great mercies will I gather you.

8 In a little wrath I hid my face from you for a moment; but with kindness of olam will I have mercy on you, says the Becoming-One your Redeemer.

9 For this is as the waters of Noah unto me: for as I have sworn that the waters of Noah should no more go over the earth; so have I sworn that I would not be angry with you, nor rebuke you.

10 For the mountains shall depart, and the hills be removed; but my kindness shall not depart from you, neither shall the covenant of my peace be removed, says the Becoming-One that has mercy on you.

11 O you afflicted, tossed with tempest, and not comforted, behold, I will lay your stones with fair colors, and lay your foundations with sapphires.

12 And I will make your windows of agates, and your gates of carbuncles, and all your borders of pleasant stones.

13 And all your children shall be taught of the Becoming-One; and great shall be the peace of your children.

14 In righteousness shall you be established: you shall be far from oppression; for you shall not fear: and from terror; for it shall not come near you.

15 Behold, they shall surely gather together, but not by me: whosoever shall gather together against you shall fall for your sake.

16 Behold, I have created the smith that blows the coals in the fire, and that brings forth an instrument for his work; and I have created the waster to destroy.

17 No weapon that is formed against you shall prosper; and every tongue that shall rise against you in judgment you shall condemn. This is the heritage of the servants of the Becoming-One, and their righteousness is of me, says the Becoming-One.

Isa 55:1 Ho, every one that thirst, you come to the waters, and he that has no money; come ye, buy, and eat; yes, come, buy wine and milk without money and without price.

2 Why do you spend money for that which is not bread? and your labor for that which satisfies not? listen diligently unto me, and eat you that which is good, and let your soul delight itself in fatness.

3 Incline your ear, and come unto me: hear, and your soul shall live; and I will make a covenant of olam with you, even the sure mercies of David.

4 Behold, I have given him for a witness to the people, a leader and commander to the people.

5 Behold, you shall call a nation that you know not, and nations that knew not you shall run unto you because of the Becoming-One your God, and for the Holy One of Israel; for he has glorified you.

6 Seek you the Becoming-One while he may be found, call you upon him while he is near:

7 Let the wicked forsake his way, and the unrighteous man his thoughts: and let him return unto the Becoming-One, and he will have mercy upon him; and to our God, for he will abundantly pardon.

8 For my thoughts are not your thoughts, neither are your ways my ways, says the Becoming-One.

9 For as the heavens are higher than the earth, so are my ways higher than your ways, and my thoughts than your thoughts.

10 For as the rain comes down, and the snow from heaven, and returns not there, but waters the earth, and makes it bring forth and bud, that it may give seed to the sower, and bread to the eater:

11 So shall my word be that goes forth out of my mouth: it shall not return unto me void, but it shall accomplish that which I please, and it shall prosper in the thing whereto I sent it.

12 For you shall go out with joy, and be led forth with peace: the mountains and the hills shall break forth before you into singing, and all the trees of the field shall clap their hands.

13 Instead of the thorn shall come up the fir tree, and instead of the brier shall come up the myrtle tree: and it shall be to the Becoming-One for a name, for a sign of olam that shall not be cut off.

Isa 56:1 Thus says the Becoming-One, Keep you judgment, and do justice: for my salvation is near to come, and my righteousness to be revealed.

2 Blessed is the man that did this, and the son of man that lays hold on it; that keeps the Sabbath from polluting it, and keeps his hand from doing any evil.

3 Neither let the son of the stranger, that has joined himself to the Becoming-One, speak, saying, The Becoming-One has utterly separated me from his people: neither let the eunuch say, Behold, I am a dry tree.

4 For thus says the Becoming-One unto the eunuchs that keep my sabbaths, and choose the things that please me, and take hold of my covenant;

5 Even unto them will I give in mine house and within my walls a place and a name better than of sons and of daughters: I will give them a name of olam, that shall not be cut off.

6 Also the sons of the stranger, that join themselves to the Becoming-One, to serve him, and to love the name of the Becoming-One, to be his servants, every one that keeps the Sabbath from polluting it, and takes hold of my covenant;

7 Even them will I bring to my holy mountain, and make them joyful in my house of prayer: their burnt offerings and their sacrifices shall be accepted upon mine altar; for mine house shall be called a house of prayer for all people.

8 My Lord(s) the Becoming-One which gathers the outcasts of Israel says, Yet will I gather others to him, beside those that are gathered unto him.

9 All you beasts of the field, come to devour, yes, all you beasts in the forest.

10 His watchmen are blind: they are all ignorant, they are all mute dogs, they cannot bark; sleeping, lying down, loving to slumber.

11 Yes, they are dogs, greedy of soul, which do not have enough, and they are shepherds that cannot understand: they all look to their own way, every one for his gain, from his end.

12 Come ye, say they, I will fetch wine, and we will fill ourselves with strong drink; and tomorrow shall be as this day, and much more abundant.

Isa 57:1 The righteous perishes, and no man lays it to heart: and merciful men are taken away, none considering that the righteous is taken away from the evil to come.

2 He shall enter into peace: they shall rest in their beds, each one walking in his uprightness.

3 But draw near here, you sons of the sorceress, the seed of the adulterer and the whore.

4 Against whom do you sport yourselves? against whom make you a wide mouth, and draw out the tongue? are you not children of transgression, a seed of falsehood,

5 Enflaming yourselves with gods under every green tree, slaying the children in the valleys under the clifts of the rocks?

6 Among the smooth stones of the stream is your portion; they, they are your lot: even to them have you poured a drink offering, you have offered a food offering. Should I receive comfort in these?

7 Upon a lofty and high mountain have you set your bed: even there went you up to offer sacrifice.

8 Behind the doors also and the posts have you set up your remembrance: for you have discovered yourself to another than me, and are gone up; you have enlarged your bed, and made you a covenant with them; you lovedst their bed where you saw it.

9 And you went to the king with ointment, and did increase your perfumes, and did send your messengers far off, and did debase yourself even unto Sheol.

10 you are wearied in the greatness of your way; yet say you not, There is no hope: you have found the life of your hand; therefore you were not grieved.

11 And of whom have you been afraid or feared, that you have lied, and have not remembered me, nor laid it to your heart? have not I held my peace even from olam, and you fear me not?

12 I will declare your righteousness, and your works; for they shall not profit you.

13 When you cry, let your companies deliver you; but the wind shall carry them all away; vanity shall take them: but he that puts his trust in me shall possess the land, and shall inherit my holy mountain.

14 And shall say, Cast you up, cast you up, prepare the way, take up the stumbling block out of the way of my people.

15 For thus says the high and lofty One that inhabits the beyond, whose name is Holy; I dwell in the high and holy place, with him also that is of a contrite and humble spirit, to revive the spirit of the humble, and to revive the heart of the contrite ones.

16 For I will not contend for olam, neither will I be completely wrath: for the spirit should fail before me, and the breath which I have made.

17 For the iniquity of his covetousness was I angry, and smote him: I hid me, and was angry, and he went on perversely in the way of his heart.

18 I have seen his ways, and will heal him: I will lead him also, and restore comforts unto him and to his mourners.

19 I create the fruit of the lips; Peace, peace to him that is far off, and to him that is near, says the Becoming-One; and I will heal him.

20 But the wicked are like the troubled sea, when it cannot rest, whose waters cast up mire and dirt.

21 There is no peace, says my God, to the wicked.

Isa 58:1 Cry aloud, spare not, lift up your voice like a trumpet, and show my people their transgression, and the house of Jacob their sins.

2 Yet they seek me daily, and delight to know my ways, as a nation that did righteousness, and forsook not the ordinance of their God: they ask of me the ordinances of justice; they take delight in approaching to God.

3 Therefore have we fasted, say they, and you see not? therefore have we afflicted our soul, and you take no knowledge? Behold, in the day of your fast you find pleasure, and exact all your labors.

4 Behold, you fast for strife and debate, and to smite with the fist of wickedness: you shall not fast as you do this day, to make your voice to be heard on high.

5 Is it such a fast that I have chosen? a day for a man to afflict his soul? is it to bow down his head as a bulrush, and to spread sackcloth and ashes under him? will you call this a fast, and an acceptable day to the Becoming-One?

6 Is not this the fast that I have chosen? to loose the bands of wickedness, to undo the heavy burdens, and to let the oppressed go free, and that you break every yoke?

7 Is it not to deal your bread to the hungry, and that you bring the poor that are afficted to your house? when you see the naked, that you cover him; and that you hide not yourself from your own flesh?

8 Then shall your light break forth as the dawn, and your health shall spring forth speedily: and your righteousness shall go before you; the glory of the Becoming-One shall be your rear-guard.

9 Then shall you call, and the Becoming-One shall answer; you shall cry, and he shall say, Here I am. If you take away from the midst of you the yoke, the putting forth of the finger, and speaking vanity;

10 And if you draw out your soul to the hungry, and satisfy the afflicted soul; then shall your light rise in darkness, and your darkness be as the noon day:

11 And the Becoming-One shall guide you continually, and satisfy your soul in drought, and make fat your bones: and you shall be like a watered garden, and like a spring of water, whose waters fail not.

12 And they that shall be of you shall build the waste places of olam: you shall raise up the foundations of many generations; and you shall be

called, The repairer of the breach, The restorer of paths to dwell in.

13 If you turn away your foot from the Sabbath, from doing your pleasure on my holy day; and call the Sabbath a delight, the holy of the Becoming-One, honorable; and shall honor him, not doing your own ways, nor finding your own pleasure, nor speaking your own words:

14 Then shall you delight yourself in the Becoming-One; and I will cause you to ride upon the high places of the earth, and feed you with the heritage of Jacob your father: for the mouth of the Becoming-One has spoken it.

Isa 59:1 Behold, the Becoming-One's hand is not shortened, that it cannot save; neither his ear heavy, that it cannot hear:

2 But your iniquities have separated between you and your God, and your sins have hid his face from you, that he will not hear.

3 For your hands are defiled with blood, and your fingers with iniquity; your lips have spoken lies, your tongue has muttered perverseness.

4 None calls for justice, nor any pleads for truth: they trust in vanity, and speak lies; they conceive mischief, and bring forth iniquity.

5 They hatch cockatrice' eggs, and weave the spider's web: he that eats of their eggs dies, and that which is crushed breaks out into a viper.

6 Their webs shall not become garments, neither shall they cover themselves with their works: their works are works of iniquity, and the act of violence is in their hands.

7 Their feet run to evil, and they make haste to shed innocent blood: their thoughts are thoughts of iniquity; wasting and destruction are in their paths.

8 The way of peace they know not; and there is no judgment in their goings: they have made them crooked paths: whosoever goes therein shall not know peace.

9 Therefore is judgment far from us, neither does justice overtake us: we wait for light, but behold darkness; for brightness, but we walk in darkness.

10 We grope for the wall like the blind, and we grope as if we had no eyes: we stumble at noon day as in the night [breeze time] we are in desolate places as dead men.

11 We roar all like bears, and mourn greatly like doves: we look for judgment, but there is none; for salvation, but it is far off from us.

12 For our transgressions are multiplied before you, and our sins testify against us: for our transgressions are with us; and as for our iniquities, we know them;

13 In transgressing and lying against the Becoming-One, and departing away from our God, speaking oppression and revolt, conceiving and uttering from the heart words of falsehood.

14 And judgment is turned away backward, and justice stands afar off: for truth is fallen in the street, and equity cannot enter.

15 Yes, truth fails; and he that departs from evil makes himself a prey: and the Becoming-One saw it, and it displeased him that there was no judgment.

16 And he saw that there was no man, and wondered that there was no intercessor: therefore his arm brought salvation unto him; and his righteousness, it sustained him.

17 For he put on righteousness as a breastplate, and a helmet of salvation upon his head; and he put on the garments of vengeance for clothing, and was clad with zeal as a cloak.

18 According to their deeds, accordingly he will repay, fury to his adversaries, recompense to his enemies; to the coastlands he will repay recompense.

19 So shall they fear the name of the Becoming-One from the west, and his glory from the rising of the sun. When the enemy shall come in like a flood, the Spirit of the Becoming-One shall lift up a standard against him.

20 And the Redeemer shall come to Zion, and unto them that turn from transgression in Jacob, says the Becoming-One.

21 As for me, this is my covenant with them, says the Becoming-One; My spirit that is upon you, and my words which I have put in your mouth, shall not depart out of your mouth, nor out of the mouth of your seed, nor out of the mouth of your seed's seed, says the Becoming-One, from henceforth and for olam.

Isa 60:1 Arise, shine; for your light is come, and the glory of the Becoming-One is risen upon you.

2 For, behold, the darkness shall cover the earth, and gross darkness the people: but the Becoming-One shall arise upon you, and his glory shall be seen upon you.

3 And the nations shall come to your light, and kings to the brightness of your rising.

4 Lift up your eyes round about, and see: all they gather themselves together, they come to you: your sons shall come from far, and your daughters shall be nursed at your side.

5 Then you shall see, and flow together, and your heart shall fear, and be enlarged; because the abundance of the sea shall be converted unto you, the forces of the nations shall come unto you.

6 The multitude of camels shall cover you, the dromedaries of Midian and Ephah; all they from Sheba shall come: they shall bring gold and incense; and they shall show forth the praises of the Becoming-One.

7 All the flocks of Kedar shall be gathered together unto you, the rams of Nebaioth shall minister unto you: they shall come up with acceptance on mine altar, and I will glorify the house of my glory.

8 Who are these that fly as a cloud, and as the doves to their windows?

9 Surely the isles shall wait for me, and the ships of Tarshish first, to bring your sons from far, their silver and their gold with them, unto the name of the Becoming-One your God, and to the Holy One of Israel, because he has glorified you.

10 And the sons of strangers shall build up your walls, and their kings shall minister unto you: for in my wrath I smote you, but in my favor have I had mercy on you.

11 Therefore your gates shall be open continually; they shall not be shut day nor night; that men may bring unto you the forces of the nations, and that their kings may be brought.

12 For the nation and kingdom that will not serve you shall perish; yes, those nations shall be utterly wasted.

13 The glory of Lebanon shall come unto you, the fir tree, the pine tree, and the box together, to beautify the place of my sanctuary; and I will make the place of my feet glorious.

14 The sons also of them that afflicted you shall come bending unto you; and all they that despised you shall bow themselves down at the soles of your feet; and they shall call you, The city of the Becoming-One, The Zion of the Holy One of Israel.

15 Whereas you have been forsaken and hated, so that no man went through you, I will make you a excellency olam, a joy of many generations.

16 you shall also suck the milk of the nations, and shall suck the breast of kings: and you shall know that I the Becoming-One am your Savior and your Redeemer, the mighty One of Jacob.

17 For brass I will bring gold, and for iron I will bring silver, and for wood brass, and for stones iron: I will also make your officers peace, and your rulers righteousness.

18 Violence shall no more be heard in your land, wasting nor destruction within your borders; but you shall call your walls Salvation, and your gates Praise.

19 The sun shall be no more your light by day; neither for brightness shall the moon give light unto you: but the Becoming-One shall be unto you a light of olam, and your God your glory.

20 your sun shall no more go down; neither shall your moon withdraw itself: for the Becoming-One shall be your light of olam, and the days of your mourning shall be ended.

21 your people also shall be all righteous: they shall inherit the land for olam, the branch of my planting, the work of my hands, that I may be glorified.

22 A little one shall become a thousand, and a small one a strong nation: I the Becoming-One will hasten it in his time.

Isa 61:1 The spirit of my Lord(s) the Becoming-One is upon me; because the Becoming-One has anointed me to preach good tidings unto the meek; he has sent me to bind up the brokenhearted, to proclaim liberty to the captives, and the opening of the prison to them that are bound;

2 To proclaim the acceptable year of the Becoming-One, and the day of vengeance of our God; to comfort all that mourn;

3 To appoint unto them that mourn in Zion, to give unto them beauty for ashes, the oil of joy for mourning, the garment of praise for the spirit of heaviness; that they might be called trees of righteousness, the planting of the Becoming-One, that he might be glorified.

4 And they shall build the wastes of olam, they shall raise up the former desolations, and they shall repair the waste cities, the desolations of many generations.

5 And strangers shall stand and feed your flocks, and the sons of the alien shall be your plowmen and your vinedressers.

6 But you shall be named the Priests of the Becoming-One: men shall call you the Ministers of our God: you shall eat the riches of the nations, and in their glory shall you boast yourselves.

7 For your shame you shall have double; and for confusion they shall rejoice in their portion: therefore in their land they shall possess the double: joy of olam shall be unto them.

8 For I the Becoming-One love judgment, I hate robbery for burnt offering; and I will direct their work in truth, and I will make a covenant of olam with them.

9 And their seed shall be known among the nations, and their offspring among the people: all that see them shall acknowledge them, that they are the seed which the Becoming-One has blessed.

10 I will greatly rejoice in the Becoming-One, my soul shall be joyful in my God; for he has clothed me with the garments of salvation, he has covered me with the robe of righteousness, as a bridegroom decks himself with ornaments, and as a bride adorns herself with her jewels.

11 For as the earth brings forth her bud, and as the garden causes the things that are sown in it to spring forth; so my Lord(s) the Becoming-One will cause righteousness and praise to spring forth before all the nations.

Isa 62:1 For Zion's sake will I not hold my peace, and for Jerusalem's sake I will not rest, until the righteousness thereof go forth as brightness, and the salvation thereof as a lamp that burns.

2 And the nations shall see your righteousness, and all kings your glory: and you shall be called by a new name, which the mouth of the Becoming-One shall name.

3 you shall also be a crown of glory in the hand of the Becoming-One, and a royal diadem in the hand of your God.

4 you shall no more be termed Forsaken; neither shall your land any more be termed Desolate: but you shall be called Hephzibah, and your land Beulah: for the Becoming-One delights in you, and your land shall be married.

5 For as a young man marries a virgin, so shall your sons marry you: and as the bridegroom rejoices over the bride, so shall your God rejoice over you.

6 I have set watchmen upon your walls, O Jerusalem, which shall always not hold their peace day nor night: you that make mention of the Becoming-One, keep not silence.

7 And give him no rest, till he establish, and till he make Jerusalem a praise in the earth.

8 The Becoming-One has sworn by his right hand, and by the arm of his strength, Surely I will no more give your corn to be food for your enemies; and the sons of the stranger shall not drink your wine, for which you have labored:

9 But they that have gathered it shall eat it and praise the Becoming-One; and they that have brought it together shall drink it in the courts of my holiness.

10 Go through, go through the gates; prepare you the way of the people; cast up, cast up the highway; gather out the stones; lift up a standard for the people.

11 Behold, the Becoming-One has proclaimed unto the end of the world, Say you to the daughter of Zion, Behold, your salvation comes; behold, his reward is with him, and his work before him.

12 And they shall call them, The holy people, The redeemed of the Becoming-One: and you shall be called, Sought out, A city not forsaken.

Isa 63:1 Who is this that comes from Edom, with dyed garments from Bozrah? this that is glorious in his apparel, travelling in the greatness of his strength? I that speak in righteousness, mighty to save.

2 Therefore are you red in your apparel, and your garments like him that treads in the winefat?

3 I have trodden the winepress alone; and of the people there was none with me: for I will tread them in mine anger, and trample them in my fury; and their blood shall be sprinkled upon my garments, and I will stain all my raiment.

4 For the day of vengeance is in mine heart, and the year of my redeemed is come.

5 And I looked, and there was none to help; and I wondered that there was none to uphold: therefore mine own arm brought salvation unto me; and my fury, it upheld me.

6 And I will tread down the people in mine anger, and make them drunk in my fury, and I will bring down their strength to the earth.

7 I will mention the loving-kindnesses of the Becoming-One, and the praises of the Becoming-One, according to all that the Becoming-One has bestowed on us, and the great goodness toward the house of Israel, which he has bestowed on them according to his mercies, and according to the multitude of his loving-kindnesses.

8 For he said, Surely they are my people, children that will not lie: so he was their Savior.

9 In all their affliction he was afflicted, and the angel of his presence saved them: in his love and in his pity he redeemed them; and he bare them, and carried them all the days of olam.

10 But they rebelled, and vexed his holy Spirit: therefore he was turned to be their enemy, and he fought against them.

11 Then he remembered the days of olam, Moses, and his people, saying, Where is he that brought them up out of the sea with the shepherd of his flock? where is he that put his holy Spirit within him?

12 That led them by the right hand of Moses with his glorious arm, dividing the water before them, to make himself a name of olam?

13 That led them through the deep, as a horse in the wilderness, that they should not stumble?

14 As a beast goes down into the valley, the Spirit of the Becoming-One caused him to rest: so did you lead your people, to make yourself a glorious name.

15 Look down from heaven, and behold from the habitation of your holiness and of your glory: where is your zeal and your strength, the sounding of your bowels and of your mercies toward me? are they restrained?

16 Doubtless you are our father, though Abraham be ignorant of us, and Israel acknowledge us not: you, O Becoming-One, are our father, our redeemer; your name is from olam.

17 O Becoming-One, why have you made us to err from your ways, and hardened our heart from your fear? Return for your servants' sake, the tribes of your inheritance.

18 The people of your holiness have possessed it but a little while: our adversaries have trodden down your sanctuary.

19 We are yours: you not for olam bare rule over them; they were not called by your name.

Isa 64:1 Oh that you would rip the heavens, that you would come down, that the mountains might flow down at your presence.

2 As when the melting fire burns, the fire causes the waters to boil, to make your name known to your adversaries, that the nations may tremble at your presence!

3 When you did terrible things which we looked not for, you came down, the mountains flowed down at your presence.

4 For since olam past men have not heard, nor perceived by the ear, neither has the eye seen, O God, beside you, what he has prepared for him that waits for him.

5 you meet him that rejoices and works righteousness, those that remember you in your ways: behold, you are angry; for we have sinned: in those is olam and we shall be saved.

6 But we are all as an unclean thing, and all our righteousness are as filthy rags; and we all do fade as a leaf; and our iniquities, like the wind, have taken us away.

7 And there is none that calls upon your name, that stirs up himself to take hold of you: for you have hid your face from us, and have consumed us, because of our iniquities.

8 But now, O Becoming-One, you are our father; we are the clay, and you our potter; and we all are the work of your hand.

9 Be not angry very great, O Becoming-One, neither remember iniquity to the beyond: behold, see, we beg you, we are all your people.

10 your holy cities are a wilderness, Zion is a wilderness, Jerusalem a desolation.

11 Our holy and our beautiful house, where our fathers praised you, is burned up with fire: and all our pleasant things are laid waste.

12 will you refrain yourself for these things, O Becoming-One? will you hold your peace, and afflict us very greatly?

Isa 65:1 I am sought of them that asked not for me; I am found of them that sought me not: I said, Behold me, behold me, unto a nation that was not called by my name.

2 I have spread out my hands all the day unto a rebellious people, which walks in a way that was not good, after their own thoughts;

3 A people that provokes me to anger continually to my face; that sacrifices in gardens, and burns incense upon altars of brick;

4 Which remain among the graves, and lodge in the monuments, which eat swine's flesh, and broth of abominable things is in their vessels;

5 Which say, Stand by thyself, come not near to me; for I am holier than you. These are a smoke in my nose, a fire that burns all the day.

6 Behold, it is written before me: I will not keep silence, but will recompense, even recompense into their bosom,

7 Your iniquities, and the iniquities of your fathers together, says the Becoming-One, which have burned incense upon the mountains, and blasphemed me upon the hills: therefore will I measure their former work into their bosom.

8 Thus says the Becoming-One, As the new wine is found in the cluster, and one said, Destroy it not; for a blessing is in it: so will I do for my servants' sakes, that I may not destroy them all.

9 And I will bring forth a seed out of Jacob, and out of Judah an inheritor of my mountains: and mine elect shall inherit it, and my servants shall dwell there.

10 And Sharon shall be a fold of flocks, and the valley of Achor a place for the herds to lie down in, for my people that have sought me.

11 But you are they that forsake the Becoming-One, that forget my holy mountain, that prepare a table for that troop, and that furnish the drink offering unto that number.

12 Therefore will I number you to the sword, and you shall all bow down to the slaughter: because when I called, you did not answer; when I spoke, you did not hear; but did evil before mine eyes, and did choose that wherein I delighted not.

13 Therefore thus says my Lord(s) the Becoming-One, Behold, my servants shall eat, but you shall be hungry: behold, my servants shall drink, but you shall be thirsty: behold, my servants shall rejoice, but you shall be ashamed:

14 Behold, my servants shall sing for joy of heart, but you shall cry for sorrow of heart, and shall howl for vexation of spirit.

15 And you shall leave your name for a oath unto my chosen: for my Lord(s) the Becoming-One shall slay you, and call his servants by another name:

16 That he who blesses himself in the earth shall bless himself in God of truth; and he that swears in the earth shall swear by God of truth; because the former troubles are forgotten, and because they are hid from mine eyes.

17 For, behold, I create new the heavens and a new earth: and the former shall not be remembered, nor come into mind.

18 But be you glad and rejoice to the beyond in that which I create: for, behold, I create Jerusalem a rejoicing, and her people a joy.

19 And I will rejoice in Jerusalem, and joy in my people: and the voice of weeping shall be no more heard in her, nor the voice of crying.

20 There shall be no more there an infant of days, nor an old man that has not filled his days: for the child shall die a son of a hundred years; but the sinner being a son of a hundred years shall be accursed.

21 And they shall build houses, and inhabit them; and they shall plant vineyards, and eat the fruit of them.

22 They shall not build, and another inhabit; they shall not plant, and another eat: for as the days of a tree are the days of my people, and mine elect shall long enjoy the work of their hands.

23 They shall not labor in vain, nor bring forth for trouble; for they are the seed of the blessed of the Becoming-One, and their offspring with them.

24 And it shall come to pass, that before they call, I will answer; and while they are yet speaking, I will hear.

25 The wolf and the lamb shall feed together, and the lion shall eat straw like the bullock: and dust shall be the serpent's food. They shall not hurt nor destroy in all my holy mountain, says the Becoming-One.

Isa 66:1 Thus says the Becoming-One, The heavens is my throne, and the earth is my footstool: where is the house that you build unto me? and where is the place of my rest?

2 For all those things has mine hand made, and all those things have been, says the Becoming-One: but to this man will I look, even to him that is poor and of a contrite spirit, and trembles at my word.

3 He that kills an ox is as if he killed a man; he that sacrifices a lamb, as if he cut off a dog's neck; he that offers an offering, as if he offered swine's blood; he that burns incense, as if he blessed an idol. Yes, they have chosen their own ways, and their soul delights in their abominations.

4 I also will choose their delusions, and will bring their fears upon them; because when I called, none did answer; when I spoke, they did not hear: but they did evil before mine eyes, and chose that in which I delighted not.

5 Hear the word of the Becoming-One, you that tremble at his word; Your brethren that hated you, that cast you out for my name's sake, said, Let the Becoming-One be glorified: but he shall appear to your joy, and they shall be ashamed.

6 A voice of noise from the city, a voice from the temple, a voice of the Becoming-One that renders recompense to his enemies.

7 Before she travailed, she brought forth; before her pain came, she delivered a man child.

8 Who has heard such a thing? who has seen such things? **Shall the earth be made to bring forth in one day? or shall a nation be born at once? for as soon as Zion travailed, she brought forth her children.**

9 Shall I bring to the birth, and not cause to bring forth? says the Becoming-One: shall I cause to bring forth, and shut the womb? says your God.

10 Rejoice you with Jerusalem, and be glad with her, all you that love her: rejoice for joy with her, all you that mourn for her:

11 That you may suck, and be satisfied with the breasts of her consolations; that you may milk out, and be delighted with the abundance of her glory.

12 For thus says the Becoming-One, Behold, I will extend peace to her like a river, and the glory of the nations like a flowing stream: then shall you suck, you shall be borne upon her sides, and be dandled upon her knees.

13 As one whom his mother comforts, so will I comfort you; and you shall be comforted in Jerusalem.

14 And when you see this, your heart shall rejoice, and your bones shall flourish like a herb: and

the hand of the Becoming-One shall be known toward his servants, and his indignation toward his enemies.

15 For, behold, the Becoming-One will come with fire, and with his chariots like a whirlwind, to render his anger with fury, and his rebuke with flames of fire.

16 For by fire and by his sword will the Becoming-One plead with all flesh: and the slain of the Becoming-One shall be many.

17 They that sanctify themselves, and purify themselves in the gardens behind one tree in the midst, eating swine's flesh, and the abomination, and the mouse, shall be consumed together, says the Becoming-One.

18 For I know their works and their thoughts: it shall come, that I will gather all nations and tongues; and they shall come, and see my glory.

19 And I will set a sign among them, and I will send those that escape of them unto the nations, to Tarshish, Pul, and Lud, that draw the bow, to Tubal, and Javan, to the isles afar off, that have not heard my fame, neither have seen my glory; and they shall declare my glory among the nations.

20 And they shall bring all your brethren for an offering unto the Becoming-One out of all nations upon horses, and in chariots, and in litters, and upon mules, and upon swift beasts, to my holy mountain Jerusalem, says the Becoming-One, as the children of Israel bring an offering in a clean vessel into the house of the Becoming-One.

21 And I will also take of them for priests and for Levites, says the Becoming-One.

22 For as the new heavens and the new earth, which I will make, shall remain before me, says the Becoming-One, so shall your seed and your name remain.

23 And it shall come to pass, that from one new moon to another, and from one Sabbath to another, shall all flesh come to worship before me, says the Becoming-One.

24 And they shall go forth, and look upon the carcases of the men that have transgressed against me: for their worm shall not die, neither shall their fire be quenched; and they shall be an abhorring unto all flesh.

Jeremiah

Jer 1:1 The words of Jeremiah the son of Hilkiah, of the priests that were in Anathoth in the land of Benjamin:

2 To whom the word of the Becoming-One came **in the days of Josiah** the son of Amon king of Judah, in the thirteenth year of his reign.**[3348 YM / 626 BC]**

3 It came also **in the days of Jehoiakim** the son of Josiah king of Judah, unto the end of the eleventh year of Zedekiah **[3388 YM]** the son of Josiah king of Judah, unto the carrying away of Jerusalem captive in the fifth month.

4 Then the word of the Becoming-One came unto me, saying,

5 Before I formed you in the belly I knew you; and before you came forth out of the womb I sanctified you, and I ordained you a prophet unto the nations.

6 Then said I, Ah, my Lord(s) the Becoming-One! behold, I cannot speak: for I am a child.

7 But the Becoming-One said unto me, Say not, I am a child: for you shall go to all that I shall send you, and whatsoever I command you you shall speak.

8 Be not afraid of their faces: for I am with you to deliver you, says the Becoming-One.

9 Then the Becoming-One put forth his hand, and touched my mouth. And the Becoming-One said unto me, Behold, I have put my words in your mouth.

10 See, I have this day set you over the nations and over the kingdoms, to root out, and to pull down, and to destroy, and to throw down, to build, and to plant.

11 Moreover the word of the Becoming-One came unto me, saying, Jeremiah, what see you? And I said, I see a rod of an almond tree.

12 Then said the Becoming-One unto me, you have well seen: for I will hasten my word to perform it.

13 And the word of the Becoming-One came unto me the second time, saying, What see you? And I said, I see a seething pot; and the face thereof is toward the north.

14 Then the Becoming-One said unto me, Out of the north an evil shall break forth upon all the inhabitants of the land.

15 For, lo, I will call all the families of the kingdoms of the north, says the Becoming-One; and they shall come, and they shall set every one his throne at the entering of the gates of Jerusalem, and against all the walls thereof round about, and against all the cities of Judah.

16 And I will utter my judgments against them touching all their wickedness, who have forsaken me, and have burned incense unto other gods, and worshiped the works of their own hands.

17 you therefore gird up your loins, and arise, and speak unto them all that I command you: be not dismayed at their faces, lest I confound you before them.

18 For, behold, I have made you this day a fortified city, and an iron pillar, and brazen walls against the whole land, against the kings of Judah, against the princes thereof, against the priests thereof, and against the people of the land.

19 And they shall fight against you; but they shall not prevail against you; for I am with you, says the Becoming-One, to deliver you.

Jer 2:1 Moreover the word of the Becoming-One came to me, saying,

2 Go and cry in the ears of Jerusalem, saying, Thus says the Becoming-One; I remember you, the kindness of your youth, the love of your espousals, when you went after me in the wilderness, in a land that was not sown.

3 Israel was holiness unto the Becoming-One, and the beginning of his increase: all that devour him shall offend; evil shall come upon them, says the Becoming-One.

4 Hear you the word of the Becoming-One, O house of Jacob, and all the families of the house of Israel:

5 Thus says the Becoming-One, What iniquity have your fathers found in me, that they are gone far from me, and have walked after vanity, and are become vain?

6 Neither said they, Where is the Becoming-One that brought us up out of the land of Egypt, that led us through the wilderness, through a land of deserts and of pits, through a land of drought, and of the shadow of death, through a land that no man passed through, and where no man dwelt?

7 And I brought you into a plentiful country, to eat the fruit thereof and the goodness thereof; but when you entered, you defiled my land, and made mine heritage an abomination.

8 The priests said not, Where is the Becoming-One? and they that handle the law knew me not: the pastors also transgressed against me, and the prophets prophesied by the lord [baal] and walked after things that do not profit.

9 Therefore I will yet plead with you, says the Becoming-One, and with your children's children will I plead.

10 For pass over the isles of Chittim, and see; and send unto Kedar, and consider diligently, and see if there be such a thing.

11 has a nation changed their gods, which are yet no gods? but my people have changed their glory for that which does not profit.

12 Be astonished, O you heavens, at this, and be horribly afraid, be you very desolate, says the Becoming-One.

13 For my people have committed two evils; they have forsaken me the fountain of living waters, and hewed them out cisterns, broken cisterns, that can hold no water.

14 Is Israel a servant? is he a home born slave? why is he spoiled?

15 The young lions roared upon him, and yelled, and they made his land waste: his cities are burned without inhabitant.

16 Also the children of Noph and Tahapanes have broken the crown of your head.

17 have you not procured this unto thyself, in that you have forsaken the Becoming-One your God, when he led you by the way?

18 And now what have you to do in the way of Egypt, to drink the waters of Sihor? or what have you to do in the way of Assyria, to drink the waters of the river?

19 your own wickedness shall correct you, and your back sliding shall reprove you: know therefore and see that it is an evil thing and bitter, that you have forsaken the Becoming-One your God, and that my fear is not in you, says my Lord(s) the Becoming-One of hosts.

20 For from olam I have broken your yoke, and burst your bands; and you said, I will not transgress; when upon every high hill and under every green tree you wandered, playing the harlot.

21 Yet I had planted you a noble vine, wholly a right seed: how then are you turned into the degenerate plant of a strange vine unto me?

22 For though you wash you with nitre, and take you much soap, yet your iniquity is marked before me, says my Lord(s) the Becoming-One.

23 How can you say, I am not polluted, I have not gone after the lords [baalim] see your way in the valley, know what you have done: you are a swift dromedary traversing her ways;

24 A wild donkey used to the wilderness, that snuffs up the wind at her soul's pleasure; in her occasion who can turn her away? all they that seek her will not weary themselves; in her month they shall find her.

25 Withhold your foot from being unshod, and your throat from thirst: but you said, There is no hope: no; for I have loved strangers, and after them will I go.

26 As the thief is ashamed when he is found, so is the house of Israel ashamed; they, their kings, their princes, and their priests, and their prophets,

27 Saying to a stock, you are my father; and to a stone, you have brought me forth: for they have turned their back unto me, and not their face: but in the time of their trouble they will say, Arise, and save us.

28 But where are your gods that you have made you? let them arise, if they can save you in the time of your trouble: for according to the number of your cities are your gods, O Judah.

29 Therefore will you plead with me? you all have transgressed against me, says the Becoming-One.

30 In vain have I struck your children; they received no correction: your own sword has devoured your prophets, like a destroying lion.

31 O generation, see you the word of the Becoming-One. Have I been a wilderness unto Israel? a land of darkness? therefore say my people, We are free; we will come no more unto you?

32 Can a maid forget her ornaments, or a bride her attire? yet my people have forgotten me days without number.

33 Why trim you your way to seek love? therefore have you also taught the wicked ones your ways.

34 Also in your skirts is found the blood of the souls of the poor innocents: I have not found it by secret search, but upon all these.

35 Yet you say, Because I am innocent, surely his anger shall turn from me. Behold, I will plead with you, because you say, I have not sinned.

36 Why gad you about so much to change your way? you also shall be ashamed of Egypt, as you were ashamed of Assyria.

37 Yes, you shall go forth from him, and your hands upon your head: for the Becoming-One has rejected your confidences, and you shall not prosper in them.

Jer 3:1 They say, If a man put away his wife, and she go from him, and become another man's, shall he return unto her again? shall not that land be greatly polluted? but you have played the harlot with many lovers; yet return again to me, says the Becoming-One.

2 Lift up your eyes unto the high places, and see where you have not been lien with. In the ways have you sat for them, as the Arabian in the wilderness; and you have polluted the land with your whoredoms and with your wickedness.

3 Therefore the showers have been withheld, and there has been no latter rain; and you had a whore's forehead, you refused to be ashamed.

4 will you not from this time cry unto me, My father, you are the guide of my youth?

5 Will he reserve his anger for olam? will he keep it to the end? Behold, you have spoken and done evil things as you could.

6 The Becoming-One said also unto me in the days of Josiah the king, have you seen that which backsliding Israel has done? she is gone up upon every high mountain and under every green tree, and there has played the harlot.

7 And I said after she had done all these things, Turn you unto me. But she returned not. And her treacherous sister Judah saw it.

8 And I saw, when for all the causes whereby backsliding Israel committed adultery I had put her away, and given her a bill of divorce; yet her treacherous sister Judah feared not, but went and played the harlot also.

9 And it came to pass through the lightness of her whoredom, that she defiled the land, and committed adultery with stones and with stocks.

10 And yet for all this her treacherous sister Judah has not turned unto me with her whole heart, but only pretended, says the Becoming-One.

11 And the Becoming-One said unto me, The backsliding Israel has justified her soul more than treacherous Judah.

12 Go and proclaim these words toward the north, and say, Return, you backsliding Israel, says the Becoming-One; and I will not cause mine anger to fall upon you: for I am merciful, says the Becoming-One, and I will not keep anger for olam.

13 Only acknowledge your iniquity, that you have transgressed against the Becoming-One your God, and have scattered your ways to the strangers under every green tree, and you have not obeyed my voice, says the Becoming-One.

14 Turn, O backsliding children, says the Becoming-One; for I am married unto you: and I will take you one of a city, and two of a family, and I will bring you to Zion:

15 And I will give you pastors according to mine heart, which shall feed you with knowledge and understanding.

16 And it shall come to pass, when you be multiplied and increased in the land, in those days, says the Becoming-One, they shall say no more, The ark of the covenant of the Becoming-One: neither shall it come to mind: neither shall they remember it; neither shall they visit it; neither shall that be done any more.

17 At that time they shall call Jerusalem the throne of the Becoming-One; and all the nations shall be gathered unto it, to the name of the Becoming-One, to Jerusalem: neither shall they walk any more after the imagination of their evil heart.

18 In those days the house of Judah shall walk with the house of Israel, and they shall come together out of the land of the north to the land that I have given for an inheritance unto your fathers.

19 But I said, How shall I put you among the children, and give you a pleasant land, a goodly heritage of the hosts of nations? and I said, you shall call me, My father; and shall not turn away from me.

20 Surely as a wife treacherously departs from her husband, so have you dealt treacherously with me, O house of Israel, says the Becoming-One.

21 A voice was heard upon the high places, weeping and supplications of the children of Israel: for they have perverted their way, and they have forgotten the Becoming-One their God.

22 Return, you backsliding children, and I will heal your backsliding. Behold, we come unto you; for you are the Becoming-One our God.

23 Truly in vain is salvation hoped for from the hills, and from the multitude of mountains: truly in the Becoming-One our God is the salvation of Israel.

24 For shame has devoured the labor of our fathers from our youth; their flocks and their herds, their sons and their daughters.

25 We lie down in our shame, and our confusion covers us: for we have sinned against the Becoming-One our God, we and our fathers, from our youth even unto this day, and have not obeyed the voice of the Becoming-One our God.

Jer 4:1 If you will return, O Israel, says the Becoming-One, return unto me: and if you will put away your abominations out of my sight, then shall you not remove.

2 And you shall swear, The Becoming-One lives, in truth, in judgment, and in righteousness; and the nations shall bless themselves in him, and in him shall they glory.

3 For thus says the Becoming-One to the men of Judah and Jerusalem, Break up your fallow ground, and sow not among thorns.

4 Circumcise yourselves to the Becoming-One, and take away the foreskins of your heart, you men of Judah and inhabitants of Jerusalem: lest my fury come forth like fire, and burn that none can quench it, because of the evil of your doings.

5 Declare you in Judah, and publish in Jerusalem; and say, Blow you the trumpet in the land: cry, gather together, and say, Assemble yourselves, and let us go into the fortified cities.

6 Set up the standard toward Zion: retire, stay not: for I will bring evil from the north, and a great destruction.

7 The lion is come up from his thicket, and the destroyer of the nations is on his way; he is gone forth from his place to make your land desolate; and your cities shall be laid waste, without an inhabitant.

8 For this gird you with sackcloth, lament and howl: for the fierce anger of the Becoming-One is not turned back from us.

9 And it shall come to pass at that day, says the Becoming-One, that the heart of the king shall perish, and the heart of the princes; and the priests shall be astonished, and the prophets shall wonder.

10 Then said I, Ah, my Lord(s) the Becoming-One! surely you have greatly deceived this people and Jerusalem, saying, you shall have peace; whereas the sword reaches unto the soul.

11 At that time shall it be said to this people and to Jerusalem, A dry wind of the high places in the wilderness toward the daughter of my people, not to fan, nor to cleanse,

12 Even a full wind from those places shall come unto me: now also will I give sentence against them.

13 Behold, he shall come up as clouds, and his chariots shall be as a whirlwind: his horses are swifter than eagles. Woe unto us! for we are spoiled.

14 O Jerusalem, wash your heart from wickedness, that you may be saved. How long shall your vain thoughts lodge within you?

15 For a voice declares from Dan, and declares affliction from mount Ephraim.

16 Make you mention to the nations; behold, publish against Jerusalem, that watchers come from a far country, and give out their voice against the cities of Judah.

17 As keepers of a field, are they against her round about; because she has been rebellious against me, says the Becoming-One.

18 your way and your doings have procured these things unto you; this is your wickedness, because it is bitter, because it reaches unto your heart.

19 My bowels, my bowels! I am pained at my very heart; my heart makes a noise in me; I cannot hold my peace, because you have heard, O my soul, the sound of the trumpet, the alarm of war.

20 Destruction upon destruction is cried; for the whole land is spoiled: suddenly are my tents spoiled, and my curtains in a moment.

21 How long shall I see the standard, and hear the sound of the trumpet?

22 For my people is foolish, they have not known me; they are sottish children, and they have none understanding: they are wise to do evil, but to do good they have no knowledge.

23 I beheld the earth, and, lo, it was without form, and void; and the heavens, and they had no light.

24 I beheld the mountains, and, lo, they trembled, and all the hills moved lightly.

25 I beheld, and, lo, there was no man, and all the birds of the heavens were fled.

26 I beheld, and, lo, the fruitful place was a wilderness, and all the cities thereof were broken

down at the presence of the Becoming-One, and by his fierce anger.

27 For thus has the Becoming-One said, The whole land shall be desolate; yet will I not make a full end.

28 For this shall the earth mourn, and the heavens above be black: because I have spoken it, I have purposed it, and will not repent, neither will I turn back from it.

29 The whole city shall flee for the noise of the horsemen and bowmen; they shall go into thickets, and climb up upon the rocks: every city shall be forsaken, and not a man dwell therein.

30 And when you are spoiled, what will you do? Though you cloth yourself with crimson, though you deck you with ornaments of gold, though you rend your face with painting, in vain shall you make yourself fair; your lovers will despise you, they will seek your soul.

31 For I have heard a voice as of a woman in travail, and the anguish as of her that brings forth her first child, the voice of the daughter of Zion, that bewails herself, that spreads her hands, saying, Woe is me now! for my soul is wearied because of murderers.

Jer 5:1 Run you back and forth through the streets of Jerusalem, and see now, and know, and seek in the broad places thereof, if you can find a man, if there be any that executes judgment, that seeks the truth; and I will pardon it.

2 And though they say, The Becoming-One lives; surely they swear falsely.

3 O Becoming-One, are not your eyes upon the truth? you have stricken them, but they have not grieved; you have consumed them, but they have refused to receive correction: they have made their faces harder than a rock; they have refused to return.

4 Therefore I said, Surely these are poor; they are foolish: for they know not the way of the Becoming-One, nor the judgment of their God.

5 I will get me unto the great men, and will speak unto them; for they have known the way of the Becoming-One, and the judgment of their God: but these have altogether broken the yoke, and burst the bonds.

6 Therefore a lion out of the forest shall slay them, and a wolf of the evenings shall spoil them, a leopard shall watch over their cities: every one that goes out there shall be torn in pieces: because their transgressions are many, and their backslidings are increased.

7 How shall I pardon you for this? your children have forsaken me, and sworn by them that are no gods: when I had fed them to the full, they then committed adultery, and assembled themselves by troops in the harlots' houses.

8 They were as fed horses in the morning: every one eyed after his neighbor's wife.

9 Shall I not visit for these things? says the Becoming-One: and shall not my soul be avenged on such a nation as this?

10 Go you up upon her walls, and destroy; but make not a full end: take away her battlements; for they are not the Becoming-One's.

11 For the house of Israel and the house of Judah have dealt very treacherously against me, says the Becoming-One.

12 They have belied the Becoming-One, and said, It is not he; neither shall evil come upon us; neither shall we see sword nor famine:

13 And the prophets shall become wind, and the word is not in them: thus shall it be done unto them.

14 Therefore thus says the Becoming-One, God of hosts, Because you speak this word, behold, I will make my words in your mouth fire, and this people wood, and it shall devour them.

15 Lo, I will bring a nation upon you from far, O house of Israel, says the Becoming-One: it is a mighty nation, it is an ancient nation, a nation whose language you know not, neither understand what they say.

16 Their quiver is as an open tomb, they are all mighty men.

17 And they shall eat up your harvest, and your bread, which your sons and your daughters should eat: they shall eat up your flocks and your herds: they shall eat up your vines and your fig trees: they shall impoverish your fenced cities, wherein you trusted, with the sword.

18 Nevertheless in those days, says the Becoming-One, I will not make a full end with you.

19 And it shall come to pass, when you shall say, Why did the Becoming-One our God all these things unto us? then shall you answer them, Like as you have forsaken me, and served strange gods in your land, so shall you serve strangers in a land that is not yours.

20 Declare this in the house of Jacob, and publish it in Judah, saying,

21 Hear now this, O foolish people, and without understanding; which have eyes, and see not; which have ears, and hear not:

22 Fear you not me? says the Becoming-One: will you not tremble at my presence, which have placed the sand for the bound of the sea by a perpetual decree, that it cannot pass it: and though the waves thereof toss themselves, yet can they not prevail; though they roar, yet can they not pass over it?

23 But this people has a revolting and a rebellious heart; they are revolted and gone.

24 Neither say they in their heart, Let us now fear the Becoming-One our God, that gives rain, both the former and the latter, in his season: he reserves unto us the appointed weeks of the harvest.

25 Your iniquities have turned away these things, and your sins have withheld good things from you.

26 For among my people are found wicked men: they lay wait, as he that sets snares; they set a trap, they catch men.

27 As a cage is full of birds, so are their houses full of deceit: therefore they are become great, and waxen rich.

28 They are waxen fat, they shine: yes, they overpass the deeds of the wicked: they judge not the cause, the cause of the fatherless, yet they prosper; and the right of the needy do they not judge.

29 Shall I not visit for these things? says the Becoming-One: shall not my soul be avenged on such a nation as this?

30 A wonderful and horrible thing is committed in the land;

31 The prophets prophesy falsely, and the priests bear rule by their means; and my people love to have it so: and what will you do in the end thereof?

Jer 6:1 O you children of Benjamin, gather yourselves to flee out of the midst of Jerusalem, and blow the trumpet in Tekoa, and set up a sign of fire in Beth-haccerem: for evil appears out of the north, and great destruction.

2 I have likened the daughter of Zion to a becoming and delicate woman.

3 The shepherds with their flocks shall come unto her; they shall pitch their tents against her round about; they shall feed every one in his place.

4 Prepare you war against her; arise, and let us go up at noon. Woe unto us! for the day goes away, for the shadows of the evening are stretched out.

5 Arise, and let us go by night, and let us destroy her palaces.

6 For thus has the Becoming-One of hosts said, Hew you down trees, and cast a mount against Jerusalem: this is the city to be visited; she is wholly oppression in the midst of her.

7 As a fountain casts out her waters, so she casts out her wickedness: violence and spoil is heard in her; before me continually is grief and wounds.

8 Be you instructed, O Jerusalem, lest my soul depart from you; lest I make you desolate, a land not inhabited.

9 Thus says the Becoming-One of hosts, They shall thoroughly glean the remnant of Israel as a vine: turn back your hand as a grape gatherer into the baskets.

10 To whom shall I speak, and give warning, that they may hear? behold, their ear is uncircumcised, and they cannot listen: behold, the word of the Becoming-One is unto them a reproach; they have no delight in it.

11 Therefore I am full of the fury of the Becoming-One; I am weary with holding in: I will pour it out upon the children abroad, and upon the assembly of young men together: for even the husband with the wife shall be taken, the aged with him that is full of days.

12 And their houses shall be turned unto others, with their fields and wives together: for I will stretch out my hand upon the inhabitants of the land, says the Becoming-One.

13 For from the least of them even unto the greatest of them every one is given to covetousness; and from the prophet even unto the priest every one deals falsely.

14 They have healed also the hurt of the daughter of my people slightly, saying, Peace, peace; when there is no peace.

15 Were they ashamed when they had committed abomination? nay, they were not at all ashamed, neither could they blush: therefore they shall fall among them that fall: at the time that I visit them they shall be cast down, says the Becoming-One.

16 Thus says the Becoming-One, Stand you in the ways, and see, and ask for the paths of olam, where is the good way, and walk therein, and you shall find rest for your souls. But they said, We will not walk therein.

17 Also I set watchmen over you, saying, listen to the sound of the trumpet. But they said, We will not listen.

18 Therefore hear, you nations, and know, O congregation, what is among them.

19 Hear, O earth: behold, I will bring evil upon this people, even the fruit of their thoughts, because they have not listened unto my words, nor to my law, but rejected it.

20 To what purpose comes there to me incense from Sheba, and the sweet cane from a far country? your burnt offerings are not acceptable, nor your sacrifices sweet unto me.

21 Therefore thus says the Becoming-One, Behold, I will lay stumbling blocks before this people, and the fathers and the sons together shall fall upon them; the neighbor and his friend shall perish.

22 Thus says the Becoming-One, Behold, a people comes from the north country, and a great nation shall be raised from the sides of the earth.

23 They shall lay hold on bow and spear; they are cruel, and have no mercy; their voice roars like the sea; and they ride upon horses, set in array as men for war against you, O daughter of Zion.

24 We have heard the fame thereof: our hands wax feeble: anguish has taken hold of us, and pain, as of a woman in travail.

25 Go not forth into the field, nor walk by the way; for the sword of the enemy and fear is on every side.

26 O daughter of my people, gird you with sackcloth, and wallow yourself in ashes: make you mourning, as for an only son, most bitter lamentation: for the spoiler shall suddenly come upon us.

27 I have set you for a tower and a fortress among my people, that you may know and try their way.

28 They are all grievous revolters, walking with slanders: they are brass and iron; they are all corrupters.

29 The bellows are burned, the lead is consumed of the fire; the founder melts in vain: for the wicked are not plucked away.

30 Reprobate silver shall men call them, because the Becoming-One has rejected them.

Jer 7:1 The word that came to Jeremiah from the Becoming-One, saying,

2 Stand in the gate of the Becoming-One's house, and proclaim there this word, and say, Hear the word of the Becoming-One, all you of Judah, that enter in at these gates to worship the Becoming-One.

3 Thus says the Becoming-One of hosts, God of Israel, Amend your ways and your doings, and I will cause you to dwell in this place.

4 Trust you not in lying words, saying, The temple of the Becoming-One, The temple of the Becoming-One, The temple of the Becoming-One, are these.

5 For if you thoroughly amend your ways and your doings; if you thoroughly execute judgment between a man and his neighbor;

6 If you oppress not the stranger, the fatherless, and the widow, and shed not innocent blood in this place, neither walk after other gods to your hurt:

7 Then will I cause you to dwell in this place, in the land that I gave to your fathers, for olam and beyond.

8 Behold, you trust in lying words, that cannot profit.

9 Will you steal, murder, and commit adultery, and swear falsely, and burn incense unto the lord [baal] and walk after other gods whom you know not;

10 And come and stand before me in this house, which is called by my name, and say, We are delivered to do all these abominations?

11 Is this house, which is called by my name, become a den of robbers in your eyes? Behold, even I have seen it, says the Becoming-One.

12 But go you now unto my place which was in Shiloh, where I set my name at the first, and see what I did to it for the wickedness of my people Israel.

13 And now, because you have done all these works, says the Becoming-One, and I spoke unto you, rising up early and speaking, but you heard not; and I called you, but you answered not;

14 Therefore will I do unto this house, which is called by my name, wherein you trust, and unto the place which I gave to you and to your fathers, as I have done to Shiloh.

15 And I will cast you out of my sight, as I have cast out all your brethren, even the whole seed of Ephraim.

16 Therefore pray not you for this people, neither lift up cry nor prayer for them, neither make intercession to me: for I will not hear you.

17 see you not what they do in the cities of Judah and in the streets of Jerusalem?

18 The children gather wood, and the fathers kindle the fire, and the women knead their dough, to make cakes to the queen of heaven, and to pour out drink offerings unto other gods, that they may provoke me to anger.

19 Do they provoke me to anger? says the Becoming-One: do they not provoke themselves to the confusion of their own faces?

20 Therefore thus says my Lord(s) the Becoming-One; Behold, mine anger and my fury shall be poured out upon this place, upon man, and upon beast, and upon the trees of the field, and upon the fruit of the ground; and it shall burn, and shall not be quenched.

21 Thus says the Becoming-One of hosts, God of Israel; Put your burnt offerings unto your sacrifices, and eat flesh.

22 For I spoke not unto your fathers, nor commanded them in the day that I brought them out of the land of Egypt, concerning burnt offerings or sacrifices:

23 But this thing commanded I them, saying, Obey my voice, and I will be your God, and you shall be my people: and walk you in all the ways that I have commanded you, that it may be well unto you.

24 But they listened not, nor inclined their ear, but walked in the counsels and in the imagination of their evil heart, and went backward, and not forward.

25 Since the day that your fathers came forth out of the land of Egypt unto this day I have even sent unto you all my servants the prophets, daily rising up early and sending them:

26 Yet they listened not unto me, nor inclined their ear, but hardened their neck: they did worse than their fathers.

27 Therefore you shall speak all these words unto them; but they will not listen to you: you shall also call unto them; but they will not answer you.

28 But you shall say unto them, This is a nation that obeys not the voice of the Becoming-One their God, nor receives correction: truth is perished, and is cut off from their mouth.

29 Cut off your hair, O Jerusalem, and cast it away, and take up a lamentation on high places; for the Becoming-One has rejected and forsaken the generation of his wrath.

30 For the children of Judah have done evil in my sight, says the Becoming-One: they have set their abominations in the house which is called by my name, to pollute it.

31 And they have built the high places of Tophet, which is in the valley of the son of Hinnom, to burn their sons and their daughters in the fire; which I commanded them not, neither came it into my heart.

32 Therefore, behold, the days come, says the Becoming-One, that it shall no more be called Tophet, nor the valley of the son of Hinnom, but the valley of slaughter: for they shall bury in Tophet, till there be no place.

33 And the carcases of this people shall be food for the fowls of the heaven, and for the beasts of the earth; and none shall fray them away.

34 Then will I cause to cease from the cities of Judah, and from the streets of Jerusalem, the voice of mirth, and the voice of gladness, the voice of the bridegroom, and the voice of the bride: for the land shall be desolate.

Jer 8:1 At that time, says the Becoming-One, they shall bring out the bones of the kings of Judah, and the bones of his princes, and the bones of the priests, and the bones of the prophets, and the bones of the inhabitants of Jerusalem, out of their graves:

2 And they shall spread them before the sun, and the moon, and all the host of heaven, whom they have loved, and whom they have served, and after whom they have walked, and whom they have sought, and whom they have worshiped: they shall not be gathered, nor be buried; they shall be for dung upon the face of the earth.

3 And death shall be chosen rather than life by all the residue of them that remain of this evil family, which remain in all the places to which I have driven them, says the Becoming-One of hosts.

4 Moreover you shall say unto them, Thus says the Becoming-One; Shall they fall, and not arise? shall he turn away, and not return?

5 Why then is this people of Jerusalem slid back by a perpetual backsliding? they hold fast deceit, they refuse to return.

6 I listened and heard, but they spoke not aright: no man repented him of his wickedness, saying, What have I done? every one turned to his course, as the horse rushes into the battle.

7 Yes, the stork in the heavens knows her appointed times; and the turtle and the crane and the

swallow observe the time of their coming; but my people know not the judgment of the Becoming-One.

8 How do you say, We are wise, and the law of the Becoming-One is with us? Lo, certainly in vain made he it; the pen of the scribes is in vain.

9 The wise men are ashamed, they are dismayed and taken: lo, they have rejected the word of the Becoming-One; and what wisdom is in them?

10 Therefore will I give their wives unto others, and their fields to them that shall inherit them: for every one from the least even unto the greatest is given to covetousness, from the prophet even unto the priest every one deals falsely.

11 For they have healed the hurt of the daughter of my people slightly, saying, Peace, peace; when there is no peace.

12 Were they ashamed when they had committed abomination? nay, they were not at all ashamed, neither could they blush: therefore shall they fall among them that fall: in the time of their visitation they shall be cast down, says the Becoming-One.

13 I will surely consume them, says the Becoming-One: there shall be no grapes on the vine, nor figs on the fig tree, and the leaf shall fade; and the things that I have given them shall pass away from them.

14 Why do we sit still? assemble yourselves, and let us enter into the fortified cities, and let us be silent there: for the Becoming-One our God has put us to silence, and given us water of gall to drink, because we have sinned against the Becoming-One.

15 We looked for peace, but no good came; and for a time of health, and behold trouble!

16 The snorting of his horses was heard from Dan: the whole land trembled at the sound of the neighing of his strong ones; for they are come, and have devoured the land, and all that is in it; the city, and those that dwell therein.

17 For, behold, I will send serpents, cockatrices, among you, which will not be charmed, and they shall bite you, says the Becoming-One.

18 When I would comfort myself against sorrow, my heart is faint in me.

19 Behold the voice of the cry of the daughter of my people because of them that dwell in a far country: Is not the Becoming-One in Zion? is not her king in her? Why have they provoked me to anger with their graven images, and with strange vanities?

20 The harvest is past, the summer is ended, and we are not saved.

21 For the hurt of the daughter of my people I am hurt; I am black; astonishment has taken hold on me.

22 Is there no balm in Gilead; is there no physician there? why then is not the health of the daughter of my people recovered?

Jer 9:1 Oh that my head were waters, and mine eyes a fountain of tears, that I might weep day and night for the slain of the daughter of my people!

2 Oh that I had in the wilderness a lodging place of wayfaring men; that I might leave my people, and go from them! for they be all adulterers, an assembly of treacherous men.

3 And they bend their tongues like their bow for lies: but they are not valiant for the truth upon the earth; for they proceed from evil to evil, and they know not me, says the Becoming-One.

4 Take you heed every one of his neighbor, and trust you not in any brother: for every brother will utterly supplant, and every neighbor will walk with slanders.

5 And they will deceive every one his neighbor, and will not speak the truth: they have taught their tongue to speak lies, and weary themselves to commit iniquity.

6 your habitation is in the midst of deceit; through deceit they refuse to know me, says the Becoming-One.

7 Therefore thus says the Becoming-One of hosts, Behold, I will melt them, and try them; for how shall I do for the daughter of my people?

8 Their tongue is as an arrow shot out; it speaks deceit: one speaks peaceably to his neighbor with his mouth, but in heart he lays his wait.

9 Shall I not visit them for these things? says the Becoming-One: shall not my soul be avenged on such a nation as this?

10 For the mountains will I take up a weeping and wailing, and for the habitations of the wilderness a lamentation, because they are burned up, so that none can pass through them; neither can men hear the voice of the cattle; both the fowl of the heavens and the beast are fled; they are gone.

11 And I will make Jerusalem heaps, and a den of monsters; and I will make the cities of Judah desolate, without an inhabitant.

12 Who is the wise man, that may understand this? and who is he to whom the mouth of the Becoming-One has spoken, that he may declare it, for what the land perishes and is burned up like a wilderness, that none passes through?

13 And the Becoming-One says, Because they have forsaken my law which I set before them, and have not obeyed my voice, neither walked therein;

14 But have walked after the imagination of their own heart, and after the lords [baalim] which their fathers taught them:

15 Therefore thus says the Becoming-One of hosts, God of Israel; Behold, I will feed them, even this people, with wormwood, and give them water of gall to drink.

16 I will scatter them also among the nations, whom neither they nor their fathers have known: and I will send a sword after them, till I have consumed them.

17 Thus says the Becoming-One of hosts, Consider ye, and call for the mourning women, that they may come; and send for cunning women, that they may come:

18 And let them make haste, and take up a wailing for us, that our eyes may run down with tears, and our eyelids gush out with waters.

19 For a voice of wailing is heard out of Zion, How are we spoiled! we are greatly confounded, because we have forsaken the land, because our dwellings have cast us out.

20 Yet hear the word of the Becoming-One, O you women, and let your ear receive the word of his

mouth, and teach your daughters wailing, and every one her neighbor lamentation.

21 For death is come up into our windows, and is entered into our palaces, to cut off the children from outside, and the young men from the streets.

22 Speak, Thus says the Becoming-One, Even the carcases of men shall fall as dung upon the open field, and as the handful after the harvestman, and none shall gather them.

23 Thus says the Becoming-One, Let not the wise man glory in his wisdom, neither let the mighty man glory in his might, let not the rich man glory in his riches:

24 But let him that glories glory in this, that he understands and knows me, that I am the Becoming-One which exercise loving-kindness, judgment, and righteousness, in the earth: for in these things I delight, says the Becoming-One.

25 Behold, the days come, says the Becoming-One, that I will punish all them which are circumcised with the uncircumcised;

26 Egypt, and Judah, and Edom, and the children of Ammon, and Moab, and all that are in the utmost corners, that dwell in the wilderness: for all these nations are uncircumcised, and all the house of Israel are uncircumcised in the heart.

Jer 10:1 Hear you the word which the Becoming-One speaks unto you, O house of Israel:

2 Thus says the Becoming-One, Learn not the way of the nations, and be not dismayed at the signs of heaven; for the nations are dismayed at them.

3 For the customs of the people are vain: for one cuts a tree out of the forest, the work of the hands of the workman, with the ax.

4 They deck it with silver and with gold; they fasten it with nails and with hammers, that it move not.

5 They are upright as the palm tree, but speak not: they must needs be borne, because they cannot go. Be not afraid of them; for they cannot do evil, neither also is it in them to do good.

6 Forasmuch as there is none like unto you, O Becoming-One; you are great, and your name is great in might.

7 Who would not fear you, O King of nations? for to you does it appertain: forasmuch as among all the wise men of the nations, and in all their kingdoms, there is none like unto you.

8 But they are altogether brutish and foolish: the stock is a doctrine of vanities.

9 Silver spread into plates is brought from Tarshish, and gold from Uphaz, the work of the workman, and of the hands of the founder: blue and purple is their clothing: they are all the work of cunning men.

10 But the Becoming-One is the true God, he is the living God, and king of olam: at his wrath the earth shall tremble, and the nations shall not be able to abide his indignation.

11 Thus shall you say unto them, The gods that have not made the heavens and the earth, even they shall perish from the earth, and from under these heavens.

12 He has made the earth by his power, he has established the world by his wisdom, and has stretched out the heavens by his discretion.

13 When he utters his voice, there is a multitude of waters in the heavens, and he causes the vapours to ascend from the ends of the earth; he makes lightning with rain, and brings forth the wind out of his treasures.

14 Every man is brutish in his knowledge: every founder is confounded by the graven image: for his molten image is falsehood, and there is no breath in them.

15 They are vanity, and the work of errors: in the time of their visitation they shall perish.

16 The portion of Jacob is not like them: for he is the former of all things; and Israel is the rod of his inheritance: The Becoming-One of hosts is his name.

17 Gather up your wares out of the land, O inhabitant of the fortress.

18 For thus says the Becoming-One, Behold, I will sling out the inhabitants of the land at this once, and will distress them, that they may find it so.

19 Woe is me for my hurt! my wound is grievous: but I said, Truly this is a grief, and I must bear it.

20 My tabernacle is spoiled, and all my cords are broken: my children are gone forth of me, and they are not: there is none to stretch forth my tent any more, and to set up my curtains.

21 For the pastors are become brutish, and have not sought the Becoming-One: therefore they shall not prosper, and all their flocks shall be scattered.

22 Behold, the noise of the bruit is come, and a great commotion out of the north country, to make the cities of Judah desolate, and a den of monsters.

23 O Becoming-One, I know that the way of man is not in himself: it is not in man that walks to direct his steps.

24 O Becoming-One, correct me, but with judgment; not in your anger, lest you bring me to nothing.

25 Pour out your fury upon the nations that know you not, and upon the families that call not on your name: for they have eaten up Jacob, and devoured him, and consumed him, and have made his habitation desolate.

Jer 11:1 The word that came to Jeremiah from the Becoming-One, saying,

2 Hear you the words of this covenant, and speak unto the men of Judah, and to the inhabitants of Jerusalem;

3 And say you unto them, Thus says the Becoming-One, God of Israel; Cursed be the man that obeys not the words of this covenant,

4 Which I commanded your fathers in the day that I brought them forth out of the land of Egypt, from the iron furnace, saying, Obey my voice, and do them, according to all which I command you: so shall you be my people, and I will be your God:

5 That I may perform the oath which I have sworn unto your fathers, to give them a land flowing with milk and honey, as it is this day. Then answered I, and said, So be it, O Becoming-One.

6 Then the Becoming-One said unto me, Proclaim all these words in the cities of Judah, and in

the streets of Jerusalem, saying, Hear you the words of this covenant, and do them.

7 For I earnestly protested unto your fathers in the day that I brought them up out of the land of Egypt, even unto this day, rising early and protesting, saying, Obey my voice.

8 Yet they obeyed not, nor inclined their ear, but walked every one in the imagination of their evil heart: therefore I will bring upon them all the words of this covenant, which I commanded them to do; but they did them not.

9 And the Becoming-One said unto me, A conspiracy is found among the men of Judah, and among the inhabitants of Jerusalem.

10 They are turned back to the iniquities of their forefathers, which refused to hear my words; and they went after other gods to serve them: the house of Israel and the house of Judah have broken my covenant which I made with their fathers.

11 Therefore thus says the Becoming-One, Behold, I will bring evil upon them, which they shall not be able to escape; and though they shall cry unto me, I will not listen unto them.

12 Then shall the cities of Judah and inhabitants of Jerusalem go, and cry unto the gods unto whom they offer incense: but they shall not save them at all in the time of their trouble.

13 For according to the number of your cities were your gods, O Judah; and according to the number of the streets of Jerusalem have you set up altars to that shameful thing, even altars to burn incense unto the lord [baal].

14 Therefore pray not you for this people, neither lift up a cry or prayer for them: for I will not hear them in the time that they cry unto me for their trouble.

15 What has my beloved to do in mine house, seeing she has worked lewdness with many, and the holy flesh is passed from you? when you do evil, then you rejoice.

16 The Becoming-One called your name, A green olive tree, fair, and of goodly fruit: with the noise of a great tumult he has kindled fire upon it, and the branches of it are broken.

17 For the Becoming-One of hosts, that planted you, has pronounced evil against you, for the evil of the house of Israel and of the house of Judah, which they have done against themselves to provoke me to anger in offering incense unto the lord [baal].

18 And the Becoming-One has given me knowledge of it, and I know it: then you showed me their doings.

19 But I was like a lamb or an ox that is brought to the slaughter; and I knew not that they had devised devices against me, saying, Let us destroy the tree with the fruit thereof, and let us cut him off from the land of the living, that his name may be no more remembered.

20 But, O Becoming-One of hosts, that judge righteously, that try the reins and the heart, let me see your vengeance on them: for unto you have I revealed my cause.

21 Therefore thus says the Becoming-One of the men of Anathoth, that seek your soul, saying, Prophesy not in the name of the Becoming-One, that you die not by our hand:

22 Therefore thus says the Becoming-One of hosts, Behold, I will punish them: the young men shall die by the sword; their sons and their daughters shall die by famine:

23 And there shall be no remnant of them: for I will bring evil upon the men of Anathoth, even the year of their visitation.

Jer 12:1 Righteous are you, O Becoming-One, when I plead with you: yet let me talk with you of your judgments: Why does the way of the wicked prosper? why are all they happy that deal very treacherously?

2 you have planted them, yes, they have taken root: they grow, yes, they bring forth fruit: you are near in their mouth, and far from their reins.

3 But you, O Becoming-One, know me: you have seen me, and tried mine heart toward you: pull them out like sheep for the slaughter, and prepare them for the day of slaughter.

4 How long shall the land mourn, and the herbs of every field wither, for the wickedness of them that dwell therein? the beasts are consumed, and the birds; because they said, He shall not see our last end.

5 If you have run with the footmen, and they have wearied you, then how can you contend with horses? and if in the land of peace, wherein you trusted, they wearied you, then how will you do in the swelling of Jordan?

6 For even your brethren, and the house of your father, even they have dealt treacherously with you; yes, they have called a multitude after you: believe them not, though they speak fair words unto you.

7 I have forsaken mine house, I have left mine heritage; I have given the dearly beloved of my soul into the hand of her enemies.

8 Mine heritage is unto me as a lion in the forest; it cries out against me: therefore have I hated it.

9 Mine heritage is unto me as a speckled bird, the birds round about are against her; come ye, assemble all the beasts of the field, come to devour.

10 Many pastors have destroyed my vineyard, they have trodden my portion under foot, they have made my pleasant portion a desolate wilderness.

11 They have made it desolate, and being desolate it mourns unto me; the whole land is made desolate, because no man lays it to heart.

12 The spoilers are come upon all high places through the wilderness: for the sword of the Becoming-One shall devour from the one end of the land even to the other end of the land: no flesh shall have peace.

13 They have sown wheat, but shall reap thorns: they have put themselves to pain, but shall not profit: and they shall be ashamed of your revenues because of the fierce anger of the Becoming-One.

14 Thus says the Becoming-One against all mine evil neighbors, that touch the inheritance which I have caused my people Israel to inherit; Behold, I will pluck them out of their land, and pluck out the house of Judah from among them.

15 And it shall come to pass, after that I have plucked them out I will return, and have compassion on them, and will bring them again, every man to his heritage, and every man to his land.

16 And it shall come to pass, if they will diligently learn the ways of my people, to swear by my name, The Becoming-One lives; as they taught my people to swear by the lord [baal] then shall they be built in the midst of my people.

17 But if they will not obey, I will utterly pluck up and destroy that nation, says the Becoming-One.

Jer 13:1 Thus says the Becoming-One unto me, Go and get you a linen girdle, and put it upon your loins, and put it not in water.

2 So I got a girdle according to the word of the Becoming-One, and put it on my loins.

3 And the word of the Becoming-One came unto me the second time, saying,

4 Take the girdle that you have got, which is upon your loins, and arise, go to Euphrates, and hide it there in a hole of the rock.

5 So I went, and hid it by Euphrates, as the Becoming-One commanded me.

6 And at the end of days, that the Becoming-One said unto me, Arise, go to Euphrates, and take the girdle from there, which I commanded you to hide there.

7 Then I went to Euphrates, and dug, and took the girdle from the place where I had hid it: and, behold, the girdle was marred, it was profitable for nothing.

8 Then the word of the Becoming-One came unto me, saying,

9 Thus says the Becoming-One, After this manner will I mar the pride of Judah, and the great pride of Jerusalem.

10 This evil people, which refuse to hear my words, which walk in the imagination of their heart, and walk after other gods, to serve them, and to worship them, shall even be as this girdle, which is good for nothing.

11 For as the girdle cleaves to the loins of a man, so have I caused to cleave unto me the whole house of Israel and the whole house of Judah, says the Becoming-One; that they might be unto me for a people, and for a name, and for a praise, and for a glory: but they would not hear.

12 Therefore you shall speak unto them this word; Thus says the Becoming-One, God of Israel, Every bottle shall be filled with wine: and they shall say unto you, Do we not certainly know that every bottle shall be filled with wine?

13 Then shall you say unto them, Thus says the Becoming-One, Behold, I will fill all the inhabitants of this land, even the kings that sit upon David's throne, and the priests, and the prophets, and all the inhabitants of Jerusalem, with drunkenness.

14 And I will dash them one against another, even the fathers and the sons together, says the Becoming-One: I will not pity, nor spare, nor have mercy, but destroy them.

15 Hear ye, and give ear; be not proud: for the Becoming-One has spoken.

16 Give glory to the Becoming-One your God, before he cause darkness, and before your feet stumble upon the breeze time of the evening mountains, and, while you look for light, he turn it into the shadow of death, and make it gross darkness.

17 But if you will not hear it, my soul shall weep in secret places for your pride; and mine eye shall weep greatly, and run down with tears, because the Becoming-One's flock is carried away captive.

18 Say unto the king and to the queen, Humble yourselves, sit down: for your crown shall come down, even the crown of your glory.

19 The cities of the south shall be shut up, and none shall open them: Judah shall be carried away captive all of it, it shall be wholly carried away captive.

20 Lift up your eyes, and behold them that come from the north: where is the flock that was given you, your beautiful flock?

21 What will you say when he shall punish you? for you have taught them to be captains, and as chief over you: shall not sorrows take you, as a woman in travail?

22 And if you say in your heart, Why come these things upon me? For the greatness of your iniquity are your skirts discovered, and your heels made bare.

23 Can the Ethiopian change his skin, or the leopard his spots? then may you also do good, that are accustomed to do evil.

24 Therefore will I scatter them as the stubble that passes away by the wind of the wilderness.

25 This is your lot, the portion of your measures from me, says the Becoming-One; because you have forgotten me, and trusted in falsehood.

26 Therefore will I discover your skirts upon your face, that your shame may appear.

27 I have seen your adulteries, and your neighings, the lewdness of your whoredom, and your abominations on the hills in the fields. Woe unto you, O Jerusalem! will you not be made clean? when shall it once be?

Jer 14:1 The word of the Becoming-One that came to Jeremiah concerning the dearth.

2 Judah mourns, and the gates thereof languish; they are black unto the ground; and the cry of Jerusalem is gone up.

3 And their nobles have sent their little ones to the waters: they came to the pits, and found no water; they returned with their vessels empty; they were ashamed and confounded, and covered their heads.

4 Because the ground is chapt, for there was no rain in the earth, the plowmen were ashamed, they covered their heads.

5 Yes, the hind also calved in the field, and forsook it, because there was no grass.

6 And the wild donkeys did stand in the high places, they snuffed up the wind like monsters; their eyes did fail, because there was no grass.

7 O Becoming-One, though our iniquities testify against us, do you it for your name's sake: for our backslidings are many; we have sinned against you.

8 O the hope of Israel, the Savior thereof in time of trouble, why should you be as a stranger in the land, and as a wayfaring man that turns aside to tarry for a night?

9 Why should you be as a man astonied, as a mighty man that cannot save? yet you, O Becoming-One, are in the midst of us, and we are called by your name; leave us not.

10 Thus says the Becoming-One unto this people, Thus have they loved to wander, they have not refrained their feet, therefore the Becoming-One does not accept them; he will now remember their iniquity, and visit their sins.

11 Then said the Becoming-One unto me, Pray not for this people for their good.

12 When they fast, I will not hear their cry; and when they offer burnt offering and an offering, I will not accept them: but I will consume them by the sword, and by the famine, and by the pestilence.

13 Then said I, Ah, my Lord(s) the Becoming-One! behold, the prophets say unto them, you shall not see the sword, neither shall you have famine; but I will give you assured peace in this place.

14 Then the Becoming-One said unto me, The prophets prophesy lies in my name: I sent them not, neither have I commanded them, neither spoke unto them: they prophesy unto you a false vision and divination, and a thing of nothing, and the deceit of their heart.

15 Therefore thus says the Becoming-One concerning the prophets that prophesy in my name, and I sent them not, yet they say, Sword and famine shall not be in this land; By sword and famine shall those prophets be consumed.

16 And the people to whom they prophesy shall be cast out in the streets of Jerusalem because of the famine and the sword; and they shall have none to bury them, them, their wives, nor their sons, nor their daughters: for I will pour their wickedness upon them.

17 Therefore you shall say this word unto them; Let mine eyes run down with tears night and day, and let them not cease: for the virgin daughter of my people is broken with a great breach, with a very grievous blow.

18 If I go forth into the field, then behold the slain with the sword! and if I enter into the city, then behold them that are sick with famine! yes, both the prophet and the priest go about into a land that they know not.

19 have you utterly rejected Judah? has your soul loathed Zion? why have you struck us, and there is no healing for us? we looked for peace, and there is no good; and for the time of healing, and behold trouble!

20 We acknowledge, O Becoming-One, our wickedness, and the iniquity of our fathers: for we have sinned against you.

21 Do not abhor us, for your name's sake, do not disgrace the throne of your glory: remember, break not your covenant with us.

22 Are there any among the vanities of the nations that can cause rain? or can the heavens give showers? are not you he, O Becoming-One our God? therefore we will wait upon you: for you have made all these things.

Jer 15:1 Then said the Becoming-One unto me, Though Moses and Samuel stood before me, yet my soul could not be toward this people: cast them out of my sight, and let them go forth.

2 And it shall come to pass, if they say unto you, To where shall we go forth? then you shall tell them, Thus says the Becoming-One; Such as are for death, to death; and such as are for the sword, to the sword; and such as are for the famine, to the famine; and such as are for the captivity, to the captivity.

3 And I will appoint over them four kinds, says the Becoming-One: the sword to slay, and the dogs to tear, and the fowls of the heaven, and the beasts of the earth, to devour and destroy.

4 And I will cause them to be removed into all kingdoms of the earth, because of Manasseh the son of Hezekiah king of Judah, for that which he did in Jerusalem.

5 For who shall have pity upon you, O Jerusalem? or who shall bemoan you? or who shall go aside to ask how you do?

6 you have forsaken me, says the Becoming-One, you are gone backward: therefore will I stretch out my hand against you, and destroy you; I am weary with repenting.

7 And I will fan them with a fan in the gates of the land; I will bereave them of children, I will destroy my people, since they return not from their ways.

8 Their widows are increased to me above the sand of the seas: I have brought upon them against the mother of the young men a spoiler at noonday: I have caused him to fall upon it suddenly, and terrors upon the city.

9 She that has borne seven languishes: she has breathed out her soul; her sun is gone down while it was yet day: she has been ashamed and confounded: and the residue of them will I deliver to the sword before their enemies, says the Becoming-One.

10 Woe is me, my mother, that you have borne me a man of strife and a man of contention to the whole earth! I have neither lent on usury, nor men have lent to me on usury; yet every one of them does curse me.

11 The Becoming-One said, Truly it shall be well with your remnant; truly I will cause the enemy to entreat you well in the time of evil and in the time of affliction.

12 Shall iron break the northern iron and the steel?

13 your substance and your treasures will I give to the spoil without price, and that for all your sins, even in all your borders.

14 And I will make you to pass with your enemies into a land which you know not: for a fire is kindled in mine anger, which shall burn upon you.

15 O Becoming-One, you know: remember me, and visit me, and revenge me of my persecutors; take me not away in your patience: know that for your sake I have permitted rebuke.

16 your words were found, and I did eat them; and your word was unto me the joy and rejoicing of mine heart: for I am called by your name, O Becoming-One, God of hosts.

17 I sat not in the assembly of the mockers, nor rejoiced; I sat alone because of your hand: for you have filled me with indignation.

18 Why is my pain perpetual, and my wound incurable, which refuses to be healed? will you be altogether unto me as a liar, and as waters that fail?

19 Therefore thus says the Becoming-One, If you return, then will I bring you again, and you shall stand before me: and if you take forth the precious

from the vile, you shall be as my mouth: let them return unto you; but return not you unto them.

20 And I will make you unto this people a fenced brazen wall: and they shall fight against you, but they shall not prevail against you: for I am with you to save you and to deliver you, says the Becoming-One.

21 And I will deliver you out of the hand of the wicked, and I will redeem you out of the hand of the terrible.

Jer 16:1 The word of the Becoming-One came also unto me, saying,

2 you shall not take you a wife, neither shall you have sons or daughters in this place.

3 For thus says the Becoming-One concerning the sons and concerning the daughters that are born in this place, and concerning their mothers that bare them, and concerning their fathers that begat them in this land;

4 They shall die of grievous deaths; they shall not be lamented; neither shall they be buried; but they shall be as dung upon the face of the earth: and they shall be consumed by the sword, and by famine; and their carcases shall be food for the fowls of heaven, and for the beasts of the earth.

5 For thus says the Becoming-One, Enter not into the house of mourning, neither go to lament nor bemoan them: for I have taken away my peace from this people, says the Becoming-One, even loving-kindness and mercies.

6 Both the great and the small shall die in this land: they shall not be buried, neither shall men lament for them, nor cut themselves, nor make themselves bald for them:

7 Neither shall men tear themselves for them in mourning, to comfort them for the dead; neither shall men give them the cup of consolation to drink for their father or for their mother.

8 you shall not also go into the house of feasting, to sit with them to eat and to drink.

9 For thus says the Becoming-One of hosts, God of Israel; Behold, I will cause to cease out of this place in your eyes, and in your days, the voice of mirth, and the voice of gladness, the voice of the bridegroom, and the voice of the bride.

10 And it shall come to pass, when you shall show this people all these words, and they shall say unto you, Why has the Becoming-One pronounced all this great evil against us? or what is our iniquity? or what is our sin that we have committed against the Becoming-One our God?

11 Then shall you say unto them, Because your fathers have forsaken me, says the Becoming-One, and have walked after other gods, and have served them, and have worshiped them, and have forsaken me, and have not kept my law;

12 And you have done worse than your fathers; for, behold, you walk every one after the imagination of his evil heart, that they may not listen unto me:

13 Therefore will I cast you out of this land into a land that you know not, neither you nor your fathers; and there shall you serve other gods day and night; where I will not show you favor.

14 Therefore, behold, the days come, says the Becoming-One, that it shall no more be said, The Becoming-One lives, that brought up the children of Israel out of the land of Egypt;

15 But, The Becoming-One lives, that brought up the children of Israel from the land of the north, and from all the lands to which he had driven them: and I will bring them again into their land that I gave unto their fathers.

16 Behold, I will send for many fishermen, says the Becoming-One, and they shall fish them; and after will I send for many hunters, and they shall hunt them from every mountain, and from every hill, and out of the holes of the rocks.

17 For mine eyes are upon all their ways: they are not hid from my face, neither is their iniquity hid from mine eyes.

18 And first I will recompense their iniquity and their sin double; because they have defiled my land, they have filled mine inheritance with the carcases of their detestable and abominable things.

19 O Becoming-One, my strength, and my fortress, and my refuge in the day of affliction, the nations shall come unto you from the ends of the earth, and shall say, Surely our fathers have inherited lies, vanity, and things wherein there is no profit.

20 Shall a man make gods unto himself, and they are no gods?

21 Therefore, behold, I will this once cause them to know, I will cause them to know mine hand and my might; and they shall know that my name is The Becoming-One.

Jer 17:1 The sin of Judah is written with a pen of iron, and with the point of a diamond: it is graven upon the table of their heart, and upon the horns of your altars;

2 As they remember their children remember they [remember] their altars and their Asherahs by the green trees upon the high hills.

3 O my mountain in the field, I will give your substance and all your treasures to the spoil, and your high places for sin, throughout all your borders.

4 And you, even thyself, shall discontinue from your heritage that I gave you; and I will cause you to serve your enemies in the land which you know not: for you have kindled a fire in mine anger, which shall burn for olam.

5 Thus says the Becoming-One; Cursed be the man that trusts in man, and makes flesh his arm, and whose heart departs from the Becoming-One.

6 For he shall be like the heath in the desert, and shall not see when good comes; but shall inhabit the parched places in the wilderness, in a salt land and not inhabited.

7 Blessed is the man that trusts in the Becoming-One, and whose hope the Becoming-One is.

8 For he shall be as a tree planted by the waters, and that spreads out her roots by the river, and shall not see when heat comes, but her leaf shall be green; and shall not be careful in the year of drought, neither shall cease from yielding fruit.

9 The heart is deceitful above all things, and desperately wicked: who can know it?

10 I the Becoming-One search the heart, I try the reins, even to give every man according to his ways, and according to the fruit of his doings.

11 As the partridge sits on eggs, and hatches them not; so he that gets riches, and not by right, shall leave them in the midst of his days, and at his end shall be a fool.

12 A glorious high throne from the beginning is the place of our sanctuary.

13 O Becoming-One, the hope of Israel, all that forsake you shall be ashamed, and they that depart from me shall be written in the earth, because they have forsaken the Becoming-One, the fountain of living waters.

14 Heal me, O Becoming-One, and I shall be healed; save me, and I shall be saved: for you are my praise.

15 Behold, they say unto me, Where is the word of the Becoming-One? let it come now.

16 As for me, I have not hurried from being a pastor to follow you: neither have I desired the woeful day; you know: that which came out of my lips was right before you.

17 Be not a terror unto me: you are my hope in the day of evil.

18 Let them be confounded that persecute me, but let not me be confounded: let them be dismayed, but let not me be dismayed: bring upon them the day of evil, and destroy them with double destruction.

19 Thus said the Becoming-One unto me; Go and stand in the gate of the children of the people, whereby the kings of Judah come in, and by the which they go out, and in all the gates of Jerusalem;

20 And say unto them, Hear you the word of the Becoming-One, you kings of Judah, and all Judah, and all the inhabitants of Jerusalem, that enter in by these gates:

21 Thus says the Becoming-One; Take heed to your souls, and bear no burden on the Sabbath day, nor bring it in by the gates of Jerusalem;

22 Neither carry forth a burden out of your houses on the Sabbath day, neither do you any work, but hallow you the Sabbath day, as I commanded your fathers.

23 But they obeyed not, neither inclined their ear, but made their neck stiff, that they might not hear, nor receive instruction.

24 And it shall come to pass, if you diligently listen unto me, says the Becoming-One, to bring in no burden through the gates of this city on the Sabbath day, but hallow the Sabbath day, to do no work therein;

25 Then shall there enter into the gates of this city kings and princes sitting upon the throne of David, riding in chariots and on horses, they, and their princes, the men of Judah, and the inhabitants of Jerusalem: and this city shall remain for olam.

26 And they shall come from the cities of Judah, and from the places about Jerusalem, and from the land of Benjamin, and from the plain, and from the mountains, and from the south, bringing burnt offerings, and sacrifices, and food offerings, and incense, and bringing sacrifices of praise, unto the house of the Becoming-One.

27 But if you will not listen unto me to hallow the Sabbath day, and not to bear a burden, even entering in at the gates of Jerusalem on the Sabbath day; then will I kindle a fire in the gates thereof, and it shall devour the palaces of Jerusalem, and it shall not be quenched.

Jer 18:1 The word which came to Jeremiah from the Becoming-One, saying,

2 Arise, and go down to the potter's house, and there I will cause you to hear my words.

3 Then I went down to the potter's house, and, behold, he worked a work on the wheels.

4 And the vessel that he made of clay was marred in the hand of the potter: so he made it again another vessel, as seemed good to the potter to make it.

5 Then the word of the Becoming-One came to me, saying,

6 O house of Israel, cannot I do with you as this potter? says the Becoming-One. Behold, as the clay is in the potter's hand, so are you in mine hand, O house of Israel.

7 At what instant I shall speak concerning a nation, and concerning a kingdom, to pluck up, and to pull down, and to destroy it;

8 If that nation, against whom I have pronounced, turn from their evil, I will repent of the evil that I thought to do unto them.

9 And at what instant I shall speak concerning a nation, and concerning a kingdom, to build and to plant it;

10 If it do evil in my sight, that it obey not my voice, then I will repent of the good, wherewith I said I would benefit them.

11 Now therefore go to, speak to the men of Judah, and to the inhabitants of Jerusalem, saying, Thus says the Becoming-One; Behold, I frame evil against you, and devise a device against you: return you now every one from his evil way, and make your ways and your doings good.

12 And they said, There is no hope: but we will walk after our own devices, and we will every one do the imagination of his evil heart.

13 Therefore thus says the Becoming-One; Ask you now among the nations, who has heard such things: the virgin of Israel has done a very horrible thing.

14 Will a man leave the snow of Lebanon which comes from the rock of the field? or shall the cold flowing waters that come from another place be forsaken?

15 Because my people has forgotten me, they have burned incense to vanity, and they have caused them to stumble in their ways from the paths of olam, to walk in paths, in a way not cast up;

16 To make their land desolate, and a hissing of olam; every one that passes thereby shall be astonished, and wag his head.

17 I will scatter them as with an east wind before the enemy; I will show them the back, and not the face, in the day of their calamity.

18 Then said they, Come, and let us devise devices against Jeremiah; for the law shall not perish from the priest, nor counsel from the wise, nor the word from the prophet. Come, and let us smite him with the tongue, and let us not give heed to any of his words.

19 Give heed to me, O Becoming-One, and listen to the voice of them that contend with me.

20 Shall evil be recompensed for good? for they have dug a pit for my soul. Remember that I stood before you to speak good for them, and to turn away your wrath from them.

21 Therefore deliver up their children to the famine, and pour out their blood by the force of the sword; and let their wives be bereaved of their children, and be widows; and let their men be put to death; let their young men be slain by the sword in battle.

22 Let a cry be heard from their houses, when you shall bring a troop suddenly upon them: for they have dug a pit to take me, and hid snares for my feet.

23 Yet, Becoming-One, you know all their counsel against me to slay me: forgive not their iniquity, neither blot out their sin from your sight, but let them be overthrown before you; deal thus with them in the time of your anger.

Jer 19:1 Thus says the Becoming-One, Go and get a potter's earthen bottle, and take of the ancients of the people, and of the ancients of the priests;

2 And go forth unto the valley of the son of Hinnom, which is by the entry of the east gate, and proclaim there the words that I shall tell you,

3 And say, Hear you the word of the Becoming-One, O kings of Judah, and inhabitants of Jerusalem; Thus says the Becoming-One of hosts, God of Israel; Behold, I will bring evil upon this place, the which whosoever hears, his ears shall tingle.

4 Because they have forsaken me, and have estranged this place, and have burned incense in it unto other gods, whom neither they nor their fathers have known, nor the kings of Judah, and have filled this place with the blood of innocents;

5 They have built also the high places of the lord [baal] to burn their sons with fire for burnt offerings unto the lord [baal] which I commanded not, nor spoke it, neither came it into my mind:

6 Therefore, behold, the days come, says the Becoming-One, that this place shall no more be called Tophet, nor The valley of the son of Hinnom, but The valley of slaughter.

7 And I will make void the counsel of Judah and Jerusalem in this place; and I will cause them to fall by the sword before their enemies, and by the hands of them that seek their souls: and their carcases will I give to be food for the fowls of the heaven, and for the beasts of the earth.

8 And I will make this city desolate, and a hissing; every one that passes thereby shall be astonished and hiss because of all the plagues thereof.

9 And I will cause them to eat the flesh of their sons and the flesh of their daughters, and they shall eat every one the flesh of his friend in the siege and straitness, wherewith their enemies, and they that seek their lives, shall straiten them.

10 Then shall you break the bottle in the sight of the men that go with you.

11 And shall say unto them, Thus says the Becoming-One of hosts; Even so will I break this people and this city, as one breaks a potter's vessel, that cannot be made whole again: and they shall bury them in Tophet, till there be no place to bury.

12 Thus will I do unto this place, says the Becoming-One, and to the inhabitants thereof, and even make this city as Tophet:

13 And the houses of Jerusalem, and the houses of the kings of Judah, shall be defiled as the place of Tophet, because of all the houses upon whose roofs they have burned incense unto all the host of heaven, and have poured out drink offerings unto other gods.

14 Then came Jeremiah from Tophet, to which the Becoming-One had sent him to prophesy; and he stood in the court of the Becoming-One's house; and said to all the people,

15 Thus says the Becoming-One of hosts, God of Israel; Behold, I will bring upon this city and upon all her towns all the evil that I have pronounced against it, because they have hardened their necks, that they might not hear my words.

Jer 20:1 Now Pashur the son of Immer the priest, who was also chief governor in the house of the Becoming-One, heard that Jeremiah prophesied these things.

2 Then Pashur smote Jeremiah the prophet, and put him in the stocks that were in the high gate of Benjamin, which was by the house of the Becoming-One.

3 And it came to pass on the next day, that Pashur brought forth Jeremiah out of the stocks. Then said Jeremiah unto him, The Becoming-One has not called your name Pashur, but Magormissabib.

4 For thus says the Becoming-One, Behold, I will make you a terror to thyself, and to all your friends: and they shall fall by the sword of their enemies, and your eyes shall behold it: and I will give all Judah into the hand of the king of Babylon, and he shall carry them captive into Babylon, and shall slay them with the sword.

5 Moreover I will deliver all the strength of this city, and all the labors thereof, and all the precious things thereof, and all the treasures of the kings of Judah will I give into the hand of their enemies, which shall spoil them, and take them, and carry them to Babylon.

6 And you, Pashur, and all that dwell in your house shall go into captivity: and you shall come to Babylon, and there you shall die, and shall be buried there, you, and all your friends, to whom you have prophesied lies.

7 O Becoming-One, you have deceived me, and I was deceived: you are stronger than I, and have prevailed: I am in derision daily, every one mocks me.

8 For since I spoke, I cried out, I cried violence and spoil; because the word of the Becoming-One was made a reproach unto me, and a derision, daily.

9 Then I said, I will not make mention of him, nor speak any more in his name. But his word was in mine heart as a burning fire shut up in my bones, and I was weary with forbearing, and I could not stay.

10 For I heard the defaming of many, fear on every side. Report, say they, and we will report it. All my familiars watched for my halting, saying, Perhaps he will be enticed, and we shall prevail against him, and we shall take our revenge on him.

11 But the Becoming-One is with me as a mighty terrible one: therefore my persecutors shall stumble, and they shall not prevail: they shall be greatly

ashamed; for they shall not prosper: their confusion of olam shall not be forgotten.

12 But, O Becoming-One of hosts, that try the righteous, and see the reins and the heart, let me see your vengeance on them: for unto you have I opened my cause.

13 Sing unto the Becoming-One, praise you the Becoming-One: for he has delivered the soul of the poor from the hand of evildoers.

14 Cursed be the day wherein I was born: let not the day wherein my mother bare me be blessed.

15 Cursed be the man who brought tidings to my father, saying, A man child is born unto you; making him very glad.

16 And let that man be as the cities which the Becoming-One overthrew, and repented not: and let him hear the cry in the morning, and the shouting at noontide;

17 Because he killed me not from the womb; or that my mother might have been my grave, and her womb to be a great olam with me.

18 Why came I forth out of the womb to see labor and sorrow, that my days should be consumed with shame?

Jer 21:1 The word which came unto Jeremiah from the Becoming-One, when king Zedekiah sent unto him Pashur the son of Melchiah, and Zephaniah the son of Maaseiah the priest, saying,

2 Inquire, I pray you, of the Becoming-One for us; for Nebuchadrezzar king of Babylon makes war against us; if so be that the Becoming-One will deal with us according to all his wondrous works, that he may go up from us.

3 Then said Jeremiah unto them, Thus shall you say to Zedekiah:

4 Thus says the Becoming-One, God of Israel; Behold, I will turn back the weapons of war that are in your hands, wherewith you fight against the king of Babylon, and against the Chaldeans, which besiege you outside the walls, and I will assemble them into the midst of this city.

5 And I myself will fight against you with an outstretched hand and with a strong arm, even in anger, and in fury, and in great wrath.

6 And I will smite the inhabitants of this city, both man and beast: they shall die of a great pestilence.

7 And afterwards, said the Becoming-One, I will give Zedekiah king of Judah , and his servants, and the people, and such as are left in this city from the pestilence, from the sword, and from the famine, into the hand of Nebuchadrezzar the king of Babylon, and into the hand of their enemies, and into the hand of those that seek their life, and he shall smite them with the edge of the sword: he shall not spare them, neither have pity, nor have mercy

8 And unto this people you shall say, Thus says the Becoming-One; Behold, I set before you the way of life, and the way of death.

9 He that abides in this city shall die by the sword, and by the famine, and by the pestilence: but he that goes out, and falls to the Chaldeans that besiege you, he shall live, and his soul shall be unto him for a prey.

10 For I have set my face against this city for evil, and not for good, says the Becoming-One: it shall be given into the hand of the king of Babylon, and he shall burn it with fire.

11 And touching the house of the king of Judah, say, Hear you the word of the Becoming-One;

12 O house of David, thus says the Becoming-One; Execute judgment in the morning, and deliver him that is spoiled out of the hand of the oppressor, lest my fury go out like fire, and burn that none can quench it, because of the evil of your doings.

13 Behold, I am against you, O inhabitant of the valley, and rock of the plain, says the Becoming-One; which say, Who shall come down against us? or who shall enter into our habitations?

14 But I will punish you according to the fruit of your doings, says the Becoming-One: and I will kindle a fire in the forest thereof, and it shall devour all things round about it.

Jer 22:1 Thus says the Becoming-One; Go down to the house of the king of Judah, and speak there this word,

2 And say, Hear the word of the Becoming-One, O king of Judah, that sit upon the throne of David, you, and your servants, and your people that enter in by these gates:

3 Thus says the Becoming-One; Execute you judgment and righteousness, and deliver the spoiled out of the hand of the oppressor: and do no wrong, do no violence to the stranger, the fatherless, nor the widow, neither shed innocent blood in this place.

4 For if you do this thing indeed, then shall there enter in by the gates of this house kings sitting upon the throne of David, riding in chariots and on horses, he, and his servants, and his people.

5 But if you will not hear these words, I swear by myself, says the Becoming-One, that this house shall become a desolation.

6 For thus says the Becoming-One unto the king's house of Judah; you are Gilead unto me, and the head of Lebanon: yet surely I will make you a wilderness, and cities which are not inhabited.

7 And I will prepare destroyers against you, every one with his weapons: and they shall cut down your choice cedars, and cast them into the fire.

8 And many nations shall pass by this city, and they shall say every man to his neighbor, Why has the Becoming-One done thus unto this great city?

9 Then they shall answer, Because they have forsaken the covenant of the Becoming-One their God, and worshiped other gods, and served them.

10 Weep you not for the dead, neither bemoan him: but weep greatly for him that goes away: for he shall return no more, nor see his native country.

11 For thus says the Becoming-One touching Shallum the son of Josiah king of Judah, which reigned instead of Josiah his father, which went forth out of this place; He shall not return there any more:

12 But he shall die in the place to which they have led him captive, and shall see this land no more.

13 Woe unto him that builds his house by unrighteousness, and his chambers by wrong; that uses his neighbor's service without wages, and gives him not for his work;

14 That said, I will build me a wide house and large chambers, and cuts him out windows; and it is covered with cedar, and painted with vermilion.

15 shall you reign, because you close yourself in cedar? did not your father eat and drink, and do judgment and justice, and then it was well with him?

16 He judged the cause of the poor and needy; then it was well with him: was not this to know me? says the Becoming-One.

17 But your eyes and your heart are not but for your covetousness, and for to shed innocent blood, and for oppression, and for violence, to do it.

18 Therefore thus says the Becoming-One concerning Jehoiakim the son of Josiah king of Judah; They shall not lament for him, saying, Ah my brother! or, Ah sister! they shall not lament for him, saying, Ah lord! or, Ah his glory!

19 He shall be buried with the burial of an donkey, drawn and cast forth beyond the gates of Jerusalem.

20 Go up to Lebanon, and cry; and lift up your voice in Bashan, and cry from the passages: for all your lovers are destroyed.

21 I spoke unto you in your prosperity; but you said, I will not hear. This has been your manner from your youth, that you obeyed not my voice.

22 The wind shall eat up all your pastors, and your lovers shall go into captivity: surely then shall you be ashamed and confounded for all your wickedness.

23 O inhabitant of Lebanon, that make your nest in the cedars, how gracious shall you be when pangs come upon you, the pain as of a woman in travail!

24 As I live, says the Becoming-One, though Coniah the son of Jehoiakim king of Judah were the signet upon my right hand, yet would I pluck you there;

25 And I will give you into the hand of them that seek your soul, and into the hand of them whose face you fear, even into the hand of Nebuchadrezzar king of Babylon, and into the hand of the Chaldeans.

26 And I will cast you out, and your mother that bare you, into another country, where you were not born; and there shall you die.

27 But to the land whereunto they lift up their soul to return, there shall they not return.

28 Is this man Coniah a despised broken idol? is he a vessel wherein is no pleasure? why are they cast out, he and his seed, and are cast into a land which they know not?

29 O earth, earth, earth, hear the word of the Becoming-One.

30 Thus says the Becoming-One, Write you this man childless, a man that shall not prosper in his days: for no man of his seed shall prosper, sitting upon the throne of David, and ruling any more in Judah.

Jer 23:1 Woe be unto the pastors that destroy and scatter the sheep of my pasture! says the Becoming-One.

2 Therefore thus says the Becoming-One, God of Israel against the pastors that feed my people; you have scattered my flock, and driven them away, and have not visited them: behold, I will visit upon you the evil of your doings, says the Becoming-One.

3 And I will gather the remnant of my flock out of all countries to which I have driven them, and will bring them again to their folds; and they shall be fruitful and increase.

4 And I will set up shepherds over them which shall feed them: and they shall fear no more, nor be dismayed, neither shall they be lacking, says the Becoming-One.

5 Behold, the days come, says the Becoming-One, that I will raise unto David a righteous Branch, and a King shall reign and prosper, and shall execute judgment and justice in the earth.

6 In his days Judah shall be saved, and Israel shall dwell safely: and this is his name whereby he shall be called, THE Becoming-One OUR RIGHTEOUSNESS.

7 Therefore, behold, the days come, says the Becoming-One, that they shall no more say, The Becoming-One lives, which brought up the children of Israel out of the land of Egypt;

8 But, The Becoming-One lives, which brought up and which led the seed of the house of Israel out of the north country, and from all countries to which I had driven them; and they shall dwell in their own land.

9 Mine heart within me is broken because of the prophets; all my bones shake; I am like a drunken man, and like a man whom wine has overcome, because of the Becoming-One, and because of the words of his holiness.

10 For the land is full of adulterers; for because of swearing the land mourns; the pleasant places of the wilderness are dried up, and their course is evil, and their force is not right.

11 For both prophet and priest are profane; yes, in my house have I found their wickedness, says the Becoming-One.

12 Therefore their way shall be unto them as slippery ways in the darkness: they shall be driven on, and fall therein: for I will bring evil upon them, even the year of their visitation, says the Becoming-One.

13 And I have seen folly in the prophets of Samaria; they prophesied in the lord [baal] and caused my people Israel to err.

14 I have seen also in the prophets of Jerusalem a horrible thing: they commit adultery, and walk in lies: they strengthen also the hands of evildoers, that none does return from his wickedness: they are all of them unto me as Sodom, and the inhabitants thereof as Gomorrah.

15 Therefore thus says the Becoming-One of hosts concerning the prophets; Behold, I will feed them with wormwood, and make them drink the water of gall: for from the prophets of Jerusalem is profaneness gone forth into all the land.

16 Thus says the Becoming-One of hosts, listen not unto the words of the prophets that prophesy unto you: they make you vain: they speak a vision of their own heart, and not out of the mouth of the Becoming-One.

17 They say still unto them that despise me, The Becoming-One has said, you shall have peace; and they say unto every one that walks after the imagination of his own heart, No evil shall come upon you.

18 For who has stood in the counsel of the Becoming-One, and has perceived and heard his word? who has marked his word, and heard it?

19 Behold, a whirlwind of the Becoming-One is gone forth in fury, even a grievous whirlwind: it shall fall grievously upon the head of the wicked.

20 The anger of the Becoming-One shall not return, until he have executed, and till he have performed the thoughts of his heart: in the end of days you shall consider it perfectly.

21 I have not sent these prophets, yet they ran: I have not spoken to them, yet they prophesied.

22 But if they had stood in my counsel, and had caused my people to hear my words, then they should have turned them from their evil way, and from the evil of their doings.

23 Am I God at hand, says the Becoming-One, and not God afar off?

24 Can any hide himself in secret places that I shall not see him? says the Becoming-One. Do not I fill the heavens and earth? says the Becoming-One.

25 I have heard what the prophets said, that prophesy lies in my name, saying, I have dreamed, I have dreamed.

26 How long shall this be in the heart of the prophets that prophesy lies? yes, they are prophets of the deceit of their own heart;

27 Which think to cause my people to forget my name by their dreams which they tell every man to his neighbor, as their fathers have forgotten my name for the lord [baal]

28 The prophet that has a dream, let him tell a dream; and he that has my word, let him speak my word faithfully. What is the chaff to the wheat? says the Becoming-One.

29 Is not my word like as a fire? says the Becoming-One; and like a hammer that breaks the rock in pieces?

30 Therefore, behold, I am against the prophets, says the Becoming-One, that steal my words every one from his neighbor.

31 Behold, I am against the prophets, says the Becoming-One, that use their tongues, and say, He says.

32 Behold, I am against them that prophesy false dreams, says the Becoming-One, and do tell them, and cause my people to err by their lies, and by their lightness; yet I sent them not, nor commanded them: therefore they shall not profit this people at all, says the Becoming-One.

33 And when this people, or the prophet, or a priest, shall ask you, saying, What is the burden of the Becoming-One? you shall then say unto them, What burden? I will even forsake you, says the Becoming-One.

34 And as for the prophet, and the priest, and the people, that shall say, The burden of the Becoming-One, I will even punish that man and his house.

35 Thus shall you say every one to his neighbor, and every one to his brother, What has the Becoming-One answered? and, What has the Becoming-One spoken?

36 And the burden of the Becoming-One shall you mention no more: for every man's word shall be his burden; for you have perverted the words of the living God, of the Becoming-One of hosts our God.

37 Thus shall you say to the prophet, What has the Becoming-One answered you? and, What has the Becoming-One spoken?

38 But since you say, The burden of the Becoming-One; therefore thus says the Becoming-One; Because you say this word, The burden of the Becoming-One, and I have sent unto you, saying, you shall not say, The burden of the Becoming-One;

39 Therefore, behold, I, even I, will utterly forget you, and I will forsake you, and the city that I gave you and your fathers, and cast you out of my presence:

40 And I will bring a reproach of olam upon you, and a shame of olam, which shall not be forgotten.

Jer 24:1 The Becoming-One showed me, and, behold, two baskets of figs were set before the temple of the Becoming-One, after that Nebuchadrezzar king of Babylon had carried away captive Jeconiah the son of Jehoiakim king of Judah, and the princes of Judah, with the carpenters and smiths, from Jerusalem, and had brought them to Babylon.

2 One basket had very good figs, even like the figs that are first ripe: and the other basket had very naughty figs, which could not be eaten, they were so bad.

3 Then said the Becoming-One unto me, What see you, Jeremiah? And I said, Figs; the good figs, very good; and the evil, very evil, that cannot be eaten, they are so evil.

4 Again the word of the Becoming-One came unto me, saying,

5 Thus says the Becoming-One, God of Israel; Like these good figs, so will I acknowledge them that are carried away captive of Judah, whom I have sent out of this place into the land of the Chaldeans for their good.

6 For I will set mine eyes upon them for good, and I will bring them again to this land: and I will build them, and not pull them down; and I will plant them, and not pluck them up.

7 And I will give them a heart to know me, that I am the Becoming-One: and they shall be my people, and I will be their God: for they shall return unto me with their whole heart.

8 And as the evil figs, which cannot be eaten, they are so evil; surely thus says the Becoming-One, So will I give Zedekiah the king of Judah, and his princes, and the residue of Jerusalem, that remain in this land, and them that dwell in the land of Egypt:

9 And I will deliver them to be removed into all the kingdoms of the earth for their hurt, to be a reproach and a proverb, a taunt and a curse, in all places to which I shall drive them.

10 And I will send the sword, the famine, and the pestilence, among them, till they be consumed from off the land that I gave unto them and to their fathers.

Jer 25:1 The word that came to Jeremiah concerning all the people of Judah **in the fourth year of Jehoiakim** the son of Josiah king of Judah, **that was the first year of Nebuchadrezzar king [sole-reign] of Babylon; [3370 YM; 604 BC]**

2 The which Jeremiah the prophet spoke unto all the people of Judah, and to all the inhabitants of Jerusalem, saying,

3 From the thirteenth year of Josiah the son of Amon king of Judah **[3348 YM]**, even unto this day, that is the **three and twentieth year**, the word of the Becoming-One has come unto me, and I have spoken unto you, rising early and speaking; but you have not listened.

4 And the Becoming-One has sent unto you all his servants the prophets, rising early and sending them; but you have not listened, nor inclined your ear to hear.

5 They said, Turn you again now every one from his evil way, and from the evil of your doings, and dwell in the land that the Becoming-One has given unto you and to your fathers for olam and beyond:

6 And go not after other gods to serve them, and to worship them, and provoke me not to anger with the works of your hands; and I will do you no hurt.

7 Yet you have not listened unto me, says the Becoming-One; that you might provoke me to anger with the works of your hands to your own hurt.

8 Therefore thus says the Becoming-One of hosts; Because you have not heard my words,

9 Behold, I will send and take all the families of the north, says the Becoming-One, and Nebuchadrezzar the king of Babylon, my servant, and will bring them against this land, and against the inhabitants thereof, and against all these nations round about, and will utterly destroy them, and make them an astonishment, and a hissing, and desolations of olam.

10 Moreover I will take from them the voice of mirth, and the voice of gladness, the voice of the bridegroom, and the voice of the bride, the sound of the millstones, and the light of the candle.

11 And this whole land shall be a desolation, and an astonishment; and these nations **shall serve the king of Babylon seventy years. [3366-3435 YM; see Chron Papers]**

12 And it shall come to pass, when seventy years are accomplished, that I will punish the king of Babylon, and that nation, says the Becoming-One, for their iniquity, and the land of the Chaldeans, and will make it desolations of olam.

13 And I will bring upon that land all my words which I have pronounced against it, even all that is written in this book, which Jeremiah has prophesied against all the nations.

14 For many nations and great kings shall serve themselves of them also: and I will recompense them according to their deeds, and according to the works of their own hands.

15 For thus says the Becoming-One, God of Israel unto me; Take the wine cup of this fury at my hand, and cause all the nations, to whom I send you, to drink it.

16 And they shall drink, and be moved, and be mad, because of the sword that I will send among them.

17 Then took I the cup at the Becoming-One's hand, and made all the nations to drink, unto whom the Becoming-One had sent me:

18 To wit, Jerusalem, and the cities of Judah, and the kings thereof, and the princes thereof, to make them a desolation, an astonishment, a hissing, and a curse; as it is this day;

19 Pharaoh king of Egypt, and his servants, and his princes, and all his people;

20 And all the mingled people, and all the kings of the land of Uz, and all the kings of the land of the Philistines, and Ashkelon, and Azzah, and Ekron, and the remnant of Ashdod,

21 Edom, and Moab, and the children of Ammon,

22 And all the kings of Tyrus, and all the kings of Zidon, and the kings of the isles which are beyond the sea,

23 Dedan, and Tema, and Buz, and all that are in the utmost corners,

24 And all the kings of Arabia, and all the kings of the mingled people that dwell in the desert,

25 And all the kings of Zimri, and all the kings of Elam, and all the kings of the Medes,

26 And all the kings of the north, far and near, one with another, and all the kingdoms of the world, which are upon the face of the earth: and the king of Sheshach shall drink after them.

27 Therefore you shall say unto them, Thus says the Becoming-One of hosts, God of Israel; Drink ye, and be drunken, and spue, and fall, and rise no more, because of the sword which I will send among you.

28 And it shall be, if they refuse to take the cup at your hand to drink, then shall you say unto them, Thus says the Becoming-One of hosts; you shall certainly drink.

29 For, lo, I begin to bring evil on the city which is called by my name, and should you be utterly unpunished? you shall not be unpunished: for I will call for a sword upon all the inhabitants of the earth, says the Becoming-One of hosts.

30 Therefore prophesy you against them all these words, and say unto them, The Becoming-One shall roar from on high, and utter his voice from his holy habitation; he shall mightily roar upon his habitation; he shall give a shout, as they that tread the grapes, against all the inhabitants of the earth.

31 A noise shall come even to the ends of the earth; for the Becoming-One has a controversy with the nations, he will plead with all flesh; he will give them that are wicked to the sword, says the Becoming-One.

32 Thus says the Becoming-One of hosts, Behold, evil shall go forth from nation to nation, and a great whirlwind shall be raised up from the coasts of the earth.

33 And the slain of the Becoming-One shall be at that day from one end of the earth even unto the other end of the earth: they shall not be lamented, neither gathered, nor buried; they shall be dung upon the ground.

34 Howl, you shepherds, and cry; and wallow yourselves in the ashes, you principal of the flock: for the days of your slaughter and of your dispersions are accomplished; and you shall fall like a pleasant vessel.

35 And the shepherds shall have no way to flee, nor the principal of the flock to escape.

36 A voice of the cry of the shepherds, and a howling of the principal of the flock, shall be heard: for the Becoming-One has spoiled their pasture.

37 And the peaceable habitations are cut down because of the fierce anger of the Becoming-One.

38 He has forsaken his covert, as the lion: for their land is desolate because of the fierceness of the oppressor, and because of his fierce anger.

Jer 26:1 In the beginning of the reign of Jehoiakim the son of Josiah king of Judah came this word from the Becoming-One, saying,

2 Thus says the Becoming-One; Stand in the court of the Becoming-One's house, and speak unto all the cities of Judah, which come to worship in the Becoming-One's house, all the words that I command you to speak unto them; diminish not a word:

3 If so be they will listen, and turn every man from his evil way, that I may repent me of the evil, which I purpose to do unto them because of the evil of their doings.

4 And you shall say unto them, Thus says the Becoming-One; If you will not listen to me, to walk in my law, which I have set before you,

5 To listen to the words of my servants the prophets, whom I sent unto you, both rising up early, and sending them, but you have not listened;

6 Then will I make this house like Shiloh, and will make this city a curse to all the nations of the earth.

7 So the priests and the prophets and all the people heard Jeremiah speaking these words in the house of the Becoming-One.

8 Now it came to pass, when Jeremiah had made an end of speaking all that the Becoming-One had commanded him to speak unto all the people, that the priests and the prophets and all the people took him, saying, in dying, you will die.[133]

9 Why have you prophesied in the name of the Becoming-One, saying, This house shall be like Shiloh, and this city shall be desolate without an inhabitant? And all the people were gathered against Jeremiah in the house of the Becoming-One.

10 When the princes of Judah heard these things, then they came up from the king's house unto the house of the Becoming-One, and sat down in the entry of the new gate of the Becoming-One's house.

11 Then spoke the priests and the prophets unto the princes and to all the people, saying, This man is worthy to die; for he has prophesied against this city, as you have heard with your ears.

12 Then spoke Jeremiah unto all the princes and to all the people, saying, The Becoming-One sent me to prophesy against this house and against this city all the words that you have heard.

13 Therefore now amend your ways and your doings, and obey the voice of the Becoming-One your God; and the Becoming-One will repent him of the evil that he has pronounced against you.

14 As for me, behold, I am in your hand: do with me as seems good and meet unto you.

15 But know you for certain, that if you put me to death, you shall surely bring innocent blood upon yourselves, and upon this city, and upon the inhabitants thereof: for of a truth the Becoming-One has sent me unto you to speak all these words in your ears.

16 Then said the princes and all the people unto the priests and to the prophets; This man is not worthy to die: for he has spoken to us in the name of the Becoming-One our God.

17 Then rose up certain of the elders of the land, and spoke to all the assembly of the people, saying,

18 Micah the Morasthite prophesied in the days of Hezekiah king of Judah, and spoke to all the people of Judah, saying, Thus says the Becoming-One of hosts; Zion shall be plowed like a field, and Jerusalem shall become heaps, and the mountain of the house as the high places of a forest.

19 Did Hezekiah king of Judah and all Judah put him at all to death? did he not fear the Becoming-One, and besought the Becoming-One, and the Becoming-One repented him of the evil which he had pronounced against them? Thus might we procure great evil against our souls.

20 And there was also a man that prophesied in the name of the Becoming-One, Urijah the son of Shemaiah of Kirjathjearim, who prophesied against this city and against this land according to all the words of Jeremiah:

21 And when Jehoiakim the king, with all his mighty men, and all the princes, heard his words, the king sought to put him to death: but when Urijah heard it, he was afraid, and fled, and went into Egypt;

22 And Jehoiakim the king sent men into Egypt, namely, Elnathan the son of Achbor, and certain men with him into Egypt.

23 And they fetched forth Urijah out of Egypt, and brought him unto Jehoiakim the king; who killed him with the sword, and cast his dead body into the graves of the common people.

24 Nevertheless the hand of Ahikam the son of Shaphan was with Jeremiah, that they should not give him into the hand of the people to put him to death.

Jer 27:1 In the beginning of the reign of Jehoiakim the son of Josiah king of Judah came this word unto Jeremiah from the Becoming-One, saying,

2 Thus says the Becoming-One to me; Make you bonds and yokes, and put them upon your neck,

3 And send them to the king of Edom, and to the king of Moab, and to the king of the Ammonites, and to the king of Tyrus, and to the king of Zidon, by the hand of the messengers which come to Jerusalem unto Zedekiah king of Judah;

4 And command them to say unto their masters, Thus says the Becoming-One of hosts, God of Israel; Thus shall you say unto your masters;

5 I have made the earth, the man and the beast that are upon the ground, by my great power and by my outstretched arm, and have given it unto whom it seemed meet unto me.

6 And now have I given all these lands into the hand of Nebuchadnezzar the king of Babylon, my servant; and the beasts of the field have I given him also to serve him.

7 And all nations shall serve him, and his son, and his son's son, until the very time of his land come: and then many nations and great kings shall serve themselves of him.

8 And it shall come to pass, that the nation and kingdom which will not serve the same Nebuchadnezzar the king of Babylon, and that will

---

[133] מוֹת תָּמוּת – "in dying, you will die" or when you die, you will be dead – a part of the group called the "dead"

not put their neck under the yoke of the king of Babylon, that nation will I punish, says the Becoming-One, with the sword, and with the famine, and with the pestilence, until I have consumed them by his hand.

9 Therefore listen not you to your prophets, nor to your diviners, nor to your dreamers, nor to your enchanters, nor to your sorcerers, which speak unto you, saying, you shall not serve the king of Babylon:

10 For they prophesy a lie unto you, to remove you far from your land; and that I should drive you out, and you should perish.

11 But the nations that bring their neck under the yoke of the king of Babylon, and serve him, those will I let remain still in their own land, says the Becoming-One; and they shall till it, and dwell therein.

12 I spoke also to Zedekiah king of Judah according to all these words, saying, Bring your necks under the yoke of the king of Babylon, and serve him and his people, and live.

13 Why will you die, you and your people, by the sword, by the famine, and by the pestilence, as the Becoming-One has spoken against the nation that will not serve the king of Babylon?

14 Therefore listen not unto the words of the prophets that speak unto you, saying, you shall not serve the king of Babylon: for they prophesy a lie unto you.

15 For I have not sent them, says the Becoming-One, yet they prophesy a lie in my name; that I might drive you out, and that you might perish, ye, and the prophets that prophesy unto you.

16 Also I spoke to the priests and to all this people, saying, Thus says the Becoming-One; listen not to the words of your prophets that prophesy unto you, saying, Behold, the vessels of the Becoming-One's house shall now shortly be brought again from Babylon: for they prophesy a lie unto you.

17 listen not unto them; serve the king of Babylon, and live: why should this city be laid waste?

18 But if they be prophets, and if the word of the Becoming-One be with them, let them now make intercession to the Becoming-One of hosts, that the vessels which are left in the house of the Becoming-One, and in the house of the king of Judah, and at Jerusalem, go not to Babylon.

19 For thus says the Becoming-One of hosts concerning the pillars, and concerning the sea, and concerning the bases, and concerning the residue of the vessels that remain in this city,

20 Which Nebuchadnezzar king of Babylon took not, when he carried away captive Jeconiah the son of Jehoiakim king of Judah from Jerusalem to Babylon, and all the nobles of Judah and Jerusalem;

21 Yes, thus says the Becoming-One of hosts, God of Israel, concerning the vessels that remain in the house of the Becoming-One, and in the house of the king of Judah and of Jerusalem;

22 They shall be carried to Babylon, and there shall they be until the day that I visit them, says the Becoming-One; then will I bring them up, and restore them to this place.

Jer 28:1 And it came to pass the same year, in the beginning of the reign of Zedekiah king of Judah, in the fourth year, and in the fifth month, that Hananiah the son of Azur the prophet, which was of Gibeon, spoke unto me in the house of the Becoming-One, in the presence of the priests and of all the people, saying,

2 Thus speaks the Becoming-One of hosts, God of Israel, saying, I have broken the yoke of the king of Babylon.

3 Within two years of days will I bring again into this place all the vessels of the Becoming-One's house, that Nebuchadnezzar king of Babylon took away from this place, and carried them to Babylon:

4 And I will bring again to this place Jeconiah the son of Jehoiakim king of Judah, with all the captives of Judah, that went into Babylon, says the Becoming-One: for I will break the yoke of the king of Babylon.

5 Then the prophet Jeremiah said unto the prophet Hananiah in the presence of the priests, and in the presence of all the people that stood in the house of the Becoming-One,

6 Even the prophet Jeremiah said, Amen: the Becoming-One do so: the Becoming-One perform your words which you have prophesied, to bring again the vessels of the Becoming-One's house, and all that is carried away captive, from Babylon into this place.

7 Nevertheless hear you now this word that I speak in your ears, and in the ears of all the people;

8 The prophets that have been before me and before you of olam prophesied both against many countries, and against great kingdoms, of war, and of evil, and of pestilence.

9 The prophet which prophesies of peace, when the word of the prophet shall come to pass, then shall the prophet be known, that the Becoming-One has truly sent him.

10 Then Hananiah the prophet took the yoke from off the prophet Jeremiah's neck, and brake it.

11 And Hananiah spoke in the presence of all the people, saying, Thus says the Becoming-One; Even so will I break the yoke of Nebuchadnezzar king of Babylon from the neck of all nations within the space of two years of days. And the prophet Jeremiah went his way.

12 Then the word of the Becoming-One came unto Jeremiah the prophet, after that Hananiah the prophet had broken the yoke from off the neck of the prophet Jeremiah, saying,

13 Go and tell Hananiah, saying, Thus says the Becoming-One; you have broken the yokes of wood; but you shall make for them yokes of iron.

14 For thus says the Becoming-One of hosts, God of Israel; I have put a yoke of iron upon the neck of all these nations, that they may serve Nebuchadnezzar king of Babylon; and they shall serve him: and I have given him the beasts of the field also.

15 Then said the prophet Jeremiah unto Hananiah the prophet, Hear now, Hananiah; The Becoming-One has not sent you; but you make this people to trust in a lie.

16 Therefore thus says the Becoming-One; Behold, I will cast you from off the face of the earth: this year you shall die, because you have taught rebellion against the Becoming-One.

17 So Hananiah the prophet died the same year in the seventh month.

Jer 29:1 Now these are the words of the letter that Jeremiah the prophet sent from Jerusalem unto the residue of the elders which were carried away captives, and to the priests, and to the prophets, and to all the people whom Nebuchadnezzar had carried away captive from Jerusalem to Babylon;

2 After that Jeconiah the king, and the queen, and the eunuchs, the princes of Judah and Jerusalem, and the carpenters, and the smiths, were departed from Jerusalem;

3 By the hand of Elasah the son of Shaphan, and Gemariah the son of Hilkiah, whom Zedekiah king of Judah sent unto Babylon to Nebuchadnezzar king of Babylon saying,

4 Thus says the Becoming-One of hosts, God of Israel, unto all that are carried away captives, whom I have caused to be carried away from Jerusalem unto Babylon;

5 Build you houses, and dwell in them; and plant gardens, and eat the fruit of them;

5 Build you houses, and dwell in them; and plant gardens, and eat the fruit of them;

6 Take you wives, and beget sons and daughters; and take wives for your sons, and give your daughters to husbands, that they may bear sons and daughters; that you may be increased there, and not diminished.

7 And seek the peace of the city to which I have caused you to be carried away captives, and pray unto the Becoming-One for it: for in the peace thereof shall you have peace.

8 For thus says the Becoming-One of hosts, God of Israel; Let not your prophets and your diviners, that be in the midst of you, deceive you, neither listen to your dreams which you cause to be dreamed.

9 For they prophesy falsely unto you in my name: I have not sent them, says the Becoming-One.

10 For thus says the Becoming-One, That after seventy years be accomplished at Babylon I will visit you, and perform my good word toward you, in causing you to return to this place.

11 For I know the thoughts that I think toward you, says the Becoming-One, thoughts of peace, and not of evil, to give you an expected end.

12 Then shall you call upon me, and you shall go and pray unto me, and I will listen unto you.

13 And you shall seek me, and find me, when you shall search for me with all your heart.

14 And I will be found of you, says the Becoming-One: and I will turn away your captivity, and I will gather you from all the nations, and from all the places to which I have driven you, says the Becoming-One; and I will bring you again into the place from where I caused you to be carried away captive.

15 Because you have said, The Becoming-One has raised us up prophets in Babylon;

16 Know that thus says the Becoming-One of the king that sits upon the throne of David, and of all the people that dwells in this city, and of your brethren that are not gone forth with you into captivity;

17 Thus says the Becoming-One of hosts; Behold, I will send upon them the sword, the famine, and the pestilence, and will make them like vile figs, that cannot be eaten, they are so evil.

18 And I will persecute them with the sword, with the famine, and with the pestilence, and will deliver them to be removed to all the kingdoms of the earth, to be a curse, and an astonishment, and a hissing, and a reproach, among all the nations to which I have driven them:

19 Because they have not listened to my words, says the Becoming-One, which I sent unto them by my servants the prophets, rising up early and sending them; but you would not hear, says the Becoming-One.

20 Hear you therefore the word of the Becoming-One, all you of the captivity, whom I have sent from Jerusalem to Babylon:

21 Thus says the Becoming-One of hosts, God of Israel, of Ahab the son of Kolaiah, and of Zedekiah the son of Maaseiah, which prophesy a lie unto you in my name; Behold, I will deliver them into the hand of Nebuchadrezzar king of Babylon; and he shall slay them before your eyes;

22 And of them shall be taken up a curse by all the captivity of Judah which are in Babylon, saying, The Becoming-One make you like Zedekiah and like Ahab, whom the king of Babylon roasted in the fire;

23 Because they have committed folly in Israel, and have committed adultery with their neighbors' wives, and have spoken lying words in my name, which I have not commanded them; even I know, and am a witness, says the Becoming-One.

24 Thus shall you also speak to Shemaiah the Nehelamite, saying,

25 Thus speaks the Becoming-One of hosts, God of Israel, saying, Because you have sent letters in your name unto all the people that are at Jerusalem, and to Zephaniah the son of Maaseiah the priest, and to all the priests, saying,

26 The Becoming-One has made you priest in the stead of Jehoiada the priest, that you should be officers in the house of the Becoming-One, for every man that is mad, and makes himself a prophet, that you should put him in prison, and in the stocks.

27 Now therefore why have you not reproved Jeremiah of Anathoth, which makes himself a prophet to you?

28 For therefore he sent unto us in Babylon, saying, This captivity is long: build you houses, and dwell in them; and plant gardens, and eat the fruit of them.

29 And Zephaniah the priest read this letter in the ears of Jeremiah the prophet.

30 Then came the word of the Becoming-One unto Jeremiah, saying,

31 Send to all them of the captivity, saying, Thus says the Becoming-One concerning Shemaiah the Nehelamite; Because that Shemaiah has prophesied unto you, and I sent him not, and he caused you to trust in a lie:

32 Therefore thus says the Becoming-One; Behold, I will punish Shemaiah the Nehelamite, and his seed: he shall not have a man to dwell among this people; neither shall he behold the good that I will do for my people, says the Becoming-One; because he has taught rebellion against the Becoming-One.

Jer 30:1 The word that came to Jeremiah from the Becoming-One, saying,

2 Thus speaks the Becoming-One, God of Israel, saying, Write you all the words that I have spoken unto you in a book.

3 For, lo, the days come, says the Becoming-One, that I will bring again the captivity of my people Israel and Judah, says the Becoming-One: and I will cause them to return to the land that I gave to their fathers, and they shall possess it.

4 And these are the words that the Becoming-One spoke concerning Israel and concerning Judah.

5 For thus says the Becoming-One; We have heard a voice of trembling, of fear, and not of peace.

6 Ask you now, and see whether a man does travail with child? therefore do I see every man with his hands on his loins, as a woman in travail, and all faces are turned into paleness?

7 Alas! for that day is great, so that none is like it: it is even the time of Jacob's trouble; but he shall be saved out of it.

8 For it shall come to pass in that day, says the Becoming-One of hosts, that I will break his yoke from off your neck, and will burst your bonds, and strangers shall no more serve themselves of him:

9 But they shall serve the Becoming-One their God, and David their king, whom I will raise up unto them.

10 Therefore fear you not, O my servant Jacob, says the Becoming-One; neither be dismayed, O Israel: for, lo, I will save you from afar, and your seed from the land of their captivity; and Jacob shall return, and shall be in rest, and be quiet, and none shall make him afraid.

11 For I am with you, says the Becoming-One, to save you: though I make a full end of all nations to which I have scattered you, yet will I not make a full end of you: but I will correct you in measure, and will not leave you altogether unpunished.

12 For thus says the Becoming-One, your bruise is incurable, and your wound is grievous.

13 There is none to plead your cause, that you may be bound up: you have no healing medicines.

14 All your lovers have forgotten you; they seek you not; for I have wounded you with the wound of an enemy, with the chastisement of a cruel one, for the multitude of your iniquity; because your sins were increased.

15 Why cry you for your affliction? your sorrow is incurable for the multitude of your iniquity: because your sins were increased, I have done these things unto you.

16 Therefore all they that devour you shall be devoured; and all your adversaries, every one of them, shall go into captivity; and they that spoil you shall be a spoil, and all that prey upon you will I give for a prey.

17 For I will restore health unto you, and I will heal you of your wounds, says the Becoming-One; because they called you an Outcast, saying, This is Zion, whom no man seeks after.

18 Thus says the Becoming-One; Behold, I will bring again the captivity of Jacob's tents, and have mercy on his dwelling places; and the city shall be built upon her own heap, and the palace shall remain after the manner thereof.

19 And out of them shall proceed thanksgiving and the voice of them that make merry: and I will multiply them, and they shall not be few; I will also glorify them, and they shall not be small.

20 Their children also shall be as aforetime, and their congregation shall be established before me, and I will punish all that oppress them.

21 And their nobles shall be of themselves, and their governor shall proceed from the midst of them; and I will cause him to draw near, and he shall approach unto me: for who is this that engaged his heart to approach unto me? says the Becoming-One.

22 And you shall be my people, and I will be your God.

23 Behold, the whirlwind of the Becoming-One goes forth with fury, a continuing whirlwind: it shall fall with pain upon the head of the wicked.

24 The fierce anger of the Becoming-One shall not return, until he have done it, and until he have performed the intents of his heart: in the end of days you shall consider it.

Jer 31:1 At the same time, says the Becoming-One, will I be God of all the families of Israel, and they shall be my people.

2 Thus says the Becoming-One, The people which were left of the sword found grace in the wilderness; even Israel, when I went to cause him to rest.

3 The Becoming-One has appeared of old unto me, saying, Yes, I have loved you with a love of olam: therefore with loving kindness have I drawn you.

4 Again I will build you, and you shall be built, O virgin of Israel: you shall again be adorned with your tabrets, and shall go forth in the dances of them that make merry.

5 you shall yet plant vines upon the mountains of Samaria: the planters shall plant, and shall eat them as common things.

6 For there shall be a day, that the watchmen upon the mount Ephraim shall cry, Arise ye, and let us go up to Zion unto the Becoming-One our God.

7 For thus says the Becoming-One; Sing with gladness for Jacob, and shout among the chief of the nations: publish ye, praise ye, and say, O Becoming-One, save your people, the remnant of Israel.

8 Behold, I will bring them from the north country, and gather them from the coasts of the earth, and with them the blind and the lame, the woman with child and her that travails with child together: a great company shall return there.

9 They shall come with weeping, and with supplications will I lead them: I will cause them to walk by the rivers of waters in a straight way, wherein they shall not stumble: for I am a father to Israel, and Ephraim is my firstborn.

10 Hear the word of the Becoming-One, O you nations, and declare it in the isles afar off, and say, He that scattered Israel will gather him, and keep him, as a shepherd does his flock.

11 For the Becoming-One has redeemed Jacob, and ransomed him from the hand of him that was stronger than he.

12 Therefore they shall come and sing in the height of Zion, and shall flow together to the goodness of the Becoming-One, for wheat, and for wine, and for oil, and for the young of the flock and of

the herd: and their soul shall be as a watered garden; and they shall not sorrow any more at all.

13 Then shall the virgin rejoice in the dance, both young men and old together: for I will turn their mourning into joy, and will comfort them, and make them rejoice from their sorrow.

14 And I will satiate the soul of the priests with fatness, and my people shall be satisfied with my goodness, says the Becoming-One.

15 Thus says the Becoming-One; A voice was heard in Ramah, lamentation, and bitter weeping; Rahel weeping for her children refused to be comforted for her children, because they were not.

16 Thus says the Becoming-One; Refrain your voice from weeping, and your eyes from tears: for your work shall be rewarded, says the Becoming-One; and they shall come again from the land of the enemy.

17 And there is hope in your end, says the Becoming-One, that your children shall come again to their own border.

18 I have surely heard Ephraim bemoaning himself thus; you have chastised me, and I was chastised, as a bullock unaccustomed to the yoke: turn you me, and I shall be turned; for you are the Becoming-One my God.

19 Surely after that I was turned, I repented; and after that I was instructed, I smote upon my thigh: I was ashamed, yes, even confounded, because I did bear the reproach of my youth.

20 Is Ephraim my dear son? is he a pleasant child? for since I spoke against him, I do earnestly remember him still: therefore my bowels are troubled for him; I will surely have mercy upon him, says the Becoming-One.

21 Set you up waymarks, make you high heaps: set your heart toward the highway, even the way which you went: turn again, O virgin of Israel, turn again to these your cities.

22 How long will you go about, O you backsliding daughter? for the Becoming-One has created a new thing in the earth, A female shall encompass with protection a man who is strong.

23 Thus says the Becoming-One of hosts, God of Israel; As yet they shall use this speech in the land of Judah and in the cities thereof, when I shall bring again their captivity; The Becoming-One bless you, O habitation of justice, and mountain of holiness.

24 And there shall dwell in Judah itself, and in all the cities thereof together, husbandmen, and they that go forth with flocks.

25 For I have satiated the weary soul, and I have replenished every sorrowful soul.

26 Upon this I awaked, and beheld; and my sleep was sweet unto me.

27 Behold, the days come, says the Becoming-One, that I will sow the house of Israel and the house of Judah with the seed of man, and with the seed of beast.

28 And it shall come to pass, that like as I have watched over them, to pluck up, and to break down, and to throw down, and to destroy, and to afflict; so will I watch over them, to build, and to plant, says the Becoming-One.

29 In those days they shall say no more, The fathers have eaten a sour grape, and the children's teeth are set on edge.

30 But every one shall die for his own iniquity: every man that eats the sour grape, his teeth shall be set on edge.

31 Behold, the days come, says the Becoming-One, that I will make a new covenant with the house of Israel, and with the house of Judah:

32 Not according to the covenant that I made with their fathers in the day that I took them by the hand to bring them out of the land of Egypt; which my covenant they broke, although I was a husband unto them, says the Becoming-One: 33 But this shall be the covenant that I will make with the house of Israel; After those days, says the Becoming-One, I will put my law in their inner thoughts, and write it in their hearts; and will be their God, and they shall be my people.

34 And they shall teach no more every man his neighbor, and every man his brother, saying, Know the Becoming-One: for they shall all know me, from the least of them unto the greatest of them, says the Becoming-One: for I will forgive their iniquity, and I will remember their sin no more.

35 Thus says the Becoming-One, which gives the sun for a light by day, and the ordinances of the moon and of the stars for a light by night, which divides the sea when the waves thereof roar; The Becoming-One of hosts is his name:

36 If those ordinances depart from before me, says the Becoming-One, then the seed of Israel also shall cease from being a nation before me for all the days.

37 Thus says the Becoming-One; If the heavens above can be measured, and the foundations of the earth searched out beneath, I will also cast off all the seed of Israel for all that they have done, says the Becoming-One.

38 Behold, the days come, says the Becoming-One, that the city shall be built to the Becoming-One from the tower of Hananeel unto the gate of the corner.

39 And the measuring line shall yet go forth over against it upon the hill Gareb, and shall compass about to Goath.

40 And the whole valley of the dead bodies, and of the ashes, and all the fields unto the brook of Kidron, unto the corner of the horse gate toward the east, shall be holy unto the Becoming-One; it shall not be plucked up, nor thrown down any more for olam.

Jer 32:1 The word that came to Jeremiah from the Becoming-One in the tenth year of Zedekiah king of Judah, which was the eighteenth year of Nebuchadrezzar. [587 BC]

2 For then the king of Babylon's army was besieging Jerusalem: and Jeremiah the prophet was shut up in the court of the prison, which was in the king of Judah's house.

3 For Zedekiah king of Judah had shut him up, saying, Why do you prophesy, and say, Thus says the Becoming-One, Behold, I will give this city into the hand of the king of Babylon, and he shall take it;

4 And Zedekiah king of Judah shall not escape out of the hand of the Chaldeans, but shall surely be

delivered into the hand of the king of Babylon, and shall speak with him mouth to mouth, and his eyes shall behold his eyes;

5 And he shall lead Zedekiah to Babylon, and there shall he be until I visit him, says the Becoming-One: though you fight with the Chaldeans, you shall not prosper.

6 And Jeremiah said, The word of the Becoming-One came unto me, saying,

7 Behold, Hanameel the son of Shallum your uncle shall come unto you, saying, Buy you my field that is in Anathoth: for the right of redemption is your to buy it.

8 So Hanameel mine uncle's son came to me in the court of the prison according to the word of the Becoming-One, and said unto me, Buy my field, I pray you, that is in Anathoth, which is in the country of Benjamin: for the right of inheritance is yours, and the redemption is yours; buy it for thyself. Then I knew that this was the word of the Becoming-One.

9 And I bought the field of Hanameel my uncle's son, that was in Anathoth, and weighed him the money, even seventeen shekels of silver.

10 And I subscribed the evidence, and sealed it, and took witnesses, and weighed him the money in the balances.

11 So I took the evidence of the purchase, both that which was sealed according to the law and custom, and that which was open:

12 And I gave the evidence of the purchase unto Baruch the son of Neriah, the son of Maaseiah, in the sight of Hanameel mine uncle's son, and in the presence of the witnesses that subscribed the book of the purchase, before all the Jews that sat in the court of the prison.

13 And I charged Baruch before them, saying,

14 Thus says the Becoming-One of hosts, God of Israel; Take these evidences, this evidence of the purchase, both which is sealed, and this evidence which is open; and put them in an earthen vessel, that they may continue many days.

15 For thus says the Becoming-One of hosts, God of Israel; Houses and fields and vineyards shall be possessed again in this land.

16 Now when I had delivered the evidence of the purchase unto Baruch the son of Neriah, I prayed unto the Becoming-One, saying,

17 Ah my Lord(s) the Becoming-One! behold, you have made the heavens and the earth by your great power and stretched out arm, and there is nothing too hard for you:

18 you show loving-kindness unto thousands, and recompense the iniquity of the fathers into the bosom of their children after them: the Great, the Mighty GOD, the Becoming-One of hosts, is his name,

19 Great in counsel, and mighty in work: for your eyes are open upon all the ways of the sons of men: to give every one according to his ways, and according to the fruit of his doings:

20 Which have set signs and wonders in the land of Egypt, even unto this day, and in Israel, and among other men; and have made you a name, as at this day;

21 And have brought forth your people Israel out of the land of Egypt with signs, and with wonders, and with a strong hand, and with a stretched out arm, and with great terror;

22 And have given them this land, which you did swear to their fathers to give them, a land flowing with milk and honey;

23 And they came in, and possessed it; but they obeyed not your voice, neither walked in your law; they have done nothing of all that you commanded them to do: therefore you have caused all this evil to come upon them:

24 Behold the mounts, they are come unto the city to take it; and the city is given into the hand of the Chaldeans, that fight against it, because of the sword, and of the famine, and of the pestilence: and what you have spoken is come to pass; and, behold, you see it.

25 And you have said unto me, O my Lord(s) the Becoming-One, Buy you the field for money, and take witnesses; for the city is given into the hand of the Chaldeans.

26 Then came the word of the Becoming-One unto Jeremiah, saying,

27 Behold, I am the Becoming-One, God of all flesh: is there anything too hard for me?

28 Therefore thus says the Becoming-One; Behold, I will give this city into the hand of the Chaldeans, and into the hand of Nebuchadrezzar king of Babylon, and he shall take it:

29 And the Chaldeans, that fight against this city, shall come and set fire on this city, and burn it with the houses, upon whose roofs they have offered incense unto the lord [baal] and poured out drink offerings unto other gods, to provoke me to anger.

30 For the children of Israel and the children of Judah have only done evil before me from their youth: for the children of Israel have only provoked me to anger with the work of their hands, says the Becoming-One.

31 For this city has been to me as a provocation of mine anger and of my fury from the day that they built it even unto this day; that I should remove it from before my face,

32 Because of all the evil of the children of Israel and of the children of Judah, which they have done to provoke me to anger, they, their kings, their princes, their priests, and their prophets, and the men of Judah, and the inhabitants of Jerusalem.

33 And they have turned unto me the back, and not the face: though I taught them, rising up early and teaching them, yet they have not listened to receive instruction.

34 But they set their abominations in the house, which is called by my name, to defile it.

35 And they built the high places of the lord [baal] which are in the valley of the son of Hinnom, to cause their sons and their daughters to pass through the fire unto Molech; which I commanded them not, neither came it into my mind, that they should do this abomination, to cause Judah to sin.

36 And now therefore thus says the Becoming-One, God of Israel, concerning this city, whereof you say, It shall be delivered into the hand of the king of Babylon by the sword, and by the famine, and by the pestilence;

37 Behold, I will gather them out of all countries, to which I have driven them in mine anger, and in my fury, and in great wrath; and I will bring them again unto this place, and I will cause them to dwell safely:

38 And they shall be my people, and I will be their God:

39 And I will give them one heart, and one way, that they may fear me for all days, for the good of them, and of their children after them:

40 And I will make a covenant of olam with them, that I will not turn away from them, to do them good; but I will put my fear in their hearts, that they shall not depart from me.

41 Yes, I will rejoice over them to do them good, and I will plant them in this land assuredly with my whole heart and with my whole soul.

42 For thus says the Becoming-One; Like as I have brought all this great evil upon this people, so will I bring upon them all the good that I have promised them.

43 And fields shall be bought in this land, whereof you say, It is desolate without man or beast; it is given into the hand of the Chaldeans.

44 Men shall buy fields for money, and subscribe evidences, and seal them, and take witnesses in the land of Benjamin, and in the places about Jerusalem, and in the cities of Judah, and in the cities of the mountains, and in the cities of the valley, and in the cities of the south: for I will cause their captivity to return, says the Becoming-One.

Jer 33:1 Moreover the word of the Becoming-One came unto Jeremiah the second time, while he was yet shut up in the court of the prison, saying,

2 Thus says the Becoming-One the maker thereof, the Becoming-One that formed it, to establish it; the Becoming-One is his name;

3 Call unto me, and I will answer you, and show you great and mighty things, which you know not.

4 For thus says the Becoming-One, God of Israel, concerning the houses of this city, and concerning the houses of the kings of Judah, which are thrown down by the mounts, and by the sword;

5 They come to fight with the Chaldeans, but it is to fill them with the dead bodies of men, whom I have slain in mine anger and in my fury, and for all whose wickedness I have hid my face from this city.

6 Behold, I will bring it health and cure, and I will cure them, and will reveal unto them the abundance of peace and truth.

7 And I will cause the captivity of Judah and the captivity of Israel to return, and will build them, as at the first.

8 And I will cleanse them from all their iniquity, whereby they have sinned against me; and I will pardon all their iniquities, whereby they have sinned, and whereby they have transgressed against me.

9 And it shall be to me a name of joy, a praise and a honor before all the nations of the earth, which shall hear all the good that I do unto them: and they shall fear and tremble for all the goodness and for all the prosperity that I procure unto it.

10 Thus says the Becoming-One; Again there shall be heard in this place, which you say shall be desolate without man and without beast, even in the cities of Judah, and in the streets of Jerusalem, that are desolate, without man, and without inhabitant, and without beast,

11 The voice of joy, and the voice of gladness, the voice of the bridegroom, and the voice of the bride, the voice of them that shall say, Praise the Becoming-One of hosts: the Becoming-One: surely good, surely mercy is for olam: and of them that shall bring the sacrifice of praise into the house of the Becoming-One. For I will cause to return the captivity of the land, as at the first, says the Becoming-One.

12 Thus says the Becoming-One of hosts; Again in this place, which is desolate without man and without beast, and in all the cities thereof, shall be a habitation of shepherds causing their flocks to lie down.

13 In the cities of the mountains, in the cities of the vale, and in the cities of the south, and in the land of Benjamin, and in the places about Jerusalem, and in the cities of Judah, shall the flocks pass again under the hands of him that tells them, says the Becoming-One.

14 Behold, the days come, says the Becoming-One, that I will perform that good thing which I have promised unto the house of Israel and to the house of Judah.

15 In those days, and at that time, will I cause the Branch of righteousness to grow up unto David; and he shall execute judgment and righteousness in the land.

16 In those days shall Judah be saved, and Jerusalem shall dwell safely: and this is the name wherewith she shall be called, The Becoming-One our righteousness.

17 For thus says the Becoming-One; David shall not lack a man to sit upon the throne of the house of Israel;

18 Neither shall the priests the Levites want a man before me to offer burnt offerings, and to kindle food offerings, and to do sacrifice all the days.

19 And the word of the Becoming-One came unto Jeremiah, saying,

20 Thus says the Becoming-One; If you can break my covenant of the day, and my covenant of the night, and that there should not be day and night in their season;

21 Then may also my covenant be broken with David my servant, that he should not have a son to reign upon his throne; and with the Levites the priests, my ministers.

22 As the host of the heavens cannot be numbered, neither the sand of the sea measured: so will I multiply the seed of David my servant, and the Levites that minister unto me.

23 Moreover the word of the Becoming-One came to Jeremiah, saying,

24 Consider you not what this people have spoken, saying, The two families which the Becoming-One has chosen, he has even cast them off? thus they have despised my people, that they should be no more a nation before them.

25 Thus says the Becoming-One; If my covenant be not with day and night, and if I have not appointed the ordinances of the heavens and earth;

26 Then will I cast away the seed of Jacob, and David my servant, so that I will not take any of his seed to be rulers over the seed of Abraham, Isaac, and Jacob: for I will cause their captivity to return, and have mercy on them.

Jer 34:1 The word which came unto Jeremiah from the Becoming-One, when Nebuchadnezzar king of Babylon, and all his army, and all the kingdoms of the earth of his dominion, and all the people, fought against Jerusalem, and against all the cities thereof, saying,

2 Thus says the Becoming-One, God of Israel; Go and speak to Zedekiah king of Judah, and tell him, Thus says the Becoming-One; Behold, I will give this city into the hand of the king of Babylon, and he shall burn it with fire:

3 And you shall not escape out of his hand, but shall surely be taken, and delivered into his hand; and your eyes shall behold the eyes of the king of Babylon, and he shall speak with you mouth to mouth, and you shall go to Babylon.

4 Yet hear the word of the Becoming-One, O Zedekiah king of Judah; Thus says the Becoming-One of you, you shall not die by the sword:

5 But you shall die in peace: and with the burnings of your fathers, the former kings which were before you, so shall they burn odors for you; and they will lament you, saying, Ah lord! for I have pronounced the word, says the Becoming-One.

6 Then Jeremiah the prophet spoke all these words unto Zedekiah king of Judah in Jerusalem,

7 When the king of Babylon's army fought against Jerusalem, and against all the cities of Judah that were left, against Lachish, and against Azekah: for these fortified cities remained of the cities of Judah.

8 This is the word that came unto Jeremiah from the Becoming-One, after that the king Zedekiah had made a covenant with all the people which were at Jerusalem, to proclaim liberty unto them;

9 That every man should let his manservant, and every man his maidservant, being a Hebrew or a Hebrewess, go free; that none should serve himself of them, to wit, of a Jew his brother.

10 Now when all the princes, and all the people, which had entered into the covenant, heard that every one should let his manservant, and every one his maidservant, go free, that none should serve themselves of them any more, then they obeyed, and let them go.

11 But afterward they turned, and caused the servants and the handmaids, whom they had let go free, to return, and brought them into subjection for servants and for handmaids.

12 Therefore the word of the Becoming-One came to Jeremiah from the Becoming-One, saying,

13 Thus says the Becoming-One, God of Israel; I made a covenant with your fathers in the day that I brought them forth out of the land of Egypt, out of the house of bondmen, saying,

14 At the end of seven years let you go every man his brother a Hebrew, which has been sold unto you; and when he has served you six years, you shall let him go free from you: but your fathers listened not unto me, neither inclined their ear.

15 And you were today turned, and had done right in my sight, in proclaiming liberty every man to his neighbor; and you had made a covenant before me in the house which is called by my name:

16 But you turned and polluted my name, and caused every man his servant, and every man his handmaid, whom he had set at liberty according to their soul, to return, and brought them into subjection, to be unto you for servants and for handmaids.

17 Therefore thus says the Becoming-One; you have not listened unto me, in proclaiming liberty, every one to his brother, and every man to his neighbor: behold, I proclaim a liberty for you, says the Becoming-One, to the sword, to the pestilence, and to the famine; and I will make you to be removed into all the kingdoms of the earth.

18 And I will give the men that have transgressed my covenant, which have not performed the words of the covenant which they had made before me, when they cut the calf in twain, and passed between the parts thereof.

19 The princes of Judah, and the princes of Jerusalem, the eunuchs, and the priests, and all the people of the land, which passed between the parts of the calf;

20 I will even give them into the hand of their enemies, and into the hand of them that seek their soul: and their dead bodies shall be for food unto the fowls of the heaven, and to the beasts of the earth.

21 And Zedekiah king of Judah and his princes will I give into the hand of their enemies, and into the hand of them that seek their soul, and into the hand of the king of Babylon's army, which are gone up from you.

22 Behold, I will command, says the Becoming-One, and cause them to return to this city; and they shall fight against it, and take it, and burn it with fire: and I will make the cities of Judah a desolation without an inhabitant.

Jer 35:1 The word which came unto Jeremiah from the Becoming-One in the days of Jehoiakim the son of Josiah king of Judah, saying,

2 Go unto the house of the Rechabites, and speak unto them, and bring them into the house of the Becoming-One, into one of the chambers, and give them wine to drink.

3 Then I took Jaazaniah the son of Jeremiah, the son of Habaziniah, and his brethren, and all his sons, and the whole house of the Rechabites;

4 And I brought them into the house of the Becoming-One, into the chamber of the sons of Hanan, the son of Igdaliah, a man of God, which was by the chamber of the princes, which was above the chamber of Maaseiah the son of Shallum, the keeper of the door:

5 And I set before the sons of the house of the Rechabites pots full of wine, and cups, and I said unto them, Drink you wine.

6 But they said, We will drink no wine: for Jonadab the son of Rechab our father commanded us, saying, you shall drink no wine, neither ye, nor your sons for olam:

7 Neither shall you build house, nor sow seed, nor plant vineyard, nor have any: but all your days you shall dwell in tents; that you may live many days in the land where you be strangers.

8 Thus have we obeyed the voice of Jonadab the son of Rechab our father in all that he has charged us, to drink no wine all our days, we, our wives, our sons, nor our daughters;

9 Nor to build houses for us to dwell in: neither have we vineyard, nor field, nor seed:

10 But we have dwelt in tents, and have obeyed, and done according to all that Jonadab our father commanded us.

11 But it came to pass, when Nebuchadrezzar king of Babylon came up into the land, that we said, Come, and let us go to Jerusalem for fear of the army of the Chaldeans, and for fear of the army of the Syrians: so we dwell at Jerusalem.

12 Then came the word of the Becoming-One unto Jeremiah, saying,

13 Thus says the Becoming-One of hosts, God of Israel; Go and tell the men of Judah and the inhabitants of Jerusalem, Will you not receive instruction to listen to my words? says the Becoming-One.

14 The words of Jonadab the son of Rechab, that he commanded his sons not to drink wine, are performed; for unto this day they drink none, but obey their father's commandment: notwithstanding I have spoken unto you, rising early and speaking; but you listened not unto me.

15 I have sent also unto you all my servants the prophets, rising up early and sending them, saying, Return you now every man from his evil way, and amend your doings, and go not after other gods to serve them, and you shall dwell in the land which I have given to you and to your fathers: but you have not inclined your ear, nor listened unto me.

16 Because the sons of Jonadab the son of Rechab have performed the commandment of their father, which he commanded them; but this people has not listened unto me:

17 Therefore thus says the Becoming-One, God of hosts, God of Israel; Behold, I will bring upon Judah and upon all the inhabitants of Jerusalem all the evil that I have pronounced against them: because I have spoken unto them, but they have not heard; and I have called unto them, but they have not answered.

18 And Jeremiah said unto the house of the Rechabites, Thus says the Becoming-One of hosts, God of Israel; Because you have obeyed the commandment of Jonadab your father, and kept all his precepts, and done according unto all that he has commanded you:

19 Therefore thus says the Becoming-One of hosts, God of Israel; Jonadab the son of Rechab shall not want a man to stand before me for all the days.

Jer 36:1 And it came to pass in the fourth year of Jehoiakim the son of Josiah king of Judah, that this word came unto Jeremiah from the Becoming-One, saying, **[3370 YM]**

2 Take you a roll of a book, and write therein all the words that I have spoken unto you against Israel, and against Judah, and against all the nations, from the day I spoke unto you, from the days of Josiah, even unto this day. [23rd yr of prophesying]

3 It may be that the house of Judah will hear all the evil which I purpose to do unto them; that they may return every man from his evil way; that I may forgive their iniquity and their sin.

4 Then Jeremiah called Baruch the son of Neriah: and Baruch wrote from the mouth of Jeremiah all the words of the Becoming-One, which he had spoken unto him, upon a roll of a book.

5 And Jeremiah commanded Baruch, saying, I am shut up; I cannot go into the house of the Becoming-One: 6 Therefore go you, and read in the roll, which you have written from my mouth, the words of the Becoming-One in the ears of the people in the Becoming-One's house upon the fasting day: and also you shall read them in the ears of all Judah that come out of their cities.

7 It may be they will present their supplication before the Becoming-One, and will return every one from his evil way: for great is the anger and the fury that the Becoming-One has pronounced against this people.

8 And Baruch the son of Neriah did according to all that Jeremiah the prophet commanded him, reading in the book the words of the Becoming-One in the Becoming-One's house.

9 And it came to pass in the fifth year of Jehoiakim the son of Josiah king of Judah, in the ninth month, that they proclaimed a fast before the Becoming-One to all the people in Jerusalem, and to all the people that came from the cities of Judah unto Jerusalem. **[3371 YM]**

10 Then read Baruch in the book the words of Jeremiah in the house of the Becoming-One, in the chamber of Gemariah the son of Shaphan the scribe, in the higher court, at the entry of the new gate of the Becoming-One's house, in the ears of all the people.

11 When Michaiah the son of Gemariah, the son of Shaphan, had heard out of the book all the words of the Becoming-One,

12 Then he went down into the king's house, into the scribe's chamber: and, lo, all the princes sat there, even Elishama the scribe, and Delaiah the son of Shemaiah, and Elnathan the son of Achbor, and Gemariah the son of Shaphan, and Zedekiah the son of Hananiah, and all the princes.

13 Then Michaiah declared unto them all the words that he had heard, when Baruch read the book in the ears of the people.

14 Therefore all the princes sent Jehudi the son of Nethaniah, the son of Shelemiah, the son of Cushi, unto Baruch, saying, Take in your hand the roll wherein you have read in the ears of the people, and come. So Baruch the son of Neriah took the roll in his hand, and came unto them.

15 And they said unto him, Sit down now, and read it in our ears. So Baruch read it in their ears.

16 Now it came to pass, when they had heard all the words, they were afraid both one and other, and said unto Baruch, We will surely tell the king of all these words.

17 And they asked Baruch, saying, Tell us now, How did you write all these words at his mouth?

18 Then Baruch answered them, He pronounced all these words unto me with his mouth, and I wrote them with ink in the book.

19 Then said the princes unto Baruch, Go, hide you, you and Jeremiah; and let no man know where you be.

20 And they went in to the king into the court, but they laid up the roll in the chamber of Elishama the scribe, and told all the words in the ears of the king.

21 So the king sent Jehudi to fetch the roll: and he took it out of Elishama the scribe's chamber. And Jehudi read it in the ears of the king, and in the ears of all the princes which stood beside the king.

22 Now the king sat in the winterhouse in the ninth month: and there was a fire on the hearth burning before him.

23 And it came to pass, that when Jehudi had read three or four leaves, he cut it with the penknife, and cast it into the fire that was on the hearth, until all the roll was consumed in the fire that was on the hearth.

24 Yet they were not afraid, nor ripped their garments, neither the king, nor any of his servants that heard all these words.

25 Nevertheless Elnathan and Delaiah and Gemariah had made intercession to the king that he would not burn the roll: but he would not hear them.

26 But the king commanded Jerahmeel the son of Hammelech, and Seraiah the son of Azriel, and Shelemiah the son of Abdeel, to take Baruch the scribe and Jeremiah the prophet: but the Becoming-One hid them.

27 Then the word of the Becoming-One came to Jeremiah, after that the king had burned the roll, and the words which Baruch wrote at the mouth of Jeremiah, saying,

28 Take you again another roll, and write in it all the former words that were in the first roll, which Jehoiakim the king of Judah has burned.

29 And you shall say to Jehoiakim king of Judah, Thus says the Becoming-One; you have burned this roll, saying, Why have you written therein, saying, The king of Babylon shall certainly come and destroy this land, and shall cause to cease from there man and beast?

30 Therefore thus says the Becoming-One of Jehoiakim king of Judah; He shall have none to sit upon the throne of David: and his dead body shall be cast out in the day to the heat, and in the night to the frost.

31 And I will punish him and his seed and his servants for their iniquity; and I will bring upon them, and upon the inhabitants of Jerusalem, and upon the men of Judah, all the evil that I have pronounced against them; but they listened not.

32 Then took Jeremiah another roll, and gave it to Baruch the scribe, the son of Neriah; who wrote therein from the mouth of Jeremiah all the words of the book which Jehoiakim king of Judah had burned in the fire: and there were added besides unto them many like words.

Jer 37:1 And king Zedekiah the son of Josiah reigned instead of Coniah the son of Jehoiakim, whom Nebuchadrezzar king of Babylon made king in the land of Judah.

2 But neither he, nor his servants, nor the people of the land, did listen unto the words of the Becoming-One, which he spoke by the prophet Jeremiah.

3 And Zedekiah the king sent Jehucal the son of Shelemiah and Zephaniah the son of Maaseiah the priest to the prophet Jeremiah, saying, Pray now unto the Becoming-One our God for us.

4 Now Jeremiah came in and went out among the people: for they had not put him into prison.

5 Then Pharaoh's army was come forth out of Egypt: and when the Chaldeans that besieged Jerusalem heard tidings of them, they departed from Jerusalem.

6 Then came the word of the Becoming-One unto the prophet Jeremiah, saying,

7 Thus says the Becoming-One, God of Israel; Thus shall you say to the king of Judah, that sent you unto me to inquire of me; Behold, Pharaoh's army, which is come forth to help you, shall return to Egypt into their own land.

8 And the Chaldeans shall come again, and fight against this city, and take it, and burn it with fire.

9 Thus says the Becoming-One; Deceive not your souls, saying, The Chaldeans shall surely depart from us: for they shall not depart.

10 For though you had struck the whole army of the Chaldeans that fight against you, and there remained but wounded men among them, yet should they rise up every man in his tent, and burn this city with fire.

11 And it came to pass, that when the army of the Chaldeans was broken up from Jerusalem for fear of Pharaoh's army,

12 Then Jeremiah went forth out of Jerusalem to go into the land of Benjamin, to separate himself there in the midst of the people.

13 And when he was in the gate of Benjamin, a captain of the ward was there, whose name was Irijah, the son of Shelemiah, the son of Hananiah; and he took Jeremiah the prophet, saying, you fall away to the Chaldeans.

14 Then said Jeremiah, It is false; I fall not away to the Chaldeans. But he listened not to him: so Irijah took Jeremiah, and brought him to the princes.

15 Therefore the princes were angry with Jeremiah, and smote him, and put him in prison in the house of Jonathan the scribe: for they had made that the prison.

16 When Jeremiah was entered into the dungeon, and into the cabins, and Jeremiah had remained there many days;

17 Then Zedekiah the king sent, and took him out: and the king asked him secretly in his house, and said, Is there any word from the Becoming-One? And Jeremiah said, There is: for, said he, you shall be delivered into the hand of the king of Babylon.

18 Moreover Jeremiah said unto king Zedekiah, What have I offended against you, or against your servants, or against this people, that you have put me in prison?

19 Where are now your prophets which prophesied unto you, saying, The king of Babylon shall not come against you, nor against this land?

20 Therefore hear now, I pray you, O my lord the king: let my supplication, I pray you, be accepted before you; that you cause me not to return to the house of Jonathan the scribe, lest I die there.

21 Then Zedekiah the king commanded that they should commit Jeremiah into the court of the prison, and that they should give him daily a piece of bread out of the bakers' street, until all the bread in the city were spent. Thus Jeremiah remained in the court of the prison.

Jer 38:1 Then Shephatiah the son of Mattan, and Gedaliah the son of Pashur, and Jucal the son of Shelemiah, and Pashur the son of Malchiah, heard the words that Jeremiah had spoken unto all the people, saying,

2 Thus says the Becoming-One, He that remains in this city shall die by the sword, by the famine, and by the pestilence: but he that goes forth to the Chaldeans shall live; for he shall have his soul for a prey, and shall live.

3 Thus says the Becoming-One, This city shall surely be given into the hand of the king of Babylon's army, which shall take it.

4 Therefore the princes said unto the king, We beg you, let this man be put to death: for thus he weakens the hands of the men of war that remain in this city, and the hands of all the people, in speaking such words unto them: for this man seeks not the welfare of this people, but the hurt.

5 Then Zedekiah the king said, Behold, he is in your hand: for the king is not he that can do anything against you.

6 Then took they Jeremiah, and cast him into the dungeon of Malchiah the son of Hammelech, that was in the court of the prison: and they let down Jeremiah with cords. And in the dungeon there was no water, but mire: so Jeremiah sunk in the mire.

7 Now when Ebedmelech the Ethiopian, one of the eunuchs which was in the king's house, heard that they had put Jeremiah in the dungeon; the king then sitting in the gate of Benjamin;

8 Ebedmelech went forth out of the king's house, and spoke to the king, saying,

9 My lord the king, these men have done evil in all that they have done to Jeremiah the prophet, whom they have cast into the dungeon; and he is like to die for hunger in the place where he is: for there is no more bread in the city.

10 Then the king commanded Ebedmelech the Ethiopian, saying, Take from hence thirty men with you, and take up Jeremiah the prophet out of the dungeon, before he die.

11 So Ebedmelech took the men with him, and went into the house of the king under the treasury, and took there old cast clouts and old rotten rags, and let them down by cords into the dungeon to Jeremiah.

12 And Ebedmelech the Ethiopian said unto Jeremiah, Put now these old cast clouts and rotten rags under your armholes under the cords. And Jeremiah did so.

13 So they drew up Jeremiah with cords, and took him up out of the dungeon: and Jeremiah remained in the court of the prison.

14 Then Zedekiah the king sent, and took Jeremiah the prophet unto him into the third entry that is in the house of the Becoming-One: and the king said unto Jeremiah, I will ask you a thing; hide nothing from me.

15 Then Jeremiah said unto Zedekiah, If I declare it unto you, will you not surely put me to death? and if I give you counsel, will you not listen unto me?

16 So Zedekiah the king swore secretly unto Jeremiah, saying, As the Becoming-One lives, that made us this soul, I will not put you to death, neither will I give you into the hand of these men that seek your soul.

17 Then said Jeremiah unto Zedekiah, Thus says the Becoming-One, God of hosts, God of Israel; If you will assuredly go forth unto the king of Babylon's princes, then your soul shall live, and this city shall not be burned with fire; and you shall live, and your house:

18 But if you will not go forth to the king of Babylon's princes, then shall this city be given into the hand of the Chaldeans, and they shall burn it with fire, and you shall not escape out of their hand.

19 And Zedekiah the king said unto Jeremiah, I am afraid of the Jews that are fallen to the Chaldeans, lest they deliver me into their hand, and they mock me.

20 But Jeremiah said, They shall not deliver you. Obey, I beg you, the voice of the Becoming-One, which I speak unto you: so it shall be well unto you, and your soul shall live.

21 But if you refuse to go forth, this is the word that the Becoming-One has showed me:

22 And, behold, all the women that are left in the king of Judah's house shall be brought forth to the king of Babylon's princes, and those women shall say, your friends have set you on, and have prevailed against you: your feet are sunk in the mire, and they are turned away back.

23 So they shall bring out all your wives and your children to the Chaldeans: and you shall not escape out of their hand, but shall be taken by the hand of the king of Babylon: and you shall cause this city to be burned with fire.

24 Then said Zedekiah unto Jeremiah, Let no man know of these words, and you shall not die.

25 But if the princes hear that I have talked with you, and they come unto you, and say unto you, Declare unto us now what you have said unto the king, hide it not from us, and we will not put you to death; also what the king said unto you:

26 Then you shall say unto them, I presented my supplication before the king, that he would not cause me to return to Jonathan's house, to die there.

27 Then came all the princes unto Jeremiah, and asked him: and he told them according to all these words that the king had commanded. So they left off speaking with him; for the matter was not perceived.

28 So Jeremiah abode in the court of the prison until the day that Jerusalem was taken: and he was there when Jerusalem was taken.

Jer 39:1 In the ninth year of Zedekiah king of Judah, in the tenth month **[3386 YM]**, came Nebuchadrezzar king of Babylon and all his army against Jerusalem, and they besieged it.

2 And in the eleventh year of Zedekiah, in the fourth month, the ninth day of the month, the city was broken up. **[3388 YM]**

3 And all the princes of the king of Babylon came in, and sat in the middle gate, even Nergalsharezer, Samgarnebo, Sarsechim, Rabsaris [or chief of the eunuchs] Nergalsharezer, Rabmag, with all the residue of the princes of the king of Babylon.

4 And it came to pass, that when Zedekiah the king of Judah saw them, and all the men of war, then they fled, and went forth out of the city by night, by

the way of the king's garden, by the gate between the two walls: and he went out the way of the plain.

5 But the Chaldeans' army pursued after them, and overtook Zedekiah in the plains of Jericho: and when they had taken him, they brought him up to Nebuchadnezzar king of Babylon to Riblah in the land of Hamath, where he gave judgment upon him.

6 Then the king of Babylon killed the sons of Zedekiah in Riblah before his eyes: also the king of Babylon killed all the nobles of Judah.

7 Moreover he put out Zedekiah's eyes, and bound him with chains, to carry him to Babylon.

8 And the Chaldeans burned the king's house, and the houses of the people, with fire, and brake down the walls of Jerusalem.

9 Then Nebuzaradan the captain of the guard carried away captive into Babylon the remnant of the people that remained in the city, and those that fell away, that fell to him, with the rest of the people that remained.

10 But Nebuzaradan the captain of the guard left of the poor of the people, which had nothing, in the land of Judah, and gave them vineyards and fields at the same day.

11 Now Nebuchadrezzar king of Babylon gave charge concerning Jeremiah to Nebuzaradan the captain of the guard, saying,

12 Take him, and look well to him, and do him no harm; but do unto him even as he shall say unto you.

13 So Nebuzaradan the captain of the guard sent, and Nebushasban, Rabsaris [or chief of the eunuchs] and Nergalsharezer, Rabmag, and all the king of Babylon's princes;

14 Even they sent, and took Jeremiah out of the court of the prison, and committed him unto Gedaliah the son of Ahikam the son of Shaphan, that he should carry him home: so he dwelt among the people.

15 Now the word of the Becoming-One came unto Jeremiah, while he was shut up in the court of the prison, saying,

16 Go and speak to Ebedmelech the Ethiopian, saying, Thus says the Becoming-One of hosts, God of Israel; Behold, I will bring my words upon this city for evil, and not for good; and they shall be accomplished in that day before you.

17 But I will deliver you in that day, says the Becoming-One: and you shall not be given into the hand of the men of whom you are afraid.

18 For I will surely deliver you, and you shall not fall by the sword, but your soul shall be for a prey unto you: because you have put your trust in me, says the Becoming-One.

Jer 40:1 The word that came to Jeremiah from the Becoming-One, after that Nebuzaradan the captain of the guard had let him go from Ramah, when he had taken him being bound in chains among all that were carried away captive of Jerusalem and Judah, which were carried away captive unto Babylon.

2 And the captain of the guard took Jeremiah, and said unto him, The Becoming-One your God has pronounced this evil upon this place.

3 Now the Becoming-One has brought it, and done according as he has said: because you have sinned against the Becoming-One, and have not obeyed his voice, therefore this thing is come upon you.

4 And now, behold, I loose you this day from the chains which were upon your hand. If it seem good unto you to come with me into Babylon, come; and I will look well unto you: but if it seem ill unto you to come with me into Babylon, forbear: behold, all the land is before you: to which it seems good and convenient for you to go, there go.

5 Now while he was not yet gone back, he said, Go back also to Gedaliah the son of Ahikam the son of Shaphan, whom the king of Babylon has made governor over the cities of Judah, and dwell with him among the people: or go wheresoever it seems convenient unto you to go. So the captain of the guard gave him victuals and a reward, and let him go.

6 Then went Jeremiah unto Gedaliah the son of Ahikam to Mizpah; and dwelt with him among the people that were left in the land.

7 Now when all the captains of the forces which were in the fields, even they and their men, heard that the king of Babylon had made Gedaliah the son of Ahikam governor in the land, and had committed unto him men, and women, and children, and of the poor of the land, of them that were not carried away captive to Babylon;

8 Then they came to Gedaliah to Mizpah, even Ishmael the son of Nethaniah, and Johanan and Jonathan the sons of Kareah, and Seraiah the son of Tanhumeth, and the sons of Ephai the Netophathite, and Jezaniah the son of a Maachathite, they and their men.

9 And Gedaliah the son of Ahikam the son of Shaphan swore unto them and to their men, saying, Fear not to serve the Chaldeans: dwell in the land, and serve the king of Babylon, and it shall be well with you.

10 As for me, behold, I will dwell at Mizpah, to serve the Chaldeans, which will come unto us: but ye, gather you wine, and summer fruits, and oil, and put them in your vessels, and dwell in your cities that you have taken.

11 Likewise when all the Jews that were in Moab, and among the Ammonites, and in Edom, and that were in all the countries, heard that the king of Babylon had left a remnant of Judah, and that he had set over them Gedaliah the son of Ahikam the son of Shaphan;

12 Even all the Jews returned out of all places to which they were driven, and came to the land of Judah, to Gedaliah, unto Mizpah, and gathered wine and summer fruits very much.

13 Moreover Johanan the son of Kareah, and all the captains of the forces that were in the fields, came to Gedaliah to Mizpah,

14 And said unto him, do you certainly know that the lord [baal] is the king of the Ammonites has sent Ishmael the son of Nethaniah to slay you soul? But Gedaliah the son of Ahikam believed them not.

15 Then Johanan the son of Kareah spoke to Gedaliah in Mizpah secretly, saying, Let me go, I pray you, and I will slay Ishmael the son of Nethaniah, and no man shall know it: why should he slay you soul, that all the Jews which are gathered unto you should be scattered, and the remnant in Judah perish?

16 But Gedaliah the son of Ahikam said unto Johanan the son of Kareah, you shall not do this thing: for you speak falsely of Ishmael.

Jer 41:1 Now it came to pass in the seventh month, that Ishmael the son of Nethaniah the son of Elishama, of the seed royal, and the princes of the king, even ten men with him, came unto Gedaliah the son of Ahikam to Mizpah; and there they did eat bread together in Mizpah.

2 Then arose Ishmael the son of Nethaniah, and the ten men that were with him, and smote Gedaliah the son of Ahikam the son of Shaphan with the sword, and killed him, whom the king of Babylon had made governor over the land.

3 Ishmael also killed all the Jews that were with him, even with Gedaliah, at Mizpah, and the Chaldeans that were found there, and the men of war.

4 And it came to pass the second day after he had slain Gedaliah, and no man knew it,

5 That there came certain from Shechem, from Shiloh, and from Samaria, even fourscore men, having their beards shaven, and their clothes rent, and having cut themselves, with offerings and incense in their hand, to bring them to the house of the Becoming-One.

6 And Ishmael the son of Nethaniah went forth from Mizpah to meet them, weeping all along as he went: and it came to pass, as he met them, he said unto them, Come to Gedaliah the son of Ahikam.

7 And it was so, when they came into the midst of the city, that Ishmael the son of Nethaniah killed them, and cast them into the midst of the pit, he, and the men that were with him.

8 But ten men were found among them that said unto Ishmael, Slay us not: for we have treasures in the field, of wheat, and of barley, and of oil, and of honey. So he forbare, and killed them not among their brethren.

9 Now the pit wherein Ishmael had cast all the dead bodies of the men, whom he had slain because of Gedaliah, was it which Asa the king had made for fear of Baasha king of Israel: and Ishmael the son of Nethaniah filled it with them that were slain.

10 Then Ishmael carried away captive all the residue of the people that were in Mizpah, even the king's daughters, and all the people that remained in Mizpah, whom Nebuzaradan the captain of the guard had committed to Gedaliah the son of Ahikam: and Ishmael the son of Nethaniah carried them away captive, and departed to go over to the Ammonites.

11 But when Johanan the son of Kareah, and all the captains of the forces that were with him, heard of all the evil that Ishmael the son of Nethaniah had done,

12 Then they took all the men, and went to fight with Ishmael the son of Nethaniah, and found him by the great waters that are in Gibeon.

13 Now it came to pass, that when all the people which were with Ishmael saw Johanan the son of Kareah, and all the captains of the forces that were with him, then they were glad.

14 So all the people that Ishmael had carried away captive from Mizpah cast about and returned, and went unto Johanan the son of Kareah.

15 But Ishmael the son of Nethaniah escaped from Johanan with eight men, and went to the Ammonites.

16 Then took Johanan the son of Kareah, and all the captains of the forces that were with him, all the remnant of the people whom he had recovered from Ishmael the son of Nethaniah, from Mizpah, after that he had slain Gedaliah the son of Ahikam, even mighty men of war, and the women, and the children, and the eunuchs, whom he had brought again from Gibeon:

17 And they departed, and dwelt in the habitation of Chimham, which is by Bethlehem, to go to enter into Egypt,

18 Because of the Chaldeans: for they were afraid of them, because Ishmael the son of Nethaniah had slain Gedaliah the son of Ahikam, whom the king of Babylon made governor in the land.

Jer 42:1 Then all the captains of the forces, and Johanan the son of Kareah, and Jezaniah the son of Hoshaiah, and all the people from the least even unto the greatest, came near,

2 And said unto Jeremiah the prophet, Let, we beseech you, our supplication be accepted before you, and pray for us unto the Becoming-One your God, even for all this remnant; for we are left but a few of many, as your eyes do behold us:

3 That the Becoming-One your God may show us the way wherein we may walk, and the thing that we may do.

4 Then Jeremiah the prophet said unto them, I have heard you; behold, I will pray unto the Becoming-One your God according to your words; and it shall come to pass, that whatsoever thing the Becoming-One shall answer you, I will declare it unto you; I will keep nothing back from you.

5 Then they said to Jeremiah, The Becoming-One be a true and faithful witness between us, if we do not even according to all things for the which the Becoming-One your God shall send you to us.

6 Whether it be good, or whether it be evil, we will obey the voice of the Becoming-One our God, to whom we send you; that it may be well with us, when we obey the voice of the Becoming-One our God.

7 And it came to pass at the end of ten days, that the word of the Becoming-One came unto Jeremiah.

8 Then called he Johanan the son of Kareah, and all the captains of the forces which were with him, and all the people from the least even to the greatest,

9 And said unto them, Thus says the Becoming-One, God of Israel, unto whom you sent me to present your supplication before him;

10 If you will still abide in this land, then will I build you, and not pull you down, and I will plant you, and not pluck you up: for I repent me of the evil that I have done unto you.

11 Be not afraid of the king of Babylon, of whom you are afraid; be not afraid of him, says the Becoming-One: for I am with you to save you, and to deliver you from his hand.

12 And I will show mercies unto you, that he may have mercy upon you, and cause you to return to your own land.

13 But if you say, We will not dwell in this land, neither obey the voice of the Becoming-One your God,

14 Saying, No; but we will go into the land of Egypt, where we shall see no war, nor hear the sound of the trumpet, nor have hunger of bread; and there will we dwell:

15 And now therefore hear the word of the Becoming-One, you remnant of Judah; Thus says the Becoming-One of hosts, God of Israel; If you wholly set your faces to enter into Egypt, and go to sojourn there;

16 Then it shall come to pass, that the sword, which you feared, shall overtake you there in the land of Egypt, and the famine, whereof you were afraid, shall follow close after you there in Egypt; and there you shall die.

17 So shall it be with all the men that set their faces to go into Egypt to sojourn there; they shall die by the sword, by the famine, and by the pestilence: and none of them shall remain or escape from the evil that I will bring upon them.

18 For thus says the Becoming-One of hosts, God of Israel; As mine anger and my fury has been poured forth upon the inhabitants of Jerusalem; so shall my fury be poured forth upon you, when you shall enter into Egypt: and you shall be an execration, and an astonishment, and a curse, and a reproach; and you shall see this place no more.

19 The Becoming-One has said concerning you, O you remnant of Judah; Go you not into Egypt: know certainly that I have admonished you this day.

20 For you dissembled in your souls, when you sent me unto the Becoming-One your God, saying, Pray for us unto the Becoming-One our God; and according unto all that the Becoming-One our God shall say, so declare unto us, and we will do it.

21 And now I have this day declared it to you; but you have not obeyed the voice of the Becoming-One your God, nor anything for the which he has sent me unto you.

22 Now therefore know certainly that you shall die by the sword, by the famine, and by the pestilence, in the place to which you desire to go and to sojourn.

Jer 43:1 And it came to pass, that when Jeremiah had made an end of speaking unto all the people all the words of the Becoming-One their God, for which the Becoming-One their God had sent him to them, even all these words,

2 Then spoke Azariah the son of Hoshaiah, and Johanan the son of Kareah, and all the proud men, saying unto Jeremiah, you speak falsely: the Becoming-One our God has not sent you to say, Go not into Egypt to sojourn there:

3 But Baruch the son of Neriah sets you on against us, for to deliver us into the hand of the Chaldeans, that they might put us to death, and carry us away captives into Babylon.

4 So Johanan the son of Kareah, and all the captains of the forces, and all the people, obeyed not the voice of the Becoming-One, to dwell in the land of Judah.

5 But Johanan the son of Kareah, and all the captains of the forces, took all the remnant of Judah, that were returned from all nations, to which they had been driven, to dwell in the land of Judah;

6 Even men, and women, and children, and the king's daughters, and every soul that Nebuzaradan the captain of the guard had left with Gedaliah the son of Ahikam the son of Shaphan, and Jeremiah the prophet, and Baruch the son of Neriah.

7 So they came into the land of Egypt: for they obeyed not the voice of the Becoming-One: thus came they even to Tahpanhes.

8 Then came the word of the Becoming-One unto Jeremiah in Tahpanhes, saying,

9 Take great stones in your hand, and hide them in the clay in the brickkiln, which is at the entry of Pharaoh's house in Tahpanhes, in the sight of the men of Judah;

10 And say unto them, Thus says the Becoming-One of hosts, God of Israel; Behold, I will send and take Nebuchadrezzar the king of Babylon, my servant, and will set his throne upon these stones that I have hid; and he shall spread his royal pavilion over them.

11 And when he comes, he shall smite the land of Egypt, and deliver such as are for death to death; and such as are for captivity to captivity; and such as are for the sword to the sword.

12 And I will kindle a fire in the houses of the gods of Egypt; and he shall burn them, and carry them away captives: and he shall array himself with the land of Egypt, as a shepherd puts on his garment; and he shall go forth from there in peace.

13 He shall break also the images of Beth-shemesh, that is in the land of Egypt; and the houses of the gods of the Egyptians shall he burn with fire.

Jer 44:1 The word that came to Jeremiah concerning all the Jews which dwell in the land of Egypt, which dwell at Migdol, and at Tahpanhes, and at Noph, and in the country of Pathros, saying,

2 Thus says the Becoming-One of hosts, God of Israel; you have seen all the evil that I have brought upon Jerusalem, and upon all the cities of Judah; and, behold, this day they are a desolation, and no man dwells therein,

3 Because of their wickedness which they have committed to provoke me to anger, in that they went to burn incense, and to serve other gods, whom they knew not, neither they, ye, nor your fathers.

4 Howbeit I sent unto you all my servants the prophets, rising early and sending them, saying, Oh, do not this abominable thing that I hate.

5 But they listened not, nor inclined their ear to turn from their wickedness, to burn no incense unto other gods.

6 Therefore my fury and mine anger was poured forth, and was kindled in the cities of Judah and in the streets of Jerusalem; and they are wasted and desolate, as at this day.

7 Therefore now thus says the Becoming-One, God of hosts, God of Israel; Why commit you this great evil against your souls, to cut off from you man and woman, child and suckling, out of Judah, to leave you none to remain;

8 In that you provoke me unto wrath with the works of your hands, burning incense unto other gods in the land of Egypt, to which you have gone to dwell, that you might cut yourselves off, and that you might be a curse and a reproach among all the nations of the earth?

9 Have you forgotten the wickedness of your fathers, and the wickedness of the kings of Judah, and the wickedness of their wives, and your own wickedness, and the wickedness of your wives, which they have committed in the land of Judah, and in the streets of Jerusalem?

10 They are not humbled even unto this day, neither have they feared, nor walked in my law, nor in my statutes, that I set before you and before your fathers.

11 Therefore thus says the Becoming-One of hosts, God of Israel; Behold, I will set my face against you for evil, and to cut off all Judah.

12 And I will take the remnant of Judah, that have set their faces to go into the land of Egypt to sojourn there, and they shall all be consumed, and fall in the land of Egypt; they shall even be consumed by the sword and by the famine: they shall die, from the least even unto the greatest, by the sword and by the famine: and they shall be an execration, and an astonishment, and a curse, and a reproach.

13 For I will punish them that dwell in the land of Egypt, as I have punished Jerusalem, by the sword, by the famine, and by the pestilence:

14 So that none of the remnant of Judah, which are gone into the land of Egypt to sojourn there, shall escape or remain, that they should return into the land of Judah, to the which they have a desire of thier soul to return to dwell there: for none shall return but such as shall escape.

15 Then all the men which knew that their wives had burned incense unto other gods, and all the women that stood by, a great multitude, even all the people that dwelt in the land of Egypt, in Pathros, answered Jeremiah, saying,

16 As for the word that you have spoken unto us in the name of the Becoming-One, we will not listen unto you.

17 But we will certainly do whatsoever thing goes forth out of our own mouth, to burn incense unto the queen of heaven, and to pour out drink offerings unto her, as we have done, we, and our fathers, our kings, and our princes, in the cities of Judah, and in the streets of Jerusalem: for then had we plenty of victuals, and were well, and saw no evil.

18 But since we left off to burn incense to the queen of heaven, and to pour out drink offerings unto her, we have wanted all things, and have been consumed by the sword and by the famine.

19 And when we burned incense to the queen of heaven, and poured out drink offerings unto her, did we make her cakes to worship her, and pour out drink offerings unto her, without our men?

20 Then Jeremiah said unto all the people, to the men, and to the women, and to all the people which had given him that answer, saying,

21 The incense that you burned in the cities of Judah, and in the streets of Jerusalem, ye, and your fathers, your kings, and your princes, and the people of the land, did not the Becoming-One remember them, and came it not into his mind?

22 So that the Becoming-One could no longer bear, because of the evil of your doings, and because of the abominations which you have committed; therefore is your land a desolation, and an astonishment, and a curse, without an inhabitant, as at this day.

23 Because you have burned incense, and because you have sinned against the Becoming-One, and have not obeyed the voice of the Becoming-One, nor walked in his law, nor in his statutes, nor in his testimonies; therefore this evil is happened unto you, as at this day.

24 Moreover Jeremiah said unto all the people, and to all the women, Hear the word of the Becoming-One, all Judah that are in the land of Egypt:

25 Thus says the Becoming-One of hosts, God of Israel, saying; you and your wives have both spoken with your mouths, and fulfilled with your hand, saying, We will surely perform our vows that we have vowed, to burn incense to the queen of heaven, and to pour out drink offerings unto her: you will surely accomplish your vows, and surely perform your vows.

26 Therefore hear you the word of the Becoming-One, all Judah that dwell in the land of Egypt; Behold, I have sworn by my great name, says the Becoming-One, that my name shall no more be named in the mouth of any man of Judah in all the land of Egypt, saying, My Lord(s) the Becoming-One lives.

27 Behold, I will watch over them for evil, and not for good: and all the men of Judah that are in the land of Egypt shall be consumed by the sword and by the famine, until there be an end of them.

28 Yet a small number that escape the sword shall return out of the land of Egypt into the land of Judah, and all the remnant of Judah, that are gone into the land of Egypt to sojourn there, shall know whose words shall stand, mine, or theirs.

29 And this shall be a sign unto you, says the Becoming-One, that I will punish you in this place, that you may know that my words shall surely stand against you for evil:

30 Thus says the Becoming-One; Behold, I will give Pharaoh-hophra king of Egypt into the hand of his enemies, and into the hand of them that seek his soul; as I gave Zedekiah king of Judah into the hand of Nebuchadrezzar king of Babylon, his enemy, and that sought his life.

Jer 45:1 The word that Jeremiah the prophet spoke unto Baruch the son of Neriah, when he had written these words in a book at the mouth of Jeremiah, in the fourth year of Jehoiakim **[3370 YM]** the son of Josiah king of Judah, saying,

2 Thus says the Becoming-One, God of Israel, unto you, O Baruch;

3 you did say, Woe is me now! for the Becoming-One has added grief to my sorrow; I fainted in my sighing, and I find no rest.

4 Thus shall you say unto him, The Becoming-One says thus; Behold, that which I have built will I break down, and that which I have planted I will pluck up, even this whole land.

5 And seek you great things for thyself? seek them not: for, behold, I will bring evil upon all flesh, says the Becoming-One: but your soul will I give unto you for a prey in all places to which you go.

Jer 46:1 The word of the Becoming-One which came to Jeremiah the prophet against the nations;

2 Against Egypt, against the army of Pharaoh-necho king of Egypt, which was by the river Euphrates in Carchemish, which Nebuchadrezzar king of Babylon smote in the fourth year of Jehoiakim the son of Josiah king of Judah. **[3370 YM / 604 BC]**

3 Order you the buckler and shield, and draw near to battle.

4 Harness the horses; and get up, you horsemen, and stand forth with your helmets; furbish the spears, and put on the brigandines.

5 Therefore have I seen them dismayed and turned away back? and their mighty ones are beaten down, and are fled apace, and look not back: for fear was round about, says the Becoming-One.

6 Let not the swift flee away, nor the mighty man escape; they shall stumble, and fall toward the north by the river Euphrates.

7 Who is this that comes up as a flood, whose waters are moved as the rivers?

8 Egypt rises up like a flood, and his waters are moved like the rivers; and he says, I will go up, and will cover the earth; I will destroy the city and the inhabitants thereof.

9 Come up, you horses; and rage, you chariots; and let the mighty men come forth; the Ethiopians and the Libyans, that handle the shield; and the Lydians, that handle and bend the bow.

10 For this is the day of my Lord(s) the Becoming-One of hosts, a day of vengeance, that he may avenge him of his adversaries: and the sword shall devour, and it shall be satisfied and filled their blood: for my Lord(s) the Becoming-One of hosts has a sacrifice in the north country by the river Euphrates.

11 Go up into Gilead, and take balm, O virgin, the daughter of Egypt: in vain shall you use many medicines; for you shall not be cured.

12 The nations have heard of your shame, and your cry has filled the land: for the mighty man has stumbled against the mighty, and they are fallen both together.

13 The word that the Becoming-One spoke to Jeremiah the prophet, how Nebuchadrezzar king of Babylon should come and smite the land of Egypt.

14 Declare you in Egypt, and publish in Migdol, and publish in Noph and in Tahpanhes: say ye, Stand firm, and prepare you; for the sword shall devour round about you.

15 Why are your valiant men swept away? they stood not, because the Becoming-One did drive them.

16 He made many to fall, yes, one fell upon another: and they said, Arise, and let us go again to our own people, and to the land of our nativity, from the oppressing sword.

17 They did cry there, Pharaoh king of Egypt is but a noise; he has passed the set time.[134]

18 As I live, says the King, whose name is the Becoming-One of hosts, Surely as Tabor is among the mountains, and as Carmel by the sea, so shall he come.

19 O you daughter dwelling in Egypt, furnish yourself to go into captivity: for Noph shall be waste and desolate without an inhabitant.

20 Egypt is like a very fair heifer, but destruction comes; it comes out of the north.

21 Also her hired men are in the midst of her like fatted bullocks; for they also are turned back, and are fled away together: they did not stand, because the day of their calamity was come upon them, and the time of their visitation.

22 The voice thereof shall go like a serpent; for they shall march with an army, and come against her with axes, as hewers of wood.

23 They shall cut down her forest, says the Becoming-One, though it cannot be searched; because they are more than the grasshoppers, and are innumerable.

24 The daughter of Egypt shall be confounded; she shall be delivered into the hand of the people of the north.

25 The Becoming-One of hosts, God of Israel, says; Behold, I will punish the multitude of No, and Pharaoh, and Egypt, with their gods, and their kings; even Pharaoh, and all them that trust in him:

26 And I will deliver them into the hand of those that seek their souls, and into the hand of Nebuchadrezzar king of Babylon, and into the hand of his servants: and afterward it shall be inhabited, as in the days of old, says the Becoming-One.

27 But fear not you, O my servant Jacob, and be not dismayed, O Israel: for, behold, I will save you from afar off, and your seed from the land of their captivity; and Jacob shall return, and be in rest and at ease, and none shall make him afraid.

28 Fear you not, O Jacob my servant, says the Becoming-One: for I am with you; for I will make a full end of all the nations to which I have driven you: but I will not make a full end of you, but correct you in measure; yet will I not leave you wholly unpunished.

Jer 47:1 The word of the Becoming-One that came to Jeremiah the prophet against the Philistines, before that Pharaoh smote Gaza.

2 Thus says the Becoming-One; Behold, waters rise up out of the north, and shall be an overflowing flood, and shall overflow the land, and all that is therein; the city, and them that dwell therein: then the men shall cry, and all the inhabitants of the land shall howl.

3 At the noise of the stamping of the hoofs of his strong horses, at the earthquake of his chariots, and at the rumbling of his wheels, the fathers shall not look back to their children for feebleness of hands;

4 Because of the day that comes to spoil all the Philistines, and to cut off from Tyrus and Zidon every helper that remains: for the Becoming-One will spoil the Philistines, the remnant of the isle of Caphtor.

5 Baldness is come upon Gaza; Ashkelon is cut off with the remnant of their valley: how long will you cut thyself?

6 O you sword of the Becoming-One, how long will it be ere you be quiet? put up yourself into your scabbard, rest, and be still.

---

[134] Appointed time or festival

7 How can it be quiet, seeing the Becoming-One has given it a charge against Ashkelon, and against the sea shore? there has he appointed it.

Jer 48:1 Against Moab thus says the Becoming-One of hosts, God of Israel; Woe unto Nebo! for it is spoiled: Kiriathaim is confounded and taken: Misgab is confounded and dismayed.

2 There shall be no more praise of Moab: in Heshbon they have devised evil against it; come, and let us cut it off from being a nation. Also you shall be silent, O Madmen; the sword shall pursue you.

3 A voice of crying shall be from Horonaim, spoiling and great destruction.

4 Moab is destroyed; her little ones have caused a cry to be heard.

5 For in the going up of Luhith continual weeping shall go up; for in the going down of Horonaim the enemies have heard a cry of destruction.

6 Flee, save your souls, and be like the heath in the wilderness.

7 For because you have trusted in your works and in your treasures, you shall also be taken: and Chemosh shall go forth into captivity with his priests and his princes together.

8 And the spoiler shall come upon every city, and no city shall escape: the valley also shall perish, and the plain shall be destroyed, as the Becoming-One has spoken.

9 Give wings unto Moab, that it may flee and get away: for the cities thereof shall be desolate, without any to dwell therein.

10 Cursed be he that did the work of the Becoming-One deceitfully, and cursed be he that keeps back his sword from blood.

11 Moab has been at ease from his youth, and he has settled on his lees, and has not been emptied from vessel to vessel, neither has he gone into captivity: therefore his taste remained in him, and his scent is not changed.

12 Therefore, behold, the days come, says the Becoming-One, that I will send unto him wanderers, that shall cause him to wander, and shall empty his vessels, and break their bottles.

13 And Moab shall be ashamed of Chemosh, as the house of Israel was ashamed of Beth-el [house of god] their confidence.

14 How say ye, We are mighty and strong men for the war?

15 Moab is spoiled, and gone up out of her cities, and his chosen young men are gone down to the slaughter, says the King, whose name is the Becoming-One of hosts.

16 The calamity of Moab is near to come, and his affliction hastens fast.

17 All you that are about him, bemoan him; and all you that know his name, say, How is the strong staff broken, and the beautiful rod!

18 you daughter that do inhabit Dibon, come down from your glory, and sit in thirst; for the spoiler of Moab shall come upon you, and he shall destroy your strong holds.

19 O inhabitant of Aroer, stand by the way, and espy; ask him that flees, and her that escapes, and say, What is done?

20 Moab is confounded; for it is broken down: howl and cry; tell you it in Arnon, that Moab is spoiled,

21 And judgment is come upon the plain country; upon Holon, and upon Jahazah, and upon Mephaath,

22 And upon Dibon, and upon Nebo, and upon Beth-diblathaim,

23 And upon Kiriathaim, and upon Beth-gamul, and upon Beth-meon,

24 And upon Kerioth, and upon Bozrah, and upon all the cities of the land of Moab, far or near.

25 The horn of Moab is cut off, and his arm is broken, says the Becoming-One.

26 Make you him drunken: for he magnified himself against the Becoming-One: Moab also shall wallow in his vomit, and he also shall be in derision.

27 For was not Israel a derision unto you? was he found among thieves? for since you spoke of him, you skipped for joy.

28 O you that dwell in Moab, leave the cities, and dwell in the rock, and be like the dove that makes her nest in the sides of the hole's mouth.

29 We have heard the pride of Moab, he is exceeding proud his loftiness, and his arrogance, and his pride, and the haughtiness of his heart.

30 I know his wrath, says the Becoming-One; but it shall not be so; his lies shall not so effect it.

31 Therefore will I howl for Moab, and I will cry out for all Moab; mine heart shall mourn for the men of Kirheres.

32 O vine of Sibmah, I will weep for you with the weeping of Jazer: your plants are gone over the sea, they reach even to the sea of Jazer: the spoiler is fallen upon your summer fruits and upon your vintage.

33 And joy and gladness is taken from the plentiful field, and from the land of Moab; and I have caused wine to fail from the winepresses: none shall tread with shouting; their shouting shall be no shouting.

34 From the cry of Heshbon even unto Elealeh, and even unto Jahaz, have they uttered their voice, from Zoar even unto Horonaim, as a heifer of three years: for the waters also of Nimrim shall be desolate.

35 Moreover I will cause to cease in Moab, says the Becoming-One, him that offers in the high places, and him that burns incense to his gods.

36 Therefore mine heart shall sound for Moab like pipes, and mine heart shall sound like pipes for the men of Kirheres: because the riches that he has gotten are perished.

37 For every head shall be bald, and every beard clipped: upon all the hands shall be cuttings, and upon the loins sackcloth.

38 There shall be lamentation generally upon all the housetops of Moab, and in the streets thereof: for I have broken Moab like a vessel wherein is no pleasure, says the Becoming-One.

39 They shall howl, saying, How is it broken down! how has Moab turned the back with shame! so shall Moab be a derision and a dismaying to all them about him.

40 For thus says the Becoming-One; Behold, he shall fly as an eagle, and shall spread his wings over Moab.

41 Kerioth is taken, and the strong holds are surprised, and the mighty men's hearts in Moab at that day shall be as the heart of a woman in her pangs.

42 And Moab shall be destroyed from being a people, because he has magnified himself against the Becoming-One.

43 Fear, and the pit, and the snare, shall be upon you, O inhabitant of Moab, says the Becoming-One.

44 He that flees from the fear shall fall into the pit; and he that gets up out of the pit shall be taken in the snare: for I will bring upon it, even upon Moab, the year of their visitation, says the Becoming-One.

45 They that fled stood under the shadow of Heshbon because of the force: but a fire shall come forth out of Heshbon, and a flame from the midst of Sihon, and shall devour the corner of Moab, and the crown of the head of the tumultuous ones.

46 Woe be unto you, O Moab! the people of Chemosh perishes: for your sons are taken captives, and your daughters captives.

47 Yet will I bring again the captivity of Moab in the end of days, says the Becoming-One. Thus far is the judgment of Moab.

Jer 49:1 Concerning the Ammonites, thus says the Becoming-One; has Israel no sons? has he no heir? why then does their king inherit Gad, and his people dwell in his cities?

2 Therefore, behold, the days come, says the Becoming-One, that I will cause an alarm of war to be heard in Rabbah of the Ammonites; and it shall be a desolate heap, and her daughters shall be burned with fire: then shall Israel be heir unto them that were his heirs, says the Becoming-One.

3 Howl, O Heshbon, for Ai is spoiled: cry, you daughters of Rabbah, gird you with sackcloth; lament, and run back and forth by the hedges; for their king shall go into captivity, and his priests and his princes together.

4 Why glory you in the valleys, your flowing valley, O backsliding daughter? that trusted in her treasures, saying, Who shall come unto me?

5 Behold, I will bring a fear upon you, says my Lord(s) the Becoming-One of hosts, from all those that be about you; and you shall be driven out every man right forth; and none shall gather up him that wanders.

6 And afterward I will bring again the captivity of the children of Ammon, says the Becoming-One.

7 Concerning Edom, thus says the Becoming-One of hosts; Is wisdom no more in Teman? is counsel perished from the prudent? is their wisdom vanished?

8 Flee ye, turn back, dwell deep, O inhabitants of Dedan; for I will bring the calamity of Esau upon him, the time that I will visit him.

9 If grapegatherers come to you, would they not leave some gleaning grapes? if thieves by night, they will destroy till they have enough.

10 But I have made Esau bare, I have uncovered his secret places, and he shall not be able to hide himself: his seed is spoiled, and his brethren, and his neighbors, and he is not.

11 Leave your fatherless children, I will preserve them alive; and let your widows trust in me.

12 For thus says the Becoming-One; Behold, they whose judgment was not to drink of the cup have assuredly drunken; and are you he that shall altogether go unpunished? you shall not go unpunished, but you shall surely drink of it.

13 For I have sworn by myself, says the Becoming-One, that Bozrah shall become a desolation, a reproach, a waste, and a curse; and all the cities thereof shall be wastes of olam.

14 I have heard a rumor from the Becoming-One, and an ambassador is sent unto the nations, saying, Gather you together, and come against her, and rise up to the battle.

15 For, lo, I will make you small among the nations, and despised among men.

16 your terribleness has deceived you, and the pride of your heart, O you that dwell in the clefts of the rock, that hold the height of the hill: though you should make your nest as high as the eagle, I will bring you down from there, says the Becoming-One.

17 Also Edom shall be a desolation: every one that goes by it shall be astonished, and shall hiss at all the plagues thereof.

18 As in the overthrow of Sodom and Gomorrah and the neighbor cities thereof, says the Becoming-One, no man shall abide there, neither shall a son of man dwell in it.

19 Behold, he shall come up like a lion from the swelling of Jordan against the habitation of the strong: but I will suddenly make him run away from her: and who is a chosen man, that I may appoint over her? for who is like me? and who will appoint me the time? and who is that shepherd that will stand before me?

20 Therefore hear the counsel of the Becoming-One, that he has taken against Edom; and his purposes, that he has purposed against the inhabitants of Teman: Surely the least of the flock shall draw them out: surely he shall make their habitations desolate with them.

21 The earth is moved at the noise of their fall, at the cry the noise thereof was heard in the boundary sea.

22 Behold, he shall come up and fly as the eagle, and spread his wings over Bozrah: and at that day shall the heart of the mighty men of Edom be as the heart of a woman in her pangs.

23 Concerning Damascus. Hamath is confounded, and Arpad: for they have heard evil tidings: they are fainthearted; there is sorrow on the sea; it cannot be quiet.

24 Damascus is grown feeble, and turns herself to flee, and fear has seized on her: anguish and sorrows have taken her, as a woman in travail.

25 How is the city of praise not left, the city of my joy!

26 Therefore her young men shall fall in her streets, and all the men of war shall be silent in that day, says the Becoming-One of hosts.

27 And I will kindle a fire in the wall of Damascus, and it shall consume the palaces of Benhadad.

28 Concerning Kedar, and concerning the kingdoms of Hazor, which Nebuchadrezzar king of Babylon shall smite, thus says the Becoming-One; Arise ye, go up to Kedar, and spoil the men of the east.

29 Their tents and their flocks shall they take away: they shall take to themselves their curtains, and all their vessels, and their camels; and they shall cry unto them, Fear is on every side.

30 Flee, get you far off, dwell deep, O you inhabitants of Hazor, says the Becoming-One; for Nebuchadrezzar king of Babylon has taken counsel against you, and has conceived a purpose against you.

31 Arise, get you up unto the wealthy nation, that dwells without care, says the Becoming-One, which have neither gates nor bars, which dwell alone.

32 And their camels shall be a booty, and the multitude of their cattle a spoil: and I will scatter into all winds them that are in the utmost corners; and I will bring their calamity from all sides thereof, says the Becoming-One.

33 And Hazor shall be a dwelling for monsters, and a desolation for olam: there shall no man abide there, nor any son of man dwell in it.

34 The word of the Becoming-One that came to Jeremiah the prophet against Elam in the beginning of the reign of Zedekiah king of Judah, saying,

35 Thus says the Becoming-One of hosts; Behold, I will break the bow of Elam, the beginning of their might.

36 And upon Elam will I bring the four winds from the four quarters of heaven, and will scatter them toward all those winds; and there shall be no nation to which the outcasts of olam shall not come.

37 For I will cause Elam to be dismayed before their enemies, and before them that seek their soul: and I will bring evil upon them, even my fierce anger, says the Becoming-One; and I will send the sword after them, till I have consumed them:

38 And I will set my throne in Elam, and will destroy from there the king and the princes, says the Becoming-One.

39 But it shall come to pass in the end of days, that I will bring again the captivity of Elam, says the Becoming-One.

Jer 50:1 The word that the Becoming-One spoke against Babylon and against the land of the Chaldeans by Jeremiah the prophet.

2 Declare you among the nations, and publish, and set up a standard; publish, and conceal not: say, Babylon is taken, Bel is confounded, Merodach is broken in pieces; her idols are confounded, her images are broken in pieces.

3 For out of the north there comes up a nation against her, which shall make her land desolate, and none shall dwell therein: they shall remove, they shall depart, both man and beast.

4 In those days, and in that time, says the Becoming-One, the children of Israel shall come, they and the children of Judah together, going and weeping: they shall go, and seek the Becoming-One their God.

5 They shall ask the way to Zion with their faces towards it, saying, Come, and let us join ourselves to the Becoming-One in a covenant of olam that shall not be forgotten.

6 My people has been lost sheep: their shepherds have caused them to go astray, they have turned them away on the mountains: they have gone from mountain to hill, they have forgotten their resting place.

7 All that found them have devoured them: and their adversaries said, We offend not, because they have sinned against the Becoming-One, the habitation of justice, even the Becoming-One, the hope of their fathers.

8 Remove out of the midst of Babylon, and go forth out of the land of the Chaldeans, and be as the he goats before the flocks.

9 For, lo, I will raise and cause to come up against Babylon an assembly of great nations from the north country: and they shall set themselves in array against her; from there she shall be taken: their arrows shall be as of a mighty expert man; none shall return in vain.

10 And Chaldea shall be a spoil: all that spoil her shall be satisfied, says the Becoming-One.

11 Because you were glad, because you rejoiced, O you destroyers of mine heritage, because you are grown fat as the heifer at grass, and bellow as bulls;

12 Your mother shall be greatly confounded; she that bare you shall be ashamed: behold, the end of the nations shall be a wilderness, a dry land, and a desert.

13 Because of the wrath of the Becoming-One it shall not be inhabited, but it shall be wholly desolate: every one that goes by Babylon shall be astonished, and hiss at all her plagues.

14 Put yourselves in array against Babylon round about: all you that bend the bow, shoot at her, spare no arrows: for she has sinned against the Becoming-One.

15 Shout against her round about: she has given her hand: her foundations are fallen, her walls are thrown down: for it is the vengeance of the Becoming-One: take vengeance upon her; as she has done, do unto her.

16 Cut off the sower from Babylon, and him that handles the sickle in the time of harvest: for fear of the oppressing sword they shall turn every one to his people, and they shall flee every one to his own land.

17 Israel is a scattered sheep; the lions have driven him away: first the king of Assyria has devoured him; and last this Nebuchadrezzar king of Babylon has broken his bones.

18 Therefore thus says the Becoming-One of hosts, God of Israel; Behold, I will punish the king of Babylon and his land, as I have punished the king of Assyria.

19 And I will bring Israel again to his habitation, and he shall feed on Carmel and Bashan, and his soul shall be satisfied upon mount Ephraim and Gilead.

20 In those days, and in that time, says the Becoming-One, the iniquity of Israel shall be sought for, and there shall be none; and the sins of Judah, and they shall not be found: for I will pardon them whom I reserve.

21 Go up against the land of Merathaim, even against it, and against the inhabitants of Pekod: waste and utterly destroy after them, says the Becoming-One, and do according to all that I have commanded you.

22 A sound of battle is in the land, and of great destruction.

23 How is the hammer of the whole earth cut asunder and broken! how is Babylon become a desolation among the nations!

24 I have laid a snare for you, and you are also taken, O Babylon, and you were not aware: you are found, and also caught, because you have striven against the Becoming-One.

25 The Becoming-One has opened his armory, and has brought forth the weapons of his indignation: for this is the work of my Lord(s) the Becoming-One of hosts in the land of the Chaldeans.

26 Come against her from the utmost border, open her storehouses: cast her up as heaps, and destroy her utterly: let nothing of her be left.

27 Slay all her bullocks; let them go down to the slaughter: woe unto them! for their day is come, the time of their visitation.

28 The voice of them that flee and escape out of the land of Babylon, to declare in Zion the vengeance of the Becoming-One our God, the vengeance of his temple.

29 Call together the archers against Babylon: all you that bend the bow, camp against it round about; let none thereof escape: recompense her according to her work; according to all that she has done, do unto her: for she has been proud against the Becoming-One, against the Holy One of Israel.

30 Therefore shall her young men fall in the streets, and all her men of war shall be silent in that day, says the Becoming-One.

31 Behold, I am against you, O you most proud, says my Lord(s) the Becoming-One of hosts: for your day is come, the time that I will visit you.

32 And the most proud shall stumble and fall, and none shall raise him up: and I will kindle a fire in his cities, and it shall devour all round about him.

33 Thus says the Becoming-One of hosts; The children of Israel and the children of Judah were oppressed together: and all that took them captives held them fast; they refused to let them go.

34 Their Redeemer is strong; the Becoming-One of hosts is his name: he shall thoroughly plead their cause, that he may give rest to the land, and disquiet the inhabitants of Babylon.

35 A sword is upon the Chaldeans, says the Becoming-One, and upon the inhabitants of Babylon, and upon her princes, and upon her wise men.

36 A sword is upon the liars; and they shall dote: a sword is upon her mighty men; and they shall be dismayed.

37 A sword is upon their horses, and upon their chariots, and upon all the mingled people that are in the midst of her; and they shall become as women: a sword is upon her treasures; and they shall be robbed.

38 A drought is upon her waters; and they shall be dried up: for it is the land of graven images, and they are mad upon their idols.

39 Therefore the wild beasts of the desert with the wild beasts of the coastlands shall dwell there, and the owls shall dwell therein: and it shall be no more inhabited completely; neither shall it be dwelt in from generation to generation.

40 As God overthrew Sodom and Gomorrah and the neighbor cities thereof, says the Becoming-One; so shall no man abide there, neither shall any son of man dwell therein.

41 Behold, a people shall come from the north, and a great nation, and many kings shall be raised up from the coasts of the earth.

42 They shall hold the bow and the lance: they are cruel, and will not show mercy: their voice shall roar like the sea, and they shall ride upon horses, every one put in array, like a man to the battle, against you, O daughter of Babylon.

43 The king of Babylon has heard the report of them, and his hands grew feeble: anguish took hold of him, and pangs as of a woman in travail.

44 Behold, he shall come up like a lion from the swelling of Jordan unto the habitation of the strong: but I will make them suddenly run away from her: and who is a chosen man, that I may appoint over her? for who is like me? and who will appoint me the time? and who is that shepherd that will stand before me?

45 Therefore hear you the counsel of the Becoming-One, that he has taken against Babylon; and his purposes, that he has purposed against the land of the Chaldeans: Surely the least of the flock shall draw them out: surely he shall make their habitation desolate with them.

46 At the noise of the taking of Babylon the earth is moved, and the cry is heard among the nations.

Jer 51:1 Thus says the Becoming-One; Behold, I will raise up against Babylon, and against them that dwell in the midst of them that rise up against me, a destroying wind;

2 And will send unto Babylon fanners [winnowers], that shall fan her, and shall empty her land: for in the day of trouble they shall be against her round about.

3 Against him that bends let the archer bend his bow, and against him that lifts himself up in his brigandine: and spare you not her young men; destroy you utterly all her host.

4 Thus the slain shall fall in the land of the Chaldeans, and they that are thrust through in her streets.

5 For Israel has not been forsaken, nor Judah of his God, of the Becoming-One of hosts; though their land was filled with sin against the Holy One of Israel.

6 Flee out of the midst of Babylon, and deliver every man his soul: be not silence in her iniquity; for this is the time of the Becoming-One's vengeance; he will render unto her a recompense.

7 Babylon has been a golden cup in the Becoming-One's hand, that made all the earth drunken: the nations have drunken of her wine; therefore the nations are mad.

8 Babylon is suddenly fallen and destroyed: howl for her; take balm for her pain, if so be she may be healed.

9 We would have healed Babylon, but she is not healed: forsake her, and let us go every one into his own country: for her judgment reaches unto heaven, and is lifted up even to the skies.

10 The Becoming-One has brought forth our righteousness: come, and let us declare in Zion the work of the Becoming-One our God.

11 Make bright the arrows; gather the shields: the Becoming-One has raised up the spirit of the kings of the Medes: for his device is against Babylon, to destroy it; because it is the vengeance of the Becoming-One, the vengeance of his temple.

12 Set up the standard upon the walls of Babylon, make the watch strong, set up the watchmen, prepare the ambushes: for the Becoming-One has both devised and done that which he spoke against the inhabitants of Babylon.

13 O you that dwell upon many waters, abundant in treasures, your end is come, and the measure of your covetousness.

14 The Becoming-One of hosts has sworn by his soul, saying, Surely I will fill you with men, as with caterpillars; and they shall lift up a shout against you.

15 He has made the earth by his power, he has established the world by his wisdom, and has stretched out the heavens by his understanding.

16 When he utters his voice, there is a multitude of waters in the heavens; and he causes the vapours to ascend from the ends of the earth: he makes lightning with rain, and brings forth the wind out of his treasures.

17 Every man is brutish by his knowledge; every founder is confounded by the graven image: for his molten image is falsehood, and there is no breath in them.

18 They are vanity, the work of errors: in the time of their visitation they shall perish.

19 The portion of Jacob is not like them; for he is the former of all things: and Israel is the rod of his inheritance: the Becoming-One of hosts is his name.

20 you are my battle ax and weapons of war: for with you will I break in pieces the nations, and with you will I destroy kingdoms;

21 And with you will I break in pieces the horse and his rider; and with you will I break in pieces the chariot and his rider;

22 With you also will I break in pieces man and woman; and with you will I break in pieces old and young; and with you will I break in pieces the young man and the maid;

23 I will also break in pieces with you the shepherd and his flock; and with you will I break in pieces the husbandman and his yoke of oxen; and with you will I break in pieces captains and rulers.

24 And I will render unto Babylon and to all the inhabitants of Chaldea all their evil that they have done in Zion in your sight, says the Becoming-One.

25 Behold, I am against you, O destroying mountain, says the Becoming-One, which destroy all the earth: and I will stretch out mine hand upon you, and roll you down from the rocks, and will make you a burnt mountain.

26 And they shall not take of you a stone for a corner, nor a stone for foundations; but you shall be desolate for olam, says the Becoming-One.

27 Set you up a standard in the land, blow the trumpet among the nations, prepare the nations against her, call together against her the kingdoms of Ararat, Minni, and Ashchenaz; appoint a captain against her; cause the horses to come up as the rough caterpillars.

28 Prepare against her the nations with the kings of the Medes, the captains thereof, and all the rulers thereof, and all the land of his dominion.

29 And the land shall tremble and sorrow: for every purpose of the Becoming-One shall be performed against Babylon, to make the land of Babylon a desolation without an inhabitant.

30 The mighty men of Babylon have forborne to fight, they have remained in their holds: their might has failed; they became as women: they have burned her dwelling places; her bars are broken.

31 One post shall run to meet another, and one messenger to meet another, to show the king of Babylon that his city is taken at one end,

32 And that the passages are stopped, and the reeds they have burned with fire, and the men of war are affrighted.

33 For thus says the Becoming-One of hosts, God of Israel; The daughter of Babylon is like a threshing floor, it is time to thresh her: yet a little while, and the time of her harvest shall come.

34 Nebuchadrezzar the king of Babylon has devoured me, he has crushed me, he has made me an empty vessel, he has swallowed me up like a monster, he has filled his belly with my delicates, he has cast me out.

35 The violence done to me and to my flesh be upon Babylon, shall the inhabitant of Zion say; and my blood upon the inhabitants of Chaldea, shall Jerusalem say.

36 Therefore thus says the Becoming-One; Behold, I will plead your cause, and take vengeance for you; and I will dry up her sea, and make her springs dry.

37 And Babylon shall become heaps, a dwelling place for monsters, an astonishment, and a hissing, without an inhabitant.

38 They shall roar together like lions: they shall yell as lions' whelps.

39 In their heat I will make their feasts, and I will make them drunken, that they may rejoice, and sleep a olam sleep, and not wake, says the Becoming-One.

40 I will bring them down like lambs to the slaughter, like rams with he goats.

41 How is Sheshach taken! and how is the praise of the whole earth surprised! how is Babylon become an astonishment among the nations!

42 The sea is come up upon Babylon: she is covered with the multitude of the waves thereof.

43 Her cities are a desolation, a dry land, and a wilderness, a land wherein no man dwells, neither does any son of man pass thereby.

44 And I will punish Bel in Babylon, and I will bring forth out of his mouth that which he has swallowed up: and the nations shall not flow together any more unto him: yes, the wall of Babylon shall fall.

45 My people, go you out of the midst of her, and deliver you every man his soul from the fierce anger of the Becoming-One.

46 And lest your heart faint, and you fear for the rumor that shall be heard in the land; a rumor shall both come one year, and after that in another year shall come a rumor, and violence in the land, ruler against ruler.

47 Therefore, behold, the days come, that I will do judgment upon the graven images of Babylon: and

her whole land shall be confounded, and all her slain shall fall in the midst of her.

48 Then the heavens and the earth, and all that is therein, shall sing for Babylon: for the spoilers shall come unto her from the north, says the Becoming-One.

49 As Babylon has caused the slain of Israel to fall, so at Babylon shall fall the slain of all the earth.

50 you that have escaped the sword, go away, stand not still: remember the Becoming-One afar off, and let Jerusalem come into your mind.

51 We are confounded, because we have heard reproach: shame has covered our faces: for strangers are come into the sanctuaries of the Becoming-One's house.

52 Therefore, behold, the days come, says the Becoming-One, that I will do judgment upon her graven images: and through all her land the wounded shall groan.

53 Though Babylon should mount up to heaven, and though she should fortify the height of her strength, yet from me shall spoilers come unto her, says the Becoming-One.

54 A sound of a cry comes from Babylon, and great destruction from the land of the Chaldeans:

55 Because the Becoming-One has spoiled Babylon, and destroyed out of her the great voice; when her waves do roar like great waters, a noise of their voice is uttered:

56 Because the spoiler is come upon her, even upon Babylon, and her mighty men are taken, every one of their bows is broken: for the Becoming-One, GOD of recompenses, shall surely requite.

57 And I will make drunk her princes, and her wise men, her captains, and her rulers, and her mighty men: and they shall sleep a olam sleep, and not wake, says the King, whose name is the Becoming-One of hosts.

58 Thus says the Becoming-One of hosts; The broad walls of Babylon shall be utterly broken, and her high gates shall be burned with fire; and the people shall labor in vain, and the folk in the fire, and they shall be weary.

59 The word which Jeremiah the prophet commanded Seraiah the son of Neriah, the son of Maaseiah, when he went with Zedekiah the king of Judah into Babylon in the fourth year of his reign. And this Seraiah was a quiet prince.

60 So Jeremiah wrote in a book all the evil that should come upon Babylon, even all these words that are written against Babylon.

61 And Jeremiah said to Seraiah, When you come to Babylon, and shall see, and shall read all these words;

62 Then shall you say, O Becoming-One, you have spoken against this place, to cut it off, that none shall remain in it, neither man nor beast, but that it shall be desolate for olam.

63 And it shall be, when you have made an end of reading this book, that you shall bind a stone to it, and cast it into the midst of Euphrates:

64 And you shall say, Thus shall Babylon sink, and shall not rise from the evil that I will bring upon her: and they shall be weary. Thus far are the words of Jeremiah.

Jer 52:1 Zedekiah was a son of one and twenty years when he began to reign, and he reigned eleven years in Jerusalem. And his mother's name was Hamutal the daughter of Jeremiah of Libnah.

2 And he did that which was evil in the eyes of the Becoming-One, according to all that Jehoiakim had done.

3 For through the anger of the Becoming-One it came to pass in Jerusalem and Judah, till he had cast them out from his presence, that Zedekiah rebelled against the king of Babylon.

4 And it came to pass in the ninth year of his reign, in the tenth month, in the tenth day of the month, that Nebuchadrezzar king of Babylon came, he and all his army, against Jerusalem, and pitched against it, and built forts against it round about. **[3386 YM]**

5 So the city was besieged unto the eleventh year of king Zedekiah. **[3388 YM]**

6 And in the fourth month, in the ninth day of the month, the famine was great in the city, so that there was no bread for the people of the land.

7 Then the city was broken up, and all the men of war fled, and went forth out of the city by night by the way of the gate between the two walls, which was by the king's garden; now the Chaldeans were by the city round about: and they went by the way of the plain.

8 But the army of the Chaldeans pursued after the king, and overtook Zedekiah in the plains of Jericho; and all his army was scattered from him.

9 Then they took the king, and carried him up unto the king of Babylon to Riblah in the land of Hamath; where he gave judgment upon him.

10 And the king of Babylon killed the sons of Zedekiah before his eyes: he killed also all the princes of Judah in Riblah.

11 Then he put out the eyes of Zedekiah; and the king of Babylon bound him in chains, and carried him to Babylon, and put him in prison till the day of his death.

12 Now in the fifth month, in the tenth *day* of the month, which *was* the nineteenth year of Nebuchadrezzar king of Babylon, came Nebuzaradan, captain of the guard, *which* served the king of Babylon, into Jerusalem, 13 And burned the house of the Becoming-One, and the king's house; and all the houses of Jerusalem, and all the houses of the great *men*, burned he with fire. [3388 YM / 586 BC]

14 And all the army of the Chaldeans, that *were* with the captain of the guard, brake down all the walls of Jerusalem round about

15 Then Nebuzaradan the captain of the guard carried away captive *certain* of the poor of the people, and the residue of the people that remained in the city, and those that fell away, that fell to the king of Babylon, and the rest of the multitude

16 But Nebuzaradan the captain of the guard left *certain* of the poor of the land for vinedressers and for husbandmen

17 Also the pillars of brass that *were* in the house of the Becoming-One, and the bases, and the brasen sea that *was* in the house of the Becoming-One, the Chaldeans brake, and carried all the brass of them to Babylon

18 The caldrons also, and the shovels, and the snuffers, and the bowls, and the spoons, and all the

vessels of brass wherewith they ministered, took they away

19 And the basins, and the firepans, and the bowls, and the caldrons, and the candlesticks, and the spoons, and the cups; that which was of gold in gold, and that which was of silver in silver, took the captain of the guard away.

20 The two pillars, one sea, and twelve brazen bulls that were under the bases, which king Solomon had made in the house of the Becoming-One: the brass of all these vessels was without weight.

21 And concerning the pillars, the height of one pillar was eighteen cubits; and a band of twelve cubits did compass it; and the thickness thereof was four fingers: it was hollow.

22 And a capital of brass was upon it; and the height of one capital was five cubits, with network and pomegranates upon the capitals round about, all of brass. The second pillar also and the pomegranates were like unto these.

23 And there were ninety and six pomegranates on a side; and all the pomegranates upon the network were a hundred round about.

24 And the captain of the guard took Seraiah the chief priest, and Zephaniah the second priest, and the three keepers of the door:

25 He took also out of the city an eunuch, which had the charge of the men of war; and seven men of them that were near the king's person, which were found in the city; and the principal scribe of the host, who mustered the people of the land; and threescore men of the people of the land, that were found in the midst of the city.

26 So Nebuzaradan the captain of the guard took them, and brought them to the king of Babylon to Riblah.

27 And the king of Babylon smote them, and put them to death in Riblah in the land of Hamath. Thus Judah was carried away captive out of his own land.

28 This is the people whom Nebuchadrezzar carried away captive: in the seventh year three thousand of Jews and three and twenty:

29 In the eighteenth year of Nebuchadrezzar he carried away captive from Jerusalem eight hundred thirty and two souls:

30 In the three and twentieth year of Nebuchadrezzar Nebuzaradan the captain of the guard carried away captive of the Jews seven hundred forty and five souls: all the souls were four thousand and six hundred. **[ab. 3392/3 YM]**

31 And it came to pass in the seven and thirtieth year of the captivity of Jehoiachin king of Judah, in the twelfth month, in the five and twentieth day of the month, that Evilmerodach king of Babylon in the first year of his reign lifted up the head of Jehoiachin king of Judah, and brought him forth out of prison, **[ab. 3414 YM; 560 BC]**

32 And spoke kindly unto him, and set his throne above the throne of the kings that were with him in Babylon,

33 And changed his prison garments: and he did continually eat bread before him all the days of his life.

34 And for his diet, there was a continual diet given him of the king of Babylon, every day a portion until the day of his death, all the days of his life.

Lamentations

Lam 1:1 How does the city sit solitary, that was full of people! how is she become as a widow! she that was great among the nations, and princess among the provinces, how is she become tributary!

2 She weeps great in the night, and her tears are on her cheeks: among all her lovers she has none to comfort her: all her friends have dealt treacherously with her, they are become her enemies.

3 Judah is gone into captivity because of affliction, and because of great servitude: she dwells among the nations, she finds no rest: all her persecutors overtook her between the straits.

4 The ways of Zion do mourn, because none come to the set times:[135] all her gates are desolate: her priests sigh, her virgins are afflicted, and she is in bitterness.

5 Her adversaries are the chief, her enemies prosper; for the Becoming-One has afflicted her for the multitude of her transgressions: her children are gone into captivity before the enemy.

6 And from the daughter of Zion all her beauty is departed: her princes are become like harts that find no pasture, and they are gone without strength before the pursuer.

7 Jerusalem remembered in the days of her affliction and of her miseries all her pleasant things that she had in the days of old, when her people fell into the hand of the enemy, and none did help her: the adversaries saw her, and did mock at her sabbaths.

8 Jerusalem has grievously sinned; therefore she is removed: all that honored her despise her, because they have seen her nakedness: yes, she sighs, and turns backward.

9 Her filthiness is in her skirts; she remembers not her last end; therefore she came down wonderfully: she had no comforter. O Becoming-One, behold my affliction: for the enemy has magnified himself.

10 The adversary has spread out his hand upon all her pleasant things: for she has seen that the nations entered into her sanctuary, whom you did command that they should not enter into your congregation.

11 All her people sigh, they seek bread; they have given their pleasant things for food to relieve the soul: see, O Becoming-One, and consider; for I am become vile.

12 Is it nothing to you, all you that pass by? behold, and see if there be any sorrow like unto my sorrow, which is done unto me, wherewith the Becoming-One has afflicted me in the day of his fierce anger.

13 From above has he sent fire into my bones, and it prevails against them: he has spread a net for my feet, he has turned me back: he has made me desolate and faint all the day.

14 The yoke of my transgressions is bound by his hand: they are woven, and come up upon my neck: he has made my strength to fall, my Lord(s) has delivered me into their hands, from whom I am not able to rise up.

15 My Lord(s) has trodden under foot all my mighty men in the midst of me: he has called a set time[136] against me to crush my young men: my Lord(s) has trodden the virgin, the daughter of Judah, as in a winepress.

16 For these things I weep; mine eye, mine eye runs down with water, because the comforter that should relieve my soul is far from me: my children are desolate, because the enemy prevailed.

17 Zion spreads forth her hands, and there is none to comfort her: the Becoming-One has commanded concerning Jacob, that his adversaries should be round about him: Jerusalem is as a menstruous woman among them.

18 The Becoming-One is righteous; for I have rebelled against his commandment: hear, I pray you, all people, and behold my sorrow: my virgins and my young men are gone into captivity.

19 I called for my lovers, but they deceived me: my priests and mine elders gave up the ghost in the city, while they sought their food to relieve their souls.

20 Behold, O Becoming-One; for I am in distress: my bowels are troubled; mine heart is turned within me; for I have grievously rebelled: abroad the sword bereaves, at home there is as death.

21 They have heard that I sigh: there is none to comfort me: all mine enemies have heard of my trouble; they are glad that you have done it: you will bring the day that you have called, and they shall be like unto me.

22 Let all their wickedness come before you; and do unto them, as you have done unto me for all my transgressions: for my sighs are many, and my heart is faint.

Lam 2:1 How has my Lord(s) covered the daughter of Zion with a cloud in his anger, and cast down from heavens unto the earth the beauty of Israel, and remembered not his footstool in the day of his anger!

2 My Lord(s) has swallowed up all the habitations of Jacob, and has not pitied: he has thrown down in his wrath the strong holds of the daughter of Judah; he has brought them down to the ground: he has polluted the kingdom and the princes thereof.

3 He has cut off in his fierce anger all the horn of Israel: he has drawn back his right hand from before the enemy, and he burned against Jacob like a flaming fire, which devours round about.

4 He has bent his bow like an enemy: he stood with his right hand as an adversary, and killed all that were pleasant to the eye in the tabernacle of the daughter of Zion: he poured out his fury like fire.

5 My Lord(s) was as an enemy: he has swallowed up Israel, he has swallowed up all her palaces: he has destroyed his strong holds, and has increased in the daughter of Judah mourning and lamentation.

---

[135] Appointed times or festivals

[136] Appointed time or festival

6 And he has violently taken away his tabernacle, as if it were of a garden: he has destroyed his set time[137] places of the assembly: the Becoming-One has caused the set times[138] and sabbaths to be forgotten in Zion, and has despised in the indignation of his anger the king and the priest.

7 My Lord(s) has cast off his altar, he has abhorred his sanctuary, he has given up into the hand of the enemy the walls of her palaces; they have made a noise in the house of the Becoming-One, as in the day of a set time.[139]

8 The Becoming-One has purposed to destroy the wall of the daughter of Zion: he has stretched out a line, he has not withdrawn his hand from destroying: therefore he made the rampart and the wall to lament; they languished together.

9 Her gates are sunk into the ground; he has destroyed and broken her bars: her king and her princes are among the nations: the law is no more; her prophets also find no vision from the Becoming-One.

10 The elders of the daughter of Zion sit upon the ground, and keep silence: they have cast up dust upon their heads; they have girded themselves with sackcloth: the virgins of Jerusalem hang down their heads to the ground.

11 Mine eyes do fail with tears, my bowels are troubled, my liver is poured upon the earth, for the destruction of the daughter of my people; because the children and the sucklings swoon in the streets of the city.

12 They say to their mothers, Where is corn and wine? when they swooned as the wounded in the streets of the city, when their soul was poured out into their mothers' bosom.

13 What thing shall I take to witness for you? what thing shall I liken to you, O daughter of Jerusalem? what shall I equal to you, that I may comfort you, O virgin daughter of Zion? for your breach is great like the sea: who can heal you?

14 your prophets have seen vain and foolish things for you: and they have not discovered your iniquity, to turn away your captivity; but have seen for you false burdens and causes of banishment.

15 All that pass by clap their hands at you; they hiss and wag their head at the daughter of Jerusalem, saying, Is this the city that men call The perfection of beauty, The joy of the whole earth?

16 All your enemies have opened their mouth against you: they hiss and gnash the teeth: they say, We have swallowed her up: certainly this is the day that we looked for; we have found, we have seen it.

17 The Becoming-One has done that which he had devised; he has fulfilled his word that he had commanded in the days of old: he has thrown down, and has not pitied: and he has caused your enemy to rejoice over you, he has set up the horn of your adversaries.

18 Their heart cried unto my Lord(s), O wall of the daughter of Zion, let tears run down like a river day and night: give yourself no rest; let not the apple of your eye cease.

19 Arise, cry out in the night: in the beginning of the watches pour out your heart like water before the face of my Lord(s): lift up your hands toward him for the soul of your young children, that faint for hunger in the top of every street.

20 Behold, O Becoming-One, and consider to whom you have done this. Shall the women eat their fruit, and children of a span long? shall the priest and the prophet be slain in the sanctuary of my Lord(s)?

21 The young and the old lie on the ground in the streets: my virgins and my young men are fallen by the sword; you have slain them in the day of your anger; you have killed, and not pitied.

22 you have called as in a set time[140] my terrors round about, so that in the day of the Becoming-One's anger none escaped nor remained: those that I have swaddled and brought up has mine enemy consumed.

Lam 3:1 I am the man that has seen affliction by the rod of his wrath.

2 He has led me, and brought me into darkness, but not into light.

3 Surely against me is he turned; he turns his hand against me all the day.

4 My flesh and my skin has he made old: he has broken my bones.

5 He has built against me, and compassed me with gall and travail.

6 He has set me in dark places, as they that be dead of olam.

7 He has hedged me about, that I cannot get out: he has made my chain heavy.

8 Also when I cry and shout, he shuts out my prayer.

9 He has enclosed my ways with hewn stone, he has made my paths crooked.

10 He was unto me as a bear lying in wait, and as a lion in secret places.

11 He has turned aside my ways, and pulled me in pieces: he has made me desolate.

12 He has bent his bow, and set me as a mark for the arrow.

13 He has caused the arrows of his quiver to enter into my reins.

14 I was a derision to all my people; and their song all the day.

15 He has filled me with bitterness, he has made me drunken with wormwood.

16 He has also broken my teeth with gravel stones, he has covered me with ashes.

17 And you have removed my soul far off from peace: I forgat prosperity.

18 And I said, My strength and my hope is perished from the Becoming-One: 19 Remembering mine affliction and my misery, the wormwood and the gall.

20 My soul has them still in remembrance, and is humbled in me.

21 This I recall to my mind, therefore I have hope.

---

[137] Appointed time or festival
[138] Appointed times or festivals
[139] Appointed time or festival
[140] Appointed time or festival

22 It is of the Becoming-One's mercies that we are not consumed, because his compassion fail not.

23 They are new every morning: great is your faithfullness.

24 The Becoming-One is my portion, says my soul; therefore will I hope in him.

25 The Becoming-One is good unto them that wait for him, to the soul that seeks him.

26 It is good that a man should both hope and quietly wait for the salvation of the Becoming-One.

27 It is good for a man that he bear the yoke in his youth.

28 He sits alone and keeps silence, because he has borne it upon him.

29 He puts his mouth in the dust; if so be there may be hope.

30 He gives his cheek to him that smites him: he is filled full with reproach.

31 For my Lord(s) will not cast off for olam:

32 But though he cause grief, yet will he have compassion according to the multitude of his mercies.

33 For he does not afflict willingly nor grieve the children of men.

34 To crush under his feet all the prisoners of the earth,

35 To turn aside the right of a man before the face of the most High,

36 To subvert a man in his cause, my Lord(s) approves not.

37 Who is he that says, and it comes to pass, when my Lord(s) commands it not?

38 Out of the mouth of the most High proceeds not evil and good?

39 Why does a living man complain, a man for the punishment of his sins?

40 Let us search and try our ways, and turn again to the Becoming-One.

41 Let us lift up our heart with our hands unto GOD in the heavens.

42 We have transgressed and have rebelled: you have not pardoned.

43 you have covered with anger, and persecuted us: you have slain, you have not pitied.

44 you have covered yourself with a cloud, that our prayer should not pass through.

45 you have made us as the offscouring and refuse in the midst of the people.

46 All our enemies have opened their mouths against us.

47 Fear and a snare is come upon us, desolation and destruction.

48 Mine eye runs down with rivers of water for the destruction of the daughter of my people.

49 Mine eye trickles down, and ceases not, without any intermission,

50 Till the Becoming-One look down, and behold from heaven.

51 Mine eye affects mine soul because of all the daughters of my city.

52 Mine enemies chased me greatly, like a bird, without cause.

53 They have cut off my life in the dungeon, and cast a stone upon me.

54 Waters flowed over mine head; then I said, I am cut off.

55 I called upon your name, O Becoming-One, out of the low dungeon.

56 you have heard my voice: hide not your ear at my breathing, at my cry.

57 you drew near in the day that I called upon you: you said, Fear not.

58 O my Lord(s), you have pleaded the causes of my soul; you have redeemed my life.

59 O Becoming-One, you have seen my wrong: judge you my cause.

60 you have seen all their vengeance and all their imaginations against me.

61 you have heard their reproach, O Becoming-One, and all their imaginations against me;

62 The lips of those that rose up against me, and their device against me all the day.

63 Behold their sitting down, and their rising up; I am their music.

64 Render unto them a recompense, O Becoming-One, according to the work of their hands.

65 Give them sorrow of heart, your curse unto them.

66 Persecute and destroy them in anger from under the heavens of the Becoming-One.

Lam 4:1 How is the gold become dim! how is the most fine gold changed! the stones of the sanctuary are poured out in the top of every street.

2 The precious sons of Zion, comparable to fine gold, how are they esteemed as earthen pitchers, the work of the hands of the potter!

3 Even the sea monsters draw out the breast, they give suck to their young ones: the daughter of my people is become cruel, like the ostriches in the wilderness.

4 The tongue of the sucking child cleaves to the roof of his mouth for thirst: the young children ask bread, and no man breaks it unto them.

5 They that did feed delicately are desolate in the streets: they that were brought up in scarlet embrace dunghills.

6 For the punishment of the iniquity of the daughter of my people is greater than the punishment of the sin of Sodom, that was overthrown as in a moment, and no hands stayed on her.

7 Her Nazarites were purer than snow, they were whiter than milk, they were more ruddy in body than rubies, their polishing was of sapphire:

8 Their visage is blacker than a coal; they are not known in the streets: their skin cleaves to their bones; it is withered, it is become like a stick.

9 They that be slain with the sword are better than they that be slain with hunger: for these pine away, stricken through for want of the fruits of the field.

10 The hands of the pitiful women have sodden their own children: they were their food in the destruction of the daughter of my people.

11 The Becoming-One has accomplished his fury; he has poured out his fierce anger, and has kindled a fire in Zion, and it has devoured the foundations thereof.

12 The kings of the earth, and all the inhabitants of the world, would not have believed that the adversary and the enemy should have entered into the gates of Jerusalem.

13 For the sins of her prophets, and the iniquities of her priests, that have shed the blood of the just in the midst of her,

14 They have wandered as blind men in the streets, they have polluted themselves with blood, so that men could not touch their garments.

15 They cried unto them, Depart ye; it is unclean; depart, depart, touch not: when they fled away and wandered, they said among the nations, They shall no more sojourn there.

16 The anger of the Becoming-One has divided them; he will no more regard them: they respected not the persons of the priests, they favored not the elders.

17 As for us, our eyes as yet failed for our vain help: in our watching we have watched for a nation that could not save us.

18 They hunt our steps, that we cannot go in our streets: our end is near, our days are fulfilled; for our end is come.

19 Our persecutors are swifter than the eagles of the heaven: they pursued us upon the mountains, they laid wait for us in the wilderness.

20 The breath of our nostrils, the anointed [Messiah] of the Becoming-One, was taken in their pits, of whom we said, Under his shadow we shall live among the nations.

21 Rejoice and be glad, O daughter of Edom, that dwell in the land of Uz; the cup also shall pass through unto you: you shall be drunken, and shall make yourself naked.

22 The punishment of your iniquity is accomplished, O daughter of Zion; he will no more carry you away into captivity: he will visit your iniquity, O daughter of Edom; he will discover your sins.

Lam 5:1 Remember, O Becoming-One, what is come upon us: consider, and behold our reproach.

2 Our inheritance is turned to strangers, our houses to aliens.

3 We are orphans and fatherless, our mothers are as widows.

4 We have drunken our water for money; our wood is sold unto us.

5 Our necks are under persecution: we labor, and have no rest.

6 We have given the hand to the Egyptians, and to the Assyrians, to be satisfied with bread.

7 Our fathers have sinned, and are not; and we have borne their iniquities.

8 Servants have ruled over us: there is none that does deliver us out of their hand.

9 We got our bread with the peril of our souls because of the sword of the wilderness.

10 Our skin was black like an oven because of the terrible famine.

11 They ravished the women in Zion, and the maids in the cities of Judah.

12 Princes are hanged up by their hand: the faces of elders were not honored.

13 They took the young men to grind, and the children fell under the wood.

14 The elders have ceased from the gate, the young men from their music.

15 The joy of our heart is ceased; our dance is turned into mourning.

16 The crown is fallen from our head: woe unto us, that we have sinned!

17 For this our heart is faint; for these things our eyes are dim.

18 Because of the mountain of Zion, which is desolate, the foxes walk upon it.

19 you, O Becoming-One, remain for olam; your throne from generation to generation.

20 Why do you forget us completely, and forsake us so long time?

21 Turn you us unto you, O Becoming-One, and we shall be turned; renew our days as of old.

22 But you have utterly rejected us; you are very angry against us.

Ezekiel

Eze 1:1 Now it came to pass in the thirtieth year [age for beginning priesthood], in the fourth month, in the fifth day of the month, as I was among the captives by the river of Chebar, that the heavens were opened, and I saw visions of God.

2 In the fifth day of the month, which was the fifth year of king Jehoiachin's captivity, **[ab. 3381 YM; 593 BC]**

3 The word of the Becoming-One came expressly unto **Ezekiel the priest**, the son of Buzi, in the land of the Chaldeans by the river Chebar; and the hand of the Becoming-One was there upon him.

4 And I looked, and, behold, a whirlwind came out of the north, a great cloud, and a fire infolding itself, and a brightness was about it, and out of the midst thereof as the color of amber, out of the midst of the fire.

5 Also out of the midst thereof came the likeness of four beasts. And this was their appearance; they had the likeness of a man.

6 And every one had four faces, and every one had four wings.

7 And their feet were straight feet; and the sole of their feet was like the sole of a calf's foot: and they sparkled like the color of burnished brass.

8 And they had the hands of a man under their wings on their four sides; and they four had their faces and their wings.

9 Their wings were joined one to another; they turned not when they went; they went every one straight forward.

10 As for the likeness of their faces, they four had the face of a man, and the face of a lion, on the right side: and they four had the face of an ox on the left side; they four also had the face of an eagle.

11 Thus were their faces: and their wings were stretched upward; two wings of every one were joined one to another, and two covered their bodies.

12 And they went every one straight forward: to which the spirit was to go, they went; and they turned not when they went.

13 As for the likeness of the beasts, their appearance was like burning coals of fire, and like the appearance of lamps: it went up and down among the beasts; and the fire was bright, and out of the fire went forth lightning.

14 And the beasts ran and returned as the appearance of a flash of lightning.

15 Now as I beheld the beasts, behold one wheel upon the earth by the beasts, with his four faces.

16 The appearance of the wheels and their work was like unto the color of a beryl: and they four had one likeness: and their appearance and their work was as it were a wheel in the middle of a wheel.

17 When they went, they went upon their four sides: and they turned not when they went.

18 As for their rings, they were so high that they were dreadful; and their rings were full of eyes round about them four.

19 And when the beasts went, the wheels went by them: and when the beasts were lifted up from the earth, the wheels were lifted up.

20 Wheresoever the spirit was to go, they went, there was their spirit to go; and the wheels were lifted up over against them: for the spirit of the beast was in the wheels.

21 When those went, these went; and when those stood, these stood; and when those were lifted up from the earth, the wheels were lifted up over against them: for the spirit of the beast was in the wheels.

22 And the likeness of the space upon the heads of the beast was as the color of the terrible crystal, stretched forth over their heads above.

23 And under the space were their wings straight, the one toward the other: every one had two, which covered on this side, and every one had two, which covered on that side, their bodies.

24 And when they went, I heard the noise of their wings, like the noise of great waters, as the voice of the Almighty, the voice of speech, as the noise of a host: when they stood, they let down their wings.

25 And there was a voice from the space that was over their heads, when they stood, and had let down their wings.

26 And above the space that was over their heads was the likeness of a throne, as the appearance of a sapphire stone: and upon the likeness of the throne was the likeness as the appearance of a man above upon it.

27 And I saw as the color of amber, as the appearance of fire round about within it, from the appearance of his loins even upward, and from the appearance of his loins even downward, I saw as it were the appearance of fire, and it had brightness round about.

28 As the appearance of the bow that is in the cloud in the day of rain, so was the appearance of the brightness round about. This was the appearance of the likeness of the glory of the Becoming-One. And when I saw it, I fell upon my face, and I heard a voice of one that spoke.

Eze 2:1 And he said unto me, Son of man, stand upon your feet, and I will speak unto you.

2 And the spirit entered into me when he spoke unto me, and set me upon my feet, that I heard him that spoke unto me.

3 And he said unto me, Son of man, I send you to the children of Israel, to a rebellious nation that has rebelled against me: they and their fathers have transgressed against me, even unto this very day.

4 For they are impudent children and stiffhearted. I do send you unto them; and you shall say unto them, Thus says my Lord(s) the Becoming-One.

5 And they, whether they will hear, or whether they will forbear, for they are a rebellious house, yet shall know that there has been a prophet among them.

6 And you, son of man, be not afraid of them, neither be afraid of their words, though briers and thorns be with you, and you do dwell among scorpions: be not afraid of their words, nor be dismayed at their looks, though they be a rebellious house.

7 And you shall speak my words unto them, whether they will hear, or whether they will forbear: for they are most rebellious.

8 But you, son of man, hear what I say unto you; Be not you rebellious like that rebellious house: open your mouth, and eat that I give you.

9 And when I looked, behold, a hand was sent unto me; and, lo, a roll of a book was therein;

10 And he spread it before me; and it was written within and without: and there was written therein lamentations, and mourning, and woe.

Eze 3:1 Moreover he said unto me, Son of man, eat that you find; eat this roll, and go speak unto the house of Israel.

2 So I opened my mouth, and he caused me to eat that roll.

3 And he said unto me, Son of man, cause your belly to eat, and fill your bowels with this roll that I give you. Then did I eat it; and it was in my mouth as honey for sweetness.

4 And he said unto me, Son of man, go, get you unto the house of Israel, and speak with my words unto them.

5 For you are not sent to a people of a strange speech and of a hard language, but to the house of Israel;

6 Not to many people of a strange speech and of a hard language, whose words you can not understand. Surely, had I sent you to them, they would have listened unto you.

7 But the house of Israel will not listen unto you; for they will not listen unto me: for all the house of Israel are impudent and hardhearted.

8 Behold, I have made your face strong against their faces, and your forehead strong against their foreheads.

9 As an adamant harder than flint I have made your forehead: fear them not, neither be dismayed at their looks, though they be a rebellious house.

10 Moreover he said unto me, Son of man, all my words that I shall speak unto you receive in your heart, and hear with your ears.

11 And go, get you to them of the captivity, unto the children of your people, and speak unto them, and tell them, Thus says my Lord(s) the Becoming-One; whether they will hear, or whether they will forbear.

12 Then the spirit took me up, and I heard behind me a voice of a great earthquake, saying, Blessed be the glory of the Becoming-One from his place.

13 I heard also the noise of the wings of the beasts that touched one another, and the noise of the wheels over against them, and a noise of a great earthquake.

14 So the spirit lifted me up, and took me away, and I went in bitterness, in the heat of my spirit; but the hand of the Becoming-One was strong upon me.

15 Then I came to them of the captivity at Tel-Abib, that dwelt by the river of Chebar [Kebar], and I sat where they sat, and remained there astonished among them seven days.

16 And it came to pass at the end of seven days, that the word of the Becoming-One came unto me, saying,

17 Son of man, I have made you a watchman unto the house of Israel: therefore hear the word at my mouth, and give them warning from me.

18 When I say unto the wicked, in dying, you will die;[141] and you give him not warning, nor speak to warn the wicked from his wicked way, to save his life; the same wicked man shall die in his iniquity; but his blood will I require at your hand.

19 Yet if you warn the wicked, and he turn not from his wickedness, nor from his wicked way, he shall die in his iniquity; but you have delivered your soul.

20 Again, When a righteous man does turn from his righteousness, and commit iniquity, and I lay a stumbling block before him, he shall die: because you have not given him warning, he shall die in his sin, and his righteousness which he has done shall not be remembered; but his blood will I require at your hand.

21 Nevertheless if you warn the righteous man, that the righteous sin not, and he does not sin, he shall surely live, because he is warned; also you have delivered your soul.

22 And the hand of the Becoming-One was there upon me; and he said unto me, Arise, go forth into the plain, and I will there talk with you.

23 Then I arose, and went forth into the plain: and, behold, the glory of the Becoming-One stood there, as the glory which I saw by the river of Chebar: and I fell on my face.

24 Then the spirit entered into me, and set me upon my feet, and spoke with me, and said unto me, Go, shut yourself within your house.

25 But you, O son of man, behold, they shall put bands upon you, and shall bind you with them, and you shall not go out among them:

26 And I will make your tongue cleave to the roof of your mouth, that you shall be mute, and shall not be to them a reprover: for they are a rebellious house.

27 But when I speak with you, I will open your mouth, and you shall say unto them, Thus says my Lord(s) the Becoming-One; He that hears, let him hear; and he that forbears, let him forbear: for they are a rebellious house.

Eze 4:1 you also, son of man, take you a tile, and lay it before you, and portray upon it the city, even Jerusalem:

2 And lay siege against it, and build a fort against it, and cast a mount against it; set the camp also against it, and set battering rams against it round about.

3 Moreover take you unto you an iron pan, and set it for a wall of iron between you and the city: and set your face against it, and it shall be besieged, and you shall lay siege against it. This shall be a sign to the house of Israel.

4 Lie you also upon your **left side**, and lay the iniquity of the house of Israel upon it: according to the number of the days that you shall lie upon it you shall bear their iniquity.

---

[141] מוֹת תָּמוּת – "in dying, you will die" or when you die, you will be dead – a part of the group called the "dead"

5 For I have laid upon you the years of their iniquity, according to the number of the days, **three hundred and ninety days**: so shall you bear the iniquity of the house of Israel.

6 And when you have accomplished them, lie again on your **right side**, and you shall bear the iniquity of the house of **Judah forty days**: I have appointed you each day for a year.

7 Therefore you shall set your face toward the siege of Jerusalem, and your arm shall be uncovered, and you shall prophesy against it.

8 And, behold, I will lay bands upon you, and you shall not turn you from one side to another, till you have ended the days of your siege.

9 Take you also unto you wheat, and barley, and beans, and lentiles, and millet, and fitches, and put them in one vessel, and make you bread thereof, according to the number of the days that you shall lie upon your side, **three hundred and ninety days shall you eat thereof**.

10 And your food which you shall eat shall be by weight, twenty shekels a day: from time to time shall you eat it.

11 you shall drink also water by measure, the sixth part of a hin: from time to time shall you drink.

12 And you shall eat it as barley cakes, and you shall bake it with dung [fuel for the fire] that comes out of man, in their sight.

13 And the Becoming-One said, Even thus shall the children of Israel eat their defiled bread among the nations, to which I will drive them.

14 Then said I, Ah my Lord(s) the Becoming-One! behold, my soul has not been polluted: for from my youth up even till now I have not eaten of that which dies of itself, or is torn in pieces; neither came there abominable flesh into my mouth.

15 Then he said unto me, Lo, I have given you cow's dung for man's dung, and you shall prepare your bread therewith.

16 Moreover he said unto me, Son of man, behold, I will break the staff of bread in Jerusalem: and they shall eat bread by weight, and with care; and they shall drink water by measure, and with astonishment:

17 That they may want bread and water, and be astonied one with another, and consume away for their iniquity.

Eze 5:1 And you, son of man, take you a sharp knife, take you a barber's razor, and cause it to pass upon your head and upon your beard: then take you balances to weigh, and divide the hair.

2 you shall burn with fire a third part in the midst of the city, **when the days of the siege are fulfilled: and you shall take a third part, and smite about it with a knife: and a third part you shall scatter in the wind; and I will draw out a sword after them.**

3 you shall also take thereof a few in number, and bind them in your skirts.

4 Then take of them again, and cast them into the midst of the fire, and burn them in the fire; for thereof shall a fire come forth into all the house of Israel.

5 Thus says my Lord(s) the Becoming-One; This is Jerusalem: I have set it in the midst of the nations and countries that are round about her.

6 And she has changed my judgments into wickedness more than the nations, and my statutes more than the countries that are round about her: for they have refused my judgments and my statutes, they have not walked in them.

7 Therefore thus says my Lord(s) the Becoming-One; Because you multiplied more than the nations that are round about you, and have not walked in my statutes, neither have kept my judgments, neither have done according to the judgments of the nations that are round about you;

8 Therefore thus says my Lord(s) the Becoming-One; Behold, I, even I, am against you, and will execute judgments in the midst of you in the sight of the nations.

9 And I will do in you that which I have not done, and whereunto I will not do any more the like, because of all your abominations.

10 Therefore the fathers shall eat the sons in the midst of you, and the sons shall eat their fathers; and I will execute judgments in you, and the whole remnant of you will I scatter into all the winds.

11 Therefore, as I live, says my Lord(s) the Becoming-One; Surely, because you have defiled my sanctuary with all your detestable things, and with all your abominations, therefore will I also diminish you; neither shall mine eye spare, neither will I have any pity.

12 A third part of you shall die with the pestilence, and with famine shall they be consumed in the midst of you: and a third part shall fall by the sword round about you; and I will scatter a third part into all the winds, and I will draw out a sword after them.

13 Thus shall mine anger be accomplished, and I will cause my fury to rest upon them, and I will be comforted: and they shall know that I the Becoming-One have spoken it in my zeal, when I have accomplished my fury in them.

14 Moreover I will make you waste, and a reproach among the nations that are round about you, in the sight of all that pass by.

15 So it shall be a reproach and a taunt, an instruction and an astonishment unto the nations that are round about you, when I shall execute judgments in you in anger and in fury and in furious rebukes. I the Becoming-One have spoken it.

16 When I shall send upon them the evil arrows of famine, which shall be for their destruction, and which I will send to destroy you: and I will increase the famine upon you, and will break your staff of bread:

17 So will I send upon you famine and evil beasts, and they shall bereave you; and pestilence and blood shall pass through you; and I will bring the sword upon you. I the Becoming-One have spoken it.

Eze 6:1 And the word of the Becoming-One came unto me, saying,

2 Son of man, set your face toward the mountains of Israel, and prophesy against them,

3 And say, you mountains of Israel, hear the word of my Lord(s) the Becoming-One; Thus says my

Lord(s) the Becoming-One to the mountains, and to the hills, to the rivers, and to the valleys; Behold, I, even I, will bring a sword upon you, and I will destroy your high places.

4 And your altars shall be desolate, and your images shall be broken: and I will cast down your slain men before your idols.

5 And I will lay the dead carcases of the children of Israel before their idols; and I will scatter your bones round about your altars.

6 In all your dwelling places the cities shall be laid waste, and the high places shall be desolate; that your altars may be laid waste and made desolate, and your idols may be broken and cease, and your images may be cut down, and your works may be abolished.

7 And the slain shall fall in the midst of you, and you shall know that I am the Becoming-One.

8 Yet will I leave a remnant, that you may have some that shall escape the sword among the nations, when you shall be scattered through the countries.

9 And they that escape of you shall remember me among the nations to which they shall be carried captives, because I am broken with their whorish heart, which has departed from me, and with their eyes, which go a whoring after their idols: and they shall loathe themselves for the evils which they have committed in all their abominations.

10 And they shall know that I am the Becoming-One, and that I have not said in vain that I would do this evil unto them.

11 Thus says my Lord(s) the Becoming-One; Smite with your hand, and stamp with your foot, and say, Alas for all the evil abominations of the house of Israel! for they shall fall by the sword, by the famine, and by the pestilence.

12 He that is far off shall die of the pestilence; and he that is near shall fall by the sword; and he that remains and is besieged shall die by the famine: thus will I accomplish my fury upon them.

13 Then shall you know that I am the Becoming-One, when their slain men shall be among their idols round about their altars, upon every high hill, in all the tops of the mountains, and under every green tree, and under every thick oak, the place where they did offer sweet aroma to all their idols.

14 So will I stretch out my hand upon them, and make the land desolate, yes, more desolate than the wilderness toward Diblath, in all their habitations: and they shall know that I am the Becoming-One.

Eze 7:1 Moreover the word of the Becoming-One came unto me, saying,

2 Also, you son of man, thus says my Lord(s) the Becoming-One unto the land of Israel; An end, the end is come upon the four corners of the land.

3 Now is the end come upon you, and I will send mine anger upon you, and will judge you according to your ways, and will recompense upon you all your abominations.

4 And mine eye shall not spare you, neither will I have pity: but I will recompense your ways upon you, and your abominations shall be in the midst of you: and you shall know that I am the Becoming-One.

5 Thus says my Lord(s) the Becoming-One; Evil, one evil, behold, is come.

6 An end is come, the end is come: it watches for you; behold, it is come.

7 The morning is come unto you, O you that dwell in the land: the time is come, the day of trouble is near, and not the sounding again of the mountains.

8 Now will I shortly pour out my fury upon you, and accomplish mine anger upon you: and I will judge you according to your ways, and will recompense you for all your abominations.

9 And mine eye shall not spare, neither will I have pity: I will recompense you according to your ways and your abominations that are in the midst of you; and you shall know that I am the Becoming-One that smites.

10 Behold the day, behold, it is come: the morning is gone forth; the rod has blossomed, pride has budded.

11 Violence is risen up into a rod of wickedness: none of them shall remain, nor of their multitude, nor of any of theirs: neither shall there be wailing for them.

12 The time is come, the day draws near: let not the buyer rejoice, nor the seller mourn: for wrath is upon all the multitude thereof.

13 For the seller shall not return to that which is sold, although they were yet alive: for the vision is touching the whole multitude thereof, which shall not return; neither shall any strengthen himself in the iniquity of his life.

14 They have blown the trumpet, even to make all ready; but none goes to the battle: for my wrath is upon all the multitude thereof.

15 The sword is outside, and the pestilence and the famine within: he that is in the field shall die with the sword; and he that is in the city, famine and pestilence shall devour him.

16 But they that escape of them shall escape, and shall be on the mountains like doves of the valleys, all of them mourning, every one for his iniquity.

17 All hands shall be feeble, and all knees shall be weak as water.

18 They shall also gird themselves with sackcloth, and horror shall cover them; and shame shall be upon all faces, and baldness upon all their heads.

19 They shall cast their silver in the streets, and their gold shall be removed: their silver and their gold shall not be able to deliver them in the day of the wrath of the Becoming-One: they shall not satisfy their souls, neither fill their bowels: because it is the stumbling block of their iniquity.

20 As for the beauty of his ornament, he set it in majesty: but they made the images of their abominations and of their detestable things therein: therefore I have set it far from them.

21 And I will give it into the hands of the strangers for a prey, and to the wicked of the earth for a spoil; and they shall pollute it.

22 My face will I turn also from them, and they shall pollute my secret place: for the robbers shall enter into it, and defile it.

23 Make a chain: for the land is full of bloody crimes, and the city is full of violence.

24 Therefore I will bring the worst of the nations, and they shall possess their houses: I will also make

the pomp of the strong to cease; and their holy places shall be defiled.

25 Destruction comes; and they shall seek peace, and there shall be none.

26 Mischief shall come upon mischief, and rumor shall be upon rumor; then shall they seek a vision of the prophet; but the law shall perish from the priest, and counsel from the ancients.

27 The king shall mourn, and the prince shall be clothed with desolation, and the hands of the people of the land shall be troubled: I will do unto them after their way, and according to their deserts will I judge them; and they shall know that I am the Becoming-One.

Eze 8:1 And it came to pass in the sixth year, in the sixth month, in the fifth day of the month, as I sat in mine house, and the elders of Judah sat before me, that the hand of my Lord(s) the Becoming-One fell there upon me. [ab, 3382 YM; 592 BC]

2 Then I beheld, and lo a likeness as the appearance of fire: from the appearance of his loins even downward, fire; and from his loins even upward, as the appearance of brightness, as the color of amber.

3 And he put forth the form of a hand, and took me by a lock of mine head; and the spirit lifted me up between the earth and the heaven, and brought me in the visions of God to Jerusalem, to the door of the inner gate that looks toward the north; where was the seat of the image of jealousy, which provokes to jealousy.

4 And, behold, the glory of God of Israel was there, according to the vision that I saw in the plain.

5 Then said he unto me, Son of man, lift up your eyes now the way toward the north. So I lifted up mine eyes the way toward the north, and behold northward at the gate of the altar this image of jealousy in the entry.

6 He said furthermore unto me, Son of man, see you what they do? even the great abominations that the house of Israel commits here, that I should go far off from my sanctuary? but turn you yet again, and you shall see greater abominations.

7 And he brought me to the door of the court; and when I looked, behold a hole in the wall.

8 Then said he unto me, Son of man, dig now in the wall: and when I had dug in the wall, behold a door.

9 And he said unto me, Go in, and behold the wicked abominations that they do here.

10 So I went in and saw; and behold every form of creeping things, and abominable beasts, and all the idols of the house of Israel, portrayed upon the wall round about.

11 And there stood before them seventy men of the ancients of the house of Israel, and in the midst of them stood Jaazaniah the son of Shaphan, with every man his censer in his hand; and a thick cloud of incense went up.

12 Then said he unto me, Son of man, have you seen what the ancients of the house of Israel do in the dark, every man in the chambers of his imagery? for they say, The Becoming-One sees us not; the Becoming-One has forsaken the earth.

13 He said also unto me, Turn you yet again, and you shall see greater abominations that they do.

14 Then he brought me to the door of the gate of the Becoming-One's house which was toward the north; and, behold, there sat women weeping for Tammuz.

15 Then said he unto me, have you seen this, O son of man? turn you yet again, and you shall see greater abominations than these.

16 And he brought me into the inner court of the Becoming-One's house, and, behold, at the door of the temple of the Becoming-One, between the porch and the altar, were about five and twenty men, with their backs toward the temple of the Becoming-One, and their faces toward the east; and they worshiped the sun toward the east.

17 Then he said unto me, have you seen this, O son of man? Is it a light thing to the house of Judah that they commit the abominations which they commit here? for they have filled the land with violence, and have returned to provoke me to anger: and, lo, they put the branch to their nose.

18 Therefore will I also deal in fury: mine eye shall not spare, neither will I have pity: and though they cry in mine ears with a loud voice, yet will I not hear them.

Eze 9:1 He cried also in mine ears with a loud voice, saying, Cause them that have charge over the city to draw near, even every man with his destroying weapon in his hand.

2 And, behold, six men came from the way of the higher gate, which lies toward the north, and every man a slaughter weapon in his hand; and one man among them was clothed with linen, with a writer's inkhorn by his side: and they went in, and stood beside the brazen altar.

3 And the glory of God of Israel was gone up from the cherub, whereupon he was, to the threshold of the house. And he called to the man clothed with linen, which had the writer's inkhorn by his side;

4 And the Becoming-One said unto him, Go through the midst of the city, through the midst of Jerusalem, and set a mark upon the foreheads of the men that sigh and that cry for all the abominations that be done in the midst thereof.

5 And to the others he said in mine hearing, Go you after him through the city, and smite: let not your eye spare, neither have you pity:

6 Slay utterly old and young, both maids, and little children, and women: but come not near any man upon whom is the mark; and begin at my sanctuary. Then they began at the ancient men which were before the house.

7 And he said unto them, Defile the house, and fill the courts with the slain: go you forth. And they went forth, and killed in the city.

8 And it came to pass, while they were slaying them, and I was left, that I fell upon my face, and cried, and said, Ah my Lord(s) the Becoming-One! will you destroy all the residue of Israel in your pouring out of your fury upon Jerusalem?

9 Then said he unto me, The iniquity of the house of Israel and Judah is exceeding great, and the land is full of blood, and the city full of perverseness:

for they say, The Becoming-One has forsaken the earth, and the Becoming-One sees not.

10 And as for me also, mine eye shall not spare, neither will I have pity, but I will recompense their way upon their head.

11 And, behold, the man clothed with linen, which had the inkhorn by his side, reported the matter, saying, I have done as you have commanded me.

Eze 10:1 Then I looked, and, behold, in the space that was above the head of the cherubs there appeared over them as it were a sapphire stone, as the appearance of the likeness of a throne.

2 And he spoke unto the man clothed with linen, and said, Go in between the wheels, even under the cherub, and fill your hand with coals of fire from between the cherubs, and scatter them over the city. And he went in in my sight.

3 Now the cherubs stood on the right side of the house, when the man went in; and the cloud filled the inner court.

4 Then the glory of the Becoming-One went up from the cherub, and stood over the threshold of the house; and the house was filled with the cloud, and the court was full of the brightness of the Becoming-One's glory.

5 And the sound of the cherubs' wings was heard even to the outer court, as the voice of the Almighty GOD when he speaks.

6 And it came to pass, that when he had commanded the man clothed with linen, saying, Take fire from between the wheels, from between the cherubs; then he went in, and stood beside the wheels.

7 And one cherub stretched forth his hand from between the cherubs unto the fire that was between the cherubs, and took thereof, and put it into the hands of him that was clothed with linen: who took it, and went out.

8 And there appeared in the cherubs the form of a man's hand under their wings.

9 And when I looked, behold the four wheels by the cherubs, one wheel by one cherub, and another wheel by another cherub: and the appearance of the wheels was as the color of a beryl stone.

10 And as for their appearances, they four had one likeness, as if a wheel had been in the midst of a wheel.

11 When they went, they went upon their four sides; they turned not as they went, but to the place to which the head looked they followed it; they turned not as they went.

12 And their whole body, and their backs, and their hands, and their wings, and the wheels, were full of eyes round about, even the wheels that they four had.

13 As for the wheels, it was cried unto them in my hearing, O wheel.

14 And every one had four faces: the first face was the face of a cherub, and the second face was the face of a man, and the third face was the face of a lion, and the fourth the face of an eagle.

15 And the cherubs were lifted up. This is the beast that I saw by the river of Chebar.

16 And when the cherubs went, the wheels went by them: and when the cherubs lifted up their wings to mount up from the earth, the same wheels also turned not from beside them.

17 When they stood, these stood; and when they were lifted up, these lifted up themselves also: for the spirit of the beast was in them.

18 Then the glory of the Becoming-One departed from off the threshold of the house, and stood over the cherubs.

19 And the cherubs lifted up their wings, and mounted up from the earth in my sight: when they went out, the wheels also were beside them, and every one stood at the door of the east gate of the Becoming-One's house; and the glory of God of Israel was over them above.

20 This is the beast that I saw under God of Israel by the river of Chebar; and I knew that they were the cherubs.

21 Every one had four faces apiece, and every one four wings; and the likeness of the hands of a man was under their wings.

22 And the likeness of their faces was the same faces which I saw by the river of Chebar, their appearances and themselves: they went every one straight forward.

Eze 11:1 Moreover the spirit lifted me up, and brought me unto the east gate of the Becoming-One's house, which looks eastward: and behold at the door of the gate five and twenty men; among whom I saw Jaazaniah the son of Azur, and Pelatiah the son of Benaiah, princes of the people.

2 Then said he unto me, Son of man, these are the men that devise mischief, and give wicked counsel in this city:

3 Which say, It is not near; let us build houses: this city is the caldron, and we be the flesh.

4 Therefore prophesy against them, prophesy, O son of man.

5 And the Spirit of the Becoming-One fell upon me, and said unto me, Speak; Thus says the Becoming-One; Thus have you said, O house of Israel: for I know the things that come into your spirit, every one of them.

6 you have multiplied your slain in this city, and you have filled the streets thereof with the slain.

7 Therefore thus says my Lord(s) the Becoming-One; Your slain whom you have laid in the midst of it, they are the flesh, and this city is the caldron: but I will bring you forth out of the midst of it.

8 you have feared the sword; and I will bring a sword upon you, says my Lord(s) the Becoming-One.

9 And I will bring you out of the midst thereof, and deliver you into the hands of strangers, and will execute judgments among you.

10 you shall fall by the sword; I will judge you in the border of Israel; and you shall know that I am the Becoming-One.

11 This city shall not be your caldron, neither shall you be the flesh in the midst thereof; but I will judge you in the border of Israel:

12 And you shall know that I am the Becoming-One: for you have not walked in my statutes, neither executed my judgments, but have done after the manners of the nations that are round about you.

13 And it came to pass, when I prophesied, that Pelatiah the son of Benaiah died. Then fell I down upon my face, and cried with a loud voice, and said, Ah my Lord(s) the Becoming-One! will you make a full end of the remnant of Israel?

14 Again the word of the Becoming-One came unto me, saying,

15 Son of man, your brethren, even your brethren, the men of your kindred, and all the house of Israel wholly, are they unto whom the inhabitants of Jerusalem have said, Get you far from the Becoming-One: unto us is this land given in possession.

16 Therefore say, Thus says my Lord(s) the Becoming-One; Although I have cast them far off among the nations, and although I have scattered them among the countries, yet will I be to them as a little sanctuary in the countries where they shall come.

17 Therefore say, Thus says my Lord(s) the Becoming-One; I will even gather you from the people, and assemble you out of the countries where you have been scattered, and I will give you the land of Israel.

18 And they shall come there, and they shall take away all the detestable things thereof and all the abominations thereof from there.

19 And I will give them one heart, and I will put a new spirit within you; and I will take the stony heart out of their flesh, and will give them a heart of flesh:

20 That they may walk in my statutes, and keep mine ordinances, and do them: and they shall be my people, and I will be their God.

21 But as for them whose heart walks after the heart of their detestable things and their abominations, I will recompense their way upon their own heads, says my Lord(s) the Becoming-One.

22 Then did the cherubs lift up their wings, and the wheels beside them; and the glory of God of Israel was over them above.

23 And the glory of the Becoming-One went up from the midst of the city, and stood upon the mountain which is on the east side of the city.

24 Afterwards the spirit took me up, and brought me in a vision by the Spirit of God into Chaldea, to them of the captivity. So the vision that I had seen went up from me.

25 Then I spoke unto them of the captivity all the things that the Becoming-One had showed me.

Eze 12:1 The word of the Becoming-One also came unto me, saying,

2 Son of man, you dwell in the midst of a rebellious house, which have eyes to see, and see not; they have ears to hear, and hear not: for they are a rebellious house.

3 Therefore, you son of man, prepare you stuff for removing, and remove by day in their sight; and you shall remove from your place to another place in their sight: it may be they will consider, though they be a rebellious house.

4 Then shall you bring forth your stuff by day in their sight, as stuff for removing: and you shall go forth at evening in their sight, as they that go forth into captivity.

5 Dig you through the wall in their sight, and carry out thereby.

6 In their sight shall you bear it upon your shoulders, and carry it forth in the twilight: you shall cover your face, that you see not the ground: for I have set you for a sign unto the house of Israel.

7 And I did so as I was commanded: I brought forth my stuff by day, as stuff for captivity, and in the even I dug through the wall with mine hand; I brought it forth in the twilight, and I bare it upon my shoulder in their sight.

8 And in the morning came the word of the Becoming-One unto me, saying,

9 Son of man, has not the house of Israel, the rebellious house, said unto you, What do you?

10 Say you unto them, Thus says my Lord(s) the Becoming-One; This burden concerns the prince in Jerusalem, and all the house of Israel that are among them.

11 Say, I am your sign: like as I have done, so shall it be done unto them: they shall remove and go into captivity.

12 And the prince that is among them shall bear upon his shoulder in the twilight, and shall go forth: they shall dig through the wall to carry out thereby: he shall cover his face, that he see not the ground with his eyes.

13 My net also will I spread upon him, and he shall be taken in my snare: and I will bring him to Babylon to the land of the Chaldeans; yet shall he not see it, though he shall die there.

14 And I will scatter toward every wind all that are about him to help him, and all his bands; and I will draw out the sword after them.

15 And they shall know that I am the Becoming-One, when I shall scatter them among the nations, and disperse them in the countries.

16 But I will leave a few men of them from the sword, from the famine, and from the pestilence; that they may declare all their abominations among the nations to which they come; and they shall know that I am the Becoming-One.

17 Moreover the word of the Becoming-One came to me, saying,

18 Son of man, eat your bread with quaking, and drink your water with trembling and with carefullness;

19 And say unto the people of the land, Thus says my Lord(s) the Becoming-One of the inhabitants of Jerusalem, and of the land of Israel; They shall eat their bread with carefullness, and drink their water with astonishment, that her land may be desolate from all that is therein, because of the violence of all them that dwell therein.

20 And the cities that are inhabited shall be laid waste, and the land shall be desolate; and you shall know that I am the Becoming-One.

21 And the word of the Becoming-One came unto me, saying,

22 Son of man, what is that proverb that you have in the land of Israel, saying, The days are prolonged, and every vision faileth?

23 Tell them therefore, Thus says my Lord(s) the Becoming-One; I will make this proverb to cease, and they shall no more use it as a proverb in Israel; but

say unto them, The days are at hand, and the effect of every vision.

24 For there shall be no more any false vision nor flattering divination within the house of Israel.

25 For I am the Becoming-One: I will speak, and the word that I shall speak shall come to pass; it shall be no more prolonged: for in your days, O rebellious house, will I say the word, and will perform it, says my Lord(s) the Becoming-One.

26 Again the word of the Becoming-One came to me, saying,

27 Son of man, behold, they of the house of Israel say, The vision that he sees is for many days to come, and he prophesies of the times that are far off.

28 Therefore say unto them, Thus says my Lord(s) the Becoming-One; There shall none of my words be prolonged any more, but the word which I have spoken shall be done, says my Lord(s) the Becoming-One.

Eze 13:1 And the word of the Becoming-One came unto me, saying,

2 Son of man, prophesy against the prophets of Israel that prophesy, and say you unto them that prophesy out of their own hearts, Hear you the word of the Becoming-One;

3 Thus says my Lord(s) the Becoming-One; Woe unto the foolish prophets, that follow their own spirit, and have seen nothing!

4 O Israel, your prophets are like the foxes in the deserts.

5 you have not gone up into the gaps, neither made up the hedge for the house of Israel to stand in the battle in the day of the Becoming-One.

6 They have seen falsely and lying divination, saying, The Becoming-One says: and the Becoming-One has not sent them: and they have made others to hope that they would confirm the word.

7 Have you not seen a false vision, and have you not spoken a lying divination, whereas you say, The Becoming-One says it; albeit I have not spoken?

8 Therefore thus says my Lord(s) the Becoming-One; Because you have spoken falsehood, and seen lies, therefore, behold, I am against you, says my Lord(s) the Becoming-One.

9 And mine hand shall be upon the prophets that see falsely, and that divine lies: they shall not be in the assembly of my people, neither shall they be written in the writing of the house of Israel, neither shall they enter into the land of Israel; and you shall know that I am my Lord(s) the Becoming-One.

10 Because, even because they have seduced my people, saying, Peace; and there was no peace; and one built up a wall, and, lo, others daubed it with untempered mortar:

11 Say unto them which daub it with untempered mortar, that it shall fall: there shall be an overflowing shower; and ye, O great hailstones, shall fall; and a stormy wind shall rend it.

12 Lo, when the wall is fallen, shall it not be said unto you, Where is the daubing wherewith you have daubed it?

13 Therefore thus says my Lord(s) the Becoming-One; I will even rend it with a stormy wind in my fury; and there shall be an overflowing shower in mine anger, and great hailstones in my fury to consume it.

14 So will I break down the wall that you have daubed with untempered mortar, and bring it down to the ground, so that the foundation thereof shall be discovered, and it shall fall, and you shall be consumed in the midst thereof: and you shall know that I am the Becoming-One.

15 Thus will I accomplish my wrath upon the wall, and upon them that have daubed it with untempered mortar, and will say unto you, The wall is no more, neither they that daubed it;

16 To wit, the prophets of Israel which prophesy concerning Jerusalem, and which see visions of peace for her, and there is no peace, says my Lord(s) the Becoming-One.

17 Likewise, you son of man, set your face against the daughters of your people, which prophesy out of their own heart; and prophesy you against them,

18 And say, Thus says my Lord(s) the Becoming-One; Woe to the women that sew pillows to all armholes, and make kerchiefs upon the head of every stature to hunt souls! Will you hunt the souls of my people, and will you save the souls alive that come unto you?

19 And will you pollute me among my people for handfuls of barley and for pieces of bread, to slay the souls that should not die, and to save the souls alive that should not live, by your lying to my people that hear your lies?

20 Therefore thus says my Lord(s) the Becoming-One; Behold, I am against your pillows, wherewith you there hunt the souls to make them fly, and I will tear them from your arms, and will let the souls go, even the souls that you hunt to make them fly.

21 Your kerchiefs also will I tear, and deliver my people out of your hand, and they shall be no more in your hand to be hunted; and you shall know that I am the Becoming-One.

22 Because with lies you have made the heart of the righteous sad, whom I have not made sad; and strengthened the hands of the wicked, that he should not return from his wicked way, by promising him life:

23 Therefore you shall see no more falsely, nor divine divinations: for I will deliver my people out of your hand: and you shall know that I am the Becoming-One.

Eze 14:1 Then came certain of the elders of Israel unto me, and sat before me.

2 And the word of the Becoming-One came unto me, saying,

3 Son of man, these men have set up their idols in their heart, and put the stumbling block of their iniquity before their face: should I be inquired of at all by them?

4 Therefore speak unto them, and say unto them, Thus says my Lord(s) the Becoming-One; Every man of the house of Israel that sets up his idols in his heart, and puts the stumbling block of his iniquity before his face, and comes to the prophet; I the Becoming-One will answer him that comes according to the multitude of his idols;

5 That I may take the house of Israel in their own heart, because they are all estranged from me through their idols.

6 Therefore say unto the house of Israel, Thus says my Lord(s) the Becoming-One; Repent, and turn yourselves from your idols; and turn away your faces from all your abominations.

7 For every one of the house of Israel, or of the stranger that sojourns in Israel, which separates himself from me, and sets up his idols in his heart, and puts the stumbling block of his iniquity before his face, and comes to a prophet to inquire of him concerning me; I the Becoming-One will answer him by myself:

8 And I will set my face against that man, and will make him a sign and a proverb, and I will cut him off from the midst of my people; and you shall know that I am the Becoming-One.

9 And if the prophet be deceived when he has spoken a thing, I the Becoming-One have deceived that prophet, and I will stretch out my hand upon him, and will destroy him from the midst of my people Israel.

10 And they shall bear the punishment of their iniquity: the punishment of the prophet shall be even as the punishment of him that seeks unto him;

11 That the house of Israel may go no more astray from me, neither be polluted any more with all their transgressions; but that they may be my people, and I may be their God, says my Lord(s) the Becoming-One.

12 The word of the Becoming-One came again to me, saying,

13 Son of man, when the land sins against me by trespassing grievously, then will I stretch out mine hand upon it, and will break the staff of the bread thereof, and will send famine upon it, and will cut off man and beast from it:

14 Though these three men, Noah, Daniel, and Job, were in it, they should deliver but their own souls by their righteousness, says my Lord(s) the Becoming-One.

15 If I cause noisome beasts to pass through the land, and they spoil it, so that it be desolate, that no man may pass through because of the beasts:

16 Though these three men were in it, as I live, says my Lord(s) the Becoming-One, they shall deliver neither sons nor daughters; they only shall be delivered, but the land shall be desolate.

17 Or if I bring a sword upon that land, and say, Sword, go through the land; so that I cut off man and beast from it:

18 Though these three men were in it, as I live, says my Lord(s) the Becoming-One, they shall deliver neither sons nor daughters, but they only shall be delivered themselves.

19 Or if I send a pestilence into that land, and pour out my fury upon it in blood, to cut off from it man and beast:

20 Though Noah, Daniel, and Job, were in it, as I live, says my Lord(s) the Becoming-One, they shall deliver neither son nor daughter; they shall but deliver their own souls by their righteousness.

21 For thus says my Lord(s) the Becoming-One; How much more when I send my four great judgments upon Jerusalem, the sword, and the famine, and the noisome beast, and the pestilence, to cut off from it man and beast?

22 Yet, behold, therein shall be left a remnant that shall be brought forth, both sons and daughters: behold, they shall come forth unto you, and you shall see their way and their doings: and you shall be comforted concerning the evil that I have brought upon Jerusalem, even concerning all that I have brought upon it.

23 And they shall comfort you, when you see their ways and their doings: and you shall know that I have not done without cause all that I have done in it, says my Lord(s) the Becoming-One.

Eze 15:1 And the word of the Becoming-One came unto me, saying,

2 Son of man, What is the vine tree more than any tree, or than a branch which is among the trees of the forest?

3 Shall wood be taken thereof to do any work? or will men take a pin of it to hang any vessel thereon?

4 Behold, it is cast into the fire for fuel; the fire devours both the ends of it, and the midst of it is burned. Is it meet for any work?

5 Behold, when it was whole, it was meet for no work: how much less shall it be meet yet for any work, when the fire has devoured it, and it is burned?

6 Therefore thus says my Lord(s), the Becoming-One; As the vine tree among the trees of the forest, which I have given to the fire for fuel, so will I give the inhabitants of Jerusalem.

7 And I will set my face against them; they shall go out from one fire, and another fire shall devour them; and you shall know that I am the Becoming-One, when I set my face against them.

8 And I will make the land desolate, because they have committed a trespass, says my Lord(s) the Becoming-One.

Eze 16:1 Again the word of the Becoming-One came unto me, saying,

2 Son of man, cause Jerusalem to know her abominations,

3 And say, Thus says my Lord(s) the Becoming-One unto Jerusalem; your birth and your nativity is of the land of Canaan; your father was an Amorite, and your mother a hittite.

4 And as for your nativity, in the day you were born your navel was not cut, neither were you washed in water to supple you; you were not salted at all, nor swaddled at all.

5 None eye pitied you, to do any of these unto you, to have compassion upon you; but you were cast out in the open field, to the loathing of your soul, in the day that you were born.

6 And when I passed by you, and saw you polluted in your own blood, I said unto you when you were in your blood, Live; yes, I said unto you when you were in your blood, Live.

7 I have caused you to multiply as the bud of the field, and you have increased and waxen great, and you are come to excellent ornaments: your breasts are fashioned, and your hair is grown, whereas you were naked and bare.

8 Now when I passed by you, and looked upon you, behold, your time was the time of love; and I

spread my skirt over you, and covered your nakedness: yes, I swore unto you, and entered into a covenant with you, says my Lord(s) the Becoming-One, and you became mine.

9 Then washed I you with water; yes, I thoroughly washed away your blood from you, and I anointed you with oil.

10 I clothed you also with broidered work, and shod you with badgers' skin, and I girded you about with fine linen, and I covered you with silk.

11 I decked you also with ornaments, and I put bracelets upon your hands, and a chain on your neck.

12 And I put a jewel on your forehead, and earrings in your ears, and a beautiful crown upon your head.

13 Thus were you decked with gold and silver; and your raiment was of fine linen, and silk, and broidered work; you did eat fine flour, and honey, and oil: and you were exceeding beautiful, and you did prosper into a kingdom.

14 And your renown went forth among the nations for your beauty: for it was perfect through my comeliness, which I had put upon you, says my Lord(s) the Becoming-One.

15 But you did trust in your own beauty, and play the harlot because of your renown, and poured out your fornications on every one that passed by; his it was.

16 And of your garments you did take, and deckedst your high places with diverse colors, and play the harlot thereupon: the like things shall not come, neither shall it be so.

17 you have also taken your fair jewels of my gold and of my silver, which I had given you, and made to yourself images of men, and did commit whoredom with them,

18 And took your broidered garments, and covered them: and you have set mine oil and mine incense before them.

19 My food also which I gave you, fine flour, and oil, and honey, wherewith I fed you, you have even set it before them for a sweet aroma: and thus it was, says my Lord(s) the Becoming-One.

20 Moreover you have taken your sons and your daughters, whom you have borne unto me, and these have you sacrificed unto them to be devoured. Is this of your whoredoms a small matter,

21 That you have slain my children, and delivered them to cause them to pass through the fire for them?

22 And in all your abominations and your whoredoms you have not remembered the days of your youth, when you were naked and bare, and were polluted in your blood.

23 And it came to pass after all your wickedness, woe, woe unto you! says my Lord(s) the Becoming-One;

24 That you have also built unto you an eminent place, and have made you a high place in every street.

25 you have built your high place at every head of the way, and have made your beauty to be abhorred, and have opened your feet to every one that passed by, and multiplied your whoredoms.

26 you have also committed fornication with the Egyptians your neighbors, great of flesh; and have increased your whoredoms, to provoke me to anger.

27 Behold, therefore I have stretched out my hand over you, and have diminished your ordinary food, and delivered you unto the soul of them that hate you, the daughters of the Philistines, which are ashamed of your lewd way.

28 you have played the whore also with the Assyrians, because you were unsatiable; yes, you have played the harlot with them, and yet could not be satisfied.

29 you have moreover multiplied your fornication in the land of Canaan unto Chaldea; and yet you were not satisfied herewith.

30 How weak is your heart, says my Lord(s) the Becoming-One, seeing you do all these things, the work of an imperious whorish woman;

31 In that you build your eminent place in the head of every way, and make your high place in every street; and have not been as a harlot, in that you scorn hire;

32 But as a wife that commits adultery, which takes strangers instead of her husband!

33 They give gifts to all whores: but you give your gifts to all your lovers, and hire them, that they may come unto you on every side for your whoredom.

34 And the contrary is in you from other women in your whoredoms, whereas none follows you to commit whoredoms: and in that you give a reward, and no reward is given unto you, therefore you are contrary.

35 Therefore, O harlot, hear the word of the Becoming-One; 36 Thus says my Lord(s) the Becoming-One; Because your filthiness was poured out, and your nakedness discovered through your whoredoms with your lovers, and with all the idols of your abominations, and by the blood of your children, which you did give unto them;

37 Behold, therefore I will gather all your lovers, with whom you have taken pleasure, and all them that you have loved, with all them that you have hated; I will even gather them round about against you, and will discover your nakedness unto them, that they may see all your nakedness.

38 And I will judge you, as women that break wedlock and shed blood are judged; and I will give you blood in fury and jealousy.

39 And I will also give you into their hand, and they shall throw down your eminent place, and shall break down your high places: they shall strip you also of your clothes, and shall take your fair jewels, and leave you naked and bare.

40 They shall also bring up a company against you, and they shall stone you with stones, and thrust you through with their swords.

41 And they shall burn your houses with fire, and execute judgments upon you in the sight of many women: and I will cause you to cease from playing the harlot, and you also shall give no hire any more.

42 So will I make my fury toward you to rest, and my jealousy shall depart from you, and I will be quiet, and will be no more angry.

43 Because you have not remembered the days of your youth, but have fretted me in all these things; behold, therefore I also will recompense your way upon your head, says my Lord(s) the Becoming-One:

and you shall not commit this lewdness above all your abominations.

44 Behold, every one that uses proverbs shall use this proverb against you, saying, As is the mother, so is her daughter.

45 you are your mother's daughter, that loathes her husband and her children; and you are the sister of your sisters, which loathed their husbands and their children: your mother was a Hittite, and your father an Amorite.

46 And your elder sister is Samaria, she and her daughters that dwell at your left hand: and your younger sister, that dwells at your right hand, is Sodom and her daughters.

47 Yet have you not walked after their ways, nor done after their abominations: but, as if that were a very little thing, you were corrupted more than they in all your ways.

48 As I live, says my Lord(s) the Becoming-One, Sodom your sister has not done, she nor her daughters, as you have done, you and your daughters.

49 Behold, this was the iniquity of your sister Sodom, pride, fullness of bread, and abundance of idleness was in her and in her daughters, neither did she strengthen the hand of the poor and needy.

50 And they were haughty, and committed abomination before me: therefore I took them away as I saw good.

51 Neither has Samaria committed half of your sins; but you have multiplied your abominations more than they, and have justified your sisters in all your abominations which you have done.

52 you also, which have judged your sisters, bear your own shame for your sins that you have committed more abominable than they: they are more righteous than you: yes, be you confounded also, and bear your shame, in that you have justified your sisters.

53 When I shall bring again their captivity, the captivity of Sodom and her daughters, and the captivity of Samaria and her daughters, then will I bring again the captivity of your captives in the midst of them:

54 That you may bear your own shame, and may be confounded in all that you have done, in that you are a comfort unto them.

55 When your sisters, Sodom and her daughters, shall return to their former estate, and Samaria and her daughters shall return to their former estate, then you and your daughters shall return to your former estate.

56 For your sister Sodom was not mentioned by your mouth in the day of your pride,

57 Before your wickedness was discovered, as at the time of your reproach of the daughters of Syria, and all that are round about her, the daughters of the Philistines, which despise you round about.

58 you have borne your lewdness and your abominations, says the Becoming-One.

59 For thus says my Lord(s) the Becoming-One; I will even deal with you as you have done, which have despised the oath in breaking the covenant.

60 Nevertheless I will remember my covenant with you in the days of your youth, and I will establish unto you a covenant of olam.

61 Then you shall remember your ways, and be ashamed, when you shall receive your sisters, your elder and your younger: and I will give them unto you for daughters, but not by your covenant.

62 And I will establish my covenant with you; and you shall know that I am the Becoming-One: 63 That you may remember, and be confounded, and not open your mouth any more because of your shame, when I atone for you for all that you have done, says my Lord(s) the Becoming-One.

Eze 17:1 And the word of the Becoming-One came unto me, saying,

2 Son of man, put forth a riddle, and speak a parable unto the house of Israel;

3 And say, Thus says my Lord(s) the Becoming-One; A great eagle with great wings, long winged, full of feathers, which had diverse colors, came unto Lebanon, and took the highest branch of the cedar:

4 He cropped off the top of his young twigs, and carried it into a land of traffic; he set it in a city of merchants.

5 He took also of the seed of the land, and planted it in a field of seed; he placed it by great waters, and set it as a willow tree.

6 And it grew, and became a spreading vine of low stature, whose branches turned toward him, and the roots thereof were under him: so it became a vine, and brought forth branches, and shot forth sprigs.

7 There was also another great eagle with great wings and many feathers: and, behold, this vine did bend her roots toward him, and shot forth her branches toward him, that he might water it by the furrows of her plantation.

8 It was planted in a good soil by great waters, that it might bring forth branches, and that it might bear fruit, that it might be a goodly vine.

9 Say you, Thus says my Lord(s) the Becoming-One; Shall it prosper? shall he not pull up the roots thereof, and cut off the fruit thereof, that it wither? it shall wither in all the leaves of her spring, even without great power or many people to pluck it up by the roots thereof.

10 Yes, behold, being planted, shall it prosper? shall it not utterly wither, when the east wind touches it? it shall wither in the furrows where it grew.

11 Moreover the word of the Becoming-One came unto me, saying,

12 Say now to the rebellious house, Don't you knowd what these things mean? tell them, Behold, the king of Babylon is come to Jerusalem, and has taken the king thereof, and the princes thereof, and led them with him to Babylon;

13 And has taken of the king's seed, and made a covenant with him, and has taken an oath of him: he has also taken the mighty of the land:

14 That the kingdom might be base, that it might not lift itself up, but that by keeping of his covenant it might stand.

15 But he rebelled against him in sending his ambassadors into Egypt, that they might give him horses and much people. Shall he prosper? shall he escape that did such things? or shall he break the covenant, and be delivered?

16 As I live, says my Lord(s) the Becoming-One, surely in the place where the king dwells that made him king, whose oath he despised, and whose covenant he brake, even with him in the midst of Babylon he shall die.

17 Neither shall Pharaoh with his mighty army and great company make for him in the war, by casting up mounts, and building forts, to cut off many souls:

18 Seeing he despised the oath by breaking the covenant, when, lo, he had given his hand, and has done all these things, he shall not escape.

19 Therefore thus says my Lord(s) the Becoming-One; As I live, surely mine oath that he has despised, and my covenant that he has broken, even it will I recompense upon his own head.

20 And I will spread my net upon him, and he shall be taken in my snare, and I will bring him to Babylon, and will judge with him there for his trespass that he has trespassed against me.

21 And all his fugitives with all his bands shall fall by the sword, and they that remain shall be scattered toward all winds: and you shall know that I the Becoming-One have spoken it.

22 Thus says my Lord(s) the Becoming-One; I will also take of the highest branch of the high cedar, and will set it; I will crop off from the top of his young twigs a tender one, and will plant it upon a high mountain and eminent:

23 In the mountain of the height of Israel will I plant it: and it shall bring forth boughs, and bear fruit, and be a goodly cedar: and under it shall dwell all fowl of every wing; in the shadow of the branches thereof shall they dwell.

24 And all the trees of the field shall know that I the Becoming-One have brought down the high tree, have exalted the low tree, have dried up the green tree, and have made the dry tree to flourish: I the Becoming-One have spoken and have done it.

Eze 18:1 The word of the Becoming-One came unto me again, saying,

2 What do you mean, that you use this proverb concerning the land of Israel, saying, The fathers have eaten sour grapes, and the children's teeth are set on edge?

3 As I live, says my Lord(s) the Becoming-One, you shall not have occasion any more to use this proverb in Israel.

4 Behold, all souls are mine; as the soul of the father, so also the soul of the son is mine: the soul that sins, it shall die.

5 But if a man be just, and do that which is lawful and right,

6 And has not eaten upon the mountains, neither has lifted up his eyes to the idols of the house of Israel, neither has defiled his neighbor's wife, neither has come near to a menstruous woman,

7 And has not oppressed any, but has restored to the debtor his pledge, has spoiled none by violence, has given his bread to the hungry, and has covered the naked with a garment;

8 He that has not given forth upon usury, neither has taken any increase, that has withdrawn his hand from iniquity, has executed true judgment between man and man,

9 has walked in my statutes, and has kept my judgments, to deal truly; he is just, he shall surely live, says my Lord(s) the Becoming-One.

10 If he beget a son that is a robber, a shedder of blood, and that did the like to any one of these things,

11 And that did not any of those duties, but even has eaten upon the mountains, and defiled his neighbor's wife,

12 has oppressed the poor and needy, has spoiled by violence, has not restored the pledge, and has lifted up his eyes to the idols, has committed abomination,

13 has given forth upon usury, and has taken increase: shall he then live? he shall not live: he has done all these abominations; he shall surely die; his blood shall be upon him.

14 Now, lo, if he beget a son, that sees all his father's sins which he has done, and considers, and did not such like,

15 That has not eaten upon the mountains, neither has lifted up his eyes to the idols of the house of Israel, has not defiled his neighbor's wife,

16 Neither has oppressed any, has not withheld the pledge, neither has spoiled by violence, but has given his bread to the hungry, and has covered the naked with a garment,

17 That has taken off his hand from the poor, that has not received usury nor increase, has executed my judgments, has walked in my statutes; he shall not die for the iniquity of his father, he shall surely live.

18 As for his father, because he cruelly oppressed, spoiled his brother by violence, and did that which is not good among his people, lo, even he shall die in his iniquity.

19 Yet say ye, Why? does not the son bear the iniquity of the father? When the son has done that which is lawful and right, and has kept all my statutes, and has done them, he shall surely live.

20 The soul that sins, it shall die. The son shall not bear the iniquity of the father, neither shall the father bear the iniquity of the son: the righteousness of the righteous shall be upon him, and the wickedness of the wicked shall be upon him.

21 But if the wicked will turn from all his sins that he has committed, and keep all my statutes, and do that which is lawful and right, he shall surely live, he shall not die.

22 All his transgressions that he has committed, they shall not be mentioned unto him: in his righteousness that he has done he shall live.

23 I have any pleasure at all that the wicked should die? says my Lord(s) the Becoming-One: and not that he should return from his ways, and live?

24 But when the righteous turns away from his righteousness, and commits iniquity, and did according to all the abominations that the wicked man does, shall he live? All his righteousness that he has done shall not be mentioned: in his trespass that he has trespassed, and in his sin that he has sinned, in them shall he die.

25 Yet you say, The way of my Lord(s) is not equal. Hear now, O house of Israel; Is not my way equal? are not your ways unequal?

26 When a righteous man turns away from his righteousness, and commits iniquity, and dies in them; for his iniquity that he has done shall he die.

27 Again, when the wicked man turns away from his wickedness that he has committed, and did that which is lawful and right, he shall save his soul alive.

28 Because he considers, and turns away from all his transgressions that he has committed, he shall surely live, he shall not die.

29 Yet says the house of Israel, The way of my Lord(s) is not equal. O house of Israel, are not my ways equal? are not your ways unequal?

30 Therefore I will judge you, O house of Israel, every one according to his ways, says my Lord(s) the Becoming-One. Repent, and turn yourselves from all your transgressions; so iniquity shall not be your ruin.

31 Cast away from you all your transgressions, whereby you have transgressed; and make you a new heart and a new spirit: for why will you die, O house of Israel?

32 For I have no pleasure in the death of him that dies, says my Lord(s) the Becoming-One: therefore turn yourselves, and live ye.

Eze 19:1 Moreover take you up a lamentation for the princes of Israel,

2 And say, What is your mother? A lioness: she lay down among lions, she nourished her whelps among young lions.

3 And she brought up one of her whelps: it became a young lion, and it learned to catch the prey; it devoured men.

4 The nations also heard of him; he was taken in their pit, and they brought him with chains unto the land of Egypt.

5 Now when she saw that she had waited, and her hope was lost, then she took another of her whelps, and made him a young lion.

6 And he went up and down among the lions, he became a young lion, and learned to catch the prey, and devoured men.

7 And he knew their desolate palaces, and he laid waste their cities; and the land was desolate, and the fullness thereof, by the noise of his roaring.

8 Then the nations set against him on every side from the provinces, and spread their net over him: he was taken in their pit.

9 And they put him in ward in chains, and brought him to the king of Babylon: they brought him into holds, that his voice should no more be heard upon the mountains of Israel.

10 your mother is like a vine in your blood, planted by the waters: she was fruitful and full of branches by reason of many waters.

11 And she had strong rods for the sceptres of them that bare rule, and her stature was exalted among the thick branches, and she appeared in her height with the multitude of her branches.

12 But she was plucked up in fury, she was cast down to the ground, and the east wind dried up her fruit: her strong rods were broken and withered; the fire consumed them.

13 And now she is planted in the wilderness, in a dry and thirsty ground.

14 And fire is gone out of a rod of her branches, which has devoured her fruit, so that she has no strong rod to be a scepter to rule. This is a lamentation, and shall be for a lamentation.

Eze 20:1 And it came to pass in the seventh year, in the fifth month, the tenth day of the month, that certain of the elders of Israel came to inquire of the Becoming-One, and sat before me. [ab. 3383 YM; 591 BC]

2 Then came the word of the Becoming-One unto me, saying,

3 Son of man, speak unto the elders of Israel, and say unto them, Thus says my Lord(s) the Becoming-One; Are you come to inquire of me? As I live, says my Lord(s) the Becoming-One, I will not be inquired of by you.

4 will you judge them, son of man, will you judge them? cause them to know the abominations of their fathers:

5 And say unto them, Thus says my Lord(s) the Becoming-One; In the day when I chose Israel, and lifted up mine hand unto the seed of the house of Jacob, and made myself known unto them in the land of Egypt, when I lifted up mine hand unto them, saying, I am the Becoming-One your God;

6 In the day that I lifted up mine hand unto them, to bring them forth of the land of Egypt into a land that I had searched for them, flowing with milk and honey, which is the glory of all lands:

7 Then said I unto them, Cast you away every man the abominations of his eyes, and defile not yourselves with the idols of Egypt: I am the Becoming-One your God.

8 But they rebelled against me, and would not listen unto me: they did not every man cast away the abominations of their eyes, neither did they forsake the idols of Egypt: then I said, I will pour out my fury upon them, to accomplish my anger against them in the midst of the land of Egypt.

9 But I worked for my name's sake, that it should not be polluted before the nations, among whom they were, in whose sight I made myself known unto them, in bringing them forth out of the land of Egypt.

10 Therefore I caused them to go forth out of the land of Egypt, and brought them into the wilderness.

11 And I gave them my statutes, and showed them my judgments, which if a man do, he shall even live in them.

12 Moreover also I gave them my sabbaths, to be a sign between me and them, that they might know that I am the Becoming-One that sanctify them.

13 But the house of Israel rebelled against me in the wilderness: they walked not in my statutes, and they despised my judgments, which if a man do, he shall even live in them; and my sabbaths they greatly polluted: then I said, I would pour out my fury upon them in the wilderness, to consume them.

14 But I worked for my name's sake, that it should not be polluted before the nations, in whose sight I brought them out.

15 Yet also I lifted up my hand unto them in the wilderness, that I would not bring them into the land which I had given them, flowing with milk and honey, which is the glory of all lands;

16 Because they despised my judgments, and walked not in my statutes, but polluted my sabbaths: for their heart went after their idols.

17 Nevertheless mine eye spared them from destroying them, neither did I make an end of them in the wilderness.

18 But I said unto their children in the wilderness, Walk you not in the statutes of your fathers, neither observe their judgments, nor defile yourselves with their idols:

19 I am the Becoming-One your God; walk in my statutes, and keep my judgments, and do them;

20 And hallow my sabbaths; and they shall be a sign between me and you, that you may know that I am the Becoming-One your God.

21 Notwithstanding the children rebelled against me: they walked not in my statutes, neither kept my judgments to do them, which if a man do, he shall even live in them; they polluted my sabbaths: then I said, I would pour out my fury upon them, to accomplish my anger against them in the wilderness.

22 Nevertheless I withdrew mine hand, and worked for my name's sake, that it should not be polluted in the sight of the nations, in whose sight I brought them forth.

23 I lifted up mine hand unto them also in the wilderness, that I would scatter them among the nations, and disperse them through the countries;

24 Because they had not executed my judgments, but had despised my statutes, and had polluted my sabbaths, and their eyes were after their fathers' idols.

25 Therefore I gave them also statutes that were not good, and judgments whereby they should not live;

26 And I polluted them in their own gifts, in that they caused to pass through the fire all that opens the womb, that I might make them desolate, to the end that they might know that I am the Becoming-One.

27 Therefore, son of man, speak unto the house of Israel, and say unto them, Thus says my Lord(s) the Becoming-One; Yet in this your fathers have blasphemed me, in that they have committed a trespass against me.

28 For when I had brought them into the land, for the which I lifted up mine hand to give it to them, then they saw every high hill, and all the thick trees, and they offered there their sacrifices, and there they presented the provocation of their offering: there also they made their sweet aroma, and poured out there their drink offerings.

29 Then I said unto them, What is the high place whereunto you go? And the name thereof is called Bamah unto this day.

30 Therefore say unto the house of Israel, Thus says my Lord(s) the Becoming-One; Are you polluted after the manner of your fathers? and commit you whoredom after their abominations?

31 For when you offer your gifts, when you make your sons to pass through the fire, you pollute yourselves with all your idols, even unto this day: and shall I be inquired of by you, O house of Israel? As I live, says my Lord(s) the Becoming-One, I will not be inquired of by you.

32 And that which comes into your spirit shall not be at all, that you say, We will be as the nations, as the families of the countries, to serve wood and stone.

33 As I live, says my Lord(s) the Becoming-One, surely with a mighty hand, and with a stretched out arm, and with fury poured out, will I rule over you:

34 And I will bring you out from the people, and will gather you out of the countries wherein you are scattered, with a mighty hand, and with a stretched out arm, and with fury poured out.

35 And I will bring you into the wilderness of the people, and there will I judge with you face to face.

36 Like as I pleaded with your fathers in the wilderness of the land of Egypt, so will I plead with you, says my Lord(s) the Becoming-One.

37 And I will cause you to pass under the rod, and I will bring you into the bond of the covenant:

38 And I will purge out from among you the rebels, and them that transgress against me: I will bring them forth out of the country where they sojourn, and they shall not enter into the land of Israel: and you shall know that I am the Becoming-One.

39 As for you, O house of Israel, thus says my Lord(s) the Becoming-One; Go ye, serve you every one his idols, and hereafter also, if you will not listen unto me: but pollute you my holy name no more with your gifts, and with your idols.

40 For in mine holy mountain, in the mountain of the height of Israel, says my Lord(s) the Becoming-One, there shall all the house of Israel, all of them in the land, serve me: there will I accept them, and there will I require your offerings, and the first of your offerings, with all your holy things.

41 I will accept you with your sweet aroma, when I bring you out from the people, and gather you out of the countries wherein you have been scattered; and I will be sanctified in you before the nations.

42 And you shall know that I am the Becoming-One, when I shall bring you into the land of Israel, into the country for the which I lifted up mine hand to give it to your fathers.

43 And there shall you remember your ways, and all your doings, wherein you have been defiled; and you shall loathe yourselves in your own sight for all your evils that you have committed.

44 And you shall know that I am the Becoming-One, when I have worked with you for my name's sake, not according to your wicked ways, nor according to your corrupt doings, O you house of Israel, says my Lord(s) the Becoming-One.

45 Moreover the word of the Becoming-One came unto me, saying,

46 Son of man, set your face toward the south, and drop your word toward the south, and prophesy against the forest of the south field;

47 And say to the forest of the south, Hear the word of the Becoming-One; Thus says my Lord(s) the Becoming-One; Behold, I will kindle a fire in you, and it shall devour every green tree in you, and every dry tree: the flaming flame shall not be quenched, and all faces from the south to the north shall be burned therein.

48 And all flesh shall see that I the Becoming-One have kindled it: it shall not be quenched.

49 Then said I, Ah my Lord(s) the Becoming-One! they say of me, does he not speak parables?

Eze 21:1 And the word of the Becoming-One came unto me, saying,

2 Son of man, set your face toward Jerusalem, and drop your word toward the holy places, and prophesy against the land of Israel,

3 And say to the land of Israel, Thus says the Becoming-One; Behold, I am against you, and will draw forth my sword out of his sheath, and will cut off from you the righteous and the wicked.

4 Seeing then that I will cut off from you the righteous and the wicked, therefore shall my sword go forth out of his sheath against all flesh from the south to the north:

5 That all flesh may know that I the Becoming-One have drawn forth my sword out of his sheath: it shall not return any more.

6 Sigh therefore, you son of man, with the breaking of your loins; and with bitterness sigh before their eyes.

7 And it shall be, when they say unto you, Why sigh you? that you shall answer, For the tidings; because it comes: and every heart shall melt, and all hands shall be feeble, and every spirit shall faint, and all knees shall be weak as water: behold, it comes, and shall be brought to pass, says my Lord(s) the Becoming-One.

8 Again the word of the Becoming-One came unto me, saying,

9 Son of man, prophesy, and say, Thus says the Becoming-One; Say, A sword, a sword is sharpened, and also furbished:

10 It is sharpened to make a great slaughter; it is furbished that it may glitter: should we then make mirth? it condemns the rod of my son, as every tree.

11 And he has given it to be furbished, that it may be handled: this sword is sharpened, and it is furbished, to give it into the hand of the slayer.

12 Cry and howl, son of man: for it shall be upon my people, it shall be upon all the princes of Israel: terrors by reason of the sword shall be upon my people: smite therefore upon your thigh.

13 Because it is a trial, and what if the sword contemn even the rod? it shall be no more, says my Lord(s) the Becoming-One.

14 you therefore, son of man, prophesy, and smite your hands together, and let the sword be doubled the third time, the sword of the slain: it is the sword of the great men that are slain, which enters into their privy chambers.

15 I have set the point of the sword against all their gates, that their heart may faint, and their ruins be multiplied: ah! it is made bright, it is wrapped up for the slaughter.

16 Go you one way or other, either on the right hand, or on the left, wheresoever your face is set.

17 I will also smite mine hands together, and I will cause my fury to rest: I the Becoming-One have said it.

18 The word of the Becoming-One came unto me again, saying,

19 Also, you son of man, appoint you two ways, that the sword of the king of Babylon may come: both twain shall come forth out of one land: and choose you a place, choose it at the head of the way to the city.

20 Appoint a way, that the sword may come to Rabbath of the Ammonites, and to Judah in Jerusalem the fortified.

21 For the king of Babylon stood at the parting of the way, at the head of the two ways, to use divination: he made his arrows bright, he consulted with images [teraphim] he looked in the liver.

22 At his right hand was the divination for Jerusalem, to appoint captains, to open the mouth in the slaughter, to lift up the voice with shouting, to appoint battering rams against the gates, to cast a mount, and to build a fort.

23 And it shall be unto them as a false divination in their sight, to them that have sworn oaths: but he will call to remembrance the iniquity, that they may be taken.

24 Therefore thus says my Lord(s) the Becoming-One; Because you have made your iniquity to be remembered, in that your transgressions are discovered, so that in all your doings your sins do appear; because, I say, that you are come to remembrance, you shall be taken with the hand.

25 And you, profane wicked prince of Israel, whose day is come, when iniquity shall have an end,

26 Thus says my Lord(s) the Becoming-One; Remove the diadem, and take off the crown: this shall not be the same: exalt him that is low, and abase him that is high.

27 I will overturn, overturn, overturn, it: and it shall be no more, until he come whose right it is; and I will give it him.

28 And you, son of man, prophesy and say, Thus says my Lord(s) the Becoming-One concerning the Ammonites, and concerning their reproach; even say you, The sword, the sword is drawn: for the slaughter it is furbished, to consume because of the glittering:

29 Whiles they see vanity unto you, whiles they divine a lie unto you, to bring you upon the necks of them that are slain, of the wicked, whose day is come, when their iniquity shall have an end.

30 Shall I cause it to return into his sheath? I will judge you in the place where you were created, in the land of your nativity.

31 And I will pour out mine indignation upon you, I will blow against you in the fire of my wrath, and deliver you into the hand of brutish men, and skillful to destroy.

32 you shall be for fuel to the fire; your blood shall be in the midst of the land; you shall be no more remembered: for I the Becoming-One have spoken it.

Eze 22:1 Moreover the word of the Becoming-One came unto me, saying,

2 Now, you son of man, will you judge, will you judge the bloody city? yes, you shall show her all her abominations.

3 Then say you, Thus says my Lord(s) the Becoming-One, The city sheds blood in the midst of it, that her time may come, and makes idols against herself to defile herself.

4 you are become guilty in your blood that you have shed; and have defiled yourself in your idols which you have made; and you have caused your days to draw near, and are come even unto your years: therefore have I made you a reproach unto the nations, and a mocking to all countries.

5 Those that be near, and those that be far from you, shall mock you, which are infamous and much vexed.

6 Behold, the princes of Israel, every one were in you to their power to shed blood.

7 In you have they set light by father and mother: in the midst of you have they dealt by oppression with the stranger: in you have they vexed the fatherless and the widow.

8 you have despised mine holy things, and have profaned my sabbaths.

9 In you are men that carry tales to shed blood: and in you they eat upon the mountains: in the midst of you they commit lewdness.

10 In you have they discovered their fathers' nakedness: in you have they humbled her that was set apart for pollution.

11 And one has committed abomination with his neighbor's wife; and another has lewdly defiled his daughter-in-law; and another in you has humbled his sister, his father's daughter.

12 In you have they taken gifts to shed blood; you have taken usury and increase, and you have greedily gained of your neighbors by extortion, and have forgotten me, says my Lord(s) the Becoming-One.

13 Behold, therefore I have struck mine hand at your dishonest gain which you have made, and at your blood which has been in the midst of you.

14 Can your heart endure, or can your hands be strong, in the days that I shall deal with you? I the Becoming-One have spoken it, and will do it.

15 And I will scatter you among the nations, and disperse you in the countries, and will consume your filthiness out of you.

16 And you shall take your inheritance in yourself in the sight of the nations, and you shall know that I am the Becoming-One.

17 And the word of the Becoming-One came unto me, saying,

18 Son of man, the house of Israel is to me become dross: all they are brass, and tin, and iron, and lead, in the midst of the furnace; they are even the dross of silver.

19 Therefore thus says my Lord(s) the Becoming-One; Because you are all become dross, behold, therefore I will gather you into the midst of Jerusalem.

20 As they gather silver, and brass, and iron, and lead, and tin, into the midst of the furnace, to blow the fire upon it, to melt it; so will I gather you in mine anger and in my fury, and I will leave you there, and melt you.

21 Yes, I will gather you, and blow upon you in the fire of my wrath, and you shall be melted in the midst thereof.

22 As silver is melted in the midst of the furnace, so shall you be melted in the midst thereof; and you shall know that I the Becoming-One have poured out my fury upon you.

23 And the word of the Becoming-One came unto me, saying,

24 Son of man, say unto her, you are the land that is not cleansed, nor rained upon in the day of indignation.

25 There is a conspiracy of her prophets in the midst thereof, like a roaring lion ravening the prey; they have devoured souls; they have taken the treasure and precious things; they have made her many widows in the midst thereof.

26 Her priests have violated my law, and have profaned mine holy things: they have put no difference between the holy and profane, neither have they showed difference between the unclean and the clean, and have hid their eyes from my sabbaths, and I am profaned among them.

27 Her princes in the midst thereof are like wolves ravening the prey, to shed blood, and to destroy souls, to get dishonest gain.

28 And her prophets have daubed them with untempered mortar, seeing vanity, and divining lies unto them, saying, Thus says my Lord(s) the Becoming-One, when the Becoming-One has not spoken.

29 The people of the land have used oppression, and exercised robbery, and have vexed the poor and needy: yes, they have oppressed the stranger wrongfully.

30 And I sought for a man among them, that should make up the hedge, and stand in the gap before me for the land, that I should not destroy it: but I found none.

31 Therefore have I poured out mine indignation upon them; I have consumed them with the fire of my wrath: their own way have I recompensed upon their heads, says my Lord(s) the Becoming-One.

Eze 23:1 The word of the Becoming-One came again unto me, saying,

2 Son of man, **there were two women**, the daughters of one mother:

3 And they committed whoredoms in Egypt; they committed whoredoms in their youth: there were their breasts pressed, and there they bruised the teats of their virginity.

4 And the names of them were Aholah the elder, and Aholibah her sister: and they were mine, and they bare sons and daughters. Thus were their names; Samaria is Aholah, and Jerusalem Aholibah.

5 And Aholah played the harlot when she was mine; and she doted on her lovers, on the Assyrians her neighbors,

6 Which were clothed with blue, captains and rulers, all of them desirable young men, horsemen riding upon horses.

7 Thus she committed her whoredoms with them, with all them that were the chosen men of Assyria, and with all on whom she doted: with all their idols she defiled herself.

8 Neither left she her whoredoms brought from Egypt: for in her youth they lay with her, and they bruised the breasts of her virginity, and poured their whoredom upon her.

9 Therefore I have delivered her into the hand of her lovers, into the hand of the Assyrians, upon whom she doted.

10 These discovered her nakedness: they took her sons and her daughters, and killed her with the sword: and she became famous among women; for they had executed judgment upon her.

11 And when her sister Aholibah saw this, she was more corrupt in her inordinate love than she, and in her whoredoms more than her sister in her whoredoms.

12 She doted upon the Assyrians her neighbors, captains and rulers clothed most gorgeously, horsemen riding upon horses, all of them desirable young men.

13 Then I saw that she was defiled, that they took both one way,

14 And that she increased her whoredoms: for when she saw men portrayed upon the wall, the images of the Chaldeans portrayed with vermilion,

15 Girded with girdles upon their loins, exceeding in dyed attire upon their heads, all of them princes to look to, after the manner of the Babylonians of Chaldea, the land of their nativity:

16 And as soon as she saw them with her eyes, she doted upon them, and sent messengers unto them into Chaldea.

17 And the Babylonians came to her into the bed of love, and they defiled her with their whoredom, and she was polluted with them, and her soul was alienated from them.

18 So she discovered her whoredoms, and discovered her nakedness: then my soul was alienated from her, like as my soul was alienated from her sister.

19 Yet she multiplied her whoredoms, in calling to remembrance the days of her youth, wherein she had played the harlot in the land of Egypt.

20 For she doted upon their paramours, whose flesh is as the flesh of donkeys, and whose issue is like the issue of horses.

21 Thus you calledst to remembrance the lewdness of your youth, in bruising your teats by the Egyptians for the paps of your youth.

22 Therefore, O Aholibah, thus says my Lord(s) the Becoming-One; Behold, I will raise up your lovers against you, from whom your soul is alienated, and I will bring them against you on every side;

23 The Babylonians, and all the Chaldeans, Pekod, and Shoa, and Koa, and all the Assyrians with them: all of them desirable young men, captains and rulers, great officers and renowned, all of them riding upon horses.

24 And they shall come against you with chariots, wagons, and wheels, and with an assembly of people, which shall set against you buckler and shield and helmet round about: and I will set judgment before them, and they shall judge you according to their judgments.

25 And I will set my jealousy against you, and they shall deal furiously with you: they shall take away your nose and your ears; and your remnant shall fall by the sword: they shall take your sons and your daughters; and your residue shall be devoured by the fire.

26 They shall also strip you out of your clothes, and take away your fair jewels.

27 Thus will I make your lewdness to cease from you, and your whoredom brought from the land of Egypt: so that you shall not lift up your eyes unto them, nor remember Egypt any more.

28 For thus says my Lord(s) the Becoming-One; Behold, I will deliver you into the hand of them whom you hate, into the hand of them from whom your soul is alienated:

29 And they shall deal with you hatefully, and shall take away all your labor, and shall leave you naked and bare: and the nakedness of your whoredoms shall be discovered, both your lewdness and your whoredoms.

30 I will do these things unto you, because you have gone a whoring after the nations, and because you are polluted with their idols.

31 you have walked in the way of your sister; therefore will I give her cup into your hand.

32 Thus says my Lord(s) the Becoming-One; you shall drink of your sister's cup deep and large: you shall be laughed to scorn and had in derision; it contains much.

33 you shall be filled with drunkenness and sorrow, with the cup of astonishment and desolation, with the cup of your sister Samaria.

34 you shall even drink it and suck it out, and you shall break the sherds thereof, and pluck off your own breasts: for I have spoken it, says my Lord(s) the Becoming-One.

35 Therefore thus says my Lord(s) the Becoming-One; Because you have forgotten me, and cast me behind your back, therefore bear you also your lewdness and your whoredoms.

36 The Becoming-One said moreover unto me; Son of man, will you judge Aholah and Aholibah? yes, declare unto them their abominations;

37 That they have committed adultery, and blood is in their hands, and with their idols have they committed adultery, and have also caused their sons, whom they bare unto me, to pass for them through the fire, to devour them.

38 Moreover this they have done unto me: they have defiled my sanctuary in the same day, and have profaned my sabbaths.

39 For when they had slain their children to their idols, then they came the same day into my sanctuary to profane it; and, lo, thus have they done in the midst of mine house.

40 And furthermore, that you have sent for men to come from far, unto whom a messenger was sent; and, lo, they came: for whom you did wash thyself, painted your eyes, and decked yourself with ornaments,

41 And sat upon a stately bed, and a table prepared before it, whereupon you have set mine incense and mine oil.

42 And a voice of a multitude being at ease was with her: and with the men of the common sort were brought Sabeans from the wilderness, which put bracelets upon their hands, and beautiful crowns upon their heads.

43 Then said I unto her that was old in adulteries, Will they now commit whoredoms with her, and she with them?

44 Yet they went in unto her, as they go in unto a woman that plays the harlot: so went they in unto Aholah and unto Aholibah, the lewd women.

45 And the righteous men, they shall judge them after the manner of adulteresses, and after the manner of women that shed blood; because they are adulteresses, and blood is in their hands.

46 For thus says my Lord(s) the Becoming-One; I will bring up a company upon them, and will give them to be removed and spoiled.

47 And the company shall stone them with stones, and dispatch them with their swords; they shall slay their sons and their daughters, and burn up their houses with fire.

48 Thus will I cause lewdness to cease out of the land, that all women may be taught not to do after your lewdness.

49 And they shall recompense your lewdness upon you, and you shall bear the sins of your idols: and you shall know that I am my Lord(s) the Becoming-One.

Eze 24:1 Again in the ninth year, in the tenth month, in the tenth day of the month, the word of the Becoming-One came unto me, saying, **[ab. 3386 YM; Dec/Jan 589/588 BC]** {warning by Ezekiel over, start of attack by Babylon}

2 Son of man, write you the name of the day, even of this same day: the king of Babylon set himself against Jerusalem this same day.

3 And utter a parable unto the rebellious house, and say unto them, Thus says my Lord(s) the Becoming-One; Set on a pot, set it on, and also pour water into it:

4 Gather the pieces thereof into it, even every good piece, the thigh, and the shoulder; fill it with the choice bones.

5 Take the choice of the flock, and burn also the bones under it, and make it boil well, and let them boil the bones of it therein.

6 Therefore thus says my Lord(s) the Becoming-One; Woe to the bloody city, to the pot whose scum is therein, and whose scum is not gone out of it! bring it out piece by piece; let no lot fall upon it.

7 For her blood is in the midst of her; she set it upon the top of a rock; she poured it not upon the ground, to cover it with dust;

8 That it might cause fury to come up to take vengeance; I have set her blood upon the top of a rock, that it should not be covered.

9 Therefore thus says my Lord(s) the Becoming-One; Woe to the bloody city! I will even make the pile for fire great.

10 Heap on wood, kindle the fire, consume the flesh, and spice it well, and let the bones be burned.

11 Then set it empty upon the coals thereof, that the brass of it may be hot, and may burn, and that the filthiness of it may be molten in it, that the scum of it may be consumed.

12 She has wearied herself with lies, and her great scum went not forth out of her: her scum shall be in the fire.

13 In your filthiness is lewdness: because I have purged you, and you were not purged, you shall not be purged from your filthiness any more, till I have caused my fury to rest upon you.

14 I the Becoming-One have spoken it: it shall come to pass, and I will do it; I will not go back, neither will I spare, neither will I repent; according to your ways, and according to your doings, shall they judge you, says my Lord(s) the Becoming-One.

15 Also the word of the Becoming-One came unto me, saying,

16 Son of man, behold, I take away from you the desire of your eyes with a blow [fatal disorder; plague; etc] yet neither shall you mourn nor weep, neither shall your tears run down.

17 Forbear to cry, make no mourning for the dead, bind the tire of your head upon you, and put on your shoes upon your feet, and cover not your lips, and eat not the bread of men.

18 So I spoke unto the people in the morning: and at evening my wife died; and I did in the morning as I was commanded.

19 And the people said unto me, will you not tell us what these things are to us, that you do so?

20 Then I answered them, The word of the Becoming-One came unto me, saying,

21 Speak unto the house of Israel, Thus says my Lord(s) the Becoming-One; Behold, I will profane my sanctuary, the excellency of your strength, the desire of your eyes, and that which your soul pities; and your sons and your daughters whom you have left shall fall by the sword.

22 And you shall do as I have done: you shall not cover your lips, nor eat the bread of men.

23 And your tires shall be upon your heads, and your shoes upon your feet: you shall not mourn nor weep; but you shall pine away for your iniquities, and mourn one toward another.

24 Thus Ezekiel is unto you a sign: according to all that he has done shall you do: and when this comes, you shall know that I am Lords the Becoming-One.

25 Also, you son of man, shall it not be in the day when I take from them their strength, the joy of their glory, the desire of their eyes, and that whereupon they set their soul, their sons and their daughters,

26 That he that escapes in that day shall come unto you, to cause you to hear it with your ears?

27 In that day shall your mouth be opened to him which is escaped, and you shall speak, and be no more mute: and you shall be a sign unto them; and they shall know that I am the Becoming-One.

Eze 25:1 The word of the Becoming-One came again unto me, saying,

2 Son of man, set your face against the **Ammonites**, and prophesy against them;

3 And say unto the Ammonites, Hear the word of my Lord(s) the Becoming-One; Thus says my Lord(s) the Becoming-One; Because you said, Aha, against my sanctuary, when it was profaned; and against the land of Israel, when it was desolate; and against the house of Judah, when they went into captivity;

4 Behold, therefore I will deliver you to the men of the east for a possession, and they shall set their palaces in you, and make their dwellings in you: they shall eat your fruit, and they shall drink your milk.

5 And I will make Rabbah a stable for camels, and the Ammonites a couching place for flocks: and you shall know that I am the Becoming-One.

6 For thus says my Lord(s) the Becoming-One; Because you have clapped your hands, and stamped with the feet, and rejoiced in soul with all your despite against the land of Israel;

7 Behold, therefore I will stretch out mine hand upon you, and will deliver you for a spoil to the nations; and I will cut you off from the people, and I

will cause you to perish out of the countries: I will destroy you; and you shall know that I am the Becoming-One.

8 Thus says my Lord(s) the Becoming-One; Because that Moab and Seir do say, Behold, the house of Judah is like unto all the nations;

9 Therefore, behold, I will open the side of Moab from the cities, from his cities which are on his frontiers, the glory of the country, Beth-jeshimoth, Baal-Meon, and Kiriathaim,

10 Unto the men of the east with the Ammonites, and will give them in possession, that the Ammonites may not be remembered among the nations.

11 And I will execute judgments upon Moab; and they shall know that I am the Becoming-One.

12 Thus says my Lord(s) the Becoming-One; Because that Edom has dealt against the house of Judah by taking vengeance, and has greatly offended, and revenged himself upon them;

13 Therefore thus says my Lord(s) the Becoming-One; I will also stretch out mine hand upon Edom, and will cut off man and beast from it; and I will make it desolate from Teman; and they of Dedan shall fall by the sword.

14 And I will lay my vengeance upon Edom by the hand of my people Israel: and they shall do in Edom according to mine anger and according to my fury; and they shall know my vengeance, says my Lord(s) the Becoming-One.

15 Thus says my Lord(s) the Becoming-One; Because the Philistines have dealt by revenge, and have taken vengeance with a despiteful soul, to destroy it for the olam hatred;

16 Therefore thus says my Lord(s) the Becoming-One; Behold, I will stretch out mine hand upon the Philistines, and I will cut off the Cherethims, and destroy the remnant of the sea coast.

17 And I will execute great vengeance upon them with furious rebukes; and they shall know that I am the Becoming-One, when I shall lay my vengeance upon them.

Eze 26:1 And it came to pass in the eleventh year, in the first day of the month, that the word of the Becoming-One came unto me, saying, **[ab. 3387/8 YM; 587/6 BC]**

2 Son of man, because that **Tyrus** has said against Jerusalem, Aha, she is broken that was the gates of the people: she is turned unto me: I shall be replenished, now she is laid waste:

3 Therefore thus says my Lord(s) the Becoming-One; Behold, I am against you, O Tyrus, and will cause many nations to come up against you, as the sea causes his waves to come up.

4 And they shall destroy the walls of Tyrus, and break down her towers: I will also scrape her dust from her, and make her like the top of a rock.

5 It shall be a place for the spreading of nets in the midst of the sea: for I have spoken it, says my Lord(s) the Becoming-One: and it shall become a spoil to the nations.

6 And her daughters which are in the field shall be slain by the sword; and they shall know that I am the Becoming-One.

7 For thus says my Lord(s) the Becoming-One; Behold, I will bring upon Tyrus Nebuchadrezzar king of Babylon, a king of kings, from the north, with horses, and with chariots, and with horsemen, and companies, and much people.

8 He shall slay with the sword your daughters in the field: and he shall make a fort against you, and cast a mount against you, and lift up the buckler against you.

9 And he shall set engines of war against your walls, and with his axes he shall break down your towers.

10 By reason of the abundance of his horses their dust shall cover you: your walls shall shake at the noise of the horsemen, and of the wheels, and of the chariots, when he shall enter into your gates, as men enter into a city wherein is made a breach.

11 With the hoofs of his horses shall he tread down all your streets: he shall slay your people by the sword, and your strong garrisons shall go down to the ground.

12 And they shall make a spoil of your riches, and make a prey of your merchandise: and they shall break down your walls, and destroy your pleasant houses: and they shall lay your stones and your timber and your dust in the midst of the water.

13 And I will cause the noise of your songs to cease; and the sound of your harps shall be no more heard.

14 And I will make you like the top of a rock: you shall be a place to spread nets upon; you shall be built no more: for I the Becoming-One have spoken it, says my Lord(s) the Becoming-One.

15 Thus says my Lord(s), the Becoming-One, to Tyrus; Shall not the isles shake at the sound of your fall, when the wounded cry, when the slaughter is made in the midst of you?

16 Then all the princes of the sea shall come down from their thrones, and lay away their robes, and put off their broidered garments: they shall clothe themselves with trembling; they shall sit upon the ground, and shall tremble at every moment, and be astonished at you.

17 And they shall take up a lamentation for you, and say to you, How are you destroyed, that were inhabited of seafaring men, the renowned city, which were strong in the sea, she and her inhabitants, which cause their terror to be on all that haunt it!

18 Now shall the isles tremble in the day of your fall; yes, the isles that are in the sea shall be troubled at your departure.

19 For thus says my Lord(s) the Becoming-One; When I shall make you a desolate city, like the cities that are not inhabited; when I shall bring up the deep upon you, and great waters shall cover you;

20 When I shall bring you down with them that descend into the pit, with the people of olam, and shall set you in the low parts of the earth, in places desolate of old, with them that go down to the pit, that you be not inhabited; and I shall set glory in the land of the living;

21 I will make you a terror, and you shall be no more: though you be sought for, yet shall you not for olam be found again, says my Lord(s) the Becoming-One.

Eze 27:1 The word of the Becoming-One came again unto me, saying,

2 Now, you son of man, **take up a lamentation for Tyrus**;

3 And say unto Tyrus, O you that are situate at the entry of the sea, which are a merchant of the people for many isles, Thus says my Lord(s) the Becoming-One; O Tyrus, you have said, I am of perfect beauty.

4 your borders are in the midst of the seas, your builders have perfected your beauty.

5 They have made all your ship boards of fir trees of Senir: they have taken cedars from Lebanon to make masts for you.

6 Of the oaks of Bashan have they made your oars; the company of the Ashurites have made your benches of ivory, brought out of the isles of Chittim.

7 Fine linen with broidered work from Egypt was that which you spread forth to be your sail; blue and purple from the isles of Elishah was that which covered you.

8 The inhabitants of Zidon and Arvad were your mariners: your wise men, O Tyrus, that were in you, were your pilots.

9 The ancients of Gebal and the wise men thereof were in you your calkers: all the ships of the sea with their mariners were in you to occupy your merchandise.

10 They of Persia and of Lud and of Phut were in your army, your men of war: they hanged the shield and helmet in you; they set forth your comeliness.

11 The men of Arvad with your army were upon your walls round about, and the Gammadims were in your towers: they hanged their shields upon your walls round about; they have made your beauty perfect.

12 Tarshish was your merchant by reason of the multitude of all kind of riches; with silver, iron, tin, and lead, they traded in your fairs.

13 Javan, Tubal, and Meshech, they were your merchants: they traded the souls of men and vessels of brass in your market.

14 They of the house of Togarmah traded in your fairs with horses and horsemen and mules.

15 The men of Dedan were your merchants; many isles were the merchandise of your hand: they brought you for a present horns of ivory and ebony.

16 Syria was your merchant by reason of the multitude of the wares of your making: they occupied in your fairs with emeralds, purple, and broidered work, and fine linen, and coral, and agate.

17 Judah, and the land of Israel, they were your merchants: they traded in your market wheat of Minnith, and Pannag, and honey, and oil, and balm.

18 Damascus was your merchant in the multitude of the wares of your making, for the multitude of all riches; in the wine of Helbon, and white wool.

19 Dan also and Javan going back and forth occupied in your fairs: bright iron, cassia, and calamus, were in your market.

20 Dedan was your merchant in precious clothes for chariots.

21 Arabia, and all the princes of Kedar, they occupied with you in lambs, and in rams, and goats: in these were they your merchants.

22 The merchants of Sheba and Raamah, they were your merchants: they occupied in your fairs with chief of all spices, and with all precious stones, and gold.

23 Haran, and Canneh, and Eden, the merchants of Sheba, Asshur, and Chilmad, were your merchants.

24 These were your merchants in all sorts of things, in blue clothes, and broidered work, and in chests of rich apparel, bound with cords, and made of cedar, among your merchandise.

25 The ships of Tarshish did sing of you in your market: and you were replenished, and made very glorious in the midst of the seas.

26 your rowers have brought you into great waters: the east wind has broken you in the midst of the seas.

27 your riches, and your fairs, your merchandise, your mariners, and your pilots, your calkers, and the occupiers of your merchandise, and all your men of war, that are in you, and in all your company which is in the midst of you, shall fall into the midst of the seas in the day of your ruin.

28 The suburbs shall shake at the sound of the cry of your pilots.

29 And all that handle the oar, the mariners, and all the pilots of the sea, shall come down from their ships, they shall stand upon the land;

30 And shall cause their voice to be heard against you, and shall cry bitterly, and shall cast up dust upon their heads, they shall wallow themselves in the ashes:

31 And they shall make themselves utterly bald for you, and gird them with sackcloth, and they shall weep for you with bitterness of soul and bitter wailing.

32 And in their wailing they shall take up a lamentation for you, and lament over you, saying, What city is like Tyrus, like the destroyed in the midst of the sea?

33 When your wares went forth out of the seas, you filled many people; you did enrich the kings of the earth with the multitude of your riches and of your merchandise.

34 In the time when you shall be broken by the seas in the depths of the waters your merchandise and all your company in the midst of you shall fall.

35 All the inhabitants of the isles shall be astonished at you, and their kings shall be greatly afraid, they shall be troubled in their countenance.

36 The merchants among the people shall hiss at you; you shall be a terror, and never shall be for olam.

Eze 28:1 The word of the Becoming-One came again unto me, saying,

2 Son of man, **say unto the prince of Tyrus**, Thus says my Lord(s) the Becoming-One; Because your heart is lifted up, and you have said, I am GOD, I sit in the seat of God, in the midst of the seas; yet you are a man, and not GOD, though you ascribe your mind as the mind of God:

3 Behold, you are wiser than Daniel; there is no secret that they can hide from you:

4 With your wisdom and with your understanding you have gotten you riches, and have gotten gold and silver into your treasures:

5 By your great wisdom and by your traffic have you increased your riches, and your mind is lifted up because of your riches:

6 Therefore thus says my Lord(s) the Becoming-One; Because you ascribe your mind as the mind of God;

7 Behold, therefore I will bring strangers upon you, the ruthless nations: and they shall draw their swords against the beauty of your wisdom, and they shall defile your brightness.

8 They shall bring you down to the pit, and you shall die the deaths of them that are slain in the midst of the seas.

9 **will you yet say before him that slays you, I am God? but you shall be a man, and no GOD, in the hand of him that slays you.**

10 you shall die the deaths of the uncircumcised by the hand of strangers: for I have spoken it, says my Lord(s) the Becoming-One.

11 Moreover the word of the Becoming-One came unto me, saying,

12 Son of man, take up a lamentation upon the king of Tyrus, and say unto him, Thus says my Lord(s) the Becoming-One; you seal up the sum, full of wisdom, and perfect in beauty.

13 **you have been in Eden the garden of God**; every precious stone was your covering, the sardius, topaz, and the diamond, the beryl, the onyx, and the jasper, the sapphire, the emerald, and the carbuncle, and gold: the workmanship of your tabrets and of your pipes was prepared in you in the day that you were created.

14 **you are the anointed cherub that covers; and I have set you so: you were upon the holy mountain of God; you have walked up and down in the midst of the stones of fire.**

15 **you were perfect in your ways from the day that you were created, till iniquity was found in you.**

16 **By the multitude of your merchandise they have filled the midst of you with violence, and you have sinned: therefore I will cast you as profane out of the mountain of God: and I will destroy you, O covering cherub, from the midst of the stones of fire.**

17 your heart was lifted up because of your beauty, you have corrupted your wisdom by reason of your brightness: I will cast you to the ground, I will lay you before kings, that they may behold you.

18 you have defiled your sanctuaries by the multitude of your iniquities, by the iniquity of your traffic; therefore will I bring forth a fire from the midst of you, it shall devour you, and I will bring you to ashes upon the earth in the sight of all them that behold you.

19 All they that know you among the people shall be astonished at you: you shall be a terror, and never shall you be for olam.

20 Again the word of the Becoming-One came unto me, saying,

21 **Son of man, set your face against Zidon**, and prophesy against it,

22 And say, Thus says my Lord(s) the Becoming-One; Behold, I am against you, O Zidon; and I will be glorified in the midst of you: and they shall know that I am the Becoming-One, when I shall have executed judgments in her, and shall be sanctified in her.

23 For I will send into her pestilence, and blood into her streets; and the wounded shall be judged in the midst of her by the sword upon her on every side; and they shall know that I am the Becoming-One.

24 And there shall be no more a pricking brier unto the house of Israel, nor any grieving thorn of all that are round about them, that despised them; and they shall know that I am my Lord(s) the Becoming-One.

25 Thus says my Lord(s) the Becoming-One; When I shall have gathered the house of Israel from the people among whom they are scattered, and shall be sanctified in them in the sight of the nations, then shall they dwell in their land that I have given to my servant Jacob.

26 And they shall dwell safely therein, and shall build houses, and plant vineyards; yes, they shall dwell with confidence, when I have executed judgments upon all those that despise them round about them; and they shall know that I am the Becoming-One their God.

Eze 29:1 In the tenth year, in the tenth month, in the twelfth day of the month, the word of the Becoming-One came unto me, saying, **[ab. 3386/7 YM; 588-587 BC]**

2 Son of man, set your face **against Pharaoh king of Egypt**, and prophesy against him, and against all Egypt:

3 Speak, and say, Thus says my Lord(s) the Becoming-One; Behold, I am against you, Pharaoh king of Egypt, the great monster that lies in the midst of his rivers, which has said, My river is mine own, and I have made it for myself.

4 But I will put hooks in your jaws, and I will cause the fish of your rivers to stick unto your scales, and I will bring you up out of the midst of your rivers, and all the fish of your rivers shall stick unto your scales.

5 And I will leave you thrown into the wilderness, you and all the fish of your rivers: you shall fall upon the open fields; you shall not be brought together, nor gathered: I have given you for food to the beasts of the field and to the fowls of the heaven.

6 And all the inhabitants of Egypt shall know that I am the Becoming-One, because they have been a staff of reed to the house of Israel.

7 When they took hold of you by your hand, you did break, and rend all their shoulder: and when they leaned upon you, you broke, and made all their loins to be at a stand.

8 Therefore thus says my Lord(s) the Becoming-One; Behold, I will bring a sword upon you, and cut off man and beast out of you.

9 And the land of Egypt shall be desolate and waste; and they shall know that I am the Becoming-One: because he has said, The river is mine, and I have made it.

10 Behold, therefore I am against you, and against your rivers, and I will make the land of Egypt utterly waste and desolate, from the tower of Syene even unto the border of Ethiopia.

11 No foot of man shall pass through it, nor foot of beast shall pass through it, neither shall it be inhabited forty years.

12 And I will make the land of Egypt desolate in the midst of the countries that are desolate, and her

cities among the cities that are laid waste shall be desolate forty years: and I will scatter the Egyptians among the nations, and will disperse them through the countries.

13 Yet thus says my Lord(s) the Becoming-One; At the end of forty years will I gather the Egyptians from the people to which they were scattered:

14 And I will bring again the captivity of Egypt, and will cause them to return into the land of Pathros, into the land of their habitation; and they shall be there a base kingdom.

15 It shall be the basest of the kingdoms; neither shall it exalt itself any more above the nations: for I will diminish them, that they shall no more rule over the nations.

16 And it shall be no more the confidence of the house of Israel, which brings their iniquity to remembrance, when they shall look after them: but they shall know that I am my Lord(s) the Becoming-One.

17 And it came to pass in the seven and twentieth year [**571 BC**], in the first month, in the first day of the month, the word of the Becoming-One came unto me, saying,

18 Son of man, Nebuchadrezzar king of Babylon caused his army to serve a great service against Tyrus: every head was made bald, and every shoulder was peeled: yet had he no wages, nor his army, for Tyrus, for the service that he had served against it:

19 Therefore thus says my Lord(s) the Becoming-One; **Behold, I will give the land of Egypt unto Nebuchadrezzar king of Babylon**; and he shall take her multitude, and take her spoil, and take her prey; and it shall be the wages for his army.

20 I have given him the land of Egypt for his labor wherewith he served against it, because they worked for me, says my Lord(s) the Becoming-One.

21 In that day will I cause the horn of the house of Israel to bud forth, and I will give you the opening of the mouth in the midst of them; and they shall know that I am the Becoming-One.

Eze 30:1 The word of the Becoming-One came again unto me, saying,

2 Son of man, prophesy and say, Thus says my Lord(s) the Becoming-One; Howl ye, Woe worth the day!

3 **For the day is near, even the day of the Becoming-One is near, a cloudy day; it shall be the time of the nations.**

4 And the sword shall come upon Egypt, and great pain shall be in Ethiopia, when the slain shall fall in Egypt, and they shall take away her multitude, and her foundations shall be broken down.

5 Ethiopia, and Libya, and Lydia, and all the mingled people, and Chub, and the men of the land that is in league, shall fall with them by the sword.

6 Thus says the Becoming-One; They also that uphold Egypt shall fall; and the pride of her power shall come down: from the tower of Syene shall they fall in it by the sword, says my Lord(s) the Becoming-One.

7 And they shall be desolate in the midst of the countries that are desolate, and her cities shall be in the midst of the cities that are wasted.

8 And they shall know that I am the Becoming-One, when I have set a fire in Egypt, and when all her helpers shall be destroyed.

9 In that day shall messengers go forth from me in ships to make the careless Ethiopians afraid, and great pain shall come upon them, as in the day of Egypt: for, lo, it comes.

10 **Thus says my Lord(s) the Becoming-One; I will also make the multitude of Egypt to cease by the hand of Nebuchadrezzar king of Babylon**.

11 He and his people with him, the terrible of the nations, shall be brought to destroy the land: and they shall draw their swords against Egypt, and fill the land with the slain.

12 And I will make the rivers dry, and sell the land into the hand of the wicked: and I will make the land waste, and all that is therein, by the hand of strangers: I the Becoming-One have spoken it.

13 Thus says my Lord(s) the Becoming-One; I will also destroy the idols, and I will cause their images to cease out of Noph; and there shall be no more a prince of the land of Egypt: and I will put a fear in the land of Egypt.

14 And I will make Pathros desolate, and will set fire in Zoan, and will execute judgments in No.

15 And I will pour my fury upon Sin, the strength of Egypt; and I will cut off the multitude of No.

16 And I will set fire in Egypt: Sin shall have great pain, and No shall be ripped asunder, and Noph shall have distresses daily.

17 The young men of Aven and of Pibeseth shall fall by the sword: and these cities shall go into captivity.

18 At Tehaphnehes also the day shall be darkened, when I shall break there the yokes of Egypt: and the pomp of her strength shall cease in her: as for her, a cloud shall cover her, and her daughters shall go into captivity.

19 Thus will I execute judgments in Egypt: and they shall know that I am the Becoming-One.

20 And it came to pass in the eleventh year, in the first month, in the seventh day of the month, that the word of the Becoming-One came unto me, saying, [585 BC]

21 Son of man, I have broken the arm of Pharaoh king of Egypt; and, lo, it shall not be bound up to be healed, to put a roller to bind it, to make it strong to hold the sword.

22 Therefore thus says my Lord(s) the Becoming-One; Behold, I am against Pharaoh king of Egypt, and will break his arms, the strong, and that which was broken; and I will cause the sword to fall out of his hand.

23 And I will scatter the Egyptians among the nations, and will disperse them through the countries.

24 And I will strengthen the arms of the king of Babylon, and put my sword in his hand: but I will break Pharaoh's arms, and he shall groan before him with the groanings of a deadly wounded man.

25 But I will strengthen the arms of the king of Babylon, and the arms of Pharaoh shall fall down; and they shall know that I am the Becoming-One, when I shall put my sword into the hand of the king of Babylon, and he shall stretch it out upon the land of Egypt.

26 And I will scatter the Egyptians among the nations, and disperse them among the countries; and they shall know that I am the Becoming-One.

Eze 31:1 And it came to pass in the eleventh year, in the third month, in the first day of the month, that the word of the BeComigOne came unto me, saying, [**ab. 3388 YM; 587/6 BC**]

2 Son of man, **speak unto Pharaoh king of Egypt, and to his multitude; Whom are you like in your greatness?**

3 **Behold, the Assyrian was a cedar in Lebanon** with fair branches, and with a shadowing shroud, and of a high stature; and his top was among the thick boughs.

4 The waters made him great, the deep set him up on high with her rivers running round about his plants, and sent out her little rivers unto all the trees of the field.

5 Therefore his height was exalted above all the trees of the field, and his boughs were multiplied, and his branches became long because of the multitude of waters, when he shot forth.

6 All the fowls of the heavens made their nests in his boughs, and under his branches did all the beasts of the field bring forth their young, and under his shadow dwelt all great nations.

7 Thus was he fair in his greatness, in the length of his branches: for his root was by great waters.

8 **The cedars in the garden of God could not hide him: the fir trees were not like his boughs, and the chestnut trees were not like his branches; nor any tree in the garden of God was like unto him in his beauty.**

9 **I have made him fair by the multitude of his branches: so that all the trees of Eden, that were in the garden of God, envied him.**

10 Therefore thus says my Lord(s) the Becoming-One; Because you have lifted up yourself in height, and he has shot up his top among the thick boughs, and his heart is lifted up in his height;

11 I have therefore delivered him into the hand of God of the nations; he shall surely deal with him: I have driven him out for his wickedness.

12 And strangers, the terrible of the nations, have cut him off, and have left him: upon the mountains and in all the valleys his branches are fallen, and his boughs are broken by all the rivers of the land; and all the people of the earth are gone down from his shadow, and have left him.

13 Upon his ruin shall all the fowls of the heavens remain, and all the beasts of the field shall be upon his branches:

14 To the end that none of all the trees by the waters exalt themselves for their height, neither shoot up their top among the thick boughs, neither their trees stand up in their height, all that drink water: for they are all delivered unto death, to the nether parts of the earth, in the midst of the children of men, with them that go down to the pit.

15 Thus says my Lord(s) the Becoming-One; In the day when he went down to Sheol I caused a mourning: I covered the deep for him, and I restrained the floods thereof, and the great waters were stayed: and I caused Lebanon to mourn for him, and all the trees of the field fainted for him.

16 **I made the nations to shake at the sound of his fall, when I cast him down to Sheol with them that descend into the pit: and all the trees of Eden, the choice and best of Lebanon, all that drink water, shall be comforted in the nether parts of the earth.**

17 They also went down into Sheol with him unto them that be slain with the sword; and they that were his arm, that dwelt under his shadow in the midst of the nations.

18 **To whom are you thus like in glory and in greatness among the trees of Eden? yet shall you be brought down with the trees of Eden unto the nether parts of the earth: you shall lie in the midst of the uncircumcised with them that be slain by the sword. This is Pharaoh and all his multitude, says my Lord(s) the Becoming-One**.

Eze 32:1 And it came to pass in the twelfth year, in the twelfth month, in the first day of the month, that the word of the Becoming-One came unto me, saying, [**ab. 3389 YM; 585 BC**]

2 Son of man, **take up a lamentation for Pharaoh king of Egypt**, and say unto him, you are like a young lion of the nations, and you are as a whale in the seas: and you came forth with your rivers, and troubled the waters with your feet, and fouled their rivers.

3 Thus says my Lord(s) the Becoming-One; I will therefore spread out my net over you with a company of many people; and they shall bring you up in my net.

4 Then will I leave you upon the land, I will cast you forth upon the open field, and will cause all the fowls of the heavens to remain upon you, and I will fill the beasts of the whole earth with you.

5 And I will lay your flesh upon the mountains, and fill the valleys with your height.

6 I will also water with your blood the land wherein you swim, even to the mountains; and the rivers shall be full of you.

7 And when I shall put you out, I will cover the heaven, and make the stars thereof dark; I will cover the sun with a cloud, and the moon shall not give her light.

8 All the bright lights of the heavens will I make dark over you, and set darkness upon your land, says my Lord(s) the Becoming-One.

9 I will also vex the hearts of many people, when I shall bring your destruction among the nations, into the countries which you have not known.

10 Yes, I will make many people amazed at you, and their kings shall be horribly afraid for you, when I shall brandish my sword before them; and they shall tremble at every moment, every man for his own soul, in the day of your fall.

11 For thus says my Lord(s) the Becoming-One; **The sword of the king of Babylon shall come upon you.**

12 By the swords of the mighty will I cause your multitude to fall, the terrible of the nations, all of them: and they shall spoil the pomp of Egypt, and all the multitude thereof shall be destroyed.

13 I will destroy also all the beasts thereof from beside the great waters; neither shall the foot of man

trouble them any more, nor the hoofs of beasts trouble them.

14 Then will I make their waters deep, and cause their rivers to run like oil, says my Lord(s) the Becoming-One.

15 When I shall make the land of Egypt desolate, and the country shall be destitute of that whereof it was full, when I shall smite all them that dwell therein, then shall they know that I am the Becoming-One.

16 This is the lamentation wherewith they shall lament her: the daughters of the nations shall lament her: they shall lament for her, even for Egypt, and for all her multitude, says my Lord(s) the Becoming-One.

17 It came to pass also in the twelfth year, in the fifteenth day of the month, that the word of the Becoming-One came unto me, saying,

18 Son of man, wail for the multitude of Egypt, and cast them down, even her, and the daughters of the famous nations, unto the nether parts of the earth, with them that go down into the pit.

19 Whom do you pass in beauty? go down, and be you laid with the uncircumcised.

20 They shall fall in the midst of them that are slain by the sword: she is delivered to the sword: draw her and all her multitudes.

21 God of the mighty shall speak to him out of the midst of Sheol with them that help him: they are gone down, they lie uncircumcised, slain by the sword.

22 Asshur is there and all her company: his graves are about him: all of them slain, fallen by the sword:

23 Whose graves are set in the sides of the pit, and her company is round about her grave: all of them slain, fallen by the sword, which caused terror in the land of the living.

24 There is Elam and all her multitude round about her grave, all of them slain, fallen by the sword, which are gone down uncircumcised into the nether parts of the earth, which caused their terror in the land of the living; yet have they borne their shame with them that go down to the pit.

25 They have set her a bed in the midst of the slain with all her multitude: her graves are round about him: all of them uncircumcised, slain by the sword: though their terror was caused in the land of the living, yet have they borne their shame with them that go down to the pit: he is put in the midst of them that be slain.

26 There is Meshech, Tubal, and all her multitude: her graves are round about him: all of them uncircumcised, slain by the sword, though they caused their terror in the land of the living.

27 And they shall not lie with the mighty that are fallen of the uncircumcised, which are gone down to Sheol with their weapons of war: and they have laid their swords under their heads, but their iniquities shall be upon their bones, though they were the terror of the mighty in the land of the living.

28 Yes, you shall be broken in the midst of the uncircumcised, and shall lie with them that are slain with the sword.

29 There is Edom, her kings, and all her princes, which with their might are laid by them that were slain by the sword: they shall lie with the uncircumcised, and with them that go down to the pit.

30 There be the princes of the north, all of them, and all the Zidonians, which are gone down with the slain; with their terror they are ashamed of their might; and they lie uncircumcised with them that be slain by the sword, and bear their shame with them that go down to the pit.

31 Pharaoh shall see them, and shall be comforted over all his multitude, even Pharaoh and all his army slain by the sword, says my Lord(s) the Becoming-One.

32 For I have caused my terror in the land of the living: and he shall be laid in the midst of the uncircumcised with them that are slain with the sword, even Pharaoh and all his multitude, says my Lord(s) the Becoming-One.

Eze 33:1 Again the word of the Becoming-One came unto me, saying,

2 Son of man, **speak to the children of your people**, and say unto them, When I bring the sword upon a land, if the people of the land take a man of their coasts, and set him for their watchman:

3 If when he sees the sword come upon the land, he blow the trumpet, and warn the people;

4 Then whosoever hears the sound of the trumpet, and takes not warning; if the sword come, and take him away, his blood shall be upon his own head.

5 He heard the sound of the trumpet, and took not warning; his blood shall be upon him. But he that takes warning shall deliver his soul.

6 But if the watchman see the sword come, and blow not the trumpet, and the people be not warned; if the sword come, and take any soul from among them, he is taken away in his iniquity; but his blood will I require at the watchman's hand.

7 So you, O son of man, I have set you a watchman unto the house of Israel; therefore you shall hear the word at my mouth, and warn them from me.

8 When I say unto the wicked, O wicked man, in dying, you will die;[142] if you do not speak to warn the wicked from his way, that wicked man shall die in his iniquity; but his blood will I require at your hand.

9 Nevertheless, if you warn the wicked of his way to turn from it; if he do not turn from his way, he shall die in his iniquity; but you have delivered your soul.

10 Therefore, O you son of man, speak unto the house of Israel; Thus you speak, saying, If our transgressions and our sins be upon us, and we pine away in them, how should we then live?

11 Say unto them, As I live, says my Lord(s) the Becoming-One, I have no pleasure in the death of the wicked; but that the wicked turn from his way and live: turn ye, turn you from your evil ways; for why will you die, O house of Israel?

12 Therefore, you son of man, say unto the children of your people, The righteousness of the righteous shall not deliver him in the day of his

---

[142] מוֹת תָּמוּת – "in dying, you will die" or when you die, you will be dead – a part of the group called the "dead"

transgression: as for the wickedness of the wicked, he shall not fall thereby in the day that he turns from his wickedness; neither shall the righteous be able to live for his righteousness in the day that he sins.

13 When I shall say to the righteous, that he shall surely live; if he trust to his own righteousness, and commit iniquity, all his righteousness shall not be remembered; but for his iniquity that he has committed, he shall die for it.

14 Again, when I say unto the wicked, in dying, you will die;[143] if he turn from his sin, and do that which is lawful and right;

15 If the wicked restore the pledge, give again that he had robbed, walk in the statutes of life, without committing iniquity; he shall surely live, he shall not die.

16 None of his sins that he has committed shall be mentioned unto him: he has done that which is lawful and right; he shall surely live.

17 Yet the children of your people say, The way of my Lord(s) is not equal: but as for them, their way is not equal.

18 When the righteous turns from his righteousness, and commits iniquity, he shall even die thereby.

19 But if the wicked turn from his wickedness, and do that which is lawful and right, he shall live thereby.

20 Yet you say, The way of my Lord(s) is not equal. O you house of Israel, I will judge you every one after his ways.

21 And it came to pass in the twelfth year of our captivity, in the tenth month, in the fifth day of the month, that one that had escaped out of Jerusalem came unto me, saying, The city is struck. [586 BC]

22 Now the hand of the Becoming-One was upon me in the evening, afore he that was escaped came; and had opened my mouth, until he came to me in the morning; and my mouth was opened, and I was no more mute.

23 Then the word of the Becoming-One came unto me, saying,

24 Son of man, they that inhabit those wastes of the land of Israel speak, saying, Abraham was one, and he inherited the land: but we are many; the land is given us for inheritance.

25 Therefore say unto them, Thus says my Lord(s) the Becoming-One; you eat with the blood, and lift up your eyes toward your idols, and shed blood: and shall you possess the land?

26 you stand upon your sword, you work abomination, and you defile every one his neighbor's wife: and shall you possess the land?

27 Say you thus unto them, Thus says my Lord(s) the Becoming-One; As I live, surely they that are in the wastes shall fall by the sword, and him that is in the open field will I give to the beasts to be devoured, and they that be in the forts and in the caves shall die of the pestilence.

28 For I will lay the land most desolate, and the pomp of her strength shall cease; and the mountains of Israel shall be desolate, that none shall pass through.

29 Then shall they know that I am the Becoming-One, when I have laid the land most desolate because of all their abominations which they have committed.

30 Also, you son of man, the children of your people still are talking against you by the walls and in the doors of the houses, and speak one to another, every one to his brother, saying, Come, I pray you, and hear what is the word that comes forth from the Becoming-One.

31 And they come unto you as the people comes, and they sit before you as my people, and they hear your words, but they will not do them: for with their mouth they show much love, but their heart goes after their covetousness.

32 And, lo, you are unto them as a very lovely song of one that has a pleasant voice, and can play well on an instrument: for they hear your words, but they do them not.

33 And when this comes to pass, lo, it will come, then shall they know that a prophet has been among them.

Eze 34:1 And the word of the Becoming-One came unto me, saying,

2 Son of man, **prophesy against the shepherds of Israel**, prophesy, and say unto them, Thus says my Lord(s), the Becoming-One, unto the shepherds; Woe be to the shepherds of Israel that do feed themselves! should not the shepherds feed the flocks?

3 you eat the fat, and you clothe you with the wool, you kill them that are fed: but you feed not the flock.

4 The diseased have you not strengthened, neither have you healed that which was sick, neither have you bound up that which was broken, neither have you brought again that which was driven away, neither have you sought that which was lost; but with force and with cruelty have you ruled them.

5 And they were scattered, because there is no shepherd: and they became food to all the beasts of the field, when they were scattered.

6 My sheep wandered through all the mountains, and upon every high hill: yes, my flock was scattered upon all the face of the earth, and none did search or seek after them.

7 Therefore, you shepherds, hear the word of the Becoming-One;

8 As I live, says my Lord(s) the Becoming-One, surely because my flock became a prey, and my flock became food to every beast of the field, because there was no shepherd, neither did my shepherds search for my flock, but the shepherds fed themselves, and fed not my flock;

9 Therefore, O you shepherds, hear the word of the Becoming-One;

10 Thus says my Lord(s) the Becoming-One; Behold, I am against the shepherds; and I will require my flock at their hand, and cause them to cease from feeding the flock; neither shall the shepherds feed themselves any more; for I will deliver my flock from their mouth, that they may not be food for them.

11 For thus says my Lord(s) the Becoming-One; Behold, I, even I, will both search my sheep, and seek them out.

---

[143] מוֹת תָּמוּת – "in dying, you will die" or when you die, you will be dead – a part of the group called the "dead"

12 As a shepherd seeks out his flock in the day that he is among his sheep that are scattered; so will I seek out my sheep, and will deliver them out of all places where they have been scattered in the cloudy and dark day.

13 And I will bring them out from the people, and gather them from the countries, and will bring them to their own land, and feed them upon the mountains of Israel by the rivers, and in all the inhabited places of the country.

14 I will feed them in a good pasture, and upon the high mountains of Israel shall their fold be: there shall they lie in a good fold, and in a fat pasture shall they feed upon the mountains of Israel.

15 I will feed my flock, and I will cause them to lie down, says my Lord(s) the Becoming-One.

16 I will seek that which was lost, and bring again that which was driven away, and will bind up that which was broken, and will strengthen that which was sick: but I will destroy the fat and the strong; I will feed them with judgment.

17 And as for you, O my flock, thus says my Lord(s) the Becoming-One; Behold, I judge between cattle and cattle, between the rams and the he goats.

18 seems it a small thing unto you to have eaten up the good pasture, but you must tread down with your feet the residue of your pastures? and to have drunk of the deep waters, but you must foul the residue with your feet?

19 And as for my flock, they eat that which you have trodden with your feet; and they drink that which you have fouled with your feet.

20 Therefore thus says my Lord(s) the, the Becoming-One, unto them; Behold, I, even I, will judge between the fat cattle and between the lean cattle.

21 Because you have thrust with side and with shoulder, and pushed all the diseased with your horns, till you have scattered them abroad;

22 Therefore will I save my flock, and they shall no more be a prey; and I will judge between cattle and cattle.

23 And I will set up one shepherd over them, and he shall feed them, even my servant David; he shall feed them, and he shall be their shepherd.

24 And I the Becoming-One will be their God, and my servant David a prince among them; I the Becoming-One have spoken it.

25 And I will make with them a covenant of peace, and will cause the evil beast to cease out of the land: and they shall dwell safely in the wilderness, and sleep in the woods.

26 And I will make them and the places round about my hill a blessing; and I will cause the shower to come down in his season; there shall be showers of blessing.

27 And the tree of the field shall yield her fruit, and the earth shall yield her increase, and they shall be safe in their land, and shall know that I am the Becoming-One, when I have broken the bands of their yoke, and delivered them out of the hand of those that served themselves of them.

28 And they shall no more be a prey to the nations, neither shall the beast of the land devour them; but they shall dwell safely, and none shall make them afraid.

29 And I will raise up for them a plant of renown, and they shall be no more consumed with hunger in the land, neither bear the shame of the nations any more.

30 Thus shall they know that I the Becoming-One their God am with them, and that they, even the house of Israel, are my people, says my Lord(s) the Becoming-One.

31 And you my flock, the flock of my pasture, are men, and I am your God, says my Lord(s) the Becoming-One.

Eze 35:1 Moreover the word of the Becoming-One came unto me, saying,

2 Son of man, **set your face against mount Seir**, and prophesy against it,

3 And say unto it, Thus says my Lord(s) the Becoming-One; Behold, O mount Seir, I am against you, and I will stretch out mine hand against you, and I will make you most desolate.

4 I will lay your cities waste, and you shall be desolate, and you shall know that I am the Becoming-One.

5 Because you have had a olam hatred, and have shed the blood of the children of Israel by the force of the sword in the time of their calamity, in the time that their iniquity had an end:

6 Therefore, as I live, says my Lord(s) the Becoming-One, I will prepare you unto blood, and blood shall pursue you: sith you have not hated blood, even blood shall pursue you.

7 Thus will I make mount Seir most desolate, and cut off from it him that passes out and him that returns.

8 And I will fill his mountains with his slain men: in your hills, and in your valleys, and in all your rivers, shall they fall that are slain with the sword.

9 I will make you desolations of olam, and your cities shall not return: and you shall know that I am the Becoming-One.

10 Because you have said, These two nations and these two countries shall be mine, and we will possess it; whereas the Becoming-One was there:

11 Therefore, as I live, says my Lord(s) the Becoming-One, I will even do according to your anger, and according to your envy which you have used out of your hatred against them; and I will make myself known among them, when I have judged you.

12 And you shall know that I am the Becoming-One, and that I have heard all your blasphemies which you have spoken against the mountains of Israel, saying, They are laid desolate, they are given us to consume.

13 Thus with your mouth you have boasted against me, and have multiplied your words against me: I have heard them.

14 Thus says my Lord(s) the Becoming-One; When the whole earth rejoices, I will make you desolate.

15 As you did rejoice at the inheritance of the house of Israel, because it was desolate, so will I do unto you: you shall be desolate, O mount Seir, and all Idumea, even all of it: and they shall know that I am the Becoming-One.

Eze 36:1 Also, you son of man, prophesy unto the mountains of Israel, and say, you mountains of Israel, hear the word of the Becoming-One: 2 Thus says my Lord(s) the Becoming-One; Because the enemy has said against you, Aha, even the olam high places are ours in possession:

3 Therefore prophesy and say, Thus says my Lord(s) the Becoming-One; Because they have made you desolate, and swallowed you up on every side, that you might be a possession unto the residue of the nations, and you are taken up in the lips of talkers, and are an infamy of the people:

4 Therefore, you mountains of Israel, hear the word of my Lord(s) the Becoming-One; Thus says my Lord(s), the Becoming-One, to the mountains, and to the hills, to the rivers, and to the valleys, to the desolate wastes, and to the cities that are forsaken, which became a prey and derision to the residue of the nations that are round about;

5 Therefore thus says my Lord(s) the Becoming-One; Surely in the fire of my jealousy have I spoken against the residue of the nations, and against all Idumea, which have appointed my land into their possession with the joy of all their heart, with despiteful souls, to cast it out for a prey.

6 **Prophesy therefore concerning the land of Israel,** and say unto the mountains, and to the hills, to the rivers, and to the valleys, Thus says my Lord(s) the Becoming-One; Behold, I have spoken in my jealousy and in my fury, because you have borne the shame of the nations:

7 Therefore thus says my Lord(s) the Becoming-One; I have lifted up mine hand, Surely the nations that are about you, they shall bear their shame.

8 But ye, O mountains of Israel, you shall shoot forth your branches, and yield your fruit to my people of Israel; for they are at hand to come.

9 For, behold, I am for you, and I will turn unto you, and you shall be tilled and sown:

10 **And I will multiply men upon you, all the house of Israel, even all of it: and the cities shall be inhabited, and the wastes shall be built:**

11 **And I will multiply upon you man and beast; and they shall increase and bring fruit: and I will settle you after your old estates, and will do better unto you than at your beginnings: and you shall know that I am the Becoming-One.**

12 Yes, I will cause men to walk upon you, even my people Israel; and they shall possess you, and you shall be their inheritance, and you shall no more henceforth bereave them of men.

13 Thus says my Lord(s) the Becoming-One; Because they say unto you, you devour up men, and have bereaved your nations;

14 Therefore you shall devour men no more, neither bereave your nations any more, says my Lord(s) the Becoming-One.

15 Neither will I cause men to hear in you the shame of the nations any more, neither shall you bear the reproach of the people any more, neither shall you cause your nations to fall any more, says my Lord(s) the Becoming-One.

16 Moreover the word of the Becoming-One came unto me, saying,

17 Son of man, when the house of Israel dwelt in their own land, they defiled it by their own way and by their doings: their way was before me as the uncleanness of a removed woman.

18 Therefore I poured my fury upon them for the blood that they had shed upon the land, and for their idols wherewith they had polluted it:

19 And I scattered them among the nations, and they were dispersed through the countries: according to their way and according to their doings I judged them.

20 And when they entered unto the nations, to which they went, they profaned my holy name, when they said to them, These are the people of the Becoming-One, and are gone forth out of his land.

21 But I had pity for mine holy name, which the house of Israel had profaned among the nations, to which they went.

22 Therefore say unto the house of Israel, Thus says my Lord(s) the Becoming-One; I do not this for your sakes, O house of Israel, but for mine holy name's sake, which you have profaned among the nations, to which you went.

23 And I will sanctify my great name, which was profaned among the nations, which you have profaned in the midst of them; and the nations shall know that I am the Becoming-One, says my Lord(s) the Becoming-One, when I shall be sanctified in you before their eyes.

24 For I will take you from among the nations, and gather you out of all countries, and will bring you into your own land.

25 Then will I sprinkle clean water upon you, and you shall be clean: from all your filthiness, and from all your idols, will I cleanse you.

26 A new heart also will I give you, and a new spirit will I put within you: and I will take away the stony heart out of your flesh, and I will give you a heart of flesh.

27 And I will put my spirit within you, and cause you to walk in my statutes, and you shall keep my judgments, and do them.

28 And you shall dwell in the land that I gave to your fathers; and you shall be my people, and I will be your God.

29 I will also save you from all your uncleannesses: and I will call for the corn, and will increase it, and lay no famine upon you.

30 And I will multiply the fruit of the tree, and the increase of the field, that you shall receive no more reproach of famine among the nations.

31 Then shall you remember your own evil ways, and your doings that were not good, and shall loathe yourselves in your own sight for your iniquities and for your abominations.

32 Not for your sakes do I this, says my Lord(s) the Becoming-One, be it known unto you: be ashamed and confounded for your own ways, O house of Israel.

33 Thus says my Lord(s) the Becoming-One; In the day that I shall have cleansed you from all your iniquities I will also cause you to dwell in the cities, and the wastes shall be built.

34 And the desolate land shall be tilled, whereas it lay desolate in the sight of all that passed by.

35 And they shall say, This land that was desolate is become like the garden of Eden; and the waste and desolate and ruined cities are become fenced, and are inhabited.

36 Then the nations that are left round about you shall know that I the Becoming-One build the ruined places, and plant that that was desolate: I the Becoming-One have spoken it, and I will do it.

37 Thus says my Lord(s) the Becoming-One; I will yet for this be inquired of by the house of Israel, to do it for them; I will increase them with men like a flock.

38 As the holy flock, as the flock of Jerusalem in her set times;[144] so shall the waste cities be filled with flocks of men: and they shall know that I am the Becoming-One.

Eze 37:1 The hand of the Becoming-One was upon me, and carried me out in the spirit of the Becoming-One, and set me down in the midst of **the valley which was full of bones**,

2 And caused me to pass by them round about: and, behold, there were very many in the open valley; and, lo, they were very dry.

3 And he said unto me, Son of man, can these bones live? And I answered, O my Lord(s) the Becoming-One, you know.

4 Again he said unto me, Prophesy upon these bones, and say unto them, O you dry bones, hear the word of the Becoming-One.

5 *Thus says my Lord(s), the Becoming-One, unto these bones; Behold, I will cause breath to enter into you, and you shall live:*

6 And I will lay tendons upon you, and will bring up flesh upon you, and cover you with skin, and put breath in you, and you shall live; and you shall know that I am the Becoming-One.

7 So I prophesied as I was commanded: and as I prophesied, there was a noise, and behold a shaking, and the bones came together, bone to his bone.

8 And when I beheld, lo, the tendons and the flesh came up upon them, and the skin covered them above: but there was no breath in them.

9 Then said he unto me, Prophesy unto the wind, prophesy, son of man, and say to the wind, Thus says my Lord(s) the Becoming-One; Come from the four winds, O breath, **and breathe upon these slain, that they may live.**

10 So I prophesied as he commanded me, and the breath came into them, and they lived, and stood up upon their feet, an exceeding great army.

11 Then he said unto me, Son of man, these bones are the whole house of Israel: behold, they say, Our bones are dried, and our hope is lost: we are cut off for our parts.

12 Therefore prophesy and say unto them, Thus says my Lord(s) the Becoming-One; Behold, O my people, I will open your graves, and cause you to come up out of your graves, and bring you into the land of Israel.

13 And you shall know that I am the Becoming-One, when I have opened your graves, O my people, and brought you up out of your graves,

14 And shall put my spirit in you, and you shall live, and I shall place you in your own land: then shall you know that I the Becoming-One have spoken it, and performed it, says the Becoming-One.

15 The word of the Becoming-One came again unto me, saying,

16 Moreover, you son of man, take you one stick, and write upon it, For Judah, and for the children of Israel his companions: then take another stick, and write upon it, For Joseph, the stick of Ephraim, and for all the house of Israel his companions:

17 And join them one to another into one stick; and they shall become one in your hand.

18 And when the children of your people shall speak unto you, saying, will you not show us what you mean by these?

19 Say unto them, Thus says my Lord(s) the Becoming-One; Behold, I will take the stick of Joseph, which is in the hand of Ephraim, and the tribes of Israel his fellows, and will put them with him, even with the stick of Judah, and make them one stick, and they shall be one in mine hand.

20 And the sticks whereon you write shall be in your hand before their eyes.

21 And say unto them, Thus says my Lord(s) the Becoming-One; Behold, I will take the children of Israel from among the nations, to which they be gone, and will gather them on every side, and bring them into their own land:

22 And I will make them one nation in the land upon the mountains of Israel; and one king shall be king to them all: and they shall be no more two nations, neither shall they be divided into two kingdoms any more at all:

23 Neither shall they defile themselves any more with their idols, nor with their detestable things, nor with any of their transgressions: but I will save them out of all their dwelling places, wherein they have sinned, and will cleanse them: so shall they be my people, and I will be their God.

24 And David my servant shall be king over them; and they all shall have one shepherd: they shall also walk in my judgments, and observe my statutes, and do them.

25 And they shall dwell in the land that I have given unto Jacob my servant, wherein your fathers have dwelt; and they shall dwell therein, even they, and their children, and their children's children for olam: and my servant David shall be their prince for olam.

26 Moreover I will make a covenant of peace with them; it shall be a covenant of olam with them: and I will place them, and multiply them, and will set my sanctuary in the midst of them for olam.

27 My tabernacle also shall be with them: yes, I will be their God, and they shall be my people.

28 And the nations shall know that I the Becoming-One do sanctify Israel, when my sanctuary shall be in the midst of them for olam.

Eze 38:1 And the word of the Becoming-One came unto me, saying,

2 Son of man, **set your face against Gog, the land of Magog, the chief prince of Meshech and Tubal, and prophesy against him**,

3 And say, Thus says my Lord(s) the Becoming-One; Behold, I am against you, O Gog, the chief prince of Meshech and Tubal:

---

[144] Appointed times or festivals

4 And I will turn you back, and put hooks into your jaws, and I will bring you forth, and all your army, horses and horsemen, all of them clothed with all sorts of armor, even a great company with bucklers and shields, all of them handling swords:

5 Persia, Ethiopia, and Libya with them; all of them with shield and helmet:

6 Gomer, and all his bands; the house of Togarmah of the north quarters, and all his bands: and many people with you.

7 Be you prepared, and prepare for thyself, you, and all your company that are assembled unto you, and be you a guard unto them.

8 After many days you shall be visited: in the end of years you shall come into the land that is brought back from the sword, and is gathered out of many people, against the mountains of Israel, which have been always waste: but it is brought forth out of the nations, and they shall dwell safely all of them.

9 you shall ascend and come like a storm, you shall be like a cloud to cover the land, you, and all your bands, and many people with you.

10 Thus says my Lord(s) the Becoming-One; It shall also come to pass, that at the same day shall things come into your mind, and you shall think an evil thought:

11 And you shall say, I will go up to the land of unwalled villages; I will go to them that are at rest, that dwell safely, all of them dwelling without walls, and having neither bars nor gates,

12 To take a spoil, and to take a prey; to turn your hand upon the desolate places that are now inhabited, and upon the people that are gathered out of the nations, which have gotten cattle and goods, that dwell in the midst of the land.

13 Sheba, and Dedan, and the merchants of Tarshish, with all the young lions thereof, shall say unto you, are you come to take a spoil? have you gathered your company to take a prey? to carry away silver and gold, to take away cattle and goods, to take a great spoil?

14 Therefore, son of man, prophesy and say unto Gog, Thus says my Lord(s) the Becoming-One; In that day when my people of Israel dwells safely, shall you not know it?

15 And you shall come from your place out of the north parts, you, and many people with you, all of them riding upon horses, a great company, and a mighty army:

16 And you shall come up against my people of Israel, as a cloud to cover the land; it shall be in the end of days, and I will bring you against my land, that the nations may know me, when I shall be sanctified in you, O Gog, before their eyes.

17 Thus says my Lord(s) the Becoming-One; are you he of whom I have spoken in old days by my servants the prophets of Israel, which prophesied in those days many years that I would bring you against them?

18 And it shall come to pass at the same day when Gog shall come against the land of Israel, says my Lord(s) the Becoming-One, that my fury shall come up in my face.

19 For in my jealousy and in the fire of my wrath have I spoken, Surely in that day there shall be a great shaking in the land of Israel;

20 So that the fishes of the sea, and the fowls of the heaven, and the beasts of the field, and all creeping things that creep upon the earth, and all the men that are upon the face of the earth, shall shake at my presence, and the mountains shall be thrown down, and the steep places shall fall, and every wall shall fall to the ground.

21 And I will call for a sword against him throughout all my mountains, says my Lord(s) the Becoming-One: every man's sword shall be against his brother.

22 And I will judge against him with pestilence and with blood; and I will rain upon him, and upon his bands, and upon the many people that are with him, an overflowing rain, and great hailstones, fire, and brimstone.

23 Thus will I magnify myself, and sanctify myself; and I will be known in the eyes of many nations, and they shall know that I am the Becoming-One.

Eze 39:1 Therefore, you son of man, prophesy against Gog, and say, Thus says my Lord(s) the Becoming-One; Behold, I am against you, O Gog, the chief prince of Meshech and Tubal:

2 And I will turn you back, and leave but the sixth part of you, and will cause you to come up from the north parts, and will bring you upon the mountains of Israel:

3 And I will smite your bow out of your left hand, and will cause your arrows to fall out of your right hand.

4 you shall fall upon the mountains of Israel, you, and all your bands, and the people that is with you: I will give you unto the ravenous birds of every sort, and to the beasts of the field to be devoured.

5 you shall fall upon the open field: for I have spoken it, says my Lord(s) the Becoming-One.

6 And I will send a fire on Magog, and among them that dwell carelessly in the isles: and they shall know that I am the Becoming-One.

7 So will I make my holy name known in the midst of my people Israel; and I will not let them pollute my holy name any more: and the nations shall know that I am the Becoming-One, the Holy One in Israel.

8 Behold, it is come, and it is done, says my Lord(s) the Becoming-One; this is the day whereof I have spoken.

9 And they that dwell in the cities of Israel shall go forth, and shall set on fire and burn the weapons, both the shields and the bucklers, the bows and the arrows, and the handstaves, and the spears, and they shall burn them with fire seven years:

10 So that they shall take no wood out of the field, neither cut down any out of the forests; for they shall burn the weapons with fire: and they shall spoil those that spoiled them, and rob those that robbed them, says my Lord(s) the Becoming-One.

11 And it shall come to pass in that day, that I will give unto Gog a place there of graves in Israel, the valley of the passengers on the east of the sea: and it shall stop the noses of the passengers: and there shall they bury Gog and all his multitude: and they shall call it The valley of Hamongog.

12 And seven months shall the house of Israel be burying of them, that they may cleanse the land.

13 Yes, all the people of the land shall bury them; and it shall be to them a renown the day that I shall be glorified, says my Lord(s) the Becoming-One.

14 And they shall sever out men of continual employment, passing through the land to bury with the passengers those that remain upon the face of the earth, to cleanse it: after the end of seven months shall they search.

15 And the passengers that pass through the land, when any sees a man's bone, then shall he set up a sign by it, till the buriers have buried it in the valley of Hamongog.

16 And also the name of the city shall be Hamonah. Thus shall they cleanse the land.

17 And, you son of man, thus says my Lord(s) the Becoming-One; Speak unto every feathered fowl, and to every beast of the field, Assemble yourselves, and come; gather yourselves on every side to my sacrifice that I do sacrifice for you, even a great sacrifice upon the mountains of Israel, that you may eat flesh, and drink blood.

18 you shall eat the flesh of the mighty, and drink the blood of the princes of the earth, of rams, of lambs, and of goats, of bullocks, all of them fatlings of Bashan.

19 And you shall eat fat till you be full, and drink blood till you be drunken, of my sacrifice which I have sacrificed for you.

20 Thus you shall be filled at my table with horses and chariots, with mighty men, and with all men of war, says my Lord(s) the Becoming-One.

21 And I will set my glory among the nations, and all the nations shall see my judgment that I have executed, and my hand that I have laid upon them.

22 So the house of Israel shall know that I am the Becoming-One their God from that day and forward.

23 And the nations shall know that the house of Israel went into captivity for their iniquity: because they trespassed against me, therefore hid I my face from them, and gave them into the hand of their enemies: so fell they all by the sword.

24 According to their uncleanness and according to their transgressions have I done unto them, and hid my face from them.

25 Therefore thus says my Lord(s) the Becoming-One; Now will I bring again the captivity of Jacob, and have mercy upon the whole house of Israel, and will be jealous for my holy name;

26 After that they have borne their shame, and all their trespasses whereby they have trespassed against me, when they dwelt safely in their land, and none made them afraid.

27 When I have brought them again from the people, and gathered them out of their enemies' lands, and am sanctified in them in the sight of many nations;

28 Then shall they know that I am the Becoming-One their God, which caused them to be led into captivity among the nations: but I have gathered them unto their own land, and have left none of them any more there.

29 Neither will I hide my face any more from them: for I have poured out my spirit upon the house of Israel, says my Lord(s) the Becoming-One.

Eze 40:1 In the five and twentieth year of our captivity, in the beginning of the year, in the tenth day of the month, in the fourteenth year after that the city was struck, in the selfsame day the hand of the Becoming-One was upon me, and brought me there. **[ab. 3402 YM; 573 BC]**

2 **In the visions of God** brought he me into the land of Israel, and set me upon a very high mountain, by which was as the frame of a city on the south.

3 And he brought me there, and, behold, there was a man, whose appearance was like the appearance of brass, with a line of flax in his hand, and a measuring reed; and he stood in the gate.

4 And the man said unto me, Son of man, behold with your eyes, and hear with your ears, and set your heart upon all that I shall show you; for to the intent that I might show them unto you are you brought here: declare all that you see to the house of Israel.

5 And behold a wall on the outside of the house round about, and in the man's hand a measuring reed of six cubits long by the cubit and a hand breadth: so he measured the breadth of the building, one reed; and the height, one reed.

6 Then came he unto the gate which looks toward the east, and went up the stairs thereof, and measured the threshold of the gate, which was one reed broad; and the other threshold of the gate, which was one reed broad.

7 And every little chamber was one reed long, and one reed broad; and between the little chambers were five cubits; and the threshold of the gate by the porch of the gate within was one reed.

8 He measured also the porch of the gate within, one reed.

9 Then measured he the porch of the gate, eight cubits; and the posts thereof, two cubits; and the porch of the gate was inward.

10 And the little chambers of the gate eastward were three on this side, and three on that side; they three were of one measure: and the posts had one measure on this side and on that side.

11 And he measured the breadth of the entry of the gate, ten cubits; and the length of the gate, thirteen cubits.

12 The space also before the little chambers was one cubit on this side, and the space was one cubit on that side: and the little chambers were six cubits on this side, and six cubits on that side.

13 He measured then the gate from the roof of one little chamber to the roof of another: the breadth was five and twenty cubits, door against door.

14 He made also posts of threescore cubits, even unto the post of the court round about the gate.

15 And from the face of the gate of the entrance unto the face of the porch of the inner gate were fifty cubits.

16 And there were narrow windows to the little chambers, and to their posts within the gate round about, and likewise to the arches: and windows were round about inward: and upon each post were palm trees.

17 Then brought he me into the outward court, and, lo, there were chambers, and a pavement made for the court round about: thirty chambers were upon the pavement.

18 And the pavement by the side of the gates over against the length of the gates was the lower pavement.

19 Then he measured the breadth from the forefront of the lower gate unto the forefront of the inner court outside, a hundred cubits eastward and northward.

20 And the gate of the outward court that looked toward the north, he measured the length thereof, and the breadth thereof.

21 And the little chambers thereof were three on this side and three on that side; and the posts thereof and the arches thereof were after the measure of the first gate: the length thereof was fifty cubits, and the breadth five and twenty cubits.

22 And their windows, and their arches, and their palm trees, were after the measure of the gate that looks toward the east; and they went up unto it by seven steps; and the arches thereof were before them.

23 And the gate of the inner court was over against the gate toward the north, and toward the east; and he measured from gate to gate a hundred cubits.

24 After that he brought me toward the south, and behold a gate toward the south: and he measured the posts thereof and the arches thereof according to these measures.

25 And there were windows in it and in the arches thereof round about, like those windows: the length was fifty cubits, and the breadth five and twenty cubits.

26 And there were seven steps to go up to it, and the arches thereof were before them: and it had palm trees, one on this side, and another on that side, upon the posts thereof.

27 And there was a gate in the inner court toward the south: and he measured from gate to gate toward the south a hundred cubits.

28 And he brought me to the inner court by the south gate: and he measured the south gate according to these measures;

29 And the little chambers thereof, and the posts thereof, and the arches thereof, according to these measures: and there were windows in it and in the arches thereof round about: it was fifty cubits long, and five and twenty cubits broad.

30 And the arches round about were five and twenty cubits long, and five cubits broad.

31 And the arches thereof were toward the utter court; and palm trees were upon the posts thereof: and the going up to it had eight steps.

32 And he brought me into the inner court toward the east: and he measured the gate according to these measures.

33 And the little chambers thereof, and the posts thereof, and the arches thereof, were according to these measures: and there were windows therein and in the arches thereof round about: it was fifty cubits long, and five and twenty cubits broad.

34 And the arches thereof were toward the outward court; and palm trees were upon the posts thereof, on this side, and on that side: and the going up to it had eight steps.

35 And he brought me to the north gate, and measured it according to these measures;

36 The little chambers thereof, the posts thereof, and the arches thereof, and the windows to it round about: the length was fifty cubits, and the breadth five and twenty cubits.

37 And the posts thereof were toward the utter court; and palm trees were upon the posts thereof, on this side, and on that side: and the going up to it had eight steps.

38 And the chambers and the entries thereof were by the posts of the gates, where they washed the burnt offering.

39 And in the porch of the gate were two tables on this side, and two tables on that side, to slay thereon the burnt offering and the sin offering and the trespass offering.

40 And at the side outside, as one goes up to the entry of the north gate, were two tables; and on the other side, which was at the porch of the gate, were two tables.

41 Four tables were on this side, and four tables on that side, by the side of the gate; eight tables, whereupon they killed their sacrifices.

42 And the four tables were of hewn stone for the burnt offering, of a cubit and a half long, and a cubit and a half broad, and one cubit high: whereupon also they laid the instruments wherewith they killed the burnt offering and the sacrifice.

43 And within were hooks, a hand broad, fastened round about: and upon the tables was the flesh of the offering.

44 And outside the inner gate were the chambers of the singers in the inner court, which was at the side of the north gate; and their prospect was toward the south: one at the side of the east gate having the prospect toward the north.

45 And he said unto me, This chamber, whose prospect is toward the south, is for the priests, the keepers of the charge of the house.

46 And the chamber whose prospect is toward the north is for the priests, the keepers of the charge of the altar: these are the sons of Zadok among the sons of Levi, which come near to the Becoming-One to minister unto him.

47 So he measured the court, a hundred cubits long, and a hundred cubits broad, foursquare; and the altar that was before the house.

48 And he brought me to the porch of the house, and measured each post of the porch, five cubits on this side, and five cubits on that side: and the breadth of the gate was three cubits on this side, and three cubits on that side.

49 The length of the porch was twenty cubits, and the breadth eleven cubits; and he brought me by the steps whereby they went up to it: and there were pillars by the posts, one on this side, and another on that side.

Eze 41:1 Afterward he brought me to the temple, and measured the posts, six cubits broad on the one side, and six cubits broad on the other side, which was the breadth of the tabernacle.

2 And the breadth of the door was ten cubits: and the sides of the door were five cubits on the one side, and five cubits on the other side: and he measured the length thereof, forty cubits: and the breadth, twenty cubits.

3 Then went he inward, and measured the post of the door, two cubits; and the door, six cubits; and the breadth of the door, seven cubits.

4 So he measured the length thereof, twenty cubits; and the breadth, twenty cubits, before the temple: and he said unto me, This is the most holy place.

5 After he measured the wall of the house, six cubits; and the breadth of every side chamber, four cubits, round about the house on every side.

6 And the side chambers were three, one over another, and thirty in order; and they entered into the wall which was of the house for the side chambers round about, that they might have hold, but they had not hold in the wall of the house.

7 And there was an enlarging, and a winding about still upward to the side chambers: for the winding about of the house went still upward round about the house: therefore the breadth of the house was still upward, and so increased from the lowest chamber to the highest by the midst.

8 I saw also the height of the house round about: the foundations of the side chambers were a full reed of six great cubits.

9 The thickness of the wall, which was for the side chamber outside, was five cubits: and that which was left was the place of the side chambers that were within.

10 And between the chambers was the wideness of twenty cubits round about the house on every side.

11 And the doors of the side chambers were toward the place that was left, one door toward the north, and another door toward the south: and the breadth of the place that was left was five cubits round about.

12 Now the building that was before the separate place at the end toward the west was seventy cubits broad; and the wall of the building was five cubits thick round about, and the length thereof ninety cubits.

13 So he measured the house, a hundred cubits long; and the separate place, and the building, with the walls thereof, a hundred cubits long;

14 Also the breadth of the face of the house, and of the separate place toward the east, a hundred cubits.

15 And he measured the length of the building over against the separate place which was behind it, and the galleries thereof on the one side and on the other side, a hundred cubits, with the inner temple, and the porches of the court;

16 The door posts, and the narrow windows, and the galleries round about on their three stories, over against the door, covered with wood round about, and from the ground up to the windows, and the windows were covered;

17 To that above the door, even unto the inner house, and outside, and by all the wall round about within and without, by measure.

18 And it was made with cherubs and palm trees, so that a palm tree was between a cherub and a cherub; and every cherub had two faces;

19 So that the face of a man was toward the palm tree on the one side, and the face of a young lion toward the palm tree on the other side: it was made through all the house round about.

20 From the ground unto above the door were cherubs and palm trees made, and on the wall of the temple.

21 The posts of the temple were squared, and the face of the sanctuary; the appearance of the one as the appearance of the other.

22 The altar of wood was three cubits high, and the length thereof two cubits; and the corners thereof, and the length thereof, and the walls thereof, were of wood: and he said unto me, This is the table that is before the Becoming-One.

23 And the temple and the sanctuary had two doors.

24 And the doors had two leaves apiece, two turning leaves; two leaves for the one door, and two leaves for the other door.

25 And there were made on them, on the doors of the temple, cherubs and palm trees, like as were made upon the walls; and there were thick planks upon the face of the porch outside.

26 And there were narrow windows and palm trees on the one side and on the other side, on the sides of the porch, and upon the side chambers of the house, and thick planks.

Eze 42:1 Then he brought me forth into the utter court, the way toward the north: and he brought me into the chamber that was over against the separate place, and which was before the building toward the north.

2 Before the length of a hundred cubits was the north door, and the breadth was fifty cubits.

3 Over against the twenty cubits which were for the inner court, and over against the pavement which was for the utter court, was gallery against gallery in three stories.

4 And before the chambers was a walk of ten cubits breadth inward, a way of one cubit; and their doors toward the north.

5 Now the upper chambers were shorter: for the galleries were higher than these, than the lower, and than the middlemost of the building.

6 For they were in three stories, but had not pillars as the pillars of the courts: therefore the building was smaller than the lowest and the middlemost from the ground.

7 And the wall that was outside over against the chambers, toward the utter court on the forepart of the chambers, the length thereof was fifty cubits.

8 For the length of the chambers that were in the utter court was fifty cubits: and, lo, before the temple were a hundred cubits.

9 And from under these chambers was the entry on the east side, as one goes into them from the utter court.

10 The chambers were in the thickness of the wall of the court toward the east, over against the separate place, and over against the building.

11 And the way before them was like the appearance of the chambers which were toward the north, as long as they, and as broad as they: and all their goings out were both according to their fashions, and according to their doors.

12 And according to the doors of the chambers that were toward the south was a door in the head of

the way, even the way directly before the wall toward the east, as one enters into them.

13 Then said he unto me, The north chambers and the south chambers, which are before the separate place, they be holy chambers, where the priests that approach unto the Becoming-One shall eat the most holy things: there shall they lay the most holy things, and the food offering, and the sin offering, and the trespass offering; for the place is holy.

14 When the priests enter therein, then shall they not go out of the holy place into the utter court, but there they shall lay their garments wherein they minister; for they are holy; and shall put on other garments, and shall approach to those things which are for the people.

15 Now when he had made an end of measuring the inner house, he brought me forth toward the gate whose prospect is toward the east, and measured it round about.

16 He measured the east wind with the measuring reed, five hundred reeds, with the measuring reed round about.

17 He measured the north wind, five hundred reeds, with the measuring reed round about.

18 He measured the south wind, five hundred reeds, with the measuring reed.

19 He turned about to the west wind, and measured five hundred reeds with the measuring reed.

20 He measured it by the four winds: it had a wall round about, five hundred reeds long, and five hundred broad, to make a separation between the sanctuary and the profane place.

Eze 43:1 Afterward he brought me to the gate, even the gate that looks toward the east:

2 And, behold, the glory of God of Israel came from the way of the east: and his voice was like a noise of many waters: and the earth shined with his glory.

3 And it was according to the appearance of the vision which I saw, even according to the vision that I saw when I came to destroy the city: **and the visions were like the vision that I saw by the river Chebar; and I fell upon my face.**

4 And the glory of the Becoming-One came into the house by the way of the gate whose prospect is toward the east.

5 So the spirit took me up, and brought me into the inner court; and, behold, the glory of the Becoming-One filled the house.

6 And I heard him speaking unto me out of the house; and the man stood by me.

7 And he said unto me, Son of man, the place of my throne, and the place of the soles of my feet, where I will dwell in the midst of the children of Israel for olam, and my holy name, shall the house of Israel no more defile, neither they, nor their kings, by their whoredom, nor by the carcases of their kings in their high places.

8 In their setting of their threshold by my thresholds, and their post by my posts, and the wall between me and them, they have even defiled my holy name by their abominations that they have committed: therefore I have consumed them in mine anger.

9 Now let them put away their whoredom, and the carcases of their kings, far from me, and I will dwell in the midst of them for olam.

10 you son of man, show the house to the house of Israel, that they may be ashamed of their iniquities: and let them measure the pattern.

11 And if they be ashamed of all that they have done, show them the form of the house, and the fashion thereof, and the goings out thereof, and the comings in thereof, and all the forms thereof, and all the ordinances thereof, and all the forms thereof, and all the laws thereof: and write it in their sight, that they may keep the whole form thereof, and all the ordinances thereof, and do them.

12 This is the law of the house; Upon the top of the mountain the whole limit thereof round about shall be most holy. Behold, this is the law of the house.

13 And these are the measures of the altar after the cubits: The cubit is a cubit and a hand breadth; even the bottom shall be a cubit, and the breadth a cubit, and the border thereof by the edge thereof round about shall be a span: and this shall be the higher place of the altar.

14 And from the bottom upon the ground even to the lower settle shall be two cubits, and the breadth one cubit; and from the lesser settle even to the greater settle shall be four cubits, and the breadth one cubit.

15 So the altar shall be four cubits; and from the altar and upward shall be four horns.

16 And the altar shall be twelve cubits long, twelve broad, square in the four squares thereof.

17 And the settle shall be fourteen cubits long and fourteen broad in the four squares thereof; and the border about it shall be half a cubit; and the bottom thereof shall be a cubit about; and his stairs shall look toward the east.

18 And he said unto me, Son of man, thus says my Lord(s) the Becoming-One; These are the ordinances of the altar in the day when they shall make it, to offer burnt offerings thereon, and to sprinkle blood thereon.

19 And you shall give to the priests the Levites that be of the seed of Zadok, which approach unto me, to minister unto me, says my Lord(s) the Becoming-One, a young bullock for a sin offering.

20 And you shall take of the blood thereof, and put it on the four horns of it, and on the four corners of the settle, and upon the border round about: thus shall you cleanse and purge it.

21 you shall take the bullock also of the sin offering, and he shall burn it in the appointed place of the house, outside the sanctuary.

22 And on the second day you shall offer a kid of the goats without blemish for a sin offering; and they shall cleanse the altar, as they did cleanse it with the bullock.

23 When you have made an end of cleansing it, you shall offer a young bullock without blemish, and a ram out of the flock without blemish.

24 And you shall offer them before the Becoming-One, and the priests shall cast salt upon

them, and they shall offer them up for a burnt offering unto the Becoming-One.

25 Seven days shall you prepare every day a goat for a sin offering: they shall also prepare a young bullock, and a ram out of the flock, without blemish.

26 Seven days shall they purge the altar and purify it; and they shall consecrate themselves.

27 And when these days are expired, it shall be, that upon the eighth day, and so forward, the priests shall make your burnt offerings upon the altar, and your peace offerings; and I will accept you, says my Lord(s) the Becoming-One.

Eze 44:1 Then he brought me back **the way of the gate of the outward sanctuary which looks toward the east; and it was shut.**

2 Then said the Becoming-One unto me; This gate shall be shut, it shall not be opened, and no man shall enter in by it; because the Becoming-One, God of Israel, has entered in by it, therefore it shall be shut.

3 It is for the prince; the prince, he shall sit in it to eat bread before the Becoming-One; he shall enter by the way of the porch of that gate, and shall go out by the way of the same.

4 Then brought he me the way of the north gate before the house: and I looked, and, behold, the glory of the Becoming-One filled the house of the Becoming-One: and I fell upon my face.

5 And the Becoming-One said unto me, Son of man, mark well, and behold with your eyes, and hear with your ears all that I say unto you concerning all the ordinances of the house of the Becoming-One, and all the laws thereof; and mark well the entering in of the house, with every going forth of the sanctuary.

6 And you shall say to the rebellious, even to the house of Israel, Thus says my Lord(s) the Becoming-One; O you house of Israel, let it suffice you of all your abominations,

7 In that you have brought into my sanctuary strangers, uncircumcised in heart, and uncircumcised in flesh, to be in my sanctuary, to pollute it, even my house, when you offer my bread, the fat and the blood, and they have broken my covenant because of all your abominations.

8 And you have not kept the charge of mine holy things: but you have set keepers of my charge in my sanctuary for yourselves.

9 Thus says my Lord(s) the Becoming-One; No stranger, uncircumcised in heart, nor uncircumcised in flesh, shall enter into my sanctuary, of any stranger that is among the children of Israel.

10 And the Levites that are gone away far from me, when Israel went astray, which went astray away from me after their idols; they shall even bear their iniquity.

11 Yet they shall be ministers in my sanctuary, having charge at the gates of the house, and ministering to the house: they shall slay the burnt offering and the sacrifice for the people, and they shall stand before them to minister unto them.

12 Because they ministered unto them before their idols, and caused the house of Israel to fall into iniquity; therefore have I lifted up mine hand against them, says my Lord(s) the Becoming-One, and they shall bear their iniquity.

13 And they shall not come near unto me, to do the office of a priest unto me, nor to come near to any of my holy things, in the most holy place: but they shall bear their shame, and their abominations which they have committed.

14 But I will make them keepers of the charge of the house, for all the service thereof, and for all that shall be done therein.

15 But the priests the Levites, the sons of Zadok, that kept the charge of my sanctuary when the children of Israel went astray from me, they shall come near to me to minister unto me, and they shall stand before me to offer unto me the fat and the blood, says my Lord(s) the Becoming-One: 16 They shall enter into my sanctuary, and they shall come near to my table, to minister unto me, and they shall keep my charge.

17 And it shall come to pass, that when they enter in at the gates of the inner court, they shall be clothed with linen garments; and no wool shall come upon them, whiles they minister in the gates of the inner court, and within.

18 They shall have linen bonnets upon their heads, and shall have linen breeches upon their loins; they shall not gird themselves with anything that causes sweat.

19 And when they go forth into the utter court, even into the utter court to the people, they shall put off their garments wherein they ministered, and lay them in the holy chambers, and they shall put on other garments; and they shall not sanctify the people with their garments.

20 Neither shall they shave their heads, nor permit their locks to grow long; they shall only poll their heads.

21 Neither shall any priest drink wine, when they enter into the inner court.

22 Neither shall they take for their wives a widow, nor her that is put away: but they shall take maidens of the seed of the house of Israel, or a widow that had a priest before.

23 And they shall teach my people the difference between the holy and profane, and cause them to discern between the unclean and the clean.

24 And in controversy they shall stand in judgment; and they shall judge it according to my judgments: and they shall keep my laws and my statutes in all mine set times;[145] and they shall hallow my sabbaths.

25 And they shall come at no dead person to defile themselves: but for father, or for mother, or for son, or for daughter, for brother, or for sister that has had no husband, they may defile themselves.

26 And after he is cleansed, they shall reckon unto him seven days.

27 And in the day that he goes into the sanctuary, unto the inner court, to minister in the sanctuary, he shall offer his sin offering, says my Lord(s) the Becoming-One.

---

[145] Appointed times or festivals

28 And it shall be unto them for an inheritance: I am their inheritance: and you shall give them no possession in Israel: I am their possession.

29 They shall eat the food offering, and the sin offering, and the trespass offering: and every dedicated thing in Israel shall be theirs.

30 And the first of all the firstfruits of all things, and every offering of all, of every sort of your offerings, shall be the priest's: you shall also give unto the priest the first of your dough, that he may cause the blessing to rest in your house.

31 The priests shall not eat of anything that is dead of itself, or torn, whether it be fowl or beast.

Eze 45:1 Moreover, when you shall divide by lot the land for inheritance, you shall offer an offering unto the Becoming-One, a holy portion of the land: the length shall be the length of five and twenty thousand reeds, and the breadth shall be ten thousand. This shall be holy in all the borders thereof round about.

2 Of this there shall be for the sanctuary five hundred in length, with five hundred in breadth, square round about; and fifty cubits round about for the suburbs thereof.

3 And of this measure shall you measure the length of five and twenty thousand, and the breadth of ten thousand: and in it shall be the sanctuary and the most holy place.

4 The holy portion of the land shall be for the priests the ministers of the sanctuary, which shall come near to minister unto the Becoming-One: and it shall be a place for their houses, and a holy place for the sanctuary.

5 And the five and twenty thousand of length, and the ten thousand of breadth, shall also the Levites, the ministers of the house, have for themselves, for a possession for twenty chambers.

6 And you shall appoint the possession of the city five thousand broad, and five and twenty thousand long, over against the offering of the holy portion: it shall be for the whole house of Israel.

7 And a portion shall be for the prince on the one side and on the other side of the offering of the holy portion, and of the possession of the city, before the offering of the holy portion, and before the possession of the city, from the west side westward, and from the east side eastward: and the length shall be over against one of the portions, from the west border unto the east border.

8 In the land shall be his possession in Israel: and my princes shall no more oppress my people; and the rest of the land shall they give to the house of Israel according to their tribes.

9 Thus says my Lord(s) the Becoming-One; Let it suffice you, O princes of Israel: remove violence and spoil, and execute judgment and justice, take away your exactions from my people, says my Lord(s) the Becoming-One.

10 you shall have just balances, and a just ephah, and a just bath.

11 The ephah and the bath shall be of one measure, that the bath may contain the tenth part of a homer, and the ephah the tenth part of a homer: the measure thereof shall be after the homer.

12 And the shekel shall be twenty gerahs: twenty shekels, five and twenty shekels, fifteen shekels, shall be your mina.

13 This is the offering that you shall offer; the sixth part of an ephah of a homer of wheat, and you shall give the sixth part of an ephah of a homer of barley:

14 Concerning the ordinance of oil, the bath of oil, you shall offer the tenth part of a bath out of the cor, which is a homer of ten baths; for ten baths are a homer:

15 And one lamb out of the flock, out of two hundred, out of the fat pastures of Israel; for a food offering, and for a burnt offering, and for peace offerings, to make atonement for them, says my Lord(s) the Becoming-One.

16 All the people of the land shall give this offering for the prince in Israel.

17 And it shall be the prince's part to give burnt offerings, and food offerings, and drink offerings, in the feasts, and in the new moons, and in the sabbaths, in all set times[146] of the house of Israel: he shall prepare the sin offering, and the food offering, and the burnt offering, and the peace offerings, to make atonement for the house of Israel.

18 Thus says my Lord(s) the Becoming-One; In the first month, in the first day of the month, you shall take a young bullock without blemish, and cleanse the sanctuary:

19 And the priest shall take of the blood of the sin offering, and put it upon the posts of the house, and upon the four corners of the settle of the altar, and upon the posts of the gate of the inner court.

20 And so you shall do the seventh day of the month for every one that errs, and for him that is simple: so shall you reconcile the house.

21 In the first month, in the fourteenth day of the month, you shall have the Passover, a feast of seven days; unleavened bread shall be eaten.

22 And upon that day shall the prince prepare for himself and for all the people of the land a bullock for a sin offering.

23 And seven days of the feast he shall prepare a burnt offering to the Becoming-One, seven bullocks and seven rams without blemish daily the seven days; and a kid of the goats daily for a sin offering.

24 And he shall prepare a food offering of an ephah for a bullock, and an ephah for a ram, and a hin of oil for an ephah.

25 In the seventh month, in the fifteenth day of the month, shall he do the like in the feast of the seven days, according to the sin offering, according to the burnt offering, and according to the food offering, and according to the oil.

Eze 46:1 Thus says my Lord(s) the Becoming-One; The gate of the inner court that looks toward the east shall be shut the six working days; but on the Sabbath day it shall be opened, and in the day of the new moon it shall be opened.

2 And the prince shall enter by the way of the porch of that gate outside, and shall stand by the post

---

[146] Appointed times or festivals

of the gate, and the priests shall prepare his burnt offering and his peace offerings, and he shall worship at the threshold of the gate: then he shall go forth; but the gate shall not be shut until the evening.

3 Likewise the people of the land shall worship at the door of this gate before the Becoming-One in the sabbaths and in the new moons.

4 And the burnt offering that the prince shall offer unto the Becoming-One in the Sabbath day shall be six lambs without blemish, and a ram without blemish.

5 And the food offering shall be an ephah for a ram, and the food offering for the lambs as he shall be able to give, and a hin of oil to an ephah.

6 And in the day of the new moon it shall be a young bullock without blemish, and six lambs, and a ram: they shall be without blemish.

7 And he shall prepare a food offering, an ephah for a bullock, and an ephah for a ram, and for the lambs according as his hand shall attain unto, and a hin of oil to an ephah.

8 And when the prince shall enter, he shall go in by the way of the porch of that gate, and he shall go forth by the way thereof.

9 But when the people of the land shall come before the Becoming-One in the set times,[147] he that enteres in by the way of the north gate to worship shall go out by the way of the south gate; and he that enters by the way of the south gate shall go forth by the way of the north gate: he shall not return by the way of the gate whereby he came in, but shall go forth over against it.

10 And the prince in the midst of them, when they go in, shall go in; and when they go forth, shall go forth.

11 And in the feasts and in the set times[148] the food offering shall be an ephah to a bullock, and an ephah to a ram, and to the lambs as he is able to give, and a hin of oil to an ephah.

12 Now when the prince shall prepare a voluntary burnt offering or peace offerings voluntarily unto the Becoming-One, one shall then open him the gate that looks toward the east, and he shall prepare his burnt offering and his peace offerings, as he did on the Sabbath day: then he shall go forth; and after his going forth one shall shut the gate.

13 you shall daily prepare a burnt offering unto the Becoming-One of a lamb of the first year without blemish: you shall prepare it every morning.

14 And you shall prepare a food offering for it every morning, the sixth part of an ephah, and the third part of a hin of oil, to temper with the fine flour; a food offering continually by a ordinance of oalm unto the Becoming-One.

15 Thus shall they prepare the lamb, and the food offering, and the oil, every morning for a continual burnt offering.

16 Thus says my Lord(s) the Becoming-One; If the prince give a gift unto any of his sons, the inheritance thereof shall be his sons'; it shall be their possession by inheritance.

17 But if he give a gift of his inheritance to one of his servants, then it shall be his to the year of liberty; after it shall return to the prince: but his inheritance shall be his sons' for them.

18 Moreover the prince shall not take of the people's inheritance by oppression, to thrust them out of their possession; but he shall give his sons inheritance out of his own possession: that my people be not scattered every man from his possession.

19 After he brought me through the entry, which was at the side of the gate, into the holy chambers of the priests, which looked toward the north: and, behold, there was a place on the two sides westward.

20 Then said he unto me, This is the place where the priests shall boil the trespass offering and the sin offering, where they shall bake the food offering; that they bear them not out into the utter court, to sanctify the people.

21 Then he brought me forth into the utter court, and caused me to pass by the four corners of the court; and, behold, in every corner of the court there was a court.

22 In the four corners of the court there were courts joined of forty cubits long and thirty broad: these four corners were of one measure.

23 And there was a row of building round about in them, round about them four, and it was made with boiling places under the rows round about.

24 Then said he unto me, These are the places of them that boil, where the ministers of the house shall boil the sacrifice of the people.

Eze 47:1 Afterward he brought me again unto the door of the house; and, behold, waters issued out from under the threshold of the house eastward: for the forefront of the house stood toward the east, and the waters came down from under from the right side of the house, at the south side of the altar.

2 Then brought he me out of the way of the gate northward, and led me about the way outside unto the utter gate by the way that looks eastward; and, behold, there ran out waters on the right side.

3 And when the man that had the line in his hand went forth eastward, he measured a thousand cubits, and he brought me through the waters; the waters were to the ankles.

4 Again he measured a thousand, and brought me through the waters; the waters were to the knees. Again he measured a thousand, and brought me through; the waters were to the loins.

5 Afterward he measured a thousand; and it was a river that I could not pass over: for the waters were risen, waters to swim in, a river that could not be passed over.

6 And he said unto me, Son of man, have you seen this? Then he brought me, and caused me to return to the brink of the river.

7 Now when I had returned, behold, at the bank of the river were very many trees on the one side and on the other.

8 Then said he unto me, These waters issue out toward the east country, and go down into the desert, and go into the sea: which being brought forth into the sea, the waters shall be healed.

9 And it shall come to pass, that every soul that lives, which moves, wheresoever the rivers shall

---

[147] Appointed time or festival
[148] Appointed time or festival

come, shall live: and there shall be a very great multitude of fish, because these waters shall come there: for they shall be healed; and every thing shall live to which the river comes.

10 And it shall come to pass, that the fishermen shall stand upon it from Engedi even unto Eneglaim; they shall be a place to spread forth nets; their fish shall be according to their kinds, as the fish of the great sea, exceeding many.

11 But the miry places thereof and the marshes thereof shall not be healed; they shall be given to salt.

12 And by the river upon the bank thereof, on this side and on that side, shall grow all trees for food, whose leaf shall not fade, neither shall the fruit thereof be consumed: it shall bring forth new fruit according to his months, because their waters they issued out of the sanctuary: and the fruit thereof shall be for food, and the leaf thereof for medicine.

13 Thus says my Lord(s) the Becoming-One; This shall be the border, whereby you shall inherit the land according to the twelve tribes of Israel: Joseph shall have two portions.

14 And you shall inherit it, one as well as another: concerning the which I lifted up mine hand to give it unto your fathers: and this land shall fall unto you for inheritance.

15 And this shall be the border of the land toward the north side, from the great sea, the way of Hethlon, as men go to Zedad;

16 Hamath, Berothah, Sibraim, which is between the border of Damascus and the border of Hamath; Hazarhatticon, which is by the coast of Hauran.

17 And the border from the sea shall be Hazarenan, the border of Damascus, and the north northward, and the border of Hamath. And this is the north side.

18 And the east side you shall measure from Hauran, and from Damascus, and from Gilead, and from the land of Israel by Jordan, from the border unto the east sea. And this is the east side.

19 And the south side southward, from Tamar even to the waters of strife [meribah] in Kadesh, the river to the great sea. And this is the south side southward.

20 The west side also shall be the great sea from the border, till a man come over against Hamath. This is the west side.

21 So shall you divide this land unto you according to the tribes of Israel.

22 And it shall come to pass, that you shall divide it by lot for an inheritance unto you, and to the strangers that sojourn among you, which shall beget children among you: and they shall be unto you as born in the country among the children of Israel; they shall have inheritance with you among the tribes of Israel.

23 And it shall come to pass, that in what tribe the stranger sojourns, there shall you give him his inheritance, says my Lord(s) the Becoming-One.

Eze 48:1 Now these are the names of the tribes. From the north end to the coast of the way of Hethlon, as one goes to Hamath, Hazarenan, the border of Damascus northward, to the coast of Hamath; for these are his sides east and west; a portion for Dan.

2 And by the border of Dan, from the east side unto the west side, a portion for Asher.

3 And by the border of Asher, from the east side even unto the west side, a portion for Naphtali.

4 And by the border of Naphtali, from the east side unto the west side, a portion for Manasseh.

5 And by the border of Manasseh, from the east side unto the west side, a portion for Ephraim.

6 And by the border of Ephraim, from the east side even unto the west side, a portion for Reuben.

7 And by the border of Reuben, from the east side unto the west side, a portion for Judah.

8 And by the border of Judah, from the east side unto the west side, shall be the offering which you shall offer of five and twenty thousand reeds in breadth, and in length as one of the other parts, from the east side unto the west side: and the sanctuary shall be in the midst of it.

9 The offering that you shall offer unto the Becoming-One shall be of five and twenty thousand in length, and of ten thousand in breadth.

10 And for them, even for the priests, shall be this holy offering; toward the north five and twenty thousand in length, and toward the west ten thousand in breadth, and toward the east ten thousand in breadth, and toward the south five and twenty thousand in length: and the sanctuary of the Becoming-One shall be in the midst thereof.

11 It shall be for the priests that are sanctified of the sons of Zadok; which have kept my charge, which went not astray when the children of Israel went astray, as the Levites went astray.

12 And this offering of the land that is offered shall be unto them a thing most holy by the border of the Levites.

13 And over against the border of the priests the Levites shall have five and twenty thousand in length, and ten thousand in breadth: all the length shall be five and twenty thousand, and the breadth ten thousand.

14 And they shall not sell of it, neither exchange, nor alienate the beginning first fruit of the land: for it is holy unto the Becoming-One.

15 And the five thousand, that are left in the breadth over against the five and twenty thousand, shall be a profane place for the city, for dwelling, and for suburbs: and the city shall be in the midst thereof.

16 And these shall be the measures thereof; the north side four thousand and five hundred, and the south side four thousand and five hundred, and on the east side four thousand and five hundred, and the west side four thousand and five hundred.

17 And the suburbs of the city shall be toward the north two hundred and fifty, and toward the south two hundred and fifty, and toward the east two hundred and fifty, and toward the west two hundred and fifty.

18 And the residue in length over against the offering of the holy portion shall be ten thousand eastward, and ten thousand westward: and it shall be over against the offering of the holy portion; and the increase thereof shall be for food unto them that serve the city.

19 And they that serve the city shall serve it out of all the tribes of Israel.

20 All the offering shall be five and twenty thousand by five and twenty thousand: you shall offer the holy offering foursquare, with the possession of the city.

21 And the residue shall be for the prince, on the one side and on the other of the holy offering, and of the possession of the city, over against the five and twenty thousand of the offering toward the east border, and westward over against the five and twenty thousand toward the west border, over against the portions for the prince: and it shall be the holy offering; and the sanctuary of the house shall be in the midst there

22 Moreover from the possession of the Levites, and from the possession of the city, being in the midst of that which is the prince's, between the border of Judah and the border of Benjamin, shall be for the prince.

23 As for the rest of the tribes, from the east side unto the west side, Benjamin shall have a portion.

24 And by the border of Benjamin, from the east side unto the west side, Simeon shall have a portion.

25 And by the border of Simeon, from the east side unto the west side, Issachar a portion.

26 And by the border of Issachar, from the east side unto the west side, Zebulun a portion.

27 And by the border of Zebulun, from the east side unto the west side, Gad a portion.

28 And by the border of Gad, at the south side southward, the border shall be even from Tamar unto the waters of strife in Kadesh, and to the river toward the great sea.

29 This is the land which you shall divide by lot unto the tribes of Israel for inheritance, and these are their portions, says my Lord(s) the Becoming-One.

30 And these are the goings out of the city on the north side, four thousand and five hundred measures.

31 And the gates of the city shall be after the names of the tribes of Israel: three gates northward; one gate of Reuben, one gate of Judah, one gate of Levi.

32 And at the east side four thousand and five hundred: and three gates; and one gate of Joseph, one gate of Benjamin, one gate of Dan.

33 And at the south side four thousand and five hundred measures: and three gates; one gate of Simeon, one gate of Issachar, one gate of Zebulun.

34 At the west side four thousand and five hundred, with their three gates; one gate of Gad, one gate of Asher, one gate of Naphtali.

35 It was round about eighteen thousand measures: and the name of the city from that day shall be, The Becoming-One is there.

Daniel

Dan 1:1 In the third year of the reign of Jehoiakim king of Judah came **Nebuchadnezzar** king of Babylon unto Jerusalem, and besieged it. **[3369 YM / 605 BC – 3rd yr of Neb. co-reign]**

2 And my Lord(s) gave Jehoiakim king of Judah into his hand, with part of the vessels of the house of God: which he carried into the land of Shinar to the house of his god; and he brought the vessels into the treasure house of his god.

3 And the king spoke unto Ashpenaz the master of his eunuchs, that he should bring certain of the children of Israel, and of the king's seed, and of the princes;

4 Children in whom was no blemish, but well favored, and skillful in all wisdom, and cunning in knowledge, and understanding science, and such as had ability in them to stand in the king's palace, and whom they might teach the learning and the tongue of the Chaldeans.

5 And the king appointed them a daily provision of the king's food, and of the wine which he drank: so nourishing them three years, that at the end thereof they might stand before the king.

6 Now among these were of the children of Judah, Daniel, Hananiah, Mishael, and Azariah:

7 Unto whom the prince of the eunuchs gave names: for he gave unto Daniel the name of Belteshazzar; and to Hananiah, of Shadrach; and to Mishael, of Meshach; and to Azariah, of Abednego.

8 But Daniel purposed in his heart that he would not defile himself with the portion of the king's food, nor with the wine which he drank: therefore he requested of the prince of the eunuchs that he might not defile himself.

9 Now God had brought Daniel into favor and tender love with the prince of the eunuchs.

10 And the prince of the eunuchs said unto Daniel, I fear my lord the king, who has appointed your food and your drink: for why should he see your faces worse liking than the children which are of your sort? then shall you make me endanger my head to the king.

11 Then said Daniel to Melzar, whom the prince of the eunuchs had set over Daniel, Hananiah, Mishael, and Azariah,

12 Prove your servants, I beg you, ten days; and let them give us pulse to eat, and water to drink.

13 Then let our countenances be looked upon before you, and the countenance of the children that eat of the portion of the king's food: and as you see, deal with your servants.

14 So he consented to them in this matter, and proved them ten days.

15 And at the end of ten days their countenances appeared fairer and fatter in flesh than all the children which did eat the portion of the king's food.

16 Thus Melzar took away the portion of their food, and the wine that they should drink; and gave them pulse.

17 As for these four children, God gave them knowledge and skill in all learning and wisdom: and Daniel had understanding in all visions and dreams.

18 Now at the end of the days that the king had said he should bring them in, then the prince of the eunuchs brought them in before Nebuchadnezzar.

19 And the king communed with them; and among them all was found none like Daniel, Hananiah, Mishael, and Azariah: therefore stood they before the king.

20 And in all matters of wisdom and understanding, that the king inquired of them, he found them ten times better than all the magicians and astrologers that were in all his realm.

21 And Daniel continued even unto the first year of king Cyrus. **[3435/6 YM / 539/8 BC]**

Dan 2:1 And in the second year of the [sole] reign of Nebuchadnezzar dreamed dreams, wherewith his spirit was troubled, and his sleep brake from him. **[3371/2 YM / 603 – 602 BC]**

2 Then the king commanded to call the magicians, and the astrologers, and the sorcerers, and the Chaldeans, for to show the king his dreams. So they came and stood before the king.

3 And the king said unto them, I have dreamed a dream, and my spirit was troubled to know the dream.

4 Then spoke the Chaldeans to the king in Aramaic, O king, live for olams tell your servants the dream, and we will show the interpretation.

5 The king answered and said to the Chaldeans, The thing is gone from me: if you will not make known unto me the dream, with the interpretation thereof, you shall be cut in pieces, and your houses shall be made a dunghill.

6 But if you show the dream, and the interpretation thereof, you shall receive of me gifts and rewards and great honor: therefore show me the dream, and the interpretation thereof.

7 They answered again and said, Let the king tell his servants the dream, and we will show the interpretation of it.

8 The king answered and said, I know of certainty that you would gain the time, because you see the thing is gone from me.

9 But if you will not make known unto me the dream, there is but one decree for you: for you have prepared lying and corrupt words to speak before me, till the time be changed: therefore tell me the dream, and I shall know that you can show me the interpretation thereof.

10 The Chaldeans answered before the king, and said, There is not a man upon the earth that can show the king's matter: therefore there is no king, nor ruler, that asked such things at any magician, or astrologer, or Chaldean.

11 And it is a rare thing that the king requires, and there is none other that can show it before the king, except the gods, whose dwelling, is not with flesh.

12 For this cause the king was angry and very furious, and commanded to destroy all the wise men of Babylon.

13 And the decree went forth that the wise men should be slain; and they sought Daniel and his fellows to be slain.

14 Then Daniel answered with counsel and wisdom to Arioch the captain of the king's guard,

which was gone forth to slay the wise men of Babylon:

15 He answered and said to Arioch the king's captain, Why is the decree so hasty from the king? Then Arioch made the thing known to Daniel.

16 Then Daniel went in, and desired of the king that he would give him time, and that he would show the king the interpretation.

17 Then Daniel went to his house, and made the thing known to Hananiah, Mishael, and Azariah, his companions:

18 That they would desire mercies of GOD of the heavens concerning this secret; that Daniel and his fellows should not perish with the rest of the wise men of Babylon.

19 Then was the secret revealed unto Daniel in a night vision. Then Daniel blessed GOD of heaven.

20 Daniel answered and said, Blessed be the name of GOD from olam and till olam: for wisdom and might are his:

21 And **he changes the times and the seasons: he removes kings, and sets up kings: he gives wisdom unto the wise, and knowledge to them that know understanding**:

22 He reveals the deep and secret things: he knows what is in the darkness, and the light dwells with him.

23 I thank you, and praise you, O you GOD of my fathers, who have given me wisdom and might, and have made known unto me now what we desired of you: for you have now made known unto us the king's matter.

24 Therefore Daniel went in unto Arioch, whom the king had ordained to destroy the wise men of Babylon: he went and said thus unto him; Destroy not the wise men of Babylon: bring me in before the king, and I will show unto the king the interpretation.

25 Then Arioch brought in Daniel before the king in haste, and said thus unto him, I have found a man of the captives of Judah, that will make known unto the king the interpretation.

26 The king answered and said to Daniel, whose name was Belteshazzar, are you able to make known unto me the dream which I have seen, and the interpretation thereof?

27 Daniel answered in the presence of the king, and said, The secret which the king has demanded cannot the wise men, the astrologers, the magicians, the soothsayers, show unto the king;

28 But there is a GOD in the heavens that reveals secrets, and makes known to the king Nebuchadnezzar what shall be in the latter days. your dream, and the visions of your head upon your bed, are these;

29 As for you, O king, your thoughts came into your mind upon your bed, what should come to pass hereafter: and he that reveals secrets makes known to you what shall come to pass.

30 But as for me, this secret is not revealed to me for any wisdom that I have more than any living, but for their sakes that shall make known the interpretation to the king, and that you might know the thoughts of your heart.

31 you, O king, look, and behold a great image. This great image, whose brightness was excellent, stood before you; and the form thereof was terrible.

32 This image's head was of fine gold, his breast and his arms of silver, his belly and his thighs of brass,

33 His legs of iron, his feet part of iron and part of clay.

34 you saw till that a stone was cut out without hands, which smote the image upon his feet that were of iron and clay, and brake them to pieces.

35 Then was the iron, the clay, the brass, the silver, and the gold, broken to pieces together, and became like the chaff of the summer threshing floors; and the wind carried them away, that no place was found for them: and the stone that smote the image became a great mountain, and filled the whole earth.

36 This is the dream; and we will tell the interpretation thereof before the king.

37 you, O king, are a king of kings: for GOD of the heavens has given you a kingdom, power, and strength, and glory.

38 And wheresoever the children of men dwell, the beasts of the field and the fowls of the heavens has he given into your hand, and has made you ruler over them all. you are this head of gold.

39 And after you shall arise another kingdom inferior to you, and another third kingdom of brass, which shall bear rule over all the earth.

40 And the fourth kingdom shall be strong as iron: forasmuch as iron breaks in pieces and subdues all things: and as iron that breaks all these, shall it break in pieces and bruise.

41 And whereas you saw the feet and toes, part of potters' clay, and part of iron, the kingdom shall be divided; but there shall be in it of the strength of the iron, forasmuch as you saw the iron mixed with miry clay.

42 And as the toes of the feet were part of iron, and part of clay, so the end of the kingdom shall be strong, and partly broken.

43 And whereas you saw iron mixed with miry clay, they shall mix themselves with the offspring of mankind:[149] but they shall not cleave one to another, even as iron is not mixed with clay.

44 And in the days of these kings shall GOD of the heavens set up a kingdom, which for olams shall not be destroyed: and the kingdom shall not be left to other people, but it shall break in pieces and consume all these kingdoms, and it shall stand for olams.

45 Forasmuch as you saw that the stone was cut out of the mountain without hands, and that it brake in pieces the iron, the brass, the clay, the silver, and the gold; the great GOD has made known to the king what shall come to pass hereafter: and the dream is certain, and the interpretation thereof sure.

46 Then the king Nebuchadnezzar fell upon his face, and worshiped Daniel, and commanded that they should offer an offering and sweet odors unto him.

47 The king answered unto Daniel, and said, Of a truth it is, that your GOD is a GOD of gods, and lord of kings, and a revealer of secrets, seeing you could reveal this secret.

---

[149] The ten toes or nations will be a mixture of races

48 Then the king made Daniel a great man, and gave him many great gifts, and made him ruler over the whole province of Babylon, and chief of the governors over all the wise men of Babylon.

49 Then Daniel requested of the king, and he set Shadrach, Meshach, and Abednego, over the affairs of the province of Babylon: but Daniel sat in the gate of the king.

Dan 3:1 Nebuchadnezzar the king made an image of gold, whose height was threescore cubits, and the breadth thereof six cubits: he set it up in the plain of Dura, in the province of Babylon.

2 Then Nebuchadnezzar the king sent to gather together the princes, the governors, and the captains, the judges, the treasurers, the councelors, the sheriffs, and all the rulers of the provinces, to come to the dedication of the image which Nebuchadnezzar the king had set up.

3 Then the princes, the governors, and captains, the judges, the treasurers, the councelors, the sheriffs, and all the rulers of the provinces, were gathered together unto the dedication of the image that Nebuchadnezzar the king had set up; and they stood before the image that Nebuchadnezzar had set up.

4 Then a herald cried aloud, To you it is commanded, O people, nations, and languages,

5 That at what time you hear the sound of the cornet, flute, harp, sackbut, psaltery, dulcimer, and all kinds of music, you fall down and worship the golden image that Nebuchadnezzar the king has set up:

6 And whoso falls not down and worships shall the same hour be cast into the midst of a burning fiery furnace.

7 Therefore at that time, when all the people heard the sound of the cornet, flute, harp, sackbut, psaltery, and all kinds of music, all the people, the nations, and the languages, fell down and worshiped the golden image that Nebuchadnezzar the king had set up.

8 Therefore at that time certain Chaldeans came near, and accused the Jews.

9 They spoke and said to the king Nebuchadnezzar, O king, live for olams.

10 you, O king, have made a decree, that every man that shall hear the sound of the cornet, flute, harp, sackbut, psaltery, and dulcimer, and all kinds of music, shall fall down and worship the golden image:

11 And whoso falls not down and worships, that he should be cast into the midst of a burning fiery furnace.

12 There are certain Jews whom you have set over the affairs of the province of Babylon, Shadrach, Meshach, and Abednego; these men, O king, have not regarded you: they serve not your gods, nor worship the golden image which you have set up.

13 Then Nebuchadnezzar in his rage and fury commanded to bring Shadrach, Meshach, and Abednego. Then they brought these men before the king.

14 Nebuchadnezzar spoke and said unto them, Is it true, O Shadrach, Meshach, and Abednego, do not you serve my gods, nor worship the golden image which I have set up?

15 Now if you be ready that at what time you hear the sound of the cornet, flute, harp, sackbut, psaltery, and dulcimer, and all kinds of music, you fall down and worship the image which I have made; well: but if you worship not, you shall be cast the same hour into the midst of a burning fiery furnace; and who is that GOD that shall deliver you out of my hands?

16 Shadrach, Meshach, and Abednego, answered and said to the king, O Nebuchadnezzar, we are not careful to answer you in this matter.

17 If it be so, our GOD whom we serve is able to deliver us from the burning fiery furnace, and he will deliver us out of your hand, O king.

18 But if not, be it known unto you, O king, that we will not serve your gods, nor worship the golden image which you have set up.

19 Then was Nebuchadnezzar full of fury, and the form of his visage was changed against Shadrach, Meshach, and Abednego: therefore he spoke, and commanded that they should heat the furnace one seven times more than it was wont to be heated.

20 And he commanded the most mighty men that were in his army to bind Shadrach, Meshach, and Abednego, and to cast them into the burning fiery furnace.

21 Then these men were bound in their coats, their hosen, and their hats, and their other garments, and were cast into the midst of the burning fiery furnace.

22 Therefore because the king's commandment was urgent, and the furnace exceeding hot, the flame of the fire killed those men that took up Shadrach, Meshach, and Abednego.

23 And these three men, Shadrach, Meshach, and Abednego, fell down bound into the midst of the burning fiery furnace.

24 Then Nebuchadnezzar the king was astonied, and rose up in haste, and spoke, and said unto his councelors, Did not we cast three men bound into the midst of the fire? They answered and said unto the king, True, O king.

25 He answered and said, Lo, I see four men loose, walking in the midst of the fire, and they have no hurt; and the form of the fourth is like the Son of GOD.

26 Then Nebuchadnezzar came near to the mouth of the burning fiery furnace, and spoke, and said, Shadrach, Meshach, and Abednego, you servants of the most high GOD, come forth, and come here. Then Shadrach, Meshach, and Abednego, came forth of the midst of the fire.

27 And the princes, governors, and captains, and the king's councelors, being gathered together, saw these men, upon whose bodies the fire had no power, nor was a hair of their head singed, neither were their coats changed, nor the smell of fire had passed on them.

28 Then Nebuchadnezzar spoke, and said, Blessed be GOD of Shadrach, Meshach, and Abednego, who has sent his angel, and delivered his servants that trusted in him, and have changed the king's word, and yielded their bodies, that they might not serve nor worship any god, except their own GOD.

29 Therefore I make a decree, That every people, nation, and language, which speak anything amiss

against GOD of Shadrach, Meshach, and Abednego, shall be cut in pieces, and their houses shall be made a dunghill: because there is no other GOD that can deliver after this sort.

30 Then the king promoted Shadrach, Meshach, and Abednego, in the province of Babylon.

Dan 4:1 Nebuchadnezzar the king, unto all people, nations, and languages, that dwell in all the earth; Peace be multiplied unto you.

2 I thought it good to show the signs and wonders that the high GOD has worked toward me.

3 How great are his signs! and how mighty are his wonders! his kingdom is a kingdom of olam, and his dominion is from generation to generation.

4 I Nebuchadnezzar was at rest in mine house, and flourishing in my palace:

5 I saw a dream which made me afraid, and the thoughts upon my bed and the visions of my head troubled me.

6 Therefore made I a decree to bring in all the wise men of Babylon before me, that they might make known unto me the interpretation of the dream.

7 Then came in the magicians, the astrologers, the Chaldeans, and the soothsayers: and I told the dream before them; but they did not make known unto me the interpretation thereof.

8 But at the last Daniel came in before me, whose name was Belteshazzar, according to the name of my god, and in whom is the spirit of the holy gods: and before him I told the dream, saying,

9 O Belteshazzar, master of the magicians, because I know that the spirit of the holy gods is in you, and no secret troubles you, tell me the visions of my dream that I have seen, and the interpretation thereof.

10 Thus were the visions of mine head in my bed; I saw, and behold, **a tree in the midst of the earth, and the height thereof was great**.

11 The tree grew, and was strong, and the height thereof reached unto heaven, and the sight thereof to the end of all the earth:

12 The leaves thereof were fair, and the fruit thereof much, and in it was food for all: the beasts of the field had shadow under it, and the fowls of the heavens dwelt in the boughs thereof, and all flesh was fed of it.

13 I saw in the visions of my head upon my bed, and, behold, a watcher and a holy one came down from heaven;

14 He cried aloud, and said thus, Hew down the tree, and cut off his branches, shake off his leaves, and scatter his fruit: let the beasts get away from under it, and the fowls from his branches:

15 Nevertheless leave the stump of his roots in the earth, even with a band of iron and brass, in the tender grass of the field; and let it be wet with the dew of heaven, and let his portion be with the beasts in the grass of the earth:

16 Let his heart be changed from man's, and let a beasts' heart be given unto him: **and let seven times pass over him**.

17 This matter is by the decree of the watchers, and the demand by the word of the holy ones: to the intent that the living may know that the most High rules in the kingdom of men, and gives it to whomsoever he will, and sets up over it the basest of men.

18 This dream I king Nebuchadnezzar have seen. Now you, O Belteshazzar, declare the interpretation thereof, forasmuch as all the wise men of my kingdom are not able to make known unto me the interpretation: but you are able; for the spirit of the holy gods is in you.

19 Then **Daniel, whose name was Belteshazzar**, was astonied for one hour, and his thoughts troubled him. The king spoke, and said, Belteshazzar, let not the dream, or the interpretation thereof, trouble you. Belteshazzar answered and said, My lord, the dream be to them that hate you, and the interpretation thereof to your enemies.

20 The tree that you saw, which grew, and was strong, whose height reached unto the heaven, and the sight thereof to all the earth;

21 Whose leaves were fair, and the fruit thereof much, and in it was food for all; under which the beasts of the field dwelt, and upon whose branches the fowls of the heavens had their habitation:

22 It is you, O king, that are grown and become strong: for your greatness is grown, and reaches unto heaven, and your dominion to the end of the earth.

23 And whereas the king saw a watcher and a holy one coming down from heaven, and saying, Hew the tree down, and destroy it; yet leave the stump of the roots thereof in the earth, even with a band of iron and brass, in the tender grass of the field; and let it be wet with the dew of heaven, and let his portion be with the beasts of the field, **till seven times pass over him**;

24 This is the interpretation, O king, and this is the decree of the most High, which is come upon my lord the king:

25 That they shall drive you from men, and your dwelling shall be with the beasts of the field, and they shall make you to eat grass as oxen, and they shall wet you with the dew of heaven, and **seven times shall pass over you**, till you know that the most High rules in the kingdom of men, and gives it to whomsoever he will.

26 And whereas they commanded to leave the stump of the tree roots; your kingdom shall be sure unto you, after that you shall have known that the heavens do rule.

27 Therefore, O king, let my counsel be acceptable unto you, and break off your sins by righteousness, and your iniquities by showing mercy to the poor; if it may be a lengthening of your tranquillity.

28 All this came upon the king Nebuchadnezzar.

29 At the end of twelve months he walked in the palace of the kingdom of Babylon.

30 The king spoke, and said, Is not this great Babylon, that I have built for the house of the kingdom by the might of my power, and for the honor of my majesty?

31 While the word was in the king's mouth, there fell a voice from heaven, saying, O king Nebuchadnezzar, to you it is spoken; The kingdom is departed from you.

32 And they shall drive you from men, and your dwelling shall be with the beasts of the field: they

shall make you to eat grass as oxen, and seven times shall pass over you, until you know that the most High rules in the kingdom of men, and gives it to whomsoever he will.

33 The same hour was the thing fulfilled upon Nebuchadnezzar: and he was driven from men, and did eat grass as oxen, and his body was wet with the dew of heaven, till his hairs were grown like eagles' feathers, and his nails like birds' claws.

34 And **at the end of the days I Nebuchadnezzar lifted up mine eyes unto heaven, and mine understanding returned unto me**, and I blessed the most High, and I praised and honored him that lives for olam, whose dominion is a dominion of olam, and his kingdom is from generation to generation:

35 And all the inhabitants of the earth are reputed as nothing: and he did according to his will in the army of heaven, and among the inhabitants of the earth: and none can stay his hand, or say unto him, What do you?

36 At the same time my reason returned unto me; and for the glory of my kingdom, mine honor and brightness returned unto me; and my councelors and my Lord(s) sought unto me; and I was established in my kingdom, and excellent majesty was added unto me.

37 Now I Nebuchadnezzar praise and extol and honor the King of heaven, all whose works are truth, and his ways judgment: and those that walk in pride he is able to abase.

Dan 5:1 Belshazzar the king made a great feast to a thousand of his lords, and drank wine before the thousand. [3435/6 YM / 538 BC]

2 Belshazzar, whiles he tasted the wine, commanded to bring the golden and silver vessels which his father Nebuchadnezzar had taken out of the temple which was in Jerusalem; that the king, and his princes, his wives, and his concubines, might drink therein.

3 Then they brought the golden vessels that were taken out of the temple of the house of GOD which was at Jerusalem; and the king, and his princes, his wives, and his concubines, drank in them.

4 They drank wine, and praised the gods of gold, and of silver, of brass, of iron, of wood, and of stone.

5 In the same hour came forth fingers of a man's hand, and wrote over against the candlestick upon the plaster of the wall of the king's palace: and the king saw the part of the hand that wrote.

6 Then the king's countenance was changed, and his thoughts troubled him, so that the joints of his loins were loosened, and his knees smote one against another.

7 The king cried aloud to bring in the astrologers, the Chaldeans, and the soothsayers. And the king spoke, and said to the wise men of Babylon, Whosoever shall read this writing, and show me the interpretation thereof, shall be clothed with scarlet, and have a chain of gold about his neck, and shall be the third ruler in the kingdom.

8 Then came in all the king's wise men: but they could not read the writing, nor make known to the king the interpretation thereof.

9 Then was king Belshazzar greatly troubled, and his countenance was changed in him, and his lords were perplexed.

10 Now the queen by reason of the words of the king and his lords came into the banquet house: and the queen spoke and said, O king, live for olams: let not your thoughts trouble you, nor let your countenance be changed:

11 There is a man in your kingdom, in whom is the spirit of the holy gods; and in the days of your father light and understanding and wisdom, like the wisdom of the gods, was found in him; whom the king Nebuchadnezzar your father, the king, I say, your father, made master of the magicians, astrologers, Chaldeans, and soothsayers;

12 Forasmuch as an excellent spirit, and knowledge, and understanding, interpreting of dreams, and showing of hard sentences, and dissolving of doubts, were found in the same Daniel, whom the king named Belteshazzar: now let Daniel be called, and he will show the interpretation.

13 Then was Daniel brought in before the king. And the king spoke and said unto Daniel, are you that Daniel, which are of the children of the captivity of Judah, whom the king my father brought out of Judah?

14 I have even heard of you, that the spirit of the God is in you, and that light and understanding and excellent wisdom is found in you.

15 And now the wise men, the astrologers, have been brought in before me, that they should read this writing, and make known unto me the interpretation thereof: but they could not show the interpretation of the thing:

16 And I have heard of you, that you can make interpretations, and dissolve doubts: now if you can read the writing, and make known to me the interpretation thereof, you shall be clothed with scarlet, and have a chain of gold about your neck, and shall be the third ruler in the kingdom.

17 Then Daniel answered and said before the king, Let your gifts be to thyself, and give your rewards to another; yet I will read the writing unto the king, and make known to him the interpretation.

18 O you king, the most high GOD gave Nebuchadnezzar your father a kingdom, and majesty, and glory, and honor:

19 And for the majesty that he gave him, all people, nations, and languages, trembled and feared before him: whom he would, he killed; and whom he would, he kept alive; and whom he would, he set up; and whom he would, he put down.

20 But when his heart was lifted up, and his mind hardened in pride, he was deposed from his kingly throne, and they took his glory from him:

21 And he was driven from the sons of men; and his heart was made like the beasts, and his dwelling was with the wild donkeys: they fed him with grass like oxen, and his body was wet with the dew of heaven; till he knew that the most high GOD ruled in the kingdom of men, and that he appoints over it whomsoever he will.

22 And you his son, O Belshazzar, have not humbled your heart, though you knew all this;

23 but you have exalted yourself against the Lord of heaven; and they have brought the vessels of His

house before you, and you and your nobles, your wives and your concubines have been drinking wine from them; and you have praised the gods of silver and gold, of bronze, iron, wood and stone, which do not see, hear or understand. But the GOD in whose hand are your life-breath and your ways, you have not glorified.

24 Then was the part of the hand sent from him; and this writing was written.

25 And this is the writing that was written, MENE, MENE, TEKEL, UPHARSIN.

26 This is the interpretation of the thing: MENE; GOD has numbered your kingdom, and finished it.

27 TEKEL; you are weighed in the balances, and are found wanting.

28 PERES; your kingdom is divided, and given to the Medes and Persians.

29 Then commanded Belshazzar, and they clothed Daniel with scarlet, and put a chain of gold about his neck, and made a proclamation concerning him, that he should be the third ruler in the kingdom.

30 In that night was Belshazzar the king of the Chaldeans slain.

31 And **Darius** the **Median** took the kingdom, being a son of about threescore and two years. **[538 BC]**

Dan 6:1 It pleased Darius to set over the kingdom a hundred and twenty princes, which should be over the whole kingdom;

2 And over these three presidents; of whom Daniel was first; that the princes might give accounts unto them, and the king should have no damage.

3 Then this Daniel was preferred above the presidents and princes, because an excellent spirit was in him; and the king thought to set him over the whole realm.

4 Then the presidents and princes sought to find occasion against Daniel concerning the kingdom; but they could find none occasion nor fault; forasmuch as he was faithful, neither was there any error or fault found in him.

5 Then said these men, We shall not find any occasion against this Daniel, except we find it against him concerning the law of his GOD.

6 Then these presidents and princes assembled together to the king, and said thus unto him, King Darius, live for olams.

7 All the presidents of the kingdom, the governors, and the princes, the councelors, and the captains, have consulted together to establish a royal statute, and to make a firm decree, that whosoever shall ask a petition of any GOD or man for thirty days, save of you, O king, he shall be cast into the den of lions.

8 Now, O king, establish the decree, and sign the writing, that it be not changed, according to the law of the Medes and Persians, which alters not.

9 Therefore king Darius signed the writing and the decree.

10 Now when Daniel knew that the writing was signed, he went into his house; and his windows being open in his chamber toward Jerusalem, he kneeled upon his knees three times a day, and prayed, and gave thanks before his GOD, as he did aforetime.

11 Then these men assembled, and found Daniel praying and making supplication before his GOD.

12 Then they came near, and spoke before the king concerning the king's decree; have you not signed a decree, that every man that shall ask a petition of any GOD or man within thirty days, save of you, O king, shall be cast into the den of lions? The king answered and said, The thing is true, according to the law of the Medes and Persians, which alters not.

13 Then answered they and said before the king, That Daniel, which is of the children of the captivity of Judah, regards not you, O king, nor the decree that you have signed, but makes his petition three times a day.

14 Then the king, when he heard these words, was greatly displeased with himself, and set his heart on Daniel to deliver him: and he labored till the going down of the sun to deliver him.

15 Then these men assembled unto the king, and said unto the king, Know, O king, that the law of the Medes and Persians is, That no decree nor statute which the king establishes may be changed.

16 Then the king commanded, and they brought Daniel, and cast him into the den of lions. Now the king spoke and said unto Daniel, your GOD whom you serve continually, he will deliver you.

17 And a stone was brought, and laid upon the mouth of the den; and the king sealed it with his own signet, and with the signet of his lords; that the purpose might not be changed concerning Daniel.

18 Then the king went to his palace, and passed the night fasting: neither were instruments of music brought before him: and his sleep went from him.

19 Then the king arose very early in the morning, and went in haste unto the den of lions.

20 And when he came to the den, he cried with a lamentable voice unto Daniel: and the king spoke and said to Daniel, O Daniel, servant of the living GOD, is your God, whom you serve continually, able to deliver you from the lions?

21 Then said Daniel unto the king, O king, live for olams.

22 My GOD has sent his angel, and has shut the lions' mouths, that they have not hurt me: forasmuch as before him innocency was found in me; and also before you, O king, have I done no hurt.

23 Then was the king exceeding glad for him, and commanded that they should take Daniel up out of the den. So Daniel was taken up out of the den, and no manner of hurt was found upon him, because he believed in his GOD.

24 And the king commanded, and they brought those men which had accused Daniel, and they cast them into the den of lions, them, their children, and their wives; and the lions had the mastery of them, and brake all their bones in pieces or ever before they came to the bottom of the den.

25 Then king Darius wrote unto all people, nations, and languages, that dwell in all the earth; Peace be multiplied unto you.

26 I make a decree, That in every dominion of my kingdom men tremble and fear before GOD of Daniel: for he is the living GOD, and stedfast for olams, and

his kingdom that which shall not be destroyed, and his dominion shall be even unto the end.

27 He delivers and rescues, and he works signs and wonders in the heavens and in earth, who has delivered Daniel from the power of the lions.

28 So this Daniel prospered in the reign of Darius, and in the reign of Cyrus the Persian.

Dan 7:1 In the first year of Belshazzar king of Babylon Daniel had a dream and visions of his head upon his bed: then he wrote the dream, and told the sum of the matters. [**3425 YM / ab. 549 BC**]

2 Daniel spoke and said, I saw in my vision by night, and, behold, the four winds of the heavens strove upon the great sea.

3 And four great beasts came up from the sea, diverse one from another.

4 The first was like a lion, and had eagle's wings: I beheld till the wings thereof were plucked, and it was lifted up from the earth, and made stand upon the feet as a man, and a man's heart was given to it.

5 And behold another beast, a second, like to a bear, and it raised up itself on one side, and it had three ribs in the mouth of it between the teeth of it: and they said thus unto it, Arise, devour much flesh.

6 After this I beheld, and lo another, like a leopard, which had upon the back of it four wings of a fowl; the beast had also four heads; and dominion was given to it.

7 After this I saw in the night visions, and behold a <u>fourth beast</u>, dreadful and terrible, and strong exceedingly; and it had great iron teeth: it devoured and brake in pieces, and stamped the residue with the feet of it: and it was diverse from all the beasts that were before it; and <u>it had ten horns</u>.

8 I considered the horns, and, behold, there came up among them a another little[150] horn, from before whom there were three of the first horns plucked up by the roots: and, behold, in this horn were eyes like the eyes of man, and a mouth speaking great[151] things.

9 I beheld till the thrones were cast down, and the Ancient of days did sit, whose garment was white as snow, and the hair of his head like the pure wool: his throne was like the fiery flame, and his wheels as burning fire.

10 A fiery stream issued and came forth from before him: a thousand, thousand ministered unto him, and multitude of multitudes stood before him: the judgment was set, and the books were opened.

11 I beheld then because of the voice of the great words which the horn spoke: I beheld even till the beast was slain, and his body destroyed, and given to the burning flame.

12 As concerning the rest of the beasts, they had their dominion taken away: yet their lives were prolonged for a season and time.

13 I saw in the night visions, and, behold, one like the Son of man came with the clouds of heaven, and came to the Ancient of days, and they brought him near before him.

14 And there was given him dominion, and glory, and a kingdom, that all people, nations, and languages, should serve him: his dominion is a dominion of olam, which shall not pass away, and his kingdom that which shall not be destroyed.

15 I Daniel was grieved in my spirit in the midst of my body, and the visions of my head troubled me.

16 I came near unto one of them that stood by, and asked him the truth of all this. So he told me, and made me know the interpretation of the things.

17 These great living beasts, which are four, are four kings, which shall arise out of the earth.

18 But the saints of the most High shall take the kingdom, and possess the kingdom for olam, even for olam and olams.

19 Then I desired to know the truth of the fourth beast, which was diverse from all the others, exceeding dreadful, whose teeth were of iron, and his nails of brass; which devoured, brake in pieces, and stamped the residue with his feet;

20 And of the ten horns that were in his head, and of the other which came up, and from before whom three fell; even of that horn that had eyes, and a mouth that spoke very great[152] things, whose appearance was greater than his fellows.[153]

21 I beheld, and the same horn made war with the saints, and prevailed against them;

22 Until the Ancient of days came, and judgment was given to the saints of the most High; and the time came that the saints possessed the kingdom.

23 Thus he said, The <u>fourth beast</u> shall be the fourth kingdom upon earth, which shall be diverse from all kingdoms, and shall devour the whole earth, and shall tread it down, and break it in pieces.

24 And the <u>ten horns</u> out of this kingdom are ten kings that shall arise: and another shall rise after them; and he shall be different[154] from the former ones, and he shall subdue three kings.

25 And he shall speak great words against the most High, and shall wear out the saints of the most High, and hopes to change times and laws: and they shall be given into his hand until a **time and times and the dividing of time**.

26 But the judgment shall sit, and they shall take away his dominion, to consume and to destroy it unto the end.

27 And the kingdom and dominion, and the greatness of the kingdom under the whole heaven, shall be given to the people of the saints of the most High, whose kingdom is a kingdom of olam, and all dominions shall serve and obey him.

28 Hitherto is the end of the matter. As for me Daniel, my thoughts much troubled me, and my countenance changed in me: but I kept the matter in my heart.

Dan 8:1 In the third year of the reign of king Belshazzar a vision appeared unto me, even unto me Daniel, after that which appeared unto me at the first. [**ab. 3427 YM / 547 BC**]

---

[150] diminished or small in size or dignity; ignoble; #2192, 6810, & 6819
[151] boastful, imposing, powerful
[152] boastful, imposing, powerful
[153] associates or comrades [greater than the other horns]
[154] Or will change

2 And I saw in a vision; and it came to pass, when I saw, that I was at Shushan in the palace, which is in the province of Elam; and I saw in a vision, and I was by the river of Ulai.

3 Then I lifted up mine eyes, and saw, and, behold, there stood before the river a ram which had two horns: and the two horns were high; but one was higher than the other, and the higher came up last.

4 I saw the ram pushing westward, and northward, and southward; so that no beasts might stand before him, neither was there any that could deliver out of his hand; but he did according to his will, and became great.

5 And as I was considering, behold, a he-goat came from the west on the face of the whole earth, and touched not the ground: and the he-goat had a conspicuous horn between his eyes.

6 And he came to the ram that had two horns, which I had seen standing before the river, and ran unto him in the fury of his power.

7 And I saw him come close unto the ram, and he was moved with choler against him, and smote the ram, and brake his two horns: and there was no power in the ram to stand before him, but he cast him down to the ground, and stamped upon him: and there was none that could deliver the ram out of his hand.

8 Therefore the he goat grew very great: and when he was strong, the great horn was broken; and for it came up four notable ones toward the four winds of heaven.

9 And out of the one of them came forth a little[155] horn, which grew exceeding great, toward the south, and toward the east, and toward the pleasant land.

10 And it grew great, even to the host of heaven; and it cast down some of the host and of the stars to the ground, and stamped upon them.

11 Yes, he magnified himself even to the prince of the host, and by him the daily sacrifice was taken away, and was cast down the holy place[156] [of God's dwelling].

12 And a host was given him against the daily sacrifice by reason of rebellion, and it cast down the truth to the ground; and it practiced, and prospered.

13 Then I heard one saint speaking, and another saint said unto that certain saint which spoke, How long shall be the vision concerning the daily sacrifice, and the rebellion of desolation, to give both the sanctuary and the host to be trodden under foot?

14 And he said unto me, Unto two thousand and three hundred evening, morning; then shall the sanctuary be cleansed.

15 And it came to pass, when I, even I Daniel, had seen the vision, and sought for the meaning, then, behold, there stood before me as the appearance of a man.

16 And I heard a man's voice between the banks of Ulai, which called, and said, Gabriel, make this man to understand the vision.

17 So he came near where I stood: and when he came, I was afraid, and fell upon my face: but he said unto me, Understand, O son of man: **for at the time of the end shall be the vision.**

18 Now as he was speaking with me, I was in a deep sleep on my face toward the ground: but he touched me, and set me upright.

19 And he said, Behold, I will make you know what shall be in the last end of the indignation: for **at the set time**[157] **the end shall be.**

20 The **ram which you saw having two horns are the kings of Media and Persia.**

21 And **the fearful he-goat is the king of Grecia: and the great horn that is between his eyes is the first king.**

22 **Now that being broken, whereas four stood up for it, four kingdoms shall stand up out of the nation, but not in his power.**

23 And in the end of their kingdom, when the rebels reach their full measure, **a king of strong presence**[158] a master of riddles[159] shall stand up.

24 And his power shall be mighty, but not by his own power: and he shall destroy extraordinarily, and shall prosper, and bring about [this prophecy], and he shall destroy the mighty and the holy people.

25 And through his skillfulness also he shall cause deceit to prosper in his hand;[B] and he shall magnify himself in his mind, and in prosperity [or in careless security or peace or without warning] shall destroy many: he shall also stand up against the Prince of princes; but he shall be broken without hand. [B He uses deceit as in the *Art of War* by Sun Tzu see: https://suntzudo.weebly.com/sun-tzu-and-deception.html]

26 And the vision of the evening and the morning which was told is true: therefore shut you up the vision; for it shall be for many days.

27 And I Daniel fainted, and was sick certain days; afterward I rose up, and did the king's business; and I was astonished at the vision, but none understood it.

Dan 9:1 In the first year of **Darius** the son of Ahasuerus, of the seed of the **Medes**, which was made king over the realm of the Chaldeans; **[3436 YM / ab. 538 BC]**

2 In the first year of his reign I Daniel understood by books the number of the years, whereof the word of the Becoming-One came to Jeremiah the prophet, that he would accomplish **seventy years** in the desolations of Jerusalem.

3 And I set my face unto my Lord(s), God, to seek by prayer and supplications, with fasting, and sackcloth, and ashes:

4 And I prayed unto the Becoming-One my God, and made my confession, and said, O my Lord, the great and dreadful GOD, keeping the covenant and

---

[155] young
[156] This means the holy place of God's dwelling (his Church or Holy Temple) by comparing in context the ten places in the Bible where the Hebrew word (מָכוֹן) for "place" occurs (Exod. 15:17, 1 Ki. 8:13, 1 Ki. 8:39, 1 Ki. 8:43, 1 Ki. 8:49, 2 Chr. 6:30, Ps. 89:15, Ps. 97:2, Isa. 4:5, Dan. 8:11).

[157] Appointed time or festival
[158] See Dan 9:26
[159] See BDB, p. 295, חִיד Strong's # H2420: "perplexing questions" or "enigmas"

mercy to them that love him, and to them that keep his commandments;

5 We have sinned, and have committed iniquity, and have done wickedly, and have rebelled, even by departing from your precepts and from your judgments:

6 Neither have we listened unto your servants the prophets, which spoke in your name to our kings, our princes, and our fathers, and to all the people of the land.

7 O my Lord(s), righteousness belongs unto you, but unto us confusion of faces, as at this day; to the men of Judah, and to the inhabitants of Jerusalem, and unto all Israel, that are near, and that are far off, through all the countries to which you have driven them, because of their trespass that they have trespassed against you.

8 O Becoming-One, to us belongs confusion of face, to our kings, to our princes, and to our fathers, because we have sinned against you.

9 To my Lord(s), our God belong mercies and forgiveness, though we have rebelled against him;

10 Neither have we obeyed the voice of the Becoming-One our God, to walk in his laws, which he set before us by his servants the prophets.

11 Yes, all Israel have transgressed your law, even by departing, that they might not obey your voice; therefore the curse is poured upon us, and the oath that is written in the law of Moses the servant of God, because we have sinned against him.

12 And he has confirmed his words, which he spoke against us, and against our judges that judged us, by bringing upon us a great evil: for under the whole heavens has not been done as has been done upon Jerusalem.

13 As it is written in the law of Moses, all this evil is come upon us: yet made we not our prayer before the Becoming-One our God, that we might turn from our iniquities, and understand your truth.

14 Therefore has the Becoming-One watched upon the evil, and brought it upon us: for the Becoming-One our God is righteous in all his works which he does: for we obeyed not his voice.

15 And now, O my Lord(s), our God, that have brought your people forth out of the land of Egypt with a mighty hand, and have gotten you renown, as at this day; we have sinned, we have done wickedly.

16 O my Lord(s), according to all your righteousness, I beg you, let your anger and your fury be turned away from your city Jerusalem, your holy mountain: because for our sins, and for the iniquities of our fathers, Jerusalem and your people are become a reproach to all that are about us.

17 Now therefore, O our God, hear the prayer of your servant, and his supplications, and cause your face to shine upon your sanctuary that is desolate, for my Lord(s)' sake.

18 O my God, incline your ear, and hear; open your eyes, and behold our desolations, and the city which is called by your name: for we do not present our supplications before you for our righteousness, but for your great mercies.

19 O my Lord(s), hear; O my Lord(s), forgive; O my Lord(s), listen and do; defer not, for your own sake, O my God: for your city and your people are called by your name.

20 And while I was speaking, and praying, and confessing my sin and the sin of my people Israel, and presenting my supplication before the Becoming-One my God for the holy mountain of my God;

21 Yes, while I was speaking in prayer, even the man Gabriel, whom I had seen in the vision at the beginning, being caused to fly swiftly, touched me about the time of the evening offering.

22 And he informed me, and talked with me, and said, O Daniel, I am now come forth to give you skill and understanding.

23 At the beginning of your supplications the commandment came forth, and I am come to show you; for you are greatly beloved: therefore understand the matter, and consider the vision.

24 Seventy weeks are determined upon your people and upon your holy city, to finish the rebellion, and to seal up sins, and to make atonement for iniquity, and to bring in righteousness of olams, and to seal up the vision and prophecy, and to anoint the most Holy.

25 Know therefore and understand, that from the going forth of the commandment to return and to rebuild Jerusalem unto the Messiah [Anointed] the Prince shall be seven weeks, and threescore and two weeks: the street shall be built again, and the wall, even in troublous times.

26 And after threescore and two weeks shall the Messiah [Anointed] be cut off, but not for Himself: and the people of the **Prince to come**[160], shall destroy the city and the sanctuary; and the end thereof shall be with a flood, and unto the end of the battle, desolations are determined.

27 And He shall confirm the covenant with many for one week: and in the midst of the week He shall cause the sacrifice and the offering to cease, and on the wing of abominations a desolator, even until the full end, and that which is decreed shall be poured upon the desolator.

Dan 10:1 In the third year of **Cyrus** king of **Persia** a thing was revealed unto Daniel, whose name was called Belteshazzar; and the thing was true, but the time appointed was long: and he understood the thing, and had understanding of the vision. **[ab. 3438 YM / ab. 536 BC]**

2 In those days I Daniel was mourning three full weeks of days.

3 I ate no pleasant bread, neither came flesh nor wine in my mouth, neither did I anoint myself at all, till three weeks of days were fulfilled.

4 And in the four and twentieth day of the first month, as I was by the side of the great river, which is Hiddekel;

5 Then I lifted up mine eyes, and looked, and behold a certain man clothed in linen, whose loins were girded with fine gold of Uphaz:

6 His body also was like the beryl, and his face as the appearance of lightning, and his eyes as lamps of fire, and his arms and his feet like in color to polished brass, and the voice of his words like the voice of a multitude.

---

[160] See Dan 8:23

7 And I Daniel alone saw the vision: for the men that were with me saw not the vision; but a great quaking fell upon them, so that they fled to hide themselves.

8 Therefore I was left alone, and saw this great vision, and there remained no strength in me: for my comeliness was turned in me into corruption, and I retained no strength.

9 Yet heard I the voice of his words: and when I heard the voice of his words, then was I in a deep sleep on my face, and my face toward the ground.

10 And, behold, a hand touched me, which set me upon my knees and upon the palms of my hands.

11 And he said unto me, O Daniel, a man greatly beloved, understand the words that I speak unto you, and stand upright: for unto you I am now sent. And when he had spoken this word unto me, I stood trembling.

12 Then said he unto me, Fear not, Daniel: for from the first day that you did set your heart to understand, and to chasten yourself before your God, your words were heard, and I am come for your words.

13 But the prince of the kingdom of Persia withstood me one and twenty days: but, lo, Michael, one of the chief princes, came to help me; and I remained there with the kings of Persia.

14 Now I am come to make you understand what shall befall your people in the end of the days: for yet the vision is for the [end of] days.

15 And when he had spoken such words unto me, I set my face toward the ground, and I became mute.

16 And, behold, one like the similitude of the sons of men touched my lips: then I opened my mouth, and spoke, and said unto him that stood before me, O my lord, by the vision my sorrows are turned upon me, and I have retained no strength.

17 For how can the servant of this my Lord(s) talk with this my lord? for as for me, straightway there remained no strength in me, neither is there breath left in me.

18 Then there came again and touched me one like the appearance of a man, and he strengthened me,

19 And said, O man greatly beloved, fear not: peace be unto you, be strong, yes, be strong. And when he had spoken unto me, I was strengthened, and said, Let my lord speak; for you have strengthened me.

20 Then said he, know you why I come unto you? and now will I return to fight with the prince of Persia: and when I am gone forth, lo, the prince of Grecia shall come.

21 But I will show you that which is noted in the scripture of truth: and there is none that holds with me in these things, but Michael your prince.

Dan 11:1 Also I in the first year of **Darius the Mede**, even I, stood to confirm and to strengthen him. [3436 YM / ab. 538 BC]

2 And now will I show you the truth. Behold, there shall stand up yet three kings in Persia; and the fourth shall be far richer than they all: and by his strength through his riches he shall stir up all against the realm of Grecia.

3 And a mighty king shall stand up, that shall rule with great dominion, and do according to his will.

4 And when he shall stand up, his kingdom shall be broken, and shall be divided toward the four winds of heaven; and not to his end [posterity] nor according to his dominion which he ruled: for his kingdom shall be plucked up, even for others beside those.

5 And the king of the south shall be strong, and one of his princes; and he shall be strong above him, and have dominion; his dominion shall be a great dominion.

6 And in the end of years they shall join themselves together; for the king's daughter of the south shall come to the king of the north to make an agreement: but she shall not retain the power of the arm; neither shall he stand, nor his arm: but she shall be given up, and they that brought her, and he that begat her, and he that strengthened her in these times.

7 But out of a branch of her roots shall one stand up in his estate, which shall come with an army, and shall enter into the fortress of the king of the north, and shall deal against them, and shall prevail:

8 And shall also carry captives into Egypt their gods, with their princes, and with their precious vessels of silver and of gold; and he shall continue more years than the king of the north.

9 So the king of the south shall come into his kingdom, and shall return into his own land.

10 But his sons shall be stirred up, and shall assemble a multitude of great forces: and one shall certainly come, and overflow, and pass through: then shall he return, and be stirred up, even to his fortress.

11 And the king of the south shall be moved with choler, and shall come forth and fight with him, even with the king of the north: and he shall set forth a great multitude; but the multitude shall be given into his hand.

12 And when he has taken away the multitude, his heart shall be lifted up; and he shall cast down multitudes: but he shall not be strengthened by it.

13 For the king of the north shall return, and shall set forth a multitude greater than the former, and at the end of times, years, he shall come with a great army and with much riches.

14 And in those times there shall many stand up against the king of the south: also the robbers of your people shall exalt themselves to establish the vision; but they shall fall.

15 So the king of the north shall come, and cast up a mount, and take the most fenced cities: and the arms of the south shall not withstand, neither his chosen people, neither shall there be any strength to withstand.

16 But he that comes against him shall do according to his own will, and none shall stand before him: and **he shall stand in the glorious land**, which by his hand shall be consumed.

17 He shall also set his face to enter with the strength of his whole kingdom, and upright ones with him; thus shall he do: and he shall give him the daughter of women, corrupting her: but she shall not stand on his side, neither be for him.

18 After this shall he turn his face unto the isles, and shall take many: but a prince for his own behalf shall cause the reproach offered by him to cease; without his own reproach he shall cause it to turn upon him.

19 Then he shall turn his face toward the fort of his own land: but he shall stumble and fall, and not be found.

20 Then shall stand up in his estate he who is taking-over,[161] overseeing,[162] the glory of the kingdom: but within few days he shall be removed, neither in anger, nor in battle.

21 And in his estate shall stand up **a despised person**, to whom they shall not give the glory of the kingdom:[163] but he shall come in suddenly, and take the kingdom by intrigue.

22 And with the arms of a flood shall they be overflown from before him, and shall be broken; yes, also the prince of the covenant.

23 And after the league [10 nations] made with him he shall work deceitfully: for he shall come up, and shall become strong with a diminished [made small: 7 nations] people.

24 He shall enter peaceably [or with ease] even upon the fat places of the province; and he shall do that which his fathers have not done, nor his fathers' fathers; he shall scatter among them the prey, and spoil, and riches: yes, and he shall forecast his devices against the strong holds, even for a time.

25 And he shall stir up his power and his courage against the king of the south with a great army; and the king of the south shall be stirred up to battle with a very great and mighty army; but he shall not stand: for they shall forecast devices against him.

26 Yes, they that feed of the portion of his food shall destroy him, and his army shall overflow: and many shall fall down slain.

27 And both these kings' hearts shall be to do mischief, and they shall speak lies at one table; but it shall not prosper: **for yet the end shall be at the set time.**[164]

28 Then shall he return into his land with great riches; and his heart shall be against the holy covenant; and he shall do exploits, and return to his own land.

29 **At the set time**[165] he shall return, and come toward the south; but it shall not be as the former, or as the latter.

30 For the ships of Chittim shall come against him: therefore he shall be grieved, and return, and have indignation against the holy covenant: so shall he do; he shall even return, and have intelligence with them that forsake the holy covenant.

31 And arms shall stand on his part, and they shall pollute the sanctuary of strength, and shall take away the daily sacrifice, and they shall place [or set up] the abomination that makes desolate.

32 And such as do wickedly against the covenant shall he corrupt by flatteries: but the people that do know their God shall be strong, and do exploits.

33 And they that understand among the people shall instruct many: yet they shall fall by the sword, and by flame, by captivity, and by spoil, many days.

34 Now when they shall fall, they shall be helped with a little help: but many shall cleave to them with flatteries.

35 And some of them of understanding shall fall, to try them, and to purge, and to make them white, **even to the time of the end: because it is yet for the set time.**[166]

36 And the king shall do according to his will; and he shall exalt himself, and shall magnify himself above every god, and shall speak marvelous things against GOD of gods, and shall prosper till the indignation be accomplished: for that which is determined shall be done.

37 Neither shall he regard God of his fathers, nor the desire of women, nor regard any god: for he shall magnify himself above all.

38 But in his estate shall he honor God of fortresses: and a god whom his fathers knew not shall he honor with gold, and silver, and with precious stones, and pleasant things.

39 Thus shall he do in the most strong holds with a strange god, whom he shall acknowledge and increase with glory: and he shall cause them to rule over many, and shall divide the land for gain.

40 And at the time of the end shall the king of the south push at him: and the king of the north shall come against him like a whirlwind, with chariots, and with horsemen, and with many ships; and he shall enter into the countries, and shall overflow and pass over.

41 He shall enter also into the glorious land, and many countries shall be overthrown: but these shall escape out of his hand, even Edom, and Moab, and the beginning of the children of Ammon.

42 He shall stretch forth his hand also upon the countries: and the land of Egypt shall not escape.

43 But he shall have power over the treasures of gold and of silver, and over all the precious things of Egypt: and the Libyans and the Ethiopians shall be at his steps.

44 But tidings out of the east and out of the north shall trouble him: therefore he shall go forth with great fury to destroy, and utterly to destroy many.

45 And he shall plant the tabernacles of his palace between the seas in the glorious holy mountain; yet he shall come to his end, and none shall help him.

Dan 12:1 And at that time shall Michael stand up, the great prince which stands for the children of your people: and **there shall be a time of trouble, such as never was since there was a nation even to that same time**: and at that time your people shall

---

[161] To "pass over" or "pass along" or "take over"; a participle verb #5674

[162] A participle verb, #5065; which means in context, someone(s) oppressing people, a taskmaster; see cf. Ex 3:7; 5:6: 5:10; Isa 9:3: 14:2, 4; Zech 9:8; 10:4; Deut 15:2, 3; Isa 3:5, 12; Zec 9:8; etc.

[163] In a democracy, one not receiving enough votes (real or fake) to win an election.

[164] Appointed time or festival

[165] Appointed time or festival

[166] Appointed time or festival

be delivered, every one that shall be found written in the book.

2 And many of them that sleep in the dust of the earth shall awake, some to life of olam, and some to shame and contempt of olam.

3 And they that be wise shall shine as the brightness of space; and they that turn many to righteousness as the stars for olam and beyond.

4 But you, O Daniel, shut up the words, and seal the book, even to the **time of the end**: many shall run back and forth, and knowledge shall be increased.

5 Then I Daniel looked, and, behold, there stood two others, the one on this side of the bank of the river, and the other on that side of the bank of the river.

6 And one said to the man clothed in linen, which was upon the waters of the river, How long shall it be to the end of these wonders?

7 And I heard the man clothed in linen, which was upon the waters of the river, when he held up his right hand and his left hand unto heaven, and swore by him that lives for olam that it shall be for a **set time, set times,**[167] **and a half**; and when he shall have accomplished to scatter the power of the holy people, all these things shall be finished.

8 And I heard, but I understood not: then said I, O my lord, what shall be the end of these things?

9 And he said, Go your way, Daniel: for the words are closed up and **sealed till the time of the end.**

10 Many shall be purified, and made white, and tried; but the wicked shall do wickedly: and none of the wicked shall understand; but the wise shall understand.

11 And from the time that the daily sacrifice shall be taken away, and to the bestowing [giving, granting] of the abomination that makes desolate, there shall be **a thousand two hundred and ninety days**.

12 Blessings[168] to he that waits, and comes to the **thousand three hundred and five and thirty days**.

13 But go you your way till the end be: for you shall rest, and stand in your lot at the end of the days.

---

[167] Appointed time(s) or festival(s)
[168] Joys or Happinesses

Hosea

Hos 1:1 The word of the Becoming-One that came unto Hosea, the son of Beeri, in the days of Uzziah, Jotham, Ahaz, and Hezekiah, kings of Judah, and in the days of Jeroboam the son of Joash, king of Israel. [747BC - ?]

2 The beginning of the word of the Becoming-One by Hosea. And the Becoming-One said to Hosea, Go, take unto you a wife of whoredoms and children of whoredoms: for the land has committed great whoredom, departing from the Becoming-One.

3 So he went and took Gomer the daughter of Diblaim; which conceived, and bare him a son.

4 And the Becoming-One said unto him, Call his name Jezreel; for yet a little while, and I will avenge the blood of Jezreel upon the house of Jehu, and will cause to cease the kingdom of the house of Israel.

5 And it shall come to pass at that day, that I will break the bow of Israel in the valley of Jezreel.

6 And she conceived again, and bare a daughter. And God said unto him, Call her name Loruhamah: for I will no more have mercy upon the house of Israel; but I will utterly take them away.

7 But I will have mercy upon the house of Judah, and will save them by the Becoming-One their God, and will not save them by bow, nor by sword, nor by battle, by horses, nor by horsemen.

8 Now when she had weaned Loruhamah, she conceived, and bare a son.

9 Then said God, Call his name Loammi: for you are not my people, and I will not be your God.

10 Yet the number of the children of Israel shall be as the sand of the sea, which cannot be measured nor numbered; and it shall come to pass, that in the place where it was said unto them, you are not my people, there it shall be said unto them, you are the sons of the living GOD.

11 Then shall the children of Judah and the children of Israel be gathered together, and appoint themselves one head, and they shall come up out of the land: for great shall be the day of Jezreel.

Hos 2:1 Say you unto your brethren, Ammi; and to your sisters, Ruhamah.

2 Plead with your mother, plead: for she is not my wife, neither I am her husband: let her therefore put away her whoredoms out of her sight, and her adulteries from between her breasts;

3 Lest I strip her naked, and set her as in the day that she was born, and make her as a wilderness, and set her like a dry land, and slay her with thirst.

4 And I will not have mercy upon her children; for they be the children of whoredoms.

5 For their mother has played the harlot: she that conceived them has done shamefully: for she said, I will go after my lovers, that give me my bread and my water, my wool and my flax, mine oil and my drink.

6 Therefore, behold, I will hedge up your way with thorns, and make a wall, that she shall not find her paths.

7 And she shall follow after her lovers, but she shall not overtake them; and she shall seek them, but shall not find them: then shall she say, I will go and return to my first husband; for then was it better with me than now.

8 For she did not know that I gave her corn, and wine, and oil, and multiplied her silver and gold, which they prepared for the lord [baal]

9 Therefore will I return, and take away my corn in the set time[169] thereof, and my wine in the season thereof, and will recover my wool and my flax given to cover her nakedness.

10 And now will I discover her lewdness in the sight of her lovers, and none shall deliver her out of mine hand.

11 I will also cause all her mirth to cease, her feast days, her new moons, and her sabbaths, and all her set times.[170]

12 And I will destroy her vines and her fig trees, whereof she has said, These are my rewards that my lovers have given me: and I will make them a forest, and the beasts of the field shall eat them.

13 And I will visit upon her the days of the lords [baalim] wherein she burned incense to them, and she decked herself with her earrings and her jewels, and she went after her lovers, and forgat me, says the Becoming-One.

14 Therefore, behold, I will allure her, and bring her into the wilderness, and speak comfortably unto her.

15 And I will give her her vineyards from there, and the valley of Achor for a door of hope: and she shall sing there, as in the days of her youth, and as in the day when she came up out of the land of Egypt.

16 And it shall be at that day, says the Becoming-One, that you shall call me Ishi; and shall call me no more my lord [baali]

17 For I will take away the names of the lords [baalim] out of her mouth, and they shall no more be remembered by their name.

18 And in that day will I make a covenant for them with the beasts of the field, and with the fowls of heaven, and with the creeping things of the ground: and I will break the bow and the sword and the battle out of the earth, and will make them to lie down safely.

19 And I will betroth you unto me for olam; yes, I will betroth you unto me in righteousness, and in judgment, and in loving-kindness, and in mercies.

20 I will even betroth you unto me in faithfullness: and you shall know the Becoming-One.

21 And it shall come to pass in that day, I will hear, says the Becoming-One, I will hear the heavens, and they shall hear the earth;

22 And the earth shall hear the corn, and the wine, and the oil; and they shall hear Jezreel.

23 And I will sow her unto me in the earth; and I will have mercy upon her that had not obtained mercy; and I will say to them which were not my

---

[169] Appointed time or festival
[170] Appointed times or festivals

people, you are my people; and they shall say, you are my God.

Hos 3:1 Then said the Becoming-One unto me, Go yet, love a woman beloved of her friend, yet an adulteress, according to the love of the Becoming-One toward the children of Israel, who look to other gods, and love flagons of wine.

2 So I bought her to me for fifteen pieces of silver, and for a homer of barley, and a half homer of barley:

3 And I said unto her, you shall abide for me many days; you shall not play the harlot, and you shall not be for another man: so will I also be for you.

4 For the children of Israel shall abide many days without a king, and without a prince, and without a sacrifice, and without an image, and without an ephod, and without teraphim:

5 Afterward shall the children of Israel return, and seek the Becoming-One their God, and David their king; and shall fear the Becoming-One and his goodness in the end of days.

Hos 4:1 Hear the word of the Becoming-One, you children of Israel: for the Becoming-One has a controversy with the inhabitants of the land, because there is no truth, nor mercy, nor knowledge of God in the land.

2 By swearing, and lying, and killing, and stealing, and committing adultery, they break out, and blood touches blood.

3 Therefore shall the land mourn, and every one that dwells therein shall languish, with the beasts of the field, and with the fowls of heaven; yes, the fishes of the sea also shall be taken away.

4 Yet let no man strive, nor reprove another: for your people are as they that strive with the priest.

5 Therefore shall you fall in the day, and the prophet also shall fall with you in the night, and I will destroy your mother.

6 My people are destroyed for lack of knowledge: because you have rejected knowledge, I will also reject you, that you shall be no priest to me: seeing you have forgotten the law of your God, I will also forget your children.

7 As they were increased, so they sinned against me: therefore will I change their glory into shame.

8 They eat up the sin of my people, and they set their soul on their iniquity.

9 And there shall be, like people, like priest: and I will punish them for their ways, and reward them their doings.

10 For they shall eat, and not have enough: they shall commit whoredom, and shall not increase: because they have left off to take heed to the Becoming-One.

11 Whoredom and wine and new wine take away the heart.

12 My people ask counsel at their stocks, and their staff declares unto them: for the spirit of whoredoms has caused them to err, and they have gone a whoring from under their God.

13 They sacrifice upon the tops of the mountains, and burn incense upon the hills, under oaks and poplars and elms, because the shadow thereof is good: therefore your daughters shall commit whoredom, and your spouses shall commit adultery.

14 I will not punish your daughters when they commit whoredom, nor your spouses when they commit adultery: for themselves are separated with whores, and they sacrifice with harlots: therefore the people that does not understand shall fall.

15 Though you, Israel, play the harlot, yet let not Judah offend; and come not you unto Gilgal, neither go you up to Beth-aven, nor swear, The Becoming-One lives.

16 For Israel slides back as a backsliding heifer: now the Becoming-One will feed them as a lamb in a large place.

17 Ephraim is joined to idols: let him alone.

18 Their drink is sour: they have committed whoredom continually: her rulers with shame do love, Give ye.

19 The wind has bound her up in her wings, and they shall be ashamed because of their sacrifices.

Hos 5:1 Hear you this, O priests; and listen, you house of Israel; and give you ear, O house of the king; for judgment is toward you, because you have been a snare on Mizpah, and a net spread upon Tabor.

2 And the revolters are profound to make slaughter, though I have been a rebuker of them all.

3 I know Ephraim, and Israel is not hid from me: for now, O Ephraim, you commit whoredom, and Israel is defiled.

4 They will not frame their doings to turn unto their God: for the spirit of whoredoms is in the midst of them, and they have not known the Becoming-One.

5 And the pride of Israel does testify to his face: therefore shall Israel and Ephraim fall in their iniquity; Judah also shall fall with them.

6 They shall go with their flocks and with their herds to seek the Becoming-One; but they shall not find him; he has withdrawn himself from them.

7 They have dealt treacherously against the Becoming-One: for they have begotten strange children: now shall a month devour them with their portions.

8 Blow you the cornet in Gibeah, and the trumpet in Ramah: cry aloud at Beth-aven, after you, O Benjamin.

9 Ephraim shall be desolate in the day of rebuke: among the tribes of Israel have I made known that which shall surely be.

10 The princes of Judah were like them that remove the bound: therefore I will pour out my wrath upon them like water.

11 Ephraim is oppressed and broken in judgment, because he willingly walked after the commandment.

12 Therefore will I be unto Ephraim as a moth, and to the house of Judah as rottenness.

13 When Ephraim saw his sickness, and Judah saw his wound, then went Ephraim to the Assyrian, and sent to king Jareb: yet could he not heal you, nor cure you of your wound.

14 For I will be unto Ephraim as a lion, and as a young lion to the house of Judah: I, even I, will tear and go away; I will take away, and none shall rescue him.

15 I will go and return to my place, till they acknowledge their offence, and seek my face: in their affliction they will seek me early.

Hos 6:1 Come, and let us return unto the Becoming-One: for he has torn, and he will heal us; he has struck, and he will bind us up.

2 After two days will he revive us: in the third day he will raise us up, and we shall live in his sight.

3 Then shall we know, if we follow on to know the Becoming-One: his going forth is prepared as the dawn; and he shall come unto us as the rain, as the latter and former rain unto the earth.

4 O Ephraim, what shall I do unto you? O Judah, what shall I do unto you? for your goodness is as a morning cloud, and as the early dew it goes away.

5 Therefore have I hewed them by the prophets; I have slain them by the words of my mouth: and your judgments are as the light that goes forth.

6 For I desired mercy, and not sacrifice; and the knowledge of God more than burnt offerings.

7 But they like men have transgressed the covenant: there have they dealt treacherously against me.

8 Gilead is a city of them that work iniquity, and is polluted with blood.

9 And as troops of robbers wait for a man, so the company of priests murder in the way by consent: for they commit lewdness.

10 I have seen a horrible thing in the house of Israel: there is the whoredom of Ephraim, Israel is defiled.

11 Also, O Judah, he has set a harvest for you, when I returned the captivity of my people.

Hos 7:1 When I would have healed Israel, then the iniquity of Ephraim was discovered, and the wickedness of Samaria: for they commit falsehood; and the thief comes in, and the troop of robbers spoils outside.

2 And they consider not in their hearts that I remember all their wickedness: now their own doings have beset them about; they are before my face.

3 They make the king glad with their wickedness, and the princes with their lies.

4 They are all adulterers, as an oven heated by the baker, who ceases from raising after he has kneaded the dough, until it be leavened.

5 In the day of our king the princes have made him sick with bottles of wine; he stretched out his hand with scorners.

6 For they have made ready their heart like an oven, whiles they lie in wait: their baker sleeps all the night; in the morning it burns as a flaming fire.

7 They are all hot as an oven, and have devoured their judges; all their kings are fallen: there is none among them that calls unto me.

8 Ephraim, he has mixed himself among the people; Ephraim is a cake not turned.

9 Strangers have devoured his strength, and he knows it not: yes, gray hairs are here and there upon him, yet he knows not.

10 And the pride of Israel testifies to his face: and they do not return to the Becoming-One their God, nor seek him for all this.

11 Ephraim also is like a silly dove without heart: they call to Egypt, they go to Assyria.

12 When they shall go, I will spread my net upon them; I will bring them down as the fowls of the heaven; I will chastise them, as their congregation has heard.

13 Woe unto them! for they have fled from me: destruction unto them! because they have transgressed against me: though I have redeemed them, yet they have spoken lies against me.

14 And they have not cried unto me with their heart, when they howled upon their beds: they assemble themselves for corn and wine, and they rebel against me.

15 Though I have bound and strengthened their arms, yet do they imagine mischief against me.

16 They return, but not to the most High: they are like a deceitful bow: their princes shall fall by the sword for the rage of their tongue: this shall be their derision in the land of Egypt.

Hos 8:1 Set the trumpet to your mouth. He shall come as an eagle against the house of the Becoming-One, because they have transgressed my covenant, and trespassed against my law.

2 Israel shall cry unto me, My God, we know you.

3 Israel has cast off the thing that is good: the enemy shall pursue him.

4 They have set up kings, but not by me: they have made princes, and I knew it not: of their silver and their gold have they made them idols, that they may be cut off.

5 your calf, O Samaria, has cast you off; mine anger is kindled against them: how long will it be ere they attain to innocency?

6 For from Israel was it also: the workman made it; therefore it is not God: but the calf of Samaria shall be broken in pieces.

7 For they have sown the wind, and they shall reap the whirlwind: it has no stalk: the bud shall yield no meal: if so be it yield, the strangers shall swallow it up.

8 Israel is swallowed up: now shall they be among the nations as a vessel wherein is no pleasure.

9 For they are gone up to Assyria, a wild donkey alone by himself: Ephraim has hired lovers.

10 Yes, though they have hired among the nations, now will I gather them, and they shall sorrow a little for the burden of the king of princes.

11 Because Ephraim has made many altars to sin, altars shall be unto him to sin.

12 I have written to him the great things of my law, but they were counted as a strange thing.

13 They sacrifice flesh for the sacrifices of my offerings, and eat it; but the Becoming-One accepts them not; now will he remember their iniquity, and visit their sins: they shall return to Egypt.

14 For Israel has forgotten his Maker, and builds temples; and Judah has multiplied fenced cities: but I will send a fire upon his cities, and it shall devour the palaces thereof.

Hos 9:1 Rejoice not, O Israel, for joy, as other people: for you have gone a whoring from your God, you have loved a reward upon every cornfloor.

2 The floor and the winepress shall not feed them, and the new wine shall fail in her.

3 They shall not dwell in the Becoming-One's land; but Ephraim shall return to Egypt, and they shall eat unclean things in Assyria.

4 They shall not offer wine offerings to the Becoming-One, neither shall they be pleasing unto him: their sacrifices shall be unto them as the bread of mourners; all that eat thereof shall be polluted: for their bread for their soul shall not come into the house of the Becoming-One.

5 What will you do in the set time,[171] and in the day of the feast of the Becoming-One?

6 For, lo, they are gone because of destruction: Egypt shall gather them up, Memphis shall bury them: the pleasant places for their silver, nettles shall possess them: thorns shall be in their tabernacles.

7 The days of visitation are come, the days of recompense are come; Israel shall know it: the prophet is a fool, the spiritual man is mad, for the multitude of your iniquity, and the great hatred.

8 The watchman of Ephraim was with my God: but the prophet is a snare of a fowler in all his ways, and hatred in the house of his God.

9 They have deeply corrupted themselves, as in the days of Gibeah: therefore he will remember their iniquity, he will visit their sins.

10 I found Israel like grapes in the wilderness; I saw your fathers as the firstripe in the fig tree at her first time: but they went to Baal-Peor, and separated themselves unto that shame; and their abominations were according as they loved.

11 As for Ephraim, their glory shall fly away like a bird, from the birth, and from the womb, and from the conception.

12 Though they bring up their children, yet will I bereave them, that there shall not be a man left: yes, woe also to them when I depart from them!

13 Ephraim, as I saw Tyrus, is planted in a pleasant place: but Ephraim shall bring forth his children to the murderer.

14 Give them, O Becoming-One: what will you give? give them a miscarrying womb and dry breasts.

15 All their wickedness is in Gilgal: for there I hated them: for the wickedness of their doings I will drive them out of mine house, I will love them no more: all their princes are revolters.

16 Ephraim is struck, their root is dried up, they shall bear no fruit: yes, though they bring forth, yet will I slay even the beloved fruit of their womb.

17 My God will cast them away, because they did not listen unto him: and they shall be wanderers among the nations.

Hos 10:1 Israel is an empty vine, he brings forth fruit unto himself: according to the multitude of his fruit he has increased the altars; according to the goodness of his land they have made goodly images.

2 Their heart is divided; now shall they be found faulty: he shall break down their altars, he shall spoil their images.

3 For now they shall say, We have no king, because we feared not the Becoming-One; what then should a king do to us?

4 They have spoken words, swearing falsely in making a covenant: thus judgment springs up as hemlock in the furrows of the field.

5 The neighbors of Samaria shall fear because of the calves of Beth-aven: for the people thereof shall mourn over it, and the priests thereof that rejoiced on it, for the glory thereof, because it is departed from it.

6 It shall be also carried unto Assyria for a present to king Jareb: Ephraim shall receive shame, and Israel shall be ashamed of his own counsel.

7 As for Samaria, her king is cut off as the foam upon the water.

8 The high places also of Aven, the sin of Israel, shall be destroyed: the thorn and the thistle shall come up on their altars; and they shall say to the mountains, Cover us; and to the hills, Fall on us.

9 O Israel, you have sinned from the days of Gibeah: there they stood: the battle in Gibeah against the children of iniquity did not overtake them.

10 It is in my desire that I should chastise them; and the people shall be gathered against them, when they shall bind themselves in their two furrows.

11 And Ephraim is as a heifer that is taught, and loves to tread out the corn; but I passed over upon her fair neck: I will make Ephraim to ride; Judah shall plow, and Jacob shall break his clods.

12 Sow to yourselves in righteousness, reap in mercy; break up your fallow ground: for it is time to seek the Becoming-One, till he come and rain righteousness upon you.

13 you have plowed wickedness, you have reaped iniquity; you have eaten the fruit of lies: because you did trust in your way, in the multitude of your mighty men.

14 Therefore shall a tumult arise among your people, and all your fortresses shall be spoiled, as Shalman spoiled Beth-arbel in the day of battle: the mother was dashed in pieces upon her children.

15 So shall Bethel do unto you because of your great wickedness: in a dawn shall the king of Israel utterly be cut off.

Hos 11:1 When Israel was a child, then I loved him, and called my son out of Egypt.

2 As they called them, so they went from them: they sacrificed unto the lords [baalim] and burned incense to graven images.

3 I taught Ephraim also to go, taking them by their arms; but they knew not that I healed them.

4 I drew them with cords of a man, with bands of love: and I was to them as they that take off the yoke on their jaws, and I laid food unto them.

5 He shall not return into the land of Egypt, but the Assyrian shall be his king, because they refused to return.

6 And the sword shall abide on his cities, and shall consume his branches, and devour them, because of their own counsels.

7 And my people are bent to backsliding from me: though they called them to the most High, none at all would exalt him.

8 How shall I give you up, Ephraim? how shall I deliver you, Israel? how shall I make you as Admah?

---

[171] Appointed time or festival

how shall I set you as Zeboim? mine heart is turned within me, my repentings are kindled together.

9 I will not execute the fierceness of mine anger, I will not return to destroy Ephraim: for I am GOD, and not man; the Holy One in the midst of you: and I will not enter into the city.

10 They shall walk after the Becoming-One: he shall roar like a lion: when he shall roar, then the children shall tremble from the west.

11 They shall tremble as a bird out of Egypt, and as a dove out of the land of Assyria: and I will place them in their houses, says the Becoming-One.

12 Ephraim compasses me about with lies, and the house of Israel with deceit: but Judah yet rules with GOD, and is faithful with the saints.

Hos 12:1 Ephraim feeds on wind, and follows after the east wind: he daily increases lies and desolation; and they do make a covenant with the Assyrians, and oil is carried into Egypt.

2 The Becoming-One has also a controversy with Judah, and will punish Jacob according to his ways; according to his doings will he recompense him.

3 He took his brother by the heel in the womb, and by his strength he had power with God:

4 Yes, he had power over the angel, and prevailed: he wept, and made supplication unto him: he found him in Bethel, and there he spoke with us;

5 Even the Becoming-One, God of hosts; the Becoming-One is his memorial.

6 Therefore turn you to your God: keep mercy and judgment, and wait on your God continually.

7 He is a merchant, the balances of deceit are in his hand: he loves to oppress.

8 And Ephraim said, Yet I am become rich, I have found me out substance: in all my labors they shall find none iniquity in me that were sin.

9 And I that am the Becoming-One your God from the land of Egypt will yet make you to dwell in tabernacles, as in the days of the set time.[172]

10 I have also spoken by the prophets, and I have multiplied visions, and used similitudes, by the ministry of the prophets.

11 Is there iniquity in Gilead? surely they are vanity: they sacrifice bullocks in Gilgal; yes, their altars are as heaps in the furrows of the fields.

12 And Jacob fled into the country of Syria, and Israel served for a wife, and for a wife he kept sheep.

13 And by a prophet the Becoming-One brought Israel out of Egypt, and by a prophet was he preserved.

14 Ephraim provoked him to anger most bitterly: therefore shall he leave his blood upon him, and his reproach shall his Lords return unto him.

Hos 13:1 When Ephraim spoke trembling, he exalted himself in Israel; but when he offended in the lord [baal] he died.

2 And now they sin more and more, and have made them molten images of their silver, and idols according to their own understanding, all of it the work of the craftsmen: they say of them, Let the men that sacrifice kiss the calves.

3 Therefore they shall be as the morning cloud, and as the early dew that passes away, as the chaff that is driven with the whirlwind out of the floor, and as the smoke out of the chimney.

4 Yet I am the Becoming-One your God from the land of Egypt, and you shall know no god but me: for there is no Savior beside me.

5 I did know you in the wilderness, in the land of great drought.

6 According to their pasture, so were they filled; they were filled, and their heart was exalted; therefore have they forgotten me.

7 Therefore I will be unto them as a lion: as a leopard by the way will I observe them:

8 I will meet them as a bear that is bereaved of her whelps, and will rend the caul of their heart, and there will I devour them like a lion: the wild liivng creatures shall tear them.

9 O Israel, you have destroyed thyself; but in me is your help.

10 I will be your king: where is any other that may save you in all your cities? and your judges of whom you said, Give me a king and princes?

11 I gave you a king in mine anger, and took him away in my wrath.

12 The iniquity of Ephraim is bound up; his sin is hid.

13 The sorrows of a travailing woman shall come upon him: he is an unwise son; for he should not stay long in the place of the breaking forth of children.

14 I will ransom them from the power of Sheol; I will redeem them from death: O death, I will be your plagues; O Sheol, I will be your destruction: repentance shall be hid from mine eyes.

15 Though he be fruitful among his brethren, an east wind shall come, the wind of the Becoming-One shall come up from the wilderness, and his spring shall become dry, and his fountain shall be dried up: he shall spoil the treasure of all pleasant vessels.

16 Samaria shall become desolate; for she has rebelled against her God: they shall fall by the sword: their infants shall be dashed in pieces, and their women with child shall be ripped up.

Hos 14:1 O Israel, return unto the Becoming-One your God; for you have fallen by your iniquity.

2 Take with you words, and turn to the Becoming-One: say unto him, Take away all iniquity, and receive us graciously: so will we render the calves of our lips.

3 Asshur shall not save us; we will not ride upon horses: neither will we say any more to the work of our hands, you are our gods: for in you the fatherless finds mercy.

4 I will heal their backsliding, I will love them freely: for mine anger is turned away from him.

5 I will be as the dew unto Israel: he shall grow as the lily, and cast forth his roots as Lebanon.

6 His branches shall spread, and his beauty shall be as the olive tree, and his smell as Lebanon.

7 They that dwell under his shadow shall return; they shall revive as the corn, and grow as the vine: the scent thereof shall be as the wine of Lebanon.

---

[172] Appointed time or festival

8 Ephraim shall say, What have I to do any more with idols? I have heard him, and observed him: I am like a green fir tree. From me is your fruit found.

9 Who is wise, and he shall understand these things? prudent, and he shall know them? for the ways of the Becoming-One are right, and the just shall walk in them: but the transgressors shall fall therein.

Joel

Joel 1:1 The word of the Becoming-One that came to Joel the son of Pethuel.

2 Hear this, you old men, and give ear, all you inhabitants of the land. Has this been in your days, or even in the days of your fathers?

3 Tell you your children of it, and let your children tell their children, and their children another generation.

4 That which the palmer worm has left has the locust eaten; and that which the locust has left has the cankerworm eaten; and that which the cankerworm has left has the caterpillar eaten.

5 Awake, you drunkards, and weep; and howl, all you drinkers of wine, because of the new wine, for it is cut off from your mouth.

6 For a nation is come up upon my land, strong, and without number, whose teeth are the teeth of a lion, and he has the cheek teeth of a great lion.

7 He has laid my vine waste, and barked my fig tree: he has made it clean bare, and cast it away; the branches thereof are made white.

8 Lament like a virgin girded with sackcloth for the husband of her youth.

9 The food offering and the drink offering is cut off from the house of the Becoming-One; the priests, the Becoming-One's ministers, mourn.

10 The field is wasted, the land mourns; for the corn is wasted: the new wine is dried up, the oil languishes.

11 Be you ashamed, O you husbandmen; howl, O you vinedressers, for the wheat and for the barley; because the harvest of the field is perished.

12 The vine is dried up, and the fig tree languishes; the pomegranate tree, the palm tree also, and the apple tree, even all the trees of the field, are withered: because joy is withered away from the sons of men.

13 Gird yourselves, and lament, you priests: howl, you ministers of the altar: come, lie all night in sackcloth, you ministers of my God: for the food offering and the drink offering is withheld from the house of your God.

14 Sanctify you a fast, call a solemn assembly, gather the elders and all the inhabitants of the land into the house of the Becoming-One your God, and cry unto the Becoming-One.

15 Alas for the day! for the day of the Becoming-One is at hand, and as a destruction from the Almighty shall it come.

16 Is not the food cut off before our eyes, yes, joy and gladness from the house of our God?

17 The seed is rotten under their clods, the garners are laid desolate, the barns are broken down; for the corn is withered.

18 How do the beasts groan! the herds of cattle are perplexed, because they have no pasture; yes, the flocks of sheep are made desolate.

19 O Becoming-One, to you will I cry: for the fire has devoured the pastures of the wilderness, and the flame has burned all the trees of the field.

20 The beasts of the field cry also unto you: for the rivers of waters are dried up, and the fire has devoured the pastures of the wilderness.

Joel 2:1 Blow you the trumpet in Zion, and sound an alarm in my holy mountain: let all the inhabitants of the land tremble: for the day of the Becoming-One comes, for it is near at hand;

2 A day of darkness and of gloominess, a day of clouds and of thick darkness, as the dawn spread upon the mountains: a great people and a strong; there has not been ever the like, neither shall be any more after it, even to the years of many generations.

3 A fire devours before them; and behind them a flame burns: the land is as the garden of Eden before them, and behind them a desolate wilderness; yes, and nothing shall escape them.

4 The appearance of them is as the appearance of horses; and as horsemen, so shall they run.

5 Like the noise of chariots on the tops of mountains shall they leap, like the noise of a flame of fire that devours the stubble, as a strong people set in battle array.

6 Before their face the people shall be much pained: all faces shall gather blackness.

7 They shall run like mighty men; they shall climb the wall like men of war; and they shall march every one on his ways, and they shall not break their ranks:

8 Neither shall one thrust another; they shall walk every one in his path: and when they fall upon the sword, they shall not be wounded.

9 They shall run back and forth in the city; they shall run upon the wall, they shall climb up upon the houses; they shall enter in at the windows like a thief.

10 The earth shall quake before them; the heavens shall tremble: the sun and the moon shall be dark, and the stars shall withdraw their shining:

11 And the Becoming-One shall utter his voice before his army: for his camp is very great: for he is strong that executes his word: for the day of the Becoming-One is great and very terrible; and who can abide it?

12 Therefore also now, says the Becoming-One, turn you even to me with all your heart, and with fasting, and with weeping, and with mourning:

13 And rend your heart, and not your garments, and turn unto the Becoming-One your God: for he is gracious and merciful, slow to anger, and of great kindness, and repents him of the evil.

14 Who knows if he will return and repent, and leave a blessing behind him; even a food offering and a drink offering unto the Becoming-One your God?

15 Blow the trumpet in Zion, sanctify a fast, call a solemn assembly:

16 Gather the people, sanctify the congregation, assemble the elders, gather the children, and those that suck the breasts: let the bridegroom go forth of his chamber, and the bride out of her closet.

17 Let the priests, the ministers of the Becoming-One, weep between the porch and the altar, and let them say, Spare your people, O Becoming-One, and give not your heritage to reproach, that the nations should rule over them: therefore should they say among the people, Where is their God?

18 Then will the Becoming-One be jealous for his land, and pity his people.

19 Yes, the Becoming-One will answer and say unto his people, Behold, I will send you corn, and wine, and oil, and you shall be satisfied therewith: and I will no more make you a reproach among the nations:

20 But I will remove far off from you the northern army, and will drive him into a land barren and desolate, with his face toward the east sea, and his hinder part toward the utmost sea, and his stink shall come up, and his ill aroma shall come up, because he has done great things.

21 Fear not, O land; be glad and rejoice: for the Becoming-One will do great things.

22 Be not afraid, you beasts of the field: for the pastures of the wilderness do spring, for the tree bears her fruit, the fig tree and the vine do yield their strength.

23 Be glad then, you children of Zion, and rejoice in the Becoming-One your God: for he has given you the former rain moderately, and he will cause to come down for you the rain, the former rain, and the latter rain in the first month.

24 And the floors shall be full of wheat, and the vats shall overflow with wine and oil.

25 And I will restore to you the years that the locust has eaten, the cankerworm, and the caterpillar, and the palmerworm, my great army which I sent among you.

26 And you shall eat in plenty, and be satisfied, and praise the name of the Becoming-One your God, that has dealt wondrously with you: and my people shall not for olam be ashamed.

27 And you shall know that I am in the midst of Israel, and that I am the Becoming-One your God, and none else: and my people shall never be ashamed.

28 And it shall come to pass afterward, that I will pour out my spirit upon all flesh; and your sons and your daughters shall prophesy, your old men shall dream dreams, your young men shall see visions:

29 And also upon the servants and upon the handmaids in those days will I pour out my spirit.

30 And I will show wonders in the heavens and in the earth, blood, and fire, and pillars of smoke.

31 The sun shall be turned into darkness, and the moon into blood, before the great and the terrible day of the Becoming-One come.

32 And it shall come to pass, that whosoever shall call on the name of the Becoming-One shall be delivered: for in mount Zion and in Jerusalem shall be deliverance, as the Becoming-One has said, and in the remnant whom the Becoming-One shall call.

Joel 3:1 For, behold, in those days, and in that time, when I shall bring again the captivity of Judah and Jerusalem,

2 I will also gather all nations, and will bring them down into the valley of Jehoshaphat, and will judge with them there for my people and for my heritage Israel, whom they have scattered among the nations, and parted my land.

3 And they have cast lots for my people; and have given a boy for a harlot, and sold a girl for wine, that they might drink.

4 Yes, and what have you to do with me, O Tyre, and Zidon, and all the coasts of Palestine? will you render me a recompense? and if you recompense me, swiftly and speedily will I return your recompense upon your own head;

5 Because you have taken my silver and my gold, and have carried into your temples my goodly pleasant things:

6 The children also of Judah and the children of Jerusalem have you sold unto the Grecians, that you might remove them far from their border.

7 Behold, I will raise them out of the place to which you have sold them, and will return your recompense upon your own head:

8 And I will sell your sons and your daughters into the hand of the children of Judah, and they shall sell them to the Sabeans, to a people far off: for the Becoming-One has spoken it.

9 Proclaim you this among the nations; Prepare war, wake up the mighty men, let all the men of war draw near; let them come up:

10 Beat your plowshares into swords, and your pruning hooks into spears: let the weak say, I am strong.

11 Assemble yourselves, and come, all you nations, and gather yourselves together round about: there cause your mighty ones to come down, O Becoming-One.

12 Let the nations be wakened, and come up to the valley of Jehoshaphat: for there will I sit to judge all the nations round about.

13 Put you in the sickle, for the harvest is ripe: come, get you down; for the press is full, the vats overflow; for their wickedness is great.

14 Multitudes, multitudes in the valley of decision: for the day of the Becoming-One is near in the valley of decision.

15 The sun and the moon shall be darkened, and the stars shall withdraw their shining.

16 The Becoming-One also shall roar out of Zion, and utter his voice from Jerusalem; and the heavens and the earth shall shake: but the Becoming-One will be the hope of his people, and the strength of the children of Israel.

17 So shall you know that I am the Becoming-One your God dwelling in Zion, my holy mountain: then shall Jerusalem be holy, and there shall no strangers pass through her any more.

18 And it shall come to pass in that day, that the mountains shall drop down new wine, and the hills shall flow with milk, and all the rivers of Judah shall flow with waters, and a fountain shall come forth of the house of the Becoming-One, and shall water the valley of Shittim.

19 Egypt shall be a desolation, and Edom shall be a desolate wilderness, for the violence against the children of Judah, because they have shed innocent blood in their land.

20 But Judah shall dwell for olam, and Jerusalem from generation to generation.

21 For I will cleanse their blood that I have not cleansed: for the Becoming-One dwells in Zion.

Amos

Amos 1:1 The words of Amos, who was among the herdmen of Tekoa, which he saw concerning Israel in the days of Uzziah king of Judah, and in the days of Jeroboam the son of Joash king of Israel, two years before the earthquake. [**ab. 794 BC ?**]

2 And he said, The Becoming-One will roar from Zion, and utter his voice from Jerusalem; and the habitations of the shepherds shall mourn, and the top of Carmel shall wither.

3 Thus says the Becoming-One; For three transgressions of Damascus, and for four, I will not turn away the punishment thereof; because they have threshed Gilead with threshing instruments of iron:

4 But I will send a fire into the house of Hazael, which shall devour the palaces of Benhadad.

5 I will break also the bar of Damascus, and cut off the inhabitant from the plain of Aven, and him that holds the scepter from the house of Eden: and the people of Syria shall go into captivity unto Kir, says the Becoming-One.

6 Thus says the Becoming-One; For three transgressions of Gaza, and for four, I will not turn away the punishment thereof; because they carried away captive the whole captivity, to deliver them up to Edom:

7 But I will send a fire on the wall of Gaza, which shall devour the palaces thereof:

8 And I will cut off the inhabitant from Ashdod, and him that holds the scepter from Ashkelon, and I will turn mine hand against Ekron: and the remnant of the Philistines shall perish, says my Lord(s) the Becoming-One.

9 Thus says the Becoming-One; For three transgressions of Tyrus, and for four, I will not turn away the punishment thereof; because they delivered up the whole captivity to Edom, and remembered not the brotherly covenant:

10 But I will send a fire on the wall of Tyrus, which shall devour the palaces thereof.

11 Thus says the Becoming-One; For three transgressions of Edom, and for four, I will not turn away the punishment thereof; because he did pursue his brother with the sword, and did cast off all pity, and his anger did tear continually, and he kept his wrath completely:

12 But I will send a fire upon Teman, which shall devour the palaces of Bozrah.

13 Thus says the Becoming-One; For three transgressions of the children of Ammon, and for four, I will not turn away the punishment thereof; because they have ripped up the women with child of Gilead, that they might enlarge their border:

14 But I will kindle a fire in the wall of Rabbah, and it shall devour the palaces thereof, with shouting in the day of battle, with a tempest in the day of the whirlwind:

15 And their king shall go into captivity, he and his princes together, says the Becoming-One.

Amos 2:1 Thus says the Becoming-One; For three transgressions of Moab, and for four, I will not turn away the punishment thereof; because he burned the bones of the king of Edom into lime:

2 But I will send a fire upon Moab, and it shall devour the palaces of Kirioth: and Moab shall die with tumult, with shouting, and with the sound of the trumpet:

3 And I will cut off the judge from the midst thereof, and will slay all the princes thereof with him, says the Becoming-One.

4 Thus says the Becoming-One; For three transgressions of Judah, and for four, I will not turn away the punishment thereof; because they have despised the law of the Becoming-One, and have not kept his commandments, and their lies caused them to err, after the which their fathers have walked:

5 But I will send a fire upon Judah, and it shall devour the palaces of Jerusalem.

6 Thus says the Becoming-One; For three transgressions of Israel, and for four, I will not turn away the punishment thereof; because they sold the righteous for silver, and the poor for a pair of shoes;

7 That pant after the dust of the earth on the head of the poor, and turn aside the way of the meek: and a man and his father will go in unto the same maid, to profane my holy name:

8 And they lay themselves down upon clothes laid to pledge by every altar, and they drink the wine of the condemned in the house of their god.

9 Yet destroyed I the Amorite before them, whose height was like the height of the cedars, and he was strong as the oaks; yet I destroyed his fruit from above, and his roots from beneath.

10 Also I brought you up from the land of Egypt, and led you forty years through the wilderness, to possess the land of the Amorite.

11 And I raised up of your sons for prophets, and of your young men for Nazarites. Is it not even thus, O you children of Israel? says the Becoming-One.

12 But you gave the Nazarites wine to drink; and commanded the prophets, saying, Prophesy not.

13 Behold, I am pressed under you, as a cart is pressed that is full of sheaves.

14 Therefore the flight shall perish from the swift, and the strong shall not strengthen his force, neither shall the mighty deliver his soul:

15 Neither shall he stand that handles the bow; and he that is swift of foot shall not deliver his soul: neither shall he that rides the horse deliver his soul.

16 And he that is courageous among the mighty shall flee away naked in that day, says the Becoming-One.

Amos 3:1 Hear this word that the Becoming-One has spoken against you, O children of Israel, against the whole family which I brought up from the land of Egypt, saying,

2 You only have I known of all the families of the earth: therefore I will punish you for all your iniquities.

3 Can two walk together, except they be agreed?

4 Will a lion roar in the forest, when he has no prey? will a young lion cry out of his den, if he have taken nothing?

5 Can a bird fall in a snare upon the earth, where no gin is for him? shall one take up a snare from the earth, and have taken nothing at all?

6 Shall a trumpet be blown in the city, and the people not be afraid? shall there be evil in a city, and the Becoming-One has not done it?

7 Surely my Lord(s), the Becoming-One, will do nothing, but he reveals his secret unto his servants the prophets.

8 The lion has roared, who will not fear? my Lord(s), the Becoming-One, has spoken, who can but prophesy?

9 Publish in the palaces at Ashdod, and in the palaces in the land of Egypt, and say, Assemble yourselves upon the mountains of Samaria, and behold the great tumults in the midst thereof, and the oppressed in the midst thereof.

10 For they know not to do right, says the Becoming-One, who store up violence and robbery in their palaces.

11 Therefore thus says my Lord(s) the Becoming-One; An adversary there shall be even round about the land; and he shall bring down your strength from you, and your palaces shall be spoiled.

12 Thus says the Becoming-One; As the shepherd takes out of the mouth of the lion two legs, or a piece of an ear; so shall the children of Israel be taken out that dwell in Samaria in the corner of a bed, and in Damascus in a couch.

13 Hear ye, and testify in the house of Jacob, says my Lord(s) the Becoming-One, God of the hosts,

14 That in the day that I shall visit the transgressions of Israel upon him I will also visit the altars of Bethel: and the horns of the altar shall be cut off, and fall to the ground.

15 And I will smite the winter house with the summer house; and the houses of ivory shall perish, and the great houses shall have an end, says the Becoming-One.

Amos 4:1 Hear this word, you kine of Bashan, that are in the mountain of Samaria, which oppress the poor, which crush the needy, which say to their masters, Bring, and let us drink.

2 My Lord(s) the Becoming-One has sworn by his holiness, that, lo, the days shall come upon you, that he will take you away with hooks, and your posterity with fish hooks.

3 And you shall go out at the breaches, every cow at that which is before her; and you shall cast them into the palace, says the Becoming-One.

4 Come to Bethel, and transgress; at Gilgal multiply transgression; for the morning bring your sacrifices, and your tithes for three days:

5 And offer a sacrifice of thanksgiving with leaven, and proclaim and publish the free offerings: for this you love, O you children of Israel, says my Lord(s) the Becoming-One.

6 And I also have given you cleanness of teeth in all your cities, and want of bread in all your places: yet have you not returned unto me, says the Becoming-One.

7 And also I have withheld the rain from you, when there were yet three months to the harvest: and I caused it to rain upon one city, and caused it not to rain upon another city: one piece was rained upon, and the piece whereupon it rained not withered.

8 So two or three cities wandered unto one city, to drink water; but they were not satisfied: yet have you not returned unto me, says the Becoming-One.

9 I have struck you with blasting and mildew: when your gardens and your vineyards and your fig trees and your olive trees increased, the palmer worm devoured them: yet have you not returned unto me, says the Becoming-One.

10 I have sent among you the pestilence after the manner of Egypt: your young men have I slain with the sword, and have taken away your horses; and I have made the stink of your camps to come up unto your nostrils: yet have you not returned unto me, says the Becoming-One.

11 I have overthrown some of you, as God overthrew Sodom and Gomorrah, and you were as a firebrand plucked out of the burning: yet have you not returned unto me, says the Becoming-One.

12 Therefore thus will I do unto you, O Israel: and because I will do this unto you, prepare to meet your God, O Israel.

13 For, lo, he that forms the mountains, and creats the wind, and declares unto man what is his thought, that makes the dawn darkness, and treads upon the high places of the earth, The Becoming-One, God of hosts, is his name.

Amos 5:1 Hear you this word which I take up against you, even a lamentation, O house of Israel.

2 The virgin of Israel is fallen; she shall no more rise: she is forsaken upon her land; there is none to raise her up.

3 For thus says my Lord(s) the Becoming-One; The city that went out by a thousand shall leave a hundred, and that which went forth by a hundred shall leave ten, to the house of Israel.

4 For thus says the Becoming-One unto the house of Israel, Seek you me, and you shall live:

5 But seek not Bethel, nor enter into Gilgal, and pass not to Beersheba: for Gilgal shall surely go into captivity, and Bethel shall come to nothing.

6 Seek the Becoming-One, and you shall live; lest he break out like fire in the house of Joseph, and devour it, and there be none to quench it in Bethel.

7 you who turn judgment to wormwood, and leave off righteousness in the earth,

8 Seek him that makes Pleiades [the seven stars] and Orion, and turns the shadow of death into the morning, and makes the day dark with night: that calls for the waters of the sea, and pours them out upon the face of the earth: The Becoming-One is his name:

9 That strengthens the spoiled against the strong, so that the spoiled shall come against the fortress.

10 They hate him that rebukes in the gate, and they abhor him that speaks uprightly.

11 Forasmuch therefore as your treading is upon the poor, and you take from him burdens of wheat: you have built houses of hewn stone, but you shall not dwell in them; you have planted pleasant vineyards, but you shall not drink wine of them.

12 For I know your manifold transgressions, and your mighty sins: they afflict the just, they take a bribe, and they turn aside the poor in the gate from their right.

13 Therefore the prudent shall keep silence in that time; for it is an evil time.

14 Seek good, and not evil, that you may live: and so the Becoming-One, God of hosts, shall be with you, as you have spoken.

15 Hate the evil, and love the good, and establish judgment in the gate: it may be that the Becoming-One, God of hosts will be gracious unto the remnant of Joseph.

16 Therefore the Becoming-One, God of hosts, my Lord(s), says thus; Wailing shall be in all streets; and they shall say in all the highways, Alas! alas! and they shall call the husbandman to mourning, and such as are skillful of lamentation to wailing.

17 And in all vineyards shall be wailing: for I will pass through you, says the Becoming-One.

18 Woe unto you that desire the day of the Becoming-One! to what end is it for you? the day of the Becoming-One is darkness, and not light.

19 As if a man did flee from a lion, and a bear met him; or went into the house, and leaned his hand on the wall, and a serpent bit him.

20 Shall not the day of the Becoming-One be darkness, and not light? even very dark, and no brightness in it?

21 I hate, I despise your feast days, and I will not smell in your solemn assemblies.

22 Though you offer me burnt offerings and your food offerings, I will not accept them: neither will I regard the peace offerings of your fat beasts.

23 Take you away from me the noise of your songs; for I will not hear the melody of your viols.

24 But let judgment run down as waters, and righteousness as a mighty stream.

25 Have you offered unto me sacrifices and offerings in the wilderness forty years, O house of Israel?

26 But you have borne the tabernacle of your Moloch and Chiun your images, the star of your god, which you made to yourselves.

27 Therefore will I cause you to go into captivity beyond Damascus, says the Becoming-One, whose name is God of hosts.

Amos 6:1 Woe to them that are at ease in Zion, and trust in the mountain of Samaria, which are named the beginning of the nations, to whom the house of Israel came!

2 Pass you unto Calneh, and see; and from there go you to Hamath the great: then go down to Gath of the Philistines: be they better than these kingdoms? or their border greater than your border?

3 you that put far away the evil day, and cause the seat of violence to come near;

4 That lie upon beds of ivory, and stretch themselves upon their couches, and eat the lambs out of the flock, and the calves out of the midst of the stall;

5 That chant to the sound of the viol, and invent to themselves instruments of music, like David;

6 That drink wine in bowls, and anoint themselves with the first ointments: but they are not grieved for the affliction of Joseph.

7 Therefore now shall they go captive with the first that go captive, and the banquet of them that stretched themselves shall be removed.

8 My Lord(s) the Becoming-One has sworn by his soul, says the Becoming-One, God of hosts, I abhor the excellency of Jacob, and hate his palaces: therefore will I deliver up the city with all that is therein.

9 And it shall come to pass, if there remain ten men in one house, that they shall die.

10 And a man's uncle shall take him up, and he that burns him, to bring out the bones out of the house, and shall say unto him that is by the sides of the house, Is there yet any with you? and he shall say, No. Then shall he say, Hold your tongue: for we may not make mention of the name of the Becoming-One.

11 For, behold, the Becoming-One commands, and he will smite the great house with breaches, and the little house with clefts.

12 Shall horses run upon the rock? will one plow there with oxen? for you have turned judgment into gall, and the fruit of righteousness into hemlock:

13 you which rejoice in a thing of nothing, which say, Have we not taken to us horns by our own strength?

14 But, behold, I will raise up against you a nation, O house of Israel, says the Becoming-One, God of hosts; and they shall afflict you from the entering in of Hemath unto the river of the wilderness.

Amos 7:1 Thus has my Lord(s), the Becoming-One, showed unto me; and, behold, he formed grasshoppers in the beginning of the shooting up of the latter growth; and, lo, it was the latter growth after the king's mowings.

2 And it came to pass, that when they had made an end of eating the grass of the land, then I said, O my Lord(s) the Becoming-One, forgive, I beg you: by whom shall Jacob arise? for he is small.

3 The Becoming-One repented for this: It shall not be, says the Becoming-One.

4 Thus has my Lord(s), the Becoming-One, showed unto me: and, behold, my Lord(s) the Becoming-One called to contend by fire, and it devoured the great deep, and did eat up a part.

5 Then said I, O my Lord(s) the Becoming-One, cease, I beg you: by whom shall Jacob arise? for he is small.

6 The Becoming-One repented for this: This also shall not be, says my Lord(s) the Becoming-One.

7 Thus he showed me: and, behold, my Lord(s) stood upon a wall made by a plumb line, with a plumb line in his hand.

8 And the Becoming-One said unto me, Amos, what see you? And I said, A plumb line. Then said my Lord(s), Behold, I will set a plumb line in the midst of my people Israel: I will not again pass by them any more:

9 And the high places of Isaac shall be desolate, and the sanctuaries of Israel shall be laid waste; and I will rise against the house of Jeroboam with the sword.

10 Then Amaziah the priest of Bethel sent to Jeroboam king of Israel, saying, Amos has conspired against you in the midst of the house of Israel: the land is not able to bear all his words.

11 For thus Amos says, Jeroboam shall die by the sword, and Israel shall surely be led away captive out of their own land.

12 Also Amaziah said unto Amos, O you seer, go, flee you away into the land of Judah, and there eat bread, and prophesy there:

13 But prophesy not again any more at Bethel: for it is the king's chapel, and it is the king's court.

14 Then answered Amos, and said to Amaziah, I was no prophet, neither was I a prophet's son; but I was a herdman, and a gatherer of sycamore fruit:

15 And the Becoming-One took me as I followed the flock, and the Becoming-One said unto me, Go, prophesy unto my people Israel.

16 Now therefore hear you the word of the Becoming-One: you say, Prophesy not against Israel, and drop not your word against the house of Isaac.

17 Therefore thus says the Becoming-One; your wife shall be a harlot in the city, and your sons and your daughters shall fall by the sword, and your land shall be divided by line; and you shall die in a polluted land: and Israel shall surely go into captivity forth of his land.

Amos 8:1 Thus has my Lord(s), the Becoming-One, showed unto me: and behold a basket of summer fruit.

2 And he said, Amos, what see you? And I said, A basket of summer fruit. Then said the Becoming-One unto me, The end is come upon my people of Israel; I will not again pass by them any more.

3 And the songs of the temple shall be howlings in that day, says my Lord(s) the Becoming-One: there shall be many dead bodies in every place; they shall cast them forth with silence.

4 Hear this, O you that swallow up the needy, even to make the poor of the land to fail,

5 Saying, When will the new moon be gone, that we may sell corn? and the Sabbath, that we may set forth wheat, making the ephah small, and the shekel great, and falsifying the balances by deceit?

6 That we may buy the poor for silver, and the needy for a pair of shoes; yes, and sell the refuse of the wheat?

7 The Becoming-One has sworn by the excellency of Jacob, Surely I will not completely forget any of their works.

8 Shall not the land tremble for this, and every one mourn that dwells therein? and it shall rise up wholly as a flood; and it shall be cast out and drowned, as by the river of Egypt.

9 And it shall come to pass in that day, says my Lord(s) the Becoming-One, that I will cause the sun to go down at noon, and I will darken the earth in the clear day:

10 And I will turn your feasts into mourning, and all your songs into lamentation; and I will bring up sackcloth upon all loins, and baldness upon every head; and I will make it as the mourning of an only son, and the end thereof as a bitter day.

11 Behold, the days come, says my Lord(s) the Becoming-One, that I will send a famine in the land, not a famine of bread, nor a thirst for water, but of hearing the words of the Becoming-One: 12 And they shall wander from sea to sea, and from the north even to the east, they shall run back and forth to seek the word of the Becoming-One, and shall not find it.

13 In that day shall the fair virgins and young men faint for thirst.

14 They that swear by the sin of Samaria, and say, your god, O Dan, lives; and, The manner of Beersheba lives; even they shall fall, and never rise up again.

Amos 9:1 I saw my Lord(s) standing upon the altar: and he said, Smite the lintel of the door, that the posts may shake: and cut them in the head, all of them; and I will slay the last of them with the sword: he that flees of them shall not flee away, and he that escapes of them shall not be delivered.

2 Though they dig into Sheol, there shall mine hand take them; though they climb up to heaven, there will I bring them down:

3 And though they hide themselves in the top of Carmel, I will search and take them out there; and though they be hid from my sight in the bottom of the sea, there will I command the serpent, and he shall bite them:

4 And though they go into captivity before their enemies, there will I command the sword, and it shall slay them: and I will set mine eyes upon them for evil, and not for good.

5 And my Lord(s), the Becoming-One of hosts, is he that touches the land, and it shall melt, and all that dwell therein shall mourn: and it shall rise up wholly like a river; and shall be drowned, as by the river of Egypt.

6 It is he that builds his stories in the heaven, and has founded his troop in the earth; he that calls for the waters of the sea, and pours them out upon the face of the earth: The Becoming-One is his name.

7 Are you not as children of the Ethiopians unto me, O children of Israel? says the Becoming-One. Have not I brought up Israel out of the land of Egypt? and the Philistines from Caphtor, and the Syrians from Kir?

8 Behold, the eyes of my Lord(s), the Becoming-One, are upon the sinful kingdom, and I will destroy it from off the face of the earth; saving that I will not utterly destroy the house of Jacob, says the Becoming-One.

9 For, lo, I will command, and I will sift the house of Israel among all nations, like as grain is sifted in a sieve, yet shall not the least grain fall upon the earth.

10 All the sinners of my people shall die by the sword, which say, The evil shall not overtake nor prevent us.

11 In that day will I raise up the tabernacle of David that is fallen, and close up the breaches thereof; and I will raise up his ruins, and I will build it as in the days of olam:

12 That they may possess the remnant of Edom, and of all the nations, which are called by my name, says the Becoming-One that did this.

13 Behold, the days come, says the Becoming-One, that the plowman shall overtake the reaper, and the treader of grapes him that sows seed; and the mountains shall drop sweet wine, and all the hills shall melt.

14 And I will bring again the captivity of my people of Israel, and they shall build the waste cities, and inhabit them; and they shall plant vineyards, and drink the wine thereof; they shall also make gardens, and eat the fruit of them.

15 And I will plant them upon their land, and they shall no more be pulled up out of their land which I have given them, says the Becoming-One your God.

Obadiah

Obad 1:1 The vision of Obadiah. Thus says my Lord(s), the Becoming-One, concerning Edom; We have heard a rumor from the Becoming-One, and an ambassador is sent among the nations, Arise ye, and let us rise up against her in battle.

2 Behold, I have made you small among the nations: you are greatly despised.

3 The pride of your heart has deceived you, you that dwell in the clefts of the rock, whose habitation is high; that says in his heart, Who shall bring me down to the ground?

4 Though you exalt yourself as the eagle, and though you set your nest among the stars, there will I bring you down, says the Becoming-One.

5 If thieves came to you, if robbers by night, how are you cut off! would they not have stolen till they had enough? if the grape gatherers came to you, would they not leave some grapes?

6 How are the things of Esau searched out! how are his hidden things sought up!

7 All the men of your confederacy have brought you even to the border: the men that were at peace with you have deceived you, and prevailed against you; they that eat your bread have laid a wound under you: there is none understanding in him.

8 Shall I not in that day, says the Becoming-One, even destroy the wise men out of Edom, and understanding out of the mount of Esau?

9 And your mighty men, O Teman, shall be dismayed, to the end that every one of the mount of Esau may be cut off by slaughter.

10 For your violence against your brother Jacob shame shall cover you, and you shall be cut off for olam.

11 In the day that you stood on the other side, in the day that the strangers carried away captive his forces, and foreigners entered into his gates, and cast lots upon Jerusalem, even you were as one of them.

12 But you should not have looked on the day of your brother in the day that he became a stranger; neither should you have rejoiced over the children of Judah in the day of their destruction; neither should you have spoken proudly in the day of distress.

13 you should not have entered into the gate of my people in the day of their calamity; yes, you should not have looked on their affliction in the day of their calamity, nor have laid hands on their substance in the day of their calamity;

14 Neither should you have stood in the crossway, to cut off those of his that did escape; neither should you have delivered up those of his that did remain in the day of distress.

15 For the day of the Becoming-One is near upon all the nations: as you have done, it shall be done unto you: your reward shall return upon your own head.

16 For as you have drunk upon my holy mountain, so shall all the nations drink continually, yes, they shall drink, and they shall swallow down, and they shall be as though they had not been.

17 But upon mount Zion shall be deliverance, and there shall be holiness; and the house of Jacob shall possess their possessions.

18 And the house of Jacob shall be a fire, and the house of Joseph a flame, and the house of Esau for stubble, and they shall kindle in them, and devour them; and there shall not be any remaining of the house of Esau; for the Becoming-One has spoken it.

19 And they of the south shall possess the mount of Esau; and they of the plain the Philistines: and they shall possess the fields of Ephraim, and the fields of Samaria: and Benjamin shall possess Gilead.

20 And the captivity of this host of the children of Israel shall possess that of the Canaanites, even unto Zarephath; and the captivity of Jerusalem, which is in Sepharad, shall possess the cities of the south.

21 And saviors shall come up on mount Zion to judge the mount of Esau; and the kingdom shall be the Becoming-One's.

Jonah

Jonah 1:1 Now the word of the Becoming-One came unto Jonah the son of Amittai, saying,

2 Arise, go to Nineveh, that great city, and cry against it; for their wickedness is come up before me.

3 But Jonah rose up to flee unto Tarshish from the presence of the Becoming-One, and went down to Joppa; and he found a ship going to Tarshish: so he paid the fare thereof, and went down into it, to go with them unto Tarshish from the presence of the Becoming-One.

4 But the Becoming-One sent out a great wind into the sea, and there was a mighty tempest in the sea, so that the ship was like to be broken.

5 Then the mariners were afraid, and cried every man unto his god, and cast forth the wares that were in the ship into the sea, to lighten it of them. But Jonah was gone down into the sides of the ship; and he lay, and was fast asleep.

6 So the shipmaster came to him, and said unto him, What do you mean, O sleeper? arise, call upon your God, if so be that God will think upon us, that we perish not.

7 And they said every one to his fellow, Come, and let us cast lots, that we may know for whose cause this evil is upon us. So they cast lots, and the lot fell upon Jonah.

8 Then said they unto him, Tell us, we pray you, for whose cause this evil is upon us; What is your occupation? and from where are you from? what is your country? and of what people are you?

9 And he said unto them, I am a Hebrew; and I fear the Becoming-One, God of heaven, which has made the sea and the dry land.

10 Then were the men exceedingly afraid, and said unto him, Why have you done this? For the men knew that he fled from the presence of the Becoming-One, because he had told them.

11 Then said they unto him, What shall we do unto you, that the sea may be calm unto us? for the sea worked, and was tempestuous.

12 And he said unto them, Take me up, and cast me forth into the sea; so shall the sea be calm unto you: for I know that for my sake this great tempest is upon you.

13 Nevertheless the men rowed hard to bring it to the land; but they could not: for the sea worked, and was tempestuous against them.

14 Therefore they cried unto the Becoming-One, and said, We beseech you, O Becoming-One, we beseech you, let us not perish for this man's soul, and lay not upon us innocent blood: for you, O Becoming-One, have done as it pleased you.

15 So they took up Jonah, and cast him forth into the sea: and the sea ceased from her raging.

16 Then the men feared the Becoming-One exceedingly, and offered a sacrifice unto the Becoming-One, and made vows.

17 Now the Becoming-One had prepared a great fish to swallow up Jonah. And Jonah was in the belly of the fish three days and three nights.

Jonah 2:1 Then Jonah prayed unto the Becoming-One his God out of the fish's belly,

2 And said, I cried by reason of mine affliction unto the Becoming-One, and he heard me; out of the belly of Sheol cried I, and you heard my voice.

3 For you had cast me into the deep, in the midst of the seas; and the floods compassed me about: all your billows and your waves passed over me.

4 Then I said, I am cast out of your sight; yet I will look again toward your holy temple.

5 The waters compassed me about, even to the soul: the depth closed me round about, the weeds were wrapped about my head.

6 I went down to the bottoms of the mountains; the earth with her bars was about me for olam: yet have you brought up my life from the pit, O Becoming-One my God.

7 When my soul fainted within me I remembered the Becoming-One: and my prayer came in unto you, into your holy temple.

8 They that observe lying vanities forsake their own mercy.

9 But I will sacrifice unto you with the voice of thanksgiving; I will pay that that I have vowed. Salvation is of the Becoming-One.

10 And the Becoming-One spoke unto the fish, and it vomited out Jonah upon the dry land.

Jonah 3:1 And the word of the Becoming-One came unto Jonah the second time, saying,

2 Arise, go unto Nineveh, that great city, and preach unto it the preaching that I bid you.

3 So Jonah arose, and went unto Nineveh, according to the word of the Becoming-One. Now Nineveh was an exceeding great city of three days' journey.

4 And Jonah began to enter into the city a day's journey, and he cried, and said, Yet forty days, and Nineveh shall be overthrown.

5 So the people of Nineveh believed God, and proclaimed a fast, and put on sackcloth, from the greatest of them even to the least of them.

6 For word came unto the king of Nineveh, and he arose from his throne, and he laid his robe from him, and covered him with sackcloth, and sat in ashes.

7 And he caused it to be proclaimed and published through Nineveh by the decree of the king and his nobles, saying, Let neither man nor beast, herd nor flock, taste anything: let them not feed, nor drink water:

8 But let man and beast be covered with sackcloth, and cry mightily unto God: yes, let them turn every one from his evil way, and from the violence that is in their hands.

9 Who can tell if God will turn and repent, and turn away from his fierce anger, that we perish not?

10 And God saw their works, that they turned from their evil way; and God repented of the evil, that he had said that he would do unto them; and he did it not.

Jonah 4:1 But it displeased Jonah exceedingly, and he was very angry.

2 And he prayed unto the Becoming-One, and said, I pray you, O Becoming-One, was not this my saying, when I was yet in my country? Therefore I fled before unto Tarshish: for I knew that you are a

gracious GOD, and merciful, slow to anger, and of great kindness, and repent you of the evil.

3 Therefore now, O Becoming-One, take, I beg you, my soul from me; for it is better for me to die than to live.

4 Then said the Becoming-One, do you well to be angry?

5 So Jonah went out of the city, and sat on the east side of the city, and there made him a booth, and sat under it in the shadow, till he might see what would become of the city.

6 And the Becoming-One God prepared a gourd, and made it to come up over Jonah, that it might be a shadow over his head, to deliver him from his grief. So Jonah was exceeding glad of the gourd.

7 But God prepared a worm when the dawn rose the next day, and it smote the gourd that it withered.

8 And it came to pass, when the sun did arise, that God prepared a vehement east wind; and the sun beat upon the head of Jonah, that he fainted, and wished in his soul to die, and said, It is better for me to die than to live.

9 And God said to Jonah, do you well to be angry for the gourd? And he said, I do well to be angry, even unto death.

10 Then said the Becoming-One, you have had pity on the gourd, for which you have not labored, neither made it grow; which came up in a night, and perished in a night:

11 And should not I spare Nineveh, that great city, wherein are more than six score thousand persons that cannot discern between their right hand and their left hand; and also much cattle?

Micah

Mic 1:1 The word of the Becoming-One that came to Micah the Morasthite in the days of Jotham, Ahaz, and Hezekiah, kings of Judah, which he saw concerning Samaria and Jerusalem. **[733- 676 BC?]**

2 Hear, all you people; listen, O earth, and all that therein is: and let my Lord(s), the Becoming-One, be witness against you, my Lord(s) from his holy temple.

3 For, behold, the Becoming-One comes forth out of his place, and will come down, and tread upon the high places of the earth.

4 And the mountains shall be molten under him, and the valleys shall be cleft, as wax before the fire, and as the waters that are poured down a steep place.

5 For the transgression of Jacob is all this, and for the sins of the house of Israel. What is the transgression of Jacob? is it not Samaria? and what are the high places of Judah? are they not Jerusalem?

6 Therefore I will make Samaria as a heap of the field, and as plantings of a vineyard: and I will pour down the stones thereof into the valley, and I will discover the foundations thereof.

7 And all the graven images thereof shall be beaten to pieces, and all the hires thereof shall be burned with the fire, and all the idols thereof will I lay desolate: for she gathered it of the hire of a harlot, and they shall return to the hire of a harlot.

8 Therefore I will wail and howl, I will go stripped and naked: I will make a wailing like the monsters, and mourning as the owls.

9 For her wound is incurable; for it is come unto Judah; he is come unto the gate of my people, even to Jerusalem.

10 Declare you it not at Gath, weep you not at all: in the house of Aphrah roll yourself in the dust.

11 Pass you away, you inhabitant of Saphir, having your shame naked: the inhabitant of Zaanan came not forth in the mourning of Beth-ezel; he shall receive of you his standing.

12 For the inhabitant of Maroth waited carefully for good: but evil came down from the Becoming-One unto the gate of Jerusalem.

13 O you inhabitant of Lachish, bind the chariot to the swift beast: she is the beginning of the sin to the daughter of Zion: for the transgressions of Israel were found in you.

14 Therefore shall you give presents to Moreshethgath: the houses of Achzib shall be a lie to the kings of Israel.

15 Yet will I bring a heir unto you, O inhabitant of Mareshah: he shall come unto Adullam the glory of Israel.

16 Make you bald, and poll you for your delicate children; enlarge your baldness as the eagle; for they are gone into captivity from you.

Mic 2:1 Woe to them that devise iniquity, and work evil upon their beds! when the morning is light, they practice it, because it is in God of their hand.

2 And they covet fields, and take them by violence; and houses, and take them away: so they oppress a man and his house, even a man and his heritage.

3 Therefore thus says the Becoming-One; Behold, against this family do I devise an evil, from which you shall not remove your necks; neither shall you go haughtily: for this time is evil.

4 In that day shall one take up a parable against you, and lament with a doleful lamentation, and say, We be utterly spoiled: he has changed the portion of my people: how has he removed it from me! turning away he has divided our fields.

5 Therefore you shall have none that shall cast a cord by lot in the congregation of the Becoming-One.

6 Prophesy you not, say they to them that prophesy: they shall not prophesy to them, that they shall not take shame.

7 O you that are named the house of Jacob, is the spirit of the Becoming-One hampered? are these his doings? do not my words do good to him that walks uprightly?

8 Even of late my people is risen up as an enemy: you pull off the robe with the garment from them that pass by securely as men averse from war.

9 The women of my people have you cast out from their pleasant houses; from their children have you taken away my glory for olam.

10 Arise ye, and depart; for this is not your rest: because it is polluted, it shall destroy you, even with a great destruction.

11 If a man walking in the spirit and falsehood do lie, saying, I will prophesy unto you of wine and of strong drink; he shall even be the prophet of this people.

12 I will surely assemble, O Jacob, all of you; I will surely gather the remnant of Israel; I will put them together as the sheep of Bozrah, as the flock in the midst of their fold: they shall make great noise by reason of the multitude of men.

13 The breaker is come up before them: they have broken up, and have passed through the gate, and are gone out by it: and their king shall pass before them, and the Becoming-One on the head of them.

Mic 3:1 And I said, Hear, I pray you, O heads of Jacob, and you princes of the house of Israel; Is it not for you to know judgment?

2 Who hate the good, and love the evil; who pluck off their skin from off them, and their flesh from off their bones;

3 Who also eat the flesh of my people, and flay their skin from off them; and they break their bones, and chop them in pieces, as for the pot, and as flesh within the caldron.

4 Then shall they cry unto the Becoming-One, but he will not hear them: he will even hide his face from them at that time, as they have behaved themselves ill in their doings.

5 Thus says the Becoming-One concerning the prophets that make my people err, that bite with their teeth, and cry, Peace; and he that puts not into their mouths, they even prepare war against him.

6 Therefore night shall be unto you, that you shall not have a vision; and it shall be dark unto you, that you shall not divine; and the sun shall go down over the prophets, and the day shall be dark over them.

7 Then shall the seers be ashamed, and the diviners confounded: yes, they shall all cover their lips; for there is no answer of God.

8 But truly I am full of power by the spirit of the Becoming-One, and of judgment, and of might, to declare unto Jacob his transgression, and to Israel his sin.

9 Hear this, I pray you, you heads of the house of Jacob, and princes of the house of Israel, that abhor judgment, and pervert all equity.

10 They build up Zion with blood, and Jerusalem with iniquity.

11 The heads thereof judge for reward, and the priests thereof teach for hire, and the prophets thereof divine for money: yet will they lean upon the Becoming-One, and say, Is not the Becoming-One among us? none evil can come upon us.

12 Therefore shall Zion for your sake be plowed as a field, and Jerusalem shall become heaps, and the mountain of the house as the high places of the forest.

Mic 4:1 But in the end of days it shall come to pass, that the mountain of the house of the Becoming-One shall be established in the top of the mountains, and it shall be exalted above the hills; and people shall flow unto it.

2 And many nations shall come, and say, Come, and let us go up to the mountain of the Becoming-One, and to the house of God of Jacob; and he will teach us of his ways, and we will walk in his paths: for the law shall go forth of Zion, and the word of the Becoming-One from Jerusalem.

3 And he shall judge among many people, and rebuke strong nations afar off; and they shall beat their swords into plowshares, and their spears into pruning hooks: nation shall not lift up a sword against nation, neither shall they learn war any more.

4 But they shall sit every man under his vine and under his fig tree; and none shall make them afraid: for the mouth of the Becoming-One of hosts has spoken it.

5 For all people will walk every one in the name of his god, but we will walk in the name of the Becoming-One our God for olam and beyond.

6 In that day, says the Becoming-One, will I assemble her that halts, and I will gather her that is driven out, and her that I have afflicted;

7 And I will make her that halted a remnant, and her that was cast far off a strong nation: and the Becoming-One shall reign over them in mount Zion from henceforth, even for olam.

8 And you, O tower of the flock, the strong hold of the daughter of Zion, unto you shall it come, even the first dominion; the kingdom shall come to the daughter of Jerusalem.

9 Now why do you cry out aloud? is there no king in you? is your counselor perished? for pangs have taken you as a woman in travail.

10 Be in pain, and labor to bring forth, O daughter of Zion, like a woman in travail: for now shall you go forth out of the city, and you shall dwell in the field, and you shall go even to Babylon; there shall you be delivered; there the Becoming-One shall redeem you from the hand of your enemies.

11 Now also many nations are gathered against you, that say, Let her be defiled, and let our eye look upon Zion.

12 But they know not the thoughts of the Becoming-One, neither understand they his counsel: for he shall gather them as the sheaves into the floor.

13 Arise and thresh, O daughter of Zion: for I will make your horn iron, and I will make your hoofs brass: and you shall beat in pieces many people: and I will consecrate their gain unto the Becoming-One, and their substance unto the Lord of the whole earth.

Mic 5:1 Now gather yourself in troops, O daughter of troops: he has laid siege against us: they shall smite the judge of Israel with a rod upon the cheek.

2 But you, Bethlehem Ephratah, though you be little among the thousands of Judah, yet out of you shall he come forth unto me that is to be ruler in Israel; whose goings forth have been from of old, from the days of olam.

3 Therefore will he give them up, until the time that she which travails has brought forth: then the remnant of his brethren shall return unto the children of Israel.

4 And he shall stand and feed in the strength of the Becoming-One, in the majesty of the name of the Becoming-One his God; and they shall abide: for now shall he be great unto the ends of the earth.

5 And this man shall be the peace, when the Assyrian shall come into our land: and when he shall tread in our palaces, then shall we raise against him seven shepherds, and eight principal men.

6 And they shall waste the land of Assyria with the sword, and the land of Nimrod in the entrances thereof: thus shall he deliver us from the Assyrian, when he comes into our land, and when he treads within our borders.

7 And the remnant of Jacob shall be in the midst of many people as a dew from the Becoming-One, as the showers upon the grass, that tarries not for man, nor waits for the sons of men.

8 And the remnant of Jacob shall be among the nations in the midst of many people as a lion among the beasts of the forest, as a young lion among the flocks of sheep: who, if he go through, both treads down, and tears in pieces, and none can deliver.

9 your hand shall be lifted up upon your adversaries, and all your enemies shall be cut off.

10 And it shall come to pass in that day, says the Becoming-One, that I will cut off your horses out of the midst of you, and I will destroy your chariots:

11 And I will cut off the cities of your land, and throw down all your strong holds:

12 And I will cut off witchcrafts out of your hand; and you shall have no more soothsayers:

13 your graven images also will I cut off, and your standing images out of the midst of you; and you shall no more worship the work of your hands.

14 And I will pluck up your Asherahs out of the midst of you: so will I destroy your cities.

15 And I will execute vengeance in anger and fury upon the nations, such as they have not heard.

Mic 6:1 Hear you now what the Becoming-One says; Arise, contend you before the mountains, and let the hills hear your voice.

2 Hear ye, O mountains, the Becoming-One's controversy, and you strong foundations of the earth:

for the Becoming-One has a controversy with his people, and he will plead with Israel.

3 O my people, what have I done unto you? and wherein have I wearied you? testify against me.

4 For I brought you up out of the land of Egypt, and redeemed you out of the house of servants; and I sent before you Moses, Aaron, and Miriam.

5 O my people, remember now what Balak king of Moab consulted, and what Balaam the son of Beor answered him from Shittim unto Gilgal; that you may know the righteousness of the Becoming-One.

6 Wherewith shall I come before the Becoming-One, and bow myself before the high God? shall I come before him with burnt offerings, with calves of a year old?

7 Will the Becoming-One be pleased with thousands of rams, or with a multitude of rivers of oil? shall I give my firstborn for my transgression, the fruit of my body for the sin of my soul?

8 He has showed you, O man, what is good; and what does the Becoming-One require of you, but to do justly, and to love mercy, and to walk humbly with your God?

9 The Becoming-One's voice cries unto the city, and the man of wisdom shall see your name: hear you the rod, and who has appointed it.

10 Are there yet the treasures of wickedness in the house of the wicked, and the scant measure that is abominable?

11 Shall I count them pure with the wicked balances, and with the bag of deceitful weights?

12 For the rich men thereof are full of violence, and the inhabitants thereof have spoken lies, and their tongue is deceitful in their mouth.

13 Therefore also will I make you sick in smiting you, in making you desolate because of your sins.

14 you shall eat, but not be satisfied; and your casting down shall be in the midst of you; and you shall take hold, but shall not deliver; and that which you deliver will I give up to the sword.

15 you shall sow, but you shall not reap; you shall tread the olives, but you shall not anoint you with oil; and sweet wine, but shall not drink wine.

16 For the statutes of Omri are kept, and all the works of the house of Ahab, and you walk in their counsels; that I should make you a desolation, and the inhabitants thereof a hissing: therefore you shall bear the reproach of my people.

Mic 7:1 Woe is me! for I am as when they have gathered the summer fruits, as the grape gleanings of the vintage: there is no cluster to eat: my soul desired the first ripe fruit.

2 The good man is perished out of the earth: and there is none upright among men: they all lie in wait for blood; they hunt every man his brother with a net.

3 That they may do evil with both hands earnestly, the prince asks, and the judge asks for a reward; and the great man, he utters his mischievous soul: so they wrap it up.

4 The best of them is as a brier: the most upright is sharper than a thorn hedge: the day of your watchmen and your visitation comes; now shall be their perplexity.

5 Trust you not in a friend, put you not confidence in a guide: keep the doors of your mouth from her that lies in your bosom.

6 For the son dishonors the father, the daughter rises up against her mother, the daughter-in-law against her mother-in-law; a man's enemies are the men of his own house.

7 Therefore I will look unto the Becoming-One; I will wait for God of my salvation: my God will hear me.

8 Rejoice not against me, O mine enemy: when I fall, I shall arise; when I sit in darkness, the Becoming-One shall be a light unto me.

9 I will bear the indignation of the Becoming-One, because I have sinned against him, until he plead my cause, and execute judgment for me: he will bring me forth to the light, and I shall behold his righteousness.

10 Then she that is mine enemy shall see it, and shame shall cover her which said unto me, Where is the Becoming-One your God? mine eyes shall behold her: now shall she be trodden down as the mire of the streets.

11 In the day that your walls are to be built, in that day shall the decree be far removed.

12 In that day also he shall come even to you from Assyria, and from the fortified cities, and from the fortress even to the river, and from sea to sea, and from mountain to mountain.

13 Notwithstanding the land shall be desolate because of them that dwell therein, for the fruit of their doings.

14 Feed your people with your rod, the flock of your heritage, which dwell solitarily in the wood, in the midst of Carmel: let them feed in Bashan and Gilead, as in the days of olam.

15 According to the days of your coming out of the land of Egypt will I show unto him marvelous things.

16 The nations shall see and be confounded at all their might: they shall lay their hand upon their mouth, their ears shall be deaf.

17 They shall lick the dust like a serpent, they shall move out of their holes like worms of the earth: they shall be afraid of the Becoming-One our God, and shall fear because of you.

18 Who is a GOD like unto you, that pardons iniquity, and passes by the transgression of the remnant of his heritage? he retains not his anger to the beyond, because he delights in mercy.

19 He will turn again, he will have compassion upon us; he will subdue our iniquities; and you will cast all their sins into the depths of the sea.

20 you will perform the truth to Jacob, and the mercy to Abraham, which you have sworn unto our fathers from the days of old.

Nahum

Nah 1:1 The burden of Nineveh. The book of the vision of Nahum the Elkoshite.

2 GOD is jealous, and the Becoming-One revenges; the Becoming-One revenges, and is furious; the Becoming-One will take vengeance on his adversaries, and he reserves wrath for his enemies.

3 The Becoming-One is slow to anger, and great in power, and will not at all acquit the wicked: the Becoming-One has his way in the whirlwind and in the storm, and the clouds are the dust of his feet.

4 He rebukes the sea, and makes it dry, and dries up all the rivers: Bashan languishes, and Carmel, and the flower of Lebanon languishes.

5 The mountains quake at him, and the hills melt, and the earth is burned at his presence, yes, the world, and all that dwell therein.

6 Who can stand before his indignation? and who can abide in the fierceness of his anger? his fury is poured out like fire, and the rocks are thrown down by him.

7 The Becoming-One is good, a strong hold in the day of trouble; and he knows them that trust in him.

8 But with an overrunning flood he will make an utter end of the place thereof, and darkness shall pursue his enemies.

9 What do you imagine against the Becoming-One? he will make an utter end: affliction shall not rise up the second time.

10 For while they be entangled together as thorns, and while they are drunken as drunkards, they shall be devoured as stubble fully dry.

11 There is one come out of you, that imagines evil against the Becoming-One, a wicked counselor.

12 Thus says the Becoming-One; Though they be quiet, and likewise many, yet thus shall they be cut down, when he shall pass through. Though I have afflicted you, I will afflict you no more.

13 For now will I break his yoke from off you, and will burst your bonds in sunder.

14 And the Becoming-One has given a commandment concerning you, that no more of your name be sown: out of the house of your gods will I cut off the graven image and the molten image: I will make your grave; for you are vile.

15 Behold upon the mountains the feet of him that brings good tidings, that declares peace! O Judah, keep your solemn feasts, perform your vows: for the wicked shall no more pass through you; he is utterly cut off.

Nah 2:1 He that dashes in pieces is come up before your face: keep the munition, watch the way, make your loins strong, fortify your power mightily.

2 For the Becoming-One has turned away the excellency of Jacob, as the excellency of Israel: for the emptiers have emptied them out, and marred their vine branches.

3 The shield of his mighty men is made red, the valiant men are in scarlet: the chariots shall be with flaming torches in the day of his preparation, and the fir trees shall be terribly shaken.

4 The chariots shall rage in the streets, they shall justle one against another in the broad ways: they shall seem like torches, they shall run like the lightning.

5 He shall recount his worthies: they shall stumble in their walk; they shall make haste to the wall thereof, and the defense shall be prepared.

6 The gates of the rivers shall be opened, and the palace shall be dissolved.

7 And Huzzab shall be led away captive, she shall be brought up, and her maids shall lead her as with the voice of doves, tabering upon their breasts.

8 But Nineveh is of old like a pool of water: yet they shall flee away. Stand, stand, shall they cry; but none shall look back.

9 Take you the spoil of silver, take the spoil of gold: for there is none end of the store and glory out of all the pleasant furniture.

10 She is empty, and void, and waste: and the heart melts, and the knees smite together, and much pain is in all loins, and the faces of them all gather blackness.

11 Where is the dwelling of the lions, and the feeding place of the young lions, where the lion, even the old lion, walked, and the lion's whelp, and none made them afraid?

12 The lion did tear in pieces enough for his whelps, and strangled for his lionesses, and filled his holes with prey, and his dens with ravin.

13 Behold, I am against you, says the Becoming-One of hosts, and I will burn her chariots in the smoke, and the sword shall devour your young lions: and I will cut off your prey from the earth, and the voice of your messengers shall no more be heard.

Nah 3:1 Woe to the bloody city! it is all full of lies and robbery; the prey departs not;

2 The noise of a whip, and the noise of the rattling of the wheels, and of the prancing horses, and of the jumping chariots.

3 The horseman lifts up both the bright sword and the glittering spear: and there is a multitude of slain, and a great number of carcases; and there is none end of their corpses; they stumble upon their corpses:

4 Because of the multitude of the whoredoms of the wellfavored harlot, the mistress of witchcrafts, that sells nations through her whoredoms, and families through her witchcrafts.

5 Behold, I am against you, says the Becoming-One of hosts; and I will discover your skirts upon your face, and I will show the nations your nakedness, and the kingdoms your shame.

6 And I will cast abominable filth upon you, and make you vile, and will set you as a gazingstock.

7 And it shall come to pass, that all they that look upon you shall flee from you, and say, Nineveh is laid waste: who will bemoan her? from where shall I seek comforters for you?

8 are you better than populous No, that was situate among the rivers, that had the waters round about it, whose rampart was the sea, and her wall was from the sea?

9 Ethiopia and Egypt were her strength, and it was infinite; Put and Lubim were your helpers.

10 Yet was she carried away, she went into captivity: her young children also were dashed in pieces at the top of all the streets: and they cast lots

for her honorable men, and all her great men were bound in chains.

11 you also shall be drunken: you shall be hid, you also shall seek strength because of the enemy.

12 All your strong holds shall be like fig trees with the firstripe figs: if they be shaken, they shall even fall into the mouth of the eater.

13 Behold, your people in the midst of you are women: the gates of your land shall be set wide open unto your enemies: the fire shall devour your bars.

14 Draw you waters for the siege, fortify your strong holds: go into clay, and tread the mortar, make strong the brickkiln.

15 There shall the fire devour you; the sword shall cut you off, it shall eat you up like the cankerworm: make yourself many as the cankerworm, make yourself many as the locusts.

16 you have multiplied your merchants above the stars of heaven: the cankerworm spoils, and flees away.

17 your crowned are as the locusts, and your captains as the great grasshoppers, which camp in the hedges in the cold day, but when the sun arises they flee away, and their place is not known where they are.

18 your shepherds slumber, O king of Assyria: your nobles shall dwell in the dust: your people is scattered upon the mountains, and no man gathers them.

19 There is no healing of your bruise; your wound is grievous: all that hear the bruit of you shall clap the hands over you; for upon whom has not your wickedness passed continually?

Habakkuk

Hab 1:1 The burden which Habakkuk the prophet did see.

2 O Becoming-One, how long shall I cry, and you will not hear! even cry out unto you of violence, and you will not save!

3 Why do you show me iniquity, and cause me to behold grievance? for spoiling and violence are before me: and there are that raise up strife and contention.

4 Therefore the law is slacked, and judgment does not completely go forth: for the wicked does compass about the righteous; therefore wrong judgment proceeds.

5 Behold you among the nations, and regard, and wonder marvelously: for I will work a work in your days, which you will not believe, though it be told you.

6 For, lo, I raise up the Chaldeans, that bitter and hasty nation, which shall march through the breadth of the land, to possess the dwelling places that are not theirs.

7 They are terrible and dreadful: their judgment and their dignity shall proceed of themselves.

8 Their horses also are swifter than the leopards, and are more fierce than the evening wolves: and their horsemen shall spread themselves, and their horsemen shall come from far; they shall fly as the eagle that hastens to eat.

9 They shall come all for violence: their faces shall sup up as the east wind, and they shall gather the captivity as the sand.

10 And they shall scoff at the kings, and the princes shall be a scorn unto them: they shall deride every strong hold; for they shall heap dust, and take it.

11 Then shall his spirit change, and he shall pass over, and offend, imputing this his power unto his god.

12 are you not from olam, O Becoming-One, my God, mine Holy One? we shall not die. O Becoming-One, you have ordained them for judgment; and, O Rock, you have established them for correction.

13 you are of purer eyes than to behold evil, and can not look on iniquity: therefore look you upon them that deal treacherously, and hold your tongue when the wicked devours the man that is more righteous than he?

14 And make men as the fishes of the sea, as the creeping things, that have no ruler over them?

15 They take up all of them with the angle, they catch them in their net, and gather them in their drag: therefore they rejoice and are glad.

16 Therefore they sacrifice unto their net, and burn incense unto their drag; because by them their portion is fat, and their food plenteous.

17 Shall they therefore empty their net, and not spare continually to slay the nations?

Hab 2:1 I will stand upon my watch, and set me upon the tower, and will watch to see what he will say unto me, and what I shall answer when I am reproved.

2 And the Becoming-One answered me, and said, Write the vision, and make it plain upon tables, that he may run that reads it.

3 For the vision is yet for a set time,[173] but at the end it shall speak, and not lie: though it tarry, wait for it; because it will surely come, it will not tarry.

4 Behold, his soul which is lifted up is not upright in him: but the just shall live by his faith.

5 Yes also, because he transgresses by wine, he is a proud man, neither keeps at home, who enlarges his soul as Sheol, and is as death, and cannot be satisfied, but gathers unto him all nations, and heaps unto him all people:

6 Shall not all these take up a parable against him, and a taunting proverb against him, and say, Woe to him that increases that which is not his! how long? and to him that loaded himself with thick clay!

7 Shall they not rise up suddenly that shall bite you, and awake that shall vex you, and you shall be for booties unto them?

8 Because you have spoiled many nations, all the remnant of the people shall spoil you; because of men's blood, and for the violence of the land, of the city, and of all that dwell therein.

9 Woe to him that covets an evil covetousness to his house, that he may set his nest on high, that he may be delivered from the power of evil!

10 you have consulted shame to your house by cutting off many people, and have sinned against your soul.

11 For the stone shall cry out of the wall, and the beam out of the timber shall answer it.

12 Woe to him that builds a town with blood, and establishes a city by iniquity!

13 Behold, is it not of the Becoming-One of hosts that the people shall labor in the very fire, and the people shall weary themselves for very vanity?

14 For the earth shall be filled with the knowledge of the glory of the Becoming-One, as the waters cover the sea.

15 Woe unto him that gives his neighbor drink, that put your bottle to him, and make him drunken also, that you may look on their nakedness!

16 you are filled with shame for glory: drink you also, and let your foreskin be uncovered: the cup of the Becoming-One's right hand shall be turned unto you, and shameful spewing shall be on your glory.

17 For the violence of Lebanon shall cover you, and the spoil of beasts, which made them afraid, because of men's blood, and for the violence of the land, of the city, and of all that dwell therein.

18 What profits the graven image that the maker thereof has graven it; the molten image, and a teacher of lies, that the maker of his work trusts therein, to make mute idols?

19 Woe unto him that says to the wood, Awake; to the mute stone, Arise, it shall teach! Behold, it is laid over with gold and silver, and there is no breath at all in the midst of it.

20 But the Becoming-One is in his holy temple: let all the earth keep silence before him.

Hab 3:1 A prayer of Habakkuk the prophet upon Shigionoth.

---

[173] Appointed time or festival

2 O Becoming-One, I have heard your speech, and was afraid: O Becoming-One, revive your work in the midst of the years, in the midst of the years make known; in wrath remember mercy.

3 God came from Teman, and the Holy One from mount Paran. Selah. His glory covered the heavens, and the earth was full of his praise.

4 And his brightness was as the light; he had horns coming out of his hand: and there was the hiding of his power.

5 Before him went the pestilence, and burning coals went forth at his feet.

6 He stood, and measured the earth: he beheld, and drove asunder the nations; and the enduring mountains were scattered, the hills of olam did bow: his ways are of olam.

7 I saw the tents of Cushan in affliction: and the curtains of the land of Midian did tremble.

8 Was the Becoming-One displeased against the rivers? was your anger against the rivers? was your wrath against the sea, that you did ride upon your horses and your chariots of salvation?

9 your bow was made quite naked, according to the oaths of the tribes, even your word. Selah. you did cleave the earth with rivers.

10 The mountains saw you, and they trembled: the overflowing of the water passed by: the deep uttered his voice, and lifted up his hands on high.

11 The sun and moon stood still in their habitation: at the light of your arrows they went, and at the shining of your glittering spear.

12 you did march through the land in indignation, you did thresh the nations in anger.

13 you went forth for the salvation of your people, even for salvation with your anointed [Messiah]; you wounded the head out of the house of the wicked, by discovering the foundation unto the neck. Selah.

14 you did strike through with his staves the head of his villages: they came out as a whirlwind to scatter me: their rejoicing was as to devour the poor secretly.

15 you did walk through the sea with your horses, through the heap of great waters.

16 When I heard, my belly trembled; my lips quivered at the voice: rottenness entered into my bones, and I trembled in myself, that I might rest in the day of trouble: when he comes up unto the people, he will invade them with his troops.

17 Although the fig tree shall not blossom, neither shall fruit be in the vines; the labor of the olive shall fail, and the fields shall yield no food; the flock shall be cut off from the fold, and there shall be no herd in the stalls:

18 Yet I will rejoice in the Becoming-One, I will joy in God of my salvation.

19 The Becoming-One, my Lord(s) is my strength, and he will make my feet like hinds' feet, and he will make me to walk upon mine high places. To the chief singer on my stringed instruments.

Zephaniah

Zeph 1:1 The word of the Becoming-One which came unto Zephaniah the son of Cushi, the son of Gedaliah, the son of Amariah, the son of Hizkiah, in the days of Josiah the son of Amon, king of Judah. **[638-608 BC?]**

2 I will utterly consume all things from off the land, says the Becoming-One.

3 I will consume man and beast; I will consume the fowls of the heaven, and the fishes of the sea, and the stumbling blocks with the wicked; and I will cut off man from off the land, says the Becoming-One.

4 I will also stretch out mine hand upon Judah, and upon all the inhabitants of Jerusalem; and I will cut off the remnant of the lord [baal] from this place, and the name of the Chemarims with the priests;

5 And them that worship the host of the heavens upon the housetops; and them that worship and that swear by the Becoming-One, and that swear by Malcham;

6 And them that are turned back from the Becoming-One; and those that have not sought the Becoming-One, nor inquired for him.

7 Hold your peace at the presence of my Lord(s) the Becoming-One: for the day of the Becoming-One is at hand: for the Becoming-One has prepared a sacrifice, he has bid his guests.

8 And it shall come to pass in the day of the Becoming-One's sacrifice, that I will punish the princes, and the king's children, and all such as are clothed with strange apparel.

9 In the same day also will I punish all those that leap on the threshold, which fill their masters' houses with violence and deceit.

10 And it shall come to pass in that day, says the Becoming-One, that there shall be the noise of a cry from the fish gate, and a howling from the second, and a great crashing from the hills.

11 Howl, you inhabitants of Maktesh, for all the merchant people are cut down; all they that bear silver are cut off.

12 And it shall come to pass at that time, that I will search Jerusalem with candles, and punish the men that are settled on their lees: that say in their heart, The Becoming-One will not do good, neither will he do evil.

13 Therefore their goods shall become a booty, and their houses a desolation: they shall also build houses, but not inhabit them; and they shall plant vineyards, but not drink the wine thereof.

14 The great day of the Becoming-One is near, it is near, and hastens greatly, even the voice of the day of the Becoming-One: the mighty man shall cry there bitterly.

15 That day is a day of wrath, a day of trouble and distress, a day of ruin and desolation, a day of darkness and gloominess, a day of clouds and thick darkness,

16 A day of the trumpet and alarm against the fenced cities, and against the high towers.

17 And I will bring distress upon men, that they shall walk like blind men, because they have sinned against the Becoming-One: and their blood shall be poured out as dust, and their flesh as the dung.

18 Neither their silver nor their gold shall be able to deliver them in the day of the Becoming-One's wrath; but the whole land shall be devoured by the fire of his jealousy: for he shall make even a speedy riddance of all them that dwell in the land.

Zeph 2:1 Gather yourselves together, yes, gather together, O nation not desired;

2 Before the decree bring forth, before the day pass as the chaff, before the fierce anger of the Becoming-One come upon you, before the day of the Becoming-One's anger come upon you.

3 Seek you the Becoming-One, all you meek of the earth, which have worked his judgment; seek righteousness, seek meekness: it may be you shall be hid in the day of the Becoming-One's anger.

4 For Gaza shall be forsaken, and Ashkelon a desolation: they shall drive out Ashdod at the noon day, and Ekron shall be rooted up.

5 Woe unto the inhabitants of the sea coast, the nation of the Cherethites! the word of the Becoming-One is against you; O Canaan, the land of the Philistines, I will even destroy you, that there shall be no inhabitant.

6 And the sea coast shall be dwellings and cottages for shepherds, and folds for flocks.

7 And the coast shall be for the remnant of the house of Judah; they shall feed thereupon: in the houses of Ashkelon shall they lie down in the evening: for the Becoming-One their God shall visit them, and turn away their captivity.

8 I have heard the reproach of Moab, and the reviling of the children of Ammon, whereby they have reproached my people, and magnified themselves against their border.

9 Therefore as I live, says the Becoming-One of hosts, God of Israel, Surely Moab shall be as Sodom, and the children of Ammon as Gomorrah, even the breeding of nettles, and salt pits, and a desolation of olam: the residue of my people shall spoil them, and the remnant of my people shall possess them.

10 This shall they have for their pride, because they have reproached and magnified themselves against the people of the Becoming-One of hosts.

11 The Becoming-One will be terrible unto them: for he will famish all the gods of the earth; and men shall worship him, every one from his place, even all the isles of the nations.

12 you Ethiopians also, you shall be slain by my sword.

13 And he will stretch out his hand against the north, and destroy Assyria; and will make Nineveh a desolation, and dry like a wilderness.

14 And flocks shall lie down in the midst of her, all the beasts of the nations: both the cormorant and the bittern shall lodge in the upper lintels of it; their voice shall sing in the windows; desolation shall be in the thresholds: for he shall uncover the cedar work.

15 This is the rejoicing city that dwelt carelessly, that said in her heart, I am, and there is none beside me: how is she become a desolation, a place for beasts to lie down in! every one that passes by her shall hiss, and wag his hand.

Zeph 3:1 Woe to her that is filthy and polluted, to the oppressing city!

2 She obeyed not the voice; she received not correction; she trusted not in the Becoming-One; she drew not near to her God.

3 Her princes within her are roaring lions; her judges are evening wolves; they gnaw not the bones till the morrow.

4 Her prophets are light and treacherous persons: her priests have polluted the sanctuary, they have done violence to the law.

5 The just Becoming-One is in the midst thereof; he will not do iniquity: every morning does he bring his judgment to light, he fails not; but the unjust knows no shame.

6 I have cut off the nations: their towers are desolate; I made their streets waste, that none passes by: their cities are destroyed, so that there is no man, that there is none inhabitant.

7 I said, Surely you will fear me, you will receive instruction; so their dwelling should not be cut off, howsoever I punished them: but they rose early, and corrupted all their doings.

8 Therefore wait you upon me, says the Becoming-One, until the day that I rise up to the prey: for my determination is to gather the nations, that I may assemble the kingdoms, to pour upon them mine indignation, even all my fierce anger: for all the earth shall be devoured with the fire of my jealousy.

9 For then will I turn to the people a pure language, to call them all by the name of the Becoming-One, to serve him with one consent.

10 From beyond the rivers of Ethiopia my suppliants, even the daughter of my dispersed, shall bring my offering.

11 In that day shall you not be ashamed for all your doings, wherein you have transgressed against me: for then I will take away out of the midst of you them that rejoice in your pride, and you shall no more be haughty because of my holy mountain.

12 I will also leave in the midst of you an afflicted and poor people, and they shall trust in the name of the Becoming-One.

13 The remnant of Israel shall not do iniquity, nor speak lies; neither shall a deceitful tongue be found in their mouth: for they shall feed and lie down, and none shall make them afraid.

14 Sing, O daughter of Zion; shout, O Israel; be glad and rejoice with all the heart, O daughter of Jerusalem.

15 The Becoming-One has taken away your judgments, he has cast out your enemy: the king of Israel, even the Becoming-One, is in the midst of you: you shall not see evil any more.

16 In that day it shall be said to Jerusalem, Fear you not: and to Zion, Let not your hands be slack.

17 The Becoming-One your God in the midst of you is mighty; he will save, he will rejoice over you with joy; he will rest in his love, he will joy over you with singing.

18 I have gathered (the) suffering ones from the appointed [or set or festival] time,[174] from your grief you were lifted up high above reproach.

19 Behold, at that time I will undo all that afflict you: and I will save her that halts, and gather her that was driven out; and I will get them praise and fame in every land where they have been put to shame.

20 At that time will I bring you again, even in the time that I gather you: for I will make you a name and a praise among all people of the earth, when I turn back your captivity before your eyes, says the Becoming-One.

---

[174] Appointed time or festival

Haggai

Hag 1:1 In the *second year of Darius* the king, in the sixth month, in the first day of the month, came the word of the Becoming-One by Haggai the prophet unto Zerubbabel the son of Shealtiel, governor of Judah, and to Joshua the son of Josedech, the high priest, saying, **[ab. 520 BC]**

2 Thus speaks the Becoming-One of hosts, saying, This people say, The time is not come, the time that the Becoming-One's house should be built.

3 Then came the word of the Becoming-One by Haggai the prophet, saying,

4 Is it time for you, O ye, to dwell in your ceiled houses, and this house lie waste?

5 Now therefore thus says the Becoming-One of hosts; Consider your ways.

6 you have sown much, and bring in little; you eat, but you have not enough; you drink, but you are not filled with drink; you clothe you, but there is none warm; and he that earns wages earns wages to put it into a bag with holes.

7 Thus says the Becoming-One of hosts; Consider your ways.

8 Go up to the mountain, and bring wood, and build the house; and I will take pleasure in it, and I will be glorified, says the Becoming-One.

9 you looked for much, and, lo, it came to little; and when you brought it home, I did blow upon it. Why? says the Becoming-One of hosts. Because of mine house that is waste, and you run every man unto his own house.

10 Therefore the heavens over you is stayed from dew, and the earth is stayed from her fruit.

11 And I called for a drought upon the land, and upon the mountains, and upon the grain, and upon the new wine, and upon the oil, and upon that which the ground brings forth, and upon men, and upon cattle, and upon all the labor of the hands.

12 Then Zerubbabel the son of Shealtiel, and Joshua the son of Josedech, the high priest, with all the remnant of the people, obeyed the voice of the Becoming-One their God, and the words of Haggai the prophet, as the Becoming-One their God had sent him, and the people did fear before the Becoming-One.

13 Then spoke Haggai the Becoming-One's messenger in the Becoming-One's message unto the people, saying, I am with you, says the Becoming-One.

14 And the Becoming-One stirred up the spirit of Zerubbabel the son of Shealtiel, governor of Judah, and the spirit of Joshua the son of Josedech, the high priest, and the spirit of all the remnant of the people; and they came and did work in the house of the Becoming-One of hosts, their God,

15 In the four and twentieth day of the sixth month, in the second year of Darius the king.

Hag 2:1 In the seventh month, in the one and twentieth day of the month, came the word of the Becoming-One by the prophet Haggai, saying, **[ab. 520 BC]**

2 Speak now to Zerubbabel the son of Shealtiel, governor of Judah, and to Joshua the son of Josedech, the high priest, and to the residue of the people, saying,

3 Who is left among you that saw this house in her first glory? and how do you see it now? is it not in your eyes in comparison of it as nothing?

4 Yet now be strong, O Zerubbabel, says the Becoming-One; and be strong, O Joshua, son of Josedech, the high priest; and be strong, all you people of the land, says the Becoming-One, and work: for I am with you, says the Becoming-One of hosts:

5 According to the word that I covenanted with you when you came out of Egypt, so my spirit remains among you: fear you not.

6 For thus says the Becoming-One of hosts; Yet once, it is a little while, and I will shake the heavens, and the earth, and the sea, and the dry land;

7 And I will shake all nations, and the desire of all nations shall come: and I will fill this house with glory, says the Becoming-One of hosts.

8 The silver is mine, and the gold is mine, says the Becoming-One of hosts.

9 The glory of this latter house shall be greater than of the former, says the Becoming-One of hosts: and in this place will I give peace, says the Becoming-One of hosts.

10 In the four and twentieth day of the ninth month, in the second year of Darius, came the word of the Becoming-One by Haggai the prophet, saying,

11 Thus says the Becoming-One of hosts; Ask now the priests concerning the law, saying,

12 If one bear holy flesh in the skirt of his garment, and with his skirt do touch bread, or pottage, or wine, or oil, or any food, shall it be holy? And the priests answered and said, No.

13 Then said Haggai, If one that is unclean by a dead soul touch any of these, shall it be unclean? And the priests answered and said, It shall be unclean.

14 Then answered Haggai, and said, So is this people, and so is this nation before me, says the Becoming-One; and so is every work of their hands; and that which they offer there is unclean.

15 And now, I pray you, consider from this day and upward, from before a stone was laid upon a stone in the temple of the Becoming-One: 16 Since those days were, when one came to a heap of twenty measures, there were but ten: when one came to the press fat for to draw out fifty vessels out of the press, there were but twenty.

17 I smote you with blasting and with mildew and with hail in all the labors of your hands; yet you turned not to me, says the Becoming-One.

18 Consider now from this day and upward, from the four and twentieth day of the ninth month, even from the day that the foundation of the Becoming-One's temple was laid, consider it.

19 Is the seed yet in the barn? yes, as yet the vine, and the fig tree, and the pomegranate, and the olive tree, has not brought forth: from this day will I bless you.

20 And again the word of the Becoming-One came unto Haggai in the four and twentieth day of the month, saying,

21 Speak to Zerubbabel, governor of Judah, saying, I will shake the heavens and the earth;

22 And I will overthrow the throne of kingdoms, and I will destroy the strength of the kingdoms of the nations; and I will overthrow the chariots, and those

that ride in them; and the horses and their riders shall come down, every one by the sword of his brother.

23 In that day, says the Becoming-One of hosts, will I take you, O Zerubbabel, my servant, the son of Shealtiel, says the Becoming-One, and will make you as a signet: for I have chosen you, says the Becoming-One of hosts.

Zechariah

Zech 1:1 In the eighth month, in the second year of Darius [ab. 3454 YM; 520 BC], came the word of the Becoming-One unto Zechariah, the son of Berechiah, the son of Iddo the prophet, saying,

2 The Becoming-One has been greatly displeased with your fathers.

3 Therefore say you unto them, Thus says the Becoming-One of hosts; Turn you unto me, says the Becoming-One of hosts, and I will turn unto you, says the Becoming-One of hosts.

4 Be you not as your fathers, unto whom the former prophets have cried, saying, Thus says the Becoming-One of hosts; Turn you now from your evil ways, and from your evil doings: but they did not hear, nor listen unto me, says the Becoming-One.

5 Your fathers, where are they? and the prophets, do they live for olam?

6 But my words and my statutes, which I commanded my servants the prophets, did they not take hold of your fathers? and they returned and said, Like as the Becoming-One of hosts thought to do unto us, according to our ways, and according to our doings, so has he dealt with us.

7 Upon the four and twentieth day of the eleventh month, which is the month Sebat, in the second year of Darius, came the word of the Becoming-One unto Zechariah, the son of Berechiah, the son of Iddo the prophet, saying,

8 I saw by night, and behold a man riding upon a red horse, and he stood among the myrtle trees that were in the bottom; and behind him were there red horses, speckled, and white.

9 Then said I, O my lord, what are these? And the angel that talked with me said unto me, I will show you what these be.

10 And the man that stood among the myrtle trees answered and said, These are they whom the Becoming-One has sent to walk back and forth through the earth.

11 And they answered the angel of the Becoming-One that stood among the myrtle trees, and said, We have walked back and forth through the earth, and, behold, all the earth sits still, and is at rest.

12 Then the angel of the Becoming-One answered and said, O Becoming-One of hosts, how long will you not have mercy on Jerusalem and on the cities of Judah, against which you have had indignation these threescore and ten years?

13 And the Becoming-One answered the angel that talked with me with good words and comfortable words.

14 So the angel that communed with me said unto me, Cry you, saying, Thus says the Becoming-One of hosts; I am jealous for Jerusalem and for Zion with a great jealousy.

15 And I am very greatly displeased with the nations that are at ease: for I was but a little displeased, and they helped forward the affliction.

16 Therefore thus says the Becoming-One; I am returned to Jerusalem with mercies: my house shall be built in it, says the Becoming-One of hosts, and a line shall be stretched forth upon Jerusalem.

17 Cry yet, saying, Thus says the Becoming-One of hosts; My cities through prosperity shall yet be spread abroad; and the Becoming-One shall yet comfort Zion, and shall yet choose Jerusalem.

18 Then lifted I up mine eyes, and saw, and behold four horns.

19 And I said unto the angel that talked with me, What be these? And he answered me, These are the horns which have scattered Judah, Israel, and Jerusalem.

20 And the Becoming-One showed me four carpenters.

21 Then said I, What come these to do? And he spoke, saying, These are the horns which have scattered Judah, so that no man did lift up his head: but these are come to fray them, to cast out the horns of the nations, which lifted up their horn over the land of Judah to scatter it.

Zech 2:1 I lifted up mine eyes again, and looked, and behold a man with a measuring line in his hand.

2 Then said I, Where are you going? And he said unto me, To measure Jerusalem, to see what is the breadth thereof, and what is the length thereof.

3 And, behold, the angel that talked with me went forth, and another angel went out to meet him,

4 And said unto him, Run, speak to this young man, saying, Jerusalem shall be inhabited as towns without walls for the multitude of men and cattle therein:

5 For I, says the Becoming-One, will be unto her a wall of fire round about, and will be the glory in the midst of her.

6 Ho, ho, come forth, and flee from the land of the north, says the Becoming-One: for I have spread you abroad as the four winds of the heaven, says the Becoming-One.

7 Deliver thyself, O Zion, that dwell with the daughter of Babylon.

8 For thus says the Becoming-One of hosts; After the glory has he sent me unto the nations which spoiled you: for he that touches you touches the apple of his eye.

9 For, behold, I will shake mine hand upon them, and they shall be a spoil to their servants: and you shall know that the Becoming-One of hosts has sent me.

10 Sing and rejoice, O daughter of Zion: for, lo, I come, and I will dwell in the midst of you, says the Becoming-One.

11 And many nations shall be joined to the Becoming-One in that day, and shall be my people: and I will dwell in the midst of you, and you shall know that the Becoming-One of hosts has sent me unto you.

12 And the Becoming-One shall inherit Judah his portion in the holy land, and shall choose Jerusalem again.

13 Be silent, O all flesh, before the Becoming-One: for he is raised up out of his holy habitation.

Zech 3:1 And he showed me Joshua the high priest standing before the angel of the Becoming-One, and Satan standing at his right hand to resist him.

2 And the Becoming-One said unto Satan, The Becoming-One rebuke you, O Satan; even the

Becoming-One that has chosen Jerusalem rebuke you: is not this a brand plucked out of the fire?

3 Now Joshua was clothed with filthy garments, and stood before the angel.

4 And he answered and spoke unto those that stood before him, saying, Take away the filthy garments from him. And unto him he said, Behold, I have caused your iniquity to pass from you, and I will clothe you with change of raiment.

5 And I said, Let them set a fair diadem upon his head. So they set a fair diadem upon his head, and clothed him with garments. And the angel of the Becoming-One stood by.

6 And the angel of the Becoming-One protested unto Joshua, saying,

7 Thus says the Becoming-One of hosts; If you will walk in my ways, and if you will keep my charge, then you shall also judge my house, and shall also keep my courts, and I will give you places to walk among these that stand by.

8 Hear now, O Joshua the high priest, you, and your fellows that sit before you: for they are men wondered at: for, behold, I will bring forth my servant the BRANCH.

9 For behold the stone that I have laid before Joshua; upon one stone shall be seven eyes: behold, I will engrave the graving thereof, says the Becoming-One of hosts, and I will remove the iniquity of that land in one day.

10 In that day, says the Becoming-One of hosts, shall you call every man his neighbor under the vine and under the fig tree.

Zech 4:1 And the angel that talked with me came again, and waked me, as a man that is wakened out of his sleep,

2 And said unto me, What see you? And I said, I have looked, and behold a candlestick all of gold, with a bowl upon the top of it, and his seven lamps thereon, and seven pipes to the seven lamps, which are upon the top thereof:

3 And two olive trees by it, one upon the right side of the bowl, and the other upon the left side thereof.

4 So I answered and spoke to the angel that talked with me, saying, What are these, my lord?

5 Then the angel that talked with me answered and said unto me, don't you know what these be? And I said, No, my lord.

6 Then he answered and spoke unto me, saying, This is the word of the Becoming-One unto Zerubbabel, saying, Not by might, nor by power, but by my spirit, says the Becoming-One of hosts.

7 Who are you, O great mountain? before Zerubbabel you shall become a plain: and he shall bring forth the headstone thereof with shouting, crying, Grace, grace unto it.

8 Moreover the word of the Becoming-One came unto me, saying,

9 The hands of Zerubbabel have laid the foundation of this house; his hands shall also finish it; and you shall know that the Becoming-One of hosts has sent me unto you.

10 For who has despised the day of small things? for they shall rejoice, and shall see the plummet in the hand of Zerubbabel with those seven; they are the eyes of the Becoming-One, which run back and forth through the whole earth.

11 Then answered I, and said unto him, What are these two olive trees upon the right side of the candlestick and upon the left side thereof?

12 And I answered again, and said unto him, What be these two olive branches which through the two golden pipes empty the golden oil out of themselves?

13 And he answered me and said, don't you know what these be? And I said, No, my lord.

14 Then said he, These are the two anointed ones, that stand by the Lord of the whole earth.

Zech 5:1 Then I turned, and lifted up mine eyes, and looked, and behold a flying roll.

2 And he said unto me, What see you? And I answered, I see a flying roll; the length thereof is twenty cubits, and the breadth thereof ten cubits.

3 Then said he unto me, This is the curse that goes forth over the face of the whole earth: for every one that steals shall be cut off as on this side according to it; and every one that swears shall be cut off as on that side according to it.

4 I will bring it forth, says the Becoming-One of hosts, and it shall enter into the house of the thief, and into the house of him that swears falsely by my name: and it shall remain in the midst of his house, and shall consume it with the timber thereof and the stones thereof.

5 Then the angel that talked with me went forth, and said unto me, Lift up now your eyes, and see what is this that goes forth.

6 And I said, What is it? And he said, This is an ephah that goes forth. He said moreover, This is their resemblance through all the earth.

7 And, behold, there was lifted up a talent of lead: and this is a woman that sits in the midst of the ephah.

8 And he said, This is wickedness. And he cast it into the midst of the ephah; and he cast the weight of lead upon the mouth thereof.

9 Then lifted I up mine eyes, and looked, and, behold, there came out two women, and the wind was in their wings; for they had wings like the wings of a stork: and they lifted up the ephah between the earth and the heaven.

10 Then said I to the angel that talked with me, To where do these bear the ephah?

11 And he said unto me, To build it a house in the land of Shinar: and it shall be established, and set there upon her own base.

Zech 6:1 And I turned, and lifted up mine eyes, and looked, and, behold, there came four chariots out from between two mountains; and the mountains were mountains of brass.

2 In the first chariot were red horses; and in the second chariot black horses;

3 And in the third chariot white horses; and in the fourth chariot dappled gray horses.

4 Then I answered and said unto the angel that talked with me, What are these, my lord?

5 And the angel answered and said unto me, These are the four spirits of the heavens, which go forth from standing before the Lord of all the earth.

6 The black horses which are therein go forth into the north country; and the white go forth after them; and the dappled go forth toward the south country.

7 And the steeds went forth, and sought to go that they might walk back and forth through the earth: and he said, Get you hence, walk back and forth through the earth. So they walked back and forth through the earth.

8 Then cried he upon me, and spoke unto me, saying, Behold, these that go toward the north country have quieted my spirit in the north country.

9 And the word of the Becoming-One came unto me, saying,

10 Take of them of the captivity, even of Heldai, of Tobijah, and of Jedaiah, which are come from Babylon, and you come the same day, and go into the house of Josiah the son of Zephaniah;

11 Then take silver and gold, and make crowns, and set them upon the head of Joshua the son of Josedech, the high priest;

12 And speak unto him, saying, Thus speaks the Becoming-One of hosts, saying, Behold the man whose name is The BRANCH; and he shall grow up out of his place, and he shall build the temple of the Becoming-One: 13 Even he shall build the temple of the Becoming-One; and he shall bear the glory, and shall sit and rule upon his throne; and he shall be a priest upon his throne: and the counsel of peace shall be between them both.

14 And the crowns shall be to Helem, and to Tobijah, and to Jedaiah, and to Hen the son of Zephaniah, for a memorial in the temple of the Becoming-One.

15 And they that are far off shall come and build in the temple of the Becoming-One, and you shall know that the Becoming-One of hosts has sent me unto you. And this shall come to pass, if you will diligently obey the voice of the Becoming-One your God.

Zech 7:1 And it came to pass in the fourth year of king Darius [3439 YM; 535 BC], that the word of the Becoming-One came unto Zechariah in the fourth day of the ninth month, even in Chisleu;

2 When they had sent unto the house of GOD Sherezer and Regem-melech, and their men, to pray before the Becoming-One,

3 And to speak unto the priests which were in the house of the Becoming-One of hosts, and to the prophets, saying, Should I weep in the fifth month, separating myself, as I have done these so many years?

4 Then came the word of the Becoming-One of hosts unto me, saying,

5 Speak unto all the people of the land, and to the priests, saying, When you fasted and mourned in the fifth and seventh month, even those seventy years, did you at all fast unto me, even to me?

6 And when you did eat, and when you did drink, did not you eat for yourselves, and drink for yourselves?

7 Should you not hear the words which the Becoming-One has cried by the former prophets, when Jerusalem was inhabited and in prosperity, and the cities thereof round about her, when men inhabited the south and the plain?

8 And the word of the Becoming-One came unto Zechariah, saying,

9 Thus speaks the Becoming-One of hosts, saying, Execute true judgment, and show mercy and compassion every man to his brother:

10 And oppress not the widow, nor the fatherless, the stranger, nor the poor; and let none of you imagine evil against his brother in your heart.

11 But they refused to listen, and pulled away the shoulder, and stopped their ears, that they should not hear.

12 Yes, they made their hearts as an adamant stone, lest they should hear the law, and the words which the Becoming-One of hosts has sent in his spirit by the former prophets: therefore came a great wrath from the Becoming-One of hosts.

13 Therefore it is come to pass, that as he cried, and they would not hear; so they cried, and I would not hear, says the Becoming-One of hosts:

14 But I scattered them with a whirlwind among all the nations whom they knew not. Thus the land was desolate after them, that no man passed through nor returned: for they laid the pleasant land desolate.

Zech 8:1 Again the word of the Becoming-One of hosts came to me, saying,

2 Thus says the Becoming-One of hosts; I was jealous for Zion with great jealousy, and I was jealous for her with great fury.

3 Thus says the Becoming-One; I am returned unto Zion, and will dwell in the midst of Jerusalem: and Jerusalem shall be called a city of truth; and the mountain of the Becoming-One of hosts the holy mountain.

4 Thus says the Becoming-One of hosts; There shall yet old men and old women dwell in the streets of Jerusalem, and every man with his staff in his hand for multitude of days.

5 And the streets of the city shall be full of boys and girls playing in the streets thereof.

6 Thus says the Becoming-One of hosts; If it be marvelous in the eyes of the remnant of this people in these days, should it also be marvelous in mine eyes? says the Becoming-One of hosts.

7 Thus says the Becoming-One of hosts; Behold, I will save my people from the east country, and from the west country;

8 And I will bring them, and they shall dwell in the midst of Jerusalem: and they shall be my people, and I will be their God, in truth and in righteousness.

9 Thus says the Becoming-One of hosts; Let your hands be strong, you that hear in these days these words by the mouth of the prophets, which were in the day that the foundation of the house of the Becoming-One of hosts was laid, that the temple might be built.

10 For before these days there was no hire for man, nor any hire for beast; neither was there any peace to him that went out or came in because of the affliction: for I set all men every one against his neighbor.

11 But now I will not be unto the residue of this people as in the former days, says the Becoming-One of hosts.

12 For the seed shall be prosperous; the vine shall give her fruit, and the ground shall give her increase,

and the heavens shall give their dew; and I will cause the remnant of this people to possess all these things.

13 And it shall come to pass, that as you were a curse among the nations, O house of Judah, and house of Israel; so will I save you, and you shall be a blessing: fear not, but let your hands be strong.

14 For thus says the Becoming-One of hosts; As I thought to punish you, when your fathers provoked me to wrath, says the Becoming-One of hosts, and I repented not:

15 So again have I thought in these days to do well unto Jerusalem and to the house of Judah: fear you not.

16 These are the things that you shall do; Speak you every man the truth to his neighbor; execute the judgment of truth and peace in your gates:

17 And let none of you imagine evil in your hearts against his neighbor; and love no false oath: for all these are things that I hate, says the Becoming-One.

18 And the word of the Becoming-One of hosts came unto me, saying,

19 Thus says the Becoming-One of hosts; The fast of the fourth month, and the fast of the fifth, and the fast of the seventh, and the fast of the tenth, shall be to the house of Judah joy and gladness, and cheerful set times;[175] therefore love the truth and peace.

20 Thus says the Becoming-One of hosts; It shall yet come to pass, that there shall come people, and the inhabitants of many cities:

21 And the inhabitants of one city shall go to another, saying, Let us go speedily to pray before the Becoming-One, and to seek the Becoming-One of hosts: I will go also.

22 Yes, many people and strong nations shall come to seek the Becoming-One of hosts in Jerusalem, and to pray before the Becoming-One.

23 Thus says the Becoming-One of hosts; In those days it shall come to pass, that ten men shall take hold out of all languages of the nations, even shall take hold of the skirt of him that is a Jew, saying, We will go with you: for we have heard that God is with you.

Zech 9:1 The burden of the word of the Becoming-One in the land of Hadrach, and Damascus shall be the rest thereof: when the eyes of man, as of all the tribes of Israel, shall be toward the Becoming-One.

2 And Hamath also shall border thereby; Tyrus, and Zidon, though it be very wise.

3 And Tyrus did build herself a strong hold, and heaped up silver as the dust, and fine gold as the mire of the streets.

4 Behold, my Lord(s) will strip her, and he will hurl her wealth into the sea; and she shall be devoured with fire.

5 Ashkelon shall see it, and fear; Gaza also shall see it, and be very sorrowful, and Ekron; for her expectation shall be ashamed; and the king shall perish from Gaza, and Ashkelon shall not be inhabited.

6 And a bastard shall dwell in Ashdod, and I will cut off the pride of the Philistines.

7 And I will take away his blood out of his mouth, and his abominations from between his teeth: but he that remains, even he, shall be for our God, and he shall be as a governor in Judah, and Ekron as a Jebusite.

8 And I will encamp about mine house because of the army, because of him that passes by, and because of him that returns: and no oppressor shall pass through them any more: for now have I seen with mine eyes.

9 Rejoice greatly, O daughter of Zion; shout, O daughter of Jerusalem: behold, your King comes unto you: he is just, and having salvation; lowly, and riding upon an donkey, and upon a colt the foal of an donkey.

10 And I will cut off the chariot from Ephraim, and the horse from Jerusalem, and the battle bow shall be cut off: and he shall speak peace unto the nations: and his dominion shall be from sea even to sea, and from the river even to the ends of the earth.

11 As for you also, by the blood of your covenant I have sent forth your prisoners out of the pit wherein is no water.

12 Turn you to the strong hold, you prisoners of hope: even today do I declare that I will render double unto you;

13 When I have bent Judah for me, filled the bow with Ephraim, and raised up your sons, O Zion, against your sons, O Greece, and made you as the sword of a mighty man.

14 And the Becoming-One shall be seen over them, and his arrow shall go forth as the lightning: and my Lord(s), the Becoming-One, shall blow the trumpet, and shall go with whirlwinds of the south.

15 The Becoming-One of hosts shall defend them; and they shall devour, and subdue with sling stones; and they shall drink, and make a noise as through wine; and they shall be filled like bowls, and as the corners of the altar.

16 And the Becoming-One their God shall save them in that day as the flock of his people: for they shall be as the stones of a crown, lifted up as an ensign upon his land.

17 For how great is his goodness, and how great is his beauty! grain shall make the young men cheerful, and new wine the maids.

Zech 10:1 Ask you of the Becoming-One rain in the time of the latter rain; so the Becoming-One shall make bright clouds, and give them showers of rain, to every one grass in the field.

2 For the idols [teraphim] have spoken vanity, and the diviners have seen a lie, and have told false dreams; they comfort in vain: therefore they went their way as a flock, they were troubled, because there was no shepherd.

3 Mine anger was kindled against the shepherds, and I punished the goats: for the Becoming-One of hosts has visited his flock the house of Judah, and has made them as his goodly horse in the battle.

4 Out of him came forth the corner, out of him the nail, out of him the battle bow, out of him every oppressor together.

5 And they shall be as mighty men, which tread down their enemies in the mire of the streets in the battle: and they shall fight, because the Becoming-One

---

[175] Appointed times or festivals

is with them, and the riders on horses shall be confounded.

6 And I will strengthen the house of Judah, and I will save the house of Joseph, and I will bring them again to place them; for I have mercy upon them: and they shall be as though I had not cast them off: for I am the Becoming-One their God, and will hear them.

7 And they of Ephraim shall be like a mighty man, and their heart shall rejoice as through wine: yes, their children shall see it, and be glad; their heart shall rejoice in the Becoming-One.

8 I will hiss for them, and gather them; for I have redeemed them: and they shall increase as they have increased.

9 And I will sow them among the people: and they shall remember me in far countries; and they shall live with their children, and turn again.

10 I will bring them again also out of the land of Egypt, and gather them out of Assyria; and I will bring them into the land of Gilead and Lebanon; and place shall not be found for them.

11 And he shall pass through the sea with affliction, and shall smite the waves in the sea, and all the deeps of the river shall dry up: and the pride of Assyria shall be brought down, and the scepter of Egypt shall depart away.

12 And I will strengthen them in the Becoming-One; and they shall walk up and down in his name, says the Becoming-One.

Zech 11:1 Open your doors, O Lebanon, that the fire may devour your cedars.

2 Howl, fir tree; for the cedar is fallen; because the mighty are spoiled: howl, O you oaks of Bashan; for the forest of the vintage is come down.

3 There is a voice of the howling of the shepherds; for their glory is spoiled: a voice of the roaring of young lions; for the pride of Jordan is spoiled.

4 Thus says the Becoming-One my God; Feed the flock of the slaughter;

5 Whose possessors slay them, and hold themselves not guilty: and they that sell them say, Blessed be the Becoming-One; for I am rich: and their own shepherds pity them not.

6 For I will no more pity the inhabitants of the land, says the Becoming-One: but, lo, I will deliver the men every one into his neighbor's hand, and into the hand of his king: and they shall smite the land, and out of their hand I will not deliver them.

7 And I will feed the flock of slaughter, even you, O poor of the flock. And I took unto me two staves; the one I called Beauty, and the other I called Bands; and I fed the flock.

8 Three shepherds also I cut off in one month; and my soul loathed them, and their soul also abhorred me.

9 Then said I, I will not feed you: that that dies, let it die; and that that is to be cut off, let it be cut off; and let the rest eat every one the flesh of another.

10 And I took my staff, even Beauty, and cut it asunder, that I might break my covenant which I had made with all the people.

11 And it was broken in that day: and so the poor of the flock that waited upon me knew that it was the word of the Becoming-One.

12 And I said unto them, If you think good, give me my price; and if not, forbear. So they weighed for my price thirty pieces of silver.

13 And the Becoming-One said unto me, Cast it unto the potter: the glorious appraised price that I was appraised at by them. And I took the thirty pieces of silver, and cast them in the house of the Becoming-One unto [as to a goal] the potter.

14 Then I cut asunder mine other staff, even Bands, that I might break the brotherhood between Judah and Israel.

15 And the Becoming-One said unto me, Take unto you yet the instruments of a foolish shepherd.

16 For, lo, I will raise up a shepherd in the land, which shall not visit those that be cut off, neither shall seek the young one, nor heal that that is broken, nor feed that that stands still: but he shall eat the flesh of the fat, and tear their claws in pieces.

17 Woe to the idol shepherd that leaves the flock! the sword shall be upon his arm, and upon his right eye: his arm shall be clean dried up, and his right eye shall be utterly darkened.

Zech 12:1 The burden of the word of the Becoming-One for Israel, says the Becoming-One, which stretches forth the heavens, and lays the foundation of the earth, and forms the spirit of man within him.

2 Behold, I will make Jerusalem a cup of trembling unto all the people round about, when they shall be in the siege both against Judah and against Jerusalem.

3 And in that day will I make Jerusalem a burdensome stone for all people: all that burden themselves with it shall be cut in pieces, though all the people of the earth be gathered together against it.

4 In that day, says the Becoming-One, I will smite every horse with astonishment, and his rider with madness: and I will open mine eyes upon the house of Judah, and will smite every horse of the people with blindness.

5 And the governors of Judah shall say in their heart, The inhabitants of Jerusalem shall be my strength in the Becoming-One of hosts their God.

6 In that day will I make the governors of Judah like a hearth of fire among the wood, and like a torch of fire in a sheaf; and they shall devour all the people round about, on the right hand and on the left: and Jerusalem shall be inhabited again in her own place, even in Jerusalem.

7 The Becoming-One also shall save the tents of Judah first, that the glory of the house of David and the glory of the inhabitants of Jerusalem do not magnify themselves against Judah.

8 In that day shall the Becoming-One defend the inhabitants of Jerusalem; and he that is feeble among them at that day shall be as David; and the house of David shall be as God, as the angel of the Becoming-One before them.

9 And it shall come to pass in that day, that I will seek to destroy all the nations that come against Jerusalem.

10 And I will pour upon the house of David, and upon the inhabitants of Jerusalem, the spirit of grace and of supplications: and they shall look upon me whom they have pierced, and they shall mourn for him, as one mourns for his only son, and shall be in

bitterness for him, as one that is in bitterness for his firstborn.

11 In that day shall there be a great mourning in Jerusalem, as the mourning of Hadad-rimmon in the valley of Megiddon.

12 And the land shall mourn, every family apart; the family of the house of David apart, and their wives apart; the family of the house of Nathan apart, and their wives apart;

13 The family of the house of Levi apart, and their wives apart; the family of Shimei apart, and their wives apart;

14 All the families that remain, every family apart, and their wives apart.

Zech 13:1 In that day there shall be a fountain opened to the house of David and to the inhabitants of Jerusalem for sin and for uncleanness.

2 And it shall come to pass in that day, says the Becoming-One of hosts, that I will cut off the names of the idols out of the land, and they shall no more be remembered: and also I will cause the prophets and the unclean spirit to pass out of the land.

3 And it shall come to pass, that when any shall yet prophesy, then his father and his mother that begat him shall say unto him, you shall not live; for you speak lies in the name of the Becoming-One: and his father and his mother that begat him shall thrust him through when he prophesies.

4 And it shall come to pass in that day, that the prophets shall be ashamed every one of his vision, when he has prophesied; neither shall they wear a rough garment to deceive:

5 But he shall say, I am no prophet, I am a husbandman; for man taught me to keep cattle from my youth.

6 And one shall say unto him, What are these wounds in your hands? Then he shall answer, Those with which I was wounded in the house of my friends.

7 Awake, O sword, against my shepherd, and against the man that is my neighbor, says the Becoming-One of hosts: smite the shepherd, and the sheep shall be scattered: and I will turn mine hand upon the little ones.

8 And it shall come to pass, that in all the land, says the Becoming-One, two parts therein shall be cut off and die; but the third shall be left therein.

9 And I will bring the third part through the fire, and will refine them as silver is refined, and will try them as gold is tried: they shall call on my name, and I will hear them: I will say, It is my people: and they shall say, The Becoming-One is my God.

Zech 14:1 Behold, the day of the Becoming-One comes, and your spoil shall be divided in the midst of you.

2 For I will gather all nations against Jerusalem to battle; and the city shall be taken, and the houses rifled, and the women ravished; and half of the city shall go forth into captivity, and the residue of the people shall not be cut off from the city.

3 Then shall the Becoming-One go forth, and fight against those nations, as when he fought in the day of battle.

4 And his feet shall stand in that day upon the mount of Olives, which is before Jerusalem on the east, and the mount of Olives shall cleave in the midst thereof toward the east and toward the west, and there shall be a very great valley; and half of the mountain shall remove toward the north, and half of it toward the south.

5 And you shall flee to the valley of the mountains; for the valley of the mountains shall reach unto Azal: yes, you shall flee, like as you fled from before the earthquake in the days of Uzziah king of Judah: and the Becoming-One my God shall come, and all the saints with you.

6 And it shall come to pass in that day, that the light shall not be clear, nor dark:

7 But it shall be one day which shall be known to the Becoming-One, not day, nor night: but it shall come to pass, that at evening time it shall be light.

8 And it shall be in that day, that living waters shall go out from Jerusalem; half of them toward the former sea, and half of them toward the hinder sea: in summer and in winter shall it be.

9 And the Becoming-One shall be king over all the earth: in that day shall there be one Becoming-One, and his name one.

10 All the land shall be turned as a plain from Geba to Rimmon south of Jerusalem: and it shall be lifted up, and inhabited in her place, from Benjamin's gate unto the place of the first gate, unto the corner gate, and from the tower of Hananeel unto the king's winepresses.

11 And men shall dwell in it, and there shall be no more utter destruction; but Jerusalem shall be safely inhabited.

12 And this shall be the plague wherewith the Becoming-One will smite all the people that have fought against Jerusalem; Their flesh shall consume away while they stand upon their feet, and their eyes shall consume away in their holes, and their tongue shall consume away in their mouth.

13 And it shall come to pass in that day, that a great tumult from the Becoming-One shall be among them; and they shall lay hold every one on the hand of his neighbor, and his hand shall rise up against the hand of his neighbor.

14 And Judah also shall fight at Jerusalem; and the wealth of all the nations round about shall be gathered together, gold, and silver, and apparel, in great abundance.

15 And so shall be the plague of the horse, of the mule, of the camel, and of the donkey, and of all the beasts that shall be in these tents, as this plague.

16 And it shall come to pass, that every one that is left of all the nations which came against Jerusalem shall even go up from year to year to worship the King, the Becoming-One of hosts, and to keep the feast of tabernacles.

17 And it shall be, that whoso will not come up of all the families of the earth unto Jerusalem to worship the King, the Becoming-One of hosts, even upon them shall be no rain.

18 And if the family of Egypt go not up, and come not, that have no rain; there shall be the plague, wherewith the Becoming-One will smite the nations that come not up to keep the feast of tabernacles.

19 This shall be the punishment of Egypt, and the punishment of all nations that come not up to keep the feast of tabernacles.

20 In that day shall there be upon the bells of the horses, Holiness unto the Becoming-One; and the pots in the Becoming-One's house shall be like the bowls before the altar.

21 Yes, every pot in Jerusalem and in Judah shall be holiness unto the Becoming-One of hosts: and all they that sacrifice shall come and take of them, and boil therein: and in that day there shall be no more the Canaanite in the house of the Becoming-One of hosts.

Malachi

Mal 1:1 The burden of the word of the Becoming-One to Israel by Malachi.

2 I have loved you, says the Becoming-One. Yet you say, Wherein have you loved us? Was not Esau Jacob's brother? says the Becoming-One: yet I loved Jacob,

3 And I hated Esau, and laid his mountains and his heritage waste for the monsters of the wilderness.

4 Whereas Edom says, We are impoverished, but we will return and build the desolate places; thus says the Becoming-One of hosts, They shall build, but I will throw down; and they shall call them, The border of wickedness, and, The people against whom the Becoming-One has indignation for olam.

5 And your eyes shall see, and you shall say, The Becoming-One will be magnified from the border of Israel.

6 A son honors his father, and a servant his master: if then I be a father, where is mine honor? and if I be a master, where is my fear? says the Becoming-One of hosts unto you, O priests, that despise my name. And you say, Wherein have we despised your name?

7 you offer polluted bread upon mine altar; and you say, Wherein have we polluted you? In that you say, The table of the Becoming-One is contemptible.

8 And if you offer the blind for sacrifice, is it not evil? and if you offer the lame and sick, is it not evil? offer it now unto your governor; will he be pleased with you, or accept your person? says the Becoming-One of hosts.

9 And now, I pray you, beseech GOD that he will be gracious unto us: this has been by your means: will he regard your persons? says the Becoming-One of hosts.

10 Who is there even among you that would shut the doors for nothing? neither do you kindle fire on mine altar for nothing. I have no pleasure in you, says the Becoming-One of hosts, neither will I accept an offering at your hand.

11 For from the rising of the sun even unto the going down of the same my name shall be great among the nations; and in every place incense shall be offered unto my name, and a pure offering: for my name shall be great among the nations, says the Becoming-One of hosts.

12 But you have profaned it, in that you say, The table of the Becoming-One is polluted; and the fruit thereof, even his food, is contemptible.

13 you said also, Behold, what a weariness is it! and you have snuffed at it, says the Becoming-One of hosts; and you brought that which was torn, and the lame, and the sick; thus you brought an offering: should I accept this of your hand? says the Becoming-One.

14 But cursed be the deceiver, which has in his flock a male, and vows, and sacrifices unto my Lord(s) a corrupt thing: for I am a great King, says the Becoming-One of hosts, and my name is dreadful among the nations.

Mal 2:1 And now, O you priests, this commandment is for you.

2 If you will not hear, and if you will not lay it to heart, to give glory unto my name, says the Becoming-One of hosts, I will even send a curse upon you, and I will curse your blessings: yes, I have cursed them already, because you do not lay it to heart.

3 Behold, I will corrupt your seed, and spread dung upon your faces, even the dung of your solemn feasts; and one shall take you away with it.

4 And you shall know that I have sent this commandment unto you, that my covenant might be with Levi, says the Becoming-One of hosts.

5 My covenant was with him of life and peace; and I gave them to him for the fear wherewith he feared me, and was afraid before my name.

6 The law of truth was in his mouth, and iniquity was not found in his lips: he walked with me in peace and equity, and did turn many away from iniquity.

7 For the priest's lips should keep knowledge, and they should seek the law at his mouth: for he is the messenger of the Becoming-One of hosts.

8 But you are departed out of the way; you have caused many to stumble at the law; you have corrupted the covenant of Levi, says the Becoming-One of hosts.

9 Therefore have I also made you contemptible and base before all the people, according as you have not kept my ways, but have been partial in the law.

10 Have we not all one father? has not one GOD created us? why do we deal treacherously every man against his brother, by profaning the covenant of our fathers?

11 Judah has dealt treacherously, and an abomination is committed in Israel and in Jerusalem; for Judah has profaned the holiness of the Becoming-One which he loved, and has married the daughter of a strange god.

12 The Becoming-One will cut off the man that did this, the master and the scholar, out of the tabernacles of Jacob, and him that offers an offering unto the Becoming-One of hosts.

13 And this have you done again, covering the altar of the Becoming-One with tears, with weeping, and with crying out, insomuch that he regards not the offering any more, or receives it with good will at your hand.

14 Yet you say, Why? Because the Becoming-One has been witness between you and the wife of your youth, against whom you have dealt treacherously: yet is she your companion, and the wife of your covenant.

15 And did not he make one? Yet had he the residue of the spirit. And why one? That he might seek a godly seed. Therefore take heed to your spirit, and let none deal treacherously against the wife of his youth.

16 For the Becoming-One, God of Israel, says that he hates putting away: for one covers violence with his garment, says the Becoming-One of hosts: therefore take heed to your spirit, that you deal not treacherously.

17 you have wearied the Becoming-One with your words. Yet you say, Wherein have we wearied him? When you say, Every one that did evil is good in the sight of the Becoming-One, and he delights in them; or, Where is God of judgment?

Mal 3:1 Behold, I will send my messenger, and he shall prepare the way before me: and the Lord, whom you seek, shall suddenly come to his temple, even the messenger of the covenant, whom you delight in: behold, he shall come, says the Becoming-One of hosts.

2 But who may abide the day of his coming? and who shall stand when he appears? for he is like a refiner's fire, and like fullers' soap:

3 And he shall sit as a refiner and purifier of silver: and he shall purify the sons of Levi, and purge them as gold and silver, that they may offer unto the Becoming-One an offering in righteousness.

4 Then shall the offering of Judah and Jerusalem be pleasant unto the Becoming-One, as in the days of olam, and as in former years.

5 And I will come near to you to judgment; and I will be a swift witness against the sorcerers, and against the adulterers, and against false swearers, and against those that oppress the hireling in his wages, the widow, and the fatherless, and that turn aside the stranger from his right, and fear not me, says the Becoming-One of hosts.

6 For I am the Becoming-One, I change not;[176] therefore you sons of Jacob are not destroyed.

7 Even from the days of your fathers you are gone away from mine ordinances, and have not kept them. Return unto me, and I will return unto you, says the Becoming-One of hosts. But you said, Wherein shall we return?

8 Will a man rob God? Yet you have robbed me. But you say, Wherein have we robbed you? In tithes and offerings.

9 you are cursed with a curse: for you have robbed me, even this whole nation.

10 Bring you all the tithes into the storehouse, that there may be food in mine house, and prove me now herewith, says the Becoming-One of hosts, if I will not open you the windows of heaven, and pour you out a blessing, that there shall not be room enough to receive it.

11 And I will rebuke the devourer for your sakes, and he shall not destroy the fruits of your ground; neither shall your vine cast her fruit before the time in the field, says the Becoming-One of hosts.

12 And all nations shall call you blessed: for you shall be a delightful land, says the Becoming-One of hosts.

13 Your words have been stout against me, says the Becoming-One. Yet you say, What have we spoken so much against you?

14 you have said, It is vain to serve God: and what profit is it that we have kept his ordinance, and that we have walked mournfully before the Becoming-One of hosts?

15 And now we call the proud happy; yes, they that work wickedness are set up; yes, they that tempt God are even delivered.

16 Then they that feared the Becoming-One spoke often one to another: and the Becoming-One listened, and heard it, and a book of remembrance was written before him for them that feared the Becoming-One, and that thought upon his name.

17 And they shall be mine, says the Becoming-One of hosts, in that day when I make up my treasure; and I will spare them, as a man spares his own son that serves him.

18 Then shall you return, and discern between the righteous and the wicked, between him that serves God and him that serves him not.

Mal 4:1 For, behold, the day comes, that shall burn as an oven; and all the proud, yes, and all that do wickedly, shall be stubble: and the day that comes shall burn them up, says the Becoming-One of hosts, that it shall leave them neither root nor branch.

2 But unto you that fear my name shall the Sun of righteousness arise with healing in his wings; and you shall go forth, and grow up as calves of the stall.

3 And you shall tread down the wicked; for they shall be ashes under the soles of your feet in the day that I shall do this, says the Becoming-One of hosts.

4 Remember you the law of Moses my servant, which I commanded unto him in Horeb for all Israel, with the statutes and judgments.

5 Behold, I will send you Elijah the prophet before the coming of the great and dreadful day of the Becoming-One: 6 And he shall turn the heart of the fathers to the children, and the heart of the children to their fathers, lest I come and smite the earth with a curse.

---

[176] His words are not changed (Psa 89:35ff), therefore Israel's seed is not destroyed (Jer 31:36-37)

Becoming-One Bible

New Testament
3rd Edition

An English Translation
of the
Holy Scriptures

Translated

by

Walter R. Dolen

Matthew

Mat 1:1 Book of the generation of Jesus Christ, Son of David, Son of Abraham.

2 Abraham begat Isaac; and Isaac begat Jacob, and Jacob begat Judah and his brethren;

3 and Judah begat Perez and Zerah of Tamar; and Perez begat Hezron, and Hezron begat Ram,

4 and Ram begat Amminadab, and Amminadab begat Nahshon, and Nahshon begat Salmon,

5 and Salmon begat Boaz of Rachab; and Boaz begat Obed of Ruth; and Obed begat Jesse,

6 and Jesse begat David the king. And David begat Solomon, of her [that had been the wife] of Uriah;

7 and Solomon begat Rehoboam, and Rehoboam begat Abijah, and Abijah begat Asa,

8 and Asa begat Jehoshaphat, and Jehoshaphat begat Joram, and Joram begat Uzziah,

9 and Uzziah begat Jotham, and Jotham begat Ahaz, and Ahaz begat Hezekiah,

10 and Hezekiah begat Manasseh, and Manasseh begat Amon, and Amon begat Josiah,

11 and Josiah begat Jeconiah and his brethren, at the time of the carrying away of Babylon.

12 **And after the carrying away of Babylon**, Jeconiah begat Shealtiel, and Shealtiel begat Zerubbabel,

13 and Zerubbabel begat Abiud, and Abiud begat Eliakim, and Eliakim begat Azor,

14 and Azor begat Zadok, and Zadok begat Akim, and Akim begat Eliud,

15 and Eliud begat Eleazar, and Eleazar begat Matthan, and Matthan begat Jacob,

16 and Jacob begat Joseph, the **father** [see Heb.] of Mary,[177] of whom was born Jesus, who is called Christ.[178]

17 All the generations, therefore, from Abraham to David [were] *fourteen* generations; and from David until the carrying away of Babylon, *fourteen* generations; **and from the carrying away of Babylon unto the Christ,** *fourteen* **generations**.

18 Now the birth of Jesus Christ was thus: His mother, Mary, that is, having been betrothed to Joseph, before they came together, she was found to be with child of the Holy Spirit.

19 But Joseph, her husband, being a righteous [man] and unwilling to expose her publicly, purposed to have put her away secretly;

20 but while he pondered on these things, behold, an angel of the Lord appeared to him in a dream, saying, Joseph, son of David, fear not to take to [you] Mary, your wife, for that which is begotten in her is of the Holy Spirit.

21 And she shall bring forth a son, and you shall call his name Jesus, for he shall save his people from their sins.

22 Now all this came to pass that that might be fulfilled which was spoken by the Lord, through the prophet, saying,

23 Behold, the virgin shall be with child, and shall bring forth a son, and they shall call his name Emmanuel, which is, being interpreted, 'the God with us.'

24 But Joseph, having awoke up from his sleep, did as the angel of the Lord had commanded him, and took to him his wife,

25 and knew her not until she had brought forth her firstborn son: and he called his name Jesus. **[7-6 BC]**

Mat 2:1 Now Jesus having been born in Bethlehem of Judea, in the days of Herod the king, behold magi from the east arrived at Jerusalem, saying,

2 Where is the king of the Jews that has been born? for we have seen his star in the east, and have come to do him homage.

3 But Herod the king having heard [of it] was troubled, and all Jerusalem with him;

4 and, assembling all the chief priests and scribes of the people, he inquired of them where the Christ should be born.

5 And they said to him, In Bethlehem of Judea; for thus it is written through the prophet:

6 And you Bethlehem, land of Judah, are in no way the least among the governors of Judah; for out of you shall go forth a leader who shall shepherd my people Israel.

7 Then Herod, having secretly called the magi, inquired of them accurately the time of the star that was appearing;

8 and having sent them to Bethlehem, said, Go, search out accurately concerning the child, and when you shall have found him, bring me back word, so that I also may come and do him homage.

9 And they having heard the king went their way; and lo, the star, which they had seen in the east, went before them until it came and stood over the place where the little child was.

10 And when they saw the star they rejoiced with exceeding great joy.

11 And having come into the house they saw the little child with Mary his mother, and falling down did him homage. And having opened their treasures, they offered to him gifts, gold, and frankincense, and myrrh.

12 And being divinely instructed in a dream not to return to Herod, they departed into their own country another way.

13 Now, they having departed, behold, an angel of the Lord appears in a dream to Joseph, saying, Arise, take to [you] the little child and his mother, and flee into Egypt, and be there until I shall tell you; for Herod will seek the little child to destroy it.

14 And, having arisen, he took to him the little child and his mother by night, and departed into Egypt.

15 And he was there until the death of Herod, that that might be fulfilled which was spoken by the

---

[177] Mary + Angel of God = 13th; Jesus = 14th generation

[178] Two Josephs: one the husband of Mary; one the father of Mary; see Hebrew texts found by Nehemia Gordon

Lord through the prophet, saying, Out of Egypt have I called my son.

16 Then Herod, seeing that he had been mocked by the magi, was greatly enraged; and sent and killed all the boys which [were] in Bethlehem, and in all its borders, from two years and under, according to the time which he had accurately inquired from the magi.

17 Then was fulfilled that which was spoken through Jeremiah the prophet, saying,

18 A voice has been heard in Rama, weeping, and great lamentation: Rachel weeping [for] her children, and would not be comforted, because they are not.

19 But Herod having died, behold, an angel of the Lord appears in a dream to Joseph in Egypt, saying,

20 Arise, take to [you] the little child and its mother, and go into the land of Israel: for they who sought the soul of the little child are dead.

21 And he arose and took to him the little child and its mother, and came into the land of Israel;

22 but having heard that 'Archelaus reigns over Judea, instead of Herod his father', he was afraid to go there; and having been divinely instructed in a dream, he went away into the parts of Galilee,

23 and came and dwelt in a town called Nazareth; so that that should be fulfilled which was spoken through the prophets, He shall be called a Nazaraene.

Mat 3:1 Now in those days comes John the Baptist, preaching in the wilderness of Judea,

2 and saying, Repent, for the kingdom of the heavens has drawn near.

3 For this is he who has been spoken of through Isaiah the prophet, saying, Voice of him that cries in the wilderness: prepare you the way of the Lord, make straight his paths.

4 And John himself had his garment of camel's hair, and a leathern girdle about his loins, and his nourishment was locusts and wild honey.

5 Then went out to him Jerusalem, and all Judea, and all the country round the Jordan,

6 and were baptized by him in the Jordan, acknowledging their sins.

7 But seeing many of the Pharisees and Sadducees coming to his baptism, he said to them, Offspring of vipers, who has forewarned you to flee from the coming wrath?

8 Produce therefore fruit worthy of repentance.

9 And do not think to say within yourselves, We have Abraham for [our] father; for I say unto you, that the God is able of these stones to raise up children to Abraham.

10 And already the axe is applied to the root of the trees; every tree therefore not producing good fruit is cut down and cast into the fire.

11 I indeed baptize you with water to repentance, but he that comes after me is mightier than I, whose sandals I am not fit to bear; he shall baptize you with the Holy Spirit and fire;

12 whose winnowing fan is in his hand, and he shall thoroughly purge his threshing-floor, and shall gather his wheat into the garner, but the chaff he will burn with fire unquenchable.

13 Then comes Jesus from Galilee to the Jordan to John, to be baptized of him;

14 but John urgently forbade him, saying, I have need to be baptized of you; and you come to me?

15 But Jesus answering said to him, Permit it now; for thus it becomes us to fulfil all righteousness. Then he permits him.

16 And Jesus, having been baptized, went up straightway from the water, and lo, the heavens were opened to him, and he saw the Spirit of the God descending as a dove, and coming upon him:

17 and behold, a voice out of the heavens saying, This is my beloved Son, in whom I have found my delight.

Mat 4:1 Then Jesus was carried up into the wilderness by the Spirit to be tempted of the devil,

2 and having fasted forty days and forty nights, afterwards he hungered.

3 And the tempter coming up to him said, If you be Son of the God, speak, that these stones may become loaves of bread.

4 But he answering said, It is written, Man shall not live by bread alone, but by every word which goes out through God's mouth.

5 Then the devil takes him to the holy city, and sets him upon the edge of the temple,

6 and says to him, If you be Son of the God cast thyself down; for it is written, He shall give charge to his angels concerning you, and on [their] hands shall they bear you, lest in anyway you strike your foot against a stone.

7 Jesus said to him, It is again written, You shall not tempt the Lord the God of you.

8 Again the devil takes him to a very high mountain, and shows him all the kingdoms of the world, and their glory,

9 and says to him, All these things will I give you if, falling down, you will do me homage.

10 Then says Jesus to him, Get you away, Satan, for it is written, You shall do homage to the Lord the God of you, and him alone shall you serve.

11 Then the devil leaves him, and behold, angels came and ministered to him.

12 But having heard that John was delivered up, he departed into Galilee:

13 and having left Nazareth, he went and dwelt at Capernaum, which is on the sea-side in the borders of Zabulon and Nepthalim,

14 that that might be fulfilled which was spoken through Isaiah the prophet, saying,

15 Land of Zabulon and land of Nepthalim, way of the sea beyond the Jordan, Galilee of the nations:

16 --the people sitting in darkness has seen a great light, and to those sitting in the country and shadow of death, to them has light sprung up.

17 From that time began Jesus to preach and to say, Repent, for the kingdom of the heavens has drawn near.

18 And walking by the sea of Galilee, he saw two brothers, Simon called Peter, and Andrew his brother, casting a net into the sea, for they were fishermen;

19 and he says to them, Come after me, and I will make you fishermen of men.

20 And they, having left their trawl-nets, immediately followed him.

21 And going on from there he saw other two brothers, James the [son] of Zebedee and John his brother, in the ship with Zebedee their father, mending their trawl-nets, and he called them;

22 and they, having left the ship and their father, immediately followed him.

23 And [Jesus] went round the whole of Galilee, teaching in their synagogues, and preaching the good news of the kingdom, and healing every disease and every bodily weakness among the people.

24 And his fame went out into the whole of Syria, and they brought to him all that were ill, suffering under various diseases and pains, and those possessed by daemons, and lunatics, and paralytics; and he healed them.

25 And great crowds followed him from Galilee, and Decapolis, and Jerusalem, and Judea, and beyond the Jordan.

Mat 5:1 But seeing the crowds, he went up into the mountain, and having sat down, his disciples came to him;

2 and, having opened his mouth, he taught them, saying,

3 Blessed [are] the poor in spirit, for theirs is the kingdom of the heavens.

4 Blessed they that mourn, for they shall be comforted.

5 Blessed the meek, for they shall inherit the earth.

6 Blessed they who hunger and thirst after righteousness, for they shall be filled.

7 Blessed the merciful, for they shall find mercy.

8 Blessed the pure in heart, for they shall see the God.

9 Blessed the peace-makers, for they shall be called sons of God.

10 Blessed they who are persecuted on account of righteousness, for theirs is the kingdom of the heavens.

11 Blessed are you when they may reproach and persecute you, and say every wicked thing against you, lying, for my sake.

12 Rejoice and exult, for your reward is great in the heavens; for thus have they persecuted the prophets who were before you.

13 You are the salt of the earth; but if the salt have become insipid, wherewith shall it be salted? It is no longer fit for anything but to be cast out and to be trodden under foot by men.

14 You are the light of the world: a city situated on the top of a mountain cannot be hid.

15 Nor do [men] light a lamp and put it under the bushel, but upon the lamp-stand, and it shines for all who are in the house.

16 Let your light thus shine before men, so that they may see your upright works, and glorify your Father who is in the heavens.

17 Think not that I am come to make void the law or the prophets; I am not come to make void, but to fulfil.[179]

18 For truly I say unto you, Until the heaven and the earth pass away, one iota or one tittle shall in no way pass from the law till all come to pass.

19 Whosoever then shall do away with one of these least commandments, and that I teach[180], shall be called least in the kingdom of the heavens; but whosoever shall practice and teach [them] he shall be called great in the kingdom of the heavens.

20 For I say unto you, that unless your righteousness surpass that of the scribes and Pharisees, you shall in no way enter into the kingdom of the heavens.

21 You have heard that it was said to the ancients, You shall not kill; but whosoever shall kill shall be subject to the judgment.

22 But I say unto you, that every one that is lightly angry with his brother shall be subject to the judgment; but whosoever shall say to his brother, Raca, shall be subject to [be called before] the Sanhedrim; but whosoever shall say, Fool, shall be subject to the penalty of the Gehenna of fire.

23 If therefore you should offer your gift at the altar, and there should remember that your brother has something against you,

24 leave there your gift before the altar, and first go, be reconciled to your brother, and then come and offer your gift.

25 Make friends with your adverse party quickly, while you are in the way with him; lest some time the adverse party deliver you to the judge, and the judge deliver you to the officer, and you be cast into prison.

26 Truly I say to you, You shall in no way come out from there till you have paid the last quarter [quadrans].

27 You have heard that it has been said, You shall not commit adultery.

28 But I say unto you, that every one who looks upon a woman to lust after her has already committed adultery with her in his heart.

29 But if your right eye be a snare to you, pluck it out and cast it from you: for it is profitable for you that one of your members perish, and not your whole body be cast into Gehenna.

30 And if your right hand be a snare to you, cut it off and cast it from you: for it is profitable for you that one of your members perish, and not your whole body be cast into Gehenna.

31 It has been said too, Whosoever shall put away his wife, let him give her a letter of divorce.

---

[179] Greek: complete, to make full
[180] A version found in the Hebrew Matthew, see Mat 28:20; 22:36-40; Mark 12:28-34; John 12:49-50; 13:34; 15:12

32 But I say unto you, that whosoever shall put away his wife, except for cause of fornication, makes her commit adultery, and whosoever marries one that is put away commits adultery.

33 Again, you have heard that it has been said to the ancients, You shall not forswear yourself, but shall render to the Lord what you have sworn.

34 But I say unto you, Do not swear at all; neither by the heaven, because it is the throne of the God;

35 nor by the earth, because it is the footstool of his feet; nor by Jerusalem, because it is the city of the great King.

36 Neither shall you swear by your head, because you can not make one hair white or black.

37 But let your word be Yes, yes; No, no; but what is more than these is from evil.

38 You have heard that it has been said, Eye for eye and tooth for tooth.

39 But I say unto you, not to resist evil; but whoever shall strike you on your right cheek, turn to him also the other;

40 and to him that would go to law with you and take your body coat, leave him your cloak also.

41 And whoever will compel you to go one mile, go with him two.

42 To him that asks of you give, and from him that desires to borrow of you turn not away.

43 You have heard that it has been said, You shall love your neighbor and hate your enemy.

44 But I say unto you, Love your enemies, [bless those who curse you] do good to those who hate you, and pray for those who [insult you and] persecute you,

45 that you may be the sons of your Father who is in the heavens; for he makes his sun rise on evil and good, and sends rain on just and unjust.

46 For if you should love those who love you, what reward have you? Do not also the tax collectors the same?

47 And if you should salute your brethren only, what do you extraordinary? Do not also the pagans the same?

48 Be you therefore perfect as your heavenly Father is perfect.

Mat 6:1 Take heed not to do your alms before men to be seen of them, otherwise you have no reward with your Father who is in the heavens.

2 When therefore you do alms, sound not a trumpet before you, as the hypocrites do in the synagogues and in the streets, so that they may have glory from men. Truly I say unto you, They have their reward.

3 But you, when you do alms, let not your left hand know what your right hand does;

4 so that your alms may be in secret, and your Father who sees in secret will render it to you.

5 And when you pray, you shall not be as the hypocrites; for they like to pray standing in the synagogues and in the corners of the streets so that they should appear to men. Truly I say unto you, They have their reward.

6 But you, when you pray, enter into your chamber, and having shut your door, pray to your Father who is in secret, and your Father who sees in secret will render it to you.

7 But when you pray, use not vain repetitions, as those who are of the pagans: for they think they shall be heard through their much speaking.

8 Be not you therefore like them, for your Father knows of what things you have need before you beg [anything] of him.

9 Thus therefore pray you: Our Father who are in the heavens, let your name be sanctified,

10 let your kingdom come, let your will be done as in heaven so upon the earth;

11 give us today our needed bread,

12 and forgive us our debts, as we also forgive our debtors,

13 and lead us not into temptation, but save us from evil.

14 For if you forgive men their offences, your heavenly Father also will forgive you [yours]

15 but if you do not forgive men their offences, neither will your Father forgive your offences.

16 And when you fast, be not as the hypocrites, downcast in countenance; for they disfigure their faces, so that they may appear fasting to men: truly I say unto you, They have their reward.

17 But you, [when] fasting, anoint your head and wash your face,

18 so that you may not appear fasting unto men, but to your Father who is in secret; and your Father who sees in secret shall render it to you.

19 Lay not up for yourselves treasures upon the earth, where moth and rust spoils, and where thieves dig through and steal;

20 but lay up for yourselves treasures in heaven, where neither moth nor rust spoils, and where thieves do not dig through nor steal;

21 for where your treasure is, there will be also your heart.

22 The lamp of the body is the eye; if therefore your eye be clear, your whole body will be light:

23 but if your eye be wicked, your whole body will be dark. If therefore the light that is in you be darkness, how great the darkness!

24 No one can serve two masters; for either he will hate the one and will love the other, or he will hold to the one and despise the other. You cannot serve God and mammon.

25 For this cause I say unto you, Do not be concerned about your soul, what you should eat and what you should drink; nor for your body what you should put on. Is not the soul more than food, and the body more than clothes?

26 Look at the birds of the heaven, that they sow not, nor reap, nor gather into granaries, and your heavenly Father nourishes them. Are you not much more excellent than they?

27 But which of you by concern can add to his growth one cubit?

28 And why are you concerned about clothing? Observe with attention the lilies of the field, how they grow: they toil not, neither do they spin;

29 but I say unto you, that not even Solomon in all his glory was clothed as one of these.

30 But if the God so clothe the herbage of the field, which is today, and tomorrow is cast into the oven, will he not much rather clothe you, O [you] of little faith?

31 Be not therefore concerned, saying, What shall we eat? or What shall we drink? or What shall we put on?

32 for all these things the nations seek after; for your heavenly Father knows that you have need of all these things.

33 But seek you first the kingdom of the God and his righteousness, and all these things shall be added unto you.

34 Be not concerned therefore for the tomorrow, for the tomorrow shall be concerned about itself. Sufficient to the day is its own evil.

Mat 7:1 Judge not, that you may not be judged;

2 for with the judgment you judge, you shall be judged; and with what measure you measured, it shall be measured to you.

3 But why look you on the straw that is in the eye of your brother, but observe not the log that is in your eye?

4 Or how will you say to your brother, Allow [me] I will cast out the straw from your eye; and behold, the beam is in your eye?

5 Hypocrite, cast out first the beam out of your eye, and then you will see clearly to cast out the straw out of the eye of your brother.

6 Give not that which is holy to the dogs, nor cast your pearls before the swine, lest they trample them with their feet, and turning round rip you.

7 Ask, and it shall be given to you. Seek, and you shall find. Knock, and it shall be opened to you.

8 For every one that asks receives; and he that seeks finds; and to him that knocks it shall be opened.

9 Or what man is there of you who, if his son shall ask of him a loaf of bread, will give him a stone;

10 and if he ask a fish, will give him a serpent?

11 If therefore you, being wicked, know [how] to give good gifts to your children, how much rather shall your Father who is in the heavens give good things to them that ask of him?

12 Therefore all things whatever you desire that men should do to you, thus do you also do to them; for this is the law and the prophets.

13 Enter in through the narrow gate, for wide the gate and broad the way that leads to destruction, and many are they who enter in through it.

14 For narrow the gate and narrow the way that leads to life, and they are few who find it.

15 But beware of false prophets, which come to you in sheep's clothing, but within are ravening wolves.

16 By their fruits you shall know them. Do [men] gather a bunch of grapes from thorns, or from thistles figs?

17 So every good tree produces good fruits, but the worthless tree produces bad fruits.

18 A good tree cannot produce bad fruits, nor a worthless tree produce good fruits.

19 Every tree not producing good fruit is cut down and cast into the fire.

20 By their fruits then surely you shall know them.

21 Not every one who says to me, Lord, Lord, shall enter into the kingdom of the heavens, but he that does the will of my Father who is in the heavens.

22 Many shall say to me in that day, Lord, Lord, have we not prophesied through your name, and through your name cast out daemons, and through your name done many works of power?

23 and then will I avow unto them, I never knew you. Depart from me, workers of lawlessness.

24 Whoever therefore hears these my words and does them, I will liken him to a prudent man, who built his house upon the rock;

25 and the rain came down, and the streams came, and the winds blew and fell upon that house, and it did not fall, for it had been founded upon the rock.

26 And every one who hears these my words and does not do them, he shall be likened to a foolish man, who built his house upon the sand;

27 and the rain came down, and the streams came, and the winds blew and beat upon that house, and it fell, and its fall was great.

28 And it came to pass, when Jesus had finished these words, the crowds were astonished at his doctrine,

29 for he taught them as having authority, and not as their scribes.

Mat 8:1 And when he had come down from the mountain, great crowds followed him.

2 And behold, a leper came up to him and did him homage, saying, Lord, if you will, you are able to cleanse me.

3 And he stretched out his hand and touched him, saying, I will; be cleansed. And immediately his leprosy was cleansed.

4 And Jesus says to him, See you tell no man, but go, show yourself to the priest, and offer the gift which Moses ordained, for a testimony to them.

5 And when he had entered into Capernaum, a centurion came to him, beseeching him,

6 and saying, Lord, my servant lies paralytic in the house, suffering grievously.

7 And Jesus says to him, I will come and heal him.

8 And the centurion answered and said, Lord, I am not fit that you should enter under my roof; but only speak a word, and my servant shall be healed.

9 For I also am a man under authority, having under me soldiers, and I say to this [one] Go, and he goes; and to another, Come, and he comes; and to my servant, Do this, and he does it.

10 And when Jesus heard it, he wondered, and said to those who followed, Truly I say unto you, Not even in Israel have I found so great faith.

11 But I say unto you, that many shall come from the rising and setting [sun] and shall lie down at table with Abraham, and Isaac, and Jacob in the kingdom of the heavens;

12 but the sons of the kingdom shall be cast out into the outer darkness: there shall be the weeping and the gnashing of teeth.

13 And Jesus said to the centurion, Go, and as you have believed, be it to you. And his servant was healed in that hour.

14 And when Jesus had come to Peter's house, he saw his mother-in-law laid down and in a fever;

15 and he touched her hand, and the fever left her, and she arose and served him.

16 And when the evening was come, they brought to him many possessed by daemons, and he cast out the spirits with a word, and healed all that were ill;

17 so that that should be fulfilled which was spoken through Isaiah the prophet, saying, Himself took our infirmities and bore our diseases.

18 And Jesus, seeing great crowds around him, commanded to depart to the other side.

19 And a scribe came up and said to him, Teacher, I will follow you wherever you may go.

20 And Jesus says to him, The foxes have holes, and the birds of the heaven nests; but the Son of man has nowhere he may lay his head.

21 But another of his disciples said to him, Lord, permit me first to go away and bury my father.

22 But Jesus said to him, Follow me, and leave the dead to bury their own dead.

23 And he went on board the ship and his disciples followed him;

24 and behold, [the water] became very agitated on the sea, so that the ship was covered by the waves; but he slept.

25 And the disciples came and awoke him, saying, Lord save: we perish.

26 And he says to them, Why are you fearful, O you of little faith? Then, having arisen, he rebuked the winds and the sea, and there was a great calm.

27 But the men were astonished, saying, What sort [of man] is this, that even the winds and the sea obey him?

28 And there met him, when he came to the other side, to the country of the Gergesenes, two possessed by daemons, coming out of the tombs, exceeding dangerous, so that no one was able to pass by that way.

29 And behold, they cried out, saying, What have we to do with you, Son of the God? have you come here before the time to torment us?

30 Now there was, a great way off from them, a herd of many swine feeding;

31 and the daemons besought him, saying, If you cast us out, send us away into the herd of swine.

32 And he said to them, Go. And they, going out, departed into the herd of swine; and lo, the whole herd [of swine] rushed down the steep slope into the sea, and died in the waters.

33 But they that fed them fled, and went away into the city and related everything, and what had happened as to those possessed by daemons.

34 And behold, the whole city went out to meet Jesus; and when they saw him, they begged him to go away out of their coasts.

Mat 9:1 And going on board the ship, he passed over and came to his own city.

2 And behold, they brought to him a paralytic, laid upon a bed; and Jesus, seeing their faith, said to the paralytic, Be of good courage, child; your sins are forgiven.

3 And behold, certain of the scribes said to themselves, This [man] blasphemes.

4 And Jesus, seeing their thoughts, said, Why do you think evil things in your hearts?

5 For which is easier: to say, Your sins are forgiven; or to say, Rise up and walk?

6 But that you may know that the Son of man has power on earth to forgive sins, then he says to the paralytic, Rise up, take up your bed and go to your house.

7 And he rose up and went to his house.

8 But the crowds seeing it were in fear, and glorified the God who gave such power to men.

9 And Jesus, passing on from there, saw a man sitting at the tax-office, called Matthew, and says to him, Follow me. And he rose up and followed him.

10 And it came to pass, as he lay at table in the house, that behold, many tax-gatherers and sinners came and lay at table with Jesus and his disciples.

11 And the Pharisees seeing it said to his disciples, Why does your teacher eat with tax-gatherers and sinners?

12 But [Jesus] hearing it, said, They that are strong have not need of a physician, but those that are ill.

13 But go and learn what that is --I will have mercy and not sacrifice; for I have not come to call righteous [men] but sinners.

14 Then come to him the disciples of John, saying, Why do we and the Pharisees often fast, but your disciples fast not?

15 And Jesus said to them, Can the sons of the bride chamber mourn so long as the bridegroom is with them? But days will come when the bridegroom will have been taken away from them, and then they will fast.

16 But no one puts a patch of new cloth on an old garment, for its filling up takes from the garment and a worse rent takes place.

17 Nor do men put new wine into old skins, otherwise the skins burst and the wine is poured out, and the skins will be destroyed; but they put new wine into new skins, and both are preserved together.

18 As he spoke these things to them, behold, a ruler coming in did homage to him, saying, My daughter has by now died; but come and lay your hand upon her and she shall live.

19 And Jesus rose up and followed him, and [so did] his disciples.

20 And behold, a woman, who had had a bloody flux [for] twelve years, came behind and touched the hem of his garment;

21 for she said within herself, If I should only touch his garment I shall be healed.

22 But Jesus turning and seeing her, said, Be of good courage, daughter; your faith has healed you. And the woman was healed from that hour.

23 And when Jesus was come to the house of the ruler, and saw the flute-players and the crowd making a tumult,

24 he said, Withdraw, for the damsel is not dead, but sleeps. And they derided him.

25 But when the crowd had been put out, he went in and took her hand; and the damsel rose up.

26 And the fame of it went out into all that land.

27 And as Jesus passed on from there, two blind [men] followed him, crying and saying, Have mercy on us, Son of David.

28 And when he was come to the house, the blind [men] came to him. And Jesus says to them, Do you believe that I am able to do this? They say to him, Yes, Lord.

29 Then he touched their eyes, saying, According to your faith, be it unto you.

30 And their eyes were opened; and Jesus charged them sharply, saying, See, let no man know it.

31 But they, when they were gone out, spread his name abroad in all that land.

32 But as these were going out, behold, they brought to him a mute man possessed by a daemon.

33 And the daemon having been cast out, the mute spoke. And the crowds were astonished, saying, It has never been seen thus in Israel.

34 But the Pharisees said, He casts out the daemons through the prince of the daemons.

35 And Jesus went round all the cities and the villages, teaching in their synagogues, and preaching the good news of the kingdom, and healing every disease and every bodily weakness.

36 But when he saw the crowds he was moved with compassion for them, because they were harassed, and cast away as sheep not having a shepherd.

37 Then says he to his disciples, The harvest is great and the workmen [are] few;

38 supplicate therefore the Lord of the harvest, that he send forth workmen unto his harvest.

Mat 10:1 And having called to him his twelve disciples, he gave them power over unclean spirits, so that they should cast them out, and heal every disease and every bodily weakness.

2 Now the names of the twelve apostles are these: first, Simon, who was called Peter, and Andrew his brother; James the [son] of Zebedee, and John his brother;

3 Philip and Bartholomew; Thomas, and Matthew the tax-gatherer; James the [son] of Alphaeus, and Lebbaeus, who was surnamed Thaddaeus;

4 Simon the Cananaean, and Judas the Iscariote, who also delivered him up.

5 These twelve Jesus sent out when he had charged them, saying, Go not off into the way of the nations, and into a city of Samaritans enter you not;

6 but go rather to the lost sheep of the house of Israel.

7 And as you go, preach, saying, The kingdom of the heavens has drawn near.

8 Heal the infirm, [raise the dead] cleanse lepers, cast out daemons: you have received freely, give freely.

9 Do not provide yourselves with gold, or silver, or brass, for your belts,

10 nor scrip for the way, nor two body coats, nor sandals, nor a staff: for the workman is worthy of his nourishment.

11 But into whatsoever city or village you enter, inquire who in it is worthy, and there remain till you go forth.

12 And as you enter into a house salute it.

13 And if the house indeed be worthy, let your peace come upon it; but if it be not worthy, let your peace return to you.

14 And whosoever shall not receive you, nor hear your words, as you go forth out of that house or city, shake off the dust of your feet.

15 Truly I say unto you, It shall be more tolerable for the land of Sodom and Gomorrha in judgment-day than for that city.

16 Behold, I send you as sheep in the midst of wolves; be therefore prudent as the serpents, and guileless as the doves.

17 But beware of men; for they will deliver you up to sanhedrims, and scourge you in their synagogues;

18 and you shall be brought before rulers and kings for my sake, for a testimony to them and to the Gentiles.

19 But when they deliver you up, be not concerned how or what you shall speak; for it shall be given to you in that hour what you shall speak.

20 For you are not the speakers, but the Spirit of your Father which speaks in you.

21 But brother shall deliver up brother to death, and father child; and children shall rise up against parents and shall put them to death;

22 and you shall be hated of all on account of my name. But he that has endured to the end, he shall be saved.

23 But when they persecute you in this city, flee to the other; for truly I say to you, You shall not have completed the cities of Israel until the Son of man be come.

24 The disciple is not above his teacher, nor the servant above his lord.

25 [It is] sufficient for the disciple that he should become as his teacher, and the servant as his lord. If they have called the master of the house Beelzebub, how much more those of his household?

26 Fear them not therefore; for there is nothing covered which shall not be revealed, and secret which shall not be known.

27 What I say to you in darkness speak in the light, and what you hear in the ear preach upon the houses.

28 And be not afraid of those who kill the body, but cannot kill the soul; but fear rather him who is able to destroy both soul and body in Gehenna.

29 Are not two sparrows sold for a quarter [quadrans] and one of them shall not fall to the ground without [knowing] your Father;

30 but of you even the hairs of the head are all numbered.

31 Fear not therefore; you are better than many sparrows.

32 Every one therefore who shall acknowledge me before men, I also will acknowledge him before my Father who is in the heavens.

33 But whosoever shall deny me before men, him will I also deny before my Father who is in the heavens.

34 Do not think that I have come to send peace upon the earth: I have not come to send peace, but a sword.

35 For I have come to set a man at variance with his father, and the daughter with her mother, and the daughter-in-law with her mother-in-law;

36 and they of his household [shall be] a man's enemies.

37 He who loves father or mother above me is not worthy of me; and he who loves son or daughter above me is not worthy of me.

38 And he who does not take up his cross and follow after me is not worthy of me.

39 He that finds his soul shall lose it, and he who has lost his soul for my sake shall find it.

40 He that receives you receives me, and he that receives me receives him that sent me.

41 He that receives a prophet in the name of a prophet, shall receive a prophet's reward; and he that receives a righteous man in the name of a righteous man, shall receive a righteous man's reward.

42 And whosoever shall give to drink to one of these little ones a cup of cold [water] only, in the name of a disciple, truly I say unto you, he shall in no way lose his reward.

Mat 11:1 And it came to pass when Jesus had finished commanding his twelve disciples, he departed from there to teach and preach in their cities.

2 But John, having heard in the prison the works of the Christ, sent by his disciples,

3 and said to him, Are you the coming [one] or are we to wait for another?

4 And Jesus answering said to them, Go, report to John what you hear and see.

5 Blind [men] see and lame walk; lepers are cleansed, and deaf hear; and dead are raised, and poor have good news preached to them:

6 and blessed is whosoever shall not be offended in me.

7 But as they went [away] Jesus began to say to the crowds concerning John, What went you out into the wilderness to see? a reed moved about by the wind?

8 But what went you out to see? a man clothed in delicate raiment? behold, those who wear delicate things are in the houses of kings.

9 But what went you out to see? a prophet? Yes, I say to you, and more than a prophet:

10 this is he of whom it is written, Behold, I send my messenger before your face, who shall prepare your way before you.

11 Truly I say to you, that there is not arisen among the born of women a greater than John the Baptist. But he who is a little one in the kingdom of the heavens is greater than he.

12 But from the days of John the Baptist until now, the kingdom of the heavens is taken by violence, and the violent seize on it.

13 For all the prophets and the law have prophesied unto John.

14 And if you will receive it, this is Elijah, who is to come.

15 He that has ears to hear, let him hear.

16 But to whom shall I liken this generation? It is like children sitting in the markets, which, calling to their companions,

17 say, We have piped to you, and you have not danced: we have mourned to you, and you have not wailed.

18 For John has come neither eating nor drinking, and they say, He has a daemon.

19 The Son of man has come eating and drinking, and they say, Behold, a man [that is] eating and wine-drinking, a friend of tax-gatherers, and of sinners: --and wisdom has been justified by her children.

20 Then began he to reproach the cities in which most of his works of power had taken place, because they had not repented.

21 Woe to you, Chorazin! woe to you Bethsaida! for if the works of power which have taken place in you, had taken place in Tyre and Sidon, they had long ago repented in sackcloth and ashes.

22 But I say to you, that it shall be more tolerable for Tyre and Sidon in judgment-day than for you.

23 And you, Capernaum, who have been raised up to heaven, shall be brought down even to Hades. For if the works of power which have taken place in you, had taken place in Sodom, it had remained until this day.

24 But I say to you, that it shall be more tolerable for the land of Sodom in judgment-day than for you.

25 At that time, Jesus answering said, I praise you, Father, Lord of the heaven and of the earth, that you have hid these things from the wise and prudent, and have revealed them to babes.

26 Yes, Father, for thus has it been well-pleasing in your sight.

27 All things have been delivered to me by my Father, and no one knows the Son but the Father, nor does any one know the Father, but the Son, and he to whom the Son may be pleased to reveal him.

28 Come to me, all you who labor and are burdened, and I will give you rest.

29 Take my yoke upon you, and learn from me; for I am meek and lowly in heart; and you shall find rest to your souls;

30 for my yoke is easy, and my burden is light.

Mat 12:1 At that time Jesus went on the sabbaths through the grain fields; and his disciples were hungry, and began to pluck the ears and to eat.

2 But the Pharisees, seeing it said to him, Behold, your disciples are doing what is not lawful to do on sabbaths.

3 But he said to them, Have you not read what David did when he was hungry, and they that were with him?

4 How he entered into the house of the God, and ate the showbread, which it was not lawful for him to eat, nor for those with him, but for the priests only?

5 Or have you not read in the law that on the sabbaths the priests in the temple profane the Sabbath, and are blameless?

6 But I say unto you, that there is here what is greater than the temple.

7 But if you had known what this means: I wish for mercy and not sacrifice, you would not have condemned the guiltless.

8 For the Son of man is Lord of the Sabbath.

9 And, going away from there, he came into their synagogue.

10 And behold, there was a man having his hand withered. And they asked him, saying, Is it lawful to heal on the sabbaths? that they might accuse him.

11 But he said to them, What man shall there be of you who has one sheep, and if this fall into a pit on the sabbaths, will not lay hold of it and raise it up?

12 How much better then is a man than a sheep! So that it is lawful to do well on the sabbaths.

13 Then he says to the man, Stretch out your hand. And he stretched it out, and it was restored sound as the other.

14 But the Pharisees, having gone out, took counsel against him, how they might destroy him.

15 But Jesus knowing it withdrew from there, and great crowds followed him; and he healed them all;

16 and charged them strictly that they should not make him publicly known:

17 that that might be fulfilled which was spoken through Isaiah the prophet, saying,

18 Behold my servant, whom I have chosen, my beloved, in whom my soul has found its delight. I will put my Spirit upon him, and he shall show forth judgment to the Gentiles.

19 He shall not strive or cry out, nor shall any one hear his voice in the streets;

20 a bruised reed shall he not break, and smoking flax shall he not quench, until he bring forth judgment unto victory;

21 and on his name shall the nations hope.

22 Then was brought to him one possessed by a daemon, blind and mute, and he healed him, so that the mute [man] spoke and saw.

23 And all the crowds were amazed and said, Is this [man] the Son of David?

24 But the Pharisees, having heard it said, This [man] does not cast out daemons, but by Beelzebub, prince of daemons.

25 But he, knowing their thoughts, said to them, Every kingdom divided against itself is brought to desolation, and every city or house divided against itself will not subsist.

26 And if Satan casts out Satan, he is divided against himself; how then shall his kingdom subsist?

27 And if I cast out daemons by Beelzebub, your sons, by whom do they cast [them] out? For this reason they shall be your judges.

28 But if I by the Spirit of God cast out daemons, then indeed the kingdom of the God is come upon you.

29 Or how can any one enter into the house of the strong [man] and plunder his goods, unless first he bind the strong [man] and then he will plunder his house.

30 He that is not with me is against me, and he that gathers not with me scatters.

31 For this reason I say unto you, Every sin and injurious speaking shall be forgiven to men, but speaking injuriously of the Spirit shall not be forgiven to men.

32 And whosoever shall have spoken a word against the Son of man, it shall be forgiven him; but whosoever shall speak against the Holy Spirit, it shall not be forgiven him, neither in this aeon, nor in the coming [one]

33 Either make the tree good, and its fruit good; or make the tree corrupt, and its fruit corrupt. For from the fruit the tree is known.

34 Offspring of vipers! how can you speak good things, being wicked? For of the abundance of the heart the mouth speaks.

35 The good man out of the good treasure brings forth good things; and the wicked man out of the wicked treasure brings forth wicked things.

36 But I say unto you, that every idle word which men shall say, they shall render an account of it in judgment-day:

37 for by your words you shall be justified, and by your words you shall be condemned.

38 Then answered him some of the scribes and Pharisees, saying, Teacher, we desire to see a sign from you.

39 But he, answering, said to them, A wicked and adulterous generation seeks after a sign, and a sign shall not be given to it except the sign of Jonah the prophet.

40 For even as Jonah was in the belly of the great fish three days and three nights, thus shall the Son of man be in the heart of the earth three days and three nights.

41 Ninevites shall stand up in the judgment with this generation, and shall condemn it: for they

repented at the preaching of Jonah; and behold, more than Jonah is here.

42 A queen of the south shall rise up in the judgment with this generation, and shall condemn it; for she came from the ends of the earth to hear the wisdom of Solomon; and behold, more than Solomon is here.

43 But when the unclean spirit has gone out of the man, he goes through dry places, seeking rest, and does not find it

44 Then he says, I will return to my house from where I came out; and having come, he finds it unoccupied, swept, and adorned.

45 Then he goes and takes with himself seven other spirits worse than himself, and entering in, they dwell there; and the last condition of that man becomes worse than the first. Thus shall it be to this wicked generation also.

46 But while he was yet speaking to the crowds, behold, his mother and his brethren stood outside, seeking to speak to him.

47 Then one said unto him, Behold, your mother and your brethren are standing outside, seeking to speak to you.

48 But he answering said to him that spoke to him, Who is my mother, and who are my brethren?

49 And, stretching out his hand to his disciples, he said, Behold my mother and my brethren;

50 for whosoever shall do the will of my Father who is in the heavens, he is my brother, and sister, and mother.

Mat 13:1 And that [same] day Jesus went out from the house and sat down by the sea.

2 And great crowds were gathered together to him, so that going on board ship himself he sat down, and the whole crowd stood on the shore.

3 And he spoke to them many things in parables, saying, Behold, the sower went out to sow:

4 and as he sowed, some [grains] fell along the way, and the birds came and devoured them;

5 and others fell upon the rocky places where they had not much earth, and immediately they sprang up out of [the ground] because of not having [any] depth of earth,

6 but when the sun rose they were burned up, and because of not having [any] root were dried up;

7 and others fell upon the thorns, and the thorns grew up and choked them;

8 and others fell upon the good ground, and produced fruit, one a hundred, one sixty, and one thirty.

9 He that has ears, let him hear.

10 And the disciples came up and said to him, Why do you speak to them in parables?

11 And he answering said to them, Because to you it is given to know the mysteries of the kingdom of the heavens, but to them it is not given;

12 for whoever has, to him shall be given, and he shall be caused to be in abundance; but he who has not, even what he has shall be taken away from him.

13 For this cause I speak to them in parables, because seeing they do not see, and hearing they do not hear nor understand;

14 and in them is fulfilled the prophecy of Isaiah, which says, Hearing you shall hear and shall not understand, and beholding you shall behold and not see;

15 for the heart of this people has grown fat, and they have heard heavily with their ears, and they have closed their eyes as asleep, lest they should see with the eyes, and hear with the ears, and understand with the heart, and should be converted, and I should heal them.

16 But blessed are your eyes because they see, and your ears because they hear;

17 for truly I say unto you, that many prophets and righteous [men] have desired to see the things which you behold and did not see [them] and to hear the things which you hear and did not hear [them]

18 You, therefore, hear the parable of the sower.

19 From every one who hears the word of the kingdom and does not understand it the wicked one comes and catches away what was sown in his heart: this is he that is sown by the wayside.

20 But he that is sown on the rocky places --this is he who hears the word and immediately receives it with joy,

21 but has no root in himself, but is for a time only; and when tribulation or persecution happens on account of the word, he is immediately offended.

22 And he that is sown among the thorns --this is he who hears the word, and the concerns of this life, and the deceit of riches choke the word, and he becomes unfruitful.

23 But he that is sown upon the good ground --this is he who hears and understands the word, who bears fruit also, and produces, one a hundred, one sixty, and one thirty.

24 Another parable set he before them, saying, The kingdom of the heavens has become like a man sowing good seed in his field;

25 but while men slept, his enemy came and sowed weeds among the wheat, and went away.

26 But when the blade shot up and produced fruit, then appeared the weeds also.

27 And the servants of the householder came up and said to him, Sir, have you not sown good seed in your field? From where came the weeds?

28 And he said to them, A man [that is] an enemy has done this. And the servants said to him, Will you then that we should go and gather it [up]

29 But he said, No; lest [in] gathering the weeds you should root up the wheat with it.

30 Permit both to grow together unto the harvest, and in time of the harvest I will say to the harvestmen, Gather first the weeds, and bind them into bundles to burn; but the wheat bring together into my granary.

31 Another parable set he before them, saying, The kingdom of the heavens is like a grain of mustard [seed] which a man took and sowed in his field;

32 which is less indeed than all seeds, but when it is grown is greater than herbs, and becomes a tree, so that the birds of heaven come and roost in its branches.

33 He spoke another parable to them: The kingdom of the heavens is like leaven, which a woman took and hid in three measures of meal until it had been all leavened.

34 All these things Jesus spoke to the crowds in parables, and outside a parable he did not speak to them,

35 so that that should be fulfilled which was spoken through the prophet, saying, I will open my mouth in parables; I will utter things hidden from the world's foundation.

36 Then, having dismissed the crowds, he went into the house; and his disciples came to him, saying, Expound to us the parable of the weeds of the field.

37 But he answering said, He that sows the good seed is the Son of man,

38 and the field is the world; and the good seed, these are the sons of the kingdom, but the weeds are the sons of the evil [one]

39 and the enemy who has sowed it is the devil [daemon other mind; devil] and the harvest is the completion of the aeon, and the harvest men are angels.

40 As then the weeds are gathered and burned in the fire, thus it shall be in the completion of the aeon.

41 The Son of man shall send his angels, and they shall gather out of his kingdom all offences, and those that practice lawlessness;

42 and they shall cast them into the furnace of fire; there shall be the weeping and the gnashing of teeth.

43 Then the righteous shall shine forth as the sun in the kingdom of their Father. He that has ears, let him hear.

44 The kingdom of the heavens is like a treasure hid in the field, which a man having found has hid, and for the joy of it goes and sells all whatever he has, and buys that field.

45 Again, the kingdom of the heavens is like a merchant seeking beautiful pearls;

46 and having found one pearl of great value, he went and sold all whatever he had and bought it.

47 Again, the kingdom of the heavens is like a weeds which has been cast into the sea, and which has gathered together of every kind,

48 which, when it has been filled, having drawn up on the shore and sat down, they gathered the good into vessels and cast the worthless out.

49 Thus shall it be in the completion of the aeon, the angels shall go forth and sever the wicked from the midst of the just,

50 and shall cast them into the furnace of fire; there shall be the weeping and the gnashing of teeth.

51 Jesus says to them, Have you understood all these things? They say to him, Yes, [lord]

52 And he said to them, For this reason every scribe discipled to the kingdom of the heavens is like a man [that is] a householder who brings out of his treasure things new and old.

53 And it came to pass when Jesus had finished these parables he withdrew from there.

54 And having come into his own country, he taught them in their synagogue, so that they were astonished, and said, From where has this [man] this wisdom and these works of power?

55 Is not this the son of the carpenter? Is not his mother called Mary, and his brethren James, and Joseph, and Simon, and Judas?

56 And his sisters, are they not all with us? From where then has this [man] all these things?

57 And they were offended in him. And Jesus said to them, A prophet is not without honor, unless in his country and in his house.

58 And he did not there perform many works of power, because of their unbelief.

Mat 14:1 At that time Herod the tetrarch heard of the fame of Jesus,

2 and said to his servants, This is John the Baptist: he is risen from the dead, and because of this these works of power display their force in him.

3 For Herod had seized John, and had bound him and put him in prison on account of Herodias the wife of Philip his brother.

4 For John said to him, It is not lawful for you to have her.

5 And [while] desiring to kill him, he feared the crowd, because they held him for a prophet.

6 But when Herod's birthday was celebrated, the daughter of Herodias danced before them, and pleased Herod;

7 whereupon he promised with oath to give her whatsoever she should ask.

8 But she, being set on by her mother, says, Give me here upon a dish the head of John the Baptist.

9 And the king was grieved; but on account of the oaths, and those lying at table with him, he commanded it to be given.

10 And he sent and beheaded John in the prison;

11 and his head was brought upon a dish, and was given to the damsel, and she carried it to her mother.

12 And his disciples came and took the body and buried it, and came and brought word to Jesus.

13 And Jesus, having heard it, went away from there by ship to a desolate place apart. And the crowds having heard [of it] followed him on foot from the cities.

14 And going out he saw a great crowd, and was moved with compassion about them, and healed their infirm.

15 But when evening was come, his disciples came to him saying, The place is desolate, and [much of] the [day] time already gone by; dismiss the crowds, that they may go into the villages and buy food for themselves.

16 But Jesus said to them, They have no need to go: give you them to eat.

17 But they say to him, We have not here except five loaves and two fishes.

18 And he said, Bring them here to me.

19 And having commanded the crowds to recline upon the grass, having taken the five loaves and the two fishes, he looked up to heaven, and blessed: and having broken the loaves, he gave [them] to the disciples, and the disciples [gave them] to the crowds.

20 And all ate and were filled, and they took up what was over and above of fragments twelve hand-baskets full.

21 But those that had eaten were about five thousand men, besides women and children.

22 And immediately he compelled the disciples to go on board ship, and to go on before him to the other side, until he should have dismissed the crowds.

23 And having dismissed the crowds, he went up into the mountain apart to pray. And when evening was come, he was alone there,

24 but the ship was already in the middle of the sea tossed by the waves, for the wind was contrary.

25 But in the fourth watch of the night he went off to them, walking on the sea.

26 And the disciples, seeing him walking on the sea, were troubled, saying, It is a ghost. And they cried out through fear.

27 But Jesus immediately spoke to them, saying, Take courage; it is I: be not afraid.

28 And Peter answering him said, Lord, if it be you, command me to come to you upon the waters.

29 And he said, Come. And Peter, having descended from the ship, walked upon the waters to go to Jesus.

30 But seeing the wind strong he was afraid; and beginning to sink he cried out, saying, Lord, save me.

31 And immediately Jesus stretched out his hand and caught hold of him, and says to him, O you of little faith, why did you doubt?

32 And when they had gone up into the ship, the wind fell.

33 But those in the ship came and did homage to him, saying, Truly you are God's Son.

34 And having crossed over they came to the land of Gennesaret.

35 And when the men of that place recognized him, they sent to that whole country around, and they brought to him all that were ill,

36 and besought him that they might only touch the hem of his garment; and as many as touched were made thoroughly well.

Mat 15:1 Then the scribes and Pharisees from Jerusalem come up to Jesus, saying,

2 Why do your disciples transgress what has been delivered by the ancients? for they do not wash their hands when they eat bread.

3 But he answering said to them, Why do you also transgress the commandment of the God on account of your traditional teaching?

4 For the God commanded saying, honor father and mother; and, He that speaks ill of father or mother, let him die the death.

5 But you say, Whosoever shall say to his father or mother, It is a gift [to God], whatsoever [it be] from me you would have received:

6 and he shall in no way honor his father or his mother; and you have made void the commandment of the God on account of your traditional teaching.

7 Hypocrites! well has Isaiah prophesied about you, saying,

8 This people honor me with the lips, but their heart is far away from me;

9 but in vain do they worship me, teaching [as] teachings commandments of men.

10 And having called to the crowd to him, he said to them, Hear and understand:

11 Not what enters into the mouth defiles the man; but what goes forth out of the mouth, this defiles the man.

12 Then his disciples, coming up, said to him, Do you know that the Pharisees, having heard this word, have been offended?

13 But he answering said, Every plant which my heavenly Father has not planted shall be rooted up.

14 Leave them alone; they are blind leaders of blind: but if blind lead blind, both will fall into a ditch.

15 And Peter answering said to him, Expound to us this parable.

16 But he said, Are you also still without intelligence?

17 Do you not yet apprehend, that everything that enters into the mouth finds its way into the belly, and is cast forth into the sewer?

18 but the things which go forth out of the mouth come out of the heart, and those defile man.

19 For out of the heart come forth evil thoughts, murders, adulteries, fornications, thefts, false witnessings, blasphemies;

20 these are the things which defile man; but the eating with unwashed hands does not defile man.

21 And Jesus, going forth from there, went away into the parts of Tyre and Sidon;

22 and lo, a Canaanitish woman, coming out from those borders, cried [to him] saying, Have pity on me, Lord, Son of David; my daughter is miserably possessed by a daemon.

23 But he did not answer her a word. And his disciples came to him, and asked him, saying, Dismiss her, for she cries after us.

24 But he answering said, I have not been sent except to the lost sheep of Israel's house.

25 But she came and did him homage, saying, Lord, help me.

26 But he answering said, It is not well to take the bread of the children and cast it to the dogs.

27 But she said, Yes, Lord; for even the dogs eat of the crumbs which fall from the table of their masters.

28 Then Jesus answering said to her, O woman, your faith is great. Be it to you as you desire. And her daughter was healed from that hour.

29 And Jesus, going away from there, came towards the sea of Galilee, and he went up into the mountain and sat down there;

30 and great crowds came to him, having with them lame, blind, mute, crippled, and many others, and they cast them at his feet, and he healed them:

31 so that the crowds wondered, seeing mute speaking, crippled made well, lame walking, and blind seeing; and they glorified the God of Israel.

32 But Jesus, having called his disciples to him, said, I have compassion on the crowd, because they have stayed with me already three days and they have not anything they can eat, and I would not send them away fasting lest they should faint on the way.

33 And his disciples say to him, From where should we have so many loaves in the wilderness as to satisfy so great a crowd?

34 And Jesus says to them, How many loaves have you? But they said, Seven, and a few small fishes.

35 And he commanded the crowds to lie down on the ground;

36 and having taken the seven loaves and the fishes, having given thanks, he broke [them] and gave [them] to his disciples, and the disciples to the crowd.

37 And all ate and were filled; and they took up what was over and above of the fragments seven baskets full;

38 but they that ate were four thousand men, besides women and children.

39 And, having dismissed the crowds, he went on board ship and came to the borders of Magadan.

Mat 16:1 And the Pharisees and Sadducees, coming to him, asked him, testing him to show them a sign out of heaven.

2 But he answering said to them, When evening is come, you say, Fine weather, for the sky is red;

3 and in the morning, A storm today, for the sky is red [and] lowering; you know [how] to discern the face of the sky, but you cannot read the signs of the times.

4 A wicked and adulterous generation seeks after a sign, and a sign shall not be given to it except the sign of Jonah. And he left them and went away.

5 And when his disciples were come to the other side, they had forgotten to take bread.

6 And Jesus said to them, See and beware of the leaven of the Pharisees and Sadducees.

7 And they reasoned among themselves, saying, Because we have taken no bread.

8 And Jesus knowing it said, Why reason you among yourselves, O you of little faith, because you have taken no bread?

9 Do you not yet understand nor remember the five loaves of the five thousand, and how many hand-baskets you took [up]

10 nor the seven loaves of the four thousand, and how many baskets you took [up]

11 How do you not understand that [it was] not concerning bread I said to you, Beware of the leaven of the Pharisees and Sadducees?

12 Then they comprehended that he did not speak of being beware of the leaven of bread, but of the doctrine of the Pharisees and Sadducees.

13 But when Jesus was come into the parts of Caesarea-Philippi, he demanded of his disciples, saying, Who do men say that I the Son of man am?

14 And they said, Some, John the Baptist; and others, Elijah; and others again, Jeremiah or one of the prophets.

15 He says to them, But you, who do you say that I am?

16 And Simon Peter answering said, You are the Christ, the Son of the living God.

17 And Jesus answering said to him, Blessed are you, Simon Bar-jona, for flesh and blood has not revealed it to you, but my Father who is in the heavens.

18 And I also, I say unto you that you are Peter, and on this rock I will build my church, and gates of Hades shall not prevail against it.

19 And I will give to you the keys of the kingdom of the heavens; and whatsoever you bind* upon the earth shall be [fut.] what was bound [perf.] in the heavens; and whatsoever you loose* on the earth shall be [fut.] what was loosened [perf.] in the heavens.[181]

20 Then he enjoined on his disciples that they should say to no man that he was the Christ.

21 From that time Jesus began to show to his disciples that he must go away to Jerusalem, and suffer many things from the elders and chief priests and scribes, and be killed, and the third day be raised.

22 And Peter taking him to [him] began to rebuke him, saying, [God] be favorable to you, Lord; this shall in no way be unto you.

23 But turning round, he said to Peter, Get away behind me, Satan; you are an offence to me, for your mind is not on the things that are of the God, but on the things that are of men.

24 Then Jesus said to his disciples, If any one desires to come after me, let him deny himself and take up his cross and follow me.

25 For whosoever shall desire to save his soul shall lose it; but whosoever shall lose his soul for my sake shall find it.

26 For what does a man profit, if he should gain the whole world and suffer the loss of his soul? or what shall a man give in exchange for his soul?

27 For the Son of man is about to come in the glory of his Father with his angels, and then he will render to each according to his doings.

28 Truly I say unto you, There are some of those standing here that shall not taste of death at all until they shall have seen the Son of man coming in his kingdom.

Mat 17:1 And after six days Jesus takes with him Peter, and James, and John his brother, and brings them up into a high mountain apart.

2 And he was transfigured before them. And his face shone as the sun, and his garments became white as the light;

---

[181] See nm30 & *New Testament*, by Williams

3 and lo, Moses and Elijah appeared to them talking with him.

4 And Peter answering said to Jesus, Lord, it is good we should be here. If you will, let us make here three tabernacles: for you one, and for Moses one, and one for Elijah.

5 While he was still speaking, behold, a bright cloud overshadowed them, and lo, a voice out of the cloud, saying, This is my beloved Son, in whom I have found my delight: hear him.

6 And the disciples hearing it fell upon their faces, and were greatly terrified.

7 And Jesus coming to [them] touched them, and said, Rise up, and be not terrified.

8 And lifting up their eyes, they saw no one but Jesus alone.

9 And as they descended from the mountain, Jesus charged them, saying, Tell the vision to no one, until the Son of man be risen up from among the dead.

10 And [his] disciples asked of him saying, Why then say the scribes that Elijah must first have come?

11 And he answering said to them, Elijah indeed comes first and will restore all things.

12 But I say unto you that Elijah has already come, and they have not known him, but have done unto him whatever they would. Thus also the Son of man is about to suffer from them.

13 Then the disciples understood that he spoke to them of John the Baptist.

14 And when they came to the crowd, a man came to him, falling on his knees before him, and saying,

15 Lord, have mercy on my son, for he is lunatic, and suffers sorely; for often he falls into the fire and often into the water.

16 And I brought him to your disciples, and they were not able to heal him.

17 And Jesus answering said, O unbelieving and perverted generation, how long shall I be with you? how long shall I bear with you? Bring him here to me.

18 And Jesus rebuked him, and the daemon went out from him, and the boy was healed from that hour.

19 Then the disciples, coming to Jesus alone, said [to him] Why were we not able to cast him out?

20 And he says to them, Because of your unbelief; for truly I say unto you, If you have faith as a grain of mustard [seed] you shall say to this mountain, Be transported over there, and it shall transport itself; and nothing shall be impossible to you.

[21 But this kind does not go out but by prayer and fasting.]

22 And while they abode in Galilee, Jesus said to them, The Son of man is about to be delivered up into the hands of men,

23 and they shall kill him; and the third day he shall be raised up. And they were greatly grieved.

24 And when they came to Capernaum, those who received the tax [didrachmas] came to Peter and said, Does your teacher not pay the tax [didrachmas]?

25 He says, Yes. And when he came into the house, Jesus anticipated him, saying, What do you think, Simon? the kings of the earth, from whom do they receive custom or tribute? from their own sons or from strangers?

26 Peter says to him, From strangers. Jesus said to him, Then are the sons free.

27 But that we may not be an offence to them, go to the sea and cast a hook, and take the first fish that comes up, and when you have opened its mouth you will find money [stater]; take that and give it to them for me and you.

Mat 18:1 In that hour the disciples came to Jesus saying, Who then is greatest in the kingdom of the heavens?

2 And Jesus having called a little child to him, set it in their midst,

3 and said, Truly I say to you, Unless you are converted and become as little children, you will not at all enter into the kingdom of the heavens.

4 Whoever therefore shall humble himself as this little child, he is the greatest in the kingdom of the heavens;

5 and whosoever shall receive one such little child in my name, receives me.

6 But whosoever shall offend one of these little ones who believe in me, it were profitable for him that a great millstone had been hanged upon his neck and he be sunk in the depths of the sea.

7 Woe to the world because of offences! For it must needs be that offences come; yet woe to that man by whom the offence comes!

8 And if your hand or your foot offend you, cut it off and cast it from you; it is good for you to enter into life lame or maimed, [rather] than having two hands or two feet to be cast into the aeonian fire.

9 And if your eye offend you, pluck it out and cast it from you; it is good for you to enter into life one-eyed, [rather] than having two eyes to be cast into the Gehenna of fire.

10 See that you do not despise one of these little ones; for I say unto you that their angels in the heavens continually behold the face of my Father who is in the heavens.

11 For the Son of man has come to save that which was lost.

12 What do you think? If a certain man should have a hundred sheep, and one of them be gone astray, does he not, leaving the ninety and nine on the mountains, go and seek the one that has gone astray?

13 And if it should come to pass that he find it, truly I say unto you, he rejoices more because of it than because of the ninety and nine not gone astray.

14 So it is not the will of your Father who is in the heavens that one of these little ones should perish.

15 But if your brother sin against you, go, reprove him between you and him alone. If he hear you, you have gained your brother.

16 But if he do not hear [you] take with you one or two besides, that every matter may stand upon the word of two witnesses or of three.

17 But if he will not listen to them, tell it to the church; and if also he will not listen to the church, let him be to you as one of the pagans and a tax-gatherer.

18 Truly I say to you, Whatsoever you shall bind on the earth shall have been bound in heaven, and whatsoever you shall loose on the earth shall have been loosened in heaven.

19 Again I say to you, that if two of you shall agree on the earth concerning any matter, whatsoever it may be that they shall ask, it shall come to them from my Father who is in the heavens.

20 For where two or three are gathered together unto my name, there I am in the midst of them.

21 Then Peter came to him and said, Lord, how often shall my brother sin against me and I forgive him? until seven times?

22 Jesus says to him, I say not to you until seven times, but until seventy times seven.

23 For this cause the kingdom of the heavens has become like a king who would reckon with his servants.

24 And having begun to reckon, one debtor of ten thousand talents was brought to him.

25 But he not having anything to pay, [his] lord commanded him to be sold, and his wife, and his children, and everything that he had, and that payment should be made.

26 The servant therefore falling down did him homage, saying, Lord, have patience with me and I will pay you all.

27 And the lord of that servant, being moved with compassion, canceled and forgave him the loan.

28 But that servant having gone out, found one of his fellow-servants who owed him a hundred denarii. And having seized him, he throttled him, saying, Pay [me] if you owe anything.

29 His fellow-servant therefore, having fallen down [at his feet] besought him, saying, Have patience with me, and I will pay you.

30 But he would not, but went away and cast him into prison, until he should pay what was owing.

31 But his fellow-servants, having seen what had taken place, were greatly grieved, and went and recounted to their lord all that had taken place.

32 Then his lord, having called him to him, says to him, Wicked servant! I forgave you all that debt because you besought me;

33 should not you also have had compassion on your fellow-servant, as I also had compassion on you?

34 And his lord being angry delivered him to the tormentors till he paid all that was owing to him.

35 Thus also my heavenly Father shall do to you if you forgive not from your hearts every one his brother.

Mat 19:1 And it came to pass, when Jesus had finished these words, he withdrew from Galilee, and came to the coasts of Judea beyond the Jordan;

2 and great crowds followed him, and he healed them there.

3 And the Pharisees came to him tempting him, and saying, Is it lawful for a man to put away his wife for every cause?

4 But he answering said [to them] Have you not read that he who made [them] from the beginning made them male and female,

5 and said, On account of this a man shall leave father and mother, and shall be united to his wife, and the two shall be one flesh?

6 so that they are no longer two, but one flesh. What therefore the God has joined together, let not man separate.

7 They say to him, Why then did Moses command to give a letter of divorce and to send [her] away?

8 He says to them, Moses, in view of your hardheartedness, allowed you to put away your wives; but from the beginning it was not thus.

9 But I say unto you, that whosoever shall put away his wife, not for fornication, and shall marry another, commits adultery; and he who marries one put away commits adultery.

10 His disciples say to him, If the case of the man be so with his wife, it is not good to marry.

11 And he said to them, All cannot receive this word, but those to whom it has been given;

12 for there are eunuchs which have been born thus from [their] mother's womb; and there are eunuchs who have been made eunuchs of men; and there are eunuchs who have made eunuchs of themselves for the sake of the kingdom of the heavens. He that is able to receive it let him receive it

13 Then there were brought to him little children that he might lay his hands on them and pray; but the disciples rebuked them.

14 But Jesus said, Permit little children, and do not hinder them from coming to me; for the kingdom of the heavens is of such:

15 and having laid his hands upon them, he departed from there.

16 And lo, one coming up said to him, Teacher, what good thing shall I do that I may have aeonian life?

17 And he said to him, Why ask me concerning goodness? One is good. But if you want to enter into life, keep the commandments.

18 He says to him, Which? And Jesus said, You shall not kill, You shall not commit adultery, You shall not steal, You shall not bear false witness,

19 honor your father and your mother, and You shall love your neighbor as yourself.

20 The young man says to him, All these have I kept; what lack I yet?

21 Jesus said to him, If you would be perfect, go, sell what you have and give to the poor, and you shall have treasure in heaven; and come, follow me.

22 But the young man, having heard the word, went away grieved, for he had large possessions.

23 And Jesus said to his disciples, Truly I say unto you, A rich man shall with difficulty enter into the kingdom of the heavens;

24 and again I say unto you, It is easier for a camel to enter a needle's eye than a rich man into the kingdom of the God.

25 And when the disciples heard it they were exceedingly astonished, saying, Who then can be saved?

26 But Jesus, looking on [them] said to them, With men this is impossible; but with God all things are possible.

27 Then Peter answering said to him, Behold, we have left all things and have followed you; what then shall happen to us?

28 And Jesus said to them, Truly I say unto you, That you who have followed me, in the regeneration when the Son of man shall sit down upon his throne of glory, you also shall sit on twelve thrones, judging the twelve tribes of Israel.

29 And every one who has left houses, or brethren, or sisters, or father, or mother, or wife, or children, or lands, for my name's sake, shall receive a hundredfold, and shall inherit aeonian life.

30 But many first shall be last, and last first.

Mat 20:1 For the kingdom of the heavens is like a householder who went out with the early morn to hire workmen for his vineyard.

2 And having agreed with the workmen for a denarius the day, he sent them into his vineyard.

3 And having gone out about the third hour, he saw others standing in the market-place idle;

4 and to them he said, Go also you into the vineyard, and whatsoever may be just I will give you. And they went their way.

5 Again, having gone out about the sixth and ninth hour, he did likewise.

6 But about the eleventh [hour] having gone out, he found others standing, and says to them, Why stand you here all the day idle?

7 They say to him, Because no man has hired us. He says to them, Go also you into the vineyard [and whatsoever may be just you shall receive]

8 But when the evening was come, the lord of the vineyard says to his steward, Call the workmen and pay [them] their wages, beginning from the last even to the first.

9 And when they [who came to work] about the eleventh hour came, they received each a denarius.

10 And when the first came, they supposed that they would receive more, and they received also themselves each a denarius.

11 And on receiving it they murmured against the master of the house,

12 saying, These last have worked one hour, and you have made them equal to us, who have borne the burden of the day and the heat.

13 But he answering said to one of them, [my] friend, I do not wrong you. Did you not agree with me for a denarius?

14 Take what is yours and go. But it is my will to give to this last even as to you:

15 is it not lawful for me to do what I will in my own affairs? Is your eye evil because I am good?

16 Thus shall the last be first, and the first last; for many are called ones, but few chosen ones.

17 And Jesus, going up to Jerusalem, took the twelve disciples with him apart in the way, and said to them,

18 Behold we go up to Jerusalem, and the Son of man will be delivered up to the chief priests and scribes, and they will condemn him to death;

19 and they will deliver him up to the Gentiles to mock and to scourge and to crucify, and the third day he shall rise again.

20 Then came to him the mother of the sons of Zebedee, with her sons, doing homage, and asking something of him.

21 And he said to her, What do you wish? She says to him, Speak [the word] that these my two sons may sit, one on your right hand and one on your left in your kingdom.

22 And Jesus answering said, You know not what you ask. Can you drink the cup which I am about to drink? They say to him, We are able.

23 [And] he says to them, You shall drink indeed my cup, but to sit on my right hand and on [my] left, is not mine to give, but to those for whom it is prepared of my Father.

24 And the ten, having heard [of it] were indignant about the two brothers.

25 But Jesus having called them to him, said, You know that the rulers of the nations exercise lordship over them, and the great exercise authority over them.

26 It shall not be thus among you, but whosoever will be great among you, shall be your servant;

27 and whosoever will be first among you, let him be your servant;

28 as indeed the Son of man did not come to be served, but to serve, and to give his soul a ransom for many.

29 And as they went out from Jericho a great crowd followed him.

30 And lo, two blind men, sitting by the wayside, having heard that Jesus was passing by, cried out saying, Have mercy on us, Lord, Son of David.

31 But the crowd rebuked them, that they might be silent. But they cried out the more, saying, Have mercy on us, Lord, Son of David.

32 And Jesus, having stopped, called them and said, What do you wish that I shall do to you?

33 They say to him, Lord, that our eyes may be opened.

34 And Jesus, moved with compassion, touched their eyes; and immediately their eyes had sight restored to them, and they followed him.

Mat 21:1 And when they drew near to Jerusalem and came to Beth-phage, at the mount of Olives, then Jesus sent two disciples,

2 saying to them, Go into the village over against you, and immediately you will find an donkey tied, and a colt with it; loose [them] and lead [them] to me.

3 And if any one say anything to you, you shall say, The Lord has need of them, and straightway he will send them.

4 But all this came to pass, that that might be fulfilled which was spoken through the prophet, saying,

5 Say to the daughter of Zion, Behold your King comes to you, meek, and mounted upon an donkey, and upon a colt the foal of an donkey.

6 But the disciples, having gone and done as Jesus had ordered them,

7 brought the donkey and the colt and put their garments upon them, and he sat on them.

8 But a very great crowd strewed their own garments on the way, and others kept cutting down branches from the trees and strewing them on the way.

9 And the crowds who went before him and who followed cried, saying, Hosanna to the Son of David; blessed [be] he who comes in the name of the Lord; hosanna in the highest.

10 And as he entered into Jerusalem, the whole city was moved, saying, Who is this?

11 And the crowds said, This is Jesus the prophet who is from Nazareth of Galilee.

12 And Jesus entered into the temple [of god] and cast out all that sold and bought in the temple, and overthrew the tables of the money-changers and the seats of those that sold the doves.

13 And he says to them, It is written, My house shall be called a house of prayer, but you have made it a den of robbers.

14 And blind and lame came to him in the temple, and he healed them.

15 And when the chief priests and the scribes saw the wonders which he worked, and the children crying in the temple and saying, Hosanna to the Son of David, they were indignant,

16 and said to him, Do you hear what these say? And Jesus says to them, Yes; have you never read, Out of the mouth of babes and sucklings you have perfected praise?

17 And leaving them he went forth out of the city to Bethany, and there he passed the night.

18 But early in the morning, as he came back into the city, he hungered.

19 And seeing one fig-tree in the way, he came to it and found on it nothing but leaves only. And he says to it, Let there be never more fruit of you into the aeon. And the fig-tree was immediately dried up.

20 And when the disciples saw it they wondered, saying, How immediately is the fig-tree dried up!

21 And Jesus answering said to them, Truly I say unto you, If you have faith, and do not doubt, not only shall you do what [is done] to the fig-tree, but even if you should say to this mountain, Be you taken away and be you cast into the sea, it shall come to pass.

22 And all things whatsoever you shall ask in prayer, believing, you shall receive.

23 And when he came into the temple, the chief priests and the elders of the people came to him [as he was] teaching, saying, By what authority do you do these things? and who gave you this authority?

24 And Jesus answering said to them, I also will ask you one thing, which if you tell me, I also will tell you by what authority I do these things:

25 The baptism of John, from where was it? of heaven or of men? And they reasoned among themselves, saying, If we should say, Of heaven, he will say to us, Why then have you not believed him?

26 but if we should say, Of men, we fear the crowd, for all hold John for a prophet.

27 And answering Jesus they said, We do not know. He also said to them, Neither do I tell you by what authority I do these things.

28 But what do you think? A man had two children, and coming to the first he said, Child, go today, work in [my] vineyard.

29 And he answering said, I will not; but afterwards repenting he went.

30 And coming to the second he said likewise; and he answering said, I [go] sir, and went not.

31 Which of the two did the will of the father? They say [to him] The first. Jesus says to them, Truly I say unto you that the tax-gatherers and the harlots go into the kingdom of the God before you.

32 For John came to you in the way of righteousness, and you believed him not; but the tax-gatherers and the harlots believed him; but even afterwards when you saw it you did not repent to believe him.

33 Hear another parable: There was a householder who planted a vineyard, and made a fence round it, and dug a winepress in it, and built a tower, and let it out to husbandmen, and left the country.

34 But when the time of fruit drew near, he sent his servants to the husbandmen to receive his fruits.

35 And the husbandmen took his servants, and beat one, killed another, and stoned another.

36 Again he sent other servants more than the first, and they did to them in like manner.

37 And at last he sent to them his son, saying, They will have respect for my son.

38 But the husbandmen, seeing the son, said among themselves, This is the heir; come, let us kill him and possess his inheritance.

39 And they took him, and cast him forth out of the vineyard, and killed him.

40 When therefore the lord of the vineyard comes, what shall he do to those husbandmen?

41 They say to him, He will miserably destroy those evil [men] and let out the vineyard to other husbandmen, who shall render him the fruits in their seasons.

42 Jesus says to them, Have you never read in the scriptures, The stone which they that builded rejected, this has become the corner-stone: this is of the Lord, and it is wonderful in our eyes?

43 Therefore I say to you, that the kingdom of the God shall be taken from you and shall be given to a nation producing the fruits of it.

44 And he that falls on this stone shall be broken, but on whomsoever it shall fall, it shall grind him to powder.

45 And the chief priests and the Pharisees, having heard his parables, knew that he spoke about them.

46 And seeking to lay hold of him, they were afraid of the crowds, because they held him to be a prophet.

Mat 22:1 And Jesus answering spoke to them again in parables, saying,

2 The kingdom of the heavens has become like a king who made a wedding feast for his son,

3 and sent his servants to call the persons invited to the wedding feast, and they would not come.

4 Again he sent other servants, saying, Say to the persons invited, Behold, I have prepared my dinner; my oxen and my fatted beasts are killed, and all things ready; come to the wedding feast.

5 But they made light of it, and went, one to his own land, and another to his commerce.

6 And the rest, laying hold of his servants, ill-treated and killed [them].

7 And [when] the king [heard of it he] was wrathful, and having sent his forces, destroyed those murderers and burned their city.

8 Then he says to his servants, The wedding feast is ready, but those invited were not worthy;

9 go therefore into the thoroughfares of the highways, and as many as you shall find invite to the wedding feast.

10 And those servants went out into the highways, and brought together all as many as they found, both evil and good; and the wedding feast was furnished with guests.

11 And the king, having gone in to see the guests, beheld there a man not clothed with a wedding garment.

12 And he says to him, [my] friend, how did you come in here not having on a wedding garment? But he was speechless.

13 Then said the king to the servants, Bind him feet and hands, and take him away, and cast him out into the outer darkness: there shall be the weeping and the gnashing of teeth.

14 For many are called ones, but few chosen ones.

15 Then went the Pharisees and held a council how they might ensnare him in speaking.

16 And they send out to him their disciples with the Herodians, saying, Teacher, we know that you are true and teach the way of the God in truth, and care not for any one, for you regard not men's person;

17 tell us therefore what you think: Is it lawful to give tribute to Caesar, or not?

18 But Jesus, knowing their wickedness, said, Why do you test me, hypocrites?

19 Show me the money of the tribute. And they presented to him a denarius.

20 And he says to them, Whose is this image and superscription?

21 They say to him, Caesar's. Then he says to them, Pay then what is Caesar's to Caesar, and what is God's to the God.

22 And when they heard him they wondered, and left him, and went away.

23 On that day came to him Sadducees, who say there is no resurrection; and they asked of him,

24 saying, Teacher, Moses said, If any one die, not having children, his brother shall marry his wife and shall raise up seed to his brother.

25 Now there were with us seven brethren; and the first having married died, and not having seed, left his wife to his brother.

26 In like manner also the second and the third, unto the seven.

27 And last of all the woman also died.

28 In the resurrection therefore of which of the seven shall she be wife, for all had her?

29 And Jesus answering said to them, You err, not knowing the scriptures nor the power of the God.

30 For in the resurrection they neither marry nor are given in marriage, but are as angels of the God in heaven.

31 But concerning the resurrection of the dead, have you not read what was spoken to you by the God, saying,

32 I am God of Abraham, and the God of Isaac, and the God of Jacob? the God is not God of the dead, but of the living.

33 And when the crowds heard it they were astonished at his doctrine.

34 But the Pharisees, having heard that he had put the Sadducees to silence, were gathered together.

35 And one of them, a lawyer, asked, testing him, and saying,

36 Teacher, which is the great commandment in the law?

37 And he said to him, You shall love the Lord the God of you with all your heart, and with all your soul, and with all your understanding.

38 This is the great and first commandment.

39 And the second is like it, You shall love your neighbor as yourself.

40 On these two commandments the whole law and the prophets hang.

41 And the Pharisees being gathered together, Jesus asked of them,

42 saying, What do you think concerning the Christ? whose son is he? They say to him, David's.

43 He says to them, How then does David in Spirit call him Lord, saying,

44 The Lord said to my Lord, Sit on my right hand until I put your enemies under your feet?

45 If therefore David call him Lord, how is he his son?

46 And no one was able to answer him a word, nor did any one dare from that day to question him any more.

Mat 23:1 Then Jesus spoke to the crowds and to his disciples,

2 saying, The scribes and the Pharisees have set themselves down in Moses' seat:

3 all things therefore, whatever he[182] [Moses] may tell you, do and keep. But do not after their [Pharisees] works, for they say and do not,

4 but bind burdens heavy and hard to bear, and lay them on the shoulders of men, but will not move them with their finger.

5 And all their works they do to be seen of men: for they make broad their phylacteries[183] and enlarge the borders [of their garments]

6 and like the chief place in feasts and the first seats in the synagogues,

7 and salutations in the market-places, and to be called of men, Rabbi, Rabbi.

8 But you, be not you called Rabbi; for one is your instructor, and all you are brethren.

9 And call not [any one] your father upon the earth; for one is your Father, he who is in the heavens.

10 Neither be called instructors, for one is your instructor, the Christ.

11 But the greatest of you shall be your servant.

12 And whoever shall exalt himself shall be humbled, and whoever shall humble himself shall be exalted.

13 But woe unto you, scribes and Pharisees, hypocrites, for you shut up the kingdom of the heavens before men; for you do not enter, nor do you permit those that are entering to go in.

14 Woe

15 Woe to you, scribes and Pharisees, hypocrites, for you compass the sea and the dry [land] to make one proselyte, and when he is become [such] you make him twofold more the son of Gehenna than yourselves.

16 Woe to you, blind guides, who say, Whosoever shall swear by the temple, it is nothing; but whosoever shall swear by the gold of the temple, he is a debtor.

17 Fools and blind, for which is greater, the gold, or the temple which sanctifies the gold?

18 And, Whosoever shall swear by the altar, it is nothing; but whosoever shall swear by the gift that is upon it is a debtor.

19 [Fools and] blind ones, for which is greater, the gift, or the altar which sanctifies the gift?

20 He therefore that swears by the altar swears by it and by all things that are upon it.

21 And he that swears by the temple swears by it and by him that dwells in it.

22 And he that swears by heaven swears by the throne of the God and by him that sits upon it.

23 Woe to you, scribes and Pharisees, hypocrites, for you pay tithes of mint and anise and cummin, and you have left aside the weightier matters of the law, judgment and mercy and faith: these you ought to have done and not have left those aside.

24 Blind guides, who strain out the gnat, but drink down the camel.

25 Woe to you, scribes and Pharisees, hypocrites, for you make clean the outside of the cup and of the dish, but within they are full of greed and intemperance.

26 Blind Pharisee, make clean first the inside of the cup and of the dish, that their outside also may become clean.

27 Woe to you, scribes and Pharisees, hypocrites, for you are like whiten tombs, which appear beautiful outwardly, but within are full of dead men's bones and all uncleanness.

28 Thus also you, outwardly you appear righteous to men, but within are full of hypocrisy and lawlessness.

29 Woe to you, scribes and Pharisees, hypocrites, for you build the tombs of the prophets and adorn the tombs of the just,

30 and you say, If we had been in the days of our fathers we would not have been partakers with them in the blood of the prophets.

31 So that you bear witness of yourselves that you are sons of those who killed the prophets:

32 and you, fill you up the measure of your fathers.

33 Serpents, offspring of vipers, how should you escape the judgment of Gehenna?

34 Therefore, behold, I send unto you prophets, and wise men, and scribes; and [some] of them you will kill and crucify, and [some] of them you will scourge in your synagogues, and will persecute from city to city;

35 so that all righteous blood shed upon the earth should come upon you, from the blood of righteous Abel to the blood of Zacharias son of Barachias, whom you killed between the temple and the altar.

36 Truly I say unto you, All these things shall come upon this generation.

37 Jerusalem, Jerusalem, [the city] that kills the prophets and stones those that are sent unto her, how often would I have gathered your children as a hen gathers her chickens under her wings, and you would not!

38 Behold, your house is left unto you desolate;

39 for I say unto you, You shall in no way see me henceforth until you say, Blessed [be] he that comes in the name of the Lord.

Mat 24:1 And Jesus went forth and went away from the temple, and his disciples came to him to point out to him the buildings of the temple.

2 And he answering said to them, Do you not see all these things? Truly I say to you, Not a stone shall be left here upon a stone which shall not be thrown down.

3 And as he was sitting upon the mount of Olives the disciples came to him privately, saying, Tell us, when shall these things be, and what is the sign of your coming and the completion of the aeon.

---

[182] As per Hebrew texts found by Nehemia Gordon
[183] Boxes containing verses, worn on the forehead and arm

4 And Jesus answering said to them, See that no one mislead you.

5 For many shall come in my name, saying, I am the Christ, and they shall mislead many.

6 But you will hear of wars and rumors of wars. See that you be not disturbed; for all [these things] must take place, but it is not yet the end.

7 For nation shall rise up against nation, and kingdom against kingdom; and there shall be famines and pestilences, and earthquakes in diverse places.

8 But all these [are the] beginning of throes.

9 Then shall they deliver you up to tribulation, and shall kill you; and you will be hated of all the nations for my name's sake.

10 And then will many be offended, and will deliver one another up, and hate one another;

11 and many false prophets shall arise and shall mislead many;

12 and because lawlessness shall prevail, the love of the most shall grow cold;

13 but he that has endured to the end, he shall be saved.

14 And these good news of the kingdom shall be preached in the whole habitable earth, for a witness to all the Gentiles, and then shall come the end.

15 When therefore you shall see the abomination of desolation, which is spoken of through Daniel the prophet, standing in [what is a] holy place, he that reads let him understand,

16 then let those who are in Judea flee to the mountains;

17 let not him that is on the house come down to take the things out of his house;

18 and let not him that is in the field turn back to take his garment.

19 But woe to those that are with child, and those that give suck in those days.

20 But pray that your flight may not be in winter time nor on Sabbath:

21 for then shall there be great tribulation, such as has not been from the beginning of the world until now, nor ever shall be;

22 and if those days had not been cut off, no flesh had been saved; but on account of the elect those days shall be cut off.

23 Then if any one say to you, Behold, here is the Christ, or here, believe it not.

24 For there shall arise false christs, and false prophets, and shall give great signs and wonders, so as to mislead, if possible, even the elect.

25 Behold, I have told you beforehand.

26 If therefore they say to you, Behold, he is in the desert, go not forth; behold, [he is] in the inner chambers, do not believe it

27 For as the lightning goes forth from the east and shines to the west, so shall be the coming of the Son of man.

28 [For] wherever the carcase is, there will be gathered the eagles.

29 But immediately after the tribulation of those days the sun shall be darkened, and the moon not give her light, and the stars shall fall from heaven, and the powers of the heavens shall be shaken.

30 And then shall appear the sign of the Son of man in heaven; and then shall all the tribes of the land lament, and they shall see the Son of man coming on the clouds of heaven with power and great glory.

31 And he shall send his angels with a great sound of trumpet, and they shall gather together his elect from the four winds, from [the one] extremity of the heavens to [the other] extremity of them.

32 But learn the parable from the fig-tree: When already its branch becomes tender and produces leaves, you know that the summer is near.

33 Thus also you, when you see all these things, know that it is near, at the doors.

34 Truly I say to you, This generation[184] will not have passed away until all these things shall have taken place.

35 The heaven and the earth shall pass away, but my words shall in no way pass away.

36 But of that day and hour no one knows, not even the angels of the heavens, but [my] Father alone.

37 But as the days of Noah, so also shall be the coming of the Son of man.

38 For as they were in the days which were before the flood, eating and drinking, marrying and giving in marriage, until the day on which Noah entered into the ark,

39 and they knew not till the flood came and took all away; thus also shall be the coming of the Son of man.

40 Then two shall be in the field, one is taken and one is left;

41 two [women] grinding at the mill, one is taken and one is left.

42 Keep awake therefore, that you do not know in what hour your Lord comes.

43 But know this, that if the master of the house had known in what watch the thief was coming, he would have watched and not have permitted his house to be dug through [into]

44 Therefore you also, be you ready, that in that hour that you think not the Son of man comes.

45 Who then is the faithful and prudent servant whom his lord has set over his household, to give them food in season?

46 Blessed is that servant whom his lord on coming shall find doing thus.

47 Truly I say unto you, that he will set him over all his substance.

48 But if that evil servant should say in his heart, My lord delays to come,

49 and begin to beat his fellow-servants, and eat and drink with the drunken;

50 the lord of that servant shall come in a day when he does not expect it, and in an hour he knows not of,

---

[184] A "seed" shall be accounted for a generation, Ps 22:30

51 and shall cut him in two and appoint his portion with the hypocrites: there shall be the weeping and the gnashing of teeth.

Mat 25:1 Then shall the kingdom of the heavens be made like to ten virgins that having taken their torches, went forth to meet the bridegroom.

2 And five of them were prudent and five foolish.

3 They that were foolish took their torches and did not take oil with them;

4 but the prudent took oil in their vessels with their torches.

5 Now the bridegroom tarrying, they all grew heavy and slept.

6 But in the middle of the night there was a cry, Behold, the bridegroom; go forth to meet him.

7 Then all those virgins arose and trimmed their torches.

8 And the foolish said to the prudent, Give us of your oil, for our torches are going out.

9 But the prudent answered saying, [We cannot,] lest it might not suffice for us and for you. Go rather to those that sell, and buy for yourselves.

10 But as they went away to buy, the bridegroom came, and the [ones that were] ready went in with him to the wedding feast, and the door was shut.

11 Afterwards come also the rest of the virgins, saying, Lord, Lord, open to us;

12 but he answering said, Truly I say unto you, I do not know you.

13 Keep awake therefore, that you not know the day nor the hour.

14 For [it is] as [if] a man going away out of a country called his own servants and delivered to them his substance.

15 And to one he gave five talents, to another two, and to another one; to each according to his particular ability, and immediately went away out of the country.

16 And he that had received the five talents went and trafficked with them, and made five other talents.

17 In like manner also he that [had received] the two, [he also] gained two others.

18 But he that had received the one went and dug in the earth, and hid the money of his lord.

19 And after a long time the lord of those servants comes and reckons with them.

20 And he that had received the five talents came to him and brought five other talents, saying, [My] lord, you delivered me five talents; behold, I have gained five other talents besides them.

21 His lord said to him, Well, good and faithful servant, you have been faithful over a few things, I will set you over many things: enter into the joy of thy lord.

22 And he also that had received the two talents came to him, and said, [My] lord, you delivered me two talents; behold, I have gained two other talents besides them.

23 His lord said to him, Well, good and faithful servant, you was faithful over a few things, I will set you over many things: enter you into the joy of thy lord.

24 And he also that had received the one talent coming to him, said, [My] lord, I knew that you are a hard man, reaping where you had not sowed, and gathering from where you had not scattered,

25 and being afraid I went away and hid thy talent in the earth; behold, you hast that which is thine.

26 And his lord answering said to him, Wicked and slothful servant, you knew that I reap where I had not sowed, and gather from where I had not scattered;

27 you ought then to have put my money to the money-changers, and when I came I should have got what is mine with interest.

28 Take therefore the talent from him, and give it to him that has the ten talents:

29 for to every one that has shall be given, and he shall be in abundance; but from him that has not, that even which he has shall be taken from him.

30 And cast out the useless servant into the outer darkness; there shall be the weeping and the gnashing of teeth.

31 But when the Son of man comes in his glory, and all the angels with him, then shall he sit down upon his throne of glory,

32 and all the nations shall be gathered before him; and he shall separate them from one another, as the shepherd separates the sheep from the goats;

33 and he will set the sheep on his right hand, and the goats on [his] left.

34 Then shall the King say to those on his right hand, Come, blessed of my Father, inherit the kingdom prepared for you from the world's foundation:

35 for I hungered, and you gave me to eat; I thirsted, and you gave me to drink; I was a stranger, and you took me in;

36 naked, and you clothed me; I was ill, and you visited me; I was in prison, and you came to me.

37 Then shall the righteous answer him saying, Lord, when did we see you hungering, and nourished you; or thirsting, and gave you to drink?

38 and when did we see you a stranger, and took you in; or naked, and clothed you?

39 and when did we see you ill, or in prison, and came to you?

40 And the King answering shall say to them, Truly, I say to you, Inasmuch as you have done it to one of the least of these my brethren, you have done it to me.

41 Then shall he say also to those on the left, Go from me, cursed, into aeonian fire, prepared for the devil and his angels:

42 for I hungered, and you gave me not to eat; I thirsted, and you gave me not to drink;

43 I was a stranger, and you took me not in; naked, and you did not clothe me; ill, and in prison, and you did not visit me.

44 Then shall they also answer saying, Lord, when saw we you hungering, or thirsting, or a stranger, or naked, or ill, or in prison, and have not ministered to you?

45 Then shall he answer them saying, Truly I say to you, Inasmuch as you have not done it to one of these least, neither have you done it to me.

46 And these shall go away into aeonian punishment, and the righteous into life aeonian.

Mat 26:1 And it came to pass when Jesus had finished all these sayings, he said to his disciples,

2 Ye know that after two days the Passover takes place, and the Son of man is delivered up to be crucified.

3 Then the chief priests and the elders of the people were gathered together to the palace of the high priest who was called Caiaphas,

4 and took counsel together in order that they might seize Jesus by subtlety and kill him;

5 but they said, Not in the feast, that there be not a tumult among the people.

6 But Jesus being in Bethany, in Simon the leper's house,

7 a woman, having an alabaster flask of very precious ointment, came to him and poured it out upon his head as he lay at table.

8 But the disciples seeing it became indignant, saying, To what end [was] this waste?

9 for this might have been sold for much and been given to the poor.

10 But Jesus knowing it said to them, Why do you trouble the woman? for she has worked a good work toward me.

11 For you have the poor always with you, but me you have not always.

12 For in pouring out this ointment on my body, she has done it for my burying.

13 Truly I say to you, Wheresoever these good news may be preached in the whole world, that also which this [woman] has done shall be spoken of for a memorial of her.

14 Then one of the twelve, he who was called Judas Iscariote, went to the chief priest

15 and said, What are you willing to give me, and I will deliver him up to you? And they appointed to him thirty pieces of silver.

16 And from that time he sought a good opportunity that he might deliver him up.

17 Now on towards the first [day] of [the feast of] unleavened bread, the disciples came to Jesus, saying, Where do you wish that we prepare for you to eat the Passover?

18 And he said, Go into the city unto such a one, and say to him, The Teacher says, My time is near, I will keep the Passover in thy house with my disciples.

19 And the disciples did as Jesus had directed them, and they prepared* the Passover.

20 And when the evening was come he lay down at table with the twelve.

21 And as they were eating he said, Truly I say to you, that one of you shall deliver me up.

22 And being exceedingly grieved they began to say to him, each of them, Is it I, Lord?

23 But he answering said, He that dips his hand with me in the dish, he it is who shall deliver me up.

24 The Son of man goes indeed, according as it is written concerning him, but woe to that man by whom the Son of man is delivered up; it were good for that man if he had not been born.

25 And Judas, who delivered him up, answering said, Is it I, Rabbi? He says to him, you hast said.

26 And as they were eating, Jesus, having taken the bread and blessed, broke it and gave it to the disciples, and said, Take, eat: this is my body.

27 And having taken the cup and given thanks, he gave it to them, saying, Drink you all of it.

28 For this is my blood, that of the [new] covenant, that shed for many for forgiveness of sins.

29 But I say to you, that I will not at all drink henceforth of this fruit of the vine, until that day when I drink it new with you in the kingdom of my Father.

30 And having sung a hymn, they went out to the mount of Olives.

31 Then says Jesus to them, All you shall be offended in me during this night. For it is written, I will smite the shepherd, and the sheep of the flock shall be scattered abroad.

32 But after that I shall be risen, I will go before you to Galilee.

33 And Peter answering said to him, If all shall be offended in you, I will never be offended.

34 Jesus said to him, Truly I say to you, that during this night, before the cock shall crow, you shalt deny me three times.

35 Peter says to him, If I should needs die with you, I will in no wise deny you. Likewise said all the disciples also.

36 Then Jesus comes with them to a place called Gethsemane, and says to the disciples, Sit here until I go away and pray yonder.

37 And taking with him Peter and the two sons of Zebedee, he began to be sorrowful and deeply depressed.

38 Then he says to them, My soul is very sorrowful even unto death; remain here and keep awake with me.

39 And going forward a little he fell upon his face, praying and saying, My Father, if it be possible let this cup pass from me; but not as I will, but as you [wilt].

40 And he comes to the disciples and finds them sleeping, and says to Peter, Thus you have not been able to watch one hour with me?

41 Keep awake and pray, that you enter not into temptation: the spirit indeed is ready, but the flesh weak.

42 Again going away a second time he prayed saying, My Father, if this cannot pass [from me] unless I drink it, thy will be done.

43 And coming he found them again sleeping, for their eyes were heavy.

44 And leaving them, he went away again and prayed the third time, saying the same thing.

45 Then he comes to the disciples and says to them, Sleep on now and take your rest; behold, the hour has drawn near, and the Son of man is delivered up into the hands of sinners.

46 Arise, let us go; behold, he that delivers me up has drawn near.

47 And while he was yet speaking, behold, Judas, one of the twelve, came, and with him a great crowd with swords and sticks from the chief priests and elders of the people.

48 Now he that delivered him up had given them a sign, saying, Whomsoever I show affection, he it is: seize him.

49 And immediately coming up to Jesus he said, Hail, Rabbi, and covered him with kisses.

50 But Jesus said to him, [My] friend, for what purpose have you come? Then coming up they laid hands upon Jesus and seized him.

51 And behold, one of those with Jesus stretched out his hand and drew his sword, and smiting the servant of the high priest took off his ear.

52 Then says Jesus to him, Return thy sword to its place; for all who take the sword shall perish by the sword.

53 Or think you that I cannot now call upon my Father, and he will furnish me more than twelve legions of angels?

54 How then should the scriptures be fulfilled that thus it must be?

55 In that hour Jesus said to the crowds, Are you come out as against a robber with swords and sticks to take me? I sat daily [with you] teaching in the temple, and you did not seize me.

56 But all this is come to pass that the scriptures of the prophets may be fulfilled. Then all the disciples left him and fled.

57 Now they that had seized Jesus led him away to Caiaphas the high priest, where the scribes and the elders were assembled.

58 And Peter followed him at a distance, even to the palace of the high priest, and entering in sat with the officers to see the end.

59 And the chief priests and the elders and the whole Sanhedrim sought false witness against Jesus, so that they might put him to death.

60 And they found none, though many false witnesses came forward. But at the last two false witnesses came forward,

61 and said, he said, I am able to destroy the temple of the God, and in three days build it.

62 And the high priest standing up said to him, Answer you nothing? What are these testifying against you?

63 But Jesus was silent. And the high priest answering said to him, I adjure you by the living God that you tell us if you are the Christ the Son of the God.

64 Jesus says to him, you hast said. Moreover, I say to you, From henceforth you shall see the Son of man sitting at the right hand of power, and coming on the clouds of heaven.

65 Then the high priest rent his clothes, saying, He has blasphemed: what need have we any more of witnesses? behold, now you have heard the blasphemy.

66 What do you think? And they answering said, He is liable to the penalty of death.

67 Then they spit in his face, and maltreated him, and some struck him with the palms of their hand,

68 saying, Prophesy to us, Christ, Who is it who struck you?

69 But Peter sat outside in the palace-court; and a maid came to him, saying, And you were with Jesus the Galilaean.

70 But he denied before all, saying, I do not know what you say.

71 And when he had gone out into the entrance, another [maid] saw him, and says to those there, This [man] also was with Jesus the Nazarene.

72 And again he denied with an oath: I do not know the man.

73 And after a little, those who stood [there], coming to him, said to Peter, Truly you too are of them, for also thy speech makes you manifest.

74 Then he began to curse and to swear, I know not the man. And immediately the cock crew.

75 And Peter remembered the word of Jesus, who had said [to him], Before the cock crow you shall deny me three times. And he went outside, and wept bitterly.

Mat 27:1 And when it was morning all the chief priests and the elders of the people took counsel against Jesus so that they might put him to death.

2 And having bound him they led him away, and delivered him up to Pontius Pilate, the governor.

3 Then Judas, who delivered him up, seeing that he had been condemned, filled with remorse, returned the thirty pieces of silver to the chief priests and the elders,

4 saying, I have sinned [in] having delivered up guiltless blood. But they said, What is that to us? see you [to that].

5 And having cast down the pieces of silver in the temple, he left the place, and went away and hanged himself.

6 And the chief priests took the pieces of silver and said, It is not lawful to cast them into the Corban,[185] since it is the price of blood.

7 And having taken counsel, they bought with them the field of the potter for a burying-ground for strangers.

8 Therefore that field has been called Blood-field unto this day.

9 Then was fulfilled that which was spoken through Jeremiah the prophet, saying, And I took the thirty pieces of silver, the price of him that was set a price on, whom [they who were] of the sons of Israel had set a price on,

10 and they gave them for the field of the potter, according as the Lord commanded me.

---

[185] Gift to God

11 But Jesus stood before the governor. And the governor questioned him, saying, Are you the King of the Jews? And Jesus said to him, You have said it.

12 And when he was accused of the chief priests and the elders, he answered nothing.

13 Then says Pilate to him, Hear you not how many things they witness against you?

14 And he answered him not so much as one word, so that the governor wondered exceedingly.

15 Now at the feast the governor was accustomed to release one prisoner to the crowd, whom they would.

16 And they had then a notable prisoner, named Barabbas.

17 They therefore being gathered together, Pilate said to them, Whom do you wish that I release to you, Barabbas, or Jesus who is called Christ?

18 For he knew that they had delivered him up through envy.

19 But, as he was sitting on the judgment-seat, his wife sent to him, saying, Have nothing to do with that righteous [man]; for I have suffered to-day many things in a dream because of him.

20 But the chief priests and the elders persuaded the crowds that they should beg for Barabbas, and destroy Jesus.

21 And the governor answering said to them, Which of the two will you that I release unto you? And they said, Barabbas.

22 Pilate says to them, What then shall I do with Jesus, who is called Christ? They all said, Let him be crucified.

23 And the governor said, What evil then has he done? But they cried more than ever, saying, Let him be crucified.

24 And Pilate, seeing that it availed nothing, but that rather a tumult was arising, having taken water, washed his hands before the crowd, saying, I am guiltless of the blood of this righteous one: see you [to it].

25 And all the people answering said, His blood [be] on us and on our children.

26 Then he released to them Barabbas; but having scourged him, he delivered up Jesus that he might be crucified.

27 Then the soldiers of the governor, having taken Jesus with [them] to the praetorium, gathered against him the whole band,

28 and having taken off his garment, put on him a scarlet cloak;

29 and having woven a crown out of thorns, they put it on his head, and a reed in his right hand; and, bowing the knee before him, they mocked him, saying, Hail, King of the Jews!

30 And having spit upon him, they took the reed and beat him on his head.

31 And when they had mocked him, they took the cloak off him, and put his own clothes on him, and led him away to crucify.

32 And as they went forth they found a man of Cyrene, Simon by name; him they compelled to go [with them] that he might bear his cross.

33 And having come to a place called Golgotha, which means Place of a skull,

34 they gave to him to drink vinegar mingled with gall; and having tasted it, he would not drink.

35 And having crucified him, they parted his clothes among [themselves], casting lots.

36 And sitting down, they kept guard over him there.

37 And they set up over his head his accusation written: This is Jesus, the King of the Jews.

38 Then are crucified with him two robbers, one on the right hand and one on the left.

39 But the passers-by reviled him, shaking their head,

40 and saying, Thou that destroy the temple and build it in three days, save thyself. If you are Son of the God, descend from the cross.

41 [And] in like manner the chief priests also, mocking, with the scribes and elders, said,

42 He saved others, himself he cannot save. He is King of Israel: let him descend now from the cross, and we will believe on him.

43 He trusted upon the God; let him save him now if he will [have] him. For he said, I am Son of God.

44 And the robbers also who had been crucified with him cast the same reproaches on him.

45 Now from the sixth hour there was darkness over the whole land until the ninth hour;

46 but about the ninth hour Jesus cried out with a loud voice, saying, Eli, Eli, lama sabachthani? that is, My God, my God, why have you forsaken me?

47 And some of those who stood there, when they heard it, said, This [man] calls for Elijah.

48 And immediately one of them running and getting a sponge, having filled it with vinegar and fixed it on a reed, gave him to drink.

49 But the rest said, Let be; let us see if Elijah comes to save him.

50 And Jesus, having again cried with a loud voice, gave up the spirit.

51 And lo, the veil of the temple was rent in two from the top to the bottom, and the earth was shaken, and the rocks were rent.

52 and the tombs were opened; and many bodies of the saints fallen asleep arose,

53 and going out of the tombs after his arising, entered into the holy city and appeared unto many.

54 But the centurion, and they who were with him on guard over Jesus, seeing the earthquake and the things that took place, feared greatly, saying, Truly this [man] was Son of God.

55 And there were there many women beholding from afar off, who had followed Jesus from Galilee ministering to him,

56 among whom was Mary of Magdala, and Mary the mother of James and Joses, and the mother of the sons of Zebedee.

57 Now when even was come there came a rich man of Arimathaea, his name Joseph, who also himself was a disciple to Jesus,

58 he, going to Pilate, begged the body of Jesus. Then Pilate commanded the body to be given up.

59 And Joseph having got the body, wrapped it in a clean linen cloth,

60 and laid it in his new tomb which he had hewn in the rock; and having rolled a great stone to the door of the tomb, went away.

61 But Mary of Magdala was there, and the other Mary, sitting opposite the tomb.

62 Now on the next day, which is after the preparation, the chief priests and the Pharisees came together to Pilate,

63 saying, Sir, we have called to mind that that deceiver said when he was still alive, After three days I arise.

64 Command therefore that the tomb be secured until the third day, lest his disciples should come and steal him away, and say to the people, He is risen from the dead; and the last error shall be worse than the first.

65 And Pilate said to them, You have a guard: go, secure it as well as you know how.

66 And they went and secured the tomb, having sealed the stone in company with the guard.

Mat 28:1 Now late in the week,[186] towards the dawn of the first of the week,[187] came Mary of Magdala and the other Mary to look at the tomb.

2 And behold, there was a great earthquake; for an angel of the Lord, descending out of heaven, came and rolled away the stone and sat upon it.

3 And his look was as lightning, and his clothing white as snow.

4 And for fear of him the guards trembled and became as dead men.

5 And the angel answering said to the women, Fear not, for I know that you seek Jesus the crucified one.

6 He is not here, for he is risen, as he said. Come, see the place where the Lord lay.

7 And go quickly and say to his disciples that he is risen from the dead; and behold, he goes before you into Galilee, there shall you see him. Behold, I have told you.

8 And going out quickly from the tomb with fear and great joy, they ran to bring his disciples word.

9 And as they went to bring his disciples word, behold also, Jesus met them, saying, Hail! And they coming up took him by the feet, and did him homage.

10 Then Jesus says to them, Fear not; go, bring word to my brethren that they go into Galilee, and there they shall see me.

11 And as they went, behold, some of the guard went into the city, and brought word to the chief priests of all that had taken place.

12 And having assembled with the elders, and having taken counsel, they gave a large sum of money to the soldiers,

13 saying, Say that his disciples coming by night stole him [while] we [were] sleeping.

14 And if this should come to the hearing of the governor, we will persuade him, and save you from all anxiety.

15 And they took the money and did as they had been taught. And this report is current among the Jews until this day.

16 But the eleven disciples went into Galilee to the mountain which Jesus had appointed them.

17 And when they saw him, they did homage to him: but some doubted.

18 And Jesus coming up spoke to them, saying, All power has been given me in heaven and upon earth.

19 Go [therefore] and make disciples of all the nations, baptizing them into the Name of the Father, and of the Son, and of the Holy Spirit;

20 teaching them to observe all things whatsoever I have commanded you. And behold, I am with you all the days, until the completion of the aeon.

---

[186] Sabbaths
[187] Sabbaths

Mark

Mark 1:1 Beginning of the good news of Jesus Christ, Son of the God;

2 as it is written in [Isaiah] the prophet, Behold, I send my messenger before thy face, who shall prepare thy way.

3 Voice of one crying in the wilderness, Prepare the way of the Lord, make his paths straight.

4 There came John baptizing in the wilderness, and preaching the baptism of repentance for forgiveness of sins.

5 And there went out to him all the district of Judea, and all they of Jerusalem, and were baptized by him in the river Jordan, confessing their sins.

6 And John was clothed in camel's hair, and a leathern girdle about his loins, and ate locusts and wild honey.

7 And he preached, saying, There comes he that is mightier than I after me, the thong of whose sandals I am not fit to stoop down and unloose.

8 I indeed have baptized you with water, but he shall baptize you with the Holy Spirit.

9 And it came to pass in those days that Jesus came from Nazareth of Galilee, and was baptized by John at the Jordan.

10 And straightway going up from the water, he saw the heavens parting asunder, and the Spirit, as a dove, descending upon him.

11 And there came a voice out of the heavens: you are my beloved Son, in you I have found my delight.

12 And immediately the Spirit drives him out into the wilderness.

13 And he was in the wilderness forty days tempted by Satan, and was with the wild beasts; and the angels ministered to him.

14 But after John was delivered up, Jesus came into Galilee preaching the good news of the kingdom of the God,

15 and saying, The time is fulfilled and the kingdom of the God has drawn near; repent and believe in the good news.

16 And walking by the sea of Galilee, he saw Simon, and Andrew, [Simon's] brother, casting out a net in the sea, for they were fishermen.

17 And Jesus said to them, Come after me, and I will make you become fishermen of men;

18 and straightway leaving their trawl-nets they followed him.

19 And going on from that place a little, he saw James the [son] of Zebedee, and John his brother, and these [were] in the ship repairing the trawl-nets;

20 and straightway he called them; and leaving their father Zebedee in the ship with the hired servants, they went away after him.

21 And they go into Capernaum. And straightway on the Sabbath he entered into the synagogue and taught.

22 And they were astonished at his doctrine, for he taught them as having authority, and not as the scribes.

23 And there was in their synagogue a man [possessed] by an unclean spirit, and he cried Eh!

24 saying, Eh! what have we to do with you, Jesus, Nazarene? Are you come to destroy us? I know you who you are, the holy one of the God.

25 And Jesus rebuked him, saying, Hold thy peace and come out of him.

26 And the unclean spirit, having torn him, and uttered a cry with a loud voice, came out of him.

27 And all were amazed, so that they questioned together among themselves, saying, What is this? what new doctrine is this? for with authority he commands even the unclean spirits, and they obey him.

28 And his fame went out straightway into the whole region of Galilee around.

29 And straightway going out of the synagogue, they came with James and John into the house of Simon and Andrew.

30 And the mother-in-law of Simon lay in a fever. And straightway they speak to him about her.

31 And he went up to [her] and raised her up, having taken her by the hand, and straightway the fever left her, and she served them.

32 But evening being come, when the sun had gone down, they brought to him all that were suffering, and those possessed by demons;

33 and the whole city was gathered together at the door.

34 And he healed many suffering from various diseases; and he cast out many daemons, and did not permit the daemons to speak because they knew him.

35 And rising in the morning long before day, he went out and went away into a desolate place, and there prayed.

36 And Simon and those with him went after him:

37 and having found him, they say to him, All seek you.

38 And he says to them, Let us go elsewhere into the neighboring country towns, that I may preach there also, for for this purpose I have come forth.

39 And he was preaching in their synagogues in the whole of Galilee, and casting out daemons.

40 And there comes to him a leper, beseeching him, and falling on his knees to him, and saying to him, If you will you can cleanse me.

41 But Jesus, moved with compassion, having stretched out his hand, touched him, and says to him, I will, be you cleansed.

42 And as he spoke straightway the leprosy left him, and he was cleansed.

43 And having sharply charged him, he straightway sent him away,

44 and says to him, See you say nothing to any one, but go, show yourself to the priest, and offer for your cleansing what Moses ordained, for a testimony to them.

45 But he, having gone forth, began to proclaim it much, and to spread the matter abroad, so that he could no longer enter openly into the city, but was

outside in desolate places, and they came to him from every side.

Mark 2:1 And he entered again into Capernaum after [several] days, and it was reported that he was at the house;

2 and straightway many were gathered together, so that there was no longer any room, not even at the door; and he spoke the word to them.

3 And there come to him [men] bringing a paralytic, borne by four;

4 and, not being able to get near to him on account of the crowd, they uncovered the roof where he was, and having dug it up they let down the couch on which the paralytic lay.

5 But Jesus, seeing their faith, says to the paralytic, Child, your sins are forgiven [you]

6 But certain of the scribes were there sitting, and reasoning in their hearts,

7 Why does this [man] thus speak? he blasphemes. Who is able to forgive sins except the God alone?

8 And straightway Jesus, knowing in his spirit that they are reasoning thus within themselves, said to them, Why reason you these things in your hearts?

9 Which is easier, to say to the paralytic, [your] sins are forgiven [you] or to say, Arise, and take up your couch and walk?

10 But that you may know that the Son of man has power on earth to forgive sins, he says to the paralytic,

11 To you I say, Arise, take up your couch and go to your house.

12 And he rose up straightway, and, having taken up his couch, went out before [them] all, so that all were amazed, and glorified the God, saying, We never saw it thus.

13 And he went out again by the sea, and all the crowd came to him, and he taught them.

14 And passing by, he saw Levi the [son] of Alphaeus sitting at the tax-office, and says to him, Follow me. And he rose up and followed him.

15 And it came to pass as he lay at table in his house, that many tax-gatherers and sinners lay at table with Jesus and his disciples; for they were many, and they followed him.

16 And the scribes and the Pharisees, seeing him eating with sinners and tax-gatherers, said to his disciples, Why [is it] that he eats and drinks with tax-gatherers and sinners?

17 And Jesus having heard it says to them, They that are strong have not need of a physician, but those who are ill. I have not come to call righteous [men] but sinners.

18 And the disciples of John and the Pharisees were fasting; and they come and say to him, Why do the disciples of John and [the disciples] of the Pharisees fast, but your disciples fast not?

19 And Jesus said to them, Can the sons of the bride-chamber fast while the bridegroom is with them? As long as they have the bridegroom with them they cannot fast.

20 But days will come when the bridegroom shall have been taken away from them, and then shall they fast in that day.

21 No one sews a patch of new cloth on an old garment: otherwise its new filling-up takes from the old [stuff] and there is a worse rent.

22 And no one puts new wine into old skins; otherwise the wine bursts the skins, and the wine is poured out, and the skins will be destroyed; but new wine is to be put into new skins.

23 And it came to pass that he went on the sabbaths through the grainfields; and his disciples began to walk on, plucking the ears.

24 And the Pharisees said to him, Behold, why do they on the sabbaths what is not lawful?

25 And he said to them, Have you never read what David did when he had need and hungered, he and those with him,

26 how he entered into the house of the God, in [the section of] Abiathar the high priest, and ate the show-bread, which it is not lawful unless for the priests to eat, and gave even to those that were with him?

27 And he said to them, The Sabbath was made on account of man, not man on account of the Sabbath;

28 so that the Son of man is lord of the Sabbath also.

Mark 3:1 And he entered again into the synagogue; and there was there a man having his hand dried up.

2 And they watched him if he would heal him on the sabbaths, that they might accuse him.

3 And he says to the man who had his hand dried up, Rise up [and come] into the midst.

4 And he says to them, Is it lawful on the sabbaths to do good or to do evil, to save a soul or to kill? But they were silent.

5 And looking round upon them with anger, distressed at the hardening of their heart, he says to the man, Stretch out your hand. And he stretched it out, and his hand was restored.

6 And the Pharisees going out straightway with the Herodians took counsel against him, how they might destroy him.

7 And Jesus withdrew with his disciples to the sea; and a great multitude from Galilee followed him, and from Judea,

8 and from Jerusalem, and from Idumaea and beyond the Jordan; and they of around Tyre and Sidon, a great multitude, having heard what things he did, came to him.

9 And he spoke to his disciples, in order that a little ship should wait upon him on account of the crowd, that they might not press upon him.

10 For he healed many, so that they beset him that they might touch him, as many as had plagues.

11 And the unclean spirits, when they beheld him, fell down before him, and cried saying, You are the Son of the God.

12 And he rebuked them much, that they might not make him manifest.

13 And he goes up into the mountain, and calls whom he himself would, and they went to him.

14 And he appointed twelve that they might be with him, and that he might send them to preach,

15 and to have power [to heal diseases, and] to cast out daemons.

16 And he gave to Simon the surname of Peter;

17 and James the [son] of Zebedee, and John the brother of James, and he gave them the surname of Boanerges, that is, Sons of thunder;

18 and Andrew, and Philip, and Bartholomew, and Matthew, and Thomas, and James the [son] of Alphaeus, and Thaddaeus, and Simon the Cananaean,

19 and Judas Iscariote, who also delivered him up. And they come to the house.

20 And again a crowd comes together, so that they cannot even eat bread.

21 And his relatives having heard [of it] went out to lay hold on him, for they said, He is out of his mind.

22 And the scribes who had come down from Jerusalem said, He has Beelzebub, and, By the prince of the daemons he casts out daemons.

23 And having called them to him, he said to them in parables, How can Satan cast out Satan?

24 And if a kingdom has become divided against itself, that kingdom cannot subsist.

25 And if a house has become divided against itself, that house cannot subsist.

26 And if Satan rise up against himself, and is divided, he cannot subsist, but has an end.

27 But no one can, having entered into his house, plunder the goods of the strong [man] unless he first bind the strong [man] and then he will plunder his house.

28 Truly I say unto you, that all sins shall be forgiven to the sons of men, and all the injurious speeches [with] which they may speak injuriously;

29 but whosoever shall speak injuriously against the Holy Spirit, to the aeon has no forgiveness; but lies under the guilt of an aeonian sin;

30 --because they said, He has an unclean spirit.

31 And his brethren and his mother come, and standing outside sent to him calling him.

32 And a crowd sat around him. And they said to him, Behold, your mother and your brethren seek you outside.

33 And he answered them, saying, Who is my mother or my brethren?

34 And looking around in a circuit at those that were sitting around him, he says, Behold my mother and my brethren:

35 for whosoever shall do the will of the God, he is my brother, and sister, and mother.

Mark 4:1 And again he began to teach by the sea. And a great crowd was gathered together to him, so that going on board ship he sat in the sea, and all the crowd were close to the sea on the land.

2 And he taught them many things in parables. And he said to them in his doctrine,

3 Listen: Behold, the sower went forth to sow.

4 And it came to pass as he sowed, one fell by the wayside, and the birds came and devoured it.

5 And another fell on the rocky ground, where it had not much earth, and immediately it sprung up out [of the ground] because it had no depth of earth;

6 and when the sun arose it was burnt up, and because of its not having any root, it withered.

7 And another fell among the thorns, and the thorns grew up and choked it, and it yielded no fruit.

8 And another fell into the good ground, and yielded fruit, growing up and increasing; and bore, one thirty, and one sixty, and one a hundred.

9 And he said, He that has ears to hear, let him hear.

10 And when he was alone, those about him with the twelve asked him [as to] the parables.

11 And he said to them, To you is given [to know] the mystery of the kingdom of the God; but to them who are outside, all things are done in parables,

12 that beholding they may behold and not see, and hearing they may hear and not understand, lest it may be, they should be converted and they should be forgiven.

13 And he says to them, Do you not know this parable? and how will you be acquainted with all the parables?

14 The sower sows the word:

15 and these are they by the wayside where the word is sown, and when they hear, immediately Satan comes and takes away the word that was sown in them.

16 And these are they in like manner who are sown upon the rocky places, who when they hear the word, immediately receive it with joy,

17 and they have no root in themselves, but are for a time: then, tribulation arising, or persecution on account of the word, immediately they are offended.

18 And others are they who are sown among the thorns: these are they who have heard the word,

19 and the cares of life, and the deceitfullness of riches, and the lusts of other things, entering in, choke the word, and it becomes unfruitful.

20 And these are they who have been sown on the good ground, such as hear the word and receive it, and bear fruit; one thirty, and one sixty, and one a hundred [fold]

21 And he said to them, Does the lamp come that it should be put under the bushel or under the couch? [is it] not that it should be set upon the lamp-stand?

22 For there is nothing hidden which shall not be made manifest; nor does any secret thing take place, but that it should come to light.

23 If any one have ears to hear, let him hear.

24 And he said to them, Take heed what you hear; with what measure you measured, it shall be measured to you; and there shall be [more] added to you.

25 For whosoever has, to him shall be given; and he who has not, even what he has shall be taken from him.

26 And he said, Thus is the kingdom of the God, as if a man should cast the seed upon the earth,

27 and should sleep and rise up night and day, and the seed should sprout and grow, he does not know how.

28 The earth bears fruit of itself, first the blade, then an ear, then full grain in the ear.

29 But when the fruit is produced, immediately he sends the sickle, for the harvest is come.

30 And he said, How should we liken the kingdom of the God, or with what comparison should we compare it?

31 As to a grain of mustard [seed] which, when it is sown upon the earth, is less than all seeds which are upon the earth,

32 and when it has been sown, mounts up and becomes greater than all herbs, and produces great branches, so that the birds of heaven can roost under its shadow.

33 And with many such parables he spoke the word to them, as they were able to hear,

34 but without a parable spoke he not to them; and in private he explained all things to his disciples.

35 And on that day, when evening was come, he says to them, Let us go over to the other side:

36 and having sent away the crowd, they take him with [them] as he was, in the ship. But other ships also were with him.

37 And there comes a violent gust of wind, and the waves beat into the ship, so that it already filled.

38 And he was in the stern sleeping on the cushion. And they awake him up and say to him, Teacher, do you not care that we are perishing?

39 And awaking up he rebuked the wind, and said to the sea, Silence; be mute. And the wind fell, and there was a great calm.

40 And he said to them, Why are you [thus] fearful? how [is it] you have not faith?

41 And they feared [with] great fear, and said one to another, Who then is this, that even the wind and the sea obey him?

Mark 5:1 And they came to the other side of the sea, to the country of the Gadarenes.

2 And immediately on his going out of the ship there met him out of the tombs a man possessed by an unclean spirit,

3 who had his dwelling in the tombs; and no one was able to bind him, not even with chains;

4 because he had been often bound with fetters and chains, and the chains had been torn asunder by him, and the fetters were shattered; and no one was able to subdue him.

5 And continually night and day, in the tombs and in the mountains, he was crying and cutting himself with stones.

6 But seeing Jesus from afar off, he ran and did him homage,

7 and crying with a loud voice he says, What have I to do with you, Jesus, Son of the Most High God? I adjure you by the God, torment me not.

8 For he said to him, Come forth, unclean spirit, out of the man.

9 And he asked him, What is your name? And he says to him, Legion is my name, because we are many.

10 And he besought him much that he would not send them away out of the country.

11 Now there was there just at the mountain a great herd of swine feeding;

12 and they besought him, saying, Send us into the swine that we may enter into them.

13 And Jesus [immediately] allowed them. And the unclean spirits going out entered into the swine, and the herd rushed down the steep slope, into the sea about two thousand, and were choked in the sea.

14 And those that were feeding them fled and reported it in the city and in the country. And they went out to see what it was that had taken place.

15 And they come to Jesus, and they see the possessed of daemons sitting [and] clothed and sensible, him that had had the legion: and they were afraid.

16 And they that had seen it related to them how it had happened to the [man] possessed by daemons, and concerning the swine.

17 And they began to beg him to depart from their coasts.

18 And as he went on board ship, the man that had been possessed by daemons besought him that he might be with him.

19 And he permitted him not, but says to him, Go to your home to your own people, and tell them how great things the Lord has done for you, and has had mercy on you.

20 And he went away and began to proclaim in the Decapolis how great things Jesus had done for him; and all wondered.

21 And Jesus having passed over in the ship again to the other side, a great crowd gathered to him; and he was by the sea.

22 And [behold] there comes one of the rulers of the synagogue, by name Jairus, and seeing him, falls down at his feet;

23 and he besought him much, saying, My little daughter is at extremity; [I pray] that you should come and lay your hands upon her so that she may be healed, and may live.

24 And he went with him, and a large crowd followed him and pressed on him.

25 And a certain woman who had had a flux of blood twelve years,

26 and had suffered much under many physicians, and had spent everything she had and had found no advantage from it, but had rather got worse,

27 having heard concerning Jesus, came in the crowd behind and touched his clothes;

28 for she said, If I shall touch but his clothes I shall be healed.

29 And immediately her fountain of blood was dried up, and she knew in her body that she was cured from the scourge.

30 And immediately Jesus, knowing in himself the power that had gone out of him, turning round in the crowd said, Who has touched my clothes?

31 And his disciples said to him, You see the crowd pressing on you, and you said, Who touched me?

32 And he looked round about to see her who had done this.

33 But the woman, frightened and trembling, knowing what had taken place in her, came and fell down before him, and told him all the truth.

34 And he said to her, Daughter, your faith has healed you; go in peace, and be well of your scourge.

35 While he was yet speaking, they come from the ruler of the synagogue's [house] saying, Your daughter has died, why trouble you the teacher any further?

36 But Jesus [immediately] having heard the word spoken, says to the ruler of the synagogue, Fear not; only believe.

37 And he permitted no one to accompany him except Peter and James, and John the brother of James.

38 And he comes to the house of the ruler of the synagogue, and sees the tumult, and people weeping and wailing greatly.

39 And entering in he says to them, Why do you make a tumult and weep? the child has not died, but sleeps.

40 And they derided him. But he, having put [them] all out, takes with him the father of the child, and the mother, and those that were with him, and enters in where the child was lying.

41 And having laid hold of the hand of the child, he says to her, Talitha koumi, which is, interpreted, Damsel, I say to you, Arise.

42 And immediately the damsel arose and walked, for she was of years twelve. And they were astonished with great astonishment.

43 And he charged them much that no one should know this; and he desired that [something] should be given her to eat.

Mark 6:1 And he went out from there and came to his own country, and his disciples follow him.

2 And when Sabbath was come he began to teach in the synagogue, and many hearing were amazed, saying, From where [has] this [man] these things? and what is the wisdom that is given to him, and such works of power are done by his hands?

3 Is not this the carpenter, the son of Mary, and brother of James, and Joses, and Judas, and Simon? and are not his sisters here with us? And they were offended in him.

4 But Jesus said to them, A prophet is not despised except in his own country, and among [his] kinsmen, and in his own house.

5 And he could not do any work of power there, except that laying his hands on a few infirm persons he healed [them]

6 And he wondered because of their unbelief. And he went round the villages in a circuit, teaching.

7 And he calls the twelve to him, and he began to send them out two [and] two, and gave to them power over the unclean spirits;

8 and he commanded them that they should take nothing for the way, except a staff only; no scrip, no bread, no money in their belt;

9 but be shod with sandals, and put not on two body-coats.

10 And he said to them, Wheresoever you shall enter into a house, there remain till you shall go from there.

11 And whatsoever place shall not receive you nor hear you, departing from there, shake off the dust which is under your feet for a testimony to them.

12 And they went forth and preached that they should change their mind [repent]

13 and they cast out many daemons, and anointed with oil many infirm, and healed them.

14 And Herod the king heard [of him], for his name had become public, and said, John the Baptist is risen from among the dead, and on this account works of power are worked by him.

15 And others said, It is Elijah; and others said, It is a prophet, as one of the prophets.

16 But Herod when he heard it said, John whom I beheaded, he it is; he is risen [from among the dead]

17 For the same Herod had sent and seized John, and had bound him in prison on account of Herodias, the wife of Philip his brother, because he had married her.

18 For John said to Herod, It is not lawful for you to have the wife of your brother.

19 But Herodias kept it [in her mind] against him, and wished to kill him, and could not:

20 for Herod feared John knowing that he was a just and holy man, and kept him safe; and having heard him, did many things, and heard him gladly.

21 And a holiday being come, when Herod, on his birthday, made a supper to his grandees, and to the commanders, and the chief [men] of Galilee;

22 and the daughter of the same Herodias having come in, and danced, pleased Herod and those that were with him at table; and the king said to the damsel, Ask of me whatsoever you will and I will give it you.

23 And he swore to her, Whatsoever you shall ask me I will give you, to half of my kingdom.

24 And she went out, and said to her mother, What should I ask? And she said, The head of John the Baptist.

25 And immediately going in with haste to the king, she asked saying, I desire that you give me directly upon a dish the head of John the Baptist.

26 And the king, [while] made very sorry, on account of the oaths and those lying at table with him would not break his word with her.

27 And immediately the king, having sent one of the guard, ordered his head to be brought. And he went out and beheaded him in the prison,

28 and brought his head upon a dish, and gave it to the damsel, and the damsel gave it to her mother.

29 And his disciples having heard it came and took up his body, and laid it in a tomb.

30 And the apostles are gathered together to Jesus. And they related to him all things, [both] what they had done and what they had taught.

31 And he said to them, Come you yourselves alone into a desolate place and rest a little. For those coming and those going were many, and they had not leisure even to eat.

32 And they went away apart into a desolate place by ship.

33 And many saw them going, and recognized them, and ran together there on foot, out of all the cities, and got [there] before them.

34 And on leaving [the ship] [Jesus] saw a great crowd, and he was moved with compassion for them, because they were as sheep not having a shepherd. And he began to teach them many things.

35 And when it was already late in the day, his disciples coming to him say, The place is desolate, and it is already late in the day;

36 send them away that they may go into the country and villages around, and buy themselves bread, for they have not anything they can eat.

37 And he answering said to them, Give you them to eat. And they say to him, Shall we go and buy two hundred denarii worth of bread and give them to eat?

38 And he says to them, How many loaves have you? Go [and] see. And when they knew they say, Five, and two fishes.

39 And he ordered them to make them all sit down by companies on the green grass.

40 And they sat down in ranks by hundreds and by fifties.

41 And having taken the five loaves and the two fishes, looking up to heaven, he blessed, and broke the loaves, and gave [them] to his disciples that they might set [them] before them. And the two fishes he divided among all.

42 And they all ate and were satisfied.

43 And they took up of fragments the fillings of twelve hand-baskets, and of the fishes.

44 And those that ate of the loaves were five thousand men.

45 And immediately he compelled his disciples to go on board ship, and to go on before to the other side to Beth-saida, while he sends the crowd away.

46 And, having dismissed them, he departed into the mountain to pray.

47 And when evening was come, the ship was in the midst of the sea, and he alone upon the land.

48 And seeing them laboring in rowing, for the wind was contrary to them, about the fourth watch of the night he comes to them walking on the sea, and would have passed them by.

49 But they, seeing him walking on the sea, thought that it was a ghost, and cried out.

50 For all saw him and were troubled. And immediately he spoke with them, and says to them, Be of good courage: it is I; be not afraid.

51 And he went up to them into the ship, and the wind fell. And they were exceedingly beyond measure astonished in themselves and wondered;

52 for they understood not through the loaves: for their heart was hardened.

53 And having passed over, they came to the land of Gennesaret and made the shore.

54 And on their coming out of the ship, immediately recognising him,

55 they ran through that whole country around, and began to carry about those that were ill on couches, where they heard that he was.

56 And wherever he entered into villages, or cities, or the country, they laid the sick in the market-places, and besought him that they might touch if it were only the hem of his garment; and as many as touched him were healed.

Mark 7:1 And the Pharisees and some of the scribes, coming from Jerusalem, are gathered together to him,

2 and seeing some of his disciples eat bread with defiled, that is, unwashed, hands,

3 for the Pharisees and all the Jews, unless they wash their hands diligently, do not eat, holding what has been delivered by the ancients;

4 and [on coming] from the market-place, unless they are washed, they do not eat; and there are many other things which they have received to hold, the washing of cups and vessels, and brazen utensils, and couches,

5 then the Pharisees and the scribes ask him, Why do your disciples not walk according to what has been delivered by the ancients, but eat the bread with defiled hands?

6 But he answering said to them, Well did Isaiah prophesy concerning you hypocrites, as it is written, This people honor me with their lips, but their heart is far away from me.

7 But in vain do they worship me, teaching [as their] teachings commandments of men.

8 [For,] leaving the commandment of the God, you hold what is delivered by men [to keep] --washing of vessels and cups, and many other such like things you do.

9 And he said to them, Well do you set aside the commandment of the God, that you may observe what is delivered by yourselves [to keep]

10 For Moses said, honor your father and your mother; and, he who speaks ill of father or mother, let him surely die.

11 But you say, If a man say to his father or his mother, [it is] corban that is, gift, whatsoever you might have profit from me by ...

12 And you no longer permit him to do anything for his father or his mother;

13 making void the word of the God by your traditional teaching which you have delivered; and many such like things you do.

14 And having called again the crowd, he said to them, Hear me, all [of you] and understand:

15 There is nothing from outside a man entering into him which can defile him; but the things which go out from him, those it is which defile the man.

16 If any one have ears to hear, let him hear.

17 And when he went indoors from the crowd, his disciples asked him concerning the parable.

18 And he says to them, Are you also thus unwise? Do you not perceive that all that is outside entering into the man cannot defile him,

19 because it does not enter into his heart but into his belly, and goes out into the sewer, purging all meats?

20 And he said, That which goes forth out of the man, that defiles the man.

21 For from within, out of the heart of men, go forth evil thoughts, adulteries, fornications, murders,

22 thefts, covetousness, wickedness, deceit, licentiousness, a wicked eye, injurious language, haughtiness, folly;

23 all these wicked things go forth from within and defile the man.

24 And he rose up and went away from there into the borders of Tyre and Sidon; and having entered into a house he would not have any one know it and he could not be hid.

25 But immediately a woman, whose little daughter had an unclean spirit, having heard of him, came and fell at his feet

26 and the woman was a Greek, Syrophenician by race, and asked him that he would cast the daemon out of her daughter.

27 But [Jesus] said to her, Permit the children to be first filled; for it is not right to take the children's bread and cast it to the dogs.

28 But she answered and says to him, Yes, Lord; for even the dogs under the table eat of the children's crumbs.

29 And he said to her, Because of this word, go your way, the daemon is gone out of your daughter.

30 And having gone away to her house she found the daemon gone out, and her daughter lying on the bed.

31 And again having left the borders of Tyre and Sidon, he came to the sea of Galilee, through the midst of the coasts of Decapolis.

32 And they bring to him a deaf [man] who could not speak right, and they beseech him that he might lay his hand on him.

33 And having taken him away from the crowd apart, he put his fingers to his ears; and having spit, he touched his tongue;

34 and looking up to heaven he groaned, and says to him, Ephphatha, that is, Be opened.

35 And immediately his ears were opened, and the band of his tongue was loosened and he spoke right.

36 And he charged them that they should speak to no one [of it] But so much the more he charged them, so much the more abundantly they proclaimed it;

37 and they were astonished above measure, saying, He does all things well; he makes both the deaf to hear, and the speechless to speak.

Mark 8:1 In those days, there being again a great crowd, and they having nothing that they could eat, having called his disciples to him, he says to them,

2 I have compassion on the crowd, because they have stayed with me already three days and they have not anything they can eat,

3 and if I should dismiss them to their home fasting, they will faint on the way; for some of them are come from far.

4 And his disciples answered him, From where shall one be able to satisfy these with bread here in a desolate place?

5 And he asked them, How many loaves have you? And they said, Seven.

6 And he commanded the crowd to sit down on the ground. And having taken the seven loaves, he gave thanks, and broke [them] and gave [them] to his disciples, that they might set [them] before [them] and they set [them] before the crowd.

7 And they had a few small fishes, and having blessed them, he desired these also to be set before [them]

8 And they ate and were satisfied. And they took up of fragments that remained seven baskets.

9 And they [that had eaten] were about four thousand; and he sent them away.

10 And immediately going on board ship with his disciples, he came into the parts of Dalmanutha.

11 And the Pharisees went out and began to dispute against him, seeking from him a sign from heaven, testing him.

12 And groaning in his spirit, he says, Why does this generation seek a sign? Truly I say unto you, A sign shall in no way be given to this generation.

13 And he left them, and going again on board ship, went away to the other side.

14 And they forgot to take bread, and except one loaf, they had not [any] with them in the ship.

15 And he charged them, saying, Take heed, beware of the leaven of the Pharisees and of the leaven of Herod.

16 And they reasoned with one another, [saying] It is because we have no bread.

17 And Jesus knowing it says to them, Why reason you because you have no bread? Do you not yet perceive nor understand? Have you your heart [yet] hardened?

18 Having eyes, see you not? and having ears, hear you not? and do you not remember?

19 When I broke the five loaves for the five thousand, how many hand-baskets full of fragments took you up? They say to him, Twelve.

20 And when the seven for the four thousand, the filling of how many baskets of fragments took you up? And they said, Seven.

21 And he said to them, How do you not yet understand?

22 And he comes to Beth-saida; and they bring him a blind man, and beseech him that he might touch him.

23 And taking hold of the hand of the blind man he led him forth out of the village, and having spit upon his eyes, he laid his hands upon him, and asked him if he beheld anything.

24 And having looked up, he said, I behold men, for I see [them] as trees, walking.

25 Then he laid his hands again upon his eyes, and he saw distinctly, and was restored and saw all things clearly.

26 And he sent him to his house, saying, Neither enter into the village, nor tell it to any one in the village.

27 And Jesus went forth and his disciples, into the villages of Caesarea-Philippi. And by the way he asked his disciples, saying unto them, Who do men say that I am?

28 And they answered him, saying, John the Baptist; and others, Elijah; but others, One of the prophets.

29 And he asked them, But you, who do you say that I am? And Peter answering says to him, You are the Christ.

30 And he charged them straitly, in order that they should tell no man about him.

31 And he began to teach them that the Son of man must suffer many things, and be rejected of the elders and of the chief priests and of the scribes, and be killed, and after three days rise [again]

32 And he spoke the thing openly. And Peter, taking him to him began to rebuke him.

33 But he, turning round and seeing his disciples, rebuked Peter, saying, Get away behind me, Satan, for your mind is not on the things that are of the God, but on the things that are of men.

34 And having called the crowd with his disciples, he said to them, Whoever desires to come after me, let him deny himself, and take up his cross and follow me.

35 For whosoever shall desire to save his soul shall lose it, but whosoever shall lose his soul for my sake and the gospel's shall save it.

36 For what shall it profit a man if he gain the whole world and suffer the loss of his soul?

37 for what should a man give in exchange for his soul?

38 For whosoever shall be ashamed of me and of my words in this adulterous and sinful generation, of him shall the Son of man also be ashamed when he shall come in the glory of his Father with the holy angels.

Mark 9:1 And he said to them, Truly I say unto you, There are some of those standing here that shall not taste death until they shall have seen the kingdom of the God come in power.

2 And after six days Jesus takes with him Peter and James and John, and takes them up on a high mountain by themselves apart. And he was transfigured before them:

3 and his garments became shining, exceeding white [as snow] such as fuller on earth could not whiten [them]

4 And there appeared to them Elijah with Moses, and they were talking with Jesus.

5 And Peter answering says to Jesus, Rabbi, it is good that we should be here; and let us make three tabernacles, for you one, and for Moses one, and for Elijah one.

6 For he knew not what he should say, for they were filled with fear.

7 And there came a cloud overshadowing them, and there came a voice out of the cloud, This is my beloved Son: hear him.

8 And suddenly having looked around, they no longer saw any one, but Jesus alone with themselves.

9 And as they descended from the mountain, he charged them that they should relate to no one what they had seen, unless when the Son of man should be risen from among the dead.

10 And they kept that saying, questioning among themselves, what rising from among the dead was.

11 And they asked him saying, Why do the scribes say that Elijah must first have come?

12 And he answering said to them, Elijah indeed, having first come, restores all things; and how is it written of the Son of man that he must suffer much, and be set at nought:

13 but I say unto you that Elijah also is come, and they have done to him whatever they would, as it is written of him.

14 And when he came to the disciples he saw a great crowd around them, and scribes disputing against them.

15 And immediately all the crowd seeing him were amazed, and running to him saluted him.

16 And he asked them, What do you question with them about?

17 And one out of the crowd answered him, Teacher, I brought to you my son, who has a mute spirit;

18 and wheresoever it seizes him it tears him, and he foams and gnashes his teeth, and he is withering away. And I spoke to your disciples, that they might cast him out, and they could not.

19 But he answering them says, O unbelieving generation! how long shall I be with you? how long shall I bear with you? bring him to me.

20 And they brought him to him. And seeing him the spirit immediately tore him; and falling upon the earth he rolled foaming.

21 And he asked his father, How long a time is it that it has been like this with him? And he said, From childhood;

22 and often it has cast him both into fire and into waters that it might destroy him: but if you could [do] anything, be moved with pity on us, and help us.

23 And Jesus said to him, The "if you are able to believe: all things are possible to him that believes.'

24 And immediately the father of the young child crying out said [with tears] I believe, help mine unbelief.

25 But Jesus, seeing that the crowd was running up together, rebuked the unclean spirit, saying to him, You mute and deaf spirit, I command you, come out of him, and enter no more into him.

26 And having cried out and torn him much, he came out; and he became as if dead, so that the most said, He is dead.

27 But Jesus, having taken hold of him by the hand, lifted him up, and he arose.

28 And when he was entered into the house, his disciples asked him privately, Why could not we cast him out?

29 And he said to them, This kind can go out by nothing but by prayer and fasting.

30 And going forth from there they went through Galilee; and he wished that no one would know it;

31 for he taught his disciples and said to them, The Son of man is delivered into men's hands, and they shall kill him; and having been killed, after three days he shall rise again.

32 But they understood not the saying, and feared to ask him.

33 And he came to Capernaum, and being in the house, he asked them, Of what were you reasoning by the way?

34 And they remained silent, for by the way they had been reasoning with one another who [was] greatest.

35 And sitting down he called the twelve; and he says to them, If any one would be first, he shall be last of all, and minister of all.

36 And taking a little child he set it in their midst, and having taken it in his arms he said to them,

37 Whosoever shall receive one of such little children in my name, receives me; and whosoever shall receive me, does not receive me, but him who sent me.

38 And John answered him saying, Teacher, we saw some one casting out daemons in your name, who does not follow us, and we forbade him, because he does not follow us.

39 But Jesus said, Forbid him not; for there is no one who shall do a miracle in my name, and be able soon [after] to speak ill of me;

40 for he who is not against us is for us.

41 For whosoever shall give you a cup of water to drink in [my] name, because you are Christ's, truly I say unto you, he shall in no way lose his reward.

42 And whosoever shall be a snare to one of the little ones who believe [in me] it were better for him if a millstone were hung about his neck, and he cast into the sea.

43 And if your hand serve as a snare to you, cut it off: it is better for you to enter into life maimed, than having your two hands to go away into Gehenna, into the fire unquenchable;

44 [where their worm dies not, and the fire is not quenched]

45 And if your foot serve as a snare to you, cut it off: it is better for you to enter into life lame, than having your two feet to be cast into Gehenna, into the fire unquenchable;

46 [where their worm dies not, and the fire is not quenched]

47 And if your eye serve as a snare to you, cast it out: it is better for you to enter into the kingdom of the God with one eye, rather than having two eyes to be cast into the Gehenna of fire,

48 where their worm dies not, and the fire is not quenched.

49 For every one shall be salted with fire, and every sacrifice shall be salted with salt.

50 Salt is good, but if the salt is become saltless, wherewith will you season it? Have salt in yourselves, and be at peace with one another.

Mark 10:1 And rising up from there he comes into the coasts of Judea, and the other side of the Jordan. And again crowds come together to him, and, as he was accustomed, again he taught them.

2 And Pharisees coming to him, asked him, Is it lawful for a man to put away [his] wife? testing him.

3 But he answering said to them, What did Moses command you?

4 And they said, Moses allowed to write a bill of divorce, and to put away.

5 And Jesus answering said to them, In view of your hard-heartedness he wrote this commandment for you;

6 but from the beginning of the creation the God made them male and female.

7 For this cause a man shall leave his father and mother and shall be united to his wife,

8 and the two shall be one flesh: so that they are no longer two but one flesh.

9 What therefore the God has joined together, let not man separate.

10 And again in the house the disciples asked him concerning this.

11 And he says to them, Whosoever shall put away his wife and shall marry another, commits adultery against her.

12 And if a woman put away her husband and shall marry another, she commits adultery.

13 And they brought little children to him that he might touch them. But the disciples rebuked those that brought [them]

14 But Jesus seeing it was indignant, and said to them, Permit the little children to come to me; forbid them not; for of such is the kingdom of the God.

15 Truly I say to you, Whosoever shall not receive the kingdom of the God as a little child, shall in no way enter into it.

16 And having taken them in his arms, having laid his hands on them, he blessed them.

17 And as he went forth into the way, a person ran up to him, and kneeling to him asked him, Good Teacher, what shall I do that I may inherit aeonian life?

18 But Jesus said to him, Why do you call me good? no one is good but one, [that is] the God.

19 You know the commandments: Do not commit adultery, Do not kill, Do not steal, Do not bear false witness, Do not defraud, honor your father and mother.

20 And he answering said to him, Teacher, all these things have I kept from my youth.

21 And Jesus looking upon him loved him, and said to him, One thing you lack: go, sell whatever you have and give to the poor, and you shall have treasure in heaven; and come, follow me, [taking up the cross]

22 But he, sad at the word, went away grieved, for he had large possessions.

23 And Jesus looking around says to his disciples, How difficultly shall they that have riches enter into the kingdom of the God!

24 And the disciples were amazed at his words. And Jesus again answering says to them, Children, how difficult it is that those who trust in riches should enter into the kingdom of the God!

25 It is easier for a camel to go through the eye of a needle than for a rich man to enter into the kingdom of the God.

26 And they were exceedingly astonished, saying to one another, And who can be saved?

27 But Jesus looking on them says, With men it is impossible, but not with the God; for all things are possible with the God.

28 Peter began to say to him, Behold, we have left all things and have followed you.

29 Jesus answering said, Truly I say to you, There is no one who has left house, or brethren, or sisters, or father, or mother, [or wife] or children, or lands, for my sake and for the sake of the gospel,

30 that shall not receive a hundredfold now in this time: houses, and brethren, and sisters, and mothers, and children, and lands, with persecutions, and in the coming aeon, aeonian life.

31 But many first shall be last, and the last first.

32 And they were in the way going up to Jerusalem, and Jesus was going on before them; and they were amazed, and were afraid as they followed. And taking the twelve again to him, he began to tell them what was going to happen to him:

33 Behold, we go up to Jerusalem, and the Son of man shall be delivered up to the chief priests and to the scribes, and they shall condemn him to death, and shall deliver him up to the Gentiles:

34 and they shall mock him, and shall scourge him, and shall spit upon him, and shall kill him; and after three days he shall rise again.

35 And there come to him James and John, the sons of Zebedee, saying [to him] Teacher, we wish that whatsoever we may ask you, you would do it for us.

36 And he said to them, What do you wish that I should do for you?

37 And they said to him, Give to us that we may sit, one on your right hand, and one on your left hand, in your glory.

38 And Jesus said to them, You do not know what you ask. Are you able to drink the cup which I drink, or be baptized with the baptism that I am baptized with?

39 And they said to him, We are able. And Jesus said to them, The cup that I drink you will drink and with the baptism that I am baptized with you will be baptized,

40 but to sit on my right hand or on my left is not mine to give, but for those for whom it is prepared.

41 And the ten having heard [of it] began to be indignant about James and John.

42 But Jesus having called them to him, says to them, You know that those who are esteemed to rule over the nations exercise lordship over them; and their great men exercise authority over them;

43 but it is not thus among you; but whosoever would be great among you, shall be your minister;

44 and whosoever would be first of you shall be servant of all.

45 For also the Son of man did not come to be ministered to, but to minister, and give his soul a ransom for many.

46 And they come to Jericho, and as he was going out from Jericho, and his disciples and a large crowd, the son of Timaeus, Bartimaeus, the blind [man] sat by the wayside begging.

47 And having heard that it was Jesus the Nazarene, he began to cry out and to say, O Son of David, Jesus, have mercy on me.

48 And many rebuked him, that he might be silent; but he cried so much the more, Son of David, have mercy on me.

49 And Jesus, standing still, desired him to be called. And they call the blind [man] saying to him, Be of good courage, rise up, he calls you.

50 And, throwing away his garment, he started up and came to Jesus.

51 And Jesus answering says to him, What do you wish that I shall do to you? And the blind [man] said to him, Rabboni, that I may see.

52 And Jesus said to him, Go, your faith has healed you. And he saw immediately, and followed him in the way.

Mark 11:1 And when they draw near to Jerusalem, to Bethphage and Bethany, at the mount of Olives, he sends two of his disciples,

2 and says to them, Go into the village which is over against you, and immediately on entering into it you will find a colt tied, upon which no [child] of man has ever sat: loose it and lead it [here]

3 And if any one say to you, Why do you do this? say, The Lord has need of it; and straightway he sends it here.

4 And they departed, and found a colt bound to the door outside at the crossway, and they loose him.

5 And some of those who stood there said to them, What are you doing, loosing the colt?

6 And they said to them as Jesus had commanded. And they let them [do it]

7 And they led the colt to Jesus, and cast their clothes upon it, and he sat on it;

8 and many scattered their clothes on the way, and others cut down branches from the trees [and went on scattering them on the way]

9 And those going on before and those following cried out, Hosanna! blessed [be] he that comes in the Lord's name.

10 Blessed [be] the coming kingdom of our father David. Hosanna in the highest!

11 And he entered into Jerusalem and into the temple; and having looked round on all things, the hour being already late, he went out to Bethany with the twelve.

12 And on the next day, when they were gone out of Bethany, he hungered.

13 And seeing from afar off a fig-tree which had leaves, he came, if perhaps he might find something on it. And having come up to it he found nothing but leaves, for it was not the time of figs.

14 And answering he said to it, Let no one eat fruit of you any more into the aeon. And his disciples heard it

15 And they come to Jerusalem, and entering into the temple, he began to cast out those who sold and who bought in the temple, and he overthrew the tables of the moneychangers and the seats of the dove-sellers,

16 and permitted not that any one should carry any package through the temple.

17 And he taught saying to them, Is it not written, My house shall be called a house of prayer for all the Gentiles? but you have made it a den of robbers.

18 And the chief priests and the scribes heard it and they sought how they might destroy him; for they feared him, because all the crowd were astonished at his doctrine.

19 And when it was evening he went forth outside the city.

20 And passing by early in the morning they saw the fig-tree dried up from the roots.

21 And Peter, remembering [what Jesus had said] says to him, Rabbi, see, the fig-tree which you cursed is dried up.

22 And Jesus answering says to them, Have faith in God.

23 Truly I say to you, that whosoever shall say to this mountain, Be you taken away and cast into the sea, and shall not doubt in his heart, but believe that what he says takes place, whatever he shall say shall come to pass for him.

24 For this reason I say to you, All things whatsoever you pray for and ask, believe that you receive it, and it shall come to pass for you.

25 And when you stand praying, forgive if you have anything against any one, that your Father also who is in the heavens may forgive you your offences.

26 But if you do not forgive, neither will your Father who is in the heavens forgive your offences.

27 And they come again to Jerusalem. And as he walked about in the temple, the chief priests and the scribes and the elders come to him,

28 and they say to him, By what authority do you do these things? and who gave you this authority, that you should do these things?

29 And Jesus answering said to them, I also will ask you one thing, and answer me, and I will tell you by what authority I do these things:

30 The baptism of John, was it of heaven, or of men? answer me.

31 And they reasoned with themselves, saying, If we should say, Of heaven, he will say, Why [then] have you not believed him?

32 but should we say, Of men --they feared the people; for all held of John that he was truly a prophet.

33 And they answering say to Jesus, We do not know. And Jesus [answering] says to them, Neither do I tell you by what authority I do these things.

Mark 12:1 And he began to say to them in parables, A man planted a vineyard, and made a fence round it and dug a wine-vat, and built a tower, and let it out to husbandmen, and left the country.

2 And he sent a servant to the husbandmen at the season, that he might receive from the husbandmen of the fruit of the vineyard.

3 But they took him, and beat him, and sent him away empty.

4 And again he sent to them another servant; and [at] him they [threw stones, and] struck him on the head, and sent him away with insult.

5 And [again] he sent another, and him they killed; and many others, beating some and killing some.

6 Having yet therefore one beloved son, he sent also him to them the last, saying, They will have respect for my son.

7 But those husbandmen said to one another, This is the heir: come, let us kill him and the inheritance will be ours.

8 And they took him and killed him, and cast him forth out of the vineyard.

9 What therefore shall the lord of the vineyard do? He will come and destroy the husbandmen, and will give the vineyard to others.

10 Have you not even read this scripture, The stone which they that built rejected, this has become the corner-stone:

11 this is of the Lord, and it is wonderful in our eyes?

12 And they sought to lay hold of him, and they feared the crowd; for they knew that he had spoken the parable of them. And they left him and went away.

13 And they send to him certain of the Pharisees and of the Herodians, that they might catch him in speaking.

14 And they come and say to him, Teacher, we know that you are true, and care not for any one; for you regard not men's person, but teach the way of the God with truth: Is it lawful to give tribute to Caesar or not?

15 Should we give, or should we not give? But he knowing their hypocrisy said unto them, Why do you test me? Bring me a denarius that I may see it

16 And they brought it And he says to them, Whose is this image and superscription? And they said to him, Caesar's.

17 And Jesus answering said to them, Pay what is Caesar's to Caesar, and what is God's to the God. And they wondered at him.

18 And Sadducees come to him, that say there is no resurrection; and they asked of him saying,

19 Teacher, Moses wrote to us that if any one's brother die, and leave a wife behind, and leave no children, that his brother shall take his wife, and raise up seed to his brother.

20 There were seven brethren; and the first took a wife, and dying did not leave seed;

21 and the second took her and died, and neither did he leave seed; and the third likewise.

22 And the seven [took her and] did not leave seed. Last of all the woman also died.

23 In the resurrection, when they shall rise again, of which of them shall she be wife, for the seven had her as wife?

24 And Jesus answering said to them, Do not you therefore err, not knowing the scriptures, nor the power of the God?

25 For when they rise from among the dead they neither marry, nor are given in marriage, but are as angels [who are] in the heavens.

26 But concerning the dead that they rise, have you not read in the book of Moses, in [the section of] the bush, how the God spoke to him, saying, I am the God of Abraham, and the God of Isaac, and the God of Jacob?

27 He is not God of the dead, but of the living. You therefore greatly err.

28 And one of the scribes who had come up, and had heard them reasoning together, perceiving that he had answered them well, asked of him, Which is the first commandment of all?

29 And Jesus answered him, the first commandment of all is Hear, Israel: the Lord our God is one Lord [see Deu 6:4: "Lord = YHWH];

30 and you shall love the Lord your God with all your heart, and with all your soul, and with all your understanding, and with all your strength. This is the first commandment.

31 And a second like it is this: You shall love your neighbor as yourself. There is not another commandment greater than these.

32 And the scribe said to him, Right, teacher; you have spoken according to the truth. For he is one, and there is none other besides him;

33 and to love him with all the heart, and with all the intelligence, and with all the soul, and with all the strength, and to love one's neighbor as one's self, is more than all the burnt-offerings and sacrifices.

34 And Jesus, seeing that he had answered wisely, said to him, You are not far from the kingdom of the God. And no one dared question him any more.

35 And Jesus answering said [as he was] teaching in the temple, How do the scribes say that the Christ is son of David?

36 [for] David himself said [speaking] in the Holy Spirit, The Lord said to my Lord, Sit on my right hand until I put your enemies [as] footstool of your feet.

37 David himself [therefore] calls him Lord, and how is he his son? And the mass of the people heard him gladly.

38 And he said to them in his doctrine, Beware of the scribes, who like to walk about in long robes, and salutations in the marketplaces,

39 and first seats in the synagogues, and first places at suppers;

40 who devour the houses of widows, and as a pretext make long prayers. These shall receive a severer judgment.

41 And Jesus, having sat down opposite the treasury, saw how the crowd was casting money into the treasury; and many rich cast in much.

42 And a poor widow came and cast in two bits [lepta] which is a quarter [quadrans]

43 And having called his disciples to him, he said to them, Truly I say unto you, This poor widow has cast in more than all who have cast into the treasury:

44 for all have cast in of that which they had in abundance, but she of her destitution has cast in all that she had, the whole of her living.

Mark 13:1 And as he was going out of the temple, one of his disciples says to him, Teacher, see what stones and what buildings!

2 And Jesus answering said to him, See you these great buildings? not a stone shall be left upon a stone, which shall not be thrown down.

3 And as he sat on the mount of Olives opposite the temple, Peter and James and John and Andrew asked him privately,

4 Tell us, when shall these things be, and what is the sign when all these things are going to be fulfilled?

5 And Jesus answering them began to say, Take heed lest any one mislead you.

6 For many shall come in my name, saying, It is I, and shall mislead many.

7 But when you shall hear of wars and rumours of wars, be not disturbed, for [this] must happen, but the end is not yet.

8 For nation shall rise up against nation, and kingdom against kingdom; and there shall be earthquakes in [different] places, and there shall be famines and troubles: these things [are the] beginnings of throes.

9 But you, take heed to yourselves, for they shall deliver you up to sanhedrims and to synagogues: you shall be beaten and brought before rulers and kings for my sake, for a testimony to them;

10 and the gospel must first be preached to all the nations.

11 But when they shall lead you away to deliver you up, be not concerned beforehand as to what you shall say, [nor prepare your discourse] but whatsoever shall be given you in that hour, that speak; for you are not the speakers, but the Holy Spirit.

12 But brother shall deliver up brother to death, and father child; and children shall rise up against parents, and cause them to be put to death.

13 And you will be hated of all on account of my name; but he that has endured to the end, he shall be saved.

14 But when you shall see the abomination of desolation standing where it should not, he that reads let him consider it then let those in Judea flee to the mountains;

15 and him that is upon the housetop not come down into the house, nor enter [into it] to take away anything out of his house;

16 and him that is in the field not return back to take his garment.

17 But woe to those that are with child and to those that give suck in those days!

18 And pray that it may not be in winter time;

19 for those days shall be distress such as there has not been the like since the beginning of creation which the God created, until now, and never shall be;

20 and if the Lord had not cut off those days, no flesh should have been saved; but on account of the elect whom he has chosen, he has cut off those days.

21 And then if any one say to you, Lo, here is the Christ, or Lo, there, believe it not.

22 For false Christs and false prophets will arise, and give signs and wonders to deceive, if possible, even the elect.

23 But do you take heed: behold, I have told you all things beforehand.

24 But in those days, after that distress, the sun shall be darkened and the moon shall not give its light;

25 and the stars of heaven shall be falling down, and the powers which are in the heavens shall be shaken;

26 and then shall they see the Son of man coming in clouds with great power and glory;

27 and then shall he send his angels and shall gather together his elect from the four winds, from end of earth to end of heaven.

28 But learn the parable from the fig-tree: when its branch already becomes tender and puts forth the leaves, you know that the summer is near.

29 Thus also you, when you see these things happening, know that it is near, at the doors.

30 Truly I say unto you, This generation[188] shall in no way pass away, till all these things take place.

31 The heaven and the earth shall pass away, but my words shall in no way pass away.

32 But of that day or of that hour no one knows, neither the angels who are in heaven, nor the Son, but the Father.

33 Take heed, watch and pray, that you do not know when the time is:

34 [it is] as a man gone out of the country, having left his house and given to his servants the authority, and to each one his work, and commanded the doorkeeper that he should watch.

35 Keep awake therefore, that you do not know when the master of the house comes: evening, or midnight, or cock-crow, or morning;

36 lest coming suddenly he find you sleeping.

37 But what I say to you, I say to all, Keep awake.

Mark 14:1 Now the Passover and the [feast of] unleavened bread was after two days. And the chief priests and the scribes were seeking how they might seize him by subtlety and kill him.

2 For they said, Not in the feast, lest perhaps there be a tumult of the people.

3 And when he was in Bethany, in the house of Simon the leper, as he lay at table, there came a woman having an alabaster flask of ointment of pure nard, very costly; and having broken the alabaster flask, she poured it out upon his head.

4 And there were some indignant in themselves, and saying, Why has this waste been made of the ointment?

5 for this ointment could have been sold for more than three hundred denarii and given to the poor. And they spoke very angrily at her.

6 But Jesus said, Let her alone; why do you trouble her? she has worked a good work as to me;

7 for you have the poor always with you, and whenever you would you can do them good; but me you have not always.

8 What she could she has done. She has beforehand anointed my body for the burial.

9 And truly I say unto you, Wheresoever these good news may be preached in the whole world, what this [woman] has done shall be also spoken of for a memorial of her.

10 And Judas Iscariote, one of the twelve, went away to the chief priests that he might deliver him up to them;

11 and they, when they heard it, rejoiced, and promised him to give money. And he sought how he could opportunely deliver him up.

12 And towards the first day of unleavened bread, when they kill the Passover, his disciples say to him, Where wish you that we go and prepare, that you may eat the Passover?

13 And he sends two of his disciples, and says to them, Go into the city, and a man shall meet you carrying a pitcher of water; follow him.

14 And wheresoever he enters, say to the master of the house, The Teacher says, Where is my guest-chamber where I may eat the Passover with my disciples?

15 and he will show you a large upper room furnished ready. There make ready for us.

16 And his disciples went away and came into the city, and found as he had said to them; and they made ready* the Passover.

17 And when evening was come, he comes with the twelve.

18 And as they lay at table and were eating, Jesus said, Truly I say to you, One of you shall deliver me up; he who is eating with me.

19 And they began to be grieved, and to say to him, one by one, Is it I? [and another, Is it I]

20 But he answered and said to them, One of the twelve, he who dips with me in the dish.

21 The Son of man goes indeed as it is written concerning him, but woe to that man by whom the Son of man is delivered up; [it were] good for that man if he had not been born.

---

[188] See Ps 22:30

22 And as they were eating, Jesus, having taken bread, when he had blessed, broke it and gave it to them, and said, Take [this] this is my body.

23 And having taken the cup, when he had given thanks, he gave it to them, and they all drank out of it.

24 And he said to them, This is my blood, that of the [new] covenant that shed for many.

25 Truly I say to you, I will no more drink at all of the fruit of the vine, until that day when I drink it new in the kingdom of the God.

26 And having sung a hymn, they went out to the mount of Olives.

27 And Jesus says to them, All you shall be offended, for it is written, I will smite the shepherd, and the sheep shall be scattered abroad.

28 But after I am risen, I will go before you into Galilee.

29 But Peter said to him, Even if all should be offended, yet not I.

30 And Jesus says to him, Truly I say to you, that you today, in this night, before the cock shall crow twice, you shall three times deny me.

31 But he said [so much] exceedingly the more, If I should have to die with you, I will in no way deny you. And likewise said they all too.

32 And they come to a place of which the name is Gethsemane, and he says to his disciples, Sit here while I shall pray.

33 And he takes with him Peter and James and John, and he began to be amazed and oppressed in spirit.

34 And he says to them, My soul is full of grief even unto death; abide here and keep awake.

35 And, going forward a little, he fell upon the earth; and he prayed that, if it were possible, the hour might pass away from him.

36 And he said, Abba, Father, all things are possible to you: take away this cup from me; but not what I will, but what you [will]

37 And he comes and finds them sleeping. And he says to Peter, Simon, do you sleep? Have you not been able to watch one hour?

38 Keep awake and pray, that you enter not into temptation. The spirit indeed is willing, but the flesh weak.

39 And going away, he prayed again, saying the same thing.

40 And returning, he found them again sleeping, for their eyes were heavy; and they knew not what they should answer him.

41 And he comes the third time and says to them, Sleep on now, and take your rest. It is enough; the hour is come; behold, the Son of man is delivered up into the hands of sinners.

42 Arise, let us go; behold, he that delivers me up has drawn near.

43 And immediately, while he was yet speaking, Judas comes up, [being] one of the twelve, and with him a great crowd, with swords and sticks, from the chief priests and the scribes and the elders.

44 Now he that delivered him up had given them a sign between them, saying, Whomsoever I shall affection for, that is he; seize him, and lead him away safely.

45 And being come, straightway coming up to him, he says, Rabbi, Rabbi; and he covered him with kisses.

46 And they laid their hands upon him and seized him.

47 But a certain one of those who stood by, having drawn his sword, struck the servant of the high priest, and took off his ear.

48 And Jesus answering said to them, Are you come out as against a robber, with swords and sticks to take me?

49 I was daily with you teaching in the temple, and you did not seize me; but [it is] that the scriptures may be fulfilled.

50 And all left him and fled.

51 And a certain young man followed him with a linen cloth cast about his naked [body] and [the young men] seize him;

52 but he, leaving the linen cloth behind him fled from them naked.

53 And they led away Jesus to the high priest. And there come together to him all the chief priests and the elders and the scribes.

54 And Peter followed him at a distance, till [he was] within the court of the high priest's palace; and he was sitting with the officers and warming himself in the light [of the fire]

55 And the chief priests and the whole Sanhedrim sought testimony against Jesus to cause him to be put to death, and did not find [any]

56 For many bore false witness against him, and their testimony did not agree.

57 And certain persons rose up and bore false witness against him, saying,

58 We heard him saying, I will destroy this temple which is made with hands, and in the course of three days I will build another not made with hands.

59 And neither thus did their testimony agree.

60 And the high priest, rising up before them all, asked Jesus, saying, Answer you nothing? What do these testify against you?

61 But he was silent, and answered nothing. Again the high priest asked him, and says to him, You are the Christ, the Son of the Blessed?

62 And Jesus said, I am, and you shall see the Son of man sitting at the right hand of power, and coming with the clouds of heaven.

63 And the high priest, having rent his clothes, says, What need have we any more of witnesses?

64 You have heard the blasphemy; what do you think? And they all condemned him to be guilty of death.

65 And some began to spit upon him, and cover up his face, and hit him, and say to him, Prophesy; and the officers struck him with the palms of their hands.

66 And Peter being below in the palace-court, there comes one of the maids of the high priest,

67 and seeing Peter warming himself, having looked at him, says, And you were with the Nazarene, Jesus.

68 But he denied, saying, I know not nor understand what you are saying. And he went out into the vestibule; and a cock crew.

69 And the maid, seeing him, again began to say to those that stood by, This is [one] of them.

70 And he again denied. And again, after a little, those that stood by said to Peter, Truly you are [one] of them, for also you are a Galilean.

71 But he began to curse and to swear, I know not this man of whom you speak.

72 And the second time a cock crew. And Peter remembered the word that Jesus said to him, Before the cock crow twice, you shall deny me three times; and when he thought thereon he wept.

Mark 15:1 And immediately in the morning the chief priests, having taken counsel with the elders and scribes and the whole Sanhedrim, bound Jesus and carried him away, and delivered him up to Pilate.

2 And Pilate asked him, Are you the King of the Jews? And he answered and said to him, You said it.

3 And the chief priests accused him urgently.

4 And Pilate asked him again, saying, Answer you nothing? See of how many things they bear witness against you.

5 But Jesus still answered nothing, so that Pilate marvelled

6 But at the feast he released to them one prisoner, whomsoever they begged [of him].

7 Now there was the [person] named Barabbas bound with those who had made insurrection with him [and] that had committed murder in the insurrection.

8 And the crowd crying out began to beg [that he would do] to them as he had always done.

9 But Pilate answered them saying, Do you wish that I release to you the King of the Jews?

10 for he knew that the chief priests had delivered him up through envy.

11 But the chief priests stirred up the crowd that he might rather release Barabbas to them.

12 And Pilate answering said to them again, What do you wish then that I do [to him] whom you call King of the Jews?

13 And they cried out again, Crucify him.

14 And Pilate said to them, What evil then has he done? But they cried out the more urgently, Crucify him.

15 And Pilate, desirous of contenting the crowd, released to them Barabbas, and delivered up Jesus, when he had scourged him, that he might be crucified.

16 And the soldiers led him away into the court which is [called the] praetorium, and they call together the whole band.

17 And they clothe him with purple, and bind round on him a crown of thorns which they had plaited.

18 And they began to salute him, Hail, King of the Jews!

19 And they struck his head with a reed, and spat on him, and, bending the knee, did him homage.

20 And when they had mocked him, they took the purple off him, and put his own clothes on him; and they lead him out that they may crucify him.

21 And they compel to go [with them] a certain passer-by, Simon, a Cyrenian, coming from the field, the father of Alexander and Rufus, that he might carry his cross.

22 And they bring him to the place [called] Golgotha, which, being interpreted, is Place of a skull.

23 And they offered him wine [to drink] medicated with myrrh; but he did not take it

24 And having crucified him, they part his clothes among [themselves] casting lots on them, what each one should take.

25 And it was the third hour, and they crucified him.

26 And the superscription of what he was accused of was written up: The King of the Jews.

27 And with him they crucify two robbers, one on his right hand, and one on his left.

28 [And the scripture was fulfilled which says, And he was reckoned with the lawless]

29 And they that passed by reviled him, shaking their heads, and saying, Aha, you that will destroy the temple and build it in three days,

30 save yourself, and descend from the cross.

31 In like manner the chief priests also, with the scribes, mocking with one another, said, He saved others; himself he cannot save.

32 Let the Christ the King of Israel descend now from the cross, that we may see and may believe. And they that were crucified with him reproached him.

33 And when the sixth hour was come, there came darkness over the whole land until the ninth hour;

34 and at the ninth hour, Jesus cried with a loud voice, [saying] Eloi, Eloi, lama sabachthani? which is, being interpreted, My God, my God ["the God of me..."], why have you forsaken me?

35 And some of those who stood by, when they heard it said, Behold, he calls for Elijah.

36 And one, running and filling a sponge with vinegar, fixed it on a reed, and gave him to drink, saying, Let alone, let us see if Elijah comes to take him down.

37 And Jesus, having uttered a loud cry, expired.

38 And the veil of the temple was rent in two from the top to the bottom.

39 And the centurion who stood by over against him, when he saw that he had expired having thus cried out, said, Truly this man was Son of God.

40 And there were women also looking on from afar off, among whom were both Mary of Magdalene, and Mary the mother of James the less and of Joses, and Salome;

41 who also, when he was in Galilee, followed him and ministered to him; and many others who came up with him to Jerusalem.

42 And when it was already evening, since it was the preparation, that is, [the day] before a Sabbath,

43 Joseph of Arimathaea, an honorable councillor, who also himself was awaiting the kingdom of the God, coming, emboldened himself and went in to Pilate and begged the body of Jesus.

44 And Pilate wondered if he were already dead; and having called to him the centurion, he inquired of him if he had long died.

45 And when he knew from the centurion, he granted the body to Joseph.

46 And having bought fine linen, [and] having taken him down, he swathed him in the fine linen, and laid him in a tomb which was cut out of rock, and rolled a stone to the door of the tomb.

47 And Mary of Magdalene and Mary the [mother] of Joses saw where he was put.

Mark 16:1 And the Sabbath being [now] past, Mary of Magdalene, and Mary the [mother] of James, and Salome, bought aromatic spices that they might come and embalm him.

2 And very early towards one of the sabbaths [of the next two Sabbath week] they come to the tomb, the sun having risen.

3 And they said to one another, Who shall roll us away the stone out of the door of the tomb?

4 And when they looked, they see that the stone has been rolled [away] for it was very great.

5 And entering into the tomb, they saw a young man sitting on the right, clothed in a white robe, and they were amazed and alarmed;

6 but he says to them, Be not alarmed. You seek Jesus, the Nazarene, the crucified one. He is risen, he is not here; behold the place where they had put him.

7 But go, tell his disciples and Peter, he goes before you into Galilee; there shall you see him, as he said to you.

8 And they went out, and fled from the tomb. And trembling and excessive amazement possessed them, and they said nothing to any one, for they were afraid.

9 Now when he had risen, very early towards the first [day] of the week,[189] he appeared first to Mary of Magdalene, out of whom he had cast seven daemons.

10 She went and brought word to those that had been with him, [who were] grieving and weeping.

11 And when these heard that he was alive and had been seen of her, they disbelieved it

12 And after these things he was manifested in another form to two of them as they walked, going into the country;

13 and they went and brought word to the rest; neither did they believe them.

14 Afterwards as they lay at table he was manifested to the eleven, and reproached [them with] their unbelief and hardness of heart, because they had not believed those who had seen him risen.

15 And he said to them, Go into all the world, and preach the good news to all the creation.

16 He that believes and is baptized shall be saved, and he that disbelieves shall be condemned.

17 And these signs shall follow those that have believed: in my name they shall cast out daemons; they shall speak with new tongues;

18 they shall take up serpents; and if they should drink any deadly thing it shall not injure them; they shall lay hands upon the infirm, and they shall be well.

19 The Lord therefore, after he had spoken to them, was taken up into heaven, and sat at the right hand of the God.

20 And they, going forth, preached everywhere, the Lord working with [them] and confirming the word by the signs following upon it

---

[189] Sabbaths or week

Luke

Luke 1:1 Forasmuch as many have undertaken to draw up an account concerning the matters fully believed among us,

2 as those who from the beginning were eye-witnesses of and attendants on the Word have delivered them to us,

3 it has seemed good to me also, accurately acquainted from the beginning with all things, to write to you with carefullness, most excellent Theophilus,

4 that you might know the certainty of those things in which you have been instructed.

5 There was in the days of Herod, the king of Judea, a certain priest, by name Zacharias, of the course of Abijah, and his wife of the daughters of Aaron, and her name Elizabeth.

6 And they were both just before the God, walking in all the commandments and ordinances of the Lord blameless.

7 And they had no child, because Elizabeth was barren, and they were both advanced in years.

8 And it came to pass, as he fulfilled his priestly service before the God in the order of his course,

9 it fell to him by lot, according to the custom of the priesthood, to enter into the temple of the Lord to burn incense.

10 And all the multitude of the people were praying outside at the hour of incense

11 And an angel of the Lord appeared to him, standing on the right of the altar of incense.

12 And Zacharias was troubled, seeing him, and fear fell upon him.

13 But the angel said to him, Fear not, Zacharias, because your supplication has been heard, and your wife Elizabeth shall bear you a son, and you shall call his name John.

14 And he shall be to you joy and rejoicing, and many shall rejoice at his birth.

15 For he shall be great before the Lord, and he shall drink no wine nor strong drink; and he shall be filled with the Holy Spirit, even from his mother's womb.

16 And many of the sons of Israel shall he turn to the Lord their God.

17 And he shall go before him in the spirit and power of Elijah, to turn hearts of fathers to children, and disobedient ones to the thoughts of just [men] to make ready for the Lord a prepared people.

18 And Zacharias said to the angel, How shall I know this, for I am an old man, and my wife advanced in years?

19 And the angel answering, said to him, I am Gabriel, who has been standing before the God, and I have been sent to speak to you, and to bring the good news to you;

20 and behold, you shall be silent and not able to speak, till the day in which these things shall take place, because you have not believed my words, which shall be fulfilled in their time.

21 And the people were awaiting Zacharias, and they wondered at his delaying in the temple.

22 But when he came out he could not speak to them, and they recognized that he had seen a vision in the temple. And he was making signs to them, and continued mute.

23 And it came to pass, when the days of his service were completed, he departed to his house.

24 Now after these days, Elizabeth his wife conceived, and hid herself five months, saying,

25 Thus has the Lord done to me in [these] days in which he looked upon [me] to take away my reproach among men.

26 But in the sixth month, the angel Gabriel was sent by the God to a city of Galilee, of which the name [was] Nazareth,

27 to a virgin betrothed to a man whose name [was] Joseph, of the house of David; and the virgin's name [was] Mary.

28 And the angel came in to her, and said, Hail, [you] favored one! the Lord is with you: [blessed are you among women]

29 But she, [seeing] [the angel] was troubled at his word, and reasoned in her mind what this salutation might be.

30 And the angel said to her, Fear not, Mary, for you have found favor with the God;

31 and behold, you shall conceive in the womb and bear a son, and you shall call his name Jesus.

32 He shall be great, and shall be called Son of the Highest; and the Lord the God shall give him the throne of David his father;

33 and he shall reign over the house of Jacob into the aeons, and of his kingdom there shall not be an end.

34 But Mary said to the angel, How shall this be, since I know not a man?

35 And the angel answering said to her, the Holy Spirit shall come upon you, and power of the Highest overshadow you, therefore the holy [one] which shall be born shall be called Son of God.

36 And behold, Elizabeth, your kinswoman, she also has conceived a son in her old age, and this is the sixth month to her that was called barren:

37 for no word shall be impossible with the God.

38 And Mary said, Behold the maid of the Lord; be it to me according to your word. And the angel departed from her.

39 And Mary, rising up in those days, went into the hill country with haste, to a city of Judah,

40 and entered into the house of Zacharias, and saluted Elizabeth.

41 And it came to pass, as Elizabeth heard the salutation of Mary, the babe leaped in her womb; and Elizabeth was filled with the Holy Spirit,

42 and cried out with a loud voice and said, Blessed [are] you among women, and blessed the fruit of your womb.

43 And why is this to me, that the mother of my Lord should come to me?

44 For behold, as the voice of your salutation sounded in my ears, the babe leaped with joy in my womb.

45 And blessed is she that has believed, for there shall be a fulfillment of the things spoken to her from the Lord.

46 And Mary said, My soul magnifies the Lord,

47 and my spirit has rejoiced in the God my Savior.

48 For he has looked upon the low estate of his maid; for behold, from henceforth all generations shall call me blessed.

49 For the Mighty One has done to me great things, and holy is his name;

50 and his mercy is to generations and generations to them that fear him.

51 He has worked strength with his arm; he has scattered haughty [ones] in the thought of their heart.

52 He has put down rulers from thrones, and exalted the lowly.

53 He has filled the hungry with good things, and sent away the rich empty.

54 He has helped Israel his servant, in order to remember mercy,

55 as he spoke to our fathers, to Abraham and to his seed into the aeon.

56 And Mary abode with her about three months, and returned to her house.

57 But the time was fulfilled for Elizabeth that she should bring forth, and she gave birth to a son.

58 And her neighbors and kinsfolk heard that the Lord had magnified his mercy with her, and they rejoiced with her.

59 And it came to pass on the eighth day they came to circumcise the child, and they called it after the name of his father, Zacharias.

60 And his mother answering said, No; but he shall be called John.

61 And they said to her, There is no one among your kinsfolk who is called by this name.

62 And they made signs to his father as to what he might wish it to be called.

63 And having asked for a writing-table, he wrote saying, John is his name. And they all wondered.

64 And his mouth was opened immediately, and his tongue, and he spoke, blessing the God.

65 And fear came upon all who dwelt round about them; and in the whole hill-country of Judea all these things were the subject of conversation.

66 And all who heard them laid them up in their heart, saying, What then will this child be? And the Lord's hand was with him.

67 And Zacharias his father was filled with the Holy Spirit, and prophesied, saying,

68 Blessed be the Lord God of Israel, because he has visited and worked redemption for his people,

69 and raised up a horn of deliverance for us in the house of David his servant;

70 as he spoke by the mouth of his holy prophets, who have been since the world began;

71 deliverance from our enemies and out of the hand of all who hate us;

72 to fulfil mercy with our fathers and remember his holy covenant

73 the oath which he swore to Abraham our father,

74 to give us, that, saved out of the hand of our enemies, we should serve him without fear

75 in piety and righteousness before him all our days.

76 And you, child, shall be called the prophet of the Highest; for you shall go before the face of the Lord to make ready his ways;

77 to give knowledge of deliverance to his people by the forgiveness of their sins

78 on account of the bowels of mercy of our God; wherein the dayspring from on high has visited us,

79 to shine upon them who were sitting in darkness and in the shadow of death, to guide our feet into the way of peace.

80 --And the child grew and was strengthened in spirit; and he was in the deserts until the day of his showing to Israel.

Luke 2:1 But it came to pass in those days that a decree went out from Caesar Augustus, that a census should be made of all the habitable world.

2 The census itself first took place when Cyrenius had the government of Syria.

3 And all went to be inscribed in the census roll, each to his own city:

4 and Joseph also went up from Galilee out of the city Nazareth to Judea, to David's city, the which is called Bethlehem, because he was of the house and family of David,

5 to be inscribed in the census roll with Mary who was betrothed to him [as his] wife, she being great with child.

6 And it came to pass, while they were there, the days of her giving birth [to her child] were fulfilled,

7 and she brought forth her first-born son, and wrapped him up in swaddling-clothes and laid him in the manger, because there was no room for them in the inn.

8 And there were shepherds in that country abiding outside, and keeping watch by night over their flock.

9 And lo, an angel of the Lord was there by them, and the glory of the Lord shone around them, and they feared [with] great fear.

10 And the angel said to them, Fear not, for behold, I announce to you good news of great joy, which shall be to all the people;

11 for today a Savior has been born to you in David's city, who is Christ the Lord.

12 And this is the sign to you: you shall find a babe wrapped in swaddling-clothes, and lying in a manger.

13 And suddenly there was with the angel a multitude of the heavenly host, praising the God and saying,

14 Glory to God in the highest, and on earth peace in men of good pleasure.

15 And it came to pass, as the angels departed from them into heaven, that the shepherds said to one another, Let us make our way now as far as

Bethlehem, and let us see this thing that is come to pass, which the Lord has made known to us.

16 And they came with haste, and found both Mary and Joseph, and the babe lying in the manger;

17 and having seen it they made known about the country the thing which had been said to them concerning this child.

18 And all who heard it wondered at the things said to them by the shepherds.

19 But Mary kept all these things [in her mind] pondering [them] in her heart.

20 And the shepherds returned, glorifying and praising the God for all things which they had heard and seen, as it had been said to them.

21 And when eight days were fulfilled for circumcising him, his name was called Jesus, which was the name given by the angel before he had been conceived in the womb.

22 And when the days were fulfilled for their purifying according to the law of Moses, they brought him to Jerusalem to present him to the Lord

23 as it is written in the law of the Lord: Every male that opens the womb shall be called holy to the Lord,

24 and to offer a sacrifice according to what is said in the law of the Lord: A pair of turtle doves, or two young pigeons.

25 And behold, there was a man in Jerusalem whose name was Simeon; and this man was just and pious, awaiting the consolation of Israel, and the Holy Spirit was upon him.

26 And it was divinely communicated to him by the Holy Spirit, that he should not see death before he should see the Lord's Christ.

27 And he came in the Spirit into the temple; and as the parents brought in the child Jesus that they might do for him according to the custom of the law,

28 he received him into his arms, and blessed the God, and said,

29 Lord, now you let your servant go, according to your word, in peace;

30 for mine eyes have seen your salvation,

31 which you have prepared before the face of all peoples;

32 a light for revelation of the Nations and the glory of your people Israel.

33 And his father and mother wondered at the things which were said concerning him.

34 And Simeon blessed them, and said to Mary his mother, Lo, this [child] is set for the fall and rising up of many in Israel, and for a sign spoken against;

35 and even a sword shall go through your own soul; so that the thoughts may be revealed from many hearts.

36 And there was a prophetess, Anna, daughter of Phanuel, of the tribe of Asher, who was far advanced in years, having lived with [her] husband seven years from her virginity,

37 and herself a widow up to eighty-four years; who did not depart from the temple, serving night and day with fasting and prayers;

38 and she coming up the same hour gave praise to the Lord, and spoke of him to all those who waited for redemption in Jerusalem.

39 And when they had completed all things according to the law of the Lord, they returned to Galilee to their own city Nazareth.

40 And the child grew and became strong [in spirit] filled with wisdom, and God's grace was upon him.

41 And his parents went yearly to Jerusalem at the feast of the Passover.

42 And when he was of years twelve, and they went up [to Jerusalem] according to the custom of the feast

43 and had completed the days, as they returned, the boy Jesus remained behind in Jerusalem, and his parents knew not [of it]

44 but, supposing him to be in the company that journeyed together, they went a day's journey, and sought him among their relations and acquaintances:

45 and not having found him they returned to Jerusalem seeking him.

46 And it came to pass, after three days they found him in the temple, sitting in the midst of the teachers and hearing them and asking them questions.

47 And all who heard him were astonished at his understanding and answers.

48 And when they saw him they were amazed: and his mother said to him, Child, why have you dealt thus with us? behold, your father and I have sought you distressed.

49 And he said to them, Why [is it] that you have sought me? did you not know that I ought to be [occupied] in my Father's business?

50 And they understood not the thing that he said to them.

51 And he went down with them and came to Nazareth, and he was in subjection to them. And his mother kept all these things in her heart.

52 And Jesus advanced in wisdom and stature, and in grace with God and men.

Luke 3:1 Now in the fifteenth year of the government of Tiberius Caesar, Pontius Pilate being governor of Judea, and Herod tetrarch of Galilee, and Philip his brother tetrarch of Ituraea and the region of Trachonitis, and Lysanias tetrarch of Abilene,

2 in the high priesthood of Annas and Caiaphas, the word of God came upon John, the son of Zacharias, in the wilderness.

3 And he came into all the district round the Jordan, preaching the baptism of repentance for the forgiveness of sins,

4 as it is written in the book of the words of Isaiah the prophet: Voice of one crying in the wilderness: Prepare you the way of the Lord, make straight his paths.

5 Every gorge shall be filled up, and every mountain and hill shall be brought low, and the crooked [places] shall become a straight [path] and the rough places smooth ways,

6 and all flesh shall see the salvation of the God.

7 He said therefore to the crowds which went out to be baptized by him, Offspring of vipers, who has forewarned you to flee from the coming wrath?

8 Produce therefore fruits worthy of repentance and begin not to say in yourselves, We have Abraham for [our] father, for I say unto you that the God is able of these stones to raise up children to Abraham.

9 And already also the axe is applied to the root of the trees; every tree therefore not producing good fruit is cut down and cast into the fire.

10 And the crowds asked him saying, What should we do then?

11 And he answering says to them, He that has two body-coats, let him give to him that has none; and he that has food, let him do likewise.

12 And tax-gatherers came also to be baptized, and they said to him, Teacher, what should we do?

13 And he said to them, Take no more [money] than what is appointed to you.

14 And persons engaged in military service also asked him saying, And we, what should we do? And he said to them, Oppress no one, nor accuse falsely, and be satisfied with your pay.

15 But as the people were in expectation, and all were reasoning in their hearts concerning John whether he might be the Christ,

16 John answered all, saying, I indeed baptize you with water, but the one coming is mightier than I, the thong of whose sandals I am not fit to unloose; he shall baptize you with the Holy Spirit and fire;

17 whose winnowing-fan is in his hand, and he will thoroughly purge his threshing-floor, and will gather the wheat into his garner, but the chaff he will burn with fire unquenchable.

18 Urging then many other things also he announced [his] good news to the people.

19 But Herod the tetrarch, being reproved by him as to Herodias, the wife of his brother, and as to all the wicked things which Herod had done,

20 added this also to all [the rest] that he shut up John in prison.

21 And it came to pass, all the people having been baptized, and Jesus having been baptized and praying, that the heaven was opened,

22 and the Holy Spirit descended in a bodily form as a dove upon him; and a voice came out of heaven, You are my beloved Son, in you I have found my delight.

23 And Jesus himself was beginning to be about of years thirty; being as was supposed son of Joseph; of Eli,

24 of Matthat, of Levi, of Melki, of Jannai, of Joseph,

25 of Mattathias, of Amos, of Nahum, of Esli, of Naggai,

26 of Maath, of Mattathias, of Semei, of Joseph, of Judah,

27 of Joanna, of Rhesa, of Zerubbabel, of Shealtiel, of Neri,

28 of Melchi, of Addi, of Cosam, of Elmodam, of Er,

29 of Jose, of Eliezer, of Jorim, of Matthat, of Levi,

30 of Simeon, of Judah, of Joseph, of Jonan, of Eliakim,

31 of Melea, of Menan, of Mattatha, of Nathan, of David,

32 of Jesse, of Obed, of Boaz, of Salmon, of Nahshon,

33 of Amminadab, of Ram, of Hezron, of Perez, of Judah,

34 of Jacob, of Isaac, of Abraham, of Terah, of Nahor,

35 of Serug, of Reu, of Peleg, of Eber, of Salah,

36 of Cainan, of Arphaxad, of Shem, of Noah, of Lamech,

37 of Methuselah, of Enoch, of Jared, of Mahalaleel, of Cainan,

38 of Enos, of Seth, of Adam, of the God.

Luke 4:1 But Jesus, full of the Holy Spirit, returned from the Jordan, and was led by the Spirit in the wilderness

2 forty days, tested of the devil, and in those days he did not eat anything, and when they were finished he hungered.

3 And the devil said to him, If you be Son of the God, speak to this stone, that it become bread.

4 And Jesus answered unto him saying, It is written, Man shall not live by bread alone, but by every word of God.

5 And the devil leading him up into a high mountain, showed him all the kingdoms of the habitable world in a moment of time.

6 And the devil said to him, I will give you all this power, and their glory; for it is given up to me, and to whomsoever I will I give it.

7 If therefore you will do homage before me, all [of it] shall be yours.

8 And Jesus answering him said, It is written, You shall do homage to the Lord your God, and him alone shall you serve.

9 And he led him to Jerusalem, and set him on the edge of the temple, and said to him, If you be Son of the God, cast yourself down hence;

10 for it is written, He shall give charge to his angels concerning you to keep you;

11 and on [their] hands shall they bear you, lest in any wise you strike your foot against a stone.

12 And Jesus answering said to him, It is said, You shall not tempt the Lord your God.

13 And the devil having completed every temptation, departed from him for a time.

14 And Jesus returned in the power of the Spirit to Galilee; and a rumor went out into the whole surrounding country about him;

15 and he taught in their synagogues, being glorified of all.

16 And he came to Nazareth, where he was brought up; and he entered, according to his custom, into the synagogue on the sabbaths, and stood up to read.

17 [And] the book of the prophet Isaiah was given to him; and having unrolled the book he found the place where it was written,

18 the Spirit of the Lord is upon me, because he has anointed me to preach good news to the poor; he has sent me to preach to captives deliverance, and to the blind sight, to send forth the crushed delivered,

19 to preach the acceptable year of the Lord.

20 And having rolled up the book, when he had delivered it up to the attendant, he sat down; and the eyes of all in the synagogue were fixed upon him.

21 And he began to say to them, Today this scripture is fulfilled in your ears.

22 And all bore witness to him, and wondered at the words of grace which were coming out of his mouth. And they said, Is not this the son of Joseph?

23 And he said to them, You will surely say to me this parable, Physician, heal yourself; whatsoever we have heard has taken place in Capernaum do here also in your own country.

24 And he said, Truly I say to you, that no prophet is acceptable in his [own] country.

25 But of a truth I say to you, There were many widows in Israel in the days of Elijah, when the heaven was shut up for three years and six months, so that a great famine came upon all the land,

26 and to none of them was Elijah sent but to Sarepta of Sidonia, to a woman [that was] a widow.

27 And there were many lepers in Israel in the time of Elisha the prophet, and none of them was cleansed but Naaman the Syrian.

28 And they were all filled with rage in the synagogue, hearing these things;

29 and rising up they cast him forth out of the city, and led him up to the brow of the mountain upon which their city was built, so that they might throw him down the cliff;

30 but he, passing through the midst of them, went his way,

31 and descended to Capernaum, a city of Galilee, and taught them on the sabbaths.

32 And they were astonished at his doctrine, for his word was with authority.

33 And there was in the synagogue a man having a spirit of an unclean daemon, and he cried with a loud voice,

34 saying, Eh! what have we to do with you, Jesus, Nazarene? have you come to destroy us? I know you who you are, the Holy [one] of the God.

35 And Jesus rebuked him, saying, Hold your peace, and come out from him. And the daemon, having thrown him down into the midst, came out from him without doing him any injury.

36 And astonishment came upon all, and they spoke to one another, saying, What word is this? for with authority and power he commands the unclean spirits, and they come out.

37 And a rumor went out into every place of the country round concerning him.

38 And rising up out of the synagogue, he entered into the house of Simon. But Simon's mother-in-law was suffering under a bad fever; and they asked him for her.

39 And standing over her, he rebuked the fever, and it left her; and forthwith standing up she served them.

40 And when the sun went down, all, as many as had persons sick with diverse diseases, brought them to him, and having laid his hands on every one of them, he healed them;

41 and daemons also went out from many, crying out and saying, You are the Son of the God. And rebuking them, he permitted them not to speak, because they knew him to be the Christ.

42 And when it was day he went out, and went into a desolate place, and the crowds sought after him, and came up to him, and [would have] kept him back that he should not go from them.

43 But he said to them, I must needs announce the good news of the kingdom of the God to the other cities also, for for this I have been sent forth.

44 And he was preaching in the synagogues of Galilee.

Luke 5:1 And it came to pass, as the crowd pressed on him to hear the word of the God, that he was standing by the lake of Gennesaret:

2 and he saw two ships standing by the lake, but the fishermen, having come down from them, were washing their nets.

3 And getting into one of the ships, which was Simon's, he asked him to draw out a little from the land; and he sat down and taught the crowds out of the ship.

4 But when he ceased speaking, he said to Simon, Draw out into the deep [water] and let down your nets for a haul.

5 And Simon answering said to him, Master, having labored through the whole night we have taken nothing, but at your word I will let down the net.

6 And having done this, they enclosed a great multitude of fishes. And their net broke.

7 And they beckoned to their partners who were in the other ship to come and help them, and they came, and filled both the ships, so that they were sinking.

8 But Simon Peter, seeing it, fell at Jesus' knees, saying, Depart from me, for I am a sinful man, Lord.

9 For astonishment had laid hold on him, and on all those who were with him, at the haul of fishes which they had taken;

10 and in like manner also on James and John, sons of Zebedee, who were partners with Simon. And Jesus said to Simon, Fear not; henceforth you shall be catching men.

11 And having run the ships on shore, leaving all they followed him.

12 And it came to pass as he was in one of the cities, that behold, there was a man full of leprosy, and seeing Jesus, falling upon his face, he besought him saying, Lord, if you will, you are able to cleanse me.

13 And stretching forth his hand he touched him, saying, I will; be you cleansed: and immediately the leprosy departed from him.

14 And he enjoined him to tell no one; but go, show yourself to the priest, and offer for your

cleansing as Moses ordained, for a testimony to them.

15 But the report concerning him was spread abroad still more, and great crowds came together to hear, and to be healed from their infirmities.

16 And he withdrew himself, and was about in the desolate [places] and praying.

17 And it came to pass on one of the days, that he was teaching, and there were Pharisees and doctors of the law sitting by, who were come out of every village of Galilee and Judea and [out of] Jerusalem; and the Lord's power was [there] to heal them.

18 And lo, men bringing upon a couch a man who was paralyzed; and they sought to bring him in, and put him before him.

19 And not finding what way to bring him in, on account of the crowd, going up on the housetop they let him down through the tiles, with his little couch, into the midst before Jesus.

20 And seeing their faith, he said, Man, your sins are forgiven you.

21 And the scribes and the Pharisees began to reason [in their minds] saying, Who is this who speaks blasphemies? Who is able to forgive sins but the God alone?

22 But Jesus, knowing their reasoning, answering said to them, Why reason you in your hearts?

23 which is easier, to say, Your sins are forgiven you; or to say, Rise up and walk?

24 But that you may know that the Son of man has power on earth to forgive sins, he said to the paralysed man, I say to you, Arise, and take up your little couch and go to your house.

25 And immediately standing up before them, having taken up that whereon he was laid, he departed to his house, glorifying the God.

26 And astonishment seized all, and they glorified the God, and were filled with fear, saying, We have seen strange things today.

27 And after these things he went forth and saw a tax-gatherer, Levi by name, sitting at the receipt of taxes, and said to him, Follow me.

28 And having left all, rising up, he followed him.

29 And Levi made a great entertainment for him in his house, and there was a great crowd of tax-gatherers and others who were at table with them.

30 And their scribes and the Pharisees murmured at his disciples, saying, Why do you eat and drink with tax-gatherers and sinners?

31 And Jesus answering said to them, They that are in sound health have not need of a physician, but those that are ill.

32 I am not come to call righteous [persons] but sinful [ones] to repentance.

33 And they said to him, Why do the disciples of John fast often and make supplications, in like manner those also of the Pharisees, but you eat and drink?

34 And he said to them, Can you make the sons of the bride chamber fast when the bridegroom is with them?

35 But days will come when also the bridegroom will have been taken away from them; then shall they fast in those days.

36 And he spoke also a parable to them: No one puts a piece of a new garment upon an old garment, otherwise he will both rip the new, and the piece which is from the new will not suit with the old.

37 And no one puts new wine into old skins, otherwise the new wine will burst the skins, and it will be poured out, and the skins will be destroyed;

38 but new wine is to be put into new skins, and both are preserved.

39 And no one having drunk old wine [straightway] wishes for new, for he says, The old is better.

Luke 6:1 And it came to pass on the second-first Sabbath, that he went through grainfields, and his disciples were plucking the ears and eating [them] rubbing [them] in their hands.

2 But some of the Pharisees said to them, Why do you do what is not lawful to do on the sabbaths?

3 And Jesus answering said to them, Have you not read so much as this, what David did when he hungered, he and those who were with him,

4 how he entered into the house of the God and took the showbread and ate, and gave to those also who were with him, which it is not lawful that [any] eat, except the priests alone?

5 And he said to them, The Son of man is Lord of the Sabbath also.

6 And it came to pass on another Sabbath also that he entered into the synagogue and taught; and there was a man there, and his right hand was withered.

7 And the scribes and the Pharisees were watching if he would heal on the Sabbath, that they might find something of which to accuse him.

8 But he knew their thoughts, and said to the man who had the withered hand, Get up, and stand in the midst. And having risen up he stood [there]

9 Jesus therefore said to them, I will ask you if it is lawful on the Sabbath to do good, or to do evil? to save a soul, or to destroy it?

10 And having looked around on them all, he said to him, Stretch out your hand. And he did [so] and his hand was restored as the other.

11 But they were filled with madness, and they spoke together among themselves what they should do to Jesus.

12 And it came to pass in those days that he went out into the mountain to pray, and he spent the night in prayer to the God.

13 And when it was day he called his disciples, and having chosen out twelve from them, whom also he named apostles:

14 Simon, to whom also he gave the name of Peter, and Andrew his brother, [and] James and John, [and] Philip and Bartholomew,

15 [and] Matthew and Thomas, James the [son] of Alphaeus and Simon who was called Zealot,

16 [and] Judas [brother] of James, and Judas Iscariote, who was also [his] betrayer;

17 and having descended with them, he stood on a level place, and a crowd of his disciples, and a great multitude of the people from all Judea and Jerusalem, and the sea coast of Tyre and Sidon, who came to hear him, and to be healed of their diseases;

18 and those that were beset by unclean spirits were healed.

19 And all the crowd sought to touch him, for power went out from him and healed all.

20 And he, lifting up his eyes upon his disciples, said, Blessed [are] you poor, for yours is the kingdom of the God.

21 Blessed you that hunger now, for you shall be filled. Blessed you that weep now, for you shall laugh.

22 Blessed are you when men shall hate you, and when they shall separate you [from them] and shall reproach [you] and cast out your name as wicked, for the Son of man's sake:

23 rejoice in that day and leap for joy, for behold, your reward is great in the heaven, for after this manner did their fathers act toward the prophets.

24 But woe to you rich, for you have received your consolation.

25 Woe to you that are filled, for you shall hunger. Woe to you who laugh now, for you shall mourn and weep.

26 Woe, when all men speak well of you, for after this manner did their fathers to the false prophets.

27 But to you that hear I say, Love your enemies; do good to those that hate you;

28 bless those that curse you; pray for those who use you despitefully.

29 To him that smites you on the cheek, offer also the other; and from him that would take away your garment, forbid not your body-coat also.

30 To every one that asks of you, give; and from him that takes away what is yours, ask it not back.

31 And as you wish that men should do to you, do you also to them in like manner.

32 And if you love those that love you, what favor is it to you? for even sinners love those that love them.

33 And if you do good to those that do good to you, what favor is it to you? for even sinners do the same.

34 And if you lend to those from whom you hope to receive, what favor is it to you? [for] even sinners lend to sinners that they may receive the like.

35 But love your enemies, and do good, and lend, expecting nothing in return, and your reward shall be great, and you shall be sons of the Highest; for he is good to the unthankful and wicked.

36 Be you therefore merciful, even as your Father also is merciful.

37 And judge not, and you shall not be judged; condemn not, and you shall not be condemned. Forgive, and it shall be forgiven to you.

38 Give, and it shall be given to you; good measure, pressed down, and shaken together, and running over, shall be given into your bosom: for with the same measure with which you measured it shall be measured to you again.

39 And he spoke also a parable to them: Can a blind [man] lead a blind [man]? shall not both fall into the ditch?

40 The disciple is not above his teacher, but every one that is perfected shall be as his teacher.

41 But why look you on the straw which is in the eye of your brother, but perceive not the beam which is in your own eye?

42 or how can you say to your brother, Brother, allow [me] I will cast out the straw that is in your eye, yourself not seeing the beam that is in your eye? Hypocrite, cast out first the beam out of your eye, and then you shall see clear to cast out the straw which is in the eye of your brother.

43 For there is no good tree which produces corrupt fruit, nor a corrupt tree which produces good fruit;

44 for every tree is known by its own fruit, for figs are not gathered from thorns, nor grapes vintaged from a bramble.

45 The good man, out of the good treasure of his heart, brings forth good; and the wicked [man] out of the wicked, brings forth what is wicked: for out of the abundance of the heart his mouth speaks.

46 And why call you me, Lord, Lord, and do not the things that I say?

47 Every one that comes to me, and hears my words and does them, I will show you to whom he is like.

48 He is like a man building a house, who dug and went deep, and laid a foundation on the rock; but a great rain coming, the stream broke upon that house, and could not shake it, for it had been founded on the rock.

49 And he that has heard and not done, is like a man who has built a house on the ground without a foundation, on which the stream broke, and immediately it fell, and the breach of that house was great.

Luke 7:1 And when he had completed all his words in the hearing of the people, he entered into Capernaum.

2 And a certain centurion's servant who was dear to him was ill and about to die;

3 and having heard of Jesus, he sent to him elders of the Jews, begging him that he might come and save his servant.

4 But they, being come to Jesus, besought him diligently, saying, He is worthy to whom you should grant this,

5 for he loves our nation, and himself has built the synagogue for us.

6 And Jesus went with them. But already, when he was not far from the house, the centurion sent to

him friends, saying to him, Lord, do not trouble yourself, for I am not worthy that you should enter under my roof.

7 Therefore neither did I count myself worthy to come to you. But say by a word and my servant shall be healed.

8 For I also am a man placed under authority, having under myself soldiers, and I say to this [one] Go, and he goes; and to another, Come, and he comes; and to my servant, Do this, and he does it

9 And Jesus hearing this wondered at him, and turning to the crowd following him said, I say to you, Not even in Israel have I found so great faith.

10 And they who had been sent returning to the house found the servant, who was ill, in good health.

11 And it came to pass afterwards he went into a city called Nain, and many of his disciples and a great crowd went with him.

12 And as he drew near to the gate of the city, behold, a dead man was carried out, the only son of his mother, and she a widow, and a very considerable crowd of the city [was] with her.

13 And the Lord, seeing her, was moved with compassion for her, and said to her, Weep not;

14 and coming up he touched the coffin, and the bearers stopped. And he said, Youth, I say to you, Wake up.

15 And the dead sat up and began to speak; and he gave him to his mother.

16 And fear seized on all, and they glorified the God, saying, A great prophet has been raised up among us; and the God has visited his people.

17 And this report went out in all Judea concerning him, and in all the surrounding country.

18 And the disciples of John brought him word concerning all these things:

19 and John, having called two of his disciples, sent to Jesus, saying, Are you he The Coming One, or are we to wait for another?

20 But the men having come to him said, John the Baptist has sent us to you, saying, Are you he The Coming One, or are we to wait for another?

21 In that hour he healed many of diseases and plagues and evil spirits, and to many blind he granted sight.

22 And Jesus answering said to them, Go, bring back word to John of what you have seen and heard: that blind see, lame walk, lepers are cleansed, deaf hear, dead are raised, poor are evangelized;

23 and blessed is whosoever shall not be offended in me.

24 And the messengers of John having departed, he began to speak to the crowds concerning John: What went you out into the wilderness to behold? a reed shaken by the wind?

25 But what went you out to see? a man clothed in delicate garments? Behold, those who are in splendid clothing and live luxuriously are in the courts of kings.

26 But what went you out to see? a prophet? Yes, I say to you, and [what is] more excellent than a prophet.

27 This is he concerning whom it is written, Behold, I send my messenger before your face, who shall prepare your way before you;

28 for I say unto you, Among them that are born of women a greater [prophet] is no one than John [the baptist] but he who is a little one in the kingdom of the God is greater than he.

29 And all the people who heard it and the tax-gatherers, justified the God, having been baptized with the baptism of John;

30 but the Pharisees and the lawyers rendered null as to themselves the counsel of the God, not having been baptized by him.

31 To whom therefore shall I liken the men of this generation, and to whom are they like?

32 They are like children sitting in the market-place, and calling one to another and saying, We have piped to you, and you have not danced; we have mourned to you, and you have not wept.

33 For John the Baptist has come neither eating bread nor drinking wine, and you say, He has a daemon.

34 The Son of man has come eating and drinking, and you say, Behold an eater and wine-drinker, a friend of tax-gatherers and sinners;

35 and wisdom has been justified of all her children.

36 But one of the Pharisees begged him that he would eat with him. And entering into the house of the Pharisee he took his place at table;

37 and behold, a woman in the city, who was a sinner, and knew that he was sitting at meat in the house of the Pharisee, having taken an alabaster box of myrrh,

38 and standing at his feet behind him weeping, began to wash his feet with tears; and she wiped them with the hairs of her head, and kissed his feet, and anointed [them] with the myrrh.

39 And the Pharisee who had invited him, seeing it, spoke with himself saying, This [person] if he were a prophet would have known who and what the woman is who touches him, for she is a sinner.

40 And Jesus answering said to him, Simon, I have somewhat to say to you. And he says, Teacher, say it

41 There were two debtors of a certain creditor: one owed five hundred denarii and the other fifty;

42 but as they had nothing to pay, he forgave both of them [their debt] [say] which of them therefore will love him most?

43 And Simon answering said, I suppose he to whom he forgave the most. And he said to him, You have rightly judged.

44 And turning to the woman he said to Simon, See you this woman? I entered into your house; you gave me not water on my feet, but she has washed my feet with tears, and wiped them with her hair.

45 You gave me not a kiss, but she from the time I came in has not ceased kissing my feet.

46 My head with oil you did not anoint, but she has anointed my feet with myrrh.

47 For which cause I say to you, Her many sins are forgiven; for she loved much; but he to whom little is forgiven loves little.

48 And he said to her, Your sins are forgiven.

49 And they that were with [them] at table began to say within themselves, Who is this who forgives also sins?

50 And he said to the woman, Your faith has saved you; go in peace.

Luke 8:1 And it came to pass afterwards that he went through [the country] city by city, and village by village, preaching and announcing the good news of the kingdom of the God; and the twelve [were] with him,

2 and certain women who had been healed of wicked spirits and infirmities, Mary who was called Magdalene, from whom seven daemons had gone out,

3 and Joanna, wife of Chuza, Herod's steward, and Susanna, and many others, who ministered to him of their substance.

4 And a great crowd coming together, and those who were coming to him out of each city, he spoke by parable:

5 The sower went out to sow his seed; and as he sowed, some fell along the way, and it was trodden under foot, and the birds of the heaven devoured it up;

6 and other fell upon the rock, and having sprung up, it was dried up because it had not moisture;

7 and other fell in the midst of the thorns, and the thorns having sprung up with it choked it;

8 and other fell into the good ground, and having sprung up bore fruit a hundredfold. As he said these things he cried, He that has ears to hear, let him hear.

9 And his disciples asked him [saying] What may this parable be?

10 And he said, To you it is given to know the mysteries of the kingdom of the God, but to the rest in parables, in order that seeing they may not see, and hearing they may not understand.

11 But the parable is this: The seed is the word of the God.

12 But those by the wayside are those who hear; then comes the devil and takes away the word from their heart that they may not believe and be saved.

13 But those upon the rock, those who when they hear receive the word with joy; and these have no root, who believe for a time, and in time of trial fall away.

14 But that that fell where the thorns were, these are they who having heard go away and are choked under cares and riches and pleasures of life, and bring no fruit to perfection.

15 But that in the good ground, these are they who in an honest and good heart, having heard the word keep it, and bring forth fruit with patience.

16 And no one having lighted a lamp covers it with a vessel or puts it under a couch, but sets it on a lamp-stand, that they who enter in may see the light.

17 For there is nothing hid which shall not become manifest, nor secret which shall not be known and come to light.

18 Take heed therefore how you hear; for whosoever has, to him shall be given, and whosoever has not, even what he seems to have shall be taken from him.

19 And his mother and his brethren came to him, and could not get to him because of the crowd.

20 And it was told him [saying] Your mother and your brethren stand outside, wishing to see you.

21 But he answering said to them, My mother and my brethren are those who hear the word of the God and do it

22 And it came to pass on one of the days, that he entered into a ship, himself and his disciples; and he said to them, Let us pass over to the other side of the lake; and they set off from shore.

23 And as they sailed, he fell asleep; and a sudden squall of wind came down on the lake, and they were filled [with water] and were in danger;

24 and coming to him they woke him up, saying, Master, master, we perish. But he, rising up, rebuked the wind and the raging of the water; and they ceased, and there was a calm.

25 And he said to them, Where is your faith? And, being afraid, they were astonished, saying to one another, Who then is this, that he commands even the winds and the water, and they obey him?

26 And they arrived in the country of the Gadarenes, which is over against Galilee.

27 And as he got out [of the ship] on the land, a certain man out of the city met him, who had daemons a long time, and put on no clothes, and did not abide in a house, but in the tombs.

28 But seeing Jesus, he cried out, and fell down before him, and with a loud voice said, What have I to do with you, Jesus Son of the Most High the God? I beseech you torment me not.

29 For he had commanded the unclean spirit to go out from the man. For very often it had seized him; and he had been bound, kept with chains and fetters; and breaking the bonds he was driven by the daemon into the deserts.

30 And Jesus asked him saying, What is your name? And he said, Legion: for many daemons had entered into him.

31 And they besought him that he would not command them to go away into the bottomless pit.

32 And there was there a herd of many swine feeding on the mountain, and they besought him that he would permit them to enter into those; and he permitted them.

33 And the daemons, going out from the man, entered into the swine, and the herd rushed down the cliff into the lake, and were choked.

34 But they that fed [them] seeing what had happened, fled, and told it to the city and to the country.

35 And they went out to see what had happened, and came to Jesus, and found the man from whom the daemons had gone out, sitting, clothed and sensible, at the feet of Jesus. And they were afraid.

36 And they also who had seen it told them how the possessed man had been healed.

37 And all the multitude of the surrounding country of the Gadarenes asked him to depart from them, for they were possessed with great fear; and he, entering into the ship, returned.

38 But the man out of whom the daemons had gone besought him that he might be with him. But he sent him away, saying,

39 Return to your house and relate how great things the God has done for you. And he went away through the whole city, publishing how great things Jesus had done for him.

40 And it came to pass when Jesus returned, the crowd received him gladly, for they were all expecting him.

41 And behold, a man came, whose name was Jairus, and he was a ruler of the synagogue, and falling at the feet of Jesus besought him to come to his house,

42 because he had an only daughter, about of years, twelve, and she was dying. And as he went the crowds thronged him.

43 And a woman who had a flux of blood since twelve years, who, having spent all her living on physicians, could not be cured by any one,

44 coming up behind, touched the hem of his garment, and immediately her flux of blood stopped.

45 And Jesus said, Who has touched me? But all denying, Peter and those with him said, Master, the crowds close you in and press upon you, and you said, Who has touched me?

46 And Jesus said, Some one has touched me, for I have known that power has gone out from me.

47 And the woman, seeing that she was not hid, came trembling, and falling down before him declared before all the people for what cause she had touched him, and how she was immediately healed.

48 And he said to her, [be of good courage] daughter; your faith has healed you; go in peace.

49 While he was yet speaking, comes some one from the ruler of the synagogue, saying to him, Your daughter is dead; do not trouble the teacher.

50 But Jesus, hearing it, answered him saying, Fear not: only believe, and she shall be made well.

51 And when he came to the house he permitted no one to go in but Peter and John and James and the father of the child and the mother.

52 And all were weeping and lamenting her. But he said, Do not weep, for she has not died, but sleeps.

53 And they derided him, knowing that she had died.

54 But he, having turned them all out and taking hold of her hand, cried saying, Child, arise.

55 And her spirit returned, and immediately she rose up; and he commanded [something] to eat to be given to her.

56 And her parents were amazed; but he enjoined them to tell no one what had happened.

Luke 9:1 And having called together the twelve, he gave them power and authority over all daemons, and to heal diseases,

2 and sent them to proclaim the kingdom of the God and to heal the sick.

3 And he said to them, Take nothing for the way, neither staff, nor scrip, nor bread, nor money; nor to have two body-coats apiece.

4 And into whatsoever house you enter, there abide and from there go forth.

5 And as many as may not receive you, going forth from that city, shake off even the dust from your feet for a witness against them.

6 And going forth they passed through the villages, announcing the good news and healing everywhere.

7 And Herod the tetrarch heard of all the things which were done [by him] and was in perplexity, because it was said by some that John was risen from among the dead,

8 and by some that Elijah had appeared, and by others that one of the old prophets had risen again.

9 And Herod said, John I have beheaded, but who is this of whom I hear such things? and he sought to see him.

10 And the apostles having returned related to him whatever they had done. And he took them and withdrew apart into [a desolate place of] a city called Bethsaida.

11 But the crowds knowing it followed him; and he received them and spoke to them of the kingdom of the God, and cured those that had need of healing.

12 But the day began to decline, and the twelve came and said to him, Send away the crowd that they may go into the villages around, and [into] the fields, and lodge and find provisions, for here we are in a desolate place.

13 And he said to them, Give you them to eat. And they said, We have not more than five loaves and two fishes, unless we should go and buy food for all this people;

14 for they were about five thousand men. And he said to his disciples, Make them sit down in companies by fifties.

15 And they did so, and made them all sit down.

16 And taking the five loaves and the two fishes, looking up to heaven he blessed them, and broke and gave to the disciples to set before the crowd.

17 And they all ate and were filled; and there was taken up of what had remained over and above to them in fragments twelve hand-baskets.

18 And it came to pass as he was praying alone, his disciples were with him, and he asked them saying, Who do the crowds say that I am?

19 But they answering said, John the Baptist; but others, Elijah; and others, that one of the old prophets has risen again.

20 And he said to them, But you, who do you say that I am? And Peter answering said, The Christ of the God.

21 But, earnestly charging them, he enjoined [them] to say this to no man,

22 saying, The Son of man must suffer many things, and be rejected of the elders and chief priests and scribes, and be killed, and the third day be raised up.

23 And he said to [them] all, If any one will come after me, let him deny himself and take up his cross daily and follow me;

24 for whosoever shall desire to save his soul shall lose it, but whosoever shall lose his soul for my sake, he shall save it.

25 For what shall a man profit if he shall have gained the whole world, and have destroyed, or come under the penalty of the loss of himself?

26 For whosoever shall have been ashamed of me and of my words, of him will the Son of man be ashamed when he shall come in his glory, and [in that] of the Father, and of the holy angels.

27 But I say unto you of a truth, There are some of those standing here who shall not taste death until they shall have seen the kingdom of the God.

28 And it came to pass after these words, about eight days, that taking Peter and John and James he went up into a mountain to pray.

29 And as he prayed the fashion of his countenance became different and his raiment white [and] effulgent.

30 And lo, two men talked with him, who were Moses and Elijah,

31 who, appearing in glory, spoke of his departure which he was about to accomplish in Jerusalem.

32 But Peter and those with him were oppressed with sleep: but having fully awoke up they saw his glory, and the two men who stood with him.

33 And it came to pass as they departed from him, Peter said to Jesus, Master, it is good for us to be here; and let us make three tabernacles, one for you, and one for Moses, and one for Elijah: not knowing what he said.

34 But as he was saying these things, there came a cloud and overshadowed them, and they feared as they entered into the cloud:

35 and there was a voice out of the cloud saying, This is my beloved [or chosen] Son: hear him.

36 And as the voice was [heard] Jesus was found alone: and they kept silence, and told no one in those days any of the things they had seen.

37 And it came to pass on the following day, when they came down from the mountain, a great crowd met him.

38 And lo, a man from the crowd cried out saying, Teacher, I beseech you look upon my son, for he is mine only child:

39 and behold, a spirit takes him, and suddenly he cries out, and it tears him with foaming, and with difficulty departs from him after crushing him.

40 And I besought your disciples that they might cast him out, and they could not.

41 And Jesus answering said, O unbelieving and perverted generation, how long shall I be with you and put up with you? Bring here your son.

42 But as he was yet coming, the daemon tore him and dragged him all together. And Jesus rebuked the unclean spirit, and healed the child and gave him back to his father.

43 And all were astonished at the glorious greatness of the God. And as all wondered at all the things which [Jesus] did, he said to his disciples,

44 Do you let these words sink into your ears. For the Son of man is about to be delivered into men's hands.

45 But they understood not this saying, and it was hid from them that they should not perceive it. And they feared to ask him concerning this saying.

46 And a reasoning came in among them, who should be the greatest of them.

47 And Jesus, seeing the reasoning of their heart, having taken a little child set it by him,

48 and said to them, Whosoever shall receive this little child in my name receives me, and whosoever shall receive me receives him that sent me. For he who is the least among you all, he is great.

49 And John answering said, Master, we saw some one casting out daemons in your name, and we forbade him, because he follows not with us.

50 And Jesus said to him, Forbid him not, for he that is not against you is for you.

51 And it came to pass when the days of his receiving up were fulfilled, that he stedfastly set his face to go to Jerusalem.

52 And he sent messengers before his face. And having gone they entered into a village of the Samaritans that they might make ready for him.

53 And they did not receive him, because his face was [turned as] going to Jerusalem.

54 And his disciples James and John seeing it said, Lord, wish you that we speak [so that] fire comes down from heaven and consume them, as also Elijah did?

55 But turning he rebuked them [and said, You know not of what spirit you are]

56 And they went to another village.

57 And it came to pass as they went in the way, one said to him, I will follow you wheresoever you go, Lord.

58 And Jesus said to him, The foxes have holes and the birds of the heaven nests, but the Son of man has not where he may lay his head.

59 And he said to another, Follow me. But he said, Lord, allow me to go first and bury my father.

60 But Jesus said to him, Permit the dead to bury their own dead, but do you go and announce the kingdom of the God.

61 And another also said, I will follow you, Lord, but first allow me to bid good-by to those at my house.

62 But Jesus said to him, No one having laid his hand on the plough and looking back is fit for the kingdom of the God.

Luke 10:1 Now after these things the Lord appointed seventy others also, and sent them two and two before his face into every city and place where he himself was about to come.

2 And he said to them, The harvest indeed is great, but the workmen few; pray therefore the Lord of the harvest that he may send out workmen into his harvest.

3 Go: behold I send you forth as lambs in the midst of wolves.

4 Carry neither purse nor scrip nor sandals, and salute no one on the way.

5 And into whatsoever house you enter, first say, Peace to this house.

6 And if a son of peace be there, your peace shall rest upon it; but if not it shall turn to you again.

7 And in the same house abide, eating and drinking such things as they have; for the workman is worthy of his hire. Remove not from house to house.

8 And into whatsoever city you may enter and they receive you, eat what is set before you,

9 and heal the sick in it, and say to them, The kingdom of the God is come near to you.

10 But into whatsoever city you may have entered and they do not receive you, go out into its streets and say,

11 Even the dust of your city, which cleaves to us on the feet, do we shake off against you; but know this, that the kingdom of the God is come near.

12 I say to you that it shall be more tolerable for Sodom in that day than for that city.

13 Woe to you, Chorazin! woe to you, Bethsaida! for if the works of power which have taken place in you had taken place in Tyre and Sidon, they had long ago repented sitting in sackcloth and ashes.

14 But it shall be more tolerable for Tyre and Sidon in the judgment than for you.

15 And you, Capernaum, who have been raised up to heaven, shall be brought down even to Hades.

16 He that hears you hears me; and he that rejects you rejects me; and he that rejects me rejects him that sent me.

17 And the seventy returned with joy, saying, Lord, even the daemons are subject to us through your name.

18 And he said to them, I am seeing Satan as lightning falling out of heaven.

19 Behold, I give you the power of treading upon serpents and scorpions and over all the power of the enemy, and nothing shall in anyway injure you.

20 Yet in this rejoice not, that the spirits are subjected to you, but rejoice that your names are written in the heavens.

21 In the same hour Jesus rejoiced in spirit and said, I praise you, Father, Lord of the heaven and of the earth, that you have hid these things from the wise and prudent, and have revealed them to babes: yes, Father, for thus has it been well-pleasing in your sight.

22 All things have been delivered to me by my Father, and no one knows who the Son is but the Father, and who the Father is but the Son, and he to whomsoever the Son is pleased to reveal him.

23 And having turned to the disciples privately he said, Blessed are the eyes which see the things that you see.

24 For I say to you that many prophets and kings have desired to see the things which you behold, and did not see [them] and to hear the things which you hear, and did not hear [them]

25 And behold, a certain lawyer stood up testing him, and saying, Teacher, what shall I do to inherit aeonian life?

26 And he said to him, What is written in the law? how do you read it?

27 But he answering said, You shall love the Lord your God with all your heart, and with all your soul, and with all your strength, and with all your understanding; and your neighbor as yourself.

28 And he said to him, You have answered right: this do and you shall live.

29 But he, desirous of justifying himself, said to Jesus, And who is my neighbor?

30 And Jesus replying said, A certain man descended from Jerusalem to Jericho and fell into [the hands of] robbers, who also, having stripped him and inflicted wounds, went away leaving him in a half-dead state.

31 And a certain priest happened to go down that way, and seeing him, passed on on the opposite side;

32 and in like manner also a Levite, being at the spot, came and looked [at him] and passed on the opposite side.

33 But a certain Samaritan journeying came to him, and seeing him was moved with compassion,

34 and came up [to him] and bound up his wounds, pouring in oil and wine; and having put him on his own beast, took him to the inn and took care of him.

35 And on the next day [as he left] taking out two denarii he gave them to the innkeeper, and said to him, Take care of him, and whatsoever you shall expend more, I will render to you on my coming back.

36 Which [now] of these three seems to you to have been neighbor of him who fell into [the hands of] the robbers?

37 And he said, He that showed him mercy. And Jesus said to him, Go, and do you likewise.

38 And it came to pass as they went that he entered into a certain village; and a certain woman, Martha by name, received him into her house.

39 And she had a sister called Mary, who also, having sat down at the feet of Jesus was listening to his word.

40 Now Martha was distracted with much serving, and coming up she said, Lord, do you not care that my sister has left me to serve alone? Speak to her therefore that she may help me.

41 But Jesus answering said to her, Martha, Martha, you are concerned and troubled about many things;

42 but there is need of one, and Mary has chosen the good part, the which shall not be taken from her.

Luke 11:1 And it came to pass as he was in a certain place praying, when he ceased, one of his disciples said to him, Lord, teach us to pray, even as John also taught his disciples.

2 And he said to them, When you pray, say, Father, your name be hallowed; your kingdom come;

3 give us our needed bread for each day;

4 and forgive us our sins, for we also forgive to every one indebted to us; and lead us not into temptation.

5 And he said to them, Who among you shall have a friend, and shall go to him at midnight and say to him, Friend, let me have three loaves,

6 since a friend of mine on a journey is come to me, and I have nothing to set before him;

7 and he within answering should say, Do not disturb me; the door is already shut, and my children are with me in bed; I cannot rise up to give it you?

8 --I say to you, Although he will not get up and give [them] to him because he is his friend, because of his shamelessness [or boldness for asking], at any rate, he will rise and give him as many as he wants.

9 And I say to you, Ask, and it shall be given to you; seek, and you shall find; knock, and it shall be opened to you.

10 For every one that asks receives; and he that seeks finds; and to him that knocks it will be opened.

11 But of whom of you that is a father shall a son ask bread, and [the father] shall give him a stone? or also a fish, and instead of a fish shall give him a serpent?

12 or if also he shall ask an egg, shall give him a scorpion?

13 If therefore you, being evil, know how to give good gifts to your children, how much rather shall the Father who is of heaven give the Holy Spirit to them that ask him?

14 And he was casting out a daemon, and it was mute; and it came to pass, the daemon being gone out, the mute [man] spoke. And the crowds wondered.

15 But some from among them said, By Beelzebub the prince of the daemons casts he out daemons.

16 And others testing him sought from him a sign out of heaven.

17 But he, knowing their thoughts, said to them, Every kingdom divided against itself is brought to desolation: and a house set against a house falls;

18 and if also Satan is divided against himself, how shall his kingdom subsist? because you say that I cast out daemons by Beelzebub.

19 But if I by Beelzebub cast out daemons, your sons --by whom do they cast [them] out? For this reason they shall be your judges.

20 But if by the finger of God I cast out daemons, then the kingdom of the God is come upon you.

21 When the strong [man] armed keeps his own house, his goods are in peace;

22 but when the stronger than he coming upon him overcomes him, he takes away his panoply in which he trusted, and he will divide the spoil [he has taken] from him.

23 He that is not with me is against me, and he that gathers not with me scatters.

24 When the unclean spirit has gone out of the man, he goes through dry places seeking rest; and not finding [any] he says, I will return to my house from what place I came out.

25 And having come, he finds it swept and adorned.

26 Then he goes and takes seven other spirits worse than himself, and entering in, they dwell there; and the last condition of that man becomes worse than the first.

27 And it came to pass as he spoke these things, a certain woman, lifting up her voice out of the crowd, said to him, Blessed is the womb that has borne you, and the breasts which you have sucked.

28 But he said, Yes rather, blessed are they who hear the word of the God and keep it

29 But as the crowds thronged together, he began to say, This generation is a wicked generation: it seeks a sign, and a sign shall not be given to it but the sign of Jonah.

30 For as Jonah was a sign to the Ninevites, thus shall also the Son of man be to this generation.

31 A queen of the south shall rise up in the judgment with the men of this generation, and shall condemn them: for she came from the ends of the earth to hear the wisdom of Solomon; and behold, more than Solomon is here.

32 Men of Nineveh shall stand up in the judgment with this generation, and shall condemn it: for they repented at the preaching of Jonah; and behold, more than Jonah is here.

33 But no one having lit a lamp sets it in secret, nor under the grain-measure, but on the lamp-stand, that they who enter in may see the light.

34 The lamp of the body is your eye: when your eye is whole, your whole body also is light; but when it is wicked, your body also is dark.

35 See therefore that the light which is in you be not darkness.

36 If therefore your whole body is light, not having any part dark, it shall be all light as when the lamp lights you with its brightness.

37 But as he spoke, a certain Pharisee asked him that he would dine with him; and entering in he placed himself at table.

38 But the Pharisee seeing it wondered that he had not first washed before dinner.

39 But the Lord said to him, Now do you Pharisees cleanse the outside of the cup and of the dish, but your inward [parts] are full of plunder and wickedness.

40 Fools, has not he who has made the outside made the inside also?

41 But rather give alms of what you have, and behold, all things are clean to you.

42 But woe unto you, Pharisees, for you pay tithes of mint and rue and every herb, and pass by the judgment and the love of the God: these you ought to have done, and not have left those aside.

43 Woe unto you, Pharisees, for you love the first seat in the synagogues and salutations in the market-places.

44 Woe unto you, for you are as the tombs which appear not, and the men walking over them do not know it

45 And one of the doctors of the law answering says to him, Teacher, in saying these things you insult us also.

46 And he said, To you also woe, doctors of the law, for you lay upon men burdens heavy to bear, and yourselves do not touch the burdens with one of your fingers.

47 Woe unto you, for you build the tombs of the prophets, but your fathers killed them.

48 You bear witness then, and consent to the works of your fathers; for they killed them, and you build [their tombs]

49 For this reason also the wisdom of the God has said, I will send to them prophets and apostles, and of these shall they kill and drive out by persecution,

50 that the blood of all the prophets which has been poured out from the foundation of the world may be required of this generation,

51 from the blood of Abel to the blood of Zacharias, who perished between the altar and the house; yes, I say to you, it shall be required of this generation.

52 Woe unto you, the doctors of the law, for you have taken away the key of knowledge; yourselves have not entered in, and those who were entering in you have hindered.

53 And as he said these things to them, the scribes and the Pharisees began to press him urgently, and to make him speak of many things;

54 watching him, [and seeking] to catch something out of his mouth, [that they might accuse him]

Luke 12:1 In those [times] the myriads of the crowd being gathered together, so that they trod one on another, he began to say to his disciples first, Beware of the leaven of the Pharisees, which is hypocrisy;

2 but there is nothing covered up which shall not be revealed, nor secret that shall not be known;

3 therefore whatever you have said in the darkness shall be heard in the light, and what you have spoken in the ear in chambers shall be proclaimed upon the housetops.

4 But I say to you, my friends, Fear not those who kill the body and after this have no more that they can do.

5 But I will show you whom you shall fear: Fear him who after he has killed has authority to cast into Gehenna; yes, I say to you, Fear him.

6 Are not five sparrows sold for two assaria? and one of them is not forgotten before the God.

7 But even the hairs of your head are all numbered. Fear not therefore, you are better than many sparrows.

8 But I say to you, Whosoever shall acknowledge me before men, the Son of man will acknowledge him also before the angels of the God;

9 but he that shall have denied me before men shall be denied before the angels of the God;

10 and whoever shall say a word against the Son of man it shall be forgiven him; but to him that speaks injuriously against the Holy Spirit it shall not be forgiven.

11 But when they bring you before the synagogues and rulers and the authorities, be not concerned how or what you shall answer, or what you shall say;

12 for the Holy Spirit shall teach you in the hour itself what should be said.

13 And a person said to him out of the crowd, Teacher, speak to my brother to divide the inheritance with me.

14 But he said to him, Man, who established me [as] a judge or a divider over you?

15 And he said to them, Take heed and keep yourselves from all covetousness, for [it is] not because a man is in abundance that his life is in his possessions.

16 And he spoke a parable to them, saying, The land of a certain rich man brought forth abundantly.

17 And he reasoned within himself saying, What shall I do? for I have not [a place] where I shall lay up my fruits.

18 And he said, This will I do: I will take away my granaries and build greater, and there I will lay up all my produce and my good things;

19 and I will say to my soul, Soul, you have much good things laid by for many years; rest yourself, eat, drink, be merry.

20 But the God said to him, Fool, this night your soul shall be required of you; and who shall own what you have prepared?

21 Thus is he who lays up treasure for himself, and is not rich toward God.

22 And he said to his disciples, For this cause I say unto you, Be not concerned for your soul, what you shall eat, nor for the body, what you shall put on.

23 The soul is more than food, and the body than raiment.

24 Consider the ravens, that they sow not nor reap; which have neither storehouse nor granary; and the God feeds them. How much better are you than the birds?

25 But which of you by being concerned can add to his stature one cubit?

26 If therefore you cannot [do] even what is least, why are you concerned about the rest?

27 Consider the lilies how they grow: they neither toil nor spin; but I say unto you, Not even Solomon in all his glory was clothed as one of these.

28 But if the God thus clothe the grass, which today is in the field and tomorrow is cast into the oven, how much rather you, O you of little faith?

29 And you, seek not what you shall eat or what you shall drink, and be not in anxiety;

30 for all these things do the nations of the world seek after, and your Father knows that you have need of these things;

31 but seek his kingdom, and [all] these things shall be added to you.

32 Fear not, little flock, for it has been the good pleasure of your Father to give you the kingdom.

33 Sell what you possess and give alms; make to yourselves purses which do not grow old, a treasure

which does not fail in the heavens, where thief does not draw near nor moth destroy.

34 For where your treasure is, there also will your heart be.

35 Let your loins be girded about, and lamps burning;

36 and be you like men who are waiting for their own lord to return from the wedding, that when he comes and knocks, they may open to him immediately.

37 Blessed are those servants whom the lord [on] coming shall find watching; truly I say unto you, that he will gird himself and make them recline at table, and coming up will serve them.

38 And if he come in the second watch, and come in the third watch, and find [them] thus, blessed are those [servants]

39 But this know, that if the master of the house had known in what hour the thief was coming, he would have watched, and not have permitted his house to be dug through.

40 And you therefore, be you ready, that in the hour in which you do not think it the Son of man comes.

41 And Peter said to him, Lord, do you say this parable to us, or also to all?

42 And the Lord said, Who then is the faithful and prudent steward, whom his lord will set over his household, to give the measure of grain in season?

43 Blessed is that servant whom his lord [on] coming shall find doing thus;

44 truly I say unto you, that he will set him over all that he has.

45 But if that servant should say in his heart, My lord delays to come, and begin to beat the menservants and the maidservants, and to eat and to drink and to be drunken,

46 the lord of that servant shall come in a day when he does not expect it, and in an hour he knows not of, and shall cut him in two and appoint his portion with the unbelievers.

47 But that servant who knew his own lord's will, and had not prepared [himself] nor done his will, shall be beaten with many [stripes]

48 but he who knew it not, and did things worthy of stripes, shall be beaten with few. And to every one to whom much has been given, much shall be required from him; and to whom [men] have committed much, they will ask from him the more.

49 I have come to cast a fire on the earth; and what will I [do] if already it has been kindled?

50 But I have a baptism to be baptized with, and how am I hampered until it shall have been accomplished!

51 Think you that I have come to give peace in the earth? No, I say to you, but rather division:

52 for from henceforth there shall be five in one house divided; three shall be divided against two, and two against three:

53 father against son, and son against father; mother against daughter, and daughter against mother; a mother-in-law against her daughter-in-law, and a daughter-in-law against her mother-in-law.

54 And he said also to the crowds, When you see a cloud rising out of the west, straightway you say, A shower is coming; and so it happens.

55 And when [you see] the south wind blow, you say, There will be heat; and it happens.

56 Hypocrites, you know how to judge of the appearance of the earth and of the heaven; how [is it then that] you do not discern this time?

57 And why among yourselves don't you judge what is right?

58 For as you go with your adverse party before a magistrate, strive in the way to be reconciled with him, lest he drag you away to the judge, and the judge shall deliver you to the officer, and the officer cast you into prison.

59 I say unto you, You shall in no way come out from there until you have paid the very last mite.

Luke 13:1 Now at the same time there were present some who told him of the Galileans whose blood Pilate mingled with [that of] their sacrifices.

2 And he answering said to them, Think you that these Galileans were sinners beyond all the Galileans because they permitted such things?

3 No, I say to you, but if you repent not, you shall all perish in the same manner.

4 Or those eighteen on whom the tower in Siloam fell and killed them, think you that they were debtors beyond all the men who dwell in Jerusalem?

5 No, I say to you, but if you repent not, you shall all perish in like manner.

6 And he spoke this parable: A certain [man] had a fig-tree planted in his vineyard, and he came seeking fruit upon it and did not find [any]

7 And he said to the vinedresser, Behold, [these] three years I come seeking fruit on this fig-tree and find none: cut it down; why does it also render the ground useless?

8 But he answering says to him, Sir, leave it alone for this year also, until I shall dig about it and put dung,

9 and if it shall bear fruit --but if not, after that you shall cut it down.

10 And he was teaching in one of the synagogues on the sabbaths.

11 And lo, [there was] a woman having a spirit of infirmity eighteen years, and she was bent together and wholly unable to lift her head up.

12 And Jesus, seeing her, called to [her] and said to her, Woman, you are loosened from your infirmity.

13 And he laid his hands upon her; and immediately she was made straight, and glorified the God.

14 But the ruler of the synagogue, indignant because Jesus healed on the Sabbath, answering said to the crowd, There are six days in which [people] ought to work; in these therefore come and be healed, and not on the Sabbath day.

15 The Lord therefore answered him and said, Hypocrites! does not each one of you on the Sabbath

loose his ox or his donkey from the manger and leading it away, water it

16 And this [woman] who is a daughter of Abraham, whom Satan has bound, lo, [these] eighteen years, ought she not to be loosened from this bond on the Sabbath day?

17 And as he said these things, all who were opposed to him were ashamed; and all the crowd rejoiced at all the glorious things which were being done by him.

18 And he said, To what is the kingdom of the God like? and to what shall I liken it?

19 It is like a grain of mustard [seed] which a man took and cast into his garden; and it grew and became a great tree, and the birds of heaven lodged in its branches.

20 And again he said, To what shall I liken the kingdom of the God?

21 It is like leaven, which a woman took and hid in three measures of meal until the whole was leavened.

22 And he went through one city and village after another, teaching, and journeying to Jerusalem.

23 And one said to him, Sir, are only a few being saved? But he said unto them,

24 Strive with earnestness to enter in through the narrow door, for many, I say to you, will seek to enter in and will not be able.

25 From the time that the master of the house shall have risen up and shall have shut the door, and you shall begin to stand outside and to knock at the door, saying, Lord, open to us; and he answering shall say to you, I know you not who you are:

26 then shall you begin to say, We have eaten in your presence and drunk, and you have taught in our streets;

27 and he shall say, I tell you, I do not know you who you are; depart from me, all workers of iniquity.

28 There shall be the weeping and the gnashing of teeth, when you shall see Abraham and Isaac and Jacob and all the prophets in the kingdom of the God, but yourselves cast out.

29 And they shall come from east and west, and from north and south, and shall lie down at table in the kingdom of the God.

30 And behold, there are last who shall be first, and there are first who shall be last.

31 The same hour certain Pharisees came up, saying to him, Get out, and go away, for Herod is desirous to kill you.

32 And he said to them, Go, tell that fox, Behold, I cast out daemons and accomplish cures today and tomorrow, and the third [day] I am perfected;

33 but I must walk today and tomorrow and the [day] following, for it must that no prophet shall perish outside of Jerusalem.

34 Jerusalem, Jerusalem, the [city] that kills the prophets and stones those that are sent unto her, how often would I have gathered your children together, as a hen her brood under her wings, and you would not.

35 Behold, your house is left unto you; and I say unto you, that you shall not see me until it come that you say, Blessed is he that comes in the name of the Lord.

Luke 14:1 And it came to pass, as he went into the house of one of the rulers, [who was] of the Pharisees, to eat bread on the Sabbath, that they were watching him.

2 And behold, there was a certain dropsical [man] before him.

3 And Jesus answering spoke unto the doctors of the law and Pharisees, saying, Is it lawful to heal on the Sabbath?

4 But they were silent. And taking him he healed him and let him go.

5 And answering he said to them, Of which of you shall have a son or ox fall into a well, that he does not straightaway pull him up on the Sabbath day?

6 And they were not able to answer him to these things.

7 And he spoke a parable to those that were invited, remarking how they chose out the first places, saying to them,

8 When you are invited by any one to a wedding, do not lay yourself down in the first place at table, lest perhaps a more honorable than you be invited by him,

9 and he who invited you and him come and say to you, Give place to this [man] and then you begin with shame to take the last place.

10 But when you have been invited, go and put yourself down in the last place, that when he who has invited you comes, he may say to you, Friend, go up higher: then shall you have honor before all that are lying at table with you;

11 for every one that exalts himself shall be abased, and he that abases himself shall be exalted.

12 And he said also to him that had invited him, When you make a dinner or a supper, call not your friends, nor your brethren, nor your kinsfolk, nor rich neighbors, lest it may be they also should invite you in return, and a recompense be made you.

13 But when you make a feast, call poor, crippled, lame, blind:

14 and you shall be blessed; for they have not [the means] to recompense you; for it shall be recompensed you in the resurrection of the just.

15 And one of those that were lying at table with [them] hearing these things, said to him, Blessed is he who shall eat bread in the kingdom of the God.

16 And he said to him, A certain man made a great supper and invited many.

17 And he sent his servant at the hour of supper to say to those who were invited, Come, for already all things are ready.

18 And all began, without exception, to excuse themselves. The first said to him, I have bought land, and I must go out and see it; I pray you hold me for excused.

19 And another said, I have bought five yoke of oxen, and I go to prove them; I ask you to excuse me.

20 And another said, I have married a wife, and on this account I cannot come.

21 And the servant came up and brought back word of these things to his lord. Then the master of the house, in anger, said to his servant, Go out quickly into the streets and lanes of the city, and bring here the poor and crippled and lame and blind.

22 And the servant said, Sir, it is done as you have commanded, and there is still room.

23 And the lord said to the servant, Go out into the ways and fences and compel to come in, that my house may be filled;

24 for I say to you, that not one of those men who were invited shall taste of my supper.

25 And great crowds went with him; and, turning round, he said to them,

26 If any man come to me, and shall not hate his own father and mother, and wife, and children, and brothers, and sisters, yes, and his own soul too, he cannot be my disciple;

27 and whoever does not carry his cross and come after me cannot be my disciple.

28 For which of you, desirous of building a tower, does not first sit down and count the cost, if he has what [is needed] to complete it;

29 in order that, having laid the foundation of it, and not being able to finish it, all who see it do not begin to mock him,

30 saying, This man began to build and was not able to finish?

31 Or what king, going on his way to engage in war with another king, does not, sitting down first, take counsel whether he is able with ten thousand to meet him coming against him with twenty thousand?

32 and if not, while he is yet far off, having sent an embassy, he asks for terms of peace.

33 Thus then every one of you who forsakes not all that is his own cannot be my disciple.

34 Salt [then] is good, but if the salt also has become flavorless, wherewith shall it be seasoned?

35 It is proper neither for land nor for dung; it is cast out. He that hath ears to hear, let him hear.

Luke 15:1 And all the tax-gatherers and the sinners were coming near to him to hear him;

2 and the Pharisees and the scribes murmured, saying, This [man] receives sinners and eats with them.

3 And he spoke to them this parable, saying,

4 What man of you having a hundred sheep, and having lost one of them, does not leave the ninety and nine in the wilderness and go after that which is lost, until he find it?

5 and having found it, he lays it upon his own shoulders, rejoicing;

6 and being come to the house, calls together the friends and the neighbors, saying to them, Rejoice with me, for I have found my lost sheep.

7 I say unto you, that thus there shall be joy in heaven for one repenting sinner, [more] than for ninety and nine righteous who have no need of repentance.

8 Or, what woman having ten drachmas, if she lose one drachma, does not light a lamp and sweep the house and seek carefully till she find it?

9 and having found it she calls together the friends and neighbors, saying, Rejoice with me, for I have found the drachma which I had lost.

10 Thus, I say unto you, there is joy before the angels of the God for one repenting sinner.

11 And he said, A certain man had two sons;

12 and the younger of them said to his father, Father, give to me the share of the property that falls [to me] And he divided to them what he was possessed of.

13 And after not many days the younger son gathering all together went away into a country a long way off, and there dissipated his property, living in debauchery.

14 But when he had spent all there arose a violent famine throughout that country, and he began to be in want.

15 And he went and joined himself to one of the citizens of that country, and he sent him into his fields to feed swine.

16 And he longed to fill his belly with the husks which the swine were eating; and no one gave to him.

17 And coming to himself, he said, How many hired servants of my father's have abundance of bread, and I perish here by famine.

18 I will rise up and go to my father, and I will say to him, Father, I have sinned against heaven and before you;

19 I am no longer worthy to be called your son: make me as one of your hired servants.

20 And he rose up and went to his own father. But while he was yet a long way off, his father saw him, and was moved with compassion, and ran, and fell upon his neck, and covered him with kisses.

21 And the son said to him, Father, I have sinned against heaven and before you; I am no longer worthy to be called your son.

22 But the father said to his servants, Bring out the best robe and clothe him in it and put a ring on his hand and sandals on his feet;

23 and bring the fatted calf and kill it, and let us eat and make merry:

24 for this my son was dead and has come to life, was lost and has been found. And they began to make merry.

25 And his elder son was in the field; and as, coming [up] he drew near to the house, he heard music and dancing.

26 And having called one of the servants, he inquired what these things might be.

27 And he said to him, Your brother is come, and your father has killed the fatted calf because he has received him safe and well.

28 But he became angry and would not go in. And his father went out and besought him.

29 But he answering said to his father, Behold, so many years I serve you, and never have I transgressed a commandment of yours; and to me

have you never given a kid that I might make merry with my friends:

30 but when this your son, who has devoured your substance with harlots, is come, you have killed for him the fatted calf.

31 But he said to him, Child, you are ever with me, and all that is mine is yours.

32 But it was right to make merry and rejoice, because this your brother was dead and has come to life again, and was lost and has been found.

Luke 16:1 And he said also to [his] disciples, There was a certain rich man who had a steward, and he was accused to him as wasting his goods.

2 And having called him, he said to him, What is this that I hear of you? give the reckoning of your stewardship, for you can be no longer steward.

3 And the steward said within himself, What shall I do; for my lord is taking the stewardship from me? I am not able to dig; I am ashamed to beg.

4 I know what I will do, that when I shall have been removed from the stewardship I may be received into their houses.

5 And having called to him each one of the debtors of his own lord, he said to the first, How much do you owe my lord?

6 And he said, A hundred baths of oil. And he said to him, Take your writing and sit down quickly and write fifty.

7 Then he said to another, And you, how much do you owe? And he said, A hundred measures of wheat. And he says to him, Take your writing and write eighty.

8 And the lord praised the unrighteous steward because he had done prudently. For the sons of this world are, for their own generation, more prudent than the sons of light.

9 And I say to you, Make to yourselves friends away from the mammon of unrighteousness [thus make friends of those of righteousness], that when it [way of mammon] fails you may be received into the aeonian tabernacles.

10 He that is faithful in the least is faithful also in much; and he that is unrighteous in the least is unrighteous also in much.

11 If therefore you have not been faithful in the unrighteous mammon, who shall entrust to you the true?

12 and if you have not been faithful in that which is another's, who shall give to you your own?

13 No servant can serve two masters, for either he will hate the one and will love the other, or he will cleave to the one and despise the other. You cannot serve God and mammon.

14 And the Pharisees also, who were covetous, heard all these things, and mocked him.

15 And he said to them, You are they who justify themselves before men, but the God knows your hearts; for what among men is highly thought of is an abomination before the God.

16 The law and the prophets [were] until John: from that time the good news of the kingdom of the God are announced, and every one forces his way into it.

17 But it is easier that the heaven and the earth should pass away than that one tittle of the law should fail.

18 Every one who puts away his wife and marries another commits adultery; and every one that marries one put away from a husband commits adultery.

19 Now there was a rich man and he was clothed in purple and fine linen, making good cheer in splendor every day.

20 And [there was] a poor man, by name Lazarus, [who] was laid at his gateway full of sores,

21 and desiring to be filled with the crumbs which fell from the table of the rich man; but the dogs also coming licked his sores.

22 And it came to pass that the poor man died, and that he was carried away by the angels into the bosom of Abraham. And the rich man also died and was buried.

23 And in Hades lifting up his eyes, being in torments, he sees Abraham afar off, and Lazarus in his bosom.

24 And he crying out said, Father Abraham, have compassion on me, and send Lazarus that he may dip the tip of his finger in water and cool my tongue, for I am suffering in this flame.

25 But Abraham said, Child, recollect that you have fully received your good things in your lifetime, and likewise Lazarus evil things. But now he is comforted here, and you are in suffering.

26 And besides all this, between us and you a great chasm is fixed, so that those who desire to pass hence to you cannot, nor do they who [desire to cross] from there pass over unto us.

27 And he said, I beseech you then, father, that you would send him to the house of my father,

28 for I have five brothers, so that he may earnestly testify to them, that they also may not come to this place of torment.

29 But Abraham says to him, They have Moses and the prophets: let them hear them.

30 But he said, No, father Abraham, but if one from the dead should go to them, they will repent.

31 And he said to him, If they hear not Moses and the prophets, not even if one rise from among the dead will they be persuaded.

Luke 17:1 And he said to his disciples, It cannot be but that offences come, but woe [to him] by whom they come!

2 It would be [more] profitable for him if a millstone were hanged about his neck and he cast into the sea, than that he should be a snare to one of these little ones.

3 Take heed to yourselves: if your brother should sin, rebuke him; and if he should repent, forgive him.

4 And if he should sin against you seven times in the day, and seven times should return to you, saying, I repent, you shall forgive him.

5 And the apostles said to the Lord, Give more faith to us.

6 But the Lord said, If you have faith as a grain of mustard [seed] you had said to this mulberry tree, Be you rooted up, and be you planted in the sea, and it would have obeyed you.

7 But which of you [is there] who, having a servant ploughing or shepherding, when he comes in out of the field, will say, Come and lie down immediately to the table?

8 But will he not say to him, Prepare what I shall sup on, and gird yourself and serve me that I may eat and drink; and after that you shall eat and drink?

9 Is he thankful to the servant because he has done what was ordered? I judge not.

10 Thus you also, when you shall have done all things that have been ordered you, say, We are unprofitable servants; we have done what it was our duty to do.

11 And it came to pass as he was going up to Jerusalem, that he passed through the midst of Samaria and Galilee.

12 And as he entered into a certain village ten leprous men met him, who stood afar off.

13 And they lifted up [their] voice saying, Jesus, Master, have compassion on us.

14 And seeing [them] he said to them, Go, show yourselves to the priests. And it came to pass as they were going they were cleansed.

15 And one of them, seeing that he was cured, turned back, glorifying the God with a loud voice,

16 and fell on [his] face at his feet giving him thanks: and he was a Samaritan.

17 And Jesus answering said, Were not the ten cleansed? but the nine, where [are they]

18 There have not been found to return and give glory to the God except this stranger.

19 And he said to him, Rise up and go your way: your faith has made you well.

20 And having been asked by the Pharisees, When is the kingdom of the God coming? he answered them and said, The kingdom of the God does not come with meticulous observation;

21 nor shall they say, Lo here, or, Lo there; for behold, the kingdom of the God is in the midst of you.

22 And he said to the disciples, Days are coming, when you shall desire to see one of the days of the Son of man, and shall not see it

23 And they will say to you, Lo here, or Lo there; go not, nor follow [them]

24 For as the lightning shines which lightens from [one end] under heaven to [the other end] under heaven, thus shall the Son of man be in his day.

25 But first he must suffer many things and be rejected of this generation.

26 And as it took place in the days of Noah, thus also shall it be in the days of the Son of man:

27 they ate, they drank, they married, they were given in marriage, until the day that Noah entered into the ark, and the flood came and destroyed all [of them]

28 and in like manner as took place in the days of Lot: they ate, they drank, they bought, they sold, they planted, they built;

29 but on the day that Lot went out from Sodom, it rained fire and sulphur from heaven, and destroyed all [of them]

30 after this [manner] shall it be in the day that the Son of man is revealed.

31 In that day, he who shall be on the housetop, and his stuff in the house, let him not go down to take it away; and he that is in the field, let him likewise not return back.

32 Remember the wife of Lot.

33 Whosoever shall seek to save his soul shall lose it, and whosoever shall lose it shall preserve it.

34 I say to you, In that night there shall be two [men] upon one bed; one shall be seized and the other shall be let go.

35 Two [women] shall be grinding together; the one shall be seized and the other shall be let go.

36 [Two men shall be in the field; the one shall be seized and the other let go]

37 And answering they say to him, Where, Lord? And he said to them, Where the body is there the eagles will be gathered together.

Luke 18:1 And he spoke also a parable to them to the purport that they should always pray and not faint,

2 saying, There was a judge in a city, not fearing the God and not respecting man:

3 and there was a widow in that city, and she came to him, saying, Avenge me of mine adverse party.

4 And he would not for a time; but afterwards he said within himself, If even I fear not the God and respect not man,

5 at any rate because this widow annoys me I will avenge her, that she may not by perpetually coming completely harass me.

6 And the Lord said, Hear what the unjust judge says.

7 And shall not the God at all avenge his elect, who cry to him day and night, and he bears long as to them?

8 I say unto you that he will avenge them speedily. But when the Son of man comes, shall he indeed find faith on the earth?

9 And he spoke this parable to some, who trusted in themselves that they were righteous and looked down upon all the rest [of men]:

10 Two men went up into the temple to pray; the one a Pharisee, and the other a tax-gatherer.

11 The Pharisee, standing, prayed thus to himself: God, I thank you that I am not as the rest of men, robbers, unjust, adulterers, or even as this tax-gatherer.

12 I fast twice in the week, I tithe everything I gain.

13 And the tax-gatherer, standing afar off, would not lift up even his eyes to heaven, but smote upon his breast, saying, O God, have compassion on me, the sinner.

14 I say unto you, This [man] went down to his house justified rather than that [other] For every one who exalts himself shall be humbled, and he that humbles himself shall be exalted.

15 And they brought to him also infants that he might touch them, but the disciples when they saw it rebuked them.

16 But Jesus calling them to him, said, Permit little children to come to me, and do not forbid them, for of such is the kingdom of the God.

17 Truly I say to you, Whosoever shall not receive the kingdom of the God as a little child shall in no way enter therein.

18 And a certain ruler asked him saying, Good teacher, having done what, shall I inherit aeonian life?

19 But Jesus said to him, Why do you call me good? There is none good but one, the God.

20 You know the commandments: Do not commit adultery, Do not kill, Do not steal, Do not bear false witness, honor your father and your mother.

21 And he said, All these things have I kept from my youth.

22 And when Jesus had heard this, he said to him, One thing is lacking to you yet: Sell all that you have and distribute to the poor, and you shall have treasure in the heavens, and come, follow me.

23 But when he heard this he became very sorrowful, for he was very rich.

24 But when Jesus saw that he became very sorrowful, he said, How difficultly shall those who have riches enter into the kingdom of the God;

25 for it is easier for a camel to enter through a needle's eye than for a rich man to enter into the kingdom of the God.

26 And those who heard it said, And who can be saved?

27 But he said, The things that are impossible with men are possible with the God.

28 And Peter said, Behold, we have left all things and have followed you.

29 And he said to them, Truly I say to you, There is no one who has left home, or parents, or brethren, or wife, or children, for the kingdom of God's sake,

30 who shall not receive manifold more at this time, and in the coming aeon, aeonian life.

31 And he took the twelve to him, and said to them, Behold, we go up to Jerusalem, and all things that are written of the Son of man by the prophets shall be accomplished;

32 for he shall be delivered up to the Gentiles, and shall be mocked, and insulted, and spit upon.

33 And when they have scourged him, they will kill him; and on the third day he will rise again.

34 And they understood nothing of these things. And this word was hidden from them, and they did not know what was said.

35 And it came to pass when he came into the neighborhood of Jericho, a certain blind man sat by the wayside begging.

36 And when he heard the crowd passing, he inquired what this might be.

37 And they told him that Jesus the Nazarene was passing by.

38 And he called out saying, Jesus, Son of David, have mercy on me.

39 And those [who were] going before rebuked him that he might be silent; but he cried out so much the more, Son of David, have mercy on me.

40 And Jesus stood still, and commanded him to be led to him. And when he drew near he asked him [saying]

41 What do you wish that I shall do to you? And he said, Lord, that I may see.

42 And Jesus said to him, See: your faith has healed you.

43 And immediately he saw, and followed him, glorifying the God. And all the people when they saw it gave praise to the God.

Luke 19:1 And he entered and passed through Jericho.

2 And behold, [there was] a man by name called Zacchaeus, and he was chief tax-gatherer, and he was rich.

3 And he sought to see Jesus who he was: and he could not for the crowd, because he was little in stature.

4 And running on before, he got up into a sycamore that he might see him, for he was going to pass that [way]

5 And when he came up to the place, Jesus looked up and saw him, and said to him, Zacchaeus, make haste and come down, for today I must remain in your house.

6 And he made haste and came down, and received him with joy.

7 And all murmured when they saw it saying, He has turned in to lodge with a sinful man.

8 But Zacchaeus stood and said to the Lord, Behold, Lord, the half of my goods I give to the poor, and if I have taken anything from any man by false accusation, I return him fourfold.

9 And Jesus said to him, Today salvation is come to this house, inasmuch as he also is a son of Abraham;

10 for the Son of man has come to seek and to save that which is lost.

11 But as they were listening to these things, he added and spoke a parable, because he was near to Jerusalem and they thought that the kingdom of the God was about to be immediately manifested.

12 He said therefore, A certain nobleman went to a distant country to receive for himself a kingdom and return.

13 And having called his own ten servants, he gave to them ten minas, and said to them, Trade while I am coming.

14 But his citizens hated him, and sent an embassy after him, saying, We do not want this [nobleman] to reign over us.

15 And it came to pass on his arrival back again, having received the kingdom, that he desired these servants to whom he gave the money to be called to

him, in order that he might know what every one had gained by trading.

16 And the first came up, saying, [my] Lord, your mina has produced ten minas.

17 And he said to him, Well [done] you good servant; because you have been faithful in that which is least, be you in authority over ten cities.

18 And the second came, saying, [my] Lord, your mina has made five minas.

19 And he said also to this one, And you, be over five cities.

20 And another came, saying, [my] Lord, lo, [there is] your mina, which I have kept laid up in a towel.

21 For I feared you because you are a harsh man: you take up what you have not laid down, and you reap what you have not sowed.

22 He says to him, Out of your mouth will I judge you, wicked servant: you knew that I am a harsh man, taking up what I have not laid down and reaping what I have not sowed.

23 And why did you not give my money to the bank; and I should have received it, at my coming, with interest?

24 And he said to those that stood by, Take from him the mina and give it to him who has the ten minas.

25 And they said to him, Lord, he has ten minas.

26 For I say unto you, that to every one that has shall be given; but from him that has not, that even which he has shall be taken from him.

27 Moreover mine enemies, who would not [have] me to reign over them, bring them here and slay [them] before me.

28 And having said these things, he went on before, going up to Jerusalem.

29 And it came to pass as he drew near to Bethphage and Bethany at the mountain called [the mount] of Olives, he sent two of his disciples,

30 saying, Go into the village over against [you] in which you will find, on entering it, a colt tied up, on which no [child] of man ever sat at any time: loose it and lead it [here]

31 And if any one ask you, Why do you loose it thus shall you say to him, Because the Lord has need of it.

32 And they that were sent, having gone their way, found as he had said to them.

33 And as they were loosing the colt, its masters said to them, Why loose you the colt?

34 And they said, Because the Lord has need of it.

35 And they led it to Jesus; and having cast their own garments on the colt, they put Jesus on it

36 And as he went, they strewed their clothes in the way.

37 And as he drew near, already at the descent of the mount of Olives, all the multitude of the disciples began, rejoicing, to praise the God with a loud voice for all the works of power which they had seen,

38 saying, Blessed the King that comes in the name of the Lord: peace in heaven, and glory in the highest.

39 And some of the Pharisees from the crowd said to him, Teacher, rebuke your disciples.

40 And he answering said to them, I say unto you, If these shall be silent, the stones will cry out.

41 And as he drew near, seeing the city, he wept over it,

42 saying, If you had known, even you, even at least in this your day, the things that are for your peace: but now they are hid from your eyes;

43 for days shall come upon you, that your enemies shall make a embankment about you, and shall close you around, and keep you in on every side,

44 and shall lay you even with the ground, and your children in you; and shall not leave in you a stone upon a stone: because you knew not the season of your visitation.

45 And entering into the temple, he began to cast out those that sold and bought in it,

46 saying to them, It is written, My house is a house of prayer, but you have made it a den of robbers.

47 And he was teaching day by day in the temple: and the chief priests and the scribes and the chief of the people sought to destroy him,

48 and did not find any way to do it, for all the people hung on him to hear [his words].

Luke 20:1 And it came to pass on one of the days, as he was teaching the people in the temple, and announcing the good news, the chief priests and the scribes with the elders came up,

2 and spoke to him saying, Tell us by what authority you do these things, or who is it who has given you this authority?

3 And he answering said to them, I also will ask you [one] thing, and tell me:

4 The baptism of John, was it of heaven or of men?

5 And they reasoned among themselves, saying, If we should say, Of heaven, he will say, Why have you not believed him?

6 but if we should say, Of men, the whole people will stone us, for they are persuaded that John was a prophet.

7 And they answered, they did not know.

8 And Jesus said to them, Neither do I tell you by what authority I do these things.

9 And he began to speak to the people this parable: A man planted a vineyard and let it out to husbandmen, and left the country for a long time.

10 And in the season he sent to the husbandmen a servant, that they might give to him of the fruit of the vineyard; but the husbandmen, having beaten him, sent him away empty.

11 And again he sent another servant; but they, having beaten him also, and cast insult upon him, sent him away empty.

12 And again he sent a third; and they, having wounded him also, cast him out.

13 And the lord of the vineyard said, What shall I do? I will send my beloved son: perhaps when they see him they will respect him.

14 But when the husbandmen saw him, they reasoned among themselves, saying, This is the heir; [come] let us kill him, that the inheritance may become ours.

15 And having cast him forth out of the vineyard, they killed him. What therefore shall the lord of the vineyard do to them?

16 He will come and destroy those husbandmen, and will give the vineyard to others. And when they heard it they said, May it never be!

17 But looking at them he said, What then is this that is written, The stone which they that built rejected, this has become the corner-stone?

18 Every one falling on this stone shall be broken, but on whomsoever it shall fall, it shall grind him to powder.

19 And the chief priests and the scribes sought the same hour to lay hands on him, and they feared the people; for they knew that he had spoken this parable of them.

20 And having watched him, they sent out spies, pretending to be just men, that they might take hold of him in [his] language, so that they might deliver him up to the power and authority of the governor.

21 And they asked him saying, Teacher, we know that you say and you teach rightly, and accept no [man's] person, but teach with truth the way of the God:

22 Is it lawful for us to give tribute to Caesar, or not?

23 But perceiving their deceit he said to them, Why do you test me?

24 Show me a denarius. Whose image and superscription has it? And answering they said, Caesar's.

25 And he said to them, Pay therefore what is Caesar's to Caesar, and what is God's to the God.

26 And they were not able to take hold of him in [his] expressions before the people, and, wondering at his answer, they were silent.

27 And some of the Sadducees, who deny that there is any resurrection, coming up [to him]

28 asked of him saying, Teacher, Moses wrote to us, If any one's brother, who has a wife, die, and he die childless, his brother shall take the wife and raise up seed to his brother.

29 There were then seven brethren: and the first, having taken a wife, died childless;

30 and the second [took the woman, and he died childless]

31 and the third took her: and in like manner also the seven left no children and died;

32 and last of all the woman also died.

33 In the resurrection therefore of which of them does she become wife, for the seven had her as wife?

34 And Jesus said to them, The sons of this world marry and are given in marriage,

35 but they who are counted worthy to have part in that world, and the resurrection from among the dead, neither marry nor are given in marriage;

36 for neither can they die any more, for they are equal to angels, and are sons of God, being sons of the resurrection.

37 But that the dead rise, even Moses showed in [the section of] the bush, when he called the Lord the God of Abraham and the God of Isaac and the God of Jacob;

38 but he is not God of the dead but of the living; for all live to him.

39 And some of the scribes answering said, Teacher, you have well spoken.

40 For they did not dare any more to ask him anything.

41 And he said to them, How do they say that the Christ is David's son,

42 and David himself says in the book of Psalms, The Lord said to my Lord, Sit at my right hand

43 until I put your enemies [as] footstool of your feet?

44 David therefore calls him Lord, and how is he his son?

45 And, as all the people were listening, he said to his disciples,

46 Beware of the scribes, who like to walk about in long robes, and who like salutations in the market-places, and first seats in the synagogues, and first places at suppers;

47 who devour the houses of widows, and as a pretext make long prayers. These shall receive a severer judgment.

Luke 21:1 And he looked up and saw the rich casting their gifts into the treasury;

2 but he saw also a certain poor widow casting therein two mites.

3 And he said, Truly I say unto you, that this poor widow has cast in more than all;

4 for all these out of their abundance have cast into the gifts [of god] but she out of her need has cast in all the living which she had.

5 And as some spoke of the temple, that it was adorned with goodly stones and consecrated offerings, he said,

6 [As to] these things which you are beholding, days are coming in which there shall not be left stone upon stone which shall not be thrown down.

7 And they asked him saying, Teacher, when then shall these things be; and what is the sign when these things are going to take place?

8 And he said, See that you be not led astray, for many shall come in my name, saying, I am [he] and the time is drawn near: go you not [therefore] after them.

9 And when you shall hear of wars and revolutions, be not terrified, for these things must first take place, but the end is not immediately.

10 Then he said to them, Nation shall rise up against nation, and kingdom against kingdom;

11 there shall be both great earthquakes in different places, and famine and pestilence; and

there shall be fearful sights and great signs from heaven.

12 But before all these things they shall lay their hands upon you and persecute you, delivering [you] up to synagogues and prisons, bringing [you] before kings and governors on account of my name;

13 but it shall turn out to you for a testimony.

14 Settle therefore in your hearts not to meditate beforehand [your] defense,

15 for I will give you a mouth and wisdom which all your oppressors shall not be able to reply to or resist.

16 But you will be delivered up even by parents and brethren and relations and friends, and they shall put to death [some] from among you,

17 and you will be hated of all for my name's sake.

18 And a hair of your head shall in no way perish.

19 By your patient endurance gain your souls.

20 But when you see Jerusalem encompassed with armies, then know that its desolation is drawn near.

21 Then let those who are in Judea flee to the mountains, and those who are in the midst of it depart out, and those who are in the country not enter into it;

22 for these are days of avenging, that all the things that are written may be accomplished.

23 But woe to them that are with child and to them who give suck in those days, for there shall be great distress upon the land and wrath upon this people.

24 And they shall fall by the edge of the sword, and be led captive into all the nations; and Jerusalem shall be trodden down of the nations until the times of the nations be fulfilled.

25 And there shall be signs in sun and moon and stars, and upon the earth distress of nations in perplexity [at] the roar of the sea and rolling waves,

26 men ready to die through fear and expectation of what is coming on the habitable earth, for the powers of the heavens shall be shaken.

27 And then shall they see the Son of man coming in a cloud with power and great glory.

28 But when these things begin to come to pass, look up and lift up your heads, because your redemption draws near.

29 And he spoke a parable to them: Behold the fig-tree and all the trees;

30 when they already sprout, you know of your own selves, [on] looking [at them] that already the summer is near.

31 So also you, when you see these things take place, know that the kingdom of the God is near.

32 Truly I say unto you, that this generation[190] shall in no way pass away until all come to pass.

33 The heaven and the earth shall pass away, but my words shall in no way pass away.

34 But take heed to yourselves lest possibly your hearts be loaded with hangovers and drinking and cares of life, and that day come upon you suddenly unawares;

35 for as a snare shall it come upon all them that dwell upon the face of the whole earth.

36 Watch therefore, praying at every season, that you may be accounted worthy to escape all these things which are about to come to pass, and to stand before the Son of man.

37 And by day he was teaching in the temple, and by night, going out, he remained abroad on the mountain called [the mount] of Olives;

38 and all the people came early in the morning to him in the temple to hear him.

Luke 22:1 Now the feast of unleavened bread, which is called the Passover, drew near,

2 and the chief priests and the scribes sought how they might kill him; for they feared the people.

3 And Satan entered into Judas, who was surnamed Iscariote, being of the number of the twelve.

4 And he went away and spoke with the chief priests and captains as to how he should deliver him up to them.

5 And they were rejoiced, and agreed to give him money.

6 And he came to an agreement to do it, and sought an opportunity to deliver him up to them away from the crowd.

7 And towards the day of unleavened bread came, in which the Passover was to be killed.

8 And he sent Peter and John, saying, Go and prepare the Passover for us, that we may eat it

9 But they said to him, Where will you that we prepare it

10 And he said to them, Behold, as you enter into the city a man will meet you, carrying an earthen pitcher of water; follow him into the house where he goes in;

11 and you shall say to the master of the house, The Teacher says to you, Where is the guest-chamber where I may eat the Passover with my disciples?

12 And he will show you a large upper room furnished: there make ready.

13 And having gone they found it as he had said to them; and they prepared* the Passover.

14 And when the hour was come, he placed himself at table, and the [twelve] apostles with him.

15 And he said to them, With desire I have desired this Passover to eat with you before I suffer.

16 Since I say unto you, that I will not eat it [Passover] until it be fulfilled in the kingdom of the God.

17 And having received a cup, when he had given thanks he said, Take this and divide it among yourselves.

18 For I say unto you, that I will not drink at all of the fruit of the vine until the kingdom of the God come.

---

[190] See Ps 22:30

19 And having taken a loaf, when he had given thanks, he broke it and gave it to them, saying, This is my body which is given for you: this do in remembrance of me.

20 In like manner also the cup, after having supper, saying, This cup is the new covenant in my blood, which is poured out for you.

21 Moreover, behold, the hand of him that delivers me up is with me on the table;

22 and the Son of man indeed goes as it is determined, but woe unto that man by whom he is delivered up.

23 And they began to question together among themselves who then it could be of them who was about to do this.

24 And there was also a strife among them which of them should be held to be the greatest.

25 And he said to them, The kings of the nations rule over them, and they that exercise authority over them are called benefactors.

26 But you [shall] not [be] thus; but let the greater among you be as the younger, and the leader as he that serves.

27 For which is greater, he that is at table or he that serves? is not he that is at table? But I am in the midst of you as the one that serves.

28 But you are they who have persevered with me in my testing.

29 And I appoint unto you, as my Father has appointed unto me, a kingdom,

30 that you may eat and drink at my table in my kingdom, and sit on thrones judging the twelve tribes of Israel.

31 And the Lord said, Simon, Simon, behold, Satan has asked to have you, to sift [you] as wheat;

32 but I have besought for you that your faith fail not; and you, when once you have been restored, confirm your brethren.

33 And he said to him, Lord, with you I am ready to go both to prison and to death.

34 And he said, I tell you, Peter, the cock shall not crow today before that you shall three times deny that you know me.

35 And he said to them, When I sent you without purse and scrip and sandals, did you lack anything? And they said, Nothing.

36 He said therefore to them, But now he that has a purse let him take it in like manner also a scrip, and he that has none let him sell his garment and buy a sword;

37 for I say unto you, that this that is written must yet be accomplished in me, And he was reckoned with the lawless: for also the things concerning me have a fulfillment.

38 And they said, Lord, behold here are two swords. And he said to them, It is enough.

39 And going forth he went according to his custom to the mount of Olives, and the disciples also followed him.

40 And when he was at the place he said to them, Pray that you enter not into temptation.

41 And he was withdrawn from them about a stone's throw, and having knelt down he prayed,

42 saying, Father, if you will remove this cup from me: --but then, not my will, but yours be done.

43 And an angel appeared to him from heaven strengthening him.

44 And being in conflict he prayed more intently. And his sweat became as great drops of blood, falling down upon the earth.

45 And rising up from his prayer, coming to the disciples, he found them sleeping from grief.

46 And he said to them, Why sleep you? rise up and pray that you enter not into temptation.

47 As he was yet speaking, behold, a crowd, and he that was called Judas, one of the twelve, went on before them, and drew near to Jesus to show affection for him.

48 And Jesus said to him, Judas, do you deliver up the Son of man with a kiss?

49 And they who were around him, seeing what was going to follow, said [to him] Lord, shall we smite with the sword?

50 And a certain one from among them smote the servant of the high priest and took off his right ear.

51 And Jesus answering said, Stop, no more of this ... and having touched his ear, he healed him.

52 And Jesus said to the chief priests and captains of the temple and elders, who were come against him, Have you come out as against a robber with swords and sticks?

53 When I was day by day with you in the temple you did not stretch out your hands against me; but this is your hour and the power of darkness.

54 And having laid hold on him, they led him [away] and they led him into the house of the high priest. And Peter followed afar off.

55 And they having lit a fire in the midst of the court and sat down together, Peter sat among them.

56 And a certain maid, having seen him sitting by the light, and having fixed her eyes upon him, said, And this [man] was with him.

57 But he denied him, saying, Woman, I do not know him.

58 And after a short time another seeing him said, And you are of them. But Peter said, Man, I am not.

59 And after the lapse of about one hour another stoutly maintained it, saying, In truth this [man] also was with him, for also he is a Galilaean.

60 And Peter said, Man, I know not what you are saying. And immediately, while he was yet speaking, the cock crew.

61 And the Lord, turning round, looked at Peter; and Peter remembered the word of the Lord, how he said to him, Before the cock crow you shall deny me three times.

62 And Peter, going forth outside, wept bitterly.

63 And the men who held him mocked him, beating him,

64 and covering him up, asked him saying, Prophesy, who is it that struck you?

65 And they said many other injurious things to him.

66 And when it was day, the elderhood of the people, both the chief priests and scribes, were gathered together, and led him into their council, saying,

67 If you are the Christ, tell us. And he said to them, If I tell you, you will not at all believe;

68 and if I should ask [you] you would not answer me at all, nor let me go;

69 but henceforth shall the Son of man be sitting on the right hand of the power of the God.

70 And they all said, You then are the Son of the God? And he said to them, You say that I am.

71 And they said, What need have we any more of witness, for we have heard ourselves out of his mouth?

Luke 23:1 And the whole multitude of them, rising up, led him to Pilate.

2 And they began to accuse him, saying, We have found this [man] perverting our nation, and forbidding to give tribute to Caesar, saying that he himself is Christ, a king.

3 And Pilate asked of him saying, Are you the king of the Jews? And he answering him said, You said it.

4 And Pilate said to the chief priests and the crowds, I find no guilt in this man.

5 But they insisted, saying, He stirs up the people, teaching throughout all Judea, beginning from Galilee even on to here.

6 But Pilate, having heard Galilee [named] asked if the man were a Galilaean;

7 and having learned that he was of Herod's jurisdiction, he sent him to Herod, who himself also was at Jerusalem in those days.

8 And when Herod saw Jesus he greatly rejoiced, for he had been a long while desirous of seeing him, because of hearing many things concerning him, and he hoped to see some sign done by him;

9 and he questioned him in many words, but he answered him nothing.

10 And the chief priests and the scribes stood and accused him violently.

11 And Herod with his troops having set him at nought and mocked him, having put a splendid robe upon him, sent him back to Pilate.

12 And Pilate and Herod became friends with one another the same day, for they had been at enmity before between themselves.

13 And Pilate, having called together the chief priests and the rulers and the people,

14 said to them, You have brought to me this man as turning away the people [to rebellion] and behold, I, having examined him before you, have found nothing criminal in this man as to the things of which you accuse him;

15 nor Herod either, for he sent him back to us, for nothing worthy of death was done by him.

16 Having chastised him therefore, I will release him.

17 Now he was obliged to release one for them at the feast.

18 But they cried out in a mass saying, Away with this [man] and release Barabbas to us;

19 who was one who, for a certain tumult which had taken place in the city, and [for] murder, had been cast into prison.

20 Pilate therefore, desirous to release Jesus, again addressed [them]

21 But they cried out in reply saying, Crucify, crucify him.

22 And he said the third time to them, What evil then has this [man] done? I have found no cause of death in him: I will chastise him therefore and release him.

23 But they were urgent with loud voices, begging that he might be crucified. And their voices [and those of the chief priests] prevailed.

24 And Pilate adjudged that what they begged should take place.

25 And he released him who, for tumult and murder, had been cast into prison, whom they begged for, and Jesus he delivered up to their will.

26 And as they led him away, they laid hold on a certain Simon, a Cyrenian, coming from the field, and put the cross upon him to bear it behind Jesus.

27 And a great multitude of the people, and of women who wailed and lamented him, followed him.

28 And Jesus turning round to them said, Daughters of Jerusalem, do not weep over me, but weep over yourselves and over your children;

29 for behold, days are coming in which they will say, Blessed [are] the barren, and wombs that have not borne, and breasts that have not given suck.

30 Then shall they begin to say to the mountains, Fall upon us; and to the hills, Cover us:

31 for if these things are done in the green tree, what shall take place in the dry?

32 Now two others also, malefactors, were led with him to be put to death.

33 And when they came to the place which is called Skull, there they crucified him, and the malefactors, one on the right hand, the other on the left.

34 And Jesus said, Father, forgive them, for they know not what they do. And, parting out his garments, they cast lots.

35 And the people stood beholding, and the rulers also [with them] sneered, saying, He has saved others; let him save himself if this is the Christ, the chosen one of the God.

36 And the soldiers also made game of him, coming up offering him vinegar,

37 and saying, If you be the king of the Jews, save yourself.

38 And there was also an inscription [written] over him in Greek, and Roman, and Hebrew letters: This is the King of the Jews.

39 Now one of the malefactors who had been hanged spoke insultingly to him, saying, Are not you the Christ? save yourself and us.

40 But the other answering rebuked him, saying, Do you too not fear the God, you that are under the same judgment?

41 and we indeed justly, for we receive the just recompense of what we have done; but this [man] has done nothing amiss.

42 And he said to Jesus, Remember me, [lord] when you come in your kingdom.

43 And Jesus said to him, Truly I say to you today, "you shall be with me in paradise."

44 And it was about the sixth hour, and there came darkness over the whole land until the ninth hour.

45 And the sun was darkened, and the veil of the temple rent in the midst.

46 And Jesus, having cried with a loud voice, said, Father, into your hands I commit my spirit. And having said this, he expired.

47 Now the centurion, seeing what took place, glorified the God, saying, In very deed this man was just.

48 And all the crowds who had come together to that sight, having seen the things that took place, returned, beating [their] breasts.

49 And all those who knew him stood afar off, the women also who had followed him from Galilee, beholding these things.

50 And behold, a man named Joseph, who was a councillor, a good man and a just

51 this [man] had not assented to their counsel and deed, of Arimathaea, a city of the Jews, who also waited, [himself also] for the kingdom of the God

52 --he having gone to Pilate begged the body of Jesus;

53 and having taken it down, wrapped it in fine linen and placed him in a tomb hewn in the rock, where no one had ever been laid.

54 And it was preparation day, and the Sabbath was coming on.

55 And women, who had come along with him out of Galilee, having followed, saw the tomb and how his body was placed.

56 And having returned they prepared aromatic spices and ointments, and rested on the Sabbath, according to the commandment.

Luke 24:1 But towards [day] one of the week [Sabbaths] very early indeed in the morning, they came to the tomb, bringing the aromatic spices which they had prepared.

2 And they found the stone rolled away from the tomb.

3 And when they had entered they found not the body of the Lord Jesus.

4 And it came to pass as they were in perplexity about it, that behold, two men suddenly stood by them in shining raiment.

5 And as they were filled with fear and bowed their faces to the ground, they said to them, Why seek you the living one among the dead?

6 He is not here, but is risen: remember how he spoke to you, being yet in Galilee,

7 saying, The Son of man must be delivered up into the hands of sinners, and be crucified, and rise the third day.

8 And they remembered his words;

9 and, returning from the tomb, related all these things to the eleven and to all the rest.

10 Now it was Mary of Magdalene, and Johanna, and Mary the [mother] of James, and the others with them, who told these things to the apostles.

11 And their words appeared in their eyes as an idle tale, and they disbelieved them.

12 But Peter, rising up, ran to the tomb, and stooping down he sees the linen clothes lying there alone, and went away home, wondering at what had happened.

13 And behold, two of them were going on that same day[191] to a village distant sixty stadia [about 7 miles] from Jerusalem, called Emmaus;

14 and they conversed with one another about all these things which had taken place.

15 And it came to pass as they talked and reasoned, that Jesus himself drawing near, went with them;

16 but their eyes were held back so as not to know him.

17 And he said to them, What discourses are these which pass between you as you walk, and are downcast?

18 And one [of them] named Cleopas, answering said to him, You sojourners alone in Jerusalem, and do not know what has taken place in it in these days?

19 And he said to them, What things? And they said to him, The things concerning Jesus the Nazarene, who was a prophet mighty in deed and word before the God and all the people;

20 and how the chief priests and our rulers delivered him up to the judgment of death and crucified him.

21 But we had hoped that he was [the one] who is about to redeem Israel. Yes, and along with all this, this brings on *the* third day since these things [v. 20] took place.

22 And certain women from among us astonished us, having been very early at the tomb,[192]

23 and, not having found his body, came, saying that they also had seen a vision of angels, who say that he is living.

24 And some of those with us went to the tomb, and found it so, as the women also had said, but him they saw not.

25 And he said to them, O senseless and slow of heart to believe in all that the prophets have spoken!

26 Ought not the Christ to have suffered these things and to enter into his glory?

27 And having begun from Moses and from all the prophets, he interpreted to them in all the scriptures the things concerning himself.

28 And they drew near to the village where they were going, and he made as though he would go farther.

29 And they constrained him, saying, Stay with us, for it is toward evening and the day is declining. And he entered in to stay with them.

30 And it came to pass as he was at table with them, having taken the bread, he blessed, and having broken it, gave it to them.

---

[191] Sunday

[192] They went to the tomb at the very end of the third day and reached the tomb right after Christ was resurrected on the very beginning of the fourth day, that is, the first day of the new week. See Chron. Papers, Part 4

31 And their eyes were opened, and they recognized him. And he disappeared from them.

32 And they said to one another, Was not our heart burning in us as he spoke to us on the way, [and] as he opened the scriptures to us?

33 And rising up the same hour, they returned to Jerusalem. And they found the eleven, and those with them, gathered together,

34 saying, The Lord is indeed risen and has appeared to Simon.

35 And they related what [had happened] on the way, and how he was made known to them in the breaking of bread.

36 And as they were saying these things, he himself stood in their midst, and says to them, Peace [be] unto you.

37 But they, being confounded and being frightened, supposed they beheld a spirit.

38 And he said to them, Why are you troubled? and why are thoughts rising in your hearts?

39 behold my hands and my feet, that it is I myself. Handle me and see, for a spirit has not flesh and bones as you see me having.

40 And having said this he showed them his hands and his feet.

41 But while they yet did not believe because of their joy, and wonderment, he said to them, Have you anything here to eat?

42 And they gave him part of a broiled fish and of a honeycomb;

43 and he took it and ate before them.

44 And he said to them, These [are] the words which I spoke to you while I was yet with you, that all that is written concerning me in the law of Moses and prophets and psalms must be fulfilled.

45 Then he opened their understanding to understand the scriptures,

46 and said to them, Thus it is written, and thus it behooved the Christ to suffer, and to rise from among the dead the third day;

47 and that repentance and forgiveness of sins should be preached in his name to all the nations beginning at Jerusalem.

48 And you are witnesses of these things.

49 And behold, I send the promise of my Father upon you; but you should remain in the city till you be clothed with power from on high.

50 And he led them out as far as Bethany, and having lifted up his hands, he blessed them.

51 And it came to pass as he was blessing them, he was separated from them and was carried up into heaven.

52 And they, having done him homage, returned to Jerusalem with great joy,

53 and were continually in the temple praising and blessing the God.

John

John 1:1 In the beginning was the Word, and the Word was toward the God, and God was the Word.

2 He was in the beginning toward the God.[193]

3 All things come to be* through him, and apart from him come to be* not one [thing] which has come to be.

4 In him was life, and the life was the light of men.

5 And the light appears in the darkness, and the darkness apprehended it not.

6 There was a man sent from God, his name John.

7 He came for witness, that he might witness concerning the light, that all might believe through him.

8 He was not the light, but [he came] that he might witness concerning the light.

9 The true light was that which, coming into the world, lightens every man.

10 He [the light] was in the world, and the world through him came to be,* and the world knew him not.

11 He came to his own, and his own received him not;

12 but as many as received him, to them gave he the power to be children of God, to those that believe into his name;

13 who [those who believe] have been born, not of blood, nor of flesh's will, nor of man's will, but of God.

14 And the Word became flesh, and dwelt among us and we have contemplated his glory, a glory as a one-of-a-kind[194] with the father, full of grace and truth;

15 John bears witness of him, and he has cried, saying, This was he of whom I said, He that comes after me is preferred before me, for he was before me;

16 for of his fullness we all have received, and grace upon grace.

17 For the law was given by Moses: grace and truth came to be* through Jesus Christ.

18 No one has seen God at any time; the one-of-a-kind[195] Son who is in the bosom of the Father, he reveals him.

19 And this is the witness of John, when the Jews sent from Jerusalem priests and Levites that they might ask him, Who are you?

20 And he acknowledged and denied not, and acknowledged, I am not the Christ.

21 And they asked him, What then? Are you Elijah? And he says, I am not. Are you the prophet? And he answered, No.

22 They said therefore to him, Who are you? that we may give an answer to those who sent us. What do you say of yourself?

23 He said, I am the voice of one crying in the wilderness, Make straight the path of the Lord, as Isaiah the prophet said.

24 And they were sent from among the Pharisees.

25 And they asked him and said to him, Why do you baptize then, if you are not the Christ, nor Elijah, nor the prophet?

26 John answered them saying, I baptize with water. In the midst of you stands, whom you do not know,

27 he who comes after me, the thong of whose sandal I am not worthy to unloose.

28 These things took place in Bethany, across the Jordan, where John was baptizing.

29 On the next day he sees Jesus coming to him, and says, Behold the Lamb of the God, who takes away the sin of the world.

30 He it is of whom I said, A man comes after me who takes a place before me, because he was before me;

31 and I knew him not; but that he might be manifested to Israel, therefore have I come baptizing with water.

32 And John bore witness, saying, I beheld the Spirit descending as a dove from heaven, and it abode upon him.

33 And I knew him not; but he who sent me to baptize with water, he said to me, Upon whom you shall see the Spirit descending and abiding on him, he it is who baptizes with the Holy Spirit.

34 And I have seen and borne witness that this is the Son of the God.

35 Again, on the next day, there stood John and two of his disciples.

36 And, looking at Jesus as he walked, he says, Behold the Lamb of the God.

37 And the two disciples heard him speaking, and followed Jesus.

38 But Jesus having turned, and seeing them following, says to them, What do you seek? And they said to him, Rabbi which, being interpreted, signifies Teacher, where do you abide?

39 He says to them, Come and see. They went therefore, and saw where he abode; and they abode with him that day. It was about the tenth hour.

40 Andrew, the brother of Simon Peter, was one of the two who heard [this] from John and followed him.

41 He first finds his own brother Simon, and says to him, We have found the Messiah which being interpreted is Christ.

42 And he led him to Jesus. Jesus looking at him said, You are Simon, the son of Jonas; you shall be called Cephas which interpreted is stone.

---

[193] "toward the God" cf John 13:3; "toward the Father" see Greek text: John 16:17; 16:28; 20:17; 1 John 2:1, the Father being the true God (YHWH), whose angel sat conversing to Moses between the cherubs, with each cherub facing *toward* the YHWH; see also John 7:33; 16:5; 16:17 in the Greek text, which may read "go to him" in English.

[194] GK: *monogenes* – unique

[195] GK: *monogenes* – unique

43 On the next day he would go forth into Galilee, and Jesus finds Philip, and says to him, Follow me.

44 And Philip was from Bethsaida, of the city of Andrew and Peter.

45 Philip finds Nathanael, and says to him, We have found him of whom Moses wrote in the law, and the prophets, Jesus, the son of Joseph, who is from Nazareth.

46 And Nathanael said to him, Can anything good come out of Nazareth? Philip says to him, Come and see.

47 Jesus saw Nathanael coming to him, and says of him, Behold [one] truly an Israelite, in whom there is no guile.

48 Nathanael says to him, From where do you know me? Jesus answered and said to him, Before that Philip called you, when you were under the fig-tree, I saw you.

49 Nathanael answered and said to him, Rabbi, you are the Son of the God, you are the King of Israel.

50 Jesus answered and said to him, Because I said to you, I saw you under the fig-tree, you believed? You shall see greater things than these.

51 And he says to him, Truly, truly, I say to you, Henceforth you shall see the heaven opened, and the angels of the God ascending and descending on the Son of man.

John 2:1 And on the third day a marriage took place in Cana of Galilee, and the mother of Jesus was there.

2 And Jesus also, and his disciples, were invited to the marriage.

3 And wine being deficient, the mother of Jesus says to him, They have no wine.

4 Jesus says to her, What have I to do with you, woman? mine hour has not yet come.

5 His mother says to the servants, Whatever he may say to you, do.

6 Now there were standing there six stone water-vessels, according to the purification of the Jews, holding two or three measures each.

7 Jesus says to them, Fill the water-vessels with water. And they filled them up to the brim.

8 And he says to them, Draw out now, and carry it to the feast-master. And they carried it

9 But when the feast-master had tasted the water which had been made wine and knew not from where it was from, but the servants knew who drew the water, the feast-master calls the bridegroom,

10 and says to him, Every man sets out first the good wine, and when [men] have well drunk, then the inferior; you have kept the good wine till now.

11 This beginning of signs did Jesus in Cana of Galilee, and manifested his glory; and his disciples believed on him.

12 After this he descended to Capernaum, he and his mother and his brethren and his disciples; and there they abode not many days.

13 And the Passover of the Jews was near, and Jesus went up to Jerusalem.

14 And he found in the temple the sellers of oxen and sheep and doves, and the money-changers sitting;

15 and, having made a scourge of cords, he cast [them] all out of the temple, both the sheep and the oxen; and he poured out the change of the money-changers, and overturned the tables,

16 and said to the sellers of doves, Take these things away; make not my Father's house a house of merchandise.

17 [And] his disciples remembered that it is written, The zeal of your house devours me.

18 The Jews therefore answered and said to him, What sign will you show to us, that you do these things?

19 Jesus answered and said to them, Destroy this temple, and in three days I will raise it up.

20 The Jews therefore said, It took forty and six years for this temple to be built, and you will raise it up in three days?

21 But he spoke of the temple of his body.

22 When therefore he was raised from among the dead, his disciples remembered that he had said this, and believed the scripture and the word which Jesus had spoken.

23 And when he was in Jerusalem, at the Passover, at the feast, many believed on his name, beholding his signs which he worked.

24 But Jesus himself did not trust himself to them, because he knew all [men]

25 and that he had not need that any should testify of man, for himself knew what was in man.

John 3:1 But there was a man from among the Pharisees, his name Nicodemus, a ruler of the Jews;

2 he came to him by night, and said to him, Rabbi, we know that you are come a teacher from God, for none can do these signs that you do unless the God be with him.

3 Jesus answered and said to him, Truly, truly, I say unto you, Except any one be born anew he cannot see the kingdom of the God.

4 Nicodemus says to him, How can a man be born being old? can he enter a second time into the womb of his mother and be born?

5 Jesus answered, Truly, truly, I say unto you, Except any one be born of water and of Spirit, he cannot enter into the kingdom of the God.

6 That which is born of the flesh is flesh; and that which is born of the Spirit is spirit.

7 Do not wonder that I said to you, It is needful that you should be born anew.

8 The wind blows where it will, and you hear its voice, but know not from where it comes and where it goes: thus is every one that is born of the Spirit.

9 Nicodemus answered and said to him, How can these things be?

10 Jesus answered and said to him, You are the teacher of Israel and know not these things!

11 Truly, truly, I say unto you, We speak that which we know, and we bear witness of that which we have seen, and you receive not our witness.

12 If I have said the earthly things to you, and you believe not, how, if I say the heavenly things to you, will you believe?

13 And no one has gone up into heaven, except he who came down* out of heaven, the Son of man [who is in heaven].

14 And as Moses lifted up the serpent in the wilderness, thus must the Son of man be lifted up,

15 that every one who believes on him may [not perish, but] have aeonian life.

16 For the God so loved the world, that he gave his one-of-a-kind[196] Son, that whosoever believes on him may not perish, but have aeonian life.

17 For the God has not sent his Son into the world that he may judge the world, but that the world may be saved through him.

18 He that believes on him is not judged: but he that believes not has been already judged, because he has not believed on the name of the one-of-a-kind[197] Son of the God.

19 And this is the judgment, that light is come into the world, and men have loved darkness rather than light; for their works were evil.

20 For every one that does evil hates the light, and does not come to the light that his works may not be shown as they are;

21 but he that practice the truth comes to the light, that his works may be manifested that they have been worked in God.

22 After these things came Jesus and his disciples into the land of Judea; and there he abode with them and baptized.

23 And John also was baptizing in Aenon, near Salim, because there was a great deal of water there; and they came to him and were baptized:

24 for John was not yet cast into prison.

25 There was therefore a reasoning of the disciples of John with a Jew about purification.

26 And they came to John and said to him, Rabbi, he who was with you beyond the Jordan, to whom you bore witness, behold, he baptizes, and all come to him.

27 John answered and said, A man can receive nothing unless it be given him out of heaven.

28 You yourselves bear me witness that I said, I am not the Christ, but, that I am sent before him.

29 He that has the bride is the bridegroom; but the friend of the bridegroom, who stands and hears him, rejoices in heart because of the voice of the bridegroom: this my joy then is fulfilled.

30 He must increase, but I must decrease.

31 He who comes from above is above all. He who has his origin in the earth is of the earth, and speaks [as] of the earth. He who comes out of heaven is above all,

32 [and] what he has seen and has heard, this he testifies; and no one receives his testimony.

33 He that has received his testimony has set to his seal that the God is true;

34 for he whom the God has sent speaks the words of the God, for the God gives not the Spirit by measure [to him].

35 The Father loves the Son, and has given all things [to be] in his hand.

36 He that believes on the Son has aeonian life, and he that is not subject to the Son shall not see life, but the wrath of the God abides upon him.

John 4:1 When therefore the Lord knew that the Pharisees had heard that Jesus makes and baptizes more disciples than John

2 however, Jesus himself did not baptize, but his disciples,

3 he left Judea and went away again unto Galilee.

4 And he had to pass through Samaria.

5 He comes therefore to a city of Samaria called Sychar, near to the land which Jacob gave to his son Joseph.

6 Now a fountain of Jacob's was there; Jesus therefore, being wearied with the way he had come, sat just as he was at the fountain. It was about the sixth hour.

7 A woman comes out of Samaria to draw water. Jesus says to her, Give me to drink

8 for his disciples had gone away into the city that they might buy provisions.

9 The Samaritan woman therefore says to him, How do you, being a Jew, ask to drink of me who am a Samaritan woman? for Jews have no intercourse with Samaritans.

10 Jesus answered and said to her, If you knew the gift of the God, and who it is that says to you, Give me to drink, you would have asked of him, and he would have given you living water.

11 The woman says to him, Sir, you have nothing to draw with, and the well is deep: from where do you get the living water?

12 Are you greater than our father Jacob, who gave us the well, and drank of it himself, and his sons, and his cattle?

13 Jesus answered and said to her, Every one who drinks of this water shall thirst again;

14 but whosoever drinks of the water which I shall give him shall never thirst into the aeon, but the water which I shall give him shall become in him a fountain of water, springing up into aeonian life.

15 The woman says to him, Sir, give me this water, that I may not thirst nor come here to draw.

16 Jesus says to her, Go, call your husband, and come here.

17 The woman answered and said, I have not a husband. Jesus says to her, You have well said, I have not a husband;

18 for you have had five husbands, and he whom now you have is not your husband: this you have spoken truly.

19 The woman says to him, Sir, I see that you are a prophet.

20 Our fathers worshiped in this mountain, and you say that in Jerusalem is the place where one must worship.

---

[196] GK: *monogenes*
[197] GK: *monogenes*

21 Jesus says to her, Woman, believe me, the hour is coming when you shall neither in this mountain nor in Jerusalem worship the Father.

22 You worship you know not what; we worship what we know, for salvation is of the Jews.

23 But the hour is coming and now is, when the true worshipers shall worship the Father in spirit and truth; for also the Father seeks such as his worshipers.

24 the God is spirit; and they who worship him must worship him in spirit and truth.

25 The woman says to him, I know that the Messiah is coming, who is called Christ; when he comes he will tell us all things.

26 Jesus says to her, I who speak to you am [he]

27 And upon this came his disciples, and wondered that he spoke with a woman; yet no one said, What do you seek? or, Why speak you with her?

28 The woman then left her waterpot and went away into the city, and says to the men,

29 Come, see a man who told me all things I had ever done: is not he the Christ?

30 They went out of the city and came to him.

31 But meanwhile the disciples asked him saying, Rabbi, eat.

32 But he said to them, I have food to eat which you do not know.

33 The disciples therefore said to one another, Has any one brought him [anything] to eat?

34 Jesus says to them, My food is that I should do the will of him that has sent me, and that I should finish his work.

35 Do not you say, that there are yet four months and the harvest comes? Behold, I say to you, Lift up your eyes and behold the fields, for they are already white to harvest.

36 He that reaps receives wages and gathers fruit unto aeonian life, that both he that sows and he that reaps may rejoice together.

37 For in this is [verified] the true saying, It is one who sows and another who reaps.

38 I have sent you to reap that on which you have not labored; others have labored, and you have entered into their labors.

39 But many of the Samaritans of that city believed on him because of the word of the woman who bore witness, He told me all things that I had ever done.

40 When therefore the Samaritans came to him they asked him to abide with them, and he abode there two days.

41 And more a great deal believed on account of his word;

42 and they said to the woman, [it is] no longer on account of your saying that we believe, for we have heard him ourselves, and we know that this is indeed the Savior of the world.

43 But after the two days he went forth from there and went away into Galilee,

44 for Jesus himself bore witness that a prophet has no honor in his own country.

45 When therefore he came into Galilee, the Galileans received him, having seen all that he had done in Jerusalem during the feast, for they also went to the feast.

46 He came therefore again to Cana of Galilee, where he made the water wine. And there was a certain nobleman in Capernaum whose son was sick.

47 He, having heard that Jesus had come out of Judea into Galilee, went to him and asked him that he would come down and heal his son, for he was about to die.

48 Jesus therefore said to him, Unless you see signs and wonders you will not believe.

49 The nobleman says to him, Sir, come down else my child die.

50 Jesus says to him, Go, your son lives. And the man believed the word which Jesus said to him, and went his way.

51 But already, as he was going down, his servants met him and brought him word saying, Your child lives.

52 He inquired therefore from them the hour at which he got better. And they said to him, Yesterday at the seventh hour the fever left him.

53 The father therefore knew that [it was] in that hour in which Jesus said to him, Your son lives; and he believed, himself and his whole house.

54 This second sign again did Jesus, being come out of Judea into Galilee.

John 5:1 After these things was a feast of the Jews, and Jesus went up to Jerusalem.

2 Now there is in Jerusalem, at the sheepgate, a pool, which is called in Hebrew, Bethesda, having five porches.

3 In these lay a multitude of sick, blind, lame, withered, [awaiting the moving of the water.

4 For an angel descended at a certain season in the pool and troubled the water. Whoever therefore first went in after the troubling of the water became well, whatever disease he labored under]

5 But there was a certain man there who had been suffering under his infirmity thirty and eight years.

6 Jesus seeing this [man] lying [there] and knowing that he was [in that state] now a great length of time, says to him, Do you want to become well?

7 The infirm [man] answered him, Sir, I have not a man, in order, when the water has been troubled, to cast me into the pool; but while I am coming another descends before me.

8 Jesus says to him, Arise, take up your couch and walk.

9 And immediately the man became well, and took up his couch and walked: and on that day was Sabbath.

10 The Jews therefore said to the healed [man] It is Sabbath, it is not permitted you to take up your couch.

11 He answered them, He that made me well, he said to me, Take up your couch and walk.

12 They asked him [therefore] Who is the man who said to you, Take up your couch and walk?

13 But he that had been healed knew not who it was, for Jesus had slid away, there being a crowd in the place.

14 After these things Jesus finds him in the temple, and said to him, Behold, you are become well: sin no more, that something worse do not happen to you.

15 The man went away and told the Jews that it was Jesus who had made him well.

16 And for this the Jews persecuted Jesus [and sought to kill him] because he had done these things on Sabbath.

17 But Jesus answered them, My Father works until now, and I work.

18 For this therefore the Jews sought the more to kill him, because he had not only violated the Sabbath, but also said that the God was his own Father, making himself equal with God.

19 Jesus therefore answered and said to them, Truly, truly, I say to you, The Son can do nothing of himself except whatever he sees the Father doing: for whatever things he does, these things also the Son does in like manner.

20 For the Father has affection for the Son and shows him all things which he himself does; and he will show him greater works than these, that you may wonder.

21 For even as the Father raises the dead and gives life, thus the Son also gives life to whom he will:

22 for neither does the Father judge any one, but has given all judgment to the Son;

23 that all may honor the Son, even as they honor the Father. He who honors not the Son, honors not the Father who has sent him.

24 Truly, truly, I say unto you, that he that hears my word, and believes him that has sent me, has aeonian life, and does not come into judgment, but is passed out of death into life.

25 Truly, truly, I say unto you, that an hour is coming, and now is, when the dead shall hear the voice of the Son of the God, and they that have heard shall live.

26 For even as the Father has life in himself, so he has given to the Son also to have life in himself,

27 and has given him authority to execute judgment [also] because he is Son of man.

28 Wonder not at this, for an hour is coming in which all who are in the tombs shall hear his voice,

29 and shall go forth; those that have practiced good, to resurrection of life, and those that have done evil, to resurrection of judgment.

30 I cannot do anything of myself; as I hear, I judge, and my judgment is righteous, because I do not seek my will, but the will of him that has sent me.

31 If I bear witness concerning myself, my witness is not true.

32 It is another who bears witness concerning me, and I know that the witness which he bears concerning me is true.

33 You have sent unto John, and he has borne witness to the truth.

34 But I do not receive witness from man, but I say this that you might be saved.

35 He was the burning and shining lamp, and you were willing for a season to rejoice in his light.

36 But I have the witness [that is] greater than that of John; for the works which the Father has given me that I should complete them, the works themselves which I do, bear witness concerning me that the Father has sent me.

37 And the Father who has sent me himself has borne witness concerning me. You have neither heard his voice at any time, nor have seen his shape,

38 and you have not his word abiding in you; for whom he hath sent, him you do not believe.

39 You search the scriptures, for you think that in them you have aeonian life, and they it is which bear witness concerning me;

40 and you will not come to me that you might have life.

41 I do not receive glory from men,

42 but I know you, that you have not the love of the God in you.

43 I come in my Father's name, and you accept me not; if another come in his own name, him you will accept.

44 How can you believe, who receive glory one of another, and seek not the glory which [comes] from the God alone?

45 Think not that I will accuse you to the Father: there is [one] who accuses you, Moses, on whom you trust;

46 for if you had believed Moses, you would have believed me, for he wrote of me.

47 But if you do not believe his writings, how shall you believe my words?

John 6:1 After these things Jesus went away beyond the sea of Galilee, [or] of Tiberias,

2 and a great crowd followed him, because they saw the signs which he worked upon the sick.

3 And Jesus went up into the mountain, and there sat with his disciples:

4 but the Passover, the feast of the Jews, was near.

5 Jesus then, lifting up his eyes and seeing that a great crowd is coming to him, says to Philip, From where shall we buy loaves that these may eat?

6 But this he said trying him, for he knew what he was going to do.

7 Philip answered him, Loaves for two hundred denarii are not sufficient for them, that each may have some little [portion]

8 One of his disciples, Andrew, Simon Peter's brother, says to him,

9 There is a little boy here who has five barley loaves and two small fishes; but this, what is it for so many?

10 [And] Jesus said, Make the men sit down. Now there was much grass in the place: the men therefore sat down, in number about five thousand.

11 And Jesus took the loaves, and having given thanks, distributed [them] to those that were set

down; and in like manner of the small fishes as much as they would.

12 And when they had been filled, he says to his disciples, Gather together the fragments which are over and above, that nothing may be lost.

13 They gathered [them] therefore together, and filled twelve hand-baskets full of fragments of the five barley loaves, which were over and above to those that had eaten.

14 The men therefore, having seen the sign which Jesus had done, said, This is truly the prophet which is coming into the world.

15 Jesus therefore knowing that they were going to come and seize him, that they might make him king, departed again to the mountain himself alone.

16 But when evening was come, his disciples went down to the sea,

17 and having gone on board ship, they went over the sea to Capernaum. And it had already become dark, and Jesus had not come to them,

18 and the sea was agitated by a strong wind blowing.

19 Having rowed then about twenty-five or thirty stadia, they see Jesus walking on the sea and coming near the ship; and they were frightened.

20 But he says to them, It is I: be not afraid.

21 They were willing therefore to receive him into the ship; and immediately the ship was at the land to which they went.

22 On the next day the crowd which stood on the other side of the sea, having seen that there was no other little ship there except that into which his disciples had got, and that Jesus had not gone with his disciples into the ship, but that his disciples had gone away alone;

23 but other little ships out of Tiberias came near to the place where they ate bread after the Lord had given thanks;

24 when therefore the crowd saw that Jesus was not there, nor his disciples, they got into the ships, and came to Capernaum, seeking Jesus.

25 And having found him the other side of the sea, they said to him, Rabbi, when did you arrive here?

26 Jesus answered them and said, Truly, truly, I say to you, You seek me not because you have seen signs, but because you have eaten of the loaves and been filled.

27 Work not [for] the food which perishes, but [for] the food which abides unto aeonian life, which the Son of man shall give to you; for him has the Father sealed the God.

28 They said therefore to him, What should we do that we may work the works of the God?

29 Jesus answered and said to them, This is the work of the God, that you believe on him whom he has sent.

30 They said therefore to him, What sign then will you do that we may see and believe you? what do you work?

31 Our fathers ate the manna in the wilderness, as it is written, He gave them bread out of heaven to eat.

32 Jesus therefore said to them, Truly, truly, I say to you, [it is] not Moses that has given you the bread out of heaven; but my Father gives you the true bread out of heaven.

33 For the bread of the God is he who comes down out of heaven and gives life to the world.

34 They said therefore to him, Lord, always give to us this bread.

35 [And] Jesus said to them, I am the bread of life: he that comes to me shall never hunger, and he that believes on me shall never thirst at any time.

36 But I have said to you, that you have also seen me and do not believe.

37 All that the Father gives me shall come to me, and him that comes to me I will not at all cast out.

38 For I am come down from heaven, not that I should do my will, but the will of him that has sent me.

39 And this is the will of him that has sent me, that of all that he has given me I should lose nothing, but should raise it up in the last day.

40 For this is the will of my Father, that every one who sees the Son, and believes on him, should have aeonian life; and I will raise him up at the last day.

41 The Jews therefore murmured about him, because he said, I am the bread which has come down out of heaven.

42 And they said, Is not this Jesus the son of Joseph, whose father and mother we have known? how then does he say, I am come down out of heaven?

43 Jesus therefore answered and said to them, Murmur not among yourselves.

44 No one can come to me except the Father who has sent me draw him, and I will raise him up in the last day.

45 It is written in the prophets, And they shall be all taught of the God. Every one that has heard from the Father and has learned, comes to me;

46 not that any one has seen the Father, except he who is of the God, he has seen the Father.

47 Truly, truly, I say to you, He that believes [on me] has aeonian life.

48 I am the bread of life.

49 Your fathers ate the manna in the wilderness and died.

50 This is the bread which comes down out of heaven, that one may eat of it and not die.

51 I am the living bread which has come down out of heaven: if any one shall have eaten of this bread he shall live into the aeon; but the bread which I shall give is my flesh, which I will give for the life of the world.

52 The Jews therefore contended among themselves, saying, How can he give us this flesh to eat?

53 Jesus therefore said to them, Truly, truly, I say unto you, Unless you shall have eaten the flesh of the Son of man, and drunk his blood, you have no life in yourselves.

54 He that eats my flesh and drinks my blood has aeonian life, and I will raise him up at the last day:

55 for my flesh is truly food and my blood is truly drink.

56 He that eats my flesh and drinks my blood dwells in me and I in him.

57 As the living Father has sent me and I live on account of the Father, he also who eats me shall live also on account of me.

58 This is the bread which has come down out of heaven. Not as the fathers ate and died: he that eats this bread shall live into the aeon.

59 These things he said in the synagogue, teaching in Capernaum.

60 Many therefore of his disciples having heard it said, This word is hard; who can hear it?

61 But Jesus, knowing in himself that his disciples murmur concerning this, said to them, Does this offend you?

62 If then you see the Son of man ascending up where he was the first?

63 It is the Spirit which gives life, the flesh profits nothing: the words which I have spoken unto you are spirit and are life.

64 But there are some of you who do not believe. For Jesus knew from the beginning who they were who did not believe, and who would deliver him up.

65 And he said, Therefore said I unto you, that no one can come to me unless it be given to him from the Father.

66 From that [time] many of his disciples went backwards and walked no more with him.

67 Jesus therefore said to the twelve, Will you also go away?

68 Simon Peter answered him, Lord, to whom shall we go? you have words of aeonian life;

69 and we have believed and known that you are the holy one of the God.

70 Jesus answered them, Have not I chosen you the twelve? and of you one is a daemon.

71 Now he spoke of Judas [the son] of Simon, Iscariote, for he [it was who] should deliver him up, being one of the twelve.

John 7:1 And after these things Jesus walked in Galilee, for he would not walk in Judea, because the Jews sought to kill him.

2 Now the tabernacles, the feast of the Jews, was near.

3 His brethren therefore said to him, Leave here and go into Judea, that your disciples also may see your works which you do;

4 for no one does anything in secret and himself seeks to be [known] in public. If you do these things, manifest yourself to the world:

5 for neither did his brethren believe on him.

6 Jesus therefore says to them, My time is not yet come, but your time is always ready.

7 The world cannot hate you, but it hates me, because I bear witness concerning it that its works are evil.

8 You, go up to this feast. I go not up to this feast, for my time is not yet fulfilled.

9 Having said these things to them he abode in Galilee.

10 But when his brethren had gone up, then he himself also went up to the feast, not openly, but as in secret.

11 The Jews therefore sought him at the feast, and said, Where is he?

12 And there was much murmuring concerning him among the crowds. Some said, He is a good [man] others said, No; but he deceives the crowd.

13 However, no one spoke openly concerning him on account of [their] fear of the Jews.

14 But when it was now the middle of the feast, Jesus went up into the temple and taught.

15 The Jews therefore wondered, saying, How does this [man] know letters, having never learned?

16 Jesus therefore answered them and said, My doctrine is not mine, but that of him that has sent me.

17 If any one desire to practice his will, he shall know concerning the doctrine, whether it is of the God, or that I speak from myself.

18 He that speaks from himself seeks his own glory; but he that seeks the glory of him that has sent him, he is true, and unrighteousness is not in him.

19 Has not Moses given you the law, and no one of you practices the law? Why do you seek to kill me?

20 The crowd answered [and said] You have a daemon: who seeks to kill you?

21 Jesus answered and said to them, I have done one work, and you all wonder.

22 Therefore Moses gave you circumcision not that it is of Moses, but of the fathers, and you circumcise a man on Sabbath.

23 If a man receives circumcision on Sabbath, that the law of Moses may not be violated, are you angry with me because I have made a man entirely sound on Sabbath?

24 Judge not according to sight, but judge righteous judgment.

25 Some therefore of those of Jerusalem said, Is not this he whom they seek to kill?

26 and behold, he speaks openly, and they say nothing to him. Have the rulers then indeed recognized that this is the Christ?

27 But this [man] we know where he is from. Now [as to] the Christ, when he comes, no one knows where he is from.

28 Jesus therefore cried out in the temple, teaching and saying, You both know me and you know where I am from; and I am not come of myself, but he that sent me is true, whom you do not know.

29 I know him, because I am from him, and he has sent me.

30 They sought therefore to take him; and no one laid his hand upon him, because his hour had not yet come.

31 But many of the crowd believed on him, and said, Will the Christ, when he comes, do more signs than those which this [man] has done?

32 The Pharisees heard the crowd murmuring these things concerning him, and the Pharisees and the chief priests sent officers that they might take him.

33 Jesus therefore said, Yet a little while I am with you, and I go toward him that has sent me.

34 You shall seek me and shall not find [me] and where I am you cannot come.

35 The Jews therefore said to one another, Where is he about to go that we shall not find him? Is he about to go to the dispersion among the Greeks, and teach the Greeks?

36 What word is this which he said, You shall seek me and shall not find [me] and where I am you cannot come?

37 In the last, the great day of the feast, Jesus stood and cried saying, If any one thirst, let him come to me and drink.

38 He that believes on me, as the scripture has said, out of his belly shall flow rivers of living water.

39 But this he said concerning the Spirit, which they that believed on him were about to receive; for the Spirit was not yet, because Jesus had not yet been glorified.

40 [Some] out of the crowd therefore, having heard this word, said, This is truly the prophet.

41 Others said, This is the Christ. Others said, Does then the Christ come out of Galilee?

42 Has not the scripture said that the Christ comes of the seed of David, and from the village of Bethlehem, where David was?

43 There was a division therefore in the crowd on account of him.

44 But some of them desired to take him, but no one laid hands upon him.

45 The officers therefore came to the chief priests and Pharisees, and they said to them, Why have you not brought him?

46 The officers answered, No man has spoke as this man [speaks].

47 The Pharisees therefore answered them, Are you also deceived?

48 Has any one of the rulers believed on him, or of the Pharisees?

49 But this crowd, which does not know the law, are accursed.

50 Nicodemus (he who came to him [Christ] the first time) says to them being one of them,

51 Does our law judge a man before it have first heard from himself, and know what he does?

52 They answered and said to him, Are you also of Galilee? Search and look, that no prophet arises out of Galilee.

53 And every one went to his home.

John 8:1 But Jesus went to the mount of Olives.

2 And early in the morning he came again into the temple, and all the people came to him; and he sat down and taught them.

3 And the scribes and the Pharisees bring [to him] a woman taken in adultery, and having set her in the midst,

4 they say to him, Teacher, this woman has been taken in the very act, committing adultery.

5 Now in the law Moses has commanded us to stone such; therefore, what do you say?

6 But this they said testing him, that they might have [something] to accuse him of. But Jesus, having stooped down, wrote with his finger on the ground.

7 But when they continued asking him, he lifted himself up and said to them, Let him that is without sin among you first cast the stone at her.

8 And again stooping down he wrote on the ground.

9 But they, having heard that went out one by one beginning from the elder ones until the last; and Jesus was left alone and the woman standing there.

10 And Jesus, lifting himself up and seeing no one but the woman, said to her, Woman, where are your accusers? Has no one condemned you?

11 And she said, No one, sir. And Jesus said to her, Neither do I condemn you: go, and sin no more.

12 Again therefore Jesus spoke to them, saying, I am the light of the world; he that follows me shall not walk in darkness, but shall have the light of life.

13 The Pharisees therefore said to him, You bear witness concerning yourself; your witness is not true.

14 Jesus answered and said to them, Even if I bear witness concerning myself, my witness is true, because I know from where I came and whither I go: but you know not from where I come and where I go.

15 You judge according to the flesh, I judge no one.

16 And if also I judge, my judgment is true, because I am not alone, but I and the Father who has sent me.

17 And in your law too it is written that the testimony of two men is true:

18 I am [one] who bear witness concerning myself, and the Father who has sent me bears witness concerning me.

19 They said to him therefore, Where is your Father? Jesus answered, You know neither me nor my Father. If you had known me, you would have known also my Father.

20 These words he spoke in the treasury, teaching in the temple; and no one took him, for his hour was not yet come.

21 He said therefore again to them, I go away, and you shall seek me, and shall die in your sin; where I go you cannot come.

22 The Jews therefore said, Will he kill himself, that he says, Where I go you cannot come?

23 And he said to them, You are from beneath; I am from above. You are of this world; I am not of this world.

24 I said therefore to you, that you shall die in your sins; for unless you shall believe that I am [he] you shall die in your sins.

25 They said therefore to him, Who are you? [and] Jesus said to them, that which I said to you from the first.

26 I have many things to say and to judge concerning you, but he that has sent me is true, and

I, what I have heard from him, these things I say to the world.

27 They knew not that he spoke to them of the Father.

28 Jesus therefore said to them, When you shall have lifted up the Son of man, then you shall know that I am [he] and that I do nothing of myself, but as the Father has taught me I speak these things.

29 And he that has sent me is with me; he has not left me alone, because I do always the things that are pleasing to him.

30 As he spoke these things many believed on him.

31 Jesus therefore said to the Jews who believed him, If you abide in my word, you are truly my disciples;

32 and you shall know the truth, and the truth shall set you free.

33 They answered him, We are Abraham's seed, and have never been under bondage to any one; how can you say, You shall become free?

34 Jesus answered them, Truly, truly, I say to you, Every one that practices sin is the servant of sin.

35 Now the servant abides not in the house into the aeon: the son abides into the aeon.

36 If therefore the Son shall set you free, you shall be really free.

37 I know that you are Abraham's seed; but you seek to kill me, because my word has no room in you.

38 I speak what I have seen with my Father, and you then do what you have seen with your father.

39 They answered and said to him, Abraham is our father. Jesus says to them, If you were Abraham's children, you would do the works of Abraham;

40 but now you seek to kill me, a man who has spoken the truth to you, which I have heard from the God: this Abraham did not do.

41 You do the works of your father. They said [therefore] to him, We are not born of fornication; we have one father, the God.

42 Jesus said to them, If the God were your father you would have loved me, for I came forth from the God and am come [from him] for neither am I come of myself, but he has sent me.

43 Why do you not know my speech? Because you cannot hear my word.

44 You are of the devil as your father, and you desire to do the lusts of your father. He was a murderer from the beginning, and has not stood in the truth, because there is no truth in him. When he speaks falsehood, he speaks of what is his own; for he is a liar and its father:

45 and because I speak the truth, you do not believe me.

46 Which of you convicts me of sin? If I speak truth, why do you not believe me?

47 He that is of the God hears the words of the God: therefore you hear [them] not, because you are not of the God.

48 The Jews answered and said to him, Are we not right, you are a Samaritan and have a daemon?

49 Jesus answered, I have not a daemon; but I honor my Father, and you dishonor me.

50 But I do not seek my own glory: there is he that seeks and judges.

51 Truly, truly, I say unto you, If any one shall keep my word, he shall not in the aeon see death.

52 The Jews therefore said to him, Now we know that you have a daemon. Abraham has died, and the prophets, and you say, If any one keep my word, he shall not in the aeon taste death.

53 Are you greater than our father Abraham, who has died? and the prophets have died: whom are you making yourself?

54 Jesus answered, If I glorify myself, my glory is nothing: it is my Father who glorifies me, of whom you say, He is our God.

55 And you know him not; but I know him; and if I said, I know him not, I should be like you, a liar. But I know him, and I keep his word.

56 Your father Abraham exulted to see my day, and he saw and rejoiced.

57 The Jews therefore said to him, You have not yet fifty years, and have you seen Abraham?

58 Jesus said to them, Truly, truly, I say unto you, Before Abraham was, I existed.

59 They took up therefore stones that they might cast [them] at him; but Jesus hid himself and went out of the temple, [going through the midst of them, and thus passed on]

John 9:1 And as he passed on, he saw a man blind from birth.

2 And his disciples asked him, saying, Rabbi, who sinned, this [man] or his parents, that he should be born blind?

3 Jesus answered, Neither has this [man] sinned nor his parents, but that the works of the God should be manifested in him.

4 I must work the works of him that has sent me while it is day. the night is coming, when no one can work.

5 As long as I am in the world, I am the light of the world.

6 Having said these things, he spat on the ground and made mud of the spittle, and put the mud, as ointment, on his eyes.

7 And he said to him, Go, wash in the pool of Siloam, which is interpreted, Sent. He went therefore and washed, and came seeing.

8 The neighbors therefore, and those who used to see him before, that he was a beggar, said, Is not this he that was sitting and begging?

9 Some said, It is he; others said, No, but he is like him: he said, It is I.

10 They said therefore to him, How have your eyes been opened?

11 He answered [and said], A man called Jesus made mud and anointed mine eyes, and said to me, Go to Siloam and wash: and having gone and washed, I saw.

12 They said therefore to him, Where is he? He says, I do not know.

13 They bring him who was before blind to the Pharisees.

14 Now it was Sabbath when Jesus made the mud and opened his eyes.

15 The Pharisees therefore also again asked him how he received his sight. And he said to them, He put mud upon mine eyes, and I washed, and I see.

16 Some of the Pharisees therefore said, This man is not from the God, for he does not keep the Sabbath. Others said, How can a sinful man perform such signs? And there was a division among them.

17 They say therefore again to the blind [man], What do you say of him, that he has opened your eyes? And he said, He is a prophet.

18 The Jews therefore did not believe concerning him that he was blind and had received sight, until they had called the parents of him that had received sight.

19 And they asked them saying, This is your son, of whom you say that he was born blind: how then does he now see?

20 His parents answered [them] and said, We know that this is our son, and that he was born blind;

21 but how he now sees we do not know, or who has opened his eyes we do not know. He is of age: ask him; he will speak concerning himself.

22 His parents said these things because they feared the Jews, for the Jews had already agreed that if any one acknowledged him [to be the] Christ, he should be excommunicated from the synagogue.

23 On this account his parents said, He is of age: ask him.

24 They called therefore a second time the man who had been blind, and said to him, Give glory to the God: we know that this man is sinful.

25 He answered therefore, If he is sinful I know not. One thing I know, that, being blind [before] now I see.

26 And they said to him again, What did he do to you? how did he open your eyes?

27 He answered them, I told you already and you did not hear: why do you desire to hear again? do you also wish to become his disciples?

28 They railed at him, and said, You are his disciple, but we are disciples of Moses.

29 We know that the God spoke to Moses; but [as to] this [man] we know not from where he is from.

30 The man answered and said to them, Now in this is a wonderful thing, that you do not know from where he is, and he has opened mine eyes.

31 [But] we know that the God does not hear sinners; but if any one be God-fearing and do his will, him he hears.

32 Since time was, it has not been heard that any one opened the eyes of one born blind.

33 If this [man] were not of God he would be able to do anything.

34 They answered and said to him, You have been wholly born in sins, and you teach us? And they cast him out.

35 Jesus heard that they had cast him out, and having found him, he said to him, You, do you believe on the Son of the God?

36 He answered and said, And who is he, Lord, that I may believe on him?

37 And Jesus said to him, You have both seen him, and he that speaks with you is he.

38 And he said, I believe, Lord: and he did him homage.

39 And Jesus said, For judgment I have come into this world, that they which see not may see, and they which see may become blind.

40 And [some] of the Pharisees who were with him heard these things, and they said to him, Are we blind also?

41 Jesus said to them, If you were blind you would not have sin; but now you say, We see, your sin remains.

John 10:1 Truly, truly, I say to you, He that enters not in by the door to the fold of the sheep, but mounts up elsewhere, he is a thief and a robber;

2 but he that enters in by the door is the shepherd of the sheep.

3 To him the doorkeeper opens; and the sheep hear his voice; and he calls his own sheep by name, and leads them out.

4 When he has put forth all his own, he goes before them, and the sheep follow him, because they know his voice.

5 But they will not follow a stranger, but will flee from him, because they know not the voice of strangers.

6 This parable spoke Jesus to them, but they did not know what it was of which he spoke to them.

7 Jesus therefore said again to them, Truly, truly, I say to you, I am the door of the sheep.

8 All whoever came before me are thieves and robbers; but the sheep did not hear them.

9 I am the door: if any one enter in by me, he shall be saved, and shall go in and shall go out and shall find pasture.

10 The thief comes not but that he may steal, and kill, and destroy: I am come that they might have life, and might have it abundantly.

11 I am the good shepherd. The good shepherd lays down his soul for the sheep:

12 but he who serves for wages, and who is not the shepherd, whose own the sheep are not, sees the wolf coming, and leaves the sheep and flees; and the wolf seizes them and scatters the sheep.

13 Now he who serves for wages flees because he serves for wages, and is not himself concerned about the sheep.

14 I am the good shepherd; and I know those that are mine, and am known of those that are mine,

15 as the Father knows me and I know the Father; and I lay down my soul for the sheep.

16 And I have other sheep which are not of this fold: those also I must bring, and they shall hear my voice; and there shall be one flock, one shepherd.

17 On this account the Father loves me, because I lay down my soul that I may take it again.

18 No one takes it from me, but I lay it down of myself. I have authority to lay it down and I have authority to take it again. I have received this commandment of my Father.

19 There was a division again among the Jews on account of these words;

20 but many of them said, He has a daemon and raves; why do you hear him?

21 Others said, These sayings are not [those] of one that is possessed by a daemon. Can a daemon open blind people's eyes?

22 Now the feast of the dedication was celebrating at Jerusalem, and it was winter.

23 And Jesus walked in the temple in the porch of Solomon.

24 The Jews therefore surrounded him, and said to him, Until when do you hold our soul in suspense? If you are the Christ, say [so] to us openly.

25 Jesus answered them, I told you, and you do not believe. The works which I do in my Father's name, these bear witness concerning me:

26 but you do not believe, for you are not of my sheep, as I told you.

27 My sheep hear my voice, and I know them, and they follow me;

28 and I give them aeonian life; and they in no way shall perish into the aeon, and no one shall seize them out of my hand.

29 My Father who has given [them] to me is greater than all, and no one can seize out of the hand of my Father.

30 I and the Father are one.

31 The Jews therefore again took stones that they might stone him.

32 Jesus answered them, Many good works have I shown you of my Father; for which work of them do you stone me?

33 The Jews answered him, For a good work we stone you not, but for blasphemy, and because you, being a man, make yourself God.

34 Jesus answered them, Is it not written in your law, I said, You are gods ["elohim" (Psalm 82:6)]?

35 If he called them gods to whom the word of the God came and the scripture cannot be broken,

36 do you say of him whom the Father has sanctified and sent into the world, You are blasphemous, because I said, I am Son of the God?

37 If I do not the works of my Father, believe me not;

38 but if I do, even if you believe me not, believe the works, that you may know [and believe] that the Father is in me and I in him.

39 They sought therefore again to take him; and he went away from out of their hand

40 and departed again beyond the Jordan to the place where John was baptizing at the first: and he abode there.

41 And many came to him, and said, John did no sign; but all things which John said of this [man] were true.

42 And many believed on him there.

John 11:1 Now there was a certain [man] sick, Lazarus of Bethany, of the village of Mary and Martha her sister.

2 It was the Mary who anointed the Lord with ointment and wiped his feet with her hair, whose brother Lazarus was sick.

3 The sisters therefore sent to him, saying, Lord, behold, he whom you like is sick.

4 But when Jesus heard it he said, This sickness is not unto death, but for the glory of the God, that the Son of the God may be glorified by it.

5 Now Jesus loved Martha, and her sister, and Lazarus.

6 When therefore he heard, He is sick, he remained two days then in the place where he was.

7 Then after this he says to his disciples, Let us go into Judea again.

8 The disciples say to him, Rabbi, [even but] now the Jews sought to stone you, and you go there again?

9 Jesus answered, Are there not twelve hours in the day? If any one walk in the day, he does not stumble, because he sees the light of this world;

10 but if any one walk in the night, he stumbles, because the light is not in him.

11 These things said he; and after this he says to them, Lazarus, our friend, is fallen asleep, but I go that I may awake him out of sleep.

12 The disciples therefore said to him, Lord, if he be fallen asleep, he will get well.

13 But Jesus spoke of his death, but they thought that he spoke of the rest of sleep.

14 Jesus therefore then said to them plainly, Lazarus has died.

15 And I rejoice on your account that I was not there, in order that you may believe. But let us go to him.

16 Thomas therefore, called Didymus, said to his fellow disciples, Let us also go, that we may die with him.

17 Jesus therefore [on] arriving found him to have been four days already in the tomb.

18 Now Bethany was near Jerusalem, about fifteen stadia off,

19 and many of the Jews came to Martha and Mary, that they might console them concerning their brother.

20 Martha then, when she heard Jesus is coming, went to meet him; but Mary sat in the house.

21 Martha therefore said to Jesus, Lord, if you had been here, my brother had not died;

22 but even now I know, that whatsoever you shall ask of the God, the God will give you.

23 Jesus says to her, Your brother shall rise again.

24 Martha says to him, I know that he will rise again in the resurrection in the last day.

25 Jesus said to her, I am the resurrection and the life: he that believes on me, though he has died, shall live;

26 and every one who lives and believes on me shall in no way die into the aeon. Do you believe this?

27 She says to him, Yes, Lord; I believe that you are the Christ, the Son of the God, who should come into the world.

28 And having said this, she went away and called her sister Mary secretly, saying, The teacher is come and calls you.

29 She, when she heard that rises up quickly and comes to him.

30 Now Jesus had not yet come into the village, but was in the place where Martha came to meet him.

31 The Jews therefore who were with her in the house and consoling her, seeing Mary that she rose up quickly and went out, followed her, saying, She goes to the tomb, that she may weep there.

32 Mary therefore, when she came where Jesus was, seeing him, fell at his feet, saying to him, Lord, if you had been here, my brother would not have died.

33 Jesus therefore, when he saw her weeping, and the Jews who came with her weeping, was deeply moved in spirit, and was troubled,

34 and said, Where have you put him? They say to him, Lord, come and see.

35 Jesus wept.

36 The Jews therefore said, Behold how he liked him!

37 But some of them said, Could not this man, who opened the eyes of the blind man, have kept this man also from dying?

38 Jesus therefore, again deeply moved in himself, comes to the tomb. Now it was a cave, and a stone lay upon it.

39 Jesus says, Take away the stone. Martha, the sister of the dead, says to him, Lord, he stinks already, for he is four days [there]

40 Jesus says to her, Did I not say to you, that if you should believe, you should see the glory of the God?

41 They took therefore the stone away. And Jesus lifted up his eyes on high and said, Father, I thank you that you have heard me;

42 but I knew that you always hear me; but on account of the crowd who stand around I have said it that they may believe that you have sent me.

43 And having said this, he cried with a loud voice, Lazarus, come forth.

44 And the dead came forth, bound feet and hands with grave clothes, and his face was bound round with a face-cloth. Jesus says to them, Set him loose and let him go.

45 Many therefore of the Jews who came to Mary and saw what he had done, believed on him;

46 but some of them went to the Pharisees and told them what Jesus had done.

47 The chief priests, therefore, and the Pharisees gathered a council, and said, What do we do? for this man does many signs.

48 If we leave him alone, all will believe on him, and the Romans will come and take away both our place and our nation.

49 But a certain one of them, Caiaphas, being high priest that year, said to them, You know nothing

50 nor consider that it is profitable for you that one man die for the people, and not that the whole nation perish.

51 But this he did not say of himself; but, being high priest that year, prophesied that Jesus was going to die for the nation;

52 and not for the nation only, but that he should also gather together into one the children of the God who were scattered abroad.

53 From that day therefore they took counsel that they might kill him.

54 Jesus therefore walked no longer openly among the Jews, but went away from there into the country near the desert, to a city called Ephraim, and there he sojourned with the disciples.

55 But the Passover of the Jews was near, and many went up to Jerusalem out of the country before the Passover, that they might purify themselves.

56 They sought therefore Jesus, and said among themselves, standing in the temple, What do you think? that he will not come to the feast?

57 Now the chief priests and the Pharisees had given commandment that if any one knew where he was, he should make it known, that they might take him.

John 12:1 Jesus therefore, six days before the Passover, came to Bethany, where was the dead [man] Lazarus, whom Jesus raised from among the dead.

2 There therefore they made him a supper, and Martha served, but Lazarus was one of those at table with him.

3 Mary therefore, having taken a pound of ointment of pure nard of great price, anointed the feet of Jesus, and wiped his feet with her hair, and the house was filled with the odor of the ointment.

4 One of his disciples therefore, Judas [son] of Simon, Iscariote, who was about to deliver him up, says,

5 Why was this ointment not sold for three hundred denarii and given to the poor?

6 But he said this, not that he cared for the poor, but because he was a thief and had the bag, and carried what was put into it

7 Jesus therefore said, Permit her to keep this for the day of my preparation for burial;

8 for you have the poor always with you, but me you have not always.

9 A great crowd therefore of the Jews knew that he was there; and they came, not because of Jesus only, but also that they might see Lazarus whom he raised from among the dead.

10 But the chief priests took counsel that they might kill Lazarus also,

11 because many of the Jews went away on his account and believed on Jesus.

12 On the next day a great crowd who came to the feast, having heard that Jesus is coming into Jerusalem,

13 took branches of palms and went out to meet him, and cried, Hosanna, blessed is he that comes in the name of the Lord, the King of Israel.

14 And Jesus, having found a young donkey, sat upon it; as it is written,

15 Fear not, daughter of Zion: behold, your King comes, sitting on a donkey's colt.

16 [Now] his disciples knew not these things at the first; but when Jesus was glorified, then they remembered that these things were written of him, and that they had done these things to him.

17 The crowd therefore that was with him bore witness because he had called Lazarus out of the tomb, and raised him from among the dead.

18 Therefore also the crowd met him because they had heard that he had done this sign.

19 The Pharisees therefore said to one another, You see that you profit nothing: behold, the world is gone after him.

20 And there were certain Greeks among those who came up that they might worship in the feast;

21 these therefore came to Philip, who was of Bethsaida of Galilee, and they asked him saying, Sir, we desire to see Jesus.

22 Philip comes and tells Andrew, [and again] Andrew comes and Philip, and they tell Jesus.

23 But Jesus answered them saying, The hour is come for the Son of man to be glorified.

24 Truly, truly, I say unto you, Except the grain falling into the ground dies, it abides alone; but if it die, it bears much fruit.

25 He that likes his soul shall lose it, and he that hates his soul in this world shall keep it to aeonian life.

26 If any one serve me, let him follow me; and where I am, there also shall be my servant. [and] if any one serve me, him shall the Father honor.

27 Now is my soul troubled, and what shall I say? Father, save me from this hour. But on account of this have I come to this hour.

28 Father, glorify your name. There came therefore a voice out of heaven, I both have glorified and will glorify it again.

29 The crowd therefore, which stood [there] and heard it said that it had thundered. Others said, An angel has spoken to him.

30 Jesus answered and said, Not on my account has this voice come, but on yours.

31 Now is the judgment of this world; now the prince of this world will be cast out.[198]

32 and I, if I be lifted up out of the earth, will draw all to me.

33 But this he said signifying by what death he was about to die.

34 The crowd answered him, We have heard out of the law that the Christ abides into the aeon; and how can you say that the Son of man must be lifted up? Who is this, the Son of man?

35 Jesus therefore said to them, Yet a little while is the light among you. Walk while you have the light, that darkness may not overtake you. And he who walks in the darkness does not know where he goes.

36 While you have the light, believe in the light, that you may become sons of light. Jesus said these things, and going away hid himself from them.

37 But though he had done so many signs before them, they believed not on him,

38 that the word of the prophet Isaiah which he said might be fulfilled, Lord, who has believed our report? and to whom has the arm of the Lord been revealed?

39 On this account they could not believe, because Isaiah said again,

40 He has blinded their eyes and hardened their heart, that they may not see with their eyes, and understand with their heart and be converted, and I should heal them.

41 These things said Isaiah because he saw his glory and spoke of him.

42 Although indeed from among the rulers also many believed on him, but on account of the Pharisees did not acknowledge him that they might not be put out of the synagogue:

43 for they loved glory from men rather than glory from the God.

44 But Jesus cried and said, He that believes on me, believes not on me, but on him that sent me;

45 and he that beholds me, beholds him that sent me.

46 I am come into the world [as] light, that every one that believes on me may not abide in darkness;

47 and if any one hear my words and do not keep [them] I judge him not, for I am not come that I might judge the world, but that I might save the world.

48 He that rejects me and does not receive my words, has him who judges him: the word which I have spoken, that shall judge him in the last day.

49 For I have not spoken from myself, but the Father who sent me has himself given me commandment what I should say and what I should speak;

50 and I know that his commandment is aeonian life. What therefore I speak, as the Father has said to me, so I speak.

John 13:1 Now before the feast of the Passover, Jesus, knowing that his hour had come that he should depart out of this world to the Father, having loved his own who were in the world, loved them to the end.

2 And during supper, the devil having already put it into the heart of Judas [son] of Simon, Iscariote, that he should deliver him up,

3 [Jesus,] knowing that the Father had given him all things into his hands, and that he came out from God and was going toward the God,

4 rises from supper and lays aside his garments, and having taken a linen towel he girded himself:

5 then he pours water into the wash-hand basin, and began to wash the feet of the disciples, and to wipe them with the linen towel with which he was girded.

---

[198] "Sent away" by force as the escape goat was sent away.

6 He comes therefore to Simon Peter; and he says to him, Lord, do you wash my feet?

7 Jesus answered and said to him, What I do you do not know now, but you shall know hereafter.

8 Peter says to him, You shall never wash my feet. Jesus answered him, Unless I wash you, you have no part with me.

9 Simon Peter says to him, Lord, not my feet only, but also my hands and my head.

10 Jesus says to him, He that is washed all over needs not to wash except his feet, but is wholly clean; and you are clean, but not all.

11 For he knew him that delivered him up: on account of this he said, You are not all clean.

12 When therefore he had washed their feet, and taken his garments, having sat down again, he said to them, Do you know what I have done to you?

13 You call me the Teacher and the Lord, and you say well, for I am [so]

14 If I therefore, the Lord and the Teacher, have washed your feet, you also ought to wash one another's feet;

15 for I have given you an example that, as I have done to you, you should do also.

16 Truly, truly, I say to you, The servant is not greater than his lord, nor the sent greater than he who has sent him.

17 If you know these things, blessed are you if you do them.

18 I speak not of you all. I know those whom I have chosen; but that the scripture might be fulfilled, He that eats bread with me has lifted up his heel against me.

19 I tell you it now before it happens, that when it happens, you may believe that I am [he]

20 Truly, truly, I say to you, He who receives whomsoever I shall send receives me; and he that receives me receives him who has sent me.

21 Having said these things, Jesus was troubled in spirit, and testified and said, Truly, truly, I say to you, that one of you shall deliver me up.

22 The disciples therefore looked one on another, uncertain of whom he spoke.

23 Now there was at table one of his disciples in the bosom of Jesus, whom Jesus loved.

24 Simon Peter makes a sign therefore to him to ask who it might be of whom he spoke.

25 But he, leaning on the breast of Jesus, says to him, Lord, who is it?

26 Jesus answers, He it is to whom I, after I have dipped the morsel, give it. And having dipped the morsel, he gives it to Judas [son] of Simon, Iscariote.

27 And, after the morsel, then entered Satan into him. Jesus therefore says to him, What you do, do quickly.

28 But none of those at table knew why he said this to him;

29 for some supposed, because Judas had the bag, that Jesus was saying to him, Buy the things of which we have need for the feast; or that he should give something to the poor.

30 Having therefore received the morsel, he went out immediately; and it was night.

31 When therefore he had gone out Jesus says, Now is the Son of man glorified* and the God is glorified* in him [Son of man].

32 If the God be glorified* in him, now the God also will glorify [fut] Himself in him [Son of man], and will glorify [fut] Himself immediately.

33 Children, yet a little while I am with you. You shall seek me; and, as I said to the Jews, Where I go you cannot come, I say to you also now.

34 A new commandment I give to you, that you love one another; as I have loved you, that you also love one another.

35 By this shall all know that you are disciples of mine, if you have love among yourselves.

36 Simon Peter says to him, Lord, where are you going? Jesus answered him, Where I go you can not follow me now, but you shall follow me after.

37 Peter says to him, Lord, why cannot I follow you now? I will lay down my soul for you.

38 Jesus answers, You will lay down your soul for me! Truly, truly, I say to you, The cock shall not crow till you have denied me three times.

John 14:1 Let not your heart be troubled; you believe on the God, believe also on me.

2 In my Father's house there are many abodes; were it not so, I had told you: for I go to prepare you a place;

3 and if I go and shall prepare you a place, I am coming again and shall receive you to myself, that where I am you also may be.

4 And you know where I go, and you know the way.

5 Thomas says to him, Lord, we know not where you are going, and how can we know the way?

6 Jesus says to him, I am the way, and the truth, and the life. No one comes to the Father unless by me.

7 If you had known me, you would have known also my Father, and henceforth you know him and have seen him.

8 Philip says to him, Lord, show us the Father and it suffices us.

9 Jesus says to him, Am I so long a time with you, and you have not known me, Philip? He that has seen me has seen the Father; and how can you say, Show us the Father?

10 Don't you believe that I am in the Father, and that the Father is in me? The words which I speak to you I do not speak from myself; but the Father who abides in me, he does the works.

11 Believe me that I am in the Father and the Father in me; but if not, believe me for the works' sake themselves.

12 Truly, truly, I say to you, He that believes on me, the works which I do shall he shall do also, and he shall do greater than these, because I go to the Father.

13 And whatsoever you shall ask in my name, this will I do, that the Father may be glorified in the Son.

14 If you shall ask anything in my name, I will do it.

15 If you love me, keep my commandments.

16 And I will ask the Father, and he will give you another Comforter, that he may be with you into the aeon,

17 the Spirit of truth, whom the world cannot receive, because it does not see him nor know him; but you know him, for he abides with you, and shall be in you.

18 I will not leave you orphans, I am coming to you.

19 Yet a little and the world sees me no longer; but you see me; because I live you also shall live.

20 In that day you shall know that I am in my Father, and you in me, and I in you.

21 He that has my commandments and keeps them, he it is that loves me; but he that loves me shall be loved by my Father, and I will love him and will manifest myself to him.

22 Judas, not the Iscariote, says to him, Lord, how is it that you will manifest yourself to us and not to the world?

23 Jesus answered and said to him, If any one love me, he will keep my word, and my Father will love him, and we will come to him and make our abode with him.

24 He that loves me not does not keep my words; and the word which you hear is not mine, but that of the Father who has sent me.

25 These things I have said to you, abiding with you;

26 but the Comforter, the Holy Spirit, whom the Father will send in my name, he shall teach you all things, and will bring to your remembrance all the things which I have said to you.

27 I leave peace with you; I give my peace to you: not as the world gives do I give to you. Let not your heart be troubled, neither let it fear.

28 You have heard that I have said unto you, I go away and I am coming to you. If you loved me you would rejoice that I go to the Father, for [my] Father is greater than I.

29 And now I have told you before it comes to pass, that when it shall have come to pass you may believe.

30 I will no longer speak much with you, for the ruler of the world comes, and in me he has nothing;

31 but that the world may know that I love the Father, and as the Father has commanded me, thus I do. Rise up, let us go from here.

John 15:1 I am the true vine, and my Father is the husbandman.

2 [As to] every branch in me not bearing fruit, he takes it away; and [as to] every one bearing fruit, he prunes it that it may bring forth more fruit.

3 You are already clean by reason of the word which I have spoken to you.

4 Abide in me and I in you. As the branch cannot bear fruit of itself unless it abide in the vine, thus neither [can] you unless you abide in me.

5 I am the vine, you [are] the branches. He that abides in me and I in him, he bears much fruit; for without me you can do nothing.

6 Unless any one abide in me he is cast out as the branch, and is dried up; and they gather them and cast them into the fire, and they are burned.

7 If you abide in me, and my words abide in you, you shall ask what you will and it shall come to pass to you.

8 In this is my Father glorified, that you bear much fruit, and you shall become disciples of mine.

9 As the Father has loved me, I also have loved you: abide in my love.

10 If you shall keep my commandments, you shall abide in my love, as I have kept my Father's commandments and abide in his love.

11 I have spoken these things to you that my joy may be in you, and your joy be full.

12 This is my commandment, that you love one another, as I have loved you.

13 No one has greater love than this, that one should lay down his soul for his friends.

14 You are my friends if you practice whatever I command you.

15 I call you no longer servants, for the servant does not know what his master is doing; but I have called you friends, for all things which I have heard of my Father I have made known to you.

16 You have not chosen me, but I have chosen you, and have set you that you should go and that you should bear fruit, and that your fruit should abide, that whatsoever you shall ask the Father in my name he may give you.

17 These things I command you, that you love one another.

18 If the world hates you, know that it has hated me before you.

19 If you were of the world, the world would like its own; but because you are not of the world, but I have chosen you out of the world, on account of this the world hates you.

20 Remember the word which I said unto you, The servant is not greater than his master. If they have persecuted me, they will also persecute you; if they have kept my word, they will keep also yours.

21 But they will do all these things to you on account of my name, because they have not known him that sent me.

22 If I had not come and spoken to them, they would have no sin; but now they have no excuse for their sin.

23 He that hates me hates also my Father.

24 If I had not done among them the works which no other one has done, they would not have sin; but now they have both seen and hated both me and my Father.

25 But that the word written in their law might be fulfilled, They hated me without a cause.

26 But when the Comforter is come, whom I will send to you from the Father, the Spirit of truth who goes forth from the Father, he shall bear witness concerning me;

27 and you too bear witness, because you are with me from the beginning.

John 16:1 These things I have spoken unto you that you may not be offended.

2 They shall put you out of the synagogues; but the hour is coming that every one who kills you will think to render service to the God;

3 and these things they will do because they have not known the Father nor me.

4 But I have spoken these things to you, that when their hour shall have come, you may remember them, that I have said [them] unto you. But I did not say these things unto you from the beginning, because I was with you.

5 But now I go toward him that has sent me, and none of you asks of me, Where do you go?

6 But because I have spoken these things to you, sorrow has filled your heart.

7 But I say the truth to you, It is profitable for you that I go away; for if I do not go away, the Comforter will not come to you; but if I go I will send him to you.

8 And having come, he will reprove the world concerning sin, and concerning righteousness, and concerning judgment:

9 of sin, because they do not believe on me;

10 of righteousness, because I go away to my Father, and you behold me no longer;

11 of judgment, because the ruler of this world is judged.

12 I have yet many things to say to you, but you cannot bear them now.

13 But when he is come, the Spirit of truth, he shall guide you into all the truth: for he shall not speak from himself; but whatsoever he shall hear he shall speak; and he will announce to you what is coming.

14 He shall glorify me, for he shall receive of mine and shall announce it to you.

15 All things that the Father has are mine; on account of this I have said that he receives of mine and shall announce it to you.

16 A little while and you do not behold me; and again a little while and you shall see me, [because I go away to the father]

17 [Some] of his disciples therefore said to one another, What is this he says to us, A little while and you do not behold me; and again a little while and you shall see me, and, Because I go away toward the Father?

18 They said therefore, What is this which he says of the little while? We do not know of what he speaks.

19 Jesus knew therefore that they desired to ask of him, and said to them, Do you inquire of this among yourselves that I said, A little while and you do not behold me; and again a little while and you shall see me?

20 Truly, truly, I say to you, that you shall weep and lament, you, but the world shall rejoice; and you will be grieved, but your grief shall be turned to joy.

21 A woman, when she gives birth to a child, has grief because her hour has come; but when the child is born, she no longer remembers the trouble, on account of the joy that a man has been born into the world.

22 And you now therefore have grief; but I will see you again, and your heart shall rejoice, and your joy no one takes from you.

23 And in that day you shall ask nothing of me: truly, truly, I say to you, Whatsoever you shall ask the Father in my name, he will give you.

24 Until now you have asked nothing in my name: ask, and you shall receive, that your joy may be full.

25 These things I have spoken to you in parables; the hour is coming that I will no longer speak to you in parables, but will declare to you openly concerning the Father.

26 In that day you shall ask in my name; and I say not to you that I will ask of the Father for you,

27 for the Father himself has affection for you, because you have had affection for me, and have believed that I came out from the God.

28 I came out from the Father and have come into the world; again, I leave the world and go toward the Father.

29 His disciples say to him, Lo, now you speak openly and utter no parable.

30 Now we know that you know all things, and have not need that any one should ask of you. By this we believe that you are come from God.

31 Jesus answered them, Do you now believe?

32 Behold, the hour is coming, and has come, that you shall be scattered, each to his own, and shall leave me alone; and [yet] I am not alone, for the Father is with me.

33 These things have I spoken to you that in me you might have peace. In the world you have tribulation; but be of good courage: I have overcome the world.

John 17:1 These things Jesus spoke, and lifted up his eyes to heaven and said, Father, the hour is come; glorify your Son, that your Son may glorify you;

2 as you have given him authority over all flesh, that all that you have given to him, he should give them aeonian life.

3 And this is the aeonian life, that they should know you, the only true God, and Jesus Christ whom you have sent.

4 I have glorified you on the earth, I have completed the work which you gave me that I should do it;

5 and now glorify me, you Father, beside yourself,[199] with the glory which I possessed[200] before the world, to be beside you[201].

6 I have manifested your name to the men whom you gave me out of the world. They were

---

[199] On the Right Side of God (Psalm 110:1)
[200] Incomplete verb, thus he possessed something before the world was, but at the time of him speaking, it was not yet fully possessed.
[201] As the Right Side of God

yours, and you gave them to me, and they have kept your word.

7 Now they have known that all things that you have given me are from you;

8 for the words which you have given me I have given them, and they have received [them] and have known truly that I came out from you, and have believed that you sent me.

9 I ask concerning them; I do not ask concerning the world, but concerning those whom you have given me, for they are yours,

10 and all that is mine is yours, and [all] that is yours is mine, and I am glorified in them.

11 And I am no longer in the world, and these are in the world, and I come to you. Holy Father, keep them in your name which you have given me, that they may be one as we.

12 When I was with them I kept them in your name; those you have given me I have guarded, and not one of them has perished, but the son of perdition, that the scripture might be fulfilled.

13 And now I come to you. And these things I speak in the world, that they may have my joy fulfilled in them.

14 I have given them your word, and the world has hated them, because they are not of the world, as I am not of the world.

15 I do not ask that you should take them out of the world, but that you should keep them out of evil.

16 They are not of the world, as I am not of the world.

17 Sanctify them by the truth: your word is truth.

18 As you have sent me into the world, I also have sent them into the world;

19 and I sanctify myself for them, that they also may be sanctified by truth.

20 And I do not ask for these only, but also for those who believe on me through their word;

21 that they may be all one, as you, Father, are in me, and I in you, that they also may be one in us, that the world may believe that you have sent me.

22 And the glory which you have given me I have given them, that they may be one, as we are one;

23 I in them and you in me, that they may be perfected into one [and] that the world may know that you have sent me, and that you have loved them as you have loved me.

24 Father, [as to] those whom you have given me, I desire that where I am they also may be with me, that they may behold my glory which you have given me, for you loved me before the foundation of the world.

25 Righteous Father, -- and the world has not known you, but I have known you, and these have known that you have sent me.

26 And I have made known to them your name, and will make it known; that the love with which you have loved me may be in them and I in them.

John 18:1 Jesus, having said these things, went out with his disciples beyond the brook Kidron, where was a garden, into which he entered, he and his disciples.

2 And Judas also, who delivered him up, knew the place, because Jesus was often there, in company with his disciples.

3 Judas therefore, having got the band, and officers of the chief priests and Pharisees, comes there with lanterns and torches and weapons.

4 Jesus therefore, knowing all things that were coming upon him, went forth and said to them, Whom do you seek?

5 They answered him, Jesus the Nazarene. Jesus says to them, I am [he] And Judas also, who delivered him up, stood with them.

6 When therefore he said to them, I am [he] they went away backward and fell to the ground.

7 He asked of them therefore again, Whom do you seek? And they said, Jesus the Nazarene.

8 Jesus answered, I told you that I am [he] if therefore you seek me, let these go away;

9 that the word might be fulfilled which he spoke, [as to] those whom you have given me, I have not lost one of them.

10 Simon Peter therefore, having a sword, drew it, and smote the servant of the high priest and cut off his right ear; and the servant's name was Malchus.

11 Jesus therefore said to Peter, Put the sword into the sheath; the cup which the Father has given me, shall I not drink it?

12 The band therefore, and the centurions, and the officers of the Jews, took Jesus and bound him:

13 and they led him away to Annas first; for he was father-in-law to Caiaphas, who was high priest that year.

14 But it was Caiaphas who counseled the Jews that it was better that one man should perish for the people.

15 Now Simon Peter followed Jesus, and the other disciple. But that disciple was known to the high priest, and went in with Jesus into the palace of the high priest;

16 but Peter stood at the door outside. The other disciple therefore, who was known to the high priest, went out and spoke to the doorkeeper and brought in Peter.

17 The maid therefore, who was the doorkeeper, says to Peter, Are you also of the disciples of this man? He says, I am not.

18 But the servants and officers, having made a fire of coals for it was cold, stood and warmed themselves; and Peter was standing with them and warming himself.

19 The high priest therefore asked of Jesus concerning his disciples and concerning his doctrine.

20 Jesus answered him, I spoke openly to the world; I taught always in the synagogue and in the temple, where all the Jews come together, and in secret I have spoken nothing.

21 Why do you ask me? Ask those who have heard, what I have spoken to them; look, they know what I have said.

22 But as he said these things, one of the officers who stood by gave a blow on the face to Jesus, saying, Answer you the high priest thus?

23 Jesus answered him, If I have spoken evil, bear witness of the evil; but if well, why do you hit me

24 Annas [then] had sent him bound to Caiaphas the high priest.

25 But Simon Peter was standing and warming himself. They said therefore to him, Are you also of his disciples? He denied, and said, I am not.

26 One of the servants of the high priest, who was kinsman of him whose ear Peter cut off, says, Did not I see you in the garden with him?

27 Peter denied therefore again, and immediately the cock crew.

28 They lead therefore Jesus from Caiaphas to the praetorium; and it was early morn. And they entered not into the praetorium, that they might not be defiled, but eat the Passover.

29 Pilate therefore went out to them and said, What accusation do you bring against this man?

30 They answered and said to him, If this [man] were not an evildoer, we should not have delivered him up to you.

31 Pilate therefore said to them, Take him, you, and judge him according to your law. The Jews therefore said to him, It is not permitted to us to put any one to death;

32 (that the word of Jesus might be fulfilled which he spoke, signifying what death he should die).

33 Pilate therefore entered again into the praetorium and called Jesus, and said to him, Are you the king of the Jews?

34 Jesus answered him. Do you say this of yourself, or have others said it to you concerning me?

35 Pilate answered, Am I a Jew? Your nation and the chief priests have delivered you up to me: what have you done?

36 Jesus answered, My kingdom is not of this world; if my kingdom were of this world, my servants had fought that I might not be delivered up to the Jews; but now my kingdom is not from here.

37 Pilate therefore said to him, You are then a king? Jesus answered, You say it that I am a king. I have been born for this, and for this I have come into the world, that I might bear witness to the truth. Every one that is of the truth hears my voice.

38 Pilate says to him, What is truth? And having said this he went out again to the Jews, and says to them, I find no fault whatever in him.

39 But you have a custom that I release [some] one to you at the Passover; will you therefore that I release unto you the king of the Jews?

40 They cried therefore again all, saying, Not this [man] but Barabbas. Now Barabbas was a robber.

John 19:1 Then Pilate therefore took Jesus and scourged him.

2 And the soldiers having plaited a crown of thorns put it on his head, and put a purple robe on him,

3 and came to him and said, Hail, king of the Jews! and gave him blows on the face.

4 And Pilate went out again and says to them, Lo, I bring him out to you, that you may know that I find in him no fault whatever.

5 Jesus therefore went forth outside, wearing the crown of thorns, and the purple robe. And he says to them, Look at the man!

6 When therefore the chief priests and the officers saw him they cried out saying, Crucify, crucify him. Pilate says to them, You take him and crucify him, for I find no fault in him.

7 The Jews answered him, We have a law, and according to [our] law he ought to die, because he made himself Son of God.

8 When Pilate therefore heard this word, he was afraid,

9 and went into the praetorium again and says to Jesus, Who are you? But Jesus gave him no answer.

10 Pilate therefore says to him, You speak not to me? Do you not know that I have authority to release you and have authority to crucify you?

11 Jesus answered, You have no authority whatever against me if it were not given to you from above. On this account he that has delivered me up to you has the greater sin.

12 From this time Pilate sought to release him; but the Jews cried out saying, If you release this [man] you are not a friend to Caesar. Every one making himself a king speaks against Caesar.

13 Pilate therefore, having heard these words, led Jesus out and sat down upon the judgment-seat, at a place called Pavement, but in Hebrew Gabbatha;

14 now it was the preparation of the Passover; it was about the sixth hour; and he says to the Jews, Behold your king!

15 But they cried out, Take him away, take him away, crucify him. Pilate says to them, Shall I crucify your king? The chief priests answered, We have no king but Caesar.

16 Then therefore he delivered him up to them, that he might be crucified; and they took Jesus and led him away.

17 And he went out, bearing his cross, to the place called [place] of a skull, which is called in Hebrew, Golgotha;

18 where they crucified him, and with him two others, [one] on this side, and [one] on that, and Jesus in the middle.

19 And Pilate wrote a title also and put it on the cross. But there was written: Jesus the Nazarene, the King of the Jews.

20 This title therefore many of the Jews read, for the place of the city where Jesus was crucified was near; and it was written in Hebrew, Greek, Latin.

21 The chief priests of the Jews therefore said to Pilate, Do not write, The king of the Jews, but that he said, I am king of the Jews.

22 Pilate answered, What I have written, I have written.

23 The soldiers therefore, when they had crucified Jesus, took his clothes, and made four parts, to each soldier a part, and the body-coat; but the body-coat was seamless, woven through the whole from the top.

24 They said therefore to one another, Let us not rip it, but let us cast lots for it, whose it shall be; that the scripture might be fulfilled which says, They parted my garments among themselves, and on my vesture they cast lots. The soldiers therefore did these things.

25 And by the cross of Jesus stood his mother, and the sister of his mother, Mary the [wife] of Clopas, and Mary of Magdalene.

26 Jesus therefore, seeing his mother, and the disciple standing by, whom he loved, says to his mother, Woman, behold your son.

27 Then he says unto the disciple, Behold your mother. And from that hour the disciple took her to his own home.

28 After this, Jesus, knowing that all things were now finished, that the scripture might be fulfilled, says, I thirst.

29 There was a vessel therefore there full of vinegar, and having filled a sponge with vinegar, and putting hyssop round it, they put it up to his mouth.

30 When therefore Jesus had received the vinegar, he said, It is finished; and having bowed his head, he delivered up his spirit.

31 The Jews therefore, that the bodies might not remain on the cross on the Sabbath, for it was the preparation, for the day of that Sabbath was a great [day], demanded of Pilate that their legs might be broken, and their bodies taken away.

32 The soldiers therefore came and broke the legs of the first and of the other that had been crucified with him;

33 but coming to Jesus, when they saw that he was already dead they did not break his legs,

34 but one of the soldiers pierced his side with a spear, and immediately there came out blood and water.

35 And he who saw it bears witness, and his witness is true, and he knows that what he says is true that you also may believe.

36 For these things took place that the scripture might be fulfilled, Not a bone of him shall be broken.

37 And again another scripture says, They shall look on him whom they pierced.

38 And after these things Joseph of Arimathaea, who was a disciple of Jesus, but secretly through fear of the Jews, demanded of Pilate that he might take the body of Jesus: and Pilate allowed it. He came therefore and took away the body of Jesus.

39 And Nicodemus also, who at first came to Jesus by night, came, bringing a mixture of myrrh and aloes, about a hundred pounds [weight]

40 They took therefore the body of Jesus and bound it up in linen with the spices, as it is the custom with the Jews to prepare for burial.

41 But there was in the place where he had been crucified a garden, and in the garden a new tomb in which no one had ever been laid.

42 There therefore, on account of the preparation of the Jews, because the tomb was near, they laid Jesus.

John 20:1 And towards first [day] of the week[202] Mary of Magdalene comes early (darkness yet taken place) to the tomb, and sees the stone taken away from the tomb.

2 She runs therefore and comes to Simon Peter, and to the other disciple, to whom Jesus had affection for, and says to them, They have taken away the Lord out of the tomb, and we know not where they have laid him.

3 Peter therefore went forth, and the other disciple, and came to the tomb.

4 And the two ran together, and the other disciple ran forward faster than Peter, and came first to the tomb,

5 and stooping down he sees the linen cloths lying; he did not however go in.

6 Simon Peter therefore comes, following him, and entered into the tomb, and sees the linen cloths lying,

7 and the face-cloth which was upon his head, not lying with the linen cloths, but folded up in a distinct place by itself.

8 Then entered in therefore the other disciple also who came first to the tomb, and he saw and believed;

9 for they had not yet known the scripture, that he must rise from among the dead.

10 The disciples therefore went away again to their own home.

11 But Mary stood at the tomb weeping outside. As therefore she wept, she stooped down into the tomb,

12 and beholds two angels sitting in white [garments] one at the head and one at the feet, where the body of Jesus had lain.

13 And they say to her, Woman, why do you weep? She says to them, Because they have taken away my Lord, and I know not where they have laid him.

14 Having said these things she turned backward and beholds Jesus standing [there] and knew not that it was Jesus.

15 Jesus says to her, Woman, why do you weep? Whom do you seek? She, supposing that it was the gardener, says to him, Sir, if you have borne him away, tell me where you have laid him, and I will take him away.

16 Jesus says to her, Mary. She, turning round, says to him in Hebrew, Rabboni, which means Teacher.

17 Jesus says to her, Touch me not, for I have not yet ascended towards my Father; but go to my

---

[202] [lit. Sabbaths]

brethren and say to them, I ascend towards my Father and your Father, and my God and your God.

18 Mary of Magdalene comes bringing word to the disciples that she had seen the Lord, and that he had said these things to her.

19 When therefore it was evening on that day, which was first [day] of the week,[203] and the doors shut where the disciples were, through fear of the Jews, Jesus came and stood in the midst, and says to them, Peace [be] to you.

20 And having said this, he showed to them his hands and his side. The disciples rejoiced therefore, having seen the Lord.

21 [Jesus] said therefore again to them, Peace [be] to you: as the Father sent me forth, I also send you.

22 And having said this, he breathed into [them] and says to them, Receive the Holy Spirit:

23 whose sins you forgive, they are forgiven, whose sins you retain, they are retained.

24 But Thomas, one of the twelve, called Didymus, was not with them when Jesus came.

25 The other disciples therefore said to him, We have seen the Lord. But he said to them, Unless I see in his hands the mark of the nails, and put my finger into the mark of the nails, and put my hand into his side, I will not believe.

26 And eight days after, his disciples were again within, and Thomas with them. Jesus comes, the doors being shut, and stood in the midst and said, Peace [be] to you.

27 Then he says to Thomas, Bring your finger here and see my hands; and bring your hand and put it into my side; and be not unbelieving, but believing.

28 Thomas answered and said to him, my Lord and my God.

29 Jesus says to him, Because you have seen me you have believed:[204] blessed they who have not seen and have believed.

30 Many other signs therefore also Jesus did before his disciples, which are not written in this book;

31 but these are written that you may believe that Jesus is the Christ, the Son of the God, and that believing you might have life in his name.

John 21:1 After these things Jesus manifested himself again to the disciples at the sea of Tiberias. And he manifested [himself] thus.

2 There were together Simon Peter, and Thomas called Didymus, and Nathanael who was of Cana of Galilee, and the [sons] of Zebedee, and two others of his disciples.

3 Simon Peter says to them, I go to fish. They say to him, We also come with you. They went forth, and went on board, and that night took nothing.

4 And early morn already breaking, Jesus stood on the shore; the disciples however did not know that it was Jesus.

5 Jesus therefore says to them, Children, have you anything to eat? They answered him, No.

6 And he said to them, Cast the net at the right side of the ship and you will find. They cast therefore, and they could no longer draw it, from the multitude of fishes.

7 That disciple therefore whom Jesus loved says to Peter, It is the Lord. Simon Peter therefore, having heard that it was the Lord, girded his overcoat [on him] for he was naked, and cast himself into the sea;

8 and the other disciples came in the small boat, for they were not far from the land, but somewhere about two hundred cubits, dragging the net of fishes.

9 When therefore they went out on the land, they see a fire of coals there, and fish laid on it, and bread.

10 Jesus says to them, Bring of the fishes which you have now taken.

11 Simon Peter went up and drew the net to the land full of great fishes, a hundred and fifty-three; and though there were so many, the net was not rent.

12 Jesus says to them, Come [and] dine. But none of the disciples dared inquire of him, Who are you? knowing that it was the Lord.

13 Jesus comes and takes the bread and gives it to them, and the fish in like manner.

14 This is already the third time that Jesus had been manifested to the disciples, being risen from among the dead.

15 When therefore they had dined, Jesus says to Simon Peter, Simon, [son] of Jonas, do you love me more than these? He says to him, Yes, Lord; you know that I like you. He says to him, Feed my lambs.

16 He says to him again a second time, Simon, [son] of Jonas, do you love me? He says to him, Yes, Lord; you know that I like you. He says to him, Shepherd my sheep.

17 He says to him the third time, Simon, [son] of Jonas, do you like me? Peter was grieved because he said to him the third time, Do you like me? and said to him, Lord, you know all things; you know that I like you. Jesus says to him, Feed my sheep.

18 Truly, truly, I say to you, When you were young, you girded yourself, and walked where you desired; but when you shall be old, you shall stretch forth your hands, and another shall gird you, and bring you where you do not desire.

19 But he said this signifying by what death he should glorify the God. And having said this, he says to him, Follow me.

20 Peter, turning round, sees the disciple whom Jesus loved following, who also leaned at supper on his breast, and said, Lord, who is it that delivers you up?

21 Peter, seeing him, says to Jesus, Lord, and what of this [man]?

22 Jesus says to him, If I wish that he abide until I come, what [is that] to you? You follow me.

23 This word therefore went out among the brethren, That disciple does not die. And Jesus did not say to him, He does not die; but, If I wish that he abide until I come, what [is that] to you?

---

[203] Lit. Sabbaths
[204] Notice, Christ does not deny that he is God.

24 This is the disciple who bears witness concerning these things, and who has written these things; and we know that his witness is true.

25 And there are also many other things which Jesus did, the which if they were written one by one, I suppose that not even the world itself would contain the books written.

Acts

Acts 1:1 I composed the first discourse, O Theophilus, concerning all things which Jesus began both to do and to teach,

2 until that day in which, having by the Holy Spirit charged the apostles whom he had chosen, he was taken up;

3 to whom also he presented himself living, after he had suffered, with many proofs; being seen by them during forty days, and speaking of the things which concern the kingdom of the God;

4 and, being assembled with them, commanded them not to depart from Jerusalem, but to await the promise of the Father, which you have heard from me.

5 For John indeed baptized with water, but you shall be baptized with the Holy Spirit after now not many days.

6 They therefore, when together, asked him saying, Lord, is it at this time that you restore the kingdom to Israel?

7 And he said to them, It is not yours to know times or seasons, which the Father has placed in his own power;

8 but you will receive the power when the Holy Spirit comes upon you, and you shall be my witnesses both in Jerusalem, and in all Judea and Samaria, and to the end of the earth.

9 And having said these things he was taken up, they beholding him and a cloud received him out of their sight.

10 And as they were gazing into heaven, as he was going, behold, also two men stood by them in white clothing,

11 who also said, Men of Galilee, why do you stand looking into heaven? This Jesus who has been taken up from you into heaven, shall thus come in the manner in which you have beheld him going into heaven.

12 Then they returned to Jerusalem from the mount called [the mount] of Olives, which is near Jerusalem, a sabbath-day's journey off.

13 And when they had come into [the city] they went up to the upper chamber, where were staying both Peter, and John, and James, and Andrew, Philip and Thomas, Bartholomew and Matthew, James [son] of Alphaeus, and Simon the zealot, and Jude [the brother] of James.

14 These gave themselves all with one accord to continual prayer, with [several] women, and Mary the mother of Jesus, and with his brethren.

15 And in those days Peter, standing up in the midst of the brethren, said, the crowd of names [who were] together [was] about a hundred and twenty,

16 Brethren, it was necessary that the scripture should have been fulfilled, which the Holy Spirit spoke before, by the mouth of David, concerning Judas, who became guide to those who took Jesus;

17 for he was numbered among us, and had received a part in this service.

18 This [man] then indeed got a field with the reward of iniquity, and, having fallen down headlong, burst in the midst, and all his bowels gushed out.

19 And it was known to all the inhabitants of Jerusalem, so that that field was called in their own dialect Aceldama; that is, field of blood.

20 For it is written in the book of Psalms, Let his homestead become desolate, and let there be no dweller in it; and, Let another take his ofice.

21 It is necessary therefore, that of the men who have assembled with us all the time in which the Lord Jesus came in and went out among us,

22 beginning from the baptism of John until the day in which he was taken up from us, one of these should be a witness with us of his resurrection.

23 And they appointed two, Joseph, who was called Barsabas, who had been surnamed Justus, and Matthias.

24 And they prayed, and said, You Lord, knower of the hearts of all, show which one of these two you have chosen,

25 to receive the lot of this service and apostleship, from which Judas transgressing fell to go to his own place.

26 And they gave lots on them, and the lot fell on Matthias, and he was numbered with the eleven apostles.

Acts 2:1 And when the day of Pentecost was in progress, they were all together in one place.

2 And there came suddenly a sound out of heaven as of a violent violent blowing, and filled all the house where they were sitting.

3 And there appeared to them parted tongues, as of fire, and being distributed (sitting down) upon each one of them.

4 And they were all filled with the Holy Spirit, and began to speak with other tongues as the Spirit gave to them to speak.

5 Now there were dwelling at Jerusalem Jews, pious men, from every nation of those under heaven.

6 But the rumor of this having spread, the multitude came together and were confounded, because each one heard them speaking in his own dialect.

7 And all were amazed and wondered, saying, Behold, are not all these who are speaking Galilaeans?

8 and how do we hear [them] each in our own dialect in which we have been born,

9 Parthians, and Medes, and Elamites, and those who inhabit Mesopotamia, and Judea, and Cappadocia, Pontus and Asia,

10 both Phrygia and Pamphylia, Egypt, and the parts of Libya which adjoin Cyrene, and the Romans sojourning [here] both Jews and proselytes,

11 Cretans and Arabians, we hear them speaking in our own tongues the great things of the God?

12 And they were all amazed and perplexed, saying one to another, What does this mean?

13 But others mocking said, They are full of new wine.

14 But Peter, standing up with the eleven, lifted up his voice and spoke to them, Men of Judea, and all you inhabitants of Jerusalem, let this be known to you, and give heed to my words:

15 for these are not full of wine, as you suppose, for it is the third hour of the day;

16 but this is that which was spoken through the prophet Joel,

17 And it shall be in the last days, says the God, that I will pour out of my Spirit upon all flesh; and your sons and your daughters shall prophesy, and your young men shall see visions, and your elders shall dream with dreams;

18 yes, even upon my servants and upon my bondwomen in those days will I pour out of my Spirit, and they shall prophesy.

19 And I will give wonders in the heaven above and signs on the earth below, blood, and fire, and vapour of smoke:

20 the sun shall be changed to darkness and the moon to blood, before the great and gloriously appearing day of the Lord come.

21 And it shall be that whosoever shall call upon the name of the Lord shall be saved.

22 Men of Israel, hear these words: Jesus the Nazarene, a man borne witness to by the God to you by works of power and wonders and signs, which the God worked by him in your midst, as yourselves know

23 --him, given up by the determinate counsel and foreknowledge of the God, you, by the hand of lawless [men] have crucified and slain.

24 Whom the God has raised up, having loosened the pains of death, inasmuch as it was not possible that he should be held by its power;

25 for David says as to him, I foresaw the Lord continually before me, because he is at my right hand that I may not be moved.

26 Therefore has my heart rejoiced and my tongue exulted; yes more, my flesh also shall dwell in hope,

27 for you will not leave my soul in Hades, nor will you give your holy one to see corruption.

28 You have made known to me the paths of life, you will fill me with joy with your countenance.

29 Brethren, let it be allowed to speak with freedom to you concerning the patriarch David, that he has both died and been buried, and his monument is among us unto this day.

30 Being therefore a prophet, and knowing that the God had sworn to him with an oath, of the fruit of his loins to set upon his throne;

31 he, seeing it before, spoke concerning the resurrection of the Christ, that neither has he been left in Hades nor his flesh seen corruption.

32 This Jesus has the God raised up, who we are all witnesses.

33 Having therefore been exalted to the right hand of the God, and having received from the Father the promise of the Holy Spirit, he has poured out this which you behold and hear.

34 For David has not ascended into the heavens, but he says himself, The Lord said unto my Lord, Sit at my right hand

35 until I have put your enemies [to be] the footstool of your feet.

36 Let the whole house of Israel therefore know assuredly that the God has made him, this Jesus whom you have crucified, both Lord and Christ.

37 And having heard it they were pricked in heart, and said to Peter and the other apostles, What shall we do, brethren?

38 And Peter said to them, repent and be baptized, each one of you, in the name of Jesus Christ, for forgiveness of sins, and you will receive the gift of the Holy Spirit.

39 For to you is the promise and to your children, and to all who are afar off, as many as the Lord our the God may call.

40 And with many other words he testified and urged them, saying, Be saved from this perverse generation.

41 Those then who had accepted his word were baptized; and there were added in that day about three thousand souls.

42 And they persevered in the doctrine and fellowship of the apostles, in breaking of bread and prayers.

43 And fear was upon every soul, and many wonders and signs took place through the means of the apostles.

44 And all that believed were together, and had all things common,

45 and sold their possessions and substance, and distributed them to all, according as any one might have need.

46 And every day, being constantly in the temple with one accord, and breaking bread in the house, they received their food with gladness and simplicity of heart,

47 praising the God, and having grace towards all the people; and the Lord added [to the church] daily those that were to be saved.

Acts 3:1 And Peter and John went up together into the temple at the hour of prayer, [which is] the ninth [hour]

2 and a certain man who was lame from his mother's womb was being carried, whom they placed every day at the gate of the temple called Beautiful, to ask alms of those who were going into the temple;

3 who, seeing Peter and John about to enter into the temple, asked to receive alms.

4 And Peter, looking stedfastly upon him with John, said, Look on us.

5 And he gave heed to them, expecting to receive something from them.

6 But Peter said, Silver and gold I have not; but what I have, this give I to you: In the name of Jesus Christ the Nazarene rise up and walk.

7 And having taken hold of him by the right hand he raised him up, and immediately his feet and ankle bones were made strong.

8 And leaping up he stood and walked, and entered with them into the temple, walking, and leaping, and praising the God.

9 And all the people saw him walking and praising the God;

10 and they recognized him, that it was he who sat for alms at the Beautiful gate of the temple; and they were filled with wonder and amazement at what had happened to him.

11 And as he held Peter and John, all the people ran together to them in the portico which is called Solomon's, greatly wondering.

12 And Peter, seeing it, answered the people, Men of Israel, why are you astonished at this? or why do you gaze on us as if we had by our own power or piety made him walk?

13 God of Abraham and Isaac and Jacob, God of our fathers, has glorified his servant Jesus, whom you delivered up, and denied him in the presence of Pilate, when he had judged that he should be let go.

14 But you denied the holy and righteous one, and asked that a man, a murderer should be granted to you;

15 but the originator of life you killed, whom the God raised from among the dead, whereof we are witnesses.

16 And, by faith in his name, his name has made this man strong whom you behold and know; and the faith which is by him [Christ] has given him this complete soundness in the presence of you all.

17 And now, brethren, I know that you did it in ignorance, as also your rulers;

18 but the God has thus fulfilled what he had announced beforehand by the mouth of all the prophets, that his Christ should suffer.

19 Repent therefore and be converted, for the blotting out of your sins, so that times of refreshing may come from the presence of the Lord,

20 and he may send Jesus Christ, who was foreordained for you,

21 whom heaven indeed must receive till the times of the restoring of all things, of which the God has spoken by the mouth of his holy prophets since time began.

22 Moses indeed said, A prophet shall the Lord your God raise up to you out of your brethren like me: him shall you hear in everything whatsoever he shall say to you.

23 And it shall be that soul that shall not hear that prophet, shall be destroyed from among the people.

24 And indeed all the prophets from Samuel and those in succession after him, as many as have spoken, have announced also these days.

25 You are the sons of the prophets and of the covenant which the God appointed to our fathers, saying to Abraham, And in your seed shall all the families of the earth be blessed.

26 To you first the God, having raised up his servant, has sent him, blessing you in turning each one [of you] from your wickedness.

Acts 4:1 And as they were speaking to the people, the priests and captain of the temple and the Sadducees came upon them,

2 being distressed on account of their teaching the people and preaching by Jesus the resurrection from among the dead;

3 and they laid hands on them, and put them in ward till the morrow; for it was already evening.

4 But many of those who had heard the word believed; and the number of the men had become [about] five thousand.

5 And it came to pass on the next day that their rulers and elders and scribes were gathered together at Jerusalem,

6 and Annas the high priest, and Caiaphas, and John, and Alexander, and as many as were of the high priestly family;

7 and having placed them in the midst they inquired, In what power or in what name have you done this?

8 Then Peter, filled with the Holy Spirit, said to them, Rulers of the people and elders [of israel]

9 if we this day are called upon to answer as to the good deed [done] to the infirm man, how he has been healed,

10 be it known to you all, and to all the people of Israel, that in the name of Jesus Christ the Nazarene, whom you have crucified, whom the God has raised from among the dead, by him this [man] stands here before you sound [in body].

11 He is the stone which has been set at nought by you the builders, which is become the corner stone.

12 And salvation is in none other, for neither is there another name under heaven which is given among men by which we can be saved.

13 But seeing the boldness of Peter and John, and perceiving that they were unlettered and uninstructed men, they wondered; and they recognized them that they were with Jesus.

14 And beholding the man who had been healed standing with them, they had nothing to reply;

15 but having commanded them to go out of the council they conferred with one another,

16 saying, What shall we do to these men? for that indeed an evident sign has come to pass through them is manifest to all that inhabit Jerusalem, and we cannot deny it.

17 But that it be not further spread among the people, let us threaten them severely no longer to speak to any man in this name.

18 And having called them, they charged them not to speak at all nor teach in the name of Jesus.

19 But Peter and John answering said to them, If it be righteous before the God to listen to you rather than to the God, judge you;

20 for as for us we cannot refrain from speaking of the things which we have seen and heard.

21 But they, having further threatened them, let them go, finding no way how they might punish them, on account of the people, because all glorified the God for what had taken place;

22 for the man on whom this sign of healing had taken place was more than of forty years old.

23 And having been let go, they came to their own [company] and reported all that the chief priests and elders had said to them.

24 And they, having heard it lifted up their voice with one accord toward the God, and said, Lord, you are God who made the heaven and the earth and the sea, and all that is in them;

25 who have said by the mouth of your servant David, Why have the nations raged haughtily and the peoples meditated vain things?

26 The kings of the earth were there, and the rulers were gathered together against the Lord and against his Christ.

27 For in truth against your holy servant Jesus, whom you had anointed, both Herod and Pontius Pilate, with the Gentiles, and peoples of Israel, have been gathered together in this city

28 to do whatever your hand and your predestinated plan should be.

29 And now, Lord, look upon their threatening, and give to your servants with all boldness to speak your word,

30 in that you stretch out your hand to heal, and that signs and wonders take place through the name of your holy servant Jesus.

31 And when they had prayed, the place in which they were assembled shook, and they were all filled with the Holy Spirit, and spoke the word of the God with boldness.

32 And the heart and soul of the multitude of those that had believed were one, and not one said that anything of what he possessed was his own, but all things were common to them;

33 and with great power did the apostles give witness of the resurrection of the Lord Jesus, and great grace was upon them all.

34 For neither was there any one in want among them; for as many as were owners of lands or houses, selling them, brought the price of what was sold

35 and laid it at the feet of the apostles; and distribution was made to each according as any one might have need.

36 And Joseph, who had been surnamed Barnabas by the apostles which is, being interpreted, Son of consolation, a Levite, Cyprian by birth,

37 being possessed of land, having sold it brought the money and laid it at the feet of the apostles.

Acts 5:1 But a certain man, Ananias by name, with Sapphira his wife, sold a possession,

2 and put aside for himself part of the price, [his] wife also being privy to it; and having brought a certain part, laid it at the feet of the apostles.

3 But Peter said, Ananias, why has Satan filled your heart that you should lie to the Holy Spirit, and put aside for yourself a part of the price of the estate?

4 While it remained did it not remain to you? and sold, was [it not] in your own power? Why is it that you have purposed this thing in your heart? You have not lied to men, but to the God.

5 And Ananias, hearing these words, fell down and expired. And great fear came upon all who heard it

6 And the young men, rising up, swathed him up for burial, and having carried him out, buried him.

7 And it came to pass about three hours afterwards, that his wife, not knowing what had happened, came in.

8 And Peter answered her, Tell me if you gave the estate for so much? And she said, Yes, for so much.

9 And Peter said to her, Why [is it] that you have agreed together to test the Spirit of the Lord? Lo, the feet of those that have buried your husband [are] at the door, and they shall carry you out.

10 And she fell down immediately at his feet and expired. And when the young men came in they found her dead; and, having carried her out, they buried her by her husband.

11 And great fear came upon all the church, and upon all who heard these things.

12 And by the hands of the apostles were many signs and wonders done among the people; and they were all with one accord in Solomon's porch,

13 but of the rest no others joined them, but the people magnified them;

14 and more believers were being added to the Lord, multitudes both of men and women;

15 so that they brought out the sick into the streets and put [them] on beds and couches, that at least the shadow of Peter, when he came, might overshadow some of them.

16 And the multitude also of the cities round about came together to Jerusalem, bringing sick persons and persons beset by unclean spirits, who were all healed.

17 And the high priest rising up, and all they that were with him, which is the sect of the Sadducees, were filled with wrath,

18 and laid hands on the apostles and put them in the public prison.

19 But an angel of the Lord during the night opened the doors of the prison, and leading them out, said,

20 Go you and stand and speak in the temple to the people all the words of this life.

21 And when they heard it, they entered very early into the temple and taught. And when the high priest was come, and they that were with him, they called together the council and all the elderhood of the sons of Israel, and sent to the prison to have them brought.

22 And when the officers came, they did not find them in the prison; and returned and reported

23 saying, We found the prison shut with all security, and the keepers standing at the doors; but when we had opened [them] within we found no one.

24 And when they heard these words, both the priest and the captain of the temple and the chief

priests were in perplexity as to them, what this would come to.

25 And some one coming reported to them, Lo, the men whom you put in the prison are in the temple, standing and teaching the people.

26 Then the captain, having gone with the officers, brought them, not with violence, for they feared the people, lest they should be stoned.

27 And they bring them and set them in the council. And the high priest asked them,

28 saying, We strictly commanded you not to teach in this name: and lo, you have filled Jerusalem with your doctrine, and purpose to bring upon us the blood of this man.

29 But Peter answering, and the apostles, said, God must be obeyed rather than men.

30 God of our fathers has raised up Jesus, whom you have slain, having hanged on a wood [cross].

31 Him has the God exalted to his right hand as Prince and Savior, to give repentance to Israel and forgiveness of sins.

32 And we are his witnesses of these things, and the Holy Spirit also, which the God has given to those that obey him.

33 But they, when they heard [these things] were cut to the heart, and took counsel to kill them.

34 But a certain [man] a Pharisee, named Gamaliel, a teacher of the law, held in honor of all the people, rose up in the council, and commanded to put the men out for a short while,

35 and said to them, Men of Israel, take heed to yourselves as regards these men what you are going to do;

36 for before these days Theudas rose up, alleging himself to be somebody, to whom a number of men, about four hundred, were joined; who was slain, and all, as many as obeyed him, were dispersed and came to nothing.

37 After him rose Judas the Galilean in the days of the census, and drew away [a number of] people after him; and he perished, and all, as many as obeyed him, were scattered abroad.

38 And now I say to you, Withdraw from these men and let them alone, for if this counsel or this work have its origin from men, it will be destroyed;

39 but if it be from God, you will not be able to put them down, lest you be found also fighters against God.

40 And they listened to his advice; and having called the apostles, they beat them, and commanded them not to speak in the name of Jesus, and dismissed them.

41 They therefore went their way from the presence of the council, rejoicing that they were counted worthy to be dishonored for the name.

42 And every day, in the temple and in the houses, they ceased not teaching and announcing the good news that Jesus [was] the Christ.

Acts 6:1 But in those days, the disciples multiplying in number, there arose a murmuring of the Hellenists against the Hebrews because their widows were overlooked in the daily ministration.

2 And the twelve, having called the multitude of the disciples to [them] said, It is not right that we, leaving the word of the God, should serve tables.

3 Look out therefore, brethren, from among yourselves seven men, well reported of, full of the [holy] Spirit and wisdom, whom we will establish over this business:

4 but we will give ourselves up to prayer and the ministry of the word.

5 And the saying pleased the whole multitude: and they chose Stephen, a man full of faith and the Holy Spirit, and Philip, and Prochorus, and Nicanor, and Timon, and Parmenas, and Nicolas, a proselyte of Antioch,

6 whom they set before the apostles; and, having prayed, they laid their hands on them.

7 And the word of the God increased; and the number of the disciples in Jerusalem was very greatly multiplied, and a great crowd of the priests obeyed the faith.

8 And Stephen, full of grace and power, worked wonders and great signs among the people.

9 And there arose up certain of those of the synagogue called of freedmen, and of Cyrenians, and of Alexandrians, and of those of Cilicia and Asia, disputing with Stephen.

10 And they were not able to resist the wisdom and the Spirit with which he spoke.

11 Then they rumor makers, who said, We have heard him speaking blasphemous words against Moses and the God.

12 And they roused the people, and the elders, and the scribes. And coming upon him, they seized him and brought him to the council.

13 And they set false witnesses, saying, This man does not cease speaking words against the holy place and the law;

14 for we have heard him saying, This Jesus the Nazarene shall destroy this place, and change the customs which Moses taught us.

15 And all who sat in the council, looking fixedly on him, saw his face as the face of an angel.

Acts 7:1 And the high priest said, Are these things then so?

2 And he said, Brethren and fathers, listen. God of glory appeared to our father Abraham when he was in Mesopotamia, before he dwelt in Haran,

3 and said to him, Go out of your land and from your kindred, and come into the land which I will show you.

4 Then going out of the land of the Chaldeans he dwelt in Haran, and from there, after his father died, he removed himself into this land in which you now dwell.

5 And he [God] did not give him an inheritance in it, not even a foot of land; but [God] promised to give it to him for a possession, and to his seed after him, when he yet had no child.

6 And the God spoke thus: His seed shall be a sojourner in a strange land, and they shall enslave and badly treated them four hundred years;

7 and the nation to which they shall be in bondage will I judge, said the God; and after these things they shall come forth and serve me in this place.

8 And he [God] gave to him the covenant of circumcision; and thus he [Abraham] begat Isaac and circumcised him the eighth day; and Isaac Jacob, and Jacob the twelve patriarchs.

9 And the patriarchs, envying Joseph, sold him away into Egypt. And the God was with him,

10 and delivered him out of all his tribulations, and gave him grace and wisdom in the sight of Pharaoh king of Egypt, and he appointed him chief over Egypt and all his house.

11 But a famine came upon all the land of Egypt and Canaan, and great distress, and our fathers found no food.

12 But Jacob, having heard of there being grain in Egypt, sent out our fathers first;

13 and the second time Joseph was made known to his brethren, and the family of Joseph became known to Pharaoh.

14 And Joseph sent and invited his father Jacob and all [his] kindred, seventy-five souls.

15 And Jacob went down into Egypt and died, he and our fathers,

16 and were carried over to Sychem and placed in the tomb which Abraham bought for a sum of money of the sons of Emmor the [father] of Sychem.

17 But as the time of promise drew near which the God had promised to Abraham, the people increased and multiplied in Egypt,

18 until another king over Egypt arose who did not know Joseph.

19 He dealt shrewdly with our race [family], and evil entreated the fathers, casting out their infants that they might not live.

20 In that time Moses was born, and was to God beautiful, who was nourished three months in the house of his father.

21 And when he was cast out, the daughter of Pharaoh took him up, and brought him up for herself [to be] for a son.

22 And Moses was instructed in all the wisdom of the Egyptians, and he was mighty in his words and deeds.

23 And when a period of forty years was fulfilled to him, it came into his heart to look upon his brethren, the sons of Israel;

24 and seeing a certain one wronged, he defended him and avenged him that was being oppressed, killing the Egyptian.

25 For he thought that his brethren would understand that the God by his hand was giving them deliverance. But they understood not.

26 And on the next day he showed himself to them as they were contending, and compelled them to make peace, saying, You are brethren, why do you wrong one another?

27 But he that was wronging his neighbor pushed him away, saying, Who established you ruler and judge over us?

28 Do you wish to kill me as you killed the Egyptian yesterday?

29 And Moses fled at this saying, and became a sojourner in the land of Madiam, where he begat two sons.

30 And when forty years were fulfilled, an angel appeared to him in the wilderness of mount Sinai, in a flame of fire of a bush.

31 And Moses seeing it wondered at the vision; and as he went up to consider it, there was a voice of the Lord,

32 I am God of your fathers, God of Abraham, and of Isaac, and of Jacob. And Moses trembled, and durst not consider it

33 And the Lord said to him, Loose the sandal of your feet, for the place on which you stand is holy ground.

34 I have surely seen the ill treatment of my people which is in Egypt, and I have heard their groan, and have come down to take them out of it; and now, come, I will send you to Egypt.

35 This Moses, whom they refused, saying, Who made you ruler and judge? him did the God send [to be] a ruler and deliverer with the hand of the angel who appeared to him in the bush.

36 He led them out, having worked wonders and signs in the land of Egypt, and in the Red sea, and in the wilderness forty years.

37 This is the Moses who said to the sons of Israel, A prophet shall the God raise up to you out of your brethren like me [him shall you hear].

38 This is he who was in the church in the wilderness, with the angel who spoke to him in the mount Sinai, and with our fathers; who received living oracles to give to us;

39 to whom our fathers would not be subject, but thrust him from them, and in their hearts turned back to Egypt,

40 saying to Aaron, Make us gods who shall go before us; for this Moses, who brought us out of the land of Egypt, we know not what has happened to him.

41 And they made a calf in those days, and offered sacrifice to the idol, and rejoiced in the works of their own hands.

42 But the God turned and delivered them up to serve the host of heaven; as it is written in the book of the prophets, Have you offered me victims and sacrifices forty years in the wilderness, O house of Israel?

43 Yes, you took up the tent of Moloch, and the star of [your] god Remphan, the forms which you made to do homage to them; and I will transport you beyond Babylon.

44 Our fathers had the tent of the testimony in the wilderness, as he that spoke to Moses commanded to make it according to the pattern which he had seen;

45 which also our fathers, receiving from their predecessors, brought in with Joshua when they entered into possession of [the lands of] the nations, whom the God drove out from the face of our fathers, until the days of David;

46 who found grace before the God, and asked to find a tabernacle for God of Jacob;

47 but Solomon built him a house.

48 But the Most High dwells not in [places] made with hands; as says the prophet,

49 The heaven is my throne and the earth the footstool of my feet: what house will you build me? says the Lord, or where [is the] place of my rest?

50 has not my hand made all these things?

51 O stiffnecked and uncircumcised in heart and ears, you do always resist the Holy Spirit; as your fathers, you also.

52 Which of the prophets have not your fathers persecuted? and they have slain those who announced beforehand concerning the coming of the Just One, of whom you have now become deliverers up and murderers!

53 who have received the law as ordained by the ministry of angels, and have not kept it

54 And hearing these things they were cut to the heart, and gnashed their teeth against him.

55 But being full of the Holy Spirit, having fixed his eyes on heaven, he saw the glory of God, and Jesus standing at the right hand of the God,

56 and said, Lo, I behold the heavens opened, and the Son of man standing at the right hand of the God.

57 And they cried out with a loud voice, and held their ears, and rushed upon him with one accord;

58 and having cast him out of the city, they stoned him. And the witnesses laid aside their clothes at the feet of a young man called Saul.

59 And they stoned Stephen, as he was praying, and saying, Lord Jesus, receive my spirit.

60 And kneeling down, he cried with a loud voice, Lord, lay not this sin to their charge. And having said this, he fell asleep.

Acts 8:1 And Saul was approving of to his killing. And on that day there arose a great persecution against the church which was in Jerusalem, and all were scattered into the countries of Judea and Samaria except the apostles.

2 And pious men buried Stephen and made great lamentation over him.

3 But Saul ravaged the church, entering into the houses one after another, and dragging off both men and women delivered them up to prison.

4 Those then that had been scattered went through [the countries] announcing the good news of the word.

5 And Philip, going down to a city of Samaria, preached the Christ to them;

6 and the crowds with one accord gave heed to the things spoken by Philip, when they heard him and saw the signs which he worked.

7 For from many who had unclean spirits they went out, crying with a loud voice; and many that were paralysed and lame were healed.

8 And there was great joy in that city.

9 But a certain man, by name Simon, had been before in the city, using magic arts, and astonishing the nation of Samaria, saying that himself was some great one.

10 To whom they had all given heed, from small to great, saying, This is the power of the God which is called great.

11 And they gave heed to him, because that for a long time he had astonished them by his magic arts.

12 But when they believed Philip announcing the good news concerning the kingdom of the God and the name of Jesus Christ, they were baptized, both men and women.

13 And Simon also himself believed; and, having been baptized, continued constantly with Philip; and, beholding the signs and great works of power which took place, was astonished.

14 And the apostles who were in Jerusalem, having heard that Samaria had received the word of the God, sent to them Peter and John;

15 who, having come down, prayed for them that they might receive the Holy Spirit;

16 for he was not yet fallen upon any of them, only they were baptized to the name of the Lord Jesus.

17 Then they laid their hands upon them, and they received the Holy Spirit.

18 But Simon, having seen that by the laying on of the hands of the apostles the [holy] Spirit was given, offered them money,

19 saying, Give to me also this power, in order that on whomsoever I may lay hands he may receive the Holy Spirit.

20 And Peter said to him, Your money go with you to destruction, because you have thought that the gift of the God can be obtained by money.

21 You have neither part nor lot in this matter, for your heart is not upright before the God.

22 Repent therefore of this your wickedness, and supplicate the Lord, if indeed the thought of your heart may be forgiven you;

23 for I see you to be in the gall of bitterness, and bond of unrighteousness.

24 And Simon answering said, Pray for me to the Lord, so that nothing may come upon me of the things of which you have spoken.

25 They therefore, having testified and spoken the word of the Lord, returned to Jerusalem, and announced the good news to many villages of the Samaritans.

26 But the angel of the Lord spoke to Philip, saying, Rise up and go southward on the way which goes down from Jerusalem to Gaza: the same is desert.

27 And he rose up and went. And lo, an Ethiopian, a eunuch, a man in power under Candace queen of the Ethiopians, who was over all her treasure, who had come to worship at Jerusalem,

28 was returning and sitting in his chariot: and he was reading the prophet Isaiah.

29 And the Spirit said to Philip, Approach and join this chariot.

30 And Philip, running up, heard him reading the prophet Isaiah, and said, Do you then know what you are reading of?

31 And he said, How should I then be able unless some one guide me? And he begged Philip to come up and sit with him.

32 And the passage of the scripture which he read was this: He was led as a sheep to slaughter, and as a lamb is mute in presence of him that shears him, thus he opens not his mouth.

33 In his humiliation his judgment has been taken away, and who shall declare his generation? for his life is taken from the earth.

34 And the eunuch answering Philip said, I ask you, concerning whom does the prophet say this? of himself or of some other?

35 And Philip, opening his mouth and beginning from that scripture, announced the good news of Jesus to him.

36 And as they went along the way, they came upon a certain water, and the eunuch says, Behold water; what hinders me being baptized?

37 [And Philip said, "If you believe with all your heart, you may." And he answered and said, "I believe that Jesus Christ is the Son of God."]

38 And he commanded the chariot to stop. And they went down both to the water, both Philip and the eunuch, and he baptized him.

39 But when they came up out of the water the Spirit of the Lord caught away Philip, and the eunuch saw him no longer, for he went on his way rejoicing.

40 And Philip was found at Azotus, and passing through he announced the good news to all the cities till he came to Caesarea.

Acts 9:1 But Saul, still breathing out threatening and slaughter against the disciples of the Lord, came to the high priest

2 and asked of him letters to Damascus, to the synagogues, so that if he found any who were of the way, both men and women, he might bring them bound to Jerusalem.

3 But as he was journeying, it came to pass that he drew near to Damascus; and suddenly there shone round about him a light out of heaven,

4 and falling on the earth he heard a voice saying to him, Saul, Saul, why do you persecute me?

5 And he said, Who are you, Lord? And he [said] I am Jesus, whom you persecute.

6 But rise up and enter into the city, and it shall be told you what you must do.

7 But the men who were traveling with him stood speechless, hearing the voice but beholding no one.

8 And Saul rose up from the earth, and his eyes being opened he saw no one. But leading him by the hand they brought him into Damascus.

9 And he was three days without seeing, and neither ate nor drank.

10 And there was a certain disciple in Damascus by name Ananias. And the Lord said to him in a vision, Ananias. And he said, Behold, [here am] I, Lord.

11 And the Lord [said] to him, Rise up and go into the street which is called Straight, and seek in the house of Judas one by name Saul, [he is] of Tarsus: for, behold, he is praying,

12 and has seen [in a vision] a man by name Ananias coming in and putting his hand on him, so that he should see.

13 And Ananias answered, Lord, I have heard from many concerning this man how much evil he has done to your saints at Jerusalem;

14 and here he has authority from the chief priests to bind all who call upon your name.

15 And the Lord said to him, Go, for this [man] is an elect vessel to me, to bear my name before both nations and kings and the sons of Israel:

16 for I will show to him how much he must suffer for my name.

17 And Ananias went and entered into the house; and laying his hands upon him he said, Saul, brother, the Lord has sent me, Jesus that appeared to you in the way in which you came, that you might see, and be filled with the Holy Spirit.

18 And straightway there fell from his eyes as it were scales, and he saw, and rising up was baptized;

19 and, having received food, got strength. And he was with the disciples who [were] in Damascus certain days.

20 And straightway in the synagogues he preached Jesus that he is the Son of the God.

21 And all who heard were astonished and said, Is not this he who destroyed in Jerusalem those who called on this name, and for this purpose, that he might bring them bound to the chief priests?

22 But Saul increased the more in power, and confounded the Jews who dwelt in Damascus, proving that this is the Christ.

23 Now when many days were fulfilled, the Jews consulted together to kill him.

24 But their plot became known to Saul. And they watched also the gates both day and night, that they might kill him;

25 but the disciples took him by night and let him down through the wall, lowering him in a basket.

26 And having arrived at Jerusalem he attempted to join himself to the disciples, and all were afraid of him, not believing that he was a disciple.

27 But Barnabas took him and brought him to the apostles, and related to them how he had seen the Lord in the way, and that he had spoken to him, and how in Damascus he had spoken boldly in the name of Jesus.

28 And he was with them coming in and going out at Jerusalem,

29 and speaking boldly in the name of the Lord. And he spoke and discussed with the Hellenists; but they sought to kill him.

30 And the brethren knowing it, brought him down to Caesarea and sent him away to Tarsus.

31 The churches then throughout the whole of Judea and Galilee and Samaria had peace, being edified and walking in the fear of the Lord, and were increased through the comfort of the Holy Spirit.

32 Now it came to pass that Peter, passing through all [quarters] descended also to the saints who inhabited Lydda.

33 And he found there a certain man, Aeneas by name, who had been lying for eight years upon a couch, who was paralyzed.

34 And Peter said to him, Aeneas, Jesus, the Christ, heals you: rise up, and make your couch for yourself. And straightway he rose up.

35 And all who inhabited Lydda and the Saron saw him, who turned to the Lord.

36 And in Joppa there was a certain female disciple, by name Tabitha, which being interpreted means Dorcas. She was full of good works and alms-deeds which she did.

37 And it came to pass in those days that she grew sick and died; and, having washed her, they put her in the upper room.

38 But Lydda being near to Joppa, the disciples having heard that Peter was there, sent two men to him, beseeching him, You must not delay coming to us.

39 And Peter rising up went with them, whom, when arrived, they brought up into the upper chamber; and all the widows stood by him weeping and showing him the body-coats and garments which Dorcas had made while she was with them.

40 But Peter, putting them all out, and kneeling down, prayed. And, turning to the body, he said, Tabitha, arise. And she opened her eyes, and, seeing Peter, sat up.

41 And having given her [his] hand, he raised her up, and having called the saints and the widows, presented her living.

42 And it became known throughout the whole of Joppa, and many believed on the Lord.

43 And it came to pass that he remained many days in Joppa with a certain Simon, a tanner.

Acts 10:1 But a certain man in Caesarea, --by name Cornelius, a centurion of the band called Italic,

2 pious, and fearing the God with all his house, [both] giving much alms to the people, and prayed to the God continually,

3 --saw plainly in a vision, about the ninth hour of the day, an angel of the God coming unto him, and saying to him, Cornelius.

4 But he, having fixed his eyes upon him, and become full of fear, said, What is it, Lord? And he said to him, Your prayers and your alms have gone up for a memorial before the God.

5 And now send men to Joppa and fetch Simon, who is surnamed Peter.

6 He lodges with a certain Simon, a tanner, whose house is by the sea.

7 And when the angel who was speaking to him had departed, having called two of his household and a pious soldier of those who were constantly with him,

8 and related all things to them, he sent them to Joppa.

9 And on the next day, as these were journeying and drawing near to the city, Peter went up on the house to pray, about the sixth hour.

10 And he became hungry and desired to eat. But as they were making ready an ecstasy came upon him:

11 and he beholds the heaven opened, and a certain vessel descending, as a great sheet, [bound] by the four corners [and] let down to the earth;

12 in which were all the quadrupeds and creeping things of the earth, and the fowls of the heaven.

13 And there was a voice to him, Rise, Peter, slay and eat.

14 And Peter said, In no way, Lord; for I have never eaten anything common or unclean.

15 And [there was] a voice again the second time to him, What the God has cleansed, do not you make unholy.

16 And this took place three times, and the vessel was straightway taken up into heaven.

17 And as Peter doubted in himself what the vision which he had seen might mean, behold also the men who were sent by Cornelius, having sought out the house of Simon, stood at the gate,

18 and having called [some one] they inquired if Simon who was surnamed Peter was lodged there.

19 But as Peter continued pondering over the vision, the Spirit said to him, Behold, three men seek you;

20 but rise up, go down, and go with them, nothing doubting, because I have sent them.

21 And Peter going down to the men said, Behold, I am he whom you seek: what is the cause for which you come?

22 And they said, Cornelius, a centurion, a righteous man, and fearing the God, and borne witness to by the whole nation of the Jews, has been divinely instructed by a holy angel to send for you to his house, and hear words from you.

23 Having therefore invited them in, he lodged them. And on the next day, rising up he went away with them, and certain of the brethren from Joppa went with him.

24 And on the next day they came to Caesarea. But Cornelius was looking for them, having called together his kinsmen and [his] intimate friends.

25 And when Peter was now coming in, Cornelius met him, and falling down did him homage.

26 But Peter made him rise, saying, Rise up: I myself also am a man.

27 And he went in, talking with him, and found many gathered together.

28 And he said to them, You know how it is unlawful for a Jew to be joined or come to one of a strange race, and to me the God has shown to call no man unholy or unclean.

29 Therefore also, having been sent for, I came without saying anything against it. I inquire therefore for what reason you have sent for me.

30 And Cornelius said, Four days ago I had been [fasting] unto this hour, and the ninth [I was]

praying in my house, and lo, a man stood before me in bright clothing,

31 and said, Cornelius, your prayer has been heard, and your alms have come in remembrance before the God.

32 Send therefore to Joppa and fetch Simon, who is surnamed Peter; he lodges in the house of Simon, a tanner, by the sea [who when he is come will speak to you].

33 Immediately therefore I sent to you, and you have well done in coming. Now therefore we are all present before the God to hear all things that are commanded you of the God.

34 And Peter opening his mouth said, Of a truth I perceive that the God is no respecter of persons,

35 but in every nation he that fears him and works righteousness is acceptable to him.

36 The word which he sent to the sons of Israel, preaching peace by Jesus Christ, he is Lord of all things,

37 you know; the testimony which has spread through the whole of Judea, beginning from Galilee after the baptism which John preached

38 --Jesus who [was] of Nazareth: how the God anointed him with the Holy Spirit and with power; who went through [all quarters] doing good, and healing all that were under the power of the devil because the God was with him.

39 We also [are] witnesses of all things which he did both in the country of the Jews and in Jerusalem; whom they also killed, having hanged him on a wood [cross].

40 This [man] the God raised up the third day and gave him to be openly seen,

41 not of all the people, but of witnesses who were chosen before of the God, us who have eaten and drunk with him after he arose from among the dead.

42 And he commanded us to preach to the people, and to testify that he it is who was appointed of the God [to be] judge of living and dead.

43 To him all the prophets bear witness that every one that believes on him will receive through his name forgiveness of sins.

44 While Peter was yet speaking these words the Holy Spirit fell upon all those who were hearing the word.

45 And the faithful of the circumcision were astonished, as many as came with Peter, that upon the nations also the gift of the Holy Spirit was poured out:

46 for they heard them speaking with tongues and magnifying the God. Then Peter answered,

47 Can any one forbid water that these should not be baptized, who have received the Holy Spirit as we also [did].

48 And he commanded them to be baptized in the name of the Lord. Then they begged him to stay some days.

Acts 11:1 And the apostles and the brethren who were in Judea heard that the nations also had received the word of the God;

2 and when Peter went up to Jerusalem, they of the circumcision contended with him,

3 saying, You visited with men uncircumcised and have eaten with them.

4 But Peter began and set forth [the matter] to them in order, saying,

5 I was in the city of Joppa praying, and in an ecstasy I saw a vision, a certain vessel descending like a great sheet, let down by four corners out of heaven, and it came even to me:

6 on which having fixed mine eyes, I considered, and saw the quadrupeds of the earth, and the wild beasts, and the creeping things, and the fowls of the heaven.

7 And I heard also a voice saying to me, Rise up, Peter, slay and eat.

8 And I said, In no way, Lord, for unholy or unclean has never entered into my mouth.

9 And a voice answered the second time out of heaven, What the God has cleansed, do not you make unholy.

10 And this took place three times, and again all was drawn up into heaven;

11 and lo, immediately three men were at the house in which I was, sent to me from Caesarea.

12 And the Spirit said to me to go with them, without misgivings. And there went with me these six brethren also, and we entered into the house of the man,

13 and he related to us how he had seen the angel in his house, standing and saying [to him] Send [men] to Joppa and fetch Simon, who is surnamed Peter,

14 who shall speak words to you whereby you shall be saved, you and all your house.

15 And as I began to speak, the Holy Spirit fell upon them even as upon us also at the beginning.

16 And I remembered the word of the Lord, how he said, John baptized with water, but you shall be baptized with the Holy Spirit.

17 If then the God has given them the same gift as also to us when we had believed on the Lord Jesus Christ, who indeed was I to be able to forbid the God?

18 And when they heard these things they held their peace, and glorified the God, saying, Then indeed the God has to the Gentiles also granted repentance to life.

19 They then who had been scattered abroad through the tribulation that took place on the occasion of Stephen, passed through [the country] to Phoenicia and Cyprus and Antioch, speaking the word to no one but to Jews alone.

20 But there were certain of them, Cyprians and Cyrenians, who entering into Antioch spoke to the Greeks also, announcing the good news of the Lord Jesus.

21 And the Lord's hand was with them, and a great number believed and turned to the Lord.

22 And the report concerning them reached the ears of the church which was in Jerusalem, and they sent out Barnabas to go through as far as Antioch:

23 who, having arrived and seeing the grace of the God, rejoiced, and urged all with purpose of heart to abide with the Lord;

24 for he was a good man and full of the Holy Spirit and of faith; and a large crowd [of people] were added to the Lord.

25 And he went away to Tarsus to seek out Saul.

26 And having found him he brought him to Antioch. And so it was with them that for a whole year they were gathered together in the church and taught a large crowd: and the disciples were first called Christians in Antioch.

27 Now in these days prophets went down from Jerusalem to Antioch;

28 and one from among them, by name Agabus, rose up and signified by the Spirit that there was going to be a great famine over all the inhabited earth, which also came to pass under Claudius.

29 And they determined, according as any one of the disciples was well off, each of them to send to the brethren who dwelt in Judea, to minister [to them]

30 which also they did, sending it to the elders by the hand of Barnabas and Saul.

Acts 12:1 At that time Herod the king laid his hands on some of those of the church to do them hurt,

2 and killed James, the brother of John, with the sword.

3 And seeing that it was pleasing to the Jews, he went on to take Peter also: and they were the days of unleavened bread:

4 whom having seized he put in prison, having delivered him to four squads of soldiers to keep, purposing after the Passover to bring him out to the people.

5 Peter therefore was kept in the prison; but unceasing prayer was made by the church toward the God concerning him.

6 And when Herod was going to bring him forth, that night Peter was sleeping between two soldiers, bound with two chains, and guards before the door kept the prison.

7 And lo, an angel of the Lord came there, and a light shone in the prison: and having struck the side of Peter, he roused him up, saying, Rise up quickly. And his chains fell off his hands.

8 And the angel said to him, Gird yourself, and bind on your sandals. And he did so. And he says to him, Cast your upper garment about you and follow me.

9 And going forth he followed him and did not know that what was happening by means of the angel was real, but supposed he saw a vision.

10 And having passed through a first and second guard, they came to the iron gate which leads into the city, which opened to them of itself; and going forth they went down one street, and immediately the angel left him.

11 And Peter, being come to himself, said, Now I know certainly that the Lord has sent forth his angel and has taken me out of the hand of Herod and all the expectation of the people of the Jews.

12 And having become clearly conscious [in himself] he came to the house of Mary, the mother of John who was surnamed Mark, where were many gathered together and praying.

13 And when he had knocked at the door of the entry, a maid came to listen, by name Rhoda;

14 and having recognized the voice of Peter, through joy did not open the entry, but running in, reported that Peter was standing before the entry.

15 And they said to her, You are mad. But she maintained that it was so. And they said, It is his angel.

16 But Peter continued knocking: and having opened, they saw him and were astonished.

17 And having made a sign to them with his hand to be silent, he related [to them] how the Lord had brought him out of prison; and he said, Report these things to James and to the brethren. And he went out and went to another place.

18 And when it was day there was no small disturbance among the soldiers, what then had become of Peter.

19 And Herod having sought him and not found him, having examined the guards, commanded [them] to be executed. And he went down from Judea to Caesarea and stayed [there]

20 And he was in bitter hostility with the Tyrians and Sidonians; but they came to him with one accord, and, having gained Blastus the king's chamberlain, sought peace, because their country was nourished by the king's.

21 And on a set day, clothed in royal apparel and sitting on the elevated seat [of honor] Herod made a public oration to them.

22 And the people cried out, A god's voice and not a man's.

23 And immediately an angel of the Lord smote him, because he did not give the glory to the God, and he expired, eaten of worms.

24 But the word of the God grew and spread itself.

25 And Barnabas and Saul returned from Jerusalem, having fulfilled the service [entrusted to them] taking also with them John, surnamed Mark.

Acts 13:1 Now there were in Antioch, in the church which was [there] prophets and teachers: Barnabas, and Simeon who was called Niger, and Lucius the Cyrenian, and Manaen, foster-brother of Herod the tetrarch, and Saul.

2 And as they were ministering to the Lord and fasting, the Holy Spirit said, Separate me now Barnabas and Saul for the work to which I have called them.

3 Then, having fasted and prayed, and having laid [their] hands on them, they let [them] go.

4 They therefore, having been sent forth by the Holy Spirit, went down to Seleucia, and from there sailed away to Cyprus.

5 And being in Salamis, they announced the word of the God in the synagogues of the Jews. And they had John also as [their] attendant.

6 And having passed through the whole island as far as Paphos, they found a certain man a magician, a false prophet, a Jew, whose name was Bar-jesus,

7 who was with the proconsul Sergius Paulus, a wise man. He, having called Barnabas and Saul to him desired to hear the word of the God.

8 But Elymas the magician (for so his name is by interpretation) opposed them, seeking to turn away the proconsul from the faith.

9 But Saul, who also is Paul, filled with the Holy Spirit, fixing his eyes upon him,

10 said, O full of all deceit and all craft: son of the daemon, enemy of all righteousness; will you not cease perverting the right paths of the Lord?

11 And now behold, the Lord's hand is upon you, and you shall be blind, not seeing the sun for a season. And immediately there fell upon him a mist and darkness; and going about he sought persons who should lead him by the hand.

12 Then the proconsul, seeing what had happened, believed, being amazed at the doctrine of the Lord.

13 And having sailed from Paphos, Paul and his company came to Perga of Pamphylia; and John separated from them and returned to Jerusalem.

14 But they, passing through from Perga, came to Antioch of Pisidia; and entering into the synagogue on the sabbaths they sat down.

15 And after the reading of the law and the prophets, the rulers of the synagogue sent to them, saying, Brethren, if you have any word of exhortation to the people, speak.

16 And Paul, rising up and making a sign with the hand, said, Israelites, and you that fear the God, listen.

17 God of this people Israel chose our fathers, and exalted the people in their sojourn in the land of Egypt, and with a high arm brought them out of it,

18 and for a time of about forty years he nursed them in the desert.

19 And having destroyed seven nations in the land of Canaan, he gave them their land as an inheritance.

20 And after these things he gave [them] judges till Samuel the prophet, [to the end of] about four hundred and fifty years.

21 And then they asked for a king, and the God gave to them Saul, son of Kis, a man of the tribe of Benjamin, during forty years.

22 And having removed him he raised up to them David for king, of whom also bearing witness he said, I have found David, the son of Jesse, a man after my heart, who shall do all my will.

23 Of this man's seed according to promise has the God brought to Israel a Savior, Jesus;

24 John having proclaimed before the face of his entry [among the people] the baptism of repentance to all the people of Israel.

25 And as John was fulfilling his course he said, Whom do you suppose that I am? I am not he. But behold, there comes one after me, the sandal of whose feet I am not worthy to loose.

26 Brethren, sons of Abraham's race, and those who among you fear the God, to you has the word of this salvation been sent:

27 for those who dwell in Jerusalem, and their rulers, not having known him, have fulfilled also the voices of the prophets which are read on every Sabbath, [by] judging him.

28 And having found no cause of death [in him] they begged of Pilate that he might be slain.

29 And when they had fulfilled all things written concerning him, they took him down from the wood [cross] and put him in a tomb;

30 but the God raised him from among the dead,

31 who appeared for many days to those who had come up with him from Galilee to Jerusalem, who are now his witnesses to the people.

32 And we declare unto you the good news of the promise made to the fathers,

33 that the God has fulfilled this to us their children, having raised up Jesus; as it is also written in the second psalm, You are my Son: this day have I begotten you.

34 But that he raised him from among the dead, no more to return to corruption, he spoke thus: I will give to you the faithful mercies of David.

35 Therefore also he says in another, You will not permit your holy one to see corruption.

36 For David indeed, having in his own generation ministered to the will of the God, fell asleep, and was added to his fathers and saw corruption.

37 But he whom the God raised up did not see corruption.

38 Be it known unto you, therefore, brethren, that through this man forgiveness of sins is preached to you,

39 and from all things from which you could not be justified in the law of Moses, in him every one that believes is justified.

40 See therefore that that which is spoken in the prophets do not come upon you.

41 Behold, you despisers, and wonder and perish; for I work a work in your days, a work which you will in no way believe if one declare it to you.

42 And as they went out they begged that these words might be spoken to them the next Sabbath.

43 And the congregation of the synagogue having broken up, many of the Jews and of the worshipping proselytes followed Paul and Barnabas, who speaking to them, persuaded them to continue in the grace of the God.

44 And on the coming Sabbath almost all the city was gathered together to hear the word of the God.

45 But the Jews, seeing the crowds, were filled with envy, and contradicted the things said by Paul, [contradicting and] speaking injuriously.

46 And Paul and Barnabas spoke boldly and said, It was necessary that the word of the God should be first spoken to you; but, since you thrust it from you, and judge yourselves unworthy of aeonian life, lo, we turn to the nations;

47 for thus has the Lord commanded us: I have set you for a light of the nations, that you should be for salvation to the end of the earth.

48 And [those of] the nations, hearing it, rejoiced, and glorified the word of the Lord, and believed, as many as were ordained to aeonian life.

49 And the word of the Lord was carried through the whole country.

50 But the Jews excited the women of the upper classes who were worshippers, and the first people of the city, and raised a persecution against Paul and Barnabas, and cast them out of their coasts.

51 But they, having shaken off the dust of their feet against them, came to Iconium.

52 And the disciples were filled with joy and the Holy Spirit.

Acts 14:1 And it came to pass in Iconium that they entered together into the synagogue of the Jews, and so spoke that a great multitude of both Jews and Greeks believed.

2 But the Jews who did not believe stirred up the souls of [those of] the nations and made [them] embittered against the brethren.

3 They stayed therefore a good while, speaking boldly, [confiding] in the Lord, who gave witness to the word of his grace, giving signs and wonders to be done by their hands.

4 And the multitude of the city was divided, and some were with the Jews and some with the apostles.

5 And when an assault was making, both of [those of] the nations and the Jews with their rulers, to do them ill and stone them,

6 they, being aware of it, fled to the cities of Lycaonia, Lystra and Derbe, and the surrounding country,

7 and there they were announcing the good news.

8 And a certain man in Lystra, impotent in his feet, sat, [being] lame from his mother's womb, who had never walked.

9 This [man] heard Paul speaking, who, fixing his eyes on him, and seeing that he had faith to be healed,

10 said with a loud voice, Rise up straight upon your feet: and he sprang up and walked.

11 But the crowds, who saw what Paul had done, lifted up their voices in Lycaonian, saying, The gods, having made themselves like men, are come down to us.

12 And they called Barnabas Jupiter, and Paul Mercury, because he took the lead in speaking.

13 And the priest of Jupiter who was before the city, having brought bulls and wreaths to the gates, would have done sacrifice along with the crowds.

14 But the apostles Barnabas and Paul, having heard it tore their garments, and rushed out to the crowd, crying

15 and saying, Men, why do you do these things? We also are men of like passions with you, preaching to you to turn from these vanities to the living the God, who made the heaven, and the earth, and the sea, and all things in them;

16 who in the past generations permitted all the nations to go in their own ways,

17 though indeed he did not leave himself without witness, doing good, and giving to you from heaven rain and fruitful seasons, filling your hearts with food and gladness.

18 And saying these things, they with difficulty kept the crowds from sacrificing to them.

19 But there came Jews from Antioch and Iconium, and having persuaded the crowds and stoned Paul, drew him out of the city, supposing him to have died.

20 But while the disciples encircled him, he rose up and entered into the city. And on the next day he went away with Barnabas to Derbe.

21 And having announced the good news to that city, and having made many disciples, they returned to Lystra, and Iconium, and Antioch,

22 establishing the souls of the disciples, urging them to abide in the faith, and that through many tribulations we must enter into the kingdom of the God.

23 And having chosen them elders in each church, having prayed with fasting, they committed them to the Lord, on whom they had believed.

24 And having passed through Pisidia they came to Pamphylia,

25 and having spoken the word in Perga, they came down to Attalia;

26 and from there they sailed away to Antioch, from where they had been committed to the grace of the God for the work which they had fulfilled.

27 And having arrived, and having brought together the church, they related to them all that the God had done with them, and that he had opened a door of faith to the Gentiles.

28 And they stayed no little time with the disciples.

Acts 15:1 And certain persons, having come down from Judea, taught the brethren, If you shall not have been circumcised according to the custom of Moses, you cannot be saved.

2 A commotion therefore having taken place, and no small discussion on the part of Paul and Barnabas against them, they arranged that Paul and Barnabas, and certain others from among them, should go up to Jerusalem to the apostles and elders about this question.

3 They therefore, having been set on their way by the church, passed through Phoenicia and Samaria, relating the conversion of [those of] the nations. And they caused great joy to all the brethren.

4 And being arrived at Jerusalem, they were received by the church, and the apostles, and the elders, and related all that the God had worked with them.

5 And some of those who were of the sect of the Pharisees, who believed, rose up from among [them]

saying that they ought to circumcise them and enjoin them to keep the law of Moses.

6 And the apostles and the elders were gathered together to see about this matter.

7 And much discussion having taken place, Peter, standing up, said to them, Brethren, you know that from the earliest days the God among you chose that the nations by my mouth should hear the word of the good news and believe.

8 And the heart-knowing God bore them witness, giving them the Holy Spirit as to us also,

9 and put no difference between us and them, having purified their hearts by faith.

10 Now therefore why tempt you the God, by putting a yoke upon the neck of the disciples, which neither our fathers nor we have been able to bear?

11 But we believe that we shall be saved by the grace of the Lord Jesus, in the same manner as they also.

12 And all the multitude kept silence and listened to Barnabas and Paul relating all the signs and wonders which the God had worked among the Gentiles by them.

13 And after they had held their peace, James answered, saying, Brethren, listen to me:

14 Simon has related how the God first visited to take out of the nations a people for his name.

15 And with this agree the words of the prophets; as it is written:

16 After these things I will return, and will rebuild the tabernacle of David which is fallen, and will rebuild its ruins, and will set it up,

17 so that the residue of men may seek out the Lord, and all the nations on whom my name is invoked, says the Lord, who does these things

18 known from the aeon (past).

19 Therefore I judge, not to trouble those who from the nations turn to the God;

20 but to write to them to abstain from pollutions of idols, and from fornication, and from what is strangled, and from blood.

21 For Moses, from generations of old, has in every city those who preach him, being read in the synagogues every Sabbath.

22 Then it seemed good to the apostles and to the elders, with the whole church, to send chosen men from among them with Paul and Barnabas to Antioch, Judas called Barsabas and Silas, leading men among the brethren,

23 having by their hand written [thus] The apostles, and the elders, and the brethren, to the brethren who are from among the nations at Antioch, and [in] Syria and Cilicia, greeting:

24 Inasmuch as we have heard that some who went out from among us have troubled you by words, upsetting your souls, [saying that you must be circumcised and keep the law] to whom we gave no commandment;

25 it seemed good to us, having arrived at a common judgment, to send chosen men to you with our beloved Barnabas and Paul,

26 men who have given up their souls for the name of our Lord Jesus Christ.

27 We have therefore sent Judas and Silas, who themselves also will tell you by word [of mouth] the same things.

28 For it has seemed good to the Holy Spirit and to us to lay upon you no greater burden than these necessary things:

29 to abstain from things sacrificed to idols, and from blood, and from what is strangled, and from fornication; keeping yourselves from which you will do well. Farewell.

30 They therefore, being let go, came to Antioch, and having gathered the multitude delivered to [them] the epistle.

31 And having read it, they rejoiced at the consolation.

32 And Judas and Silas, being themselves also prophets, urged the brethren with much discourse, and strengthened them.

33 And having passed some time [there] they were let go in peace from the brethren to those who sent them.

34 [But it seemed good to Silas to remain there.]

35 And Paul and Barnabas stayed in Antioch, teaching and announcing the good news, with many others also, of the word of the Lord.

36 But after certain days Paul said to Barnabas, Let us return now and visit the brethren in every city where we have announced the word of the Lord, [and see] how they are getting on.

37 And Barnabas proposed to take with [them] John also, called Mark;

38 but Paul thought it not well to take with them him who had abandoned them, [going back] from Pamphylia, and had not gone with them to the work.

39 There arose therefore a sharp disagreement, so that they separated from one another; and Barnabas taking Mark sailed away to Cyprus;

40 but Paul having chosen Silas went forth, committed by the brethren to the grace of the God.

41 And he passed through Syria and Cilicia, confirming the churches.

Acts 16:1 And he came to Derbe and Lystra: and behold, a certain disciple was there, by name Timothy, son of a Jewish believing woman, but his father a Greek,

2 who had a [good] testimony of the brethren in Lystra and Iconium.

3 Him would Paul have go forth with him, and took [him and] circumcised him on account of the Jews who were in those places, for they all knew his father that he was a Greek.

4 And as they passed through the cities they instructed them to observe the decrees determined on by the apostles and elders who were in Jerusalem.

5 The churches therefore were confirmed in the faith, and increased in number every day.

6 And having passed through Phrygia and the Galatian country, having been forbidden by the Holy Spirit to speak the word in Asia,

7 having come down to Mysia, they attempted to go to Biyournia, but the Spirit of Jesus did not allow them;

8 and having passed by Mysia they descended to Troas.

9 And a vision appeared to Paul in the night: There was a certain Macedonian man, standing and beseeching him, and saying, Pass over into Macedonia and help us.

10 And when he had seen the vision, immediately we sought to go forth to Macedonia, concluding that the Lord had called us to announce to them the good news.

11 Having sailed therefore away from Troas, we went in a straight course to Samothracia, and on the next day to Neapolis,

12 and from there to Philippi, which is the first city of that part of Macedonia, a colony. And we were staying in that city certain days.

13 And on the sabbaths we went outside the gate by the river, where it was the custom for prayer to be, and we sat down and spoke to the women who had assembled.

14 And a certain woman, by name Lydia, a seller of purple, of the city of Thyatira, who worshiped the God, heard; whose heart the Lord opened to attend to the things spoken by Paul.

15 And when she had been baptized and her house, she besought [us] saying, If you have judged me to be faithful to the Lord, come into my house and abide [there]. And she constrained us.

16 And it came to pass as we were going to prayer that a certain female slave, having a spirit of Python, met us, who brought much profit to her masters by prophesying.

17 She, having followed Paul and us, cried saying, These men are servants of the Most High God, who announce to you the way of salvation.

18 And this she did many days. And Paul, being distressed, turned, and said to the spirit, I enjoin you in the name of Jesus Christ to come out of her. And it came out the same hour.

19 And her masters, seeing that the hope of their gains was gone, having seized Paul and Silas, dragged [them] into the market before the magistrates;

20 and having brought them up to the magistrates, said, These men utterly trouble our city, being Jews,

21 and announce customs which it is not lawful for us to receive nor practice, being Romans.

22 And the crowd rose up too against them; and the magistrates having torn off their clothes, commanded to scourge them.

23 And having laid many stripes upon them they cast [them] into prison, charging the jailor to keep them safely;

24 who, having received such a charge, cast them into the inner prison, and secured their feet to the stocks.

25 And at midnight Paul and Silas, in praying, were praising the God with singing, and the prisoners listened to them.

26 And suddenly there was a great earthquake, so that the foundations of the prison shook, and all the doors were immediately opened, and the bonds of all loosened.

27 And the jailor being awakened out of his sleep, and seeing the doors of the prison opened, having drawn a sword was going to kill himself, thinking the prisoners had fled.

28 But Paul called out with a loud voice, saying, Do yourself no harm, for we are all here.

29 And having asked for lights, he rushed in, and, trembling, fell down before Paul and Silas.

30 And leading them out said, Sirs, what must I do that I may be saved?

31 And they said, Believe on the Lord Jesus and you shall be saved, you and your house.

32 And they spoke to him the word of the Lord, with all that were in his house.

33 And he took them the same hour of the night and washed [them] from their stripes; and was baptized, he and all his straightaway.

34 And having brought them into his house he laid the table [for them] and rejoiced with all his house, having believed in God.

35 And when it was day, the magistrates sent the officers saying, Let those men go.

36 And the jailor reported these words to Paul: The magistrates have sent that you may be let go. Now therefore go out and depart in peace.

37 But Paul said to them, Having beaten us publicly without a trial, us who are Romans, they have cast us into prison, and now they thrust us out secretly? no, indeed, but let them come themselves and bring us out.

38 And the officers reported these words to the magistrates. And they were afraid when they heard they were Romans.

39 And they came and besought them, and having brought them out, asked them to go out of the city.

40 And having gone out of the prison, they came to Lydia; and having seen the brethren, they urged them and went away.

Acts 17:1 And having journeyed through Amphipolis and Apollonia, they came to Thessalonica, where was the synagogue of the Jews.

2 And according to Paul's custom he went in among them, and on three sabbaths reasoned with them from the scriptures,

3 opening and laying down that the Christ must have suffered and risen up from among the dead, and that this is the Christ, Jesus whom I announce to you.

4 And some of them believed, and joined themselves to Paul and Silas, and of the Greeks who worshiped, a great multitude, and of the chief women not a few.

5 But the Jews having been stirred up to jealousy, and taken to [themselves] certain wicked men of the lowest uproar, and having got a crowd together, set the city in confusion; and having beset

the house of Jason sought to bring them out to the people;

6 and not having found them, dragged Jason and certain brethren before the politarchs, crying out, These [men] that have set the world in tumult, are come here also,

7 whom Jason has received; and these all do contrary to the decrees of Caesar, saying, that there is another king, Jesus.

8 And they troubled the crowd and the politarchs when they heard these things.

9 And having taken security of Jason and the rest, they let them go.

10 But the brethren immediately sent away, in the night, Paul and Silas to Berea; who, being arrived, went away into the synagogue of the Jews.

11 And these were more noble than those in Thessalonica, receiving the word with all readiness of mind, daily searching the scriptures if these things were so.

12 Therefore many from among them believed, and of Grecian women of the upper classes and men not a few.

13 But when the Jews from Thessalonica knew that the word of the God was announced in Berea also by Paul, they came there also, stirring up the crowds.

14 And then immediately the brethren sent away Paul to go as to the sea; but Silas and Timothy abode there.

15 But they that conducted Paul brought him as far as Athens; and, having received a commandment to Silas and Timothy, that they should come to him as quickly as possible, they departed.

16 But in Athens, while Paul was waiting for them, his spirit was painfully excited in him seeing the city given up to idolatry.

17 He reasoned therefore in the synagogue with the Jews, and those who worshiped, and in the market-place every day with those he met with.

18 But some also of the Epicurean and Stoic philosophers were conversing with him. And some said, What would this chatterer say? and some, He seems to be an announcer of foreign daemons, because he announced the good news of Jesus and the resurrection [to them]

19 And having taken hold on him they brought him to Areopagus, saying, Might we know what is this new doctrine which is spoken by you.

20 For you bring certain strange things to our ears. We wish therefore to know what these things may mean.

21 Now all the Athenians and the strangers sojourning there spent their time in nothing else than to tell and to hear the news.

22 And Paul standing in the midst of Areopagus said, Athenians, in every way I see you given up to daemon worship;

23 for, passing through and beholding your shrines, I found also an altar on which was inscribed, To the unknown God. Whom therefore you reverence, not knowing him, him I announce to you.

24 God who has made the world and all things which are in it, he, being Lord of heaven and earth, does not dwell in temples made with hands,

25 nor is served by men's hands as needing something, himself giving to all life and breath and all things;

26 and has made of one blood every nation of men to dwell upon the whole face of the earth, having determined their appointed times and boundaries of their dwelling,

27 that they may seek the God; if indeed they might feel after him and find him, although he is not far from each one of us:

28 for in him we live and move and exist; as also some of the poets among you have said, For we are also his family [race; offspring; kindred].

29 Being then the children of God, we ought not to think that the Godhood is like gold or silver or stone, an image formed by the art and thought of man.

30 the God therefore, having overlooked the times of ignorance, now declaring to men that they shall all everywhere repent.

31 because he has set a day in which he is going to judge the habitable earth in righteousness by the man whom he has appointed, giving the proof [of it] to all [in], having raised him from among the dead.

32 And when they heard [of the] resurrection of the dead, some mocked, and some said, We will hear you again also concerning this.

33 Thus Paul went out of their midst.

34 But some men joining themselves to him believed; among whom also was Dionysius the Areopagite, and a woman by name Damaris, and others with them.

Acts 18:1 And after these things, having left Athens, he came to Corinth;

2 and finding a certain Jew by name Aquila, of Pontus by race, just come from Italy, and Priscilla his wife, because Claudius had ordered all the Jews to leave Rome, came to them,

3 and because they were of the same trade abode with them, and worked. For they were tent-makers by trade.

4 And he reasoned in the synagogue every Sabbath, and persuaded Jews and Greeks.

5 And when both Silas and Timothy came down from Macedonia, Paul was pressed in respect of the word, testifying to the Jews that Jesus was the Christ.

6 But as they opposed and spoke injuriously, he shook his clothes, and said to them, Your blood be upon your own head: I am pure; from henceforth I will go to the nations.

7 And departing from there he came to the house of a certain [man] by name Justus, who worshiped the God, whose house adjoined the synagogue.

8 But Crispus the ruler of the synagogue believed in the Lord with all his house; and many of the Corinthians hearing, believed, and were baptized.

9 And the Lord said by vision in the night to Paul, Fear not, but speak and be not silent;

10 because I am with you, and no one shall set upon you to injure you; because I have much people in this city.

11 And he remained [there] a year and six months, teaching among them the word of the God.

12 But when Gallio was proconsul of Achaia, the Jews with one consent rose against Paul and led him to the judgment-seat,

13 saying, This [man] persuades men to worship the God contrary to the law.

14 But as Paul was going to open his mouth, Gallio said to the Jews, If indeed it was some wrong or wicked criminality, O Jews, of reason I should have borne with you;

15 but if it be questions about words, and names, and the law that you have, see to it yourselves; [for] I do not intend to be judge of these things.

16 And he drove them from the judgment-seat.

17 And having all laid hold on Sosthenes the ruler of the synagogue, they beat him before the judgment-seat. And Gallio troubled himself about none of these things.

18 And Paul, having yet stayed [there] many days, took leave of the brethren and sailed from there to Syria, and with him Priscilla and Aquila, having shorn his head in Cenchrea, for he had a vow;

19 and he arrived at Ephesus, and left them there. But entering himself into the synagogue he reasoned with the Jews.

20 And when they asked him that he would remain for a longer time [with them] he did not accede,

21 but bade them farewell, saying, [I must by all means keep the coming feast at Jerusalem]. I will return to you again, if the God wills it: and he sailed away from Ephesus.

22 And landing at Caesarea, and having gone up and saluted the church, he went down to Antioch.

23 And having stayed [there] some time, he went forth, passing in order through the country of Galatia and Phrygia, establishing all the disciples.

24 But a certain Jew, Apollos by name, an Alexandrian by race, an eloquent man, who was mighty in the scriptures, arrived at Ephesus.

25 He was instructed in the way of the Lord, and being fervent in his spirit, he spoke and taught exactly the things concerning Jesus, knowing only the baptism of John.

26 And he began to speak boldly in the synagogue. And Aquila and Priscilla, having heard him, took him to [them] and unfolded to him the way of the God more exactly.

27 And when he purposed to go into Achaia, the brethren wrote to the disciples engaging them to receive him, who, having come, contributed much to those who believed through grace.

28 For he with great force convinced the Jews publicly, showing by the scriptures that Jesus was the Christ.

Acts 19:1 And it came to pass, while Apollos was at Corinth, Paul, having passed through the upper districts, came to Ephesus, and finding certain disciples,

2 he said to them, Did you receive the Holy Spirit when you had believed? And they [said] to him, No, we have not even heard whether there is a Holy Spirit.

3 And he said, To what then were you baptized? And they said, To the baptism of John.

4 And Paul said, John indeed baptized [with] the baptism of repentance saying to the people that they should believe on him that was coming after him, that is, on Jesus.

5 And when they heard that, they were baptized to the name of the Lord Jesus.

6 And Paul having laid [his] hands on them, the Holy Spirit came upon them, and they spoke with tongues and prophesied.

7 And all the men were about twelve.

8 And entering into the synagogue, he spoke boldly during three months, reasoning and persuading [the things] concerning the kingdom of the God.

9 But when some were hardened and disbelieved, speaking evil of the way before the multitude, he left them and separated the disciples, reasoning daily in the school of Tyrannus.

10 And this took place for two years, so that all that inhabited Asia heard the word of the Lord, both Jews and Greeks.

11 And the God worked no ordinary miracles by the hands of Paul,

12 so that even napkins or aprons were brought from his body [and put] upon the sick, and the diseases left them, and the wicked spirits went out.

13 And certain of the Jewish exorcists also, who went about, took in hand to call upon those who had wicked spirits the name of the Lord Jesus, saying, I adjure you by Jesus, whom Paul preaches.

14 And there were certain [men] seven sons of Sceva, Jewish high priest, who were doing this.

15 But the wicked spirit answering said to them, Jesus I know, and Paul I am acquainted with; but you, who are you?

16 And the man in whom the wicked spirit was leaped upon them, and having mastered both, prevailed against them, so that they fled out of that house naked and wounded.

17 And this became known to all, both Jews and Greeks, who inhabited Ephesus, and fear fell upon all of them, and the name of the Lord Jesus was magnified.

18 And many of those that believed came acknowledging and declaring their deeds.

19 And many of those that practiced curious arts brought their books [of charms] and burnt them before all. And they reckoned up the prices of them, and found it fifty thousand pieces of silver.

20 Thus with might the word of the Lord increased and prevailed.

21 And when these things were fulfilled, Paul purposed in his spirit to go to Jerusalem, passing

through Macedonia and Achaia, saying, After I have been there I must see Rome also.

22 And having sent into Macedonia two of those ministering to him, Timothy and Erastus, he remained himself awhile in Asia.

23 And there took place at that time no small disturbance about the way.

24 For a certain [man] by name Demetrius, a silver-beater, making silver temples of Artemis, brought no small gain to the artisans;

25 whom having brought together, and those who worked in such things, he said, Men, you know that our well-living arises from this work,

26 and you see and hear that this Paul has persuaded and turned away a great crowd, not only of Ephesus, but almost of all Asia, saying that they are no gods which are made with hands.

27 Now not only there is danger for us that our business come into discredit, but also that the temple of the great goddess Artemis be counted for nothing, and that her greatness should be destroyed whom the whole of Asia and the world reveres.

28 And having heard [this] and being filled with rage, they cried out, saying, Great is Artemis of the Ephesians.

29 And the [whole] city was filled with confusion, and they rushed with one accord to the theater, having seized and carried off with [them] Gaius and Aristarchus, Macedonians, fellow-travelers of Paul.

30 But Paul intending to go in to the people, the disciples permitted him not;

31 and some of the Asiarchs also, who were his friends, sent to him and urged him not to throw himself into the theater.

32 Different persons therefore cried out some different thing; for the assembly was tumultuous, and the most did not know for what cause they had come together.

33 But from among the crowd they put forward Alexander, the Jews pushing him forward. And Alexander, beckoning with his hand, would have made a defense to the people.

34 But, recognizing that he was a Jew, there was one cry from all, shouting for about two hours, Great is Artemis of the Ephesians.

35 And the town clerk, having quieted the crowd, said, Ephesians, what man is there then who does not know that the city of the Ephesians is temple-keeper of Artemis the great, and of the [image] which fell down from heaven?

36 These things therefore being undeniable, it is necessary that you should be calm and do nothing rash.

37 For you have brought these men, [who are] neither temple-plunderers, nor do speak blasphemous of your goddess.

38 If therefore Demetrius and the artisans who [are] with him have a matter against any one, the courts are being held, and there are proconsuls: let them accuse one another.

39 But if you inquire anything concerning other matters, it will be settled in the regular assembly.

40 For also we are in danger to be put in accusation for sedition for this [affair] of today, no cause existing in reference to which we shall be able to give a reason for this concourse.

41 And having said these things, he dismissed the assembly.

Acts 20:1 But after the tumult had ceased, Paul having called the disciples to him, and embraced them went away to go to Macedonia.

2 And having passed through those parts, and having urged them with much discourse, he came to Greece.

3 And having spent three months [there] a treacherous plot against him having been set on foot by the Jews, as he was going to sail to Syria, the resolution was adopted of returning through Macedonia.

4 And there accompanied him as far as Asia, Sopater [son] of Pyrrhus, a Berean; and of Thessalonians, Aristarchus and Secundus, and Gaius and Timothy of Derbe, and of Asia, Tychicus and Trophimus.

5 These going before waited for us in Troas;

6 but we sailed away from Philippi after the days of unleavened bread, and we came to them to Troas in five days, where we spent seven days.

7 And in one of the sabbaths, we being assembled to break bread, Paul discoursed to them, about to depart on the next day. And he prolonged the discourse till midnight.

8 And there were many lights in the upper room where we were assembled.

9 And a certain youth, by name Eutychus, sitting at the window-opening, overpowered by deep sleep, while Paul discoursed very much at length, having been overpowered by the sleep, fell from the third story down to the bottom, and was taken up dead.

10 But Paul descending fell upon him, and enfolding him [in his arms], said, Be not troubled, for his soul is in him.

11 And having gone up, and having broken the bread, and eaten, and having long spoken until daybreak, so he went away.

12 And they took the boy away alive, and were greatly comforted.

13 And we, having gone before on board ship, sailed off to Assos, going to take in Paul there; for so he had directed, he himself being about to go on foot.

14 And when he met with us at Assos, having taken him on board, we came to Mitylene;

15 and having sailed from there, on the next day arrived opposite Chios, and the next day put in at Samos; and having stayed at Trogyllium, the next day we came to Miletus:

16 for Paul thought it desirable to sail by Ephesus, so that he might not be made to spend time in Asia; for he hastened, if it was possible for him, to be in Jerusalem on the day of the Pentecost.

17 But from Miletus having sent to Ephesus, he called over [to him] the elders of the church.

18 And when they were come to him, he said to them, You know how I was with you all the time from the first day that I arrived in Asia,

19 serving the Lord with all lowliness, and tears, and trials, which happened to me through the plots of the Jews;

20 how I held back nothing of what is profitable, so as not to announce it to you, and to teach you publicly and in every house,

21 testifying to both Jews and Greeks repentance towards the God, and faith towards our Lord Jesus Christ.

22 And now, behold, bound in my spirit I go to Jerusalem, not knowing what things shall happen to me in it;

23 only that the Holy Spirit testifies to me in every city, saying that bonds and tribulations await me.

24 But I make no account of my soul as dear to myself, so that I finish my course, and the ministry which I have received of the Lord Jesus, to testify the good news of the grace of the God.

25 And now, behold, I know that you all, among whom I have gone about preaching the kingdom [of god] shall see my face no more.

26 Therefore I witness to you this day, that I am clean from the blood of all,

27 for I have not shrunk from announcing to you all the counsel of the God.

28 Take heed therefore to yourselves, and to all the flock, wherein the Holy Spirit has set you as overseers, to shepherd the church of the God, which he has purchased with the blood of his own.

29 For I know this that there will come in among you after my departure grievous wolves, not sparing the flock;

30 and from among your own selves shall rise up men speaking perverted things to draw away the disciples after them.

31 Therefore keep awake, remembering that for three years, night and day, I ceased not admonishing each one [of you] with tears.

32 And now I commit you to the God, and to the word of his grace, which is able to build [you] up and give [to you] an inheritance among all the sanctified.

33 I have coveted the silver or gold or clothing of no one.

34 Yourselves know that these hands have ministered to my wants, and to those who were with me.

35 I have showed you all things, that thus laboring [we] ought to come in aid of the weak, and to remember the words of the Lord Jesus, that he himself said, It is more blessed to give than to receive.

36 And having said these things, he knelt down and prayed with them all.

37 And they all wept sore; and falling upon the neck of Paul they ardently kissed him,

38 specially pained by the word which he had said, that they would no more see his face. And they went down with him to the ship.

Acts 21:1 And when, having gone away from them, we at last sailed away, we came by a direct course to Cos, and on the next day to Rhodes, and from there to Patara.

2 And having found a ship passing over into Phoenicia, we went on board and sailed;

3 and having sighted Cyprus, and left it on the left hand, we sailed to Syria, and made the land at Tyre, for there the ship was to discharge her cargo.

4 And having found out the disciples, we remained there seven days; who said to Paul by the Spirit not to go up to Jerusalem.

5 But when we had completed the days, we set out and took our journey, all of them accompanying us, with wives and children, till [we were] out of the city. And kneeling down upon the shore we prayed.

6 And having embraced one another, we went on board ship, and they returned home.

7 And we, having completed the voyage, arrived from Tyre at Ptolemais, and having saluted the brethren, we remained one day with them.

8 And leaving on the next day, we came to Caesarea; and entering into the house of Philip the evangelist, who was of the seven, we abode with him.

9 Now this man had four virgin daughters who prophesied.

10 And as we stayed there many days, a certain man, by name Agabus, a prophet, came down from Judea,

11 and coming to us and taking the girdle of Paul, and having bound his own hands and feet, said, Thus says the Holy Spirit, The man whose this girdle is shall the Jews thus bind in Jerusalem, and deliver him up into the hands of the Nations.

12 And when we heard these things, both we and those of the place besought him not to go up to Jerusalem.

13 But Paul answered, What are you doing, weeping and breaking my heart? for I am ready not only to be bound, but also to die at Jerusalem for the name of the Lord Jesus.

14 And when he would not be persuaded, we were silent, saying, The will of the Lord be done.

15 And after these days, having got our effects ready, we went up to Jerusalem.

16 And [some] of the disciples from Caesarea went with us, bringing [with them] a certain Mnason, a Cyprian, an old disciple, with whom we were to lodge.

17 And when we arrived at Jerusalem the brethren gladly received us.

18 And on the next day Paul went in with us to James, and all the elders came there.

19 And having saluted them, he related one by one the things which the God had worked among the Gentiles by his ministry.

20 And they having heard it glorified the God, and said to him, You see, brother, how many myriads there are of the Jews who have believed, and all are zealous of the law.

21 And they have been informed concerning you, that you teach all the Jews among the nations

apostasy from Moses, saying that they should not circumcise their children, nor walk in the customs.

22 What is it then? a multitude must necessarily come together, for they will hear that you have come.

23 This do therefore that we say to you: We have four men who have a vow on them;

24 take these and be purified with them, and pay their expenses, that they may have their heads shaved; and all will know that [of those things] of which they have been informed about you nothing is [true], but that you yourself also walk orderly, keeping the law.

25 But concerning [those of] the nations who have believed, we have written, deciding that they should [observe no such thing, only to] keep themselves both from things offered to idols, and from blood, and from things strangled, and from fornication.

26 Then Paul, taking the men, on the next day, having been purified, entered with them into the temple, signifying the time the days of the purification would be fulfilled, until the offering was offered for every one of them.

27 And when the seven days were nearly completed, the Jews from Asia, having seen him in the temple, set all the crowd in a tumult, and laid hands upon him,

28 crying, Israelites, help! this is the man who teaches all everywhere against the people, and the law, and this place, and has brought Greeks too into the temple, and profaned this holy place.

29 For they had before seen Trophimus the Ephesian with him in the city, whom they supposed that Paul had brought into the temple.

30 And the whole city was moved, and there was a concourse of the people; and having laid hold on Paul they drew him out of the temple, and immediately the doors were shut.

31 And as they were seeking to kill him, a representation came to the centurions of the band that the whole of Jerusalem was in a tumult;

32 who, taking with him immediately soldiers and centurions, ran down upon them. But they, seeing the centurions and the soldiers, ceased beating Paul.

33 Then the centurions came up and laid hold upon him, and commanded him to be bound with two chains, and inquired who he might be, and what he had done.

34 And different persons cried some different thing in the crowd. But he, not being able to know the certainty on account of the uproar, commanded him to be brought into the fortress.

35 But when he got upon the stairs it was so that he was borne by the soldiers on account of the violence of the crowd.

36 For the multitude of the people followed, crying, Away with him.

37 But as he was about to be led into the fortress, Paul says to the centurions, Is it allowed me to say something to you? And he said, Do you know Greek?

38 You are not then that Egyptian who before these days raised a sedition and led out into the wilderness the four thousand men of the assassins?

39 But Paul said, I am a Jew of Tarsus, citizen of no insignificant city of Cilicia, and I beseech of you, allow me to speak to the people.

40 And when he had allowed him, Paul, standing on the stairs, beckoned with his hand to the people; and a great silence having been made, he addressed them in the Hebrew tongue, saying,

Acts 22:1 Brethren and fathers, hear my defense which I now make to you.

2 And hearing that he addressed them in the Hebrew tongue, they kept the more quiet; and he says,

3 I am a Jew, born in Tarsus of Cilicia, but brought up in this city, at the feet of Gamaliel, educated according to the exactness of the law of our fathers, being zealous for the God, as you are all this day;

4 who have persecuted this way unto death, binding and delivering up to prisons both men and women;

5 as also the high priest bears me witness, and all the elderhood: from whom also, having received letters to the brethren, I went to Damascus to bring those also who were there, bound, to Jerusalem, to be punished.

6 And it came to pass, as I was journeying and drawing near to Damascus, that, about mid-day, there suddenly shone out of heaven a great light round about me.

7 And I fell to the ground, and heard a voice saying to me, Saul, Saul, why do you persecute me?

8 And I answered, Who are you, Lord? And he said to me, I am Jesus the Nazarene, whom you persecute.

9 But they that were with me beheld the light, [and were filled with fear] but heard not the voice of him that was speaking to me.

10 And I said, What shall I do, Lord? And the Lord said to me, Rise up, and go to Damascus, and there it shall be told you of all things which it is appointed you to do.

11 And as I could not see, through the glory of that light, being led by the hand of those who were with me, I came to Damascus.

12 And a certain Ananias, a pious man according to the law, borne witness to by all the Jews who dwelt [there]

13 coming to me and standing by me, said to me, Brother Saul, receive your sight. And I, in the same hour, received my sight and saw him.

14 And he said, God of our fathers has chosen you beforehand to know his will, and to see the just one, and to hear a voice out of his mouth;

15 for you shall be a witness for him to all men of what you have seen and heard.

16 And now why do you linger? Arise and get baptized, and have your sins washed away, calling on his name.

17 And it came to pass when I had returned to Jerusalem, and as I was praying in the temple, that I became in ecstasy,

18 and saw him saying to me, Make haste and go quickly out of Jerusalem, for they will not receive your testimony concerning me.

19 And I said, Lord, they themselves know that I was imprisoning and beating in every synagogue those that believe on you;

20 and when the blood of your witness Stephen was shed, I also myself was standing by and consenting, and kept the clothes of them who killed him.

21 And he said to me, Go, for I will send you to the nations afar off.

22 And they (crowd) heard him until this word, and lifted up their voice, saying, Away with such a one as that from the earth, for it was not fit he should live.

23 And as they were crying, and throwing away their clothes, and casting dust into the air,

24 the centurions commanded him to be brought into the fortress, saying that he should be examined by scourging, that he might ascertain for what cause they cried thus against him.

25 But as they stretched him forward with the thongs, Paul said to the centurion who stood [by] Is it lawful for you to scourge a man [who is] a Roman and uncondemned?

26 And the centurion, having heard it, went and reported it to the centurions, saying, What are you going to do? for this man is a Roman.

27 And the centurions coming up said to him, Tell me, Are you a Roman? And he said, Yes.

28 And the centurions answered, I, for a great sum, bought this citizenship. And Paul said, But I was born [a citizen].

29 Immediately therefore those who were going to examine him left him, and the centurions also was afraid when he ascertained that he was a Roman, and because he had bound him.

30 And on the next day, desirous to know the certainty [of the matter] why he was accused of the Jews, he loosened him, and commanded the chief priests and all the council to meet, and having brought Paul down set him before them.

Acts 23:1 And Paul, fixing his eyes on the council, said, Brethren, I have walked in all good conscience with the God unto this day.

2 But the high priest Ananias commanded those standing by him to smite his mouth.

3 Then Paul said to him, the God will smite you, whiten wall. And you, do you sit judging me according to the law, and breaking the law commanding me to be struck?

4 And those that stood by said, Do you rail against the high priest of the God?

5 And Paul said, I was not conscious, brethren, that he was high priest; for it is written, You shall not speak evilly of the ruler of your people.

6 But Paul, knowing that the one part [of them] were of the Sadducees and the other of the Pharisees, cried out in the council, Brethren, I am a Pharisee, son of Pharisees: I am judged concerning the hope and resurrection of the dead.

7 And when he had spoken this, there was a tumult of the Pharisees and the Sadducees, and the multitude was divided.

8 For Sadducees say there is no resurrection, nor angel, nor spirit; but Pharisees acknowledge both of them.

9 And there was a great clamor, and the scribes of the Pharisees' part rising up contended, saying, We find nothing evil in this man; and if a spirit has spoken to him, or an angel ...

10 And a great tumult having arisen, the centurions, fearing lest Paul should have been torn in pieces by them, commanded the troop to come down and take him by force from the midst of them, and to bring him into the fortress.

11 But the following night the Lord stood by him, and said, Be of good courage; for as you have testified the things concerning me at Jerusalem, so you must bear witness at Rome also.

12 And when it was day, the Jews, having banded together, put themselves under a curse, saying that they would neither eat nor drink till they should kill Paul.

13 And they were more than forty who had joined together in this oath;

14 and they went to the chief priests and elders, and said, We have cursed ourselves with a curse to taste nothing until we kill Paul.

15 Now therefore do you with the council make a representation to the centurions so that he may bring him down to you, as about to determine more precisely what concerns him, and we, before he draws near, are ready to kill him.

16 But Paul's sister's son, having heard of the lying in wait, came and entered into the fortress and reported it to Paul.

17 And Paul, having called one of the centurions, said, Take this youth to the centurions, for he has something to report to him.

18 He therefore, having taken him with him led him to the centurions, and says, The prisoner Paul called me to him and asked me to lead this youth to you, who has something to say to you.

19 And the centurions having taken him by the hand, and having gone apart in private, inquired, What is it that you have to report to me?

20 And he said, The Jews have agreed together to make a request to you, that you may bring Paul down tomorrow into the council, as about to inquire something more precise concerning him.

21 Do not you then be persuaded by them, for there lie in wait for him of them more than forty men, who have put themselves under a curse neither to eat nor drink till they kill him; and now they are ready waiting the promise from you.

22 The centurions then dismissed the youth, commanding him, Utter to no one that you have represented these things to me.

23 And having called to him certain two of the centurions, he said, Prepare two hundred soldiers

that they may go as far as Caesarea, and seventy horsemen, and two hundred light-armed footmen, for the third hour of the night.

24 And [he commanded them] to provide beasts, that they might set Paul on them and carry him safe through to Felix the governor,

25 having written a letter, having this form:

26 Claudius Lysias to the most excellent governor Felix, greeting.

27 This man, having been taken by the Jews, and being about to be killed by them, I came up with the military and took out [of their hands] having learned that he was a Roman.

28 And desiring to know the charge on which they accused him, I brought him down to their council;

29 whom I found to be accused of questions of their law, but to have no charge laid against him [making him] worthy of death or of bonds.

30 But having received information of a plot about to be put in execution against the man [by the Jews] I have immediately sent him to you, commanding also his accusers to say before you the things that are against him. [farewell]

31 The soldiers therefore, according to what was commanded them, took Paul and brought him by night to Antipatris,

32 and on the next day, having left the horsemen to go with him, returned to the fortress.

33 And these, having entered into Caesarea, and given up the letter to the governor, presented Paul also to him.

34 And having read it and asked of what province he was, and learned that [he was] of Cilicia,

35 he said, I will hear you fully when your accusers also are arrived. And he commanded him to be kept in Herod's praetorium.

Acts 24:1 And after five days came down the high priest Ananias, with the elders, and a certain orator called Tertullus, and laid their information against Paul before the governor.

2 And he having been called, Tertullus began to accuse, saying, Seeing we enjoy great peace through you, and that excellent measures are executed for this nation by your forethought,

3 we receive it always and everywhere, most excellent Felix, with all thankfullness.

4 But that I may not too much intrude on your time, I beseech you to hear us briefly in your kindness.

5 For finding this man a pest, and moving sedition among all the Jews throughout the world, and a leader of the sect of the Nazaraeans;

6 who also attempted to profane the temple; whom we also had seized, [and would have judged according to our law;

7 but Lysias, the centurions, coming up, took him away with great force out of our hands,

8 having commanded his accusers to come to you] of whom you can yourself, in examining him know the certainty of all these things of which we accuse him.

9 And the Jews also joined in pressing the matter against [Paul] saying that these things were so.

10 But Paul, the governor having beckoned to him to speak, answered, Knowing that for many years you have been judge to this nation, I answer readily as to the things which concern myself.

11 As you may know that there are not more than twelve days since I went up to worship at Jerusalem,

12 and neither in the temple did they find me discoursing to any one, or making any tumultuous gathering together of the crowd, nor in the synagogues, nor in the city;

13 neither can they make good the things of which they now accuse me.

14 But this I avow to you, that in the way which they call sect, so I serve my fathers' God, believing all things which are written throughout the law, and in the prophets;

15 having hope towards the God, which they themselves also receive, that there is to be a resurrection both of just and unjust.

16 For this cause I also exercise [myself] to have in everything a conscience without offence toward the God and men.

17 And after a lapse of many years I arrived, bringing alms to my nation, and offerings.

18 Whereupon they found me purified in the temple, with neither crowd nor tumult. But it was certain Jews from Asia,

19 who ought to appear before you and accuse, if they have anything against me;

20 or let these themselves say what wrong they found in me when I stood before the council,

21 [other] than concerning this one voice which I cried standing among them: I am judged this day by you touching the resurrection of the dead.

22 And Felix, knowing accurately the things concerning the way, adjourned them, saying, When Lysias the commander is come down, I will determine your affair;

23 ordering the centurion to keep him, and that he should have freedom, and to hinder none of his friends to minister to him.

24 And after certain days, Felix having arrived with Drusilla his wife, who was a Jewess, he sent for Paul and heard him concerning the faith in Christ.

25 And as he reasoned concerning righteousness, and temperance, and the judgment about to come, Felix, being filled with fear, answered, Go for the present, and when I get an opportunity I will send for you;

26 hoping at the same time that money would be given him by Paul: therefore also he sent for him the oftener and communed with him.

27 But when two years were completed, Felix was relieved by Porcius Festus as his successor; and Felix, desirous to oblige the Jews, to acquire their favor, left Paul bound.

Acts 25:1 Festus therefore, being come into the province, after three days went up to Jerusalem from Caesarea.

2 And the chief priests and the chief of the Jews laid information before him against Paul, and besought him,

3 asking as a grace against him that he would send for him to Jerusalem, laying people in wait to kill him on the way.

4 Festus therefore answered that Paul should be kept at Caesarea, and that he himself was about to leave shortly.

5 Therefore, he said, Let the influential men among you go there with me, and if there is anything wrong about the man, let them prosecute him.

6 And having remained among them not more than eight or ten days, he went down to Caesarea; and on the next day, having sat down on the judgment-seat, commanded Paul to be brought.

7 And when he was come, the Jews who were come down from Jerusalem stood round, bringing many and grievous charges which they were not able to prove:

8 Paul answering for himself, Neither against the law of the Jews, nor against the temple, nor against Caesar, have I offended [in] anything.

9 But Festus, desirous of obliging the Jews, to acquire their favor, answering Paul, said, Are you willing to go up to Jerusalem, there to be judged before me concerning these things?

10 But Paul said, I am standing before the judgment-seat of Caesar, where I ought to be judged. To the Jews have I done no wrong, as you also very well know.

11 If then I have done any wrong and committed anything worthy of death, I do not refuse to die; but if there is nothing of those things of which they accuse me, no man can give me up to them. I appeal to Caesar.

12 Then Festus, having conferred with the council, answered, You have appealed to Caesar. To Caesar shall you go.

13 And when certain days had elapsed, Agrippa the king and Bernice arrived at Caesarea to salute Festus.

14 And when they had spent many days there, Festus laid before the king the matters relating to Paul, saying, There is a certain man left prisoner by Felix,

15 concerning whom, when I was at Jerusalem, the chief priests and the elders of the Jews laid information, requiring judgment against him:

16 to whom I answered, It is not the custom of the Romans to give up any man before that the accused have the accusers face to face, and he have got opportunity of defense touching the charge.

17 When therefore they had come together here, without putting it off, I sat the next day on the judgment-seat and commanded the man to be brought:

18 concerning whom the accusers, standing up, brought no such accusation of guilt as I supposed;

19 but had against him certain questions of their own system of worship, and concerning a certain Jesus who is dead, whom Paul affirmed to be living.

20 And as I myself was at a loss as to an inquiry into these things, I said, Was he willing to go to Jerusalem and there to be judged concerning these things?

21 But Paul having appealed to be kept for the examination of Augustus, I commanded him to be kept till I shall send him to Caesar.

22 And Agrippa [said] to Festus, I myself also would desire to hear the man. Tomorrow, said he, you shall hear him.

23 On the next day therefore, Agrippa being come, and Bernice, with great pomp, and having entered into the hall of audience, with the officers and the men of distinction of the city, and Festus having given command, Paul was brought.

24 And Festus said, King Agrippa, and all men who are here present with us, you see this person, concerning whom all the multitude of the Jews applied to me both in Jerusalem and here, crying out against him that he ought not to live any longer.

25 But I, having found that he had done nothing worthy of death, and this [man] himself having appealed to Augustus, I have decided to send him;

26 concerning whom I have nothing certain to write to my lord. Therefore I have brought him before you, and specially before you, king Agrippa, so that an examination having been gone into I may have something to write:

27 for it seems to me senseless, sending a prisoner, not also to signify the charges against him.

Acts 26:1 And Agrippa said to Paul, It is permitted you to speak for yourself. Then Paul stretching out his hand answered in his defense:

2 I count myself happy, king Agrippa, in having to answer today before you concerning all of which I am accused by the Jews,

3 especially because you are acquainted with all the customs and questions which are among the Jews; therefore I beseech you to hear me patiently.

4 My manner of life then from my youth, which from its commencement was passed among my nation in Jerusalem, know all the Jews,

5 who knew me before from the outset [of my life] if they would bear witness, that according to the strictest sect of our religion I lived a Pharisee.

6 And now I stand to be judged because of the hope of the promise made by the God to our fathers,

7 to which our whole twelve tribes serving incessantly day and night hope to arrive; about which hope, O king, I am accused of the Jews.

8 Why should it be judged a thing incredible in your sight if the God raises the dead?

9 I indeed myself thought that I ought to do much against the name of Jesus the Nazarene.

10 Which also I did in Jerusalem, and myself shut up in prisons many of the saints, having received the authority from the chief priests; and when they were put to death I gave my vote.

11 And often punishing them in all the synagogues, I compelled them to blaspheme. And, being exceedingly furious against them, I persecuted them even to cities out [of our own land].

12 And when, [engaged] in this, I was journeying to Damascus, with authority and power from the chief priests,

13 at mid-day, on the way, I saw, O king, a light above the brightness of the sun, shining from heaven round about me and those who were journeying with me.

14 And, when we were all fallen to the ground, I heard a voice saying to me in the Hebrew tongue, Saul, Saul, why persecute you me? [it is] hard for you to kick against goads.

15 And I said, Who are you, Lord? And the Lord said, I am Jesus whom you persecute:

16 but rise up and stand on your feet; for, for this purpose have I appeared to you, to appoint you to be a servant and a witness both of what you have seen, and of what I shall appear to you in,

17 taking you out from among the people, and the nations, to whom I send you,

18 to open their eyes, that they may turn from darkness to light, and from the power of Satan to the God, that they may receive forgiveness of sins and inheritance among them that are sanctified by faith in me.

19 Whereupon, king Agrippa, I was not disobedient to the heavenly vision;

20 but have, first to those both in Damascus and Jerusalem, and to all the region of Judea, and to the Gentiles, announced that they should repent and turn to the God, doing works worthy of repentance

21 On account of these things the Jews, having seized me in the temple, attempted to lay hands on and destroy me.

22 Having therefore met with the help which is from the God, I have stood firm unto this day, witnessing both to small and great, saying nothing else than those things which both the prophets and Moses have said should happen,

23 [namely,] that Christ should suffer; through resurrection from the dead, and that he would be the first to proclaim the light both to the people [of Judah] and to the Gentiles.

24 And as he answered for his defense with these things, Festus says with a loud voice, You are mad, Paul; much learning turns you to madness.

25 But Paul said, I am not mad, most excellent Festus, but utter words of truth and soberness;

26 for the king is informed about these things, to whom also I speak with all freedom. For I am persuaded that of these things nothing is hidden from him; for this was not done in a corner.

27 King Agrippa, You believe the prophets? I know that you believe.

28 And Agrippa [said] to Paul, In a little you will persuade me to become a Christian.

29 And Paul [said] I wish to God, both in little and in much, that not only you, but all who have heard me this day, should become such as I also am, except these bonds.

30 And the king stood up, and the governor and Bernice, and those who sat with them,

31 and having gone aside, they spoke to one another saying, This man does nothing worthy of death or of bonds.

32 And Agrippa said to Festus, This man might have been let go if he had not appealed to Caesar.

Acts 27:1 But when it had been determined that we should sail to Italy, they delivered up Paul and certain other prisoners to a centurion, by name Julius, of Augustus' company.

2 And going on board a ship of Adramyttium about to navigate by the places along Asia, we set sail, Aristarchus, a Macedonian of Thessalonica, being with us.

3 And the next day we arrived at Sidon. And Julius treated Paul kindly and permitted him to go to his friends and refresh himself.

4 And setting sail from there we sailed under the sheltered side of Cyprus, because the winds were contrary.

5 And having sailed over the waters of Cilicia and Pamphylia we came to Myra in Lycia:

6 and there the centurion having found a ship of Alexandria sailing to Italy, he made us go on board her.

7 And sailing slowly for many days, and having with difficulty got abreast of Cnidus, the wind not permitting us, we sailed under the sheltered side of Crete abreast of Salmone;

8 and coasting it with difficulty we came to a certain place called Fair Havens, near to which was the city of Lasaea.

9 And much time having now been spent, and navigation being already dangerous, because the fast also was already past, Paul counseled them,

10 saying, Men, I perceive that the navigation will be with disaster and much loss, not only of the cargo and the ship, but also of our lives.

11 But the centurion believed rather the helmsman and the shipowner than what was said by Paul.

12 And the harbor being ill adapted to winter in, the most counseled to set sail from there, if perhaps they might reach Phoenice to winter in, a port of Crete looking north-east and south-east.

13 And the south wind blowing gently, supposing that they had gained their object, having weighed anchor they sailed close in shore along Crete.

14 But not long after, there came a hurricane, called Euroclydon [northeaster wind].

15 And the ship being caught and driven, and not able to bring her head to the wind, letting her go, we were driven [before it].

16 But running under the sheltered side of a certain island called Clauda, we were with difficulty able to make ourselves masters of the boat;

17 which having hoisted up, they used helps, undergirding the ship; and fearing lest they should run into Syrtis and run aground, and having lowered the gear they were so driven.

18 But the storm being extremely violent on us, on the next day they threw cargo overboard,

19 and on the third day with their own hands they cast away the ship furniture.

20 And neither sun nor stars appearing for many days, and no small storm lying on us, in the end all hope of our being saved was taken away.

21 And when they had been a long while without taking food, Paul then standing up in the midst of them said, You ought, O men, to have listened to me, and not have made sail from Crete and have gained this disaster and loss.

22 And now I exhort you to be of good courage, for there shall be no loss at all of soul of any of you, only of the ship.

23 For an angel of God, whose I am and whom I serve, stood by me this night,

24 saying, Fear not, Paul; you must stand before Caesar; and behold, the God has granted to you all those that sail with you.

25 Therefore be of good courage, men, for I believe the God that thus it shall be, as it has been said to me.

26 But we must be cast ashore on a certain island.

27 And when the fourteenth night was come, we being driven about in Adria, towards the middle of the night the sailors supposed that some land neared them,

28 and having dropped a weighted line found twenty fathoms, and having gone a little farther and having again dropped a weighted line, they found fifteen fathoms;

29 and fearing lest we should be cast on rocky places, casting four anchors out of the stern, they wished that day were come.

30 But the sailors wishing to flee out of the ship, and having let down the boat into the sea under pretext of being about to carry out anchors from the bow [front of ship],

31 Paul said to the centurion and the soldiers, Unless these abide in the ship you cannot be saved.

32 Then the soldiers cut away the ropes of the boat and let her fall.

33 And while it was drawing on to daylight, Paul urged them all to partake of food, saying, You have passed the fourteenth day watching in expectation without taking food.

34 Therefore I exhort you to partake of food, for this has to do with your safety; for not a hair from the head of any one of you shall perish.

35 And, having said these things and taken a loaf, he gave thanks to the God before all, and having broken it began to eat.

36 And all taking courage, themselves also took food.

37 And we were in the ship, all the souls, two hundred and seventy-six.

38 And having satisfied themselves with food, they lightened the ship, casting out the wheat into the sea.

39 And when it was day they did not recognize the land; but they perceived a certain bay having a shore, which they thought, if they should be able, they could run the ship ashore;

40 and, having cast off the anchors, they left [them] in the sea, at the same time loosening the lashings of the rudders, and hoisting the foresail to the wind, they made for the strand.

41 And falling into a place where two seas met they ran the ship aground, and the bow having stuck itself fast remained unmoved, but the stern was broken by the force of the waves.

42 And the counsel of the soldiers was that they should kill the prisoners, lest any one should swim off and escape.

43 But the centurion, desirous of saving Paul, hindered them of their purpose, and commanded those who were able to swim, casting themselves first [into the sea] to get out on land;

44 and the rest, some on boards, some on some of the things [that came] from the ship; and thus it came to pass that all got safe to land.

Acts 28:1 And when we got safely to land we then knew that the island was called Melita.

2 But the barbarians showed us uncommon kindness; for, having kindled a fire, they took us all in because of the rain that was falling and because of the cold.

3 And Paul having gathered a [certain] quantity of sticks together in a bundle and laid it on the fire, a viper coming out from the heat seized his hand.

4 And when the barbarians saw the beast hanging from his hand, they said to one another, This man is certainly a murderer, whom, [though] saved out of the sea, Nemesis has not allowed to live.

5 He however, having shaken off the beast into the fire, felt no harm.

6 But they expected that he would have swollen or fallen down suddenly dead. But when they had expected a long time and saw nothing unusual happen to him, changing their opinion, they said he was a god.

7 Now in the country surrounding that place were the lands belonging to the chief man of the island, by name Publius, who received us and gave [us] hospitality three days in a very friendly way.

8 And it happened that the father of Publius lay ill of fever and dysentery; to whom Paul entered in, and having prayed and laid his hands on him cured him.

9 But this having taken place, the rest also who had sicknesses in the island came and were healed:

10 who also honored us with many honors, and on our leaving they made presents to us of what should minister to our wants.

11 And after three months we sailed in a ship which had wintered in the island, an Alexandrian, with the Dioscuri for its ensign.

12 And having come to Syracuse we remained three days.

13 Therefore, going in a circuitous course, we arrived at Rhegium; and after one day, the wind having changed to south, on the second day we came to Puteoli,

14 where, having found brethren, we were asked to stay with them seven days. And thus we went to Rome.

15 And the brethren, when they heard about us, came from there as far as the Market of Appius and Three Inns to meet us; and when Paul saw them, he thanked God and took courage.

16 And when we came to Rome, [the centurion delivered up the prisoners to the praetorian prefect, but] Paul was allowed to remain by himself with the soldier who kept him.

17 And it came to pass after three days, that he called together those who were the chief of the Jews; and when they had come together he said to them, Brethren, I having done nothing against the people or the customs of our forefathers, have been delivered a prisoner from Jerusalem into the hands of the Romans,

18 who having examined me were minded to let me go, because there was nothing worthy of death in me.

19 But when the Jews objected, I was forced to appeal to Caesar, not that I had any accusation against my nation.

20 For this cause therefore I have called you to [me] to see and to speak to you; for on account of the hope of Israel I have this chain about me.

21 And they said to him, For our part, we have neither received letters from Judea concerning you, nor has any one of the brethren who has arrived reported or said anything evil concerning you.

22 But we desire to hear from you what your views are; for concerning this sect, it is known to us that it is spoken against everywhere.

23 And having appointed him a day many came to him to the lodging, to whom he expounded, testifying of the kingdom of the God, and persuading them concerning Jesus, both from the law of Moses and the prophets, from early morning to evening.

24 And some were persuaded of the things which were said, but some disbelieved.

25 And being disagreed among themselves they left; Paul having spoken one word, Well spoke the Holy Spirit through Isaiah the prophet to our fathers,

26 saying, Go to this people, and say, Hearing you shall hear and not understand, and seeing you shall see and not perceive.

27 For the heart of this people has become fat, and they hear heavily with their ears, and they have closed their eyes; lest they should see with their eyes, and hear with their ears, and understand with their heart, and be converted, and I should heal them.

28 Be it known to you therefore, that this salvation of the God has been sent to the Gentiles; they also will hear it

29 [And he having said this, the Jews went away, having great reasoning among themselves]

30 And he remained two whole years in his own hired lodging, and received all who came to him,

31 preaching the kingdom of the God, and teaching the things concerning the Lord Jesus Christ, with all freedom unhindered.

Romans

Rom 1:1 Paul, servant of Jesus Christ, a called apostle, separated to God's good news,

2 which he had before promised by his prophets in holy writings,

3 concerning his Son the one coming out of David's seed according to flesh,

4 marked out Son of God in power, according to the Spirit of holiness, by resurrection of the dead Jesus Christ our Lord;

5 by whom we have received grace and apostleship in behalf of his name, for obedience of faith among all the Gentiles,

6 among whom are you also the called of Jesus Christ:

7 to all that are in Rome, beloved of God, called saints: Grace to you and peace from God our Father and [our] Lord Jesus Christ.

8 First, I thank my God through Jesus Christ for you all, that your faith is proclaimed in the whole world.

9 For the God is my witness, whom I serve in my spirit in the good news of his Son, how unceasingly I make mention of you,

10 always beseeching at my prayers, if any way now at least I may be prospered by the will of the God to come to you.

11 For I greatly desire to see you, that I may impart to you some spiritual gift to establish you;

12 that is, to have mutual comfort among you, each by the faith [which is] in the other, both yours and mine.

13 But I do not wish you to be ignorant, brethren, that I often proposed to come to you, and have been hindered until the present time, that I might have some fruit among you too, even as among the other Gentiles also.

14 I am a debtor both to Greeks and barbarians, both to wise and unwise:

15 so, as far as depends on me, I am ready to announce the good news to you also who [are] in Rome.

16 For I am not ashamed of the good news; for it is God's power to salvation, to every one that believes, both to Jew first and to Greek:

17 For the righteousness of God is revealed from faith to faith; according as it is written, But the just shall live by faith.

18 For there is revealed wrath of God from heaven upon all impiety, and unrighteousness of men holding the truth in unrighteousness.

19 Because what is known of God is manifest among them, for God has manifested it to them,

20 --for from the creation of the cosmos the invisible things of him are perceived, being understood by the mind through the things that are made, both his perpetual[1] power and Godhood, -- so as to render them inexcusable.

21 Because, knowing the God, they glorified him not as God, neither were thankful; but fell into folly in their thoughts, and their heart without understanding was darkened:

22 professing themselves to be wise, they became fools,

23 and changed the glory of the incorruptible God into the likeness of an image of corruptible man and of birds and quadrupeds and reptiles.

24 Therefore the God gave them up [also] in the lusts of their hearts to uncleanness, to dishonor their bodies between themselves:

25 who changed the truth of the God into falsehood, and dishonored and served the creature more than him who had created it who is blessed into the aeons. Amen.

26 For this reason the God gave them up to vile lusts; for both their females changed the natural use into that contrary to nature;

27 and in like manner the males also, leaving the natural use of the female, were inflamed in their lust towards one another; males with males working shame, and receiving in themselves the reward of their error which was fit.

28 And according as they did not think good to have the God in [their] knowledge, the God gave them up to a reprobate mind to practice improper things;

29 being filled with all unrighteousness, wickedness, greed, evil; full of envy, murder, strife, deceit, malice; [they are] gossips,

30 slanderers, haters of God, insolent, arrogant, boastful, inventors of evil, disobedient to parents,

31 without understanding, untrustworthy, unloving, unmerciful;

32 who knowing the righteous judgment of the God, that they who do such things are worthy of death, not only, practice them, but are consenting to those who do [them].

Rom 2:1 Therefore you have no excuse, O man, every one who judges, for in that in which you judge another, you condemn yourself; for you that judge do the same things.

2 But we know that the judgment of the God is according to truth upon those who do such things.

3 And think you this, O man, who judges those that do such things, and practices them [yourself] that you shall escape the judgment of the God?

4 or despises you the riches of his goodness, and forbearance, and patience, not knowing that the goodness of God leads you to repentance.

5 but, according to your hardness and unrepentant heart, treasure up to yourself wrath, in the day of wrath and revelation of the righteous judgment of the God,

6 who shall render to each according to his works:

7 to them who, in patient continuance of good works, seek for glory and honor and incorruptibility, aeonian life.

---

[1] See note for Jude 1:6

8 But to those that are contentious, and are disobedient to the truth, but obey unrighteousness, [there shall be] wrath and indignation,

9 tribulation and distress, on every soul of man that works evil, both of Jew first, and of Greek;

10 but glory and honor and peace to every one that works good, both to Jew first and to Greek:

11 for there is no partiality of persons with God.

12 For as many as have sinned without law shall perish also without law; and as many as have sinned under law shall be judged by law,

13 for not the hearers of the law [are] just before God, but the doers of the law shall be justified.

14 For when [those of the] nations, which have no law, practice by nature the things of the law, these, having no law, are a law to themselves;

15 who show the work of the law written in their hearts, their conscience also bearing witness, and their thoughts accusing or else excusing themselves between themselves;

16 in the day when God shall judge the secrets of men, according to my good news, by Jesus Christ.

17 But if you are named a Jew, and rest in the law, and make your boast in God,

18 and know the will, and discerning approve the things that are more excellent, being instructed out of the law;

19 and have confidence that you yourself are a leader of the blind, a light of those who [are] in darkness,

20 an instructor of the foolish, a teacher of babes, having the form of knowledge and of truth in the law:

21 you then that teach another, do you not teach yourself? you that preach not to steal, do you steal?

22 you that say [man should] not commit adultery, do you commit adultery? you that abhor idols, do you commit sacrilege?

23 you who boast in law, do you by transgression of the law dishonor God?

24 For the name of God is blasphemed on your account among the Gentiles, according as it is written.

25 For circumcision indeed profits if you keep the law; but if you be a law-transgressor, your circumcision is become uncircumcision.

26 If therefore the uncircumcision keep the requirements of the law, shall not his uncircumcision be reckoned for circumcision,

27 and he who is physically uncircumcised, if he keeps the Law, will he not judge you who though having the letter [of the Law] and circumcision are a transgressor of the Law?

28 For he is not a Jew who is one outwardly, nor is circumcision that which is outward in the flesh.

29 But he is a Jew who is one inwardly; and circumcision is that which is of the heart, by the Spirit, not by the letter; and his praise is not from men, but from God.

Rom 3:1 What then is the superiority of the Jew? or what the profit of circumcision?

2 Much every way: and first, indeed, that to them were entrusted the oracles of God.

3 For what? if some have not believed, shall their unbelief supersede the faith of God?

4 Far be the thought: but let God be true, and every man false; according as it is written, So that you should be justified in your words, and should overcome when you are in judgment.

5 But if our unrighteousness commend God's righteousness, what shall we say? Is God unrighteous who inflicts wrath? I speak according to man.

6 Far be the thought: since how shall God judge the world?

7 For if the truth of God, in my lie, has more abounded to his glory, why yet am I also judged as a sinner?

8 And why not say (as we are blasphemously charged and as some claim that we say), Let us do evil that good may come ? Their condemnation is just.

9 What then? are we better? No, in no way: for we have before charged both Jews and Greeks with being all under sin:

10 according as it is written, There is not a righteous [man] not even one;

11 there is not the [man] that understands, there is not one that seeks after God.

12 All have gone out of the way, they have together become unprofitable; there is not one that practice goodness, there is not so much as one:

13 their throat is an open tomb; with their tongues they have used deceit; asps' poison is under their lips:

14 whose mouth is full of cursing and bitterness;

15 swift their feet to shed blood;

16 ruin and misery [are] in their ways,

17 and way of peace they have not known:

18 there is no fear of God before their eyes.

19 Now we know that whatever the things the law says, it speaks to those under the law, that every mouth may be stopped, and all the world be under judgment to God.

20 Therefore by works of law no flesh shall be justified before him; for by law is knowledge of sin.

21 But now apart from the law the righteousness of God is manifested, being witnessed by the law and the prophets;

22 righteousness of God by faith of Jesus Christ towards all, and upon all those who believe: for there is no difference;

23 for all have sinned, and come short of the glory of God;

24 being justified freely by his grace through the redemption which is in Christ Jesus;

25 whom God has set forth as a mercy-seat, through faith in his blood, for the showing forth of his righteousness, in respect of the passing by the sins that had taken place before, through the forbearance of God;

26 for the showing forth of his righteousness in the present time, so that he should be just, and justify him that is of the faith of Jesus.

27 Where then is boasting? It has been excluded. By what law? of works? No, but by law of faith;

28 for we reckon that a man is justified by faith, without works of law.

29 Is [God] God of Jews only? is he not of the nations also? Yes, of nations also:

30 since indeed [it is] one God who shall justify the circumcision on the principle of faith, and uncircumcision by faith.

31 Do we then supersede the law by faith? Far be the thought: [no] but we establish law.

Rom 4:1 What shall we say about Abraham our father according to flesh?

2 For if Abraham has been justified on the principle of works, he has something to boast: but not before God;

3 for what does the scripture say? And Abraham believed God, and it was reckoned to him as righteousness.

4 Now to him that works, the reward is not reckoned as of grace, but of debt:

5 but to him who does not work, but believes on him who justifies the ungodly, his faith is reckoned as righteousness.

6 Even as David also declares the blessedness of the man to whom God reckons righteousness without works:

7 Blessed [they] whose lawlessness have been forgiven, and whose sins have been covered:

8 blessed the man to whom the Lord shall not at all reckon sin.

9 [Does] this blessedness then [rest] on the circumcision, or also on the uncircumcision? For we say that faith has been reckoned to Abraham as righteousness.

10 How then has it been reckoned? when he was in circumcision, or in uncircumcision? Not in circumcision, but in uncircumcision.

11 And he received the sign of circumcision [as] seal of the righteousness of faith which [he had] being in uncircumcision, that he might be the father of all them that believe being in uncircumcision, that righteousness might be reckoned to them also;

12 and father of circumcision, not only to those who are of the circumcision, but to those also who walk in the steps of the uncircumcised faith, as our father Abraham.

13 For [it was] not by law that the promise was to Abraham, or to his seed, that he should be heir of the world, but by righteousness of faith.

14 For if they which [are] of law be heirs, faith is superseded, and the promise made of no effect.

15 For law works wrath; but where no law is neither [is there] transgression.

16 Therefore [it is] on the principle of faith, that [it might be] according to grace, in order to the promise being sure to all the seed, not to that only which is of the law, but to that also which is of Abraham's faith, who is father of us all,

17 according as it is written, I have made you father of many nations, before God whom he believed, who gives life to the dead, and calls the things which be not as being;

18 who against hope believed in hope to his becoming father of many nations, according to that which was spoken, So shall your seed be:

19 and not being weak in faith, he considered not his own body already as good as dead, being about a hundred years, and the deadness of Sarah's womb,

20 and hesitated not at the promise of God through unbelief; but found strength in faith, giving glory to God;

21 and being fully persuaded that what he has promised he is able also to do;

22 therefore also it was reckoned to him as righteousness.

23 Now it was not written on his account alone that it was reckoned to him,

24 but on ours also, to whom, believing on him who has raised from among the dead Jesus our Lord,

25 who has been delivered for our offences and has been raised for our justification, it will be reckoned.

Rom 5:1 Therefore having been justified on the principle of faith, we have peace toward the God through our Lord Jesus Christ;

2 by whom we have also access by faith into this grace in which we stand, and we boast in hope of the glory of God.

3 And not only that but we also boast in tribulations, knowing that tribulation works endurance;

4 and endurance, experience; and experience, hope;

5 and hope does not make ashamed, because the love of God is shed abroad in our hearts by the Holy Spirit which has been given to us:

6 for we being still without strength, in the due time Christ has died for the ungodly.

7 For scarcely for the just [man] will one die, for perhaps for the good [man] some one might also dare to die;

8 but God commends his love to us, in that, we being still sinners, Christ has died for us.

9 Much rather therefore, having been now justified in [the power of] his blood, we shall be saved by him from wrath.

10 For if, being enemies, we have been reconciled to God through the death of his Son, much rather, having been reconciled, we shall be saved in [the power of] his life.

11 And not only that but [we are] making our boast in God, through our Lord Jesus Christ, through whom now we have received the reconciliation.

12 For this [cause] even as by one man sin entered into the world, and by sin death; and thus death passed upon all men, for that all have sinned:

13 for until the law, sin was in the world; but sin is not put to account when there is no law;

14 but death reigned from Adam until Moses, even upon those who had not sinned in the likeness

of Adam's transgression, who is the type of him to come.

15 But grace not as the transgression. For if by the offence of the one, many have died, much more has the grace of God, and the free gift in grace in the one man, Jesus Christ, abounded unto the many.

16 The gift [of grace] is not like the one transgression. For on the one hand, the judgment arose from the one transgression resulting in condemnation; but on the other hand, the gift [of grace] arose from many transgressions resulting in justification.

17 For if by the one transgression the death reigned through the one [transgression], much more shall those who receive the abundance of grace, and of the gift of righteousness, reign in life by the one Jesus Christ:

18 so then by one transgression, all men to condemnation, so by one righteousness, all men into justification of life.

19 For as indeed by the disobedience of the one man the many have been constituted sinners, so also by the obedience of the one the many will be constituted righteous.

20 But law came in, in order that the transgression might abound; but where sin abounded grace has super-abounded,

21 in order that, even as sin has reigned in [the power of] death, so also grace might reign through righteousness to aeonian life through Jesus Christ our Lord.

Rom 6:1 What then shall we say? Should we continue in sin that grace may abound?

2 Far be the thought. We who have died to sin, how shall we still live in it?

3 Are you ignorant that we, as many as have been baptized unto Christ Jesus, have been baptized unto his death?

4 We have been buried therefore with him by baptism unto death, in order that, even as Christ has been raised up from among the dead through the glory of the Father, so we also should walk in newness of life.

5 For if we are become identified with him in the likeness of his death, so also we shall be of [his] resurrection;

6 knowing this, that our old man has been crucified with him that the body of sin be superseded, that we should no longer serve sin.

7 For he that has died is justified from sin.

8 Now if we have died with Christ, we believe that we shall also live with him,

9 knowing that Christ having been raised up from among the dead dies no more: death has dominion over him no more.

10 For in that he has died, he has died to sin once for all; but in that he lives, he lives to God.

11 So also you, reckon yourselves dead to sin and alive to God in Christ Jesus.

12 Let not sin therefore reign in your mortal body to obey its lusts.

13 Neither yield your members instruments of unrighteousness to sin, but yield yourselves to God as alive from among the dead, and your members instruments of righteousness to God.

14 For sin shall not have dominion over you, for you are not under law but under grace.

15 What then? should we sin because we are not under law but under grace? Far be the thought.

16 Don't you know that to whom you yield yourselves servants for obedience, you are servants to him whom you obey, whether of sin unto death, or of obedience unto righteousness?

17 But thanks [be] to God, that you were servants of sin, but have obeyed from the heart the form of teaching into which you were instructed.

18 Now, having got your freedom from sin, you have become servants to righteousness.

19 I speak humanly on account of the weakness of your flesh. For even as you have yielded your members in bondage to uncleanness and to lawlessness unto lawlessness, so now yield your members in bondage to righteousness unto holiness.

20 For when you were servants of sin you were free from righteousness.

21 What fruit therefore had you then in the things of which you are now ashamed? for the end of them is death.

22 But now, having got your freedom from sin, and having become servants to God, you have your fruit unto holiness, and the end, aeonian life.

23 For the wages of sin is death; but the act of grace of God, aeonian life in Christ Jesus our Lord.

Rom 7:1 Are you ignorant, brethren, for I speak to those knowing law, that law rules over a man as long as he lives?

2 For the married woman is bound by law to her husband so long as he is alive; but if the husband should die, she supersedes from the law of the husband:

3 so then, the husband being alive, she shall be called an adulteress if she be to another man; but if the husband should die, she is free from the law, so as not to be an adulteress, though she be to another man.

4 So that, my brethren, you also have been made dead to the law by the body of the Christ, to be to another, who has been raised up from among the dead, in order that we might bear fruit to God.

5 For when we were in the flesh the passions of sins, which [were] by the law, worked in our members to bring forth fruit to death;

6 but now we supersede from the law, having died to that in which we were held, so that we should serve in newness of spirit, and not in oldness of letter.

7 What shall we say then? is the law sin? Far be the thought. But I had not known sin, unless by law: for I would not have had conscience of lust unless the law had said, You shall not lust;

8 but sin, being induced by the commandment, worked in me every lust; for without law sin [was] dead.

9 But I was alive without law once; but the commandment having come, sin revived, but I died.

10 And the commandment, which [was] for life, was found, [as] to me, itself [to be] unto death:

11 for sin, being induced by the commandment, deceived me, and by it killed [me].

12 So that the law indeed is holy, and the commandment holy, and just, and good.

13 Did then that which is good become death to me? Far be the thought. But sin, that it might appear sin, working death to me by that which is good; in order that sin by the commandment might become exceeding sinful.

14 For we know that the law is spiritual: but I am fleshly, sold under sin.

15 For that which I do, I do not know: for not what I wish, this I do; but what I hate, this I practice.

16 But if what I do not want, this I practice, I consent to the law that [it is] right.

17 Now then [it is] no longer I that do it, but the sin that dwells in me.

18 For I know that in me, that is, in my flesh, good does not dwell: for the wish [to do good] is there with me, but to do right [I find] not.

19 For I do not practice the good that I wish; but the evil I do not wish, that I do.

20 But if what I do not wish, this I practice, [it is] no longer I that do it, but the sin that dwells in me.

21 I find then this law for me: the willingness to practice what is right, yet alongside this there is evil.

22 For I delight in the law of God according to the inward man:

23 but I see another law in my members, warring in opposition to the law of my mind, and bringing me into captivity to the law of sin which exists in my members.

24 O wretched man that I am, who shall deliver me out of this body of death?

25 I thank God, through Jesus Christ our Lord. So then I myself with the mind serve God's law; but with the flesh sin's law.

Rom 8:1 [There is] then now no condemnation to those in Christ Jesus.

2 For the law of the Spirit of life in Christ Jesus has set me free from the law of sin and of death.

3 For what the law could not do, in that it was weak through the flesh, God, having sent his own Son, in likeness of flesh of sin, and for sin, has condemned sin in the flesh,

4 in order that the righteous requirement of the law should be fulfilled in us, who do not walk according to flesh but according to Spirit.

5 For they that are according to flesh mind the things of the flesh; and they that are according to Spirit, the things of the Spirit.

6 For the mind of the flesh is death; but the mind of the Spirit life and peace.

7 Because the mind of the flesh is enmity against God: for it is not subject to the law of God; for neither indeed can it be:

8 and they that are in flesh cannot please God.

9 But you are not in flesh but in Spirit, if indeed God's Spirit dwell in you; but if any one has not the Spirit of Christ he is not of him:

10 but if Christ be in you, the body is dead through sin, but the Spirit is life through righteousness.

11 But if the Spirit of him that has raised up Jesus from among the dead dwell in you, he that has raised up Christ from among the dead shall quicken your mortal bodies also on account of his Spirit which dwells in you.

12 So then, brethren, we are debtors, not to the flesh, to live according to flesh;

13 for if you live according to flesh, you are about to die; but if, by the Spirit, you put to death the deeds of the body, you shall live:

14 for as many as are led by the Spirit of God, these are sons of God.

15 For you have not received a spirit of bondage again for fear, but you have received a spirit of adoption, whereby we cry, Abba, Father.

16 The very Spirit testifies to our Spirit, that we are children of God.

17 And if children, heirs also: heirs of God, and joint heirs with Christ; if indeed we suffer with him that we may also be glorified with him.

18 For I reckon that the sufferings of this present time are not worthy [to be compared] with the coming glory to be revealed to us.

19 The creation awaits in eager expectation for the revelation of the sons of God;

20 for the creation has been made subject to futility; not of its will, but by reason of him who has subjected [the same] in hope

21 that the creation itself also shall be set free from the bondage of corruption into the liberty of the glory of the children of God.

22 For we know that the whole creation groans together and travails in pain together until now.

23 And not only that but even we ourselves, who have the first-fruits of the Spirit, we also ourselves groan in ourselves, awaiting adoption, [that is] the redemption of our body.

24 For we have been saved in hope; but hope seen is not hope; for what any one sees, why does he also hope?

25 But if what we see not, we hope, we expect in patience.

26 And in like manner the Spirit joins also its help to our weakness; for we do not know what we should pray for as is fitting, but the Spirit itself makes intercession with groanings which cannot be uttered.

27 But he who searches the hearts knows what is the mind of the Spirit, because he intercedes for saints according to God.

28 But we do know that all things work together for good to those who love God, to those who are called according to purpose.

29 Because whom he foreknows,* he also predestinates* to conform to the image of his Son, so that he should be the firstborn among many brethren.

30 But whom he predestinates,* these also he calls;* and whom he calls,* these also he justifies;* but whom he justifies,* these also he has glorifies.*

31 What shall we then say to these things? If God is for us, who is against us?

32 He who, yes, has not spared his own Son, but delivered him up for us all, how shall he not also with him grant us all things?

33 Who shall bring an accusation against God's elect? [it is] God who justifies:

34 who is he that condemns? [it is] Christ who has died, but rather has been [also] raised up; who is also at the right hand of God; who also intercedes for us.

35 Who shall separate us from the love of Christ? tribulation or distress, or persecution, or famine, or nakedness, or danger, or sword?

36 According as it is written, For your sake we are put to death all the day long; we have been reckoned as sheep for slaughter.

37 But in all these things we more than conquer through him that has loved us.

38 For I am persuaded that neither death, nor life, nor angels, nor principalities, nor things present, nor things to come, nor powers,

39 nor height, nor depth, nor any other creation, shall be able to separate us from the love of God, which is in Christ Jesus our Lord.

Rom 9:1 I say the truth in Christ, I lie not, my conscience bearing witness with me in the Holy Spirit,

2 that I have great grief and uninterrupted pain in my heart,

3 for I have wished, I myself, to be a curse from the Christ for my brethren, my kinsmen, according to flesh;

4 who are Israelites; whose is the adoption, and the glory, and the covenants and the law-giving, and the service, and the promises;

5 whose are the fathers; and of whom, as according to flesh, is the Christ, who is over all, God blessed into the aeons. Amen.

6 Not however as though the word of God had failed; for all are not Israel which are of Israel;

7 nor because they are seed of Abraham [are] all children: but, In Isaac shall a seed be called to you.

8 That is, [they that are] the children of the flesh, these [are] not the children of God; but the children of the promise are reckoned as seed.

9 For this word is of promise, According to this time I will come, and there shall be a son to Sarah.

10 And not only that but Rebecca having conceived by one, Isaac our father,

11 [the children] indeed being not yet born, or having done anything good or worthless that the purpose of God according to election might abide, not of works, but of him that calls,

12 it was said to her, The greater shall serve the less:

13 according as it is written, I have loved Jacob, and I have hated Esau.

14 What shall we say then? [is there] unrighteousness with God? Far be the thought.

15 For he says to Moses, I will show mercy to whom I will show mercy, and I will feel compassion for whom I will feel compassion.

16 So then [it is] not of him that wills, nor of him that runs, but of God that shows mercy.

17 For the scripture says to Pharaoh, For this very thing I have raised you up from among [men] that I might thus show in you my power, and so that my name should be declared in all the earth.

18 So then, to whom he will he shows mercy, and whom he will he hardens.

19 You will say to me then, Why does he yet find fault? for who resists his purpose?

20 Aye, but you, O man, who are you that answer again to God? Shall the thing formed say to him that has formed it, Why have you made me thus?

21 Or has not the potter authority over the clay, out of the same lump to make one vessel to honor, and another to dishonor?

22 And if God, wished to show his wrath and to make his power known, endured with much patience vessels of wrath fitted for destruction;

23 and that he might make known the riches of his glory upon vessels of mercy, which he had before prepared for glory,

24 us, whom he has also called, not only from among the Jews, but also from among the nations?

25 As he says also in Hosea, I will call not-my-people My people; and the-not-beloved Beloved.

26 And it shall be, in the place where it was said to them, You [are] not my people, there shall they be called Sons of the living God.

27 But Isaiah cries concerning Israel, Should the number of the children of Israel be as the sand of the sea, the remnant shall be saved:

28 The Lord will execute his word on the earth quickly and completely.

29 And according as Isaiah said before, Unless the Lord of hosts had left us a seed, we had been as Sodom, and made like even as Gomorrha.

30 What then shall we say? That [they of the] nations, who did not follow after righteousness, have attained righteousness, but the righteousness that is on the principle of faith.

31 But Israel, pursuing after a law of righteousness, has not attained to that law.

32 Why so? Because [it was] not on the principle of faith, but as of works. They have stumbled at the stumbling stone,

33 according as it is written, Behold, I place in Zion a stone of stumbling and rock of offence: and he that believes on him shall not be ashamed.

Rom 10:1 Brethren, the delight of my own heart and my supplication which [I address] toward the God for them is for salvation.

2 For I bear them witness that they have zeal for God, but not according to knowledge.

3 For they, being ignorant of God's righteousness, and seeking to establish their own

[righteousness] have not submitted to the righteousness of God.

4 For Christ is the fulfillment of the law for righteousness to every one that believes.

5 For Moses lays down in writing the righteousness which is of the law, The man who has practiced those things shall live by them.

6 But the righteousness of faith speaks thus: Do not say in your heart, Who shall ascend to the heavens? that is, to bring Christ down;

7 or, Who shall descend into the abyss? that is, to bring up Christ from among the dead.

8 But what do you say? The word is near you, in your mouth and in your heart: that is, the word of faith, which we preach:

9 that if you shall acknowledge with your mouth Jesus as Lord, and shall believe in your heart that God has raised him from among the dead, you shall be saved.

10 For with the heart is belief toward righteousness; and with the mouth acknowledgment made toward salvation.

11 For the scripture says, No one believing on him shall be ashamed.

12 For there is no difference of Jew and Greek; for the same Lord of all is rich towards all that call upon him.

13 For every one whosoever, who shall call on the name of the Lord, shall be saved.

14 How then shall they call upon him in whom they have not believed? and how shall they believe on him of whom they have not heard? and how shall they hear without one who preaches?

15 and how shall they preach unless they have been sent? according as it is written, How beautiful the feet of them that announce good news of peace, of them that announce good news of good things!

16 But they have not all obeyed the good news. For Isaiah says, Lord, who has believed our report?

17 So faith then is by a report, but the report by God's word.

18 But I say, Have they not heard? Yes, surely, Their voice has gone out into all the earth, and their words to the end of the habitable world.

19 But I say, Has not Israel known? First, Moses says, I will provoke you to jealousy through [them that are] not a nation: through a nation without understanding I will anger you.

20 But Isaiah is very bold, and says, I have been found by those not seeking me; I have become manifest to those not inquiring after me.

21 But unto Israel he says, All the day long I have stretched out my hands unto a people disobeying and opposing.

Rom 11:1 I say then, Has God cast away his people? Far be the thought. For I also am an Israelite, of the seed of Abraham, of the tribe of Benjamin.

2 God has not cast away his people whom he foreknew. Don't you know what the scripture says about Elijah, how he pleads with God against Israel?

3 Lord, they have killed your prophets, they have dug down your altars; and I have been left alone, and they seek my soul.

4 But what says the divine answer to him? I have left to myself seven thousand men, who have not bowed knee to the lord [baal].

5 Thus, then, in the present time also there has been a remnant according to election of grace.

6 But if by grace, no longer of works: since [otherwise] grace is no more grace.

7 What then? What Israel seeks for, that he has not obtained; but the election has obtained, and the rest have been blinded,

8 according as it is written, God has given to them a spirit of slumber, eyes not to see, and ears not to hear, unto this day.

9 And David says, Let their table be for a snare, and for a trap, and for a stumbling block, and for a recompense to them:

10 let their eyes be darkened not to see, and bow down their back always.

11 I say then, Have they stumbled in order that they might fall? Far be the thought: but by their fall there is salvation to the Gentiles to provoke them [Jews] to jealousy.

12 But if their fall [be the] world's wealth, and their loss the wealth of the nations, how much rather their fullness?

13 For I speak to you, the Gentiles, inasmuch as I am apostle of nations, I glorify my ministry;

14 if by any means I shall provoke to jealousy [them which are] my flesh, and shall save some from among them.

15 For if their casting away [be the] world's reconciliation, what [their] reception but life from among the dead?

16 Now if the first-fruit [be] holy, the lump also; and if the root [be] holy, the branches also.

17 Now if some of the branches have been broken out, and you, being a wild olive tree, have been grafted in among them, and have become a fellow-partaker of the root and of the fatness of the olive tree,

18 boast not against the branches; but if you boast, [it is] not you that bear the root, but the root you.

19 You will say then, The branches have been broken out in order that I might be grafted in.

20 Right: they have been broken off through unbelief, and you stand through faith. Be not high-minded, but fear:

21 For if God did not spare the natural branches, He will not spare you, either.

22 Behold then the goodness and severity of God: upon them who have fallen, severity; upon you goodness of God, if you shall abide in goodness, since [otherwise] you also will be cut away.

23 And they too, if they abide not in unbelief, shall be grafted in; for God is able again to graft them in.

24 For if you were cut off from what is by nature a wild olive tree, and were grafted contrary to nature into a cultivated olive tree, how much more will

these who are the natural branches be grafted into their own olive tree?

25 For I do not wish you to be ignorant, brethren, of this revealed-mystery, that you may not be wise in your own conceits, that blindness in part has happened to Israel, until the fullness of the nations be come in;

26 and so all Israel shall be saved. According as it is written, The deliverer shall come out of Zion; he shall turn away ungodliness from Jacob.

27 And this is the covenant from me to them, when I shall have taken away their sins.

28 As regards the good news, [they are] enemies on your account; but as regards election, beloved on account of the fathers.

29 For the gifts and the calling of God are irrevocable

30 For as indeed you [also] once have not believed in God, but now have been objects of mercy through the unbelief of these;

31 so these also have now not believed in your mercy, in order that they also may be objects of mercy.

32 For God hath shut up together all in unbelief, in order that he might show mercy to all.

33 O depth of riches both of the wisdom and knowledge of God! how unsearchable his judgments, and untraceable his ways!

34 For who has known the mind of the Lord, or who has been his counselor?

35 or who has first given to him, and it shall be rendered to him?

36 For out of him, and through him, and into him all things: to him be glory into the aeons. Amen.

Rom 12:1 I beseech you therefore, brethren, by the compassion of God, to present your bodies a living sacrifice, holy, acceptable to God, [which is] your reasonable service.

2 And be not conformed to this world, but be transformed by the renewing of [your] mind, that you may prove what is the good and acceptable and perfect will of God.

3 For I say, through the grace which has been given to me, to every one that is among you, not to have high thoughts above what he should think; but to think so as to be wise, as God has dealt to each a measure of faith.

4 For, as in one body we have many members, but all the members have not the same office;

5 thus we many, are one body in Christ, and each one members, one of the other.

6 But having different gifts, according to the grace which has been given to us, whether prophecy, [let us prophesy] according to the proportion of faith;

7 or service, in service; or he that teaches, in teaching;

8 or he that exhorts, in exhortation; he that gives, in simplicity; he that leads, with diligence; he that shows mercy, with cheerfullness.

9 Let love be sincere; abhorring evil; cleaving to good:

10 as to brotherly-love, kindly affectionate towards one another: as to honor, each taking the lead in paying it to the other:

11 as to diligent zealousness, not slothful; in spirit fervent; serving the Lord.

12 As regards hope, rejoicing: as regards tribulation, enduring: as regards prayer, persevering:

13 distributing to the necessities of the saints; given to hospitality.

14 Bless them that persecute you; bless, and curse not.

15 Rejoice with those that rejoice, weep with those that weep.

16 Have the same respect one for another, not minding high things, but going along with the lowly: be not wise in your own eyes:

17 recompensing to no one evil for evil: providing things honest before all men:

18 if possible, as far as depends on you, living in peace with all men;

19 not avenging yourselves, beloved, but give place to wrath; for it is written, Vengeance [belongs] to me, I will recompense, says the Lord.

20 If therefore your enemy should hunger, feed him; if he should thirst, give him drink; for, so doing, you shall heap coals of fire upon his head.

21 Be not overcome by evil, but overcome evil with good.

Rom 13:1 Let every soul be subject to the authorities that are above him. For there is no authority except from God; and those that exist are set up by God.

2 So that he that sets himself in opposition to the authority resists the ordinance of God; and they who [thus] resist shall bring sentence of guilt on themselves.

3 For rulers are not a cause of fear for good behavior, but for evil. Do you want to have no fear of authority? Do what is good and you will have praise from the same;

4 for it is God's minister to you for good. But if you practice evil, fear; for it bears not the sword in vain; for it is God's minister, an avenger for wrath to him that does evil.

5 Therefore it is necessary to be subject, not only on account of wrath, but also on account of conscience.

6 For on this account you pay tribute also; for they are God's officers, attending continually on this very thing.

7 Render to all their dues: to whom tribute [is due] tribute; to whom custom, custom; to whom fear, fear; to whom honor, honor.

8 Owe no one anything, unless to love one another: for he that loves another has fulfilled the law.

9 For, You shall not commit adultery, You shall not kill, You shall not steal, You shall not lust; and if there be any other commandment, it is summed up in this word, namely, You shall love your neighbor as yourself.

10 Love works no evil to its neighbor; love therefore performs the fulfillment of the law.

11 This also, knowing the time, that it is already time that we should be aroused out of sleep; for now is our salvation nearer than when we believed.

12 The night is far spent, and the day is near; let us cast away therefore the works of darkness, and let us put on the armor of light.

13 Let us behave properly as in the day, not in carousing and drunkenness, not in sexual promiscuity and sensuality, not in strife and jealousy.

14 But put on the Lord Jesus Christ, and make no provision for the flesh in regard to its lusts.

Rom 14:1 Now welcome the one who is weak in faith, but not for the purpose of passing judgment on his opinions.

2 One man is assured that he may eat all things; but the weak eats herbs.

3 Let not him that eats make little of him that eats not; and let not him that eats not judge him that eats: for God has received him.

4 Who are you that judge the servant of another? to his own master he stands or falls. And he shall be made to stand; for the Lord is able to make him stand.

5 One man esteems one day more than another day; another esteems every day [alike]. Let each be fully persuaded in his own mind.

6 He that regards the day, regards it to the Lord. And he that eats, eats to the Lord, for he gives God thanks; and he that does not eat, to the Lord he does not eat, and gives God thanks.

7 For none of us lives to himself, and none dies to himself.

8 For both if we should live, [it is] to the Lord we live; and if we should die, [it is] to the Lord we die: both if we should live then, and if we should die, we are the Lord's.

9 For to this [end] Christ has died and lived [again] that he might rule over both dead and living.

10 But you, why judge you your brother? or again, you, why do you make little of your brother? for we shall all be placed before the judgment-seat of God.

11 For it is written, I live, says the Lord, that to me shall bow every knee, and every tongue shall acknowledge to God.

12 So then each of us shall give an account concerning himself to God.

13 Let us no longer therefore judge one another; but judge you this rather, not to put a stumbling-block or a trap before his brother.

14 I know, and am persuaded in the Lord Jesus, that nothing is unclean of itself; except to him who reckons anything to be unclean, to that man [it is] unclean.

15 For if on account of meat your brother is grieved, you walk no longer according to love. Destroy not him with your meat for whom Christ has died.

16 Therefore do not let what is for you a good thing be spoken of as evil;

17 for the kingdom of the God is not eating and drinking, but righteousness, and peace, and joy in the Holy Spirit.

18 For he who in this way serves Christ is acceptable to God and approved by men.

19 So then let us pursue the things which tend to peace, and things whereby one shall build up another.

20 For the sake of meat do not destroy the work of God. All things indeed [are] pure; but [it is] evil to that man who eats while stumbling [in doing so]

21 [It is] right not to eat meat, nor drink wine, nor [do anything] in which your brother stumbles, or is offended, or is weak.

22 The faith which you have, have as your own conviction before God. Happy is he who does not condemn himself in what he approves.

23 But he who doubts is condemned if he eats, because [he eats] not from faith; and whatever is not from faith is sin.

Rom 15:1 But we ought, we that are strong, to bear the infirmities of the weak, and not to please ourselves.

2 Let each one of us please his neighbor with a view to what is good, to edification.

3 For the Christ also did not please himself; but according as it is written, The reproaches of them that reproach you have fallen upon me.

4 For as many things as have been written before have been written for our instruction, that through endurance and through encouragement of the scriptures we might have hope.

5 Now God of endurance and of encouragement give to you to be like-minded one toward another, according to Christ Jesus;

6 that you may with one accord, with one mouth, glorify God and Father of our Lord Jesus Christ.

7 Therefore receive you one another, according as the Christ also has received you to the glory of God.

8 For I say that Jesus Christ became a minister of the circumcision for the truth of God, to confirm the promises of the fathers;

9 and that the Gentiles should glorify God for mercy; according as it is written, For this cause I will acknowledge you among the Gentiles, and will sing to your name.

10 And again he says, Rejoice, Gentiles, with his people.

11 And again, Praise the Lord, all [you] Gentiles, and let all the peoples praise him.

12 And again, Isaiah says, There shall be the root of Jesse, and one that arises, to rule over the Gentiles: in him shall the Gentiles hope.

13 Now God of hope fill you with all joy and peace in believing, so that you should abound in hope by the power of the Holy Spirit.

14 But I am persuaded, my brethren, I myself also, concerning you, that yourselves also are full of

goodness, filled with all knowledge, able also to admonish one another.

15 But I have written to you the more boldly, in part, as putting you in mind, because of the grace given to me by God,

16 for me to be minister of Christ Jesus to the nations, carrying on as a sacrificial service the good news of God, in order that the offering up of the nations might be acceptable, sanctified by the Holy Spirit.

17 Therefore in Christ Jesus I have found reason for boasting in things pertaining to God.

18 For I will not dare to speak anything of the things which Christ has not worked by me, for the obedience of the nations, by word and deed,

19 in the power of signs and wonders, in the power of the Spirit of God; so that I, from Jerusalem, and in a circuit round to Illyricum, have fully preached the good news of the Christ;

20 and so aiming to announce the good news, not where Christ has been named, that I might not build upon another's foundation;

21 but according as it is written, To whom there was nothing told concerning him, they shall see; and they that have not heard shall understand.

22 Therefore also I have been often hindered from coming to you.

23 But now, having no longer place in these regions, and having great desire to come to you these many years,

24 whenever I should go to Spain; for I hope to see you as I go through, and by you to be set forward there, if first I shall have been in part filled with your company;

25 but now I go to Jerusalem, ministering to the saints;

26 for Macedonia and Achaia have been well pleased to make a certain contribution for the poor of the saints who [are] in Jerusalem.

27 They have been well pleased indeed, and they are their debtors; for if the nations have participated in their spiritual things, they ought also in fleshly things minister to them.

28 Having finished this therefore, and having sealed to them this fruit, I will set off by you into Spain.

29 But I know that, coming to you, I shall come in the fullness of the blessing of Christ.

30 But I beseech you, brethren, by our Lord Jesus Christ, and by the love of the Spirit, that you strive together with me in prayers for me toward the God;

31 that I may be saved from those that do not believe in Judea; and that my ministry for Jerusalem may be acceptable to the saints;

32 in order that I may come to you in joy by God's will, and that I may be refreshed with you.

33 And God of peace be with you all. Amen.

Rom 16:1 But I recommend to you Phoebe, our sister, who is minister of the church which is in Cenchrea;

2 that you may receive her in the Lord worthily of saints, and that you may assist her in whatever matter she has need of you; for she also has been a helper of many, and of myself.

3 Salute Prisca and Aquila, my fellow-workmen in Christ Jesus,

4 who for my soul risked their own neck; to whom not I only am thankful, but also all the churches of the nations,

5 and the church at their house. Salute Epaenetus, my beloved, who is the first-fruit of Asia for Christ.

6 Salute Maria, who labored much for you.

7 Salute Andronicus and Junias, my kinsmen and fellow-captives, who are of note among the apostles; who were also in Christ before me.

8 Salute Amplias, my beloved in the Lord.

9 Salute Urbanus, our fellow-workman in Christ, and Stachys, my beloved.

10 Salute Apelles, approved in Christ. Salute those who belong to Aristobulus.

11 Salute Herodion, my kinsman. Salute those who belong to Narcissus, who are in the Lord.

12 Salute Tryphaena and Tryphosa, who labor in the Lord. Salute Persis, the beloved, who has labored much in the Lord.

13 Salute Rufus, chosen in the Lord; and his mother and mine.

14 Salute Asyncritus, Phlegon, Hermes, Patrobas, Hermas, and the brethren with them.

15 Salute Philologus, and Julia, Nereus, and his sister, and Olympas, and all the saints with them.

16 Salute one another with a holy kiss. All the churches of Christ salute you.

17 But I beseech you, brethren, to consider those who create divisions and occasions of falling, contrary to the doctrine which you have learnt, and turn away from them.

18 For such serve not our Lord Christ, but their own belly, and by good words and fair speeches deceive the hearts of the unsuspecting.

19 For your obedience has reached to all. I rejoice therefore as it regards you; but I wish you to be wise [as] to that which is good, and simple [as] to evil.

20 But God of peace shall bruise Satan under your feet shortly. The grace of our Lord Jesus Christ [be] with you.

21 Timothy, my fellow-workman, and Lucius, and Jason, and Sosipater, my kinsmen, salute you.

22 I Tertius, who have written this epistle, salute you in the Lord.

23 Gaius, my host and of the whole church, salutes you. Erastus, the steward of the city, salutes you, and the brother Quartus.

24 The grace of our Lord Jesus Christ [be] with you all. Amen.

25 Now to him that is able to establish you, according to my good news and the preaching of Jesus Christ, according to the revelation of the revealed-mystery, as to which silence has been kept to the aeonian times,

26 but [which] has now been made manifest, and by prophetic scriptures, according to commandment of the aeonian God [God of aeonian] made known for obedience of faith to all the nations

27 To the only wise God, through Jesus Christ, to whom be glory into the aeons. Amen.

1 Corinthians

1 Cor 1:1 Paul, a called apostle of Jesus Christ, by God's will, and Sosthenes the brother,

2 to the church of God which is in Corinth, to [those] sanctified in Christ Jesus, called saints, with all that in every place call on the name of our Lord Jesus Christ, both theirs and ours:

3 Grace to you and peace from God our Father, and the Lord Jesus Christ.

4 I thank my God always about you, in respect of the grace of God given to you in Christ Jesus;

5 that in everything you have been enriched in him, in all word and all knowledge,

6 according as the testimony of the Christ has been confirmed in you,

7 so that you come short in no gift, awaiting the revelation of our Lord Jesus Christ;

8 who shall also confirm you to the end, unimpeachable in the day of our Lord Jesus Christ.

9 God is faithful, by whom you have been called into the fellowship of his Son Jesus Christ our Lord.

10 Now I urge you, brethren, by the name of our Lord Jesus Christ, that you all say the same thing, and that there be not among you divisions; but that you be perfectly united in the same mind and in the same opinion.

11 For it has been shown to me concerning you, my brethren, by those of [the house of] Chloe, that there are strifes among you.

12 But I speak of this, that each of you says, I am of Paul, and I of Apollos, and I of Cephas, and I of Christ.

13 Is the Christ divided? has Paul been crucified for you? or have you been baptized unto the name of Paul?

14 I thank God that I have baptized none of you, unless Crispus and Gaius,

15 that no one may say that I have baptized unto my own name.

16 Yes, I baptized also the house of Stephanas; for the rest I know not if I have baptized any other.

17 For Christ has not sent me to baptize, but to preach good news; not in wisdom of word, that the cross of the Christ may not be made vain.

18 For the word of the cross is to them that perish foolishness, but to us that are saved it is God's power.

19 For it is written, I will destroy the wisdom of the wise, and set aside the understanding of the understanding ones.

20 Where [is the] wise? where scribe? where disputer of this world? has not God made foolish the wisdom of the world?

21 For since, in the wisdom of God, the world by wisdom has not known God, God has been pleased by the foolishness of the preaching to save those that believe.

22 Since Jews indeed ask for signs, and Greeks seek wisdom;

23 but we preach Christ crucified, to Jews an offence, and to Gentiles foolishness;

24 but to those that [are] called, both Jews and Greeks, Christ God's power and God's wisdom.

25 Because the foolishness of God is wiser than men, and the weakness of God is stronger than men.

26 For consider your calling, brethren, that [there are] not many wise according to flesh, not many powerful, not many noblemen.

27 But God has chosen the foolish things of the world, that he may put to shame the wise; and God has chosen the weak things of the world, that he may put to shame the strong things;

28 and the ignoble things of the world, and the despised, has God chosen, [and] things that are not, that he may supersede the things that are;

29 so that no flesh should boast before God.

30 But of him are you in Christ Jesus, who has been made to us wisdom from God, and righteousness, and holiness, and redemption;

31 that according as it is written, He that boasts, let him boast in the Lord.

1 Cor 2:1 And I, when I came to you, brethren, announcing to you the revealed-mystery of God, I came not in excellency of word, or wisdom,.

2 For I did not judge to know anything among you except Jesus Christ, and him crucified.

3 And I was with you in weakness and in fear and in much trembling;

4 and my word and my preaching, not in persuasive words of wisdom, but in demonstration of the Spirit and of power;

5 that your faith might not stand in men's wisdom, but in God's power.

6 But we speak wisdom among the perfect; but wisdom not of this world, nor of the rulers of this world, who are being superseded.

7 But we speak God's wisdom in a revealed-mystery, that hidden [wisdom] which God had predestinated before the aeons for our glory:

8 which none of the princes of this aeon knew, for had they known, they would not have crucified the Lord of glory;

9 but according as it is written, Things which eye has not seen, and ear not heard, and which have not come into man's heart, which God has prepared for them that love him,

10 but God has revealed to us by his Spirit; for the Spirit searches all things, even the depths of God.

11 For who of men has known the things of a man except the spirit of the man which is in him? thus also the things of God knows no one except the Spirit of God.

12 But we have received, not the spirit of the world, but the Spirit which is of God, that we may know the things which have been freely given to us of God:

13 which also we speak, not in words taught by human wisdom, but in those taught by the Spirit, communicating spiritual by spiritual.

14 But the natural man does not receive the things of the Spirit of God, for they are folly to him; and he cannot know, because they are spiritually discerned;

15 the spiritual discerns all things, but the very spiritual essence is not discerned by anyone.

16 For who has known the mind of the Lord, who shall instruct him? But we have the mind of Christ.

1 Cor 3:1 And I, brethren, have not been able to speak to you as to spiritual, but as to fleshly; as to babes in Christ.

2 I have given you milk to drink, not meat, for you have not yet been able, nor indeed are you yet able;

3 for you are yet carnal. For whereas [there are] among you emulation and strife, are you not carnal, and walk according to man?

4 For when one says, I am of Paul, and another, I of Apollos, are you not men?

5 Who then is Apollos, and who Paul? Ministering servants, through whom you have believed, and as the Lord has given to each.

6 I have planted; Apollos watered; but God has given the increase.

7 So that neither the planter is anything, nor the waterer; but God the giver of the increase.

8 But the planter and the waterer are one; but each shall receive his own reward according to his own labor.

9 For we are God's fellow-workmen; you are God's field, God's building.

10 According to the grace of God which has been given to me, as a wise architect, I have laid the foundation, but another builds upon it. But let each see how he builds upon it.

11 For other foundation can no man lay besides that which is laid, which is Jesus Christ.

12 Now if any one build upon [this] foundation, gold, silver, precious stones, wood, grass, straw,

13 the work of each shall be made manifest; for the day [of judgment] shall declare it because it is revealed in fire; and the fire shall try the work of each for what it is.

14 If the work of any one which he has built upon [the foundation] shall abide, he shall receive a reward.

15 If the work of any one shall be consumed, he shall suffer loss, but he shall be saved, but so as through the fire.

16 Do you not know that you are the temple of God, and that the Spirit of God dwells in you?

17 If any one corrupt the temple of God, him shall God destroy; for the temple of God is holy, and such are you.

18 Let no one deceive himself: if any one thinks himself to be wise among you in this world, let him become foolish, that he may be wise.

19 For the wisdom of this world is foolishness before God. For it is written, He takes the wise in their own craftiness.

20 And again, the Lord knows the reasoning of the wise that they are vain.

21 So that let no one boast in men; for all things are yours.

22 Whether Paul, or Apollos, or Cephas, or the world, or life, or death, or things present, or things coming, all are yours;

23 and yours Christ's; and Christ, God's.

1 Cor 4:1 Let a man so account of us as servants of Christ, and stewards of the revealed-mysteries of God.

2 Here, further, it is sought in stewards, that a man be found faithful.

3 But for me it is the very smallest matter that I be examined of you or of man's court. Nor do I even examine myself.

4 For I am conscious of nothing in myself; but I am not justified by this: but he that examines me is the Lord.

5 So do not judge anything before the time, until the Lord shall come, who shall also both bring to light the hidden things of darkness, and shall make manifest the counsels of hearts; and then shall each have [his] praise from God.

6 Now these things, brethren, I have transferred, in their application, to myself and Apollos, for your sakes, that you may learn in us the [lesson of] not [letting your thoughts go] above what is written, so that no one of you will become arrogant in behalf of one against the other.

7 For who makes you to differ? and what have you which you have not received? but if also you have received, why do you boast as not receiving?

8 Already you are filled; already you have been enriched; you have reigned without us; and I wish that you reigned, that we also might reign with you.

9 For, I think, God has exhibited us apostles last of all, as men condemned to death; because we have become a spectacle to the world, both to angels and to men.

10 We [are] fools for Christ's sake, but you prudent in Christ: we weak, but you strong: you glorious, but we in dishonor.

11 To the present hour we both hunger and thirst, and are in nakedness, and maltreated, and wander without a home,

12 and labor, working with our own hands. Railed at, we bless; persecuted, we suffer it

13 insulted, we entreat: we are become as the scum of the world, the refuse of all, until now.

14 Not as chiding do I write these things to you, but as my beloved children I admonish.

15 For if you should have ten thousand instructors in Christ, yet not many fathers; for in Christ Jesus I have begotten you through the good news.

16 I entreat you therefore, be my imitators.

17 For this reason I have sent to you Timothy, who is my beloved and faithful child in the Lord, who shall put you in mind of my ways [as] they [are] in Christ, according as I teach everywhere in every church.

18 But some have been puffed up, as if I were not coming to you;

19 but I will come quickly to you, if the Lord will; and I will know, not the word of those that are puffed up, but the power.

20 For the kingdom of the God is not in word, but in power.

21 What do you wish? that I come to you with a rod; or in love, and [in] a spirit of meekness?

1 Cor 5:1 It is universally reported [that there is] fornication among you, and such fornication as is not even among the Gentiles, so that one should have his father's wife.

2 And you are puffed up, and you have not rather mourned, in order that he that has done this deed might be taken away out of the midst of you.

3 For I, [as] absent in body but present in spirit, have already judged as present,

4 [to deliver] in the name of our Lord Jesus Christ you and my spirit being gathered together, with the power of our Lord Jesus Christ, him that has so worked this:

5 to deliver him to Satan for destruction of the flesh, that the spirit may be saved in the day of the Lord Jesus.

6 Your boasting is not good. Do you not know that a little leaven leavens the whole lump?

7 Purge out the old leaven, that you may be a new lump, according as you are unleavened. For also our Passover, Christ, has been sacrificed;

8 so that let us celebrate the feast, not with old leaven, nor with leaven of malice and wickedness, but with unleavened [bread] of sincerity and truth.

9 I have written to you in the epistle not to mix with fornicators;

10 not altogether with the fornicators of this world, or with the greedy and extortionists, or idolaters, since [then] you would have to go out of the world.

11 But now I have written to you, if any one called brother be fornicator, or greedy, or idolater, or abusive, or a drunkard, or extortionists, not to mix with him with such a one not even to eat.

12 For what have I to do with judging those outside also? you, do not you judge them that are within?

13 But those outside God judges. Remove the wicked person from among yourselves.

1 Cor 6:1 Dare any one of you, having a matter against another, prosecute his suit before the unjust, and not before the saints?

2 Do you not then know that the saints shall judge the world? and if the world is judged by you, are you unworthy of the smallest judgments?

3 Do you not know that we shall judge angels? and not then matters of this life?

4 So if you have law courts dealing with matters of this life, do you appoint them as judges who are of no account in the church?

5 I speak to you [to put you] to shame. Thus there is not a wise person among you, not even one, who shall be able to decide between his brethren!

6 But brother prosecutes his suit with brother, and that before unbelievers.

7 Already indeed then it is altogether a fault in you that you have suits between yourselves. Why do you not rather suffer wrong? Why are you not rather defrauded?

8 But you do wrong, and defraud, and this [your] brethren.

9 Do you not know that the unrighteous shall not inherit the kingdom of God? Do not err: neither fornicators, nor idolaters, nor adulterers, nor effeminate dressing men, nor homosexuals,

10 nor thieves, nor covetous, nor drunkards, nor abusive persons, nor the extortionists, shall inherit the kingdom of God.

11 And these things were some of you; but you have been washed, but you have been sanctified, but you have been justified in the name of the Lord Jesus, and by the Spirit of our God.

12 All things are lawful to me, but all things do not profit; all things are lawful to me, but I will not be brought under the power of any.

13 Meats for the belly, and the belly for meats; but God will supersede both it and them: but the body is not for fornication, but for the Lord, and the Lord for the body.

14 And God has both raised up the Lord, and will raise us up from among [the dead] by his power.

15 Do you not know that your bodies are members of Christ? Shall I then, taking the members of the Christ, make [them] members of a harlot? Far be the thought.

16 Do you not know that he [that is] joined to the harlot is one body? for the two, he says, shall be one flesh.

17 But he that is joined to the Lord is one Spirit.

18 Flee fornication. Every sin which a man may practice is outside the body, but he that commits fornication sins against his own body.

19 Do you not know that your body is the temple of the Holy Spirit which is in you, which you have of God; and you are not your own?

20 for you have been bought with a price: glorify now then God in your body.

1 Cor 7:1 But concerning the things of which you have written [to me] [it is] good for a man not to touch a woman;

2 but on account of fornications, let each have his own wife, and each [woman] have her own husband.

3 Let the husband render her due to the wife, and in like manner the wife to the husband.

4 The wife has not authority over her own body, but the husband: in like manner also the husband has not authority over his own body, but the wife.

5 Deprive not one another, unless, it may be, by consent for a time, that you may devote yourselves to prayer, and again be together, that Satan tempt you not because of your weaknesses.

6 But this I say, as concession, not as commanding it

7 Now I wish all men to be even as myself: but every one has his own gift of God: one man thus, and another thus.

8 But I say to the unmarried and to the widows, It is good for them that they remain even as I.

9 But if they have not control over themselves, let them marry; for it is better to marry than to burn.

10 But to the married I enjoin, not I, but the Lord, Let not wife be separated from husband;

11 but if also she shall have been separated, let her remain unmarried, or be reconciled to her husband; and let not the husband leave the wife.

12 But as to the rest, I say, not the Lord, If any brother have an unbelieving wife, and she consent to dwell with him, let him not leave her.

13 And a woman who has an unbelieving husband, and he consents to dwell with her, let her not leave [her] husband.

14 For the unbelieving husband is sanctified in the wife, and the unbelieving wife is sanctified in the brother; since [otherwise] indeed your children are unclean, but now they are holy.

15 But if the unbeliever go away, let them go away; a brother or a sister is not bound in such [cases], for God has called us in peace.

16 For what know you, O wife, if you shall save your husband? or what know you, O husband, if you shall save your wife?

17 However, as the Lord has divided to each, as God has called each, so let him walk; and thus I ordain in all the churches.

18 Has any one been called circumcised? let him not become uncircumcised: has any one been called in uncircumcision? let him not be circumcised.

19 Circumcision is nothing, and uncircumcision is nothing; but keeping God's commandments.

20 Let each abide in that calling in which he has been called.

21 Have you been called [being] a servant, let it not concern you; but and if you can become free, do it rather.

22 For the servant that is called in the Lord is the Lord's freedman; in like manner [also] the freeman being called is Christ's servant.

23 You have been bought with a price; do not be the servants of men.

24 Let each, wherein he is called, brethren, therein abide with God.

25 But concerning virgins, I have no commandment of the Lord; but I give my opinion, as having received mercy of the Lord to be faithful.

26 I think then that this is good, on account of the present necessity, that [it is] good for a man to remain so as he is.

27 Are you bound to a wife? seek not to be loosened; are you free from a wife? do not seek a wife.

28 But if you should also marry, you have not sinned; and if the virgin marry, they have not sinned: but such shall have tribulation in the flesh; but I spare you.

29 But this I say, brethren, the time is shorter. From now on, they who have wives, be as not having,

30 and they that weep, as not weeping; and they that rejoice, as not rejoicing; and they that buy, as not possessing;

31 and they that use the world, as not abusing it as their own; for the way of this world passes.

32 But I wish you to be without anxiety. The unmarried is concerned for the things of the Lord, how he shall please the Lord;

33 but he that has married is concerned for the things of the world, how he shall please his wife.

34 There is a difference between the wife and the virgin. The unmarried is concerned for the things of the Lord, that she may be holy both in body and spirit; but she that has married is concerned for the things of the world, how she shall please her husband.

35 But I say this for your own profit; not that I may set a snare before you, but for what is seemly, and waiting on the Lord without distraction.

36 But if any one think that he behaves unseemly to her virgin, if she be beyond the flower of her age, and so it must be, let him do what he will, he does not sin: let them marry.

37 But he who stands firm in his heart, having no need, but has authority over his own will, and has judged this in his heart to keep his own virginity, he does well.

38 So that he that marries does well; and he that does not marry does better.

39 A wife is bound for whatever time her husband lives; but if the husband be fallen asleep, she is free to be married to whom she will, only in the Lord.

40 But she is happier if she so remain, according to my judgment; but I think that I also have God's Spirit.

1 Cor 8:1 But concerning things sacrificed to idols, we know, for we all have knowledge: knowledge puffs up, but love edifies.

2 If any one think he knows anything, he knows nothing yet as he ought to know it.

3 But if any one love God, he is known of him:

4 --concerning then the eating of things sacrificed to idols, we know that an idol is nothing in the world, and that there is no other God except one.

5 For if indeed there are [those] called gods, whether in heaven or on earth, as there are gods many, and lords many,

6 yet to us, one God, the Father, out of whom all things, and we into him; and one Lord, Jesus Christ, through whom all things, and we through him.

7 But knowledge is not in all: but some, with conscience of the idol, until now eat as of a thing sacrificed to idols; and their conscience, being weak, is defiled.

8 But meat does not commend us to God; neither if we should not eat do we come short; nor if we should eat have we an advantage.

9 But see lest anyway this your right [to eat] itself be a stumbling-block to the weak.

10 For if any one see you, who have knowledge, sitting at table in an idol-house, shall not his conscience, he being weak, be emboldened to eat the things sacrificed to the idol?

11 and the weak, the brother for whose sake Christ died, will perish through your knowledge.

12 Now, thus sinning against the brethren, and wounding their weak conscience, you sin against Christ.

13 Therefore if meat be a trap to my brother, I will eat no flesh into the aeon, that I may not be a trap to my brother.

1 Cor 9:1 Am I not free? am I not an apostle? have I not seen Jesus our Lord? are not you my work in the Lord?

2 If I am not an apostle to others, yet at any rate I am to you: for the seal of mine apostleship are you in the Lord.

3 My defense to those who examine me is this:

4 Have we not a right to eat and to drink?

5 have we not a right to take round a sister [as] wife, as also the other apostles, and the brethren of the Lord, and Cephas?

6 Or I alone and Barnabas, have we not a right not to work?

7 Who ever carries on war at his own expense? Who plants a vineyard and does not eat of its fruit? or who herds a flock and does not eat of the milk of the flock?

8 Do I speak these things as a man, or does not the law also say these things?

9 For in the law of Moses it is written, You shall not muzzle the ox that is treading out grain. Is God occupied with the oxen,

10 or does he say this for our sakes? For for our sakes it has been written, that the plougher should plough in hope, and he that treads out grain, in hope of partaking of it.

11 If we have sown to you spiritual things, [is it a] great [thing] if we shall reap your carnal things?

12 If others partake of this right over you, should not rather we? But we have not used this right, but we bear all things, that we may put no hindrance in the way of the good news from the Christ.

13 Do you not know that they who labor [at] sacred things eat of the [offerings offered in the] temple; they that attend at the altar partake with the altar?

14 So also the Lord has ordained to those that announce the good news to live of the good news.

15 But I have used none of these things. Now I have not written these things that it should be thus in my case; for [it were] good for me rather to die than that any one should make vain my boast.

16 For if I announce the good news, I have nothing to boast of; for a necessity is laid upon me; for it is woe to me if I should not announce the good news.

17 For if I do this voluntarily, I have a reward; but if not of my own will, I am entrusted with an administration.

18 What is the reward then that I have? That in announcing the good news I make the good news costless [to others] so as not to have made use, as belonging to me, of my right in [announcing] the good news.

19 For being free from all, I have made myself servant to all, that I might gain the most [possible].

20 And I became to the Jews as a Jew, in order that I might gain the Jews: to those under law, as under law, not being myself under law, in order that I might gain those under law:

21 to those without law, as without law, not as without law to God, but as legitimately subject to Christ, in order that I might gain [those] without law.

22 I become to the weak, [as] weak, in order that I might gain the weak. To all I have become all things, in order that at all events I might save some.

23 And I do all things for the sake of the good news, that I may be fellow-partaker with them.

24 Don't you know that they all run in the race, but only one receives the prize? Thus run in order that you may obtain.

25 But every one that contends [for a prize] is temperate in all things: they then indeed that they may receive a corruptible crown, but we an incorruptible.

26 I therefore thus run, not as uncertain; but I combat, so as not to be boxing the air.

27 But I buffet my body, and lead it captive, lest [after] having preached to others I should be myself rejected.

1 Cor 10:1 For I would not have you ignorant, brethren, that all our fathers were under the cloud, and all passed through the sea;

2 and all were baptized* unto Moses in the cloud and in the sea;

3 and all eat* the same spiritual food,

4 and all drink* the same spiritual drink, for they will drink [imp.] of a spiritual rock which followed [them] now the rock was the Christ;

5 yet the God was not pleased with the most of them, for they were scattered in the desert.

6 But these things happened [as] types of us, that we should not be lusting after evil things, as they also lusted.

7 Neither be you idolaters, as some of them; as it is written, The people sat down to eat and to drink, and rose up to play.

8 Neither let us commit fornication, as some of them committed fornication, and fell in one day three and twenty thousand.

9 Neither let us test the Lord [YHWH, Ex 17:2], as some of them tested, and perished by serpents.

10 Neither murmur you, as some of them murmured, and perished by the destroyer.

11 Now all these things happened to them [as] types, and have been written for our admonition, upon whom the ends of the aeons are come.

12 So let him that thinks that he stands take heed lest he fall.

13 No trial has taken you but such as is according to any man; and God is faithful, who will not permit you to be tested above what you are able [to bear] but will with the trial make the escape also, so that [you] should be able to bear it

14 Therefore, my beloved, flee from idolatry.

15 I speak as to wise men; you judge what I say.

16 The cup of blessing which we bless, is it not the communion of the blood of the Christ? The bread which we break, is it not the communion of the body of the Christ?

17 Because we, [being] many, are one loaf, one body; for we all partake of that one loaf.

18 See Israel according to flesh: are not they who eat the sacrifices in communion with the altar?

19 What then do I say? that what is sacrificed to an idol is anything, or that an idol is anything?

20 But that what [the nations] sacrifice they sacrifice to daemons, and not to God. Now I do not wish you to be in communion with daemons.

21 You cannot drink the Lord's cup, and the cup of daemons: you cannot partake of the Lord's table, and of the table of daemons.

22 Do we provoke the Lord to jealousy? are we stronger than he?

23 All things are lawful, but all are not profitable; all things are lawful, but all do not edify.

24 Let no one seek his own, but that of the other.

25 Everything sold in the shambles eat, making no inquiry for conscience sake.

26 For the earth is the Lord's and its fullness.

27 But if any one of the unbelievers invite you, and you want to go, all that is set before you eat, making no inquiry for conscience sake.

28 But if any one say to you, This is offered to holy purposes, do not eat, for his sake that pointed it out, and conscience sake;

29 but conscience, I mean, not your own, but that of the other: for why is my liberty judged by another conscience?

30 If I partake with thanksgiving, why am I spoken evil of for what I give thanks for?

31 Whether therefore you eat, or drink, or whatever you do, do all things to God's glory.

32 Give no occasion to stumbling, whether to Jews, or Greeks, or the church of God.

33 Even as I also please all in all things; not seeking my own profit, but that of the many, that they may be saved.

1 Cor 11:1 Be my imitators, even as I also am of Christ.

2 Now I praise you, that in all things you are mindful of me; and that as I have directed you, you keep the directions.

3 But I wish you to know that the Christ is the head of every man, but woman's head is the man, and the Christ's head God.

4 Every man praying or prophesying, having [anything] on his head, puts his head to shame.

5 But every woman praying or prophesying with her head uncovered puts her own head to shame; for it is one and the same as a shaved [woman].

6 For if a woman be not covered, let her hair also be cut off. But if [it be] shameful to a woman to have her hair cut off or to be shaved, let her be covered.

7 For man indeed ought not to have his head covered, being God's image and glory; but woman is man's glory.

8 For man is not of woman, but woman of man.

9 For also man was not created for the sake of the woman, but woman for the sake of the man.

10 Therefore ought the woman to have authority on her head, on account of the angels.

11 However, neither is woman apart from man, nor man apart from woman, in the Lord.

12 For as the woman is out of the man, so also is the man through the woman, but all things out of God.

13 Judge in yourselves: is it becoming that a woman should pray to God uncovered?

14 Does not even nature itself teach you, that man, if he have long hair, it is a dishonor to him?

15 But woman, if she have long hair, [it is] glory to her; for the long hair is given [to her] in lieu of a veil.

16 But if any one think to be contentious, we have no such custom, nor the churches of God.

17 But [in] prescribing [to you on] this [which I now enter on] I do not praise, [namely] that you come together, not for the better, but for the worse.

18 For first, when you come together in church, I hear there exist divisions among you, and I partly give credit [to it].

19 For there must also be sects among you, that the approved may become manifest among you.

20 When you come therefore together into one place, it is not to eat the Lord's supper?

21 For each one in eating takes his own supper before [others] and one is hungry and another drinks to excess.

22 Have you not then houses for eating and drinking? or do you despise the church of God, and put to shame them who have not? What shall I say to you? shall I praise you? In this [point] I do not praise.

23 For I received from the Lord, that which I also delivered to you, that the Lord Jesus, in the night in which he was delivered up, took bread,

24 and having given thanks broke it and said, This is my body, which is for you: this do in remembrance of me.

25 In like manner also the cup, after having supped, saying, This cup is the new covenant in my blood: this do, as often as you shall drink it in remembrance of me.

26 For as often as you shall eat this bread, and drink the cup, you announce the death of the Lord, until he come.

27 So that whosoever shall eat the bread, or drink the cup of the Lord, unworthily, shall be guilty in respect of the body and of the blood of the Lord.

28 But let a man prove himself, and thus eat of the bread, and drink of the cup.

29 For the eater and drinker eats and drinks judgment to himself, not distinguishing the body.

30 On this account many among you [are] weak and infirm, and a good many are fallen asleep.

31 But if we judged ourselves, so were we not judged.

32 But being judged, we are disciplined of the Lord, that we may not be condemned with the world.

33 So that, my brethren, when you come together to eat, wait for one another.

34 If any one be hungry, let him eat at home, that you may not come together for judgment. But the other things, whenever I come, I will set in order.

1 Cor 12:1 But concerning spiritual things brethren, I do not wish you to be ignorant.

2 You know that when you were [of the] nations [you were] led away to mute idols, in whatever way you might be led.

3 I give you therefore to know, that no one, speaking in [the power of the] Spirit of God, says, Curse [on] Jesus; and no one can say, Lord Jesus, unless in [the power of the] Holy Spirit.

4 But there are distinctions of gifts, but the same Spirit;

5 and there are distinctions of services, but the same Lord;

6 and there are distinctions of operations, but the same God who operates all things in all.

7 But each manifestation of the Spirit is given for profit.

8 For to one, by the Spirit, is given the word of wisdom; and to another the word of knowledge, according to the same Spirit;

9 and to a different one faith, in the same Spirit; and to another gifts of healing in the same Spirit;

10 and to another operations of miracles; and to another prophecy; and to another discerning of spirits; and to a different one different kinds of tongues; and to another interpretation of tongues.

11 But all these things operates the one and the same Spirit, dividing to each in particular according as he pleases.

12 For even as the body is one and has many members, but all the members of the body, being many, are one body, so also is the Christ.

13 For also in [the power of] one Spirit we have all been baptized into one body, whether Jews or Greeks, whether servants or free, and have all been given to drink of one Spirit.

14 For also the body is not one member but many.

15 If the foot say, Because I am not a hand I am not of the body, is it on account of this not of the body?

16 And if the ear say, Because I am not an eye I am not of the body, is it because of this outside the body?

17 If the whole body, [were] an eye, where the hearing? if all hearing, where the smelling?

18 But now God has set the members, each one of them in the body, according as it has pleased him.

19 But if all were one body part, where is the body?

20 But now the members [are] many, and the body one.

21 The eye cannot say to the hand, I have no need of you; or again, the head to the feet, I have no need of you.

22 But much rather, the members of the body which seem to be weaker are necessary;

23 and those [parts] of the body which we esteem to be the more void of honor, these we clothe with more abundant honor; and our unbecoming [parts] have more abundant comeliness;

24 but our becoming [parts] have not need. But God has tempered the body together, having given more abundant honor to [the part] that lacked;

25 that there might be no division in the body, but that the members might have the same concern one for another.

26 And if one member suffer, all the members suffer with it and if one member be glorified, all the members rejoice with it

27 Now you are Christ's body, and members in particular.

28 And God has set certain in the church: first, apostles; secondly, prophets; thirdly, teachers; then miraculous powers; then gifts of healings; helpers; directors; different tongues.

29 [Are] all apostles? [are] all prophets? [are] all teachers? [are] all [in possession of] miraculous powers?

30 have all gifts of healings? do all speak with tongues? do all interpret?

31 But desire earnestly the greater gifts, and yet show I unto you a way of more surpassing excellence.

1 Cor 13:1 If I speak with the tongues of men and of angels, but have not love, I am become sounding brass or a clanging cymbal.

2 And if I have prophecy, and know all revealable-mysteries and all knowledge, and if I have all faith, so as to remove mountains, but have not love, I am nothing.

3 And if I shall dole out all my goods in food, and if I deliver up my body that I may be burned, but have not love, I profit nothing.

4 <u>Love is</u> patience, is kind; love is not jealous, not boastful, not arrogant,

5 [Love] is not rude, not self-centered, is not quickly provoked, does not reckon[1] the evil,

6 [Love] does not rejoice in the time of injustice, but rejoices with the truth,

7 [Love] covers all [sin[2]], believes all [good], hopes all [good], endures all [evil].

8 Love never fails; but whether [gifts of] prophecies, they shall be superseded[3]; or [gifts of] tongues, they shall cease; or [gift of] knowledge, it shall be superseded[3].

9 For we know in part, and we prophesy in part:

10 but when that which is perfect has come, that which is in part shall be superseded[3].

---

[1] Keep an account of the evil of others, or possibly think the evil

[2] See Prov 10:12

[3] "the basic sense *cause to be idle* or *useless*, the term always denotes a nonphysical destruction by means of a superior force coming in to replace the force previously in effect, as e.g. light destroys darkness"

11 When I was a child, I spoke as a child, I felt as a child, I reasoned as a child; when I became a man, I have superseded[3] what belonged to the child.

12 For we see now through a dim window obscurely, but later face to face; now I know partially, but then I shall know according as I also have been known.

13 And now abide faith, hope, love; these three things; and the greater of these is love.

1 Cor 14:1 Follow after love, and be zealous of spiritual [things] so that you may prophesy [teach].

2 For he that speaks with a tongue does not speak to men but to God: for no one hears; but in spirit he speaks revealed-mysteries.

3 But he that prophesies speaks to men [in] edification, and encouragement, and consolation.

4 He that speaks with a tongue[1] edifies himself; but he that prophesies edifies the church.

5 Now I wish that you should all speak with tongues, but rather that you should prophesy [teach]. But greater is he that prophesies than he that speaks with tongues, unless he interpret, that the church may receive edification.

6 And now, brethren, if I come to you speaking with tongues, what shall I profit you, unless I shall speak to you either in revelation, or in knowledge, or in prophecy, or in doctrine?

7 Even lifeless things giving a sound, whether pipe or harp, if they give not distinction to the sounds, how shall it be known what is piped or harped?

8 For also, if the trumpet give an uncertain sound, who shall prepare himself for war?

9 Thus also you with the tongue, unless you give a distinct speech, how shall it be known what is spoken? for you will be speaking to the air.

10 There are, perhaps, a great many kinds of languages in the world, and no kind is without meaning.

11 If then I do not know the meaning of the language, I will be a barbarian to the speaker, and the speaker will be a barbarian to me.

12 Thus you also, since you are desirous of spiritual things, seek that you may abound for the edification of the church.

13 Therefore let him that speaks with a tongue pray that he may interpret.

14 For if I pray with a tongue, my spirit prays, but my understanding is unfruitful.

15 What is it then? I will pray with the spirit, but I will pray also with the understanding; I will sing with the spirit, but I will sing also with the understanding.

16 Since otherwise, if you bless with the spirit [because you speak in a tongue no others understand], how shall he who does not understand [your tongue] say, Amen, at your giving of thanks, since he does not know what you say?

17 For you indeed give thanks well, but the other is not edified.

18 I thank God I speak in tongues more than all of you:

19 but in the church I desire to speak five words with my understanding, that I may instruct others also, [rather] than ten thousand words in a tongue.

20 Brethren, be not children in [your] minds, but in malice be babes; but in [your] minds be grown [men].

21 It is written in the law, By people of other tongues, and by strange lips, will I speak to this people; and neither will they hear me, says the Lord.

22 So that tongues are for a sign, not to those who believe, but to unbelievers; but prophecy, not to unbelievers, but to those who believe.

23 If therefore the whole church come together in one place, and all speak with tongues, and the unskilled [in the language] enter in, or unbelievers, will not they say you are mad?

24 But if all prophesy [teach], and some unbeliever or unskilled come in, he is reproved by all [the words], he is judged by all [the words];

25 the secrets of his heart are manifested; and thus, falling upon [his] face, he will do homage to God, reporting that God is indeed among you.

26 What is it then, brethren? whenever you come together, each [of you] has a psalm, has a teaching, has a tongue, has a revelation, has an interpretation. Let all things be done to edification.

27 If any one speak with a tongue, [let it be] two, or at the most three, and separately, and let one interpret;

28 but if there be no interpreter, let him be silent in the church, and let him speak to himself and to God.

29 And let two or three prophets [teachers] speak, and let the others judge.

30 But if there be a revelation to another sitting [there] let the first be silent.

31 For you can all prophesy [teach] one by one, that all may learn and all be encouraged.

32 And spirits of prophets are subject to prophets.

33 For God is not of disorder but of peace, as in all the churches of the saints.

34 Let [your] women be silent in the churches, for it is not permitted to them to speak; but to be in subjection, as the law also says.

35 But if they wish to learn anything, let them ask their own husbands at home; for it is a shame for a woman to speak in church.

36 Did the word of God go out from you, or did it come to you only?

37 If any one thinks himself to be a prophet or spiritual, let him recognize the things that I write to you, that it is the Lord's commandment.

38 But if any be ignorant, let him be ignorant.

39 So that, brethren, desire to prophesy [teach], and do not forbid the speaking with tongues.

40 But let all things be done fitting and with order.

---

[1] That no one can understand

1 Cor 15:1 But I make known to you, brethren, the good news which I announced to you, which also you received, in which also you stand,

2 by which also you are saved, if you hold fast the word which I announced to you as the good news, unless indeed you have believed in vain.

3 For I delivered to you, in the first place, what also I had received, that Christ died for our sins, according to the scriptures;

4 and that he was buried; and that he was raised the third day, according to the scriptures;

5 and that he appeared to Cephas, then to the twelve.

6 Then he appeared to above five hundred brethren at once, of whom the most remain until now, but some also have fallen asleep.

7 Then he appeared to James; then to all the apostles;

8 and last of all, as to an abortion, he appeared to me also.

9 For I am the least of the apostles, who am not fit to be called apostle, because I have persecuted the church of God.

10 But by God's grace I am what I am; and his grace, which [was] towards me, has not been vain; but I have labored more abundantly than they all, but not I, but the grace of God which [was] with me.

11 Whether, therefore, I or they, thus we preach, and thus you have believed.

12 Now if Christ is preached that he is raised from among the dead, how can some among you say that there is not a resurrection of [those that are] dead?

13 But if there is not a resurrection of [those that are] dead, neither is Christ raised:

14 but if Christ is not raised, then, indeed, vain also is our preaching, and vain also your faith.

15 And we are found also false witnesses of God; for we have witnessed concerning God that he raised the Christ, whom he has not raised if indeed [those that are] dead are not raised.

16 For if [those that are] dead are not raised, neither is Christ raised;

17 but if Christ be not raised, your faith is vain; you are yet in your sins.

18 Then indeed also those who have fallen asleep in Christ have perished.

19 If in this life only we have hope in [a dead] Christ, we are the most miserable of all men.

20 But now Christ is raised from among the dead, first-fruit of those fallen asleep.

21 For since by man [came] death, by man also resurrection of [those that are] dead.

22 For as in the Adam all die, thus also in the Christ all shall be made alive.

23 But each in his own rank [or order]: the first-fruit, Christ; then those that are of the Christ at his coming.

24 Then the end, when he gives up the kingdom to him [who is] God and Father; when he supersedes all rule and all authority and power.

25 For he must reign until he put all enemies under his feet.

26 the last enemy that is superseded is death.

27 For he [God] has put all things in subjection under his [Christ's] feet. But when he says that all things are put in subjection, [it is] evident that [it is] except him [Father] who put all things in subjection to him [Christ].

28 But when all things shall have been brought into subjection to him [Christ], then the Son also himself shall be placed in subjection to him [Father] who put all things in subjection to him [Christ], that the God may be the all in all.

29 Since what shall the baptized for the dead do if [those that are] dead rise not at all? why also are they baptized for them?

30 Why do we also endanger ourselves every hour?

31 Daily I face death, by your boasting which I have in Christ Jesus our Lord.

32 If, [to speak] after the manner of man, I have fought with beasts in Ephesus, what is the profit to me if [those that are] dead do not rise? let us eat and drink; for tomorrow we die.

33 Be not deceived: evil company corrupt good habits.

34 Awake up righteously, and sin not; for some are ignorant of God: I speak to you as a matter of shame.

35 But some one will say, How are the dead raised? and with what body do they come?

36 Fool; what you sow is not quickened unless it die.

37 And what you sow, you sow not the body that shall be, but a bare grain: it may be of wheat, or one of the rest:

38 and God gives to it a body as he has pleased, and to each of the seeds its own body.

39 Every flesh is not the same flesh, but one is of men, and another flesh of beasts, and another [flesh] of birds, and another of fish.

40 And [there are] heavenly bodies, and earthly bodies: but different is the glory of the heavenly, different that of the earthly:

41 one the sun's glory, and another the moon's glory, and another the stars' glory; for star differs from star in glory.

42 Thus also is the resurrection of the dead. It is sown in corruption, it is raised in incorruptibility.

43 It is sown in dishonor, it is raised in glory. It is sown in weakness, it is raised in power.

44 It is sown a natural body, it is raised a spiritual body: if there is a natural body, there is also a spiritual [one]

45 Thus also it is written, The first man Adam became a living soul; the last Adam in spirit being made alive.

46 But that which is spiritual [was] not first, but that which is natural, then that which is spiritual:

47 the first man out of the earth, made of dust; the second man, out of heaven.

48 Such as he made of dust, such also those made of dust; and such as the heavenly [one] such also the heavenly [ones]

49 And as we have borne the image of the [one] made of dust, we shall bear also the image of the heavenly [one].

50 But this I say, brethren, that flesh and blood cannot inherit God's kingdom, nor does corruption inherit incorruptibility.

51 Behold, I tell you a revealed-mystery: We shall not all fall asleep, but we shall all be changed,

52 in an instant, in the twinkling of an eye, at the last trumpet; for the trumpet shall sound, and the dead shall be raised incorruptible, and we shall be changed.

53 For this corruptible must put on incorruptibility, and this mortal put on immortality.

54 But when this corruptible shall have put on incorruptibility, and this mortal shall have put on immortality, then shall come to pass the word written: Death has been swallowed up in victory.

55 Where, O death, is your sting? where, O death, your victory?

56 Now the sting of death is sin, and the power of sin the law;

57 but thanks to God, who gives us the victory by our Lord Jesus Christ.

58 So then, my beloved brethren, be firm, immovable, abounding always in the work of the Lord, knowing that your toil is not in vain in the Lord.

1 Cor 16:1 Now concerning the collection for the saints, as I directed the churches of Galatia, so do you do also.

2 On one of the sabbaths let each of you put by at home, laying up [in] whatever [degree] he may have prospered, that there may be no collections when I come.

3 And when I am arrived, whomsoever you shall approve, these I will send with letters to carry your bounty to Jerusalem:

4 and if it be suitable that I also should go, they shall go with me.

5 But I will come to you when I shall have gone through Macedonia; for I do go through Macedonia.

6 But perhaps I will stay with you, or even winter with you, that you may set me forward wheresoever I may go.

7 For I will not see you now in passing, for I hope to remain a certain time with you, if the Lord permit.

8 But I remain in Ephesus until Pentecost.

9 For a great door is opened to me and a great working one, but adversaries many.

10 Now if Timothy come, see that he may be with you without fear; for he works the work of the Lord, even as I.

11 Let not therefore any one despise him; but set him forward in peace, that he may come to me; for I expect him with the brethren.

12 Now concerning the brother Apollos, I begged him much that he would go to you with the brethren; but it was not at all [his] will to go now; but he will come when he shall have good opportunity.

13 Keep awake; stand firm in the faith; stand like men; be strong.

14 Let all things you do be done in love.

15 But I beseech you, brethren, you know the house of Stephanas, that it is the first-fruit of Achaia, and they have devoted themselves to the saints for service,

16 that you should also be subject to such, and to every one joined in the work and laboring.

17 But I rejoice in the coming of Stephanas and Fortunatus and Achaicus; because they have supplied what was lacking on your part.

18 For they have refreshed my spirit and yours: so recognize such persons.

19 The churches of Asia salute you. Aquila and Priscilla, with the church in their house, salute you much in the Lord.

20 All the brethren salute you. Salute one another with a holy kiss.

21 The salutation of [me] Paul with my own hand.

22 If any one like not the Lord [Jesus Christ] let him be cursed.

23 The grace of the Lord Jesus Christ [be] with you.

24 My love [be] with you all in Christ Jesus. Amen.

2 Corinthians

2 Cor 1:1 Paul, apostle of Jesus Christ by God's will, and the brother Timothy, to the church of God which is in Corinth, with all the saints who are in the whole of Achaia.

2 Grace to you, and peace from God our Father, and the Lord Jesus Christ.

3 Blessed [be] God and Father of our Lord Jesus Christ, the Father of compassion, and God of all encouragement;

4 who encourages us in all our tribulation, that we may be able to encourage those who are in any tribulation whatever, through the encouragement with which we ourselves are encouraged of God.

5 Because, even as the sufferings of the Christ abound towards us, so through the Christ does our encouragement also abound.

6 But whether we are in tribulation, [it is] for your encouragement and salvation, worked in the endurance of the same sufferings which we also suffer,

7 and our hope for you is sure; or whether we are encouraged, [it is] for your encouragement and salvation: knowing that as you are partakers of the sufferings, so also of the encouragement.

8 For we do not wish you to be ignorant, brethren, as to our tribulation which happened [to us] in Asia, that we were excessively pressed beyond [our] power, so as to despair even of living.

9 But we ourselves had the sentence of death in ourselves, that we should not have our trust in ourselves, but in God who raises the dead;

10 who has delivered us from so great a death, and does deliver; in whom we confide that he will also yet deliver;

11 you also laboring together by supplication for us that the gift towards us, through means of many persons, may be the subject of the thanksgiving of many for us.

12 For our boasting is this, the testimony of our conscience, that in simplicity and sincerity before God, not in fleshly wisdom but in God's grace, we have had our behavior in the world, and more abundantly towards you.

13 For we do not write other things to you but what you well know and recognize; and I hope that you will recognize to the end,

14 even as also you have recognized us in part, that we are your boast, even as you [are] ours in the day of the Lord Jesus.

15 And with this confidence I purposed to come to you previously, that you might have a second grace;

16 and to pass through to Macedonia by you, and again from Macedonia to come to you, and to be set forward by you to Judea.

17 Having therefore this purpose, did I then use lightness? Or what I purpose, do I purpose according to flesh, that there should be with me yes yes, and no no?

18 Now God is faithful, that our word to you is not yes and no.

19 For the Son of God, Jesus Christ, he who has been preached by us among you by me and Silvanus and Timothy, did not become yes and no, but yes is in him.

20 For whatever promises of God [there are] in him is the yes, and in him the amen, for glory to God by us.

21 Now he that establishes us with you in Christ, and has anointed us, is God,

22 who also has sealed us, and given the earnest of the Spirit in our hearts.

23 But I call God to witness upon my soul that to spare you I have not yet come to Corinth.

24 Not that we rule over your faith, but are fellow-workmen of your joy: for by faith you stand.

2 Cor 2:1 But I have judged this with myself, not to come back to you in grief.

2 For if I grieve you, who also is it that gladdens me, if not he that is grieved through me?

3 And I have written this very [letter] [to you] that coming I may not have grief from those from whom I ought to have joy; trusting in you all that my joy is that of you all.

4 For out of much tribulation and distress of heart I wrote to you, with many tears; not that you may be grieved, but that you may know the love which I have very abundantly towards you.

5 But if any has caused sorrow, he has caused sorrow not to me, but in some degree-- in order not to say too much-- to all of you.

6 Sufficient to such a one is this rebuke which [has been inflicted] by the majority;

7 so that on the contrary you should rather show grace and encourage, lest perhaps such a one should be swallowed up with excessive grief.

8 Therefore I exhort you to assure him of [your] love.

9 For to this end also I have written, that I might know, by putting you to the test, if as to everything you are obedient.

10 But to whom you forgive anything, I also; for I also, what I have forgiven, if I have forgiven anything, [it is] for your sakes in the person of Christ;

11 that we might not have Satan get an advantage against us, for we are not ignorant of his thoughts.

12 Now when I came to Troas for the good news of the Christ, a door also being opened to me in the Lord,

13 I had no rest in my spirit at not finding Titus my brother; but bidding them good-by, I came away to Macedonia.

14 But thanks [be] to God, who always leads us in triumph in the Christ, and makes manifest the aroma of his knowledge through us in every place.

15 For we are a sweet aroma of Christ to God, in the saved and in those that perish:

16 to the one an aroma from death unto death, but to the others an aroma from life unto life; and who is sufficient for these things?

17 For we do not, as the many, make a trade of the word of God; but as of sincerity, but as of God, before God, we speak in Christ.

2 Cor 3:1 Do we begin again to commend ourselves? or do we need, as some, commendatory letters to you, or [commendatory] from you?

2 You are our letter, written in our hearts, known and read of all men,

3 being manifested to be Christ's epistle ministered by us, written, not with ink, but the Spirit of the living God; not on stone tables, but on fleshy tables of the heart.

4 And such confidence have we through the Christ toward the God:

5 not that we are competent of ourselves to think anything as of ourselves, but our competency is of God;

6 who has also made us competent, [as] ministers of the new covenant not of letter, but of spirit. For the letter kills, but the Spirit gives life.

7 But if the ministry of death, in letters, graven in stones, began with glory, so that the children of Israel could not fix their eyes on the face of Moses, on account of the glory of his face, [a glory] which is being superseded;

8 how shall not rather the ministry of the Spirit subsist in glory?

9 For if the ministry of condemnation [be] glory, much rather the ministry of righteousness abounds in glory.

10 For also that [which was] glorified is not glorified in this respect, on account of the surpassing glory.

11 For if that superseded [was introduced] with glory, much rather that which abides [subsists] in glory.

12 Having therefore such hope, we use much boldness:

13 and not according as Moses put a veil on his own face, so that the children of Israel should not fix their eyes on the fulfillment of that superseded.

14 But their thoughts have been darkened, for unto this day the same veil remains unremoved in reading the old covenant, which in Christ is superseded.

15 But unto this day, when Moses is read, the veil lies upon their heart.

16 But when he shall turn to the Lord, the veil is taken away.

17 Now the Lord is the Spirit, but where the Spirit of the Lord [is there is] liberty.

18 But we all, looking on the glory of the Lord, with unveiled face, are transformed according to the same image from glory to glory, even as by the Lord the Spirit.

2 Cor 4:1 Therefore, having this ministry, as we have had mercy shown us, we faint not.

2 But we have renounced the things hidden because of shame, not walking in craftiness or adulterating the word of God, but by the manifestation of truth commending ourselves to every man's conscience in the sight of God.

3 But if also our gospel is veiled, it is veiled in those that are lost;

4 in whom **God of this world**[1] has blinded the thoughts of the unbelieving, so that the radiancy of the good news of the glory of the Christ, who is the image of God, should not shine forth [for them].

5 For we do not preach ourselves, but Christ Jesus Lord, and ourselves your servants for Jesus' sake.

6 Because [it is] God who spoke that out of darkness light should shine who has shone in our hearts for the shining forth of the knowledge of the glory of God in the face of [Jesus] Christ.

7 But we have this treasure in clay vessels, that the all-surpassing power may be of God, and not from us:

8 every way afflicted, but not crushed; seeing no apparent escape, but our way not entirely shut up;

9 persecuted, but not abandoned; cast down, but not destroyed;

10 always bearing about in the body the dying of Jesus, that the life also of Jesus may be manifested in our body;

11 for we who live are always delivered unto death on account of Jesus, that the life also of Jesus may be manifested in our mortal flesh;

12 so that death works in us, but life in you.

13 And having the same spirit of faith, according to what is written, I have believed, therefore have I spoken; we also believe, therefore also we speak;

14 knowing that he who has raised the Lord Jesus shall raise us also with Jesus, and shall present [us] with you.

15 For all things [are] for your sakes, that the grace abounding through the many may cause thanksgiving to abound to the glory of God.

16 Therefore we faint not; but if indeed our outward man is consumed, yet the inward is renewed day by day.

17 For our momentary [and] light affliction works for us in surpassing measure an aeonian weight of glory;

18 while we look not at the things that are seen, but at the things that are not seen; for the things that are seen [are] for a time, but those that are not seen [are] aeonian.

2 Cor 5:1 For we know that if our earthly tabernacle house be destroyed, we have a building from God, a house not made with hands, aeonian in the heavens.

2 For indeed in this we groan, earnestly desiring to have put on our house which is from heaven;

3 if indeed being also clothed we shall not be found naked.

4 For indeed we who are in the tabernacle groan, being burdened; while yet we do not wish to

---

[1] Satan, see Eph 2:2; John 12:31; Col 1:13; 2 Tim 2:26; 1 John 5:19

be unclothed, but clothed, that [what is] mortal may be swallowed up by life.

5 Now he that has worked us for this very thing is God, who also has given to us the down payment of the Spirit.

6 Therefore [we are] always confident, and know that while present in the body we are absent from the Lord,

7 for we walk by faith, not by sight;

8 we are confident, I say, and pleased rather to be absent from the body and present with the Lord.

9 Therefore also we are zealous, whether present or absent, to be agreeable to him.

10 For we must all be manifested before the judgment-seat of the Christ, that each may receive the things [done] in the body, according to those he has done, whether [it be] good or evil.

11 Knowing therefore the terror of the Lord we persuade men, but have been manifested to God, and I hope also that we have been manifested in your consciences.

12 [For] we are not again recommending ourselves to you, but [we are] giving to you occasion of boast in our behalf, that you may have [such] with those boasting in appearance, and not in heart.

13 For whether we are beside ourselves, [it is] to God; or are sober, [it is] for you.

14 For the love of the Christ constrains us, having judged this: that one died for all, then all have died;

15 and he died for all, that they who live should no longer live to themselves, but to him who died for them and has been raised.

16 So that we henceforth know no one according to flesh; but if even we have known Christ according to flesh, yet now we know [him thus] no longer.

17 So if any one [be] in Christ, [there is] a new creation; the old things have passed away; behold all things have become new:

18 and all things [are] out of the God who has reconciled us to himself through [Jesus] Christ, and given to us the ministry of that reconciliation:

19 how that God was in Christ, reconciling the world to himself, not reckoning to them their offences; and putting in us the word of that reconciliation.

20 We are ambassadors therefore for Christ, God as [it were] beseeching by us, we entreat for Christ, Be reconciled to God.

21 Him who knew not sin he was made sin for us, that we might become God's righteousness in him.

2 Cor 6:1 But [as] fellow-workmen, we also beseech that you receive not the grace of God in vain:

2 for he says, I have listened to you in an accepted time, and I have helped you in a day of salvation: behold, now [is the] well-accepted time; behold, now the day of salvation:

3 giving no manner of offence in anything, that the ministry be not blamed;

4 but in everything commending ourselves as God's ministers, in much endurance, in afflictions, in necessities, in difficulties,

5 in stripes, in prisons, in riots, in labors, in watching, in fasting,

6 in pureness, in knowledge, in patience, in kindness, in the Holy Spirit, in love which is not hypocritical,

7 in the word of truth, in the power of God; through the arms of righteousness on the right hand and left,

8 through glory and dishonor, through evil report and good report: as deceivers, and true;

9 as unknown, and well known; as dying, and behold, we live; as disciplined, and not put to death;

10 as grieved, but always rejoicing; as poor, but enriching many; as having nothing, and possessing all things.

11 Our mouth is opened to you, Corinthians, our heart is expanded.

12 You are not crushed in us, but you are crushed in your affections;

13 but for a awarding exchange, I speak as to children, let your heart also expand itself.

14 Be not diversely yoked with unbelievers; for what participation [is there] between righteousness and lawlessness? or what fellowship of light with darkness?

15 and what consent of Christ with Belial [Satan], or what part for a believer along with an unbeliever?

16 and what agreement of God's temple with idols? for you are the living God's temple; according as God has said, I will dwell among them, and walk among [them] and I will be their God, and they shall be to me a people.

17 Therefore come out from the midst of them, and be separated, says the Lord, and touch not [what is] unclean, and I will receive you;

18 and I will be to you for a Father, and you shall be to me for sons and daughters, says the Lord Almighty.

2 Cor 7:1 Having therefore these promises, beloved, let us purify ourselves from every pollution of flesh and spirit, perfecting holiness in God's fear.

2 Receive us: we have injured no one, we have ruined no one, we have made gain of no one.

3 I do not speak for condemnation, for I have already said that you are in our hearts, to die together, and live together.

4 Great is my boldness towards you, great my exulting in respect of you; I am filled with encouragement; I overabound in joy under all our affliction.

5 For indeed, when we came into Macedonia, our flesh had no rest, but [we were] afflicted in every way; outside were combats, within fears.

6 But he who encourages those that are [brought] low, [even] God, encouraged us by the coming of Titus;

7 and not by his coming only, but also through the encouragement with which he was encouraged

as to you; relating to us your ardent desire, your mourning, your zeal for me; so that I the more rejoiced.

8 For if also I grieved you in the letter, I do not regret it if even I have regretted it; for I see that that letter, if even [it were] only for a time, grieved you.

9 Now I rejoice, not that you have been grieved, but that you have been grieved to repentance for you have been grieved according to God, that in nothing you might be injured by us.

10 For grief according to God works repentance to salvation, never to be regretted; but the grief of the world works death.

11 For, behold, this same thing, your being grieved according to God, how much diligence it worked in you, but [what] excusing [of yourselves], but [what] indignation, but [what] fear, but [what] ardent desire, but [what] zeal, but [what] vengeance: in every way you have proved yourselves to be pure in the matter.

12 So then, if also I wrote to you, [it was] not for the sake of him that injured, nor for the sake of him that was injured, but for the sake of our diligent zeal for you being manifested to you before God.

13 For this reason we have been encouraged. And we the rather rejoiced in our encouragement more abundantly by reason of the joy of Titus, because his spirit has been refreshed by you all.

14 Because if I boasted to him anything about you, I have not been put to shame; but as we have spoken to you all things in truth, so also our boasting to Titus has been the truth;

15 and his affections are more abundantly towards you, calling to mind the obedience of you all, how with fear and trembling you received him.

16 I rejoice that in everything I am confident as to you.

2 Cor 8:1 But we make known to you, brethren, the grace of God bestowed in the churches of Macedonia;

2 that in a great trial of affliction the abundance of their joy and their deep poverty has abounded to the riches of their liberality.

3 For according to [their] power, I bear witness, and beyond [their] power, [they were] willing of their own accord,

4 begging of us with much entreaty [to give effect to] the grace and fellowship of the service which [was to be rendered] to the saints.

5 And not according as we hoped, but they gave themselves first to the Lord, and to us by God's will.

6 So that we begged Titus that, according as he had before begun, so he would also complete as to you this grace also;

7 but even as you abound in every way, in faith, and word, and knowledge, and all diligence, and in love from you to us, that you may abound in this grace also.

8 I do not speak as commanding it but through the zeal of others, and proving the genuineness of your love.

9 For you know the grace of our Lord Jesus Christ, that for your sakes he, being rich, became poor, in order that you by his poverty might be enriched.

10 And I give [my] opinion in this, for this is profitable for you who began before, not only to do, but also to be willing, a year ago.

11 But now also complete the doing of it; so that as [there was] the readiness to be willing, so also to complete out of what you have.

12 For if the readiness be there, [a man is] accepted according to what he may have, not according to what he has not.

13 For [it is] not in order that there may be ease for others, and for you distress,

14 but [on the principle] of equality; in the present time your abundance for their lack, that their abundance may be for your lack, so that there should be equality.

15 According as it is written, He who [gathered] much had no excess, and he who [gathered] little was nothing short.

16 But thanks [be] to God, who gives the same diligent zeal for you in the heart of Titus.

17 For he received indeed the entreaty, but, being full of zeal, he went of his own accord to you;

18 but we have sent with him the brother whose praise is in the good news through all the churches;

19 and not only [so] but is also chosen by the churches as our fellow-traveller with this grace, ministered by us to the glory of the Lord himself, and [a witness of] our readiness;

20 avoiding this, that any one should blame us in this abundance [which is] administered by us;

21 for we provide for things honest, not only before the Lord, but also before men.

22 And we have sent with them our brother whom we have often proved to be of diligent zeal in many things, and now more diligently zealous through the great confidence [he has] as to you.

23 Whether as regards Titus, [he is] my companion and fellow-laborer in your behalf; or our [other] brethren, [they are] apostles of the churches, to Christ's glory.

24 Show therefore to them, before the churches, the proof of your love, and of our boasting about you.

2 Cor 9:1 For concerning the ministration which is for the saints, it is superfluous my writing to you.

2 For I know your readiness, which I boast of you to Macedonians, that Achaia is prepared since a year ago, and the zeal [reported] of you has stimulated the mass [of the brethren]

3 But I have sent the brethren, in order that our boasting about you may not be made void in this respect, in order that, as I have said, you may be prepared;

4 lest haply, if Macedonians come with me and find you unprepared, we, that we say not you, may be put to shame in this confidence.

5 I thought it necessary therefore to beg the brethren that they would come to you, and complete beforehand your fore-announced blessing, that this may be ready thus as blessing, and not as got out of you.

6 But this [is true] he that sows sparingly shall reap also sparingly; and he that sows in [the spirit of] blessing shall reap also in blessing:

7 each according as he is purposed in his heart; not grieving, or of necessity; for God loves a cheerful giver.

8 But God is able to make every gracious gift abound towards you, that, having in every way always all-sufficiency, you may abound to every good work:

9 according as it is written, He has scattered abroad, he has given to the poor, his righteousness remains into the aeon.

10 Now he that supplies seed to the sower and bread for eating shall supply and make abundant your sowing, and increase the fruits of your righteousness:

11 enriched in every way unto all liberality, which works through us thanksgiving to God.

12 Because the ministration of this service is not only filling up the measure of what is lacking to the saints, but also abounding by many thanksgivings to God;

13 they glorifying God through the proof of this ministration, by reason of your subjection, by profession, to the good news of the Christ, and your free-hearted liberality in sharing towards them and towards all;

14 and in their supplication for you, full of ardent desire for you, on account of the exceeding grace of God [which is] upon you.

15 Thanks [be] to God for his unspeakable free gift.

2 Cor 10:1 But I myself, Paul, entreat you by the meekness and gentleness of the Christ, who, as to appearance, [when present] I am lowly among you, but absent I am bold towards you;

2 but I beseech that present I may not be bold with the confidence with which I think to be daring towards some who think of us as walking according to flesh.

3 For walking in flesh, we do not war according to flesh.

4 For the arms of our warfare [are] not fleshly, but powerful according to God to the overthrow of strongholds;

5 overthrowing reasoning and every high thing that lifts itself up against the knowledge of God, and leading captive every thought into the obedience of the Christ;

6 and having in readiness to avenge all disobedience when your obedience shall have been fulfilled.

7 Do you look at what concerns appearance? If any one has confidence in himself that he is of Christ, let him think this again in himself, that even as he is of Christ, so also [are] we.

8 For and if I should boast even somewhat more abundantly of our authority, which the Lord has given [to us] for building up and not for your overthrowing, I shall not be put to shame;

9 that I may not seem as if I was frightening you by letters:

10 because his letters, he says, [are] weighty and strong, but his presence in the body weak, and his speech naught.

11 Let such a one think this, that such as we are in word by letters [when] absent, such also present in deed.

12 For we dare not class ourselves or compare ourselves with some who commend themselves; but these, measuring themselves by themselves, and comparing themselves with themselves, are not wise.

13 Now we will not boast out of measure, but according to the measure of the rule which God of measure has apportioned to us, to reach to you also.

14 For we do not, as not reaching to you, overstretch ourselves, for we have come to you also in the good news of the Christ;

15 not boasting out of measure in other people's labors, but having hope, your faith increasing, to be enlarged among you, according to our rule, yet more abundantly

16 to announce the good news to that [which is] beyond you, not to be boasting in another's territory.

17 But he that boasts, let him boast in the Lord.

18 For not he that commends himself is approved, but whom the Lord commends.

2 Cor 11:1 I wish you would bear with me [in] a little folly; but indeed bear with me.

2 For I am jealous as to you with a jealousy [which is] of God; for I have espoused you unto one man, to present [you] a chaste virgin to Christ.

3 But I fear lest by any means, as the serpent deceived Eve by his craft, [so] your thoughts should be corrupted from simplicity as to the Christ.

4 For if indeed he that comes preaches another Jesus, whom we have not preached, or you get a different Spirit, which you have not got, or a different good news, which you have not received, you might well bear with it

5 For I reckon that in nothing I am inferior to those who are super apostles.

6 But if [I am] a simple person in speech, yet not in knowledge, but in everything making [the truth] manifest in all things to you.

7 Have I committed sin, abasing myself in order that you might be exalted, because I freely announced to you the good news of God?

8 I robbed other churches, receiving hire for ministry towards you.

9 And being present with you and lacking, I did not lazily burden any one, for the brethren who came from Macedonia supplied what I lacked, and in everything I kept myself from being a burden to you, and will keep myself.

10 the truth of Christ is in me that this boasting shall not be stopped as to me in the regions of Achaia.

11 Why? because I do not love you? God knows.

12 But what I do, I will also do, that I may cut off the opportunity of those wishing [for] an opportunity, that wherein they boast they may be found even as we.

13 For such [are] false apostles, deceitful workers, transforming themselves into apostles of Christ.

14 No wonder, for even Satan disguises himself as an angel of light.

15 It is no great thing therefore if his ministers also transform themselves as ministers of righteousness; whose end shall be according to their works.

16 Again I say, Let not any one think me to be a fool; but if otherwise, receive me then even as a fool, that I also may boast myself a little.

17 What I speak I do not speak according to the Lord, but as in folly, in this confidence of boasting.

18 Since many boast according to flesh, I also will boast.

19 For you bear fools readily, being wise.

20 For you bear if any one bring you into bondage, if any one devour [you] if any one get [your money] if any one exalt himself, if any one beat you on the face.

21 I speak as to dishonor, as though we had been weak; but wherein any one is daring, I speak in folly, I also am daring.

22 Are they Hebrews? I also. Are they Israelites? I also. Are they seed of Abraham? I also.

23 Are they ministers of Christ? I speak as being beside myself I above measure [so] in labors exceedingly abundant, in stripes to excess, in prisons exceedingly abundant, in [near] deaths often.

24 From the Jews five times have I received forty [stripes] except one.

25 Three times have I been scourged, once I have been stoned, three times I have suffered shipwreck, a night and day I passed in the deep:

26 in journeying often, in perils of rivers, in perils of robbers, in perils from [my own] race, in perils from the nations, in perils in the city, in perils in the desert, in perils on the sea, in perils among false brethren;

27 in labor and toil, in watching often, in hunger and thirst, in fasting often, in cold and nakedness.

28 Besides those things that are outside, the crowd [of cares] pressing on me daily, the burden of all the churches.

29 Who is weak, and I am not weak? Who has stumbled (into sin), am I not on fire?

30 If it is needful to boast, I will boast in the things which concern my weakness.

31 God and Father of the Lord Jesus knows --he who is blessed into the aeons --that I do not lie.

32 In Damascus the ethnarch of Aretas the king kept the city of the Damascenes shut up, wishing to take me;

33 and through a window in a basket I was let down by the wall, and escaped his hands.

2 Cor 12:1 Well, it is not of profit to me to boast, but I will continue on with visions and revelations of the Lord.

2 I know a man in Christ, fourteen years ago, whether in the body I know not, or out of the body I know not, God knows; such [a one] caught up to the third heaven.

3 And I know such a man, whether in the body or out of the body I know not, God knows;

4 that he was caught up into paradise, and heard unspeakable things said which it is not allowed to man to utter.

5 Of such [a one] I will boast, but of myself I will not boast, unless in my weaknesses.

6 For if I shall desire to boast, I shall not be a fool; for I will say the truth; but I forbear, lest any one should think as to me above what he sees me [to be] or whatever he may hear of me.

7 And that I might not be exalted by the exceeding greatness of the revelations, there was given to me a thorn for the flesh, an angel of Satan that he might torment me, that I might not be exalted.

8 For this I three times besought the Lord that it might depart from me.

9 And he said to me, My grace is sufficient for you; for [my] power is perfected in weakness. Most gladly therefore will I rather boast in my weaknesses, that the power of the Christ may dwell upon me.

10 Therefore I take pleasure in weaknesses, in insults, in necessities, in persecutions, in difficulties for Christ: for when I am weak, then I am powerful.

11 I have become a fool; you have compelled me; for I ought to have been commended by you; for I have been nothing behind those who were super apostles, if also I am nothing.

12 The signs indeed of the apostle were worked among you in all endurance, signs, and wonders, and works of power.

13 For in what is it that you have been inferior to the other churches, unless that I myself have not been in laziness a charge upon you? Forgive me this injury.

14 Behold, this third time I am ready to come to you, and I will not be in laziness a charge; for I do not seek yours, but you; for the children ought not to lay up for the parents, but the parents for the children.

15 Now I shall most gladly spend and be utterly spent for your souls, if even in abundantly loving you I should be less loved.

16 But be it so. I did not burden you, but being crafty I took you by guile.

17 Did I make gain of you by any of those whom I have sent to you?

18 I begged Titus, and sent the brother with him, did Titus at all make gain of you? have we not walked in the same spirit? [have we] not in the same steps?

19 You have long been supposing that we excuse ourselves to you: we speak before God in Christ; and all things, beloved, for your building up.

20 For I fear lest perhaps coming I find you not such as I wish, and that I be found by you such as you do not wish: lest [there might be] strife, jealousies, angers, contentions, evil speaking, whisperings, puffing up, disturbances;

21 lest my God should humble me as to you when I come again, and that I shall grieve over many of those who have sinned before, and have not repented as to the uncleanness and fornication and licentiousness which they have practiced.

2 Cor 13:1 This third time I am coming to you. In the mouth of two or three witnesses shall every matter be established.

2 I have declared beforehand, and I say beforehand as present the second time, and now absent, to those that have sinned before, and to all the rest, that if I come again I will not spare.

3 Since you seek a proof of Christ speaking in me, who is not weak towards you, but is powerful among you,

4 for if indeed he has been crucified in weakness, yet he lives by God's power; for indeed we are weak in him, but we shall live with him by God's power towards you,

5 examine your own selves if you be in the faith; prove your own selves: do you not recognize yourselves, that Jesus Christ is in you, unless indeed you be reprobates?

6 Now I hope that you will know that we are not reprobates.

7 But we pray toward the God that you may do nothing evil; not that we may appear approved, but that you may do what is right, and we be as reprobates.

8 For we can do nothing against the truth, but for the truth.

9 For we rejoice when we may be weak and you may be powerful. But this also we pray for, your perfecting.

10 On this account I write these things being absent, that being present I may not be harsh according to the authority which the Lord has given me for building up, and not for overthrowing.

11 For the rest, brethren, rejoice; be perfected; be encouraged; be of one mind; be at peace; and God of love and peace shall be with you.

12 Salute one another with a holy kiss.

13 All the saints salute you.

14 The grace of the Lord Jesus Christ, and the love of God, and the communion of the Holy Spirit, [be] with you all.

Galatians

Gal 1:1 Paul, apostle, not from men nor through man, but through Jesus Christ, and God the Father who raised him from among the dead,

2 and all the brethren with me, to the churches of Galatia.

3 Grace to you, and peace, from God the Father, and our Lord Jesus Christ,

4 who gave himself for our sins, so that he should deliver us out of the present evil world, according to the will of our God and Father;

5 to whom [be] glory into the aeons of aeons. Amen.

6 I wonder that you thus quickly change, from him that called you in Christ's grace, to a different gospel,

7 which is not another [one] but there are some that trouble you, and desire to pervert the good news of the Christ.

8 But if even we or an angel out of heaven announce as good news to you [anything] besides what we have announced as good news to you, let him be accursed.

9 As we have said before, now also again I say, If any one announce to you as good news [anything] besides what you have received, let him be accursed.

10 For do I now seek to satisfy men or God? or do I seek to please men? If I were yet pleasing men, I were not Christ's servant.

11 But I let you know, brethren, [as to] the good news which were announced by me, that they are not according to man.

12 For neither did I receive them from man, neither was I taught [them] but by revelation of Jesus Christ.

13 For you have heard [what was] my behavior formerly in Judaism, that I excessively persecuted the church of God, and ravaged it;

14 and advanced in Judaism beyond many contemporaries in my nation, being exceedingly zealous of the doctrines of my fathers.

15 But when God, who set me apart [even] from my mother's womb, and called [me] by his grace,

16 was pleased to reveal his Son in me, that I may announce him as good news among the Gentiles, immediately I took not counsel with flesh and blood,

17 nor went I up to Jerusalem to those [who were] apostles before me; but I went to Arabia, and again returned to Damascus.

18 Then after three years I went up to Jerusalem to make acquaintance with Peter, and I remained with him fifteen days;

19 but I saw none other of the apostles, but James the brother of the Lord.

20 Now what I write to you, behold, before God, I do not lie.

21 Then I came into the regions of Syria and Cilicia.

22 But I was unknown personally to the churches of Judea which [are] in Christ;

23 only they were hearing that he who persecuted us formerly now announces the good news of the faith which formerly he ravaged:

24 and they glorified God in me.

Gal 2:1 Then after a lapse of fourteen years I went up again to Jerusalem with Barnabas, taking Titus also with [me]

2 and I went up according to revelation, and I laid before them the good news which I preach among the Gentiles, but privately to those conspicuous [among them] lest in any way I run or had run in vain;

3 but neither was Titus, who was with me, being a Greek, compelled to be circumcised;

4 and [it was] on account of the infiltration of false brethren, who infiltrated to spy on our liberty which we have in Christ Jesus, that they might bring us into bondage;

5 to whom we did not yield in subjection for an hour, that the truth of the good news might remain with you.

6 But from those who looked as being important – whatsoever they were, it makes no difference to me: God does not accept man's person; for to me these conferred nothing;

7 but, on the contrary, seeing that the good news of the uncircumcision were confided to me, even as to Peter that of the circumcision,

8 for he that worked in Peter for the apostleship of the circumcision worked also in me towards the Nations,

9 and recognizing the grace given to me, James and Cephas and John, who looked like pillars [in the Church], gave to me and Barnabas the right hands of fellowship, that we [should go] to the nations, and they to the circumcision;

10 only that we should remember the poor, which I was diligent to do.

11 But when Peter came to Antioch, I withstood him to the face, because he was to be condemned:

12 For prior to the coming of certain men from James, he used to eat with the Gentiles; but when they came, he began to withdraw and hold himself aloof, fearing the party of the circumcision.

13 and the rest of the Jews also played the same dissembling part with him; so that even Barnabas was carried away too by their dissimulation.

14 But when I saw that they do not walk straightforward, according to the truth of the good news, I said to Peter before all, If you, being a Jew, live as the nations and not as the Jews, how do you compel the nations to Judaize?

15 We, Jews by nature, and not sinners of the nations,

16 but knowing that a man is not justified on the principle of works of law [nor] but by the faith of Jesus Christ, we also have believed on Christ Jesus, that we might be justified on the principle of the faith of Christ; and not of works of law; because on the principle of works of law no flesh shall be justified.

17 Now if in seeking to be justified in Christ we also have been found sinners, then is Christ minister of sin? Far be the thought.

18 For if the things I have thrown down, these I build again, I constitute myself a transgressor.

19 For I, through law, have died to law, that I may live to God.

20 I am crucified with Christ, and no longer do I live, but Christ lives in me; but [in] that I now live in flesh, I live by faith, the [faith] of the Son of God, who has loved me and given himself for me.

21 I do not set aside the grace of God; for if righteousness is by law, then Christ has died for nothing.

Gal 3:1 O senseless Galatians, who has bewitched you; to whom, as before your very eyes, Jesus Christ has been portrayed, crucified [among you]

2 This only I wish to learn of you, Have you received the Spirit on the principle of works of law, or of the report of faith?

3 Are you so senseless? having begun in Spirit, are you going to be made perfect in flesh?

4 Have you suffered so many things in vain, if indeed also in vain?

5 He therefore who ministers to you the Spirit, and works miracles among you, [is it] on the principle of works of law, or of the report of faith?

6 Even as Abraham believed God, and it was reckoned to him as righteousness.

7 Know then that they that are on the principle of faith, these are Abraham's sons;

8 and the scripture, foreseeing that God would justify the nations on the principle of faith, announced beforehand the good news to Abraham: In you all the nations shall be blessed.

9 So that they who are on the principle of faith are blessed with believing Abraham.

10 For as many as are on the principle of works of law are under curse. For it is written, Cursed is every one who does not continue in all things which [are] written in the book of the law to do them;

11 but that by law no one is justified with God is evident, because The just shall live on the principle of faith;

12 but the law is not on the principle of faith; but, He that shall have done these things shall live by them.

13 Christ has redeemed us out of the curse of the law, having become a curse for us, for it is written, Cursed is every one hanged upon a tree,

14 that the blessing of Abraham might come to the nations in Christ Jesus, that we might receive the promise of the Spirit through faith.

15 Brethren, I speak according to man, even man's confirmed covenant no one sets aside, or adds other dispositions to.

16 But to Abraham were the promises addressed, and to his seed: he does not say, And to seeds, as of many; but as of one, And to your seed; which is Christ.

17 Now I say this, A covenant confirmed beforehand by God, the law, which took place four hundred and thirty years after, does not annul, so as to supersede the promise.

18 For if the inheritance [be] on the principle of law, [it is] no longer on the principle of promise; but God gave it in grace to Abraham by promise.

19 Why then the law? It was added for the sake of transgressions, until the seed came to whom the promise was made, ordained through angels in the hand of a mediator.

20 But a mediator is not of one, but God is one.

21 is then the law against the promises of God? Far be the thought. For if a law had been given able to quicken, then indeed righteousness were on the principle of law;

22 but the scripture has shut up all things under sin, that the promise, on the principle of faith of Jesus Christ, should be given to those that believe.

23 But before faith came, we were guarded under law, shut up to faith [which was] about to be revealed.

24 So that the law has been our tutor up to Christ, that we might be justified on the principle of faith.

25 But, faith having come, we are no longer under a tutor;

26 for you are all God's sons by faith in Christ Jesus.

27 For you, as many as have been baptized unto Christ, have put on Christ.

28 There is no Jew nor Greek; there is no servant nor freeman; there is no male and female; for you are all one in Christ Jesus:

29 but if you [are] of Christ, then you are Abraham's seed, heirs according to promise.

Gal 4:1 Now I say, As long as the heir is a child, he differs nothing from a servant, though he be lord of all;

2 but he is under guardians and stewards until the period fixed by the father.

3 So we also, when we were children, were held in bondage under the principles of the world;

4 but when the fullness of the time had come, God sent forth his Son, who came into existence out of woman, born under the law,

5 that he might redeem those under law, that we might receive sonship.

6 But because you are sons, God has sent out the Spirit of his Son into our hearts, crying, Abba, Father.

7 So you are no longer servant, but son; but if son, heir also through God.

8 But then indeed, not knowing God, you were in bondage to those who by nature are not gods;

9 but now, knowing God, but rather being known by God, how do you turn again to the weak and beggarly principles to which you desire to be again anew in bondage?

10 You observe days and months and times and years.

11 I am afraid of you, lest indeed I have labored in vain as to you.

12 Be as I am for I also am as you, brethren, I beseech you: you have not at all wronged me.

13 But you know that in weakness of the flesh I announced the good news to you at the first;

14 and my trial, which [was] in my flesh, you did not slight nor reject with contempt; but you received me as an angel of God, as Christ Jesus.

15 What then [was] your blessedness? for I bear you witness that, if possible, plucking out your own eyes you would have given [them] to me.

16 So I have become your enemy in speaking the truth to you?

17 They are not rightly zealous after you, but desire to shut you out [from us] that you may be zealous after them.

18 But [it is] right to be zealous at all times in what is right, and not only when I am present with you

19 --my children, of whom I again travail in birth until Christ shall have been formed in you:

20 and I should wish to be present with you now, and change my voice, for I am perplexed as to you.

21 Tell me, you who are desirous of being under law, do you not listen to the law?

22 For it is written that Abraham had two sons; one of the maid servant, and one of the free woman.

23 But he [that was] of the maid servant was born according to flesh, and he [that was] of the free woman through the promise.

24 Which things have an allegorical sense; for these are two covenants, one from mount Sinai, gendering to bondage, which is Hagar.

25 For Hagar is mount Sinai in Arabia, and corresponds to Jerusalem which is now, for she is in bondage with her children;

26 but the Jerusalem above is free, which is our mother.

27 For it is written, Rejoice, you barren that bear not; break out and cry, you that travail not; because the children of the desolate are more numerous than [those] of her that has a husband.

28 But you, brethren, after the pattern of Isaac, are children of promise.

29 But as then he that was born according to flesh persecuted him [that was born] according to Spirit, so also [it is] now.

30 But what says the scripture? Cast out the maid servant and her son; for the son of the maid servant shall not inherit with the son of the free woman.

31 So then, brethren, we are not the maid servant's children, but [children] of the free woman.

Gal 5:1 Christ has set us free in freedom; stand firm therefore, and be not held again in a yoke of bondage.

2 Behold, I, Paul, say to you, that if you are circumcised, Christ shall profit you nothing.

3 And I witness again to every man [who is] circumcised, that he is debtor to do the whole law.

4 You have superseded from the Christ as separated [from him] as many as are justified by law; you have fallen from grace.

5 For we, by the Spirit, on the principle of faith, await the hope of righteousness.

6 For in Christ Jesus neither circumcision has any force, nor uncircumcision; but faith working through love.

7 You ran well; who has stopped you that you should not obey the truth?

8 The persuasibleness is not of him that calls you.

9 A little leaven leavens the whole lump.

10 I have confidence as to you in the Lord, that you will have no other mind; and he that is troubling you shall bear the guilt [of it] whosoever he may be.

11 But I, brethren, if I yet preach circumcision, why am I yet persecuted? Then perhaps the stumbling block of the cross has been superseded.

12 I wish that they would even cut themselves off who throw you into confusion.

13 For you have been called to liberty, brethren; only [do] not [turn] liberty into an opportunity to the flesh, but by love serve one another.

14 For the whole law is fulfilled in one word, You shall love your neighbor as yourself;

15 but if you bite and devour one another, see that you are not consumed one of another.

16 But I say, Walk in the Spirit, and you shall no way fulfil the flesh's lust.

17 For the flesh lusts against the Spirit, and the Spirit against the flesh: and these things are opposed one to the other, that you should not do those things which you desire;

18 but if you are led by the Spirit, you are not under law.

19 Now the works of the flesh are manifest, which are fornication, uncleanness, licentiousness,

20 idolatry, sorcery, hatred, strife, jealousies, angers, contentions, disputes, schools of opinion,

21 envy, murders, drunkenness, revels, and things like these; as to which I tell you beforehand, even as I also have said before, that they who do such things shall not inherit God's kingdom.

22 But the fruit of the Spirit is love, joy, peace, patience, kindness, goodness, fidelity,

23 meekness, self-control: against such things there is no law.

24 But they that [are] of the Christ have crucified the flesh with the passions and the lusts.

25 If we live by the Spirit, let us walk also by the Spirit.

26 Let us not become vain-glorious, provoking one another, envying one another.

Gal 6:1 Brethren, if even a man be taken in some fault, you who are spiritual restore such a one in a spirit of meekness, considering yourself lest you also be tempted.

2 Bear one another's burdens, and thus fulfil the law of the Christ.

3 For if any man reputes himself to be something, being nothing, he deceives himself;

4 but let each prove his own work, and then he will have his boast in what belongs to himself alone, and not in what belongs to another.

5 For each shall bear his own burden.

6 Let him that is taught in the word communicate to him that teaches in all good things.

7 Be not deceived: God is not mocked; for whatever a man shall sow, that also shall he reap.

8 For he that sows to his own flesh, shall reap corruption from the flesh; but he that sows to the Spirit, from the Spirit shall reap aeonian life:

9 but let us not lose heart in doing good; for in due time, if we do not faint, we shall reap.

10 So then, as we have occasion, let us do good towards all, and specially towards those of the household of faith.

11 See how long a letter I have written to you with my own hand.

12 As many as desire to have a fair appearance in the flesh, these compel you to be circumcised, only that they may not be persecuted because of the cross of Christ.

13 For neither do they that are circumcised themselves keep the law; but they wish you to be circumcised, that they may boast in your flesh.

14 But far be it from me to boast except in the cross of our Lord Jesus Christ, through whom the world is crucified to me, and I to the world.

15 For [in Christ Jesus] neither is circumcision anything, nor uncircumcision; but new creation.

16 And as many as shall walk by this rule, peace upon them and mercy, and upon the Israel of God.

17 For the rest let no one trouble me, for I bear in my body the brands of the Lord Jesus.

18 The grace of our Lord Jesus Christ [be] with your spirit, brethren. Amen.

Ephesians

Eph 1:1 Paul, apostle of Jesus Christ by God's will, to the saints and faithful in Christ Jesus who are at Ephesus.

2 Grace to you and peace from God our Father, and the Lord Jesus Christ.

3 Blessed [be] God and Father of our Lord Jesus Christ, who has blessed us with every spiritual blessing in the heavenlies in Christ;

4 according as he has chosen us in him before the foundation of the cosmos, that we should be holy and blameless before him in love;

5 having been predestinated for adoption through Jesus Christ to himself, according to the good pleasure of his will,

6 to the praise of the glory of his grace, wherein he has taken us into grace in the Beloved:

7 in whom we have redemption through his blood, the forgiveness of offences, according to the riches of his grace;

8 which he has caused to abound towards us in all wisdom and intelligence,

9 having made known to us the revealed-mystery of his will, according to his good pleasure which he purposed in himself

10 for the plan of the fullness of times; to gather up all things in the Christ, the things in the heavens and the things upon the earth; in him,

11 in whom we have also obtained an inheritance, being predestinated according to the purpose of him who works all things according to the counsel of his own will,

12 that we should be to the praise of his glory who have first trusted in the Christ:

13 in whom you also [have trusted] having heard the word of the truth, the good news of your salvation; in whom also, having believed, you have been sealed with the Holy Spirit of promise,

14 who is the down payment [earnest money] of our inheritance to the redemption of the acquired possession to the praise of his glory.

15 Therefore I also, having heard of the faith in the Lord Jesus which is in you, and the love which [you have] towards all the saints,

16 do not cease giving thanks for you, making mention [of you] at my prayers,

17 that God of our Lord Jesus Christ, the Father of glory, would give you the spirit of wisdom and revelation in the full knowledge of him,

18 being enlightened in the eyes of your heart, so that you should know what is the hope of his calling, [and] what the riches of the glory of his inheritance in the saints,

19 and what the surpassing greatness of his power towards us who believe, according to the engery of the might of his strength,

20 [in] which he worked in the Christ [in] raising him from among the dead, and he set him down at his right hand in the heavenlies,

21 above every principality, and authority, and power, and dominion, and every name named, not only in this aeon, but also in that to come;

22 and subjected* all things under his feet, and gave him [to be] head over all things to the church,

23 which is his body, the fullness of him who fills all in all:

Eph 2:1 and you, being dead in your offences and sins

2 --in which you once walked according to the aeon of this world, according to the ruler of the authority of the air, the spirit who now works in the sons of disobedience:

3 among whom we also all had our behavior in the lusts of our flesh, doing what the flesh and the thoughts willed to do, and were children, by nature, of wrath, even as the rest:

4 but God, being rich in mercy, because of his great love wherewith he loved us,

5 we too being dead in offences, has quickened us with the Christ, you are saved by grace,

6 and has raised [us] up together, and has made [us] sit down together in the heavenlies in Christ Jesus,

7 that he might display in the coming aeons the surpassing riches of his grace in kindness towards us in Christ Jesus.

8 For you are saved by grace, through faith; and this not of yourselves; it is God's gift:

9 not on the principle of works, that no one might boast.

10 For we are his workmanship, having been created in Christ Jesus for good works, which God has before prepared that we should walk in them.

11 Therefore remember that you, once nations in the flesh, who [are] called uncircumcision by that called circumcision in the flesh done with the hand;

12 that you were at that time without Christ, aliens from the commonwealth of Israel, and strangers to the covenants of promise, having no hope, and without God in the world:

13 but now in Christ Jesus you who once were afar off are become near by the blood of the Christ.

14 For he is our peace, who has made both one, and has broken down the middle wall of enclosure,

15 having superseded the enmity in his flesh, the law of commandments in ordinances, that he might form the two in himself into one new man, making peace;

16 and might reconcile both in one body to God by the cross, having by it slain the enmity;

17 and, coming, he has preached the good news of peace to you who [were] afar off, and [the good news of] peace to those [who were] near.

18 For through him we have both access by one Spirit to the Father.

19 So then you are no longer strangers and foreigners, but you are fellow-citizens of the saints, and of the family of God,

20 being built upon the foundation of the apostles and prophets, Jesus Christ himself being the corner-stone,

21 in whom all a building [with stones] fitted together increases into a holy temple in the Lord;

22 in whom you also are being built together for a habitation of God in the Spirit.

Eph 3:1 For this reason I Paul, prisoner of the Christ Jesus for you nations,

2 if indeed you have heard of the plan of the grace of God which has been given to me towards you,

3 that by revelation the revealed-mystery has been made known to me, according as I have written before briefly,

4 by which, in reading it, you can understand my knowledge in the revealed-mystery of the Christ,

5 which in other generations has not been made known to the sons of men, as it has now been revealed to his holy apostles and prophets in [the power of the] Spirit,

6 that [they who are of] the nations should be joint heirs, and a joint body, and joint partakers of [his] promise in Christ Jesus by the good news;

7 of which I am become minister according to the gift of the grace of God given to me, according to the energy of his power.

8 To me, less than the least of all saints, has this grace been given, to announce among the Gentiles the good news of the unsearchable riches of the Christ,

9 and to enlighten all [with the knowledge of] what is the plan of the revealed-mystery hidden throughout the aeons in God, who has created all things,

10 in order that now to the principalities and authorities in the heavenlies might be made known through the church the diverse wisdom of God,

11 according to the purpose of the aeons, which he purposed in Christ Jesus our Lord,

12 in whom we have boldness and access in confidence by the faith of him.

13 Therefore I beseech [you] not to faint through my tribulations for you, which is your glory.

14 For this reason I bow my knees to the Father [of our Lord Jesus Christ]

15 of whom every family in the heavens and on earth is named,

16 in order that he may give you according to the riches of his glory, to be strengthened with power by his Spirit in the inner man;

17 that the Christ may dwell, through faith, in your hearts, being rooted and founded in love,

18 in order that you may be fully able to apprehend with all the saints what is the breadth and length and depth and height;

19 and to know the love of the Christ which surpasses knowledge; that you may be filled [even] to all the fullness of God.

20 But to him that is able to do far exceedingly above all which we ask or think, according to the power which works in us,

21 to him be glory in the church in Christ Jesus unto all generations of the aeon of aeons. Amen.

Eph 4:1 I, the prisoner in the Lord, urge you therefore to walk worthy of the calling wherewith you have been called,

2 with all lowliness and meekness, with patience, bearing with one another in love;

3 using diligence to keep the unity of the Spirit in the uniting bond of peace.

4 [There is] one body and one Spirit, as you have been also called in one hope of your calling;

5 one Lord, one faith, one baptism;

6 one God and Father of all, who is over all, and through all, and in us all.

7 But to each one of us has been given grace according to the measure of the gift of the Christ.

8 Therefore he says, Having ascended up on high, he has led captivity captive, and has given gifts to men.

9 But that he ascended, what is it but that he also descended into the lower parts of the earth [in death]?

10 He that descended is the same who has also ascended up above all the heavens, that he might fill all things;

11 and he has given some apostles, and some prophets, and some evangelists, and some shepherds and teachers,

12 for the perfecting of the saints; with a view to the work of the ministry, with a view to the edifying of the body of Christ;

13 until we all arrive at the unity of the faith and of the knowledge of the Son of God, at the full-grown man, at the measure of the stature of the fullness of the Christ;

14 in order that we may be no longer babes, tossed and carried about by every wind of that teaching [which is] in the trickery of men, in cunning craftiness of delusion.

15 but, holding the truth in love, we may grow up to him in all things, who is the head, the Christ:

16 from whom the whole body, fitting together, and uniting together through the supply of each connection, according to the energy in [its] measure of each single part, the growth of the body forming itself in love.

17 This I say therefore, and testify in the Lord, that you should no longer walk as [the rest of] the nations walk in the vanity of their mind,

18 being darkened in understanding, alienated from the life of God by reason of the ignorance which is in them, by reason of the hardness of their hearts,

19 who having cast off all feeling, have given themselves up to lasciviousness, to work all uncleanness with greedy unsatisfied lust.

20 But you have not learnt Christ in this way,

21 if you have heard him and been instructed in him according as the truth is in Jesus;

22 [namely] your having put off the former behavior of the old man which corrupts itself according to the deceitful lusts;

23 and being renewed in the spirit of your mind;

24 and [your] having put on the new man, which according to God is created in truthful righteousness and holiness.

25 Therefore, having put off falsehood, speak truth every one with his neighbor, because we are members one of another.

26 Be angry, but do not sin; let not the sun set upon your wrath,

27 neither give room for the devil.

28 Let the stealer steal no more, but rather let him work, working what is honest with his hands, that he may have to share to him that has need.

29 Let no corrupt word go out of your mouth, but if [there be a word] be it a good one for needful edification, that it may give grace to those that hear it.

30 And do not grieve the Holy Spirit of God, with which you have been sealed for the day of redemption.

31 Let all bitterness, and heat of passion, and wrath, and clamor, and injurious language, be removed from you, with all malice;

32 and be to one another kind, compassionate, forgiving one another, so as God also in Christ has forgiven you.

Eph 5:1 Be you therefore imitators of God, as beloved children,

2 and walk in love, even as the Christ loved us, and delivered himself up for us, an offering and sacrifice to God for a sweet-smelling aroma.

3 But fornication and all uncleanness or unbridled lust, let it not be even named among you, as it becomes saints;

4 and filthiness and foolish talking, or jesting, which are not fitting; but rather thanksgiving.

5 For this you are [well] informed of, knowing that no fornicator, or unclean person, or person of unbridled lust, who is an idolater, has inheritance in the kingdom of the Christ and God.

6 Let no one deceive you with vain words, for on account of these things the wrath of God comes upon the sons of disobedience.

7 Be not fellow-partakers with them;

8 for you were once darkness, but now light in the Lord; walk as children of light,

9 for the fruit of the light is in all goodness and righteousness and truth,

10 proving what is agreeable to the Lord;

11 and do not have fellowship with the unfruitful works of darkness, but rather also reprove [them],

12 for the things that are done by them in secret it is shameful even to say.

13 But all things having their true character exposed by the light are made manifest; for that which makes everything manifest is light.

14 Therefore he says, Wake up, [you] that sleep, and arise up from among the dead, and the Christ shall shine upon you.

15 See therefore how you walk carefully, not as unwise but as wise,

16 redeeming the time, because the days are evil.

17 For this reason be not foolish, but understanding what is the will of the Lord.

18 And be not drunk with wine, in which is debauchery; but be filled with the Spirit,

19 speaking to yourselves in psalms and hymns and spiritual songs, singing and chanting with your heart to the Lord;

20 giving thanks at all times for all things to him [who is] God and the Father in the name of our Lord Jesus Christ,

21 submitting yourselves to one another in the fear of Christ.

22 Wives, [submit yourselves] to your own husbands, as to the Lord,

23 for a husband is head of the wife, as also the Christ is head of the church. He is Savior of the body.

24 But even as the church is subjected to the Christ, so also wives to their own husbands in everything.

25 Husbands, love your own wives, even as the Christ also loved the church, and has delivered himself up for it,

26 in order that he might sanctify it, purifying it by the washing of water by the word,

27 that he might present the church to himself glorious, having no spot, or wrinkle, or any of such things; but that it might be holy and blameless.

28 So ought men also to love their own wives as their own bodies: he that loves his own wife loves himself.

29 For no one has ever hated his own flesh, but nourishes and cherishes it, even as also the Christ the church;

30 for we are members of his body; [we are of his flesh, and of his bones]

31 Because of this a man shall leave his father and mother, and shall be united to his wife, and the two shall be one flesh.

32 This revealed-mystery is great, but I speak as to Christ, and as to the church.

33 But you also, every one of you, let each so love his own wife as himself; but as to the wife [I speak] that she may fear the husband.

Eph 6:1 Children, obey your parents in the Lord, for this is just.

2 honor your father and your mother, which is the first commandment with a promise,

3 that it may be well with you, and that you may be long-lived on the earth.

4 And [you] fathers, do not provoke your children to anger, but bring them up in the discipline and admonition of the Lord.

5 Servants, obey masters according to flesh, with fear and trembling, in simplicity of your heart as to the Christ;

6 not with eye-service as men-pleasers; but as servants of Christ, doing the will of God from the soul,

7 serving with good will as to the Lord, and not to men;

8 knowing that whatever good each shall do, this he shall receive of the Lord, whether bond or free.

9 And, masters, do the same things towards them, giving up threatening, knowing that both their and your Master is in heaven, and there is no partiality of persons with him.

10 For the rest, brethren, be strong in the Lord, and in the might of his strength.

11 Put on the armor of God, that you may be able to stand against the schemes of the devil,

12 because our fight is not against flesh and blood, but against principalities, against authorities, against the universal lords of this darkness, against spiritual [power] of wickedness in the heavenlies.

13 For this reason take [to you] the armor of God, that you may be able to withstand in the evil day, and, having accomplished all things, to stand.

14 Stand therefore, having girt about your loins with truth, and having put on the breastplate of righteousness,

15 and shod your feet with the preparation of the good news of peace:

16 besides all [these] having taken the shield of faith with which you will be able to quench all the inflamed darts of the wicked one.

17 Have also the helmet of salvation, and the sword of the Spirit, which is God's word;

18 praying at all times, with all prayer and supplication in the Spirit, and watching unto this very thing with all perseverance and supplication for all the saints;

19 and for me in order that utterance may be given to me in the opening of my mouth to make known with boldness the revealed-mystery of the good news,

20 for which I am an ambassador [bound] with a chain, that I may be bold in it as I ought to speak.

21 But in order that you also may know what concerns me, how I am getting on, Tychicus, the beloved brother and faithful minister in the Lord, shall make all things known to you;

22 whom I have sent to you for this very thing, that you may know of our affairs and that he may encourage your hearts.

23 Peace to the brethren, and love with faith, from God the Father and the Lord Jesus Christ.

24 Grace with all them that love our Lord Jesus Christ in incorruptibility.

Philippians

Phil 1:1 Paul and Timothy, servants of Jesus Christ, to all the saints in Christ Jesus who are in Philippi, with the overseers [bishops] and ministers [deacons];

2 grace to you, and peace from God our Father and the Lord Jesus Christ.

3 I thank my God for my whole remembrance of you,

4 constantly in my every supplication, making the supplication for you all with joy,

5 because of your fellowship with the gospel, from the first day until now;

6 having confidence of this very thing, that he who has begun in you a good work will complete it unto Jesus Christ's day:

7 as it is righteous for me to think this as to you all, because you have me in your hearts, and that both in my bonds and in the defense and confirmation of the good news you are all participators in my grace.

8 For God is my witness how I long after you all in the affection of Christ Jesus.

9 And this I pray, that your love may abound yet more and more in full knowledge and all intelligence,

10 that you may judge of and approve the things that are more excellent, in order that you may be pure and without offence for Christ's day,

11 being complete as regards the fruit of righteousness, which is by Jesus Christ, to God's glory and praise.

12 Now I want you to know, brethren, that my circumstances have turned out for the greater progress of the good news,

13 so that my bonds in Christ have become manifest in all of the praetorium and to all others;

14 and that the most of the brethren, trusting in the Lord through my bonds, dare more abundantly to speak the word of God fearlessly.

15 Some indeed also for envy and strife, but some also for good will, preach the Christ.

16 These indeed out of love, knowing that I am set for the defense of the good news;

17 but those out of contention, announce the Christ, not purely, supposing to arouse tribulation for my bonds.

18 What is it then? at any rate, in every way, whether in pretext or in truth, Christ is announced; and in this I rejoice, yes, also I will rejoice;

19 for I know that this shall turn out for me to salvation, through your prayers and the supply of the Spirit of Jesus Christ;

20 according to my earnest expectation and hope, that in nothing I shall be ashamed, but in all boldness, as always, now also Christ shall be magnified in my body whether by life or by death.

21 For to me to live is Christ, and to die is gain;

22 but I live on in the flesh, this is for me fruitful labor, and so I do not know what to choose.

23 But I am pressed by both, having the desire for departure and being with Christ [in Spirit], [for this is] very much better,

24 remaining in the flesh [which is] more necessary for your sakes;

25 and having confidence of this, I know that I shall remain and abide along with you all, for your progress and joy in faith;

26 that your boasting may abound in Christ Jesus through me by my presence again with you.

27 Only conduct yourselves worthily of the good news of the Christ, in order that whether coming and seeing you, or absent, I may hear of what concerns you, that you stand firm in one spirit, with one soul, laboring together in the same conflict with the faith of the good news;

28 and not frightened in anything by the opponents, which is to them a sign of destruction, but of your salvation, and that from God;

29 because to you has been given, as regards Christ, not only the believing on him but the suffering for him also,

30 having the same conflict which you have seen in me, and now hear of in me.

Phil 2:1 If then [there be] any comfort in Christ, if any consolation of love, if any fellowship of the Spirit, if any emotions and compassion,

2 fulfil my joy, that you may think the same thing, having the same love, joined in soul, thinking one thing;

3 [let] nothing [be] in the spirit of strife or vain glory, but, in lowliness of mind, each esteeming the other as more excellent than themselves;

4 regarding not each his own [qualities] but each those of others also.

5 For let this mind be in you which [was] also in Christ Jesus;

6 who, being in a form of God, found it not robbery to be equal to God;[1]

7 but de-emphasized himself, taking a form of a servant, being born in human likeness;

8 and being found in human form, humbled himself, becoming obedient even unto death, and [that the] death of the cross.

9 Therefore also God highly exalted him, and granted him a name, that which is above every name,

10 so that in the name of Jesus every knee should bow: those of heaven, those on the earth, and those under the earth,

11 and every tongue acknowledges* that Lord Jesus Christ into the Glory of God the Father.

12 So that, my beloved, even as you have always obeyed, not as in my presence only, but now much rather in my absence, work out your own salvation with fear and trembling,

13 for it is God who works in you both the willing and the working according to [his] good pleasure.

---

[1] John 5:18

14 Do all things without murmuring and reasoning,

15 that you may be harmless and simple, irreproachable children of God in the midst of a crooked and perverted generation; among whom you appear as lights in the world,

16 holding forth the word of life, so as to be a boast for me in Christ's day, that I have not run in vain nor labored in vain.

17 But if also I am poured out as a drink offering on the sacrifice and ministration of your faith, I rejoice, and rejoice in common with you all.

18 In like manner do you also rejoice, and rejoice with me.

19 But I hope in the Lord Jesus to send Timothy to you shortly, that I also may be refreshed, knowing how you are getting along.

20 For I have no one like-minded who will care with genuine feeling how you get on.

21 For all seek their own things, not the things of Jesus Christ.

22 But you know of his proven worth, that he served with me in the furtherance of the gospel like a child serving his father.

23 Him therefore I hope to send immediately, as soon as I shall see how it goes with me:

24 but I trust in the Lord that I myself also shall soon come;

25 but I have thought it necessary to send to you Epaphroditus, my brother and fellow-workman and fellow-soldier, but your messenger and minister to my need,

26 since he had a longing desire after you all, and was distressed because you had heard that he was sick;

27 for he was also sick close to death, but God had mercy on him, and not indeed on him alone, but also on me, that I might not have sorrow upon sorrow.

28 I have sent him therefore the more diligently, that seeing him you might again rejoice, and that I might be the less sorrowful.

29 Receive him therefore in the Lord with all joy, and hold such in honor;

30 because for the sake of the work he drew near even to death, venturing his soul that he might fill up what lacked in your ministration toward me.

Phil 3:1 For the rest, my brethren, rejoice in the Lord: to write the same things to you, to me is not irksome, and for you safe.

2 Beware of dogs, beware of evil workmen, beware of false circumcision.

3 For we are the circumcision, who worship by the Spirit of God, and boast in Christ Jesus, and do not trust in flesh.

4 although I myself might have confidence even in the flesh. If anyone else has a mind to put confidence in the flesh, I far more:

5 as to circumcision, the eighth day; of the race of Israel, of the tribe of Benjamin, Hebrew of Hebrews; as to the law, a Pharisee;

6 as to zeal, persecuting the church; as to righteousness which is in the law, found blameless;

7 but what things were gain to me these I counted as loss, on account of Christ.

8 But surely I count also all things to be loss on account of the excellency of the knowledge of Christ Jesus my Lord, through whom I have suffered the loss of all, and count them to be filth, that I may gain Christ;

9 and that I may be found in him, not having my righteousness, which [would be] on the principle of law, but that which is by faith of Christ, the righteousness which is of God through faith,

10 to know him, and the power of his resurrection, and the fellowship of his sufferings, being conformed to his death,

11 if any way I arrive at the resurrection from among the dead.

12 Not that I have already obtained [the prize] or am already perfected; but I pursue, if also I may get possession [of it] seeing that also I have been taken possession of by Christ [Jesus]

13 Brethren, I do not count to have got possession myself; but one thing -- forgetting the things behind, and stretching out to the things before,

14 I pursue, [looking] towards the goal, for the prize of the calling on high of God in Christ Jesus.

15 As many therefore as [are] perfect, let us be thus minded; and if you are any otherwise minded, this also God shall reveal to you.

16 But whereto we have attained, [let us] walk in the same steps.

17 Be imitators [all] together of me, brethren, and fix your eyes on those walking thus as you have us for a model;

18 for many walk of whom I have told you often, and now tell you even weeping, that they [are] the enemies of the cross of Christ:

19 whose end is destruction, whose god is the belly, and [their] glory in their shame, who mind earthly things:

20 for our commonwealth has its existence in the heavens, from which also we await the Lord Jesus Christ [as] Savior,

21 who shall transform our body of humiliation into conformity to his body of glory, according to the energy of the power which he has even to subdue all things to himself.

Phil 4:1 So that, my brethren, beloved and longed for, my joy and crown, thus stand firm in the Lord, beloved.

2 I urge Euodia, and exhort Syntyche, to be of the same mind in the Lord;

3 yes, I ask you also, true yoke fellow, assist them, who have contended along with me in the good news, with Clement also, and my other fellow-laborers, whose names [are] in the book of life.

4 Rejoice in the Lord always: again I will say, Rejoice.

5 Let your gentleness be known of all men. The Lord is near.

6 Be concerned about nothing; but in everything, by prayer and prayer with thanksgiving, let your requests be made known toward the God;

7 and the peace of God, which surpasses every understanding, shall guard your hearts and your thoughts by Christ Jesus.

8 For the rest, brethren, whatsoever things [are] true, whatsoever things [are] noble, whatsoever things [are] just, whatsoever things [are] pure, whatsoever things [are] amiable, whatsoever things [are] of good report; if [there be] any virtue and if any praise, think on these things.

9 What you have both learned, and received, and heard, and seen in me, these things do; and God of peace shall be with you.

10 But I rejoiced in the Lord greatly, that now however at length you have revived your thinking of me, though surely you did also think [of me] but lacked opportunity.

11 Not that I speak as regards privation, for as to me I have learnt in those circumstances in which I am, to be satisfied in myself.

12 I know both how to be abased and I know how to abound. In everything and in all things I am initiated both to be full and to be hungry, both to abound and to suffer privation.

13 I have strength for all things in him that gives me power.

14 But you have done well in taking part in my affliction.

15 And know also you, O Philippians, that in the beginning of the gospel, when I came out of Macedonia, no church shared with me in the way of giving and receiving except you alone;

16 for also in Thessalonica once and even twice you sent to me for my need.

17 Not that I seek a gift, but I seek fruit abounding to your account.

18 But I have all things in full supply and abound; I am full, having received of Epaphroditus the things [sent] from you, an odour of sweet aroma, an acceptable sacrifice, agreeable to God.

19 But my God shall abundantly supply all your need according to his riches in glory in Christ Jesus.

20 But to our God and Father [be] glory into the aeons of aeons. Amen.

21 Salute every saint in Christ Jesus. The brethren who [are] with me salute you.

22 All the saints salute you, and specially those of the household of Caesar.

23 The grace of the Lord Jesus Christ [be] with your spirit. Amen.

Colossians

Col 1:1 Paul, apostle of Christ Jesus, by God's will, and Timothy the brother,

2 to the holy and faithful brethren in Christ which [are] in Colosse. Grace to you and peace from God our Father [and Lord Jesus Christ]

3 We give thanks to God and Father of our Lord Jesus Christ continually [when] praying for you,

4 having heard of your faith in Christ Jesus, and the love which you have towards all the saints,

5 on account of the hope which is laid up for you in the heavens; of which you heard before in the word of the truth of the good news,

6 which are come to you, as in all the world, and are bearing fruit and growing, even as also among you, from the day you heard and knew indeed the grace of God, in truth:

7 even as you learned from Epaphras our beloved fellow-servant, who is a faithful minister of Christ for you,

8 who has also manifested to us your love in the Spirit.

9 For this reason we also, from the day we heard [of your faith and love] do not cease praying and asking for you, to the end that you may be filled with the full knowledge of his will, in all wisdom and spiritual understanding,

10 [so as] to walk worthily of the Lord unto all well-pleasing, bearing fruit in every good work, and growing by the true knowledge of God;

11 strengthened with all power according to the might of his glory unto all patience and endurance with joy;

12 giving thanks to the Father, who has made us fit for sharing the portion of the saints in light,

13 who has delivered us from the authority of darkness, and translated [us] into the kingdom of the Son of his love:

14 in whom we have redemption, the forgiveness of sins;

15 who is the image of the invisible God, firstborn of all creation;

16 because in him being created* all things, the things in the heavens and the things upon the earth, the visible and the invisible, whether thrones, or lordships, or principalities, or authorities: all things have been created through him and into him.

17 And he is before all, and all things come together in him.

18 And he is the head of the body, the church; who is the beginning, firstborn from among the dead, that he becomes* the first place in all things:

19 it pleased [God] that in him [Christ] all the fullness was to dwell,

20 and through him [Christ] to reconcile all things into himself [God], having made peace by the blood of his cross –through him, whether the things on the earth or the things in the heavens.

21 And you, who once were alienated and enemies in mind by wicked works, yet now has been reconciled

22 in the body of his flesh through death; to present you holy and unblamable and beyond reproach.

23 if indeed you abide in the faith founded and firm, and not moved away from the hope of the good news, which you have heard, which have been proclaimed in the whole creation under heaven, of which I Paul became minister.

24 Now I rejoice in my sufferings for your sake, and in my flesh I do my share on behalf of His body, which is the church, in filling up what is lacking in Christ's afflictions.

25 of which I became minister, according to the management of God which is given me towards you to complete the word of God,

26 the revealed-mystery which was hidden from aeons and from generations, but has now been made manifest to his saints;

27 to whom God would make known what are the riches of the glory of this revealed-mystery among the Gentiles, which is Christ in you the hope of glory:

28 whom we announce, admonishing every man, and teaching every man, in all wisdom, to the end that we may present every man perfect in Christ.

29 Whereunto also I word, combating according to his energy, which works in me in power.

Col 2:1 For I would have you know what combat I have for you, and those in Laodicea, and as many as have not seen my face in flesh;

2 to the end that their hearts may be encouraged, being united together in love, and unto all riches of the full assurance of understanding, to the full knowledge of the revealed-mystery of God;

3 in which are hid all the treasures of wisdom and of knowledge.

4 And I say this to the end that no one may delude you by persuasive speech.

5 For if indeed in the flesh I am absent, yet I am with you in spirit, rejoicing and seeing your order, and the firmness of your faith in Christ.

6 As therefore you have received the Christ, Jesus the Lord, walk in him,

7 rooted and built up in him, and assured in the faith, even as you have been taught, abounding in it with thanksgiving.

8 See that there be no one who shall lead you away as a prey through philosophy and vain deceit, according to the teaching of men, according to the elements of the world, and not according to Christ.

9 For in him dwells all the fullness of the Godhood in form of a body;

10 and you are complete in him, who is the head of all principality and authority,

11 in whom also you have been circumcised with circumcision not done by hand, in the putting off of the body of the flesh, in the circumcision of the Christ;

12 buried with him in baptism, in which you have been also raised with him through faith of the energy of God who raised him from among the dead.

13 And you, being dead in offences and in the uncircumcision of your flesh, he has quickened together with him, having forgiven us all the offences;

14 having canceled the handwriting in ordinances which [stood out] against us, which was contrary to us, he has taken it also out of the way, having nailed it to the cross;

15 having disarmed principalities and authorities, he made public display of them, triumphing over them triumph by it.

16 Let none therefore judge you in meat or in drink, or in matter of feast, or new moon, or sabbaths,

17 which are a shadow of things to come: the body of Christ [is the things to come].

18 Let no one keep defrauding you of your prize by delighting in self-abasement and the worship of the angels, taking his stand on visions he has seen, inflated without cause by his fleshly mind,

19 and not holding fast the head [Christ], from whom all the body, ministered to and united together by the joints and bands, increases with the increase of God.

20 If you have died with Christ from the elements of the world, why as [if] alive in the world do you subject yourselves to ordinances?

21 Do not handle, do not taste, do not touch,

22 which all refer to things destined to perish with use)-- in accordance with the commandments and teachings of men?

23 These are matters which have the appearance of wisdom in self-made religion and self-abasement and severe treatment of the body, but are of no value against indulgence of the flesh.

Col 3:1 If therefore you have been raised with the Christ, seek the things [which are] above, where the Christ is, sitting at the right hand of God:

2 have your mind on the things [that are] above, not on the things [that are] on the earth;

3 for you have died, and your life is hid with the Christ in God.

4 When the Christ is manifested who is our life, then shall you also be manifested with him in glory.

5 Put to death therefore your members which [are] upon the earth, fornication, uncleanness, vile passions, evil lust, and unbridled desire, which is idolatry.

6 On account of which things the wrath of God comes upon the sons of disobedience.

7 In which you also once walked when you lived in these things.

8 But now, put off, you also, all [these] things, wrath, anger, malice, blasphemy, vile language out of your mouth.

9 Do not lie to one another, having put off the old man with his deeds,

10 and having put on the new, renewed into full knowledge according to the image of him that has created him;

11 wherein there is not Greek and Jew, circumcision and uncircumcision, barbarian, Scythian, servant, freeman; but Christ is everything, and in all.

12 Put on therefore, as the elect of God, holy and beloved, affection of compassion, kindness, lowliness, meekness, endurance;

13 forbearing one another, and forgiving one another, if any should have a complaint against any; even as the Christ has forgiven you, so also you do.

14 And to all these [add] love, which is the bond of perfectness.

15 And let the peace of Christ preside in your hearts, to which also you have been called in one body, and be thankful.

16 Let the word of the Christ dwell in you richly, in all wisdom teaching and admonishing one another, in psalms, hymns, spiritual songs, singing with grace in your hearts to God.

17 And everything, whatever you may do in word or in deed, [do] all things in the name of the Lord Jesus, giving thanks to God the Father by him.

18 Wives, be subject to [your] husbands, as is fitting in the Lord.

19 Husbands, love your wives, and be not bitter against them.

20 Children, obey your parents in all things, for this is well-pleasing in the Lord.

21 Fathers, do not vex your children, to the end that they be not disheartened.

22 Servants, obey in all things your masters according to flesh; not with eye-services, as men-pleasers, but in simplicity of heart, fearing the Lord.

23 Whatsoever you do, labor at it soulfully, as [doing it] to the Lord, and not to men;

24 knowing that of the Lord you shall receive the reward of the inheritance; you serve the Lord Christ.

25 For he that does a wrong shall receive the wrong he has done, and there is no respect of persons.

Col 4:1 Masters, give to servants what is just and fair, knowing that you also have a Master in the heavens.

2 Persevere in prayer, watching in it with thanksgiving;

3 praying at the same time for us also, that God may open to us a door of the word to speak the revealed-mystery of Christ, on account of which also I am bound,

4 to the end that I may make it manifest as I ought to speak.

5 Walk in wisdom towards those outside, redeeming opportunities.

6 [Let] your word [be] always with grace, seasoned with salt, [so as] to know how you ought to answer each one.

7 Tychicus, the beloved brother and faithful minister and fellow-servant in the Lord, will make known to you all that concerns me;

8 whom I have sent to you for this very purpose, that he might know your state, and that he might encourage your hearts:

9 with Onesimus, the faithful and beloved brother, who is [one] of you. They shall make known to you everything here.

10 Aristarchus my fellow-captive salutes you, and Mark, Barnabas's cousin, concerning whom you have received orders, if he comes to you, receive him,

11 and Jesus called Justus, who are of the circumcision. These [are the] only fellow-workers for the kingdom of the God who have been a consolation to me.

12 Epaphras, who is [one] of you, the servant of Christ Jesus, salutes you, always combating earnestly for you in prayers, to the end that you may stand perfect and complete in all the will of God.

13 For I bear him witness that he labors much for you, and them in Laodicea, and them in Hierapolis.

14 Luke, the beloved physician, salutes you, and Demas.

15 Salute the brethren in Laodicea, and Nymphas, and the church which is in his house.

16 And when the letter has been read among you, cause that it be read also in the church of Laodiceans, and that you also read that from Laodicea.

17 And say to Archippus, Take heed to the ministry which you have received in the Lord, to the end that you fulfil it.

18 The salutation by the hand of me Paul. Remember my bonds. Grace [be] with you.

1 Thessalonians

1 Thes 1:1 Paul and Silvanus and Timothy to the church of Thessalonians in God the Father and the Lord Jesus Christ. Grace to you and peace.

2 We give thanks to God always for you all, making mention of you at our prayers,

3 remembering unceasingly your work of faith, and labor of love, and enduring constancy of hope, of our Lord Jesus Christ, before our God and Father;

4 knowing, brethren beloved by God, your election.

5 For our good news were not with you in word only, but also in power, and in the Holy Spirit, and in much assurance; even as you know what we were among you for your sakes:

6 and you became our imitators, and of the Lord, having accepted the word in much tribulation with joy of the Holy Spirit,

7 so that you became models to all that believe in Macedonia and in Achaia:

8 for the word of the Lord sounded out from you, not only in Macedonia and Achaia, but in every place your faith which is toward the God has gone abroad, so that we have no need to say anything;

9 for they themselves relate concerning the reception we had from you, and how you turned toward the God from idols to serve a living and true God,

10 and to await his Son from the heavens, whom he raised from among the dead, Jesus, our deliverer from the coming wrath.

1 Thes 2:1 For you know yourselves, brethren, our reception we had from you, that it has not been in vain;

2 but, having suffered before and been insulted, even as you know, in Philippi, we were bold in our God to speak unto you the good news of God with much earnest striving.

3 For our exhortation [was] not of deceit, nor of uncleanness, nor in guile;

4 but even as we have been approved of God to have the good news entrusted to us, so we speak; not as pleasing men, but God, who proves our hearts.

5 For we have not at any time been with flattering discourse, even as you know, nor with a pretext for covetousness, God is witness;

6 nor seeking glory from men, neither from you nor from others, when we might have been a charge as Christ's apostles;

7 but have been gentle in the midst of you, as a nurse would cherish her own children.

8 Thus, yearning over you, we had found our delight in having imparted to you not only the good news of God, but our own souls also, because you had become beloved of us.

9 For you remember, brethren, our labor and work: working night and day, not to be chargeable to any one of you, we have preached to you the good news of God.

10 You [are] witnesses, and God, how piously and righteously and blamelessly we have conducted ourselves with you that believe:

11 just as you know how we were exhorting and encouraging and imploring each one of you as a father would his own children,

12 that you should walk worthy of God, who calls you to his own kingdom and glory.

13 And for this cause we also give thanks to God unceasingly that, having received the word of the report of God by us, you accepted, not men's word, but, even as it is truly, God's word, which also works in you who believe.

14 For you, brethren, have become imitators of the churches of God which are in Judea in Christ Jesus; for you also have suffered the same things of your own countrymen as also they of the Jews,

15 who have both slain the Lord Jesus and the prophets, and have driven us out by persecution, and do not please God, and [are] against all men,

16 forbidding us to speak to the Gentiles that they may be saved, that they may fill up their sins always: but wrath has come upon them to the uttermost.

17 But we, brethren, having been bereaved of you and separated for a little moment in person, not in heart, have used more abundant diligence to see your face with much desire;

18 therefore we have desired to come to you, even I Paul, both once and twice, and Satan has hindered us.

19 For what is our hope, or joy, or crown of boasting? [are] not you also before our Lord Jesus at his coming?

20 for you are our glory and joy.

1 Thes 3:1 Therefore when we could endure it no longer, we thought it best to be left behind at Athens alone,

2 and sent Timothy, our brother and fellow-workman under God in the good news of Christ, to confirm you and encourage [you] concerning your faith,

3 that no one might be moved by these afflictions. For yourselves know that we are appointed to this;

4 for also, when we were with you, we told you beforehand we are about to be in tribulation, even as also it came to pass, and you know.

5 For this reason I also, no longer able to refrain myself, sent to know your faith, lest perhaps the tempter had tempted you, and our labor should be come to nothing.

6 But Timothy having just come to us from you, and brought to us the good news of your faith and love, and that you have always good remembrance of us, desiring much to see us, even as we also you;

7 for this reason we have been comforted in you, brethren, in all our distress and tribulation, through your faith,

8 because now we live if you stand firm in the Lord.

9 For what thanksgiving can we render to God for you, for all the joy wherewith we rejoice on account of you before our God,

10 night and day beseeching exceedingly to the end that we may see your face, and perfect what is lacking in your faith?

11 But our God and Father himself, and our Lord Jesus, direct our way to you.

12 But you, may the Lord make to exceed and abound in love toward one another, and toward all, even as we also towards you,

13 in order to the confirming of your hearts unblamable in holiness before our God and Father at the coming of our Lord Jesus with all his saints.

1 Thes 4:1 For the rest, then, brethren, we beg you and exhort you in the Lord Jesus, even as you have received from us how you ought to walk and please God, even as you also do walk, that you would abound still more.

2 For you know what charges we gave you through the Lord Jesus.

3 For this is the will of God, [even] your sanctification, that you should abstain from fornication;

4 that each of you know how to possess his own vessel in sanctification and honor,

5 not in passionate desire, even as the nations who know not God,

6 not overstepping the rights of and wronging his brother in the matter, because the Lord is the avenger of all these things, even as we also told you before, and have fully testified.

7 For God has not called us to uncleanness, but in sanctification.

8 He therefore that disregards, disregards, not man, but God, who has given also his Holy Spirit to you.

9 Now concerning brotherly love you have no need that we should write to you, for you yourselves are taught of God to love one another.

10 For also you do this towards all the brethren in the whole of Macedonia; but we exhort you, brethren, to abound still more,

11 and to seek earnestly to be quiet and mind your own affairs, and work with your [own] hands, even as we charged you,

12 that you may walk reputably towards those outside, and may have need of no one.

13 But we do not want you to be uninformed, brethren, about those who are asleep, so that you will not grieve as do the rest who have no hope.

14 For if we believe that Jesus has died and has risen again, so also God will bring with him those who have fallen asleep through Jesus.

15 For this we say to you in the word of the Lord, that we, the living, who remain to the coming of the Lord, are in no way to precede those who have fallen asleep;

16 for the Lord himself, with an assembling shout, with archangel's voice and with trump of God, shall descend from heaven; and the dead in Christ shall rise first;

17 then we, the living who remain, shall be caught up together with them in the clouds, to meet the Lord in the air; and thus we shall be always with the Lord.

18 So encourage one another with these words.

1 Thes 5:1 But concerning the times and the seasons, brethren, you have no need that you should be written to,

2 for you know perfectly well yourselves, that the day of the Lord so comes as a thief by night.

3 When they may say, Peace and safety, then sudden destruction comes upon them, as travail upon her that is with child; and they shall in no way escape.

4 But you, brethren, are not in darkness, that the day should overtake you as a thief:

5 for all you are sons of light and sons of day; we are not of night nor of darkness.

6 So then do not let us sleep as the rest do, but let us watch and be sober;

7 for they that sleep sleep by night, and they that drink drink by night;

8 but we being of the day, let us be sober, putting on the breastplate of faith and love, and a helmet, the hope of salvation;

9 because God has not set us for wrath, but for obtaining salvation through our Lord Jesus Christ,

10 who has died for us, that whether we may be watching or sleep [dead, 4:15], we may live together with him.

11 Therefore encourage one another, and build up each one the other, even as also you do.

12 But we beg you, brethren, to know those who labor among you, and take the lead among you in the Lord, and admonish you,

13 and to regard them exceedingly in love on account of their work. Be in peace among yourselves.

14 But we exhort you, brethren, admonish the disorderly, comfort the faint-hearted, sustain the weak, be patient towards all.

15 See that no one render to any evil for evil, but pursue always what is good towards one another and towards all;

16 rejoice always;

17 pray unceasingly;

18 in everything give thanks, for this is the will of God in Christ Jesus towards you;

19 quench not the Spirit;

20 do not lightly esteem prophecies;

21 but prove all things, keep the good;

22 stay away from every form of wickedness.

23 Now God of peace himself sanctify you wholly: and your whole spirit, and soul, and body be preserved blameless at the coming of our Lord Jesus Christ.

24 He is faithful who calls you, who will also perform it

25 Brethren, pray for us.

26 Greet all the brethren with a holy kiss.

27 I adjure you by the Lord that the letter be read to all the [holy] brethren.

28 The grace of our Lord Jesus Christ [be] with you.

2 Thessalonians

2 Thes 1:1 Paul and Silvanus and Timothy to the church of Thessalonians in God our Father and the Lord Jesus Christ.

2 Grace to you, and peace from God our Father, and the Lord Jesus Christ.

3 We ought to thank God always for you, brethren, even as it is fit, because your faith increases exceedingly, and the love of each one of you towards one another abounds;

4 so that we ourselves make our boast in you in the churches of God for your endurance and faith in all your persecutions and tribulations, which you are sustaining;

5 a manifest token of the righteous judgment of the God, to the end that you should be counted worthy of the kingdom of the God, for the sake of which you also suffer;

6 if at least [it is a] righteous thing with God to render tribulation to those that trouble you,

7 and to you that are troubled rest with us, at the revelation of the Lord Jesus from heaven, with the angels of his power,

8 in flaming fire taking vengeance on those who know not God, and those who do not obey the good news of our Lord Jesus Christ;

9 who shall pay the penalty of aeonian destruction from the presence of the Lord, and from the glory of his might,

10 when he shall have come to be glorified in his saints, and admired by all that have believed, for our testimony to you has been believed, in that day.

11 To which end we also pray always for you, that our God may count you worthy of the calling, and fulfil all the good pleasure of [his] goodness and the work of faith with power,

12 so that the name of our Lord Jesus [Christ] may be glorified in you and you in him, according to the grace of our God, and of the Lord Jesus Christ.

2 Thes 2:1 Now we beg you, brethren, regarding the coming of our Lord Jesus Christ and our gathering together to him,

2 that you not be quickly shaken from your composure or be disturbed either by a spirit or a message or a letter as if from us, to the effect that the day of the Lord has come.

3 Let not any one deceive you in any manner, because [it will not be] unless the apostasy [defection] first comes, and the lawless one has been revealed, the son of destruction;

4 who opposes and exalts himself on high against all called God, or object of veneration; so that he himself sits down in the temple of the God, showing himself that he is God.

5 Do you not remember that, being yet with you, I said these things to you?

6 And now you know that which restrains, that he should be revealed in his own time.

7 For the revealed-mystery of lawlessness already works; only [there is] he who restrains [God] now until out of the midst he be created,

8 and then the lawless one shall be revealed, whom the Lord Jesus shall consume with the breath of his mouth, and shall supersede by the appearing of his coming;

9 whose coming [the lawless one] is according to the energy of Satan in all power and signs and wonders of falsehood,

10 and in all deceit of unrighteousness to them that perish, because they have not received the love of the truth that they might be saved.

11 And for this reason the God sends to them an energetic delusion into believing the falsehood [v. 9],

12 that all might be judged who have not believed the truth, but have found pleasure in unrighteousness.

13 But we ought to give thanks to God always for you, brethren beloved of the Lord, that the God has chosen you from the beginning to salvation in sanctification of the Spirit and belief of the truth:

14 whereto he has called you by our good news, to the obtaining of the glory of our Lord Jesus Christ.

15 So then, brethren, stand firm, and hold fast the instructions which you have been taught, whether by word or by our letter.

16 But our Lord Jesus Christ himself, and our God and Father, who has loved us, and given [us] aeonian comfort and good hope by grace,

17 encourage your hearts, and establish you in every good work and word.

2 Thes 3:1 Finally, brethren, pray for us, that the word of the Lord may run and be glorified, even as also with you;

2 and that we may be delivered from bad and evil men, for faith is not [the portion] of all.

3 But the Lord is faithful, who shall establish you and keep [you] from evil.

4 But we trust in the Lord as to you, that the things which we enjoin, you both do and will do.

5 But the Lord direct your hearts into the love of the God, and into the patience of the Christ.

6 Now we enjoin you, brethren, in the name of our Lord Jesus Christ, that you withdraw from every brother walking disorderly and not according to the instruction which he received from us.

7 For you know yourselves how you ought to imitate us, because we have not walked disorderly among you;

8 nor have we eaten bread from any one without cost; but in toil and hardship working night and day not to be chargeable to any one of you:

9 not because we do not have the right to this, but in order to offer ourselves as a model for you, so that you would follow our example.

10 For also when we were with you we commanded you this, that if any man does not like to work, neither let him eat.

11 For we hear that [there are] some walking among you disorderly, not working at all, but busybodies.

12 Now such we command and urge in the Lord Jesus Christ, that working quietly they eat their own bread.

13 But you, brethren, do not faint in well-doing.

14 But if any one obey not our word by the letter, mark that man, and do not keep company with him, that he may be ashamed of himself;

15 and do not esteem him as an enemy, but admonish him as a brother.

16 But the Lord of peace himself give you peace continually in every way. The Lord [be] with you all.

17 The salutation by the hand of me, Paul, which is the mark in every letter; so I write.

18 The grace of our Lord Jesus Christ [be] with you all.

1 Timothy

1 Tim 1:1 Paul, apostle of Jesus Christ, according to the command of God our Savior, and of Christ Jesus our hope,

2 to Timothy, [my] true child in faith: grace, mercy, peace, from God our Father and Christ Jesus our Lord.

3 Even as I begged you to remain in Ephesus, [when I was] going to Macedonia, that you might enjoin some not to teach other doctrines,

4 nor to turn their minds to fables and endless genealogies, which bring debate rather than [further] God's plan which is in faith.

5 But the end of what is commanded is love out of a pure heart and a good conscience and sincere faith;

6 which [things] some having missed, have turned aside to vain discourse,

7 desiring to be law-teachers, not understanding either what they say or concerning what they [so] strenuously affirm.

8 Now we know that the law is good if any one uses it lawfully,

9 knowing this, that law has not its application to a righteous person, but to the lawless and insubordinate, to the impious and sinful, to the unholy and profane, to killer of fathers and killer of mothers; to murderers,

10 fornicators, homosexual, kidnappers, liars, oath breakers; and if any other thing is opposed to sound teaching,

11 according to the good news of the glory of the blessed God, with which I have been entrusted.

12 And I thank Christ Jesus our Lord, who has strengthened me, for that he counted me faithful, putting me into the ministry;

13 who before was a blasphemer and persecutor, and an insolent overbearing [man], but mercy was shown me because I did it ignorantly, in unbelief.

14 But the grace of our Lord surpassingly super-abounded with faith and love, which is in Christ Jesus.

15 Faithful is the word, and worthy of full acceptance, that Christ Jesus came into the world to save sinners, of whom I am the first.

16 But for this reason mercy was shown me, that in me, the first, Jesus Christ might display the whole endurance, for a delineation of those about to believe on him to aeonian life.

17 Now to the King of the aeons, the immortal, invisible, only God, honor and glory into the aeons of aeons. Amen.

18 This command I entrust to you, Timothy, my son, in accordance with the prophecies previously made concerning you, that by them you fight the good fight,

19 maintaining faith and a good conscience; which some, having put away, have made shipwreck as to faith;

20 of whom is Hymenaeus and Alexander, whom I have delivered to Satan, that they may be taught by discipline not to blaspheme.

1 Tim 2:1 I exhort therefore, first of all, that supplications, prayers, intercessions, thanksgivings be made for all men;

2 for kings and all that are in dignity, that we may lead a quiet and tranquil life in all piety and gravity;

3 for this is good and acceptable before our Savior God,

4 who desires that all men should be saved and come to the knowledge of the truth.

5 For one God, and the one mediator of God and of men, the man Christ Jesus,

6 who gave himself a ransom for all, the testimony [to be rendered] in its own appointed times;

7 to which I have been appointed a herald and apostle, I speak the truth, I do not lie, a teacher of the nations in faith and truth.

8 I wish therefore that the men pray in every place, lifting up pious hands, without wrath or reasoning.

9 In like manner also that the women in decent deportment and dress adorn themselves with modesty and discretion, not with plaited [hair] and gold, or pearls, or costly clothing,

10 but, what becomes women making profession of the fear of God, by good works.

11 Let a woman learn in quietness in all subjection;

12 but I do not permit a woman to teach nor to exercise authority over man, but to be in quietness;

13 for Adam was formed first, then Eve:

14 and Adam was not deceived; but the woman, having been deceived, was in transgression.

15 But she shall be preserved in childbearing, if they continue in faith and love and holiness with discretion.

1 Tim 3:1 The word is faithful: if any one aspires to exercise oversight, he desires a good work.

2 The overseer then must be irreproachable, husband of one wife, sober, discreet, decorous, hospitable, apt to teach;

3 not given to excesses from wine, not contentious, but mild, not a brawler, not fond of money,

4 conducting his own house well, having [his] children in subjection with all gravity;

5 but if one does not know how to conduct his own house, how shall he take care of the church of God?

6 not a novice, that he may not, being inflated, fall into the fault of the devil.

7 But it is necessary that he should have also a good testimony from those outside, that he may fall not into reproach and the snare of the devil.

8 Ministers, in like manner, honorable, not double-tongued, not given to much wine, not seeking gain by base means,

9 holding the revealed-mystery of the faith in a pure conscience.

10 And let these be first proved, then let them minister, being without reproach.

11 The women in like manner honorable, not slanderers, sober, faithful in all things.

12 Let the ministers be husbands of one wife, conducting [their] children and their own houses well:

13 for those who shall have ministered well obtain for themselves a good degree, and much boldness in faith which is in Christ Jesus.

14 These things I write to you, hoping to come to you more quickly;

15 but if I delay, in order that you may know how one ought to conduct oneself in God's house, which is the church of the living God, the pillar and base of the truth.

16 And knowing that the revealed-mystery of piety is great. God has been manifested in flesh, has been justified in the Spirit, seen by angels, has been preached among the Gentiles, has been believed on in the world, has been received up in glory.

1 Tim 4:1 But the Spirit speaks expressly, that in latter times some shall depart from the faith, giving their mind to deceiving spirits and teachings of daemons

2 speaking lies in hypocrisy, branded [as with hot iron] as to their own conscience,

3 forbidding to marry, [bidding] to abstain from meats, which God has created for receiving with thanksgiving for them who are faithful and know the truth.

4 For every creation of God is good, and nothing is to be rejected, being received with thanksgiving;

5 for it is sanctified by God's word and prayer.

6 Laying these things before the brethren, you will be a good minister of Christ Jesus, nourished with the words of the faith and of the good teaching which you have fully followed up.

7 But profane and old wives' fables avoid, but exercise yourself unto piety;

8 for bodily exercise is profitable for a little, but piety is profitable for everything, having promise of life, of the present one, and of that to come.

9 The word is faithful and worthy of all acceptance;

10 for this we labor and suffer reproach, because we hope in a living God, who is preserver of all men, specially of those that believe.

11 Command and teach these things.

12 Let no one despise your youth, but be a model of the believers, in word, in conduct, in love, in faith, in purity.

13 Till I come, give yourself to reading, to exhortation, to teaching.

14 Be not negligent of the gift [that is] in you, which has been given to you through prophecy, with laying on of the hands of the elderhood.

15 Occupy yourself with these things; be wholly in them, that your progress may be manifest to all.

16 Give heed to yourself and to the teaching; continue in them; for, doing this, you shall save both yourself and those that hear you.

1 Tim 5:1 Rebuke not an elder sharply, but urge him as a father, younger [men] as brethren,

2 elder women as mothers, younger women as sisters, with all purity.

3 honor widows who are really widows;

4 but if any widow have children or descendants, let them learn first to be pious as regards their own house, and to render a return on their side to [their] parents; for this is acceptable in the sight of the God.

5 Now she who is a widow indeed, and is left alone, has put [her] hope in God, and continues in supplications and prayers night and day.

6 But she that lives in habits of self-indulgence is dead [while] living.

7 And these things enjoin, that they may be irreproachable.

8 But if any one does not provide for his own, and specially for those of [his] house, he has denied the faith, and is worse than the unbeliever.

9 Let a widow be put upon the list, being of not less than sixty years, [having been] wife of one man,

10 borne witness to in good works, if she have brought up children, if she have exercised hospitality, if she have washed saints' feet, if she have imparted relief to the distressed, if she have diligently followed every good work.

11 But younger widows decline; for when they grow wanton against Christ, they desire to marry,

12 being guilty, because they have cast off their first faith.

13 And, at the same time, they learn also [to be] idle, going about to people's houses; and not only idle, but also gossipers and meddlers, speaking things not becoming.

14 I wish therefore that the younger marry, bear children, rule the house, give no occasion to the adversary in respect of reproach.

15 For already some have turned aside after Satan.

16 If any believing man or woman have widows, let them impart relief to them, and let not the church be charged, that it may impart relief to those [that are] widows indeed.

17 Let the elders who take the lead [among the saints] be well esteemed worthy of double honor, specially those laboring in word and teaching;

18 for the scripture says, You shall not muzzle an ox that treads out grain, and, The workman is worthy of his hire.

19 Against an elder receive not an accusation unless where there are two or three witnesses.

20 Those that sin rebuke before all, that the rest also may have fear.

21 I testify before God and Christ Jesus and the elect angels, that you keep these things without prejudice, doing nothing by partiality.

22 Lay hands quickly on no man, nor partake in others' sins. Keep yourself pure.

23 Drink no longer only water, but use a little wine on account of your stomach and your frequent illnesses.

24 Of some men the sins are manifest beforehand, going before to judgment, and some also they follow after.

25 In like manner good works also are manifest beforehand, and those [works] that are contrary cannot be hidden.

1 Tim 6:1 Let as many servants as are under yoke count their own masters worthy of all honor, that the name of the God and the teaching be not blasphemed.

2 And they that have believing masters, let them not despise [them] because they are brethren; but let them the rather serve them with subjection, because they are faithful and beloved, who profit by the good and ready service. These things teach and exhort.

3 If any one teach differently, and do not agree to sound words, those of our Lord Jesus Christ, and the teaching which is according to piety,

4 he is conceited and understands nothing; but he has a morbid interest in controversial questions and disputes about words, out of which arise envy, strife, abusive language, evil suspicions,

5 constant quarreling of men corrupted in mind and destitute of the truth, holding gain to be [the end of] piety.

6 But piety with contentment is great gain.

7 For we have brought nothing into the world: that neither can we carry anything out.

8 But having sustenance and covering, we will be content with these.

9 But those who desire to be rich fall into temptation and a snare, and many unwise and hurtful lusts, which plunge men into destruction and ruin.

10 For the love of money is a root of every evil; which some having aspired after, have wandered from the faith, and pierced themselves with many sorrows.

11 But you, O man of God, flee these things, and pursue righteousness, piety, faith, love, endurance, meekness of spirit.

12 Strive earnestly in the good conflict of faith. Lay hold of aeonian life, to which you have been called, and have acknowledged the good acknowledgment before many witnesses.

13 I enjoin you before God who preserves all things in life, and Christ Jesus who witnessed before Pontius Pilate the good acknowledgment,

14 that you keep the commandment spotless, irreproachable, until the appearing of our Lord Jesus Christ;

15 which in its own time the blessed and only Ruler shall show, the King of those that reign, and Lord of those that exercise lordship;

16 who only has immortality, dwelling in unapproachable light; whom no man has seen, nor is able to see; to whom [be] honor and aeonian might. Amen.

17 Enjoin on those rich in the present aeon, not to be high-minded, nor to trust on the uncertainty of riches; but in God who affords us all things richly for our enjoyment;

18 to do good, to be rich in good works, to be generous, ready to share [of their substance]

19 laying by for themselves a good foundation for the future, that they may lay hold of [what is] really life.

20 O Timothy, keep the entrusted deposit, avoiding profane, vain babbling, and oppositions of false-named knowledge,

21 of which some having made profession, have missed the faith. Grace [be] with you.

2 Timothy

2 Tim 1:1 Paul, apostle of Jesus Christ by God's will, according to promise of life, which is in Christ Jesus,

2 to Timothy, my beloved child: grace, mercy, peace, from God the Father, and Christ Jesus our Lord.

3 I am thankful to God, whom I serve from my forefathers with pure conscience, how unceasingly I have the remembrance of you in my prayers night and day,

4 earnestly desiring to see you, remembering your tears, that I may be filled with joy;

5 calling to mind the sincere faith which is in you, which dwelt first in your grandmother Lois, and in your mother Eunice, and I am persuaded that in you also.

6 For which cause I put you in mind to rekindle the gift of the God which is in you by the putting on of my hands.

7 For God has not given us a spirit of cowardice, but of power, and of love, and of wise discretion.

8 Be not therefore ashamed of the testimony of our Lord, nor of me his prisoner; but suffer evil along with the good news, according to the power of God;

9 who has saved us, and has called us with a holy calling, not according to our works, but according to his own purpose and grace, which was given to us in Christ Jesus before the aeons of time,

10 but has been made manifest now by the appearing of our Savior Jesus Christ, who has superseded death, and brought to light life and immortality by the good news;

11 to which I have been appointed a herald and apostle and teacher of the nations.

12 For which cause also I suffer these things; but I am not ashamed; for I know whom I have believed, and am persuaded that he is able to keep for that day the deposit I have entrusted to him.

13 Have an outline of sound words, which you have heard of me, in faith and love which are in Christ Jesus.

14 Keep, by the Holy Spirit which dwells in us, the good deposit entrusted.

15 You know this, that all who are in Asia, of whom is Phygellus and Hermogenes, have turned away from me.

16 The Lord grant mercy to the house of Onesiphorus, for he has often refreshed me, and has not been ashamed of my chain;

17 but being in Rome sought me out very diligently, and found me

18 --the Lord grant to him to find mercy from the Lord in that day --and how much service he rendered in Ephesus you know best.

2 Tim 2:1 You therefore, my child, be strong in the grace which is in Christ Jesus.

2 And the things you have heard of me in the presence of many witnesses, these entrust to faithful men, such as shall be competent to instruct others also.

3 Take your share in suffering as a good soldier of Jesus Christ.

4 No one going as a soldier entangles himself with the affairs of life, that he may please him who has enlisted him as a soldier.

5 And if also any one competes [in the games] he is not crowned unless he competes by the rules.

6 The husbandman must labor before partaking of the fruits.

7 Think about what I saying, for the Lord will give you understanding in all things.

8 Remember Jesus Christ raised from among the dead, of the seed of David, according to my good news,

9 in which I suffer even unto bonds as an evil-doer: but the word of the God is not bound.

10 For this cause I endure all things for the sake of the elect, that they also may obtain the salvation which is in Christ Jesus with aeonian glory.

11 The word is faithful; for if we have died together with him, we shall also live together;

12 if we endure, we shall also reign together; if we deny, he also will deny us;

13 if we are unfaithful, he abides faithful, for he cannot deny himself.

14 Of these things put in remembrance, testifying earnestly before the Lord not to have disputes of words, profitable for nothing, to the subversion of the hearers.

15 Strive diligently to present yourself approved to God, a workman that has not to be ashamed, cutting in a straight line the word of truth.

16 But profane and vain babbling shun, for they will advance to greater impiety,

17 and their word will spread as a gangrene; of whom is Hymenaeus and Philetus;

18 [men] who as to the truth have gone astray, saying that the resurrection has taken place already; and overthrow the faith of some.

19 Yet the firm foundation of the God stands, having this seal, the Lord knows those that are his; and, Let every one who names the name of the Lord withdraw from iniquity.

20 But in a great house there are not only gold and silver vessels, but also wooden and earthen; and some to honor, and some to dishonor.

21 If therefore one shall have purified himself from these, [in separating himself from them] he shall be a vessel to honor, sanctified, serviceable to the Master, prepared for every good work.

22 But youthful lusts flee, and pursue righteousness, faith, love, peace, with those that call upon the Lord out of a pure heart.

23 But foolish and senseless questioning avoid, knowing that they beget contentions.

24 And a servant of the Lord ought not to contend, but be gentle towards all; apt to teach; forbearing;

25 in meekness setting right those who oppose, if God perhaps may sometime give them repentance to acknowledgment of the truth,

26 and they may come to their senses and escape from the snare of the devil, having been held captive by him to do his will.

2 Tim 3:1 But this know, that in the last days difficult times shall be there;

2 for men shall be lovers of self, lovers of money, boastful, arrogant, evil speakers, disobedient to parents, ungrateful, profane,

3 unloving, unforgiving, slanderers, without self-control, savage, having no love for what is good,

4 traitors, reckless, of vain pretensions, lovers of pleasure rather than lovers of God;

5 having a form of piety but denying the power of it: and from these turn away.

6 For of these are they who are getting into houses, and leading captive silly women, loaded with sins, led by various lusts,

7 always learning, and never able to come to the knowledge of the truth.

8 Now in the same manner in which Jannes and Jambres withstood Moses, thus these also withstand the truth; men corrupted in mind, found worthless as regards the faith.

9 But they shall not advance farther; for their folly shall be completely manifest to all, as that of those [Jannes & Jambres] also became.

10 But you have been thoroughly acquainted with my teaching, conduct, purpose, faith, patience, love, endurance,

11 persecutions, sufferings: what [sufferings] happened to me in Antioch, in Iconium, in Lystra; what persecutions I endured; and the Lord delivered me out of all.

12 And all indeed who desire to live piously in Christ Jesus will be persecuted.

13 But wicked men and juggling impostors shall advance in evil, leading and being led astray.

14 But you, abide in those things which you have learned, and you have been fully persuaded, knowing from whom you have learned,

15 and that from a child you have known the sacred letters, which are able to make you wise unto salvation, through faith which is in Christ Jesus.

16 Every scripture is divinely inspired, and profitable for teaching, for conviction, for correction, for instruction in righteousness;

17 that the man of the God may be complete, fully fitted to every good work.

2 Tim 4:1 I testify before God and Christ Jesus, who is about to judge living and dead, by his appearing and his kingdom,

2 proclaim the word; be urgent in season and out of season, convict, rebuke, encourage, with all patience and doctrine.

3 For the time shall be when they will not bear sound teaching; but according to their own lusts will heap up to themselves teachers, having an itching ear;

4 and they will turn away their ear from the truth, and will have turned aside to fables.

5 But you, be sober in all things, bear evils, do the work of an evangelist, fill up the full measure of your ministry.

6 For I am already being poured out, and the time of my release [from this life] is come.

7 I have combated the good combat, I have finished the race, I have kept the faith.

8 Henceforth the crown of righteousness is laid up for me, which the Lord, the righteous Judge, will render to me in that day; but not only to me, but also to all who love his appearing.

9 Use diligence to come to me quickly;

10 for Demas has forsaken me, having loved the present aeon, and is gone to Thessalonica; Crescens to Galatia, Titus to Dalmatia.

11 Luke alone is with me. Take Mark, and bring him with yourself, for he is serviceable to me for ministry.

12 But Tychicus I have sent to Ephesus.

13 The cloak which I left behind [me] in Troas at Carpus's, bring when you come, and the books, especially the parchments.

14 Alexander the smith did many evil things against me. The Lord will render to him according to his works.

15 Against whom be you also on your guard, for he has greatly withstood our words.

16 At my first defense no man stood with me, but all deserted me. May it not be imputed to them.

17 But the Lord stood with me and gave me power, that through me the proclamation might be fully made, and all the nations should hear; and I was delivered out of the lion's mouth.

18 The Lord shall deliver me from every wicked work, and shall preserve me for his heavenly kingdom; to whom be glory into the aeons of aeons. Amen.

19 Salute Prisca and Aquila, and the house of Onesiphorus.

20 Erastus remained in Corinth, but Trophimus I left behind in Miletus sick.

21 Use diligence to come before winter. Eubulus salutes you, and Pudens, and Linus, and Claudia, and the brethren all.

22 The Lord Jesus Christ [be] with your spirit. Grace [be] with you.

Titus

Titus 1:1 Paul, servant of God, and apostle of Jesus Christ according to the faith of God's elect, and knowledge of the truth which is according to piety;

2 in the hope of aeonian life, which God, who cannot lie, promised before the aeons of time,

3 but has manifested in its own due season his word, in the proclamation with which I have been entrusted, according to the commandment of our Savior God;

4 to Titus, my own child according to the faith common [to us]. Grace and peace from God the Father, and Christ Jesus our Savior.

5 For this cause I left you in Crete, that you might go on to set right what remained [unordered] and establish elders in each city, as I had directed you:

6 if any one be free from all charge [against him] husband of one wife, having believing children not accused of excess or unruly.

7 For the overseer must be free from all charge [against him] as God's steward; not headstrong, not passionate, not disorderly through wine, not a striker, not seeking gain by base means;

8 but hospitable, a lover of goodness, discreet, just, pious, temperate,

9 clinging to the faithful word according to the doctrine taught, that he may be able both to encourage with sound teaching and refute gainsayers.

10 For there are many and disorderly vain speakers and deceivers of people's minds, specially those of the circumcision,

11 who must have their mouths stopped, who subvert whole houses, teaching things which ought not [to be taught] for the sake of base gain.

12 One of themselves, a prophet of their own, has said, Cretans are always liars, evil wild beasts, lazy gluttons.

13 This testimony is true; for which cause rebuke them severely, that they may be sound in the faith,

14 not turning [their] minds to Jewish fables and commandments of men turning away from the truth.

15 All things are pure to the pure; but to the defiled and unbelieving nothing is pure; but both their mind and their conscience are defiled.

16 They profess to know God, but in works deny him being abominable, and disobedient, and found worthless as to every good work.

Titus 2:1 But you speak the things that become sound teaching;

2 that the elder men be sober, honorable, discreet, sound in faith, in love, in patience;

3 that the elder women in like manner be reverent, not slanderers, not enslaved to much wine, teachers of what is right;

4 that they may admonish the young women to be attached to their husbands, to be attached to their children,

5 discreet, chaste, diligent in home work, good, subject to their own husbands, that the word of the God may not be evil spoken of.

6 The younger men in like manner exhort to be discreet:

7 in all things affording yourself as a pattern of good works; in teaching uncorruptedness, dignified,

8 a sound word, not to be condemned; that he who is opposed may be ashamed, having no evil thing to say about us:

9 servants to be subject to their own masters, to make themselves acceptable in everything; not contradicting;

10 not robbing [their masters] but showing all good fidelity, that they may adorn the teaching which is of our Savior God in all things.

11 For the grace of the God which carries with it salvation for all men has appeared,

12 teaching us that, having denied impiety and worldly lusts, we should live soberly, and justly, and piously in the present course of things,

13 awaiting the blessed hope and appearing of the glory of our great God and Savior Jesus Christ;

14 who gave himself for us, that he might redeem us from all lawlessness, and purify to himself a peculiar people, zealous for good works.

15 These things speak, and exhort, and rebuke with all authority. Let no one despise you.

Titus 3:1 Put them in mind to be subject to rulers, to authorities, to be obedient, to be ready to do every good work,

2 to speak evil of no one, not to be contentious, mild, showing all meekness towards all men.

3 For we were once ourselves also without intelligence, disobedient, wandering in error, serving various lusts and pleasures, living in malice and envy, hateful, [and] hating one another.

4 But when the kindness of God our Savior and His love for mankind appeared,

5 He saved us, not on the basis of deeds which we have done in righteousness, but according to His mercy, by the washing of regeneration and renewing by the Holy Spirit,

6 which he poured out on us richly through Jesus Christ our Savior;

7 that, having been justified by his grace, we should become heirs according to the hope of aeonian life.

8 The word is faithful, and I desire that you insist strenuously on these things, that they who have believed God may take care to pay diligent attention to good works. These things are good and profitable to men.

9 But foolish questions, and genealogies, and strifes, and contentions about the law, shun; for they are unprofitable and vain.

10 A heretical man after a first and second admonition be done with,

11 knowing that such a one is perverted, and sins, being self-condemned.

12 When I shall send Artemas to you, or Tychicus, use diligence to come to me to Nicopolis; for I have decided to winter there.

13 Zenas the lawyer and Apollos set forward diligently on their way, that nothing may be lacking to them;

14 and let ours also learn to apply themselves to good works for necessary wants, that they may not be unfruitful.

15 All with me salute you. Salute those who brotherly-loves us in the faith. Grace [be] with you all.

Philemon

Phile 1:1 Paul, prisoner of Christ Jesus, and Timothy the brother, to Philemon the beloved and our fellow-workman,

2 and to the sister Apphia and to Archippus our fellow-soldier, and to the church which is in your house.

3 Grace to you and peace from God our Father, and the Lord Jesus Christ.

4 I thank my God, always making mention of you at my prayers,

5 hearing of your love and the faith which you have towards the Lord Jesus, and towards all the saints,

6 that your fellowship in the faith should become effective in the acknowledgment of every good thing which is in us towards Christ [Jesus].

7 For we have great thankfullness and encouragement through your love, because the affection of the saints are refreshed by you, brother.

8 Therefore having much boldness in Christ to enjoin you what is fitting,

9 for love's sake I rather exhort, being such a one as Paul the aged, and now also prisoner of Jesus Christ.

10 I exhort you for my child, whom I have begotten in [my] bonds, Onesimus,

11 once useless to you, but now of service to you and to me:

12 whom I have sent back to you: [but do you receive] him, that is, my affection:

13 whom I was desirous of keeping with myself, that for you he might minister to me in the bonds of the good news;

14 but I have wished to do nothing without your consent, that your good might not be as of necessity but of willingness:

15 for perhaps for this reason he has been separated [from you] for a time, that you might possess him fully aeonianly;

16 not any longer as a servant, but above a servant, a beloved brother, specially to me, and how much rather to you, both in the flesh and in the Lord?

17 If therefore you hold me to be a partner [with you] receive him as me;

18 but if he have wronged you anything or owe anything [to you] put this to my account.

19 I Paul have written it with mine own hand; I will repay it (that I say not to you that you owe even your own self also to me).

20 Yes, brother, I would have profit of you in the Lord: refresh my affection in Christ.

21 Being confident of your obedience, I have written to you, knowing that you will do even more than I say.

22 But prepare me also a lodging; for I hope that I shall be granted to you through your prayers.

23 Epaphras salutes you, my fellow-prisoner in Christ Jesus;

24 Mark, Aristarchus, Demas, Luke, my fellow-workmen.

25 The grace of our Lord Jesus Christ be with your spirit.

Hebrews

Heb 1:1 Little by little, and in different ways, long ago the God spoke to the fathers in the prophets,

2 in the time of the last days this very [God] speaks to us in his Son, for whom he appointed * heir of all things, and on account of he makes * the aeons;

3 who being the brightness of the glory and the exact representation of the essence of the very [God], and upholding all things by the word of power of the very [God], when He makes * purification for the sins, He sits * down at the right hand of the Majesty on high,

4 taking a place so much better than the angels, as he inherits a name more excellent than they.

5 For to which of the angels did He ever say, You are my son, today I have begotten you? And again, I will be a father to him and he shall be a Son to me?

6 and again, when he brings in the firstborn into the habitable world, he says, And let all God's angels worship him.

7 And as to the angels he says, Who makes his angels spirits and his ministers a flame of fire;

8 but as to the Son, Your throne, O God, is to the aeon of the aeon, and a scepter of uprightness is the scepter of your kingdom.

9 You have loved righteousness and have hated lawlessness; therefore God, your God, has anointed you with oil of gladness above your companions.

10 And, You in the beginning, Lord, have founded the earth, and works of your hands are the heavens.

11 They shall perish, but you continue still; and they all shall grow old as a garment,

12 and as a covering shall you roll them up, and they shall be changed; but you are the very[1], and your years shall not fail.

13 But as to which of the angels said he ever, Sit at my right hand until I put your enemies a footstool of your feet?

14 Are they not all ministering spirits, sent out for service for those who shall inherit salvation?

Heb 2:1 For this reason we should give heed more abundantly to the things [we have] heard, lest in any way we should slip away.

2 For if the word which was spoken by angels was firm, and every transgression and disobedience received just retribution,

3 how shall we escape if we have been negligent of such a great salvation, which, having had its commencement in being spoken of by the Lord, has been confirmed to us by those who have heard;

4 God bearing, besides, witness with [them] to it both by signs and wonders, and various acts of power, and distributions of the Holy Spirit, according to his will?

5 For he has not subjected to angels the habitable world which is to come, of which we speak;

6 but one has testified somewhere, saying, What is man, that you remember him, or son of man that you visit him?

7 You have made him a little inferior to the angels; you have crowned him with glory and honor, [and have set him over the works of your hands]

8 you have subjected all things under his feet. For in subjecting all things to him, he has left nothing unsubject to him. But now we see not yet all things subjected to him,

9 but we see Jesus, who [was] made a little inferior to angels on account of the suffering of death, crowned with glory and honor; so that by the grace of God he should taste death for every thing.

10 For it was fitting for Him, for whom are all things, and through whom are all things, in bringing many sons to glory, to perfect the author of their salvation through sufferings.

11 For both he that sanctifies and those sanctified are all out of one; for which cause he is not ashamed to call them brethren,

12 saying, I will declare your name to my brethren; in the midst of the church will I sing your praises.

13 And again, I will trust in him. And again, Behold, I and the children which God has given me.

14 Since therefore the children partake of blood and flesh, he also, in like manner, took part in the same, that through death he might supersede him who has the power of death, that is, the devil.

15 and might set free all those who through fear of death through the whole of their life were subject to bondage.

16 For he does not indeed take hold of angels, but he takes hold of the seed of Abraham.

17 Therefore it behoved him in all things to be made like to his brethren, that he might be a merciful and faithful high priest in things relating to the God, to make reconciliation for the sins of the people;

18 for, in that himself has suffered, being tested, he is able to help those that are being tested.

Heb 3:1 Therefore holy brethren, partakers of the heavenly calling, consider the Apostle and High Priest of our allegiance, Jesus,

2 who is faithful to him that has appointed him, as Moses also in all his house.

3 For he has been counted worthy of greater glory than Moses, by how much he that has built it has more honor than the house.

4 For every house is built by some one; but he who has built all things is God.

5 And Moses indeed [was] faithful in all his house, as a ministering servant, for a testimony of the things to be spoken afterward;

6 but Christ, as Son over his family, whose family we are, if indeed we hold fast the boldness and the boast of hope firm to the end.

---

[1] An intensive pronoun to emphasize identity

7 Therefore, as the Holy Spirit says, Today if you will hear his voice,

8 harden not your hearts, as in the rebellion, in the day of trials in the wilderness;

9 where your fathers tested [me] by proving [me] and saw my works forty years.

10 Therefore, I was wrathful with this generation, and said, They always err in heart; and they have not known my ways;

11 so I swore in my wrath, If they shall enter into my rest.

12 See, brethren, lest there be in any one of you a wicked heart of unbelief, in turning away from the living God.

13 But encourage yourselves each day, as long as it is called Today, that none of you be hardened by the deceitfullness of sin.

14 For we are become companions of the Christ if indeed we hold the beginning of the assurance firm to the end;

15 in that it is said, Today if you will hear his voice, do not harden your hearts, as in the rebellion;

16 for who was it, who, having heard, rebelled? Indeed, did not all those who came out of Egypt led by Moses?

17 And with whom was he wrathful forty years? [was it] not with those who had sinned, whose carcases fell in the wilderness?

18 And to whom he swore that they should not enter into his rest, but to those who had not listened to the word?

19 And we see that they could not enter in on account of unbelief;

Heb 4:1 Let us therefore fear, lest, a promise remains for entering into his rest, any one of you might seem to have come up short.

2 For indeed we have had good news presented to us, even as they also; but the word of the report did not profit them, not being mixed with faith in those who heard.

3 For we enter into the rest who have believed; as he said, As I have sworn in my wrath, If they shall enter into my rest; although the works had been completed from the foundation of the world.

4 For he has said somewhere of the seventh [day] thus, And God rested on the seventh day from all his works:

5 and in this again, If they shall enter into my rest.

6 Seeing therefore it remains that some enter into it, and those who first received the good news did not enter in on account of not hearing the word,

7 again he determines a certain day, saying, in David, 'Today', after so long a time; according as it has been said before, Today, if you will hear his voice, harden not your hearts.

8 For if Joshua had brought them into rest, he would not have spoken afterwards about another day.

9 There remains then a Sabbath for the people of the God.

10 For he that has entered into his rest, he also has rested from his works, as God did from his own.

11 Let us therefore use diligence to enter into that rest, that no one may fall after the same example of not hearing the word.

12 For the word of the God is living and operative, and sharper than any two-edged sword, and penetrating to the division of soul and spirit, both of joints and marrow, and a discerner of the thoughts and intents of the heart.

13 And there is nothing of the creation hidden before him; but all things are naked and laid bare to his eyes, with whom we have to do.

14 Having therefore a great high priest who has passed through the heavens, Jesus the Son of the God, let us hold fast the allegiance.

15 For we have not a high priest not able to sympathize with our weaknesses, but tested in all things in like manner, without sin.

16 Let us approach therefore with boldness to the throne of grace, so that we may receive mercy and find grace to help in time of need.

Heb 5:1 For every high priest taken from among men is established for men in things relating toward the God, that he may offer both gifts and sacrifices for sins;

2 being able to exercise forbearance towards the ignorant and misguided, since he himself also is clothed with weakness;

3 and, on account of this [infirmity] he ought, even as for the people, so also for himself, to offer for sins.

4 And no one takes the honor to himself but [as] called by God, even as Aaron also.

5 Thus the Christ also has not glorified himself to be made a high priest; but he who had said to him, You are my Son, I have today begotten you.

6 Even as also in another [place] he says, You are a priest into the aeon according to the order of Melchisedec.

7 Who in the days of his flesh, having offered up both supplications and entreaties to him who was able to save him out of death, with strong crying and tears; and having been heard because of his piety;

8 though he were Son, he learned obedience from the things which he suffered;

9 and having been perfected, became to all them that obey him, author of aeonian salvation;

10 addressed by God [as] high priest according to the order of Melchisedec.

11 Concerning whom we have much to say, and hard to be interpreted in speaking [of it] since you are become dull in hearing.

12 For when for the time you ought to be teachers, you have again need that [one] should teach you what [are] the elements of the beginning of the oracles of the God, and are become such as have need of milk, [and] not of solid food.

13 For every one that partakes of milk is unskilled in the word of righteousness, for he is a babe;

14 but solid food belongs to full-grown men, who, because of use, have their senses exercised for distinguishing both good and evil.

Heb 6:1 Therefore, leaving the word of the beginning of the Christ, let us go on [to what belongs] to full growth, not laying again a foundation of repentance from dead works and faith in God,

2 of the doctrine of washing, and of laying on of hands, and of resurrection of the dead, and of aeonian judgment;

3 and this will we do if God permit.

4 For it is impossible to renew again to repentance those once enlightened, and who have tasted of the heavenly gift, and have been made partakers of the Holy Spirit,

5 and have tasted the good word of God, and the works of power of the aeon to come,

6 and have fallen away, crucifying for themselves the Son of the God, and making a show of him.

7 For ground which drinks the rain which comes often upon it, and produces useful herbs for those for who also it is tilled, partakes of blessing from God;

8 but bringing forth thorns and briars, it is found worthless and near to a curse, whose end is to be burned.

9 But we are persuaded concerning you, beloved, better things, and connected with salvation, even if we speak thus.

10 For God is not unrighteous to forget your work, and the love which you have shown to his name, having ministered to the saints, and [still] ministering.

11 But we desire earnestly that each one of you show the same diligence to the full assurance of hope unto the end;

12 that you be not sluggish, but imitators of those who through faith and patience have been inheritors of the promises.

13 For God, having promised to Abraham, since he had no greater to swear by, swore by himself,

14 saying, Surely blessing I will bless you, and multiplying I will multiply you;

15 and thus, having had long patience, he got the promise.

16 For men indeed swear by a greater, and an oath for confirmation is to them an end of all strife.

17 Wherein God, willing to show more abundantly to the heirs of the promise the unchangeableness of his purpose, intervened by an oath,

18 that by two unchangeable things, in which [it was] impossible that God should lie, we might have a strong encouragement, who have fled for refuge to lay hold on the hope set before us,

19 which we have as anchor of the soul, both secure and firm, and entering within the veil,

20 where Jesus is entered as forerunner for us, become into the aeon a high priest according to the order of Melchisedec.

Heb 7:1 For this Melchisedec, King of Salem, priest of the most high God, who met Abraham returning from smiting the kings, and blessed him;

2 to whom Abraham gave also the tenth portion of all; first being interpreted King of righteousness, and then also King of Salem, which is King of peace;

3 without father, without mother, without genealogy; having neither beginning of days nor end of life, but like to the Son of the God, abides a priest continually.

4 Now consider how great this [personage] was, to whom [even] the patriarch Abraham gave a tenth out of the spoils.

5 And they indeed from among the sons of Levi, who receive the priesthood, have commandment to take tithes from the people according to the law, that is from their brethren, though these are come out of the loins of Abraham:

6 but he who has no genealogy from them collected a tithe from Abraham, and blessed him who had the promises.

7 But beyond all dispute, the inferior is blessed by the better.

8 In this case mortal men receive tithes, but in that case one receives them, of whom it is witnessed that he lives on.

9 and, so to speak, through Abraham, Levi also, who received tithes, has been made to pay tithes.

10 For he was yet in the loins of his father when Melchisedec met him.

11 If indeed then perfection were by the Levitical priesthood, for the people had their law given to them in connection with it, what need [was there] still that a different priest should arise according to the order of Melchisedec, and not be named after the order of Aaron?

12 For, the priesthood being changed, there takes place of necessity a change of law also.

13 For he, of whom these things are said, belongs to a different tribe, of which no one has [ever] been attached to the service of the altar.

14 For it is clear that our Lord has sprung out of Judah, as to which tribe Moses spoke nothing as to priests.

15 And it is yet more abundantly evident, since a different priest arises according to the likeness of Melchisedec,

16 who has been such, not according to law of fleshly commandment, but according to power of indestructible life.

17 For it is borne witness, You are a priest into the aeon according to the order of Melchisedec.

18 For there is a setting aside of the former commandment for its weakness and unprofitableness,

19 for the law perfected nothing, and the introduction of a better hope by which we draw near to God.

20 And by how much [it was] not without the swearing of an oath;

21 for they are become priests without the swearing of an oath, but he with the swearing of an oath, by him who said, as to him, The Lord has

sworn, and will not repent. You are a priest into the aeon [according to the order of Melchisedec],

22 by so much Jesus became surety of a better covenant

23 And they have been many priests, on account of being hindered from continuing by death;

24 but he, because of his continuing into the aeon, has the priesthood unchangeable.

25 Therefore also he is able to save completely those who approach by him to God, always living to intercede for them.

26 For such a high priest became us, holy, harmless, undefiled, separated from sinners, and become higher than the heavens:

27 who has not day by day need, as the high priests, first to offer up sacrifices for his own sins, then [for] those of the people; for this he did once for all [in] having offered up himself.

28 For the law constitutes men high priests, having infirmity; but the word of the swearing of the oath which is with the law, a Son fulfills into the aeon.

Heb 8:1 Now the main point in what has been said is this: we have such a high priest, who has taken His seat at the right hand of the throne of the Majesty in the heavens,

2 minister of the holy places and of the true tabernacle, which the Lord has pitched, not man.

3 For every high priest is appointed for the offering both of gifts and sacrifices; therefore it is needful that this one also should have something which he may offer.

4 If then indeed he were upon earth, he would not even be a priest, there being those who offer the gifts according to the law,

5 who serve a copy and shadow of heavenly things, according as Moses was told [when] he made the tabernacle; for See, says He, that you make all things according to the pattern which has been shown to you in the mountain.

6 But now he has got a more excellent ministry, by so much as he is mediator of a better covenant which is established on the footing of better promises.

7 For if that first was faultless, a place would not have been sought for a second.

8 For finding fault, he says to them, Behold, days come, says the Lord, and I will made a new covenant as regards the house of Israel, and as regards the house of Judah;

9 not according to the covenant which I made to their fathers in the day of my taking their hand to lead them out of the land of Egypt; because they did not continue in my covenant and I did not regard them, says the Lord.

10 Because this is the covenant that I will give to the house of Israel after those days, says the Lord: Giving my laws into their mind, I will write them also upon their hearts; and I will be to them for God, and they shall be to me for a nation.

11 And they shall not teach each his fellow-citizen, and each his brother, saying, Know the Lord; because all shall know me in themselves, from the little one unto the great among them.

12 Because I will be merciful to their unrighteousness, and their sins and their lawlessness I will never remember any more.

13 In that he says New, he has made the first old; but that which grows old and aged is near disappearing.

Heb 9:1 The first therefore also indeed had ordinances of service, and the sanctuary, a worldly one.

2 For a tabernacle was set up; the first, in which [were] both the candlestick and the table and the showbread, which is called Holy;

3 but after the second veil a tabernacle which is called Holy of holies,

4 having a golden censer, and the ark of the covenant covered round in every part with gold, in which [were] the golden pot that had the manna, and the rod of Aaron that had sprouted, and the tables of the covenant,

5 and above over it the cherubs of glory shadowing the mercy-seat; concerning which it is not now [the time] to speak in detail.

6 Now these things being thus ordered, into the first tabernacle the priests enter at all times, accomplishing the services;

7 but into the second, the high priest only, once a year, not without blood, which he offers for himself and for the errors of the people;

8 the Holy Spirit showing this, that the way of the [holy of] holies has not yet been made manifest while as yet the first tabernacle was standing;

9 the which is an image for the present time, according to which both gifts and sacrifices, unable to perfect as to conscience him that worshiped, are offered,

10 [consisting] only of meats and drinks and diverse washing, ordinances of flesh, imposed until the time of setting things right.

11 But Christ being high priest of the good things to come, by the better and more perfect tabernacle not made with hand, that is, not of this creation,

12 nor by blood of goats and calves, but by his own blood, has entered in once for all into the [holy of] holies, having found an aeonian redemption.

13 For if the blood of goats and bulls, and a heifer's ashes sprinkling the defiled, sanctifies for the purity of the flesh,

14 how much rather shall the blood of the Christ, who by the aeonian Spirit offered himself spotless to God, purify your conscience from dead works to worship the living God?

15 And for this reason he is mediator of a new covenant so that, death having taken place for redemption of the transgressions under the first covenant, the called might receive the promise of the aeonian inheritance.

16 For where a covenant, the death of the covenant maker must come.

17 For a covenant is of force when men are dead, since it is in no way of force while the covenant maker is alive.

18 Therefore neither the first was inaugurated without blood.

19 For every commandment having been spoken according to the law by Moses to all the people; having taken the blood of calves and goats, with water and scarlet wool and hyssop, he sprinkled both the book itself and all the people,

20 saying, This is the blood of the covenant which God has commanded to you.

21 And the tabernacle too and all the vessels of service he sprinkled in like manner with blood;

22 and almost all things are purified with blood according to the law, and without blood-shedding there is no forgiveness.

23 [It was] necessary then that the figurative representations of the things in the heavens should be purified with these; but the heavenly things themselves with sacrifices better than these.

24 For the Christ is not entered into holy places made with hand, figures of the true, but into heaven itself, now to appear before the presence of the God for us:

25 nor in order that he should offer himself often, as the high priest enters into the holy places every year with blood not his own;

26 since he had [then] been obliged often to suffer from the foundation of the world. But now once in the end of the aeons, he has been appeared for the putting away of sin by his sacrifice.

27 And forasmuch as it is the portion of men once to die, and after this judgment;

28 thus the Christ also, having been once offered to bear the sins of many, shall appear to those that look for him the second time without sin for salvation.

Heb 10:1 For the law, having a shadow of the coming good things, not the image itself of the things, can never, by the same sacrifices which they offer continually yearly, perfect those who approach.

2 Since, would they not indeed have ceased being offered, on account of the worshipers once purged having no longer any conscience of sins?

3 But in these [there is] a calling to mind of sins yearly.

4 For blood of bulls and goats is incapable of taking away sins.

5 Therefore coming into the world he says, Sacrifice and offering you wished not; but you have prepared me a body.

6 You took no pleasure in burnt-offerings and sacrifices for sin.

7 Then he said, Lo, I come (in the roll of the book it is written of me) to do, O God, your will.

8 So first he said, Sacrifices and offerings and burnt-offerings and sacrifices for sin you wished not, neither took pleasure in which are offered according to the law;

9 Then he said, Lo, I come to do your will. He takes away the first that he may establish the second;

10 by which desire [will] we have been sanctified through the offering of the body of Jesus Christ once for all.

11 And every priest stands daily ministering, and offering often the same sacrifices, which can never take away sins.

12 But he, having offered one sacrifice for sins, sat down in perpetuity at the right hand of the God,

13 waiting from henceforth until his enemies be set a footstool of his feet.

14 For by one offering he has fulfilled in perpetuity the sanctifying.

15 And the Holy Spirit also bears us witness, for after what was said:

16 This is the covenant which I will establish towards them after those days, says the Lord: Giving my laws into their hearts, I will write them also in their thinking;

17 and their sins and their lawlessness I will not remember any more.

18 But where there is forgiveness of these, [there is] no longer a sacrifice for sin.

19 Having therefore, brethren, boldness for entering into the [holy of] holies by the blood of Jesus,

20 the new and living way which he has dedicated for us through the veil, that is, his flesh,

21 and [having] a great priest over the house of the God,

22 let us approach with a true heart, in full assurance of faith, sprinkled as to our hearts from a wicked conscience, and washed as to our body with pure water.

23 Let us hold fast the allegiance of the hope unwavering, for he is faithful who has promised;

24 and let us consider one another for provoking to love and good works;

25 not forsaking the assembling of ourselves together, as the custom is with some; but encouraging [one another] and by so much the more as you see the day drawing near.

26 For where we sin wilfully after receiving the knowledge of the truth, there no longer remains any sacrifice for sins,

27 but a certain fearful expectation of judgment, and heat of fire about to devour the adversaries.

28 Any one that has disregarded Moses' law dies without mercy on [the testimony of] two or three witnesses:

29 of how much worse punishment, think you, shall he be judged worthy who has trodden under foot the Son of the God, and esteemed the blood of the covenant whereby he has been sanctified, common, and has insulted the Spirit of grace?

30 For we know him that said, To me [belongs] vengeance; I will recompense, says the Lord: and again, The Lord shall judge his people.

31 [It is] a fearful thing falling into the hands of the living God.

32 But call to mind the earlier days in which, having been enlightened, you endured much conflict of sufferings;

33 on the one hand, when you were made a spectacle both in reproaches and afflictions; and on the other, when you became partakers with those who were passing through them.

34 For you both sympathized with prisoners and accepted with joy the plunder of your goods, knowing that you have for yourselves a better substance, and an abiding one.

35 Cast not away your confidence, which has great reward.

36 For you have need of endurance in order that, having done the will of the God, you may receive the promise.

37 For yet a very little while, he that comes will come, and will not delay.

38 But the just shall live by faith; and, if he draw back, my soul does not take pleasure in him.

39 But we are not drawers back to destruction, but of faith to saving the soul.

Heb 11:1 Now faith is the assurance of things hoped for, the proof of things not seen.

2 For in this the elders have obtained testimony.

3 By faith we understand that the aeons were framed by the word of God, so that what is seen, was not made out of what was visible.

4 By faith Abel offered to God a more excellent sacrifice than Cain, by which he obtained testimony of being righteous, God bearing testimony to his gifts, and by it, having died, he yet speaks.

5 By faith Enoch was translated that he should not see death; and was not found, because God had translated him; for before [his] translation he has the testimony that he had pleased God.

6 But without faith [it is] impossible to please him. For he that draws near to God must believe that he is, and that he is a rewarder of them who seek him out.

7 By faith, Noah, being warned concerning things not yet seen, moved with fear, prepared an ark for the saving of his house; by which he condemned the world, and became heir of the righteousness which is according to faith.

8 By faith Abraham, being called, obeyed to go out into the place which he was to receive for an inheritance, and went out, not knowing where he was going.

9 By faith he sojourned as a stranger in the land of promise as a foreign country, having dwelt in tents with Isaac and Jacob, the heirs with him of the same promise;

10 for he waited for the city which has foundations, of which God is the architect and builder.

11 By faith also Sarah herself received strength for the conception of seed, and that beyond the time [of having babies]; since she counted him faithful who promised.

12 Therefore, also there have been born of one (and him as good as dead), even as the stars of heaven in multitude, and as the countless sand which is by the sea shore.

13 All these died in faith, not having received the promises, but having seen them from afar off and embraced [them] and acknowledged that they were strangers and sojourners on the earth.

14 For they who say such things show clearly that they seek [their] country.

15 And if they had called to mind that from where they went out from, they had opportunity to have returned;

16 but now they seek a better, that is, a heavenly; therefore God is not ashamed of them, to be called their God; for he has prepared for them a city.

17 By faith Abraham, [when] tried, offered up Isaac, and he who had received to himself the promises offered up his one-of-a-kind[1] [son].

18 as to whom it had been said, In Isaac shall your seed be called:

19 counting that God [was] able to raise him even from among the dead, from which he also received him as a type.

20 By faith Isaac blessed Jacob and Esau concerning things to come.

21 By faith Jacob [when] dying blessed each of the sons of Joseph, and worshiped [while leaning] on the top of his staff.

22 By faith Joseph [when] dying called to mind the going forth of the sons of Israel, and gave commandment concerning his bones.

23 By faith Moses, being born, was hid three months by his parents, because they saw the child beautiful; and they did not fear the injunction of the king.

24 By faith Moses, when he had become great, refused to be called son of Pharaoh's daughter;

25 choosing rather to suffer affliction along with the people of the God than to have the temporary pleasure of sin;

26 esteeming the reproach of the Christ greater riches than the treasures of Egypt, for he was fixed on the reward.

27 By faith he left Egypt, not fearing the wrath of the king; for he persevered, as seeing him who is invisible.

28 By faith he celebrated the Passover and the sprinkling of the blood, that the destroyer of the firstborn might not touch them.

29 By faith they passed through the Red sea as through dry land; the Egyptians tried but were swallowed up.

30 By faith the walls of Jericho fell, having been encircled for seven days.

31 By faith Rahab the harlot did not perish along with the unbelieving, having received the spies in peace.

32 And what more do I say? For the time would fail me telling of Gideon, and Barak, and Samson, and

---

[1] GK: *monogenes*

Jephthah, and David and Samuel, and of the prophets:

33 who by faith overcame kingdoms, worked righteousness, obtained promises, stopped lions' mouths,

34 quenched the power of fire, escaped the edge of the sword, became strong out of weakness, became mighty in war, made the armies of strangers run way.

35 Women received their dead again by resurrection; and others were tortured, not having accepted deliverance, that they might get a better resurrection;

36 and others underwent trial of mocking and scourging, yes, and of bonds and imprisonment.

37 They were stoned, were sawn asunder, were tempted, died by the death of the sword; they went about in sheepskins, in goatskins, destitute, afflicted, evil treated,

38 of whom the world was not worthy, wandering in deserts and mountains, and [in] dens and caverns of the earth.

39 And all of these, having obtained witness through faith, did not receive the promise,

40 God having foreseen some better thing for us, that they should not be made perfect without us.

Heb 12:1 Let us also therefore, having so great a cloud of witnesses surrounding us, laying aside every weight, and sin which so easily entangles us, run with endurance the race that lies before us,

2 looking fixed on Jesus the leader and finisher of faith: who, in view of the joy lying before him, endured the cross, having despised the shame, and is set down at the right hand of the throne of the God.

3 For consider well him who endured such hostility from sinners against himself, that you be not weary, fainting in your souls.

4 You have not yet resisted unto blood, wrestling against sin.

5 And have you forgotten the exhortation which speaks to you as to sons: My son, despise not the chastening of the Lord, nor faint [when] reproved by him;

6 for whom the Lord loves, he disciplines, and scourges every son whom he receives.

7 You endure for discipline, God conducts himself towards you as towards sons; for who is the son that the father disciplines not?

8 But if you are without disciplining, of which all have been made partakers, then are you bastards, and not sons.

9 Moreover we have had the fathers of our flesh for discipline, and we respected [them], shall we not much rather be in subjection to the Father of spirits, and live?

10 For they indeed disciplined for a few days, as seemed good to them; but he for profit, in order to share his holiness.

11 But no disciplining at the time seems to be [a matter] of joy, but of grief; but afterwards yields the peaceful fruit of righteousness to those exercised by it.

12 Therefore, lift up the hands that hang down, and the feeble knees;

13 and walk straight, for that which is lame be not turned aside; but that rather that it may be healed.

14 Pursue peace with all, and holiness, without which no one shall see the Lord:

15 watching lest [there be] any one who lacks the grace of the God; lest any root of bitterness springing up trouble [you] and many be defiled by it;

16 lest [there be] any fornicator, or profane person, as Esau, who for one meal sold his birthright;

17 for you know that also afterwards, desiring to inherit the blessing, he was rejected, for he found no place for repentance although he sought it earnestly with tears.

18 For you have not come to [the mount] that was touched and was on fire, and to obscurity, and darkness, and tempest,

19 and trumpet's sound, and voice of words; which they heard, begged that the word not be addressed to them any more:

20 for they were not able to bear what was commanded: And if a beast should touch the mountain, it shall be stoned;

21 and, so fearful was the sight, Moses said, I am exceedingly afraid and full of trembling;

22 but you have come to mount Zion; and to the city of the living God, heavenly Jerusalem; and to myriads of angels,

23 the universal gathering; and to the church of the firstborn [who are] registered in heaven; and to God, judge of all; and to the spirits of just [men] made perfect;

24 and to Jesus, mediator of a new covenant and to the blood of sprinkling, speaking better than Abel.

25 See that you refuse not him that speaks. For, if those did not escape who had refused him, who uttered the oracles on earth, much more we who turn away from him [who does so] from heaven:

26 whose voice then shook the earth; but now he has promised, saying, Yet once will I shake not only the earth, but also the heaven.

27 But this, Yet once, signifies the removing of what is shaken, as being made, that what is not shaken may remain.

28 Therefore, let us, receiving a kingdom not to be shaken, have grace, by which let us serve God acceptably with reverence and fear.

29 For also our God is a consuming fire.

Heb 13:1 Let brotherly love abide.

2 Be not forgetful of hospitality; for by it some have unawares entertained angels.

3 Remember prisoners, as bound with [them], those that are evil-treated, as being yourselves also in the body.

4 [Let] marriage [be held] every way in honor, and the bed [be] undefiled; for fornicators and adulterers will God judge.

5 [Let your] behavior [be] without love of money, satisfied with [your] present circumstances;

for he has said, I will not leave you, neither will I forsake you.

6 So that, taking courage, we may say, The Lord is my helper, and I will not be afraid: what will man do unto me?

7 Remember your leaders who have spoken to you the word of the God; and considering the result of their conduct, imitate their faith.

8 Jesus Christ is the very[1] yesterday, and today, and into the aeons.

9 Be not carried away with various and strange doctrines; for [it is] good that the heart be confirmed with grace, not meats; those who have walked in [other things besides grace] were not benefitted by [them].

10 We have an altar of which they have no right to eat who serve the tabernacle;

11 for of their animals' blood is carried [as sacrifices for sin] into the [holy of] holies by the high priest, and the bodies are burned outside the camp.

12 Therefore, also Jesus, that he might sanctify the people by his own blood, suffered outside the gate:

13 therefore let us go forth to him outside the camp, bearing his reproach:

14 for we have here no abiding city, but we seek the coming one.

15 By him therefore let us offer the sacrifice of praise continually to God, that is, the fruit of the lips acknowledging his name.

16 But of doing good and sharing [of your substance] be not forgetful, for with such sacrifices God is well pleased.

17 Obey your leaders and submit to them, for they keep watch over your souls as those who will give an account. Let them do this with joy and not with grief, for this would be unprofitable for you.

18 Pray for us: for we persuade ourselves that we have a good conscience, in all things desirous to walk rightly.

19 But I much more beseech [you] to do this, that I may quickly be restored to you.

20 But God of peace, who brought again from among the dead our Lord Jesus, the great shepherd of the sheep, in blood of the aeonian covenant,

21 perfect you in every good work to the doing of his will, doing in you what is pleasing before him through Jesus Christ; to whom [be] glory into the aeons of aeons. Amen.

22 But I beseech you, brethren, bear the word of exhortation, for it is but in few words that I have written to you.

23 Know that our brother Timothy is set at liberty; with whom, if he should come soon, I will see you.

24 Salute all your leaders, and all the saints. They from Italy salute you.

25 Grace [be] with you all. Amen.

---

[1] An intensive pronoun to emphasize identity

James

James 1:1 James, servant of God and of the Lord Jesus Christ, to the twelve tribes which are in the dispersion, greeting.

2 Count it all joy, my brethren, when you fall into various trials,

3 knowing that the proving of your faith works patience.

4 But let endurance have [its] perfect work, that you may be perfect and complete, lacking nothing.

5 But if any one of you lack wisdom, let him ask God, who gives to all freely and reproaches not, and it shall be given to him:

6 but let him ask in faith, nothing doubting. For he that doubts is like a wave of the sea driven by the wind and tossed about;

7 for let not that man think that he shall receive anything from the Lord;

8 [he is] a double-minded man, unstable in all his ways.

9 But let the brother of low degree glory in his elevation,

10 and the rich in his humiliation, because as the grass's flower he will pass away.

11 For the sun has risen with its burning heat, and has withered the grass, and its flower has fallen, and the comeliness of its look has perished: thus the rich also shall wither in his goings.

12 Blessed [is the] man who endures trial; for, having been proved, he shall receive the crown of life, which He has promised to them that love him.

13 Let no man, being tempted, say, I am tempted from God. For God cannot be tempted by evil things, and himself tempts no one.

14 But every one is tempted, drawn away, and enticed by his own lust;

15 then lust, having conceived, gives birth to sin; but sin fully completed brings forth death.

16 Do not err, my beloved brethren.

17 Every good gift and every perfect gift comes down from above, from the Father of lights, with whom is no variation nor shadow of turning.

18 According to his own he will begat us by the word of truth, that we should be a certain first-fruits of his creatures.

19 So that, my beloved brethren, let every man be swift to hear, slow to speak, slow to wrath;

20 for man's wrath does not work God's righteousness.

21 Therefore, laying aside all filthiness and abounding of wickedness, accept with meekness the implanted word, which is able to save your souls.

22 But be you doers of the word and not hearers only, fooling yourselves.

23 For if any man be a hearer of the word and not a doer, he is like to a man considering his natural face in a mirror:

24 for he has considered himself and is gone away, and straightway he has forgotten what he was like.

25 But he that fixes his view on the perfect law, that of liberty, and abides in it being not a forgetful hearer but a doer of the work, he shall be blessed in his doing.

26 If any one think himself to be religious, not bridling his tongue, but deceiving his heart, this man's religion is vain.

27 Pure and undefiled religion before God and the Father is this: to visit orphans and widows in their affliction, to keep oneself unspotted from the world.

James 2:1 My brethren, do not have the faith of our Lord Jesus Christ, [lord] of glory, with partiality.

2 for if there come unto your synagogue a man with a gold ring in fine clothing and a poor man also come in with poor clothing,

3 and you look upon him who wears the splendid apparel, and say, Sit here in a good place, and say to the poor, Stand there, or sit here under my footstool:

4 have you not made a difference among yourselves, and become judges having evil thoughts?

5 Hear, my beloved brethren: Has not God chosen the poor as to the world, rich in faith, and heirs of the kingdom, which he has promised to them that love him?

6 But you have despised the poor [man]. Do not the rich oppress you, and [do not] they drag you before the tribunals?

7 And [do not] they blaspheme the excellent name which has been called upon you?

8 If indeed you keep the royal law according to the scripture, You shall love your neighbor as yourself, you do well.

9 But if you are partial, you commit sin, being convicted by the law as transgressors.

10 For whoever shall keep the whole law and shall offend in one [point] he has come under the guilt of [breaking] all.

11 For he who said, You shall not commit adultery, said also, You shall not kill. Now if you do not commit adultery, but kill, you have become a transgressor of the law.

12 So speak, and so act, as those that are to be judged by the law of liberty;

13 for judgment [will be] without mercy to him that has shown no mercy. Mercy glories over judgment.

14 What is the profit, my brethren, if any one say he have faith, but have not works? can faith save him?

15 Now if a brother or a sister is naked and destitute of daily food,

16 and one from among you say to them, Go in peace, be warmed and filled; but give not to them the needful things for the body, what is the profit?

17 So also faith, if it have not works, is dead by itself.

18 But some will say, You have faith and I have works. Show me your faith without works, and I from my works will show you my faith.

19 You believe that God is one. You do well. The daemons even believe, and tremble.

20 But know this, O vain man, that faith without works is dead?

21 Was not Abraham our father justified by works when he had offered Isaac his son upon the altar?

22 You see that faith worked with his works, and that by works faith was perfected.

23 And the scripture was fulfilled which says, Abraham believed God, and it was reckoned to him as righteousness, and he was called Friend of God.

24 You see that a man is justified on the principle of works, and not on the principle of faith only.

25 But was not in like manner also Rahab the harlot justified on the principle of works, when she had received the messengers and put [them] forth by another way?

26 For as the body without a spirit is dead, so also faith without works is dead.

James 3:1 Let there be not too many teachers, my brethren, knowing that we shall receive greater judgment.

2 For we all often offend. If any one offend not in word, he is a perfect man, able to bridle the whole body too.

3 Behold, we put the bits in the mouths of the horses, that they may obey us, and we turn round their whole bodies.

4 Behold also the ships, which are so great, and driven by violent winds, are turned about by a very small rudder, where the desire of the helmsman wishes.

5 Thus also the tongue is a little member, and boasts great things. See how little a fire, how large a wood it kindles!

6 and the tongue is fire, the world of unrighteousness; the tongue is set in our members, the defiler of the whole body, and which sets fire to the course of nature, and is set on fire by Gehenna.

7 For every species both of beasts and of birds, both of creeping things and of sea animals, is tamed and has been tamed by the human species;

8 but the tongue can no one among men tame; [it is] an unsettled evil, full of death-bringing poison.

9 With it we bless the Lord and Father, and with it we curse men made after the likeness of God.

10 Out of the same mouth goes forth blessing and cursing. It is not right, my brethren, that these things should be thus.

11 Does the fountain, out of the same opening, pour forth sweet and bitter?

12 Can, my brethren, a fig produce olives, or a vine figs? Neither [can] salt [water] make sweet water.

13 Who is wise and understanding among you; let him show out of good behavior his works in meekness of wisdom;

14 but if you have bitter emulation and strife in your hearts, do not boast and lie against the truth.

15 This is not the wisdom which comes down from above, but earthly, natural, daemonish.

16 For where emulation and strife [are] there is disorder and every evil thing.

17 But the wisdom from above first is pure, then peaceful, gentle, yielding, full of mercy and good fruits, unquestioning, without hypocrisy.

18 But the fruit of righteousness in peace is sown for them that make peace.

James 4:1 From where [come] wars and from where fighting among you? [is it] not from your lusts, which war in your members?

2 You lust and have not: you kill and are full of envy, and cannot obtain; you fight and war; you do not have because you ask not.

3 You ask and receive not, because you ask evilly, that you may consume it in your lusts.

4 Adulteresses, don't you know that friendship with the world is enmity with God? Whoever therefore is minded to be the friend of the world is constituted enemy of the God.

5 Think you that the scripture speaks in vain? Does the Spirit which lives in us deeply envy?

6 But he gives more grace. Therefore he says, God sets himself against the proud, but gives grace to the lowly.

7 Subject yourselves therefore to God. Resist the devil and he will flee from you.

8 Draw near to God, and he will draw near to you. Cleanse [your] hands, sinners, and purify [your] hearts, you double-minded.

9 Be wretched, and mourn, and weep: let your laughter be turned to mourning, and [your] joy to heaviness.

10 Humble yourselves before the Lord, and he shall exalt you.

11 Speak not against one another, brethren. He that speaks against [his] brother, or judges his brother, speaks against the law and judges the law. But if you judge the law, you are not a doer of the law, but judge.

12 One is the lawgiver and judge, who is able to save and to destroy: but who are you who judges your neighbor?

13 Come now, you who say, Today or tomorrow will we go into such a city and spend a year there, and traffic and make gain,

14 you who do not know what will be on the next day, [for] what is your life? It is even a vapor, appearing for a little while, and then disappearing,

15 instead of your saying, If the Lord should [so] will and we should live, we will also do this or that.

16 But now you glory in your vaulting: all such glorying is evil.

17 To him therefore who knows how to do good, and does it not, to him it is sin.

James 5:1 Come now, you rich, weep, howling over your miseries that [are] coming upon [you]

2 Your wealth is become rotten, and your garments moth-eaten.

3 Your gold and silver is eaten away, and their rust shall be for a witness against you, and shall eat

your flesh as fire. You have heaped up treasure in the last days.

4 Behold, the wages of your laborers, who have harvested your fields, wrongfully kept back by you, cry, and the cries of those that have reaped are entered into the ears of the Lord of Sabbath.

5 You have lived luxuriously on the earth and indulged yourselves; you have nourished your hearts [as] in a day of slaughter;

6 you have condemned, you have killed the just; he does not resist you.

7 Have patience, therefore, brethren, till the coming of the Lord. Behold, the laborer awaits the precious fruit of the earth, having patience for it until it receive the early and the latter rain.

8 You also have patience: establish your hearts, for the coming of the Lord is drawn near.

9 Complain not one against another, brethren, that you be not judged. Behold, the judge stands before the door.

10 Take [as] an example, brethren, of suffering and having patience, the prophets, who have spoken in the name of the Lord.

11 Behold, we call them blessed who have endured. You have heard of the endurance of Job, and seen the outcome of the Lord; that the Lord is full of tender compassion and pitiful.

12 But before all things, my brethren, swear not, neither by heaven, nor by the earth, nor by any other oath; but let your yes be yes, and your no, no, that you do not fall under judgment.

13 Does any one among you suffer evil? let him pray. Is any happy? let him sing psalms.

14 Is any sick among you? let him call to him the elders of the church, and let them pray over him, anointing him with oil in the name of the Lord;

15 and the prayer of faith shall heal the sick, and the Lord shall raise him up; and if he be one who has committed sins, it shall be forgiven him.

16 Acknowledge therefore your offences to one another, and pray for one another, that you may be healed. the fervent prayer of the righteous [man] has much power.

17 Elijah was a man of like passions to us, and he prayed with prayer that it should not rain; and it did not rain upon the earth three years and six months;

18 and again he prayed, and the heaven gave rain, and the earth caused its fruit to spring forth.

19 My brethren, if any one among you error from the truth, and one bring him back,

20 let him know that he that brings back a sinner from the error of his way shall save a soul from death and shall cover a multitude of sins.

1 Peter

1 Pet 1:1 Peter, apostle of Jesus Christ, to the sojourners of the dispersion of Pontus, Galatia, Cappadocia, Asia, and Biyournia,

2 elect according to the foreknowledge of God the Father, by sanctification of the Spirit, unto the obedience and sprinkling of the blood of Jesus Christ: Grace to you and peace be multiplied.

3 Blessed [be] God and Father of our Lord Jesus Christ, who, according to his great mercy, has begotten us again to a living hope through the resurrection of Jesus Christ from among the dead,

4 to an incorruptible and undefiled and unfading inheritance, reserved in the heavens for you,

5 who are kept guarded by the power of God through faith for salvation ready to be revealed in the last time.

6 Wherein you exult, for a little while at present, if needed, put to grief by various trials,

7 that the proving of your faith, much more precious than of gold which perishes, though it be proved by fire, be found to praise and glory and honor in the revelation of Jesus Christ:

8 whom, having not seen, you love; on whom [though] not now looking, but believing, you exult with joy unspeakable and filled with the glory,

9 receiving the end of your faith, the salvation of [your] souls.

10 Concerning which salvation prophets, who have prophesied of the grace towards you, sought out and searched out;

11 searching what, or what manner of time, the Spirit of Christ which [was] in them pointed out, testifying before of the sufferings which [belonged] to Christ, and the glories after these.

12 To whom it was revealed, that not to themselves but to you they ministered those things, which have now been announced to you by those who have declared to you the good news by the Holy Spirit, sent from heaven, which angels desire to look into.

13 Therefore, having girded up the loins of your mind, [be] sober [and] hope with perfect steadfastness in the grace brought to you at the revelation of Jesus Christ;

14 as children of obedience, not conformed to [your] former lusts in your ignorance;

15 but as he who has called you is holy, be you also holy in all [your] behavior;

16 because it is written, Be you holy, for I am holy.

17 And if you address as Father him who, without regard of persons, judges according to the work of each, pass your time of sojourn in fear,

18 knowing that you were not redeemed with perishable things like silver or gold from your futile way of life inherited from your forefathers,

19 but by precious blood, as of a lamb without blemish and without spot, [the blood] of Christ,

20 foreknown indeed before the foundation of the cosmos, but who has been manifested at the end of times for your sakes,

21 who by him do believe on God, who has raised him from among the dead and given him glory, that your faith and hope should be in God.

22 Having purified your souls by obedience to the truth to sincere brotherly love, love one another out of a pure heart fervently;

23 being born again, not of corruptible seed, but of incorruptible, by the living and abiding word of God.

24 Because all flesh is as grass, and all its glory as the flower of grass. The grass has withered and [its] flower has fallen;

25 but the word of the Lord abides into the aeon. And this is the word which in the good news is preached to you.

1 Pet 2:1 Laying aside therefore all malice and all deceit and hypocrisies and envy and all slander,

2 as newborn babes desire earnestly the pure mental milk of the word, that by it you may grow up to salvation,

3 if indeed you have tasted that the Lord is good.

4 To whom coming, a living stone, cast away indeed as worthless by men, but with God chosen, precious,

5 yourselves also, as living stones, are being built up a spiritual house, a holy priesthood, to offer spiritual sacrifices acceptable to God by Jesus Christ.

6 Because it is contained in the scripture: Behold, I lay in Zion a corner stone, elect, precious: and he that believes on him shall not be put to shame.

7 To you therefore who believe is the preciousness; but to the disobedient, the stone which the builders cast away as worthless, this is become head of the corner,

8 and a stone of stumbling and rock of offence; [who] stumble at the word, being disobedient to which also they have been appointed.

9 But you [are] a chosen family [race], a kingly priesthood, a holy nation, a people for a possession, that you might set forth the excellencies of him who has called you out of darkness to his wonderful light;

10 who once [were] not a people, but now God's people; who were not enjoying mercy, but now have found mercy.

11 Beloved, I exhort [you] as strangers and sojourners, to abstain from fleshly lusts, which war against the soul;

12 having your behavior honest among the Gentiles, that [as to that] in which they speak against you as evildoers, they may through [your] good works, [themselves] witnessing [them] glorify God in the day of visitation.

13 Be in subjection [therefore] to every human institution for the Lord's sake; whether to the king as supreme,

14 or to rulers as sent by him, for vengeance on evildoers, and praise to them that do well.

15 Because so is the will of the God, that by well-doing you put to silence the ignorance of senseless men;

16 as free, and not as having liberty as a cloak of malice, but as God's servants.

17 Show honor to all, love the brotherhood, fear God, honor the king.

18 Servants, [be] subject with all fear to your masters, not only to the good and gentle, but also to the ill-tempered.

19 For this is acceptable, if one, for conscience sake towards God, endure griefs, suffering unjustly.

20 For what glory [is it] if sinning and being maltreated you shall bear it, but if, doing good and suffering, you shall bear it this is acceptable with God.

21 For to this have you been called; for Christ also has suffered for you, leaving you a model that you should follow in his steps:

22 who did no sin, neither was guile found in his mouth;

23 who, [when] reviled, reviled not again; [when] suffering, threatened not; but gave [himself] over into the hands of him who judges righteously;

24 who himself bore our sins in his body on the wood [cross], in order that, being dead to sins, we may live to righteousness: by whose stripes you have been healed.

25 For you were going astray as sheep, but have now returned to the shepherd and overseer of your souls.

1 Pet 3:1 Likewise, wives, [be] subject to your own husbands, that, even if any are disobedient to the word, they may be gained without the word by the behavior of the wives,

2 having witnessed your pure behavior [carried out] in fear;

3 whose adorning let it not be that outward one of tressing of hair, and wearing gold, or putting on apparel;

4 but the hidden man of the heart, in the incorruptible [ornament] of a meek and quiet spirit, which in the sight of the God is of great price.

5 For thus also the holy women who have hoped in God heretofore adorned themselves, being subject to their own husbands;

6 as Sarah obeyed Abraham, calling him lord; whose children you have become, doing good, and not fearing with any kind of terror.

7 [You] husbands likewise, dwell with [them] according to knowledge, as with a weaker, [even] the female, vessel, giving [them] honor, as also fellow-heirs of the grace of life, that your prayers be not hindered.

8 Finally, [be] all of one mind, sympathizing, full of brotherly love, tender hearted, humble minded;

9 not rendering evil for evil, or railing for railing; but on the contrary, blessing [others] because you have been called to this, that you should inherit blessing.

10 For he that wishes live and to see good days, let him cause his tongue to cease from evil and his lips that they speak no guile.

11 And let him avoid evil, and do good; let him seek peace and pursue it;

12 because the eyes of the Lord [are] on the righteous, and his ears towards their prayers; but the face of the Lord is against them that do evil.

13 And who shall injure you if you have become imitators of that which is good?

14 But if also you should suffer for righteousness' sake, blessed [are ye] but be not afraid of their fear, neither be troubled;

15 but sanctify the Lord the Christ in your hearts, and [be] always prepared to [give] an answer [to] every one that asks you to give an account of the hope that is in you, but with meekness and fear;

16 having a good conscience, that [as to that] in which they speak against you as evildoers, they may be ashamed who revile your good behavior in Christ.

17 For [it is] better, if the will of the God should will it, to suffer [as] well-doers than [as] evildoers;

18 for Christ indeed has once suffered for sins, the just for the unjust, that he might bring us to God; being put to death in flesh, but made alive in the Spirit,

19 in which also going he preached to the spirits in prison,

20 who before were disobedient, when the patience of the God waited in the days of Noah while the ark was preparing, into which few, that is, eight souls, were saved through water:

21 Corresponding [type] to that, baptism now saves you -- not the removal of dirt from the flesh, but an appeal to God for a good conscience – through the resurrection of Jesus Christ,

22 who is at the right hand of God, gone into heaven, angels and authorities and powers being subjected to him.

1 Pet 4:1 Christ, then, having suffered for us in the flesh, do you also arm yourselves with the same mind; for he that has suffered in the flesh has ceased with sin,

2 no longer to live the rest of [his] time in the flesh to men's lusts, but to God's will.

3 For the time past is sufficient [for us] to have worked the will of the Nations, walking in lasciviousness, lusts, wine-drinking, revels, drinking, and unholy idolatries.

4 Wherein they think it strange that you run not with [them] to the same sink of corruption, speaking injuriously [of you]

5 who shall render account to him who is ready to judge the living and the dead.

6 For to this [end] were the good news preached to the dead also, that they might be judged, as regards men, after the flesh, but live, as regards God, after the Spirit.

7 But the end of all things is drawn near: be sober therefore, and be watchful unto prayers;

8 but before all things having fervent love among yourselves, because love covers a multitude of sins;

9 hospitable one to another, without murmuring;

10 each according as he has received a gift, ministering it to one another, as good stewards of the various grace of God.

11 If any one speak – as oracles of God; if any one minister – as of strength which the God supplies; that the God in all things may be glorified through Jesus Christ, to whom is the glory and the might into the aeons of aeons. Amen.

12 Beloved, take not [as] strange the fire [of persecution] which has taken place among you for [your] trial, as if a strange thing was happening to you;

13 but as you have share in the sufferings of Christ, rejoice, that in the revelation of his glory also you may rejoice with exultation.

14 If you are reproached in the name of Christ, blessed [are ye] for the [spirit] of glory and the Spirit of the God rests upon you: [on their part he is blasphemed, but on your part he is glorified]

15 Let none of you suffer indeed as murderer, or thief, or evildoer, or as overseer of other people's matters;

16 but if as a Christian, let him not be ashamed, but glorify God in this name.

17 For the time for the judgment begins from the house of the God, but if first from us, what [shall be] the end of those who obey not the good news of the God?

18 And if the righteous is saved with difficulty, where shall the impious and the sinner appear?

19 Therefore, also let them who suffer according to the will of the God commit their souls in well-doing to a faithful Creator.

1 Pet 5:1 The elders which [are] among you I exhort, who [I am their] fellow-elder and witness of the sufferings of the Christ, who also [I am] partaker of the glory about to be revealed:

2 shepherd the flock of the God which is among you, exercising oversight, not by necessity, but willingly; not for base gain, but readily;

3 not as if being lord of your possessions, but being examples for the flock.

4 And when the chief shepherd is manifested you shall receive the unfading crown of glory.

5 Likewise [you] younger, be subject to the elder, and all of you bind on humility towards one another; for God sets himself against the proud, but to the humble gives grace.

6 Humble yourselves therefore under the mighty hand of the God, that he may exalt you in [the due] time;

7 having cast all your care upon him, for he cares about you.

8 Be vigilant, watch. Your adversary the devil as a roaring lion walks about seeking whom he may devour.

9 Whom resist, steadfast in faith, knowing that the selfsame sufferings are accomplished in your brotherhood which is in the world.

10 But God of all grace who has called you to his aeonian glory in Christ Jesus, when you have suffered for a little while, himself shall make perfect, establish, strengthen, stabilize:

11 to him [be] the glory and the might into the aeons of the aeons. Amen.

12 By Silvanus, the faithful brother, as I suppose, I have written to you briefly; urging and testifying that this is the true grace of the God in which you stand.

13 She that is elected with [you] in Babylon salutes you, and Marcus my son.

14 Salute one another with a kiss of love. Peace be with you all who [are] in Christ.

2 Peter

2 Pet 1:1 Simon Peter, servant and apostle of Jesus Christ, to them that have received the same precious faith with us through the righteousness of our God and Savior Jesus Christ:

2 Grace and peace be multiplied to you in the knowledge of the God and of Jesus our Lord.

3 As his divine power has given to us all things which relate to life and godliness, through the knowledge of him that has called us by glory and virtue,

4 through which he has given to us the greatest and precious promises, that through these you may become partakers of the divine nature, having escaped the corruption that is in the world through lust.

5 But for this very reason also, using all diligence, in your faith have virtue, in virtue knowledge,

6 in knowledge temperance, in temperance endurance, in endurance godliness,

7 in godliness brotherly love, in brotherly love love:

8 for these things existing and abounding in you make [you] to be neither idle nor unfruitful as regards the knowledge of our Lord Jesus Christ;

9 for he with whom these things are not present is blind, short-sighted, and has forgotten the purging of his former sins.

10 Therefore, rather, brethren, use diligence to make your calling and election sure, for doing these things you will never fall;

11 for thus shall the entrance into the aeonian kingdom of our Lord and Savior Jesus Christ be richly furnished unto you.

12 Therefore, I will be careful to put you always in mind of these things, although knowing [them] and established in the present truth.

13 But I account it right, as long as I am in this tabernacle, to stir you up by putting [you] in remembrance,

14 knowing that the putting off of my tabernacle is soon [to take place] as also our Lord Jesus Christ has manifested to me;

15 but I will use diligence, that after my departure you should have also, at any time, [in your power] to call to mind these things.

16 For we have not made known to you the power and coming of our Lord Jesus Christ, following cleverly imagined fables, but having been eyewitnesses of his majesty.

17 For he received from God the Father honor and glory, such a voice being uttered to him by the excellent glory: This is my beloved Son, in whom I have found my delight;

18 and this voice we heard uttered from heaven, being with him on the holy mountain.

19 And we have the prophetic word [made] surer, to which you do well taking heed as to a lamp shining in an obscure place until the day dawn and the morning star arise in your hearts;

20 knowing this first, that no prophecy of scripture is ascertained from its own private interpretation,

21 for prophecy was not uttered by the will of man, but holy men from God spoke under the power of the Holy Spirit.

2 Pet 2:1 But there were false prophets also among the people, as there shall be also among you false teachers, who shall bring in by the way destructive heresies, and deny the master that bought them, bringing upon themselves swift destruction;

2 and many shall follow their dissolute ways, through whom the way of the truth shall be blasphemed.

3 And through covetousness, with well-turned words, will they make merchandise of you: for whom judgment of old is not idle, and their destruction slumbers not.

4 For if God spares* not the angels who sin* but casts* them chained into the hell [Tartarus] of darkness; to be kept* for judgment;

5 and spared not the old world, but preserved Noah, the eighth, a preacher of righteousness, having brought in the flood upon the world of the ungodly;

6 and having reduced the cities of Sodom and Gomorrha to ashes, condemned [them] with an overthrow, setting [them as] an example to those that should [afterwards] live an ungodly life;

7 and saved righteous Lot, distressed with the abandoned behavior of the godless,

8 for the righteous man through seeing and hearing, dwelling among them, tormented [his] righteous soul day after day because of [their] lawless works,

9 the Lord knows [how] to deliver the godly out of trial, and to keep the unjust to the day of judgment [to be] punished;

10 and specially those who walk after the flesh in the lust of uncleanness, and despise lordship. Bold [are they] self-willed; they do n ot fear speaking wrongly of dignities:

11 when angels, who are greater in might and power, do not bring against them, before the Lord, an blasphemous charge.

12 But these, as natural animals without reason, made to be caught and destroyed, speaking blasphemy in things they are ignorant of, shall also perish in their own corruption,

13 receiving the reward of unrighteousness; accounting daily indulgence pleasure; spots and blemishes, rioting in their own deceits, feasting with you;

14 having eyes full of adultery, and that cease not from sin, alluring unestablished souls; having a heart practiced in covetousness, children of curse;

15 having left the straight way they have gone astray, having followed in the path of Balaam [the son] of Beor, who loved the reward of unrighteousness;

16 but had reproof of his own wickedness the mute donkey speaking with man's voice forbade the folly of the prophet.

17 These are springs without water, and mists driven by storm, to whom the gloom of darkness is reserved [into the aeonian].

18 For speaking out arrogant words of vanity they entice by fleshly desires, by sensuality, those who barely escape from the ones who live in error,

19 promising them liberty, while they themselves are slaves of corruption; for by whom a man is subdued, by him is he also brought into slavery.

20 For if after having escaped the pollution of the world through the knowledge of the Lord and Savior Jesus Christ, again entangled, they are subdued by these, their last state is worse than the first.

21 For it were better for them not to have known the way of righteousness, than having known it to turn back from the holy commandment delivered to them.

22 But that [word] of the true proverb has happened to them: the dog [has] turned back to his own vomit; and, the washed sow to [her] rolling in mud.

2 Pet 3:1 This, a second letter, beloved, I have written to you, in [both] which I stir up, in the way of putting you in remembrance, your pure mind,

2 to be mindful of the words spoken before by the holy prophets, and of the commandment of the Lord and Savior by your apostles;

3 knowing this first, that there shall come at the close of the days mockers with mocking, walking according to their own lusts,

4 and saying, Where is the promise of his coming? for from the time the fathers fell asleep all things remain thus from the beginning of the creation.

5 For this is hidden from them through their own wilfullness, that heavens were of old, and an earth, having its subsistence out of water and in water, by the word of the God,

6 through which the world, was deluged with water, perished.

7 But the present heavens and the earth by his word are laid up in store, kept for fire unto a day of judgment and destruction of ungodly men.

8 But let not this one thing be hidden from you, beloved, that **one day with the Lord is as a thousand years, and a thousand years as one day**.

9 The Lord does not delay his promise, as some account of delay, but is patient towards you, not willing that any should perish, but that all should come to repentance.

10 But the day of the Lord will come as a thief, in which the heavens will pass away with a rushing noise, and the elements, burning with heat, shall be dissolved, and the earth and the works in it shall be burnt up.

11 Since in this way all things are dissolving, what sort of people ought you to be in holy conduct and godliness,

12 waiting for and hastening the coming of the day of the God, by reason of which the heavens, being on fire, shall be dissolved, and the elements, burning with heat, shall melt?

13 But, according to his promise, we wait for new heavens and a new earth, wherein dwells righteousness.

14 Therefore, beloved, as you wait for these things, be diligent to be found of him in peace, without spot and blameless;

15 and account the endurance of our Lord [to be] salvation; according as our beloved brother Paul also has written to you according to the wisdom given to him,

16 as also in all [his] epistles, speaking in them of these things; among which some things are hard to be understood, which the untaught and ill-established distort, as also the other scriptures, to their own destruction.

17 You therefore, beloved, knowing [these] things before, take care lest, being led away along with the error of the wicked, you should fall from your own steadfastness:

18 but grow in grace, and in the knowledge of our Lord and Savior Jesus Christ. To him [be] glory both now and to the day of the aeon. Amen.

1 John

1 John 1:1 That which was from the beginning, that which we have heard, which we have seen with our eyes; that which we looked upon, and our hands handled, concerning the word of life;

2 and the life has been manifested, and we have seen, and bear witness, and report to you the aeonian life, which was toward the Father, and has been manifested to us:

3 that which we have seen and heard we report to you, that you also may have fellowship with us; and our fellowship is indeed with the Father, and with his Son Jesus Christ.

4 And these things write we to you that your joy may be full.

5 And this is the message which we have heard from him, and declare to you, that God is light, and in him is no darkness at all.

6 If we say that we have fellowship with him, and walk in darkness, we lie, and do not practice the truth.

7 But if we walk in the light as he is in the light, we have fellowship with one another, and the blood of Jesus Christ his Son cleanses us from all sin.

8 If we say that we have no sin, we deceive ourselves, and the truth is not in us.

9 If we acknowledge our sins, he is faithful and righteous to forgive us [our] sins, and cleanse us from all unrighteousness.

10 If we say that we have not sinned, we make him a liar, and his word is not in us.

1 John 2:1 My children, these things I write to you in order that you may not sin; and if any one sin, we have a patron toward the Father, Jesus Christ the righteous;

2 and he is the reconciliation for our sins; but not for ours alone, but also for the whole world.

3 And hereby we know that we know him, if we keep his commandments.

4 He that says, I know him, and does not keep his commandments, is a liar, and the truth is not in him;

5 but whoever keeps his word, in him truly the love of the God is perfected. Hereby we know that we are in him.

6 He that says he abides in him ought, even as he walked, himself also [so] to walk.

7 Beloved, I write no new commandment to you, but an old commandment, which you have had from the beginning. The old commandment is the word which you heard.

8 Again, I write a new commandment to you, which thing is true in him and in you, because the darkness is passing and the true light already shines.

9 He who says he is in the light, and hates his brother, is in the darkness until now.

10 He that loves his brother abides in light, and there is no occasion of stumbling in him.

11 But he that hates his brother is in the darkness, and walks in the darkness, and knows not where he goes, because the darkness has blinded his eyes.

12 I write to you, children, because [your] sins are forgiven you for his name's sake.

13 I write to you, fathers, because you have known him [that is] from the beginning. I write to you, young men, because you have overcome the wicked [one] I write to you, little children, because you have known the Father.

14 I have written to you, fathers, because you have known him [that is] from the beginning. I have written to you, young men, because you are strong, and the word of the God abides in you, and you have overcome the wicked [one]

15 Love not the world, nor the things in the world. If any one love the world, the love of the Father is not in him;

16 because all that is in the world, the lust of the flesh, and the lust of the eyes, and the pride of life, is not of the Father, but is of the world.

17 And the world is passing, and its lust, but he that does the will of the God abides into the aeon.

18 Little children, it is the last hour, and, according as you have heard that antichrist comes, even now there have come many antichrists, therefore we know that it is the last hour.

19 They went out from among us, but they were not of us; for if they had been of us, they would have surely remained with us, but that they might be made manifest that none are of us.

20 And you have the oil from the holy [one] and you know all things.

21 I have not written to you because you do not know the truth, but because you know it, and that no lie is of the truth.

22 Who is the liar but he who denies that Jesus is the Christ? He is the antichrist who denies the Father and the Son.

23 Whoever denies the Son has not the Father either; he who acknowledges the Son has the Father also.

24 As for you let that which you have heard from the beginning abide in you: if what you have heard from the beginning abides in you, you also shall abide in the Son and in the Father.

25 And this is the promise which he has promised us, aeonian life.

26 These things have I written to you concerning those who lead you astray:

27 and yourselves, the oil which you have received from him abides in you, and you have not need that any one should teach you; but as the same oil teaches you all things, and is true and is not a lie, and even as it has taught you, you shall abide in him.

28 Now, little children, abide in Him, so that when He appears, we may have confidence and not shrink away from Him in shame at His coming.

29 If you know that he is righteous, know that every one who practice righteousness is begotten of him.

1 John 3:1 See what love the Father has given to us, that we should be called the children of God. For this reason the world knows us not, because it knew him not.

2 Beloved, now are we children of God, and what we shall be has not yet been manifested; we know that if it is manifested we shall be like him, for we shall see him as he is.

3 And every one that has this hope in him purifies himself, even as he is pure.

4 Every one that practice sin practice also lawlessness; and sin is lawlessness.

5 And you know that he has been manifested that he might take away our sins; and in him sin is not.

6 Whoever abides in him, does not sin: whoever sins, has not seen him or known him.

7 Children, let no man lead you astray; he that practice righteousness is righteous, even as he is righteous.

8 He that practice sin is of the devil, for from the beginning the devil sins. To this end the Son of the God has been manifested, that he might undo the works of the devil.

9 Whoever has been begotten of the God does not practice sin, because his seed abides in him, and he cannot sin, because he has been begotten of the God.

10 By this the children of God and the children of the devil are obvious: anyone who does not practice righteousness is not of God, nor the one who does not love his brother.

11 For this is the message which you have heard from the beginning, that we should love one another:

12 not as Cain was of the wicked one, and killed his brother; and why did he kill him? because his works were wicked, and those of his brother righteous.

13 Do not wonder, brethren, if the world hate you.

14 We know that we have passed from death to life, because we love the brethren. He who does not love [his] brother abides in death.

15 Every one that hates his brother is a murderer, and you know that no murderer has aeonian life abiding in him.

16 Hereby we have known love, because he has laid down his soul for us; and we ought for the brethren to lay down [our] souls.

17 But whoever has the world's goods, and sees his brother in need and closes his heart against him, how does the love of God abide in him?

18 Children, let us not love with word, nor with tongue, but in deed and in truth.

19 We will know by this that we are of the truth, and will assure our heart before Him

20 – in whatever our heart condemns us; for God is greater than our heart and knows all things.

21 Beloved, if our heart does not condemn us, we have confidence before God;

22 and whatsoever we ask we receive from him, because we keep his commandments, and practice the things which are pleasing in his sight.

23 And this is his commandment, that we believe on the name of his Son Jesus Christ, and that we love one another, even as he has given us commandment.

24 And he that keeps his commandments abides in him, and he in him. And hereby we know that he abides in us, by the Spirit which he has given to us.

1 John 4:1 Beloved, believe not every spirit, but prove the spirits, if they are of the God; because many false prophets are gone out into the world.

2 Hereby you know the Spirit of the God: every spirit which acknowledges Jesus Christ has come in flesh is of the God;

3 and every spirit which does not acknowledge Jesus Christ has come in flesh is not of the God: and this is that [spirit] of the antichrist, of which you have heard that it comes, and now it is already in the world.

4 You are of the God, children, and have overcome them, because greater is he that is in you than he that is in the world.

5 They are of the world; for this reason they speak of the world, and the world hears them.

6 We are of the God; he that knows God hears us; he who is not of the God does not hear us. From this we know the spirit of truth and the spirit of error.

7 Beloved, let us love one another; because love is of the God, and every one that loves has been begotten of the God, and knows God.

8 He that loves not has not known God; for God is love.

9 Herein as to us has been manifested the love of the God, that God has sent his one-of-a-kind[1] Son into the world, that we might live through him.

10 Herein is love, not that we loved God, but that he loved us, and sent his Son a reconciliation for our sins.

11 Beloved, if God has so loved us, we also ought to love one another.

12 No one has seen God at any time: if we love one another, God abides in us, and his love is perfected in us.

13 Hereby we know that we abide in him and he in us, that he has given to us his Spirit.

14 And we have seen, and testify, that the Father has sent the Son [as] Savior of the world.

15 Whosoever shall acknowledge that Jesus is the Son of the God, God abides in him, and he in God.

16 And we have known and have believed the love which God has to us. God is love, and he that abides in love abides in God, and God in him.

17 Herein has love been perfected with us that we may have boldness in the day of judgment, that even as he is, we also are in this world.

18 There is no fear in love, but perfect love casts out fear; for fear has torment, and he that fears has not been made perfect in love.

19 We love because he has first loved us.

20 If any one say, I love God, and hate his brother, he is a liar: for he that loves not his brother

---

[1] GK: *monogenes*

whom he has seen, how can he love God whom he has not seen?

21 And this commandment have we from him, That he that loves God love also his brother.

1 John 5:1 Every one that believes that Jesus is the Christ is begotten of the God; and every one that loves him [Christ] that has begotten loves also him [brother] that is begotten of him.

2 Hereby we know that we love the children of the God, when we love God and keep his commandments.

3 For this is the love of the God, that we keep his commandments; and his commandments are not grievous.

4 For all that has been begotten of the God gets the victory over the world; and this is the victory which has gotten the victory over the world, our faith.

5 Who is he that gets the victory over the world, but he that believes that Jesus is the Son of the God?

6 This is he that came by water and blood, Jesus the Christ; not by water only, but by water and blood. And it is the Spirit that bears witness, for the Spirit is the truth.

7 For they that bear witness are three:

8 the Spirit, and the water, and the blood; and the three agree in one.

9 If we receive the witness of men, the witness of the God is greater. For this is the witness of the God [which] he has witnessed concerning his Son.

10 He that believes into the Son of the God has the witness in himself; he that does not believe God has made him a liar, because he has not believed in the witness which God has witnessed concerning his Son.

11 And this is the witness, that God has given to us aeonian life; and this life is in his Son.

12 He that has the Son has life: he that has not the Son of the God has not life.

13 These things have I written to you that you may know that you have aeonian life who believe on the name of the Son of the God.

14 And this is the boldness which we have towards him, that if we ask him anything according to his will he hears us.

15 And if we know that he hears us, whatsoever we ask, we know that we have the petitions which we have asked of him.

16 If any one see his brother sinning a sin not unto death, he shall ask, and he shall give him life, for those that do not sin unto death. There is a sin to death: I do not say of that that he should make a request.

17 Every unrighteousness is sin; and there is a sin not to death.

18 We know that every one begotten of the God does not sin [to death in the aeon], but he that has been begotten of the God keeps himself, and the wicked [one] does not touch him.

19 We know that we are of the God, and the whole world lies in the evil.

20 And we know that the Son of the God has come, and has given us an understanding that we should know him that is true; and we are in him that is true, in his Son Jesus Christ. He is the true God and aeonian life.

21 Children, keep yourselves from idols.

2 John

2 John 1:1 The elder to the elect lady and her children, whom I love in truth, and not I only but also all who have known the truth,

2 for the truth's sake which abides in us and shall be with us into the aeon.

3 Grace shall be with you, mercy, peace from God the Father, and from the Lord Jesus Christ, the Son of the Father, in truth and love.

4 I rejoiced greatly that I have found your children walking in truth, as we have received commandment from the Father.

5 And now I beseech you, lady, not as writing to you a new commandment, but that which we have had from the beginning, that we should love one another.

6 And this is love, that we should walk according to his commandments. This is the commandment, according as you have heard from the beginning, that you might walk in it.

7 For many deceivers have gone out into the world, they who do not acknowledge Jesus Christ coming in flesh – this is the deceiver and the antichrist.

8 See to yourselves, that we may not lose what we have worked, but may receive full wages.

9 Whosoever goes forward and abides not in the doctrine of the Christ has not God. He that abides in the doctrine, he has both the Father and the Son.

10 If any one come to you and bring not this doctrine, do not receive him into the house, and greet him not;

11 for he who greets him partakes in his wicked works.

12 Having many things to write to you, I would not with paper and ink; but hope to come to you, and to speak mouth to mouth, that our joy may be full.

13 The children of your elect sister greet you.

3 John

3 John 1:1 The elder to the beloved Gaius, whom I love in truth.

2 Beloved, I desire that in all things you should prosper and be in health, even as your soul prospers.

3 For I rejoiced exceedingly when the brethren came and bore testimony to your truth, even as you walk in truth.

4 I have no greater joy than these things that I hear of my children walking in the truth.

5 Beloved, you do faithfully [in] whatever you may have worked towards the brethren and that strangers,

6 and they have testified to your love before the church. You will do well to send them on their way in a manner worthy of God.

7 For they went out for the sake of the Name, accepting nothing from the pagans.

8 We therefore ought to receive such, that we may be fellow-workers with the truth.

9 I wrote something to the church; but Diotrephes, who loves to have the first place among them, receives us not.

10 For this reason, if I come, I will bring to remembrance his works which he does, babbling against us with wicked words; and not content with these, neither does he himself receive the brethren; and those who would he prevents, and casts [them] out of the church.

11 Beloved, do not imitate what is evil, but what is good. He that does good is of the God. He that does evil has not seen God.

12 Demetrius has witness borne to him by all, and by the truth itself; and we also bear witness, and you know that our witness is true.

13 I had many things to write to you, but I will not with ink and pen write to you;

14 but I hope soon to see you, and we will speak mouth to mouth. Peace [be] to you. The friends greet you. Greet the friends by name.

Jude

Jude 1:1 Jude, servant of Jesus Christ, and brother of James, to the called ones beloved in God the Father and preserved in Jesus Christ:

2 Mercy to you, and peace, and love be multiplied.

3 Beloved, using all diligence to write to you of our common salvation, I have been trying to write to you urging [you] to contend earnestly for the faith once delivered to the saints.

4 For certain men have got in unnoticed, they who of old were marked out beforehand to this sentence, ungodly [persons] turning the grace of our God into wantonness, and denying our only Master and Lord Jesus Christ.

5 But I would put you in remembrance, you who once knew all things, that the Lord, having saved a people out of the land of Egypt, in the second place destroyed those who had not believed.

6 And angels who had not kept their own original state, but had abandoned their beginning, for the judgment of the great day; chained perpetually[1] under gloomy darkness, he keeps [them].

7 as Sodom and Gomorrah, and the cities around them, committing greedily fornication, in like manner with them, and going after other flesh, lie there as an example, undergoing the judgment of aeonian fire.

8 Yet in like manner these dreamers also defile the flesh, and despise authority, and speak against dignities.

9 But Michael the archangel, when disputing with the devil he reasoned about the body of Moses, did not dare to bring a railing judgment against him [devil], but said, the Lord rebuke you.

10 But these, whatever things they know not, they speak against; but as the irrational animals, they understand by instinct, in these things they corrupt themselves.

11 Woe to them! because they have gone in the way of Cain, and given themselves up to the error of Balaam for reward, and perished in the rebellion of Korah.

12 These are spots in your love-feasts, feasting together [with you] without fear, pasturing themselves; clouds without water, carried along by the winds; autumn trees without fruit, twice dead, rooted up;

13 raging waves of the sea, foaming out their own shames; wandering stars, to whom has been reserved the gloom of darkness into the aeon.

14 And Enoch, the seventh from Adam, prophesied also as to these, saying, Behold, the Lord has come amidst his holy myriads,

15 to execute judgment upon all, and to convict all the ungodly of all their ungodly deeds which they have done in an ungodly way, and of all the harsh things which ungodly sinners have spoken against Him.

16 These are murmurers, complainers, walking after their lusts; and their mouth speaks swelling words, admiring persons for the sake of profit.

17 But you, beloved, remember the words spoken before by the apostles of our Lord Jesus Christ,

18 that they said to you, that at the end of the time there should be mockers, walking after their own lusts of ungodliness.

19 These are they who set [themselves] apart, natural [men] not having the Spirit.

20 But you, beloved, building yourselves up on your most holy faith, praying in the Holy Spirit,

21 keep yourselves in the love of God, awaiting the mercy of our Lord Jesus Christ unto aeonian life.

22 And some having compassion, making a difference,

23 but others save with fear, snatching [them] out of the fire; hating even the garment spotted by the flesh.

24 But to him that is able to keep you without stumbling, and to set [you] with exultation blameless before his glory,

25 to the only God our Savior, through Jesus Christ our Lord, [be] glory, majesty, might, and authority, from before the whole aeon, and now, and to all the aeons. Amen.

---

[1] Strong's # 126 (from #104) = always, continual, perpetual, not necessarily "forever." See NM24.

Revelation

Rev 1:1 Revelation of Jesus Christ, which the God gave to Him, to show to his servants what must shortly take place; and he signified it by sending his angel, to his servant John,

2 who testified the word of the God, and the testimony of Jesus Christ, all things that he saw.

3 Happy is he that reads [Spiritually], and they that hear the words of the prophecy, and keep the things written in it; for the time is near.

4 John to the seven churches which [are] in Asia: Grace to you and peace from him who is, and who was, and who is coming[1]; and from the seven Spirits which [are] before his throne;

5 and from Jesus Christ, the faithful witness, the firstborn from the dead, and the prince of the kings of the earth. To him who loves us, and has washed us from our sins in his blood,

6 and made us a kingdom, priests to his God and Father: to him [be] the glory and the might into the aeons of aeons. Amen.

7 Behold, he comes with the clouds, and every eye shall see him, and they which have pierced him, and all the tribes of the land shall wail because of him. Yes. Amen.

8 I am the Alpha and the Omega, says the Lord the God, he who is, and who was, and who is coming[1], the Almighty.

9 I John, your brother and fellow-partaker in the tribulation and kingdom and patience, in Jesus, was in the island called Patmos, for the word of the God, and for the testimony of Jesus.

10 I became in the Spirit on the Lord's day, and I heard behind me a great voice as of a trumpet,

11 saying, What you see write in a book, and send to the seven churches: to Ephesus, and to Smyrna, and to Pergamos, and to Thyatira, and to Sardis, and to Philadelphia, and to Laodicea.

12 And I turned back to see the voice which spoke with me; and having turned, I saw seven golden lamps,

13 and in the midst of the [seven] lamps [one] like the Son of man, clothed with a garment reaching to the feet, and girt about at the breasts with a golden girdle:

14 his head and hair white like white wool, as snow; and his eyes as a flame of fire;

15 and his feet like fine brass, as burning in a furnace; and his voice as the voice of many waters;

16 and having in his right hand seven stars; and out of his mouth a sharp two-edged sword going forth; and his appearance as the sun shines in its power.

17 And when I saw him I fell at his feet as dead; and he laid his right hand upon me, saying, Fear not; I am the first and the last,

18 and the living one: and I became dead, and behold, I am living into the aeons of aeons, and have the keys of death and of Hades.

19 Write therefore what you have seen* and the things that are, and the things that are about to be after these.

20 The revealed-mystery of the seven stars which you have seen on my right hand, and the seven golden lamps. --The seven stars are angels of the seven churches; and the seven lamps are seven churches.

Rev 2:1 To the angel of the church in Ephesus write: These things says he that holds the seven stars in his right hand, who walks in the midst of the seven golden lamps:

2 I know your works and labor, and your endurance, and that you can not bear evil, and you have tried them who call themselves apostles, and are not, and have found them liars;

3 and endure, and have borne for my name's sake, and have not wearied:

4 but I have against you, that you have left your first love.

5 Remember therefore from where you are fallen, and repent and do the first works: but if not, I am coming to you, and I will remove your lamp out of its place, except you shall repent.

6 But this you have, that you hate the works of the Nicolaitans, which I also hate.

7 He that has an ear, let him hear what the Spirit says to the churches. To him that overcomes, I will give to him to eat of the tree of life which is in the paradise of the God.

8 And to the angel of the church in Smyrna write: These things says the first and the last, who became dead, and lived:

9 I know your tribulation and your poverty; but you are rich; and the railing of those who say that they themselves are Jews, and are not, but a synagogue of Satan.

10 Fear nothing of what you are about to suffer. Behold, the devil is about to cast of you into prison, that you may be tried; and you shall have tribulation ten days. Be you faithful unto death, and I will give to you the crown of life.

11 He that has an ear, let him hear what the Spirit says to the churches. He that overcomes shall in no way be injured of the second death.

12 And to the angel of the church in Pergamos write: These things says he that has the sharp two-edged sword:

13 I know where you dwell, where the throne of Satan is and you hold fast my name, and have not denied my faith, even in the days in which Antipas my faithful witness [was] who was slain among you, where Satan dwells.

14 But I have a few things against you: that you have there those who hold the doctrine of Balaam, who taught Balak to cast a snare before the sons of Israel, to eat of idol sacrifices and commit fornication.

---

[1] Becoming-One

15 So you also have those who hold the doctrine of Nicolaitans in like manner.

16 Repent therefore: but if not, I come to you quickly, and I will make war with them with the sword of my mouth.

17 He that has an ear, let him hear what the Spirit says to the churches. To him that overcomes, to him will I give of the hidden manna; and I will give to him a white stone, and on the stone a new name written, which no one knows but he that receives it

18 And to the angel of the church in Thyatira write: These things says the Son of the God, he that has his eyes as a flame of fire, and his feet [are] like fine brass:

19 I know your works, and love, and faith, and service, and your endurance, and your last works [to be] more than the first.

20 But I have against you that you permitted the woman Jezebel, she who calls herself prophetess, and she teaches and leads astray my servants to commit fornication and eat of idol sacrifices.

21 And I gave her time that she should repent, but she was not willing to repent of her fornication.

22 Behold, I cast her into a bed, and those that commit adultery with her into great tribulation, unless they repent of her works,

23 and her children will I kill with death; and all the churches shall know that I am he that searches the reins and the hearts; and I will give to you each according to your works.

24 But to you I say, the rest who [are] in Thyatira, as many as have not this doctrine, who have not known the depths of Satan, as they say, I do not cast upon you any other burden;

25 but what you have hold fast till I shall come.

26 And he that overcomes, and he that keeps unto the end my works, to him will I give authority over the nations,

27 and he shall shepherd them with an iron rod; as vessels of pottery are they broken in pieces, as I also have received from my Father;

28 and I will give to him the morning star.

29 He that has an ear, let him hear what the Spirit says to the churches.

Rev 3:1 And to the angel of the church in Sardis write: These things says he that has the seven Spirits of the God, and the seven stars: I know your works, that you have a name that you live, and are dead.

2 Be watchful, and strengthen the things that remain, which are about to die, for I have not found your works complete before my God.

3 Remember therefore how you have received and heard, and keep it and repent, If therefore you shall not watch, I will come [upon you] as a thief, and you shall not know at what hour I shall come upon you.

4 But you have a few names in Sardis which have not defiled their garments, and they shall walk with me in white, because they are worthy.

5 He that overcomes, he shall be clothed in white garments, and I will not blot his name out of the book of life, and will acknowledge his name before my Father and before his angels.

6 He that has an ear, let him hear what the Spirit says to the churches.

7 And to the angel of the church in Philadelphia write: These things says the holy, the true; he that has the key of David, he who opens and no one shall shut, and shuts and no one shall open:

8 I know your works: behold, I have set before you an opened door, which no one can shut, [I know] that you have little power, and have kept my word, and have not denied my name.

9 Behold, I make them of the synagogue of Satan who say that they are Jews, and are not, but lie; behold, I will cause that they shall come and shall do homage before your feet, and shall know that I have loved you.

10 Because you have kept the word of my patience, I also will preserve you out of the hour of trial, which is about to come upon the whole habitable world, to try them that dwell upon the earth.

11 I come quickly: hold fast what you have, that no one take your crown.

12 He that overcomes, him will I make a pillar in the temple of my God, and he shall go no more at all out; and I will write upon him the name of my God, and the name of the city of my God, the new Jerusalem, which comes down out of heaven, from my God, and my new name.

13 He that has an ear, let him hear what the Spirit says to the churches.

14 And to the angel of the church in Laodicea write: These things says the Amen, the faithful and true witness, the beginning of the creation of the God:

15 I know your works, that you are neither cold nor hot; I wish you were cold or hot.

16 Thus because you are lukewarm, and neither cold nor hot, I am about to spit you out of my mouth.

17 Because you say, I am rich, and am grown rich, and have need of nothing, and know not that you are the wretched and the miserable, and poor, and blind, and naked;

18 I counsel you to buy of me gold purified by fire, that you may be rich; and white garments, that you may be clothed, and that the shame of your nakedness may not be made manifest; and eye-salve to anoint your eyes, that you may see.

19 I rebuke and discipline as many as I brotherly-love; be zealous therefore and repent.

20 Behold, I stand at the door and am knocking; if any one hear my voice and open the door, I will come in unto him and supper with him, and he with me.

21 He that overcomes, to him will I give to sit with me in my throne; as I also have overcome, and have sat down with my Father in his throne.

22 He that has an ear, let him hear what the Spirit says to the churches.

Rev 4:1 After these things I saw, and behold, a door opened in heaven, and the first voice which I heard as of a trumpet speaking with me, saying, Come up here, and I will show you the things which must take place after these things.

2 Immediately I became in the Spirit; and behold, a throne stood in the heaven, and upon the throne one sitting,

3 and he [that was] sitting like in appearance to a stone of jasper and a sardius, and a rainbow round the throne like in appearance to an emerald.

4 And around the throne twenty-four thrones, and on the thrones twenty-four elders sitting, clothed with white garments; and on their heads golden crowns.

5 And out of the throne go forth lightning, and voices, and thunders; and seven lamps of fire, burning before the throne, which are the seven Spirits of the God;

6 and before the throne, as a glass sea, like crystal. And in the midst of the throne, and around the throne, four beasts, full of eyes, before and behind;

7 and the first beast like a lion, and the second beast like a calf, and the third beast having the face as of a man, and the fourth beast like a flying eagle.

8 And the four beasts, each one of them having respectively six wings; round and within they are full of eyes; and they cease not day and night saying, Holy, holy, holy, Lord the God Almighty, who was, and who is, and who is coming[1].

9 And when the beasts shall give glory and honor and thanksgiving to him that sits upon the throne, who lives into the aeons of aeons;

10 the twenty-four elders shall fall before him that sits upon the throne, and do homage to him that lives into the aeons of aeons, and shall cast their crowns before the throne, saying,

11 You are worthy, O Lord and O God, to receive glory and honor and power; for you have created all things, and for your will they were, and they have been created.

Rev 5:1 And I saw on the right hand of him that sat upon the throne a book, written within and on the back, sealed with seven seals.

2 And I saw a strong angel proclaiming with a loud voice, Who is worthy to open the book, and to break its seals?

3 And no one was able in the heaven, or upon the earth, or underneath the earth, to open the book, or to look at it.

4 And I wept much because no one had been found worthy to open the book nor to look at it.

5 And one of the elders says to me, Do not weep. Behold, the lion which is of the tribe of Judah, the root of David, has overcome [so as] to open the book, and its seven seals.

6 And I saw in the midst of the throne and of the four beasts, and in the midst of the elders, a Lamb standing, as slain, having seven horns and seven eyes, which are the seven Spirits of the God [which are] sent into all the earth:

7 and one came and took it out of the right hand of him that sat upon the throne.

8 And when he took the book, the four beasts and the twenty-four elders fell before the Lamb, having each a harp and golden bowls full of incenses, which are the prayers of the saints.

9 And they sing a new song, saying, You are worthy to take the book, and to open its seals; because you have been slain, and have redeemed to God, by your blood, out of every tribe, and tongue, and people, and nation,

10 and made them to our God kings and priests; and they shall reign upon the earth.

11 And I saw, and I heard the voice of many angels around the throne and the beasts and the elders; and their number was ten thousands of ten thousands and thousands of thousands;

12 saying with a loud voice, Worthy is the Lamb that has been slain, to receive power, and riches, and wisdom, and strength, and honor, and glory, and blessing.

13 And all creation which is in the heaven and upon the earth and under the earth, and [those that are] upon the sea, and all things in them, heard I saying, To him that sits upon the throne, and to the Lamb, blessing, and honor, and glory, and might, into the aeons of aeons.

14 And the four beasts said, Amen; and the elders fell down and did homage.

Rev 6:1 And I saw when the Lamb opened one of the seven seals, and I heard one of the four beasts saying, as a voice of thunder, Come [and see]

2 And I saw: and behold, a white horse, and he that sat upon it having a bow; and a crown was given to him, and he went forth conquering and that he might conquer.

3 And when it opened the second seal, I heard the second beast saying, Come [and see]

4 And another, a red horse, went forth; and to him that sat upon it, to him it was given to take peace from the earth, and that they should slay one another; and there was given to him a great sword.

5 And when it opened the third seal, I heard the third beast saying, Come [and see] And I saw: and behold, a black horse, and he that sat upon it having a balance in his hand.

6 And I heard as a voice in the midst of the four beasts saying, A quart [choenix] of wheat for a day's wage [denarius], and three quarts [choenixes] of barley for a day's wage [denarius]: and do not injure the oil and the wine.

7 And when it opened the fourth seal, I heard [the voice of] the fourth beast saying, Come [and see]

8 And I saw: and behold, a pale horse, and he that sat upon it, his name [was] Death, and Sheol followed with him; and authority was given to him over the fourth of the earth to slay with sword, and with hunger, and with death, and by the beasts of the earth.

---

[1] Becoming-One

9 And when it opened the fifth seal, I saw underneath the altar the souls of them that had been slain for the word of the God, and for the testimony which they held;

10 and they cried with a loud voice, saying, How long, O sovereign Ruler, holy and true, do you not judge and avenge our blood on them that dwell upon the earth?

11 And there was given to them, to each one a white robe; and it was said to them that they should rest yet a little while, until both their fellow-servants and their brethren, who were about to be killed as they, should be fulfilled.

12 And I saw when it opened the sixth seal, and there was a great earthquake; and the sun became black as hair sackcloth, and the whole moon became as blood,

13 and the stars of heaven fell upon the earth, as a fig tree, shaken by a great wind, casts its unseasonable figs.

14 And the heaven was removed as a book rolled up, and every mountain and island were removed out of their places.

15 And the kings of the earth, and the great, and the commanders, and the rich, and the strong, and every servant and freeman, hid themselves in the caves and in the rocks of the mountains;

16 and they say to the mountains and to the rocks, Fall on us, and have us hidden from the face of him that sits upon the throne, and from the wrath of the Lamb;

17 because the great day of his wrath is come, and who is able to stand?

Rev 7:1 And after this I saw four angels standing upon the four corners of the earth, holding fast the four winds of the earth, that no wind might blow upon the earth, nor upon the sea, nor upon any tree.

2 And I saw another angel ascending from the sunrising, having the seal of the living God; and he cried with a loud voice to the four angels to whom it had been given to hurt the earth and the sea,

3 saying, Hurt not the earth, nor the sea, nor the trees, until we shall have sealed the servants of our God upon their foreheads.

4 And I heard the number of the sealed, a hundred [and] forty-four thousand, sealed out of every tribe of the sons of Israel:

5 out of the tribe of Judah, twelve thousand sealed; out of the tribe of Reuben, twelve thousand; out of the tribe of Gad, twelve thousand;

6 out of the tribe of Aser, twelve thousand; out of the tribe of Nepthalim, twelve thousand; out of the tribe of Manasseh, twelve thousand;

7 out of the tribe of Simeon, twelve thousand; out of the tribe of Levi, twelve thousand; out of the tribe of Issachar, twelve thousand;

8 out of the tribe of Zabulun, twelve thousand; out of the tribe of Joseph, twelve thousand; out of the tribe of Benjamin, twelve thousand sealed.

9 After these things I saw, and lo, a great crowd, which no one could number, out of every nation and tribes and peoples and tongues, standing before the throne, and before the Lamb, clothed with white robes, and palm branches in their hands.

10 And they cry with a loud voice, saying, Salvation to our God who sits upon the throne, and to the Lamb.

11 And all the angels stood around the throne, and the elders, and the four beasts, and fell before the throne upon their faces, and worshiped the God,

12 saying, Amen: Blessing, and glory, and wisdom, and thanksgiving, and honor, and power, and strength, to our God, into the aeons of aeons. Amen.

13 And one of the elders answered, saying to me, These who are clothed with white robes, who are they, and from where came they?

14 And I said to him, My lord, you know. And he said to me, These are they who come out of the great tribulation, and have washed their robes, and have made them white in the blood of the Lamb.

15 Therefore are they before the throne of the God, and serve him day and night in his temple, and he that sits upon the throne shall spread his tabernacle over them.

16 They shall not hunger any more, neither shall they thirst any more, nor shall the sun at all fall on them, nor any burning heat;

17 because the Lamb which is in the midst of the throne shall shepherd them, and shall lead them to fountains of waters of life, and the God shall wipe away every tear from their eyes.

Rev 8:1 And when it opened the seventh seal, there was silence in the heaven about half an hour.

2 And I saw the seven angels who stand before the God, and seven trumpets were given to them.

3 And another angel came and stood at the altar, having a golden censer; and much incense was given to him, that he might add to the prayers of all saints at the golden altar which [was] before the throne.

4 And the smoke of the incense went up with the prayers of the saints, out of the hand of the angel before the God.

5 And the angel took the censer, and filled it from the fire of the altar, and cast it on the earth: and there were voices, and thunders and lightning, and an earthquake.

6 And the seven angels who had the seven trumpets prepared themselves that they might sound with [their] trumpets.

7 And the first sounded [his] trumpet: and there was hail and fire, mingled with blood, and they were cast upon the earth; and the third part of the earth was burnt up, and the third part of the trees was burnt up, and all green grass was burnt up.

8 And the second angel sounded [his] trumpet: and as a great mountain burning with fire was cast into the sea, and the third part of the sea became blood;

9 and the third part of the creation which were in the sea which had soul died; and the third part of the ships were destroyed.

10 And the third angel sounded [his] trumpet: and there fell out of the heaven a great star, burning as a torch, and it fell upon the third part of the rivers, and upon the fountains of waters.

11 And the name of the star is called Wormwood; and the third part of the waters became wormwood, and many of the men died of the waters because they were made bitter.

12 And the fourth angel sounded [his] trumpet: and the third part of the sun was struck, and the third part of the moon, and the third part of the stars; so that the third part of them should be darkened, and that the day should not appear [for] the third part of it, and the night the same.

13 And I saw, and I heard an eagle flying in mid-heaven, saying with a loud voice, Woe, woe, woe, to them that dwell upon the earth, for the remaining voices of the trumpet of the three angels who are about to sound.

Rev 9:1 And the fifth angel sounded [his] trumpet: and I saw a star out of the heaven fallen to the earth; and there was given to it the key of the pit of the abyss.

2 And it opened the pit of the abyss; and there went up smoke out of the pit as the smoke of a great furnace; and the sun and the air were darkened with the smoke of the pit.

3 And out of the smoke came forth locusts on the earth, and power was given to them as the scorpions of the earth have power;

4 and it was said to them, that they should not injure the grass of the earth, nor any green thing, nor any tree, but the men who have not the seal of the God on their foreheads:

5 and it was given to them that they should not kill them, but that they should be tormented five months; and their torment [was] as the torment of a scorpion when it strikes a man.

6 And in those days shall men seek death, and shall in no way find it; and shall desire to die, and death flees from them.

7 And the likenesses of the locusts [were] like to horses prepared for war; and upon their heads as crowns like gold, and their faces as faces of men;

8 and they had hair as women's hair, and their teeth were as of lions,

9 and they had breastplates as breastplates of iron, and the sound of their wings [was] as the sound of chariots of many horses running to war;

10 and they have tails like scorpions, and stings; and their power [was] in their tails to hurt men five months.

11 They have a king over them, the angel of the abyss: his name in Hebrew, Abaddon, and in Greek he has [for] name Apollyon.

12 The first woe has passed. Behold, there come yet two woes after these things.

13 And the sixth angel sounded [his] trumpet: and I heard a voice from the four horns of the golden altar which is before the God,

14 saying to the sixth angel that had the trumpet, Loose the four angels which are bound at the great river Euphrates.

15 And the four angels were let loose, who are prepared for the hour and day and month and year, that they might slay the third part of men;

16 and the number of the hosts of horse [was] twice ten thousand times ten thousand. I heard their number.

17 And thus I saw the horses in the vision, and those that sat upon them, having breastplates of fire and jacinth and brimstone; and the heads of the horses [were] as heads of lions, and out of their mouths goes out fire and smoke and brimstone.

18 By these three plagues were the third part of men killed, by the fire and the smoke and the brimstone which goes out of their mouths.

19 For the power of the horses is in their mouth and in their tails: for their tails [are] like serpents, having heads, and with them they injure.

20 And the rest of men who were not killed with these plagues repented not of the works of their hands, that they should not worship daemons, and the golden and silver and brazen and stone and wooden idols, which can neither see nor hear nor walk.

21 And they repented not of their murders, nor of their drugs, nor of their fornication, nor of their thefts.

Rev 10:1 And I saw another strong angel coming down out of the heaven, clothed with a cloud, and the rainbow upon his head, and his appearance as the sun, and his feet as pillars of fire,

2 and having in his hand a little opened book. And he set his right foot on the sea, and the left upon the earth,

3 and cried with a loud voice as a lion roars. And when he cried, the seven thunders uttered their own voices.

4 And when the seven thunders spoke, I was about to write: and I heard a voice out of the heaven saying, Seal the things which the seven thunders have spoken, and write them not.

5 And the angel whom I saw stand on the sea and on the earth lifted up his right hand to the heaven,

6 and swore by him that lives into the aeons of aeons, who created the heaven and the things that are in it, and the earth and the things that are in it, and the sea and the things that are in it, that there should be no longer delay;

7 but in the days of the voice of the seventh angel, when he is about to sound the trumpet, the revealed-mystery of the God also shall be completed, as he has made known the good news to his own servants the prophets.

8 And the voice which I heard out of the heaven [was] again speaking with me, and saying, Go, take the little book which is opened in the hand of the angel who is standing on the sea and on the earth.

9 And I went to the angel, saying to him to give me the little book. And he says to me, Take and eat it

up: and it shall make your belly bitter, but in your mouth it shall be sweet as honey.

10 And I took the little book out of the hand of the angel, and ate it up; and it was in my mouth as honey, sweet; and when I had eaten it my belly was made bitter.

11 And it was said to me, You must prophesy [teach] again to peoples and Gentiles and tongues and many kings.

Rev 11:1 And there was given to me a reed like a staff, saying, Rise, and measure the temple of the God, and the altar, and them that worship in it.

2 And the court which is outside the temple cast out, and measure it not; because it has been given to the Gentiles, and the holy city shall they tread under foot **forty-two months**.

3 And I will give [power] to my two witnesses, and they shall prophesy [teach] a **thousand two hundred [and] sixty days**, clothed in sackcloth.

4 These are the two olive trees and the two lamps which stand before the Lord of the earth;

5 and if any one wills to injure them, fire goes out of their mouth, and devours their enemies. And if any one wills to injure them, thus must he be killed.

6 These have power to shut the heaven that no rain may fall during the days of their prophecy; and they have power over the waters to turn them into blood, and to smite the earth as often as they will with every plague.

7 And when they shall have finished* their testimony, the beast who comes up out of the abyss shall make war with them, and shall conquer them, and shall kill them:

8 and their bodies [shall be] on the street of the great city, which is called spiritually Sodom and Egypt, where also their Lord was crucified.

9 And [men] of the peoples and tribes and tongues and nations see their bodies three days and a half, and they do not permit their bodies to be put into a tomb.

10 And they that dwell upon the earth rejoice over them, and are full of delight, and shall send gifts one to another, because these, the two prophets, tormented them that dwell upon the earth.

11 And after the three days and a half the spirit of life from the God came into them, and they stood upon their feet; and great fear fell upon those beholding them.

12 And I heard a great voice out of the heaven saying to them, Come up here; and they went up to the heaven in the cloud, and their enemies beheld them.

13 And in that hour there was a great earthquake, and the tenth of the city fell, and seven thousand names of men were slain in the earthquake. And the remnant were filled with fear, and gave glory to God of the heaven.

14 The second woe has passed; behold, the third woe comes quickly.

15 And the seventh angel sounded [his] trumpet: and there were great voices in the heaven, saying, The kingdom of the world of our Lord and of his Christ is come, and he shall reign into the aeons of aeons.

16 And the twenty-four elders, who sit on their thrones before the God, fell upon their faces, and worshiped God,

17 saying, We give you thanks, Lord the God Almighty, [he] who is, and who was, that you have taken your great power and have reigned.

18 And the nations have been full of wrath, and your wrath is come, and the time of the dead to be judged, and to give the reward to your servants the prophets, and to the saints, and to those who fear your name, small and great; and to destroy those that destroy the earth.

19 And the temple of the God in the heaven was opened, and the ark of his covenant was seen in his temple: and there were lightning, and voices, and thunders, and an earthquake, and great hail.

Rev 12:1 And a great sign was seen in the heaven: a woman clothed with the sun, and the moon under her feet, and upon her head a crown of twelve stars;

2 and being with child she cried, [being] in travail, and in pain to bring forth.

3 And another sign was seen in the heaven: and behold, a great red dragon, having seven heads and ten horns, and on his heads seven diadems;

4 and his tail draws the third part of the stars of the heaven; and he cast them to the earth. And the dragon stood before the woman who was about to bring forth, in order that when she brought forth he might devour her child.

5 And she brought forth* a male son, who shall shepherd all the nations with an iron rod; and her child was caught up toward the God and to his throne.

6 And the woman fled into the wilderness, where she has there a place prepared of the God, that they should nourish her there a thousand two hundred [and] sixty days.

7 And there was war in the heaven: Michael and his angels went to war with the dragon. And the dragon fought, and his angels;

8 and he prevailed not, nor was their place found any more in the heaven.

9 And the great dragon was cast out, the ancient serpent, he who is called the Devil and Satan, he who deceives the whole habitable world, he was cast out into the earth, and his angels were cast out with him.

10 And I heard a great voice in the heaven saying, Now is come the salvation and the power and the kingdom of our God, and the authority of his Christ; for the accuser of our brethren has been cast out, who accused them before our God day and night:

11 and they have overcome him by reason of the blood of the Lamb, and by reason of the word of their testimony, and have not loved their souls even unto death.

12 Therefore be full of delight, you heavens, and you that dwell in them. Woe to the earth and to the

sea, because the devil has come down to you, having great rage, knowing he has a short time.

13 And when the dragon saw that he had been cast out[aor.] into the earth, he persecuted the woman which bore the male [child]

14 And there were given to the woman the two wings of the great eagle, that she might fly into the desert into her place, where she is nourished there a **time, and times, and half a time**, from the face of the serpent.

15 And the serpent cast out of his mouth behind the woman water as a river, that he might make her be [as] one carried away by a river.

16 And the earth helped the woman, and the earth opened its mouth and swallowed the river which the dragon cast out of his mouth.

17 And the dragon was angry with the woman, and went to make war with the remnant of her seed, who keep the commandments of the God, and have the testimony of Jesus.

Rev 13:1 And I stood upon the sand of the sea; and I saw a <u>beast</u> rising out of the sea, <u>having ten horns</u> <u>and</u> <u>seven heads, and upon its horns ten diadems</u>, and upon its heads names of blasphemy.

2 And the beast which I saw was like to a leopardess, and its feet as of a bear, and its mouth as a lion's mouth; and the dragon gave to it his power, and his throne, and great authority;

3 and one of his heads [was] as slain to death, and his wound of death had been healed: and the whole earth wondered after the beast.

4 And they did homage to the dragon, because he gave the authority to the beast; and they did homage to the beast, saying, Who is like to the beast? and who can make war with it?

5 And there was given to it a mouth, speaking great things and blasphemies; and there was given to it authority to pursue its career **forty-two months**.

6 And it opened its mouth for blasphemies toward the God, to blaspheme his name and his tabernacle, and those who have their tabernacle in the heaven.

7 And there was given to it to make war with the saints, and to overcome them; and there was given to it authority over every tribe, and people, and tongue, and nation;

8 and all that dwell on the earth shall do it homage, [every one] whose name had not been written from the founding of the world in the book of life of the slain Lamb.

9 If any one has an ear, let him hear.

10 If any one [leads] into captivity, he goes into captivity. If any one shall kill with the sword, he must with the sword be killed. Here is the endurance and the faith of the saints.

11 And I saw another beast rising out of the earth; and it had two horns like to a lamb, and spoke as a dragon;

12 and it exercises all the authority of the first beast before it, and causes the earth and those that dwell in it to do homage to the first beast, whose wound of death was healed.

13 And it works great signs, that it should cause even fire to come down from heaven to the earth before men.

14 And it deceives those that dwell upon the earth by reason of the signs which it was given to it to work before the beast, saying to those that dwell upon the earth to make an image to the beast, which has the wound of the sword, and lived.

15 And it was given to it to give breath to the image of the beast, that the image of the beast should also speak, and should cause that as many as should not do homage to the image of the beast should be killed.

16 And it causes all, the small and the great, and the rich and the poor, and the free and the servants, that they should give them a mark upon their right hand or upon their forehead;

17 and that no one should be able to buy or sell except he that had the mark, the name of the beast, or the number of its name.

18 Here is wisdom. He that has understanding let him count the number of the beast: for it is a man's number; and its number is six hundred [and] sixty-six.

Rev 14:1 And I saw, and behold, the Lamb standing upon mount Zion, and with him a hundred [and] forty-four thousand, having his name and the name of his Father written upon their foreheads.

2 And I heard a voice out of the heaven as a voice of many waters, and as a voice of great thunder. And the voice which I heard [was] as of harp-singers harping with their harps;

3 and they sing a new song before the throne, and before the four beasts and the elders. And no one could learn that song except the hundred [and] forty-four thousand who were bought from the earth.

4 These are they who have not been defiled with women, for they are virgins: these are they who follow the Lamb wheresoever it goes. These have been bought from men [as] first-fruit to God and to the Lamb:

5 and in their mouths was no lie found; [for] they are blameless.

6 And I saw another angel flying in mid-heaven, having the aeonian good news to announce to those settled on the earth, and to every nation and tribe and tongue and people,

7 saying with a loud voice, Fear the God and give him glory, for the hour of his judgment has come; and do homage to him who has made the heaven and the earth and the sea and fountains of waters.

8 And another, a second, angel followed, saying, Great Babylon has fallen, has fallen, which of the wine of the fury of her fornication has made all nations drink.

9 And another, a third, angel followed them, saying with a loud voice, If any one do homage to the beast and its image, and receive a mark upon his forehead or upon his hand,

10 he also shall drink of the wine of the fury of the God prepared unmixed in the cup of his wrath, and he shall be tormented in fire and brimstone before the holy angels and before the Lamb.

11 And the smoke of their torment goes up into the aeons of aeons, and they have no rest day and night who do homage to the beast and to its image, and if any one receive the mark of its name.

12 Here is the endurance of the saints, who keep the commandments of the God and the faith of Jesus.

13 And I heard a voice out of the heaven saying, Write, Happy the dead who die in the Lord from henceforth. Yes, says the Spirit, that they may rest from their labors; for their works follow with them.

14 And I saw, and behold, a white cloud, and on the cloud one sitting like the Son of man, having upon his head a golden crown, and in his hand a sharp sickle.

15 And another angel came out of the temple, crying with a loud voice to him that sat on the cloud, Send your sickle and reap; for the hour of reaping is come, for the harvest of the earth is dried [or ripe when applied to grain].

16 And he that sat on the cloud put his sickle on the earth, and the earth was reaped.

17 And another angel came out of the temple which is in the heaven, he also having a sharp sickle.

18 And another angel came out of the altar, having power over fire, and called with a loud cry to him that had the sharp sickle, saying, Send your sharp sickle, and gather the clusters of the vine of the earth; for her grapes are fully ripened.

19 And the angel put his sickle to the earth, and gathered the vine of the earth, and cast [the bunches] into the great wine-press of the fury of the God;

20 and the wine-press was trodden outside the city, and blood went out of the wine-press to the bits of the horses for a thousand six hundred stadia.

Rev 15:1 And I saw another sign in the heaven, great and wonderful: seven angels having seven plagues, the last; for in them the fury of the God is completed.

2 And I saw as a glass sea, mingled with fire, and those that had gained the victory over the beast, and over its image, and over the number of its name, standing upon the glass sea, having harps of the God.

3 And they sing the song of Moses servant of the God, and the song of the Lamb, saying, Great and wonderful [are] your works, Lord the God Almighty; righteous and true [are] your ways, O King of nations.

4 Who shall not fear [you] O Lord, and glorify your name? for [you] only [are] holy; for all nations shall come and do homage before you; for your righteousness have been made manifest.

5 And after these things I saw, and the temple of the tabernacle of witness in the heaven was opened;

6 and the seven angels who had the seven plagues came out of the temple, clothed in pure bright linen, and girded about the breasts with golden girdles.

7 And one of the four beasts gave to the seven angels seven golden bowls, full of the fury of the God, who lives into the aeons of aeons.

8 And the temple was filled with smoke from the glory of the God and from his power: and no one could enter into the temple until the seven plagues of the seven angels were completed.

Rev 16:1 And I heard a great voice out of the temple, saying to the seven angels, Go and pour out the seven bowls of the fury of the God upon the earth.

2 And the first went and poured out his bowl on the earth; and there came an evil and grievous sore upon the men that had the mark of the beast, and those who worshiped its image.

3 And the second poured out his bowl on the sea; and it became blood, as of a dead man; and every living soul died in the sea.

4 And the third poured out his bowl on the rivers, and [on] the fountains of waters; and they became blood.

5 And I heard the angel of the waters saying, You are righteous, who are and was, the holy one, that you have judged so;

6 for they have poured out the blood of saints and prophets, and you have given them blood to drink; they are worthy.

7 And I heard the altar saying, Yes, Lord the God Almighty, true and righteous [are] your judgments.

8 And the fourth poured out his bowl on the sun; and it was given to it to burn men with fire.

9 And the men were burnt with great heat, and blasphemed the name of the God, who had authority over these plagues, and did not repent to give him glory.

10 And the fifth poured out his bowl on the throne of the beast; and its kingdom became darkened; and they gnawed their tongues with distress,

11 and blasphemed the God of the heaven for their distresses and their sores, and did not repent of their works.

12 And the sixth poured out his bowl on the great river Euphrates; and its water was dried up, that the way of the kings from the rising of the sun might be prepared.

13 And I saw out of the mouth of the dragon, and out of the mouth of the beast, and out of the mouth of the false prophet, three unclean spirits, as frogs;

14 for they are the spirits of daemons, doing signs; which go out to the kings of the whole habitable world to gather them together to the war of that great day of the God the Almighty.

15 Behold, I come as a thief. Happy is he that watches and keeps his garments, that he may not walk naked, and that they [may not] see his shame.

16 And he gathered them together to the place called in Hebrew, Armagedon.

17 And the seventh poured out his bowl on the air; and there came out a great voice from the temple of the heaven, from the throne, saying, It is done.

18 And there were lightning, and voices, and thunders; and there was a great earthquake, such as was not since men were upon the earth, such an earthquake, so great.

19 And the great city was [divided] into three parts; and the cities of the nations fell: and great Babylon was remembered before the God to give her the cup of the wine of the fury of his wrath.

20 And every island fled, and mountains were not found;

21 and a great hail, as of a talent weight, comes down out of the heaven upon men; and men blasphemed the God because of the plague of hail, for the plague of it is exceeding great.

Rev 17:1 And one of the seven angels, which had the seven bowls, came and spoke with me, saying, Come here, I will show you the sentence of the great harlot who sits upon the many waters;

2 with whom the kings of the earth have committed fornication; and they that dwell on the earth have been made drunk with the wine of her fornication.

3 And he carried me away in spirit to a desert; and I saw a <u>woman</u> sitting <u>upon</u> a <u>scarlet beast</u>, full of names of blasphemy, <u>having seven heads and ten horns</u>.

4 And the woman was clothed in purple and scarlet, and had ornaments of gold and precious stones and pearls, having a golden cup in her hand full of abominations and the unclean things of her fornication;

5 and upon her forehead a name written, Mystery, great Babylon, the mother of the harlots, and of the abominations of the earth.

6 And I saw the woman drunk with the blood of the saints, and with the blood of the witnesses of Jesus. And I wondered, seeing her, with great wonder.

7 And the angel said to me, Why have you wondered? I will tell you the revealed-mystery of the woman, and of the beast which carries her, which has the seven heads and the ten horns.

8 The beast which you saw was, and is not, and is about to come up out of the abyss and go into destruction: and they who dwell on the earth, whose names are not written from the founding of the world in the book of life, shall wonder, seeing the beast, that it was, and is not, and shall be present.

9 Here is the mind that has wisdom: The seven heads are seven mountains, whereon the woman sits.

10 And there are seven kings: five have fallen, one is, the other has not yet come; and when he comes he must remain [only] a little while.

11 And the beast that was and is not, he also is an eighth, and is of the seven, and goes into destruction.

12 And the ten horns which you saw are ten kings, which have not yet received a kingdom, but receive authority as kings one hour with the beast.

13 These have one mind, and give their power and authority to the beast.

14 These shall make war with the Lamb, and the Lamb shall overcome them; for he is Lord of lords and King of kings: and they [that are] with him called, and chosen, and faithful.

15 And he says to me, The waters which you saw, where the harlot sits, are peoples and multitudes and nations and tongues.

16 And the ten horns which you saw, and the beast, these shall hate the harlot, and shall make her desolate and naked, and shall eat her flesh, and shall burn her with fire;

17 for the God has given to their hearts to do his mind, and to act with one mind, and to give their kingdom to the beast until the words of the God shall be fulfilled.

18 And the woman which you saw is the great city, which has kingship over the kings of the earth.

Rev 18:1 After these things I saw another angel descending out of the heaven, having great authority: and the earth was lightened with his glory.

2 And he cried with a strong voice, saying, Great Babylon has fallen, has fallen, and has become the habitation of daemons, and a hold of every unclean spirit, and a hold of every unclean and hated bird;

3 because all the nations have drunk of the wine of the fury of her fornication; and the kings of the earth have committed fornication with her, and the merchants of the earth have been enriched through the might of her luxury.

4 And I heard another voice out of the heaven saying, Come out of her, my people, that you have not fellowship in her sins, and that you do not receive of her plagues:

5 for her sins have been heaped on one another up to the heaven, and the God has remembered her unrighteousness.

6 Reward her even as she has recompensed; and double [to her] double, according to her works. In the cup which she has mixed, mix to her double.

7 So much as she has glorified herself and lived luxuriously, so much torment and grief give to her. Because she says in her heart, I sit a queen, and I am not a widow; and I shall in no way see grief:

8 for this reason in one day shall her plagues come, death and grief and famine, and she shall be burnt with fire; for strong [is the] Lord the God who has judged her.

9 And the kings of the earth, who have committed fornication, and lived luxuriously with her, shall weep and wail over her, when they see the smoke of her burning,

10 standing afar off, through fear of her torment, saying, Woe, woe, the great city, Babylon, the strong city! for in one hour your judgment is come.

11 And the merchants of the earth weep and grieve over her, because no one buys their cargoes any more;

12 cargoes of gold, and silver, and precious stones, and pearl, and fine linen, and purple, and silk, and scarlet dye, and all thyine wood, and every

article in ivory, and every article in most precious wood, and in brass, and in iron, and in marble,

13 and cinnamon, and amomum, and incense, and unguent, and frankincense, and wine, and oil, and fine flour, and wheat, and cattle, and sheep, and of horses, and of chariots, and of bodies, and souls of men.

14 And the ripe fruits which were the lust of your soul have departed from you, and all fair and splendid things have perished from you, and they shall not find them any more at all.

15 The merchants of these things, who had been enriched through her, shall stand afar off through fear of her torment, weeping and grieving,

16 saying, Woe, woe, the great city, which [was] clothed with fine linen and purple and scarlet, and had ornaments of gold and precious stones and pearls!

17 for in one hour so great riches has been made desolate. And every steersman, and every one who sailed to any place, and sailors, and all who exercise their calling on the sea, stood afar off,

18 and cried, seeing the smoke of her burning, saying, What [city] is like to the great city?

19 and cast dust upon their heads, and cried, weeping and grieving, saying, Woe, woe, the great city, in which all that had ships in the sea were enriched through her costliness! for in one hour she has been made desolate.

20 Rejoice over her, heaven, and [you] saints and apostles and prophets; for the God has judged your judgment upon her.

21 And a strong angel took up a stone, as a great millstone, and cast it into the sea, saying, Thus with violence shall Babylon the great city be cast down, and shall be found no more at all;

22 and voice of harp-singers and musicians and flute-players and trumpeters shall not be heard any more at all in you, and no artificer of any are shall be found any more at all in you, and voice of millstone shall be heard no more at all in you,

23 and light of lamp shall shine no more at all in you, and voice of bridegroom and bride shall be heard no more at all in you; for your merchants were the great ones of the earth; for by your sorcery [through drugs] have all the nations been deceived.

24 And in her was found the blood of prophets and saints, and of all the slain upon the earth.

Rev 19:1 After these things I heard as a loud voice of a great multitude in the heaven, saying, Hallelujah: the salvation and the glory and the power of our God:

2 for true and righteous [are] his judgments; for he has judged the great harlot which corrupted the earth with her fornication, and has avenged the blood of his servants at her hand.

3 And a second time they said, Hallelujah. And her smoke goes up into the aeons of aeons.

4 And the twenty-four elders and the four beasts fell down and did homage to God who sits upon the throne, saying, Amen, Hallelujah.

5 And a voice came out of the throne, saying, Praise our God, all you his servants, [and] you that fear him, small and great.

6 And I heard as a voice of a great crowd, and as a voice of many waters, and as a voice of strong thunders, saying, Hallelujah, for the Lord our God the Almighty has taken to himself kingly power.

7 Let us rejoice and exult, and give him glory; for the marriage of the Lamb is come, and his wife has made herself ready.

8 And it was given to her that she should be clothed in fine linen, bright [and] pure; for the fine linen is the righteousness of the saints.

9 And he says to me, Write, Happy [are] they who are called to the supper of the marriage of the Lamb. And he says to me, These are the true words of the God.

10 And I fell before his feet to do him homage. And he says to me, See [you do it] not. I am your fellow-servant, and [the fellow-servant] of your brethren who have the testimony of Jesus. Do homage to God. For the spirit of prophecy is the testimony of Jesus.

11 And I saw the heaven opened, and behold, a white horse, and one sitting on it, [called] Faithful and True, and he judges and makes war in righteousness.

12 And his eyes are a flame of fire, and upon his head many diadems, having a name written which no one knows but himself;

13 and [he is] clothed with a garment dipped in blood; and his name is called, The Word of the God.

14 And the armies which [are] in the heaven followed him upon white horses, clad in white, pure, fine linen.

15 And out of his mouth goes a sharp [two edged] sword, that with it he might smite the nations; and he shall shepherd them with an iron rod; and he treads the wine-press of the fury of the wrath of the God the Almighty.

16 And he has upon his garment, and upon his thigh, a name written, King of kings, and Lord of lords.

17 And I saw an angel standing in the sun; and he cried with a loud voice, saying to all the birds that fly in mid-heaven, Come, gather yourselves to the great supper of the God,

18 that you may eat flesh of kings, and flesh of officers, and flesh of strong men, and flesh of horses and of those that sit upon them, and flesh of all, both free and bond, and small and great.

19 And I saw the beast and the kings of the earth and their armies gathered together to make war against him that sat upon the horse, and against his army.

20 And the beast was taken* and the false prophet that [was] with him, who worked the signs before him by which he deceived them that received the mark of the beast, and those that worship his image. Alive were both cast into the lake of fire which burns with brimstone;

21 and the rest were slain with the sword of him that sat upon the horse, which goes out of his mouth; and all the birds were filled with their flesh.

Rev 20:1 And I saw an angel descending from heaven, having the key of the abyss, and a great chain in his hand.

2 And he laid hold of the dragon, the ancient serpent who is the Devil and Satan, and bound him a **thousand years**,

3 and cast him into the abyss, and shut it and sealed it over him, that he should not any more deceive the nations until the **thousand years** were completed; (after these things he must be released for a little time.)

4 And I saw thrones; and they sat upon them, and judgment was given to them; and the souls of those beheaded on account of the testimony of Jesus, and on account of the word of the God; and those who had not done homage to the beast nor to his image, and had not received the mark on their forehead and hand; and they lived and reigned with the Christ a **thousand years**:

5 (the rest of the dead did not live until the **thousand years** had been completed.) This is the first resurrection.

6 Happy and holy he who has part in the first resurrection: over these the second death has no power; but they shall be priests of the God and of the Christ, and shall reign with him a **thousand years**.

7 (And when the **thousand years** have been completed, Satan shall be released from his prison.)

8 and [Satan] shall go out to deceive the nations which [are] in the four corners of the earth, Gog and Magog, to gather them together to the war, whose number is as the sand of the sea.

9 And they went up on the breadth of the earth, and surrounded the camp of the saints and the beloved city: and fire came down and devoured them.

10 And the devil who deceived them was cast into the lake of fire and brimstone, and where the beast and the false prophet; and they shall be tormented day and night into the aeons of aeons.

11 And I saw a great white throne, and him that sat on it, from whose face the earth and the heaven fled, and place was not found for them.

12 And I saw the dead, great and small, standing before the throne, and books were opened; and another book was opened, which is the book of life. And the dead were judged out of the things written in the books according to their works.

13 And the sea gave up the dead which [were] in it, and death and Hades gave up the dead which [were] in them; and they were judged each according to their works:

14 and death and Hades were cast into the lake of fire. This is the second death, [even] the lake of fire.

15 And if any one was not found written in the book of life, he was cast into the lake of fire.

Rev 21:1 And I saw a new heaven and a new earth; for the first heaven and the first earth had passed away, and the sea exists no more.

2 And I saw the holy city, new Jerusalem, coming down out of the heaven from the God, prepared as a bride adorned for her husband.

3 And I heard a loud voice out of the heaven, saying, Behold, the tabernacle of the God is with men, and he shall tabernacle with them, and they shall be his people, and the God himself shall be with them, their God.

4 And he shall wipe away every tear from their eyes; and death shall not exist any more, nor grief, nor crying, nor distress shall exist any more, for the former things have passed away.

5 And he that sat on the throne said, Behold, I make all things new. And he says [to me] Write, for these words are true and faithful.

6 And he said to me, It is done. I am the Alpha and the Omega, the beginning and the end. I will give to him that thirsts of the fountain of the water of life freely.

7 He that overcomes shall inherit these things[1], and I will be to him God, and he shall be to me son.

8 But to the fearful and unbelieving, [and sinners] and those who make themselves abominable, and murderers, and fornicators, and pharmacists (sorcerers), and idolaters, and all liars, their part is in the lake which burns with fire and brimstone; which is the second death.

9 And there came one of the seven angels which had had the seven bowls full of the seven last plagues, and spoke with me, saying, Come here, I will show you the bride, the Lamb's wife.

10 And he carried me away in the Spirit, [and set me] on a great and high mountain, and showed me the holy city, Jerusalem, coming down out of the heaven from the God,

11 having the glory of the God. Her shining [was] like a most precious stone, as a crystal-like jasper stone;

12 having a great and high wall; having twelve gates, and at the gates twelve angels, and names inscribed, which are those of the twelve tribes of the sons of Israel.

13 On the east three gates; and on the north three gates; and on the south three gates; and on the west three gates.

14 And the wall of the city had twelve foundations, and on them twelve names of the twelve apostles of the Lamb.

15 And he that spoke with me had a golden reed [as] a measure, that he might measure the city, and its gates, and its wall.

16 And the city lies four-square, and its length is as much as the breadth. And he measured the city with the reed --twelve thousand stadia: the length and the breadth and height of it are equal.

---

[1] All things, see v. 21:5

17 And he measured its wall, a hundred [and] forty-four cubits, a man's measure, that is, the angel's.

18 And the building of its wall [was] jasper; and the city pure gold, like pure glass:

19 the foundations of the wall of the city [were] adorned with every precious stone: the first foundation, jasper; the second, sapphire; the third, chalcedony; the fourth, emerald;

20 the fifth, sardonyx; the sixth, sardius; the seventh, chrysolite; the eighth, beryl; the ninth, topaz; the tenth, chrysoprasus; the eleventh, jacinth; the twelfth, ameyourst.

21 And the twelve gates, twelve pearls; each one of the gates, respectively, was of one pearl; and the street of the city pure gold, as transparent glass.

22 And I saw no temple in it; for the Lord the God Almighty is its temple, and the Lamb.

23 And the city has no need of the sun nor of the moon, that they should shine for it; for the glory of the God has enlightened it, and the lamp thereof is the Lamb.

24 And the nations shall walk by its light; and the kings of the earth bring their glory to it.

25 And its gates shall not be shut at all by day, for night shall not be there.

26 And they shall bring the glory and the honor of the nations to it.

27 And nothing common, nor that makes an abomination and a lie, shall at all enter into it; but those only who [are] written in the book of life of the Lamb.

Rev 22:1 And he showed me a river of water of life, bright as crystal, going out of the throne of the God and of the Lamb.

2 In the midst of its street, and of the river, on this side and on that side, the tree of life, producing twelve fruits, in each month yielding its fruit; and the leaves of the tree for healing of the nations.

3 And no curse shall be any more; and the throne of the God and of the Lamb shall be in it; and his servants shall serve him,

4 and they shall see his face; and his name is on their foreheads.

5 And night shall not be any more, and no need of a lamp, and light of the sun; for the Lord the God shall shine upon them, and they shall reign into the aeons of aeons.

6 And he said to me, These words [are] faithful and true; and the Lord the God of the spirits of the prophets has sent his angel to show to his servants the things which must soon come to pass.

7 And behold, I come quickly. Happy is he who keeps the words of the prophecy of this book.

8 And I, John, [was] he who heard and saw these things. And when I heard and saw, I fell down to do homage before the feet of the angel who showed me these things.

9 And he says to me, See [you do it] not. I am your fellow-servant, and [the fellow-servant] of your brethren the prophets, and of those who keep the words of this book. Do homage to God.

10 And he says to me, Seal not the words of the prophecy of this book. The time is near.

11 Let him that does unrighteously do unrighteously still; and let the filthy make himself filthy still; and let him that is righteous practice righteousness still; and he that is holy, let him be sanctified still.

12 Behold, I come quickly, and my reward with me, to render to every one as his work shall be.

13 I am the Alpha and the Omega, the first and the last, the beginning and the end.

14 Happy [are] they that wash their robes, that they may have right to the tree of life, and that they should go in by the gates into the city.

15 Outside [are] the dogs, and the pharmacists (sorcerers), and the fornicators, and the murderers, and the idolaters, and every one that likes and makes a lie.

16 I Jesus have sent mine angel to testify these things to you in the churches. I am the root and family [offspring] of David, the bright [and] morning star.

17 And the Spirit and the bride say, Come. And let him that hears say, Come. And let him that is athirst come; he that will, let him take the water of life freely.

18 I testify to every one who hears the words of the prophecy of this book, If any one shall add to these things, the God shall add to him the plagues which are written in this book.

19 And if any one take from the words of the book of this prophecy, the God shall take away his part from the tree of life, and out of the holy city, which are written in this book.

20 He that testifies these things says, Yes, I come quickly. Amen; come, Lord Jesus.

21 The grace of the Lord Jesus Christ [be] with all the saints.

About the Author

Walter Dolen is an author who uses the scientific method[1] to research the material for his books. He has researched and written on science, chronology, philosophy, psychology, theology, religion, sex differences, feminism and so forth. The author questions everything and from this he writes his books. For more info on the author see:

www.walterdolen.com or www.walterdolen.ws

---

[1] (1) Perceive a problem; (2) examine and analyze all the available evidence; (3) examine and imagine different hypotheses in attempt to solve the problem in a logical manner; (4) form a theory that answers the problem; (5) test the theory; (6) always have an open mind for better theories or answers to the problem; (7) change the theory if new evidence is inconsistent to your prior theory.

www.ingramcontent.com/pod-product-compliance
Lightning Source LLC
Chambersburg PA
CBHW081411230426
43668CB00016B/2206